The Stock Car
Racing Encyclopedia

THE
STOCK CAR
RACING
ENCYCLOPEDIA

Edited by Peter Golenbock and Greg Fielden

Macmillan ▪ USA

MACMILLAN

A Simon & Schuster Macmillan Company
1633 Broadway
New York, NY 10019

Macmillan is a registered trademark of Macmillan, Inc.

Original concept developed by Neil Reshen & Dawn Reshen-Doty of Benay Enterprises, Inc.

Copyright © 1997 Benay Enterprises, Inc.

Library of Congress Cataloging-in-Publication Data

The stock car racing encyclopedia : the complete record of America's most popular sport / edited by Peter Golenbock and Greg Fielden.
   p. cm.
  ISBN 0-02-860859-3
  1. Stock car racing—United States—Encyclopedias. 2. Stock car racing—United States—Records. 3. Automobile racing drivers—United States—Biography. I. Golenbock, Peter, 1946– . II. Fielden, Greg.
GV1029.9.S74S764 1997
796.72—dc21   96-52887
                                                    CIP

Electronic book design and composition by Stephen Ogata

First Edition
10 9 8 7 6 5 4 3 2 1

Printed in the United States of America

CONTENTS

PREFACE

When Macmillan first published *The Baseball Encyclopedia* in 1969, it sparked an interest in baseball history and statistics that continues to this day. With this first edition of *The Stock Car Racing Encyclopedia*, fans of this popular sport have a comprehensive reference book of their own. Every driver who ever competed in a race is listed—from Paul Aars to Ralph Zrimsek. The same way that baseball fans can look up the career records of their favorite players in *The Baseball Encyclopedia*, racing fans can get all the season and career totals for their favorite drivers. Other sections include career leaders, year-by-year breakdowns of the top fifty drivers, a section on car owners, and results of every NASCAR race from 1949 through the end of the 1996 season.

Arriving at the Bottom Line

The inaugural Winston Cup Series event, then named the Strictly Stock Division, was staged on a rutted, dusty track in Charlotte, North Carolina, on June 19, 1949.

Over nearly fifty years, NASCAR's unique brand of motorsports has grown from a playground for daring moonshine runners to the slick production we all enjoy today. This is the first encyclopedia to document Winston Cup racing over the years.

Definitive statistical records were seldom compiled in NASCAR's early years. A number of discrepancies have surfaced over the years—from driver records to race wins to money earnings. For instance, NASCAR awarded ten driver victories for the eight races contested in 1949. Tim Flock and June Cleveland were given credit for winning races that were not part of the championship tour in 1949. In fact, the events Flock and Cleveland won were not even sanctioned by NASCAR.

Records for this *Stock Car Racing Encyclopedia* have been tabulated from all events that have been part of the Winston Cup championship season—races that offer championship points. Finish positions in events such as the Winston Select All-Star race and Busch Clash do not count; however, following NASCAR's procedure in recent years, earnings from these events are included in the total money won.

Allison's 85 Wins

Interpretation is a key word when tabulating NASCAR statistics. At times NASCAR has interpreted an event one way, then corrected it years later—without making necessary adjustments in similar or identical circumstances. Clearly, the most glaring inconsistency concerns Bobby Allison, long noted in "official" records as having eighty-four career Winston Cup victories. He actually won eighty-five races, but his victory in the August 6, 1971, race at Winston-Salem, North Carolina, was never properly credited to him. Allison drove a Mustang to victory that day in an event that had both Winston Cup and Grand American cars competing. Allison was not competing for Winston Cup points, but he was competing in the Winston Cup race. NASCAR declared Allison the winner of the event, but that victory has never been reflected in his personal Winston Cup record sheet. His victory is reflected in this *Encyclopedia*. This *Encyclopedia* lists an official winner for each and every event that NASCAR regards as a Winston Cup point-paying event.

NASCAR did not originally credit Allison with a victory because he drove a Mustang. However, in today's official NASCAR records, the Mustang that Allison drove is listed as a bona fide Winston Cup victory for Ford. It is inconsistent for the driver who drove the Mustang not to be credited with his victory. Two years earlier, Grand American cars competed with the Winston Cuppers, and NASCAR officially credited all drivers with official starts—despite the fact that the Grand American drivers were not competing for points.

Fixing Things Later—Partially

There are a number of gray areas that have surfaced in NASCAR's record keeping. Ray Elder won the 1971 500-miler at Riverside, California, but was not originally credited with the victory. Elder was competing for Winston West points rather than Winston Cup (similar to Allison), and his victory was not credited until 1976, five years *after* he won the race. On-the-spot calculations by NASCAR in 1971 did not credit a race winner unless he was competing for Winston Cup points.

That was a direct turnaround from NASCAR's interpretation during the 1960s. A number of races had been won by IndyCar drivers (A. J. Foyt, Dan Gurney, Johnny Rutherford, Mario Andretti, etc.) who were not competing for Winston Cup points, but they received credit for winning a Winston Cup event when they indeed won the event. Many races have been won by drivers who failed to mail in an entry form, and thus did not compete for Winston Cup points, but their victories also counted.

In 1971, the record keepers got lost in the gray areas. Ray Elder, Bobby Allison, and Tiny Lund won races when they were competing for points in divisions other than the Winston Cup. While Elder's victory was appropriately adjusted five years later, no adjustments were made for Bobby Allison and Tiny Lund, who won twice in Camaros. Lund's pair of wins currently count as Winston Cup wins for Chevrolet, but not for the man who won driving the Camaros. This discrepancy has been addressed in this Encyclopedia. When a man won a race, he has been awarded credit for winning that race.

This is essentially the way NASCAR interprets its races today. At Phoenix, Arizona, and Sears Point, California, a number of drivers competing for Winston West points compete with the Winston Cup regulars. If a Winston West driver happened to win the Phoenix or Sears Point event, he received Winston West points, and he also received credit for winning a Winston Cup event.

Sweepstakes Races

In the late 1950s, NASCAR conducted a number of "Sweepstakes" races, events that grouped two, sometimes three, different divisions. The Grand National hardtops (today's Winston Cup), Convertibles, and NASCAR Short Track Division (a separate series that competed on tracks shorter than a half-mile) cars all competed together. NASCAR's interpretation during that era was to credit the winner of the race with a victory *only* if he was in a Grand National (Winston Cup) car. If a Convertible car won the race, the highest Grand National finisher (sometimes, but not always) received credit for the win. In 1957, Whitey Norman received credit for winning a Sweepstakes race at Langhorne, Pennsylvania, when he finished second to Gwyn Staley's Convertible. Norman's victory was credited in the 1958 NASCAR *Record Book*, but his lone win had disappeared by 1959. Since Norman didn't actually win a race, NASCAR dropped his name from the victory list. And his name fails to show up anywhere in the Winston Cup kingdom as winning a race. Simply said, Whitey Norman finished second in the 1957 Langhorne race, and second place is what he is credited with in this *Encyclopedia*. In NASCAR's official records, no driver is credited with winning the 1957 Langhorne event.

In a 1959 Sweepstakes event staged in California, Harlan Richardson was the highest-finishing Grand National (Winston Cup) driver, but he finished in 16th place, 94 laps behind Parnelli Jones, who won the race in a Short Track Division car. For this event, NASCAR immediately credited Jones with winning the race, not Richardson, who was the highest-finishing Grand National driver. Yet for another Sweepstakes race in the same year, Bob Welborn won at Weaverville, North Carolina, in a Convertible, but NASCAR failed to credit him with a victory. Same year, but different interpretations in virtually identical situations.

Sound confusing? It has been, and interpretations today have contributed to that. In NASCAR's defense, there have been varying types of races throughout the years. In the 1950s, foreign cars were eligible in certain NASCAR Grand National (now Winston Cup) events. In fact, a Jaguar driven by Al Keller won NASCAR's first venture in road racing (on the airport runways at Linden, New Jersey, in 1954). A Volkswagen actually competed in an event at Langhorne. Corvettes, MGs, and Sprites also competed on occasion. NASCAR also had frequent personnel changes in its statistical department, and succeeding individuals had little definitive or historical background data to rely on. Thus, different evaluations in similar situations surfaced through the years. It is understandable that a number of these discrepancies have crept into the charted and uncharted records. NASCAR's annual Record Book did not begin publishing year-by-year driver records until 1969.

A Start is a Start

The Stock Car Racing Encyclopedia has credited drivers with finish positions regardless of the points, if any, they were competing for. A start is a start, a win is a win, and all drivers receive credit accordingly.

Post-season winnings have been credited for all years in this *Encyclopedia*. In the first two decades of Winston Cup racing, post-season awards were not officially credited to a driver's statistical record by the sanctioning body—only the winnings earned in the actual races were so credited. Beginning in 1971, the post-season Winston awards were counted in official NASCAR records, but not the NASCAR point money or any other post-season awards. Special event winnings were not counted until the mid-1980s. When Dale Earnhardt won the Busch Clash in 1980, the $50,000 he won was not credited to his annual or career earnings. When Earnhardt won the 1988 Busch Clash, the $75,000 he won that day was credited to him in official NASCAR records. In an effort to maintain consistency, all post-season and special event earnings have been credited to the driver.

From 1976–78, NASCAR failed to credit contingency awards for each and every race to any driver. It seems odd that David Pearson could win a 500-mile race at Darlington as late as 1976 and only get credit for the $11,670 in official NASCAR winnings. With the predetermined contingency money added, Pearson actually won $17,570. This practice by NASCAR was effective for only three years. In this *Encyclopedia*, the contingency money has been credited to the drivers during those years.

And in 1956

An unusual and unprecedented incident occurred in the 1956 season that has only recently been uncovered. A 300-mile event was staged at Langhorne, Pennsylvania. Five hundred points were originally awarded for first place with a drop of twenty points for each descending position. After NASCAR had released the official box score, it was determined that the Langhorne contest should have awarded 620 points for the winner with a drop of 24 points for each place in the finishing order. Speedy Thompson finished in third place and was originally awarded 460 points. After the "clerical error" was detected by NASCAR, Thompson's new point total should have been 572 points, an increase of 112 points. When NASCAR updated the new point totals, Thompson was credited with only 112 points, instead of 572. The error resulted in Thompson finishing third in the final point standings rather than second. It is odd that this error was never detected at the time. In this *Encyclopedia*, Thompson has been credited with finishing second in the final 1956 point standings.

In NASCAR's official final 1956 point standings, Tom Harbison was officially credited with 1,248 points, ranking him 39th overall. Harbison never competed in a Grand National (now Winston Cup) race and, accordingly, is not listed as ranking 39th in the 1956 season in this *Encyclopedia*.

Rankings

Driver rankings in this *Encyclopedia* reflect the driver's position in the final season point standings. Tie-breakers have been applied in all cases, but there are some instances where there have been absolute ties. For example, A. J. Foyt and Gary Bradberry tied for 70th in the 1994 final point standings. Each had one start and finished in 30th place, earning 73 points. That is regarded as an absolute tie.

In most cases, applying NASCAR's procedure for breaking ties will do just that—break the tie. If one or more drivers accumulate the same number of points, the driver with the highest finishing position gets the nod. If two drivers tie for the championship, the title goes to the driver who posts the most victories. If that number is the same, the procedure falls back to the driver finishing second the most times, and so on.

Pole Winners

Pole winners have been credited per NASCAR's structure for awarding poles. The procedure—or interpretation—has changed only once during the history of Winston Cup Grand National racing. Since 1990, the driver who registered the fastest run under the clock during the first round of qualifying has earned the pole position. On a number of occasions since 1990, the pole-winning driver has had an incident in practice before the race that forced him and his team to unload a backup car for the race. Prior to 1990, when a primary car was withdrawn from a race, the driver lost the pole.

The most memorable example of a driver losing the pole came in qualifying for the 1983 Daytona 500. Cale Yarborough zipped through the timing lights at 200.503 mph on his first of two qualifying laps, but flipped his Chevrolet on the second lap, destroying the car. His time, fastest in the first qualifying round, earned him the pole. However, the pole-winning car had suffered irreparable damage and team owner Harry Ranier made the decision to withdraw the car. The official pole for the 1983 Daytona 500 went to the second-fastest qualifier, Ricky Rudd, who had posted a 198.864 mph lap. Yarborough had to requalify in the backup car, and he wound up winning the Daytona 500 six days later. But he didn't get credit for winning the pole.

Another similar ruling occurred in the inaugural Talladega 500 in 1969. Charlie Glotzbach had earned the pole with a qualifying lap of 199.466 mph, but when his car was withdrawn in the driver's boycott of the event, Bobby Isaac went down on record as winning the pole with a speed of 196.386 mph. Isaac had posted the seventh-fastest qualifying lap in the first round of time trials, but since the first six cars were withdrawn, Isaac officially wound up with the pole.

A Few Incompletes

During the formative years, record-keeping for NASCAR Grand National (now Winston Cup) racing was not as thorough as it is today, and many of the records have been discarded. Our records are 99% complete, but some of the drivers' finishing positions for 1951 have not been determined. Often a top-ten finishing order was released, but other competitors who started the race were not assigned finishing positions in any particular order. On a few occasions, the number of drivers and the number of starters were not the same. Some positions have been left blank. For these events, a driver has simply been listed as competing in the race without a definite finish position.

Lap Leaders

NASCAR did not include lap leaders for the Winston Cup Grand National events until the early 1970s. Through years of research, most of the lap leaders in each race have been determined. Not surprisingly, statistics for the early years have been the most difficult to locate. In events where complete lap leaders are not available, the winning driver is credited with leading one lap—the last one. The final lap is the only one that is assured. Accordingly, the figures for lap leaders for the early years are quite low. Lee Petty, Herb Thomas, the Flock brothers, and many others certainly led more laps than are indicated, but until the missing links are found, there is little else that can be done.

We have uncovered most of the race results from the beginning of NASCAR's elite stock car racing series, but we are interested in any additional information that you, the reader, may have. We not only invite you to contribute any additional information, we encourage it.

—Greg Fielden

ACKNOWLEDGMENTS

This book would not be complete without our acknowledgment of all the people who tirelessly worked to make this first edition a reality.

First, our thanks to Jeanine Bucek, the editor who gave this book a home at Macmillan, and to Ken Samelson, the editor who drove this project across the finish line.

Neil Reshen and Dawn Reshen-Doty of Benay Enterprises, Inc., would like to thank Carolyn Jack, Linda Cooke & Suzanne Hilton for all of their help and assistance.

Peter Golenbock wishes to thank the following for their many kindnesses: Jonathan Mauk, the curator of NASCAR's photo library, for helping supply the photos for this book, and Donna Freismuth, Tom Cotter, Humpy Wheeler, Jimmy Johnson, Ed Carroll, Ralph Moody, and Tim Flock for their longtime support and assistance, and to all those racers, crew chiefs, mechanics, and other friends in NASCAR who have been so kind to me over the years.

Greg Fielden expresses his special thanks to P.J. Hollebrand and Allan E. Brown for their invaluable assistance with this project, and to Jon Mauk, Fletcher Williams, Tim and Frances Flock, Hank Schoolfield, Larry Jendras Jr., Doris Roberts, Dink Gardner, Tim Milecki, Bob Wecks, Lawson Diggett, Houston Lawing, Patricia Fielden, Don O'Reilly, K.C. Breslauer, Halifax Historical Society, Morris and Jeanne Metcalfe, Paul Dalton, Dorothy Davis, Owen Kearns Jr., Mitzi Teague, Fred Bince, Dave Rodman, Larry Belewski, Ken Clapp, Chris Economaki, and Marty Little.

On the editorial and production side, we would like to thank publisher Natalie Chapman, George Yates of Yates Engineering Systems, Seiji Ogata, Chris Dreyer, Cheryl Mamaril, Helen Chin, Barry Rogers, Sheri Hyman, Christina Sheldon, and Bob Cherry.

INTRODUCTION
A Brief History of Stock Car Racing
By Peter Golenbock

The Bootleggers

When the sport of stock car racing first began to organize itself in the late '40s, the leading drivers were mostly bootleggers, men who ran whiskey from illegal stills to hundreds of markets across the Southeast. They were the real Dukes of Hazzard, only there was nothing funny about their business. Driving at high speeds at night, often with the police in pursuit, was dangerous. Jail and loss of livelihood were the penalties for losing the race.

The bootleggers had faster cars. They could go 95 miles an hour in first gear, 115 in second. Few police cars could go faster than 95. The bootleggers' cars also had better equipment, notably special springs and shocks for handling on the turns. Parts were imported from California, where the hot rod was king.

The local sheriffs were intent on catching bootleggers not so much because selling untaxed whiskey was illegal, but because if the sheriff could catch his prey, he then could sell the car at auction and reap half the returns. Often the bootlegger bought back his own car, and the cat-and-mouse game began anew.

Sheriffs went to great lengths to corral the faster, better-handling cars. Some tried attaching a cowcatcherlike device (like a large ice tongs) to the bumper. The trick was to catch a bootlegger with a full load going up a hill and clamp onto the car before he could get away. To combat the clamp, the bootleggers resorted to putting the bumpers on with coat-hanger wire. They'd latch on, the bootlegger would floor it, and the fender would roll under the front wheels of the revenuer's car and get tangled. By the time the revenuer got the bumper free, the whiskey runner was long gone.

Other sheriffs relied on their marksmanship, shooting the bootlegger's radiator with a shotgun. Some bootleggers countered by installing a steel plate to protect the radiator, others put the radiator in the trunk and ran air scoops from the front to cool the engine.

To keep the sheriffs from catching them, the bootleggers had tricks of their own. They made bootleg turns, spinning 180 degrees and driving off in the other direction; spilled oil on the roads; tried smokescreens; created roads where there were none; and devised a system of using a second car to block the sheriff while the car with the load got away. The old Burt Reynolds—Jackie Gleason *Smokey and the Bandit* movies weren't far off the mark. To stay in business, the kingpins also paid off the sheriffs, something even the movies didn't talk about.

Tim Flock, NASCAR champion in 1952 and 1955, came from a family of bootleggers-racers (along with brothers Fonty and Bob). Tim recalled that the first race among the bootleggers was held in the mid-1930s in a cow pasture in the town of Stockbridge, Georgia, about fifteen miles outside Atlanta.

"We didn't have no tickets, no safety equipment, no fences, no nothing. Just a bunch of these bootleggers who'd been arguing all week about who had the fastest car would get together and prove it."

According to Flock, the participants formed a track by running around and around an oval about a half-mile round until the tires dug up enough dirt to make the course visible.

"These guys would run and bet against their own cars, betting who had the fastest car. That night they'd be hauling liquor in the same car. About fifty people saw this dust cloud and came up trying to see what was causing it." The next time, the crowd swelled to a hundred. Then it tripled. Before long, the cars were racing every Sunday. (According to Flock, the car owners would buy four tires from Sears & Roebuck on Saturday, race them on Sunday, and bring them back on Monday. "Naw, I don't know how they got wore out so fast.") By the 1940s, a crowd of five thousand at a stock car race was not uncommon.

Among the moonshine haulers famed for their racing skills were such racers as the three Flock brothers, who worked for their uncle, Peachtree Williams, one of the biggest bootleggers in the state of Georgia; Curtis Turner; Bob Smith; the Martin boys; Clay Earles, the owner of the Martinsville Speedway; Buddy Shuman, who was once shot in the neck while running moonshine; Wendell Scott, an African-American racer who was once arrested when he had to swerve at high speed to avoid hitting a bunch of drunks walking on the highway and skidded off the road into a house; and the most famous of them all, Junior Johnson, who drove hundreds of sorties delivering moonshine. Johnson, dubbed the Last American Hero by author Tom Wolfe, was often chased by the law but was never caught behind the wheel of a car.

"Making moonshine was a hand-me-down trade that came down through the generations," said Johnson. "By the time one was too old to make it, another had already picked it up. It was important that the location of the still be kept secret, because the revenuers were out there looking for it. Sometimes the moonshiners put [the stills] underground, put them in buildings. They would be back in the woods where no one could see them or find them. There were a lot of ways to conceal them. It was a cat-and-mouse game."

The bootleggers knew the names of the revenuers and vice versa. Several years before he obtained a driver's license, Johnson was driving from his home in Ronda, North Carolina, to cities such as Lexington, High Point, Greensboro, Winston-Salem, and Charlotte. Like the other bootleggers, Johnson learned how to make the motors fast and how to make the cars drive well. Two or three times a night, every night, Johnson and the others made their runs. "It was hard, dangerous, scary work," said Johnson. "I did that from the time I was thirteen until I was in the mid-twenties, 365 days a year, seven or eight times a week, probably more."

Johnson drove his first stock car race at age sixteen at a North Wilkesboro dirt track in a race among the local bootleggers. His brother and he had fixed up the car, and when they got to the track his brother told him, "You drive." He did, with the same reckless abandon he had demonstrated on his moonshine runs.

Recalled Ralph Moody, "Back then the drivers were rough, boy. There was always some kind of fight going on. They'd wangbang out there, but if someone figured it was a little bit out of line, if the guy figured you were too rough, there was a fight."

Moody recalled the time Junior Johnson and Lee Petty were running at the old Fairgrounds at Charlotte. The race was fifty laps, and Johnson was winning about three-quarters of the way through. Petty couldn't catch him, so he kept banging into Johnson's left rear, trying to spin him out and knock him out of the way. Finally, Petty managed to cut Johnson's tire.

Johnson was driving for the Wood brothers, and when he came into pit, he told Glen and Leonard Wood, "Put a tire on it."

Glen said, "Oh, no. Oh, no." Moody, standing next to Glen, asked him, "Oh, no?" Said Glen, "We're in for it now."

Said Moody, "They put a tire on it, and Junior went out there, and he sailed around there, and here came Lee Petty. Junior let Petty by and ran him down the end of the racetrack and never shut it down and ran him off the end of the big pigpen out there and over the wall. Petty went sailing clear out of the racetrack! The race was coming to an end, and Junior knocked him out just so Lee couldn't win it."

The first big race Johnson drove was at Darlington in 1952, a 200-mile Modified-Sportsman race hastily added to the NASCAR schedule to compete with an IndyCar race slated for Raleigh, North Carolina, on the July 4th weekend. The race lacked the flair of a late model event because Bill France, who ran NASCAR, the top racing body in the area, favored using new cars in his races. "He felt people could relate to the new cars," said Johnson. "If you were driving a '51 Ford, and a '51 Ford was running on the racetrack, you could relate to it better than to a '34 Ford modified to run. France was the one who started NASCAR, and he had a lot to do with everybody's career in racing. I don't think there's a single soul in racing today who Bill France Sr. wasn't a big booster in their career."

NASCAR's Founding Father

William Henry Getty France was 25 years old when he moved from Washington, D.C., to Daytona Beach, Florida, in 1934 to escape the ice and cold of the north. France had two middle names because his parents hoped the Getty name would bring their son riches. He had been into cars since high school, when he and a buddy named Hugh Ostermeyer built a canvas-covered race car with a Model T engine capable of running 90 miles an hour.

In Washington, D.C., he had worked in car garages and service stations, driven in sprint car races, won, and too often got burned by promoters who skipped out with the proceeds.

He remembered one race in 1930 in a town called Pikesville, Maryland, where a winning purse of $500 was trumpeted. He finished fourth. When he went for his prize money, he was told the winner got $50 and he $10. France, angry, wanted to know why, when the purse was supposed to be $500. He was told that the larger purse had been announced as a ploy to impress the fans.

He had been working for a service station, and during winter his job was to venture out onto the street and restart dead batteries. France knew his future was in fixing cars, and he decided that if he were going to be laying on his back, he wanted to be where he could feel warm and comfortable. He had heard talk of how fast Florida was developing. Florida was his destination. Exactly where in Florida, however, he wasn't sure.

France, his wife, Annie, and their infant son, Bill Jr., headed south in his Hupmobile. On a beautiful fall day they stopped their car on the sands of Daytona Beach to go swimming. The beauty of the place charmed them. Bill and Annie decided to end their journey. They rented a little, one-bedroom, furnished house for $15 a month. France got a job first as a house painter, and soon thereafter as a mechanic at J. Saxton Lloyd's Buick-Pontiac-Cadillac garage.

In March 1935, with France in attendance, Sir Malcolm Campbell drove his supercharged V-8 to a land-speed record of 276 miles an hour on the sands of Daytona Beach. The problem for Campbell and other land-speed racers was that though the Daytona Beach sand was wide, flat, firm, and long enough for most races, Campbell's incredible speed made racing there too dangerous. He needed a longer, flatter, smoother, less windy course.

Later that year, Campbell took his Bluebird to the beds of Utah's Bonneville Salt Flats and broke the record at 301 miles an hour. Daytona Beach was abandoned forever as the land-speed capital.

In an effort to resuscitate the city's racing reputation and a flagging economy, Daytona city officials staged a AAA-sanctioned 250-mile stock car race for all comers on March 8, 1936. The man in charge was a well-known racing promoter named Sig Haugdahl. He devised a combination beach-road race with the backstretch and turns on the sand and the front straightaway on the paved street closest to the beach.

It was a handicap race with the slower qualifiers leaving the line first. Twenty-seven drivers entered, including France, who drove a Ford owned by a man named Glen Brooks. France started tenth, leaving about eight minutes after the slowest Willys.

The initial race had some problems. The worst was if you drove too slow, you got stuck in the sand; if you went too fast, you risked turning over.

The heaviest cars got stuck in the sand, and because speeds were slower than expected, the tide came in before the race was over. The north turn was completely blocked with stuck cars at around the two-hundred-mile mark when the officials called it.

Shortened prematurely, it took several days for racing officials to figure out that Milt "Red" Marion had won. Bill France, who swore he passed Marion a couple of times, was awarded fifth place, twelve laps back. Marion won $1,700 in prize money and France received $375. At that time the minimum wage was $14.50 a week.

The other negative was that because there was no way to fence in the entire course, thousands of spectators watched the race without paying. The city fathers lost $22,000 on the promotion.

The following year the Elks Club took a crack at the promotion, running a fifty-mile race to ensure the tides wouldn't be a factor. The crowd was so anemic the winning driver was awarded a purse of $43. The Elks were dissuaded from ever doing that again.

The Chamber of Commerce needed to find a person or group to promote the race. It asked France, whose Pure Oil gas station on Main Street had become a headquarters for the local racers, if he knew anyone who might be interested in putting on the race.

France had been racing a 1937 Ford coupe owned by a local restaurant owner named Charlie Reese on the weekends. Reese asked France if he would have an interest in taking on the promotion.

France foresaw that the race had a future if run right. He saw that when a motorcycle race was organized, fans flocked to see it. He figured the lack of success of the stock car event was a result of inadequate or inept promotion.

France told Reese, "I can get the cars and the drivers, but I don't have any money."

Replied Reese, "I'll put up the money and you can do the work." France agreed, and that first year sold forty-five hundred tickets at fifty cents apiece. The next year they raised ticket prices to a dollar, and after donating 10 percent to the Bundles for Britain campaign, France and Reese split $2,000. The annual beach race at Daytona was saved.

Bill France Organizes

On December 12, 1947, Bill France gathered racing promoters from around the Southeast for a meeting at the Ebony Bar atop the Streamline Hotel in Daytona Beach. France saw the need to set up an organization of promoters, mechanics, and drivers to regulate the sport.

Acutely aware that unscrupulous promoters were negatively affecting the image of the sport, Bill France believed that an association of racing promoters was needed for the sport to grow. To enhance competition, France wanted to see a set of rules that would keep the cars, and the competition, uniform. His other goals were to provide insurance for the drivers and to inaugurate a point system so drivers could compete for a driving championship.

France had attempted to promote his beach race as a "national championship" only to be told he could not do that unless he had rules, a point championship, and an organization that crossed more than one state line. The rebuff likely was the impetus for his call to organize. Yet as far back as 1938, when France began promoting the race on the beach at Daytona, he had expressed his belief that the sport was in need of a set of rules to keep cars uniform and the competition equal.

At the end of that 1938 beach race, the first racer to cross the finish line was driver Smokey Purser. After Purser received the checkered flag, he drove away from the beach and out of sight. The race's technical director, Ed Parkinson, figured Purser was hiding something. Purser was promptly disqualified.

During the organization meeting France expressed his feeling that the first and foremost goal should be equal competition. He sought to codify the rules to help reduce cheating. If this was to be "stock" car racing, each car mechanic had to know what he could or could not do. France knew it wouldn't be possible to catch everyone, but he knew he had to at least try to curb the most flagrant abusers.

As part of the new organization, France said, he wanted the sport to be able to list its champions, to memorialize their records and their earnings. As a promoter France was aware of the importance of records and statistics, and he kept records of who led after each lap as a clever way of involving local merchants in his races.

Among the prizes France had awarded in the 1938 race on the beach at Daytona to lap leaders were a bottle of rum, $2.50 credit at a local men's clothing store, a box of fancy Hav-a-Tampa cigars, a case of Pennzoil motor oil, a pair of $5 sunglasses from Walgreen's, two cases of Blue Ribbon beer, and a $25 credit on any automobile in Dick Rose's used car lot. This element of sponsor involvement has never changed. The only difference today is the amount awarded by sponsors.

France made one other proposal, one that was to distance and distinguish his new organization from all other racing groups. It was the notion of only allowing new cars in the races. France told the other promoters, "We need to think about our image. If you race a junky-looking automobile—even if you take a new Cadillac, take the bumpers off, and let it get real dirty—then in people's minds it would still be a jalopy.

"We need to have races for the most modern automobiles available. Plain, ordinary working people have to be able to associate with the cars. Standard street stock cars are what we should be running."

France's reasoning bordered on genius. He could not have foreseen a day when the car manufacturers would pump millions of dollars into racing but, ultimately, that was the result of his thinking. When, in 1950, Joe Littlejohn drove his Olds 88 Rocket 98.840 miles an hour to win the pole in France's beach race, it gave a big boost to Olds 88 sales. No new cars were made during World War II (nor was there any auto racing; Bill France built sub chasers during the war) but once the war ended, the car manufacturers used racing to sell and promote their products as Hudsons, Chevys, Chryslers, and Fords vied on the NASCAR circuit. The dealers' slogan became, "Win on Sunday, sell on Monday."

At that historic meeting Bill France was named president of the organization. When a name for the organization was requested, the first suggestion was NSCRA, the National Stock Car Racing Association. But a small group in Georgia already had the name, and so driver-mechanic Red Vogt suggested an alternative, the National Association for Stock Car Automobile Racing. There was some concern that NASCAR sounded a lot like Nash Car (Nash was a minor auto manufacturer), but the recommendation was seconded and passed.

The group needed money to incorporate. Louis Ossinsky, a Daytona Beach attorney who was a customer at Bill France's gas station, volunteered to do the work. The incorporation date was February 21, 1948. Its headquarters were located at 88 Main Street.

In order to give this new organization some publicity and clout, France hired the world-famous endurance record driver Erwin "Cannonball" Baker to be NASCAR's Commissioner of Racing. Baker, who knew cars, was known to be fair, and his authority gave the new organization needed prestige.

The First "New Car" Race

The first "new car" race was held at the Charlotte Speedway on June 19, 1949. It called for two hundred laps over the three-quarter-mile dirt oval. Beside Fords, Oldsmobiles, Buicks, and Chryslers, there were Hudsons, Lincolns, a Mercury, and even a Kaiser. Under the new rules set down by Bill France and NASCAR, the cars had to come off the showroom floor. There could be no tampering, no souping up of the engines. For this season, the oldest a competing car could be was a 1946 model.

The Charlotte race, the first ever in the Grand National championship series, was won by Glenn Dunnaway in a '47 Ford owned by Hubert Westmoreland. After the race inspectors discovered a wedge that had been placed to stiffen the rear springs of Dunnaway's car. The car had been used during the week for bootlegging. The use of a wedge was typical in bootleggers' cars, but it was in violation of NASCAR's rules. Dunnaway was disqualified; the victory and the $2,000 first-place prize money were given to Jim Roper, who drove a '49 Lincoln.

The other drivers, among them Tim and Fonty Flock and Red Byron, were convinced that Dunnaway hadn't known about the wedge and chipped in part of their purses. Dunnaway went home richer than if he had won.

Car owner Hubert Westmoreland sued, claiming his car was stock and demanding his prize money. Discussing the illegal wedge in court, the lawyer for NASCAR kept repeating the term "bootlegger" over and over. NASCAR won the case.

The era during which most of the cars were owned by bootleggers had come to an end.

The Early Sponsors

In 1955 a millionaire by the name of Carl Kiekhaefer entered the sport. He owned the Mercury Outboard motor company, and he chose to race Chrysler cars. Kiekhaefer's initial reason for entering racing was to learn more about motors in order to improve his boat engines. He also advertised his product, writing "Mercury Outboards" on the side of his car in big block letters. When it became clear that Kiekhaefer's advertising was selling a lot of Mercury cars, he changed the lettering to read "Kiekhaefer Outboards."

Carl Kiekhaefer changed the face of racing. He spent a great deal of money preparing his car, paid his driver Tim Flock

a lord's salary of $40,000 a year, and dominated the '55 season, winning 18 poles and 18 Grand National races.

The next year Kiekhaefer sponsored as many as six drivers, including Buck Baker, Tim Flock, Speedy Thompson, and Charlie Scott, the first African American to compete at NASCAR's elite level. Kiekhaefer's cars won twenty-one of the first twenty-five races in 1956. From March 25 through May 30, Kiekhaefer's cars won sixteen consecutive races, still a record for a car owner. But Kiefhaefer made the lives of his drivers intolerable. He ordered them around, prevented them from sleeping with their wives the night before the race, and made them fill out reports after a race. When Tim Flock quit early in the 1956 season and his replacement, Herb Thomas, also quit Kiekhaefer late that summer, the team suffered during the last part of the season, winning only four of the final twenty starts. In two years Kiekhaefer's cars won fifty-two of the ninety races entered, but he had become disillusioned and he retired from racing forever at the end of 1956. Many years later, Kiekhaefer was elected to the Hall of Fame.

Because of Kiekhaefer's success selling outboard motors (and Mercury cars) through his racing exposure, in 1957 General Motors and Ford decided to get involved in racing big time. The factories spent a lot of money preparing their cars. On the Chevy payroll were some of the top drivers, including Buck Baker, Speedy Thompson, Jack Smith, Rex White, and Frankie Schneider. Ford picked John Holman to run its team, and Holman hired as his drivers Fireball Roberts, Curtis Turner, Joe Weatherly, Bill Amick, Marvin Panch, and Ralph Moody. Driving for Pontiac were Banjo Matthews and Cotton Owens. Billy Myers and Jim Paschal drove for Mercury. Lee Petty and Ralph Earnhardt drove Oldsmobiles, and Johnny Allen drove for Plymouth. Everyone else ran independently on the cheap.

It was a very exciting time in racing, but the infusion of car factory money was short lived. On May 19, 1957, in a race at Martinsville, Billy Myers and Tom Pistone collided. Myers's Mercury hurtled the retaining wall and hit four spectators standing near a sign that read "No Spectators Allowed." Among the four spectators was eight-year-old Alvin Helsabeck, who had to undergo brain surgery. The headlines were on front pages across America. The car companies were horrified by the negative publicity.

Two weeks later, the car companies completely withdrew their sponsorship and support. The drivers suddenly found themselves the owners of their cars. The withdrawal of the factories was a shock, but Bill France was undeterred. NASCAR needed an infusion of excitement to hold the fans' interest, and France himself provided the electric jolt to the fortunes of NASCAR with the opening in February of 1959 of the Daytona International Speedway.

The Age of the Superspeedway

During a poker game in 1949, stock car race promoter Harold Brasington proposed that an asphalt track be built near his home in Darlington, South Carolina. Brasington had visited the Indianapolis Speedway, and he envisioned building a similar track for stock cars.

Brasington took a huge risk but with the advance sale of $25,000 worth of tickets, he was able to complete construction. Brasington, who had competed in Bill France's beach races in Daytona, originally gave the race sanction to the Central States Racing Association, but when he found himself short on drivers, he called France and invited him to view the site. France, impressed, pledged his NASCAR drivers.

On September 4, 1950, Darlington International Raceway's first Southern 500 was staged, four hundred laps around a mile-and-a-quarter paved track. Seventy-five cars competed. It took fifteen days to qualify the field. There were few hotels to accommodate the crowds, but that first year 25,000 fans flocked to see the race.

The favorites were Red Byron and Curtis Turner, but the winner was Johnny "Madman" Mantz from Long Beach, California. Mantz qualified forty-third, but he won because his car was light and, through his Indy racing, he had connections with tire people in Dayton, Ohio, and was able to put heavy-duty truck tires, similar to Indy-style tires, on his car.

During the race Mantz changed tires but three times. The cars using standard tires had to change tires as many as twenty-four times. Twenty-two cars had blowouts. Mantz averaged 75.25 miles an hour to win.

When he crossed the finish line, the second car, driven by Glenn "Fireball" Roberts, was nine laps back. The co-owners of Mantz's 1950 Plymouth, which was used to run business errands during the week, were mechanic Hubert Westmoreland, NASCAR starter and flagman Alvin Hawkins, and Bill France.

Bill France became enamored of the superspeedway concept. He had been trying to coerce the ruling political body of Daytona Beach to allow him to build a similar facility since 1949. He felt that stock car racing needed a track that was wide and banked so cars could run in different grooves and pass in the turns. IndyCar racing had been king up to that time, but France believed the Indy track too narrow for stock car racing; the cars would have to run single file around the turns, and because the track was flat, the wear on the cars would be too great.

France wanted to build a paved track at Daytona because he foresaw that the growth in popularity of his beach race would soon clash with the growth of the beach community. In anticipation of the day when he would be barred from staging his race, he began lobbying for a permanent facility in order to make sure Daytona Beach didn't lose motor sports racing.

A Racing and Recreation District was formed, land was bought, and France got a ninety-nine-year lease. The chairman of the commission was J. Saxton Lloyd, who owned the Buick and Cadillac dealership where France had worked when he first moved to Daytona Beach.

France sold 300,000 shares of stock at one dollar a share and then had to borrow $600,000 from oil millionaire Clint Murchison and his financial advisor, Howard Sluyter. France could have built a conventional track with the original money, but he was so committed to his vision of a banked track that he refused to compromise. He went deep into personal debt to see the realization of his dream.

France started selling tickets and used a lot of the ticket money for construction costs. His track was such a success that he paid off the original $600,000 loan only ten years after the Daytona International Speedway opened.

When the Daytona International Speedway opened in 1959, the drivers marveled. Where Darlington was a fast mile-and-three-eighths track, Daytona was two-and-a-half miles around, and with its long straightaways, breathtaking speeds of over 140 miles an hour were attainable.

Said Speedway President Jim Foster, "Mr. France had something that none of the others had, and that was vision. Bill France was a visionary. He saw where the sport was going to go, and he believed in it strongly, risked every penny he had. When he built his Speedway, he went deep in debt, and for years afterward was besieged by creditors. And when the others were selling their Daytona Speedway stock, he bought. And Daytona was a huge success, and he built the Talladega track, and he bought Darlington, and he bought Watkins Glen, and it's all because Bill France had this vision. Bill France was the one who took on the risk. It's the risktakers who become wealthy. And mostly it's those who refused to take that risk who were left bitter and angry."

Concluded Foster, "Without Bill France, there would have been no NASCAR, would have been no racing as we know it today."

At Daytona, cars could go thirty to forty miles an hour faster than they had driven before. All the drivers felt like rookies on the new track. Said driver Jimmy Thompson about the new track, "There have been other tracks that separated the men from the boys. This is the track that will separate the brave from the weak after the boys are gone."

When driver Lee Petty saw the huge track at Daytona for the first time, he realized that his world of short-track, dirt-track racing soon would be coming to an end.

"We knew stock car racing was never going to be the same again," he said.

The Early Legends

Smokey Yunick was a controversial owner-mechanic genius who was renowned for his innovative engine and chassis designs. His cars won scores of races with Herb Thomas, and later he won with drivers Paul Goldsmith, Fireball Roberts, and Marcin Panch.

Said Yunick about Thomas, who during the week was a dirt farmer, "Herb Thomas could really drive. He was smart in the race. He knew how to pace himself. He was as good as they came, and they have never given him enough credit for his ability."

Another of Yunick's favorites was old breed Buck Baker, driving champion in 1956 and 1957 (winner of forty-six races).

Said Yunick, "Buck was a wild son of a bitch. He had a nasty streak. When he got drunk, he'd show off. He was bad about fighting, and when he got drunk he was a nasty son of a bitch."

That's the way it was back then, rough and tumble. Ralph Moody, who began racing in the 1930s, remembers the old timers. An itinerant race driver, Moody settled in the Charlotte area in 1956. Moody became partners with a man named John Holman, and the new concern began under the name Holman & Moody, which quickly became the premier car-building firm in racing. At its peak in 1960 Holman & Moody built four hundred race cars. Holman was the businessman, Moody the brains of the operation.

Driving for the Holman–Moody team were most of the legendary drivers of the period: Curtis Turner, Joe Weatherly, Marvin Panch, Fireball Roberts, Freddy Lorenzen, and Junior Johnson.

The stories told about these legendary racers reflect a period in America that today seems long gone. The Depression created a class of hungry, often fierce, competitive men without formal educations who dragged themselves up by their bootstraps and retained that inner drive, even after they attained success.

Lee Petty, who won fifty-four races, came from a farming background. During the Depression he sold biscuits and later had a small trucking business. He turned to racing and, like many before and after him, found out just how tough it was to be an independent owner-driver. Petty, unlike most of the others, was a family man and too serious about winning races to party late into the night. He was also a churlish despot who would do anything to win. One time in the mid-1950s, Petty put wing nuts and armor plating on the side of his Oldsmobile, so that anytime his car brushed against the side of another car, he'd shred the opponent's sheet metal. Charlton Heston's enemy had done that to him during the chariot race in *Ben-Hur*; Lee Petty did it for real.

One time during a race at High Point, Petty came into the pits. His son, Richard, a member of the pit crew, climbed up on the hood to wipe the mud off the windshield. The crew finished changing tires, and without saying a word to Richard, Lee Petty drove away, with a petrified Richard still on the car, hanging on. Lee drove one entire lap before he returned to the pit road to let Richard off. After the race, he cussed out the boy. When Richard himself began to race, there were times when Lee bumped him and caused him to crash, so great was Lee's desire to win.

Unlike the serious Petty, life for Curtis Turner (seventeen wins), Joe Weatherly (twenty-five wins), and Fireball Roberts (thirty-three wins) was a never-ending string of parties and competitions that ended in their early deaths.

On the track Turner was a fearsome competitor who would think nothing of forcing you off the track if you were in his way. Turner had a feel for how far he could push his race car. He could get his car completely sideways at 135 miles an hour and save it, where other drivers would lose control.

Off the track Turner loved women, V.O. and 7-Up, and flying. He had a saying, "If you feel bad enough before you start a race, nothing can happen to bother you." Turner, the quintessential partier, wouldn't invite you back to his fourteen-acre home if you didn't get drunk at one of his parties, which might last a week. At one shindig Joe Weatherly was seen using a fire extinguisher to serve drinks in flower vases. Young girls danced on tables. Guests lay on the floor passed out. Said Tim Flock, "Curtis was a party man."

Turner was a businessman who made, and then lost, millions. He sold timber, owned movie theaters, and with Bruton Smith built the Charlotte Motor Speedway, before it went broke. Humpy Wheeler, who later became president of the Speedway, often said that Turner's mistake was trying to mix racing with business.

In 1961 Turner sought to organize the NASCAR drivers for the Teamsters Union. Turner wanted the drivers to receive 40 percent of the gate receipts. He was also hoping Teamster boss Jimmy Hoffa would help him save his failing track. But in return for their support, Hoffa had Turner ask for parimutuel betting on the races.

Turner had once teamed with NASCAR head Bill France in a Pan American Road Race, and he had saved their lives when he averted a plunge off a steep cliff by driving the car into the rocks on the other side of the road. Despite their shared past, France broke Turner's efforts, threatening to close the tracks, find new drivers and put the old ones out of work. Turner found himself isolated. France banned Turner from racing for life but after four years, Turner begged forgiveness, and France allowed him to return.

Turner, an expert pilot, often took businessmen up in his airplane to sell them timber. According to Tim Flock, he'd have them so scared they would be afraid to look out the window. Said Flock, "He would fly over the worst timber in the world and say, 'There's some damn fine timber down there,' and they'd say, 'Okay. Okay. Can we go back down to the ground now?' And that's why he sold so much timber."

A jokester, Turner had the habit of turning off one of the two engines in mid-flight and pretending he didn't know what was wrong. He would say to a passenger who had never flown before, "Go ahead, you fly it."

Turner died on a Sunday afternoon in October 1970 when his Aerocommander crashed into a hill near Du Bois, Pennsylvania, twenty minutes after takeoff. His body was found a half-block away in the woods. The passenger, golf pro Clarence King, was strapped in the cockpit seat. Speculation was that while Curtis was sleeping off a toot in the back, King suffered a heart attack, and the plane crashed.

Turner's sidekick was Little Joe Weatherly. They were the Don Quixote and Sancho Panza of stock car racing, drinking buddies, hell raisers. Weatherly, who got his start driving motorcycles, loved to play practical jokes. He had a stuffed mongoose in a box, and he'd pop it open and scare the unsuspecting. He wore one suit that was half gray and half red.

Weatherly spoke in short, staccato bursts, and when he got excited ran his words together and talked "four thousand miles an hour," according to Humpy Wheeler, who recalled the night Weatherly bet Fireball Roberts that Roberts couldn't back up his brand-new, black and gold Pontiac at a high speed. Roberts, of course, took the bet. They marked a course, at the end of which were three-foot-high wooden telephone poles that Weatherly had made invisible by painting them black.

Wheeler was sitting in the back seat when Roberts flew backward, hit an unseen pole, and bent the back of the car almost in half. Wheeler, who was lucky he wasn't killed, had a sore neck for a week.

Because Weatherly was very superstitious, other drivers drove him crazy by throwing peanuts onto his seat before a race. He also thought the color green brought him bad luck so, of course, they were always bringing him something green.

Weatherly also loved to fly, even though he never learned how to make flight plans or use the instruments, including the radio. Sometimes he flew in a direction opposite of what he was intending. One time on a trip to Dayton, Ohio, he was quite surprised when he passed by the top of the Empire State Building in New York. On another trip, from Darlington to Charlotte, he ended up in Spartanburg.

Joe Weatherly died on January 19, 1964, at Riverside, California, during the fifth race of the season. Little Joe was trying to catch the eventual winner, Dan Gurney, but the brakes of his Mercury failed, and Weatherly went wide into the dangerous turn six and hit the wall on the left side. He wasn't going more than eighty-five miles an hour, but the impact caused his head to fly out the driver's window, and his skull slapped against the concrete wall, killing him. His was the first death in a Grand National Race in seven years.

Glenn "Fireball" Roberts, perhaps the first superstar in stock car racing, received what proved to be fatal burns in a fiery crash at Charlotte on May 24, 1964, four months after Weatherly's fatal crash. Roberts, who had won thirty-three races in a career that began in 1947, was talking of retirement at the time of his death. He had started young and was able to beat all comers until a young driver named Fred Lorenzen challenged him and proved himself superior. On the day Roberts was severely burned, according to Lorenzen, Roberts didn't want to race. Weatherly's death still haunted him, and the fire to race had burned itself out. His desire was gone.

Banjo Matthews, then a driver and later one of the sport's most famous body fabricators until his death in October 1996, remembers that Roberts was losing his skills. He had spun out on superspeedways during practice a couple of times. Roberts, who had socked away a lot of money, talked to Matthews about retiring. He talked of going to work for a beer distributorship to do public relations. According to fellow driver and friend Neil Castles, he intended to become a radio broadcaster. He had been taking a course in public speaking.

The night before the accident, Roberts and Ned Jarrett sat poolside at a motel and talked. Roberts said his competitive edge was missing. He talked about quitting. For Roberts, the thrill was ebbing. His nerves were beginning to jangle.

The morning of Roberts's crash, Banjo Matthews helped Roberts put on his uniform. Roberts complained that the flame retardant fiberglass in the uniform made him break out in a rash. As a result, he cut his sleeves off. According to Matthews, Roberts told him he didn't feel up to racing.

"Glenn," said Mathews, "get your ass up and go get in your car and go home."

"I can't do that," said Roberts. Matthews wanted to know why.

"Because all these people are here to see me race," Roberts said. He said he also felt obligated to Ford and his sponsors.

During the race at Charlotte, Junior Johnson hooked the rear of Ned Jarrett's car, spinning out both cars. Roberts came down the straightaway, swerved to avoid Johnson and Jarrett, and smashed into an opening in the concrete wall. After the car became airborn, it turned upside down and the fuel tank broke open, with the fuel cascading into the car. Back then there was no rubber bladder or fuel cell to prevent spilled gas. When the car came to a stop, the fuel began to pool around the car.

Suddenly, the lavender car with the white number "22" ignited. Fire raged. Roberts, strapped in the car, knew to hold his breath to keep the flames from searing his lungs. As the conflagration burned all around Roberts, Ned Jarrett tried to pull him out.

"My God, Ned," said Roberts, "help me. I'm on fire."

The heroic Jarrett finally did pull him out, burning his own hands. Once he got Roberts out, he began tearing off the driver's clothing. Roberts, still conscious, helped him. The rescue squad finished, and the racer was taken by helicopter to Charlotte Memorial Hospital. He was burned over 80 percent of his body.

For a while it looked like Roberts would make it, despite his third-degree burns. "He is a remarkable patient," announced his doctors, who after several weeks said he was improving. But after an operation to remove burned skin on June 30, his condition worsened. Pneumonia set in. He lapsed into a coma and never regained consciousness. Glenn "Fireball" Roberts died on July 2, 1964, of the burns, pneumonia, and blood poisoning.

After the funeral, a relative complained: "Want to hear about bad taste? Glenn gets burned to death, and the mortuary sends the family a smoked ham. That's the goddam South for you."

Two years after Roberts' death, Ned Jarrett, who won NASCAR's racing championship in 1961 and 1965, retired. In thirteen years Jarrett had won fifty races, tied for seventh on the list with Junior Johnson. Ironically, it was Ned Jarrett who entered the broadcasting profession, where he has been an analyst for CBS, ESPN, and TNN ever since.

The King

On the heels of the deaths of Turner, Weatherly, and Roberts came a new generation of racers led by Lee Petty's son, Richard, whose driving skill would take stock car racing to its next plateau. Beginning in 1958, the year before his father won the initial Daytona 500 race, Richard would go on to become the Babe Ruth of stock car racing. Long before his retirement in 1992 he would be called simply The King. Over a driving career spanning thirty-five years, Richard Petty would win an incredible two hundred NASCAR Winston Cup Grand National races and seven times be named driving champion (1964, 1967, 1971, 1972, 1974, 1975, and 1979).

Perhaps the most famous race Richard Petty didn't win came in the Daytona 500 in 1976 when he and rival David Pearson drove side by side toward the checkered flag. Coming out of turn two, Pearson shot his Mercury around Petty's Dodge. Pearson, in the lead, drifted high into turn three. Petty tried to duck down low and, as they came off turn four, they were door to door, inches apart. Then they collided. Out of control, Pearson hit the wall nose first, clipping Petty's rear bumper. Both cars went skidding out of control.

Petty's Dodge stopped on the infield grass, a hundred yards from the finish line. His engine was dead. It could not be restarted. Pearson had come to a stop at the foot of the pit road, perhaps a couple of hundred yards from the finish.

Working the starter over and over, Pearson was able to get his car to jump ahead a foot or two at a time until he was able to cross the line. No other car was on the lead lap, so Petty was awarded second place even though he had completed but 199 laps. That race is considered the most dramatic finish in superspeedway history.

After the race Petty was asked what he was thinking while the crash was taking place.

"Well," he said in his most endearing manner, "I wasn't exactly hollering, 'Hooray for me.'"

Three years later Petty was the beneficiary of another renowned Daytona 500 crash, which occurred on the last lap when Cale Yarborough and Donnie Allison tangled and wrecked each other's cars, allowing Petty to roar across the finish line with the 1979 Daytona victory.

In all Richard Petty won the Daytona 500 in 1964, 1966, 1971, 1973, 1974, 1979, and 1981. He won roughly one-third of the races at Daytona during the years in which he dominated NASCAR racing.

And yet, despite his immense popularity, Richard Petty never shunned a request for an interview or for an autograph as he became the unofficial ambassador of stock car racing. When interviewed in 1992, he said with a smile, "You know, there is no man on earth who has been interviewed more times than I have." Who else might have been in the running for such a distinction? Muhammad Ali? He retired a long time ago. Charles Lindbergh? Elvis? They were recluses much of their lives. John Wayne? Movie stars were kept from the press by agents and bodyguards. Other famous American athletes, like Mickey Mantle, Willie Mays, and Hank Aaron shunned the press whenever possible. Few of the newcomers in any sport seem to embrace the media and the fans. Even Michael Jordan, as great a player as he is, seems uncomfortable in an uncontrolled interview situation.

Richard Petty, the winningest stock car driver of all time, courted the press and repaid his legions of fans for their loyalty by allowing them easy access. Millions of Richard Petty autographs grace walls all across America. For all those reasons, he will always be regarded as The King.

The Crown Princes

Petty's duels with such drivers as David Pearson, Bobby Allison, and Cale Yarborough were classics. Pearson (105 NASCAR wins), Allison (85 wins), and Yarborough (83 wins) are currently ranked second, third, and fifth respectively in wins on the all-time driver's list.

If Richard Petty was The King, David Pearson was Crown Prince, the winner of the NASCAR championship in 1966, 1968, and 1969. Said Petty, "David was the best I ever ran with." A quiet man who was uncomfortable in public, David Pearson was most at home behind the wheel of a race car, and it didn't matter what sort of track it was. Said Petty, "David loved to drive the race car, but that's all he wanted to do with it. He wasn't interested in the PR part, wasn't interested in making anything out of it. All he loved was to drive the race car, and he was super. He could win on quarter-mile dirt tracks, quarter-mile asphaults, superspeedways, road courses—it didn't make any difference." Pearson retired in 1987.

Bobby Allison, who came from Hueytown, Alabama, won the championship in 1983 and finished second five times, often by miniscule margins. Allison, who was one of the most popular drivers in racing history, was so infatuated with racing that he would run forty to fifty short-track events in addition to his NASCAR duties. Racing has been his whole life. Allsion's career was cut short in 1988 when he was T-boned at the door and suffered a severe blow to his head in a crash at Pocono. Had the accident not happened, Allison might well be driving today.

Cale Yarborough, champion in 1976, 1977, and 1978, was a down-home South Carolina farmer best known for his competitiveness. Like Turner and Weatherly, Yarborough loved flying and other thrilling things such as wrestling an alligator and skydiving. He also loved to fight, and his fistic confrontation with the Allison brothers, Bobby and Donnie, at the end of the 1979 Daytona 500 became the stuff of legends. The first driver to qualify at over 200 miles an hour at Daytona (in 1984), Yarborough ran so hard his crew chief had to tell him to slow down for him to run faster. If his car was loose, his crew learned it had better bring him in, or else he would keep driving hard, risking a collision with a wall. Regardless of how far back Yarborough might be in a race, he never gave up. Yarborough retired in 1988.

The Era of the Sponsors

Junior Johnson and Ralph Seagraves from R.J. Reynolds were good old mountain buddies, and after Johnson asked Seagraves if R.J. Reynolds would be interested in putting up $800,000 to sponsor his car, Seagraves told Johnson that R.J. Reynolds wanted to spend closer to $400 million, because the federal government had forbidden the tobacco company from placing its ads on TV and radio and in magazines, and it was looking for a new avenue for its advertising.

Johnson brought Seagraves to see Bill France Sr. After R.J. Reynolds sponsored the first Winston 500 at Talladega, and then the Winston Western 500 at Riverside, California, the company agreed to put up the prize money for the NASCAR point fund—the monetary prizes for the top drivers. After several years, the name of the competition was changed from the Winston Cup Grand National Championship to the Winston Cup Series, the name it is known by today.

Before R.J. Reynolds became involved, most of the sponsors had been automobile related: Champion spark plugs, Goodyear, Firestone, STP, Purolator, and service stations such as Pure Oil Company. Once Winston came in and started using racing in its marketing and had almost instant success, the beer companies such as Falstaff, Miller, and Coors got involved.

The real phenomenon came along about 1984. About then NASCAR made it known that 48 percent of older race fans were women. As a result, Gatorade came in as a sponsor, and they now sponsor the Gatorade circle of champions. At the same time Procter & Gamble came in, along with Crisco, Tide, Hanes Pantyhose, and even candy bars. From then on corporations brought store managers and presidents of chains to every major race and began entertaining them. As more and more sponsors saw the sales of their products soar because of their connection to NASCAR racing, the sport enjoyed a prosperity never equaled in its history.

Jaws

A young driver by the name of Dale Earnhardt surprised everyone when he became the first driver in NASCAR history to follow rookie-of-the-year honors (1979) with a driving championship (1980). But the newcomer who most rattled the older generation of racers and race fans was brash Darrell Waltrip, who arrived on the NASCAR scene from Nashville with a vocal message to the veterans, "Look out." In one race at North Wilkesboro in 1979, the cocky Waltrip kept ramming into the rear of Bobby Allison's car, warning the veteran driver to move out of his way. On the radio Waltrip's crew chief warned him not to do that, but an arrogant Waltrip, who was nicknamed "Jaws" by Cale Yarborough for his ability to run his mouth, replied, "He'll take it. There ain't nothing he can do about it." About that time Allison let off the gas and let Waltrip pass. Then the angry Allison put the youngster into the wall.

Waltrip would brag that he was better than his older competitors, and in time he was, breaking the monopoly of the older drivers by winning the NASCAR championship in 1981, 1982, and 1985. Though fans booed Waltrip and threw things at him, it was Darrell Waltrip who broke the hold of the older vets and led the way for the new generation of drivers who included Dale Earnhardt, Tim Richmond, Davey Allison, Terry Labonte (1996 and 1984 champion), Mark Martin, Rusty Wallace (1989 champion), Kyle Petty, and Ernie Irvan.

Another driver who began racing in the late 1970s and who made his mark is Bill Elliott, who earned the driving title in 1988. Elliott earned fame by winning The Winston Million—an award of $1 million for winning three of the Big Four races (Daytona 500, Winston 500, and Southern 500) in 1985. That year he also set the race speed mark of 186.288 miles an hour in winning at Talladega. Elliott, who is from Dawsonville, Georgia, is one of the most popular drivers in racing history.

The Intimidator

Dale Earnhardt, who is loved and hated by more racing fans than any other driver, is the son of Ralph Earnhardt, a champion dirt track racer. Like his father, Dale runs with a fearless intensity that can at times be intimidating. If a driver doesn't get out of his way, Earnhardt has been known to take the air off the offender's spoiler and send him into the wall. His father often told him, "Establish your territory." That's exactly what Earnhardt has done, winning the NASCAR driving championship in 1980, 1986, 1987, 1990, 1991, 1993, and 1994.

Tragedy

The race world was shocked and saddened when two of Earnhardt's top challengers, Alan Kulwicki and Davey Allison, met early deaths in 1993 in separate air accidents. The following year Neil Bonnett died in a crash at Daytona.

In 1990 Alan Kulwicki was offered $1 million to drive for car owner Junior Johnson but the brash independent turned down the offer. Said Kulwicki, "I figured I could make pretty good money and be happy running my own team. If I drove for him, maybe I'd be happy and maybe I wouldn't."

Kulwicki, who began driving in 1985 with a used car and two crew members, believed he could win a championship as owner of his own race team. Everyone thought he was foolish not to take the money and run for Johnson. But Alan Kulwicki was a maverick, a racer who listened to his heart, who did things his way. Just two years later Kulwicki was battling Bill Elliott for the title. To win, he needed to finish the final race in Atlanta with the most laps led, even if Elliott won the race. Elliott did win, but Kulwicki, who led the most laps and finished second, won the title by ten points over Elliott. Said Kulwicki after the race, "When I moved down South years ago, this was my dream. I came here in a pick-up truck and a trailer. I want to thank the many people who helped me along the way."

Alan Kulwicki was the toast of racing, but his reign was short-lived. One of the perks of Kulwicki's winning the championship was that he was given the use of a plane owned by his sponsor, Hooters restaurants. On April 1, 1993, his plane mysteriously crashed en route to the track in Bristol, Tennessee. Kulwicki and three others aboard were killed.

Davey Allison, who was NASCAR rookie-of-the-year in 1987 was well on his way to a driving championship in 1992 when, at Pocono in July, he and Darrell Waltrip collided and Allison's car shot off the track, flipped backwards, and tumbled wildly. He suffered two fractures of his right forearm and a broken right wrist and collarbone. Despite the serious injuries, a valiant Allison was in the car to start the race the following week at Talladega. He let Bobby Hillin take over after the first caution. Then on Friday, August 13, 1992, Davey's brother, Clifford, was killed in a crash at the Michigan International Speedway. Distraught and in mourning, Davey went to Michigan, drove the entire four-hundred-mile race, and finished fifth. Going into the final race of the season in Atlanta, a top-five finish by Allison would have given him the championship, but a collision with Ernie Irvan late in the race eliminated him and allowed Alan Kulwicki to earn the 1992 driving title.

Allison was again in contention to win the championship in 1993, but on June 21, 1993, he was flying his helicopter to the Talledega track when he miscalculated on landing, the copter's back rotor hit a chain-link fence, and the machine fell sideways to the ground, killing him and badly injuring his close friend Red Farmer. The loss of Kulwicki and then Allison in such close proximity cast a pall over the entire sport.

Neil Bonnett, an Alabaman who was like family to the Allisons, began racing in 1973 and won 18 Winston Cup races before his 1990 retirement, which was prompted by a series of serious injuries that put him in the hospital seven years in a row. The crash that sent him into retirement occurred during the 1990 TranSouth 500 at Darlington. Head injuries prevented him from recognizing his family. When he recovered, Bonnett became an integral part of racing's coverage on CBS and TNN, but the lure of the track became too great. In 1993 Bonnett decided to return to racing. On February 11, 1994, while practicing for the Daytona 500, he apparently lost control of his car on the high-banked turn four, skidded almost sideways, and slammed into the outside wall nearly head-on. He suffered massive head injuries and died.

A Miraculous Escape

Racing nearly claimed the life of another top racer, Ernie Irvan, who began driving for the Morgan-McClure team in 1990. Irvan quickly became known for a reckless style that caused several crashes, including one at Darlington that seriously injured Neil Bonnett. His nickname is Swervin' Irvan. And then in 1991 Irvan won the Daytona 500 and established himself as a force. His driving style never wavered, and when the other drivers blamed him for a multicar crash at Talladega and another at Pocono, Irvan took the unusual step of apologizing for being "overaggressive" just before the second race at Talladega. That afternoon Irvan was hit from the rear, his car spun out, and there was another pile-up. This time, though, no one complained.

After the death of Davey Allison, Irvan was hired by Robert Yates to drive Allison's Havoline\Texaco 28 car. Irvan was the favorite to win the championship in 1994 when, on August 21, while Irvan was driving at 165 miles an hour around the Michigan International Speedway, a tire flattened, steering became impossible, and his car shot into a cement wall. His skull was fractured, his lungs collapsed, and recovery looked bleak. But the indominable Irvan—miraculously—didn't die, and after ten days in a coma, he awoke to tell the world that he had no intentions of quitting the sport. No one thought it possible he would ever race again, but he returned to racing in 1995, and astounded everyone by racing competitively, even while wearing an eye-patch.

As racing enters a new season, veterans such as Dale Earnhardt, Mark Martin, Sterling Marlin, Geoff Bodine, Ricky Rudd, Bill Elliott, Kyle Petty (Richard's son and Lee's grandson), Rusty Wallace, Dale Jarrett, and Terry Labonte are among a large group of competitors capable of winning races. As always there will be young drivers pushing to topple them, led by Jeff Gordon, Jeff Purvis, and Bobby Labonte. Some of the names may change, but as NASCAR spreads to new sites in states like New Hampshire, Indiana, and Texas, the lure of stock car racing grows every year.

PART 1
THE RECORDS

CAREER RECORDS— DRIVERS

RACES STARTED

1.	Richard Petty	1,184
2.	Dave Marcis	816
3.	Bobby Allison	718
4.	Buddy Baker	699
5.	Darrell Waltrip	689
6.	J.D. McDuffie	653
7.	Buck Baker	636
8.	James Hylton	601
9.	David Pearson	574
10.	Ricky Rudd	562
11.	Buddy Arrington	560
12.	Cale Yarborough	559
13.	Dale Earnhardt	542
	Terry Labonte	542
15.	Elmo Langley	536
16.	Benny Parsons	526
17.	Neil Castles	497
18.	Bill Elliott	495
	Wendell Scott	495
20.	Harry Gant	474
21.	Kyle Petty	469
22.	Jimmy Means	455
23.	Cecil Gordon	450
24.	Morgan Shepherd	445
25.	Geoff Bodine	443
26.	Lee Petty	427
27.	Jim Paschal	422
28.	G.C. Spencer	415
29.	Frank Warren	396
30.	Rusty Wallace	393

WINS

1.	Richard Petty	200
2.	David Pearson	105
3.	Bobby Allison	85
4.	Darrell Waltrip	84
5.	Cale Yarborough	83
6.	Dale Earnhardt	70
7.	Lee Petty	54
8.	Ned Jarrett	50
	Junior Johnson	50
10.	Herb Thomas	48
11.	Buck Baker	46
	Rusty Wallace	46
13.	Bill Elliott	40
14.	Tim Flock	39
15.	Bobby Isaac	37
16.	Fireball Roberts	33
17.	Rex White	28
18.	Fred Lorenzen	26
19.	Jim Paschal	25
	Joe Weatherly	25
21.	Benny Parsons	21
	Jack Smith	21
23.	Speedy Thompson	20
24.	Davey Allison	19
	Buddy Baker	19
	Fonty Flock	19
	Jeff Gordon	19
28.	Geoff Bodine	18

	Neil Bonnett	18
	Harry Gant	18
	Terry Labonte	18
	Mark Martin	18
33.	Marvin Panch	17
	Ricky Rudd	17
	Curtis Turner	17
36.	Dick Hutcherson	14
	Ernie Irvan	14
	LeeRoy Yarbrough	14
39.	Dick Rathmann	13
	Tim Richmond	13
41.	Donnie Allison	10
42.	Paul Goldsmith	9
	Cotton Owens	9
	Bob Welborn	9
45.	Dale Jarrett	8
	Kyle Petty	8
47.	Darel Dieringer	7
	A. J. Foyt	7
	Jim Reed	7
	Marshall Teague	7
51.	Sterling Marlin	6
52.	Dan Gurney	5
	Alan Kulwicki	5
	Tiny Lund	5
	Dave Marcis	5
	Ralph Moody	5
57.	Lloyd Dane	4
	Bob Flock	4
	Charlie Glotzbach	4
	Eddie Gray	4
	Pete Hamilton	4
	Parnelli Jones	4
	Bobby Labonte	4
	Hershel McGriff	4
	Eddie Pagan	4
	Ken Schrader	4
	Morgan Shepherd	4
	Nelson Stacy	4
	Billy Wade	4
	Glen Wood	4
71.	Bill Blair	3
	Dick Linder	3
	Frank Mundy	3
	Gwyn Staley	3
75.	Johnny Beauchamp	2
	Red Byron	2
	Derrike Cope	2
	Ray Elder	2
	James Hylton	2
	Bobby Johns	2
	Joe Lee Johnson	2
	Al Keller	2
	Elmo Langley	2
	Danny Letner	2
	Billy Myers	2
	Jimmy Pardue	2
	Tom Pistone	2
	Marvin Porter	2
	Gober Sosebee	2
	Jimmy Spencer	2
	Emanuel Zervakis	2
92.	Johnny Allen	1
	Bill Amick	1

	Mario Andretti	1
	Earl Balmer	1
	Brett Bodine	1
	Ron Bouchard	1
	Richard Brickhouse	1
	Dick Brooks	1
	Bob Burdick	1
	Marvin Burke	1
	Ward Burton	1
	Neil Cole	1
	Jim Cook	1
	Mark Donohue	1
	Joe Eubanks	1
	Lou Figaro	1
	Jimmy Florian	1
	Larry Frank	1
	Danny Graves	1
	Royce Haggerty	1
	Bobby Hamilton	1
	Bobby Hillin	1
	Jim Hurtubise	1
	John Kieper	1
	Harold Kite	1
	Paul Lewis	1
	Johnny Mantz	1
	Sam McQuagg	1
	Lloyd Moore	1
	Norm Nelson	1
	Bill Norton	1
	Phil Parsons	1
	Dick Passwater	1
	Lennie Pond	1
	Bill Rexford	1
	Jody Ridley	1
	Shorty Rollins	1
	Jim Roper	1
	Earl Ross	1
	John Rostek	1
	Johnny Rutherford	1
	Greg Sacks	1
	Leon Sales	1
	Frankie Schneider	1
	Wendell Scott	1
	Buddy Shuman	1
	John Soares	1
	Lake Speed	1
	Chuck Stevenson	1
	Donald Thomas	1
	Tommy Thompson	1
	Art Watts	1
	Danny Weinberg	1
	Jack White	1

TOP 5 FINISHES

1.	Richard Petty	555
2.	Bobby Allison	336
3.	David Pearson	301
4.	Darrell Waltrip	274
5.	Cale Yarborough	255
6.	Dale Earnhardt	249
7.	Buck Baker	246
8.	Lee Petty	231
9.	Buddy Baker	202
10.	Benny Parsons	199
11.	Ned Jarrett	185

12. Terry Labonte	158
13. Jim Paschal	149
14. Bill Elliott	146
15. Ricky Rudd	143
16. James Hylton	140
17. Bobby Isaac	134
18. Rusty Wallace	132
19. Harry Gant	123
20. Herb Thomas	122
21. Junior Johnson	121
22. Mark Martin	115
23. Rex White	110
24. Joe Weatherly	105
25. Tim Flock	102
26. Marvin Panch	96
27. Geoff Bodine	94
Dave Marcis	94
Jack Smith	94
30. Fireball Roberts	93

TOP 10 FINISHES

1. Richard Petty	712
2. Bobby Allison	446
3. Darrell Waltrip	384
4. Buck Baker	372
5. David Pearson	366
6. Dale Earnhardt	354
7. Lee Petty	332
8. Cale Yarborough	318
9. Buddy Baker	311
10. James Hylton	301
11. Terry Labonte	289
12. Benny Parsons	283
13. Ricky Rudd	282
14. Bill Elliott	257
15. Ned Jarrett	239
16. Jim Paschal	230
17. Dave Marcis	222
18. Rusty Wallace	209
19. Harry Gant	208
20. Elmo Langley	193
21. Mark Martin	182
22. Neil Castles	178
23. Geoff Bodine	171
24. Bobby Isaac	170
25. Morgan Shepherd	165
26. Rex White	163
27. Neil Bonnett	156
Herb Thomas	156
29. Joe Weatherly	153
30. Dick Brooks	150

POLES

1. Richard Petty	126
2. David Pearson	113
3. Cale Yarborough	70
4. Bobby Allison	59
Darrell Waltrip	59
6. Bobby Isaac	50
7. Bill Elliott	48
8. Junior Johnson	47
9. Buck Baker	44
10. Buddy Baker	40
11. Tim Flock	39
12. Herb Thomas	38

13. Rex White	36
14. Geoff Bodine	35
Ned Jarrett	35
Fireball Roberts	35
17. Fonty Flock	33
Fred Lorenzen	33
19. Mark Martin	32
20. Terry Labonte	25
21. Alan Kulwicki	24
Jack Smith	24
23. Ricky Rudd	23
24. Dale Earnhardt	22
Dick Hutcherson	22
26. Marvin Panch	21
27. Neil Bonnett	20
Benny Parsons	20
29. Joe Weatherly	19

WINNINGS

1. Dale Earnhardt	28,695,088
2. Bill Elliott	16,236,933
3. Darrell Waltrip	15,674,704
4. Terry Labonte	14,629,863
5. Rusty Wallace	14,460,947
6. Mark Martin	11,981,873
7. Ricky Rudd	11,641,931
8. Geoff Bodine	10,385,370
9. Jeff Gordon	10,346,804
10. Sterling Marlin	8,958,496
11. Ken Schrader	8,831,281
12. Richard Petty	8,541,218
13. Harry Gant	8,524,844
14. Dale Jarrett	8,064,780
15. Kyle Petty	7,911,332
16. Bobby Allison	7,673,808
17. Morgan Shepherd	7,468,422
18. Ernie Irvan	7,336,109
19. Davey Allison	6,689,154
20. Cale Yarborough	5,645,887
21. Michael Waltrip	5,391,672
22. Dave Marcis	5,246,691
23. Brett Bodine	5,135,005
24. Alan Kulwicki	5,059,052
25. Benny Parsons	4,426,287
26. Lake Speed	4,207,595
27. Neil Bonnett	3,998,470
28. Buddy Baker.	3,995,500
29. Rick Mast	3,920,492
30. Ted Musgrave	3,904,480

LAPS COMPLETED

1. Richard Petty	307,836
2. Dave Marcis	213,241
3. Darrell Waltrip	206,128
4. Bobby Allison	197,438
5. Dale Earnhardt	163,781
6. Ricky Rudd	163,415
7. James Hylton	160,733
8. Terry Labonte	160,064
9. Buddy Baker	151,129
10. J. D. McDuffie	148,694
11. Buddy Arrington	147,899
12. Bill Elliott	146,659
13. Cale Yarborough	144,552
14. David Pearson	135,020

15. Benny Parsons	134,540
16. Kyle Petty	134,344
17. Harry Gant	133,629
18. Geoff Bodine	125,882
19. Morgan Shepherd	120,924
20. Elmo Langley	119,706
21. Rusty Wallace	115,519
22. Jimmy Means	113,945
23. Cecil Gordon	112,908
24. Buck Baker	109,256
25. Sterling Marlin	105,753
26. Ken Schrader	105,237
27. Wendell Scott	102,435
28. Neil Bonnett	96,021
29. Mark Martin	95,996
30. Michael Waltrip	95,343

LAPS LED

1. Richard Petty	52,194
2. Cale Yarborough	31,776
3. Bobby Allison	27,539
4. David Pearson	25,425
5. Dale Earnhardt	24,624
6. Darrell Waltrip	22,988
7. Bobby Isaac	13,229
8. Rusty Wallace	13,212
9. Junior Johnson	12,651
10. Buddy Baker	9,748
11. Bill Elliott	9,720
12. Ned Jarrett	9,468
13. Geoff Bodine	8,550
14. Harry Gant	8,445
15. Fred Lorenzen	8,131
16. Tim Flock	6,937
17. Benny Parsons	6,860
18. Neil Bonnett	6,382
19. Herb Thomas	6,197
20. Ricky Rudd	6,162
21. Fireball Roberts	5,970
22. Mark Martin	5,859
23. Terry Labonte	5,833
24. Buck Baker	5,662
25. Jeff Gordon	5,590
26. Davey Allison	4,978
27. Ernie Irvan	4,817
28. Lee Petty	4,787
29. Curtis Turner	4,771
30. Donnie Allison	4,642

RACES LED

1. Richard Petty	599
2. Bobby Allison	414
3. Darrell Waltrip	386
4. Dale Earnhardt	356
5. Cale Yarborough	340
6. David Pearson	329
7. Buddy Baker	242
8. Bill Elliott	202
9. Terry Labonte	200
10. Geoff Bodine	199
11. Harry Gant	192
Benny Parsons	192
13. Dave Marcis	186
14. Rusty Wallace	182
15. Ricky Rudd	172

16. Neil Bonnett	155	
Bobby Isaac	155	
18. Mark Martin	142	
19. Junior Johnson	138	
20. Ken Schrader	115	
21. Ned Jarrett	111	
22. Donnie Allison	105	
23. Buck Baker	104	
Morgan Shepherd	102	
25. Ernie Irvan	101	
26. Davey Allison	97	
27. Lee Petty	93	
28. Sterling Marlin	91	
29. Fireball Roberts	90	
30. Kyle Petty	86	

CONSECUTIVE RACES LED

1. Bobby Allison	39	1971–72
2. Darrell Waltrip	25	1981–82
Cale Yarborough	25	1976
4. Richard Petty	22	1972–73
Cale Yarborough	22	1977–78
6. Dale Earnhardt	20	1986–87
Dale Earnhardt	20	1987–88
8. Jeff Gordon	19	1995
9. Geoff Bodine	17	1986
David Pearson	17	1969
11. Richard Petty	16	1974
Darrell Waltrip	16	1980–81
Cale Yarborough	16	1978
14. Bobby Isaac	15	1972
Richard Petty	15	1971
16. Bobby Allison	14	1981
Bill Elliott	14	1988
Tim Flock	14	1955
Terry Labonte	14	1984–85
Richard Petty	14	1971–72
Darrell Waltrip	14	1978
Darrell Waltrip	14	1979
Darrell Waltrip	14	1982
Darrell Waltrip	14	1985–86
Cale Yarborough	14	1974
Cale Yarborough	14	1978–79
Cale Yarborough	14	1980

CONSECUTIVE RACES STARTED

1. Terry Labonte	537
2. Dale Earnhardt	514
3. Richard Petty	513
4. Ricky Rudd	475
5. Darrell Waltrip	431
6. Bill Elliott	395
7. Rusty Wallace	383
8. Bobby Allison	374
9. Ken Schrader	354
10. Michael Waltrip	324
11. Benny Parsons	321
12. Sterling Marlin	297
13. Dave Marcis	284
14. Mark Martin	268
15. Harry Gant	264
16. Richard Childress	256
17. Morgan Shepherd	240
18. Dale Jarrett	219
19. Geoff Bodine	212

20. Buddy Arrington	205
21. J.D. McDuffie	195
22. Cecil Gordon	193
23. Alan Kulwicki	190
24. Darrell Waltrip	189
25. Rick Mast	187
26. James Hylton	183
27. Kyle Petty	176
28. Geoff Bodine	170
29. Brett Bodine	169
Tim Richmond	169
Cale Yarborough	169

CONSECUTIVE RACES WON

1. Richard Petty	10	1967
2. Bobby Allison	5	1971
Richard Petty	5	1971
4. Dale Earnhardt	4	1987
Bill Elliott	4	1992
Harry Gant	4	1991
Mark Martin	4	1993
David Pearson	4	1966
David Pearson	4	1968
Billy Wade	4	1964
Darrell Waltrip	4	1981
Cale Yarborough	4	1976

CONSECUTIVE YEARS RACING

1. Richard Petty	35	1958–92
2. Buddy Baker	30	1959–88
Cale Yarborough	30	1959–88
4. Dave Marcis	29	1968–96
5. A.J. Foyt	28	1963–90
6. David Pearson	27	1960–86
7. Elmo Langley	26	1954–79
J.D. McDuffie	26	1966–91
9. Buddy Arrington	25	1964–88
Buck Baker	25	1949–73
Darrell Waltrip	25	1972–96
12. Bobby Allison	24	1965–88
13. Dale Earnhardt	22	1975–96
Harry Gant	22	1973–94
Ricky Rudd	22	1975–96
16. Bill Elliott	21	1976–96
17. Benny Parsons	20	1969–88
Jim Paschal	20	1949–68
G.C. Spencer	20	1958–77
20. Terry Labonte	19	1978–96
Tiny Lund	19	1955–73
Sterling Marlin	19	1978–96
Bill Schmitt	19	1975–93
24. Donnie Allison	18	1966–83
James Hylton	18	1966–83
Jimmy Means	18	1976–93
Kyle Petty	18	1979–96
Frank Warren	18	1963–80

WIN PERCENT (100 RACES MIN.)

1. Herb Thomas	21%
Tim Flock	21%
3. David Pearson	18%
4. Richard Petty	17%
5. Fred Lorenzen	16%
Fireball Roberts	16%
Junior Johnson	16%

8. Jeff Gordon	15%
Cale Yarborough	15%
10. Ned Jarrett	14%
Dick Hutcherson	14%
12. Dale Earnhardt	13%
Lee Petty	13%
14. Fonty Flock	12%
Darrell Waltrip	12%
Rex White	12%
Bobby Isaac	12%
Bobby Allison	12%
Rusty Wallace	12%
20. Joe Weatherly	11%
21. Dick Rathmann	10%
Speedy Thompson	10%
Davey Allison	10%
24. Curtis Turner	9%
25. Bill Elliott	8%
Jack Smith	8%
Marvin Panch	8%
28. Buck Baker	7%
Paul Goldsmith	7%
LeeRoy Yarbrough	7%

AVERAGE FINISH

1. Lee Petty	7.600
2. Dick Hutcherson	8.670
3. Rex White	8.983
4. Herb Thomas	9.017
5. Ned Jarrett	9.153
6. Tim Flock	9.465
7. Joe Weatherly	10.052
8. Dale Earnhardt	10.731
9. Dick Rathmann	10.734
10. David Pearson	11.033
11. Richard Petty	11.259
12. Buck Baker	11.365
13. Bobby Allison	11.494
14. Marvin Panch	11.676
15. Speedy Thompson	11.848
16. Fonty Flock	12.175
17. Bob Welborn	12.317
18. Jack Smith	12.420
19. Jim Paschal	12.533
20. Cale Yarborough	12.574
21. Bobby Isaac	12.854
22. Bill Elliott	12.984
23. Darrell Waltrip	13.097
24. Fireball Roberts	13.209
25. Mark Martin	13.218
26. Jeff Gordon	13.234
27. Larry Thomas	13.286
28. Cotton Owens	13.288
29. Fred Lorenzen	13.304
30. Terry Labonte	13.507

PERFORMANCE POINTS* (1949–1996)

1. Richard Petty	3,645
2. David Pearson	2,045
3. Bobby Allison	1,993
4. Darrell Waltrip	1,642
5. Cale Yarborough	1,559
6. Dale Earnhardt	1,452
7. Lee Petty	1,269
8. Buck Baker	1,262

9.	Ned Jarrett	1,044
10.	Buddy Baker	916
11.	Benny Parsons	866
12.	Rusty Wallace	832
13.	Bill Elliott	827
14.	Herb Thomas	796
15.	Bobby Isaac	795
16.	Junior Johnson	778
17.	Jim Paschal	755
18.	Terry Labonte	739
19.	Tim Flock	645
	Ricky Rudd	645
21.	Rex White	637
22.	Harry Gant	618
23.	Mark Martin	592
24.	Joe Weatherly	590
25.	Fireball Roberts	577
26.	James Hylton	514
	Marvin Panch	514
28.	Jack Smith	502
29.	Geoff Bodine	484
30.	Fred Lorenzen	454

Points are based on an International Point System on 10–6 - 4 - 3 - 2 - 1 breakdown for the first six finishers in every event. It is the most effective method of ranking individuals based on performance.

SINGLE SEASON RECORDS—DRIVERS

WINS

1.	Richard Petty	1967	27
2.	Richard Petty	1971	21
3.	Tim Flock	1955	18
	Richard Petty	1970	18
5.	Bobby Isaac	1969	17
6.	David Pearson	1968	16
	Richard Petty	1968	16
8.	Ned Jarrett	1964	15
	David Pearson	1966	15
10.	Buck Baker	1956	14
	Richard Petty	1963	14
12.	Ned Jarrett	1965	13
	Junior Johnson	1965	13
	Richard Petty	1975	13
15.	Herb Thomas	1953	12
	Herb Thomas	1954	12
	Darrell Waltrip	1981	12
	Darrell Waltrip	1982	12
19.	Bobby Allison	1971	11
	Dale Earnhardt	1987	11
	Bill Elliott	1985	11
	Bobby Isaac	1970	11
	David Pearson	1969	11
	David Pearson	1973	11
	Lee Petty	1959	11

MONEY

1.	Jeff Gordon	1995	$4,347,343
2.	Terry Labonte	1996	4,030,648
3.	Jeff Gordon	1996	3,428,485
4.	Dale Earnhardt	1994	3,400,733
5.	Dale Earnhardt	1993	3,353,789
6.	Dale Earnhardt	1990	3,308,056
7.	Dale Earnhardt	1995	3,154,241
8.	Dale Jarrett	1996	2,985,415
9.	Bill Elliott	1985	2,433,187
10.	Dale Earnhardt	1991	2,416,685
11.	Alan Kulwicki	1992	2,322,561
12.	Dale Earnhardt	1996	2,285,926
13.	Sterling Marlin	1995	2,253,502
14.	Rusty Wallace	1989	2,237,950
15.	Dale Earnhardt	1987	2,069,243
16.	Rusty Wallace	1994	1,959,072
17.	Davey Allison	1992	1,955,628
18.	Mark Martin	1995	1,893,519
19.	Mark Martin	1996	1,887,396
20.	Jeff Gordon	1994	1,799,523
21.	Dale Earnhardt	1986	1,768,880
22.	Davey Allison	1991	1,712,924
23.	Rusty Wallace	1993	1,702,154
24.	Bill Elliott	1992	1,692,381
25.	Ernie Irvan	1996	1,683,313
26.	Mark Martin	1994	1,678,906
27.	Rusty Wallace	1996	1,665,315
28.	Mark Martin	1993	1,657,662
29.	Rusty Wallace	1995	1,642,230
30.	Bill Elliott	1987	1,599,210

LAPS LED

1.	Richard Petty	1967	5,537
2.	Bobby Isaac	1969	5,072
3.	Richard Petty	1970	5,007
4.	Richard Petty	1971	4,932
5.	Bobby Allison	1972	4,343
6.	Richard Petty	1968	4,242
7.	Junior Johnson	1965	3,998
8.	David Pearson	1968	3,950
9.	Cale Yarborough	1976	3,791
10.	Cale Yarborough	1974	3,630
11.	Cale Yarborough	1978	3,587
12.	Bobby Allison	1971	3,582
13.	Richard Petty	1964	3,534
14.	Tim Flock	1955	3,495
15.	Dale Earnhardt	1987	3,358
16.	Ned Jarrett	1964	3,304
17.	Cale Yarborough	1977	3,218
18.	Bobby Isaac	1970	3,188
19.	David Pearson	1966	3,174
20.	Cale Yarborough	1973	3,167
21.	Richard Petty	1975	3,158
22.	Richard Petty	1974	3,100
23.	Darrell Waltrip	1982	3,027
24.	David Pearson	1969	3,018
25.	Richard Petty	1966	2,924
26.	Rusty Wallace	1993	2,860
27.	Cale Yarborough	1980	2,810
28.	Richard Petty	1969	2,778
29.	Dale Earnhardt	1989	2,735
30.	David Pearson	1973	2,658

MILES LED

1.	Bobby Allison	1972	4,117
2.	Bobby Allison	1971	4,042
3.	Cale Yarborough	1978	3,867
4.	Richard Petty	1971	3,721
5.	Richard Petty	1967	3,666
6.	Richard Petty	1970	3,633

7.	Cale Yarborough	1976	3,576
8.	Jeff Gordon	1995	3,458
9.	Dale Earnhardt	1987	3,399
10.	Cale Yarborough	1974	3,374
11.	Richard Petty	1975	3,319
12.	David Pearson	1973	3,275
13.	Richard Petty	1974	3,256
14.	Bobby Allison	1982	3,217
15.	Dale Earnhardt	1990	3,203
16.	Bill Elliott	1985	3,188
17.	Cale Yarborough	1980	3,155
18.	Richard Petty	1964	3,065
19.	Cale Yarborough	1977	3,054
20.	Cale Yarborough	1973	2,727
21.	Bobby Isaac	1969	2,688
22.	Darrell Waltrip	1982	2,672
23.	Darrell Waltrip	1979	2,629
24.	Dale Earnhardt	1989	2,624
25.	Rusty Wallace	1989	2,549
26.	Dale Earnhardt	1993	2,485
27.	Tim Flock	1955	2,477
28.	Junior Johnson	1965	2,449
29.	Dale Earnhardt	1986	2,439
30.	Ernie Irvan	1994	2,419

LAPS COMPLETED

1.	David Pearson	1969	14,270
2.	Richard Petty	1964	14,041
3.	Richard Petty	1971	13,739
4.	James Hylton	1969	13,540
5.	Ned Jarrett	1965	13,525
6.	Ned Jarrett	1964	13,325
7.	David Pearson	1964	13,225
8.	David Pearson	1968	13,097
9.	Bobby Isaac	1968	12,947
10.	James Hylton	1971	12,785
11.	Richard Petty	1967	12,739
12.	Bobby Isaac	1970	12,726
13.	James Hylton	1970	12,712
14.	Neil Castles	1969	12,661
15.	Richard Petty	1969	12,589
16.	Elmo Langley	1969	12,531
17.	Cecil Gordon	1971	12,468
18.	Bobby Allison	1970	12,452
19.	Joe Weatherly	1962	12,431
20.	Bobby Isaac	1969	12,308
21.	Richard Petty	1968	12,254
22.	Richard Petty	1963	12,183
23.	Jabe Thomas	1969	12,025
24.	Clyde Lynn	1968	12,013
25.	Wendell Scott	1969	11,856
26.	Ned Jarrett	1963	11,845
27.	Bobby Allison	1971	11,716
28.	John Sears	1969	11,620
29.	Dick Hutcherson	1965	11,610
30.	Richard Petty	1962	11,544

MILES DRIVEN

1.	Richard Petty	1971	12,870
2.	James Hylton	1971	12,718
3.	Bobby Allison	1971	12,122
4.	Ricky Rudd	1994	12,046
5.	Cecil Gordon	1971	12,034
6.	Darrell Waltrip	1994	12,026
7.	Richard Petty	1972	11,996
8.	Morgan Shepherd	1994	11,950

9.	Sterling Marlin	1995	11,936
10.	Ted Musgrave	1995	11,822
11.	Dale Earnhardt	1993	11,808
12.	Bobby Allison	1972	11,801
13.	Darrell Waltrip	1979	11,768
14.	Ken Schrader	1994	11,740
15.	Dale Earnhardt	1995	11,714
16.	Michael Waltrip	1994	11,666
17.	Bobby Allison	1981	11,609
18.	Jeff Gordon	1995	11,608
19.	Geoff Bodine	1995	11,571
20.	Rusty Wallace	1995	11,563
21.	Bobby Hamilton	1995	11,555
22.	Jeff Gordon	1994	11,548
23.	Morgan Shepherd	1995	11,547
24.	Bobby Allison	1983	11,526
25.	Dale Earnhardt	1996	11,523
26.	Terry Labonte	1996	11,522
27.	Bill Elliott	1988	11,521
28.	Ken Schrader	1996	11,499
29.	Mark Martin	1990	11,487
30.	Dale Earnhardt	1991	11,435

POLES

1.	Bobby Isaac	1969	20
2.	Richard Petty	1967	19
3.	Tim Flock	1955	18
4.	Richard Petty	1966	16
5.	Cale Yarborough	1980	14
	David Pearson	1969	14
7.	Bobby Isaac	1970	13
8.	Bobby Allison	1972	12
	Buck Baker	1956	12
	Fonty Flock	1951	12
	David Pearson	1964	12
	David Pearson	1968	12
	Richard Petty	1968	12
	Herb Thomas	1953	12
15.	Bill Elliott	1985	11
	David Pearson	1974	11
	Darrell Waltrip	1981	11
18.	Junior Johnson	1961	10
	Junior Johnson	1965	10
	Herb Thomas	1952	10

TOP 5 FINISHES

1.	Ned Jarrett	1965	42
	David Pearson	1969	42
3.	Ned Jarrett	1964	40
4.	Joe Weatherly	1962	39
5.	Richard Petty	1967	38
	Richard Petty	1971	38
7.	Richard Petty	1964	37
8.	David Pearson	1968	36
9.	Tim Flock	1955	32
	Dick Hutcherson	1965	32
	Bobby Isaac	1970	32
	Ned Jarrett	1963	32
	Richard Petty	1962	32
14.	Buck Baker	1956	31
	Richard Petty	1968	31
	Richard Petty	1969	31
17.	Bobby Allison	1970	30
	Buck Baker	1957	30
	Richard Petty	1963	30
20.	Bobby Isaac	1969	29

	David Pearson	1964	29
	Rex White	1961	29
23.	Lee Petty	1958	28
24.	Bobby Allison	1971	27
	James Hylton	1969	27
	Bobby Isaac	1968	27
	Lee Petty	1959	27
	Richard Petty	1970	27
	Jack Smith	1962	27
	Herb Thomas	1953	27

TOP 10 FINISHES

1.	Ned Jarrett	1964	45
	Ned Jarrett	1965	45
	Joe Weatherly	1962	45
4.	David Pearson	1969	44
5.	Lee Petty	1958	43
	Richard Petty	1964	43
7.	David Pearson	1964	42
8.	Richard Petty	1971	41
9.	Richard Petty	1967	40
10.	Buck Baker	1956	39
	James Hylton	1967	39
	James Hylton	1969	39
	James Hylton	1970	39
	Ned Jarrett	1963	39
	Richard Petty	1962	39
	Richard Petty	1963	39
17.	Buck Baker	1957	38
	Bobby Isaac	1970	38
	David Pearson	1968	38
	Richard Petty	1969	38
	Rex White	1961	38
22.	Dick Hutcherson	1965	37
	James Hylton	1971	37
24.	Bobby Isaac	1968	36
	Herb Thomas	1956	36

RACES LED

1.	Richard Petty	1967	41
	Richard Petty	1971	41
3.	David Pearson	1969	39
4.	Bobby Isaac	1969	38
5.	David Pearson	1968	37
6.	Bobby Isaac	1970	35
	Richard Petty	1968	35
8.	Tim Flock	1955	33
	Richard Petty	1964	33
10.	Richard Petty	1969	32
	Richard Petty	1970	32
12.	Bobby Allison	1971	31
	David Pearson	1964	31
14.	Bobby Allison	1972	30
	Ned Jarrett	1964	30
	Junior Johnson	1965	30
	Richard Petty	1972	30
18.	Jeff Gordon	1995	29
	Ned Jarrett	1965	29
	Richard Petty	1963	29
21.	Darrell Waltrip	1980	28
	Cale Yarborough	1976	28
	Cale Yarborough	1977	28
	Cale Yarborough	1978	28
	Cale Yarborough	1980	28
26.	Dale Earnhardt	1987	27

	Darrell Waltrip	1981	27
	Darrell Waltrip	1982	27

WIN PERCENT (MIN. 10 STARTS)

1.	David Pearson	1973	61%
2.	Fireball Roberts	1958	60%
3.	Richard Petty	1967	56%
4.	Fred Lorenzen	1964	50%
5.	Tim Flock	1955	46%
	Richard Petty	1971	46%
7.	David Pearson	1976	45%
	Richard Petty	1970	45%
9.	Richard Petty	1975	43%
10.	Darrell Waltrip	1982	40%
11.	Bill Elliott	1985	39%
	Darrell Waltrip	1981	39%
13.	Dale Earnhardt	1987	38%
14.	David Pearson	1974	37%
15.	Junior Johnson	1965	36%
	Joe Weatherly	1961	36%
	David Pearson	1966	36%
18.	David Pearson	1972	35%
	Herb Thomas	1954	35%
20.	Bobby Isaac	1969	34%
21.	David Pearson	1968	33%
	Richard Petty	1974	33%
	Marshall Teague	1951	33%
	Rusty Wallace	1993	33%
	Cale Yarborough	1974	33%
	Cale Yarborough	1978	33%
	Richard Petty	1968	33%
28.	Herb Thomas	1953	32%
	Bobby Allison	1972	32%
	Jeff Gordon	1996	32%

AVERAGE FINISH (MIN. 10 STARTS)

1.	Richard Petty	1971	4.217
2.	Cale Yarborough	1977	4.500
3.	Tim Flock	1955	4.590
4.	Buck Baker	1957	4.675
5.	Richard Petty	1972	4.677
6.	Lee Petty	1953	4.833
7.	Ned Jarrett	1965	4.907
8.	Joe Weatherly	1962	4.962
9.	Fireball Roberts	1958	5.000
10.	Richard Petty	1967	5.021
11.	Herb Thomas	1953	5.216
12.	David Pearson	1969	5.275
13.	Bobby Allison	1972	5.323
14.	Rex White	1960	5.325
15.	Lee Petty	1954	5.647
16.	Dick Rathmann	1954	5.750
17.	David Pearson	1968	5.833
18.	Dale Earnhardt	1987	5.931
19.	Cale Yarborough	1978	6.033
20.	Lee Petty	1959	6.167
21.	Lee Petty	1958	6.320
22.	Lee Petty	1949	6.333
23.	David Pearson	1966	6.381
24.	Richard Petty	1979	6.387
25.	Mark Martin	1990	6.552
26.	Lee Petty	1952	6.563
27.	Bill Elliott	1988	6.586
28.	Richard Petty	1975	6.633
29.	Buck Baker	1955	6.667
30.	Cale Yarborough	1974	6.667

CAREER RECORDS— OWNERS

RACES STARTED

1.	Petty Enterprises	1,635
2.	Bud Moore	911
3.	Wood Bros.	896
4.	Junior Johnson	750
5.	Junie Donlavey	717
6.	Elmo Langley	675
7.	James Hylton	634
8.	Richard Childress	628
9.	Dave Marcis	627
10.	Buddy Arrington	584
11.	Billy Hagan	546
12.	Buck Baker	525
13.	L. G.DeWitt	521
14.	J D McDuffie	488
15.	Henley Gray	476
16.	D. K. Ulrich	469
17.	Wendell Scott	465
18.	G. C. Spencer	451
18.	Jimmy Means	435
19.	Don Robertson	431
20.	Bobby Allison	429
22.	Cecil Gordon	406
23.	Harry Melling	389
24.	Rick Hendrick	384
25.	DiGard	371
26.	Stavola Brothers	368
27.	Holman-Moody	366
28.	Larry McClure	354
29.	Cotton Owens	353
30.	Bob Rahilly & Butch Mock	350

WINS

1.	Petty Enterprises	266
2.	Junior Johnson	119
3.	Wood Bros.	97
4.	Holman-Moody	93
5.	Bud Moore	63
6.	Richard Childress	63
7.	Rick Hendrick	60
8.	Carl Kiekhaefer	52
9.	Herb Thomas	44
10.	Nord Krauskopf	43
	DiGard	43
12.	Cotton Owens	39
13.	Harry Melling	34
14.	Roger Penske	33
15.	Bondy Long	31
16.	Robert Yates	27
17.	Rex White	26
18.	Harry Ranier	24
19.	Frank Christian	22
20.	Pete DePaolo	21
	Richard Howard	21
22.	Rex Lovette	20
	Ted Chester	20
	Raymond Beadle	20
25.	Jack Roush	18
26.	Jack Smith	15
27.	Ray Fox	14
	Bobby Allison	14
29.	J. H. Petty	13
	Larry McClure	13
	Buck Baker	13

TOP 5 FINISHES

1.	Petty Enterprises	871
2.	Junior Johnson	417
3.	Wood Bros.	323
4.	Bud Moore	308
5.	Rick Hendrick	294
6.	Holman-Moody	281
7.	Richard Childress	211
8.	Cotton Owens	179
9.	L. G. DeWitt	177
10.	Nord Krauskopf	171
11.	Buck Baker	159
12.	DiGard	158
13.	Jack Roush	128
14.	Herb Thomas	118
15.	Carl Kiekhaefer	116
16.	Bondy Long	115
17.	Harry Melling	114
18.	Roger Penske	113
19.	Harry Ranier	107
20.	Robert Yates	102
21.	Bobby Allison	101
	Billy Hagan	101
23.	James Hylton	94
24.	Rex White	89
25.	Frank Christian	85
26.	Pete DePaolo	80
27.	Jack Smith	79
28.	Raymond Beadle	73
29.	J. H. Petty	68
	Hal Needham	68

TOP 10 FINISHES

1.	Petty Enterprises	1,195
2.	Junior Johnson	556
3.	Rick Hendrick	493
4.	Wood Bros.	477
5.	Bud Moore	476
6.	Richard Childress	357
7.	Holman-Moody	331
8.	Buck Baker	330
9.	L. G. DeWitt	315
10.	Cotton Owens	246
11.	James Hylton	237
12.	Billy Hagan	236
13.	Nord Krauskopf	214
	Junie Donlavey	214
15.	Jack Roush	212
16.	DiGard	211
17.	Harry Melling	180
18.	Herb Thomas	158
19.	Roger Penske	156
20.	Bobby Allison	155
	Wendell Scott	155
22.	Harry Ranier	146
23.	Robert Yates	142
24.	Carl Kiekhaefer	138
25.	Bondy Long	136
26.	G. C. Spencer	133
27.	Elmo Langley	132
28.	Raymond Beadle	130
29.	Dave Marcis	128
30.	Rex White	123

POLES

1.	Petty Enterprises	150
2.	Wood Bros.	118
3.	Junior Johnson	106
4.	Holman-Moody	83
5.	Rick Hendrick	75
6.	Nord Krauskopf	67
7.	Carl Kiekhaefer	50
8.	Bud Moore	48
9.	Harry Melling	40
10.	Harry Ranier	39
11.	Jack Roush	36
	Cotton Owens	36
13.	Herb Thomas	34
14.	Frank Christian	31
15.	Bondy Long	28
16.	Rex White	26
	DiGard	26
18.	Alan Kulwicki	24
	Richard Childress	24
20.	Richard Howard	23
21.	Jack Smith	22
22.	Rex Lovette	21
23.	Bobby Allison	20
24.	Pete DePaolo	18
	Ray Fox	18
26.	Robert Yates	17
27.	Smokey Yunick	16
	Buck Baker	16
	Roger Penske	16
30.	Billy Hagan	15

LAPS COMPLETED

1.	Petty Enterprises	471,974
2.	Junior Johnson	295,136
3.	Rick Hendrick	289,466
4.	Bud Moore	253,664
5.	Wood Bros.	244,570
6.	Richard Childress	190,281
7.	Junie Donlavey	190,248
8.	James Hylton	171,126
9.	Elmo Langley	165,647
10.	Dave Marcis	164,965
11.	Billy Hagan	157,574
12.	Buddy Arrington	156,200
13.	Stavola Brothers	139,299
14.	L. G. DeWitt	135,176
15.	Jack Roush	134,180
16.	Buck Baker	133,944
17.	Holman-Moody	120,432
18.	J. D. McDuffie	119,110
19.	Don Robertson	116,035
20.	Harry Melling	115,404
21.	Bobby Allison	110,474
22.	Jimmy Means	109,180
23.	Cecil Gordon	107,152
24.	D.K. Ulrich	107,070
25.	DiGard	106,157
26.	Henley Gray	103,089
27.	Wendell Scott	101,505
28.	Bob Rahilly & Butch Mock	99,434
29.	Larry McClure	95,664
30.	Richard Jackson	95,063

LAPS LED

1.	Petty Enterprises	59,638
2.	Junior Johnson	40,377
3.	Holman-Moody	24,412
4.	Wood Bros.	24,285
5.	Richard Childress	21,614
6.	Rick Hendrick	18,257

7.	Bud Moore	17,110
8.	Nord Krauskopf	15,705
9.	DiGard	14,277
10.	Richard Howard	10,209
11.	Roger Penske	9,630
12.	Cotton Owens	9,560
13.	Carl Kiekhaefer	8,255
14.	Harry Melling	8,129
15.	Robert Yates	7,908
16.	Bondy Long	7,381
17.	Harry Ranier	7,029
18.	Rex Lovette	6,741
19.	Jack Roush	6,005
20.	Raymond Beadle	5,968
21.	Herb Thomas	5,899
22.	Bobby Allison	5,495
23.	Hal Needham	4,962
24.	Ray Fox	4,709
25.	L. G. DeWitt	4,344
26.	Banjo Matthews	3,910
27.	Frank Christian	3,896
28.	Rex White	3,805
29.	Billy Hagan	3,550
30.	Felix Sabates	3,326

RACES LED

1.	Petty Enterprises	719
2.	Junior Johnson	510
3.	Wood Bros.	396
4.	Bud Moore	335
5.	Richard Childress	309
6.	Rick Hendrick	299
7.	Holman-Moody	243
8.	DiGard	227
9.	Nord Krauskopf	198
10.	Cotton Owens	157
11.	Harry Melling	152
12.	Harry Ranier	147
	Jack Roush	147
14.	Billy Hagan	146
15.	Roger Penske	141
16.	Robert Yates	132
17.	L. G. DeWitt	128
18.	Dave Marcis	120
19.	Raymond Beadle	114
20.	Bobby Allison	112
21.	Hal Needham	111
22.	Larry McClure	105
23.	Hoss Ellington	99
24.	Bondy Long	90
25.	Banjo Matthews	77
26.	Carl Kiekhaefer	75
	Richard Howard	75
	Herb Thomas	75
29.	Alan Kulwicki	73
	Kenny Bernstein	73

WIN PERCENT (100 STARTS MIN.)

1.	Holman-Moody	26%
2.	Herb Thomas	21%
3.	Petty Enterprises	16%
	Junior Johnson	16%
	Rick Hendrick	16%
6.	Bondy Long	15%
	Rex White	15%
8.	Frank Christian	14%
9.	Nord Krauskopf	13%
10.	Roger Penske	12%
	DiGard	12%
12.	Robert Yates	11%
	Cotton Owens	11%
	Wood Bros.	11%
15.	Richard Childress	10%
	J. H. Petty	10%
17.	Harry Ranier	9%
	Harry Melling	9%
	Charles Robinson	9%
	Raymond Beadle	9%
21.	Ray Fox	8%
	Jack Smith	8%
23.	Bud Moore	7%
	M. C. Anderson	7%
	Jack Roush	7%
26.	Ray Nichels	6%
27.	Banjo Matthews	5%
28.	Leo Jackson	4%
	Rod Osterlund	4%
	Joe Gibbs	4%

AVERAGE FINISH (100 STARTS MIN.)

1.	Rex White	8.831
2.	Bondy Long	9.668
3.	Charles Robinson	9.748
4.	Holman-Moody	10.761
5.	J. H. Petty	11.161
6.	Nord Krauskopf	11.610
7.	Cotton Owens	11.648
8.	Petty Enterprises	11.984
9.	Richard Childress	12.204
10.	Jack Smith	12.567
11.	Junior Johnson	12.781
12.	L. G. DeWitt	12.855
13.	Raymond Beadle	13.372
14.	DiGard	13.404
15.	Herman Beam	13.618
16.	Wood Bros.	13.628
17.	Robert Yates	13.675
18.	Harry Ranier	13.820
19.	Roger Penske	13.942
20.	Henry Woodfield	13.965
21.	Wade Younts	14.039
22.	Rick Hendrick	14.089
23.	Clyde Lynn	14.176
24.	Jack Roush	14.321
25.	Bud Moore	14.402
26.	Harry Melling	14.524
27.	Wendell Scott	14.736
28.	M. C. Anderson	14.902
29.	Buck Baker	15.086
30.	Rod Osterlund	15.378

SINGLE SEASON RECORDS—OWNERS

WINS

1.	Carl Kiekhaefer	1956	30
2.	Petty Enterprises	1967	27
3.	Carl Kiekhaefer	1955	22
	Petty Enterprises	1971	22
5.	Petty Enterprises	1970	19
5.	Petty Enterprises	1963	19
7.	Holman-Moody	1968	17
	Nord Krauskopf	1969	17
9.	Petty Enterprises	1968	16
10.	Cotton Owens	1966	15
11.	Bondy Long	1964	14
12.	Petty Enterprises	1975	13
	Rex Lovette	1965	13
	Holman-Moody	1965	13
	Bondy Long	1965	13
16.	Junior Johnson	1982	12
	Junior Johnson	1981	12
	Rick Hendrick	1996	12
	Herb Thomas	1954	12
	Herb Thomas	1953	12
21.	Wood Bros.	1973	11
	Harry Melling	1985	11
	Holman-Moody	1963	11
	Richard Childress	1987	11
	Petty Enterprises	1959	11
	Nord Krauskopf	1970	11
	Holman-Moody	1969	11
	Petty Enterprises	1962	11

LAPS LED

1.	Petty Enterprises	1971	5,625
2.	Petty Enterprises	1967	5,538
3.	Petty Enterprises	1970	5,140
4.	Nord Krauskopf	1969	5,072
5.	Richard Howard & Junior Johnson	1972	4,398
6.	Holman-Moody	1968	4,287
7.	Petty Enterprises	1968	4,242
8.	Carl Kiekhaefer	1956	4,228
9.	Rex Lovette	1965	4,170
10.	Carl Kiekhaefer	1955	4,027
11.	Junior Johnson	1976	3,791
12.	Petty Enterprises	1964	3,710
13.	Junior Johnson	1978	3,587
14.	Richard Childress	1987	3,358
15.	Rick Hendrick	1996	3,334
16.	Holman-Moody	1963	3,276
16.	Rick Hendrick	1995	3,276
18.	Junior Johnson	1977	3,218
19.	Nord Krauskopf	1970	3,188
20.	Cotton Owens	1966	3,174
21.	Richard Howard & Junior Johnson	1973	3,167
22.	Petty Enterprises	1975	3,158
23.	Petty Enterprises	1974	3,100
24.	Holman-Moody	1965	3,086
25.	Bondy Long	1964	3,071
26.	Petty Enterprises	1966	3,037
27.	Junior Johnson	1982	3,028
28.	Holman-Moody	1969	3,025
29.	Holman-Moody	1971	2,873
30.	Roger Penske	1993	2,860

MILES LED

1.	Petty Enterprises	1971	4,691
2.	Petty Enterprises	1970	4,286
3.	Rick Hendrick	1995	4,194
4.	Richard Howard & Junior Johnson	1972	4,117
5.	Junior Johnson	1978	3,867
6.	Rick Hendrick	1996	3,697
7.	Petty Enterprises	1967	3,669
8.	Rick Hendrick	1986	3,646
9.	Junior Johnson	1976	3,576
10.	Holman-Moody	1971	3,468
11.	Richard Childress	1987	3,399
12.	Petty Enterprises	1964	3,347

13. Petty Enterprises	1975	3,319
14. Wood Bros.	1973	3,275
15. Petty Enterprises	1974	3,256
16. DiGard	1982	3,217
17. Richard Childress	1990	3,203
18. Harry Melling	1985	3,188
19. Junior Johnson	1980	3,155
20. Junior Johnson	1977	3,054
21. Carl Kiekhaefer	1955	3,026
22. Wood Bros.	1972	2,873
23. Carl Kiekhaefer	1956	2,769
24. Richard Howard	1973	2,727
25. Nord Krauskopf	1969	2,688
26. Junior Johnson	1982	2,675
27. Richard Childress	1989	2,624
28. Holman-Moody	1963	2,588
29. Holman-Moody	1968	2,554
30. Raymond Beadle	1989	2,549

Laps Completed

1. Rick Hendrick	1990	30,006
2. Rick Hendrick	1996	28,156
3. Rick Hendrick	1994	28,130
4. Rick Hendrick	1989	27,745
5. Rick Hendrick	1988	27,205
6. Rick Hendrick	1995	27,031
7. Jack Roush	1996	27,008
8. Rick Hendrick	1993	26,059
9. Rick Hendrick	1987	24,996
10. Petty Enterprises	1963	22,021
11. Buck Baker	1965	21,684
12. Carl Kiekhaefer	1956	20,937
13. Petty Enterprises	1964	20,386
14. Cotton Owens	1964	20,382
15. Buck Baker	1966	20,340
16. Bill Seifert	1969	20,047
17. Petty Enterprises	1960	19,035
18. Jack Roush	1995	18,973
19. Junior Johnson	1984	18,590
20. Jack Roush	1994	18,474
21. Stavola Brothers	1988	18,363
22. Petty Enterprises	1971	18,353
23. Junior Johnson	1991	18,089
24. Felix Sabates	1993	18,065
25. Petty Enterprises	1962	18,011
26. Robert Yates	1996	17,925
27. Rick Hendrick	1991	17,892
28. Junior Johnson	1992	17,882
29. Jack Roush	1993	17,792
30. Petty Enterprises	1983	17,784

Miles Driven

1. Rick Hendrick	1990	36,777
2. Rick Hendrick	1994	34,601
3. Rick Hendrick	1996	33,883
4. Rick Hendrick	1989	33,292
5. Rick Hendrick	1995	33,150
6. Jack Roush	1996	33,005
7. Rick Hendrick	1988	32,906
8. Rick Hendrick	1987	31,979
9. Rick Hendrick	1993	31,717
10. Jack Roush	1995	23,249
11. Stavola Brothers	1988	21,945
12. Jack Roush	1994	21,908
13. Junior Johnson	1991	21,881

14. Junior Johnson	1992	21,868
15. Felix Sabates	1993	21,737
16. Junior Johnson	1993	21,546
17. Robert Yates	1996	21,400
18. Rick Hendrick	1991	21,268
19. Junior Johnson	1985	21,259
20. Jack Roush	1993	21,162
21. Junior Johnson	1984	20,900
22. Stavola Brothers	1989	20,841
23. Junior Johnson	1994	20,816
24. Rick Hendrick	1986	20,476
25. Petty Enterprises	1971	20,383
26. Jack Roush	1992	20,383
27. Rick Hendrick	1992	20,334
28. Petty Enterprises	1983	20,132
29. Bill & Mickey Stavola	1986	19,906
30. Junior Johnson	1995	19,721

Poles

1. Carl Kiekhaefer	1955	25
Carl Kiekhaefer	1956	25
3. Nord Krauskopf	1969	20
4. Petty Enterprises	1967	19
5. Rick Hendrick	1986	16
Petty Enterprises	1966	16
7. Holman-Moody	1965	15
8. Junior Johnson	1980	14
Holman-Moody	1969	14
9. Nord Krauskopf	1970	13
11. Junior Johnson &		
Richard Howard	1972	12
Frank Christian	1951	12
Holman-Moody	1968	12
Petty Enterprises	1968	12
Cotton Owens	1964	12
16. Wood Bros.	1974	11
Harry Melling	1985	11
Herb Thomas	1952	11
Junior Johnson	1981	11
Herb Thomas	1953	11
Rex Lovette	1965	11
Petty Enterprises	1970	11
23. Rick Hendrick	1995	10
Petty Enterprises	1971	10
Bondy Long	1965	10

Top 5 Finishes

1. Carl Kiekhaefer	1956	74
2. Petty Enterprises	1963	51
3. Petty Enterprises	1971	50
4. Petty Enterprises	1964	49
5. Rick Hendrick	1996	45
6. Petty Enterprises	1967	43
Holman-Moody	1965	43
8. Carl Kiekhaefer	1955	42
Holman-Moody	1969	42
10. Pete DePaolo	1956	41
Petty Enterprises	1960	41
Bondy Long	1965	41
13. Petty Enterprises	1962	40
14. Cotton Owens	1964	39
15. Holman-Moody	1968	38
Bud Moore	1962	38
15. Bondy Long	1964	38
18. Holman-Moody	1963	37

19. Petty Enterprises	1970	34
20. Pete DePaolo	1957	33
Rick Hendrick	1989	33
Rick Hendrick	1995	33
Petty Enterprises	1959	33
24. Nord Krauskopf	1970	32
25. Petty Enterprises	1968	31
Petty Enterprises	1969	31
27. Charles Robinson	1963	30

Top 10 Finishes

1. Carl Kiekhaefer	1956	92
2. Petty Enterprises	1960	70
3. Petty Enterprises	1963	65
4. Pete DePaolo	1956	61
5. Petty Enterprises	1964	60
6. Cotton Owens	1964	59
7. Rick Hendrick	1996	58
8. Petty Enterprises	1971	56
8. Buck Baker	1965	56
10. Petty Enterprises	1962	54
11. Rick Hendrick	1995	50
12. Holman-Moody	1963	49
Holman-Moody	1965	49
14. Rick Hendrick	1988	47
Petty Enterprises	1958	47
16. Rick Hendrick	1994	46
Carl Kiekhaefer	1955	46
18. Rick Hendrick	1990	45
Petty Enterprises	1967	45
Bondy Long	1965	45
21. Petty Enterprises	1959	44
Bud Moore	1962	44
Holman-Moody	1969	44
24. Rick Hendrick	1989	43
Bondy Long	1964	43
26. Jack Roush	1996	42
27. Petty Enterprises	1970	41
B. G. Holloway	1961	41
Holman-Moody	1968	41
30. Pete DePaolo	1957	40
Rick Hendrick	1993	40

Races Led

1. Petty Enterprises	1971	44
2. Petty Enterprises	1967	42
3. Carl Kiekhaefer	1956	40
Holman-Moody	1969	40
5. Holman-Moody	1968	38
Nord Krauskopf	1969	38
7. Petty Enterprises	1970	36
8. Carl Kiekhaefer	1955	35
Nord Krauskopf	1970	35
Petty Enterprises	1968	35
Petty Enterprises	1964	35
12. Holman-Moody	1965	34
13. Cotton Owens	1964	33
14. Petty Enterprises	1969	32
Petty Enterprises	1963	32
16. Petty Enterprises	1972	31
Rick Hendrick	1996	31
Rex Lovette	1965	31
19. Junior Johnson &		
Richard Howard	1972	30
Rick Hendrick	1995	30

21.	Holman-Moody	1971	29
	Bondy Long	1965	29
23.	Rick Hendrick	1986	28
	Junior Johnson	1976	28
	Junior Johnson	1977	28
	Junior Johnson	1978	28
	Junior Johnson	1980	28

WIN PERCENT

1.	Wood Bros.	1973	61%
2.	Carl Kiekhaefer	1956	59%
3.	Carl Kiekhaefer	1955	56%
4.	Pete DePaolo	1957	56%
5.	Petty Enterprises	1967	55%
6.	Petty Enterprises	1970	49%
7.	Petty Enterprises	1971	47%
8.	Wood Bros.	1976	45%
9.	Petty Enterprises	1975	43%
10.	Holman-Moody	1964	41%
11.	Richard Howard	1974	40%
	Junior Johnson	1982	40%
13.	Harry Melling	1985	39%
14.	Wood Bros.	1972	39%
15.	Junior Johnson	1981	39%

	Rick Hendrick	1996	39%
17.	Holman-Moody	1963	38%
	Richard Childress	1987	38%
19.	Wood Bros.	1974	37%
20.	Holman-Moody	1968	36%
21.	Cotton Owens	1966	36%
22.	Marshall Teague	1951	35%
	Herb Thomas	1954	35%
24.	Rex Lovette	1965	35%
25.	Wood Bros.	1965	35%
	Wood Bros.	1968	35%
27.	Bud Moore	1961	35%
28.	Petty Enterprises	1963	35%
29.	Nord Krauskopf	1969	34%

AVERAGE FINISH

1.	Bobby Allison	1970	4.409
2.	Junior Johnson	1977	4.500
3.	Rex White	1960	4.919
4.	Bondy Long	1965	5.037
5.	Petty Enterprises	1971	5.094
6.	Bud Moore	1962	5.096
7.	Wood Bros.	1963	5.160
8.	Buck Baker	1957	5.720

9.	Petty Enterprises	1967	5.818
10.	Richard Childress	1987	5.931
11.	Junior Johnson	1978	6.033
12.	Holman-Moody	1969	6.113
13.	Junior Johnson &		
	Richard Howard	1972	6.152
14.	Wood Bros.	1972	6.158
15.	Harry Ranier	1981	6.300
16.	Junior Johnson &		
	Richard Howard	1974	6.563
17.	Jack Roush	1990	6.571
18.	Harry Melling	1988	6.586
19.	Petty Enterprises	1975	6.633
20.	Nord Krauskopf	1970	6.809
21.	Wood Bros.	1976	6.864
22.	Rex White	1961	6.935
23.	DiGard	1979	7.000
24.	Raymond Beadle	1988	7.069
25.	Petty Enterprises	1952	7.241
26.	Harry Ranier	1984	7.375
27.	Richard Childress	1986	7.379
28.	J.H. Petty	1961	7.400
29.	Cotton Owens	1966	7.477
30.	Petty Enterprises	1977	7.533

Key

BUICK	Buick
CHEV	Chevrolet
CHRYS	Chrysler
DODG	Dodge
FORD	Ford
HUDS	Hudson
JAG	Jaguar
LINC	Lincoln
MATA	Matador (AMC)
MERC	Mercury
NASH	Nash
OLDS	Oldsmobile
PLYM	Plymouth
PONT	Pontiac
STUD	Studebaker

WINNERS BY CAR MANUFACTURER

Year	Buick	Chev	Chrys	Dodg	Ford	Huds	JAG	Linc	Mata	Merc	Nash	Olds	Plym	Pont	Stud	Total
1949	0	0	0	0	0	0	0	2	0	0	0	5	1	0	0	8
1950	0	0	0	0	1	0	0	2	0	2	0	10	4	0	0	19
1951	0	0	1	0	0	12	0	0	0	2	1	20	2	0	3	41
1952	0	0	1	0	0	27	0	0	0	0	0	3	3	0	0	34
1953	0	0	0	6	0	22	0	0	0	0	0	9	0	0	0	37
1954	0	0	7	1	0	17	1	0	0	0	0	11	0	0	0	37
1955	2	2	27	1	2	1	0	0	0	0	0	10	0	0	0	45
1956	0	3	22	11	14	0	0	0	0	5	0	1	0	0	0	56
1957	0	21	0	0	26	0	0	0	0	0	0	4	0	2	0	53
1958	0	24	0	0	17	0	0	0	0	0	0	7	0	3	0	51
1959	0	16	0	0	16	0	0	0	0	0	0	4	7	1	0	44
1960	0	13	0	1	15	0	0	0	0	0	0	0	8	7	0	44
1961	0	11	1	0	7	0	0	0	0	0	0	0	3	30	0	52
1962	0	14	0	0	6	0	0	0	0	0	0	0	11	22	0	53
1963	0	7	0	0	23	0	0	0	0	1	0	0	19	5	0	55
1964	0	1	0	14	30	0	0	0	0	5	0	0	12	0	0	62
1965	0	0	0	2	48	0	0	0	0	1	0	0	4	0	0	55
1966	0	3	0	18	10	0	0	0	0	2	0	0	16	0	0	49
1967	0	3	0	5	10	0	0	0	0	0	0	0	31	0	0	49
1968	0	1	0	5	20	0	0	0	0	7	0	0	16	0	0	49
1969	0	0	0	22	26	0	0	0	0	4	0	0	2	0	0	54
1970	0	0	0	17	6	0	0	0	0	4	0	0	21	0	0	48
1971	0	3	0	8	5	0	0	0	0	10	0	0	22	0	0	48
1972	0	10	0	4	0	0	0	0	0	9	0	0	8	0	0	31
1973	0	7	0	8	0	0	0	0	1	11	0	0	1	0	0	28
1974	0	12	0	10	0	0	0	0	1	7	0	0	0	0	0	30
1975	0	6	0	14	4	0	0	0	3	3	0	0	0	0	0	30
1976	0	13	0	6	1	0	0	0	0	10	0	0	0	0	0	30
1977	0	21	0	7	0	0	0	0	0	2	0	0	0	0	0	30
1978	0	10	0	0	5	0	0	0	0	4	0	11	0	0	0	30
1979	0	18	0	0	5	0	0	0	0	3	0	5	0	0	0	31
1980	0	22	0	0	4	0	0	0	0	2	0	3	0	0	0	31
1981	22	1	0	0	7	0	0	0	0	0	0	0	0	1	0	31
1982	25	3	0	0	2	0	0	0	0	0	0	0	0	0	0	30
1983	6	15	0	0	4	0	0	0	0	0	Olds	0	0	5	0	30
1984	2	21	0	0	4	0	0	0	0	0	0	0	0	3	0	30
1985	0	14	0	0	14	0	0	0	0	0	0	0	0	0	0	28
1986	3	18	0	0	5	0	0	0	0	0	0	1	0	2	0	29
1987	1	15	0	0	11	0	0	0	0	0	0	0	0	2	0	29
1988	2	8	0	0	9	0	0	0	0	0	0	2	0	8	0	29
1989	1	13	0	0	8	0	0	0	0	0	0	1	0	6	0	29
1990	1	13	0	0	11	0	0	0	0	0	0	1	0	3	0	29
1991	0	11	0	0	10	0	0	0	0	0	0	5	0	3	0	29
1992	0	8	0	0	16	0	0	0	0	0	0	2	0	3	0	29
1993	0	9	0	0	10	0	0	0	0	0	0	0	0	11	0	30
1994	0	11	0	0	20	0	0	0	0	0	0	0	0	0	0	31
1995	0	21	0	0	8	0	0	0	0	0	0	0	0	2	0	31
1996	0	17	0	0	13	0	0	0	0	0	0	0	0	1	0	31
Total	65	439	59	160	453	79	1	4	5	94	1	115	191	120	3	1789

Derived from winning cars of each and every Winston Cup race from 1949–1996

*All T-Bird victories count as Ford victories (T-Bird was listed separately in 1959).

**2 Camaro wins in 1971 count as Chevrolet; 1 Mustang win in 1971 counts as Ford.

PART 2
YEAR BY YEAR

Driver	Starts	Poles	Finish						Laps	Laps Led	Races Led	Winston Cup Points	$
			1	2	3	4	5	6–10					

1970

	Driver	Starts	Poles	1	2	3	4	5	6–10	Laps	Laps Led	Races Led	Winston Cup Points	$
1.	Bobby Isaac	47	13	11	9	5	4	3	6	12,726	3,188	35	3,911	199,600
2.	Bobby Allison	46	5	3	15	8	4	0	5	12,452	1,246	22	3,860	149,745
3.	James Hylton	47	1	1	4	2	8	7	17	12,712	199	8	3,788	78,201
4.	Richard Petty	40	9	18	5	0	0	4	4	10,536	5,007	32	3,447	151,124
5.	Neil Castles	47	0	0	1	4	3	4	12	10,297	31	2	3,158	49,746

Key

STARTS	Number of starts that year
POLES	Number of poles that year
FINISH	
1	Number of first place finishes that year
2	Number of second place finishes that year
3	Number of third place finishes that year
4	Number of fourth place finishes that year
5	Number of fifth place finishes that year
6–10	Number of sixth through tenth place finishes that year
LAPS	Number of laps completed that year
LAPS LED	Number of laps led that year
RACES LED	Number of races led that year
WINSTON CUP POINTS	Winston Cup points that year
$	Winnings for that year
N/A	Information not available

The left-hand pages list the drivers ranked one through fifty for that year based on Winston Cup points. The right-hand page lists the top thirty leaders for that year in the following categories: laps completed, laps led, miles led, miles driven, and races led. Please note that some of the top thirty leaders in the preceding five categories may not have been ranked in the top fifty drivers (based on Winston Cup points) for that year.

*Please note that due to incomplete lap leader records for the years 1949–67, the figures for the Laps Led, Miles Led, and Races Led categories cannot be endorsed as absolute totals for those years. The statistics given here simply represent the most accurate figures given the information available.

Driver	Starts	Poles	Finish 1	2	3	4	5	6–10	Laps	Laps Led	Races Led	Winston Cup Points	$
1949													
1. Red Byron	6	1	2	0	2	0	0	0	633	103	2	842.5	5,800
2. Lee Petty	6	0	1	2	0	0	0	2	890	1	1	725	3,855
3. Bob Flock	6	1	2	1	0	0	0	0	728	27	4	704	4,870
4. Bill Blair	6	0	0	0	0	0	3	2	613	325	2	567.5	1,280
5. Fonty Flock	6	0	0	1	1	1	0	0	304	85	1	554.5	2,015
6. Curtis Turner	6	1	1	0	0	0	0	3	564	78	2	430	2,675
7. Ray Erickson	4	0	0	1	1	0	0	1	713	0	0	422	1,460
8. Tim Flock	5	0	0	1	0	0	1	1	347	0	0	421	1,510
9. Glenn Dunnaway	6	0	0	0	1	0	0	2	594	1	1	384	810
10. Frank Mundy	4	0	0	0	1	1	0	0	274	0	0	370	1,160
11. Bill Snowden	4	0	0	0	0	0	1	2	182	0	0	315	660
12. Bill Rexford	3	0	0	0	1	0	1	0	370	0	0	286	785
13. Sara Christian	6	0	0	0	0	0	1	1	606	0	0	282	760
14. Clyde Minter	2	0	0	0	0	2	0	0	386	0	0	280	760
15. Gober Sosebee	3	1	0	1	0	0	0	1	170	34	1	265	1,305
16. Jim Roper	2	0	1	0	0	0	0	0	197	47	1	253	2,130
17. Sam Rice	2	0	0	0	0	2	0	0	192	0	0	231	680
18. Jack White	1	0	1	0	0	0	0	0	200	66	1	200	1,580
19. Dick Linder	3	0	0	1	0	0	0	0	416	0	0	180.5	830
20. Billy Rafter	1	0	0	0	1	0	0	0	N/A	0	0	160	480
21. Archie Smith	2	0	0	0	0	0	0	2	161	0	0	145	225
22. Joe Littlejohn	1	0	0	0	0	1	0	0	40	0	0	140	300
23. Jack Russell	3	0	0	0	0	0	0	2	178	0	0	140	175
24. Mike Eagan	1	0	0	0	0	1	0	0	N/A	0	0	140	300
25. Herb Thomas	4	0	0	0	0	0	1	0	197	0	0	132	225
26. Sterling Long	2	0	0	0	0	0	0	1	N/A	0	0	100	150
27. Frank Christian	1	0	0	0	0	0	0	1	N/A	0	0	100	175
28. Frankie Schneider	1	0	0	0	0	0	0	1	N/A	0	0	100	150
29. Lloyd Moore	1	0	0	0	0	0	0	1	186	0	0	100	150
30. Roy Hall	1	0	0	0	0	0	0	1	196	0	0	100	150
31. Slick Smith	4	0	0	0	0	0	0	0	277	0	0	99	275
32. Al Keller	1	0	0	0	0	0	0	0	185	0	0	90	200
33. John Wright	1	0	0	0	0	0	0	1	179	0	0	80	100
34. Al Bonnell	2	1	0	0	0	0	0	0	183	0	0	80	150
35. Otis Martin	4	0	0	0	0	0	0	1	66	0	0	69.5	200
36. Jimmy Thompson	2	0	0	0	0	0	0	2	N/A	0	0	65	175
37. Charles Muscatel	1	0	0	0	0	0	0	1	N/A	0	0	60	75
38. Raymond Lewis	1	0	0	0	0	0	0	1	194	0	0	60	75
39. Al Wagoner	1	0	0	0	0	0	0	1	178	0	0	60	75
40. George Lewis	1	0	0	0	0	0	0	1	168	0	0	40	50
41. Lou Volk	1	0	0	0	0	0	0	1	182	0	0	30	125
42. Buddy Helms	1	0	0	0	0	0	0	1	N/A	0	0	27.5	75
43. Bob Apperson	3	0	0	0	0	0	0	0	191	0	0	25	150
44. Bill Bennett	1	0	0	0	0	0	0	0	181	0	0	24	100
45. Ted Chamberlain	2	0	0	0	0	0	0	0	148	0	0	24	100
46. Buck Baker	2	0	0	0	0	0	0	0	N/A	0	0	20	50
47. Jack Etheridge	1	0	0	0	0	0	0	1	N/A	0	0	20	75
48. Ellis Pearce	1	0	0	0	0	0	0	1	N/A	0	0	20	50
49. Bobby Greene	2	0	0	0	0	0	0	0	148	0	0	19.5	50
50. Ken Wagner	3	1	0	0	0	0	0	0	412	0	0	19	100

LAPS COMPLETED

1.	Lee Petty	890
2.	Bob Flock	728
3.	Ray Erickson	713
4.	Red Byron	633
5.	Bill Blair	613
6.	Sara Christian	606
7.	Glenn Dunnaway	594
8.	Curtis Turner	564
9.	Dick Linder	416
10.	Ken Wagner	412
11.	Clyde Minter	386
12.	Bill Rexford	370
13.	Tim Flock	347
14.	Fonty Flock	304
15.	Slick Smith	277
16.	Frank Mundy	274
17.	Jack White	200
18.	Jim Roper	197
	Herb Thomas	197
20.	Roy Hall	196
21.	Raymond Lewis	194
22.	Sam Rice	192
23.	Bob Apperson	191
24.	Lloyd Moore	186
25.	Al Keller	185
26.	Al Bonnell	183
27.	Bill Snowden	182
	Lou Volk	182
29.	Bill Bennett	181
30.	Budd Olsen	180

LAPS LED

1.	Bill Blair	325
2.	Red Byron	103
3.	Fonty Flock	85
4.	Curtis Turner	78
5.	Jack White	66
6.	Jim Roper	47
7.	Gober Sosebee	34
8.	Bob Flock	27
9.	Glenn Dunnaway	1
	Lee Petty	1

MILES LED

1.	Bill Blair	199
2.	Gober Sosebee	141
3.	Red Byron	73
4.	Curtis Turner	69
5.	Fonty Flock	43
6.	Jim Roper	35
7.	Jack White	33
8.	Bob Flock	16
9.	Glenn Dunnaway	1
	Lee Petty	1

MILES DRIVEN

1.	Red Byron	582
2.	Bob Flock	574
3.	Lee Petty	565
4.	Bill Blair	551
5.	Sara Christian	417
6.	Tim Flock	415
7.	Curtis Turner	382
8.	Frank Mundy	381
9.	Ray Erickson	357
10.	Glenn Dunnaway	347
11.	Dick Linder	289
12.	Bill Rexford	274
13.	Ken Wagner	206
14.	Clyde Minter	193
15.	Al Keller	185
16.	Al Bonnell	183
17.	Lou Volk	182
18.	Bill Bennett	181
19.	Budd Olsen	180
20.	Dick Zimmerman	178
21.	Erwin Blatt	176
22.	Louise Smith	175
23.	Don Cecchini	173
24.	Lee Schmidt	171
25.	Gober Sosebee	170
26.	Ken Marriott	169
	Ed Tyson	169
28.	Ken Schroeder	168
29.	Tommy Coates	167
30.	Wally Campbell	166
	Joe Littlejohn	166

RACES LED

1.	Bob Flock	4
2.	Bill Blair	2
	Red Byron	2
	Curtis Turner	2
3.	Harold Dunnaway	1
	Fonty Flock	1
	Lee Petty	1
	Jim Roper	1
	Gober Sosebee	1
	Jack White	1

Driver	Starts	Poles	Finish 1	2	3	4	5	6–10	Laps	Laps Led	Races Led	Winston Cup Points	$
1950													
1. Bill Rexford	17	0	1	0	1	2	1	6	1,302	98	2	1,959	5,750
2. Fireball Roberts	9	1	1	2	1	0	0	1	1,138	60	3	1,848.5	6,800
3. Lee Petty	17	0	1	1	2	3	2	4	1,558	43	1	1,590	7,120
4. Lloyd Moore	16	0	1	2	3	1	0	3	1,358	57	2	1,398	5,235
5. Curtis Turner	16	4	4	1	1	1	0	0	1,626	1,110	12	1,375.5	8,080
6. Johnny Mantz	3	0	1	0	0	0	0	1	400	351	1	1,282	10,810
7. Chuck Mahoney	11	1	0	1	1	0	1	3	705	18	1	1,217.5	2,250
8. Dick Linder	13	5	3	1	1	0	0	3	1,437	460	5	1,121	5,695
9. Jimmy Florian	10	1	1	0	1	1	0	3	1,060	40	1	801	2,730
10. Bill Blair	16	0	1	2	0	0	2	2	1,550	218	3	766	4,400
11. Herb Thomas	13	0	1	0	2	1	0	2	719	176	2	590.5	2,645
12. Buck Baker	9	1	0	1	1	0	0	3	587	10	1	531.5	2,145
13. Cotton Owens	3	0	0	0	0	0	0	1	511	23	1	500	1,100
14. Fonty Flock	7	2	1	0	0	1	0	1	951	369	4	458.5	2,195
15. Weldon Adams	4	0	0	0	1	0	1	1	560	0	0	440	1,205
16. Tim Flock	12	1	1	0	0	3	0	3	1,403	190	2	437.5	3,980
17. Clyde Minter	8	0	0	0	1	0	2	0	665	0	0	427	1,155
18. Dick Burns	8	0	0	0	0	1	1	1	323	0	0	341.5	780
19. Art Lamey	4	0	0	0	0	0	2	1	N/A	0	0	320	655
20. Bob Flock	4	0	0	1	0	0	0	2	595	5	1	314	1,155
21. George Hartley	8	0	0	0	0	0	0	2	371	0	0	298	875
22. Gayle Warren	10	0	0	0	0	0	1	1	429	10	1	287	550
23. Frank Mundy	8	0	0	0	0	0	0	3	310	0	0	275.5	550
24. Jim Paschal	6	0	0	1	0	0	0	1	669	0	0	220.5	850
25. Jack White	7	0	0	0	0	0	1	1	712	0	0	211.5	525
26. Pappy Hough	5	0	0	0	0	0	0	2	296	0	0	207.5	325
27. Ray Duhigg	5	0	0	0	0	0	1	1	N/A	0	0	202.5	450
28. Leon Sales	2	0	1	0	0	0	0	0	227	18	1	200	1,000
29. Jimmy Thompson	4	0	0	0	0	0	0	3	522	0	0	200	525
30. Harold Kite	3	0	1	0	0	0	0	0	382	38	1	187	1,550
31. Neil Cole	2	0	0	0	0	0	1	0	N/A	0	0	183.5	300
32. Jack Smith	3	0	0	1	0	0	0	0	376	45	1	180	775
33. Bucky Sager	2	0	0	1	0	0	0	0	N/A	146	1	180	750
34. Red Harvey	1	0	0	1	0	0	0	0	N/A	1	1	180	750
34. Ted Swaim	1	0	0	1	0	0	0	0	200	0	0	180	750
36. Buck Barr	2	0	0	0	1	0	0	1	N/A	0	0	180	575
37. Pepper Cunningham	2	0	0	0	0	0	0	2	130	0	0	177.5	300
38. Ewell Weddle	3	0	0	0	1	0	0	0	158	0	0	173.5	600
39. Donald Thomas	2	0	0	0	0	0	0	2	141	0	0	164	300
40. Bill Snowden	4	0	0	0	0	0	1	1	532	0	0	163	325
41. Jimmie Lewallen	3	0	0	0	0	1	0	0	330	0	0	140	400
42. Chuck James	1	0	0	0	0	1	0	0	N/A	0	0	140	400
43. Dick Clothier	5	0	0	0	0	0	0	2	194	0	0	133.5	350
44. Paul Parks	6	0	0	0	0	0	0	1	95	0	0	124.5	375
45. Al Gross	3	0	0	0	0	1	0	0	182	0	0	124	550
46. Jack Reynolds	2	0	0	0	0	0	1	0	N/A	0	0	120	300
47. Jim Delaney	2	0	0	0	0	0	0	1	N/A	0	0	114	175
48. Carl Renner	2	0	0	0	0	0	0	1	N/A	0	0	108	250
49. Jack Holloway	2	0	0	0	0	0	0	2	192	0	0	107.5	225
50. Bob Dickson	6	0	0	0	0	0	0	2	627	0	0	105	275
51. J. C. Van Landingham	1	0	0	0	0	0	1	0	48	0	0	105	450

LAPS COMPLETED

1.	Curtis Turner	1,626
2.	Lee Petty	1,558
3.	Bill Blair	1,550
4.	Dick Linder	1,437
5.	Tim Flock	1,403
6.	Lloyd Moore	1,358
7.	Bill Rexford	1,302
8.	Fireball Roberts	1,138
9.	Jimmy Florian	1,060
10.	Fonty Flock	951
11.	Glenn Dunnaway	866
12.	Herb Thomas	719
13.	Jack White	712
14.	Chuck Mahoney	705
15.	Jim Paschal	669
16.	Clyde Minter	665
17.	Red Byron	634
18.	Bob Dickson	627
19.	Bob Flock	595
20.	Buck Baker	587
21.	Bob Apperson	573
22.	Weldon Adams	560
23.	Ted Chamberlain	541
24.	Bill Snowden	532
25.	Johnny Grubb	530
26.	Jimmy Thompson	522
27.	Cotton Owens	511
28.	Elmer Wilson	497
29.	Gayle Warren	429
30.	Bob Smith	419

LAPS LED

1.	Curtis Turner	1,110
2.	Dick Linder	460
3.	Fonty Flock	369
4.	Johnny Mantz	351
5.	Bill Blair	218
6.	Tim Flock	190
7.	Herb Thomas	176
8.	Bucky Sager	146
9.	Bill Rexford	98
10.	Red Byron	85
11.	Fireball Roberts	60
12.	Lloyd Moore	57
13.	Jack Smith	45
14.	Lee Petty	43
15.	Jimmy Florian	40
16.	Harold Kite	38
17.	Ray Erickson	31
18.	Cotton Owens	23
19.	Chuck Mahoney	18
	Leon Sales	18
21.	Pee Wee Martin	12
22.	Buck Baker	10
	Gayle Warren	10
24.	Bob Flock	5
25.	Gober Sosebee	4
26.	Red Harvey	1

MILES LED

1.	Curtis Turner	689
2.	Johnny Mantz	439
3.	Fonty Flock	326
4.	Dick Linder	230
5.	Harold Kite	158
6.	Tim Flock	152
7.	Bill Blair	130
8.	Red Byron	94
9.	Herb Thomas	88
10.	Bucky Sager	73
11.	Bill Rexford	58
12.	Fireball Roberts	56
13.	Lee Petty	43
14.	Ray Erickson	31
15.	Cotton Owens	29
16.	Lloyd Moore	29
17.	Jack Smith	28
18.	Jimmy Florian	20
19.	Pee Wee Martin	12
20.	Leon Sales	11
21.	Chuck Mahoney	9
22.	Buck Baker	5
	Gober Sosebee	5
	Gayle Warren	5
25.	Bob Flock	4
26.	Red Harvey	1

MILES DRIVEN

1.	Lee Petty	1,407
2.	Curtis Turner	1,390
3.	Tim Flock	1,275
4.	Bill Blair	1,253
5.	Bill Rexford	1,146
6.	Fonty Flock	1,077
7.	Fireball Roberts	1,065
8.	Dick Linder	1,060
9.	Lloyd Moore	1,046
10.	Jack White	850
11.	Jimmy Florian	850
12.	Red Byron	835
13.	Bob Flock	781
14.	Glenn Dunnaway	731
15.	Cotton Owens	727
16.	Chuck Mahoney	638
17.	Bob Apperson	631
18.	Harold Kite	618
19.	Buck Baker	605
20.	Jim Paschal	571
21.	Bill Snowden	568
22.	Jack Smith	561
23.	Weldon Adams	555
24.	Billy Carden	548
25.	Clyde Minter	546
26.	Gober Sosebee	543
27.	Johnny Grubb	541
28.	Ted Chamberlain	539
29.	Al Keller	538
30.	Elmer Wilson	519

RACES LED

1.	Curtis Turner	12
2.	Dick Linder	5
3.	Fonty Flock	4
4.	Bill Blair	3
	Red Byron	3
	Fireball Roberts	3
7.	Tim Flock	2
	Lloyd Moore	2
	Bill Rexford	2
	Herb Thomas	2

1951

Driver	Starts	Poles	Finish 1	2	3	4	5	6–10	Laps	Laps Led	Races Led	Winston Cup Points	$
1. Herb Thomas	35	4	7	1	3	4	1	2	2,159	954	10	4,208.45	20,850
2. Fonty Flock	34	15	8	2	4	5	1	2	2,788	2,068	21	4,062.25	15,200
3. Tim Flock	30	6	7	5	3	3	1	2	2,408	844	12	3,722.5	14,545
4. Lee Petty	32	0	1	4	2	1	3	8	1,248	99	1	2,392.25	7,340
5. Frank Mundy	27	4	3	2	1	2	1	3	874	445	5	1,963.5	7,085
6. Buddy Shuman	7	0	0	0	1	0	0	6	391	0	0	1,368.75	2,830
7. Jesse James Taylor	10	0	0	1	0	0	0	2	519	104	3	1,214	3,750
8. Dick Rathmann	15	0	0	3	1	0	0	3	231	0	0	1,040	3,225
9. Bill Snowden	12	0	0	0	0	2	1	6	383	0	0	1,009.25	2,640
10. Joe Eubanks	12	0	0	1	2	0	0	0	490	7	1	1,005.5	3,415
11. Lloyd Moore	22	0	0	0	1	0	3	4	322	0	0	996.5	2,600
12. Fireball Roberts	9	0	0	1	0	0	1	1	825	0	0	930	1,190
13. Jimmie Lewallen	12	0	0	0	2	0	2	4	613	0	0	874.25	2,430
14. Bob Flock	17	1	1	2	0	1	0	5	1,028	133	5	869	3,680
15. Jim Paschal	16	0	0	0	1	3	0	3	767	33	1	858.5	2,450
16. Bill Blair	18	0	0	1	1	2	0	3	815	0	0	840	2,710
17. Gober Sosebee	10	1	0	3	0	0	1	1	717	7	1	784	2,710
18. Erick Erickson	12	0	0	1	1	0	2	2	859	0	0	723.5	2,435
19. Tommy Thompson	5	0	1	0	0	0	0	1	398	58	1	755	5,510
20. Donald Thomas	17	0	0	0	1	0	3	4	479	0	0	743.5	2,060
21. Johnny Mantz	6	0	0	1	1	0	0	2	332	28	1	725	2,025
22. Lou Figaro	13	1	1	0	0	2	0	1	431	200	1	684.2	2,135
23. Buck Baker	11	0	0	0	1	0	3	1	338	0	0	644.5	1,650
24. Dick Meyer	6	0	0	1	0	0	2	1	N/A	82	1	626.5	1,650
25. Harold Kite	2	0	0	0	0	0	0	1	384	0	0	625	800
26. Billy Carden	11	2	0	0	1	1	0	3	519	58	1	509.75	1,460
27. Jimmy Florian	9	0	0	0	0	2	0	3	N/A	0	0	462.5	1,100
28. Jim Fiebelkorn	17	0	0	1	0	0	0	3	984	0	0	455	1,355
29. Ronnie Kohler	5	0	0	0	2	0	0	1	N/A	0	0	432	1,100
30. Danny Weinberg	6	0	1	0	0	0	1	1	297	1	1	423.5	1,470
31. Pappy Hough	9	0	0	0	0	0	1	3	N/A	0	0	423	760
32. Woody Brown	3	0	0	0	1	0	1	0	14	0	0	421	1,125
33. Neil Cole	5	1	1	1	0	0	1	0	399	45	1	382	2,050
34. Paul Newkirk	1	0	0	0	0	0	1	0	241	0	0	375	500
35. John McGinley	6	0	0	1	0	1	0	0	224	0	0	372.5	1,300
36. Marvin Panch	3	0	0	1	0	0	0	1	N/A	0	0	371.5	1,075
37. Oda Greene	6	0	0	0	1	0	1	1	173	0	0	366.5	825
38. Jack Goodwin	3	0	0	0	0	0	0	1	617	0	0	362.5	725
39. Jack Smith	7	0	0	1	1	0	0	0	480	0	0	360.5	1,275
40. Robert Caswell	3	0	0	1	0	0	0	0	247	0	0	350	1,325
41. Lloyd Dane	7	0	0	0	1	1	0	1	447	0	0	323.5	975
42. Cotton Owens	5	0	0	0	0	0	1	2	370	0	0	312.5	225
43. Fred Steinbroner	6	0	0	0	0	1	1	1	198	0	0	306.5	700
44. Ewell Weddle	7	0	0	0	0	0	0	2	743	0	0	293.5	435
45. George Seeger	9	0	0	0	1	0	0	2	705	0	0	278	910
46. Sam Hawks	3	0	0	0	0	1	0	0	N/A	0	0	262.5	650
47. Don Bailey	10	0	0	0	0	1	0	1	151	0	0	239.5	625
48. Bud Farrell	5	0	0	0	0	1	0	1	373	0	0	227.5	700
49. Harvey Riley	8	0	0	0	0	0	1	1	606	0	0	262.5	475
50. Fred Lee	6	0	0	0	0	1	0	1	98	0	0	224	450

LAPS COMPLETED

1.	Fonty Flock	2,788
2.	Tim Flock	2,408
3.	Herb Thomas	2,159
4.	Marshall Teague	1,611
5.	Lee Petty	1,248
6.	Curtis Turner	1,164
7.	Bob Flock	1,028
8.	Jim Fiebelkorn	984
9.	Frank Mundy	874
10.	Erick Erickson	859
11.	Fireball Roberts	825
12.	Bill Blair	815
13.	Jim Paschal	767
14.	Ewell Weddle	743
15.	Gober Sosebee	717
16.	George Seeger	705
17.	Jack Goodwin	617
18.	Jimmie Lewallen	613
19.	Red Byron	609
	Billy Myers	609
21.	Harvey Riley	606
22.	Iggy Katona	559
23.	Slick Smith	529
24.	Billy Carden	519
	Jesse James Taylor	519
26.	Jim Delaney	494
27.	Joe Eubanks	490
28.	Jack Smith	480
29.	Earl Moss	479
	Donald Thomas	479

LAPS LED

1.	Fonty Flock	2,068
2.	Herb Thomas	954
3.	Tim Flock	844
4.	Marshall Teague	789
5.	Curtis Turner	513
6.	Frank Mundy	445
7.	Lou Figaro	200
8.	Marvin Burke	156
9.	Bob Flock	133
10.	Jesse James Taylor	104
11.	Lee Petty	99
12.	Dick Meyer	82
13.	Billy Carden	58
	Jim Reed	58
	Tommy Thompson	58
16.	Neil Cole	45
17.	Jim Paschal	33
18.	Johnny Mantz	28
19.	Billy Myers	23
20.	Bill Norton	19
	Leonard Tippett	19
22.	Joe Eubanks	7
	Gober Sosebee	7
24.	Hershel McGriff	1
	John Soares	1
	Danny Weinberg	1

MILES LED

1.	Fonty Flock	1,339
2.	Herb Thomas	782
3.	Tim Flock	607
4.	Marshall Teague	531
5.	Curtis Turner	361
6.	Frank Mundy	261
7.	Lou Figaro	100
8.	Marvin Burke	98
9.	Bob Flock	82
10.	Tommy Thompson	58
11.	Jesse James Taylor	57
12.	Lee Petty	50
13.	Billy Carden	44
14.	Dick Meyer	41
15.	Jim Reed	29
16.	Neil Cole	23
17.	Jim Paschal	17
18.	Johnny Mantz	14
19.	Billy Myers	12
20.	Bill Norton	10
	Leonard Tippett	10
22.	Joe Eubanks	7
	Gober Sosebee	7
24.	Hershel McGriff	1
25.	John Soares	1
26.	Danny Weinberg	1

MILES DRIVEN

1.	Fonty Flock	2,068
2.	Tim Flock	1,773
3.	Herb Thomas	1,686
4.	Marshall Teague	1,417
5.	Lee Petty	1,168
6.	Curtis Turner	948
7.	Bob Flock	927
8.	Jim Fiebelkorn	913
9.	Jim Paschal	846
10.	Erick Erickson	832
11.	Ewell Weddle	799
12.	Bill Blair	755
13.	Fireball Roberts	738
14.	Jack Goodwin	712
15.	Gober Sosebee	711
16.	Billy Myers	702
17.	Red Byron	701
18.	George Seeger	697
19.	Jimmie Lewallen	671
20.	Iggy Katona	643
21.	Harvey Riley	624
22.	Billy Carden	613
23.	Slick Smith	593
24.	Frank Mundy	579
25.	Jesse James Taylor	566
26.	Donald Thomas	563
27.	Hershel McGriff	561
28.	Jack Smith	552
29.	Tommy Melvin	551
30.	Leon Sales	548

RACES LED

1.	Fonty Flock	21
2.	Tim Flock	12
3.	Herb Thomas	10
4.	Marshall Teague	8
5.	Curtis Turner	6
6.	Bob Flock	5
	Frank Mundy	5
8.	Jesse James Taylor	3

1952

Driver	Starts	Poles	Finish 1	2	3	4	5	6–10	Laps	Laps Led	Races Led	Winston Cup Points	$
1. Tim Flock	33	4	8	5	2	7	0	3	5,345	1,469	16	6,858.5	22,890
2. Herb Thomas	32	10	8	7	3	0	1	3	5,134	1,509	16	6,752.5	18,965
3. Lee Petty	32	0	3	6	5	5	2	6	5,094	193	7	6,498.5	16,876
4. Fonty Flock	29	7	2	6	2	2	2	3	3,906	984	10	5,183.5	19,112
5. Dick Rathmann	27	2	5	1	4	0	4	0	3,607	701	10	3,952.5	11,248
6. Bill Blair	19	1	1	3	4	2	0	3	2,427	120	4	3,449	7,899
7. Joe Eubanks	19	0	0	0	1	1	2	5	2,626	0	0	3,090.5	3,630
8. Ray Duhigg	18	0	0	0	2	1	1	6	2,823	0	0	2,986.5	3,811
9. Donald Thomas	21	1	1	1	1	1	1	9	2,623	9	1	2,574	4,477
10. Buddy Shuman	15	0	1	1	0	0	1	4	1,785	65	2	2,483	4,587
11. Ted Chamberlain	18	0	0	0	0	0	0	6	3,053	0	0	2,208	1,277
12. Buck Baker	14	2	1	0	0	2	0	3	1,550	139	3	2,159	3,187
13. Perk Brown	19	1	0	0	2	0	1	3	2,336	0	0	2,151.5	2,187
14. Jimmie Lewallen	20	0	0	0	0	1	1	5	2,327	0	0	2,033	2,052
15. Bub King	10	0	0	0	1	1	0	3	1,743	0	0	1,993	2,737
16. Herschel Buchanan	5	0	0	0	1	1	2	1	1,302	0	0	1,868	2,468
17. Johnny Patterson	5	0	0	1	0	0	1	0	1,054	0	0	1,708	3,618
18. Jim Paschal	15	0	0	0	0	1	0	6	1,705	0	0	1,694	1,483
19. Neil Cole	11	0	0	0	1	0	0	6	1,579	0	0	1,618	1,793
20. Lloyd Moore	8	0	0	1	0	1	0	2	1,457	0	0	1,513.5	2,193
21. Gene Comstock	8	0	0	0	0	1	0	2	1,496	0	0	1,339	785
22. Banjo Matthews	3	0	0	0	0	0	1	0	667	0	0	1,240	1,000
23. Ralph Liguori	12	0	0	0	0	1	0	5	1,671	0	0	1,230	920
24. Jack Reynolds	10	0	0	0	0	2	0	4	1,335	0	0	1,177.5	1,450
25. Dick Passwater	6	0	0	0	0	0	1	2	1,366	0	0	1,148	945
26. Bucky Sager	10	0	0	0	0	1	0	2	1,545	0	0	1,119.5	710
27. Frankie Schneider	6	0	0	0	1	2	0	1	411	0	0	931	1,350
28. Otis Martin	5	0	0	0	0	0	0	2	620	0	0	873.5	275
29. Coleman Lawrence	8	0	0	0	0	0	0	3	1,326	0	0	846	375
30. Ed Samples	8	0	0	1	1	0	0	2	614	0	0	827	1,535
31. Fred Dove	8	0	0	0	0	0	0	3	919	0	0	780	390
32. Slick Smith	5	0	0	0	0	0	0	3	613	0	0	746	725
33. Iggy Katona	5	0	0	0	0	0	0	2	1,067	0	0	742	525
34. Jack Smith	8	1	0	0	0	0	0	2	883	186	1	729	820
35. Tommy Moon	6	1	0	1	0	0	1	1	487	0	0	726	1,145
36. Rollin Smith	1	0	0	0	0	0	0	0	385	0	0	700	350
37. Speedy Thompson	2	0	0	0	0	0	0	0	409	0	0	656	305
38. Jimmy Thompson	1	0	0	0	0	0	0	0	383	0	0	650	300
39. Bud Farrell	6	0	0	0	0	0	0	2	881	0	0	648	325
40. Weldon Adams	6	0	0	0	0	0	0	2	708	0	0	634	275
41. Clyde Minter	5	0	0	0	0	0	0	3	620	0	0	632	375
42. Elton Hildreth	6	0	0	0	0	0	0	1	815	0	0	614	375
43. Dave Terrell	5	0	0	0	0	0	1	2	477	0	0	612	475
44. Tommy Thompson	5	0	0	0	0	0	0	1	553	20	1	602.5	525
45. Bob Moore (OH)	5	0	0	0	1	0	0	2	524	0	0	579.5	575
46. Jim Reed	7	0	0	0	0	0	1	2	597	0	0	567	475
47. E. C. Ramsey	7	0	0	0	0	0	0	0	826	0	0	560	260
48. Jimmy Florian	6	0	0	0	0	0	0	2	283	0	0	551	175
49. Ed Benedict	5	0	0	0	0	0	1	1	633	0	0	526	360
50. Curtis Turner	7	0	0	0	0	0	1	0	500	12	1	505	265

LAPS COMPLETED		LAPS LED		MILES LED		MILES DRIVEN		RACES LED	
1. Tim Flock	5,345	1. Herb Thomas	1,509	1. Tim Flock	904	1. Tim Flock	3,564	1. Tim Flock	16
2. Herb Thomas	5,134	2. Tim Flock	1,469	2. Herb Thomas	875	2. Herb Thomas	3,475	Herb Thomas	16
3. Lee Petty	5,094	3. Fonty Flock	984	3. Fonty Flock	870	3. Lee Petty	3,439	3. Fonty Flock	10
4. Fonty Flock	3,906	4. Dick Rathmann	701	4. Dick Rathmann	519	4. Fonty Flock	2,767	Dick Rathmann	10
5. Dick Rathmann	3,607	5. Marshall Teague	236	5. Marshall Teague	248	5. Dick Rathmann	2,539	5. Lee Petty	7
6. Ted Chamberlain	3,053	6. Gober Sosebee	215	6. Lee Petty	141	6. Ted Chamberlain	2,181	6. Bill Blair	4
7. Ray Duhigg	2,823	7. Lee Petty	193	7. Gober Sosebee	119	7. Joe Eubanks	2,066	7. Buck Baker	3
8. Joe Eubanks	2,626	8. Jack Smith	186	8. Bill Blair	111	8. Ray Duhigg	2,029	Gober Sosebee	3
9. Donald Thomas	2,623	9. Buck Baker	139	9. Jack Smith	93	9. Donald Thomas	1,928	9. Buddy Shuman	2
10. Bill Blair	2,427	10. Bill Blair	120	10. Buck Baker	91	10. Bill Blair	1,920	Marshall Teague	2
11. Perk Brown	2,336	11. Buddy Shuman	65	11. Buddy Shuman	33	11. Jimmie Lewallen	1,638		
12. Jimmie Lewallen	2,327	12. Tommy Thompson	20	12. Tommy Thompson	25	12. Perk Brown	1,458		
13. Buddy Shuman	1,785	13. Fireball Roberts	15	13. Fireball Roberts	19	13. Bub King	1,419		
14. Bub King	1,743	14. George Gallup	13	14. Roscoe Thompson	11	14. Buddy Shuman	1,413		
15. Jim Paschal	1,705	15. Curtis Turner	12	15. Donald Thomas	9	15. Buck Baker	1,273		
16. Ralph Liguori	1,671	16. Roscoe Thompson	11	16. George Gallup	7	16. Ralph Liguori	1,236		
17. Neil Cole	1,579	17. Donald Thomas	9	17. Curtis Turner	6	17. Gene Comstock	1,185		
18. Buck Baker	1,550	18. Bob Flock	1	18. Bob Flock	1	18. Jim Paschal	1,109		
19. Bucky Sager	1,545					19. Dick Passwater	1,085		
20. Gene Comstock	1,496					20. Lloyd Moore	1,084		
21. Lloyd Moore	1,457					21. Bucky Sager	1,068		
22. Dick Passwater	1,366					22. Herschel Buchanan	1,068		
23. Jack Reynolds	1,335					23. Coleman Lawrence	1,045		
24. Coleman Lawrence	1,326					24. Neil Cole	982		
25. Herschel Buchanan	1,302					25. Pat Kirkwood	972		
26. Iggy Katona	1,067					26. Iggy Katona	925		
27. Johnny Patterson	1,054					27. Jack Reynolds	901		
28. Fred Dove	919					28. Johnny Patterson	879		
29. Jack Smith	883					29. Jack Smith	820		
30. Bud Farrell	881					30. E. C. Ramsey	693		

Driver	Starts	Poles	Finish 1	2	3	4	5	6–10	Laps	Laps Led	Races Led	Winston Cup Points	$
1. Herb Thomas	37	11	12	8	3	3	1	4	4,292	1,420	23	8,460	28,910
2. Lee Petty	36	0	5	4	10	4	3	6	3,021	209	6	7,814	18,447
3. Dick Rathmann	34	2	5	12	1	2	1	3	2,545	542	8	7,362	20,245
4. Buck Baker	33	4	4	2	3	4	3	9	1,619	564	9	6,713	18,167
5. Fonty Flock	33	3	4	5	4	3	1	0	1,999	581	10	6,174	17,756
6. Tim Flock	26	5	1	1	2	3	4	7	1,990	289	8	5,011	8,282
7. Jim Paschal	24	1	1	0	1	2	2	3	1,179	73	1	4,211	5,571
8. Joe Eubanks	24	1	0	1	2	4	0	8	718	82	2	3,603	5,254
9. Jimmie Lewallen	22	0	0	1	2	0	4	6	908	0	0	3,508	4,222
10. Curtis Turner	19	3	1	0	1	1	0	2	1,396	191	4	3,373	4,347
11. Speedy Thompson	7	0	2	2	1	0	0	2	1,257	99	4	2,958	6,547
12. Slick Smith	23	1	0	0	0	0	0	10	592	4	1	2,670	2,302
13. Elton Hildreth	25	0	0	0	0	1	0	4	821	0	0	2,625	1,997
14. Gober Sosebee	17	0	0	1	1	0	0	7	943	73	1	2,525	2,722
15. Bill Blair	21	0	1	0	2	0	3	2	1,043	51	2	2,457	4,535
16. Fred Dove	20	0	0	0	0	0	0	4	742	0	0	1,997	1,240
17. Bub King	14	0	0	0	0	0	0	5	1,029	0	0	1,624	1,036
18. Gene Comstock	13	0	0	0	0	0	0	3	756	0	0	1,519	990
19. Donald Thomas	17	0	0	0	0	0	0	4	1,034	0	0	1,408	1,765
20. Ralph Liguori	12	0	0	0	0	0	2	1	407	0	0	1,336	1,098
21. Pop McGinnis	13	0	0	0	0	0	2	3	775	13	1	1,113	975
22. Otis Martin	8	0	0	0	0	0	0	2	519	0	0	1,068	610
23. Andy Winfree	7	0	0	0	0	0	0	3	277	0	0	954	300
24. Bob Welborn	11	0	0	0	0	1	1	4	617	0	0	761	1,160
25. Johnny Patterson	11	0	0	0	0	0	1	1	534	0	0	753	645
26. Ted Chamberlain	9	0	0	0	0	0	0	3	572	0	0	738	500
27. Neil Roberts	2	0	0	0	0	0	0	1	335	0	0	738	400
28. Buddy Shuman	5	0	0	0	0	0	0	0	342	0	0	713	395
29. Arden Mounts	10	0	0	0	0	0	0	1	792	0	0	644	395
30. Bobby Myers	2	0	0	0	0	0	0	1	321	0	0	644	390
31. Clyde Minter	8	0	0	0	0	0	0	3	591	0	0	636	405
32. George Osborne	2	0	0	0	0	0	0	0	477	0	0	612	300
33. Jim Reed	3	0	0	0	0	1	0	0	260	0	0	590	635
34. Gordon Bracken	6	0	0	0	0	0	0	1	221	0	0	538	215
35. Don Oldenberg	4	0	0	0	0	0	1	1	223	0	0	527	375
36. C. H. Dingler	5	0	0	0	0	0	0	3	119	0	0	520	250
37. Elbert Allen	4	0	0	0	0	0	0	2	N/A	0	0	488	250
38. Mike Magill	3	0	0	0	0	0	0	0	244	0	0	486	235
39. Lloyd Hulette	1	0	0	0	0	0	0	0	328	0	0	486	250
40. Bill Harrison	3	0	0	0	0	0	0	3	N/A	0	0	480	450
41. Tommy Thompson	3	0	0	0	1	0	0	0	39	0	0	463	865
42. Coleman Lawrence	8	0	0	0	0	0	0	1	263	0	0	446	250
43. Dub Livingston	6	0	0	0	0	0	0	1	309	0	0	435	225
44. Buck Smith	5	0	0	0	0	0	0	1	N/A	0	0	400	175
45. Jimmy Ayers	4	0	0	0	0	0	0	2	N/A	0	0	384	150
46. Bob Walden	4	0	0	0	0	0	0	2	325	0	0	356	250
47. Eddie Skinner	4	0	0	0	0	0	0	1	N/A	0	0	352	200
48. Bill Adams	2	0	0	0	0	0	0	1	36	0	0	346	250
49. Mel Krueger	3	0	0	0	0	0	0	1	N/A	0	0	336	175
50. Johnny Beauchamp	3	0	0	0	0	0	0	1	N/A	0	0	328	150

1953

Laps Completed

1. Herb Thomas — 4,292
2. Lee Petty — 3,021
3. Dick Rathmann — 2,545
4. Fonty Flock — 1,999
5. Tim Flock — 1,990
6. Buck Baker — 1,619
7. Curtis Turner — 1,396
8. Speedy Thompson — 1,257
9. Jim Paschal — 1,179
10. Bill Blair — 1,043
11. Donald Thomas — 1,034
12. Bub King — 1,029
13. Dick Passwater — 993
14. Gober Sosebee — 943
15. Jimmie Lewallen — 908
16. Elton Hildreth — 821
17. Arden Mounts — 792
18. Pop McGinnis — 775
19. Gene Comstock — 756
20. Fred Dove — 742
21. Joe Eubanks — 718
22. Bob Welborn — 617
23. Slick Smith — 592
24. Clyde Minter — 591
25. Ted Chamberlain — 572
26. Johnny Patterson — 534
27. Otis Martin — 519
28. Herschel Buchanan — 506
29. Ray Duhigg — 489
30. Ralph Dyer — 480

Laps Led

1. Herb Thomas — 1,420
2. Fonty Flock — 581
3. Buck Baker — 564
4. Dick Rathmann — 542
5. Tim Flock — 289
6. Lee Petty — 209
7. Curtis Turner — 191
8. Hershel McGriff — 101
9. Speedy Thompson — 99
10. Joe Eubanks — 82
11. Jim Paschal — 73
    Gober Sosebee — 73
13. Bill Blair — 51
14. Fireball Roberts — 41
15. Pop McGinnis — 13
16. Slick Smith — 4
17. Dick Passwater — 3

Miles Led

1. Herb Thomas — 916
2. Fonty Flock — 539
3. Buck Baker — 522
4. Dick Rathmann — 434
5. Tim Flock — 214
6. Curtis Turner — 149
7. Lee Petty — 118
8. Hershel McGriff — 101
9. Speedy Thompson — 77
10. Fireball Roberts — 56
11. Bill Blair — 54
12. Joe Eubanks — 41
13. Jim Paschal — 37
    Gober Sosebee — 37
15. Pop McGinnis — 10
16. Slick Smith — 4
17. Dick Passwater — 2

Miles Driven

1. Herb Thomas — 3,107
2. Lee Petty — 2,201
3. Dick Rathmann — 2,002
4. Tim Flock — 1,774
5. Fonty Flock — 1,626
6. Buck Baker — 1,550
7. Curtis Turner — 1,370
8. Speedy Thompson — 1,229
9. Jim Paschal — 1,218
10. Dick Passwater — 1,125
11. Donald Thomas — 1,119
12. Bill Blair — 1,100
13. Bub King — 1,013
14. Gober Sosebee — 928
15. Gene Comstock — 895
16. Jimmie Lewallen — 791
17. Elton Hildreth — 785
18. Arden Mounts — 759
19. Slick Smith — 755
20. Fred Dove — 720
21. Pop McGinnis — 664
22. Otis Martin — 608
23. Joe Eubanks — 588
24. George Osborne — 528
25. Clyde Minter — 519
26. Dick Meyer — 488
27. Buddy Shuman — 481
28. Bob Welborn — 466
29. Neil Roberts — 461
30. Dick Allwine — 456

Races Led

1. Herb Thomas — 23
2. Fonty Flock — 10
3. Buck Baker — 9
4. Tim Flock — 8
   Dick Rathmann — 8
6. Lee Petty — 6
7. Speedy Thompson — 4
   Curtis Turner — 4
9. Bill Blair — 2
   Joe Eubanks — 2

1954

	Driver	Starts	Poles	Finish 1	2	3	4	5	6–10	Laps	Laps Led	Races Led	Winston Cup Points	$
1.	Lee Petty	34	3	7	5	5	4	3	8	5,903	681	12	8,649	21,127
2.	Herb Thomas	34	8	12	4	1	2	0	8	5,605	1,366	18	8,366	30,975
3.	Buck Baker	34	7	4	7	6	3	3	5	5,726	768	14	6,893	19,368
4.	Dick Rathmann	32	4	3	5	8	6	1	3	5,286	729	11	6,760	16,264
5.	Joe Eubanks	33	0	0	1	2	5	3	13	5,167	0	0	5,467	8,559
6.	Hershel McGriff	24	5	4	3	5	0	1	4	3,891	122	6	5,137	13,250
7.	Jim Paschal	27	2	1	0	1	1	2	6	3,546	193	1	3,903	5,451
8.	Jimmie Lewallen	22	0	0	2	0	0	3	5	2,963	0	0	3,233	4,694
9.	Curtis Turner	10	1	1	1	2	1	2	1	1,678	277	3	2,994	10,120
10.	Ralph Liguori	23	1	0	0	1	0	1	10	3,461	0	0	2,905	3,495
11.	Blackie Pitt	27	0	0	0	0	0	0	6	3,731	0	0	2,661	1,925
12.	Dave Terrell	30	0	0	0	0	0	0	8	3,876	0	0	2,645	2,225
13.	Bill Blair	19	0	0	0	0	0	2	8	2,853	7	1	2,362	2,650
14.	Laird Bruner	24	0	0	0	0	0	2	4	3,052	0	0	2,243	2,080
15.	Gober Sosebee	18	1	1	0	1	1	1	3	1,970	170	2	2,114	3,150
16.	John Soares	9	0	1	0	1	0	0	2	1,947	211	1	2,072	3,262
17.	Marvin Panch	10	1	0	2	1	0	0	4	2,100	17	1	1,935	4,747
18.	Eddie Skinner	15	0	0	0	0	0	0	1	2,044	0	0	1,794	1,017
19.	Joel Million	9	0	0	0	0	0	0	1	1,298	0	0	1,779	1,092
20.	Elton Hildreth	14	0	0	0	0	0	0	2	1,519	0	0	1,710	1,152
21.	Arden Mounts	12	0	0	0	0	0	0	1	1,592	0	0	1,705	875
22.	Fireball Roberts	5	0	0	0	0	0	0	2	811	0	0	1,648	1,080
23.	Speedy Thompson	7	0	0	0	0	1	0	2	949	0	0	1,480	1,165
24.	Johnny Patterson	4	0	0	0	0	1	0	0	582	0	0	1,417	1,240
25.	Erick Erickson	6	0	0	0	0	0	1	2	1,398	0	0	1,337	1,365
26.	Ray Duhigg	12	0	0	0	0	1	1	3	1,458	0	0	1,245	1,375
27.	Slick Smith	6	0	0	0	0	1	0	1	698	0	0	1,122	950
28.	Clyde Minter	12	0	0	0	0	0	0	6	1,653	0	0	1,116	900
29.	Gwyn Staley	2	0	0	0	0	0	0	1	357	0	0	1,088	670
30.	Lloyd Dane	4	0	0	1	0	0	2	1	1,268	180	1	984	1,600
31.	Donald Thomas	9	0	0	1	0	1	1	1	1,175	53	1	980	1,675
32.	Ted Chamberlain	10	0	0	0	0	0	0	1	1,596	0	0	920	475
33.	Danny Letner	4	1	1	0	1	0	0	1	1,058	142	2	915	1,975
34.	Elmo Langley	2	0	0	0	0	0	0	0	340	0	0	864	450
35.	Tim Flock	5	1	0	1	0	0	0	2	800	180	1	860	1,050
36.	Fred Dove	12	0	0	0	0	0	0	2	1,428	0	0	832	525
37.	Bill Widenhouse	6	0	0	0	0	0	0	0	987	0	0	805	425
38.	Gene Comstock	1	0	0	0	0	0	0	0	334	0	0	780	400
39.	Walt Flinchum	8	0	0	0	0	0	0	2	1,123	0	0	756	425
40.	Charlie Cregar	5	0	0	0	0	0	0	0	857	8	1	716	405
41.	Bill Amick	6	0	0	1	0	0	0	0	884	9	1	700	250
42.	Harvey Eakin	7	0	0	0	0	0	0	0	741	0	0	698	425
43.	Lou Figaro	3	0	0	0	0	0	0	2	461	0	0	690	425
44.	Ken Fisher	5	0	0	0	0	0	0	1	879	0	0	668	400
45.	Jim Reed	9	0	0	0	0	0	2	1	1,083	0	0	631	965
46.	Russ Hepler	6	0	0	0	0	1	0	0	691	0	0	624	525
46.	Allen Adkins	2	0	0	0	1	1	0	0	545	0	0	624	1,150
48.	Van Van Wey	3	0	0	0	0	0	0	0	629	0	0	602	495
49.	Tony Nelson	3	0	0	0	0	0	0	1	995	0	0	568	325
50.	John Dodd Jr.	1	0	0	0	0	0	0	1	161	0	0	552	150

LAPS COMPLETED		LAPS LED		MILES LED		MILES DRIVEN		RACES LED	
1. Lee Petty	5,903	1. Herb Thomas	1,366	1. Herb Thomas	1,030	1. Lee Petty	4,060	1. Herb Thomas	18
2. Buck Baker	5,726	2. Buck Baker	768	2. Lee Petty	677	2. Herb Thomas	3,998	2. Buck Baker	14
3. Herb Thomas	5,605	3. Dick Rathmann	729	3. Buck Baker	503	3. Buck Baker	3,893	3. Lee Petty	12
4. Dick Rathmann	5,286	4. Lee Petty	681	4. Dick Rathmann	398	4. Dick Rathmann	3,629	4. Dick Rathmann	11
5. Joe Eubanks	5,167	5. Al Keller	378	5. Curtis Turner	376	5. Joe Eubanks	3,542	5. Hershel McGriff	6
6. Hershel McGriff	3,891	6. Curtis Turner	277	6. Al Keller	237	6. Hershel McGriff	2,743	6. Al Keller	5
7. Dave Terrell	3,876	7. Jim Paschal	193	7. Gober Sosebee	99	7. Dave Terrell	2,608	7. Curtis Turner	3
8. Blackie Pitt	3,731	8. Lloyd Dane	180	8. Jim Paschal	97	8. Blackie Pitt	2,507	8. Danny Letner	2
9. Jim Paschal	3,546	Tim Flock	180	9. Lloyd Dane	90	9. Jim Paschal	2,492	Gober Sosebee	2
10. Ralph Liguori	3,461	10. Gober Sosebee	170	Tim Flock	90	10. Ralph Liguori	2,447		
11. Laird Bruner	3,052	11. Danny Letner	142	11. Hershel McGriff	80	11. Laird Bruner	2,338		
12. Jimmie Lewallen	2,963	12. Hershel McGriff	122	12. Danny Letner	71	12. Jimmie Lewallen	2,206		
13. Bill Blair	2,853	13. Donald Thomas	53	13. Donald Thomas	53	13. Bill Blair	1,893		
14. Marvin Panch	2,100	14. Marvin Panch	17	14. Bill Amick	12	14. Marvin Panch	1,779		
15. Eddie Skinner	2,044	15. Fonty Flock	15	15. Charlie Cregar	11	15. Eddie Skinner	1,659		
16. Gober Sosebee	1,970	16. Bill Amick	9	16. Marvin Panch	9	16. Curtis Turner	1,497		
17. John Soares	1,947	17. Charlie Cregar	8	17. Fonty Flock	8	17. Ted Chamberlain	1,423		
18. Al Keller	1,811	18. Bill Blair	7	18. Pop McGinnis	6	18. Elton Hildreth	1,420		
19. Curtis Turner	1,678	19. Pop McGinnis	4	19. Bill Blair	4	19. Gober Sosebee	1,376		
20. Clyde Minter	1,653					20. John Soares	1,374		
21. Ted Chamberlain	1,596					21. Al Keller	1,372		
22. Arden Mounts	1,592					22. Joel Million	1,324		
23. Elton Hildreth	1,519					23. Arden Mounts	1,317		
24. Ray Duhigg	1,458					24. Erick Erickson	1,191		
25. Fred Dove	1,428					25. Bill Widenhouse	999		
26. Erick Erickson	1,398					26. Fireball Roberts	975		
27. Joel Million	1,298					27. Speedy Thompson	942		
28. Lloyd Dane	1,268					28. Ray Duhigg	938		
29. Bob Welborn	1,251					29. Harvey Eakin	915		
30. Ben Gregory	1,232					30. Charlie Cregar	877		

1955

Driver	Starts	Poles	Finish 1	2	3	4	5	6–10	Laps	Laps Led	Races Led	Winston Cup Points	$
1. Tim Flock	39	20	18	5	5	1	3	1	6,208	3,495	33	9,596	37,780
2. Buck Baker	42	2	3	6	6	4	5	10	6,705	808	9	8,088	19,771
3. Lee Petty	42	1	6	4	5	4	1	10	6,328	769	6	7,194	18,920
4. Bob Welborn	32	1	0	1	4	4	3	13	5,291	31	1	5,460	10,147
5. Herb Thomas	23	2	3	3	3	3	2	1	3,248	250	7	5,186	18,024
6. Junior Johnson	36	2	5	1	2	1	3	6	4,620	790	7	4,810	13,803
7. Eddie Skinner	38	0	0	0	0	0	4	11	5,473	0	0	4,652	4,737
8. Jim Paschal	36	2	3	3	3	2	1	8	4,751	306	7	4,572	10,586
9. Jimmie Lewallen	33	1	0	2	0	4	2	8	4,028	0	0	4,526	6,440
10. Gwyn Staley	24	1	0	1	2	2	2	7	3,196	33	1	4,360	6,547
11. Fonty Flock	31	5	3	5	2	0	2	2	3,482	430	7	4,266	13,100
12. Dave Terrell	25	0	0	0	2	0	1	7	3,199	9	1	3,170	3,655
13. Jimmy Massey	11	0	0	0	1	1	2	4	1,906	0	0	2,924	3,510
14. Marvin Panch	10	0	0	2	0	2	0	0	1,597	15	1	2,812	4,385
15. Speedy Thompson	15	0	2	1	0	0	0	2	1,918	222	2	2,452	7,090
16. Jim Reed	14	0	0	1	0	1	2	0	1,691	32	1	2,416	2,703
17. Gene Simpson	22	0	0	0	0	0	1	6	2,667	0	0	2,388	2,158
18. Dick Rathmann	20	3	0	2	2	3	0	1	2,296	176	5	2,298	4,368
19. Ralph Liguori	12	0	0	0	0	0	0	6	1,402	0	0	2,124	1,973
20. Joe Eubanks	14	0	0	0	0	0	0	4	1,607	0	0	2,028	2,008
21. Blackie Pitt	20	0	0	0	0	0	0	7	2,532	0	0	1,992	1,785
22. Harvey Henderson	17	0	0	0	0	0	1	5	2,284	0	0	1,930	1,810
23. Banks Simpson	7	0	0	0	0	0	0	0	1,103	0	0	1,852	870
24. Dink Widenhouse	15	1	0	0	0	0	0	6	1,743	0	0	1,752	1,660
25. John Dodd Jr.	13	0	0	0	0	0	1	6	1,653	0	0	1,496	1,695
26. Bill Widenhouse	5	0	0	0	0	0	1	2	799	2	1	1,444	1,065
27. Lou Spears	3	0	0	0	0	0	0	1	708	0	0	1,272	810
28. Larry Flynn	1	0	0	0	0	0	1	0	359	0	0	1,260	1,175
29. Cotton Owens	2	0	0	0	0	0	1	1	549	0	0	1,248	900
30. Gordon Smith	15	0	0	0	0	0	0	2	1,584	0	0	1,212	975
31. Billy Carden	13	0	0	0	0	2	0	1	1,589	0	0	1,172	1,340
32. Arden Mounts	12	1	0	0	0	0	0	4	1,560	0	0	1,170	1,025
33. Joel Million	8	0	0	1	0	1	0	4	973	0	0	1,136	1,685
34. Curtis Turner	9	0	0	1	1	2	0	0	928	14	1	1,120	2,605
35. John Lindsay	6	0	0	0	0	0	0	3	853	0	0	1,052	575
36. Nace Mattingly	3	0	0	0	3	0	1	0	696	0	0	992	700
37. Bill Blair	12	0	0	0	0	0	0	0	1,320	0	0	974	440
38. Donald Thomas	10	0	0	0	0	2	0	2	1,320	0	0	932	1,240
39. Ed Cole Jr.	13	0	0	0	0	0	0	0	1,442	0	0	924	645
40. Mack Hanbury	8	0	0	0	0	0	0	2	807	0	0	900	575
41. Danny Letner	4	0	1	0	1	0	0	0	614	34	1	892	1,780
42. George Parrish	12	0	0	0	0	0	0	1	1,057	0	0	880	750
43. Banjo Matthews	3	0	0	0	0	0	0	2	734	0	0	860	745
44. Carl Krueger	7	0	0	0	0	0	1	0	955	0	0	748	585
45. Ted Cannady	9	0	0	0	0	0	0	0	812	0	0	744	450
46. Allen Adkins	4	0	0	1	0	0	1	0	601	79	1	740	1,160
47. Joe Weatherly	6	0	0	0	0	1	0	3	994	140	1	724	2,575
48. John McVitty	7	0	0	0	0	0	0	2	951	0	0	684	550
49. Lloyd Dane	5	0	0	0	1	0	0	1	545	5	1	674	780
50. Fred Dove	7	0	0	0	1	0	0	2	830	0	0	668	750

LAPS COMPLETED

1.	Buck Baker	6,705
2.	Lee Petty	6,328
3.	Tim Flock	6,208
4.	Eddie Skinner	5,473
5.	Bob Welborn	5,291
6.	Jim Paschal	4,751
7.	Junior Johnson	4,620
8.	Jimmie Lewallen	4,028
9.	Fonty Flock	3,482
10.	Herb Thomas	3,248
11.	Dave Terrell	3,199
12.	Gwyn Staley	3,196
13.	Gene Simpson	2,667
14.	Blackie Pitt	2,532
15.	Dick Rathmann	2,296
16.	Harvey Henderson	2,284
17.	Speedy Thompson	1,918
18.	Jimmy Massey	1,906
19.	Dink Widenhouse	1,743
20.	Jim Reed	1,691
21.	John Dodd Jr.	1,653
22.	Joe Eubanks	1,607
23.	Marvin Panch	1,597
24.	Billy Carden	1,589
25.	Gordon Smith	1,584
26.	Arden Mounts	1,560
27.	Ed Cole Jr.	1,442
28.	Ralph Liguori	1,402
29.	Bill Blair	1,320
	Donald Thomas	1,320

LAPS LED

1.	Tim Flock	3,495
2.	Buck Baker	808
3.	Junior Johnson	790
4.	Lee Petty	769
5.	Fonty Flock	430
6.	Jim Paschal	306
7.	Herb Thomas	250
8.	Speedy Thompson	222
9.	Dick Rathmann	176
10.	Joe Weatherly	140
11.	Norm Nelson	106
12.	John Kieper	89
13.	Allen Adkins	79
14.	Ed Brown	44
15.	Danny Letner	34
16.	Gwyn Staley	33
17.	Jim Reed	32
18.	Bob Welborn	31
19.	Bill Amick	28
20.	Marvin Panch	15
21.	Curtis Turner	14
22.	Dave Terrell	9
23.	Lloyd Dane	5
24.	Fireball Roberts	4
25.	Bill Widenhouse	2

MILES LED

1.	Tim Flock	2,479
2.	Buck Baker	459
3.	Fonty Flock	445
4.	Junior Johnson	395
5.	Lee Petty	385
6.	Speedy Thompson	269
7.	Herb Thomas	216
8.	Joe Weatherly	193
9.	Jim Paschal	179
10.	Dick Rathmann	122
11.	Norm Nelson	106
12.	John Kieper	89
13.	Allen Adkins	40
14.	Ed Brown	22
15.	Curtis Turner	19
16.	Danny Letner	17
17.	Gwyn Staley	17
18.	Jim Reed	16
19.	Bob Welborn	16
20.	Bill Amick	14
21.	Dave Terrell	9
22.	Marvin Panch	8
23.	Fireball Roberts	6
24.	Lloyd Dane	5
25.	Bill Widenhouse	3

MILES DRIVEN

1.	Buck Baker	4,781
2.	Tim Flock	4,576
3.	Lee Petty	4,423
4.	Bob Welborn	3,638
5.	Eddie Skinner	3,629
6.	Jim Paschal	3,222
7.	Junior Johnson	3,153
8.	Jimmie Lewallen	2,959
9.	Herb Thomas	2,707
10.	Fonty Flock	2,565
11.	Dave Terrell	2,452
12.	Gwyn Staley	2,236
13.	Gene Simpson	2,001
14.	Speedy Thompson	1,835
15.	Blackie Pitt	1,744
16.	Jimmy Massey	1,721
17.	Marvin Panch	1,654
18.	Dick Rathmann	1,601
19.	Joe Eubanks	1,487
20.	Ralph Liguori	1,422
21.	Banks Simpson	1,377
22.	Harvey Henderson	1,344
23.	Jim Reed	1,265
24.	Bill Blair	1,227
25.	Dink Widenhouse	1,185
26.	Billy Carden	1,168
27.	Arden Mounts	1,050
28.	Bobby Waddell	942
29.	John Dodd Jr.	915
30.	Gordon Smith	910

RACES LED

1.	Tim Flock	33
2.	Buck Baker	9
3.	Fonty Flock	7
	Junior Johnson	7
	Jim Paschal	7
	Herb Thomas	7
7.	Lee Petty	6
8.	Dick Rathmann	5
9.	Speedy Thompson	2

1956

Driver	Starts	Poles	Finish						Laps	Laps Led	Races Led	Winston Cup Points	$
			1	2	3	4	5	6–10					
1. Buck Baker	48	13	14	7	3	4	3	8	8,495	1,401	23	9,252	34,077
2. Speedy Thompson	42	6	8	5	5	4	2	5	6,957	2,023	23	8,788	27,169
3. Herb Thomas	48	3	5	2	4	7	4	14	7,854	522	8	8,710	19,352
4. Lee Petty	47	1	2	1	6	2	6	11	7,507	252	6	8,324	15,338
5. Jim Paschal	42	1	1	8	2	4	2	10	6,626	212	6	7,878	17,204
6. Billy Myers	42	1	2	6	3	1	1	9	6,270	103	4	6,976	15,830
7. Fireball Roberts	33	3	5	1	2	7	2	5	5,695	470	10	5,794	14,742
8. Ralph Moody	35	5	4	5	2	1	1	8	5,258	312	6	5,528	15,493
9. Tim Flock	22	5	4	1	3	2	1	3	3,076	445	9	5,062	15,769
10. Marvin Panch	20	1	1	2	5	2	0	3	3,298	150	6	4,680	11,520
11. Rex White	24	1	0	0	2	0	1	11	4,240	0	0	4,642	5,334
12. Johnny Allen	32	0	0	0	0	0	2	9	4,888	0	0	4,024	4,559
13. Paul Goldsmith	9	0	1	0	0	2	1	2	2,292	182	1	3,788	8,569
14. Gwyn Staley	22	0	0	0	0	2	3	8	3,506	0	0	3,550	5,159
15. Joe Eubanks	26	2	0	0	3	0	4	6	3,398	107	2	3,284	5,584
16. Joe Weatherly	17	1	0	1	1	3	1	6	2,745	20	1	3,084	5,251
17. Bill Amick	13	0	0	1	3	1	2	3	2,446	10	2	3,048	5,381
18. Jim Reed	11	2	0	1	1	2	1	0	1,505	286	3	2,890	5,077
19. Tiny Lund	21	0	0	0	0	1	0	7	3,988	0	0	2,754	2,811
20. Curtis Turner	13	0	1	3	0	0	0	1	1,967	287	3	2,580	14,541
21. Jack Smith	15	0	1	0	0	0	0	5	2,669	234	2	2,320	3,825
22. Billy Carden	23	0	0	0	0	0	0	4	2,831	0	0	2,108	2,175
23. Lloyd Dane	10	0	2	0	1	2	0	4	1,706	91	2	2,106	4,370
24. Frank Mundy	9	1	0	1	1	0	1	2	1,589	0	0	1,836	3,585
25. Bobby Johns	9	0	0	0	0	0	0	3	1,537	0	0	1,832	1,450
26. Blackie Pitt	27	0	0	0	0	0	0	5	2,702	0	0	1,760	1,545
27. Harold Hardesty	9	0	0	1	0	0	1	4	1,761	0	0	1,724	2,380
28. Al Watkins	14	0	0	0	0	0	0	4	2,065	0	0	1,710	1,185
29. Chuck Meekins	7	0	0	1	1	1	0	3	1,241	43	3	1,656	2,815
30. Harvey Henderson	18	0	0	0	0	0	0	4	2,477	0	0	1,634	1,310
31. Bill Champion	14	0	0	0	0	0	0	4	2,297	0	0	1,632	1,570
32. Eddie Pagan	8	2	1	1	0	0	2	0	1,366	31	2	1,598	4,095
33. Pat Kirkwood	3	0	0	0	1	0	0	1	715	0	0	1,540	2,025
34. Clyde Palmer	11	0	0	2	1	0	1	2	1,730	296	2	1,516	2,755
35. John Kieper	8	3	1	1	1	1	0	3	1,479	67	2	1,506	3,250
36. Johnny Dodson	11	0	0	0	0	0	0	4	1,842	0	0	1,488	1,450
37. Bill Blair	9	0	0	0	0	0	0	4	1,275	0	0	1,284	1,005
38. Junior Johnson	13	1	0	1	0	0	0	0	1,131	60	2	1,272	1,350
39. Ed Cole	12	0	0	0	0	0	0	1	1,486	0	0	1,200	950
40. Brownie King	15	0	0	0	0	0	0	0	1,994	0	0	1,140	925
41. Scotty Cain	4	0	0	0	0	0	1	3	701	0	0	1,124	1,235
42. Allen Adkins	6	0	0	0	0	0	1	2	1,016	0	0	1,104	1,465
43. Bobby Keck	15	0	0	0	0	0	0	3	2,236	0	0	1,076	950
44. Gordon Haines	7	0	0	1	0	1	0	2	1,067	66	1	1,066	1,500
45. Bob Keefe	7	0	0	0	0	1	0	1	1,200	0	0	1,066	1,040
46. Dick Beaty	15	0	0	0	0	0	0	3	1,513	0	0	1,036	910
47. Jim Blomgren	6	0	0	0	0	0	0	1	841	0	0	992	475
48. Ed Negre	5	0	0	0	0	1	1	2	936	200	2	952	1,255
49. Jimmy Massey	7	0	0	0	0	1	2	1	1,140	0	0	950	1,545
50. Fonty Flock	7	2	1	0	0	0	0	3	629	150	2	946	1,780

LAPS COMPLETED

1.	Buck Baker	8,495
2.	Herb Thomas	7,854
3.	Lee Petty	7,507
4.	Speedy Thompson	6,957
5.	Jim Paschal	6,626
6.	Billy Myers	6,270
7.	Fireball Roberts	5,695
8.	Ralph Moody	5,258
9.	Johnny Allen	4,888
10.	Rex White	4,240
11.	Tiny Lund	3,988
12.	Gwyn Staley	3,506
13.	Joe Eubanks	3,398
14.	Marvin Panch	3,298
15.	Tim Flock	3,076
16.	Billy Carden	2,831
17.	Joe Weatherly	2,745
18.	Blackie Pitt	2,702
19.	Jack Smith	2,669
20.	Harvey Henderson	2,477
21.	Bill Amick	2,446
22.	Bill Champion	2,297
23.	Paul Goldsmith	2,292
24.	Bobby Keck	2,236
25.	Al Watkins	2,065
26.	Brownie King	1,994
27.	Curtis Turner	1,967
28.	Johnny Dodson	1,842
29.	Harold Hardesty	1,761
30.	Clyde Palmer	1,730

LAPS LED

1.	Speedy Thompson	2,023
2.	Buck Baker	1,401
3.	Herb Thomas	522
4.	Fireball Roberts	470
5.	Tim Flock	445
6.	Ralph Moody	312
7.	Clyde Palmer	296
8.	Curtis Turner	287
9.	Jim Reed	286
10.	Lee Petty	252
11.	Jack Smith	234
12.	Jim Paschal	212
13.	Ed Negre	200
14.	Paul Goldsmith	182
15.	Fonty Flock	150
	Marvin Panch	150
17.	Joe Eubanks	107
18.	Billy Myers	103
19.	Lloyd Dane	91
20.	Royce Haggerty	72
21.	John Kieper	67
22.	Gordon Haines	66
23.	Junior Johnson	60
24.	Chuck Stevenson	54
25.	Chuck Meekins	43
26.	Eddie Pagan	31
27.	Joe Weatherly	20
28.	Ralph Earnhardt	15
29.	Bill Amick	10
30.	Bill Hyde	1

MILES LED

1.	Speedy Thompson	1,145
2.	Buck Baker	1,052
3.	Tim Flock	454
4.	Fireball Roberts	395
5.	Curtis Turner	340
6.	Herb Thomas	261
7.	Marvin Panch	247
8.	Jim Paschal	227
9.	Paul Goldsmith	182
10.	Ralph Moody	176
11.	Clyde Palmer	148
12.	Jim Reed	144
13.	Chuck Stevenson	135
14.	Lee Petty	127
15.	Jack Smith	117
16.	Fonty Flock	109
17.	Ed Negre	100
18.	Lloyd Dane	59
19.	Joe Eubanks	56
20.	Billy Myers	51
21.	John Kieper	43
22.	Royce Haggerty	36
23.	Chuck Meekins	35
24.	Gordon Haines	33
25.	Eddie Pagan	31
26.	Junior Johnson	28
27.	Joe Weatherly	10
28.	Ralph Earnhardt	6
29.	Bill Amick	5
30.	Bill Hyde	1

MILES DRIVEN

1.	Buck Baker	5,460
2.	Herb Thomas	5,062
3.	Lee Petty	4,954
4.	Speedy Thompson	4,646
5.	Jim Paschal	4,543
6.	Billy Myers	4,231
7.	Fireball Roberts	3,789
8.	Ralph Moody	3,506
9.	Johnny Allen	3,349
10.	Rex White	2,978
11.	Tim Flock	2,696
12.	Joe Eubanks	2,529
13.	Marvin Panch	2,502
14.	Tiny Lund	2,466
15.	Gwyn Staley	2,404
16.	Paul Goldsmith	2,090
17.	Joe Weatherly	1,997
18.	Jack Smith	1,916
19.	Billy Carden	1,881
20.	Blackie Pitt	1,754
21.	Bill Amick	1,631
22.	Bill Champion	1,626
23.	Harvey Henderson	1,597
24.	Jim Reed	1,514
25.	Frank Mundy	1,479
26.	Curtis Turner	1,431
27.	Clyde Palmer	1,381
28.	Al Watkins	1,380
29.	Johnny Dodson	1,379
30.	Harold Hardesty	1,350

RACES LED

1.	Buck Baker	23
	Speedy Thompson	23
3.	Fireball Roberts	10
4.	Tim Flock	9
5.	Herb Thomas	8
6.	Ralph Moody	6
	Marvin Panch	6
	Jim Paschal	6
	Lee Petty	6
10.	Billy Myers	4
11.	Chuck Meekins	3
	Jim Reed	3
	Curtis Turner	3
14.	Bill Amick	2
	Lloyd Dane	2
	Joe Eubanks	2
	Fonty Flock	2
	Royce Haggerty	2
	Junior Johnson	2
14.	John Kieper	2
	Ed Negre	2
	Eddie Pagan	2
	Clyde Palmer	2
	Jack Smith	2

Driver	Starts	Poles	Finish 1	2	3	4	5	6–10	Laps	Laps Led	Races Led	Winston Cup Points	$
1957													
1. Buck Baker	40	6	10	7	4	5	4	8	8,058	858	15	10,716	30,764
2. Marvin Panch	42	4	6	3	6	6	1	5	6,890	449	12	9,956	24,307
3. Speedy Thompson	38	4	2	4	3	4	3	6	6,301	648	8	8,560	26,841
4. Lee Petty	41	3	4	4	3	3	6	13	7,466	449	11	8,528	18,326
5. Jack Smith	39	2	4	1	2	3	7	8	6,589	429	9	8,464	14,562
6. Fireball Roberts	42	4	8	6	2	1	4	6	6,891	1,107	16	8,268	19,829
7. Johnny Allen	42	1	0	0	1	1	2	13	6,033	0	0	7,068	9,815
8. L. D. Austin	40	0	0	0	0	0	1	12	6,920	0	0	6,532	6,485
9. Brownie King	36	0	0	0	0	0	1	15	5,756	0	0	5,740	5,589
10. Jim Paschal	35	0	0	1	2	3	3	8	4,999	0	0	5,124	7,079
11. Tiny Lund	32	3	0	0	3	1	2	9	4,922	209	2	4,848	6,424
12. Billy Myers	28	0	0	0	0	4	0	5	3,923	201	1	4,640	6,566
13. Paul Goldsmith	25	4	4	4	1	1	0	5	3,759	588	10	4,188	12,734
14. Cotton Owens	17	1	1	1	0	0	1	3	2,300	179	3	4,032	12,784
15. Eddie Pagan	15	2	3	3	3	1	1	0	2,611	3	3	3,612	7,274
16. Bill Amick	21	2	1	3	4	0	0	4	3,364	12	2	3,512	8,073
17. Dick Beaty	20	0	0	0	0	0	1	6	3,202	0	0	3,220	3,648
18. Jim Reed	6	0	0	0	1	1	0	1	892	11	2	2,836	3,408
19. Clarence DeZalia	25	0	0	0	0	0	0	6	4,059	0	0	2,828	3,308
20. Frankie Schneider	10	1	0	1	0	2	0	3	1,781	37	1	2,516	4,588
21. Rex White	9	1	0	1	0	3	0	2	1,585	193	2	2,508	3,870
22. Curtis Turner	10	1	0	2	0	0	0	2	1,397	109	4	2,356	4,830
23. George Green	17	0	0	0	0	1	0	3	2,668	0	0	2,216	2,240
24. Whitey Norman	13	0	0	1	0	0	0	3	2,437	0	0	1,920	3,990
25. Lloyd Dane	10	1	1	5	1	0	0	3	1,296	1	1	1,852	4,985
26. Jimmie Lewallen	7	0	0	0	0	0	0	0	895	0	0	1,796	1,030
27. Johnny Mackison	5	0	0	0	0	0	1	1	769	0	0	1,764	1,330
28. Bobby Keck	16	0	0	0	0	0	0	2	2,144	0	0	1,740	1,525
29. Billy Carden	3	0	0	0	0	0	0	2	625	0	0	1,600	1,675
30. Bill Benson	11	0	0	0	0	0	0	2	1,320	0	0	1,592	1,090
31. Dick Getty	10	0	0	0	0	0	3	5	1,174	0	0	1,504	1,890
32. Scotty Cain	11	0	0	0	0	3	0	4	1,151	0	0	1,492	1,165
33. Roy Tyner	10	0	0	0	0	0	0	2	1,705	0	0	1,468	1,020
34. T. A. Toomes	11	0	0	0	0	0	0	1	1,920	0	0	1,404	1,450
35. Possum Jones	6	0	0	0	0	0	0	4	1,443	0	0	1,360	2,375
36. Huck Spaulding	8	0	0	0	3	0	0	3	1,006	0	0	1,240	1,120
37. Ralph Earnhardt	9	0	0	0	0	0	0	3	1,465	0	0	1,180	1,150
38. George Seeger	6	0	0	1	3	1	0	0	764	19	1	1,108	2,740
39. Ken Rush	16	1	0	0	1	0	0	5	2,266	0	0	1,104	2,045
40. Peck Peckham	10	0	0	0	0	0	0	0	1,060	0	0	1,064	950
41. Bill Champion	10	0	0	0	0	0	0	1	1,663	0	0	956	1,125
42. Chuck Hansen	7	0	0	0	0	0	0	0	990	0	0	900	510
43. Danny Graves	7	1	1	0	1	0	1	1	787	1	1	880	1,895
44. Marvin Porter	6	0	1	1	0	0	0	1	771	1	1	872	1,770
45. Eddie Skinner	4	0	0	0	0	0	0	0	833	0	0	848	605
46. Jimmy Thompson	2	0	0	0	0	0	0	0	352	0	0	816	325
47. Parnelli Jones	10	1	1	0	0	0	0	2	743	1	1	812	1,625
48. Bobby Johns	1	0	0	0	0	0	0	0	335	0	0	800	225
49. Don Porter	6	0	0	0	0	0	0	4	722	0	0	784	810
50. Joe Weatherly	14	0	0	1	3	0	1	2	2,059	3	1	776	5,240

LAPS COMPLETED

1.	Buck Baker	8,058
2.	Lee Petty	7,466
3.	L. D. Austin	6,920
4.	Fireball Roberts	6,891
5.	Marvin Panch	6,890
6.	Jack Smith	6,589
7.	Speedy Thompson	6,301
8.	Johnny Allen	6,033
9.	Brownie King	5,756
10.	Jim Paschal	4,999
11.	Tiny Lund	4,922
12.	Clarence DeZalia	4,059
13.	Billy Myers	3,923
14.	Paul Goldsmith	3,759
15.	Bill Amick	3,364
16.	Dick Beaty	3,202
17.	George Green	2,668
18.	Eddie Pagan	2,611
19.	Gwyn Staley	2,449
20.	Whitey Norman	2,437
21.	Cotton Owens	2,300
22.	Ken Rush	2,266
23.	Bobby Keck	2,144
24.	Joe Weatherly	2,059
25.	T. A. Toomes	1,920
26.	Frankie Schneider	1,781
27.	Roy Tyner	1,705
28.	Bill Champion	1,663
29.	Rex White	1,585
30.	Ralph Earnhardt	1,465

LAPS LED

1.	Fireball Roberts	1,107
2.	Buck Baker	858
3.	Speedy Thompson	648
4.	Paul Goldsmith	588
5.	Bob Welborn	457
6.	Marvin Panch	449
	Lee Petty	449
8.	Jack Smith	429
9.	Tiny Lund	209
10.	Billy Myers	201
11.	Gwyn Staley	196
12.	Rex White	193
13.	Cotton Owens	179
14.	Curtis Turner	109
15.	Ralph Moody	100
	Art Watts	100
17.	Banjo Matthews	56
18.	Frankie Schneider	37
19.	George Seeger	19
20.	Bill Amick	12
21.	Jim Reed	11
22.	Jimmy Massey	7
23.	Eddie Pagan	3
	Joe Weatherly	3
25.	Lloyd Dane	1
	Danny Graves	1
	Parnelli Jones	1
	Bobby Myers	1
	Marvin Porter	1

MILES LED

1.	Fireball Roberts	714
2.	Speedy Thompson	503
3.	Buck Baker	501
4.	Paul Goldsmith	484
5.	Marvin Panch	330
6.	Jack Smith	275
7.	Bob Welborn	240
8.	Lee Petty	219
9.	Cotton Owens	213
10.	Curtis Turner	133
11.	Gwyn Staley	133
12.	Tiny Lund	105
13.	Billy Myers	101
14.	Rex White	97
15.	Ralph Moody	50
	Art Watts	50
17.	George Seeger	48
18.	Frankie Schneider	37
19.	Banjo Matthews	35
20.	Jim Reed	11
21.	Bill Amick	6
22.	Jimmy Massey	4
23.	Eddie Pagan	2
24.	Bobby Myers	1
25.	Joe Weatherly	1
26.	Danny Graves	1
27.	Parnelli Jones	1
28.	Lloyd Dane	1
29.	Marvin Porter	1

MILES DRIVEN

1.	Buck Baker	4,844
2.	Lee Petty	4,595
3.	Marvin Panch	4,401
4.	Fireball Roberts	4,269
5.	L. D. Austin	4,132
6.	Jack Smith	3,969
7.	Speedy Thompson	3,903
8.	Johnny Allen	3,876
9.	Brownie King	3,464
10.	Tiny Lund	3,024
11.	Jim Paschal	2,947
12.	Paul Goldsmith	2,495
13.	Billy Myers	2,441
14.	Clarence DeZalia	2,119
15.	Bill Amick	2,067
16.	Dick Beaty	2,061
17.	Eddie Pagan	1,802
18.	Cotton Owens	1,769
19.	Whitey Norman	1,614
20.	Gwyn Staley	1,516
21.	George Green	1,485
22.	Bobby Keck	1,419
23.	Ken Rush	1,397
24.	Possum Jones	1,395
25.	Joe Weatherly	1,350
26.	Curtis Turner	1,304
27.	Frankie Schneider	1,248
28.	Bill Champion	1,167
29.	Rex White	1,144
30.	Roy Tyner	1,099

RACES LED

1.	Fireball Roberts	16
2.	Buck Baker	15
3.	Marvin Panch	12
4.	Lee Petty	11
5.	Paul Goldsmith	10
6.	Jack Smith	9
7.	Speedy Thompson	8
8.	Gwyn Staley	4
	Curtis Turner	4
10.	Cotton Owens	3
	Eddie Pagan	3
12.	Bill Amick	2
	Tiny Lund	2
	Jim Reed	2
	Bob Welborn	2
	Rex White	2

1958

Driver	Starts	Poles	1	2	3	4	5	6–10	Laps	Laps Led	Races Led	Winston Cup Points	$
1. Lee Petty	50	4	7	5	4	9	3	15	9,173	439	14	12,232	26,565
2. Buck Baker	44	3	3	10	4	2	4	12	7,827	364	8	11,588	25,841
3. Speedy Thompson	37	7	4	2	7	2	3	5	6,450	230	7	8,792	17,295
4. Shorty Rollins	29	0	1	1	3	5	2	10	5,324	87	4	8,124	13,399
5. Jack Smith	39	4	2	5	2	3	3	6	5,750	381	7	7,666	12,634
6. L. D. Austin	46	0	0	0	0	0	0	10	6,903	0	0	6,972	6,246
7. Rex White	22	7	2	4	6	0	1	4	3,848	471	7	6,552	12,233
8. Junior Johnson	27	0	6	2	3	1	0	4	4,244	317	9	6,380	13,809
9. Eddie Pagan	27	2	0	2	1	1	7	7	3,961	57	2	4,910	7,472
10. Jim Reed	17	2	4	0	5	1	0	2	3,693	692	4	4,762	9,644
11. Fireball Roberts	10	0	6	1	1	0	0	1	2,491	877	7	4,420	32,219
12. Bobby Keck	30	0	0	0	0	0	0	7	4,345	0	0	4,240	3,459
13. Herman Beam	20	0	0	0	0	0	0	1	3,651	0	0	4,224	2,599
14. Herb Estes	11	0	0	0	0	0	0	4	2,202	0	0	4,048	2,509
15. Clarence DeZalia	27	0	0	0	0	0	0	6	4,073	0	0	3,448	3,004
16. Doug Cox	14	0	0	1	0	1	1	6	2,479	0	0	3,736	3,404
17. Cotton Owens	29	2	1	4	2	1	0	9	3,700	241	5	3,716	6,579
18. Marvin Panch	11	2	0	1	1	1	2	0	1,833	157	3	3,424	4,114
19. Billy Rafter	19	0	0	0	0	0	1	7	3,160	0	0	2,916	2,799
20. Curtis Turner	17	1	3	2	0	1	2	2	3,068	827	6	2,856	10,029
21. Lloyd Dane	5	0	0	1	0	0	0	1	1,084	0	0	2,844	2,490
22. Bob Duell	7	1	0	1	1	0	1	3	1,273	0	0	2,740	2,415
23. Jimmy Thompson	8	0	0	0	0	2	0	1	1,281	0	0	2,540	3,275
24. Fred Harb	25	0	0	0	1	2	1	3	3,651	0	0	2,484	3,320
25. Tiny Lund	22	2	0	0	2	1	1	3	3,506	14	1	2,436	3,155
26. Bill Poor	24	0	0	0	0	0	1	6	3,880	0	0	2,292	3,115
27. Gene White	9	0	0	0	0	0	0	2	1,641	0	0	2,040	1,400
28. Joe Weatherly	15	1	1	1	0	2	1	2	2,692	104	3	2,032	6,330
29. Johnny Mackison	11	0	0	0	1	0	1	1	1,423	0	0	1,680	1,255
30. Jim Parsley	10	0	0	0	0	0	0	4	1,720	0	0	1,488	1,135
31. Al White	9	0	0	0	0	0	0	1	1,483	0	0	1,464	920
32. Jimmy Massey	9	1	0	0	0	0	1	2	1,612	0	0	1,300	1,625
33. Parnelli Jones	3	2	1	0	0	0	0	0	587	148	2	1,140	1,010
34. Joe Eubanks	7	0	1	0	0	1	0	1	956	38	2	1,120	2,070
35. Brownie King	24	0	0	0	0	0	0	5	3,926	0	0	1,116	3,045
36. G. C. Spencer	1	0	0	0	0	0	0	0	343	0	0	1,040	315
37. Richard Petty	9	0	0	0	0	0	0	1	977	0	0	1,016	760
38. Billy Carden	13	0	0	0	0	0	0	2	1,469	0	0	1,012	815
39. Elmo Langley	9	0	0	0	0	0	1	2	1,240	0	0	980	1,090
40. Buzz Woodward	9	0	0	0	0	0	0	2	1,508	0	0	964	1,195
41. Possum Jones	11	1	0	0	0	0	1	2	1,870	28	1	960	1,790
42. Jim Paschal	6	1	1	0	0	1	0	2	1,105	150	1	928	1,670
43. Chuck Hansen	7	0	0	0	0	0	0	1	1,011	0	0	916	580
44. Eddie Gray	3	0	1	0	0	0	0	0	437	43	1	910	3,375
45. Peck Peckham	11	0	0	0	0	0	0	2	1,263	0	0	868	835
46. Lennie Page	8	0	0	0	0	0	0	2	901	0	0	836	760
47. Bob Keefe	2	0	0	0	0	0	1	1	276	0	0	782	925
48. R. L. Combs	9	0	0	0	0	0	0	1	1,062	0	0	760	805
49. Volney Schulze	7	0	0	0	0	0	0	0	725	0	0	680	490
50. Dean Layfield	7	0	0	0	0	0	0	0	522	0	0	664	370

LAPS COMPLETED

1.	Lee Petty	9,173
2.	Buck Baker	7,827
3.	L. D. Austin	6,903
4.	Speedy Thompson	6,450
5.	Jack Smith	5,750
6.	Shorty Rollins	5,324
7.	Bobby Keck	4,345
8.	Junior Johnson	4,244
9.	Clarence DeZalia	4,073
10.	Eddie Pagan	3,961
11.	Brownie King	3,926
12.	Bill Poor	3,880
13.	Rex White	3,848
14.	Bob Welborn	3,770
15.	Cotton Owens	3,700
16.	Jim Reed	3,693
17.	Herman Beam	3,651
	Fred Harb	3,651
19.	Tiny Lund	3,506
20.	Shep Langdon	3,220
21.	Billy Rafter	3,160
22.	Roy Tyner	3,148
23.	Curtis Turner	3,068
24.	Joe Weatherly	2,692
25.	Johnny Allen	2,613
26.	Fireball Roberts	2,491
27.	Doug Cox	2,479
28.	Glen Wood	2,348
29.	Herb Estes	2,202
30.	Bob Walden	2,104

LAPS LED

1.	Fireball Roberts	877
2.	Curtis Turner	827
3.	Jim Reed	692
4.	Bob Welborn	579
5.	Rex White	471
6.	Lee Petty	439
7.	Jack Smith	381
8.	Buck Baker	364
9.	Glen Wood	360
10.	Junior Johnson	317
11.	Cotton Owens	241
12.	Speedy Thompson	230
13.	Marvin Panch	157
14.	Jim Paschal	150
15.	Parnelli Jones	148
16.	Frankie Schneider	106
17.	Joe Weatherly	104
18.	Shorty Rollins	87
19.	Eddie Pagan	57
20.	Eddie Gray	43
21.	Paul Goldsmith	39
22.	Joe Eubanks	38
23.	Possum Jones	28
24.	Tim Flock	25
25.	Tiny Lund	14
26.	George Dunn	10

MILES LED

1.	Fireball Roberts	867
2.	Curtis Turner	534
3.	Parnelli Jones	388
4.	Jack Smith	254
5.	Bob Welborn	249
6.	Jim Reed	245
7.	Buck Baker	223
8.	Junior Johnson	207
9.	Lee Petty	187
10.	Rex White	186
11.	Glen Wood	184
12.	Paul Goldsmith	160
13.	Cotton Owens	148
14.	Speedy Thompson	141
15.	Marvin Panch	118
16.	Eddie Gray	113
17.	Joe Weatherly	53
18.	Joe Eubanks	47
19.	Shorty Rollins	43
20.	Eddie Pagan	40
21.	Frankie Schneider	40
22.	Jim Paschal	38
23.	Tim Flock	25
24.	Tiny Lund	13
25.	Possum Jones	9
26.	George Dunn	3

MILES DRIVEN

1.	Lee Petty	5,671
2.	Buck Baker	4,726
3.	Speedy Thompson	3,944
4.	L. D. Austin	3,898
5.	Jack Smith	3,711
6.	Shorty Rollins	3,201
7.	Junior Johnson	2,797
8.	Eddie Pagan	2,607
9.	Jim Reed	2,474
10.	Clarence DeZalia	2,412
11.	Herman Beam	2,251
12.	Bobby Keck	2,219
13.	Cotton Owens	2,208
14.	Fireball Roberts	2,197
15.	Bob Welborn	2,190
16.	Curtis Turner	2,190
17.	Brownie King	2,153
18.	Rex White	2,122
19.	Joe Weatherly	2,120
20.	Tiny Lund	1,991
21.	Roy Tyner	1,951
22.	Bill Poor	1,947
23.	Fred Harb	1,840
24.	Herb Estes	1,658
25.	Shep Langdon	1,648
26.	Doug Cox	1,592
27.	Marvin Panch	1,576
28.	Billy Rafter	1,529
29.	Johnny Allen	1,483
30.	Wilbur Rakestraw	1,443

RACES LED

1.	Lee Petty	14
2.	Junior Johnson	9
3.	Buck Baker	8
4.	Fireball Roberts	7
	Jack Smith	7
	Speedy Thompson	7
	Bob Welborn	7
	Rex White	7
9.	Curtis Turner	6
10.	Cotton Owens	5
11.	Jim Reed	4
	Shorty Rollins	4
	Glen Wood	4
14.	Marvin Panch	3
	Joe Weatherly	3
16.	Joe Eubanks	2
	Parnelli Jones	2
	Eddie Pagan	2

1959

Driver	Starts	Poles	Finish 1	2	3	4	5	6–10	Laps	Laps Led	Races Led	Winston Cup Points	$
1. Lee Petty	42	2	11	5	7	4	0	8	8,278	1,011	16	11,792	49,220
2. Cotton Owens	37	2	1	4	2	2	4	9	6,733	209	4	9,962	14,640
3. Speedy Thompson	29	1	0	1	0	2	2	4	4,785	228	3	7,684	6,816
4. Herman Beam	30	0	0	0	0	0	1	11	6,034	0	0	7,396	6,380
5. Buck Baker	35	4	1	2	6	1	4	5	6,056	183	5	7,170	11,061
6. Tom Pistone	22	0	2	2	4	2	2	6	3,902	181	7	7,050	12,725
7. L. D. Austin	35	0	0	0	0	0	0	13	6,481	0	0	6,519	4,671
8. Jack Smith	21	3	4	1	2	2	0	3	3,594	222	7	6,150	13,290
9. Jim Reed	14	1	3	0	1	1	2	2	2,512	289	5	5,744	23,534
10. Rex White	23	5	5	2	2	1	1	2	4,744	826	9	5,526	12,360
11. Junior Johnson	28	1	5	1	3	3	2	1	4,433	166	7	4,864	9,675
12. Shep Langdon	21	0	0	0	0	0	0	6	3,976	0	0	4,768	3,526
13. G. C. Spencer	28	0	0	0	0	1	0	4	4,552	0	0	4,260	3,701
14. Tommy Irwin	25	1	0	1	2	3	4	6	4,410	174	2	3,876	9,190
15. Richard Petty	21	0	0	1	3	1	1	3	3,648	7	1	3,694	8,111
16. Fireball Roberts	8	3	1	0	0	0	0	3	1,445	147	3	3,676	10,661
17. Bob Welborn	29	5	3	1	3	3	0	3	3,895	176	7	3,588	6,491
18. Joe Weatherly	17	0	0	2	0	1	3	4	2,776	189	7	3,404	9,816
19. Bobby Johns	8	1	0	0	1	0	0	1	1,911	129	2	2,732	5,951
20. Tiny Lund	27	0	0	2	0	3	0	5	4,837	0	0	2,634	4,941
21. Bob Burdick	6	2	0	1	0	0	0	3	912	25	1	2,392	10,050
22. Larry Frank	15	0	0	1	0	1	2	5	3,300	39	1	2,256	5,993
23. Bobby Keck	18	0	0	0	0	0	0	0	2,484	0	0	2,186	1,270
24. Curtis Turner	10	1	2	1	0	1	0	0	1,293	438	5	2,088	3,845
25. Jim Paschal	6	0	0	2	0	0	1	1	1,485	0	0	1,792	2,980
26. Buddy Baker	12	0	0	0	0	1	0	4	1,639	0	0	1,692	1,705
27. Shorty Rollins	10	0	0	0	0	0	0	4	1,391	0	0	1,600	1,500
28. Elmo Langley	13	0	0	0	1	0	0	1	1,694	0	0	1,568	2,286
29. Jimmy Thompson	5	0	0	0	0	0	0	1	1,002	0	0	1,528	1,580
30. Brownie King	18	0	0	0	0	0	1	4	3,247	0	0	1,480	1,875
31. Tim Flock	2	0	0	0	0	0	0	1	223	0	0	1,464	850
32. Joe Eubanks	13	0	0	1	0	0	1	5	1,279	0	0	1,432	2,000
33. Roy Tyner	28	0	0	1	0	3	3	7	5,234	0	0	1,416	5,425
34. Charlie Cregar	3	0	0	0	0	0	0	0	496	0	0	1,408	550
35. Dick Freeman	3	0	0	0	0	0	0	0	695	0	0	1,352	475
36. Raul Cilloniz	2	0	0	0	0	0	0	0	229	0	0	1,272	550
37. Ned Jarrett	17	2	2	1	1	0	0	3	2,929	2	2	1,248	3,860
38. Dave White	5	0	0	0	0	0	0	1	1,253	0	0	1,228	660
39. Dick Joslin	4	0	0	0	0	0	0	0	338	0	0	1,224	485
40. Tommy Thompson	3	0	0	0	0	0	0	0	367	0	0	1,168	510
41. Harvey Hege	10	0	0	0	0	0	0	3	1,485	0	0	1,152	955
42. Eduardo Dibos	3	0	0	0	0	0	2	0	181	0	0	1,128	1,050
43. Bill Champion	1	0	0	0	0	0	0	0	343	0	0	1,120	500
44. Joe Caspolich	1	0	0	0	0	0	0	0	342	0	0	1,040	470
45. Jim Austin	5	0	0	0	0	0	0	0	784	0	0	1,016	440
46. Marvin Porter	7	0	0	0	1	1	0	2	1,696	0	0	984	1,940
47. Jim McGuirk	4	0	0	0	0	0	0	0	314	0	0	928	325
48. Harlan Richardson	10	0	0	0	0	0	0	2	1,893	0	0	924	1,120
49. Al White	5	0	0	0	0	0	0	0	826	0	0	872	575
50. Richard Riley	10	0	0	0	0	0	0	2	1,433	0	0	760	910

LAPS COMPLETED		LAPS LED		MILES LED		MILES DRIVEN		RACES LED	
1. Lee Petty	8,278	1. Lee Petty	1,011	1. Lee Petty	614	1. Lee Petty	4,977	1. Lee Petty	16
2. Cotton Owens	6,733	2. Rex White	826	2. Fireball Roberts	320	2. Cotton Owens	4,397	2. Rex White	9
3. L. D. Austin	6,481	3. Curtis Turner	438	3. Rex White	269	3. Herman Beam	4,011	3. Tom Pistone	7
4. Buck Baker	6,056	4. Jim Reed	289	4. Jim Reed	267	4. Buck Baker	3,606	Jack Smith	7
5. Herman Beam	6,034	5. Speedy Thompson	228	5. Curtis Turner	252	5. L. D. Austin	3,603	Joe Weatherly	7
6. Roy Tyner	5,234	6. Jack Smith	222	6. Jack Smith	246	6. Speedy Thompson	3,436	Bob Welborn	7
7. Tiny Lund	4,837	7. Cotton Owens	209	7. Tom Pistone	240	7. Roy Tyner	3,405	7. Buck Baker	5
8. Speedy Thompson	4,785	8. Joe Weatherly	189	8. Johnny Beauchamp	175	8. Rex White	3,039	Junior Johnson	5
9. Rex White	4,744	9. Buck Baker	183	9. Cotton Owens	173	9. Tiny Lund	2,972	Jim Reed	5
10. G. C. Spencer	4,552	10. Tom Pistone	181	10. Bob Welborn	153	10. Tom Pistone	2,966	Curtis Turner	5
11. Junior Johnson	4,433	11. Bob Welborn	176	11. Joe Weatherly	120	11. Tommy Irwin	2,847	Cotton Owens	4
12. Tommy Irwin	4,410	12. Tommy Irwin	174	12. Bobby Johns	114	12. Junior Johnson	2,745	12. Fireball Roberts	3
13. Glen Wood	4,186	13. Junior Johnson	166	13. Speedy Thompson	113	13. Jack Smith	2,735	Speedy Thompson	3
14. Shep Langdon	3,976	14. Fireball Roberts	147	14. Buck Baker	89	14. Larry Frank	2,647	14. Johnny Beauchamp	2
15. Tom Pistone	3,902	15. Johnny Beauchamp	130	15. Tommy Irwin	87	15. G. C. Spencer	2,553	Tommy Irwin	2
16. Bob Welborn	3,895	16. Bobby Johns	129	16. Junior Johnson	78	16. Richard Petty	2,419	Ned Jarrett	2
17. Richard Petty	3,648	17. Glen Wood	98	17. Banjo Matthews	76	17. Bob Welborn	2,364	Bobby Johns	2
18. Jack Smith	3,594	18. Banjo Matthews	55	18. Glen Wood	49	18. Glen Wood	2,292	Glen Wood	2
19. George Green	3,337	19. Larry Frank	39	19. Bob Burdick	34	19. Shep Langdon	2,259		
20. Larry Frank	3,300	20. Bob Burdick	25	20. Larry Frank	20	20. Joe Weatherly	2,105		
21. Brownie King	3,247	21. Richard Petty	7	21. Fritz Wilson	10	21. Jim Reed	2,071		
22. Ned Jarrett	2,929	22. Fritz Wilson	4	22. Richard Petty	10	22. Joe Lee Johnson	2,007		
23. Joe Weatherly	2,776	23. Dick Bailey	3	23. Dick Bailey	1	23. George Green	1,966		
24. Joe Lee Johnson	2,743	Russ Gemberling	3	Russ Gemberling	1	24. Brownie King	1,903		
25. Fred Harb	2,689	25. Eddie Gray	1			25. Ken Rush	1,533		
26. Jim Reed	2,512	Joe Lee Johnson	1			26. Fireball Roberts	1,489		
27. Bobby Keck	2,484	Parnelli Jones	1			27. Ned Jarrett	1,489		
28. Ken Rush	2,388					28. Bobby Johns	1,440		
29. Bobby Johns	1,911					29. Gene White	1,319		
30. Harlan Richardson	1,893					30. Elmo Langley	1,314		

1960

Driver	Starts	Poles	Finish 1	2	3	4	5	6–10	Laps	Laps Led	Races Led	Winston Cup Points	$
1. Rex White	40	3	6	6	7	4	2	10	8,921	541	11	21,164	57,525
2. Richard Petty	40	2	3	6	3	3	1	14	8,189	447	6	17,228	41,873
3. Bobby Johns	19	0	1	2	1	3	1	2	3,695	438	6	14,964	46,115
4. Buck Baker	37	2	2	1	3	1	8	9	7,271	213	4	14,674	38,399
5. Ned Jarrett	40	5	5	3	4	4	4	6	7,399	382	11	14,660	25,438
6. Lee Petty	39	3	5	7	2	6	1	9	7,518	515	10	14,510	31,283
7. Junior Johnson	34	3	3	2	4	2	3	4	5,096	320	7	9,932	38,990
8. Emanuel Zervakis	14	1	0	0	1	1	0	8	3,382	0	0	9,720	12,124
9. Jim Paschal	10	0	0	0	2	1	0	4	2,752	11	1	8,968	15,096
10. Banjo Matthews	12	0	0	0	0	0	0	4	1,894	9	1	8,458	15,617
11. Johnny Beauchamp	11	0	1	1	0	0	1	2	2,669	1	1	8,306	17,374
12. Herman Beam	26	0	0	0	0	1	0	5	5,348	0	0	7,776	5,916
13. Joe Lee Johnson	22	0	1	1	1	1	2	2	3,453	48	1	7,352	34,519
14. Jack Smith	13	4	3	1	2	0	1	0	2,198	514	10	6,944	24,721
15. Fred Lorenzen	10	0	0	0	2	0	1	2	2,086	93	1	6,764	9,136
16. Bob Welborn	15	0	0	1	0	2	3	4	2,809	94	2	6,732	6,194
17. Jimmy Pardue	32	0	0	0	0	0	1	10	5,004	0	0	6,682	5,610
18. Tom Pistone	21	0	0	0	1	0	1	6	4,137	183	4	6,572	6,714
19. Johnny Allen	10	0	0	1	0	0	1	3	1,820	0	0	6,506	14,789
20. Joe Weatherly	24	0	3	2	0	2	0	4	4,294	246	6	6,380	20,124
21. Doug Yates	24	1	0	0	2	1	0	5	4,030	39	1	6,374	5,205
22. L. D. Austin	27	0	0	0	0	0	1	9	4,822	0	0	6,180	4,785
23. David Pearson	22	1	0	1	0	1	1	4	3,885	0	0	5,956	5,030
24. Gerald Duke	11	0	0	0	0	1	0	6	2,062	0	0	5,950	5,930
25. Speedy Thompson	9	0	2	0	0	1	1	1	1,646	217	2	5,658	18,035
26. Marvin Panch	11	0	0	0	0	0	0	1	1,482	22	1	5,268	3,225
27. Paul Lewis	22	0	0	0	0	0	0	4	3,690	0	0	5,212	3,535
28. Curtis Crider	24	0	0	0	0	0	0	2	3,985	0	0	4,720	3,645
29. Fireball Roberts	9	6	2	0	0	0	0	1	1,338	578	9	4,700	19,895
30. Shorty Rollins	4	0	0	0	0	0	0	1	952	0	0	4,374	2,120
31. Possum Jones	13	0	0	3	1	0	0	1	2,594	0	0	4,270	6,330
32. Tiny Lund	8	0	0	0	0	0	0	2	1,254	0	0	4,124	2,440
33. G. C. Spencer	26	0	0	0	0	1	1	4	4,907	0	0	3,986	3,910
34. Larry Frank	10	0	0	0	0	0	0	2	1,927	11	1	3,634	2,440
35. Herb Tillman	9	0	0	0	0	0	0	0	1,705	0	0	3,504	2,605
36. Curtis Turner	9	1	0	0	3	0	0	1	1,090	106	2	3,300	3,220
37. Bunkie Blackburn	20	0	0	0	0	0	1	3	2,789	0	0	3,252	3,400
38. Buddy Baker	15	0	0	0	0	0	0	1	2,149	0	0	3,070	1,745
39. Cotton Owens	14	3	1	3	1	0	0	0	2,121	185	7	3,050	14,065
40. Charley Griffith	5	0	0	0	0	0	0	0	599	0	0	2,684	1,300
41. Wilbur Rakestraw	12	0	0	0	0	0	0	1	1,862	0	0	2,676	2,695
42. Jimmy Massey	6	0	0	1	1	0	0	1	1,392	26	1	2,662	3,310
43. Jimmy Thompson	9	0	0	0	0	0	0	0	1,944	0	0	2,472	1,940
44. Jim Reed	8	0	0	0	1	0	0	0	1,175	28	1	2,340	2,240
45. Jim Cook	3	1	1	0	0	0	0	0	560	0	0	2,178	1,600
46. Ernie Gahan	2	0	0	0	0	0	0	0	818	0	0	2,080	625
47. Elmo Henderson	6	0	0	0	0	0	0	0	870	0	0	2,072	1,425
48. Bob Burdick	2	0	0	0	0	0	0	1	71	0	0	1,970	850
49. Roz Howard	3	0	0	0	0	0	0	2	676	0	0	1,810	1,490
50. Bob Potter	3	0	0	0	0	0	0	1	708	0	0	1,800	640

LAPS COMPLETED		LAPS LED		MILES LED		MILES DRIVEN		RACES LED	
1. Rex White	8,921	1. Glen Wood	766	1. Fireball Roberts	918	1. Rex White	6,916	1. Ned Jarrett	11
2. Richard Petty	8,189	2. Fireball Roberts	578	2. Jack Smith	786	2. Richard Petty	6,015	Rex White	11
3. Lee Petty	7,518	3. Rex White	541	3. Bobby Johns	462	3. Buck Baker	5,854	3. Lee Petty	10
4. Ned Jarrett	7,399	4. Lee Petty	515	4. Richard Petty	418	4. Ned Jarrett	5,479	Jack Smith	10
5. Buck Baker	7,271	5. Jack Smith	514	5. Rex White	396	5. Lee Petty	5,389	5. Fireball Roberts	9
6. Herman Beam	5,348	6. Richard Petty	447	6. Lee Petty	358	6. Herman Beam	4,730	6. Junior Johnson	7
7. Junior Johnson	5,096	7. Bobby Johns	438	7. Junior Johnson	307	7. L. D. Austin	3,996	Cotton Owens	7
8. Jimmy Pardue	5,004	8. Ned Jarrett	382	8. Cotton Owens	286	8. G. C. Spencer	3,822	8. Bobby Johns	6
9. G. C. Spencer	4,907	9. Junior Johnson	320	9. Joe Weatherly	268	9. Bobby Johns	3,815	Richard Petty	6
10. L. D. Austin	4,822	10. Joe Weatherly	246	10. Buck Baker	262	10. Joe Weatherly	3,804	Joe Weatherly	6
11. Joe Weatherly	4,294	11. Speedy Thompson	217	11. Glen Wood	233	11. Junior Johnson	3,797	11. Glen Wood	5
12. Tom Pistone	4,137	12. Buck Baker	213	12. Tom Pistone	161	12. David Pearson	3,768	12. Buck Baker	4
13. Doug Yates	4,030	13. Cotton Owens	185	13. Ned Jarrett	153	13. Tom Pistone	3,728	Tom Pistone	4
14. Curtis Crider	3,985	14. Tom Pistone	183	14. Speedy Thompson	153	14. Jimmy Pardue	3,704	14. Mel Larson	2
15. David Pearson	3,885	15. Curtis Turner	106	15. Lloyd Dane	125	15. Emanuel Zervakis	3,457	Marvin Porter	2
16. Bobby Johns	3,695	16. Bob Welborn	94	16. Marvin Porter	81	16. Doug Yates	3,262	John Rostek	2
17. Paul Lewis	3,690	17. Fred Lorenzen	93	17. Curtis Turner	74	17. Curtis Crider	2,973	Speedy Thompson	2
18. Joe Lee Johnson	3,453	18. Lloyd Dane	89	18. Joe Johnson	72	18. Banjo Matthews	2,815	Curtis Turner	2
19. Emanuel Zervakis	3,382	19. John Rostek	65	John Rostek	72	19. Jim Paschal	2,713	Bob Welborn	2
20. Fred Harb	3,269	20. Marvin Porter	61	20. Jim Reed	56	20. Joe Lee Johnson	2,651		
21. Bob Welborn	2,809	21. Joe Johnson	48	21. Bob Welborn	47	21. Jack Smith	2,570		
22. Bunkie Blackburn	2,789	22. Doug Yates	39	22. Fred Lorenzen	47	22. Paul Lewis	2,562		
23. Jim Paschal	2,752	23. Jim Reed	28	23. Scotty Cain	27	23. Bob Welborn	2,533		
24. Johnny Beauchamp	2,669	24. Jimmy Massey	26	24. Parnelli Jones	25	24. Johnny Beauchamp	2,530		
25. Tommy Irwin	2,659	25. Parnelli Jones	25	25. Mel Larson	24	25. Fred Lorenzen	2,521		
26. Possum Jones	2,594	26. Marvin Panch	22	26. Doug Yates	20	26. Johnny Allen	2,501		
27. Neil Castles	2,293	27. Scotty Cain	19	27. Larry Frank	17	27. Larry Frank	2,379		
28. Glen Wood	2,206	Mel Larson	19	28. Jimmy Massey	13	28. Cotton Owens	2,362		
29. Jack Smith	2,198	29. Larry Frank	11	29. Frank Secrist	11	29. Marvin Panch	2,322		
30. Buddy Baker	2,149	Jim Paschal	11	30. Marvin Panch	11	30. Jimmy Thompson	2,288		

Driver	Starts	Poles	Finish 1	2	3	4	5	6–10	Laps	Laps Led	Races Led	Winston Cup Points	$
1961													
1. Ned Jarrett	46	4	1	4	8	4	6	11	9,813	606	9	27,272	41,056
2. Rex White	47	7	7	8	8	2	4	9	10,307	1,224	15	26,442	56,395
3. Emanuel Zervakis	38	1	2	1	3	5	8	9	9,198	386	2	22,312	27,281
4. Joe Weatherly	25	4	9	3	0	1	1	4	5,790	809	18	17,894	47,079
5. Fireball Roberts	22	6	2	4	2	2	3	1	5,075	1,002	13	17,600	50,267
6. Junior Johnson	41	10	7	3	2	3	1	6	7,016	2,373	23	17,178	28,541
7. Jack Smith	25	0	2	2	4	1	1	4	4,695	278	4	15,186	21,410
8. Richard Petty	42	2	2	4	4	5	3	5	7,866	703	7	14,984	25,239
9. Jim Paschal	23	1	2	4	1	2	3	4	5,464	209	4	13,922	18,100
10. Buck Baker	42	1	1	1	3	4	2	4	7,195	114	3	13,746	13,697
11. Jimmy Pardue	44	0	0	0	0	1	2	13	7,757	0	0	13,408	10,562
12. Johnny Allen	22	1	0	0	2	0	1	8	4,508	3	1	13,114	13,127
13. David Pearson	19	1	3	0	2	1	1	1	3,087	247	5	13,088	51,911
14. Bob Welborn	14	0	0	1	2	0	0	4	2,996	104	4	12,570	13,487
15. Herman Beam	41	0	0	0	0	1	0	13	8,827	0	0	11,382	9,392
16. Nelson Stacy	15	0	1	0	1	2	0	4	3,024	144	4	10,436	27,608
17. Ralph Earnhardt	8	0	0	1	1	0	0	3	1,664	90	3	10,182	11,473
18. Marvin Panch	9	1	1	1	0	1	0	3	1,517	129	2	9,392	30,478
19. Fred Lorenzen	15	4	3	1	0	1	1	0	2,657	781	10	9,316	30,395
20. G. C. Spencer	31	0	0	0	0	3	0	15	6,221	0	0	9,128	7,363
21. Curtis Crider	41	0	0	0	0	0	1	1	5,882	0	0	8,414	7,420
22. Cotton Owens	17	2	4	3	1	2	1	0	2,694	58	5	8,032	11,890
23. Tiny Lund	10	0	0	0	0	0	0	2	2,583	0	0	7,740	5,545
24. Bobby Johns	14	1	0	0	0	1	0	2	2,674	52	2	7,590	5,010
25. L. D. Austin	20	0	0	0	0	0	0	8	4,802	0	0	7,306	4,530
26. Tommy Irwin	26	0	0	2	0	1	0	5	3,748	166	1	7,300	7,170
27. Doug Yates	32	0	0	0	0	0	2	8	5,058	0	0	5,878	1,090
28. Paul Lewis	21	0	0	0	0	0	0	5	3,669	0	0	5,712	4,095
29. Bob Barron	31	0	0	0	0	0	0	5	5,005	0	0	5,412	3,725
30. Elmo Langley	15	0	0	0	0	0	1	4	2,826	0	0	5,376	3,530
31. Banjo Matthews	14	0	0	0	0	1	0	2	2,019	197	6	4,924	5,560
32. Wendell Scott	23	0	0	0	0	0	0	5	4,364	0	0	4,726	3,240
33. Jim Reed	8	0	0	2	0	0	1	1	1,735	32	1	4,705	3,350
34. Fred Harb	27	0	0	0	0	1	0	7	4,039	0	0	4,526	3,460
35. Darel Dieringer	7	0	0	0	0	0	1	1	1,008	0	0	4,416	3,150
36. Bob Burdick	5	0	1	0	0	1	0	2	1,086	44	2	4,382	18,750
37. Lee Reitzel	17	0	0	0	0	0	0	3	2,566	0	0	4,380	2,910
38. Tom Pistone	4	0	0	0	0	0	0	3	576	0	0	3,766	2,050
39. Buddy Baker	14	0	0	0	0	0	1	2	2,370	0	0	3,668	4,965
40. Roscoe Thompson	6	0	0	0	0	0	0	2	721	0	0	3,602	2,535
41. Woodie Wilson	5	0	0	0	0	0	0	1	828	0	0	3,580	2,625
42. Larry Frank	8	0	0	0	0	0	0	1	978	0	0	3,162	2,380
43. Larry Thomas	14	0	0	0	0	0	0	4	2,830	0	0	3,140	2,015
44. Harry Leake	15	0	0	0	0	0	0	7	2,375	0	0	3,092	2,000
45. Paul Goldsmith	2	0	0	0	1	0	0	1	239	0	0	2,930	6,050
46. Joe Lee Johnson	9	0	0	0	0	0	0	3	1,276	0	0	2,700	2,615
47. Bill Morgan	5	0	0	0	0	0	0	1	1,132	0	0	2,430	1,900
48. Theodore Hunt	7	0	0	0	0	0	0	0	940	0	0	2,430	2,750
49. Marvin Porter	8	0	0	0	0	0	1	0	1,096	0	0	2,326	2,070
50. Joe Eubanks	2	0	0	0	0	0	0	0	448	0	0	2,320	1,475

Laps Completed

1. Rex White — 10,307
2. Ned Jarrett — 9,813
3. Emanuel Zervakis — 9,198
4. Herman Beam — 8,827
5. Richard Petty — 7,866
6. Jimmy Pardue — 7,757
7. Buck Baker — 7,195
8. Junior Johnson — 7,016
9. G. C. Spencer — 6,221
10. Curtis Crider — 5,882
11. Joe Weatherly — 5,790
12. Jim Paschal — 5,464
13. Fireball Roberts — 5,075
14. Doug Yates — 5,058
15. Bob Barron — 5,005
16. L. D. Austin — 4,802
17. Jack Smith — 4,695
18. Johnny Allen — 4,508
19. Wendell Scott — 4,364
20. Fred Harb — 4,039
21. Tommy Irwin — 3,748
22. Paul Lewis — 3,669
23. David Pearson — 3,087
24. Nelson Stacy — 3,024
25. Bob Welborn — 2,996
26. Larry Thomas — 2,830
27. Elmo Langley — 2,826
28. Cotton Owens — 2,694
29. Bobby Johns — 2,674
30. Fred Lorenzen — 2,657

Laps Led

1. Junior Johnson — 2,373
2. Rex White — 1,224
3. Fireball Roberts — 1,002
4. Joe Weatherly — 809
5. Fred Lorenzen — 781
6. Richard Petty — 703
7. Ned Jarrett — 606
8. Emanuel Zervakis — 386
9. Jack Smith — 278
10. David Pearson — 247
11. Jim Paschal — 209
12. Banjo Matthews — 197
13. Tommy Irwin — 166
14. Curtis Turner — 151
15. Nelson Stacy — 144
16. Glen Wood — 138
17. Marvin Panch — 129
18. Lee Petty — 126
19. Buck Baker — 114
20. Bob Welborn — 104
21. Ralph Earnhardt — 90
22. Eddie Gray — 75
23. Cotton Owens — 58
24. Bobby Johns — 52
25. Bob Burdick — 44
26. Jim Reed — 32
27. Bill Amick — 25
28. Johnny Allen — 3

Miles Led

1. Fireball Roberts — 1,590
2. Junior Johnson — 1,258
3. Fred Lorenzen — 699
4. Rex White — 627
5. Richard Petty — 456
6. Joe Weatherly — 455
7. David Pearson — 381
8. Banjo Matthews — 323
9. Ned Jarrett — 317
10. Nelson Stacy — 214
11. Curtis Turner — 186
12. Jack Smith — 144
13. Ralph Earnhardt — 134
14. Bob Welborn — 129
15. Emanuel Zervakis — 103
16. Jim Paschal — 102
17. Marvin Panch — 99
18. Tommy Irwin — 83
19. Eddie Gray — 75
20. Bob Burdick — 66
21. Lee Petty — 63
22. Buck Baker — 57
23. Cotton Owens — 37
24. Glen Wood — 35
25. Bobby Johns — 32
26. Bill Amick — 25
27. Jim Reed — 8
28. Johnny Allen — 4

Miles Driven

1. Rex White — 7,542
2. Ned Jarrett — 7,184
3. Emanuel Zervakis — 6,664
4. Herman Beam — 6,403
5. Jimmy Pardue — 5,628
6. Richard Petty — 5,392
7. Joe Weatherly — 5,329
8. Junior Johnson — 5,228
9. Buck Baker — 5,226
10. Fireball Roberts — 5,033
11. Johnny Allen — 4,493
12. Curtis Crider — 4,186
13. Jack Smith — 4,098
14. G. C. Spencer — 3,824
15. Jim Paschal — 3,665
16. David Pearson — 3,449
17. Bob Welborn — 3,424
18. L. D. Austin — 3,402
19. Nelson Stacy — 3,281
20. Tommy Irwin — 3,235
21. Bobby Johns — 3,084
22. Fred Lorenzen — 3,040
23. Elmo Langley — 3,012
24. Banjo Matthews — 3,010
25. Doug Yates — 2,992
26. Bob Barron — 2,870
27. Paul Lewis — 2,803
28. Tiny Lund — 2,756
29. Marvin Panch — 2,576
30. Ralph Earnhardt — 2,522

Races Led

1. Junior Johnson — 23
2. Joe Weatherly — 18
3. Rex White — 15
4. Fireball Roberts — 13
5. Fred Lorenzen — 10
6. Ned Jarrett — 9
7. Richard Petty — 7
8. Banjo Matthews — 6
9. Cotton Owens — 5
   David Pearson — 5
   Curtis Turner — 5
12. Jim Paschal — 4
    Jack Smith — 4
    Nelson Stacy — 4
    Bob Welborn — 4
16. Buck Baker — 3
    Ralph Earnhardt — 3
18. Bob Burdick — 2
    Bobby Johns — 2
    Marvin Panch — 2
    Lee Petty — 2
    Emanuel Zervakis — 2

Driver	Starts	Poles	Finish						Laps	Laps Led	Races Led	Winston Cup Points	$
			1	2	3	4	5	6–10					

1962

Driver	Starts	Poles	1	2	3	4	5	6–10	Laps	Laps Led	Races Led	Winston Cup Points	$
1. Joe Weatherly	52	7	9	12	10	3	5	6	12,431	1,014	17	30,836	70,743
2. Richard Petty	52	5	8	9	8	5	2	7	11,544	1,396	19	28,440	60,764
3. Ned Jarrett	52	4	6	2	3	3	5	16	11,296	866	11	25,336	43,444
4. Jack Smith	51	7	5	6	5	8	3	8	10,781	894	9	22,870	34,748
5. Rex White	37	9	8	3	3	1	3	5	7,683	1,129	15	19,424	36,246
6. Jim Paschal	39	0	4	4	3	3	3	7	8,311	856	9	18,128	27,348
7. Fred Lorenzen	19	3	2	2	4	1	2	1	4,435	471	9	17,554	46,100
8. Fireball Roberts	19	9	3	3	0	2	1	3	4,312	960	12	16,380	66,152
9. Marvin Panch	17	0	0	2	3	0	0	3	3,642	172	4	15,138	26,746
10. David Pearson	12	0	0	0	0	1	0	6	2,690	280	4	14,404	19,032
11. Herman Beam	51	1	0	0	0	0	0	18	11,217	0	0	13,650	12,571
12. Curtis Crider	52	0	0	0	1	1	1	15	10,051	0	0	13,050	12,016
13. Buck Baker	37	0	0	1	3	2	0	8	6,707	18	2	12,838	12,787
14. Larry Frank	19	0	1	0	0	0	1	6	3,566	85	1	12,814	32,987
15. Bob Welborn	25	0	0	1	0	2	2	7	5,654	0	0	12,368	10,347
16. George Green	46	0	0	0	0	0	1	14	9,279	0	0	12,132	9,221
17. Larry Thomas	37	0	0	0	0	2	1	9	7,268	0	0	11,946	9,486
18. Thomas Cox	42	0	0	0	0	1	2	17	8,370	0	0	11,688	10,181
19. Jimmy Pardue	29	0	1	1	1	1	1	11	7,274	200	3	11,414	12,066
20. Junior Johnson	23	2	1	2	2	1	1	1	3,663	648	11	11,140	34,841
21. Nelson Stacy	15	0	3	1	0	0	1	2	3,484	371	4	10,934	43,080
22. Wendell Scott	41	1	0	0	2	1	1	15	8,542	0	0	9,906	7,133
23. Buddy Baker	31	0	0	0	1	2	2	5	5,454	0	0	9,828	7,578
24. G. C. Spencer	42	0	0	0	0	2	4	7	7,300	0	0	9,788	7,995
25. Bunkie Blackburn	10	0	0	0	0	1	0	2	2,325	0	0	8,016	5,890
26. Johnny Allen	20	1	1	0	0	3	1	3	4,094	288	4	7,602	7,230
27. Emanuel Zervakis	11	0	0	0	0	0	0	2	2,151	5	1	6,406	4,545
28. Bobby Johns	13	0	1	0	1	0	0	1	2,745	614	8	5,670	15,863
29. Ralph Earnhardt	17	0	0	0	1	0	1	4	2,022	0	0	5,472	4,545
30. Cotton Owens	16	1	0	2	2	2	1	1	2,000	36	2	4,984	5,905
31. Banjo Matthews	5	2	0	1	0	0	0	1	532	145	3	4,956	11,375
32. Sherman Utsman	12	0	0	0	0	0	1	3	3,293	0	0	4,896	3,580
33. Darel Dieringer	14	1	0	0	0	0	1	2	3,179	17	1	4,548	4,880
34. Tiny Lund	10	0	0	0	0	0	0	1	2,487	8	1	4,384	2,880
35. Stick Elliott	21	0	0	0	0	0	0	2	3,028	0	0	4,254	3,928
36. LeeRoy Yarbrough	12	0	0	0	0	0	1	0	1,478	0	0	4,240	3,285
37. Tommy Irwin	20	0	0	1	0	1	0	7	2,982	10	1	3,980	3,305
38. Ed Livingston	13	0	0	0	0	0	0	0	1,758	0	0	3,604	2,940
39. Fred Harb	21	0	0	0	0	0	0	3	2,763	0	0	3,430	2,220
40. Elmo Langley	6	0	0	0	0	0	0	0	774	0	0	2,556	1,795
41. Bill Morton	5	0	0	0	0	0	0	2	1,359	0	0	2,522	1,350
42. Speedy Thompson	3	0	0	0	0	0	0	1	443	0	0	2,522	1,400
43. Jimmy Thompson	3	0	0	0	0	0	0	0	847	0	0	2,346	1,650
44. Red Foote	4	0	0	0	0	0	0	0	939	0	0	2,274	1,600
45. Ernie Gahan	3	0	0	0	0	0	0	1	284	0	0	2,092	725
46. Billy Wade	4	0	0	0	0	0	0	2	1,054	0	0	2,008	1,350
47. Jim Cushman	4	0	0	0	0	0	0	1	782	0	0	1,954	850
48. Bill Wimble	2	0	0	0	0	0	0	0	231	0	0	1,944	675
49. Troy Ruttman	1	0	0	0	0	0	1	0	218	0	0	1,890	1,750
50. Cale Yarborough	8	0	0	0	0	0	0	1	727	0	0	1,884	2,725

LAPS COMPLETED

1.	Joe Weatherly	12,431
2.	Richard Petty	11,544
3.	Ned Jarrett	11,296
4.	Herman Beam	11,217
5.	Jack Smith	10,781
6.	Curtis Crider	10,051
7.	George Green	9,279
8.	Wendell Scott	8,542
9.	Thomas Cox	8,370
10.	Jim Paschal	8,311
11.	Rex White	7,683
12.	G. C. Spencer	7,300
13.	Jimmy Pardue	7,274
14.	Larry Thomas	7,268
15.	Buck Baker	6,707
16.	Bob Welborn	5,654
17.	Buddy Baker	5,454
18.	Fred Lorenzen	4,435
19.	Fireball Roberts	4,312
20.	Johnny Allen	4,094
21.	Junior Johnson	3,663
22.	Marvin Panch	3,642
23.	Larry Frank	3,566
24.	Nelson Stacy	3,484
25.	Sherman Utsman	3,293
26.	Darel Dieringer	3,179
27.	Stick Elliott	3,028
28.	Tommy Irwin	2,982
29.	Fred Harb	2,763
30.	Bobby Johns	2,745

LAPS LED

1.	Richard Petty	1,396
2.	Rex White	1,129
3.	Joe Weatherly	1,014
4.	Fireball Roberts	960
5.	Jack Smith	894
6.	Ned Jarrett	866
7.	Jim Paschal	856
8.	Junior Johnson	648
9.	Bobby Johns	614
10.	Fred Lorenzen	471
11.	Nelson Stacy	371
12.	Johnny Allen	288
13.	David Pearson	280
14.	Jimmy Pardue	200
15.	Marvin Panch	172
16.	Banjo Matthews	145
17.	Larry Frank	85
18.	Cotton Owens	36
19.	Buck Baker	18
20.	Darel Dieringer	17
21.	Tommy Irwin	10
22.	Tiny Lund	8
23.	Emanuel Zervakis	5

MILES LED

1.	Fireball Roberts	1,113
2.	Richard Petty	809
3.	Joe Weatherly	643
4.	Junior Johnson	638
5.	Bobby Johns	501
6.	Rex White	451
7.	Jim Paschal	434
8.	David Pearson	413
9.	Fred Lorenzen	388
10.	Ned Jarrett	376
11.	Jack Smith	353
12.	Banjo Matthews	290
13.	Marvin Panch	235
14.	Nelson Stacy	212
15.	Jimmy Pardue	205
16.	Larry Frank	117
17.	Johnny Allen	104
18.	Darel Dieringer	23
19.	Cotton Owens	20
20.	Tiny Lund	12
21.	Buck Baker	9
22.	Emanuel Zervakis	8
23.	Tommy Irwin	5

MILES DRIVEN

1.	Joe Weatherly	8,001
2.	Richard Petty	7,558
3.	Ned Jarrett	7,209
4.	Herman Beam	7,140
5.	Jack Smith	7,110
6.	Curtis Crider	6,431
7.	George Green	5,896
8.	Jim Paschal	5,868
9.	Rex White	5,760
10.	Buck Baker	5,035
11.	Thomas Cox	4,990
12.	Larry Thomas	4,889
13.	Jimmy Pardue	4,855
14.	G. C. Spencer	4,791
15.	Bob Welborn	4,558
16.	Fred Lorenzen	4,372
17.	Wendell Scott	4,211
18.	Buddy Baker	4,139
19.	Fireball Roberts	4,068
20.	Marvin Panch	3,758
21.	David Pearson	3,552
22.	Larry Frank	3,506
23.	Johnny Allen	3,401
24.	Junior Johnson	3,224
25.	Nelson Stacy	3,171
26.	Darel Dieringer	2,986
27.	Bobby Johns	2,976
28.	Bunkie Blackburn	2,705
29.	Tiny Lund	2,580
30.	Emanuel Zervakis	2,357

RACES LED

1.	Richard Petty	19
2.	Joe Weatherly	17
3.	Rex White	15
4.	Fireball Roberts	12
5.	Ned Jarrett	11
	Junior Johnson	11
7.	Fred Lorenzen	9
	Jim Paschal	9
	Jack Smith	9
10.	Bobby Johns	8
11.	Johnny Allen	4
	Marvin Panch	4
	David Pearson	4
	Nelson Stacy	4
15.	Banjo Matthews	3
	Jimmy Pardue	3
17.	Buck Baker	2
	Cotton Owens	2

Driver	Starts	Poles	Finish 1	2	3	4	5	6–10	Laps	Laps Led	Races Led	Winston Cup Points	$
1963													
1. Joe Weatherly	53	6	3	5	5	5	2	15	11,343	878	12	33,398	74,624
2. Richard Petty	54	8	14	9	2	4	1	9	12,183	2,316	29	31,170	55,964
3. Fred Lorenzen	29	9	6	8	3	0	4	2	7,484	2,419	20	29,684	122,588
4. Ned Jarrett	53	5	8	7	5	7	5	7	11,845	1,897	18	27,214	45,844
5. Fireball Roberts	20	2	4	2	0	4	1	3	4,643	692	12	22,642	73,060
6. Jimmy Pardue	52	1	1	0	1	4	1	13	9,719	74	3	22,228	20,359
7. Darel Dieringer	20	0	1	0	1	3	2	8	5,513	84	3	21,418	29,725
8. David Pearson	41	2	0	3	2	5	3	6	8,697	178	6	21,156	24,986
9. Rex White	25	3	0	3	2	0	0	9	5,595	171	6	20,976	27,241
10. Tiny Lund	22	0	1	1	1	1	1	7	5,093	127	5	19,624	49,397
11. Buck Baker	47	0	1	3	6	2	5	13	9,505	63	2	18,114	18,616
12. Junior Johnson	33	9	7	2	2	0	2	1	5,671	2,396	21	17,720	67,351
13. Marvin Panch	12	3	1	2	5	1	0	3	3,510	291	6	17,156	39,102
14. Nelson Stacy	12	0	0	0	1	2	1	5	2,816	76	2	14,974	18,266
15. Wendell Scott	47	0	0	0	0	0	1	14	9,459	0	0	14,814	10,966
16. Billy Wade	31	0	0	1	0	2	1	10	6,008	21	2	14,646	15,204
17. Curtis Crider	49	0	0	0	1	0	1	13	8,859	0	0	13,996	11,644
18. G. C. Spencer	31	0	0	1	1	1	1	8	4,888	30	3	13,744	13,514
19. Jim Paschal	32	1	5	3	5	2	0	3	6,915	400	12	13,456	20,979
20. Bobby Isaac	27	0	0	0	1	0	2	4	4,989	30	1	12,858	9,529
21. Bobby Johns	12	0	0	0	1	0	2	3	2,433	84	3	12,652	15,915
22. Larry Thomas	32	0	0	0	2	1	3	7	6,991	0	0	11,010	8,945
23. Stick Elliott	28	0	0	0	0	0	0	7	4,693	0	0	9,582	6,235
24. Jack Smith	29	2	0	0	0	1	3	7	5,300	25	2	8,218	8,645
25. Cale Yarborough	18	0	0	0	0	0	3	4	4,519	0	0	8,062	5,550
26. LeeRoy Yarbrough	14	1	0	0	0	0	1	4	2,564	8	1	7,872	6,680
27. Herman Beam	25	0	0	0	0	0	0	6	5,061	0	0	7,742	5,255
28. Larry Frank	11	0	0	0	1	1	0	0	2,392	5	1	7,582	5,450
29. Larry Manning	23	0	0	0	0	1	0	8	5,158	0	0	6,952	5,405
30. Ed Livingston	20	0	0	0	0	0	0	1	3,294	0	0	6,818	4,930
31. Neil Castles	28	0	0	0	0	1	1	6	4,093	0	0	5,928	5,165
32. Tommy Irwin	7	0	0	0	1	0	1	3	1,528	0	0	5,176	2,655
33. Reb Wickersham	14	0	0	0	0	0	0	1	3,501	0	0	4,812	3,800
34. Worth McMillion	15	0	0	0	0	0	0	4	4,177	0	0	4,614	3,145
35. Bob James	10	0	0	0	0	0	0	0	1,414	0	0	4,316	3,375
36. Roy Mayne	20	0	0	0	0	0	1	3	3,857	0	0	4,188	3,490
37. Bob Cooper	9	0	0	0	0	0	0	1	1,559	0	0	4,164	3,115
38. Jimmy Massey	15	0	0	0	0	1	0	7	3,179	0	0	4,016	2,870
39. Elmo Langley	11	0	0	0	0	0	1	1	2,196	0	0	3,982	2,170
40. Bob Welborn	11	0	0	1	2	1	0	0	2,221	0	0	3,484	4,830
41. Fred Harb	16	0	0	1	0	1	0	5	2,563	0	0	3,286	2,720
42. Dave MacDonald	2	0	0	1	0	0	0	0	323	92	1	2,944	5,330
43. Major Melton	17	0	0	0	0	0	0	0	2,780	0	0	2,806	1,910
44. Sal Tovella	3	0	0	0	0	0	0	0	346	0	0	2,570	1,300
45. Ron Hornaday	2	0	0	0	0	0	0	1	316	0	0	2,520	1,600
46. J. D. McDuffie	12	0	0	0	0	0	0	3	1,918	0	0	2,498	1,620
47. Bob Perry	5	0	0	0	0	0	0	0	668	0	0	2,478	1,550
48. Bunkie Blackburn	7	0	0	0	0	0	0	1	909	0	0	2,454	2,525
49. Bill Foster	10	0	0	0	0	0	0	2	1,628	0	0	2,168	1,410
50. Bud Harless	5	0	0	0	0	0	0	1	1,508	0	0	2,156	1,550

LAPS COMPLETED		LAPS LED		MILES LED		MILES DRIVEN		RACES LED	
1. Richard Petty	12,183	1. Fred Lorenzen	2,419	1. Junior Johnson	2,258	1. Joe Weatherly	8,407	1. Richard Petty	29
2. Ned Jarrett	11,845	2. Junior Johnson	2,396	2. Fred Lorenzen	1,654	2. Ned Jarrett	7,938	2. Junior Johnson	21
3. Joe Weatherly	11,343	3. Richard Petty	2,316	3. Richard Petty	1,164	3. Richard Petty	7,873	3. Fred Lorenzen	20
4. Jimmy Pardue	9,719	4. Ned Jarrett	1,897	4. Ned Jarrett	792	4. Jimmy Pardue	7,295	4. Ned Jarrett	18
5. Buck Baker	9,505	5. Joe Weatherly	878	5. Fireball Roberts	621	5. David Pearson	6,503	5. Jim Paschal	12
6. Wendell Scott	9,459	6. Fireball Roberts	692	6. Joe Weatherly	530	6. Fred Lorenzen	6,472	Fireball Roberts	12
7. Curtis Crider	8,859	7. Jim Paschal	400	7. Dan Gurney	324	7. Wendell Scott	6,165	Joe Weatherly	12
8. David Pearson	8,697	8. Marvin Panch	291	8. Marvin Panch	312	8. Buck Baker	5,702	8. Marvin Panch	6
9. Fred Lorenzen	7,484	9. Glen Wood	268	9. Dave MacDonald	248	9. Rex White	5,490	David Pearson	6
10. Larry Thomas	6,991	10. David Pearson	178	10. Jim Paschal	211	10. Fireball Roberts	5,470	Rex White	6
11. Jim Paschal	6,915	11. Rex White	171	11. Darel Dieringer	168	11. Darel Dieringer	5,432	11. Tiny Lund	5
12. Billy Wade	6,008	12. Tiny Lund	127	12. Bobby Johns	148	12. Curtis Crider	5,402	12. Darel Dieringer	3
13. Junior Johnson	5,671	13. Dan Gurney	120	13. Rex White	139	13. Billy Wade	4,989	A. J. Foyt	3
14. Rex White	5,595	14. Dave MacDonald	92	14. Parnelli Jones	105	14. Tiny Lund	4,881	Paul Goldsmith	3
15. Darel Dieringer	5,513	15. Darel Dieringer	84	15. Tiny Lund	105	15. Junior Johnson	4,723	Bobby Johns	3
16. Jack Smith	5,300	Bobby Johns	84	16. A. J. Foyt	104	16. Jim Paschal	4,592	Jimmy Pardue	3
17. Larry Manning	5,158	17. Nelson Stacy	76	17. David Pearson	84	17. Bobby Isaac	4,299	G. C. Spencer	3
18. Tiny Lund	5,093	18. Jimmy Pardue	74	18. Glen Wood	67	18. Larry Thomas	4,209	18. Buck Baker	2
19. Herman Beam	5,061	19. A. J. Foyt	64	19. Nelson Stacy	65	19. G. C. Spencer	4,004	Jack Smith	2
20. Bobby Isaac	4,989	20. Buck Baker	63	20. G. C. Spencer	57	20. Stick Elliott	3,766	Nelson Stacy	2
21. G. C. Spencer	4,888	21. Parnelli Jones	39	21. Paul Goldsmith	48	21. Marvin Panch	3,742	Billy Wade	2
22. Stick Elliott	4,693	22. Bobby Isaac	30	22. Buck Baker	32	22. Jack Smith	3,625	Glen Wood	2
23. Fireball Roberts	4,643	G. C. Spencer	30	23. Billy Wade	27	23. Herman Beam	3,476		
24. Cale Yarborough	4,519	24. Jack Smith	25	24. Jimmy Pardue	19	24. Bobby Johns	3,383		
25. Worth McMillion	4,177	25. Paul Goldsmith	22	25. Bobby Isaac	15	25. Cale Yarborough	3,298		
26. Neil Castles	4,093	26. Billy Wade	21	Johnny Rutherford	15	26. Ed Livingston	3,196		
27. Roy Mayne	3,857	27. LeeRoy Yarbrough	8	27. Larry Frank	13	27. Nelson Stacy	3,179		
28. Marvin Panch	3,510	28. Johnny Rutherford	6	28. Jack Smith	12	28. Larry Manning	2,980		
29. Reb Wickersham	3,501	29. Larry Frank	5	29. LeeRoy Yarbrough	4	29. Larry Frank	2,735		
30. Ed Livingston	3,294					30. Reb Wickersham	2,577		

Driver	Starts	Poles	Finish 1	2	3	4	5	6–10	Laps	Laps Led	Races Led	Winston Cup Points	$
1964													
1. Richard Petty	61	9	9	14	12	0	2	6	14,041	3,534	33	40,252	114,772
2. Ned Jarrett	59	9	15	7	5	7	6	5	13,325	3,304	30	34,950	71,925
3. David Pearson	61	12	8	8	4	7	2	13	13,225	2,256	31	32,146	45,542
4. Billy Wade	35	5	4	0	4	3	1	13	7,627	954	14	28,474	36,095
5. Jimmy Pardue	50	2	0	2	4	4	4	10	9,412	237	5	26,570	41,598
6. Curtis Crider	59	0	0	0	1	1	5	23	11,443	0	0	25,606	22,171
7. Jim Paschal	22	0	1	3	1	2	3	5	6,030	155	4	25,450	60,116
8. Larry Thomas	43	0	0	1	3	2	3	18	10,025	0	0	22,950	21,226
9. Buck Baker	34	0	2	3	3	3	4	3	7,263	159	5	22,366	43,781
10. Marvin Panch	31	5	3	7	3	4	1	3	6,499	648	10	21,480	34,836
11. Darel Dieringer	27	1	1	0	1	2	2	7	5,662	238	5	19,972	20,685
12. Wendell Scott	56	0	1	0	0	6	1	17	10,752	27	1	19,574	16,495
13. Fred Lorenzen	16	7	8	1	0	1	0	0	4,426	2,375	11	18,098	73,860
14. Junior Johnson	29	5	3	2	4	3	0	3	6,298	1,116	15	17,066	26,975
15. LeeRoy Yarbrough	34	0	2	3	2	3	1	4	5,896	200	5	16,172	16,630
16. Roy Tyner	46	0	0	0	0	0	0	17	7,327	0	0	13,922	11,488
17. Neil Castles	58	0	0	0	0	0	1	23	8,336	0	0	13,372	14,318
18. Bobby Isaac	19	0	1	3	0	1	0	2	3,163	134	6	13,252	26,733
19. Cale Yarborough	24	0	0	0	0	0	2	7	4,990	10	1	12,618	10,378
20. Tiny Lund	22	0	0	0	2	0	1	6	3,551	14	1	12,598	9,913
21. Doug Cooper	39	0	0	0	1	2	1	7	5,549	0	0	11,942	10,445
22. Paul Goldsmith	14	2	0	0	3	0	0	1	2,281	319	8	11,700	20,835
23. J. T. Putney	17	0	0	0	1	0	0	5	4,226	0	0	10,744	7,295
24. Larry Frank	12	0	0	0	0	0	0	3	1,483	0	0	10,314	7,830
25. Jack Anderson	31	0	0	0	0	1	0	3	4,402	0	0	10,040	8,510
26. G. C. Spencer	20	0	0	0	1	0	3	2	3,601	0	0	10,012	9,490
27. Fireball Roberts	9	0	1	2	1	0	1	1	1,702	17	2	9,900	28,345
28. Rex White	6	0	0	0	1	0	1	1	1,444	27	1	8,222	12,310
29. Dave MacDonald	5	0	0	1	0	0	0	2	661	0	0	7,650	9,195
30. Worth McMillion	18	0	0	0	0	0	0	6	4,681	0	0	7,586	4,700
31. Buddy Baker	33	0	0	0	1	1	1	4	3,239	0	0	7,314	8,460
32. Bunkie Blackburn	14	0	0	0	0	1	0	3	2,295	0	0	7,264	6,630
33. Bill McMahan	20	0	0	0	0	0	1	3	4,134	0	0	7,240	7,205
34. Buddy Arrington	27	0	0	0	0	0	2	7	5,172	0	0	6,364	4,715
35. Earl Balmer	10	0	0	0	0	1	1	2	2,771	1	1	6,170	5,795
36. Bob Derrington	18	0	0	0	0	0	0	2	1,897	1	1	5,896	2,755
37. Bobby Johns	12	0	0	0	0	0	0	2	1,806	0	0	5,436	5,700
38. E. J. Trivette	26	0	0	0	0	0	0	3	2,969	0	0	5,118	5,495
39. Doug Moore	24	0	0	0	0	0	0	6	3,894	0	0	4,970	5,175
40. Ken Spikes	6	0	0	0	0	0	0	1	1,018	0	0	4,934	3,100
41. Earl Brooks	28	0	0	0	0	0	0	8	3,988	0	0	4,820	3,925
42. Elmo Langley	14	0	0	0	0	0	0	5	2,739	0	0	4,400	3,905
43. Roy Mayne	14	0	0	0	0	0	1	1	2,207	0	0	4,278	4,705
44. Gene Hobby	18	0	0	0	0	0	0	3	4,013	0	0	4,054	2,795
45. Doug Yates	15	1	0	1	0	0	2	4	2,573	9	1	3,778	3,290
46. Ralph Earnhardt	11	0	0	0	0	1	0	0	1,107	0	0	3,720	3,290
47. Bob Cooper	13	0	0	0	0	0	0	1	783	0	0	3,602	3,360
48. Joe Weatherly	5	0	0	1	0	1	0	1	768	84	1	3,132	5,290
49. Sam McQuagg	5	0	0	0	0	0	0	0	653	0	0	2,928	1,700
50. Bobby Keck	10	0	0	0	0	1	1	3	2,137	0	0	2,754	2,850

LAPS COMPLETED		LAPS LED		MILES LED		MILES DRIVEN		RACES LED	
1. Richard Petty	14,041	1. Richard Petty	3,534	1. Richard Petty	3,065	1. Richard Petty	9,480	1. Richard Petty	33
2. Ned Jarrett	13,325	2. Ned Jarrett	3,304	2. Fred Lorenzen	1,651	2. David Pearson	8,906	2. David Pearson	31
3. David Pearson	13,225	3. Fred Lorenzen	2,375	3. Ned Jarrett	1,567	3. Ned Jarrett	8,785	3. Ned Jarrett	30
4. Curtis Crider	11,443	4. David Pearson	2,256	4. David Pearson	1,196	4. Curtis Crider	7,872	4. Junior Johnson	15
5. Wendell Scott	10,752	5. Junior Johnson	1,116	5. Billy Wade	543	5. Larry Thomas	6,957	5. Billy Wade	14
6. Larry Thomas	10,025	6. Billy Wade	954	6. Junior Johnson	509	6. Billy Wade	6,724	6. Fred Lorenzen	11
7. Jimmy Pardue	9,412	7. Marvin Panch	648	7. Paul Goldsmith	495	7. Jimmy Pardue	6,613	7. Marvin Panch	10
8. Neil Castles	8,336	8. Paul Goldsmith	319	8. Marvin Panch	400	8. Wendell Scott	6,466	8. Paul Goldsmith	8
9. Billy Wade	7,627	9. Darel Dieringer	238	9. Dan Gurney	383	9. Buck Baker	6,080	9. Bobby Isaac	6
10. Roy Tyner	7,327	10. Jimmy Pardue	237	10. Bobby Isaac	248	10. Jim Paschal	5,531	10. Buck Baker	5
11. Buck Baker	7,263	11. LeeRoy Yarbrough	200	11. Jim Paschal	229	11. Darel Dieringer	5,364	Darel Dieringer	5
12. Marvin Panch	6,499	12. Buck Baker	159	12. Buck Baker	203	12. Marvin Panch	5,031	Jimmy Pardue	5
13. Junior Johnson	6,298	13. Jim Paschal	155	13. Jimmy Pardue	200	13. Roy Tyner	4,641	LeeRoy Yarbrough	5
14. Jim Paschal	6,030	14. Dan Gurney	142	14. Darel Dieringer	139	14. LeeRoy Yarbrough	4,477	14. Jim Paschal	4
15. LeeRoy Yarbrough	5,896	15. Bobby Isaac	134	15. LeeRoy Yarbrough	108	15. Junior Johnson	4,474	15. A. J. Foyt	2
16. Darel Dieringer	5,662	16. Bob Welborn	125	16. Bob Welborn	63	16. Fred Lorenzen	4,181	Dick Hutcherson	2
17. Doug Cooper	5,549	17. Joe Weatherly	84	17. Fireball Roberts	47	17. Neil Castles	4,158	Fireball Roberts	2
18. Buddy Arrington	5,172	18. Dick Hutcherson	75	18. Joe Weatherly	42	18. Cale Yarborough	4,121		
19. Cale Yarborough	4,990	19. Cotton Owens	54	19. Rex White	41	19. Doug Cooper	3,863		
20. Worth McMillion	4,681	20. Wendell Scott	27	20. A. J. Foyt	40	20. Tiny Lund	3,662		
21. Fred Lorenzen	4,426	Rex White	27	21. Dick Hutcherson	38	21. J. T. Putney	3,370		
22. Jack Anderson	4,402	22. Jack Smith	20	22. Cotton Owens	27	22. Jack Anderson	3,365		
23. J. T. Putney	4,226	23. Fireball Roberts	17	23. Parnelli Jones	24	23. Bobby Isaac	3,360		
24. Bill McMahan	4,134	24. A. J. Foyt	16	24. Wendell Scott	14	24. Paul Goldsmith	2,903		
25. Gene Hobby	4,013	25. Tiny Lund	14	25. Jack Smith	10	25. Bill McMahan	2,897		
26. Earl Brooks	3,988	26. Cale Yarborough	10	26. Tiny Lund	7	26. G. C. Spencer	2,803		
27. Doug Moore	3,894	27. Parnelli Jones	9	27. Cale Yarborough	5	27. Worth McMillion	2,756		
28. G. C. Spencer	3,601	Doug Yates	9	28. Doug Yates	5	28. Buddy Arrington	2,504		
29. Tiny Lund	3,551	29. Glen Wood	5	29. Jim Hurtubise	3	29. Larry Frank	2,366		
30. Buddy Baker	3,239	30. Jim Hurtubise	2	30. Bob Derrington	3	30. Bunkie Blackburn	2,329		

1965

Driver	Starts	Poles	1	2	3	4	5	6–10	Laps	Laps Led	Races Led	Winston Cup Points	$
1. Ned Jarrett	54	9	13	13	10	4	2	3	13,525	2,244	29	38,824	93,625
2. Dick Hutcherson	52	10	9	9	8	4	2	5	11,610	2,065	23	35,790	57,851
3. Darel Dieringer	35	2	1	4	2	3	0	5	6,845	737	10	24,696	52,214
4. G. C. Spencer	47	1	0	3	4	3	4	11	9,092	90	5	24,314	29,775
5. Marvin Panch	20	5	4	1	4	1	2	2	4,743	856	12	22,798	64,027
6. Bob Derrington	51	0	0	0	1	0	2	16	10,374	0	0	21,394	20,120
7. J. T. Putney	40	0	0	1	3	4	2	14	7,932	0	0	20,928	22,329
8. Neil Castles	51	0	0	0	1	1	4	22	9,768	0	0	20,848	22,329
9. Buddy Baker	42	0	0	2	4	2	4	5	6,969	0	0	20,672	26,837
10. Cale Yarborough	46	0	1	3	1	5	3	8	7,734	166	8	20,192	26,587
11. Wendell Scott	52	0	0	0	0	2	2	17	9,759	0	0	19,902	18,639
12. Junior Johnson	36	10	13	2	1	2	0	1	7,144	3,998	30	18,486	62,216
13. Fred Lorenzen	17	6	4	1	0	0	0	1	3,677	981	12	18,448	80,615
14. Paul Lewis	24	1	0	0	0	1	2	10	5,954	0	0	18,118	13,247
15. E. J. Trivette	39	0	0	0	0	0	0	7	7,485	0	0	13,450	13,248
16. Larry Hess	10	0	0	0	0	0	0	3	2,347	0	0	13,148	9,260
17. Buck Baker	31	0	0	2	0	0	1	9	5,266	0	0	13,136	21,580
18. Jimmy Helms	39	0	0	0	0	0	0	4	5,731	0	0	12,996	12,050
19. Doug Cooper	30	0	0	0	0	1	0	8	5,281	0	0	12,920	12,380
20. Bobby Johns	13	0	0	2	2	0	1	0	2,696	37	6	12,842	24,930
21. Tiny Lund	30	0	1	1	1	4	1	9	5,224	209	2	12,820	11,750
22. Buddy Arrington	31	0	0	0	1	1	4	4	5,274	0	0	11,744	11,600
23. Earl Balmer	9	0	0	1	0	1	0	2	1,320	32	6	11,636	19,045
24. Sam McQuagg	14	0	0	0	1	0	1	3	2,458	31	1	11,460	10,555
25. Elmo Langley	34	0	0	0	2	1	0	6	5,698	19	1	10,982	10,555
26. Henley Gray	38	0	0	0	0	0	1	6	5,291	0	0	9,552	8,320
27. Roy Mayne	14	0	0	0	0	1	0	4	2,463	0	0	8,838	9,060
28. Junior Spencer	21	0	0	0	0	0	1	6	4,062	0	0	8,436	9,345
29. H. B. Bailey	5	0	0	0	0	0	1	2	810	0	0	7,340	5,000
30. Wayne Smith	25	0	0	0	0	0	0	2	3,744	0	0	7,326	6,790
31. Donald Tucker	9	0	0	0	0	1	0	2	1,597	0	0	7,118	5,680
32. Tom Pistone	33	1	0	1	0	1	2	4	3,334	0	0	6,598	10,050
33. Bub Strickler	9	0	0	0	0	0	0	2	1,572	0	0	6,540	5,275
34. Bobby Allison	8	0	0	0	0	0	0	3	799	0	0	6,152	4,780
35. Jim Paschal	10	0	0	0	1	2	1	0	2,403	99	3	6,046	7,805
36. Roy Tyner	28	0	0	0	0	1	0	5	3,448	0	0	5,882	6,505
37. LeeRoy Yarbrough	14	0	0	0	0	1	1	1	1,747	42	2	5,852	5,905
38. Richard Petty	14	7	4	4	2	0	0	0	3,697	1,169	8	5,638	16,450
39. Curtis Turner	7	0	1	0	1	0	1	0	1,360	256	2	5,542	17,440
40. David Pearson	14	1	2	2	2	1	1	3	3,242	744	8	5,464	8,925
41. Clyde Lynn	24	0	0	0	0	0	0	9	4,522	0	0	5,414	4,545
42. Gene Black	18	0	0	0	0	0	0	4	4,167	0	0	4,970	6,080
43. Ned Setzer	8	0	0	0	0	0	0	3	862	0	0	4,828	4,805
44. Stick Elliott	15	0	0	1	0	1	0	1	2,082	0	0	4,332	4,985
45. Reb Wickersham	7	0	0	0	0	0	0	2	906	0	0	4,322	4,410
46. Frank Warren	4	0	0	0	0	0	0	1	769	0	0	3,814	2,880
47. Worth McMillion	10	0	0	0	0	0	0	2	2,290	0	0	3,794	2,590
48. Lionel Johnson	8	0	0	0	0	0	0	2	1,663	0	0	3,510	3,105
49. Bud Moore	14	1	0	1	1	1	0	4	1,687	93	2	3,216	3,434
50. Sonny Hutchins	10	0	0	0	0	0	1	1	2,272	0	0	3,118	3,780

LAPS COMPLETED		LAPS LED		MILES LED		MILES DRIVEN		RACES LED	
1. Ned Jarrett	13,525	1. Junior Johnson	3,998	1. Junior Johnson	2,449	1. Ned Jarrett	9,121	1. Junior Johnson	30
2. Dick Hutcherson	11,610	2. Ned Jarrett	2,244	2. Ned Jarrett	1,143	2. Dick Hutcherson	8,131	2. Ned Jarrett	29
3. Bob Derrington	10,374	3. Dick Hutcherson	2,065	3. Dick Hutcherson	1,000	3. Bob Derrington	6,777	3. Dick Hutcherson	23
4. Neil Castles	9,768	4. Richard Petty	1,169	4. Fred Lorenzen	998	4. Neil Castles	6,555	4. Fred Lorenzen	12
5. Wendell Scott	9,759	5. Fred Lorenzen	981	5. Marvin Panch	985	5. G. C. Spencer	6,506	Marvin Panch	12
6. G. C. Spencer	9,092	6. Marvin Panch	856	6. Darel Dieringer	765	6. Wendell Scott	6,451	6. Darel Dieringer	10
7. J. T. Putney	7,932	7. David Pearson	744	7. Richard Petty	535	7. Darel Dieringer	5,806	7. David Pearson	8
8. Cale Yarborough	7,734	8. Darel Dieringer	737	8. David Pearson	380	8. J. T. Putney	5,680	Richard Petty	8
9. E. J. Trivette	7,485	9. Curtis Turner	256	9. Dan Gurney	340	9. Cale Yarborough	5,396	Cale Yarborough	8
10. Junior Johnson	7,144	10. Tiny Lund	209	10. A. J. Foyt	286	10. Buddy Baker	5,394	10. Earl Balmer	6
11. Buddy Baker	6,969	11. Bobby Isaac	183	11. Cale Yarborough	277	11. Paul Lewis	5,057	Bobby Johns	6
12. Darel Dieringer	6,845	12. Cale Yarborough	166	12. Curtis Turner	265	12. Junior Johnson	5,040	12. G. C. Spencer	5
13. Paul Lewis	5,954	13. A. J. Foyt	161	13. Tiny Lund	105	13. E. J. Trivette	4,935	13. A. J. Foyt	3
14. Jimmy Helms	5,731	14. Dan Gurney	126	14. Jim Paschal	98	14. Marvin Panch	4,716	Jim Paschal	3
15. Elmo Langley	5,698	15. Jim Paschal	99	15. Parnelli Jones	97	15. Buck Baker	4,173	15. Bobby Isaac	2
16. Henley Gray	5,291	16. Bud Moore	93	16. Bobby Isaac	68	16. Fred Lorenzen	3,998	Tiny Lund	2
17. Doug Cooper	5,281	17. G. C. Spencer	90	17. LeeRoy Yarbrough	63	17. Jimmy Helms	3,987	Bud Moore	2
18. Buddy Arrington	5,274	18. LeeRoy Yarbrough	42	18. Earl Balmer	55	18. Doug Cooper	3,909	Curtis Turner	2
19. Buck Baker	5,266	19. Bobby Johns	37	19. Larry Frank	50	19. Elmo Langley	3,816	LeeRoy Yarbrough	2
20. Tiny Lund	5,224	20. Parnelli Jones	36	20. Bud Moore	47	20. Buddy Arrington	3,545		
21. Marvin Panch	4,743	21. Larry Frank	33	21. Bobby Johns	43	21. Larry Hess	3,543		
22. Clyde Lynn	4,522	22. Earl Balmer	32	22. Sam McQuagg	43	22. Tiny Lund	3,427		
23. Gene Black	4,167	23. Sam McQuagg	31	23. G. C. Spencer	38	23. Henley Gray	3,225		
24. Junior Spencer	4,062	24. Elmo Langley	19	24. Elmo Langley	7	24. Junior Spencer	3,127		
25. Wayne Smith	3,744	25. Doug Yates	13	25. Doug Yates	7	25. Gene Black	3,011		
26. Richard Petty	3,697					26. Bobby Johns	2,941		
27. Fred Lorenzen	3,677					27. Sam McQuagg	2,922		
28. Roy Tyner	3,448					28. Wayne Smith	2,475		
29. Tom Pistone	3,334					29. Roy Mayne	2,449		
30. David Pearson	3,242					30. Jim Paschal	2,210		

1966

Driver	Starts	Poles	1	2	3	4	5	6–10	Laps	Laps Led	Races Led	Winston Cup Points	$
1. David Pearson	42	7	15	5	5	1	0	7	10,781	3,174	25	35,638	78,194
2. James Hylton	41	1	0	4	6	7	3	12	10,804	155	3	33,688	38,723
3. Richard Petty	39	16	8	9	3	0	0	2	8,737	2,924	26	22,952	94,666
4. Henley Gray	45	0	0	0	0	1	3	14	10,719	0	0	22,468	21,901
5. Paul Goldsmith	21	1	3	3	2	1	2	0	5,097	452	10	22,078	54,609
6. Wendell Scott	45	0	0	0	1	1	1	14	9,793	0	0	21,702	23,052
7. John Sears	46	0	0	1	1	4	5	19	9,981	109	2	21,432	25,192
8. J. T. Putney	39	0	0	1	2	1	0	5	7,836	32	2	21,208	18,653
9. Neil Castles	41	0	0	1	1	3	2	10	8,824	0	0	20,446	19,035
10. Bobby Allison	33	4	3	0	4	1	2	5	6,949	714	6	19,910	23,420
11. Elmo Langley	47	1	2	1	1	4	4	8	9,461	308	5	19,116	22,455
12. Darel Dieringer	25	0	3	3	0	1	0	2	4,818	515	8	18,214	52,530
13. Ned Jarrett	21	0	0	0	3	1	1	3	4,584	167	3	17,616	23,255
14. Jim Paschal	18	2	2	0	1	2	1	4	5,008	759	7	16,404	30,985
15. Sam McQuagg	16	0	1	0	1	0	2	3	3,575	175	3	16	29,530
16. Paul Lewis	21	0	1	1	6	1	0	5	6,260	67	2	15,352	17,827
17. Marvin Panch	14	0	1	0	1	2	0	2	2,808	183	5	15,308	38,432
18. Cale Yarborough	14	0	0	2	0	1	0	4	3,831	252	4	15,188	24,077
19. G. C. Spencer	20	0	0	3	0	0	3	3	4,701	2	1	15,028	26,722
20. Clyde Lynn	40	0	0	1	0	0	0	14	9,384	0	0	14,856	13,222
21. Buck Baker	36	0	0	3	0	2	2	7	6,725	0	0	14,504	13,860
22. Buddy Baker	41	1	0	1	0	0	0	6	6,361	142	4	14,302	21,325
23. Fred Lorenzen	11	2	2	1	0	1	2	0	3,066	782	7	12,454	36,310
24. Curtis Turner	21	2	0	1	1	3	0	1	3,697	385	11	12,266	16,890
25. Roy Mayne	18	0	0	0	0	0	1	4	4,052	0	0	11,074	9,940
26. LeeRoy Yarbrough	9	2	1	0	0	1	0	2	1,545	364	5	10,528	23,925
27. J. D. McDuffie	36	0	0	0	0	0	1	8	7,166	0	0	9,572	8,545
28. Dick Hutcherson	14	2	3	0	2	1	2	1	3,152	400	7	9,392	22,985
29. Tiny Lund	31	1	1	2	1	0	1	5	4,306	654	6	9,332	11,880
30. Blackie Watt	20	0	0	0	0	0	0	9	4,067	0	0	8,518	7,000
31. Frank Warren	11	0	0	0	0	0	0	1	1,989	0	0	8,334	6,740
32. Buddy Arrington	25	0	0	0	0	0	0	3	3,607	0	0	7,636	8,510
33. Wayne Smith	23	0	0	0	0	0	0	1	4,108	0	0	7,442	9,835
34. Jimmy Helms	29	0	0	0	0	0	0	0	3,186	0	0	6,530	5,815
35. Stick Elliott	19	0	0	0	0	1	0	2	3,285	0	0	6,358	7,335
36. Earl Balmer	9	0	1	0	0	0	1	0	1,388	4	2	5,794	7,935
37. Tom Pistone	28	4	0	3	1	0	2	0	4,090	385	8	5,788	7,765
38. Johnny Wynn	21	0	0	0	0	0	0	5	3,245	0	0	5,644	4,650
39. Larry Manning	13	0	0	0	0	1	0	0	2,769	0	0	4,964	3,920
40. Larry Hess	13	0	0	0	0	0	0	0	1,830	0	0	4,928	5,290
41. Roy Tyner	26	0	0	0	0	0	0	4	3,511	0	0	4,248	4,435
43. Bill Seifert	15	0	0	0	0	0	0	4	3,322	0	0	4,128	3,830
44. Bob Derrington	11	0	0	0	0	0	0	1	1,156	0	0	4,122	2,730
45. Joel Davis	21	0	0	0	0	1	0	2	2,977	0	0	4,066	4,685
46. Paul Connors	3	0	0	0	0	0	0	1	668	0	0	3,986	2,820
47. Jabe Thomas	13	0	0	0	0	0	0	0	1,559	0	0	3,820	3,580
48. Doug Cooper	21	0	0	0	1	1	1	1	3,177	0	0	3,808	5,185
49. Junior Johnson	7	3	0	0	0	0	1	0	1,813	467	6	3,750	3,610
50. Larry Frank	2	0	0	0	0	0	0	2	232	0	0	3,738	1,575

LAPS COMPLETED		LAPS LED		MILES LED		MILES DRIVEN		RACES LED	
1. James Hylton	10,804	1. David Pearson	3,174	1. Richard Petty	2,355	1. James Hylton	8,498	1. Richard Petty	26
2. David Pearson	10,781	2. Richard Petty	2,924	2. David Pearson	1,680	2. David Pearson	8,409	2. David Pearson	25
3. Henley Gray	10,719	3. Fred Lorenzen	782	3. Fred Lorenzen	642	3. Henley Gray	7,402	3. Curtis Turner	11
4. John Sears	9,981	4. Jim Paschal	759	4. LeeRoy Yarbrough	543	4. Wendell Scott	6,914	4. Paul Goldsmith	10
5. Wendell Scott	9,793	5. Bobby Allison	714	5. Paul Goldsmith	537	5. John Sears	6,632	5. Darel Dieringer	8
6. Elmo Langley	9,461	6. Tiny Lund	654	6. Jim Paschal	481	6. J. T. Putney	6,460	Tom Pistone	8
7. Clyde Lynn	9,384	7. Darel Dieringer	515	7. Dan Gurney	400	7. Richard Petty	6,458	7. Dick Hutcherson	7
8. Neil Castles	8,824	8. Junior Johnson	467	8. Darel Dieringer	376	8. Elmo Langley	6,372	Fred Lorenzen	7
9. Richard Petty	8,737	9. Paul Goldsmith	452	9. Sam McQuagg	373	9. Neil Castles	6,126	Jim Paschal	7
10. J. T. Putney	7,836	10. Dick Hutcherson	400	10. Curtis Turner	346	10. Clyde Lynn	5,789	10. Bobby Allison	6
11. J. D. McDuffie	7,166	11. Tom Pistone	385	11. Dick Hutcherson	321	11. Paul Goldsmith	5,382	Junior Johnson	6
12. Bobby Allison	6,949	Curtis Turner	385	12. Cale Yarborough	318	12. Bobby Allison	5,370	Tiny Lund	6
13. Buck Baker	6,725	13. LeeRoy Yarbrough	364	13. Bobby Allison	309	13. Jim Paschal	5,264	13. Elmo Langley	5
14. Buddy Baker	6,361	14. Elmo Langley	308	14. Tiny Lund	302	14. Buddy Baker	4,890	Marvin Panch	5
15. Paul Lewis	6,260	15. Cale Yarborough	252	15. Jim Hurtubise	256	15. Buck Baker	4,882	LeeRoy Yarbrough	5
16. Paul Goldsmith	5,097	16. Marvin Panch	183	16. Junior Johnson	244	16. Paul Lewis	4,742	16. Buddy Baker	4
17. Jim Paschal	5,008	17. Sam McQuagg	175	17. Marvin Panch	227	17. Darel Dieringer	4,545	Jim Hurtubise	4
18. Darel Dieringer	4,818	18. Ned Jarrett	167	18. Buddy Baker	185	18. Ned Jarrett	4,336	Cale Yarborough	4
19. G. C. Spencer	4,701	19. Jim Hurtubise	158	19. Tom Pistone	147	19. J. D. McDuffie	4,255	19. James Hylton	3
20. Ned Jarrett	4,584	20. James Hylton	155	20. Elmo Langley	125	20. G. C. Spencer	4,252	Ned Jarrett	3
21. Tiny Lund	4,306	21. Dan Gurney	148	21. Ned Jarrett	72	21. Curtis Turner	4,120	Sam McQuagg	3
22. Wayne Smith	4,108	22. Buddy Baker	142	22. James Hylton	48	22. Roy Mayne	4,051	22. Earl Balmer	2
23. Tom Pistone	4,090	23. John Sears	109	23. John Sears	47	23. Cale Yarborough	3,944	Bobby Isaac	2
24. Blackie Watt	4,067	24. Paul Lewis	67	24. Paul Lewis	37	24. Sam McQuagg	3,906	Gordon Johncock	2
25. Roy Mayne	4,052	25. J. T. Putney	32	25. Gordon Johncock	32	25. Marvin Panch	3,843	Paul Lewis	2
26. Cale Yarborough	3,831	26. Bobby Isaac	21	26. J. T. Putney	16	26. Wayne Smith	3,655	J. T. Putney	2
27. Curtis Turner	3,697	Gordon Johncock	21	27. Bobby Isaac	16	27. Tiny Lund	3,625	John Sears	2
28. Buddy Arrington	3,607	28. Don White	8	28. Don White	12	28. Fred Lorenzen	3,425		
29. Sam McQuagg	3,575	29. Earl Balmer	4	29. Bunkie Blackburn	10	29. Don White	3,199		
30. Roy Tyner	3,511	Bunkie Blackburn	4	30. Earl Balmer	7	30. Buddy Arrington	3,054		

1967

Driver	Starts	Poles	Finish 1	2	3	4	5	6–10	Laps	Laps Led	Races Led	Winston Cup Points	$
1. Richard Petty	48	19	27	7	2	1	1	2	12,739	5,537	41	42,472	150,197
2. James Hylton	46	1	0	3	3	12	8	13	11,526	109	5	36,444	49,732
3. Dick Hutcherson	33	9	2	9	7	3	1	3	8,893	1,455	21	33,658	85,160
4. Bobby Allison	45	2	6	4	5	4	2	6	10,157	1,554	21	30,812	58,250
5. John Sears	41	1	0	1	3	3	2	16	10,031	59	4	29,078	28,937
6. Jim Paschal	45	1	4	5	5	3	3	5	9,402	1,074	16	27,624	60,123
7. David Pearson	22	2	2	4	3	2	0	2	5,638	667	13	26,302	72,651
8. Neil Castles	36	0	0	0	0	2	2	12	7,140	0	0	23,218	20,683
9. Elmo Langley	45	0	0	1	3	2	4	14	9,652	0	0	22,286	23,898
10. Wendell Scott	45	0	0	0	0	0	0	11	9,217	0	0	20,700	19,510
11. Paul Goldsmith	21	0	0	2	3	1	1	1	4,851	398	7	20,402	38,732
12. Darel Dieringer	19	6	1	3	3	0	1	1	4,537	765	11	20,194	34,710
13. Clyde Lynn	44	0	0	0	0	2	3	17	9,556	0	0	20,016	19,520
14. Bobby Isaac	12	0	0	1	0	0	2	2	2,625	65	3	19,698	24,475
15. Buddy Baker	20	0	1	1	2	2	0	1	3,905	480	8	18,600	46,950
16. Donnie Allison	20	0	0	1	0	2	1	3	4,336	158	2	18,298	17,614
17. Henley Gray	43	0	0	0	0	0	0	10	7,864	0	0	17,502	15,987
18. J. T. Putney	29	0	0	0	1	0	0	9	6,050	0	0	16,752	15,687
19. Tiny Lund	19	0	0	0	0	1	3	1	3,587	36	3	16,292	17,332
20. Cale Yarborough	16	4	2	3	1	1	0	1	3,728	908	9	16,228	57,912
21. G. C. Spencer	29	0	0	0	3	0	2	5	4,947	0	0	15,240	20,225
22. Bill Seifert	41	0	0	0	0	0	0	12	8,171	0	0	14,676	11,905
23. Charlie Glotzbach	9	0	0	0	0	3	0	2	1,783	4	1	11,444	14,790
24. Frank Warren	12	0	0	0	0	0	0	1	1,805	0	0	9,992	9,185
25. Earl Brooks	34	1	0	0	0	0	0	8	5,373	24	1	9,952	8,610
26. Buddy Arrington	15	0	0	0	0	0	1	4	2,972	0	0	9,768	7,720
27. Buck Baker	21	0	0	0	0	0	0	5	4,544	0	0	9,450	7,560
28. Wayne Smith	27	0	0	0	0	0	0	2	4,364	0	0	9,372	10,225
29. Fred Lorenzen	5	0	1	1	0	0	0	0	895	23	4	9,268	17,875
30. Roy Mayne	14	0	0	0	0	0	0	1	2,209	3	1	9,262	8,830
31. Bobby Wawak	14	0	0	0	0	0	0	3	2,225	0	0	9,078	8,070
32. Friday Hassler	21	0	0	0	0	1	2	6	4,309	12	1	8,820	10,265
33. Paul Lewis	14	0	0	1	0	0	2	5	2,959	4	1	8,492	8,620
34. Sonny Hutchins	7	0	0	0	0	0	0	2	998	0	0	8,448	6,385
35. Bud Moore	6	0	0	0	0	0	2	1	1,351	0	0	7,812	7,200
36. Sam McQuagg	15	0	0	2	3	2	1	0	2,244	11	3	7,400	9,845
37. LeeRoy Yarbrough	15	0	1	0	2	0	0	1	2,647	34	4	7,012	15,325
38. Don Biederman	22	0	0	0	0	0	0	1	2,679	0	0	5,850	5,935
39. Ramo Stott	3	0	0	0	0	0	0	1	588	0	0	5,676	3,335
40. George Davis	21	0	0	0	0	0	1	5	3,342	0	0	5,434	4,400
41. Jack Harden	10	0	0	0	0	0	0	0	1,393	0	0	5,254	4,450
42. Paul Dean Holt	24	0	0	0	0	0	0	1	3,165	0	0	5,006	4,220
43. Roy Tyner	27	0	0	0	0	0	0	1	2,966	0	0	4,936	8,170
44. Bill Champion	11	0	0	0	0	0	0	0	1,889	0	0	4,040	6,205
45. Dick Johnson	23	0	0	0	0	0	0	0	2,636	0	0	3,954	5,070
46. George Poulos	23	0	0	0	0	0	0	1	2,872	0	0	3,780	3,040
47. Bill Dennis	3	0	0	0	0	0	0	0	1,012	0	0	3,730	2,335
48. Doug Cooper	21	0	0	0	0	0	2	3	3,351	0	0	3,666	5,665
49. Ed Negre	14	0	0	0	0	0	0	0	1,439	0	0	3,578	3,805
50. H. B. Bailey	3	0	0	0	0	0	0	0	322	0	0	3,482	3,850

LAPS COMPLETED			LAPS LED			MILES LED			MILES DRIVEN			RACES LED	
1.	Richard Petty	12,739	1.	Richard Petty	5,537	1.	Richard Petty	3,666	1.	Richard Petty	9,387	1.	Richard Petty	41
2.	James Hylton	11,526	2.	Bobby Allison	1,554	2.	Cale Yarborough	1,035	2.	James Hylton	8,534	2.	Bobby Allison	21
3.	Bobby Allison	10,157	3.	Dick Hutcherson	1,455	3.	Dick Hutcherson	909	3.	Bobby Allison	7,686		Dick Hutcherson	21
4.	John Sears	10,031	4.	Jim Paschal	1,074	4.	Jim Paschal	879	4.	John Sears	7,468	4.	Jim Paschal	16
5.	Elmo Langley	9,652	5.	Cale Yarborough	908	5.	Bobby Allison	808	5.	Dick Hutcherson	7,278	5.	David Pearson	13
6.	Clyde Lynn	9,556	6.	Darel Dieringer	765	6.	Buddy Baker	637	6.	Jim Paschal	7,228	6.	Darel Dieringer	11
7.	Jim Paschal	9,402	7.	David Pearson	667	7.	David Pearson	576	7.	Elmo Langley	6,781	7.	Cale Yarborough	9
8.	Wendell Scott	9,217	8.	Buddy Baker	480	8.	Darel Dieringer	570	8.	Wendell Scott	6,639	8.	Buddy Baker	8
9.	Dick Hutcherson	8,893	9.	Paul Goldsmith	398	9.	Parnelli Jones	340	9.	Clyde Lynn	6,551	9.	Paul Goldsmith	7
10.	Bill Seifert	8,171	10.	Donnie Allison	158	10.	Mario Andretti	337	10.	David Pearson	5,940	10.	A. J. Foyt	5
11.	Henley Gray	7,864	11.	Mario Andretti	137	11.	Paul Goldsmith	239	11.	Henley Gray	5,859		James Hylton	5
12.	Neil Castles	7,140	12.	Parnelli Jones	126	12.	Bobby Isaac	132	12.	Neil Castles	5,749	12.	Fred Lorenzen	4
13.	J. T. Putney	6,050	13.	James Hylton	109	13.	A. J. Foyt	105	13.	Paul Goldsmith	5,409		John Sears	4
14.	David Pearson	5,638	14.	Bobby Isaac	65	14.	Dan Gurney	97	14.	Bill Seifert	5,133		LeeRoy Yarbrough	4
15.	Earl Brooks	5,373	15.	John Sears	59	15.	LeeRoy Yarbrough	64	15.	Darel Dieringer	4,906	15.	Mario Andretti	3
16.	G. C. Spencer	4,947	16.	A. J. Foyt	57	16.	Fred Lorenzen	55	16.	J. T. Putney	4,817		Bobby Isaac	3
17.	Paul Goldsmith	4,851	17.	Dan Gurney	36	17.	Donnie Allison	54	17.	Donnie Allison	4,537		Tiny Lund	3
18.	Buck Baker	4,544		Tiny Lund	36	18.	James Hylton	32	18.	G. C. Spencer	4,156		Sam McQuagg	3
19.	Darel Dieringer	4,537	19.	LeeRoy Yarbrough	34	19.	Tiny Lund	24	19.	Buddy Baker	4,135	19.	Donnie Allison	2
20.	Wayne Smith	4,364	20.	Earl Brooks	24	20.	John Sears	17	20.	Bobby Isaac	3,927			
21.	Donnie Allison	4,336	21.	Fred Lorenzen	23	21.	Curtis Turner	15	21.	Cale Yarborough	3,668			
22.	Friday Hassler	4,309	22.	Friday Hassler	12	22.	Earl Brooks	12	22.	Wayne Smith	3,629			
23.	Buddy Baker	3,905	23.	Jack Bowsher	11	23.	Jack Bowsher	11	23.	Earl Brooks	3,536			
24.	Cale Yarborough	3,728		Sam McQuagg	11	24.	Sam McQuagg	9	24.	Tiny Lund	3,251			
25.	Tiny Lund	3,587	25.	Red Farmer	7	25.	Red Farmer	7	25.	Buck Baker	3,156			
26.	Doug Cooper	3,351	26.	Curtis Turner	6	26.	Charlie Glotzbach	6	26.	Friday Hassler	3,091			
27.	George Davis	3,342	27.	Charlie Glotzbach	4		Friday Hassler	6	27.	LeeRoy Yarbrough	2,894			
28.	Paul Dean Holt	3,165		Paul Lewis	4		Paul Lewis	6	28.	Frank Warren	2,668			
29.	Buddy Arrington	2,972	29.	Roy Mayne	3	29.	Whitey Gerkin	2	29.	Buddy Arrington	2,635			
30.	Roy Tyner	2,966	30.	Whitey Gerkin	2	30.	Roy Mayne	1	30.	Paul Lewis	2,593			

Driver	Starts	Poles	Finish						Laps	Laps Led	Races Led	Winston Cup Points	$
			1	2	3	4	5	6–10					

1968

	Driver	Starts	Poles	1	2	3	4	5	6–10	Laps	Laps Led	Races Led	Winston Cup Points	$
1.	David Pearson	48	12	16	12	4	2	2	2	13,097	3,950	37	3,499	133,065
2.	Bobby Isaac	49	3	3	9	7	4	4	9	12,947	1,384	20	3,373	60,342
3.	Richard Petty	49	12	16	6	5	2	2	4	12,254	4,242	35	3,123	99,535
4.	Clyde Lynn	49	0	0	0	0	1	1	23	12,013	0	0	3,041	29,226
5.	John Sears	49	0	0	0	1	1	3	19	11,077	0	0	3,017	29,179
6.	Elmo Langley	48	0	0	0	1	1	4	22	11,149	0	0	2,823	25,832
7.	James Hylton	41	0	0	1	4	8	3	12	10,058	15	3	2,719	32,608
8.	Jabe Thomas	48	0	0	0	0	0	1	14	11,194	0	0	2,687	21,166
9.	Wendell Scott	48	0	0	0	0	0	0	10	10,231	0	0	2,685	20,498
10.	Roy Tyner	48	0	0	0	0	2	2	10	8,789	0	0	2,504	20,247
11.	Bobby Allison	37	2	2	4	4	6	2	2	8,781	690	13	2,454	52,288
12.	Neil Castles	44	0	0	0	2	1	1	11	9,082	0	0	2,330	19,507
13.	Buddy Baker	38	4	1	4	6	3	2	2	7,949	564	12	2,310	56,023
14.	Bill Seifert	44	0	0	0	0	0	1	8	8,033	0	0	2,175	18,403
15.	Earl Brooks	40	0	0	0	0	0	0	5	6,507	0	0	1,957	14,233
16.	LeeRoy Yarbrough	26	6	2	3	6	1	3	1	6,423	1,300	14	1,894	87,920
17.	Cale Yarborough	21	4	6	2	1	0	3	0	5,661	1,215	16	1,804	138,052
18.	Paul Dean Holt	40	0	0	0	0	0	0	0	5,863	0	0	1,723	8,986
19.	Charlie Glotzbach	22	3	1	3	1	4	1	2	4,871	291	5	1,693	43,101
20.	Henley Gray	30	0	0	0	0	0	0	6	6,072	0	0	1,559	12,566
21.	Darel Dieringer	18	1	0	1	0	3	1	3	4,409	159	2	1,525	28,215
22.	Tiny Lund	17	0	0	0	1	1	3	5	4,547	1	1	1,443	17,775
23.	G. C. Spencer	26	0	0	0	0	1	0	5	4,380	0	0	1,401	10,120
24.	J. D. McDuffie	32	0	0	0	0	0	0	9	5,587	0	0	1,370	8,335
25.	Donnie Allison	13	1	1	1	3	0	0	3	3,829	284	6	1,307	50,815
26.	Stan Meserve	31	0	0	0	0	0	0	1	4,283	0	0	1,274	7,475
27.	Friday Hassler	20	0	0	0	0	2	1	5	5,012	0	0	1,224	12,000
28.	Bill Champion	18	0	0	0	0	0	0	2	3,505	0	0	1,155	10,170
29.	Bud Moore	16	0	0	1	0	1	0	7	3,399	51	2	1,086	12,325
30.	Paul Goldsmith	15	0	0	1	0	0	1	2	2,793	304	8	1,020	24,365
31.	Ed Negre	24	0	0	0	0	0	0	1	2,930	0	0	928	4,985
32.	Pete Hamilton	16	0	0	1	0	0	2	3	3,555	42	3	919	7,920
33.	Wayne Smith	18	0	0	0	0	0	0	1	2,456	0	0	901	7,235
34.	Dave Marcis	10	0	0	0	0	0	0	2	3,240	0	0	851	7,099
35.	Don Tarr	12	0	0	0	0	0	0	0	1,941	0	0	827	7,510
36.	E. J. Trivette	13	0	0	0	0	0	0	0	2,684	0	0	821	8,295
37.	Dick Johnson	11	0	0	0	0	0	0	0	2,187	0	0	735	5,920
38.	Bob Cooper	14	0	0	0	0	0	0	1	2,170	0	0	668	4,485
39.	Buck Baker	17	0	0	0	0	0	1	2	2,675	0	0	650	3,580
40.	Walson Gardner	14	0	0	0	0	0	0	2	3,546	0	0	640	4,275
41.	Larry Manning	12	0	0	0	0	0	0	0	2,151	0	0	640	6,995
42.	Frank Warren	10	0	0	0	0	0	0	1	1,643	0	0	611	5,365
43.	Jerry Grant	7	0	0	0	0	0	0	1	971	1	1	559	5,665
44.	Frog Fagan	12	0	0	0	0	0	0	1	1,808	0	0	531	3,680
45.	Richard Brickhouse	7	0	0	0	0	1	0	1	1,571	0	0	514	7,190
46.	Jim Hurtubise	6	0	0	0	0	0	0	1	982	0	0	504	4,490
47.	Curtis Turner	6	0	0	0	0	1	0	3	1,448	0	0	456	5,850
48.	Bobby Johns	7	0	0	0	0	0	0	0	750	0	0	453	5,010
49.	Eddie Yarboro	6	0	0	0	0	0	0	0	2,109	0	0	447	2,255
50.	Red Farmer	7	0	0	0	0	1	0	0	928	1	1	407	4,810

LAPS COMPLETED

1. David Pearson — 13,097
2. Bobby Isaac — 12,947
3. Richard Petty — 12,254
4. Clyde Lynn — 12,013
5. Jabe Thomas — 11,194
6. Elmo Langley — 11,149
7. John Sears — 11,077
8. Wendell Scott — 10,231
9. James Hylton — 10,058
10. Neil Castles — 9,082
11. Roy Tyner — 8,789
12. Bobby Allison — 8,781
13. Bill Seifert — 8,033
14. Buddy Baker — 7,949
15. Earl Brooks — 6,507
16. LeeRoy Yarbrough — 6,423
17. Henley Gray — 6,072
18. Paul Dean Holt — 5,863
19. Cale Yarborough — 5,661
20. J. D. McDuffie — 5,587
21. Friday Hassler — 5,012
22. Charlie Glotzbach — 4,871
23. Tiny Lund — 4,547
24. Darel Dieringer — 4,409
25. G. C. Spencer — 4,380
26. Stan Meserve — 4,283
27. Donnie Allison — 3,829
28. Pete Hamilton — 3,555
29. Walson Gardner — 3,546
30. Bill Champion — 3,505

LAPS LED

1. Richard Petty — 4,242
2. David Pearson — 3,950
3. Bobby Isaac — 1,384
4. LeeRoy Yarbrough — 1,300
5. Cale Yarborough — 1,215
6. Bobby Allison — 690
7. Buddy Baker — 564
8. Paul Goldsmith — 304
9. Charlie Glotzbach — 291
10. Donnie Allison — 284
11. Darel Dieringer — 159
12. Dan Gurney — 124
13. Bud Moore — 51
14. Parnelli Jones — 49
15. Tom Pistone — 43
16. Pete Hamilton — 42
17. Mario Andretti — 20
18. James Hylton — 15
19. Butch Hartman — 10
20. Ray Hendrick — 7
21. Sam McQuagg — 5
22. Red Farmer — 1
 Jerry Grant — 1
 Tiny Lund — 1

MILES LED

1. David Pearson — 2,336
2. Richard Petty — 2,241
3. Cale Yarborough — 1,505
4. LeeRoy Yarbrough — 1,409
5. Bobby Isaac — 736
6. Buddy Baker — 503
7. Bobby Allison — 450
8. Donnie Allison — 338
9. Dan Gurney — 335
10. Charlie Glotzbach — 283
11. Paul Goldsmith — 209
12. Darel Dieringer — 158
13. Parnelli Jones — 132
14. Mario Andretti — 51
15. Bud Moore — 50
16. Pete Hamilton — 30
17. Tom Pistone — 23
18. Butch Hartman — 18
19. James Hylton — 18
20. Sam McQuagg — 8
21. Ray Hendrick — 4
22. Red Farmer — 2
 Jerry Grant — 2
24. Tiny Lund — 1

MILES DRIVEN

1. David Pearson — 9,568
2. Bobby Isaac — 9,160
3. Richard Petty — 8,907
4. Clyde Lynn — 8,897
5. John Sears — 7,861
6. Elmo Langley — 7,786
7. Bobby Allison — 7,420
8. Jabe Thomas — 7,362
9. Wendell Scott — 7,348
10. James Hylton — 7,285
11. LeeRoy Yarbrough — 5,897
12. Bill Seifert — 5,864
13. Roy Tyner — 5,857
14. Cale Yarborough — 5,747
15. Buddy Baker — 5,728
16. Neil Castles — 5,455
17. Darel Dieringer — 4,972
18. Charlie Glotzbach — 4,791
19. Henley Gray — 4,580
20. Earl Brooks — 4,396
21. Tiny Lund — 4,381
22. Friday Hassler — 4,245
23. Donnie Allison — 4,107
24. Bill Champion — 3,547
25. Paul Goldsmith — 3,505
26. Paul Dean Holt — 3,498
27. G. C. Spencer — 3,276
28. Bud Moore — 3,219
29. Dave Marcis — 3,179
30. J. D. McDuffie — 3,020

RACES LED

1. David Pearson — 37
2. Richard Petty — 35
3. Bobby Isaac — 20
4. Cale Yarborough — 16
5. LeeRoy Yarbrough — 14
6. Bobby Allison — 13
7. Buddy Baker — 12
8. Paul Goldsmith — 8
9. Donnie Allison — 6
10. Charlie Glotzbach — 5
11. Pete Hamilton — 3
 James Hylton — 3
13. Mario Andretti — 2
 Darel Dieringer — 2
 Butch Hartman — 2
 Bud Moore — 2
 Tom Pistone — 2

1969

Driver	Starts	Poles	Finish 1	2	3	4	5	6–10	Laps	Laps Led	Races Led	Winston Cup Points	$
1. David Pearson	51	14	11	18	9	2	2	2	14,270	3,018	39	4,170	229,760
2. Richard Petty	50	6	10	9	9	0	3	7	12,589	2,778	32	3,813	129,906
3. James Hylton	52	0	0	4	9	8	6	12	13,540	162	12	3,750	114,416
4. Neil Castles	51	0	0	2	1	4	6	16	12,661	29	1	3,530	54,367
5. Elmo Langley	52	1	0	0	1	6	6	15	12,531	40	1	3,383	73,092
6. Bobby Isaac	50	21	17	3	5	3	1	4	12,308	5,072	38	3,301	92,074
7. John Sears	52	0	0	1	3	7	6	10	11,620	18	3	3,166	52,281
8. Jabe Thomas	51	0	0	0	0	0	0	12	12,025	0	0	3,103	44,989
9. Wendell Scott	51	0	0	0	0	0	0	11	11,856	0	0	3,015	47,451
10. Cecil Gordon	51	0	0	0	0	0	1	7	10,745	0	0	3,002	39,679
11. E. J. Trivette	49	0	0	0	0	0	0	15	11,110	0	0	2,988	35,896
12. Bill Champion	49	0	0	0	0	0	1	9	10,582	0	0	2,813	33,656
13. Bill Seifert	50	0	0	0	0	1	0	14	9,728	0	0	2,765	44,361
14. J. D. McDuffie	50	0	0	0	0	0	0	12	10,173	0	0	2,741	30,861
15. Ben Arnold	48	0	0	0	0	0	0	8	10,334	0	0	2,736	33,256
16. LeeRoy Yarbrough	30	0	7	2	0	6	1	5	8,190	1,155	17	2,712	193,211
17. Henley Gray	48	0	0	0	0	0	0	5	8,954	0	0	2,517	29,335
18. Earl Brooks	49	0	0	0	0	0	1	5	8,719	0	0	2,454	34,793
19. Dave Marcis	37	0	0	0	1	2	0	8	7,099	22	3	2,348	32,383
20. Bobby Allison	27	1	5	3	1	2	2	2	6,445	1,251	15	2,055	69,483
21. Dick Brooks	28	0	0	0	1	0	2	9	5,741	2	1	1,780	28,187
22. Buddy Baker	18	3	0	2	4	1	2	2	4,177	770	14	1,769	62,928
23. Cale Yarborough	19	6	2	2	1	2	0	1	4,341	946	16	1,715	74,240
24. Donnie Allison	16	2	1	2	4	1	2	1	3,893	400	10	1,662	78,055
25. Richard Brickhouse	24	0	1	0	0	0	1	7	3,629	34	2	1,660	45,637
26. G. C. Spencer	26	0	0	0	0	2	2	4	4,823	0	0	1,562	21,660
27. Ed Negre	31	0	0	0	0	0	0	4	4,556	0	0	1,465	15,160
28. Friday Hassler	18	0	0	0	0	0	0	7	4,607	3	1	1,421	17,690
29. Frank Warren	23	0	0	0	0	0	0	1	3,343	0	0	1,299	15,677
30. Hoss Ellington	15	0	0	0	0	0	0	4	2,988	0	0	1,210	16,552
31. Roy Tyner	21	0	0	0	0	0	0	1	3,285	0	0	1,191	12,302
32. Ed Hessert	16	0	0	0	0	0	0	4	2,635	1	1	1,113	17,690
33. Buddy Arrington	16	0	0	0	0	0	2	4	3,758	0	0	1,099	12,975
34. Dick Johnson	22	0	0	0	0	0	0	4	3,803	0	0	1,055	11,182
35. Buddy Young	21	0	0	0	0	0	1	5	4,510	0	0	981	15,542
36. Dub Simpson	20	0	0	0	0	0	0	0	2,923	0	0	959	12,915
37. Charlie Glotzbach	12	2	0	2	0	2	1	1	2,823	171	8	944	36,090
38. Roy Mayne	13	0	0	0	0	0	0	0	2,855	0	0	922	10,340
39. Wayne Smith	16	0	0	0	0	0	0	2	2,692	0	0	922	10,610
40. Paul Goldsmith	11	0	0	0	3	1	0	1	1,999	20	4	892	22,305
41. Don Tarr	12	0	0	0	0	0	0	3	1,754	6	1	855	13,720
42. Ken Meisenhelder	16	0	0	0	0	0	0	0	1,832	0	0	627	5,630
43. Pete Hazelwood	16	0	0	0	0	0	0	1	2,367	0	0	598	4,160
44. Sonny Hutchins	8	0	0	2	0	0	0	0	1,694	0	0	535	9,552
45. Wayne Gillette	16	0	0	0	0	0	0	0	887	0	0	509	5,827
46. Paul Dean Holt	14	0	0	0	0	0	0	0	1,408	0	0	485	4,442
47. Johnny Halford	8	0	0	0	0	0	0	0	1,881	0	0	465	4,200
49. Ray Elder	4	0	0	0	0	0	0	4	642	0	0	433	7,200
49. John Kennedy	9	0	0	0	0	0	0	0	1,085	0	0	417	6,462
50. Dick Poling	12	0	0	0	0	0	0	0	1,305	0	0	408	5,467

Laps Completed		Laps Led		Miles Led		Miles Driven		Races Led	
1. David Pearson	14,270	1. Bobby Isaac	5,072	1. Bobby Isaac	2,688	1. David Pearson	11,369	1. David Pearson	39
2. James Hylton	13,540	2. David Pearson	3,018	2. David Pearson	2,179	2. James Hylton	10,937	2. Bobby Isaac	38
3. Neil Castles	12,661	3. Richard Petty	2,778	3. Richard Petty	1,940	3. Richard Petty	10,520	3. Richard Petty	32
4. Richard Petty	12,589	4. Bobby Allison	1,251	4. LeeRoy Yarbrough	1,740	4. Neil Castles	10,290	4. LeeRoy Yarbrough	17
5. Elmo Langley	12,531	5. LeeRoy Yarbrough	1,155	5. Cale Yarborough	1,289	5. Jabe Thomas	9,868	5. Cale Yarborough	16
6. Bobby Isaac	12,308	6. Cale Yarborough	946	6. Bobby Allison	927	6. Elmo Langley	9,812	6. Bobby Allison	15
7. Jabe Thomas	12,025	7. Buddy Baker	770	7. Buddy Baker	898	7. Bobby Isaac	9,329	7. Buddy Baker	14
8. Wendell Scott	11,856	8. Donnie Allison	400	8. Donnie Allison	607	8. Bill Champion	9,254	8. James Hylton	12
9. John Sears	11,620	9. Charlie Glotzbach	171	9. Charlie Glotzbach	284	9. Wendell Scott	9,165	9. Donnie Allison	10
10. E. J. Trivette	11,110	10. James Hylton	162	10. Jim Vandiver	271	10. E. J. Trivette	9,046	10. Charlie Glotzbach	8
11. Cecil Gordon	10,745	11. Jim Vandiver	102	11. A. J. Foyt	170	11. Cecil Gordon	9,016	11. Paul Goldsmith	4
12. Bill Champion	10,582	12. A. J. Foyt	63	12. James Hylton	98	12. John Sears	8,916	12. Dave Marcis	3
13. Ben Arnold	10,334	13. Elmo Langley	40	13. Richard Brickhouse	90	13. LeeRoy Yarbrough	8,717	John Sears	3
14. J. D. McDuffie	10,173	14. Richard Brickhouse	34	14. Tiny Lund	74	14. Ben Arnold	8,493	14. Richard Brickhouse	2
15. Bill Seifert	9,728	15. Neil Castles	29	15. Pete Hamilton	35	15. J. D. McDuffie	7,913	A. J. Foyt	2
16. Henley Gray	8,954	16. Tiny Lund	28	16. Paul Goldsmith	35	16. Bill Seifert	7,475	Bobby Unser	2
17. Earl Brooks	8,719	17. Dave Marcis	22	17. Dave Marcis	32	17. Henley Gray	7,326		
18. LeeRoy Yarbrough	8,190	18. Paul Goldsmith	20	18. Elmo Langley	20	18. Earl Brooks	7,077		
19. Dave Marcis	7,099	19. John Sears	18	19. Mario Andretti	19	19. Dave Marcis	6,930		
20. Bobby Allison	6,445	20. Pete Hamilton	14	20. Don Tarr	16	20. Bobby Allison	6,582		
21. Dick Brooks	5,741	21. Mario Andretti	7	21. Neil Castles	12	21. Dick Brooks	6,255		
22. G. C. Spencer	4,823	22. Don Tarr	6	22. Ramo Stott	11	22. Cale Yarborough	5,482		
23. Friday Hassler	4,607	23. Ramo Stott	4	23. John Sears	11	23. Buddy Baker	5,210		
24. Ed Negre	4,556	24. Friday Hassler	3	24. Friday Hassler	6	24. Donnie Allison	5,106		
25. Buddy Young	4,510	25. Dick Brooks	2	25. Dick Brooks	5	25. Friday Hassler	4,665		
26. Cale Yarborough	4,341	Bobby Unser	2	26. Bobby Unser	5	26. Richard Brickhouse	4,630		
27. Buddy Baker	4,177	27. Ed Hessert	1	27. Ed Hessert	2	27. Hoss Ellington	4,136		
28. Donnie Allison	3,893					28. G. C. Spencer	3,982		
29. Dick Johnson	3,803					29. Charlie Glotzbach	3,957		
30. Buddy Arrington	3,758					30. Frank Warren	3,892		

1970

Driver	Starts	Poles	Finish 1	2	3	4	5	6–10	Laps	Laps Led	Races Led	Winston Cup Points	$
1. Bobby Isaac	47	13	11	9	5	4	3	6	12,726	3,188	35	3,911	199,600
2. Bobby Allison	46	5	3	15	8	4	0	5	12,452	1,246	22	3,860	149,745
3. James Hylton	47	1	1	4	2	8	7	17	12,712	199	8	3,788	78,201
4. Richard Petty	40	9	18	5	0	0	4	4	10,536	5,007	32	3,447	151,124
5. Neil Castles	47	0	0	1	4	3	4	12	10,297	31	2	3,158	49,746
6. Elmo Langley	47	0	0	0	1	0	0	18	10,672	0	0	3,154	45,193
7. Jabe Thomas	46	0	0	0	0	0	0	23	10,928	0	0	3,120	42,958
8. Benny Parsons	45	1	0	1	2	4	5	11	9,164	164	6	2,993	59,402
9. Dave Marcis	47	0	0	0	3	0	4	8	8,909	14	1	2,820	41,111
10. Frank Warren	46	1	0	0	0	0	0	2	7,709	71	1	2,697	35,161
11. Cecil Gordon	44	0	0	0	0	1	1	9	8,424	0	0	2,514	32,713
12. John Sears	40	1	0	0	0	3	1	3	7,777	10	1	2,465	32,675
13. Dick Brooks	34	0	0	2	5	4	4	3	6,821	194	6	2,460	53,754
14. Wendell Scott	41	0	0	0	0	0	0	9	8,276	0	0	2,425	28,518
15. Bill Champion	38	0	0	0	0	0	0	6	7,493	0	0	2,350	30,943
16. J. D. McDuffie	36	0	0	0	0	0	1	9	8,461	0	0	2,079	24,905
17. Ben Arnold	29	0	0	0	0	0	0	3	6,838	0	0	1,997	25,805
18. Bill Seifert	39	0	0	0	0	0	1	3	5,189	0	0	1,962	25,647
19. Henley Gray	34	0	0	0	0	0	0	2	6,134	0	0	1,871	23,130
20. Friday Hassler	26	0	0	0	0	0	1	5	5,439	56	1	1,831	27,535
21. Pete Hamilton	16	1	3	1	3	0	3	2	4,069	338	9	1,819	131,406
22. Joe Frasson	21	0	0	0	0	0	0	2	4,866	0	0	1,723	20,172
23. David Pearson	19	2	1	2	2	4	0	2	4,210	580	11	1,716	87,118
24. Buddy Baker	18	1	1	2	0	1	2	2	3,611	485	11	1,555	63,510
25. Bill Dennis	25	0	0	0	0	0	0	5	4,014	0	0	1,432	15,630
26. Ed Negre	31	0	0	0	0	0	0	1	3,336	0	0	1,413	14,580
27. G. C. Spencer	20	0	0	0	0	2	1	6	4,618	0	0	1,410	17,915
28. Charlie Glotzbach	19	4	2	0	3	2	0	1	3,396	417	16	1,358	50,649
29. Roy Mayne	16	0	0	0	0	0	0	3	3,731	0	0	1,333	16,910
30. Bill Shirey	29	0	0	0	0	0	0	1	3,691	0	0	1,244	12,215
31. Raymond Williams	21	0	0	0	0	0	0	0	3,641	0	0	1,204	12,535
32. Larry Baumel	23	1	0	0	0	0	0	1	2,731	0	0	1,138	16,645
33. Buddy Arrington	19	0	0	0	0	0	0	2	2,855	0	0	1,087	16,845
34. Cale Yarborough	19	5	3	4	3	0	1	2	5,034	906	14	1,016	115,875
35. Don Tarr	17	0	0	0	0	0	0	5	2,471	5	1	995	16,592
36. Johnny Halford	25	0	0	0	0	0	0	1	3,619	16	1	975	15,645
37. Earl Brooks	21	0	0	0	0	0	0	1	1,779	0	0	884	10,340
38. Coo Coo Marlin	13	0	0	0	0	0	0	4	2,531	0	0	876	14,799
39. Ron Keselowski	17	0	0	0	0	0	0	1	2,339	9	1	855	11,985
40. Donnie Allison	19	0	3	0	2	3	2	2	5,252	697	10	841	96,081
41. Ken Meisenhelder	19	0	0	0	0	0	0	2	2,717	0	0	812	7,020
42. Roy Tyner	14	0	0	0	0	0	0	3	1,890	0	0	631	5,565
43. LeeRoy Yarbrough	19	2	1	1	4	2	0	3	4,250	284	12	625	61,930
44. Dick May	16	0	0	0	0	0	0	0	1,028	0	0	551	4,510
45. Jim Vandiver	14	0	0	0	0	0	0	5	2,634	6	1	519	16,080
46. John Kenney	11	0	0	0	0	0	0	0	1,385	0	0	457	4,115
47. Dub Simpson	6	0	0	0	0	0	0	1	1,155	0	0	367	4,510
48. Lee Roy Carrigg	9	0	0	0	0	0	0	0	1,002	0	0	355	4,130
49. Joe Phipps	7	0	0	0	0	0	0	0	1,506	0	0	325	4,090
50. Wayne Smith	8	0	0	0	0	0	0	0	593	0	0	300	4,505

LAPS COMPLETED		LAPS LED		MILES LED		MILES DRIVEN		RACES LED	
1. Bobby Isaac	12,726	1. Richard Petty	5,007	1. Richard Petty	3,633	1. Bobby Isaac	11,251	1. Bobby Isaac	35
2. James Hylton	12,712	2. Bobby Isaac	3,188	2. Bobby Isaac	1,883	2. James Hylton	11,223	2. Richard Petty	32
3. Bobby Allison	12,452	3. Bobby Allison	1,246	3. Cale Yarborough	1,048	3. Bobby Allison	11,164	3. Bobby Allison	22
4. Jabe Thomas	10,928	4. Cale Yarborough	906	4. Bobby Allison	972	4. Richard Petty	9,811	4. Charlie Glotzbach	16
5. Elmo Langley	10,672	5. Donnie Allison	697	5. David Pearson	898	5. Jabe Thomas	9,510	5. Cale Yarborough	14
6. Richard Petty	10,536	6. David Pearson	580	6. Buddy Baker	883	6. Elmo Langley	9,319	6. LeeRoy Yarbrough	12
7. Neil Castles	10,297	7. Buddy Baker	485	7. Donnie Allison	782	7. Neil Castles	9,154	7. Buddy Baker	11
8. Benny Parsons	9,164	8. Charlie Glotzbach	417	8. Pete Hamilton	745	8. Benny Parsons	8,725	David Pearson	11
9. Dave Marcis	8,909	9. Pete Hamilton	338	9. Charlie Glotzbach	730	9. Dave Marcis	8,041	9. Donnie Allison	10
10. J. D. McDuffie	8,461	10. LeeRoy Yarbrough	284	10. LeeRoy Yarbrough	387	10. John Sears	7,939	10. Pete Hamilton	9
11. Cecil Gordon	8,424	11. James Hylton	199	11. Parnelli Jones	231	11. Frank Warren	7,763	11. James Hylton	8
12. Wendell Scott	8,276	12. Dick Brooks	194	12. James Hylton	126	12. Dick Brooks	6,996	12. Dick Brooks	6
13. John Sears	7,777	13. Benny Parsons	164	13. Dick Brooks	114	13. Wendell Scott	6,949	Benny Parsons	6
14. Frank Warren	7,709	14. Parnelli Jones	88	14. Benny Parsons	112	14. Cecil Gordon	6,872	14. Neil Castles	2
15. Bill Champion	7,493	15. Frank Warren	71	15. A. J. Foyt	92	15. Bill Champion	6,864	Fred Lorenzen	2
16. Ben Arnold	6,838	16. Friday Hassler	56	16. Fred Lorenzen	75	16. Ben Arnold	6,746	Tiny Lund	2
17. Dick Brooks	6,821	17. Fred Lorenzen	50	17. Frank Warren	36	17. Friday Hassler	6,518		
18. Henley Gray	6,134	18. A. J. Foyt	35	18. Friday Hassler	33	18. J. D. McDuffie	6,287		
19. Friday Hassler	5,439	19. Neil Castles	31	19. Tiny Lund	18	19. Cale Yarborough	6,237		
20. Donnie Allison	5,252	20. Johnny Halford	16	20. Jim Paschal	17	20. Joe Frasson	6,230		
21. Bill Seifert	5,189	21. Dave Marcis	14	21. Dave Marcis	14	21. Pete Hamilton	6,210		
22. Cale Yarborough	5,034	22. Jim Paschal	11	22. Don Tarr	13	22. Buddy Baker	5,874		
23. Joe Frasson	4,866	23. John Sears	10	23. Neil Castles	13	23. David Pearson	5,815		
24. G. C. Spencer	4,618	24. Ron Keselowski	9	24. Jim Vandiver	9	24. Donnie Allison	5,674		
25. LeeRoy Yarbrough	4,250	25. Tiny Lund	7	25. Johnny Halford	8	25. LeeRoy Yarbrough	5,438		
26. David Pearson	4,210	26. Jim Vandiver	6	26. Richard Brickhouse	5	26. Charlie Glotzbach	5,258		
27. Pete Hamilton	4,069	27. Don Tarr	5	27. Roger McCluskey	5	27. Henley Gray	5,249		
28. Bill Dennis	4,014	28. Richard Brickhouse	2	28. John Sears	5	28. Bill Seifert	5,196		
29. Roy Mayne	3,731	Roger McCluskey	2	Ramo Stott	5	29. Roy Mayne	4,764		
30. Bill Shirey	3,691	Ramo Stott	2	30. Ron Keselowski	5	30. G. C. Spencer	4,091		

Driver	Starts	Poles	Finish						Laps	Laps Led	Races Led	Winston Cup Points	$
			1	2	3	4	5	6–10					

1971

	Driver	Starts	Poles	1	2	3	4	5	6–10	Laps	Laps Led	Races Led	Winston Cup Points	$
1.	Richard Petty	46	9	21	8	7	2	0	3	13,739	4,932	41	4,435	351,071
2.	James Hylton	46	1	0	2	3	5	4	23	12,785	105	5	4,071	90,282
3.	Cecil Gordon	46	0	0	0	2	2	2	15	12,468	0	0	3,677	69,080
4.	Bobby Allison	42	9	11	7	3	5	1	4	11,716	3,582	31	3,636	254,316
5.	Elmo Langley	46	0	0	3	1	3	4	12	11,299	48	1	3,356	57,037
6.	Jabe Thomas	43	0	0	0	0	1	1	13	11,360	0	0	3,200	48,241
7.	Bill Champion	45	0	0	0	0	0	3	11	10,518	0	0	3,058	43,769
8.	Frank Warren	47	0	0	0	0	0	1	9	8,984	0	0	2,886	40,072
9.	J. D. McDuffie	43	0	0	0	1	0	1	6	9,389	5	1	2,862	35,578
10.	Walter Ballard	41	0	0	0	1	1	1	8	9,419	0	0	2,633	30,974
11.	Benny Parsons	35	0	1	2	5	1	4	5	7,981	144	4	2,611	55,896
12.	Ed Negre	43	0	0	0	0	0	0	2	8,359	0	0	2,528	29,738
13.	Bill Seifert	37	0	0	0	0	0	0	4	6,552	0	0	2,403	33,220
14.	Henley Gray	39	0	0	0	0	0	0	4	7,684	0	0	2,392	31,789
15.	Buddy Baker	19	1	1	6	5	0	1	3	4,814	727	15	2,358	115,150
16.	Friday Hassler	29	2	0	1	2	0	1	9	5,650	68	3	2,277	37,305
17.	Earl Brooks	35	0	0	0	0	1	0	3	6,657	0	0	2,205	25,360
18.	Bill Dennis	28	1	0	0	1	1	2	6	6,111	47	2	2,181	29,420
19.	Wendell Scott	37	0	0	0	0	0	0	4	7,791	0	0	2,180	21,701
20.	John Sears	37	0	0	0	0	0	0	3	7,512	0	0	2,167	26,735
21.	Dave Marcis	29	2	0	1	1	4	3	5	6,460	331	8	2,049	37,582
22.	Neil Castles	38	0	0	0	0	1	0	9	6,946	10	1	2,036	22,939
23.	Bobby Isaac	25	5	4	4	2	4	2	1	6,856	1,753	17	1,819	106,526
24.	Pete Hamilton	22	2	1	0	5	4	1	1	4,525	224	14	1,739	60,440
25.	Joe Frasson	17	0	0	0	0	0	1	3	3,752	0	0	1,619	20,975
26.	Ben Arnold	18	0	0	0	0	0	0	3	4,130	0	0	1,618	18,491
27.	Ron Keselowski	20	0	0	0	0	0	0	6	3,046	0	0	1,446	17,680
28.	Bill Shirey	27	0	0	0	0	0	0	2	3,667	0	0	1,303	9,160
29.	Donnie Allison	13	5	1	1	1	2	2	2	3,017	806	8	1,280	69,995
30.	Dean Dalton	19	0	0	0	0	0	0	1	3,487	0	0	1,276	13,910
31.	Raymond Williams	20	0	0	0	0	0	0	0	2,822	0	0	1,270	14,585
32.	Dick May	22	0	0	0	0	0	0	1	2,527	0	0	1,090	9,225
33.	Charlie Roberts	19	0	0	0	0	0	0	2	2,795	0	0	1,053	12,470
34.	G. C. Spencer	17	0	0	0	0	0	2	4	3,325	12	1	1,008	11,470
35.	Richard Brown	13	0	0	0	0	0	0	2	2,454	0	0	967	11,940
36.	Dick Brooks	20	0	0	1	5	0	3	3	4,495	16	5	939	32,921
37.	Larry Baumel	16	0	0	0	0	0	0	1	2,245	0	0	904	10,910
38.	Maynard Troyer	13	0	0	0	0	1	0	2	1,617	0	0	879	13,115
39.	Roy Mayne	11	0	0	0	0	0	0	1	1,918	0	0	852	10,330
40.	Ken Meisenhelder	15	0	0	0	0	0	0	1	2,194	0	0	797	5,405
41.	Tommy Gale	9	0	0	0	0	0	0	1	1,616	0	0	729	8,800
42.	Charlie Glotzbach	20	4	1	2	0	3	1	3	4,735	805	10	699	38,605
43.	Bill Hollar	11	0	0	0	0	0	0	1	2,095	0	0	644	4,275
44.	Marv Acton	11	0	0	0	0	0	0	0	1,421	0	0	627	8,620
45.	Fred Lorenzen	14	1	0	1	0	2	4	2	3,229	152	6	611	45,100
46.	Richard Childress	12	0	0	0	0	0	0	0	1,394	0	0	601	3,855
47.	Paul Tyler	10	0	0	0	0	0	0	0	1,521	0	0	561	6,360
48.	Jim Vandiver	7	0	0	0	0	0	1	3	1,423	0	0	553	13,575
49.	Coo Coo Marlin	12	0	0	0	0	0	0	0	1,495	0	0	527	9,085
50.	Eddie Yarboro	7	0	0	0	0	0	0	0	1,624	0	0	497	3,685

LAPS COMPLETED		LAPS LED		MILES LED		MILES DRIVEN		RACES LED	
1. Richard Petty	13,739	1. Richard Petty	4,932	1. Bobby Allison	4,042	1. Richard Petty	12,870	1. Richard Petty	41
2. James Hylton	12,785	2. Bobby Allison	3,582	2. Richard Petty	3,721	2. James Hylton	12,718	2. Bobby Allison	31
3. Cecil Gordon	12,468	3. Bobby Isaac	1,753	3. Bobby Isaac	1,224	3. Bobby Allison	12,122	3. Bobby Isaac	17
4. Bobby Allison	11,716	4. Donnie Allison	806	4. Buddy Baker	1,021	4. Cecil Gordon	12,034	4. Buddy Baker	15
5. Jabe Thomas	11,360	5. Charlie Glotzbach	805	5. Donnie Allison	985	5. Elmo Langley	10,489	5. Pete Hamilton	14
6. Elmo Langley	11,299	6. Buddy Baker	727	6. A. J. Foyt	780	6. Jabe Thomas	9,816	6. Charlie Glotzbach	10
7. Bill Champion	10,518	7. A. J. Foyt	392	7. Charlie Glotzbach	695	7. Bill Champion	9,714	David Pearson	10
8. Walter Ballard	9,419	8. Dave Marcis	331	8. Pete Hamilton	365	8. J. D. McDuffie	9,170	8. Donnie Allison	8
9. J. D. McDuffie	9,389	9. Tiny Lund	258	9. David Pearson	257	9. Frank Warren	8,599	Dave Marcis	8
10. Frank Warren	8,984	10. David Pearson	252	10. Dave Marcis	227	10. Walter Ballard	8,035	10. Tiny Lund	7
11. Ed Negre	8,359	11. Pete Hamilton	224	11. Fred Lorenzen	225	11. Buddy Baker	7,813	11. Fred Lorenzen	6
12. Benny Parsons	7,981	12. Fred Lorenzen	152	12. Ray Elder	183	12. Benny Parsons	7,633	12. Dick Brooks	5
13. Wendell Scott	7,791	13. Benny Parsons	144	13. Tiny Lund	122	13. Bobby Isaac	7,602	James Hylton	5
14. Henley Gray	7,684	14. James Hylton	105	14. Benny Parsons	79	14. Ed Negre	7,547	14. A. J. Foyt	4
15. John Sears	7,512	15. Ray Elder	70	15. James Hylton	63	15. Henley Gray	7,504	Benny Parsons	4
16. Neil Castles	6,946	16. Friday Hassler	68	16. Friday Hassler	44	16. Bill Seifert	7,151	16. Friday Hassler	3
17. Bobby Isaac	6,856	17. Jim Paschal	50	17. LeeRoy Yarbrough	32	17. Friday Hassler	7,130	17. Bill Dennis	2
18. Earl Brooks	6,657	18. Elmo Langley	48	18. Jim Paschal	27	18. Bill Dennis	6,976	Ray Elder	2
19. Bill Seifert	6,552	19. Bill Dennis	47	19. Bill Dennis	25	19. Pete Hamilton	6,890	Hershel McGriff	2
20. Dave Marcis	6,460	20. LeeRoy Yarbrough	26	20. Dick Brooks	21	20. Wendell Scott	6,819	Jim Paschal	2
21. Bill Dennis	6,111	21. Dick Brooks	16	21. Cale Yarborough	20	21. John Sears	6,815	LeeRoy Yarbrough	2
22. Friday Hassler	5,650	22. Cale Yarborough	13	22. Elmo Langley	16	22. Dave Marcis	6,689		
23. Buddy Baker	4,814	23. G. C. Spencer	12	23. G. C. Spencer	12	23. Earl Brooks	6,548		
24. Charlie Glotzbach	4,735	24. H. B. Bailey	11	24. Hershel McGriff	10	24. Ben Arnold	6,172		
25. Pete Hamilton	4,525	25. Neil Castles	10	25. H. B. Bailey	6	25. Joe Frasson	5,698		
26. Dick Brooks	4,495	26. J. D. McDuffie	5	26. Neil Castles	4	26. Neil Castles	5,620		
27. Ben Arnold	4,130	27. Hershel McGriff	4	27. J. D. McDuffie	2	27. Fred Lorenzen	5,038		
28. Tiny Lund	3,783					28. Dick Brooks	4,784		
29. Joe Frasson	3,752					29. Charlie Glotzbach	4,695		
30. Bill Shirey	3,667					30. Donnie Allison	4,327		

Driver	Starts	Poles	Finish						Laps	Laps Led	Races Led	Winston Cup Points	$
			1	2	3	4	5	6–10					

1972

	Driver	Starts	Poles	1	2	3	4	5	6–10	Laps	Laps Led	Races Led	Winston Cup Points	$
1.	Richard Petty	31	3	8	9	5	2	1	3	10,282	2,093	30	8,701	339,405
2.	Bobby Allison	31	12	10	12	2	1	0	2	10,063	4,343	30	8,573	348,939
3.	James Hylton	31	0	1	0	0	5	3	14	9,672	111	4	8,158	126,705
4.	Cecil Gordon	31	0	0	0	0	1	3	12	9,033	3	2	7,326	73,126
5.	Benny Parsons	31	0	0	1	0	8	1	9	7,922	19	2	6,844	102,043
6.	Walter Ballard	31	0	0	0	0	0	0	7	8,460	0	0	6,781	59,745
7.	Elmo Langley	30	0	0	0	0	0	1	8	8,150	0	0	6,656	59,644
8.	John Sears	28	0	0	0	0	0	2	5	7,882	0	0	6,298	51,314
9.	Dean Dalton	29	0	0	0	0	0	0	4	7,533	0	0	6,295	42,299
10.	Ben Arnold	26	0	0	0	0	0	0	7	6,976	0	0	6,179	44,547
11.	Frank Warren	30	0	0	0	0	0	0	2	7,091	0	0	5,788	45,048
12.	Jabe Thomas	28	0	0	0	0	0	0	4	7,132	0	0	5,772	43,438
13.	Bill Champion	29	0	0	0	0	0	0	4	7,044	0	0	5,740	42,242
14.	Raymond Williams	28	0	0	0	0	0	0	5	6,759	0	0	5,712	37,000
15.	Dave Marcis	27	0	0	0	2	1	2	6	6,708	4	2	5,459	45,012
16.	Charlie Roberts	26	0	0	0	0	0	0	1	6,437	0	0	5,354	32,488
17.	Henley Gray	28	0	0	0	0	0	0	2	6,121	0	0	5,093	38,461
18.	J. D. McDuffie	27	0	0	0	0	0	1	1	6,231	0	0	5,075	36,833
19.	Bobby Isaac	27	9	1	3	5	0	1	0	5,636	1,326	20	5,050	133,257
20.	David Pearson	17	4	6	1	3	2	0	1	4,902	1,571	16	4,718	142,440
21.	Ed Negre	26	0	0	0	0	0	0	0	5,755	0	0	4,696	30,538
22.	Buddy Arrington	20	0	0	0	0	0	1	9	5,503	0	0	4,555	28,700
23.	Larry Smith	23	0	0	0	• 0	0	0	7	4,320	0	0	4,173	24,215
24.	Buddy Baker	17	1	2	1	4	1	0	1	4,641	594	14	3,936	102,540
25.	Coo Coo Marlin	20	0	0	0	1	1	0	3	4,092	31	5	3,852	28,124
26.	David Ray Boggs	24	0	0	0	0	0	0	0	3,968	0	0	3,739 •	19,489
27.	Ron Keselowski	22	0	0	0	0	0	1	2	3,398	0	0	3,475	21,905
28.	Joe Frasson	16	0	0	0	1	0	0	3	3,013	9	2	3,152	21,570
29.	Richard Brown	16	0	0	0	0	0	1	0	3,403	0	0	2,939	19,283
30.	Neil Castles	21	0	0	0	0	0	0	1	4,075	0	0	2,789	18,760
31.	Jim Vandiver	16	0	0	0	2	0	0	1	2,871	6	1	2,514	27,983
32.	Clarence Lovell	12	0	0	0	0	0	0	0	2,202	0	0	2,360	10,770
33.	David Sisco	12	0	0	0	0	0	0	2	2,067	0	0	2,310	13,700
34.	LeeRoy Yarbrough	18	0	0	0	1	2	2	4	4,174	8	4	2,157	40,705
35.	George Althiede	11	0	0	0	0	0	0	0	1,578	0	0	1,916	10,405
36.	Donnie Allison	10	0	0	0	1	0	1	1	1,385	35	4	1,849	16,826
37.	Richard Childress	15	0	0	0	0	0	0	0	1,681	0	0	1,521	7,245
38.	Bill Shirey	13	0	0	0	0	0	0	0	1,812	0	0	1,468	8,070
39.	Fred Lorenzen	8	0	0	0	0	3	0	1	1,801	4	1	1,333	19,505
40.	Wendell Scott	6	0	0	0	0	0	0	0	1,763	0	0	1,317	5,830
41.	Tommy Gale	6	0	0	0	0	0	0	0	1,144	0	0	1,298	7,197
42.	Bill Dennis	11	0	0	0	1	0	1	0	2,327	2	1	1,279	9,604
43.	G. C. Spencer	10	0	0	0	0	0	0	1	1,492	0	0	1,238	8,040
44.	Dick May	6	0	0	0	0	0	0	1	955	0	0	1,229	5,370
45.	Hershel McGriff	4	0	0	0	0	0	2	1	727	3	1	1,199	12,290
46.	Les Covey	7	0	0	0	0	0	0	0	1,347	0	0	1,128	5,070
47.	Johnny Halford	5	0	0	0	0	0	0	1	1,032	0	0	1,103	4,955
48.	Pete Hamilton	5	0	0	0	0	0	1	0	1,044	8	2	1,083	8,005
49.	Dick Brooks	14	0	0	0	0	0	0	1	1,156	3	2	1,023	14,146
50.	Eddie Yarboro	6	0	0	0	0	0	0	0	1,728	0	0	1,007	3,435

LAPS COMPLETED

1. Richard Petty — 10,282
2. Bobby Allison — 10,063
3. James Hylton — 9,672
4. Cecil Gordon — 9,033
5. Walter Ballard — 8,460
6. Elmo Langley — 8,150
7. Benny Parsons — 7,922
8. John Sears — 7,882
9. Dean Dalton — 7,533
10. Jabe Thomas — 7,132
11. Frank Warren — 7,091
12. Bill Champion — 7,044
13. Ben Arnold — 6,976
14. Raymond Williams — 6,759
15. Dave Marcis — 6,708
16. Charlie Roberts — 6,437
17. J. D. McDuffie — 6,231
18. Henley Gray — 6,121
19. Ed Negre — 5,755
20. Bobby Isaac — 5,636
21. Buddy Arrington — 5,503
22. David Pearson — 4,902
23. Buddy Baker — 4,641
24. Larry Smith — 4,320
25. LeeRoy Yarbrough — 4,174
26. Coo Coo Marlin — 4,092
27. Neil Castles — 4,075
28. David Ray Boggs — 3,968
29. Richard Brown — 3,403
30. Ron Keselowski — 3,398

LAPS LED

1. Bobby Allison — 4,343
2. Richard Petty — 2,093
3. David Pearson — 1,571
4. Bobby Isaac — 1,326
5. Buddy Baker — 594
6. A. J. Foyt — 344
7. James Hylton — 111
8. Ray Elder — 50
9. Donnie Allison — 35
10. Coo Coo Marlin — 31
11. Benny Parsons — 19
12. Joe Frasson — 9
    Cale Yarborough — 9
14. Pete Hamilton — 8
    LeeRoy Yarbrough — 8
16. Darrell Waltrip — 7
17. H. B. Bailey — 6
    Jim Vandiver — 6
19. Fred Lorenzen — 4
    Dave Marcis — 4
21. Dick Brooks — 3
    Cecil Gordon — 3
    Hershel McGriff — 3
    Ramo Stott — 3
25. Bill Dennis — 2

MILES LED

1. Bobby Allison — 4,117
2. David Pearson — 2,292
3. Richard Petty — 2,252
4. Bobby Isaac — 1,515
5. Buddy Baker — 925
6. A. J. Foyt — 834
7. James Hylton — 291
8. Ray Elder — 131
9. Donnie Allison — 75
10. Coo Coo Marlin — 41
11. Benny Parsons — 39
12. Pete Hamilton — 21
13. Darrell Waltrip — 19
14. Joe Frasson — 18
15. Fred Lorenzen — 11
16. Cale Yarborough — 9
17. H. B. Bailey — 8
    Jim Vandiver — 8
19. Ramo Stott — 8
20. Hershel McGriff — 8
21. LeeRoy Yarbrough — 7
22. Dave Marcis — 6
23. Dick Brooks — 4
24. Cecil Gordon — 4
25. Bill Dennis — 2

MILES DRIVEN

1. Richard Petty — 11,996
2. Bobby Allison — 11,801
3. James Hylton — 11,431
4. Cecil Gordon — 10,421
5. Walter Ballard — 9,748
6. Benny Parsons — 9,463
7. Elmo Langley — 9,459
8. Dean Dalton — 9,068
9. John Sears — 8,994
10. Ben Arnold — 8,935
11. Frank Warren — 8,404
12. Jabe Thomas — 8,207
13. Bill Champion — 8,121
14. Raymond Williams — 8,079
15. Charlie Roberts — 7,728
16. Dave Marcis — 7,522
17. Henley Gray — 7,307
18. J. D. McDuffie — 7,094
19. Buddy Arrington — 7,008
20. Bobby Isaac — 6,872
21. Ed Negre — 6,702
22. David Pearson — 6,593
23. Buddy Baker — 6,030
24. Larry Smith — 5,831
25. Coo Coo Marlin — 5,383
26. David Ray Boggs — 5,164
27. Ron Keselowski — 4,976
28. LeeRoy Yarbrough — 4,866
29. Joe Frasson — 4,638
30. Richard Brown — 4,190

RACES LED

1. Bobby Allison — 30
   Richard Petty — 30
3. Bobby Isaac — 20
4. David Pearson — 16
5. Buddy Baker — 14
6. A. J. Foyt — 6
7. Coo Coo Marlin — 5
8. Donnie Allison — 4
   James Hylton — 4
   LeeRoy Yarbrough — 4
11. Dick Brooks — 2
    Ray Elder — 2
    Joe Frasson — 2
    Cecil Gordon — 2
    Pete Hamilton — 2
    Dave Marcis — 2
    Benny Parsons — 2

1973

Driver	Starts	Poles	Finish 1	2	3	4	5	6–10	Laps	Laps Led	Races Led	Winston Cup Points	$
1. Benny Parsons	28	0	1	3	3	3	5	6	9,311	374	8	7,173	182,321
2. Cale Yarborough	28	5	4	6	4	1	1	3	9,314	3,167	21	7,106	267,513
3. Cecil Gordon	28	0	0	0	1	1	6	10	8,995	5	3	7,046	102,120
4. James Hylton	28	0	0	0	0	1	0	10	9,324	1	1	6,972	82,512
5. Richard Petty	28	3	6	6	1	2	0	2	8,644	1,815	16	6,877	234,389
6. Buddy Baker	27	5	2	4	6	4	0	4	8,369	975	14	6,327	190,531
7. Bobby Allison	27	6	2	2	6	4	1	1	8,072	870	20	6,272	161,818
8. Walter Ballard	28	0	0	0	0	0	0	4	8,048	5	1	5,955	53,875
9. Elmo Langley	27	0	0	0	0	0	0	4	8,016	0	0	5,826	49,542
10. J. D. McDuffie	27	0	0	0	0	0	3	7	7,388	11	2	5,743	56,140
11. Jabe Thomas	25	0	0	0	0	0	0	1	7,205	0	0	5,637	42,955
12. Buddy Arrington	26	0	0	0	0	0	1	3	7,476	0	0	5,483	40,877
13. David Pearson	18	8	11	2	1	0	0	0	5,338	2,658	16	5,382	228,408
14. Henley Gray	24	0	0	0	0	0	0	4	7,517	0	0	5,215	34,112
15. Richard Childress	25	0	0	0	0	1	0	1	6,918	1	1	5,169	37,880
16. Frank Warren	26	0	0	0	0	0	0	0	6,713	0	0	4,992	36,551
17. David Sisco	23	0	0	0	0	1	1	4	6,552	12	2	4,986	36,205
18. Ed Negre	24	0	0	0	0	0	1	1	6,230	0	0	4,942	34,235
19. Dean Dalton	26	0	0	0	0	0	0	2	5,889	0	0	4,712	35,954
20. Charlie Roberts	24	0	0	0	0	0	0	0	7,017	0	0	4,695	32,144
21. Bill Champion	26	0	0	0	0	0	0	1	5,103	0	0	4,447	31,828
22. Coo Coo Marlin	21	0	0	0	1	0	0	7	5,454	16	3	4,233	29,997
23. Lennie Pond	23	0	0	0	0	1	0	8	5,850	4	2	4,013	25,155
24. Dave Marcis	23	0	0	0	0	1	2	3	4,905	0	0	3,973	30,253
25. Raymond Williams	22	0	0	0	0	0	0	3	4,684	0	0	3,708	22,728
26. Bobby Isaac	19	0	0	2	1	2	0	1	4,177	62	7	3,352	84,550
27. Dick Brooks	14	0	1	0	1	0	1	6	3,448	25	3	3,200	55,369
28. Darrell Waltrip	19	0	0	1	0	0	0	4	3,783	50	3	2,968	42,466
29. Joe Frasson	14	0	0	0	1	1	0	2	2,732	1	1	2,952	25,884
30. Vic Parsons	18	0	0	0	0	0	0	6	3,498	0	0	2,929	18,200
31. Jim Vandiver	10	0	0	0	0	0	0	4	2,431	0	0	2,508	18,586
32. John Sears	17	0	0	0	0	0	0	0	3,568	0	0	2,465	16,890
33. Larry Smith	11	0	0	0	0	0	0	1	2,103	0	0	2,367	14,090
34. Rick Newsom	12	0	0	0	0	0	0	0	3,209	0	0	1,931	8,530
35. Donnie Allison	14	0	0	1	1	0	0	3	2,904	44	3	1,755	41,246
36. D. K. Ulrich	11	0	0	0	0	0	0	0	2,006	0	0	1,543	3,955
37. G. C. Spencer	10	0	0	0	0	0	0	1	1,459	0	0	1,503	12,013
38. Mel Larson	10	0	0	0	0	0	0	0	2,160	0	0	1,182	8,235
39. Johnny Barnes	8	0	0	0	0	0	0	0	1,416	0	0	1,174	8,585
40. Eddie Bond	6	0	0	0	0	0	0	0	1,407	0	0	1,163	6,901
41. Earle Canavan	5	0	0	0	0	0	0	0	1,223	0	0	1,144	4,980
42. Earl Brooks	9	0	0	0	0	0	0	0	2,267	0	0	1,075	4,880
43. Charlie Glotzbach	5	0	0	0	0	0	0	1	1,048	11	2	903	6,451
44. Randy Tissot	3	0	0	0	0	0	0	0	816	0	0	887	4,245
45. Ron Keselowski	5	0	0	0	0	0	1	0	733	0	0	879	6,060
46. Jimmy Crawford	4	0	0	0	0	0	0	0	1,053	0	0	846	4,059
47. Richard Brown	13	0	0	0	0	0	0	0	1,260	0	0	827	7,340
48. Clarence Lovell	4	0	0	0	0	1	0	1	661	0	0	813	9,175
49. Bill Dennis	4	0	0	0	0	0	0	2	1,430	0	0	809	4,225
50. Jack McCoy	3	0	0	0	0	0	1	2	797	0	0	793	5,270

Laps Completed

1.	James Hylton	9,324
2.	Cale Yarborough	9,314
3.	Benny Parsons	9,311
4.	Cecil Gordon	8,995
5.	Richard Petty	8,644
6.	Buddy Baker	8,369
7.	Bobby Allison	8,072
8.	Walter Ballard	8,048
9.	Elmo Langley	8,016
10.	Henley Gray	7,517
11.	Buddy Arrington	7,476
12.	J. D. McDuffie	7,388
13.	Jabe Thomas	7,205
14.	Charlie Roberts	7,017
15.	Richard Childress	6,918
16.	Frank Warren	6,713
17.	David Sisco	6,552
18.	Ed Negre	6,230
19.	Dean Dalton	5,889
20.	Lennie Pond	5,850
21.	Coo Coo Marlin	5,454
22.	David Pearson	5,338
23.	Bill Champion	5,103
24.	Dave Marcis	4,905
25.	Raymond Williams	4,684
26.	Bobby Isaac	4,177
27.	Darrell Waltrip	3,783
28.	John Sears	3,568
29.	Vic Parsons	3,498
30.	Dick Brooks	3,448

Laps Led

1.	Cale Yarborough	3,167
2.	David Pearson	2,658
3.	Richard Petty	1,815
4.	Buddy Baker	975
5.	Bobby Allison	870
6.	Benny Parsons	374
7.	Mark Donohue	138
8.	Bobby Isaac	62
9.	Darrell Waltrip	50
10.	Donnie Allison	44
11.	Dick Brooks	25
12.	Coo Coo Marlin	16
13.	David Sisco	12
14.	Charlie Glotzbach	11
	J. D. McDuffie	11
16.	Charles Barrett	9
17.	Walter Ballard	5
	Cecil Gordon	5
19.	Lennie Pond	4
20.	Dick Trickle	2
21.	Richard Childress	1
	Joe Frasson	1
	James Hylton	1
	Marty Robbins	1
	Ramo Stott	1

Miles Led

1.	David Pearson	3,275
2.	Cale Yarborough	2,727
3.	Richard Petty	1,642
4.	Buddy Baker	1,597
5.	Bobby Allison	1,023
6.	Mark Donohue	362
7.	Benny Parsons	236
8.	Donnie Allison	109
9.	Darrell Waltrip	90
10.	Bobby Isaac	81
11.	Dick Brooks	65
12.	Coo Coo Marlin	41
13.	J. D. McDuffie	29
14.	Charles Barrett	24
15.	David Sisco	19
16.	Charlie Glotzbach	15
17.	Walter Ballard	13
18.	Cecil Gordon	9
19.	Lennie Pond	8
20.	Dick Trickle	3
21.	Richard Childress	3
	James Hylton	3
	Marty Robbins	3
	Ramo Stott	3
25.	Joe Frasson	2

Miles Driven

1.	Benny Parsons	10,047
2.	James Hylton	10,044
3.	Cecil Gordon	9,988
4.	Cale Yarborough	9,737
5.	Richard Petty	9,286
6.	Buddy Baker	8,908
7.	Bobby Allison	8,646
8.	Walter Ballard	8,626
9.	Elmo Langley	8,377
10.	J. D. McDuffie	8,129
11.	Jabe Thomas	7,910
12.	Buddy Arrington	7,876
13.	Henley Gray	7,608
14.	Richard Childress	7,456
15.	David Pearson	7,182
16.	Ed Negre	7,180
17.	Frank Warren	7,171
18.	David Sisco	7,140
19.	Charlie Roberts	6,848
20.	Dean Dalton	6,825
21.	Bill Champion	6,364
22.	Coo Coo Marlin	5,937
23.	Lennie Pond	5,472
24.	Dave Marcis	5,448
25.	Darrell Waltrip	5,352
26.	Raymond Williams	5,220
27.	Dick Brooks	4,947
28.	Bobby Isaac	4,536
29.	Joe Frasson	4,379
30.	Vic Parsons	4,017

Races Led

1.	Cale Yarborough	21
2.	Bobby Allison	20
3.	David Pearson	16
	Richard Petty	16
5.	Buddy Baker	14
6.	Benny Parsons	8
7.	Bobby Isaac	7
8.	Donnie Allison	3
	Dick Brooks	3
	Cecil Gordon	3
	Coo Coo Marlin	3
	Darrell Waltrip	3
13.	Charlie Glotzbach	2
	J. D. McDuffie	2
	Lennie Pond	2
	David Sisco	2

1974

Driver	Starts	Poles	Finish 1	2	3	4	5	6–10	Laps	Laps Led	Races Led	Winston Cup Points	$
1. Richard Petty	30	7	10	8	4	0	0	1	9,097	3,100	24	5,037	432,020
2. Cale Yarborough	30	3	10	4	5	1	1	1	9,398	3,630	26	4,470	363,782
3. David Pearson	19	11	7	5	2	1	0	0	4,630	1,168	18	2,389	252,819
4. Bobby Allison	27	3	2	3	5	2	5	0	7,523	900	20	2,019	178,437
5. Benny Parsons	30	0	0	2	2	5	2	3	8,120	87	11	1,591	185,080
6. Dave Marcis	30	0	0	0	0	2	4	12	8,658	12	2	1,378	83,377
7. Buddy Baker	19	2	0	4	5	1	1	1	4,346	381	13	1,016	151,025
8. Earl Ross	21	0	1	1	1	1	1	5	5,860	127	6	1,009	81,199
9. Cecil Gordon	30	0	0	0	0	1	0	9	7,396	2	2	1,000	66,166
10. David Sisco	28	0	0	0	1	1	0	7	7,483	43	4	956	58,313
11. James Hylton	29	0	0	0	0	0	1	7	6,774	29	6	924	61,385
12. J. D. McDuffie	30	0	0	0	0	0	0	7	8,283	1	1	920	59,535
13. Frank Warren	29	0	0	0	0	0	1	1	7,342	0	0	820	55,779
14. Richie Panch	28	0	0	0	1	0	1	5	6,257	1	1	775	52,713
15. Walter Ballard	27	0	0	0	0	0	1	5	6,820	2	1	748	54,039
16. Richard Childress	29	0	0	0	0	0	0	3	5,138	0	0	735	50,249
17. Donnie Allison	21	2	0	1	1	2	2	4	5,101	182	10	728	60,315
18. Lennie Pond	22	0	0	0	0	1	4	6	6,684	17	6	723	55,990
19. Darrell Waltrip	16	1	0	1	3	2	1	4	4,649	103	5	609	67,775
20. Tony Bettenhausen Jr.	27	0	0	0	0	0	0	1	5,548	0	0	601	38,995
21. Jackie Rogers	22	0	0	0	0	0	0	6	4,555	1	1	587	32,367
22. Coo Coo Marlin	23	0	0	0	0	1	0	4	5,623	28	7	581	41,759
23. Ed Negre	26	0	0	0	0	0	0	0	5,302	0	0	534	24,622
24. Bob Burcham	20	0	0	0	0	1	0	4	4,819	2	1	445	27,923
25. Elmo Langley	23	0	0	0	0	0	0	3	5,589	0	0	433	24,722
26. Charlie Glotzbach	14	0	0	0	0	4	0	1	3,582	126	5	293	33,072
27. Dick Brooks	16	0	0	0	0	0	0	3	2,951	1	1	267	22,760
28. Joe Frasson	14	0	0	0	0	0	0	3	2,141	13	3	240	22,629
29. George Follmer	13	1	0	0	0	1	2	2	3,086	27	2	230	53,780
30. Buddy Arrington	16	0	0	0	0	0	0	4	4,781	0	0	221	21,510
31. Bill Champion	18	0	0	0	0	0	0	0	2,324	0	0	207	13,480
32. D. K. Ulrich	15	0	0	0	0	0	0	0	3,194	0	0	155	11,955
33. Bobby Isaac	11	0	0	1	0	0	0	4	1,907	11	4	152	22,642
34. Travis Tiller	14	0	0	0	0	0	0	0	2,446	0	0	146	11,410
35. Roy Mayne	11	0	0	0	0	0	0	0	1,681	0	0	141	15,284
36. Dean Dalton	14	0	0	0	0	0	0	0	2,414	6	1	125	12,375
37. Neil Castles	14	0	0	0	0	0	0	0	1,422	0	0	123	12,479
38. G. C. Spencer	10	0	0	0	0	0	0	1	1,205	3	1	96	12,985
39. Ramo Stott	6	0	0	0	1	0	0	3	1,414	0	0	82	23,705
40. Jim Vandiver	7	0	0	0	0	0	0	1	1,061	1	1	71	15,909
41. Dan Daughtry	8	0	0	0	0	0	0	1	772	6	2	63	12,413
42. Jabe Thomas	10	0	0	0	0	0	0	1	1,504	0	0	49	7,445
43. Gary Bettenhausen	5	0	0	0	0	1	0	2	986	35	1	49	10,350
44. A. J. Foyt	4	0	0	0	0	1	1	0	612	70	3	41	15,560
45. Jerry Schild	5	0	0	0	0	0	0	1	1,142	0	0	35	8,395
46. Earle Canavan	6	0	0	0	0	0	0	0	1,477	0	0	34	6,570
47. Dick Trickle	3	0	0	0	0	0	0	3	1,201	0	0	24	10,828
48. Marty Robbins	4	0	0	0	0	0	1	1	550	0	0	23	5,734
49. Alton Jones	5	0	0	0	0	0	1	1	1,163	0	0	20	4,080
50. Hershel McGriff	5	0	0	0	0	0	0	1	559	0	0	20	8,585

LAPS COMPLETED

1. Cale Yarborough — 9,398
2. Richard Petty — 9,097
3. Dave Marcis — 8,658
4. J. D. McDuffie — 8,283
5. Benny Parsons — 8,120
6. Bobby Allison — 7,523
7. David Sisco — 7,483
8. Cecil Gordon — 7,396
9. Frank Warren — 7,342
10. Walter Ballard — 6,820
11. James Hylton — 6,774
12. Lennie Pond — 6,684
13. Richie Panch — 6,257
14. Earl Ross — 5,860
15. Coo Coo Marlin — 5,623
16. Elmo Langley — 5,589
17. Tony Bettenhausen Jr. — 5,548
18. Ed Negre — 5,302
19. Richard Childress — 5,138
20. Donnie Allison — 5,101
21. Bob Burcham — 4,819
22. Buddy Arrington — 4,781
23. Darrell Waltrip — 4,649
24. David Pearson — 4,630
25. Jackie Rogers — 4,555
26. Buddy Baker — 4,346
27. Charlie Glotzbach — 3,582
28. D. K. Ulrich — 3,194
29. George Follmer — 3,086
30. Dick Brooks — 2,951

LAPS LED

1. Cale Yarborough — 3,630
2. Richard Petty — 3,100
3. David Pearson — 1,168
4. Bobby Allison — 900
5. Buddy Baker — 381
6. Donnie Allison — 182
7. Earl Ross — 127
8. Charlie Glotzbach — 126
9. Darrell Waltrip — 103
10. Benny Parsons — 87
11. Sonny Hutchins — 79
12. A. J. Foyt — 70
13. David Sisco — 43
14. Gary Bettenhausen — 35
15. James Hylton — 29
16. Coo Coo Marlin — 28
17. George Follmer — 27
18. Lennie Pond — 17
19. Joe Frasson — 13
20. Dave Marcis — 12
21. Bobby Isaac — 11
22. Jimmy Hensley — 9
23. Grant Adcox — 8
    Randy Tissot — 8
25. Dean Dalton — 6
    Dan Daughtry — 6
27. Jack McCoy — 4
28. Johnny Rutherford — 3
    G. C. Spencer — 3

MILES LED

1. Cale Yarborough — 3,374
2. Richard Petty — 3,256
3. David Pearson — 1,876
4. Bobby Allison — 1,091
5. Buddy Baker — 657
6. Donnie Allison — 318
7. Charlie Glotzbach — 177
8. A. J. Foyt — 150
9. Darrell Waltrip — 138
10. Gary Bettenhausen — 93
11. Earl Ross — 92
12. Benny Parsons — 78
13. George Follmer — 72
14. David Sisco — 69
15. Coo Coo Marlin — 68
16. James Hylton — 61
17. Sonny Hutchins — 41
18. Joe Frasson — 25
19. Bobby Isaac — 23
20. Randy Tissot — 21
21. Dave Marcis — 16
22. Dan Daughtry — 15
23. Grant Adcox — 12
24. Lennie Pond — 12
25. Jack McCoy — 10
26. Johnny Rutherford — 7
27. Bob Burcham — 5
28. Walter Ballard — 5
29. Jimmy Hensley — 5
30. G. C. Spencer — 4

MILES DRIVEN

1. Cale Yarborough — 11,058
2. Richard Petty — 10,830
3. Dave Marcis — 9,966
4. J. D. McDuffie — 9,518
5. Bobby Allison — 9,154
6. Cecil Gordon — 9,079
7. David Sisco — 9,012
8. Frank Warren — 8,993
9. Benny Parsons — 8,865
10. James Hylton — 7,969
11. David Pearson — 7,746
12. Earl Ross — 7,644
13. Walter Ballard — 7,246
14. Lennie Pond — 7,191
15. Richie Panch — 6,872
16. Jackie Rogers — 6,677
17. Richard Childress — 6,484
18. Bob Burcham — 6,405
19. Ed Negre — 6,344
20. Coo Coo Marlin — 6,261
21. Tony Bettenhausen Jr. — 6,151
22. Darrell Waltrip — 6,013
23. Buddy Baker — 5,890
24. Elmo Langley — 5,852
25. Donnie Allison — 5,761
26. Buddy Arrington — 4,797
27. Dick Brooks — 4,097
28. Charlie Glotzbach — 3,950
29. George Follmer — 3,747
30. Joe Frasson — 3,671

RACES LED

1. Cale Yarborough — 26
2. Richard Petty — 24
3. Bobby Allison — 20
4. David Pearson — 18
5. Buddy Baker — 13
6. Benny Parsons — 11
7. Donnie Allison — 10
8. Coo Coo Marlin — 7
9. James Hylton — 6
    Lennie Pond — 6
    Earl Ross — 6
12. Charlie Glotzbach — 5
    Darrell Waltrip — 5
14. Bobby Isaac — 4
    David Sisco — 4
16. A. J. Foyt — 3
    Joe Frasson — 3
18. Dan Daughtry — 2
    George Follmer — 2
    Cecil Gordon — 2
    Dave Marcis — 2
    Johnny Rutherford — 2

1975

Driver	Starts	Poles	Finish 1	2	3	4	5	6–10	Laps	Laps Led	Races Led	Winston Cup Points	$
1. Richard Petty	30	3	13	5	3	0	0	3	9,082	3,158	26	4,783	481,751
2. Dave Marcis	30	4	1	1	5	6	3	2	8,324	458	17	4,061	240,646
3. James Hylton	30	0	0	0	0	1	1	14	9,650	11	4	3,914	113,642
4. Benny Parsons	30	3	1	3	3	3	1	6	8,198	496	16	3,820	214,354
5. Richard Childress	30	0	0	0	0	1	1	13	9,433	3	2	3,818	96,780
6. Cecil Gordon	30	0	0	1	1	2	3	9	8,577	6	2	3,702	101,467
7. Darrell Waltrip	28	2	2	2	2	3	2	3	7,240	562	13	3,462	160,192
8. Elmo Langley	29	0	0	0	0	0	2	5	8,601	0	0	3,399	67,600
9. Cale Yarborough	27	3	3	3	3	3	1	0	7,353	2,542	20	3,295	214,691
10. Dick Brooks	25	0	0	1	2	3	0	9	7,344	60	4	3,182	93,001
11. Walter Ballard	30	0	0	0	0	0	0	3	7,518	16	2	3,151	55,696
12. Frank Warren	27	0	0	0	0	0	0	0	7,758	0	0	3,148	55,671
13. David Sisco	28	0	0	0	1	0	1	5	7,572	37	4	3,116	62,186
14. David Pearson	21	7	3	6	2	2	0	1	5,653	1,323	18	3,057	192,141
15. Buddy Baker	23	3	4	2	4	1	1	1	6,281	788	18	3,050	236,351
16. Bruce Hill	26	0	0	0	0	0	3	8	7,088	2	2	3,002	79,428
17. Ed Negre	29	0	0	0	0	0	0	4	7,191	2	1	2,982	49,629
18. J. D. McDuffie	26	0	0	0	0	0	1	5	5,832	0	0	2,745	50,937
19. Buddy Arrington	25	0	0	0	0	0	0	3	7,786	0	0	2,654	45,893
20. Coo Coo Marlin	23	0	0	0	1	0	3	7	5,199	25	5	2,584	60,013
21. Lennie Pond	22	0	0	3	0	1	2	3	5,859	275	8	2,540	59,265
22. Jabe Thomas	21	0	0	0	0	0	0	2	5,822	0	0	2,252	22,390
23. Carl Adams	20	0	0	0	0	0	0	4	5,332	0	0	2,182	24,865
24. Bobby Allison	19	3	3	3	1	2	1	0	4,268	578	14	2,181	122,435
25. Bruce Jacobi	15	0	0	0	0	0	0	3	3,863	0	0	1,732	29,455
26. Dean Dalton	16	0	0	0	0	0	0	3	3,800	0	0	1,486	19,430
27. D. K. Ulrich	16	0	0	0	0	0	0	1	3,448	0	0	1,453	16,525
28. Donnie Allison	14	2	0	0	2	0	1	3	2,819	33	5	1,376	45,595
29. Richie Panch	14	0	0	0	0	0	1	3	2,276	8	3	1,243	32,585
30. Jim Vandiver	13	0	0	0	0	1	0	3	2,929	1	1	1,228	24,200
31. Bill Champion	13	0	0	0	0	0	0	0	2,690	0	0	1,218	11,340
32. Earle Canavan	12	0	0	0	0	0	0	0	1,601	0	0	1,062	9,725
33. Grant Adcox	11	0	0	0	0	0	0	1	1,620	0	0	1,020	16,540
34. Joe Mihalic	10	0	0	0	0	0	0	1	1,939	0	0	957	12,910
35. Joe Frasson	9	0	0	0	0	0	0	1	1,352	1	1	939	11,975
36. Travis Tiller	10	0	0	0	0	0	0	0	1,958	0	0	922	7,780
37. Rick Newsom	10	0	0	0	0	0	0	0	1,672	0	0	877	9,370
38. Ferrel Harris	10	0	0	0	0	0	0	0	2,357	0	0	797	16,165
39. Henley Gray	9	0	0	0	0	0	0	1	2,179	2	1	747	8,785
40. G. C. Spencer	9	0	0	0	0	0	0	1	906	11	1	634	14,945
41. Dick May	9	0	0	0	0	0	0	1	1,688	0	0	631	11,020
42. Earl Brooks	7	0	0	0	0	0	0	0	1,229	0	0	534	4,900
43. Neil Castles	7	0	0	0	0	0	0	0	578	0	0	529	4,190
44. Jackie Rogers	8	0	0	0	0	0	0	1	913	2	1	502	11,000
45. Harry Jefferson	5	0	0	0	0	0	0	2	1,036	0	0	455	11,395
46. Tommy Gale	5	0	0	0	0	0	0	0	585	0	0	437	6,570
47. Ricky Rudd	4	0	0	0	0	0	0	1	1,025	0	0	431	4,345
48. Bobby Isaac	6	0	0	0	0	0	0	1	1,101	0	0	405	6,695
49. Dick Skillen	5	0	0	0	0	0	0	0	1,052	0	0	389	4,865
50. Ray Elder	3	0	0	0	0	1	0	0	368	1	1	372	8,020

LAPS COMPLETED

1.	James Hylton	9,650
2.	Richard Childress	9,433
3.	Richard Petty	9,082
4.	Elmo Langley	8,601
5.	Cecil Gordon	8,577
6.	Dave Marcis	8,324
7.	Benny Parsons	8,198
8.	Buddy Arrington	7,786
9.	Frank Warren	7,758
10.	David Sisco	7,572
11.	Walter Ballard	7,518
12.	Cale Yarborough	7,353
13.	Dick Brooks	7,344
14.	Darrell Waltrip	7,240
15.	Ed Negre	7,191
16.	Bruce Hill	7,088
17.	Buddy Baker	6,281
18.	Lennie Pond	5,859
19.	J. D. McDuffie	5,832
20.	Jabe Thomas	5,822
21.	David Pearson	5,653
22.	Carl Adams	5,332
23.	Coo Coo Marlin	5,199
24.	Bobby Allison	4,268
25.	Bruce Jacobi	3,863
26.	Dean Dalton	3,800
27.	D. K. Ulrich	3,448
28.	Jim Vandiver	2,929
29.	Donnie Allison	2,819
30.	Bill Champion	2,690

LAPS LED

1.	Richard Petty	3,158
2.	Cale Yarborough	2,542
3.	David Pearson	1,323
4.	Buddy Baker	788
5.	Bobby Allison	578
6.	Darrell Waltrip	562
7.	Benny Parsons	496
8.	Dave Marcis	458
9.	Lennie Pond	275
10.	A. J. Foyt	186
11.	Dick Brooks	60
12.	David Sisco	37
13.	Donnie Allison	33
14.	Coo Coo Marlin	25
15.	Jimmy Insolo	18
16.	Walter Ballard	16
17.	Neil Bonnett	12
18.	James Hylton	11
	G. C. Spencer	11
20.	Richie Panch	8
21.	Cecil Gordon	6
22.	Hershel McGriff	4
23.	Richard Childress	3
24.	Darel Dieringer	2
	Sonny Easley	2
	Henley Gray	2
	Bruce Hill	2
	Ed Negre	2
	Marty Robbins	2
24.	Jackie Rogers	2

MILES LED

1.	Richard Petty	3,319
2.	Cale Yarborough	2,075
3.	David Pearson	2,022
4.	Buddy Baker	1,645
5.	Bobby Allison	1,055
6.	Dave Marcis	432
7.	Benny Parsons	392
8.	Darrell Waltrip	367
9.	A. J. Foyt	299
10.	Lennie Pond	171
11.	Dick Brooks	103
12.	Donnie Allison	86
13.	David Sisco	72
14.	Coo Coo Marlin	56
15.	Jimmy Insolo	47
16.	Neil Bonnett	32
17.	James Hylton	27
18.	G. C. Spencer	15
19.	Richie Panch	14
20.	Cecil Gordon	11
21.	Walter Ballard	11
22.	Richard Childress	7
23.	Hershel McGriff	6
24.	Darel Dieringer	5
	Marty Robbins	5
	Jackie Rogers	5
27.	Sonny Easley	5
28.	Henley Gray	4
	Ed Negre	4
30.	Bruce Hill	3

MILES DRIVEN

1.	James Hylton	11,032
2.	Richard Childress	10,925
3.	Richard Petty	10,846
4.	Elmo Langley	9,884
5.	Dave Marcis	9,789
6.	Cecil Gordon	9,683
7.	Frank Warren	9,123
8.	David Pearson	8,579
9.	David Sisco	8,455
10.	Benny Parsons	8,454
11.	Walter Ballard	8,254
12.	Buddy Arrington	8,170
13.	Buddy Baker	8,113
14.	Cale Yarborough	8,100
15.	Dick Brooks	8,052
16.	Bruce Hill	7,868
17.	Ed Negre	7,725
18.	Darrell Waltrip	7,425
19.	J. D. McDuffie	7,054
20.	Coo Coo Marlin	6,400
21.	Lennie Pond	6,361
22.	Bobby Allison	6,226
23.	Carl Adams	5,827
24.	Bruce Jacobi	5,767
25.	Jabe Thomas	5,661
26.	Dean Dalton	4,236
27.	D. K. Ulrich	4,093
28.	Donnie Allison	3,971
29.	Ferrel Harris	3,854
30.	Jim Vandiver	3,625

RACES LED

1.	Richard Petty	26
2.	Cale Yarborough	20
3.	Buddy Baker	18
	David Pearson	18
5.	Dave Marcis	17
6.	Benny Parsons	16
7.	Bobby Allison	14
8.	Darrell Waltrip	13
9.	Lennie Pond	8
10.	Donnie Allison	5
	A. J. Foyt	5
	Coo Coo Marlin	5
13.	Dick Brooks	4
	James Hylton	4
	David Sisco	4
16.	Richie Panch	3
17.	Walter Ballard	2
	Richard Childress	2
	Cecil Gordon	2
	Bruce Hill	2

1976

Driver	Starts	Poles	Finish 1	2	3	4	5	6–10	Laps	Laps Led	Races Led	Winston Cup Points	$
1. Cale Yarborough	30	2	9	6	3	2	2	1	9,269	3,791	28	4,644	453,405
2. Richard Petty	30	1	3	9	3	4	0	3	8,941	1,269	23	4,449	374,806
3. Benny Parsons	30	2	2	2	7	2	5	5	8,679	455	15	4,304	270,043
4. Bobby Allison	30	3	0	2	6	5	2	4	8,735	360	18	4,097	230,170
5. Lennie Pond	30	0	0	2	0	4	4	9	8,182	217	10	3,930	159,701
6. Dave Marcis	30	7	3	0	1	2	3	7	8,355	893	20	3,875	218,250
7. Buddy Baker	30	2	1	3	1	4	7	0	7,335	1,028	15	3,745	239,922
8. Darrell Waltrip	30	3	1	3	4	1	1	2	7,780	534	10	3,505	204,193
9. David Pearson	22	8	10	3	2	1	0	2	6,194	1,213	19	3,483	346,890
10. Dick Brooks	28	0	0	0	1	1	1	15	7,542	16	2	3,447	111,880
11. Richard Childress	30	0	0	0	0	0	0	11	8,147	0	0	3,428	85,780
12. J. D. McDuffie	30	0	0	0	0	0	1	7	7,954	0	0	3,400	82,240
13. James Hylton	30	0	0	0	0	1	1	3	8,125	14	4	3,380	78,705
14. D. K. Ulrich	30	0	0	0	0	0	0	2	8,489	0	0	3,280	69,435
15. Cecil Gordon	30	0	0	0	0	0	0	5	7,387	7	3	3,247	73,830
16. Frank Warren	30	0	0	0	0	0	0	3	8,063	0	0	3,240	67,732
17. David Sisco	28	0	0	0	0	0	0	7	7,111	6	3	2,994	62,622
18. Skip Manning	27	0	0	0	0	0	0	4	6,913	0	0	2,931	61,537
19. Ed Negre	28	0	0	0	0	0	0	2	6,153	0	0	2,709	50,919
20. Buddy Arrington	25	0	0	0	0	0	0	3	6,256	0	0	2,573	56,647
21. Terry Bivins	18	0	0	0	0	0	1	5	5,237	6	1	2,099	44,070
22. Bobby Wawak	19	0	0	0	0	0	0	9	4,888	0	0	2,062	31,415
23. Bruce Hill	22	0	0	0	0	0	0	4	3,469	3	1	1,995	43,705
24. Jimmy Means	19	0	0	0	0	0	0	0	4,336	1	1	1,752	20,945
25. Dick May	18	0	0	0	0	0	0	0	4,595	0	0	1,719	29,425
26. Walter Ballard	14	0	0	0	0	0	0	3	4,168	0	0	1,554	16,380
27. Henley Gray	16	0	0	0	0	0	0	0	2,993	0	0	1,425	15,090
28. Coo Coo Marlin	12	0	0	0	0	0	0	6	3,074	0	0	1,412	39,485
29. Gary Myers	15	0	0	0	0	0	0	0	3,077	0	0	1,296	11,430
30. Jackie Rogers	11	0	0	0	0	0	0	3	2,439	3	2	1,173	21,215
31. Grant Adcox	11	0	0	0	0	0	0	2	3,126	0	0	1,163	25,715
32. Neil Bonnett	14	0	0	0	0	0	1	3	2,377	1	1	1,130	31,800
33. Tommy Gale	12	0	0	0	0	0	0	0	2,205	0	0	1,005	18,955
34. Donnie Allison	9	0	1	0	1	0	0	3	2,178	104	4	988	48,455
35. Joe Mihalic	9	0	0	0	0	0	0	0	2,171	0	0	981	12,925
36. Elmo Langley	7	0	0	0	0	0	0	1	2,451	0	0	824	7,515
37. Travis Tiller	9	0	0	0	0	0	0	0	2,012	0	0	816	6,310
38. Sonny Easley	7	0	0	0	0	0	0	2	1,861	0	0	772	11,290
39. Joe Frasson	9	0	0	0	0	0	0	1	863	1	1	707	12,075
40. Jabe Thomas	6	0	0	0	0	0	0	0	1,944	0	0	648	6,160
41. Bill Elliott	8	0	0	0	0	0	0	0	1,047	0	0	635	11,635
42. Dean Dalton	6	0	0	0	0	0	0	0	1,433	0	0	633	7,245
43. Earle Canavan	7	0	0	0	0	0	0	0	1,687	0	0	610	6,035
44. Rick Newsom	7	0	0	0	0	0	0	0	1,604	0	0	607	5,520
45. Tighe Scott	6	0	0	0	0	0	0	1	697	0	0	566	15,520
46. Terry Ryan	5	0	0	0	0	0	1	2	603	1	1	558	24,940
47. Darrell Bryant	8	0	0	0	0	0	0	1	1,678	0	0	546	11,925
48. Buck Baker	8	0	0	0	0	0	0	1	1,977	0	0	513	12,655
49. Chuck Bown	5	0	0	0	0	0	0	0	568	3	1	481	5,480
50. Baxter Price	6	0	0	0	0	0	0	0	1,680	0	0	479	3,010

LAPS COMPLETED

1.	Cale Yarborough	9,269
2.	Richard Petty	8,941
3.	Bobby Allison	8,735
4.	Benny Parsons	8,679
5.	D. K. Ulrich	8,489
6.	Dave Marcis	8,355
7.	Lennie Pond	8,182
8.	Richard Childress	8,147
9.	James Hylton	8,125
10.	Frank Warren	8,063
11.	J. D. McDuffie	7,954
12.	Darrell Waltrip	7,780
13.	Dick Brooks	7,542
14.	Cecil Gordon	7,387
15.	Buddy Baker	7,335
16.	David Sisco	7,111
17.	Skip Manning	6,913
18.	Buddy Arrington	6,256
19.	David Pearson	6,194
20.	Ed Negre	6,153
21.	Terry Bivins	5,237
22.	Bobby Wawak	4,888
23.	Dick May	4,595
24.	Jimmy Means	4,336
25.	Walter Ballard	4,168
26.	Bruce Hill	3,469
27.	Grant Adcox	3,126
28.	Gary Myers	3,077
29.	Coo Coo Marlin	3,074
30.	Henley Gray	2,993

LAPS LED

1.	Cale Yarborough	3,791
2.	Richard Petty	1,269
3.	David Pearson	1,213
4.	Buddy Baker	1,028
5.	Dave Marcis	893
6.	Darrell Waltrip	534
7.	Benny Parsons	455
8.	Bobby Allison	360
9.	Lennie Pond	217
10.	Donnie Allison	104
11.	A. J. Foyt	79
12.	Dick Brooks	16
13.	James Hylton	14
14.	Cecil Gordon	7
15.	Terry Bivins	6
	David Sisco	6
17.	Chuck Bown	3
	Bruce Hill	3
	Jackie Rogers	3
	Chuck Wahl	3
21.	David Hobbs	2
22.	Neil Bonnett	1
	Joe Frasson	1
	Jimmy Means	1
	Terry Ryan	1

MILES LED

1.	Cale Yarborough	3,576
2.	David Pearson	2,219
3.	Buddy Baker	1,537
4.	Richard Petty	1,453
5.	Dave Marcis	1,043
6.	Bobby Allison	556
7.	Benny Parsons	454
8.	Darrell Waltrip	341
9.	A. J. Foyt	199
10.	Lennie Pond	193
11.	Donnie Allison	150
12.	James Hylton	35
13.	Cecil Gordon	18
14.	Terry Bivins	15
15.	David Sisco	14
16.	Dick Brooks	10
17.	Chuck Bown	8
	Chuck Wahl	8
19.	Jackie Rogers	7
20.	Bruce Hill	6
21.	David Hobbs	5
22.	Jimmy Means	3
	Terry Ryan	3
24.	Neil Bonnett	2
	Joe Frasson	2

MILES DRIVEN

1.	Cale Yarborough	10,547
2.	Benny Parsons	10,403
3.	Richard Petty	10,345
4.	Bobby Allison	10,203
5.	Lennie Pond	10,055
6.	D. K. Ulrich	9,932
7.	Frank Warren	9,898
8.	Richard Childress	9,779
9.	Dave Marcis	9,733
10.	J. D. McDuffie	9,664
11.	James Hylton	9,331
12.	David Pearson	9,048
13.	Cecil Gordon	8,757
14.	Buddy Baker	8,610
15.	Dick Brooks	8,585
16.	Skip Manning	8,298
17.	David Sisco	8,101
18.	Darrell Waltrip	8,088
19.	Ed Negre	7,221
20.	Buddy Arrington	6,737
21.	Bobby Wawak	6,231
22.	Terry Bivins	5,816
23.	Dick May	5,365
24.	Bruce Hill	5,138
25.	Jimmy Means	5,117
26.	Grant Adcox	4,643
27.	Coo Coo Marlin	4,309
28.	Jackie Rogers	3,874
29.	Henley Gray	3,599
30.	Walter Ballard	3,542

RACES LED

1.	Cale Yarborough	28
2.	Richard Petty	23
3.	Dave Marcis	20
4.	David Pearson	19
5.	Bobby Allison	18
6.	Buddy Baker	15
	Benny Parsons	15
8.	Lennie Pond	10
	Darrell Waltrip	10
10.	Donnie Allison	4
	James Hylton	4
12.	A. J. Foyt	3
	Cecil Gordon	3
	David Sisco	3
15.	Dick Brooks	2
	Jackie Rogers	2

Driver	Starts	Poles	Finish 1	2	3	4	5	6–10	Laps	Laps Led	Races Led	Winston Cup Points	$
1977													
1. Cale Yarborough	30	3	9	6	4	3	3	2	9,747	3,218	28	5,000	561,642
2. Richard Petty	30	5	5	6	6	2	1	3	8,840	1,403	24	4,614	406,608
3. Benny Parsons	30	3	4	3	10	0	3	2	9,410	1,399	25	4,570	359,341
4. Darrell Waltrip	30	3	6	4	3	1	2	8	9,301	948	23	4,498	324,814
5. Buddy Baker	30	0	0	1	1	4	3	11	8,084	52	7	3,961	224,847
6. Dick Brooks	29	0	0	1	0	1	5	13	8,191	8	2	3,742	151,374
7. James Hylton	30	0	0	0	0	0	0	11	8,375	3	1	3,476	108,392
8. Bobby Allison	30	0	0	1	0	2	2	10	7,024	102	9	3,467	94,575
9. Richard Childress	30	0	0	0	0	0	0	11	7,973	27	4	3,463	97,012
10. Cecil Gordon	30	0	0	0	0	0	0	2	8,133	0	0	3,294	86,312
11. Buddy Arrington	28	0	0	0	0	0	0	5	8,601	0	0	3,247	88,887
12. J. D. McDuffie	30	0	0	0	0	0	0	4	8,252	1	1	3,236	85,227
13. David Pearson	22	5	2	7	2	2	3	0	5,694	868	17	3,227	221,272
14. Skip Manning	28	0	0	0	1	0	0	7	7,533	13	1	3,120	111,317
15. D. K. Ulrich	30	0	0	0	0	0	0	0	6,735	0	0	2,901	69,677
16. Frank Warren	29	0	0	0	0	0	0	1	6,466	1	1	2,876	67,945
17. Ricky Rudd	25	0	0	0	0	1	0	9	6,233	13	3	2,810	75,905
18. Neil Bonnett	23	6	2	0	1	1	1	4	5,893	493	11	2,649	122,615
19. Jimmy Means	26	0	0	0	0	0	0	6	6,010	0	0	2,640	52,505
20. Tighe Scott	26	0	0	0	0	0	1	0	6,134	0	0	2,628	63,225
21. Sam Sommers	23	1	0	0	0	1	1	6	5,764	28	3	2,517	54,525
22. Ed Negre	24	0	0	0	0	0	0	0	5,523	0	0	2,214	42,665
23. Janet Guthrie	19	0	0	0	0	0	0	4	5,031	5	1	2,037	37,945
24. Donnie Allison	17	3	2	2	1	4	0	1	4,133	1,163	13	1,970	146,435
25. Dave Marcis	18	0	0	0	0	4	1	2	4,386	92	7	1,931	72,605
26. Tommy Gale	18	0	0	0	0	0	0	0	4,402	0	0	1,689	39,190
27. Dick May	13	0	0	0	0	0	0	0	3,977	0	0	1,324	21,690
28. Henley Gray	14	0	0	0	0	0	0	0	3,049	0	0	1,214	18,610
29. Bruce Hill	16	0	0	0	0	0	0	4	2,883	4	1	1,213	25,035
30. Lennie Pond	14	0	0	0	0	2	2	2	3,154	5	3	1,193	49,440
31. Butch Hartman	11	0	0	0	0	0	0	2	2,005	0	0	1,116	18,615
32. Ferrel Harris	11	0	0	0	0	0	0	0	2,979	0	0	1,088	19,365
33. Baxter Price	12	0	0	0	0	0	0	0	2,566	0	0	1,086	10,890
34. Coo Coo Marlin	11	0	0	0	0	1	0	4	2,930	1	1	1,004	42,450
35. Bill Elliott	10	0	0	0	0	0	0	2	2,082	0	0	926	20,075
36. Gary Myers	10	0	0	0	0	0	0	0	2,648	0	0	888	10,975
37. David Sisco	10	0	0	0	0	0	0	0	2,030	0	0	847	13,920
38. Terry Bivins	8	0	0	0	0	0	0	1	2,002	0	0	841	14,920
39. G. C. Spencer	8	0	0	0	0	0	0	1	1,817	0	0	785	15,755
40. Terry Ryan	7	0	0	0	0	0	0	1	1,142	0	0	702	12,405
41. Joe Mihalic	8	0	0	0	0	0	0	0	1,550	0	0	683	7,650
42. Elmo Langley	7	0	0	0	0	0	0	0	1,395	0	0	634	5,855
43. Dean Dalton	8	0	0	0	0	0	0	0	1,100	0	0	620	6,255
44. Earl Brooks	6	0	0	0	0	0	0	0	1,260	0	0	552	3,045
45. Bobby Wawak	8	0	0	0	0	0	0	0	1,633	0	0	522	13,455
46. Harold Miller	6	0	0	0	0	0	0	0	1,267	0	0	470	8,480
47. Junior Miller	5	0	0	0	0	0	0	0	1,028	0	0	467	2,475
48. Ramo Stott	5	0	0	0	0	0	0	0	688	0	0	440	10,170
49. Grant Adcox	6	0	0	0	0	0	0	0	776	0	0	413	8,750
50. Sonny Easley	3	0	0	0	0	0	1	1	360	0	0	386	9,490

LAPS COMPLETED

1.	Cale Yarborough	9,747
2.	Benny Parsons	9,410
3.	Darrell Waltrip	9,301
4.	Richard Petty	8,840
5.	Buddy Arrington	8,601
6.	James Hylton	8,375
7.	J. D. McDuffie	8,252
8.	Dick Brooks	8,191
9.	Cecil Gordon	8,133
10.	Buddy Baker	8,084
11.	Richard Childress	7,973
12.	Skip Manning	7,533
13.	Bobby Allison	7,024
14.	D. K. Ulrich	6,735
15.	Frank Warren	6,466
16.	Ricky Rudd	6,233
17.	Tighe Scott	6,134
18.	Jimmy Means	6,010
19.	Neil Bonnett	5,893
20.	Sam Sommers	5,764
21.	David Pearson	5,694
22.	Ed Negre	5,523
23.	Janet Guthrie	5,031
24.	Tommy Gale	4,402
25.	Dave Marcis	4,386
26.	Donnie Allison	4,133
27.	Dick May	3,977
28.	Lennie Pond	3,154
29.	Henley Gray	3,049
30.	Ferrel Harris	2,979

LAPS LED

1.	Cale Yarborough	3,218
2.	Richard Petty	1,403
3.	Benny Parsons	1,399
4.	Donnie Allison	1,163
5.	Darrell Waltrip	948
6.	David Pearson	868
7.	Neil Bonnett	493
8.	Bobby Allison	102
9.	Dave Marcis	92
10.	Buddy Baker	52
11.	Sam Sommers	28
12.	Richard Childress	27
13.	A. J. Foyt	20
14.	Skip Manning	13
	Ricky Rudd	13
16.	Dick Brooks	8
17.	Janet Guthrie	5
	Lennie Pond	5
19.	Bruce Hill	4
20.	James Hylton	3
21.	Coo Coo Marlin	1
	J. D. McDuffie	1
	Frank Warren	1

MILES LED

1.	Cale Yarborough	3,054
2.	Richard Petty	1,995
3.	Benny Parsons	1,629
4.	Donnie Allison	1,612
5.	David Pearson	1,153
6.	Darrell Waltrip	1,006
7.	Neil Bonnett	485
8.	Dave Marcis	157
9.	Buddy Baker	123
10.	Bobby Allison	118
11.	A. J. Foyt	50
12.	Sam Sommers	48
13.	Skip Manning	35
14.	Ricky Rudd	27
15.	Richard Childress	22
16.	Janet Guthrie	13
17.	Bruce Hill	11
18.	Dick Brooks	10
19.	James Hylton	8
20.	Lennie Pond	7
21.	J. D. McDuffie	3
22.	Frank Warren	3
23.	Coo Coo Marlin	2

MILES DRIVEN

1.	Cale Yarborough	11,382
2.	Benny Parsons	10,755
3.	Darrell Waltrip	10,589
4.	Richard Petty	10,418
5.	Buddy Arrington	10,037
6.	Buddy Baker	9,876
7.	J. D. McDuffie	9,688
8.	Cecil Gordon	9,604
9.	James Hylton	9,591
10.	Dick Brooks	9,511
11.	Richard Childress	9,411
12.	Skip Manning	8,355
13.	David Pearson	8,180
14.	Frank Warren	8,107
15.	Bobby Allison	7,822
16.	D. K. Ulrich	7,648
17.	Ricky Rudd	7,509
18.	Tighe Scott	7,467
19.	Sam Sommers	7,080
20.	Jimmy Means	6,759
21.	Neil Bonnett	6,390
22.	Janet Guthrie	6,182
23.	Tommy Gale	6,071
24.	Ed Negre	6,040
25.	Donnie Allison	5,910
26.	Dave Marcis	5,499
27.	Dick May	4,476
28.	Bruce Hill	4,290
29.	Coo Coo Marlin	4,210
30.	Lennie Pond	3,713

RACES LED

1.	Cale Yarborough	28
2.	Benny Parsons	25
3.	Richard Petty	24
4.	Darrell Waltrip	23
5.	David Pearson	17
6.	Donnie Allison	13
7.	Neil Bonnett	11
8.	Bobby Allison	9
9.	Buddy Baker	7
	Dave Marcis	7
11.	Richard Childress	4
12.	A. J. Foyt	3
	Lennie Pond	3
	Ricky Rudd	3
	Sam Sommers	3
16.	Dick Brooks	2

75

Driver	Starts	Poles	Finish						Laps	Laps Led	Races Led	Winston Cup Points	$
			1	2	3	4	5	6–10					

1978

	Driver	Starts	Poles	1	2	3	4	5	6–10	Laps	Laps Led	Races Led	Winston Cup Points	$
1.	Cale Yarborough	30	8	10	6	1	5	1	1	9,758	3,587	28	4,841	623,506
2.	Bobby Allison	30	1	5	3	4	0	2	8	9,283	1,043	19	4,367	411,517
3.	Darrell Waltrip	30	2	6	6	4	1	2	1	9,445	2,171	26	4,362	413,908
4.	Benny Parsons	30	2	3	3	6	2	1	6	9,609	824	21	4,350	329,993
5.	Dave Marcis	30	0	0	1	3	8	2	10	9,672	115	12	4,335	205,871
6.	Richard Petty	30	0	0	3	3	3	2	6	8,904	419	15	3,949	242,273
7.	Lennie Pond	28	5	1	2	2	1	5	8	8,443	319	12	3,794	181,096
8.	Dick Brooks	30	0	0	0	0	1	4	12	8,689	24	2	3,769	137,590
9.	Buddy Arrington	30	0	0	0	0	0	1	6	9,580	0	0	3,626	112,960
10.	Richard Childress	30	0	0	0	1	0	0	11	8,946	52	4	3,566	108,702
11.	J. D. McDuffie	30	1	0	0	0	0	1	5	7,300	15	4	3,255	86,857
12.	Neil Bonnett	30	3	0	1	1	2	3	5	6,278	316	6	3,129	162,742
13.	Tighe Scott	29	0	0	0	0	0	0	7	6,626	3	1	3,110	87,912
14.	Frank Warren	30	0	0	0	0	0	0	0	8,481	0	0	3,036	68,173
15.	Dick May	28	0	0	0	0	0	0	2	7,221	0	0	2,936	65,291
16.	David Pearson	22	7	4	2	1	1	3	0	5,375	757	13	2,756	198,775
17.	Jimmy Means	27	0	0	0	0	0	0	2	7,083	0	0	2,756	61,725
18.	Ronnie Thomas	27	0	0	0	0	0	0	2	7,287	0	0	2,733	75,815
19.	Cecil Gordon	26	0	0	0	0	0	0	1	6,773	0	0	2,641	53,815
20.	Tommy Gale	26	0	0	0	0	0	0	0	6,980	0	0	2,639	60,765
21.	Roger Hamby	26	0	0	0	0	0	0	2	7,181	0	0	2,617	41,315
22.	D. K. Ulrich	22	0	0	0	0	0	0	3	6,175	1	1	2,452	54,550
23.	Baxter Price	24	0	0	0	0	0	0	0	7,343	0	0	2,418	36,560
24.	Buddy Baker	19	1	0	1	1	1	1	4	4,319	354	10	2,130	111,765
25.	Donnie Allison	17	0	1	2	2	1	1	1	3,876	209	12	1,993	127,475
26.	James Hylton	19	0	0	0	0	0	0	4	5,774	16	2	1,965	48,045
27.	Gary Myers	19	0	0	0	0	0	0	0	5,524	0	0	1,915	22,140
28.	Ed Negre	21	0	0	0	0	0	0	1	4,826	0	0	1,857	28,995
29.	Skip Manning	17	0	0	0	0	1	0	3	4,410	0	0	1,802	55,470
30.	Grant Adcox	14	0	0	0	0	0	1	2	3,072	0	0	1,802	37,100
31.	Ricky Rudd	13	0	0	0	0	0	0	4	2,535	16	5	1,260	50,630
32.	Bruce Hill	14	0	0	0	0	0	0	2	2,805	0	0	1,214	25,770
33.	Bill Elliott	10	0	0	0	0	0	0	5	2,278	0	0	1,176	42,215
34.	Al Holbert	12	0	0	0	0	0	0	3	2,479	0	0	1,142	31,075
35.	Ferrel Harris	14	0	0	0	0	0	0	5	2,915	0	0	1,066	39,685
36.	Coo Coo Marlin	9	0	0	0	0	0	0	2	1,518	4	2	765	19,415
37.	Blackie Wangerin	10	0	0	0	0	0	0	0	1,342	0	0	760	13,515
38.	Bobby Wawak	8	0	0	0	0	0	0	0	1,512	0	0	680	5,870
39.	Terry Labonte	5	0	0	0	0	1	0	2	1,849	0	0	659	21,395
40.	Ralph Jones	7	0	0	0	0	0	0	0	1,871	0	0	634	6,305
41.	Janet Guthrie	7	0	0	0	0	0	0	1	1,147	0	0	592	17,120
42.	Earle Canavan	9	0	0	0	0	0	0	0	2,111	0	0	559	8,740
43.	Dale Earnhardt	5	0	0	0	0	1	0	1	1,359	0	0	558	20,745
44.	Roland Wlodyka	6	0	0	0	0	0	0	0	1,172	0	0	549	9,910
45.	Joe Frasson	5	0	0	0	0	0	0	0	1,436	0	0	533	9,210
46.	Nelson Oswald	6	0	0	0	0	0	0	0	1,103	0	0	501	2,955
47.	Joe Mihalic	6	0	0	0	0	0	0	0	1,216	0	0	419	6,030
48.	Jim Thirkettle	3	0	0	0	0	0	0	2	393	1	1	389	6,850
49.	Jimmy Insolo	3	0	0	0	0	0	0	2	345	5	2	369	8,665
50.	Satch Worley	4	0	0	0	0	0	0	1	1,298	0	0	368	6,205

LAPS COMPLETED

1.	Cale Yarborough	9,758
2.	Dave Marcis	9,672
3.	Benny Parsons	9,609
4.	Buddy Arrington	9,580
5.	Darrell Waltrip	9,445
6.	Bobby Allison	9,283
7.	Richard Childress	8,946
8.	Richard Petty	8,904
9.	Dick Brooks	8,689
10.	Frank Warren	8,481
11.	Lennie Pond	8,443
12.	Baxter Price	7,343
13.	J. D. McDuffie	7,300
14.	Ronnie Thomas	7,287
15.	Dick May	7,221
16.	Roger Hamby	7,181
17.	Jimmy Means	7,083
18.	Tommy Gale	6,980
19.	Cecil Gordon	6,773
20.	Tighe Scott	6,626
21.	Neil Bonnett	6,278
22.	D. K. Ulrich	6,175
23.	James Hylton	5,774
24.	Gary Myers	5,524
25.	David Pearson	5,375
26.	Ed Negre	4,826
27.	Skip Manning	4,410
28.	Buddy Baker	4,319
29.	Donnie Allison	3,876
30.	Grant Adcox	3,072

LAPS LED

1.	Cale Yarborough	3,587
2.	Darrell Waltrip	2,171
3.	Bobby Allison	1,043
4.	Benny Parsons	824
5.	David Pearson	757
6.	Richard Petty	419
7.	Buddy Baker	354
8.	Lennie Pond	319
9.	Neil Bonnett	316
10.	Donnie Allison	209
11.	Dave Marcis	115
12.	Richard Childress	52
13.	Harry Gant	45
14.	Dick Brooks	24
15.	James Hylton	16
	Ricky Rudd	16
17.	J. D. McDuffie	15
18.	Jimmy Insolo	5
19.	Coo Coo Marlin	4
20.	Tighe Scott	3
21.	Richard White	2
22.	Jim Thirkettle	1
	D. K. Ulrich	1

MILES LED

1.	Cale Yarborough	3,867
2.	Darrell Waltrip	2,200
3.	Bobby Allison	1,517
4.	David Pearson	1,163
5.	Benny Parsons	767
6.	Buddy Baker	675
7.	Richard Petty	585
8.	Donnie Allison	342
9.	Lennie Pond	233
10.	Neil Bonnett	193
11.	Dave Marcis	144
12.	Richard Childress	30
13.	Ricky Rudd	26
14.	Dick Brooks	24
15.	Harry Gant	24
16.	J. D. McDuffie	18
17.	James Hylton	16
18.	Jimmy Insolo	13
19.	Coo Coo Marlin	6
20.	Richard White	5
21.	Tighe Scott	3
22.	Jim Thirkettle	3
23.	D. K. Ulrich	2

MILES DRIVEN

1.	Cale Yarborough	11,366
2.	Dave Marcis	10,992
3.	Benny Parsons	10,832
4.	Buddy Arrington	10,739
5.	Darrell Waltrip	10,541
6.	Bobby Allison	10,539
7.	Richard Petty	10,162
8.	Richard Childress	10,060
9.	Dick Brooks	10,023
10.	Frank Warren	9,827
11.	Lennie Pond	9,412
12.	Tommy Gale	8,867
13.	J. D. McDuffie	8,715
14.	Dick May	8,622
15.	Tighe Scott	8,223
16.	Jimmy Means	7,992
17.	Ronnie Thomas	7,769
18.	Roger Hamby	7,688
19.	Baxter Price	7,610
20.	David Pearson	7,602
21.	D. K. Ulrich	7,425
22.	Cecil Gordon	7,191
23.	Neil Bonnett	6,760
24.	Buddy Baker	6,594
25.	Gary Myers	6,134
26.	Donnie Allison	6,128
27.	Skip Manning	5,486
28.	James Hylton	5,018
29.	Ed Negre	4,950
30.	Grant Adcox	4,586

RACES LED

1.	Cale Yarborough	28
2.	Darrell Waltrip	26
3.	Benny Parsons	21
4.	Bobby Allison	19
5.	Richard Petty	15
6.	David Pearson	13
7.	Donnie Allison	12
	Dave Marcis	12
	Lennie Pond	12
10.	Buddy Baker	10
11.	Neil Bonnett	6
12.	Ricky Rudd	5
13.	Richard Childress	4
	J. D. McDuffie	4
15.	Dick Brooks	2
	James Hylton	2
	Jimmy Insolo	2
	Coo Coo Marlin	2

1979

Driver	Starts	Poles	Finish 1	2	3	4	5	6–10	Laps	Laps Led	Races Led	Winston Cup Points	$
1. Richard Petty	31	1	5	7	2	4	5	4	9,367	1,150	16	4,830	561,934
2. Darrell Waltrip	31	5	7	4	5	1	2	3	9,994	2,128	26	4,819	557,012
3. Bobby Allison	31	3	5	7	2	4	0	4	9,885	1,854	24	4,633	428,801
4. Cale Yarborough	31	1	4	2	6	4	3	3	9,677	1,323	22	4,604	440,129
5. Benny Parsons	31	1	2	2	2	5	5	5	9,335	736	12	4,256	264,930
6. Joe Millikan	31	1	0	1	1	0	3	15	9,122	188	8	4,014	229,713
7. Dale Earnhardt	27	4	1	1	3	4	2	6	8,340	604	16	3,749	274,810
8. Richard Childress	31	0	0	0	0	0	1	10	9,109	13	2	3,735	132,922
9. Ricky Rudd	28	0	0	0	2	0	2	13	8,836	22	4	3,642	150,898
10. Terry Labonte	31	0	0	0	1	0	1	11	8,766	8	4	3,615	134,653
11. Buddy Arrington	31	0	0	0	1	0	0	6	8,452	2	1	3,589	131,833
12. D. K. Ulrich	31	0	0	0	0	0	0	5	8,995	0	0	3,508	113,458
13. J. D. McDuffie	31	0	0	0	0	0	1	6	8,014	116	3	3,473	113,478
14. James Hylton	30	0	0	0	0	0	0	5	8,658	11	4	3,405	97,428
15. Buddy Baker	26	7	3	2	3	3	1	3	6,107	1,083	20	3,249	342,148
16. Frank Warren	31	0	0	0	0	0	0	3	8,477	0	0	3,199	94,539
17. Ronnie Thomas	30	0	0	0	0	0	0	3	6,928	1	1	2,912	100,079
18. Tommy Gale	27	0	0	0	0	0	0	1	7,054	0	0	2,795	72,809
19. Cecil Gordon	28	0	0	0	0	0	0	0	7,419	0	0	2,737	66,275
20. Dave Marcis	25	0	0	0	0	0	1	5	6,842	20	4	2,736	56,434
21. Harry Gant	25	1	0	0	0	0	0	5	6,226	29	4	2,664	47,185
22. Dick Brooks	27	0	0	0	1	0	0	7	6,307	16	1	2,622	61,985
23. Jimmy Means	27	0	0	0	0	0	0	1	5,431	0	0	2,575	55,560
24. Donnie Allison	20	1	0	2	1	2	2	3	4,841	293	9	2,508	144,770
25. Baxter Price	24	0	0	0	0	0	0	0	6,791	0	0	2,364	45,165
26. Neil Bonnett	21	4	3	0	0	1	0	2	4,213	569	14	2,223	151,235
27. Tighe Scott	17	0	0	0	0	1	0	6	3,834	0	0	1,879	88,010
28. Bill Elliott	14	0	0	1	0	0	0	4	3,691	8	3	1,548	58,200
29. Lennie Pond	15	0	0	0	0	0	0	2	3,043	14	2	1,415	42,970
30. Dick May	19	0	0	0	0	0	0	0	3,387	0	0	1,390	26,345
31. Roger Hamby	12	0	0	0	0	0	0	0	2,974	0	0	1,231	21,000
32. David Pearson	9	2	1	2	0	1	0	1	2,271	264	6	1,203	99,180
33. Coo Coo Marlin	7	0	0	0	0	0	0	2	907	0	0	613	27,540
34. Bruce Hill	7	0	0	0	0	0	0	0	1,352	0	0	594	17,260
35. Blackie Wangerin	7	0	0	0	0	0	0	0	894	0	0	571	14,300
36. Grant Adcox	6	0	0	0	0	0	0	0	1,132	5	1	560	15,290
37. Kyle Petty	5	0	0	0	0	0	0	1	1,069	0	0	559	10,810
38. Chuck Bown	7	0	0	0	0	0	0	2	1,388	0	0	523	31,380
39. John Anderson	4	0	0	0	0	0	1	0	1,263	1	1	496	11,210
40. Ralph Jones	6	0	0	0	0	0	0	0	729	0	0	477	12,785
41. Earle Canavan	7	0	0	0	0	0	0	0	698	0	0	456	6,675
42. Slick Johnson	4	0	0	0	0	0	0	1	1,039	0	0	431	5,360
43. Nelson Oswald	6	0	0	0	0	0	0	0	842	0	0	431	3,610
44. Dave Watson	4	0	0	0	0	0	0	1	1,092	7	2	413	7,170
45. Al Holbert	6	0	0	0	0	0	0	0	938	5	1	402	14,170
46. Bobby Wawak	4	0	0	0	0	0	0	0	740	0	0	376	7,295
47. Jody Ridley	3	0	0	0	0	0	1	1	787	0	0	374	11,245
48. Bill Hollar	5	0	0	0	0	0	0	0	552	0	0	371	2,545
49. Rick Newsom	4	0	0	0	0	0	0	0	484	0	0	355	5,530
50. Bill Schmitt	3	0	0	0	0	1	0	0	325	0	0	342	11,695

LAPS COMPLETED

1. Darrell Waltrip — 9,994
2. Bobby Allison — 9,885
3. Cale Yarborough — 9,677
4. Richard Petty — 9,367
5. Benny Parsons — 9,335
6. Joe Millikan — 9,122
7. Richard Childress — 9,109
8. D. K. Ulrich — 8,995
9. Ricky Rudd — 8,836
10. Terry Labonte — 8,766
11. James Hylton — 8,658
12. Frank Warren — 8,477
13. Buddy Arrington — 8,452
14. Dale Earnhardt — 8,340
15. J. D. McDuffie — 8,014
16. Cecil Gordon — 7,419
17. Tommy Gale — 7,054
18. Ronnie Thomas — 6,928
19. Dave Marcis — 6,842
20. Baxter Price — 6,791
21. Dick Brooks — 6,307
22. Harry Gant — 6,226
23. Buddy Baker — 6,107
24. Jimmy Means — 5,431
25. Donnie Allison — 4,841
26. Neil Bonnett — 4,213
27. Tighe Scott — 3,834
28. Bill Elliott — 3,691
29. Dick May — 3,387
30. Lennie Pond — 3,043

LAPS LED

1. Darrell Waltrip — 2,128
2. Bobby Allison — 1,854
3. Cale Yarborough — 1,323
4. Richard Petty — 1,150
5. Buddy Baker — 1,083
6. Benny Parsons — 736
7. Dale Earnhardt — 604
8. Neil Bonnett — 569
9. Donnie Allison — 293
10. David Pearson — 264
11. Joe Millikan — 188
12. J. D. McDuffie — 116
13. Harry Gant — 29
14. Ricky Rudd — 22
15. Dave Marcis — 20
16. Dick Brooks — 16
17. Lennie Pond — 14
18. Richard Childress — 13
19. James Hylton — 11
    Sterling Marlin — 11
21. Bill Elliott — 8
    Terry Labonte — 8
23. A. J. Foyt — 7
    Dave Watson — 7
25. Geoff Bodine — 6
26. Grant Adcox — 5
    Al Holbert — 5
28. Buddy Arrington — 2
    Bill Green — 2

MILES LED

1. Darrell Waltrip — 2,629
2. Bobby Allison — 1,796
3. Cale Yarborough — 1,592
4. Buddy Baker — 1,276
5. Neil Bonnett — 1,058
6. Richard Petty — 1,000
7. Dale Earnhardt — 775
8. Benny Parsons — 769
9. Donnie Allison — 492
10. David Pearson — 359
11. Joe Millikan — 154
12. J. D. McDuffie — 70
13. Dick Brooks — 40
14. Harry Gant — 32
15. Ricky Rudd — 30
16. Lennie Pond — 23
17. A. J. Foyt — 18
18. Dave Marcis — 17
19. Terry Labonte — 16
20. Geoff Bodine — 15
21. Grant Adcox — 13
22. Al Holbert — 13
23. James Hylton — 13
24. Bill Elliott — 12
25. Dave Watson — 12
26. Richard Childress — 10
27. Sterling Marlin — 7
28. Buddy Arrington — 5
29. Bill Green — 4
30. Ronnie Thomas — 2

MILES DRIVEN

1. Darrell Waltrip — 11,768
2. Bobby Allison — 11,237
3. Cale Yarborough — 11,192
4. Richard Petty — 10,933
5. Benny Parsons — 10,574
6. Joe Millikan — 10,509
7. Richard Childress — 10,442
8. Buddy Arrington — 10,333
9. Frank Warren — 10,046
10. D. K. Ulrich — 10,043
11. Ricky Rudd — 9,917
12. Terry Labonte — 9,886
13. J. D. McDuffie — 9,634
14. James Hylton — 9,603
15. Dale Earnhardt — 9,357
16. Cecil Gordon — 8,163
17. Tommy Gale — 8,092
18. Ronnie Thomas — 7,840
19. Dave Marcis — 7,634
20. Dick Brooks — 7,422
21. Buddy Baker — 7,421
22. Harry Gant — 7,367
23. Baxter Price — 6,665
24. Donnie Allison — 6,345
25. Jimmy Means — 6,317
26. Neil Bonnett — 6,132
27. Tighe Scott — 5,684
28. Bill Elliott — 4,822
29. Lennie Pond — 3,864
30. Dick May — 3,714

RACES LED

1. Darrell Waltrip — 26
2. Bobby Allison — 24
3. Cale Yarborough — 22
4. Buddy Baker — 20
5. Dale Earnhardt — 16
   Richard Petty — 16
7. Neil Bonnett — 14
8. Benny Parsons — 12
9. Donnie Allison — 9
10. Joe Millikan — 8
11. David Pearson — 6
12. Harry Gant — 4
    James Hylton — 4
    Terry Labonte — 4
    Dave Marcis — 4
    Ricky Rudd — 4
17. Bill Elliott — 3
    J. D. McDuffie — 3
19. Richard Childress — 2
    A. J. Foyt — 2
    Lennie Pond — 2
    Dave Watson — 2

1980

	Driver	Starts	Poles	Finish 1	2	3	4	5	6–10	Laps	Laps Led	Races Led	Winston Cup Points	$
1.	Dale Earnhardt	31	0	5	3	4	3	4	5	9,615	1,185	25	4,661	671,991
2.	Cale Yarborough	31	14	6	4	4	4	1	3	9,440	2,810	28	4,642	567,891
3.	Benny Parsons	31	2	3	3	2	4	4	5	8,676	659	19	4,278	411,519
4.	Richard Petty	31	0	2	4	3	2	4	4	9,314	713	23	4,255	397,318
5.	Darrell Waltrip	31	5	5	3	2	6	0	1	9,015	2,023	28	4,239	405,711
6.	Bobby Allison	31	2	4	2	4	1	1	6	8,244	948	18	4,019	378,970
7.	Jody Ridley	31	0	0	0	0	0	2	16	9,579	2	2	3,972	204,883
8.	Terry Labonte	31	0	1	0	1	1	3	10	8,760	46	6	3,766	222,502
9.	Dave Marcis	31	0	0	0	1	2	1	10	9,012	94	14	3,745	150,165
10.	Richard Childress	31	0	0	0	0	0	0	10	8,693	21	6	3,742	157,420
11.	Harry Gant	31	0	0	3	2	2	2	5	7,986	263	10	3,703	177,150
12.	Buddy Arrington	31	0	0	0	0	0	0	7	8,765	0	0	3,461	120,355
13.	James Hylton	31	0	0	0	0	0	0	4	9,232	26	1	3,449	109,230
14.	Ronnie Thomas	30	0	0	0	0	0	0	4	7,522	0	0	3,066	94,730
15.	Cecil Gordon	29	0	0	0	0	0	0	3	7,864	0	0	2,993	83,300
16.	J. D. McDuffie	31	0	0	0	0	0	0	3	6,044	0	0	2,968	82,402
17.	Jimmy Means	28	0	0	0	0	0	0	0	7,684	0	0	2,947	105,628
18.	Tommy Gale	29	0	0	0	0	0	0	0	7,605	0	0	2,885	84,279
19.	Neil Bonnett	22	0	2	4	1	1	2	3	5,173	331	14	2,865	231,854
20.	Roger Hamby	25	0	0	0	0	0	0	0	6,777	0	0	2,606	51,534
21.	Buddy Baker	19	6	2	2	4	2	0	2	5,042	671	15	2,603	275,200
22.	Lake Speed	19	0	0	0	0	0	0	5	4,019	2	1	1,853	69,670
23.	Slick Johnson	18	0	0	0	0	0	0	5	4,724	7	2	1,851	35,460
24.	John Anderson	20	0	0	0	0	0	0	2	4,282	0	0	1,805	48,265
25.	Bobby Wawak	19	0	0	0	0	0	0	1	4,065	0	0	1,742	21,080
26.	Donnie Allison	18	1	0	0	1	0	2	3	3,794	231	7	1,730	92,640
27.	Dick Brooks	19	0	0	0	0	0	2	3	3,978	6	1	1,698	60,700
28.	Kyle Petty	15	0	0	0	0	0	0	6	3,722	0	0	1,690	36,045
29.	Baxter Price	18	0	0	0	0	0	0	0	4,890	0	0	1,689	26,615
30.	Lennie Pond	17	0	0	0	1	1	0	5	3,396	68	6	1,558	62,265
31.	Junior Miller	16	0	0	0	0	0	0	0	3,848	0	0	1,402	23,420
32.	Dick May	21	0	0	0	0	0	0	2	5,767	0	0	1,323	42,945
33.	Joe Millikan	12	0	0	0	0	1	1	4	2,796	5	3	1,274	74,765
34.	Bill Elliott	12	0	0	0	0	0	0	4	2,572	4	4	1,232	42,545
35.	Ricky Rudd	13	0	0	0	0	1	0	2	2,719	7	2	1,213	50,500
36.	Bill Elswick	12	0	0	0	0	0	0	0	2,717	0	0	1,053	15,600
37.	David Pearson	9	1	1	2	1	0	0	1	1,787	172	7	1,004	102,730
38.	D. K. Ulrich	11	0	0	0	0	0	0	1	1,734	0	0	935	23,055
39.	Tighe Scott	10	0	0	0	0	0	1	1	1,066	4	1	791	21,925
40.	Frank Warren	7	0	0	0	0	0	0	0	1,591	0	0	559	18,375
41.	Tim Richmond	5	0	0	0	0	0	0	0	1,359	0	0	527	14,925
42.	Bill Schmitt	4	0	0	0	0	0	1	0	579	0	0	503	21,610
43.	Buck Simmons	6	0	0	0	0	0	0	0	1,333	0	0	495	6,365
44.	Rick Newsom	6	0	0	0	0	0	0	0	1,179	0	0	483	3,830
45.	Dave Dion	4	0	0	0	0	0	0	1	1,075	0	0	441	5,015
46.	Don Whittington	7	0	0	0	0	0	0	1	659	0	0	429	17,610
47.	Steve Moore	4	0	0	0	0	0	0	0	735	0	0	412	9,040
48.	Tommy Houston	4	0	0	0	0	0	0	0	1,170	10	1	396	5,020
49.	Sterling Marlin	5	0	0	0	0	0	0	2	1,311	0	0	387	29,810
50.	Bruce Hill	6	0	0	0	0	0	0	0	418	0	0	348	7,540

LAPS COMPLETED

1. Dale Earnhardt — 9,615
2. Jody Ridley — 9,579
3. Cale Yarborough — 9,440
4. Richard Petty — 9,314
5. James Hylton — 9,232
6. Darrell Waltrip — 9,015
7. Dave Marcis — 9,012
8. Buddy Arrington — 8,765
9. Terry Labonte — 8,760
10. Richard Childress — 8,693
11. Benny Parsons — 8,676
12. Bobby Allison — 8,244
13. Harry Gant — 7,986
14. Cecil Gordon — 7,864
15. Jimmy Means — 7,684
16. Tommy Gale — 7,605
17. Ronnie Thomas — 7,522
18. Roger Hamby — 6,777
19. J. D. McDuffie — 6,044
20. Dick May — 5,767
21. Neil Bonnett — 5,173
22. Buddy Baker — 5,042
23. Baxter Price — 4,890
24. Slick Johnson — 4,724
25. John Anderson — 4,282
26. Bobby Wawak — 4,065
27. Lake Speed — 4,019
28. Dick Brooks — 3,978
29. Junior Miller — 3,848
30. Donnie Allison — 3,794

LAPS LED

1. Cale Yarborough — 2,810
2. Darrell Waltrip — 2,023
3. Dale Earnhardt — 1,185
4. Bobby Allison — 948
5. Richard Petty — 713
6. Buddy Baker — 671
7. Benny Parsons — 659
8. Neil Bonnett — 331
9. Harry Gant — 263
10. Donnie Allison — 231
11. David Pearson — 172
12. Dave Marcis — 94
13. Lennie Pond — 68
14. Terry Labonte — 46
15. James Hylton — 26
16. Richard Childress — 21
17. Tommy Houston — 10
18. Slick Johnson — 7
    Ricky Rudd — 7
20. Dick Brooks — 6
21. Joe Millikan — 5
    Connie Saylor — 5
23. Bill Elliott — 4
    Kenny Hemphill — 4
    Tighe Scott — 4
26. Roy Smith — 3
27. Jody Ridley — 2
    Lake Speed — 2

MILES LED

1. Cale Yarborough — 3,155
2. Darrell Waltrip — 2,300
3. Dale Earnhardt — 1,426
4. Buddy Baker — 1,156
5. Bobby Allison — 930
6. Benny Parsons — 753
7. Neil Bonnett — 598
8. Richard Petty — 544
9. David Pearson — 273
10. Donnie Allison — 258
11. Harry Gant — 257
12. Dave Marcis — 108
13. Terry Labonte — 54
14. Lennie Pond — 48
15. James Hylton — 39
16. Richard Childress — 28
17. Tighe Scott — 11
18. Ricky Rudd — 11
19. Dick Brooks — 9
20. Slick Johnson — 9
21. Roy Smith — 8
22. Bill Elliott — 8
23. Connie Saylor — 8
24. Tommy Houston — 5
25. Lake Speed — 5
26. Joe Millikan — 5
27. Jody Ridley — 4
28. Kenny Hemphill — 4

MILES DRIVEN

1. Dale Earnhardt — 11,136
2. Cale Yarborough — 11,015
3. Jody Ridley — 10,976
4. Richard Childress — 10,692
5. James Hylton — 10,547
6. Richard Petty — 10,147
7. Benny Parsons — 10,035
8. Terry Labonte — 9,951
9. Buddy Arrington — 9,936
10. Dave Marcis — 9,790
11. Darrell Waltrip — 9,763
12. Ronnie Thomas — 9,081
13. Bobby Allison — 9,027
14. Cecil Gordon — 8,978
15. Jimmy Means — 8,890
16. Tommy Gale — 8,813
17. Harry Gant — 8,774
18. Roger Hamby — 7,588
19. Neil Bonnett — 7,503
20. J. D. McDuffie — 7,407
21. Buddy Baker — 6,952
22. Dick May — 6,360
23. Lake Speed — 6,271
24. Donnie Allison — 5,197
25. Dick Brooks — 5,106
26. John Anderson — 5,087
27. Kyle Petty — 4,941
28. Baxter Price — 4,929
29. Slick Johnson — 4,731
30. Lennie Pond — 4,512

RACES LED

1. Darrell Waltrip — 28
   Cale Yarborough — 28
3. Dale Earnhardt — 25
4. Richard Petty — 23
5. Benny Parsons — 19
6. Bobby Allison — 18
7. Buddy Baker — 15
8. Neil Bonnett — 14
   Dave Marcis — 14
10. Harry Gant — 10
11. Donnie Allison — 7
    David Pearson — 7
13. Richard Childress — 6
    Terry Labonte — 6
    Lennie Pond — 6
16. Bill Elliott — 4
17. Joe Millikan — 3
18. Slick Johnson — 2
    Jody Ridley — 2
    Ricky Rudd — 2
    Connie Saylor — 2

Driver	Starts	Poles	Finish 1	2	3	4	5	6–10	Laps	Laps Led	Races Led	Winston Cup Points	$
1981													
1. Darrell Waltrip	31	11	12	6	3	0	0	4	9,575	2,517	27	4,880	799,134
2. Bobby Allison	31	2	5	7	4	3	2	5	10,098	1,182	23	4,827	680,957
3. Harry Gant	31	3	0	7	1	4	1	5	9,082	1,169	20	4,210	280,047
4. Terry Labonte	31	2	0	1	3	2	2	9	9,074	114	14	4,052	348,703
5. Jody Ridley	31	0	1	0	0	1	1	15	8,971	28	6	4,002	267,605
6. Ricky Rudd	31	3	0	3	4	3	4	3	8,942	443	12	3,988	395,685
7. Dale Earnhardt	31	0	0	2	3	2	2	8	8,134	300	12	3,975	353,972
8. Richard Petty	31	0	3	1	4	3	1	4	7,276	546	21	3,880	396,072
9. Dave Marcis	31	1	0	0	2	1	1	5	8,004	178	15	3,507	162,213
10. Benny Parsons	31	0	3	0	3	0	4	2	6,709	537	10	3,449	311,093
11. Buddy Arrington	31	0	0	0	0	0	0	7	8,344	0	0	3,381	133,928
12. Kyle Petty	31	0	0	0	0	0	1	9	7,402	20	3	3,335	117,433
13. Morgan Shepherd	29	1	1	0	0	2	0	7	7,441	518	6	3,261	170,473
14. Jimmy Means	30	0	0	0	0	0	0	2	8,647	0	0	3,142	105,628
15. Tommy Gale	30	0	0	0	0	0	0	0	9,015	2	1	3,140	110,518
16. Tim Richmond	29	0	0	0	0	0	0	6	8,266	24	2	3,091	96,448
17. J. D. McDuffie	28	0	0	0	0	0	0	1	7,110	8	2	2,996	105,499
18. Lake Speed	27	0	0	0	0	0	0	6	6,757	14	2	2,817	94,069
19. James Hylton	28	0	0	0	0	0	0	0	7,051	12	2	2,753	87,305
20. Joe Millikan	23	0	0	0	1	0	2	7	6,735	15	4	2,682	148,400
21. Ron Bouchard	22	1	1	0	0	1	3	7	6,155	12	2	2,594	152,855
22. Neil Bonnett	22	1	3	1	0	3	0	1	4,917	1,549	16	2,449	181,670
23. Cecil Gordon	25	0	0	0	0	0	0	0	5,587	0	0	2,320	55,980
24. Cale Yarborough	18	2	2	1	2	0	1	4	4,922	769	13	2,201	150,840
25. Richard Childress	21	0	0	0	0	1	0	0	5,218	16	3	2,144	71,125
26. Ronnie Thomas	23	0	0	0	0	0	0	0	5,756	0	0	2,138	53,605
27. Buddy Baker	16	0	0	1	0	2	3	3	3,562	110	9	1,904	115,095
28. Joe Ruttman	17	0	0	1	0	0	1	5	4,194	106	7	1,851	137,275
29. Mike Alexander	19	0	0	0	0	0	0	3	4,340	4	1	1,784	34,055
30. Bill Elliott	13	1	0	0	0	1	0	6	2,777	33	3	1,442	70,320
31. Bobby Wawak	14	0	0	0	0	0	0	1	2,734	0	0	1,212	21,790
32. D. K. Ulrich	15	0	0	0	0	1	0	0	4,504	0	0	1,191	38,095
33. Johnny Rutherford	12	0	0	0	0	0	1	1	2,432	5	1	1,140	38,095
34. Lennie Pond	12	0	0	0	0	0	0	0	3,083	0	0	1,100	29,045
35. Elliott Forbes-Robinson	11	0	0	0	0	0	0	3	2,169	0	0	1,020	27,350
36. Rick Newsom	9	0	0	0	0	0	0	0	1,676	0	0	768	8,625
37. Dick May	9	0	0	0	0	0	0	1	1,843	0	0	754	26,380
38. Stan Barrett	10	0	0	0	0	0	0	1	1,559	4	2	718	28,540
39. Connie Saylor	7	0	0	0	0	0	0	0	1,267	0	0	664	19,715
40. Gary Balough	10	0	0	0	0	0	0	1	2,267	1	1	656	34,430
41. Rick Wilson	8	0	0	0	0	0	0	0	989	7	2	639	15,625
42. Mark Martin	5	2	0	0	1	0	0	1	1,478	76	2	615	13,950
43. Bruce Hill	8	0	0	0	0	0	0	0	880	0	0	596	15,485
44. Donnie Allison	6	0	0	0	0	0	1	0	1,306	2	1	527	38,745
45. Geoff Bodine	5	0	0	0	0	0	0	1	945	14	2	420	15,000
46. Joe Fields	6	0	0	0	0	0	0	0	1,681	0	0	418	7,750
47. Jack Ingram	5	0	0	0	0	0	0	1	822	0	0	377	9,965
48. Randy Ogden	4	0	0	0	0	0	0	0	577	0	0	367	3,905
49. Jim Robinson	3	0	0	0	0	0	0	2	264	0	0	351	9,505
50. Don Waterman	3	0	0	0	0	0	0	1	301	1	1	351	8,570

LAPS COMPLETED		LAPS LED		MILES LED		MILES DRIVEN		RACES LED	
1. Bobby Allison	10,098	1. Darrell Waltrip	2,517	1. Darrell Waltrip	2,330	1. Bobby Allison	11,609	1. Darrell Waltrip	27
2. Darrell Waltrip	9,575	2. Neil Bonnett	1,549	2. Neil Bonnett	2,055	2. Darrell Waltrip	10,974	2. Bobby Allison	23
3. Harry Gant	9,082	3. Bobby Allison	1,182	3. Bobby Allison	1,762	3. Terry Labonte	10,530	3. Richard Petty	21
4. Terry Labonte	9,074	4. Harry Gant	1,169	4. Harry Gant	1,191	4. Jody Ridley	10,528	4. Harry Gant	20
5. Tommy Gale	9,015	5. Cale Yarborough	769	5. Cale Yarborough	1,023	5. Harry Gant	10,253	5. Neil Bonnett	16
6. Jody Ridley	8,971	6. Richard Petty	546	6. Richard Petty	772	6. Dale Earnhardt	10,062	6. Dave Marcis	15
7. Ricky Rudd	8,942	7. Benny Parsons	537	7. Benny Parsons	519	7. Tommy Gale	9,926	7. Terry Labonte	14
8. Jimmy Means	8,647	8. Morgan Shepherd	518	8. Dale Earnhardt	479	8. Ricky Rudd	9,879	8. Cale Yarborough	13
9. Buddy Arrington	8,344	9. Ricky Rudd	443	9. Ricky Rudd	359	9. Buddy Arrington	9,443	9. Dale Earnhardt	12
10. Tim Richmond	8,266	10. Dale Earnhardt	300	10. Morgan Shepherd	288	10. Jimmy Means	9,393	Ricky Rudd	12
11. Dale Earnhardt	8,134	11. Dave Marcis	178	11. Buddy Baker	272	11. Dave Marcis	9,255	11. Benny Parsons	10
12. Dave Marcis	8,004	12. Terry Labonte	114	12. Terry Labonte	227	12. Tim Richmond	9,076	12. Buddy Baker	9
13. Morgan Shepherd	7,441	13. Buddy Baker	110	13. Joe Ruttman	157	13. J. D. McDuffie	8,871	13. Joe Ruttman	7
14. Kyle Petty	7,402	14. Joe Ruttman	106	14. Dave Marcis	143	14. Richard Petty	8,602	14. Jody Ridley	6
15. Richard Petty	7,276	15. Mark Martin	76	15. David Pearson	55	15. James Hylton	8,509	Morgan Shepherd	6
16. J. D. McDuffie	7,110	16. David Pearson	48	16. Bill Elliott	44	16. Kyle Petty	8,483	16. Joe Millikan	4
17. James Hylton	7,051	17. Bill Elliott	33	17. Mark Martin	42	17. Morgan Shepherd	7,919	17. Richard Childress	3
18. Lake Speed	6,757	18. Butch Lindley	28	18. Richard Childress	41	18. Lake Speed	7,557	Bill Elliott	3
19. Joe Millikan	6,735	Jody Ridley	28	19. Lake Speed	35	19. Benny Parsons	7,515	David Pearson	3
20. Benny Parsons	6,709	20. Tim Richmond	24	20. Kyle Petty	33	20. Joe Millikan	7,270	Kyle Petty	3
21. Ron Bouchard	6,155	21. Kyle Petty	20	21. Jody Ridley	30	21. Cale Yarborough	7,134	21. Stan Barrett	2
22. Ronnie Thomas	5,756	22. Richard Childress	16	22. James Hylton	27	22. Ron Bouchard	6,978	Geoff Bodine	2
23. Cecil Gordon	5,587	23. Joe Millikan	15	23. Tim Richmond	22	23. Cecil Gordon	6,872	Ron Bouchard	2
24. Richard Childress	5,218	24. Geoff Bodine	14	24. Joe Millikan	21	24. Richard Childress	6,468	Tommy Ellis	2
25. Cale Yarborough	4,922	Lake Speed	14	25. J. D. McDuffie	20	25. Neil Bonnett	6,365	James Hylton	2
26. Neil Bonnett	4,917	26. Ron Bouchard	12	26. Ron Bouchard	19	26. Ronnie Thomas	5,928	Butch Lindley	2
27. D. K. Ulrich	4,504	James Hylton	12	27. Geoff Bodine	18	27. Buddy Baker	5,811	21. Mark Martin	2
28. Mike Alexander	4,340	28. J. D. McDuffie	8	28. Rick Wilson	17	28. Joe Ruttman	5,588	J. D. McDuffie	2
29. Joe Ruttman	4,194	29. Rick Wilson	7	29. Butch Lindley	15	29. Mike Alexander	4,886	Tim Richmond	2
30. Buddy Baker	3,562	30. Johnny Rutherford	5			30. D. K. Ulrich	4,507	Lake Speed	2
								Rick Wilson	2

1982

Driver	Starts	Poles	Finish 1	2	3	4	5	6–10	Laps	Laps Led	Races Led	Winston Cup Points	$
1. Darrell Waltrip	30	7	12	1	3	0	1	3	9,455	3,027	27	4,489	923,151
2. Bobby Allison	30	1	8	2	1	2	1	6	9,184	2,423	24	4,417	795,078
3. Terry Labonte	30	3	0	6	2	6	3	4	8,900	263	17	4,211	398,635
4. Harry Gant	30	1	2	2	3	1	1	7	8,454	420	17	3,877	337,582
5. Richard Petty	30	0	0	5	2	1	1	7	7,834	355	18	3,814	465,793
6. Dave Marcis	30	0	1	1	0	0	0	12	8,370	56	10	3,666	249,027
7. Buddy Arrington	30	0	0	0	0	0	0	8	9,336	6	4	3,642	178,159
8. Ron Bouchard	30	1	0	0	2	1	0	12	8,048	1	1	3,545	375,759
9. Ricky Rudd	30	2	0	2	0	3	1	7	7,753	140	8	3,537	217,140
10. Morgan Shepherd	29	2	0	0	1	1	4	7	7,708	211	12	3,451	166,030
11. Jimmy Means	30	0	0	0	0	0	0	2	8,837	2	1	3,423	154,460
12. Dale Earnhardt	30	1	1	1	3	2	0	5	7,208	1,062	18	3,402	400,880
13. Jody Ridley	30	0	0	0	0	0	0	10	7,983	4	4	3,333	308,664
14. Mark Martin	30	0	0	0	0	0	2	6	7,449	4	3	3,042	142,710
15. Kyle Petty	29	0	0	1	0	1	0	2	6,414	13	3	3,024	126,285
16. Joe Ruttman	29	0	0	0	1	2	2	2	7,354	178	6	3,021	191,634
17. Neil Bonnett	25	0	1	0	2	1	3	3	6,730	412	12	2,966	158,197
18. Benny Parsons	23	3	0	0	4	3	3	3	5,631	253	8	2,892	252,267
19. J. D. McDuffie	30	0	0	0	0	0	0	1	6,695	1	1	2,886	112,744
20. Lake Speed	30	0	0	0	0	0	0	5	5,830	0	0	2,850	118,457
21. Tommy Gale	26	0	0	0	0	0	0	0	7,566	1	1	2,698	101,485
22. Geoff Bodine	25	2	0	0	1	2	1	6	6,518	118	6	2,654	247,750
23. Buddy Baker	23	1	0	1	0	0	3	7	5,672	103	12	2,591	253,675
24. D. K. Ulrich	25	0	0	0	0	0	0	1	7,102	0	0	2,566	78,120
25. Bill Elliott	21	1	0	3	3	1	1	1	5,540	151	9	2,558	201,030
26. Tim Richmond	26	1	2	2	0	1	2	5	6,834	321	13	2,497	175,980
27. Cale Yarborough	16	2	3	2	1	2	0	0	3,439	379	12	2,022	231,590
28. James Hylton	13	0	0	0	0	0	0	0	4,208	0	0	1,514	49,130
29. Slick Johnson	17	0	0	0	0	0	0	1	3,826	3	2	1,261	44,190
30. Ronnie Thomas	18	0	0	0	0	0	0	0	3,243	0	0	1,093	23,570
31. Bobby Wawak	10	0	0	0	0	0	0	0	2,489	2	1	1,002	23,660
32. Brad Teague	9	0	0	0	0	0	0	0	3,052	0	0	966	14,300
33. Lennie Pond	13	0	0	0	0	0	0	2	2,490	1	1	756	45,715
34. Rick Wilson	8	0	0	0	0	0	0	2	1,404	0	0	731	33,230
35. Joe Millikan	8	0	0	0	0	0	0	2	2,408	5	1	678	56,230
36. Rick Newsom	8	0	0	0	0	0	0	0	1,143	0	0	619	12,390
37. David Pearson	6	2	0	0	1	0	1	0	1,019	7	2	613	55,945
38. Gary Balough	5	0	0	0	0	0	0	1	1,359	0	0	564	35,735
39. Lowell Cowell	5	0	0	0	0	0	0	0	862	0	0	554	26,215
40. Philip Duffie	5	0	0	0	0	0	0	0	1,166	0	0	542	10,910
41. H. B. Bailey	6	0	0	0	0	0	0	0	1,016	0	0	462	9,455
42. Butch Lindley	4	0	0	1	0	0	0	0	1,020	165	2	435	16,695
43. Dean Combs	5	0	0	0	0	0	0	0	639	0	0	431	7,940
44. Delma Cowart	5	0	0	0	0	0	0	0	775	0	0	410	11,855
45. Donnie Allison	9	0	0	0	0	0	0	3	1,818	1	1	406	38,180
46. Bobby Hillin Jr.	5	0	0	0	0	0	0	0	917	0	0	379	9,830
47. Roy Smith	3	0	0	0	0	0	0	2	394	0	0	375	26,770
48. Dick Brooks	5	0	0	0	0	0	0	0	517	0	0	347	9,470
49. Connie Saylor	7	0	0	0	0	0	0	0	1,450	3	1	335	16,225
50. Darryl Sage	5	0	0	0	0	0	0	0	1,572	0	0	324	4,970

LAPS COMPLETED

1.	Darrell Waltrip	9,455
2.	Buddy Arrington	9,336
3.	Bobby Allison	9,184
4.	Terry Labonte	8,900
5.	Jimmy Means	8,837
6.	Harry Gant	8,454
7.	Dave Marcis	8,370
8.	Ron Bouchard	8,048
9.	Jody Ridley	7,983
10.	Richard Petty	7,834
11.	Ricky Rudd	7,753
12.	Morgan Shepherd	7,708
13.	Tommy Gale	7,566
14.	Mark Martin	7,449
15.	Joe Ruttman	7,354
16.	Dale Earnhardt	7,208
17.	D. K. Ulrich	7,102
18.	Tim Richmond	6,834
19.	Neil Bonnett	6,730
20.	J. D. McDuffie	6,695
21.	Geoff Bodine	6,518
22.	Kyle Petty	6,414
23.	Lake Speed	5,830
24.	Buddy Baker	5,672
25.	Benny Parsons	5,631
26.	Bill Elliott	5,540
27.	James Hylton	4,208
28.	Slick Johnson	3,826
29.	Cale Yarborough	3,439
30.	Ronnie Thomas	3,243

LAPS LED

1.	Darrell Waltrip	3,027
2.	Bobby Allison	2,423
3.	Dale Earnhardt	1,062
4.	Harry Gant	420
5.	Neil Bonnett	412
6.	Cale Yarborough	379
7.	Richard Petty	355
8.	Tim Richmond	321
9.	Terry Labonte	263
10.	Benny Parsons	253
11.	Morgan Shepherd	211
12.	Joe Ruttman	178
13.	Butch Lindley	165
14.	Bill Elliott	151
15.	Ricky Rudd	140
16.	Geoff Bodine	118
17.	Buddy Baker	103
18.	Dave Marcis	56
19.	Kyle Petty	13
20.	David Pearson	7
21.	Buddy Arrington	6
22.	Rodney Combs	5
	Joe Millikan	5
	Jim Sauter	5
25.	Mark Martin	4
	Steve Moore	4
	Jody Ridley	4
28.	Slick Johnson	3
	Connie Saylor	3
30.	Jimmy Means	2
	Bobby Wawak	2

MILES LED

1.	Bobby Allison	3,217
2.	Darrell Waltrip	2,672
3.	Dale Earnhardt	1,176
4.	Richard Petty	685
5.	Cale Yarborough	639
6.	Neil Bonnett	490
7.	Tim Richmond	433
8.	Harry Gant	420
9.	Terry Labonte	377
10.	Benny Parsons	362
11.	Bill Elliott	234
12.	Buddy Baker	174
13.	Morgan Shepherd	161
14.	Joe Ruttman	154
15.	Geoff Bodine	129
16.	Dave Marcis	88
17.	Butch Lindley	87
18.	Ricky Rudd	83
19.	Kyle Petty	25
20.	Buddy Arrington	14
21.	Jim Sauter	13
22.	Steve Moore	11
23.	David Pearson	10
24.	Mark Martin	10
25.	Rodney Combs	8
26.	Jody Ridley	6
27.	Jimmy Means	5
28.	Joe Millikan	5
29.	Slick Johnson	4
	Connie Saylor	4

MILES DRIVEN

1.	Bobby Allison	10,860
2.	Buddy Arrington	10,840
3.	Darrell Waltrip	10,597
4.	Jimmy Means	10,273
5.	Terry Labonte	10,259
6.	Dave Marcis	9,642
7.	Harry Gant	9,641
8.	Richard Petty	9,024
9.	Jody Ridley	8,789
10.	Ricky Rudd	8,680
11.	Morgan Shepherd	8,620
12.	Tommy Gale	8,607
13.	Ron Bouchard	8,543
14.	Mark Martin	8,321
15.	Tim Richmond	8,246
16.	Joe Ruttman	8,033
17.	Geoff Bodine	7,939
18.	Neil Bonnett	7,903
19.	Bill Elliott	7,886
20.	J. D. McDuffie	7,851
21.	Dale Earnhardt	7,787
22.	Kyle Petty	7,720
23.	D. K. Ulrich	7,587
24.	Buddy Baker	7,393
25.	Benny Parsons	7,314
26.	Lake Speed	6,856
27.	Cale Yarborough	5,642
28.	James Hylton	4,332
29.	Slick Johnson	4,229
30.	Bobby Wawak	3,981

RACES LED

1.	Darrell Waltrip	27
2.	Bobby Allison	24
3.	Dale Earnhardt	18
	Richard Petty	18
5.	Harry Gant	17
	Terry Labonte	17
7.	Tim Richmond	13
8.	Buddy Baker	12
	Neil Bonnett	12
	Morgan Shepherd	12
	Cale Yarborough	12
12.	Dave Marcis	10
13.	Bill Elliott	9
14.	Benny Parsons	8
	Ricky Rudd	8
16.	Geoff Bodine	6
	Joe Ruttman	6
18.	Buddy Arrington	4
	Jody Ridley	4
20.	Mark Martin	3
	Kyle Petty	3
22.	Slick Johnson	2
	Butch Lindley	2
	David Pearson	2

1983

Driver	Starts	Poles	Finish 1	2	3	4	5	6–10	Laps	Laps Led	Races Led	Winston Cup Points	$
1. Bobby Allison	30	0	6	5	6	1	0	7	10,038	1,755	25	4,667	883,010
2. Darrell Waltrip	30	7	6	8	4	2	2	3	9,403	2,363	22	4,620	865,185
3. Bill Elliott	30	0	1	4	1	3	3	10	9,536	173	15	4,279	514,030
4. Richard Petty	30	0	3	1	1	1	3	12	9,439	279	16	4,042	508,884
5. Terry Labonte	30	3	1	0	0	4	6	9	8,498	434	13	4,004	388,419
6. Neil Bonnett	30	4	2	1	2	5	0	7	9,418	650	15	3,842	453,586
7. Harry Gant	30	0	1	1	3	1	4	6	9,024	60	10	3,790	414,353
8. Dale Earnhardt	30	0	2	3	0	3	1	5	7,701	1,027	19	3,732	465,203
9. Ricky Rudd	30	4	2	1	1	1	2	7	8,581	871	13	3,693	275,400
10. Tim Richmond	30	4	1	1	4	1	3	5	7,176	590	15	3,612	262,139
11. Dave Marcis	30	0	0	0	0	0	0	7	7,771	24	6	3,361	306,355
12. Joe Ruttman	30	2	0	0	1	3	0	6	7,887	397	10	3,342	223,809
13. Kyle Petty	30	0	0	0	0	0	0	2	8,345	13	5	3,261	163,848
14. Dick Brooks	30	0	0	0	0	0	2	4	7,866	108	6	3,230	180,556
15. Buddy Arrington	30	0	0	0	0	0	0	2	8,933	1	1	3,158	138,429
16. Ron Bouchard	28	1	0	0	0	1	0	6	7,187	22	4	3,113	159,173
17. Geoff Bodine	28	1	0	1	0	2	2	4	7,042	490	13	3,019	209,611
18. Jimmy Means	28	0	0	0	0	0	0	3	8,269	2	1	2,983	132,915
19. Sterling Marlin	30	0	0	0	0	0	0	1	8,053	0	0	2,980	148,253
20. Morgan Shepherd	25	0	0	1	1	1	0	10	6,309	5	4	2,733	287,326
21. Buddy Baker	21	1	1	1	2	0	1	7	5,111	174	7	2,621	216,355
22. Ronnie Thomas	26	0	0	0	0	0	0	0	7,141	1	1	2,515	47,190
23. Tommy Gale	28	0	0	0	0	0	0	1	6,540	0	0	2,507	88,305
24. D. K. Ulrich	22	0	0	0	0	0	0	2	6,983	0	0	2,400	85,245
25. Trevor Boys	23	0	0	0	0	0	0	1	5,907	3	2	2,293	87,555
26. J. D. McDuffie	25	0	0	0	0	0	0	0	5,890	0	0	2,197	73,425
27. Lake Speed	18	0	0	0	1	1	0	3	4,933	22	2	2,114	78,220
28. Cale Yarborough	16	3	4	0	0	0	0	4	3,783	608	13	1,960	265,035
29. Benny Parsons	16	0	0	2	1	0	1	1	2,847	116	7	1,657	129,760
30. Mark Martin	16	0	0	0	1	0	0	2	4,130	1	1	1,627	99,055
31. Ronnie Hopkins Jr.	13	0	0	0	0	0	0	0	2,563	0	0	1,147	26,455
32. Jody Ridley	10	0	0	0	0	0	0	3	1,963	0	0	1,050	45,710
33. David Pearson	10	0	0	0	1	0	0	3	1,643	18	1	943	71,720
34. Lennie Pond	10	0	0	0	0	0	0	2	2,288	3	1	887	41,530
35. Ken Ragan	8	0	0	0	0	0	0	0	1,984	0	0	836	27,905
36. Bobby Wawak	9	0	0	0	0	0	0	0	2,167	0	0	825	19,130
37. Bobby Hillin Jr.	12	0	0	0	0	0	0	0	2,791	0	0	737	30,275
38. Slick Johnson	10	0	0	0	0	0	0	0	2,330	0	0	705	13,665
39. Mike Potter	11	0	0	0	0	0	0	0	1,916	0	0	662	20,375
40. Cecil Gordon	8	0	0	0	0	0	0	0	1,831	0	0	649	17,340
41. Rick Newsom	6	0	0	0	0	0	0	0	2,097	0	0	573	14,445
42. Dean Combs	5	0	0	0	0	0	0	1	1,296	0	0	500	21,370
43. Phil Parsons	5	0	0	0	0	0	0	0	887	0	0	458	23,850
44. Bob Senneker	5	0	0	0	0	0	0	0	1,317	0	0	436	11,355
45. Jerry Bowman	5	0	0	0	0	0	0	0	1,183	0	0	419	8,610
46. Clark Dwyer	5	0	0	0	0	0	0	1	851	0	0	411	14,570
47. Greg Sacks	5	0	0	0	0	0	0	0	638	0	0	359	8,060
48. Rick McCray	4	0	0	0	0	0	0	0	760	0	0	313	3,710
49. Delma Cowart	4	0	0	0	0	0	0	0	643	0	0	277	7,750
50. Philip Duffie	4	0	0	0	0	0	0	0	750	0	0	265	6,480

LAPS COMPLETED

1.	Bobby Allison	10,038
2.	Bill Elliott	9,536
3.	Richard Petty	9,439
4.	Neil Bonnett	9,418
5.	Darrell Waltrip	9,403
6.	Harry Gant	9,024
7.	Buddy Arrington	8,933
8.	Ricky Rudd	8,581
9.	Terry Labonte	8,498
10.	Kyle Petty	8,345
11.	Jimmy Means	8,269
12.	Sterling Marlin	8,053
13.	Joe Ruttman	7,887
14.	Dick Brooks	7,866
15.	Dave Marcis	7,771
16.	Dale Earnhardt	7,701
17.	Ron Bouchard	7,187
18.	Tim Richmond	7,176
19.	Ronnie Thomas	7,141
20.	Geoff Bodine	7,042
21.	D. K. Ulrich	6,983
22.	Tommy Gale	6,540
23.	Morgan Shepherd	6,309
24.	Trevor Boys	5,907
25.	J. D. McDuffie	5,890
26.	Buddy Baker	5,111
27.	Lake Speed	4,933
28.	Mark Martin	4,130
29.	Cale Yarborough	3,783
30.	Benny Parsons	2,847

LAPS LED

1.	Darrell Waltrip	2,363
2.	Bobby Allison	1,755
3.	Dale Earnhardt	1,027
4.	Ricky Rudd	871
5.	Neil Bonnett	650
6.	Cale Yarborough	608
7.	Tim Richmond	590
8.	Geoff Bodine	490
9.	Terry Labonte	434
10.	Joe Ruttman	397
11.	Richard Petty	279
12.	Buddy Baker	174
13.	Bill Elliott	173
14.	Benny Parsons	116
15.	Dick Brooks	108
16.	Harry Gant	60
17.	Dave Marcis	24
18.	Ron Bouchard	22
	Lake Speed	22
20.	David Pearson	18
21.	Kyle Petty	13
22.	Butch Lindley	7
23.	Morgan Shepherd	5
24.	Trevor Boys	3
	Lennie Pond	3
26.	Jimmy Means	2
27.	Buddy Arrington	1
	Mark Martin	1
	Ronnie Thomas	1

MILES LED

1.	Bobby Allison	2,093
2.	Darrell Waltrip	1,815
3.	Cale Yarborough	993
4.	Dale Earnhardt	876
5.	Tim Richmond	861
6.	Neil Bonnett	768
7.	Ricky Rudd	707
8.	Geoff Bodine	699
9.	Terry Labonte	676
10.	Richard Petty	526
11.	Joe Ruttman	466
12.	Buddy Baker	375
13.	Bill Elliott	249
14.	Benny Parsons	232
15.	Dick Brooks	168
16.	Harry Gant	82
17.	Ron Bouchard	52
18.	Lake Speed	48
19.	Dave Marcis	39
20.	Kyle Petty	29
21.	David Pearson	25
22.	Morgan Shepherd	8
23.	Lennie Pond	8
24.	Trevor Boys	6
25.	Jimmy Means	5
26.	Butch Lindley	4
27.	Ronnie Thomas	3
28.	Buddy Arrington	2
29.	Mark Martin	1

MILES DRIVEN

1.	Bobby Allison	11,526
2.	Bill Elliott	11,272
3.	Richard Petty	10,696
4.	Darrell Waltrip	10,546
5.	Neil Bonnett	10,451
6.	Harry Gant	10,193
7.	Buddy Arrington	10,009
8.	Ricky Rudd	9,907
9.	Terry Labonte	9,774
10.	Kyle Petty	9,436
11.	Dave Marcis	9,171
12.	Sterling Marlin	9,166
13.	Jimmy Means	8,974
14.	Dale Earnhardt	8,946
15.	Dick Brooks	8,872
16.	Joe Ruttman	8,817
17.	Ron Bouchard	8,315
18.	Tim Richmond	8,218
19.	D. K. Ulrich	7,875
20.	Tommy Gale	7,814
21.	Ronnie Thomas	7,705
22.	Morgan Shepherd	7,613
23.	Geoff Bodine	7,328
24.	Lake Speed	6,928
25.	Trevor Boys	6,896
26.	Buddy Baker	6,816
27.	J. D. McDuffie	6,524
28.	Cale Yarborough	5,975
29.	Mark Martin	5,545
30.	Benny Parsons	5,285

RACES LED

1.	Bobby Allison	25
2.	Darrell Waltrip	22
3.	Dale Earnhardt	19
4.	Richard Petty	16
5.	Neil Bonnett	15
	Bill Elliott	15
	Tim Richmond	15
8.	Geoff Bodine	13
	Terry Labonte	13
	Ricky Rudd	13
	Cale Yarborough	13
12.	Harry Gant	10
	Joe Ruttman	10
14.	Buddy Baker	7
	Benny Parsons	7
16.	Dick Brooks	6
	Dave Marcis	6
18.	Kyle Petty	5
19.	Ron Bouchard	4
	Morgan Shepherd	4
21.	Trevor Boys	2
	Lake Speed	2

Driver	Starts	Poles	Finish						Laps	Laps Led	Races Led	Winston Cup Points	$
			1	2	3	4	5	6–10					

1984

	Driver	Starts	Poles	1	2	3	4	5	6–10	Laps	Laps Led	Races Led	Cup Points	$
1.	Terry Labonte	30	3	2	6	6	2	1	7	9,886	880	26	4,508	767,716
2.	Harry Gant	30	3	3	6	0	5	1	8	9,899	1,186	19	4,443	673,060
3.	Bill Elliott	30	4	3	1	4	4	1	11	9,848	570	17	4,377	680,344
4.	Dale Earnhardt	30	0	2	4	2	0	4	10	9,584	446	16	4,265	634,671
5.	Darrell Waltrip	30	4	7	2	3	1	0	7	9,464	2,030	22	4,230	731,023
6.	Bobby Allison	30	0	2	1	2	4	4	5	9,051	1,160	23	4,094	641,049
7.	Ricky Rudd	30	4	1	1	3	1	1	9	9,271	566	8	3,918	497,779
8.	Neil Bonnett	30	1	0	2	0	2	3	7	9,126	641	11	3,802	282,533
9.	Geoff Bodine	30	3	3	0	1	2	1	7	8,848	686	12	3,734	413,748
10.	Richard Petty	30	0	2	0	0	2	1	8	8,835	275	8	3,643	257,932
11.	Ron Bouchard	30	0	0	1	2	1	1	6	9,200	111	8	3,609	246,510
12.	Tim Richmond	30	0	1	3	0	0	2	5	8,225	58	7	3,505	345,848
13.	Dave Marcis	30	0	0	0	0	3	0	6	9,383	30	5	3,416	330,766
14.	Rusty Wallace	30	0	0	0	0	1	1	2	8,868	11	7	3,316	201,739
15.	Dick Brooks	30	0	0	0	1	0	0	4	8,157	185	3	3,265	192,407
16.	Kyle Petty	30	0	0	0	0	0	1	5	8,400	2	1	3,159	329,920
17.	Trevor Boys	30	0	0	0	0	0	0	1	8,719	20	3	3,040	165,376
18.	Joe Ruttman	29	1	0	0	0	0	0	8	6,635	55	4	2,945	168,433
19.	Greg Sacks	29	0	0	0	0	0	0	1	6,348	0	0	2,545	75,184
20.	Buddy Arrington	26	0	0	0	0	0	0	0	7,323	0	0	2,504	128,802
21.	Buddy Baker	21	1	0	1	2	0	1	8	6,213	84	2	2,477	151,635
22.	Cale Yarborough	16	4	3	1	3	1	2	0	4,387	736	12	2,448	403,853
23.	Clark Dwyer	26	0	0	0	0	0	0	0	7,025	1	1	2,374	114,335
24.	Phil Parsons	22	0	0	0	0	0	0	3	6,286	4	1	2,290	90,700
25.	Jimmy Means	22	0	0	0	0	0	0	0	7,044	0	0	2,218	105,105
26.	Lake Speed	19	0	0	0	1	0	1	5	4,814	122	5	2,023	98,320
27.	Benny Parsons	14	2	1	1	0	1	4	3	2,877	407	6	1,865	241,665
28.	Mike Alexander	19	0	0	0	0	0	0	1	4,656	0	0	1,862	94,820
29.	Morgan Shepherd	20	0	0	0	0	0	0	1	5,134	1	1	1,811	59,670
30.	Ronnie Thomas	21	0	0	0	0	0	0	0	4,976	2	1	1,775	79,325
31.	Tommy Ellis	20	0	0	0	0	0	0	1	5,010	1	1	1,738	44,315
32.	Bobby Hillin Jr.	16	0	0	0	0	0	0	0	3,452	0	0	1,477	45,020
33.	Tommy Gale	16	0	0	0	0	0	0	0	4,248	0	0	1,426	69,385
34.	J. D. McDuffie	16	0	0	0	0	0	0	0	4,064	0	0	1,366	50,320
35.	Jody Ridley	14	0	0	0	0	0	0	3	2,891	4	2	1,288	64,135
36.	Doug Heveron	16	0	0	0	0	0	0	0	3,553	7	1	1,265	39,950
37.	Sterling Marlin	14	0	0	0	0	0	0	2	2,737	0	0	1,207	54,355
38.	Lennie Pond	12	0	0	0	0	0	0	2	3,590	0	0	923	54,200
39.	Dean Combs	12	0	0	0	0	0	0	0	2,399	0	0	903	22,385
40.	Ken Ragan	10	0	0	0	0	0	0	0	1,839	1	1	873	37,045
41.	David Pearson	11	0	0	0	0	0	0	3	1,630	10	3	812	54,125
42.	D. K. Ulrich	9	0	0	0	0	0	0	0	2,565	0	0	810	31,040
43.	Connie Saylor	8	0	0	0	0	0	0	0	1,193	1	1	367	19,675
44.	Jerry Bowman	5	0	0	0	0	0	0	0	834	0	0	362	6,265
45.	Elliott Forbes-Robinson	5	0	0	0	0	0	0	0	895	0	0	349	11,335
46.	Jeff Hooker	4	0	0	0	0	0	0	0	980	0	0	322	4,495
47.	Bobby Wawak	4	0	0	0	0	0	0	0	874	0	0	307	8,575
48.	Dick May	3	0	0	0	0	0	0	0	1,274	0	0	300	5,325
49.	Dean Roper	3	0	0	0	0	0	0	0	500	0	0	294	19,150
50.	Bobby Gerhart	4	0	0	0	0	0	0	0	655	0	0	262	7,585

LAPS COMPLETED

1.	Harry Gant	9,899
2.	Terry Labonte	9,886
3.	Bill Elliott	9,848
4.	Dale Earnhardt	9,584
5.	Darrell Waltrip	9,464
6.	Dave Marcis	9,383
7.	Ricky Rudd	9,271
8.	Ron Bouchard	9,200
9.	Neil Bonnett	9,126
10.	Bobby Allison	9,051
11.	Rusty Wallace	8,868
12.	Geoff Bodine	8,848
13.	Richard Petty	8,835
14.	Trevor Boys	8,719
15.	Kyle Petty	8,400
16.	Tim Richmond	8,225
17.	Dick Brooks	8,157
18.	Buddy Arrington	7,323
19.	Jimmy Means	7,044
20.	Clark Dwyer	7,025
21.	Joe Ruttman	6,635
22.	Greg Sacks	6,348
23.	Phil Parsons	6,286
24.	Buddy Baker	6,213
25.	Morgan Shepherd	5,134
26.	Tommy Ellis	5,010
27.	Ronnie Thomas	4,976
28.	Lake Speed	4,814
29.	Mike Alexander	4,656
30.	Cale Yarborough	4,387

LAPS LED

1.	Darrell Waltrip	2,030
2.	Harry Gant	1,186
3.	Bobby Allison	1,160
4.	Terry Labonte	880
5.	Cale Yarborough	736
6.	Geoff Bodine	686
7.	Neil Bonnett	641
8.	Bill Elliott	570
9.	Ricky Rudd	566
10.	Dale Earnhardt	446
11.	Benny Parsons	407
12.	Richard Petty	275
13.	Dick Brooks	185
14.	Lake Speed	122
15.	Ron Bouchard	111
16.	Buddy Baker	84
17.	Tim Richmond	58
18.	Joe Ruttman	55
19.	Dave Marcis	30
20.	Trevor Boys	20
21.	Rusty Wallace	11
22.	David Pearson	10
23.	Doug Heveron	7
24.	Jim Bown	4
	Phil Parsons	4
	Jody Ridley	4
27.	Kyle Petty	2
	Ronnie Thomas	2

MILES LED

1.	Darrell Waltrip	1,577
2.	Harry Gant	1,511
3.	Cale Yarborough	1,485
4.	Bobby Allison	1,216
5.	Terry Labonte	1,140
6.	Bill Elliott	814
7.	Benny Parsons	709
8.	Dale Earnhardt	663
9.	Geoff Bodine	562
10.	Richard Petty	458
11.	Neil Bonnett	409
12.	Ricky Rudd	338
13.	Buddy Baker	223
14.	Dick Brooks	188
15.	Lake Speed	147
16.	Ron Bouchard	142
17.	Tim Richmond	63
18.	Dave Marcis	46
19.	Joe Ruttman	36
20.	Trevor Boys	30
21.	David Pearson	24
22.	Doug Heveron	18
23.	Rusty Wallace	12
24.	Phil Parsons	11
25.	Jim Bown	10
26.	Jody Ridley	6
27.	Kyle Petty	5
28.	Clark Dwyer	3
	Tommy Ellis	3
	Ken Ragan	3

MILES DRIVEN

1.	Harry Gant	11,395
2.	Bill Elliott	11,385
3.	Terry Labonte	11,236
4.	Dale Earnhardt	10,850
5.	Ricky Rudd	10,584
6.	Bobby Allison	10,545
7.	Ron Bouchard	10,504
8.	Neil Bonnett	10,460
9.	Darrell Waltrip	10,440
10.	Dave Marcis	10,387
11.	Geoff Bodine	10,064
12.	Rusty Wallace	10,024
13.	Trevor Boys	9,970
14.	Richard Petty	9,917
15.	Tim Richmond	9,416
16.	Dick Brooks	9,320
17.	Kyle Petty	9,302
18.	Buddy Arrington	8,295
19.	Joe Ruttman	8,161
20.	Clark Dwyer	8,059
21.	Greg Sacks	7,781
22.	Phil Parsons	7,762
23.	Jimmy Means	7,482
24.	Buddy Baker	7,447
25.	Cale Yarborough	7,140
26.	Lake Speed	6,752
27.	Ronnie Thomas	5,761
28.	Mike Alexander	5,694
29.	Bobby Hillin Jr.	5,655
30.	Morgan Shepherd	5,478

RACES LED

1.	Terry Labonte	26
2.	Bobby Allison	23
3.	Darrell Waltrip	22
4.	Harry Gant	19
5.	Bill Elliott	17
6.	Dale Earnhardt	16
7.	Geoff Bodine	12
	Cale Yarborough	12
9.	Neil Bonnett	11
10.	Ron Bouchard	8
	Richard Petty	8
	Ricky Rudd	8
13.	Tim Richmond	7
	Rusty Wallace	7
15.	Benny Parsons	6
16.	Dave Marcis	5
	Lake Speed	5
18.	Joe Ruttman	4
19.	Trevor Boys	3
	Dick Brooks	3
	David Pearson	3
22.	Buddy Baker	2
	Jody Ridley	2

Driver	Starts	Poles	Finish						Laps	Laps Led	Races Led	Winston Cup Points	$
			1	2	3	4	5	6–10					

1985

Driver	Starts	Poles	1	2	3	4	5	6–10	Laps	Laps Led	Races Led	Winston Cup Points	$
1. Darrell Waltrip	28	5	3	6	6	2	1	3	8,932	969	21	4,292	1,318,375
2. Bill Elliott	28	12	11	2	0	2	1	2	8,724	1,920	19	4,191	2,433,187
3. Harry Gant	28	3	3	5	3	1	2	5	8,806	1,270	20	4,033	804,287
4. Neil Bonnett	28	1	2	2	3	1	3	7	8,675	618	15	3,902	530,145
5. Geoff Bodine	28	3	0	3	3	2	2	4	8,719	692	18	3,862	565,868
6. Ricky Rudd	28	0	1	2	1	5	4	6	8,475	329	6	3,857	512,441
7. Terry Labonte	28	4	1	2	3	1	1	9	7,973	563	14	3,683	694,510
8. Dale Earnhardt	28	1	4	0	0	4	2	6	8,231	1,237	17	3,561	546,596
9. Kyle Petty	28	0	0	1	1	1	4	5	8,796	75	6	3,528	296,367
10. Lake Speed	28	0	0	1	0	1	0	12	8,308	8	4	3,507	300,326
11. Tim Richmond	28	0	0	1	1	1	0	10	8,199	377	12	3,413	290,284
12. Bobby Allison	28	0	0	0	3	3	1	4	7,656	422	14	3,312	272,536
13. Ron Bouchard	28	0	0	1	1	2	1	7	7,723	77	5	3,267	240,304
14. Richard Petty	28	0	0	0	1	0	0	12	7,767	105	7	3,140	306,142
15. Bobby Hillin Jr.	28	0	0	0	0	0	0	5	8,636	2	2	3,091	145,070
16. Ken Schrader	28	0	0	0	0	0	0	3	7,786	4	1	3,024	211,523
17. Buddy Baker	28	0	0	0	0	2	0	5	6,296	4	2	2,986	235,480
18. Dave Marcis	28	0	0	0	0	0	0	5	7,319	30	4	2,871	173,467
19. Rusty Wallace	28	0	0	0	0	0	2	6	7,271	28	1	2,867	233,670
20. Buddy Arrington	26	0	0	0	0	0	0	1	7,809	1	1	2,780	153,222
21. Phil Parsons	28	0	0	0	0	0	0	4	6,678	1	1	2,740	104,840
22. Clark Dwyer	28	0	0	0	0	0	0	0	7,205	0	0	2,641	128,710
23. Jimmy Means	28	0	0	0	0	0	0	0	6,774	0	0	2,548	132,130
24. Eddie Bierschwale	26	0	0	0	0	0	0	0	6,559	0	0	2,396	102,650
25. Greg Sacks	20	0	1	0	0	0	0	4	4,855	36	3	1,944	234,141
26. Cale Yarborough	16	0	2	2	2	0	0	1	3,450	664	11	1,861	310,465
27. J. D. McDuffie	23	0	0	0	0	0	0	0	4,667	0	0	1,853	84,965
28. Trevor Boys	20	0	0	0	0	0	0	0	3,673	3	1	1,461	76,325
29. Benny Parsons	14	0	0	0	0	0	1	5	2,230	8	3	1,427	94,450
30. Joe Ruttman	16	0	0	0	0	0	1	3	3,378	5	1	1,410	81,425
31. Morgan Shepherd	16	0	0	0	0	0	1	1	2,951	1	1	1,406	55,985
32. Bobby Wawak	14	0	0	0	0	0	0	0	3,157	0	0	1,226	42,165
33. Lennie Pond	12	0	0	0	0	0	0	0	2,831	3	2	1,107	70,640
34. Tommy Ellis	14	0	0	0	0	0	0	1	2,853	0	0	1,100	27,695
35. Mike Alexander	11	0	0	0	0	0	0	0	2,336	0	0	1,046	43,765
36. David Pearson	12	0	0	0	0	0	0	1	1,418	2	1	879	55,625
37. Sterling Marlin	8	0	0	0	0	0	0	0	1,321	1	1	645	31,155
38. Don Hume	7	0	0	0	0	0	0	0	2,057	0	0	637	22,230
39. Ronnie Thomas	7	0	0	0	0	0	0	0	1,510	0	0	631	10,505
40. Alan Kulwicki	5	0	0	0	0	0	0	0	1,843	0	0	509	10,290
41. Rick Newsom	6	0	0	0	0	0	0	0	834	0	0	450	8,690
42. Mike Potter	6	0	0	0	0	0	0	0	1,434	0	0	443	10,855
43. Jerry Bowman	5	0	0	0	0	0	0	0	1,326	0	0	434	8,665
44. Bobby Gerhart	5	0	0	0	0	0	0	0	1,166	0	0	422	7,400
45. A. J. Foyt	7	0	0	0	0	0	1	0	966	2	2	410	29,750
46. Phil Good	4	0	0	0	0	0	0	0	1,339	0	0	406	6,870
47. Ken Ragan	7	0	0	0	0	0	0	0	1,359	0	0	356	35,995
48. Slick Johnson	6	0	0	0	0	0	0	0	1,608	0	0	343	24,995
49. Connie Saylor	5	0	0	0	0	0	0	0	456	0	0	296	8,915
50. Jim Sauter	3	0	0	0	0	0	0	0	565	0	0	267	15,465

LAPS COMPLETED

1.	Darrell Waltrip	8,932
2.	Harry Gant	8,806
3.	Kyle Petty	8,796
4.	Bill Elliott	8,724
5.	Geoff Bodine	8,719
6.	Neil Bonnett	8,675
7.	Bobby Hillin Jr.	8,636
8.	Ricky Rudd	8,475
9.	Lake Speed	8,308
10.	Dale Earnhardt	8,231
11.	Tim Richmond	8,199
12.	Terry Labonte	7,973
13.	Buddy Arrington	7,809
14.	Ken Schrader	7,786
15.	Richard Petty	7,767
16.	Ron Bouchard	7,723
17.	Bobby Allison	7,656
18.	Dave Marcis	7,319
19.	Rusty Wallace	7,271
20.	Clark Dwyer	7,205
21.	Jimmy Means	6,774
22.	Phil Parsons	6,678
23.	Eddie Bierschwale	6,559
24.	Buddy Baker	6,296
25.	Greg Sacks	4,855
26.	J. D. McDuffie	4,667
27.	Trevor Boys	3,673
28.	Cale Yarborough	3,450
29.	Joe Ruttman	3,378
30.	Bobby Wawak	3,157

LAPS LED

1.	Bill Elliott	1,920
2.	Harry Gant	1,270
3.	Dale Earnhardt	1,237
4.	Darrell Waltrip	969
5.	Geoff Bodine	692
6.	Cale Yarborough	664
7.	Neil Bonnett	618
8.	Terry Labonte	563
9.	Bobby Allison	422
10.	Tim Richmond	377
11.	Ricky Rudd	329
12.	Richard Petty	105
13.	Ron Bouchard	77
14.	Kyle Petty	75
15.	Greg Sacks	36
16.	Dave Marcis	30
17.	Rusty Wallace	28
18.	Benny Parsons	8
	Lake Speed	8
20.	Joe Ruttman	5
21.	Buddy Baker	4
	Ken Schrader	4
23.	Trevor Boys	3
	Lennie Pond	3
25.	A. J. Foyt	2
	Bobby Hillin Jr.	2
	David Pearson	2
28.	Buddy Arrington	1
	Sterling Marlin	1
	Phil Parsons	1
	Morgan Shepherd	1

MILES LED

1.	Bill Elliott	3,188
2.	Harry Gant	1,266
3.	Cale Yarborough	1,138
4.	Dale Earnhardt	1,092
5.	Darrell Waltrip	1,005
6.	Geoff Bodine	858
7.	Terry Labonte	730
8.	Neil Bonnett	722
9.	Tim Richmond	305
10.	Bobby Allison	294
11.	Ricky Rudd	288
12.	Greg Sacks	90
13.	Ron Bouchard	86
14.	Kyle Petty	82
15.	Richard Petty	76
16.	Dave Marcis	27
17.	Benny Parsons	20
18.	Rusty Wallace	15
19.	Lake Speed	14
20.	Joe Ruttman	13
21.	Trevor Boys	8
22.	Lennie Pond	7
23.	A. J. Foyt	5
24.	David Pearson	5
25.	Buddy Baker	4
26.	Buddy Arrington	3
27.	Ken Schrader	3
28.	Bobby Hillin Jr.	2
29.	Phil Parsons	1
30.	Sterling Marlin	1

MILES DRIVEN

1.	Darrell Waltrip	10,910
2.	Bill Elliott	10,727
3.	Geoff Bodine	10,711
4.	Kyle Petty	10,377
5.	Neil Bonnett	10,350
6.	Ricky Rudd	10,281
7.	Bobby Hillin Jr.	10,204
8.	Harry Gant	10,177
9.	Lake Speed	9,937
10.	Buddy Arrington	9,644
11.	Terry Labonte	9,603
12.	Tim Richmond	9,489
13.	Ken Schrader	9,356
14.	Bobby Allison	9,336
15.	Dale Earnhardt	9,149
16.	Ron Bouchard	8,961
17.	Richard Petty	8,858
18.	Dave Marcis	8,729
19.	Clark Dwyer	8,550
20.	Rusty Wallace	8,376
21.	Buddy Baker	8,250
22.	Eddie Bierschwale	7,752
23.	Phil Parsons	7,602
24.	Jimmy Means	7,512
25.	Greg Sacks	6,425
26.	Cale Yarborough	5,669
27.	J. D. McDuffie	5,531
28.	Joe Ruttman	4,599
29.	Bobby Wawak	4,452
30.	Trevor Boys	4,400

RACES LED

1.	Darrell Waltrip	21
2.	Harry Gant	20
3.	Bill Elliott	19
4.	Geoff Bodine	18
5.	Dale Earnhardt	17
6.	Neil Bonnett	15
7.	Bobby Allison	14
	Terry Labonte	14
9.	Tim Richmond	12
10.	Cale Yarborough	11
11.	Richard Petty	7
12.	Kyle Petty	6
	Ricky Rudd	6
14.	Ron Bouchard	5
15.	Dave Marcis	4
	Lake Speed	4
17.	Benny Parsons	3
	Greg Sacks	3
19.	Buddy Baker	2
	A. J. Foyt	2
	Bobby Hillin Jr.	2
	Lennie Pond	2

Driver	Starts	Poles	Finish 1	2	3	4	5	6–10	Laps	Laps Led	Races Led	Winston Cup Points	$
1986													
1. Dale Earnhardt	29	1	5	5	3	1	2	7	9,212	2,127	26	4,468	1,768,880
2. Darrell Waltrip	29	1	3	2	4	6	6	1	8,327	573	21	4,180	1,099,735
3. Tim Richmond	29	8	7	4	0	1	1	4	8,544	1,006	21	4,174	973,221
4. Bill Elliott	29	4	2	0	2	1	3	8	8,549	511	15	3,844	1,049,142
5. Ricky Rudd	29	1	2	4	2	3	0	6	8,120	525	7	3,823	671,548
6. Rusty Wallace	29	0	2	0	0	2	0	12	8,486	427	8	3,762	557,354
7. Bobby Allison	29	0	1	2	1	1	1	9	8,391	127	11	3,698	503,095
8. Geoff Bodine	29	9	2	2	5	1	0	5	7,791	1,676	25	3,678	795,111
9. Bobby Hillin Jr.	29	0	1	0	1	2	0	10	8,121	25	4	3,546	448,452
10. Kyle Petty	29	0	1	0	1	0	2	10	8,546	17	6	3,537	403,242
11. Harry Gant	29	2	0	3	1	3	2	4	7,965	646	17	3,498	583,024
12. Terry Labonte	29	1	1	2	2	0	0	5	8,284	565	10	3,473	522,235
13. Neil Bonnett	28	0	1	1	1	1	2	6	7,691	323	16	3,369	485,930
14. Richard Petty	29	0	0	1	2	1	0	7	7,639	153	7	3,314	280,657
15. Joe Ruttman	29	0	0	2	0	0	3	9	7,732	55	5	3,295	259,263
16. Ken Schrader	29	0	0	0	0	0	0	4	8,047	2	2	3,052	235,904
17. Dave Marcis	29	0	0	0	0	0	1	3	7,316	63	11	2,912	220,461
18. Morgan Shepherd	27	0	1	0	1	2	0	4	6,358	357	13	2,896	244,146
19. Michael Waltrip	28	0	0	0	0	0	0	0	7,952	6	4	2,853	108,767
20. Buddy Arrington	26	0	0	0	0	0	0	0	8,152	4	1	2,776	186,588
21. Alan Kulwicki	23	0	0	0	0	1	0	3	7,872	14	6	2,705	94,450
22. Jimmy Means	26	0	0	0	0	0	0	0	6,472	5	3	2,495	157,940
23. Tommy Ellis	24	0	0	0	0	0	0	3	6,559	50	5	2,393	78,310
24. Buddy Baker	17	0	0	0	1	2	3	0	3,964	45	5	1,924	138,600
25. Eddie Bierschwale	24	0	0	0	0	0	0	0	5,558	1	1	1,860	98,110
26. J. D. McDuffie	20	0	0	0	0	0	0	0	4,750	1	1	1,825	106,115
27. Phil Parsons	17	0	0	0	0	0	1	4	3,404	1	1	1,742	84,680
28. Rick Wilson	17	0	0	0	0	0	0	4	3,265	7	1	1,698	88,820
29. Cale Yarborough	16	1	0	0	2	0	0	3	3,467	110	4	1,642	137,010
30. Benny Parsons	16	1	0	0	0	0	2	2	2,620	13	7	1,555	176,985
31. Ron Bouchard	17	0	0	0	0	0	0	2	3,654	1	1	1,553	106,835
32. Chet Fillip	17	0	0	0	0	0	0	0	3,276	0	0	1,433	36,110
33. Jody Ridley	12	0	0	0	0	0	0	1	3,183	0	0	1,213	84,380
34. Trevor Boys	14	0	0	0	0	0	0	0	3,210	2	1	1,064	74,645
35. Doug Heveron	13	0	0	0	0	0	0	0	2,536	1	1	1,052	74,030
36. Sterling Marlin	10	0	0	1	0	1	0	2	1,738	21	3	989	113,070
37. D. K. Ulrich	10	0	0	0	0	0	0	0	2,159	0	0	804	47,795
38. Pancho Carter	9	0	0	0	0	0	0	0	1,423	3	2	706	56,355
39. Ken Ragan	7	0	0	0	0	0	0	0	1,284	1	1	627	33,890
40. Lake Speed	5	0	0	0	0	0	0	2	1,779	10	2	608	82,800
41. Greg Sacks	8	0	0	0	0	0	0	1	1,181	0	0	579	64,810
42. Ronnie Thomas	6	0	0	0	0	0	0	0	973	0	0	504	25,215
43. Bobby Wawak	6	0	0	0	0	0	0	0	1,270	0	0	480	10,155
44. Rodney Combs	5	0	0	0	0	0	0	0	909	4	1	421	12,180
45. Derrike Cope	5	0	0	0	0	0	0	1	1,101	0	0	400	8,025
46. James Hylton	4	0	0	0	0	0	0	0	544	0	0	386	22,090
47. Davey Allison	5	0	0	0	0	0	0	1	1,435	13	1	364	24,190
48. Mark Martin	5	0	0	0	0	0	0	0	1,342	0	0	364	20,515
49. Jim Sauter	8	0	0	0	0	0	0	0	1,285	2	1	361	52,020
50. A. J. Foyt	5	0	0	0	0	0	0	0	640	1	1	355	24,135

LAPS COMPLETED		LAPS LED		MILES LED		MILES DRIVEN		RACES LED	
1. Dale Earnhardt	9,212	1. Dale Earnhardt	2,127	1. Dale Earnhardt	2,439	1. Dale Earnhardt	11,164	1. Dale Earnhardt	26
2. Bill Elliott	8,549	2. Geoff Bodine	1,676	2. Geoff Bodine	2,055	2. Bill Elliott	10,591	2. Geoff Bodine	25
3. Kyle Petty	8,546	3. Tim Richmond	1,006	3. Tim Richmond	1,591	3. Tim Richmond	10,526	3. Tim Richmond	21
4. Tim Richmond	8,544	4. Harry Gant	646	4. Bill Elliott	972	4. Rusty Wallace	10,416	Darrell Waltrip	21
5. Rusty Wallace	8,486	5. Darrell Waltrip	573	5. Harry Gant	786	5. Kyle Petty	10,338	5. Harry Gant	17
6. Bobby Allison	8,391	6. Terry Labonte	565	6. Terry Labonte	596	6. Ricky Rudd	10,193	6. Neil Bonnett	16
7. Darrell Waltrip	8,327	7. Ricky Rudd	525	7. Darrell Waltrip	549	7. Bobby Hillin Jr.	9,978	7. Bill Elliott	15
8. Terry Labonte	8,284	8. Bill Elliott	511	8. Morgan Shepherd	418	8. Darrell Waltrip	9,946	8. Morgan Shepherd	13
9. Buddy Arrington	8,152	9. Rusty Wallace	427	9. Neil Bonnett	372	9. Bobby Allison	9,928	9. Bobby Allison	11
10. Bobby Hillin Jr.	8,121	10. Morgan Shepherd	357	10. Ricky Rudd	366	10. Ken Schrader	9,697	Dave Marcis	11
11. Ricky Rudd	8,120	11. Neil Bonnett	323	11. Rusty Wallace	257	11. Terry Labonte	9,588	11. Terry Labonte	10
12. Ken Schrader	8,047	12. Richard Petty	153	12. Cale Yarborough	176	12. Harry Gant	9,565	12. Rusty Wallace	8
13. Harry Gant	7,965	13. Bobby Allison	127	13. Bobby Allison	171	13. Buddy Arrington	9,457	13. Benny Parsons	7
14. Michael Waltrip	7,952	14. Cale Yarborough	110	14. Richard Petty	128	14. Geoff Bodine	9,359	Richard Petty	7
15. Alan Kulwicki	7,872	15. Dave Marcis	63	15. Buddy Baker	107	15. Michael Waltrip	9,295	Ricky Rudd	7
16. Geoff Bodine	7,791	16. Joe Ruttman	55	16. Bobby Hillin Jr.	60	16. Neil Bonnett	8,990	16. Alan Kulwicki	6
17. Joe Ruttman	7,732	17. Tommy Ellis	50	17. Sterling Marlin	54	17. Richard Petty	8,949	Kyle Petty	6
18. Neil Bonnett	7,691	18. Buddy Baker	45	18. Dave Marcis	50	18. Joe Ruttman	8,707	18. Buddy Baker	5
19. Richard Petty	7,639	19. Bobby Hillin Jr.	25	19. Joe Ruttman	38	19. Alan Kulwicki	8,602	Tommy Ellis	5
20. Dave Marcis	7,316	20. Sterling Marlin	21	20. Tommy Ellis	37	20. Dave Marcis	8,520	Joe Ruttman	5
21. Tommy Ellis	6,559	21. Kyle Petty	17	21. Davey Allison	35	21. Morgan Shepherd	8,346	21. Bobby Hillin Jr.	4
22. Jimmy Means	6,472	22. Alan Kulwicki	14	22. Kyle Petty	28	22. Jimmy Means	8,102	Michael Waltrip	4
23. Morgan Shepherd	6,358	23. Davey Allison	13	23. Benny Parsons	25	23. Tommy Ellis	7,334	Cale Yarborough	4
24. Eddie Bierschwale	5,558	Benny Parsons	13	24. Alan Kulwicki	22	24. Eddie Bierschwale	6,983	24. Sterling Marlin	3
25. J. D. McDuffie	4,750	25. Lake Speed	10	25. Rick Wilson	19	25. Buddy Baker	6,465	Jimmy Means	3
26. Buddy Baker	3,964	26. Rick Wilson	7	26. Lake Speed	13	26. Phil Parsons	6,151	26. Phil Barkdoll	2
27. Ron Bouchard	3,654	27. Michael Waltrip	6	27. Michael Waltrip	11	27. Cale Yarborough	5,828	Pancho Carter	2
28. Cale Yarborough	3,467	28. Jimmy Means	5	28. Rodney Combs	11	28. Rick Wilson	5,309	Ken Schrader	2
29. Phil Parsons	3,404	29. Buddy Arrington	4	29. Buddy Arrington	10	29. Benny Parsons	5,098	Lake Speed	2
30. Chet Fillip	3,276	Rodney Combs	4	30. Phil Barkdoll	8	30. Ron Bouchard	5,093		

Driver	Starts	Poles	Finish 1	2	3	4	5	6–10	Laps	Laps Led	Races Led	Winston Cup Points	$
1987													
1. Dale Earnhardt	29	1	11	5	1	2	2	3	9,043	3,358	27	4,696	2,069,243
2. Bill Elliott	29	8	6	3	1	5	1	4	8,902	1,399	22	4,207	1,599,210
3. Terry Labonte	29	4	1	2	2	5	3	9	8,609	592	16	4,007	805,054
4. Darrell Waltrip	29	0	1	1	1	2	1	10	8,996	311	14	3,911	511,768
5. Rusty Wallace	29	1	2	3	2	1	1	7	8,323	450	15	3,818	690,652
6. Ricky Rudd	29	0	2	2	4	1	1	3	8,206	505	12	3,742	653,508
7. Kyle Petty	29	0	1	1	4	0	0	8	8,523	103	7	3,737	544,437
8. Richard Petty	29	0	0	1	3	2	3	5	8,306	38	8	3,708	445,227
9. Bobby Allison	29	1	1	1	0	1	1	9	7,962	331	10	3,530	515,894
10. Ken Schrader	29	1	0	0	0	0	1	9	8,162	154	10	3,405	375,918
11. Sterling Marlin	29	0	0	0	1	2	1	4	8,356	68	6	3,381	306,412
12. Neil Bonnett	26	0	0	0	4	1	0	10	7,834	120	10	3,352	401,541
13. Geoff Bodine	29	2	0	1	1	0	1	7	7,638	342	13	3,328	449,816
14. Phil Parsons	29	0	0	0	0	1	0	6	8,216	18	2	3,327	180,261
15. Alan Kulwicki	29	3	0	1	0	1	1	6	7,758	102	8	3,238	369,889
16. Benny Parsons	29	0	0	3	0	1	2	3	6,975	87	9	3,215	566,484
17. Morgan Shepherd	29	1	0	1	1	1	4	4	6,410	164	7	3,099	317,034
18. Dave Marcis	29	0	0	0	2	0	0	5	6,880	84	9	3,080	256,354
19. Bobby Hillin Jr.	29	0	0	0	0	0	1	3	6,889	1	1	3,027	346,735
20. Michael Waltrip	29	0	0	0	0	0	0	1	7,790	1	1	2,840	205,370
21. Davey Allison	22	5	2	3	0	0	4	1	5,511	710	11	2,824	361,060
22. Harry Gant	29	1	0	0	0	0	0	4	6,497	71	3	2,725	197,645
23. Jimmy Means	28	0	0	0	0	0	0	1	6,339	21	1	2,483	154,055
24. Buddy Baker	20	0	0	1	1	1	0	7	4,509	91	7	2,373	255,320
25. Buddy Arrington	20	0	0	0	0	0	0	0	5,746	0	0	1,885	115,300
26. Dale Jarrett	24	0	0	0	0	0	0	2	4,788	0	0	1,840	143,405
27. Steve Christman	20	0	0	0	0	0	0	0	4,404	0	0	1,727	54,965
28. Rick Wilson	19	0	0	0	0	0	0	1	3,530	20	1	1,723	65,935
29. Cale Yarborough	16	0	0	0	0	1	1	2	2,671	11	2	1,450	111,025
30. J. D. McDuffie	17	0	0	0	0	0	0	0	3,459	0	0	1,361	45,555
31. Lake Speed	13	0	0	0	1	0	0	4	2,591	1	1	1,345	110,810
32. Brett Bodine	14	0	0	0	0	0	0	0	2,908	20	3	1,271	71,460
33. Greg Sacks	16	0	0	0	0	0	0	0	2,705	1	1	1,200	54,815
34. Eddie Bierschwale	14	0	0	0	0	0	0	0	3,560	0	0	1,162	66,790
35. Rodney Combs	14	0	0	0	0	0	0	0	2,752	0	0	1,098	90,990
36. Tim Richmond	8	1	2	0	0	1	0	1	1,199	161	6	1,063	151,850
37. Derrike Cope	11	0	0	0	0	0	0	0	1,631	0	0	797	33,750
38. Mark Stahl	9	0	0	0	0	0	0	0	1,635	0	0	687	32,850
39. Bobby Wawak	8	0	0	0	0	0	0	0	1,648	0	0	638	22,505
40. D. K. Ulrich	7	0	0	0	0	0	0	0	1,876	0	0	625	30,915
41. Ken Ragan	6	0	0	0	0	0	0	0	1,259	0	0	549	30,575
42. Connie Saylor	10	0	0	0	0	0	0	0	1,775	0	0	486	59,455
43. Jerry Cranmer	5	0	0	0	0	0	0	0	1,914	0	0	482	20,660
44. Trevor Boys	10	0	0	0	0	0	0	0	2,312	5	2	460	59,240
45. Mike Potter	6	0	0	0	0	0	0	0	1,285	0	0	456	13,290
46. Slick Johnson	8	0	0	0	0	0	0	0	2,113	3	2	444	40,630
47. Ron Bouchard	5	0	0	0	0	0	0	1	917	0	0	440	24,105
48. H. B. Bailey	5	0	0	0	0	0	0	0	1,150	0	0	428	18,885
49. A. J. Foyt	6	0	0	0	0	0	0	0	748	2	2	409	21,075
50. Larry Pearson	4	0	0	0	0	0	0	1	1,162	1	1	401	18,555

LAPS COMPLETED		LAPS LED		MILES LED		MILES DRIVEN		RACES LED	
1. Dale Earnhardt	9,043	1. Dale Earnhardt	3,358	1. Dale Earnhardt	3,399	1. Darrell Waltrip	11,034	1. Dale Earnhardt	27
2. Darrell Waltrip	8,996	2. Bill Elliott	1,399	2. Bill Elliott	2,040	2. Dale Earnhardt	10,898	2. Bill Elliott	22
3. Bill Elliott	8,902	3. Davey Allison	710	3. Davey Allison	1,152	3. Bill Elliott	10,422	3. Terry Labonte	16
4. Terry Labonte	8,609	4. Terry Labonte	592	4. Rusty Wallace	656	4. Kyle Petty	10,399	4. Rusty Wallace	15
5. Kyle Petty	8,523	5. Ricky Rudd	505	5. Terry Labonte	586	5. Sterling Marlin	10,304	5. Darrell Waltrip	14
6. Sterling Marlin	8,356	6. Rusty Wallace	450	6. Ricky Rudd	553	6. Terry Labonte	10,157	6. Geoff Bodine	13
7. Rusty Wallace	8,323	7. Geoff Bodine	342	7. Geoff Bodine	448	7. Richard Petty	9,985	7. Ricky Rudd	12
8. Richard Petty	8,306	8. Bobby Allison	331	8. Bobby Allison	422	8. Ken Schrader	9,900	8. Davey Allison	11
9. Phil Parsons	8,216	9. Darrell Waltrip	311	9. Tim Richmond	404	9. Ricky Rudd	9,891	9. Bobby Allison	10
10. Ricky Rudd	8,206	10. Morgan Shepherd	164	10. Ken Schrader	242	10. Phil Parsons	9,672	Neil Bonnett	10
11. Ken Schrader	8,162	11. Tim Richmond	161	11. Darrell Waltrip	188	11. Rusty Wallace	9,668	Ken Schrader	10
12. Bobby Allison	7,962	12. Ken Schrader	154	12. Buddy Baker	179	12. Bobby Allison	9,599	12. Dave Marcis	9
13. Neil Bonnett	7,834	13. Neil Bonnett	120	13. Morgan Shepherd	154	13. Alan Kulwicki	9,119	Benny Parsons	9
14. Michael Waltrip	7,790	14. Kyle Petty	103	14. Neil Bonnett	132	14. Neil Bonnett	9,072	14. Alan Kulwicki	8
15. Alan Kulwicki	7,758	15. Alan Kulwicki	102	15. Dave Marcis	122	15. Benny Parsons	8,864	Richard Petty	8
16. Geoff Bodine	7,638	16. Buddy Baker	91	16. Benny Parsons	116	16. Michael Waltrip	8,848	16. Buddy Baker	7
17. Benny Parsons	6,975	17. Benny Parsons	87	17. Kyle Petty	114	17. Geoff Bodine	8,753	Kyle Petty	7
18. Bobby Hillin Jr.	6,889	18. Dave Marcis	84	18. Alan Kulwicki	70	18. Dave Marcis	8,749	Morgan Shepherd	7
19. Dave Marcis	6,880	19. Harry Gant	71	19. Richard Petty	69	19. Bobby Hillin Jr.	8,559	19. Sterling Marlin	6
20. Harry Gant	6,497	20. Sterling Marlin	68	20. Sterling Marlin	46	20. Davey Allison	8,518	Tim Richmond	6
21. Morgan Shepherd	6,410	21. Richard Petty	38	21. Harry Gant	38	21. Morgan Shepherd	7,975	21. Brett Bodine	3
22. Jimmy Means	6,339	22. Jimmy Means	21	22. Brett Bodine	33	22. Harry Gant	7,921	Harry Gant	3
23. Buddy Arrington	5,746	23. Brett Bodine	20	23. Rick Wilson	30	23. Jimmy Means	7,282	23. Trevor Boys	2
24. Davey Allison	5,511	Rick Wilson	20	24. Brad Teague	26	24. Buddy Baker	7,163	A. J. Foyt	2
25. Dale Jarrett	4,788	25. Phil Parsons	18	25. Cale Yarborough	21	25. Buddy Arrington	6,792	Slick Johnson	2
26. Buddy Baker	4,509	26. Brad Teague	17	26. George Follmer	21	26. Dale Jarrett	5,680	Phil Parsons	2
27. Steve Christman	4,404	27. Cale Yarborough	11	27. Phil Parsons	16	27. Rick Wilson	5,575	Cale Yarborough	2
28. Eddie Bierschwale	3,560	28. George Follmer	8	28. Trevor Boys	12	28. Steve Christman	5,100		
29. Rick Wilson	3,530	29. Trevor Boys	5	29. Jimmy Means	11	29. Cale Yarborough	4,519		
30. J. D. McDuffie	3,459	30. Slick Johnson	3	30. Slick Johnson	6	30. Brett Bodine	4,485		

Driver	Starts	Poles	Finish						Laps	Laps Led	Races Led	Winston Cup Points	$
			1	2	3	4	5	6-10					

1988

	Driver	Starts	Poles	1	2	3	4	5	6-10	Laps	Laps Led	Races Led	Winston Cup Points	$
1.	Bill Elliott	29	6	6	2	2	4	1	7	9,647	1,598	20	4,488	1,554,639
2.	Rusty Wallace	29	2	6	5	4	2	2	4	9,222	908	18	4,484	1,411,567
3.	Dale Earnhardt	29	0	3	2	3	3	2	6	9,561	1,808	20	4,256	1,214,089
4.	Terry Labonte	29	1	1	2	3	4	1	7	9,206	207	17	4,007	950,781
5.	Ken Schrader	29	2	1	1	0	1	1	13	9,115	151	13	3,858	631,544
6.	Geoff Bodine	29	3	1	1	4	1	3	6	8,995	464	15	3,799	570,643
7.	Darrell Waltrip	29	2	2	1	1	2	4	4	9,065	520	18	3,764	731,659
8.	Davey Allison	29	3	2	2	3	2	3	4	8,333	611	14	3,631	844,532
9.	Phil Parsons	29	0	1	1	2	1	1	9	8,494	108	10	3,630	532,043
10.	Sterling Marlin	29	0	0	1	1	0	4	7	8,798	332	13	3,621	521,464
11.	Ricky Rudd	29	2	1	3	1	1	0	5	8,867	695	16	3,547	410,954
12.	Bobby Hillin Jr.	29	0	0	0	1	0	0	6	9,383	70	4	3,446	330,217
13.	Kyle Petty	29	0	0	0	0	0	2	6	8,883	67	3	3,296	377,092
14.	Alan Kulwicki	29	4	1	2	1	1	2	2	8,149	134	8	3,176	448,547
15.	Mark Martin	29	1	0	1	0	2	0	7	7,615	123	5	3,142	223,630
16.	Neil Bonnett	27	0	2	0	0	1	0	4	8,017	324	7	3,040	440,139
17.	Lake Speed	29	0	1	1	0	1	1	3	7,005	368	6	2,984	260,500
18.	Michael Waltrip	29	0	0	1	0	0	0	2	7,734	6	2	2,949	240,400
19.	Dave Marcis	29	0	0	0	0	0	0	2	8,178	62	7	2,854	212,485
20.	Brett Bodine	29	0	0	0	1	1	0	3	7,789	200	5	2,828	433,658
21.	Rick Wilson	28	1	0	1	0	1	0	3	6,870	152	4	2,762	209,925
22.	Richard Petty	29	0	0	0	1	0	0	4	6,207	11	3	2,644	190,155
23.	Dale Jarrett	29	0	0	0	0	0	0	1	6,556	5	2	2,622	118,640
24.	Benny Parsons	27	0	0	0	0	0	0	1	7,420	82	3	2,559	210,755
25.	Ken Bouchard	24	0	0	0	0	0	0	1	7,281	4	1	2,378	109,410
26.	Ernie Irvan	25	0	0	0	0	0	0	0	7,337	1	1	2,319	96,370
27.	Harry Gant	24	0	0	0	0	0	0	3	5,896	343	8	2,266	173,325
28.	Morgan Shepherd	23	2	0	1	0	1	0	4	4,601	127	5	2,193	197,425
29.	Buddy Baker	17	0	0	0	0	0	0	7	4,445	42	7	2,056	184,200
30.	Jimmy Means	27	0	0	0	0	0	0	0	5,172	12	4	2,045	139,290
31.	Derrike Cope	26	0	0	0	0	0	0	0	4,772	0	0	1,985	132,835
32.	Mike Alexander	16	0	0	0	1	0	1	4	4,677	51	5	1,931	200,709
33.	Bobby Allison	13	0	1	1	0	0	1	3	4,303	104	4	1,654	409,295
34.	Eddie Bierschwale	20	0	0	0	0	0	0	0	4,106	0	0	1,481	59,355
35.	Rodney Combs	19	0	0	0	0	0	0	0	3,693	0	0	1,468	54,150
36.	Brad Noffsinger	17	0	0	0	0	0	0	0	3,555	1	1	1,316	54,645
37.	Greg Sacks	15	0	0	0	0	0	0	3	3,543	1	1	1,237	105,579
38.	Cale Yarborough	10	0	0	0	0	0	0	3	1,653	6	2	940	66,065
39.	Joe Ruttman	12	0	0	0	0	0	0	1	1,899	0	0	803	46,455
40.	Brad Teague	13	0	0	0	0	0	0	0	3,408	0	0	802	53,105
41.	Jimmy Horton	8	0	0	0	0	0	0	0	2,007	0	0	647	23,575
42.	A. J. Foyt	7	0	0	0	0	0	0	0	920	9	3	523	29,660
43.	H. B. Bailey	7	0	0	0	0	0	0	0	1,180	0	0	478	15,775
44.	Jim Sauter	9	0	0	0	0	0	0	0	2,413	6	1	463	35,040
45.	Chad Little	4	0	0	0	0	0	0	0	1,089	3	1	405	14,225
46.	Buddy Arrington	4	0	0	0	0	0	0	0	760	0	0	352	22,165
47.	Ken Ragan	5	0	0	0	0	0	0	0	731	0	0	314	15,755
48.	Dana Patten	4	0	0	0	0	0	0	0	1,059	0	0	313	9,595
49.	Rick Jeffrey	4	0	0	0	0	0	0	0	978	0	0	307	25,535
50.	Mickey Gibbs	5	0	0	0	0	0	0	0	636	2	1	283	12,850

LAPS COMPLETED

1.	Bill Elliott	9,647
2.	Dale Earnhardt	9,561
3.	Bobby Hillin Jr.	9,383
4.	Rusty Wallace	9,222
5.	Terry Labonte	9,206
6.	Ken Schrader	9,115
7.	Darrell Waltrip	9,065
8.	Geoff Bodine	8,995
9.	Kyle Petty	8,883
10.	Ricky Rudd	8,867
11.	Sterling Marlin	8,798
12.	Phil Parsons	8,494
13.	Davey Allison	8,333
14.	Dave Marcis	8,178
15.	Alan Kulwicki	8,149
16.	Neil Bonnett	8,017
17.	Brett Bodine	7,789
18.	Michael Waltrip	7,734
19.	Mark Martin	7,615
20.	Benny Parsons	7,420
21.	Ernie Irvan	7,337
22.	Ken Bouchard	7,281
23.	Lake Speed	7,005
24.	Rick Wilson	6,870
25.	Dale Jarrett	6,556
26.	Richard Petty	6,207
27.	Harry Gant	5,896
28.	Jimmy Means	5,172
29.	Derrike Cope	4,772
30.	Mike Alexander	4,677

LAPS LED

1.	Dale Earnhardt	1,808
2.	Bill Elliott	1,598
3.	Rusty Wallace	908
4.	Ricky Rudd	695
5.	Davey Allison	611
6.	Darrell Waltrip	520
7.	Geoff Bodine	464
8.	Lake Speed	368
9.	Harry Gant	343
10.	Sterling Marlin	332
11.	Neil Bonnett	324
12.	Terry Labonte	207
13.	Brett Bodine	200
14.	Rick Wilson	152
15.	Ken Schrader	151
16.	Alan Kulwicki	134
17.	Morgan Shepherd	127
18.	Mark Martin	123
19.	Phil Parsons	108
20.	Bobby Allison	104
21.	Benny Parsons	82
22.	Bobby Hillin Jr.	70
23.	Kyle Petty	67
24.	Dave Marcis	62
25.	Mike Alexander	51
26.	Buddy Baker	42
27.	Butch Miller	18
28.	Jimmy Means	12
29.	Richard Petty	11
30.	A. J. Foyt	9

MILES LED

1.	Bill Elliott	1,851
2.	Dale Earnhardt	1,792
3.	Rusty Wallace	1,311
4.	Darrell Waltrip	881
5.	Geoff Bodine	796
6.	Davey Allison	674
7.	Ricky Rudd	564
8.	Lake Speed	382
9.	Sterling Marlin	365
10.	Ken Schrader	359
11.	Neil Bonnett	284
12.	Brett Bodine	274
13.	Phil Parsons	252
14.	Bobby Allison	241
15.	Terry Labonte	232
16.	Harry Gant	229
17.	Rick Wilson	224
18.	Mark Martin	140
19.	Morgan Shepherd	139
20.	Benny Parsons	121
21.	Alan Kulwicki	120
22.	Bobby Hillin Jr.	66
23.	Buddy Baker	61
24.	Mike Alexander	58
25.	Dave Marcis	44
26.	Kyle Petty	38
27.	Richard Petty	27
28.	Jimmy Means	17
29.	A. J. Foyt	17
30.	Cale Yarborough	15

MILES DRIVEN

1.	Bill Elliott	11,521
2.	Dale Earnhardt	11,314
3.	Rusty Wallace	11,180
4.	Bobby Hillin Jr.	11,179
5.	Ken Schrader	11,033
6.	Terry Labonte	11,032
7.	Darrell Waltrip	10,786
8.	Geoff Bodine	10,559
9.	Kyle Petty	10,514
10.	Ricky Rudd	10,428
11.	Sterling Marlin	10,383
12.	Phil Parsons	10,287
13.	Michael Waltrip	10,041
14.	Davey Allison	9,740
15.	Dave Marcis	9,545
16.	Alan Kulwicki	9,317
17.	Mark Martin	9,193
18.	Brett Bodine	9,155
19.	Neil Bonnett	9,131
20.	Ernie Irvan	8,845
21.	Benny Parsons	8,744
22.	Rick Wilson	8,703
23.	Lake Speed	8,534
24.	Ken Bouchard	8,480
25.	Dale Jarrett	8,161
26.	Richard Petty	7,619
27.	Harry Gant	6,867
28.	Jimmy Means	6,589
29.	Derrike Cope	6,535
30.	Buddy Baker	6,481

RACES LED

1.	Dale Earnhardt	20
	Bill Elliott	20
3.	Rusty Wallace	18
	Darrell Waltrip	18
5.	Terry Labonte	17
6.	Ricky Rudd	16
7.	Geoff Bodine	15
8.	Davey Allison	14
9.	Sterling Marlin	13
	Ken Schrader	13
11.	Phil Parsons	10
12.	Harry Gant	8
	Alan Kulwicki	8
14.	Buddy Baker	7
	Neil Bonnett	7
	Dave Marcis	7
17.	Lake Speed	6
18.	Mike Alexander	5
	Brett Bodine	5
	Mark Martin	5
	Morgan Shepherd	5
22.	Bobby Allison	4
	Bobby Hillin Jr.	4
	Jimmy Means	4
	Rick Wilson	4
26.	A. J. Foyt	3
	Benny Parsons	3
	Kyle Petty	3
	Richard Petty	3
30.	Dale Jarrett	2
	Michael Waltrip	2
	Cale Yarborough	2

Driver	Starts	Poles	Finish						Laps	Laps Led	Races Led	Winston Cup Points	$
			1	2	3	4	5	6–10	Laps				

1989

Driver	Starts	Poles	1	2	3	4	5	6–10	Laps	Laps Led	Races Led	Winston Cup Points	$
1. Rusty Wallace	29	4	6	4	0	2	1	7	9,104	2,021	23	4,176	2,237,950
2. Dale Earnhardt	29	2	5	3	5	1	0	5	9,112	2,735	22	4,164	1,432,230
3. Mark Martin	29	6	1	5	6	1	1	4	9,010	480	16	4,053	1,016,850
4. Darrell Waltrip	29	0	6	2	2	2	2	4	9,333	758	17	3,971	1,312,479
5. Ken Schrader	29	4	1	1	3	4	1	4	8,675	364	17	3,876	1,037,941
6. Bill Elliott	29	2	3	0	1	3	1	6	9,037	380	11	3,774	849,370
7. Harry Gant	29	0	1	3	1	2	2	5	8,627	440	11	3,610	639,792
8. Ricky Rudd	29	0	1	0	2	3	1	8	9,326	247	7	3,608	533,624
9. Geoff Bodine	29	3	1	1	3	3	1	2	9,051	511	14	3,600	619,494
10. Terry Labonte	29	0	2	2	1	1	3	2	8,306	104	10	3,569	703,806
11. Davey Allison	29	1	2	1	0	2	2	6	8,287	241	13	3,481	640,956
12. Sterling Marlin	29	0	0	1	1	0	2	9	8,840	42	6	3,422	473,267
13. Morgan Shepherd	29	1	0	2	0	1	2	8	7,590	137	6	3,403	544,255
14. Alan Kulwicki	29	6	0	4	0	0	1	4	8,324	564	14	3,236	501,295
15. Dick Trickle	28	0	0	0	3	1	2	3	8,504	80	8	3,203	343,728
16. Bobby Hillin Jr.	28	0	0	0	0	0	1	6	8,377	26	4	3,139	283,181
17. Rick Wilson	29	0	0	0	0	1	1	5	8,004	29	5	3,119	312,402
18. Michael Waltrip	29	0	0	0	0	0	0	5	8,372	9	4	3,057	249,233
19. Brett Bodine	29	0	0	0	0	0	1	5	8,202	2	2	3,051	281,274
20. Neil Bonnett	26	0	0	0	0	0	0	11	7,795	23	6	2,995	271,628
21. Phil Parsons	29	0	0	0	1	0	1	1	7,735	39	4	2,933	285,012
22. Ernie Irvan	29	0	0	0	0	0	0	4	8,286	69	4	2,919	155,329
23. Larry Pearson	29	0	0	0	0	0	0	2	7,993	5	2	2,860	156,060
24. Dale Jarrett	29	0	0	0	0	0	2	3	7,798	99	3	2,789	232,317
25. Dave Marcis	27	0	0	0	0	0	0	1	7,866	16	5	2,715	196,161
26. Hut Stricklin	27	0	0	0	0	1	0	3	7,557	3	1	2,705	152,504
27. Lake Speed	24	0	0	0	0	0	1	4	7,028	11	4	2,550	201,977
28. Derrike Cope	23	0	0	0	0	0	0	4	5,382	5	3	2,180	125,630
29. Richard Petty	25	0	0	0	0	0	0	0	5,567	9	1	2,148	133,050
30. Kyle Petty	19	0	0	0	0	1	0	4	5,207	16	1	2,099	117,027
31. Jimmy Means	22	0	0	0	0	0	0	0	4,868	4	1	1,698	65,005
32. Greg Sacks	20	0	0	0	0	0	0	2	4,955	110	4	1,565	113,535
33. Jim Sauter	17	0	0	0	0	0	0	2	3,974	8	1	1,510	73,832
34. Jimmy Spencer	17	0	0	0	0	0	0	3	3,544	0	0	1,445	121,065
35. Rick Mast	13	0	0	0	0	0	0	1	4,160	14	2	1,315	128,102
36. Eddie Bierschwale	16	0	0	0	0	0	0	1	3,829	2	1	1,306	82,695
37. Ben Hess	9	0	0	0	0	0	0	0	3,194	0	0	921	48,490
38. Chad Little	8	0	0	0	0	0	0	0	1,936	0	0	602	44,690
39. Butch Miller	9	0	0	0	0	0	0	0	1,129	0	0	576	22,520
40. A. J. Foyt	7	0	0	0	0	0	0	0	860	6	2	527	31,995
41. Mickey Gibbs	7	0	0	0	0	0	0	0	1,363	0	0	508	27,040
42. Rodney Combs	9	0	0	0	0	0	0	0	1,657	0	0	470	36,090
43. Joe Ruttman	9	0	0	0	0	0	0	1	1,704	0	0	469	64,645
44. J. D. McDuffie	7	0	0	0	0	0	0	0	1,381	0	0	457	27,720
45. Phil Barkdoll	4	0	0	0	0	0	0	0	658	2	1	378	29,050
46. Jimmy Horton	5	0	0	0	0	0	0	0	955	0	0	377	19,232
47. Dick Johnson	4	0	0	0	0	0	0	0	497	0	0	322	11,515
48. Ken Bouchard	4	0	0	0	0	0	0	0	911	0	0	313	33,930
49. Terry Byers	3	0	0	0	0	0	0	0	773	0	0	306	15,400
50. Darin Brassfield	3	0	0	0	0	0	0	0	275	0	0	306	10,852

LAPS COMPLETED

1.	Darrell Waltrip	9,333
2.	Ricky Rudd	9,326
3.	Dale Earnhardt	9,112
4.	Rusty Wallace	9,104
5.	Geoff Bodine	9,051
6.	Bill Elliott	9,037
7.	Mark Martin	9,010
8.	Sterling Marlin	8,840
9.	Ken Schrader	8,675
10.	Harry Gant	8,627
11.	Dick Trickle	8,504
12.	Bobby Hillin Jr.	8,377
13.	Michael Waltrip	8,372
14.	Alan Kulwicki	8,324
15.	Terry Labonte	8,306
16.	Davey Allison	8,287
17.	Ernie Irvan	8,286
18.	Brett Bodine	8,202
19.	Rick Wilson	8,004
20.	Larry Pearson	7,993
21.	Dave Marcis	7,866
22.	Dale Jarrett	7,798
23.	Neil Bonnett	7,795
24.	Phil Parsons	7,735
25.	Morgan Shepherd	7,590
26.	Hut Stricklin	7,557
27.	Lake Speed	7,028
28.	Richard Petty	5,567
29.	Derrike Cope	5,382
30.	Kyle Petty	5,207

LAPS LED

1.	Dale Earnhardt	2,735
2.	Rusty Wallace	2,021
3.	Darrell Waltrip	758
4.	Alan Kulwicki	564
5.	Geoff Bodine	511
6.	Mark Martin	480
7.	Harry Gant	440
8.	Bill Elliott	380
9.	Ken Schrader	364
10.	Ricky Rudd	247
11.	Davey Allison	241
12.	Morgan Shepherd	137
13.	Greg Sacks	110
14.	Terry Labonte	104
15.	Dale Jarrett	99
16.	Dick Trickle	80
17.	Ernie Irvan	69
18.	Sterling Marlin	42
19.	Phil Parsons	39
20.	Rick Wilson	29
21.	Bobby Hillin Jr.	26
22.	Neil Bonnett	23
23.	Dave Marcis	16
	Kyle Petty	16
25.	Rick Mast	14
26.	Lake Speed	11
27.	Richard Petty	9
	Michael Waltrip	9
29.	Jim Sauter	8
30.	A. J. Foyt	6

MILES LED

1.	Dale Earnhardt	2,624
2.	Rusty Wallace	2,549
3.	Darrell Waltrip	766
4.	Ken Schrader	723
5.	Alan Kulwicki	610
6.	Mark Martin	604
7.	Harry Gant	577
8.	Bill Elliott	573
9.	Geoff Bodine	450
10.	Davey Allison	446
11.	Ricky Rudd	363
12.	Morgan Shepherd	346
13.	Terry Labonte	240
14.	Dick Trickle	108
15.	Greg Sacks	68
16.	Sterling Marlin	60
17.	Dale Jarrett	55
18.	Phil Parsons	54
19.	Bobby Hillin Jr.	53
20.	Rick Wilson	52
21.	Kyle Petty	40
22.	Ernie Irvan	38
23.	Neil Bonnett	37
24.	Dave Marcis	26
25.	Rick Mast	25
26.	Michael Waltrip	22
27.	Lake Speed	21
28.	Richard Petty	14
29.	A. J. Foyt	13
30.	Jimmy Means	11

MILES DRIVEN

1.	Ricky Rudd	11,075
2.	Darrell Waltrip	10,984
3.	Bill Elliott	10,834
4.	Dale Earnhardt	10,796
5.	Rusty Wallace	10,781
6.	Ken Schrader	10,780
7.	Mark Martin	10,716
8.	Sterling Marlin	10,578
9.	Geoff Bodine	10,533
10.	Brett Bodine	10,354
11.	Bobby Hillin Jr.	10,296
12.	Harry Gant	10,293
13.	Michael Waltrip	10,112
14.	Davey Allison	10,111
15.	Dick Trickle	10,075
16.	Rick Wilson	9,990
17.	Dave Marcis	9,984
18.	Ernie Irvan	9,961
19.	Morgan Shepherd	9,908
20.	Terry Labonte	9,771
21.	Larry Pearson	9,735
22.	Alan Kulwicki	9,560
23.	Neil Bonnett	9,488
24.	Phil Parsons	9,319
25.	Hut Stricklin	9,285
26.	Dale Jarrett	9,178
27.	Lake Speed	8,245
28.	Richard Petty	7,927
29.	Kyle Petty	7,345
30.	Derrike Cope	6,863

RACES LED

1.	Rusty Wallace	23
2.	Dale Earnhardt	22
3.	Ken Schrader	17
	Darrell Waltrip	17
5.	Mark Martin	16
6.	Geoff Bodine	14
	Alan Kulwicki	14
8.	Davey Allison	13
9.	Bill Elliott	11
	Harry Gant	11
11.	Terry Labonte	10
12.	Dick Trickle	8
13.	Ricky Rudd	7
14.	Neil Bonnett	6
	Sterling Marlin	6
	Morgan Shepherd	6
17.	Dave Marcis	5
	Rick Wilson	5
19.	Bobby Hillin Jr.	4
	Ernie Irvan	4
	Phil Parsons	4
	Greg Sacks	4
	Lake Speed	4
	Michael Waltrip	4
25.	Derrike Cope	3
	Dale Jarrett	3
27.	Brett Bodine	2
	A. J. Foyt	2
	Rick Mast	2
	Larry Pearson	2

Driver	Starts	Poles	Finish 1	2	3	4	5	6–10	Laps	Laps Led	Races Led	Winston Cup Points	$
1990													
1. Dale Earnhardt	29	5	9	3	3	1	2	5	9,162	2,438	22	4,430	3,308,056
2. Mark Martin	29	4	3	5	4	2	2	7	9,636	451	15	4,404	1,302,958
3. Geoff Bodine	29	2	3	3	2	3	0	8	8,852	976	21	4,017	1,131,222
4. Bill Elliott	29	2	1	4	1	5	1	4	9,349	1,182	13	3,999	1,090,730
5. Morgan Shepherd	29	0	1	2	2	0	2	9	8,794	202	8	3,689	666,915
6. Rusty Wallace	29	2	2	3	2	0	2	7	8,459	1,137	16	3,676	954,129
7. Ricky Rudd	29	2	1	0	3	2	2	7	8,664	180	7	3,601	573,650
8. Alan Kulwicki	29	1	1	1	1	1	1	8	8,635	400	10	3,599	550,936
9. Ernie Irvan	29	3	1	2	1	1	1	7	8,991	280	10	3,593	535,280
10. Ken Schrader	29	3	0	2	2	1	2	7	8,649	242	12	3,572	769,934
11. Kyle Petty	29	2	1	0	0	1	0	12	8,795	852	12	3,501	746,326
12. Brett Bodine	29	1	1	0	2	2	0	4	9,097	216	7	3,440	442,681
13. Davey Allison	29	0	2	0	1	0	2	5	9,154	222	8	3,423	640,684
14. Sterling Marlin	29	0	0	0	1	1	3	5	8,310	71	6	3,387	369,167
15. Terry Labonte	29	0	0	1	0	3	0	5	8,518	9	3	3,371	450,230
16. Michael Waltrip	29	0	0	0	1	2	2	5	8,226	17	4	3,251	395,507
17. Harry Gant	28	0	1	0	1	1	3	3	7,441	53	9	3,182	522,519
18. Derrike Cope	29	0	2	0	0	0	0	4	7,961	109	6	3,140	569,451
19. Bobby Hillin Jr.	29	0	0	0	0	0	1	3	8,281	60	5	3,048	339,366
20. Darrell Waltrip	23	0	0	1	1	2	1	7	8,138	297	9	3,013	520,420
21. Dave Marcis	29	0	0	0	0	0	0	0	8,906	8	4	2,944	242,724
22. Dick Trickle	29	1	0	0	1	0	1	2	8,311	82	4	2,863	350,990
23. Rick Wilson	29	0	0	0	0	0	1	2	8,036	0	0	2,666	242,067
24. Jimmy Spencer	26	0	0	0	0	0	0	2	7,576	10	5	2,579	219,775
25. Dale Jarrett	24	0	0	0	0	1	0	6	6,801	73	4	2,558	214,495
26. Richard Petty	29	0	0	0	0	0	0	1	7,438	5	1	2,556	169,465
27. Butch Miller	23	0	0	0	0	0	0	1	6,891	4	4	2,377	151,941
28. Hut Stricklin	24	0	0	0	0	0	0	2	5,947	1	1	2,316	169,199
29. Jimmy Means	27	0	0	0	0	0	0	0	7,419	0	0	2,271	135,165
30. Rob Moroso	25	0	0	0	0	0	0	1	5,666	9	3	2,184	162,002
31. Rick Mast	20	0	0	0	0	0	0	1	5,335	0	0	1,719	112,875
32. Greg Sacks	16	1	0	2	0	0	0	2	3,790	107	4	1,663	216,148
33. Chad Little	18	0	0	0	0	0	0	0	4,822	0	0	1,632	80,140
34. Jack Pennington	14	0	0	0	0	0	0	0	3,450	7	2	1,278	95,860
35. Larry Pearson	9	0	0	0	0	0	0	0	2,871	0	0	822	72,305
36. Jimmy Horton	9	0	0	0	0	0	0	0	2,264	0	0	756	72,375
37. Mickey Gibbs	9	0	0	0	0	0	0	0	1,837	1	1	755	38,665
38. Mike Alexander	7	0	0	0	0	0	0	0	2,392	0	0	682	41,080
39. Phil Parsons	9	0	0	0	0	0	0	0	2,240	0	0	632	90,010
40. J. D. McDuffie	8	0	0	0	0	0	0	0	1,301	0	0	557	26,170
41. Buddy Baker	8	0	0	0	0	0	0	0	1,326	1	1	498	40,085
42. Lake Speed	6	0	0	0	0	0	0	0	835	3	1	479	75,537
43. Neil Bonnett	5	0	0	0	0	0	0	0	1,179	0	0	455	62,600
44. Mark Stahl	5	0	0	0	0	0	0	0	1,268	0	0	371	18,470
45. Bill Venturini	4	0	0	0	0	0	0	0	702	0	0	349	22,970
46. Rodney Combs	5	0	0	0	0	0	0	0	988	0	0	323	23,365
47. Irv Hoerr	2	0	0	0	0	0	0	2	164	3	1	281	14,775
48. Tommy Kendall	3	0	0	0	0	0	0	1	613	4	1	281	14,120
49. Ted Musgrave	4	0	0	0	0	0	0	0	786	0	0	280	17,190
50. Chuck Bown	3	0	0	0	0	0	0	0	951	0	0	276	10,150

LAPS COMPLETED

1.	Mark Martin	9,636
2.	Bill Elliott	9,349
3.	Dale Earnhardt	9,162
4.	Davey Allison	9,154
5.	Brett Bodine	9,097
6.	Ernie Irvan	8,991
7.	Dave Marcis	8,906
8.	Geoff Bodine	8,852
9.	Kyle Petty	8,795
10.	Morgan Shepherd	8,794
11.	Ricky Rudd	8,664
12.	Ken Schrader	8,649
13.	Alan Kulwicki	8,635
14.	Terry Labonte	8,518
15.	Rusty Wallace	8,459
16.	Dick Trickle	8,311
17.	Sterling Marlin	8,310
18.	Bobby Hillin Jr.	8,281
19.	Michael Waltrip	8,226
20.	Darrell Waltrip	8,138
21.	Rick Wilson	8,036
22.	Derrike Cope	7,961
23.	Jimmy Spencer	7,576
24.	Harry Gant	7,441
25.	Richard Petty	7,438
26.	Jimmy Means	7,419
27.	Butch Miller	6,891
28.	Dale Jarrett	6,801
29.	Hut Stricklin	5,947
30.	Rob Moroso	5,666

LAPS LED

1.	Dale Earnhardt	2,438
2.	Bill Elliott	1,182
3.	Rusty Wallace	1,137
4.	Geoff Bodine	976
5.	Kyle Petty	852
6.	Mark Martin	451
7.	Alan Kulwicki	400
8.	Darrell Waltrip	297
9.	Ernie Irvan	280
10.	Ken Schrader	242
11.	Davey Allison	222
12.	Brett Bodine	216
13.	Morgan Shepherd	202
14.	Ricky Rudd	180
15.	Derrike Cope	109
16.	Greg Sacks	107
17.	Dick Trickle	82
18.	Dale Jarrett	73
19.	Sterling Marlin	71
20.	Bobby Hillin Jr.	60
21.	Harry Gant	53
22.	Michael Waltrip	17
23.	Jimmy Spencer	10
24.	Terry Labonte	9
	Rob Moroso	9
26.	Dave Marcis	8
27.	Jack Pennington	7
28.	Richard Petty	5

MILES LED

1.	Dale Earnhardt	3,203
2.	Bill Elliott	1,512
3.	Rusty Wallace	1,311
4.	Geoff Bodine	1,141
5.	Kyle Petty	845
6.	Mark Martin	556
7.	Alan Kulwicki	396
8.	Morgan Shepherd	288
9.	Ken Schrader	284
10.	Ernie Irvan	284
11.	Greg Sacks	256
12.	Davey Allison	241
13.	Darrell Waltrip	212
14.	Ricky Rudd	182
15.	Brett Bodine	174
16.	Derrike Cope	127
17.	Sterling Marlin	97
18.	Harry Gant	85
19.	Dick Trickle	81
20.	Bobby Hillin Jr.	70
21.	Dale Jarrett	44
22.	Michael Waltrip	30
23.	Jimmy Spencer	23
24.	Rob Moroso	23
25.	Terry Labonte	21
26.	Jack Pennington	18
27.	A. J. Foyt	11
28.	Mike Chase	10
	Tommy Kendall	10
30.	Richard Petty	10

MILES DRIVEN

1.	Mark Martin	11,487
2.	Bill Elliott	11,087
3.	Dale Earnhardt	10,955
4.	Brett Bodine	10,878
5.	Davey Allison	10,816
6.	Alan Kulwicki	10,655
7.	Geoff Bodine	10,646
8.	Dave Marcis	10,611
9.	Morgan Shepherd	10,575
10.	Kyle Petty	10,496
11.	Ernie Irvan	10,413
12.	Ricky Rudd	10,392
13.	Terry Labonte	10,143
14.	Sterling Marlin	10,139
15.	Michael Waltrip	10,124
16.	Bobby Hillin Jr.	10,086
17.	Rusty Wallace	10,073
18.	Ken Schrader	9,948
19.	Dick Trickle	9,827
20.	Harry Gant	9,669
21.	Derrike Cope	9,654
22.	Rick Wilson	9,305
23.	Darrell Waltrip	9,190
24.	Richard Petty	9,063
25.	Jimmy Spencer	8,929
26.	Jimmy Means	8,650
27.	Butch Miller	8,648
28.	Hut Stricklin	7,941
29.	Dale Jarrett	7,699
30.	Rob Moroso	6,900

RACES LED

1.	Dale Earnhardt	22
2.	Geoff Bodine	21
3.	Rusty Wallace	16
4.	Mark Martin	15
5.	Bill Elliott	13
6.	Kyle Petty	12
	Ken Schrader	12
8.	Ernie Irvan	10
	Alan Kulwicki	10
10.	Harry Gant	9
	Darrell Waltrip	9
12.	Davey Allison	8
	Morgan Shepherd	8
14.	Brett Bodine	7
	Ricky Rudd	7
16.	Derrike Cope	6
	Sterling Marlin	6
18.	Bobby Hillin Jr.	5
	Jimmy Spencer	5
20.	Dale Jarrett	4
	Dave Marcis	4
	Butch Miller	4
	Greg Sacks	4
	Dick Trickle	4
	Michael Waltrip	4
26.	Terry Labonte	3
	Rob Moroso	3
28.	Jack Pennington	2

Driver	Starts	Poles	Finish 1	2	3	4	5	6–10	Laps	Laps Led	Races Led	Winston Cup Points	$

1991

Driver	Starts	Poles	1	2	3	4	5	6–10	Laps	Laps Led	Races Led	Winston Cup Points	$
1. Dale Earnhardt	29	0	4	3	4	1	2	7	9,541	1,125	20	4,287	2,416,685
2. Ricky Rudd	29	1	1	3	0	2	3	8	9,561	425	13	4,092	1,093,765
3. Davey Allison	29	3	5	4	2	1	0	4	8,770	1,528	23	4,088	1,712,924
4. Harry Gant	29	1	5	2	3	4	1	2	9,428	1,684	17	3,985	1,194,033
5. Ernie Irvan	29	1	2	3	0	4	2	8	8,720	584	16	3,925	1,079,017
6. Mark Martin	29	5	1	1	5	4	3	3	8,927	663	15	3,914	1,039,991
7. Sterling Marlin	29	2	0	2	1	1	3	9	9,205	201	8	3,839	633,690
8. Darrell Waltrip	29	0	2	2	1	0	0	12	9,229	203	12	3,711	604,854
9. Ken Schrader	29	0	2	2	2	1	3	8	8,331	440	16	3,690	772,434
10. Rusty Wallace	29	2	2	0	3	2	2	5	8,316	524	14	3,582	502,073
11. Bill Elliott	29	2	1	2	1	0	2	6	9,030	211	6	3,535	705,605
12. Morgan Shepherd	29	0	0	0	2	2	0	10	9,021	86	5	3,438	521,147
13. Alan Kulwicki	29	4	1	0	1	1	1	7	8,507	233	9	3,354	595,614
14. Geoff Bodine	27	2	1	2	1	1	1	6	7,997	152	12	3,277	625,256
15. Michael Waltrip	29	2	0	0	1	0	3	8	8,394	292	11	3,254	440,812
16. Hut Stricklin	29	0	0	1	0	2	0	4	8,813	69	7	3,199	426,524
17. Dale Jarrett	29	0	1	0	0	0	2	5	7,767	47	7	3,124	444,256
18. Terry Labonte	29	1	0	0	0	0	1	6	7,989	52	2	3,024	348,898
19. Brett Bodine	29	1	0	1	0	1	0	4	7,873	163	3	2,980	376,220
20. Joe Ruttman	29	0	0	0	1	0	0	3	8,974	11	1	2,938	361,661
21. Rick Mast	29	0	0	0	0	1	0	2	8,861	32	3	2,918	344,020
22. Bobby Hamilton	28	0	0	0	0	0	0	4	8,304	7	3	2,915	259,105
23. Ted Musgrave	29	0	0	0	0	0	0	0	9,074	6	5	2,841	200,910
24. Richard Petty	29	0	0	0	0	0	0	1	8,341	1	1	2,817	268,035
25. Jimmy Spencer	29	0	0	0	1	0	0	5	7,627	330	6	2,790	283,620
26. Rick Wilson	29	0	0	0	0	0	0	0	7,966	10	1	2,723	241,375
27. Chad Little	28	0	0	0	0	0	0	1	7,784	21	3	2,678	184,190
28. Derrike Cope	28	0	0	0	0	1	0	1	6,784	0	0	2,516	419,380
29. Dave Marcis	27	0	0	0	0	0	0	1	7,271	3	3	2,374	219,760
30. Bobby Hillin Jr.	22	0	0	0	0	0	0	1	6,152	10	1	2,317	251,645
31. Kyle Petty	18	2	1	1	0	0	0	2	6,631	553	7	2,078	413,727
32. Lake Speed	20	0	0	0	0	0	0	0	4,513	0	0	1,742	149,300
33. Jimmy Means	20	0	0	0	0	0	0	0	4,425	3	3	1,562	111,210
34. Mickey Gibbs	15	0	0	0	0	0	0	0	4,078	0	0	1,401	100,360
35. Dick Trickle	14	0	0	0	0	0	0	1	3,650	0	0	1,258	129,125
36. Stanley Smith	12	0	0	0	0	0	0	0	1,932	12	1	893	56,915
37. Larry Pearson	11	0	0	0	0	0	0	0	1,543	0	0	848	56,570
38. Wally Dallenbach Jr.	11	0	0	0	0	0	0	0	2,070	0	0	803	54,020
39. Greg Sacks	11	0	0	0	0	0	0	0	2,101	0	0	791	84,215
40. Buddy Baker	6	0	0	0	0	0	0	0	845	0	0	552	58,060
41. Jimmy Hensley	4	0	0	0	0	0	0	1	1,708	0	0	488	32,125
42. Eddie Bierschwale	5	0	0	0	0	0	0	0	1,112	0	0	431	55,025
43. Jim Sauter	6	0	0	0	0	0	0	0	1,012	0	0	423	47,395
44. Kenny Wallace	5	0	0	0	0	0	0	0	1,544	1	1	412	58,325
45. Jeff Purvis	6	0	0	0	0	0	0	0	888	0	0	399	42,910
46. Phil Barkdoll	4	0	0	0	0	0	0	0	646	0	0	364	41,655
47. Mike Chase	5	0	0	0	0	0	0	0	804	0	0	356	22,700
48. J. D. McDuffie	5	0	0	0	0	0	0	0	732	0	0	335	19,795
49. Bill Sedgwick	3	0	0	0	0	0	0	0	848	0	0	324	15,150
50. Randy LaJoie	4	0	0	0	0	0	0	0	1,080	0	0	304	23,875

LAPS COMPLETED

1.	Ricky Rudd	9,561
2.	Dale Earnhardt	9,541
3.	Harry Gant	9,428
4.	Darrell Waltrip	9,229
5.	Sterling Marlin	9,205
6.	Ted Musgrave	9,074
7.	Bill Elliott	9,030
8.	Morgan Shepherd	9,021
9.	Joe Ruttman	8,974
10.	Mark Martin	8,927
11.	Rick Mast	8,861
12.	Hut Stricklin	8,813
13.	Davey Allison	8,770
14.	Ernie Irvan	8,720
15.	Alan Kulwicki	8,507
16.	Michael Waltrip	8,394
17.	Richard Petty	8,341
18.	Ken Schrader	8,331
19.	Rusty Wallace	8,316
20.	Bobby Hamilton	8,304
21.	Geoff Bodine	7,997
22.	Terry Labonte	7,989
23.	Rick Wilson	7,966
24.	Brett Bodine	7,873
25.	Chad Little	7,784
26.	Dale Jarrett	7,767
27.	Jimmy Spencer	7,627
28.	Dave Marcis	7,271
29.	Derrike Cope	6,784
30.	Kyle Petty	6,631

LAPS LED

1.	Harry Gant	1,684
2.	Davey Allison	1,528
3.	Dale Earnhardt	1,125
4.	Mark Martin	663
5.	Ernie Irvan	584
6.	Kyle Petty	553
7.	Rusty Wallace	524
8.	Ken Schrader	440
9.	Ricky Rudd	425
10.	Jimmy Spencer	330
11.	Michael Waltrip	292
12.	Alan Kulwicki	233
13.	Bill Elliott	211
14.	Darrell Waltrip	203
15.	Sterling Marlin	201
16.	Brett Bodine	163
17.	Geoff Bodine	152
18.	Morgan Shepherd	86
19.	Hut Stricklin	69
20.	Terry Labonte	52
21.	Dale Jarrett	47
22.	Rick Mast	32
23.	Chad Little	21
24.	Tommy Kendall	12
	Stanley Smith	12
26.	Joe Ruttman	11
27.	Bobby Hillin Jr.	10
	Rick Wilson	10
29.	Bobby Hamilton	7
30.	Ted Musgrave	6

MILES LED

1.	Davey Allison	1,879
2.	Dale Earnhardt	1,525
3.	Harry Gant	1,477
4.	Mark Martin	926
5.	Ernie Irvan	919
6.	Ken Schrader	667
7.	Kyle Petty	667
8.	Rusty Wallace	516
9.	Ricky Rudd	421
10.	Michael Waltrip	406
11.	Bill Elliott	353
12.	Sterling Marlin	335
13.	Darrell Waltrip	260
14.	Geoff Bodine	213
15.	Jimmy Spencer	211
16.	Alan Kulwicki	152
17.	Hut Stricklin	130
18.	Brett Bodine	96
19.	Morgan Shepherd	89
20.	Dale Jarrett	80
21.	Rick Mast	73
22.	Terry Labonte	64
23.	Tommy Kendall	30
24.	Joe Ruttman	28
25.	Chad Little	26
26.	Bobby Hillin Jr.	15
27.	Stanley Smith	12
28.	Ted Musgrave	12
29.	Rick Wilson	10
30.	Bobby Hamilton	9

MILES DRIVEN

1.	Dale Earnhardt	11,435
2.	Ricky Rudd	11,427
3.	Sterling Marlin	11,207
4.	Harry Gant	11,124
5.	Darrell Waltrip	10,900
6.	Bill Elliott	10,826
7.	Mark Martin	10,810
8.	Joe Ruttman	10,774
9.	Rick Mast	10,650
10.	Davey Allison	10,610
11.	Ted Musgrave	10,579
12.	Morgan Shepherd	10,479
13.	Ernie Irvan	10,465
14.	Hut Stricklin	10,433
15.	Bobby Hamilton	10,187
16.	Rusty Wallace	10,147
17.	Alan Kulwicki	10,145
18.	Ken Schrader	9,841
19.	Michael Waltrip	9,757
20.	Rick Wilson	9,694
21.	Richard Petty	9,644
22.	Terry Labonte	9,615
23.	Geoff Bodine	9,589
24.	Chad Little	9,528
25.	Dale Jarrett	9,438
26.	Dave Marcis	9,173
27.	Brett Bodine	9,048
28.	Jimmy Spencer	8,581
29.	Derrike Cope	8,448
30.	Bobby Hillin Jr.	8,351

RACES LED

1.	Davey Allison	23
2.	Dale Earnhardt	20
3.	Harry Gant	17
4.	Ernie Irvan	16
	Ken Schrader	16
6.	Mark Martin	15
7.	Rusty Wallace	14
8.	Ricky Rudd	13
9.	Geoff Bodine	12
	Darrell Waltrip	12
11.	Michael Waltrip	11
12.	Alan Kulwicki	9
13.	Sterling Marlin	8
14.	Dale Jarrett	7
	Kyle Petty	7
	Hut Stricklin	7
17.	Bill Elliott	6
	Jimmy Spencer	6
19.	Morgan Shepherd	5
	Ted Musgrave	5
21.	Brett Bodine	3
	Bobby Hamilton	3
	Chad Little	3
	Dave Marcis	3
	Rick Mast	3
	Jimmy Means	3
27.	Terry Labonte	2

1992

Driver	Starts	Poles	Finish 1	2	3	4	5	6–10	Laps	Laps Led	Races Led	Winston Cup Points	$
1. Alan Kulwicki	29	6	2	3	2	2	2	6	8,991	1,235	20	4,078	2,322,561
2. Bill Elliott	29	2	5	2	3	1	3	3	9,115	1,273	18	4,068	1,692,381
3. Davey Allison	29	2	5	1	1	5	3	2	8,976	1,377	18	4,015	1,955,628
4. Harry Gant	29	0	2	3	2	0	3	5	9,197	407	15	3,955	1,122,776
5. Kyle Petty	29	3	2	0	4	3	0	8	9,059	970	8	3,945	1,107,063
6. Mark Martin	29	1	2	5	2	1	0	7	8,954	533	17	3,887	1,000,571
7. Ricky Rudd	29	1	1	0	2	3	3	9	8,968	331	9	3,735	793,903
8. Terry Labonte	29	0	0	1	0	2	1	12	8,912	43	4	3,674	600,381
9. Darrell Waltrip	29	1	3	2	3	0	2	3	8,706	513	14	3,659	876,492
10. Sterling Marlin	29	5	0	3	0	1	2	7	8,462	218	8	3,603	649,048
11. Ernie Irvan	29	3	3	2	1	2	1	2	8,561	477	17	3,580	996,885
12. Dale Earnhardt	29	1	1	2	2	1	0	9	8,694	487	10	3,574	915,463
13. Rusty Wallace	29	1	1	2	1	1	0	7	8,759	673	11	3,556	657,925
14. Morgan Shepherd	29	0	0	2	0	0	1	8	9,093	60	3	3,549	634,222
15. Brett Bodine	29	1	0	0	1	1	0	11	8,581	237	11	3,491	495,224
16. Geoff Bodine	29	0	2	0	2	2	1	4	8,222	474	5	3,437	716,583
17. Ken Schrader	29	1	0	0	2	1	1	7	8,425	83	5	3,404	639,679
18. Ted Musgrave	29	0	0	0	0	0	1	6	9,253	11	3	3,315	449,121
19. Dale Jarrett	29	0	0	1	1	0	0	6	8,586	99	5	3,251	418,648
20. Dick Trickle	29	0	0	0	0	0	3	6	8,259	5	2	3,097	429,521
21. Derrike Cope	29	0	0	0	0	0	0	3	8,483	0	0	3,033	277,215
22. Rick Mast	29	1	0	0	0	0	0	1	8,123	0	0	2,830	350,740
23. Michael Waltrip	29	0	0	0	0	1	0	1	8,474	3	1	2,825	410,545
24. Wally Dallenbach Jr.	29	0	0	0	0	0	1	0	8,118	0	0	2,799	220,245
25. Bobby Hamilton	29	0	0	0	0	0	0	2	8,998	0	0	2,787	367,065
26. Richard Petty	29	0	0	0	0	0	0	0	7,977	5	1	2,731	348,870
27. Hut Stricklin	28	0	0	0	0	0	0	4	7,928	60	2	2,689	336,965
28. Jimmy Hensley	22	0	0	0	0	0	0	4	6,804	22	3	2,410	247,660
29. Dave Marcis	29	0	0	0	0	0	0	0	6,739	0	0	2,348	218,045
30. Greg Sacks	20	0	0	0	0	0	0	0	4,926	6	1	1,759	178,120
31. Chad Little	19	0	0	0	0	0	0	1	5,114	0	0	1,669	145,805
32. Jimmy Means	22	0	0	0	0	0	0	0	4,370	0	0	1,531	133,160
33. Jimmy Spencer	12	0	0	0	0	2	1	0	3,803	1	1	1,284	183,585
34. Bobby Hillin Jr.	13	0	0	0	0	0	0	0	2,728	0	0	1,135	102,160
35. Stanley Smith	14	0	0	0	0	0	0	0	2,685	0	0	959	89,650
36. Mike Potter	11	0	0	0	0	0	0	0	1,869	0	0	806	74,710
37. Jim Sauter	9	0	0	0	0	0	0	0	2,829	0	0	729	56,045
38. Lake Speed	9	0	0	0	0	0	0	0	2,248	0	0	726	49,545
39. Jimmy Horton	9	0	0	0	0	0	0	0	2,166	0	0	660	50,125
40. Bob Schacht	9	0	0	0	0	0	0	0	1,363	2	1	611	58,815
41. Charlie Glotzbach	7	0	0	0	0	0	0	0	1,528	0	0	592	48,060
42. James Hylton	8	0	0	0	0	0	0	0	611	0	0	476	37,910
43. Andy Belmont	8	0	0	0	0	0	0	0	784	0	0	467	39,820
44. Jeff Purvis	6	0	0	0	0	0	0	0	1,418	0	0	453	45,545
45. Dave Mader III	5	0	0	0	0	0	0	0	1,387	7	1	436	69,635
46. Jerry O'Neil	6	0	0	0	0	0	0	0	958	0	0	429	32,370
47. Eddie Bierschwale	4	0	0	0	0	0	0	0	628	0	0	277	25,995
48. Buddy Baker	3	0	0	0	0	0	0	0	547	0	0	255	49,500
49. Rich Bickle	3	0	0	0	0	0	0	0	816	0	0	252	13,370
50. Mike Wallace	3	0	0	0	0	0	0	0	1,042	0	0	249	17,415

LAPS COMPLETED

1.	Ted Musgrave	9,253
2.	Harry Gant	9,197
3.	Bill Elliott	9,115
4.	Morgan Shepherd	9,093
5.	Kyle Petty	9,059
6.	Bobby Hamilton	8,998
7.	Alan Kulwicki	8,991
8.	Davey Allison	8,976
9.	Ricky Rudd	8,968
10.	Mark Martin	8,954
11.	Terry Labonte	8,912
12.	Rusty Wallace	8,759
13.	Darrell Waltrip	8,706
14.	Dale Earnhardt	8,694
15.	Dale Jarrett	8,586
16.	Brett Bodine	8,581
17.	Ernie Irvan	8,561
18.	Derrike Cope	8,483
19.	Michael Waltrip	8,474
20.	Sterling Marlin	8,462
21.	Ken Schrader	8,425
22.	Dick Trickle	8,259
23.	Geoff Bodine	8,222
24.	Rick Mast	8,123
25.	Wally Dallenbach Jr.	8,118
26.	Richard Petty	7,977
27.	Hut Stricklin	7,928
28.	Jimmy Hensley	6,804
29.	Dave Marcis	6,739
30.	Chad Little	5,114

LAPS LED

1.	Davey Allison	1,377
2.	Bill Elliott	1,273
3.	Alan Kulwicki	1,235
4.	Kyle Petty	970
5.	Rusty Wallace	673
6.	Mark Martin	533
7.	Darrell Waltrip	513
8.	Dale Earnhardt	487
9.	Ernie Irvan	477
10.	Geoff Bodine	474
11.	Harry Gant	407
12.	Ricky Rudd	331
13.	Brett Bodine	237
14.	Sterling Marlin	218
15.	Dale Jarrett	99
16.	Ken Schrader	83
17.	Morgan Shepherd	60
	Hut Stricklin	60
19.	Terry Labonte	43
20.	Jimmy Hensley	22
21.	Ted Musgrave	11
22.	Dave Mader III	7
23.	Greg Sacks	6
24.	Richard Petty	5
	Dick Trickle	5
26.	Michael Waltrip	3
27.	Bob Schacht	2
28.	Jimmy Spencer	1

MILES LED

1.	Davey Allison	2,315
2.	Bill Elliott	1,493
3.	Alan Kulwicki	1,304
4.	Kyle Petty	1,070
5.	Ernie Irvan	803
6.	Mark Martin	690
7.	Rusty Wallace	571
8.	Harry Gant	504
9.	Dale Earnhardt	466
10.	Sterling Marlin	436
11.	Darrell Waltrip	394
12.	Ricky Rudd	390
13.	Geoff Bodine	288
14.	Brett Bodine	177
15.	Dale Jarrett	150
16.	Ken Schrader	126
17.	Terry Labonte	78
18.	Morgan Shepherd	71
19.	Hut Stricklin	61
20.	Jimmy Hensley	32
21.	Ted Musgrave	23
22.	Richard Petty	13
23.	Dick Trickle	10
24.	Greg Sacks	9
25.	Michael Waltrip	8
26.	Dave Mader III	4
27.	Bob Schacht	3
28.	Jimmy Spencer	2

MILES DRIVEN

1.	Harry Gant	11,220
2.	Bill Elliott	11,124
3.	Davey Allison	10,998
4.	Ted Musgrave	10,988
5.	Kyle Petty	10,940
6.	Alan Kulwicki	10,852
7.	Morgan Shepherd	10,839
8.	Bobby Hamilton	10,736
9.	Mark Martin	10,670
10.	Terry Labonte	10,612
11.	Rusty Wallace	10,450
12.	Dale Jarrett	10,295
13.	Sterling Marlin	10,286
14.	Ernie Irvan	10,279
15.	Ricky Rudd	10,269
16.	Darrell Waltrip	10,248
17.	Dale Earnhardt	10,198
18.	Michael Waltrip	10,184
19.	Derrike Cope	10,174
20.	Brett Bodine	10,021
21.	Rick Mast	9,985
22.	Dick Trickle	9,883
23.	Ken Schrader	9,815
24.	Geoff Bodine	9,780
25.	Wally Dallenbach Jr.	9,714
26.	Richard Petty	9,624
27.	Hut Stricklin	9,260
28.	Jimmy Hensley	8,491
29.	Dave Marcis	8,477
30.	Chad Little	6,707

RACES LED

1.	Alan Kulwicki	20
2.	Davey Allison	18
	Bill Elliott	18
4.	Ernie Irvan	17
	Mark Martin	17
6.	Harry Gant	15
7.	Darrell Waltrip	14
8.	Brett Bodine	11
	Rusty Wallace	11
10.	Dale Earnhardt	10
11.	Ricky Rudd	9
12.	Sterling Marlin	8
	Kyle Petty	8
14.	Geoff Bodine	5
	Dale Jarrett	5
	Ken Schrader	5
17.	Terry Labonte	4
18.	Jimmy Hensley	3
	Morgan Shepherd	3
	Ted Musgrave	3
21.	Hut Stricklin	2
	Dick Trickle	2

Driver	Starts	Poles	Finish 1	2	3	4	5	6–10	Laps	Laps Led	Races Led	Winston Cup Points	$
1993													
1. Dale Earnhardt	30	3	6	5	3	3	0	4	9,787	1,475	21	4,526	3,353,789
2. Rusty Wallace	30	3	10	4	2	1	2	2	9,641	2,860	20	4,446	1,702,154
3. Mark Martin	30	5	5	3	1	1	2	7	9,381	1,353	20	4,150	1,657,662
4. Dale Jarrett	30	0	1	1	4	5	2	5	9,149	263	15	4,000	1,242,394
5. Kyle Petty	30	1	1	1	2	2	3	6	9,259	526	13	3,860	914,662
6. Ernie Irvan	29	4	3	4	3	0	2	2	8,185	1,112	18	3,834	1,400,468
7. Morgan Shepherd	30	0	1	1	0	1	0	12	9,442	92	9	3,807	782,523
8. Bill Elliott	30	2	0	1	2	2	1	9	9,329	14	4	3,774	955,859
9. Ken Schrader	30	6	0	2	2	3	2	6	8,877	286	14	3,715	952,748
10. Ricky Rudd	30	0	1	1	1	3	3	5	8,635	136	7	3,644	752,562
11. Harry Gant	30	1	0	0	1	2	1	8	8,843	265	8	3,524	772,832
12. Jimmy Spencer	30	0	0	1	2	2	0	5	8,848	64	4	3,496	686,026
13. Darrell Waltrip	30	0	0	0	2	1	1	6	9,194	151	9	3,479	746,646
14. Jeff Gordon	30	1	0	2	1	1	3	4	8,390	230	14	3,447	765,168
15. Sterling Marlin	30	0	0	1	0	0	0	7	9,153	341	6	3,355	628,835
16. Geoff Bodine	30	1	1	0	1	0	0	7	8,496	102	11	3,338	783,762
17. Michael Waltrip	30	0	0	0	0	0	0	5	9,379	40	6	3,291	529,923
18. Terry Labonte	30	0	0	0	0	0	0	10	8,866	55	3	3,280	531,717
19. Bobby Labonte	30	1	0	0	0	0	0	6	9,295	33	7	3,221	395,660
20. Brett Bodine	29	2	0	1	0	0	2	6	8,120	102	7	3,183	582,014
21. Rick Mast	30	0	0	0	0	0	1	4	8,488	32	4	3,001	568,095
22. Wally Dallenbach Jr.	30	0	0	1	0	0	0	3	8,411	3	2	2,978	474,340
23. Kenny Wallace	30	0	0	0	0	0	0	3	8,806	1	1	2,893	330,325
24. Hut Stricklin	30	0	0	0	0	1	0	1	8,356	98	3	2,866	494,600
25. Ted Musgrave	29	0	0	0	0	0	2	3	8,530	8	3	2,853	458,615
26. Derrike Cope	30	0	0	0	0	0	0	1	8,406	38	3	2,787	402,515
27. Bobby Hillin Jr.	30	0	0	0	0	0	0	0	8,343	3	1	2,717	263,540
28. Rick Wilson	29	0	0	0	0	0	0	1	8,117	1	1	2,647	299,725
29. Phil Parsons	26	0	0	0	0	0	0	2	6,331	3	1	2,454	293,725
30. Dick Trickle	26	0	0	0	0	0	1	1	7,003	3	1	2,224	24,065
31. Davey Allison	16	0	1	1	2	1	1	2	5,061	276	9	2,104	513,585
32. Jimmy Hensley	21	0	0	0	0	0	0	2	5,843	1	1	2,001	368,150
33. Dave Marcis	23	0	0	0	0	0	0	0	6,233	14	3	1,970	202,305
34. Lake Speed	21	0	0	0	0	0	0	1	5,852	2	1	1,956	319,800
35. Greg Sacks	19	0	0	0	0	0	0	1	5,251	1	1	1,730	168,055
36. Jimmy Means	18	0	0	0	0	0	0	0	4,765	2	2	1,471	148,205
37. Bobby Hamilton	15	0	0	0	0	0	0	1	3,989	0	0	1,348	142,740
38. Jimmy Horton	13	0	0	0	0	0	0	0	2,198	0	0	841	115,105
39. Jeff Purvis	8	0	0	0	0	0	0	0	2,491	3	2	774	108,545
40. Todd Bodine	10	0	0	0	0	0	0	0	2,393	0	0	715	63,245
41. Alan Kulwicki	5	0	0	0	1	1	0	1	1,588	4	2	625	165,470
42. P. J. Jones	6	0	0	0	0	0	0	1	710	0	0	498	53,370
43. Joe Ruttman	5	0	0	0	0	0	1	0	1,133	0	0	417	70,700
44. Joe Nemechek	5	0	0	0	0	0	0	0	1,114	0	0	389	56,580
45. Loy Allen Jr.	5	0	0	0	0	0	0	0	878	0	0	362	34,695
46. Mike Wallace	4	0	0	0	0	0	0	0	1,287	0	0	343	30,125
47. Jim Sauter	4	0	0	0	0	0	0	0	769	0	0	295	48,860
48. Rich Bickle	5	0	0	0	0	0	0	0	842	1	1	292	36,095
49. Rick Carelli	3	0	0	0	0	0	0	0	499	0	0	258	19,650
50. John Andretti	4	0	0	0	0	0	0	0	874	0	0	250	24,915

LAPS COMPLETED

1.	Dale Earnhardt	9,787
2.	Rusty Wallace	9,641
3.	Morgan Shepherd	9,442
4.	Mark Martin	9,381
5.	Michael Waltrip	9,379
6.	Bill Elliott	9,329
7.	Bobby Labonte	9,295
8.	Kyle Petty	9,259
9.	Darrell Waltrip	9,194
10.	Sterling Marlin	9,153
11.	Dale Jarrett	9,149
12.	Ken Schrader	8,877
13.	Terry Labonte	8,866
14.	Jimmy Spencer	8,848
15.	Harry Gant	8,843
16.	Kenny Wallace	8,806
17.	Ricky Rudd	8,635
18.	Ted Musgrave	8,530
19.	Geoff Bodine	8,496
20.	Rick Mast	8,488
21.	Wally Dallenbach Jr.	8,411
22.	Derrike Cope	8,406
23.	Jeff Gordon	8,390
24.	Hut Stricklin	8,356
25.	Bobby Hillin Jr.	8,343
26.	Ernie Irvan	8,185
27.	Brett Bodine	8,120
28.	Rick Wilson	8,117
29.	Dick Trickle	7,003
30.	Phil Parsons	6,331

LAPS LED

1.	Rusty Wallace	2,860
2.	Dale Earnhardt	1,475
3.	Mark Martin	1,353
4.	Ernie Irvan	1,112
5.	Kyle Petty	526
6.	Sterling Marlin	341
7.	Ken Schrader	286
8.	Davey Allison	276
9.	Harry Gant	265
10.	Dale Jarrett	263
11.	Jeff Gordon	230
12.	Darrell Waltrip	151
13.	Ricky Rudd	136
14.	Brett Bodine	102
	Geoff Bodine	102
16.	Hut Stricklin	98
17.	Morgan Shepherd	92
18.	Jimmy Spencer	64
19.	Terry Labonte	55
20.	Michael Waltrip	40
21.	Derrike Cope	38
22.	Bobby Labonte	33
23.	Rick Mast	32
24.	Bill Elliott	14
	Dave Marcis	14
26.	Ted Musgrave	8
27.	Alan Kulwicki	4

MILES LED

1.	Dale Earnhardt	2,485
2.	Rusty Wallace	2,333
3.	Mark Martin	1,792
4.	Ernie Irvan	1,257
5.	Kyle Petty	831
6.	Dale Jarrett	466
7.	Harry Gant	339
8.	Ken Schrader	332
9.	Sterling Marlin	319
10.	Jeff Gordon	303
11.	Davey Allison	254
12.	Ricky Rudd	240
13.	Geoff Bodine	161
14.	Darrell Waltrip	149
15.	Morgan Shepherd	125
16.	Brett Bodine	122
17.	Derrike Cope	89
18.	Hut Stricklin	70
19.	Jimmy Spencer	63
20.	Michael Waltrip	49
21.	Terry Labonte	35
22.	Bobby Labonte	35
23.	Rick Mast	23
24.	Bill Elliott	22
25.	Dave Marcis	16
26.	Ted Musgrave	13
27.	Bobby Hillin Jr.	8
28.	Alan Kulwicki	5
29.	Phil Parsons	5
30.	Lake Speed	4

MILES DRIVEN

1.	Dale Earnhardt	11,808
2.	Morgan Shepherd	11,406
3.	Dale Jarrett	11,335
4.	Bill Elliott	11,335
5.	Rusty Wallace	11,231
6.	Sterling Marlin	11,221
7.	Kyle Petty	11,186
8.	Michael Waltrip	11,146
9.	Mark Martin	11,106
10.	Ken Schrader	10,994
11.	Bobby Labonte	10,937
12.	Harry Gant	10,867
13.	Jimmy Spencer	10,823
14.	Darrell Waltrip	10,817
15.	Terry Labonte	10,641
16.	Kenny Wallace	10,551
17.	Ted Musgrave	10,397
18.	Rick Wilson	10,330
19.	Ricky Rudd	10,265
20.	Hut Stricklin	10,211
21.	Geoff Bodine	10,198
22.	Ernie Irvan	10,136
23.	Jeff Gordon	10,066
24.	Wally Dallenbach Jr.	10,056
25.	Derrike Cope	9,965
26.	Rick Mast	9,802
27.	Bobby Hillin Jr.	9,768
28.	Brett Bodine	9,382
29.	Dick Trickle	8,376
30.	Phil Parsons	8,041

RACES LED

1.	Dale Earnhardt	21
2.	Mark Martin	20
	Rusty Wallace	20
4.	Ernie Irvan	18
5.	Dale Jarrett	15
6.	Jeff Gordon	14
	Ken Schrader	14
8.	Kyle Petty	13
9.	Geoff Bodine	11
10.	Davey Allison	9
	Morgan Shepherd	9
	Darrell Waltrip	9
13.	Harry Gant	8
14.	Brett Bodine	7
	Bobby Labonte	7
	Ricky Rudd	7
17.	Sterling Marlin	6
	Michael Waltrip	6
19.	Bill Elliott	4
	Rick Mast	4
	Jimmy Spencer	4
22.	Derrike Cope	3
	Terry Labonte	3
	Dave Marcis	3
	Hut Stricklin	3
	Ted Musgrave	3
27.	Wally Dallenbach Jr.	2
	Alan Kulwicki	2
	Jimmy Means	2
	Jeff Purvis	2

Driver	Starts	Poles	Finish 1	2	3	4	5	6–10	Laps	Laps Led	Races Led	Winston Cup Points	$

1994

Driver	Starts	Poles	1	2	3	4	5	6–10	Laps	Laps Led	Races Led	Winston Cup Points	$
1. Dale Earnhardt	31	2	4	7	6	1	2	5	9,546	1,013	23	4,694	3,400,733
2. Mark Martin	31	1	2	4	2	4	3	5	9,549	733	18	4,250	1,678,906
3. Rusty Wallace	31	2	8	3	1	4	1	3	9,281	2,142	19	4,207	1,959,072
4. Ken Schrader	31	0	0	1	2	4	2	9	9,704	222	9	4,060	1,211,062
5. Ricky Rudd	31	1	1	0	0	3	2	9	9,728	192	10	4,050	1,079,441
6. Morgan Shepherd	31	0	0	2	2	1	4	7	9,788	80	10	4,029	1,119,038
7. Terry Labonte	31	0	3	1	1	0	1	8	9,149	487	8	3,876	1,150,921
8. Jeff Gordon	31	1	2	1	1	2	1	7	9,277	446	17	3,776	1,799,523
9. Darrell Waltrip	31	0	0	0	2	2	0	9	9,905	60	8	3,688	854,280
10. Bill Elliott	31	1	1	1	3	0	1	6	9,172	62	8	3,617	951,679
11. Lake Speed	31	0	0	0	1	1	2	5	9,111	39	5	3,565	845,963
12. Michael Waltrip	31	0	0	0	1	0	1	7	9,508	8	5	3,512	720,426
13. Ted Musgrave	31	3	0	0	0	0	1	7	9,237	50	4	3,477	669,687
14. Sterling Marlin	31	1	1	1	1	0	2	6	9,184	144	11	3,443	1,140,683
15. Kyle Petty	31	0	0	0	0	1	1	5	9,085	7	2	3,339	818,832
16. Dale Jarrett	30	0	1	0	0	2	1	5	8,410	55	8	3,298	893,754
17. Geoff Bodine	31	5	3	1	1	1	1	3	8,150	1,744	20	3,297	1,287,626
18. Rick Mast	31	1	0	1	3	0	0	6	8,756	166	8	3,238	733,361
19. Brett Bodine	31	0	0	1	0	0	0	5	8,931	55	6	3,159	801,944
20. Todd Bodine	30	0	0	0	1	0	1	5	8,475	60	5	3,048	504,316
21. Bobby Labonte	31	0	0	0	0	0	1	1	8,541	3	2	3,038	550,305
22. Ernie Irvan	20	5	3	6	2	0	2	2	5,357	1,781	17	3,026	1,311,522
23. Bobby Hamilton	30	0	0	0	0	0	0	1	8,337	24	4	2,749	514,520
24. Jeff Burton	30	0	0	0	0	2	0	1	7,752	122	4	2,726	594,700
25. Harry Gant	30	1	0	0	0	0	0	7	7,329	94	3	2,720	556,020
26. Hut Stricklin	29	0	0	0	0	0	0	1	8,562	26	2	2,711	333,495
27. Joe Nemechek	29	0	0	0	1	0	0	2	7,951	22	2	2,673	386,315
28. Steve Grissom	27	0	0	0	0	0	0	3	7,966	1	1	2,660	300,915
29. Jimmy Spencer	29	1	2	0	0	1	0	1	6,904	47	6	2,613	479,235
30. Derrike Cope	30	0	0	0	0	0	0	2	8,506	11	2	2,612	398,436
31. Greg Sacks	31	1	0	0	0	0	0	3	8,266	38	8	2,593	411,728
32. John Andretti	29	0	0	0	0	0	0	0	7,508	41	4	2,299	391,920
33. Mike Wallace	22	0	0	0	0	0	1	0	6,672	13	1	2,191	265,115
34. Dick Trickle	25	0	0	0	0	0	0	1	6,423	1	1	2,019	244,806
35. Ward Burton	26	1	0	1	0	0	0	1	5,230	74	5	1,971	304,700
36. Dave Marcis	23	0	0	0	0	0	0	1	5,914	17	4	1,910	261,650
37. Jeremy Mayfield	20	0	0	0	0	0	0	0	5,581	0	0	1,673	226,265
38. Wally Dallenbach Jr.	14	0	0	0	0	1	0	2	3,568	1	1	1,493	241,492
39. Loy Allen Jr.	19	3	0	0	0	0	0	0	4,446	12	3	1,468	216,751
40. Kenny Wallace	12	0	0	0	0	1	0	2	4,426	4	3	1,413	235,005
41. Jimmy Hensley	17	0	0	0	0	0	0	0	3,861	4	3	1,394	203,520
42. Chuck Bown	13	1	0	0	0	0	0	1	3,714	0	0	1,211	225,260
43. Rich Bickle	12	0	0	0	0	0	0	0	2,087	0	0	849	115,575
44. Bobby Hillin Jr.	9	0	0	0	0	0	0	0	2,007	2	1	749	125,340
45. Brad Teague	8	0	0	0	0	0	0	0	1,959	0	0	548	59,990
46. Jeff Purvis	7	0	0	0	0	0	0	0	1,081	0	0	484	78,755
47. Billy Standridge	8	0	0	0	0	0	0	0	1,260	0	0	404	56,405
48. Randy LaJoie	3	0	0	0	0	0	0	0	1,010	0	0	312	30,565
49. Rick Carelli	4	0	0	0	0	0	0	0	958	0	0	283	31,975
50. Phil Parsons	3	0	0	0	0	0	0	0	757	0	0	243	21,415

LAPS COMPLETED		LAPS LED		MILES LED		MILES DRIVEN		RACES LED	
1. Darrell Waltrip	9,905	1. Rusty Wallace	2,142	1. Ernie Irvan	2,419	1. Ricky Rudd	12,046	1. Dale Earnhardt	23
2. Morgan Shepherd	9,788	2. Ernie Irvan	1,781	2. Rusty Wallace	2,113	2. Darrell Waltrip	12,026	2. Geoff Bodine	20
3. Ricky Rudd	9,728	3. Geoff Bodine	1,744	3. Geoff Bodine	2,027	3. Morgan Shepherd	11,950	3. Rusty Wallace	19
4. Ken Schrader	9,704	4. Dale Earnhardt	1,013	4. Dale Earnhardt	1,322	4. Ken Schrader	11,740	4. Mark Martin	18
5. Mark Martin	9,549	5. Mark Martin	733	5. Mark Martin	926	5. Michael Waltrip	11,666	5. Jeff Gordon	17
6. Dale Earnhardt	9,546	6. Terry Labonte	487	6. Jeff Gordon	658	6. Jeff Gordon	11,548	Ernie Irvan	17
7. Michael Waltrip	9,508	7. Jeff Gordon	446	7. Terry Labonte	442	7. Dale Earnhardt	11,409	7. Sterling Marlin	11
8. Rusty Wallace	9,281	8. Ken Schrader	222	8. Ken Schrader	294	8. Mark Martin	11,403	8. Ricky Rudd	10
9. Jeff Gordon	9,277	9. Ricky Rudd	192	9. Sterling Marlin	235	9. Bill Elliott	11,380	Morgan Shepherd	10
10. Ted Musgrave	9,237	10. Rick Mast	166	10. Ricky Rudd	226	10. Terry Labonte	11,313	10. Ken Schrader	9
11. Sterling Marlin	9,184	11. Sterling Marlin	144	11. Rick Mast	201	11. Lake Speed	11,291	11. Bill Elliott	8
12. Bill Elliott	9,172	12. Jeff Burton	122	12. Jeff Burton	187	12. Kyle Petty	11,104	Dale Jarrett	8
13. Terry Labonte	9,149	13. Harry Gant	94	13. Todd Bodine	112	13. Sterling Marlin	10,841	Terry Labonte	8
14. Lake Speed	9,111	14. Morgan Shepherd	80	14. Jimmy Spencer	109	14. Ted Musgrave	10,817	Rick Mast	8
15. Kyle Petty	9,085	15. Ward Burton	74	15. Ward Burton	109	15. Brett Bodine	10,772	Greg Sacks	8
16. Brett Bodine	8,931	16. Bill Elliott	62	16. Bill Elliott	108	16. Rick Mast	10,753	Darrell Waltrip	8
17. Rick Mast	8,756	17. Todd Bodine	60	17. Morgan Shepherd	97	17. Rusty Wallace	10,730	17. Brett Bodine	6
18. Hut Stricklin	8,562	Darrell Waltrip	60	18. Brett Bodine	85	18. Hut Stricklin	10,585	Jimmy Spencer	6
19. Bobby Labonte	8,541	19. Brett Bodine	55	19. Darrell Waltrip	77	19. Todd Bodine	10,478	19. Todd Bodine	5
20. Derrike Cope	8,506	Dale Jarrett	55	20. Dale Jarrett	69	20. Bobby Labonte	10,456	Ward Burton	5
21. Todd Bodine	8,475	21. Ted Musgrave	50	21. Greg Sacks	63	21. Dale Jarrett	10,441	Lake Speed	5
22. Dale Jarrett	8,410	22. Jimmy Spencer	47	22. John Andretti	62	22. Jeff Burton	10,225	Michael Waltrip	5
23. Bobby Hamilton	8,337	23. John Andretti	41	23. Harry Gant	62	23. Bobby Hamilton	10,220	23. John Andretti	4
24. Greg Sacks	8,266	24. Lake Speed	39	24. Lake Speed	56	24. Greg Sacks	10,041	Jeff Burton	4
25. Geoff Bodine	8,150	25. Greg Sacks	38	25. Ted Musgrave	42	25. Geoff Bodine	9,771	Bobby Hamilton	4
26. Steve Grissom	7,966	26. Hut Stricklin	26	26. Loy Allen Jr.	27	26. Steve Grissom	9,740	Dave Marcis	4
27. Joe Nemechek	7,951	27. Bobby Hamilton	24	27. Dave Marcis	27	27. Derrike Cope	9,718	Ted Musgrave	4
28. Jeff Burton	7,752	28. Joe Nemechek	22	28. Derrike Cope	24	28. Harry Gant	9,570	28. Loy Allen Jr.	3
29. John Andretti	7,508	29. Dave Marcis	17	29. Bobby Hamilton	23	29. Joe Nemechek	9,486	Harry Gant	3
30. Harry Gant	7,329	30. Mike Wallace	13	30. Mike Wallace	20	30. John Andretti	8,920	Jimmy Hensley	3
								Kenny Wallace	3

Driver	Starts	Poles	Finish 1	2	3	4	5	6–10	Laps	Laps Led	Races Led	Winston Cup Points	$

1995

Driver	Starts	Poles	1	2	3	4	5	6–10	Laps	Laps Led	Races Led	Winston Cup Points	$
1. Jeff Gordon	31	9	7	4	5	0	1	6	9,405	2,600	29	4,614	4,347,343
2. Dale Earnhardt	31	3	5	6	5	1	2	4	9,625	1,583	24	4,580	3,154,241
3. Sterling Marlin	31	1	3	2	0	3	1	13	9,728	472	12	4,361	2,253,502
4. Mark Martin	31	4	4	1	4	1	3	9	9,393	740	14	4,320	1,893,519
5. Rusty Wallace	31	0	2	4	6	2	1	4	9,497	1,066	17	4,240	1,642,837
6. Terry Labonte	31	1	3	4	2	3	2	3	9,076	438	11	4,146	1,558,659
7. Ted Musgrave	31	1	0	2	2	2	1	6	9,580	43	6	3,949	1,147,445
8. Bill Elliott	31	2	0	0	0	2	2	7	8,995	123	8	3,746	996,816
9. Ricky Rudd	31	2	1	0	1	4	4	6	8,813	368	11	3,734	1,337,703
10. Bobby Labonte	31	2	3	3	0	0	1	7	9,019	278	14	3,718	1,413,682
11. Morgan Shepherd	31	0	0	1	1	1	1	6	9,275	31	8	3,618	996,374
12. Michael Waltrip	31	0	0	0	1	0	1	6	9,222	45	12	3,601	898,338
13. Dale Jarrett	31	1	1	1	2	1	4	5	8,671	324	8	3,584	1,363,158
14. Bobby Hamilton	31	0	0	1	0	2	1	6	9,421	131	7	3,576	804,505
15. Derrike Cope	31	0	0	1	0	0	1	6	9,335	70	4	3,384	683,075
16. Geoff Bodine	31	0	0	0	0	0	1	3	9,257	13	4	3,357	1,011,090
17. Ken Schrader	31	1	0	0	1	1	0	8	8,550	238	9	3,221	886,566
18. John Andretti	31	1	0	0	0	1	0	4	8,412	77	9	3,140	593,542
19. Darrell Waltrip	31	1	0	0	1	3	0	4	8,222	168	8	3,075	850,632
20. Brett Bodine	31	0	0	0	0	0	0	2	9,159	6	1	2,958	893,029
21. Rick Mast	31	1	0	0	0	0	0	3	8,560	143	3	2,984	749,550
22. Ward Burton	29	0	1	0	0	1	1	3	7,744	173	4	2,926	634,655
23. Lake Speed	31	0	0	0	0	0	0	2	9,073	17	1	2,921	529,435
24. Ricky Craven	31	0	0	0	0	0	0	4	8,711	6	4	2,883	597,054
25. Dick Trickle	31	0	0	0	0	0	0	1	8,941	5	1	2,875	694,920
26. Jimmy Spencer	29	0	0	0	0	0	0	4	8,682	4	2	2,809	504,560
27. Steve Grissom	29	0	0	0	0	0	1	3	8,279	17	2	2,757	509,047
28. Joe Nemechek	29	0	0	0	0	1	0	3	8,504	1	1	2,742	428,925
29. Robert Pressley	31	0	0	0	0	0	0	1	8,191	37	3	2,663	695,875
30. Kyle Petty	30	0	1	0	0	0	0	4	8,127	311	4	2,635	698,875
31. Jeremy Mayfield	27	0	0	0	0	0	0	1	7,943	79	3	2,637	436,805
32. Jeff Burton	29	0	0	0	0	0	1	1	8,050	4	2	2,556	628,270
33. Todd Bodine	28	0	0	0	0	1	0	2	6,684	19	2	2,372	664,620
34. Mike Wallace	26	0	0	0	0	0	0	1	6,819	1	1	2,175	428,006
35. Dave Marcis	28	0	0	0	0	0	0	0	7,319	3	2	2,126	337,853
36. Hut Stricklin	24	1	0	0	0	1	1	3	5,513	45	4	2,052	486,065
37. Bobby Hillin Jr.	18	0	0	0	0	0	0	1	4,410	1	1	1,888	244,270
38. Elton Sawyer	20	0	0	0	0	0	0	0	4,573	0	0	1,499	416,490
39. Greg Sacks	20	0	0	0	0	0	0	0	4,682	0	0	1,349	323,720
40. Randy LaJoie	14	0	0	0	0	0	0	0	3,606	0	0	1,133	281,945
41. Loy Allen Jr.	11	0	0	0	0	0	0	1	2,707	18	1	890	186,670
42. Kenny Wallace	11	0	0	0	0	0	0	0	3,127	0	0	878	151,700
43. Chuck Bown	9	0	0	0	0	0	0	0	2,068	0	0	818	99,995
44. Jimmy Hensley	9	0	0	0	0	0	0	0	1,512	0	0	558	161,025
45. Rich Bickle	8	0	0	0	0	0	0	0	1,995	2	1	538	153,250
46. Davy Jones	7	0	0	0	0	0	0	0	1,680	0	0	520	109,925
47. Jeff Purvis	7	0	0	0	0	0	0	0	951	0	0	391	93,875
48. Ernie Irvan	3	0	0	0	0	0	0	2	924	142	2	354	54,875
49. Steve Kinser	5	0	0	0	0	0	0	0	958	0	0	287	105,224
50. Wally Dallenbach Jr.	2	0	0	1	0	0	0	0	131	21	1	221	63,900

LAPS COMPLETED

1.	Sterling Marlin	9,728
2.	Dale Earnhardt	9,625
3.	Ted Musgrave	9,580
4.	Rusty Wallace	9,497
5.	Bobby Hamilton	9,421
6.	Jeff Gordon	9,405
7.	Mark Martin	9,393
8.	Derrike Cope	9,335
9.	Morgan Shepherd	9,275
10.	Geoff Bodine	9,257
11.	Michael Waltrip	9,222
12.	Brett Bodine	9,159
13.	Terry Labonte	9,076
14.	Lake Speed	9,073
15.	Bobby Labonte	9,019
16.	Bill Elliott	8,995
17.	Dick Trickle	8,941
18.	Ricky Rudd	8,813
19.	Ricky Craven	8,711
20.	Jimmy Spencer	8,682
21.	Dale Jarrett	8,671
22.	Rick Mast	8,560
23.	Ken Schrader	8,550
24.	Joe Nemechek	8,504
25.	John Andretti	8,412
26.	Steve Grissom	8,279
27.	Darrell Waltrip	8,222
28.	Robert Pressley	8,191
29.	Kyle Petty	8,127
30.	Jeff Burton	8,050

LAPS LED

1.	Jeff Gordon	2,600
2.	Dale Earnhardt	1,583
3.	Rusty Wallace	1,066
4.	Mark Martin	740
5.	Sterling Marlin	472
6.	Terry Labonte	438
7.	Ricky Rudd	368
8.	Dale Jarrett	324
9.	Kyle Petty	311
10.	Bobby Labonte	278
11.	Ken Schrader	238
12.	Ward Burton	173
13.	Darrell Waltrip	168
14.	Rick Mast	143
15.	Ernie Irvan	142
16.	Bobby Hamilton	131
17.	Bill Elliott	123
18.	Jeremy Mayfield	79
19.	John Andretti	77
20.	Derrike Cope	70
21.	Hut Stricklin	45
	Michael Waltrip	45
23.	Ted Musgrave	43
24.	Robert Pressley	37
25.	Morgan Shepherd	31
26.	Wally Dallenbach Jr.	21
27.	Todd Bodine	19
28.	Loy Allen Jr.	18
29.	Steve Grissom	17
	Lake Speed	17

MILES LED

1.	Jeff Gordon	3,458
2.	Dale Earnhardt	1,739
3.	Mark Martin	1,015
4.	Sterling Marlin	964
5.	Rusty Wallace	943
6.	Ricky Rudd	511
7.	Bobby Labonte	417
8.	Ken Schrader	400
9.	Dale Jarrett	373
10.	Terry Labonte	336
11.	Kyle Petty	293
12.	Bill Elliott	259
13.	Ward Burton	196
14.	Rick Mast	147
15.	Bobby Hamilton	133
16.	Ernie Irvan	130
17.	Darrell Waltrip	109
18.	John Andretti	94
19.	Michael Waltrip	68
20.	Hut Stricklin	66
21.	Jeremy Mayfield	60
22.	Ted Musgrave	56
23.	Derrike Cope	54
24.	Wally Dallenbach Jr.	51
25.	Morgan Shepherd	51
26.	Loy Allen Jr.	48
27.	Todd Bodine	27
28.	Robert Pressley	27
29.	Geoff Bodine	22
30.	Steve Grissom	12

MILES DRIVEN

1.	Sterling Marlin	11,936
2.	Ted Musgrave	11,822
3.	Dale Earnhardt	11,714
4.	Jeff Gordon	11,608
5.	Geoff Bodine	11,571
6.	Rusty Wallace	11,563
7.	Bobby Hamilton	11,555
8.	Morgan Shepherd	11,547
9.	Mark Martin	11,427
10.	Michael Waltrip	11,399
11.	Terry Labonte	11,376
12.	Lake Speed	11,196
13.	Dick Trickle	11,094
14.	Ricky Craven	11,086
15.	Brett Bodine	11,084
16.	Bill Elliott	11,073
17.	Derrike Cope	11,039
18.	Bobby Labonte	10,974
19.	Ricky Rudd	10,834
20.	Rick Mast	10,599
21.	Jimmy Spencer	10,484
22.	Jeremy Mayfield	10,440
23.	Dale Jarrett	10,417
24.	Steve Grissom	10,299
25.	Joe Nemechek	10,223
26.	Jeff Burton	10,193
27.	John Andretti	10,178
28.	Ken Schrader	10,166
29.	Kyle Petty	10,077
30.	Robert Pressley	10,006

RACES LED

1.	Jeff Gordon	29
2.	Dale Earnhardt	24
3.	Rusty Wallace	17
4.	Bobby Labonte	14
	Mark Martin	14
6.	Sterling Marlin	12
	Michael Waltrip	12
	Terry Labonte	11
	Ricky Rudd	11
10.	John Andretti	9
	Ken Schrader	9
12.	Bill Elliott	8
	Dale Jarrett	8
	Morgan Shepherd	8
	Darrell Waltrip	8
16.	Bobby Hamilton	7
17.	Ted Musgrave	6
18.	Geoff Bodine	4
	Ward Burton	4
	Derrike Cope	4
	Ricky Craven	4
	Kyle Petty	4
	Hut Stricklin	4
24.	Rick Mast	3
	Jeremy Mayfield	3
	Robert Pressley	3

1996

Driver	Starts	Poles	Finish 1	2	3	4	5	6–10	Laps	Laps Led	Races Led	Winston Cup Points	$
1. Terry Labonte	31	4	2	7	5	1	6	3	9,443	973	22	4,657	4,030,648
2. Jeff Gordon	31	5	10	3	4	2	2	3	8,972	2,314	25	4,620	3,428,485
3. Dale Jarrett	31	2	4	7	4	2	0	4	9,307	755	20	4,568	2,985,418
4. Dale Earnhardt	31	2	2	3	3	4	1	4	9,530	614	18	4,327	2,285,926
5. Mark Martin	31	4	0	4	5	3	2	9	9,064	702	16	4,278	1,887,396
6. Ricky Rudd	31	0	1	2	1	1	0	11	9,281	151	12	3,845	1,503,025
7. Rusty Wallace	31	0	5	1	0	1	1	10	8,383	964	13	3,717	1,665,315
8. Sterling Marlin	31	0	2	0	1	1	1	5	8,877	331	10	3,682	1,588,425
9. Bobby Hamilton	31	2	1	0	1	0	1	8	9,153	648	11	3,639	1,151,235
10. Ernie Irvan	31	1	2	2	0	6	2	4	8,618	370	15	3,632	1,683,313
11. Bobby Labonte	31	4	1	1	0	1	2	9	8,916	337	13	3,590	1,475,196
12. Ken Schrader	31	0	0	0	1	1	1	7	9,408	45	7	3,540	1,089,603
13. Jeff Burton	30	1	0	0	1	3	2	6	8,592	210	7	3,538	884,303
14. Michael Waltrip	31	0	0	0	0	0	1	10	9,279	18	5	3,535	1,182,811
15. Jimmy Spencer	31	0	0	0	0	1	1	7	9,339	156	7	3,476	1,090,876
16. Ted Musgrave	31	1	0	0	1	1	0	5	9,352	5	3	3,466	961,512
17. Geoff Bodine	31	0	1	0	1	0	0	4	8,918	90	7	3,218	1,031,762
18. Rick Mast	31	0	0	0	0	1	0	4	8,972	1	1	3,190	924,559
19. Morgan Shepherd	31	0	0	0	0	0	1	4	8,976	50	4	3,133	719,059
20. Ricky Craven	31	2	0	0	2	0	1	2	8,561	136	9	3,078	941,959
21. Johnny Benson Jr.	30	1	0	0	0	0	1	5	8,507	105	4	3,004	947,080
22. Hut Stricklin	31	0	0	1	0	0	0	0	8,620	163	3	2,854	631,055
23. Lake Speed	31	0	0	0	0	0	0	2	8,493	10	3	2,834	817,175
24. Brett Bodine	30	0	0	0	0	0	0	1	8,732	3	2	2,814	767,716
25. Wally Dallenbach Jr.	30	0	0	0	1	0	0	2	8,191	0	0	2,786	837,001
26. Jeremy Mayfield	30	1	0	0	0	1	1	0	7,814	20	4	2,721	592,853
27. Kyle Petty	28	0	0	0	0	0	0	2	8,081	72	5	2,696	689,041
28. Kenny Wallace	30	0	0	0	0	0	0	2	8,415	7	2	2,694	457,665
29. Darrell Waltrip	31	0	0	0	0	0	0	2	7,766	2	2	2,657	740,185
30. Bill Elliott	24	0	0	0	0	0	0	6	7,439	108	7	2,627	716,506
31. John Andretti	30	0	0	0	0	0	2	1	7,850	32	5	2,621	688,511
32. Robert Pressley	30	0	0	0	0	1	1	1	7,948	110	7	2,485	690,465
33. Ward Burton	27	1	0	0	0	0	0	4	6,544	54	4	2,411	873,619
34. Joe Nemechek	29	0	0	0	0	0	0	2	8,110	2	1	2,391	666,247
35. Derrike Cope	29	0	0	0	0	0	0	3	7,329	28	2	2,374	675,781
36. Dick Trickle	26	0	0	0	0	0	0	1	6,694	2	1	2,131	404,927
37. Bobby Hillin Jr.	26	0	0	0	0	0	0	0	7,164	4	1	2,128	395,224
38. Dave Marcis	27	0	0	0	0	0	0	0	7,202	20	8	2,047	435,177
39. Steve Grissom	13	0	0	0	0	0	1	1	3,169	12	1	1,188	314,983
40. Todd Bodine	10	0	0	0	0	0	0	1	3,210	1	1	991	198,525
41. Mike Wallace	11	0	0	0	0	0	0	0	2,876	3	1	799	169,082
42. Greg Sacks	9	0	0	0	0	0	0	0	2,196	3	1	710	207,755
43. Elton Sawyer	9	0	0	0	0	0	0	0	2,448	0	0	705	129,618
44. Chad Little	9	0	0	0	0	0	0	0	1,816	0	0	627	164,752
45. Loy Allen Jr.	9	0	0	0	0	0	0	0	1,439	0	0	603	130,667
46. Gary Bradberry	9	0	0	0	0	0	0	0	2,212	0	0	591	155,785
47. Mike Skinner	5	0	0	0	0	0	0	0	1,459	10	1	529	65,850
48. Jeff Purvis	4	0	0	0	0	0	0	0	532	0	0	328	91,127
49. Jeff Green	4	0	0	0	0	0	0	0	813	0	0	247	46,875
50. Randy MacDonald	3	0	0	0	0	0	0	0	680	0	0	228	33,910

LAPS COMPLETED

#	Driver	Laps
1.	Dale Earnhardt	9,530
2.	Terry Labonte	9,443
3.	Ken Schrader	9,408
4.	Ted Musgrave	9,352
5.	Jimmy Spencer	9,339
6.	Dale Jarrett	9,307
7.	Ricky Rudd	9,281
8.	Michael Waltrip	9,279
9.	Bobby Hamilton	9,153
10.	Mark Martin	9,064
11.	Morgan Shepherd	8,976
12.	Jeff Gordon	8,972
	Rick Mast	8,972
14.	Geoff Bodine	8,918
15.	Bobby Labonte	8,916
16.	Sterling Marlin	8,877
17.	Brett Bodine	8,732
18.	Hut Stricklin	8,620
19.	Ernie Irvan	8,618
20.	Jeff Burton	8,592
21.	Ricky Craven	8,561
22.	Johnny Benson Jr.	8,507
23.	Lake Speed	8,493
24.	Kenny Wallace	8,415
25.	Rusty Wallace	8,383
26.	Wally Dallenbach Jr.	8,191
27.	Joe Nemechek	8,110
28.	Kyle Petty	8,081
29.	Robert Pressley	7,948
30.	John Andretti	7,850

LAPS LED

#	Driver	Laps
1.	Jeff Gordon	2,314
2.	Terry Labonte	973
3.	Rusty Wallace	964
4.	Dale Jarrett	755
5.	Mark Martin	702
6.	Bobby Hamilton	648
7.	Dale Earnhardt	614
8.	Ernie Irvan	370
9.	Bobby Labonte	337
10.	Sterling Marlin	331
11.	Jeff Burton	210
12.	Hut Stricklin	163
13.	Jimmy Spencer	156
14.	Ricky Rudd	151
15.	Ricky Craven	136
16.	Robert Pressley	110
17.	Bill Elliott	108
18.	Johnny Benson Jr.	105
19.	Geoff Bodine	90
20.	Kyle Petty	72
21.	Ward Burton	54
22.	Morgan Shepherd	50
23.	Ken Schrader	45
24.	John Andretti	32
25.	Derrike Cope	28
26.	Dave Marcis	20
	Jeremy Mayfield	20
28.	Michael Waltrip	18
29.	Steve Grissom	12
30.	Mike Skinner	10
	Lake Speed	10

MILES LED

#	Driver	Miles
1.	Jeff Gordon	2,386
2.	Terry Labonte	1,214
3.	Mark Martin	1,092
4.	Dale Jarrett	1,023
5.	Dale Earnhardt	929
6.	Rusty Wallace	787
7.	Sterling Marlin	646
8.	Bobby Labonte	497
9.	Bobby Hamilton	460
10.	Ernie Irvan	457
11.	Hut Stricklin	245
12.	Johnny Benson Jr.	215
13.	Ricky Rudd	186
14.	Ricky Craven	181
15.	Jeff Burton	179
16.	Jimmy Spencer	174
17.	Geoff Bodine	134
18.	Bill Elliott	134
19.	Robert Pressley	108
20.	Morgan Shepherd	99
21.	Ken Schrader	95
22.	John Andretti	73
23.	Derrike Cope	66
24.	Ward Burton	62
25.	Kyle Petty	48
26.	Jeremy Mayfield	45
27.	Michael Waltrip	43
28.	Dave Marcis	37
29.	Steve Grissom	32
30.	Lake Speed	21

MILES DRIVEN

#	Driver	Miles
1.	Dale Earnhardt	11,523
2.	Terry Labonte	11,522
3.	Ken Schrader	11,499
4.	Ricky Rudd	11,400
5.	Ted Musgrave	11,388
6.	Jimmy Spencer	11,238
7.	Dale Jarrett	11,180
8.	Michael Waltrip	11,165
9.	Geoff Bodine	11,067
10.	Mark Martin	11,066
11.	Rick Mast	10,936
12.	Bobby Hamilton	10,896
13.	Morgan Shepherd	10,720
14.	Brett Bodine	10,718
15.	Hut Stricklin	10,632
16.	Sterling Marlin	10,582
17.	Bobby Labonte	10,570
18.	Jeff Burton	10,551
19.	Jeff Gordon	10,517
20.	Johnny Benson Jr.	10,483
21.	Wally Dallenbach Jr.	10,417
22.	Ricky Craven	10,229
23.	Ernie Irvan	10,220
24.	Rusty Wallace	10,159
25.	Lake Speed	10,027
26.	John Andretti	9,912
27.	Kenny Wallace	9,896
28.	Joe Nemechek	9,710
29.	Kyle Petty	9,682
30.	Robert Pressley	9,678

RACES LED

#	Driver	Races
1.	Jeff Gordon	25
2.	Terry Labonte	22
3.	Dale Jarrett	20
4.	Dale Earnhardt	18
5.	Mark Martin	16
6.	Ernie Irvan	15
7.	Bobby Labonte	13
	Rusty Wallace	13
9.	Ricky Rudd	12
10.	Bobby Hamilton	11
11.	Sterling Marlin	10
12.	Ricky Craven	9
13.	Dave Marcis	8
14.	Geoff Bodine	7
	Jeff Burton	7
	Bill Elliott	7
	Robert Pressley	7
	Ken Schrader	7
	Jimmy Spencer	7
20.	John Andretti	5
	Kyle Petty	5
	Michael Waltrip	5
23.	Ward Burton	4
	Jeremy Mayfield	4
	Morgan Shepherd	4
	Johnny Benson Jr.	4
27.	Lake Speed	3
	Hut Stricklin	3
	Ted Musgrave	3

PART 3
THE DRIVERS

Year	Rank	Starts	Poles	Finish						Laps	Laps Led	Races Led	Miles	$
				1	2	3	4	5	6–10					
Richard Petty				Richard Lee Petty (The King) B: 7/2/1937 Racing Hometown: Randleman, NC										
1969	2	50	6	10	9	9	0	3	7	12,589	2,778	32	10,520	129,906
1970	4	40	9	18	5	0	0	4	4	10,536	**5,007**	32	9,811	151,124
1971	1	46	9	21	8	7	2	0	3	**13,739**	4,932	41[1]	**12,870**[1]	351,071
1972	1	31	3	8	9	5	2	1	3	**10,282**	2,093	30	**11,996**	339,405
1991	24	29	0	0	0	0	0	0	1	8,341	1	1	9,644	268,035
1992	26	29	0	0	0	0	0	0	0	7,977	5	1	9,624	348,870
Lifetime		1184	126	200	157	104	52	42	157	307,836	52,134	599	303,662	$8,541,218
		1st	**1st**	**1st**						**1st**	**1st**	**1st**	**1st**	

Key

RANK	Rank that year as according to Winston Cup Points
STARTS	Number of starts that year
POLES	Number of poles that year
FINISH	
1	Number of first place finishes that year
2	Number of second place finishes that year
3	Number of third place finishes that year
4	Number of fourth place finishes that year
5	Number of fifth place finishes that year
6–10	Number of sixth through tenth place finishes that year
LAPS	Number of laps completed that year (a blank entry indicates that the information is not available or incomplete)
LAPS LED	Number of laps led that year
RACES LED	Number of races led that year
MILES	Number of miles driven that year (a blank entry indicates that the information is not available or incomplete)
$	Winnings for that year (includes post-season and special event earnings)
N/A	Information not available or incomplete
NR	Not ranked, no points at season's end

Yearly Leaders. Statistics that appear in boldface indicate the driver led all others that year in a particular statistical category. Petty, for example, drove more laps than anyone else in 1971 with 13,739.

All-Time Yearly Leaders. Indicated by the small number "1" that appears next to the statistic. Petty, for example, has a one next to his races led total of 41 in 1971. This means that no one else has ever led more races in a single season.

Lifetime Leaders. Indicated by the figure that appears beneath the line showing the driver's lifetime totals. Petty has a "1st" shown beneath his 1st place finishes total. This indicates that Petty has won more races in his career than anyone else.

*Please note a driver will occasionally win money without having any starts. The winnings were derived from special events which were not part of the official NASCAR Winston Cup schedule.

*Please also note that the above record is incomplete and shown here for example purposes only.

Year	Rank	Starts	Poles	Finish 1	2	3	4	5	6–10	Laps	Laps Led	Races Led	Miles	$

Paul Aars

Paul Aars
Racing Hometown: San Mateo, CA

Year	Rank	Starts	Poles	1	2	3	4	5	6–10	Laps	Laps Led	Races Led	Miles	$
1958	67	1	0	0	0	0	0	0	1	168	0	0	442	200
Lifetime		1	0	0	0	0	0	0	1	168	0	0	442	$200

Bobby Abel

Robert Abel
B: 4/20/1930 D: 1/31/1995
Racing Hometown: Wrightsville, PA

Year	Rank	Starts	Poles	1	2	3	4	5	6–10	Laps	Laps Led	Races Led	Miles	$
1957	NR	1	0	0	0	0	0	0	0	57	0	0	57	0
Lifetime		1	0	0	0	0	0	0	0	57	0	0	57	$0

Marv Acton

Marv Acton
B: 2/3/1944
Racing Hometown: Porterville, CA

Year	Rank	Starts	Poles	1	2	3	4	5	6–10	Laps	Laps Led	Races Led	Miles	$
1971	44	11	0	0	0	0	0	0	0	1,421	0	0	2,399	8,620
1974	NR	1	0	0	0	0	0	0	0	66	0	0	41	365
1977	92	2	0	0	0	0	0	0	0	359	0	0	202	945
Lifetime		14	0	0	0	0	0	0	0	1,846	0	0	2,642	$9,930

Bill Adams

William Adams
Racing Hometown: Ambridge, PA

Year	Rank	Starts	Poles	1	2	3	4	5	6–10	Laps	Laps Led	Races Led	Miles	$
1953	48	2	0	0	0	0	0	0	1	36	0	0	148	250
Lifetime		2	0	0	0	0	0	0	1	36	0	0	148	$250

Boyd Adams

Boyd Adams
Racing Hometown: Nashville, TN

Year	Rank	Starts	Poles	1	2	3	4	5	6–10	Laps	Laps Led	Races Led	Miles	$
1965	135	1	0	0	0	0	0	0	0	15	0	0	8	100
Lifetime		1	0	0	0	0	0	0	0	15	0	0	8	$100

Carl Adams

Carl Adams
B: 4/24/1942
Racing Hometown: National City, CA

Year	Rank	Starts	Poles	1	2	3	4	5	6–10	Laps	Laps Led	Races Led	Miles	$
1972	75	2	0	0	0	0	0	0	1	320	0	0	818	3,170
1973	69	2	0	0	0	0	0	0	0	290	0	0	760	2,030
1974	51	4	0	0	0	0	0	0	0	667	0	0	1,413	5,100
1975	23	20	0	0	0	0	0	0	4	5,332	0	0	5,827	25,220
Lifetime		28	0	0	0	0	0	0	5	6,609	0	0	8,817	$35,520

Eddie Adams

Edward Adams
Racing Hometown: Rising Sun, MD

Year	Rank	Starts	Poles	1	2	3	4	5	6–10	Laps	Laps Led	Races Led	Miles	$
1950	NR	1	0	0	0	0	0	0	0		0	0		0
1952	102	1	0	0	0	0	0	0	0	128	0	0	128	25
Lifetime		2	0	0	0	0	0	0	0	128	0	0	128	$25

Joe Bill Adams

Joseph William Adams
Racing Hometown: Mt. Airy, NC

Year	Rank	Starts	Poles	1	2	3	4	5	6–10	Laps	Laps Led	Races Led	Miles	$
1965	137	2	0	0	0	0	0	0	1	244	0	0	99	450
Lifetime		2	0	0	0	0	0	0	1	244	0	0	99	$450

Serge Adams

Serge Adams
Racing Hometown: Montreal, Ont., Canada

Year	Rank	Starts	Poles	1	2	3	4	5	6–10	Laps	Laps Led	Races Led	Miles	$
1968	68	3	0	0	0	0	0	0	0	368	0	0	440	1,260
Lifetime		3	0	0	0	0	0	0	0	368	0	0	440	$1,260

Weldon Adams

Weldon Adams
B: 1938 D: 5/9/1995
Racing Hometown: Augusta, GA

Year	Rank	Starts	Poles	1	2	3	4	5	6–10	Laps	Laps Led	Races Led	Miles	$
1950	15	4	0	0	0	1	0	1	1	560	0	0	555	1,205
1951	N/A	11	0	0	0	0	0	0	2	246	0	0	237	425
1952	40	6	0	0	0	0	0	0	2	708	0	0	537	275
1953	150	2	0	0	0	0	0	0	0	217	0	0	298	135

Year	Rank	Starts	Poles		Finish						Laps	Laps Led	Races Led	Miles	$
				1	2	3	4	5	6–10		Laps	Led	Led	Miles	$

Weldon Adams *continued*

Year	Rank	Starts	Poles	1	2	3	4	5	6–10	Laps	Laps Led	Races Led	Miles	$
1962	115	1	0	0	0	0	0	0	0	90	0	0	45	85
1964	129	1	0	0	0	0	0	0	0	2	0	0	6	525
Lifetime		25	0	0	0	1	0	1	5	1,823	0	0	1,678	$2,650

Grant Adcox

Grant Adcox
B: 1/2/1950   D: 11/19/1989   *Killed in Atlanta NASCAR race.*
Racing Hometown: Chattanooga, TN

Year	Rank	Starts	Poles	1	2	3	4	5	6–10	Laps	Laps Led	Races Led	Miles	$
1974	54	4	0	0	0	0	0	0	0	979	8	1	1,375	6,240
1975	33	11	0	0	0	0	0	0	1	1,620	0	0	2,798	16,980
1976	31	11	0	0	0	0	0	0	2	3,126	0	0	4,643	26,115
1977	49	6	0	0	0	0	0	0	0	776	0	0	1,482	8,750
1978	30	14	0	0	0	0	0	1	2	3,072	0	0	4,586	37,100
1979	36	6	0	0	0	0	0	0	0	1,132	5	1	2,104	15,290
1983	95T	1	0	0	0	0	0	0	0	1	0	0	3	1,790
1984	91T	1	0	0	0	0	0	0	0	1	0	0	3	1,800
1985	70	2	0	0	0	0	0	0	0	169	0	0	426	4,590
1986	101T	1	0	0	0	0	0	0	0	154	0	0	385	3,395
1987	—	0												1,700
1989	51	3	0	0	0	0	0	0	0	541	0	0	1,188	11,815
Lifetime		60	0	0	0	0	0	1	5	11,571	13	2	18,993	$134,815

Allen Adkins

Allen Adkins
B: 3/29/1929
Racing Hometown: Clovis, CA

Year	Rank	Starts	Poles	1	2	3	4	5	6–10	Laps	Laps Led	Races Led	Miles	$
1954	46	2	0	0	0	1	1	0	0	545	0	0	397	1,150
1955	46	4	0	0	1	0	0	1	0	601	79	1	502	1,160
1956	42	6	0	0	0	0	0	1	2	1,016	0	0	1,101	1,465
1957	95	2	0	0	0	0	0	0	1	252	0	0	193	350
Lifetime		14	0	0	1	1	1	2	3	2,414	79	1	2,192	$3,775

Blair Aiken

Blair Aiken
B: 9/2/1956
Racing Hometown: Lakeport, CA

Year	Rank	Starts	Poles	1	2	3	4	5	6–10	Laps	Laps Led	Races Led	Miles	$
1985	72	2	0	0	0	0	0	0	0	135	0	0	354	2,020
Lifetime		2	0	0	0	0	0	0	0	135	0	0	354	$2,020

Thomas Aiken

Thomas Aiken
Racing Hometown: Atlanta, GA

Year	Rank	Starts	Poles	1	2	3	4	5	6–10	Laps	Laps Led	Races Led	Miles	$
1958	121	1	0	0	0	0	0	0	0	93	0	0	93	110
Lifetime		1	0	0	0	0	0	0	0	93	0	0	93	$110

Chuck Akerblade

Chuck Akerblade
Racing Hometown: Portland, OR

Year	Rank	Starts	Poles	1	2	3	4	5	6–10	Laps	Laps Led	Races Led	Miles	$
1956	169	1	0	0	0	0	0	0	0	238	0	0	119	100
Lifetime		1	0	0	0	0	0	0	0	238	0	0	119	$100

Will Albright

Will Albright
Racing Hometown: Graham, NC

Year	Rank	Starts	Poles	1	2	3	4	5	6–10	Laps	Laps Led	Races Led	Miles	$
1950	136	1	0	0	0	0	0	0	0	43	0	0	179	50
Lifetime		1	0	0	0	0	0	0	0	43	0	0	179	$50

Ronnie Alderman

Ronnie Alderman

Year	Rank	Starts	Poles	1	2	3	4	5	6–10	Laps	Laps Led	Races Led	Miles	$
1973	118	1	0	0	0	0	0	0	0	34	0	0	89	655
Lifetime		1	0	0	0	0	0	0	0	34	0	0	89	$655

John Alexander

John Alexander
B: 5/22/1954
Racing Hometown: Elmira, NY

Year	Rank	Starts	Poles	1	2	3	4	5	6–10	Laps	Laps Led	Races Led	Miles	$
1990	101	1	0	0	0	0	0	0	0	35	0	0	85	2,210
Lifetime		1	0	0	0	0	0	0	0	35	0	0	85	$2,210

Year	Rank	Starts	Poles	Finish 1	2	3	4	5	6–10	Laps	Laps Led	Races Led	Miles	$

Mike Alexander

Mike Alexander
B: 7/31/1957
Racing Hometown: Franklin, TN

Year	Rank	Starts	Poles	1	2	3	4	5	6–10	Laps	Laps Led	Races Led	Miles	$
1980	NR	1	0	0	0	0	0	0	1	409	0	0	244	3,130
1981	29	19	0	0	0	0	0	0	3	4,340	4	1	4,886	34,055
1984	28	19	0	0	0	0	0	0	1	4,656	0	0	5,694	94,820
1985	35	11	0	0	0	0	0	0	0	2,336	0	0	3,410	43,765
1988	32	16	0	0	0	1	0	1	4	4,677	51	5	6,004	200,709
1989	81T	1	0	0	0	0	0	0	0	188	0	0	470	16,275
1990	38	7	0	0	0	0	0	0	0	2,392	0	0	2,325	41,080
Lifetime		74	0	0	0	1	0	1	9	18,998	55	6	23,032	$423,995

Elbert Allen

Elbert Allen
Racing Hometown: Atlanta, GA

Year	Rank	Starts	Poles	1	2	3	4	5	6–10	Laps	Laps Led	Races Led	Miles	$
1953	37	4	0	0	0	0	0	0	2		0	0		250
1954	79	4	0	0	0	0	0	0	0	472	0	0	401	100
Lifetime		8	0	0	0	0	0	0	2	472	0	0	401	$350

Johnny Allen

John Harold Allen
B: 9/17/1934
Racing Hometown: Greenville, SC

Year	Rank	Starts	Poles	1	2	3	4	5	6–10	Laps	Laps Led	Races Led	Miles	$
1955	114	1	0	0	0	0	0	0	0	169	0	0	254	195
1956	12	32	0	0	0	0	0	2	9	4,888	0	0	3,349	4,559
1957	7	42	1	0	0	1	1	2	13	6,033	0	0	3,876	9,815
1958	NR	22	0	0	0	1	0	1	4	2,613	0	0	1,483	2,240
1959	NR	5	0	0	0	1	0	0	0	522	0	0	883	2,525
1960	19	10	0	0	1	0	0	1	3	1,820	0	0	2,501	14,789
1961	12	22	1	0	0	2	0	1	8	4,508	3	1	4,493	13,127
1962	26	20	1	1	0	0	3	1	3	4,094	288	4	3,401	7,230
1963	59	8	0	0	0	0	0	0	1	743	0	0	951	2,325
1964	60	4	0	0	0	0	0	0	1	484	0	0	586	1,775
1965	82	2	0	0	0	0	0	0	0	120	0	0	300	1,235
1966	68	3	0	0	0	0	0	0	0	598	0	0	633	1,585
1967	104	2	0	0	0	0	0	0	0	137	0	0	170	1,565
Lifetime		173	3	1	1	5	4	8	42	26,729	291	5	22,880	$62,965

Loy Allen Jr.

Loy Allen Jr.
B: 4/7/1966
Racing Hometown: Raleigh, NC

Year	Rank	Starts	Poles	1	2	3	4	5	6–10	Laps	Laps Led	Races Led	Miles	$
1993	45	5	0	0	0	0	0	0	0	878	0	0	1,537	34,695
1994	39	19	3	0	0	0	0	0	0	4,446	12	3	6,776	216,751
1995	41	11	0	0	0	0	0	0	1	2,707	18	1	4,182	186,670
1996	45	9	0	0	0	0	0	0	0	1,439	0	0	2,772	130,667
Lifetime		44	3	0	0	0	0	0	1	9,470	30	4	15,267	$568,783

Olin Allen

Olin Allen
Racing Hometown: Macon, GA

Year	Rank	Starts	Poles	1	2	3	4	5	6–10	Laps	Laps Led	Races Led	Miles	$
1952	108	1	0	0	0	0	0	0	0	182	0	0	91	25
Lifetime		1	0	0	0	0	0	0	0	182	0	0	91	$25

Bobby Allison

Robert Arthur Allison
B: 12/3/1937
Racing Hometown: Hueytown, AL

Year	Rank	Starts	Poles	1	2	3	4	5	6–10	Laps	Laps Led	Races Led	Miles	$
1961	106	4	0	0	0	0	0	0	0	359	0	0	751	650
1965	34	8	0	0	0	0	0	0	3	799	0	0	1,324	4,780
1966	10	33	4	3	0	4	1	2	5	6,949	714	6	5,370	23,420
1967	4	45	2	6	4	5	4	2	6	10,157	1,554	21	7,686	58,250
1968	11	37	2	2	4	4	6	2	2	8,781	690	13	7,420	52,288
1969	20	27	1	5	3	1	2	2	2	6,445	1,251	15	6,582	69,483
1970	2	46	5	3	15	8	4	0	5	12,452	1,246	**22**	11,164	149,745
1971	4	42	9	11	7	3	5	1	4	11,716	3,582	31	12,122	254,316
1972	2	31	12	10	12	2	1	0	2	10,063	**4,343**	**30**	11,801	348,939
1973	7	27	6	2	2	6	4	1	1	8,072	870	20	8,646	161,818
1974	4	27	3	2	3	5	2	5	0	7,523	900	20	9,154	178,437

Year	Rank	Starts	Poles	Finish 1	2	3	4	5	6–10	Laps	Laps Led	Races Led	Miles	$

Bobby Allison *continued*

Year	Rank	Starts	Poles	1	2	3	4	5	6–10	Laps	Laps Led	Races Led	Miles	$
1975	24	19	3	3	3	1	2	1	0	4,268	578	14	6,226	126,735
1976	4	30	2	0	2	6	5	2	4	8,735	360	18	10,203	230,170
1977	8	30	0	0	1	0	2	2	10	7,024	102	9	7,822	94,575
1978	2	30	1	5	3	4	0	2	8	9,283	1,043	19	10,539	411,517
1979	3	31	3	5	7	2	4	0	4	9,885	1,854	24	11,237	428,801
1980	6	31	2	4	2	4	1	1	6	8,244	948	18	9,027	378,970
1981	2	31	2	5	7	4	3	2	5	10,098	1,182	23	**11,609**	680,957
1982	2	30	1	8	2	1	2	1	6	9,184	2,423	24	**10,860**	795,078
1983	1	30	0	6	5	6	1	0	7	10,038	1,755	**25**	11,526	883,010
1984	6	30	0	2	1	2	4	4	5	9,051	1,160	23	10,545	641,049
1985	12	28	0	0	0	3	3	1	4	7,656	422	14	9,336	272,536
1986	7	29	0	1	2	1	1	1	9	8,391	127	11	9,928	503,095
1987	9	29	1	1	1	0	1	1	9	7,962	331	10	9,599	515,894
1988	33	13	0	1	1	0	0	1	3	4,303	104	4	4,762	409,295
Lifetime		718	59	85	87	72	58	34	110	197,438	27,539	414	215,239	$7,673,808
		3rd	**4th**	**3rd**						**4th**	**3rd**	**2nd**	**4th**	

Davey Allison

David Carl Allison
B: 2/25/1961   D: 7/13/1993   *Killed @ Talladega in helicopter mishap.*
Racing Hometown: Hueytown, AL

Year	Rank	Starts	Poles	1	2	3	4	5	6–10	Laps	Laps Led	Races Led	Miles	$
1985	71	3	0	0	0	0	0	0	1	539	0	0	1,025	11,715
1986	47	5	0	0	0	0	0	0	1	1,435	13	1	1,368	8,070
1987	21	22	5	2	3	0	0	4	1	5,511	710	11	8,518	361,060
1988	8	29	3	2	2	3	2	3	4	8,333	611	14	9,740	844,532
1989	11	29	1	2	1	0	2	2	6	8,287	241	13	10,111	640,956
1990	13	29	0	2	0	1	0	2	5	9,154	222	8	10,816	640,684
1991	3	29	3	5	4	2	1	0	4	8,770	1,528	**23**	10,610	1,712,924
1992	3	29	2	5	1	1	5	3	2	8,976	**1,377**	18	10,998	1,955,628
1993	31	16	0	1	1	2	1	1	2	5,061	276	9	6,214	513,585
Lifetime		191	14	19	12	9	11	15	26	56,066	4,978	97	69,400	$6,689,154

Donnie Allison

Donald Allison
B: 9/7/1939
Racing Hometown: Hueytown, AL

Year	Rank	Starts	Poles	1	2	3	4	5	6–10	Laps	Laps Led	Races Led	Miles	$
1966	64	2	0	0	0	0	0	0	1	664	0	0	757	2,180
1967	16	20	0	0	1	0	2	1	3	4,336	158	2	4,537	17,614
1968	25	13	1	1	1	3	0	0	3	3,829	284	6	4,107	50,815
1969	24	16	2	1	2	4	1	2	1	3,893	400	10	5,106	78,055
1970	40	19	1	3	0	2	3	2	2	5,252	697	10	5,674	96,081
1971	29	13	5	1	1	1	2	2	2	3,017	806	8	4,327	69,995
1972	36	10	0	0	0	1	0	1	1	1,385	35	4	2,667	16,826
1973	35	14	0	0	1	1	0	0	3	2,904	44	3	3,690	41,246
1974	17	21	2	0	1	1	2	2	4	5,101	182	10	5,761	60,315
1975	28	14	2	0	0	2	0	1	3	2,819	33	5	3,971	49,080
1976	34	9	0	1	0	1	0	0	3	2,178	104	4	3,254	48,455
1977	24	17	3	2	2	1	4	0	1	4,133	1,163	13	5,910	146,435
1978	25	17	0	1	2	2	1	1	1	3,876	209	12	6,128	127,475
1979	24	20	1	0	2	1	2	2	3	4,841	293	9	6,345	144,770
1980	26	18	1	0	0	1	0	2	3	3,794	231	7	5,197	92,640
1981	44	6	0	0	0	0	0	1	0	1,306	2	1	2,082	38,745
1982	41	9	0	0	0	0	0	0	3	1,818	1	1	2,541	38,180
1983	NR	2	0	0	0	0	0	0	0	138	0	0	339	6,375
1986	114T	1	0	0	0	0	0	0	0	131	0	0	179	1,840
1987	—	0												1,050
1988	81	1	0	0	0	0	0	0	0	114	0	0	228	6,700
Lifetime		242	18	10	13	21	17	17	37	55,529	4,642	105	72,799	$1,134,872

Dick Allwine

Richard Allwine
Racing Hometown: Greensburg, PA

Year	Rank	Starts	Poles	1	2	3	4	5	6–10	Laps	Laps Led	Races Led	Miles	$
1953	52	3	0	0	0	0	0	0	1	382	0	0	456	605
1955	202	1	0	0	0	0	0	0	0	202	0	0	278	50
1956	95	2	0	0	0	0	0	0	0	294	0	0	294	200
Lifetime		6	0	0	0	0	0	0	1	878	0	0	1,028	$855

Year	Rank	Starts	Poles	Finish 1	2	3	4	5	6–10	Laps	Laps Led	Races Led	Miles	$

Dave Alonzo

David Alonzo
Racing Hometown: Mt. View, CA

Year	Rank	Starts	Poles	1	2	3	4	5	6–10	Laps	Laps Led	Races Led	Miles	$
1969	72	2	0	0	0	0	0	0	0	486	0	0	504	1,555
1970	67	2	0	0	0	0	0	0	0	160	0	0	420	2,260
Lifetime		4	0	0	0	0	0	0	0	646	0	0	924	$3,815

George Alsobrook

George L. Alsobrook
B: 2/23/1934
Racing Hometown: Hiram, GA

Year	Rank	Starts	Poles	1	2	3	4	5	6–10	Laps	Laps Led	Races Led	Miles	$
1958	123	1	0	0	0	0	0	0	0	54	0	0	27	70
1959	NR	4	0	0	0	0	0	0	1	936	0	0	723	1,150
1961	69	8	0	0	0	0	0	0	1	938	0	0	736	1,825
1962	69	5	0	0	0	0	0	0	1	406	0	0	723	925
Lifetime		18	0	0	0	0	0	0	3	2,334	0	0	2,209	$3,970

George Althiede

George J. Althiede
B: 1/6/1933
Racing Hometown: Morristown, TN

Year	Rank	Starts	Poles	1	2	3	4	5	6–10	Laps	Laps Led	Races Led	Miles	$
1971	55	5	0	0	0	0	0	0	0	840	0	0	1,857	4,620
1972	35	11	0	0	0	0	0	0	0	1,578	0	0	2,760	10,405
Lifetime		16	0	0	0	0	0	0	0	2,418	0	0	4,617	$15,025

Bernard Alvarez

Bernard V. Alvarez
B: 12/14/1939
Racing Hometown: Jacksonville, FL

Year	Rank	Starts	Poles	1	2	3	4	5	6–10	Laps	Laps Led	Races Led	Miles	$
1964	90	7	0	0	0	0	0	0	0	162	0	0	127	650
1965	115	2	0	0	0	0	0	0	0	9	0	0	7	600
Lifetime		9	0	0	0	0	0	0	0	171	0	0	134	$1,250

Pancho Alvarez

Pancho Alvarez
Racing Hometown: Tampa, FL

Year	Rank	Starts	Poles	1	2	3	4	5	6–10	Laps	Laps Led	Races Led	Miles	$
1952	191T	1	0	0	0	0	0	0	0		0	0		25
Lifetime		1	0	0	0	0	0	0	0		0	0		$25

Bill Amberg

William Amberg
Racing Hometown: Oakland, CA

Year	Rank	Starts	Poles	1	2	3	4	5	6–10	Laps	Laps Led	Races Led	Miles	$
1951	NR	1	0	0	0	0	0	0	0	94	0	0	59	25
Lifetime		1	0	0	0	0	0	0	0	94	0	0	59	$25

Bill Amick

William Amick
B: 11/16/1925
Racing Hometown: Portland, OR

Year	Rank	Starts	Poles	1	2	3	4	5	6–10	Laps	Laps Led	Races Led	Miles	$
1954	41	6	0	0	1	0	0	0	0	884	9	1	867	1,750
1955	76	4	2	0	0	0	1	1	0	485	28	1	388	710
1956	17	13	0	0	1	3	1	2	3	2,446	10	2	1,631	5,381
1957	16	21	2	1	3	4	0	0	4	3,364	12	2	2,067	8,073
1961	187	1	1	0	0	0	0	0	0	25	25	1	25	25
1963	67	1	0	0	0	0	0	0	1	142	0	0	383	1,000
1964	52	1	0	0	0	0	1	0	0	181	0	0	489	2,470
1965	72	1	0	0	0	0	0	0	0	95	0	0	257	620
Lifetime		48	5	1	5	7	3	3	8	7,622	84	7	6,107	$19,420

Art Anderson

Arthur Anderson
Racing Hometown: Syracuse, NY

Year	Rank	Starts	Poles	1	2	3	4	5	6–10	Laps	Laps Led	Races Led	Miles	$
1957	NR	1	0	0	0	0	0	0	0	14	0	0	14	50
Lifetime		1	0	0	0	0	0	0	0	14	0	0	14	$50

Axel Anderson

Axel Anderson
B: 7/21/1921   D: 9/14/1994
Racing Hometown: Patchogue, NY

Year	Rank	Starts	Poles	1	2	3	4	5	6–10	Laps	Laps Led	Races Led	Miles	$
1955	133	2	0	0	0	0	0	0	0	152	0	0	267	225

Year	Rank	Starts	Poles	Finish						Laps	Laps Led	Races Led	Miles	$
				1	2	3	4	5	6–10					

Axel Anderson *continued*

Year	Rank	Starts	Poles	1	2	3	4	5	6–10	Laps	Laps Led	Races Led	Miles	$
1958	100	3	0	0	0	0	0	0	0	203	0	0	178	155
Lifetime		5	0	0	0	0	0	0	0	355	0	0	445	$380

Bob Anderson

Robert Anderson
Racing Hometown: Sandstrom, VA

Year	Rank	Starts	Poles	1	2	3	4	5	6–10	Laps	Laps Led	Races Led	Miles	$
1956	NR	1	0	0	0	0	0	0	0	9	0	0	9	40
Lifetime		1	0	0	0	0	0	0	0	9	0	0	9	$40

Carl Anderson

Carl Anderson
Racing Hometown: Arlington, VA

Year	Rank	Starts	Poles	1	2	3	4	5	6–10	Laps	Laps Led	Races Led	Miles	$
1956	165	1	0	0	0	0	0	0	1	173	0	0	87	200
1957	198T	1	0	0	0	0	0	0	0	56	0	0	28	0
Lifetime		2	0	0	0	0	0	0	1	229	0	0	115	$200

Dave Anderson

David Anderson
Racing Hometown: Birmingham, AL

Year	Rank	Starts	Poles	1	2	3	4	5	6–10	Laps	Laps Led	Races Led	Miles	$
1951	N/A	1	0	0	0	0	0	0	0	335	0	0	419	50
Lifetime		1	0	0	0	0	0	0	0	335	0	0	419	$50

Eddie Anderson

Edward Anderson
B: 1927   D: 5/1/1995
Racing Hometown: Blue Island, IL

Year	Rank	Starts	Poles	1	2	3	4	5	6–10	Laps	Laps Led	Races Led	Miles	$
1951	N/A	5	0	0	0	0	0	0	0	8	0	0	6	110
Lifetime		5	0	0	0	0	0	0	0	8	0	0	6	$110

Fuzzy Anderson

Fuzzy Anderson

Year	Rank	Starts	Poles	1	2	3	4	5	6–10	Laps	Laps Led	Races Led	Miles	$
1951	N/A	3	0	0	0	0	0	0	0		0	0		100
Lifetime		3	0	0	0	0	0	0	0		0	0		$100

Jack Anderson

Jack Anderson
B: 7/26/1936
Racing Hometown: Pearisburg, VA

Year	Rank	Starts	Poles	1	2	3	4	5	6–10	Laps	Laps Led	Races Led	Miles	$
1963	98	3	0	0	0	0	0	0	0	532	0	0	231	475
1964	25	31	0	0	0	0	1	0	3	4,402	0	0	3,365	8,510
1965	90	2	0	0	0	0	0	0	0	18	0	0	45	1,220
Lifetime		36	0	0	0	0	1	0	3	4,952	0	0	3,641	$10,205

Jess Anderson

Jess Anderson
Racing Hometown: Burbank, CA

Year	Rank	Starts	Poles	1	2	3	4	5	6–10	Laps	Laps Led	Races Led	Miles	$
1951	N/A	1	0	0	0	0	0	0	0		0	0		25
Lifetime		1	0	0	0	0	0	0	0		0	0		$25

John Anderson

John B. Anderson
B: 4/20/1944   D: 7/31/1986   *Killed in highway crash in Charlotte, NC.*
Racing Hometown: Massilon, OH

Year	Rank	Starts	Poles	1	2	3	4	5	6–10	Laps	Laps Led	Races Led	Miles	$
1979	39	4	0	0	0	0	0	1	0	1,263	1	1	1,757	11,210
1980	24	20	0	0	0	0	0	0	2	4,282	0	0	5,087	48,265
1981	NR	3	0	0	0	0	0	0	0	583	0	0	772	8,615
1982	83	4	0	0	0	0	0	0	0	625	0	0	1,108	11,855
1983	NR	1	0	0	0	0	0	0	0	317	0	0	476	1,350
Lifetime		32	0	0	0	0	0	1	2	7,070	1	1	9,200	$81,295

Johnny Anderson

John Anderson
B: 7/24/1942
Racing Hometown: Palmdale, CA

Year	Rank	Starts	Poles	1	2	3	4	5	6–10	Laps	Laps Led	Races Led	Miles	$
1971	NR	1	0	0	0	0	0	0	0	34	0	0	89	690
1972	67	4	0	0	0	0	0	0	0	385	0	0	969	4,600
1973	80	2	0	0	0	0	0	0	0	186	0	0	487	1,840
1974	84	2	0	0	0	0	0	0	0	154	0	0	403	2,130
Lifetime		9	0	0	0	0	0	0	0	759	0	0	1948	$9,260

Year	Rank	Starts	Poles	Finish 1	2	3	4	5	6–10	Laps	Laps Led	Races Led	Miles	$

Ken Anderson

Kenneth Anderson
Racing Hometown: Mt. Croghan, SC

Year	Rank	Starts	Poles	1	2	3	4	5	6–10	Laps	Laps Led	Races Led	Miles	$
1964	89	3	0	0	0	0	0	0	0	848	0	0	463	450
Lifetime		3	0	0	0	0	0	0	0	848	0	0	463	$450

Ole Anderson

Ole Anderson

Year	Rank	Starts	Poles	1	2	3	4	5	6–10	Laps	Laps Led	Races Led	Miles	$
1956	272T	1	0	0	0	0	0	0	0	9	0	0	9	40
Lifetime		1	0	0	0	0	0	0	0	9	0	0	9	$40

John Andretti

John Andrew Andretti
B: 3/12/1963
Racing Hometown: Bethlehem, PA

Year	Rank	Starts	Poles	1	2	3	4	5	6–10	Laps	Laps Led	Races Led	Miles	$
1993	50	4	0	0	0	0	0	0	0	874	0	0	895	24,915
1994	32	29	0	0	0	0	0	0	0	7,508	41	4	8,920	391,920
1995	18	31	1	0	0	0	1	0	4	8,412	77	9	10,178	593,542
1996	31	30	0	0	0	0	0	2	1	7,850	32	5	9,912	688,511
Lifetime		94	1	0	0	0	1	2	5	24,644	150	18	29,905	$1,709,066

Mario Andretti

Mario Gabriel Andretti
B: 2/28/1940
Racing Hometown: Nazareth, PA

Year	Rank	Starts	Poles	1	2	3	4	5	6–10	Laps	Laps Led	Races Led	Miles	$
1966	NR	4	0	0	0	0	0	0	0	300	1	1	781	2,140
1967	NR	6	0	1	0	0	0	0	2	867	137	3	1,757	52,165
1968	NR	3	0	0	0	0	0	0	0	297	20	2	751	2,845
1969	NR	1	0	0	0	0	0	0	0	132	7	1	356	925
Lifetime		14	0	1	0	0	0	0	2	1,596	165	7	3,645	$58,075

Ed Andrews

Edward Andrews
Racing Hometown: San Francisco, CA

Year	Rank	Starts	Poles	1	2	3	4	5	6–10	Laps	Laps Led	Races Led	Miles	$
1960	92	1	0	0	0	0	0	0	0	150	0	0	210	350
Lifetime		1	0	0	0	0	0	0	0	150	0	0	210	$350

Tommy Andrews

Thomas Andrews
B: 3/15/1936
Racing Hometown: Huntsville, AL

Year	Rank	Starts	Poles	1	2	3	4	5	6–10	Laps	Laps Led	Races Led	Miles	$
1971	NR	2	0	0	0	0	0	0	0	251	0	0	79	450
Lifetime		2	0	0	0	0	0	0	0	251	0	0	79	$450

Wayne Andrews

Wayne Earl Andrews
B: 8/18/1938
Racing Hometown: Siler City, NC

Year	Rank	Starts	Poles	1	2	3	4	5	6–10	Laps	Laps Led	Races Led	Miles	$
1971	NR	5	0	0	0	0	0	1	2	1,372	0	0	600	1,780
1973	125	1	0	0	0	0	0	0	0	5	0	0	8	1,005
Lifetime		6	0	0	0	0	0	1	2	1,377	0	0	608	$2,785

Don Angel

Donald Angel
Racing Hometown: Miami, FL

Year	Rank	Starts	Poles	1	2	3	4	5	6–10	Laps	Laps Led	Races Led	Miles	$
1958	NR	3	0	0	0	0	0	0	0	401	0	0	241	210
1959	NR	2	0	0	0	0	0	0	0	167	0	0	100	100
Lifetime		5	0	0	0	0	0	0	0	568	0	0	341	$310

Bob Apperson

Robert Apperson
Racing Hometown: Charlottesville, VA

Year	Rank	Starts	Poles	1	2	3	4	5	6–10	Laps	Laps Led	Races Led	Miles	$
1949	43	2	0	0	0	0	0	0	0	191	0	0	96	100
1950	67	7	0	0	0	0	0	0	0	573	0	0	631	200
1952	197	1	0	0	0	0	0	0	0		0	0		25
Lifetime		10	0	0	0	0	0	0	0	764	0	0	727	$325

Nelson Applegate

Nelson Applegate
B: 1925   D: 1979
Racing Hometown: Denville, NJ

Year	Rank	Starts	Poles	1	2	3	4	5	6–10	Laps	Laps Led	Races Led	Miles	$
1951	N/A	3	0	0	0	0	0	0	0		0	0		60

Year	Rank	Starts	Poles	Finish 1	2	3	4	5	6–10	Laps	Laps Led	Races Led	Miles	$

Nelson Applegate *continued*

Year	Rank	Starts	Poles	1	2	3	4	5	6–10	Laps	Laps Led	Races Led	Miles	$
1952	89	2	0	0	0	0	0	0	1	313	0	0	219	160
Lifetime		5	0	0	0	0	0	0	1	313	0	0	219	$220

Bob Appleton

Robert Appleton
Racing Hometown: N. Tonawanda, NY

Year	Rank	Starts	Poles	1	2	3	4	5	6–10	Laps	Laps Led	Races Led	Miles	$
1949	69	1	0	0	0	0	0	0	0		0	0		50
Lifetime		1	0	0	0	0	0	0	0		0	0		$50

Sam Ard

Samuel J. Ard
B: 2/14/1939
Racing Hometown: Asheboro, NC

Year	Rank	Starts	Poles	1	2	3	4	5	6–10	Laps	Laps Led	Races Led	Miles	$
1984	NR	1	0	0	0	0	0	0	0	1	0	0	1	1,100
Lifetime		1	0	0	0	0	0	0	0	1	0	0	1	$1,100

Frank Arford

Frank Arford
D: 6/20/1953 *Killed qualifying for Langhorne NASCAR race.*
Racing Hometown: Indianapolis, IN

Year	Rank	Starts	Poles	1	2	3	4	5	6–10	Laps	Laps Led	Races Led	Miles	$
1953	NR	4	0	0	0	0	0	0	0	255	0	0	261	100
Lifetime		4	0	0	0	0	0	0	0	255	0	0	261	$100

Russell Armentrout

Russell Armentrout

Year	Rank	Starts	Poles	1	2	3	4	5	6–10	Laps	Laps Led	Races Led	Miles	$
1953	NR	2	0	0	0	0	0	0	0	60	0		60	50
Lifetime		2	0	0	0	0	0	0	0	60	0		60	$50

Ben Arnold

Ben Robert Arnold
B: 7/30/1936
Racing Hometown: Fairfield, AL

Year	Rank	Starts	Poles	1	2	3	4	5	6–10	Laps	Laps Led	Races Led	Miles	$
1968	51	10	0	0	0	0	0	0	0	1,413	0	0	1,236	2,785
1969	15	48	0	0	0	0	0	0	8	10,334	0	0	8,493	33,256
1970	17	29	0	0	0	0	0	0	3	6,838	0	0	6,746	25,805
1971	26	18	0	0	0	0	0	0	3	4,130	0	0	6,172	18,491
1972	10	26	0	0	0	0	0	0	7	6,976	0	0	8,935	44,547
1973	127	1	0	0	0	0	0	0	0	9	0	0	24	885
Lifetime		132	0	0	0	0	0	0	21	29,700	0	0	31,605	$125,769

Pete Arnold

Peter Andrew Arnold
B: 8/31/1943
Racing Hometown: Bellaire, TX

Year	Rank	Starts	Poles	1	2	3	4	5	6–10	Laps	Laps Led	Races Led	Miles	$
1971	85	1	0	0	0	0	0	0	0	58	0	0	29	340
Lifetime		1	0	0	0	0	0	0	0	58	0	0	29	$340

Ralph Arnold

Ralph Arnold
Racing Hometown: Los Angeles, CA

Year	Rank	Starts	Poles	1	2	3	4	5	6–10	Laps	Laps Led	Races Led	Miles	$
1969	NR	1	0	0	0	0	0	0	0	43	0	0	116	765
Lifetime		1	0	0	0	0	0	0	0	43	0	0	116	$765

Buddy Arrington

Buddy Rogers Arrington
B: 7/26/1938
Racing Hometown: Martinsville, VA

Year	Rank	Starts	Poles	1	2	3	4	5	6–10	Laps	Laps Led	Races Led	Miles	$
1964	34	27	0	0	0	0	0	2	7	5,172	0	0	2,504	5,315
1965	22	31	0	0	0	1	1	4	4	5,274	0	0	3,545	11,600
1966	32	25	0	0	0	0	0	0	3	3,607	0	0	3,054	8,980
1967	26	15	0	0	0	0	0	1	4	2,972	0	0	2,635	7,820
1968	NR	1	0	0	0	0	0	0	0	186	0	0	465	2,350
1969	33	16	0	0	0	0	0	2	4	3,758	0	0	3,557	12,975
1970	33	19	0	0	0	0	0	0	2	2,855	0	0	3,638	16,845
1971	NR	1	0	0	0	0	0	0	0	472	0	0	248	650
1972	22	20	0	0	0	0	0	1	9	5,503	0	0	7,008	29,050
1973	12	26	0	0	0	0	0	1	3	7,476	0	0	7,876	40,877
1974	30	16	0	0	0	0	0	0	4	4,781	0	0	4,797	22,085
1975	19	25	0	0	0	0	0	0	3	7,786	0	0	8,170	45,893

Year	Rank	Starts	Poles	Finish						Laps	Laps Led	Races Led	Miles	$
				1	2	3	4	5	6–10					

Buddy Arrington *continued*

Year	Rank	Starts	Poles	1	2	3	4	5	6–10	Laps	Laps Led	Races Led	Miles	$
1976	20	25	0	0	0	0	0	0	3	6,256	0	0	6,737	56,647
1977	11	28	0	0	0	0	0	0	5	8,601	0	0	10,037	88,887
1978	9	30	0	0	0	0	0	1	6	9,580	0	0	10,739	112,960
1979	11	31	0	0	0	1	0	0	6	8,452	2	1	10,333	131,833
1980	12	31	0	0	0	0	0	0	7	8,765	0	0	9,936	120,355
1981	11	31	0	0	0	0	0	0	7	8,344	0	0	9,443	133,928
1982	7	30	0	0	0	0	0	0	8	9,336	6	4	10,840	178,159
1983	15	30	0	0	0	0	0	0	2	8,933	1	1	10,009	138,429
1984	20	26	0	0	0	0	0	0	0	7,323	0	0	8,295	128,802
1985	20	26	0	0	0	0	0	0	1	7,809	1	1	9,644	153,222
1986	20	26	0	0	0	0	0	0	0	8,152	4	1	9,457	186,588
1987	25	20	0	0	0	0	0	0	0	5,746	0	0	6,792	115,300
1988	46	4	0	0	0	0	0	0	0	760	0	0	1,549	22,165
Lifetime		560	0	0	0	2	1	12	88	147,899	14	8	161,308	$1,771,715

Joey Arrington

Joseph Arrington
B: 7/25/1956
Racing Hometown: Rocky Mount, VA

Year	Rank	Starts	Poles	1	2	3	4	5	6–10	Laps	Laps Led	Races Led	Miles	$
1974	97	2	0	0	0	0	0	0	0	342	0	0	214	985
1975	99	2	0	0	0	0	0	0	0	91	0	0	87	1,060
1978	60	3	0	0	0	0	0	0	0	690	0	0	706	2,790
1979	109	1	0	0	0	0	0	0	0	42	0	0	42	650
1980	84T	1	0	0	0	0	0	0	0	368	0	0	199	2,030
Lifetime		9	0	0	0	0	0	0	0	1,533	0	0	1,248	$7,515

Woody Arrington

Woodrow Arrington
Racing Hometown: Aberdeen, NC

Year	Rank	Starts	Poles	1	2	3	4	5	6–10	Laps	Laps Led	Races Led	Miles	$
1955	240T	1	0	0	0	0	0	0	0	4	0	0	4	0
Lifetime		1	0	0	0	0	0	0	0	4	0	0	4	$0

Bob Ashbrook

Robert Harold Ashbrook
B: 3/20/1929
Racing Hometown: Akron, OH

Year	Rank	Starts	Poles	1	2	3	4	5	6–10	Laps	Laps Led	Races Led	Miles	$
1969	57	2	0	0	0	0	0	0	0	200	0	0	399	1,587
1970	108T	1	0	0	0	0	0	0	0	44	0	0	110	220
Lifetime		3	0	0	0	0	0	0	0	244	0	0	509	$1,807

George Ashbrook

George Ashbrook
Racing Hometown: Akron, OH

Year	Rank	Starts	Poles	1	2	3	4	5	6–10	Laps	Laps Led	Races Led	Miles	$
1969	75T	1	0	0	0	0	0	0	0	262	0	0	262	540
Lifetime		1	0	0	0	0	0	0	0	262	0	0	262	$540

Bruce Atchley

Bruce H. Atchley
Racing Hometown: Loudon, TN

Year	Rank	Starts	Poles	1	2	3	4	5	6–10	Laps	Laps Led	Races Led	Miles	$
1952	60	6	0	0	0	0	0	0	0	307	0	0	187	200
Lifetime		6	0	0	0	0	0	0	0	307	0	0	187	$200

Irv Atkinson

Irv Atkinson
Racing Hometown: Grand Rapids, MI

Year	Rank	Starts	Poles	1	2	3	4	5	6–10	Laps	Laps Led	Races Led	Miles	$
1954	NR	1	0	0	0	0	0	0	0	35	0	0	18	0
Lifetime		1	0	0	0	0	0	0	0	35	0	0	18	$0

Ray Atkinson

Raymond Atkinson
Racing Hometown: Indianapolis, IN

Year	Rank	Starts	Poles	1	2	3	4	5	6–10	Laps	Laps Led	Races Led	Miles	$
1952	NR	1	0	0	0	0	0	0	0	255	0	0	128	25
Lifetime		1	0	0	0	0	0	0	0	255	0	0	128	$25

W. H. Atkinson

W. H. Atkinson III
Racing Hometown: Bunnell, FL

Year	Rank	Starts	Poles	1	2	3	4	5	6–10	Laps	Laps Led	Races Led	Miles	$
1956	276	1	0	0	0	0	0	0	0			0		0
Lifetime		1	0	0	0	0	0	0	0			0		$0

Year	Rank	Starts	Poles	Finish 1	2	3	4	5	6–10	Laps	Laps Led	Races Led	Miles	$

Roger Attard

Roger Attard
Racing Hometown: Highland Park, MI

Year	Rank	Starts	Poles	1	2	3	4	5	6–10	Laps	Laps Led	Races Led	Miles	$
1952	185	1	0	0	0	0	0	0	0	25	0	0	25	0
Lifetime		1	0	0	0	0	0	0	0	25	0	0	25	$0

Buzz Auckland

Buzz Auckland
Racing Hometown: Southampton, PA

Year	Rank	Starts	Poles	1	2	3	4	5	6–10	Laps	Laps Led	Races Led	Miles	$
1956	290	1	0	0	0	0	0	0	0	43	0	0	43	0
Lifetime		1	0	0	0	0	0	0	0	43	0	0	43	$0

Reggie Ausmus

Reginald Ausmus

Year	Rank	Starts	Poles	1	2	3	4	5	6–10	Laps	Laps Led	Races Led	Miles	$
1956	266T	1	0	0	0	0	0	0	0	138	0	0	138	40
1957	114T	2	0	0	0	0	0	0	0	256	0	0	128	150
Lifetime		3	0	0	0	0	0	0	0	394	0	0	266	$190

Gene Austin

Gene Austin
Racing Hometown: Mexico, NY

Year	Rank	Starts	Poles	1	2	3	4	5	6–10	Laps	Laps Led	Races Led	Miles	$
1950	52	2	0	0	0	0	0	0	1	0	0	0	0	175
Lifetime		2	0	0	0	0	0	0	1	0	0	0	0	$175

Jack Austin

Jack Austin
Racing Hometown: Gardena, CA

Year	Rank	Starts	Poles	1	2	3	4	5	6–10	Laps	Laps Led	Races Led	Miles	$
1959	NR	1	0	0	0	0	0	0	0	54	0	0	54	75
Lifetime		1	0	0	0	0	0	0	0	54	0	0	54	$75

Jim Austin

James Austin
Racing Hometown: Boynton Beach, FL

Year	Rank	Starts	Poles	1	2	3	4	5	6–10	Laps	Laps Led	Races Led	Miles	$
1959	45	5	0	0	0	0	0	0	0	784	0	0	413	440
1960	97	2	0	0	0	0	0	0	0	199	0	0	124	310
Lifetime		7	0	0	0	0	0	0	0	983	0	0	537	$750

L. D. Austin

L. D. Austin
B: 8/17/1918   *Deceased*
Racing Hometown: Greenville, SC

Year	Rank	Starts	Poles	1	2	3	4	5	6–10	Laps	Laps Led	Races Led	Miles	$
1957	8	40	0	0	0	0	0	1	12	6,920	0	0	4,132	6,485
1958	6	46	0	0	0	0	0	0	10	6,903	0	0	3,898	6,246
1959	7	35	0	0	0	0	0	0	13	6,481	0	0	3,603	4,671
1960	22	27	0	0	0	0	0	1	9	4,822	0	0	3,996	4,885
1961	25	20	0	0	0	0	0	0	8	4,802	0	0	3,402	4,530
1962	NR	1	0	0	0	0	0	0	0	53	0	0	27	0
Lifetime		169	0	0	0	0	0	2	52	29,981	0	0	19,057	$26,817

Paul Austin

Paul Austin
Racing Hometown: Asheville, NC

Year	Rank	Starts	Poles	1	2	3	4	5	6–10	Laps	Laps Led	Races Led	Miles	$
1951	N/A	1	0	0	0	0	0	0	0		0	0		25
Lifetime		1	0	0	0	0	0	0	0		0	0		$25

Scott Autrey

Scott Autrey
B: 7/9/1953
Racing Hometown: San Angelo, TX

Year	Rank	Starts	Poles	1	2	3	4	5	6–10	Laps	Laps Led	Races Led	Miles	$
1985	88T	1	0	0	0	0	0	0	0	79	0	0	207	1,125
Lifetime		1	0	0	0	0	0	0	0	79	0	0	207	$1,125

Jimmy Ayers

James Ayers
B: 4/2/1917
Racing Hometown: Gardendale, AL

Year	Rank	Starts	Poles	1	2	3	4	5	6–10	Laps	Laps Led	Races Led	Miles	$
1950	NR	1	0	0	0	0	0	0	0		0	0		0
1951	71	7	0	0	0	0	0	0	5	225	0	0	281	500
1952	101	3	0	0	0	0	0	0	0	179	0	0	90	85
1953	45	4	0	0	0	0	0	0	2		0	0		175
1954	171	2	0	0	0	0	0	0	0	219	0	0	178	75

Year	Rank	Starts	Poles	Finish						Laps	Laps Led	Races Led	Miles	$
				1	2	3	4	5	6–10					

Jimmy Ayers *continued*

Year	Rank	Starts	Poles	1	2	3	4	5	6–10	Laps	Laps Led	Races Led	Miles	$
1955	72	2	0	0	0	0	0	0	1	277	0	0	292	350
Lifetime		19	0	0	0	0	0	0	8	900	0	0	840	$1,185

Bill Bade

William Bade
    Racing Hometown: Redondo Beach, CA

Year	Rank	Starts	Poles	1	2	3	4	5	6–10	Laps	Laps Led	Races Led	Miles	$
1954	85	3	0	0	0	0	0	0	1	832	0	0	488	190
1956	224	1	0	0	0	0	0	0	0	214	0	0	214	40
1957	146	2	0	0	0	0	0	0	0	194	0	0	97	90
1958	171	1	0	0	0	0	0	0	0	28	0	0	28	25
Lifetime		7	0	0	0	0	0	0	1	1,268	0	0	827	$345

George Bagnell

George Bagnell
    B: 1926

Year	Rank	Starts	Poles	1	2	3	4	5	6–10	Laps	Laps Led	Races Led	Miles	$
1950	NR	1	0	0	0	0	0	0	0		0	0		0
Lifetime		1	0	0	0	0	0	0	0		0	0		$0

Dick Bailey

Richard Bailey
    B: 1922
    Racing Hometown: Grove City, PA

Year	Rank	Starts	Poles	1	2	3	4	5	6–10	Laps	Laps Led	Races Led	Miles	$
1951	N/A	2	0	0	0	0	0	0	0		0	0		25
1958	18	1	0	0	0	0	0	0	0	33	0	0	135	75
1959	NR	1	1	0	0	0	0	0	0	54	3	1	14	50
Lifetime		4	1	0	0	0	0	0	0	87	3	1	149	$150

Don Bailey

Donald Bailey
    B: 1927
    Racing Hometown: Brockway, PA

Year	Rank	Starts	Poles	1	2	3	4	5	6–10	Laps	Laps Led	Races Led	Miles	$
1951	47	10	0	0	0	0	1	0	1	151	0	0	76	625
1956	270T	1	0	0	0	0	0	0	0		0		0	25
1957	160T	1	0	0	0	0	0	0	0	62	0	0	62	75
Lifetime		12	0	0	0	0	1	0	1	213	0	0	138	$700

H. B. Bailey

Herring Burl Bailey
    B: 11/15/1936
    Racing Hometown: Houston, TX

Year	Rank	Starts	Poles	1	2	3	4	5	6–10	Laps	Laps Led	Races Led	Miles	$
1962	128	1	0	0	0	0	0	0	0	101	0	0	152	300
1963	53	2	0	0	0	0	0	0	0	226	0	0	565	775
1964	136	2	0	0	0	0	0	0	0	141	0	0	195	900
1965	29	5	0	0	0	0	0	1	2	810	0	0	1,338	5,000
1966	66	4	0	0	0	0	0	0	0	450	0	0	671	2,745
1967	50	3	0	0	0	0	0	0	0	322	0	0	676	3,850
1968	81	2	0	0	0	0	0	0	0	187	0	0	264	1,250
1969	53	6	0	0	0	0	0	0	1	638	0	0	1,303	5,880
1970	NR	1	0	0	0	0	0	0	0	180	0	0	246	995
1971	NR	4	0	0	0	0	0	0	0	657	11	1	480	1,490
1972	58	5	0	0	0	0	0	1	0	1,167	6	1	1,654	8,010
1973	77	2	0	0	0	0	0	0	0	243	0	0	483	1,935
1975	114T	1	0	0	0	0	0	0	0	1	0	0	1	1,330
1979	56	4	0	0	0	0	0	0	0	738	0	0	1,175	5,835
1981	55	4	0	0	0	0	0	0	0	605	0	0	989	7,465
1982	42	6	0	0	0	0	0	0	0	1,016	0	0	1,612	9,455
1983	61	2	0	0	0	0	0	0	0	684	0	0	1,033	4,110
1984	58	2	0	0	0	0	0	0	0	529	0	0	770	5,640
1985	88T	2	0	0	0	0	0	0	0	206	0	0	299	3,065
1986	52	4	0	0	0	0	0	0	0	918	1	1	1,289	9,225
1987	48	5	0	0	0	0	0	0	0	1,150	0	0	1,691	18,885
1988	43	7	0	0	0	0	0	0	0	1,180	0	0	1,788	15,775
1989	60	2	0	0	0	0	0	0	0	487	0	0	787	9,595
1990	65	3	0	0	0	0	0	0	0	421	0	0	608	9,615
1991	53	3	0	0	0	0	0	0	0	545	0	0	981	13,095
1992	95T	1	0	0	0	0	0	0	0	8	0	0	16	7,755
1993	60	2	0	0	0	0	0	0	0	238	0	0	442	12,750
Lifetime		85	0	0	0	0	0	2	3	13,848	18	3	21,505	$166,725

Year	Rank	Starts	Poles	Finish 1	2	3	4	5	6–10	Laps	Laps Led	Races Led	Miles	$

Buck Baity

Buck Baity
Racing Hometown: Yadkinsville, NC

Year	Rank	Starts	Poles	1	2	3	4	5	6–10	Laps	Laps Led	Races Led	Miles	$
1951	N/A	1	0	0	0	0	0	0	0	248	0	0	310	0
Lifetime		1	0	0	0	0	0	0	0	248	0	0	310	$0

Bill Baker

William Baker
B: 6/19/1931
Racing Hometown: Pismo Beach, CA

Year	Rank	Starts	Poles	1	2	3	4	5	6–10	Laps	Laps Led	Races Led	Miles	$
1977	69	2	0	0	0	0	0	0	0	142	0	0	372	2,540
1978	101	1	0	0	0	0	0	0	0	20	0	0	52	550
Lifetime		3	0	0	0	0	0	0	0	162	0	0	424	$3,090

Bobby Baker

Robert Baker

Year	Rank	Starts	Poles	1	2	3	4	5	6–10	Laps	Laps Led	Races Led	Miles	$
1987	80	1	0	0	0	0	0	0	0	380	0	0	238	3,500
Lifetime		1	0	0	0	0	0	0	0	380	0	0	238	$3,500

Bryan Baker

Bryan Scott Baker
B: 6/8/1961
Racing Hometown: Charlotte, NC

Year	Rank	Starts	Poles	1	2	3	4	5	6–10	Laps	Laps Led	Races Led	Miles	$
1986	107T	1	0	0	0	0	0	0	0	252	0	0	252	3,985
Lifetime		1	0	0	0	0	0	0	0	252	0	0	252	$3,985

Buck Baker

Elzie Wylie Baker
B: 3/4/1919
Racing Hometown: Charlotte, NC

Year	Rank	Starts	Poles	1	2	3	4	5	6–10	Laps	Laps Led	Races Led	Miles	$
1949	48	2	0	0	0	0	0	0	0		0	0		50
1950	12	9	1	0	1	1	0	0	3	587	10	1	605	2,145
1951	23	11	0	0	0	1	0	3	1	338	0	0	407	1,800
1952	12	14	2	1	0	0	2	0	3	1,550	139	3	1,273	3,187
1953	4	33	4	4	2	3	4	3	9	1,619	564	9	1,550	18,167
1954	3	34	7	4	7	6	3	3	5	5,726	768	14	3,893	19,368
1955	2	42	2	3	6	6	4	5	10	**6,705**	808	9	**4,781**	19,771
1956	1	48	12	14	7	3	4	3	8	**8,495**	1,401	**23**	**5,460**	34,077
1957	1	40	6	10	7	4	5	4	8	**8,058**	858	15	**4,844**	30,764
1958	2	44	3	3	10	4	2	4	12	7,827	364	8	4,726	25,841
1959	5	35	4	1	2	6	1	4	5	6,056	183	5	3,606	11,061
1960	4	37	2	2	1	3	1	8	9	7,271	213	4	5,854	38,399
1961	10	42	1	1	1	3	4	2	4	7,195	114	3	5,226	13,697
1962	13	37	0	0	1	3	2	0	8	6,707	18	2	5,035	12,787
1963	11	47	0	1	3	6	2	5	13	9,505	63	2	5,702	18,616
1964	9	34	0	2	3	3	3	4	3	7,263	159	5	6,080	43,781
1965	17	31	0	0	2	0	0	1	9	5,266	0	0	4,173	21,580
1966	21	36	0	0	3	0	2	2	7	6,725	0	0	4,882	14,900
1967	27	21	0	0	0	0	0	0	5	4,544	0	0	3,156	7,730
1968	40	17	0	0	0	0	0	1	2	2,675	0	0	1,560	3,580
1969	NR	1	0	0	0	0	0	0	0	108	0	0	287	1,300
1970	NR	1	0	0	0	0	0	0	0	267	0	0	267	610
1971	NR	6	0	0	0	0	1	0	1	1,775	0	0	835	2,345
1972	NR	5	0	0	0	0	0	0	0	660	0	0	722	3,255
1973	101	1	0	0	0	0	0	0	0	357	0	0	363	670
1976	48	8	0	0	0	0	0	0	1	1,977	0	0	2,678	12,655
Lifetime		636	44	46	56	52	40	52	126	109,256	5,662	103	77,965	$362,136
		7th	**9th**											

Buddy Baker

Elzie Wylie Baker Jr.
B: 1/25/1941
Racing Hometown: Charlotte, NC

Year	Rank	Starts	Poles	1	2	3	4	5	6–10	Laps	Laps Led	Races Led	Miles	$
1959	26	12	0	0	0	0	1	0	4	1,639	0	0	876	1,705
1960	38	15	0	0	0	0	0	0	1	2,149	0	0	1,881	1,745
1961	31	14	0	0	0	0	0	1	2	2,370	0	0	2,434	4,965
1962	23	31	0	0	0	1	2	2	5	5,454	0	0	4,139	7,578
1963	52	8	0	0	0	0	1	0	1	1,478	0	0	1,098	2,665
1964	31	33	0	0	0	1	1	1	4	3,239	0	0	2,246	8,460
1965	9	42	0	0	2	4	2	4	5	6,969	0	0	5,394	26,837
1966	22	41	1	0	1	0	0	0	6	6,361	142	4	4,890	21,335

Year	Rank	Starts	Poles	Finish						Laps	Laps Led	Races Led	Miles	$
				1	2	3	4	5	6–10	Laps	Led	Led	Miles	$

Buddy Baker *continued*

Year	Rank	Starts	Poles	1	2	3	4	5	6–10	Laps	Laps Led	Races Led	Miles	$
1967	15	20	0	1	1	2	2	0	1	3,905	480	8	4,135	46,950
1968	13	38	4	1	4	6	3	2	2	7,949	564	12	5,728	56,023
1969	22	18	3	0	2	4	1	2	2	4,177	770	14	5,210	63,525
1970	24	18	1	1	2	0	1	2	2	3,611	485	11	5,874	63,778
1971	15	19	1	1	6	5	0	1	3	4,814	727	15	7,813	115,150
1972	24	17	1	2	1	4	1	0	1	4,641	594	14	6,030	103,140
1973	6	27	5	2	4	6	4	0	4	8,369	975	14	8,908	190,531
1974	7	19	2	0	4	5	1	1	1	4,346	381	13	5,890	151,025
1975	15	23	3	4	2	4	1	1	1	6,281	788	18	8,113	236,351
1976	7	30	2	1	3	1	4	7	0	7,335	1,028	15	8,610	239,922
1977	5	30	0	0	1	1	4	3	11	8,084	52	7	9,876	224,847
1978	24	19	1	0	1	1	1	1	4	4,319	354	10	6,594	111,765
1979	15	26	7	3	2	3	3	1	3	6,107	1,083	20	7,421	342,148
1980	21	19	6	2	2	4	2	0	2	5,042	671	15	6,952	275,200
1981	27	16	0	0	1	0	2	3	3	3,562	110	9	5,811	115,095
1982	23	23	1	0	1	0	0	3	7	5,672	103	12	7,393	253,675
1983	21	21	1	1	1	2	0	1	7	5,111	174	7	6,816	216,355
1984	21	21	1	0	1	2	0	1	8	6,213	84	2	7,447	151,635
1985	17	28	0	0	0	0	2	0	5	6,296	4	2	8,250	235,480
1986	24	17	0	0	0	1	2	3	0	3,964	45	5	6,465	138,600
1987	24	20	0	0	1	1	1	0	7	4,509	91	7	7,163	255,320
1988	29	17	0	0	0	0	0	0	7	4,445	42	7	6,481	184,200
1990	41	8	0	0	0	0	0	0	0	1,326	1	1	2,353	40,085
1991	40	6	0	0	0	0	0	0	0	845	0	0	1,958	58,060
1992	48	3	0	0	0	0	0	0	0	547	0	0	1,227	49,500
1994	—	0												1,850
Lifetime		699	40	19	43	58	42	40	109	151,129	9,748	242	181,473	$3,995,500
		4th	**10th**							**9th**	**10th**	**7th**	**9th**	

Charlie Baker

Charles Baker Jr.
B: 1962
Racing Hometown: New Oxford, PA

Year	Rank	Starts	Poles	1	2	3	4	5	6–10	Laps	Laps Led	Races Led	Miles	$
1982	NR	3	0	0	0	0	0	0	0	444	0	0	1,025	5,235
1986	92T	1	0	0	0	0	0	0	0	457	0	0	465	2,500
1987	68	2	0	0	0	0	0	0	0	610	0	0	695	7,915
1988	87T	1	0	0	0	0	0	0	0	136	0	0	138	3,190
1989	57	3	0	0	0	0	0	0	0	255	0	0	611	16,370
1990	77	2	0	0	0	0	0	0	0	84	0	0	85	5,325
Lifetime		12	0	0	0	0	0	0	0	1,986	0	0	3,019	$40,535

Gary Baker

Gary Baker
B: 5/28/1946
Racing Hometown: Nashville, TN

Year	Rank	Starts	Poles	1	2	3	4	5	6–10	Laps	Laps Led	Races Led	Miles	$
1980	NR	1	0	0	0	0	0	0	0	145	0	0	386	4,040
Lifetime		1	0	0	0	0	0	0	0	145	0	0	386	$4,040

Jim Baker

James Baker
Racing Hometown: Atlanta, GA

Year	Rank	Starts	Poles	1	2	3	4	5	6–10	Laps	Laps Led	Races Led	Miles	$
1953	117T	1	0	0	0	0	0	0	0		0	0		25
Lifetime		1	0	0	0	0	0	0	0		0	0		$25

Randy Baker

Randall Baker
B: 1958
Racing Hometown: Charlotte, NC

Year	Rank	Starts	Poles	1	2	3	4	5	6–10	Laps	Laps Led	Races Led	Miles	$
1982	84T	1	0	0	0	0	0	0	0	347	0	0	353	1,300
1984	54	3	0	0	0	0	0	0	0	553	0	0	826	6,400
1985	NR	1	0	0	0	0	0	0	0	453	0	0	453	2,025
1986	83	2	0	0	0	0	0	0	0	328	0	0	499	2,790
1987	NR	2	0	0	0	0	0	0	0	653	0	0	986	13,060
1988	82	1	0	0	0	0	0	0	0	135	0	0	184	4,355
1991	58	2	0	0	0	0	0	0	0	689	0	0	941	13,055
1992	75	1	0	0	0	0	0	0	0	459	0	0	467	8,700
1996	67	1	0	0	0	0	0	0	0	51	0	0	78	12,550
Lifetime		14	0	0	0	0	0	0	0	3,668	0	0	4,787	$64,235

Year	Rank	Starts	Poles	Finish						Laps	Laps Led	Races Led	Miles	$
				1	2	3	4	5	6–10					

W. E. Baker

William E. Baker Jr. (Bill)
Racing Hometown: New Zion, SC

Year	Rank	Starts	Poles	1	2	3	4	5	6–10	Laps	Laps Led	Races Led	Miles	$
1952	82	1	0	0	0	0	0	0	0	368	0	0	460	90
Lifetime		1	0	0	0	0	0	0	0	368	0	0	460	$90

Ivan Baldwin

Ivan Baldwin
B: 8/26/1946   D: 9/29/1996
Racing Hometown: Modesto, CA

Year	Rank	Starts	Poles	1	2	3	4	5	6–10	Laps	Laps Led	Races Led	Miles	$
1971	NR	3	0	0	0	0	0	0	0	272	0	0	692	3,535
1972	98	1	0	0	0	0	0	0	0	123	0	0	322	1,120
1975	112	2	0	0	0	0	0	0	0	9	0	0	24	1,040
Lifetime		6	0	0	0	0	0	0	0	404	0	0	1,038	$5,695

Rick Baldwin

Richard Baldwin
B: 1955
Racing Hometown: Corpus Christi, TX

Year	Rank	Starts	Poles	1	2	3	4	5	6–10	Laps	Laps Led	Races Led	Miles	$
1981	NR	1	0	0	0	0	0	0	0	149	0	0	298	1,550
1982	76	1	0	0	0	0	0	0	0	323	0	0	485	6,065
1983	69	5	0	0	0	0	0	0	0	818	0	0	1,222	15,140
1985	64	2	0	0	0	0	0	0	0	458	0	0	765	3,035
1986	NR	2	0	0	0	0	0	0	0	393	0	0	260	6,905
Lifetime		11	0	0	0	0	0	0	0	2,141	0	0	3,030	$32,695

Roger Baldwin

Roger Baldwin
Racing Hometown: Belmont, NC

Year	Rank	Starts	Poles	1	2	3	4	5	6–10	Laps	Laps Led	Races Led	Miles	$
1957	NR	2	0	0	0	0	0	0	0	337	0	0	337	200
Lifetime		2	0	0	0	0	0	0	0	337	0	0	337	$200

F. Ballantine

F. Ballantine

Year	Rank	Starts	Poles	1	2	3	4	5	6–10	Laps	Laps Led	Races Led	Miles	$
1954	NR	1	0	0	0	0	0	0	0	9	0	0	18	25
Lifetime		1	0	0	0	0	0	0	0	9	0	0	18	$25

Walter Ballard

Walter H. Ballard
B: 1/12/1933
Racing Hometown: Houston, TX

Year	Rank	Starts	Poles	1	2	3	4	5	6–10	Laps	Laps Led	Races Led	Miles	$
1966	92	1	0	0	0	0	0	0	0	234	0	0	322	525
1971	10	41	0	0	0	1	1	1	8	9,419	0	0	8,035	30,974
1972	6	31	0	0	0	0	0	0	7	8,460	0	0	9,748	59,745
1973	8	28	0	0	0	0	0	0	4	8,048	5	1	8,626	53,875
1974	15	27	0	0	0	0	0	1	5	6,820	2	1	7,246	54,039
1975	11	30	0	0	0	0	0	0	3	7,518	16	2	8,254	55,696
1976	26	14	0	0	0	0	0	0	3	4,168	0	0	3,542	16,380
1977	54	3	0	0	0	0	0	0	0	752	0	0	738	5,175
1978	96T	0	0	0	0	0	0	0	0	0	0	0	0	505
Lifetime		175	0	0	0	1	1	2	30	45,419	23	4	46,511	$270,708

Claude Ballot-Lena

Claude Ballot-Lena
Racing Hometown: Paris, France

Year	Rank	Starts	Poles	1	2	3	4	5	6–10	Laps	Laps Led	Races Led	Miles	$
1978	NR	4	0	0	0	0	0	0	0	460	0	0	1,186	7,770
1979	NR	2	0	0	0	0	0	0	0	251	0	0	463	3,020
Lifetime		6	0	0	0	0	0	0	0	711	0	0	1,649	$10,790

Earl Balmer

Earl Franklin Balmer
B: 12/13/1935
Racing Hometown: Floyds Knob, IN

Year	Rank	Starts	Poles	1	2	3	4	5	6–10	Laps	Laps Led	Races Led	Miles	$
1959	54	2	0	0	0	0	0	0	0	436	0	0	423	250
1964	35	10	0	0	0	0	1	1	2	2,771	1	1	2,052	5,795
1965	23	9	0	0	1	0	1	0	2	1,320	32	6	2,174	19,045
1966	36	9	0	1	0	0	0	1	0	1,388	4	2	2,097	7,935
1967	100	1	0	0	0	0	0	0	0	102	0	0	140	625
1968	NR	1	0	0	0	0	0	0	0	59	0	0	89	1,075
Lifetime		32	0	1	1	0	2	2	4	6,076	37	9	6,974	$34,725

Year	Rank	Starts	Poles	Finish						Laps	Laps Led	Races Led	Miles	$
				1	2	3	4	5	6–10	Laps	Led	Led	Miles	$

Gary Balough

Gary Balough
B: 9/16/1947
Racing Hometown: Ft. Lauderdale, FL

Year	Rank	Starts	Poles	1	2	3	4	5	6–10	Laps	Laps Led	Races Led	Miles	$
1979	89	3	0	0	0	0	0	0	0	216	0	0	540	6,015
1980	108	1	0	0	0	0	0	0	0	16	0	0	24	610
1981	40	10	0	0	0	0	0	0	1	2,267	1	1	3,232	34,430
1982	38	5	0	0	0	0	0	0	1	1,359	0	0	1,608	35,735
1991	74T	2	0	0	0	0	0	0	0	44	0	0	68	9,010
1992	93T	1	0	0	0	0	0	0	0	131	0	0	197	7,700
Lifetime		22	0	0	0	0	0	0	2	4,033	1	1	5,669	$93,500

John Banks

John Banks
Racing Hometown: Windsor, Ont., Canada,

Year	Rank	Starts	Poles	1	2	3	4	5	6–10	Laps	Laps Led	Races Led	Miles	$
1974	NR	1	0	0	0	0	0	0	0	14	0	0	28	835
1975	86T	3	0	0	0	0	0	0	0	478	0	0	816	2,760
Lifetime		4	0	0	0	0	0	0	0	492	0	0	844	$3,595

Phil Barkdoll

Phillip Barkdoll
B: 9/9/1937
Racing Hometown: Phoenix, AZ

Year	Rank	Starts	Poles	1	2	3	4	5	6–10	Laps	Laps Led	Races Led	Miles	$
1984	65	2	0	0	0	0	0	0	0	212	0	0	564	5,075
1985	69	2	0	0	0	0	0	0	0	200	0	0	532	5,525
1986	103	2	0	0	0	0	0	0	0	249	3	2	662	6,045
1987	98T	1	0	0	0	0	0	0	0	27	0	0	72	6,000
1988	52	3	0	0	0	0	0	0	0	465	0	0	1,220	22,145
1989	45	4	0	0	0	0	0	0	0	658	2	1	1,702	29,050
1990	64	3	0	0	0	0	0	0	0	202	0	0	524	24,160
1991	46	4	0	0	0	0	0	0	0	646	0	0	1,674	41,655
1992	55	2	0	0	0	0	0	0	0	354	0	0	885	33,255
1994	—	0												1,850
1995	—	0												2,450
Lifetime		23	0	0	0	0	0	0	0	3,013	5	3	7,836	$177,210

Bill Barker

William Barker
Racing Hometown: Greenville, PA

Year	Rank	Starts	Poles	1	2	3	4	5	6–10	Laps	Laps Led	Races Led	Miles	$
1952	79	2	0	0	0	0	0	0	0	376	0	0	301	75
1954	99	4	0	0	0	0	0	0	0	364	0	0	279	35
Lifetime		6	0	0	0	0	0	0	0	740	0	0	580	$110

Curley Barker

Curley Barker
Racing Hometown: Tillemook, OR

Year	Rank	Starts	Poles	1	2	3	4	5	6–10	Laps	Laps Led	Races Led	Miles	$
1956	58	4	0	0	0	2	0	1	1	840	0	0	420	1,395
Lifetime		4	0	0	0	2	0	1	1	840	0	0	420	$1,395

John Barker

John Barker
Racing Hometown: Hickory, NC

Year	Rank	Starts	Poles	1	2	3	4	5	6–10	Laps	Laps Led	Races Led	Miles	$
1949	66	1	0	0	0	0	0	0	0		0	0		50
1951	N/A	7	0	0	0	0	0	0	0	471	0	0	526	175
Lifetime		8	0	0	0	0	0	0	0	471	0	0	526	$225

Johnny Barnes

John Barnes
B: 4/24/1942
Racing Hometown: Port Charlotte, FL

Year	Rank	Starts	Poles	1	2	3	4	5	6–10	Laps	Laps Led	Races Led	Miles	$
1971	NR	1	0	0	0	0	0	0	0	23	0	0	61	615
1973	39	8	0	0	0	0	0	0	0	1,416	0	0	2,174	8,890
1974	65	4	0	0	0	0	0	0	0	135	0	0	171	2,515
Lifetime		13	0	0	0	0	0	0	0	1,574	0	0	2,406	$12,020

Jerry Barnett

Jerry Barnett
B: 12/17/1951
Racing Hometown: Bonita, CA

Year	Rank	Starts	Poles	1	2	3	4	5	6–10	Laps	Laps Led	Races Led	Miles	$
1971	NR	2	0	0	0	0	0	0	0	118	0	0	256	1,260
Lifetime		2	0	0	0	0	0	0	0	118	0	0	256	$1,260

Year	Rank	Starts	Poles	1	2	3	4	5	6–10	Laps	Laps Led	Races Led	Miles	$

Dick Baron

Richard Baron
Racing Hometown: Sacramento, CA

Year	Rank	Starts	Poles	1	2	3	4	5	6–10	Laps	Laps Led	Races Led	Miles	$
1961	189	1	0	0	0	0	0	0	0	5	0	0	5	25
Lifetime		1	0	0	0	0	0	0	0	5	0	0	5	$25

Buck Barr

Buck Barr
Racing Hometown: Zanesville, OH

Year	Rank	Starts	Poles	1	2	3	4	5	6–10	Laps	Laps Led	Races Led	Miles	$
1950	36	2	0	0	0	1	0	0	1		0	0		575
Lifetime		2	0	0	0	1	0	0	1		0	0		$575

Charles Barrett

Charles Barrett
B: 11/28/1944
Racing Hometown: Cleveland, GA

Year	Rank	Starts	Poles	1	2	3	4	5	6–10	Laps	Laps Led	Races Led	Miles	$
1973	65	4	0	0	0	0	0	0	1	726	9	1	1,298	5,610
Lifetime		4	0	0	0	0	0	0	1	726	9	1	1,298	$5,610

Stan Barrett

Stanley Barrett
B: 6/26/1943
Racing Hometown: Bishop, CA

Year	Rank	Starts	Poles	1	2	3	4	5	6–10	Laps	Laps Led	Races Led	Miles	$
1980	NR	3	0	0	0	0	0	0	1	987	0	0	1,454	13,760
1981	38	10	0	0	0	0	0	0	1	1,559	4	2	3,265	28,540
1982	96	1	0	0	0	0	0	0	0	65	0	0	163	5,585
1989	61	4	0	0	0	0	0	0	0	391	0	0	613	11,500
1990	74	1	0	0	0	0	0	0	0	74	0	0	186	6,300
Lifetime		19	0	0	0	0	0	0	2	3,076	4	2	5,680	$65,685

Bob Barron

Dr. Robert Barron
B: 1/13/1921
Racing Hometown: Bradenton, FL

Year	Rank	Starts	Poles	1	2	3	4	5	6–10	Laps	Laps Led	Races Led	Miles	$
1960	140	1	0	0	0	0	0	0	0	186	0	0	279	900
1961	29	31	0	0	0	0	0	0	5	5,005	0	0	2,870	3,825
Lifetime		32	0	0	0	0	0	0	5	5,191	0	0	3,149	$4,725

Chester Barron

Charles Barron
Racing Hometown: Cornelia, GA

Year	Rank	Starts	Poles	1	2	3	4	5	6–10	Laps	Laps Led	Races Led	Miles	$
1956	144	2	0	0	0	0	0	0	1	207	0	0	152	150
1958	NR	1	0	0	0	0	0	0	0	49	0	0	49	75
1959	NR	3	0	0	0	0	0	0	1	271	0	0	175	275
Lifetime		6	0	0	0	0	0	0	2	527	0	0	376	$500

Paul Barrow

Paul Barrow
Racing Hometown: Sycamore, IL

Year	Rank	Starts	Poles	1	2	3	4	5	6–10	Laps	Laps Led	Races Led	Miles	$
1962	64	2	0	0	0	0	0	0	0	189	0	0	473	500
Lifetime		2	0	0	0	0	0	0	0	189	0	0	473	$500

Charles Barry

Charles Barry
Racing Hometown: Syracuse, NY

Year	Rank	Starts	Poles	1	2	3	4	5	6–10	Laps	Laps Led	Races Led	Miles	$
1952	78	3	0	0	0	0	0	0	0	312	0	0	162	75
1953	NR	1	0	0	0	0	0	0	1		0	0		100
Lifetime		4	0	0	0	0	0	0	1	312	0	0	162	$175

Paul Bass

Paul Bass
Racing Hometown: Indianapolis, IN

Year	Rank	Starts	Poles	1	2	3	4	5	6–10	Laps	Laps Led	Races Led	Miles	$
1959	NR	1	0	0	0	0	0	0	0	52	0	0	130	100
Lifetime		1	0	0	0	0	0	0	0	52	0	0	130	$100

Mike Batinick

Michael Batinick
Racing Hometown: Campbell, CA

Year	Rank	Starts	Poles	1	2	3	4	5	6–10	Laps	Laps Led	Races Led	Miles	$
1958	62	2	0	0	0	0	0	0	0	257	0	0	528	240
Lifetime		2	0	0	0	0	0	0	0	257	0	0	528	$240

Year	Rank	Starts	Poles	Finish						Laps	Laps Led	Races Led	Miles	$
				1	2	3	4	5	6–10	Laps	Led	Led	Miles	$

George Bauer

George Bauer
Racing Hometown: Covington, KY

Year	Rank	Starts	Poles	1	2	3	4	5	6–10	Laps	Laps Led	Races Led	Miles	$
1969	NR	2	0	0	0	0	0	0	0	203	0	0	508	2,410
Lifetime		2	0	0	0	0	0	0	0	203	0	0	508	$2,410

Ed Baugess

Edward Baugess

Year	Rank	Starts	Poles	1	2	3	4	5	6–10	Laps	Laps Led	Races Led	Miles	$
1983	90T	1	0	0	0	0	0	0	0	13	0	0	8	725
Lifetime		1	0	0	0	0	0	0	0	13	0	0	8	$725

Larry Baumel

Lawrence Allan Baumel
B: 5/26/1944
Racing Hometown: Sparta, WI

Year	Rank	Starts	Poles	1	2	3	4	5	6–10	Laps	Laps Led	Races Led	Miles	$
1969	59	6	0	0	0	0	0	0	0	964	0	0	682	2,760
1970	32	23	1	0	0	0	0	0	1	2,731	0	0	3,697	16,645
1971	37	16	0	0	0	0	0	0	1	2,245	0	0	2,998	10,910
Lifetime		45	1	0	0	0	0	0	2	5,940	0	0	7,376	$30,290

Ray Baxter

Raymond Baxter
Racing Hometown: Bronx, NY

Year	Rank	Starts	Poles	1	2	3	4	5	6–10	Laps	Laps Led	Races Led	Miles	$
1956	239T	1	0	0	0	0	0	0	0	55	0	0	55	50
Lifetime		1	0	0	0	0	0	0	0	55	0	0	55	$50

Harold Beal

Harold Beal (Hal)
Racing Hometown: Portland, OR

Year	Rank	Starts	Poles	1	2	3	4	5	6–10	Laps	Laps Led	Races Led	Miles	$
1956	66	5	0	0	0	0	1	0	2	781	0	0	398	915
1957	69	4	0	0	0	0	0	0	1	429	0	0	236	400
1963	83	1	0	0	0	0	0	0	0	164	0	0	443	425
Lifetime		10	0	0	0	0	1	0	3	1,374	0	0	1,077	$1,740

Herman Beam

Herman Beam
B: 12/11/1929   D: 1980
Racing Hometown: Johnson City, TN

Year	Rank	Starts	Poles	1	2	3	4	5	6–10	Laps	Laps Led	Races Led	Miles	$
1957	NR	1	0	0	0	0	0	0	0		0	0		50
1958	13	20	0	0	0	0	0	0	1	3,651	0	0	2,251	2,599
1959	4	30	0	0	0	0	0	1	11	6,034	0	0	4,011	6,380
1960	12	26	0	0	0	0	1	0	5	5,348	0	0	4,730	5,916
1961	15	41	0	0	0	0	1	0	13	8,827	0	0	6,403	9,392
1962	11	51	0	0	0	0	0	0	18	11,217	0	0	7,140	12,571
1963	27	25	0	0	0	0	0	0	6	5,061	0	0	3,476	5,255
Lifetime		194	0	0	0	0	2	1	54	40,138	0	0	28,010	$42,163

Nix Beard

Nix Beard
Racing Hometown: Germantown, OH

Year	Rank	Starts	Poles	1	2	3	4	5	6–10	Laps	Laps Led	Races Led	Miles	$
1950	126T	1	0	0	0	0	0	0	0		0	0		0
Lifetime		1	0	0	0	0	0	0	0		0	0		$0

Byron Beatty

Byron Beatty

Year	Rank	Starts	Poles	1	2	3	4	5	6–10	Laps	Laps Led	Races Led	Miles	$
1950	NR	1	0	0	0	0	0	0	0	351	0	0	439	0
Lifetime		1	0	0	0	0	0	0	0	351	0	0	439	$0

Dick Beaty

Richard Beaty
B: 12/16/1924
Racing Hometown: Charlotte, NC

Year	Rank	Starts	Poles	1	2	3	4	5	6–10	Laps	Laps Led	Races Led	Miles	$
1955	203	1	0	0	0	0	0	0	0	184	0	0	253	50
1956	46	15	0	0	0	0	0	0	3	1,513	0	0	1,091	910
1957	17	20	0	0	0	0	0	1	6	3,202	0	0	2,061	3,648
1958	89	2	0	0	0	0	0	0	0	448	0	0	224	150
Lifetime		38	0	0	0	0	0	1	9	5,347	0	0	3,628	$4,558

Johnny Beauchamp

John Beauchamp
B: 3/23/1923   D: 4/17/1981
Racing Hometown: Harlan, IA

Year	Rank	Starts	Poles	1	2	3	4	5	6–10	Laps	Laps Led	Races Led	Miles	$
1953	50	3	0	0	0	0	0	0	1		0	0		150

Year	Rank	Starts	Poles	Finish						Laps	Laps Led	Races Led	Miles	$
				1	2	3	4	5	6–10					

Johnny Beauchamp *continued*

Year	Rank	Starts	Poles	1	2	3	4	5	6–10	Laps	Laps Led	Races Led	Miles	$
1957	66	1	0	0	1	0	0	0	0	39	0	0	160	2,450
1959	NR	7	0	1	2	0	0	0	0	1,107	130	2	1,146	10,465
1960	11	11	0	1	1	0	0	1	2	2,669	1	1	2,530	17,374
1961	166	1	0	0	0	0	0	0	0	37	0	0	93	75
Lifetime		23	0	2	4	0	0	1	3	3,852	131	3	3,929	$30,514

Bob Beck

Robert Beck
Racing Hometown: Buffalo, NY

Year	Rank	Starts	Poles	1	2	3	4	5	6–10	Laps	Laps Led	Races Led	Miles	$
1955	158	2	0	0	0	0	0	0	0	223	0	0	144	75
Lifetime		2	0	0	0	0	0	0	0	223	0	0	144	$75

Randy Becker

Randall Becker
B: 10/2/1952
Racing Hometown: Highland, CA

Year	Rank	Starts	Poles	1	2	3	4	5	6–10	Laps	Laps Led	Races Led	Miles	$
1982	103	2	0	0	0	0	0	0	0	116	0	0	304	1,640
1983	70	2	0	0	0	0	0	0	0	139	0	0	364	3,650
Lifetime		4	0	0	0	0	0	0	0	255	0	0	668	$5,290

Christine Beckers

Christine Beckers
Racing Hometown: Brussels, Belgium

Year	Rank	Starts	Poles	1	2	3	4	5	6–10	Laps	Laps Led	Races Led	Miles	$
1977	NR	1	0	0	0	0	0	0	0	33	0	0	83	695
Lifetime		1	0	0	0	0	0	0	0	33	0	0	83	$695

Troy Beebe

Troy Beebe
B: 1/5/1962
Racing Hometown: Modesto, CA

Year	Rank	Starts	Poles	1	2	3	4	5	6–10	Laps	Laps Led	Races Led	Miles	$
1989	75T	1	0	0	0	0	0	0	0	72	0	0	181	2,605
1990	71	4	0	0	0	0	0	0	0	584	0	0	1,001	19,675
Lifetime		5	0	0	0	0	0	0	0	656	0	0	1,182	$22,280

Earl Beer

Earl Beer
Racing Hometown: Brooklyn, NY

Year	Rank	Starts	Poles	1	2	3	4	5	6–10	Laps	Laps Led	Races Led	Miles	$
1954	NR	1	0	0	0	0	0	0	0	46	0	0	92	100
Lifetime		1	0	0	0	0	0	0	0	46	0	0	92	$100

George Behlman

George Behlman
B: 4/22/1944
Racing Hometown: Lemon Grove, CA

Year	Rank	Starts	Poles	1	2	3	4	5	6–10	Laps	Laps Led	Races Led	Miles	$
1973	100	1	0	0	0	0	0	0	0	137	0	0	359	875
1974	124	1	0	0	0	0	0	0	0	25	0	0	66	695
Lifetime		2	0	0	0	0	0	0	0	162	0	0	424	$1,570

Leo Beiethaupt

Leo Beiethaupt
Racing Hometown: Los Angeles, CA

Year	Rank	Starts	Poles	1	2	3	4	5	6–10	Laps	Laps Led	Races Led	Miles	$
1951	N/A	1	0	0	0	0	0	0	1		0	0		100
Lifetime		1	0	0	0	0	0	0	1		0	0		$100

Sam Beler

Samuel Beler
Racing Hometown: Lakewood, CA

Year	Rank	Starts	Poles	1	2	3	4	5	6–10	Laps	Laps Led	Races Led	Miles	$
1976	109T	1	0	0	0	0	0	0	0	15	0	0	39	585
Lifetime		1	0	0	0	0	0	0	0	15	0	0	39	$585

John Belgard

John E. Belgard
Racing Hometown: Hyattsville, MD

Year	Rank	Starts	Poles	1	2	3	4	5	6–10	Laps	Laps Led	Races Led	Miles	$
1949	NR	1	0	0	0	0	0	0	0		0	0		0
Lifetime		1	0	0	0	0	0	0	0		0	0		$0

Joe Bell

Joseph Bell
Racing Hometown: N. Tarrytown, NY

Year	Rank	Starts	Poles	1	2	3	4	5	6–10	Laps	Laps Led	Races Led	Miles	$
1954	186	1	0	0	0	0	0	0	0	48	0	0	48	0
Lifetime		1	0	0	0	0	0	0	0	48	0	0	48	$0

Year	Rank	Starts	Poles	Finish 1	2	3	4	5	6–10	Laps	Laps Led	Races Led	Miles	$

Phillips Bell

Phillips Bell
Racing Hometown: Manasquan, NJ

Year	Rank	Starts	Poles	1	2	3	4	5	6–10	Laps	Laps Led	Races Led	Miles	$
1954	NR	1	0	0	0	0	0	0	0	45	0	0	90	75
Lifetime		1	0	0	0	0	0	0	0	45	0	0	90	$75

Joe Bellinato

Joseph Bellinato
Racing Hometown: Singac, NJ

Year	Rank	Starts	Poles	1	2	3	4	5	6–10	Laps	Laps Led	Races Led	Miles	$
1951	224	1	0	0	0	0	0	0	0		0	0		25
Lifetime		1	0	0	0	0	0	0	0		0	0		$25

Andy Belmont

Andrew Belmont
B: 11/20/1957
Racing Hometown: Langhorne, PA

Year	Rank	Starts	Poles	1	2	3	4	5	6–10	Laps	Laps Led	Races Led	Miles	$
1989	86	1	0	0	0	0	0	0	0	373	0	0	373	2,150
1990	—	0												3,250
1991	89	1	0	0	0	0	0	0	0	11	0	0	11	3,450
1992	43	8	0	0	0	0	0	0	0	784	0	0	1,548	39,820
Lifetime		10	0	0	0	0	0	0	0	1,168	0	0	1,932	$48,670

Ed Benedict

Edward Benedict
Racing Hometown: Miamisburg, OH

Year	Rank	Starts	Poles	1	2	3	4	5	6–10	Laps	Laps Led	Races Led	Miles	$
1951	88	6	0	0	0	0	0	0	1	445	0	0	538	300
1952	49	5	0	0	0	0	0	1	1	633	0	0	380	360
1953	73	1	0	0	0	0	0	0	1	189	0	0	95	125
Lifetime		12	0	0	0	0	0	1	3	1,267	0	0	1,012	$785

Corey Benjamin

Corey Benjamin
Racing Hometown: Rising Sun, MD

Year	Rank	Starts	Poles	1	2	3	4	5	6–10	Laps	Laps Led	Races Led	Miles	$
1956	261	1	0	0	0	0	0	0	0	34	0	0	34	50
Lifetime		1	0	0	0	0	0	0	0	34	0	0	34	$50

Jerry Benjamin

Jerry Benjamin
Racing Hometown: Rising Sun, MD

Year	Rank	Starts	Poles	1	2	3	4	5	6–10	Laps	Laps Led	Races Led	Miles	$
1955	226	1	0	0	0	0	0	0	0	71	0	0	71	50
1957	191	3	0	0	0	0	0	0	0	200	0	0	157	125
1958	173	1	0	0	0	0	0	0	0	26	0	0	13	10
Lifetime		5	0	0	0	0	0	0	0	297	0	0	241	$185

Arnold Bennett

Arnold Bennett
Racing Hometown: Battle Creek, MI

Year	Rank	Starts	Poles	1	2	3	4	5	6–10	Laps	Laps Led	Races Led	Miles	$
1970	113	1	0	0	0	0	0	0	0	1	0	0	3	0
Lifetime		1	0	0	0	0	0	0	0	1	0	0	3	$0

Bill Bennett

William Bennett
Racing Hometown: Rehoboth Beach, NJ

Year	Rank	Starts	Poles	1	2	3	4	5	6–10	Laps	Laps Led	Races Led	Miles	$
1949	45	1	0	0	0	0	0	0	0	181	0	0	181	100
Lifetime		1	0	0	0	0	0	0	0	181	0	0	181	$100

Bud Bennett

Bud Bennett
Racing Hometown: Grand Rapids, MI

Year	Rank	Starts	Poles	1	2	3	4	5	6–10	Laps	Laps Led	Races Led	Miles	$
1954	NR	1	0	0	0	0	0	0	0	167	0	0	84	25
Lifetime		1	0	0	0	0	0	0	0	167	0	0	84	$25

Harry Bennett

Harry Bennett
Racing Hometown: St. Claire Shores, MI

Year	Rank	Starts	Poles	1	2	3	4	5	6–10	Laps	Laps Led	Races Led	Miles	$
1953	169	1	0	0	0	0	0	0	0		0	0		25
Lifetime		1	0	0	0	0	0	0	0		0	0		$25

Jim Bennett

James Bennett
D: 11/11/1990
Racing Hometown: Jonesboro, GA

Year	Rank	Starts	Poles	1	2	3	4	5	6–10	Laps	Laps Led	Races Led	Miles	$
1961	82	2	0	0	0	0	0	0	0	170	0	0	351	500

Year	Rank	Starts	Poles	Finish						Laps	Laps Led	Races Led	Miles	$
				1	2	3	4	5	6–10					

Jim Bennett *continued*

Year	Rank	Starts	Poles	1	2	3	4	5	6–10	Laps	Laps Led	Races Led	Miles	$
1962	63	5	0	0	0	0	0	1	1	402	0	0	341	950
Lifetime		7	0	0	0	0	0	1	1	572	0	0	692	$1,450

Russell Bennett

Russell Horace Bennett
B: 12/29/1920
Racing Hometown: Milford, DE

Year	Rank	Starts	Poles	1	2	3	4	5	6–10	Laps	Laps Led	Races Led	Miles	$
1950	90	2	0	0	0	0	0	0	0	123	0	0	123	100
Lifetime		2	0	0	0	0	0	0	0	123	0	0	123	$100

Norm Benning

Norman Benning
B: 1/16/1952
Racing Hometown: Level Green, PA

Year	Rank	Starts	Poles	1	2	3	4	5	6–10	Laps	Laps Led	Races Led	Miles	$
1989	53	3	0	0	0	0	0	0	0	653	0	0	880	6,875
1993	87T	1	0	0	0	0	0	0	0	1	0	0	1	6,410
1994	—	0												2,400
1995	—	0												1,600
Lifetime		4	0	0	0	0	0	0	0	654	0	0	881	$17,285

Bill Benson

William Benson
Racing Hometown: Far Rockaway, NY

Year	Rank	Starts	Poles	1	2	3	4	5	6–10	Laps	Laps Led	Races Led	Miles	$
1957	30	11	0	0	0	0	0	0	2	1,320	0	0	827	1,090
1958	53	5	0	0	0	0	0	0	0	549	0	0	375	220
Lifetime		16	0	0	0	0	0	0	2	1,869	0	0	1,202	$1,310

Johnny Benson

Johnny Benson Sr.
B: 4/24/1937
Racing Hometown: Grand Rapids, MI

Year	Rank	Starts	Poles	1	2	3	4	5	6–10	Laps	Laps Led	Races Led	Miles	$
1973	97	1	0	0	0	0	0	0	0	185	0	0	370	850
Lifetime		1	0	0	0	0	0	0	0	185	0	0	370	$850

Johnny Benson Jr.

Johnny Benson Jr.
B: 6/27/63
Racing Hometown: Grand Rapids, MI

Year	Rank	Starts	Poles	1	2	3	4	5	6–10	Laps	Laps Led	Races Led	Miles	$
1996	21	30	1	0	0	0	0	1	5	8,507	105	4	10,483	947,080
Lifetime		30	1	0	0	0	0	1	5	8,507	105	4	10,483	$947,080

Tiny Benson

Tiny Benson
Racing Hometown: Syracuse, NY

Year	Rank	Starts	Poles	1	2	3	4	5	6–10	Laps	Laps Led	Races Led	Miles	$
1958	73	4	0	0	0	0	0	0	2	445	0	0	182	450
1959	NR	2	0	0	0	0	0	0	2	298	0	0	205	350
Lifetime		6	0	0	0	0	0	0	4	743	0	0	387	$800

Roy Bentley

Roy Bentley
D: circa 1977 *Killed in highway crash.*
Racing Hometown: Florence, SC

Year	Rank	Starts	Poles	1	2	3	4	5	6–10	Laps	Laps Led	Races Led	Miles	$
1950	NR	1	0	0	0	0	0	0	0	319	0	0	399	0
1953	161	1	0	0	0	0	0	0	0	220	0	0	220	25
1955	197	1	0	0	0	0	0	0	0	317	0	0	436	60
1956	139	3	0	0	0	0	0	0	0	329	0	0	292	200
Lifetime		6	0	0	0	0	0	0	0	1,185	0	0	1,347	$285

Clarence Benton

Clarence Benton
Racing Hometown: N. Wilkesboro, NC

Year	Rank	Starts	Poles	1	2	3	4	5	6–10	Laps	Laps Led	Races Led	Miles	$
1949	NR	1	0	0	0	0	0	0	0		0	0		0
Lifetime		1	0	0	0	0	0	0	0		0	0		$0

Ben Benz

Ben Benz *Real Name*: Bernard Friedland
Racing Hometown: Far Rockaway, NY

Year	Rank	Starts	Poles	1	2	3	4	5	6–10	Laps	Laps Led	Races Led	Miles	$
1958	82	4	0	0	0	0	0	0	2	831	0	0	408	400

Year	Rank	Starts	Poles	Finish 1	2	3	4	5	6–10	Laps	Laps Led	Races Led	Miles	$

Ben Benz *continued*

Year	Rank	Starts	Poles	1	2	3	4	5	6–10	Laps	Laps Led	Races Led	Miles	$
1959	62	5	0	0	0	0	0	0	2	665	0	0	740	625
Lifetime		9	0	0	0	0	0	0	4	1,496	0	0	1,148	$1,025

Leo Bergeron

Leo Bergeron
Racing Hometown: Montreal, Que., Canada

Year	Rank	Starts	Poles	1	2	3	4	5	6–10	Laps	Laps Led	Races Led	Miles	$
1953	121	2	0	0	0	0	0	0	0		0	0		65
Lifetime		2	0	0	0	0	0	0	0		0	0		$65

Ed Bergin

Edward Bergin

Year	Rank	Starts	Poles	1	2	3	4	5	6–10	Laps	Laps Led	Races Led	Miles	$
1955	198	1	0	0	0	0	0	0	0	302	0	0	415	160
Lifetime		1	0	0	0	0	0	0	0	302	0	0	415	$160

Gene Bergin

Eugene Bergin
B: 1933
Racing Hometown: Enfield, CT

Year	Rank	Starts	Poles	1	2	3	4	5	6–10	Laps	Laps Led	Races Led	Miles	$
1956	219	2	0	0	0	0	0	0	0	384	0	0	500	310
Lifetime		2	0	0	0	0	0	0	0	384	0	0	500	$310

Ed Berrier

Edward Berrier
B: 11/8/1961
Racing Hometown: Winston-Salem, NC

Year	Rank	Starts	Poles	1	2	3	4	5	6–10	Laps	Laps Led	Races Led	Miles	$
1995	57	1	0	0	0	0	0	0	0	358	0	0	489	15,460
1996	66	1	0	0	0	0	0	0	0	57	0	0	78	9,895
Lifetime		2	0	0	0	0	0	0	0	415	0	0	567	$25,355

Max Berrier

Max Berrier
B: 2/1/1936
Racing Hometown: Wallburg, NC

Year	Rank	Starts	Poles	1	2	3	4	5	6–10	Laps	Laps Led	Races Led	Miles	$
1955	NR	2	0	0	0	0	0	0	0	232	0	0	116	100
1957	129	2	0	0	0	0	0	0	0	0	0	0	0	50
1959	NR	2	0	0	0	0	0	0	0	214	0	0	64	110
1972	NR	1	0	0	0	0	0	0	0	349	0	0	218	740
Lifetime		7	0	0	0	0	0	0	0	795	0	0	398	$1,000

Robert Berrier

Robert Berrier
Racing Hometown: Winston-Salem, NC

Year	Rank	Starts	Poles	1	2	3	4	5	6–10	Laps	Laps Led	Races Led	Miles	$
1961	NR	1	0	0	0	0	0	0	0	137	0	0	34	110
1962	NR	1	0	0	0	0	0	0	0	100	0	0	25	250
Lifetime		2	0	0	0	0	0	0	0	237	0	0	59	$360

Randy Bethea

Randolph Bethea
Racing Hometown: Johnson City, TN

Year	Rank	Starts	Poles	1	2	3	4	5	6–10	Laps	Laps Led	Races Led	Miles	$
1975	109T	1	0	0	0	0	0	0	0	251	0	0	377	1,055
Lifetime		1	0	0	0	0	0	0	0	251	0	0	377	$1,055

Fred Bethune

Frederick Bethune
Racing Hometown: Wyandotte, MI

Year	Rank	Starts	Poles	1	2	3	4	5	6–10	Laps	Laps Led	Races Led	Miles	$
1952	63	2	0	0	0	0	0	0	1	377	0	0	293	125
Lifetime		2	0	0	0	0	0	0	1	377	0	0	293	$125

Gary Bettenhausen

Gary Clyde Bettenhausen
B: 11/18/1941
Racing Hometown: Monrovia, IN

Year	Rank	Starts	Poles	1	2	3	4	5	6–10	Laps	Laps Led	Races Led	Miles	$
1967	NR	3	0	0	0	0	0	0	1	124	0	0	310	1,680
1974	43	5	0	0	0	0	1	0	2	986	35	1	2,100	12,750
Lifetime		8	0	0	0	0	1	0	3	1,110	35	1	2,410	$14,430

Year	Rank	Starts	Poles	Finish						Laps	Laps Led	Races Led	Miles	$
				1	2	3	4	5	6–10					

Tony Bettenhausen Jr.

Tony Lee Bettenhausen Jr.
B: 10/31/1950
Racing Hometown: Indianapois, IN

Year	Rank	Starts	Poles	1	2	3	4	5	6–10	Laps	Laps Led	Races Led	Miles	$
1973	54	5	0	0	0	0	0	0	0	863	0	0	1,319	5,015
1974	20	27	0	0	0	0	0	0	1	5,548	0	0	6,151	38,995
1982	NR	1	0	0	0	0	0	0	0	139	0	0	278	3,215
Lifetime		33	0	0	0	0	0	0	1	6,550	0	0	7,747	$47,225

Jim Bickerstaff

James Bickerstaff
Racing Hometown: Pittsburgh, PA

Year	Rank	Starts	Poles	1	2	3	4	5	6–10	Laps	Laps Led	Races Led	Miles	$
1959	NR	1	0	0	0	0	0	0	0	12	0	0	3	50
Lifetime		1	0	0	0	0	0	0	0	12	0	0	3	$50

Rich Bickle

Richard Bickle Jr.
B: 5/13/1961
Racing Hometown: Edgerton, WI

Year	Rank	Starts	Poles	1	2	3	4	5	6–10	Laps	Laps Led	Races Led	Miles	$
1989	62	2	0	0	0	0	0	0	0	355	0	0	540	4,185
1990	84T	1	0	0	0	0	0	0	0	195	0	0	488	19,120
1991	51	3	0	0	0	0	0	0	0	1,118	0	0	1,404	16,125
1992	49	3	0	0	0	0	0	0	0	816	0	0	881	13,370
1993	48	5	0	0	0	0	0	0	0	842	1	1	1,356	36,305
1994	43	12	0	0	0	0	0	0	0	2,087	0	0	3,616	116,625
1995	45	8	0	0	0	0	0	0	0	1,995	2	1	2,400	153,250
Lifetime		34	0	0	0	0	0	0	0	7,408	3	2	10,684	$358,980

Andy Biddle

Andrew Biddle
Racing Hometown: Grand Rapids, MI

Year	Rank	Starts	Poles	1	2	3	4	5	6–10	Laps	Laps Led	Races Led	Miles	$
1954	NR	1	0	0	0	0	0	0	0	142	0	0	71	25
Lifetime		1	0	0	0	0	0	0	0	142	0	0	71	$25

Don Biederman

Donald Biederman
Racing Hometown: Port Credit, Ont., Canada

Year	Rank	Starts	Poles	1	2	3	4	5	6–10	Laps	Laps Led	Races Led	Miles	$
1966	58	14	0	0	0	0	0	0	0	2,169	0	0	1,285	2,215
1967	38	22	0	0	0	0	0	0	1	2,679	0	0	2,231	5,935
1968	77	2	0	0	0	0	0	0	0	252	0	0	372	1,210
1969	88	4	0	0	0	0	0	0	1	566	0	0	687	1,960
Lifetime		42	0	0	0	0	0	0	2	5,666	0	0	4,576	$11,320

Eddie Bierschwale

Edward Bierschwale
B: 6/29/1959
Racing Hometown: San Antonio, TX

Year	Rank	Starts	Poles	1	2	3	4	5	6–10	Laps	Laps Led	Races Led	Miles	$
1983	51	3	0	0	0	0	0	0	0	524	0	0	888	3,665
1984	66	2	0	0	0	0	0	0	0	317	0	0	583	3,495
1985	24	26	0	0	0	0	0	0	0	6,559	0	0	7,752	109,625
1986	25	24	0	0	0	0	0	0	0	5,558	1	1	6,983	98,110
1987	34	14	0	0	0	0	0	0	0	3,560	0	0	4,062	66,790
1988	34	20	0	0	0	0	0	0	0	4,106	0	0	6,117	59,355
1989	36	16	0	0	0	0	0	0	1	3,829	2	1	4,974	82,695
1990	54	3	0	0	0	0	0	0	0	665	0	0	1,264	28,540
1991	42	5	0	0	0	0	0	0	0	1,112	0	0	2,127	55,025
1992	47	4	0	0	0	0	0	0	0	628	0	0	1,092	25,995
Lifetime		117	0	0	0	0	0	0	1	26,858	3	2	35,841	$533,295

Tom Bigelow

Thomas Allan Bigelow
B: 10/31/1939
Racing Hometown: Winchester, IN

Year	Rank	Starts	Poles	1	2	3	4	5	6–10	Laps	Laps Led	Races Led	Miles	$
1986	121T	1	0	0	0	0	0	0	0	58	0	0	88	985
Lifetime		1	0	0	0	0	0	0	0	58	0	0	88	$985

Fred Bince

Fred Lee Bince
Raced as Fred Lee in 1951, Sam Lamm in 1954 and 1956
B: 9/28/1923
Racing Hometown: Los Angeles, CA

Year	Rank	Starts	Poles	1	2	3	4	5	6–10	Laps	Laps Led	Races Led	Miles	$
1951	50	6	0	0	0	0	1	0	1	98	0	0	49	525

Year	Rank	Starts	Poles	Finish 1	2	3	4	5	6–10	Laps	Laps Led	Races Led	Miles	$

Fred Bince *continued*

Year	Rank	Starts	Poles	1	2	3	4	5	6–10	Laps	Laps Led	Races Led	Miles	$
1954	NR	2	0	0	0	0	0	0	0	426	0	0	326	50
1956	289	1	0	0	0	0	0	0	0	3	0	0	8	30
Lifetime		9	0	0	0	0	1	0	1	527	0	0	383	$605

Art Binkley

Arthur Binkley
B: 12/19/1920
Racing Hometown: New Albany, IN

1954	NR	1	0	0	0	0	0	0	0	21	0	0	86	0
1956	NR	1	0	0	0	0	0	0	0	349	0	0	175	150
1957	NR	3	0	0	0	0	0	0	0	690	0	0	495	390
Lifetime		5	0	0	0	0	0	0	0	1,060	0	0	755	$540

Gordon Birkett

Gordon Birkett
Racing Hometown: Tappahannock, VA

| 1971 | NR | 2 | 0 | 0 | 0 | 0 | 0 | 0 | 0 | 263 | 0 | 0 | 123 | 635 |
| **Lifetime** | | 2 | 0 | 0 | 0 | 0 | 0 | 0 | 0 | 263 | 0 | 0 | 123 | $635 |

Gordon Bishop

Gordon Bishop
Racing Hometown: Anniston, AL

| 1952 | 125 | 2 | 0 | 0 | 0 | 0 | 0 | 0 | 0 | | 0 | 0 | | 25 |
| **Lifetime** | | 2 | 0 | 0 | 0 | 0 | 0 | 0 | 0 | | 0 | 0 | | $25 |

Terry Bivins

Terry Bivins
B: 9/13/1943
Racing Hometown: Shawnee Mission, KS

1975	78	2	0	0	0	0	0	0	1	562	0	0	758	2,735
1976	21	18	0	0	0	0	0	1	5	5,237	6	1	5,816	44,070
1977	38	8	0	0	0	0	0	0	1	2,002	0	0	2,195	15,645
Lifetime		28	0	0	0	0	0	1	7	7,801	6	1	8,769	$62,450

Don Black

Donald Black
Racing Hometown: Parker, PA

| 1951 | N/A | 1 | 0 | 0 | 0 | 0 | 0 | 0 | 0 | | 0 | 0 | | 25 |
| **Lifetime** | | 1 | 0 | 0 | 0 | 0 | 0 | 0 | 0 | | 0 | 0 | | $25 |

Gene Black

Francis Eugene Black II
B: 9/23/1943
Racing Hometown: Arden, NC

1965	42	18	0	0	0	0	0	0	4	4,167	0	0	3,011	6,080
1966	55	12	0	0	0	0	0	0	2	1,713	0	0	1,216	3,765
1968	65	7	0	0	0	0	0	0	0	762	0	0	336	805
Lifetime		37	0	0	0	0	0	0	6	6,642	0	0	4,563	$10,650

Sonny Black

Robert Black
B: 1926   D: 9/18/1964   *Killed in practice @ 5-Flags Speedway in Pensacola, FL.*
Racing Hometown: Forrest Park, GA

1951	N/A	4	0	0	0	0	0	0	2	73	0	0	91	175
1955	170T	1	0	0	0	0	0	0	0	181	0	0	91	50
1956	209T	1	0	0	0	0	0	0	0	79	0	0	79	50
Lifetime		6	0	0	0	0	0	0	2	333	0	0	261	$275

Bunkie Blackburn

James Ronald Blackburn
B: 4/22/1936
Racing Hometown: Fayetteville, NC

1960	37	20	0	0	0	0	0	1	3	2,789	0	0	2,110	3,600
1961	108	5	0	0	0	0	0	0	0	478	0	0	485	1,175
1962	25	10	0	0	0	0	1	0	2	2,325	0	0	2,705	5,890
1963	48	7	0	0	0	0	0	0	1	909	0	0	1,220	2,525
1964	32	14	0	0	0	0	1	0	3	2,295	0	0	2,329	6,630
1965	70	6	0	0	0	0	0	0	1	371	0	0	637	3,420
1966	57	8	0	0	0	0	0	1	0	770	4	1	1,151	5,900

Year	Rank	Starts	Poles	1	2	Finish 3	4	5	6–10	Laps	Laps Led	Races Led	Miles	$

Bunkie Blackburn *continued*

Year	Rank	Starts	Poles	1	2	3	4	5	6–10	Laps	Laps Led	Races Led	Miles	$
1970	NR	1	0	0	0	0	0	0	0	35	0	0	36	620
Lifetime		71	0	0	0	0	3	1	10	9,972	4	1	10,673	$29,760

Gene Blackburn

Gene Blackburn
Racing Hometown: Bristol, TN

Year	Rank	Starts	Poles	1	2	3	4	5	6–10	Laps	Laps Led	Races Led	Miles	$
1961	178	1	0	0	0	0	0	0	0	117	0	0	59	100
1962	113	1	0	0	0	0	0	0	0	274	0	0	137	150
Lifetime		2	0	0	0	0	0	0	0	391	0	0	196	$250

Glenn Blackman

Glenn Blackman
Racing Hometown: Columbia, SC

Year	Rank	Starts	Poles	1	2	3	4	5	6–10	Laps	Laps Led	Races Led	Miles	$
1955	212	1	0	0	0	0	0	0	0		0	0		0
Lifetime		1	0	0	0	0	0	0	0		0	0		$0

Bill Blackwell

William Blackwell

Year	Rank	Starts	Poles	1	2	3	4	5	6–10	Laps	Laps Led	Races Led	Miles	$
1954	NR	1	0	0	0	0	0	0	0	4	0	0	2	0
Lifetime		1	0	0	0	0	0	0	0	4	0	0	2	$0

Dick Blackwell

Samuel Richard Blackwell
B: 1920
Racing Hometown: Startex, SC

Year	Rank	Starts	Poles	1	2	3	4	5	6–10	Laps	Laps Led	Races Led	Miles	$
1956	159	3	0	0	0	0	0	0	0	192	0	0	154	60
1959	80	3	0	0	0	0	0	0	0	544	0	0	487	250
Lifetime		6	0	0	0	0	0	0	0	736	0	0	641	$310

Bill Blair

William Ivey Blair
B: 7/14/1911   D: 11/2/1995
Racing Hometown: High Point, NC

Year	Rank	Starts	Poles	1	2	3	4	5	6–10	Laps	Laps Led	Races Led	Miles	$
1949	4	6	0	0	0	0	0	3	2	613	**325**	2	551	1,280
1950	10	16	0	1	2	0	0	2	2	1,550	218	3	1,253	4,400
1951	16	18	0	0	1	1	2	0	3	815	0	0	755	2,725
1952	6	19	1	1	3	4	2	0	3	2,427	120	4	1,920	7,899
1953	15	21	0	1	0	2	0	3	2	1,043	51	2	1,100	4,535
1954	13	19	0	0	0	0	0	2	8	2,853	7	1	1,893	2,650
1955	37	12	0	0	0	0	0	0	0	1,320	0	0	1,227	565
1956	37	9	0	0	0	0	0	0	4	1,275	0	0	1,164	1,005
1957	157	1	0	0	0	0	0	0	0	63	0	0	87	100
1958	NR	2	0	0	0	0	0	0	0	147	0	0	137	200
Lifetime		123	1	3	6	7	4	10	24	12,106	721	12	10,086	$24,919

Gene Blair

Gene Blair
B: 1933   D: 8/18/1962   *Killed in Midget race @ Cattaraugus Fairgrounds in Little Valley, NY.*
Racing Hometown: Buffalo, NY

Year	Rank	Starts	Poles	1	2	3	4	5	6–10	Laps	Laps Led	Races Led	Miles	$
1957	NR	1	0	0	0	0	0	0	0	32	0	0	74	110
Lifetime		1	0	0	0	0	0	0	0	32	0	0	74	$110

T. L. Blakely

Terrance L. Blakely (Terry)
Racing Hometown: Birmingham, MI

Year	Rank	Starts	Poles	1	2	3	4	5	6–10	Laps	Laps Led	Races Led	Miles	$
1966	148	1	0	0	0	0	0	0	0	10	0	0	25	0
Lifetime		1	0	0	0	0	0	0	0	10	0	0	25	$0

Pug Blalock

Silas Blalock
Racing Hometown: Decatur, GA

Year	Rank	Starts	Poles	1	2	3	4	5	6–10	Laps	Laps Led	Races Led	Miles	$
1951	N/A	3	0	0	0	0	0	0	1		0	0		100
Lifetime		3	0	0	0	0	0	0	1		0	0		$100

Leonard Blanchard

Charles Leonard Blanchard
B: 11/20/1936
Racing Hometown: Jackson, KY

Year	Rank	Starts	Poles	1	2	3	4	5	6–10	Laps	Laps Led	Races Led	Miles	$
1970	NR	2	0	0	0	0	0	0	0	92	0	0	230	1,135

Year	Rank	Starts	Poles	Finish						Laps	Laps Led	Races Led	Miles	$
				1	2	3	4	5	6–10					

Leonard Blanchard *continued*

Year	Rank	Starts	Poles	1	2	3	4	5	6–10	Laps	Laps Led	Races Led	Miles	$
1971	86	1	0	0	0	0	0	0	0	46	0	0	115	255
1972	—	0												220
Lifetime		3	0	0	0	0	0	0	0	138	0	0	345	$1,610

Dave Blaney

David Blaney
B: 10/24/1962
Racing Hometown: Hartford, OH

Year	Rank	Starts	Poles	1	2	3	4	5	6–10	Laps	Laps Led	Races Led	Miles	$
1992	79T	1	0	0	0	0	0	0	0	371	0	0	377	4,500
Lifetime		1	0	0	0	0	0	0	0	371	0	0	377	$4,500

Lem Blankenship

Lem Blankenship
B: 2/6/1945
Racing Hometown: Keokuk, IA

Year	Rank	Starts	Poles	1	2	3	4	5	6–10	Laps	Laps Led	Races Led	Miles	$
1972	NR	1	0	0	0	0	0	0	0	50	0	0	76	855
Lifetime		1	0	0	0	0	0	0	0	50	0	0	76	$855

Charlie Blanton

Charles Ken Blanton
B: 12/29/1935
Racing Hometown: Gaffney, SC

Year	Rank	Starts	Poles	1	2	3	4	5	6–10	Laps	Laps Led	Races Led	Miles	$
1973	82	1	0	0	0	0	0	0	0	351	0	0	527	1,825
1974	129T	1	0	0	0	0	0	0	0	231	0	0	235	720
1977	—	0												600
1978	NR	1	0	0	0	0	0	0	0	52	0	0	53	590
Lifetime		3	0	0	0	0	0	0	0	634	0	0	814	$3,735

Erwin Blatt

Erwin Blatt
Racing Hometown: Hamburg, PA

Year	Rank	Starts	Poles	1	2	3	4	5	6–10	Laps	Laps Led	Races Led	Miles	$
1949	60	1	0	0	0	0	0	0	0	176	0	0	176	50
1952	68	2	0	0	0	0	0	0	0	566	0	0	650	160
1958	132T	1	0	0	0	0	0	0	0	28	0	0	80	85
Lifetime		4	0	0	0	0	0	0	0	770	0	0	906	$295

Charles Blewitt

Charles Blewitt (Chuck)
Racing Hometown: Brooklyn, NY

Year	Rank	Starts	Poles	1	2	3	4	5	6–10	Laps	Laps Led	Races Led	Miles	$
1954	142	1	0	0	0	0	0	0	0	207	0	0	207	50
1956	93	2	0	0	0	0	0	0	0	411	0	0	327	200
1957	141	3	0	0	0	0	0	0	0	205	0	0	107	150
Lifetime		6	0	0	0	0	0	0	0	823	0	0	640	$400

Bill Block

William Block
Racing Hometown: Winston-Salem, NC

Year	Rank	Starts	Poles	1	2	3	4	5	6–10	Laps	Laps Led	Races Led	Miles	$
1962	NR	1	0	0	0	0	0	0	0	32	0	0	8	75
Lifetime		1	0	0	0	0	0	0	0	32	0	0	8	$75

Bruce Blodgett

Bruce Blodgett
B: 11/25/1945
Racing Hometown: Fresno, CA

Year	Rank	Starts	Poles	1	2	3	4	5	6–10	Laps	Laps Led	Races Led	Miles	$
1976	NR	1	0	0	0	0	0	0	0	447	0	0	235	800
Lifetime		1	0	0	0	0	0	0	0	447	0	0	235	$800

Jim Blomgren

James Blomgren
Racing Hometown: El Monte, CA

Year	Rank	Starts	Poles	1	2	3	4	5	6–10	Laps	Laps Led	Races Led	Miles	$
1956	47	6	0	0	0	0	0	0	1	841	0	0	820	635
1957	71	4	0	0	0	0	0	1	0	356	0	0	320	520
1958	179	1	0	0	0	0	0	0	0	8	0	0	8	0
1959	109	1	0	0	0	0	0	0	0	49	0	0	49	50
1960	84	3	0	0	0	0	0	0	2	288	0	0	332	400
1961	92	4	0	0	0	0	1	0	1	401	0	0	406	590
1964	104	1	0	0	0	0	0	0	0	94	0	0	254	500
Lifetime		20	0	0	0	0	1	1	4	2,037	0	0	2,187	$2,695

Year	Rank	Starts	Poles	Finish 1	2	3	4	5	6–10	Laps	Laps Led	Races Led	Miles	$

Larry Bock

Lawrence Bock
Racing Hometown: Miskawaka, IN

Year	Rank	Starts	Poles	1	2	3	4	5	6–10	Laps	Laps Led	Races Led	Miles	$
1969	NR	1	0	0	0	0	0	0	0	85	0	0	226	1,225
Lifetime		1	0	0	0	0	0	0	0	85	0	0	226	$1,225

Brett Bodine

Brett E. Bodine
B: 1/11/1959
Racing Hometown: Chemung, NY

Year	Rank	Starts	Poles	1	2	3	4	5	6–10	Laps	Laps Led	Races Led	Miles	$
1986	92T	1	0	0	0	0	0	0	0	394	0	0	591	10,100
1987	32	14	0	0	0	0	0	0	0	2,908	20	3	4,485	51,145
1988	20	29	0	0	0	1	1	0	3	7,789	200	5	9,155	433,658
1989	19	29	0	0	0	0	0	1	5	8,202	2	2	10,354	281,274
1990	12	29	1	1	0	2	2	0	4	9,097	216	7	10,878	442,681
1991	19	29	1	0	1	0	1	0	4	7,873	163	3	9,048	376,220
1992	15	29	1	0	0	1	1	0	11	8,581	237	11	10,021	495,224
1993	20	29	2	0	1	0	0	2	6	8,120	102	7	9,382	582,014
1994	19	31	0	0	1	0	0	0	5	8,931	55	6	10,772	801,944
1995	20	31	0	0	0	0	0	0	2	9,159	6	1	11,084	893,029
1996	24	30	0	0	0	0	0	0	1	8,732	3	2	10,718	767,716
Lifetime		281	5	1	3	4	5	3	41	79,786	1,004	47	96,487	$5,135,005

Geoff Bodine

Geoffrey Bodine
B: 4/18/1949
Racing Hometown: Chemung, NY

Year	Rank	Starts	Poles	1	2	3	4	5	6–10	Laps	Laps Led	Races Led	Miles	$
1979	81	3	0	0	0	0	0	0	0	443	6	1	631	4,820
1981	45	5	0	0	0	0	0	0	1	945	14	2	1,388	15,000
1982	22	25	2	0	0	1	2	1	6	6,518	118	6	7,939	247,750
1983	17	28	1	0	1	0	2	2	4	7,042	490	13	7,328	209,611
1984	9	30	3	3	0	1	2	1	7	8,848	686	12	10,064	413,748
1985	5	28	3	0	3	3	2	2	4	8,719	692	18	10,711	565,868
1986	8	29	8	2	2	5	1	0	5	7,791	1,676	25	9,359	795,111
1987	13	29	2	0	1	1	0	1	7	7,638	342	13	8,753	449,816
1988	6	29	3	1	1	4	1	3	6	8,995	464	15	10,559	570,643
1989	9	29	3	1	1	3	3	1	2	9,051	511	14	10,533	619,494
1990	3	29	2	3	3	2	3	0	8	8,852	976	21	10,646	1,131,222
1991	14	27	2	1	2	1	1	1	6	7,997	152	12	9,589	625,256
1992	16	29	0	2	0	2	2	1	4	8,222	474	5	9,780	716,583
1993	16	30	1	1	0	1	0	0	7	8,496	102	11	10,198	783,762
1994	17	31	5	3	1	1	1	1	3	8,150	1,744	20	9,771	1,287,626
1995	16	31	0	0	0	0	0	1	3	9,257	13	4	11,571	1,011,090
1996	17	31	0	1	0	1	0	0	4	8,918	90	7	11,067	1,031,762
Lifetime		443	35	18	15	26	20	15	77	125,882	8,550	199	149,885	$10,385,370
												10th		8th

Todd Bodine

Todd Bodine
B: 2/27/1964
Racing Hometown: Chemung, NY

Year	Rank	Starts	Poles	1	2	3	4	5	6–10	Laps	Laps Led	Races Led	Miles	$
1992	87T	1	0	0	0	0	0	0	0	16	0	0	39	3,485
1993	40	10	0	0	0	0	0	0	0	2,393	0	0	2,310	63,245
1994	20	30	0	0	0	1	0	1	5	8,475	60	5	10,478	504,316
1995	33	28	0	0	0	0	1	0	2	6,684	19	2	9,058	664,620
1996	40	10	0	0	0	0	0	0	1	3,210	1	1	4,184	198,525
Lifetime		79	0	0	0	1	1	1	8	20,778	80	8	26,069	$1,434,191

Tommy Boger

Thomas Boger
B: 1925
Racing Hometown: Concord, NC

Year	Rank	Starts	Poles	1	2	3	4	5	6–10	Laps	Laps Led	Races Led	Miles	$
1953	174	1	0	0	0	0	0	0	0	32	0	0	131	25
Lifetime		1	0	0	0	0	0	0	0	32	0	0	131	$25

David Ray Boggs

David Ray Boggs
B: 9/8/1943
Racing Hometown: Morrisville, NC

Year	Rank	Starts	Poles	1	2	3	4	5	6–10	Laps	Laps Led	Races Led	Miles	$
1971	55	7		0	0	0	0	0	2	1,985	0	0	1,711	4,969

Year	Rank	Starts	Poles	Finish 1	2	3	4	5	6–10	Laps	Laps Led	Races Led	Miles	$

David Ray Boggs *continued*

Year	Rank	Starts	Poles	1	2	3	4	5	6–10	Laps	Laps Led	Races Led	Miles	$
1972	26	24	0	0	0	0	0	0	0	3,968	0	0	5,164	19,769
1973	NR	1	0	0	0	0	0	0	0	116	0	0	158	1,535
Lifetime		32	0	0	0	0	0	0	2	6,069	0	0	7,034	$26,273

Fred Boggs

Fred J. Boggs
Racing Hometown: Warsaw, IN

Year	Rank	Starts	Poles	1	2	3	4	5	6–10	Laps	Laps Led	Races Led	Miles	$
1957	180	1	0	0	0	0	0	0	0		0	0		25
Lifetime		1	0	0	0	0	0	0	0		0	0		$25

Pete Boland

Peter Boland
Racing Hometown: Charleston, SC

Year	Rank	Starts	Poles	1	2	3	4	5	6–10	Laps	Laps Led	Races Led	Miles	$
1961	139	2	0	0	0	0	0	0	0	217	0	0	126	110
1964	116	3	0	0	0	0	0	0	0	7	0	0	6	200
Lifetime		5	0	0	0	0	0	0	0	224	0	0	132	$310

Bill Boldt

William Boldt
Racing Hometown: Torrance, CA

Year	Rank	Starts	Poles	1	2	3	4	5	6–10	Laps	Laps Led	Races Led	Miles	$
1958	98	2	0	0	0	0	0	0	1	244	0	0	490	210
1965	123	1	0	0	0	0	0	0	0	19	0	0	51	500
Lifetime		3	0	0	0	0	0	0	1	263	0	0	542	$710

Aubrey Boles

Aubrey Boles
Racing Hometown: High Point, NC

Year	Rank	Starts	Poles	1	2	3	4	5	6–10	Laps	Laps Led	Races Led	Miles	$
1959	NR	4	0	0	0	0	0	0	1	796	0	0	398	300
1960	150	1	0	0	0	0	0	0	0	97	0	0	49	50
Lifetime		5	0	0	0	0	0	0	1	893	0	0	447	$350

Fred Boles

Fred Boles
Racing Hometown: Greenville, SC

Year	Rank	Starts	Poles	1	2	3	4	5	6–10	Laps	Laps Led	Races Led	Miles	$
1959	NR	1	0	0	0	0	0	0	0	165	0	0	83	85
Lifetime		1	0	0	0	0	0	0	0	165	0	0	83	$85

Bob Bolheimer

Robert Bolheimer
Racing Hometown: Raleigh, NC

Year	Rank	Starts	Poles	1	2	3	4	5	6–10	Laps	Laps Led	Races Led	Miles	$
1958	139	2	0	0	0	0	0	0	0	209	0	0	215	100
Lifetime		2	0	0	0	0	0	0	0	209	0	0	215	$100

Al Bolinger

Al Bolinger

Year	Rank	Starts	Poles	1	2	3	4	5	6–10	Laps	Laps Led	Races Led	Miles	$
1954	NR	1	0	0	0	0	0	0	0	103	0	0	52	25
Lifetime		1	0	0	0	0	0	0	0	103	0	0	52	$25

Toy Bolton

Lee Roy Bolton (Lefty)
Racing Hometown: Gastonia, NC

Year	Rank	Starts	Poles	1	2	3	4	5	6–10	Laps	Laps Led	Races Led	Miles	$
1964	140	1	0	0	0	0	0	0	0	48	0	0	24	0
1966	87	3	0	0	0	0	0	0	2	455	0	0	217	880
Lifetime		4	0	0	0	0	0	0	2	503	0	0	241	$880

Les Bomar

Les Bomar
Racing Hometown: Los Angeles, CA

Year	Rank	Starts	Poles	1	2	3	4	5	6–10	Laps	Laps Led	Races Led	Miles	$
1951	N/A	4	0	0	0	0	0	0	0		0	0		100
Lifetime		4	0	0	0	0	0	0	0		0	0		$100

Tony Bonadies

Anthony Bonadies
B: 12/29/1916   D: 7/5/1964   *Killed in ARDC Midget race @ Williams Grove, PA.*
Racing Hometown: Bronx, NY

Year	Rank	Starts	Poles	1	2	3	4	5	6–10	Laps	Laps Led	Races Led	Miles	$
1952	145	2	0	0	0	0	0	0	0	523	0	0	611	360
Lifetime		2	0	0	0	0	0	0	0	523	0	0	611	$360

Year	Rank	Starts	Poles	Finish						Laps	Laps Led	Races Led	Miles	$
				1	2	3	4	5	6–10	Laps	Led	Led	Miles	$

Crash Bond

Lowell E. Bond
Racing Hometown: Nashville, TN

Year	Rank	Starts	Poles	1	2	3	4	5	6–10	Laps	Laps Led	Races Led	Miles	$
1961	132	1	0	0	0	0	0	0	0	367	0	0	184	150
Lifetime		1	0	0	0	0	0	0	0	367	0	0	184	$150

Eddie Bond

Edward Bond
B: 11/12/1930
Racing Hometown: Bedford, IN

Year	Rank	Starts	Poles	1	2	3	4	5	6–10	Laps	Laps Led	Races Led	Miles	$
1973	40	6	0	0	0	0	0	0	0	1,407	0	0	2,287	7,216
1974	—	0												335
Lifetime		6	0	0	0	0	0	0	0	1,407	0	0	2,287	$7,551

Bob Bondurant

Robert L. Bondurant
B: 4/27/1933
Racing Hometown: Sonoma, CA

Year	Rank	Starts	Poles	1	2	3	4	5	6–10	Laps	Laps Led	Races Led	Miles	$
1963	149	1	0	0	0	0	0	0	0	44	0	0	119	200
1965	105	1	0	0	0	0	0	0	0	47	0	0	127	520
1981	80	2	0	0	0	0	0	0	0	207	0	0	542	2,430
Lifetime		4	0	0	0	0	0	0	0	298	0	0	788	$3,150

Al Bonnell

Al Bonnell
B: 1/26/1909   D: 1/12/1980
Racing Hometown: Erie, PA

Year	Rank	Starts	Poles	1	2	3	4	5	6–10	Laps	Laps Led	Races Led	Miles	$
1949	34	2	1	0	0	0	0	0	1	183	0	0	183	150
Lifetime		2	1	0	0	0	0	0	1	183	0	0	183	$150

Bill Bonner

William Bonner
Racing Hometown: Los Angeles, CA

Year	Rank	Starts	Poles	1	2	3	4	5	6–10	Laps	Laps Led	Races Led	Miles	$
1950	112T	1	0	0	0	0	0	0	0		0	0		0
Lifetime		1	0	0	0	0	0	0	0		0	0		$0

Neil Bonnett

Lawrence Neil Bonnett
B: 7/30/1946   D: 2/11/1994   *Killed in practice for Daytona 500.*
Racing Hometown: Bessemer, AL

Year	Rank	Starts	Poles	1	2	3	4	5	6–10	Laps	Laps Led	Races Led	Miles	$
1974	87	2	0	0	0	0	0	0	0	97	0	0	258	2,560
1975	NR	2	0	0	0	0	0	0	0	474	12	1	483	2,705
1976	32	14	1	0	0	0	0	1	3	2,377	1	1	3,323	32,275
1977	18	23	6	2	0	1	1	1	4	5,893	493	11	6,390	122,615
1978	12	30	3	0	1	1	2	3	5	6,278	316	6	6,760	162,742
1979	26	21	4	3	0	0	1	0	2	4,213	569	14	6,132	151,235
1980	19	22	0	2	4	1	1	2	3	5,173	331	14	7,503	231,854
1981	22	22	1	3	1	0	3	0	1	4,917	1,549	16	6,365	181,670
1982	17	25	0	1	0	2	1	3	3	6,730	412	12	7,903	158,197
1983	6	30	4	2	1	2	5	0	7	9,418	650	15	10,451	453,586
1984	8	30	0	0	2	0	2	3	7	9,126	641	11	10,460	282,533
1985	4	28	1	2	2	3	1	3	7	8,675	618	15	10,350	530,145
1986	13	28	0	1	1	1	1	2	6	7,691	323	16	8,990	485,930
1987	12	26	0	0	0	4	1	0	10	7,834	120	10	9,072	401,541
1988	16	27	0	2	0	0	1	0	4	8,017	324	7	9,131	440,139
1989	20	26	0	0	0	0	0	0	11	7,795	23	6	9,488	271,628
1990	43	5	0	0	0	0	0	0	0	1,179	0	0	1,635	62,600
1993	67T	2	0	0	0	0	0	0	0	134	0	0	353	14,515
Lifetime		363	20	18	12	15	20	18	73	96,021	6,382	155	115,046	$3,998,470

Joe Booher

Joseph Booher
B: 2/22/1941   D: 2/12/1993   *Killed in Dash race @ Daytona.*
Racing Hometown: W. Lafayette, IN

Year	Rank	Starts	Poles	1	2	3	4	5	6–10	Laps	Laps Led	Races Led	Miles	$
1975	—	0												335
1977	—	0												575
1978	NR	3	0	0	0	0	0	0	0	595	0	0	769	3,205
1980	56	6	0	0	0	0	0	0	0	1,273	0	0	1,674	15,930
1981	82	4	0	0	0	0	0	0	0	581	0	0	1,259	4,995
1982	NR	2	0	0	0	0	0	0	0	371	0	0	832	4,850
1983	NR	1	0	0	0	0	0	0	0	2	0	0	3	1,435

Year	Rank	Starts	Poles	Finish 1	2	3	4	5	6–10	Laps	Laps Led	Races Led	Miles	$

Joe Booher *continued*

Year	Rank	Starts	Poles	1	2	3	4	5	6–10	Laps	Laps Led	Races Led	Miles	$
1984	—	0												1,650
1985	65	2	0	0	0	0	0	0	0	358	0	0	801	3,685
1986	71	2	0	0	0	0	0	0	0	556	0	0	556	8,930
1987	—	0												2,000
1988	87T	1	0	0	0	0	0	0	0	272	0	0	272	3,295
1990	—	0												1,000
1992	—	0												2,300
Lifetime		21	0	0	0	0	0	0	0	4,008	0	0	6,165	$54,185

Bud Boone

Bud Boone
Racing Hometown: Warren, OH

Year	Rank	Starts	Poles	1	2	3	4	5	6–10	Laps	Laps Led	Races Led	Miles	$
1950	68T	1	0	0	0	0	0	0	1	0	0	0	0	75
Lifetime		1	0	0	0	0	0	0	1	0	0	0	0	$75

Ernie Boost

Ernie Boost
Racing Hometown: Cleveland, OH

Year	Rank	Starts	Poles	1	2	3	4	5	6–10	Laps	Laps Led	Races Led	Miles	$
1952	NR	3	0	0	0	0	0	0	1	381	0	0	232	100
Lifetime		3	0	0	0	0	0	0	1	381	0	0	232	$100

Bobby Booth

Robert Booth
Racing Hometown: Hapeville, GA

Year	Rank	Starts	Poles	1	2	3	4	5	6–10	Laps	Laps Led	Races Led	Miles	$
1951	N/A	3	0	0	0	0	0	0	0	156	0	0	169	25
Lifetime		3	0	0	0	0	0	0	0	156	0	0	169	$25

John Borden

John Borden
Racing Hometown: Lancaster, NY

Year	Rank	Starts	Poles	1	2	3	4	5	6–10	Laps	Laps Led	Races Led	Miles	$
1950	82	2	0	0	0	0	0	0	0		0	0		50
Lifetime		2	0	0	0	0	0	0	0		0	0		$50

John Borneman

John Borneman Jr.
B: 4/19/1949
Racing Hometown: El Cajon, CA

Year	Rank	Starts	Poles	1	2	3	4	5	6–10	Laps	Laps Led	Races Led	Miles	$
1977	96T	1	0	0	0	0	0	0	0	150	0	0	375	1,200
1978	61	3	0	0	0	0	0	0	0	305	0	0	777	3,320
1979	98T	1	0	0	0	0	0	0	0	79	0	0	207	1,305
1980	81	2	0	0	0	0	0	0	0	84	0	0	220	1,250
1981	73T	1	0	0	0	0	0	0	0	116	0	0	304	3,140
Lifetime		8	0	0	0	0	0	0	0	734	0	0	1,883	$10,215

Joe Bossard

Joseph Bossard
Racing Hometown: Little Falls, NJ

Year	Rank	Starts	Poles	1	2	3	4	5	6–10	Laps	Laps Led	Races Led	Miles	$
1954	91	2	0	0	0	0	0	0	0	206	0	0	168	50
Lifetime		2	0	0	0	0	0	0	0	206	0	0	168	$50

Jim Bossic

James Bossic
Racing Hometown: Montgomery, AL

Year	Rank	Starts	Poles	1	2	3	4	5	6–10	Laps	Laps Led	Races Led	Miles	$
1955	NR	1	0	0	0	0	0	0	0		0	0		25
Lifetime		1	0	0	0	0	0	0	0		0	0		$25

Tommy Bostick

Thomas P. Bostick
Racing Hometown: Bennettsville, SC

Year	Rank	Starts	Poles	1	2	3	4	5	6–10	Laps	Laps Led	Races Led	Miles	$
1966	122	1	0	0	0	0	0	0	0	42	0	0	42	500
Lifetime		1	0	0	0	0	0	0	0	42	0	0	42	$500

Rodney Bottinger

Rodney Bottinger
Racing Hometown: Charleston, SC

Year	Rank	Starts	Poles	1	2	3	4	5	6–10	Laps	Laps Led	Races Led	Miles	$
1964	NR	3	0	0	0	0	0	0	0	17	0	0	9	300
Lifetime		3	0	0	0	0	0	0	0	17	0	0	9	$300

Year	Rank	Starts	Poles	Finish 1	2	3	4	5	6–10	Laps	Laps Led	Races Led	Miles	$

Ken Bouchard

Kenneth P. Bouchard
B: 4/6/1955
Racing Hometown: Fitchburg, MA

Year	Rank	Starts	Poles	1	2	3	4	5	6–10	Laps	Laps Led	Races Led	Miles	$
1987	93	1	0	0	0	0	0	0	0	158	0	0	316	2,075
1988	25	24	0	0	0	0	0	0	1	7,281	4	1	8,480	109,410
1989	48	4	0	0	0	0	0	0	0	911	0	0	1,373	33,930
1993	52	3	0	0	0	0	0	0	0	503	0	0	849	25,785
1994	69	1	0	0	0	0	0	0	0	280	0	0	426	675
1995	—	0												2,100
Lifetime		33	0	0	0	0	0	0	1	9,133	4	1	11,445	$173,975

Ron Bouchard

Ronald Bouchard
B: 11/23/1948
Racing Hometown: Fitchburg, MA

Year	Rank	Starts	Poles	1	2	3	4	5	6–10	Laps	Laps Led	Races Led	Miles	$
1981	21	22	1	1	0	0	1	3	7	6,155	12	2	6,978	152,855
1982	8	30	1	0	0	2	1	0	12	8,048	1	1	8,543	375,759
1983	16	28	1	0	0	0	1	0	6	7,187	22	4	8,315	159,173
1984	11	30	0	0	1	2	1	1	6	9,200	111	8	10,504	246,510
1985	13	28	0	0	1	1	2	1	7	7,723	77	5	8,961	240,304
1986	31	17	0	0	0	0	0	0	2	3,654	1	1	5,093	106,835
1987	47	5	0	0	0	0	0	0	1	917	0	0	1,446	24,105
Lifetime		160	3	1	2	5	6	5	41	42,884	224	21	49,840	$1,305,541

Smokey Boutwell

Nathan Boutwell   D: 9/29/1993
Racing Hometown: Pelham, NH

Year	Rank	Starts	Poles	1	2	3	4	5	6–10	Laps	Laps Led	Races Led	Miles	$
1964	62	2	0	0	0	0	0	0	0	217	0	0	543	1,100
Lifetime		2	0	0	0	0	0	0	0	217	0	0	543	$1,100

Eliso Bowie

Eliso Bowie
Racing Hometown: San Mateo, CA

Year	Rank	Starts	Poles	1	2	3	4	5	6–10	Laps	Laps Led	Races Led	Miles	$
1955	223	1	0	0	0	0	0	0	0	172	0	0	172	90
Lifetime		1	0	0	0	0	0	0	0	172	0	0	172	$90

Bill Bowman

William Bowman
Racing Hometown: Aberdeen, MD

Year	Rank	Starts	Poles	1	2	3	4	5	6–10	Laps	Laps Led	Races Led	Miles	$
1955	81	3	0	0	0	0	0	0	2	675	0	0	610	610
1956	176T	1	0	0	0	0	0	0	1	181	0	0	91	100
1957	60	4	0	0	0	0	0	0	1	817	0	0	463	510
Lifetime		8	0	0	0	0	0	0	4	1,673	0	0	1,163	$1,220

Jerry Bowman

Jerry Bowman
B: 3/9/1962
Racing Hometown: Havre de Grace, MD

Year	Rank	Starts	Poles	1	2	3	4	5	6–10	Laps	Laps Led	Races Led	Miles	$
1982	NR	1	0	0	0	0	0	0	0	53	0	0	81	765
1983	45	5	0	0	0	0	0	0	0	1,183	0	0	1,553	8,610
1984	44	5	0	0	0	0	0	0	0	834	0	0	1,000	8,115
1985	43	5	0	0	0	0	0	0	0	1,326	0	0	1,628	8,665
1986	85	2	0	0	0	0	0	0	0	255	0	0	255	2,125
1987	92	1	0	0	0	0	0	0	0	161	0	0	161	1,450
Lifetime		19	0	0	0	0	0	0	0	3,812	0	0	4,678	$29,730

Dick Bown

Richard Bown
B: 8/12/1928
Racing Hometown: Portland, OR

Year	Rank	Starts	Poles	1	2	3	4	5	6–10	Laps	Laps Led	Races Led	Miles	$
1961	143	1	0	0	0	0	0	0	0	133	0	0	186	250
1965	98	1	0	0	0	0	0	0	0	47	0	0	127	525
1969	NR	1	0	0	0	0	0	0	0	160	0	0	432	1,230
1970	51	6	0	0	0	0	0	0	1	836	0	0	1,187	4,275
1971	NR	4	0	0	0	0	0	0	0	414	0	0	941	4,500
1972	59	3	0	0	0	0	0	0	0	459	0	0	1,181	4,465
1973	75	2	0	0	0	0	0	0	0	196	0	0	514	1,860
1974	90	2	0	0	0	0	0	0	0	68	0	0	178	1,655
1975	104	1	0	0	0	0	0	0	0	17	0	0	45	775
Lifetime		21	0	0	0	0	0	0	1	2,330	0	0	4,790	$19,535

Year	Rank	Starts	Poles	Finish						Laps	Laps Led	Races Led	Miles	$
				1	2	3	4	5	6–10					

Jim Bown

James Bown
B: 6/24/1960
Racing Hometown: Portland, OR

Year	Rank	Starts	Poles	1	2	3	4	5	6–10	Laps	Laps Led	Races Led	Miles	$
1981	75	2	0	0	0	0	0	0	0	48	0	0	126	1,415
1982	56	2	0	0	0	0	0	0	1	204	0	0	534	4,490
1983	74	2	0	0	0	0	0	0	0	118	0	0	309	2,125
1984	69	2	0	0	0	0	0	0	0	132	4	1	346	2,330
1985	59	2	0	0	0	0	0	0	0	185	0	0	485	4,860
1986	112	1	0	0	0	0	0	0	0	81	0	0	212	1,175
1987	91	2	0	0	0	0	0	0	0	264	0	0	668	8,850
1988	76	2	0	0	0	0	0	0	0	86	0	0	122	3,325
1989	59	4	0	0	0	0	0	0	0	664	0	0	786	15,750
1990	61	4	0	0	0	0	0	0	0	910	0	0	1,058	18,330
1996	—	0												3,572
Lifetime		23	0	0	0	0	0	0	1	2,692	4	1	4,646	$66,222

Chuck Bown

Richard Charles Bown
B: 2/22/1954
Racing Hometown: Portland, OR

Year	Rank	Starts	Poles	1	2	3	4	5	6–10	Laps	Laps Led	Races Led	Miles	$
1972	69	3	0	0	0	0	0	0	0	391	0	0	1,005	3,710
1973	73	2	0	0	0	0	0	0	1	204	0	0	534	2,305
1974	93	3	0	0	0	0	0	0	0	114	0	0	297	2,070
1975	57	5	0	0	0	0	0	0	0	415	0	0	634	5,160
1976	49	5	0	0	0	0	0	0	0	568	3	1	1,192	5,480
1977	59	3	0	0	0	0	0	0	0	180	0	0	468	7,270
1978	56	4	0	0	0	0	0	0	0	539	0	0	732	3,585
1979	38	7	0	0	0	0	0	0	2	1,388	0	0	2,143	31,380
1980	51	8	0	0	0	0	0	0	0	1,060	0	0	1,905	13,145
1981	67	3	0	0	0	0	0	0	0	631	0	0	860	4,725
1990	50	3	0	0	0	0	0	0	0	951	0	0	1,280	10,150
1991	76	1	0	0	0	0	0	0	0	391	0	0	244	7,325
1993	71	1	0	0	0	0	0	0	0	306	0	0	306	6,610
1994	42	13	1	0	0	0	0	0	1	3,714	0	0	4,176	225,260
1995	43	9	0	0	0	0	0	0	0	2,068	0	0	3,026	99,995
1996	53	3	0	0	0	0	0	0	0	338	0	0	723	38,867
Lifetime		73	1	0	0	0	0	0	4	13,424	3	1	19,974	$467,037

Jack Bowsher

Jack Bowsher
B: 10/2/1930
Racing Hometown: Springfield, OH

Year	Rank	Starts	Poles	1	2	3	4	5	6–10	Laps	Laps Led	Races Led	Miles	$
1966	NR	2	0	0	0	0	0	0	0	775	0	0	932	1,710
1967	NR	2	0	0	0	0	0	0	0	207	11	1	302	1,705
Lifetime		4	0	0	0	0	0	0	0	982	11	1	1,234	$3,415

Jim Boyd

Jim Boyd
B: 3/31/1920
Racing Hometown: Cottonwood, CA

Year	Rank	Starts	Poles	1	2	3	4	5	6–10	Laps	Laps Led	Races Led	Miles	$
1975	71	2	0	0	0	0	0	0	0	203	0	0	524	2,335
Lifetime		2	0	0	0	0	0	0	0	203	0	0	524	$2,335

Frank Boylan

Frank Boylan
Racing Hometown: Ashtabula, OH

Year	Rank	Starts	Poles	1	2	3	4	5	6–10	Laps	Laps Led	Races Led	Miles	$
1950	92	2	0	0	0	0	0	0	0	196	0	0	98	50
Lifetime		2	0	0	0	0	0	0	0	196	0	0	98	$50

Bobby Boyles

Robert Boyles

Year	Rank	Starts	Poles	1	2	3	4	5	6–10	Laps	Laps Led	Races Led	Miles	$
1970	NR	1	0	0	0	0	0	0	0	3	0	0	1	200
Lifetime		1	0	0	0	0	0	0	0	3	0	0	1	$200

Buddie Boys

Buddie Boys
B: 1926
Racing Hometown: Alsa Craig, Ont., Canada

Year	Rank	Starts	Poles	1	2	3	4	5	6–10	Laps	Laps Led	Races Led	Miles	$
1984	84	1	0	0	0	0	0	0	0	178	0	0	181	1,055

Year	Rank	Starts	Poles	Finish						Laps	Laps Led	Races Led	Miles	$
				1	2	3	4	5	6–10					

Buddie Boys *continued*

Year	Rank	Starts	Poles	1	2	3	4	5	6–10	Laps	Laps Led	Races Led	Miles	$
1986	98	2	0	0	0	0	0	0	0	91	0	0	168	2,480
Lifetime		3	0	0	0	0	0	0	0	269	0	0	349	$3,535

Trevor Boys

Trevor Boys
B: 11/3/1957
Racing Hometown: Alsa Craig, Ont., Canada

Year	Rank	Starts	Poles	1	2	3	4	5	6–10	Laps	Laps Led	Races Led	Miles	$
1982	86	1	0	0	0	0	0	0	0	105	0	0	275	1,200
1983	25	23	0	0	0	0	0	0	1	5,907	3	2	6,896	87,555
1984	17	30	0	0	0	0	0	0	1	8,719	20	3	9,970	165,376
1985	28	20	0	0	0	0	0	0	0	3,673	3	1	4,400	76,325
1986	34	14	0	0	0	0	0	0	0	3,210	2	1	3,501	74,645
1987	44	10	0	0	0	0	0	0	0	2,312	5	2	3,132	59,240
1988	65	2	0	0	0	0	0	0	0	505	0	0	804	17,960
1989	NR	1	0	0	0	0	0	0	0	118	2	1	295	3,775
1990	—	0												1,800
1993	79	1	0	0	0	0	0	0	0	38	1	1	95	6,510
1994	—	0												2,500
Lifetime		102	0	0	0	0	0	0	2	24,587	36	11	29,368	$496,886

Geoff Brabham

Geoffrey Brabham
B: 3/20/1952
Racing Hometown: Sydney, Australia

Year	Rank	Starts	Poles	1	2	3	4	5	6–10	Laps	Laps Led	Races Led	Miles	$
1994	76T	1	0	0	0	0	0	0	0	127	0	0	318	27,400
Lifetime		1	0	0	0	0	0	0	0	127	0	0	318	$27,400

Bruno Bracchy *See* Johnny Frank

Bobby Brack

Robert Frederick Brack
B: 8/20/1938
Racing Hometown: Miami, FL

Year	Rank	Starts	Poles	1	2	3	4	5	6–10	Laps	Laps Led	Races Led	Miles	$
1971	58	5	0	0	0	0	0	0	0	946	0	0	1,610	4,608
1979	122	1	0	0	0	0	0	0	0	70	1	1	105	930
Lifetime		6	0	0	0	0	0	0	0	1,016	1	1	1,715	$5,538

Gordon Bracken

Gordon W. Bracken Jr.
Racing Hometown: Barnesville, GA

Year	Rank	Starts	Poles	1	2	3	4	5	6–10	Laps	Laps Led	Races Led	Miles	$
1953	34	6	0	0	0	0	0	0	1	221	0	0	221	215
Lifetime		6	0	0	0	0	0	0	1	221	0	0	221	$215

Gary Bradberry

Gary Bradberry
B: 1/27/1961
Racing Hometown: Chelsea, AL

Year	Rank	Starts	Poles	1	2	3	4	5	6–10	Laps	Laps Led	Races Led	Miles	$
1994	70T	1	0	0	0	0	0	0	0	276	0	0	420	6,600
1995	52	4	0	0	0	0	0	0	0	604	0	0	803	36,075
1996	46	9	0	0	0	0	0	0	0	2,212	0	0	2,827	155,785
Lifetime		14	0	0	0	0	0	0	0	3,092	0	0	4,050	$198,460

Melvin Bradley

Melvin Bradley
Racing Hometown: Richmond, VA

Year	Rank	Starts	Poles	1	2	3	4	5	6–10	Laps	Laps Led	Races Led	Miles	$
1962	59	3	0	0	0	0	1	0	1	1,007	0	0	445	990
1967	85	3	0	0	0	0	0	0	1	549	0	0	321	525
Lifetime		6	0	0	0	0	1	0	2	1,556	0	0	766	$1,515

Eddie Bradshaw

Edward Bradshaw
Racing Hometown: Bakersfield, CA

Year	Rank	Starts	Poles	1	2	3	4	5	6–10	Laps	Laps Led	Races Led	Miles	$
1974	105	1	0	0	0	0	0	0	1	123	0	0	322	1,375
1975	96	1	0	0	0	0	0	0	0	63	0	0	165	820
1976	70	2	0	0	0	0	0	0	0	224	0	0	587	2,685
1977	72	2	0	0	0	0	0	0	1	152	0	0	394	2,920

Year	Rank	Starts	Poles	Finish						Laps	Laps Led	Races Led	Miles	$
				1	2	3	4	5	6–10					

Eddie Bradshaw *continued*

Year	Rank	Starts	Poles	1	2	3	4	5	6–10	Laps	Laps Led	Races Led	Miles	$
1978	100	1	0	0	0	0	0	0	0	15	0	0	39	600
Lifetime		7	0	0	0	0	0	0	2	577	0	0	1,507	$8,400

Art Brady

Arthur Brady
Racing Hometown: Peoria, IL

Year	Rank	Starts	Poles	1	2	3	4	5	6–10	Laps	Laps Led	Races Led	Miles	$
1962	71	2	0	0	0	0	0	0	0	179	0	0	448	450
Lifetime		2	0	0	0	0	0	0	0	179	0	0	448	$450

Lonnie Bragg

Lonnie Bragg
Racing Hometown: Terre Haute, IN

Year	Rank	Starts	Poles	1	2	3	4	5	6–10	Laps	Laps Led	Races Led	Miles	$
1953	NR	1	0	0	0	0	0	0	0	149	0	0	205	105
Lifetime		1	0	0	0	0	0	0	0	149	0	0	205	$105

Whitey Brainerd

Whitey Brainerd
Racing Hometown: Monroe, CT

Year	Rank	Starts	Poles	1	2	3	4	5	6–10	Laps	Laps Led	Races Led	Miles	$
1954	67	2	0	0	0	0	0	0	1	317	0	0	224	175
Lifetime		2	0	0	0	0	0	0	1	317	0	0	224	$175

Al Brand

Clarence Brand
Racing Hometown: Inglewood, CA

Year	Rank	Starts	Poles	1	2	3	4	5	6–10	Laps	Laps Led	Races Led	Miles	$
1961	111	3	0	0	0	0	0	0	0	205	0	0	179	155
1963	152	1	0	0	0	0	0	0	0	1	0	0	3	200
1964	133	1	0	0	0	0	0	0	0	7	0	0	19	500
Lifetime		5	0	0	0	0	0	0	0	213	0	0	201	$855

Don Branson

Donald Branson
Racing Hometown: Charleston, SC

Year	Rank	Starts	Poles	1	2	3	4	5	6–10	Laps	Laps Led	Races Led	Miles	$
1964	92	8	0	0	0	0	0	0	0	271	0	0	116	660
Lifetime		8	0	0	0	0	0	0	0	271	0	0	116	$660

Wally Branston

Walter Branston
Racing Hometown: Toronto, Ont., Canada

Year	Rank	Starts	Poles	1	2	3	4	5	6–10	Laps	Laps Led	Races Led	Miles	$
1954	211	1	0	0	0	0	0	0	0	52	0	0	26	0
Lifetime		1	0	0	0	0	0	0	0	52	0	0	26	$0

Bruce Brantley

Bruce Brantley
Racing Hometown: Chamblee, GA

Year	Rank	Starts	Poles	1	2	3	4	5	6–10	Laps	Laps Led	Races Led	Miles	$
1962	126	1	0	0	0	0	0	0	0	139	0	0	209	275
1963	91	4	0	0	0	0	0	0	1	231	0	0	146	840
Lifetime		5	0	0	0	0	0	0	1	370	0	0	354	$1,115

Frank Brantley

Frank Meyer Brantley
B: 11/10/1932
Racing Hometown: Savannah, GA

Year	Rank	Starts	Poles	1	2	3	4	5	6–10	Laps	Laps Led	Races Led	Miles	$
1962	NR	1	0	0	0	0	0	0	0	164	0	0	82	85
1964	101	2	0	0	0	0	0	0	0	262	0	0	131	290
Lifetime		3	0	0	0	0	0	0	0	426	0	0	213	$375

Everett Brashear

Everett Brashear
Racing Hometown: Beaumont, TX

Year	Rank	Starts	Poles	1	2	3	4	5	6–10	Laps	Laps Led	Races Led	Miles	$
1957	183	1	0	0	0	0	0	0	0		0	0		25
Lifetime		1	0	0	0	0	0	0	0		0	0		$25

Darin Brassfield

Darin Brassfield
B: 9/16/1960
Racing Hometown: Los Gatos, CA

Year	Rank	Starts	Poles	1	2	3	4	5	6–10	Laps	Laps Led	Races Led	Miles	$
1989	50	3	0	0	0	0	0	0	0	275	0	0	486	10,852
Lifetime		3	0	0	0	0	0	0	0	275	0	0	486	$10,852

Year	Rank	Starts	Poles	Finish						Laps	Laps Led	Races Led	Miles	$
				1	2	3	4	5	6–10					

Bill Braun

William Braun
Racing Hometown: Paterson, NJ

Year	Rank	Starts	Poles	1	2	3	4	5	6–10	Laps	Laps Led	Races Led	Miles	$
1951	139T	1	0	0	0	0	0	0	1		0	0		50
Lifetime		1	0	0	0	0	0	0	1		0	0		$50

Jim Bray

James Bray
Racing Hometown: S. Port Credit, Ont., Canada

Year	Rank	Starts	Poles	1	2	3	4	5	6–10	Laps	Laps Led	Races Led	Miles	$
1962	76	3	0	0	0	0	0	0	0	362	0	0	175	300
1963	109	2	0	0	0	0	0	0	0	377	0	0	120	225
1964	69	4	0	0	0	0	0	0	0	167	0	0	452	1,875
1965	93	2	0	0	0	0	0	0	0	6	0	0	15	1,190
1974	62	4	0	0	0	0	0	0	0	388	0	0	395	2,880
Lifetime		15	0	0	0	0	0	0	0	1,300	0	0	1,158	$6,470

Victor Brenzelli

Victor Brenzelli
Racing Hometown: Atlanta, GA

Year	Rank	Starts	Poles	1	2	3	4	5	6–10	Laps	Laps Led	Races Led	Miles	$
1951	N/A	1	0	0	0	0	0	0	0		0	0		25
Lifetime		1	0	0	0	0	0	0	0		0	0		$25

Bobby Brewer

George Robert Brewer
B: 8/11/1929
Racing Hometown: Winston-Salem, NC

Year	Rank	Starts	Poles	1	2	3	4	5	6–10	Laps	Laps Led	Races Led	Miles	$
1969	NR	1	0	0	0	0	0	0	0	9	0	0	24	975
Lifetime		1	0	0	0	0	0	0	0	9	0	0	24	$975

E. J. Brewer

Emery J. Brewer
Racing Hometown: Winston-Salem, NC

Year	Rank	Starts	Poles	1	2	3	4	5	6–10	Laps	Laps Led	Races Led	Miles	$
1957	NR	1	0	0	0	0	0	0	0	138	0	0	69	110
1958	129	5	0	0	0	0	0	0	1	486	0	0	390	490
Lifetime		6	0	0	0	0	0	0	1	624	0	0	459	$600

Richard Brickhouse

Richard Fleming Brickhouse
B: 10/27/1939
Racing Hometown: Rocky Point, NC

Year	Rank	Starts	Poles	1	2	3	4	5	6–10	Laps	Laps Led	Races Led	Miles	$
1968	45	7	0	0	0	0	1	0	1	1,571	0	0	1,977	7,190
1969	25	24	0	1	0	0	0	1	7	3,629	34	2	4,630	45,637
1970	58	5	0	0	0	0	0	1	1	409	2	1	902	6,925
1979	126T	1	0	0	0	0	0	0	0	15	0	0	23	870
1982	89	2	0	0	0	0	0	0	0	557	0	0	673	2,610
Lifetime		39	0	1	0	0	1	2	9	6,181	36	3	8,204	$63,232

Kenneth Bridge

Kenneth Bridge
Racing Hometown: Thompsonville, CT

Year	Rank	Starts	Poles	1	2	3	4	5	6–10	Laps	Laps Led	Races Led	Miles	$
1954	190	1	0	0	0	0	0	0	0	5	0	0	5	0
Lifetime		1	0	0	0	0	0	0	0	5	0	0	5	$0

Johnny Bridgers

John F. Bridgers
Racing Hometown: Rowland, NC

Year	Rank	Starts	Poles	1	2	3	4	5	6–10	Laps	Laps Led	Races Led	Miles	$
1952	163	1	0	0	0	0	0	0	0	244	0	0	305	0
1953	151	1	0	0	0	0	0	0	0	279	0	0	384	120
Lifetime		2	0	0	0	0	0	0	0	523	0	0	689	$120

Buck Brigance

Buck Brigance
Racing Hometown: Charlotte, NC

Year	Rank	Starts	Poles	1	2	3	4	5	6–10	Laps	Laps Led	Races Led	Miles	$
1958	NR	1	0	0	0	0	0	0	0	109	0	0	55	70
1959	87	13	0	0	0	0	0	0	1	1,835	0	0	907	890
1960	NR	2	0	0	0	0	0	0	1	297	0	0	149	210
Lifetime		16	0	0	0	0	0	0	2	2,241	0	0	1,110	$1,170

Mason Bright

Mason Bright
B: 1929
Racing Hometown: Detroit, MI

Year	Rank	Starts	Poles	1	2	3	4	5	6–10	Laps	Laps Led	Races Led	Miles	$
1953	171	1	0	0	0	0	0	0	0	33	0	0	135	25

Year	Rank	Starts	Poles	Finish						Laps	Laps Led	Races Led	Miles	$
				1	2	3	4	5	6–10					

Mason Bright *continued*

Year	Rank	Starts	Poles	1	2	3	4	5	6–10	Laps	Laps Led	Races Led	Miles	$
1954	NR	2	0	0	0	0	0	0	0	200	0	0	226	50
Lifetime		3	0	0	0	0	0	0	0	233	0	0	361	$75

Kenny Brightbill

Kenneth Brightbill
Racing Hometown: Sinking Springs, PA

Year	Rank	Starts	Poles	1	2	3	4	5	6–10	Laps	Laps Led	Races Led	Miles	$
1974	106	2	0	0	0	0	0	0	2	663	0	0	944	3,950
1975	77	1	0	0	0	0	0	0	1	480	0	0	480	2,000
1977	77	2	0	0	0	0	0	0	0	206	0	0	497	1,950
1978	NR	1	0	0	0	0	0	0	0	177	0	0	443	1,130
Lifetime		6	0	0	0	0	0	0	3	1,526	0	0	2,363	$9,030

Charles Brinkley

Charles Brinkley
Racing Hometown: Memphis, TN

Year	Rank	Starts	Poles	1	2	3	4	5	6–10	Laps	Laps Led	Races Led	Miles	$
1954	NR	2	0	0	0	0	0	0	0	319	0	0	445	100
Lifetime		2	0	0	0	0	0	0	0	319	0	0	445	$100

Maudis Brissette

Maudis Brissette
Racing Hometown: Bailey, NC

Year	Rank	Starts	Poles	1	2	3	4	5	6–10	Laps	Laps Led	Races Led	Miles	$
1951	209T	1	0	0	0	0	0	0	0		0	0		25
Lifetime		1	0	0	0	0	0	0	0		0	0		$25

Ronnie Bristow

Ronald Bristow
Racing Hometown: Aberdeen, CA

Year	Rank	Starts	Poles	1	2	3	4	5	6–10	Laps	Laps Led	Races Led	Miles	$
1963	121	2	0	0	0	0	0	0	0	112	0	0	48	485
Lifetime		2	0	0	0	0	0	0	0	112	0	0	48	$485

Leonard Brock

Leonard Brock (Lee)
Racing Hometown: Niota, TN

Year	Rank	Starts	Poles	1	2	3	4	5	6–10	Laps	Laps Led	Races Led	Miles	$
1968	94	3	0	0	0	0	0	0	0	17	0	0	8	175
Lifetime		3	0	0	0	0	0	0	0	17	0	0	8	$175

Pete Brock

Peter Brock
Racing Hometown: Riverside, CA

Year	Rank	Starts	Poles	1	2	3	4	5	6–10	Laps	Laps Led	Races Led	Miles	$
1963	89	1	0	0	0	0	0	0	0	134	0	0	362	350
Lifetime		1	0	0	0	0	0	0	0	134	0	0	362	$350

Barry Brooks

Barry Brooks
Racing Hometown: Ft. Mill, SC

Year	Rank	Starts	Poles	1	2	3	4	5	6–10	Laps	Laps Led	Races Led	Miles	$
1965	87	4	0	0	0	0	0	0	0	131	0	0	76	1,450
Lifetime		4	0	0	0	0	0	0	0	131	0	0	76	$1,450

Dick Brooks

Richard Brooks
B: 4/14/1942
Racing Hometown: Porterville, CA

Year	Rank	Starts	Poles	1	2	3	4	5	6–10	Laps	Laps Led	Races Led	Miles	$
1969	21	28	0	0	0	1	0	2	9	5,741	2	1	6,255	28,187
1970	13	34	0	0	2	5	4	4	3	6,821	194	6	6,996	53,754
1971	36	20	0	0	1	5	0	3	3	4,495	16	5	4,784	32,936
1972	49	14	0	0	0	0	0	0	1	1,156	3	2	2,169	14,146
1973	27	14	0	1	0	1	0	1	6	3,448	25	3	4,947	55,369
1974	27	16	0	0	0	0	0	0	3	2,951	1	1	4,097	22,760
1975	10	25	0	0	1	2	3	0	9	7,344	60	4	8,052	93,001
1976	10	28	0	0	0	1	1	1	15	7,542	16	2	8,585	111,880
1977	6	29	0	0	1	0	1	5	13	8,191	8	2	9,511	151,374
1978	8	30	0	0	0	0	1	4	12	8,689	24	2	10,023	137,590
1979	22	27	0	0	0	1	0	0	7	6,307	16	1	7,422	61,985
1980	27	19	0	0	0	0	0	2	3	3,978	6	1	5,106	60,700
1981	61	5	0	0	0	0	0	0	0	1,397	1	1	2,065	14,845
1982	48	5	0	0	0	0	0	0	0	517	0	0	688	9,470
1983	14	30	0	0	0	0	0	2	4	7,866	108	6	8,872	180,556
1984	15	30	0	0	0	1	0	0	4	8,157	185	3	9,320	192,407

Year	Rank	Starts	Poles	Finish						Laps	Laps Led	Races Led	Miles	$
				1	2	3	4	5	6–10					

Dick Brooks *continued*

Year	Rank	Starts	Poles	1	2	3	4	5	6–10	Laps	Laps Led	Races Led	Miles	$
1985	53	4	0	0	0	0	0	0	1	1,076	0	0	1,572	29,340
Lifetime		358	0	1	5	17	10	24	93	85,676	665	40	100,464	$1,250,300

Earl Brooks

Earl Lee Brooks
B: 8/11/1929
Racing Hometown: Lynchburg, VA

Year	Rank	Starts	Poles	1	2	3	4	5	6–10	Laps	Laps Led	Races Led	Miles	$
1962	58	8	0	0	0	0	0	0	3	946	0	0	451	745
1963	93	3	0	0	0	0	0	1	0	783	0	0	354	725
1964	41	28	0	0	0	0	0	0	8	3,988	0	0	1,834	3,925
1965	139	1	0	0	0	0	0	0	0	0	0	0	0	100
1966	63	9	0	0	0	0	0	0	1	1,769	0	0	1,198	3,470
1967	25	34	0	0	0	0	0	0	8	5,373	24	1	3,536	8,610
1968	15	40	0	0	0	0	0	0	5	6,507	0	0	4,396	14,233
1969	18	49	0	0	0	0	0	1	5	8,719	0	0	7,077	34,793
1970	37	21	0	0	0	0	0	0	1	1,779	0	0	1,891	10,360
1971	17	35	0	0	0	0	1	0	3	6,657	0	0	6,548	25,360
1972	73	6	0	0	0	0	0	0	0	609	0	0	593	3,215
1973	42	9	0	0	0	0	0	0	0	2,267	0	0	1,396	4,880
1974	115	1	0	0	0	0	0	0	0	1	0	0	1	1,100
1975	42	7	0	0	0	0	0	0	0	1,229	0	0	1,376	4,900
1976	63	4	0	0	0	0	0	0	0	1,230	0	0	1,340	5,225
1977	44	6	0	0	0	0	0	0	0	1,260	0	0	949	3,045
1979	NR	1	0	0	0	0	0	0	0	79	0	0	49	405
Lifetime		262	0	0	0	0	1	2	34	43,196	24	1	32,989	$125,091

Gary Brooks

Gary Brooks

Year	Rank	Starts	Poles	1	2	3	4	5	6–10	Laps	Laps Led	Races Led	Miles	$
1991	87T	1	0	0	0	0	0	0	0	11	0	0	11	3,425
Lifetime		1	0	0	0	0	0	0	0	11	0	0	11	$3,425

Tex Brooks

Tex Brooks
Racing Hometown: Yonkers, NY

Year	Rank	Starts	Poles	1	2	3	4	5	6–10	Laps	Laps Led	Races Led	Miles	$
1954	100	2	0	0	0	0	0	0	0	57	0	0	93	35
Lifetime		2	0	0	0	0	0	0	0	57	0	0	93	$35

Willard Brooks

Willard Brooks
Racing Hometown: Mobile, AL

Year	Rank	Starts	Poles	1	2	3	4	5	6–10	Laps	Laps Led	Races Led	Miles	$
1951	N/A	1	0	0	0	0	0	0	0		0	0		25
Lifetime		1	0	0	0	0	0	0	0		0	0		$25

Wayne Broome

Wayne Broome
Racing Hometown: Mt. Gilead, NC

Year	Rank	Starts	Poles	1	2	3	4	5	6–10	Laps	Laps Led	Races Led	Miles	$
1979	115	2	0	0	0	0	0	0	0	125	0	0	318	2,140
Lifetime		2	0	0	0	0	0	0	0	125	0	0	318	$2,140

Bill Brown

William Brown (Slim)
Racing Hometown: Paterson, NJ

Year	Rank	Starts	Poles	1	2	3	4	5	6–10	Laps	Laps Led	Races Led	Miles	$
1952	154T	1	0	0	0	0	0	0	0	111	0	0	56	25
1954	NR	1	0	0	0	0	0	0	0	41	0	0	21	0
1955	166T	1	0	0	0	0	0	0	0	169	0	0	85	60
1959	NR	1	0	0	0	0	0	0	1	183	0	0	46	165
Lifetime		4	0	0	0	0	0	0	1	504	0	0	208	$250

Bill Brown

William Brown
Racing Hometown: Chicago, IL

Year	Rank	Starts	Poles	1	2	3	4	5	6–10	Laps	Laps Led	Races Led	Miles	$
1956	238	1	0	0	0	0	0	0	0	235	0	0	323	250
Lifetime		1	0	0	0	0	0	0	0	235	0	0	323	$250

Brownie Brown

Brownie Brown
Racing Hometown: Las Vegas, NV

Year	Rank	Starts	Poles	1	2	3	4	5	6–10	Laps	Laps Led	Races Led	Miles	$
1960	NR	1	0	0	0	0	0	0	0	12	0	0	17	0

Year	Rank	Starts	Poles	Finish						Laps	Laps Led	Races Led	Miles	$
				1	2	3	4	5	6–10					

Brownie Brown *continued*

Year	Rank	Starts	Poles	1	2	3	4	5	6–10	Laps	Laps Led	Races Led	Miles	$
1961	NR	1	0	0	0	0	0	0	0	6	0	0	8	0
Lifetime		2	0	0	0	0	0	0	0	18	0	0	25	$0

Cannonball Brown

Thomas Brown
Racing Hometown: Atlanta, GA

Year	Rank	Starts	Poles	1	2	3	4	5	6–10	Laps	Laps Led	Races Led	Miles	$
1958	NR	2	0	0	0	0	0	0	0	104	0	0	99	50
Lifetime		2	0	0	0	0	0	0	0	104	0	0	99	$50

Chester Brown

Chester Brown
Racing Hometown: Greenville, SC

Year	Rank	Starts	Poles	1	2	3	4	5	6–10	Laps	Laps Led	Races Led	Miles	$
1955	NR	1	0	0	0	0	0	0	0	20	0	0	10	0
Lifetime		1	0	0	0	0	0	0	0	20	0	0	10	$0

Ed Brown

Edwin Brown
B: 3/15/1920
Racing Hometown: Merridian, CA

Year	Rank	Starts	Poles	1	2	3	4	5	6–10	Laps	Laps Led	Races Led	Miles	$
1955	53	4	0	0	0	0	0	0	2	584	44	1	488	450
1956	244	1	0	0	0	0	0	0	0	72	0	0	180	55
1957	142	1	0	0	0	0	0	0	0	52	0	0	130	115
1961	151	1	0	0	0	0	0	0	0	74	0	0	74	50
1965	64	1	0	0	0	0	0	0	0	151	0	0	408	605
1968	88	1	0	0	0	0	0	0	0	73	0	0	197	615
Lifetime		9	0	0	0	0	0	0	2	1,006	44	1	1,477	$1,890

Len Brown

Leonard Brown
Racing Hometown: Lambertville, NJ

Year	Rank	Starts	Poles	1	2	3	4	5	6–10	Laps	Laps Led	Races Led	Miles	$
1949	NR	1	0	0	0	0	0	0	0	158	0	0	158	25
1950	81	3	0	0	0	0	0	0	0	290	0	0	205	175
1951	N/A	1	0	0	0	0	0	0	0		0	0		10
Lifetime		5	0	0	0	0	0	0	0	448	0	0	363	$210

Merritt Brown

Merritt L. Brown
Racing Hometown: Daytona Beach, FL

Year	Rank	Starts	Poles	1	2	3	4	5	6–10	Laps	Laps Led	Races Led	Miles	$
1952	169	1	0	0	0	0	0	0	0	28	0	0	35	0
1953	NR	1	0	0	0	0	0	0	0	20	0	0	28	100
Lifetime		2	0	0	0	0	0	0	0	48	0	0	63	$100

Mike Brown

Mike A. Brown (Nick)
Racing Hometown: Royal Oak, MI

Year	Rank	Starts	Poles	1	2	3	4	5	6–10	Laps	Laps Led	Races Led	Miles	$
1954	122	2	0	0	0	0	0	0	0	149	0	0	201	50
Lifetime		2	0	0	0	0	0	0	0	149	0	0	201	$50

Perk Brown

Real Name: Jack B. Thomasson
B: 2/10/1925
Racing Hometown: Spray, NC

Year	Rank	Starts	Poles	1	2	3	4	5	6–10	Laps	Laps Led	Races Led	Miles	$
1952	13	19	1	0	0	2	0	1	3	2,336	0	0	1,458	2,187
1953	NR	2	0	0	0	0	0	0	0	14	0	0	57	25
1954	115	3	0	0	0	0	0	0	0	346	0	0	212	75
1955	131	2	0	0	0	0	0	0	1	275	0	0	138	150
1963	112	2	0	0	0	0	0	0	1	233	0	0	69	300
Lifetime		28	1	0	0	2	0	1	5	3,204	0	0	1,933	$2,360

Richard Brown

Richard Brown
Racing Hometown: Los Angeles, CA

Year	Rank	Starts	Poles	1	2	3	4	5	6–10	Laps	Laps Led	Races Led	Miles	$
1954	NR	1	0	0	0	0	0	0	0	118	0	0	59	0
1963	77	1	0	0	0	0	0	0	0	166	0	0	448	425
Lifetime		2	0	0	0	0	0	0	0	284	0	0	507	$425

Year	Rank	Starts	Poles	Finish						Laps	Laps Led	Races Led	Miles	$
				1	2	3	4	5	6–10					

Richard Brown

Richard D. Brown
B: 4/9/1940
Racing Hometown: Claremont, NC

Year	Rank	Starts	Poles	1	2	3	4	5	6–10	Laps	Laps Led	Races Led	Miles	$
1971	35	13	0	0	0	0	0	0	2	2,454	0	0	3,080	11,940
1972	29	16	0	0	0	0	0	1	0	3,403	0	0	4,190	20,233
1973	47	13	0	0	0	0	0	0	0	1,260	0	0	771	7,340
1974	133	1	0	0	0	0	0	0	0	51	0	0	51	595
1975	63	4	0	0	0	0	0	0	0	365	0	0	218	1,660
1976	66	3	0	0	0	0	0	0	0	591	0	0	340	1,310
Lifetime		50	0	0	0	0	0	1	2	8,124	0	0	8,650	$43,078

Robert Brown

Robert Sydney Brown (Bob)
B: 7/4/1943
Racing Hometown: Milan, TN

Year	Rank	Starts	Poles	1	2	3	4	5	6–10	Laps	Laps Led	Races Led	Miles	$
1971	61	5	0	0	0	0	0	0	0	462	0	0	335	1,335
1972	103	2	0	0	0	0	0	0	0	324	0	0	175	710
1973	106	2	0	0	0	0	0	0	0	353	0	0	210	590
Lifetime		9	0	0	0	0	0	0	0	1,139	0	0	721	$2,635

Woody Brown

Woodward Brown
Racing Hometown: Oakland, CA

Year	Rank	Starts	Poles	1	2	3	4	5	6–10	Laps	Laps Led	Races Led	Miles	$
1951	32	3	0	0	0	1	0	1	0	14	0	0	7	1,225
1954	60	4	0	0	0	0	0	0	0	991	0	0	613	175
Lifetime		7	0	0	0	1	0	1	0	1,005	0	0	620	$1,400

Richard Brownlee

Richard Brownlee
Racing Hometown: Greensboro, NC

Year	Rank	Starts	Poles	1	2	3	4	5	6–10	Laps	Laps Led	Races Led	Miles	$
1954	NR	1	0	0	0	0	0	0	0	74	0	0	37	25
1955	57	7	0	0	0	0	0	0	0	681	0	0	359	315
Lifetime		8	0	0	0	0	0	0	0	755	0	0	396	$340

Rodney Bruce

Rodney Bruce
Racing Hometown: Hampton, VA

Year	Rank	Starts	Poles	1	2	3	4	5	6–10	Laps	Laps Led	Races Led	Miles	$
1970	NR	1	0	0	0	0	0	0	0	261	0	0	103	225
Lifetime		1	0	0	0	0	0	0	0	261	0	0	103	$225

Laird Bruner

Laird Bruner
Racing Hometown: Rockwood, PA

Year	Rank	Starts	Poles	1	2	3	4	5	6–10	Laps	Laps Led	Races Led	Miles	$
1953	152	1	0	0	0	0	0	0	0	142	0	0	195	105
1954	14	24	0	0	0	0	0	2	4	3,052	0	0	2,338	2,080
Lifetime		25	0	0	0	0	0	2	4	3,194	0	0	2,533	$2,080

Andy Bruni

Andrew Bruni
Racing Hometown: Grand Rapids, MI

Year	Rank	Starts	Poles	1	2	3	4	5	6–10	Laps	Laps Led	Races Led	Miles	$
1954	NR	1	0	0	0	0	0	0	0	34	0	0	17	0
Lifetime		1	0	0	0	0	0	0	0	34	0	0	17	$0

Darrell Bryant

Darrell Bryant
B: 10/6/1940
Racing Hometown: Thomasville, NC

Year	Rank	Starts	Poles	1	2	3	4	5	6–10	Laps	Laps Led	Races Led	Miles	$
1964	95	5	0	0	0	0	0	0	1	366	0	0	177	725
1965	91	3	0	0	0	0	0	0	0	102	0	0	69	755
1966	100	2	0	0	0	0	0	0	0	243	0	0	139	670
1976	47	8	0	0	0	0	0	0	1	1,678	0	0	2,105	11,925
Lifetime		18	0	0	0	0	0	0	2	2,389	0	0	2,490	$13,925

Kirk Bryant

Kirk Bryant
B: 4/27/1962
Racing Hometown: Thomasville, NC

Year	Rank	Starts	Poles	1	2	3	4	5	6–10	Laps	Laps Led	Races Led	Miles	$
1986	58	4	0	0	0	0	0	0	0	842	0	0	978	26,335
1987	95	1	0	0	0	0	0	0	0	205	0	0	208	3,015
Lifetime		5	0	0	0	0	0	0	0	1,047	0	0	1,187	$29,350

Year	Rank	Starts	Poles	Finish						Laps	Laps Led	Races Led	Miles	$
				1	2	3	4	5	6–10	Laps	Led	Led	Miles	$

Herschel Buchanan

Herschel Buchanan
B: 1908
Racing Hometown: Shreveport, LA

Year	Rank	Starts	Poles	1	2	3	4	5	6–10	Laps	Laps Led	Races Led	Miles	$
1950	53	2	0	0	0	0	0	0	1	3	0	0	13	200
1951	N/A	1	0	0	0	0	0	0	0		0	0		0
1952	16	5	0	0	0	1	1	2	1	1,302	0	0	1,068	2,468
1953	NR	14	0	0	0	1	2	1	2	506	0	0	456	2,050
1954	53	1	0	0	0	0	0	1	0	160	0	0	240	500
Lifetime		23	0	0	0	2	3	4	4	1,971	0	0	1,776	$4,950

Julian Buesink

Julian Buesink
B: 1910
Racing Hometown: Findlay Park, NY

Year	Rank	Starts	Poles	1	2	3	4	5	6–10	Laps	Laps Led	Races Led	Miles	$
1951	N/A	1	0	0	0	0	0	0	0		0	0		0
Lifetime		1	0	0	0	0	0	0	0		0	0		$0

Andy Buffington

Andrew Buffington
Racing Hometown: Forrest Park, GA

Year	Rank	Starts	Poles	1	2	3	4	5	6–10	Laps	Laps Led	Races Led	Miles	$
1964	106	1	0	0	0	0	0	0	1	173	0	0	87	175
Lifetime		1	0	0	0	0	0	0	1	173	0	0	87	$175

George Bumgardner

George Bumgardner
Racing Hometown: Sarasota Springs, NY

Year	Rank	Starts	Poles	1	2	3	4	5	6–10	Laps	Laps Led	Races Led	Miles	$
1957	NR	1	0	0	0	0	0	0	0	111	0	0	111	100
Lifetime		1	0	0	0	0	0	0	0	111	0	0	111	$100

Paul Bumhaver

Paul Bumhaver
Racing Hometown: Mansfield, OH

Year	Rank	Starts	Poles	1	2	3	4	5	6–10	Laps	Laps Led	Races Led	Miles	$
1966	108	2	0	0	0	0	0	0	0	548	0	0	274	500
Lifetime		2	0	0	0	0	0	0	0	548	0	0	274	$500

Hully Bunn

Hully Bunn
B: 4/14/1920
Racing Hometown: Bristol, CT

Year	Rank	Starts	Poles	1	2	3	4	5	6–10	Laps	Laps Led	Races Led	Miles	$
1951	N/A	1	0	0	0	0	0	0	0		0	0		25
Lifetime		1	0	0	0	0	0	0	0		0	0		$25

Ann Bunselmeyer

Ann Bunselmeyer
Racing Hometown: Elmsford, NY

Year	Rank	Starts	Poles	1	2	3	4	5	6–10	Laps	Laps Led	Races Led	Miles	$
1950	126T	1	0	0	0	0	0	0	0		0	0		0
Lifetime		1	0	0	0	0	0	0	0		0	0		$0

Clarence Burch

Clarence Burch
Racing Hometown: Durham, NC

Year	Rank	Starts	Poles	1	2	3	4	5	6–10	Laps	Laps Led	Races Led	Miles	$
1954	194	1	0	0	0	0	0	0	0	58	0	0	58	50
Lifetime		1	0	0	0	0	0	0	0	58	0	0	58	$50

Bob Burcham

Robert Burcham
B: 8/22/1935
Racing Hometown: Rossville, GA

Year	Rank	Starts	Poles	1	2	3	4	5	6–10	Laps	Laps Led	Races Led	Miles	$
1968	103	2	0	0	0	0	0	0	0	366	0	0	183	515
1969	NR	1	0	0	0	0	0	0	0	2	0	0	5	900
1974	24	20	0	0	0	0	1	0	4	4,819	2	1	6,405	27,923
1975	55	3	0	0	0	0	0	0	0	733	0	0	1,289	6,895
1976	55	5	0	0	0	0	0	0	0	621	0	0	1,108	6,465
1977	68	2	0	0	0	0	0	0	1	408	0	0	808	13,825
1978	86T	1	0	0	0	0	0	0	0	243	0	0	332	2,790
1979	65	2	0	0	0	0	0	0	0	356	0	0	826	6,565
Lifetime		36	0	0	0	0	1	0	5	7,548	2	1	10,955	$65,878

Year	Rank	Starts	Poles	Finish 1	2	3	4	5	6–10	Laps	Laps Led	Races Led	Miles	$

Bob Burdick

Robert Burdick
B: 10/20/1936
Racing Hometown: Omaha, NE

Year	Rank	Starts	Poles	1	2	3	4	5	6–10	Laps	Laps Led	Races Led	Miles	$
1959	21	6	2	0	1	0	0	0	3	912	25	1	1,000	10,050
1960	93	2	0	0	0	0	0	0	1	71	0	0	178	850
1961	36	5	0	1	0	0	1	0	1	1,086	44	2	1,798	18,750
1962	85	2	0	0	0	0	0	0	1	95	0	0	238	625
Lifetime		15	2	1	1	0	1	0	6	2,164	69	3	3,213	$29,900

Bud Burdick

Bud Burdick
Racing Hometown: Omaha, NE

Year	Rank	Starts	Poles	1	2	3	4	5	6–10	Laps	Laps Led	Races Led	Miles	$
1960	48	2	0	0	0	0	0	0	1	236	0	0	590	750
Lifetime		2	0	0	0	0	0	0	1	236	0	0	590	$750

Marvin Burke

Marvin Burke
Racing Hometown: Pittsburg, CA

Year	Rank	Starts	Poles	1	2	3	4	5	6–10	Laps	Laps Led	Races Led	Miles	$
1951	N/A	1	0	1	0	0	0	0	0	250	156	1	156	1,875
Lifetime		1	0	1	0	0	0	0	0	250	156	1	156	$1,875

Gordon Burkett

Gordon Burkett
Racing Hometown: Huntington, WV

Year	Rank	Starts	Poles	1	2	3	4	5	6–10	Laps	Laps Led	Races Led	Miles	$
1971	78	1	0	0	0	0	0	0	0	220	0	0	100	360
Lifetime		1	0	0	0	0	0	0	0	220	0	0	100	$360

Bob Burkhart

Robert Burkhart

Year	Rank	Starts	Poles	1	2	3	4	5	6–10	Laps	Laps Led	Races Led	Miles	$
1950	NR	1	0	0	0	0	0	0	0		0	0		0
Lifetime		1	0	0	0	0	0	0	0		0	0		$0

Charles Burnett

Charles Burnett
Racing Hometown: Warner Robbins, GA

Year	Rank	Starts	Poles	1	2	3	4	5	6–10	Laps	Laps Led	Races Led	Miles	$
1968	66	2	0	0	0	0	0	0	0	215	0	0	469	1,765
Lifetime		2	0	0	0	0	0	0	0	215	0	0	469	$1,765

Frank Burnett

Frank Burnett
Racing Hometown: Modesto, CA

Year	Rank	Starts	Poles	1	2	3	4	5	6–10	Laps	Laps Led	Races Led	Miles	$
1967	93	1	0	0	0	0	0	0	0	60	0	0	162	500
1968	85	1	0	0	0	0	0	0	0	92	0	0	248	640
1969	NR	1	0	0	0	0	0	0	0	80	0	0	216	785
Lifetime		3	0	0	0	0	0	0	0	232	0	0	626	$1,925

Jerry Burnett

Jerry Burnett
Racing Hometown: New Ellington, SC

Year	Rank	Starts	Poles	1	2	3	4	5	6–10	Laps	Laps Led	Races Led	Miles	$
1962	116T	1	0	0	0	0	0	0	0	143	0	0	57	75
Lifetime		1	0	0	0	0	0	0	0	143	0	0	57	$75

Dick Burns

Richard Burns
Racing Hometown: Braddock, PA

Year	Rank	Starts	Poles	1	2	3	4	5	6–10	Laps	Laps Led	Races Led	Miles	$
1950	18	8	0	0	0	0	1	1	1	323	0	0	162	780
1956	209T	1	0	0	0	0	0	0	0	148	0	0	74	50
Lifetime		9	0	0	0	0	1	1	1	471	0	0	236	$780

Herbert Burns

Herbert Burns
Racing Hometown: Tampa, FL

Year	Rank	Starts	Poles	1	2	3	4	5	6–10	Laps	Laps Led	Races Led	Miles	$
1950	58	2	0	0	0	0	0	0	2		0	0		150
Lifetime		2	0	0	0	0	0	0	2		0	0		$150

Carl Burris

Carl Burris
B: 1924
Racing Hometown: Leaksville, NC

Year	Rank	Starts	Poles	1	2	3	4	5	6–10	Laps	Laps Led	Races Led	Miles	$
1953	NR	2	0	0	0	0	0	1	0	194	0	0	97	225
1954	156T	1	0	0	0	0	0	0	0	150	0	0	75	0
1958	NR	4	0	0	0	0	0	0	1	502	0	0	257	375

Year	Rank	Starts	Poles	Finish 1	2	3	4	5	6–10	Laps	Laps Led	Races Led	Miles	$

Carl Burris *continued*

Year	Rank	Starts	Poles	1	2	3	4	5	6–10	Laps	Laps Led	Races Led	Miles	$
1959	113	1	0	0	0	0	0	0	0	2	0	0	3	150
1960	143	2	0	0	0	0	0	0	0	81	0	0	151	200
Lifetime		10	0	0	0	0	0	1	1	929	0	0	582	$950

Clarence Burris

Clarence Burris
Racing Hometown: Heidelberg, PA

1949	53	1	0	0	0	0	0	0	0	165	0	0	83	50
Lifetime		1	0	0	0	0	0	0	0	165	0	0	83	$50

Bill Burton

William Burton
Racing Hometown: Marcy, NY

1950	129T	1	0	0	0	0	0	0	0		0	0		0
Lifetime		1	0	0	0	0	0	0	0		0	0		$0

Jeff Burton

Jeff Burton
B: 6/29/1967
Racing Hometown: South Boston, VA

1993	83T	1	0	0	0	0	0	0	0	86	0	0	91	9,550
1994	24	30	0	0	0	0	2	0	1	7,752	122	4	10,225	594,700
1995	32	29	0	0	0	0	0	1	1	8,050	4	2	10,193	628,270
1996	13	30	1	0	0	1	3	2	6	8,592	210	7	10,551	884,303
Lifetime		90	1	0	0	1	5	3	8	24,480	336	13	31,059	$2,116,823

Ward Burton

Ward Burton
B: 10/25/1961
Racing Hometown: South Boston, VA

1994	35	26	1	0	1	0	0	0	1	5,230	74	5	6,180	304,700
1995	22	29	0	1	0	0	1	1	3	7,744	173	4	9,889	634,655
1996	33	27	1	0	0	0	0	0	4	6,544	54	4	8,845	873,619
Lifetime		82	2	1	1	0	1	1	8	19,518	301	13	24,913	$1,812,974

George Bush

George Bush
Racing Hometown: Hamburg, NY

1952	52	5	0	0	0	0	0	0	3	598	0	0	488	330
Lifetime		5	0	0	0	0	0	0	3	598	0	0	488	$330

Darrell Busham

Darrell Busham
Racing Hometown: Jeffersonville, IN

1979	NR	1	0	0	0	0	0	0	0	101	0	0	60	385
Lifetime		1	0	0	0	0	0	0	0	101	0	0	60	$385

Bill Butts

William Butts
B: 9/3/1937
Racing Hometown: El Cajon, CA

1972	76	2	0	0	0	0	0	0	0	313	0	0	798	3,060
Lifetime		2	0	0	0	0	0	0	0	313	0	0	798	$3,060

Terry Byers

Terry Byers
B: 1/23/1950
Racing Hometown: Wollongong, NSW, Australia

1989	49	3	0	0	0	0	0	0	0	773	0	0	1,554	15,400
1990	103	2	0	0	0	0	0	0	0	41	0	0	63	7,525
1995	—	0												2,700
Lifetime		5	0	0	0	0	0	0	0	814	0	0	1,616	$25,625

Danny Byrd

Daniel Byrd
B: 8/3/1937
Racing Hometown: Taylor, MI

1965	85	4	0	0	0	0	0	1	0	294	0	0	210	1,075
Lifetime		4	0	0	0	0	0	1	0	294	0	0	210	$1,075

Year	Rank	Starts	Poles	Finish						Laps	Laps Led	Races Led	Miles	$
				1	2	3	4	5	6–10	Laps	Led	Led	Miles	$

Jim Byrd

James Byrd
Racing Hometown: Los Angeles, CA

Year	Rank	Starts	Poles	1	2	3	4	5	6–10	Laps	Laps Led	Races Led	Miles	$
1951	N/A	3	0	0	0	0	0	0	1		0	0		150
Lifetime		3	0	0	0	0	0	0	1		0	0		$150

Red Byron

Robert N. Byron Jr.
B: 3/12/1915   D: 11/11/1960   *Died in hotel @ Chicago.*
Racing Hometown: Anniston, AL

Year	Rank	Starts	Poles	1	2	3	4	5	6–10	Laps	Laps Led	Races Led	Miles	$
1949	1	6	1	2	0	2	0	0	0	633	103	2	**582**	5,800
1950	NR	4	1	0	1	1	1	0	0	634	85	3	835	3,325
1951	NR	5	0	0	0	0	1	0	1	609	0	0	701	975
Lifetime		15	2	2	1	3	2	0	1	1,876	188	5	2,117	$10,100

Scotty Cain

Scott Cain
B: 8/11/1920
Racing Hometown: Venice, CA

Year	Rank	Starts	Poles	1	2	3	4	5	6–10	Laps	Laps Led	Races Led	Miles	$
1956	41	4	0	0	0	0	0	1	3	701	0	0	698	1,235
1957	32	11	0	0	0	0	3	0	4	1,151	0	0	782	2,005
1958	NR	1	0	0	0	0	0	0	1	176	0	0	463	275
1959	79	2	0	0	1	0	0	0	0	467	0	0	247	700
1960	79	4	0	0	1	1	0	0	0	351	19	1	324	1,225
1961	91	4	0	0	0	0	0	0	1	218	0	0	335	705
1963	84	2	0	0	0	0	0	0	0	229	0	0	618	575
1965	57	1	0	0	0	0	0	0	1	172	0	0	464	1,175
1966	127	1	0	0	0	0	0	0	0	20	0	0	54	525
1967	49	1	0	0	0	0	0	0	1	171	0	0	462	1,400
1968	74	1	0	0	0	0	0	0	1	167	0	0	451	1,150
1969	63	1	0	0	0	0	0	0	1	170	0	0	459	1,450
1970	111	2	0	0	0	0	0	0	0	60	0	0	157	1,495
1971	NR	1	0	0	0	0	0	0	1	143	0	0	375	1,270
Lifetime		36	0	0	2	1	3	1	14	4,196	19	1	5,888	$15,185

Leo Caldwell

Leo Caldwell
B: 1926
Racing Hometown: Perrysburg, OH

Year	Rank	Starts	Poles	1	2	3	4	5	6–10	Laps	Laps Led	Races Led	Miles	$
1950	84T	1	0	0	0	0	0	0	0		0	0		50
1951	NR	1	0	0	0	0	0	0	0		0	0		25
1952	87	2	0	0	0	0	0	0	0		0	0		75
Lifetime		4	0	0	0	0	0	0	0		0	0		$150

Hal Callentine

Hal Callentine
Racing Hometown: Palo Cedro, CA

Year	Rank	Starts	Poles	1	2	3	4	5	6–10	Laps	Laps Led	Races Led	Miles	$
1979	104T	2	0	0	0	0	0	0	0	279	0	0	708	4,065
Lifetime		2	0	0	0	0	0	0	0	279	0	0	708	$4,065

John Callis

John Callis
B: 5/31/1949
Racing Hometown: Orlando, FL

Year	Rank	Starts	Poles	1	2	3	4	5	6–10	Laps	Laps Led	Races Led	Miles	$
1980	91	2	0	0	0	0	0	0	0	464	0	0	472	1,500
1982	58	3	0	0	0	0	0	0	0	352	0	0	507	2,675
1983	72	2	0	0	0	0	0	0	0	525	0	0	671	2,775
Lifetime		7	0	0	0	0	0	0	0	1,341	0	0	1,649	$6,950

Bob Cameron

Robert Cameron
B: 12/18/1927
Racing Hometown: Kenmore, NY

Year	Rank	Starts	Poles	1	2	3	4	5	6–10	Laps	Laps Led	Races Led	Miles	$
1949	62T	1	0	0	0	0	0	0	0		0	0		50
1953	NR	1	0	0	0	0	0	0	1		0	0		150
Lifetime		2	0	0	0	0	0	0	1		0	0		$200

Gordon Campbell

Gordon Campbell

Year	Rank	Starts	Poles	1	2	3	4	5	6–10	Laps	Laps Led	Races Led	Miles	$
1956	171	1	0	0	0	0	0	0	0	74	0	0	185	75
Lifetime		1	0	0	0	0	0	0	0	74	0	0	185	$75

Year	Rank	Starts	Poles	Finish						Laps	Laps Led	Races Led	Miles	$
				1	2	3	4	5	6–10	Laps	Led	Led	Miles	$

Kim Campbell

Kim Campbell

Year	Rank	Starts	Poles	1	2	3	4	5	6–10	Laps	Laps Led	Races Led	Miles	$
1991	79	1	0	0	0	0	0	0	0	64	0	0	155	3,725
Lifetime		1	0	0	0	0	0	0	0	64	0	0	155	$3,725

Ray Campbell

Raymond Campbell
Racing Hometown: Tonawanda, NY

Year	Rank	Starts	Poles	1	2	3	4	5	6–10	Laps	Laps Led	Races Led	Miles	$
1957	NR	1	0	0	0	0	0	0	0	77	0	0	77	135
1958	134T	1	0	0	0	0	0	0	0	150	0	0	75	70
Lifetime		2	0	0	0	0	0	0	0	227	0	0	152	$205

Wally Campbell

Wally Campbell
B: 7/16/1926   D: 7/17/1954   *Killed in sprint car @ Salem, IN, during practice.*
Racing Hometown: Trenton, NJ

Year	Rank	Starts	Poles	1	2	3	4	5	6–10	Laps	Laps Led	Races Led	Miles	$
1949	NR	1	0	0	0	0	0	0	0	166	0	0	166	25
1950	NR	2	1	0	0	0	0	0	0	309	0	0	386	175
1951	NR	5	0	0	0	0	0	0	0	21	0	0	11	85
1953	NR	3	0	0	0	0	0	0	0	4	0	0	16	50
Lifetime		11	1	0	0	0	0	0	0	500	0	0	579	$335

Ed Camrud

Edward Camrud
Racing Hometown: Phoenix, AZ

Year	Rank	Starts	Poles	1	2	3	4	5	6–10	Laps	Laps Led	Races Led	Miles	$
1951	N/A	1	0	0	0	0	0	0	1		0	0		100
Lifetime		1	0	0	0	0	0	0	1		0	0		$100

Frank Canale

Frank Canale
Racing Hometown: Toledo, OH

Year	Rank	Starts	Poles	1	2	3	4	5	6–10	Laps	Laps Led	Races Led	Miles	$
1950	NR	1	0	0	0	0	0	0	0	74	0	0	37	0
Lifetime		1	0	0	0	0	0	0	0	74	0	0	37	$0

Earle Canavan

Earle Samuel Canavan
B: 12/5/1938
Racing Hometown: Ft. Johnson, NY

Year	Rank	Starts	Poles	1	2	3	4	5	6–10	Laps	Laps Led	Races Led	Miles	$
1969	NR	1	0	0	0	0	0	0	0	62	0	0	165	1,100
1971	63	5	0	0	0	0	0	0	0	375	0	0	483	2,530
1972	62	7	0	0	0	0	0	0	0	777	0	0	1,027	5,858
1973	41	5	0	0	0	0	0	0	0	1,223	0	0	1,674	4,980
1974	46	6	0	0	0	0	0	0	0	1,477	0	0	2,106	6,915
1975	32	12	0	0	0	0	0	0	0	1,601	0	0	1,861	9,725
1976	43	7	0	0	0	0	0	0	0	1,687	0	0	1,609	6,035
1977	56	5	0	0	0	0	0	0	0	646	0	0	783	4,390
1978	42	9	0	0	0	0	0	0	0	2,111	0	0	2,451	8,865
1979	41	7	0	0	0	0	0	0	0	698	0	0	1,032	6,675
1982	102	2	0	0	0	0	0	0	0	76	0	0	108	2,380
1985	91T	1	0	0	0	0	0	0	0	53	0	0	53	875
1986	114T	1	0	0	0	0	0	0	0	165	0	0	168	1,475
Lifetime		68	0	0	0	0	0	0	0	10,951	0	0	13,521	$61,803

Ted Cannady

Theodore H. Cannady
Racing Hometown: Collinsville, VA

Year	Rank	Starts	Poles	1	2	3	4	5	6–10	Laps	Laps Led	Races Led	Miles	$
1955	45	9	0	0	0	0	0	0	0	812	0	0	705	450
1956	92	6	0	0	0	0	0	0	0	814	0	0	484	260
Lifetime		15	0	0	0	0	0	0	0	1,626	0	0	1,189	$710

Ben Cannaziaro

Benjamin Cannaziaro
B: 5/17/1910
Racing Hometown: Trenton, NJ

Year	Rank	Starts	Poles	1	2	3	4	5	6–10	Laps	Laps Led	Races Led	Miles	$
1949	NR	1	0	0	0	0	0	0	0	159	0	0	159	25
Lifetime		1	0	0	0	0	0	0	0	159	0	0	159	$25

Billy Cantrell

William Cantrell
B: 1915
Racing Hometown: Anaheim, CA

Year	Rank	Starts	Poles	1	2	3	4	5	6–10	Laps	Laps Led	Races Led	Miles	$
1957	122	1	0	0	0	0	0	0	0	53	0	0	133	110

Year	Rank	Starts	Poles	Finish 1	2	3	4	5	6–10	Laps	Laps Led	Races Led	Miles	$

Billy Cantrell *continued*

Year	Rank	Starts	Poles	1	2	3	4	5	6–10	Laps	Laps Led	Races Led	Miles	$
1965	NR	1	0	0	0	0	0	0	0	2	0	0	5	500
Lifetime		2	0	0	0	0	0	0	0	55	0	0	138	$610

Jimmy Lee Capps

Jimmy Lee Capps
B: 3/12/1938
Racing Hometown: Jacksonville, FL

Year	Rank	Starts	Poles	1	2	3	4	5	6–10	Laps	Laps Led	Races Led	Miles	$
1964	123	1	0	0	0	0	0	0	0	50	0	0	25	50
1976	54	4	0	0	0	0	0	0	1	505	0	0	1,229	6,950
1977	57	3	0	0	0	0	0	0	0	815	0	0	1,097	4,800
1978	63	3	0	0	0	0	0	0	0	586	0	0	701	3,880
Lifetime		11	0	0	0	0	0	0	1	1,956	0	0	3,052	$15,680

John Capps

John Capps
Racing Hometown: Greensboro, NC

Year	Rank	Starts	Poles	1	2	3	4	5	6–10	Laps	Laps Led	Races Led	Miles	$
1955	NR	1	0	0	0	0	0	0	0	17	0	0	17	25
Lifetime		1	0	0	0	0	0	0	0	17	0	0	17	$25

Carl Carday

Carl Carday

Year	Rank	Starts	Poles	1	2	3	4	5	6–10	Laps	Laps Led	Races Led	Miles	$
1966	NR	1	0	0	0	0	0	0	0	119	0	0	321	530
1967	NR	1	0	0	0	0	0	0	0	0	0	0	0	500
Lifetime		2	0	0	0	0	0	0	0	119	0	0	321	$1,030

Billy Carden

William Carden
B: 4/1/1924
Racing Hometown: Mableton, GA

Year	Rank	Starts	Poles	1	2	3	4	5	6–10	Laps	Laps Led	Races Led	Miles	$
1949	72	1	0	0	0	0	0	0	0		0	0		50
1950	93	3	0	0	0	0	0	0	0	368	0	0	548	75
1951	26	11	3	0	0	1	1	0	3	519	58	1	613	1,535
1952	74	3	0	0	0	0	0	0	0	186	0	0	93	50
1955	31	13	0	0	0	0	2	0	1	1,589	0	0	1,168	1,340
1956	22	23	0	0	0	0	0	0	4	2,831	0	0	1,881	2,175
1957	29	3	0	0	0	0	0	0	2	625	0	0	751	1,675
1958	38	13	0	0	0	0	0	0	2	1,469	0	0	804	1,215
1959	NR	3	0	0	0	0	0	0	1	364	0	0	574	375
Lifetime		73	3	0	0	1	3	0	13	7,951	58	1	6,432	$8,490

Pete Cardenas

Peter Cardenas
Racing Hometown: Long Beach, CA

Year	Rank	Starts	Poles	1	2	3	4	5	6–10	Laps	Laps Led	Races Led	Miles	$
1957	201T	1	0	0	0	0	0	0	0	9	0	0	9	0
Lifetime		1	0	0	0	0	0	0	0	9	0	0	9	$0

Rick Carelli

Richard Carelli
B: 11/9/1955
Racing Hometown: Arvada, CO

Year	Rank	Starts	Poles	1	2	3	4	5	6–10	Laps	Laps Led	Races Led	Miles	$
1992	74	2	0	0	0	0	0	0	0	58	0	0	145	9,005
1993	49	3	0	0	0	0	0	0	0	499	0	0	671	19,650
1994	49	4	0	0	0	0	0	0	0	958	0	0	1,165	33,675
Lifetime		9	0	0	0	0	0	0	0	1,515	0	0	1,980	$62,330

Frank Carlin

Frank Carlin

Year	Rank	Starts	Poles	1	2	3	4	5	6–10	Laps	Laps Led	Races Led	Miles	$
1951	N/A	1	0	0	0	0	0	0	0	0	0	0	0	0
Lifetime		1	0	0	0	0	0	0	0	0	0	0	0	$0

Harold Carmac

Harold Carmac
Racing Hometown: Ramseur, NC

Year	Rank	Starts	Poles	1	2	3	4	5	6–10	Laps	Laps Led	Races Led	Miles	$
1962	75	2	0	0	0	0	0	0	1	172	0	0	86	525
Lifetime		2	0	0	0	0	0	0	1	172	0	0	86	$525

Year	Rank	Starts	Poles	Finish						Laps	Laps Led	Races Led	Miles	$
				1	2	3	4	5	6–10	Laps	Led	Led	Miles	$

Bob Carpenter
Robert Carpenter
Racing Hometown: Wabash, IN

Year	Rank	Starts	Poles	1	2	3	4	5	6–10	Laps	Laps Led	Races Led	Miles	$
1951	N/A	1	0	0	0	0	0	0	0		0	0		25
Lifetime		1	0	0	0	0	0	0	0		0	0		$25

Erwin Carpenter
Erwin Carpenter
Racing Hometown: Rock Hill, SC

Year	Rank	Starts	Poles	1	2	3	4	5	6–10	Laps	Laps Led	Races Led	Miles	$
1959	NR	1	0	0	0	0	0	0	0	299	0	0	150	75
Lifetime		1	0	0	0	0	0	0	0	299	0	0	150	$75

Don Carr
Donald Carr
Racing Hometown: Detroit, MI

Year	Rank	Starts	Poles	1	2	3	4	5	6–10	Laps	Laps Led	Races Led	Miles	$
1956	129	5	0	0	0	0	0	0	0	499	0	0	364	210
Lifetime		5	0	0	0	0	0	0	0	499	0	0	364	$210

Jack Carr
Jack Carr
Racing Hometown: Atlanta, GA

Year	Rank	Starts	Poles	1	2	3	4	5	6–10	Laps	Laps Led	Races Led	Miles	$
1950	NR	2	0	0	0	0	0	0	0	52	0	0	65	0
Lifetime		2	0	0	0	0	0	0	0	52	0	0	65	$0

Lee Roy Carrigg
Lee Roy Carrigg
B: 2/22/1942
Racing Hometown: Elloree, SC

Year	Rank	Starts	Poles	1	2	3	4	5	6–10	Laps	Laps Led	Races Led	Miles	$
1970	48	9	0	0	0	0	0	0	0	1,002	0	0	1,021	4,130
Lifetime		9	0	0	0	0	0	0	0	1,002	0	0	1,021	$4,130

Bob Carroll
Robert Carroll
Racing Hometown: Portland, OR

Year	Rank	Starts	Poles	1	2	3	4	5	6–10	Laps	Laps Led	Races Led	Miles	$
1956	NR	1	0	0	0	0	0	0	0	62	0	0	31	50
Lifetime		1	0	0	0	0	0	0	0	62	0	0	31	$50

Lynn Carroll
Lynn Carroll

Year	Rank	Starts	Poles	1	2	3	4	5	6–10	Laps	Laps Led	Races Led	Miles	$
1978	NR	1	0	0	0	0	0	0	0	445	0	0	237	650
Lifetime		1	0	0	0	0	0	0	0	445	0	0	237	$650

Jim Carrusso
James Carrusso
Racing Hometown: Sewickley, PA

Year	Rank	Starts	Poles	1	2	3	4	5	6–10	Laps	Laps Led	Races Led	Miles	$
1949	NR	2	0	0	0	0	0	0	0	67	0	0	34	25
Lifetime		2	0	0	0	0	0	0	0	67	0	0	34	$25

Hank Carruthers
Rankin Carruthers
Racing Hometown: Haw River, NC

Year	Rank	Starts	Poles	1	2	3	4	5	6–10	Laps	Laps Led	Races Led	Miles	$
1952	147T	1	0	0	0	0	0	0	0	18	0	0	18	25
Lifetime		1	0	0	0	0	0	0	0	18	0	0	18	$25

Crash Carson
Crash Carson

Year	Rank	Starts	Poles	1	2	3	4	5	6–10	Laps	Laps Led	Races Led	Miles	$
1955	227T	1	0	0	0	0	0	0	0	8	0	0	8	40
Lifetime		1	0	0	0	0	0	0	0	8	0	0	8	$40

Dick Carter
Richard Carter
B: 1935   D: 8/14/1965   *Killed @ Grand Rapids, MI, Super Modified race.*
Racing Hometown: San Leandro, CA

Year	Rank	Starts	Poles	1	2	3	4	5	6–10	Laps	Laps Led	Races Led	Miles	$
1954	132	3	0	0	0	0	0	0	0	376	0	0	265	65
1958	144	1	0	0	0	0	0	0	0	86	0	0	86	50
1959	115	2	0	0	0	0	0	0	0	269	0	0	131	125
1961	NR	1	0	0	0	0	0	0	0	119	0	0	167	100
Lifetime		7	0	0	0	0	0	0	0	850	0	0	649	$340

Year	Rank	Starts	Poles	Finish 1	2	3	4	5	6–10	Laps	Laps Led	Races Led	Miles	$

Duane Carter

Duane C. Carter
B: 5/5/1913   D: 3/7/1993
Racing Hometown: Fresno, CA

Year	Rank	Starts	Poles	1	2	3	4	5	6–10	Laps	Laps Led	Races Led	Miles	$
1950	56T	1	0	0	0	0	0	0	1		0	0		125
Lifetime		1	0	0	0	0	0	0	1		0	0		$125

Pancho Carter

Duane C. Carter Jr.
B: 6/11/1950
Racing Hometown: Brownsburg, IN

Year	Rank	Starts	Poles	1	2	3	4	5	6–10	Laps	Laps Led	Races Led	Miles	$
1985	NR	1	0	0	0	0	0	0	0	336	0	0	459	2,755
1986	38	9	0	0	0	0	0	0	0	1,423	3	2	2,689	56,355
1990	90	1	0	0	0	0	0	0	0	298	0	0	454	3,040
1992	82	1	0	0	0	0	0	0	0	297	0	0	446	3,735
1994	60	1	0	0	0	0	0	0	0	322	0	0	490	9,130
1995	63T	1	0	0	0	0	0	0	0	180	0	0	450	8,475
Lifetime		14	0	0	0	0	0	0	0	2,856	3	2	4,987	$83,490

Rags Carter

Allen Carter
B: 12/2/1928   D: 5/23/1993
Racing Hometown: Miami Springs, FL

Year	Rank	Starts	Poles	1	2	3	4	5	6–10	Laps	Laps Led	Races Led	Miles	$
1952	NR	1	0	0	0	0	0	0	1	183	0	0	92	150
Lifetime		1	0	0	0	0	0	0	1	183	0	0	92	$150

Raymond Carter

Raymond Carter
Racing Hometown: Henry, VA

Year	Rank	Starts	Poles	1	2	3	4	5	6–10	Laps	Laps Led	Races Led	Miles	$
1964	114T	1	0	0	0	0	0	0	0	37	0	0	12	100
1965	62	9	0	0	0	0	0	0	2	638	0	0	617	2,145
Lifetime		10	0	0	0	0	0	0	2	675	0	0	629	$2,245

Fats Caruso

Mario Caruso
D: 1993
Racing Hometown: Shrewsburg, NY

Year	Rank	Starts	Poles	1	2	3	4	5	6–10	Laps	Laps Led	Races Led	Miles	$
1966	114	1	0	0	0	0	0	0	0	167	0	0	56	130
1967	122	1	0	0	0	0	0	0	0	96	0	0	32	100
Lifetime		2	0	0	0	0	0	0	0	263	0	0	88	$230

Jerry Carver

Gerald Carver
Racing Hometown: Canfield, OH

Year	Rank	Starts	Poles	1	2	3	4	5	6–10	Laps	Laps Led	Races Led	Miles	$
1951	N/A	2	0	0	0	0	0	0	0		0	0		50
Lifetime		2	0	0	0	0	0	0	0		0	0		$50

Joe Carver

Joseph Carver

Year	Rank	Starts	Poles	1	2	3	4	5	6–10	Laps	Laps Led	Races Led	Miles	$
1951	N/A	1	0	0	0	0	0	0	0		0	0		25
Lifetime		1	0	0	0	0	0	0	0		0	0		$25

Walt Carver

Walter Carver

Year	Rank	Starts	Poles	1	2	3	4	5	6–10	Laps	Laps Led	Races Led	Miles	$
1952	NR	1	0	0	0	0	0	0	1	188	0	0	94	50
Lifetime		1	0	0	0	0	0	0	1	188	0	0	94	$50

Joe Caspolich

Joseph Caspolich
B: 1929
Racing Hometown: Gulfport, MS

Year	Rank	Starts	Poles	1	2	3	4	5	6–10	Laps	Laps Led	Races Led	Miles	$
1957	156	1	0	0	0	0	0	0	0	66	0	0	91	200
1959	44	1	0	0	0	0	0	0	0	342	0	0	470	470
1960	51	5	0	0	0	0	0	0	0	838	0	0	1,542	1,965
1961	160	1	0	0	0	0	0	0	0	50	0	0	69	200
Lifetime		8	0	0	0	0	0	0	0	1,296	0	0	2,172	$2,835

Neil Castles

Henry Neil Castles (Soapy)
B: 10/1/1934
Racing Hometown: Charlotte, NC

Year	Rank	Starts	Poles	1	2	3	4	5	6–10	Laps	Laps Led	Races Led	Miles	$
1957	123	5	0	0	0	0	0	0	0	492	0	0	359	475

Year	Rank	Starts	Poles	Finish						Laps	Laps Led	Races Led	Miles	$
				1	2	3	4	5	6–10	Laps	Led	Led	Miles	$

Neil Castles *continued*

Year	Rank	Starts	Poles	1	2	3	4	5	6–10	Laps	Laps Led	Races Led	Miles	$
1958	NR	15	0	0	0	0	0	0	0	1,797	0	0	993	805
1959	77	5	0	0	0	0	0	0	0	754	0	0	458	410
1960	145	18	0	0	0	0	0	0	5	2,293	0	0	1,162	2,125
1962	NR	8	0	0	0	0	0	0	1	547	0	0	240	620
1963	31	28	0	0	0	0	1	1	6	4,093	0	0	2,330	5,590
1964	17	58	0	0	0	0	0	1	23	8,336	0	0	4,158	14,318
1965	8	51	0	0	0	1	1	4	22	9,768	0	0	6,555	22,329
1966	9	41	0	0	1	1	3	2	10	8,824	0	0	6,126	19,035
1967	8	36	0	0	0	0	2	2	12	7,140	0	0	5,749	21,283
1968	12	44	0	0	0	2	1	1	11	9,082	0	0	5,455	19,507
1969	4	51	0	0	2	1	4	6	16	12,661	29	1	10,290	54,367
1970	5	47	0	0	1	4	3	4	12	10,297	31	2	9,154	49,746
1971	22	38	0	0	0	0	1	0	9	6,946	10	1	5,620	22,939
1972	30	21	0	0	0	0	0	0	1	4,075	0	0	3,936	18,985
1973	55	8	0	0	0	0	0	0	0	869	0	0	803	7,074
1974	37	14	0	0	0	0	0	0	0	1,422	0	0	1,303	12,479
1975	43	7	0	0	0	0	0	0	0	578	0	0	513	4,510
1976	NR	2	0	0	0	0	0	0	0	147	0	0	100	930
Lifetime		497	0	0	4	9	16	21	128	90,121	70	4	65,304	$277,527

Robert Caswell

Robert E. Caswell (Bill)
Racing Hometown: Walnut Creek, CA

Year	Rank	Starts	Poles	1	2	3	4	5	6–10	Laps	Laps Led	Races Led	Miles	$
1951	40	3	0	0	1	0	0	0	0	247	0	0	154	1,325
1953	122T	1	0	0	0	0	0	0	0		0	0		25
1954	59	3	0	0	0	0	0	0	1	751	0	0	498	225
Lifetime		7	0	0	1	0	0	0	1	998	0	0	652	$1,550

Larry Caudill

Lawrence Caudill
B: 6/29/1948
Racing Hometown: N. Wilkesboro, NC

Year	Rank	Starts	Poles	1	2	3	4	5	6–10	Laps	Laps Led	Races Led	Miles	$
1987	NR	1	0	0	0	0	0	0	0	470	0	0	470	4,725
Lifetime		1	0	0	0	0	0	0	0	470	0	0	470	$4,725

Charlie Causey

Charles Causey
Racing Hometown: Rome, GA

Year	Rank	Starts	Poles	1	2	3	4	5	6–10	Laps	Laps Led	Races Led	Miles	$
1952	187	1	0	0	0	0	0	0	0	7	0	0	7	25
1953	104	3	0	0	0	0	0	0	0	35	0	0	144	50
Lifetime		4	0	0	0	0	0	0	0	42	0	0	151	$75

George Cavana

George A. Cavana
Racing Hometown: S. Glastonbury, CT

Year	Rank	Starts	Poles	1	2	3	4	5	6–10	Laps	Laps Led	Races Led	Miles	$
1951	N/A	1	0	0	0	0	0	0	0		0	0		50
Lifetime		1	0	0	0	0	0	0	0		0	0		$50

Don Cecchini

Donald Cecchini
Racing Hometown: Philadelphia, PA

Year	Rank	Starts	Poles	1	2	3	4	5	6–10	Laps	Laps Led	Races Led	Miles	$
1949	69	1	0	0	0	0	0	0	0	173	0	0	173	50
1950	NR	1	0	0	0	0	0	0	0		0	0		0
Lifetime		2	0	0	0	0	0	0	0	173	0	0	173	$50

Bud Chaddock

Bud Chaddock
Racing Hometown: Parkersburg, WV

Year	Rank	Starts	Poles	1	2	3	4	5	6–10	Laps	Laps Led	Races Led	Miles	$
1954	177	1	0	0	0	0	0	0	0	66	0	0	99	50
Lifetime		1	0	0	0	0	0	0	0	66	0	0	99	$50

Floyd Chaddock

Floyd Chaddock
Racing Hometown: Parkersburg, WV

Year	Rank	Starts	Poles	1	2	3	4	5	6–10	Laps	Laps Led	Races Led	Miles	$
1955	231	1	0	0	0	0	0	0	0	35	0	0	144	35
Lifetime		1	0	0	0	0	0	0	0	35	0	0	144	$35

Year	Rank	Starts	Poles	Finish						Laps	Laps Led	Races Led	Miles	$
				1	2	3	4	5	6–10					

Hank Chaffee

Hank Chaffee
Racing Hometown: Dundee, NY

Year	Rank	Starts	Poles	1	2	3	4	5	6–10	Laps	Laps Led	Races Led	Miles	$
1954	156T	1	0	0	0	0	0	0	0	157	0	0	79	0
Lifetime		1	0	0	0	0	0	0	0	157	0	0	79	$0

Ray Chaike

Ramon Chaike
Racing Hometown: Mt. Healthy, OH

Year	Rank	Starts	Poles	1	2	3	4	5	6–10	Laps	Laps Led	Races Led	Miles	$
1955	180	1	0	0	0	0	0	0	0	37	0	0	152	50
1956	74	3	0	0	0	0	0	0	0	554	0	0	339	225
Lifetime		4	0	0	0	0	0	0	0	591	0	0	491	$275

Gerald Chamberlain

Gerald Chamberlain
Racing Hometown: Everett, PA

Year	Rank	Starts	Poles	1	2	3	4	5	6–10	Laps	Laps Led	Races Led	Miles	$
1969	89	2	0	0	0	0	0	0	1	324	0	0	453	2,225
Lifetime		2	0	0	0	0	0	0	1	324	0	0	453	$2,225

Ted Chamberlain

Theodore Carl Chamberlain
B: 5/15/1906   D: 1968
Racing Hometown: St. Petersburg, FL

Year	Rank	Starts	Poles	1	2	3	4	5	6–10	Laps	Laps Led	Races Led	Miles	$
1949	44	2	0	0	0	0	0	0	0	148	0	0	74	100
1950	61	5	0	0	0	0	0	0	2	541	0	0	539	225
1951	N/A	3	0	0	0	0	0	0	1	340	0	0	425	175
1952	11	18	0	0	0	0	0	0	6	3,053	0	0	2,181	1,277
1953	26	9	0	0	0	0	0	0	3	572	0	0	442	500
1954	32	10	0	0	0	0	0	0	1	1,596	0	0	1,423	475
1955	227T	1	0	0	0	0	0	0	0	67	0	0	67	50
1957	NR	5	0	0	0	0	0	0	1	903	0	0	738	550
1958	51	9	0	0	0	0	0	0	1	809	0	0	403	680
1959	NR	1	0	0	0	0	0	0	0	68	0	0	17	50
Lifetime		63	0	0	0	0	0	0	15	8,097	0	0	6,309	$4,082

Charlie Chamblee

Charles Chamblee
Racing Hometown: Arab, AL

Year	Rank	Starts	Poles	1	2	3	4	5	6–10	Laps	Laps Led	Races Led	Miles	$
1980	NR	1	0	0	0	0	0	0	0	298	0	0	454	2,825
1981	NR	1	0	0	0	0	0	0	0	10	0	0	6	830
Lifetime		2	0	0	0	0	0	0	0	308	0	0	460	$3,655

Bill Champion

William Champion
B: 10/16/1921   D: 5/20/1991
Racing Hometown: Norfolk, VA

Year	Rank	Starts	Poles	1	2	3	4	5	6–10	Laps	Laps Led	Races Led	Miles	$
1951	N/A	1	0	0	0	0	0	0	1		0	0		50
1955	80	1	0	0	0	0	0	0	0	346	0	0	476	195
1956	31	14	0	0	0	0	0	0	4	2,297	0	0	1,626	1,570
1957	41	10	0	0	0	0	0	0	1	1,663	0	0	1,167	1,125
1959	43	1	0	0	0	0	0	0	0	343	0	0	472	500
1962	121	2	0	0	0	0	0	0	0	55	0	0	41	400
1965	116	1	0	0	0	0	0	0	0	109	0	0	36	100
1966	61	9	0	0	0	0	0	0	0	1,120	0	0	1,220	3,735
1967	44	11	0	0	0	0	0	0	0	1,889	0	0	2,027	6,205
1968	28	18	0	0	0	0	0	0	2	3,505	0	0	3,547	10,170
1969	12	49	0	0	0	0	0	1	9	10,582	0	0	9,254	33,656
1970	15	38	0	0	0	0	0	0	6	7,493	0	0	6,864	30,943
1971	7	45	0	0	0	0	0	3	11	10,518	0	0	9,714	43,769
1972	13	29	0	0	0	0	0	0	4	7,044	0	0	8,121	42,242
1973	21	26	0	0	0	0	0	0	1	5,103	0	0	6,364	32,138
1974	31	18	0	0	0	0	0	0	0	2,324	0	0	2,262	13,825
1975	31	13	0	0	0	0	0	0	0	2,690	0	0	2,777	12,400
1976	64	3	0	0	0	0	0	0	0	530	0	0	317	2,575
Lifetime		289	0	0	0	0	0	4	39	57,611	0	0	56,284	$235,598

Charlie Chapman

Charles Chapman
Racing Hometown: Compton, CA

Year	Rank	Starts	Poles	1	2	3	4	5	6–10	Laps	Laps Led	Races Led	Miles	$
1960	89	1	0	0	0	0	0	0	0	152	0	0	213	400
1961	81	6	0	0	0	0	0	0	0	702	0	0	515	610
Lifetime		7	0	0	0	0	0	0	0	854	0	0	727	$1,010

Hank Chapman

Hank Chapman
Racing Hometown: Aurora, IL

Year	Rank	Starts	Poles	1	2	3	4	5	6–10	Laps	Laps Led	Races Led	Miles	$
1957	182	1	0	0	0	0	0	0	0		0	0		25
Lifetime		1	0	0	0	0	0	0	0		0	0		$25

Johnny Chapman

Johnny Dale Chapman
B: 12/14/1967
Racing Hometown: Statesville, NC

Year	Rank	Starts	Poles	1	2	3	4	5	6–10	Laps	Laps Led	Races Led	Miles	$
1993	81T	1	0	0	0	0	0	0	0	368	0	0	374	9,126
1995	—	0												2,500
Lifetime		1	0	0	0	0	0	0	0	368	0	0	374	$11,626

J. R. Charbonneau

Jean R. Charbonneau

Year	Rank	Starts	Poles	1	2	3	4	5	6–10	Laps	Laps Led	Races Led	Miles	$
1982	NR	1	0	0	0	0	0	0	0	118	0	0	118	650
Lifetime		1	0	0	0	0	0	0	0	118	0	0	118	$650

Rene Charland

Joseph Maurice Charland
B: 11/13/1928
Racing Hometown: Agawam, MA

Year	Rank	Starts	Poles	1	2	3	4	5	6–10	Laps	Laps Led	Races Led	Miles	$
1964	119	1	0	0	0	0	0	0	0	9	0	0	2	100
1965	108	2	0	0	0	0	0	0	0	26	0	0	30	1,005
1966	83	5	0	0	0	1	0	0	0	452	0	0	185	1,590
1971	NR	1	0	0	0	0	0	0	0	33	0	0	12	100
Lifetime		9	0	0	0	1	0	0	0	520	0	0	229	$2,795

Mike Chase

Michael Chase
B: 4/17/1952
Racing Hometown: Bakersfield, CA

Year	Rank	Starts	Poles	1	2	3	4	5	6–10	Laps	Laps Led	Races Led	Miles	$
1990	57	3	0	0	0	0	0	0	0	340	4	1	647	11,500
1991	47	5	0	0	0	0	0	0	0	804	0	0	1,505	22,700
1992	84T	1	0	0	0	0	0	0	0	69	0	0	174	6,330
1993	87T	1	0	0	0	0	0	0	0	87	0	0	87	6,015
1994	56	3	0	0	0	0	0	0	0	463	0	0	706	38,190
Lifetime		13	0	0	0	0	0	0	0	1,763	4	1	3,119	$84,735

Ray Chase

Raymond Chase
Racing Hometown: Portland, OR

Year	Rank	Starts	Poles	1	2	3	4	5	6–10	Laps	Laps Led	Races Led	Miles	$
1951	N/A	6	0	0	0	0	0	0	0	354	0	0	399	100
1952	137	1	0	0	0	0	0	0	0	173	0	0	173	25
Lifetime		7	0	0	0	0	0	0	0	527	0	0	572	$125

Bob Chauncey

Robert Chauncey
Racing Hometown: Chicago, IL

Year	Rank	Starts	Poles	1	2	3	4	5	6–10	Laps	Laps Led	Races Led	Miles	$
1956	246T	1	0	0	0	0	0	0	0	78	0	0	39	50
Lifetime		1	0	0	0	0	0	0	0	78	0	0	39	$50

Tru Cheek

Truceson Burgess Cheek
B: 6/11/1937
Racing Hometown: Sylmar, CA

Year	Rank	Starts	Poles	1	2	3	4	5	6–10	Laps	Laps Led	Races Led	Miles	$
1971	NR	1	0	0	0	0	0	0	0	57	0	0	149	750
1972	NR	1	0	0	0	0	0	0	0	12	0	0	31	645
Lifetime		2	0	0	0	0	0	0	0	69	0	0	181	$1,395

Bill Cheesbourg

William Cheesbourg
B: 6/12/1927   D: 11/6/1995
Racing Hometown: Tucson, AZ

Year	Rank	Starts	Poles	1	2	3	4	5	6–10	Laps	Laps Led	Races Led	Miles	$
1951	N/A	2	0	0	0	0	0	0	0		0	0		50
Lifetime		2	0	0	0	0	0	0	0		0	0		$50

Tom Cherry

Thomas Cherry
B: 1911   D: 7/6/1990
Racing Hometown: Muncie, IN

Year	Rank	Starts	Poles	1	2	3	4	5	6–10	Laps	Laps Led	Races Led	Miles	$
1953	58	1	0	0	0	0	0	0	1	38	0	0	156	180
Lifetime		1	0	0	0	0	0	0	0	1	38	0	0	156	$180

Year	Rank	Starts	Poles	Finish 1	2	3	4	5	6–10	Laps	Laps Led	Races Led	Miles	$

Ann Chester

Ann Chester
Racing Hometown: Buffalo, NY

Year	Rank	Starts	Poles	1	2	3	4	5	6–10	Laps	Laps Led	Races Led	Miles	$
1950	NR	2	0	0	0	0	0	0	0	92	0	0	46	0
Lifetime		2	0	0	0	0	0	0	0	92	0	0	46	$0

Bill Chevalier

William J. Chevalier
B: 2/14/1922
Racing Hometown: Sayerville, NJ

Year	Rank	Starts	Poles	1	2	3	4	5	6–10	Laps	Laps Led	Races Led	Miles	$
1954	NR	2	0	0	0	0	0	0	0	66	0	0	99	25
1971	NR	1	0	0	0	0	0	0	1	188	0	0	282	620
Lifetime		3	0	0	0	0	0	0	1	254	0	0	381	$645

Lloyd Chick

Lloyd Chick
Racing Hometown: Chicago, IL

Year	Rank	Starts	Poles	1	2	3	4	5	6–10	Laps	Laps Led	Races Led	Miles	$
1954	175	1	0	0	0	0	0	0	0	94	0	0	141	50
1955	113	2	0	0	0	0	0	0	1	245	0	0	123	125
Lifetime		3	0	0	0	0	0	0	1	339	0	0	264	$175

Richard Childress

Richard Reed Childress
B: 9/21/1945
Racing Hometown: Winston-Salem, NC

Year	Rank	Starts	Poles	1	2	3	4	5	6–10	Laps	Laps Led	Races Led	Miles	$
1969	NR	1	0	0	0	0	0	0	0	80	0	0	213	1,175
1971	46	12	0	0	0	0	0	0	0	1,394	0	0	1,006	3,855
1972	37	15	0	0	0	0	0	0	0	1,681	0	0	1,652	7,245
1973	15	25	0	0	0	0	1	0	1	6,918	1	1	7,456	37,880
1974	16	29	0	0	0	0	0	0	3	5,138	0	0	6,484	50,249
1975	5	30	0	0	0	0	1	1	13	9,433	3	2	10,925	96,780
1976	11	30	0	0	0	0	0	0	11	8,147	0	0	9,779	85,780
1977	9	30	0	0	0	0	0	0	11	7,973	27	4	9,411	97,012
1978	10	30	0	0	0	1	0	0	11	8,946	52	4	10,060	108,702
1979	8	31	0	0	0	0	0	1	10	9,109	13	2	10,442	132,922
1980	10	31	0	0	0	0	0	0	10	8,693	21	6	10,692	157,420
1981	25	21	0	0	0	0	1	0	0	5,218	16	3	6,468	71,125
Lifetime		285	0	0	0	1	3	2	70	72,730	133	22	84,587	$850,145

Ronnie Childress

Ronald Childress
Racing Hometown: Winston-Salem, NC

Year	Rank	Starts	Poles	1	2	3	4	5	6–10	Laps	Laps Led	Races Led	Miles	$
1974	139	1	0	0	0	0	0	0	0	43	0	0	27	325
Lifetime		1	0	0	0	0	0	0	0	43	0	0	27	$325

Jack Choquette

Jack Choquette
B: 1928
Racing Hometown: Montclair, NJ

Year	Rank	Starts	Poles	1	2	3	4	5	6–10	Laps	Laps Led	Races Led	Miles	$
1955	54	4	0	0	1	0	0	0	0	469	0	0	371	825
1956	164	2	0	0	0	0	0	0	1	173	0	0	87	100
Lifetime		6	0	0	1	0	0	0	1	642	0	0	458	$925

Chauncey Christ

Chauncey Christ

Year	Rank	Starts	Poles	1	2	3	4	5	6–10	Laps	Laps Led	Races Led	Miles	$
1958	147	1	0	0	0	0	0	0	0	85	0	0	85	50
Lifetime		1	0	0	0	0	0	0	0	85	0	0	85	$50

Frank Christian

Frank E. Christian
Deceased
Racing Hometown: Atlanta, GA

Year	Rank	Starts	Poles	1	2	3	4	5	6–10	Laps	Laps Led	Races Led	Miles	$
1949	26T	1	0	0	0	0	0	0	1		0	0		175
Lifetime		1	0	0	0	0	0	0	1		0	0		$175

Sara Christian

Sara Christian
B: 1920 *Deceased*
Racing Hometown: Atlanta, GA

Year	Rank	Starts	Poles	1	2	3	4	5	6–10	Laps	Laps Led	Races Led	Miles	$
1949	13	6	0	0	0	0	0	1	1	606	0	0	417	760
1950	107T	1	0	0	0	0	0	0	0		0	0		50
Lifetime		7	0	0	0	0	0	1	1	606	0	0	417	$810

Year	Rank	Starts	Poles	Finish						Laps	Laps Led	Races Led	Miles	$
				1	2	3	4	5	6–10	Laps	Led	Led	Miles	$

Steve Christman

Steve Christman
B: 9/22/1947
Racing Hometown: Ft. Wayne, IN

Year	Rank	Starts	Poles	1	2	3	4	5	6–10	Laps	Laps Led	Races Led	Miles	$
1987	27	20	0	0	0	0	0	0	0	4,404	0	0	5,100	54,965
Lifetime		20	0	0	0	0	0	0	0	4,404	0	0	5,100	$54,965

J. Christopher

J. Christopher

Year	Rank	Starts	Poles	1	2	3	4	5	6–10	Laps	Laps Led	Races Led	Miles	$
1954	NR	1	0	0	0	0	0	0	0	23	0	0	46	0
Lifetime		1	0	0	0	0	0	0	0	23	0	0	46	$0

Ronnie Chumley

Ronald B. Chumley
B: 1/18/1935
Racing Hometown: Houston, TX

Year	Rank	Starts	Poles	1	2	3	4	5	6–10	Laps	Laps Led	Races Led	Miles	$
1964	NR	2	0	0	0	0	0	0	0	59	0	0	148	850
1966	105	2	0	0	0	0	0	0	0	42	0	0	105	1,130
1971	70	2	0	0	0	0	0	0	0	291	0	0	378	990
1972	94	1	0	0	0	0	0	0	0	200	0	0	400	645
Lifetime		7	0	0	0	0	0	0	0	592	0	0	1,031	$3,615

Obie Chupp

Obie Chupp
Racing Hometown: Columbus, GA

Year	Rank	Starts	Poles	1	2	3	4	5	6–10	Laps	Laps Led	Races Led	Miles	$
1953	NR	1	0	0	0	0	0	0	0	36	0	0	148	50
Lifetime		1	0	0	0	0	0	0	0	36	0	0	148	$50

Jerry Churchill

Gerald Eugene Churchill
B: 9/18/1938
Racing Hometown: Dearborne, MI

Year	Rank	Starts	Poles	1	2	3	4	5	6–10	Laps	Laps Led	Races Led	Miles	$
1971	68	6	0	0	0	0	0	0	0	664	0	0	299	1,815
1984	85T	1	0	0	0	0	0	0	0	118	0	0	118	3,120
Lifetime		7	0	0	0	0	0	0	0	782	0	0	417	$4,935

Raul Cilloniz

Raul Cilloniz
B: 1929
Racing Hometown: Lima, Peru

Year	Rank	Starts	Poles	1	2	3	4	5	6–10	Laps	Laps Led	Races Led	Miles	$
1959	NR	2	0	0	0	0	0	0	0	229	0	0	573	550
Lifetime		2	0	0	0	0	0	0	0	229	0	0	573	$550

Bill Cintia

William Cintia
Racing Hometown: Waterbury, CT

Year	Rank	Starts	Poles	1	2	3	4	5	6–10	Laps	Laps Led	Races Led	Miles	$
1951	N/A	1	0	0	0	0	0	0	1		0	0		50
Lifetime		1	0	0	0	0	0	0	1		0	0		$50

Buck Clardy

Buck Clardy
B: 6/22/1925
Racing Hometown: Greenville, SC

Year	Rank	Starts	Poles	1	2	3	4	5	6–10	Laps	Laps Led	Races Led	Miles	$
1951	N/A	1	0	0	0	0	0	0	0		0	0		25
Lifetime		1	0	0	0	0	0	0	0		0	0		$25

Bill Claren

William Claren
B: 5/31/1925
Racing Hometown: Montclair, NJ

Year	Rank	Starts	Poles	1	2	3	4	5	6–10	Laps	Laps Led	Races Led	Miles	$
1954	NR	1	0	0	0	0	0	0	1	49	0	0	98	275
Lifetime		1	0	0	0	0	0	0	1	49	0	0	98	$275

George Clark

George Clark
Racing Hometown: Hartford, CT

Year	Rank	Starts	Poles	1	2	3	4	5	6–10	Laps	Laps Led	Races Led	Miles	$
1951	N/A	1	0	0	0	0	0	0	0		0	0		25
1953	96	1	0	0	0	0	0	0	0		0	0		35
1954	81	1	0	0	0	0	0	0	0	179	0	0	90	25
Lifetime		3	0	0	0	0	0	0	0	179	0	0	90	$85

Year	Rank	Starts	Poles	Finish 1	2	3	4	5	6–10	Laps	Laps Led	Races Led	Miles	$

Jim Clark

James Clark
Racing Hometown: Ft. Worth, TX

Year	Rank	Starts	Poles	1	2	3	4	5	6–10	Laps	Laps Led	Races Led	Miles	$
1952	104T	1	0	0	0	0	0	0	0	135	0	0	68	25
1954	52	6	0	0	0	0	0	0	1	721	0	0	508	400
Lifetime		7	0	0	0	0	0	0	1	856	0	0	576	$425

Jimmy Clark

Jimmy Clark
B: 3/14/1936 D: 4/7/1968 *Killed in German Grand Prix @ Hockenheim, Germany.*
Racing Hometown: Dunn, Scotland

Year	Rank	Starts	Poles	1	2	3	4	5	6–10	Laps	Laps Led	Races Led	Miles	$
1967	NR	1	0	0	0	0	0	0	0	144	0	0	144	665
Lifetime		1	0	0	0	0	0	0	0	144	0	0	144	$665

Joe Clark

Joseph Clark
Racing Hometown: Neptune Beach, CA

Year	Rank	Starts	Poles	1	2	3	4	5	6–10	Laps	Laps Led	Races Led	Miles	$
1961	164	2	0	0	0	0	0	0	0	56	0	0	61	25
1964	84	6	0	0	0	0	0	0	0	272	0	0	208	2,250
1965	120	1	0	0	0	0	0	0	0	41	0	0	111	500
1966	132	1	0	0	0	0	0	0	0	4	0	0	11	500
1967	97	1	0	0	0	0	0	0	0	52	0	0	140	500
1968	114	1	0	0	0	0	0	0	0	0	0	0	0	500
1970	NR	1	0	0	0	0	0	0	1	136	0	0	356	1,215
1971	NR	1	0	0	0	0	0	0	0	21	0	0	55	1,065
Lifetime		14	0	0	0	0	0	0	1	582	0	0	942	$6,555

Paul Clark

Paul Clark
Racing Hometown: Mansfield, OH

Year	Rank	Starts	Poles	1	2	3	4	5	6–10	Laps	Laps Led	Races Led	Miles	$
1963	96	4	0	0	0	0	0	0	0	470	0	0	370	875
Lifetime		4	0	0	0	0	0	0	0	470	0	0	370	$875

Ray Clark

Raymond Clark
B: 1922 D: 8/24/1958 *Killed in race @ Ferndale, CA, Fairgrounds.*
Racing Hometown: Tucson, AZ

Year	Rank	Starts	Poles	1	2	3	4	5	6–10	Laps	Laps Led	Races Led	Miles	$
1955	128	2	0	0	0	0	0	0	0	193	0	0	142	50
Lifetime		2	0	0	0	0	0	0	0	193	0	0	142	$50

Sherman Clark

Sherman Clark
Racing Hometown: Yorba Linda, CA

Year	Rank	Starts	Poles	1	2	3	4	5	6–10	Laps	Laps Led	Races Led	Miles	$
1955	103	2	0	0	0	0	1	0	0	214	0	0	214	380
1956	80	5	0	0	0	0	0	0	2	405	0	0	428	425
1957	112	1	0	0	0	0	0	0	0	54	0	0	135	115
Lifetime		8	0	0	0	0	1	0	2	673	0	0	777	$920

Allan Clarke

Allan Clarke
Racing Hometown: Miami, FL

Year	Rank	Starts	Poles	1	2	3	4	5	6–10	Laps	Laps Led	Races Led	Miles	$
1952	73	3	0	0	0	0	0	0	1	170	0	0	85	125
1953	144T	1	0	0	0	0	0	0	0	76	0	0	38	25
1954	NR	1	0	0	0	0	0	0	0	166	0	0	83	25
1955	166T	1	0	0	0	0	0	0	0	179	0	0	90	25
Lifetime		6	0	0	0	0	0	0	1	591	0	0	296	$200

George Clarke

George Clarke
Racing Hometown: E. Hartford, CT

Year	Rank	Starts	Poles	1	2	3	4	5	6–10	Laps	Laps Led	Races Led	Miles	$
1953	NR	1	0	0	0	0	0	0	0		0	0		25
1954	NR	1	0	0	0	0	0	0	0	44	0	0	88	25
Lifetime		2	0	0	0	0	0	0	0	44	0	0	88	$50

Jack Clarke

Jack Clarke

Year	Rank	Starts	Poles	1	2	3	4	5	6–10	Laps	Laps Led	Races Led	Miles	$
1954	NR	3	0	0	0	0	0	0	0	401	0	0	268	65
Lifetime		3	0	0	0	0	0	0	0	401	0	0	268	$65

				Finish							Laps	Races		
Year	Rank	Starts	Poles	1	2	3	4	5	6–10	Laps	Led	Led	Miles	$

Johnny Clements
John Clements
Racing Hometown: Burlington, NC

1963	128	1	0	0	0	0	0	0	0	132	0	0	66	100
Lifetime		1	0	0	0	0	0	0	0	132	0	0	66	$100

Roger Clemmens
Roger Clemmens
Racing Hometown: Greensboro, NC

1957	NR	1	0	0	0	0	0	0	0		0	0		0
Lifetime		1	0	0	0	0	0	0	0		0	0		$0

Bill Cleveland
William Cleveland
Racing Hometown: Teaneck, NJ

1953	77	2	0	0	0	0	0	0	1		0	0		50
1954	167	2	0	0	0	0	0	0	0	224	0	0	187	60
Lifetime		4	0	0	0	0	0	0	1	224	0	0	187	$110

June Cleveland
Glen Cleveland
D: 9/28/1991
Racing Hometown: McBean, GA

1950	102	2	0	0	0	0	0	0	0	130	0	0	251	50
1951	N/A	1	0	0	0	0	0	0	0		0	0		25
1952	56	5	0	0	0	0	1	0	1	655	0	0	517	510
1953	158	1	0	0	0	0	0	0	0		0	0		25
Lifetime		9	0	0	0	0	1	0	1	785	0	0	768	$610

Fuzzy Clifton
Donald R. Clifton
Racing Hometown: King, NC

1959	NR	1	0	0	0	0	0	0	1	214	0	0	86	140
Lifetime		1	0	0	0	0	0	0	1	214	0	0	86	$140

Ernie Cline
Ernest Cline
Racing Hometown: Winston-Salem, NC

1980	NR	1	0	0	0	0	0	0	0	74	0	0	75	610
1981	97	1	0	0	0	0	0	0	0	77	0	0	41	550
1982	94	1	0	0	0	0	0	0	0	154	0	0	157	900
1983	94	1	0	0	0	0	0	0	0	35	0	0	36	910
Lifetime		4	0	0	0	0	0	0	0	340	0	0	309	$2,970

Gene Cline
Gene Cline
B: 5/30/1930
Racing Hometown: Rome, GA

1966	59	13	0	0	0	0	0	0	2	2,125	0	0	1,451	3,945
Lifetime		13	0	0	0	0	0	0	2	2,125	0	0	1,451	$3,945

Bill Clinton
William Clinton
Racing Hometown: San Fernando, CA

1961	126	3	0	0	0	0	0	0	0	183	0	0	102	145
1963	76	2	0	0	0	0	0	0	0	247	0	0	667	725
1964	85	1	0	0	0	0	0	0	0	150	0	0	405	525
Lifetime		6	0	0	0	0	0	0	0	580	0	0	1,173	$1,395

Dick Clothier
Richard Clothier
Racing Hometown: Fulton, NJ

1950	43	5	0	0	0	0	0	0	2	194	0	0	115	350
Lifetime		5	0	0	0	0	0	0	2	194	0	0	115	$350

Byron Clouse
Byron Clouse

1953	NR	1	0	0	0	0	0	0	1		0	0		125
Lifetime		1	0	0	0	0	0	0	1		0	0		$125

Year	Rank	Starts	Poles	Finish 1	2	3	4	5	6–10	Laps	Laps Led	Races Led	Miles	$

Tommy Coates
Thomas Coates
Racing Hometown: Trenton, NJ

Year	Rank	Starts	Poles	1	2	3	4	5	6–10	Laps	Laps Led	Races Led	Miles	$
1949	77	1	0	0	0	0	0	0	0	167	0	0	167	50
1950	N/A	1	0	0	0	0	0	0	0		0	0		50
1951	NR	1	0	0	0	0	0	0	0		0	0		10
Lifetime		3	0	0	0	0	0	0	0	167	0	0	167	$110

Shelby Colby
Sheldon Colby

Year	Rank	Starts	Poles	1	2	3	4	5	6–10	Laps	Laps Led	Races Led	Miles	$
1954	NR	1	0	0	0	0	0	0	0	82	0	0	41	0
Lifetime		1	0	0	0	0	0	0	0	82	0	0	41	$0

Ed Cole
Edward Cole Jr.
Racing Hometown: Pinehurst, NC

Year	Rank	Starts	Poles	1	2	3	4	5	6–10	Laps	Laps Led	Races Led	Miles	$
1955	39	13	0	0	0	0	0	0	0	1,442	0	0	801	695
1956	39	12	0	0	0	0	0	0	1	1,486	0	0	1,012	950
1957	144	1	0	0	0	0	0	0	0	163	0	0	82	100
Lifetime		26	0	0	0	0	0	0	1	3,091	0	0	1,894	$1,745

Fred Cole
Fred Cole

Year	Rank	Starts	Poles	1	2	3	4	5	6–10	Laps	Laps Led	Races Led	Miles	$
1954	NR	1	0	0	0	0	0	0	0	44	0	0	88	100
Lifetime		1	0	0	0	0	0	0	0	44	0	0	88	$100

George Cole
George Cole
Racing Hometown: Rhinebeck, NY

Year	Rank	Starts	Poles	1	2	3	4	5	6–10	Laps	Laps Led	Races Led	Miles	$
1954	154T	1	0	0	0	0	0	0	0	159	0	0	80	25
Lifetime		1	0	0	0	0	0	0	0	159	0	0	80	$25

Hal Cole
Harold Cole
Racing Hometown: South Gate, CA

Year	Rank	Starts	Poles	1	2	3	4	5	6–10	Laps	Laps Led	Races Led	Miles	$
1951	N/A	3	0	0	0	0	0	0	1		0	0		200
Lifetime		3	0	0	0	0	0	0	1		0	0		$200

Neil Cole
Neil Cole
B: 5/27/1926
Racing Hometown: Oakland, NJ

Year	Rank	Starts	Poles	1	2	3	4	5	6–10	Laps	Laps Led	Races Led	Miles	$
1950	31	2	0	0	0	0	0	1	0		0	0		300
1951	33	5	1	1	1	0	0	1	0	399	45	1	200	2,050
1952	19	11	0	0	0	1	0	0	6	1,579	0	0	982	1,793
1953	165T	1	0	0	0	0	0	0	0		0	0		25
Lifetime		19	1	1	1	1	0	2	6	1,978	45	1	1,181	$4,168

Bob Coleman
Robert Coleman
Racing Hometown: Memphis, TN

Year	Rank	Starts	Poles	1	2	3	4	5	6–10	Laps	Laps Led	Races Led	Miles	$
1955	150	1	0	0	0	0	0	0	0	152	0	0	228	95
Lifetime		1	0	0	0	0	0	0	0	152	0	0	228	$95

Earl Coleman
Earl H. Coleman Jr.
Racing Hometown: Atlanta, GA

Year	Rank	Starts	Poles	1	2	3	4	5	6–10	Laps	Laps Led	Races Led	Miles	$
1951	N/A	1	0	0	0	0	0	0	0		0	0		0
Lifetime		1	0	0	0	0	0	0	0		0	0		$0

Bob Collins
Robert Collins
Racing Hometown: Norton, VA

Year	Rank	Starts	Poles	1	2	3	4	5	6–10	Laps	Laps Led	Races Led	Miles	$
1950	84T	1	0	0	0	0	0	0	0	133	0	0	67	50
Lifetime		1	0	0	0	0	0	0	0	133	0	0	67	$50

Gary Collins
Gary Collins
B: 1/24/1960
Racing Hometown: Bakersfield, CA

Year	Rank	Starts	Poles	1	2	3	4	5	6–10	Laps	Laps Led	Races Led	Miles	$
1988	80	1	0	0	0	0	0	0	0	212	0	0	212	2,525

Year	Rank	Starts	Poles	Finish						Laps	Laps Led	Races Led	Miles	$
				1	2	3	4	5	6–10					

Gary Collins *continued*

Year	Rank	Starts	Poles	1	2	3	4	5	6–10	Laps	Laps Led	Races Led	Miles	$
1990	91T	1	0	0	0	0	0	0	0	280	0	0	280	3,125
1991	91	1	0	0	0	0	0	0	0	61	0	0	61	3,250
1994	79	1	0	0	0	0	0	0	0	43	0	0	108	7,100
Lifetime		4	0	0	0	0	0	0	0	596	0	0	661	$16,000

Roy Collins

Roy Collins
Racing Hometown: Garden City, MI

Year	Rank	Starts	Poles	1	2	3	4	5	6–10	Laps	Laps Led	Races Led	Miles	$
1971	NR	1	0	0	0	0	0	0	0	7	0	0	18	1,040
Lifetime		1	0	0	0	0	0	0	0	7	0	0	18	$1,040

Leland Colvin

Leland Colvin Sr.
Racing Hometown: Darlington, SC

Year	Rank	Starts	Poles	1	2	3	4	5	6–10	Laps	Laps Led	Races Led	Miles	$
1951	N/A	4	0	0	0	0	0	0	1		0	0		150
Lifetime		4	0	0	0	0	0	0	1		0	0		$150

Leland Colvin Jr.

Leland Colvin Jr.
Racing Hometown: Camden, SC

Year	Rank	Starts	Poles	1	2	3	4	5	6–10	Laps	Laps Led	Races Led	Miles	$
1964	114T	1	0	0	0	0	0	0	0	118	0	0	59	100
Lifetime		1	0	0	0	0	0	0	1	118	0	0	59	$100

Sam Colvin

Samuel Eugene Colvin
B: 7/21/1934
Racing Hometown: Greenville, SC

Year	Rank	Starts	Poles	1	2	3	4	5	6–10	Laps	Laps Led	Races Led	Miles	$
1958	117	1	0	0	0	0	0	0	0	185	0	0	93	125
Lifetime		1	0	0	0	0	0	0	0	185	0	0	93	$125

Dean Combs

Dean Combs
B: 2/23/1952
Racing Hometown: N. Wilkesboro, NC

Year	Rank	Starts	Poles	1	2	3	4	5	6–10	Laps	Laps Led	Races Led	Miles	$
1981	NR	2	0	0	0	0	0	0	0	183	0	0	149	1,155
1982	44	5	0	0	0	0	0	0	0	639	0	0	1,100	7,940
1983	42	5	0	0	0	0	0	0	1	1,296	0	0	1,995	21,370
1984	39	12	0	0	0	0	0	0	0	2,399	0	0	3,152	22,385
Lifetime		24	0	0	0	0	0	0	1	4,517	0	0	6,396	$52,850

George Combs

George Combs
Racing Hometown: Pittsburgh, PA

Year	Rank	Starts	Poles	1	2	3	4	5	6–10	Laps	Laps Led	Races Led	Miles	$
1955	170T	1	0	0	0	0	0	0	0	27	0	0	14	50
Lifetime		1	0	0	0	0	0	0	0	27	0	0	14	$50

R. L. Combs

R. L. Combs
Racing Hometown: N. Wilkesboro, NC

Year	Rank	Starts	Poles	1	2	3	4	5	6–10	Laps	Laps Led	Races Led	Miles	$
1957	138	3	0	0	0	0	0	0	0	123	0	0	62	210
1958	48	9	0	0	0	0	0	0	1	1,062	0	0	473	805
1959	104	9	0	0	0	0	0	0	1	1,478	0	0	665	735
Lifetime		21	0	0	0	0	0	0	2	2,663	0	0	1,200	$1,730

Rodney Combs

Rodney Combs
B: 3/27/1950
Racing Hometown: Cincinnati, OH

Year	Rank	Starts	Poles	1	2	3	4	5	6–10	Laps	Laps Led	Races Led	Miles	$
1982	7i	1	0	0	0	0	0	0	1	325	5	1	495	2,900
1983	87	1	0	0	0	0	0	0	0	320	0	0	480	1,725
1984	NR	1	0	0	0	0	0	0	0	192	0	0	384	1,750
1986	44	5	0	0	0	0	0	0	0	909	4	1	1,767	12,180
1987	35	14	0	0	0	0	0	0	0	2,752	0	0	4,409	90,990
1988	35	19	0	0	0	0	0	0	0	3,693	0	0	4,907	54,150
1989	42	9	0	0	0	0	0	0	0	1,657	0	0	2,109	36,090
1990	46	5	0	0	0	0	0	0	0	988	0	0	1,407	23,365
Lifetime		55	0	0	0	0	0	0	1	10,836	9	2	15,959	$223,150

Year	Rank	Starts	Poles	Finish 1	2	3	4	5	6–10	Laps	Laps Led	Races Led	Miles	$

Stacy Compton

Stacy Compton
B: 5/26/67
Racing Hometown: Lynchburg, VA

Year	Rank	Starts	Poles	1	2	3	4	5	6–10	Laps	Laps Led	Races Led	Miles	$
1996	56	2	0	0	0	0	0	0	0	756	0	0	397	18,115
Lifetime		2	0	0	0	0	0	0	0	756	0	0	397	$18,115

Gene Comstock

Gene Comstock
B: 2/21/1909   D: 2/1/1980
Racing Hometown: Chesapeake, OH

Year	Rank	Starts	Poles	1	2	3	4	5	6–10	Laps	Laps Led	Races Led	Miles	$
1950	NR	1	0	0	0	0	0	0	0	355	0	0	444	0
1951	N/A	4	0	0	0	0	0	0	0	357	0	0	446	125
1952	21	8	0	0	0	0	1	0	2	1,496	0	0	1,185	785
1953	18	13	0	0	0	0	0	0	3	756	0	0	895	990
1954	38	1	0	0	0	0	0	0	0	334	0	0	459	400
1955	183	2	0	0	0	0	0	0	0	239	0	0	380	250
Lifetime		29	0	0	0	0	1	0	5	3,537	0	0	3,809	$2,550

Doug Congden

Douglas Congden

Year	Rank	Starts	Poles	1	2	3	4	5	6–10	Laps	Laps Led	Races Led	Miles	$
1952	NR	1	0	0	0	0	0	0	0	30	0	0	15	25
Lifetime		1	0	0	0	0	0	0	0	30	0	0	15	$25

Jack Conley

Jack Conley
Racing Hometown: Brighton, MI

Year	Rank	Starts	Poles	1	2	3	4	5	6–10	Laps	Laps Led	Races Led	Miles	$
1954	NR	1	0	0	0	0	0	0	0	37	0	0	152	50
Lifetime		1	0	0	0	0	0	0	0	37	0	0	152	$50

Lee Connell

Lee Connell
Racing Hometown: Monroe, NC

Year	Rank	Starts	Poles	1	2	3	4	5	6–10	Laps	Laps Led	Races Led	Miles	$
1951	N/A	1	0	0	0	0	0	0	0	58	0	0	73	0
Lifetime		1	0	0	0	0	0	0	0	58	0	0	73	$0

Bob Connor

Robert Connor
Racing Hometown: Saugus, CA

Year	Rank	Starts	Poles	1	2	3	4	5	6–10	Laps	Laps Led	Races Led	Miles	$
1957	192	1	0	0	0	0	0	0	0	88	0	0	44	25
1965	69	1	0	0	0	0	0	0	0	115	0	0	311	580
Lifetime		2	0	0	0	0	0	0	0	203	0	0	355	$605

Paul Connors

Paul H. Connors Jr.
Racing Hometown: West Palm Beach, FL

Year	Rank	Starts	Poles	1	2	3	4	5	6–10	Laps	Laps Led	Races Led	Miles	$
1966	46	3	0	0	0	0	0	0	1	668	0	0	737	2,820
1969	82	1	0	0	0	0	0	0	0	31	0	0	78	635
1970	84	1	0	0	0	0	0	0	0	134	0	0	183	890
Lifetime		5	0	0	0	0	0	0	1	833	0	0	997	$4,345

Al Conroy

Al Conroy
Racing Hometown: Chicago, IL

Year	Rank	Starts	Poles	1	2	3	4	5	6–10	Laps	Laps Led	Races Led	Miles	$
1952	161	1	0	0	0	0	0	0	0	308	0	0	385	150
Lifetime		1	0	0	0	0	0	0	0	308	0	0	385	$150

Jim Conway

James Conway
Racing Hometown: Greenville, SC

Year	Rank	Starts	Poles	1	2	3	4	5	6–10	Laps	Laps Led	Races Led	Miles	$
1965	131	1	0	0	0	0	0	0	0	1	0	0	2	500
1967	101	1	0	0	0	0	0	0	0	215	0	0	108	100
Lifetime		2	0	0	0	0	0	0	0	216	0	0	109	$600

Bill Cook

William Cook

Year	Rank	Starts	Poles	1	2	3	4	5	6–10	Laps	Laps Led	Races Led	Miles	$
1960	NR	1	0	0	0	0	0	0	0	137	0	0	192	200
Lifetime		1	0	0	0	0	0	0	0	137	0	0	192	$200

Year	Rank	Starts	Poles	Finish 1	2	3	4	5	6–10	Laps	Laps Led	Races Led	Miles	$

Dick Cook
Richard Cook
Racing Hometown: Lakewood, CA

Year	Rank	Starts	Poles	1	2	3	4	5	6–10	Laps	Laps Led	Races Led	Miles	$
1961	96	3	0	0	0	0	0	0	0	273	0	0	353	490
Lifetime		3	0	0	0	0	0	0	0	273	0	0	353	$490

Jim Cook
James V. Cook
B: 8/15/1922
Racing Hometown: High Point, NC

Year	Rank	Starts	Poles	1	2	3	4	5	6–10	Laps	Laps Led	Races Led	Miles	$
1950	NR	1	0	0	0	0	0	0	0		0	0		0
Lifetime		1	0	0	0	0	0	0	0		0	0		$0

Jim Cook
James Cook
Racing Hometown: Norwalk, CA

Year	Rank	Starts	Poles	1	2	3	4	5	6–10	Laps	Laps Led	Races Led	Miles	$
1954	82	4	0	0	0	0	0	0	1	985	0	0	585	165
1955	225	1	0	0	0	0	0	0	0	110	0	0	110	40
1956	87	6	0	0	0	0	0	1	0	663	0	0	638	540
1957	NR	5	0	0	0	0	0	0	0	371	0	0	335	290
1958	72	2	0	0	0	0	1	0	0	258	0	0	519	455
1959	90	2	0	0	0	0	0	0	1	357	0	0	195	325
1960	45	3	1	1	0	0	0	0	0	560	1	1	778	1,600
1961	75	4	0	0	0	0	1	0	1	314	0	0	421	925
1963	75	2	0	0	0	0	0	0	0	274	0	0	740	625
1964	55	4	0	0	0	0	0	0	0	396	0	0	580	1,550
1965	121	1	0	0	0	0	0	0	0	36	0	0	97	550
1966	129	1	0	0	0	0	0	0	0	14	0	0	38	500
1967	77	1	0	0	0	0	0	0	0	92	0	0	248	530
1968	75	1	0	0	0	0	0	0	0	162	0	0	437	1,000
1969	NR	1	0	0	0	0	0	0	0	3	0	0	8	750
1970	86	1	0	0	0	0	0	0	0	94	0	0	246	925
Lifetime		39	1	1	0	0	2	1	3	4,689	0	0	5,975	$10,770

Mel Cook
Mel Cook
Racing Hometown: Cincinnati, OH

Year	Rank	Starts	Poles	1	2	3	4	5	6–10	Laps	Laps Led	Races Led	Miles	$
1952	NR	1	0	0	0	0	0	0	0	38	0	0	19	25
Lifetime		1	0	0	0	0	0	0	0	38	1	1	19	$25

Smokey Cook
Fred Cook
Racing Hometown: Winston-Salem, NC

Year	Rank	Starts	Poles	1	2	3	4	5	6–10	Laps	Laps Led	Races Led	Miles	$
1960	126	1	0	0	0	0	0	0	0	1	0	0	0	140
1963	NR	1	0	0	0	0	0	0	0	12	0	0	3	75
Lifetime		2	0	0	0	0	0	0	0	13	0	0	3	$215

Bill Cooper
William Cooper
B: 8/22/1946
Racing Hometown: Phoenix, AZ

Year	Rank	Starts	Poles	1	2	3	4	5	6–10	Laps	Laps Led	Races Led	Miles	$
1989	96T	1	0	0	0	0	0	0	0	61	0	0	154	2,360
Lifetime		1	0	0	0	0	0	0	0	61	0	0	154	$2,360

Bob Cooper
Robert Cooper
B: 11/13/1935
Racing Hometown: Gastonia, NC

Year	Rank	Starts	Poles	1	2	3	4	5	6–10	Laps	Laps Led	Races Led	Miles	$
1962	52	13	0	0	0	0	0	0	1	1,644	0	0	883	1,300
1963	37	9	0	0	0	0	0	0	1	1,559	0	0	1,889	3,115
1964	47	13	0	0	0	0	0	0	1	783	0	0	803	4,510
1965	84	4	0	0	0	0	0	0	1	697	0	0	252	600
1966	86	2	0	0	0	0	0	0	1	634	0	0	317	500
1967	64	7	0	0	0	0	0	0	2	1,195	0	0	743	2,345
1968	39	14	0	0	0	0	0	0	1	2,170	0	0	1,415	4,540
1969	98	1	0	0	0	0	0	0	0	55	0	0	83	675
Lifetime		63	0	0	0	0	0	0	8	8,737	0	0	6,385	$17,585

Year	Rank	Starts	Poles	Finish						Laps	Laps Led	Races Led	Miles	$
				1	2	3	4	5	6–10					

Doug Cooper

Ben Douglas Cooper
B: 9/9/1938   D: 9/3/1987
Racing Hometown: Gastonia, NC

Year	Rank	Starts	Poles	1	2	3	4	5	6–10	Laps	Laps Led	Races Led	Miles	$
1963	95	2	0	0	0	1	0	0	0	154	0	0	139	750
1964	21	39	0	0	0	1	2	1	7	5,549	0	0	3,863	10,445
1965	19	30	0	0	0	0	1	0	8	5,281	0	0	3,909	12,380
1966	48	21	0	0	0	1	1	1	1	3,177	0	0	2,097	5,235
1967	48	21	0	0	0	0	0	2	3	3,351	0	0	2,091	5,665
1968	112	1	0	0	0	0	0	0	0	206	0	0	103	275
Lifetime		114	0	0	0	3	4	4	19	17,718	0	0	12,202	$34,750

Edward Cooper

Edward Cooper
B: 12/26/1946
Racing Hometown: Clark Lake, MI

Year	Rank	Starts	Poles	1	2	3	4	5	6–10	Laps	Laps Led	Races Led	Miles	$
1985	91T	1	0	0	0	0	0	0	0	7	0	0	14	1,375
1990	76	2	0	0	0	0	0	0	0	94	0	0	188	8,225
Lifetime		3	0	0	0	0	0	0	0	101	0	0	202	$9,600

Elmer Cooper

Elmer Cooper
Racing Hometown: Winston-Salem, NC

Year	Rank	Starts	Poles	1	2	3	4	5	6–10	Laps	Laps Led	Races Led	Miles	$
1953	NR	1	0	0	0	0	0	0	0	271	0	0	373	110
Lifetime		1	0	0	0	0	0	0	0	271	0	0	373	$110

Jim Cooper

James Cooper
Racing Hometown: Winston-Salem, NC

Year	Rank	Starts	Poles	1	2	3	4	5	6–10	Laps	Laps Led	Races Led	Miles	$
1954	209	1	0	0	0	0	0	0	0	141	0	0	71	0
Lifetime		1	0	0	0	0	0	0	0	141	0	0	71	$0

Derrike Cope

Derrike Cope
B: 11/3/1958
Racing Hometown: Spanaway, WA

Year	Rank	Starts	Poles	1	2	3	4	5	6–10	Laps	Laps Led	Races Led	Miles	$
1982	101	1	0	0	0	0	0	0	0	42	0	0	110	625
1984	57	3	0	0	0	0	0	0	0	370	0	0	631	6,500
1985	55	2	0	0	0	0	0	0	0	206	0	0	540	7,100
1986	45	5	0	0	0	0	0	0	1	1,101	0	0	1,349	8,025
1987	37	11	0	0	0	0	0	0	0	1,631	0	0	1,977	33,750
1988	31	26	0	0	0	0	0	0	0	4,772	0	0	6,535	132,835
1989	29	23	0	0	0	0	0	0	4	5,382	5	3	6,863	125,630
1990	18	29	0	2	0	0	0	0	4	7,961	109	6	9,654	569,451
1991	28	28	0	0	0	0	1	0	1	6,784	0	0	8,448	419,380
1992	21	29	0	0	0	0	0	0	3	8,483	0	0	10,174	277,215
1993	26	30	0	0	0	0	0	0	1	8,406	38	3	9,965	402,515
1994	30	30	0	0	0	0	0	0	2	8,506	11	2	9,718	398,436
1995	15	31	0	0	1	0	0	1	6	9,335	70	4	11,039	683,075
1996	35	29	0	0	0	0	0	0	3	7,329	28	2	8,831	675,781
Lifetime		277	0	2	1	0	1	1	25	70,308	261	20	85,833	$3,740,318

Ernie Cope

Ernest Cope
B: 7/17/1969
Racing Hometown: Tacoma, WA

Year	Rank	Starts	Poles	1	2	3	4	5	6–10	Laps	Laps Led	Races Led	Miles	$
1995	71	1	0	0	0	0	0	0	0	19	0	0	19	8,605
Lifetime		1	0	0	0	0	0	0	0	19	0	0	19	$8,605

Marvin Copple

Marvin Copple
Racing Hometown: Lincoln, NE

Year	Rank	Starts	Poles	1	2	3	4	5	6–10	Laps	Laps Led	Races Led	Miles	$
1953	69T	1	0	0	0	0	0	1	0		0	0		200
1955	136	1	0	0	0	0	0	0	0	37	0	0	152	85
Lifetime		2	0	0	0	0	0	1	0	37	0	0	152	$285

George Cork

George Cork (Guy)
Racing Hometown: Newark, NJ

Year	Rank	Starts	Poles	1	2	3	4	5	6–10	Laps	Laps Led	Races Led	Miles	$
1956	75	4	0	0	0	0	0	0	0	905	0	0	619	375
Lifetime		4	0	0	0	0	0	0	0	905	0	0	619	$375

Year	Rank	Starts	Poles	Finish 1	2	3	4	5	6–10	Laps	Laps Led	Races Led	Miles	$

Bill Corley

William Corley
Racing Hometown: Phoenix, AZ

Year	Rank	Starts	Poles	1	2	3	4	5	6–10	Laps	Laps Led	Races Led	Miles	$
1958	176	1	0	0	0	0	0	0	0	7	0	0	29	0
Lifetime		1	0	0	0	0	0	0	0	7	0	0	29	$0

Bill Cornwall

William Cornwall
Racing Hometown: Harvey, IL

1954	203	1	0	0	0	0	0	0	0	18	0	0	74	0
Lifetime		1	0	0	0	0	0	0	0	18	0	0	74	$0

Tony Correnti

Anthony Correnti
Racing Hometown: Newark, NJ

1951	N/A	1	0	0	0	0	0	0	0		0	0		10
Lifetime		1	0	0	0	0	0	0	0		0	0		$10

Joe Cote

Joseph Cote
Racing Hometown: N. Charleston, SC

1964	118	4	0	0	0	0	0	0	0	23	0	0	12	350
Lifetime		4	0	0	0	0	0	0	0	23	0	0	12	$350

Vince Cougineri

Vince Cougineri

1956	103	1	0	0	0	0	0	0	0	256	0	0	256	150
Lifetime		1	0	0	0	0	0	0	0	256	0	0	256	$150

Bobby Courtwright

Robert Courtwright
B: 11/6/1923   D: 9/6/1988
Racing Hometown: Butler, NJ

1950	62T	1	0	0	0	0	0	0	1	189	0	0	95	125
1952	55	4	0	0	0	0	0	1	0	424	0	0	218	275
1954	95	1	0	0	0	0	0	0	0	107	0	0	107	25
Lifetime		6	0	0	0	0	0	1	1	720	0	0	419	$425

Les Covey

Les Fred Covey
B: 5/5/1939
Racing Hometown: Paris, Ont., Canada

1972	46	7	0	0	0	0	0	0	0	1,347	0	0	1,540	5,070
Lifetime		7	0	0	0	0	0	0	0	1,347	0	0	1,540	$5,070

Delma Cowart

Clinton Cowart
B: 7/6/1941
Racing Hometown: Savannah, GA

1981	NR	1	0	0	0	0	0	0	0	315	0	0	479	1,940
1982	45	5	0	0	0	0	0	0	0	775	0	0	1,466	11,855
1983	49	4	0	0	0	0	0	0	0	643	0	0	1,141	7,750
1984	64	2	0	0	0	0	0	0	0	533	0	0	803	5,720
1985	79	2	0	0	0	0	0	0	0	71	0	0	183	9,930
1986	60	3	0	0	0	0	0	0	0	403	0	0	977	7,595
1987	NR	1	0	0	0	0	0	0	0	180	0	0	479	4,640
1989	—	0												1,400
1990	—	0												1,500
1991	—	0												1,750
1992	54	3	0	0	0	0	0	0	0	498	0	0	950	33,470
1993	—	0												2,300
1994	—	0												2,300
1995	—	0												2,150
1996	—	0												3,440
Lifetime		21	0	0	0	0	0	0	0	3,418	0	0	6,478	$97,740

Lowell Cowell

Lowell Cowell
B: 1945
Racing Hometown: Morganton, WV

1981	56	4	0	0	0	0	0	0	0	812	0	0	1,220	8,055

Year	Rank	Starts	Poles	Finish 1	2	3	4	5	6–10	Laps	Laps Led	Races Led	Miles	$

Lowell Cowell *continued*

Year	Rank	Starts	Poles	1	2	3	4	5	6–10	Laps	Laps Led	Races Led	Miles	$
1982	39	5	0	0	0	0	0	0	0	862	0	0	2,210	27,365
1983	NR	1	0	0	0	0	0	0	0	93	0	0	247	3,335
1984	—	0												1,550
Lifetime		10	0	0	0	0	0	0	0	1,767	0	0	3,677	$40,305

A. J. Cox

Aubrey Johnson Cox
B: 9/8/1927
Racing Hometown: Wilmington, DE

Year	Rank	Starts	Poles	1	2	3	4	5	6–10	Laps	Laps Led	Races Led	Miles	$
1971	81	1	0	0	0	0	0	0	0	82	0	0	82	615
1972	NR	1	0	0	0	0	0	0	0	2	0	0	3	325
Lifetime		2	0	0	0	0	0	0	0	84	0	0	85	$940

Buddy Cox

Buddy Cox
Racing Hometown: Dayton, OH

Year	Rank	Starts	Poles	1	2	3	4	5	6–10	Laps	Laps Led	Races Led	Miles	$
1952	NR	1	0	0	0	0	0	0	0	29	0	0	15	25
Lifetime		1	0	0	0	0	0	0	0	29	0	0	15	$25

Doug Cox

William Douglas Cox
Racing Hometown: Greenville, SC

Year	Rank	Starts	Poles	1	2	3	4	5	6–10	Laps	Laps Led	Races Led	Miles	$
1955	139	2	0	0	0	0	0	0	0	406	0	0	400	200
1956	111	3	1	0	0	0	0	1	1	511	0	0	231	460
1957	84	3	0	0	0	0	0	1	0	230	0	0	176	460
1958	16	14	0	0	1	0	1	1	6	2,479	0	0	1,592	3,404
1959	NR	4	0	0	0	0	0	0	2	532	0	0	266	380
1961	88	5	0	0	0	0	0	0	0	367	0	0	190	510
Lifetime		31	1	0	1	0	1	3	9	4,525	0	0	2,855	$5,414

James Cox

James Cox
B: 12/13/1945
Racing Hometown: Radford, VA

Year	Rank	Starts	Poles	1	2	3	4	5	6–10	Laps	Laps Led	Races Led	Miles	$
1969	60	8	0	0	0	0	0	0	0	606	0	0	299	1,935
1970	64	7	0	0	0	0	0	0	0	318	0	0	210	2,755
1971	75	5	0	0	0	0	0	0	0	531	0	0	327	1,650
1972	105	2	0	0	0	0	0	0	0	527	0	0	323	1,220
Lifetime		22	0	0	0	0	0	0	0	1,982	0	0	1,159	$7,560

Thomas Cox

Thomas Clarkston Cox
B: 2/24/1936
Racing Hometown: Asheboro, NC

Year	Rank	Starts	Poles	1	2	3	4	5	6–10	Laps	Laps Led	Races Led	Miles	$
1962	18	42	0	0	0	0	1	2	17	8,370	0	0	4,990	10,181
1963	133	2	0	0	0	0	0	0	0	8	0	0	12	700
Lifetime		44	0	0	0	0	1	2	17	8,378	0	0	5,002	$10,881

Johnny Coy

John Coy
B: 1925
Racing Hometown: Merrick, NY

Year	Rank	Starts	Poles	1	2	3	4	5	6–10	Laps	Laps Led	Races Led	Miles	$
1956	194	1	0	0	0	0	0	0	0	197	0	0	197	175
Lifetime		1	0	0	0	0	0	0	0	197	0	0	197	$175

Johnny Coy Jr.

John Coy Jr.
B: 1949
Racing Hometown: Freeport, NY

Year	Rank	Starts	Poles	1	2	3	4	5	6–10	Laps	Laps Led	Races Led	Miles	$
1984	NR	1	0	0	0	0	0	0	0	416	0	0	416	1,090
1986	73	2	0	0	0	0	0	0	0	591	0	0	593	9,200
Lifetime		4	0	0	0	0	0	0	0	1,007	0	0	1,009	$10,290

Gene Coyle

Gene Coyle
B: 1955   D: 5/13/1991
Racing Hometown: Piscataway, NJ

Year	Rank	Starts	Poles	1	2	3	4	5	6–10	Laps	Laps Led	Races Led	Miles	$
1984	NR	2	0	0	0	0	0	0	0	619	0	0	895	4,840
Lifetime		2	0	0	0	0	0	0	0	619	0	0	895	$4,840

Year	Rank	Starts	Poles	Finish 1	2	3	4	5	6–10	Laps	Laps Led	Races Led	Miles	$

Lamar Crabtree

Lamar Crabtree
Racing Hometown: Pensacola, FL

Year	Rank	Starts	Poles	1	2	3	4	5	6–10	Laps	Laps Led	Races Led	Miles	$
1951	84T	1	0	0	0	0	0	0	1		0	0		200
1952	110	2	0	0	0	0	0	0	0	349	0	0	365	25
1953	97T	1	0	0	0	0	0	0	0	0	0	0	0	25
Lifetime		4	0	0	0	0	0	0	1	349	0	0	365	$250

Herb Craig

Herbert Craig
Racing Hometown: Keithville, LA

Year	Rank	Starts	Poles	1	2	3	4	5	6–10	Laps	Laps Led	Races Led	Miles	$
1950	120T	1	0	0	0	0	0	0	0		0	0		0
Lifetime		1	0	0	0	0	0	0	0		0	0		$0

Jim Cramblitt

James Cramblitt
Racing Hometown: Baltimore, MD

Year	Rank	Starts	Poles	1	2	3	4	5	6–10	Laps	Laps Led	Races Led	Miles	$
1955	162	2	0	0	0	0	0	0	0	200	0	0	111	75
Lifetime		2	0	0	0	0	0	0	0	200	0	0	111	$75

Pappy Crane

H. T. Crane
Racing Hometown: Long Beach, MS

Year	Rank	Starts	Poles	1	2	3	4	5	6–10	Laps	Laps Led	Races Led	Miles	$
1960	99	2	0	0	0	0	0	0	1	270	0	0	313	340
Lifetime		2	0	0	0	0	0	0	1	270	0	0	313	$340

Willie Crane

William Crane
Racing Hometown: Springfield, MO

Year	Rank	Starts	Poles	1	2	3	4	5	6–10	Laps	Laps Led	Races Led	Miles	$
1968	87	1	0	0	0	0	0	0	0	300	0	0	450	875
Lifetime		1	0	0	0	0	0	0	0	300	0	0	450	$875

Jerry Cranmer

Gerald Cranmer
Racing Hometown: Atlantic City, NJ

Year	Rank	Starts	Poles	1	2	3	4	5	6–10	Laps	Laps Led	Races Led	Miles	$
1986	56	5	0	0	0	0	0	0	0	1,727	0	0	1,771	23,510
1987	43	5	0	0	0	0	0	0	0	1,914	0	0	1,278	20,660
Lifetime		10	0	0	0	0	0	0	0	3,641	0	0	3,050	$44,170

Ricky Craven

Richard Craven
B: 5/24/1966
Racing Hometown: Newburgh, ME

Year	Rank	Starts	Poles	1	2	3	4	5	6–10	Laps	Laps Led	Races Led	Miles	$
1991	82T	1	0	0	0	0	0	0	0	221	0	0	225	3,750
1995	24	31	0	0	0	0	0	0	4	8,711	6	4	11,086	597,054
1996	20	31	2	0	0	2	0	1	2	8,561	136	9	10,229	941,959
Lifetime		63	2	0	0	2	0	1	6	17,493	142	13	21,540	$1,542,763

Freddie Crawford

Fred Crawford

Year	Rank	Starts	Poles	1	2	3	4	5	6–10	Laps	Laps Led	Races Led	Miles	$
1990	NR	1	0	0	0	0	0	0	0	6	0	0	6	2,775
Lifetime		1	0	0	0	0	0	0	0	6	0	0	6	$2,775

Herb Crawford

Herbert Crawford
Racing Hometown: San Diego, CA

Year	Rank	Starts	Poles	1	2	3	4	5	6–10	Laps	Laps Led	Races Led	Miles	$
1955	135	3	0	0	0	0	0	0	1	338	0	0	251	150
1956	288	1	0	0	0	0	0	0	0	63	0	0	158	40
Lifetime		4	0	0	0	0	0	0	1	401	0	0	409	$190

Jimmy Crawford

James Harrison Crawford
B: 7/12/1944
Racing Hometown: East Point, GA

Year	Rank	Starts	Poles	1	2	3	4	5	6–10	Laps	Laps Led	Races Led	Miles	$
1970	69	3	0	0	0	0	0	0	0	292	0	0	526	1,795
1971	74	3	0	0	0	0	0	0	0	110	0	0	284	1,575
1972	89	1	0	0	0	0	0	0	0	181	0	0	481	1,695
1973	46	4	0	0	0	0	0	0	0	1,053	0	0	1,228	4,059
1974	56	4	0	0	0	0	0	0	0	559	0	0	903	5,965
Lifetime		15	0	0	0	0	0	0	0	2,195	0	0	3,421	$15,089

Year	Rank	Starts	Poles	Finish						Laps	Laps Led	Races Led	Miles	$
				1	2	3	4	5	6–10					

Spook Crawford
Ankrum Crawford
Racing Hometown: Fayetteville, NC

Year	Rank	Starts	Poles	1	2	3	4	5	6–10	Laps	Laps Led	Races Led	Miles	$
1956	NR	1	0	0	0	0	0	0	0	13	0	0	7	50
1957	NR	1	0	0	0	0	0	0	0	34	0	0	78	125
1958	132T	1	0	0	0	0	0	0	0	152	0	0	76	85
1960	88	3	0	0	0	0	0	0	1	439	0	0	212	320
Lifetime		6	0	0	0	0	0	0	1	638	0	0	373	$580

Walt Crawford
Walter Crawford
Racing Hometown: Greenville, SC

Year	Rank	Starts	Poles	1	2	3	4	5	6–10	Laps	Laps Led	Races Led	Miles	$
1950	104	1	0	0	0	0	0	0	0	358	0	0	448	0
Lifetime		1	0	0	0	0	0	0	0	358	0	0	448	$0

Charlie Cregar
Charles Cregar
Racing Hometown: Bloomsbury, NJ

Year	Rank	Starts	Poles	1	2	3	4	5	6–10	Laps	Laps Led	Races Led	Miles	$
1954	40	5	0	0	0	0	0	0	0	857	8	1	877	405
1955	213	2	0	0	0	0	0	0	0	47	0	0	60	0
1956	232	2	0	0	0	0	0	0	0	74	0	0	37	0
1957	57	3	0	0	0	0	0	0	3	356	0	0	178	500
1958	156	1	0	0	0	0	0	0	0	127	0	0	127	100
1959	NR	3	0	0	0	0	0	0	0	496	0	0	725	560
Lifetime		16	0	0	0	0	0	0	3	1,957	8	1	2,004	$1,565

Curtis Crider
Curtis Wade Crider (Crawfish)
B: 10/7/1930
Racing Hometown: Abbeyville, SC

Year	Rank	Starts	Poles	1	2	3	4	5	6–10	Laps	Laps Led	Races Led	Miles	$
1959	NR	4	0	0	0	0	0	0	1	453	0	0	227	375
1960	28	24	0	0	0	0	0	0	2	3,985	0	0	2,973	3,645
1961	21	41	0	0	0	0	0	1	1	5,882	0	0	4,186	7,420
1962	12	52	0	0	0	1	1	1	15	10,051	0	0	6,431	12,016
1963	17	49	0	0	0	1	0	1	13	8,859	0	0	5,402	11,644
1964	6	59	0	0	0	1	1	5	23	11,443	0	0	7,872	22,171
1965	NR	3	0	0	0	0	1	0	1	785	0	0	455	1,200
Lifetime		232	0	0	0	3	3	8	56	41,458	0	0	27,546	$58,471

Bud Crothers
Bud Crothers
Racing Hometown: Piedmont, SC

Year	Rank	Starts	Poles	1	2	3	4	5	6–10	Laps	Laps Led	Races Led	Miles	$
1959	60	3	0	0	0	0	0	0	1	867	0	0	712	475
Lifetime		3	0	0	0	0	0	0	1	867	0	0	712	$475

Ray Crowley
Raymond Crowley
Racing Hometown: Chicago, IL

Year	Rank	Starts	Poles	1	2	3	4	5	6–10	Laps	Laps Led	Races Led	Miles	$
1956	294T	1	0	0	0	0	0	0	0	36	0	0	18	100
Lifetime		1	0	0	0	0	0	0	0	36	0	0	18	$100

Ronnie Croy
Ronald Croy
Racing Hometown: Pearisburg, VA

Year	Rank	Starts	Poles	1	2	3	4	5	6–10	Laps	Laps Led	Races Led	Miles	$
1964	141	1	0	0	0	0	0	0	0	11	0	0	6	150
Lifetime		1	0	0	0	0	0	0	0	11	0	0	6	$150

Tommie Crozier
Thomas Crozier
Racing Hometown: Roanoke, VA

Year	Rank	Starts	Poles	1	2	3	4	5	6–10	Laps	Laps Led	Races Led	Miles	$
1984	80T	1	0	0	0	0	0	0	0	277	0	0	277	990
1985	54	3	0	0	0	0	0	0	0	516	0	0	560	4,895
1986	86	2	0	0	0	0	0	0	0	354	0	0	359	2,475
1989	70	2	0	0	0	0	0	0	0	112	0	0	136	4,600
Lifetime		8	0	0	0	0	0	0	0	1,259	0	0	1,332	$12,960

Jack Culpepper
Jack Culpepper
Racing Hometown: West Palm Beach, FL

Year	Rank	Starts	Poles	1	2	3	4	5	6–10	Laps	Laps Led	Races Led	Miles	$
1953	NR	1	0	0	0	0	0	0	0	119	0	0	60	25
Lifetime		1	0	0	0	0	0	0	0	119	0	0	60	$25

Year	Rank	Starts	Poles	Finish						Laps	Laps Led	Races Led	Miles	$
				1	2	3	4	5	6–10					

Jack Cumiford

Jack Cumiford
  Racing Hometown: Grand Rapids, MI

Year	Rank	Starts	Poles	1	2	3	4	5	6–10	Laps	Laps Led	Races Led	Miles	$
1954	NR	1	0	0	0	0	0	0	0	170	0	0	85	25
Lifetime		1	0	0	0	0	0	0	0	170	0	0	85	$25

Richard Cummings

Richard Cummings (Red)
  B: 2/26/1924
  Racing Hometown: Beverley, MA

Year	Rank	Starts	Poles	1	2	3	4	5	6–10	Laps	Laps Led	Races Led	Miles	$
1950	NR	1	0	0	0	0	0	0	0		0	0		0
Lifetime		1	0	0	0	0	0	0	0		0	0		$0

Pepper Cunningham

William Cunningham
  Racing Hometown: Trenton, NJ

Year	Rank	Starts	Poles	1	2	3	4	5	6–10	Laps	Laps Led	Races Led	Miles	$
1949	NR	1	0	0	0	0	0	0	0	134	0	0	134	0
1950	37	2	0	0	0	0	0	0	2	130	0	0	130	300
1951	N/A	4	0	0	0	0	0	0	0		0	0		85
1952	NR	1	0	0	0	0	0	0	0		0	0		25
1953	56	1	0	0	0	0	0	0	0		0	0		50
1954	NR	0	0	0	0	0	0	0	0	0	0	0	0	0
1955	237	1	0	0	0	0	0	0	0	3	0	0	3	0
Lifetime		10	0	0	0	0	0	0	2	267	0	0	267	$460

Danny Curley

Daniel Curley

Year	Rank	Starts	Poles	1	2	3	4	5	6–10	Laps	Laps Led	Races Led	Miles	$
1954	NR	1	0	0	0	0	0	0	0	125	0	0	63	25
Lifetime		1	0	0	0	0	0	0	0	125	0	0	63	$25

Floyd Curtis

Floyd Curtis
  Racing Hometown: Rossville, GA

Year	Rank	Starts	Poles	1	2	3	4	5	6–10	Laps	Laps Led	Races Led	Miles	$
1954	88	2	0	0	0	0	0	0	1	270	0	0	181	125
1955	219	1	0	0	0	0	0	0	0	10	0	0	15	40
Lifetime		3	0	0	0	0	0	0	1	280	0	0	196	$165

Jim Cushman

James Cushman
  B: 4/24/1929
  Racing Hometown: Lansing, MI

Year	Rank	Starts	Poles	1	2	3	4	5	6–10	Laps	Laps Led	Races Led	Miles	$
1956	264T	1	0	0	0	0	0	0	0	0	0	0	0	50
1962	47	4	0	0	0	0	0	0	1	782	0	0	883	850
1963	62	2	0	0	0	0	0	0	0	211	0	0	528	625
Lifetime		7	0	0	0	0	0	0	1	993	0	0	1,411	$1,525

Steve Dabb

Steve Dabb

Year	Rank	Starts	Poles	1	2	3	4	5	6–10	Laps	Laps Led	Races Led	Miles	$
1951	N/A	1	0	0	0	0	0	0	0		0	0		25
Lifetime		1	0	0	0	0	0	0	0		0	0		$25

Fred Dagavar

Fred Dagavar
  Racing Hometown: Philadelphia, PA

Year	Rank	Starts	Poles	1	2	3	4	5	6–10	Laps	Laps Led	Races Led	Miles	$
1950	118	1	0	0	0	0	0	0	0		0	0		50
Lifetime		1	0	0	0	0	0	0	0		0	0		$50

Clyde Dagit

Clyde A. Dagit
  B: 10/10/1941
  Racing Hometown: Pekin, IL

Year	Rank	Starts	Poles	1	2	3	4	5	6–10	Laps	Laps Led	Races Led	Miles	$
1974	117	1	0	0	0	0	0	0	0	183	0	0	366	1,020
1975	82T	1	0	0	0	0	0	0	0	418	0	0	425	1,400
Lifetime		2	0	0	0	0	0	0	0	601	0	0	791	$2,420

Don Dahle

Donald Dahle
  Racing Hometown: Clarion, PA

Year	Rank	Starts	Poles	1	2	3	4	5	6–10	Laps	Laps Led	Races Led	Miles	$
1959	NR	1	0	0	0	0	0	0	1	192	0	0	48	200
Lifetime		1	0	0	0	0	0	0	1	192	0	0	48	$200

Year	Rank	Starts	Poles	Finish 1	2	3	4	5	6–10	Laps	Laps Led	Races Led	Miles	$

Chuck Daigh

Charles George Daigh
Racing Hometown: Long Beach, CA

Year	Rank	Starts	Poles	1	2	3	4	5	6–10	Laps	Laps Led	Races Led	Miles	$
1963	131	1	0	0	0	0	0	0	0	37	0	0	93	75
1964	125T	1	0	0	0	0	0	0	0	62	0	0	167	500
Lifetime		2	0	0	0	0	0	0	0	99	0	0	260	$575

Darrell Dake

Darrell Dake
B: 8/11/1927
Racing Hometown: Cedar Rapids, IA

Year	Rank	Starts	Poles	1	2	3	4	5	6–10	Laps	Laps Led	Races Led	Miles	$
1960	56	2	0	0	0	0	0	0	1	235	0	0	588	575
1961	157	2	0	0	0	0	0	0	0	54	0	0	135	200
Lifetime		4	0	0	0	0	0	0	1	289	0	0	723	$775

Wally Dallenbach

Wallace Paul Dallenbach
B: 12/12/1936
Racing Hometown: E. Brunswick, NJ

Year	Rank	Starts	Poles	1	2	3	4	5	6–10	Laps	Laps Led	Races Led	Miles	$
1962	81	2	0	0	0	0	0	0	1	92	0	0	230	650
1964	112	1	0	0	0	0	0	0	0	142	0	0	71	110
1974	NR	1	0	0	0	0	0	0	0	125	0	0	188	1,395
Lifetime		5	0	0	0	0	0	0	1	359	0	0	489	$2,155

Wally Dallenbach Jr.

Wallace Paul Dallenbach Jr.
B: 5/23/1963
Racing Hometown: Basalt, CO

Year	Rank	Starts	Poles	1	2	3	4	5	6–10	Laps	Laps Led	Races Led	Miles	$
1991	38	11	0	0	0	0	0	0	0	2,070	0	0	3,244	54,020
1992	24	29	0	0	0	0	0	1	0	8,118	0	0	9,714	220,245
1993	22	30	0	0	1	0	0	0	3	8,411	3	2	10,056	474,340
1994	38	14	0	0	0	0	1	0	2	3,568	1	1	5,323	241,492
1995	50	2	0	0	1	0	0	0	0	131	21	1	324	63,900
1996	25	30	0	0	0	1	0	0	2	8,191	0	0	10,417	837,001
Lifetime		116	0	0	2	1	1	1	7	30,489	25	4	39,078	$1,890,998

Dean Dalton

Dean Dalton
B: 6/18/1945
Racing Hometown: Asheville, NC

Year	Rank	Starts	Poles	1	2	3	4	5	6–10	Laps	Laps Led	Races Led	Miles	$
1971	30	19	0	0	0	0	0	0	1	3,487	0	0	4,311	13,910
1972	9	29	0	0	0	0	0	0	4	7,533	0	0	9,068	42,299
1973	19	26	0	0	0	0	0	0	2	5,889	0	0	6,825	40,269
1974	36	14	0	0	0	0	0	0	0	2,414	6	1	2,303	12,485
1975	26	16	0	0	0	0	0	0	3	3,800	0	0	4,236	20,365
1976	42	6	0	0	0	0	0	0	0	1,433	0	0	1,853	7,245
1977	43	8	0	0	0	0	0	0	0	1,100	0	0	1,304	6,255
Lifetime		118	0	0	0	0	0	0	10	25,656	6	1	29,901	$142,828

Roxy Dancy

Roxy R. Dancy
Racing Hometown: Shreveport, LA

Year	Rank	Starts	Poles	1	2	3	4	5	6–10	Laps	Laps Led	Races Led	Miles	$
1953	NR	1	0	0	0	0	0	0	0		0	0		25
Lifetime		1	0	0	0	0	0	0	0		0	0		$25

Lloyd Dane

Lloyd Dane
B: 8/9/1925
Racing Hometown: Eldon, MO

Year	Rank	Starts	Poles	1	2	3	4	5	6–10	Laps	Laps Led	Races Led	Miles	$
1951	41	7	0	0	0	1	0	0	1	447	0	0	421	1,025
1954	NR	4	0	0	1	0	0	2	1	1,268	180	1	756	1,600
1955	49	5	0	0	0	1	0	0	1	545	5	1	446	780
1956	23	10	0	2	0	1	2	0	4	1,706	91	2	1,257	4,370
1957	25	10	1	1	5	1	0	0	3	1,296	1	1	863	4,985
1958	21	5	0	0	1	0	0	0	1	1,084	0	0	1,198	2,490
1959	86	2	0	0	1	0	0	0	1	578	0	0	286	1,100
1960	75	3	0	0	0	1	0	1	0	323	89	1	375	950
1961	74	4	0	1	0	0	0	0	1	396	1	1	443	1,390
1963	90	2	0	0	0	0	0	0	0	139	0	0	375	550
1964	79	1	0	0	0	0	0	0	0	154	0	0	416	525
Lifetime		53	1	4	8	5	3	3	13	7,936	367	7	6,836	$19,765

Year	Rank	Starts	Poles	Finish						Laps	Laps Led	Races Led	Miles	$
				1	2	3	4	5	6–10					

Charles Danello
Clayton Danello
Racing Hometown: Hartford, CT

Year	Rank	Starts	Poles	1	2	3	4	5	6–10	Laps	Laps Led	Races Led	Miles	$
1955	93	2	0	0	0	0	0	0	0	335	0	0	274	225
Lifetime		2	0	0	0	0	0	0	0	335	0	0	274	$225

Dan Danello
Daniel Danello
Racing Hometown: Hartford, CT

Year	Rank	Starts	Poles	1	2	3	4	5	6–10	Laps	Laps Led	Races Led	Miles	$
1954	181	1	0	0	0	0	0	0	0	199	0	0	199	50
Lifetime		1	0	0	0	0	0	0	0	199	0	0	199	$50

Ronnie Daniel
Ronald Lee Daniel
B: 8/5/1937
Racing Hometown: Lynchburg, VA

Year	Rank	Starts	Poles	1	2	3	4	5	6–10	Laps	Laps Led	Races Led	Miles	$
1971	88	1	0	0	0	0	0	0	0	16	0	0	6	200
1972	85	2	0	0	0	0	0	0	0	490	0	0	471	1,360
1973	66	5	0	0	0	0	0	0	0	1,148	0	0	624	2,480
Lifetime		8	0	0	0	0	0	0	0	1,654	0	0	1,101	$4,040

Dan Daniels
Daniel Daniels
Racing Hometown: Batavia, NY

Year	Rank	Starts	Poles	1	2	3	4	5	6–10	Laps	Laps Led	Races Led	Miles	$
1951	N/A	2	0	0	0	0	0	0	0		0	0		50
Lifetime		2	0	0	0	0	0	0	0		0	0		$50

Quinton Daniels
Quinton Daniels
Racing Hometown: Tyler, TX

Year	Rank	Starts	Poles	1	2	3	4	5	6–10	Laps	Laps Led	Races Led	Miles	$
1951	108	7	0	0	0	0	0	0	1		0	0		250
Lifetime		7	0	0	0	0	0	0	1		0	0		$250

Jim Danielson
James C. Danielson
B: 12/11/1930
Racing Hometown: Chico, CA

Year	Rank	Starts	Poles	1	2	3	4	5	6–10	Laps	Laps Led	Races Led	Miles	$
1972	80	2	0	0	0	0	0	0	0	282	0	0	717	3,140
1973	86	1	0	0	0	0	0	0	1	176	0	0	461	1,520
1974	104	1	0	0	0	0	0	0	0	178	0	0	466	1,425
1976	99T	1	0	0	0	0	0	0	0	39	0	0	102	890
Lifetime		5	0	0	0	0	0	0	1	675	0	0	1,746	$6,975

Frank Danley See Danny Graves

Bay Darnell
Wilber Darnell
B: 2/4/1931
Racing Hometown: Lake Bluff, IL

Year	Rank	Starts	Poles	1	2	3	4	5	6–10	Laps	Laps Led	Races Led	Miles	$
1954	NR	1	0	0	0	0	0	0	0	18	0	0	9	0
1964	NR	1	0	0	0	0	0	0	0	205	0	0	308	625
1967	117	1	0	0	0	0	0	0	0	123	0	0	185	600
Lifetime		3	0	0	0	0	0	0	0	346	0	0	501	$1,225

Reitzel Darner
Reitzel Darner
Racing Hometown: Asheboro, NC

Year	Rank	Starts	Poles	1	2	3	4	5	6–10	Laps	Laps Led	Races Led	Miles	$
1956	135	1	0	0	0	0	0	0	0	441	0	0	221	100
Lifetime		1	0	0	0	0	0	0	0	441	0	0	221	$100

Gene Darragh
Eugene Darragh
Racing Hometown: Tampa, FL

Year	Rank	Starts	Poles	1	2	3	4	5	6–10	Laps	Laps Led	Races Led	Miles	$
1950	NR	1	0	0	0	0	0	0	0	323	0	0	404	0
1951	N/A	1	0	0	0	0	0	0	0	309	0	0	386	50
1952	103	3	0	0	0	0	0	0	0	237	0	0	228	60
1953	NR	1	0	0	0	0	0	0	0		0	0		0
Lifetime		6	0	0	0	0	0	0	0	869	0	0	1,018	$110

Year	Rank	Starts	Poles	Finish						Laps	Laps Led	Races Led	Miles	$
				1	2	3	4	5	6–10					

Hugh Darragh

Hugh Darragh
Racing Hometown: Ebenezer, NY

Year	Rank	Starts	Poles	1	2	3	4	5	6–10	Laps	Laps Led	Races Led	Miles	$
1950	106	3	0	0	0	0	0	0	0	142	0	0	71	0
Lifetime		3	0	0	0	0	0	0	0	142	0	0	71	$0

Dan Daughtry

Daniel Daughtry
B: 4/10/1940
Racing Hometown: Punta Gorda, FL

Year	Rank	Starts	Poles	1	2	3	4	5	6–10	Laps	Laps Led	Races Led	Miles	$
1974	41	8	0	0	0	0	0	0	1	772	6	2	1,321	12,413
1975	103	2	0	0	0	0	0	0	0	9	0	0	23	2,530
Lifetime		10	0	0	0	0	0	0	1	781	6	2	1,344	$14,943

Bill Davis

William Davis
Racing Hometown: West Palm Beach, FL

Year	Rank	Starts	Poles	1	2	3	4	5	6–10	Laps	Laps Led	Races Led	Miles	$
1952	96	1	0	0	0	0	0	0	1		0	0		75
Lifetime		1	0	0	0	0	0	0	1		0	0		$75

Bob Davis

Robert W. Davis
B: 3/21/1925
Racing Hometown: Lighthouse Point, FL

Year	Rank	Starts	Poles	1	2	3	4	5	6–10	Laps	Laps Led	Races Led	Miles	$
1973	111	1	0	0	0	0	0	0	0	93	0	0	247	1,140
Lifetime		1	0	0	0	0	0	0	0	93	0	0	247	$1,140

Gene Davis

Gene Davis
Racing Hometown: Santa Monica, CA

Year	Rank	Starts	Poles	1	2	3	4	5	6–10	Laps	Laps Led	Races Led	Miles	$
1963	129	1	0	0	0	0	0	0	0	95	0	0	257	200
1965	55	1	0	0	0	0	0	1	0	177	0	0	478	1,850
Lifetime		2	0	0	0	0	0	1	0	272	0	0	734	$2,050

George Davis

George Davis
B: 5/29/1938
Racing Hometown: Adelphi, MD

Year	Rank	Starts	Poles	1	2	3	4	5	6–10	Laps	Laps Led	Races Led	Miles	$
1967	40	21	0	0	0	0	0	1	5	3,342	0	0	1,866	4,400
1968	56	6	0	0	0	0	0	0	1	576	0	0	362	1,915
1969	NR	1	0	0	0	0	0	0	0	24	0	0	24	400
Lifetime		28	0	0	0	0	0	1	6	3,942	0	0	2,252	$6,675

Jeff Davis

Jeffrey Davis
B: 1/29/1959
Racing Hometown: Anaheim, CA

Year	Rank	Starts	Poles	1	2	3	4	5	6–10	Laps	Laps Led	Races Led	Miles	$
1992	76	1	0	0	0	0	0	0	0	299	0	0	299	4,785
1993	93T	1	0	0	0	0	0	0	0	46	0	0	116	6,560
Lifetime		2	0	0	0	0	0	0	0	345	0	0	415	$11,345

Joel Davis

Joel Davis
B: 1/25/1941
Racing Hometown: Tenneville, GA

Year	Rank	Starts	Poles	1	2	3	4	5	6–10	Laps	Laps Led	Races Led	Miles	$
1963	102	3	0	0	0	0	0	0	0	280	0	0	140	245
1966	45	21	0	0	0	0	1	0	2	2,977	0	0	1,690	4,885
1967	50	6	0	0	0	0	0	0	2	888	0	0	773	1,825
Lifetime		30	0	0	0	0	1	0	4	4,145	0	0	2,604	$6,955

Keith Davis

Keith Davis
Racing Hometown: Hueytown, AL

Year	Rank	Starts	Poles	1	2	3	4	5	6–10	Laps	Laps Led	Races Led	Miles	$
1979	90	2	0	0	0	0	0	0	0	45	0	0	103	2,310
Lifetime		2	0	0	0	0	0	0	0	45	0	0	103	$2,310

Ray Davis

Raymond Davis

Year	Rank	Starts	Poles	1	2	3	4	5	6–10	Laps	Laps Led	Races Led	Miles	$
1957	167	1	0	0	0	0	0	0	0	78	0	0	39	50
Lifetime		1	0	0	0	0	0	0	0	78	0	0	39	$50

Year	Rank	Starts	Poles	Finish						Laps	Laps Led	Races Led	Miles	$
				1	2	3	4	5	6–10					

Walt Davis
Walter Davis
Racing Hometown: Oakland, CA

Year	Rank	Starts	Poles	1	2	3	4	5	6–10	Laps	Laps Led	Races Led	Miles	$
1951	N/A	2	0	0	0	0	0	0	2			0	0	150
Lifetime		2	0	0	0	0	0	0	2			0	0	$150

Bob Dawson
Robert Dawson
Racing Hometown: Orlando, FL

Year	Rank	Starts	Poles	1	2	3	4	5	6–10	Laps	Laps Led	Races Led	Miles	$
1955	110	2	0	0	0	0	0	0	0	190	0	0	228	75
Lifetime		2	0	0	0	0	0	0	0	190	0	0	228	$75

Chick Dawson
Chick Dawson
Racing Hometown: Richmond, VA

Year	Rank	Starts	Poles	1	2	3	4	5	6–10	Laps	Laps Led	Races Led	Miles	$
1955	244	1	0	0	0	0	0	0	0	11	0	0	6	0
Lifetime		1	0	0	0	0	0	0	0	11	0	0	6	$0

Tom Dawson
Thomas Dawson
Racing Hometown: Philadelphia, PA

Year	Rank	Starts	Poles	1	2	3	4	5	6–10	Laps	Laps Led	Races Led	Miles	$
1952	84T	1	0	0	0	0	0	0	1	134	0	0	134	150
Lifetime		1	0	0	0	0	0	0	1	134	0	0	134	$150

Bill Deakin
William Deakin

Year	Rank	Starts	Poles	1	2	3	4	5	6–10	Laps	Laps Led	Races Led	Miles	$
1952	97	1	0	0	0	0	0	0	0	225	0	0	225	50
Lifetime		1	0	0	0	0	0	0	0	225	0	0	225	$50

Dizzy Dean
Dizzy Dean
Racing Hometown: Millers, MD

Year	Rank	Starts	Poles	1	2	3	4	5	6–10	Laps	Laps Led	Races Led	Miles	$
1954	215T	1	0	0	0	0	0	0	0	1	0	0	1	0
Lifetime		1	0	0	0	0	0	0	0	1	0	0	1	$0

O. A. Dean
O. A. Dean
Racing Hometown: Mobile, AL

Year	Rank	Starts	Poles	1	2	3	4	5	6–10	Laps	Laps Led	Races Led	Miles	$
1951	N/A	1	0	0	0	0	0	0	0			0	0	25
Lifetime		1	0	0	0	0	0	0	0			0	0	$25

Al DeAngelo
Al DeAngelo
B: 1927
Racing Hometown: Flushing, NY

Year	Rank	Starts	Poles	1	2	3	4	5	6–10	Laps	Laps Led	Races Led	Miles	$
1966	143	1	0	0	0	0	0	0	0	23	0	0	5	0
Lifetime		1	0	0	0	0	0	0	0	23	0	0	5	$0

Duke DeBrizzi
Charles DeBrizzi
B: 3/13/1928
Racing Hometown: Jamesburg, NY

Year	Rank	Starts	Poles	1	2	3	4	5	6–10	Laps	Laps Led	Races Led	Miles	$
1957	94	3	0	0	0	0	0	0	0	622	0	0	363	225
Lifetime		3	0	0	0	0	0	0	0	622	0	0	363	$225

Billy DeCoster
William DeCoster
B: 1938
Racing Hometown: Basking Ridge, NJ

Year	Rank	Starts	Poles	1	2	3	4	5	6–10	Laps	Laps Led	Races Led	Miles	$
1965	61	2	0	0	0	0	0	0	0	252	0	0	378	800
Lifetime		2	0	0	0	0	0	0	0	252	0	0	378	$800

Bob Deehan
Robert Deehan

Year	Rank	Starts	Poles	1	2	3	4	5	6–10	Laps	Laps Led	Races Led	Miles	$
1954	NR	1	0	0	0	0	0	0	0	213	0	0	213	40
Lifetime		1	0	0	0	0	0	0	0	213	0	0	213	$40

Frank Deiny
Frank Deiny
D: 1986
Racing Hometown: Los Angeles, CA

Year	Rank	Starts	Poles	1	2	3	4	5	6–10	Laps	Laps Led	Races Led	Miles	$
1963	NR	1	0	0	0	0	0	0	0	44	0	0	119	200

Year	Rank	Starts	Poles	Finish						Laps	Laps Led	Races Led	Miles	$
				1	2	3	4	5	6–10					

Frank Deiny *continued*

Year	Rank	Starts	Poles	1	2	3	4	5	6–10	Laps	Laps Led	Races Led	Miles	$
1964	NR	1	0	0	0	0	0	0	0	9	0	0	24	500
1970	NR	1	0	0	0	0	0	0	0	4	0	0	10	800
Lifetime		3	0	0	0	0	0	0	0	57	0	153	$1,500	

Bill Delaney

William Delaney
Racing Hometown: Winston-Salem, NC

Year	Rank	Starts	Poles	1	2	3	4	5	6–10	Laps	Laps Led	Races Led	Miles	$
1962	NR	1	0	0	0	0	0	0	0	3	0	0	1	60
Lifetime		1	0	0	0	0	0	0	0	3	0	0	1	$60

Jim Delaney

James Delaney
B: 1929   D: 4/5/1991
Racing Hometown: Lyndhurst, NJ

Year	Rank	Starts	Poles	1	2	3	4	5	6–10	Laps	Laps Led	Races Led	Miles	$
1949	NR	1	0	0	0	0	0	0	0	0	0	0	0	0
1950	47	2	0	0	0	0	0	0	1	0	0	0	0	175
1951	64	7	0	0	0	0	0	1	1	494	0	0	468	375
1957	135	1	0	0	0	0	0	0	0	0	0	0	0	75
Lifetime		11	0	0	0	0	0	1	2	494	0	0	468	$625

Rex DeLewis

Rex DeLewis
Racing Hometown: Dayton, OH

Year	Rank	Starts	Poles	1	2	3	4	5	6–10	Laps	Laps Led	Races Led	Miles	$
1955	185	1	0	0	0	0	0	0	0	42	0	0	42	0
Lifetime		1	0	0	0	0	0	0	0	42	0	0	42	$0

Rick DeLewis

Richard DeLewis
Racing Hometown: Dearborne, MI

Year	Rank	Starts	Poles	1	2	3	4	5	6–10	Laps	Laps Led	Races Led	Miles	$
1955	189	2	0	0	0	0	0	0	0	122	0	0	105	50
Lifetime		2	0	0	0	0	0	0	0	122	0	0	105	$50

Joe Deloach

Joseph Deloach
Racing Hometown: Blackville, SC

Year	Rank	Starts	Poles	1	2	3	4	5	6–10	Laps	Laps Led	Races Led	Miles	$
1952	104T	1	0	0	0	0	0	0	0	135	0	0	68	50
Lifetime		1	0	0	0	0	0	0	0	135	0	0	68	$50

Mal Delometer

Mal Delometer

Year	Rank	Starts	Poles	1	2	3	4	5	6–10	Laps	Laps Led	Races Led	Miles	$
1963	NR	1	0	0	0	0	0	0	0	183	0	0	92	120
Lifetime		1	0	0	0	0	0	0	0	183	0	0	92	$120

Matthew DeMatthews

Matthew DeMatthews

Year	Rank	Starts	Poles	1	2	3	4	5	6–10	Laps	Laps Led	Races Led	Miles	$
1962	NR	1	0	0	0	0	0	0	0	2	0	0	3	400
Lifetime		1	0	0	0	0	0	0	0	2	0	0	3	$400

Phil Demola

Phillip Demola
Racing Hometown: Nutley, NJ

Year	Rank	Starts	Poles	1	2	3	4	5	6–10	Laps	Laps Led	Races Led	Miles	$
1953	134T	1	0	0	0	0	0	0	0		0	0		25
Lifetime		1	0	0	0	0	0	0	0		0	0		$25

Dick Denise

Richard Denise
Racing Hometown: Rochester, NY

Year	Rank	Starts	Poles	1	2	3	4	5	6–10	Laps	Laps Led	Races Led	Miles	$
1956	NR	1	0	0	0	0	0	0	0	41	0	0	21	50
Lifetime		1	0	0	0	0	0	0	0	41	0	0	21	$50

Jack Deniston

Jack Deniston
Racing Hometown: Arlington, VA

Year	Rank	Starts	Poles	1	2	3	4	5	6–10	Laps	Laps Led	Races Led	Miles	$
1962	127	1	0	0	0	0	0	0	0	81	0	0	27	50
1963	125	1	0	0	0	0	0	0	0	187	0	0	47	135
Lifetime		2	0	0	0	0	0	0	0	268	0	0	74	$185

Year	Rank	Starts	Poles	1	2	Finish 3	4	5	6–10	Laps	Laps Led	Races Led	Miles	$

Arnold Denley

Arnold Denley
Racing Hometown: Memphis, TN

Year	Rank	Starts	Poles	1	2	3	4	5	6–10	Laps	Laps Led	Races Led	Miles	$
1956	266T	1	0	0	0	0	0	0	0	5	0	0	8	150
Lifetime		1	0	0	0	0	0	0	0	5	0	0	8	$150

F. L. Denney

F. L. Denney
Racing Hometown: Ft. Worth, TX

Year	Rank	Starts	Poles	1	2	3	4	5	6–10	Laps	Laps Led	Races Led	Miles	$
1950	107T	1	0	0	0	0	0	0	0		0	0		50
Lifetime		1	0	0	0	0	0	0	0		0	0		$50

Bill Dennis

William C Dennis
B: 12/9/1935
Racing Hometown: Glen Allen, VA

Year	Rank	Starts	Poles	1	2	3	4	5	6–10	Laps	Laps Led	Races Led	Miles	$
1962	107	1	0	0	0	0	0	0	0	268	0	0	134	150
1967	47	3	0	0	0	0	0	0	0	1,012	0	0	1,160	2,335
1969	62	3	0	0	0	0	0	0	0	276	0	0	209	1,655
1970	25	25	0	0	0	0	0	0	5	4,014	0	0	3,748	15,670
1971	18	28	1	0	0	1	1	2	6	6,111	47	2	6,976	29,420
1972	42	11	0	0	0	1	0	1	0	2,327	2	1	2,249	10,949
1973	49	4	0	0	0	0	0	0	2	1,430	0	0	1,114	4,225
1974	60	3	0	0	0	0	0	0	2	1,118	0	0	1,147	7,775
1976	92T	1	0	0	0	0	0	0	0	313	0	0	470	1,385
1978	105T	1	0	0	0	0	0	0	0	66	0	0	99	1,560
1979	70	2	0	0	0	0	0	0	0	387	0	0	777	12,645
1980	—	0												1,200
1981	81	1	0	0	0	0	0	0	0	327	0	0	491	3,200
Lifetime		83	1	0	0	2	1	3	15	17,649	49	3	18,573	$92,169

Lloyd Dennis

Lloyd Dennis
Racing Hometown: Salisbury, NC

Year	Rank	Starts	Poles	1	2	3	4	5	6–10	Laps	Laps Led	Races Led	Miles	$
1951	N/A	1	0	0	0	0	0	0	0	39	0	0	29	10
Lifetime		1	0	0	0	0	0	0	0	39	0	0	29	$10

Jim Derhaag

James Derhaag

Year	Rank	Starts	Poles	1	2	3	4	5	6–10	Laps	Laps Led	Races Led	Miles	$
1991	69	1	0	0	0	0	0	0	0	88	0	0	214	5,120
Lifetime		1	0	0	0	0	0	0	0	88	0	0	214	$5,120

Zeke DeRose

Zeke DeRose
Racing Hometown: Paterson, NJ

Year	Rank	Starts	Poles	1	2	3	4	5	6–10	Laps	Laps Led	Races Led	Miles	$
1952	133T	1	0	0	0	0	0	0	0	168	0	0	84	25
Lifetime		1	0	0	0	0	0	0	0	168	0	0	84	$25

Benny DeRosier

Benoit DeRosier
Racing Hometown: New Britain, CT

Year	Rank	Starts	Poles	1	2	3	4	5	6–10	Laps	Laps Led	Races Led	Miles	$
1956	132	4	0	0	0	0	0	0	0	236	0	0	236	200
Lifetime		4	0	0	0	0	0	0	0	236	0	0	236	$200

Ernie Derr

Ernie Derr
B: 1922
Racing Hometown: Keokuk, IA

Year	Rank	Starts	Poles	1	2	3	4	5	6–10	Laps	Laps Led	Races Led	Miles	$
1953	NR	1	0	0	0	0	0	0	0		0	0		25
Lifetime		1	0	0	0	0	0	0	0		0	0		$25

Bob Derrington

Robert Elbert Derrington
B: 11/22/1930
Racing Hometown: Houston, TX

Year	Rank	Starts	Poles	1	2	3	4	5	6–10	Laps	Laps Led	Races Led	Miles	$
1964	36	18	0	0	0	0	0	0	2	1,897	1	1	1,819	3,580
1965	6	51	0	0	0	1	0	2	16	10,374	0	0	6,777	20,120
1966	44	11	0	0	0	0	0	0	1	1,156	0	0	1,260	3,840
Lifetime		80	0	0	0	1	0	2	19	13,427	1	1	9,856	$25,605

Year	Rank	Starts	Poles	Finish 1	2	3	4	5	6–10	Laps	Laps Led	Races Led	Miles	$

Leroy DeShields

Leroy DeShields
Racing Hometown: Oklahoma City, OK

Year	Rank	Starts	Poles	1	2	3	4	5	6–10	Laps	Laps Led	Races Led	Miles	$
1956	291	1	0	0	0	0	0	0	0	75	0	0	75	35
Lifetime		1	0	0	0	0	0	0	0	75	0	0	75	$35

Geoffrey Dessault

Geoffrey Dessault
Racing Hometown: Victoriaville, Ont., Canada

Year	Rank	Starts	Poles	1	2	3	4	5	6–10	Laps	Laps Led	Races Led	Miles	$
1953	NR	1	0	0	0	0	0	0	0		0	0		50
Lifetime		1	0	0	0	0	0	0	0		0	0		$50

Tony DeStafano

Anthony DeStafano

Year	Rank	Starts	Poles	1	2	3	4	5	6–10	Laps	Laps Led	Races Led	Miles	$
1955	169	1	0	0	0	0	0	0	0	103	0	0	103	25
Lifetime		1	0	0	0	0	0	0	0	103	0	0	103	$25

Dennis DeVea

Dennis DeVea
B: 3/15/1948
Racing Hometown: Joliet, IL

Year	Rank	Starts	Poles	1	2	3	4	5	6–10	Laps	Laps Led	Races Led	Miles	$
1982	NR	1	0	0	0	0	0	0	0	185	1	1	370	1,670
Lifetime		1	0	0	0	0	0	0	0	185	1	1	370	$1,670

Bob Devine

Robert Devine
Racing Hometown: New Fairfield, CT

Year	Rank	Starts	Poles	1	2	3	4	5	6–10	Laps	Laps Led	Races Led	Miles	$
1961	128	1	0	0	0	0	0	0	0	92	0	0	23	150
1962	80	2	0	0	0	0	0	0	0	453	0	0	151	240
Lifetime		3	0	0	0	0	0	0	0	545	0	0	174	$390

Ed DeWolff

Edward DeWolff
Racing Hometown: Lodi, NJ

Year	Rank	Starts	Poles	1	2	3	4	5	6–10	Laps	Laps Led	Races Led	Miles	$
1953	59	3	0	0	0	0	0	0	1		0	0		110
1954	166	2	0	0	0	0	0	0	0	95	0	0	49	10
Lifetime		5	0	0	0	0	0	0	1	95	0	0	49	$120

Clarence DeZalia

Clarence DeZalia
B: 10/1/1919
Racing Hometown: Aberdeen, MD

Year	Rank	Starts	Poles	1	2	3	4	5	6–10	Laps	Laps Led	Races Led	Miles	$
1955	94	5	0	0	0	0	0	0	0	691	0	0	610	200
1957	19	25	0	0	0	0	0	0	6	4,059	0	0	2,119	3,308
1958	15	27	0	0	0	0	0	0	6	4,073	0	0	2,412	3,004
1959	102	1	0	0	0	0	0	0	0	136	0	0	45	60
Lifetime		58	0	0	0	0	0	0	12	8,959	0	0	5,185	$6,572

Oliver Dial

Oliver Dial
Racing Hometown: S. Norfolk, VA

Year	Rank	Starts	Poles	1	2	3	4	5	6–10	Laps	Laps Led	Races Led	Miles	$
1951	N/A	2	0	0	0	0	0	0	0	355	0	0	444	100
Lifetime		2	0	0	0	0	0	0	0	355	0	0	444	$100

Bud Diamond

Bud Diamond
Racing Hometown: Long Beach, CA

Year	Rank	Starts	Poles	1	2	3	4	5	6–10	Laps	Laps Led	Races Led	Miles	$
1954	131	2	0	0	0	0	0	0	0	277	0	0	139	25
Lifetime		2	0	0	0	0	0	0	0	277	0	0	139	$25

Eduardo Dibos

Eduardo Dibos (Chi Chi)
Deceased
Racing Hometown: Lima, Peru

Year	Rank	Starts	Poles	1	2	3	4	5	6–10	Laps	Laps Led	Races Led	Miles	$
1959	42	3	0	0	0	0	0	2	0	181	0	0	453	1,050
Lifetime		3	0	0	0	0	0	2	0	181	0	0	453	$1,050

Year	Rank	Starts	Poles	Finish 1	2	3	4	5	6–10	Laps	Laps Led	Races Led	Miles	$

Eddie Dickerson

Edward Dickerson
B: 7/17/1955
Racing Hometown: Milford, DE

Year	Rank	Starts	Poles	1	2	3	4	5	6–10	Laps	Laps Led	Races Led	Miles	$
1980	73	2	0	0	0	0	0	0	0	787	0	0	632	1,590
Lifetime		2	0	0	0	0	0	0	0	787	0	0	632	$1,590

Bob Dickson

Robert Dickson
Racing Hometown: Salem, NJ

Year	Rank	Starts	Poles	1	2	3	4	5	6–10	Laps	Laps Led	Races Led	Miles	$
1950	51	6	0	0	0	0	0	0	2	627	0	0	380	275
1951	N/A	1	0	0	0	0	0	0	0	0	0	0	0	25
Lifetime		7	0	0	0	0	0	0	2	627	0	0	380	$300

Larry Dickson

Lawrence Dickson
B: 9/8/1938
Racing Hometown: Marietta, OH

Year	Rank	Starts	Poles	1	2	3	4	5	6–10	Laps	Laps Led	Races Led	Miles	$
1972	NR	1	0	0	0	0	0	0	0	103	0	0	258	1,535
1973	—	0												310
Lifetime		1	0	0	0	0	0	0	0	103	0	0	258	$1,845

Darel Dieringer

Darel E. Dieringer
B: 6/1/1926   D: 10/28/1989
Racing Hometown: Indianapolis, IN

Year	Rank	Starts	Poles	1	2	3	4	5	6–10	Laps	Laps Led	Races Led	Miles	$
1957	59	9	0	0	0	0	0	0	3	1,262	0	0	849	1,210
1958	131	2	0	0	0	0	0	0	0	125	0	0	102	110
1961	35	7	0	0	0	0	0	1	1	1,008	0	0	1,735	3,150
1962	33	14	1	0	0	0	0	1	2	3,179	17	1	2,986	5,000
1963	7	20	0	1	0	1	3	2	8	5,513	84	3	5,432	29,725
1964	11	27	1	1	0	1	2	2	7	5,662	238	5	5,364	20,685
1965	3	35	2	1	4	2	3	0	5	6,845	737	10	5,806	52,214
1966	12	25	0	3	3	0	1	0	2	4,818	515	8	4,545	52,530
1967	12	19	6	1	3	3	0	1	1	4,537	765	11	4,906	34,710
1968	21	18	1	0	1	0	3	1	3	4,409	159	2	4,972	28,215
1969	NR	1	0	0	0	0	0	0	0	119	0	0	60	250
1975	54	4	0	0	0	0	0	0	2	923	2	1	1,629	10,530
Lifetime		181	11	7	11	7	12	8	34	38,400	2,517	41	38,385	$241,054

Bob Dietrich

Robert Dietrich
Racing Hometown: Pittsburgh, PA

Year	Rank	Starts	Poles	1	2	3	4	5	6–10	Laps	Laps Led	Races Led	Miles	$
1951	68	2	0	0	0	0	0	0	2		0	0		225
Lifetime		2	0	0	0	0	0	0	2		0	0		$225

Ernie Dietzman

Ernest Dietzman
Racing Hometown: Phoenix, AZ

Year	Rank	Starts	Poles	1	2	3	4	5	6–10	Laps	Laps Led	Races Led	Miles	$
1951	N/A	1	0	0	0	0	0	0	0		0	0		25
Lifetime		1	0	0	0	0	0	0	0		0	0		$25

Tom Dill

Thomas Dill
Racing Hometown: Harbor Creek, PA

Year	Rank	Starts	Poles	1	2	3	4	5	6–10	Laps	Laps Led	Races Led	Miles	$
1961	71	3	0	0	0	0	0	0	0	273	0	0	631	630
Lifetime		3	0	0	0	0	0	0	0	273	0	0	631	$630

Jim Dimeo

James Dimeo
Racing Hometown: Gastonia, NC

Year	Rank	Starts	Poles	1	2	3	4	5	6–10	Laps	Laps Led	Races Led	Miles	$
1964	97	3	0	0	0	0	0	0	1	368	0	0	136	385
Lifetime		3	0	0	0	0	0	0	1	368	0	0	136	$385

Chick DiNatale

Chick DiNatale
Racing Hometown: Trenton, NJ

Year	Rank	Starts	Poles	1	2	3	4	5	6–10	Laps	Laps Led	Races Led	Miles	$
1949	NR	1	0	0	0	0	0	0	0	96	0	0	96	0
Lifetime		1	0	0	0	0	0	0	0	96	0	0	96	$0

Year	Rank	Starts	Poles	Finish 1	2	3	4	5	6–10	Laps	Laps Led	Races Led	Miles	$

Rocky DiNatale

Rocky DiNatale
Racing Hometown: Trenton, NJ

Year	Rank	Starts	Poles	1	2	3	4	5	6–10	Laps	Laps Led	Races Led	Miles	$
1951	NR	1	0	0	0	0	0	0	0	0	0	0	0	25
Lifetime		1	0	0	0	0	0	0	0	0	0	0	0	$25

John Dineen

John Dineen
B: 4/3/1946
Racing Hometown: El Cajon, CA

Year	Rank	Starts	Poles	1	2	3	4	5	6–10	Laps	Laps Led	Races Led	Miles	$
1976	95	1	0	0	0	0	0	0	0	73	0	0	191	1,040
1977	84T	1	0	0	0	0	0	0	0	89	0	0	233	1,400
Lifetime		2	0	0	0	0	0	0	0	162	0	0	424	$2,440

C. H. Dingler

Charles H. Dingler (Charlie)
Racing Hometown: Birmingham, AL

Year	Rank	Starts	Poles	1	2	3	4	5	6–10	Laps	Laps Led	Races Led	Miles	$
1951	N/A	3	0	0	0	0	0	0	0		0	0		100
1952	153	1	0	0	0	0	0	0	0	160	0	0	80	35
1953	36	5	0	0	0	0	0	0	3	119	0	0	60	275
1954	118	3	0	0	0	0	0	0	1	383	0	0	348	175
1955	NR	1	0	0	0	0	0	0	0	8	0	0	4	0
1956	96	3	0	0	0	0	0	0	0	181	0	0	239	200
Lifetime		16	0	0	0	0	0	0	4	851	0	0	730	$785

Harry Dinwiddie

Harry Dinwiddie
Racing Hometown: Oneida, TN

Year	Rank	Starts	Poles	1	2	3	4	5	6–10	Laps	Laps Led	Races Led	Miles	$
1980	82	1	0	0	0	0	0	0	0	173	0	0	460	5,250
1981	—	0												600
Lifetime		1	0	0	0	0	0	0	0	173	0	0	460	$5,850

Dave Dion

David F. Dion
B: 11/30/1943
Racing Hometown: Hudson, NH

Year	Rank	Starts	Poles	1	2	3	4	5	6–10	Laps	Laps Led	Races Led	Miles	$
1978	69	4	0	0	0	0	0	0	0	335	0	0	314	2,285
1979	72	2	0	0	0	0	0	0	0	528	0	0	284	1,265
1980	45	4	0	0	0	0	0	0	1	1,075	0	0	1,171	5,015
1981	94	1	0	0	0	0	0	0	0	143	0	0	78	615
1983	90T	1	0	0	0	0	0	0	0	50	0	0	27	700
Lifetime		12	0	0	0	0	0	0	1	2,131	0	0	1,873	$9,880

Francis Dionne

Francis Dionne
Racing Hometown: Philadelphia, PA

Year	Rank	Starts	Poles	1	2	3	4	5	6–10	Laps	Laps Led	Races Led	Miles	$
1956	262	1	0	0	0	0	0	0	0	2	0	0	2	150
Lifetime		1	0	0	0	0	0	0	0	2	0	0	2	$150

Sam DiRusso

Samuel DiRusso
Racing Hometown: Sandbury, MA

Year	Rank	Starts	Poles	1	2	3	4	5	6–10	Laps	Laps Led	Races Led	Miles	$
1951	NR	1	0	0	0	0	0	0	0		0	0		25
1953	NR	2	0	0	0	0	0	0	1	213	0	0	225	75
Lifetime		3	0	0	0	0	0	0	1	213	0	0	225	$100

Al Disney

Al Disney
Racing Hometown: Silver Spring, MD

Year	Rank	Starts	Poles	1	2	3	4	5	6–10	Laps	Laps Led	Races Led	Miles	$
1961	142	1	0	0	0	0	0	0	0	214	0	0	107	125
Lifetime		1	0	0	0	0	0	0	0	214	0	0	107	$125

Pete Diviney

Peter Diviney
Racing Hometown: St. Claire Shores, MI

Year	Rank	Starts	Poles	1	2	3	4	5	6–10	Laps	Laps Led	Races Led	Miles	$
1956	125	2	0	0	0	0	0	0	0	378	0	0	189	150
1957	200	1	0	0	0	0	0	0	0	13	0	0	13	0
Lifetime		3	0	0	0	0	0	0	0	391	0	0	202	$150

Ben Dixon

Benjamin Dixon
Racing Hometown: Shelby, NC

Year	Rank	Starts	Poles	1	2	3	4	5	6–10	Laps	Laps Led	Races Led	Miles	$
1951	N/A	1	0	0	0	0	0	0	0		0	0		0

Year	Rank	Starts	Poles	Finish						Laps	Laps Led	Races Led	Miles	$
				1	2	3	4	5	6–10	Laps	Led	Led	Miles	$

Ben Dixon *continued*

Year	Rank	Starts	Poles	1	2	3	4	5	6–10	Laps	Laps Led	Races Led	Miles	$
1953	NR	1	0	0	0	0	0	0	0	187	0	0	257	105
Lifetime		2	0	0	0	0	0	0	0	187	0	0	257	$105

Dick Dixon

Richard Dixon
B: 1929 D: 5/28/1967 *Killed in Modified race @ Thompson, CT.*
Racing Hometown: Warehouse Point, CT

Year	Rank	Starts	Poles	1	2	3	4	5	6–10	Laps	Laps Led	Races Led	Miles	$
1960	119	2	0	0	0	0	0	0	0	181	0	0	453	250
1962	NR	1	0	0	0	0	0	0	0	23	0	0	12	75
1965	NR	8	0	0	0	2	1	2	2	2,029	0	0	733	2,215
Lifetime		11	0	0	0	2	1	2	2	2,233	0	0	1,197	$2,540

John Dodd Sr.

John Dodd Sr.
B: 1913
Racing Hometown: Glen Burnie, MD

Year	Rank	Starts	Poles	1	2	3	4	5	6–10	Laps	Laps Led	Races Led	Miles	$
1953	NR	1	0	0	0	0	0	0			0	0		35
1954	207	2	0	0	0	0	0	0	1	302	0	0	271	300
1955	164T	2	0	0	0	0	0	0	0	292	0	0	160	100
1956	297T	1	0	0	0	0	0	0	0	28	0	0	14	0
1957	130	1	0	0	0	0	0	0	1	189	0	0	95	140
1958	83	1	0	0	0	0	0	0	0	290	0	0	290	150
1959	NR	3	0	0	0	0	0	0	1	704	0	0	352	540
Lifetime		11	0	0	0	0	0	0	3	1,805	0	0	1,181	$1,265

John Dodd Jr.

John Dodd Jr.
B: 5/14/1933
Racing Hometown: Baltimore, MD

Year	Rank	Starts	Poles	1	2	3	4	5	6–10	Laps	Laps Led	Races Led	Miles	$
1954	50	1	0	0	0	0	0	0	1	161	0	0	81	150
1955	25	13	0	0	0	0	0	1	6	1,653	0	0	915	1,695
1956	158	4	0	0	0	0	0	0	1	372	0	0	180	100
1957	NR	1	0	0	0	0	0	0	0	67	0	0	34	25
1960	NR	2	0	0	0	0	0	0	0	51	0	0	54	50
1962	108	2	0	0	0	0	0	0	0	78	0	0	127	625
Lifetime		23	0	0	0	0	0	1	8	2,382	0	0	1,390	$2,645

Randy Dodd

Randall Dodd
Racing Hometown: Newhall, CA

Year	Rank	Starts	Poles	1	2	3	4	5	6–10	Laps	Laps Led	Races Led	Miles	$
1967	108	1	0	0	0	0	0	0	0	47	0	0	127	500
1969	NR	1	0	0	0	0	0	0	0	143	0	0	386	950
1970	83	2	0	0	0	0	0	0	0	183	0	0	479	1,715
Lifetime		4	0	0	0	0	0	0	0	373	0	0	992	$3,165

Johnny Dodson

Johnny Frank Dodson
B: 4/24/1931
Racing Hometown: King, NC

Year	Rank	Starts	Poles	1	2	3	4	5	6–10	Laps	Laps Led	Races Led	Miles	$
1956	36	11	0	0	0	0	0	0	4	1,842	0	0	1,379	1,450
1957	121	4	0	0	0	0	0	0	1	404	0	0	326	715
Lifetime		15	0	0	0	0	0	0	5	2,246	0	0	1,706	$2,165

Russ Dohlen

Russell Dohlen

Year	Rank	Starts	Poles	1	2	3	4	5	6–10	Laps	Laps Led	Races Led	Miles	$
1957	NR	1	0	0	0	0	0	0	0		0	0		0
Lifetime		1	0	0	0	0	0	0	0		0	0		$0

Johnny Dollar

John Dollar
Racing Hometown: Bay Shore, NY

Year	Rank	Starts	Poles	1	2	3	4	5	6–10	Laps	Laps Led	Races Led	Miles	$
1960	144	2	0	0	0	0	0	0	0	8	0	0	17	200
Lifetime		2	0	0	0	0	0	0	0	8	0	0	17	$200

Jack Donohue

Jack Donohue
B: 1945
Racing Hometown: Nobleton, Ont., Canada

Year	Rank	Starts	Poles	1	2	3	4	5	6–10	Laps	Laps Led	Races Led	Miles	$
1974	98	2	0	0	0	0	0	0	0	333	0	0	237	1,020

Year	Rank	Starts	Poles	Finish 1	2	3	4	5	6–10	Laps	Laps Led	Races Led	Miles	$

Jack Donohue *continued*

Year	Rank	Starts	Poles	1	2	3	4	5	6–10	Laps	Laps Led	Races Led	Miles	$
1976	65	3	0	0	0	0	0	0	0	888	0	0	896	2,680
Lifetime		5	0	0	0	0	0	0	0	1,221	0	0	1,132	$3,700

Mark Donohue

Mark Donohue
B: 3/18/1937   D: 8/19/1975   *Killed in practice for South African Grand Prix.*
Racing Hometown: Newtowne Square, PA

Year	Rank	Starts	Poles	1	2	3	4	5	6–10	Laps	Laps Led	Races Led	Miles	$
1972	NR	4	0	0	0	0	0	0	0	390	0	0	669	5,580
1973	NR	2	0	1	0	0	0	0	0	393	138	1	803	16,120
Lifetime		6	0	1	0	0	0	0	0	783	138	1	1,473	$21,700

Jim Donovan

James Donovan
Racing Hometown: Chicago, IL

Year	Rank	Starts	Poles	1	2	3	4	5	6–10	Laps	Laps Led	Races Led	Miles	$
1956	151	2	0	0	0	0	0	0	0	247	0	0	152	200
Lifetime		2	0	0	0	0	0	0	0	247	0	0	152	$200

Paul Dorrity

Paul Dorrity
B: 10/19/1943
Racing Hometown: Modesto, CA

Year	Rank	Starts	Poles	1	2	3	4	5	6–10	Laps	Laps Led	Races Led	Miles	$
1968	99	1	0	0	0	0	0	0	0	28	0	0	76	500
1969	NR	1	0	0	0	0	0	0	0	129	0	0	348	850
1970	77	1	0	0	0	0	0	0	0	0	0	0	0	615
1971	NR	2	0	0	0	0	0	0	0	74	0	0	194	1,685
1972	84	2	0	0	0	0	0	0	0	208	0	0	545	1,860
Lifetime		7	0	0	0	0	0	0	0	439	0	0	1,163	$5,510

Eldon Dotson

Eldon Dotson
Racing Hometown: Allen, TX

Year	Rank	Starts	Poles	1	2	3	4	5	6–10	Laps	Laps Led	Races Led	Miles	$
1985	78	2	0	0	0	0	0	0	0	104	0	0	153	2,805
Lifetime		2	0	0	0	0	0	0	0	104	0	0	153	$2,805

Frank Douglas

Frank Douglas
Racing Hometown: Albuquerque, NM

Year	Rank	Starts	Poles	1	2	3	4	5	6–10	Laps	Laps Led	Races Led	Miles	$
1955	178T	1	0	0	0	0	0	0	0	89	0	0	89	25
Lifetime		1	0	0	0	0	0	0	0	89	0	0	89	$25

Red Douglass

R. W. Douglass
B: 1920
Racing Hometown: New Albany, OH

Year	Rank	Starts	Poles	1	2	3	4	5	6–10	Laps	Laps Led	Races Led	Miles	$
1953	163	1	0	0	0	0	0	0	0	33	0	0	135	25
Lifetime		1	0	0	0	0	0	0	0	33	0	0	135	$25

Fred Dove

Fred Dove
Racing Hometown: Martinsville, VA

Year	Rank	Starts	Poles	1	2	3	4	5	6–10	Laps	Laps Led	Races Led	Miles	$
1952	31	8	0	0	0	0	0	0	3	919	0	0	692	390
1953	16	20	0	0	0	0	0	0	4	742	0	0	720	1,240
1954	36	12	0	0	0	0	0	0	2	1,428	0	0	869	525
1955	51	7	0	0	0	1	0	0	2	830	0	0	416	750
Lifetime		47	0	0	0	1	0	0	11	3,919	0	0	2,696	$2,905

Red Dowdy

Red Dowdy
Racing Hometown: Dallas, TX

Year	Rank	Starts	Poles	1	2	3	4	5	6–10	Laps	Laps Led	Races Led	Miles	$
1953	NR	1	0	0	0	0	0	0	0		0	0		25
Lifetime		1	0	0	0	0	0	0	0		0	0		$25

Fred Drake

Fred Drake
Racing Hometown: Trenton, NJ

Year	Rank	Starts	Poles	1	2	3	4	5	6–10	Laps	Laps Led	Races Led	Miles	$
1972	NR	1	0	0	0	0	0	0	0	93	0	0	140	345
Lifetime		1	0	0	0	0	0	0	0	93	0	0	140	$345

Year	Rank	Starts	Poles	Finish 1	2	3	4	5	6–10	Laps	Laps Led	Races Led	Miles	$

Tom Drake

Thomas Drake
Racing Hometown: Los Angeles, CA

Year	Rank	Starts	Poles	1	2	3	4	5	6–10	Laps	Laps Led	Races Led	Miles	$
1954	NR	1	0	0	0	0	0	0	0	444	0	0	222	50
Lifetime		1	0	0	0	0	0	0	0	444	0	0	222	$50

Jerry Draper

Jerry Draper
Racing Hometown: Silvis, IL

Year	Rank	Starts	Poles	1	2	3	4	5	6–10	Laps	Laps Led	Races Led	Miles	$
1953	102	1	0	0	0	0	0	0	0	0	0	0	0	25
1958	141	3	0	0	0	0	0	0	0	488	0	0	430	250
1959	NR	6	0	0	0	0	0	0	3	1,049	0	0	503	640
Lifetime		10	0	0	0	0	0	0	3	1,537	0	0	932	$915

John DuBoise

John DuBoise
B: 4/26/1919
Racing Hometown: Paterson, NJ

Year	Rank	Starts	Poles	1	2	3	4	5	6–10	Laps	Laps Led	Races Led	Miles	$
1950	73	2	0	0	0	0	0	0	0	367	0	0	459	250
1951	66	3	0	0	0	0	1	0	0	211	0	0	179	400
1952	159	2	0	0	0	0	0	0	0	203	0	0	128	50
Lifetime		7	0	0	0	0	1	0	0	781	0	0	766	$700

Don Duckworth

Donald Duckworth
B: 1928
Racing Hometown: Graycourt, SC

Year	Rank	Starts	Poles	1	2	3	4	5	6–10	Laps	Laps Led	Races Led	Miles	$
1955	204	1	0	0	0	0	0	0	0	147	0	0	202	50
Lifetime		1	0	0	0	0	0	0	0	147	0	0	202	$50

Bob Duell

Robert Duell
Racing Hometown: Warren, PA

Year	Rank	Starts	Poles	1	2	3	4	5	6–10	Laps	Laps Led	Races Led	Miles	$
1956	78	6	0	0	0	0	0	1	0	642	0	0	443	670
1957	76	5	0	0	0	0	0	0	0	503	0	0	476	260
1958	22	7	1	0	1	1	0	1	3	1,273	0	0	969	2,415
1959	108	4	0	0	0	0	0	0	0	672	0	0	578	650
1960	64	6	0	0	0	0	0	0	1	422	0	0	531	935
Lifetime		28	1	0	1	1	0	2	4	3,512	0	0	2,997	$4,930

Philip Duffie

Philip Duffie
Racing Hometown: Augusta, GA

Year	Rank	Starts	Poles	1	2	3	4	5	6–10	Laps	Laps Led	Races Led	Miles	$
1982	40	5	0	0	0	0	0	0	0	1,166	0	0	2,273	13,755
1983	50	4	0	0	0	0	0	0	0	750	0	0	1,168	7,730
1984	—	0												2,750
1988	77T	1	0	0	0	0	0	0	0	332	0	0	454	4,540
1989	—	0												1,200
1990	68	2	0	0	0	0	0	0	0	191	0	0	419	10,930
1991	—	0												2,000
Lifetime		12	0	0	0	0	0	0	0	2,439	0	0	4,314	$42,905

Art Dugan

Arthur Dugan

Year	Rank	Starts	Poles	1	2	3	4	5	6–10	Laps	Laps Led	Races Led	Miles	$
1954	NR	1	0	0	0	0	0	0	0	165	0	0	83	25
Lifetime		1	0	0	0	0	0	0	0	165	0	0	83	$25

Bobby Dugan

Robert Dugan
Racing Hometown: Waukegan, IL

Year	Rank	Starts	Poles	1	2	3	4	5	6–10	Laps	Laps Led	Races Led	Miles	$
1952	77	2	0	0	0	0	0	0	0	275	0	0	138	75
Lifetime		2	0	0	0	0	0	0	0	275	0	0	138	$75

Yvon DuHamel

Yvon DuHamel
Racing Hometown: Ville LaSalle, Que., Canada

Year	Rank	Starts	Poles	1	2	3	4	5	6–10	Laps	Laps Led	Races Led	Miles	$
1973	109	1	0	0	0	0	0	0	1	381	0	0	238	800
Lifetime		1	0	0	0	0	0	0	1	381	0	0	238	$800

Year	Rank	Starts	Poles	Finish 1	2	3	4	5	6–10	Laps	Laps Led	Races Led	Miles	$

Ray Duhigg

Raymond Duhigg
B: 1929   D: 10/9/1955   *Killed in race @ Salem, IN.*
Racing Hometown: Toledo, OH

Year	Rank	Starts	Poles	1	2	3	4	5	6–10	Laps	Laps Led	Races Led	Miles	$
1950	27	5	0	0	0	0	0	1	1		0	0		450
1951	N/A	6	0	0	0	0	0	0	0	213	0	0	190	150
1952	8	18	0	0	0	2	1	1	6	2,823	0	0	2,029	3,811
1953	NR	12	0	0	0	2	2	0	4	489	0	0	411	2,765
1954	NR	12	0	0	0	0	1	1	3	1,458	0	0	938	1,375
1955	86	1	0	0	0	1	0	0	0	39	0	0	160	1,000
Lifetime		54	0	0	0	5	4	3	14	5,022	0	0	3,727	$9,551

Gerald Duke

Gerald Duke
B: 1928
Racing Hometown: College Park, GA

Year	Rank	Starts	Poles	1	2	3	4	5	6–10	Laps	Laps Led	Races Led	Miles	$
1959	51	1	0	0	0	0	0	0	0	249	0	0	125	125
1960	24	11	0	0	0	0	1	0	6	2,062	0	0	2,017	5,930
1961	176	1	0	0	0	0	0	0	0	39	0	0	20	50
1962	84	4	0	0	0	0	0	0	0	607	0	0	754	800
Lifetime		17	0	0	0	0	1	0	6	2,957	0	0	2,915	$6,905

George Dunn

George Dunn
B: 1931
Racing Hometown: Raleigh, NC

Year	Rank	Starts	Poles	1	2	3	4	5	6–10	Laps	Laps Led	Races Led	Miles	$
1958	75	10	1	0	1	0	1	1	3	1,747	10	1	939	1,880
1959	NR	1	0	0	0	0	0	0	0	145	0	0	48	130
1962	92	1	0	0	0	0	1	0	0	108	0	0	27	305
Lifetime		12	1	0	1	0	2	1	3	2,000	10	1	1,015	$2,315

Huey Dunn

Huey Dunn
Racing Hometown: Charlotte, NC

Year	Rank	Starts	Poles	1	2	3	4	5	6–10	Laps	Laps Led	Races Led	Miles	$
1950	75	1	0	0	0	0	0	0	1	172	0	0	129	75
Lifetime		1	0	0	0	0	0	0	1	172	0	0	129	$75

Jim Dunn

James Dunn
Racing Hometown: Beaverdam, VA

Year	Rank	Starts	Poles	1	2	3	4	5	6–10	Laps	Laps Led	Races Led	Miles	$
1958	163	1	0	0	0	0	0	0	0	21	0	0	55	100
Lifetime		1	0	0	0	0	0	0	0	21	0	0	55	$100

Glenn Dunnaway

Henry Glenn Dunnaway
B: 1915   D: 3/15/1964   *Killed @ train crossing in Camden, SC.*
Racing Hometown: Gastonia, NC

Year	Rank	Starts	Poles	1	2	3	4	5	6–10	Laps	Laps Led	Races Led	Miles	$
1949	9	6	0	0	0	1	0	0	2	594	1	1	347	810
1950	NR	7	0	0	1	0	1	0	1	866	0	0	731	1,275
1951	89	6	0	0	0	0	0	0	2		0	0		275
Lifetime		19	0	0	1	1	1	0	5	1,460	1	1	1,078	$2,360

Harold Dunnaway

Harold Dunnaway
B: 10/7/1933
Racing Hometown: Gastonia, NC

Year	Rank	Starts	Poles	1	2	3	4	5	6–10	Laps	Laps Led	Races Led	Miles	$
1966	123	1	0	0	0	0	0	0	0	14	0	0	14	560
Lifetime		1	0	0	0	0	0	0	0	14	0	0	14	$560

Gary DuPuis

Gary DuPuis
Racing Hometown: Deland, FL

Year	Rank	Starts	Poles	1	2	3	4	5	6–10	Laps	Laps Led	Races Led	Miles	$
1970	89	1	0	0	0	0	0	0	0	78	0	0	195	735
Lifetime		1	0	0	0	0	0	0	0	78	0	0	195	$735

Ralph Dutton

Ralph Dutton
Racing Hometown: Chilhowie, VA

Year	Rank	Starts	Poles	1	2	3	4	5	6–10	Laps	Laps Led	Races Led	Miles	$
1953	125	4	0	0	0	0	0	0	0	46	0	0	23	100
1954	145T	1	0	0	0	0	0	0	0	70	0	0	44	25
Lifetime		5	0	0	0	0	0	0	0	116	0	0	67	$125

Year	Rank	Starts	Poles	Finish 1	2	3	4	5	6–10	Laps	Laps Led	Races Led	Miles	$

Doug Duvall
Douglas Duvall
Racing Hometown: Winston-Salem, NC

Year	Rank	Starts	Poles	1	2	3	4	5	6–10	Laps	Laps Led	Races Led	Miles	$
1962	NR	1	0	0	0	0	0	0	0	59	0	0	15	160
Lifetime		1	0	0	0	0	0	0	0	59	0	0	15	$160

Red Duvall
Duane Michael Duvall
B: 10/7/1923   D: 1/12/1994
Racing Hometown: Hammond, IN

Year	Rank	Starts	Poles	1	2	3	4	5	6–10	Laps	Laps Led	Races Led	Miles	$
1951	52	2	0	0	0	1	0	0	1		0	0		550
1952	54	4	0	0	0	0	0	0	2	538	0	0	372	275
1953	72	1	0	0	0	0	0	0	0	37	0	0	152	75
1954	NR	1	0	0	0	0	0	0	0	49	0	0	25	0
Lifetime		8	0	0	0	1	0	0	3	624	0	0	548	$900

Clark Dwyer
Clark Dwyer
B: 1/12/1964
Racing Hometown: Littleton, CO

Year	Rank	Starts	Poles	1	2	3	4	5	6–10	Laps	Laps Led	Races Led	Miles	$
1983	46	5	0	0	0	0	0	0	1	851	0	0	1,412	14,570
1984	23	26	0	0	0	0	0	0	0	7,025	1	1	8,059	114,335
1985	22	28	0	0	0	0	0	0	0	7,205	0	0	8,550	128,710
1986	—	0												1,800
Lifetime		59	0	0	0	0	0	0	1	15,081	1	1	18,021	$259,415

Carson Dyer
Carson Dyer
Racing Hometown: Atlanta, GA

Year	Rank	Starts	Poles	1	2	3	4	5	6–10	Laps	Laps Led	Races Led	Miles	$
1950	NR	1	0	0	0	0	0	0	0	310	0	0	388	0
1951	N/A	3	0	0	0	0	0	0	0		0	0		60
1952	84T	1	0	0	0	0	0	0	1	283	0	0	142	170
Lifetime		5	0	0	0	0	0	0	1	593	0	0	530	$230

Charles Dyer
Charles Dyer
B: 11/10/1917   D: 5/24/1957   *Died of heart attack in late model race @ Fredericksburg, VA.*
Racing Hometown: North Bergen, NJ

Year	Rank	Starts	Poles	1	2	3	4	5	6–10	Laps	Laps Led	Races Led	Miles	$
1955	70	3	0	0	0	0	0	0	2	446	0	0	268	350
Lifetime		3	0	0	0	0	0	0	2	446	0	0	268	$350

Ralph Dyer
Ralph Dyer
Racing Hometown: Shreveport, LA

Year	Rank	Starts	Poles	1	2	3	4	5	6–10	Laps	Laps Led	Races Led	Miles	$
1950	94T	1	0	0	0	0	0	0	0		0	0		50
1953	NR	6	0	0	0	0	0	0	3	480	0	0	384	600
Lifetime		7	0	0	0	0	0	0	3	480	0	0	384	$650

Dick Eagan
Clayton Richard Eagan
B: 6/12/1919
Racing Hometown: Springdale, CT

Year	Rank	Starts	Poles	1	2	3	4	5	6–10	Laps	Laps Led	Races Led	Miles	$
1950	NR	1	0	0	0	0	0	0	0		0	0		0
1951	51	3	0	0	0	1	0	0	1		0	0		625
1952	NR	2	0	0	0	0	0	0	1		0	0		100
Lifetime		6	0	0	0	1	0	0	2		0	0		$725

Mike Eagan
Michael P. Eagan
B: 8/2/1926
Racing Hometown: Dunkirk, NY

Year	Rank	Starts	Poles	1	2	3	4	5	6–10	Laps	Laps Led	Races Led	Miles	$
1949	22T	1	0	0	0	0	1	0	0		0	0		300
Lifetime		1	0	0	0	0	1	0	0		0	0		$300

Harvey Eakin
Harvey Eakin
Racing Hometown: Baltimore, MD

Year	Rank	Starts	Poles	1	2	3	4	5	6–10	Laps	Laps Led	Races Led	Miles	$
1954	42	7	0	0	0	0	0	0	0	741	0	0	915	425
1955	106	3	0	0	0	0	0	0	0	307	0	0	416	210
1956	175	2	0	0	0	0	0	0	0	278	0	0	278	100

Year	Rank	Starts	Poles	1	2	3	4	5	6–10	Laps	Laps Led	Races Led	Miles	$

Harvey Eakin *continued*

Year	Rank	Starts	Poles	1	2	3	4	5	6–10	Laps	Laps Led	Races Led	Miles	$
1957	56	5	0	0	0	0	0	0	0	763	0	0	575	375
Lifetime		17	0	0	0	0	0	0	0	2,089	0	0	2,184	$1,110

Danny Eames

Daniel Eames
B: 1918
Racing Hometown: Long Beach, CA

Year	Rank	Starts	Poles	1	2	3	4	5	6–10	Laps	Laps Led	Races Led	Miles	$
1958	NR	1	0	0	0	0	0	0	0	147	0	0	387	185
Lifetime		1	0	0	0	0	0	0	0	147	0	0	387	$185

Jerry Earl

Jerry Earl
Racing Hometown: Rochester, NY

Year	Rank	Starts	Poles	1	2	3	4	5	6–10	Laps	Laps Led	Races Led	Miles	$
1953	80T	1	0	0	0	0	0	0	1		0	0		100
Lifetime		1	0	0	0	0	0	0	1		0	0		$100

Dale Earnhardt

Ralph Dale Earnhardt
B: 4/29/1951
Racing Hometown: Kannapolis, NC

Year	Rank	Starts	Poles	1	2	3	4	5	6–10	Laps	Laps Led	Races Led	Miles	$
1975	NR	1	0	0	0	0	0	0	0	355	0	0	533	2,425
1976	103	2	0	0	0	0	0	0	0	416	0	0	630	3,085
1977	117	1	0	0	0	0	0	0	0	25	0	0	38	1,375
1978	43	5	0	0	0	0	1	0	1	1,359	0	0	2,370	20,745
1979	7	27	4	1	1	3	4	2	6	8,340	604	16	9,357	274,810
1980	1	31	0	5	3	4	3	4	5	**9,615**	1,185	25	**11,136**	671,991
1981	7	31	0	0	2	3	2	2	8	8,134	300	12	10,062	353,972
1982	12	30	1	1	1	3	2	0	5	7,208	1,062	18	7,787	400,880
1983	8	30	0	2	3	0	3	1	5	7,701	1,027	19	8,946	465,203
1984	4	30	0	2	4	2	0	4	10	9,584	446	16	10,850	634,671
1985	8	28	1	4	0	0	4	2	6	8,231	1,237	17	9,149	546,596
1986	1	29	1	5	5	3	1	2	7	**9,212**	2,127	**26**	**11,164**	1,768,880
1987	1	29	1	11	5	1	2	2	3	**9,043**	3,358	**27**	10,898	2,069,243
1988	3	29	0	3	2	3	3	2	6	9,561	**1,808**	**20**	11,314	1,214,089
1989	2	29	0	5	3	5	1	0	5	9,112	**2,735**	22	10,796	1,432,230
1990	1	29	4	9	3	3	1	2	5	9,162	**2,438**	22	10,955	3,308,056
1991	1	29	0	4	3	4	1	2	7	9,541	1,125	20	**11,435**	2,416,685
1992	12	29	1	1	2	2	1	0	9	8,694	487	10	10,198	915,463
1993	1	30	2	6	5	3	3	0	4	**9,787**	1,475	**21**	**11,808**	3,353,789
1994	1	31	2	4	7	6	1	2	5	9,546	1,013	**23**	11,409	3,400,733
1995	2	31	3	5	6	5	1	2	4	9,625	1,583	24	11,714	3,154,241
1996	4	31	2	2	3	3	4	1	4	**9,530**	614	18	**11,523**	2,285,926
Lifetime		542	22	70	58	53	38	30	105	163,781	24,624	356	194,069	$28,695,088
				6th						5th	5th	4th	6th	1st

Ralph Earnhardt

Ralph Lee Earnhardt
B: 2/29/1928   D: 9/26/1973
Racing Hometown: Kannapolis, NC

Year	Rank	Starts	Poles	1	2	3	4	5	6–10	Laps	Laps Led	Races Led	Miles	$
1956	148	1	1	0	1	0	0	0	0	250	15	1	100	625
1957	37	9	0	0	0	0	0	0	3	1,465	0	0	764	1,150
1961	17	8	0	0	1	1	0	0	3	1,664	90	3	2,522	11,473
1962	29	17	0	0	0	1	0	1	4	2,022	0	0	2,159	4,545
1963	94	5	0	0	0	0	0	0	0	491	0	0	767	1,995
1964	46	11	0	0	0	0	1	0	0	1,107	0	0	1,055	3,290
Lifetime		51	1	0	2	2	1	1	10	6,999	105	4	7,366	$22,050

Sonny Easley

Lynwood Easley
B: 6/5/1939   D: 1/15/1978   *Killed @ Riverside, CA.*
Racing Hometown: Van Nuys, CA

Year	Rank	Starts	Poles	1	2	3	4	5	6–10	Laps	Laps Led	Races Led	Miles	$
1972	113	1	0	0	0	0	0	0	0	35	0	0	92	670
1973	90	2	0	0	0	0	0	0	0	144	0	0	377	2,015
1974	61	3	0	0	0	0	0	0	1	415	0	0	1,074	4,800
1975	66	3	0	0	0	0	0	0	0	136	2	1	355	2,405
1976	38	7	0	0	0	0	0	0	2	1,861	0	0	2,137	11,290
1977	50	3	0	0	0	0	0	1	1	360	0	0	925	9,490
Lifetime		19	0	0	0	0	0	1	4	2,951	2	1	4,960	$30,670

Year	Rank	Starts	Poles	Finish 1	2	3	4	5	6–10	Laps	Laps Led	Races Led	Miles	$

Doug Easton
Douglas Easton
B: 3/12/1931
Racing Hometown: Horse Cave, NY

Year	Rank	Starts	Poles	1	2	3	4	5	6–10	Laps	Laps Led	Races Led	Miles	$
1969	NR	1	0	0	0	0	0	0	0	0	0	0	0	875
Lifetime		1	0	0	0	0	0	0	0	0	0	0	0	$875

Tom Edmonds
Thomas Edmonds
Racing Hometown: Los Angeles, CA

Year	Rank	Starts	Poles	1	2	3	4	5	6–10	Laps	Laps Led	Races Led	Miles	$
1959	NR	1	0	0	0	0	0	0	0	239	0	0	96	75
Lifetime		1	0	0	0	0	0	0	0	239	0	0	96	$75

Frank Edwards
Frank Edwards
Racing Hometown: Chicago, IL

Year	Rank	Starts	Poles	1	2	3	4	5	6–10	Laps	Laps Led	Races Led	Miles	$
1956	195T	1	0	0	0	0	0	0	0	182	0	0	91	100
Lifetime		1	0	0	0	0	0	0	0	182	0	0	91	$100

J. D. Edwards
J. D. Edwards
Racing Hometown: Albemarle, NC

Year	Rank	Starts	Poles	1	2	3	4	5	6–10	Laps	Laps Led	Races Led	Miles	$
1949	54	1	0	0	0	0	0	0	0		0	0		50
Lifetime		1	0	0	0	0	0	0	0		0	0		$50

Jonathan Lee Edwards
Jonathan Lee Edwards
B: 1958
Racing Hometown: Lake Wylie, SC

Year	Rank	Starts	Poles	1	2	3	4	5	6–10	Laps	Laps Led	Races Led	Miles	$
1985	68	2	0	0	0	0	0	0	0	633	0	0	640	3,220
1986	53	4	0	0	0	0	0	0	0	1,114	0	0	1,405	8,030
1987	78	2	0	0	0	0	0	0	0	226	0	0	309	6,155
Lifetime		8	0	0	0	0	0	0	0	1,973	0	0	2,355	$17,405

Marion Edwards
Marion Edwards
D: 1973
Racing Hometown: Hialeah, FL

Year	Rank	Starts	Poles	1	2	3	4	5	6–10	Laps	Laps Led	Races Led	Miles	$
1952	NR	1	0	0	0	0	0	1	0	183	0	0	92	200
1953	116	2	0	0	0	0	0	0	0	197	0	0	210	50
1955	NR	1	0	0	0	0	0	0	0	180	0	0	90	25
Lifetime		4	0	0	0	0	0	1	0	560	0	0	392	$275

Don Eggert
Donald Eggert
Racing Hometown: Jamestown, NY

Year	Rank	Starts	Poles	1	2	3	4	5	6–10	Laps	Laps Led	Races Led	Miles	$
1951	N/A	7	0	0	0	0	0	0	2		0	0		275
Lifetime		7	0	0	0	0	0	0	2		0	0		$275

Bob Eichlor
Robert Eichlor
Racing Hometown: Oklahoma City, OK

Year	Rank	Starts	Poles	1	2	3	4	5	6–10	Laps	Laps Led	Races Led	Miles	$
1960	138	1	0	0	0	0	0	0	0	39	0	0	59	200
Lifetime		1	0	0	0	0	0	0	0	39	0	0	59	$200

Howard Elder
Howard Elder
Racing Hometown: Jacksonville, FL

Year	Rank	Starts	Poles	1	2	3	4	5	6–10	Laps	Laps Led	Races Led	Miles	$
1949	NR	1	0	0	0	0	0	0	0		0	0		25
Lifetime		1	0	0	0	0	0	0	0		0	0		$25

Ray Elder
Raymond Marvin Elder
B: 8/19/1942
Racing Hometown: Carruthers, CA

Year	Rank	Starts	Poles	1	2	3	4	5	6–10	Laps	Laps Led	Races Led	Miles	$
1967	114	1	0	0	0	0	0	0	0	23	0	0	62	500
1968	96	1	0	0	0	0	0	0	0	37	0	0	100	500
1969	48	4	0	0	0	0	0	0	4	642	0	0	1,523	7,200
1970	53	4	0	0	0	0	0	0	1	441	0	0	1,127	4,570
1971	NR	4	0	1	1	0	0	0	1	564	70	2	1,439	30,595
1972	52	3	0	1	0	0	1	1	0	493	50	2	1,268	23,165

Year	Rank	Starts	Poles	Finish 1	2	3	4	5	6–10	Laps	Laps Led	Races Led	Miles	$

Ray Elder *continued*

Year	Rank	Starts	Poles	1	2	3	4	5	6–10	Laps	Laps Led	Races Led	Miles	$
1973	58	3	0	0	0	1	0	0	0	381	0	0	977	9,225
1974	95	2	0	0	0	0	0	0	0	37	0	0	94	1,435
1975	50	3	0	0	0	0	1	0	0	368	1	1	956	8,020
1976	58	2	0	0	0	0	2	0	0	254	0	0	665	11,715
1977	105	1	0	0	0	0	0	0	0	14	0	0	37	625
1978	64	3	0	0	0	0	0	0	1	108	0	0	283	5,305
Lifetime		31	0	2	1	1	4	1	7	3,362	121	5	8,531	$102,855

Vic Elford

Victor Elford
B: 6/10/1935
Racing Hometown: South London, England

Year	Rank	Starts	Poles	1	2	3	4	5	6–10	Laps	Laps Led	Races Led	Miles	$
1969	NR	2	0	0	0	0	0	0	0	236	0	0	590	2,950
1971	NR	1	0	0	0	0	0	0	0	46	0	0	115	220
1972	NR	1	0	0	0	0	0	0	1	182	0	0	455	3,445
Lifetime		4	0	0	0	0	0	0	1	464	0	0	1,160	$6,615

Hoss Ellington

Charles Everett Ellington
B: 5/12/1935
Racing Hometown: Wilmington, NC

Year	Rank	Starts	Poles	1	2	3	4	5	6–10	Laps	Laps Led	Races Led	Miles	$
1968	61	3	0	0	0	0	0	0	0	494	0	0	703	2,395
1969	30	15	0	0	0	0	0	0	4	2,988	0	0	4,136	16,552
1970	55	3	0	0	0	0	0	0	0	728	0	0	875	3,133
Lifetime		21	0	0	0	0	0	0	4	4,210	0	0	5,714	$22,080

Bill Elliott

William Clyde Elliott
B: 10/8/1955
Racing Hometown: Dawsonville, GA

Year	Rank	Starts	Poles	1	2	3	4	5	6–10	Laps	Laps Led	Races Led	Miles	$
1976	41	8	0	0	0	0	0	0	0	1,047	0	0	1,452	11,635
1977	35	10	0	0	0	0	0	0	2	2,082	0	0	3,319	20,075
1978	33	10	0	0	0	0	0	0	5	2,278	0	0	4,099	42,215
1979	28	14	0	0	1	0	0	0	4	3,691	8	3	4,822	58,215
1980	34	12	0	0	0	0	0	0	4	2,572	4	4	4,324	44,005
1981	30	13	1	0	0	0	1	0	6	2,777	33	3	4,444	70,320
1982	25	21	1	0	3	3	1	1	1	5,540	151	9	7,886	201,030
1983	3	30	0	1	4	1	3	3	10	9,536	173	15	11,272	514,030
1984	3	30	4	3	1	4	4	1	11	9,848	570	17	11,385	680,344
1985	2	28	11	11	2	0	2	1	2	8,724	**1,920**	19	10,727	2,433,187
1986	4	29	4	2	0	2	1	3	8	8,549	511	15	10,591	1,049,142
1987	2	29	8	6	3	1	5	1	4	8,902	1,399	22	10,422	1,599,210
1988	1	29	6	6	2	2	4	1	7	**9,647**	1,598	**20**	**11,521**	1,554,639
1989	6	29	2	3	0	1	3	1	6	9,037	380	11	10,834	849,370
1990	4	29	2	1	4	1	5	1	4	9,349	1,182	13	11,087	1,090,730
1991	11	29	2	1	2	1	0	2	6	9,030	211	6	10,826	705,605
1992	2	29	2	5	2	3	1	3	3	9,115	1,273	18	11,124	1,692,381
1993	8	30	2	0	1	2	2	1	9	9,329	14	4	11,335	955,859
1994	10	31	1	1	1	3	0	1	6	9,172	62	8	11,380	951,679
1995	8	31	2	0	0	0	2	2	7	8,995	123	8	11,073	996,816
1996	30	24	0	0	0	0	0	0	6	7,439	108	7	8,641	716,506
Lifetime		495	48	40	26	24	34	22	111	146,659	9,720	202	182,563	$16,236,933
			7th									8th	8th	3rd

Brent Elliott

Brent Elliott
B: 1959
Racing Hometown: Denton, NC

Year	Rank	Starts	Poles	1	2	3	4	5	6–10	Laps	Laps Led	Races Led	Miles	$
1984	80T	1	0	0	0	0	0	0	0	203	0	0	127	835
1985	63	3	0	0	0	0	0	0	0	837	0	0	469	3,210
1986	100	1	0	0	0	0	0	0	0	325	0	0	203	950
Lifetime		5	0	0	0	0	0	0	0	1,365	0	0	799	$4,995

Stick Elliott

Gene Hampton Elliott
B: 7/27/1934   D: 11/1/1980
Racing Hometown: Shelby, NC

Year	Rank	Starts	Poles	1	2	3	4	5	6–10	Laps	Laps Led	Races Led	Miles	$
1962	35	21	0	0	0	0	0	0	2	3,028	0	0	2,317	3,928

Year	Rank	Starts	Poles	Finish						Laps	Laps Led	Races Led	Miles	$
				1	2	3	4	5	6–10					

Stick Elliott *continued*

Year	Rank	Starts	Poles	1	2	3	4	5	6–10	Laps	Laps Led	Races Led	Miles	$
1963	23	28	0	0	0	0	0	0	7	4,693	0	0	3,766	6,235
1964	91	7	0	0	0	0	0	0	0	211	0	0	244	1,450
1965	44	15	0	0	1	0	1	0	1	2,082	0	0	1,562	5,235
1966	35	19	0	0	0	0	1	0	2	3,285	0	0	2,716	7,335
1967	58	1	0	0	0	0	0	0	0	370	0	0	555	1,650
1971	NR	2	0	0	0	0	0	0	0	598	0	0	687	1,818
Lifetime		93	0	0	1	0	2	0	12	14,267	0	0	11,847	$27,651

Tommie Elliott

Thomas D. Elliott
B: 12/27/1935   D: 6/18/1989
Racing Hometown: Bloomfield, NJ

Year	Rank	Starts	Poles	1	2	3	4	5	6–10	Laps	Laps Led	Races Led	Miles	$
1951	152	2	0	0	0	0	0	0	0	0	0	0	0	50
1954	62	3	0	0	0	0	0	0	3	546	0	0	273	400
1957	NR	1	0	0	0	0	0	0	1	281	0	0	281	500
1958	172	1	0	0	0	0	0	0	0	40	0	0	20	0
Lifetime		7	0	0	0	0	0	0	4	867	0	0	574	$950

James Ellis

James Ellis
Racing Hometown: Mobile, AL

Year	Rank	Starts	Poles	1	2	3	4	5	6–10	Laps	Laps Led	Races Led	Miles	$
1951	160T	1	0	0	0	0	0	0	0		0	0		25
Lifetime		1	0	0	0	0	0	0	0		0	0		$25

Tommy Ellis

Thomas W. Ellis
B: 8/8/1947
Racing Hometown: Richmond, VA

Year	Rank	Starts	Poles	1	2	3	4	5	6–10	Laps	Laps Led	Races Led	Miles	$
1976	92T	1	0	0	0	0	0	0	0	429	0	0	429	1,335
1981	62	4	0	0	0	0	1	0	0	651	2	2	767	13,475
1982	75	2	0	0	0	0	0	0	0	642	0	0	348	4,170
1983	79	1	0	0	0	0	0	0	0	386	0	0	579	4,350
1984	31	20	0	0	0	0	0	0	1	5,010	1	1	5,356	44,315
1985	34	14	0	0	0	0	0	0	1	2,853	0	0	3,505	27,695
1986	23	24	0	0	0	0	0	0	3	6,559	50	5	7,334	78,310
1987	55	4	0	0	0	0	0	0	0	564	0	0	661	17,735
1988	91	2	0	0	0	0	0	0	0	178	0	0	267	3,125
1989	66	3	0	0	0	0	0	0	0	996	0	0	885	15,385
1990	NR	1	0	0	0	0	0	0	0	285	0	0	205	3,050
1991	70	2	0	0	0	0	0	0	0	887	0	0	1,085	13,250
Lifetime		78	0	0	0	0	1	0	5	19,440	53	8	21,500	$226,195

Pee Wee Ellwanger

Ronald Gene Ellwanger
B: 8/12/1935
Racing Hometown: Roanoke, VA

Year	Rank	Starts	Poles	1	2	3	4	5	6–10	Laps	Laps Led	Races Led	Miles	$
1965	83	4	0	0	0	0	0	0	0	345	0	0	173	575
1966	138	1	0	0	0	0	0	0	0	127	0	0	64	250
Lifetime		5	0	0	0	0	0	0	0	472	0	0	236	$825

Al Elmore

Al Elmore
Racing Hometown: Bishopville, SC

Year	Rank	Starts	Poles	1	2	3	4	5	6–10	Laps	Laps Led	Races Led	Miles	$
1979	87T	1	0	0	0	0	0	0	0	389	0	0	232	1,265
1983	NR	4	0	0	0	0	0	0	0	1,151	0	0	1,384	13,155
Lifetime		5	0	0	0	0	0	0	0	1,540	0	0	1,616	$14,420

Ray Elston *See* Leslie Young

Bill Elswick

William Elswick
B: 2/23/1948
Racing Hometown: N. Miami, FL

Year	Rank	Starts	Poles	1	2	3	4	5	6–10	Laps	Laps Led	Races Led	Miles	$
1979	62	3	0	0	0	0	0	0	0	1,112	0	0	842	3,400
1980	36	12	0	0	0	0	0	0	0	2,717	0	0	2,363	15,600

Year	Rank	Starts	Poles	1	2	3	4	5	6–10	Laps	Laps Led	Races Led	Miles	$

Bill Elswick *continued*

Year	Rank	Starts	Poles	1	2	3	4	5	6–10	Laps	Laps Led	Races Led	Miles	$
1981	85	3	0	0	0	0	0	0	0	662	0	0	1,345	20,100
Lifetime		18	0	0	0	0	0	0	0	4,491	0	0	4,549	$39,100

Jack Ely

Jack Ely
B: 7/21/1957
Racing Hometown: Bethel, CT

Year	Rank	Starts	Poles	1	2	3	4	5	6–10	Laps	Laps Led	Races Led	Miles	$
1986	94	2	0	0	0	0	0	0	0	329	0	0	823	5,145
1989	96T	1	0	0	0	0	0	0	0	204	0	0	204	1,800
Lifetime		3	0	0	0	0	0	0	0	533	0	0	1,027	$6,945

Bun Emery

Laurice Emery
Racing Hometown: Chicago, IL

Year	Rank	Starts	Poles	1	2	3	4	5	6–10	Laps	Laps Led	Races Led	Miles	$
1956	225T	1	0	0	0	0	0	0	0	364	0	0	182	200
Lifetime		1	0	0	0	0	0	0	0	364	0	0	182	$200

Bud Emra

Bud Emra
Racing Hometown: Portland, OR

Year	Rank	Starts	Poles	1	2	3	4	5	6–10	Laps	Laps Led	Races Led	Miles	$
1956	62	1	0	0	0	0	0	0	0	116	0	0	58	50
1957	NR	4	0	0	0	0	0	0	3	479	0	0	269	665
Lifetime		5	0	0	0	0	0	0	3	595	0	0	327	$715

Vallie Engelauf

Vallie Engelauf
Racing Hometown: Riverside, CA

Year	Rank	Starts	Poles	1	2	3	4	5	6–10	Laps	Laps Led	Races Led	Miles	$
1968	93	1	0	0	0	0	0	0	0	38	0	0	103	505
Lifetime		1	0	0	0	0	0	0	0	38	0	0	103	$505

Bob England

Robert England
B: 1/29/1935
Racing Hometown: Daly City, CA

Year	Rank	Starts	Poles	1	2	3	4	5	6–10	Laps	Laps Led	Races Led	Miles	$
1969	NR	1	0	0	0	0	0	0	0	1	0	0	3	750
1970	112	2	0	0	0	0	0	0	0	126	0	0	330	1,740
1971	NR	4	0	0	0	0	0	0	0	477	0	0	1,160	4,105
Lifetime		7	0	0	0	0	0	0	0	604	0	0	1,493	$6,595

George England

George England
Racing Hometown: Dallas, TX

Year	Rank	Starts	Poles	1	2	3	4	5	6–10	Laps	Laps Led	Races Led	Miles	$
1966	76	1	0	0	0	0	0	0	0	293	0	0	440	745
1967	73	5	0	0	0	0	0	0	1	748	0	0	780	3,050
1968	100	1	0	0	0	0	0	0	0	235	0	0	118	275
1974	81	3	0	0	0	0	0	0	0	184	0	0	178	1,485
Lifetime		10	0	0	0	0	0	0	1	1,460	0	0	1,515	$5,555

Bud Erb

Herbert Erb
Racing Hometown: Mobile, AL

Year	Rank	Starts	Poles	1	2	3	4	5	6–10	Laps	Laps Led	Races Led	Miles	$
1951	N/A	3	0	0	0	0	0	0	0		0	0		100
Lifetime		3	0	0	0	0	0	0	0		0	0		$100

Erick Erickson

Erick Erickson
B: 11/8/1916 *Deceased*
Racing Hometown: Lancaster, CA

Year	Rank	Starts	Poles	1	2	3	4	5	6–10	Laps	Laps Led	Races Led	Miles	$
1951	18	12	0	0	1	1	0	2	2	859	0	0	832	2,435
1954	25	6	0	0	0	0	0	1	2	1,398	0	0	1,191	1,365
1955	211	2	0	0	0	0	0	0	0	74	0	0	74	30
1956	72	5	0	0	0	0	0	0	1	736	0	0	639	365
Lifetime		25	0	0	1	1	0	3	5	3,067	0	0	2,735	$3,985

John Erickson

John Erickson
Racing Hometown: Jackson, MS

Year	Rank	Starts	Poles	1	2	3	4	5	6–10	Laps	Laps Led	Races Led	Miles	$
1954	96	1	0	0	0	0	0	0	0	137	0	0	206	100
Lifetime		1	0	0	0	0	0	0	0	137	0	0	206	$100

Year	Rank	Starts	Poles	Finish						Laps	Laps Led	Races Led	Miles	$
				1	2	3	4	5	6–10					

Ray Erickson

Raymond Erickson
B: 4/15/1918
Racing Hometown: Chicago, IL

Year	Rank	Starts	Poles	1	2	3	4	5	6–10	Laps	Laps Led	Races Led	Miles	$
1949	7	4	0	0	1	1	0	0	1	713	0	0	357	1,460
1950	115	2	0	0	0	0	0	0	0	137	31	1	131	50
1951	203	3	0	0	0	0	0	0	0	120	0	0	90	70
1952	NR	2	0	0	0	0	0	0	0	184	0	0	184	60
1953	NR	1	0	0	0	0	0	0	0	0	0	0	0	25
Lifetime		12	0	0	1	1	0	0	1	1,154	31	1	761	$1,665

Mike Ernest

Michael Ernest
Racing Hometown: Wadsworth, OH

Year	Rank	Starts	Poles	1	2	3	4	5	6–10	Laps	Laps Led	Races Led	Miles	$
1951	N/A	1	0	0	0	0	0	0	0	0	0	0	0	10
1952	NR	1	0	0	0	0	0	0	0	168	0	0	84	50
Lifetime		2	0	0	0	0	0	0	0	168	0	0	84	$60

Bill Ervin

William Ervin
Racing Hometown: Tellico Plains, TN

Year	Rank	Starts	Poles	1	2	3	4	5	6–10	Laps	Laps Led	Races Led	Miles	$
1967	57	18	0	0	0	0	0	0	0	1,804	0	0	926	2,005
1968	64	5	0	0	0	0	0	0	0	785	0	0	393	700
1969	NR	1	0	0	0	0	0	0	0	161	0	0	81	100
Lifetime		24	0	0	0	0	0	0	0	2,750	0	0	1,399	$2,805

Wimpy Ervin

Paul Ervin
B: 12/24/1917
Racing Hometown: Bloomfield, NJ

Year	Rank	Starts	Poles	1	2	3	4	5	6–10	Laps	Laps Led	Races Led	Miles	$
1951	N/A	4	0	0	0	0	0	0	1		0	0		175
1952	171	2	0	0	0	0	0	0	0	217	0	0	217	35
1953	NR	2	0	0	0	0	0	0	1		0	0		110
1954	NR	2	0	0	0	0	0	0	0	132	0	0	164	25
Lifetime		10	0	0	0	0	0	0	2	349	0	0	381	$345

Larry Esau

Larry George Esau
B: 5/8/1947
Racing Hometown: San Diego, CA

Year	Rank	Starts	Poles	1	2	3	4	5	6–10	Laps	Laps Led	Races Led	Miles	$
1972	102	1	0	0	0	0	0	0	0	118	0	0	309	1,080
1974	120	1	0	0	0	0	0	0	0	47	0	0	123	825
1975	82T	1	0	0	0	0	0	0	0	135	0	0	354	1,535
1976	86T	1	0	0	0	0	0	0	0	169	0	0	443	1,745
Lifetime		4	0	0	0	0	0	0	0	469	0	0	1,229	$5,185

Ron Esau

Ronald Esau
B: 10/9/1954
Racing Hometown: Lakeside, CA

Year	Rank	Starts	Poles	1	2	3	4	5	6–10	Laps	Laps Led	Races Led	Miles	$
1975	91T	1	0	0	0	0	0	0	0	96	0	0	252	1,125
1976	77	2	0	0	0	0	0	0	0	160	0	0	419	2,310
1983	83	2	0	0	0	0	0	0	0	70	0	0	183	1,575
1984	62	2	0	0	0	0	0	0	0	170	0	0	445	2,660
1985	100	1	0	0	0	0	0	0	0	10	0	0	26	2,925
1986	113	2	0	0	0	0	0	0	0	168	0	0	440	10,625
1987	NR	1	0	0	0	0	0	0	0	90	0	0	236	4,165
1988	69	2	0	0	0	0	0	0	0	231	0	0	594	9,335
1989	71	3	0	0	0	0	0	0	0	326	0	0	543	8,670
1990	80	1	0	0	0	0	0	0	0	383	0	0	287	3,050
Lifetime		17	0	0	0	0	0	0	0	1,704	0	0	3,426	$46,440

Bob Esposito

Robert Esposito
Racing Hometown: Chicago, IL

Year	Rank	Starts	Poles	1	2	3	4	5	6–10	Laps	Laps Led	Races Led	Miles	$
1956	184T	1	0	0	0	0	0	0	0	189	0	0	95	100
Lifetime		1	0	0	0	0	0	0	0	189	0	0	95	$100

Curtis Estes

Curtis Estes
Racing Hometown: Norfolk, VA

Year	Rank	Starts	Poles	1	2	3	4	5	6–10	Laps	Laps Led	Races Led	Miles	$
1953	108T	1	0	0	0	0	0	0	0		0	0		25
Lifetime		1	0	0	0	0	0	0	0		0	0		$25

Year	Rank	Starts	Poles	Finish						Laps	Laps Led	Races Led	Miles	$
				1	2	3	4	5	6–10					

Herbert Estes

Herbert Estes (Tootle)
D: 8/20/1982   *Died 2 hours after winning Late Model race at Bulls Gap, TN.*
Racing Hometown: Knoxville, TN

Year	Rank	Starts	Poles	1	2	3	4	5	6–10	Laps	Laps Led	Races Led	Miles	$
1956	184T	1	0	0	0	0	0	0	0	178	0	0	89	100
1958	14	11	0	0	0	0	0	0	4	2,202	0	0	1,658	2,509
Lifetime		12	0	0	0	0	0	0	4	2,380	0	0	1,747	$2,609

Jack Etheridge

Jack A. Etheridge
B: 4/24/1916
Racing Hometown: Jacksonville, FL

Year	Rank	Starts	Poles	1	2	3	4	5	6–10	Laps	Laps Led	Races Led	Miles	$
1949	46T	1	0	0	0	0	0	0	1		0	0		75
1967	95	3	0	0	0	0	0	0	0	160	0	0	84	645
1969	94T	1	0	0	0	0	0	0	0	7	0	0	4	100
Lifetime		5	0	0	0	0	0	0	1	167	0	0	88	$820

Joe Eubanks

Joseph F. Eubanks
B: 8/9/1925   D: 6/21/1971
Racing Hometown: Spartanburg, SC

Year	Rank	Starts	Poles	1	2	3	4	5	6–10	Laps	Laps Led	Races Led	Miles	$
1950	91	1	0	0	0	0	0	0	0	359	0	0	449	0
1951	10	12	0	0	1	2	0	0	0	490	7	1	513	3,415
1952	7	19	0	0	0	1	1	2	5	2,626	0	0	2,066	3,630
1953	8	24	1	0	1	2	4	0	8	718	82	2	588	5,254
1954	5	33	0	0	1	2	5	3	13	5,167	0	0	3,542	8,559
1955	20	14	0	0	0	0	0	0	4	1,607	0	0	1,487	2,008
1956	15	26	2	0	0	3	0	4	6	3,398	107	2	2,529	5,584
1957	124	1	0	0	0	0	0	0	1	180	0	0	90	100
1958	34	7	0	1	0	0	1	0	1	956	38	2	737	2,070
1959	32	13	0	0	1	0	0	1	5	1,279	0	0	945	2,000
1960	57	7	0	0	0	0	0	1	1	822	0	0	687	1,310
1961	50	2	0	0	0	0	0	0	0	448	0	0	672	1,475
Lifetime		159	3	1	4	10	11	11	44	18,050	234	7	14,303	$35,405

Rod Eulenfeld

Ludwig Everard Eulenfeld
B: 12/20/1935
Racing Hometown: Jacksonville, FL

Year	Rank	Starts	Poles	1	2	3	4	5	6–10	Laps	Laps Led	Races Led	Miles	$
1964	139	1	0	0	0	0	0	0	0	1	0	0	1	50
1965	110T	1	0	0	0	0	0	0	0		0	0		100
1968	67	2	0	0	0	0	0	0	0	229	0	0	464	2,150
1970	99	1	0	0	0	0	0	0	0	80	0	0	44	390
1971	79	1	0	0	0	0	0	0	0	293	0	0	446	1,135
1972	—	0												200
Lifetime		6	0	0	0	0	0	0	0	603	0	0	955	$4,025

Ernest Eury

Ernest Eury
Racing Hometown: Concord, NC

Year	Rank	Starts	Poles	1	2	3	4	5	6–10	Laps	Laps Led	Races Led	Miles	$
1966	74	8	0	0	0	0	0	0	1	1,221	0	0	660	1,190
1971	87	1	0	0	0	0	0	0	0	1	0	0	1	200
Lifetime		9	0	0	0	0	0	0	1	1,222	0	0	660	$1,390

Jim Ewing

James Ewing
Racing Hometown: Akron, OH

Year	Rank	Starts	Poles	1	2	3	4	5	6–10	Laps	Laps Led	Races Led	Miles	$
1954	145T	1	0	0	0	0	0	0	0	100	0	0	50	25
Lifetime		1	0	0	0	0	0	0	0	100	0	0	50	$25

Ben Eyerly

Benjamin Eyerly
Racing Hometown: Portland, OR

Year	Rank	Starts	Poles	1	2	3	4	5	6–10	Laps	Laps Led	Races Led	Miles	$
1957	171	1	0	0	0	0	0	0	0	41	0	0	21	50
Lifetime		1	0	0	0	0	0	0	0	41	0	0	21	$50

David Ezell

David Ezell
B: 6/19/1928
Racing Hometown: Jacksonville, FL

Year	Rank	Starts	Poles	1	2	3	4	5	6–10	Laps	Laps Led	Races Led	Miles	$
1952	86	1	0	0	0	1	0	0	0	153	0	0	77	450
1956	268	1	0	0	0	0	0	0	0		0	0		50

Year	Rank	Starts	Poles	Finish 1	2	3	4	5	6–10	Laps	Laps Led	Races Led	Miles	$

David Ezell *continued*

Year	Rank	Starts	Poles	1	2	3	4	5	6–10	Laps	Laps Led	Races Led	Miles	$
1961	172	1	0	0	0	0	0	0	0	87	0	0	44	50
Lifetime		3	0	0	0	1	0	0	0	240	0	0	120	$550

Art Faber

Arthur Faber
Racing Hometown: Parsippany, NJ

Year	Rank	Starts	Poles	1	2	3	4	5	6–10	Laps	Laps Led	Races Led	Miles	$
1954	208	1	0	0	0	0	0	0	0	61	0	0	31	10
Lifetime		1	0	0	0	0	0	0	0	61	0	0	31	$10

Fred Faber

Fred Faber
Racing Hometown: Rochester, NY

Year	Rank	Starts	Poles	1	2	3	4	5	6–10	Laps	Laps Led	Races Led	Miles	$
1951	N/A	1	0	0	0	0	0	0	0		0	0		25
Lifetime		1	0	0	0	0	0	0	0		0	0		$25

Frog Fagan

Harold P. Fagan
B: 3/11/1940   D: 8/6/1993
Racing Hometown: Willowdale, Ont., Canada

Year	Rank	Starts	Poles	1	2	3	4	5	6–10	Laps	Laps Led	Races Led	Miles	$
1967	101	5	0	0	0	0	0	0	0	309	0	0	210	600
1968	44	12	0	0	0	0	0	0	1	1,808	0	0	1,343	3,680
1970	96	2	0	0	0	0	0	0	0	179	0	0	466	1,925
1971	89	1	0	0	0	0	0	0	0	1	0	0	0	100
Lifetime		20	0	0	0	0	0	0	1	2,297	0	0	2,019	$6,305

Joy Fair

Joy Fair
B: 9/11/1930
Racing Hometown: Pontiac Springs, MI

Year	Rank	Starts	Poles	1	2	3	4	5	6–10	Laps	Laps Led	Races Led	Miles	$
1956	163	2	0	0	0	0	0	0	1	192	0	0	96	100
Lifetime		2	0	0	0	0	0	0	1	192	0	0	96	$100

Cy Fairchild

Cyrus Fairchild
B: 10/11/1936
Racing Hometown: Saginaw, MI

Year	Rank	Starts	Poles	1	2	3	4	5	6–10	Laps	Laps Led	Races Led	Miles	$
1966	146T	1	0	0	0	0	0	0	0	18	0	0	45	0
Lifetime		1	0	0	0	0	0	0	0	18	0	0	45	$0

Len Fanelli

Leonard Fanelli
B: 7/1/1912
Racing Hometown: New Rochelle, NY

Year	Rank	Starts	Poles	1	2	3	4	5	6–10	Laps	Laps Led	Races Led	Miles	$
1951	N/A	1	0	0	0	0	0	0	0		0	0		50
Lifetime		1	0	0	0	0	0	0	0		0	0		$50

Ray Fanning

Raymond Fanning
Racing Hometown: Baltimore, MD

Year	Rank	Starts	Poles	1	2	3	4	5	6–10	Laps	Laps Led	Races Led	Miles	$
1958	NR	1	0	0	0	0	0	0	1	157	0	0	79	130
1959	97	1	0	0	0	0	0	0	0	117	0	0	59	60
Lifetime		2	0	0	0	0	0	0	1	274	0	0	137	$190

Cotton Farmer

Al Farmer
Racing Hometown: New Ellington, SC

Year	Rank	Starts	Poles	1	2	3	4	5	6–10	Laps	Laps Led	Races Led	Miles	$
1964	108	2	0	0	0	0	0	0	0	289	0	0	136	260
Lifetime		2	0	0	0	0	0	0	0	289	0	0	136	$260

Freddie Farmer

Fred Farmer
Racing Hometown: Los Angeles, CA

Year	Rank	Starts	Poles	1	2	3	4	5	6–10	Laps	Laps Led	Races Led	Miles	$
1951	102T	5	0	0	0	0	0	0	1	447	0	0	540	250
Lifetime		5	0	0	0	0	0	0	1	447	0	0	540	$250

Red Farmer

Charles Lawrence Farmer
B: 10/15/1932
Racing Hometown: Hialeah, FL

Year	Rank	Starts	Poles	1	2	3	4	5	6–10	Laps	Laps Led	Races Led	Miles	$
1953	176	1	0	0	0	0	0	0	0	12	0	0	49	0

Year	Rank	Starts	Poles	Finish						Laps	Laps Led	Races Led	Miles	$
				1	2	3	4	5	6–10					

Red Farmer *continued*

Year	Rank	Starts	Poles	1	2	3	4	5	6–10	Laps	Laps Led	Races Led	Miles	$
1956	154	3	0	0	0	0	0	0	0	324	0	0	162	125
1960	131	2	0	0	0	0	0	0	0	103	0	0	258	250
1962	90	2	0	0	0	0	0	0	0	72	0	0	180	535
1965	104	1	0	0	0	0	0	0	0	3	0	0	8	1,070
1967	54	4	0	0	0	0	0	0	0	610	7	1	749	2,925
1968	50	7	0	0	0	0	1	0	0	928	1	1	849	4,810
1969	92	1	0	0	0	0	0	0	0	101	0	0	51	100
1971	NR	3	0	0	0	0	0	0	1	213	0	0	533	2,835
1972	63	5	0	0	0	0	1	0	0	474	0	0	1,101	9,575
1973	72	3	0	0	0	0	0	0	0	247	0	0	647	4,235
1974	76	2	0	0	0	0	0	0	0	329	0	0	875	2,860
1975	97	2	0	0	0	0	0	0	0	44	0	0	117	2,245
Lifetime		36	0	0	0	0	2	0	1	3,460	8	2	5,577	$31,565

Jack Farnell

Jack Farnell
Racing Hometown: College Park, NY

Year	Rank	Starts	Poles	1	2	3	4	5	6–10	Laps	Laps Led	Races Led	Miles	$
1954	NR	1	0	0	0	0	0	0	0	10	0	0	20	25
Lifetime		1	0	0	0	0	0	0	0	10	0	0	20	$25

Bubba Farr

Marion Farr
B: 1921
Racing Hometown: Augusta, GA

Year	Rank	Starts	Poles	1	2	3	4	5	6–10	Laps	Laps Led	Races Led	Miles	$
1962	116T	1	0	0	0	0	0	0	0	22	0	0	11	75
1963	120	2	0	0	0	0	0	0	0	34	0	0	85	550
Lifetime		3	0	0	0	0	0	0	0	56	0	0	96	$625

Bud Farrell

George Farrell
Racing Hometown: Red Bank, NJ

Year	Rank	Starts	Poles	1	2	3	4	5	6–10	Laps	Laps Led	Races Led	Miles	$
1951	48	5	0	0	0	0	1	0	1	373	0	0	466	700
1952	39	6	0	0	0	0	0	0	2	881	0	0	621	325
Lifetime		11	0	0	0	0	1	0	3	1,254	0	0	1,087	$1,025

Jack Farris

Jack Farris
B: 1929
Racing Hometown: New Paris, OH

Year	Rank	Starts	Poles	1	2	3	4	5	6–10	Laps	Laps Led	Races Led	Miles	$
1955	232	1	0	0	0	0	0	0	0	30	0	0	123	25
Lifetime		1	0	0	0	0	0	0	0	30	0	0	123	$25

Lew Fattman

Lew Fattman
Racing Hometown: Greenville, PA

Year	Rank	Starts	Poles	1	2	3	4	5	6–10	Laps	Laps Led	Races Led	Miles	$
1950	NR	1	0	0	0	0	0	0	0	105	0	0	53	0
Lifetime		1	0	0	0	0	0	0	0	105	0	0	53	$0

Lee Faulk

Lee Faulk
Racing Hometown: Crossville, TN

Year	Rank	Starts	Poles	1	2	3	4	5	6–10	Laps	Laps Led	Races Led	Miles	$
1988	66	3	0	0	0	0	0	0	0	841	0	0	858	9,320
Lifetime		3	0	0	0	0	0	0	0	841	0	0	858	$9,320

Bill Faulkner

William Faulkner
Racing Hometown: Richmond, VA

Year	Rank	Starts	Poles	1	2	3	4	5	6–10	Laps	Laps Led	Races Led	Miles	$
1962	NR	1	0	0	0	0	0	0	0	43	0	0	11	125
Lifetime		1	0	0	0	0	0	0	0	43	0	0	11	$125

Doc Faustina

Dr. Leonard Manuel Faustina
B: 2/1/1939
Racing Hometown: Las Vegas, NV

Year	Rank	Starts	Poles	1	2	3	4	5	6–10	Laps	Laps Led	Races Led	Miles	$
1971	65	3	0	0	0	0	0	0	0	402	0	0	864	2,745
1972	61	5	0	0	0	0	0	0	0	607	0	0	1,161	3,850
1975	91T	1	0	0	0	0	0	0	0	116	0	0	290	880

Year	Rank	Starts	Poles	Finish						Laps	Laps Led	Races Led	Miles	$
				1	2	3	4	5	6–10					

Doc Faustina *continued*

Year	Rank	Starts	Poles	1	2	3	4	5	6–10	Laps	Laps Led	Races Led	Miles	$
1976	96T	1	0	0	0	0	0	0	0	378	0	0	378	1,115
Lifetime		10	0	0	0	0	0	0	0	1,503	0	0	2,693	$8,590

Lou Faver

Louis Faver
Racing Hometown: Irvington, NJ

Year	Rank	Starts	Poles	1	2	3	4	5	6–10	Laps	Laps Led	Races Led	Miles	$
1953	182	1	0	0	0	0	0	0	0	12	0	0	12	25
Lifetime		1	0	0	0	0	0	0	0	12	0	0	12	$25

Pat Fay

Patrick Fay
B: 3/31/1944
Racing Hometown: Gustine, CA

Year	Rank	Starts	Poles	1	2	3	4	5	6–10	Laps	Laps Led	Races Led	Miles	$
1970	NR	1	0	0	0	0	0	0	0	24	0	0	63	655
1971	NR	3	0	0	0	0	0	0	1	248	0	0	636	3,635
Lifetime		4	0	0	0	0	0	0	1	272	0	0	699	$4,290

Gary Fedewa

Gary Fedewa
B: 1/1/1944
Racing Hometown: Lansing, MI

Year	Rank	Starts	Poles	1	2	3	4	5	6–10	Laps	Laps Led	Races Led	Miles	$
1986	51	4	0	0	0	0	0	0	0	819	0	0	1,229	7,230
1987	86	1	0	0	0	0	0	0	0	355	0	0	355	1,650
Lifetime		5	0	0	0	0	0	0	0	1,174	0	0	1,584	$8,880

Tim Fedewa

Timothy Fedewa
B: 5/9/1967
Racing Hometown: Holt, MI

Year	Rank	Starts	Poles	1	2	3	4	5	6–10	Laps	Laps Led	Races Led	Miles	$
1994	64	1	0	0	0	0	0	0	0	487	0	0	487	8,565
Lifetime		1	0	0	0	0	0	0	0	487	0	0	487	$8,565

Paul Feldner

Paul J. Feldner
B: 2/14/1935
Racing Hometown: Richfield, WI

Year	Rank	Starts	Poles	1	2	3	4	5	6–10	Laps	Laps Led	Races Led	Miles	$
1970	NR	2	0	0	0	0	0	0	1	214	0	0	535	1,490
1972	NR	1	0	0	0	0	0	0	0	198	0	0	396	750
Lifetime		3	0	0	0	0	0	0	1	412	0	0	931	$2,240

Dick Fellows

Richard Fellows
Racing Hometown: Minneapolis, MN

Year	Rank	Starts	Poles	1	2	3	4	5	6–10	Laps	Laps Led	Races Led	Miles	$
1953	86T	1	0	0	0	0	0	0	1		0	0		75
Lifetime		1	0	0	0	0	0	0	1		0	0		$75

Ron Fellows

Ronald Fellows
B: 9/28/1959
Racing Hometown: Toronto, Ont., Canada

Year	Rank	Starts	Poles	1	2	3	4	5	6–10	Laps	Laps Led	Races Led	Miles	$
1995	63T	1	0	0	0	0	0	0	0	40	0	0	98	9,035
Lifetime		1	0	0	0	0	0	0	0	40	0	0	98	$9,035

Gene Felton

Gene Felton
B: 5/11/1936
Racing Hometown: Marietta, GA

Year	Rank	Starts	Poles	1	2	3	4	5	6–10	Laps	Laps Led	Races Led	Miles	$
1976	88T	1	0	0	0	0	0	0	0	308	0	0	469	1,635
Lifetime		1	0	0	0	0	0	0	0	308	0	0	469	$1,635

Ed Ferree

Edward Ferree
B: 3/16/1952
Racing Hometown: Saxonburg, PA

Year	Rank	Starts	Poles	1	2	3	4	5	6–10	Laps	Laps Led	Races Led	Miles	$
1992	77T	1	0	0	0	0	0	0	0	50	0	0	123	4,035
1993	58	2	0	0	0	0	0	0	0	511	0	0	571	12,865
Lifetime		3	0	0	0	0	0	0	0	561	0	0	694	$16,900

Year	Rank	Starts	Poles	1	2	3	4	5	6–10	Laps	Laps Led	Races Led	Miles	$

Bill Ferrier
William Ferrier
Racing Hometown: Fillmore, CA

Year	Rank	Starts	Poles	1	2	3	4	5	6–10	Laps	Laps Led	Races Led	Miles	$
1961	118	2	0	0	0	0	0	0	0	214	0	0	148	130
Lifetime		2	0	0	0	0	0	0	0	214	0	0	148	$130

Paul Fess
Paul Fess
Racing Hometown: Mt. Pleasant, PA

Year	Rank	Starts	Poles	1	2	3	4	5	6–10	Laps	Laps Led	Races Led	Miles	$
1978	NR	1	0	0	0	0	0	0	0	75	0	0	188	835
1979	76	2	0	0	0	0	0	0	0	232	0	0	532	4,860
Lifetime		3	0	0	0	0	0	0	0	307	0	0	719	$5,695

Jim Fiebelkorn
James Fiebelkorn
Racing Hometown: Randolph, NY

Year	Rank	Starts	Poles	1	2	3	4	5	6–10	Laps	Laps Led	Races Led	Miles	$
1951	28	17	0	0	1	0	0	0	3	984	0	0	913	1,355
1952	183	1	0	0	0	0	0	0	0	35	0	0	35	0
Lifetime		18	0	0	1	0	0	0	3	1,019	0	0	948	$1,355

Wayne Fielden
Wayne Fielden
Racing Hometown: Knoxville, TN

Year	Rank	Starts	Poles	1	2	3	4	5	6–10	Laps	Laps Led	Races Led	Miles	$
1956	130T	2	0	0	0	0	0	0	1	361	0	0	181	200
Lifetime		2	0	0	0	0	0	0	1	361	0	0	181	$200

Bo Fields
Elmer Fields
Racing Hometown: Alger, AL

Year	Rank	Starts	Poles	1	2	3	4	5	6–10	Laps	Laps Led	Races Led	Miles	$
1954	105	1	0	0	0	0	0	0	0	137	0	0	206	200
1955	124	3	0	0	0	0	0	0	0	347	0	0	292	100
Lifetime		4	0	0	0	0	0	0	0	484	0	0	498	$300

Joe Fields
Joe Fields *Real Name*: J. E. Liesfeld Jr.
B: 6/26/1948
Racing Hometown: Montpelier, VA

Year	Rank	Starts	Poles	1	2	3	4	5	6–10	Laps	Laps Led	Races Led	Miles	$
1981	46	6	0	0	0	0	0	0	0	1,681	0	0	1,160	7,750
1982	91	3	0	0	0	0	0	0	0	738	0	0	397	2,610
1983	78	3	0	0	0	0	0	0	0	1,064	0	0	787	4,315
1984	63	2	0	0	0	0	0	0	0	661	0	0	661	1,915
1986	NR	1	0	0	0	0	0	0	0	0	0	0	0	875
Lifetime		15	0	0	0	0	0	0	0	4,144	0	0	3,005	$17,465

Lawrence Fields
Lawrence D. Fields (Junior)
B: 8/19/1934
Racing Hometown: Greensboro, NC

Year	Rank	Starts	Poles	1	2	3	4	5	6–10	Laps	Laps Led	Races Led	Miles	$
1971	83	1	0	0	0	0	0	0	0	31	0	0	31	570
1979	98T	1	0	0	0	0	0	0	0	379	0	0	205	1,385
Lifetime		2	0	0	0	0	0	0	0	410	0	0	236	$1,955

Wade Fields
Wade Fields
Racing Hometown: Sanford, NC

Year	Rank	Starts	Poles	1	2	3	4	5	6–10	Laps	Laps Led	Races Led	Miles	$
1951	N/A	6	0	0	0	0	0	0	0	268	0	0	335	175
1956	237	1	0	0	0	0	0	0	0	244	0	0	336	50
Lifetime		7	0	0	0	0	0	0	0	512	0	0	671	$225

Lou Figaro
Lou Figaro
B: 10/12/1917   D: 10/25/1954   *Died after crash in 10/24/54 NASCAR Grand National Race @ North Wilkesboro.*
Racing Hometown: Inglewood, CA

Year	Rank	Starts	Poles	1	2	3	4	5	6–10	Laps	Laps Led	Races Led	Miles	$
1951	22	13	1	1	0	0	2	0	1	431	200	1	331	2,200
1954	43	3	0	0	0	0	0	0	2	461	0	0	403	425
Lifetime		16	1	1	0	0	2	0	3	892	200	1	734	$2,625

Chet Fillip
Chet Fillip
B: 4/4/1957
Racing Hometown: San Angelo, TX

Year	Rank	Starts	Poles	1	2	3	4	5	6–10	Laps	Laps Led	Races Led	Miles	$
1985	80	1	0	0	0	0	0	0	0	308	0	0	469	1,425

Year	Rank	Starts	Poles	Finish						Laps	Laps Led	Races Led	Miles	$
				1	2	3	4	5	6–10					

Chet Fillip *continued*

Year	Rank	Starts	Poles	1	2	3	4	5	6–10	Laps	Laps Led	Races Led	Miles	$
1986	32	17	0	0	0	0	0	0	0	3,276	0	0	4,550	36,110
1987	56	6	0	0	0	0	0	0	0	895	0	0	1,624	35,565
Lifetime		24	0	0	0	0	0	0	0	4,479	0	0	6,643	$73,100

Bob Finale

Robert Finale

Year	Rank	Starts	Poles	1	2	3	4	5	6–10	Laps	Laps Led	Races Led	Miles	$
1958	NR	1	0	0	0	0	0	0	1	138	0	0	46	165
Lifetime		1	0	0	0	0	0	0	1	138	0	0	46	$165

John Findlay

John Findlay

Year	Rank	Starts	Poles	1	2	3	4	5	6–10	Laps	Laps Led	Races Led	Miles	$
1957	91	3	0	0	0	0	0	0	1	382	0	0	191	320
1958	61	4	0	0	0	0	0	1	0	674	0	0	320	530
1959	NR	1	0	0	0	0	0	0	0	116	0	0	58	50
Lifetime		8	0	0	0	0	0	1	1	1,172	0	0	569	$900

Jimmy Finger

James Finger
Racing Hometown: Austin, TX

Year	Rank	Starts	Poles	1	2	3	4	5	6–10	Laps	Laps Led	Races Led	Miles	$
1971	NR	1	0	0	0	0	0	0	0	18	0	0	36	530
1972	83	2	0	0	0	0	0	0	0	214	0	0	535	3,830
1979	64	3	0	0	0	0	0	0	0	152	0	0	398	5,020
1980	84T	1	0	0	0	0	0	0	0	181	0	0	362	2,200
Lifetime		7	0	0	0	0	0	0	0	565	0	0	1,331	$11,580

Phil Finney

Phillip W. Finney
B: 4/20/1950
Racing Hometown: Merritt Island, FL

Year	Rank	Starts	Poles	1	2	3	4	5	6–10	Laps	Laps Led	Races Led	Miles	$
1971	71	1	0	0	0	0	0	0	0	357	0	0	193	400
1972	107	1	0	0	0	0	0	0	0	321	0	0	174	450
1973	NR	1	0	0	0	0	0	0	0	55	0	0	146	910
1974	114	1	0	0	0	0	0	0	0	100	0	0	266	1,010
1977	110T	1	0	0	0	0	0	0	0	148	0	0	225	1,145
1980	78T	2	0	0	0	0	0	0	0	188	0	0	476	3,850
Lifetime		7	0	0	0	0	0	0	0	1,169	0	0	1,481	$7,765

Ed Fiola

Edward Fiola
B: 1928
Racing Hometown: Turtle Creek, PA

Year	Rank	Starts	Poles	1	2	3	4	5	6–10	Laps	Laps Led	Races Led	Miles	$
1957	106	2	0	0	0	0	0	0	0	127	0	0	127	75
Lifetime		2	0	0	0	0	0	0	0	127	0	0	127	$75

B. Fisher

B. Fisher

Year	Rank	Starts	Poles	1	2	3	4	5	6–10	Laps	Laps Led	Races Led	Miles	$
1954	NR	1	0	0	0	0	0	0	0	29	0	0	58	0
Lifetime		1	0	0	0	0	0	0	0	29	0	0	58	$0

Bobby Fisher

Robert D. Fisher
Racing Hometown: Vero Beach, FL

Year	Rank	Starts	Poles	1	2	3	4	5	6–10	Laps	Laps Led	Races Led	Miles	$
1978	109	2	0	0	0	0	0	0	0	33	0	0	22	1,410
1979	116T	1	0	0	0	0	0	0	0	136	0	0	204	1,720
Lifetime		3	0	0	0	0	0	0	0	169	0	0	226	$3,130

Cal Fisher

Cal Fisher
Racing Hometown: Lexington, NE

Year	Rank	Starts	Poles	1	2	3	4	5	6–10	Laps	Laps Led	Races Led	Miles	$
1951	N/A	1	0	0	0	0	0	0	0		0	0		25
Lifetime		1	0	0	0	0	0	0	0		0	0		$25

Jack Fisher

Jack Fisher
Racing Hometown: Moline, IL

Year	Rank	Starts	Poles	1	2	3	4	5	6–10	Laps	Laps Led	Races Led	Miles	$
1952	111	2	0	0	0	0	0	0	0	307	0	0	307	60
Lifetime		2	0	0	0	0	0	0	0	307	0	0	307	$60

Year	Rank	Starts	Poles	Finish 1	2	3	4	5	6–10	Laps	Laps Led	Races Led	Miles	$

Ken Fisher

Kenneth Fisher
Racing Hometown: Hamburg, NY

Year	Rank	Starts	Poles	1	2	3	4	5	6–10	Laps	Laps Led	Races Led	Miles	$
1954	44	5	0	0	0	0	0	0	1	879	0	0	657	400
1955	73	9	0	0	0	0	0	0	1	453	0	0	292	175
Lifetime		14	0	0	0	0	0	0	2	1,332	0	0	949	$575

Terry Fisher

Terry Fisher
B: 5/24/1962
Racing Hometown: Sandy, OR

Year	Rank	Starts	Poles	1	2	3	4	5	6–10	Laps	Laps Led	Races Led	Miles	$
1989	79	1	0	0	0	0	0	0	0	72	0	0	181	2,825
1990	72	1	0	0	0	0	0	0	0	74	0	0	186	4,575
1993	83T	1	0	0	0	0	0	0	0	132	0	0	132	6,040
1995	67	1	0	0	0	0	0	0	0	57	0	0	144	9,760
Lifetime		4	0	0	0	0	0	0	0	335	0	0	644	$23,200

Woody Fisher

Woodrow Fisher
Racing Hometown: Ormond Beach, FL

Year	Rank	Starts	Poles	1	2	3	4	5	6–10	Laps	Laps Led	Races Led	Miles	$
1978	66	3	0	0	0	0	0	0	0	383	0	0	510	4,250
1979	—	0												800
Lifetime		3	0	0	0	0	0	0	0	383	0	0	510	$5,050

John Fite

John Fite
Racing Hometown: Liberty, SC

Year	Rank	Starts	Poles	1	2	3	4	5	6–10	Laps	Laps Led	Races Led	Miles	$
1956	152	3	0	0	0	0	0	0	0	388	0	0	218	200
Lifetime		3	0	0	0	0	0	0	0	388	0	0	218	$200

Jim Fitzgerald

James Fitzgerald
B: 12/1/1921   D: 11/8/1987   *Killed in Florida road race.*
Racing Hometown: Pittsburgh, PA

Year	Rank	Starts	Poles	1	2	3	4	5	6–10	Laps	Laps Led	Races Led	Miles	$
1986	120	1	0	0	0	0	0	0	0	28	0	0	73	925
1987	77	1	0	0	0	0	0	0	0	93	0	0	244	1,675
Lifetime		2	0	0	0	0	0	0	0	121	0	0	317	$2,600

Pat Flaherty

Patrick Flaherty
B: 1/6/1926
Racing Hometown: Chicago, IL

Year	Rank	Starts	Poles	1	2	3	4	5	6–10	Laps	Laps Led	Races Led	Miles	$
1951	N/A	1	0	0	0	0	0	0	0	13	0	0	13	0
Lifetime		1	0	0	0	0	0	0	0	13	0	0	13	$0

Walt Flanders

Walter Flanders
Racing Hometown: Detroit, MI

Year	Rank	Starts	Poles	1	2	3	4	5	6–10	Laps	Laps Led	Races Led	Miles	$
1951	N/A	1	0	0	0	0	0	0	0	145	0	0	145	10
Lifetime		1	0	0	0	0	0	0	0	145	0	0	145	$10

Bill Flatcher

William Flatcher
Racing Hometown: Phoenix, AZ

Year	Rank	Starts	Poles	1	2	3	4	5	6–10	Laps	Laps Led	Races Led	Miles	$
1951	N/A	1	0	0	0	0	0	0	0		0	0		25
Lifetime		1	0	0	0	0	0	0	0		0	0		$25

Al Fleming

Al Fleming
Racing Hometown: Richmond, VA

Year	Rank	Starts	Poles	1	2	3	4	5	6–10	Laps	Laps Led	Races Led	Miles	$
1952	160	1	0	0	0	0	0	0	0	336	0	0	420	210
Lifetime		1	0	0	0	0	0	0	0	336	0	0	420	$210

Bobby Fleming

Robert Winfield Fleming
B: 3/20/1941
Racing Hometown: Danville, VA

Year	Rank	Starts	Poles	1	2	3	4	5	6–10	Laps	Laps Led	Races Led	Miles	$
1969	NR	1	0	0	0	0	0	0	0	146	0	0	388	1,400
1974	96	2	0	0	0	0	0	0	0	394	0	0	210	1,025
Lifetime		3	0	0	0	0	0	0	0	540	0	0	598	$2,425

Year	Rank	Starts	Poles	Finish 1	2	3	4	5	6–10	Laps	Laps Led	Races Led	Miles	$

George Fleming

George Fleming
Racing Hometown: Silver Spring, MD

Year	Rank	Starts	Poles	1	2	3	4	5	6–10	Laps	Laps Led	Races Led	Miles	$
1952	200	1	0	0	0	0	0	0	0		0	0		0
1953	172	1	0	0	0	0	0	0	0	33	0	0	135	25
1957	NR	1	0	0	0	0	0	0	0	174	0	0	87	135
Lifetime		3	0	0	0	0	0	0	0	207	0	0	222	$160

Jack Fleming

Jack Fleming
Racing Hometown: Panama, NY

Year	Rank	Starts	Poles	1	2	3	4	5	6–10	Laps	Laps Led	Races Led	Miles	$
1951	N/A	1	0	0	0	0	0	0	0		0	0		10
Lifetime		1	0	0	0	0	0	0	0		0	0		$10

Eddie Flemke

Edward A. Flemke
B: 8/12/1930   D: 3/30/1984
Racing Hometown: New Britain, CT

Year	Rank	Starts	Poles	1	2	3	4	5	6–10	Laps	Laps Led	Races Led	Miles	$
1961	120	1	0	0	0	0	0	0	0	231	0	0	58	175
Lifetime		1	0	0	0	0	0	0	0	231	0	0	58	$175

Walt Flinchum

Walter Flinchum
Racing Hometown: Summerfield, NC

Year	Rank	Starts	Poles	1	2	3	4	5	6–10	Laps	Laps Led	Races Led	Miles	$
1954	39	8	0	0	0	0	0	0	2	1,123	0	0	689	425
Lifetime		8	0	0	0	0	0	0	2	1,123	0	0	689	$425

Bob Flock

Robert Newman Flock
B: 4/16/1918   D: 5/16/1964
Racing Hometown: Atlanta, GA

Year	Rank	Starts	Poles	1	2	3	4	5	6–10	Laps	Laps Led	Races Led	Miles	$
1949	3	6	1	2	1	0	0	0	0	728	27	**4**	574	4,870
1950	20	4	0	0	1	0	0	0	2	595	5	1	781	1,155
1951	14	17	1	1	2	0	1	0	5	1,028	133	5	927	3,680
1952	73	2	0	1	0	0	0	0	0	538	1	1	523	1,060
1954	NR	2	0	0	0	0	0	0	0	167	0	0	84	25
1955	62	1	0	0	0	0	0	1	0	195	0	0	293	650
1956	77	4	0	0	0	0	0	1	0	442	0	0	397	485
Lifetime		36	2	4	4	0	1	2	7	3,693	166	11	3,576	$11,925

Fonty Flock

Truman Fontell Flock
B: 3/21/1921   D: 7/15/1972
Racing Hometown: Decatur, GA

Year	Rank	Starts	Poles	1	2	3	4	5	6–10	Laps	Laps Led	Races Led	Miles	$
1949	5	6	0	0	1	1	1	0	0	304	85	1	153	2,015
1950	14	7	2	1	0	0	1	0	1	951	369	4	1,077	2,195
1951	2	34	12	8	2	4	5	1	2	**2,788**	**2,068**	**21**	**2,068**	15,200
1952	4	29	7	2	6	2	2	2	3	3,906	984	10	2,767	19,112
1953	5	33	3	4	5	4	3	1	0	1,999	581	10	1,626	17,756
1954	NR	5	0	0	1	0	0	1	0	657	15	1	425	1,000
1955	11	31	7	3	5	2	0	2	2	3,482	430	7	2,565	13,100
1956	50	7	2	1	0	0	0	0	3	629	150	2	490	1,780
1957	63	2	0	0	0	1	0	0	0	18	0	0	25	1,600
Lifetime		154	33	19	20	14	12	7	11	14,734	4,682	56	11,196	$73,758

Tim Flock

Julius Timothy Flock
B: 5/11/1924
Racing Hometown: Atlanta, GA

Year	Rank	Starts	Poles	1	2	3	4	5	6–10	Laps	Laps Led	Races Led	Miles	$
1949	8	5	0	0	1	0	0	1	1	347	0	0	415	1,510
1950	16	12	1	1	0	0	3	0	3	1,403	190	2	1,275	3,980
1951	3	30	6	7	5	3	3	1	2	2,408	844	12	1,773	14,545
1952	1	33	4	8	5	2	7	0	3	**5,345**	1,469	**16**	**3,564**	22,890
1953	6	26	4	1	1	2	3	4	7	1,990	289	8	1,774	8,282
1954	35	5	1	0	1	0	0	0	2	800	180	1	791	1,050
1955	1	39	18	18	5	5	1	3	1	6,208	**3,495**	33	4,576	37,780
1956	9	22	5	4	1	3	2	1	3	3,076	445	9	2,696	15,769
1957	93	1	0	0	0	0	0	0	0		0	0		135
1958	NR	3	0	0	0	0	0	0	0	167	25	1	176	410
1959	31	2	0	0	0	0	0	0	1	223	0	0	558	850

Year	Rank	Starts	Poles	Finish 1	2	3	4	5	6–10	Laps	Laps Led	Races Led	Miles	$

Tim Flock *continued*

Year	Rank	Starts	Poles	1	2	3	4	5	6–10	Laps	Laps Led	Races Led	Miles	$
1960	63	2	0	0	0	0	0	0	1	235	0	0	348	850
1961	NR	7	0	0	0	0	0	0	3	1,227	0	0	1,398	1,605
Lifetime		187	39	39	19	15	19	10	27	23,429	6,937	82	19,343	$109,656

Jimmy Florian

James Frank Florian
B: 9/25/1923
Racing Hometown: Cleveland, OH

Year	Rank	Starts	Poles	1	2	3	4	5	6–10	Laps	Laps Led	Races Led	Miles	$
1950	9	10	1	1	0	1	1	0	3	1,060	40	1	850	2,730
1951	27	9	0	0	0	0	2	0	3	0	0	0	0	1,100
1952	48	6	0	0	0	0	0	0	2	283	0	0	188	175
1954	NR	1	0	0	0	0	0	0	0	34	0	0	139	25
Lifetime		26	1	1	0	1	3	0	8	1,377	40	1	1,178	$4,030

Bill Flowers

William Flowers

Year	Rank	Starts	Poles	1	2	3	4	5	6–10	Laps	Laps Led	Races Led	Miles	$
1989	96T	1	0	0	0	0	0	0	0	2	0	0	2	1,800
Lifetime		1	0	0	0	0	0	0	0	2	0	0	2	$1,800

Jack Flynn

Jack Flynn

Year	Rank	Starts	Poles	1	2	3	4	5	6–10	Laps	Laps Led	Races Led	Miles	$
1951	80	2	0	0	0	0	0	0	1		0	0		225
Lifetime		2	0	0	0	0	0	0	1		0	0		$225

Larry Flynn

Lawrence Flynn
Racing Hometown: Holly Hill, FL

Year	Rank	Starts	Poles	1	2	3	4	5	6–10	Laps	Laps Led	Races Led	Miles	$
1955	28	1	0	0	0	0	0	1	0	359	0	0	494	1,175
1956	153	2	0	0	0	0	0	0	0	402	0	0	395	250
1959	53	4	0	0	0	0	0	0	0	206	0	0	283	275
1961	101	1	0	0	0	0	0	0	0	195	0	0	268	200
Lifetime		8	0	0	0	0	0	1	0	1,162	0	0	1,440	$1,900

Sonny Fogle

Samuel Fogle
Racing Hometown: Columbia, SC

Year	Rank	Starts	Poles	1	2	3	4	5	6–10	Laps	Laps Led	Races Led	Miles	$
1963	66	8	0	0	0	0	0	0	0	779	0	0	382	600
Lifetime		8	0	0	0	0	0	0	0	779	0	0	382	$600

Dick Foley

Richard A. Foley Jr.
Racing Hometown: Montreal, Que., Canada

Year	Rank	Starts	Poles	1	2	3	4	5	6–10	Laps	Laps Led	Races Led	Miles	$
1957	186	1	0	0	0	0	0	0	0	0	0	0	0	0
1958	111	1	0	0	0	0	0	0	0	34	0	0	139	75
1959	55	3	0	0	0	0	0	0	0	226	0	0	565	250
1960	101	2	0	0	0	0	0	0	1	69	0	0	173	325
Lifetime		7	0	0	0	0	0	0	0	329	0	0	877	$650

George Follmer

George Follmer
B: 1/27/1934
Racing Hometown: Arcadia, CA

Year	Rank	Starts	Poles	1	2	3	4	5	6–10	Laps	Laps Led	Races Led	Miles	$
1972	120	1	0	0	0	0	0	0	0	4	0	0	10	1,440
1974	29	13	1	0	0	0	1	2	2	3,086	27	2	3,747	53,780
1975	75	2	0	0	0	0	0	0	0	105	0	0	267	2,370
1986	76	2	0	0	0	0	0	0	0	130	0	0	324	3,885
1987	69	2	0	0	0	0	0	0	0	122	8	1	320	2,880
Lifetime		20	1	0	0	0	1	2	2	3,447	35	3	4,668	$63,255

Ronnie Fones

Ralston Fones
Racing Hometown: Landover, MD

Year	Rank	Starts	Poles	1	2	3	4	5	6–10	Laps	Laps Led	Races Led	Miles	$
1961	144	2	0	0	0	0	0	0	0	217	0	0	75	185
1962	88T	2	0	0	0	0	0	0	0	434	0	0	145	200
Lifetime		4	0	0	0	0	0	0	0	651	0	0	219	$385

Year	Rank	Starts	Poles	Finish						Laps	Laps Led	Races Led	Miles	$
				1	2	3	4	5	6–10	Laps	Led	Led	Miles	$

Red Foote
Melvin K. Foote
B: 11/27/1927
Racing Hometown: Southington, CT

Year	Rank	Starts	Poles	1	2	3	4	5	6–10	Laps	Laps Led	Races Led	Miles	$
1962	44	4	0	0	0	0	0	0	0	939	0	0	1,367	1,600
1963	80	3	0	0	0	0	0	0	0	316	0	0	625	950
1965	134	3	0	0	0	0	0	0	0	181	0	0	88	420
Lifetime		10	0	0	0	0	0	0	0	1,436	0	0	2,080	$2,970

Elliott Forbes-Robinson
Elliott Forbes-Robinson
B: 10/31/1943
Racing Hometown: La Crescenta, CA

Year	Rank	Starts	Poles	1	2	3	4	5	6–10	Laps	Laps Led	Races Led	Miles	$
1977	67	3	0	0	0	0	0	0	0	571	0	0	716	3,575
1981	35	11	0	0	0	0	0	0	3	2,169	0	0	3,495	27,350
1982	68	2	0	0	0	0	0	0	0	174	0	0	447	7,985
1983	101T	1	0	0	0	0	0	0	0	36	0	0	90	5,550
1984	45	5	0	0	0	0	0	0	0	895	0	0	1,513	11,335
Lifetime		22	0	0	0	0	0	0	3	3,845	0	0	6,261	$55,795

Henry Ford
Henry Ford
Racing Hometown: Memphis, TN

Year	Rank	Starts	Poles	1	2	3	4	5	6–10	Laps	Laps Led	Races Led	Miles	$
1955	66	5	0	0	0	0	0	0	0	579	0	0	345	190
Lifetime		5	0	0	0	0	0	0	0	579	0	0	345	$190

John Ford
John Ford
Racing Hometown: Harrisburg, PA

Year	Rank	Starts	Poles	1	2	3	4	5	6–10	Laps	Laps Led	Races Led	Miles	$
1954	183	1	0	0	0	0	0	0	0	198	0	0	198	50
Lifetime		1	0	0	0	0	0	0	0	198	0	0	198	$50

Nick Fornoro
Nofri Samuel Fornoro
B: 10/23/1920
Racing Hometown: Danbury, CT

Year	Rank	Starts	Poles	1	2	3	4	5	6–10	Laps	Laps Led	Races Led	Miles	$
1953	NR	1	0	0	0	0	0	0	1	181	0	0	181	200
Lifetime		1	0	0	0	0	0	0	1	181	0	0	181	$200

Roy Forsythe
Roy Forsythe

Year	Rank	Starts	Poles	1	2	3	4	5	6–10	Laps	Laps Led	Races Led	Miles	$
1951	N/A	1	0	0	0	0	0	0	0		0	0		25
Lifetime		1	0	0	0	0	0	0	0		0	0		$25

Curt Foss
Curtis Foss
Racing Hometown: South Wales, NY

Year	Rank	Starts	Poles	1	2	3	4	5	6–10	Laps	Laps Led	Races Led	Miles	$
1949	NR	1	0	0	0	0	0	0	0	68	0	0	34	0
1950	129T	1	0	0	0	0	0	0	0	158	0	0	79	0
Lifetime		2	0	0	0	0	0	0	0	226	0	0	113	$0

Bill Foster
William Foster
Racing Hometown: High Point, NC

Year	Rank	Starts	Poles	1	2	3	4	5	6–10	Laps	Laps Led	Races Led	Miles	$
1961	170	1	0	0	0	0	0	0	0	61	0	0	61	25
1962	68	5	0	0	0	0	0	0	1	1,230	0	0	740	800
1963	49	10	0	0	0	0	0	0	2	1,628	0	0	1,049	1,410
Lifetime		16	0	0	0	0	0	0	3	2,919	0	0	1,850	$2,235

Billy Foster
William Foster
B: 9/18/1937   D: 1/20/1967   *Killed in practice for NASCAR Riverside race after earning the 9th starting position.*
Racing Hometown: Victoria, B.C., Canada

Year	Rank	Starts	Poles	1	2	3	4	5	6–10	Laps	Laps Led	Races Led	Miles	$
1966	NR	1	0	0	0	0	0	0	1	181	0	0	489	1,275
Lifetime		1	0	0	0	0	0	0	1	181	0	0	489	$1,275

Earl Foushee
Earl Foushee
Racing Hometown: Durham, NC

Year	Rank	Starts	Poles	1	2	3	4	5	6–10	Laps	Laps Led	Races Led	Miles	$
1953	160	1	0	0	0	0	0	0	0	256	0	0	256	50
Lifetime		1	0	0	0	0	0	0	0	256	0	0	256	$50

Year	Rank	Starts	Poles	Finish						Laps	Laps Led	Races Led	Miles	$
				1	2	3	4	5	6–10					

Bobby Fox

Robert Fox
B: 3/12/1948
Racing Hometown: Bremerton, WA

Year	Rank	Starts	Poles	1	2	3	4	5	6–10	Laps	Laps Led	Races Led	Miles	$
1984	79	1	0	0	0	0	0	0	0	352	0	0	358	1,495
Lifetime		1	0	0	0	0	0	0	0	352	0	0	358	$1,495

George Fox

George Fox
Racing Hometown: Wilkesboro, NC

Year	Rank	Starts	Poles	1	2	3	4	5	6–10	Laps	Laps Led	Races Led	Miles	$
1962	138	1	0	0	0	0	0	0	0	3	0	0	2	50
Lifetime		1	0	0	0	0	0	0	0	3	0	0	2	$50

Jackie Fox

Jack Fox
Racing Hometown: Asheville, NC

Year	Rank	Starts	Poles	1	2	3	4	5	6–10	Laps	Laps Led	Races Led	Miles	$
1967	120	2	0	0	0	0	0	0	0	57	0	0	23	0
Lifetime		2	0	0	0	0	0	0	0	57	0	0	23	$0

Jim Fox

James Fox
Racing Hometown: Rochester, NY

Year	Rank	Starts	Poles	1	2	3	4	5	6–10	Laps	Laps Led	Races Led	Miles	$
1953	NR	1	0	0	0	0	0	0	0		0	0		25
Lifetime		1	0	0	0	0	0	0	0		0	0		$25

Leon Fox

Leon Fox
B: 12/17/1937
Racing Hometown: Bremerton, WA

Year	Rank	Starts	Poles	1	2	3	4	5	6–10	Laps	Laps Led	Races Led	Miles	$
1973	96	1	0	0	0	0	0	0	0	139	0	0	364	925
1974	112	1	0	0	0	0	0	0	0	113	0	0	296	1,210
Lifetime		2	0	0	0	0	0	0	0	252	0	0	660	$2,135

Stan Fox

Stan Fox *Real Name*: Stanley Cole Fuchs
B: 7/7/1952
Racing Hometown: Janesville, WI

Year	Rank	Starts	Poles	1	2	3	4	5	6–10	Laps	Laps Led	Races Led	Miles	$
1992	68	2	0	0	0	0	0	0	0	146	0	0	359	11,750
Lifetime		2	0	0	0	0	0	0	0	146	0	0	359	$11,750

A. J. Foyt

Anthony Joseph Foyt Jr.
B: 1/16/1935
Racing Hometown: Houston, TX

Year	Rank	Starts	Poles	1	2	3	4	5	6–10	Laps	Laps Led	Races Led	Miles	$
1963	NR	5	0	0	1	1	0	0	0	639	64	3	1,509	8,850
1964	NR	6	0	1	0	0	1	0	0	851	16	2	1,785	15,950
1965	NR	4	0	1	0	0	0	0	2	685	161	3	1,390	12,040
1966	NR	4	0	0	0	0	0	0	0	141	0	0	350	2,390
1967	NR	7	0	0	1	0	1	0	0	1,060	57	5	1,534	8,035
1968	NR	4	0	0	0	0	0	0	1	572	0	0	1,105	4,975
1969	NR	4	1	0	1	0	2	0	0	522	63	2	1,254	17,375
1970	NR	3	0	1	0	0	0	0	0	298	35	1	768	21,210
1971	NR	7	4	2	1	1	0	0	0	1,134	392	4	2,124	88,574
1972	NR	6	3	2	2	0	1	0	0	1,417	344	6	2,778	101,340
1973	NR	3	0	0	0	0	1	0	0	467	0	0	943	8,555
1974	44	4	0	0	0	0	1	1	0	612	70	3	1,360	17,110
1975	NR	7	0	0	0	0	0	1	0	1,420	186	5	2,462	17,155
1976	NR	5	1	0	0	0	1	0	0	581	79	3	1,335	15,610
1977	NR	6	1	0	0	0	0	1	2	1,058	20	3	2,165	29,200
1978	NR	2	0	0	0	1	0	0	0	255	0	0	667	24,875
1979	NR	2	0	0	0	1	0	0	1	356	7	2	890	41,690
1980	101	1	0	0	0	0	0	0	0	69	0	0	173	3,575
1981	59	3	0	0	0	0	0	0	1	530	0	0	1,007	9,210
1982	70	2	0	0	0	0	0	0	0	162	0	0	388	9,405
1983	76	3	0	0	0	0	0	0	0	406	0	0	890	22,935
1984	76	3	0	0	0	0	0	0	0	224	0	0	418	8,830
1985	45	7	0	0	0	0	0	1	0	966	2	2	1,781	29,750
1986	50	5	0	0	0	0	0	0	0	640	1	1	1,220	24,135
1987	49	6	0	0	0	0	0	0	0	748	2	2	1,274	21,075

Year	Rank	Starts	Poles	Finish						Laps	Laps Led	Races Led	Miles	$
				1	2	3	4	5	6–10	Laps	Led	Led	Miles	$

A. J. Foyt *continued*

Year	Rank	Starts	Poles	1	2	3	4	5	6–10	Laps	Laps Led	Races Led	Miles	$
1988	42	7	0	0	0	0	0	0	0	920	9	3	1,992	29,660
1989	40	7	0	0	0	0	0	0	0	860	6	2	1,869	31,995
1990	62	3	0	0	0	0	0	0	0	301	4	1	782	26,725
1992	70	1	0	0	0	0	0	0	0	195	0	0	488	23,055
1993	—	0												2,400
1994	70T	1	0	0	0	0	0	0	0	156	0	0	390	29,000
Lifetime		128	10	7	6	4	8	4	7	18,245	1,518	53	37,092	$706,684

Len Fraker

Leon Fraker
Racing Hometown: Puente, CA

Year	Rank	Starts	Poles	1	2	3	4	5	6–10	Laps	Laps Led	Races Led	Miles	$
1956	NR	1	0	0	0	0	0	0	0	10	0	0	25	30
Lifetime		1	0	0	0	0	0	0	0	10	0	0	25	$30

Glenn Francis

Glenn Francis
B: 5/22/1942
Racing Hometown: Bakersfield, CA

Year	Rank	Starts	Poles	1	2	3	4	5	6–10	Laps	Laps Led	Races Led	Miles	$
1970	NR	1	0	0	0	0	0	0	0	95	0	0	249	805
1971	NR	1	0	0	0	0	0	0	0	27	0	0	71	1,015
1973	79	2	0	0	0	0	0	0	0	187	0	0	490	2,010
1974	79	2	0	0	0	0	0	0	0	258	0	0	659	2,700
1975	67	2	0	0	0	0	0	0	0	181	0	0	474	2,660
1976	99T	1	0	0	0	0	0	0	0	125	0	0	313	1,065
1977	106T	1	0	0	0	0	0	0	0	9	0	0	24	640
1980	102T	1	0	0	0	0	0	0	0	91	0	0	228	1,025
1982	78	1	0	0	0	0	0	0	0	113	0	0	296	1,650
1983	59	2	0	0	0	0	0	0	0	179	0	0	469	2,775
1984	74	1	0	0	0	0	0	0	0	91	0	0	238	1,475
1985	76	1	0	0	0	0	0	0	0	84	0	0	220	1,665
Lifetime		16	0	0	0	0	0	0	0	1,440	0	0	3,730	$19,485

Tom Francis

Thomas Francis

Year	Rank	Starts	Poles	1	2	3	4	5	6–10	Laps	Laps Led	Races Led	Miles	$
1955	146	1	0	0	0	0	0	0	0	95	0	0	95	90
1956	287	1	0	0	0	0	0	0	0	68	0	0	170	40
Lifetime		2	0	0	0	0	0	0	0	163	0	0	265	$130

Bob Francy

Robert Francy
Racing Hometown: Phoenix, AZ

Year	Rank	Starts	Poles	1	2	3	4	5	6–10	Laps	Laps Led	Races Led	Miles	$
1956	246T	1	0	0	0	0	0	0	0	91	0	0	46	0
Lifetime		1	0	0	0	0	0	0	0	91	0	0	46	$0

Johnny Frank

Johnny Frank *Real Name*: Bruno Bracchy
Racing Hometown: Far Rockaway, NY

Year	Rank	Starts	Poles	1	2	3	4	5	6–10	Laps	Laps Led	Races Led	Miles	$
1957	NR	1	0	0	0	0	0	0	0	111	0	0	111	75
Lifetime		1	0	0	0	0	0	0	0	111	0	0	111	$75

Larry Frank

Larry S. Frank
B: 4/29/1931
Racing Hometown: Indianapolis, IN

Year	Rank	Starts	Poles	1	2	3	4	5	6–10	Laps	Laps Led	Races Led	Miles	$
1956	NR	1	0	0	0	0	0	0	0	77	0	0	39	50
1957	NR	4	0	0	0	0	0	0	0	1,113	0	0	935	995
1958	137	11	0	0	0	1	0	0	3	2,099	0	0	1,259	2,590
1959	22	15	0	0	1	0	1	2	5	3,300	39	1	2,647	5,993
1960	34	10	0	0	0	0	0	0	2	1,927	11	1	2,379	2,440
1961	42	8	0	0	0	0	0	0	1	978	0	0	1,585	2,380
1962	14	19	0	1	0	0	0	1	6	3,566	85	1	3,506	32,987
1963	28	11	0	0	0	1	1	0	0	2,392	5	1	2,735	5,450
1964	24	12	0	0	0	0	0	0	3	1,483	0	0	2,366	7,830
1965	53	9	0	0	0	0	1	0	0	1,009	33	1	1,200	5,080
1966	50	2	0	0	0	0	0	0	2	232	0	0	580	1,575
Lifetime		102	0	1	1	2	3	3	22	18,176	173	5	19,231	$65,718

Year	Rank	Starts	Poles	1	2	Finish 3	4	5	6–10	Laps	Laps Led	Races Led	Miles	$

Allen Franklin

Allen Franklin
Racing Hometown: Skygusty, WV

Year	Rank	Starts	Poles	1	2	3	4	5	6–10	Laps	Laps Led	Races Led	Miles	$
1961	173	2	0	0	0	0	0	0	0	8	0	0	4	225
Lifetime		2	0	0	0	0	0	0	0	8	0	0	4	$225

Ray Franklin

Raymond Franklin
Racing Hometown: Hawthorne, CA

Year	Rank	Starts	Poles	1	2	3	4	5	6–10	Laps	Laps Led	Races Led	Miles	$
1957	173	1	0	0	0	0	0	0	0	42	0	0	105	60
Lifetime		1	0	0	0	0	0	0	0	42	0	0	105	$60

Joe Frasson

Joseph R. Frasson
B: 9/3/1935
Racing Hometown: Golden Valley, MN

Year	Rank	Starts	Poles	1	2	3	4	5	6–10	Laps	Laps Led	Races Led	Miles	$
1969	NR	1	0	0	0	0	0	0	0	3	0	0	8	825
1970	22	21	0	0	0	0	0	0	2	4,866	0	0	6,230	20,172
1971	25	17	0	0	0	0	0	1	3	3,752	0	0	5,698	20,975
1972	28	16	0	0	0	1	0	0	3	3,013	9	2	4,638	21,645
1973	29	14	0	0	0	1	1	0	2	2,732	1	1	4,379	25,884
1974	28	14	0	0	0	0	0	0	3	2,141	13	3	3,671	22,629
1975	35	9	0	0	0	0	0	0	1	1,352	1	1	2,018	11,975
1976	39	9	0	0	0	0	0	0	1	863	1	1	1,510	13,565
1977	93T	1	0	0	0	0	0	0	0	126	0	0	335	2,050
1978	45	5	0	0	0	0	0	0	0	1,436	0	0	1,878	9,210
Lifetime		107	0	0	0	2	1	1	15	20,284	25	8	30,365	$148,930

Pete Frazee

Peter Frazee
B: 11/2/1926
Racing Hometown: Rahway, N J

Year	Rank	Starts	Poles	1	2	3	4	5	6–10	Laps	Laps Led	Races Led	Miles	$
1958	66	2	0	0	0	0	0	0	0	517	0	0	432	310
Lifetime		2	0	0	0	0	0	0	0	517	0	0	432	$310

Fred Frazier

Fred Frazier
Racing Hometown: Weldon, NC

Year	Rank	Starts	Poles	1	2	3	4	5	6–10	Laps	Laps Led	Races Led	Miles	$
1956	130T	2	0	0	0	0	0	0	1	288	0	0	144	200
Lifetime		2	0	0	0	0	0	0	1	288	0	0	144	$200

Dick Freeman

Richard Freeman
B: 1931
Racing Hometown: Dayton, OH

Year	Rank	Starts	Poles	1	2	3	4	5	6–10	Laps	Laps Led	Races Led	Miles	$
1954	NR	1	0	0	0	0	0	0	0	20	0	0	10	0
1959	NR	3	0	0	0	0	0	0	0	695	0	0	800	475
1960	124	2	0	0	0	0	0	0	0	41	0	0	103	250
Lifetime		6	0	0	0	0	0	0	0	756	0	0	912	$725

Doug French

Douglas French
B: 5/16/1959
Racing Hometown: Howell, NJ

Year	Rank	Starts	Poles	1	2	3	4	5	6–10	Laps	Laps Led	Races Led	Miles	$
1987	87	1	0	0	0	0	0	0	0	75	0	0	41	895
Lifetime		1	0	0	0	0	0	0	0	75	0	0	41	$895

Jim Frey

James Frey
Racing Hometown: North Wilkesboro, NC

Year	Rank	Starts	Poles	1	2	3	4	5	6–10	Laps	Laps Led	Races Led	Miles	$
1954	NR	1	0	0	0	0	0	0	0	52	0	0	33	0
Lifetime		1	0	0	0	0	0	0	0	52	0	0	33	$0

Lamoine Frey

Lamoine Frey
Racing Hometown: Sacramento, CA

Year	Rank	Starts	Poles	1	2	3	4	5	6–10	Laps	Laps Led	Races Led	Miles	$
1957	85	3	0	0	0	0	0	0	2	330	0	0	189	350
Lifetime		3	0	0	0	0	0	0	2	330	0	0	189	$350

Year	Rank	Starts	Poles	Finish						Laps	Laps Led	Races Led	Miles	$
				1	2	3	4	5	6–10	Laps	Led	Led	Miles	$

Billy Fritts

William Fritts
Racing Hometown: Chester, NJ

Year	Rank	Starts	Poles	1	2	3	4	5	6–10	Laps	Laps Led	Races Led	Miles	$
1953	122T	1	0	0	0	0	0	0	0		0	0		25
Lifetime		1	0	0	0	0	0	0	0		0	0		$25

Ted Fritz

Theodore Fritz
B: 5/13/1936
Racing Hometown: Modesto, CA

Year	Rank	Starts	Poles	1	2	3	4	5	6–10	Laps	Laps Led	Races Led	Miles	$
1975	109T	1	0	0	0	0	0	0	0	10	0	0	26	620
Lifetime		1	0	0	0	0	0	0	0	10	0	0	26	$620

Steve Froines

Steve Froines
Racing Hometown: Lafayette, CA

Year	Rank	Starts	Poles	1	2	3	4	5	6–10	Laps	Laps Led	Races Led	Miles	$
1970	88	2	0	0	0	0	0	0	0	86	0	0	225	1,520
Lifetime		2	0	0	0	0	0	0	0	86	0	0	225	$1,520

Dudley Froy

Dudley Froy
Racing Hometown: Tucson, AZ

Year	Rank	Starts	Poles	1	2	3	4	5	6–10	Laps	Laps Led	Races Led	Miles	$
1951	N/A	2	0	0	0	0	0	0	0		0	0		50
Lifetime		2	0	0	0	0	0	0	0		0	0		$50

Herb Fry

Herbert Fry
Racing Hometown: Wayne, WV

Year	Rank	Starts	Poles	1	2	3	4	5	6–10	Laps	Laps Led	Races Led	Miles	$
1952	94	1	0	0	0	0	0	0	0	366	0	0	458	95
Lifetime		1	0	0	0	0	0	0	0	366	0	0	458	$95

Freddy Fryar

Freddy George Fryar
B: 2/15/1936
Racing Hometown: Baton Rouge, LA

Year	Rank	Starts	Poles	1	2	3	4	5	6–10	Laps	Laps Led	Races Led	Miles	$
1956	209T	1	0	0	0	0	0	0	0	183	0	0	92	100
1959	NR	1	0	0	0	0	0	0	0	53	0	0	27	0
1961	168	1	0	0	0	0	0	0	0	116	0	0	174	200
1970	68	1	0	0	0	0	0	0	1	182	0	0	484	3,000
1971	NR	2	0	0	0	0	0	0	0	238	0	0	595	2,010
Lifetime		6	0	0	0	0	0	0	1	772	0	0	1,371	$5,310

Harold Fryar

Harold Fryar
Racing Hometown: Chattanooga, TN

Year	Rank	Starts	Poles	1	2	3	4	5	6–10	Laps	Laps Led	Races Led	Miles	$
1962	110T	1	0	0	0	0	0	0	0	187	0	0	62	110
Lifetime		1	0	0	0	0	0	0	0	187	0	0	62	$110

Tetsuo Fuchigami *See George Tet*

Stanley Fuchs *See Stan Fox*

Dusty Fuller

Dusty Fuller

Year	Rank	Starts	Poles	1	2	3	4	5	6–10	Laps	Laps Led	Races Led	Miles	$
1955	NR	1	0	0	0	0	0	0	0	197	0	0	197	40
Lifetime		1	0	0	0	0	0	0	0	197	0	0	197	$40

Jeff Fuller

Jeffrey Carl Fuller
B: 3/27/1957
Racing Hometown: Auburn, MA

Year	Rank	Starts	Poles	1	2	3	4	5	6–10	Laps	Laps Led	Races Led	Miles	$
1992	77T	1	0	0	0	0	0	0	0	386	0	0	290	4,000
Lifetime		1	0	0	0	0	0	0	0	386	0	0	290	$4,000

Year	Rank	Starts	Poles	Finish 1	2	3	4	5	6–10	Laps	Laps Led	Races Led	Miles	$

Buck Fulp

John Fulp
B: 1938
Racing Hometown: Anderson, SC

Year	Rank	Starts	Poles	1	2	3	4	5	6–10	Laps	Laps Led	Races Led	Miles	$
1961	122	1	0	0	0	0	0	0	1	65	0	0	98	175
Lifetime		1	0	0	0	0	0	0	1	65	0	0	98	$175

Al Funderburk

Alfred W. Funderburk
Racing Hometown: Tampa, FL

Year	Rank	Starts	Poles	1	2	3	4	5	6–10	Laps	Laps Led	Races Led	Miles	$
1952	NR	1	0	0	0	0	0	0	1		0	0		50
Lifetime		1	0	0	0	0	0	0	1		0	0		$50

Troy Funk

Troy Funk

Year	Rank	Starts	Poles	1	2	3	4	5	6–10	Laps	Laps Led	Races Led	Miles	$
1958	148	1	0	0	0	0	0	0	0	64	0	0	32	50
Lifetime		1	0	0	0	0	0	0	0	64	0	0	32	$50

Niles Gage

Niles Henry Gage Jr.
B: 11/23/1934
Racing Hometown: Milton, ME

Year	Rank	Starts	Poles	1	2	3	4	5	6–10	Laps	Laps Led	Races Led	Miles	$
1968	117	1	0	0	0	0	0	0	0	274	0	0	91	155
Lifetime		1	0	0	0	0	0	0	0	274	0	0	91	$155

Ernie Gahan

Ernest E. Gahan
B: 10/12/1926
Racing Hometown: Dover, NH

Year	Rank	Starts	Poles	1	2	3	4	5	6–10	Laps	Laps Led	Races Led	Miles	$
1960	46	2	0	0	0	0	0	0	0	818	0	0	759	625
1961	90	5	0	0	0	0	0	0	1	707	0	0	348	750
1962	45	3	0	0	0	0	0	0	1	284	0	0	604	725
1966	119T	1	0	0	0	0	0	0	0	114	0	0	38	115
Lifetime		11	0	0	0	0	0	0	2	1,923	0	0	1,749	$2,215

Harry Gailey

James Harry Gailey
B: 2/24/1936
Racing Hometown: Clermont, GA

Year	Rank	Starts	Poles	1	2	3	4	5	6–10	Laps	Laps Led	Races Led	Miles	$
1971	NR	1	0	0	0	0	0	0	0	141	0	0	375	990
Lifetime		1	0	0	0	0	0	0	0	141	0	0	375	$990

Dexter Gainey

Dexter L. Gainey
B: 11/3/1930
Racing Hometown: Taylors, SC

Year	Rank	Starts	Poles	1	2	3	4	5	6–10	Laps	Laps Led	Races Led	Miles	$
1968	123	2	0	0	0	0	0	0	0	142	0	0	92	650
Lifetime		2	0	0	0	0	0	0	0	142	0	0	92	$650

Bill Galdarisi

William Galdarisi
Racing Hometown: Hermosa Beach, CA

Year	Rank	Starts	Poles	1	2	3	4	5	6–10	Laps	Laps Led	Races Led	Miles	$
1954	110	1	0	0	0	0	0	0	0	445	0	0	223	100
Lifetime		1	0	0	0	0	0	0	0	445	0	0	223	$100

Tommy Gale

Thomas J. Gale
B: 9/10/1934
Racing Hometown: McKeesport, PA

Year	Rank	Starts	Poles	1	2	3	4	5	6–10	Laps	Laps Led	Races Led	Miles	$
1968	NR	1	0	0	0	0	0	0	0	172	0	0	172	760
1969	90	1	0	0	0	0	0	0	0	46	0	0	115	290
1970	52	5	0	0	0	0	0	0	1	391	0	0	659	3,135
1971	41	9	0	0	0	0	0	0	1	1,616	0	0	2,969	8,800
1972	41	6	0	0	0	0	0	0	0	1,144	0	0	1,959	7,477
1973	57	5	0	0	0	0	0	0	0	451	0	0	982	5,680
1975	46	5	0	0	0	0	0	0	0	585	0	0	1,104	6,970
1976	33	12	0	0	0	0	0	0	0	2,205	0	0	3,202	19,325
1977	26	18	0	0	0	0	0	0	0	4,402	0	0	6,071	39,865
1978	20	26	0	0	0	0	0	0	0	6,980	0	0	8,867	60,765
1979	18	27	0	0	0	0	0	0	1	7,054	0	0	8,092	73,029
1980	18	29	0	0	0	0	0	0	0	7,605	0	0	8,813	84,279
1981	15	30	0	0	0	0	0	0	0	9,015	2	1	9,926	110,518
1982	21	26	0	0	0	0	0	0	0	7,566	1	1	8,607	101,485

Year	Rank	Starts	Poles	Finish 1	2	3	4	5	6–10	Laps	Laps Led	Races Led	Miles	$

Tommy Gale *continued*

Year	Rank	Starts	Poles	1	2	3	4	5	6–10	Laps	Laps Led	Races Led	Miles	$
1983	23	28	0	0	0	0	0	0	1	6,540	0	0	7,814	88,305
1984	33	16	0	0	0	0	0	0	0	4,248	0	0	5,268	69,385
1986	NR	1	0	0	0	0	0	0	0	175	0	0	466	5,845
Lifetime		245	0	0	0	0	0	0	4	60,195	3	2	75,084	$685,913

Homer Galloway

Homer Galloway
Racing Hometown: Hartsville, SC

Year	Rank	Starts	Poles	1	2	3	4	5	6–10	Laps	Laps Led	Races Led	Miles	$
1961	140T	1	0	0	0	0	0	0	0	127	0	0	42	110
Lifetime		1	0	0	0	0	0	0	0	127	0	0	42	$110

George Gallup

George L. Gallup
D: 1960   *Killed while flagging short track race @ Menands NY (Empire Raceway).*
Racing Hometown: Oneonta, NY

Year	Rank	Starts	Poles	1	2	3	4	5	6–10	Laps	Laps Led	Races Led	Miles	$
1952	72	4	0	0	0	0	0	0	1	441	13	1	356	175
1953	NR	1	0	0	0	0	0	0	0	36	0	0	148	50
Lifetime		5	0	0	0	0	0	0	1	477	13	1	504	$225

Dan Galullo

Daniel Galullo

Year	Rank	Starts	Poles	1	2	3	4	5	6–10	Laps	Laps Led	Races Led	Miles	$
1956	246T	1	0	0	0	0	0	0	0	34	0	0	17	25
Lifetime		1	0	0	0	0	0	0	0	34	0	0	17	$25

Harry Gant

Harry Phil Gant
B: 1/10/1940
Racing Hometown: Taylorsville, NC

Year	Rank	Starts	Poles	1	2	3	4	5	6–10	Laps	Laps Led	Races Led	Miles	$
1973	85	1	0	0	0	0	0	0	0	307	0	0	461	2,260
1974	64	3	0	0	0	0	0	0	1	790	0	0	846	4,784
1975	105T	1	0	0	0	0	0	0	0	306	0	0	459	1,130
1976	84	1	0	0	0	0	0	0	1	387	0	0	581	5,430
1977	100T	1	0	0	0	0	0	0	0	266	0	0	399	1,460
1978	53	5	0	0	0	0	0	0	1	873	45	1	1,230	14,150
1979	21	25	1	0	0	0	0	0	5	6,226	29	4	7,367	47,185
1980	11	31	0	0	3	2	2	2	5	7,986	263	10	8,774	177,150
1981	3	31	3	0	7	1	4	1	5	9,082	1,169	20	10,253	280,047
1982	4	30	1	2	2	3	1	1	7	8,454	420	17	9,641	337,582
1983	7	30	0	1	1	3	1	4	6	9,024	60	10	10,193	414,353
1984	2	30	3	3	6	0	5	1	8	**9,899**	1,186	19	**11,395**	673,060
1985	3	28	3	3	5	3	1	2	5	8,806	1,270	20	10,177	804,287
1986	11	29	2	0	3	1	3	2	4	7,965	646	17	9,565	583,024
1987	22	29	1	0	0	0	0	0	4	6,497	71	3	7,921	197,645
1988	27	24	0	0	0	0	0	0	3	5,896	343	8	6,867	173,325
1989	7	29	0	1	3	1	2	2	5	8,627	440	11	10,293	639,792
1990	17	28	0	1	0	1	1	3	3	7,441	53	9	9,669	522,519
1991	4	29	1	5	2	3	4	1	2	9,428	**1,684**	17	11,124	1,194,033
1992	4	29	0	2	3	2	0	3	5	9,197	407	15	**11,220**	1,122,776
1993	11	30	1	0	0	1	2	1	8	8,843	265	8	10,867	772,832
1994	25	30	1	0	0	0	0	0	7	7,329	94	3	9,570	556,020
Lifetime		474	17	18	35	21	26	23	85	133,629	8,445	192	158,871	$8,524,844

Ruben Garcia

Ruben Garcia
B: 4/1/1946
Racing Hometown: South El Monte, CA

Year	Rank	Starts	Poles	1	2	3	4	5	6–10	Laps	Laps Led	Races Led	Miles	$
1984	70	2	0	0	0	0	0	0	0	121	0	0	317	1,885
1985	56	2	0	0	0	0	0	0	0	196	0	0	514	6,525
1986	72	2	0	0	0	0	0	0	0	169	0	0	443	4,530
1987	70	2	0	0	0	0	0	0	0	116	0	0	304	4,180
1988	89T	1	0	0	0	0	0	0	0	27	0	0	71	3,380
Lifetime		9	0	0	0	0	0	0	0	629	0	0	1,648	$20,500

Arnold Gardner

Arnold Gardner
B: 12/25/1926   D: 2/1994
Racing Hometown: Batavia, IL

Year	Rank	Starts	Poles	1	2	3	4	5	6–10	Laps	Laps Led	Races Led	Miles	$
1960	96	4	0	0	0	0	0	0	0	614	0	0	904	575
Lifetime		4	0	0	0	0	0	0	0	614	0	0	904	$575

Year	Rank	Starts	Poles	Finish						Laps	Laps Led	Races Led	Miles	$
				1	2	3	4	5	6–10					

Bud Gardner

Bud Gardner

Year	Rank	Starts	Poles	1	2	3	4	5	6–10	Laps	Laps Led	Races Led	Miles	$
1958	NR	1	0	0	0	0	0	0	0	127	0	0	42	100
Lifetime		1	0	0	0	0	0	0	0	127	0	0	42	$100

Frank Gardner

Frank Gardner
Racing Hometown: Australia

Year	Rank	Starts	Poles	1	2	3	4	5	6–10	Laps	Laps Led	Races Led	Miles	$
1968	NR	1	0	0	0	0	0	0	0	1	0	0	1	515
Lifetime		1	0	0	0	0	0	0	0	1	0	0	1	$515

Johnny Gardner

John Gardner
Racing Hometown: Rock Hill, SC

Year	Rank	Starts	Poles	1	2	3	4	5	6–10	Laps	Laps Led	Races Led	Miles	$
1958	146	14	0	0	0	0	0	0	0	1,510	0	0	894	780
Lifetime		14	0	0	0	0	0	0	0	1,510	0	0	894	$780

Slick Gardner

Slick Gardner
B: 12/24/1946
Racing Hometown: Buellton, CA

Year	Rank	Starts	Poles	1	2	3	4	5	6–10	Laps	Laps Led	Races Led	Miles	$
1973	126	1	0	0	0	0	0	0	0	9	0	0	24	990
Lifetime		1	0	0	0	0	0	0	0	9	0	0	24	$990

Walson Gardner

William Walson Gardner
B: 8/21/1932
Racing Hometown: Laurinburg, NC

Year	Rank	Starts	Poles	1	2	3	4	5	6–10	Laps	Laps Led	Races Led	Miles	$
1965	107	2	0	0	0	0	0	0	0	61	0	0	31	200
1967	NR	1	0	0	0	0	0	0	0	47	0	0	24	150
1968	38	14	0	0	0	0	0	0	2	3,546	0	0	2,203	4,275
1969	55	7	0	0	0	0	0	0	0	1,299	0	0	650	2,115
Lifetime		24	0	0	0	0	0	0	2	4,953	0	0	2,907	$6,740

Nick Garin

Nick Garin
Racing Hometown: Oakdale, PA

Year	Rank	Starts	Poles	1	2	3	4	5	6–10	Laps	Laps Led	Races Led	Miles	$
1949	62	1	0	0	0	0	0	0	0	142	0	0	71	50
1951	N/A	1	0	0	0	0	0	0	0	0	0	0		0
Lifetime		2	0	0	0	0	0	0	0	142	0	0	71	$50

Dick Garlington

Richard Garlington
Racing Hometown: Atlanta, GA

Year	Rank	Starts	Poles	1	2	3	4	5	6–10	Laps	Laps Led	Races Led	Miles	$
1954	192T	2	0	0	0	0	0	0	0	46	0	0	155	25
Lifetime		2	0	0	0	0	0	0	0	46	0	0	155	$25

Cliff Garner

Clifford Garner
B: 1937
Racing Hometown: Los Angeles, CA

Year	Rank	Starts	Poles	1	2	3	4	5	6–10	Laps	Laps Led	Races Led	Miles	$
1966	88	1	0	0	0	0	0	0	0	98	0	0	265	500
1967	113	1	0	0	0	0	0	0	0	25	0	0	68	500
1969	NR	1	0	0	0	0	0	0	0	48	0	0	130	775
1972	NR	1	0	0	0	0	0	0	0	185	0	0	463	1,495
Lifetime		4	0	0	0	0	0	0	0	356	0	0	924	$3,270

Rat Garner

Rat Garner
Racing Hometown: Asheboro, NC

Year	Rank	Starts	Poles	1	2	3	4	5	6–10	Laps	Laps Led	Races Led	Miles	$
1956	140T	1	0	0	0	0	0	0	0	216	0	0	216	225
Lifetime		1	0	0	0	0	0	0	0	216	0	0	216	$225

Chuck Garrett

Charles Garrett
Racing Hometown: Sharon, PA

Year	Rank	Starts	Poles	1	2	3	4	5	6–10	Laps	Laps Led	Races Led	Miles	$
1950	62T	1	0	0	0	0	0	0	1		0	0		100
1952	NR	1	0	0	0	0	0	0	0	109	0	0	109	0
1954	NR	1	0	0	0	0	0	0	1	149	0	0	75	200
Lifetime		3	0	0	0	0	0	0	2	258	0	0	184	$300

Year	Rank	Starts	Poles	Finish						Laps	Laps Led	Races Led	Miles	$
				1	2	3	4	5	6–10					

Steve Garrett

Steve Garrett
Racing Hometown: Winston-Salem, NC

Year	Rank	Starts	Poles	1	2	3	4	5	6–10	Laps	Laps Led	Races Led	Miles	$
1962	NR	1	0	0	0	0	0	0	0	40	0	0	10	75
Lifetime		1	0	0	0	0	0	0	0	40	0	0	10	$75

Charles Gattalia

Charles Gattalia
Racing Hometown: New Haven, CT

Year	Rank	Starts	Poles	1	2	3	4	5	6–10	Laps	Laps Led	Races Led	Miles	$
1951	54	6	0	0	1	0	0	0	0		0	0		775
1952	NR	8	0	0	0	0	0	0	3	810	0	0	565	485
Lifetime		14	0	0	1	0	0	0	3	810	0	0	565	$1,260

Louis Gatto

Louis Gatto
Racing Hometown: Bloomfield, NJ

Year	Rank	Starts	Poles	1	2	3	4	5	6–10	Laps	Laps Led	Races Led	Miles	$
1978	102T	1	0	0	0	0	0	0	0	5	0	0	5	500
1979	83	2	0	0	0	0	0	0	0	31	0	0	39	1,445
Lifetime		3	0	0	0	0	0	0	0	36	0	0	44	$1,945

Ron Gautsche

Rolland Gautsche
B: 7/6/1935
Racing Hometown: Truckee, CA

Year	Rank	Starts	Poles	1	2	3	4	5	6–10	Laps	Laps Led	Races Led	Miles	$
1971	NR	3	0	0	0	0	0	0	0	176	0	0	460	2,935
1972	87	2	0	0	0	0	0	0	0	215	0	0	544	2,735
Lifetime		5	0	0	0	0	0	0	0	391	0	0	1,004	$5,670

Scott Gaylord

Scott Gaylord
B: 8/12/1958
Racing Hometown: Lakewood, CO

Year	Rank	Starts	Poles	1	2	3	4	5	6–10	Laps	Laps Led	Races Led	Miles	$
1991	80T	1	0	0	0	0	0	0	0	61	0	0	154	3,625
1992	87T	1	0	0	0	0	0	0	0	124	0	0	124	4,265
1993	74T	1	0	0	0	0	0	0	0	75	0	0	184	5,935
1996	65	1	0	0	0	0	0	0	0	67	0	0	169	10,095
Lifetime		4	0	0	0	0	0	0	0	327	0	0	630	$23,920

Jack Gaynor

Jack Gaynor
Racing Hometown: Los Angeles, CA

Year	Rank	Starts	Poles	1	2	3	4	5	6–10	Laps	Laps Led	Races Led	Miles	$
1951	N/A	1	0	0	0	0	0	0	0		0	0		25
Lifetime		1	0	0	0	0	0	0	0		0	0		$25

Bill Gazaway

William Gazaway
B: 4/13/1905
Racing Hometown: Atlanta, GA

Year	Rank	Starts	Poles	1	2	3	4	5	6–10	Laps	Laps Led	Races Led	Miles	$
1960	NR	1	0	0	0	0	0	0	0	1	0	0	2	200
Lifetime		1	0	0	0	0	0	0	0	1	0	0	2	$200

Bud Geiselman

Bud Geiselman
Racing Hometown: Raleigh, NC

Year	Rank	Starts	Poles	1	2	3	4	5	6–10	Laps	Laps Led	Races Led	Miles	$
1955	206T	1	0	0	0	0	0	0	0	164	0	0	82	50
1956	205	2	0	0	0	0	0	0	0	173	0	0	173	50
Lifetime		3	0	0	0	0	0	0	0	337	0	0	255	$100

Victor Geisler

Victor Geisler
Racing Hometown: Cullman, AL

Year	Rank	Starts	Poles	1	2	3	4	5	6–10	Laps	Laps Led	Races Led	Miles	$
1954	206	1	0	0	0	0	0	0	0	2	0	0	8	0
Lifetime		1	0	0	0	0	0	0	0	2	0	0	8	$0

Roy Gemberling

Roy Gemberling
B: 1923
Racing Hometown: Kent, OH

Year	Rank	Starts	Poles	1	2	3	4	5	6–10	Laps	Laps Led	Races Led	Miles	$
1964	117	1	0	0	0	0	0	0	0	34	0	0	85	100
Lifetime		1	0	0	0	0	0	0	0	34	0	0	85	$100

Year	Rank	Starts	Poles	Finish						Laps	Laps Led	Races Led	Miles	$
				1	2	3	4	5	6–10					

Russ Gemberling

Russell Gemberling
Racing Hometown: Kent, OH

Year	Rank	Starts	Poles	1	2	3	4	5	6–10	Laps	Laps Led	Races Led	Miles	$
1959	117	1	0	0	0	0	0	0	0	127	3	1	32	85
Lifetime		1	0	0	0	0	0	0	0	127	3	1	32	$85

Tony Genove

Anthony Genove

Year	Rank	Starts	Poles	1	2	3	4	5	6–10	Laps	Laps Led	Races Led	Miles	$
1949	NR	1	0	0	0	0	0	0	0		0	0		0
Lifetime		1	0	0	0	0	0	0	0		0	0		$0

J. W. Gentry

J. W. Gentry
Racing Hometown: Shreveport, LA

Year	Rank	Starts	Poles	1	2	3	4	5	6–10	Laps	Laps Led	Races Led	Miles	$
1953	NR	1	0	0	0	0	0	0	0		0	0		25
Lifetime		1	0	0	0	0	0	0	0		0	0		$25

Doug George

Douglas George
B: 11/5/1960
Racing Hometown: Atwater, CA

Year	Rank	Starts	Poles	1	2	3	4	5	6–10	Laps	Laps Led	Races Led	Miles	$
1995	55	2	0	0	0	0	0	0	0	251	0	0	362	18,610
Lifetime		2	0	0	0	0	0	0	0	251	0	0	362	$18,610

Benny Georgeson

Benjamin Georgeson
Racing Hometown: Ft. Lauderdale, FL

Year	Rank	Starts	Poles	1	2	3	4	5	6–10	Laps	Laps Led	Races Led	Miles	$
1949	NR	1	0	0	0	0	0	0	0		0	0		0
Lifetime		1	0	0	0	0	0	0	0		0	0		$0

Bobby Gerhart

Robert Gerhart
B: 7/21/1958
Racing Hometown: Lebanon, PA

Year	Rank	Starts	Poles	1	2	3	4	5	6–10	Laps	Laps Led	Races Led	Miles	$
1983	82	2	0	0	0	0	0	0	0	69	0	0	173	2,550
1984	50	4	0	0	0	0	0	0	0	655	0	0	813	7,585
1985	44	5	0	0	0	0	0	0	0	1,166	0	0	1,503	7,400
1986	57	4	0	0	0	0	0	0	0	575	0	0	1,178	6,535
1987	74	2	0	0	0	0	0	0	0	169	0	0	423	3,665
1988	55	2	0	0	0	0	0	0	0	377	0	0	943	5,050
1989	72	1	0	0	0	0	0	0	0	193	0	0	483	4,575
1990	91T	1	0	0	0	0	0	0	0	151	0	0	151	4,550
1992	57	3	0	0	0	0	0	0	0	350	0	0	904	15,810
Lifetime		24	0	0	0	0	0	0	0	3,705	0	0	6,569	$57,720

Whitey Gerkin

William Gerkin
B: 5/26/1930   D: 10/8/1973   *Died from injuries at Illiana Speedway 10/7/73.*
Racing Hometown: Melrose Park, IL

Year	Rank	Starts	Poles	1	2	3	4	5	6–10	Laps	Laps Led	Races Led	Miles	$
1960	59	2	0	0	0	0	0	0	0	233	0	0	583	400
1963	140	1	0	0	0	0	0	0	0	23	0	0	58	75
1967	NR	2	0	0	0	0	0	0	0	407	2	1	408	1,410
Lifetime		5	0	0	0	0	0	0	0	663	2	1	1,048	$1,885

Wally Gervais

Wally Gervais
Racing Hometown: Portland, OR

Year	Rank	Starts	Poles	1	2	3	4	5	6–10	Laps	Laps Led	Races Led	Miles	$
1956	162	3	0	0	0	0	0	0	0	110	0	0	82	140
Lifetime		3	0	0	0	0	0	0	0	110	0	0	82	$140

Ernie Gesell

Ernest Gesell
Racing Hometown: Trenton, NJ

Year	Rank	Starts	Poles	1	2	3	4	5	6–10	Laps	Laps Led	Races Led	Miles	$
1959	NR	1	0	0	0	0	0	0	1	115	0	0	115	200
Lifetime		1	0	0	0	0	0	0	1	115	0	0	115	$200

Dick Getty

Richard Getty
Racing Hometown: Van Nuys, CA

Year	Rank	Starts	Poles	1	2	3	4	5	6–10	Laps	Laps Led	Races Led	Miles	$
1956	201	3	0	0	0	0	0	0	0	186	0	0	217	90

Year	Rank	Starts	Poles	Finish						Laps	Laps Led	Races Led	Miles	$
				1	2	3	4	5	6–10	Laps	Led	Led	Miles	$

Dick Getty *continued*

Year	Rank	Starts	Poles	1	2	3	4	5	6–10	Laps	Laps Led	Races Led	Miles	$
1957	31	10	0	0	0	0	0	3	5	1,174	0	0	786	1,890
1959	121	2	0	0	0	0	0	0	0	138	0	0	59	175
1960	135	2	0	0	0	0	0	0	0	198	0	0	254	385
1961	93	4	0	0	0	0	0	0	0	310	0	0	331	500
1962	60	5	0	0	0	0	0	0	2	525	0	0	213	675
Lifetime		26	0	0	0	0	0	3	7	2,531	0	0	1,860	$3,715

Vince Giamformaggio

Vincent Giamformaggio
Racing Hometown: Santa Fe Springs, CA

Year	Rank	Starts	Poles	1	2	3	4	5	6–10	Laps	Laps Led	Races Led	Miles	$
1977	106T	1	0	0	0	0	0	0	0	93	0	0	233	850
1978	93T	1	0	0	0	0	0	0	0	41	0	0	107	805
1979	74	2	0	0	0	0	0	0	0	139	0	0	361	4,295
1980	90	1	0	0	0	0	0	0	0	109	0	0	286	2,260
Lifetime		5	0	0	0	0	0	0	0	382	0	0	987	$8,210

Mickey Gibbs

Mickey Gibbs
B: 3/15/1958
Racing Hometown: Glencoe, AL

Year	Rank	Starts	Poles	1	2	3	4	5	6–10	Laps	Laps Led	Races Led	Miles	$
1988	50	5	0	0	0	0	0	0	0	636	2	1	1,134	14,750
1989	41	7	0	0	0	0	0	0	0	1,363	0	0	1,927	27,040
1990	37	9	0	0	0	0	0	0	0	1,837	1	1	2,541	38,665
1991	34	15	0	0	0	0	0	0	0	4,078	0	0	5,308	100,360
Lifetime		36	0	0	0	0	0	0	0	7,914	3	2	10,910	$180,815

Shorty Gibbs

Sidney Gibbs
Racing Hometown: Greenville, SC

Year	Rank	Starts	Poles	1	2	3	4	5	6–10	Laps	Laps Led	Races Led	Miles	$
1952	99	2	0	0	0	0	0	0	0	87	0	0	53	50
Lifetime		2	0	0	0	0	0	0	0	87	0	0	53	$50

Herb Gibson

Herbert Gibson
Racing Hometown: Charlotte, NC

Year	Rank	Starts	Poles	1	2	3	4	5	6–10	Laps	Laps Led	Races Led	Miles	$
1956	264T	1	0	0	0	0	0	0	0	21	0	0	32	50
1957	165T	1	0	0	0	0	0	0	0	0	0	0	0	75
Lifetime		2	0	0	0	0	0	0	0	21	0	0	32	$125

Mark Gibson

Mark Gibson
B: 8/14/1957
Racing Hometown: Daytona Beach, FL

Year	Rank	Starts	Poles	1	2	3	4	5	6–10	Laps	Laps Led	Races Led	Miles	$
1987	96T	1	0	0	0	0	0	0	0	204	0	0	204	1,300
1989	91T	1	0	0	0	0	0	0	0	100	0	0	250	5,030
1990	—		0											1,050
1992	—		0											1,900
Lifetime		2	0	0	0	0	0	0	0	304	0	0	454	$9,280

Tom Gifford

Thomas Gifford
Racing Hometown: Providence, RI

Year	Rank	Starts	Poles	1	2	3	4	5	6–10	Laps	Laps Led	Races Led	Miles	$
1951	N/A	1	0	0	0	0	0	0	0		0	0		0
1952	157	3	0	0	0	0	0	0	0	53	0	0	27	50
Lifetime		4	0	0	0	0	0	0	0	53	0	0	27	$50

Art Gill

Arthur Gill
Racing Hometown: Mantua, OH

Year	Rank	Starts	Poles	1	2	3	4	5	6–10	Laps	Laps Led	Races Led	Miles	$
1950	70	3	0	0	0	0	0	0	0	360	0	0	180	125
Lifetime		3	0	0	0	0	0	0	0	360	0	0	180	$125

Jim Gillette

James Gillette
Racing Hometown: Roanoke, VA

Year	Rank	Starts	Poles	1	2	3	4	5	6–10	Laps	Laps Led	Races Led	Miles	$
1954	108	2	0	0	0	0	0	0	0	441	0	0	477	140
Lifetime		2	0	0	0	0	0	0	0	441	0	0	477	$140

Year	Rank	Starts	Poles	Finish 1	2	3	4	5	6–10	Laps	Laps Led	Races Led	Miles	$

Mel Gillette

Mel Gillette
Racing Hometown: Howell, MI

Year	Rank	Starts	Poles	1	2	3	4	5	6–10	Laps	Laps Led	Races Led	Miles	$
1969	NR	1	0	0	0	0	0	0	0	50	0	0	100	720
Lifetime		1	0	0	0	0	0	0	0	50	0	0	100	$720

Wayne Gillette

Elias Wayne Gillette
B: 7/17/1938
Racing Hometown: Atlanta, GA

Year	Rank	Starts	Poles	1	2	3	4	5	6–10	Laps	Laps Led	Races Led	Miles	$
1969	45	16	0	0	0	0	0	0	0	887	0	0	981	6,127
Lifetime		16	0	0	0	0	0	0	0	887	0	0	981	$6,127

Elmer Gilliam

Elmer Gilliam
Racing Hometown: Morristown, TN

Year	Rank	Starts	Poles	1	2	3	4	5	6–10	Laps	Laps Led	Races Led	Miles	$
1965	NR	1	0	0	0	0	0	0	0	1	0	0	1	100
1967	NR	3	0	0	0	0	0	0	0	9	0	0	6	325
Lifetime		4	0	0	0	0	0	0	0	10	0	0	6	$425

Jim Gilliam

James Gilliam
Racing Hometown: N. Hollywood, CA

Year	Rank	Starts	Poles	1	2	3	4	5	6–10	Laps	Laps Led	Races Led	Miles	$
1974	113	1	0	0	0	0	0	0	0	76	0	0	199	1,025
Lifetime		1	0	0	0	0	0	0	0	76	0	0	199	$1,025

Butch Gilliland

Butch Gilliland
B: 2/25/1958
Racing Hometown: Anaheim, CA

Year	Rank	Starts	Poles	1	2	3	4	5	6–10	Laps	Laps Led	Races Led	Miles	$
1990	84T	1	0	0	0	0	0	0	0	71	0	0	179	4,200
1991	78	1	0	0	0	0	0	0	0	299	0	0	299	3,750
1992	65	2	0	0	0	0	0	0	0	347	0	0	431	10,990
1993	78	1	0	0	0	0	0	0	0	71	0	0	179	6,765
1994	67	1	0	0	0	0	0	0	0	72	0	0	181	7,755
1995	69	1	0	0	0	0	0	0	0	19	0	0	48	9,760
Lifetime		7	0	0	0	0	0	0	0	879	0	0	1,317	$43,220

Charles Gillman

Charles M. Gillman Jr.
Racing Hometown: Pleasant Point, NJ

Year	Rank	Starts	Poles	1	2	3	4	5	6–10	Laps	Laps Led	Races Led	Miles	$
1951	N/A	2	0	0	0	0	0	0	1		0	0		125
Lifetime		2	0	0	0	0	0	0	1		0	0		$125

Joe Gillow

Joseph Gillow

Year	Rank	Starts	Poles	1	2	3	4	5	6–10	Laps	Laps Led	Races Led	Miles	$
1952	NR	1	0	0	0	0	0	0	0	20	0	0	10	25
Lifetime		1	0	0	0	0	0	0	0	20	0	0	10	$25

Dick Girvin

Richard Girvin
Racing Hometown: South Norfolk, VA

Year	Rank	Starts	Poles	1	2	3	4	5	6–10	Laps	Laps Led	Races Led	Miles	$
1953	140T	1	0	0	0	0	0	0	0		0	0		25
Lifetime		1	0	0	0	0	0	0	0		0	0		$25

Frank Gise

Frank Gise
Racing Hometown: New Point, IN

Year	Rank	Starts	Poles	1	2	3	4	5	6–10	Laps	Laps Led	Races Led	Miles	$
1951	N/A	2	0	0	0	0	0	0	1	215	0	0	269	100
Lifetime		2	0	0	0	0	0	0	1	215	0	0	269	$100

Don Glass

Donald Glass

Year	Rank	Starts	Poles	1	2	3	4	5	6–10	Laps	Laps Led	Races Led	Miles	$
1953	NR	1	0	0	0	0	0	0	0		0	0		75
Lifetime		1	0	0	0	0	0	0	0		0	0		$75

Charlie Glotzbach

Charles Lee Glotzbach
B: 6/19/1938
Racing Hometown: Edwardsville, IN

Year	Rank	Starts	Poles	1	2	3	4	5	6–10	Laps	Laps Led	Races Led	Miles	$
1960	136	2	0	0	0	0	0	0	0	266	0	0	399	400

Year	Rank	Starts	Poles	Finish 1	2	3	4	5	6–10	Laps	Laps Led	Races Led	Miles	$

Charlie Glotzbach *continued*

Year	Rank	Starts	Poles	1	2	3	4	5	6–10	Laps	Laps Led	Races Led	Miles	$
1961	56	4	0	0	0	0	0	0	0	344	0	0	653	755
1967	23	9	0	0	0	0	3	0	2	1,783	4	1	2,461	14,870
1968	19	22	2	1	3	1	4	1	2	4,871	332	5	4,791	43,101
1969	37	12	1	0	2	0	2	1	1	2,823	171	8	3,957	37,515
1970	28	19	5	2	0	3	2	0	1	3,396	427	16	5,258	50,749
1971	42	20	4	1	2	0	3	1	3	4,735	805	10	4,695	38,880
1972	65	3	0	0	1	1	0	0	0	709	0	0	1,150	26,175
1973	43	5	0	0	0	0	0	0	1	1,048	11	2	1,307	6,451
1974	26	14	0	0	0	0	4	0	1	3,582	126	5	3,950	34,172
1975	111	2	0	0	0	0	0	0	1	454	1	1	681	6,390
1976	109T	1	0	0	0	0	0	0	0	121	0	0	182	1,535
1981	88T	1	0	0	0	0	0	0	0	218	0	0	327	1,275
1989	—	0												1,700
1990	70	3	0	0	0	0	0	0	0	651	0	0	649	16,555
1992	41	7	0	0	0	0	0	0	0	1,528	0	0	2,564	48,060
Lifetime		124	12	4	8	5	18	3	12	26,529	1,877	48	33,022	$328,583

Gene Glover

Eugene Glover
B: 11/20/1934
Racing Hometown: Kingsport, TN

Year	Rank	Starts	Poles	1	2	3	4	5	6–10	Laps	Laps Led	Races Led	Miles	$
1957	150	1	0	0	0	0	0	0	0	104	0	0	52	100
Lifetime		1	0	0	0	0	0	0	0	104	0	0	52	$100

Fred Goad

Fred Goad
Racing Hometown: Woodlawn, VA

Year	Rank	Starts	Poles	1	2	3	4	5	6–10	Laps	Laps Led	Races Led	Miles	$
1965	118	2	0	0	0	0	0	0	0	9	0	0	11	515
Lifetime		2	0	0	0	0	0	0	0	9	0	0	11	$515

P. E. Godfrey

P. E. Godfrey
Racing Hometown: Charlotte, NC

Year	Rank	Starts	Poles	1	2	3	4	5	6–10	Laps	Laps Led	Races Led	Miles	$
1950	NR	1	0	0	0	0	0	0	0	278	0	0	348	0
Lifetime		1	0	0	0	0	0	0	0	278	0	0	348	$0

Paul Goldsmith

Paul Goldsmith
B: 10/2/1927
Racing Hometown: St. Claire Shores, MI

Year	Rank	Starts	Poles	1	2	3	4	5	6–10	Laps	Laps Led	Races Led	Miles	$
1956	13	9	0	1	0	0	2	1	2	2,292	182	1	2,090	8,569
1957	13	25	4	4	4	1	1	0	5	3,759	588	10	2,495	12,734
1958	NR	2	1	1	0	0	0	0	1	178	39	1	206	4,690
1961	45	2	0	0	0	1	0	0	1	239	0	0	598	6,050
1962	51	1	0	0	0	0	0	0	1	218	0	0	327	1,375
1963	NR	6	1	0	1	0	0	0	0	545	22	3	1,058	4,170
1964	22	14	2	0	0	3	0	0	1	2,281	319	8	2,903	20,835
1966	5	21	1	3	3	2	1	2	0	5,097	452	10	5,382	54,609
1967	11	21	0	0	2	3	1	1	1	4,851	398	7	5,409	38,732
1968	30	15	0	0	1	0	0	1	2	2,793	304	8	3,505	24,365
1969	40	11	0	0	0	3	1	0	1	1,999	20	4	2,970	22,850
Lifetime		127	9	9	11	13	6	5	15	24,252	2,324	52	26,943	$198,979

Tubby Gonzales

Elar Gonzales
B: 10/21/1919
Racing Hometown: Houston, TX

Year	Rank	Starts	Poles	1	2	3	4	5	6–10	Laps	Laps Led	Races Led	Miles	$
1961	84	5	0	0	0	0	1	0	0	598	0	0	889	1,300
1962	NR	4	0	0	0	0	0	0	0	422	0	0	629	1,050
Lifetime		9	0	0	0	0	1	0	0	1,020	0	0	1,518	$2,350

Phil Good

Phillip Good
B: 1/27/1955
Racing Hometown: Williamsburg, VA

Year	Rank	Starts	Poles	1	2	3	4	5	6–10	Laps	Laps Led	Races Led	Miles	$
1984	NR	1	0	0	0	0	0	0	0	331	0	0	331	1,065
1985	46	4	0	0	0	0	0	0	0	1,339	0	0	1,331	6,870
1986	81	2	0	0	0	0	0	0	0	439	0	0	254	2,825

Year	Rank	Starts	Poles	Finish						Laps	Laps Led	Races Led	Miles	$
				1	2	3	4	5	6–10	Laps				

Phil Good *continued*

Year	Rank	Starts	Poles	1	2	3	4	5	6–10	Laps	Laps Led	Races Led	Miles	$
1987	101T	1	0	0	0	0	0	0	0	10	0	0	24	1,435
Lifetime		8	0	0	0	0	0	0	0	2,119	0	0	1,940	$12,195

Dick Goode

Richard Goode
B: 12/1/1927   D: 11/5/1992
Racing Hometown: Mishawaka, IN

Year	Rank	Starts	Poles	1	2	3	4	5	6–10	Laps	Laps Led	Races Led	Miles	$
1963	100	2	0	0	0	0	0	0	1	107	0	0	268	700
Lifetime		2	0	0	0	0	0	0	1	107	0	0	268	$700

Gene Goodman

Gene Goodman

Year	Rank	Starts	Poles	1	2	3	4	5	6–10	Laps	Laps Led	Races Led	Miles	$
1956	146	1	0	0	0	0	0	0	0	130	0	0	195	75
Lifetime		1	0	0	0	0	0	0	0	130	0	0	195	$75

Jack Goodwin

Jack Goodwin
B: 1929
Racing Hometown: Birmingham, MI

Year	Rank	Starts	Poles	1	2	3	4	5	6–10	Laps	Laps Led	Races Led	Miles	$
1956	140T	1	0	0	0	0	0	0	0	58	0	0	238	200
1957	145	1	0	0	0	0	0	0	0	0	0	0	0	60
Lifetime		2	0	0	0	0	0	0	0	58	0	0	238	$260

Jack Goodwin

Jack Goodwin
Racing Hometown: Berkeley, CA

Year	Rank	Starts	Poles	1	2	3	4	5	6–10	Laps	Laps Led	Races Led	Miles	$
1951	38	3	0	0	0	0	0	0	1	617	0	0	712	725
1952	195	1	0	0	0	0	0	0	0	0	0	0	0	25
1965	141	1	0	0	0	0	0	0	0	0	0	0	0	0
1966	121	1	0	0	0	0	0	0	0	35	0	0	88	100
Lifetime		6	0	0	0	0	0	0	1	652	0	0	800	$850

Clyde Goons

Clyde Goons

Year	Rank	Starts	Poles	1	2	3	4	5	6–10	Laps	Laps Led	Races Led	Miles	$
1958	NR	1	0	0	0	0	0	0	0	69	0	0	23	85
Lifetime		1	0	0	0	0	0	0	0	69	0	0	23	$85

Cecil Gordon

Cecil Owen Gordon
B: 6/21/1941
Racing Hometown: Horse Shoe, NC

Year	Rank	Starts	Poles	1	2	3	4	5	6–10	Laps	Laps Led	Races Led	Miles	$
1968	55	9	0	0	0	0	0	0	0	1,144	0	0	762	2,295
1969	10	51	0	0	0	0	0	1	7	10,745	0	0	9,016	39,679
1970	11	44	0	0	0	0	1	1	9	8,424	0	0	6,872	32,713
1971	3	46	0	0	0	2	2	2	15	12,468	0	0	12,034	69,080
1972	4	31	0	0	0	0	1	3	12	9,033	3	2	10,421	73,126
1973	3	28	0	0	0	1	1	6	10	8,995	5	3	9,988	102,120
1974	9	30	0	0	0	0	1	0	9	7,396	2	2	9,079	66,166
1975	6	30	0	0	1	1	2	3	9	8,577	6	2	9,683	101,467
1976	15	30	0	0	0	0	0	0	5	7,387	7	3	8,757	73,830
1977	10	30	0	0	0	0	0	0	2	8,133	0	0	9,604	86,312
1978	19	26	0	0	0	0	0	0	1	6,773	0	0	7,191	53,815
1979	19	28	0	0	0	0	0	0	0	7,419	0	0	8,163	67,180
1980	15	29	0	0	0	0	0	0	3	7,864	0	0	8,978	83,300
1981	23	25	0	0	0	0	0	0	0	5,587	0	0	6,872	55,980
1982	82	4	0	0	0	0	0	0	0	1,125	0	0	1,445	13,920
1983	40	8	0	0	0	0	0	0	0	1,831	0	0	3,021	17,340
1985	NR	1	0	0	0	0	0	0	0	7	0	0	4	2,640
Lifetime		450	0	0	1	4	8	16	82	112,908	23	12	121,891	$940,963

Jeff Gordon

Jeffrey Michael Gordon
B: 8/4/1971
Racing Hometown: Pittsboro, IN

Year	Rank	Starts	Poles	1	2	3	4	5	6–10	Laps	Laps Led	Races Led	Miles	$
1992	79T	1	0	0	0	0	0	0	0	164	0	0	250	6,285
1993	14	30	1	0	2	1	1	3	4	8,390	230	14	10,066	765,168
1994	8	31	1	2	1	1	2	1	7	9,277	446	17	11,548	1,799,523
1995	1	31	8	7	4	5	0	1	6	9,405	**2,600**	**29**	11,608	4,347,343

Year	Rank	Starts	Poles	Finish 1	2	3	4	5	6–10	Laps	Laps Led	Races Led	Miles	$

Jeff Gordon *continued*

Year	Rank	Starts	Poles	1	2	3	4	5	6–10	Laps	Laps Led	Races Led	Miles	$
1996	2	31	5	10	3	4	2	2	3	8,972	**2,314**	25	10,517	3,428,485
Lifetime		124	15	19	10	11	5	7	20	36,208	5,590	85	43,989	$10,346,804
														9th

Lee Gordon

Donald Lee Gordon
B: 2/4/1936
Racing Hometown: Horse Shoe, NC

Year	Rank	Starts	Poles	1	2	3	4	5	6–10	Laps	Laps Led	Races Led	Miles	$
1969	NR	1	0	0	0	0	0	0	0	160	0	0	80	100
1970	NR	7	0	0	0	0	0	0	0	755	0	0	354	1,770
Lifetime		8	0	0	0	0	0	0	0	915	0	0	434	$1,870

Robby Gordon

Robert Gordon
B: 1/2/1969
Racing Hometown: Cerritos, CA

Year	Rank	Starts	Poles	1	2	3	4	5	6–10	Laps	Laps Led	Races Led	Miles	$
1991	55	2	0	0	0	0	0	0	0	584	0	0	781	27,265
1993	93T	1	0	0	0	0	0	0	0	55	0	0	146	17,665
1994	76T	1	0	0	0	0	0	0	0	69	0	0	138	7,965
1996	57	3	0	0	0	0	0	0	0	344	0	0	447	33,915
Lifetime		7	0	0	0	0	0	0	0	1,052	0	0	1,512	$86,810

Wally Gore

Wally Gore
Racing Hometown: Arlington, VA

Year	Rank	Starts	Poles	1	2	3	4	5	6–10	Laps	Laps Led	Races Led	Miles	$
1957	NR	1	0	0	0	0	0	0	0	203	0	0	81	110
Lifetime		1	0	0	0	0	0	0	0	203	0	0	81	$110

Bob Gossett

Robert Gossett
Racing Hometown: Greenville, SC

Year	Rank	Starts	Poles	1	2	3	4	5	6–10	Laps	Laps Led	Races Led	Miles	$
1961	177	1	0	0	0	0	0	0	0	19	0	0	10	0
Lifetime		1	0	0	0	0	0	0	0	19	0	0	10	$0

Herb Gott

Herbert Gott
Racing Hometown: Toledo, OH

Year	Rank	Starts	Poles	1	2	3	4	5	6–10	Laps	Laps Led	Races Led	Miles	$
1951	N/A	1	0	0	0	0	0	0	0		0	0		25
Lifetime		1	0	0	0	0	0	0	0		0	0		$25

Ken Goudermoat

Kenneth Goudermoat
Racing Hometown: Altamont, NY

Year	Rank	Starts	Poles	1	2	3	4	5	6–10	Laps	Laps Led	Races Led	Miles	$
1955	208	1	0	0	0	0	0	0	0	118	0	0	59	50
Lifetime		1	0	0	0	0	0	0	0	118	0	0	59	$50

Junie Gough

Junie Gough
B: 4/19/1925
Racing Hometown: Rising Sun, MD

Year	Rank	Starts	Poles	1	2	3	4	5	6–10	Laps	Laps Led	Races Led	Miles	$
1955	206T	1	0	0	0	0	0	0	0	150	0	0	75	50
Lifetime		1	0	0	0	0	0	0	0	150	0	0	75	$50

Harry Goularte

Harry Goularte
B: 7/29/1956
Racing Hometown: Morgan Hill, CA

Year	Rank	Starts	Poles	1	2	3	4	5	6–10	Laps	Laps Led	Races Led	Miles	$
1977	91	1	0	0	0	0	0	0	0	81	0	0	212	900
1978	76	2	0	0	0	0	0	0	0	185	0	0	473	1,930
1979	104T	1	0	0	0	0	0	0	0	82	0	0	215	1,460
1984	61	2	0	0	0	0	0	0	0	172	0	0	451	3,490
1987	65	2	0	0	0	0	0	0	0	171	0	0	448	4,770
Lifetime		8	0	0	0	0	0	0	0	691	0	0	1,799	$12,550

Bob Gould

Robert Gould
Racing Hometown: Andalusia, AL

Year	Rank	Starts	Poles	1	2	3	4	5	6–10	Laps	Laps Led	Races Led	Miles	$
1955	161	2	0	0	0	0	0	0	0	102	0	0	94	75
Lifetime		2	0	0	0	0	0	0	0	102	0	0	94	$75

Year	Rank	Starts	Poles	Finish						Laps	Laps Led	Races Led	Miles	$
				1	2	3	4	5	6–10					

Johnny Gouveia

Johnny Gouveia
B: 7/23/1927
Racing Hometown: New Bedford, MA

Year	Rank	Starts	Poles	1	2	3	4	5	6–10	Laps	Laps Led	Races Led	Miles	$
1952	168	1	0	0	0	0	0	0	0	61	0	0	76	0
1955	82	4	0	0	0	0	0	0	1	614	0	0	307	260
Lifetime		5	0	0	0	0	0	0	1	675	0	0	383	$260

Scott Gow

Scott Gow

Year	Rank	Starts	Poles	1	2	3	4	5	6–10	Laps	Laps Led	Races Led	Miles	$
1952	NR	1	0	0	0	0	0	0	0	46	0	0	23	25
Lifetime		1	0	0	0	0	0	0	0	46	0	0	23	$25

Matthew Gowan

Matthew Gowan
Racing Hometown: Highland Falls, NY

Year	Rank	Starts	Poles	1	2	3	4	5	6–10	Laps	Laps Led	Races Led	Miles	$
1953	138	2	0	0	0	0	0	0	0	250	0	0	344	110
1954	125	1	0	0	0	0	0	0	0	53	0	0	53	25
Lifetime		3	0	0	0	0	0	0	0	303	0	0	397	$135

Ron Grable

Ronald Grable
Racing Hometown: Belmont, CA

Year	Rank	Starts	Poles	1	2	3	4	5	6–10	Laps	Laps Led	Races Led	Miles	$
1971	NR	1	0	0	0	0	0	0	0	77	0	0	202	1,160
Lifetime		1	0	0	0	0	0	0	0	77	0	0	202	$1,160

Don Graham

Donald Graham
B: 10/5/1943
Racing Hometown: Rio Linda, CA

Year	Rank	Starts	Poles	1	2	3	4	5	6–10	Laps	Laps Led	Races Led	Miles	$
1977	100T	1	0	0	0	0	0	0	0	118	0	0	295	1,000
1978	86T	1	0	0	0	0	0	0	0	75	0	0	197	875
1979	101T	1	0	0	0	0	0	0	0	100	0	0	262	1,495
Lifetime		3	0	0	0	0	0	0	0	293	0	0	754	$3,370

Frank Graham

Frank Graham
B: 7/27/1940
Racing Hometown: Charleston Heights, SC

Year	Rank	Starts	Poles	1	2	3	4	5	6–10	Laps	Laps Led	Races Led	Miles	$
1961	175	1	0	0	0	0	0	0	0	140	0	0	210	300
1962	100T	1	0	0	0	0	0	0	1	178	0	0	89	175
1963	111	3	0	0	0	0	0	0	0	99	0	0	245	1,050
1964	NR	3	0	0	0	0	0	0	0	410	0	0	206	820
Lifetime		8	0	0	0	0	0	0	1	827	0	0	750	$2,345

Jim Graham

James Graham
Racing Hometown: Rockville, MD

Year	Rank	Starts	Poles	1	2	3	4	5	6–10	Laps	Laps Led	Races Led	Miles	$
1954	56	2	0	0	0	0	0	0	1	530	0	0	385	400
1956	105	3	0	0	0	1	0	0	0	317	0	0	173	595
Lifetime		5	0	0	0	1	0	0	1	847	0	0	558	$995

Russ Graham

Russell Graham (Bud)
Racing Hometown: Murrayville, PA

Year	Rank	Starts	Poles	1	2	3	4	5	6–10	Laps	Laps Led	Races Led	Miles	$
1955	59	5	0	0	0	0	0	0	0	735	0	0	702	375
1956	124	2	0	0	0	0	0	0	0	153	0	0	163	100
Lifetime		7	0	0	0	0	0	0	0	888	0	0	865	$475

Ron Grana

Ronald C. Grana
B: 3/4/1940
Racing Hometown: Farmington, MI

Year	Rank	Starts	Poles	1	2	3	4	5	6–10	Laps	Laps Led	Races Led	Miles	$
1969	67	1	0	0	0	0	0	0	0	162	0	0	324	1,275
1970	87	3	0	0	0	0	0	0	1	243	0	0	546	2,165
1971	NR	1	0	0	0	0	0	0	0	187	0	0	381	920
1972	NR	1	0	0	0	0	0	0	0	31	0	0	62	690
Lifetime		6	0	0	0	0	0	0	1	623	0	0	1,313	$5,050

Year	Rank	Starts	Poles	Finish 1	2	3	4	5	6–10	Laps	Laps Led	Races Led	Miles	$

Coleman Grant

Coleman L. Grant (Crash)
Racing Hometown: High Point, NC

Year	Rank	Starts	Poles	1	2	3	4	5	6–10	Laps	Laps Led	Races Led	Miles	$
1950	NR	1	0	0	0	0	0	0	0		0	0		0
1951	237T	1	0	0	0	0	0	0	0		0	0		25
1952	70	4	0	0	0	0	0	0	0	421	0	0	263	100
Lifetime		6	0	0	0	0	0	0	0	421	0	0	263	$125

Jerry Grant

Jerry Grant
B: 1/23/1935
Racing Hometown: Escondido, CA

Year	Rank	Starts	Poles	1	2	3	4	5	6–10	Laps	Laps Led	Races Led	Miles	$
1965	54	3	0	0	0	0	0	0	1	327	0	0	851	2,150
1966	65	3	0	0	0	0	0	1	0	433	1	1	854	3,180
1967	NR	4	0	0	0	0	0	1	0	312	0	0	727	5,520
1968	43	7	0	0	0	0	0	0	1	971	1	1	1,312	5,665
1973	NR	1	0	0	0	0	0	0	0	4	0	0	10	1,015
1974	121	1	0	0	0	0	0	0	0	45	0	0	118	775
Lifetime		19	0	0	0	0	0	2	2	2,092	2	2	3,873	$18,305

Danny Graves

Danny Graves *Real Name*: Frank Danley
D: 1987 *Killed in bar-room brawl.*
Racing Hometown: Modesto, CA

Year	Rank	Starts	Poles	1	2	3	4	5	6–10	Laps	Laps Led	Races Led	Miles	$
1957	43	7	1	1	0	1	0	1	1	787	1	1	473	1,895
1958	150	2	0	0	0	0	0	0	0	90	0	0	198	125
Lifetime		9	1	1	0	1	0	1	1	877	1	1	671	$2,020

Bob Gray

Robert Gray
Racing Hometown: Charleston, SC

Year	Rank	Starts	Poles	1	2	3	4	5	6–10	Laps	Laps Led	Races Led	Miles	$
1964	135	1	0	0	0	0	0	0	0	2	0	0	3	400
Lifetime		1	0	0	0	0	0	0	0	2	0	0	3	$400

Don Gray

Donald Gray
D: 1994
Racing Hometown: Indianapolis, IN

Year	Rank	Starts	Poles	1	2	3	4	5	6–10	Laps	Laps Led	Races Led	Miles	$
1957	NR	3	0	0	0	0	0	0	0	549	0	0	604	325
1958	125	2	0	0	0	0	0	0	0	264	0	0	120	115
Lifetime		5	0	0	0	0	0	0	0	813	0	0	724	$440

Eddie Gray

Edward Gray
B: 1920 D: 10/25/1969 *Died of heart attack; had suffered ailment in Sportsman race @ Riverside 1/18/69.*
Racing Hometown: Gardena, CA

Year	Rank	Starts	Poles	1	2	3	4	5	6–10	Laps	Laps Led	Races Led	Miles	$
1957	55	5	0	0	0	0	0	1	1	525	0	0	421	755
1958	44	3	0	1	0	0	0	0	0	437	43	1	807	3,375
1959	76	2	0	1	0	0	0	0	0	317	1	1	187	870
1960	76	4	0	0	0	0	0	0	1	279	0	0	395	580
1961	64	4	1	2	1	0	0	0	0	509	76	2	532	3,485
1963	103	1	0	0	0	0	0	0	0	131	0	0	354	225
1964	63	1	0	0	0	0	0	0	0	174	0	0	470	650
1965	56	1	0	0	0	0	0	0	1	176	0	0	475	1,300
1966	110	1	0	0	0	0	0	0	0	43	0	0	116	500
Lifetime		22	1	4	1	0	0	1	3	2,591	120	4	3,756	$11,740

Henley Gray

Clarence Henley Gray
B: 1/3/1933
Racing Hometown: Rome, GA

Year	Rank	Starts	Poles	1	2	3	4	5	6–10	Laps	Laps Led	Races Led	Miles	$
1964	NR	1	0	0	0	0	0	0	0	126	0	0	63	100
1965	26	38	0	0	0	0	0	1	6	5,291	0	0	3,225	8,320
1966	4	45	0	0	0	0	1	3	14	10,719	0	0	7,402	21,901
1967	17	43	0	0	0	0	0	0	10	7,864	0	0	5,859	15,987
1968	20	30	0	0	0	0	0	0	6	6,072	0	0	4,580	12,566
1969	17	48	0	0	0	0	0	0	5	8,954	0	0	7,326	29,335
1970	19	34	0	0	0	0	0	0	2	6,134	0	0	5,249	23,130
1971	14	39	0	0	0	0	0	0	4	7,684	0	0	7,504	31,789

Year	Rank	Starts	Poles	Finish 1	2	3	4	5	6–10	Laps	Laps Led	Races Led	Miles	$

Henley Gray *continued*

Year	Rank	Starts	Poles	1	2	3	4	5	6–10	Laps	Laps Led	Races Led	Miles	$
1972	17	28	0	0	0	0	0	0	2	6,121	0	0	7,307	38,461
1973	14	24	0	0	0	0	0	0	4	7,517	0	0	7,608	34,467
1974	55	5	0	0	0	0	0	0	1	1,342	0	0	1,193	5,185
1975	39	9	0	0	0	0	0	0	1	2,179	2	1	2,472	10,050
1976	27	16	0	0	0	0	0	0	0	2,993	0	0	3,599	15,780
1977	28	14	0	0	0	0	0	0	0	3,049	0	0	2,666	18,610
Lifetime		374	0	0	0	0	1	4	55	76,045	2	1	66,054	$265,687

Steve Gray

Steve Gray
B: 8/11/1956
Racing Hometown: Rome, GA

Year	Rank	Starts	Poles	1	2	3	4	5	6–10	Laps	Laps Led	Races Led	Miles	$
1979	126T	1	0	0	0	0	0	0	0	1	0	0	3	1,305
1980	NR	1	0	0	0	0	0	0	0	35	0	0	35	450
1982	90	1	0	0	0	0	0	0	0	103	0	0	258	1,250
1983	86	3	0	0	0	0	0	0	0	853	0	0	853	3,525
1984	83	1	0	0	0	0	0	0	0	178	0	0	445	1,675
1985	NR	1	0	0	0	0	0	0	0	151	0	0	378	1,970
Lifetime		8	0	0	0	0	0	0	0	1,321	0	0	1,971	$10,175

Vince Gray

Vincent Gray

Year	Rank	Starts	Poles	1	2	3	4	5	6–10	Laps	Laps Led	Races Led	Miles	$
1954	NR	1	0	0	0	0	0	0	0	34	0	0	68	0
Lifetime		1	0	0	0	0	0	0	0	34	0	0	68	$0

Bob Greeley

Robert Greeley
Racing Hometown: Auburn, ME

Year	Rank	Starts	Poles	1	2	3	4	5	6–10	Laps	Laps Led	Races Led	Miles	$
1972	100	1	0	0	0	0	0	0	0	182	0	0	273	500
Lifetime		1	0	0	0	0	0	0	0	182	0	0	273	$500

Bill Green

William Green
B: 1946
Racing Hometown: Edgewood, KY

Year	Rank	Starts	Poles	1	2	3	4	5	6–10	Laps	Laps Led	Races Led	Miles	$
1978	96T	1	0	0	0	0	0	0	0	0	0	0	0	400
1979	NR	1	0	0	0	0	0	0	0	76	2	1	152	1,745
1980	—		0											900
Lifetime		2	0	0	0	0	0	0	0	76	2	1	152	$3,045

George Green

George Green
B: 9/15/1927
Racing Hometown: Johnson City, TN

Year	Rank	Starts	Poles	1	2	3	4	5	6–10	Laps	Laps Led	Races Led	Miles	$
1956	76	6	0	0	0	0	0	0	0	867	0	0	468	550
1957	23	17	0	0	0	0	1	0	3	2,668	0	0	1,485	2,240
1958	NR	12	0	0	0	0	0	0	0	1,304	0	0	563	655
1959	107	18	0	0	0	0	0	0	5	3,337	0	0	1,966	2,385
1960	98	3	0	0	0	0	0	0	0	237	0	0	327	360
1961	52	11	0	0	0	0	1	0	2	1,926	0	0	1,186	1,635
1962	16	46	0	0	0	0	0	1	14	9,279	0	0	5,896	9,221
1963	88	3	0	0	0	0	0	0	2	569	0	0	198	425
Lifetime		116	0	0	0	0	2	1	26	20,187	0	0	12,088	$16,460

Jeff Green

Jeff Green
B: 9/6/1962
Racing Hometown: Owensboro, KY

Year	Rank	Starts	Poles	1	2	3	4	5	6–10	Laps	Laps Led	Races Led	Miles	$
1994	51	3	0	0	0	0	0	0	0	717	0	0	741	20,270
1996	49	4	0	0	0	0	0	0	0	813	0	0	966	46,875
Lifetime		7	0	0	0	0	0	0	0	1,530	0	0	1,707	$67,145

Jerry Green

Jerry Green
Racing Hometown: Nashville, TN

Year	Rank	Starts	Poles	1	2	3	4	5	6–10	Laps	Laps Led	Races Led	Miles	$
1958	NR	1	0	0	0	0	0	0	0	154	0	0	77	65
Lifetime		1	0	0	0	0	0	0	0	154	0	0	77	$65

Year	Rank	Starts	Poles	Finish 1	2	3	4	5	6–10	Laps	Laps Led	Races Led	Miles	$

Bobby Greene
Robert Greene
B: 6/12/1925
Racing Hometown: Siler City, NC

| 1949 | 49 | 2 | 0 | 0 | 0 | 0 | 0 | 0 | 0 | 148 | 0 | 0 | 74 | 50 |
| Lifetime | | 2 | 0 | 0 | 0 | 0 | 0 | 0 | 0 | 148 | 0 | 0 | 74 | $50 |

Oda Greene
Oda Greene
B: 9/23/1928
Racing Hometown: Toledo, OH

1951	37	6	0	0	0	1	0	1	1	173	0	0	173	850
1952	NR	1	0	0	0	0	0	0	0	134	0	0	67	25
Lifetime		7	0	0	0	1	0	1	1	307	0	0	240	$875

John Greenwood
John Greenwood
B: 1945
Racing Hometown: Troy, MI

| 1980 | NR | 2 | 0 | 0 | 0 | 0 | 0 | 0 | 0 | 174 | 0 | 0 | 411 | 2,730 |
| Lifetime | | 2 | 0 | 0 | 0 | 0 | 0 | 0 | 0 | 174 | 0 | 0 | 411 | $2,730 |

Bob Greer
Robert Greer
Racing Hometown: Hubbard, OH

1950	NR	1	0	0	0	0	0	0	0	56	0	0	28	0
1951	N/A	5	0	0	0	0	0	0	0	126	0	0	126	60
Lifetime		6	0	0	0	0	0	0	0	182	0	0	154	$60

Bill Greever
William Greever
Racing Hometown: Bluefield, WV

1949	75	1	0	0	0	0	0	0	0	134	0	0	67	0
1950	120T	1	0	0	0	0	0	0	0	128	0	0	64	0
Lifetime		2	0	0	0	0	0	0	0	262	0	0	131	$0

Peter Gregg
Peter Holden Gregg
B: 5/4/1940   D: 12/16/1980   *Suicide.*
Racing Hometown: Jacksonville, FL

| 1973 | 120 | 1 | 0 | 0 | 0 | 0 | 0 | 0 | 0 | 34 | 0 | 0 | 51 | 775 |
| Lifetime | | 1 | 0 | 0 | 0 | 0 | 0 | 0 | 0 | 34 | 0 | 0 | 51 | $775 |

Ben Gregory
Benjamin Gregory
Racing Hometown: Crockett, CA

1951	NR	1	0	0	0	0	0	0	0		0	0		50
1954	NR	4	0	0	0	0	2	0	0	1,232	0	0	730	825
1955	142	1	0	0	0	0	0	0	1	96	0	0	96	200
Lifetime		6	0	0	0	0	2	0	1	1,328	0	0	826	$1,075

Buzz Gregory
Buzz Gregory
D: 1993
Racing Hometown: Speedway City, IN

| 1966 | 96 | 2 | 0 | 0 | 0 | 0 | 0 | 0 | 0 | 563 | 0 | 0 | 282 | 500 |
| Lifetime | | 2 | 0 | 0 | 0 | 0 | 0 | 0 | 0 | 563 | 0 | 0 | 282 | $500 |

George Gregory
George Gregory

| 1955 | 240T | 1 | 0 | 0 | 0 | 0 | 0 | 0 | 0 | 82 | 0 | 0 | 41 | 25 |
| Lifetime | | 1 | 0 | 0 | 0 | 0 | 0 | 0 | 0 | 82 | 0 | 0 | 41 | $25 |

Allan Grice
Allan Grice
B: 1943
Racing Hometown: Australia

1987	NR	1	0	0	0	0	0	0	0	161	0	0	242	1,700
1989	93T	1	0	0	0	0	0	0	0	294	0	0	441	1,900
Lifetime		2	0	0	0	0	0	0	0	455	0	0	683	$3,600

Year	Rank	Starts	Poles	Finish 1	2	3	4	5	6–10	Laps	Laps Led	Races Led	Miles	$

Dick Grice
Richard Grice
Racing Hometown: Asheville, NC

Year	Rank	Starts	Poles	1	2	3	4	5	6–10	Laps	Laps Led	Races Led	Miles	$
1954	NR	1	0	0	0	0	0	0	0	52	0	0	26	0
Lifetime		1	0	0	0	0	0	0	0	52	0	0	26	$0

Charlie Griffin
Charles Griffin
Racing Hometown: Roanoke, VA

Year	Rank	Starts	Poles	1	2	3	4	5	6–10	Laps	Laps Led	Races Led	Miles	$
1975	76	2	0	0	0	0	0	0	0	82	0	0	52	720
Lifetime		2	0	0	0	0	0	0	0	82	0	0	52	$720

Jerry Griffin
Jerry Griffin

Year	Rank	Starts	Poles	1	2	3	4	5	6–10	Laps	Laps Led	Races Led	Miles	$
1970	NR	1	0	0	0	0	0	0	0	94	0	0	246	790
Lifetime		1	0	0	0	0	0	0	0	94	0	0	246	$790

Charley Griffith
Charles Griffith
B: 9/4/1929
Racing Hometown: Chattanooga, TN

Year	Rank	Starts	Poles	1	2	3	4	5	6–10	Laps	Laps Led	Races Led	Miles	$
1958	65	2	0	0	0	0	0	0	0	211	0	0	150	215
1959	NR	6	0	0	0	1	0	0	2	438	0	0	697	4,955
1960	40	5	0	0	0	0	0	0	0	599	0	0	921	1,300
1962	87	3	0	0	0	0	0	0	0	229	0	0	299	625
1963	135	1	0	0	0	0	0	0	0	182	0	0	91	60
Lifetime		17	0	0	0	1	0	0	2	1,659	0	0	2,158	$7,155

Jimmy Griggs
James Griggs
Racing Hometown: Donelson, TN

Year	Rank	Starts	Poles	1	2	3	4	5	6–10	Laps	Laps Led	Races Led	Miles	$
1963	117	1	0	0	0	0	0	0	0	304	0	0	152	240
Lifetime		1	0	0	0	0	0	0	0	304	0	0	152	$240

Hank Grilliott
Hank Grilliott
Racing Hometown: Atlanta, GA

Year	Rank	Starts	Poles	1	2	3	4	5	6–10	Laps	Laps Led	Races Led	Miles	$
1962	136	1	0	0	0	0	0	0	0	1	0	0	1	150
Lifetime		1	0	0	0	0	0	0	0	1	0	0	1	$150

Al Grinnan
Alfred Grinnan
B: 1931
Racing Hometown: Fredericksburg, VA

Year	Rank	Starts	Poles	1	2	3	4	5	6–10	Laps	Laps Led	Races Led	Miles	$
1971	NR	1	0	0	0	0	0	0	0	459	0	0	249	495
Lifetime		1	0	0	0	0	0	0	0	459	0	0	249	$495

Steve Grissom
Stephen Todd Grissom
B: 6/26/1963
Racing Hometown: Gadsden, AL

Year	Rank	Starts	Poles	1	2	3	4	5	6–10	Laps	Laps Led	Races Led	Miles	$
1990	78T	1	0	0	0	0	0	0	0	322	0	0	490	4,275
1993	74T	1	0	0	0	0	0	0	0	260	0	0	260	6,485
1994	28	27	0	0	0	0	0	0	3	7,966	1	1	9,740	300,915
1995	27	29	0	0	0	0	0	1	3	8,279	17	2	10,299	509,047
1996	39	13	0	0	0	0	0	1	1	3,169	12	1	4,302	314,983
Lifetime		71	0	0	0	0	0	2	7	19,996	30	4	25,092	$1,135,705

Al Gristermacher *See* Al White

Pat Grogan
Patrick Grogan
Racing Hometown: Kinston, NC

Year	Rank	Starts	Poles	1	2	3	4	5	6–10	Laps	Laps Led	Races Led	Miles	$
1956	270T	2	0	0	0	0	0	0	0	223	0	0	299	50
Lifetime		2	0	0	0	0	0	0	0	223	0	0	299	$50

Jerry Groh
Jerry Groh
Racing Hometown: Dayton, OH

Year	Rank	Starts	Poles	1	2	3	4	5	6–10	Laps	Laps Led	Races Led	Miles	$
1951	N/A	2	0	0	0	0	0	0	0		0	0		50
Lifetime		2	0	0	0	0	0	0	0		0	0		$50

Year	Rank	Starts	Poles	Finish						Laps	Laps Led	Races Led	Miles	$
				1	2	3	4	5	6–10					

Al Gross

Al Gross
Racing Hometown: Tampa, FL

Year	Rank	Starts	Poles	1	2	3	4	5	6–10	Laps	Laps Led	Races Led	Miles	$
1950	45	3	0	0	0	0	1	0	0	182	0	0	267	550
Lifetime		3	0	0	0	0	1	0	0	182	0	0	267	$550

Bill Gross

William Gross
Racing Hometown: Philadelphia, PA

Year	Rank	Starts	Poles	1	2	3	4	5	6–10	Laps	Laps Led	Races Led	Miles	$
1955	127	3	0	0	0	0	0	0	0	352	0	0	220	125
Lifetime		3	0	0	0	0	0	0	0	352	0	0	220	$125

Bob Grossman

Robert Grossman
B: 1912
Racing Hometown: West Nyack, NY

Year	Rank	Starts	Poles	1	2	3	4	5	6–10	Laps	Laps Led	Races Led	Miles	$
1954	NR	1	0	0	0	0	1	0	0	49	0	0	98	400
1965	NR	1	0	0	0	0	0	0	0	13	0	0	30	175
Lifetime		2	0	0	0	0	1	0	0	62	0	0	128	$575

Johnny Grubb

John R. Grubb
B: 4/23/1914
Racing Hometown: Beckley, WV

Year	Rank	Starts	Poles	1	2	3	4	5	6–10	Laps	Laps Led	Races Led	Miles	$
1950	55	4	0	0	0	0	0	0	1	530	0	0	541	575
1951	192T	1	0	0	0	0	0	0	0		0	0		25
Lifetime		5	0	0	0	0	0	0	1	530	0	0	541	$600

Cecil Grubbs

Cecil Grubbs

Year	Rank	Starts	Poles	1	2	3	4	5	6–10	Laps	Laps Led	Races Led	Miles	$
1958	NR	1	0	0	0	0	0	0	0	79	0	0	49	50
Lifetime		1	0	0	0	0	0	0	0	79	0	0	49	$50

Tom Guffy

Thomas Guffy

Year	Rank	Starts	Poles	1	2	3	4	5	6–10	Laps	Laps Led	Races Led	Miles	$
1961	184	1	0	0	0	0	0	0	0	29	0	0	41	0
Lifetime		1	0	0	0	0	0	0	0	29	0	0	41	$0

Joe Guide

Joseph Guide Jr.
Racing Hometown: Memphis, TN

Year	Rank	Starts	Poles	1	2	3	4	5	6–10	Laps	Laps Led	Races Led	Miles	$
1952	152	2	0	0	0	0	0	0	0	200	0	0	250	0
1953	106	2	0	0	0	0	0	0	0	147	0	0	300	150
1954	162	2	0	0	0	0	0	0	0	160	0	0	331	75
1955	77	2	0	0	0	0	0	0	0	275	0	0	413	360
1956	140T	1	0	0	0	0	0	0	0	141	0	0	212	200
Lifetime		9	0	0	0	0	0	0	0	923	0	0	1,505	$785

Dick Gulstrand

Richard Gulstrand
Racing Hometown: Manhattan Beach, CA

Year	Rank	Starts	Poles	1	2	3	4	5	6–10	Laps	Laps Led	Races Led	Miles	$
1965	68	1	0	0	0	0	0	0	0	151	0	0	408	615
1966	94	1	0	0	0	0	0	0	0	65	0	0	176	500
1970	NR	2	0	0	0	0	0	1	1	309	0	0	810	3,890
1971	NR	2	0	0	0	0	0	0	0	251	0	0	637	2,775
1972	115	1	0	0	0	0	0	0	0	28	0	0	73	740
Lifetime		7	0	0	0	0	0	1	1	804	0	0	2,103	$8,520

John Gunn

John Gunn

Year	Rank	Starts	Poles	1	2	3	4	5	6–10	Laps	Laps Led	Races Led	Miles	$
1981	87	1	0	0	0	0	0	0	0	67	0	0	176	2,225
Lifetime		1	0	0	0	0	0	0	0	67	0	0	176	$2,225

Larry Gunselman

Lawrence Gunselman
Racing Hometown: Snohomish, WA

Year	Rank	Starts	Poles	1	2	3	4	5	6–10	Laps	Laps Led	Races Led	Miles	$
1996	62	1	0	0	0	0	0	0	0	70	0	0	176	10,200
Lifetime		1	0	0	0	0	0	0	0	70	0	0	176	$10,200

Year	Rank	Starts	Poles	Finish 1	2	3	4	5	6–10	Laps	Laps Led	Races Led	Miles	$

Dan Gurney

Daniel Sexton Gurney
B: 4/13/1931
Racing Hometown: Costa Mesa, CA

Year	Rank	Starts	Poles	1	2	3	4	5	6–10	Laps	Laps Led	Races Led	Miles	$
1962	77	2	0	0	0	0	1	0	0	174	0	0	435	700
1963	NR	3	1	1	0	0	0	2	0	424	120	1	1,097	18,250
1964	NR	4	0	1	0	0	0	0	1	433	142	1	1,103	14,770
1965	NR	1	0	1	0	0	0	0	0	185	126	1	500	13,625
1966	NR	1	0	1	0	0	0	0	0	185	148	1	500	18,445
1967	NR	1	0	0	0	0	0	0	0	143	36	1	386	990
1968	NR	1	1	1	0	0	0	0	0	186	124	1	502	21,250
1969	NR	1	0	0	0	0	0	0	0	66	0	0	178	980
1970	NR	1	1	0	0	0	0	0	1	180	0	0	472	2,400
1980	NR	1	0	0	0	0	0	0	0	79	0	0	207	1,105
Lifetime		16	3	5	0	0	1	2	2	2,055	696	6	5,379	$92,515

Janet Guthrie

Janet Guthrie
B: 3/7/1938
Racing Hometown: New York, NY

Year	Rank	Starts	Poles	1	2	3	4	5	6–10	Laps	Laps Led	Races Led	Miles	$
1976	NR	5	0	0	0	0	0	0	0	1,183	0	0	2,015	8,179
1977	23	19	0	0	0	0	0	0	4	5,031	5	1	6,182	38,045
1978	41	7	0	0	0	0	0	0	1	1,147	0	0	2,406	18,745
1980	69	2	0	0	0	0	0	0	0	327	0	0	818	15,065
Lifetime		33	0	0	0	0	0	0	5	7,688	5	1	11,420	$80,034

C. B. Gwynn

Clayborne Beattie Gwynn
B: 10/24/1935
Racing Hometown: Marion, VA

Year	Rank	Starts	Poles	1	2	3	4	5	6–10	Laps	Laps Led	Races Led	Miles	$
1969	NR	1	0	0	0	0	0	0	0	73	0	0	194	1,150
Lifetime		1	0	0	0	0	0	0	0	73	0	0	194	$1,150

Alton Haddock

John Alton Haddock
B: 8/16/1915
Racing Hometown: Greenville, SC

Year	Rank	Starts	Poles	1	2	3	4	5	6–10	Laps	Laps Led	Races Led	Miles	$
1950	NR	2	0	0	0	0	0	0	0	139	0	0	293	125
1951	N/A	2	0	0	0	0	0	0	1	136	0	0	136	100
Lifetime		4	0	0	0	0	0	0	1	275	0	0	429	$225

Bob Haden

Robert Haden
Racing Hometown: Scottsville, NY

Year	Rank	Starts	Poles	1	2	3	4	5	6–10	Laps	Laps Led	Races Led	Miles	$
1954	212	1	0	0	0	0	0	0	0	23	0	0	12	0
Lifetime		1	0	0	0	0	0	0	0	23	0	0	12	$0

Billy Hagan

William Joseph Hagan
B: 3/22/1932
Racing Hometown: Lafayette, LA

Year	Rank	Starts	Poles	1	2	3	4	5	6–10	Laps	Laps Led	Races Led	Miles	$
1969	NR	1	0	0	0	0	0	0	1	155	0	0	412	1,750
1975	84T	1	0	0	0	0	0	0	0	175	0	0	466	1,770
1979	94T	1	0	0	0	0	0	0	0	185	0	0	370	3,280
Lifetime		3	0	0	0	0	0	0	1	515	0	0	1,248	$6,800

Budd Hagelin

Budd Hagelin
B: 12/8/1944
Racing Hometown: Camden, NJ

Year	Rank	Starts	Poles	1	2	3	4	5	6–10	Laps	Laps Led	Races Led	Miles	$
1976	82	1	0	0	0	0	0	0	0	409	0	0	409	1,040
Lifetime		1	0	0	0	0	0	0	0	409	0	0	409	$1,040

Al Hager

Al Hager
Racing Hometown: Florissant, MO

Year	Rank	Starts	Poles	1	2	3	4	5	6–10	Laps	Laps Led	Races Led	Miles	$
1955	92	1	0	0	0	0	0	0	0	176	0	0	264	125
Lifetime		1	0	0	0	0	0	0	0	176	0	0	264	$125

Year	Rank	Starts	Poles	Finish						Laps	Laps Led	Races Led	Miles	$
				1	2	3	4	5	6–10					

Dick Hagey

Richard Hagey
　　Racing Hometown: Philadelphia, PA

Year	Rank	Starts	Poles	1	2	3	4	5	6–10	Laps	Laps Led	Races Led	Miles	$
1953	NR	1	0	0	0	0	0	0	0		0	0		40
Lifetime		1	0	0	0	0	0	0	0		0	0		$40

Royce Haggerty

Royce C. Haggerty
　　Racing Hometown: Portland, OR

Year	Rank	Starts	Poles	1	2	3	4	5	6–10	Laps	Laps Led	Races Led	Miles	$
1955	111	1	0	0	0	0	0	0	0	228	0	0	228	100
1956	59	6	1	1	0	0	0	0	1	1,017	72	2	610	1,720
1957	143	2	0	0	0	0	0	0	0	172	0	0	86	185
Lifetime		9	1	1	0	0	0	0	1	1,417	72	2	924	$2,005

Neil Haight

Neil Haight
　　Racing Hometown: Buffalo, NY

Year	Rank	Starts	Poles	1	2	3	4	5	6–10	Laps	Laps Led	Races Led	Miles	$
1958	113	2	0	0	0	0	0	0	0	132	0	0	39	195
Lifetime		2	0	0	0	0	0	0	0	132	0	0	39	$195

Jimmy Hailey

James Hailey
　　Racing Hometown: Winston-Salem, NC

Year	Rank	Starts	Poles	1	2	3	4	5	6–10	Laps	Laps Led	Races Led	Miles	$
1974	131	1	0	0	0	0	0	0	0	421	0	0	228	615
Lifetime		1	0	0	0	0	0	0	0	421	0	0	228	$615

Gordon Haines

Gordon Haines
　　Racing Hometown: Yakima, WA

Year	Rank	Starts	Poles	1	2	3	4	5	6–10	Laps	Laps Led	Races Led	Miles	$
1956	44	7	0	0	1	0	1	0	2	1,067	66	1	715	1,500
Lifetime		7	0	0	1	0	1	0	2	1,067	66	1	715	$1,500

Ted Hairfield

Theodore Hairfield
　　B: 12/18/1931
　　Racing Hometown: Richmond, VA

Year	Rank	Starts	Poles	1	2	3	4	5	6–10	Laps	Laps Led	Races Led	Miles	$
1963	106	2	0	0	0	0	0	0	0	50	0	0	125	675
Lifetime		2	0	0	0	0	0	0	0	50	0	0	125	$675

Ed Hale

Edward Hale
　　Racing Hometown: Lakeside, CA

Year	Rank	Starts	Poles	1	2	3	4	5	6–10	Laps	Laps Led	Races Led	Miles	$
1979	87T	1	0	0	0	0	0	0	0	85	0	0	223	2,045
1980	99	1	0	0	0	0	0	0	0	37	0	0	97	1,200
Lifetime		2	0	0	0	0	0	0	0	122	0	0	320	$3,245

Robert Hale

Robert Hale (Bob)
　　Racing Hometown: Tucson, AZ

Year	Rank	Starts	Poles	1	2	3	4	5	6–10	Laps	Laps Led	Races Led	Miles	$
1969	NR	1	0	0	0	0	0	0	0	24	0	0	65	750
1970	NR	1	0	0	0	0	0	0	0	123	0	0	322	915
Lifetime		2	0	0	0	0	0	0	0	147	0	0	387	$1,665

Johnny Halford

Johnny Lain Halford
　　B: 10/15/1930
　　Racing Hometown: Spartanburg, SC

Year	Rank	Starts	Poles	1	2	3	4	5	6–10	Laps	Laps Led	Races Led	Miles	$
1969	47	8	0	0	0	0	0	0	0	1,881	0	0	1,494	4,200
1970	36	25	0	0	0	0	0	0	0	3,619	16	1	4,057	15,654
1971	NR	2	0	0	0	0	0	0	0	308	0	0	513	1,719
1972	47	5	0	0	0	0	0	0	1	1,032	0	0	1,574	4,955
1978	NR	1	0	0	0	0	0	0	0	84	0	0	85	610
Lifetime		41	0	0	0	0	0	0	1	6,924	16	1	7,723	$27,138

Bill Hall

William Hall
　　Racing Hometown: Haw River, NC

Year	Rank	Starts	Poles	1	2	3	4	5	6–10	Laps	Laps Led	Races Led	Miles	$
1957	198T	1	0	0	0	0	0	0	0	25	0	0	13	50
Lifetime		1	0	0	0	0	0	0	0	25	0	0	13	$50

Year	Rank	Starts	Poles	Finish						Laps	Laps Led	Races Led	Miles	$
				1	2	3	4	5	6–10					

Buck Hall

Buck Hall
  Racing Hometown: Burlington, NC

Year	Rank	Starts	Poles	1	2	3	4	5	6–10	Laps	Laps Led	Races Led	Miles	$
1956	253	1	0	0	0	0	0	0	0	11	0	0	10	25
Lifetime		1	0	0	0	0	0	0	0	11	0	0	10	$25

Dana Hall

Dana Hall
  Racing Hometown: Gastonia, NC

Year	Rank	Starts	Poles	1	2	3	4	5	6–10	Laps	Laps Led	Races Led	Miles	$
1965	129	1	0	0	0	0	0	0	0	1	0	0	3	500
Lifetime		1	0	0	0	0	0	0	0	1	0	0	3	$500

Don Hall

Donald Hall
  B: 9/2/1943
  Racing Hometown: Puyallup, WA

Year	Rank	Starts	Poles	1	2	3	4	5	6–10	Laps	Laps Led	Races Led	Miles	$
1974	116	1	0	0	0	0	0	0	0	102	0	0	255	1,100
1975	80	1	0	0	0	0	0	0	0	188	0	0	470	2,225
Lifetime		2	0	0	0	0	0	0	0	290	0	0	725	$3,325

Roy Hall

Roy Hall
  B: 1921   D: 3/14/1991
  Racing Hometown: Atlanta, GA

Year	Rank	Starts	Poles	1	2	3	4	5	6–10	Laps	Laps Led	Races Led	Miles	$
1949	26T	1	0	0	0	0	0	0	1	196	0	0	98	150
1952	165	1	0	0	0	0	0	0	0	182	0	0	228	0
Lifetime		2	0	0	0	0	0	0	1	378	0	0	326	$150

Shane Hall

Shane Hall
  B: 8/25/1969
  Racing Hometown: Simpsonville, SC

Year	Rank	Starts	Poles	1	2	3	4	5	6–10	Laps	Laps Led	Races Led	Miles	$
1995	65T	1	0	0	0	0	0	0	0	205	0	0	208	13,975
Lifetime		1	0	0	0	0	0	0	0	205	0	0	208	$13,975

Dick Hallock

Richard M. Hallock
  Racing Hometown: Walden, NY

Year	Rank	Starts	Poles	1	2	3	4	5	6–10	Laps	Laps Led	Races Led	Miles	$
1950	NR	1	0	0	0	0	0	0	0		0	0		0
1954	133	3	0	0	0	0	0	0	0	388	0	0	342	150
1955	134	3	0	0	0	0	0	0	1	321	0	0	245	150
Lifetime		7	0	0	0	0	0	0	1	709	0	0	586	$300

Roy Hallquist

Roy Hallquist
  Racing Hometown: Stratford, CT

Year	Rank	Starts	Poles	1	2	3	4	5	6–10	Laps	Laps Led	Races Led	Miles	$
1962	100T	1	0	0	0	0	0	0	1	183	0	0	46	175
1963	122T	1	0	0	0	0	0	0	0	34	0	0	97	130
1966	78	4	0	0	0	0	2	0	0	547	0	0	335	895
1968	113	1	0	0	0	0	0	0	0	51	0	0	51	250
1969	58	3	0	0	0	0	0	0	0	260	0	0	259	1,070
Lifetime		10	0	0	0	0	2	0	1	1,075	0	0	787	$2,520

Joe Halton

Joseph Halton
  Racing Hometown: High Point, NC

Year	Rank	Starts	Poles	1	2	3	4	5	6–10	Laps	Laps Led	Races Led	Miles	$
1959	NR	6	0	0	0	0	0	0	1	898	0	0	365	465
Lifetime		6	0	0	0	0	0	0	1	898	0	0	365	$465

Jeff Halverson

Jeffrey Halverson
  Racing Hometown: Three Rivers, MI

Year	Rank	Starts	Poles	1	2	3	4	5	6–10	Laps	Laps Led	Races Led	Miles	$
1979	123T	1	0	0	0	0	0	0	0	1	0	0	1	490
Lifetime		1	0	0	0	0	0	0	0	1	0	0	1	$490

Ed Hamanard

Edward Hamanard
  Racing Hometown: Rome, NY

Year	Rank	Starts	Poles	1	2	3	4	5	6–10	Laps	Laps Led	Races Led	Miles	$
1950	NR	1	0	0	0	0	0	0	0	68	0	0	34	0
Lifetime		1	0	0	0	0	0	0	0	68	0	0	34	$0

Year	Rank	Starts	Poles	Finish 1	2	3	4	5	6–10	Laps	Laps Led	Races Led	Miles	$

J. V. Hamby

John V. Hamby
Racing Hometown: Columbia, SC

Year	Rank	Starts	Poles	1	2	3	4	5	6–10	Laps	Laps Led	Races Led	Miles	$
1958	NR	2	0	0	0	0	0	0	1	237	0	0	119	200
1961	105	4	0	0	0	0	0	0	0	745	0	0	382	450
1962	79	3	0	0	0	0	0	0	0	638	0	0	300	315
1964	87	5	0	0	0	0	0	0	1	484	0	0	173	735
Lifetime		14	0	0	0	0	0	0	2	2,104	0	0	974	$1,700

Roger Hamby

Roger Hamby
B: 7/2/1943
Racing Hometown: Ferguson, NC

Year	Rank	Starts	Poles	1	2	3	4	5	6–10	Laps	Laps Led	Races Led	Miles	$
1977	89	2	0	0	0	0	0	0	0	614	0	0	605	2,275
1978	21	26	0	0	0	0	0	0	2	7,181	0	0	7,688	41,565
1979	31	12	0	0	0	0	0	0	0	2,974	0	0	2,736	21,660
1980	20	25	0	0	0	0	0	0	0	6,777	0	0	7,588	51,534
1981	90	1	0	0	0	0	0	0	0	72	0	0	144	2,450
Lifetime		66	0	0	0	0	0	0	2	17,618	0	0	18,762	$119,484

Bobby Hamilton

Robert Hamilton
B: 5/29/1957
Racing Hometown: Nashville, TN

Year	Rank	Starts	Poles	1	2	3	4	5	6–10	Laps	Laps Led	Races Led	Miles	$
1989	89	1	0	0	0	0	0	0	0	215	5	1	215	3,075
1990	66	3	0	0	0	0	0	0	0	407	0	0	611	13,065
1991	22	28	0	0	0	0	0	0	4	8,304	7	3	10,187	259,105
1992	25	29	0	0	0	0	0	0	2	8,998	0	0	10,736	367,065
1993	37	15	0	0	0	0	0	0	1	3,989	0	0	5,277	142,740
1994	23	30	0	0	0	0	0	0	1	8,337	24	4	10,220	514,520
1995	14	31	0	0	1	0	2	1	6	9,421	131	7	11,555	804,505
1996	9	31	2	1	0	1	0	1	8	9,153	648	11	10,896	1,151,235
Lifetime		168	2	1	1	1	2	2	22	48,824	815	26	59,698	$3,255,310

Don Hamilton

Donald Hamilton
Racing Hometown: Portland, OR

Year	Rank	Starts	Poles	1	2	3	4	5	6–10	Laps	Laps Led	Races Led	Miles	$
1956	243	2	0	0	0	0	0	0	0	70	0	0	35	0
Lifetime		2	0	0	0	0	0	0	0	70	0	0	35	$0

Pete Hamilton

Peter Goodwill Hamilton
B: 7/20/1942
Racing Hometown: Dedham, MA

Year	Rank	Starts	Poles	1	2	3	4	5	6–10	Laps	Laps Led	Races Led	Miles	$
1968	32	16	0	0	1	0	0	2	3	3,555	42	3	2,592	8,239
1969	NR	3	0	0	0	0	0	1	1	421	14	1	724	5,435
1970	21	16	1	3	1	3	0	3	2	4,069	338	9	6,210	131,406
1971	24	22	2	1	0	5	4	1	1	4,525	224	14	6,890	60,440
1972	48	5	0	0	0	0	0	1	0	1,044	8	2	1,630	8,005
1973	114	2	0	0	0	0	0	0	0	71	0	0	140	2,905
Lifetime		64	3	4	2	8	4	8	7	13,685	626	29	18,185	$216,330

Bill Hammersley

William Hammersley (Red)
B: 5/30/1908
Racing Hometown: Mariners Harbor, NY

Year	Rank	Starts	Poles	1	2	3	4	5	6–10	Laps	Laps Led	Races Led	Miles	$
1952	129T	1	0	0	0	0	0	0	0	172	0	0	86	25
1953	179	1	0	0	0	0	0	0	0		0	0		25
Lifetime		2	0	0	0	0	0	0	0	172	0	0	86	$50

Carl Hammill

Carl Hammill
Racing Hometown: Santa Rosa, CA

Year	Rank	Starts	Poles	1	2	3	4	5	6–10	Laps	Laps Led	Races Led	Miles	$
1955	224	1	0	0	0	0	0	0	0	144	0	0	144	40
1956	97	2	0	0	0	0	0	0	0	321	0	0	321	160
Lifetime		3	0	0	0	0	0	0	0	465	0	0	465	$200

Art Hammond

Arthur Hammond
Racing Hometown: Rome, NY

Year	Rank	Starts	Poles	1	2	3	4	5	6–10	Laps	Laps Led	Races Led	Miles	$
1950	129T	1	0	0	0	0	0	0	0		0	0		0
Lifetime		1	0	0	0	0	0	0	0		0	0		$0

Year	Rank	Starts	Poles	Finish						Laps	Laps Led	Races Led	Miles	$
				1	2	3	4	5	6–10					

Keith Hamner

Keith Hamner
  Racing Hometown: Elkin, WV

Year	Rank	Starts	Poles	1	2	3	4	5	6–10	Laps	Laps Led	Races Led	Miles	$
1952	61	1	0	0	0	0	0	0	0	375	0	0	469	90
1953	84	2	0	0	0	0	0	0	1	33	0	0	135	75
Lifetime		3	0	0	0	0	0	0	1	408	0	0	604	$165

Andy Hampton

Andrew T. Hampton
  B: 11/30/1928
  Racing Hometown: Louisville, KY

Year	Rank	Starts	Poles	1	2	3	4	5	6–10	Laps	Laps Led	Races Led	Miles	$
1959	67	1	0	0	0	0	0	0	0	76	0	0	38	50
1968	NR	1	0	0	0	0	0	0	1	193	0	0	483	2,525
1969	NR	2	0	0	0	0	0	0	1	197	0	0	493	2,500
Lifetime		4	0	0	0	0	0	0	2	466	0	0	1,013	$5,075

John Hamson

John Hamson
  Racing Hometown: Santa Barbara, CA

Year	Rank	Starts	Poles	1	2	3	4	5	6–10	Laps	Laps Led	Races Led	Miles	$
1976	105T	1	0	0	0	0	0	0	0	26	0	0	68	790
Lifetime		1	0	0	0	0	0	0	0	26	0	0	68	$790

Mack Hanbury

Mack Hanbury
  Racing Hometown: Hyattsville, MD

Year	Rank	Starts	Poles	1	2	3	4	5	6–10	Laps	Laps Led	Races Led	Miles	$
1955	40	8	0	0	0	0	0	0	2	807	0	0	584	575
1966	107	2	0	0	0	0	0	0	0	220	0	0	78	225
Lifetime		10	0	0	0	0	0	0	2	1,027	0	0	662	$800

Richard Hancock

Richard Hancock

Year	Rank	Starts	Poles	1	2	3	4	5	6–10	Laps	Laps Led	Races Led	Miles	$
1951	N/A	1	0	0	0	0	0	0	0		0	0		25
Lifetime		1	0	0	0	0	0	0	0		0	0		$25

Jeff Handy

H. L. Handy
  Racing Hometown: Charlotte, NC

Year	Rank	Starts	Poles	1	2	3	4	5	6–10	Laps	Laps Led	Races Led	Miles	$
1975	86T	1	0	0	0	0	0	0	0	174	0	0	463	1,820
1976	NR	1	0	0	0	0	0	0	0	3	0	0	2	370
Lifetime		2	0	0	0	0	0	0	0	177	0	0	465	$2,190

Frank Hannellburg

Frank Hannellburg

Year	Rank	Starts	Poles	1	2	3	4	5	6–10	Laps	Laps Led	Races Led	Miles	$
1954	NR	1	0	0	0	0	0	0	0	147	0	0	74	0
Lifetime		1	0	0	0	0	0	0	0	147	0	0	74	$0

Chuck Hansen

Charles H. Hansen
  Racing Hometown: Whiteford, MD

Year	Rank	Starts	Poles	1	2	3	4	5	6–10	Laps	Laps Led	Races Led	Miles	$
1954	72	6	0	0	0	0	0	0	1	694	0	0	520	225
1955	61	4	0	0	0	0	0	0	2	624	0	0	312	250
1956	269	1	0	0	0	0	0	0	0	66	0	0	66	50
1957	42	7	0	0	0	0	0	0	0	990	0	0	734	510
1958	43	7	0	0	0	0	0	0	1	1,011	0	0	659	580
Lifetime		25	0	0	0	0	0	0	4	3,385	0	0	2,291	$1,615

Jerry Hansen

Jerry Hansen
  Racing Hometown: Bremen, GA

Year	Rank	Starts	Poles	1	2	3	4	5	6–10	Laps	Laps Led	Races Led	Miles	$
1974	69	3	0	0	0	0	0	0	0	221	0	0	543	3,230
1980	—	0												600
Lifetime		3	0	0	0	0	0	0	0	221	0	0	543	$3,830

Walt Hansgen

Walter Hansgen
  B: 10/28/1919   D: 4/7/1966   *Died from injuries suffered 4/2/66 while practicing for LeMans 24-hour race.*
  Racing Hometown: Westfield, NJ

Year	Rank	Starts	Poles	1	2	3	4	5	6–10	Laps	Laps Led	Races Led	Miles	$
1964	NR	2	0	0	0	2	0	0	0	113	0	0	286	1,100
1965	NR	1	0	0	0	0	0	0	1	58	0	0	133	355
Lifetime		3	0	0	0	2	0	0	1	171	0	0	420	$1,455

Year	Rank	Starts	Poles	Finish						Laps	Laps Led	Races Led	Miles	$
				1	2	3	4	5	6–10	Laps	Led	Led	Miles	$

Fred Harb

Fareed Joseph Harb Jr.
B: 6/14/1930
Racing Hometown: High Point, NC

Year	Rank	Starts	Poles	1	2	3	4	5	6–10	Laps	Laps Led	Races Led	Miles	$
1955	106	2	0	0	0	0	0	0	0	276	0	0	185	135
1956	217	3	0	0	0	0	0	0	0	231	0	0	101	100
1957	NR	3	0	0	0	0	0	0	0	322	0	0	161	360
1958	24	25	0	0	0	1	2	1	3	3,651	0	0	1,840	3,315
1959	106	19	0	0	0	1	0	1	4	2,689	0	0	1,277	1,875
1960	60	20	0	0	0	0	0	2	5	3,269	0	0	1,467	2,780
1961	34	27	0	0	0	0	1	0	7	4,039	0	0	2,022	3,460
1962	39	21	0	0	0	0	0	0	3	2,763	0	0	1,190	2,220
1963	41	16	0	0	1	0	1	0	5	2,563	0	0	1,053	2,720
1964	99	3	0	0	0	0	0	1	1	550	0	0	138	555
1965	71	5	0	0	0	0	0	1	1	766	0	0	291	840
Lifetime		144	0	0	1	2	4	6	29	21,119	0	0	9,724	$18,360

Jack Harden

John Harden
B: 4/23/1934
Racing Hometown: Huntsville, AL

Year	Rank	Starts	Poles	1	2	3	4	5	6–10	Laps	Laps Led	Races Led	Miles	$
1967	42	10	0	0	0	0	0	0	0	1,393	0	0	1,958	4,450
Lifetime		10	0	0	0	0	0	0	0	1,393	0	0	1,958	$4,450

Harold Hardesty

Harold Hardesty
Racing Hometown: Pasco, WA

Year	Rank	Starts	Poles	1	2	3	4	5	6–10	Laps	Laps Led	Races Led	Miles	$
1956	27	9	0	0	1	0	0	1	4	1,761	0	0	1,350	2,380
1957	105	4	0	0	0	0	0	0	0	303	0	0	166	205
1958	107	1	0	0	0	0	0	1	0	98	0	0	98	300
1968	89	1	0	0	0	0	0	0	0	67	0	0	181	575
1969	NR	1	0	0	0	0	0	0	1	163	0	0	440	1,250
Lifetime		16	0	0	1	0	0	2	5	2,392	0	0	2,235	$4,710

J. E. Hardie

J. E. Hardie
Racing Hometown: Tabor City, NC

Year	Rank	Starts	Poles	1	2	3	4	5	6–10	Laps	Laps Led	Races Led	Miles	$
1950	NR	1	0	0	0	0	0	0	0	317	0	0	396	0
1951	N/A	1	0	0	0	0	0	0	0	339	0	0	424	50
1952	119	2	0	0	0	0	0	0	0	69	0	0	86	25
Lifetime		4	0	0	0	0	0	0	0	725	0	0	906	$75

Charles Hardiman

Charles Hardiman
Racing Hometown: Goodlettesville, TN

Year	Rank	Starts	Poles	1	2	3	4	5	6–10	Laps	Laps Led	Races Led	Miles	$
1954	74	1	0	0	0	0	0	0	0	146	0	0	219	200
Lifetime		1	0	0	0	0	0	0	0	146	0	0	219	$200

John Harkins

John Harkins

Year	Rank	Starts	Poles	1	2	3	4	5	6–10	Laps	Laps Led	Races Led	Miles	$
1975	NR	1	0	0	0	0	0	0	0	382	0	0	382	800
Lifetime		1	0	0	0	0	0	0	0	382	0	0	382	$800

Bud Harless

Pearley Jackson Harless
B: 1/21/1924
Racing Hometown: Gilbert, WV

Year	Rank	Starts	Poles	1	2	3	4	5	6–10	Laps	Laps Led	Races Led	Miles	$
1953	134T	1	0	0	0	0	0	0	0	168	0	0	84	25
1954	75	5	0	0	0	0	0	0	0	482	0	0	364	75
1955	98	4	0	0	0	0	0	0	1	324	0	0	294	210
1963	50	5	0	0	0	0	0	0	1	1,508	0	0	958	1,550
1964	67	8	0	0	0	0	0	0	0	1,373	0	0	712	2,330
1965	77	5	0	0	0	0	0	0	0	849	0	0	621	2,065
Lifetime		28	0	0	0	0	0	0	2	4,704	0	0	3,032	$6,255

Marshall Harless

Marshall Harless
Racing Hometown: Gilbert, WV

Year	Rank	Starts	Poles	1	2	3	4	5	6–10	Laps	Laps Led	Races Led	Miles	$
1954	154T	1	0	0	0	0	0	0	0	82	0	0	82	25
Lifetime		1	0	0	0	0	0	0	0	82	0	0	82	$25

Year	Rank	Starts	Poles	Finish						Laps	Laps Led	Races Led	Miles	$
				1	2	3	4	5	6–10					

Allan Harley

Allan Harley
Racing Hometown: Bristol, VA

Year	Rank	Starts	Poles	1	2	3	4	5	6–10	Laps	Laps Led	Races Led	Miles	$
1962	130	2	0	0	0	0	0	0	0	15	0	0	8	150
Lifetime		2	0	0	0	0	0	0	0	15	0	0	8	$150

Rock Harn

Otis A. Harn
B: 7/29/1924
Racing Hometown: North Augusta, SC

Year	Rank	Starts	Poles	1	2	3	4	5	6–10	Laps	Laps Led	Races Led	Miles	$
1962	129	1	0	0	0	0	0	0	0	2	0	0	1	50
1965	101	2	0	0	0	0	0	0	0	331	0	0	167	745
1966	145	1	0	0	0	0	0	0	0	33	0	0	83	0
Lifetime		4	0	0	0	0	0	0	0	366	0	0	251	$795

Leon Harrell

Leon Harrell
Racing Hometown: Asheville, NC

Year	Rank	Starts	Poles	1	2	3	4	5	6–10	Laps	Laps Led	Races Led	Miles	$
1951	N/A	1	0	0	0	0	0	0	0		0	0		25
Lifetime		1	0	0	0	0	0	0	0		0	0		$25

Red Harrelson

Raymond Harrelson
Racing Hometown: Pensacola, FL

Year	Rank	Starts	Poles	1	2	3	4	5	6–10	Laps	Laps Led	Races Led	Miles	$
1951	N/A	1	0	0	0	0	0	0	0		0	0		25
1952	98	2	0	0	0	0	0	0	0	73	0	0	39	75
Lifetime		3	0	0	0	0	0	0	0	73	0	0	39	$100

Bob Harris

Robert Harris
B: 9/11/1926
Racing Hometown: Greensboro, NC

Year	Rank	Starts	Poles	1	2	3	4	5	6–10	Laps	Laps Led	Races Led	Miles	$
1953	NR	1	0	0	0	0	0	0	0		0	0		35
Lifetime		1	0	0	0	0	0	0	0		0	0		$35

Ferrel Harris

Ferrel Harris
B: 10/8/1940
Racing Hometown: Pikeville, KY

Year	Rank	Starts	Poles	1	2	3	4	5	6–10	Laps	Laps Led	Races Led	Miles	$
1975	38	10	0	0	0	0	0	0	0	2,357	0	0	3,854	16,165
1976	80	2	0	0	0	0	0	0	0	217	0	0	565	3,360
1977	32	11	0	0	0	0	0	0	0	2,979	0	0	2,560	19,365
1978	35	14	0	0	0	0	0	0	5	2,915	0	0	4,372	39,685
1979	NR	1	0	0	0	0	0	0	0	2	0	0	3	2,060
1980	NR	2	0	0	0	0	0	0	0	359	0	0	512	4,025
1982	NR	1	0	0	0	0	0	0	0	146	0	0	388	3,975
1983	—	0												2,350
Lifetime		41	0	0	0	0	0	0	5	8,975	0	0	12,255	$90,985

Runt Harris

Gayther Wallace Harris
B: 6/4/1927   D: 6/30/1990
Racing Hometown: Fredericksburg, VA

Year	Rank	Starts	Poles	1	2	3	4	5	6–10	Laps	Laps Led	Races Led	Miles	$
1950	129T	1	0	0	0	0	0	0	0	41	0	0	21	0
1957	158	1	0	0	0	0	0	0	0	50	0	0	69	100
1959	NR	1	0	0	0	0	0	1	0	193	0	0	97	250
1960	109	3	0	0	0	0	0	0	0	391	0	0	233	350
1962	109	2	0	0	0	0	0	0	0	130	0	0	51	100
Lifetime		8	0	0	0	0	0	1	0	805	0	0	470	$800

Bill Harrison

William J. Harrison
B: 9/2/1910   D: 11/0/1993
Racing Hometown: Topeka, KS

Year	Rank	Starts	Poles	1	2	3	4	5	6–10	Laps	Laps Led	Races Led	Miles	$
1949	NR	1	0	0	0	0	0	0	0		0	0		25
1950	135	2	0	0	0	0	0	0	0	38	0	0	29	0
1951	N/A	1	0	0	0	0	0	0	0	133	0	0	100	25
1953	40	3	0	0	0	0	0	0	3		0	0		450
1954	210	1	0	0	0	0	0	0	0		0	0		0

Year	Rank	Starts	Poles	Finish						Laps	Laps Led	Races Led	Miles	$
				1	2	3	4	5	6–10	Laps	Led	Led	Miles	$

Bill Harrison *continued*

Year	Rank	Starts	Poles	1	2	3	4	5	6–10	Laps	Laps Led	Races Led	Miles	$
1955	108	2	0	0	0	0	0	0	1	279	0	0	140	125
Lifetime		10	0	0	0	0	0	0	4	450	0	0	268	$625

Jack Harrison

Jack Harrison
B: 1930   D: 11/11/1956   *Died of ulcers @ age 26.*
Racing Hometown: W. Newton, IN

Year	Rank	Starts	Poles	1	2	3	4	5	6–10	Laps	Laps Led	Races Led	Miles	$
1952	NR	1	0	0	0	0	0	0	0	277	0	0	139	50
1954	NR	1	0	0	0	0	0	0	0	19	0	0	19	25
Lifetime		2	0	0	0	0	0	0	0	296	0	0	158	$75

Joe Harrison

Joseph Harrison
Racing Hometown: Syracuse, NY

Year	Rank	Starts	Poles	1	2	3	4	5	6–10	Laps	Laps Led	Races Led	Miles	$
1950	NR	1	0	0	0	0	0	0	0	3	0	0	13	25
Lifetime		1	0	0	0	0	0	0	0	3	0	0	13	$25

Tubby Harrison

Tubby Harrison
Racing Hometown: Topeka, KS

Year	Rank	Starts	Poles	1	2	3	4	5	6–10	Laps	Laps Led	Races Led	Miles	$
1953	53T	2	0	0	0	0	0	0	2		0	0		150
Lifetime		2	0	0	0	0	0	0	2		0	0		$150

Jack Hart

Jack Hart
B: 1926
Racing Hometown: Boothwyn, PA

Year	Rank	Starts	Poles	1	2	3	4	5	6–10	Laps	Laps Led	Races Led	Miles	$
1960	116	1	0	0	0	0	0	0	0	76	0	0	19	145
1961	NR	1	0	0	0	0	0	0	0	52	0	0	13	60
Lifetime		2	0	0	0	0	0	0	0	128	0	0	32	$205

Jim Hart

James Hart
Racing Hometown: Newark, NJ

Year	Rank	Starts	Poles	1	2	3	4	5	6–10	Laps	Laps Led	Races Led	Miles	$
1951	N/A	1	0	0	0	0	0	0	0		0	0		25
Lifetime		1	0	0	0	0	0	0	0		0	0		$25

George Hartley

George Hartley
Racing Hometown: Erie, PA

Year	Rank	Starts	Poles	1	2	3	4	5	6–10	Laps	Laps Led	Races Led	Miles	$
1950	21	8	0	0	0	0	0	0	2	371	0	0	464	875
Lifetime		8	0	0	0	0	0	0	2	371	0	0	464	$875

Butch Hartman

Larry Hartman
B: 5/11/1940   D: 12/22/1994
Racing Hometown: Zanesville, OH

Year	Rank	Starts	Poles	1	2	3	4	5	6–10	Laps	Laps Led	Races Led	Miles	$
1966	NR	1	0	0	0	0	0	0	0	307	0	0	461	875
1968	NR	5	0	0	0	0	0	0	2	1,458	10	2	2,278	6,455
1972	NR	1	0	0	0	0	0	1	0	326	0	0	489	3,570
1977	31	11	0	0	0	0	0	0	2	2,005	0	0	3,690	18,615
1978	104	1	0	0	0	0	0	0	0	121	0	0	184	640
1979	86	1	0	0	0	0	0	0	0	351	0	0	479	2,225
Lifetime		20	0	0	0	0	0	1	4	4,568	10	2	7,581	$32,380

Walt Hartman

Walter Hartman
Racing Hometown: Chattanooga, TN

Year	Rank	Starts	Poles	1	2	3	4	5	6–10	Laps	Laps Led	Races Led	Miles	$
1951	N/A	3	0	0	0	0	0	0	0		0	0		75
Lifetime		3	0	0	0	0	0	0	0		0	0		$75

Billie Harvey

William Harvey
B: 1950
Racing Hometown: Delray Beach, FL

Year	Rank	Starts	Poles	1	2	3	4	5	6–10	Laps	Laps Led	Races Led	Miles	$
1980	87	4	0	0	0	0	0	0	0	805	0	0	1,691	7,995

Year	Rank	Starts	Poles	Finish 1	2	3	4	5	6–10	Laps	Laps Led	Races Led	Miles	$

Billie Harvey *continued*

Year	Rank	Starts	Poles	1	2	3	4	5	6–10	Laps	Laps Led	Races Led	Miles	$
1981	91	2	0	0	0	0	0	0	0	60	0	0	150	3,915
1982	104T	1	0	0	0	0	0	0	0	6	0	0	15	3,875
1983	NR	1	0	0	0	0	0	0	0	1	0	0	3	1,730
Lifetime		8	0	0	0	0	0	0	0	872	0	0	1,859	$17,515

Gordon Harvey

Gordon Harvey
B: 1920
Racing Hometown: Sayerville, NJ

Year	Rank	Starts	Poles	1	2	3	4	5	6–10	Laps	Laps Led	Races Led	Miles	$
1951	N/A	1	0	0	0	0	0	0	0		0	0		0
Lifetime		1	0	0	0	0	0	0	0		0	0		$0

Red Harvey

Red Harvey
Racing Hometown: Dayton, OH

Year	Rank	Starts	Poles	1	2	3	4	5	6–10	Laps	Laps Led	Races Led	Miles	$
1950	34T	1	0	0	1	0	0	0	0		1	1		750
1951	N/A	1	0	0	0	0	0	0	1		0	0		100
Lifetime		2	0	0	1	0	0	0	1		1	1		$750

Walt Harvey

Walter Harvey
Racing Hometown: Greenboro, NC

Year	Rank	Starts	Poles	1	2	3	4	5	6–10	Laps	Laps Led	Races Led	Miles	$
1954	150	1	0	0	0	0	0	0	0	284	0	0	391	120
Lifetime		1	0	0	0	0	0	0	0	284	0	0	391	$120

Bill Hasley

William Hasley
Racing Hometown: Sacramento, CA

Year	Rank	Starts	Poles	1	2	3	4	5	6–10	Laps	Laps Led	Races Led	Miles	$
1958	143	2	0	0	0	0	0	0	0	154	0	0	322	125
Lifetime		2	0	0	0	0	0	0	0	154	0	0	322	$125

Friday Hassler

Raymond Hassler
B: 6/29/1935   D: 2/17/1972   *Killed in 125-mile qualifying race @ Daytona.*
Racing Hometown: Chattanooga, TN

Year	Rank	Starts	Poles	1	2	3	4	5	6–10	Laps	Laps Led	Races Led	Miles	$
1960	87	2	0	0	0	0	0	0	0	251	0	0	377	425
1961	53	7	0	0	0	0	0	0	1	939	0	0	1,513	2,175
1962	114	2	0	0	0	0	0	0	0	257	0	0	321	300
1966	56	9	0	0	0	0	0	1	2	2,431	0	0	1,797	4,290
1967	32	21	0	0	0	0	1	2	6	4,309	12	1	3,091	10,270
1968	27	20	0	0	0	0	2	1	5	5,012	0	0	4,245	12,000
1969	28	18	0	0	0	0	0	0	7	4,607	3	1	4,665	18,000
1970	20	26	0	0	0	0	0	1	5	5,439	56	1	6,518	27,535
1971	16	29	2	0	1	2	0	1	9	5,650	68	3	7,130	37,305
1972	93	1	0	0	0	0	0	0	1	137	0	0	359	2,225
Lifetime		135	2	0	1	2	3	6	36	29,032	139	6	30,015	$114,525

Barney Hatchell

Barney Hatchell

Year	Rank	Starts	Poles	1	2	3	4	5	6–10	Laps	Laps Led	Races Led	Miles	$
1958	103	2	0	0	0	0	0	0	0	281	0	0	141	160
Lifetime		2	0	0	0	0	0	0	0	281	0	0	141	$160

Jake Hatcher

Joseph C. Hatcher
Racing Hometown: Pensacola, FL

Year	Rank	Starts	Poles	1	2	3	4	5	6–10	Laps	Laps Led	Races Led	Miles	$
1956	184T	1	0	0	0	0	0	0	0	172	0	0	86	100
Lifetime		1	0	0	0	0	0	0	0	172	0	0	86	$100

Curley Hatfield

Ewell Hatfield
Racing Hometown: Wharncliffe, WV

Year	Rank	Starts	Poles	1	2	3	4	5	6–10	Laps	Laps Led	Races Led	Miles	$
1955	196	1	0	0	0	0	0	0	0	319	0	0	439	60
1956	NR	2	0	0	0	0	0	0	0	191	0	0	156	150
Lifetime		3	0	0	0	0	0	0	0	510	0	0	595	$210

Jack Hauher

Jack Hauher
Racing Hometown: Buffalo, NY

Year	Rank	Starts	Poles	1	2	3	4	5	6–10	Laps	Laps Led	Races Led	Miles	$
1952	140T	1	0	0	0	0	0	0	0	26	0	0	13	25
Lifetime		1	0	0	0	0	0	0	0	26	0	0	13	$25

Year	Rank	Starts	Poles	Finish 1	2	3	4	5	6–10	Laps	Laps Led	Races Led	Miles	$

Dave Haupt *See* Joe Kelly

Ted Hauser
Theodore Hauser

Year	Rank	Starts	Poles	1	2	3	4	5	6–10	Laps	Laps Led	Races Led	Miles	$
1957	NR	1	0	0	0	0	0	0	0	43	0	0	43	100
Lifetime		1	0	0	0	0	0	0	0	43	0	0	43	$100

Bob Havenmann
Robert Havenmann
Racing Hometown: Eureka, CA

Year	Rank	Starts	Poles	1	2	3	4	5	6–10	Laps	Laps Led	Races Led	Miles	$
1954	68	2	0	0	0	0	0	0	1	694	0	0	347	275
1955	69	3	0	0	0	0	0	0	2	506	0	0	410	400
1956	107	4	0	0	0	0	0	0	1	496	0	0	366	290
1957	136T	1	0	0	0	0	0	0	0	117	0	0	73	100
1958	130	1	0	0	0	0	0	0	0	91	0	0	91	100
Lifetime		11	0	0	0	0	0	0	4	1,904	0	0	1,287	$1,165

John Haver
John Haver
Racing Hometown: Weimar, TX

Year	Rank	Starts	Poles	1	2	3	4	5	6–10	Laps	Laps Led	Races Led	Miles	$
1976	107T	1	0	0	0	0	0	0	0	49	0	0	98	780
1979	NR	1	0	0	0	0	0	0	0	36	0	0	72	950
1982	—	0												750
Lifetime		2	0	0	0	0	0	0	0	85	0	0	170	$2,480

Jeff Hawkins
Jeffrey Hawkins
Racing Hometown: Greenville, SC

Year	Rank	Starts	Poles	1	2	3	4	5	6–10	Laps	Laps Led	Races Led	Miles	$
1965	81	6	0	0	0	0	0	0	0	322	0	0	261	2,160
1966	79	2	0	0	0	0	0	1	1	360	0	0	180	425
1968	119	1	0	0	0	0	0	0	0	107	0	0	54	100
Lifetime		9	0	0	0	0	0	1	1	789	0	0	495	$2,685

Lewis Hawkins
Lewis Hawkins
Racing Hometown: Spartanburg, SC

Year	Rank	Starts	Poles	1	2	3	4	5	6–10	Laps	Laps Led	Races Led	Miles	$
1950	124	1	0	0	0	0	0	0	0		0	0		50
Lifetime		1	0	0	0	0	0	0	0		0	0		$50

Sam Hawks
Samuel Hawks
Racing Hometown: Modesto, CA

Year	Rank	Starts	Poles	1	2	3	4	5	6–10	Laps	Laps Led	Races Led	Miles	$
1951	46	3	0	0	0	0	1	0	0		0	0		800
1954	87	3	0	0	0	0	0	0	1	677	0	0	440	265
Lifetime		6	0	0	0	0	1	0	1	677	0	0	440	$1,065

J. T. Hayes
J. T. Hayes
Racing Hometown: Corinth, MS

Year	Rank	Starts	Poles	1	2	3	4	5	6–10	Laps	Laps Led	Races Led	Miles	$
1990	102	1	0	0	0	0	0	0	0	10	0	0	10	2,700
Lifetime		1	0	0	0	0	0	0	0	10	0	0	10	$2,700

Ronnie Hayes
Ronald Hayes
Racing Hometown: Rochester, NY

Year	Rank	Starts	Poles	1	2	3	4	5	6–10	Laps	Laps Led	Races Led	Miles	$
1954	NR	1	0	0	0	0	0	0	0	43	0	0	22	0
Lifetime		1	0	0	0	0	0	0	0	43	0	0	22	$0

Stew Hayes
Stewart Hayes
Racing Hometown: Rochester, NY

Year	Rank	Starts	Poles	1	2	3	4	5	6–10	Laps	Laps Led	Races Led	Miles	$
1952	133T	1	0	0	0	0	0	0	0	156	0	0	78	25
Lifetime		1	0	0	0	0	0	0	0	156	0	0	78	$25

Bill Hazel
William Hazel

Year	Rank	Starts	Poles	1	2	3	4	5	6–10	Laps	Laps Led	Races Led	Miles	$
1957	81	1	0	0	0	0	0	0	0	96	0	0	144	175
Lifetime		1	0	0	0	0	0	0	0	96	0	0	144	$175

241

Year	Rank	Starts	Poles	Finish						Laps	Laps Led	Races Led	Miles	$
				1	2	3	4	5	6–10					

Pete Hazelwood

Charles Hazelwood
Racing Hometown: Cartersville, GA

Year	Rank	Starts	Poles	1	2	3	4	5	6–10	Laps	Laps Led	Races Led	Miles	$
1969	43	16	0	0	0	0	0	0	1	2,367	0	0	1,163	4,390
1970	81	3	0	0	0	0	0	0	0	51	0	0	26	620
Lifetime		19	0	0	0	0	0	0	1	2,418	0	0	1,189	$5,010

Louis Headley

Louis M. Headley
Racing Hometown: Plymouth Meeting, PA

Year	Rank	Starts	Poles	1	2	3	4	5	6–10	Laps	Laps Led	Races Led	Miles	$
1955	234	1	0	0	0	0	0	0	0	3	0	0	12	0
1956	294T	1	0	0	0	0	0	0	0	1	0	0	1	25
Lifetime		2	0	0	0	0	0	0	0	4	0	0	13	$25

Gil Hearne

Gilbert Hearne
B: 1939
Racing Hometown: Wrightstown, NJ

Year	Rank	Starts	Poles	1	2	3	4	5	6–10	Laps	Laps Led	Races Led	Miles	$
1965	112T	1	0	0	0	0	0	0	0	172	0	0	57	100
1966	117	2	0	0	0	0	0	0	0	319	0	0	160	100
Lifetime		3	0	0	0	0	0	0	0	491	0	0	217	$200

Allen Heath

Allen Heath
B: 1/18/1918
Racing Hometown: Saskatoon, Saskatchewan, Canada,

Year	Rank	Starts	Poles	1	2	3	4	5	6–10	Laps	Laps Led	Races Led	Miles	$
1951	N/A	4	0	0	0	0	0	0	0		0	0		100
1954	NR	1	0	0	0	0	0	0	0	52	0	0	26	0
Lifetime		5	0	0	0	0	0	0	0	52	0	0	26	$100

Jim Heath

James Heath
Racing Hometown: Oakland, CA

Year	Rank	Starts	Poles	1	2	3	4	5	6–10	Laps	Laps Led	Races Led	Miles	$
1954	101	2	0	0	0	0	0	0	1	436	0	0	323	140
Lifetime		2	0	0	0	0	0	0	1	436	0	0	323	$140

Jay Hedgecock

Wesley Hedgecock
B: 2/28/1955
Racing Hometown: High Point, NC

Year	Rank	Starts	Poles	1	2	3	4	5	6–10	Laps	Laps Led	Races Led	Miles	$
1993	72T	1	0	0	0	0	0	0	0	372	0	0	233	4,780
1994	58	2	0	0	0	0	0	0	0	537	0	0	287	9,475
1995	—	0												2,300
Lifetime		3	0	0	0	0	0	0	0	909	0	0	520	$16,555

Gene Hege

Gene Hege
Racing Hometown: Columbia, SC

Year	Rank	Starts	Poles	1	2	3	4	5	6–10	Laps	Laps Led	Races Led	Miles	$
1958	154	1	0	0	0	0	0	0	0	85	0	0	43	0
Lifetime		1	0	0	0	0	0	0	0	85	0	0	43	$0

Harvey Hege

Harvey Hege
Racing Hometown: Thomasville, NC

Year	Rank	Starts	Poles	1	2	3	4	5	6–10	Laps	Laps Led	Races Led	Miles	$
1958	152	13	0	0	0	0	0	0	2	1,498	0	0	786	1,200
1959	41	10	0	0	0	0	0	0	3	1,485	0	0	765	955
1960	NR	1	0	0	0	0	0	0	0	62	0	0	31	100
1961	145	1	0	0	0	0	0	0	0	166	0	0	42	100
Lifetime		25	0	0	0	0	0	0	5	3,211	0	0	1,624	$2,355

Marvin Heinis

Marvin Heinis
Racing Hometown: Sylmar, CA

Year	Rank	Starts	Poles	1	2	3	4	5	6–10	Laps	Laps Led	Races Led	Miles	$
1961	137	2	0	0	0	0	0	0	0	132	0	0	187	200
Lifetime		2	0	0	0	0	0	0	0	132	0	0	187	$200

Greg Heller

Gregory Heller
Racing Hometown: Dubois, PA

Year	Rank	Starts	Poles	1	2	3	4	5	6–10	Laps	Laps Led	Races Led	Miles	$
1977	98T	1	0	0	0	0	0	0	0	110	0	0	275	680

Year	Rank	Starts	Poles	Finish						Laps	Laps Led	Races Led	Miles	$
				1	2	3	4	5	6–10					

Greg Heller *continued*

Year	Rank	Starts	Poles	1	2	3	4	5	6–10	Laps	Laps Led	Races Led	Miles	$
1978	NR	1	0	0	0	0	0	0	0	250	0	0	250	575
Lifetime		2	0	0	0	0	0	0	0	360	0	0	525	$1,255

Buddy Helms

Buddy Helms
Racing Hometown: Charlotte, NC

Year	Rank	Starts	Poles	1	2	3	4	5	6–10	Laps	Laps Led	Races Led	Miles	$
1949	42	1	0	0	0	0	0	0	1		0	0		75
1950	NR	3	0	0	0	0	0	0	0	36	0	0	18	0
1951	N/A	1	0	0	0	0	0	0	0	132	0	0	99	25
Lifetime		5	0	0	0	0	0	0	1	168	0	0	117	$100

Jimmy Helms

James Helms
B: 8/7/1935
Racing Hometown: Charlotte, NC

Year	Rank	Starts	Poles	1	2	3	4	5	6–10	Laps	Laps Led	Races Led	Miles	$
1964	54	18	0	0	0	0	0	0	2	750	0	0	386	4,180
1965	18	39	0	0	0	0	0	0	4	5,731	0	0	3,987	12,050
1966	34	29	0	0	0	0	0	0	0	3,186	0	0	2,709	5,915
1967	78	2	0	0	0	0	0	0	1	607	0	0	304	640
Lifetime		88	0	0	0	0	0	0	7	10,274	0	0	7,385	$22,785

Kenny Hemphill

Kenneth Hemphill
B: 1951
Racing Hometown: Vandergrift, PA

Year	Rank	Starts	Poles	1	2	3	4	5	6–10	Laps	Laps Led	Races Led	Miles	$
1980	62	5	0	0	0	0	0	0	1	884	4	1	1,493	8,970
Lifetime		5	0	0	0	0	0	0	1	884	4	1	1,493	$8,970

Elmo Henderson

Elmo Henderson
Racing Hometown: Spartanburg, SC

Year	Rank	Starts	Poles	1	2	3	4	5	6–10	Laps	Laps Led	Races Led	Miles	$
1959	81	2	0	0	0	0	0	0	0	176	0	0	102	200
1960	47	6	0	0	0	0	0	0	0	870	0	0	1,083	1,425
1961	77	4	0	0	0	0	0	0	1	583	0	0	782	835
1964	59	8	0	0	0	0	0	1	2	661	0	0	362	2,175
1965	99	1	0	0	0	0	0	0	0	101	0	0	51	130
Lifetime		21	0	0	0	0	0	1	3	2,391	0	0	2,378	$4,715

Harvey Henderson

Harvey Henderson
Racing Hometown: Beltsville, MD

Year	Rank	Starts	Poles	1	2	3	4	5	6–10	Laps	Laps Led	Races Led	Miles	$
1952	120T	1	0	0	0	0	0	0	0		0	0		25
1955	22	17	0	0	0	0	0	1	5	2,284	0	0	1,344	1,810
1956	30	18	0	0	0	0	0	0	4	2,477	0	0	1,597	1,360
1957	NR	1	0	0	0	0	0	0	0	172	0	0	86	100
1958	120	2	0	0	0	0	0	0	0	160	0	0	58	125
1961	163	1	0	0	0	0	0	0	0	153	0	0	77	75
Lifetime		40	0	0	0	0	0	1	9	5,246	0	0	3,162	$3,495

Rick Henderson

Richard Henderson
Racing Hometown: Petaluma, CA

Year	Rank	Starts	Poles	1	2	3	4	5	6–10	Laps	Laps Led	Races Led	Miles	$
1954	109	3	0	0	0	0	0	0	0	609	0	0	404	65
Lifetime		3	0	0	0	0	0	0	0	609	0	0	404	$65

Ray Hendrick

Raymond D. Hendrick
B: 4/1/1929   D: 9/28/1990
Racing Hometown: Richmond, VA

Year	Rank	Starts	Poles	1	2	3	4	5	6–10	Laps	Laps Led	Races Led	Miles	$
1956	228	2	0	0	0	0	0	0	0	177	0	0	231	100
1962	83	2	0	0	0	0	0	0	0	714	0	0	357	275
1963	87	2	0	0	0	0	0	1	1	573	0	0	238	625
1967	112	1	0	0	0	0	0	0	0	107	0	0	54	175
1968	95	4	0	0	0	0	0	1	3	1,295	7	1	627	1,470
1969	75T	1	0	0	0	0	0	0	0	351	0	0	176	490
1971	NR	1	0	0	0	0	0	0	0	295	0	0	300	665

Year	Rank	Starts	Poles	Finish 1	2	3	4	5	6–10	Laps	Laps Led	Races Led	Miles	$

Ray Hendrick *continued*

Year	Rank	Starts	Poles	1	2	3	4	5	6–10	Laps	Laps Led	Races Led	Miles	$
1972	NR	1	0	0	0	0	0	0	0	311	0	0	163	625
1973	88	2	0	0	0	0	0	0	0	613	0	0	324	1,950
1974	128	1	0	0	0	0	0	0	0	179	0	0	94	620
Lifetime		17	0	0	0	0	0	2	4	4,615	7	1	2,564	$6,995

Rick Hendrick

Joseph R. Hendrick III
B: 7/12/1949
Racing Hometown: Charlotte, NC

Year	Rank	Starts	Poles	1	2	3	4	5	6–10	Laps	Laps Led	Races Led	Miles	$
1987	NR	1	0	0	0	0	0	0	0	75	0	0	197	1,150
1988	63	1	0	0	0	0	0	0	0	94	0	0	246	2,550
Lifetime		2	0	0	0	0	0	0	0	169	0	0	443	$3,700

Roy Lee Hendrick

Roy Lee Hendrick
B: 12/25/1953
Racing Hometown: Richmond, VA

Year	Rank	Starts	Poles	1	2	3	4	5	6–10	Laps	Laps Led	Races Led	Miles	$
1986	119	1	0	0	0	0	0	0	0	91	0	0	91	875
Lifetime		1	0	0	0	0	0	0	0	91	0	0	91	$875

Jim Hendrickson

James Hendrickson
Racing Hometown: Deer Park, NY

Year	Rank	Starts	Poles	1	2	3	4	5	6–10	Laps	Laps Led	Races Led	Miles	$
1961	117	2	0	0	0	0	0	0	0	208	0	0	349	275
Lifetime		2	0	0	0	0	0	0	0	208	0	0	349	$275

J. C. Hendrix

J. C. Hendrix
Racing Hometown: Griffin, GA

Year	Rank	Starts	Poles	1	2	3	4	5	6–10	Laps	Laps Led	Races Led	Miles	$
1959	52	3	0	0	0	0	0	0	1	361	0	0	274	360
1961	67	2	0	0	0	0	0	0	1	456	0	0	684	1,175
1962	94	1	0	0	0	0	0	0	0	379	0	0	237	250
Lifetime		6	0	0	0	0	0	0	2	1,196	0	0	1,194	$1,785

Jimmy Hensley

James Hensley Jr.
B: 10/11/1945
Racing Hometown: Ridgeway, VA

Year	Rank	Starts	Poles	1	2	3	4	5	6–10	Laps	Laps Led	Races Led	Miles	$
1972	99	2	0	0	0	0	0	1	0	548	0	0	288	1,900
1973	103	1	0	0	0	0	0	0	1	485	0	0	255	1,550
1974	83	2	0	0	0	0	0	0	1	668	9	1	351	2,260
1975	98	2	0	0	0	0	0	0	1	534	0	0	280	1,860
1976	68	2	0	0	0	0	0	0	1	474	0	0	249	2,150
1977	60	2	0	0	0	0	0	0	1	812	0	0	426	2,680
1981	NR	1	0	0	0	0	0	0	1	487	0	0	256	4,650
1982	NR	3	0	0	0	0	0	0	1	791	0	0	417	3,205
1984	NR	4	0	0	0	0	0	0	0	1,484	0	0	793	12,895
1986	54	3	0	0	0	0	0	0	0	1,194	0	0	634	11,755
1988	NR	1	0	0	0	0	0	0	0	290	0	0	153	4,245
1989	—	0	1	0	0	0	0	0	0	0	0	0	0	0
1990	88	2	0	0	0	0	0	0	0	692	0	0	820	7,475
1991	41	4	0	0	0	0	0	0	1	1,708	0	0	1,491	32,125
1992	28	22	0	0	0	0	0	0	4	6,804	22	3	8,491	247,660
1993	32	21	0	0	0	0	0	0	2	5,843	1	1	6,929	368,150
1994	41	17	0	0	0	0	0	0	0	3,861	4	3	5,750	203,520
1995	44	9	0	0	0	0	0	0	0	1,512	0	0	2,434	161,025
Lifetime		98	1	0	0	0	0	1	14	28,187	36	8	30,015	$1,069,105

Bill Henson

William Henson
Racing Hometown: Birmingham, AL

Year	Rank	Starts	Poles	1	2	3	4	5	6–10	Laps	Laps Led	Races Led	Miles	$
1950	NR	1	0	0	0	0	0	0	0	200	0	0	250	100
1955	NR	1	0	0	0	0	0	0	0	109	0	0	109	25
Lifetime		2	0	0	0	0	0	0	0	309	0	0	359	$125

Bernie Hentges

Bernard Hentges
Racing Hometown: Anoka, MN

Year	Rank	Starts	Poles	1	2	3	4	5	6–10	Laps	Laps Led	Races Led	Miles	$
1957	187	1	0	0	0	0	0	0	0		0	0		0

Year	Rank	Starts	Poles	1	2	3	4	5	6–10	Laps	Laps Led	Races Led	Miles	$

Bernie Hentges *continued*

Year	Rank	Starts	Poles	1	2	3	4	5	6–10	Laps	Laps Led	Races Led	Miles	$
1959	78	2	0	0	0	0	0	0	0	176	0	0	440	210
Lifetime		3	0	0	0	0	0	0	0	176	0	0	440	$210

Russ Hepler

Russell Hepler
B: 1923   D: 1969
Racing Hometown: Clarion, PA

Year	Rank	Starts	Poles	1	2	3	4	5	6–10	Laps	Laps Led	Races Led	Miles	$
1951	N/A	1	0	0	0	0	0	0	1		0	0		50
1952	113	2	0	0	0	0	0	0	0	166	0	0	97	25
1954	47	6	0	0	0	0	1	0	0	691	0	0	510	525
1957	90	4	1	0	0	0	0	0	0	365	0	0	206	345
Lifetime		13	1	0	0	0	1	0	1	1,222	0	0	812	$945

Tommy Herbert

Thomas Herbert
B: 1922
Racing Hometown: Delray Beach, FL

Year	Rank	Starts	Poles	1	2	3	4	5	6–10	Laps	Laps Led	Races Led	Miles	$
1956	275	1	0	0	0	0	0	0	0		0	0		0
1960	127	2	0	0	0	0	0	0	0	155	0	0	388	250
Lifetime		3	0	0	0	0	0	0	0	155	0	0	388	$250

Terry Herman

Terry Herman
Racing Hometown: Sonora, CA

Year	Rank	Starts	Poles	1	2	3	4	5	6–10	Laps	Laps Led	Races Led	Miles	$
1981	NR	2	0	0	0	0	0	0	0	238	0	0	631	7,035
1982	NR	1	0	0	0	0	0	0	0	113	0	0	296	4,220
Lifetime		3	0	0	0	0	0	0	0	351	0	0	927	$11,255

Ronnie Herra

Ronald Herra

Year	Rank	Starts	Poles	1	2	3	4	5	6–10	Laps	Laps Led	Races Led	Miles	$
1956	260	1	0	0	0	0	0	0	0	34	0	0	34	50
Lifetime		1	0	0	0	0	0	0	0	34	0	0	34	$50

Skimp Hersey

John Edward Hersey
B: 2/8/1913   D: 6/12/1950   *Died from burns suffered @ Lakewood Speedway 6/11/50.*
Racing Hometown: St. Augustine, FL

Year	Rank	Starts	Poles	1	2	3	4	5	6–10	Laps	Laps Led	Races Led	Miles	$
1949	NR	1	0	0	0	0	0	0	0		0	0		25
Lifetime		1	0	0	0	0	0	0	0		0	0		$25

Ben Hess

Benjamin Hess
B: 12/20/1964
Racing Hometown: Dayton, OH

Year	Rank	Starts	Poles	1	2	3	4	5	6–10	Laps	Laps Led	Races Led	Miles	$
1988	67	1	0	0	0	0	0	0	0	472	0	0	472	3,370
1989	37	9	0	0	0	0	0	0	0	3,194	0	0	3,818	48,490
1990	89	1	0	0	0	0	0	0	0	169	0	0	338	4,275
1995	59	1	0	0	0	0	0	0	0	196	0	0	490	35,785
Lifetime		12	0	0	0	0	0	0	0	4,031	0	0	5,118	$86,920

Larry Hess

Lawrence Hess
B: 5/3/1935
Racing Hometown: Salisbury, NC

Year	Rank	Starts	Poles	1	2	3	4	5	6–10	Laps	Laps Led	Races Led	Miles	$
1965	16	10	0	0	0	0	0	0	3	2,347	0	0	3,543	9,260
1966	40	13	0	0	0	0	0	0	0	1,830	0	0	2,160	5,290
1967	109	2	0	0	0	0	0	0	0	58	0	0	82	900
1968	109	1	0	0	0	0	0	0	0	0	0	0	0	460
1969	81	1	0	0	0	0	0	0	0	122	0	0	183	1,325
Lifetime		27	0	0	0	0	0	0	3	4,357	0	0	5,968	$17,235

Ed Hessert

Dr. Edmond C. Hessert
B: 6/25/1932   *Deceased*
Racing Hometown: Trenton, NJ

Year	Rank	Starts	Poles	1	2	3	4	5	6–10	Laps	Laps Led	Races Led	Miles	$
1969	32	16	0	0	0	0	0	0	4	2,635	1	1	3,301	17,690
1970	82	2	0	0	0	0	0	0	0	105	0	0	203	495

Year	Rank	Starts	Poles	Finish 1	2	3	4	5	6–10	Laps	Laps Led	Races Led	Miles	$

Ed Hessert *continued*

Year	Rank	Starts	Poles	1	2	3	4	5	6–10	Laps	Laps Led	Races Led	Miles	$
1971	82	2	0	0	0	0	0	0	0	108	0	0	55	415
1972	114	2	0	0	0	0	0	0	0	157	0	0	343	1,505
Lifetime		22	0	0	0	0	0	0	4	3,005	1	1	3,901	$17,690

Tom Hessert

Thomas Hessert
B: 4/1/1951
Racing Hometown: Trenton, NJ

Year	Rank	Starts	Poles	1	2	3	4	5	6–10	Laps	Laps Led	Races Led	Miles	$
1982	100	1	0	0	0	0	0	0	0	8	0	0	20	950
Lifetime		1	0	0	0	0	0	0	0	8	0	0	20	$950

Doug Heveron

Douglas Heveron
B: 3/29/1964
Racing Hometown: Liverpool, NY

Year	Rank	Starts	Poles	1	2	3	4	5	6–10	Laps	Laps Led	Races Led	Miles	$
1984	36	16	0	0	0	0	0	0	0	3,553	7	1	4,864	39,950
1985	97	2	0	0	0	0	0	0	0	238	0	0	595	11,015
1986	35	13	0	0	0	0	0	0	0	2,536	1	1	3,409	74,030
1989	—	0												1,100
Lifetime		31	0	0	0	0	0	0	0	6,327	8	2	8,868	$126,095

Bud Hickey

Bud Hickey

Year	Rank	Starts	Poles	1	2	3	4	5	6–10	Laps	Laps Led	Races Led	Miles	$
1985	95T	1	0	0	0	0	0	0	0	40	0	0	105	950
Lifetime		1	0	0	0	0	0	0	0	40	0	0	105	$950

Lester Hicks

Lester Hicks
Racing Hometown: Bristol, VA

Year	Rank	Starts	Poles	1	2	3	4	5	6–10	Laps	Laps Led	Races Led	Miles	$
1962	119	2	0	0	0	0	0	0	0	264	0	0	132	150
Lifetime		2	0	0	0	0	0	0	0	264	0	0	132	$150

Bill Hidden

William Hidden
Racing Hometown: Portland, OR

Year	Rank	Starts	Poles	1	2	3	4	5	6–10	Laps	Laps Led	Races Led	Miles	$
1957	114T	2	0	0	0	0	0	0	0	121	0	0	89	150
Lifetime		2	0	0	0	0	0	0	0	121	0	0	89	$150

Boyce Hildreth

Boyce Hildreth
Racing Hometown: Greensboro, NC

Year	Rank	Starts	Poles	1	2	3	4	5	6–10	Laps	Laps Led	Races Led	Miles	$
1955	214	2	0	0	0	0	0	0	0	46	0	0	24	50
Lifetime		2	0	0	0	0	0	0	0	46	0	0	24	$50

Don Hildreth

Donald Hildreth
Racing Hometown: Portland, OR

Year	Rank	Starts	Poles	1	2	3	4	5	6–10	Laps	Laps Led	Races Led	Miles	$
1956	214T	1	0	0	0	0	0	0	0	140	0	0	70	50
Lifetime		1	0	0	0	0	0	0	0	140	0	0	70	$50

Elton Hildreth

Elton C. Hildreth
B: 1918
Racing Hometown: Bridgeton, NJ

Year	Rank	Starts	Poles	1	2	3	4	5	6–10	Laps	Laps Led	Races Led	Miles	$
1952	42	6	0	0	0	0	0	0	1	815	0	0	608	375
1953	13	25	0	0	0	0	1	0	4	821	0	0	785	1,997
1954	20	14	0	0	0	0	0	0	2	1,519	0	0	1,420	1,152
1955	156	3	0	0	0	0	0	0	0	130	0	0	79	100
1956	257	1	0	0	0	0	0	0	0	122	0	0	122	75
1957	257	2	0	0	0	0	0	0	0	153	0	0	153	150
Lifetime		51	0	0	0	0	1	0	7	3,560	0	0	3,167	$3,524

Bruce Hill

Bruce Hill
B: 7/9/1949
Racing Hometown: Topeka, KS

Year	Rank	Starts	Poles	1	2	3	4	5	6–10	Laps	Laps Led	Races Led	Miles	$
1974	101	1	0	0	0	0	0	0	0	189	0	0	473	1,575

Year	Rank	Starts	Poles	Finish						Laps	Laps Led	Races Led	Miles	$
				1	2	3	4	5	6–10					

Bruce Hill *continued*

Year	Rank	Starts	Poles	1	2	3	4	5	6–10	Laps	Laps Led	Races Led	Miles	$
1975	16	26	0	0	0	0	0	3	8	7,088	2	2	7,868	79,428
1976	23	22	0	0	0	0	0	0	4	3,469	3	1	5,138	43,705
1977	29	16	0	0	0	0	0	0	4	2,883	4	1	4,290	25,035
1978	32	14	0	0	0	0	0	0	2	2,805	0	0	3,796	26,445
1979	34	7	0	0	0	0	0	0	0	1,352	0	0	2,693	17,265
1980	50	6	0	0	0	0	0	0	0	418	0	0	808	7,540
1981	43	8	0	0	0	0	0	0	0	880	0	0	1,514	15,485
Lifetime		100	0	0	0	0	0	3	18	19,084	9	4	26,579	$216,478

Charlie Hill

Charles Hill
Racing Hometown: Winston-Salem, NC

Year	Rank	Starts	Poles	1	2	3	4	5	6–10	Laps	Laps Led	Races Led	Miles	$
1952	NR	1	0	0	0	0	0	0	0	217	0	0	217	50
Lifetime		1	0	0	0	0	0	0	0	217	0	0	217	$50

Cliff Hill

Clifford Hill

Year	Rank	Starts	Poles	1	2	3	4	5	6–10	Laps	Laps Led	Races Led	Miles	$
1961	152	1	0	0	0	0	0	0	0	31	0	0	80	50
Lifetime		1	0	0	0	0	0	0	0	31	0	0	80	$50

Frank Hill

Frank Hill

Year	Rank	Starts	Poles	1	2	3	4	5	6–10	Laps	Laps Led	Races Led	Miles	$
1978	NR	1	0	0	0	0	0	0	0	37	0	0	98	1,280
Lifetime		1	0	0	0	0	0	0	0	37	0	0	98	$1,280

Fred Hill

Fred Hill
Racing Hometown: Houston, TX

Year	Rank	Starts	Poles	1	2	3	4	5	6–10	Laps	Laps Led	Races Led	Miles	$
1971	NR	1	0	0	0	0	0	0	0	116	0	0	58	350
Lifetime		1	0	0	0	0	0	0	0	116	0	0	58	$350

Herb Hill

Herbert Hill
Racing Hometown: Las Vegas, NV

Year	Rank	Starts	Poles	1	2	3	4	5	6–10	Laps	Laps Led	Races Led	Miles	$
1955	187	1	0	0	0	0	0	0	0	70	0	0	70	40
Lifetime		1	0	0	0	0	0	0	0	70	0	0	70	$40

Jerry Hill

Jerry Hill
B: 7/25/1961
Racing Hometown: Brandywine, MD

Year	Rank	Starts	Poles	1	2	3	4	5	6–10	Laps	Laps Led	Races Led	Miles	$
1991	72	2	0	0	0	0	0	0	0	52	0	0	52	6,975
1992	51	4	0	0	0	0	0	0	0	520	0	0	554	17,705
1993	67T	2	0	0	0	0	0	0	0	353	0	0	359	13,885
1994	—		0											5,600
Lifetime		8	0	0	0	0	0	0	0	925	0	0	965	$44,165

Morris Hill

Morris Hill
Racing Hometown: Montgomery, AL

Year	Rank	Starts	Poles	1	2	3	4	5	6–10	Laps	Laps Led	Races Led	Miles	$
1955	NR	1	0	0	0	0	0	0	0	0	0	0	0	25
Lifetime		1	0	0	0	0	0	0	0	0	0	0	0	$25

Ray Hill

Raymond Hill
B: Medford, MA

Year	Rank	Starts	Poles	1	2	3	4	5	6–10	Laps	Laps Led	Races Led	Miles	$
1951	NR	1	0	0	0	0	0	0	0		0	0		25
Lifetime		1	0	0	0	0	0	0	0		0	0		$25

Ray Hill

Raymond Hill
B: 9/20/1931
Racing Hometown: Concord, NC

Year	Rank	Starts	Poles	1	2	3	4	5	6–10	Laps	Laps Led	Races Led	Miles	$
1966	73	6	0	0	0	0	0	0	3	1,430	0	0	604	1,045
1967	123	1	0	0	0	0	0	0	0	91	0	0	46	275
1968	NR	1	0	0	0	0	0	0	0	1	0	0	1	100
Lifetime		8	0	0	0	0	0	0	3	1,522	0	0	651	$1,420

Year	Rank	Starts	Poles	Finish 1	2	3	4	5	6–10	Laps	Laps Led	Races Led	Miles	$

Andy Hillenburg

Andrew Hillenburg
B: 4/30/1963
Racing Hometown: Indianapolis, IN

Year	Rank	Starts	Poles	1	2	3	4	5	6–10	Laps	Laps Led	Races Led	Miles	$
1991	64T	2	0	0	0	0	0	0	0	320	0	0	484	7,520
1993	91T	1	0	0	0	0	0	0	0	242	0	0	363	4,365
1995	65T	1	0	0	0	0	0	0	0	157	0	0	393	17,320
1996	—	0												1,000
Lifetime		4	0	0	0	0	0	0	0	719	0	0	1,240	$30,205

Harvey Hilligas

Harvey Hilligas
Racing Hometown: Philadelphia, PA

Year	Rank	Starts	Poles	1	2	3	4	5	6–10	Laps	Laps Led	Races Led	Miles	$
1949	NR	1	0	0	0	0	0	0	0	162	0	0	162	25
Lifetime		1	0	0	0	0	0	0	0	162	0	0	162	$25

Bobby Hillin Jr.

Robert Hillin Jr.
B: 6/5/1964
Racing Hometown: Midland, TX

Year	Rank	Starts	Poles	1	2	3	4	5	6–10	Laps	Laps Led	Races Led	Miles	$
1982	46	5	0	0	0	0	0	0	0	917	0	0	1,515	9,830
1983	37	12	0	0	0	0	0	0	0	2,791	0	0	4,199	31,425
1984	32	16	0	0	0	0	0	0	0	3,452	0	0	5,655	45,020
1985	15	28	0	0	0	0	0	0	5	8,636	2	2	10,204	145,070
1986	9	29	0	1	0	1	2	0	10	8,121	25	4	9,978	448,452
1987	19	29	0	0	0	0	0	1	3	6,889	1	1	8,559	346,735
1988	12	29	0	0	0	1	0	0	6	9,383	70	4	11,179	330,217
1989	16	28	0	0	0	0	0	1	6	8,377	26	4	10,296	283,181
1990	19	29	0	0	0	0	0	1	3	8,281	60	5	10,086	339,366
1991	30	22	0	0	0	0	0	0	1	6,152	10	1	8,351	251,645
1992	34	13	0	0	0	0	0	0	0	2,728	0	0	4,635	102,160
1993	27	30	0	0	0	0	0	0	0	8,343	3	1	9,768	263,540
1994	44	9	0	0	0	0	0	0	0	2,007	2	1	3,171	125,340
1995	37	18	0	0	0	0	0	0	1	4,410	1	1	6,351	244,270
1996	37	26	0	0	0	0	0	0	0	7,164	4	1	8,870	395,224
Lifetime		323	0	1	0	2	2	3	35	87,651	204	25	112,818	$3,361,475

Jimmy Hindman

James Hindman

Year	Rank	Starts	Poles	1	2	3	4	5	6–10	Laps	Laps Led	Races Led	Miles	$
1979	NR	1	0	0	0	0	0	0	0	2	0	0	1	350
Lifetime		1	0	0	0	0	0	0	0	2	0	0	1	$350

Joe Hines

Joseph Charleton Hines Jr.
B: 8/24/1937
Racing Hometown: Statesboro, GA

Year	Rank	Starts	Poles	1	2	3	4	5	6–10	Laps	Laps Led	Races Led	Miles	$
1969	NR	1	0	0	0	0	0	0	0	38	0	0	76	800
1970	107	1	0	0	0	0	0	0	0	43	0	0	108	245
1971	90	1	0	0	0	0	0	0	0	1	0	0	3	0
Lifetime		3	0	0	0	0	0	0	0	82	0	0	186	$1,045

Rudy Hires

Rudolph Hires
Racing Hometown: Norfolk, VA

Year	Rank	Starts	Poles	1	2	3	4	5	6–10	Laps	Laps Led	Races Led	Miles	$
1951	N/A	1	0	0	0	0	0	0	0	82	0	0	103	0
1952	162	1	0	0	0	0	0	0	0	267	0	0	334	50
Lifetime		2	0	0	0	0	0	0	0	349	0	0	436	$50

Dave Hirschfield

Dave Harry Hirschfield
B: 7/5/1930
Racing Hometown: Midlothian, IL

Year	Rank	Starts	Poles	1	2	3	4	5	6–10	Laps	Laps Led	Races Led	Miles	$
1960	128	2	0	0	0	0	0	0	0	50	0	0	125	100
Lifetime		2	0	0	0	0	0	0	0	50	0	0	125	$100

Butch Hirst

John Hirst
B: 8/29/1940
Racing Hometown: Orange City, FL

Year	Rank	Starts	Poles	1	2	3	4	5	6–10	Laps	Laps Led	Races Led	Miles	$
1970	56	5	0	0	0	0	0	0	0	663	0	0	1,398	5,414
1971	NR	1	0	0	0	0	0	0	0	2	0	0	5	0
Lifetime		6	0	0	0	0	0	0	0	665	0	0	1,403	$5,414

Year	Rank	Starts	Poles	Finish 1	2	3	4	5	6–10	Laps	Laps Led	Races Led	Miles	$

Mike Hiss

Michael Hiss
B: 7/7/1941
Racing Hometown: Norwalk, CT

Year	Rank	Starts	Poles	1	2	3	4	5	6–10	Laps	Laps Led	Races Led	Miles	$
1976	NR	1	0	0	0	0	0	0	0	169	0	0	423	1,365
Lifetime		1	0	0	0	0	0	0	0	169	0	0	423	$1,365

George Hixon

George Hixon
Racing Hometown: Soddy-Daisy, TN

Year	Rank	Starts	Poles	1	2	3	4	5	6–10	Laps	Laps Led	Races Led	Miles	$
1967	NR	1	0	0	0	0	0	0	0	187	0	0	94	120
Lifetime		1	0	0	0	0	0	0	0	187	0	0	94	$120

Dutch Hoag

Donald Hoag
B: 11/2/1926
Racing Hometown: Penn Yan, NY

Year	Rank	Starts	Poles	1	2	3	4	5	6–10	Laps	Laps Led	Races Led	Miles	$
1952	114T	1	0	0	0	0	0	0	0	163	0	0	82	25
1955	112	2	0	0	0	0	0	0	1	285	0	0	143	200
1957	NR	1	0	0	0	0	0	0	0	85	0	0	85	0
Lifetime		4	0	0	0	0	0	0	1	533	0	0	309	$225

Chuck Hobbs

Charles Hobbs
Racing Hometown: Gibson, OH

Year	Rank	Starts	Poles	1	2	3	4	5	6–10	Laps	Laps Led	Races Led	Miles	$
1957	181	1	0	0	0	0	0	0	0		0	0		25
Lifetime		1	0	0	0	0	0	0	0		0	0		$25

David Hobbs

David Wishart Hobbs
B: 6/9/1939
Racing Hometown: Upper Buddington, England

Year	Rank	Starts	Poles	1	2	3	4	5	6–10	Laps	Laps Led	Races Led	Miles	$
1976	NR	2	0	0	0	0	0	0	0	255	2	1	544	3,030
Lifetime		2	0	0	0	0	0	0	0	255	2	1	544	$3,030

Gene Hobby

Eugene Hobby
B: 10/17/1937
Racing Hometown: Henderson, NC

Year	Rank	Starts	Poles	1	2	3	4	5	6–10	Laps	Laps Led	Races Led	Miles	$
1964	44	18	0	0	0	0	0	0	3	4,013	0	0	1,804	2,795
1965	51	15	0	0	0	0	1	0	1	1,979	0	0	971	2,560
1966	135	2	0	0	0	0	0	0	0	34	0	0	12	0
Lifetime		35	0	0	0	0	1	0	4	6,026	0	0	2,788	$5,355

Cotton Hodges

James Elmer Hodges
B: 5/12/1926
Racing Hometown: Hollywood, FL

Year	Rank	Starts	Poles	1	2	3	4	5	6–10	Laps	Laps Led	Races Led	Miles	$
1953	173	1	0	0	0	0	0	0	0	32	0	0	131	25
1954	NR	1	0	0	0	0	0	0	0	164	0	0	82	25
1963	145	1	0	0	0	0	0	0	0	9	0	0	5	50
Lifetime		3	0	0	0	0	0	0	0	205	0	0	218	$100

Irv Hoerr

Irv Hoerr
B: 1947
Racing Hometown: Peoria, IL

Year	Rank	Starts	Poles	1	2	3	4	5	6–10	Laps	Laps Led	Races Led	Miles	$
1987	NR	1	0	0	0	0	0	0	0	114	0	0	299	1,705
1990	47	2	0	0	0	0	0	0	2	164	3	1	405	14,775
1991	52	3	0	0	0	0	0	0	0	243	0	0	608	11,125
1992	95T	1	0	0	0	0	0	0	0	42	0	0	106	4,725
Lifetime		7	0	0	0	0	0	0	2	563	3	1	1,418	$32,330

Charlie Hoff

Charles Hoff
Racing Hometown: Bloomfield, NJ

Year	Rank	Starts	Poles	1	2	3	4	5	6–10	Laps	Laps Led	Races Led	Miles	$
1953	127T	1	0	0	0	0	0	0	0		0	0		25
Lifetime		1	0	0	0	0	0	0	0		0	0		$25

Dick Hoffman

Richard Hoffman

Year	Rank	Starts	Poles	1	2	3	4	5	6–10	Laps	Laps Led	Races Led	Miles	$
1957	164	1	0	0	0	0	0	0	0	50	0	0	125	60
Lifetime		1	0	0	0	0	0	0	0	50	0	0	125	$60

Year	Rank	Starts	Poles	Finish 1	2	3	4	5	6–10	Laps	Laps Led	Races Led	Miles	$

Don Hoffman
Donald Hoffman
Racing Hometown: Des Moines, IA

Year	Rank	Starts	Poles	1	2	3	4	5	6–10	Laps	Laps Led	Races Led	Miles	$
1975	NR	1	0	0	0	0	0	0	0	178	0	0	445	1,650
Lifetime		1	0	0	0	0	0	0	0	178	0	0	445	$1,650

John Hoffman
John Hoffman
Racing Hometown: Charlotte, NC

Year	Rank	Starts	Poles	1	2	3	4	5	6–10	Laps	Laps Led	Races Led	Miles	$
1963	146	1	0	0	0	0	0	0	0	51	0	0	13	100
Lifetime		1	0	0	0	0	0	0	0	51	0	0	13	$100

Bob Hogle
Robert Hogle
B: 1934
Racing Hometown: Buena Park, CA

Year	Rank	Starts	Poles	1	2	3	4	5	6–10	Laps	Laps Led	Races Led	Miles	$
1959	NR	2	0	0	0	0	0	0	0	429	0	0	184	165
1960	149	1	0	0	0	0	0	0	0	3	0	0	4	0
Lifetime		3	0	0	0	0	0	0	0	432	0	0	188	$165

Al Holbert
Alvah R. Holbert
B: 11/11/1946   D: 9/30/1988   *Killed in private plane crash.*
Racing Hometown: Warrington, PA

Year	Rank	Starts	Poles	1	2	3	4	5	6–10	Laps	Laps Led	Races Led	Miles	$
1976	NR	1	0	0	0	0	0	0	0	7	0	0	11	855
1978	34	12	0	0	0	0	0	0	3	2,479	0	0	3,919	31,075
1979	45	6	0	0	0	0	0	0	1	938	5	1	1,620	14,170
Lifetime		19	0	0	0	0	0	0	4	3,424	5	1	5,549	$46,100

Gene Holcomb
Gene Holcomb
Racing Hometown: Aberdeen, MD

Year	Rank	Starts	Poles	1	2	3	4	5	6–10	Laps	Laps Led	Races Led	Miles	$
1954	161	2	0	0	0	0	0	0	0	369	0	0	283	50
1955	145	2	0	0	0	0	0	0	0	188	0	0	147	25
Lifetime		4	0	0	0	0	0	0	0	557	0	0	430	$75

Jerry Holden
Jerry Holden
Racing Hometown: Springfield, MO

Year	Rank	Starts	Poles	1	2	3	4	5	6–10	Laps	Laps Led	Races Led	Miles	$
1986	NR	1	0	0	0	0	0	0	0	100	0	0	100	1,200
1987	105	2	0	0	0	0	0	0	0	141	0	0	362	4,100
Lifetime		3	0	0	0	0	0	0	0	241	0	0	462	$5,300

Joe Holder
Joseph Holder
Racing Hometown: Franklinton, NC

Year	Rank	Starts	Poles	1	2	3	4	5	6–10	Laps	Laps Led	Races Led	Miles	$
1965	114	2	0	0	0	0	0	0	0	135	0	0	47	200
1966	146T	1	0	0	0	0	0	0	0	2	0	0	1	0
Lifetime		3	0	0	0	0	0	0	0	137	0	0	48	$200

Bill Holland
William A. Holland
B: 12/18/1907   D: 5/19/1984
Racing Hometown: Bridgeport, CT

Year	Rank	Starts	Poles	1	2	3	4	5	6–10	Laps	Laps Led	Races Led	Miles	$
1951	55	7	0	0	0	0	1	0	1	224	0	0	191	435
1952	179	1	0	0	0	0	0	0	0	123	0	0	123	25
Lifetime		8	0	0	0	0	1	0	1	347	0	0	314	$460

Bill Hollar
William Mack Hollar
B: 9/6/1938
Racing Hometown: Burlington, NC

Year	Rank	Starts	Poles	1	2	3	4	5	6–10	Laps	Laps Led	Races Led	Miles	$
1970	66	3	0	0	0	0	0	0	1	792	0	0	414	970
1971	43	11	0	0	0	0	0	0	1	2,095	0	0	1,602	4,275
1972	112	1	0	0	0	0	0	0	0	64	0	0	128	705
1973	89	1	0	0	0	0	0	0	0	419	0	0	419	1,060
1975	60	3	0	0	0	0	0	0	0	1,107	0	0	777	1,865
1976	115T	1	0	0	0	0	0	0	0	2	0	0	5	540
1978	72	3	0	0	0	0	0	0	0	90	0	0	62	1,360
1979	48	5	0	0	0	0	0	0	0	552	0	0	381	2,545
1980	92T	1	0	0	0	0	0	0	0	281	0	0	152	600
Lifetime		29	0	0	0	0	0	0	2	5,402	0	0	3,940	$13,920

Year	Rank	Starts	Poles	Finish 1	2	3	4	5	6–10	Laps	Laps Led	Races Led	Miles	$

Armond Holley

Armond Holley
B: 7/19/1934
Racing Hometown: Columbus, MS

Year	Rank	Starts	Poles	1	2	3	4	5	6–10	Laps	Laps Led	Races Led	Miles	$
1967	69	5	0	0	0	0	0	0	0	378	0	0	451	2,775
Lifetime		5	0	0	0	0	0	0	0	378	0	0	451	$2,775

Claude Holliday

Claude Holliday (Buck)
Racing Hometown: Waddington, NY

Year	Rank	Starts	Poles	1	2	3	4	5	6–10	Laps	Laps Led	Races Led	Miles	$
1957	NR	1	0	0	0	0	0	0	0	12	0	0	28	50
Lifetime		1	0	0	0	0	0	0	0	12	0	0	28	$50

Red Hollingsworth

Red Hollingsworth
Racing Hometown: Chattanooga, TN

Year	Rank	Starts	Poles	1	2	3	4	5	6–10	Laps	Laps Led	Races Led	Miles	$
1961	154	3	0	0	0	0	0	0	0	70	0	0	173	450
Lifetime		3	0	0	0	0	0	0	0	70	0	0	173	$450

Jack Holloway

Jack Holloway
Racing Hometown: Winston-Salem, NC

Year	Rank	Starts	Poles	1	2	3	4	5	6–10	Laps	Laps Led	Races Led	Miles	$
1950	49	2	0	0	0	0	0	0	2	192	0	0	96	225
1951	N/A	3	0	0	0	0	0	0	0	0	0	0	0	75
1952	205	1	0	0	0	0	0	0	0	12	0	0	6	25
Lifetime		6	0	0	0	0	0	0	2	204	0	0	102	$325

Bill Holluck

William Holluck
Racing Hometown: Martinsville, VA

Year	Rank	Starts	Poles	1	2	3	4	5	6–10	Laps	Laps Led	Races Led	Miles	$
1951	N/A	1	0	0	0	0	0	0	0		0	0		25
Lifetime		1	0	0	0	0	0	0	0		0	0		$25

Elgin Holmes

Elgin Holmes
Racing Hometown: Miami, FL

Year	Rank	Starts	Poles	1	2	3	4	5	6–10	Laps	Laps Led	Races Led	Miles	$
1956	254	1	0	0	0	0	0	0	0	71	0	0	178	50
1957	195	1	0	0	0	0	0	0	0	14	0	0	35	35
1958	134T	1	0	0	0	0	0	0	0	91	0	0	91	75
Lifetime		3	0	0	0	0	0	0	0	176	0	0	304	$160

Harland Holmes

Harland Holmes
Racing Hometown: Lewiston, NY

Year	Rank	Starts	Poles	1	2	3	4	5	6–10	Laps	Laps Led	Races Led	Miles	$
1950	100	3	0	0	0	0	0	0	0	177	0	0	89	50
Lifetime		3	0	0	0	0	0	0	0	177	0	0	89	$50

Hop Holmes

Preston Holmes
B: 1933   D: 7/4/1989
Racing Hometown: Loris, SC

Year	Rank	Starts	Poles	1	2	3	4	5	6–10	Laps	Laps Led	Races Led	Miles	$
1965	109	1	0	0	0	0	0	0	0	71	0	0	36	100
Lifetime		1	0	0	0	0	0	0	0	71	0	0	36	$100

Paul Dean Holt

Paul Dean Holt
B: 3/30/1936
Racing Hometown: Sweetwater, TN

Year	Rank	Starts	Poles	1	2	3	4	5	6–10	Laps	Laps Led	Races Led	Miles	$
1966	98	4	0	0	0	0	0	0	0	213	0	0	87	475
1967	41	24	0	0	0	0	0	0	1	3,165	0	0	1,962	4,330
1968	18	40	0	0	0	0	0	0	0	5,863	0	0	3,498	8,986
1969	46	14	0	0	0	0	0	0	0	1,408	0	0	1,016	4,442
1975	96	2	0	0	0	0	0	0	0	120	0	0	72	685
1977	96T	1	0	0	0	0	0	0	0	47	0	0	28	275
Lifetime		85	0	0	0	0	0	0	1	10,816	0	0	6,663	$17,715

Willard Holt

Willard Holt
Racing Hometown: Cincinnati, OH

Year	Rank	Starts	Poles	1	2	3	4	5	6–10	Laps	Laps Led	Races Led	Miles	$
1955	157	1	0	0	0	0	0	0	0	37	0	0	152	50
Lifetime		1	0	0	0	0	0	0	0	37	0	0	152	$50

Year	Rank	Starts	Poles	Finish 1	2	3	4	5	6–10	Laps	Laps Led	Races Led	Miles	$

Frank Holzhauer

Frank Holzhauer
Racing Hometown: Lakewood, NJ

Year	Rank	Starts	Poles	1	2	3	4	5	6–10	Laps	Laps Led	Races Led	Miles	$
1951	N/A	1	0	0	0	0	0	0	0		0	0		25
Lifetime		1	0	0	0	0	0	0	0		0	0		$25

Hooker Hood

Clarence Caldwell Hood
B: 4/9/1926
Racing Hometown: Memphis, TN

Year	Rank	Starts	Poles	1	2	3	4	5	6–10	Laps	Laps Led	Races Led	Miles	$
1954	112	2	0	0	0	0	0	0	0	248	0	0	244	75
1955	75	3	0	0	0	0	0	0	0	256	0	0	420	175
Lifetime		5	0	0	0	0	0	0	0	504	0	0	665	$250

Jeff Hooker

Jeffrey Hooker
Racing Hometown: Valley City, OH

Year	Rank	Starts	Poles	1	2	3	4	5	6–10	Laps	Laps Led	Races Led	Miles	$
1984	46	4	0	0	0	0	0	0	0	980	0	0	861	4,495
1985	NR	1	0	0	0	0	0	0	0	11	0	0	15	1,100
Lifetime		5	0	0	0	0	0	0	0	991	0	0	876	$5,595

Lance Hooper

Lance Hooper
B: 6/1/1967
Racing Hometown: Palmdale, CA

Year	Rank	Starts	Poles	1	2	3	4	5	6–10	Laps	Laps Led	Races Led	Miles	$
1996	61	1	0	0	0	0	0	0	0	302	0	0	302	9,645
Lifetime		1	0	0	0	0	0	0	0	302	0	0	302	$9,645

Carl Hoover

Carl Hoover

Year	Rank	Starts	Poles	1	2	3	4	5	6–10	Laps	Laps Led	Races Led	Miles	$
1955	238	1	0	0	0	0	0	0	0	35	0	0	35	20
Lifetime		1	0	0	0	0	0	0	0	35	0	0	35	$20

Ronnie Hopkins Jr.

Ronald Hopkins Jr.
B: 1962
Racing Hometown: Greenville, SC

Year	Rank	Starts	Poles	1	2	3	4	5	6–10	Laps	Laps Led	Races Led	Miles	$
1983	31	13	0	0	0	0	0	0	0	2,563	0	0	3,101	26,455
Lifetime		13	0	0	0	0	0	0	0	2,563	0	0	3,101	$26,455

Jim Hopkinson

James Hopkinson
B: 12/13/1942
Racing Hometown: Carmichael, CA

Year	Rank	Starts	Poles	1	2	3	4	5	6–10	Laps	Laps Led	Races Led	Miles	$
1980	95	1	0	0	0	0	0	0	0	42	0	0	110	750
Lifetime		1	0	0	0	0	0	0	0	42	0	0	110	$750

Ron Hornaday

Ronald Hornaday
B: 1/13/1931
Racing Hometown: San Fernando, CA

Year	Rank	Starts	Poles	1	2	3	4	5	6–10	Laps	Laps Led	Races Led	Miles	$
1955	175T	1	0	0	0	0	0	0	0	90	0	0	90	25
1957	132T	1	0	0	0	0	0	0	0	95	0	0	95	100
1958	145	2	0	0	0	0	0	0	0	53	0	0	60	125
1959	NR	1	0	0	0	0	0	0	0	325	0	0	130	75
1960	83	3	0	0	0	0	1	0	0	283	0	0	328	610
1961	103	4	0	0	0	0	0	1	0	283	0	0	219	325
1963	45	2	0	0	0	0	0	0	1	316	0	0	853	1,600
1966	62	1	0	0	0	0	0	0	1	171	0	0	462	900
1971	NR	1	0	0	0	0	0	0	0	177	0	0	443	1,750
1973	113	1	0	0	0	0	0	0	0	62	0	0	162	685
Lifetime		17	0	0	0	0	1	1	2	1,855	0	0	2,841	$6,195

Ron Hornaday Jr.

Ronald Lee Hornaday Jr.
B: 6/20/1958
Racing Hometown: Palmdale, CA

Year	Rank	Starts	Poles	1	2	3	4	5	6–10	Laps	Laps Led	Races Led	Miles	$
1992	64	2	0	0	0	0	0	0	0	373	0	0	482	11,290
1993	69	1	0	0	0	0	0	0	0	307	0	0	307	6,660
1994	61	2	0	0	0	0	0	0	0	350	1	1	431	13,710

Year	Rank	Starts	Poles	Finish						Laps	Laps Led	Races Led	Miles	$
				1	2	3	4	5	6–10					

Ron Hornaday Jr. *continued*

Year	Rank	Starts	Poles	1	2	3	4	5	6–10	Laps	Laps Led	Races Led	Miles	$
1995	58	1	0	0	0	0	0	0	0	307	0	0	307	9,660
Lifetime		6	0	0	0	0	0	0	0	1,337	1	1	1,527	$41,320

Jimmy Horton

James Horton
B: 7/3/1956
Racing Hometown: Folsom, N J

Year	Rank	Starts	Poles	1	2	3	4	5	6–10	Laps	Laps Led	Races Led	Miles	$
1987	67	2	0	0	0	0	0	0	0	256	0	0	640	4,405
1988	41	8	0	0	0	0	0	0	0	2,007	0	0	2,894	23,575
1989	46	5	0	0	0	0	0	0	0	955	0	0	1,391	19,232
1990	36	9	0	0	0	0	0	0	0	2,264	0	0	3,545	72,375
1991	—	0												2,400
1992	39	9	0	0	0	0	0	0	0	2,166	0	0	2,874	50,125
1993	38	13	0	0	0	0	0	0	0	2,198	0	0	3,632	115,105
1994	62	1	0	0	0	0	0	0	0	199	0	0	498	33,485
1995	61T	1	0	0	0	0	0	0	0	192	0	0	480	16,550
Lifetime		48	0	0	0	0	0	0	0	10,237	0	0	15,953	$337,252

Lee Hough

Lee Hough
Racing Hometown: Princeton, NJ

Year	Rank	Starts	Poles	1	2	3	4	5	6–10	Laps	Laps Led	Races Led	Miles	$
1950	NR	2	0	0	0	0	0	0	0	60	0	0	30	0
Lifetime		2	0	0	0	0	0	0	0	60	0	0	30	$0

Pappy Hough

Roscoe Morris Hough
B: 11/22/1902 D: 6/17/1996
Racing Hometown: Paterson, N J

Year	Rank	Starts	Poles	1	2	3	4	5	6–10	Laps	Laps Led	Races Led	Miles	$
1950	26	5	0	0	0	0	0	0	2	296	0	0	215	325
1951	31	9	0	0	0	0	0	1	3		0	0		950
1952	NR	4	0	0	0	0	0	0	1	565	0	0	393	250
1955	85	3	0	0	0	0	0	0	0	422	0	0	256	160
Lifetime		21	0	0	0	0	0	1	6	1,283	0	0	864	$1,660

Kevin Housby

Kevin Housby
B: 1956
Racing Hometown: Des Moines, IA

Year	Rank	Starts	Poles	1	2	3	4	5	6–10	Laps	Laps Led	Races Led	Miles	$
1979	92T	1	0	0	0	0	0	0	0	149	0	0	396	3,190
1980	75	3	0	0	0	0	0	0	0	524	0	0	1,006	6,165
1981	103	1	0	0	0	0	0	0	0	53	0	0	133	2,480
Lifetime		5	0	0	0	0	0	0	0	726	0	0	1,535	$11,835

Chuck Housley

Chuck Housley
Racing Hometown: Columbus, GA

Year	Rank	Starts	Poles	1	2	3	4	5	6–10	Laps	Laps Led	Races Led	Miles	$
1953	65	2	0	0	0	0	0	0	0		0	0		50
Lifetime		2	0	0	0	0	0	0	0		0	0		$50

Tommy Houston

Thomas C. Houston
B: 1/29/1945
Racing Hometown: Hickory, NC

Year	Rank	Starts	Poles	1	2	3	4	5	6–10	Laps	Laps Led	Races Led	Miles	$
1980	48	4	0	0	0	0	0	0	0	1,170	10	1	949	5,020
1981	52	7	0	0	0	0	0	0	0	2,219	0	0	1,902	20,760
1982	88	1	0	0	0	0	0	0	0	238	0	0	129	875
1985	91T	1	0	0	0	0	0	0	0	47	0	0	64	1,645
Lifetime		13	0	0	0	0	0	0	0	3,674	10	1	3,044	$28,300

Roz Howard

Roz Howard
Racing Hometown: Macon, GA

Year	Rank	Starts	Poles	1	2	3	4	5	6–10	Laps	Laps Led	Races Led	Miles	$
1956	57	1	0	0	0	0	0	0	0	343	0	0	472	250
1958	NR	2	0	0	0	0	0	0	1	300	0	0	150	215
1960	49	3	0	0	0	0	0	0	2	676	0	0	535	1,490
Lifetime		6	0	0	0	0	0	0	3	1,319	0	0	1,157	$1,955

Year	Rank	Starts	Poles	Finish 1	2	3	4	5	6–10	Laps	Laps Led	Races Led	Miles	$

Zane Howell

Zane Howell
Racing Hometown: South Bend, IN

Year	Rank	Starts	Poles	1	2	3	4	5	6–10	Laps	Laps Led	Races Led	Miles	$
1952	NR	1	0	0	0	0	0	0	0	109	0	0	55	25
Lifetime		1	0	0	0	0	0	0	0	109	0	0	55	$25

Augie Howerton

August Howerton
Racing Hometown: Tulsa, OK

Year	Rank	Starts	Poles	1	2	3	4	5	6–10	Laps	Laps Led	Races Led	Miles	$
1956	NR	1	0	0	0	0	0	0	1	181	0	0	91	150
Lifetime		1	0	0	0	0	0	0	1	181	0	0	91	$150

Ed Howland

Edward Howland

Year	Rank	Starts	Poles	1	2	3	4	5	6–10	Laps	Laps Led	Races Led	Miles	$
1970	NR	1	0	0	0	0	0	0	0	91	0	0	238	760
Lifetime		1	0	0	0	0	0	0	0	91	0	0	238	$760

John Hren

John Hren
Racing Hometown: Bloomington, CA

Year	Rank	Starts	Poles	1	2	3	4	5	6–10	Laps	Laps Led	Races Led	Miles	$
1972	110	1	0	0	0	0	0	0	0	45	0	0	118	720
1973	115	1	0	0	0	0	0	0	0	58	0	0	152	1,020
Lifetime		2	0	0	0	0	0	0	0	103	0	0	270	$1,740

Jack Hubbard

Jack Hubbard

Year	Rank	Starts	Poles	1	2	3	4	5	6–10	Laps	Laps Led	Races Led	Miles	$
1955	210	1	0	0	0	0	0	0	0	56	0	0	84	50
Lifetime		1	0	0	0	0	0	0	0	56	0	0	84	$50

Chuck Huckabee

Chuck Huckabee (Huck)
Racing Hometown: Chattanooga, TN

Year	Rank	Starts	Poles	1	2	3	4	5	6–10	Laps	Laps Led	Races Led	Miles	$
1963	105	3	0	0	0	0	0	0	1	171	0	0	86	450
1964	NR	9	0	0	0	0	0	0	0	788	0	0	306	830
Lifetime		12	0	0	0	0	0	0	1	959	0	0	391	$1,280

Cliff Hucul

Clifford Hucul
B: 8/21/1948
Racing Hometown: Prince George, B.C., Canada

Year	Rank	Starts	Poles	1	2	3	4	5	6–10	Laps	Laps Led	Races Led	Miles	$
1986	91	2	0	0	0	0	0	0	0	229	0	0	232	2,325
Lifetime		2	0	0	0	0	0	0	0	229	0	0	232	$2,325

Skip Hudson

Skip Hudson
B: 1932
Racing Hometown: Arlington, CA

Year	Rank	Starts	Poles	1	2	3	4	5	6–10	Laps	Laps Led	Races Led	Miles	$
1963	147	1	0	0	0	0	0	0	0	75	0	0	203	275
1964	57	1	0	0	0	0	0	0	1	178	0	0	481	1,075
1965	79	1	0	0	0	0	0	0	0	90	0	0	243	635
1966	126	1	0	0	0	0	0	0	0	30	0	0	81	500
Lifetime		4	0	0	0	0	0	0	1	373	0	0	1,007	$2,485

Jerry Hufflin

Jerry Calvin Hufflin
B: 6/4/1944
Racing Hometown: Greenville, SC

Year	Rank	Starts	Poles	1	2	3	4	5	6–10	Laps	Laps Led	Races Led	Miles	$
1974	100	2	0	0	0	0	0	0	0	262	0	0	155	900
1990	98T	1	0	0	0	0	0	0	0	130	0	0	130	2,750
Lifetime		3	0	0	0	0	0	0	0	392	0	0	285	$3,650

Stuart Huffman

Alan Stuart Huffman
Racing Hometown: Newton, NC

Year	Rank	Starts	Poles	1	2	3	4	5	6–10	Laps	Laps Led	Races Led	Miles	$
1980	96T	2	0	0	0	0	0	0	0	517	0	0	535	1,310
Lifetime		2	0	0	0	0	0	0	0	517	0	0	535	$1,310

George Hufford

George Hufford
Racing Hometown: McKeesport, PA

Year	Rank	Starts	Poles	1	2	3	4	5	6–10	Laps	Laps Led	Races Led	Miles	$
1952	151	3	0	0	0	0	0	0	0	192	0	0	96	75
Lifetime		3	0	0	0	0	0	0	0	192	0	0	96	$75

Year	Rank	Starts	Poles	Finish 1	2	3	4	5	6–10	Laps	Laps Led	Races Led	Miles	$

Ray Hughes

Raymond Hughes
Racing Hometown: Asheboro, NC

Year	Rank	Starts	Poles	1	2	3	4	5	6–10	Laps	Laps Led	Races Led	Miles	$
1962	56	6	0	0	0	0	0	0	2	1,289	0	0	536	965
1963	126T	1	0	0	0	0	0	0	0	183	0	0	46	110
Lifetime		7	0	0	0	0	0	0	2	1,472	0	0	582	$1,075

Lloyd Hulette

Lloyd Hulette
Racing Hometown: Cincinnati, OH

Year	Rank	Starts	Poles	1	2	3	4	5	6–10	Laps	Laps Led	Races Led	Miles	$
1953	39	1	0	0	0	0	0	0	0	328	0	0	451	250
Lifetime		1	0	0	0	0	0	0	0	328	0	0	451	$250

Jim Hull

James Hull
B: 1952
Racing Hometown: Clarkston, MI

Year	Rank	Starts	Poles	1	2	3	4	5	6–10	Laps	Laps Led	Races Led	Miles	$
1985	86T	1	0	0	0	0	0	0	0	68	0	0	136	1,570
1986	99	1	0	0	0	0	0	0	0	191	0	0	382	5,390
Lifetime		2	0	0	0	0	0	0	0	259	0	0	518	$6,960

Don Hume

Donald Hume
B: 5/8/1938
Racing Hometown: Belvedere, NJ

Year	Rank	Starts	Poles	1	2	3	4	5	6–10	Laps	Laps Led	Races Led	Miles	$
1964	137	2	0	0	0	0	0	0	0	18	0	0	26	900
1965	66	4	0	0	0	0	0	0	0	640	0	0	916	2,720
1981	NR	1	0	0	0	0	0	0	0	101	0	0	103	590
1984	NR	1	0	0	0	0	0	0	0	299	0	0	455	1,595
1985	38	7	0	0	0	0	0	0	0	2,057	0	0	1,906	22,230
Lifetime		15	0	0	0	0	0	0	0	3,115	0	0	3,406	$28,035

Lee Humphers

Lee Humphers
Racing Hometown: San Pablo, CA

Year	Rank	Starts	Poles	1	2	3	4	5	6–10	Laps	Laps Led	Races Led	Miles	$
1957	152T	1	0	0	0	0	0	0	0	91	0	0	91	50
Lifetime		1	0	0	0	0	0	0	0	91	0	0	91	$50

Dave Humphrey

David Humphrey

Year	Rank	Starts	Poles	1	2	3	4	5	6–10	Laps	Laps Led	Races Led	Miles	$
1951	N/A	1	0	0	0	0	0	0	0		0	0		0
Lifetime		1	0	0	0	0	0	0	0		0	0		$0

Bob Hundley

Robert Hundley
Racing Hometown: Richmond, VA

Year	Rank	Starts	Poles	1	2	3	4	5	6–10	Laps	Laps Led	Races Led	Miles	$
1959	NR	1	0	0	0	0	0	0	0	141	0	0	71	100
Lifetime		1	0	0	0	0	0	0	0	141	0	0	71	$100

Curtis Hunt

Curtis Hunt
Racing Hometown: Greensboro, NC

Year	Rank	Starts	Poles	1	2	3	4	5	6–10	Laps	Laps Led	Races Led	Miles	$
1951	N/A	1	0	0	0	0	0	0	0	15	0	0	15	25
Lifetime		1	0	0	0	0	0	0	0	15	0	0	15	$25

Fred Hunt

Fred Hunt
Racing Hometown: Tracy, CA

Year	Rank	Starts	Poles	1	2	3	4	5	6–10	Laps	Laps Led	Races Led	Miles	$
1956	182	2	0	0	0	0	0	0	0	118	0	0	99	100
1957	195	1	0	0	0	0	0	0	0	20	0	0	50	50
Lifetime		3	0	0	0	0	0	0	0	138	0	0	149	$150

T. C. Hunt

Theodore C. Hunt
B: 4/7/1926   D: 3/1/1995
Racing Hometown: Atlanta, GA

Year	Rank	Starts	Poles	1	2	3	4	5	6–10	Laps	Laps Led	Races Led	Miles	$
1960	100	3	0	0	0	0	0	0	0	353	0	0	497	600
1961	48	7	0	0	0	0	0	0	0	940	0	0	1,445	2,750
1962	62	9	0	0	0	0	0	0	2	920	0	0	614	1,340

Year	Rank	Starts	Poles	Finish 1	2	3	4	5	6–10	Laps	Laps Led	Races Led	Miles	$

T. C. Hunt *continued*

Year	Rank	Starts	Poles	1	2	3	4	5	6–10	Laps	Laps Led	Races Led	Miles	$
1963	60	3	0	0	0	0	0	0	0	754	0	0	947	865
1965	78	1	0	0	0	0	0	0	0	214	0	0	321	550
1969	NR	1	0	0	0	0	0	0	0	53	0	0	141	1,050
Lifetime		24	0	0	0	0	0	0	2	3,234	0	0	3,966	$7,155

Bob Hunter

Robert Hunter
Racing Hometown: Indianapolis, IN

Year	Rank	Starts	Poles	1	2	3	4	5	6–10	Laps	Laps Led	Races Led	Miles	$
1953	NR	1	0	0	0	0	0	0	0	210	0	0	289	105
Lifetime		1	0	0	0	0	0	0	0	210	0	0	289	$105

Jim Hunter

James Hunter
B: 1936
Racing Hometown: Knoxville, TN

Year	Rank	Starts	Poles	1	2	3	4	5	6–10	Laps	Laps Led	Races Led	Miles	$
1965	96	1	0	0	0	0	1	0	0	191	0	0	96	300
1966	139	1	0	0	0	0	0	0	0	8	0	0	4	0
1967	91	3	1	0	0	1	0	0	0	382	0	0	191	720
Lifetime		5	1	0	0	1	1	0	0	581	0	0	291	$1,020

Jim Hurlbert

James Hurlbert
Racing Hometown: Mahomet, IL

Year	Rank	Starts	Poles	1	2	3	4	5	6–10	Laps	Laps Led	Races Led	Miles	$
1974	—	0												325
1979	106T	1	0	0	0	0	0	0	0	150	0	0	300	1,400
1980	107	1	0	0	0	0	0	0	0	33	0	0	83	2,950
1982	NR	1	0	0	0	0	0	0	0	1	0	0	3	1,430
1984	—	0												1,450
Lifetime		3	0	0	0	0	0	0	0	184	0	0	385	$7,555

Mark Hurley

Harry Mark Hurley
B: 12/12/1936
Racing Hometown: Johnson City, TN

Year	Rank	Starts	Poles	1	2	3	4	5	6–10	Laps	Laps Led	Races Led	Miles	$
1961	135	1	0	0	0	0	0	0	0	224	0	0	90	125
1962	99	3	0	0	0	0	0	0	0	289	0	0	145	100
1963	92	3	0	0	0	0	1	0	0	668	0	0	274	635
1964	71	9	0	0	0	0	0	0	1	1,082	0	0	504	1,770
Lifetime		16	0	0	0	0	1	0	1	2,263	0	0	1,011	$2,630

Bob Hurt

Robert Hurt
Racing Hometown: Richmond, VA

Year	Rank	Starts	Poles	1	2	3	4	5	6–10	Laps	Laps Led	Races Led	Miles	$
1963	NR	1	0	0	0	0	0	0	0	144	0	0	48	75
Lifetime		1	0	0	0	0	0	0	0	144	0	0	48	$75

Jim Hurtubise

James Ernest Hurtubise
B: 12/5/1932   D: 1/6/1989
Racing Hometown: N. Tonawanda, NY

Year	Rank	Starts	Poles	1	2	3	4	5	6–10	Laps	Laps Led	Races Led	Miles	$
1957	99	2	0	0	0	0	0	0	1	244	0	0	122	210
1963	NR	4	0	0	0	0	0	0	0	583	0	0	1,196	1,300
1964	NR	1	0	0	0	0	0	0	0	77	2	1	116	585
1966	NR	6	0	1	1	0	0	1	2	1,215	158	4	2,434	25,010
1967	NR	2	0	0	0	0	0	0	1	196	0	0	490	2,600
1968	46	6	0	0	0	0	0	0	1	982	0	0	1,520	4,490
1969	NR	1	0	0	0	0	0	0	0	63	0	0	168	1,125
1970	63	2	0	0	0	0	0	0	1	211	0	0	528	2,575
1971	84	3	0	0	0	0	0	0	1	290	0	0	682	4,100
1972	NR	1	0	0	0	0	0	0	0	100	0	0	250	1,700
1974	78	2	0	0	0	0	0	0	0	344	0	0	633	5,200
1976	88T	1	0	0	0	0	0	0	0	180	0	0	450	3,975
1977	58	4	0	0	0	0	0	0	0	235	0	0	570	5,110
1978	—	0												700
1979	—	0												835
Lifetime		35	0	1	1	0	0	1	7	4,720	160	5	9,157	$59,515

Year	Rank	Starts	Poles	Finish						Laps	Laps Led	Races Led	Miles	$
				1	2	3	4	5	6–10	Laps	Led	Led	Miles	$

Joe Dean Huss

Joe Dean Huss
B: 3/8/1939
Racing Hometown: Roanoke Rapids, NC

Year	Rank	Starts	Poles	1	2	3	4	5	6–10	Laps	Laps Led	Races Led	Miles	$
1971	NR	3	0	0	0	0	0	0	0	1,242	0	0	671	1,435
Lifetime		3	0	0	0	0	0	0	0	1,242	0	0	671	$1,435

Dick Hutcherson

Richard Leon Hutcherson
B: 11/30/1931
Racing Hometown: Keokuk, IA

Year	Rank	Starts	Poles	1	2	3	4	5	6–10	Laps	Laps Led	Races Led	Miles	$
1964	76	4	2	0	1	0	0	1	0	592	75	2	362	1,585
1965	2	52	9	9	9	8	4	2	5	11,610	2,065	23	8,131	57,851
1966	28	14	2	3	0	2	1	2	1	3,152	400	7	3,042	22,985
1967	3	33	9	2	9	7	3	1	3	8,893	1,455	21	7,278	85,160
Lifetime		103	22	14	19	17	8	6	9	24,247	3,995	53	18,812	$167,581

Ron Hutcherson

Ronald Hutcherson
B: 4/24/1943
Racing Hometown: Keokuk, IA

Year	Rank	Starts	Poles	1	2	3	4	5	6–10	Laps	Laps Led	Races Led	Miles	$
1972	NR	1	0	0	0	0	0	0	0	29	0	0	29	550
1977	NR	5	0	0	0	0	0	0	1	1,104	0	0	2,075	26,210
1978	68	3	0	0	0	0	1	0	0	388	0	0	870	24,720
1979	NR	1	0	0	0	0	0	0	0	0	0	0	0	1,165
Lifetime		10	0	0	0	0	1	0	1	1,521	0	0	2,975	$52,645

Sonny Hutchins

Ernest Lloyd Hutchins
B: 5/17/1929
Racing Hometown: Richmond, VA

Year	Rank	Starts	Poles	1	2	3	4	5	6–10	Laps	Laps Led	Races Led	Miles	$
1955	242T	1	0	0	0	0	0	0	0	15	0	0	8	0
1965	50	10	0	0	0	0	0	1	1	2,272	0	0	1,332	3,780
1966	83	4	0	0	0	0	0	0	0	222	0	0	318	2,190
1967	34	7	0	0	0	0	0	0	2	998	0	0	1,711	6,385
1968	62	4	0	0	0	0	0	0	0	420	0	0	528	2,810
1969	44	8	0	0	2	0	0	0	0	1,694	0	0	1,640	9,565
1970	78	2	0	0	0	0	0	1	0	722	0	0	612	2,575
1973	112	1	0	0	0	0	0	0	0	254	0	0	138	440
1974	132	1	0	0	0	0	0	0	0	150	79	1	79	590
Lifetime		38	0	0	2	0	0	2	3	6,747	79	1	6,365	$28,140

Randy Hutchison

Ivan Randall Hutchison
B: 8/25/1948
Racing Hometown: Newport News, VA

Year	Rank	Starts	Poles	1	2	3	4	5	6–10	Laps	Laps Led	Races Led	Miles	$
1971	NR	6	0	0	0	0	0	0	1	1,233	0	0	556	2,010
1974	134	1	0	0	0	0	0	0	0	66	0	0	35	730
Lifetime		7	0	0	0	0	0	0	1	1,299	0	0	590	$2,740

Bill Hyde

William Hyde
Racing Hometown: Portland, OR

Year	Rank	Starts	Poles	1	2	3	4	5	6–10	Laps	Laps Led	Races Led	Miles	$
1955	102	1	0	0	1	0	0	0	0	109	0	0	109	820
1956	55	6	0	0	0	0	0	0	3	770	1	1	644	910
Lifetime		7	0	0	1	0	0	0	3	879	1	1	753	$1,730

James Hylton

James Harvey Hylton
B: 8/26/1935
Racing Hometown: Inman, SC

Year	Rank	Starts	Poles	1	2	3	4	5	6–10	Laps	Laps Led	Races Led	Miles	$
1964	NR	3	0	0	0	0	0	0	0	47	0	0	72	350
1966	2	41	1	0	4	6	7	3	12	**10,804**	155	3	**8,498**	38,723
1967	2	46	1	0	3	3	12	8	13	11,526	109	5	8,534	49,732
1968	7	41	0	0	1	4	8	3	12	10,058	15	3	7,285	32,608
1969	3	52	0	0	4	9	8	6	12	13,540	162	12	10,937	114,416
1970	3	47	1	1	4	2	8	7	17	12,712	199	8	11,223	78,201
1971	2	46	1	0	2	3	5	4	23	12,785	105	5	12,718	90,282
1972	3	31	0	1	0	0	5	3	14	9,672	111	4	11,431	126,705
1973	4	28	0	0	0	0	1	0	10	**9,324**	1	1	10,044	82,512

Year	Rank	Starts	Poles	Finish						Laps	Laps Led	Races Led	Miles	$
				1	2	3	4	5	6–10					

James Hylton *continued*

Year	Rank	Starts	Poles	1	2	3	4	5	6–10	Laps	Laps Led	Races Led	Miles	$
1974	11	29	0	0	0	0	0	1	7	6,774	29	6	7,969	61,385
1975	3	30	0	0	0	0	1	1	14	**9,650**	11	4	**11,032**	113,642
1976	13	30	0	0	0	0	1	1	3	8,125	14	4	9,331	78,705
1977	7	30	0	0	0	0	0	0	11	8,375	3	1	9,591	108,392
1978	26	19	0	0	0	0	0	0	4	5,774	16	2	5,018	48,045
1979	14	30	0	0	0	0	0	0	5	8,658	11	4	9,603	98,333
1980	13	31	0	0	0	0	0	0	4	9,232	26	1	10,547	109,230
1981	19	28	0	0	0	0	0	0	0	7,051	12	2	8,509	87,305
1982	28	13	0	0	0	0	0	0	0	4,208	0	0	4,332	50,630
1983	NR	2	0	0	0	0	0	0	0	556	0	0	662	12,105
1985	NR	1	0	0	0	0	0	0	0	201	0	0	201	3,945
1986	46	4	0	0	0	0	0	0	0	544	0	0	576	22,090
1987	79	2	0	0	0	0	0	0	0	93	0	0	99	2,550
1989	74	2	0	0	0	0	0	0	0	38	0	0	43	3,775
1990	NR	1	0	0	0	0	0	0	0	202	0	0	202	2,800
1991	54	4	0	0	0	0	0	0	0	87	0	0	113	14,190
1992	42	8	0	0	0	0	0	0	0	611	0	0	1,100	37,910
1993	64T	2	0	0	0	0	0	0	0	86	0	0	109	17,295
1995	—	0												3,950
Lifetime		601	4	2	18	27	56	37	161	160,733	979	65	159,778	$1,489,806
		8th								**7th**				

Jimmy Ingalls

James Ingalls
Racing Hometown: Boca Raton, FL

Year	Rank	Starts	Poles	1	2	3	4	5	6–10	Laps	Laps Led	Races Led	Miles	$
1983	81	2	0	0	0	0	0	0	0	901	0	0	901	3,080
1984	68	3	0	0	0	0	0	0	0	491	0	0	597	8,865
Lifetime		5	0	0	0	0	0	0	0	1,392	0	0	1,498	$11,945

Bill Ingram

William Ingram
B: 6/15/1954
Racing Hometown: Acworth, GA

Year	Rank	Starts	Poles	1	2	3	4	5	6–10	Laps	Laps Led	Races Led	Miles	$
1989	78	1	0	0	0	0	0	0	0	181	0	0	481	3,875
Lifetime		1	0	0	0	0	0	0	0	181	0	0	481	$3,875

Jack Ingram

Jack Ingram
B: 12/28/1936
Racing Hometown: Asheville, NC

Year	Rank	Starts	Poles	1	2	3	4	5	6–10	Laps	Laps Led	Races Led	Miles	$
1965	140	1	0	0	0	0	0	0	0	4	0	0	2	100
1966	119T	1	0	0	0	0	0	0	0	14	0	0	5	100
1967	87	4	0	0	1	0	0	0	0	506	0	0	218	1,165
1968	63	4	0	0	0	0	0	0	2	805	0	0	385	1,150
1979	63	4	0	0	0	0	0	0	0	532	0	0	661	4,240
1981	48	5	0	0	0	0	0	0	1	822	0	0	1,285	9,965
1984	—	0												2,450
Lifetime		19	0	0	1	0	0	0	3	2,683	0	0	2,556	$19,170

Jim Ingram

James Ingram
Racing Hometown: Cheraw, SC

Year	Rank	Starts	Poles	1	2	3	4	5	6–10	Laps	Laps Led	Races Led	Miles	$
1980	86	1	0	0	0	0	0	0	0	437	0	0	437	1,435
Lifetime		1	0	0	0	0	0	0	0	437	0	0	437	$1,435

Jimmy Ingram

James Ingram
Racing Hometown: Jacksonville, FL

Year	Rank	Starts	Poles	1	2	3	4	5	6–10	Laps	Laps Led	Races Led	Miles	$
1951	N/A	1	0	0	0	0	0	0	0		0	0		25
1952	166	1	0	0	0	0	0	0	0	91	0	0	114	0
Lifetime		2	0	0	0	0	0	0	0	91	0	0	114	$25

Tommy Ingram

Thomas Ingram
D: 4/17/1995
Racing Hometown: Asheville, NC

Year	Rank	Starts	Poles	1	2	3	4	5	6–10	Laps	Laps Led	Races Led	Miles	$
1967	106	2	0	0	0	0	0	0	0	58	0	0	73	1,060
Lifetime		2	0	0	0	0	0	0	0	58	0	0	73	$1,060

Year	Rank	Starts	Poles	Finish 1	2	3	4	5	6–10	Laps	Laps Led	Races Led	Miles	$

Jimmy Insolo

James Edward Insolo
B: 2/4/1943
Racing Hometown: Mission Hills, CA

Year	Rank	Starts	Poles	1	2	3	4	5	6–10	Laps	Laps Led	Races Led	Miles	$
1970	85	2	0	0	0	0	0	0	0	137	0	0	359	1,635
1971	NR	3	0	0	0	0	0	0	0	349	0	0	892	3,790
1972	97	1	0	0	0	0	0	0	0	130	0	0	341	835
1973	62	2	0	0	0	0	1	1	0	335	0	0	878	6,295
1974	67	3	0	0	0	0	0	0	0	338	1	1	867	3,360
1975	53	4	0	0	0	0	0	0	1	296	18	1	717	5,640
1976	61	3	0	0	0	1	0	0	1	454	0	0	1,169	12,105
1977	109	2	0	0	0	0	1	0	0	97	0	0	254	4,490
1978	49	3	0	0	0	0	0	0	2	345	5	2	880	10,665
1979	55	3	0	0	0	0	0	0	0	192	0	0	499	6,905
1981	NR	1	0	0	0	0	0	0	0	41	0	0	107	755
1982	NR	1	0	0	0	0	0	0	0	89	0	0	233	2,470
1983	104	1	0	0	0	0	0	0	0	1	0	0	3	840
Lifetime		29	0	0	0	1	2	1	4	2,804	24	4	7,199	$59,785

Bubba Into

James Into
B: 1938
Racing Hometown: Hardeeville, SC

Year	Rank	Starts	Poles	1	2	3	4	5	6–10	Laps	Laps Led	Races Led	Miles	$
1964	134	2	0	0	0	0	0	0	0	185	0	0	93	210
Lifetime		2	0	0	0	0	0	0	0	185	0	0	93	$210

Innes Ireland

Robert MacGregor Innes Ireland
B: 6/12/1930   D: 10/23/1993
Racing Hometown: Prestiegne Rads, United Kingdom

Year	Rank	Starts	Poles	1	2	3	4	5	6–10	Laps	Laps Led	Races Led	Miles	$
1967	NR	2	0	0	0	0	0	0	1	165	0	0	413	1,265
Lifetime		2	0	0	0	0	0	0	1	165	0	0	413	$1,265

Ernie Irvan

Ernie Irvan
B: 1/13/1959
Racing Hometown: Modesto, CA

Year	Rank	Starts	Poles	1	2	3	4	5	6–10	Laps	Laps Led	Races Led	Miles	$
1987	52	5	0	0	0	0	0	0	1	1,341	1	1	1,311	23,050
1988	26	25	0	0	0	0	0	0	0	7,337	1	1	8,845	96,370
1989	22	29	0	0	0	0	0	0	4	8,286	69	4	9,961	155,329
1990	9	29	3	1	2	1	1	1	7	8,991	280	10	10,413	535,280
1991	5	29	1	2	3	0	4	2	8	8,720	584	16	10,465	1,079,017
1992	11	29	3	3	2	1	2	1	2	8,561	477	17	10,279	996,885
1993	6	29	4	3	4	3	0	2	2	8,185	1,112	18	10,136	1,400,468
1994	22	20	5	3	6	2	0	2	2	5,357	1,781	17	7,643	1,311,522
1995	48	3	0	0	0	0	0	0	2	924	142	2	945	54,875
1996	10	31	1	2	2	0	6	2	4	8,618	370	15	10,220	1,683,313
Lifetime		229	17	14	19	7	13	10	32	66,320	4,817	101	80,218	$7,336,109

Billy Irvin

William Irvin
Racing Hometown: Baltimore, MD

Year	Rank	Starts	Poles	1	2	3	4	5	6–10	Laps	Laps Led	Races Led	Miles	$
1954	NR	7	0	0	0	0	0	0	0	846	0	0	585	125
Lifetime		7	0	0	0	0	0	0	0	846	0	0	585	$125

Tommy Irwin

Thomas Irwin
B: 4/27/1928
Racing Hometown: Keyesville, VA

Year	Rank	Starts	Poles	1	2	3	4	5	6–10	Laps	Laps Led	Races Led	Miles	$
1958	NR	5	0	0	0	1	1	0	1	1,255	0	0	689	1,280
1959	14	25	1	0	1	2	3	4	6	4,410	174	2	2,847	9,190
1960	55	16	1	0	0	0	3	1	7	2,659	0	0	1,641	2,805
1961	26	26	0	0	2	0	1	0	5	3,748	166	1	3,235	7,170
1962	37	20	0	0	1	0	1	0	7	2,982	10	1	1,637	3,775
1963	32	7	0	0	0	1	0	1	3	1,528	0	0	1,105	2,655
Lifetime		99	2	0	4	4	9	6	29	16,582	350	4	11,154	$26,400

Bobby Isaac

Robert Vance Isaac
B: 8/1/1932   D: 8/14/1977
Racing Hometown: Catawba, NC

Year	Rank	Starts	Poles	1	2	3	4	5	6–10	Laps	Laps Led	Races Led	Miles	$
1961	158T	1	0	0	0	0	0	0	0	2	0	0	3	50

Year	Rank	Starts	Poles	1	2	3	4	5	6–10	Laps	Laps Led	Races Led	Miles	$

Bobby Isaac *continued*

Year	Rank	Starts	Poles	1	2	3	4	5	6–10	Laps	Laps Led	Races Led	Miles	$
1963	28	27	0	0	0	1	0	2	4	4,989	30	1	4,299	9,529
1964	18	19	0	1	3	0	1	0	2	3,163	134	6	3,360	26,733
1965	75	4	1	0	1	0	0	0	0	699	183	2	472	1,860
1966	53	9	0	0	1	1	0	0	1	1,387	21	2	1,388	5,530
1967	14	12	0	0	1	0	0	2	2	2,625	65	3	3,927	24,475
1968	2	49	3	3	9	7	4	4	9	12,947	1,384	20	9,160	60,342
1969	6	50	**20**[1]	17	3	5	3	1	4	12,308	**5,072**	38	9,329	92,074
1970	1	47	13	11	9	5	4	3	6	**12,726**	3,188	**35**	**11,251**	199,600
1971	23	25	5	4	4	2	4	2	1	6,856	1,753	17	7,602	106,526
1972	19	27	8	1	3	5	0	1	0	5,636	1,326	20	6,872	133,257
1973	26	19	0	0	2	1	2	0	1	4,177	62	7	4,536	84,550
1974	33	11	0	0	1	0	0	0	4	1,907	11	4	2,490	22,642
1975	48	6	0	0	0	0	0	0	1	1,101	0	0	1,214	6,695
1976	114	2	0	0	0	0	0	0	1	512	0	0	540	4,190
Lifetime		308	50	37	37	27	18	15	36	71,035	13,229	155	66,442	$778,053
			6th								7th			

Larry Isley

Lawrence Isley
Racing Hometown: Burlington, NC

Year	Rank	Starts	Poles	1	2	3	4	5	6–10	Laps	Laps Led	Races Led	Miles	$
1979	101T	1	0	0	0	0	0	0	0	256	0	0	160	925
Lifetime		1	0	0	0	0	0	0	0	256	0	0	160	$925

Don Israel

Donald Israel
Racing Hometown: Asheville, NC

Year	Rank	Starts	Poles	1	2	3	4	5	6–10	Laps	Laps Led	Races Led	Miles	$
1966	106	1	0	0	0	0	0	0	1	188	0	0	94	150
Lifetime		1	0	0	0	0	0	0	1	188	0	0	94	$150

Wayne Jacks

Wayne Jacks
B: 2/21/1949
Racing Hometown: Las Vegas, NV

Year	Rank	Starts	Poles	1	2	3	4	5	6–10	Laps	Laps Led	Races Led	Miles	$
1993	91T	1	0	0	0	0	0	0	0	48	0	0	48	5,980
Lifetime		1	0	0	0	0	0	0	0	48	0	0	48	$5,980

Burt Jackson

Burt Jackson
Racing Hometown: Los Angeles, CA

Year	Rank	Starts	Poles	1	2	3	4	5	6–10	Laps	Laps Led	Races Led	Miles	$
1951	N/A	1	0	0	0	0	0	0	1		0	0		100
Lifetime		1	0	0	0	0	0	0	1		0	0		$100

Charlie Jackson

Charles Jackson
Racing Hometown: Indianapolis, IN

Year	Rank	Starts	Poles	1	2	3	4	5	6–10	Laps	Laps Led	Races Led	Miles	$
1956	90	5	0	0	0	0	0	0	2	635	0	0	336	260
Lifetime		5	0	0	0	0	0	0	2	635	0	0	336	$260

Ed Jackson

Edward Jackson
Racing Hometown: Syracuse, NY

Year	Rank	Starts	Poles	1	2	3	4	5	6–10	Laps	Laps Led	Races Led	Miles	$
1950	112T	1	0	0	0	0	0	0	0		0	0		0
1957	NR	1	0	0	0	0	0	0	0	72	0	0	72	110
Lifetime		2	0	0	0	0	0	0	0	72	0	0	72	$110

Lacy Jackson

Lacy Jackson
Racing Hometown: N. Augusta, SC

Year	Rank	Starts	Poles	1	2	3	4	5	6–10	Laps	Laps Led	Races Led	Miles	$
1953	149	1	0	0	0	0	0	0	0	288	0	0	396	130
Lifetime		1	0	0	0	0	0	0	0	288	0	0	396	$130

Bruce Jacobi

Bruce Jacobi
B: 6/23/1935   D: 2/4/1987   *Died of injuries suffered @ Daytona 1983.*
Racing Hometown: Indianapolis, IN

Year	Rank	Starts	Poles	1	2	3	4	5	6–10	Laps	Laps Led	Races Led	Miles	$
1975	25	15	0	0	0	0	0	0	3	3,863	0	0	5,767	29,455
1976	73	3	0	0	0	0	0	0	0	621	0	0	788	3,735

Year	Rank	Starts	Poles	Finish						Laps	Laps Led	Races Led	Miles	$
				1	2	3	4	5	6–10	Laps	Led	Led	Miles	$

Bruce Jacobi *continued*

Year	Rank	Starts	Poles	1	2	3	4	5	6–10	Laps	Laps Led	Races Led	Miles	$
1979	—	0												1,050
1980	92T	1	0	0	0	0	0	0	0	189	0	0	378	985
1981	NR	1	0	0	0	0	0	0	0	117	0	0	293	955
1983	—	0												500
Lifetime		20	0	0	0	0	0	0	3	4,790	0	0	7,226	$36,680

Al Jacobs

Al Jacobs
  Racing Hometown: Gardena, CA

Year	Rank	Starts	Poles	1	2	3	4	5	6–10	Laps	Laps Led	Races Led	Miles	$
1951	N/A	3	0	0	0	0	0	0	0		0	0		100
Lifetime		3	0	0	0	0	0	0	0		0	0		$100

Jake Jacobs

Warren Jacobs
  B: 1928
  Racing Hometown: Providence, RI

Year	Rank	Starts	Poles	1	2	3	4	5	6–10	Laps	Laps Led	Races Led	Miles	$
1957	116	1	0	0	0	0	0	0	0	58	0	0	58	100
Lifetime		1	0	0	0	0	0	0	0	58	0	0	58	$100

Lawrence Jacquelin

Lawrence Jacquelin
  Racing Hometown: New Haven, CT

Year	Rank	Starts	Poles	1	2	3	4	5	6–10	Laps	Laps Led	Races Led	Miles	$
1952	190	1	0	0	0	0	0	0	0	34	0	0	34	0
Lifetime		1	0	0	0	0	0	0	0	34	0	0	34	$0

Carl Jaemar

Carl Jaemar

Year	Rank	Starts	Poles	1	2	3	4	5	6–10	Laps	Laps Led	Races Led	Miles	$
1961	129	1	0	0	0	0	0	0	1	95	0	0	95	100
Lifetime		1	0	0	0	0	0	0	1	95	0	0	95	$100

Bill James

William James
  Racing Hometown: Lectonia, OH

Year	Rank	Starts	Poles	1	2	3	4	5	6–10	Laps	Laps Led	Races Led	Miles	$
1952	117	1	0	0	0	0	0	0	0	117	0	0	117	25
Lifetime		1	0	0	0	0	0	0	0	117	0	0	117	$25

Bob James

Robert James
  Racing Hometown: Cuyahoga Falls, OH

Year	Rank	Starts	Poles	1	2	3	4	5	6–10	Laps	Laps Led	Races Led	Miles	$
1951	N/A	1	0	0	0	0	0	0	0	55	0	0	28	25
1963	35	10	0	0	0	0	0	0	0	1,414	0	0	2,068	3,375
Lifetime		11	0	0	0	0	0	0	0	1,469	0	0	2,096	$3,400

Chuck James

Charles James
  Racing Hometown: Columbiana, OH

Year	Rank	Starts	Poles	1	2	3	4	5	6–10	Laps	Laps Led	Races Led	Miles	$
1950	42	1	0	0	0	0	1	0	0		0	0		400
Lifetime		1	0	0	0	0	1	0	0		0	0		$400

Dave James

David James
  Racing Hometown: Venice, CA

Year	Rank	Starts	Poles	1	2	3	4	5	6–10	Laps	Laps Led	Races Led	Miles	$
1958	52	2	0	0	0	0	0	0	2	262	0	0	538	300
1959	116	2	0	0	0	0	0	0	1	489	0	0	217	400
1964	124	1	0	0	0	0	0	0	0	79	0	0	213	500
1966	131	1	0	0	0	0	0	0	0	4	0	0	11	500
1968	72	1	0	0	0	0	0	0	1	171	0	0	462	1,250
1969	NR	1	0	0	0	0	0	0	0	5	0	0	14	850
Lifetime		8	0	0	0	0	0	0	4	1,010	0	0	1,454	$3,800

Frank James

Frank Edwin James
  B: 3/19/1938
  Racing Hometown: Bakersfield, CA

Year	Rank	Starts	Poles	1	2	3	4	5	6–10	Laps	Laps Led	Races Led	Miles	$
1970	79	2	0	0	0	0	0	0	0	257	0	0	673	1,915
1971	NR	3	0	0	0	0	0	0	1	409	0	0	1,050	3,890
1972	79	2	0	0	0	0	0	0	1	259	0	0	679	2,195
Lifetime		7	0	0	0	0	0	0	2	925	0	0	2,402	$8,000

Year	Rank	Starts	Poles	1	2	3	4	5	6–10	Laps	Laps Led	Races Led	Miles	$

Mike James

Markey L. James
B: 11/4/1941
Racing Hometown: Medford, OR

Year	Rank	Starts	Poles	1	2	3	4	5	6–10	Laps	Laps Led	Races Led	Miles	$
1971	NR	1	0	0	0	0	0	0	0	1	0	0	3	615
1972	88	2	0	0	0	0	0	0	0	180	0	0	450	2,620
1973	102	1	0	0	0	0	0	0	0	129	0	0	338	1,065
1974	119	1	0	0	0	0	0	0	0	103	0	0	270	995
Lifetime		5	0	0	0	0	0	0	0	413	0	0	1,061	$5,295

Walt James

Walter James
B: 1923
Racing Hometown: Saucier, MS

Year	Rank	Starts	Poles	1	2	3	4	5	6–10	Laps	Laps Led	Races Led	Miles	$
1957	196	1	0	0	0	0	0	0	0	14	0	0	35	35
Lifetime		1	0	0	0	0	0	0	0	14	0	0	35	$35

Frank Jamison

Frank Jamison
Racing Hometown: Quarryville, PA

Year	Rank	Starts	Poles	1	2	3	4	5	6–10	Laps	Laps Led	Races Led	Miles	$
1956	122	3	0	0	0	0	0	0	1	315	0	0	229	350
1957	139	2	0	0	0	0	0	0	0	87	0	0	81	150
Lifetime		5	0	0	0	0	0	0	1	402	0	0	309	$500

Roy Janelle

Roy Janelle
B: 1918
Racing Hometown: Depew, NY

Year	Rank	Starts	Poles	1	2	3	4	5	6–10	Laps	Laps Led	Races Led	Miles	$
1951	N/A	1	0	0	0	0	0	0	0		0	0		0
1952	146	1	0	0	0	0	0	0	0		0	0		25
Lifetime		2	0	0	0	0	0	0	0		0	0		$25

Bill Jarlick

William Jarlick
Racing Hometown: Westchester, CA

Year	Rank	Starts	Poles	1	2	3	4	5	6–10	Laps	Laps Led	Races Led	Miles	$
1957	125	2	0	0	0	0	0	0	1	115	0	0	106	100
1958	106	2	0	0	0	0	0	0	1	111	0	0	137	250
1959	119	2	0	0	0	0	0	0	0	360	0	0	152	100
Lifetime		6	0	0	0	0	0	0	2	586	0	0	395	$450

Dale Jarrett

Dale Arnold Jarrett
B: 11/26/1956
Racing Hometown: Hickory, NC

Year	Rank	Starts	Poles	1	2	3	4	5	6–10	Laps	Laps Led	Races Led	Miles	$
1984	72	3	0	0	0	0	0	0	0	796	0	0	798	7,305
1986	107T	1	0	0	0	0	0	0	0	69	0	0	37	990
1987	26	24	0	0	0	0	0	0	2	4,788	0	0	5,680	143,405
1988	23	29	0	0	0	0	0	0	1	6,556	5	2	8,161	118,640
1989	24	29	0	0	0	0	0	2	3	7,798	99	3	9,178	232,317
1990	25	24	0	0	0	0	1	0	6	6,801	73	4	7,699	214,495
1991	17	29	0	1	0	0	0	2	5	7,767	47	7	9,438	444,256
1992	19	29	0	0	1	1	0	0	6	8,586	99	5	10,295	418,648
1993	4	30	0	1	1	4	5	2	5	9,149	263	15	11,335	1,242,394
1994	16	30	0	1	0	0	2	1	5	8,410	55	8	10,441	893,754
1995	13	31	1	1	1	2	1	4	5	8,671	324	8	10,417	1,363,158
1996	3	31	2	4	7	4	2	0	4	9,307	755	20	11,180	2,985,418
Lifetime		290	3	8	10	11	11	11	42	78,698	1,720	72	94,658	$8,064,780

Glenn Jarrett

Glenn Jarrett
B: 8/11/1950
Racing Hometown: Conover, NC

Year	Rank	Starts	Poles	1	2	3	4	5	6–10	Laps	Laps Led	Races Led	Miles	$
1978	85	1	0	0	0	0	0	0	0	317	0	0	476	2,940
1979	118T	2	0	0	0	0	0	0	0	330	0	0	416	2,745
1980	NR	2	0	0	0	0	0	0	0	209	0	0	502	4,435
1981	58	3	0	0	0	0	0	0	0	679	0	0	864	12,650
1982	104T	1	0	0	0	0	0	0	0	35	0	0	53	735
1983	95T	1	0	0	0	0	0	0	0	24	0	0	60	1,200
1985	—	0												4,200
Lifetime		10	0	0	0	0	0	0	0	1,594	0	0	2,370	$28,905

Year	Rank	Starts	Poles	Finish						Laps	Laps Led	Races Led	Miles	$
				1	2	3	4	5	6–10					

Ned Jarrett

Ned Miller Jarrett
B: 10/12/1932
Racing Hometown: Neton, NC

Year	Rank	Starts	Poles	1	2	3	4	5	6–10	Laps	Laps Led	Races Led	Miles	$
1953	68	2	0	0	0	0	0	0	0	8	0	0	11	125
1954	147	2	0	0	0	0	0	0	0	273	0	0	151	25
1955	173	3	0	0	0	0	0	0	0	403	0	0	491	260
1956	166	2	0	0	0	0	0	0	0	244	0	0	140	60
1957	169	1	0	0	0	0	0	0	0	7	0	0	4	50
1959	37	17	0	2	1	1	0	0	3	2,929	2	2	1,489	3,860
1960	5	40	5	5	3	4	4	4	6	7,399	382	11	5,479	25,438
1961	1	46	4	1	4	8	4	6	11	9,813	606	9	7,184	41,056
1962	3	52	4	6	2	3	3	5	16	11,296	866	11	7,209	43,444
1963	4	53	4	8	7	5	7	5	7	11,845	1,897	18	7,938	45,844
1964	2	59	9	15	7	5	7	6	5	13,325	3,304	30	8,785	71,925
1965	1	54	9	13	13	10	4	2	3	**13,525**	2,244	29	**9,121**	93,625
1966	13	21	0	0	0	3	1	1	3	4,584	167	3	4,336	23,255
Lifetime		352	35	50	37	39	30	29	54	75,651	9,468	111	52,337	$348,967
				8th										

Bob Jarvis

Dr. Robert D. Jarvis
Racing Hometown: Greenville, SC

Year	Rank	Starts	Poles	1	2	3	4	5	6–10	Laps	Laps Led	Races Led	Miles	$
1982	92	2	0	0	0	0	0	0	0	192	0	0	204	2,895
Lifetime		2	0	0	0	0	0	0	0	192	0	0	204	$2,895

Harry Jefferson

Harry Jefferson
B: 11/2/1946
Racing Hometown: Naches, WA

Year	Rank	Starts	Poles	1	2	3	4	5	6–10	Laps	Laps Led	Races Led	Miles	$
1973	117	1	0	0	0	0	0	0	0	37	0	0	97	1,015
1974	52	4	0	0	0	0	0	0	1	457	0	0	775	6,083
1975	45	5	0	0	0	0	0	0	2	1,036	0	0	1,787	11,395
1976	111T	1	0	0	0	0	0	0	0	14	0	0	37	535
1977	88	1	0	0	0	0	0	0	0	195	0	0	488	1,600
Lifetime		12	0	0	0	0	0	0	3	1,739	0	0	3,183	$20,628

Rick Jeffrey

Richard Jeffrey
B: 1951
Racing Hometown: Prospect, KY

Year	Rank	Starts	Poles	1	2	3	4	5	6–10	Laps	Laps Led	Races Led	Miles	$
1987	82	1	0	0	0	0	0	0	0	391	0	0	391	1,800
1988	49	4	0	0	0	0	0	0	0	978	0	0	1,767	25,535
1989	87T	1	0	0	0	0	0	0	0	191	0	0	382	3,125
1990	87	1	0	0	0	0	0	0	0	467	0	0	475	5,300
1991	—	0												2,700
Lifetime		7	0	0	0	0	0	0	0	2,027	0	0	3,015	$38,460

Bob Jeffries

Robert Jeffries
Racing Hometown: Detroit, MI

Year	Rank	Starts	Poles	1	2	3	4	5	6–10	Laps	Laps Led	Races Led	Miles	$
1951	N/A	2	0	0	0	0	0	0	0	225	0	0	225	35
Lifetime		2	0	0	0	0	0	0	0	225	0	0	225	$35

Dick Jennette

Richard Jennette
Racing Hometown: Whitmore Lake, MI

Year	Rank	Starts	Poles	1	2	3	4	5	6–10	Laps	Laps Led	Races Led	Miles	$
1954	NR	1	0	0	0	0	0	0	0	115	0	0	58	25
Lifetime		1	0	0	0	0	0	0	0	115	0	0	58	$25

John Jennings

John Jennings
Racing Hometown: Fayetteville, NC

Year	Rank	Starts	Poles	1	2	3	4	5	6–10	Laps	Laps Led	Races Led	Miles	$
1970	71	6	0	0	0	0	0	0	0	610	0	0	281	1,515
Lifetime		6	0	0	0	0	0	0	0	610	0	0	281	$1,515

Bill Jennings

William Jennings
B: 3/27/1926
Racing Hometown: Syracuse, NY

Year	Rank	Starts	Poles	1	2	3	4	5	6–10	Laps	Laps Led	Races Led	Miles	$
1953	86T	1	0	0	0	0	0	0	1		0	0		75
Lifetime		1	0	0	0	0	0	0	1		0	0		$75

Year	Rank	Starts	Poles	1	2	3	4	5	6–10	Laps	Laps Led	Races Led	Miles	$

Joe Jernigan

Joseph Stanley Jernigan (Little Joe)
B: 5/23/1915   D: 6/23/1951   *Killed at Royall Speedway in Richmond, VA.*
Racing Hometown: Norfolk, VA

Year	Rank	Starts	Poles	1	2	3	4	5	6–10	Laps	Laps Led	Races Led	Miles	$
1950	87	2	0	0	0	0	0	0	0	166	0	0	296	100
1951	N/A	2	0	0	0	0	0	0	0		0	0		25
Lifetime		4	0	0	0	0	0	0	0	166	0	0	296	$125

Dick Jerrett

Richard Jerrett
Racing Hometown: Mexico, NY

Year	Rank	Starts	Poles	1	2	3	4	5	6–10	Laps	Laps Led	Races Led	Miles	$
1950	NR	3	0	0	0	0	0	0	2	184	0	0	92	175
Lifetime		3	0	0	0	0	0	0	2	184	0	0	92	$175

Tom Jerris

Thomas Jerris
Racing Hometown: Pittsburgh, PA

Year	Rank	Starts	Poles	1	2	3	4	5	6–10	Laps	Laps Led	Races Led	Miles	$
1951	76	1	0	0	0	0	0	1	0		0	0		250
Lifetime		1	0	0	0	0	0	1	0		0	0		$250

Paul Jett

Paul Jett
Racing Hometown: San Antonio, TX

Year	Rank	Starts	Poles	1	2	3	4	5	6–10	Laps	Laps Led	Races Led	Miles	$
1972	72	2	0	0	0	0	0	0	1	391	0	0	895	2,495
Lifetime		2	0	0	0	0	0	0	1	391	0	0	895	$2,495

Fran Jischke

Francis Jischke
Racing Hometown: Rochester, NY

Year	Rank	Starts	Poles	1	2	3	4	5	6–10	Laps	Laps Led	Races Led	Miles	$
1951	N/A	1	0	0	0	0	0	0	0		0	0		25
1952	129T	1	0	0	0	0	0	0	0	158	0	0	79	25
1954	217	1	0	0	0	0	0	0	0	22	0	0	11	0
Lifetime		3	0	0	0	0	0	0	0	180	0	0	90	$50

Gordon Johncock

Gordon Walter Johncock
B: 8/5/1936
Racing Hometown: Coldwater, MI

Year	Rank	Starts	Poles	1	2	3	4	5	6–10	Laps	Laps Led	Races Led	Miles	$
1966	NR	5	0	0	0	0	1	0	1	1,139	21	2	1,673	5,485
1967	NR	6	0	0	0	0	0	1	0	685	1	1	930	4,945
1972	NR	2	0	0	0	0	0	0	0	226	0	0	430	1,384
1973	NR	6	0	0	0	0	1	0	0	1,307	0	0	1,802	10,600
1975	NR	1	0	0	0	0	0	0	0	47	0	0	125	1,230
1976	NR	1	0	0	0	0	0	0	0	41	0	0	62	870
Lifetime		21	0	0	0	0	2	1	1	3,445	22	3	5,022	$24,514

Bobby Johns

Robert James Johns
B: 5/22/1934
Racing Hometown: Miami, Fl

Year	Rank	Starts	Poles	1	2	3	4	5	6–10	Laps	Laps Led	Races Led	Miles	$
1956	25	9	0	0	0	0	0	0	3	1,537	0	0	1,091	1,450
1957	48	1	0	0	0	0	0	0	0	335	0	0	461	225
1958	NR	3	0	0	0	0	1	0	0	894	0	0	835	1,625
1959	19	8	1	0	0	1	0	0	1	1,911	129	2	1,440	5,951
1960	3	19	0	1	2	1	3	1	2	3,695	438	6	3,815	46,115
1961	24	14	1	0	0	0	1	0	2	2,674	52	2	3,084	5,010
1962	28	13	0	1	0	1	0	0	1	2,745	614	8	2,976	15,863
1963	21	12	0	0	0	1	0	2	3	2,433	84	3	3,383	15,915
1964	37	12	0	0	0	0	0	0	2	1,806	0	0	1,859	5,700
1965	20	13	0	0	2	2	0	1	0	2,696	37	6	2,941	24,930
1966	60	11	0	0	0	0	0	0	1	1,419	0	0	1,236	5,245
1967	52	11	0	0	0	0	0	0	0	1,279	0	0	1,301	6,405
1968	48	7	0	0	0	0	0	0	0	750	0	0	1,108	5,010
1969	54	8	0	0	0	0	0	0	0	1,075	0	0	1,185	5,875
Lifetime		141	2	2	4	6	5	4	15	25,249	1,354	27	26,714	$103,819

Don Johns

Donald Johns
B: 1934   D: 8/25/1962   *Killed in race @ Minnesota Fairgrounds in St. Paul, MN.*
Racing Hometown: Belflower, CA

Year	Rank	Starts	Poles	1	2	3	4	5	6–10	Laps	Laps Led	Races Led	Miles	$
1957	111	2	0	0	0	0	0	0	1	255	0	0	128	200
Lifetime		2	0	0	0	0	0	0	1	255	0	0	128	$200

Year	Rank	Starts	Poles	Finish						Laps	Laps Led	Races Led	Miles	$
				1	2	3	4	5	6–10					

Ken Johns
Kenneth Johns
Racing Hometown: Ft. Worth, TX

Year	Rank	Starts	Poles	1	2	3	4	5	6–10	Laps	Laps Led	Races Led	Miles	$
1955	58	2	0	0	0	0	0	0	2	249	0	0	326	300
Lifetime		2	0	0	0	0	0	0	2	249	0	0	326	$300

Squirt Johns
Squirt Johns

Year	Rank	Starts	Poles	1	2	3	4	5	6–10	Laps	Laps Led	Races Led	Miles	$
1958	NR	2	0	0	0	0	0	0	0	105	0	0	35	90
Lifetime		2	0	0	0	0	0	0	0	105	0	0	35	$90

Amos Johnson
Amos Neill Johnson Jr.
B: 4/9/1941
Racing Hometown: Raleigh, NC

Year	Rank	Starts	Poles	1	2	3	4	5	6–10	Laps	Laps Led	Races Led	Miles	$
1969	NR	1	0	0	0	0	0	0	0	147	0	0	391	1,450
Lifetime		1	0	0	0	0	0	0	0	147	0	0	391	$1,450

Bob Johnson
Robert Johnson
Racing Hometown: Tampa, FL

Year	Rank	Starts	Poles	1	2	3	4	5	6–10	Laps	Laps Led	Races Led	Miles	$
1951	N/A	1	0	0	0	0	0	0	0	214	0	0	268	0
Lifetime		1	0	0	0	0	0	0	0	214	0	0	268	$0

Cal Johnson
Cal Johnson
Racing Hometown: Ashland, VA

Year	Rank	Starts	Poles	1	2	3	4	5	6–10	Laps	Laps Led	Races Led	Miles	$
1951	86	2	0	0	0	0	0	0	2		0	0		150
Lifetime		2	0	0	0	0	0	0	2		0	0		$150

Dick Johnson
Richard Myron Johnson
B: 1/9/1928
Racing Hometown: Elverta, CA

Year	Rank	Starts	Poles	1	2	3	4	5	6–10	Laps	Laps Led	Races Led	Miles	$
1967	45	23	0	0	0	0	0	0	0	2,636	0	0	1,647	5,070
1968	37	11	0	0	0	0	0	0	0	2,187	0	0	2,040	5,920
1969	34	22	0	0	0	0	0	0	4	3,803	0	0	2,910	11,477
Lifetime		56	0	0	0	0	0	0	4	8,626	0	0	6,597	$22,467

Dick Johnson
Richard Johnson
B: 1945
Racing Hometown: Brisbane, QLD, Australia

Year	Rank	Starts	Poles	1	2	3	4	5	6–10	Laps	Laps Led	Races Led	Miles	$
1989	47	4	0	0	0	0	0	0	0	497	0	0	1,269	11,515
1990	63	3	0	0	0	0	0	0	0	166	0	0	300	10,550
Lifetime		7	0	0	0	0	0	0	0	663	0	0	1,569	$22,065

Don Johnson
Donald Johnson

Year	Rank	Starts	Poles	1	2	3	4	5	6–10	Laps	Laps Led	Races Led	Miles	$
1954	NR	1	0	0	0	0	0	0	0	39	0	0	78	0
Lifetime		1	0	0	0	0	0	0	0	39	0	0	78	$0

Fred Johnson
Fred Johnson
B: 12/9/1929 *Deceased*
Racing Hometown: Hamptonville, NC

Year	Rank	Starts	Poles	1	2	3	4	5	6–10	Laps	Laps Led	Races Led	Miles	$
1949	NR	2	0	0	0	0	0	0	0		0	0		0
1950	60	2	0	0	0	0	0	0	1	244	0	0	197	125
1955	186	2	0	0	0	0	0	0	0	258	0	0	345	460
1956	106	1	0	0	0	0	0	0	1	60	0	0	246	325
Lifetime		7	0	0	0	0	0	0	2	562	0	0	787	$910

Gary Johnson
Gary Johnson
B: 5/12/1940
Racing Hometown: Modesto, CA

Year	Rank	Starts	Poles	1	2	3	4	5	6–10	Laps	Laps Led	Races Led	Miles	$
1976	79	1	0	0	0	0	0	0	0	72	0	0	189	840
1977	74	2	0	0	0	0	0	0	0	126	0	0	330	2,445
1978	102T	1	0	0	0	0	0	0	0	3	0	0	8	500
Lifetime		4	0	0	0	0	0	0	0	201	0	0	527	$3,785

Year	Rank	Starts	Poles	Finish 1	2	3	4	5	6–10	Laps	Laps Led	Races Led	Miles	$

Hubert Johnson

Hubert Johnson

Year	Rank	Starts	Poles	1	2	3	4	5	6–10	Laps	Laps Led	Races Led	Miles	$
1960	NR	1	0	0	0	0	0	0	0	105	0	0	53	50
Lifetime		1	0	0	0	0	0	0	0	105	0	0	53	$50

Jerry Johnson

Jerry Johnson
Racing Hometown: Torrance, CA

Year	Rank	Starts	Poles	1	2	3	4	5	6–10	Laps	Laps Led	Races Led	Miles	$
1958	NR	1	0	0	0	0	0	0	0	93	0	0	93	100
Lifetime		1	0	0	0	0	0	0	0	93	0	0	93	$100

Joe Lee Johnson

Joe Lee Johnson
B: 9/11/1929
Racing Hometown: Chattanooga, TN

Year	Rank	Starts	Poles	1	2	3	4	5	6–10	Laps	Laps Led	Races Led	Miles	$
1957	92	2	0	0	0	0	0	0	0	63	0	0	95	175
1958	91	6	0	0	0	0	0	1	2	989	0	0	732	1,210
1959	70	12	0	1	0	0	1	1	3	2,743	1	1	2,007	6,807
1960	13	22	0	1	1	1	1	2	2	3,453	48	1	2,651	34,519
1961	46	9	0	0	0	0	0	0	3	1,276	0	0	1,461	2,615
1962	93	4	0	0	0	0	0	0	0	381	0	0	191	340
Lifetime		55	0	2	1	1	2	4	10	8,905	49	2	7,137	$45,666

Junior Johnson

Robert Glenn Johnson
B: 6/28/1931
Racing Hometown: Ronda, NC

Year	Rank	Starts	Poles	1	2	3	4	5	6–10	Laps	Laps Led	Races Led	Miles	$
1953	NR	1	0	0	0	0	0	0	0	222	0	0	305	110
1954	55	4	1	0	0	0	0	1	0	535	0	0	389	550
1955	6	36	2	5	1	2	1	3	6	4,620	790	7	3,153	13,803
1956	38	13	1	0	1	0	0	0	0	1,131	60	2	955	1,350
1957	154	1	0	0	0	0	0	0	0	102	0	0	64	50
1958	8	27	0	6	2	3	1	0	4	4,244	317	9	2,797	13,809
1959	11	28	1	5	1	3	3	2	1	4,433	166	7	2,745	9,675
1960	7	34	3	3	2	4	2	3	4	5,096	320	7	3,797	38,990
1961	6	41	10	7	3	2	3	1	6	7,016	**2,373**	**23**	5,228	28,541
1962	20	23	2	1	2	2	1	1	1	3,663	648	11	3,224	34,841
1963	12	33	9	7	2	2	0	2	1	5,671	2,396	21	4,723	67,351
1964	14	29	5	3	2	4	3	0	3	6,298	1,116	15	4,474	26,975
1965	12	36	10	13	2	1	2	0	1	7,144	**3,998**	**30**	5,040	62,216
1966	49	7	3	0	0	0	0	1	0	1,813	467	6	1,160	3,610
Lifetime		313	47	50	18	23	16	14	27	51,988	12,651	138	38,054	$301,871
			8th	8th								9th		

Ken Johnson

Kenneth Johnson
Racing Hometown: Jamestown, NY

Year	Rank	Starts	Poles	1	2	3	4	5	6–10	Laps	Laps Led	Races Led	Miles	$
1956	NR	1	0	0	0	0	0	0	0	127	0	0	64	100
1958	NR	1	0	0	0	1	0	0	0	149	0	0	50	375
1959	59	4	0	0	0	0	0	0	1	408	0	0	366	370
1960	NR	4	0	0	0	0	0	0	0	317	0	0	721	460
1961	154	2	0	0	0	0	0	0	0	36	0	0	90	250
Lifetime		12	0	0	0	1	0	0	1	1,037	0	0	1,290	$1,555

Lionel Johnson

Lionel Barbour Johnson
B: 10/16/1928
Racing Hometown: Unionville, VA

Year	Rank	Starts	Poles	1	2	3	4	5	6–10	Laps	Laps Led	Races Led	Miles	$
1965	48	8	0	0	0	0	0	0	2	1,663	0	0	1,338	3,165
1966	91	5	0	0	0	0	0	0	0	328	0	0	274	1,895
Lifetime		13	0	0	0	0	0	0	2	1,991	0	0	1,611	$5,060

Lou Johnson

Louis Johnson
Racing Hometown: Wilmington, DE

Year	Rank	Starts	Poles	1	2	3	4	5	6–10	Laps	Laps Led	Races Led	Miles	$
1953	78	2	0	0	0	0	0	0	0		0	0		50
Lifetime		2	0	0	0	0	0	0	0		0	0		$50

Slick Johnson

Julius David Johnson III
B: 2/23/1948   D: 2/14/1990   *Died of injuries suffered in ARCA 200 @ Daytona on 2/11/90.*
Racing Hometown: Florence, SC

Year	Rank	Starts	Poles	1	2	3	4	5	6–10	Laps	Laps Led	Races Led	Miles	$
1979	42	4	0	0	0	0	0	0	1	1,039	0	0	1,134	5,360

Year	Rank	Starts	Poles	Finish						Laps	Laps Led	Races Led	Miles	$
				1	2	3	4	5	6–10					

Slick Johnson *continued*

Year	Rank	Starts	Poles	1	2	3	4	5	6–10	Laps	Laps Led	Races Led	Miles	$
1980	23	18	0	0	0	0	0	0	5	4,724	7	2	4,731	35,460
1981	65	4	0	0	0	0	0	0	0	611	0	0	752	4,150
1982	29	17	0	0	0	0	0	0	1	3,826	3	2	4,229	44,190
1983	38	10	0	0	0	0	0	0	0	2,330	0	0	2,501	14,155
1984	NR	1	0	0	0	0	0	0	0	70	0	0	96	1,495
1985	48	6	0	0	0	0	0	0	0	1,608	0	0	2,327	24,995
1986	—	0												1,100
1987	46	8	0	0	0	0	0	0	0	2,113	3	2	1,839	40,630
Lifetime		68	0	0	0	0	0	0	7	16,321	13	6	17,609	$171,535

Ray Johnstone

Raymond Johnstone
B: 6/19/1928
Racing Hometown: San Bernadino, CA

Year	Rank	Starts	Poles	1	2	3	4	5	6–10	Laps	Laps Led	Races Led	Miles	$
1969	NR	1	0	0	0	0	0	0	0	163	0	0	440	1,225
1970	NR	1	0	0	0	0	0	0	0	26	0	0	68	660
1971	NR	3	0	0	0	0	0	0	0	211	0	0	541	3,405
1972	109	1	0	0	0	0	0	0	0	62	0	0	162	725
Lifetime		6	0	0	0	0	0	0	0	462	0	0	1,212	$6,015

Carl Joiner

Carl Joiner
B: 5/12/1924
Racing Hometown: Portland, OR

Year	Rank	Starts	Poles	1	2	3	4	5	6–10	Laps	Laps Led	Races Led	Miles	$
1957	NR	1	0	0	0	0	0	0	0	18	0	0	9	100
1961	109	1	0	0	0	0	0	0	0	125	0	0	175	100
1963	104	1	0	0	0	0	0	0	0	143	0	0	386	375
1966	125	1	0	0	0	0	0	0	0	41	0	0	111	500
1968	111	1	0	0	0	0	0	0	0	3	0	0	8	500
1970	104T	1	0	0	0	0	0	0	0	23	0	0	60	800
1971	NR	3	0	0	0	0	0	0	1	385	0	0	987	4,250
1972	77	2	0	0	0	0	0	1	0	283	0	0	741	3,420
1973	116	1	0	0	0	0	0	0	0	46	0	0	121	1,015
1975	91T	1	0	0	0	0	0	0	0	87	0	0	228	895
1976	78	2	0	0	0	0	0	0	0	227	0	0	581	2,155
1977	102T	1	0	0	0	0	0	0	0	10	0	0	26	740
Lifetime		16	0	0	0	0	0	1	1	1,391	0	0	3,433	$14,850

Jerry Jolly

Jerry Jolly
B: 8/12/1941
Racing Hometown: Denver, CO

Year	Rank	Starts	Poles	1	2	3	4	5	6–10	Laps	Laps Led	Races Led	Miles	$
1978	70	3	0	0	0	0	0	0	0	307	0	0	652	5,740
1979	101T	1	0	0	0	0	0	0	0	99	0	0	263	3,275
1984	89	1	0	0	0	0	0	0	0	10	0	0	26	715
Lifetime		5	0	0	0	0	0	0	0	416	0	0	941	$9,730

Alton Jones

Alton Jones
B: 8/27/1941
Racing Hometown: Pleasant Grove, AL

Year	Rank	Starts	Poles	1	2	3	4	5	6–10	Laps	Laps Led	Races Led	Miles	$
1970	NR	1	0	0	0	0	0	0	0	155	0	0	412	1,485
1973	74	5	0	0	0	0	0	0	1	686	0	0	807	4,195
1974	49	5	0	0	0	0	0	1	1	1,163	0	0	1,095	4,745
1975	62	2	0	0	0	0	0	0	1	790	0	0	471	1,935
Lifetime		13	0	0	0	0	0	1	3	2,794	0	0	2,785	$12,360

Bill Jones

William Jones

Year	Rank	Starts	Poles	1	2	3	4	5	6–10	Laps	Laps Led	Races Led	Miles	$
1958	NR	1	0	0	0	0	0	0	0	160	0	0	421	195
Lifetime		1	0	0	0	0	0	0	0	160	0	0	421	$195

Britton Jones

Britton Jones
Racing Hometown: Las Vegas, NV

Year	Rank	Starts	Poles	1	2	3	4	5	6–10	Laps	Laps Led	Races Led	Miles	$
1955	239	1	0	0	0	0	0	0	0	11	0	0	11	20
Lifetime		1	0	0	0	0	0	0	0	11	0	0	11	$20

Year	Rank	Starts	Poles	Finish 1	2	3	4	5	6–10	Laps	Laps Led	Races Led	Miles	$

Bud Jones

Bud Jones
Racing Hometown: Wilkesboro, NC

Year	Rank	Starts	Poles	1	2	3	4	5	6–10	Laps	Laps Led	Races Led	Miles	$
1953	NR	1	0	0	0	0	0	0	0	36	0	0	23	25
Lifetime		1	0	0	0	0	0	0	0	36	0	0	23	$25

Davy Jones

Duane Davy Jones
B: 6/1/1964
Racing Hometown: Chicago, IL

Year	Rank	Starts	Poles	1	2	3	4	5	6–10	Laps	Laps Led	Races Led	Miles	$
1995	46	7	0	0	0	0	0	0	0	1,680	0	0	2,359	109,925
Lifetime		7	0	0	0	0	0	0	0	1,680	0	0	2,359	$109,925

Frank Jones

Frank Jones
Racing Hometown: Seattle, WA

Year	Rank	Starts	Poles	1	2	3	4	5	6–10	Laps	Laps Led	Races Led	Miles	$
1968	90	1	0	0	0	0	0	0	0	55	0	0	149	520
Lifetime		1	0	0	0	0	0	0	0	55	0	0	149	$520

Guy Jones

Guy Jones
Racing Hometown: South Gate, CA

Year	Rank	Starts	Poles	1	2	3	4	5	6–10	Laps	Laps Led	Races Led	Miles	$
1968	NR	1	0	0	0	0	0	0	0	109	0	0	294	650
1969	NR	1	0	0	0	0	0	0	0	8	0	0	22	800
Lifetime		2	0	0	0	0	0	0	0	117	0	0	316	$1,450

Hap Jones

Vivien S. Jones
B: 4/18/1927
Racing Hometown: Jackson Center, PA

Year	Rank	Starts	Poles	1	2	3	4	5	6–10	Laps	Laps Led	Races Led	Miles	$
1951	84T	1	0	0	0	0	0	0	1		0	0		200
1954	NR	1	0	0	0	0	0	0	0	31	0	0	127	0
Lifetime		2	0	0	0	0	0	0	1	31	0	0	127	$200

Harvey Jones

Harvey Jones
B: 1924
Racing Hometown: Tallahassee, FL

Year	Rank	Starts	Poles	1	2	3	4	5	6–10	Laps	Laps Led	Races Led	Miles	$
1965	97	1	0	0	0	0	0	1	0	195	0	0	98	275
Lifetime		1	0	0	0	0	0	1	0	195	0	0	98	$275

Henry Jones

Henry Jones
Racing Hometown: Manhattan, KS

Year	Rank	Starts	Poles	1	2	3	4	5	6–10	Laps	Laps Led	Races Led	Miles	$
1979	58	3	0	0	0	0	0	0	0	77	0	0	43	1,160
1980	106	4	0	0	0	0	0	0	0	376	0	0	850	4,725
1981	79	1	0	0	0	0	0	0	0	363	0	0	197	765
Lifetime		8	0	0	0	0	0	0	0	816	0	0	1,090	$6,650

James Jones

James Jones
Racing Hometown: Goldsboro, NC

Year	Rank	Starts	Poles	1	2	3	4	5	6–10	Laps	Laps Led	Races Led	Miles	$
1956	214T	1	0	0	0	0	0	0	0	169	0	0	85	100
1958	NR	1	0	0	0	0	0	0	0	212	0	0	212	100
Lifetime		2	0	0	0	0	0	0	0	381	0	0	297	$200

Jim Jones

James Jones
B: 1922
Racing Hometown: Osceola, AR

Year	Rank	Starts	Poles	1	2	3	4	5	6–10	Laps	Laps Led	Races Led	Miles	$
1954	NR	1	0	0	0	0	0	0	0	7	0	0	4	0
Lifetime		1	0	0	0	0	0	0	0	7	0	0	4	$0

Joe Jones

Joseph Jones
Racing Hometown: Winston-Salem, NC

Year	Rank	Starts	Poles	1	2	3	4	5	6–10	Laps	Laps Led	Races Led	Miles	$
1961	70	9	0	0	0	0	0	0	0	895	0	0	639	1,065
1962	103	2	0	0	0	0	0	0	0	250	0	0	125	100
1963	122T	1	0	0	0	0	0	0	0	186	0	0	47	130
Lifetime		12	0	0	0	0	0	0	0	1,331	0	0	810	$1,295

Year	Rank	Starts	Poles	1	2	3	4	5	6–10	Laps	Laps Led	Races Led	Miles	$

Owen Jones
Owen Jones
Racing Hometown: Cleveland, OH

| 1951 | N/A | 2 | 0 | 0 | 0 | 0 | 0 | 0 | 0 | | 0 | 0 | | 50 |
| Lifetime | | 2 | 0 | 0 | 0 | 0 | 0 | 0 | 0 | | 0 | 0 | | $50 |

P. J. Jones
P. J. Jones
B: 4/23/1969
Racing Hometown: Rolling Hills, CA

1993	42	6	0	0	0	0	0	0	1	710	0	0	1,447	53,370
1994	59	2	0	0	0	0	0	0	0	370	0	0	467	23,045
Lifetime		8	0	0	0	0	0	0	1	1,080	0	0	1,914	$76,415

Parnelli Jones
Rufus Parnell Jones
B: 8/12/1933
Racing Hometown: Torrance, CA

1956	67	3	0	0	1	0	0	0	0	591	0	0	564	1,705
1957	47	10	1	1	0	0	0	0	2	743	1	1	582	1,625
1958	33	3	2	1	0	0	0	0	0	587	148	2	954	1,010
1959	94	2	0	1	0	0	0	0	0	560	1	1	268	1,905
1960	91	3	0	0	0	0	0	0	1	204	25	1	371	465
1963	NR	4	0	0	0	0	0	0	1	444	39	1	993	2,000
1964	NR	4	0	0	0	0	0	0	1	202	9	1	502	2,110
1965	NR	1	0	0	0	0	0	0	0	37	36	1	100	980
1967	NR	1	0	1	0	0	0	0	0	185	126	1	500	18,720
1968	NR	1	0	0	0	1	0	0	0	186	49	1	502	5,600
1969	NR	1	0	0	0	0	0	0	0	22	0	0	59	770
1970	NR	1	0	0	0	0	0	0	0	168	88	1	440	1,275
Lifetime		34	3	4	1	1	0	0	5	3,929	522	11	5,834	$38,165

Pee Wee Jones
Phillip Jones
B: 3/31/1928
Racing Hometown: Clemmons, NC

1955	148T	2	0	0	0	0	0	0	0	204	0	0	102	50
1956	128	3	0	0	0	0	0	0	0	549	0	0	327	125
1957	NR	1	0	0	0	0	0	0	0	262	0	0	262	225
1959	NR	1	0	0	0	0	0	0	0	150	0	0	38	50
Lifetime		7	0	0	0	0	0	0	0	1,165	0	0	729	$450

Possum Jones
Lewis V. Jones
B: 1/16/1932
Racing Hometown: Mango, FL

1952	164	1	0	0	0	0	0	0	0	193	0	0	241	0
1955	199	1	0	0	0	0	0	0	0	276	0	0	380	60
1956	137	1	0	0	0	0	0	0	0	336	0	0	462	110
1957	35	6	0	0	0	0	0	0	4	1,443	0	0	1,395	2,375
1958	41	11	1	0	0	0	0	1	2	1,870	28	1	1,254	1,790
1959	112	1	0	0	0	0	0	0	0	74	0	0	102	295
1960	31	13	0	0	3	1	0	0	1	2,594	0	0	2,127	6,330
1963	61	7	0	0	0	0	0	0	1	917	0	0	763	1,880
1964	94	5	0	0	0	0	0	0	0	531	0	0	227	740
1965	136	1	0	0	0	0	0	0	0		0	0		100
Lifetime		47	1	0	3	1	0	1	8	8,234	28	1	6,951	$13,680

Ralph Jones
Ralph Jones
B: 1/20/1944
Racing Hometown: Upton, KY

1977	51	4	0	0	0	0	0	0	0	871	0	0	645	3,395
1978	40	7	0	0	0	0	0	0	0	1,871	0	0	1,856	6,305
1979	40	6	0	0	0	0	0	0	0	729	0	0	1,171	12,785
1980	94	2	0	0	0	0	0	0	0	547	0	0	780	4,335
1983	—	0												1,250
1984	—	0												2,350
1987	—	0												1,900
1988	74	1	0	0	0	0	0	0	0	190	0	0	475	11,645
Lifetime		20	0	0	0	0	0	0	0	4,208	0	0	4,928	$43,965

Year	Rank	Starts	Poles	Finish						Laps	Laps Led	Races Led	Miles	$
				1	2	3	4	5	6–10					

Richard Jones

Richard Jones

Year	Rank	Starts	Poles	1	2	3	4	5	6–10	Laps	Laps Led	Races Led	Miles	$
1954	NR	1	0	0	0	0	0	0	0	1	0	0	2	0
Lifetime		1	0	0	0	0	0	0	0	1	0	0	2	$0

Ed Jordan

Edward Jordan
Racing Hometown: Houston, TX

Year	Rank	Starts	Poles	1	2	3	4	5	6–10	Laps	Laps Led	Races Led	Miles	$
1966	104	3	0	0	0	0	0	0	0	147	0	0	73	460
Lifetime		3	0	0	0	0	0	0	0	147	0	0	73	$460

Bill Joslin

William Joslin
Racing Hometown: Fayetteville, NC

Year	Rank	Starts	Poles	1	2	3	4	5	6–10	Laps	Laps Led	Races Led	Miles	$
1950	110	2	0	0	0	0	0	0	0		0	0		25
1951	N/A	4	0	0	0	0	0	0	0	108	0	0	54	100
Lifetime		6	0	0	0	0	0	0	0	108	0	0	54	$125

Dick Joslin

Richard Joslin
B: 9/18/1926   D: 1/23/1972
Racing Hometown: Orlando, FL

Year	Rank	Starts	Poles	1	2	3	4	5	6–10	Laps	Laps Led	Races Led	Miles	$
1955	95	1	0	0	0	0	0	0	1	38	0	0	156	425
1957	128	1	0	0	0	0	0	0	1	48	0	0	77	100
1958	177	1	0	0	0	0	0	0	0	6	0	0	25	0
1959	NR	4	0	0	0	0	0	0	0	338	0	0	793	485
1960	73	3	0	0	0	0	0	0	0	302	0	0	755	535
Lifetime		10	0	0	0	0	0	0	2	732	0	0	1,805	$1,545

Claude Joyce

Claude Joyce
Racing Hometown: Kernersville, NC

Year	Rank	Starts	Poles	1	2	3	4	5	6–10	Laps	Laps Led	Races Led	Miles	$
1951	N/A	1	0	0	0	0	0	0	0		0	0		0
Lifetime		1	0	0	0	0	0	0	0		0	0		$0

Stuart Joyce

Stuart Joyce
B: 1917   D: 1/11/1981
Racing Hometown: Wannamaker, IN

Year	Rank	Starts	Poles	1	2	3	4	5	6–10	Laps	Laps Led	Races Led	Miles	$
1952	53	1	0	0	0	0	0	0	1	229	0	0	229	200
Lifetime		1	0	0	0	0	0	0	1	229	0	0	229	$200

J. L. Justice

J. L. Justice
Racing Hometown: Raleigh, NC

Year	Rank	Starts	Poles	1	2	3	4	5	6–10	Laps	Laps Led	Races Led	Miles	$
1953	126	3	0	0	0	0	0	0	0	226	0	0	307	145
Lifetime		3	0	0	0	0	0	0	0	226	0	0	307	$145

Jack Kabat

Jack Kabat
Racing Hometown: Cleveland, OH

Year	Rank	Starts	Poles	1	2	3	4	5	6–10	Laps	Laps Led	Races Led	Miles	$
1950	56T	1	0	0	0	0	0	0	1		0	0		125
1951	N/A	1	0	0	0	0	0	0	0		0	0		25
Lifetime		2	0	0	0	0	0	0	1		0	0		$150

Dick Kable

Richard Kable
Racing Hometown: Cleveland, OH

Year	Rank	Starts	Poles	1	2	3	4	5	6–10	Laps	Laps Led	Races Led	Miles	$
1954	NR	1	0	0	0	0	0	0	0	168	0	0	84	0
Lifetime		1	0	0	0	0	0	0	0	168	0	0	84	$0

Hoss Kagle

Ralph Kagle
B: 1928
Racing Hometown: Mt. Ranier, MD

Year	Rank	Starts	Poles	1	2	3	4	5	6–10	Laps	Laps Led	Races Led	Miles	$
1956	NR	1	0	0	0	0	0	0	0	135	0	0	135	100
1961	136	1	0	0	0	0	0	0	0	2	0	0	1	125
Lifetime		2	0	0	0	0	0	0	0	137	0	0	136	$225

Year	Rank	Starts	Poles	Finish 1	2	3	4	5	6–10	Laps	Laps Led	Races Led	Miles	$

Reds Kagle
Richard H. Kagle
B: 4/20/1932
Racing Hometown: Greenbelt, MD

Year	Rank	Starts	Poles	1	2	3	4	5	6–10	Laps	Laps Led	Races Led	Miles	$
1954	86	1	0	0	0	0	0	0	0	220	0	0	220	175
1956	191	2	0	0	0	0	0	0	0	202	0	0	85	60
1957	172	1	0	0	0	0	0	0	0	23	0	0	12	25
1958	NR	14	0	0	0	0	0	2	5	1,642	0	0	896	1,750
1959	91	4	0	0	0	0	1	0	0	627	0	0	340	525
1961	54	3	0	0	0	0	0	0	1	720	0	0	963	1,495
Lifetime		25	0	0	0	0	1	2	6	3,434	0	0	2,515	$4,030

H. R. Kahl
H. R. Kahl
Racing Hometown: Cathedral City, CA

Year	Rank	Starts	Poles	1	2	3	4	5	6–10	Laps	Laps Led	Races Led	Miles	$
1954	135	2	0	0	0	0	0	0	0	225	0	0	113	25
Lifetime		2	0	0	0	0	0	0	0	225	0	0	113	$25

Red Kalajainen
Red Kalajainen

Year	Rank	Starts	Poles	1	2	3	4	5	6–10	Laps	Laps Led	Races Led	Miles	$
1958	155	1	0	0	0	0	0	0	0	68	0	0	27	25
Lifetime		1	0	0	0	0	0	0	0	68	0	0	27	$25

Frank Kapack
Frank Kapack

Year	Rank	Starts	Poles	1	2	3	4	5	6–10	Laps	Laps Led	Races Led	Miles	$
1953	NR	1	0	0	0	0	0	0	0		0	0		25
Lifetime		1	0	0	0	0	0	0	0		0	0		$25

Iggy Katona
Egnatius Katona
B: 8/16/1916
Racing Hometown: Willis, MI

Year	Rank	Starts	Poles	1	2	3	4	5	6–10	Laps	Laps Led	Races Led	Miles	$
1951	131	5	0	0	0	0	0	0	0	559	0	0	643	150
1952	33	5	0	0	0	0	0	0	2	1,067	0	0	925	525
1965	65	1	0	0	0	0	0	0	1	251	0	0	377	850
1966	81	1	0	0	0	0	0	0	0	286	0	0	429	715
1974	102	1	0	0	0	0	0	0	0	181	0	0	481	1,675
Lifetime		13	0	0	0	0	0	0	3	2,344	0	0	2,855	$3,915

Frank Katucka
Frank Katucka

Year	Rank	Starts	Poles	1	2	3	4	5	6–10	Laps	Laps Led	Races Led	Miles	$
1953	NR	1	0	0	0	0	0	0	0		0	0		25
Lifetime		1	0	0	0	0	0	0	0		0	0		$25

Bob Kauf
Robert C. Kauf
B: 4/1/1942
Racing Hometown: Pacoima, CA

Year	Rank	Starts	Poles	1	2	3	4	5	6–10	Laps	Laps Led	Races Led	Miles	$
1971	NR	2	0	0	0	0	0	0	0	64	0	0	168	1,675
1972	90	2	0	0	0	0	0	0	0	178	0	0	445	2,500
1973	NR	1	0	0	0	0	0	0	0	9	0	0	24	1,015
Lifetime		5	0	0	0	0	0	0	0	251	0	0	637	$5,190

Blaine Kauffman
Blaine Kauffman
Racing Hometown: Burton, OH

Year	Rank	Starts	Poles	1	2	3	4	5	6–10	Laps	Laps Led	Races Led	Miles	$
1966	136	1	0	0	0	0	0	0	0	33	0	0	83	0
1968	70	2	0	0	0	0	0	0	0	710	0	0	480	750
Lifetime		3	0	0	0	0	0	0	0	743	0	0	562	$750

Brent Keading
Brent Keading

Year	Rank	Starts	Poles	1	2	3	4	5	6–10	Laps	Laps Led	Races Led	Miles	$
1990	86	1	0	0	0	0	0	0	0	304	0	0	304	3,230
Lifetime		1	0	0	0	0	0	0	0	304	0	0	304	$3,230

William Kearney
William Kearney
Racing Hometown: Calumet, IL

Year	Rank	Starts	Poles	1	2	3	4	5	6–10	Laps	Laps Led	Races Led	Miles	$
1954	NR	1	0	0	0	0	0	0	0	28	0	0	115	0
Lifetime		1	0	0	0	0	0	0	0	28	0	0	115	$0

Year	Rank	Starts	Poles	Finish						Laps	Laps Led	Races Led	Miles	$
				1	2	3	4	5	6–10					

Bobby Keck

Robert Keck
Racing Hometown: Graham, NC

Year	Rank	Starts	Poles	1	2	3	4	5	6–10	Laps	Laps Led	Races Led	Miles	$
1956	43	15	0	0	0	0	0	0	3	2,236	0	0	1,309	1,250
1957	28	16	0	0	0	0	0	0	2	2,144	0	0	1,419	1,525
1958	12	30	0	0	0	0	0	0	7	4,345	0	0	2,219	3,459
1959	23	18	0	0	0	0	0	0	0	2,484	0	0	1,152	1,270
1963	65	9	0	0	0	0	0	0	2	935	0	0	458	1,530
1964	50	10	0	0	0	0	1	1	3	2,137	0	0	1,407	2,850
Lifetime		98	0	0	0	0	1	1	17	14,281	0	0	7,963	$11,884

Bob Keefe

Robert Keefe
Racing Hometown: Yakima, WA

Year	Rank	Starts	Poles	1	2	3	4	5	6–10	Laps	Laps Led	Races Led	Miles	$
1956	45	7	0	0	0	0	1	0	1	1,200	0	0	779	1,040
1957	97	3	0	0	0	0	0	0	1	367	0	0	184	440
1958	47	2	0	0	0	0	0	1	1	276	0	0	571	925
1959	NR	1	0	0	0	0	0	1	0	459	0	0	184	500
Lifetime		13	0	0	0	0	1	2	3	2,302	0	0	1,717	$2,905

Dick Keene

Richard Keene

Year	Rank	Starts	Poles	1	2	3	4	5	6–10	Laps	Laps Led	Races Led	Miles	$
1954	NR	1	0	0	0	0	0	0	0	31	0	0	62	0
Lifetime		1	0	0	0	0	0	0	0	31	0	0	62	$0

Tex Keene

Tex Keene
B: 12/26/1917
Racing Hometown: Marietta, GA

Year	Rank	Starts	Poles	1	2	3	4	5	6–10	Laps	Laps Led	Races Led	Miles	$
1950	NR	2	0	0	0	0	0	0	0	229	0	0	286	0
Lifetime		2	0	0	0	0	0	0	0	229	0	0	286	$0

Al Keller

Al Keller
B: 4/11/1920   D: 11/19/1961   *Killed in Indy Car race @ Phoenix Fairgrounds.*
Racing Hometown: Buffalo, NY

Year	Rank	Starts	Poles	1	2	3	4	5	6–10	Laps	Laps Led	Races Led	Miles	$
1949	32	1	0	0	0	0	0	0	1	185	0	0	185	200
1950	125	3	0	0	0	0	0	0	0	328	0	0	538	50
1952	64	4	0	0	0	0	0	0	0	328	0	0	164	125
1953	107	4	0	0	0	0	0	0	0	73	0	0	37	115
1954	NR	13	1	2	2	0	2	0	3	1,811	378	5	1,372	5,135
1956	69	4	0	0	1	0	0	0	1	446	0	0	247	1,300
Lifetime		29	1	2	3	0	2	0	5	3,171	378	5	2,543	$6,925

Duke Keller

Duke Keller

Year	Rank	Starts	Poles	1	2	3	4	5	6–10	Laps	Laps Led	Races Led	Miles	$
1952	206T	1	0	0	0	0	0	0	0	6	0	0	3	25
Lifetime		1	0	0	0	0	0	0	0	6	0	0	3	$25

Frank Keller

Frank Keller

Year	Rank	Starts	Poles	1	2	3	4	5	6–10	Laps	Laps Led	Races Led	Miles	$
1950	94T	1	0	0	0	0	0	0	0		0	0		50
Lifetime		1	0	0	0	0	0	0	0		0	0		$50

Pete Keller

Peter Keller
B: 11/13/1929
Racing Hometown: Columbia, SC

Year	Rank	Starts	Poles	1	2	3	4	5	6–10	Laps	Laps Led	Races Led	Miles	$
1950	NR	1	0	0	0	0	0	0	0	281	0	0	351	0
Lifetime		1	0	0	0	0	0	0	0	281	0	0	351	$0

Calvin Kelly

Calvin Kelly
Racing Hometown: Greenville, SC

Year	Rank	Starts	Poles	1	2	3	4	5	6–10	Laps	Laps Led	Races Led	Miles	$
1966	NR	2	0	0	0	0	0	0	0	41	0	0	103	1,120
Lifetime		2	0	0	0	0	0	0	0	41	0	0	103	$1,120

Joe Kelly

Joe Kelly *Real Name*: Dave Haupt
Racing Hometown: Quakertown, PA

Year	Rank	Starts	Poles	1	2	3	4	5	6–10	Laps	Laps Led	Races Led	Miles	$
1961	87	2	0	0	0	0	0	0	0	200	0	0	500	300

Year	Rank	Starts	Poles	Finish 1	2	3	4	5	6–10	Laps	Laps Led	Races Led	Miles	$

Joe Kelly *continued*

| 1963 | 130 | 1 | 0 | 0 | 0 | 0 | 0 | 0 | 0 | 120 | 0 | 0 | 60 | 85 |
| **Lifetime** | | 3 | 0 | 0 | 0 | 0 | 0 | 0 | 0 | 320 | 0 | 0 | 560 | $385 |

Pete Kelly
Peter Kelly
   Racing Hometown: Columbus, GA

1952	132	2	0	0	0	0	0	0	0	231	0	0	237	35
1959	NR	2	0	0	0	0	0	0	0	44	0	0	95	150
Lifetime		4	0	0	0	0	0	0	0	275	0	0	332	$185

Ray Kelly
Raymond Kelly
   B: 12/29/1946   D: 4/17/1992
   Racing Hometown: West Covina, CA

| 1986 | 116T | 1 | 0 | 0 | 0 | 0 | 0 | 0 | 0 | 36 | 0 | 0 | 94 | 850 |
| **Lifetime** | | 1 | 0 | 0 | 0 | 0 | 0 | 0 | 0 | 36 | 0 | 0 | 94 | $850 |

Jerry Kemp
Jerry Kemp
   D: 1/1995
   Racing Hometown: St. Louis, MO

| 1950 | NR | 1 | 0 | 0 | 0 | 0 | 0 | 0 | 0 | 315 | 0 | 0 | 394 | 0 |
| **Lifetime** | | 1 | 0 | 0 | 0 | 0 | 0 | 0 | 0 | 315 | 0 | 0 | 394 | $0 |

Mike Kempton
Michael John Kempton
   B: 1/21/1947
   Racing Hometown: Merriam, KS

1977	75	2	0	0	0	0	0	0	0	336	0	0	450	2,555
1979	73	2	0	0	0	0	0	0	0	499	0	0	487	1,605
1983	—	0												2,550
Lifetime		4	0	0	0	0	0	0	0	835	0	0	937	$6,710

Tommy Kendall
Thomas Kendall
   B: 10/17/1966
   Racing Hometown: LeCanada, CA

1987	NR	1	0	0	0	0	0	0	0	26	0	0	68	950
1988	64	1	0	0	0	0	0	0	0	94	1	1	246	3,400
1989	NR	1	0	0	0	0	0	0	0	79	1	1	192	3,015
1990	48	3	0	0	0	0	0	0	1	613	4	1	820	14,120
1991	63	1	0	0	0	0	0	0	0	74	12	1	186	12,450
1992	66	1	0	0	0	0	0	0	0	74	0	0	186	6,755
1993	54	2	0	0	0	0	0	0	0	158	0	0	392	32,190
1994	63	1	0	0	0	0	0	0	0	88	0	0	216	9,435
1996	60	1	0	0	0	0	0	0	1	73	4	1	184	20,730
Lifetime		12	0	0	0	0	0	0	1	1,279	22	5	2,490	$103,045

Bob Kennedy
Robert Kennedy
   Racing Hometown: Philipsburg, NJ

| 1954 | 179 | 1 | 0 | 0 | 0 | 0 | 0 | 0 | 0 | 46 | 0 | 0 | 46 | 0 |
| **Lifetime** | | 1 | 0 | 0 | 0 | 0 | 0 | 0 | 0 | 46 | 0 | 0 | 46 | $0 |

Bob Kennedy
Robert Kennedy
   B: 5/13/1936
   Racing Hometown: Thousand Oaks, CA

| 1983 | 84 | 1 | 0 | 0 | 0 | 0 | 0 | 0 | 0 | 89 | 0 | 0 | 233 | 1,990 |
| **Lifetime** | | 1 | 0 | 0 | 0 | 0 | 0 | 0 | 0 | 89 | 0 | 0 | 233 | $1,990 |

John Kennedy
John Kennedy
   Racing Hometown: Villa Park, IL

1969	49	8	0	0	0	0	0	0	0	1,084	0	0	1,675	6,462
1977	106T	1	0	0	0	0	0	0	0	66	0	0	132	880
1978	51	4	0	0	0	0	0	0	0	296	0	0	350	2,900

Year	Rank	Starts	Poles	Finish						Laps	Laps Led	Races Led	Miles	$
				1	2	3	4	5	6–10					

John Kennedy *continued*

Year	Rank	Starts	Poles	1	2	3	4	5	6–10	Laps	Laps Led	Races Led	Miles	$
1979	52	5	0	0	0	0	0	0	0	600	0	0	942	4,515
Lifetime		19	0	0	0	0	0	0	0	2,046	0	0	3,099	$14,757

Ted Kennedy

Theodore Kennedy

Year	Rank	Starts	Poles	1	2	3	4	5	6–10	Laps	Laps Led	Races Led	Miles	$
1986	74	2	0	0	0	0	0	0	0	172	0	0	451	3,255
1990	104	1	0	0	0	0	0	0	0	11	0	0	28	3,225
Lifetime		3	0	0	0	0	0	0	0	183	0	0	478	$6,480

John Kenney

John Golden Kenney Jr.
B: 2/28/1943
Racing Hometown: Poquoson, VA

Year	Rank	Starts	Poles	1	2	3	4	5	6–10	Laps	Laps Led	Races Led	Miles	$
1969	97	2	0	0	0	0	0	0	0	5	0	0	7	1,395
1970	46	11	0	0	0	0	0	0	0	1,385	0	0	675	4,115
Lifetime		13	0	0	0	0	0	0	0	1,390	0	0	682	$5,510

Al Kent

Al Kent
Racing Hometown: Richmond, VA

Year	Rank	Starts	Poles	1	2	3	4	5	6–10	Laps	Laps Led	Races Led	Miles	$
1953	117T	1	0	0	0	0	0	0	0		0	0		25
Lifetime		1	0	0	0	0	0	0	0		0	0		$25

Don Kent

Donald Kent
Racing Hometown: Dayton, OH

Year	Rank	Starts	Poles	1	2	3	4	5	6–10	Laps	Laps Led	Races Led	Miles	$
1952	NR	1	0	0	0	0	0	0	0	255	0	0	128	25
Lifetime		1	0	0	0	0	0	0	0	255	0	0	128	$25

Gary Kershaw

Gary Kershaw
Racing Hometown: Canada

Year	Rank	Starts	Poles	1	2	3	4	5	6–10	Laps	Laps Led	Races Led	Miles	$
1981	73T	1	0	0	0	0	0	0	0	117	0	0	307	1,800
Lifetime		1	0	0	0	0	0	0	0	117	0	0	307	$1,800

Bob Keselowski

Robert Keselowski
B: 8/1/1951
Racing Hometown: Rochester Hills, CA

Year	Rank	Starts	Poles	1	2	3	4	5	6–10	Laps	Laps Led	Races Led	Miles	$
1994	81T	1	0	0	0	0	0	0	0	17	0	0	43	7,150
Lifetime		1	0	0	0	0	0	0	0	17	0	0	43	$7,150

Ron Keselowski

Ronald William Keselowski
B: 9/12/1946
Racing Hometown: Troy, MI

Year	Rank	Starts	Poles	1	2	3	4	5	6–10	Laps	Laps Led	Races Led	Miles	$
1970	39	17	0	0	0	0	0	0	1	2,339	9	1	2,842	11,985
1971	27	20	0	0	0	0	0	0	6	3,046	0	0	4,248	17,680
1972	27	22	0	0	0	0	0	1	2	3,398	0	0	4,976	22,175
1973	45	5	0	0	0	0	0	1	0	733	0	0	1,293	6,060
1974	59	4	0	0	0	0	0	0	0	456	0	0	797	5,160
Lifetime		68	0	0	0	0	0	2	9	9,972	9	1	14,157	$63,035

Tip R. Key

Tip R. Key
Racing Hometown: Hannibal, MO

Year	Rank	Starts	Poles	1	2	3	4	5	6–10	Laps	Laps Led	Races Led	Miles	$
1951	N/A	1	0	0	0	0	0	0	0		0	0		25
Lifetime		1	0	0	0	0	0	0	0		0	0		$25

Jerry Keyes

Jerry Keyes
Racing Hometown: Encino, CA

Year	Rank	Starts	Poles	1	2	3	4	5	6–10	Laps	Laps Led	Races Led	Miles	$
1954	NR	1	0	0	0	0	0	0	0	338	0	0	169	25
Lifetime		1	0	0	0	0	0	0	0	338	0	0	169	$25

Year	Rank	Starts	Poles	Finish						Laps	Laps Led	Races Led	Miles	$
				1	2	3	4	5	6–10	Laps				

John Kieper

John Kieper
B: 2/12/1932
Racing Hometown: Portland, OR

Year	Rank	Starts	Poles	1	2	3	4	5	6–10	Laps	Laps Led	Races Led	Miles	$
1954	NR	1	0	0	0	0	0	0	0	420	0	0	210	25
1955	56	2	0	0	1	0	0	0	0	323	89	1	323	1,500
1956	35	8	4	1	1	1	1	0	3	1,479	67	2	917	3,250
1957	152T	1	0	0	0	0	0	0	0	6	0	0	3	50
1975	86T	2	0	0	0	0	0	0	0	191	0	0	490	2,110
1976	111T	1	0	0	0	0	0	0	0	62	0	0	155	710
1977	113T	1	0	0	0	0	0	0	0	50	0	0	125	740
Lifetime		16	4	1	2	1	1	0	3	2,531	156	3	2,223	$8,385

J. Kilgore

J. Kilgore

Year	Rank	Starts	Poles	1	2	3	4	5	6–10	Laps	Laps Led	Races Led	Miles	$
1954	NR	1	0	0	0	0	0	0	0	45	0	0	90	130
Lifetime		1	0	0	0	0	0	0	0	45	0	0	90	$130

Glenn Killian

Glenn Killian
Racing Hometown: Hickory, NC

Year	Rank	Starts	Poles	1	2	3	4	5	6–10	Laps	Laps Led	Races Led	Miles	$
1962	133	1	0	0	0	0	0	0	0	3	0	0	1	50
Lifetime		1	0	0	0	0	0	0	0	3	0	0	1	$50

Don Kimberling

Donald Kimberling
Racing Hometown: Tyronne, PA

Year	Rank	Starts	Poles	1	2	3	4	5	6–10	Laps	Laps Led	Races Led	Miles	$
1958	140	1	0	0	0	0	0	0	0	7	0	0	10	100
Lifetime		1	0	0	0	0	0	0	0	7	0	0	10	$100

Oma Kimbrough

Oma Kimbrough
B: 3/29/1951
Racing Hometown: Tyronne, PA

Year	Rank	Starts	Poles	1	2	3	4	5	6–10	Laps	Laps Led	Races Led	Miles	$
1989	87T	1	0	0	0	0	0	0	0	64	0	0	155	2,135
1990	98T	1	0	0	0	0	0	0	0	40	0	0	97	2,240
1991	73	1	0	0	0	0	0	0	0	80	0	0	194	3,620
Lifetime		3	0	0	0	0	0	0	0	184	0	0	447	$7,995

Bill Kimmel

William J. Kimmel
B: 9/13/1928
Racing Hometown: Clarksville, IN

Year	Rank	Starts	Poles	1	2	3	4	5	6–10	Laps	Laps Led	Races Led	Miles	$
1969	NR	2	0	0	0	0	0	0	0	39	0	0	98	1,100
1970	108T	1	0	0	0	0	0	0	0	41	0	0	103	220
Lifetime		3	0	0	0	0	0	0	0	80	0	0	200	$1,320

Marty Kinerk

Marty Kinerk
Racing Hometown: South Gate, CA

Year	Rank	Starts	Poles	1	2	3	4	5	6–10	Laps	Laps Led	Races Led	Miles	$
1969	NR	1	0	0	0	0	0	0	0	40	0	0	108	755
1971	NR	1	0	0	0	0	0	0	0	91	0	0	228	1,450
Lifetime		2	0	0	0	0	0	0	0	131	0	0	336	$2,205

Al King

Al King
Racing Hometown: St. Louis, MO

Year	Rank	Starts	Poles	1	2	3	4	5	6–10	Laps	Laps Led	Races Led	Miles	$
1951	N/A	1	0	0	0	0	0	0	0	71	0	0	71	25
Lifetime		1	0	0	0	0	0	0	0	71	0	0	71	$25

Brownie King

Herman H. King
B: 1/31/1934
Racing Hometown: Johnson City, TN

Year	Rank	Starts	Poles	1	2	3	4	5	6–10	Laps	Laps Led	Races Led	Miles	$
1956	40	15	0	0	0	0	0	0	0	1,994	0	0	1,322	925
1957	9	36	0	0	0	0	0	1	15	5,756	0	0	3,464	5,589
1958	35	24	0	0	0	0	0	0	5	3,926	0	0	2,153	3,205
1959	30	18	0	0	0	0	0	1	4	3,247	0	0	1,903	1,875
1960	113	3	0	0	0	0	0	0	1	410	0	0	647	465

Year	Rank	Starts	Poles	Finish						Laps	Laps Led	Races Led	Miles	$
				1	2	3	4	5	6–10					

Brownie King *continued*

Year	Rank	Starts	Poles	1	2	3	4	5	6–10	Laps	Laps Led	Races Led	Miles	$
1961	183	1	0	0	0	0	0	0	0	442	0	0	221	250
Lifetime		97	0	0	0	0	0	2	25	15,775	0	0	9,710	$12,309

Bub King
T. L. King
   Racing Hometown: Corbin, KY

Year	Rank	Starts	Poles	1	2	3	4	5	6–10	Laps	Laps Led	Races Led	Miles	$
1950	NR	1	0	0	0	0	0	0	0	329	0	0	411	0
1951	60	9	0	0	0	0	0	0	2	247	0	0	260	450
1952	15	10	0	0	0	1	1	0	3	1,743	0	0	1,419	2,737
1953	17	14	0	0	0	0	0	0	5	1,029	0	0	1,013	1,036
1954	141	1	0	0	0	0	0	0	0	34	0	0	17	25
Lifetime		35	0	0	0	1	1	0	10	3,382	0	0	3,120	$3,773

Byron King
Byron King
   Racing Hometown: Orlando, FL

Year	Rank	Starts	Poles	1	2	3	4	5	6–10	Laps	Laps Led	Races Led	Miles	$
1954	NR	1	0	0	0	0	0	0	0	37	0	0	152	60
Lifetime		1	0	0	0	0	0	0	0	37	0	0	152	$60

J. W. King
J. W. King
   Racing Hometown: Atlanta, GA

Year	Rank	Starts	Poles	1	2	3	4	5	6–10	Laps	Laps Led	Races Led	Miles	$
1969	NR	1	0	0	0	0	0	0	0	26	0	0	69	1,000
Lifetime		1	0	0	0	0	0	0	0	26	0	0	69	$1,000

Max King
Max King
   B: 6/4/1913
   Racing Hometown: Cartersville, GA

Year	Rank	Starts	Poles	1	2	3	4	5	6–10	Laps	Laps Led	Races Led	Miles	$
1953	134T	1	0	0	0	0	0	0	0		0	0		25
Lifetime		1	0	0	0	0	0	0	0		0	0		$25

Steve Kinser
Steve Kinser
   B: 6/5/1954
   Racing Hometown: Bloomington, IN

Year	Rank	Starts	Poles	1	2	3	4	5	6–10	Laps	Laps Led	Races Led	Miles	$
1993	—	0												2,000
1995	49	5	0	0	0	0	0	0	0	958	0	0	948	105,224
Lifetime		5	0	0	0	0	0	0	0	958	0	0	948	$107,224

Pat Kirkwood
Patrick Kirkwood
   Racing Hometown: Ft. Worth, TX

Year	Rank	Starts	Poles	1	2	3	4	5	6–10	Laps	Laps Led	Races Led	Miles	$
1949	NR	1	0	0	0	0	0	0	0		0	0		0
1952	NR	4	1	0	0	1	0	1	0	764	0	0	972	1,215
1956	33	3	0	0	0	1	0	0	1	715	0	0	928	2,025
1957	178	1	0	0	0	0	0	0	0		0	0		50
Lifetime		9	1	0	0	2	0	1	1	1,479	0	0	1,900	$3,290

Ken Kiser
Kenneth Kiser

Year	Rank	Starts	Poles	1	2	3	4	5	6–10	Laps	Laps Led	Races Led	Miles	$
1954	NR	1	0	0	0	0	0	0	0	164	0	0	82	25
Lifetime		1	0	0	0	0	0	0	0	164	0	0	82	$25

Harold Kite
Harold Kite
   B: 11/12/1921 D: 10/17/1965 *Killed in NASCAR race @ Charlotte, NC.*
   Racing Hometown: East Point, GA

Year	Rank	Starts	Poles	1	2	3	4	5	6–10	Laps	Laps Led	Races Led	Miles	$
1950	30	3	0	1	0	0	0	0	0	382	38	1	618	1,550
1951	25	2	0	0	0	0	0	0	1	384	0	0	480	800
1955	181	2	0	0	0	0	0	0	0	279	0	0	387	110
1956	184T	1	0	0	0	0	0	0	0	178	0	0	89	110
1965	133	1	0	0	0	0	0	0	0	1	0	0	2	410
Lifetime		9	0	1	0	0	0	0	1	1,224	38	1	1,575	$2,980

Mike Kittlekow
Michael Kittlekow

Year	Rank	Starts	Poles	1	2	3	4	5	6–10	Laps	Laps Led	Races Led	Miles	$
1971	NR	1	0	0	0	0	0	0	0	38	0	0	100	1,015
Lifetime		1	0	0	0	0	0	0	0	38	0	0	100	$1,015

Year	Rank	Starts	Poles	Finish 1	2	3	4	5	6–10	Laps	Laps Led	Races Led	Miles	$

Dick Klank
Richard Klank

Year	Rank	Starts	Poles	1	2	3	4	5	6–10	Laps	Laps Led	Races Led	Miles	$
1957	131	7	0	0	0	0	0	0	1	942	0	0	631	565
Lifetime		7	0	0	0	0	0	0	1	942	0	0	631	$565

Mike Klapak
Michael Klapak
B: 3/8/1913
Racing Hometown: Warren, OH

Year	Rank	Starts	Poles	1	2	3	4	5	6–10	Laps	Laps Led	Races Led	Miles	$
1950	98	4	0	0	0	0	0	0	0	158	0	0	79	50
1951	N/A	5	0	0	0	0	0	0	1	0	0	0	0	150
1952	199	1	0	0	0	0	0	0	0	0	0	0	0	0
1953	NR	2	0	0	0	0	0	0	2	0	0	0	0	250
Lifetime		12	0	0	0	0	0	0	3	158	0	0	79	$450

Charles Kleber
Charles Kleber

Year	Rank	Starts	Poles	1	2	3	4	5	6–10	Laps	Laps Led	Races Led	Miles	$
1951	209T	1	0	0	0	0	0	0	0		0	0		25
Lifetime		1	0	0	0	0	0	0	0		0	0		$25

Ken Klutz
Kenneth Klutz
Racing Hometown: Salisbury, NC

Year	Rank	Starts	Poles	1	2	3	4	5	6–10	Laps	Laps Led	Races Led	Miles	$
1951	N/A	1	0	0	0	0	0	0	0	95	0	0	71	25
Lifetime		1	0	0	0	0	0	0	0	95	0	0	71	$25

Peter Knab
Peter C. Knab
B: 1938
Racing Hometown: Dayton, OH

Year	Rank	Starts	Poles	1	2	3	4	5	6–10	Laps	Laps Led	Races Led	Miles	$
1977	78	3	0	0	0	0	0	0	0	507	0	0	1,017	6,865
Lifetime		3	0	0	0	0	0	0	0	507	0	0	1,017	$6,865

Fred Knapp
Fred Knapp
Racing Hometown: Jamestown, NY

Year	Rank	Starts	Poles	1	2	3	4	5	6–10	Laps	Laps Led	Races Led	Miles	$
1957	120	2	0	0	0	0	0	0	1	216	0	0	128	240
Lifetime		2	0	0	0	0	0	0	1	216	0	0	128	$240

Art Knoll
Arthur Knoll
Racing Hometown: Pittsburgh, PA

Year	Rank	Starts	Poles	1	2	3	4	5	6–10	Laps	Laps Led	Races Led	Miles	$
1951	NR	1	0	0	0	0	0	0	0		0	0		25
Lifetime		1	0	0	0	0	0	0	0		0	0		$25

Rick Knoop
Richard Knoop
B: 7/8/1953
Racing Hometown: Atherton, CA

Year	Rank	Starts	Poles	1	2	3	4	5	6–10	Laps	Laps Led	Races Led	Miles	$
1981	NR	1	0	0	0	0	0	0	0	197	0	0	394	3,405
1986	95	1	0	0	0	0	0	0	0	88	0	0	214	6,995
1987	81	3	0	0	0	0	0	0	0	686	0	0	1,025	21,875
Lifetime		5	0	0	0	0	0	0	0	971	0	0	1,632	$32,275

Barry Knowlton
Barry Knowlton

Year	Rank	Starts	Poles	1	2	3	4	5	6–10	Laps	Laps Led	Races Led	Miles	$
1957	174	1	0	0	0	0	0	0	0	73	0	0	37	50
Lifetime		1	0	0	0	0	0	0	0	73	0	0	37	$50

Red Knuter
Red Knuter
Racing Hometown: North Platte, NE

Year	Rank	Starts	Poles	1	2	3	4	5	6–10	Laps	Laps Led	Races Led	Miles	$
1953	108T	1	0	0	0	0	0	0	0		0	0		25
Lifetime		1	0	0	0	0	0	0	0		0	0		$25

Bud Kohler
Bud Kohler
B: 2/15/1921
Racing Hometown: Blue Island, IL

Year	Rank	Starts	Poles	1	2	3	4	5	6–10	Laps	Laps Led	Races Led	Miles	$
1952	176	1	0	0	0	0	0	0	0	140	0	0	140	25
Lifetime		1	0	0	0	0	0	0	0	140	0	0	140	$25

Year	Rank	Starts	Poles	Finish						Laps	Laps Led	Races Led	Miles	$
				1	2	3	4	5	6–10	Laps	Led	Led	Miles	$

Ronnie Kohler
Ronald W. Kohler
B: 5/28/1927
Racing Hometown: Paterson, NJ

Year	Rank	Starts	Poles	1	2	3	4	5	6–10	Laps	Laps Led	Races Led	Miles	$
1951	29	5	0	0	0	2	0	0	1		0	0		1,100
1952	80	2	0	0	0	0	0	1	0	253	0	0	127	225
1953	NR	4	0	0	0	0	0	1	0		0	0		425
1954	103	2	0	0	0	0	0	0	1	368	0	0	276	150
Lifetime		13	0	0	0	2	0	2	2	621	0	0	403	$1,875

Bob Korf
Robert Korf
Racing Hometown: Long Beach, CA

Year	Rank	Starts	Poles	1	2	3	4	5	6–10	Laps	Laps Led	Races Led	Miles	$
1956	101	1	0	0	0	0	0	0	1		0	0		400
Lifetime		1	0	0	0	0	0	0	1		0	0		$400

Bob Kosiski
Robert Kosiski
Racing Hometown: Omaha, NE

Year	Rank	Starts	Poles	1	2	3	4	5	6–10	Laps	Laps Led	Races Led	Miles	$
1960	110	2	0	0	0	0	0	0	0	163	0	0	408	250
Lifetime		2	0	0	0	0	0	0	0	163	0	0	408	$250

Dick Kranzler
Richard E. Kranzler
B: 11/26/1938
Racing Hometown: Santa Susana, CA

Year	Rank	Starts	Poles	1	2	3	4	5	6–10	Laps	Laps Led	Races Led	Miles	$
1970	75	1	0	0	0	0	0	0	0	148	0	0	388	1,100
1971	NR	3	0	0	0	0	0	0	0	215	0	0	562	3,105
1972	68	3	0	0	0	0	0	0	0	391	0	0	1,008	3,635
1973	107	1	0	0	0	0	0	0	0	108	0	0	283	890
1979	114	1	0	0	0	0	0	0	0	23	0	0	60	700
Lifetime		9	0	0	0	0	0	0	0	885	0	0	2,301	$9,430

Buddy Krebs
Buddy Krebs
Racing Hometown: E. Hartford, CT

Year	Rank	Starts	Poles	1	2	3	4	5	6–10	Laps	Laps Led	Races Led	Miles	$
1953	117T	1	0	0	0	0	0	0	0		0	0		25
1956	282	1	0	0	0	0	0	0	0		0	0		0
Lifetime		2	0	0	0	0	0	0	0		0	0		$25

Fred Krebs
Fred Krebs

Year	Rank	Starts	Poles	1	2	3	4	5	6–10	Laps	Laps Led	Races Led	Miles	$
1955	229	1	0	0	0	0	0	0	0	50	0	0	50	50
Lifetime		1	0	0	0	0	0	0	0	50	0	0	50	$50

John Krebs
John Krebs
B: 10/1/1950
Racing Hometown: Roseville, CA

Year	Rank	Starts	Poles	1	2	3	4	5	6–10	Laps	Laps Led	Races Led	Miles	$
1982	67	2	0	0	0	0	0	0	0	127	0	0	333	1,750
1983	92	1	0	0	0	0	0	0	0	60	0	0	157	1,100
1984	78	2	0	0	0	0	0	0	0	54	0	0	141	1,790
1985	81T	1	0	0	0	0	0	0	0	73	0	0	191	2,250
1986	87	2	0	0	0	0	0	0	0	94	0	0	246	2,075
1987	88T	1	0	0	0	0	0	0	0	80	0	0	210	1,125
1988	73	1	0	0	0	0	0	0	0	92	0	0	241	1,600
1989	91T	1	0	0	0	0	0	0	0	65	0	0	164	3,000
1990	67	2	0	0	0	0	0	0	0	366	0	0	477	8,435
1991	84	1	0	0	0	0	0	0	0	57	1	1	144	3,525
1992	61	2	0	0	0	0	0	0	0	380	0	0	489	12,990
1993	61	2	0	0	0	0	0	0	0	154	0	0	386	16,455
1994	80	1	0	0	0	0	0	0	0	18	1	1	45	8,100
Lifetime		19	0	0	0	0	0	0	0	1,620	2	2	3,225	$64,195

Ed Kretz
Edward Kretz
Racing Hometown: Monterey, CA

Year	Rank	Starts	Poles	1	2	3	4	5	6–10	Laps	Laps Led	Races Led	Miles	$
1956	279	1	0	0	0	0	0	0	0		0	0		0
Lifetime		1	0	0	0	0	0	0	0		0	0		$0

Year	Rank	Starts	Poles	Finish 1	2	3	4	5	6–10	Laps	Laps Led	Races Led	Miles	$
Jeff Krogh				Jeffrey Krogh B: 3/21/1972 Racing Hometown: Kamiah, ID										
1996	59	2	0	0	0	0	0	0	0	222	0	0	330	19,680
Lifetime		2	0	0	0	0	0	0	0	222	0	0	330	$19,680
Stan Kross				Stanley Kross Racing Hometown: Salem, IN										
1954	66	5	0	0	0	0	0	0	1	135	0	0	215	150
Lifetime		5	0	0	0	0	0	0	1	135	0	0	215	$150
Carl Krueger				Carl Krueger Racing Hometown: Newton, PA										
1955	44	7	0	0	0	0	0	1	1	955	0	0	534	585
Lifetime		7	0	0	0	0	0	1	1	955	0	0	534	$585
Mel Krueger				Mel Krueger Racing Hometown: Anita, IA										
1953	49	3	0	0	0	0	0	0	1		0	0		175
1954	117	2	0	0	0	0	0	0	0	208	0	0	226	50
Lifetime		5	0	0	0	0	0	0	1	208	0	0	226	$225
Alan Kulwicki				Alan Dennis Kulwicki B: 12/14/1954 D: 4/1/1993 *Killed in private plane crash en route to Bristol.* Racing Hometown: Greenfield, WI										
1985	40	5	0	0	0	0	0	0	0	1,843	0	0	1,991	10,290
1986	21	23	0	0	0	0	1	0	3	7,872	14	6	8,602	94,450
1987	15	29	3	0	1	0	1	1	6	7,758	102	8	9,119	369,889
1988	14	29	4	1	2	1	1	2	2	8,149	134	8	9,317	448,547
1989	14	29	6	0	4	0	0	1	4	8,324	564	14	9,560	501,295
1990	8	29	1	1	1	1	1	1	8	8,635	400	10	10,655	550,936
1991	13	29	4	1	0	1	1	1	7	8,507	233	9	10,145	595,614
1992	1	29	6	2	3	2	2	2	6	8,991	1,235	**20**	10,852	2,322,561
1993	41	5	0	0	0	1	1	0	1	1,588	4	2	1,995	165,470
Lifetime		207	24	5	11	6	8	8	37	61,667	2,686	77	72,236	$5,059,052
Joe Kusler				Joseph Kusler Racing Hometown: Franklin, NJ										
1952	147T	1	0	0	0	0	0	0	0	164	0	0	82	25
Lifetime		1	0	0	0	0	0	0	0	164	0	0	82	$25
Bud Kutina				Bud Kutina Racing Hometown: Rochester, MN										
1955	118	1	0	0	0	0	0	0	0	38	0	0	156	140
Lifetime		1	0	0	0	0	0	0	0	38	0	0	156	$140
Kuzie Kuzmanich				Kuzie Kuzmanich Racing Hometown: Portland, OR										
1960	106	2	0	0	0	0	0	0	1	115	0	0	124	350
1961	125	1	0	0	0	0	0	0	1	97	0	0	97	150
Lifetime		3	0	0	0	0	0	0	2	212	0	0	221	$500
Bobby Labonte				Robert Allen Labonte B: 5/8/1964 Racing Hometown: Corpus Christi, TX										
1991	66	2	0	0	0	0	0	0	0	128	0	0	168	8,350
1993	19	30	1	0	0	0	0	0	6	9,295	33	7	10,937	395,660
1994	21	31	0	0	0	0	0	1	1	8,541	3	2	10,456	550,305
1995	10	31	2	3	3	0	0	1	7	9,019	278	14	10,974	1,413,682
1996	11	31	4	1	1	0	1	2	9	8,916	337	13	10,570	1,475,196
Lifetime		125	7	4	4	0	1	4	23	35,899	651	36	43,105	$3,843,193

Year	Rank	Starts	Poles	Finish 1	2	3	4	5	6–10	Laps	Laps Led	Races Led	Miles	$

Terry Labonte

Terrence Lee Labonte
B: 11/16/1956
Racing Hometown: Corpus Christi, TX

Year	Rank	Starts	Poles	1	2	3	4	5	6–10	Laps	Laps Led	Races Led	Miles	$
1978	39	5	0	0	0	0	1	0	2	1,849	0	0	1,879	21,395
1979	10	31	0	0	0	1	0	1	11	8,766	8	4	9,886	134,653
1980	8	31	0	1	0	1	1	3	10	8,760	46	6	9,951	222,502
1981	4	31	2	0	1	3	2	2	9	9,074	114	14	10,530	348,703
1982	3	30	2	0	6	2	6	3	4	8,900	263	17	10,259	398,635
1983	5	30	3	1	0	0	4	6	9	8,498	434	13	9,774	388,419
1984	1	30	2	2	6	6	2	1	7	9,886	880	26	11,236	767,716
1985	7	28	4	1	2	3	1	1	9	7,973	563	14	9,603	694,510
1986	12	29	1	1	2	2	0	0	5	8,284	565	10	9,588	522,235
1987	3	29	4	1	2	2	5	3	9	8,609	592	16	10,157	805,054
1988	4	29	1	1	2	3	4	1	7	9,206	207	17	11,032	950,781
1989	10	29	0	2	2	1	1	3	2	8,306	104	10	9,771	703,806
1990	15	29	0	0	1	0	3	0	5	8,518	9	3	10,143	450,230
1991	18	29	1	0	0	0	0	1	6	7,989	52	2	9,615	348,898
1992	8	29	0	0	1	0	2	1	12	8,912	43	4	10,612	600,381
1993	18	30	0	0	0	0	0	0	10	8,866	55	3	10,641	531,717
1994	7	31	0	3	1	1	0	1	8	9,149	487	8	11,313	1,150,921
1995	6	31	1	3	4	2	3	2	3	9,076	438	11	11,376	1,558,659
1996	1	31	4	2	7	5	1	6	3	9,443	973	22	11,522	4,030,648
Lifetime		542	25	18	37	32	36	35	131	160,064	5,833	200	188,890	$14,629,863
										8th		**9th**	**7th**	**4th**

Rick Lach

Richard Lach

Year	Rank	Starts	Poles	1	2	3	4	5	6–10	Laps	Laps Led	Races Led	Miles	$
1986	121T	1	0	0	0	0	0	0	0	20	0	0	52	825
Lifetime		1	0	0	0	0	0	0	0	20	0	0	52	$825

Jim Lacy

James Lacy
B: 1926
Racing Hometown: N. Bellmore, NY

Year	Rank	Starts	Poles	1	2	3	4	5	6–10	Laps	Laps Led	Races Led	Miles	$
1953	66	3	0	0	0	0	0	0	0		0	0		125
1954	NR	1	0	0	0	0	0	0	0	3	0	0	3	0
Lifetime		4	0	0	0	0	0	0	0	3	0	0	3	$125

Arnold Ladd

Arnold Ladd

Year	Rank	Starts	Poles	1	2	3	4	5	6–10	Laps	Laps Led	Races Led	Miles	$
1954	NR	1	0	0	0	0	0	0	0	41	0	0	82	45
Lifetime		1	0	0	0	0	0	0	0	41	0	0	82	$45

Scott Lagasse

Scott Lagasse
B: 2/20/1959
Racing Hometown: St. Augustine, FL

Year	Rank	Starts	Poles	1	2	3	4	5	6–10	Laps	Laps Led	Races Led	Miles	$
1993	59	1	0	0	0	0	0	0	0	90	0	0	221	7,800
1994	75	1	0	0	0	0	0	0	0	65	0	0	159	6,055
Lifetime		2	0	0	0	0	0	0	0	155	0	0	380	$13,855

Bill LaGrance

William LaGrance
Racing Hometown: Greensboro, NC

Year	Rank	Starts	Poles	1	2	3	4	5	6–10	Laps	Laps Led	Races Led	Miles	$
1951	NR	1	0	0	0	0	0	0	0		0	0		25
Lifetime		1	0	0	0	0	0	0	0		0	0		$25

Randy LaJoie

Randall LaJoie
B: 8/28/1961
Racing Hometown: Norwalk, CT

Year	Rank	Starts	Poles	1	2	3	4	5	6–10	Laps	Laps Led	Races Led	Miles	$
1985	NR	1	0	0	0	0	0	0	0	319	0	0	486	8,325
1986	107T	1	0	0	0	0	0	0	0	144	0	0	360	3,315
1988	NR	1	0	0	0	0	0	0	0	89	0	0	89	1,460
1989	83T	1	0	0	0	0	0	0	0	178	0	0	445	5,175
1990	73	2	0	0	0	0	0	0	0	177	0	0	438	6,675
1991	50	4	0	0	0	0	0	0	0	1,080	0	0	1,447	23,875
1994	48	3	0	0	0	0	0	0	0	1,010	0	0	1,390	30,565
1995	40	14	0	0	0	0	0	0	0	3,606	0	0	4,490	281,945
Lifetime		27	0	0	0	0	0	0	0	6,603	0	0	9,144	$361,335

Year	Rank	Starts	Poles	Finish						Laps	Laps Led	Races Led	Miles	$
				1	2	3	4	5	6–10	Laps	Led	Led	Miles	$

Ben Lalomia

Ben Lalomia
B: 3/29/1919
Racing Hometown: Buffalo, NY

Year	Rank	Starts	Poles	1	2	3	4	5	6–10	Laps	Laps Led	Races Led	Miles	$
1951	N/A	1	0	0	0	0	0	0	0		0	0		25
Lifetime		1	0	0	0	0	0	0	0		0	0		$25

Morris Lamb

Morris Lamb
Racing Hometown: Germantown, OH

Year	Rank	Starts	Poles	1	2	3	4	5	6–10	Laps	Laps Led	Races Led	Miles	$
1950	137T	1	0	0	0	0	0	0	0		0	0		0
Lifetime		1	0	0	0	0	0	0	0		0	0		$0

Wayne Lambath

R. Wayne Lambath
Racing Hometown: Winston-Salem, NC

Year	Rank	Starts	Poles	1	2	3	4	5	6–10	Laps	Laps Led	Races Led	Miles	$
1961	174	1	0	0	0	0	0	0	0	117	0	0	59	125
Lifetime		1	0	0	0	0	0	0	0	117	0	0	59	$125

Art Lamey

Arthur Lamey
D: 8/30/1983
Racing Hometown: Racine, WI

Year	Rank	Starts	Poles	1	2	3	4	5	6–10	Laps	Laps Led	Races Led	Miles	$
1950	19	4	0	0	0	0	0	2	1		0	0		655
Lifetime		4	0	0	0	0	0	2	1		0	0		$655

Sam Lamm *See* Fred Bince

Jim Lamport

James Lamport
Racing Hometown: Pittsburg, CA

Year	Rank	Starts	Poles	1	2	3	4	5	6–10	Laps	Laps Led	Races Led	Miles	$
1959	NR	1	0	0	0	0	0	0	0	414	0	0	166	150
Lifetime		1	0	0	0	0	0	0	0	414	0	0	166	$150

Furman Lancaster

Furman Lancaster
Racing Hometown: Atlanta, GA

Year	Rank	Starts	Poles	1	2	3	4	5	6–10	Laps	Laps Led	Races Led	Miles	$
1951	N/A	1	0	0	0	0	0	0	1	140	0	0	140	100
Lifetime		1	0	0	0	0	0	0	1	140	0	0	140	$100

Junie Lancaster

Junie Lancaster

Year	Rank	Starts	Poles	1	2	3	4	5	6–10	Laps	Laps Led	Races Led	Miles	$
1954	NR	1	0	0	0	0	0	0	0	202	0	0	202	50
Lifetime		1	0	0	0	0	0	0	0	202	0	0	202	$50

Tommy Lane

Thomas Lane

Year	Rank	Starts	Poles	1	2	3	4	5	6–10	Laps	Laps Led	Races Led	Miles	$
1951	138	2	0	0	0	0	0	0	1		0	0		125
Lifetime		2	0	0	0	0	0	0	1		0	0		$125

Shep Langdon

Shepard Langdon
Racing Hometown: Angier, NC

Year	Rank	Starts	Poles	1	2	3	4	5	6–10	Laps	Laps Led	Races Led	Miles	$
1957	NR	2	0	0	0	0	0	0	0	268	0	0	268	0
1958	NR	18	0	0	0	0	0	0	1	3,220	0	0	1,648	1,645
1959	12	21	0	0	0	0	0	0	6	3,976	0	0	2,259	3,526
1960	65	4	0	0	0	0	0	0	1	588	0	0	756	635
Lifetime		45	0	0	0	0	0	0	8	8,052	0	0	4,931	$5,806

Elmo Langley

Elmo Harrell Langley
B: 8/22/1929 D: 11/21/1996
Racing Hometown: Landover, MD

Year	Rank	Starts	Poles	1	2	3	4	5	6–10	Laps	Laps Led	Races Led	Miles	$
1954	34	2	0	0	0	0	0	0	0	340	0	0	466	450
1955	100	4	0	0	0	0	0	0	1	518	0	0	370	350
1956	NR	1	0	0	0	0	0	0	0	338	0	0	465	140
1957	132T	1	0	0	0	0	0	0	0	189	0	0	95	150
1958	39	9	0	0	0	0	0	1	2	1,240	0	0	874	1,090
1959	28	13	0	0	0	1	0	0	1	1,694	0	0	1,314	2,280

Year	Rank	Starts	Poles	Finish						Laps	Laps Led	Races Led	Miles	$
				1	2	3	4	5	6–10					

Elmo Langley *continued*

Year	Rank	Starts	Poles	1	2	3	4	5	6–10	Laps	Laps Led	Races Led	Miles	$
1960	54	11	0	0	0	0	0	0	0	1,234	0	0	1,195	1,640
1961	30	15	0	0	0	0	0	1	4	2,826	0	0	3,012	3,530
1962	40	6	0	0	0	0	0	0	0	774	0	0	1,086	1,795
1963	39	11	0	0	0	0	0	1	1	2,196	0	0	1,513	2,170
1964	42	14	0	0	0	0	0	0	5	2,739	0	0	1,658	3,905
1965	25	34	0	0	0	2	1	0	6	5,698	19	1	3,816	10,895
1966	11	47	1	2	1	1	4	4	8	9,461	308	5	6,372	22,455
1967	9	45	0	0	1	3	2	4	14	9,652	0	0	6,781	23,898
1968	6	48	0	0	0	1	1	4	22	11,149	0	0	7,786	25,832
1969	5	52	0	0	0	1	6	6	15	12,531	40	1	9,812	73,092
1970	6	47	0	0	0	1	0	0	18	10,672	0	0	9,319	45,193
1971	5	46	0	0	3	1	3	4	12	11,299	48	1	10,489	57,037
1972	7	30	0	0	0	0	0	1	8	8,150	0	0	9,459	59,644
1973	9	27	0	0	0	0	0	0	4	8,016	0	0	8,377	49,892
1974	25	23	0	0	0	0	0	0	3	5,589	0	0	5,852	24,722
1975	8	29	0	0	0	0	0	2	5	8,601	0	0	9,884	67,600
1976	36	7	0	0	0	0	0	0	1	2,451	0	0	1,368	7,515
1977	42	7	0	0	0	0	0	0	0	1,395	0	0	812	5,855
1978	65	3	0	0	0	0	0	0	0	482	0	0	326	2,765
1979	82	3	0	0	0	0	0	0	0	466	0	0	253	3,010
1981	69	1	0	0	0	0	0	0	0	6	0	0	6	575
Lifetime		536	1	2	5	11	17	28	130	119,706	415	8	102,760	$497,480

Sonny Lanphear

Hugh Lanphear
Racing Hometown: Charlotte, NC

Year	Rank	Starts	Poles	1	2	3	4	5	6–10	Laps	Laps Led	Races Led	Miles	$
1966	75	12	0	0	0	0	0	0	1	618	0	0	339	2,270
Lifetime		12	0	0	0	0	0	0	1	618	0	0	339	$2,270

John Lansaw

John Lansaw
Racing Hometown: Anaheim, CA

Year	Rank	Starts	Poles	1	2	3	4	5	6–10	Laps	Laps Led	Races Led	Miles	$
1955	168	1	0	0	0	0	0	0	0	74	0	0	74	50
1956	242	2	0	0	0	0	0	0	0	133	0	0	124	35
Lifetime		3	0	0	0	0	0	0	0	207	0	0	198	$85

Nick Lari

Nicholas Lari
Racing Hometown: Santa Monica, CA

Year	Rank	Starts	Poles	1	2	3	4	5	6–10	Laps	Laps Led	Races Led	Miles	$
1956	229	1	0	0	0	0	0	0	0	155	0	0	78	50
Lifetime		1	0	0	0	0	0	0	0	155	0	0	78	$50

Glen Larsen

Glen G. Larsen
Racing Hometown: Aurora, IL

Year	Rank	Starts	Poles	1	2	3	4	5	6–10	Laps	Laps Led	Races Led	Miles	$
1952	91T	1	0	0	0	0	0	0	1	171	0	0	86	125
Lifetime		1	0	0	0	0	0	0	1	171	0	0	86	$125

Mel Larson

Mel Larson
B: 10/1/1929
Racing Hometown: Phoenix, AZ

Year	Rank	Starts	Poles	1	2	3	4	5	6–10	Laps	Laps Led	Races Led	Miles	$
1955	143	2	0	0	0	0	0	0	1	230	0	0	135	150
1956	99	6	0	0	0	0	0	0	1	504	0	0	471	385
1957	119	11	1	0	0	0	0	1	5	1,295	0	0	761	1,235
1958	68	4	0	0	0	0	0	0	1	546	0	0	412	280
1959	92	2	0	0	0	0	0	0	2	529	0	0	258	350
1960	66	4	1	0	1	0	0	0	1	465	19	2	835	1,325
1970	NR	1	0	0	0	0	0	0	1	133	0	0	348	1,115
1972	95	4	0	0	0	0	0	0	0	609	0	0	1,336	3,630
1973	38	10	0	0	0	0	0	0	0	2,160	0	0	1,999	8,255
1975	NR	1	0	0	0	0	0	0	0	36	0	0	72	665
1978	77	2	0	0	0	0	0	0	0	169	0	0	407	2,290
Lifetime		47	2	0	1	0	0	1	12	6,676	19	2	7,035	$19,680

Eddie LaRue

Edward LaRue

Year	Rank	Starts	Poles	1	2	3	4	5	6–10	Laps	Laps Led	Races Led	Miles	$
1951	N/A	1	0	0	0	0	0	0	0		0	0		25
Lifetime		1	0	0	0	0	0	0	0		0	0		$25

Year	Rank	Starts	Poles	Finish						Laps	Laps Led	Races Led	Miles	$
				1	2	3	4	5	6–10					

Roland LaRue
Roland LaRue
Racing Hometown: Mantica, OH

Year	Rank	Starts	Poles	1	2	3	4	5	6–10	Laps	Laps Led	Races Led	Miles	$
1954	126T	1	0	0	0	0	0	0	0	118	0	0	59	25
Lifetime		1	0	0	0	0	0	0	0	118	0	0	59	$25

Cecil Lassiter
Cecil Lassiter

Year	Rank	Starts	Poles	1	2	3	4	5	6–10	Laps	Laps Led	Races Led	Miles	$
1956	115	1	0	0	0	0	0	0	0	235	0	0	235	100
Lifetime		1	0	0	0	0	0	0	0	235	0	0	235	$100

Bill Latham
William Latham
Racing Hometown: Birmingham, AL

Year	Rank	Starts	Poles	1	2	3	4	5	6–10	Laps	Laps Led	Races Led	Miles	$
1961	124	1	0	0	0	0	0	0	0	440	0	0	220	250
1966	NR	2	0	0	0	0	0	0	0	160	0	0	54	200
Lifetime		3	0	0	0	0	0	0	0	600	0	0	274	$450

Patrick Latimer
Patrick Latimer

Year	Rank	Starts	Poles	1	2	3	4	5	6–10	Laps	Laps Led	Races Led	Miles	$
1987	103T	1	0	0	0	0	0	0	0	38	0	0	39	1,250
Lifetime		1	0	0	0	0	0	0	0	38	0	0	39	$1,250

Gene Laughlin
Glenn Laughlin
Racing Hometown: Akron, OH

Year	Rank	Starts	Poles	1	2	3	4	5	6–10	Laps	Laps Led	Races Led	Miles	$
1954	156T	2	0	0	0	0	0	0	0	94	0	0	107	0
Lifetime		2	0	0	0	0	0	0	0	94	0	0	107	$0

Harry LaVois
Harry LaVois
Racing Hometown: Newark, NJ

Year	Rank	Starts	Poles	1	2	3	4	5	6–10	Laps	Laps Led	Races Led	Miles	$
1954	NR	1	0	0	0	0	0	1	0	49	0	0	98	275
Lifetime		1	0	0	0	0	0	1	0	49	0	0	98	$275

Clare Lawicki
Clare Lawicki
Racing Hometown: Roseville, MI

Year	Rank	Starts	Poles	1	2	3	4	5	6–10	Laps	Laps Led	Races Led	Miles	$
1954	NR	1	0	0	0	0	0	0	0	175	0	0	88	25
Lifetime		1	0	0	0	0	0	0	0	175	0	0	88	$25

Bill Lawrence
William Lawrence
Racing Hometown: Martinsville, VA

Year	Rank	Starts	Poles	1	2	3	4	5	6–10	Laps	Laps Led	Races Led	Miles	$
1951	N/A	1	0	0	0	0	0	0	0		0	0		25
Lifetime		1	0	0	0	0	0	0	0		0	0		$25

Coleman Lawrence
Coleman Lawrence
Racing Hometown: Martinsville, VA

Year	Rank	Starts	Poles	1	2	3	4	5	6–10	Laps	Laps Led	Races Led	Miles	$
1951	78	6	0	0	0	0	0	0	2	130	0	0	130	250
1952	29	8	0	0	0	0	0	0	3	1,326	0	0	1,045	375
1953	42	8	0	0	0	0	0	0	1	263	0	0	263	250
Lifetime		22	0	0	0	0	0	0	6	1,719	0	0	1,438	$875

Dick Lawrence
Richard Lawrence

Year	Rank	Starts	Poles	1	2	3	4	5	6–10	Laps	Laps Led	Races Led	Miles	$
1969	NR	1	0	0	0	0	0	0	0	108	0	0	287	1,275
Lifetime		1	0	0	0	0	0	0	0	108	0	0	287	$1,275

Jack Lawrence
Jack Lawrence
B: 10/13/1941
Racing Hometown: Grand Rapids, MI

Year	Rank	Starts	Poles	1	2	3	4	5	6–10	Laps	Laps Led	Races Led	Miles	$
1953	90	2	0	0	0	0	0	0	0	101	0	0	51	50
1958	116	1	0	0	0	0	0	0	1	177	0	0	89	140
Lifetime		3	0	0	0	0	0	0	1	278	0	0	139	$190

Leonard Lawrence
Leonard Lawrence
Racing Hometown: Tampa, FL

Year	Rank	Starts	Poles	1	2	3	4	5	6–10	Laps	Laps Led	Races Led	Miles	$
1953	113	2	0	0	0	0	0	0	0		0	0		50
Lifetime		2	0	0	0	0	0	0	0		0	0		$50

Year	Rank	Starts	Poles	Finish						Laps	Laps Led	Races Led	Miles	$
				1	2	3	4	5	6–10					

Mike Laws

Michael Laws
B: 10/7/1957
Racing Hometown: Orlando, FL

Year	Rank	Starts	Poles	1	2	3	4	5	6–10	Laps	Laps Led	Races Led	Miles	$
1986	78	2	0	0	0	0	0	0	0	422	0	0	698	3,095
Lifetime		2	0	0	0	0	0	0	0	422	0	0	698	$3,095

Dean Layfield

Dean Layfield
B: 4/6/1919 D: 8/25/1961 *Died of injuries from 8/20/61 Super Modified race @ Perry Raceway in Perry, NY.*
Racing Hometown: Wellsville, NY

Year	Rank	Starts	Poles	1	2	3	4	5	6–10	Laps	Laps Led	Races Led	Miles	$
1957	NR	1	0	0	0	0	1	0	0	97	0	0	97	295
1958	50	7	0	0	0	0	0	0	0	522	0	0	433	370
Lifetime		8	0	0	0	0	1	0	0	619	0	0	530	$665

Harry Leake

Harry Leake
Racing Hometown: Lewisville, NC

Year	Rank	Starts	Poles	1	2	3	4	5	6–10	Laps	Laps Led	Races Led	Miles	$
1958	NR	2	0	0	0	0	0	0	0	336	0	0	123	115
1961	44	15	0	0	0	0	0	0	7	2,375	0	0	1,107	2,000
1962	61	5	0	0	0	0	0	0	1	669	0	0	278	525
Lifetime		22	0	0	0	0	0	0	8	3,380	0	0	1,507	$2,640

Dawson Lechlider

F. Dawson Lechlider
Racing Hometown: Silver Spring, MD

Year	Rank	Starts	Poles	1	2	3	4	5	6–10	Laps	Laps Led	Races Led	Miles	$
1951	N/A	4	0	0	0	0	0	0	0	49	0	0	49	75
Lifetime		4	0	0	0	0	0	0	0	49	0	0	49	$75

Thomas Lechlider

Thomas Lee Lechlider
Racing Hometown: Silver Spring, MD

Year	Rank	Starts	Poles	1	2	3	4	5	6–10	Laps	Laps Led	Races Led	Miles	$
1952	194	1	0	0	0	0	0	0	0		0	0		25
Lifetime		1	0	0	0	0	0	0	0		0	0		$25

Bill Ledbetter

William Ledbetter
Racing Hometown: Los Angeles, CA

Year	Rank	Starts	Poles	1	2	3	4	5	6–10	Laps	Laps Led	Races Led	Miles	$
1951	81	3	0	0	0	0	0	0	1		0	0		250
Lifetime		3	0	0	0	0	0	0	1		0	0		$250

Max Ledbetter

Max Ledbetter
Racing Hometown: Franklin, NC

Year	Rank	Starts	Poles	1	2	3	4	5	6–10	Laps	Laps Led	Races Led	Miles	$
1966	70	9	0	0	0	0	0	0	1	1,752	0	0	882	1,110
1967	53	10	0	0	0	0	0	0	4	2,394	0	0	1,171	2,325
1968	120T	1	0	0	0	0	0	0	0	134	0	0	67	100
1969	NR	1	0	0	0	0	0	0	0	91	0	0	46	260
Lifetime		21	0	0	0	0	0	0	5	4,371	0	0	2,165	$3,795

Bobby Lee

Robert Lee
Racing Hometown: Sumter, SC

Year	Rank	Starts	Poles	1	2	3	4	5	6–10	Laps	Laps Led	Races Led	Miles	$
1958	64	5	0	0	0	0	0	0	0	532	0	0	568	285
Lifetime		5	0	0	0	0	0	0	0	532	0	0	568	$285

Doc Lee

Doc Lee

Year	Rank	Starts	Poles	1	2	3	4	5	6–10	Laps	Laps Led	Races Led	Miles	$
1961	NR	1	0	0	0	0	0	0	0	135	0	0	34	75
Lifetime		1	0	0	0	0	0	0	0	135	0	0	34	$75

Fred Lee *See* Fred Bince

Hank Lee

Edward Franklin Lee
B: 1928 D: 6/4/1952 *Died of heart attack.*
Racing Hometown: Mobile, AL

Year	Rank	Starts	Poles	1	2	3	4	5	6–10	Laps	Laps Led	Races Led	Miles	$
1951	N/A	1	0	0	0	0	0	0	0		0	0		25

Year	Rank	Starts	Poles	Finish						Laps	Laps Led	Races Led	Miles	$
				1	2	3	4	5	6–10					

Hank Lee *continued*

Year	Rank	Starts	Poles	1	2	3	4	5	6–10	Laps	Laps Led	Races Led	Miles	$
1952	NR	2	0	0	0	0	0	0	0	114	0	0	104	50
Lifetime		3	0	0	0	0	0	0	0	114	0	0	104	$75

Jim Lee

James Lee
Racing Hometown: Vista, CA

Year	Rank	Starts	Poles	1	2	3	4	5	6–10	Laps	Laps Led	Races Led	Miles	$
1974	127	1	0	0	0	0	0	0	0	21	0	0	55	650
1982	69	2	0	0	0	0	0	0	0	125	0	0	328	1,760
Lifetime		3	0	0	0	0	0	0	0	146	0	0	383	$2,410

Russ Lee

Russell Lee
Racing Hometown: Robbinsdale, MN

Year	Rank	Starts	Poles	1	2	3	4	5	6–10	Laps	Laps Led	Races Led	Miles	$
1950	NR	1	0	0	0	0	0	0	0	38	0	0	158	25
Lifetime		1	0	0	0	0	0	0	0	38	0	0	158	$25

Ted Lee

Theodore Lee
Racing Hometown: Encino, CA

Year	Rank	Starts	Poles	1	2	3	4	5	6–10	Laps	Laps Led	Races Led	Miles	$
1953	79	4	0	0	0	0	0	0	0	294	0	0	387	125
1954	NR	2	0	0	0	0	0	0	0	492	0	0	328	65
Lifetime		6	0	0	0	0	0	0	0	786	0	0	715	$190

Marion Leech

Marion Leech
Racing Hometown: Evansville, IN

Year	Rank	Starts	Poles	1	2	3	4	5	6–10	Laps	Laps Led	Races Led	Miles	$
1952	NR	1	0	0	0	0	0	0	0	117	0	0	59	25
Lifetime		1	0	0	0	0	0	0	0	117	0	0	59	$25

Herb Legg

Herbert Legg
Racing Hometown: Rochester, NY

Year	Rank	Starts	Poles	1	2	3	4	5	6–10	Laps	Laps Led	Races Led	Miles	$
1952	147T	1	0	0	0	0	0	0	0	133	0	0	67	25
Lifetime		1	0	0	0	0	0	0	0	133	0	0	67	$25

Irv Leitch

Irving Leitch
Racing Hometown: Glenshaw, PA

Year	Rank	Starts	Poles	1	2	3	4	5	6–10	Laps	Laps Led	Races Led	Miles	$
1950	NR	1	0	0	0	0	0	0	0	113	0	0	57	0
1951	N/A	1	0	0	0	0	0	0	0		0	0		25
Lifetime		2	0	0	0	0	0	0	0	113	0	0	57	$25

Butch Leitzinger

Butch Leitzinger
B: 2/8/1969
Racing Hometown: State College, PA

Year	Rank	Starts	Poles	1	2	3	4	5	6–10	Laps	Laps Led	Races Led	Miles	$
1994	72T	1	0	0	0	0	0	0	0	81	0	0	198	6,330
1995	54	1	0	0	0	0	0	0	0	90	0	0	221	17,060
1996	58	1	0	0	0	0	0	0	0	90	0	0	221	22,705
Lifetime		3	0	0	0	0	0	0	0	261	0	0	639	$46,095

Larry LeMay

Lawrence LeMay
B: 10/25/1949
Racing Hometown: Mt. Clemens, MI

Year	Rank	Starts	Poles	1	2	3	4	5	6–10	Laps	Laps Led	Races Led	Miles	$
1976	75	2	0	0	0	0	0	0	0	460	0	0	280	975
1977	79	2	0	0	0	0	0	0	0	288	0	0	177	710
Lifetime		4	0	0	0	0	0	0	0	748	0	0	457	$1,685

Albert Lemieux

Albert Lemieux
Racing Hometown: Montreal, Que., Canada

Year	Rank	Starts	Poles	1	2	3	4	5	6–10	Laps	Laps Led	Races Led	Miles	$
1952	NR	1	0	0	0	0	0	0	1	121	0	0	61	50
Lifetime		1	0	0	0	0	0	0	1	121	0	0	61	$50

Eddie Lenz

Edward Lenz
Racing Hometown: Colden, NY

Year	Rank	Starts	Poles	1	2	3	4	5	6–10	Laps	Laps Led	Races Led	Miles	$
1951	N/A	1	0	0	0	0	0	0	0		0	0		25

Year	Rank	Starts	Poles	Finish						Laps	Laps Led	Races Led	Miles	$
				1	2	3	4	5	6–10					

Eddie Lenz *continued*

Year	Rank	Starts	Poles	1	2	3	4	5	6–10	Laps	Laps Led	Races Led	Miles	$
1952	N/A	1	0	0	0	0	0	0	0	55	0	0	28	25
Lifetime		2	0	0	0	0	0	0	0	55	0	0	28	$50

Joe Leonard

Joseph Paul Leonard
B: 8/4/1934
Racing Hometown: San Diego, CA

Year	Rank	Starts	Poles	1	2	3	4	5	6–10	Laps	Laps Led	Races Led	Miles	$
1969	NR	1	0	0	0	0	0	0	0	47	0	0	118	720
Lifetime		1	0	0	0	0	0	0	0	47	0	0	118	$720

Tracy Leslie

Tracy Leslie
B: 10/24/1957
Racing Hometown: Mt. Clemens, MI

Year	Rank	Starts	Poles	1	2	3	4	5	6–10	Laps	Laps Led	Races Led	Miles	$
1989	56	2	0	0	0	0	0	0	0	557	0	0	934	8,800
1990	69	3	0	0	0	0	0	0	0	316	0	0	504	11,740
1996	—	0												3,672
Lifetime		5	0	0	0	0	0	0	0	873	0	0	1,438	$24,212

Danny Letner

Daniel Letner
Racing Hometown: Downey, CA

Year	Rank	Starts	Poles	1	2	3	4	5	6–10	Laps	Laps Led	Races Led	Miles	$
1951	87	5	0	0	0	0	0	0	2	153	0	0	153	225
1954	33	4	1	1	0	1	0	0	1	1,058	142	2	674	1,975
1955	41	4	0	1	0	1	0	0	0	614	34	1	514	1,780
1956	127	6	0	0	0	0	0	0	0	585	0	0	705	410
1957	70	5	0	0	0	0	0	0	1	546	0	0	350	500
1959	NR	1	0	0	0	0	0	0	0	224	0	0	90	100
1961	NR	1	0	0	0	1	0	0	0	175	0	0	245	750
1963	55	1	0	0	0	0	0	0	1	179	0	0	483	950
Lifetime		27	1	2	0	3	0	0	5	3,534	176	3	3,214	$6,690

Jimmie Lewallen

James Edward Lewallen
B: 8/22/1919   D: 10/16/1995
Racing Hometown: Archdale, NC

Year	Rank	Starts	Poles	1	2	3	4	5	6–10	Laps	Laps Led	Races Led	Miles	$
1949	NR	3	0	0	0	0	0	0	0		0	0		25
1950	41	3	0	0	0	0	1	0	0	330	0	0	413	400
1951	13	12	0	0	0	2	0	2	4	613	0	0	671	2,430
1952	14	20	0	0	0	0	1	1	5	2,327	0	0	1,638	2,052
1953	9	22	0	0	1	2	0	4	6	908	0	0	791	4,222
1954	8	22	0	0	2	0	0	3	5	2,963	0	0	2,206	4,694
1955	9	33	1	0	2	0	4	2	8	4,028	0	0	2,959	6,440
1956	56	11	0	0	0	0	1	0	0	742	0	0	413	1,150
1957	26	7	0	0	0	0	0	0	0	895	0	0	865	1,030
1958	NR	1	0	0	0	0	0	0	0	389	0	0	195	210
1959	NR	6	0	0	0	0	0	0	1	509	0	0	198	350
1960	NR	2	0	0	0	0	0	0	0	63	0	0	16	215
Lifetime		142	1	0	5	4	7	12	29	13,767	0	0	10,363	$23,218

Emory Lewis

Emory Lewis
Racing Hometown: Winchester, KY

Year	Rank	Starts	Poles	1	2	3	4	5	6–10	Laps	Laps Led	Races Led	Miles	$
1953	NR	2	0	0	0	0	0	0	1	387	0	0	364	255
1954	NR	5	0	0	0	0	0	0	2	422	0	0	378	475
Lifetime		7	0	0	0	0	0	0	3	809	0	0	742	$730

Skip Lewis

George Lewis
Racing Hometown: Dayton, NY

Year	Rank	Starts	Poles	1	2	3	4	5	6–10	Laps	Laps Led	Races Led	Miles	$
1949	40	1	0	0	0	0	0	0	1	168	0	0	84	50
Lifetime		1	0	0	0	0	0	0	1	168	0	0	84	$50

Herb Lewis

Herbert Lewis
Racing Hometown: Nashville, TN

Year	Rank	Starts	Poles	1	2	3	4	5	6–10	Laps	Laps Led	Races Led	Miles	$
1959	65	1	0	0	0	0	0	0	0	221	0	0	111	100
Lifetime		1	0	0	0	0	0	0	0	221	0	0	111	$100

Year	Rank	Starts	Poles	Finish						Laps	Laps Led	Races Led	Miles	$
				1	2	3	4	5	6–10					

Paul Lewis

William Paul Lewis
B: 9/28/1932
Racing Hometown: Johnson City, TN

Year	Rank	Starts	Poles	1	2	3	4	5	6–10	Laps	Laps Led	Races Led	Miles	$
1960	27	22	0	0	0	0	0	0	4	3,690	0	0	2,562	3,535
1961	28	21	0	0	0	0	0	0	5	3,669	0	0	2,803	4,095
1962	55	6	0	0	0	0	0	0	0	945	0	0	989	1,695
1963	138	1	0	0	0	0	0	0	0	2	0	0	3	500
1964	142	1	0	0	0	0	0	0	0	27	0	0	17	150
1965	14	24	1	0	0	0	1	2	10	5,954	0	0	5,057	13,247
1966	16	21	0	1	1	6	1	0	5	6,260	67	2	4,742	17,827
1967	33	14	0	0	1	0	0	2	5	2,959	4	1	2,593	8,720
1968	71	4	0	0	0	0	0	1	0	584	0	0	571	3,100
Lifetime		114	1	1	2	6	2	5	29	24,090	71	3	19,337	$52,869

Raymond Lewis

Raymond Lewis
Racing Hometown: War, WV

Year	Rank	Starts	Poles	1	2	3	4	5	6–10	Laps	Laps Led	Races Led	Miles	$
1949	37T	1	0	0	0	0	0	0	1	194	0	0	97	75
Lifetime		1	0	0	0	0	0	0	1	194	0	0	97	$75

Frank Lies

Frank Lies
Racing Hometown: Wichita, KS

Year	Rank	Starts	Poles	1	2	3	4	5	6–10	Laps	Laps Led	Races Led	Miles	$
1958	158	1	0	0	0	0	0	0	0	33	0	0	33	100
Lifetime		1	0	0	0	0	0	0	0	33	0	0	33	$100

Ralph Liguori

Ralph Liguori
B: 10/10/1926
Racing Hometown: Bronx, NY

Year	Rank	Starts	Poles	1	2	3	4	5	6–10	Laps	Laps Led	Races Led	Miles	$
1951	N/A	1	0	0	0	0	0	0	0	20	0	0	10	0
1952	23	12	0	0	0	0	1	0	5	1,671	0	0	1,236	920
1953	20	12	0	0	0	0	0	2	1	407	0	0	377	1,098
1954	10	23	0	0	0	1	0	1	10	3,461	0	0	2,447	3,495
1955	19	12	0	0	0	0	0	0	6	1,402	0	0	1,422	1,973
1956	51	16	0	0	0	0	0	0	3	1,382	0	0	1,093	1,210
Lifetime		76	0	0	0	1	1	3	25	8,343	0	0	6,585	$8,696

Bill Lillenthal

William Lillenthal
Racing Hometown: East Randolph, NY

Year	Rank	Starts	Poles	1	2	3	4	5	6–10	Laps	Laps Led	Races Led	Miles	$
1951	N/A	1	0	0	0	0	0	0	0		0	0		50
Lifetime		1	0	0	0	0	0	0	0		0	0		$50

Dick Linder

Richard R. Linder
B: 4/6/1923   D: 4/19/1959   *Killed in IndyCar race @ Trenton, NJ.*
Racing Hometown: Pittsburgh, PA

Year	Rank	Starts	Poles	1	2	3	4	5	6–10	Laps	Laps Led	Races Led	Miles	$
1949	19	3	0	0	1	0	0	0	0	416	0	0	289	830
1950	8	13	5	3	1	1	0	0	3	1,437	460	5	1,060	5,695
1951	N/A	10	0	0	0	0	0	0	2	21	0	0	11	375
1953	97T	1	0	0	0	0	0	0	0	176	0	0	88	25
1956	281	1	0	0	0	0	0	0	0	0	0	0	0	0
Lifetime		28	5	3	2	1	0	0	5	2,050	460	5	1,447	$6,925

Gus Linder

Gus Linder
Racing Hometown: Pittsburgh, PA

Year	Rank	Starts	Poles	1	2	3	4	5	6–10	Laps	Laps Led	Races Led	Miles	$
1951	219T	1	0	0	0	0	0	0	0		0	0		25
Lifetime		1	0	0	0	0	0	0	0		0	0		$25

Butch Lindley

Clyde Lindley
B: 3/25/1948   D: 6/6/1990   *Died from injuries in All Pro race @ Bradenton, FL.*
Racing Hometown: Greenville, SC

Year	Rank	Starts	Poles	1	2	3	4	5	6–10	Laps	Laps Led	Races Led	Miles	$
1979	111T	1	0	0	0	0	0	0	0	82	0	0	43	570
1981	60	3	0	0	0	0	0	0	0	559	28	2	323	2,375
1982	43	4	0	0	1	0	0	0	0	1,020	165	2	547	16,695
1983	56	2	0	0	0	0	0	0	0	518	7	1	279	3,535

Year	Rank	Starts	Poles	Finish 1	2	3	4	5	6–10	Laps	Laps Led	Races Led	Miles	$

Butch Lindley *continued*

Year	Rank	Starts	Poles	1	2	3	4	5	6–10	Laps	Laps Led	Races Led	Miles	$
1985	NR	1	0	0	0	0	0	0	0	352	0	0	191	1,365
Lifetime		11	0	0	1	0	0	0	0	2,531	200	5	1,383	$24,540

John Lindsay

John Lindsay
Racing Hometown: Jersey City, NJ

Year	Rank	Starts	Poles	1	2	3	4	5	6–10	Laps	Laps Led	Races Led	Miles	$
1954	NR	1	0	0	0	0	0	0	0	197	0	0	197	50
1955	35	6	0	0	0	0	0	0	3	853	0	0	630	575
1956	63	5	0	0	0	0	0	0	1	715	0	0	585	425
1958	85	3	0	0	0	0	0	0	1	476	0	0	262	310
Lifetime		15	0	0	0	0	0	0	5	2,241	0	0	1,673	$1,360

Jim Lineberger

James Lineberger
Racing Hometown: Hickory, NC

Year	Rank	Starts	Poles	1	2	3	4	5	6–10	Laps	Laps Led	Races Led	Miles	$
1969	83T	1	0	0	0	0	0	0	0	131	0	0	197	925
Lifetime		1	0	0	0	0	0	0	0	131	0	0	197	$925

Bob Link

Robert Link
Racing Hometown: Walnut Creek, CA

Year	Rank	Starts	Poles	1	2	3	4	5	6–10	Laps	Laps Led	Races Led	Miles	$
1968	105	1	0	0	0	0	0	0	0	14	0	0	38	500
Lifetime		1	0	0	0	0	0	0	0	14	0	0	38	$500

Robert Link

Robert Link
Racing Hometown: Macon, GA

Year	Rank	Starts	Poles	1	2	3	4	5	6–10	Laps	Laps Led	Races Led	Miles	$
1969	NR	1	0	0	0	0	0	0	0	62	0	0	167	775
Lifetime		1	0	0	0	0	0	0	0	62	0	0	167	$775

Terry Link

Terry Link
B: 8/13/1952
Racing Hometown: Daytona Beach, FL

Year	Rank	Starts	Poles	1	2	3	4	5	6–10	Laps	Laps Led	Races Led	Miles	$
1974	86	2	0	0	0	0	0	0	0	146	0	0	388	2,520
1975	117	1	0	0	0	0	0	0	0	6	0	0	16	895
Lifetime		3	0	0	0	0	0	0	0	152	0	0	404	$3,415

Jim Linke

James Linke
Racing Hometown: Jamesburg, NY

Year	Rank	Starts	Poles	1	2	3	4	5	6–10	Laps	Laps Led	Races Led	Miles	$
1957	72	4	0	0	0	0	0	0	1	361	0	0	282	400
1958	80	3	0	0	0	0	0	0	0	397	0	0	308	170
Lifetime		7	0	0	0	0	0	0	1	758	0	0	590	$570

Bennis Listman

Bennis Listman

Year	Rank	Starts	Poles	1	2	3	4	5	6–10	Laps	Laps Led	Races Led	Miles	$
1971	NR	1	0	0	0	0	0	0	0	6	0	0	1	100
Lifetime		1	0	0	0	0	0	0	0	6	0	0	1	$100

Chad Little

Chad Little
B: 4/29/1963
Racing Hometown: Spokane, WA

Year	Rank	Starts	Poles	1	2	3	4	5	6–10	Laps	Laps Led	Races Led	Miles	$
1986	70	2	0	0	0	0	0	0	0	145	0	0	380	6,065
1987	59	2	0	0	0	0	0	0	0	211	0	0	553	8,810
1988	45	4	0	0	0	0	0	0	0	1,089	3	1	1,435	14,225
1989	38	8	0	0	0	0	0	0	0	1,936	0	0	2,594	44,690
1990	33	18	0	0	0	0	0	0	0	4,822	0	0	6,411	80,140
1991	27	28	0	0	0	0	0	0	1	7,784	21	3	9,528	184,190
1992	31	19	0	0	0	0	0	0	1	5,114	0	0	6,707	145,805
1993	51	3	0	0	0	0	0	0	0	775	0	0	1,361	41,040
1994	68	1	0	0	0	0	0	0	0	196	1	1	490	30,805
1995	53	2	0	0	0	0	0	0	0	195	0	0	508	22,775
1996	44	9	0	0	0	0	0	0	0	1,816	0	0	2,396	164,752
Lifetime		96	0	0	0	0	0	0	2	24,083	25	5	32,362	$743,297

Year	Rank	Starts	Poles	Finish 1	2	3	4	5	6–10	Laps	Laps Led	Races Led	Miles	$

Chuck Little

Charles M. Little
B: 6/1/1944   D: 5/19/1995
Racing Hometown: Spokane, WA

Year	Rank	Starts	Poles	1	2	3	4	5	6–10	Laps	Laps Led	Races Led	Miles	$
1975	100T	1	0	0	0	0	0	0	0	35	0	0	92	875
Lifetime		1	0	0	0	0	0	0	0	35	0	0	92	$875

Mike Little

Michael Little
B: 1914
Racing Hometown: Johnstown, PA

Year	Rank	Starts	Poles	1	2	3	4	5	6–10	Laps	Laps Led	Races Led	Miles	$
1951	N/A	1	0	0	0	0	0	0	0	0	0	0	0	25
1952	191T	1	0	0	0	0	0	0	0	62	0	0	31	25
Lifetime		2	0	0	0	0	0	0	0	62	0	0	31	$50

Jim Little

James Little
Racing Hometown: Schenectady, NY

Year	Rank	Starts	Poles	1	2	3	4	5	6–10	Laps	Laps Led	Races Led	Miles	$
1951	N/A	1	0	0	0	0	0	0	1		0	0		100
Lifetime		1	0	0	0	0	0	0	1		0	0		$100

Joe Littlejohn

Joseph Littlejohn
B: 1908   D: 7/29/1989
Racing Hometown: Spartanburg, SC

Year	Rank	Starts	Poles	1	2	3	4	5	6–10	Laps	Laps Led	Races Led	Miles	$
1949	22T	1	0	0	0	0	1	0	0	40	0	0	166	300
1950	NR	1	1	0	0	0	0	0	0	7	0	0	29	25
Lifetime		2	1	0	0	0	1	0	0	47	0	0	195	$325

Virgil Livengood

Virgil Livengood
Racing Hometown: Mankota, MN

Year	Rank	Starts	Poles	1	2	3	4	5	6–10	Laps	Laps Led	Races Led	Miles	$
1950	NR	1	0	0	0	0	0	0	0	338	0	0	423	0
1953	57	3	0	0	0	0	0	0	1	7	0	0	4	100
1954	199	1	0	0	0	0	0	0	0	35	0	0	144	25
Lifetime		5	0	0	0	0	0	0	1	380	0	0	570	$125

Dub Livingston

Dub Livingston
Racing Hometown: Gadsden, AL

Year	Rank	Starts	Poles	1	2	3	4	5	6–10	Laps	Laps Led	Races Led	Miles	$
1952	NR	1	0	0	0	0	0	0	0	152	0	0	76	25
1953	43	6	0	0	0	0	0	0	1	309	0	0	252	225
Lifetime		7	0	0	0	0	0	0	1	461	0	0	328	$250

Ed Livingston

Edward Livingston
B: 10/17/1935
Racing Hometown: Folly Beach, SC

Year	Rank	Starts	Poles	1	2	3	4	5	6–10	Laps	Laps Led	Races Led	Miles	$
1961	62	10	0	0	0	0	0	0	0	1,477	0	0	2,201	1,945
1962	38	13	0	0	0	0	0	0	0	1,758	0	0	2,146	2,940
1963	30	20	0	0	0	0	0	0	1	3,294	0	0	3,196	4,930
1964	93	4	0	0	0	0	1	0	0	213	0	0	116	1,375
Lifetime		47	0	0	0	0	1	0	1	6,742	0	0	7,658	$11,090

Jim Locke

James Locke
Racing Hometown: Circleville, OH

Year	Rank	Starts	Poles	1	2	3	4	5	6–10	Laps	Laps Led	Races Led	Miles	$
1962	125	1	0	0	0	0	0	0	0	140	0	0	210	225
Lifetime		1	0	0	0	0	0	0	0	140	0	0	210	$225

Les Loeser

Lester Loeser
Racing Hometown: Modesto, CA

Year	Rank	Starts	Poles	1	2	3	4	5	6–10	Laps	Laps Led	Races Led	Miles	$
1970	94T	1	0	0	0	0	0	0	0	38	0	0	100	830
1972	96	1	0	0	0	0	0	0	0	164	0	0	410	1,745
Lifetime		2	0	0	0	0	0	0	0	202	0	0	510	$2,575

Owen Loggins

Owen Loggins
Racing Hometown: Lafayette, CA

Year	Rank	Starts	Poles	1	2	3	4	5	6–10	Laps	Laps Led	Races Led	Miles	$
1955	90	3	0	0	0	0	0	0	0	341	0	0	326	150

Year	Rank	Starts	Poles	Finish 1	2	3	4	5	6–10	Laps	Laps Led	Races Led	Miles	$

Owen Loggins *continued*

Year	Rank	Starts	Poles	1	2	3	4	5	6–10	Laps	Laps Led	Races Led	Miles	$
1956	300	1	0	0	0	0	0	0	0	0	0	0	0	0
1958	167	1	0	0	0	0	0	0	0	25	0	0	66	175
1959	103	1	0	0	0	0	0	0	0	57	0	0	57	100
1960	112	1	0	0	0	0	0	0	0	126	0	0	176	100
Lifetime		7	0	0	0	0	0	0	0	549	0	0	625	$525

Lella Lombardi

Lella Lombardi
B: 3/26/1943   D: 3/1992   *Died of cancer.*
Racing Hometown: Frugarolo, Italy

Year	Rank	Starts	Poles	1	2	3	4	5	6–10	Laps	Laps Led	Races Led	Miles	$
1977	NR	1	0	0	0	0	0	0	0	103	0	0	258	785
Lifetime		1	0	0	0	0	0	0	0	103	0	0	258	$785

Bill Lone

William Raymond Lone
Racing Hometown: Glen Burnie, MD

Year	Rank	Starts	Poles	1	2	3	4	5	6–10	Laps	Laps Led	Races Led	Miles	$
1954	NR	1	0	0	0	0	0	0	0	209	0	0	209	150
1957	NR	1	0	0	0	0	0	0	0	167	0	0	84	100
Lifetime		2	0	0	0	0	0	0	0	376	0	0	293	$250

Bill Long

W. G. Long
Racing Hometown: Charlotte, NC

Year	Rank	Starts	Poles	1	2	3	4	5	6–10	Laps	Laps Led	Races Led	Miles	$
1950	54	1	0	0	0	0	0	0	1	141	0	0	71	175
Lifetime		1	0	0	0	0	0	0	1	141	0	0	71	$175

Gene Long

Gene Long
Racing Hometown: Artesia, CA

Year	Rank	Starts	Poles	1	2	3	4	5	6–10	Laps	Laps Led	Races Led	Miles	$
1957	113	1	0	0	0	0	0	0	1	112	0	0	56	250
Lifetime		1	0	0	0	0	0	0	1	112	0	0	56	$250

Lucky Long

William G. Long
Racing Hometown: Lakewood, CA

Year	Rank	Starts	Poles	1	2	3	4	5	6–10	Laps	Laps Led	Races Led	Miles	$
1956	209T	1	0	0	0	0	0	0	0	180	0	0	90	50
1957	201T	1	0	0	0	0	0	0	0	24	0	0	12	0
1958	63	2	0	0	0	0	0	0	0	252	0	0	524	300
1959	83	2	0	0	0	0	0	1	1	554	0	0	280	700
Lifetime		6	0	0	0	0	0	1	1	1,010	0	0	906	$1,050

Sterling Long

Sterling Long
Racing Hometown: Charlotte, NC

Year	Rank	Starts	Poles	1	2	3	4	5	6–10	Laps	Laps Led	Races Led	Miles	$
1949	30	2	0	0	0	0	0	0	1		0	0		150
1950	NR	1	0	0	0	0	0	0	0		0	0		0
Lifetime		3	0	0	0	0	0	0	1		0	0		$150

Jimmy Longo

James Longo
Racing Hometown: Hubbard, OH

Year	Rank	Starts	Poles	1	2	3	4	5	6–10	Laps	Laps Led	Races Led	Miles	$
1951	N/A	1	0	0	0	0	0	0	0		0	0		25
Lifetime		1	0	0	0	0	0	0	0		0	0		$25

Al Loquasto

Al Loquasto
B: 6/21/1943   D: 8/7/1991   *Killed in private plane crash.*
Racing Hometown: Easton, PA

Year	Rank	Starts	Poles	1	2	3	4	5	6–10	Laps	Laps Led	Races Led	Miles	$
1981	NR	1	0	0	0	0	0	0	0	184	0	0	460	2,345
1982	81	5	0	0	0	0	0	0	0	519	0	0	1,228	14,090
Lifetime		6	0	0	0	0	0	0	0	703	0	0	1,688	$16,435

Fred Lorenzen

Fred Lorenzen
B: 12/30/1934
Racing Hometown: Elmhurst, IL

Year	Rank	Starts	Poles	1	2	3	4	5	6–10	Laps	Laps Led	Races Led	Miles	$
1956	120	7	0	0	0	0	0	0	0	778	0	0	420	235
1960	15	10	0	0	0	2	0	1	2	2,086	93	1	2,521	9,136

Year	Rank	Starts	Poles	Finish						Laps	Laps Led	Races Led	Miles	$
				1	2	3	4	5	6–10	Laps	Led	Led	Miles	$

Fred Lorenzen *continued*

Year	Rank	Starts	Poles	1	2	3	4	5	6–10	Laps	Laps Led	Races Led	Miles	$
1961	19	15	4	3	1	0	1	1	0	2,657	781	10	3,040	30,395
1962	7	19	3	2	2	4	1	2	1	4,435	471	9	4,372	46,100
1963	3	29	9	6	8	3	0	4	2	7,484	**2,419**	20	6,472	122,588
1964	13	16	7	8	1	0	1	0	0	4,426	2,375	11	4,181	73,860
1965	13	17	6	4	1	0	0	0	1	3,677	981	12	3,998	80,615
1966	23	11	2	2	1	0	1	2	0	3,066	782	7	3,425	37,305
1967	29	5	0	1	1	0	0	0	0	895	23	4	1,411	19,125
1970	54	7	1	0	0	1	0	0	0	1,165	50	2	1,720	12,610
1971	45	14	1	0	1	0	2	4	2	3,229	152	6	5,038	45,100
1972	39	8	0	0	0	0	3	0	1	1,801	4	1	2,833	19,505
Lifetime		158	33	26	16	10	9	14	9	35,699	8,131	83	39,429	$496,574

Ken Love

Kenneth Love
Racing Hometown: Chicago Heights, IL

Year	Rank	Starts	Poles	1	2	3	4	5	6–10	Laps	Laps Led	Races Led	Miles	$
1956	192	3	0	0	0	0	0	0	0	278	0	0	328	200
1957	177	1	0	0	0	0	0	0	0		0	0		60
1958	78	3	0	0	0	0	0	0	0	125	0	0	156	135
Lifetime		7	0	0	0	0	0	0	0	403	0	0	484	$395

Gene Lovelace

Gene Lovelace
D: 7/3/1970   *Died of heart attack during race at Southside Speedway in Richmond, VA.*
Racing Hometown: Newport News, VA

Year	Rank	Starts	Poles	1	2	3	4	5	6–10	Laps	Laps Led	Races Led	Miles	$
1964	110	1	0	0	0	0	0	0	0	125	0	0	50	130
Lifetime		1	0	0	0	0	0	0	0	125	0	0	50	$130

Clarence Lovell

Clarence Lovell
B: 6/19/1946   D: 5/11/1973   *Killed in highway crash.*
Racing Hometown: San Antonio, TX

Year	Rank	Starts	Poles	1	2	3	4	5	6–10	Laps	Laps Led	Races Led	Miles	$
1972	32	12	0	0	0	0	0	0	0	2,202	0	0	3,586	10,770
1973	48	4	0	0	0	0	1	0	1	661	0	0	1,162	9,475
Lifetime		16	0	0	0	0	1	0	1	2,863	0	0	4,748	$20,245

Bosco Lowe

William B. Lowe
B: 3/27/1943
Racing Hometown: Fairview, NC

Year	Rank	Starts	Poles	1	2	3	4	5	6–10	Laps	Laps Led	Races Led	Miles	$
1967	96	2	0	0	0	0	0	0	1	333	0	0	143	340
1968	91	2	0	0	0	0	0	0	0	258	0	0	136	225
1982	NR	1	0	0	0	0	0	0	0	381	0	0	572	4,550
1983	100	1	0	0	0	0	0	0	0	36	0	0	90	5,350
1985	NR	1	0	0	0	0	0	0	0	171	0	0	455	6,825
Lifetime		7	0	0	0	0	0	0	1	1,179	0	0	1,396	$17,290

Harold Lucas

Harold Lucas

Year	Rank	Starts	Poles	1	2	3	4	5	6–10	Laps	Laps Led	Races Led	Miles	$
1951	N/A	1	0	0	0	0	0	0	0		0	0		25
Lifetime		1	0	0	0	0	0	0	0		0	0		$25

Keith Lucas

Keith Lucas
Racing Hometown: Sperry, IA

Year	Rank	Starts	Poles	1	2	3	4	5	6–10	Laps	Laps Led	Races Led	Miles	$
1953	91T	1	0	0	0	0	0	0	1		0	0		50
Lifetime		1	0	0	0	0	0	0	1		0	0		$50

Glenn Luce

Glenn Luce
Racing Hometown: Strong, ME

Year	Rank	Starts	Poles	1	2	3	4	5	6–10	Laps	Laps Led	Races Led	Miles	$
1968	120T	1	0	0	0	0	0	0	0	223	0	0	74	125
Lifetime		1	0	0	0	0	0	0	0	223	0	0	74	$125

Jim Luke

James Luke
Racing Hometown: Utica, NY

Year	Rank	Starts	Poles	1	2	3	4	5	6–10	Laps	Laps Led	Races Led	Miles	$
1954	163	1	0	0	0	0	0	0	0	154	0	0	77	0
Lifetime		1	0	0	0	0	0	0	0	154	0	0	77	$0

Year	Rank	Starts	Poles	Finish 1	2	3	4	5	6–10	Laps	Laps Led	Races Led	Miles	$

Tiny Lund

DeWayne Louis Lund
B: 3/3/1936 D: 8/17/1975 *Killed in Talladega 500.*
Racing Hometown: Cross, SC

Year	Rank	Starts	Poles	1	2	3	4	5	6–10	Laps	Laps Led	Races Led	Miles	$
1955	217	1	0	0	0	0	0	0	0	65	0	0	98	60
1956	19	21	0	0	0	0	1	0	7	3,988	0	0	2,466	2,811
1957	11	32	3	0	0	3	1	2	9	4,922	209	2	3,024	6,424
1958	25	22	2	0	0	2	1	1	3	3,506	14	1	1,991	3,155
1959	20	27	0	0	2	0	3	0	5	4,837	0	0	2,972	4,941
1960	32	8	0	0	0	0	0	0	2	1,254	0	0	1,706	2,440
1961	23	10	0	0	0	0	0	0	2	2,583	0	0	2,756	5,545
1962	34	10	0	0	0	0	0	0	0	2,487	8	1	2,580	2,880
1963	10	22	0	1	1	1	1	1	7	5,093	127	5	4,881	49,397
1964	20	22	0	0	0	2	0	1	6	3,551	14	1	3,662	9,913
1965	21	30	0	1	1	1	4	1	9	5,224	209	2	3,427	11,750
1966	29	31	1	1	2	1	0	1	5	4,306	654	6	3,625	11,880
1967	19	19	0	0	0	0	1	3	1	3,587	36	3	3,251	17,332
1968	22	17	0	0	0	1	1	3	5	4,547	1	1	4,381	17,785
1969	NR	1	0	0	0	0	0	0	1	152	28	1	404	1,675
1970	NR	5	0	0	0	0	2	0	0	819	7	2	1,540	11,365
1971	NR	15	0	2	3	0	1	0	3	3,783	258	7	3,255	18,965
1972	104	4	0	0	0	0	0	0	0	638	0	0	704	2,345
1973	94	5	0	0	0	0	0	0	0	388	0	0	409	4,420
1975	116	1	0	0	0	0	0	0	0	6	0	0	16	620
Lifetime		303	6	5	9	11	16	13	65	55,736	1,565	32	47,147	$185,703

Dave Lundman

David Lundman
Racing Hometown: Libertyville, IL

Year	Rank	Starts	Poles	1	2	3	4	5	6–10	Laps	Laps Led	Races Led	Miles	$
1956	207	1	0	0	0	0	0	0	0		0	0		60
Lifetime		1	0	0	0	0	0	0	0		0	0		$60

Leon Lundy

Leon Lundy
Racing Hometown: Philadelphia, PA

Year	Rank	Starts	Poles	1	2	3	4	5	6–10	Laps	Laps Led	Races Led	Miles	$
1953	71	1	0	0	0	0	0	0	0	0	0	0	0	75
1954	184	1	0	0	0	0	0	0	0	192	0	0	192	50
1955	NR	1	0	0	0	0	0	0	0	193	0	0	193	150
Lifetime		3	0	0	0	0	0	0	0	385	0	0	385	$275

Tom Lupo

Thomas Lupo
Racing Hometown: Green Sea, SC

Year	Rank	Starts	Poles	1	2	3	4	5	6–10	Laps	Laps Led	Races Led	Miles	$
1956	235	1	0	0	0	0	0	0	0	313	0	0	430	50
Lifetime		1	0	0	0	0	0	0	0	313	0	0	430	$50

Frank Luptow

Frank Luptow
B: 1914 D: 9/21/1952 *Killed at Lakewood Speedway in Atlanta during AAA Stock car race.*
Racing Hometown: Tampa, FL

Year	Rank	Starts	Poles	1	2	3	4	5	6–10	Laps	Laps Led	Races Led	Miles	$
1950	128	1	0	0	0	0	0	0	0	43	0	0	179	50
1951	69	4	0	0	0	0	0	1	0	161	0	0	125	250
Lifetime		5	0	0	0	0	0	1	0	204	0	0	305	$300

Louis Luther

Louis Luther

Year	Rank	Starts	Poles	1	2	3	4	5	6–10	Laps	Laps Led	Races Led	Miles	$
1951	N/A	1	0	0	0	0	0	0	0		0	0		25
Lifetime		1	0	0	0	0	0	0	0		0	0		$25

Bill Lutz

William F. Lutz
B: 4/30/1929
Racing Hometown: Louisville, KY

Year	Rank	Starts	Poles	1	2	3	4	5	6–10	Laps	Laps Led	Races Led	Miles	$
1956	NR	1	0	0	0	0	0	0	0	63	0	0	32	50
1957	75	1	0	0	0	0	0	0	1		0	0		600
1960	129	2	0	0	0	0	0	0	0	88	0	0	220	250
Lifetime		4	0	0	0	0	0	0	1	151	0	0	252	$900

Year	Rank	Starts	Poles	Finish 1	2	3	4	5	6–10	Laps	Laps Led	Races Led	Miles	$

Harold Lutz

Harold Lutz
Racing Hometown: Louisville, KY

Year	Rank	Starts	Poles	1	2	3	4	5	6–10	Laps	Laps Led	Races Led	Miles	$
1954	NR	1	0	0	0	0	0	0	0	11	0	0	17	50
Lifetime		1	0	0	0	0	0	0	0	11	0	0	17	$50

Ralph Lyden

Ralph Lyden
Racing Hometown: Indianapolis, IN

Year	Rank	Starts	Poles	1	2	3	4	5	6–10	Laps	Laps Led	Races Led	Miles	$
1950	129T	1	0	0	0	0	0	0	0		0	0		0
Lifetime		1	0	0	0	0	0	0	0		0	0		$0

Norman Lynch

Norman Lynch
Racing Hometown: Columbus, OH

Year	Rank	Starts	Poles	1	2	3	4	5	6–10	Laps	Laps Led	Races Led	Miles	$
1952	178	1	0	0	0	0	0	0	0	130	0	0	130	25
Lifetime		1	0	0	0	0	0	0	0	130	0	0	130	$25

Sandy Lynch

Sandy Neal Lynch
B: 5/24/1922
Racing Hometown: Jacksonville, FL

Year	Rank	Starts	Poles	1	2	3	4	5	6–10	Laps	Laps Led	Races Led	Miles	$
1951	N/A	2	0	0	0	0	0	0	0	215	0	0	269	25
Lifetime		2	0	0	0	0	0	0	0	215	0	0	269	$25

L. Lyndstrom

L. Lyndstrom

Year	Rank	Starts	Poles	1	2	3	4	5	6–10	Laps	Laps Led	Races Led	Miles	$
1959	NR	1	0	0	0	0	0	0	0	99	0	0	25	60
Lifetime		1	0	0	0	0	0	0	0	99	0	0	25	$60

Clyde Lynn

Clyde Lynn
B: 3/3/1936   D: 11/1/1996
Racing Hometown: Christiansburg, VA

Year	Rank	Starts	Poles	1	2	3	4	5	6–10	Laps	Laps Led	Races Led	Miles	$
1965	41	24	0	0	0	0	0	0	9	4,522	0	0	2,067	4,545
1966	20	40	0	0	1	0	0	0	14	9,384	0	0	5,789	13,222
1967	13	44	0	0	0	0	2	3	17	9,556	0	0	6,551	19,520
1968	4	49	0	0	0	0	1	1	23	12,013	0	0	8,897	29,226
1969	87	3	0	0	0	0	0	0	1	688	0	0	386	1,915
1970	NR	1	0	0	0	0	0	0	1	386	0	0	241	625
1971	80	3	0	0	0	0	0	0	0	508	0	0	271	1,080
1976	96T	1	0	0	0	0	0	0	0	123	0	0	66	735
Lifetime		165	0	0	1	0	3	4	65	37,180	0	0	24,267	$66,511

John Lyons

John Lyons

Year	Rank	Starts	Poles	1	2	3	4	5	6–10	Laps	Laps Led	Races Led	Miles	$
1971	NR	1	0	0	0	0	0	0	0	35	0	0	92	700
Lifetime		1	0	0	0	0	0	0	0	35	0	0	92	$700

Paul Lyons

Paul Lyons
Racing Hometown: Winston-Salem, NC

Year	Rank	Starts	Poles	1	2	3	4	5	6–10	Laps	Laps Led	Races Led	Miles	$
1961	NR	1	0	0	0	0	0	0	0	4	0	0	1	0
1962	NR	1	0	0	0	0	0	0	0	9	0	0	2	25
Lifetime		2	0	0	0	0	0	0	0	13	0	0	3	$25

Art MacBurney

Arthur MacBurney

Year	Rank	Starts	Poles	1	2	3	4	5	6–10	Laps	Laps Led	Races Led	Miles	$
1955	122	1	0	0	0	0	0	0	0	204	0	0	204	175
Lifetime		1	0	0	0	0	0	0	0	204	0	0	204	$175

Dave MacDonald

David MacDonald
B: 7/23/1937   D: 5/30/1964   *Killed in Indianapolis 500.*
Racing Hometown: El Monte, CA

Year	Rank	Starts	Poles	1	2	3	4	5	6–10	Laps	Laps Led	Races Led	Miles	$
1963	42	2	0	0	1	0	0	0	0	323	92	1	872	5,330
1964	29	5	0	0	1	0	0	0	2	661	0	0	1,599	9,195
Lifetime		7	0	0	2	0	0	0	2	984	92	1	2,471	$14,525

Year	Rank	Starts	Poles	Finish						Laps	Laps Led	Races Led	Miles	$
				1	2	3	4	5	6–10					

Eddie MacDonald

Edward MacDonald
Racing Hometown: Tifton, GA

Year	Rank	Starts	Poles	1	2	3	4	5	6–10	Laps	Laps Led	Races Led	Miles	$
1966	54	3	0	0	0	0	0	0	1	492	0	0	870	2,110
Lifetime		3	0	0	0	0	0	0	1	492	0	0	870	$2,110

Randy MacDonald

Randall MacDonald
B: 7/26/1962
Racing Hometown: Oshawa, Ont., Canada,

Year	Rank	Starts	Poles	1	2	3	4	5	6–10	Laps	Laps Led	Races Led	Miles	$
1994	65	1	0	0	0	0	0	0	0	466	0	0	474	8,200
1995	—	0												5,150
1996	50	3	0	0	0	0	0	0	0	680	0	0	1,285	33,910
Lifetime		4	0	0	0	0	0	0	0	1,146	0	0	1,759	$47,260

Johnny Mackison

John Mackison
B: 9/27/1935
Racing Hometown: Delta, PA

Year	Rank	Starts	Poles	1	2	3	4	5	6–10	Laps	Laps Led	Races Led	Miles	$
1957	27	5	0	0	0	0	0	1	1	769	0	0	693	1,330
1958	29	11	0	0	0	1	0	1	1	1,423	0	0	1,074	1,255
Lifetime		16	0	0	0	1	0	2	2	2,192	0	0	1,766	$2,585

Dave Mader

David Mader Jr.
B: 10/19/1930
Racing Hometown: Birmingham, AL

Year	Rank	Starts	Poles	1	2	3	4	5	6–10	Laps	Laps Led	Races Led	Miles	$
1961	61	6	0	0	0	0	0	0	0	638	0	0	791	880
Lifetime		6	0	0	0	0	0	0	0	638	0	0	791	$880

Dave Mader III

David Mader III
B: 6/30/1955
Racing Hometown: Maylene, AL

Year	Rank	Starts	Poles	1	2	3	4	5	6–10	Laps	Laps Led	Races Led	Miles	$
1988	72	1	0	0	0	0	0	0	0	271	0	0	144	1,565
1989	75T	1	0	0	0	0	0	0	0	480	0	0	488	2,675
1990	75	1	0	0	0	0	0	0	0	323	0	0	492	4,525
1991	61	2	0	0	0	0	0	0	0	515	0	0	753	10,210
1992	45	5	0	0	0	0	0	0	0	1,387	7	1	1,389	69,635
Lifetime		10	0	0	0	0	0	0	0	2,976	7	1	3,266	$88,610

Paul Magee

Paul Magee
Racing Hometown: Scio, OH

Year	Rank	Starts	Poles	1	2	3	4	5	6–10	Laps	Laps Led	Races Led	Miles	$
1952	114T	1	0	0	0	0	0	0	0	173	0	0	87	25
Lifetime		1	0	0	0	0	0	0	0	173	0	0	87	$25

Jocko Maggiacomo

Chauncey Maggiacomo
B: 11/30/1947
Racing Hometown: Poughkeepsie, NY

Year	Rank	Starts	Poles	1	2	3	4	5	6–10	Laps	Laps Led	Races Led	Miles	$
1977	80	3	0	0	0	0	0	0	0	467	0	0	806	2,080
1978	105T	1	0	0	0	0	0	0	0	45	0	0	113	815
1979	106T	1	0	0	0	0	0	0	0	172	0	0	430	1,105
1980	80	2	0	0	0	0	0	0	0	280	0	0	283	2,325
1981	98T	1	0	0	0	0	0	0	0	189	0	0	189	540
1982	61	4	0	0	0	0	0	0	0	411	0	0	546	3,525
1983	60	3	0	0	0	0	0	0	0	312	0	0	722	4,900
1984	—	0												1,650
1986	96	2	0	0	0	0	0	0	0	14	0	0	35	2,695
1987	62	3	0	0	0	0	0	0	0	233	0	0	582	4,885
1988	57	3	0	0	0	0	0	0	0	125	0	0	320	6,455
Lifetime		23	0	0	0	0	0	0	0	2,248	0	0	4,024	$30,975

Mike Magill

Michael Magill
B: 2/8/1920
Racing Hometown: Haddonville, NJ

Year	Rank	Starts	Poles	1	2	3	4	5	6–10	Laps	Laps Led	Races Led	Miles	$
1952	NR	2	0	0	0	0	0	0	0	50	0	0	50	25

Year	Rank	Starts	Poles	Finish						Laps	Laps Led	Races Led	Miles	$
				1	2	3	4	5	6–10					

Mike Magill *continued*

Year	Rank	Starts	Poles	1	2	3	4	5	6–10	Laps	Laps Led	Races Led	Miles	$
1953	38	3	0	0	0	0	0	0	0	244	0	0	336	235
Lifetime		5	0	0	0	0	0	0	0	294	0	0	386	$260

Emory Mahon

Emory Mahon
Racing Hometown: Warren, PA

Year	Rank	Starts	Poles	1	2	3	4	5	6–10	Laps	Laps Led	Races Led	Miles	$
1955	117	2	0	0	0	0	0	0	1	256	0	0	165	200
1957	NR	1	0	0	0	0	0	0	0	3	0	0	3	50
1958	NR	2	0	0	0	0	1	0	0	149	0	0	50	270
Lifetime		5	0	0	0	0	1	0	1	408	0	0	218	$520

Chuck Mahoney

Charles Mahoney
B: 3/3/1920
Racing Hometown: Rome, NY

Year	Rank	Starts	Poles	1	2	3	4	5	6–10	Laps	Laps Led	Races Led	Miles	$
1949	71	1	0	0	0	0	0	0	0		0	0		0
1950	7	11	1	0	1	1	0	1	3	705	18	1	638	2,550
1951	N/A	1	0	0	0	0	0	0	1		0	0		75
1952	203	1	0	0	0	0	0	0	0		0	0		25
1956	167	2	0	0	0	0	0	0	0	219	0	0	110	200
Lifetime		16	1	0	1	1	0	1	4	924	18	1	748	$2,850

Jimmy Mairs

James Mairs
Racing Hometown: Wheaton, MD

Year	Rank	Starts	Poles	1	2	3	4	5	6–10	Laps	Laps Led	Races Led	Miles	$
1956	283	1	0	0	0	0	0	0	0		0	0		0
1959	NR	1	0	0	0	0	0	0	0	202	0	0	101	75
1961	89	3	0	0	0	0	0	0	2	293	0	0	73	510
Lifetime		5	0	0	0	0	0	0	2	495	0	0	174	$585

Bill Majot

William E. Majot
Racing Hometown: Toledo, OH

Year	Rank	Starts	Poles	1	2	3	4	5	6–10	Laps	Laps Led	Races Led	Miles	$
1951	N/A	3	0	0	0	0	0	0	0	233	0	0	233	75
Lifetime		3	0	0	0	0	0	0	0	233	0	0	233	$75

Jim Malloy

James Malloy
B: 5/23/1932   D: 5/18/1972   *Died of injuries suffered practicing for Indy 500 (5/14/72).*
Racing Hometown: Denver, CO

Year	Rank	Starts	Poles	1	2	3	4	5	6–10	Laps	Laps Led	Races Led	Miles	$
1966	NR	1	0	0	0	0	0	0	0	37	0	0	93	100
Lifetime		1	0	0	0	0	0	0	0	37	0	0	93	$100

Art Malone

Arthur Malone
B: 6/3/1936
Racing Hometown: Lutz, FL

Year	Rank	Starts	Poles	1	2	3	4	5	6–10	Laps	Laps Led	Races Led	Miles	$
1961	100	1	0	0	0	0	0	0	1	484	0	0	242	500
1962	65	1	0	0	0	0	0	0	1	95	0	0	238	600
Lifetime		2	0	0	0	0	0	0	2	579	0	0	480	$1,100

Bob Malzahn

Robert Malzahn
B: 1931
Racing Hometown: Miami, FL

Year	Rank	Starts	Poles	1	2	3	4	5	6–10	Laps	Laps Led	Races Led	Miles	$
1958	NR	1	0	0	0	0	0	0	0	33	0	0	33	0
Lifetime		1	0	0	0	0	0	0	0	33	0	0	33	$0

Bill Mann

William Mann
Racing Hometown: Gothenburg, NE

Year	Rank	Starts	Poles	1	2	3	4	5	6–10	Laps	Laps Led	Races Led	Miles	$
1953	97T	1	0	0	0	0	0	0	0		0	0		25
Lifetime		1	0	0	0	0	0	0	0		0	0		$25

Year	Rank	Starts	Poles	Finish						Laps	Laps Led	Races Led	Miles	$
				1	2	3	4	5	6–10					

Larry Mann

Lawrence Mann
D: 9/14/1952   *Killed in NASCAR race @ Langhorne.*
Racing Hometown: Yonkers, NY

Year	Rank	Starts	Poles	1	2	3	4	5	6–10	Laps	Laps Led	Races Led	Miles	$
1952	NR	6	0	0	0	0	0	0	0	767	0	0	632	135
Lifetime		6	0	0	0	0	0	0	0	767	0	0	632	$135

John Manning

John Manning
Racing Hometown: Axton, VA

Year	Rank	Starts	Poles	1	2	3	4	5	6–10	Laps	Laps Led	Races Led	Miles	$
1950	112T	1	0	0	0	0	0	0	0	95	0	0	48	0
Lifetime		1	0	0	0	0	0	0	0	95	0	0	48	$0

Larry Manning

Lawrence N. Manning
B: 10/4/1942
Racing Hometown: Salisbury, NC

Year	Rank	Starts	Poles	1	2	3	4	5	6–10	Laps	Laps Led	Races Led	Miles	$
1963	29	23	0	0	0	0	1	0	8	5,158	0	0	2,980	5,405
1964	75	5	0	0	0	0	0	0	3	971	0	0	438	910
1965	NR	10	0	0	0	0	0	0	1	1,683	0	0	1,062	2,465
1966	39	13	0	0	0	0	1	0	0	2,769	0	0	1,689	4,070
1967	79	6	0	0	0	0	0	0	0	630	0	0	508	2,575
1968	41	12	0	0	0	0	0	0	0	2,151	0	0	2,270	6,995
1970	100	1	0	0	0	0	0	0	0	83	0	0	52	755
1974	135	1	0	0	0	0	0	0	0	1	0	0	1	580
Lifetime		71	0	0	0	0	2	0	12	13,446	0	0	8,999	$23,755

Skip Manning

Skip Manning
B: 4/23/1945
Racing Hometown: Bogalusa, LA

Year	Rank	Starts	Poles	1	2	3	4	5	6–10	Laps	Laps Led	Races Led	Miles	$
1975	61	5	0	0	0	0	0	0	0	995	0	0	1,794	9,705
1976	18	27	0	0	0	0	0	0	4	6,913	0	0	8,298	61,537
1977	14	28	0	0	0	1	0	0	7	7,533	13	1	8,355	111,317
1978	29	17	0	0	0	0	1	0	3	4,410	0	0	5,486	55,470
1979	91	2	0	0	0	0	0	0	0	182	0	0	326	5,880
Lifetime		79	0	0	0	1	1	0	14	20,033	13	1	24,259	$243,909

George Mantooth

George Edward Mantooth
B: 6/7/1925
Racing Hometown: Concord, NC

Year	Rank	Starts	Poles	1	2	3	4	5	6–10	Laps	Laps Led	Races Led	Miles	$
1949	NR	1	0	0	0	0	0	0	0		0	0		0
1956	302	1	0	0	0	0	0	0	0	43	0	0	22	0
Lifetime		2	0	0	0	0	0	0	0	43	0	0	22	$0

Johnny Mantz

John Mantz
B: 9/18/1918   D: 10/25/1972   *Killed in highway crash.*
Racing Hometown: Long Beach, CA

Year	Rank	Starts	Poles	1	2	3	4	5	6–10	Laps	Laps Led	Races Led	Miles	$
1950	6	3	0	1	0	0	0	0	1	400	351	1	500	10,810
1951	21	6	0	0	1	1	0	0	2	332	28	1	354	2,025
1955	116	2	0	0	0	0	0	0	1	148	0	0	171	245
1956	98	1	0	0	0	1	0	0	0	79	0	0	198	1,130
Lifetime		12	0	1	1	2	0	0	4	959	379	2	1,223	$14,210

Dave Marburger

David Marburger
Racing Hometown: Reading, PA

Year	Rank	Starts	Poles	1	2	3	4	5	6–10	Laps	Laps Led	Races Led	Miles	$
1959	NR	1	0	0	0	0	0	0	0	22	0	0	11	0
Lifetime		1	0	0	0	0	0	0	0	22	0	0	11	$0

Dave Marcis

David A. Marcis
B: 3/1/1941
Racing Hometown: Wausau, WI

Year	Rank	Starts	Poles	1	2	3	4	5	6–10	Laps	Laps Led	Races Led	Miles	$
1968	34	10	0	0	0	0	0	0	2	3,240	0	0	3,179	8,199
1969	19	37	0	0	0	1	2	0	8	7,099	22	3	6,930	32,383
1970	9	47	0	0	0	3	0	4	8	8,909	14	1	8,041	41,111
1971	21	29	2	0	1	1	4	3	5	6,460	331	8	6,689	37,582
1972	15	27	0	0	0	2	1	2	6	6,708	4	2	7,522	45,012

Year	Rank	Starts	Poles	Finish 1	2	3	4	5	6–10	Laps	Laps Led	Races Led	Miles	$

Dave Marcis *continued*

Year	Rank	Starts	Poles	1	2	3	4	5	6–10	Laps	Laps Led	Races Led	Miles	$
1973	24	23	0	0	0	0	1	2	3	4,905	0	0	5,448	30,253
1974	6	30	0	0	0	0	2	4	12	8,658	12	2	9,966	83,377
1975	2	30	4	1	1	5	6	3	2	8,324	458	17	9,789	240,646
1976	6	30	7	3	0	1	2	3	7	8,355	893	20	9,733	218,250
1977	25	18	0	0	0	0	4	1	2	4,386	92	7	5,499	72,605
1978	5	30	0	0	1	3	8	2	10	9,672	115	12	10,992	205,871
1979	20	25	0	0	0	0	0	1	5	6,842	20	4	7,634	56,434
1980	9	31	0	0	0	1	2	1	10	9,012	94	14	9,790	150,165
1981	9	31	1	0	0	2	1	1	5	8,004	178	15	9,255	162,213
1982	6	30	0	1	1	0	0	0	12	8,370	56	10	9,642	249,027
1983	11	30	0	0	0	0	0	0	7	7,771	24	6	9,171	306,355
1984	13	30	0	0	0	0	3	0	6	9,383	30	5	10,387	330,766
1985	18	28	0	0	0	0	0	0	5	7,319	30	4	8,729	173,467
1986	17	29	0	0	0	0	0	1	3	7,316	63	11	8,520	220,461
1987	18	29	0	0	0	2	0	0	5	6,880	84	9	8,749	256,354
1988	19	29	0	0	0	0	0	0	2	8,178	62	7	9,545	212,485
1989	25	27	0	0	0	0	0	0	1	7,866	16	5	9,984	196,161
1990	21	29	0	0	0	0	0	0	0	8,906	8	4	10,611	242,724
1991	29	27	0	0	0	0	0	0	1	7,271	3	3	9,173	219,760
1992	29	29	0	0	0	0	0	0	0	6,739	0	0	8,477	218,045
1993	33	23	0	0	0	0	0	0	0	6,233	14	3	7,818	202,305
1994	36	23	0	0	0	0	0	0	1	5,914	17	4	7,762	261,650
1995	35	28	0	0	0	0	0	0	0	7,319	3	2	9,225	337,853
1996	38	27	0	0	0	0	0	0	0	7,202	20	8	8,698	435,177
Lifetime		816	14	5	4	21	36	28	128	213,241	2,663	186	246,957	$5,246,691
		2nd								**2nd**			**2nd**	

Howard Mark

Howard Mark
Racing Hometown: Deland, FL

Year	Rank	Starts	Poles	1	2	3	4	5	6–10	Laps	Laps Led	Races Led	Miles	$
1986	116T	1	0	0	0	0	0	0	0	14	0	0	14	875
Lifetime		1	0	0	0	0	0	0	0	14	0	0	14	$875

Curtis Markham

Curtis Markham
B: 9/21/1959
Racing Hometown: Fredericksburg, VA

Year	Rank	Starts	Poles	1	2	3	4	5	6–10	Laps	Laps Led	Races Led	Miles	$
1987	90	4	0	0	0	0	0	0	0	704	0	0	679	12,620
1994	78	1	0	0	0	0	0	0	0	32	0	0	49	8,325
Lifetime		5	0	0	0	0	0	0	0	736	0	0	728	$20,945

Peck Markota

Peck Markota
Racing Hometown: Gardena, CA

Year	Rank	Starts	Poles	1	2	3	4	5	6–10	Laps	Laps Led	Races Led	Miles	$
1958	87	1	0	0	0	0	0	0	0	98	0	0	258	100
Lifetime		1	0	0	0	0	0	0	0	98	0	0	258	$100

Ed Markstellar

Edward Markstellar
Racing Hometown: E. Patchogue, NY

Year	Rank	Starts	Poles	1	2	3	4	5	6–10	Laps	Laps Led	Races Led	Miles	$
1960	111	2	0	0	0	0	0	0	0	34	0	0	58	325
1961	78	4	0	0	0	0	0	0	0	616	0	0	991	700
Lifetime		6	0	0	0	0	0	0	0	650	0	0	1,049	$1,025

Coo Coo Marlin

Clifton Burton Marlin
B: 1/3/1932
Racing Hometown: Columbia, TN

Year	Rank	Starts	Poles	1	2	3	4	5	6–10	Laps	Laps Led	Races Led	Miles	$
1966	103	1	0	0	0	0	0	0	1	375	0	0	188	375
1967	88	3	0	0	0	0	0	0	0	158	0	0	155	755
1969	52	7	0	0	0	0	0	0	2	993	0	0	1,285	5,680
1970	38	13	0	0	0	0	0	0	4	2,531	0	0	3,825	14,799
1971	49	12	0	0	0	0	0	0	0	1,495	0	0	2,334	9,135
1972	25	20	0	0	0	1	1	0	3	4,092	31	5	5,383	28,924
1973	22	21	0	0	0	1	0	0	7	5,454	16	3	5,937	29,997
1974	22	23	0	0	0	0	1	0	4	5,623	28	7	6,261	41,944
1975	20	23	0	0	0	1	0	3	7	5,199	25	5	6,400	60,013
1976	28	12	0	0	0	0	0	0	6	3,074	0	0	4,309	39,485

Year	Rank	Starts	Poles	Finish						Laps	Laps Led	Races Led	Miles	$
				1	2	3	4	5	6–10					

Coo Coo Marlin *continued*

Year	Rank	Starts	Poles	1	2	3	4	5	6–10	Laps	Laps Led	Races Led	Miles	$
1977	34	11	0	0	0	0	1	0	4	2,930	1	1	4,210	42,450
1978	36	9	0	0	0	0	0	0	2	1,518	4	2	2,372	19,415
1979	33	7	0	0	0	0	0	0	2	907	0	0	1,989	27,540
1980	54	3	0	0	0	0	0	0	0	377	0	0	978	8,400
Lifetime		165	0	0	0	3	3	3	42	34,726	105	23	45,625	$328,912

Jack Marlin

Jack Marlin
Racing Hometown: Nashville, TN

Year	Rank	Starts	Poles	1	2	3	4	5	6–10	Laps	Laps Led	Races Led	Miles	$
1968	NR	1	0	0	0	0	0	0	1	237	0	0	119	300
Lifetime		1	0	0	0	0	0	0	1	237	0	0	119	$300

Sterling Marlin

Sterling Marlin
B: 6/30/1957
Racing Hometown: Columbia, TN

Year	Rank	Starts	Poles	1	2	3	4	5	6–10	Laps	Laps Led	Races Led	Miles	$
1976	101	1	0	0	0	0	0	0	0	55	0	0	33	565
1978	67	2	0	0	0	0	0	0	1	591	0	0	708	10,320
1979	85	1	0	0	0	0	0	0	0	341	11	1	203	505
1980	49	5	0	0	0	0	0	0	2	1,311	0	0	1,762	29,810
1981	93	2	0	0	0	0	0	0	0	437	0	0	435	1,955
1982	NR	1	0	0	0	0	0	0	0	256	0	0	384	4,015
1983	19	30	0	0	0	0	0	0	1	8,053	0	0	9,166	148,253
1984	37	14	0	0	0	0	0	0	2	2,737	0	0	3,983	54,355
1985	37	8	0	0	0	0	0	0	0	1,321	1	1	2,348	31,155
1986	36	10	0	0	1	0	1	0	2	1,738	21	3	3,225	113,070
1987	11	29	0	0	0	1	2	1	4	8,356	68	6	10,304	306,412
1988	10	29	0	0	1	1	0	4	7	8,798	332	13	10,383	521,464
1989	12	29	0	0	1	1	0	2	9	8,840	42	6	10,578	473,267
1990	14	29	0	0	0	1	1	3	5	8,310	71	6	10,139	369,167
1991	7	29	2	0	2	1	1	3	9	9,205	201	8	11,207	633,690
1992	10	29	5	0	3	0	1	2	7	8,462	218	8	10,286	649,048
1993	15	30	0	0	1	0	0	0	7	9,153	341	6	11,221	628,835
1994	14	31	1	1	1	1	0	2	6	9,184	144	11	10,841	1,140,683
1995	3	31	1	3	2	0	3	1	13	**9,728**	472	12	**11,936**	2,253,502
1996	8	31	0	2	0	1	1	1	5	8,877	331	10	10,582	1,588,425
Lifetime		371	9	6	12	7	10	19	80	105,753	2,253	91	129,725	$8,958,496
														10th

Gene Marmor

Gene Marmor
Racing Hometown: Northlake, IL

Year	Rank	Starts	Poles	1	2	3	4	5	6–10	Laps	Laps Led	Races Led	Miles	$
1960	67	4	0	0	0	0	0	0	1	732	0	0	836	775
Lifetime		4	0	0	0	0	0	0	1	732	0	0	836	$775

Ken Marriott

Kenneth Marriott
B: 1920
Racing Hometown: Baltimore, MD

Year	Rank	Starts	Poles	1	2	3	4	5	6–10	Laps	Laps Led	Races Led	Miles	$
1949	73	1	0	0	0	0	0	0	0	169	0	0	169	50
1950	NR	1	0	0	0	0	0	0	0	0	0	0	0	0
1953	NR	1	0	0	0	0	0	0	0	0	0	0	0	40
1957	NR	1	0	0	0	0	0	0	1	281	0	0	281	600
1959	NR	1	0	0	0	0	0	0	0	1	0	0	3	100
Lifetime		5	0	0	0	0	0	0	1	451	0	0	453	$790

Jack Marsh

Jack Marsh

Year	Rank	Starts	Poles	1	2	3	4	5	6–10	Laps	Laps Led	Races Led	Miles	$
1957	79	3	0	0	0	0	0	0	1	489	0	0	262	365
Lifetime		3	0	0	0	0	0	0	1	489	0	0	262	$365

Sam Marshall

Samuel Marshall
Racing Hometown: Jacksonville, FL

Year	Rank	Starts	Poles	1	2	3	4	5	6–10	Laps	Laps Led	Races Led	Miles	$
1949	NR	1	0	0	0	0	0	0	0	0	0	0	0	0
Lifetime		1	0	0	0	0	0	0	0	0	0	0	0	$0

Year	Rank	Starts	Poles	Finish						Laps	Laps Led	Races Led	Miles	$
				1	2	3	4	5	6–10					

Bobby Marshman

Robert Marshman
B: 9/24/1936   D: 12/4/1964   *Killed in test session at Phoenix Int'l Raceway 11/27/64.*
Racing Hometown: Pottstown, PA

Year	Rank	Starts	Poles	1	2	3	4	5	6–10	Laps	Laps Led	Races Led	Miles	$
1964	NR	2	0	0	0	0	0	0	1	56	0	0	140	925
Lifetime		2	0	0	0	0	0	0	1	56	0	0	140	$925

Dick Martin

Richard Martin
Racing Hometown: Toledo, OH

Year	Rank	Starts	Poles	1	2	3	4	5	6–10	Laps	Laps Led	Races Led	Miles	$
1952	109	2	0	0	0	0	0	0	0	72	0	0	36	50
Lifetime		2	0	0	0	0	0	0	0	72	0	0	36	$50

Joe Martin

Joseph H. Martin
Racing Hometown: Lewes, DE

Year	Rank	Starts	Poles	1	2	3	4	5	6–10	Laps	Laps Led	Races Led	Miles	$
1954	NR	1	0	0	0	0	0	0	0	85	0	0	85	0
Lifetime		1	0	0	0	0	0	0	0	85	0	0	85	$0

John Martin

John Martin
B: 3/20/1939
Racing Hometown: Irvine, CA

Year	Rank	Starts	Poles	1	2	3	4	5	6–10	Laps	Laps Led	Races Led	Miles	$
1967	NR	2	0	0	0	0	0	0	0	154	0	0	363	1,120
1974	58	4	0	0	0	0	0	0	0	283	0	0	639	4,465
1975	NR	1	0	0	0	0	0	0	0	53	0	0	133	850
Lifetime		7	0	0	0	0	0	0	0	490	0	0	1,134	$6,435

Mark Martin

Mark Martin
B: 1/9/1959
Racing Hometown: Batesville, AR

Year	Rank	Starts	Poles	1	2	3	4	5	6–10	Laps	Laps Led	Races Led	Miles	$
1981	42	5	2	0	0	1	0	0	1	1,478	76	2	829	13,950
1982	14	30	0	0	0	0	0	2	6	7,449	4	3	8,321	142,710
1983	30	16	0	0	0	1	0	0	2	4,130	1	1	5,545	99,665
1986	48	5	0	0	0	0	0	0	0	1,342	0	0	1,955	20,515
1987	101T	1	0	0	0	0	0	0	0	68	0	0	102	3,550
1988	15	29	1	0	1	0	2	0	7	7,615	123	5	9,193	223,630
1989	3	29	6	1	5	6	1	1	4	9,010	480	16	10,716	1,016,850
1990	2	29	3	3	5	4	2	2	7	**9,636**	451	15	**11,487**	1,302,958
1991	6	29	5	1	1	5	4	3	3	8,927	663	15	10,810	1,039,991
1992	6	29	1	2	5	2	1	0	7	8,954	533	17	10,670	1,000,571
1993	3	30	5	5	3	1	1	2	7	9,381	1,353	20	11,106	1,657,662
1994	2	31	1	2	4	2	4	3	5	9,549	733	18	11,403	1,678,906
1995	4	31	4	4	1	4	1	3	9	9,393	740	14	11,427	1,893,519
1996	5	31	4	0	4	5	3	2	9	9,064	702	16	11,066	1,887,396
Lifetime		325	32	18	29	31	19	18	67	95,996	5,859	142	114,629	$11,981,873
														6th

Otis Martin

Otis Mason Martin
B: 3/1/1918   *Deceased*
Racing Hometown: Bassett, VA

Year	Rank	Starts	Poles	1	2	3	4	5	6–10	Laps	Laps Led	Races Led	Miles	$
1949	35	4	0	0	0	0	0	0	1	66	0	0	33	200
1950	66	1	0	0	0	0	0	0	1	47	0	0	196	175
1951	N/A	2	0	0	0	0	0	0	0			0	0	50
1952	28	5	0	0	0	0	0	0	2	620	0	0	560	275
1953	22	8	0	0	0	0	0	0	2	519	0	0	608	610
1954	123	3	0	0	0	0	0	0	0	414	0	0	637	225
Lifetime		23	0	0	0	0	0	0	6	1,666	0	0	2,035	$1,535

Pee Wee Martin

Leonard Martin
B: 6/29/1922   *Deceased*
Racing Hometown: Bassett, VA

Year	Rank	Starts	Poles	1	2	3	4	5	6–10	Laps	Laps Led	Races Led	Miles	$
1949	NR	1	0	0	0	0	0	0	0			0	0	0
1950	83	2	0	0	0	0	0	0	0	344	12	1	430	150
Lifetime		3	0	0	0	0	0	0	0	344	12	1	430	$150

Year	Rank	Starts	Poles	Finish						Laps	Laps Led	Races Led	Miles	$
				1	2	3	4	5	6–10					

Virgil Martin

Virgil Martin

Year	Rank	Starts	Poles	1	2	3	4	5	6–10	Laps	Laps Led	Races Led	Miles	$
1955	194	1	0	0	0	0	0	0	0	62	0	0	62	20
Lifetime		1	0	0	0	0	0	0	0	62	0	0	62	$20

Larry Marx

Lawrence Marx
Racing Hometown: Buffalo, NY

Year	Rank	Starts	Poles	1	2	3	4	5	6–10	Laps	Laps Led	Races Led	Miles	$
1956	NR	1	0	0	0	0	0	0	0	78	0	0	39	100
Lifetime		1	0	0	0	0	0	0	0	78	0	0	39	$100

George Masker

George Masker

Year	Rank	Starts	Poles	1	2	3	4	5	6–10	Laps	Laps Led	Races Led	Miles	$
1950	NR	1	0	0	0	0	0	0	0		0	0		0
Lifetime		1	0	0	0	0	0	0	0		0	0		$0

Buck Mason

Buck Mason
Racing Hometown: Richmond, VA

Year	Rank	Starts	Poles	1	2	3	4	5	6–10	Laps	Laps Led	Races Led	Miles	$
1953	62	2	0	0	0	0	0	0	0	0	0	0	0	75
1954	151T	1	0	0	0	0	0	0	0	283	0	0	389	110
Lifetime		3	0	0	0	0	0	0	0	283	0	0	389	$185

Bill Massey

William Carl Massey
B: 1929   D: 8/22/1965   *Killed when hit in head with chair leg in tavern.*
Racing Hometown: Rural Hall, NC

Year	Rank	Starts	Poles	1	2	3	4	5	6–10	Laps	Laps Led	Races Led	Miles	$
1956	203T	1	0	0	0	0	0	0	0	176	0	0	88	100
1957	147	2	0	0	0	0	0	0	0	215	0	0	124	200
1960	120	1	0	0	0	0	0	0	0	71	0	0	18	130
Lifetime		4	0	0	0	0	0	0	0	462	0	0	229	$430

Ed Massey

Edsel Massey
Racing Hometown: Birmingham, AL

Year	Rank	Starts	Poles	1	2	3	4	5	6–10	Laps	Laps Led	Races Led	Miles	$
1951	N/A	3	0	0	0	0	0	0	1		0	0		150
1953	139	2	0	0	0	0	0	0	0		0	0		50
1954	172	1	0	0	0	0	0	0	0	127	0	0	191	50
1956	294T	1	0	0	0	0	0	0	0	76	0	0	38	0
Lifetime		7	0	0	0	0	0	0	1	203	0	0	229	$250

Jimmy Massey

James Massey
B: 12/1/1929
Racing Hometown: Mebane, NC

Year	Rank	Starts	Poles	1	2	3	4	5	6–10	Laps	Laps Led	Races Led	Miles	$
1955	13	11	0	0	0	1	1	2	4	1,906	0	0	1,721	3,510
1956	49	7	0	0	0	0	1	2	1	1,140	0	0	717	1,545
1957	NR	2	0	0	1	0	0	0	1	652	7	1	345	2,115
1958	32	9	1	0	0	0	0	1	2	1,612	0	0	1,114	1,625
1960	42	6	0	0	1	1	0	0	1	1,392	26	1	1,299	3,310
1963	38	15	0	0	0	0	1	0	7	3,179	0	0	1,433	2,870
1964	143	1	0	0	0	0	0	0	0	0	0	0	0	0
Lifetime		51	1	0	2	2	3	5	16	9,881	33	2	6,629	$14,565

Sam Massey

Samuel Massey
Racing Hometown: Atlanta, GA

Year	Rank	Starts	Poles	1	2	3	4	5	6–10	Laps	Laps Led	Races Led	Miles	$
1959	NR	1	0	0	0	0	0	0	0	73	0	0	73	110
Lifetime		1	0	0	0	0	0	0	0	73	0	0	73	$110

Bill Massuch

William Massuch
Racing Hometown: Lansing, MI

Year	Rank	Starts	Poles	1	2	3	4	5	6–10	Laps	Laps Led	Races Led	Miles	$
1969	74	1	0	0	0	0	0	0	0	157	0	0	314	1,075
Lifetime		1	0	0	0	0	0	0	0	157	0	0	314	$1,075

Rick Mast

Richard K. Mast
B: 3/4/1957
Racing Hometown: Rockbridge Baths, VA

Year	Rank	Starts	Poles	1	2	3	4	5	6–10	Laps	Laps Led	Races Led	Miles	$
1988	NR	2	0	0	0	0	0	0	0	512	2	1	527	9,190

Year	Rank	Starts	Poles	Finish						Laps	Laps Led	Races Led	Miles	$
				1	2	3	4	5	6–10					

Rick Mast *continued*

Year	Rank	Starts	Poles	1	2	3	4	5	6–10	Laps	Laps Led	Races Led	Miles	$
1989	35	13	0	0	0	0	0	0	1	4,160	14	2	4,439	128,102
1990	31	20	0	0	0	0	0	0	1	5,335	0	0	5,744	112,875
1991	21	29	0	0	0	0	1	0	2	8,861	32	3	10,650	344,020
1992	22	29	1	0	0	0	0	0	1	8,123	0	0	9,985	350,740
1993	21	30	0	0	0	0	0	1	4	8,488	32	4	9,802	568,095
1994	18	31	1	0	1	3	0	0	6	8,756	166	8	10,753	733,361
1995	21	31	1	0	0	0	0	0	3	8,560	143	3	10,599	749,550
1996	18	31	0	0	0	0	1	0	4	8,972	1	1	10,936	924,559
Lifetime		216	3	0	1	3	2	1	22	61,767	390	22	73,436	$3,920,492

Gary Mathieson

Gary Mathieson
Racing Hometown: Norwalk, CT

Year	Rank	Starts	Poles	1	2	3	4	5	6–10	Laps	Laps Led	Races Led	Miles	$
1954	92	1	0	0	0	0	0	0	1	114	0	0	114	100
Lifetime		1	0	0	0	0	0	0	1	114	0	0	114	$100

Lyle Matlock

Lyle Matlock
Racing Hometown: Los Altos, CA

Year	Rank	Starts	Poles	1	2	3	4	5	6–10	Laps	Laps Led	Races Led	Miles	$
1956	222	2	0	0	0	0	0	0	0	142	0	0	73	50
1957	201T	1	0	0	0	0	0	0	0	47	0	0	24	0
Lifetime		3	0	0	0	0	0	0	0	189	0	0	97	$50

Bob Matson

Robert Matson (Bud)
Racing Hometown: Cleveland Heights, OH

Year	Rank	Starts	Poles	1	2	3	4	5	6–10	Laps	Laps Led	Races Led	Miles	$
1951	N/A	1	0	0	0	0	0	0	0		0	0		25
Lifetime		1	0	0	0	0	0	0	0		0	0		$25

Banjo Matthews

Edwin Keith Matthews
B: 2/14/1932   D: 10/2/1996
Racing Hometown: Asheville, NC

Year	Rank	Starts	Poles	1	2	3	4	5	6–10	Laps	Laps Led	Races Led	Miles	$
1952	22	3	0	0	0	0	0	1	0	667	0	0	628	1,000
1955	43	3	0	0	0	0	0	0	2	734	0	0	672	745
1956	117	1	0	0	0	0	0	0	0	149	0	0	224	200
1957	58	5	1	0	0	1	0	0	0	713	56	1	404	855
1958	95	3	0	0	0	0	0	0	0	90	0	0	93	190
1959	61	4	0	0	0	0	0	0	0	654	55	1	483	1,990
1960	10	12	0	0	0	0	0	0	4	1,894	9	1	2,815	15,617
1961	31	14	0	0	0	0	1	0	2	2,019	197	6	3,010	5,610
1962	31	5	2	0	1	0	0	0	1	532	145	3	1,098	11,375
1963	57	1	0	0	0	0	0	0	0	358	0	0	537	700
Lifetime		51	3	0	1	1	1	1	9	7,810	462	12	9,963	$38,282

Frank Matthews

Frank Matthews
Racing Hometown: Dallas, TX

Year	Rank	Starts	Poles	1	2	3	4	5	6–10	Laps	Laps Led	Races Led	Miles	$
1949	59	1	0	0	0	0	0	0	0		0	0		50
Lifetime		1	0	0	0	0	0	0	0		0	0		$50

Gary Matthews

Gary Matthews
Racing Hometown: Fresno, CA

Year	Rank	Starts	Poles	1	2	3	4	5	6–10	Laps	Laps Led	Races Led	Miles	$
1974	123	1	0	0	0	0	0	0	0	37	0	0	97	725
1975	64	2	0	0	0	0	0	0	1	298	0	0	781	3,795
1976	90	2	0	0	0	0	0	0	0	209	0	0	548	2,410
1977	93T	1	0	0	0	0	0	0	0	91	0	0	238	1,225
Lifetime		6	0	0	0	0	0	0	1	635	0	0	1,664	$8,155

Nace Mattingly

P. A. Mattingly
Racing Hometown: Leonardtown, MD

Year	Rank	Starts	Poles	1	2	3	4	5	6–10	Laps	Laps Led	Races Led	Miles	$
1955	36	3	0	0	0	0	0	1	0	696	0	0	653	700
1956	231	3	0	0	0	0	0	1	0	311	0	0	219	410
1957	103	4	0	0	0	0	0	0	0	658	0	0	614	400
1958	119	4	0	0	0	0	0	0	1	325	0	0	145	285
1960	NR	2	0	0	0	0	0	0	1	361	0	0	181	285

Year	Rank	Starts	Poles	Finish						Laps	Laps Led	Races Led	Miles	$
				1	2	3	4	5	6–10	Laps	Led	Led	Miles	$

Nace Mattingly *continued*

Year	Rank	Starts	Poles	1	2	3	4	5	6–10	Laps	Laps Led	Races Led	Miles	$
1963	108	1	0	0	0	0	0	0	1	288	0	0	108	240
Lifetime		17	0	0	0	0	0	2	3	2,639	0	0	1,921	$2,320

Bobby Mausgrover

Robert H. Mausgrover
B: 3/27/1940
Racing Hometown: Keokuk, IA

Year	Rank	Starts	Poles	1	2	3	4	5	6–10	Laps	Laps Led	Races Led	Miles	$
1967	90	4	0	0	0	0	0	0	1	610	0	0	448	1,800
1968	73	4	0	0	0	0	0	0	0	298	0	0	173	1,235
1969	51	13	0	0	0	0	0	0	0	1,192	0	0	1,082	5,305
1970	65	3	0	0	0	0	0	0	0	103	0	0	179	2,710
1971	52	12	0	0	0	0	0	0	0	1,418	0	0	1,562	6,140
1972	55	6	0	0	0	0	0	0	0	655	0	0	1,214	5,100
1973	60	4	0	0	0	0	0	0	0	678	0	0	999	3,510
Lifetime		46	0	0	0	0	0	0	1	4,954	0	0	5,657	$25,800

Dick May

Richard Shelton May
B: 11/7/1930
Racing Hometown: Watertown, NY

Year	Rank	Starts	Poles	1	2	3	4	5	6–10	Laps	Laps Led	Races Led	Miles	$
1970	44	16	0	0	0	0	0	0	0	1,028	0	0	689	5,195
1971	32	22	0	0	0	0	0	0	1	2,527	0	0	2,518	9,225
1972	44	6	0	0	0	0	0	0	1	955	0	0	1,793	5,870
1973	71	4	0	0	0	0	0	0	0	337	0	0	566	3,605
1974	75	2	0	0	0	0	0	0	0	350	0	0	924	3,310
1975	41	9	0	0	0	0	0	0	1	1,688	0	0	2,344	11,525
1976	25	18	0	0	0	0	0	0	0	4,595	0	0	5,365	29,425
1977	27	13	0	0	0	0	0	0	0	3,977	0	0	4,476	22,265
1978	15	28	0	0	0	0	0	0	2	7,221	0	0	8,622	65,291
1979	30	19	0	0	0	0	0	0	0	3,387	0	0	3,714	27,320
1980	32	21	0	0	0	0	0	0	2	5,767	0	0	6,360	42,945
1981	37	9	0	0	0	0	0	0	1	1,843	0	0	3,173	30,315
1982	55	8	0	0	0	0	0	0	0	1,930	0	0	2,522	16,810
1983	64	5	0	0	0	0	0	0	0	1,100	0	0	1,384	7,390
1984	48	3	0	0	0	0	0	0	0	1,274	0	0	1,282	5,325
1985	NR	2	0	0	0	0	0	0	0	665	0	0	636	2,825
Lifetime		185	0	0	0	0	0	0	8	38,644	0	0	46,367	$288,641

Gary Mayeda

Gary Mayeda
Racing Hometown: Riverside, CA

Year	Rank	Starts	Poles	1	2	3	4	5	6–10	Laps	Laps Led	Races Led	Miles	$
1984	NR	1	0	0	0	0	0	0	0	21	0	0	55	2,215
Lifetime		1	0	0	0	0	0	0	0	21	0	0	55	$2,215

Jim Mayes

James Mayes
Racing Hometown: Princeton, IN

Year	Rank	Starts	Poles	1	2	3	4	5	6–10	Laps	Laps Led	Races Led	Miles	$
1951	N/A	1	0	0	0	0	0	0	0		0	0		50
1952	196	1	0	0	0	0	0	0	0		0	0		25
Lifetime		2	0	0	0	0	0	0	0		0	0		$75

Jeremy Mayfield

Jeremy Mayfield
B: 5/27/1969
Racing Hometown: Owensboro, KY

Year	Rank	Starts	Poles	1	2	3	4	5	6–10	Laps	Laps Led	Races Led	Miles	$
1993	74T	1	0	0	0	0	0	0	0	324	0	0	486	4,830
1994	37	20	0	0	0	0	0	0	0	5,581	0	0	7,313	226,265
1995	31	27	0	0	0	0	0	0	1	7,943	79	3	10,440	436,805
1996	26	30	1	0	0	0	1	1	0	7,814	20	4	9,408	592,853
Lifetime		78	1	0	0	0	1	1	1	21,662	99	7	27,647	$1,260,753

Roy Mayne

Roy Elwood Mayne
B: 5/16/1935
Racing Hometown: Sumter, SC

Year	Rank	Starts	Poles	1	2	3	4	5	6–10	Laps	Laps Led	Races Led	Miles	$
1963	36	20	0	0	0	0	0	1	3	3,857	0	0	1,944	3,490
1964	43	14	0	0	0	0	0	1	1	2,207	0	0	1,457	4,705
1965	27	14	0	0	0	0	1	0	4	2,463	0	0	2,449	9,060
1966	25	18	0	0	0	0	0	1	4	4,052	0	0	4,051	10,390

Year	Rank	Starts	Poles	Finish						Laps	Laps Led	Races Led	Miles	$
				1	2	3	4	5	6–10	Laps	Led	Led	Miles	$

Roy Mayne *continued*

Year	Rank	Starts	Poles	1	2	3	4	5	6–10	Laps	Laps Led	Races Led	Miles	$
1967	30	14	0	0	0	0	0	0	1	2,209	3	1	2,574	8,930
1968	115	1	0	0	0	0	0	0	0	77	0	0	116	775
1969	38	13	0	0	0	0	0	0	0	2,855	0	0	2,788	10,340
1970	29	16	0	0	0	0	0	0	3	3,731	0	0	4,764	16,910
1971	39	11	0	0	0	0	0	0	1	1,918	0	0	2,662	10,330
1972	86	4	0	0	0	0	0	0	0	362	0	0	518	2,990
1973	93	3	0	0	0	0	0	0	1	658	0	0	1,091	5,470
1974	35	11	0	0	0	0	0	0	0	1,681	0	0	2,856	15,589
Lifetime		139	0	0	0	0	1	3	18	26,070	3	1	27,270	$98,979

Harold Mays

Harold Mays (Lucky)
Racing Hometown: Augusta, GA

Year	Rank	Starts	Poles	1	2	3	4	5	6–10	Laps	Laps Led	Races Led	Miles	$
1951	147T	1	0	0	0	0	0	0	0		0	0		50
1952	174	1	0	0	0	0	0	0	0	1	0	0	1	60
Lifetime		2	0	0	0	0	0	0	0	1	0	0	1	$110

G. McBride

G. McBride

Year	Rank	Starts	Poles	1	2	3	4	5	6–10	Laps	Laps Led	Races Led	Miles	$
1954	NR	1	0	0	0	0	0	0	0	35	0	0	70	30
Lifetime		1	0	0	0	0	0	0	0	35	0	0	70	$30

Hub McBride

Hub McBride
Racing Hometown: Decatur, GA

Year	Rank	Starts	Poles	1	2	3	4	5	6–10	Laps	Laps Led	Races Led	Miles	$
1950	NR	1	0	0	0	0	0	0	0	341	0	0	426	0
1953	NR	1	0	0	0	0	0	0	0	29	0	0	119	25
Lifetime		2	0	0	0	0	0	0	0	370	0	0	545	$25

Robin McCall

Robin McCall
B: 1964
Racing Hometown: San Antonio, TX

Year	Rank	Starts	Poles	1	2	3	4	5	6–10	Laps	Laps Led	Races Led	Miles	$
1982	74	2	0	0	0	0	0	0	0	154	0	0	308	2,395
Lifetime		2	0	0	0	0	0	0	0	154	0	0	308	$2,395

Buzz McCann

Harold McCann
Racing Hometown: St. Paul, MN

Year	Rank	Starts	Poles	1	2	3	4	5	6–10	Laps	Laps Led	Races Led	Miles	$
1960	NR	1	0	0	0	0	0	0	0	8	0	0	20	0
1961	190	1	0	0	0	0	0	0	0	1	0	0	3	0
Lifetime		2	0	0	0	0	0	0	0	9	0	0	23	$0

Buck McCardell

Buck McCardell
Racing Hometown: Conowingo, MD

Year	Rank	Starts	Poles	1	2	3	4	5	6–10	Laps	Laps Led	Races Led	Miles	$
1950	NR	1	0	0	0	0	0	0	0		0	0		0
1952	144	3	0	0	0	0	0	0	0	49	0	0	49	60
Lifetime		4	0	0	0	0	0	0	0	49	0	0	49	$60

Norm McCarthy

Norm McCarthy
B: 1924   D: 1992
Racing Hometown: Bedford, OH

Year	Rank	Starts	Poles	1	2	3	4	5	6–10	Laps	Laps Led	Races Led	Miles	$
1951	N/A	3	0	0	0	0	0	0	1		0	0		125
Lifetime		3	0	0	0	0	0	0	1		0	0		$125

Jack McClure

Jack McClure
Racing Hometown: Columbia, SC

Year	Rank	Starts	Poles	1	2	3	4	5	6–10	Laps	Laps Led	Races Led	Miles	$
1951	N/A	2	0	0	0	0	0	0	0		0	0		25
Lifetime		2	0	0	0	0	0	0	0		0	0		$25

Jeff McClure

Jeff McClure
B: 1/22/1967
Racing Hometown: Harrisburg, NC

Year	Rank	Starts	Poles	1	2	3	4	5	6–10	Laps	Laps Led	Races Led	Miles	$
1992	79T	1	0	0	0	0	0	0	0	173	0	0	346	5,990
Lifetime		1	0	0	0	0	0	0	0	173	0	0	346	$5,990

Year	Rank	Starts	Poles	Finish						Laps	Laps Led	Races Led	Miles	$
				1	2	3	4	5	6–10					

Roger McCluskey

Roger F. McCluskey
B: 8/24/1930   D: 8/29/1993
Racing Hometown: Tucson, AZ

Year	Rank	Starts	Poles	1	2	3	4	5	6–10	Laps	Laps Led	Races Led	Miles	$
1969	NR	1	0	0	0	0	0	0	0	100	0	0	270	825
1970	NR	1	0	0	1	0	0	0	0	193	2	1	506	9,000
1972	NR	1	0	0	0	0	0	0	0	241	0	0	362	1,586
1977	NR	1	0	0	0	0	0	0	0	20	0	0	50	700
Lifetime		4	0	0	1	0	0	0	0	554	2	1	1,187	$12,111

Jim McCorkindale

James McCorkindale

Year	Rank	Starts	Poles	1	2	3	4	5	6–10	Laps	Laps Led	Races Led	Miles	$
1958	165	1	0	0	0	0	0	0	0	120	0	0	316	110
Lifetime		1	0	0	0	0	0	0	0	120	0	0	316	$110

Jack D. McCoy

Jack D. McCoy
Racing Hometown: Ashland, OR

Year	Rank	Starts	Poles	1	2	3	4	5	6–10	Laps	Laps Led	Races Led	Miles	$
1956	227	1	0	0	0	0	0	0	0	125	0	0	125	50
1957	68	5	0	0	0	0	0	1	0	553	0	0	277	520
1958	54	2	0	0	0	0	0	0	1	198	0	0	493	550
1959	114	1	0	0	0	0	0	0	0	42	0	0	42	50
Lifetime		9	0	0	0	0	0	1	1	918	0	0	937	$1,170

Jack McCoy

Jack McCoy
B: 3/24/1938
Racing Hometown: Bakersfield, CA

Year	Rank	Starts	Poles	1	2	3	4	5	6–10	Laps	Laps Led	Races Led	Miles	$
1963	150	1	0	0	0	0	0	0	0	1	0	0	3	200
1966	80	1	0	0	0	0	0	0	0	123	0	0	332	540
1967	82	1	0	0	0	0	0	0	0	88	0	0	238	575
1968	82T	1	0	0	0	0	0	0	0	118	0	0	319	725
1969	NR	2	0	0	0	0	0	0	1	257	0	0	533	2,750
1970	92	2	0	0	0	0	0	0	1	207	0	0	542	2,740
1971	NR	3	0	0	0	0	0	0	0	443	0	0	1,138	4,315
1972	82	3	0	0	0	0	0	0	0	228	0	0	575	4,070
1973	50	3	0	0	0	0	0	1	2	797	0	0	1,106	5,270
1974	72	3	0	0	0	0	0	0	0	175	4	1	453	3,390
Lifetime		20	0	0	0	0	0	1	4	2,437	4	1	5,239	$24,575

Rick McCray

Richard McCray
B: 6/12/1956
Racing Hometown: Bloomington, CA

Year	Rank	Starts	Poles	1	2	3	4	5	6–10	Laps	Laps Led	Races Led	Miles	$
1978	57	3	0	0	0	0	0	0	0	220	0	0	575	4,585
1979	110	1	0	0	0	0	0	0	0	31	0	0	81	750
1980	66	3	0	0	0	0	0	0	0	238	0	0	601	3,415
1981	88T	1	0	0	0	0	0	0	0	66	0	0	173	1,655
1982	54	2	0	0	0	0	0	0	0	151	0	0	396	3,355
1983	48	4	0	0	0	0	0	0	0	760	0	0	629	3,710
1984	71	2	0	0	0	0	0	0	0	102	0	0	267	2,170
1985	99	2	0	0	0	0	0	0	0	47	0	0	123	1,665
1986	84	2	0	0	0	0	0	0	0	123	0	0	322	4,910
1987	72	2	0	0	0	0	0	0	0	151	0	0	396	6,300
1988	83T	1	0	0	0	0	0	0	0	46	0	0	121	1,140
1989	83T	1	0	0	0	0	0	0	0	72	0	0	181	3,200
Lifetime		24	0	0	0	0	0	0	0	2,007	0	0	3,864	$36,855

Tex McCullough

Tex McCullough
Racing Hometown: Asheville, NC

Year	Rank	Starts	Poles	1	2	3	4	5	6–10	Laps	Laps Led	Races Led	Miles	$
1966	124	1	0	0	0	0	0	0	0	5	0	0	5	535
Lifetime		1	0	0	0	0	0	0	0	5	0	0	5	$535

John McDaniel

John L. McDaniel
Racing Hometown: West Palm Beach, FL

Year	Rank	Starts	Poles	1	2	3	4	5	6–10	Laps	Laps Led	Races Led	Miles	$
1958	86	3	0	0	0	0	0	0	0	279	0	0	167	100
Lifetime		3	0	0	0	0	0	0	0	279	0	0	167	$100

Year	Rank	Starts	Poles	Finish						Laps	Laps Led	Races Led	Miles	$
				1	2	3	4	5	6–10					

Bill McDonald

William A. McDonald
Racing Hometown: Buffalo, NY

Year	Rank	Starts	Poles	1	2	3	4	5	6–10	Laps	Laps Led	Races Led	Miles	$
1961	181	1	0	0	0	0	0	0	0	180	0	0	90	100
1962	112	2	0	0	0	0	0	0	0	121	0	0	61	100
Lifetime		3	0	0	0	0	0	0	0	301	0	0	151	$200

Eddie McDonald

Edward McDonald
Racing Hometown: Gainesville, FL

Year	Rank	Starts	Poles	1	2	3	4	5	6–10	Laps	Laps Led	Races Led	Miles	$
1958	NR	1	0	0	0	0	0	0	0	177	0	0	89	100
Lifetime		1	0	0	0	0	0	0	0	177	0	0	89	$100

Neil McDonald

Neil McDonald
Racing Hometown: Ridgefield, NJ

Year	Rank	Starts	Poles	1	2	3	4	5	6–10	Laps	Laps Led	Races Led	Miles	$
1953	NR	1	0	0	0	0	0	0	0		0	0		25
Lifetime		1	0	0	0	0	0	0	0		0	0		$25

Stewart McDonald

Stewart McDonald
Racing Hometown: Miami, FL

Year	Rank	Starts	Poles	1	2	3	4	5	6–10	Laps	Laps Led	Races Led	Miles	$
1953	103	1	0	0	0	0	0	0	0	271	0	0	271	50
Lifetime		1	0	0	0	0	0	0	0	271	0	0	271	$50

Charles McDuffie

Charles McDuffie
Racing Hometown: Yorktown Heights, NY

Year	Rank	Starts	Poles	1	2	3	4	5	6–10	Laps	Laps Led	Races Led	Miles	$
1954	197	2	0	0	0	0	0	0	0	150	0	0	75	0
Lifetime		2	0	0	0	0	0	0	0	150	0	0	75	$0

Glenn McDuffie

Glenn McDuffie
Racing Hometown: Raleigh, NC

Year	Rank	Starts	Poles	1	2	3	4	5	6–10	Laps	Laps Led	Races Led	Miles	$
1975	NR	1	0	0	0	0	0	0	0	431	0	0	438	1,130
1976	98	1	0	0	0	0	0	0	0	205	0	0	208	730
Lifetime		2	0	0	0	0	0	0	0	636	0	0	647	$1,860

J. D. McDuffie

John Delphus McDuffie
B: 12/5/1938 D: 8/11/1991 *Killed at Watkins Glen.*
Racing Hometown: Sanford, NC

Year	Rank	Starts	Poles	1	2	3	4	5	6–10	Laps	Laps Led	Races Led	Miles	$
1963	46	12	0	0	0	0	0	0	3	1,918	0	0	765	1,620
1966	27	36	0	0	0	0	0	1	8	7,166	0	0	4,255	8,545
1967	NR	1	0	0	0	0	0	0	0	137	0	0	69	150
1968	24	32	0	0	0	0	0	0	9	5,587	0	0	3,020	8,355
1969	14	50	0	0	0	0	0	0	12	10,173	0	0	7,913	30,861
1970	16	36	0	0	0	0	0	1	9	8,461	0	0	6,287	24,905
1971	9	43	0	0	0	1	0	1	6	9,389	5	1	9,170	35,578
1972	18	27	0	0	0	0	0	1	1	6,231	0	0	7,094	36,833
1973	10	27	0	0	0	0	0	3	7	7,388	11	2	8,129	56,140
1974	12	30	0	0	0	0	0	0	7	8,283	1	1	9,518	59,535
1975	18	26	0	0	0	0	0	1	5	5,832	0	0	7,054	50,937
1976	12	30	0	0	0	0	0	1	7	7,954	0	0	9,664	82,240
1977	12	30	0	0	0	0	0	0	4	8,252	1	1	9,688	85,227
1978	11	30	1	0	0	0	0	1	5	7,300	15	4	8,715	86,857
1979	13	31	0	0	0	0	0	1	6	8,014	116	3	9,634	113,478
1980	16	31	0	0	0	0	0	0	3	6,044	0	0	7,407	82,402
1981	17	28	0	0	0	0	0	0	1	7,110	8	2	8,871	105,499
1982	19	30	0	0	0	0	0	0	1	6,695	1	1	7,851	112,744
1983	26	25	0	0	0	0	0	0	0	5,890	0	0	6,524	75,125
1984	34	16	0	0	0	0	0	0	0	4,064	0	0	3,422	54,170
1985	27	23	0	0	0	0	0	0	0	4,667	0	0	5,531	84,965
1986	26	20	0	0	0	0	0	0	0	4,750	1	1	5,083	106,115
1987	30	17	0	0	0	0	0	0	0	3,459	0	0	4,060	45,555
1988	61	2	0	0	0	0	0	0	0	516	1	1	573	3,750
1989	44	7	0	0	0	0	0	0	0	1,381	0	0	1,847	27,745
1990	40	8	0	0	0	0	0	0	0	1,301	0	0	1,657	27,570
1991	48	5	0	0	0	0	0	0	0	732	0	0	1,142	20,495
Lifetime		653	1	0	0	1	0	11	94	148,694	160	17	154,944	$1,427,396
		6th								10th				

Year	Rank	Starts	Poles	Finish 1	2	3	4	5	6–10	Laps	Laps Led	Races Led	Miles	$

Jeff McDuffie

Jeff McDuffie
B: 3/31/1962
Racing Hometown: Sanford, NC

Year	Rank	Starts	Poles	1	2	3	4	5	6–10	Laps	Laps Led	Races Led	Miles	$
1980	53	3	0	0	0	0	0	0	0	1,138	0	0	869	2,725
1982	80	1	0	0	0	0	0	0	0	377	0	0	236	1,005
1985	NR	1	0	0	0	0	0	0	0	445	0	0	445	1,875
Lifetime		5	0	0	0	0	0	0	0	1,960	0	0	1,549	$5,605

Bob McElee

Robert McElee

Year	Rank	Starts	Poles	1	2	3	4	5	6–10	Laps	Laps Led	Races Led	Miles	$
1981	NR	2	0	0	0	0	0	0	1	803	0	0	460	5,450
Lifetime		2	0	0	0	0	0	0	1	803	0	0	460	$5,450

Jim McElreath

Jim McElreath
B: 2/18/1928
Racing Hometown: Arlington, TX

Year	Rank	Starts	Poles	1	2	3	4	5	6–10	Laps	Laps Led	Races Led	Miles	$
1964	NR	3	0	0	0	0	0	0	0	336	0	0	667	1,350
1971	NR	1	0	0	0	0	0	0	0	88	0	0	220	1,440
Lifetime		4	0	0	0	0	0	0	0	424	0	0	887	$2,790

John McFadden

John McFadden
B: 11/4/1951
Racing Hometown: Forrest City, NC

Year	Rank	Starts	Poles	1	2	3	4	5	6–10	Laps	Laps Led	Races Led	Miles	$
1982	87	1	0	0	0	0	0	0	0	368	0	0	196	655
1983	57	3	0	0	0	0	0	0	0	289	0	0	181	2,260
1989	67	2	0	0	0	0	0	0	0	213	0	0	291	6,879
1992	52	5	0	0	0	0	0	0	0	37	0	0	53	21,810
Lifetime		11	0	0	0	0	0	0	0	907	0	0	721	$31,604

Bill McGee

William McGee
Racing Hometown: Zanesville, OH

Year	Rank	Starts	Poles	1	2	3	4	5	6–10	Laps	Laps Led	Races Led	Miles	$
1950	NR	1	0	0	0	0	0	0	0		0	0		0
Lifetime		1	0	0	0	0	0	0	0		0	0		$0

Ron McGee

Ronald McGee
B: 12/27/1947
Racing Hometown: Sunnyvale, CA

Year	Rank	Starts	Poles	1	2	3	4	5	6–10	Laps	Laps Led	Races Led	Miles	$
1977	102T	1	0	0	0	0	0	0	0	103	0	0	258	950
Lifetime		1	0	0	0	0	0	0	0	103	0	0	258	$950

John McGinley

John McGinley
B: 1925
Racing Hometown: Chicora, PA

Year	Rank	Starts	Poles	1	2	3	4	5	6–10	Laps	Laps Led	Races Led	Miles	$
1951	35	6	0	0	1	0	1	0	0	224	0	0	224	1,175
1954	70	4	0	0	0	0	0	0	1	435	0	0	249	350
1955	NR	1	0	0	0	0	0	0	0	157	0	0	79	60
Lifetime		11	0	0	1	0	1	0	1	816	0	0	552	$1,585

Billy McGinnis

William McGinnis
Racing Hometown: Griffin, GA

Year	Rank	Starts	Poles	1	2	3	4	5	6–10	Laps	Laps Led	Races Led	Miles	$
1976	NR	1	0	0	0	0	0	0	0	15	0	0	23	805
1977	NR	1	0	0	0	0	0	0	0	264	0	0	402	2,295
1978	92	1	0	0	0	0	0	0	0	221	0	0	336	875
Lifetime		3	0	0	0	0	0	0	0	500	0	0	761	$3,975

Pop McGinnis

Glenn McGinnis
Racing Hometown: Huntington, WV

Year	Rank	Starts	Poles	1	2	3	4	5	6–10	Laps	Laps Led	Races Led	Miles	$
1952	91T	1	0	0	0	0	0	0	1	180	0	0	90	125
1953	21	13	0	0	0	0	0	2	3	775	13	1	664	975
1954	78	4	0	0	0	0	0	0	1	536	4	1	618	315
1955	140	2	0	0	0	0	0	0	0	201	0	0	116	100
1964	138	1	0	0	0	0	0	0	0	238	0	0	104	200
1970	103	1	0	0	0	0	0	0	1	274	0	0	120	330
Lifetime		22	0	0	0	0	0	2	6	2,204	17	2	1,712	$2,045

Year	Rank	Starts	Poles	Finish						Laps	Laps Led	Races Led	Miles	$
				1	2	3	4	5	6–10					

John McGorrien

John McGorrien

Year	Rank	Starts	Poles	1	2	3	4	5	6–10	Laps	Laps Led	Races Led	Miles	$
1953	NR	1	0	0	0	0	0	0	0		0	0		50
Lifetime		1	0	0	0	0	0	0	0		0	0		$50

Steve McGrath

Steve McGrath
B: 4/28/1924
Racing Hometown: New Canaan, CT

Year	Rank	Starts	Poles	1	2	3	4	5	6–10	Laps	Laps Led	Races Led	Miles	$
1953	75	3	0	0	0	0	0	0	0		0	0		90
1960	133	1	0	0	0	0	0	0	0	188	0	0	259	200
Lifetime		4	0	0	0	0	0	0	0	188	0	0	259	$290

Joe Bill McGraw

Joseph William McGraw
Racing Hometown: Syracuse, NY

Year	Rank	Starts	Poles	1	2	3	4	5	6–10	Laps	Laps Led	Races Led	Miles	$
1956	NR	5	0	0	0	0	0	0	1	424	0	0	212	500
Lifetime		5	0	0	0	0	0	0	1	424	0	0	212	$500

Mickey McGreevey

Mickey McGreevey (Mike)
B: 1/3/1926
Racing Hometown: Hayward, CA

Year	Rank	Starts	Poles	1	2	3	4	5	6–10	Laps	Laps Led	Races Led	Miles	$
1955	101	1	0	0	0	0	0	0	0	232	0	0	232	150
1957	87	3	0	0	0	0	0	0	0	189	0	0	205	235
Lifetime		4	0	0	0	0	0	0	0	421	0	0	437	$385

Hershel McGriff

Hershel McGriff
B: 12/14/1927
Racing Hometown: Bridal Veil, OR

Year	Rank	Starts	Poles	1	2	3	4	5	6–10	Laps	Laps Led	Races Led	Miles	$
1950	NR	1	0	0	0	0	0	0	1	374	0	0	468	500
1951	N/A	4	0	0	0	0	1	0	0	463	1	1	561	1,260
1952	NR	2	0	0	0	0	0	0	1	283	0	0	261	325
1953	51	2	0	0	0	0	0	0	0	274	101	1	274	125
1954	6	24	5	4	3	5	0	1	4	3,891	122	6	2,743	13,250
1971	NR	3	0	0	0	0	0	0	0	397	4	2	1,021	3,860
1972	45	4	0	0	0	0	0	2	1	727	3	1	1,728	12,290
1973	51	3	0	0	0	0	0	1	1	426	0	0	1,093	8,690
1974	50	5	0	0	0	0	0	0	1	559	0	0	1,198	8,585
1975	70	5	0	0	0	0	0	0	1	652	4	1	1,353	7,995
1976	102	2	0	0	0	0	0	0	0	179	0	0	456	1,655
1977	65	2	0	0	0	0	0	0	1	120	0	0	314	3,240
1978	83	2	0	0	0	0	0	0	1	208	0	0	545	4,490
1980	59	3	0	0	0	0	0	0	0	307	0	0	785	3,280
1981	66	3	0	0	0	0	0	0	0	80	1	1	210	2,170
1982	73	2	0	0	0	0	0	0	0	115	0	0	301	1,545
1983	53	2	0	0	0	0	0	0	1	191	0	0	500	5,650
1984	67	2	0	0	0	0	0	0	1	149	1	1	390	3,815
1985	66	2	0	0	0	0	0	0	0	178	0	0	466	2,835
1986	77	2	0	0	0	0	0	0	0	170	0	0	445	4,080
1987	66	2	0	0	0	0	0	0	0	101	0	0	265	7,530
1988	53	3	0	0	0	0	0	0	0	316	0	0	524	5,960
1989	65	1	0	0	0	0	0	0	0	74	0	0	186	5,075
1990	105	1	0	0	0	0	0	0	0	2	0	0	5	3,225
1991	60	2	0	0	0	0	0	0	0	361	0	0	454	7,475
1992	97	1	0	0	0	0	0	0	0	19	0	0	48	4,725
1993	95	1	0	0	0	0	0	0	0	27	0	0	68	6,560
Lifetime		86	5	4	3	5	1	4	14	10,643	237	14	16,663	$130,190

Norman McGriff

Norman McGriff
B: 9/6/1933
Racing Hometown: Portland, OR

Year	Rank	Starts	Poles	1	2	3	4	5	6–10	Laps	Laps Led	Races Led	Miles	$
1957	65	3	0	0	0	0	0	0	2	342	0	0	198	370
Lifetime		3	0	0	0	0	0	0	2	342	0	0	198	$370

Jim McGuirk

James McGuirk
Racing Hometown: Vero Beach, FL

Year	Rank	Starts	Poles	1	2	3	4	5	6–10	Laps	Laps Led	Races Led	Miles	$
1959	47	4	0	0	0	0	0	0	0	314	0	0	590	325
1962	82	2	0	0	0	0	0	0	0	196	0	0	490	500

Year	Rank	Starts	Poles	Finish						Laps	Laps Led	Races Led	Miles	$
				1	2	3	4	5	6–10					

Jim McGuirk *continued*

Year	Rank	Starts	Poles	1	2	3	4	5	6–10	Laps	Laps Led	Races Led	Miles	$
1963	58	3	0	0	0	0	0	0	0	212	0	0	530	1,200
Lifetime		9	0	0	0	0	0	0	0	722	0	0	1,610	$1,975

Sumner McKnight

Sumner McKnight
B: 9/9/1946
Racing Hometown: Newport Beach, CA

Year	Rank	Starts	Poles	1	2	3	4	5	6–10	Laps	Laps Led	Races Led	Miles	$
1977	102T	1	0	0	0	0	0	0	0	15	0	0	39	650
1983	55	2	0	0	0	0	0	0	0	204	0	0	534	5,275
1984	56	2	0	0	0	0	0	0	0	192	0	0	503	5,140
1985	73	1	0	0	0	0	0	0	0	91	0	0	238	3,985
Lifetime		6	0	0	0	0	0	0	0	502	0	0	1,315	$15,050

Jim McLain

James McLain
Racing Hometown: Wilkesboro, NC

Year	Rank	Starts	Poles	1	2	3	4	5	6–10	Laps	Laps Led	Races Led	Miles	$
1954	174	1	0	0	0	0	0	0	0	112	0	0	168	50
1955	123	3	0	0	0	0	0	0	0	118	0	0	271	110
Lifetime		4	0	0	0	0	0	0	0	230	0	0	439	$160

Mike McLaughlin

Michael McLaughlin
B: 10/6/1956
Racing Hometown: Waterloo, NY

Year	Rank	Starts	Poles	1	2	3	4	5	6–10	Laps	Laps Led	Races Led	Miles	$
1994	55	2	0	0	0	0	0	0	0	386	0	0	529	17,975
Lifetime		2	0	0	0	0	0	0	0	386	0	0	529	$17,975

Don McLeish

Donald McLeish
Racing Hometown: Los Angeles, CA

Year	Rank	Starts	Poles	1	2	3	4	5	6–10	Laps	Laps Led	Races Led	Miles	$
1951	N/A	1	0	0	0	0	0	0	0		0	0		25
Lifetime		1	0	0	0	0	0	0	0		0	0		$25

Bill McMahan

William McMahan
Racing Hometown: Dandridge, TN

Year	Rank	Starts	Poles	1	2	3	4	5	6–10	Laps	Laps Led	Races Led	Miles	$
1964	33	20	0	0	0	0	0	1	3	4,134	0	0	2,897	7,205
1965	119	1	0	0	0	0	0	0	0		0	0		100
Lifetime		21	0	0	0	0	0	1	3	4,134	0	0	2,897	$7,305

Allen McMillion

Allen McMillion
Racing Hometown: Amelia, VA

Year	Rank	Starts	Poles	1	2	3	4	5	6–10	Laps	Laps Led	Races Led	Miles	$
1965	103	1	0	0	0	0	0	0	0	236	0	0	79	110
1966	NR	1	0	0	0	0	0	0	0	250	0	0	125	150
Lifetime		2	0	0	0	0	0	0	0	486	0	0	204	$260

Worth McMillion

Hollingsworth McMillion
B: 10/8/1926
Racing Hometown: Amelia, VA

Year	Rank	Starts	Poles	1	2	3	4	5	6–10	Laps	Laps Led	Races Led	Miles	$
1962	72	4	0	0	0	0	0	0	0	1,105	0	0	517	675
1963	34	15	0	0	0	0	0	0	4	4,177	0	0	2,412	3,145
1964	30	18	0	0	0	0	0	0	6	4,681	0	0	2,756	4,710
1965	47	10	0	0	0	0	0	0	2	2,290	0	0	1,289	2,590
1966	52	9	0	0	0	0	0	0	3	2,311	0	0	1,282	2,440
1967	83	2	0	0	0	0	0	0	2	497	0	0	249	775
1968	NR	3	0	0	0	0	0	1	0	772	0	0	474	875
1969	77	1	0	0	0	0	0	0	0	328	0	0	164	480
Lifetime		62	0	0	0	0	0	1	17	16,161	0	0	9,142	$15,220

Sam McQuagg

Samuel David McQuagg
B: 11/11/1937
Racing Hometown: Columbus, GA

Year	Rank	Starts	Poles	1	2	3	4	5	6–10	Laps	Laps Led	Races Led	Miles	$
1962	106	1	0	0	0	0	0	0	0	51	0	0	26	120
1964	49	5	0	0	0	0	0	0	0	653	0	0	842	1,700
1965	24	14	0	0	0	1	0	1	3	2,458	31	1	2,922	10,555
1966	15	16	0	1	0	1	0	2	3	3,575	175	3	3,906	29,530

Year	Rank	Starts	Poles	Finish 1	2	3	4	5	6–10	Laps	Laps Led	Races Led	Miles	$

Sam McQuagg *continued*

Year	Rank	Starts	Poles	1	2	3	4	5	6–10	Laps	Laps Led	Races Led	Miles	$
1967	36	15	0	0	0	0	2	1	0	2,244	11	3	2,508	10,045
1968	54	5	0	0	0	0	0	0	2	1,045	5	1	1,566	4,960
1969	70	3	0	0	0	0	0	0	2	1,056	0	0	845	2,625
1974	56	3	0	0	0	0	0	0	2	698	1	1	1,221	6,460
Lifetime		62	0	1	0	2	2	4	12	11,780	223	9	13,834	$65,995

John McVitty

John McVitty
B: 1925   D: 4/21/1956   *Killed qualifying at Langhorne.*
Racing Hometown: Mamaroneck, NY

Year	Rank	Starts	Poles	1	2	3	4	5	6–10	Laps	Laps Led	Races Led	Miles	$
1955	48	7	0	0	0	0	0	0	2	951	0	0	559	550
1956	116	4	0	0	0	0	0	0	1	431	0	0	228	250
Lifetime		11	0	0	0	0	0	0	3	1,382	0	0	787	$800

Bill Meacham

William Meacham
B: 4/13/1960
Racing Hometown: Pineville, NC

Year	Rank	Starts	Poles	1	2	3	4	5	6–10	Laps	Laps Led	Races Led	Miles	$
1990	94T	1	0	0	0	0	0	0	0	87	0	0	65	2,425
1991	68	2	0	0	0	0	0	0	0	146	0	0	159	6,535
Lifetime		3	0	0	0	0	0	0	0	233	0	0	225	$8,960

Leon Meadows

Leon Meadows
Racing Hometown: Kokomo, IN

Year	Rank	Starts	Poles	1	2	3	4	5	6–10	Laps	Laps Led	Races Led	Miles	$
1952	181	1	0	0	0	0	0	0	0	67	0	0	67	25
Lifetime		1	0	0	0	0	0	0	0	67	0	0	67	$25

Jimmy Means

James Means
B: 5/29/1950
Racing Hometown: Huntsville, AL

Year	Rank	Starts	Poles	1	2	3	4	5	6–10	Laps	Laps Led	Races Led	Miles	$
1976	24	19	0	0	0	0	0	0	0	4,336	1	1	5,117	20,945
1977	19	26	0	0	0	0	0	0	6	6,010	0	0	6,759	52,505
1978	17	27	0	0	0	0	0	0	2	7,083	0	0	7,992	61,725
1979	23	27	0	0	0	0	0	0	1	5,431	0	0	6,317	55,560
1980	17	28	0	0	0	0	0	0	0	7,684	0	0	8,890	105,628
1981	14	30	0	0	0	0	0	0	2	8,647	0	0	9,393	105,628
1982	11	30	0	0	0	0	0	0	2	8,837	2	1	10,273	154,460
1983	18	28	0	0	0	0	0	0	3	8,269	2	1	8,974	132,915
1984	25	22	0	0	0	0	0	0	0	7,044	0	0	7,432	105,105
1985	23	28	0	0	0	0	0	0	0	6,774	0	0	7,512	132,140
1986	22	26	0	0	0	0	0	0	0	6,472	5	3	8,102	157,940
1987	23	28	0	0	0	0	0	0	1	6,339	21	1	7,282	154,055
1988	30	27	0	0	0	0	0	0	0	5,172	12	4	6,589	139,290
1989	31	22	0	0	0	0	0	0	0	4,868	4	1	6,288	65,005
1990	29	27	0	0	0	0	0	0	0	7,419	0	0	8,650	135,165
1991	33	20	0	0	0	0	0	0	0	4,425	3	3	6,580	111,210
1992	32	22	0	0	0	0	0	0	0	4,370	0	0	5,165	133,160
1993	36	18	0	0	0	0	0	0	0	4,765	2	2	5,644	148,205
Lifetime		455	0	0	0	0	0	0	17	113,945	52	17	133,009	$2,588,616

Bill Meazel

William Meazel
Racing Hometown: Nacogdoches, TX

Year	Rank	Starts	Poles	1	2	3	4	5	6–10	Laps	Laps Led	Races Led	Miles	$
1979	118T	1	0	0	0	0	0	0	0	46	0	0	92	1,000
1982	—	0												2,750
Lifetime		1	0	0	0	0	0	0	0	46	0	0	92	$3,750

Chuck Meekins

Charles Meekins
Racing Hometown: Los Angeles, CA

Year	Rank	Starts	Poles	1	2	3	4	5	6–10	Laps	Laps Led	Races Led	Miles	$
1951	58	5	0	0	1	0	0	0	0	202	0	0	102	700
1954	NR	3	0	0	0	0	0	0	1	719	0	0	479	300
1955	230	3	0	0	0	0	1	0	0	467	0	0	369	450
1956	29	7	0	0	1	1	1	0	3	1,241	43	3	1,015	2,815
1957	51	6	0	0	0	1	2	0	1	563	0	0	434	1,280
Lifetime		24	0	0	2	2	4	0	5	3,192	43	3	2,398	$5,545

Year	Rank	Starts	Poles	Finish 1	2	3	4	5	6–10	Laps	Laps Led	Races Led	Miles	$

John Meekins

John Meekins
Racing Hometown: Los Angeles, CA

Year	Rank	Starts	Poles	1	2	3	4	5	6–10	Laps	Laps Led	Races Led	Miles	$
1950	NR	1	0	0	0	0	0	0	0		0	0		0
Lifetime		1	0	0	0	0	0	0	0		0	0		$0

John Meggers

John Charles Meggers
B: 12/8/1928
Racing Hometown: Washington, DC

Year	Rank	Starts	Poles	1	2	3	4	5	6–10	Laps	Laps Led	Races Led	Miles	$
1953	NR	5	0	0	0	0	0	0	3		0	0		350
Lifetime		5	0	0	0	0	0	0	3		0	0		$350

Ken Meisenhelder

Kenneth Anthony Meisenhelder
B: 12/17/1942
Racing Hometown: Springfield, MA

Year	Rank	Starts	Poles	1	2	3	4	5	6–10	Laps	Laps Led	Races Led	Miles	$
1968	118	1	0	0	0	0	0	0	0	103	0	0	93	100
1969	42	16	0	0	0	0	0	0	0	1,832	0	0	1,305	5,630
1970	41	19	0	0	0	0	0	0	2	2,717	0	0	1,842	7,020
1971	40	15	0	0	0	0	0	0	1	2,194	0	0	1,544	5,405
Lifetime		51	0	0	0	0	0	0	3	6,846	0	0	4,783	$18,155

Johnny Mello

John Mello
Racing Hometown: Hanford, CA

Year	Rank	Starts	Poles	1	2	3	4	5	6–10	Laps	Laps Led	Races Led	Miles	$
1960	148	1	0	0	0	0	0	0	0	22	0	0	31	0
Lifetime		1	0	0	0	0	0	0	0	22	0	0	31	$0

Major Melton

Major Melton
B: 1/25/1930
Racing Hometown: Laurinburg, NC

Year	Rank	Starts	Poles	1	2	3	4	5	6–10	Laps	Laps Led	Races Led	Miles	$
1963	43	17	0	0	0	0	0	0	0	2,780	0	0	1,287	1,910
1964	58	3	0	0	0	0	0	0	1	737	0	0	648	1,100
Lifetime		20	0	0	0	0	0	0	1	3,517	0	0	1,935	$3,010

Tommy Melvin

Thomas Melvin
Racing Hometown: Oconomowoc, WI

Year	Rank	Starts	Poles	1	2	3	4	5	6–10	Laps	Laps Led	Races Led	Miles	$
1950	88	1	0	0	0	0	0	0	0		0	0		50
1951	NR	3	0	0	0	0	0	0	0	459	0	0	551	75
Lifetime		4	0	0	0	0	0	0	0	459	0	0	551	$125

Francisco Menendez *See* Frank Mundy

Joe Merola

Joseph Merola
Racing Hometown: Wilkensberg, PA

Year	Rank	Starts	Poles	1	2	3	4	5	6–10	Laps	Laps Led	Races Led	Miles	$
1949	55T	1	0	0	0	0	0	0	0	161	0	0	81	50
1950	NR	2	0	0	0	0	0	0	0		0	0		0
1951	N/A	4	0	0	0	0	0	0	1	472	0	0	522	175
Lifetime		7	0	0	0	0	0	0	1	633	0	0	602	$225

Charles Merrill

Charles Merrill
Racing Hometown: Mobile, AL

Year	Rank	Starts	Poles	1	2	3	4	5	6–10	Laps	Laps Led	Races Led	Miles	$
1954	139	1	0	0	0	0	0	0	0	129	0	0	194	50
Lifetime		1	0	0	0	0	0	0	0	129	0	0	194	$50

Stan Meserve

Stanley Rexford Meserve
B: 8/23/1941
Racing Hometown: Winslow, ME

Year	Rank	Starts	Poles	1	2	3	4	5	6–10	Laps	Laps Led	Races Led	Miles	$
1968	26	31	0	0	0	0	0	0	1	4,283	0	0	2,759	7,475
Lifetime		31	0	0	0	0	0	0	1	4,283	0	0	2,759	$7,475

Chuck Mesler

Chuck Mesler
Racing Hometown: Ecorse, MI

Year	Rank	Starts	Poles	1	2	3	4	5	6–10	Laps	Laps Led	Races Led	Miles	$
1956	209T	1	0	0	0	0	0	0	0	175	0	0	88	100
Lifetime		1	0	0	0	0	0	0	0	175	0	0	88	$100

Al Metz

Al Metz Jr.
Racing Hometown: Masury, OH

Year	Rank	Starts	Poles	1	2	3	4	5	6–10	Laps	Laps Led	Races Led	Miles	$
1954	113T	1	0	0	0	0	0	0	0	131	0	0	66	25
Lifetime		1	0	0	0	0	0	0	0	131	0	0	66	$25

Jim Metzler

James Metzler
B: 3/10/1912
Racing Hometown: Pottersville, NJ

Year	Rank	Starts	Poles	1	2	3	4	5	6–10	Laps	Laps Led	Races Led	Miles	$
1951	N/A	1	0	0	0	0	0	0	0		0	0		10
Lifetime		1	0	0	0	0	0	0	0		0	0		$10

Bill Meyer

William Meyer
Racing Hometown: Anaheim, CA

Year	Rank	Starts	Poles	1	2	3	4	5	6–10	Laps	Laps Led	Races Led	Miles	$
1965	124	1	0	0	0	0	0	0	0	19	0	0	51	500
Lifetime		1	0	0	0	0	0	0	0	19	0	0	51	$500

Dick Meyer

Richard Meyer
D: 9/16/1953   *Killed in highway crash en route from Detroit race to pregnant wife.*
Racing Hometown: Porterville, CA

Year	Rank	Starts	Poles	1	2	3	4	5	6–10	Laps	Laps Led	Races Led	Miles	$
1951	24	6	0	0	1	0	0	2	1		82	1		1,650
1952	112	1	0	0	0	0	0	0	0		0	0		50
1953	NR	1	0	0	0	0	1	0	0	355	0	0	488	1,000
Lifetime		8	0	0	1	0	1	2	1	355	82	1	488	$2,600

Hylan Micka

Hylan Micka

Year	Rank	Starts	Poles	1	2	3	4	5	6–10	Laps	Laps Led	Races Led	Miles	$
1958	NR	1	0	0	0	0	0	0	0	66	0	0	174	150
Lifetime		1	0	0	0	0	0	0	0	66	0	0	174	$150

Charlie Mincey

Charles Mincey
Racing Hometown: Acworth, GA

Year	Rank	Starts	Poles	1	2	3	4	5	6–10	Laps	Laps Led	Races Led	Miles	$
1954	107	1	0	0	0	0	0	0	1	184	0	0	92	100
1956	184T	1	0	0	0	0	0	0	0	91	0	0	91	75
1958	NR	1	0	0	0	0	0	1	0	148	0	0	148	550
Lifetime		3	0	0	0	0	0	1	1	423	0	0	331	$725

Joe Mihalic

Joseph Mihalic
B: 11/8/1926
Racing Hometown: Pittsburgh, PA

Year	Rank	Starts	Poles	1	2	3	4	5	6–10	Laps	Laps Led	Races Led	Miles	$
1974	53	5	0	0	0	0	0	0	1	1,725	0	0	1,570	7,595
1975	34	10	0	0	0	0	0	0	1	1,939	0	0	2,694	13,385
1976	35	9	0	0	0	0	0	0	0	2,171	0	0	3,129	12,925
1977	41	8	0	0	0	0	0	0	0	1,550	0	0	2,137	8,275
1978	47	6	0	0	0	0	0	0	0	1,216	0	0	1,537	6,030
Lifetime		38	0	0	0	0	0	0	2	8,601	0	0	11,067	$48,210

Walter Milczarski

Walter Milczarski

Year	Rank	Starts	Poles	1	2	3	4	5	6–10	Laps	Laps Led	Races Led	Miles	$
1954	NR	1	0	0	0	0	0	0	0	142	0	0	71	0
Lifetime		1	0	0	0	0	0	0	0	142	0	0	71	$0

Ken Miles

Kenneth Miles
B: 11/1/1918   D: 8/17/1966   *Killed @ Riverside testing Ford Formula J car.*
Racing Hometown: Hollywood, CA

Year	Rank	Starts	Poles	1	2	3	4	5	6–10	Laps	Laps Led	Races Led	Miles	$
1963	NR	1	0	0	0	0	0	0	0	139	0	0	375	710
Lifetime		1	0	0	0	0	0	0	0	139	0	0	375	$710

Year	Rank	Starts	Poles	Finish 1	2	3	4	5	6–10	Laps	Laps Led	Races Led	Miles	$

Jim Millard

James Millard
Racing Hometown: Hollywood, FL

Year	Rank	Starts	Poles	1	2	3	4	5	6–10	Laps	Laps Led	Races Led	Miles	$
1952	91T	1	0	0	0	0	0	0	1		0	0		100
Lifetime		1	0	0	0	0	0	0	1		0	0		$100

Al Miller

Al Miller
Racing Hometown: Detroit, MI

Year	Rank	Starts	Poles	1	2	3	4	5	6–10	Laps	Laps Led	Races Led	Miles	$
1951	N/A	1	0	0	0	0	0	0	0	115	0	0	115	0
Lifetime		1	0	0	0	0	0	0	0	115	0	0	115	$0

Bill Miller

William Miller
B: 1915   D: 12/31/1952
Racing Hometown: Evansville, IN

Year	Rank	Starts	Poles	1	2	3	4	5	6–10	Laps	Laps Led	Races Led	Miles	$
1951	65	6	0	0	0	0	0	0	2		0	0		350
1952	83	4	0	0	0	0	0	0	0	547	0	0	562	125
Lifetime		10	0	0	0	0	0	0	2	547	0	0	562	$475

Butch Miller

Henry Miller
B: 6/5/1952
Racing Hometown: Coopersville, MI

Year	Rank	Starts	Poles	1	2	3	4	5	6–10	Laps	Laps Led	Races Led	Miles	$
1986	75	3	0	0	0	0	0	0	0	799	0	0	891	5,085
1987	100	2	0	0	0	0	0	0	0	215	0	0	307	3,145
1988	NR	2	0	0	0	0	0	0	0	790	18	1	497	5,905
1989	39	9	0	0	0	0	0	0	0	1,129	0	0	1,194	22,520
1990	27	23	0	0	0	0	0	0	1	6,891	4	4	8,648	151,941
1994	53	2	0	0	0	0	0	0	0	842	0	0	982	17,335
Lifetime		41	0	0	0	0	0	0	1	10,666	22	5	12,519	$198,931

Charlie Miller

Charles Miller
B: 1912   D: 9/24/1955   *Killed in Sprint Car race @ Shelby, NC.*
Racing Hometown: Allentown, PA

Year	Rank	Starts	Poles	1	2	3	4	5	6–10	Laps	Laps Led	Races Led	Miles	$
1953	NR	1	0	0	0	0	0	0	0		0	0		100
Lifetime		1	0	0	0	0	0	0	0		0	0		$100

Chris Miller

Christopher Miller
Racing Hometown: Seven Valleys, PA

Year	Rank	Starts	Poles	1	2	3	4	5	6–10	Laps	Laps Led	Races Led	Miles	$
1954	185	1	0	0	0	0	0	0	0	126	0	0	126	0
Lifetime		1	0	0	0	0	0	0	0	126	0	0	126	$0

Dick Miller

Richard Miller
Racing Hometown: Los Angeles, CA

Year	Rank	Starts	Poles	1	2	3	4	5	6–10	Laps	Laps Led	Races Led	Miles	$
1961	NR	2	0	0	0	0	0	0	0	134	0	0	136	140
Lifetime		2	0	0	0	0	0	0	0	134	0	0	136	$140

Jim Miller

James Miller

Year	Rank	Starts	Poles	1	2	3	4	5	6–10	Laps	Laps Led	Races Led	Miles	$
1951	N/A	1	0	0	0	0	0	0	0		0	0		0
Lifetime		1	0	0	0	0	0	0	0		0	0		$0

Johnny Miller

John Miller
Racing Hometown: Kannapolis, NC

Year	Rank	Starts	Poles	1	2	3	4	5	6–10	Laps	Laps Led	Races Led	Miles	$
1960	118	2	0	0	0	0	0	0	0	207	0	0	307	500
Lifetime		2	0	0	0	0	0	0	0	207	0	0	307	$500

Junior Miller

Junior Miller
B: 4/6/1951
Racing Hometown: Winston-Salem, NC

Year	Rank	Starts	Poles	1	2	3	4	5	6–10	Laps	Laps Led	Races Led	Miles	$
1976	67	2	0	0	0	0	0	0	0	744	0	0	465	1,325
1977	46	5	0	0	0	0	0	0	0	1,028	0	0	648	2,475
1978	71	2	0	0	0	0	0	0	0	498	0	0	359	2,110
1980	31	16	0	0	0	0	0	0	0	3,848	0	0	3,139	23,420
1981	68	2	0	0	0	0	0	0	0	276	0	0	190	3,130
Lifetime		27	0	0	0	0	0	0	0	6,394	0	0	4,802	$32,460

Year	Rank	Starts	Poles	Finish						Laps	Laps Led	Races Led	Miles	$
				1	2	3	4	5	6–10	Laps	Led	Led	Miles	$

Kirby Miller

Kirby Miller
Racing Hometown: Canoga Park, CA

Year	Rank	Starts	Poles	1	2	3	4	5	6–10	Laps	Laps Led	Races Led	Miles	$
1958	126	1	0	0	0	0	0	0	0	152	0	0	400	110
1959	NR	1	0	0	0	0	0	0	0	47	0	0	19	150
Lifetime		2	0	0	0	0	0	0	0	199	0	0	419	$260

Larry Miller

Larry Martin Miller
B: 8/22/1934
Racing Hometown: Taylors, SC

Year	Rank	Starts	Poles	1	2	3	4	5	6–10	Laps	Laps Led	Races Led	Miles	$
1967	52	15	0	0	0	0	0	0	1	1,558	0	0	704	2,075
Lifetime		15	0	0	0	0	0	0	1	1,558	0	0	704	$2,075

Mike Miller

Michael Miller
Racing Hometown: Wisconsin Rapids, WI

Year	Rank	Starts	Poles	1	2	3	4	5	6–10	Laps	Laps Led	Races Led	Miles	$
1980	83	2	0	0	0	0	0	0	0	176	0	0	267	2,145
1989	93T	1	0	0	0	0	0	0	0	137	0	0	274	3,075
Lifetime		3	0	0	0	0	0	0	0	313	0	0	541	$5,220

Nels Miller

Nels Miller

Year	Rank	Starts	Poles	1	2	3	4	5	6–10	Laps	Laps Led	Races Led	Miles	$
1973	119	1	0	0	0	0	0	0	0	19	0	0	50	900
Lifetime		1	0	0	0	0	0	0	0	19	0	0	50	$900

Scott Miller

Scott Miller
B: 8/23/1957
Racing Hometown: Garden Grove, CA

Year	Rank	Starts	Poles	1	2	3	4	5	6–10	Laps	Laps Led	Races Led	Miles	$
1981	95	1	0	0	0	0	0	0	0	69	0	0	181	805
1982	77	1	0	0	0	0	0	0	0	90	0	0	236	1,495
1983	71	2	0	0	0	0	0	0	0	173	0	0	453	2,400
1984	73	2	0	0	0	0	0	0	0	98	0	0	257	1,815
Lifetime		6	0	0	0	0	0	0	0	430	0	0	1,127	$6,515

T. R. Miller

T. R. Miller
Racing Hometown: High Point, NC

Year	Rank	Starts	Poles	1	2	3	4	5	6–10	Laps	Laps Led	Races Led	Miles	$
1961	148	1	0	0	0	0	0	0	0	96	0	0	24	75
Lifetime		1	0	0	0	0	0	0	0	96	0	0	24	$75

V. E. Miller

V. E. Miller

Year	Rank	Starts	Poles	1	2	3	4	5	6–10	Laps	Laps Led	Races Led	Miles	$
1951	N/A	1	0	0	0	0	0	0	0		0	0		25
Lifetime		1	0	0	0	0	0	0	0		0	0		$25

Harold Miller

William Miller
B: 10/19/1950
Racing Hometown: Emerson, GA

Year	Rank	Starts	Poles	1	2	3	4	5	6–10	Laps	Laps Led	Races Led	Miles	$
1975	52	5	0	0	0	0	0	0	0	455	0	0	980	4,520
1976	57	3	0	0	0	0	0	0	0	499	0	0	1,184	4,885
1977	46	6	0	0	0	0	0	0	0	1,267	0	0	2,276	8,480
Lifetime		14	0	0	0	0	0	0	0	2,221	0	0	4,440	$17,885

Ken Milligan

Kenneth Milligan
Racing Hometown: Knoxville, TN

Year	Rank	Starts	Poles	1	2	3	4	5	6–10	Laps	Laps Led	Races Led	Miles	$
1956	79	4	0	0	0	0	0	0	1	347	0	0	267	300
Lifetime		4	0	0	0	0	0	0	1	347	0	0	267	$300

Joe Millikan

Joseph Millikan
B: 4/30/1950
Racing Hometown: Randleman, NC

Year	Rank	Starts	Poles	1	2	3	4	5	6–10	Laps	Laps Led	Races Led	Miles	$
1974	NR	1	0	0	0	0	0	0	0	456	0	0	464	1,150
1979	6	31	1	0	1	1	0	3	15	9,122	188	8	10,509	229,713
1980	33	12	0	0	0	0	1	1	4	2,796	5	3	2,936	74,765
1981	20	23	0	0	0	1	0	2	7	6,735	15	4	7,270	148,400
1982	35	8	0	0	0	0	0	0	2	2,408	5	1	2,453	62,325
1983	NR	1	0	0	0	0	0	0	0	384	0	0	240	1,475

Year	Rank	Starts	Poles	Finish 1	2	3	4	5	6–10	Laps	Laps Led	Races Led	Miles	$

Joe Millikan *continued*

Year	Rank	Starts	Poles	1	2	3	4	5	6–10	Laps	Laps Led	Races Led	Miles	$
1984	75	2	0	0	0	0	0	0	0	512	0	0	606	5,645
1986	88	2	0	0	0	0	0	0	0	59	0	0	56	1,950
Lifetime		80	1	0	1	2	1	6	28	22,472	213	16	24,533	$525,423

Joel Million

Joel Million
Racing Hometown: Richmond, KY

Year	Rank	Starts	Poles	1	2	3	4	5	6–10	Laps	Laps Led	Races Led	Miles	$
1954	19	9	0	0	0	0	0	0	1	1,298	0	0	1,324	1,092
1955	33	8	0	0	1	0	1	0	4	973	0	0	624	1,685
1956	218	2	0	0	0	0	0	0	0	175	0	0	88	50
Lifetime		19	0	0	1	0	1	0	5	2,446	0	0	2,035	$2,827

Curley Mills

Curley Mills
Racing Hometown: Charlotte, NC

Year	Rank	Starts	Poles	1	2	3	4	5	6–10	Laps	Laps Led	Races Led	Miles	$
1967	81	4	0	0	0	0	0	0	2	500	0	0	243	580
Lifetime		4	0	0	0	0	0	0	2	500	0	0	243	$580

Billy Minter

William Minter
Racing Hometown: Martinsville, VA

Year	Rank	Starts	Poles	1	2	3	4	5	6–10	Laps	Laps Led	Races Led	Miles	$
1954	104	4	0	0	0	0	0	0	0	412	0	0	248	75
Lifetime		4	0	0	0	0	0	0	0	412	0	0	248	$75

Clyde Minter

Clyde Minter
B: 10/15/1921   D: 12/21/1971
Racing Hometown: Martinsville, VA

Year	Rank	Starts	Poles	1	2	3	4	5	6–10	Laps	Laps Led	Races Led	Miles	$
1949	14	2	0	0	0	0	2	0	0	386	0	0	193	760
1950	17	8	0	0	0	1	0	2	0	665	0	0	546	1,155
1951	N/A	6	0	0	0	0	0	0	1	81	0	0	66	150
1952	41	5	0	0	0	0	0	0	3	620	0	0	442	375
1953	31	8	0	0	0	0	0	0	3	591	0	0	519	405
1954	28	12	0	0	0	0	0	0	6	1,653	0	0	870	900
1955	152T	1	0	0	0	0	0	0	1	178	0	0	89	100
Lifetime		42	0	0	0	1	2	2	14	4,174	0	0	2,725	$3,845

Pat Mintey

Patrick N. Mintey
B: 5/25/1947
Racing Hometown: Arleta, CA

Year	Rank	Starts	Poles	1	2	3	4	5	6–10	Laps	Laps Led	Races Led	Miles	$
1981	101	1	0	0	0	0	0	0	0	40	0	0	105	850
1983	77	2	0	0	0	0	0	0	0	76	0	0	199	1,875
Lifetime		3	0	0	0	0	0	0	0	116	0	0	304	$2,725

Walter Minx

Walter Minx

Year	Rank	Starts	Poles	1	2	3	4	5	6–10	Laps	Laps Led	Races Led	Miles	$
1949	NR	1	0	0	0	0	0	0	0	25	0	0	25	0
Lifetime		1	0	0	0	0	0	0	0	25	0	0	25	$0

Artie Mitchell

Artie Mitchell
Racing Hometown: Savannah, GA

Year	Rank	Starts	Poles	1	2	3	4	5	6–10	Laps	Laps Led	Races Led	Miles	$
1954	156T	1	0	0	0	0	0	0	0	9	0	0	5	0
Lifetime		1	0	0	0	0	0	0	0	9	0	0	5	$0

Bill Mitchell

William Mitchell

Year	Rank	Starts	Poles	1	2	3	4	5	6–10	Laps	Laps Led	Races Led	Miles	$
1958	166	1	0	0	0	0	0	0	0	107	0	0	282	100
Lifetime		1	0	0	0	0	0	0	0	107	0	0	282	$100

Clyde Mitchell

Clyde Mitchell
Racing Hometown: Los Angeles, CA

Year	Rank	Starts	Poles	1	2	3	4	5	6–10	Laps	Laps Led	Races Led	Miles	$
1956	173T	1	0	0	0	0	0	0	0	216	0	0	216	50
1957	160T	1	0	0	0	0	0	0	0	50	0	0	125	60
1960	NR	2	0	0	0	0	0	0	1	135	0	0	135	190
Lifetime		4	0	0	0	0	0	0	1	401	0	0	476	$300

Year	Rank	Starts	Poles	Finish						Laps	Laps Led	Races Led	Miles	$
				1	2	3	4	5	6–10					

Dick Mitchell
Richard Mitchell
Racing Hometown: Torrance, CA

Year	Rank	Starts	Poles	1	2	3	4	5	6–10	Laps	Laps Led	Races Led	Miles	$
1963	107	1	0	0	0	0	0	0	0	126	0	0	340	200
1964	82	1	0	0	0	0	0	0	0	152	0	0	410	525
Lifetime		2	0	0	0	0	0	0	0	278	0	0	751	$725

Mike Mitchell
Michael Mitchell
Racing Hometown: Los Angeles, CA

Year	Rank	Starts	Poles	1	2	3	4	5	6–10	Laps	Laps Led	Races Led	Miles	$
1961	NR	1	0	0	0	0	0	0	0	5	0	0	13	50
Lifetime		1	0	0	0	0	0	0	0	5	0	0	13	$50

Herk Moak
Herbert Moak
Racing Hometown: Albany, NY

Year	Rank	Starts	Poles	1	2	3	4	5	6–10	Laps	Laps Led	Races Led	Miles	$
1955	190T	1	0	0	0	0	0	0	0	132	0	0	66	50
Lifetime		1	0	0	0	0	0	0	0	132	0	0	66	$50

Ethel Mobley
Ethel Mobley
B: 3/8/1920 D: 6/26/1984
Racing Hometown: Atlanta, GA

Year	Rank	Starts	Poles	1	2	3	4	5	6–10	Laps	Laps Led	Races Led	Miles	$
1949	52	2	0	0	0	0	0	0	0		0	0		50
Lifetime		2	0	0	0	0	0	0	0		0	0		$50

Butch Mock
Royce Mock III
B: 4/8/1952
Racing Hometown: N. Miami, FL

Year	Rank	Starts	Poles	1	2	3	4	5	6–10	Laps	Laps Led	Races Led	Miles	$
1978	89	2	0	0	0	0	0	0	0	564	0	0	853	2,390
1979	126T	1	0	0	0	0	0	0	0	38	0	0	95	3,035
Lifetime		3	0	0	0	0	0	0	0	602	0	0	948	$5,425

Johnny Mock
John Mock
Racing Hometown: Eureka, KS

Year	Rank	Starts	Poles	1	2	3	4	5	6–10	Laps	Laps Led	Races Led	Miles	$
1955	152T	1	0	0	0	0	0	0	1	183	0	0	92	100
Lifetime		1	0	0	0	0	0	0	1	183	0	0	92	$100

Dick Moffitt
Richard Moffitt

Year	Rank	Starts	Poles	1	2	3	4	5	6–10	Laps	Laps Led	Races Led	Miles	$
1951	N/A	4	0	0	0	0	0	0	2	142	0	0	71	300
Lifetime		4	0	0	0	0	0	0	2	142	0	0	71	$300

Patty Moise
Patricia Moise
B: 12/19/1960
Racing Hometown: Jacksonville, FL

Year	Rank	Starts	Poles	1	2	3	4	5	6–10	Laps	Laps Led	Races Led	Miles	$
1987	94	1	0	0	0	0	0	0	0	53	0	0	129	1,690
1988	59	2	0	0	0	0	0	0	0	241	0	0	596	10,370
1989	69	2	0	0	0	0	0	0	0	33	0	0	88	7,680
Lifetime		5	0	0	0	0	0	0	0	327	0	0	813	$19,740

Chris Monoleos
Christopher Monoleos
B: 4/26/1938
Racing Hometown: Burbank, CA

Year	Rank	Starts	Poles	1	2	3	4	5	6–10	Laps	Laps Led	Races Led	Miles	$
1979	121	1	0	0	0	0	0	0	0	2	0	0	5	550
Lifetime		1	0	0	0	0	0	0	0	2	0	0	5	$550

Phil Montague
Philip Montague

Year	Rank	Starts	Poles	1	2	3	4	5	6–10	Laps	Laps Led	Races Led	Miles	$
1969	NR	1	0	0	0	0	0	0	0	8	0	0	12	230
Lifetime		1	0	0	0	0	0	0	0	8	0	0	12	$230

Jack Montgangelo
Jack Montgangelo

Year	Rank	Starts	Poles	1	2	3	4	5	6–10	Laps	Laps Led	Races Led	Miles	$
1956	161	1	0	0	0	0	0	0	0	206	0	0	206	100
Lifetime		1	0	0	0	0	0	0	0	206	0	0	206	$100

Year	Rank	Starts	Poles	Finish 1	2	3	4	5	6–10	Laps	Laps Led	Races Led	Miles	$

Henry Montgomery

Henry Montgomery
Racing Hometown: Tampa, FL

Year	Rank	Starts	Poles	1	2	3	4	5	6–10	Laps	Laps Led	Races Led	Miles	$
1963	134	1	0	0	0	0	0	0	0	166	0	0	50	75
Lifetime		1	0	0	0	0	0	0	0	166	0	0	50	$75

Ralph Moody

Ralph Moody
B: 9/10/1917
Racing Hometown: Taunton, MA

Year	Rank	Starts	Poles	1	2	3	4	5	6–10	Laps	Laps Led	Races Led	Miles	$
1956	8	35	5	4	5	2	1	1	8	5,258	312	6	3,506	15,493
1957	NR	10	0	1	0	2	2	0	0	1,039	100	1	560	2,905
1959	NR	1	0	0	0	0	0	0	1	197	0	0	99	200
1962	137	1	0	0	0	0	0	0	0	1	0	0	1	75
Lifetime		47	5	5	5	4	3	1	9	6,495	412	7	4,165	$18,673

Tommy Moon

Thomas Moon
B: 4/16/1925
Racing Hometown: Jacksonville, FL

Year	Rank	Starts	Poles	1	2	3	4	5	6–10	Laps	Laps Led	Races Led	Miles	$
1951	83	2	0	0	0	0	0	0	1		0	0		225
1952	35	6	1	0	1	0	0	1	1	487	0	0	428	1,145
1953	178	1	0	0	0	0	0	0	0	5	0	0	21	0
1954	111	1	0	0	0	0	0	0	1	179	0	0	90	100
Lifetime		10	1	0	1	0	0	1	3	671	0	0	538	$1,470

Bill Moore

William Moore
Racing Hometown: Phoenix, AZ

Year	Rank	Starts	Poles	1	2	3	4	5	6–10	Laps	Laps Led	Races Led	Miles	$
1954	NR	1	0	0	0	0	0	0	1	183	0	0	92	100
1956	88	6	0	0	0	0	0	0	2	633	0	0	574	485
1957	197	1	0	0	0	0	0	0	0	7	0	0	18	35
Lifetime		8	0	0	0	0	0	0	3	823	0	0	683	$620

Bob Moore

Robert F. Moore
B: 6/1/1921
Racing Hometown: Kent, OH

Year	Rank	Starts	Poles	1	2	3	4	5	6–10	Laps	Laps Led	Races Led	Miles	$
1950	NR	2	0	0	0	0	0	0	0		0	0		0
1951	N/A	2	0	0	0	0	0	0	0		0	0		25
1952	45	5	0	0	0	1	0	0	2	524	0	0	270	575
Lifetime		9	0	0	0	1	0	0	2	524	0	0	270	$600

Bob Moore

Robert Moore
Racing Hometown: Tampa, FL

Year	Rank	Starts	Poles	1	2	3	4	5	6–10	Laps	Laps Led	Races Led	Miles	$
1952	NR	1	0	0	0	0	0	0	1		0	0		50
Lifetime		1	0	0	0	0	0	0	1		0	0		$50

Bob Moore

Robert Moore
Racing Hometown: Macon, GA

Year	Rank	Starts	Poles	1	2	3	4	5	6–10	Laps	Laps Led	Races Led	Miles	$
1968	58	4	0	0	0	0	0	0	1	1,033	0	0	1,057	2,745
Lifetime		4	0	0	0	0	0	0	1	1,033	0	0	1,057	$2,745

Bunk Moore

Samuel Marion Moore
B: 1925   D: circa 1987
Racing Hometown: Indian Trail, NC

Year	Rank	Starts	Poles	1	2	3	4	5	6–10	Laps	Laps Led	Races Led	Miles	$
1955	148T	2	0	0	0	0	0	0	0	199	0	0	100	50
1956	62	5	0	0	0	0	0	1	1	736	0	0	416	845
1958	NR	1	0	0	0	0	0	0	0	141	0	0	88	70
1959	73	10	0	0	0	0	0	0	0	1,350	0	0	684	530
1960	115	3	0	0	0	0	0	0	0	416	0	0	411	285
1961	153	2	0	0	0	0	0	0	0	273	0	0	137	150
1966	111T	1	0	0	0	0	0	0	0	101	0	0	51	100
Lifetime		24	0	0	0	0	0	1	1	3,216	0	0	1,886	$2,030

Charles Moore

Charles Moore
Racing Hometown: West Asheville, NC

Year	Rank	Starts	Poles	1	2	3	4	5	6–10	Laps	Laps Led	Races Led	Miles	$
1951	N/A	1	0	0	0	0	0	0	0		0	0		25
Lifetime		1	0	0	0	0	0	0	0		0	0		$25

Year	Rank	Starts	Poles	Finish						Laps	Laps Led	Races Led	Miles	$
				1	2	3	4	5	6–10	Laps	Led	Led	Miles	$

Doug Moore

Douglas Beall Moore
Racing Hometown: Chattanooga, TN

Year	Rank	Starts	Poles	1	2	3	4	5	6–10	Laps	Led	Led	Miles	$
1964	39	24	0	0	0	0	0	0	6	3,894	0	0	1,870	5,175
1965	67	5	0	0	0	0	0	0	0	664	0	0	452	1,160
Lifetime		29	0	0	0	0	0	0	6	4,558	0	0	2,322	$6,335

Fred Moore

Fred Moore (Red)
Racing Hometown: Pensacola, FL

Year	Rank	Starts	Poles	1	2	3	4	5	6–10	Laps	Led	Led	Miles	$
1951	N/A	1	0	0	0	0	0	0	0	112	0	0	140	0
1953	63	2	0	0	0	0	0	0	1	0	0	0	0	75
Lifetime		3	0	0	0	0	0	0	1	112	0	0	140	$75

Lloyd Moore

Lloyd D. Moore
B: 6/8/1912
Racing Hometown: Frewsburg, NY

Year	Rank	Starts	Poles	1	2	3	4	5	6–10	Laps	Led	Led	Miles	$
1949	26T	1	0	0	0	0	0	0	1	186	0	0	93	150
1950	4	16	0	1	2	3	1	0	3	1,358	57	2	1,046	5,235
1951	11	22	0	0	0	1	0	3	4	322	0	0	332	2,600
1952	20	8	0	0	1	0	1	0	2	1,457	0	0	1,084	2,193
1955	91	2	0	0	0	0	0	0	0	439	0	0	567	235
Lifetime		49	0	1	3	4	2	3	10	3,762	57	2	3,122	$10,413

Pat Moore

Murray Moore
Racing Hometown: Clymer, NY

Year	Rank	Starts	Poles	1	2	3	4	5	6–10	Laps	Led	Led	Miles	$
1960	151	1	0	0	0	0	0	0	0	72	0	0	36	50
Lifetime		1	0	0	0	0	0	0	0	72	0	0	36	$50

Bud Moore

Paul Moore (Little Bud)
B: 12/7/1941
Racing Hometown: Charleston, SC

Year	Rank	Starts	Poles	1	2	3	4	5	6–10	Laps	Led	Led	Miles	$
1964	102	3	0	0	0	0	0	0	0	209	0	0	229	700
1965	49	14	1	0	1	1	1	0	4	1,687	93	2	804	3,435
1966	115	1	0	0	0	0	0	0	0	35	0	0	18	100
1967	35	6	0	0	0	0	0	2	1	1,351	0	0	1,681	7,200
1968	29	16	0	0	1	0	1	0	7	3,399	51	2	3,219	12,325
1973	110	1	0	0	0	0	0	0	0	174	0	0	238	1,225
Lifetime		41	1	0	2	1	2	2	12	6,855	144	4	6,188	$24,985

Steve Moore

Steve Moore
B: 11/6/1958
Racing Hometown: Carrollton, GA

Year	Rank	Starts	Poles	1	2	3	4	5	6–10	Laps	Led	Led	Miles	$
1977	NR	1	0	0	0	0	0	0	0	139	0	0	370	2,165
1978	90	1	0	0	0	0	0	0	0	150	0	0	399	1,590
1979	94T	1	0	0	0	0	0	0	0	170	0	0	452	2,415
1980	47	4	0	0	0	0	0	0	0	735	0	0	1,469	9,040
1981	—	0												3,155
1982	59	4	0	0	0	0	0	0	0	456	4	1	727	7,975
1983	65	2	0	0	0	0	0	0	0	316	0	0	714	5,215
1984	60	2	0	0	0	0	0	0	0	237	0	0	622	6,245
1987	—	0												1,150
1988	51	3	0	0	0	0	0	0	0	726	0	0	1,069	20,290
Lifetime		18	0	0	0	0	0	0	0	2,929	4	1	5,822	$59,240

Rocky Moran

William James Moran
B: 2/3/1951
Racing Hometown: Arcadia, CA

Year	Rank	Starts	Poles	1	2	3	4	5	6–10	Laps	Led	Led	Miles	$
1978	62	3	0	0	0	0	0	0	0	289	0	0	735	3,195
Lifetime		3	0	0	0	0	0	0	0	289	0	0	735	$3,195

Harold Morese

Harold Morese
D: 2/22/1953   *Killed in AAA race at Carrell Speedway, Gardena, CA.*

Year	Rank	Starts	Poles	1	2	3	4	5	6–10	Laps	Led	Led	Miles	$
1952	NR	1	0	0	0	0	0	0	0	186	0	0	93	25
Lifetime		1	0	0	0	0	0	0	0	186	0	0	93	$25

Year	Rank	Starts	Poles	Finish						Laps	Laps Led	Races Led	Miles	$
				1	2	3	4	5	6–10					

Jerry Morese

Jerry Morese
Racing Hometown: Newark, NJ

Year	Rank	Starts	Poles	1	2	3	4	5	6–10	Laps	Laps Led	Races Led	Miles	$
1951	70	2	0	0	0	0	0	1	0		0	0		275
1956	184T	1	0	0	0	0	0	0	0	184	0	0	92	100
Lifetime		3	0	0	0	0	0	1	0	184	0	0	92	$375

Tony Moretti

Anthony Moretti

Year	Rank	Starts	Poles	1	2	3	4	5	6–10	Laps	Laps Led	Races Led	Miles	$
1957	170	1	0	0	0	0	0	0	0	19	0	0	10	50
Lifetime		1	0	0	0	0	0	0	0	19	0	0	10	$50

Bill Morgan

Herbert William Morgan
Racing Hometown: Fairfax, VA

Year	Rank	Starts	Poles	1	2	3	4	5	6–10	Laps	Laps Led	Races Led	Miles	$
1953	86T	1	0	0	0	0	0	0	1	185	0	0	93	100
1954	187	1	0	0	0	0	0	0	0	44	0	0	44	0
1957	101	1	0	0	0	0	0	0	0	223	0	0	223	100
1960	125	1	0	0	0	0	0	0	1	183	0	0	92	130
1961	47	5	0	0	0	0	0	0	1	1,132	0	0	1,179	1,900
Lifetime		9	0	0	0	0	0	0	3	1,767	0	0	1,630	$2,105

Lee Morgan

Lee Morgan

Year	Rank	Starts	Poles	1	2	3	4	5	6–10	Laps	Laps Led	Races Led	Miles	$
1950	NR	1	0	0	0	0	0	0	0	342	0	0	428	0
Lifetime		1	0	0	0	0	0	0	0	342	0	0	428	$0

Sonny Morgan

Sonny Morgan
B: 1935
Racing Hometown: Beaumont, TX

Year	Rank	Starts	Poles	1	2	3	4	5	6–10	Laps	Laps Led	Races Led	Miles	$
1957	184	1	0	0	0	0	0	0	0		0	0		25
Lifetime		1	0	0	0	0	0	0	0		0	0		$25

Wayne Morgan

Wayne Morgan

Year	Rank	Starts	Poles	1	2	3	4	5	6–10	Laps	Laps Led	Races Led	Miles	$
1978	82	2	0	0	0	0	0	0	0	19	0	0	12	785
Lifetime		2	0	0	0	0	0	0	0	19	0	0	12	$785

Wes Morgan

Wister Lewis Morgan
B: 9 or 11/22/1922
Racing Hometown: Alexandria, VA

Year	Rank	Starts	Poles	1	2	3	4	5	6–10	Laps	Laps Led	Races Led	Miles	$
1960	74	2	0	0	0	0	0	0	0	277	0	0	378	350
1961	107	3	0	0	0	0	0	0	1	493	0	0	573	405
Lifetime		5	0	0	0	0	0	0	1	770	0	0	950	$755

Rob Moroso

Robert Moroso
B: 9/28/1968   D: 9/30/1990   *Killed in highway crash.*
Racing Hometown: Madison, CT

Year	Rank	Starts	Poles	1	2	3	4	5	6–10	Laps	Laps Led	Races Led	Miles	$
1988	54	2	0	0	0	0	0	0	0	473	0	0	585	5,750
1989	63	2	0	0	0	0	0	0	0	583	0	0	671	4,725
1990	30	25	0	0	0	0	0	0	1	5,666	9	3	6,900	162,002
Lifetime		29	0	0	0	0	0	0	1	6,722	9	3	8,156	$172,477

Buckshot Morris

Riley Morris
Racing Hometown: Atlanta, GA

Year	Rank	Starts	Poles	1	2	3	4	5	6–10	Laps	Laps Led	Races Led	Miles	$
1949	NR	2	0	0	0	0	0	0	0		0	0		0
Lifetime		2	0	0	0	0	0	0	0		0	0		$0

Bill Morton

Robert William Morton
B: 7/22/1938
Racing Hometown: Church Hill, TN

Year	Rank	Starts	Poles	1	2	3	4	5	6–10	Laps	Laps Led	Races Led	Miles	$
1955	144	2	0	0	0	0	0	0	0	288	0	0	267	110
1957	77	5	0	0	0	0	0	0	4	653	0	0	365	600
1958	110	8	0	0	0	0	0	0	0	1,370	0	0	917	1,045
1959	71	3	0	0	0	0	0	0	0	398	0	0	218	100
1961	60	6	0	0	0	0	0	0	3	1,879	0	0	932	1,615

Year	Rank	Starts	Poles	Finish						Laps	Laps Led	Races Led	Miles	$
				1	2	3	4	5	6–10					

Bill Morton *continued*

Year	Rank	Starts	Poles	1	2	3	4	5	6–10	Laps	Led	Led	Miles	$
1962	42	5	0	0	0	0	0	0	2	1,359	0	0	1,255	1,350
1963	155	1	0	0	0	0	0	0	0	115	0	0	58	125
1965	58	5	0	0	0	0	0	0	0	601	0	0	832	2,590
Lifetime		35	0	0	0	0	0	0	9	6,663	0	0	4,842	$7,535

Walt Mortz

Walter Mortz

Year	Rank	Starts	Poles	1	2	3	4	5	6–10	Laps	Led	Led	Miles	$
1957	NR	1	0	0	0	0	0	0	0	15	0	0	35	100
Lifetime		1	0	0	0	0	0	0	0	15	0	0	35	$100

Earl Mosbach

Earl Mosbach

Year	Rank	Starts	Poles	1	2	3	4	5	6–10	Laps	Led	Led	Miles	$
1957	165T	1	0	0	0	0	0	0	0	55	0	0	28	50
Lifetime		1	0	0	0	0	0	0	0	55	0	0	28	$50

Earl Moss

Earl Moss
B: 7/28/1925   D: 9/23/1994
Racing Hometown: Creedmoor, NC

Year	Rank	Starts	Poles	1	2	3	4	5	6–10	Laps	Led	Led	Miles	$
1951	N/A	5	0	0	0	0	0	0	1	479	0	0	515	310
1952	104T	1	0	0	0	0	0	0	0	162	0	0	81	25
1953	162	1	0	0	0	0	0	0	0	190	0	0	190	25
1956	198	2	0	0	0	0	0	0	0	84	0	0	67	125
1959	NR	2	0	0	0	0	0	0	1	279	0	0	140	140
Lifetime		11	0	0	0	0	0	0	2	1,194	0	0	992	$625

David Mote

David George Mote
B: 10/3/1940
Racing Hometown: Siler City, NC

Year	Rank	Starts	Poles	1	2	3	4	5	6–10	Laps	Led	Led	Miles	$
1968	76	7	0	0	0	0	0	0	0	396	0	0	376	1,150
Lifetime		7	0	0	0	0	0	0	0	396	0	0	376	$1,150

Lothar Motschenbacher

Lothar Motschenbacher
B: 11/19/1938
Racing Hometown: Cologne, Germany

Year	Rank	Starts	Poles	1	2	3	4	5	6–10	Laps	Led	Led	Miles	$
1970	NR	1	0	0	0	0	0	0	0	7	0	0	18	800
Lifetime		1	0	0	0	0	0	0	0	7	0	0	18	$800

Arden Mounts

Arden Mounts
Deceased
Racing Hometown: Gilbert, WV

Year	Rank	Starts	Poles	1	2	3	4	5	6–10	Laps	Led	Led	Miles	$
1953	29	10	0	0	0	0	0	0	1	792	0	0	759	395
1954	21	12	0	0	0	0	0	0	1	1,592	0	0	1,317	875
1955	32	12	0	0	0	0	0	0	4	1,560	0	0	1,050	1,025
1956	136	3	0	0	0	0	0	0	0	545	0	0	381	210
Lifetime		37	0	0	0	0	0	0	6	4,489	0	0	3,506	$2,505

Pete Moxley

Peter Moxley
Racing Hometown: Delta, PA

Year	Rank	Starts	Poles	1	2	3	4	5	6–10	Laps	Led	Led	Miles	$
1954	196	2	0	0	0	0	0	0	0	149	0	0	75	10
Lifetime		2	0	0	0	0	0	0	0	149	0	0	75	$10

Larry Moyer

Lawrence Moyer
Racing Hometown: Ft. Wayne, IN

Year	Rank	Starts	Poles	1	2	3	4	5	6–10	Laps	Led	Led	Miles	$
1988	79	1	0	0	0	0	0	0	0	148	0	0	370	4,255
Lifetime		1	0	0	0	0	0	0	0	148	0	0	370	$4,255

Roy Mulligan

Roy Mulligan
B: 1940   D: 6/30/1975   *Electrocuted.*
Racing Hometown: Birmingham, AL

Year	Rank	Starts	Poles	1	2	3	4	5	6–10	Laps	Led	Led	Miles	$
1971	NR	1	0	0	0	0	0	0	0	83	0	0	221	1,450
Lifetime		1	0	0	0	0	0	0	0	83	0	0	221	$1,450

Year	Rank	Starts	Poles	Finish						Laps	Laps Led	Races Led	Miles	$
				1	2	3	4	5	6–10					

Jack Mulrain

Jack Mulrain
Racing Hometown: Elizabeth, NJ

Year	Rank	Starts	Poles	1	2	3	4	5	6–10	Laps	Laps Led	Races Led	Miles	$
1952	120T	1	0	0	0	0	0	0	0	173	0	0	87	25
Lifetime		1	0	0	0	0	0	0	0	173	0	0	87	$25

Frank Mundy

Frank Mundy *Real Name*: Francisco Melendez
B: 6/18/1918
Racing Hometown: Atlanta, GA

Year	Rank	Starts	Poles	1	2	3	4	5	6–10	Laps	Laps Led	Races Led	Miles	$
1949	10	4	0	0	0	1	1	0	0	274	0	0	381	1,160
1950	23	8	0	0	0	0	0	0	3	310	0	0	283	550
1951	5	27	4	3	2	1	2	1	3	874	445	5	579	7,085
1952	NR	5	0	0	0	0	0	0	2	536	0	0	462	275
1956	24	9	2	0	1	1	0	1	2	1,589	0	0	1,479	3,585
Lifetime		53	6	3	3	3	3	2	10	3,583	445	5	3,185	$12,655

Jim Mundy

James Mundy
Racing Hometown: Columbia, SC

Year	Rank	Starts	Poles	1	2	3	4	5	6–10	Laps	Laps Led	Races Led	Miles	$
1956	239T	1	0	0	0	0	0	0	0	104	0	0	78	50
Lifetime		1	0	0	0	0	0	0	0	104	0	0	78	$50

Dutch Munsinger

Dutch Munsinger
Racing Hometown: Tabor, IA

Year	Rank	Starts	Poles	1	2	3	4	5	6–10	Laps	Laps Led	Races Led	Miles	$
1954	178	1	0	0	0	0	0	0	0	46	0	0	69	0
1955	125	2	0	0	0	0	0	0	1	145	0	0	121	150
1956	292	1	0	0	0	0	0	0	0	69	0	0	69	25
Lifetime		4	0	0	0	0	0	0	1	260	0	0	259	$175

Terry Murchison

Terry Murchison
Racing Hometown: Rome, GA

Year	Rank	Starts	Poles	1	2	3	4	5	6–10	Laps	Laps Led	Races Led	Miles	$
1965	138	1	0	0	0	0	0	0	0	2	0	0	1	250
Lifetime		1	0	0	0	0	0	0	0	2	0	0	1	$250

Jim Murray

James Murray
Racing Hometown: Illinois

Year	Rank	Starts	Poles	1	2	3	4	5	6–10	Laps	Laps Led	Races Led	Miles	$
1955	105	2	0	0	0	0	0	1	0	165	0	0	197	330
Lifetime		2	0	0	0	0	0	1	0	165	0	0	197	$330

Ralph Murray

Ralph Murray

Year	Rank	Starts	Poles	1	2	3	4	5	6–10	Laps	Laps Led	Races Led	Miles	$
1956	301	1	0	0	0	0	0	0	0	2	0	0	1	0
Lifetime		1	0	0	0	0	0	0	0	2	0	0	1	$0

Charles Muscatel

Charles Muscatel
Racing Hometown: Lambertville, NJ

Year	Rank	Starts	Poles	1	2	3	4	5	6–10	Laps	Laps Led	Races Led	Miles	$
1949	37T	1	0	0	0	0	0	0	1		0	0		75
1950	NR	1	0	0	0	0	0	0	0	26	0	0	26	0
Lifetime		2	0	0	0	0	0	0	1	26	0	0	26	$75

Elmer Musclow

Elmer Musclow
Racing Hometown: Rochester, NY

Year	Rank	Starts	Poles	1	2	3	4	5	6–10	Laps	Laps Led	Races Led	Miles	$
1953	127T	1	0	0	0	0	0	0	0		0	0		25
1954	134	1	0	0	0	0	0	0	0	171	0	0	86	25
Lifetime		2	0	0	0	0	0	0	0	171	0	0	86	$50

Ted Musgrave

Ted Musgrave

Year	Rank	Starts	Poles	1	2	3	4	5	6–10	Laps	Laps Led	Races Led	Miles	$
1990	49	4	0	0	0	0	0	0	0	786	0	0	1,019	17,190
1991	23	29	0	0	0	0	0	0	0	9,074	6	5	10,579	200,910
1992	18	29	0	0	0	0	0	1	6	**9,253**	11	3	10,988	449,121
1993	25	29	0	0	0	0	0	2	3	8,530	8	3	10,397	458,615
1994	13	31	3	0	0	0	0	1	7	9,237	50	4	10,817	669,687

Year	Rank	Starts	Poles	Finish 1	2	3	4	5	6–10	Laps	Laps Led	Races Led	Miles	$

Ted Musgrave *continued*

Year	Rank	Starts	Poles	1	2	3	4	5	6–10	Laps	Laps Led	Races Led	Miles	$
1995	7	31	1	0	2	2	2	1	6	9,580	43	6	11,822	1,147,445
1996	16	31	1	0	0	1	1	0	5	9,352	5	3	11,388	961,512
Lifetime		184	5	0	2	3	3	5	27	55,812	123	24	67,009	$3,904,480

Billy Myers

William Wade Myers
B: 10/19/1924   D: 4/12/1958   *Died of heart attack while racing @ Winston-Salem, NC.*
Racing Hometown: Germanton, NC

Year	Rank	Starts	Poles	1	2	3	4	5	6–10	Laps	Laps Led	Races Led	Miles	$
1951	59	8	0	0	0	1	0	0	1	609	23	1	702	925
1952	NR	1	0	0	0	0	0	0	0	220	0	0	220	50
1955	78	3	0	0	0	0	0	0	1	512	0	0	555	240
1956	6	42	1	2	6	3	1	1	9	6,270	103	4	4,231	15,830
1957	12	28	0	0	0	0	4	0	5	3,923	201	1	2,441	6,566
1958	162	2	0	0	0	0	0	0	0	28	0	0	115	50
Lifetime		84	1	2	6	4	5	1	16	11,562	327	6	8,265	$23,661

Bob Myers

Robert Myers
Racing Hometown: Calumet City, IL

Year	Rank	Starts	Poles	1	2	3	4	5	6–10	Laps	Laps Led	Races Led	Miles	$
1951	164	1	0	0	0	0	0	0	0	230	0	0	230	50
Lifetime		1	0	0	0	0	0	0	0	230	0	0	230	$50

Bobby Myers

Robert Harris Myers
B: 6/27/1927   D: 9/2/1957   *Killed in Darlington's Southern 500.*
Racing Hometown: Winston-Salem, NC

Year	Rank	Starts	Poles	1	2	3	4	5	6–10	Laps	Laps Led	Races Led	Miles	$
1951	208	2	0	0	0	0	0	0	0	199	0	0	199	50
1952	158	1	0	0	0	0	0	0	0	145	0	0	181	0
1953	30	2	0	0	0	0	0	0	1	321	0	0	441	390
1956	61	8	0	0	0	0	0	0	2	980	0	0	714	600
1957	126	2	0	0	0	0	0	0	0	53	1	1	50	335
Lifetime		15	0	0	0	0	0	0	3	1,698	1	1	1,585	$1,375

Gary Myers

Gary Myers
B: 2/20/1940
Racing Hometown: Huntsville, AL

Year	Rank	Starts	Poles	1	2	3	4	5	6–10	Laps	Laps Led	Races Led	Miles	$
1971	NR	1	0	0	0	0	0	0	1	474	0	0	216	500
Lifetime		1	0	0	0	0	0	0	1	474	0	0	216	$500

Gary Myers

Gary Burton Myers
B: 3/4/1950
Racing Hometown: Walnut Grove, NC

Year	Rank	Starts	Poles	1	2	3	4	5	6–10	Laps	Laps Led	Races Led	Miles	$
1974	125	2	0	0	0	0	0	0	0	35	0	0	36	1,425
1976	29	15	0	0	0	0	0	0	0	3,077	0	0	2,799	11,430
1977	36	10	0	0	0	0	0	0	0	2,648	0	0	2,691	10,975
1978	27	19	0	0	0	0	0	0	0	5,524	0	0	6,134	22,140
Lifetime		46	0	0	0	0	0	0	0	11,284	0	0	11,660	$45,970

Randy Myers

Randall Myers

Year	Rank	Starts	Poles	1	2	3	4	5	6–10	Laps	Laps Led	Races Led	Miles	$
1977	NR	1	0	0	0	0	0	0	0	377	0	0	383	1,000
Lifetime		1	0	0	0	0	0	0	0	377	0	0	383	$1,000

Ronny Myers

Ronald Myers
Racing Hometown: Los Angeles, CA

Year	Rank	Starts	Poles	1	2	3	4	5	6–10	Laps	Laps Led	Races Led	Miles	$
1959	NR	1	0	0	0	0	0	0	0	369	0	0	148	100
Lifetime		1	0	0	0	0	0	0	0	369	0	0	148	$100

Joe Nagle

Joseph Nagle
Racing Hometown: Dayton, OH

Year	Rank	Starts	Poles	1	2	3	4	5	6–10	Laps	Laps Led	Races Led	Miles	$
1950	68T	1	0	0	0	0	0	0	1		0	0		75
Lifetime		1	0	0	0	0	0	0	1		0	0		$75

Year	Rank	Starts	Poles	Finish						Laps	Laps Led	Races Led	Miles	$
				1	2	3	4	5	6–10	Laps	Led	Led	Miles	$

Burrhead Nantz

Homer Nantz
Racing Hometown: Mooresville, NC

Year	Rank	Starts	Poles	1	2	3	4	5	6–10	Laps	Laps Led	Races Led	Miles	$
1960	117	3	0	0	0	0	0	0	0	66	0	0	133	300
Lifetime		3	0	0	0	0	0	0	0	66	0	0	133	$300

Harold Nash

Harold Nash
Racing Hometown: Atlanta, GA

Year	Rank	Starts	Poles	1	2	3	4	5	6–10	Laps	Laps Led	Races Led	Miles	$
1953	180	2	0	0	0	0	0	0	0		0	0		50
1954	192T	2	0	0	0	0	0	0	0	27	0	0	111	0
Lifetime		4	0	0	0	0	0	0	0	27	0	0	111	$50

Johnny Nave

John Nave
Racing Hometown: Jonesboro, GA

Year	Rank	Starts	Poles	1	2	3	4	5	6–10	Laps	Laps Led	Races Led	Miles	$
1958	NR	1	0	0	0	0	0	0	0	70	0	0	63	70
1962	132	2	0	0	0	0	0	0	0	170	0	0	106	200
1964	NR	1	0	0	0	0	0	0	0	2	0	0	1	250
Lifetime		4	0	0	0	0	0	0	0	242	0	0	170	$520

Brian Naylor

Brian Naylor
Racing Hometown: Stockport, England

Year	Rank	Starts	Poles	1	2	3	4	5	6–10	Laps	Laps Led	Races Led	Miles	$
1961	156	2	0	0	0	0	0	0	0	86	0	0	215	200
Lifetime		2	0	0	0	0	0	0	0	86	0	0	215	$200

Al Neal

Al Neal
Racing Hometown: N. Linthonium, MD

Year	Rank	Starts	Poles	1	2	3	4	5	6–10	Laps	Laps Led	Races Led	Miles	$
1954	189	1	0	0	0	0	0	0	0	13	0	0	13	0
Lifetime		1	0	0	0	0	0	0	0	13	0	0	13	$0

Chuck Neale

Charles Neale
Racing Hometown: Grand Rapids, MI

Year	Rank	Starts	Poles	1	2	3	4	5	6–10	Laps	Laps Led	Races Led	Miles	$
1954	NR	1	0	0	0	0	0	0	0	170	0	0	85	25
Lifetime		1	0	0	0	0	0	0	0	170	0	0	85	$25

Ed Negre

Ed Charles Negre
B: 7/16/1929
Racing Hometown: Kelso, WA

Year	Rank	Starts	Poles	1	2	3	4	5	6–10	Laps	Laps Led	Races Led	Miles	$
1955	83T	1	0	0	0	0	0	0	1	239	0	0	239	200
1956	48	5	0	0	0	0	1	1	2	936	200	2	597	1,255
1957	NR	6	0	0	0	0	0	1	2	519	0	0	307	825
1961	113	2	0	0	0	0	0	0	1	308	0	0	258	260
1967	49	14	0	0	0	0	0	0	0	1,439	0	0	1,100	3,805
1968	31	24	0	0	0	0	0	0	1	2,930	0	0	1,487	5,085
1969	27	31	0	0	0	0	0	0	4	4,556	0	0	3,477	15,615
1970	26	31	0	0	0	0	0	0	1	3,336	0	0	2,700	14,580
1971	12	43	0	0	0	0	0	0	2	8,359	0	0	7,547	29,738
1972	21	26	0	0	0	0	0	0	0	5,755	0	0	6,702	30,783
1973	18	24	0	0	0	0	0	1	1	6,230	0	0	7,180	34,235
1974	23	26	0	0	0	0	0	0	0	5,302	0	0	6,344	24,942
1975	17	29	0	0	0	0	0	0	4	7,191	2	1	7,725	49,629
1976	19	28	0	0	0	0	0	0	2	6,153	0	0	7,221	50,919
1977	22	24	0	0	0	0	0	0	0	5,523	0	0	6,040	42,665
1978	28	21	0	0	0	0	0	0	1	4,826	0	0	4,950	29,145
1979	51	3	0	0	0	0	0	0	0	849	0	0	1,387	11,215
Lifetime		338	0	0	0	0	1	3	22	64,451	202	3	65,263	$344,896

Jess Nelson

Jess Nelson
Racing Hometown: Sacramento, CA

Year	Rank	Starts	Poles	1	2	3	4	5	6–10	Laps	Laps Led	Races Led	Miles	$
1956	214T	1	0	0	0	0	0	0	0	88	0	0	88	50
Lifetime		1	0	0	0	0	0	0	0	88	0	0	88	$50

Norm Nelson

Norm Nelson
B: 1/30/1923   D: 11/8/1988
Racing Hometown: Racine, WI

Year	Rank	Starts	Poles	1	2	3	4	5	6–10	Laps	Laps Led	Races Led	Miles	$
1955	68	2	1	1	0	0	0	0	0	273	106	1	354	1,420

Year	Rank	Starts	Poles	Finish 1	2	3	4	5	6–10	Laps	Laps Led	Races Led	Miles	$

Norm Nelson *continued*

Year	Rank	Starts	Poles	1	2	3	4	5	6–10	Laps	Laps Led	Races Led	Miles	$
1966	NR	1	0	0	0	0	0	0	1	176	0	0	475	1,000
1967	NR	1	0	0	0	1	0	0	0	183	0	0	494	5,250
1968	NR	1	0	0	0	0	0	0	0	87	0	0	235	720
Lifetime		5	1	1	0	1	0	0	1	719	106	1	1,558	$8,390

Tony Nelson

Tony Nelson
Racing Hometown: Ventura, CA

Year	Rank	Starts	Poles	1	2	3	4	5	6–10	Laps	Laps Led	Races Led	Miles	$
1954	49	3	0	0	0	0	0	0	1	995	0	0	616	325
Lifetime		3	0	0	0	0	0	0	1	995	0	0	616	$325

Joe Nemechek

Joseph Frank Nemechek III
B: 9/26/1963
Racing Hometown: Naples, FL

Year	Rank	Starts	Poles	1	2	3	4	5	6–10	Laps	Laps Led	Races Led	Miles	$
1993	44	5	0	0	0	0	0	0	0	1,114	0	0	1,516	56,580
1994	27	29	0	0	0	1	0	0	2	7,951	22	2	9,486	389,565
1995	28	29	0	0	0	0	1	0	3	8,504	1	1	10,223	428,925
1996	34	29	0	0	0	0	0	0	2	8,110	2	1	9,710	666,247
Lifetime		92	0	0	0	1	1	0	7	25,679	25	4	30,936	$1,541,317

Archie Nepstad

Archie Nepstad
Racing Hometown: Rochester, MN

Year	Rank	Starts	Poles	1	2	3	4	5	6–10	Laps	Laps Led	Races Led	Miles	$
1955	235	1	0	0	0	0	0	0	0	41	0	0	41	25
Lifetime		1	0	0	0	0	0	0	0	41	0	0	41	$25

Joe Edd Neubert

Joe Edd Neubert
Racing Hometown: Knoxville, TN

Year	Rank	Starts	Poles	1	2	3	4	5	6–10	Laps	Laps Led	Races Led	Miles	$
1967	99	3	0	0	0	0	0	0	1	254	0	0	127	465
Lifetime		3	0	0	0	0	0	0	1	254	0	0	127	$465

Al Neves

Al Neves
Racing Hometown: Oakland, CA

Year	Rank	Starts	Poles	1	2	3	4	5	6–10	Laps	Laps Led	Races Led	Miles	$
1954	137	2	0	0	0	0	0	0	0	455	0	0	333	65
Lifetime		2	0	0	0	0	0	0	0	455	0	0	333	$65

Paul Newkirk

Paul Newkirk
Racing Hometown: Cedar Rapids, IA

Year	Rank	Starts	Poles	1	2	3	4	5	6–10	Laps	Laps Led	Races Led	Miles	$
1951	34	1	0	0	0	0	0	1	0	241	0	0	241	500
1952	184	1	0	0	0	0	0	0	0	27	0	0	27	0
1953	112	1	0	0	0	0	0	0	0		0	0		25
Lifetime		3	0	0	0	0	0	1	0	268	0	0	268	$525

Homer Newland

Homer Newland
B: 2/17/1930
Racing Hometown: Dearborne, MI

Year	Rank	Starts	Poles	1	2	3	4	5	6–10	Laps	Laps Led	Races Led	Miles	$
1955	215	1	0	0	0	0	0	0	0	120	0	0	60	25
1969	65	2	0	0	0	0	0	0	0	179	0	0	393	1,875
Lifetime		3	0	0	0	0	0	0	0	299	0	0	453	$1,900

Gus Newman

Gus Newman
Racing Hometown: Las Vegas, NV

Year	Rank	Starts	Poles	1	2	3	4	5	6–10	Laps	Laps Led	Races Led	Miles	$
1961	130	2	0	0	0	0	0	0	0	40	0	0	93	130
Lifetime		2	0	0	0	0	0	0	0	40	0	0	93	$130

Rick Newsom

Rickey Lyle Newsom
B: 3/19/1950   D: 8/16/1988   *Killed in private plane crash.*
Racing Hometown: Ft. Mill, SC

Year	Rank	Starts	Poles	1	2	3	4	5	6–10	Laps	Laps Led	Races Led	Miles	$
1972	91	1	0	0	0	0	0	0	0	231	0	0	462	800
1973	34	12	0	0	0	0	0	0	0	3,209	0	0	2,551	8,530
1974	92	2	0	0	0	0	0	0	0	535	0	0	507	1,425
1975	37	10	0	0	0	0	0	0	0	1,672	0	0	1,695	9,780

Year	Rank	Starts	Poles	Finish						Laps	Laps Led	Races Led	Miles	$
				1	2	3	4	5	6–10	Laps	Led	Led	Miles	$

Rick Newsom *continued*

Year	Rank	Starts	Poles	1	2	3	4	5	6–10	Laps	Laps Led	Races Led	Miles	$
1976	44	7	0	0	0	0	0	0	0	1,604	0	0	1,392	5,520
1977	NR	7	0	0	0	0	0	0	0	1,240	0	0	888	3,260
1979	49	4	0	0	0	0	0	0	0	484	0	0	1,236	5,530
1980	44	6	0	0	0	0	0	0	0	1,179	0	0	790	3,830
1981	36	9	0	0	0	0	0	0	0	1,676	0	0	1,741	8,625
1982	36	8	0	0	0	0	0	0	0	1,143	0	0	1,931	12,390
1983	41	6	0	0	0	0	0	0	0	2,097	0	0	1,699	14,895
1984	82	1	0	0	0	0	0	0	0	242	0	0	246	2,835
1985	41	6	0	0	0	0	0	0	0	834	0	0	1,105	12,840
1986	69	3	0	0	0	0	0	0	0	358	0	0	447	4,185
Lifetime		82	0	0	0	0	0	0	0	16,504	0	0	16,690	$94,445

A. F. Nichols

A. F. Nichols
Racing Hometown: Atlanta, GA

Year	Rank	Starts	Poles	1	2	3	4	5	6–10	Laps	Laps Led	Races Led	Miles	$
1962	NR	1	0	0	0	0	0	0	0	1	0	0	2	200
Lifetime		1	0	0	0	0	0	0	0	1	0	0	2	$200

Nick Nicolette

Nicholas Nicolette
Racing Hometown: Belleville, NJ

Year	Rank	Starts	Poles	1	2	3	4	5	6–10	Laps	Laps Led	Races Led	Miles	$
1951	N/A	1	0	0	0	0	0	0	0		0	0		10
1953	115	2	0	0	0	0	0	0	0		0	0		65
Lifetime		3	0	0	0	0	0	0	0		0	0		$75

Wayne Niedecken

Wayne Niedecken
B: 4/8/1931   D: 3/22/1993
Racing Hometown: Pensacola, FL

Year	Rank	Starts	Poles	1	2	3	4	5	6–10	Laps	Laps Led	Races Led	Miles	$
1953	NR	1	0	0	0	0	0	0	0		0	0		25
Lifetime		1	0	0	0	0	0	0	0		0	0		$25

Stan Noble

Stanley Noble
Racing Hometown: Gardena, CA

Year	Rank	Starts	Poles	1	2	3	4	5	6–10	Laps	Laps Led	Races Led	Miles	$
1951	N/A	3	0	0	0	0	0	0	0		0	0		75
Lifetime		3	0	0	0	0	0	0	0		0	0		$75

Don Noel

Donald E. Noel
B: 6/29/1929
Racing Hometown: Arletto, CA

Year	Rank	Starts	Poles	1	2	3	4	5	6–10	Laps	Laps Led	Races Led	Miles	$
1960	71	3	0	0	0	0	0	1	0	240	0	0	309	725
1961	66	4	0	0	2	0	0	1	0	493	0	0	518	1,705
1963	86	2	0	0	0	0	0	0	0	259	0	0	699	800
1964	NR	1	0	0	0	0	0	0	0	10	0	0	27	500
1967	74	1	0	0	0	0	0	0	0	131	0	0	354	625
1968	98	1	0	0	0	0	0	0	0	31	0	0	84	575
1970	106	2	0	0	0	0	0	0	0	38	0	0	100	1,450
1971	NR	3	0	0	0	0	0	0	0	164	0	0	425	3,235
1972	92	2	0	0	0	0	0	0	0	159	0	0	413	2,585
1973	104	1	0	0	0	0	0	0	0	119	0	0	312	770
1977	110T	1	0	0	0	0	0	0	0	0	0	0	0	500
1978	91	2	0	0	0	0	0	0	0	180	0	0	453	1,765
1979	116T	1	0	0	0	0	0	0	0	15	0	0	39	700
Lifetime		24	0	0	2	0	0	2	0	1,839	0	0	3,732	$15,935

Brad Noffsinger

Brad Noffsinger
B: 8/29/1960
Racing Hometown: Huntington Beach, CA

Year	Rank	Starts	Poles	1	2	3	4	5	6–10	Laps	Laps Led	Races Led	Miles	$
1988	36	17	0	0	0	0	0	0	0	3,555	1	1	5,513	54,645
Lifetime		17	0	0	0	0	0	0	0	3,555	1	1	5,513	$54,645

G. T. Nolan

G. Thomas Nolan (Tommy)
Racing Hometown: Jetersville, VA

Year	Rank	Starts	Poles	1	2	3	4	5	6–10	Laps	Laps Led	Races Led	Miles	$
1965	74	8	0	0	0	0	0	0	1	1,018	0	0	563	1,165
1966	93	3	0	0	0	0	0	0	0	486	0	0	199	305

Year	Rank	Starts	Poles	Finish						Laps	Laps Led	Races Led	Miles	$
				1	2	3	4	5	6–10					

G. T. Nolan *continued*

Year	Rank	Starts	Poles	1	2	3	4	5	6–10	Laps	Laps Led	Races Led	Miles	$
1967	105	1	0	0	0	0	0	0	0	144	0	0	130	100
1968	122	1	0	0	0	0	0	0	0	123	0	0	62	110
Lifetime		13	0	0	0	0	0	0	1	1,771	0	0	952	$1,680

Whitey Norman

William G. Norman
B: 4/14/1926
Racing Hometown: Winston-Salem, NC

Year	Rank	Starts	Poles	1	2	3	4	5	6–10	Laps	Laps Led	Races Led	Miles	$
1956	180T	1	0	0	0	0	0	0	1	150	0	0	94	100
1957	24	13	0	0	1	0	0	0	3	2,437	0	0	1,614	3,990
1958	138	9	0	0	0	0	2	0	1	1,348	0	0	752	1,635
1959	NR	6	0	0	0	0	0	0	0	899	0	0	403	445
Lifetime		29	0	0	1	0	2	0	5	4,834	0	0	2,862	$6,170

Ed Normi

Edward Normi
D: 1993
Racing Hometown: Petaluma, CA

Year	Rank	Starts	Poles	1	2	3	4	5	6–10	Laps	Laps Led	Races Led	Miles	$
1954	124	2	0	0	0	0	0	0	0	313	0	0	176	65
1955	NR	1	0	0	0	0	0	0	0	237	0	0	237	250
Lifetime		3	0	0	0	0	0	0	0	550	0	0	413	$315

Chick Norris

Chick Norris
Racing Hometown: Pittsburgh, PA

Year	Rank	Starts	Poles	1	2	3	4	5	6–10	Laps	Laps Led	Races Led	Miles	$
1955	178T	1	0	0	0	0	0	0	0	10	0	0	5	50
Lifetime		1	0	0	0	0	0	0	0	10	0	0	5	$50

Paul Norris

Paul Norris
Racing Hometown: Concord, NC

Year	Rank	Starts	Poles	1	2	3	4	5	6–10	Laps	Laps Led	Races Led	Miles	$
1960	139	1	0	0	0	0	0	0	0	1	0	0	2	200
Lifetime		1	0	0	0	0	0	0	0	1	0	0	2	$200

Bill Norton

William Norton
Racing Hometown: Gardena, CA

Year	Rank	Starts	Poles	1	2	3	4	5	6–10	Laps	Laps Led	Races Led	Miles	$
1951	N/A	3	0	1	0	1	0	0	1	200	19	1	100	1,675
1953	NR	1	0	0	0	0	0	0	0	241	0	0	331	110
Lifetime		4	0	1	0	1	0	0	1	441	19	1	431	$1,785

George Norton

George Norton
Racing Hometown: Pacoima, CA

Year	Rank	Starts	Poles	1	2	3	4	5	6–10	Laps	Laps Led	Races Led	Miles	$
1957	109	3	0	0	0	0	0	0	1	192	0	0	116	235
1958	79	2	0	0	0	0	0	0	0	248	0	0	512	170
1959	NR	1	0	0	0	0	0	0	0	73	0	0	29	50
Lifetime		6	0	0	0	0	0	0	1	513	0	0	657	$455

Jack Norton

James Norton
Racing Hometown: Long Beach, CA

Year	Rank	Starts	Poles	1	2	3	4	5	6–10	Laps	Laps Led	Races Led	Miles	$
1960	130	1	0	0	0	0	0	0	0	65	0	0	65	100
1961	83	4	0	0	0	0	0	0	1	352	0	0	418	590
1963	118	1	0	0	0	0	0	0	0	140	0	0	378	325
Lifetime		6	0	0	0	0	0	0	1	557	0	0	861	$1,015

James Norton

James Norton
Racing Hometown: Dallas, GA

Year	Rank	Starts	Poles	1	2	3	4	5	6–10	Laps	Laps Led	Races Led	Miles	$
1960	NR	5	0	0	0	0	0	0	1	814	0	0	352	540
1963	142	1	0	0	0	0	0	0	0	84	0	0	126	275
Lifetime		6	0	0	0	0	0	0	1	898	0	0	478	$815

George Norvath

George Norvath

Year	Rank	Starts	Poles	1	2	3	4	5	6–10	Laps	Laps Led	Races Led	Miles	$
1954	NR	1	0	0	0	0	0	0	0	143	0	0	72	10
Lifetime		1	0	0	0	0	0	0	0	143	0	0	72	$10

Year	Rank	Starts	Poles	Finish						Laps	Laps Led	Races Led	Miles	$
				1	2	3	4	5	6–10					

Tom Nundy

Thomas Nundy

Year	Rank	Starts	Poles	1	2	3	4	5	6–10	Laps	Laps Led	Races Led	Miles	$
1958	NR	1	0	0	0	0	0	0	0	34	0	0	11	65
Lifetime		1	0	0	0	0	0	0	0	34	0	0	11	$65

Jack O'Brien

Jack O'Brien
Racing Hometown: Pittsburgh, PA

Year	Rank	Starts	Poles	1	2	3	4	5	6–10	Laps	Laps Led	Races Led	Miles	$
1949	NR	2	0	0	0	0	0	0	0	115	0	0	58	0
Lifetime		2	0	0	0	0	0	0	0	115	0	0	58	$0

Don O'Dell

Donald O'Dell
Racing Hometown: Blue Island, IL

Year	Rank	Starts	Poles	1	2	3	4	5	6–10	Laps	Laps Led	Races Led	Miles	$
1960	142	1	0	0	0	0	0	0	0	90	0	0	135	200
1961	127	2	0	0	0	0	0	0	1	48	0	0	120	340
Lifetime		3	0	0	0	0	0	0	1	138	0	0	255	$540

Joe Bill O'Dell

Joseph William O'Dell
Racing Hometown: Baltimore, MD

Year	Rank	Starts	Poles	1	2	3	4	5	6–10	Laps	Laps Led	Races Led	Miles	$
1953	96	5	0	0	0	0	0	0	1	183	0	0	92	210
1954	94	4	0	0	0	0	0	0	0	556	0	0	382	75
1956	269	1	0	0	0	0	0	0	0	37	0	0	19	60
1957	104	1	0	0	0	0	0	0	0	222	0	0	222	0
Lifetime		11	0	0	0	0	0	0	1	998	0	0	714	$345

Rick O'Dell

Richard O'Dell
B: 10/26/1948
Racing Hometown: Victoria, B.C., Canada

Year	Rank	Starts	Poles	1	2	3	4	5	6–10	Laps	Laps Led	Races Led	Miles	$
1981	76	1	0	0	0	0	0	0	0	86	0	0	225	2,145
Lifetime		1	0	0	0	0	0	0	0	86	0	0	225	$2,145

Jerry O'Neil

Jerry O'Neil
B: 3/28/1956
Racing Hometown: Auburn, NY

Year	Rank	Starts	Poles	1	2	3	4	5	6–10	Laps	Laps Led	Races Led	Miles	$
1989	52	4	0	0	0	0	0	0	0	1,026	0	0	1,255	10,865
1990	51	4	0	0	0	0	0	0	0	423	0	0	985	29,580
1992	46	6	0	0	0	0	0	0	0	958	0	0	1,644	32,370
1993	64T	2	0	0	0	0	0	0	0	320	0	0	476	15,400
1994	—	0												2,500
Lifetime		16	0	0	0	0	0	0	0	2,727	0	0	4,361	$90,715

Dan Obrist

Daniel Obrist
B: 9/27/1946
Racing Hometown: Portland, OR

Year	Rank	Starts	Poles	1	2	3	4	5	6–10	Laps	Laps Led	Races Led	Miles	$
1995	70	1	0	0	0	0	0	0	0	7	0	0	18	9,760
Lifetime		1	0	0	0	0	0	0	0	7	0	0	18	$9,760

Larry Odo

Lawrence Odo
B: 9/28/1922
Racing Hometown: Chicago, IL

Year	Rank	Starts	Poles	1	2	3	4	5	6–10	Laps	Laps Led	Races Led	Miles	$
1956	NR	1	0	0	0	0	0	0	0	361	0	0	181	150
1959	NR	1	0	0	0	0	0	0	0	3	0	0	8	100
Lifetime		2	0	0	0	0	0	0	0	364	0	0	188	$250

Randy Ogden

Randall Ogden
Racing Hometown: Woodward, OK

Year	Rank	Starts	Poles	1	2	3	4	5	6–10	Laps	Laps Led	Races Led	Miles	$
1979	NR	3	0	0	0	0	0	0	0	473	0	0	737	2,465
1980	72	3	0	0	0	0	0	0	0	135	0	0	267	2,385
1981	49	4	0	0	0	0	0	0	0	577	0	0	762	3,905
Lifetime		10	0	0	0	0	0	0	0	1,185	0	0	1,766	$8,755

Year	Rank	Starts	Poles	Finish						Laps	Laps Led	Races Led	Miles	$
				1	2	3	4	5	6–10					

Don Oldenberg

Donald Oldenberg
B: 12/18/1922   D: 12/13/1983
Racing Hometown: Highland, IN

Year	Rank	Starts	Poles	1	2	3	4	5	6–10	Laps	Laps Led	Races Led	Miles	$
1951	63	3	0	0	0	0	0	1	1		0	0		375
1952	186	1	0	0	0	0	0	0	0		0	0		25
1953	35	4	0	0	0	0	0	1	1	223	0	0	245	375
1954	NR	6	0	0	0	0	0	0	3	806	0	0	715	900
1955	88	2	0	0	0	0	0	0	2	260	0	0	178	350
1956	206	3	0	0	0	0	0	0	0	495	0	0	341	200
1957	98	1	0	0	0	0	0	0	0	0	0	0	0	100
Lifetime		20	0	0	0	0	0	2	7	1,784	0	0	1,479	$2,325

Jack Oldenhage

Jack Oldenhage
Racing Hometown: Merced, CA

Year	Rank	Starts	Poles	1	2	3	4	5	6–10	Laps	Laps Led	Races Led	Miles	$
1957	86	3	0	0	0	0	0	0	1	354	0	0	177	250
Lifetime		3	0	0	0	0	0	0	1	354	0	0	177	$250

Barney Oldfield

Bernard Oldfield
(Not to be confused with the legendary Barney Oldfield from the early 1900s.)
Racing Hometown: Asheboro, NC

Year	Rank	Starts	Poles	1	2	3	4	5	6–10	Laps	Laps Led	Races Led	Miles	$
1957	118	1	0	0	0	0	0	0	0	356	0	0	178	150
Lifetime		1	0	0	0	0	0	0	0	356	0	0	178	$150

Charles Oldham

Charles T. Oldham
Racing Hometown: Manning, SC

Year	Rank	Starts	Poles	1	2	3	4	5	6–10	Laps	Laps Led	Races Led	Miles	$
1956	272T	1	0	0	0	0	0	0	0		0	0		25
Lifetime		1	0	0	0	0	0	0	0		0	0		$25

Jackie Oliver

Jack Keith Oliver
B: 8/14/1943
Racing Hometown: Walton-on-Thames, England

Year	Rank	Starts	Poles	1	2	3	4	5	6–10	Laps	Laps Led	Races Led	Miles	$
1971	NR	1	0	0	0	0	0	0	0	117	0	0	234	605
1972	NR	7	0	0	0	0	1	0	0	1,034	0	0	1,486	11,575
Lifetime		8	0	0	0	0	1	0	0	1,151	0	0	1,720	$12,180

Jerry Oliver

Jerry Dennis Oliver
B: 1/18/1944
Racing Hometown: Concord, CA

Year	Rank	Starts	Poles	1	2	3	4	5	6–10	Laps	Laps Led	Races Led	Miles	$
1966	77	1	0	0	0	0	0	0	0	144	0	0	389	560
1967	65	1	0	0	0	0	0	0	0	160	0	0	432	800
1968	92	1	0	0	0	0	0	0	0	39	0	0	105	510
1969	NR	1	0	0	0	0	0	0	0	48	0	0	130	770
1970	70	2	0	0	0	0	0	0	1	268	0	0	702	2,175
1971	NR	2	0	0	0	0	0	1	0	192	0	0	503	2,970
1972	NR	1	0	0	0	0	0	0	0	122	0	0	320	1,100
Lifetime		9	0	0	0	0	0	1	1	973	0	0	2,581	$8,885

Budd Olsen

Budd Olsen
B: 10/16/1924   D: 12/26/1991
Racing Hometown: Paulsboro, NJ

Year	Rank	Starts	Poles	1	2	3	4	5	6–10	Laps	Laps Led	Races Led	Miles	$
1949	51	1	0	0	0	0	0	0	0	180	0	0	180	75
1961	NR	1	0	0	0	0	0	0	0	168	0	0	42	175
Lifetime		2	0	0	0	0	0	0	0	348	0	0	222	$250

Bill Olson

William Olson

Year	Rank	Starts	Poles	1	2	3	4	5	6–10	Laps	Laps Led	Races Led	Miles	$
1958	88	1	0	0	0	0	0	0	0	162	0	0	426	130
Lifetime		1	0	0	0	0	0	0	0	162	0	0	426	$130

Keith Olson

Keith Olson

Year	Rank	Starts	Poles	1	2	3	4	5	6–10	Laps	Laps Led	Races Led	Miles	$
1957	NR	1	0	0	0	0	0	0	0	17	0	0	9	100
Lifetime		1	0	0	0	0	0	0	0	17	0	0	9	$100

Year	Rank	Starts	Poles	Finish 1	2	3	4	5	6–10	Laps	Laps Led	Races Led	Miles	$

Ollie Olson
A. A. Olson
Racing Hometown: Richmond, VA

Year	Rank	Starts	Poles	1	2	3	4	5	6–10	Laps	Laps Led	Races Led	Miles	$
1953	165T	1	0	0	0	0	0	0	0		0	0		25
Lifetime		1	0	0	0	0	0	0	0		0	0		$25

Jan Opperman
Jan Opperman
B: 2/9/1939
Racing Hometown: Beaver Crossing, NE

Year	Rank	Starts	Poles	1	2	3	4	5	6–10	Laps	Laps Led	Races Led	Miles	$
1974	103	1	0	0	0	0	0	0	1	188	0	0	470	1,850
Lifetime		1	0	0	0	0	0	0	1	188	0	0	470	$1,850

Jim Ord
James Ord

Year	Rank	Starts	Poles	1	2	3	4	5	6–10	Laps	Laps Led	Races Led	Miles	$
1955	87	2	0	0	0	0	0	0	1	217	0	0	192	225
Lifetime		2	0	0	0	0	0	0	1	217	0	0	192	$225

Bobby Ore
Robert Ore
Racing Hometown: Gunter, TX

Year	Rank	Starts	Poles	1	2	3	4	5	6–10	Laps	Laps Led	Races Led	Miles	$
1974	137	1	0	0	0	0	0	0	0	297	0	0	177	440
Lifetime		1	0	0	0	0	0	0	0	297	0	0	177	$440

Gibb Orr
Gibb Orr
B: 1918
Racing Hometown: Niles, OH

Year	Rank	Starts	Poles	1	2	3	4	5	6–10	Laps	Laps Led	Races Led	Miles	$
1952	95	2	0	0	0	0	0	0	0	197	0	0	120	25
Lifetime		2	0	0	0	0	0	0	0	197	0	0	120	$25

Phil Orr
Phillip Orr
Racing Hometown: Winter Park, FL

Year	Rank	Starts	Poles	1	2	3	4	5	6–10	Laps	Laps Led	Races Led	Miles	$
1957	96	1	0	0	0	0	0	0	0		0	0		110
1958	84	1	0	0	0	0	0	0	0	31	0	0	127	50
Lifetime		2	0	0	0	0	0	0	0	31	0	0	127	$160

Red Ortwein
Myron Ortwein
Racing Hometown: San Lorenzo, CA

Year	Rank	Starts	Poles	1	2	3	4	5	6–10	Laps	Laps Led	Races Led	Miles	$
1954	170	2	0	0	0	0	0	0	0	338	0	0	241	40
Lifetime		2	0	0	0	0	0	0	0	338	0	0	241	$40

Bill Osborne
William Osborne
Racing Hometown: Pensacola, FL

Year	Rank	Starts	Poles	1	2	3	4	5	6–10	Laps	Laps Led	Races Led	Miles	$
1950	NR	1	0	0	0	0	0	0	0	311	0	0	389	100
1951	67	1	0	0	0	0	1	0	0	148	0	0	111	300
1956	155	1	0	0	0	0	0	0	0	128	0	0	192	75
Lifetime		3	0	0	0	0	1	0	0	587	0	0	692	$475

Bill Osborne
William Osborne
B: 11/24/1946
Racing Hometown: Rialto, CA

Year	Rank	Starts	Poles	1	2	3	4	5	6–10	Laps	Laps Led	Races Led	Miles	$
1971	NR	2	0	0	0	0	0	0	0	61	0	0	157	1,870
1972	117	1	0	0	0	0	0	0	0	36	0	0	90	1,440
1974	85	2	0	0	0	0	0	0	0	164	0	0	418	1,875
1975	73T	2	0	0	0	0	0	0	0	192	0	0	503	2,230
1977	NR	1	0	0	0	0	0	0	0	188	0	0	470	1,350
1980	88	2	0	0	0	0	0	0	0	42	0	0	75	1,075
1985	60	2	0	0	0	0	0	0	0	198	0	0	519	3,605
1986	NR	1	0	0	0	0	0	0	0	38	0	0	100	850
Lifetime		16	0	0	0	0	1	0	0	1,506	0	0	3,023	$14,295

Bob Osborne
Robert Osborne

Year	Rank	Starts	Poles	1	2	3	4	5	6–10	Laps	Laps Led	Races Led	Miles	$
1957	82	2	0	0	0	0	0	0	0	80	0	0	158	135
1958	168	1	0	0	0	0	0	0	0	16	0	0	42	100
Lifetime		3	0	0	0	0	0	0	0	96	0	0	200	$235

Year	Rank	Starts	Poles	Finish						Laps	Laps Led	Races Led	Miles	$
				1	2	3	4	5	6–10	Laps	Led	Led	Miles	$

George Osborne

George Osborne
Racing Hometown: Winchester, KY

Year	Rank	Starts	Poles	1	2	3	4	5	6–10	Laps	Laps Led	Races Led	Miles	$
1953	32	2	0	0	0	0	0	0	0	477	0	0	528	300
1954	204	1	0	0	0	0	0	0	0	16	0	0	66	0
Lifetime		3	0	0	0	0	0	0	0	493	0	0	594	$300

Johnny Osteen

John Osteen
Racing Hometown: Orlando, FL

Year	Rank	Starts	Poles	1	2	3	4	5	6–10	Laps	Laps Led	Races Led	Miles	$
1956	280	1	0	0	0	0	0	0	0		0	0		0
Lifetime		1	0	0	0	0	0	0	0		0	0		$0

Don Ostendorf

Donald Ostendorf
Racing Hometown: North Platte, NE

Year	Rank	Starts	Poles	1	2	3	4	5	6–10	Laps	Laps Led	Races Led	Miles	$
1953	127T	1	0	0	0	0	0	0	0	0	0	0	0	25
Lifetime		1	0	0	0	0	0	0	0	0	0	0	0	$25

Billy Oswald

William Oswald
Racing Hometown: New York, NY

Year	Rank	Starts	Poles	1	2	3	4	5	6–10	Laps	Laps Led	Races Led	Miles	$
1953	NR	1	0	0	0	0	0	0	1	174	0	0	174	150
1963	135T	1	0	0	0	0	0	0	0	61	0	0	31	60
Lifetime		2	0	0	0	0	0	0	1	235	0	0	205	$210

Nelson Oswald

Nelson Oswald
Racing Hometown: Jamestown, NC

Year	Rank	Starts	Poles	1	2	3	4	5	6–10	Laps	Laps Led	Races Led	Miles	$
1978	46	6	0	0	0	0	0	0	0	1,103	0	0	781	3,530
1979	43	6	0	0	0	0	0	0	0	842	0	0	1,000	3,610
1980	78T	2	0	0	0	0	0	0	0	184	0	0	374	2,520
Lifetime		14	0	0	0	0	0	0	0	2,129	0	0	2,154	$9,660

L. D. Ottinger

Lloyd Dolph Ottinger
B: 12/30/1938
Racing Hometown: Newport, TN

Year	Rank	Starts	Poles	1	2	3	4	5	6–10	Laps	Laps Led	Races Led	Miles	$
1966	144	1	0	0	0	0	0	0	0	32	0	0	16	0
1973	56	3	0	0	1	0	0	0	1	813	0	0	955	7,452
1974	62	4	0	0	0	0	0	0	0	290	0	0	395	4,985
1984	77	2	0	0	0	0	0	0	0	695	0	0	714	7,650
Lifetime		10	0	0	1	0	0	0	1	1,830	0	0	2,080	$20,087

Frank Oviado

Frank Oviado
Racing Hometown: Phoenix, AZ

Year	Rank	Starts	Poles	1	2	3	4	5	6–10	Laps	Laps Led	Races Led	Miles	$
1951	NR	1	0	0	0	0	0	0	0		0	0		25
Lifetime		1	0	0	0	0	0	0	0		0	0		$25

Cotton Owens

Everett Owens
B: 5/21/1924
Racing Hometown: Spartanburg, SC

Year	Rank	Starts	Poles	1	2	3	4	5	6–10	Laps	Laps Led	Races Led	Miles	$
1950	13	3	0	0	0	0	0	0	1	511	23	1	727	1,100
1951	42	5	0	0	0	0	0	1	2	370	0	0	463	725
1952	65	4	0	0	0	0	0	0	1	391	0	0	202	200
1953	76	1	0	0	0	0	0	0	0	274	0	0	274	50
1954	84	4	0	0	0	0	0	0	1	530	0	0	475	175
1955	29	2	0	0	0	0	0	1	1	549	0	0	584	900
1956	52	8	0	0	0	0	0	1	3	1,126	0	0	663	870
1957	14	17	1	1	1	0	0	1	3	2,300	179	3	1,769	12,784
1958	17	29	2	1	4	2	1	0	9	3,700	241	5	2,208	6,579
1959	2	37	2	1	4	2	2	4	9	6,733	209	4	4,397	14,640
1960	39	14	3	1	3	1	0	0	0	2,121	185	7	2,362	14,065
1961	22	17	2	4	3	1	2	1	0	2,694	58	5	2,124	11,890
1962	30	16	1	0	2	2	2	1	1	2,000	36	2	1,515	5,905
1963	114T	1	0	0	0	0	0	0	1	170	0	0	85	175
1964	80	2	0	1	1	0	0	0	0	466	54	1	299	3,400
Lifetime		160	11	9	18	8	7	10	32	23,935	985	28	18,147	$73,458

Year	Rank	Starts	Poles	Finish						Laps	Laps Led	Races Led	Miles	$
				1	2	3	4	5	6–10					

Augie Pabst

August Pabst
B: 1933
Racing Hometown: Milwaukee, WI

Year	Rank	Starts	Poles	1	2	3	4	5	6–10	Laps	Laps Led	Races Led	Miles	$
1963	NR	1	0	0	0	0	0	0	0	18	0	0	49	250
Lifetime		1	0	0	0	0	0	0	0	18	0	0	49	$250

Ken Pace

Kenneth Pace
Racing Hometown: Martinsville, VA

Year	Rank	Starts	Poles	1	2	3	4	5	6–10	Laps	Laps Led	Races Led	Miles	$
1954	NR	2	0	0	0	0	0	0	0	258	0	0	144	25
1955	155	2	0	0	0	0	0	0	0	160	0	0	80	25
Lifetime		4	0	0	0	0	0	0	0	418	0	0	224	$50

Sammy Packard

Samuel Packard
Racing Hometown: Barrington, RI

Year	Rank	Starts	Poles	1	2	3	4	5	6–10	Laps	Laps Led	Races Led	Miles	$
1951	N/A	2	0	0	0	0	0	0	0		0	0		50
1961	115	1	0	0	0	0	0	0	1	444	0	0	111	275
1962	NR	1	0	0	0	0	0	0	0	45	0	0	23	110
Lifetime		4	0	0	0	0	0	0	1	489	0	0	134	$435

Eddie Pagan

Edward Pagan
B: 8/1/1918   D: 8/1/1984
Racing Hometown: Lynwood, CA

Year	Rank	Starts	Poles	1	2	3	4	5	6–10	Laps	Laps Led	Races Led	Miles	$
1954	80	2	0	0	0	0	0	0	0	682	0	0	453	140
1955	107	2	0	0	0	0	0	0	0	287	0	0	287	120
1956	32	8	2	1	1	0	0	2	0	1,366	31	2	1,037	4,095
1957	15	15	2	3	3	3	1	1	0	2,611	3	3	1,802	7,274
1958	9	27	2	0	2	1	1	7	7	3,961	57	2	2,607	7,472
1959	NR	1	0	0	0	0	0	0	1	439	0	0	176	375
1961	68	5	0	0	0	0	0	1	3	581	0	0	657	985
1962	98	1	0	0	0	0	0	0	0	354	0	0	177	250
1963	132	1	0	0	0	0	0	0	0	137	0	0	370	325
Lifetime		62	6	4	6	4	2	11	11	10,418	91	7	7,564	$21,036

Marian Pagan

Marian Pagan (Mopsie)
Racing Hometown: Lynwood, CA

Year	Rank	Starts	Poles	1	2	3	4	5	6–10	Laps	Laps Led	Races Led	Miles	$
1954	NR	1	0	0	0	0	0	0	0	261	0	0	131	25
Lifetime		1	0	0	0	0	0	0	0	261	0	0	131	$25

Arthur Page

Arthur Page
Racing Hometown: Charlotte, NC

Year	Rank	Starts	Poles	1	2	3	4	5	6–10	Laps	Laps Led	Races Led	Miles	$
1965	112T	1	0	0	0	0	0	0	0	43	0	0	22	100
Lifetime		1	0	0	0	0	0	0	0	43	0	0	22	$100

Lennie Page

Lennie Page
Racing Hometown: Buffalo, NY

Year	Rank	Starts	Poles	1	2	3	4	5	6–10	Laps	Laps Led	Races Led	Miles	$
1956	NR	1	0	0	0	0	0	0	1	180	0	0	90	250
1957	73	4	0	0	0	0	0	0	1	396	0	0	332	410
1958	46	8	0	0	0	0	0	0	2	901	0	0	355	760
1959	72	2	0	0	0	0	0	0	1	251	0	0	143	280
1960	61	5	0	0	0	0	0	0	2	774	0	0	616	1,050
Lifetime		20	0	0	0	0	0	0	7	2,502	0	0	1,536	$2,750

Mike Page

Michael Page
Racing Hometown: Richmond, VA

Year	Rank	Starts	Poles	1	2	3	4	5	6–10	Laps	Laps Led	Races Led	Miles	$
1966	109	1	0	0	0	0	0	0	0	132	0	0	119	100
Lifetime		1	0	0	0	0	0	0	0	132	0	0	119	$100

Pete Page

Peter Page
Racing Hometown: Nashville, TN

Year	Rank	Starts	Poles	1	2	3	4	5	6–10	Laps	Laps Led	Races Led	Miles	$
1951	N/A	1	0	0	0	0	0	0	0		0	0		25
Lifetime		1	0	0	0	0	0	0	0		0	0		$25

Year	Rank	Starts	Poles	1	2	3	4	5	6–10	Laps	Laps Led	Races Led	Miles	$

Harold Painter

William Harold Painter
Racing Hometown: Greenville, NC

Year	Rank	Starts	Poles	1	2	3	4	5	6–10	Laps	Laps Led	Races Led	Miles	$
1965	132	1	0	0	0	0	0	0	0		0	0		100
Lifetime		1	0	0	0	0	0	0	0		0	0		$100

Bud Palmer

Bud Palmer
Racing Hometown: Nassau, NY

Year	Rank	Starts	Poles	1	2	3	4	5	6–10	Laps	Laps Led	Races Led	Miles	$
1955	188	1	0	0	0	0	0	0	0	36	0	0	148	35
1956	274	1	0	0	0	0	0	0	0		0	0		0
Lifetime		2	0	0	0	0	0	0	0	36	0	0	148	$35

Clyde Palmer

Clyde Palmer
Racing Hometown: Monte Vista, CA

Year	Rank	Starts	Poles	1	2	3	4	5	6–10	Laps	Laps Led	Races Led	Miles	$
1954	NR	2	0	0	0	0	1	0	1	526	0	0	263	450
1955	115	2	0	0	0	1	0	0	0	154	0	0	154	470
1956	34	11	0	0	2	1	0	1	2	1,730	296	2	1,381	2,755
1957	67	6	0	0	0	1	0	0	0	578	0	0	380	795
1961	188	1	0	0	0	0	0	0	0	16	0	0	16	25
Lifetime		22	0	0	2	3	1	1	3	3,004	296	2	2,193	$4,495

Ernest Palmer

Ernest Palmer
Racing Hometown: Nassau, NY

Year	Rank	Starts	Poles	1	2	3	4	5	6–10	Laps	Laps Led	Races Led	Miles	$
1954	202	1	0	0	0	0	0	0	0	20	0	0	82	0
Lifetime		1	0	0	0	0	0	0	0	20	0	0	82	$0

Norm Palmer

Norm Palmer
B: 5/30/1940 *Killed in late 1980s. Drove off cliff, then struck by Mack truck after climbing to safety.*
Racing Hometown: Torrance, CA

Year	Rank	Starts	Poles	1	2	3	4	5	6–10	Laps	Laps Led	Races Led	Miles	$
1977	55	3	0	0	0	0	0	0	1	239	0	0	620	4,560
1978	73	2	0	0	0	0	0	0	0	119	0	0	312	2,100
1979	79T	1	0	0	0	0	0	0	1	91	0	0	238	2,500
1985	98	1	0	0	0	0	0	0	0	22	0	0	58	745
Lifetime		7	0	0	0	0	0	0	2	471	0	0	1,227	$9,905

Marvin Panch

Marvin Richard Panch
B: 5/28/1926
Racing Hometown: Oakland, CA

Year	Rank	Starts	Poles	1	2	3	4	5	6–10	Laps	Laps Led	Races Led	Miles	$
1951	36	3	0	0	1	0	0	0	1		0	0		1,075
1953	60	2	0	0	0	0	0	0	0	275	0	0	378	160
1954	17	10	1	0	2	1	0	0	4	2,100	17	1	1,779	4,747
1955	14	10	0	0	2	0	2	0	0	1,597	15	1	1,654	4,385
1956	10	20	1	1	2	5	2	0	3	3,298	150	6	2,502	11,520
1957	2	42	4	6	3	6	6	1	5	6,890	449	12	4,401	24,307
1958	18	11	2	0	1	1	1	2	0	1,833	157	3	1,576	4,114
1959	66	4	0	0	0	0	0	0	0	640	0	0	860	1,050
1960	26	11	0	0	0	0	0	0	1	1,482	22	1	2,322	3,225
1961	18	9	1	1	1	0	1	0	3	1,517	129	2	2,576	30,478
1962	9	17	0	0	2	3	0	0	3	3,642	172	4	3,758	26,746
1963	13	12	2	1	2	5	1	0	3	3,510	291	6	3,742	39,102
1964	10	31	5	3	7	3	4	1	3	6,499	648	10	5,031	34,836
1965	5	20	5	4	1	4	1	2	2	4,743	856	12	4,716	64,027
1966	17	14	0	1	0	1	2	0	2	2,808	183	5	3,843	38,432
Lifetime		216	21	17	24	29	20	6	30	40,834	3,089	63	39,135	$288,204

Richie Panch

Richard Panch
B: 5/28/1954   D: 9/2/1985   *Killed in private plane crash.*
Racing Hometown: Daytona Beach, FL

Year	Rank	Starts	Poles	1	2	3	4	5	6–10	Laps	Laps Led	Races Led	Miles	$
1973	70	4	0	0	0	0	0	0	0	510	0	0	654	4,510
1974	14	28	0	0	0	1	0	1	5	6,257	1	1	6,872	52,713
1975	29	14	0	0	0	0	0	1	3	2,276	8	3	3,132	32,585
1976	92T	1	0	0	0	0	0	0	0	252	0	0	384	1,035
Lifetime		47	0	0	0	1	0	2	8	9,295	9	4	11,041	$90,843

Year	Rank	Starts	Poles	Finish						Laps	Laps Led	Races Led	Miles	$
				1	2	3	4	5	6–10	Laps	Led	Led	Miles	$

Jimmy Pardue

James Mansfield Pardue
B: 10/26/1930   D: 9/22/1964   *Killed @ Charlotte in tire test.*
Racing Hometown: N. Wilkesboro, NC

Year	Rank	Starts	Poles	1	2	3	4	5	6–10	Laps	Laps Led	Races Led	Miles	$
1955	245	1	0	0	0	0	0	0	0	10	0	0	5	0
1956	145	2	0	0	0	0	0	0	0	170	0	0	85	200
1959	NR	7	0	0	0	0	0	0	1	657	0	0	308	515
1960	17	32	0	0	0	0	0	1	10	5,004	0	0	3,704	5,610
1961	11	44	0	0	0	0	1	2	13	7,757	0	0	5,628	10,562
1962	19	29	0	1	1	1	1	1	11	7,274	200	3	4,855	12,066
1963	6	52	1	1	0	1	4	1	13	9,719	74	3	7,295	20,359
1964	5	50	2	0	2	4	4	4	10	9,412	237	5	6,613	41,598
Lifetime		217	3	2	3	6	10	9	58	40,003	511	11	28,493	$90,910

Stan Parker

Stanley L. Parker
Racing Hometown: Maitland, FL

Year	Rank	Starts	Poles	1	2	3	4	5	6–10	Laps	Laps Led	Races Led	Miles	$
1963	NR	1	0	0	0	0	0	0	0	59	0	0	18	0
Lifetime		1	0	0	0	0	0	0	0	59	0	0	18	$0

Bill Parks

William Parks

Year	Rank	Starts	Poles	1	2	3	4	5	6–10	Laps	Laps Led	Races Led	Miles	$
1956	193	2	0	0	0	0	0	0	0	205	0	0	205	110
Lifetime		2	0	0	0	0	0	0	0	205	0	0	205	$110

Paul Parks

Paul Parks
Racing Hometown: Columbus, OH

Year	Rank	Starts	Poles	1	2	3	4	5	6–10	Laps	Laps Led	Races Led	Miles	$
1950	44	6	0	0	0	0	0	0	1	95	0	0	95	375
1951	N/A	1	0	0	0	0	0	0	0	0	0	0	0	25
1953	181	1	0	0	0	0	0	0	0	33	0	0	17	25
1960	NR	3	0	0	0	0	0	0	0	273	0	0	537	250
1961	155	2	0	0	0	0	0	0	0	208	0	0	520	200
Lifetime		13	0	0	0	0	0	0	1	609	0	0	1,168	$800

Bud Parnell

William Parnell
Racing Hometown: College Park, GA

Year	Rank	Starts	Poles	1	2	3	4	5	6–10	Laps	Laps Led	Races Led	Miles	$
1960	85	4	0	0	0	0	0	0	1	407	0	0	204	280
Lifetime		4	0	0	0	0	0	0	1	407	0	0	204	$280

Stan Parnell

Stanley Parnell
Racing Hometown: Albany, GA

Year	Rank	Starts	Poles	1	2	3	4	5	6–10	Laps	Laps Led	Races Led	Miles	$
1952	126T	1	0	0	0	0	0	0	0	159	0	0	80	50
Lifetime		1	0	0	0	0	0	0	0	159	0	0	80	$50

Wendell Parnell

Wendell Parnell

Year	Rank	Starts	Poles	1	2	3	4	5	6–10	Laps	Laps Led	Races Led	Miles	$
1969	NR	1	0	0	0	0	0	0	0	87	0	0	235	795
Lifetime		1	0	0	0	0	0	0	0	87	0	0	235	$795

Dick Parran

Richard Parran
Racing Hometown: Raleigh, NC

Year	Rank	Starts	Poles	1	2	3	4	5	6–10	Laps	Laps Led	Races Led	Miles	$
1958	169	1	0	0	0	0	0	0	0	22	0	0	22	0
Lifetime		1	0	0	0	0	0	0	0	22	0	0	22	$0

Lee Parris

Lee Parris

Year	Rank	Starts	Poles	1	2	3	4	5	6–10	Laps	Laps Led	Races Led	Miles	$
1960	NR	1	0	0	0	0	0	0	0	129	0	0	65	100
Lifetime		1	0	0	0	0	0	0	0	129	0	0	65	$100

George Parrish

George W. Parrish
Racing Hometown: Henderson, NC

Year	Rank	Starts	Poles	1	2	3	4	5	6–10	Laps	Laps Led	Races Led	Miles	$
1954	73	3	0	0	0	0	0	0	0	440	0	0	482	185
1955	42	12	0	0	0	0	0	0	1	1,057	0	0	606	750
1957	108	5	0	0	0	0	0	0	0	483	0	0	472	525
1958	136	1	0	0	0	0	0	0	0	7	0	0	2	50
Lifetime		21	0	0	0	0	0	0	1	1,987	0	0	1,561	$1,500

Year	Rank	Starts	Poles	1	2	3	4	5	6–10	Laps	Laps Led	Races Led	Miles	$

Frank Parry

Frank Parry

Year	Rank	Starts	Poles	1	2	3	4	5	6–10	Laps	Laps Led	Races Led	Miles	$
1955	NR	1	0	0	0	0	0	0	0	205	0	0	205	50
Lifetime		1	0	0	0	0	0	0	0	205	0	0	205	$50

Gene Parry

Gene Parry

Year	Rank	Starts	Poles	1	2	3	4	5	6–10	Laps	Laps Led	Races Led	Miles	$
1953	NR	1	0	0	0	0	0	0	0		0	0		25
Lifetime		1	0	0	0	0	0	0	0		0	0		$25

Jim Parsley

James Parsley
Racing Hometown: Wheaton, MD

Year	Rank	Starts	Poles	1	2	3	4	5	6–10	Laps	Laps Led	Races Led	Miles	$
1958	30	10	0	0	0	0	0	0	4	1,720	0	0	760	1,135
1959	NR	1	0	0	0	0	0	0	1	177	0	0	89	150
Lifetime		11	0	0	0	0	0	0	5	1,897	0	0	848	$1,285

Benny Parsons

Benny Parsons
B: 7/12/1941
Racing Hometown: Ellerbe, NC

Year	Rank	Starts	Poles	1	2	3	4	5	6–10	Laps	Laps Led	Races Led	Miles	$
1964	120	1	0	0	0	0	0	0	0	258	0	0	129	250
1969	56	4	0	0	0	1	0	1	1	568	0	0	1,259	7,650
1970	8	45	1	0	1	2	4	5	11	9,164	164	6	8,725	59,402
1971	11	35	0	1	2	5	1	4	5	7,981	144	4	7,633	55,896
1972	5	31	0	0	1	0	8	1	9	7,922	19	2	9,463	102,043
1973	1	28	0	1	3	3	3	5	6	9,311	374	8	**10,047**	182,321
1974	5	30	0	0	2	2	5	2	3	8,120	87	11	8,865	185,080
1975	4	30	3	1	3	3	3	1	6	8,198	496	16	8,454	214,354
1976	3	30	2	2	2	7	2	5	5	8,679	455	15	10,403	270,043
1977	3	30	3	4	3	10	0	3	2	9,410	1,399	25	10,755	359,341
1978	4	30	2	3	3	6	2	1	6	9,609	824	21	10,832	329,993
1979	5	31	1	2	2	2	5	5	5	9,335	736	12	10,574	264,930
1980	3	31	2	3	3	2	4	4	5	8,676	659	19	10,035	411,519
1981	10	31	0	3	0	3	0	4	2	6,709	537	10	7,515	311,093
1982	18	23	3	0	0	4	3	3	3	5,631	253	8	7,314	252,267
1983	29	16	0	0	2	1	0	1	1	2,847	116	7	5,285	129,760
1984	27	14	2	1	1	0	1	4	3	2,877	407	6	5,451	241,665
1985	29	14	0	0	0	0	0	1	5	2,230	8	3	4,279	94,450
1986	30	16	1	0	0	0	0	2	2	2,620	13	7	5,098	176,985
1987	16	29	0	0	3	0	1	2	3	6,975	87	9	8,864	566,484
1988	24	27	0	0	0	0	0	0	1	7,420	82	3	8,744	210,755
Lifetime		526	20	21	31	51	42	54	84	134,540	6,860	192	159,725	$4,426,287

Goldie Parsons

Gloria Parsons
B: 1941
Racing Hometown: Clemmons, NC

Year	Rank	Starts	Poles	1	2	3	4	5	6–10	Laps	Laps Led	Races Led	Miles	$
1965	NR	1	0	0	0	0	0	0	0	242	0	0	81	100
Lifetime		1	0	0	0	0	0	0	0	242	0	0	81	$100

Phil Parsons

Phillip Parsons
B: 6/21/1957
Racing Hometown: Denver, NC

Year	Rank	Starts	Poles	1	2	3	4	5	6–10	Laps	Laps Led	Races Led	Miles	$
1983	43	5	0	0	0	0	0	0	0	887	0	0	1,696	23,850
1984	24	22	0	0	0	0	0	0	3	6,286	4	1	7,762	90,700
1985	21	28	0	0	0	0	0	0	4	6,678	1	1	7,602	105,060
1986	27	17	0	0	0	0	0	1	4	3,404	1	1	6,151	85,030
1987	14	29	0	0	0	0	1	0	6	8,216	18	2	9,672	180,261
1988	9	29	0	1	1	2	1	1	9	8,494	108	10	10,287	532,043
1989	21	29	0	0	0	1	0	1	1	7,735	39	4	9,319	285,012
1990	39	9	0	0	0	0	0	0	0	2,240	0	0	2,767	90,010
1991	—	0												2,300
1992	53	2	0	0	0	0	0	0	1	567	0	0	872	58,475
1993	29	26	0	0	0	0	0	0	2	6,331	3	1	8,041	293,725
1994	50	3	0	0	0	0	0	0	0	757	0	0	922	21,415
1995	60	2	0	0	0	0	0	0	0	36	0	0	81	41,450
Lifetime		201	0	1	1	3	2	3	30	51,631	174	20	65,172	$1,809,331

Year	Rank	Starts	Poles	Finish						Laps	Laps Led	Races Led	Miles	$
				1	2	3	4	5	6–10					

Vic Parsons

Victor Arthur Parsons
B: 11/29/1939
Racing Hometown: Willowdale, Ont., Canada

Year	Rank	Starts	Poles	1	2	3	4	5	6–10	Laps	Laps Led	Races Led	Miles	$
1972	NR	1	0	0	0	0	0	0	1	380	0	0	238	800
1973	30	18	0	0	0	0	0	0	6	3,498	0	0	4,017	18,200
Lifetime		19	0	0	0	0	0	0	7	3,878	0	0	4,255	$19,000

Jim Paschal

James Roy Paschal
B: 12/5/1926
Racing Hometown: High Point, NC

Year	Rank	Starts	Poles	1	2	3	4	5	6–10	Laps	Laps Led	Races Led	Miles	$
1949	NR	1	0	0	0	0	0	0	0		0	0		0
1950	24	6	0	0	1	0	0	0	1	669	0	0	571	850
1951	15	16	0	0	0	1	3	0	3	767	33	1	846	2,450
1952	18	15	0	0	0	0	1	0	6	1,705	0	0	1,109	1,483
1953	7	24	1	1	0	1	2	2	3	1,179	73	1	1,218	5,571
1954	7	27	2	1	0	1	1	2	6	3,546	193	1	2,492	5,451
1955	8	36	2	3	3	3	2	1	8	4,751	306	7	3,222	10,586
1956	5	42	1	1	8	2	4	2	10	6,626	212	6	4,544	17,204
1957	10	35	0	0	1	2	3	3	8	4,999	0	0	2,947	7,079
1958	42	6	1	1	0	0	1	0	2	1,105	150	1	918	1,670
1959	25	6	0	0	2	0	0	1	1	1,485	0	0	1,012	2,980
1960	9	10	0	0	0	2	1	0	4	2,752	11	1	2,713	15,096
1961	9	23	1	2	4	1	2	3	4	5,464	209	4	3,665	18,100
1962	6	39	0	4	4	3	3	3	7	8,311	856	9	5,868	27,348
1963	19	32	1	5	3	5	2	0	3	6,915	400	12	4,592	20,979
1964	7	22	0	1	3	1	2	3	5	6,030	155	4	5,531	60,116
1965	35	10	0	0	0	1	2	1	0	2,403	99	3	2,210	7,805
1966	14	18	2	2	0	1	2	1	4	5,008	759	7	5,264	30,985
1967	6	45	1	4	5	5	3	3	5	9,402	1,074	16	7,228	60,123
1968	104	1	0	0	0	0	0	0	0	171	0	0	91	275
1970	NR	1	0	0	0	0	0	0	0	325	11	1	488	1,800
1971	NR	6	0	0	0	2	0	0	1	1,746	50	2	1,153	4,215
1972	NR	1	0	0	0	0	0	0	0	338	0	0	507	1,825
Lifetime		422	12	25	34	31	34	25	81	75,697	4,591	76	58,188	$303.991

John Paschall

John Paschall
Racing Hometown: Hibernia, NJ

Year	Rank	Starts	Poles	1	2	3	4	5	6–10	Laps	Laps Led	Races Led	Miles	$
1959	68	1	0	0	0	0	0	0	0	67	0	0	168	100
Lifetime		1	0	0	0	0	0	0	0	67	0	0	168	$100

Ed Paskovich

Edward Paskovich
Racing Hometown: Hackensack, NJ

Year	Rank	Starts	Poles	1	2	3	4	5	6–10	Laps	Laps Led	Races Led	Miles	$
1953	NR	2	0	0	0	0	0	0	0		0	0		50
1954	168	3	0	0	0	0	0	0	0	260	0	0	179	10
1955	89	5	0	0	0	0	0	0	1	333	0	0	346	300
Lifetime		10	0	0	0	0	0	0	1	593	0	0	525	$360

Dick Passwater

Richard Passwater
B: 1926
Racing Hometown: Indianapolis, IN

Year	Rank	Starts	Poles	1	2	3	4	5	6–10	Laps	Laps Led	Races Led	Miles	$
1952	25	6	0	0	0	0	0	1	2	1,366	0	0	1,085	945
1953	NR	14	0	1	0	0	3	2	5	993	3	1	1,125	4,555
Lifetime		20	0	1	0	0	3	3	7	2,359	3	1	2,210	$5,500

Dana Patten

Dana Patten
Racing Hometown: Enfield, NH

Year	Rank	Starts	Poles	1	2	3	4	5	6–10	Laps	Laps Led	Races Led	Miles	$
441988	48	4	0	0	0	0	0	0	0	1,059	0	0	1,446	9,595
Lifetime		4	0	0	0	0	0	0	0	1,059	0	0	1,446	$9,595

Johnny Patterson

John Patterson
B: 1931   D: 7/5/1969
Racing Hometown: Huntington, WV

Year	Rank	Starts	Poles	1	2	3	4	5	6–10	Laps	Laps Led	Races Led	Miles	$
1952	17	5	0	0	1	0	0	1	0	1,054	0	0	879	3,618
1953	25	11	0	0	0	0	0	1	1	534	0	0	410	645
1952	24	4	0	0	0	0	1	0	0	582	0	0	759	1,240

Year	Rank	Starts	Poles	Finish						Laps	Laps Led	Races Led	Miles	$
				1	2	3	4	5	6–10	Laps	Led	Led	Miles	$

Johnny Patterson *continued*

Year	Rank	Starts	Poles	1	2	3	4	5	6–10	Laps	Laps Led	Races Led	Miles	$
1955	104	1	0	0	0	0	0	0	0	342	0	0	470	225
1956	53	3	0	0	0	0	0	0	1	563	0	0	582	425
1959	111	1	0	0	0	0	0	0	0	180	0	0	248	150
Lifetime		25	0	0	1	0	1	2	2	3,255	0	0	3,347	$6,303

Don Patton

Donald Patton

Year	Rank	Starts	Poles	1	2	3	4	5	6–10	Laps	Laps Led	Races Led	Miles	$
1969	NR	1	0	0	0	0	0	0	0	441	0	0	242	500
Lifetime		1	0	0	0	0	0	0	0	441	0	0	242	$500

Donny Paul

Donald Paul
B: 1/2/1961
Racing Hometown: Berrien Springs, MI

Year	Rank	Starts	Poles	1	2	3	4	5	6–10	Laps	Laps Led	Races Led	Miles	$
1984	93	1	0	0	0	0	0	0	0	1	0	0	2	2,755
1985	90	1	0	0	0	0	0	0	0	156	0	0	234	2,620
1986	—	0												2,450
1987	98T	1	0	0	0	0	0	0	0	104	0	0	208	4,015
Lifetime		3	0	0	0	0	0	0	0	261	0	0	444	$11,840

John Paul Jr.

John Paul Jr.
B: 2/19/1960
Racing Hometown: Lawrenceville, GA

Year	Rank	Starts	Poles	1	2	3	4	5	6–10	Laps	Laps Led	Races Led	Miles	$
1991	56	2	0	0	0	0	0	0	0	167	0	0	411	8,460
Lifetime		2	0	0	0	0	0	0	0	167	0	0	411	$8,460

Kenny Paulsen

Kenneth Paulsen
Racing Hometown: Stone Park, IL

Year	Rank	Starts	Poles	1	2	3	4	5	6–10	Laps	Laps Led	Races Led	Miles	$
1956	284	1	0	0	0	0	0	0	0	40	0	0	20	50
Lifetime		1	0	0	0	0	0	0	0	40	0	0	20	$50

Ellis Pearce

Ellis Pearce (Buttercup)
Racing Hometown: Jacksonville, FL

Year	Rank	Starts	Poles	1	2	3	4	5	6–10	Laps	Laps Led	Races Led	Miles	$
1949	46T	1	0	0	0	0	0	0	1		0	0		50
Lifetime		1	0	0	0	0	0	0	1		0	0		$50

David Pearson

David Gene Pearson
B: 12/22/1934
Racing Hometown: Spartanburg, SC

Year	Rank	Starts	Poles	1	2	3	4	5	6–10	Laps	Laps Led	Races Led	Miles	$
1960	23	22	1	0	1	0	1	1	4	3,885	0	0	3,768	5,030
1961	13	19	1	3	0	2	1	1	1	3,087	247	5	3,449	51,911
1962	10	12	0	0	0	0	1	0	6	2,690	280	4	3,552	19,032
1963	8	41	2	0	3	2	5	3	6	8,697	178	6	6,503	24,986
1964	3	61	12	8	8	4	7	2	13	13,225	2,256	31	8,906	45,542
1965	40	14	1	2	2	2	1	1	3	3,242	744	8	1,803	8,925
1966	1	42	7	15	5	5	1	0	7	10,781	**3,174**	25	8,409	78,194
1967	7	22	2	2	4	3	2	0	2	5,638	667	13	5,940	72,651
1968	1	48	14	16	12	4	2	2	2	**13,097**	3,950	**37**	9,568	133,065
1969	1	51	14	11	18	9	2	2	2	**14,270**¹	3,018	**39**	11,369	229,760
1970	23	19	2	1	2	2	4	0	2	4,210	580	11	5,815	87,493
1971	51	17	2	2	4	0	2	0	1	2,998	252	10	3,118	32,010
1972	20	17	4	6	1	3	2	0	1	4,902	1,571	16	6,593	142,440
1973	13	18	8	11	2	1	0	0	0	5,338	2,658	16	7,182	228,408
1974	3	19	11	7	5	2	1	0	0	4,630	1,168	18	7,746	252,819
1975	14	21	7	3	6	2	2	0	1	5,653	1,323	18	8,579	192,141
1976	9	22	8	10	3	2	1	0	2	6,194	1,213	19	9,048	346,890
1977	13	22	5	2	7	2	2	3	0	5,694	868	17	8,180	221,272
1978	16	22	7	4	2	1	1	3	0	5,375	757	13	7,602	198,775
1979	32	9	2	1	2	0	1	0	1	2,271	264	6	3,228	99,180
1980	37	9	1	1	2	1	0	0	1	1,787	172	7	3,252	102,730
1981	70	6	1	0	0	0	0	0	2	1,309	48	3	1,876	17,150
1982	37	6	2	0	0	1	0	1	0	1,019	7	2	1,721	55,945
1983	33	10	0	0	0	1	0	0	3	1,643	18	1	3,094	71,720
1984	41	11	1	0	0	0	0	0	3	1,630	10	3	2,949	54,125
1985	36	12	0	0	0	0	0	0	1	1,418	2	1	2,641	55,625

Year	Rank	Starts	Poles	Finish						Laps	Laps Led	Races Led	Miles	$
				1	2	3	4	5	6–10					

David Pearson *continued*

Year	Rank	Starts	Poles	1	2	3	4	5	6–10	Laps	Laps Led	Races Led	Miles	$
1986	82	2	0	0	0	0	0	0	1	337	0	0	605	8,405
Lifetime		574	113	105	89	49	39	19	65	135,020	25,425	329	146,497	$2,836,224
		9th	**2nd**	**2nd**							**4th**	**6th**		

Dell Pearson

Dell Pearson
Racing Hometown: Portland, OR

Year	Rank	Starts	Poles	1	2	3	4	5	6–10	Laps	Laps Led	Races Led	Miles	$
1951	73	8	0	0	1	0	0	0	2	310	0	0	310	900
Lifetime		8	0	0	1	0	0	0	2	310	0	0	310	$900

Hugh Pearson

Hugh Pearson
B: 4/15/1947
Racing Hometown: Bakersfield, CA

Year	Rank	Starts	Poles	1	2	3	4	5	6–10	Laps	Laps Led	Races Led	Miles	$
1973	105	2	0	0	0	0	0	0	0	94	0	0	246	1,720
1974	91	2	0	0	0	0	0	0	0	116	0	0	302	1,385
1975	72	2	0	0	0	0	0	0	0	218	0	0	553	2,550
1976	81	2	0	0	0	0	0	0	0	115	0	0	301	1,930
1977	83	1	0	0	0	0	0	0	1	114	0	0	299	2,490
Lifetime		9	0	0	0	0	0	0	1	657	0	0	1,701	$10,075

Larry Pearson

Lawrence Pearson
B: 11/2/1953
Racing Hometown: Spartanburg, SC

Year	Rank	Starts	Poles	1	2	3	4	5	6–10	Laps	Laps Led	Races Led	Miles	$
1986	79	2	0	0	0	0	0	0	0	358	0	0	566	14,310
1987	50	4	0	0	0	0	0	0	1	1,162	1	1	1,435	18,555
1988	62	2	0	0	0	0	0	0	0	281	0	0	427	3,705
1989	23	29	0	0	0	0	0	0	2	7,993	5	2	9,735	156,060
1990	35	9	0	0	0	0	0	0	0	2,871	0	0	3,220	72,305
1991	37	11	0	0	0	0	0	0	0	1,543	0	0	2,662	56,570
Lifetime		57	0	0	0	0	0	0	3	14,208	6	3	18,046	$303,490

Sam Pearson

Samuel Pearson

Year	Rank	Starts	Poles	1	2	3	4	5	6–10	Laps	Laps Led	Races Led	Miles	$
1954	NR	1	0	0	0	0	0	0	0	150	0	0	75	25
Lifetime		1	0	0	0	0	0	0	0	150	0	0	75	$25

Peck Peckham

Sewell Peckham
Racing Hometown: Old Bridge, NJ

Year	Rank	Starts	Poles	1	2	3	4	5	6–10	Laps	Laps Led	Races Led	Miles	$
1954	97	3	0	0	0	0	0	0	0	354	0	0	239	35
1956	150	3	0	0	0	0	0	0	0	301	0	0	225	225
1957	40	10	0	0	0	0	0	0	0	1,060	0	0	716	950
1958	45	11	0	0	0	0	0	0	0	1,263	0	0	834	835
Lifetime		27	0	0	0	0	0	0	0	2,978	0	0	2,013	$2,045

Ken Pedersen

Kenneth Pedersen
B: 1959
Racing Hometown: San Rafael, CA

Year	Rank	Starts	Poles	1	2	3	4	5	6–10	Laps	Laps Led	Races Led	Miles	$
1995	68	1	0	0	0	0	0	0	0	25	0	0	63	9,760
Lifetime		1	0	0	0	0	0	0	0	25	0	0	63	$9,760

Nestor Peles

Nestor Peles
Racing Hometown: Glen Campbell, PA

Year	Rank	Starts	Poles	1	2	3	4	5	6–10	Laps	Laps Led	Races Led	Miles	$
1977	110T	2	0	0	0	0	0	0	0	209	0	0	473	1,330
1978	56	3	0	0	0	0	0	0	0	979	0	0	1,249	3,280
1979	96T	1	0	0	0	0	0	0	0	465	0	0	465	1,765
1980	96T	1	0	0	0	0	0	0	0	207	0	0	207	600
Lifetime		7	0	0	0	0	0	0	0	1,860	0	0	2,394	$6,975

Steve Peles

Steve Peles
B: 1961
Racing Hometown: Glen Campbell, PA

Year	Rank	Starts	Poles	1	2	3	4	5	6–10	Laps	Laps Led	Races Led	Miles	$
1979	69	2	0	0	0	0	0	0	0	641	0	0	922	2,180

Year	Rank	Starts	Poles	Finish						Laps	Laps Led	Races Led	Miles	$
				1	2	3	4	5	6–10	Laps	Led	Led	Miles	$

Steve Peles *continued*

Year	Rank	Starts	Poles	1	2	3	4	5	6–10	Laps	Led	Led	Miles	$
1980	—	0												935
Lifetime		2	0	0	0	0	0	0	0	641	0	0	922	$3,115

Gene Peltier

Gene Peltier
Racing Hometown: South Gate, CA

Year	Rank	Starts	Poles	1	2	3	4	5	6–10	Laps	Led	Led	Miles	$
1959	NR	1	0	0	0	0	0	0	0	36	0	0	14	50
Lifetime		1	0	0	0	0	0	0	0	36	0	0	14	$50

Dean Pelton

Dean Pelton
Racing Hometown: Takoma Park, MD

Year	Rank	Starts	Poles	1	2	3	4	5	6–10	Laps	Led	Led	Miles	$
1954	69	3	0	0	0	0	0	0	0	620	0	0	605	155
Lifetime		3	0	0	0	0	0	0	0	620	0	0	605	$155

Charles Pemberton

Charles Pemberton
Racing Hometown: San Jose, CA

Year	Rank	Starts	Poles	1	2	3	4	5	6–10	Laps	Led	Led	Miles	$
1954	63	2	0	0	0	0	0	0	1	525	0	0	381	200
Lifetime		2	0	0	0	0	0	0	1	525	0	0	381	$200

Joe Penland

Joseph Penland
B: 1935
Racing Hometown: Caycee, SC

Year	Rank	Starts	Poles	1	2	3	4	5	6–10	Laps	Led	Led	Miles	$
1962	102	3	0	0	0	0	0	0	0	379	0	0	190	235
1964	125T	1	0	0	0	0	0	0	0	4	0	0	12	525
1965	89	3	0	0	0	0	0	0	0	112	0	0	60	1,260
Lifetime		7	0	0	0	0	0	0	0	495	0	0	262	$2,020

Jack Pennington

Jack Pennington
Racing Hometown: Augusta, GA

Year	Rank	Starts	Poles	1	2	3	4	5	6–10	Laps	Led	Led	Miles	$
1989	75T	2	0	0	0	0	0	0	0	580	0	0	743	4,475
1990	34	14	0	0	0	0	0	0	0	3,450	7	2	5,902	95,860
Lifetime		16	0	0	0	0	0	0	0	4,030	7	2	6,645	$100,335

Bob Penrod

Robert Penrod
Racing Hometown: Atlanta, GA

Year	Rank	Starts	Poles	1	2	3	4	5	6–10	Laps	Led	Led	Miles	$
1984	90	1	0	0	0	0	0	0	0	55	0	0	84	955
Lifetime		1	0	0	0	0	0	0	0	55	0	0	84	$955

Buck Peralta

Buck Peralta
B: 11/11/1934
Racing Hometown: Lake Oswego, OR

Year	Rank	Starts	Poles	1	2	3	4	5	6–10	Laps	Led	Led	Miles	$
1974	107	1	0	0	0	0	0	0	0	121	0	0	317	1,250
Lifetime		1	0	0	0	0	0	0	0	121	0	0	317	$1,250

Bob Perry

Robert Perry
D: 1992
Racing Hometown: Hawthorne, CA

Year	Rank	Starts	Poles	1	2	3	4	5	6–10	Laps	Led	Led	Miles	$
1957	89	1	0	0	0	0	0	0	0	71	0	0	71	50
1958	128	2	0	0	0	0	0	0	0	121	0	0	317	200
1959	75	3	0	0	0	0	0	0	1	509	0	0	317	500
1960	78	3	0	0	0	0	0	0	1	256	0	0	314	475
1961	76	4	0	0	0	0	0	1	2	424	0	0	452	840
1963	47	5	0	0	0	0	0	0	0	668	0	0	1,325	1,550
1965	130	1	0	0	0	0	0	0	0	1	0	0	3	500
Lifetime		19	0	0	0	0	0	1	4	2,050	0	0	2,799	$4,115

Dale Perry

Dale Perry

Year	Rank	Starts	Poles	1	2	3	4	5	6–10	Laps	Led	Led	Miles	$
1985	84T	1	0	0	0	0	0	0	0	57	0	0	149	880
Lifetime		1	0	0	0	0	0	0	0	57	0	0	149	$880

Year	Rank	Starts	Poles	Finish						Laps	Laps Led	Races Led	Miles	$
				1	2	3	4	5	6–10					

Rod Perry

Marion Perry
B: 1924   D: 5/5/1992
Racing Hometown: Miami, FL

Year	Rank	Starts	Poles	1	2	3	4	5	6–10	Laps	Laps Led	Races Led	Miles	$
1957	NR	1	0	0	0	0	0	0	0		0	0		100
Lifetime		1	0	0	0	0	0	0	0		0	0		$100

Steve Perry

Steve Perry
B: 4/22/1955
Racing Hometown: Dallas, TX

Year	Rank	Starts	Poles	1	2	3	4	5	6–10	Laps	Laps Led	Races Led	Miles	$
1991	77	1	0	0	0	0	0	0	0	244	0	0	244	4,150
Lifetime		1	0	0	0	0	0	0	0	244	0	0	244	$4,150

Dominic Persicketti

Dominic Persicketti
Racing Hometown: Trenton, NJ

Year	Rank	Starts	Poles	1	2	3	4	5	6–10	Laps	Laps Led	Races Led	Miles	$
1954	188	1	0	0	0	0	0	0	0	25	0	0	25	0
1959	74	2	0	0	0	0	0	0	1	581	0	0	359	450
1961	NR	1	0	0	0	0	0	0	1	450	0	0	113	300
1963	141	1	0	0	0	0	0	0	0	16	0	0	8	50
Lifetime		5	0	0	0	0	0	0	2	1,072	0	0	505	$800

Natz Peters

Ronald Nathen Peters
Racing Hometown: Pinellas Park, FL

Year	Rank	Starts	Poles	1	2	3	4	5	6–10	Laps	Laps Led	Races Led	Miles	$
1983	93	1	0	0	0	0	0	0	0	103	0	0	103	800
1984	—	0												1,700
Lifetime		1	0	0	0	0	0	0	0	103	0	0	103	$2,500

M. R. Peterson

M. R. Peterson (Eric)
Racing Hometown: Brooklyn, NY

Year	Rank	Starts	Poles	1	2	3	4	5	6–10	Laps	Laps Led	Races Led	Miles	$
1954	NR	1	0	0	0	0	0	0	0	6	0	0	12	0
Lifetime		1	0	0	0	0	0	0	0	6	0	0	12	$0

Terry Petris

Terry Petris
B: 6/28/1951
Racing Hometown: Bakersfield, CA

Year	Rank	Starts	Poles	1	2	3	4	5	6–10	Laps	Laps Led	Races Led	Miles	$
1986	80	2	0	0	0	0	0	0	0	149	0	0	390	3,110
1988	NR	1	0	0	0	0	0	0	0	52	0	0	136	1,150
Lifetime		3	0	0	0	0	0	0	0	201	0	0	527	$4,260

Gene Petro

Eugene Petro
Racing Hometown: Columbus, IN

Year	Rank	Starts	Poles	1	2	3	4	5	6–10	Laps	Laps Led	Races Led	Miles	$
1966	NR	1	0	0	0	0	0	0	0	35	0	0	88	100
Lifetime		1	0	0	0	0	0	0	0	35	0	0	88	$100

Paul Pettitt

Paul Pettitt
Racing Hometown: Danbury, CT

Year	Rank	Starts	Poles	1	2	3	4	5	6–10	Laps	Laps Led	Races Led	Miles	$
1950	NR	1	0	0	0	0	0	0	0		0	0		0
1951	191	4	0	0	0	0	0	0	0		0	0		50
1952	NR	3	0	0	0	0	0	0	0	198	0	0	116	60
1954	77	2	0	0	0	0	0	1	0	166	0	0	149	325
1955	154	2	0	0	0	0	0	0	0	50	0	0	25	100
Lifetime		12	0	0	0	0	0	1	0	414	0	0	290	$535

J. H. Petty

Julian H. Petty (Julie)
Racing Hometown: Greensboro, NC

Year	Rank	Starts	Poles	1	2	3	4	5	6–10	Laps	Laps Led	Races Led	Miles	$
1952	NR	1	0	0	0	0	0	0	1	193	0	0	97	125
1955	182	2	0	0	0	0	0	0	0	5	0	0	3	75
Lifetime		3	0	0	0	0	0	0	1	198	0	0	99	$200

Kyle Petty

Kyle Petty
B: 6/2/1960
Racing Hometown: Randleman, NC

Year	Rank	Starts	Poles	1	2	3	4	5	6–10	Laps	Laps Led	Races Led	Miles	$
1979	37	5	0	0	0	0	0	0	1	1,069	0	0	2,111	10,810

Year	Rank	Starts	Poles		Finish					Laps	Laps Led	Races Led	Miles	$
				1	2	3	4	5	6–10					

Kyle Petty *continued*

Year	Rank	Starts	Poles	1	2	3	4	5	6–10	Laps	Laps Led	Races Led	Miles	$
1980	28	15	0	0	0	0	0	0	6	3,722	0	0	4,941	36,350
1981	12	31	0	0	0	0	0	1	9	7,402	20	3	8,483	117,433
1982	15	29	0	0	1	0	1	0	2	6,414	13	3	7,720	126,285
1983	13	30	0	0	0	0	0	0	2	8,345	13	5	9,436	163,848
1984	16	30	0	0	0	0	0	1	5	8,400	2	1	9,302	329,920
1985	9	28	0	0	1	1	1	4	5	8,796	75	6	10,377	296,367
1986	10	29	0	1	0	1	0	2	10	8,546	17	6	10,338	403,242
1987	7	29	0	1	1	4	0	0	8	8,523	103	7	10,399	544,437
1988	13	29	0	0	0	0	0	2	6	8,883	67	3	10,514	377,092
1989	30	19	0	0	0	0	1	0	4	5,207	16	1	7,345	117,022
1990	11	29	2	1	0	0	1	0	12	8,795	852	12	10,496	746,326
1991	31	18	2	1	1	0	0	0	2	6,631	553	7	6,556	413,727
1992	5	29	3	2	0	4	3	0	8	9,059	970	8	10,940	1,107,063
1993	5	30	1	1	1	2	2	3	6	9,259	526	13	11,186	914,662
1994	15	31	0	0	0	0	1	1	5	9,085	7	2	11,104	818,832
1995	30	30	0	1	0	0	0	0	4	8,127	311	4	10,077	698,875
1996	27	28	0	0	0	0	0	0	2	8,081	72	5	9,682	689,041
Lifetime		469	8	8	5	12	10	14	97	134,344	3,617	86	161,006	$7,911,332

Lee Petty

Lee Arnold Petty
B: 3/14/1914
Racing Hometown: Randleman, NC

Year	Rank	Starts	Poles	1	2	3	4	5	6–10	Laps	Laps Led	Races Led	Miles	$
1949	2	6	0	1	2	0	0	0	2	**890**	1	1	565	3,855
1950	3	17	0	1	1	2	3	2	4	1,558	43	1	**1,407**	7,120
1951	4	32	0	1	4	2	1	3	8	1,248	99	1	1,168	7,400
1952	3	32	0	3	6	5	5	2	6	5,094	193	7	3,439	16,876
1953	2	36	0	5	4	10	4	3	6	3,021	209	6	2,201	18,447
1954	1	34	3	7	5	5	4	3	8	**5,903**	681	12	**4,060**	21,127
1955	3	42	1	6	4	5	4	1	10	6,328	769	6	4,423	18,920
1956	4	47	1	2	1	6	2	6	11	7,507	252	6	4,954	15,338
1957	4	41	3	4	4	3	3	6	13	7,466	449	11	4,595	18,326
1958	1	50	4	7	5	4	9	3	15	**9,173**	439	**14**	5,671	26,565
1959	1	42	2	11	5	7	4	0	8	8,278	**1,011**	**16**	4,977	49,220
1960	6	39	3	5	7	2	6	1	9	7,518	515	10	5,389	31,283
1961	104	3	1	1	0	1	0	0	0	433	126	2	291	1,260
1962	73	1	0	0	0	0	0	1	0	499	0	0	250	750
1963	82	3	0	0	0	0	1	0	1	291	0	0	179	600
1964	109	2	0	0	0	0	0	0	0	28	0	0	30	250
Lifetime		427	18	54	48	52	46	31	101	65,235	4,787	93	43,597	$237,337
				7th										

Maurice Petty

Maurice Petty
B: 3/27/1939
Racing Hometown: Randleman, NC

Year	Rank	Starts	Poles	1	2	3	4	5	6–10	Laps	Laps Led	Races Led	Miles	$
1960	94	2	0	0	0	0	0	0	2	375	0	0	142	290
1961	59	9	0	0	0	1	1	0	2	1,207	0	0	611	1,460
1962	57	5	0	0	0	0	1	1	1	800	0	0	443	965
1963	74	4	0	0	0	0	0	1	1	654	0	0	238	575
1964	61	6	0	0	0	0	1	1	3	1,130	0	0	587	1,540
Lifetime		26	0	0	0	1	3	3	9	4,166	0	0	2,021	$4,830

Richard Petty

Richard Lee Petty (The King)
B: 7/2/1937
Racing Hometown: Randleman, NC

Year	Rank	Starts	Poles	1	2	3	4	5	6–10	Laps	Laps Led	Races Led	Miles	$
1958	37	9	0	0	0	0	0	0	1	977	0	0	410	760
1959	15	21	0	0	1	3	1	1	3	3,648	7	1	2,419	8,111
1960	2	40	2	3	6	3	3	1	14	8,189	447	6	6,015	41,873
1961	8	42	2	2	4	4	5	3	5	7,866	703	7	5,392	25,239
1962	2	52	4	8	9	8	5	2	7	11,544	**1,396**	19	7,558	60,764
1963	2	54	8	14	9	2	4	1	9	**12,183**	2,316	29	7,873	55,964
1964	1	61	9	9	14	12	0	2	6	**14,041**	3,534	33	**9,480**	114,772
1965	38	14	7	4	4	2	0	0	0	3,697	1,169	8	1,693	16,450
1966	3	39	16	8	9	3	0	0	2	8,737	2,924	**26**	6,458	94,666
1967	1	48	19	27[1]	7	2	1	1	2	**12,739**	5,537[1]	41[1]	9,387	150,197
1968	3	49	12	16	6	5	2	2	4	12,254	**4,542**	35	8,907	99,535
1969	2	50	6	10	9	9	0	3	7	12,589	2,778	32	10,520	129,906

Year	Rank	Starts	Poles	Finish 1	2	3	4	5	6–10	Laps	Laps Led	Races Led	Miles	$

Richard Petty *continued*

Year	Rank	Starts	Poles	1	2	3	4	5	6–10	Laps	Laps Led	Races Led	Miles	$
1970	4	40	9	18	5	0	0	4	4	10,536	**5,007**	32	9,811	151,124
1971	1	46	9	21	8	7	2	0	3	**13,739**	4,932	41[1]	12,870[1]	351,071
1972	1	31	3	8	9	5	2	1	3	**10,282**	2,093	**30**	**11,996**	339,405
1973	5	28	3	6	6	1	2	0	2	8,644	1,815	16	9,286	234,389
1974	1	30	7	10	8	4	0	0	1	9,097	3,100	24	10,830	432,020
1975	1	30	3	13	5	3	0	0	3	9,082	**3,158**	**26**	10,846	481,751
1976	2	30	1	3	9	3	4	0	3	8,941	1,269	23	10,345	374,806
1977	2	30	5	5	6	6	2	1	3	8,840	1,403	24	10,418	406,608
1978	6	30	0	0	3	3	3	2	6	8,904	419	15	10,162	242,273
1979	1	31	1	5	7	2	4	5	4	9,367	1,150	16	10,933	561,934
1980	4	31	0	2	4	3	2	4	4	9,314	713	23	10,147	397,318
1981	8	31	0	3	1	4	3	1	4	7,276	546	21	8,602	396,072
1982	5	30	0	0	5	2	1	1	7	7,834	355	18	9,024	465,793
1983	4	30	0	3	1	1	1	3	12	9,439	279	16	10,696	508,884
1984	10	30	0	2	0	0	2	1	8	8,835	275	8	9,917	257,932
1985	14	28	0	0	0	1	0	0	12	7,767	105	7	8,858	306,142
1986	14	29	0	0	1	2	1	0	7	7,639	153	7	8,949	280,657
1987	8	29	0	0	1	3	2	3	5	8,306	38	8	9,985	445,227
1988	22	29	0	0	0	1	0	0	4	6,207	11	3	7,619	190,155
1989	29	25	0	0	0	0	0	0	0	5,567	9	1	7,927	133,050
1990	26	29	0	0	0	0	0	0	1	7,438	5	1	9,063	169,465
1991	24	29	0	0	0	0	0	0	1	8,341	1	1	9,644	268,035
1992	26	29	0	0	0	0	0	0	0	7,977	5	1	9,624	348,870
Lifetime		1184	126	200	157	104	52	42	157	307,836	52,194	599	303,662	$8,541,218
		1st	**1st**	**1st**						**1st**	**1st**	**1st**	**1st**	

Ritchie Petty

Ritchie Petty
B: 6/20/1968
Racing Hometown: Randleman, NC

Year	Rank	Starts	Poles	1	2	3	4	5	6–10	Laps	Laps Led	Races Led	Miles	$
1993	53	3	0	0	0	0	0	0	0	364	0	0	950	22,990
1994	81T	1	0	0	0	0	0	0	0	73	0	0	183	10,455
1995	—	0												2,050
Lifetime		4	0	0	0	0	0	0	0	437	0	0	1,133	$35,495

Eddie Pettyjohn

Edward Pettyjohn
Racing Hometown: Milton, DE

Year	Rank	Starts	Poles	1	2	3	4	5	6–10	Laps	Laps Led	Races Led	Miles	$
1973	76	2	0	0	0	0	0	0	1	491	0	0	491	2,145
1974	94	2	0	0	0	0	0	0	0	297	1	1	297	2,885
Lifetime		4	0	0	0	0	0	0	1	788	1	1	788	$5,030

Steve Pfeifer

Steve Pfeifer
B: 10/4/1938
Racing Hometown: San Francisco, CA

Year	Rank	Starts	Poles	1	2	3	4	5	6–10	Laps	Laps Led	Races Led	Miles	$
1978	99	1	0	0	0	0	0	0	0	98	0	0	245	955
1979	84	3	0	0	0	0	0	0	0	368	0	0	565	4,220
1980	77	2	0	0	0	0	0	0	0	157	0	0	411	1,805
1981	86	2	0	0	0	0	0	0	0	175	0	0	459	4,135
Lifetime		8	0	0	0	0	0	0	0	798	0	0	1,679	$11,115

Howard Phillippi

Howard Phillippi
Racing Hometown: Torrance, CA

Year	Rank	Starts	Poles	1	2	3	4	5	6–10	Laps	Laps Led	Races Led	Miles	$
1954	NR	2	0	0	0	0	0	0	0	264	0	0	232	40
1956	157	4	0	0	0	0	0	0	0	501	0	0	398	125
1957	100	3	0	0	0	0	0	0	1	334	0	0	167	200
1958	92	2	0	0	0	0	0	0	1	190	0	0	55	320
Lifetime		11	0	0	0	0	0	0	2	1,289	0	0	852	$685

Larry Phillips

Larry Gene Phillips
B: 7/3/1942
Racing Hometown: Springfield, MO

Year	Rank	Starts	Poles	1	2	3	4	5	6–10	Laps	Laps Led	Races Led	Miles	$
1976	NR	1	0	0	0	0	0	0	0	188	0	0	470	1,990
Lifetime		1	0	0	0	0	0	0	0	188	0	0	470	$1,990

Year	Rank	Starts	Poles	1	2	3	4	5	6–10	Laps	Laps Led	Races Led	Miles	$

Joe Phipps
Joseph D. Phipps
Racing Hometown: Newark, DE

Year	Rank	Starts	Poles	1	2	3	4	5	6–10	Laps	Laps Led	Races Led	Miles	$
1970	49	7	0	0	0	0	0	0	0	1,506	0	0	1,583	4,090
1971	77	2	0	0	0	0	0	0	0	73	0	0	53	920
Lifetime		9	0	0	0	0	0	0	0	1,579	0	0	1,635	$5,010

Paul Phipps
Paul Phipps

Year	Rank	Starts	Poles	1	2	3	4	5	6–10	Laps	Laps Led	Races Led	Miles	$
1954	NR	1	0	0	0	0	0	0	0	167	0	0	84	25
Lifetime		1	0	0	0	0	0	0	0	167	0	0	84	$25

Bob Pickell
Robert Pickell
Racing Hometown: Flemington, NJ

Year	Rank	Starts	Poles	1	2	3	4	5	6–10	Laps	Laps Led	Races Led	Miles	$
1967	76	3	0	0	0	0	0	0	0	467	0	0	304	1,600
Lifetime		3	0	0	0	0	0	0	0	467	0	0	304	$1,600

Wilbur Pickett
Dr. Wilbur Pickett
B: 1/3/1930
Racing Hometown: Daytona Beach, FL

Year	Rank	Starts	Poles	1	2	3	4	5	6–10	Laps	Laps Led	Races Led	Miles	$
1969	NR	1	0	0	0	0	0	0	0	92	0	0	245	1,250
Lifetime		1	0	0	0	0	0	0	0	92	0	0	245	$1,250

Andy Pierce
Andrew Pierce
Racing Hometown: Gardena, CA

Year	Rank	Starts	Poles	1	2	3	4	5	6–10	Laps	Laps Led	Races Led	Miles	$
1951	N/A	3	1	0	0	0	0	0	0	98	0	0	49	75
Lifetime		3	1	0	0	0	0	0	0	98	0	0	49	$75

Jug Pierce
Jug Pierce

Year	Rank	Starts	Poles	1	2	3	4	5	6–10	Laps	Laps Led	Races Led	Miles	$
1958	NR	1	0	0	0	0	0	0	0	53	0	0	18	50
Lifetime		1	0	0	0	0	0	0	0	53	0	0	18	$50

Ed Pimm
Edward George Pimm
B: 5/3/1956
Racing Hometown: Newburg, NY

Year	Rank	Starts	Poles	1	2	3	4	5	6–10	Laps	Laps Led	Races Led	Miles	$
1987	63	3	0	0	0	0	0	0	0	243	1	1	595	8,010
1988	60	2	0	0	0	0	0	0	0	502	0	0	794	13,350
Lifetime		5	0	0	0	0	0	0	0	745	1	1	1,388	$21,360

Tom Pistone
Thomas Pistone (Tiger)
B: 3/17/1929
Racing Hometown: Chicago, IL

Year	Rank	Starts	Poles	1	2	3	4	5	6–10	Laps	Laps Led	Races Led	Miles	$
1955	NR	1	0	0	0	0	0	0	0	28	0	0	18	0
1956	252	3	0	0	0	0	0	0	0	355	0	0	158	125
1957	61	2	0	0	0	1	0	0	0	588	0	0	294	1,260
1959	6	22	0	2	2	4	2	2	6	3,902	181	7	2,966	12,725
1960	18	21	0	0	0	1	0	1	6	4,137	183	4	3,728	6,714
1961	38	4	0	0	0	0	0	0	3	576	0	0	1,081	2,050
1962	131	1	0	0	0	0	0	0	0	2	0	0	5	250
1965	32	33	1	0	1	0	1	2	4	3,334	0	0	1,906	10,050
1966	37	28	4	0	3	1	0	2	0	4,090	385	8	2,221	7,775
1967	68	9	0	0	0	1	0	0	4	1,455	0	0	753	2,495
1968	52	7	0	0	0	1	1	1	1	1,531	43	2	747	2,250
Lifetime		131	5	2	6	9	4	8	24	19,998	792	21	13,875	$45,694

Ted Pitcher
Theodore Pitcher

Year	Rank	Starts	Poles	1	2	3	4	5	6–10	Laps	Laps Led	Races Led	Miles	$
1955	120	2	0	0	0	0	0	0	0	219	0	0	110	110
Lifetime		2	0	0	0	0	0	0	0	219	0	0	110	$110

Blackie Pitt
William H. Pitt
B: 3/18/1925
Racing Hometown: Rocky Mount, NC

Year	Rank	Starts	Poles	1	2	3	4	5	6–10	Laps	Laps Led	Races Led	Miles	$
1954	11	27	0	0	0	0	0	0	6	3,731	0	0	2,507	1,925

Year	Rank	Starts	Poles	Finish						Laps	Laps Led	Races Led	Miles	$
				1	2	3	4	5	6–10					

Blackie Pitt *continued*

Year	Rank	Starts	Poles	1	2	3	4	5	6–10	Laps	Laps Led	Races Led	Miles	$
1955	21	20	0	0	0	0	0	0	7	2,532	0	0	1,744	1,835
1956	26	27	0	0	0	0	0	0	5	2,702	0	0	1,754	1,545
1958	69	7	0	0	0	0	0	0	1	361	0	0	217	315
Lifetime		81	0	0	0	0	0	0	19	9,326	0	0	6,222	$5,410

Brownie Pitt

Brownie Pitt
Racing Hometown: Rocky Mount, NC

Year	Rank	Starts	Poles	1	2	3	4	5	6–10	Laps	Laps Led	Races Led	Miles	$
1956	NR	1	0	0	0	0	0	0	0	49	0	0	44	100
Lifetime		1	0	0	0	0	0	0	0	49	0	0	44	$100

Chuck Pittinger

Chuck Pittinger

Year	Rank	Starts	Poles	1	2	3	4	5	6–10	Laps	Laps Led	Races Led	Miles	$
1981	NR	1	0	0	0	0	0	0	0	80	0	0	210	1,155
Lifetime		1	0	0	0	0	0	0	0	80	0	0	210	$1,155

Clyde Pittinger

Clyde Pittinger
Racing Hometown: Newton, NJ

Year	Rank	Starts	Poles	1	2	3	4	5	6–10	Laps	Laps Led	Races Led	Miles	$
1952	NR	3	0	0	0	0	0	0	0	703	0	0	633	140
Lifetime		3	0	0	0	0	0	0	0	703	0	0	633	$140

Art Plas

Arthur Plas
Racing Hometown: Eryia, OH

Year	Rank	Starts	Poles	1	2	3	4	5	6–10	Laps	Laps Led	Races Led	Miles	$
1951	N/A	1	0	0	0	0	0	0	0		0	0		25
1952	NR	1	0	0	0	0	0	0	0	46	0	0	23	25
Lifetime		2	0	0	0	0	0	0	0	46	0	0	23	$50

Ray Platte

Raymond Platte
B: 1926   D: 7/21/1963   *Died from injuries in modified race @ S. Boston, VA, 7/20/63.*
Racing Hometown: Norfolk, VA

Year	Rank	Starts	Poles	1	2	3	4	5	6–10	Laps	Laps Led	Races Led	Miles	$
1955	195	1	0	0	0	0	0	0	0	339	0	0	466	100
Lifetime		1	0	0	0	0	0	0	0	339	0	0	466	$100

Dave Pletcher

David Pletcher
B: 1/26/1952
Racing Hometown: Clearwater, FL

Year	Rank	Starts	Poles	1	2	3	4	5	6–10	Laps	Laps Led	Races Led	Miles	$
1987	73	2	0	0	0	0	0	0	0	210	0	0	548	4,915
1988	77T	1	0	0	0	0	0	0	0	464	0	0	472	2,015
Lifetime		3	0	0	0	0	0	0	0	674	0	0	1,020	$6,930

Jerry Plotts

Jerry Plotts
Racing Hometown: Sacramento, CA

Year	Rank	Starts	Poles	1	2	3	4	5	6–10	Laps	Laps Led	Races Led	Miles	$
1961	186	1	0	0	0	0	0	0	0	30	0	0	30	25
Lifetime		1	0	0	0	0	0	0	0	30	0	0	30	$25

Charles Poalillo

Charles Poalillo

Year	Rank	Starts	Poles	1	2	3	4	5	6–10	Laps	Laps Led	Races Led	Miles	$
1984	NR	1	0	0	0	0	0	0	0	159	0	0	398	2,050
1985	NR	1	0	0	0	0	0	0	0	22	0	0	55	1,395
Lifetime		2	0	0	0	0	0	0	0	181	0	0	453	$3,445

Bill Polich

William Polich
Racing Hometown: Dana Point, CA

Year	Rank	Starts	Poles	1	2	3	4	5	6–10	Laps	Laps Led	Races Led	Miles	$
1976	74	2	0	0	0	0	0	0	0	167	0	0	438	2,155
Lifetime		2	0	0	0	0	0	0	0	167	0	0	438	$2,155

Dick Poling

Richard Poling
Racing Hometown: Sumter, SC

Year	Rank	Starts	Poles	1	2	3	4	5	6–10	Laps	Laps Led	Races Led	Miles	$
1969	50	12	0	0	0	0	0	0	0	1,305	0	0	1,630	5,467
1971	66	3	0	0	0	0	0	0	0	249	0	0	393	915
Lifetime		15	0	0	0	0	0	0	0	1,554	0	0	2,022	$6,382

Year	Rank	Starts	Poles	Finish						Laps	Laps Led	Races Led	Miles	$
				1	2	3	4	5	6–10	Laps				

Tony Polito

Tony Polito
Racing Hometown: Pompton Lakes, NJ

Year	Rank	Starts	Poles	1	2	3	4	5	6–10	Laps	Laps Led	Races Led	Miles	$
1953	144T	1	0	0	0	0	0	0	0		0	0		25
Lifetime		1	0	0	0	0	0	0	0		0	0		$25

Hank Pollard

Hank Pollard

Year	Rank	Starts	Poles	1	2	3	4	5	6–10	Laps	Laps Led	Races Led	Miles	$
1952	NR	1	0	0	0	0	0	0	0	4	0	0	2	25
Lifetime		1	0	0	0	0	0	0	0	4	0	0	2	$25

Larry Pollard

Lawrence Pollard
B: 5/5/1954
Racing Hometown: Victoria, B.C., Canada

Year	Rank	Starts	Poles	1	2	3	4	5	6–10	Laps	Laps Led	Races Led	Miles	$
1987	NR	4	0	0	0	0	0	0	0	1,415	0	0	1,324	19,130
Lifetime		4	0	0	0	0	0	0	0	1,415	0	0	1,324	$19,130

Al Pombo

Al Pombo
B: 1928
Racing Hometown: Fresno, CA

Year	Rank	Starts	Poles	1	2	3	4	5	6–10	Laps	Laps Led	Races Led	Miles	$
1956	199	2	0	0	0	0	0	0	0	334	0	0	273	90
1960	134	1	0	0	0	0	0	0	0	52	0	0	52	50
Lifetime		3	0	0	0	0	0	0	0	386	0	0	325	$140

Lennie Pond

Lennie Pond
B: 8/11/1940
Racing Hometown: Ettrick, VA

Year	Rank	Starts	Poles	1	2	3	4	5	6–10	Laps	Laps Led	Races Led	Miles	$
1969	83T	1	0	0	0	0	0	0	0	73	0	0	74	650
1970	NR	1	0	0	0	0	0	0	0	88	0	0	134	1,020
1973	23	23	0	0	0	0	1	0	8	5,850	4	2	5,472	25,610
1974	18	22	0	0	0	0	1	4	6	6,684	17	6	7,191	55,990
1975	21	22	0	0	3	0	1	2	3	5,859	275	8	6,361	59,265
1976	5	30	0	0	2	0	4	4	9	8,182	217	10	10,055	159,701
1977	30	14	0	0	0	0	2	2	2	3,154	5	3	3,713	49,440
1978	7	28	5	1	2	2	1	5	8	8,443	319	12	9,412	181,096
1979	29	15	0	0	0	0	0	0	2	3,043	14	2	3,864	42,970
1980	30	17	0	0	0	1	1	0	5	3,396	68	6	4,512	62,265
1981	34	12	0	0	0	0	0	0	0	3,083	0	0	3,446	29,045
1982	33	13	0	0	0	0	0	0	2	2,490	1	1	3,193	45,715
1983	34	10	0	0	0	0	0	0	2	2,288	3	1	2,911	41,530
1984	38	12	0	0	0	0	0	0	2	3,590	0	0	3,350	54,200
1985	33	12	0	0	0	0	0	0	2	2,831	3	2	4,320	70,640
1988	NR	1	0	0	0	0	0	0	0	383	0	0	208	2,375
1989	64	1	0	0	0	0	0	0	0	394	0	0	296	3,475
Lifetime		234	5	1	7	3	11	17	49	59,831	926	53	68,510	$884,987

Bobby Poole

Robert Poole

Year	Rank	Starts	Poles	1	2	3	4	5	6–10	Laps	Laps Led	Races Led	Miles	$
1973	NR	1	0	0	0	0	0	0	0	2	0	0	1	250
Lifetime		1	0	0	0	0	0	0	0	2	0	0	1	$250

Junior Pooler

Junior Pooler

Year	Rank	Starts	Poles	1	2	3	4	5	6–10	Laps	Laps Led	Races Led	Miles	$
1951	N/A	1	0	0	0	0	0	0	0		0	0		25
Lifetime		1	0	0	0	0	0	0	0	0	0	0	0	$25

Bill Poor

C. William Poor Jr.
Racing Hometown: Wheaton, MO

Year	Rank	Starts	Poles	1	2	3	4	5	6–10	Laps	Laps Led	Races Led	Miles	$
1956	NR	1	0	0	0	0	0	0	0	364	0	0	182	200
1957	NR	2	0	0	0	0	0	0	0	167	0	0	84	160
1958	26	24	0	0	0	0	0	1	6	3,880	0	0	1,947	3,115
1959	93	4	0	0	0	0	0	0	0	484	0	0	219	190
Lifetime		31	0	0	0	0	0	1	6	4,895	0	0	2,431	$3,665

Year	Rank	Starts	Poles	1	2	3	4	5	6–10	Laps	Laps Led	Races Led	Miles	$

Don Porter

Donald Porter
B: 1927   D: 7/13/1958   *Killed in race @ Portland, OR.*
Racing Hometown: Redding, CA

Year	Rank	Starts	Poles	1	2	3	4	5	6–10	Laps	Laps Led	Races Led	Miles	$
1956	160	3	0	0	0	0	0	0	0	179	0	0	140	100
1957	49	6	0	0	0	0	0	0	4	722	0	0	456	810
Lifetime		9	0	0	0	0	0	0	4	901	0	0	596	$910

Lloyd Porter

Lloyd Porter

Year	Rank	Starts	Poles	1	2	3	4	5	6–10	Laps	Laps Led	Races Led	Miles	$
1951	N/A	3	0	0	0	0	0	0	0		0	0		75
Lifetime		3	0	0	0	0	0	0	0		0	0		$75

Marvin Porter

Marvin Porter
B: 1924
Racing Hometown: Lakewood, CA

Year	Rank	Starts	Poles	1	2	3	4	5	6–10	Laps	Laps Led	Races Led	Miles	$
1957	44	6	0	1	1	0	0	0	1	771	1	1	632	1,770
1958	NR	6	0	0	0	0	0	0	2	542	0	0	433	565
1959	46	7	0	0	0	1	1	0	2	1,696	0	0	706	1,940
1960	69	3	0	1	0	0	0	0	0	223	61	2	295	2,100
1961	49	8	0	0	0	0	0	1	0	1,096	0	0	1,252	2,070
1963	79	2	0	0	0	0	0	0	0	202	0	0	545	1,100
1964	56	1	0	0	0	0	0	0	1	179	0	0	483	1,150
1967	115	1	0	0	0	0	0	0	0	15	0	0	41	500
Lifetime		34	0	2	1	1	1	1	6	4,724	62	3	4,387	$11,195

Randy Porter

Randall Porter
B: 7/6/1964
Racing Hometown: Greenville, SC

Year	Rank	Starts	Poles	1	2	3	4	5	6–10	Laps	Laps Led	Races Led	Miles	$
1992	62T	2	0	0	0	0	0	0	0	502	0	0	962	12,475
Lifetime		2	0	0	0	0	0	0	0	502	0	0	962	$12,475

Sam Posey

Samuel Posey
B: 5/26/1944
Racing Hometown: Sharon, CT

Year	Rank	Starts	Poles	1	2	3	4	5	6–10	Laps	Laps Led	Races Led	Miles	$
1970	NR	1	0	0	0	0	0	0	0	82	0	0	215	900
Lifetime		1	0	0	0	0	0	0	0	82	0	0	215	$900

Bob Potter

Robert Potter
Racing Hometown: Duluth, MN

Year	Rank	Starts	Poles	1	2	3	4	5	6–10	Laps	Laps Led	Races Led	Miles	$
1959	105	2	0	0	0	0	0	0	0	46	0	0	115	150
1960	50	3	0	0	0	0	0	0	1	708	0	0	822	640
Lifetime		5	0	0	0	0	0	0	1	754	0	0	937	$790

John Potter

John Potter
Racing Hometown: Inglewood, CA

Year	Rank	Starts	Poles	1	2	3	4	5	6–10	Laps	Laps Led	Races Led	Miles	$
1959	85	2	0	0	0	0	0	0	2	549	0	0	277	550
1960	114	2	0	0	0	0	0	0	0	126	0	0	158	150
Lifetime		4	0	0	0	0	0	0	2	675	0	0	435	$700

Mike Potter

Michael Potter
B: 7/4/1949
Racing Hometown: Johnson City, TN

Year	Rank	Starts	Poles	1	2	3	4	5	6–10	Laps	Laps Led	Races Led	Miles	$
1979	67	4	0	0	0	0	0	0	0	1,021	0	0	835	3,165
1980	64	3	0	0	0	0	0	0	0	450	0	0	535	2,370
1981	92	6	0	0	0	0	0	0	0	1,051	0	0	1,351	14,500
1982	97	2	0	0	0	0	0	0	0	322	0	0	645	3,535
1983	39	11	0	0	0	0	0	0	0	1,916	0	0	2,321	21,275
1984	NR	1	0	0	0	0	0	0	0	9	0	0	9	710
1985	42	6	0	0	0	0	0	0	0	1,434	0	0	1,721	10,855
1986	67	3	0	0	0	0	0	0	0	470	0	0	476	5,890
1987	45	6	0	0	0	0	0	0	0	1,285	0	0	1,388	13,290
1988	83T	1	0	0	0	0	0	0	0	44	0	0	110	3,000
1989	93T	1	0	0	0	0	0	0	0	137	0	0	187	2,455
1990	60	3	0	0	0	0	0	0	0	463	0	0	652	11,275
1992	36	11	0	0	0	0	0	0	0	1,869	0	0	3,151	74,710

Year	Rank	Starts	Poles	Finish						Laps	Laps Led	Races Led	Miles	$
				1	2	3	4	5	6–10	Laps	Led	Led	Miles	$

Mike Potter *continued*

Year	Rank	Starts	Poles	1	2	3	4	5	6–10	Laps	Laps Led	Races Led	Miles	$
1993	66	2	0	0	0	0	0	0	0	236	0	0	241	14,715
Lifetime		60	0	0	0	0	0	0	0	10,707	0	0	13,623	$181,795

George Poulos

George Poulos
B: 5/21/1932
Racing Hometown: Charlotte, NC

Year	Rank	Starts	Poles	1	2	3	4	5	6–10	Laps	Laps Led	Races Led	Miles	$
1967	46	23	0	0	0	0	0	0	1	2,872	0	0	1,457	3,040
Lifetime		23	0	0	0	0	0	0	1	2,872	0	0	1,457	$3,040

Charles Powell

Charles Powell
Racing Hometown: Paramont, CA

Year	Rank	Starts	Poles	1	2	3	4	5	6–10	Laps	Laps Led	Races Led	Miles	$
1965	127	1	0	0	0	0	0	0	0	1	0	0	3	500
1966	134	1	0	0	0	0	0	0	0	1	0	0	3	500
Lifetime		2	0	0	0	0	0	0	0	2	0	0	5	$1,000

Floyd Powell

John Floyd Powell
B: 1931   D: 8/23/1963   *Killed by brother-in-law Melvin Easler.*
Racing Hometown: Chesnee, SC

Year	Rank	Starts	Poles	1	2	3	4	5	6–10	Laps	Laps Led	Races Led	Miles	$
1962	110T	1	0	0	0	0	0	0	0	142	0	0	71	110
1963	69	5	0	0	0	0	0	0	2	543	0	0	667	1,315
Lifetime		6	0	0	0	0	0	0	2	685	0	0	738	$1,425

Frank Powell

Frank Powell
Racing Hometown: Pittsburgh, PA

Year	Rank	Starts	Poles	1	2	3	4	5	6–10	Laps	Laps Led	Races Led	Miles	$
1955	175T	1	0	0	0	0	0	0	0	23	0	0	12	50
Lifetime		1	0	0	0	0	0	0	0	23	0	0	12	$50

Macon Powers

Macon Powers
Racing Hometown: Vinton, VA

Year	Rank	Starts	Poles	1	2	3	4	5	6–10	Laps	Laps Led	Races Led	Miles	$
1950	129T	1	0	0	0	0	0	0	0	125	0	0	63	0
Lifetime		1	0	0	0	0	0	0	0	125	0	0	63	$0

Bill Pratt

William Pratt

Year	Rank	Starts	Poles	1	2	3	4	5	6–10	Laps	Laps Led	Races Led	Miles	$
1970	NR	1	0	0	0	0	0	0	0	5	0	0	13	630
Lifetime		1	0	0	0	0	0	0	0	5	0	0	13	$630

Hal Prentice

Hal Prentice
Racing Hometown: Ferndale, MI

Year	Rank	Starts	Poles	1	2	3	4	5	6–10	Laps	Laps Led	Races Led	Miles	$
1955	220	1	0	0	0	0	0	0	0	197	0	0	197	90
Lifetime		1	0	0	0	0	0	0	0	197	0	0	197	$90

Bob Presnell

Robert Presnell
Racing Hometown: Lenoir, NC

Year	Rank	Starts	Poles	1	2	3	4	5	6–10	Laps	Laps Led	Races Led	Miles	$
1961	99	5	0	0	0	0	0	0	1	494	0	0	201	520
Lifetime		5	0	0	0	0	0	0	1	494	0	0	201	$520

Robert Pressley

Robert E. Pressley
B: 4/8/1959
Racing Hometown: Asheville, NC

Year	Rank	Starts	Poles	1	2	3	4	5	6–10	Laps	Laps Led	Races Led	Miles	$
1994	57	3	0	0	0	0	0	0	0	587	0	0	947	39,485
1995	29	31	0	0	0	0	0	0	1	8,191	37	3	10,006	695,875
1996	32	30	0	0	0	0	1	1	1	7,948	110	7	9,678	690,465
Lifetime		64	0	0	0	0	1	1	2	16,726	147	10	20,631	$1,425,825

Albert Price

Albert Price
Racing Hometown: Greensboro, NC

Year	Rank	Starts	Poles	1	2	3	4	5	6–10	Laps	Laps Led	Races Led	Miles	$
1952	NR	1	0	0	0	0	0	0	0	37	0	0	37	25
Lifetime		1	0	0	0	0	0	0	0	37	0	0	37	$25

Year	Rank	Starts	Poles	Finish						Laps	Laps Led	Races Led	Miles	$
				1	2	3	4	5	6–10					

Baxter Price

Baxter Larry Price
B: 11/29/1938
Racing Hometown: Monroe, NC

Year	Rank	Starts	Poles	1	2	3	4	5	6–10	Laps	Laps Led	Races Led	Miles	$
1973	122	1	0	0	0	0	0	0	0	3	0	0	2	325
1975	59	3	0	0	0	0	0	0	0	331	0	0	548	1,685
1976	50	6	0	0	0	0	0	0	0	1,680	0	0	1,432	3,730
1977	33	12	0	0	0	0	0	0	0	2,566	0	0	2,706	10,890
1978	23	24	0	0	0	0	0	0	0	7,343	0	0	7,610	35,420
1979	25	24	0	0	0	0	0	0	0	6,791	0	0	6,665	45,165
1980	29	18	0	0	0	0	0	0	0	4,890	0	0	4,929	26,625
1981	96	2	0	0	0	0	0	0	0	17	0	0	11	4,000
Lifetime		90	0	0	0	0	0	0	0	23,621	0	0	23,903	$127,840

Bob Price

Robert Price
Racing Hometown: Burbank, CA

Year	Rank	Starts	Poles	1	2	3	4	5	6–10	Laps	Laps Led	Races Led	Miles	$
1958	159	2	0	0	0	0	0	0	0	146	0	0	382	110
1959	120	2	0	0	0	0	0	0	0	427	0	0	176	225
1960	80	3	0	0	0	0	0	0	0	258	0	0	314	445
1961	114	2	0	0	0	0	0	0	1	204	0	0	150	180
Lifetime		9	0	0	0	0	0	0	1	1,035	0	0	1,022	$960

Don Price

Donald Price
Racing Hometown: Trevose, PA

Year	Rank	Starts	Poles	1	2	3	4	5	6–10	Laps	Laps Led	Races Led	Miles	$
1952	126T	1	0	0	0	0	0	0	0	116	0	0	116	25
1953	143	1	0	0	0	0	0	0	0	0	0	0	0	50
Lifetime		2	0	0	0	0	0	0	0	116	0	0	116	$75

Frank Price

Frank Price
Racing Hometown: Pittston, PA

Year	Rank	Starts	Poles	1	2	3	4	5	6–10	Laps	Laps Led	Races Led	Miles	$
1953	NR	2	0	0	0	0	0	0	0		0	0		125
Lifetime		2	0	0	0	0	0	0	0		0	0		$125

Mike Price

Michael Price
Racing Hometown: Atlanta, GA

Year	Rank	Starts	Poles	1	2	3	4	5	6–10	Laps	Laps Led	Races Led	Miles	$
1959	NR	1	0	0	0	0	0	0	0	72	0	0	72	50
Lifetime		1	0	0	0	0	0	0	0	72	0	0	72	$50

Walt Price

Walter Price
B: 3/15/1935
Racing Hometown: San Fernando, CA

Year	Rank	Starts	Poles	1	2	3	4	5	6–10	Laps	Laps Led	Races Led	Miles	$
1964	128	1	0	0	0	0	0	0	0	43	0	0	116	500
1966	73	1	0	0	0	0	0	0	0	154	0	0	416	575
1967	103	1	0	0	0	0	0	0	0	51	0	0	138	500
1974	89	2	0	0	0	0	0	0	0	136	0	0	349	1,800
Lifetime		5	0	0	0	0	0	0	0	384	0	0	1,019	$3,375

Charles Prickett

Charles Prickett
Racing Hometown: Sanger, CA

Year	Rank	Starts	Poles	1	2	3	4	5	6–10	Laps	Laps Led	Races Led	Miles	$
1967	63	1	0	0	0	0	0	0	1	162	0	0	437	1,000
Lifetime		1	0	0	0	0	0	0	1	162	0	0	437	$1,000

Clyde Prickett

Clyde Prickett
Racing Hometown: Fresno, CA

Year	Rank	Starts	Poles	1	2	3	4	5	6–10	Laps	Laps Led	Races Led	Miles	$
1966	130	1	0	0	0	0	0	0	0	11	0	0	30	500
1967	75	1	0	0	0	0	0	0	0	104	0	0	281	610
1968	80	1	0	0	0	0	0	0	0	140	0	0	378	700
Lifetime		3	0	0	0	0	0	0	0	255	0	0	689	$1,810

Cotton Priddy

Thomas Priddy
B: 1929   D: 6/1956   *Killed in NASCAR Race @ LeHi, AR.*
Racing Hometown: Lousiville, KY

Year	Rank	Starts	Poles	1	2	3	4	5	6–10	Laps	Laps Led	Races Led	Miles	$
1953	131	2	0	0	0	0	0	0	0	35	0	0	144	75

Year	Rank	Starts	Poles	Finish						Laps	Laps Led	Races Led	Miles	$
				1	2	3	4	5	6–10					

Cotton Priddy *continued*

Year	Rank	Starts	Poles	1	2	3	4	5	6–10	Laps	Laps Led	Races Led	Miles	$
1956	250T	1	0	0	0	0	0	0	0	38	0	0	57	50
Lifetime		3	0	0	0	0	0	0	0	73	0	0	201	$125

Bob Prince

Robert Prince
   Racing Hometown: Detroit, MI

Year	Rank	Starts	Poles	1	2	3	4	5	6–10	Laps	Laps Led	Races Led	Miles	$
1951	N/A	1	0	0	0	0	0	0	0	199	0	0	199	25
Lifetime		1	0	0	0	0	0	0	0	199	0	0	199	$25

Talmadge Prince

Talmadge Prince (Tab)
   B: 1937   D: 2/19/1970   *Killed in Daytona 125-mile qualifying race.*
   Racing Hometown: Dublin, GA

Year	Rank	Starts	Poles	1	2	3	4	5	6–10	Laps	Laps Led	Races Led	Miles	$
1970	NR	1	0	0	0	0	0	0	0	18	0	0	45	0
Lifetime		1	0	0	0	0	0	0	0	18	0	0	45	$0

Joe Prismo

Joseph Prismo

Year	Rank	Starts	Poles	1	2	3	4	5	6–10	Laps	Laps Led	Races Led	Miles	$
1956	149	1	0	0	0	0	0	0	1	246	0	0	123	200
Lifetime		1	0	0	0	0	0	0	0	1	246	0	0	123	$200

Clem Proctor

Clem Proctor
   B: 10/16/1928   D: 1/1995
   Racing Hometown: Compton, CA

Year	Rank	Starts	Poles	1	2	3	4	5	6–10	Laps	Laps Led	Races Led	Miles	$
1960	NR	1	0	0	0	0	0	0	0	338	0	0	465	500
1961	112	2	0	0	0	0	0	0	1	100	0	0	105	250
1963	72	2	0	0	0	0	0	0	0	260	0	0	702	850
1964	130	1	0	0	0	0	0	0	0	15	0	0	41	500
1966	82	1	0	0	0	0	0	0	0	114	0	0	308	600
1972	111	1	0	0	0	0	0	0	0	37	0	0	97	685
1973	124	1	0	0	0	0	0	0	0	5	0	0	13	1,015
Lifetime		9	0	0	0	0	0	0	1	869	0	0	1,730	$4,400

Bob Pronger

Robert Pronger
   B: 1/22/1922   D: 6/17/1971   *Declared missing after disappearing at the hands of mafia agents.*
   Racing Hometown: Blue Island, IL

Year	Rank	Starts	Poles	1	2	3	4	5	6–10	Laps	Laps Led	Races Led	Miles	$
1951	N/A	1	0	0	0	0	0	0	0	332	0	0	415	50
1952	139	2	0	0	0	0	0	0	0	189	0	0	224	25
1953	177	1	1	0	0	0	0	0	0	5	0	0	21	0
1958	151	2	0	0	0	0	0	0	0	16	0	0	66	25
1959	84	2	0	0	0	0	0	0	0	156	0	0	390	125
1961	165	1	0	0	0	0	0	0	0	37	0	0	93	85
Lifetime		9	1	0	0	0	0	0	0	735	0	0	1,208	$310

Oren Prosser

Oren Prosser
   B: 1941
   Racing Hometown: Granada Hills, CA

Year	Rank	Starts	Poles	1	2	3	4	5	6–10	Laps	Laps Led	Races Led	Miles	$
1961	161T	1	0	0	0	0	0	0	0	73	0	0	73	50
1963	137	1	0	0	0	0	0	0	0	95	0	0	257	200
1964	113	1	0	0	0	0	0	0	0	87	0	0	235	500
Lifetime		3	0	0	0	0	0	0	0	255	0	0	564	$750

Bill Pruitt

William Pruitt
   Racing Hometown: Detroit, MI

Year	Rank	Starts	Poles	1	2	3	4	5	6–10	Laps	Laps Led	Races Led	Miles	$
1952	NR	1	0	0	0	0	0	0	0	169	0	0	169	25
Lifetime		1	0	0	0	0	0	0	0	169	0	0	169	$25

Don Pruitt

Donald Pruitt
   Racing Hometown: Burbank, CA

Year	Rank	Starts	Poles	1	2	3	4	5	6–10	Laps	Laps Led	Races Led	Miles	$
1974	126	1	0	0	0	0	0	0	0	28	0	0	73	670
Lifetime		1	0	0	0	0	0	0	0	28	0	0	73	$670

Year	Rank	Starts	Poles	Finish 1	2	3	4	5	6–10	Laps	Laps Led	Races Led	Miles	$

Ervin Pruitt

Ervin Pruitt
B: 5/11/1940
Racing Hometown: Spartanburg, SC

Year	Rank	Starts	Poles	1	2	3	4	5	6–10	Laps	Laps Led	Races Led	Miles	$
1968	79	5	0	0	0	0	0	0	1	1,376	0	0	766	1,930
1969	64	4	0	0	0	0	0	0	1	565	0	0	371	850
Lifetime		9	0	0	0	0	0	0	2	1,941	0	0	1,137	$2,780

Ray Pruitt

Raymond Pruitt
Racing Hometown: Yorktown, PA

Year	Rank	Starts	Poles	1	2	3	4	5	6–10	Laps	Laps Led	Races Led	Miles	$
1951	N/A	2	0	0	0	0	0	0	0	93	0	0	70	35
Lifetime		2	0	0	0	0	0	0	0	93	0	0	70	$35

Sherral Pruitt

Sherral Pruitt
Racing Hometown: Spartanburg, SC

Year	Rank	Starts	Poles	1	2	3	4	5	6–10	Laps	Laps Led	Races Led	Miles	$
1969	93	1	0	0	0	0	0	0	0	10	0	0	5	100
Lifetime		1	0	0	0	0	0	0	0	10	0	0	5	$100

Smokey Purser

Carl Daniel Purser
B: Late 1800s   D: 5/30/1964
Racing Hometown: Lumber City, GA

Year	Rank	Starts	Poles	1	2	3	4	5	6–10	Laps	Laps Led	Races Led	Miles	$
1952	NR	1	0	0	0	0	0	0	0		0	0		0
Lifetime		1	0	0	0	0	0	0	0		0	0		$0

Jeff Purvis

Jeffrey Thomas Purvis
B: 2/19/1959
Racing Hometown: Clarksville, TN

Year	Rank	Starts	Poles	1	2	3	4	5	6–10	Laps	Laps Led	Races Led	Miles	$
1990	56	5	0	0	0	0	0	0	0	900	0	0	747	14,370
1991	45	6	0	0	0	0	0	0	0	888	0	0	1,486	42,910
1992	44	6	0	0	0	0	0	0	0	1,418	0	0	1,280	45,545
1993	39	8	0	0	0	0	0	0	0	2,491	3	2	2,741	108,545
1994	46	7	0	0	0	0	0	0	0	1,081	0	0	2,259	78,755
1995	47	7	0	0	0	0	0	0	0	951	0	0	1,928	93,875
1996	48	4	0	0	0	0	0	0	0	532	0	0	1,364	91,127
Lifetime		43	0	0	0	0	0	0	0	8,261	3	2	11,806	$475,127

Don Puskarich

Donald Puskarich
B: 2/26/1939
Racing Hometown: Garden Grove, CA

Year	Rank	Starts	Poles	1	2	3	4	5	6–10	Laps	Laps Led	Races Led	Miles	$
1975	65	3	0	0	0	0	0	0	0	184	0	0	480	3,060
1976	62	3	0	0	0	0	0	0	0	343	0	0	876	3,770
1977	82	2	0	0	0	0	0	0	0	51	0	0	134	1,520
1978	98	1	0	0	0	0	0	0	0	36	0	0	94	700
1979	111T	1	0	0	0	0	0	0	0	47	0	0	123	855
1980	61	3	0	0	0	0	0	0	0	201	0	0	526	3,835
1981	47	3	0	0	0	0	0	0	0	211	0	0	553	4,770
1982	84T	1	0	0	0	0	0	0	0	87	0	0	228	1,870
Lifetime		17	0	0	0	0	0	0	0	1,160	0	0	3,014	$20,380

J. T. Putney

Julian Taylor Putney
B: 10/5/1928
Racing Hometown: Arden, NC

Year	Rank	Starts	Poles	1	2	3	4	5	6–10	Laps	Laps Led	Races Led	Miles	$
1964	23	17	0	0	0	1	0	0	5	4,226	0	0	3,370	7,295
1965	7	40	0	0	1	3	4	2	14	7,932	0	0	5,680	22,329
1966	8	39	0	0	1	2	1	0	5	7,836	32	2	6,460	18,653
1967	18	29	0	0	0	1	0	0	9	6,050	0	0	4,817	15,687
Lifetime		125	0	0	2	7	5	2	33	26,044	32	2	20,327	$63,964

Bud Rackley

Bud Rackley
Racing Hometown: Houston, TX

Year	Rank	Starts	Poles	1	2	3	4	5	6–10	Laps	Laps Led	Races Led	Miles	$
1955	NR	1	0	0	0	0	0	0	0	44	0	0	61	50
Lifetime		1	0	0	0	0	0	0	0	44	0	0	61	$50

Year	Rank	Starts	Poles	Finish 1	2	3	4	5	6–10	Laps	Laps Led	Races Led	Miles	$

Francis Radaker

Francis Radaker
  Racing Hometown: DuBoise, PA

Year	Rank	Starts	Poles	1	2	3	4	5	6–10	Laps	Laps Led	Races Led	Miles	$
1952	204	1	0	0	0	0	0	0	0	64	0	0	32	25
Lifetime		1	0	0	0	0	0	0	0	64	0	0	32	$25

Paul Radford

James Paul Radford
  B: 8/1932
  Racing Hometown: Ferrum, VA

Year	Rank	Starts	Poles	1	2	3	4	5	6–10	Laps	Laps Led	Races Led	Miles	$
1974	136	1	0	0	0	0	0	0	0	20	0	0	11	750
Lifetime		1	0	0	0	0	0	0	0	20	0	0	11	$750

Jack Radtke

Jack Radtke
  Racing Hometown: Grays Lake, IL

Year	Rank	Starts	Poles	1	2	3	4	5	6–10	Laps	Laps Led	Races Led	Miles	$
1955	109	1	0	0	0	0	0	0	1	38	0	0	156	150
1956	123	1	0	0	0	0	0	0	0		0	0		110
Lifetime		2	0	0	0	0	0	0	1	38	0	0	156	$260

Billy Rafter

William Fred Rafter
  B: 7/31/1929 *Deceased*
  Racing Hometown: Clarence Center, NY

Year	Rank	Starts	Poles	1	2	3	4	5	6–10	Laps	Laps Led	Races Led	Miles	$
1949	20	1	0	0	0	1	0	0	0		0	0		480
1953	144T	1	0	0	0	0	0	0	0		0	0		25
1954	201	1	0	0	0	0	0	0	0	32	0	0	131	0
1956	73	9	0	0	0	0	0	0	1	1,140	0	0	623	975
1957	127	4	0	0	0	0	0	0	1	250	0	0	304	440
1958	19	19	0	0	0	0	0	1	7	3,160	0	0	1,529	2,799
Lifetime		35	0	0	0	1	0	1	9	4,582	0	0	2,587	$4,330

Ken Ragan

Kenneth Ragan
  B: 9/12/1950
  Racing Hometown: Unadilla, GA

Year	Rank	Starts	Poles	1	2	3	4	5	6–10	Laps	Laps Led	Races Led	Miles	$
1983	35	8	0	0	0	0	0	0	0	1,984	0	0	3,526	27,905
1984	40	10	0	0	0	0	0	0	0	1,839	1	1	3,467	37,045
1985	47	7	0	0	0	0	0	0	0	1,359	0	0	2,255	35,995
1986	39	7	0	0	0	0	0	0	0	1,284	1	1	2,503	33,890
1987	41	6	0	0	0	0	0	0	0	1,259	0	0	2,354	30,575
1988	47	5	0	0	0	0	0	0	0	731	0	0	1,426	15,755
1989	54	3	0	0	0	0	0	0	0	550	0	0	922	7,295
1990	55	4	0	0	0	0	0	0	0	398	0	0	745	23,020
Lifetime		50	0	0	0	0	0	0	0	9,404	2	2	17,200	$211,480

Walt Ragan

Walter Ragan
  Racing Hometown: Conowingo, MD

Year	Rank	Starts	Poles	1	2	3	4	5	6–10	Laps	Laps Led	Races Led	Miles	$
1952	NR	1	0	0	0	0	0	0	0	13	0	0	13	25
Lifetime		1	0	0	0	0	0	0	0	13	0	0	13	$25

Lloyd Ragon

Lloyd M. Ragon
  Racing Hometown: Syracuse, NY

Year	Rank	Starts	Poles	1	2	3	4	5	6–10	Laps	Laps Led	Races Led	Miles	$
1958	77	2	0	0	0	0	0	0	1	34	0	0	139	230
Lifetime		2	0	0	0	0	0	0	1	34	0	0	139	$230

Buddy Ragsdale

Buddy Ragsdale

Year	Rank	Starts	Poles	1	2	3	4	5	6–10	Laps	Laps Led	Races Led	Miles	$
1958	NR	1	0	0	0	0	0	0	0	130	0	0	130	150
Lifetime		1	0	0	0	0	0	0	0	130	0	0	130	$150

Bobby Rahal

Robert Woodward Rahal
  B: 1/10/1953
  Racing Hometown: Dublin, OH

Year	Rank	Starts	Poles	1	2	3	4	5	6–10	Laps	Laps Led	Races Led	Miles	$
1984	91T	1	0	0	0	0	0	0	0	44	0	0	115	875
Lifetime		1	0	0	0	0	0	0	0	44	0	0	115	$875

Year	Rank	Starts	Poles	Finish						Laps	Laps Led	Races Led	Miles	$
				1	2	3	4	5	6–10					

Ansel Rakestraw

Ansel Rakestraw
Racing Hometown: Hiram, GA

Year	Rank	Starts	Poles	1	2	3	4	5	6–10	Laps	Laps Led	Races Led	Miles	$
1956	NR	1	0	0	0	0	0	0	0	48	0	0	197	100
1957	NR	2	0	0	0	0	0	0	0	276	0	0	138	200
Lifetime		3	0	0	0	0	0	0	0	324	0	0	335	$300

Benny Rakestraw

Benjamin Rakestraw
Racing Hometown: Dallas, GA

Year	Rank	Starts	Poles	1	2	3	4	5	6–10	Laps	Laps Led	Races Led	Miles	$
1956	NR	1	0	0	0	0	0	0	1	156	0	0	78	100
1958	174	5	0	0	0	0	0	0	1	756	0	0	384	400
1959	NR	7	0	0	0	0	1	0	0	1,144	0	0	774	1,165
Lifetime		13	0	0	0	0	1	0	2	2,056	0	0	1,236	$1,665

Tyre Rakestraw

Tyrell Rakestraw
Racing Hometown: Hiram, GA

Year	Rank	Starts	Poles	1	2	3	4	5	6–10	Laps	Laps Led	Races Led	Miles	$
1953	NR	1	0	0	0	0	0	0	0	308	0	0	424	160
Lifetime		1	0	0	0	0	0	0	0	308	0	0	424	$160

Wilbur Rakestraw

Wilbur Rakestraw
B: 6/6/1928
Racing Hometown: Dallas, GA

Year	Rank	Starts	Poles	1	2	3	4	5	6–10	Laps	Laps Led	Races Led	Miles	$
1956	NR	1	0	0	0	0	0	0	0	29	0	0	15	100
1958	NR	9	0	0	0	0	1	0	2	1,688	0	0	1,443	1,655
1959	NR	3	0	0	0	0	0	0	1	413	0	0	815	1,025
1960	41	12	0	0	0	0	0	0	1	1,862	0	0	2,038	2,695
1961	95	5	0	0	0	0	0	0	1	360	0	0	306	635
Lifetime		30	0	0	0	0	1	0	5	4,352	0	0	4,616	$6,110

Tom Raley

Thomas E. Raley
B: 12/16/1936
Racing Hometown: North Beach, MD

Year	Rank	Starts	Poles	1	2	3	4	5	6–10	Laps	Laps Led	Races Led	Miles	$
1967	84	9	0	0	0	0	0	0	0	632	0	0	363	925
Lifetime		9	0	0	0	0	0	0	0	632	0	0	363	$925

Ted Rambo

Theodore Rambo
Racing Hometown: New Bloomington, OH

Year	Rank	Starts	Poles	1	2	3	4	5	6–10	Laps	Laps Led	Races Led	Miles	$
1954	71	5	0	0	0	0	0	0	1	296	0	0	260	200
Lifetime		5	0	0	0	0	0	0	1	296	0	0	260	$200

Nick Rampling

Nicholas Rampling
Racing Hometown: Cooksville, Ont., Canada

Year	Rank	Starts	Poles	1	2	3	4	5	6–10	Laps	Laps Led	Races Led	Miles	$
1966	97	3	0	0	0	0	0	0	0	472	0	0	209	230
Lifetime		3	0	0	0	0	0	0	0	472	0	0	209	$230

E. C. Ramsey

E. C. Ramsey
Racing Hometown: Greenville, SC

Year	Rank	Starts	Poles	1	2	3	4	5	6–10	Laps	Laps Led	Races Led	Miles	$
1952	47	7	0	0	0	0	0	0	0	826	0	0	693	260
Lifetime		7	0	0	0	0	0	0	0	826	0	0	693	$260

Darvin Randahl

Darvin Randahl
Racing Hometown: Rio, WI

Year	Rank	Starts	Poles	1	2	3	4	5	6–10	Laps	Laps Led	Races Led	Miles	$
1956	65	7	0	0	0	0	0	0	1	492	0	0	301	710
Lifetime		7	0	0	0	0	0	0	1	492	0	0	301	$710

Maurice Randall

Maurice Randall
B: 11/28/1952
Racing Hometown: Charlotte, MI

Year	Rank	Starts	Poles	1	2	3	4	5	6–10	Laps	Laps Led	Races Led	Miles	$
1984	NR	1	0	0	0	0	0	0	0	50	0	0	30	1,010
1985	67	3	0	0	0	0	0	0	0	104	0	0	107	3,450
Lifetime		4	0	0	0	0	0	0	0	154	0	0	137	$4,460

Year	Rank	Starts	Poles	Finish 1	2	3	4	5	6–10	Laps	Laps Led	Races Led	Miles	$

Roscoe Rann

Roscoe Rann
Racing Hometown: Memphis, TN

Year	Rank	Starts	Poles	1	2	3	4	5	6–10	Laps	Led	Led	Miles	$
1954	NR	1	0	0	0	0	0	0	0	33	0	0	50	100
1955	97	2	0	0	0	0	0	0	0	271	0	0	407	110
Lifetime		3	0	0	0	0	0	0	0	304	0	0	456	$210

Jim Raptis

James Al Raptis
B: 6/21/1947
Racing Hometown: Woodstock, GA

Year	Rank	Starts	Poles	1	2	3	4	5	6–10	Laps	Led	Led	Miles	$
1977	95	3	0	0	0	0	0	0	0	116	0	0	252	2,530
Lifetime		3	0	0	0	0	0	0	0	116	0	0	252	$2,530

Dick Rathmann

Richard R. Rathmann *Born as:* Jim Rathmann *(swapped identities with brother in 1940s).*
B: 1/6/1924
Racing Hometown: Los Angeles, CA

Year	Rank	Starts	Poles	1	2	3	4	5	6–10	Laps	Led	Led	Miles	$
1951	8	15	0	0	3	1	0	0	3	231	0	0	131	3,225
1952	5	27	2	5	1	4	0	4	0	3,607	701	10	2,539	11,248
1953	3	34	1	5	12	1	2	1	3	2,545	542	8	2,002	20,245
1954	4	32	4	3	5	8	6	1	3	5,286	729	11	3,629	16,264
1955	18	20	3	0	2	2	3	0	1	2,296	176	5	1,601	4,368
Lifetime		128	10	13	23	16	11	6	10	13,965	2,148	34	9,902	$55,350

Jim Rathmann

James Rathmann *Born as:* Dick Rathmann *(swapped identities with brother in 1940s).*
B: 7/16/1928
Racing Hometown: Alhambra, CA

Year	Rank	Starts	Poles	1	2	3	4	5	6–10	Laps	Led	Led	Miles	$
1949	NR	1	0	0	0	0	0	0	0		0	0		0
1950	89	1	0	0	0	0	0	0	0	46	0	0	192	50
1951	N/A	1	0	0	0	0	0	0	0	76	0	0	76	0
Lifetime		3	0	0	0	0	0	0	0	122	0	0	268	$50

Ken Rauch

Kenneth Rauch

Year	Rank	Starts	Poles	1	2	3	4	5	6–10	Laps	Led	Led	Miles	$
1952	NR	1	0	0	0	0	0	0	0	133	0	0	67	25
Lifetime		1	0	0	0	0	0	0	0	133	0	0	67	$25

Bob Rauscher

Robert Rauscher

Year	Rank	Starts	Poles	1	2	3	4	5	6–10	Laps	Led	Led	Miles	$
1957	83	3	0	0	0	0	0	1	1	329	0	0	195	435
Lifetime		3	0	0	0	0	0	1	1	329	0	0	195	$435

John Ray

John Ray
Racing Hometown: Des Moines, IA

Year	Rank	Starts	Poles	1	2	3	4	5	6–10	Laps	Led	Led	Miles	$
1953	NR	1	0	0	0	0	0	0	0	202	0	0	202	25
Lifetime		1	0	0	0	0	0	0	0	202	0	0	202	$25

Johnny Ray

John Ray
B: 3/25/1937
Racing Hometown: Eastaboga, AL

Year	Rank	Starts	Poles	1	2	3	4	5	6–10	Laps	Led	Led	Miles	$
1974	80	2	0	0	0	0	0	0	0	252	0	0	670	2,435
1975	69	4	0	0	0	0	0	0	0	247	0	0	577	3,435
1976	83	2	0	0	0	0	0	0	0	145	0	0	367	3,005
Lifetime		8	0	0	0	0	0	0	0	644	0	0	1,614	$8,875

Joie Ray

Joie Ray
Racing Hometown: Portland, OR

Year	Rank	Starts	Poles	1	2	3	4	5	6–10	Laps	Led	Led	Miles	$
1952	NR	1	0	0	0	0	0	0	0		0	0		0
Lifetime		1	0	0	0	0	0	0	0		0	0		$0

Leo Ray

Leo Ray
Racing Hometown: Rapid City, SD

Year	Rank	Starts	Poles	1	2	3	4	5	6–10	Laps	Led	Led	Miles	$
1953	80T	1	0	0	0	0	0	0	1		0	0		100
Lifetime		1	0	0	0	0	0	0	0	1		0	0	$100

Year	Rank	Starts	Poles	Finish						Laps	Laps Led	Races Led	Miles	$
				1	2	3	4	5	6–10	Laps	Led	Led	Miles	$

Lee Raymond

Lee Raymond
B: 10/2/1954
Racing Hometown: Dayton, OH

Year	Rank	Starts	Poles	1	2	3	4	5	6–10	Laps	Laps Led	Races Led	Miles	$
1989	NR	1	0	0	0	0	0	0	0	189	0	0	473	18,030
Lifetime		1	0	0	0	0	0	0	0	189	0	0	473	$18,030

Bob Read

Robert Read
Racing Hometown: Blairstown, NJ

Year	Rank	Starts	Poles	1	2	3	4	5	6–10	Laps	Laps Led	Races Led	Miles	$
1950	NR	1	0	0	0	0	0	0	0		0	0		25
1951	N/A	1	0	0	0	0	0	0	0		0	0		10
Lifetime		2	0	0	0	0	0	0	0		0	0		$35

Jim Reed

James Reed
B: 2/21/1926
Racing Hometown: Peekskill, NY

Year	Rank	Starts	Poles	1	2	3	4	5	6–10	Laps	Laps Led	Races Led	Miles	$
1951	56	4	0	0	1	0	0	0	0	199	58	1	100	675
1952	46	7	0	0	0	0	0	1	2	597	0	0	336	475
1953	33	3	0	0	0	0	1	0	0	260	0	0	358	635
1954	45	9	0	0	0	0	0	2	1	1,083	0	0	815	965
1955	16	14	0	0	1	0	1	2	0	1,691	32	1	1,265	2,710
1956	18	11	2	0	1	1	2	1	0	1,505	286	3	1,514	5,077
1957	18	6	0	0	0	1	1	0	1	892	11	2	980	3,408
1958	10	17	2	4	0	5	1	0	2	3,693	692	4	2,474	9,644
1959	9	14	1	3	0	1	1	2	2	2,512	289	5	2,071	23,534
1960	44	8	0	0	0	1	0	0	0	1,175	28	1	1,670	2,240
1961	33	8	0	0	2	0	0	1	1	1,735	32	1	1,717	3,350
1962	70	4	0	0	0	0	0	1	0	919	0	0	781	1,030
1963	139	1	0	0	0	0	0	0	0	29	0	0	15	50
Lifetime		106	5	7	5	9	7	10	9	16,290	1,428	18	14,095	$53,793

Mark Reed

Mark Reed
B: 2/19/1969
Racing Hometown: Bakersfield, CA

Year	Rank	Starts	Poles	1	2	3	4	5	6–10	Laps	Laps Led	Races Led	Miles	$
1990	94T	1	0	0	0	0	0	0	0	269	0	0	269	3,100
1991	82T	1	0	0	0	0	0	0	0	177	0	0	177	3,375
Lifetime		2	0	0	0	0	0	0	0	446	0	0	446	$6,475

Bo Reeder

Bo Reeder
Racing Hometown: Compton, CA

Year	Rank	Starts	Poles	1	2	3	4	5	6–10	Laps	Laps Led	Races Led	Miles	$
1967	66	1	0	0	0	0	0	0	0	159	0	0	429	700
1968	108	1	0	0	0	0	0	0	0	4	0	0	11	500
Lifetime		2	0	0	0	0	0	0	0	163	0	0	440	$1,200

Ken Reeder

Kenneth Reeder
Racing Hometown: McConnellsburg, PA

Year	Rank	Starts	Poles	1	2	3	4	5	6–10	Laps	Laps Led	Races Led	Miles	$
1954	126T	1	0	0	0	0	0	0	0	179	0	0	90	25
Lifetime		1	0	0	0	0	0	0	0	179	0	0	90	$25

Nat Reeder

Nat Reeder
Racing Hometown: Hollywood, CA

Year	Rank	Starts	Poles	1	2	3	4	5	6–10	Laps	Laps Led	Races Led	Miles	$
1965	63	1	0	0	0	0	0	0	0	100	0	0	270	625
Lifetime		1	0	0	0	0	0	0	0	100	0	0	270	$625

Walt Regan

Walter Regan

Year	Rank	Starts	Poles	1	2	3	4	5	6–10	Laps	Laps Led	Races Led	Miles	$
1952	88	1	0	0	0	0	0	0	0	225	0	0	225	50
1955	190T	1	0	0	0	0	0	0	0	162	0	0	81	50
Lifetime		2	0	0	0	0	0	0	0	387	0	0	306	$100

Jim Reich

James Reich
B: 11/5/1942
Racing Hometown: Turlock, CA

Year	Rank	Starts	Poles	1	2	3	4	5	6–10	Laps	Laps Led	Races Led	Miles	$
1982	57	2	0	0	0	0	0	0	1	202	0	0	529	4,865
Lifetime		2	0	0	0	0	0	0	1	202	0	0	529	$4,865

Year	Rank	Starts	Poles	Finish						Laps	Laps Led	Races Led	Miles	$
				1	2	3	4	5	6–10	Laps	Led	Led	Miles	$

Hassell Reid

Hassell Reid
  Racing Hometown: Winston-Salem, NC

Year	Rank	Starts	Poles	1	2	3	4	5	6–10	Laps	Laps Led	Races Led	Miles	$
1954	143	3	0	0	0	0	0	0	0	262	0	0	141	100
Lifetime		3	0	0	0	0	0	0	0	262	0	0	141	$100

Dave Reiley

David Reiley

Year	Rank	Starts	Poles	1	2	3	4	5	6–10	Laps	Laps Led	Races Led	Miles	$
1951	N/A	1	0	0	0	0	0	0	0		0	0		0
Lifetime		1	0	0	0	0	0	0	0		0	0		$0

Lee Reitzel

Dr. Lee L. Reitzel
  B: 9/14/1932   D: 9/24/1965
  Racing Hometown: Charlotte, NC

Year	Rank	Starts	Poles	1	2	3	4	5	6–10	Laps	Laps Led	Races Led	Miles	$
1961	37	17	0	0	0	0	0	0	3	2,566	0	0	2,039	2,910
1962	66	8	0	0	0	0	0	0	1	1,056	0	0	863	1,205
1963	99	4	0	0	0	0	0	0	0	496	0	0	275	875
Lifetime		29	0	0	0	0	0	0	4	4,118	0	0	3,177	$4,990

Bill Remaly

William Remaly

Year	Rank	Starts	Poles	1	2	3	4	5	6–10	Laps	Laps Led	Races Led	Miles	$
1951	N/A	1	0	0	0	0	0	0	0	80	0	0	80	25
Lifetime		1	0	0	0	0	0	0	0	80	0	0	80	$25

B. E. Renfro

B. E. Renfro
  Racing Hometown: Charlotte, NC

Year	Rank	Starts	Poles	1	2	3	4	5	6–10	Laps	Laps Led	Races Led	Miles	$
1949	NR	2	0	0	0	0	0	0	0		0	0		25
Lifetime		2	0	0	0	0	0	0	0		0	0		$25

Carl Renner

Carl Renner
  Racing Hometown: Toledo, OH

Year	Rank	Starts	Poles	1	2	3	4	5	6–10	Laps	Laps Led	Races Led	Miles	$
1950	48	2	0	0	0	0	0	0	1		0	0		250
Lifetime		2	0	0	0	0	0	0	1		0	0		$250

A. J. Reno

Arthur J. Reno
  Racing Hometown: Dawsonville, VA

Year	Rank	Starts	Poles	1	2	3	4	5	6–10	Laps	Laps Led	Races Led	Miles	$
1974	NR	1	0	0	0	0	0	0	0	15	0	0	40	760
1975	90	1	0	0	0	0	0	0	0	170	0	0	452	1,670
Lifetime		2	0	0	0	0	0	0	0	185	0	0	492	$2,430

Bob Reuther

Robert Reuther
  B: 9/12/1927
  Racing Hometown: Nashville, TN

Year	Rank	Starts	Poles	1	2	3	4	5	6–10	Laps	Laps Led	Races Led	Miles	$
1951	NR	1	0	0	0	0	0	0	0		0	0		25
1959	58	1	0	0	0	0	0	0	1	284	0	0	142	250
1960	NR	1	0	0	0	0	0	0	0	285	0	0	143	140
Lifetime		3	0	0	0	0	0	0	1	569	0	0	285	$415

Buzzie Reutimann

Emile Reutimann
  B: 5/7/1941
  Racing Hometown: Harrisburg, PA

Year	Rank	Starts	Poles	1	2	3	4	5	6–10	Laps	Laps Led	Races Led	Miles	$
1963	119	1	0	0	0	0	0	0	1	192	0	0	58	140
Lifetime		1	0	0	0	0	0	0	1	192	0	0	58	$140

Melvin Revis

Melvin W. Revis
  Racing Hometown: Spartanburg, SC

Year	Rank	Starts	Poles	1	2	3	4	5	6–10	Laps	Laps Led	Races Led	Miles	$
1979	NR	1	0	0	0	0	0	0	0	76	0	0	41	410
1980	104	1	0	0	0	0	0	0	0	23	0	0	31	1,115
Lifetime		2	0	0	0	0	0	0	0	99	0	0	72	$1,525

Bill Rexford

William J. Rexford
  B: 3/14/1927   D: 4/18/1994
  Racing Hometown: Conowango Valley, NY

Year	Rank	Starts	Poles	1	2	3	4	5	6–10	Laps	Laps Led	Races Led	Miles	$
1949	12	3	0	0	0	1	0	1	0	370	0	0	274	785
1950	1	17	0	1	0	1	2	1	6	1,302	98	2	1,146	5,800

Year	Rank	Starts	Poles	Finish						Laps	Laps Led	Races Led	Miles	$
				1	2	3	4	5	6–10					

Bill Rexford *continued*

Year	Rank	Starts	Poles	1	2	3	4	5	6–10	Laps	Laps Led	Races Led	Miles	$
1951	72	11	1	0	0	0	0	0	1	354	0	0	308	450
1952	NR	3	0	0	0	0	0	0	1	396	0	0	239	150
1953	NR	2	0	0	0	0	0	1	1	173	0	0	173	350
Lifetime		36	1	1	0	2	2	3	9	2,595	98	2	2,140	$7,535

Don Reynolds

Donald Reynolds
Racing Hometown: Cabazon, CA

Year	Rank	Starts	Poles	1	2	3	4	5	6–10	Laps	Laps Led	Races Led	Miles	$
1974	76	2	0	0	0	0	0	0	1	303	0	0	772	2,600
1975	86T	1	0	0	0	0	0	0	0	110	0	0	288	1,230
1976	91	1	0	0	0	0	0	0	0	83	0	0	217	1,140
Lifetime		4	0	0	0	0	0	0	1	496	0	0	1,278	$4,970

Jack Reynolds

Jack Reynolds
B: 4/17/1928
Racing Hometown: Hawthorne, NJ

Year	Rank	Starts	Poles	1	2	3	4	5	6–10	Laps	Laps Led	Races Led	Miles	$
1950	46	2	0	0	0	0	0	1	0		0	0		300
1951	79	2	0	0	0	0	0	0	1		0	0		175
1952	24	10	0	0	0	0	2	0	4	1,335	0	0	901	1,450
Lifetime		14	0	0	0	0	2	1	5	1,335	0	0	901	$1,850

John Rezek

John Rezek
Racing Hometown: Alvin, TX

Year	Rank	Starts	Poles	1	2	3	4	5	6–10	Laps	Laps Led	Races Led	Miles	$
1979	66	4	0	0	0	0	0	0	0	584	0	0	1,012	5,585
Lifetime		4	0	0	0	0	0	0	0	584	0	0	1,012	$5,585

Jim Rhoades

James Rhoades
Racing Hometown: Hanover, MD

Year	Rank	Starts	Poles	1	2	3	4	5	6–10	Laps	Laps Led	Races Led	Miles	$
1956	112	5	0	0	0	0	0	0	1	454	0	0	340	335
1958	94	1	0	0	0	0	0	0	0	208	0	0	208	150
Lifetime		6	0	0	0	0	0	0	1	662	0	0	548	$485

Willy T. Ribbs

Willy Theodore Ribbs
B: 1/3/1956
Racing Hometown: San Jose, CA

Year	Rank	Starts	Poles	1	2	3	4	5	6–10	Laps	Laps Led	Races Led	Miles	$
1986	65	3	0	0	0	0	0	0	0	516	0	0	540	3,520
Lifetime		3	0	0	0	0	0	0	0	516	0	0	540	$3,520

Hank Ribet

Henry Ribet
Racing Hometown: Palm Beach, FL

Year	Rank	Starts	Poles	1	2	3	4	5	6–10	Laps	Laps Led	Races Led	Miles	$
1953	168	1	0	0	0	0	0	0	0	68	0	0	34	25
Lifetime		1	0	0	0	0	0	0	0	68	0	0	34	$25

Ken Rice

Kenneth Rice

Year	Rank	Starts	Poles	1	2	3	4	5	6–10	Laps	Laps Led	Races Led	Miles	$
1967	NR	3	0	0	0	0	0	0	0	22	0	0	8	200
Lifetime		3	0	0	0	0	0	0	0	22	0	0	8	$200

Sam Rice

John Sam Rice
Racing Hometown: Martinsville, VA

Year	Rank	Starts	Poles	1	2	3	4	5	6–10	Laps	Laps Led	Races Led	Miles	$
1949	17	2	0	0	0	0	2	0	0	192	0	0	96	680
Lifetime		2	0	0	0	0	2	0	0	192	0	0	96	$680

Leo Richards

Leo Richards
Racing Hometown: Gardner, MA

Year	Rank	Starts	Poles	1	2	3	4	5	6–10	Laps	Laps Led	Races Led	Miles	$
1952	133T	1	0	0	0	0	0	0	0		0	0		25
Lifetime		1	0	0	0	0	0	0	0		0	0		$25

Harlan Richardson

Harlan Richardson
Racing Hometown: Houston, TX

Year	Rank	Starts	Poles	1	2	3	4	5	6–10	Laps	Laps Led	Races Led	Miles	$
1959	48	10	0	0	0	0	0	0	2	1,893	0	0	948	1,120

Year	Rank	Starts	Poles	Finish 1	2	3	4	5	6–10	Laps	Laps Led	Races Led	Miles	$

Harlan Richardson *continued*

Year	Rank	Starts	Poles	1	2	3	4	5	6–10	Laps	Laps Led	Races Led	Miles	$
1961	134	4	0	0	0	0	0	0	0	284	0	0	640	525
1962	NR	1	0	0	0	0	0	0	0	17	0	0	43	50
Lifetime		15	0	0	0	0	0	0	2	2,194	0	0	1,630	$1,695

Jack Richardson

Jack Richardson
    Racing Hometown: Phoenix, AZ

Year	Rank	Starts	Poles	1	2	3	4	5	6–10	Laps	Laps Led	Races Led	Miles	$
1955	184	1	0	0	0	0	0	0	0	50	0	0	25	25
1956	297T	1	0	0	0	0	0	0	0	8	0	0	4	0
Lifetime		2	0	0	0	0	0	0	0	58	0	0	29	$25

Woody Richmond

Woody Richmond
    Racing Hometown: Jacksonville, FL

Year	Rank	Starts	Poles	1	2	3	4	5	6–10	Laps	Laps Led	Races Led	Miles	$
1955	190T	1	0	0	0	0	0	0	0	33	0	0	17	25
Lifetime		1	0	0	0	0	0	0	0	33	0	0	17	$25

Larry Richardson

Lawrence Richardson
    Racing Hometown: Gunter, TX

Year	Rank	Starts	Poles	1	2	3	4	5	6–10	Laps	Laps Led	Races Led	Miles	$
1974	129T	1	0	0	0	0	0	0	0	36	0	0	90	670
Lifetime		1	0	0	0	0	0	0	0	36	0	0	90	$670

Paul Richardson

Paul Richardson

Year	Rank	Starts	Poles	1	2	3	4	5	6–10	Laps	Laps Led	Races Led	Miles	$
1952	NR	1	0	0	0	0	0	0	0	39	0	0	24	25
Lifetime		1	0	0	0	0	0	0	0	39	0	0	24	$25

Cliff Richmond

Clifford Richmond
    Racing Hometown: San Luis Obispo, CA

Year	Rank	Starts	Poles	1	2	3	4	5	6–10	Laps	Laps Led	Races Led	Miles	$
1955	126	2	0	0	0	0	0	0	0	246	0	0	167	50
Lifetime		2	0	0	0	0	0	0	0	246	0	0	167	$50

Tim Richmond

Timothy Richmond
    B: 6/7/1955   D: 8/13/1989   *Died of AIDS.*
    Racing Hometown: Ashland, OH

Year	Rank	Starts	Poles	1	2	3	4	5	6–10	Laps	Laps Led	Races Led	Miles	$
1980	41	5	0	0	0	0	0	0	0	1,359	0	0	1,650	14,925
1981	16	29	0	0	0	0	0	0	6	8,266	24	2	9,076	96,448
1982	26	26	1	2	2	0	1	2	5	6,834	321	13	8,246	181,830
1983	10	30	4	1	1	4	1	3	5	7,176	590	15	8,218	262,139
1984	12	30	0	1	3	0	0	2	5	8,225	58	7	9,416	345,848
1985	11	28	0	0	1	1	1	0	10	8,199	377	12	9,489	290,284
1986	3	29	8	7	4	0	1	1	4	8,544	1,006	21	10,526	973,221
1987	36	8	1	2	0	0	1	0	1	1,199	161	6	2,858	151,850
Lifetime		185	14	13	11	5	5	8	36	49,802	2,537	76	59,479	$2,316,545

Dick Richter

Richard Richter

Year	Rank	Starts	Poles	1	2	3	4	5	6–10	Laps	Laps Led	Races Led	Miles	$
1951	NR	1	0	0	0	0	0	0	0		0	0		0
Lifetime		1	0	0	0	0	0	0	0		0	0		$0

Judge Rider

Judge Rider
    Racing Hometown: Dahlonega, GA

Year	Rank	Starts	Poles	1	2	3	4	5	6–10	Laps	Laps Led	Races Led	Miles	$
1956	236	1	0	0	0	0	0	0	0	258	0	0	355	50
Lifetime		1	0	0	0	0	0	0	0	258	0	0	355	$50

Sam Rider

Samuel Rider

Year	Rank	Starts	Poles	1	2	3	4	5	6–10	Laps	Laps Led	Races Led	Miles	$
1949	NR	1	0	0	0	0	0	0	0		0	0		50
Lifetime		1	0	0	0	0	0	0	0		0	0		$50

Jody Ridley

Jody Ridley
    B: 5/19/1942
    Racing Hometown: Chatsworth, GA

Year	Rank	Starts	Poles	1	2	3	4	5	6–10	Laps	Laps Led	Races Led	Miles	$
1973	59	3	0	0	0	0	0	1	0	690	0	0	982	7,120

Year	Rank	Starts	Poles	Finish						Laps	Laps Led	Races Led	Miles	$
				1	2	3	4	5	6–10					

Jody Ridley *continued*

Year	Rank	Starts	Poles	1	2	3	4	5	6–10	Laps	Laps Led	Races Led	Miles	$
1974	88	2	0	0	0	0	0	0	0	163	0	0	205	2,935
1975	NR	3	0	0	0	0	0	0	0	421	0	0	631	3,315
1977	86	1	0	0	0	0	0	0	0	316	0	0	481	2,080
1979	47	3	0	0	0	0	0	1	1	787	0	0	1,403	11,245
1980	7	31	0	0	0	0	0	2	16	9,579	2	2	10,976	204,883
1981	5	31	0	1	0	0	1	1	15	8,971	28	6	10,528	267,605
1982	13	30	0	0	0	0	0	0	10	7,983	4	4	8,789	308,664
1983	32	10	0	0	0	0	0	0	3	1,963	0	0	3,494	45,710
1984	35	14	0	0	0	0	0	0	3	2,891	4	2	4,810	64,135
1985	—	0												1,300
1986	33	12	0	0	0	0	0	0	1	3,183	0	0	4,055	84,380
1989	—	0												3,800
Lifetime		140	0	1	0	0	1	5	49	36,947	38	14	46,353	$1,007,172

Hilly Rife

Hillen Rife
Racing Hometown: New Oxford, PA

Year	Rank	Starts	Poles	1	2	3	4	5	6–10	Laps	Laps Led	Races Led	Miles	$
1954	179T	1	0	0	0	0	0	0	0	174	0	0	87	0
Lifetime		1	0	0	0	0	0	0	0	174	0	0	87	$0

John Riggi

John Riggi
Racing Hometown: Heidelberg, PA

Year	Rank	Starts	Poles	1	2	3	4	5	6–10	Laps	Laps Led	Races Led	Miles	$
1949	NR	1	0	0	0	0	0	0	0	33	0	0	17	0
Lifetime		1	0	0	0	0	0	0	0	33	0	0	17	$0

Tommy Riggins

Thomas Riggins
B: 1951
Racing Hometown: Jacksonville, FL

Year	Rank	Starts	Poles	1	2	3	4	5	6–10	Laps	Laps Led	Races Led	Miles	$
1986	89	1	0	0	0	0	0	0	0	89	0	0	216	3,525
1990	53	4	0	0	0	0	0	0	0	469	0	0	952	12,140
Lifetime		5	0	0	0	0	0	0	0	558	0	0	1,168	$15,665

L. C. Rigsby

L. C. Rigsby
Racing Hometown: Orlando, FL

Year	Rank	Starts	Poles	1	2	3	4	5	6–10	Laps	Laps Led	Races Led	Miles	$
1952	202	1	0	0	0	0	0	0	0		0	0		0
Lifetime		1	0	0	0	0	0	0	0		0	0		$0

Eddie Riker

Edward Riker
Racing Hometown: Boonton, NJ

Year	Rank	Starts	Poles	1	2	3	4	5	6–10	Laps	Laps Led	Races Led	Miles	$
1953	67	2	0	0	0	0	0	0	1		0	0		185
1954	NR	4	0	0	0	0	0	0	0	455	0	0	411	235
1960	108	1	0	0	0	0	0	0	0	61	0	0	122	110
Lifetime		7	0	0	0	0	0	0	1	516	0	0	533	$530

Bob Riley

Robert Riley
Racing Hometown: Norwalk, CT

Year	Rank	Starts	Poles	1	2	3	4	5	6–10	Laps	Laps Led	Races Led	Miles	$
1980	NR	2	0	0	0	0	0	0	0	196	0	0	408	1,625
1981	72	3	0	0	0	0	0	0	0	139	0	0	265	1,975
1982	—	0												2,050
1983	62	3	0	0	0	0	0	0	0	329	0	0	491	3,530
1984	NR	1	0	0	0	0	0	0	0	179	0	0	448	1,735
1985	NR	1	0	0	0	0	0	0	0	449	0	0	449	2,100
Lifetime		10	0	0	0	0	0	0	0	1,292	0	0	2,060	$13,015

Bud Riley

Harvey Riley
Racing Hometown: Los Angeles, CA

Year	Rank	Starts	Poles	1	2	3	4	5	6–10	Laps	Laps Led	Races Led	Miles	$
1951	49	8	0	0	0	0	0	1	1	606	0	0	624	575
Lifetime		8	0	0	0	0	0	1	1	606	0	0	624	$575

Richard Riley

Richard Riley
Racing Hometown: Charlotte, NC

Year	Rank	Starts	Poles	1	2	3	4	5	6–10	Laps	Laps Led	Races Led	Miles	$
1956	180T	1	0	0	0	0	0	0	1	141	0	0	71	100

Year	Rank	Starts	Poles	Finish 1	2	3	4	5	6–10	Laps	Laps Led	Races Led	Miles	$

Richard Riley *continued*

Year	Rank	Starts	Poles	1	2	3	4	5	6–10	Laps	Laps Led	Races Led	Miles	$
1959	50	10	0	0	0	0	0	0	2	1,433	0	0	767	910
1960	81	4	0	0	0	0	0	0	1	609	0	0	563	600
Lifetime		15	0	0	0	0	0	0	4	2,183	0	0	1,400	$1,610

Bud Rinaldo

Bud Rinaldo
Racing Hometown: Shreveport, LA

Year	Rank	Starts	Poles	1	2	3	4	5	6–10	Laps	Laps Led	Races Led	Miles	$
1953	NR	1	0	0	0	0	0	0	0		0	0		25
Lifetime		1	0	0	0	0	0	0	0		0	0		$25

Tommy Ringstaff

Thomas Ringstaff
Racing Hometown: Catlettsburg, KY

Year	Rank	Starts	Poles	1	2	3	4	5	6–10	Laps	Laps Led	Races Led	Miles	$
1955	99	3	0	0	0	0	0	0	1	225	0	0	199	125
Lifetime		3	0	0	0	0	0	0	1	225	0	0	199	$125

Gene Riniker

Gene Riniker
Racing Hometown: Riverside, CA

Year	Rank	Starts	Poles	1	2	3	4	5	6–10	Laps	Laps Led	Races Led	Miles	$
1975	79	1	0	0	0	0	0	0	1	138	0	0	362	1,735
Lifetime		1	0	0	0	0	0	0	1	138	0	0	362	$1,735

Laurent Rioux

Laurent Rioux
Racing Hometown: Montreal, Que., Canada

Year	Rank	Starts	Poles	1	2	3	4	5	6–10	Laps	Laps Led	Races Led	Miles	$
1983	NR	2	0	0	0	0	0	0	0	884	0	0	674	4,565
1984	NR	1	0	0	0	0	0	0	0	424	0	0	431	5,745
Lifetime		3	0	0	0	0	0	0	0	1,308	0	0	1,105	$10,310

Michael Ritch

Michael Ritch
B: 2/24/1973
Racing Hometown: High Point, NC

Year	Rank	Starts	Poles	1	2	3	4	5	6–10	Laps	Laps Led	Races Led	Miles	$
1995	61T	1	0	0	0	0	0	0	0	226	0	0	226	12,655
Lifetime		1	0	0	0	0	0	0	0	226	0	0	226	$12,655

Tom Rivers

Thomas Rivers
Racing Hometown: Oakhurst, NJ

Year	Rank	Starts	Poles	1	2	3	4	5	6–10	Laps	Laps Led	Races Led	Miles	$
1954	NR	1	0	0	0	0	0	0	0	45	0	0	90	175
Lifetime		1	0	0	0	0	0	0	0	45	0	0	90	$175

Hank Rivet

Henry Rivet
Racing Hometown: Roanoke, VA

Year	Rank	Starts	Poles	1	2	3	4	5	6–10	Laps	Laps Led	Races Led	Miles	$
1953	NR	1	0	0	0	0	0	0	0	32	0	0	131	25
Lifetime		1	0	0	0	0	0	0	0	32	0	0	131	$25

Tom Roa

Thomas Roa
Racing Hometown: Compton, CA

Year	Rank	Starts	Poles	1	2	3	4	5	6–10	Laps	Laps Led	Races Led	Miles	$
1967	116	1	0	0	0	0	0	0	0	9	0	0	24	500
Lifetime		1	0	0	0	0	0	0	0	9	0	0	24	$500

Bert Robbins

Bertrand B. Robbins
B: 3/6/1931
Racing Hometown: Washington, DC

Year	Rank	Starts	Poles	1	2	3	4	5	6–10	Laps	Laps Led	Races Led	Miles	$
1964	86	2	0	0	0	0	0	1	0	918	0	0	401	600
1965	80	5	0	0	0	0	0	0	2	479	0	0	241	1,240
Lifetime		7	0	0	0	0	0	1	2	1,397	0	0	641	$1,840

Marty Robbins

Martin David Robbins *Real Last Name:* Robinson
B: 9/26/1925   D: 12/8/1982
Racing Hometown: Glendale, AZ

Year	Rank	Starts	Poles	1	2	3	4	5	6–10	Laps	Laps Led	Races Led	Miles	$
1966	140	1	0	0	0	0	0	0	0	48	0	0	24	100
1968	78	1	0	0	0	0	0	0	0	312	0	0	468	1,525
1970	94T	1	0	0	0	0	0	0	0	105	0	0	158	1,160

Year	Rank	Starts	Poles	Finish						Laps	Laps Led	Races Led	Miles	$
				1	2	3	4	5	6–10	Laps	Led	Led	Miles	$

Marty Robbins *continued*

Year	Rank	Starts	Poles	1	2	3	4	5	6–10	Laps	Laps Led	Races Led	Miles	$
1971	69	5	0	0	0	0	0	0	1	1,295	0	0	1,984	7,152
1972	54	5	0	0	0	0	0	0	2	1,096	0	0	1,864	7,950
1973	83	4	0	0	0	0	0	0	1	334	1	1	829	5,395
1974	48	4	0	0	0	0	0	1	1	550	0	0	1,343	5,734
1975	81	2	0	0	0	0	0	0	0	65	2	1	172	3,160
1977	76	2	0	0	0	0	0	0	0	229	0	0	482	2,590
1978	84	1	0	0	0	0	0	0	0	171	0	0	455	2,240
1979	68	3	0	0	0	0	0	0	0	235	0	0	520	3,120
1980	71	4	0	0	0	0	0	0	0	529	0	0	1,188	7,520
1982	79	2	0	0	0	0	0	0	0	134	0	0	248	2,055
Lifetime		35	0	0	0	0	0	1	5	5,103	3	2	9,734	$49,701

Bob Roberts

Robert Roberts

Year	Rank	Starts	Poles	1	2	3	4	5	6–10	Laps	Laps Led	Races Led	Miles	$
1960	NR	1	0	0	0	0	0	0	0	10	0	0	5	50
Lifetime		1	0	0	0	0	0	0	0	10	0	0	5	$50

Charlie Roberts

Charles Douglas Roberts
B: 10/28/1940
Racing Hometown: Anniston, AL

Year	Rank	Starts	Poles	1	2	3	4	5	6–10	Laps	Laps Led	Races Led	Miles	$
1970	76	3	0	0	0	0	0	0	0	95	0	0	149	1,470
1971	33	19	0	0	0	0	0	0	2	2,795	0	0	3,684	12,470
1972	16	26	0	0	0	0	0	0	1	6,437	0	0	7,728	32,488
1973	20	24	0	0	0	0	0	0	0	7,017	0	0	6,848	32,469
1974	71	3	0	0	0	0	0	0	0	226	0	0	471	3,940
Lifetime		75	0	0	0	0	0	0	3	16,570	0	0	18,880	$82,837

Cliff Roberts

Clifford Roberts
Racing Hometown: Oakland, CA

Year	Rank	Starts	Poles	1	2	3	4	5	6–10	Laps	Laps Led	Races Led	Miles	$
1954	98	2	0	0	0	0	0	0	0	616	0	0	308	50
Lifetime		2	0	0	0	0	0	0	0	616	0	0	308	$50

Fireball Roberts

Edward Glenn Roberts
B: 1/20/1929   D: 7/2/1964   *Died of injuries after crash @ Charlotte (5/24/64).*
Racing Hometown: Daytona Beach, FL

Year	Rank	Starts	Poles	1	2	3	4	5	6–10	Laps	Laps Led	Races Led	Miles	$
1950	2	9	1	1	2	1	0	0	1	1,138	60	3	1,065	6,800
1951	12	9	0	0	1	0	0	1	1	825	0	0	738	1,685
1952	59	7	0	0	0	0	0	0	1	443	15	1	436	199
1953	132	2	0	0	0	0	0	0	0	352	41	1	426	365
1954	22	5	0	0	0	0	0	0	2	811	0	0	975	1,080
1955	201	2	1	0	0	0	0	0	0	69	4	1	201	140
1956	7	33	3	5	1	2	7	2	5	5,695	470	10	3,789	14,742
1957	6	42	4	8	6	2	1	4	6	6,891	**1,107**	**16**	4,269	19,829
1958	11	10	0	6	1	1	0	0	1	2,491	**877**	7	2,197	32,219
1959	16	8	3	1	0	0	0	0	3	1,445	147	3	1,489	10,865
1960	29	9	6	2	0	0	0	0	1	1,338	578	9	2,072	19,895
1961	5	22	6	2	4	2	2	3	1	5,075	1,002	13	5,033	50,267
1962	8	19	9	3	3	0	2	1	3	4,312	960	12	4,068	66,152
1963	5	20	2	4	2	0	4	1	3	4,643	692	12	5,470	73,060
1964	27	9	0	1	2	1	0	1	1	1,702	17	2	2,013	28,345
Lifetime		206	35	33	22	9	16	13	29	37,230	5,970	90	34,242	$325,643

Gene Roberts

Gene Roberts
Racing Hometown: Rochelle Park, NJ

Year	Rank	Starts	Poles	1	2	3	4	5	6–10	Laps	Laps Led	Races Led	Miles	$
1954	136	1	0	0	0	0	0	0	0	168	0	0	84	25
Lifetime		1	0	0	0	0	0	0	0	168	0	0	84	$25

Johnny Roberts

Johnny Roberts
B: 5/31/1924   D: 7/25/1965   *Killed @ Lincoln Speedway in New Oxford, PA in Modified race.*
Racing Hometown: Brooklyn, MD

Year	Rank	Starts	Poles	1	2	3	4	5	6–10	Laps	Laps Led	Races Led	Miles	$
1953	167	2	0	0	0	0	0	0	0	33	0	0	135	50
1954	148	2	0	0	0	0	0	0	0	160	0	0	159	25
1955	60	4	0	0	0	0	0	0	1	600	0	0	406	250
1956	114	4	0	0	0	0	0	0	0	461	0	0	215	210

Year	Rank	Starts	Poles	Finish						Laps	Laps Led	Races Led	Miles	$
				1	2	3	4	5	6–10	Laps	Led	Led	Miles	$

Johnny Roberts *continued*

Year	Rank	Starts	Poles	1	2	3	4	5	6–10	Laps	Laps Led	Races Led	Miles	$
1961	167	1	0	0	0	0	0	0	0	113	0	0	57	75
Lifetime		13	0	0	0	0	0	0	1	1,367	0	0	972	$610

Neil Roberts

Neil Roberts
Racing Hometown: Atlanta, GA

Year	Rank	Starts	Poles	1	2	3	4	5	6–10	Laps	Laps Led	Races Led	Miles	$
1951	N/A	1	0	0	0	0	0	0	0		0	0		50
1953	27	2	0	0	0	0	0	0	1	335	0	0	461	400
Lifetime		3	0	0	0	0	0	0	1	335	0	0	461	$450

Ralph Roberts

Ralph Roberts

Year	Rank	Starts	Poles	1	2	3	4	5	6–10	Laps	Laps Led	Races Led	Miles	$
1958	NR	1	0	0	0	0	0	0	0	160	0	0	421	120
Lifetime		1	0	0	0	0	0	0	0	160	0	0	421	$120

Odie Robertson

Odie Robertson
Racing Hometown: Littleton, CO

Year	Rank	Starts	Poles	1	2	3	4	5	6–10	Laps	Laps Led	Races Led	Miles	$
1974	111	1	0	0	0	0	0	0	0	89	0	0	233	1,075
Lifetime		1	0	0	0	0	0	0	0	89	0	0	233	$1,075

Jim Robinson

James Robinson
B: 1/28/1946
Racing Hometown: N. Hollywood, CA

Year	Rank	Starts	Poles	1	2	3	4	5	6–10	Laps	Laps Led	Races Led	Miles	$
1979	57	3	0	0	0	0	0	0	0	193	0	0	493	3,005
1980	58	3	0	0	0	0	0	0	0	288	0	0	742	4,300
1981	50	3	0	0	0	0	0	0	2	264	0	0	692	9,505
1982	66	2	0	0	0	0	0	0	0	150	0	0	393	2,220
1983	52	2	0	0	0	0	0	0	0	204	0	0	534	6,075
1984	55	2	0	0	0	0	0	0	0	189	0	0	495	7,560
1985	52	2	0	0	0	0	0	0	0	209	0	0	548	10,820
1986	66	2	0	0	0	0	0	0	0	192	0	0	503	9,300
1987	64	2	0	0	0	0	0	0	0	157	0	0	411	5,685
Lifetime		21	0	0	0	0	0	0	2	1,846	0	0	4,812	$58,470

Robbie Robinson

Robert Robinson
Racing Hometown: Fleming, OH

Year	Rank	Starts	Poles	1	2	3	4	5	6–10	Laps	Laps Led	Races Led	Miles	$
1952	NR	4	0	0	0	0	0	0	0	300	0	0	160	75
Lifetime		4	0	0	0	0	0	0	0	300	0	0	160	$75

Pedro Rodriguez

Pedro Rodriguez
B: 1/18/1940   D: 7/11/1971   *Killed in West German Grand Prix.*
Racing Hometown: Mexico City, Mexico

Year	Rank	Starts	Poles	1	2	3	4	5	6–10	Laps	Laps Led	Races Led	Miles	$
1959	NR	1	0	0	0	0	0	0	1	144	0	0	144	300
1963	NR	1	0	0	0	0	0	0	0	54	0	0	135	400
1965	NR	1	0	0	0	0	0	1	0	391	0	0	587	3,425
1971	NR	3	0	0	0	0	0	0	0	228	0	0	570	3,150
Lifetime		6	0	0	0	0	0	1	1	817	0	0	1,436	$7,275

Robert Roeber

Robert Roeber (Bob)
Racing Hometown: Posen, IL

Year	Rank	Starts	Poles	1	2	3	4	5	6–10	Laps	Laps Led	Races Led	Miles	$
1961	133	2	0	0	0	0	0	0	0	208	0	0	520	315
Lifetime		2	0	0	0	0	0	0	0	208	0	0	520	$315

Jerry Roedell

Jerry Roedell
Racing Hometown: Peoria, IL

Year	Rank	Starts	Poles	1	2	3	4	5	6–10	Laps	Laps Led	Races Led	Miles	$
1960	141	1	0	0	0	0	0	0	0	168	0	0	252	200
Lifetime		1	0	0	0	0	0	0	0	168	0	0	252	$200

Don Rogala

Donald Rogala
Racing Hometown: Erie, PA

Year	Rank	Starts	Poles	1	2	3	4	5	6–10	Laps	Laps Led	Races Led	Miles	$
1949	NR	1	0	0	0	0	0	0	1	167	0	0	84	50
Lifetime		1	0	0	0	0	0	0	0	1	167	0	0	84	$50

Year	Rank	Starts	Poles	Finish 1	2	3	4	5	6–10	Laps	Laps Led	Races Led	Miles	$

Jackie Rogers

Julius Franklin Rogers III
B: 5/6/1943
Racing Hometown: Wilmington, NC

Year	Rank	Starts	Poles	1	2	3	4	5	6–10	Laps	Laps Led	Races Led	Miles	$
1974	21	22	0	0	0	0	0	0	6	4,555	1	1	6,677	32,367
1975	44	8	0	0	0	0	0	0	1	913	2	1	1,746	11,000
1976	30	11	0	0	0	0	0	0	3	2,439	3	2	3,874	21,215
Lifetime		41	0	0	0	0	0	0	10	7,907	6	4	12,298	$64,582

Joe Rogers

Joseph Rogers
D: 6/24/1951 *Killed at Arlington Downs Speedway.*
Racing Hometown: Tampa, FL

Year	Rank	Starts	Poles	1	2	3	4	5	6–10	Laps	Laps Led	Races Led	Miles	$
1951	N/A	1	0	0	0	0	0	0	0		0	0		25
Lifetime		1	0	0	0	0	0	0	0		0	0		$25

John Rogers

John A. Rogers (Buck)
Racing Hometown: Crystal Lake, IL

Year	Rank	Starts	Poles	1	2	3	4	5	6–10	Laps	Laps Led	Races Led	Miles	$
1962	124	1	0	0	0	0	0	0	0	35	0	0	88	50
1963	110	2	0	0	0	0	0	0	0	109	0	0	273	625
Lifetime		3	0	0	0	0	0	0	0	144	0	0	361	$675

Johnny Rogers

John Rogers
Racing Hometown: Trenton, NJ

Year	Rank	Starts	Poles	1	2	3	4	5	6–10	Laps	Laps Led	Races Led	Miles	$
1949	NR	1	0	0	0	0	0	0	0		0	0		0
Lifetime		1	0	0	0	0	0	0	0		0	0		$0

George Rogge

George Rogge
Racing Hometown: Palo Alto, CA

Year	Rank	Starts	Poles	1	2	3	4	5	6–10	Laps	Laps Led	Races Led	Miles	$
1954	NR	1	0	0	0	0	0	0	0	64	0	0	64	40
Lifetime		1	0	0	0	0	0	0	0	64	0	0	64	$40

Jimmy Roland

James Roland
Racing Hometown: Newberry, SC

Year	Rank	Starts	Poles	1	2	3	4	5	6–10	Laps	Laps Led	Races Led	Miles	$
1955	129	2	0	0	0	0	0	0	1	324	0	0	282	150
Lifetime		2	0	0	0	0	0	0	1	324	0	0	282	$150

Joe Roletto

Joseph Roletto

Year	Rank	Starts	Poles	1	2	3	4	5	6–10	Laps	Laps Led	Races Led	Miles	$
1955	159T	1	0	0	0	0	0	0	0	212	0	0	212	50
Lifetime		1	0	0	0	0	0	0	0	212	0	0	212	$50

Shorty Rollins

Lloyd George Rollins
B: 4/3/1929
Racing Hometown: Corpus Christi, TX

Year	Rank	Starts	Poles	1	2	3	4	5	6–10	Laps	Laps Led	Races Led	Miles	$
1958	4	29	0	1	1	3	5	2	10	5,324	87	4	3,201	13,399
1959	27	10	0	0	0	0	0	0	4	1,391	0	0	1,122	1,500
1960	30	4	0	0	0	0	0	0	1	952	0	0	1,480	2,120
Lifetime		43	0	1	1	3	5	2	15	7,667	87	4	5,803	$17,019

Gene Romero

Gene Romero
B: 1946
Racing Hometown: San Luis Obispo, CA

Year	Rank	Starts	Poles	1	2	3	4	5	6–10	Laps	Laps Led	Races Led	Miles	$
1972	106	1	0	0	0	0	0	0	0	105	0	0	263	1,620
Lifetime		1	0	0	0	0	0	0	0	105	0	0	263	$1,620

Jim Romine

James Romine
Racing Hometown: Youngstown, OH

Year	Rank	Starts	Poles	1	2	3	4	5	6–10	Laps	Laps Led	Races Led	Miles	$
1951	N/A	3	0	0	0	0	0	0	1		0	0		150
1954	NR	1	0	0	0	0	0	0	0	25	0	0	102	0
Lifetime		4	0	0	0	0	0	0	1	25	0	0	102	$150

Year	Rank	Starts	Poles	Finish						Laps	Laps Led	Races Led	Miles	$
				1	2	3	4	5	6–10					

Slim Rominger

Slim Rominger
Racing Hometown: Clemmons, NC

Year	Rank	Starts	Poles	1	2	3	4	5	6–10	Laps	Laps Led	Races Led	Miles	$
1953	148	2	0	0	0	0	0	0	0	153	0	0	147	125
Lifetime		2	0	0	0	0	0	0	0	153	0	0	147	$125

Ed Rooney

Edward Rooney Jr.
Racing Hometown: Somerville, NJ

Year	Rank	Starts	Poles	1	2	3	4	5	6–10	Laps	Laps Led	Races Led	Miles	$
1951	N/A	1	0	0	0	0	0	0	0		0	0		25
Lifetime		1	0	0	0	0	0	0	0		0	0		$25

Dean Roper

Dean Roper
B: 12/26/1938
Racing Hometown: Fair Grove, MO

Year	Rank	Starts	Poles	1	2	3	4	5	6–10	Laps	Laps Led	Races Led	Miles	$
1983	54	2	0	0	0	0	0	0	0	364	0	0	937	16,485
1984	49	3	0	0	0	0	0	0	0	500	0	0	1,274	19,150
1985	—	0												3,550
Lifetime		5	0	0	0	0	0	0	0	864	0	0	2,211	$39,185

Jim Roper

James Chris Roper
B: 8/13/1916
Racing Hometown: Halstead, KS

Year	Rank	Starts	Poles	1	2	3	4	5	6–10	Laps	Laps Led	Races Led	Miles	$
1949	16	2	0	1	0	0	0	0	0	197	47	1	148	2,050
Lifetime		2	0	1	0	0	0	0	0	197	47	1	148	$2,050

Frank Ropp

Frank Ropp

Year	Rank	Starts	Poles	1	2	3	4	5	6–10	Laps	Laps Led	Races Led	Miles	$
1954	NR	1	0	0	0	0	0	0	0	163	0	0	82	25
Lifetime		1	0	0	0	0	0	0	0	163	0	0	82	$25

Mickey Rorer

Mickey Rorer
Racing Hometown: Quakertown, PA

Year	Rank	Starts	Poles	1	2	3	4	5	6–10	Laps	Laps Led	Races Led	Miles	$
1953	85	2	0	0	0	0	0	0	0		0	0		60
Lifetime		2	0	0	0	0	0	0	0		0	0		$60

Bob Rose

Robert Rose
Racing Hometown: Inglewood, CA

Year	Rank	Starts	Poles	1	2	3	4	5	6–10	Laps	Laps Led	Races Led	Miles	$
1954	NR	1	0	0	0	0	0	0	0	393	0	0	197	25
1957	NR	2	0	0	0	0	0	0	0	195	0	0	145	175
1959	56	3	0	0	0	0	0	0	0	182	0	0	441	150
Lifetime		6	0	0	0	0	0	0	0	770	0	0	782	$350

Gene Rose

Gene Rose

Year	Rank	Starts	Poles	1	2	3	4	5	6–10	Laps	Laps Led	Races Led	Miles	$
1955	137	1	0	0	0	0	0	0	0	160	0	0	240	95
Lifetime		1	0	0	0	0	0	0	0	160	0	0	240	$95

Howard Rose

Howard Rose
B: 12/18/1963
Racing Hometown: Ashland, KY

Year	Rank	Starts	Poles	1	2	3	4	5	6–10	Laps	Laps Led	Races Led	Miles	$
1986	110	1	0	0	0	0	0	0	0	241	0	0	241	1,200
Lifetime		1	0	0	0	0	0	0	0	241	0	0	241	$1,200

Ralph Rose

Ralph Rose
Racing Hometown: S. Norfolk, VA

Year	Rank	Starts	Poles	1	2	3	4	5	6–10	Laps	Laps Led	Races Led	Miles	$
1953	53T	2	0	0	0	0	0	0	2		0	0		150
Lifetime		2	0	0	0	0	0	0	2		0	0		$150

Sam Rose

Samuel Rose
Racing Hometown: San Bernadino, CA

Year	Rank	Starts	Poles	1	2	3	4	5	6–10	Laps	Laps Led	Races Led	Miles	$
1968	86	1	0	0	0	0	0	0	0	92	0	0	248	630
1969	NR	1	0	0	0	0	0	0	0	65	0	0	176	775

Year	Rank	Starts	Poles	Finish						Laps	Laps Led	Races Led	Miles	$
				1	2	3	4	5	6–10	Laps	Led	Led	Miles	$

Sam Rose *continued*

Year	Rank	Starts	Poles	1	2	3	4	5	6–10	Laps	Laps Led	Races Led	Miles	$
1970	74	1	0	0	0	0	0	0	0	157	0	0	411	1,175
Lifetime		3	0	0	0	0	0	0	0	314	0	0	835	$2,580

H. G. Rosier

Howard G. Rosier Jr.
Racing Hometown: North Augusta, SC

Year	Rank	Starts	Poles	1	2	3	4	5	6–10	Laps	Laps Led	Races Led	Miles	$
1962	53	5	0	0	0	0	0	0	1	772	0	0	807	1,505
1963	97	3	0	0	0	0	1	0	0	228	0	0	172	850
Lifetime		8	0	0	0	0	1	0	1	1,000	0	0	979	$2,355

Bob Ross

Robert Ross
Racing Hometown: Lakewood, CA

Year	Rank	Starts	Poles	1	2	3	4	5	6–10	Laps	Laps Led	Races Led	Miles	$
1956	68	3	0	0	0	0	0	0	2	601	0	0	418	575
1957	53	3	0	0	0	0	0	0	3	396	0	0	314	720
1958	96	2	0	0	1	0	0	0	0	135	0	0	192	600
1959	82	2	0	0	0	0	2	0	0	582	0	0	293	935
1960	105	3	0	0	0	0	0	0	0	105	0	0	117	250
1961	110	2	1	0	1	0	0	0	0	112	0	0	117	800
1963	70	2	0	0	0	0	0	0	1	315	0	0	851	1,525
Lifetime		17	1	0	2	0	2	0	6	2,246	0	0	2,302	$5,405

Brian Ross

Brian J. Ross
B: 11/4/1944
Racing Hometown: Ballston Spa, NY

Year	Rank	Starts	Poles	1	2	3	4	5	6–10	Laps	Laps Led	Races Led	Miles	$
1990	83	1	0	0	0	0	0	0	0	175	0	0	350	3,775
1991	87T	1	0	0	0	0	0	0	0	37	0	0	37	6,075
Lifetime		2	0	0	0	0	0	0	0	212	0	0	387	$9,850

Dick Ross

Richard Ross
Racing Hometown: Havre de Grace, MD

Year	Rank	Starts	Poles	1	2	3	4	5	6–10	Laps	Laps Led	Races Led	Miles	$
1954	165	2	0	0	0	0	0	0	0	341	0	0	271	50
Lifetime		2	0	0	0	0	0	0	0	341	0	0	271	$50

Earl Ross

Earl Ross
B: 9/4/1941
Racing Hometown: Alsa Craig, Ont., Canada

Year	Rank	Starts	Poles	1	2	3	4	5	6–10	Laps	Laps Led	Races Led	Miles	$
1973	68	3	0	0	0	0	0	0	0	335	0	0	797	4,005
1974	8	21	0	1	1	1	1	1	5	5,860	127	6	7,644	81,199
1975	NR	1	0	0	0	0	0	0	0	372	0	0	558	2,965
1976	115T	1	0	0	0	0	0	0	0	28	0	0	70	2,025
1978	—	0												500
Lifetime		26	0	1	1	1	1	1	5	6,595	127	6	9,069	$90,694

Jim Ross

James Ross
Racing Hometown: Detroit, MI

Year	Rank	Starts	Poles	1	2	3	4	5	6–10	Laps	Laps Led	Races Led	Miles	$
1951	N/A	2	0	0	0	0	0	0	0		0	0		50
Lifetime		2	0	0	0	0	0	0	0		0	0		$50

John Ross

John Ross
Racing Hometown: Syracuse, NY

Year	Rank	Starts	Poles	1	2	3	4	5	6–10	Laps	Laps Led	Races Led	Miles	$
1953	NR	1	0	0	0	0	0	0	0		0	0		25
Lifetime		1	0	0	0	0	0	0	0		0	0		$25

Mario Rossi

Mario Rossi
B: 11/17/1932
Racing Hometown: Trenton, NJ

Year	Rank	Starts	Poles	1	2	3	4	5	6–10	Laps	Laps Led	Races Led	Miles	$
1955	83T	1	0	0	0	0	0	0	1	223	0	0	223	200
1956	258	1	0	0	0	0	0	0	0	97	0	0	97	60
1958	60	2	0	0	0	0	0	0	0	501	0	0	475	220
Lifetime		4	0	0	0	0	0	0	1	821	0	0	795	$480

Year	Rank	Starts	Poles	Finish 1	2	3	4	5	6–10	Laps	Laps Led	Races Led	Miles	$

John Rostek

John Rostek
B: 11/12/1925
Racing Hometown: Ft. Collins, CO

Year	Rank	Starts	Poles	1	2	3	4	5	6–10	Laps	Laps Led	Races Led	Miles	$
1960	NR	5	1	1	0	1	0	0	1	658	65	2	688	2,060
1963	68	1	0	0	0	0	0	0	0	172	0	0	464	500
Lifetime		6	1	1	0	1	0	0	1	830	65	2	1,152	$2,560

Gil Roth

Dr. Gilbert Roth

Year	Rank	Starts	Poles	1	2	3	4	5	6–10	Laps	Laps Led	Races Led	Miles	$
1982	99	1	0	0	0	0	0	0	0	91	0	0	91	615
Lifetime		1	0	0	0	0	0	0	0	91	0	0	91	$615

Tom Rotsell

Thomas Rotsell

Year	Rank	Starts	Poles	1	2	3	4	5	6–10	Laps	Laps Led	Races Led	Miles	$
1986	101T	1	0	0	0	0	0	0	0	84	0	0	204	2,080
1987	84T	1	0	0	0	0	0	0	0	84	0	0	204	2,110
1988	71	1	0	0	0	0	0	0	0	90	0	0	219	2,470
Lifetime		3	0	0	0	0	0	0	0	258	0	0	626	$6,660

Jack Rounds

Jack Rounds
B: 12/2/1930
Racing Hometown: Huntington, WV

Year	Rank	Starts	Poles	1	2	3	4	5	6–10	Laps	Laps Led	Races Led	Miles	$
1958	71	1	0	0	0	0	0	0	0	167	0	0	439	150
Lifetime		1	0	0	0	0	0	0	0	167	0	0	439	$150

Lloyd Ruby

Lloyd Ruby
B: 1/12/1928
Racing Hometown: Wichita Falls, TX

Year	Rank	Starts	Poles	1	2	3	4	5	6–10	Laps	Laps Led	Races Led	Miles	$
1967	NR	1	0	0	0	0	0	0	0	96	0	0	259	565
Lifetime		1	0	0	0	0	0	0	0	96	0	0	259	$565

Al Rudd Jr.

Al Rudd Jr.
Racing Hometown: Chesapeake, VA

Year	Rank	Starts	Poles	1	2	3	4	5	6–10	Laps	Laps Led	Races Led	Miles	$
1979	NR	1	0	0	0	0	0	0	0	39	0	0	78	740
Lifetime		1	0	0	0	0	0	0	0	39	0	0	78	$740

Ricky Rudd

Richard Lee Rudd
B: 9/12/1956
Racing Hometown: Chesapeake, VA

Year	Rank	Starts	Poles	1	2	3	4	5	6–10	Laps	Laps Led	Races Led	Miles	$
1975	47	4	0	0	0	0	0	0	1	1,025	0	0	886	4,345
1976	53	4	0	0	0	0	0	0	1	876	0	0	1,527	7,525
1977	17	25	0	0	0	0	1	0	9	6,233	13	3	7,509	75,905
1978	31	13	0	0	0	0	0	0	4	2,535	16	5	4,334	50,630
1979	9	28	0	0	0	2	0	2	13	8,836	22	4	9,917	150,898
1980	35	13	0	0	0	0	1	0	2	2,719	7	2	4,149	50,500
1981	6	31	3	0	3	4	3	4	3	8,942	443	12	9,879	395,685
1982	9	30	2	0	2	0	3	1	7	7,753	140	8	8,680	217,140
1983	9	30	4	2	1	1	1	2	7	8,581	871	13	9,907	275,400
1984	7	30	4	1	1	3	1	1	9	9,271	566	8	10,584	497,779
1985	6	28	0	1	2	1	5	4	6	8,475	329	6	10,281	512,441
1986	5	29	1	2	4	2	3	0	6	8,120	525	7	10,193	671,548
1987	6	29	0	2	2	4	1	1	3	8,206	505	12	9,891	653,508
1988	11	29	2	1	3	1	1	0	5	8,867	695	16	10,428	410,954
1989	8	29	0	1	0	2	3	1	8	9,326	247	7	**11,075**	533,624
1990	7	29	2	1	0	3	2	2	7	8,664	180	7	10,392	573,650
1991	2	29	1	1	3	0	2	3	8	**9,561**	425	13	11,427	1,093,765
1992	7	29	1	1	0	2	3	3	9	8,968	331	9	10,269	793,903
1993	10	30	0	1	1	1	3	3	5	8,635	136	7	10,265	752,562
1994	5	31	1	1	0	0	3	2	9	9,728	192	10	**12,046**	1,079,441
1995	9	31	2	1	0	1	4	4	6	8,813	368	11	10,834	1,337,703
1996	6	31	0	1	2	1	1	0	11	9,281	151	12	11,400	1,503,025
Lifetime		562	23	17	24	28	41	33	139	163,415	6,162	172	195,874	$11,641,931
		10th									**6th**		**7th**	

Year	Rank	Starts	Poles	Finish 1	2	3	4	5	6–10	Laps	Laps Led	Races Led	Miles	$

Charlie Rudolph

Charles Rudolph
B: 1958
Racing Hometown: Newark, NJ

Year	Rank	Starts	Poles	1	2	3	4	5	6–10	Laps	Laps Led	Races Led	Miles	$
1987	51	4	0	0	0	0	0	0	0	924	0	0	1,583	9,995
Lifetime		4	0	0	0	0	0	0	0	924	0	0	1,583	$9,995

Don Rudolph

Donald Rudolph
Racing Hometown: Newark, NJ

Year	Rank	Starts	Poles	1	2	3	4	5	6–10	Laps	Laps Led	Races Led	Miles	$
1951	N/A	1	0	0	0	0	0	0	0		0	0		10
1952	180	1	0	0	0	0	0	0	0	82	0	0	82	25
Lifetime		2	0	0	0	0	0	0	0	82	0	0	82	$35

Bob Ruppert

Robert Ruppert
Racing Hometown: Las Vegas, NV

Year	Rank	Starts	Poles	1	2	3	4	5	6–10	Laps	Laps Led	Races Led	Miles	$
1955	121	1	0	0	0	0	0	0	1	102	0	0	102	200
1956	138	2	0	0	0	0	0	0	0	164	0	0	278	150
Lifetime		3	0	0	0	0	0	0	1	266	0	0	380	$350

Dan Rush

Daniel Rush
Racing Hometown: Rome, GA

Year	Rank	Starts	Poles	1	2	3	4	5	6–10	Laps	Laps Led	Races Led	Miles	$
1951	N/A	1	0	0	0	0	0	0	0		0	0		25
Lifetime		1	0	0	0	0	0	0	0		0	0		$25

Ermon Rush

Ermon Rush
Racing Hometown: Thomasville, NC

Year	Rank	Starts	Poles	1	2	3	4	5	6–10	Laps	Laps Led	Races Led	Miles	$
1953	74	3	0	0	0	0	0	0	0		0	0		75
1959	NR	1	0	0	0	0	0	0	0	188	0	0	47	140
Lifetime		4	0	0	0	0	0	0	0	188	0	0	47	$215

Ken Rush

Samuel Kenneth Rush
B: 9/14/1931
Racing Hometown: High Point, NC

Year	Rank	Starts	Poles	1	2	3	4	5	6–10	Laps	Laps Led	Races Led	Miles	$
1957	39	16	1	0	0	1	0	0	5	2,266	0	0	1,397	2,045
1958	160	11	1	0	0	0	0	0	3	1,625	0	0	828	1,640
1959	NR	12	0	0	1	0	1	0	1	2,388	0	0	1,533	2,095
1961	51	6	0	0	0	0	0	1	1	1,586	0	0	1,065	2,325
1962	104	1	0	0	0	0	0	0	0	463	0	0	232	150
1964	70	8	0	0	0	0	1	0	1	768	0	0	398	1,640
1971	NR	1	0	0	0	0	0	0	0	117	0	0	29	240
1972	NR	1	0	0	0	0	0	0	0	149	0	0	224	1,625
Lifetime		56	2	0	1	1	2	1	11	9,362	0	0	5,706	$11,760

Rusty Rushton

Russell Rushton
Racing Hometown: Pawtucket, RI

Year	Rank	Starts	Poles	1	2	3	4	5	6–10	Laps	Laps Led	Races Led	Miles	$
1951	N/A	2	0	0	0	0	0	0	0		0	0		50
Lifetime		2	0	0	0	0	0	0	0		0	0		$50

Hank Russ

Hank Russ
Racing Hometown: Saginaw, MI

Year	Rank	Starts	Poles	1	2	3	4	5	6–10	Laps	Laps Led	Races Led	Miles	$
1951	N/A	1	0	0	0	0	0	0	0		0	0		25
1954	N/A	1	0	0	0	0	0	0	0	165	0	0	83	25
Lifetime		2	0	0	0	0	0	0	0	165	0	0	83	$50

Fred Russell

Fred Russell
Racing Hometown: Oakland, CA

Year	Rank	Starts	Poles	1	2	3	4	5	6–10	Laps	Laps Led	Races Led	Miles	$
1951	N/A	1	0	0	0	0	0	0	1		0	0		75
Lifetime		1	0	0	0	0	0	0	1		0	0		$75

Jack Russell

Jack Russell
Racing Hometown: Erie, PA

Year	Rank	Starts	Poles	1	2	3	4	5	6–10	Laps	Laps Led	Races Led	Miles	$
1949	24	3	0	0	0	0	0	0	2	178	0	0	89	175

Year	Rank	Starts	Poles	Finish 1	2	3	4	5	6–10	Laps	Laps Led	Races Led	Miles	$

Jack Russell *continued*

Year	Rank	Starts	Poles	1	2	3	4	5	6–10	Laps	Laps Led	Races Led	Miles	$
1950	116T	1	0	0	0	0	0	0	0		0	0		0
1958	NR	1	0	0	0	0	0	0	0	74	0	0	74	100
Lifetime		5	0	0	0	0	0	0	2	252	0	0	163	$275

Jim Russell

James Russell
  Racing Hometown: Odessa, TX

Year	Rank	Starts	Poles	1	2	3	4	5	6–10	Laps	Laps Led	Races Led	Miles	$
1957	190	4	0	0	0	0	0	0	0	263	0	0	148	150
Lifetime		4	0	0	0	0	0	0	0	263	0	0	148	$150

Jerry Russo

Jerry Russo

Year	Rank	Starts	Poles	1	2	3	4	5	6–10	Laps	Laps Led	Races Led	Miles	$
1951	N/A	1	0	0	0	0	0	0	0		0	0		25
Lifetime		1	0	0	0	0	0	0	0		0	0		$25

Johnny Rutherford

John Sherman Rutherford III
  B: 3/12/1938
  Racing Hometown: Ft. Worth, TX

Year	Rank	Starts	Poles	1	2	3	4	5	6–10	Laps	Laps Led	Races Led	Miles	$
1963	NR	2	0	1	0	0	0	0	1	236	6	1	590	2,350
1964	NR	3	0	0	0	0	0	0	1	280	0	0	700	2,175
1965	NR	1	0	0	0	0	0	0	0	298	0	0	447	650
1966	NR	2	0	0	0	0	0	0	0	150	0	0	375	1,210
1972	NR	1	0	0	0	0	0	0	0	224	0	0	448	1,280
1973	NR	1	0	0	0	0	0	0	0	471	0	0	479	1,325
1974	82	3	0	0	0	0	0	0	0	325	3	2	611	5,164
1975	NR	4	0	0	0	0	0	0	0	189	0	0	337	4,925
1976	NR	2	0	0	0	0	0	0	0	347	0	0	660	2,745
1977	NR	3	0	0	0	0	0	0	0	193	0	0	452	4,150
1981	33	12	0	0	0	0	0	1	1	2,432	5	1	3,793	38,095
1988	89T	1	0	0	0	0	0	0	0	155	0	0	155	3,775
Lifetime		35	0	1	0	0	0	1	3	5,300	14	4	9,045	$67,844

Joe Ruttman

Joseph Ruttman
  B: 10/28/1944
  Racing Hometown: Upland, CA

Year	Rank	Starts	Poles	1	2	3	4	5	6–10	Laps	Laps Led	Races Led	Miles	$
1963	56	1	0	0	0	0	0	0	1	176	0	0	475	850
1964	127	1	0	0	0	0	0	0	0	46	0	0	124	500
1977	84T	1	0	0	0	0	0	0	0	196	0	0	490	2,035
1980	NR	1	0	0	0	0	0	0	0	29	0	0	73	1,055
1981	28	17	0	0	1	0	0	1	5	4,194	106	7	5,588	137,275
1982	16	29	0	0	0	1	2	2	2	7,354	178	6	8,033	191,634
1983	12	30	2	0	0	1	3	0	6	7,887	397	10	8,817	223,809
1984	18	29	1	0	0	0	0	0	8	6,635	55	4	8,161	168,433
1985	30	16	0	0	0	0	0	1	3	3,378	5	1	4,599	81,425
1986	15	29	0	0	2	0	0	3	9	7,732	55	5	8,707	259,263
1987	NR	4	0	0	0	0	0	0	2	963	0	0	1,380	28,405
1988	39	12	0	0	0	0	0	0	1	1,899	0	0	3,422	46,455
1989	43	9	0	0	0	0	0	0	1	1,704	0	0	2,673	64,645
1990	81T	1	0	0	0	0	0	0	0	196	0	0	490	22,950
1991	20	29	0	0	0	1	0	0	3	8,974	11	1	10,774	361,661
1992	84T	1	0	0	0	0	0	0	0	213	0	0	320	5,250
1993	43	5	0	0	0	0	0	1	0	1,133	0	0	1,597	70,700
1994	54	2	0	0	0	0	0	0	0	527	0	0	990	39,695
1995	56	1	0	0	0	0	0	0	0	200	0	0	500	40,135
1996	—	0												3,522
Lifetime		218	3	0	3	3	5	8	41	53,436	807	34	67,211	$1,749,697

Troy Ruttman

Troy Ruttman
  B: 3/11/1930
  Racing Hometown: Mooreland, OK

Year	Rank	Starts	Poles	1	2	3	4	5	6–10	Laps	Laps Led	Races Led	Miles	$
1962	49	1	0	0	0	0	0	1	0	218	0	0	327	1,750
1963	NR	5	0	0	0	1	0	0	2	796	0	0	1,699	6,430
1964	NR	1	0	0	0	0	0	0	1	177	0	0	478	850
Lifetime		7	0	0	0	1	0	1	3	1,191	0	0	2,504	$9,030

Year	Rank	Starts	Poles	Finish						Laps	Laps Led	Races Led	Miles	$
				1	2	3	4	5	6–10					

Hal Ruyle
Hal Ruyle
Racing Hometown: St. Louis, MO

Year	Rank	Starts	Poles	1	2	3	4	5	6–10	Laps	Laps Led	Races Led	Miles	$
1954	NR	1	0	0	0	0	0	0	0	178	0	0	89	25
Lifetime		1	0	0	0	0	0	0	0	178	0	0	89	$25

Kelly Ryan
Kelly Ryan

Year	Rank	Starts	Poles	1	2	3	4	5	6–10	Laps	Laps Led	Races Led	Miles	$
1962	NR	1	0	0	0	0	0	0	0	34	0	0	9	75
Lifetime		1	0	0	0	0	0	0	0	34	0	0	9	$75

Terry Ryan
Terry Ryan
B: 5/13/1938
Racing Hometown: Davenport, IA

Year	Rank	Starts	Poles	1	2	3	4	5	6–10	Laps	Laps Led	Races Led	Miles	$
1976	46	5	0	0	0	0	0	1	2	603	1	1	1,516	24,940
1977	40	7	0	0	0	0	0	0	1	1,142	0	0	2,240	12,405
1980	—	0												970
Lifetime		12	0	0	0	0	0	1	3	1,745	1	1	3,756	$38,315

Red Ryder
Samuel Ryder
Racing Hometown: Athol Springs, NY

Year	Rank	Starts	Poles	1	2	3	4	5	6–10	Laps	Laps Led	Races Led	Miles	$
1950	NR	1	0	0	0	0	0	0	0		0	0		0
1951	N/A	1	0	0	0	0	0	0	0		0	0		25
Lifetime		2	0	0	0	0	0	0	0		0	0		$25

Mike Saathoff
Michael Saathoff
Racing Hometown: Los Angeles, CA

Year	Rank	Starts	Poles	1	2	3	4	5	6–10	Laps	Laps Led	Races Led	Miles	$
1961	149	1	0	0	0	0	0	0	0	129	0	0	181	200
Lifetime		1	0	0	0	0	0	0	0	129	0	0	181	$200

Greg Sacks
Gregory Sacks
B: 11/3/1952
Racing Hometown: Mattituck, NY

Year	Rank	Starts	Poles	1	2	3	4	5	6–10	Laps	Laps Led	Races Led	Miles	$
1983	47	5	0	0	0	0	0	0	0	638	0	0	1,202	8,060
1984	19	29	0	0	0	0	0	0	1	6,348	0	0	7,781	75,184
1985	25	20	0	1	0	0	0	0	4	4,855	36	3	6,425	234,141
1986	41	8	0	0	0	0	0	0	1	1,181	0	0	1,743	64,810
1987	33	16	0	0	0	0	0	0	0	2,705	1	1	4,254	54,815
1988	37	15	0	0	0	0	0	0	3	3,543	1	1	4,499	105,579
1989	32	20	0	0	0	0	0	0	2	4,955	110	4	5,692	113,535
1990	32	16	1	0	2	0	0	0	2	3,790	107	4	5,401	216,148
1991	39	11	0	0	0	0	0	0	0	2,101	0	0	3,161	84,215
1992	30	20	0	0	0	0	0	0	0	4,926	6	1	6,502	178,120
1993	35	19	0	0	0	0	0	0	1	5,251	1	1	7,219	168,055
1994	31	31	1	0	0	0	0	0	3	8,266	38	8	10,041	411,728
1995	39	20	0	0	0	0	0	0	0	4,682	0	0	5,633	323,720
1996	42	9	0	0	0	0	0	0	0	2,196	3	1	3,614	207,755
Lifetime		239	2	1	2	0	0	0	17	55,437	303	24	73,167	$2,245,865

Hermie Sadler
Herman Sadler
B: 4/24/1969
Racing Hometown: Emporia, VA

Year	Rank	Starts	Poles	1	2	3	4	5	6–10	Laps	Laps Led	Races Led	Miles	$
1996	63T	1	0	0	0	0	0	0	0	349	0	0	349	13,055
Lifetime		1	0	0	0	0	0	0	0	349	0	0	349	$13,055

Darryl Sage
Darryl Sage
B: 5/8/1965
Racing Hometown: Murfreesboro, TN

Year	Rank	Starts	Poles	1	2	3	4	5	6–10	Laps	Laps Led	Races Led	Miles	$
1982	50	5	0	0	0	0	0	0	0	1,572	0	0	1,148	4,970
1983	85	3	0	0	0	0	0	0	0	638	0	0	675	3,610
Lifetime		8	0	0	0	0	0	0	0	2,210	0	0	1,823	$8,580

Bucky Sager
John Sager
Racing Hometown: Toledo, OH

Year	Rank	Starts	Poles	1	2	3	4	5	6–10	Laps	Laps Led	Races Led	Miles	$
1950	33	2	0	0	1	0	0	0	0		146	1		750

Year	Rank	Starts	Poles			Finish				Laps	Laps Led	Races Led	Miles	$
				1	2	3	4	5	6–10					

Bucky Sager *continued*

Year	Rank	Starts	Poles	1	2	3	4	5	6–10	Laps	Laps Led	Races Led	Miles	$
1951	N/A	1	0	0	0	0	0	0	0		0	0		25
1952	26	10	0	0	0	0	1	0	2	1,545	0	0	1,068	710
1954	NR	3	0	0	0	0	0	0	0	190	0	0	221	50
Lifetime		16	0	0	1	0	1	0	2	1,735	146	1	1,289	$1,460

Bob Said

Boris Said
B: 1922
Racing Hometown: Greenwich, CT

Year	Rank	Starts	Poles	1	2	3	4	5	6–10	Laps	Laps Led	Races Led	Miles	$
1959	NR	1	0	0	0	0	0	0	0	42	0	0	105	100
Lifetime		1	0	0	0	0	0	0	0	42	0	0	105	$100

Gary Sain

Gary L. Sain
Racing Hometown: Hickory, NC

Year	Rank	Starts	Poles	1	2	3	4	5	6–10	Laps	Laps Led	Races Led	Miles	$
1962	74	5	0	0	0	0	0	0	0	986	0	0	533	700
1963	64	7	0	0	0	0	0	0	1	994	0	0	523	700
1967	86	4	0	0	0	0	0	0	1	399	0	0	271	2,335
Lifetime		16	0	0	0	0	0	0	2	2,379	0	0	1,327	$3,735

Leon Sales

Leon J. Sales
B: 10/4/1923   D: 4/27/1981
Racing Hometown: Winston-Salem, NC

Year	Rank	Starts	Poles	1	2	3	4	5	6–10	Laps	Laps Led	Races Led	Miles	$
1950	28	2	0	1	0	0	0	0	0	227	18	1	139	1,000
1951	N/A	4	0	0	0	0	0	0	2	452	0	0	548	850
1952	188	2	0	0	0	0	0	0	0		0	0		25
Lifetime		8	0	1	0	0	0	0	2	679	18	1	687	$1,875

Ed Samples

Edward Samples
B: 1/31/1921   D: 6/10/1991
Racing Hometown: Atlanta, GA

Year	Rank	Starts	Poles	1	2	3	4	5	6–10	Laps	Laps Led	Races Led	Miles	$
1951	61	4	0	0	0	0	0	0	2	15	0	0	11	285
1952	30	8	0	0	1	1	0	0	2	614	0	0	370	1,535
1954	NR	1	0	0	0	0	0	0	0	36	0	0	148	40
Lifetime		13	0	0	1	1	0	0	4	665	0	0	529	$1,860

Jesse Samples

Jesse Samples
Racing Hometown: Atlanta, GA

Year	Rank	Starts	Poles	1	2	3	4	5	6–10	Laps	Laps Led	Races Led	Miles	$
1965	106	1	0	0	0	0	0	0	0	198	0	0	297	495
Lifetime		1	0	0	0	0	0	0	0	198	0	0	297	$495

Jesse Samples Jr.

Jesse Samples Jr.
B: 1968
Racing Hometown: Atlanta, GA

Year	Rank	Starts	Poles	1	2	3	4	5	6–10	Laps	Laps Led	Races Led	Miles	$
1987	76	2	0	0	0	0	0	0	0	164	0	0	106	4,610
Lifetime		2	0	0	0	0	0	0	0	164	0	0	106	$4,610

Bob Sampson

Robert Sampson
Racing Hometown: Levittown, PA

Year	Rank	Starts	Poles	1	2	3	4	5	6–10	Laps	Laps Led	Races Led	Miles	$
1953	NR	1	0	0	0	0	0	0	0	172	0	0	86	25
1954	200	1	0	0	0	0	0	0	0	32	0	0	131	0
Lifetime		2	0	0	0	0	0	0	0	204	0	0	217	$25

Charles Sanchez

Charles Sanchez
Racing Hometown: Ripon, CA

Year	Rank	Starts	Poles	1	2	3	4	5	6–10	Laps	Laps Led	Races Led	Miles	$
1958	109	1	0	0	0	0	0	0	1	98	0	0	98	250
1959	117	1	0	0	0	0	0	0	0	35	0	0	35	25
Lifetime		2	0	0	0	0	0	0	1	133	0	0	133	$275

August Sand

August Sand
Racing Hometown: Pittsburgh, PA

Year	Rank	Starts	Poles	1	2	3	4	5	6–10	Laps	Laps Led	Races Led	Miles	$
1959	NR	1	0	0	0	0	0	0	0	133	0	0	33	100
Lifetime		1	0	0	0	0	0	0	0	133	0	0	33	$100

Year	Rank	Starts	Poles	Finish						Laps	Laps Led	Races Led	Miles	$
				1	2	3	4	5	6–10					

Ronnie Sanders

Ronald Sanders
B: 12/5/1945
Racing Hometown: Fayetteville, GA

Year	Rank	Starts	Poles	1	2	3	4	5	6–10	Laps	Laps Led	Races Led	Miles	$
1981	77	1	0	0	0	0	0	0	0	191	0	0	478	7,635
1982	—	0												1,550
1983	—	0												950
1987	NR	1	0	0	0	0	0	0	0	195	0	0	488	13,930
1988	—	0												1,300
1989	83T	1	0	0	0	0	0	0	0	184	0	0	460	12,570
1993	—	0												2,650
Lifetime		3	0	0	0	0	0	0	0	570	0	0	1,425	$40,585

Rusty Sanders

Rusty Sanders
Racing Hometown: Bakersfield, CA

Year	Rank	Starts	Poles	1	2	3	4	5	6–10	Laps	Laps Led	Races Led	Miles	$
1976	104	1	0	0	0	0	0	0	0	29	0	0	76	815
Lifetime		1	0	0	0	0	0	0	0	29	0	0	76	$815

Scott Sandman

Scott Sandman
Racing Hometown: Pittsburgh, PA

Year	Rank	Starts	Poles	1	2	3	4	5	6–10	Laps	Laps Led	Races Led	Miles	$
1959	NR	1	0	0	0	0	0	0	0	20	0	0	5	50
Lifetime		1	0	0	0	0	0	0	0	20	0	0	5	$50

Bobby Sands

Robert Sands
Racing Hometown: Henryville, IN

Year	Rank	Starts	Poles	1	2	3	4	5	6–10	Laps	Laps Led	Races Led	Miles	$
1980	100	1	0	0	0	0	0	0	0	2	0	0	1	450
Lifetime		1	0	0	0	0	0	0-	0	2	0	0	1	$450

Dick Sanford

Richard Sanford
Racing Hometown: Ramsey, NJ

Year	Rank	Starts	Poles	1	2	3	4	5	6–10	Laps	Laps Led	Races Led	Miles	$
1954	119T	1	0	0	0	0	0	0	0	180	0	0	90	25
Lifetime		1	0	0	0	0	0	0	0	180	0	0	90	$25

Ed Sanger

Edward Sanger
B: 1940
Racing Hometown: Waterloo, IA

Year	Rank	Starts	Poles	1	2	3	4	5	6–10	Laps	Laps Led	Races Led	Miles	$
1985	81T	1	0	0	0	0	0	0	0	358	0	0	224	910
Lifetime		1	0	0	0	0	0	0	0	358	0	0	224	$910

Dick Santee

Richard Santee
Racing Hometown: Fullerton, CA

Year	Rank	Starts	Poles	1	2	3	4	5	6–10	Laps	Laps Led	Races Led	Miles	$
1959	NR	1	0	0	0	0	0	0	0	407	0	0	163	130
1961	116	1	0	0	0	0	0	0	0	159	0	0	223	400
Lifetime		2	0	0	0	0	0	0	0	566	0	0	385	$530

Marshall Sargent

Marshall Sargent
D: 10/19/1990
Racing Hometown: Salinas, CA

Year	Rank	Starts	Poles	1	2	3	4	5	6–10	Laps	Laps Led	Races Led	Miles	$
1957	64	5	0	0	0	0	0	0	2	541	0	0	334	575
1958	164	1	0	0	0	0	0	0	0	135	0	0	355	110
1960	146	1	0	0	0	0	0	0	0	1	0	0	1	25
1961	86	3	0	0	0	0	0	0	0	369	0	0	690	450
1963	NR	1	0	0	0	0	0	0	0	157	0	0	424	375
1964	107	1	0	0	0	0	0	0	1	77	0	0	39	150
Lifetime		12	0	0	0	0	0	0	3	1,280	0	0	1,842	$1,685

Don Satterfield

Donald Satterfield
B: 11/9/1953
Racing Hometown: Spartanburg, SC

Year	Rank	Starts	Poles	1	2	3	4	5	6–10	Laps	Laps Led	Races Led	Miles	$
1981	NR	1	0	0	0	0	0	0	0	1	0	0	1	450
1983	NR	3	0	0	0	0	0	0	0	645	0	0	359	2,555
Lifetime		4	0	0	0	0	0	0	0	646	0	0	359	$3,005

Year	Rank	Starts	Poles	Finish						Laps	Laps Led	Races Led	Miles	$
				1	2	3	4	5	6–10					

Sandy Satullo

S. Sandy Satullo II
B: 1954
Racing Hometown: Fairview Park, OH

Year	Rank	Starts	Poles	1	2	3	4	5	6–10	Laps	Laps Led	Races Led	Miles	$
1979	77	2	0	0	0	0	0	0	0	210	0	0	429	2,360
1981	98T	1	0	0	0	0	0	0	0	68	0	0	181	1,500
Lifetime		3	0	0	0	0	0	0	0	278	0	0	610	$3,860

Joe Saunders

Joseph Saunders
Racing Hometown: Syracuse, NY

Year	Rank	Starts	Poles	1	2	3	4	5	6–10	Laps	Laps Led	Races Led	Miles	$
1957	NR	1	0	0	0	0	0	0	0	19	0	0	19	50
Lifetime		1	0	0	0	0	0	0	0	19	0	0	19	$50

Jim Sauter

James Sauter
B: 6/1/1943
Racing Hometown: Necedah, WI

Year	Rank	Starts	Poles	1	2	3	4	5	6–10	Laps	Laps Led	Races Led	Miles	$
1980	109	1	0	0	0	0	0	0	0	33	0	0	50	900
1982	62	3	0	0	0	0	0	0	1	511	5	1	961	23,270
1983	68	5	0	0	0	0	0	0	0	1,414	0	0	1,830	26,910
1984	88	3	0	0	0	0	0	0	0	737	0	0	1,152	18,015
1985	50	3	0	0	0	0	0	0	0	565	0	0	1,107	15,465
1986	49	8	0	0	0	0	0	0	0	1,285	2	1	2,705	52,020
1987	53	3	0	0	0	0	0	0	1	781	0	0	1,364	28,655
1988	44	9	0	0	0	0	0	0	0	2,413	6	1	3,196	38,090
1989	33	17	0	0	0	0	0	0	2	3,974	8	1	5,116	73,832
1990	58	3	0	0	0	0	0	0	0	712	0	0	1,172	14,175
1991	43	6	0	0	0	0	0	0	0	1,012	0	0	1,843	47,395
1992	37	9	0	0	0	0	0	0	0	2,829	0	0	2,434	58,995
1993	47	4	0	0	0	0	0	0	0	769	0	0	1,505	51,960
1994	—	0												5,300
1995	—	0												2,400
1996	52	2	0	0	0	0	0	0	0	633	0	0	631	51,172
Lifetime		76	0	0	0	0	0	0	4	17,668	21	4	25,067	$508,554

Swede Savage

David Earle Savage Jr.
B: 8/26/1946   D: 7/2/1973   *Died from injuries in 1973 Indy 500.*
Racing Hometown: Santa Ana, CA

Year	Rank	Starts	Poles	1	2	3	4	5	6–10	Laps	Laps Led	Races Led	Miles	$
1967	70	3	0	0	0	0	0	0	2	1,091	0	0	571	1,275
1968	84	2	0	0	0	1	0	0	0	841	0	0	592	2,635
1969	NR	4	0	0	0	0	0	1	1	924	0	0	1,074	5,120
Lifetime		9	0	0	0	1	0	1	3	2,856	0	0	2,237	$9,030

Elton Sawyer

Everett Elton Sawyer
B: 11/5/1959
Racing Hometown: Chesapeake, VA

Year	Rank	Starts	Poles	1	2	3	4	5	6–10	Laps	Laps Led	Races Led	Miles	$
1995	38	20	0	0	0	0	0	0	0	4,573	0	0	6,185	416,490
1996	43	9	0	0	0	0	0	0	0	2,448	0	0	3,330	129,618
Lifetime		29	0	0	0	0	0	0	0	7,021	0	0	9,516	$546,108

Lucky Sawyer

Richard Sawyer
Racing Hometown: Baltimore, MD

Year	Rank	Starts	Poles	1	2	3	4	5	6–10	Laps	Laps Led	Races Led	Miles	$
1952	131	3	0	0	0	0	0	0	0	333	0	0	315	110
1953	105	4	0	0	0	0	0	0	0	27	0	0	96	75
1957	193	2	0	0	0	0	0	0	0	81	0	0	49	50
1958	178	1	0	0	0	0	0	0	0	12	0	0	6	10
Lifetime		10	0	0	0	0	0	0	0	453	0	0	465	$245

Connie Saylor

Connie Saylor
B: 6/3/1940   D: 2/4/1993
Racing Hometown: Johnson City, TN

Year	Rank	Starts	Poles	1	2	3	4	5	6–10	Laps	Laps Led	Races Led	Miles	$
1978	54	3	0	0	0	0	0	0	1	820	0	0	1,237	9,115
1979	75	2	0	0	0	0	0	0	0	262	0	0	565	5,130
1980	67	5	0	0	0	0	0	0	0	1,171	5	2	1,729	10,285
1981	39	7	0	0	0	0	0	0	0	1,267	0	0	2,139	19,715

Year	Rank	Starts	Poles	Finish						Laps	Laps Led	Races Led	Miles	$
				1	2	3	4	5	6–10					

Connie Saylor *continued*

Year	Rank	Starts	Poles	1	2	3	4	5	6–10	Laps	Laps Led	Races Led	Miles	$
1982	49	7	0	0	0	0	0	0	0	1,450	3	1	1,704	18,025
1983	101T	2	0	0	0	0	0	0	0	175	0	0	441	8,060
1984	43	8	0	0	0	0	0	0	0	1,193	1	1	2,166	23,175
1985	49	5	0	0	0	0	0	0	0	456	0	0	871	10,815
1986	59	7	0	0	0	0	0	0	0	1,760	0	0	2,846	34,970
1987	42	10	0	0	0	0	0	0	0	1,775	0	0	2,776	59,455
1988	68	2	0	0	0	0	0	0	0	496	0	0	544	12,210
1989	—	0												2,000
Lifetime		58	0	0	0	0	0	0	1	10,825	9	4	17,018	$212,955

John Scarfo

John Scarfo
Racing Hometown: Detroit, MI

Year	Rank	Starts	Poles	1	2	3	4	5	6–10	Laps	Laps Led	Races Led	Miles	$
1952	177	1	0	0	0	0	0	0	0	135	0	0	135	25
Lifetime		1	0	0	0	0	0	0	0	135	0	0	135	$25

Bob Schacht

Robert Schacht
B: 1/24/1950
Racing Hometown: Lombard, IL

Year	Rank	Starts	Poles	1	2	3	4	5	6–10	Laps	Laps Led	Races Led	Miles	$
1981	71	2	0	0	0	0	0	0	0	241	0	0	263	1,290
1982	52	3	0	0	0	0	0	0	0	576	0	0	318	2,880
1988	70	3	0	0	0	0	0	0	0	165	0	0	171	5,170
1989	57	2	0	0	0	0	0	0	0	602	0	0	818	5,475
1990	—	0												1,900
1992	40	9	0	0	0	0	0	0	0	1,363	2	1	2,320	58,815
1993	55	3	0	0	0	0	0	0	0	272	0	0	365	25,965
1994	83	1	0	0	0	0	0	0	0	11	0	0	28	7,560
Lifetime		23	0	0	0	0	0	0	0	3,230	2	1	4,283	$109,055

Bill Schade

William C. Schade
Racing Hometown: Irwin, PA

Year	Rank	Starts	Poles	1	2	3	4	5	6–10	Laps	Laps Led	Races Led	Miles	$
1951	N/A	2	0	0	0	0	0	0	0		0	0		50
Lifetime		2	0	0	0	0	0	0	0		0	0		$50

John Schelesky

John Schelesky
Racing Hometown: Pittsburgh, PA

Year	Rank	Starts	Poles	1	2	3	4	5	6–10	Laps	Laps Led	Races Led	Miles	$
1950	NR	1	0	0	0	0	0	0	0		0	0		25
Lifetime		1	0	0	0	0	0	0	0		0	0		$25

Milford Schell

Milford Schell
Racing Hometown: Erie, PA

Year	Rank	Starts	Poles	1	2	3	4	5	6–10	Laps	Laps Led	Races Led	Miles	$
1950	NR	1	0	0	0	0	0	0	0	104	0	0	52	0
Lifetime		1	0	0	0	0	0	0	0	104	0	0	52	$0

Norman Schihl

Norman Schihl
Racing Hometown: Toronto, Ont., Canada

Year	Rank	Starts	Poles	1	2	3	4	5	6–10	Laps	Laps Led	Races Led	Miles	$
1956	NR	1	0	0	0	0	0	0	0	349	0	0	175	150
Lifetime		1	0	0	0	0	0	0	0	349	0	0	175	$150

Jerry Schild

Jerry Schild
Racing Hometown: Houston, TX

Year	Rank	Starts	Poles	1	2	3	4	5	6–10	Laps	Laps Led	Races Led	Miles	$
1974	45	5	0	0	0	0	0	0	1	1,142	0	0	1,750	8,396
Lifetime		5	0	0	0	0	0	0	1	1,142	0	0	1,750	$8,396

Robin Schildnecht

Robin Schildnecht
B: 12/24/1953
Racing Hometown: Louisville, KY

Year	Rank	Starts	Poles	1	2	3	4	5	6–10	Laps	Laps Led	Races Led	Miles	$
1977	87	2	0	0	0	0	0	0	0	581	0	0	344	2,075
Lifetime		2	0	0	0	0	0	0	0	581	0	0	344	$2,075

Year	Rank	Starts	Poles	Finish 1	2	3	4	5	6–10	Laps	Laps Led	Races Led	Miles	$

Harry Schilling

Harry Schilling
Racing Hometown: Iseton, CA

Year	Rank	Starts	Poles	1	2	3	4	5	6–10	Laps	Laps Led	Races Led	Miles	$
1971	NR	3	0	0	0	0	0	0	0	222	0	0	561	3,395
1972	71	3	0	0	0	0	0	0	0	587	0	0	923	2,399
1974	122	1	0	0	0	0	0	0	0	65	0	0	170	1,005
Lifetime		7	0	0	0	0	0	0	0	874	0	0	1,654	$6,799

Don Schissler

Donald Schissler
B: 1934
Racing Hometown: Detroit, MI

Year	Rank	Starts	Poles	1	2	3	4	5	6–10	Laps	Laps Led	Races Led	Miles	$
1967	94	2	0	0	0	0	0	0	0	176	0	0	124	1,015
1969	NR	1	0	0	0	0	0	0	0	0	0	0	0	850
Lifetime		3	0	0	0	0	0	0	0	176	0	0	124	$1,865

Joe Schlesser

Joseph Schlesser
B: 1928   D: 7/7/1968   *Killed in 1968 French Grand Prix.*
Racing Hometown: Neuilly-sur-Seine, France

Year	Rank	Starts	Poles	1	2	3	4	5	6–10	Laps	Laps Led	Races Led	Miles	$
1964	NR	2	0	0	0	0	0	0	1	231	0	0	578	1,350
Lifetime		2	0	0	0	0	0	0	1	231	0	0	578	$1,350

Lee Schmidt

Lee Schmidt
B: 2/5/1919
Racing Hometown: Milwaukee, WI

Year	Rank	Starts	Poles	1	2	3	4	5	6–10	Laps	Laps Led	Races Led	Miles	$
1949	70	1	0	0	0	0	0	0	0	171	0	0	171	50
1950	NR	1	0	0	0	0	0	0	0	40	0	0	167	25
Lifetime		2	0	0	0	0	0	0	0	211	0	0	338	$75

Bill Schmitt

William Schmitt
B: 2/13/1936
Racing Hometown: Redding, CA

Year	Rank	Starts	Poles	1	2	3	4	5	6–10	Laps	Laps Led	Races Led	Miles	$
1975	58	3	0	0	0	0	0	0	1	293	0	0	764	3,970
1976	72	2	0	0	0	0	0	0	1	318	0	0	816	3,360
1977	64	3	0	0	0	0	0	0	0	144	0	0	375	3,285
1978	52	3	0	0	0	0	0	0	1	304	0	0	773	8,430
1979	50	3	0	0	0	0	1	0	0	325	0	0	828	11,695
1980	42	4	0	0	0	0	0	1	0	579	0	0	1,473	21,610
1981	53	3	0	0	0	0	0	0	0	257	1	1	673	6,610
1982	64	2	0	0	0	0	0	0	0	186	0	0	487	2,210
1983	67	2	0	0	0	0	0	0	1	107	0	0	280	4,520
1984	59	2	0	0	0	0	0	0	0	125	0	0	328	5,270
1985	61	2	0	0	0	0	0	0	0	157	0	0	411	5,640
1986	64	2	0	0	0	0	0	0	0	207	0	0	542	7,840
1987	75	2	0	0	0	0	0	0	0	99	0	0	259	2,500
1988	56	2	0	0	0	0	0	0	0	252	0	0	406	6,245
1989	55	2	0	0	0	0	0	0	0	380	0	0	491	7,920
1990	59	2	0	0	0	0	0	0	0	384	0	0	496	11,525
1991	57	2	0	0	0	0	0	0	0	210	0	0	322	10,605
1992	62T	2	0	0	0	0	0	0	0	282	0	0	393	13,095
1993	77	1	0	0	0	0	0	0	0	71	0	0	179	6,815
Lifetime		44	0	0	0	0	1	1	4	4,680	1	1	10,299	$143,145

Frankie Schneider

Franklin Schneider
B: 8/11/1926
Racing Hometown: Lambertville, NJ

Year	Rank	Starts	Poles	1	2	3	4	5	6–10	Laps	Laps Led	Races Led	Miles	$
1949	26T	1	0	0	0	0	0	0	1		0	0		150
1950	80	1	0	0	0	0	0	0	0		0	0		50
1951	N/A	1	0	0	0	0	0	0	0		0	0		10
1952	27	6	0	0	0	1	2	0	1	411	0	0	211	1,350
1953	NR	1	0	0	0	0	0	0	0		0	0		100
1957	20	10	1	0	1	0	2	0	3	1,781	37	1	1,248	4,588
1958	NR	7	0	1	1	0	3	0	0	1,215	106	1	606	1,970
Lifetime		27	1	1	2	1	7	0	5	3,407	143	2	2,064	$8,218

Year	Rank	Starts	Poles	Finish						Laps	Laps Led	Races Led	Miles	$
				1	2	3	4	5	6–10					

Lee Schneider

Lee Schneider
Racing Hometown: Glenshaw, PA

Year	Rank	Starts	Poles	1	2	3	4	5	6–10	Laps	Laps Led	Races Led	Miles	$
1951	N/A	1	0	0	0	0	0	0	0	64	0	0	48	25
Lifetime		1	0	0	0	0	0	0	0	64	0	0	48	$25

Terry Schoonover

Terry L. Schoonover
D: 11/11/1984 *Killed in Atlanta 500.*
Racing Hometown: Royal Palm Beach, FL

Year	Rank	Starts	Poles	1	2	3	4	5	6–10	Laps	Laps Led	Races Led	Miles	$
1984	85T	2	0	0	0	0	0	0	0	543	0	0	614	2,585
Lifetime		2	0	0	0	0	0	0	0	543	0	0	614	$2,585

Ken Schrader

Ken Schrader
B: 5/29/1955
Racing Hometown: Fenton, MO

Year	Rank	Starts	Poles	1	2	3	4	5	6–10	Laps	Laps Led	Races Led	Miles	$
1984	53	5	0	0	0	0	0	0	0	1,508	0	0	1,632	16,425
1985	16	28	0	0	0	0	0	0	3	7,786	4	1	9,356	211,523
1986	16	29	0	0	0	0	0	0	4	8,047	2	2	9,697	235,904
1987	10	29	1	0	0	0	0	1	9	8,162	154	10	9,900	375,918
1988	5	29	2	1	1	0	1	1	13	9,115	151	13	11,033	631,544
1989	5	29	4	1	1	3	4	1	4	8,675	364	17	10,780	1,037,941
1990	10	29	3	0	2	2	1	2	7	8,649	242	12	9,948	769,934
1991	9	29	0	2	2	2	1	3	8	8,331	440	16	9,841	772,434
1992	17	29	1	0	0	2	1	1	7	8,425	83	5	9,815	639,679
1993	9	30	6	0	2	2	3	2	6	8,877	286	14	10,994	952,748
1994	4	31	0	0	1	2	4	2	9	9,704	222	9	11,740	1,211,062
1995	17	31	1	0	0	1	1	0	8	8,550	238	10	10,166	886,566
1996	12	31	0	0	0	1	1	1	7	9,408	45	7	11,499	1,089,603
Lifetime		359	18	4	9	15	17	14	85	105,237	2,231	115	126,402	$8,831,281

Chuck Schroedel

Chuck Schroedel

Year	Rank	Starts	Poles	1	2	3	4	5	6–10	Laps	Laps Led	Races Led	Miles	$
1987	103T	1	0	0	0	0	0	0	0	8	0	0	19	1,375
Lifetime		1	0	0	0	0	0	0	0	8	0	0	19	$1,375

Dorsey Schroeder

Dorsey Schroeder
B: 2/5/1953
Racing Hometown: Baldwin, MO

Year	Rank	Starts	Poles	1	2	3	4	5	6–10	Laps	Laps Led	Races Led	Miles	$
1991	59	2	0	0	0	0	0	0	0	92	3	1	222	14,145
1992	60	2	0	0	0	0	0	0	0	372	0	0	758	36,135
1993	62	2	0	0	0	0	0	0	0	69	0	0	174	16,315
1996	55	1	0	0	0	0	0	0	0	90	1	1	221	22,745
Lifetime		7	0	0	0	0	0	0	0	623	4	2	1,374	$89,340

Ken Schroeder

Kenneth Schroeder
Racing Hometown: Jamestown, NY

Year	Rank	Starts	Poles	1	2	3	4	5	6–10	Laps	Laps Led	Races Led	Miles	$
1949	76	1	0	0	0	0	0	0	0	168	0	0	168	50
Lifetime		1	0	0	0	0	0	0	0	168	0	0	168	$50

Walt Schubert

Walter Schubert
Racing Hometown: Cold Spring, NY

Year	Rank	Starts	Poles	1	2	3	4	5	6–10	Laps	Laps Led	Races Led	Miles	$
1955	159T	1	0	0	0	0	0	0	0	196	0	0	196	75
1956	86	4	0	0	0	0	0	0	1	413	0	0	324	375
Lifetime		5	0	0	0	0	0	0	1	609	0	0	520	$450

Fritz Schultz

Fritz Schultz
Racing Hometown: Adenau, Germany

Year	Rank	Starts	Poles	1	2	3	4	5	6–10	Laps	Laps Led	Races Led	Miles	$
1971	NR	1	0	0	0	0	0	0	0	45	0	0	113	205
Lifetime		1	0	0	0	0	0	0	0	45	0	0	113	$205

Larry Schultz

Lawrence Schultz
Racing Hometown: Highland Falls, NY

Year	Rank	Starts	Poles	1	2	3	4	5	6–10	Laps	Laps Led	Races Led	Miles	$
1953	NR	2	0	0	0	0	0	0	0		0	0		65
Lifetime		2	0	0	0	0	0	0	0		0	0		$65

Year	Rank	Starts	Poles	Finish						Laps	Laps Led	Races Led	Miles	$
				1	2	3	4	5	6–10					

Volney Schulze

Volney E. Schulze
Racing Hometown: Silver Spring, MD

Year	Rank	Starts	Poles	1	2	3	4	5	6–10	Laps	Laps Led	Races Led	Miles	$
1954	214	1	0	0	0	0	0	0	0	46	0	0	23	0
1955	67	6	0	0	0	0	0	0	1	674	0	0	456	300
1957	78	3	0	0	0	0	0	0	1	530	0	0	380	340
1958	49	7	0	0	0	0	0	0	0	725	0	0	370	490
Lifetime		17	0	0	0	0	0	0	2	1,975	0	0	1,228	$1,130

Bobby Schuyler

Robert Schuyler
Racing Hometown: Islip, NY

Year	Rank	Starts	Poles	1	2	3	4	5	6–10	Laps	Laps Led	Races Led	Miles	$
1964	NR	1	0	0	0	0	0	0	0	3	0	0	1	100
Lifetime		1	0	0	0	0	0	0	0	3	0	0	1	$100

Bob Schwingle

Robert Schwingle
Racing Hometown: Naples, NJ

Year	Rank	Starts	Poles	1	2	3	4	5	6–10	Laps	Laps Led	Races Led	Miles	$
1952	140T	1	0	0	0	0	0	0	0	142	0	0	71	25
1954	140	1	0	0	0	0	0	0	0	165	0	0	83	25
Lifetime		2	0	0	0	0	0	0	0	307	0	0	154	$50

Bill Scott

William Scott
Racing Hometown: Winston-Salem, NC

Year	Rank	Starts	Poles	1	2	3	4	5	6–10	Laps	Laps Led	Races Led	Miles	$
1959	69	6	0	0	0	0	0	0	2	805	0	0	452	430
Lifetime		6	0	0	0	0	0	0	2	805	0	0	452	$430

Bill Scott

William Scott
B: 10/10/1948
Racing Hometown: San Bernadino, CA

Year	Rank	Starts	Poles	1	2	3	4	5	6–10	Laps	Laps Led	Races Led	Miles	$
1970	NR	1	0	0	0	0	0	0	0	6	0	0	16	635
Lifetime		1	0	0	0	0	0	0	0	6	0	0	16	$635

Bill Scott

William Scott
Racing Hometown: Brevard, NC

Year	Rank	Starts	Poles	1	2	3	4	5	6–10	Laps	Laps Led	Races Led	Miles	$
1982	93	1	0	0	0	0	0	0	0	75	0	0	200	2,825
1983	—	0												1,900
1985	NR	1	0	0	0	0	0	0	0	71	0	0	178	1,615
Lifetime		9	0	0	0	0	0	0	2	957	0	0	845	$6,340

Billy Scott

William Scott
B: 8/9/1935
Racing Hometown: Union, SC

Year	Rank	Starts	Poles	1	2	3	4	5	6–10	Laps	Laps Led	Races Led	Miles	$
1973	84	1	0	0	0	0	0	0	0	340	0	0	510	1,850
1974	109	1	0	0	0	0	0	0	0	262	0	0	393	1,625
Lifetime		2	0	0	0	0	0	0	0	602	0	0	903	$3,475

Bob Scott

Robert Scott
B: 10/4/1928   D: 7/5/1954   *Killed in IndyCar race @ Darlington.*
Racing Hometown: Los Angeles, CA

Year	Rank	Starts	Poles	1	2	3	4	5	6–10	Laps	Laps Led	Races Led	Miles	$
1950	137T	1	0	0	0	0	0	0	0		0	0		0
Lifetime		1	0	0	0	0	0	0	0		0	0		$0

Charlie Scott

Charles Scott
Racing Hometown: College Park, GA

Year	Rank	Starts	Poles	1	2	3	4	5	6–10	Laps	Laps Led	Races Led	Miles	$
1956	173T	1	0	0	0	0	0	0	0		0	0		75
Lifetime		1	0	0	0	0	0	0	0		0	0		$75

FiFi Scott

FiFi Scott
Racing Hometown: W. Sacramento, CA

Year	Rank	Starts	Poles	1	2	3	4	5	6–10	Laps	Laps Led	Races Led	Miles	$
1955	216	2	0	0	0	0	0	0	0	216	0	0	145	25
Lifetime		2	0	0	0	0	0	0	0	216	0	0	145	$25

Year	Rank	Starts	Poles	Finish						Laps	Laps Led	Races Led	Miles	$
				1	2	3	4	5	6–10					

Harry Scott

Harry Scott

Year	Rank	Starts	Poles	1	2	3	4	5	6–10	Laps	Laps Led	Races Led	Miles	$
1951	N/A	1	0	0	0	0	0	0	1		0	0		100
Lifetime		1	0	0	0	0	0	0	1		0	0		$100

Herbert Scott

Herbert W. Scott
B: 1926
Racing Hometown: Wexford, PA

Year	Rank	Starts	Poles	1	2	3	4	5	6–10	Laps	Laps Led	Races Led	Miles	$
1962	NR	1	0	0	0	0	0	0	0	79	0	0	20	175
Lifetime		1	0	0	0	0	0	0	0	79	0	0	20	$175

Lyle Scott

Lyle Scott
Racing Hometown: Port Washington, NY

Year	Rank	Starts	Poles	1	2	3	4	5	6–10	Laps	Laps Led	Races Led	Miles	$
1950	59	6	0	0	0	0	0	0	1	380	0	0	223	225
1951	N/A	2	0	0	0	0	0	0	1		0	0		125
1953	91T	1	0	0	0	0	0	0	1		0	0		50
1956	233T	1	0	0	0	0	0	0	0		0	0		60
Lifetime		10	0	0	0	0	0	0	3	380	0	0	223	$460

Tighe Scott

Tighe Scott
B: 6/2/1949
Racing Hometown: Pen Argyle, PA

Year	Rank	Starts	Poles	1	2	3	4	5	6–10	Laps	Laps Led	Races Led	Miles	$
1976	45	6	0	0	0	0	0	0	1	697	0	0	1,703	15,520
1977	20	26	0	0	0	0	0	1	0	6,134	0	0	7,467	63,225
1978	13	29	0	0	0	0	0	0	7	6,626	3	1	8,223	87,912
1979	27	17	0	0	0	0	1	0	6	3,834	0	0	5,684	88,010
1980	39	10	0	0	0	0	0	1	1	1,066	4	1	1,968	21,925
1982	NR	1	0	0	0	0	0	0	0	81	0	0	203	5,050
Lifetime		89	0	0	0	0	1	2	15	18,438	7	2	25,247	$281,642

Wendell Scott

Wendell Oliver Scott
B: 8/29/1921   D: 12/23/1990
Racing Hometown: Danville, VA

Year	Rank	Starts	Poles	1	2	3	4	5	6–10	Laps	Laps Led	Races Led	Miles	$
1961	32	23	0	0	0	0	0	0	5	4,364	0	0	2,217	3,240
1962	22	41	1	0	0	2	1	1	15	8,542	0	0	4,211	7,133
1963	15	47	0	0	0	0	0	1	14	9,459	0	0	6,165	10,966
1964	12	56	0	1	0	0	6	1	17	10,752	27	1	6,466	16,495
1965	11	52	0	0	0	0	2	2	17	9,759	0	0	6,451	18,639
1966	6	45	0	0	0	1	1	1	14	9,793	0	0	6,914	23,052
1967	10	45	0	0	0	0	0	0	11	9,217	0	0	6,639	19,510
1968	9	48	0	0	0	0	0	0	10	10,231	0	0	7,348	20,498
1969	9	51	0	0	0	0	0	0	11	11,856	0	0	9,165	47,451
1970	14	41	0	0	0	0	0	0	9	8,276	0	0	6,949	28,518
1971	19	37	0	0	0	0	0	0	4	7,791	0	0	6,819	21,701
1972	40	6	0	0	0	0	0	0	0	1,763	0	0	1,926	5,830
1973	61	3	0	0	0	0	0	0	0	632	0	0	915	3,530
Lifetime		495	1	1	0	3	10	6	127	102,435	27	1	72,186	$226,563

Arley Scranton

Arley Scranton
Racing Hometown: Compton, CA

Year	Rank	Starts	Poles	1	2	3	4	5	6–10	Laps	Laps Led	Races Led	Miles	$
1954	NR	1	0	0	0	0	0	0	0	413	0	0	207	25
1956	NR	1	0	0	0	0	0	0	0	9	0	0	23	20
1957	175T	1	0	0	0	0	0	0	0	25	0	0	25	25
1958	158	2	0	0	0	0	0	0	0	17	0	0	17	100
1959	118	2	0	0	0	0	0	0	0	361	0	0	158	100
1961	NR	1	0	0	0	0	0	0	0	3	0	0	8	0
1966	133	1	0	0	0	0	0	0	0	3	0	0	8	500
Lifetime		9	0	0	0	0	0	0	0	831	0	0	444	$770

Rick Scribner

Richard Scribner
B: 2/10/1952
Racing Hometown: Orangevale, CA

Year	Rank	Starts	Poles	1	2	3	4	5	6–10	Laps	Laps Led	Races Led	Miles	$
1992	72	2	0	0	0	0	0	0	0	75	0	0	178	9,025
Lifetime		2	0	0	0	0	0	0	0	75	0	0	178	$9,025

Year	Rank	Starts	Poles	Finish						Laps	Laps Led	Races Led	Miles	$
				1	2	3	4	5	6–10	Laps	Led	Led	Miles	$

Ed Sczech

Edward Sczech
B: 2/1/1944
Racing Hometown: San Antonio, TX

Year	Rank	Starts	Poles	1	2	3	4	5	6–10	Laps	Laps Led	Races Led	Miles	$
1973	53	4	0	0	0	0	0	0	0	558	0	0	1,137	4,270
Lifetime		4	0	0	0	0	0	0	0	558	0	0	1,137	$4,270

James Sears

James Sidney Sears
B: 11/11/1940   D: 8/3/1973   *Killed at Starlite Speedway in Monroe, NC.*
Racing Hometown: Rockingham, NC

Year	Rank	Starts	Poles	1	2	3	4	5	6–10	Laps	Laps Led	Races Led	Miles	$
1967	NR	1	0	0	0	0	0	0	0	72	0	0	72	505
1968	110	1	0	0	0	0	0	0	0	92	0	0	92	710
1969	83T	1	0	0	0	0	0	0	0	247	0	0	247	725
1970	102	2	0	0	0	0	0	0	2	641	0	0	552	1,665
1971	NR	1	0	0	0	0	0	0	0	9	0	0	9	545
Lifetime		6	0	0	0	0	0	0	2	1,061	0	0	972	$4,150

John Sears

John Hamilton Sears
B: 5/9/1936
Racing Hometown: Ellerbe, NC

Year	Rank	Starts	Poles	1	2	3	4	5	6–10	Laps	Laps Led	Races Led	Miles	$
1964	65	6	0	0	0	0	0	0	3	1,200	0	0	581	1,130
1965	95	2	0	0	0	0	0	0	1	281	0	0	94	650
1966	7	46	0	0	1	1	4	5	19	9,981	109	2	6,632	25,192
1967	5	41	1	0	1	3	3	2	16	10,031	59	4	7,468	28,937
1968	5	49	0	0	0	1	1	3	19	11,077	0	0	7,861	29,179
1969	7	52	0	0	1	3	7	6	10	11,620	18	3	8,916	52,281
1970	12	40	1	0	0	0	3	1	3	7,777	10	1	7,939	32,675
1971	20	37	0	0	0	0	0	0	3	7,512	0	0	6,815	26,735
1972	8	28	0	0	0	0	0	2	5	7,882	0	0	8,994	51,314
1973	32	17	0	0	0	0	0	0	0	3,568	0	0	3,332	16,890
Lifetime		318	2	0	3	8	18	19	79	70,929	196	10	58,632	$264,983

Ken Seibel

Kenneth Seibel
Racing Hometown: Syracuse, NY

Year	Rank	Starts	Poles	1	2	3	4	5	6–10	Laps	Laps Led	Races Led	Miles	$
1956	NR	1	0	0	0	0	0	0	0	134	0	0	134	100
Lifetime		1	0	0	0	0	0	0	0	134	0	0	134	$100

Frank Secrist

Frank Secrist
B: 1930
Racing Hometown: Oildale, CA

Year	Rank	Starts	Poles	1	2	3	4	5	6–10	Laps	Laps Led	Races Led	Miles	$
1956	250T	1	0	0	0	0	0	0	0	207	0	0	207	40
1957	168	2	0	0	0	0	0	0	0	104	0	0	100	95
1960	122	2	1	0	0	0	0	0	0	105	8	1	123	175
1961	97	3	0	0	0	0	1	0	0	249	0	0	313	750
Lifetime		8	1	0	0	0	1	0	0	665	8	1	743	$1,060

Bill Sedgwick

William Sedgwick
B: 3/19/1955
Racing Hometown: Granada Hills, CA

Year	Rank	Starts	Poles	1	2	3	4	5	6–10	Laps	Laps Led	Races Led	Miles	$
1989	99	1	0	0	0	0	0	0	0	170	0	0	170	3,525
1990	52	3	0	0	0	0	0	0	0	730	0	0	653	11,355
1991	49	3	0	0	0	0	0	0	0	848	0	0	740	15,150
1992	56	2	0	0	0	0	0	0	0	373	0	0	485	16,365
1993	72T	1	0	0	0	0	0	0	0	73	0	0	184	8,140
Lifetime		10	0	0	0	0	0	0	0	2,194	0	0	2,232	$54,535

George Seeger

George Seeger
Racing Hometown: Whittier, CA

Year	Rank	Starts	Poles	1	2	3	4	5	6–10	Laps	Laps Led	Races Led	Miles	$
1951	45	9	0	0	0	1	0	0	2	705	0	0	697	910
1954	NR	2	0	0	0	0	0	1	0	669	0	0	335	350
1956	89	2	0	0	0	0	0	0	1	205	0	0	322	400
1957	38	6	0	0	1	3	1	0	0	764	19	1	520	2,740
Lifetime		19	0	0	1	4	1	1	3	2,343	19	1	1,874	$4,325

Year	Rank	Starts	Poles	Finish 1	2	3	4	5	6–10	Laps	Laps Led	Races Led	Miles	$

John Seeley

John Seeley
Racing Hometown: Frewsburg, NY

Year	Rank	Starts	Poles	1	2	3	4	5	6–10	Laps	Laps Led	Races Led	Miles	$
1958	NR	1	0	0	0	0	0	1	0	143	0	0	48	245
1959	89	1	0	0	0	0	0	0	0	160	0	0	80	125
Lifetime		2	0	0	0	0	0	1	0	303	0	0	128	$370

Bob Seharns

Robert Seharns

Year	Rank	Starts	Poles	1	2	3	4	5	6–10	Laps	Laps Led	Races Led	Miles	$
1958	NR	1	0	0	0	0	0	0	0	131	0	0	44	130
Lifetime		1	0	0	0	0	0	0	0	131	0	0	44	$130

Bill Seifert

William John Seifert
B: 7/2/1939
Racing Hometown: Skyland, NC

Year	Rank	Starts	Poles	1	2	3	4	5	6–10	Laps	Laps Led	Races Led	Miles	$
1966	43	15	0	0	0	0	0	0	4	3,322	0	0	1,706	3,830
1967	22	41	0	0	0	0	0	0	12	8,171	0	0	5,133	11,910
1968	14	44	0	0	0	0	0	1	8	8,033	0	0	5,864	18,403
1969	13	50	0	0	0	0	1	0	14	9,728	0	0	7,475	44,361
1970	18	39	0	0	0	0	0	1	3	5,189	0	0	5,196	25,647
1971	13	37	0	0	0	0	0	0	4	6,552	0	0	7,151	33,220
1972	74	6	0	0	0	0	0	0	1	472	0	0	652	7,290
1977	71	2	0	0	0	0	0	0	0	346	0	0	540	2,270
1979	123T	1	0	0	0	0	0	0	0	32	0	0	64	960
Lifetime		235	0	0	0	0	1	2	46	41,845	0	0	33,781	$147,891

Al Self

Al Self
Racing Hometown: Venice, CA

Year	Rank	Starts	Poles	1	2	3	4	5	6–10	Laps	Laps Led	Races Led	Miles	$
1960	77	2	0	0	0	0	0	0	1	227	0	0	290	550
1963	151	1	0	0	0	0	0	0	0	1	0	0	3	200
1964	132	1	0	0	0	0	0	0	0	9	0	0	24	500
1965	92	1	0	0	0	0	0	0	0	49	0	0	132	500
Lifetime		5	0	0	0	0	0	0	1	286	0	0	449	$1,750

Jack Sellers

Jack Sellers
B: 7/27/1944
Racing Hometown: Sacramento, CA

Year	Rank	Starts	Poles	1	2	3	4	5	6–10	Laps	Laps Led	Races Led	Miles	$
1990	NR	1	0	0	0	0	0	0	0	41	0	0	103	3,225
1992	93T	1	0	0	0	0	0	0	0	48	0	0	121	4,725
Lifetime		2	0	0	0	0	0	0	0	89	0	0	224	$7,950

Mack Sellers

Mark Sellers
Racing Hometown: Spartanburg, SC

Year	Rank	Starts	Poles	1	2	3	4	5	6–10	Laps	Laps Led	Races Led	Miles	$
1969	78	3	0	0	0	0	0	0	0	164	0	0	82	450
Lifetime		3	0	0	0	0	0	0	0	164	0	0	82	$450

Bob Senneker

Robert Senneker
B: 12/12/1944
Racing Hometown: Dorr, MI

Year	Rank	Starts	Poles	1	2	3	4	5	6–10	Laps	Laps Led	Races Led	Miles	$
1968	NR	1	0	0	0	0	0	0	0	182	0	0	455	3,200
1970	80	1	0	0	0	0	0	0	0	175	0	0	357	775
1981	NR	1	0	0	0	0	0	0	0	256	0	0	384	1,975
1983	44	5	0	0	0	0	0	0	0	1,317	0	0	2,186	11,355
Lifetime		8	0	0	0	0	0	0	0	1,930	0	0	3,382	$17,285

Harry Sents

Harry Sents
Racing Hometown: Glen Aubrey, NY

Year	Rank	Starts	Poles	1	2	3	4	5	6–10	Laps	Laps Led	Races Led	Miles	$
1950	105	2	0	0	0	0	0	0	0	145	0	0	73	25
Lifetime		2	0	0	0	0	0	0	0	145	0	0	73	$25

Frank Sessoms

Frank Marvin Sessoms
B: 1/29/1933
Racing Hometown: Darlington, SC

Year	Rank	Starts	Poles	1	2	3	4	5	6–10	Laps	Laps Led	Races Led	Miles	$
1962	88T	2	0	0	0	0	0	0	0	319	0	0	160	185

Year	Rank	Starts	Poles	Finish						Laps	Laps Led	Races Led	Miles	$
				1	2	3	4	5	6–10					

Frank Sessoms *continued*

Year	Rank	Starts	Poles	1	2	3	4	5	6–10	Laps	Laps Led	Races Led	Miles	$
1969	NR	1	0	0	0	0	0	0	0	128	0	0	340	1,325
1971	NR	2	0	0	0	0	0	0	2	852	0	0	496	1,180
Lifetime		5	0	0	0	0	0	0	2	1,299	0	0	996	$2,690

Ned Setzer

Ned Setzer
D: 7/29/1975
Racing Hometown: Claremont, NC

Year	Rank	Starts	Poles	1	2	3	4	5	6–10	Laps	Laps Led	Races Led	Miles	$
1965	43	8	0	0	0	0	0	0	3	862	0	0	859	4,805
1966	101	2	0	0	0	0	0	0	0	147	0	0	368	1,200
Lifetime		10	0	0	0	0	0	0	3	1,009	0	0	1,227	$6,005

Leland Sewell

Leland Sewell
Racing Hometown: Memphis, TN

Year	Rank	Starts	Poles	1	2	3	4	5	6–10	Laps	Laps Led	Races Led	Miles	$
1954	176	1	0	0	0	0	0	0	0	84	0	0	126	50
1955	96	1	0	0	0	0	0	0	0	176	0	0	264	125
Lifetime		2	0	0	0	0	0	0	0	260	0	0	390	$175

Buster Sexton

Wilson Sexton
Racing Hometown: Duncan, SC

Year	Rank	Starts	Poles	1	2	3	4	5	6–10	Laps	Laps Led	Races Led	Miles	$
1966	111T	1	0	0	0	0	0	0	0	183	0	0	92	100
1967	124	1	0	0	0	0	0	0	0	15	0	0	8	100
1969	94T	1	0	0	0	0	0	0	0	9	0	0	5	0
Lifetime		3	0	0	0	0	0	0	0	207	0	0	104	$200

Ralph Shaffer

Ralph Shaffer
Racing Hometown: Monticello, IL

Year	Rank	Starts	Poles	1	2	3	4	5	6–10	Laps	Laps Led	Races Led	Miles	$
1955	233	1	0	0	0	0	0	0	0	16	0	0	66	0
Lifetime		1	0	0	0	0	0	0	0	16	0	0	66	$0

Herb Shannon

Herbert Shannon
B: 9/1/1931
Racing Hometown: Peoria, IL

Year	Rank	Starts	Poles	1	2	3	4	5	6–10	Laps	Laps Led	Races Led	Miles	$
1960	NR	1	0	0	0	0	0	0	0	184	0	0	276	350
1965	NR	2	0	0	0	0	0	0	0	110	0	0	275	1,130
Lifetime		3	0	0	0	0	0	0	0	294	0	0	551	$1,480

Scott Sharp

Scott Sharp
B: 2/14/1968
Racing Hometown: E. Norwalk, CT

Year	Rank	Starts	Poles	1	2	3	4	5	6–10	Laps	Laps Led	Races Led	Miles	$
1992	69	1	0	0	0	0	0	0	0	51	0	0	125	7,155
Lifetime		1	0	0	0	0	0	0	0	51	0	0	125	$7,155

Bob Shaw

William B. Shaw
Racing Hometown: Warren, OH

Year	Rank	Starts	Poles	1	2	3	4	5	6–10	Laps	Laps Led	Races Led	Miles	$
1951	N/A	1	0	0	0	0	0	0	0		0	0		10
1952	172	1	0	0	0	0	0	0	0	112	0	0	56	25
Lifetime		2	0	0	0	0	0	0	0	112	0	0	56	$35

Ernie Shaw

Ernest Anthony Shaw
B: 10/9/1942
Racing Hometown: Winston-Salem, NC

Year	Rank	Starts	Poles	1	2	3	4	5	6–10	Laps	Laps Led	Races Led	Miles	$
1969	NR	1	0	0	0	0	0	0	0	149	0	0	396	1,500
1971	NR	2	0	0	0	0	0	0	1	578	0	0	312	775
1974	68	4	0	0	0	0	0	0	0	842	0	0	538	2,280
1976	NR	1	0	0	0	0	0	0	0	372	0	0	202	700
1979	92T	1	0	0	0	0	0	0	0	368	0	0	230	625
Lifetime		9	0	0	0	0	0	0	1	2,309	0	0	1,677	$5,880

Year	Rank	Starts	Poles	Finish						Laps	Laps Led	Races Led	Miles	$
				1	2	3	4	5	6–10					

Graham Shaw

J. Graham Shaw
B: 7/8/1937
Racing Hometown: Columbia, SC

Year	Rank	Starts	Poles	1	2	3	4	5	6–10	Laps	Laps Led	Races Led	Miles	$
1964	66	2	0	0	0	0	0	0	0	127	0	0	379	1,000
Lifetime		2	0	0	0	0	0	0	0	127	0	0	379	$1,000

Lloyd Shaw

Lloyd Shaw
Racing Hometown: Toronto, Ont., Canada

Year	Rank	Starts	Poles	1	2	3	4	5	6–10	Laps	Laps Led	Races Led	Miles	$
1953	NR	1	1	0	0	0	0	0	0		0	0		40
Lifetime		1	1	0	0	0	0	0	0		0	0		$40

Ace Shearer

Ace Shearer
Racing Hometown: Erie, PA

Year	Rank	Starts	Poles	1	2	3	4	5	6–10	Laps	Laps Led	Races Led	Miles	$
1950	137T	1	0	0	0	0	0	0	0	129	0	0	65	0
Lifetime		1	0	0	0	0	0	0	0	129	0	0	65	$0

Eddie Sheeler

Eddie Sheeler
Racing Hometown: Chicago, IL

Year	Rank	Starts	Poles	1	2	3	4	5	6–10	Laps	Laps Led	Races Led	Miles	$
1951	N/A	2	0	0	0	0	0	0	0		0	0		75
Lifetime		2	0	0	0	0	0	0	0		0	0		$75

Ralph Sheeler

Ralph Sheeler
B: 11/10/1910
Racing Hometown: Paterson, NJ

Year	Rank	Starts	Poles	1	2	3	4	5	6–10	Laps	Laps Led	Races Led	Miles	$
1953	61	3	0	0	0	0	0	0	0		0	0		85
Lifetime		3	0	0	0	0	0	0	0		0	0		$85

Kirk Shelmerdine

Kirk Shelmerdine
B: 3/8/1958
Racing Hometown: Philadelphia, PA

Year	Rank	Starts	Poles	1	2	3	4	5	6–10	Laps	Laps Led	Races Led	Miles	$
1981	NR	1	0	0	0	0	0	0	0	2	0	0	4	950
1994	66	1	0	0	0	0	0	0	0	179	0	0	476	11,265
Lifetime		2	0	0	0	0	0	0	0	181	0	0	480	$12,215

Ron Shephard

Ronald Shephard

Year	Rank	Starts	Poles	1	2	3	4	5	6–10	Laps	Laps Led	Races Led	Miles	$
1986	104T	1	0	0	0	0	0	0	0	282	0	0	153	3,145
1987	71	2	0	0	0	0	0	0	0	198	0	0	462	3,745
Lifetime		3	0	0	0	0	0	0	0	480	0	0	615	$6,890

Morgan Shepherd

Clay Morgan Shepherd
B: 10/21/1941
Racing Hometown: Conover, NC

Year	Rank	Starts	Poles	1	2	3	4	5	6–10	Laps	Laps Led	Races Led	Miles	$
1970	90	3	0	0	0	0	0	0	0	522	0	0	241	965
1977	53	3	0	0	0	0	0	0	1	1,114	0	0	1,433	7,465
1978	75	2	0	0	0	0	0	0	0	397	0	0	604	8,115
1979	—	0												255
1981	13	29	1	1	0	0	2	0	7	7,441	518	6	7,919	170,473
1982	10	29	2	0	0	1	1	4	7	7,708	211	12	8,620	166,030
1983	20	25	0	0	1	1	1	0	10	6,309	5	4	7,613	287,326
1984	29	20	0	0	0	0	0	0	1	5,134	1	1	5,478	59,670
1985	31	16	0	0	0	0	0	1	1	2,951	1	1	4,059	55,985
1986	18	27	0	1	0	1	2	0	4	6,358	357	13	8,346	244,146
1987	17	29	1	0	1	1	1	4	4	6,410	164	7	7,975	317,034
1988	28	23	2	0	1	0	1	0	4	4,601	127	5	6,076	197,425
1989	13	29	1	0	2	0	1	2	8	7,590	137	6	9,908	544,255
1990	5	29	0	1	2	2	0	2	9	8,794	202	8	10,575	666,915
1991	12	29	0	0	0	2	2	0	10	9,021	86	5	10,479	521,147
1992	14	29	0	0	2	0	0	1	8	9,093	60	3	10,839	634,222
1993	7	30	0	1	1	0	1	0	12	9,442	92	9	11,406	782,523
1994	6	31	0	0	2	2	1	4	7	9,788	80	10	11,950	1,119,038
1995	11	31	0	0	1	1	1	1	6	9,275	31	8	11,547	966,374
1996	19	31	0	0	0	0	0	1	4	8,976	50	4	10,720	719,059
Lifetime		445	7	4	13	11	14	20	103	120,924	2,122	102	145,787	$7,468,422

Year	Rank	Starts	Poles	Finish						Laps	Laps Led	Races Led	Miles	$
				1	2	3	4	5	6–10					

Joe Sheppard

Joseph Sheppard
B: 1929
Racing Hometown: Trenton, NJ

Year	Rank	Starts	Poles	1	2	3	4	5	6–10	Laps	Laps Led	Races Led	Miles	$
1954	151T	1	0	0	0	0	0	0	0	215	0	0	296	75
Lifetime		1	0	0	0	0	0	0	0	215	0	0	296	$75

Lou Sherman

Louis Sherman
Racing Hometown: Portland, OR

Year	Rank	Starts	Poles	1	2	3	4	5	6–10	Laps	Laps Led	Races Led	Miles	$
1956	64	5	0	0	0	1	0	0	1	837	0	0	531	810
Lifetime		5	0	0	0	1	0	0	1	837	0	0	531	$810

Ray Sherman

Raymond Sherman
Racing Hometown: Shermont, DE

Year	Rank	Starts	Poles	1	2	3	4	5	6–10	Laps	Laps Led	Races Led	Miles	$
1953	NR	1	0	0	0	0	0	0	0		0	0		40
Lifetime		1	0	0	0	0	0	0	0		0	0		$40

James Shields

James Shields
Racing Hometown: Rochester, NY

Year	Rank	Starts	Poles	1	2	3	4	5	6–10	Laps	Laps Led	Races Led	Miles	$
1951	N/A	1	0	0	0	0	0	0	0		0	0		25
Lifetime		1	0	0	0	0	0	0	0		0	0		$25

Harry Shipe

Harry Shipe
Racing Hometown: Silver Spring, MD

Year	Rank	Starts	Poles	1	2	3	4	5	6–10	Laps	Laps Led	Races Led	Miles	$
1970	97	2	0	0	0	0	0	0	0	45	0	0	65	450
Lifetime		2	0	0	0	0	0	0	0	45	0	0	65	$450

Bill Shirey

William L. Shirey
B: 2/28/1932
Racing Hometown: Detroit, MI

Year	Rank	Starts	Poles	1	2	3	4	5	6–10	Laps	Laps Led	Races Led	Miles	$
1969	61	3	0	0	0	0	0	0	0	418	0	0	332	1,315
1970	30	29	0	0	0	0	0	0	1	3,691	0	0	2,542	12,390
1971	28	27	0	0	0	0	0	0	2	3,667	0	0	2,574	9,160
1972	38	13	0	0	0	0	0	0	0	1,812	0	0	1,951	8,070
Lifetime		72	0	0	0	0	0	0	3	9,588	0	0	7,399	$30,935

Barney Shore

Bernard Shore
Racing Hometown: Lewisville, NC

Year	Rank	Starts	Poles	1	2	3	4	5	6–10	Laps	Laps Led	Races Led	Miles	$
1958	170	12	0	0	0	0	0	1	2	1,741	0	0	835	1,320
1959	NR	6	0	0	0	0	0	0	2	628	0	0	212	425
1960	NR	1	0	0	0	0	0	0	0	93	0	0	47	50
Lifetime		19	0	0	0	0	0	1	4	2,462	0	0	1,094	$1,795

Chuck Shove

Charles Shove
Racing Hometown: Portland, OR

Year	Rank	Starts	Poles	1	2	3	4	5	6–10	Laps	Laps Led	Races Led	Miles	$
1963	148	1	0	0	0	0	0	0	0	74	0	0	200	200
Lifetime		1	0	0	0	0	0	0	0	74	0	0	200	$200

Dick Shuebruk

Richard Shuebruk
Racing Hometown: Boston, MA

Year	Rank	Starts	Poles	1	2	3	4	5	6–10	Laps	Laps Led	Races Led	Miles	$
1950	NR	1	0	0	0	0	0	0	0		0	0		0
Lifetime		1	0	0	0	0	0	0	0		0	0		$0

Buddy Shuman

Lewis Grier Shuman
B: 9/8/1915   D: 11/13/1955   *Died in a hotel fire in Hickory, NC.*
Racing Hometown: Charlotte, NC

Year	Rank	Starts	Poles	1	2	3	4	5	6–10	Laps	Laps Led	Races Led	Miles	$
1951	6	7	0	0	0	1	0	0	6	391	0	0	489	2,830
1952	10	15	0	1	1	0	0	1	4	1,785	65	2	1,413	4,587
1953	28	5	0	0	0	0	0	0	0	342	0	0	481	430
1955	138	2	0	0	0	0	0	0	2	379	0	0	190	350
Lifetime		29	0	1	1	1	0	1	12	2,897	65	2	2,573	$8,197

Year	Rank	Starts	Poles	Finish						Laps	Laps Led	Races Led	Miles	$
				1	2	3	4	5	6–10	Laps	Led	Led	Miles	$

Larry Shurter

Larry Shurter
B: 9/27/1917
Racing Hometown: West Shokan, NY

Year	Rank	Starts	Poles	1	2	3	4	5	6–10	Laps	Laps Led	Races Led	Miles	$
1950	NR	1	0	0	0	0	0	0	0	37	0	0	154	25
1952	69	4	0	0	0	0	0	0	0	138	0	0	107	125
Lifetime		5	0	0	0	0	0	0	0	175	0	0	261	$150

Leo Sigman

Leo Sigman
Racing Hometown: Marion, VA

Year	Rank	Starts	Poles	1	2	3	4	5	6–10	Laps	Laps Led	Races Led	Miles	$
1951	N/A	2	0	0	0	0	0	0	0		0	0		50
Lifetime		2	0	0	0	0	0	0	0		0	0		$50

Jim Sills

James Sills
Racing Hometown: Rio Linda, CA

Year	Rank	Starts	Poles	1	2	3	4	5	6–10	Laps	Laps Led	Races Led	Miles	$
1956	133	1	0	0	0	0	0	0	0	76	0	0	190	150
Lifetime		1	0	0	0	0	0	0	0	76	0	0	190	$150

Don Simkins

Donald Simkins
Racing Hometown: Orcutt, CA

Year	Rank	Starts	Poles	1	2	3	4	5	6–10	Laps	Laps Led	Races Led	Miles	$
1970	NR	1	0	0	0	0	0	0	0	127	0	0	333	965
Lifetime		1	0	0	0	0	0	0	0	127	0	0	333	$965

David Simko

David Simko
B: 11/26/1954
Racing Hometown: Clarkston, MI

Year	Rank	Starts	Poles	1	2	3	4	5	6–10	Laps	Laps Led	Races Led	Miles	$
1982	106	2	0	0	0	0	0	0	0	100	0	0	203	3,200
1983	98T	1	0	0	0	0	0	0	0	154	0	0	234	3,815
1984	NR	1	0	0	0	0	0	0	0	189	0	0	378	4,000
1986	104T	1	0	0	0	0	0	0	0	170	0	0	340	1,625
1987	54	4	0	0	0	0	0	0	0	850	0	0	1,211	9,330
1988	NR	1	0	0	0	0	0	0	0	9	0	0	18	2,450
Lifetime		10	0	0	0	0	0	0	0	1,472	0	0	2,384	$24,420

Buck Simmons

Buck Simmons
B: 7/31/1946
Racing Hometown: Baldwin, GA

Year	Rank	Starts	Poles	1	2	3	4	5	6–10	Laps	Laps Led	Races Led	Miles	$
1979	71	2	0	0	0	0	0	0	0	438	0	0	787	3,025
1980	43	6	0	0	0	0	0	0	0	1,333	0	0	1,308	7,145
Lifetime		8	0	0	0	0	0	0	0	1,771	0	0	2,095	$10,170

Dick Simon

Richard Raymond Simon
B: 9/21/1933
Racing Hometown: Seattle, WA

Year	Rank	Starts	Poles	1	2	3	4	5	6–10	Laps	Laps Led	Races Led	Miles	$
1973	NR	2	0	0	0	0	0	0	1	264	0	0	689	3,700
1974	NR	1	0	0	0	0	0	0	0	96	0	0	240	3,410
Lifetime		3	0	0	0	0	0	0	1	360	0	0	929	$7,110

Rick Simon

Richard Simon
Racing Hometown: Portland, OR

Year	Rank	Starts	Poles	1	2	3	4	5	6–10	Laps	Laps Led	Races Led	Miles	$
1957	NR	1	0	0	0	0	0	0	0	23	0	0	12	100
Lifetime		1	0	0	0	0	0	0	0	23	0	0	12	$100

Banks Simpson

Banks Simpson
B: 11/4/1916
Racing Hometown: Concord, NC

Year	Rank	Starts	Poles	1	2	3	4	5	6–10	Laps	Laps Led	Races Led	Miles	$
1955	23	7	0	0	0	0	0	0	0	1,103	0	0	1,377	870
Lifetime		7	0	0	0	0	0	0	0	1,103	0	0	1,377	$870

Dub Simpson

Clifford Walker Simpson
B: 1936
Racing Hometown: Charlotte, NC

Year	Rank	Starts	Poles	1	2	3	4	5	6–10	Laps	Laps Led	Races Led	Miles	$
1967	NR	1	0	0	0	0	0	0	0	89	0	0	134	865

Year	Rank	Starts	Poles	1	2	3	4	5	6–10	Laps	Laps Led	Races Led	Miles	$

Dub Simpson *continued*

Year	Rank	Starts	Poles	1	2	3	4	5	6–10	Laps	Laps Led	Races Led	Miles	$
1968	57	4	0	0	0	0	0	1	0	721	0	0	589	1,850
1969	36	20	0	0	0	0	0	0	0	2,923	0	0	2,998	12,915
1970	47	6	0	0	0	0	0	0	1	1,155	0	0	1,111	4,510
1971	59	11	0	0	0	0	0	0	0	621	0	0	654	5,400
1972	78	5	0	0	0	0	0	0	0	563	0	0	637	3,525
1974	NR	1	0	0	0	0	0	0	0	157	0	0	94	340
Lifetime		48	0	0	0	0	0	1	1	6,229	0	0	6,217	$29,405

Gene Simpson

Gene Simpson
Racing Hometown: Meadville, PA

Year	Rank	Starts	Poles	1	2	3	4	5	6–10	Laps	Laps Led	Races Led	Miles	$
1955	17	22	0	0	0	0	0	1	6	2,667	0	0	2,001	2,158
1956	140T	1	0	0	0	0	0	0	0		0	0		100
Lifetime		23	0	0	0	0	0	1	6	2,667	0	0	2,001	$2,258

Jack Simpson

Jack Simpson
Racing Hometown: Montreal, Que., Canada

Year	Rank	Starts	Poles	1	2	3	4	5	6–10	Laps	Laps Led	Races Led	Miles	$
1973	108	1	0	0	0	0	0	0	0	104	0	0	272	725
1974	118	1	0	0	0	0	0	0	0	105	0	0	275	875
1978	86T	1	0	0	0	0	0	0	0	74	0	0	194	1,105
Lifetime		3	0	0	0	0	0	0	0	283	0	0	741	$2,705

Wallace Simpson

Wallace Simpson
Racing Hometown: Macon, GA

Year	Rank	Starts	Poles	1	2	3	4	5	6–10	Laps	Laps Led	Races Led	Miles	$
1954	NR	1	0	0	0	0	0	0	0	143	0	0	72	25
Lifetime		1	0	0	0	0	0	0	0	143	0	0	72	$25

Wimpy Sipple

Elwin Sipple
Racing Hometown: Fairport, NY

Year	Rank	Starts	Poles	1	2	3	4	5	6–10	Laps	Laps Led	Races Led	Miles	$
1953	140T	1	0	0	0	0	0	0	0		0	0		25
Lifetime		1	0	0	0	0	0	0	0		0	0		$25

David Sisco

David Sisco
B: 6/26/1937
Racing Hometown: Nashville, TN

Year	Rank	Starts	Poles	1	2	3	4	5	6–10	Laps	Laps Led	Races Led	Miles	$
1971	57	4	0	0	0	0	0	0	0	853	0	0	1,019	3,625
1972	33	12	0	0	0	0	0	0	2	2,067	0	0	3,269	14,490
1973	17	23	0	0	0	0	1	1	4	6,552	12	2	7,140	36,205
1974	10	28	0	0	0	1	1	0	7	7,483	43	4	9,012	58,313
1975	13	28	0	0	0	1	0	1	5	7,572	37	4	8,455	62,186
1976	17	28	0	0	0	0	0	0	7	7,111	6	3	8,101	62,622
1977	37	10	0	0	0	0	0	0	0	2,030	0	0	2,186	14,520
Lifetime		133	0	0	0	2	2	2	25	33,668	98	13	39,182	$251,961

Jerry Sisco

Jerry Lee Sisco
B: 8/1/1941
Racing Hometown: Nashville, TN

Year	Rank	Starts	Poles	1	2	3	4	5	6–10	Laps	Laps Led	Races Led	Miles	$
1974	NR	1	0	0	0	0	0	0	0	142	0	0	85	295
1976	60	3	0	0	0	0	0	0	0	781	0	0	797	3,070
Lifetime		4	0	0	0	0	0	0	0	923	0	0	882	$3,365

Marvin Sjolin

Marvin Sjolin
Racing Hometown: Highland, CA

Year	Rank	Starts	Poles	1	2	3	4	5	6–10	Laps	Laps Led	Races Led	Miles	$
1969	NR	1	0	0	0	0	0	0	0	132	0	0	356	925
Lifetime		1	0	0	0	0	0	0	0	132	0	0	356	$925

Buren Skeen

Buren Skeen
B: 1937   D: 9/13/1965   *Died from injuries suffered @ Darlington 9/6/65.*
Racing Hometown: Denton, NC

Year	Rank	Starts	Poles	1	2	3	4	5	6–10	Laps	Laps Led	Races Led	Miles	$
1965	60	8	0	0	0	0	0	1	2	1,319	0	0	676	2,875
Lifetime		8	0	0	0	0	0	1	2	1,319	0	0	676	$2,875

Year	Rank	Starts	Poles	Finish						Laps	Laps Led	Races Led	Miles	$
				1	2	3	4	5	6–10					

Dick Skillen

Dr. Richard Skillen
B: 8/5/1945
Racing Hometown: Claremont, NH

Year	Rank	Starts	Poles	1	2	3	4	5	6–10	Laps	Laps Led	Races Led	Miles	$
1974	66	3	0	0	0	0	0	0	0	908	0	0	1,137	3,740
1975	49	5	0	0	0	0	0	0	0	1,052	0	0	1,333	4,865
1976	51	5	0	0	0	0	0	0	0	810	0	0	1,716	8,250
1977	113T	1	0	0	0	0	0	0	0	38	0	0	101	1,830
1980	96T	1	0	0	0	0	0	0	0	76	0	0	202	2,785
1982	—	0												550
1983	101T	1	0	0	0	0	0	0	0	1	0	0	3	2,050
1985	75	1	0	0	0	0	0	0	0	167	0	0	444	5,720
1986	—	0												1,800
Lifetime		17	0	0	0	0	0	0	0	3,052	0	0	4,936	$31,590

Eddie Skinner

Edward Skinner
Racing Hometown: Yerrington, NV

Year	Rank	Starts	Poles	1	2	3	4	5	6–10	Laps	Laps Led	Races Led	Miles	$
1953	47	4	0	0	0	0	0	0	1		0	0		200
1954	18	15	0	0	0	0	0	0	1	2,044	0	0	1,659	1,017
1955	7	38	0	0	0	0	0	4	11	5,473	0	0	3,629	4,737
1956	118	6	0	0	0	0	0	0	0	427	0	0	242	200
1957	45	4	0	0	0	0	0	0	0	833	0	0	534	605
1958	58	5	0	0	0	0	0	0	0	750	0	0	440	420
Lifetime		72	0	0	0	0	0	4	13	9,527	0	0	6,504	$7,179

J. R. Skinner

J. R. Skinner
Racing Hometown: Northridge, CA

Year	Rank	Starts	Poles	1	2	3	4	5	6–10	Laps	Laps Led	Races Led	Miles	$
1971	NR	1	0	0	0	0	0	0	0	17	0	0	45	640
Lifetime		1	0	0	0	0	0	0	0	17	0	0	45	$640

Mike Skinner

Michael Curtis Skinner
B: 6/28/1957
Racing Hometown: Ontario, CA

Year	Rank	Starts	Poles	1	2	3	4	5	6–10	Laps	Laps Led	Races Led	Miles	$
1986	61	3	0	0	0	0	0	0	0	807	0	0	635	4,255
1990	96	1	0	0	0	0	0	0	0	230	0	0	234	2,825
1991	64T	2	0	0	0	0	0	0	0	350	0	0	362	8,505
1992	59	2	0	0	0	0	0	0	0	929	0	0	945	13,450
1993	80	1	0	0	0	0	0	0	0	145	0	0	198	5,180
1994	72T	1	0	0	0	0	0	0	0	469	0	0	477	9,550
1996	47	5	0	0	0	0	0	0	0	1,459	10	1	1,742	65,850
Lifetime		15	0	0	0	0	0	0	0	4,389	10	1	4,593	$109,615

Otis Skinner

Otis Skinner
Racing Hometown: Riverside, CA

Year	Rank	Starts	Poles	1	2	3	4	5	6–10	Laps	Laps Led	Races Led	Miles	$
1958	57	1	0	0	0	0	0	0	1	178	0	0	468	325
Lifetime		1	0	0	0	0	0	0	1	178	0	0	468	$325

Joe Skovron

Joseph Skovron
Racing Hometown: Greenville, RI

Year	Rank	Starts	Poles	1	2	3	4	5	6–10	Laps	Laps Led	Races Led	Miles	$
1951	N/A	1	0	0	0	0	0	0	0		0	0		0
Lifetime		1	0	0	0	0	0	0	0		0	0		$0

Ann Slaasted

Ann Slaasted
Racing Hometown: Racine, WI

Year	Rank	Starts	Poles	1	2	3	4	5	6–10	Laps	Laps Led	Races Led	Miles	$
1950	NR	1	0	0	0	0	0	0	0		0	0		0
Lifetime		1	0	0	0	0	0	0	0		0	0		$0

Sandy Slack

Everett Slack
Racing Hometown: N. Platte, NE

Year	Rank	Starts	Poles	1	2	3	4	5	6–10	Laps	Laps Led	Races Led	Miles	$
1953	91T	1	0	0	0	0	0	0	1		0	0		50
Lifetime		1	0	0	0	0	0	0	1		0	0		$50

Year	Rank	Starts	Poles	Finish						Laps	Laps Led	Races Led	Miles	$
				1	2	3	4	5	6–10	Laps				

Wayne Slark
Wayne Slark

Year	Rank	Starts	Poles	1	2	3	4	5	6–10	Laps	Laps Led	Races Led	Miles	$
1986	116T	1	0	0	0	0	0	0	0	96	0	0	98	4,055
Lifetime		1	0	0	0	0	0	0	0	96	0	0	98	$4,055

Bob Slawinski
Robert Slawinski
Racing Hometown: Harper Woods, MI

Year	Rank	Starts	Poles	1	2	3	4	5	6–10	Laps	Laps Led	Races Led	Miles	$
1982	98	1	0	0	0	0	0	0	0	56	0	0	149	1,745
Lifetime		1	0	0	0	0	0	0	0	56	0	0	149	$1,745

Robert Slensby
Robert C. Slensby
Racing Hometown: Pensacola, FL

Year	Rank	Starts	Poles	1	2	3	4	5	6–10	Laps	Laps Led	Races Led	Miles	$
1954	173	1	0	0	0	0	0	0	0	117	0	0	176	50
1956	195T	1	0	0	0	0	0	0	0	117	0	0	59	100
Lifetime		2	0	0	0	0	0	0	0	234	0	0	234	$150

Bill Small
William Small
Racing Hometown: Newhall, CA

Year	Rank	Starts	Poles	1	2	3	4	5	6–10	Laps	Laps Led	Races Led	Miles	$
1968	102	1	0	0	0	0	0	0	0	16	0	0	43	500
Lifetime		1	0	0	0	0	0	0	0	16	0	0	43	$500

Al Smith
Al Smith
B: 1/30/1929
Racing Hometown: Daytona, OH

Year	Rank	Starts	Poles	1	2	3	4	5	6–10	Laps	Laps Led	Races Led	Miles	$
1952	NR	1	0	0	0	0	0	0	0	125	0	0	63	25
Lifetime		1	0	0	0	0	0	0	0	125	0	0	63	$25

Archie Smith
Archie Smith
Racing Hometown: Denton, NC

Year	Rank	Starts	Poles	1	2	3	4	5	6–10	Laps	Laps Led	Races Led	Miles	$
1949	21	2	0	0	0	0	0	0	2	161	0	0	81	225
Lifetime		2	0	0	0	0	0	0	2	161	0	0	81	$225

Barney Smith
Barney Smith
Racing Hometown: Macon, GA

Year	Rank	Starts	Poles	1	2	3	4	5	6–10	Laps	Laps Led	Races Led	Miles	$
1950	77	1	0	0	0	0	0	0	0	366	0	0	458	275
1951	N/A	2	0	0	0	0	0	0	0		0	0		75
1952	58	3	0	0	0	0	0	0	2	647	0	0	324	285
Lifetime		6	0	0	0	0	0	0	2	1,013	0	0	781	$635

Bill Smith
William Smith
Racing Hometown: Hillside, NJ

Year	Rank	Starts	Poles	1	2	3	4	5	6–10	Laps	Laps Led	Races Led	Miles	$
1954	NR	3	0	0	0	0	0	0	1	828	0	0	456	340
Lifetime		3	0	0	0	0	0	0	1	828	0	0	456	$340

Bill Smith
William Smith
Racing Hometown: Kannapolis, NC

Year	Rank	Starts	Poles	1	2	3	4	5	6–10	Laps	Laps Led	Races Led	Miles	$
1962	120	1	0	0	0	0	0	0	0	60	0	0	30	200
Lifetime		1	0	0	0	0	0	0	0	60	0	0	30	$200

Billy Smith
William Smith
Racing Hometown: Hampton, VA

Year	Rank	Starts	Poles	1	2	3	4	5	6–10	Laps	Laps Led	Races Led	Miles	$
1979	120	1	0	0	0	0	0	0	0	179	0	0	245	1,575
Lifetime		1	0	0	0	0	0	0	0	179	0	0	245	$1,575

Bob Smith
Robert Smith
Racing Hometown: Rinet, VA

Year	Rank	Starts	Poles	1	2	3	4	5	6–10	Laps	Laps Led	Races Led	Miles	$
1949	NR	2	0	0	0	0	0	0	0		0	0		25
1950	NR	2	0	0	0	0	0	0	0	419	0	0	458	0
Lifetime		4	0	0	0	0	0	0	0	419	0	0	458	$25

Year	Rank	Starts	Poles	Finish						Laps	Laps Led	Races Led	Miles	$
				1	2	3	4	5	6–10					

Buck Smith

James Smith
Racing Hometown: Martinsville, VA

Year	Rank	Starts	Poles	1	2	3	4	5	6–10	Laps	Laps Led	Races Led	Miles	$
1953	44	5	0	0	0	0	0	0	1		0	0		175
Lifetime		5	0	0	0	0	0	0	1		0	0		$175

Dick Smith

Richard Smith
Racing Hometown: Lakewood, CA

Year	Rank	Starts	Poles	1	2	3	4	5	6–10	Laps	Laps Led	Races Led	Miles	$
1960	NR	2	0	0	0	0	0	0	2	262	0	0	330	750
1961	95	3	0	0	0	1	0	0	0	191	0	0	218	475
Lifetime		5	0	0	0	1	0	0	2	453	0	0	548	$1,225

Frank Smith

Frank Smith
B: 12/16/1901
Racing Hometown: Denton, NC

Year	Rank	Starts	Poles	1	2	3	4	5	6–10	Laps	Laps Led	Races Led	Miles	$
1949	61	2	0	0	0	0	0	0	0		0	0		50
Lifetime		2	0	0	0	0	0	0	0		0	0		$50

Frank Smith

Frank Smith
Racing Hometown: Memphis, TN

Year	Rank	Starts	Poles	1	2	3	4	5	6–10	Laps	Laps Led	Races Led	Miles	$
1954	83	1	0	0	0	0	0	0	0	144	0	0	216	100
Lifetime		1	0	0	0	0	0	0	0	144	0	0	216	$100

Freddy Smith

William Freddy Smith
B: 12/22/1946
Racing Hometown: Kings Mountain, NC

Year	Rank	Starts	Poles	1	2	3	4	5	6–10	Laps	Laps Led	Races Led	Miles	$
1979	NR	2	0	0	0	0	0	0	0	765	0	0	936	2,950
Lifetime		2	0	0	0	0	0	0	0	765	0	0	936	$2,950

Garland Smith

Garland Smith
Racing Hometown: Greensboro, NC

Year	Rank	Starts	Poles	1	2	3	4	5	6–10	Laps	Laps Led	Races Led	Miles	$
1949	NR	1	0	0	0	0	0	0	0		0	0		25
Lifetime		1	0	0	0	0	0	0	0		0	0		$25

Gordon Smith

Gordon Smith
Racing Hometown: Enfield, NC

Year	Rank	Starts	Poles	1	2	3	4	5	6–10	Laps	Laps Led	Races Led	Miles	$
1955	30	15	0	0	0	0	0	0	2	1,584	0	0	910	975
Lifetime		15	0	0	0	0	0	0	2	1,584	0	0	910	$975

Harold Smith

Harold Wayne Smith
B: 1927
Racing Hometown: Dayton, OH

Year	Rank	Starts	Poles	1	2	3	4	5	6–10	Laps	Laps Led	Races Led	Miles	$
1959	64	2	0	0	0	0	0	0	0	194	0	0	485	160
1960	NR	2	0	0	0	0	0	0	0	105	0	0	263	200
1966	51	3	0	0	0	0	1	0	0	703	0	0	962	4,195
1968	82T	1	0	0	0	0	0	0	0	244	0	0	366	1,850
1970	98	1	0	0	0	0	0	0	0	30	0	0	60	635
Lifetime		9	0	0	0	0	1	0	0	1,276	0	0	2,135	$7,040

Jack Smith

Jack Smith
Racing Hometown: New Jersey

Year	Rank	Starts	Poles	1	2	3	4	5	6–10	Laps	Laps Led	Races Led	Miles	$
1953	N/A	1	0	0	0	0	0	0	0		0	0		25
Lifetime		1	0	0	0	0	0	0	0		0	0		$25

Jack Smith

Jack Thomas Smith
B: 5/24/1924
Racing Hometown: Sandy Springs, GA

Year	Rank	Starts	Poles	1	2	3	4	5	6–10	Laps	Laps Led	Races Led	Miles	$
1949	58	1	0	0	0	0	0	0	0		0	0		50
1950	32	3	0	0	1	0	0	0	0	376	45	1	561	775
1951	39	7	0	0	1	1	0	0	0	480	0	0	552	1,275
1952	34	8	1	0	0	0	0	0	2	883	186	1	820	820
1954	64	6	0	0	0	0	0	0	1	381	0	0	423	500

Jack Smith *continued*

Year	Rank	Starts	Poles	1	2	3	4	5	6–10	Laps	Laps Led	Races Led	Miles	$
1955	141	2	0	0	0	0	0	0	2	386	0	0	193	400
1956	21	15	0	1	0	0	0	0	5	2,669	234	2	1,916	3,825
1957	5	39	2	4	1	2	3	7	8	6,589	429	9	3,969	14,562
1958	5	39	4	2	5	2	3	3	6	5,750	381	7	3,711	12,634
1959	8	21	3	4	1	2	2	0	3	3,594	222	7	2,735	13,290
1960	14	13	4	3	1	2	0	1	0	2,198	514	10	2,570	24,721
1961	7	25	0	2	2	4	1	1	4	4,695	278	4	4,098	21,410
1962	4	51	7	5	6	5	8	3	8	10,781	894	9	7,110	34,748
1963	24	29	2	0	0	0	1	3	7	5,300	25	2	3,625	8,885
1964	81	4	1	0	1	1	0	0	0	459	20	1	240	1,575
Lifetime		263	24	21	19	19	18	18	46	44,541	3,228	50	32,521	$139,470

Jerry Smith

Jerry Smith
Racing Hometown: Chattanooga, TN

Year	Rank	Starts	Poles	1	2	3	4	5	6–10	Laps	Laps Led	Races Led	Miles	$
1959	NR	2	0	0	0	0	0	0	0	644	0	0	322	215
1962	NR	1	0	0	0	0	0	0	0	109	0	0	36	60
Lifetime		3	0	0	0	0	0	0	0	753	0	0	358	$275

John Smith

John W. Smith
Racing Hometown: Baltimore, MD

Year	Rank	Starts	Poles	1	2	3	4	5	6–10	Laps	Laps Led	Races Led	Miles	$
1954	113T	1	0	0	0	0	0	0	0	174	0	0	87	25
Lifetime		1	0	0	0	0	0	0	0	174	0	0	87	$25

John Smith

John Smith
Racing Hometown: San Jose, CA

Year	Rank	Starts	Poles	1	2	3	4	5	6–10	Laps	Laps Led	Races Led	Miles	$
1957	163	1	0	0	0	0	0	0	0	61	0	0	31	50
Lifetime		1	0	0	0	0	0	0	0	61	0	0	31	$50

Larry Smith

Larry Grayson Smith
B: 6/16/1942   D: 8/12/1973   *Killed in Talladega 500.*
Racing Hometown: Lenoir, NC

Year	Rank	Starts	Poles	1	2	3	4	5	6–10	Laps	Laps Led	Races Led	Miles	$
1971	54	4	0	0	0	0	0	0	1	896	0	0	1,699	5,058
1972	23	23	0	0	0	0	0	0	7	4,320	0	0	5,831	24,215
1973	33	11	0	0	0	0	0	0	1	2,103	0	0	3,562	14,090
Lifetime		38	0	0	0	0	0	0	9	7,319	0	0	11,092	$43,363

Louise Smith

Louise Smith
B: 7/31/1916
Racing Hometown: Greenville, SC

Year	Rank	Starts	Poles	1	2	3	4	5	6–10	Laps	Laps Led	Races Led	Miles	$
1949	67	3	0	0	0	0	0	0	0	175	0	0	175	75
1950	109	5	0	0	0	0	0	0	0	84	0	0	84	25
1952	173	3	0	0	0	0	0	0	0	118	0	0	101	85
Lifetime		11	0	0	0	0	0	0	0	377	0	0	360	$185

Paul Smith

Paul Smith
Racing Hometown: Dayton, OH

Year	Rank	Starts	Poles	1	2	3	4	5	6–10	Laps	Laps Led	Races Led	Miles	$
1950	74	3	0	0	0	0	0	0	1		0	0		50
Lifetime		3	0	0	0	0	0	0	1		0	0		$50

Perry Smith

Perry Smith
D: 12/8/1951   *Killed in private plane crash while flying an 80-year-old woman to Chicago for medical treatment.*
Racing Hometown: W. Columbia, SC

Year	Rank	Starts	Poles	1	2	3	4	5	6–10	Laps	Laps Led	Races Led	Miles	$
1951	N/A	1	0	0	0	0	1	0	0		0	0		300
Lifetime		1	0	0	0	0	1	0	0		0	0		$300

R. K. Smith

R. K. Smith

Year	Rank	Starts	Poles	1	2	3	4	5	6–10	Laps	Laps Led	Races Led	Miles	$
1991	92	1	0	0	0	0	0	0	0	2	0	0	5	3,475
1992	83	1	0	0	0	0	0	0	0	70	0	0	176	4,880
Lifetime		2	0	0	0	0	0	0	0	72	0	0	181	$8,355

Year	Rank	Starts	Poles	Finish						Laps	Laps Led	Races Led	Miles	$
				1	2	3	4	5	6–10					

Ralph Smith

Ralph Smith
Racing Hometown: Roswell, GA

Year	Rank	Starts	Poles	1	2	3	4	5	6–10	Laps	Laps Led	Races Led	Miles	$
1962	96	2	0	0	0	0	0	0	0	684	0	0	342	300
Lifetime		2	0	0	0	0	0	0	0	684	0	0	342	$300

Rollin Smith

Rollin Smith
Racing Hometown: N. Manchester, IN

Year	Rank	Starts	Poles	1	2	3	4	5	6–10	Laps	Laps Led	Races Led	Miles	$
1950	NR	1	0	0	0	0	0	0	0	208	0	0	260	0
1952	36	1	0	0	0	0	0	0	0	385	0	0	481	350
Lifetime		2	0	0	0	0	0	0	0	593	0	0	741	$350

Roy Smith

Wilroy Clarence Smith
B: 8/6/1944
Racing Hometown: Victoria, B.C., Canada

Year	Rank	Starts	Poles	1	2	3	4	5	6–10	Laps	Laps Led	Races Led	Miles	$
1975	NR	1	0	0	0	0	0	0	0	62	0	0	155	900
1976	69	3	0	0	0	0	0	0	0	225	0	0	569	4,285
1977	62	3	0	0	0	0	0	0	0	205	0	0	532	5,365
1978	78	1	0	0	0	0	0	0	1	115	0	0	301	2,300
1979	100	1	0	0	0	0	0	0	0	193	0	0	483	2,690
1980	60	3	0	0	0	0	0	0	0	223	3	1	576	4,045
1981	57	3	0	0	0	0	0	0	1	178	0	0	466	8,695
1982	47	3	0	0	0	0	0	0	2	394	0	0	1,009	26,770
1983	95T	1	0	0	0	0	0	0	0	36	0	0	94	2,025
1984	NR	1	0	0	0	0	0	0	0	70	0	0	183	2,475
1987	83	2	0	0	0	0	0	0	0	29	0	0	76	2,325
1988	58	2	0	0	0	0	0	0	0	303	1	1	441	4,550
1989	80	2	0	0	0	0	0	0	0	86	0	0	156	7,820
Lifetime		26	0	0	0	0	0	0	4	2,119	4	2	5,041	$74,245

Ruel Smith

Ruel Smith
Racing Hometown: Mobile, AL

Year	Rank	Starts	Poles	1	2	3	4	5	6–10	Laps	Laps Led	Races Led	Miles	$
1950	NR	2	0	0	0	0	0	0	0	336	0	0	385	0
1951	N/A	1	0	0	0	0	0	0	0		0	0		25
Lifetime		3	0	0	0	0	0	0	0	336	0	0	385	$25

Sam Smith

Sam Smith
Racing Hometown: Greensboro, NC

Year	Rank	Starts	Poles	1	2	3	4	5	6–10	Laps	Laps Led	Races Led	Miles	$
1954	126T	1	0	0	0	0	0	0	0	137	0	0	69	25
Lifetime		1	0	0	0	0	0	0	0	137	0	0	69	$25

Samuel Smith

Samuel Hollis Smith (Sam)
B: 1936   D: 5/7/1982
Racing Hometown: Union, SC

Year	Rank	Starts	Poles	1	2	3	4	5	6–10	Laps	Laps Led	Races Led	Miles	$
1965	102	1	0	0	0	0	0	0	0	108	0	0	54	110
Lifetime		1	0	0	0	0	0	0	0	108	0	0	54	$110

Slick Smith

Ebenezer Smith
Deceased
Racing Hometown: Atlanta, GA

Year	Rank	Starts	Poles	1	2	3	4	5	6–10	Laps	Laps Led	Races Led	Miles	$
1949	31	4	0	0	0	0	0	0	1	277	0	0	139	275
1950	103	5	0	0	0	0	0	0	0	375	0	0	457	25
1951	90	4	0	0	0	0	0	0	0	529	0	0	593	315
1952	32	5	0	0	0	0	0	0	3	613	0	0	516	725
1953	12	23	1	0	0	0	0	0	10	592	4	1	755	2,302
1954	27	6	0	0	0	0	1	0	1	698	0	0	688	950
1955	193	3	0	0	0	0	0	0	2	424	0	0	434	525
Lifetime		50	1	0	0	0	1	0	17	3,508	4	1	3,581	$5,117

Snuffy Smith

Snuffy Smith
Racing Hometown: Hickory, NC

Year	Rank	Starts	Poles	1	2	3	4	5	6–10	Laps	Laps Led	Races Led	Miles	$
1953	122T	1	0	0	0	0	0	0	0		0	0		25
Lifetime		1	0	0	0	0	0	0	0		0	0		$25

Year	Rank	Starts	Poles	Finish 1	2	3	4	5	6–10	Laps	Laps Led	Races Led	Miles	$

Stanley Smith

Stanley Smith
B: 1949
Racing Hometown: Chelsea, AL

Year	Rank	Starts	Poles	1	2	3	4	5	6–10	Laps	Laps Led	Races Led	Miles	$
1990	98T	1	0	0	0	0	0	0	0	54	0	0	144	4,285
1991	36	12	0	0	0	0	0	0	0	1,932	12	1	3,201	56,915
1992	35	14	0	0	0	0	0	0	0	2,685	0	0	4,009	89,650
1993	89T	1	0	0	0	0	0	0	0	68	0	0	181	9,790
Lifetime		28	0	0	0	0	0	0	0	4,739	12	1	7,534	$160,640

Wayne Smith

Howard Wayne Smith
B: 4/12/1939
Racing Hometown: Advance, NC

Year	Rank	Starts	Poles	1	2	3	4	5	6–10	Laps	Laps Led	Races Led	Miles	$
1965	30	25	0	0	0	0	0	0	2	3,744	0	0	2,475	6,790
1966	33	23	0	0	0	0	0	0	1	4,108	0	0	3,655	9,930
1967	28	27	0	0	0	0	0	0	2	4,364	0	0	3,629	10,225
1968	33	18	0	0	0	0	0	0	1	2,456	0	0	2,019	7,235
1969	39	16	0	0	0	0	0	0	2	2,692	0	0	2,961	10,610
1970	50	8	0	0	0	0	0	0	0	593	0	0	813	4,505
1971	67	2	0	0	0	0	0	0	0	67	0	0	39	660
1972	81	3	0	0	0	0	0	0	1	270	0	0	624	3,445
Lifetime		122	0	0	0	0	0	0	9	18,294	0	0	16,217	$53,200

Tom Sneva

Thomas E. Sneva
B: 6/1/1948
Racing Hometown: Spokane, WA

Year	Rank	Starts	Poles	1	2	3	4	5	6–10	Laps	Laps Led	Races Led	Miles	$
1977	NR	1	0	0	0	0	0	0	0	194	0	0	291	1,150
1981	—	0												815
1982	53	3	0	0	0	0	0	0	0	520	0	0	840	15,585
1983	75	2	0	0	0	0	0	0	1	274	0	0	648	29,740
1985	NR	1	0	0	0	0	0	0	0	138	0	0	210	2,655
1987	88T	1	0	0	0	0	0	0	0	182	0	0	455	11,135
Lifetime		8	0	0	0	0	0	0	1	1,308	0	0	2,444	$61,080

Les Snow

Leslie Snow Jr.
B: 9/20/1925
Racing Hometown: Bloomington, IL

Year	Rank	Starts	Poles	1	2	3	4	5	6–10	Laps	Laps Led	Races Led	Miles	$
1951	77	2	0	0	0	0	0	0	1	222	0	0	222	375
1969	NR	1	0	0	0	0	0	0	0	2	0	0	5	925
Lifetime		3	0	0	0	0	0	0	1	224	0	0	227	$1,300

Bill Snowden

William Snowden
B: 5/6/1910   D: 1/1959
Racing Hometown: St. Augustine, FL

Year	Rank	Starts	Poles	1	2	3	4	5	6–10	Laps	Laps Led	Races Led	Miles	$
1949	11	4	0	0	0	0	0	1	2	182	0	0	91	660
1950	40	4	0	0	0	0	0	1	1	532	0	0	568	325
1951	9	12	0	0	0	0	2	1	6	383	0	0	479	2,640
1952	62	4	0	0	0	0	0	0	1	384	0	0	237	290
Lifetime		24	0	0	0	0	2	3	10	1,481	0	0	1,375	$3,915

John Soares

John Soares
Racing Hometown: Oakland, CA

Year	Rank	Starts	Poles	1	2	3	4	5	6–10	Laps	Laps Led	Races Led	Miles	$
1951	N/A	3	0	0	0	0	0	0	0		0	0		175
1954	16	9	0	1	0	1	0	0	2	1,947	211	1	1,374	3,262
1955	209	1	0	0	0	0	0	0	0	86	0	0	86	25
Lifetime		13	0	1	0	1	0	0	2	2,033	211	1	1,460	$3,462

John Soares Jr.

John Soares Jr.
B: 5/18/1942
Racing Hometown: Hayward, CA

Year	Rank	Starts	Poles	1	2	3	4	5	6–10	Laps	Laps Led	Races Led	Miles	$
1970	NR	1	0	0	0	0	1	0	0	141	0	0	369	3,415
1971	NR	4	0	0	0	0	0	0	1	764	0	0	1,280	4,855

Year	Rank	Starts	Poles	Finish						Laps	Laps Led	Races Led	Miles	$
				1	2	3	4	5	6–10					

John Soares Jr. *continued*

Year	Rank	Starts	Poles	1	2	3	4	5	6–10	Laps	Laps Led	Races Led	Miles	$
1972	70	3	0	0	0	0	0	0	0	337	0	0	861	4,315
1973	99	2	0	0	0	0	0	0	0	122	0	0	320	1,980
1975	105T	1	0	0	0	0	0	0	0	18	0	0	47	670
1985	62	2	0	0	0	0	0	0	0	192	0	0	503	3,100
Lifetime		13	0	0	0	0	1	0	1	1,766	0	0	3,883	$18,335

Jay Sommers

Jay Sommers
Racing Hometown: Mt. Clemens, MI

Year	Rank	Starts	Poles	1	2	3	4	5	6–10	Laps	Laps Led	Races Led	Miles	$
1988	83T	1	0	0	0	0	0	0	0	280	0	0	280	1,510
Lifetime		1	0	0	0	0	0	0	0	280	0	0	280	$1,510

Joe Sommers

Joseph Sommers
Racing Hometown: Newark, NJ

Year	Rank	Starts	Poles	1	2	3	4	5	6–10	Laps	Laps Led	Races Led	Miles	$
1951	N/A	1	0	0	0	0	0	0	1		0	0		75
Lifetime		1	0	0	0	0	0	0	1		0	0		$75

Sam Sommers

Cecil Franklin Sommers
B: 9/17/1939
Racing Hometown: Savannah, GA

Year	Rank	Starts	Poles	1	2	3	4	5	6–10	Laps	Laps Led	Races Led	Miles	$
1976	52	5	0	0	0	0	0	0	1	1,000	0	0	1,534	8,930
1977	21	23	1	0	0	0	1	1	6	5,764	28	3	7,080	54,625
1978	81	2	0	0	0	0	0	0	0	512	0	0	748	3,565
Lifetime		30	1	0	0	0	1	1	7	7,276	28	3	9,362	$67,120

Dick Soper

Richard Soper

Year	Rank	Starts	Poles	1	2	3	4	5	6–10	Laps	Laps Led	Races Led	Miles	$
1950	NR	1	0	0	0	0	0	0	0	282	0	0	353	0
Lifetime		1	0	0	0	0	0	0	0	282	0	0	353	$0

Jack Soper

Jack George Soper
Racing Hometown: Charlotte, NC

Year	Rank	Starts	Poles	1	2	3	4	5	6–10	Laps	Laps Led	Races Led	Miles	$
1966	142	1	0	0	0	0	0	0	0	25	0	0	5	0
Lifetime		1	0	0	0	0	0	0	0	25	0	0	5	$0

David Sosebee

David Sosebee
B: 12/8/1955
Racing Hometown: Dawsonville, GA

Year	Rank	Starts	Poles	1	2	3	4	5	6–10	Laps	Laps Led	Races Led	Miles	$
1979	78	3	0	0	0	0	0	0	0	547	0	0	892	2,910
1986	90	2	0	0	0	0	0	0	0	267	0	0	404	2,310
1987	61	3	0	0	0	0	0	0	0	570	0	0	1,013	25,030
1988	75	2	0	0	0	0	0	0	0	289	0	0	499	7,560
Lifetime		10	0	0	0	0	0	0	0	1,673	0	0	2,807	$37,810

Gober Sosebee

Gober Sosebee
B: 10/15/1915   D: 11/11/1996   *Killed in farming accident.*
Racing Hometown: Atlanta, GA

Year	Rank	Starts	Poles	1	2	3	4	5	6–10	Laps	Laps Led	Races Led	Miles	$
1949	15	3	1	0	1	0	0	0	1	170	34	1	170	1,305
1950	NR	2	0	0	0	0	0	0	0	385	4	1	543	315
1951	17	10	1	0	3	0	0	1	1	717	7	1	711	2,710
1952	90	9	0	1	0	0	0	3	1	744	215	3	556	2,125
1953	14	17	0	0	1	1	0	0	7	943	73	1	928	2,722
1954	15	18	1	1	0	1	1	1	3	1,970	170	2	1,376	3,150
1955	64	6	0	0	0	0	2	0	0	344	0	0	218	775
1958	112	5	1	0	0	0	0	0	3	692	0	0	476	695
1959	NR	1	0	0	0	0	0	0	0	44	0	0	110	100
Lifetime		71	4	2	5	2	3	5	16	6,009	503	9	5,087	$13,897

Jim Southard

James Southard
B: 1933
Racing Hometown: Marietta, GA

Year	Rank	Starts	Poles	1	2	3	4	5	6–10	Laps	Laps Led	Races Led	Miles	$
1984	51	4	0	0	0	0	0	0	0	1,113	0	0	1,653	9,515

Year	Rank	Starts	Poles	Finish 1	2	3	4	5	6–10	Laps	Laps Led	Races Led	Miles	$

Jim Southard *continued*

Year	Rank	Starts	Poles	1	2	3	4	5	6–10	Laps	Laps Led	Races Led	Miles	$
1985	NR	1	0	0	0	0	0	0	0	431	0	0	438	1,970
Lifetime		5	0	0	0	0	0	0	0	1,544	0	0	2,091	$11,485

Nick Spano
Nicholas Spano
Racing Hometown: Montclair, NJ

Year	Rank	Starts	Poles	1	2	3	4	5	6–10	Laps	Laps Led	Races Led	Miles	$
1954	156T	1	0	0	0	0	0	0	0	147	0	0	74	10
Lifetime		1	0	0	0	0	0	0	0	147	0	0	74	$10

Tony Spanos
Anthony Spanos
Racing Hometown: Australia

Year	Rank	Starts	Poles	1	2	3	4	5	6–10	Laps	Laps Led	Races Led	Miles	$
1987	NR	1	0	0	0	0	0	0	0	386	0	0	203	3,455
1988	—	0												1,400
1989	—	0												1,500
Lifetime		1	0	0	0	0	0	0	0	386	0	0	203	$6,355

Huck Spaulding
Huck Spaulding
Racing Hometown: Coxsackie, NY

Year	Rank	Starts	Poles	1	2	3	4	5	6–10	Laps	Laps Led	Races Led	Miles	$
1957	36	8	0	0	0	0	0	0	3	1,006	0	0	659	1,130
1958	153	1	0	0	0	0	0	0	0		0	0		50
Lifetime		9	0	0	0	0	0	0	3	1,006	0	0	659	$1,180

Jack Spearman
Jack Spearman

Year	Rank	Starts	Poles	1	2	3	4	5	6–10	Laps	Laps Led	Races Led	Miles	$
1954	NR	1	0	0	0	0	0	0	0	39	0	0	78	0
Lifetime		1	0	0	0	0	0	0	0	39	0	0	78	$0

Lou Spears
Louis Spears
Racing Hometown: Ardmore, PA

Year	Rank	Starts	Poles	1	2	3	4	5	6–10	Laps	Laps Led	Races Led	Miles	$
1955	27	3	0	0	0	0	0	0	1	708	0	0	748	810
1956	208	3	0	0	0	0	0	0	0	406	0	0	495	175
1957	NR	3	0	0	0	0	0	0	0	351	0	0	172	235
Lifetime		9	0	0	0	0	0	0	1	1,465	0	0	1,416	$1,220

Lake Speed
Lake Chambers Speed
B: 1/17/1948
Racing Hometown: Jackson, MS

Year	Rank	Starts	Poles	1	2	3	4	5	6–10	Laps	Laps Led	Races Led	Miles	$
1980	22	19	0	0	0	0	0	0	5	4,019	2	1	6,271	70,640
1981	18	27	0	0	0	0	0	0	6	6,757	14	2	7,557	95,690
1982	20	30	0	0	0	0	0	0	5	5,830	0	0	6,856	118,457
1983	27	18	0	0	0	1	1	0	3	4,933	22	2	6,928	78,220
1984	26	19	0	0	0	1	0	1	5	4,814	122	5	6,752	98,320
1985	10	28	0	0	1	0	1	0	12	8,308	8	4	9,937	300,326
1986	40	5	0	0	0	0	0	0	2	1,779	10	2	2,271	82,800
1987	31	13	0	0	0	1	0	0	4	2,591	1	1	4,433	110,810
1988	17	29	0	1	1	0	1	1	3	7,005	368	6	8,534	260,500
1989	27	24	0	0	0	0	0	1	4	7,028	11	4	8,245	201,977
1990	42	6	0	0	0	0	0	0	0	835	3	1	1,753	75,537
1991	32	20	0	0	0	0	0	0	0	4,513	0	0	5,052	149,300
1992	38	9	0	0	0	0	0	0	0	2,248	0	0	3,200	52,645
1993	34	21	0	0	0	0	0	0	1	5,852	2	1	7,217	319,800
1994	11	31	0	0	0	1	1	2	5	9,111	39	5	11,291	845,963
1995	23	31	0	0	0	0	0	0	2	9,073	17	1	11,196	529,435
1996	23	31	0	0	0	0	0	0	2	8,493	10	3	10,027	817,175
Lifetime		361	0	1	2	4	4	5	59	93,189	629	38	117,519	$4,207,595

Sam Speers
Samuel Speers

Year	Rank	Starts	Poles	1	2	3	4	5	6–10	Laps	Laps Led	Races Led	Miles	$
1956	176T	1	0	0	0	0	0	0	1	119	0	0	74	125
Lifetime		1	0	0	0	0	0	0	1	119	0	0	74	$125

Cy Spencer
Cyrus Spencer

Year	Rank	Starts	Poles	1	2	3	4	5	6–10	Laps	Laps Led	Races Led	Miles	$
1956	225T	1	0	0	0	0	0	0	0	34	0	0	17	50
Lifetime		1	0	0	0	0	0	0	0	34	0	0	17	$50

Year	Rank	Starts	Poles	Finish 1	2	3	4	5	6–10	Laps	Laps Led	Races Led	Miles	$

Ed Spencer

Edward Spencer
Racing Hometown: Nanticolte, PA

Year	Rank	Starts	Poles	1	2	3	4	5	6–10	Laps	Laps Led	Races Led	Miles	$
1953	153	1	0	0	0	0	0	0	0		0	0		25
Lifetime		1	0	0	0	0	0	0	0		0	0		$25

G. C. Spencer

Grover Clinton Spencer
B: 7/9/1925
Racing Hometown: Jonesboro, TN

Year	Rank	Starts	Poles	1	2	3	4	5	6–10	Laps	Laps Led	Races Led	Miles	$
1958	36	1	0	0	0	0	0	0	0	343	0	0	472	315
1959	13	28	0	0	0	0	1	0	4	4,552	0	0	2,553	3,701
1960	33	26	0	0	0	0	1	1	4	4,907	0	0	3,822	3,910
1961	20	31	0	0	0	0	3	0	15	6,221	0	0	3,824	7,363
1962	24	42	0	0	0	0	2	4	7	7,300	0	0	4,791	8,260
1963	18	31	0	0	1	1	1	1	8	4,888	30	3	4,004	13,514
1964	26	20	0	0	0	1	0	3	2	3,601	0	0	2,803	9,490
1965	4	47	1	0	3	4	3	4	11	9,092	90	5	6,506	29,775
1966	19	20	0	0	3	0	0	3	3	4,701	2	1	4,252	26,722
1967	21	29	0	0	0	3	0	2	5	4,947	0	0	4,156	20,225
1968	23	26	0	0	0	0	1	0	5	4,380	0	0	3,276	10,120
1969	26	26	0	0	0	0	2	2	4	4,823	0	0	3,982	21,675
1970	27	20	0	0	0	0	2	1	6	4,618	0	0	4,091	17,915
1971	34	17	0	0	0	0	0	2	4	3,325	12	1	2,869	11,470
1972	43	10	0	0	0	0	0	0	1	1,492	0	0	1,611	8,040
1973	37	10	0	0	0	0	0	0	1	1,459	0	0	2,036	12,013
1974	38	10	0	0	0	0	0	0	1	1,205	3	1	1,721	12,985
1975	40	9	0	0	0	0	0	0	1	906	11	1	1,663	14,945
1976	59	4	0	0	0	0	0	0	0	501	0	0	941	4,965
1977	39	8	0	0	0	0	0	0	1	1,817	0	0	2,908	15,755
Lifetime		415	1	0	7	9	16	23	83	75,078	148	12	62,282	$253,158

Jimmy Spencer

James Peter Spencer
B: 2/15/1957
Racing Hometown: Berwick, PA

Year	Rank	Starts	Poles	1	2	3	4	5	6–10	Laps	Laps Led	Races Led	Miles	$
1989	34	17	0	0	0	0	0	0	3	3,544	0	0	4,558	121,065
1990	24	26	0	0	0	0	0	0	2	7,576	10	5	8,929	219,775
1991	25	29	0	0	0	1	0	0	5	7,627	330	6	8,581	283,620
1992	33	12	0	0	0	0	2	1	0	3,803	1	1	4,176	186,085
1993	12	30	0	0	1	2	2	0	5	8,848	64	4	10,823	686,026
1994	29	29	1	2	0	0	1	0	1	6,904	47	6	8,732	479,235
1995	26	29	0	0	0	0	0	0	4	8,682	4	2	10,484	506,860
1996	15	31	0	0	0	0	1	1	7	9,339	156	7	11,238	1,090,876
Lifetime		203	1	2	1	3	6	2	27	56,323	612	31	67,520	$3,573,542

Junior Spencer

Henry Spencer
B: 8/27/1937
Racing Hometown: Hamlin, WV

Year	Rank	Starts	Poles	1	2	3	4	5	6–10	Laps	Laps Led	Races Led	Miles	$
1964	83	3	0	0	0	0	0	0	0	1,172	0	0	558	670
1965	28	21	0	0	0	0	0	1	6	4,062	0	0	3,127	9,345
1971	NR	1	0	0	0	0	0	0	0	112	0	0	51	310
Lifetime		25	0	0	0	0	0	1	6	5,346	0	0	3,736	$9,920

Steve Spencer

Steve Spencer
B: 1946
Racing Hometown: Old Hickory, TN

Year	Rank	Starts	Poles	1	2	3	4	5	6–10	Laps	Laps Led	Races Led	Miles	$
1979	59	2	0	0	0	0	0	0	0	556	0	0	331	2,270
1980	NR	3	0	0	0	0	0	0	0	599	0	0	344	2,050
1981	78	3	0	0	0	0	0	0	0	1,038	0	0	747	5,805
Lifetime		8	0	0	0	0	0	0	0	2,193	0	0	1,422	$10,125

Craig Spetman

Craig Spetman
Racing Hometown: Council Bluffs, IA

Year	Rank	Starts	Poles	1	2	3	4	5	6–10	Laps	Laps Led	Races Led	Miles	$
1985	94	1	0	0	0	0	0	0	0	188	0	0	188	1,150
Lifetime		1	0	0	0	0	0	0	0	188	0	0	188	$1,150

Year	Rank	Starts	Poles	Finish 1	2	3	4	5	6–10	Laps	Laps Led	Races Led	Miles	$

Ken Spikes

Kenneth Spikes
Racing Hometown: Cordele, GA

Year	Rank	Starts	Poles	1	2	3	4	5	6–10	Laps	Laps Led	Races Led	Miles	$
1964	40	6	0	0	0	0	0	0	1	1,018	0	0	1,570	3,100
1967	72	9	0	0	0	0	0	0	0	621	0	0	817	4,245
1970	104T	1	0	0	0	0	0	0	0	116	0	0	309	890
Lifetime		16	0	0	0	0	0	0	1	1,755	0	0	2,695	$8,235

Richard Spittle

Richard Spittle
Racing Hometown: Mineral Springs, NC

Year	Rank	Starts	Poles	1	2	3	4	5	6–10	Laps	Laps Led	Races Led	Miles	$
1958	142	1	0	0	0	0	0	0	0	125	0	0	63	50
Lifetime		1	0	0	0	0	0	0	0	125	0	0	63	$50

J. C. Spradley

J. C. Spradley
Racing Hometown: Gloverville, SC

Year	Rank	Starts	Poles	1	2	3	4	5	6–10	Laps	Laps Led	Races Led	Miles	$
1969	72	1	0	0	0	0	0	0	0	203	0	0	279	1,075
Lifetime		1	0	0	0	0	0	0	0	203	0	0	279	$1,075

Dean Sprague

Dean Sprague
Racing Hometown: Belmont, NY

Year	Rank	Starts	Poles	1	2	3	4	5	6–10	Laps	Laps Led	Races Led	Miles	$
1951	N/A	1	0	0	0	0	0	0	0	46	0	0	35	25
Lifetime		1	0	0	0	0	0	0	0	46	0	0	35	$25

Jack Sprague

Jack Sprague
B: 8/8/1964
Racing Hometown: Spring Lake, MI

Year	Rank	Starts	Poles	1	2	3	4	5	6–10	Laps	Laps Led	Races Led	Miles	$
1996	54	2	0	0	0	0	0	0	0	333	2	1	345	22,720
Lifetime		2	0	0	0	0	0	0	0	333	2	1	345	$22,720

Robert Sprague

Robert Sprague
Racing Hometown: New York

Year	Rank	Starts	Poles	1	2	3	4	5	6–10	Laps	Laps Led	Races Led	Miles	$
1950	84T	1	0	0	0	0	0	0	0		0	0		50
Lifetime		1	0	0	0	0	0	0	0		0	0		$50

Robert Sprague

Robert Sprague
B: 12/26/1959
Racing Hometown: North Bend, OR

Year	Rank	Starts	Poles	1	2	3	4	5	6–10	Laps	Laps Led	Races Led	Miles	$
1991	86	1	0	0	0	0	0	0	0	54	1	1	136	3,500
Lifetime		1	0	0	0	0	0	0	0	54	1	1	136	$3,500

Walt Sprague

Walter D. Sprague
B: 1936   D: 8/24/1951   *Killed @ Monroe County Fairgrounds in Rochester, NY.*
Racing Hometown: Wellsville, NY

Year	Rank	Starts	Poles	1	2	3	4	5	6–10	Laps	Laps Led	Races Led	Miles	$
1951	N/A	7	0	0	0	0	0	0	2	113	0	0	113	385
Lifetime		7	0	0	0	0	0	0	2	113	0	0	113	$385

Ray Springer

Raymond Springer
Racing Hometown: Freeport, IL

Year	Rank	Starts	Poles	1	2	3	4	5	6–10	Laps	Laps Led	Races Led	Miles	$
1953	97T	1	0	0	0	0	0	0	0		0	0		25
Lifetime		1	0	0	0	0	0	0	0		0	0		$25

Don Sprouse

Donald W. Sprouse
B: 1942
Racing Hometown: Greenville, SC

Year	Rank	Starts	Poles	1	2	3	4	5	6–10	Laps	Laps Led	Races Led	Miles	$
1980	55	4	0	0	0	0	0	0	0	1,312	0	0	745	2,880
1981	63	2	0	0	0	0	0	0	0	570	0	0	663	6,850
Lifetime		6	0	0	0	0	0	0	0	1,882	0	0	1,408	$9,730

Year	Rank	Starts	Poles	Finish 1	2	3	4	5	6–10	Laps	Laps Led	Races Led	Miles	$

Dick Stacey

Richard Stacey
Racing Hometown: Detroit, MI

Year	Rank	Starts	Poles	1	2	3	4	5	6–10	Laps	Laps Led	Races Led	Miles	$
1952	118	1	0	0	0	0	0	0	0	175	0	0	175	25
Lifetime		1	0	0	0	0	0	0	0	175	0	0	175	$25

Bill Stacy

William Stacy
Racing Hometown: Garden Grove, CA

Year	Rank	Starts	Poles	1	2	3	4	5	6–10	Laps	Laps Led	Races Led	Miles	$
1956	286	1	0	0	0	0	0	0	0	70	0	0	175	50
Lifetime		1	0	0	0	0	0	0	0	70	0	0	175	$50

Nelson Stacy

William Nelson Stacy
B: 12/28/1921   D: 5/14/1986
Racing Hometown: Cincinnati, OH

Year	Rank	Starts	Poles	1	2	3	4	5	6–10	Laps	Laps Led	Races Led	Miles	$
1952	NR	1	0	0	0	0	0	0	0	277	0	0	139	50
1961	16	15	0	1	0	1	2	0	4	3,024	144	4	3,281	27,608
1962	21	15	0	3	1	0	0	1	2	3,484	371	4	3,171	43,080
1963	14	12	0	0	0	1	2	1	5	2,816	76	2	3,179	20,025
1964	NR	1	0	0	0	0	0	0	0	5	0	0	7	500
1965	94	1	0	0	0	0	0	0	0	83	0	0	208	480
Lifetime		45	0	4	1	2	4	2	11	9,689	591	10	9,984	$91,743

Mark Stahl

Mark Stahl
B: 8/12/1951
Racing Hometown: San Diego, CA

Year	Rank	Starts	Poles	1	2	3	4	5	6–10	Laps	Laps Led	Races Led	Miles	$
1981	84	1	0	0	0	0	0	0	0	109	0	0	286	1,080
1982	72	2	0	0	0	0	0	0	0	109	0	0	286	4,240
1983	66	2	0	0	0	0	0	0	0	622	0	0	363	1,970
1984	52	3	0	0	0	0	0	0	0	842	0	0	892	6,985
1985	77	1	0	0	0	0	0	0	0	375	0	0	563	6,750
1986	62	3	0	0	0	0	0	0	0	719	0	0	889	7,290
1987	38	9	0	0	0	0	0	0	0	1,635	0	0	2,643	32,850
1988	83T	1	0	0	0	0	0	0	0	233	0	0	237	2,815
1989	81T	1	0	0	0	0	0	0	0	176	0	0	468	7,285
1990	44	5	0	0	0	0	0	0	0	1,268	0	0	1,890	19,770
1991	67	2	0	0	0	0	0	0	0	30	0	0	35	12,755
Lifetime		30	0	0	0	0	0	0	0	6,118	0	0	8,552	$103,790

Gwyn Staley

Gwyn Edward Staley
B: 7/6/1927   D: 3/23/1958   *Killed in NASCAR Convertible race @ Richmond.*
Racing Hometown: Burlington, NC

Year	Rank	Starts	Poles	1	2	3	4	5	6–10	Laps	Laps Led	Races Led	Miles	$
1951	N/A	2	0	0	0	0	0	0	0	303	0	0	379	75
1952	166	1	0	0	0	0	0	0	0	74	0	0	93	0
1953	144T	1	0	0	0	0	0	0	0	0	0	0	0	25
1954	29	2	0	0	0	0	0	0	1	357	0	0	480	670
1955	10	24	1	0	1	2	2	2	7	3,196	33	1	2,236	6,547
1956	14	22	0	0	0	0	2	3	8	3,506	0	0	2,404	5,159
1957	151	13	2	3	1	0	2	1	2	2,449	196	4	1,516	9,080
1958	55	4	0	0	1	0	2	1	0	336	0	0	255	1,730
Lifetime		69	3	3	3	2	8	7	18	10,221	229	5	7,361	$23,286

Willard Starney

Willard Starney
Racing Hometown: Greenville, SC

Year	Rank	Starts	Poles	1	2	3	4	5	6–10	Laps	Laps Led	Races Led	Miles	$
1955	NR	1	0	0	0	0	0	0	0	187	0	0	94	60
Lifetime		1	0	0	0	0	0	0	0	187	0	0	94	$60

Bill Stammer

William Stammer
Racing Hometown: Pasadena, CA

Year	Rank	Starts	Poles	1	2	3	4	5	6–10	Laps	Laps Led	Races Led	Miles	$
1951	N/A	4	0	0	0	0	0	0	2		0	0		200
1954	93	2	0	0	0	0	0	0	0	631	0	0	316	75
1955	63	2	0	0	0	0	0	0	2	338	0	0	338	400
1956	200	2	0	0	0	0	0	0	0	131	0	0	241	140
Lifetime		10	0	0	0	0	0	0	4	1,100	0	0	894	$815

Year	Rank	Starts	Poles	Finish						Laps	Laps Led	Races Led	Miles	$
				1	2	3	4	5	6–10					

Bob Stanclift

Robert Stanclift
Racing Hometown: Long Beach, CA

Year	Rank	Starts	Poles	1	2	3	4	5	6–10	Laps	Laps Led	Races Led	Miles	$
1955	130	2	0	0	0	0	0	0	1	135	0	0	135	140
1956	230	1	0	0	0	0	0	0	0	72	0	0	180	40
Lifetime		3	0	0	0	0	0	0	1	207	0	0	315	$180

Billy Standridge

William Standridge
B: 11/27/1953
Racing Hometown: Shelby, NC

Year	Rank	Starts	Poles	1	2	3	4	5	6–10	Laps	Laps Led	Races Led	Miles	$
1994	47	8	0	0	0	0	0	0	0	1,260	0	0	1,706	58,605
1995	51	2	0	0	0	0	0	0	0	594	0	0	859	22,595
1996	51	3	0	0	0	0	0	0	0	789	0	0	1,123	27,780
Lifetime		13	0	0	0	0	0	0	0	2,643	0	0	3,688	$108,980

Paul Stanley

Paul Stanley
Racing Hometown: Martinsville, VA

Year	Rank	Starts	Poles	1	2	3	4	5	6–10	Laps	Laps Led	Races Led	Miles	$
1951	N/A	2	0	0	0	0	0	0	0		0	0		50
Lifetime		2	0	0	0	0	0	0	0		0	0		$50

Sam Stanley

Samuel Stanley
Racing Hometown: Newhall, CA

Year	Rank	Starts	Poles	1	2	3	4	5	6–10	Laps	Laps Led	Races Led	Miles	$
1965	59	1	0	0	0	0	0	0	1	172	0	0	464	1,050
1972	116	1	0	0	0	0	0	0	0	17	0	0	45	655
Lifetime		2	0	0	0	0	0	0	1	189	0	0	509	$1,705

Don Stanyer

Donald Stanyer

Year	Rank	Starts	Poles	1	2	3	4	5	6–10	Laps	Laps Led	Races Led	Miles	$
1956	285	1	0	0	0	0	0	0	0	70	0	0	175	40
Lifetime		1	0	0	0	0	0	0	0	70	0	0	175	$40

Jim Stapley

James Stapley
Racing Hometown: Phoenix, AZ

Year	Rank	Starts	Poles	1	2	3	4	5	6–10	Laps	Laps Led	Races Led	Miles	$
1956	293	1	0	0	0	0	0	0	0	51	0	0	51	0
Lifetime		1	0	0	0	0	0	0	0	51	0	0	51	$0

Charles Stark

Charles Stark
Racing Hometown: Tampa, FL

Year	Rank	Starts	Poles	1	2	3	4	5	6–10	Laps	Laps Led	Races Led	Miles	$
1952	154T	1	0	0	0	0	0	0	0		0	0		25
Lifetime		1	0	0	0	0	0	0	0		0	0		$25

Fred Starr

Fred Starr
Racing Hometown: Brooklyn, NY

Year	Rank	Starts	Poles	1	2	3	4	5	6–10	Laps	Laps Led	Races Led	Miles	$
1954	116	2	0	0	0	0	0	0	0	169	0	0	85	35
Lifetime		2	0	0	0	0	0	0	0	169	0	0	85	$35

Stan Starr Jr.

Stanley Monroe Starr Jr.
B: 8/11/1943
Racing Hometown: Madison, TN

Year	Rank	Starts	Poles	1	2	3	4	5	6–10	Laps	Laps Led	Races Led	Miles	$
1969	NR	1	0	0	0	0	0	0	0	82	0	0	218	1,200
Lifetime		1	0	0	0	0	0	0	0	82	0	0	218	$1,200

J. O. Staton

Joseph O. Staton
Racing Hometown: Greenville, SC

Year	Rank	Starts	Poles	1	2	3	4	5	6–10	Laps	Laps Led	Races Led	Miles	$
1952	67	7	0	0	0	0	0	0	1	331	0	0	185	250
Lifetime		7	0	0	0	0	0	0	1	331	0	0	185	$250

Al Stearn

Al Stearn
Racing Hometown: Syracuse, NY

Year	Rank	Starts	Poles	1	2	3	4	5	6–10	Laps	Laps Led	Races Led	Miles	$
1957	NR	1	0	0	0	0	0	0	0	57	0	0	57	100
Lifetime		1	0	0	0	0	0	0	0	57	0	0	57	$100

Year	Rank	Starts	Poles	Finish 1	2	3	4	5	6–10	Laps	Laps Led	Races Led	Miles	$

Johnny Steele

John Steele
B: 12/20/1934
Racing Hometown: Carmichael, CA

Year	Rank	Starts	Poles	1	2	3	4	5	6–10	Laps	Laps Led	Races Led	Miles	$
1965	125	1	0	0	0	0	0	0	0	16	0	0	43	500
1966	69	2	0	0	0	0	0	0	0	325	0	0	523	900
1967	92	5	0	0	0	0	0	0	0	402	0	0	254	900
1968	97	1	0	0	0	0	0	0	0	33	0	0	89	500
1969	NR	1	0	0	0	0	0	0	0	3	0	0	8	750
1971	NR	1	0	0	0	0	0	0	0	79	0	0	198	1,375
Lifetime		11	0	0	0	0	0	0	0	858	0	0	1,115	$4,925

Tim Steele

Timothy Steele
B: 3/1/1968
Racing Hometown: Coopersville, MI

Year	Rank	Starts	Poles	1	2	3	4	5	6–10	Laps	Laps Led	Races Led	Miles	$
1994	52	5	0	0	0	0	0	0	0	391	0	0	807	65,000
Lifetime		5	0	0	0	0	0	0	0	391	0	0	807	$65,000

Fred Steinbroner

Fred Steinbroner
Racing Hometown: Los Angeles, CA

Year	Rank	Starts	Poles	1	2	3	4	5	6–10	Laps	Laps Led	Races Led	Miles	$
1951	43	6	0	0	0	0	1	1	1	198	0	0	99	700
1955	151	1	0	0	0	0	0	0	0	84	0	0	84	80
1956	223	1	0	0	0	0	0	0	0	72	0	0	180	40
Lifetime		8	0	0	0	0	1	1	1	354	0	0	363	$795

Lyle Stelter

Lyle Stelter
Racing Hometown: Phoenix, AZ

Year	Rank	Starts	Poles	1	2	3	4	5	6–10	Laps	Laps Led	Races Led	Miles	$
1960	NR	2	0	0	0	0	0	0	0	130	0	0	164	160
1963	116	2	0	0	0	0	0	0	0	304	0	0	85	175
1966	NR	2	0	0	0	0	0	0	0	38	0	0	35	0
Lifetime		6	0	0	0	0	0	0	0	472	0	0	285	$335

Tommy Stenger

Thomas Stenger
Racing Hometown: Dayton, OH

Year	Rank	Starts	Poles	1	2	3	4	5	6–10	Laps	Laps Led	Races Led	Miles	$
1951	N/A	1	0	0	0	0	0	0	0		0	0		25
Lifetime		1	0	0	0	0	0	0	0		0	0		$25

Dirk Stephens

Dirk Stephens
B: 6/13/1963
Racing Hometown: Tumwater, WA

Year	Rank	Starts	Poles	1	2	3	4	5	6–10	Laps	Laps Led	Races Led	Miles	$
1993	63	2	0	0	0	0	0	0	0	96	0	0	205	12,880
Lifetime		2	0	0	0	0	0	0	0	96	0	0	205	$12,880

Tojo Stephens

Tojo Stephens
Racing Hometown: Dunn, NC

Year	Rank	Starts	Poles	1	2	3	4	5	6–10	Laps	Laps Led	Races Led	Miles	$
1955	NR	1	0	0	0	0	0	0	0	291	0	0	400	60
Lifetime		1	0	0	0	0	0	0	0	291	0	0	400	$60

Nero Steptoe

Nero Steptoe
Racing Hometown: Albany, GA

Year	Rank	Starts	Poles	1	2	3	4	5	6–10	Laps	Laps Led	Races Led	Miles	$
1953	NR	1	0	0	0	0	0	0	0		0	0		25
1954	NR	1	0	0	0	0	0	0	0	35	0	0	144	25
1962	86	3	0	0	0	0	0	0	0	168	0	0	64	275
Lifetime		5	0	0	0	0	0	0	0	203	0	0	208	$325

Glenn Steurer

Glenn Steurer
B: 6/3/1955
Racing Hometown: Canoga Park, CA

Year	Rank	Starts	Poles	1	2	3	4	5	6–10	Laps	Laps Led	Races Led	Miles	$
1985	51	2	0	0	0	0	0	0	0	211	0	0	553	6,850
1986	63	2	0	0	0	0	0	0	1	210	0	0	550	10,755
1987	NR	1	0	0	0	0	0	0	0	19	0	0	50	925
Lifetime		5	0	0	0	0	0	0	1	440	0	0	1,153	$18,530

Year	Rank	Starts	Poles	Finish						Laps	Laps Led	Races Led	Miles	$
				1	2	3	4	5	6–10					

Bugs Stevens

Bugs Stevens *Real Name:* Carl S. Berghman
B: 5/11/1934
Racing Hometown: Rehoboth, MA

Year	Rank	Starts	Poles	1	2	3	4	5	6–10	Laps	Laps Led	Races Led	Miles	$
1970	61	3	0	0	0	0	0	0	1	458	0	0	682	6,145
Lifetime		3	0	0	0	0	0	0	1	458	0	0	682	$6,145

Chuck Stevenson

Charles J. Stevenson
B: 10/15/1919 D: 8/1995
Racing Hometown: Sidney, MT

Year	Rank	Starts	Poles	1	2	3	4	5	6–10	Laps	Laps Led	Races Led	Miles	$
1955	218	1	0	0	0	0	0	0	0	43	0	0	65	60
1956	94	1	0	1	0	0	0	0	0	80	54	1	200	1,570
Lifetime		2	0	1	0	0	0	0	0	123	54	1	265	$1,630

Jim Stewart

James Stewart
Racing Hometown: Sacramento, CA

Year	Rank	Starts	Poles	1	2	3	4	5	6–10	Laps	Laps Led	Races Led	Miles	$
1961	140T	1	0	0	0	0	0	0	0	93	0	0	93	100
Lifetime		1	0	0	0	0	0	0	0	93	0	0	93	$100

Joe Stewart

Joseph Stewart
Racing Hometown: Memphis, TN

Year	Rank	Starts	Poles	1	2	3	4	5	6–10	Laps	Laps Led	Races Led	Miles	$
1956	233T	1	0	0	0	0	0	0	0	57	0	0	86	50
Lifetime		1	0	0	0	0	0	0	0	57	0	0	86	$50

Pete Stewart

Marvin Peter Stewart
B: 8/12/1931
Racing Hometown: Statesville, NC

Year	Rank	Starts	Poles	1	2	3	4	5	6–10	Laps	Laps Led	Races Led	Miles	$
1953	NR	1	0	0	0	0	0	0	0	20	0	0	13	25
1954	195	1	0	0	0	0	0	0	0	77	0	0	39	0
1956	108	3	0	0	0	0	0	0	0	756	0	0	356	235
1957	NR	1	0	0	0	0	0	0	0	25	0	0	13	0
1963	124	2	0	0	0	0	0	0	0	78	0	0	109	150
1964	51	7	0	0	0	0	0	0	0	1,243	0	0	879	2,365
1965	100	2	0	0	0	0	0	0	0	2	0	0	5	1,165
Lifetime		17	0	0	0	0	0	0	0	2,201	0	0	1,412	$3,940

H. F. Stickleather

H. F. Stickleather
Racing Hometown: Charlotte, NC

Year	Rank	Starts	Poles	1	2	3	4	5	6–10	Laps	Laps Led	Races Led	Miles	$
1949	62T	1	0	0	0	0	0	0	0	167	0	0	84	50
Lifetime		1	0	0	0	0	0	0	0	167	0	0	84	$50

Bill Stickler

William Stickler
Racing Hometown: Gardena, CA

Year	Rank	Starts	Poles	1	2	3	4	5	6–10	Laps	Laps Led	Races Led	Miles	$
1951	N/A	2	0	0	0	0	0	0	0		0	0		50
Lifetime		2	0	0	0	0	0	0	0		0	0		$50

Ernie Stierly

Ernest Stierly
B: 12/29/1930
Racing Hometown: Vancouver, WA

Year	Rank	Starts	Poles	1	2	3	4	5	6–10	Laps	Laps Led	Races Led	Miles	$
1976	107T	1	0	0	0	0	0	0	0	21	0	0	55	765
1977	81	2	0	0	0	0	0	0	0	137	0	0	352	1,805
1978	74	2	0	0	0	0	0	0	0	141	0	0	369	2,520
Lifetime		5	0	0	0	0	0	0	0	299	0	0	777	$5,090

Billy Stiles

William Stiles
Racing Hometown: Charlotte, NC

Year	Rank	Starts	Poles	1	2	3	4	5	6–10	Laps	Laps Led	Races Led	Miles	$
1966	141	1	0	0	0	0	0	0	0	4	0	0	1	0
Lifetime		1	0	0	0	0	0	0	0	4	0	0	1	$0

Chuck Stimus

Charles Stimus
Racing Hometown: Rochester, NY

Year	Rank	Starts	Poles	1	2	3	4	5	6–10	Laps	Laps Led	Races Led	Miles	$
1951	N/A	1	0	0	0	0	0	0	1		0	0		150
Lifetime		1	0	0	0	0	0	0	1		0	0		$150

Year	Rank	Starts	Poles	1	2	3	4	5	6–10	Laps	Laps Led	Races Led	Miles	$

Don Stives
Donald Stives
Racing Hometown: Hightstown, NJ

Year	Rank	Starts	Poles	1	2	3	4	5	6–10	Laps	Laps Led	Races Led	Miles	$
1967	98	3	0	0	0	0	0	0	1	188	0	0	49	510
Lifetime		3	0	0	0	0	0	0	1	188	0	0	49	$510

Harold Stockton
Harold Stockton
Racing Hometown: Franklin, NC

Year	Rank	Starts	Poles	1	2	3	4	5	6–10	Laps	Laps Led	Races Led	Miles	$
1967	80	6	0	0	0	0	0	0	0	626	0	0	287	705
Lifetime		6	0	0	0	0	0	0	0	626	0	0	287	$705

Virgil Stockton
Virgil Stockton
Racing Hometown: Melvindale, MI

Year	Rank	Starts	Poles	1	2	3	4	5	6–10	Laps	Laps Led	Races Led	Miles	$
1953	127T	1	0	0	0	0	0	0	0	0	0	0	0	25
1954	NR	4	0	0	0	0	0	0	1	463	0	0	232	175
Lifetime		5	0	0	0	0	0	0	1	463	0	0	232	$200

Gene Stokes
Gene Stokes
Racing Hometown: Hemingway, SC

Year	Rank	Starts	Poles	1	2	3	4	5	6–10	Laps	Laps Led	Races Led	Miles	$
1961	131	2	0	0	0	0	0	0	0	96	0	0	144	250
Lifetime		2	0	0	0	0	0	0	0	96	0	0	144	$250

Mike Stolarcyk
Michael Stolarcyk

Year	Rank	Starts	Poles	1	2	3	4	5	6–10	Laps	Laps Led	Races Led	Miles	$
1985	86T	1	0	0	0	0	0	0	0	116	0	0	290	1,615
Lifetime		1	0	0	0	0	0	0	0	116	0	0	290	$1,615

Steve Stolarek
Steve Stolarek
Racing Hometown: Minneapolis, MN

Year	Rank	Starts	Poles	1	2	3	4	5	6–10	Laps	Laps Led	Races Led	Miles	$
1977	113T	1	0	0	0	0	0	0	0	21	0	0	21	490
1978	—	0												400
Lifetime		1	0	0	0	0	0	0	0	21	0	0	21	$890

Rolf Stommelen
Rolf-Johann Stommelen
B: 7/11/1943 D: 4/24/1983 *Killed @ Riverside, CA.*
Racing Hometown: Siegen, Germany

Year	Rank	Starts	Poles	1	2	3	4	5	6–10	Laps	Laps Led	Races Led	Miles	$
1971	NR	1	0	0	0	0	0	0	0	53	0	0	141	790
Lifetime		1	0	0	0	0	0	0	0	53	0	0	141	$790

Charlie Stone
Charles Stone
Racing Hometown: Austell, GA

Year	Rank	Starts	Poles	1	2	3	4	5	6–10	Laps	Laps Led	Races Led	Miles	$
1958	93	1	0	0	0	0	0	0	0	35	0	0	144	100
Lifetime		1	0	0	0	0	0	0	0	35	0	0	144	$100

Dick Stone
Richard Stone
Racing Hometown: Novelty, OH

Year	Rank	Starts	Poles	1	2	3	4	5	6–10	Laps	Laps Led	Races Led	Miles	$
1951	N/A	4	0	0	0	0	0	0	1		0	0		125
1954	163T	1	0	0	0	0	0	0	0	12	0	0	6	0
Lifetime		5	0	0	0	0	0	0	1	12	0	0	6	$125

Roland Stone
Roland Stone
Racing Hometown: Galax, VA

Year	Rank	Starts	Poles	1	2	3	4	5	6–10	Laps	Laps Led	Races Led	Miles	$
1950	NR	1	0	0	0	0	0	0	0		0	0		0
Lifetime		1	0	0	0	0	0	0	0		0	0		$0

Ramo Stott
Ramo E. Stott
B: 4/6/1934
Racing Hometown: Keokuk, IA

Year	Rank	Starts	Poles	1	2	3	4	5	6–10	Laps	Laps Led	Races Led	Miles	$
1967	39	3	0	0	0	0	0	0	1	588	0	0	1,082	3,335
1969	69	3	0	0	0	1	0	0	1	375	4	1	968	8,785
1970	60	3	0	0	0	0	0	0	3	424	2	1	1,089	4,875
1971	64	3	0	0	0	0	0	0	1	476	0	0	1,075	3,715

| Year | Rank | Starts | Poles | Finish |||||| Laps | Laps Led | Races Led | Miles | $ |
				1	2	3	4	5	6–10					

Ramo Stott *continued*

Year	Rank	Starts	Poles	1	2	3	4	5	6–10	Laps	Laps Led	Races Led	Miles	$
1972	66	5	0	0	1	1	0	0	1	1,113	3	1	1,965	19,655
1973	52	4	0	0	0	0	0	0	2	488	1	1	1,109	8,440
1974	39	6	0	0	0	1	0	0	3	1,414	0	0	2,481	23,705
1975	68	2	0	0	0	0	0	1	0	259	0	0	657	13,030
1976	NR	1	1	0	0	0	0	0	0	113	0	0	283	6,830
1977	48	5	0	0	0	0	0	0	0	688	0	0	1,438	10,170
1984	—	0												2,550
Lifetime		35	1	0	1	3	0	1	12	5,938	10	4	12,145	$105,090

Joel Stowe

Joel Stowe
Racing Hometown: Waxhaw, NC

Year	Rank	Starts	Poles	1	2	3	4	5	6–10	Laps	Laps Led	Races Led	Miles	$
1980	89	2	0	0	0	0	0	0	0	835	0	0	694	4,685
1981	NR	1	0	0	0	0	0	0	0	14	0	0	7	540
1982	NR	1	0	0	0	0	0	0	0	57	0	0	36	2,305
Lifetime		4	0	0	0	0	0	0	0	906	0	0	737	$7,530

Don Strain

Donald Strain
Racing Hometown: Pittsburgh, PA

Year	Rank	Starts	Poles	1	2	3	4	5	6–10	Laps	Laps Led	Races Led	Miles	$
1959	NR	1	0	0	0	0	0	0	1	181	0	0	45	140
Lifetime		1	0	0	0	0	0	0	1	181	0	0	45	$140

Harold Strapp

Harold Strapp

Year	Rank	Starts	Poles	1	2	3	4	5	6–10	Laps	Laps Led	Races Led	Miles	$
1951	N/A	1	0	0	0	0	0	0	0		0	0		10
Lifetime		1	0	0	0	0	0	0	0		0	0		$10

Victor Strassburg

Victor Strassburg
Racing Hometown: Niagara Falls, NY

Year	Rank	Starts	Poles	1	2	3	4	5	6–10	Laps	Laps Led	Races Led	Miles	$
1953	156	1	0	0	0	0	0	0	0		0	0		25
Lifetime		1	0	0	0	0	0	0	0		0	0		$25

Al Straub

Allen Straub
B: 11/9/1940
Racing Hometown: Louisville, KY

Year	Rank	Starts	Poles	1	2	3	4	5	6–10	Laps	Laps Led	Races Led	Miles	$
1969	NR	1	0	0	0	0	0	0	0	9	0	0	24	950
1971	NR	1	0	0	0	0	0	0	0	48	0	0	22	300
Lifetime		2	0	0	0	0	0	0	0	57	0	0	46	$1,250

Jim Street

James Street
Racing Hometown: Winston-Salem, NC

Year	Rank	Starts	Poles	1	2	3	4	5	6–10	Laps	Laps Led	Races Led	Miles	$
1962	NR	1	0	0	0	0	0	0	0	8	0	0	2	50
Lifetime		1	0	0	0	0	0	0	0	8	0	0	2	$50

Bub Strickler

Early Harry Strickler
B: 12/18/1938
Racing Hometown: Timberville, VA

Year	Rank	Starts	Poles	1	2	3	4	5	6–10	Laps	Laps Led	Races Led	Miles	$
1965	33	9	0	0	0	0	0	0	2	1,572	0	0	1,909	5,275
1966	NR	3	0	0	0	0	0	0	0	230	0	0	239	585
1970	91	1	0	0	0	0	0	0	0	316	0	0	198	455
1971	NR	1	0	0	0	0	0	0	0	1	0	0	3	1,000
1979	123T	1	0	0	0	0	0	0	0	67	0	0	68	550
1980	NR	5	0	0	0	0	0	0	0	1,199	0	0	733	3,980
Lifetime		20	0	0	0	0	0	0	2	3,385	0	0	3,149	$11,845

Hut Stricklin

Waymond Lane Stricklin Jr.
B: 6/24/1961
Racing Hometown: Calera, AL

Year	Rank	Starts	Poles	1	2	3	4	5	6–10	Laps	Laps Led	Races Led	Miles	$
1987	58	3	0	0	0	0	0	0	0	912	0	0	1,009	6,085
1989	26	27	0	0	0	0	1	0	3	7,557	3	1	9,285	152,504
1990	28	24	0	0	0	0	0	0	2	5,947	1	1	7,941	169,199
1991	16	29	0	0	1	0	2	0	4	8,813	69	7	10,433	426,524

Year	Rank	Starts	Poles	Finish						Laps	Laps Led	Races Led	Miles	$
				1	2	3	4	5	6–10					

Hut Stricklin *continued*

Year	Rank	Starts	Poles	1	2	3	4	5	6–10	Laps	Laps Led	Races Led	Miles	$
1992	27	28	0	0	0	0	0	0	4	7,928	60	2	9,260	336,965
1993	24	30	0	0	0	0	1	0	1	8,356	98	3	10,211	494,600
1994	26	29	0	0	0	0	0	0	1	8,562	26	2	10,585	333,495
1995	36	24	1	0	0	0	1	1	3	5,513	45	4	7,311	486,065
1996	22	31	0	0	1	0	0	0	0	8,620	163	3	10,632	631,055
Lifetime		225	1	0	2	0	5	1	18	62,208	465	23	76,667	$3,036,492

D. Wayne Strout

D. Wayne Strout
B: 1951
Racing Hometown: Dallas, TX

Year	Rank	Starts	Poles	1	2	3	4	5	6–10	Laps	Laps Led	Races Led	Miles	$
1987	84T	1	0	0	0	0	0	0	0	381	0	0	381	1,700
Lifetime		1	0	0	0	0	0	0	0	381	0	0	381	$1,700

Don Stumpf

Donald Stumpf
B: 1927   D: 12/11/1991
Racing Hometown: Ridgefield Park, NJ

Year	Rank	Starts	Poles	1	2	3	4	5	6–10	Laps	Laps Led	Races Led	Miles	$
1953	153	1	0	0	0	0	0	0	0		0	0		25
Lifetime		1	0	0	0	0	0	0	0		0	0		$25

Frank Stutts

Frank Stutts
Racing Hometown: Mooresville, NC

Year	Rank	Starts	Poles	1	2	3	4	5	6–10	Laps	Laps Led	Races Led	Miles	$
1954	NR	3	0	0	0	0	0	0	0	426	0	0	452	125
Lifetime		3	0	0	0	0	0	0	0	426	0	0	452	$125

Johnny Sudderth

John Sudderth
B: 7/11/1929
Racing Hometown: Atlanta, GA

Year	Rank	Starts	Poles	1	2	3	4	5	6–10	Laps	Laps Led	Races Led	Miles	$
1960	86	3	0	0	0	0	0	0	0	351	0	0	676	515
1961	169	1	0	0	0	0	0	0	0	22	0	0	33	200
1962	95	3	0	0	0	0	0	0	0	261	0	0	392	895
1963	143	1	0	0	0	0	0	0	0	16	0	0	24	250
Lifetime		8	0	0	0	0	0	0	0	650	0	0	1,124	$1,860

Tom Suligoy

Thomas Suligoy
Racing Hometown: Joilet, IL

Year	Rank	Starts	Poles	1	2	3	4	5	6–10	Laps	Laps Led	Races Led	Miles	$
1951	N/A	1	0	0	0	0	0	0	0	115	0	0	115	0
Lifetime		1	0	0	0	0	0	0	0	115	0	0	115	$0

Bill Sullivan

William Sullivan

Year	Rank	Starts	Poles	1	2	3	4	5	6–10	Laps	Laps Led	Races Led	Miles	$
1956	156	2	0	0	0	0	0	0	0	278	0	0	154	100
Lifetime		2	0	0	0	0	0	0	0	278	0	0	154	$100

Danny Sullivan

Daniel John Sullivan III (Danny)
B: 3/9/1950
Racing Hometown: Louisville, KY

Year	Rank	Starts	Poles	1	2	3	4	5	6–10	Laps	Laps Led	Races Led	Miles	$
1994	74	1	0	0	0	0	0	0	0	152	0	0	380	22,750
Lifetime		1	0	0	0	0	0	0	0	152	0	0	380	$22,750

Ross Surgenor

Ross Surgenor
Racing Hometown: Victoria, B.C., Canada

Year	Rank	Starts	Poles	1	2	3	4	5	6–10	Laps	Laps Led	Races Led	Miles	$
1974	99	2	0	0	0	0	0	0	0	134	0	0	351	2,095
Lifetime		2	0	0	0	0	0	0	0	134	0	0	351	$2,095

Parks Surratt

Parks Surratt
Racing Hometown: Gaffney, SC

Year	Rank	Starts	Poles	1	2	3	4	5	6–10	Laps	Laps Led	Races Led	Miles	$
1953	114	3	0	0	0	0	0	0	0	271	0	0	153	75
1954	76	4	0	0	0	0	0	0	0	649	0	0	325	100
Lifetime		7	0	0	0	0	0	0	0	920	0	0	478	$175

Year	Rank	Starts	Poles	Finish						Laps	Laps Led	Races Led	Miles	$
				1	2	3	4	5	6–10					

Len Sutton

Leonard Sutton
B: 8/9/1925
Racing Hometown: Portland, OR

Year	Rank	Starts	Poles	1	2	3	4	5	6–10	Laps	Laps Led	Races Led	Miles	$
1956	168	1	0	0	0	0	0	0	0	238	0	0	119	150
1963	NR	4	0	0	0	0	0	0	0	274	0	0	570	1,175
Lifetime		5	0	0	0	0	0	0	0	512	0	0	689	$1,325

Lem Svajian

Lem Svajian
Racing Hometown: Detroit, MI

Year	Rank	Starts	Poles	1	2	3	4	5	6–10	Laps	Laps Led	Races Led	Miles	$
1957	179	1	0	0	0	0	0	0	0		0	0		50
Lifetime		1	0	0	0	0	0	0	0		0	0		$50

Ted Swaim

Ted Swaim
Racing Hometown: Winston-Salem, NC

Year	Rank	Starts	Poles	1	2	3	4	5	6–10	Laps	Laps Led	Races Led	Miles	$
1950	34T	1	0	0	1	0	0	0	0	200	0	0	100	750
1951	N/A	2	0	0	0	0	0	0	0	360	0	0	450	75
1952	175	1	0	0	0	0	0	0	0	65	0	0	65	25
Lifetime		4	0	0	1	0	0	0	0	625	0	0	615	$750

Ted Sweeney

Ted Sweeney
Racing Hometown: Portland, OR

Year	Rank	Starts	Poles	1	2	3	4	5	6–10	Laps	Laps Led	Races Led	Miles	$
1956	134	3	0	0	0	0	0	0	0	377	0	0	196	150
Lifetime		3	0	0	0	0	0	0	0	377	0	0	196	$150

Nolan Swift

Nolan Swift
B: 1923
Racing Hometown: Syracuse, NY

Year	Rank	Starts	Poles	1	2	3	4	5	6–10	Laps	Laps Led	Races Led	Miles	$
1956	119	2	0	0	0	0	0	0	1	174	0	0	156	175
Lifetime		2	0	0	0	0	0	0	1	174	0	0	156	$175

Jeff Swindell

Jeffrey Swindell
B: 1960
Racing Hometown: Memphis, TN

Year	Rank	Starts	Poles	1	2	3	4	5	6–10	Laps	Laps Led	Races Led	Miles	$
1986	111	1	0	0	0	0	0	0	0	227	0	0	345	1,160
1987	96T	1	0	0	0	0	0	0	0	102	0	0	271	6,630
Lifetime		2	0	0	0	0	0	0	0	329	0	0	617	$7,790

Sammy Swindell

Samuel Alan Swindell
B: 10/26/1955
Racing Hometown: Bartlett, TN

Year	Rank	Starts	Poles	1	2	3	4	5	6–10	Laps	Laps Led	Races Led	Miles	$
1985	84T	1	0	0	0	0	0	0	0	242	0	0	368	1,175
1991	90	1	0	0	0	0	0	0	0	28	0	0	70	16,500
Lifetime		2	0	0	0	0	0	0	0	270	0	0	438	$17,675

Joe Sykes

Joseph Sykes
Racing Hometown: Buffalo, NY

Year	Rank	Starts	Poles	1	2	3	4	5	6–10	Laps	Laps Led	Races Led	Miles	$
1955	NR	1	0	0	0	0	0	0	0	69	0	0	69	0
1956	NR	1	0	0	0	0	0	0	0	166	0	0	83	100
Lifetime		2	0	0	0	0	0	0	0	235	0	0	152	$100

G. T. Tallas

George T. Tallas
B: 1/31/1944
Racing Hometown: Sun Valley, CA

Year	Rank	Starts	Poles	1	2	3	4	5	6–10	Laps	Laps Led	Races Led	Miles	$
1970	93	2	0	0	0	0	0	0	0	139	0	0	364	1,585
1971	NR	2	0	0	0	0	0	0	0	189	0	0	491	2,490
1972	108	1	0	0	0	0	0	0	0	88	0	0	220	1,620
1974	—	0												320
1975	102	1	0	0	0	0	0	0	0	28	0	0	73	1,170
Lifetime		6	0	0	0	0	0	0	0	444	0	0	1,149	$7,185

Year	Rank	Starts	Poles	Finish						Laps	Laps Led	Races Led	Miles	$
				1	2	3	4	5	6–10					

Bill Tanner

William Tanner
Racing Hometown: Newton, PA

Year	Rank	Starts	Poles	1	2	3	4	5	6–10	Laps	Laps Led	Races Led	Miles	$
1954	191	1	0	0	0	0	0	0	0	4	0	0	4	0
1955	71	5	0	0	0	0	0	0	1	423	0	0	443	475
1956	202	2	0	0	0	0	0	0	0	230	0	0	230	75
Lifetime		8	0	0	0	0	0	0	1	657	0	0	677	$550

Frank Tanner

Frank Tanner
Racing Hometown: Charleston, SC

Year	Rank	Starts	Poles	1	2	3	4	5	6–10	Laps	Laps Led	Races Led	Miles	$
1964	103	4	0	0	0	0	0	0	0	9	0	0	7	300
Lifetime		4	0	0	0	0	0	0	0	9	0	0	7	$300

Tony Tantarelli

Anthony Tantarelli
Racing Hometown: Columbus, OH

Year	Rank	Starts	Poles	1	2	3	4	5	6–10	Laps	Laps Led	Races Led	Miles	$
1968	101	1	0	0	0	0	0	0	0	74	0	0	111	650
Lifetime		1	0	0	0	0	0	0	0	74	0	0	111	$650

Gene Tapia

Gene Tapia
Racing Hometown: Mobile, AL

Year	Rank	Starts	Poles	1	2	3	4	5	6–10	Laps	Laps Led	Races Led	Miles	$
1951	181	3	0	0	0	0	0	0	0		0	0		75
1953	134T	1	0	0	0	0	0	0	0		0	0		25
Lifetime		4	0	0	0	0	0	0	0		0	0		$100

Don Tarr

Dr. Donald F. Tarr
B: 5/4/1929
Racing Hometown: Miami Beach, FL

Year	Rank	Starts	Poles	1	2	3	4	5	6–10	Laps	Laps Led	Races Led	Miles	$
1967	89	3	0	0	0	0	0	0	0	621	0	0	506	1,580
1968	35	12	0	0	0	0	0	0	0	1,941	0	0	2,415	7,510
1969	41	12	0	0	0	0	0	0	3	1,754	6	1	3,122	13,950
1970	35	17	0	0	0	0	0	0	5	2,471	5	1	3,415	16,592
1971	62	4	0	0	0	0	0	0	1	496	0	0	771	3,995
Lifetime		48	0	0	0	0	0	0	9	7,283	11	2	10,229	$43,627

Robert Tartaglia

Robert Tartaglia
B: 4/19/1959
Racing Hometown: Reedley, CA

Year	Rank	Starts	Poles	1	2	3	4	5	6–10	Laps	Laps Led	Races Led	Miles	$
1979	106T	1	0	0	0	0	0	0	0	47	0	0	123	825
1981	102	1	0	0	0	0	0	0	0	4	0	0	10	500
Lifetime		2	0	0	0	0	0	0	0	51	0	0	134	$1,325

Al Tasnady

Alex Tasnady
B: 3/4/1929 D: 12/1988
Racing Hometown: Vineland, NJ

Year	Rank	Starts	Poles	1	2	3	4	5	6–10	Laps	Laps Led	Races Led	Miles	$
1957	188	1	0	0	0	0	0	0	0		0	0		0
1960	NR	1	0	0	0	0	0	0	0	172	0	0	86	110
1967	119	1	0	0	0	0	0	0	0	89	0	0	89	275
Lifetime		3	0	0	0	0	0	0	0	261	0	0	175	$385

Jim Tatum

James Tatum
Racing Hometown: Jacksonville, FL

Year	Rank	Starts	Poles	1	2	3	4	5	6–10	Laps	Laps Led	Races Led	Miles	$
1965	NR	1	0	0	0	0	0	0	0	103	0	0	34	100
1966	85	4	0	0	0	0	0	0	0	351	0	0	174	445
Lifetime		5	0	0	0	0	0	0	0	454	0	0	208	$545

Bill Taylor

William L. Taylor
Racing Hometown: Concord, NC

Year	Rank	Starts	Poles	1	2	3	4	5	6–10	Laps	Laps Led	Races Led	Miles	$
1957	NR	1	0	0	0	0	0	0	0	223	0	0	223	100
1959	NR	3	0	0	0	0	0	0	0	827	0	0	433	310
Lifetime		4	0	0	0	0	0	0	0	1,050	0	0	656	$410

Year	Rank	Starts	Poles	Finish						Laps	Laps Led	Races Led	Miles	$
				1	2	3	4	5	6–10	Laps	Led	Led	Miles	$

Billy Taylor
William Taylor
Racing Hometown: Yanceville, NC

Year	Rank	Starts	Poles	1	2	3	4	5	6–10	Laps	Laps Led	Races Led	Miles	$
1969	86	2	0	0	0	0	0	0	0	65	0	0	163	1,140
Lifetime		2	0	0	0	0	0	0	0	65	0	0	163	$1,140

Don Taylor
Donald Taylor
Racing Hometown: Torrance, CA

Year	Rank	Starts	Poles	1	2	3	4	5	6–10	Laps	Laps Led	Races Led	Miles	$
1959	98	2	0	0	0	0	0	0	0	430	0	0	214	200
Lifetime		2	0	0	0	0	0	0	0	430	0	0	214	$200

Graham Taylor
Graham Taylor
B: 2/3/1939
Racing Hometown: Port Royal, PA

Year	Rank	Starts	Poles	1	2	3	4	5	6–10	Laps	Laps Led	Races Led	Miles	$
1992	71	2	0	0	0	0	0	0	0	17	0	0	17	8,595
1993	89T	1	0	0	0	0	0	0	0	3	0	0	8	6,210
Lifetime		3	0	0	0	0	0	0	0	20	0	0	25	$14,805

Jesse James Taylor
Jesse James Taylor
B: 1919
Racing Hometown: Macon, GA

Year	Rank	Starts	Poles	1	2	3	4	5	6–10	Laps	Laps Led	Races Led	Miles	$
1950	NR	1	0	0	0	0	0	0	0	329	0	0	411	0
1951	7	10	0	0	1	0	0	0	2	519	104	3	566	3,750
1956	126	3	0	0	0	0	0	0	0	269	0	0	186	250
1958	NR	1	0	0	0	0	0	0	0	95	0	0	131	100
1961	171	1	0	0	0	0	0	0	0	10	0	0	15	250
Lifetime		16	0	0	1	0	0	0	2	1,222	104	3	1,309	$3,825

Ken Taylor
Kenneth Taylor
Racing Hometown: Louisville, KY

Year	Rank	Starts	Poles	1	2	3	4	5	6–10	Laps	Laps Led	Races Led	Miles	$
1954	NR	1	0	0	0	0	0	0	0	137	0	0	69	25
Lifetime		1	0	0	0	0	0	0	0	137	0	0	69	$25

T. W. Taylor
T. W. Taylor
B: 1/25/1955
Racing Hometown: Chester, VA

Year	Rank	Starts	Poles	1	2	3	4	5	6–10	Laps	Laps Led	Races Led	Miles	$
1992	84T	1	0	0	0	0	0	0	0	138	0	0	367	6,045
1993	56	3	0	0	0	0	0	0	0	280	1	1	391	21,605
1994	—	0												2,700
Lifetime		4	0	0	0	0	0	0	0	418	1	1	758	$30,350

Brad Teague
Brad Teague
B: 12/9/1947
Racing Hometown: Johnson City, TN

Year	Rank	Starts	Poles	1	2	3	4	5	6–10	Laps	Laps Led	Races Led	Miles	$
1982	32	9	0	0	0	0	0	0	0	3,052	0	0	2,611	14,750
1986	68	3	0	0	0	0	0	0	0	419	0	0	321	3,860
1987	57	5	0	0	0	0	0	0	0	915	17	1	1,176	15,045
1988	40	13	0	0	0	0	0	0	0	3,408	0	0	3,643	53,105
1989	68	2	0	0	0	0	0	0	0	733	0	0	628	4,830
1991	71	1	0	0	0	0	0	0	0	322	0	0	483	6,175
1992	58	2	0	0	0	0	0	0	0	603	0	0	611	15,780
1993	85T	1	0	0	0	0	0	0	0	13	0	0	18	7,710
1994	45	8	0	0	0	0	0	0	0	1,959	0	0	2,094	62,790
1995	—	0												1,000
Lifetime		44	0	0	0	0	0	0	0	11,424	17	1	11,583	$185,045

Kerry Teague
Kerry Teague
B: 1/12/1961
Racing Hometown: Concord, NC

Year	Rank	Starts	Poles	1	2	3	4	5	6–10	Laps	Laps Led	Races Led	Miles	$
1991	85	1	0	0	0	0	0	0	0	124	0	0	186	9,125
1992	67	2	0	0	0	0	0	0	0	137	0	0	325	26,235
1993	57	2	0	0	0	0	0	0	0	223	0	0	558	17,350
1994	—	0												2,000

Year	Rank	Starts	Poles	Finish						Laps	Laps Led	Races Led	Miles	$
				1	2	3	4	5	6–10	Laps	Led	Led	Miles	$

Kerry Teague *continued*

Year	Rank	Starts	Poles	1	2	3	4	5	6–10	Laps	Laps Led	Races Led	Miles	$
1995	—	0												2,250
Lifetime		5	0	0	0	0	0	0	0	484	0	0	1,069	$56,960

Marshall Teague

Marshall Teague
B: 2/17/1922   D: 2/11/1959   *Killed in test session @ Daytona.*
Racing Hometown: Daytona Beach, FL

Year	Rank	Starts	Poles	1	2	3	4	5	6–10	Laps	Laps Led	Races Led	Miles	$
1949	62T	1	0	0	0	0	0	0	0		0	0		50
1950	119	3	0	0	0	0	0	0	0	240	0	0	329	50
1951	NR	15	1	5	0	2	0	0	2	1,611	789	8	1,417	7,410
1952	NR	4	1	2	0	0	0	0	0	317	236	2	299	2,550
Lifetime		23	2	7	0	2	0	0	2	2,168	1,025	10	2,045	$10,060

Ted Tedrow

Theodore Tedrow
Racing Hometown: Mobile, AL

Year	Rank	Starts	Poles	1	2	3	4	5	6–10	Laps	Laps Led	Races Led	Miles	$
1951	N/A	1	0	0	0	0	0	0	0		0	0		25
Lifetime		1	0	0	0	0	0	0	0		0	0		$25

Al Terrell

Al Terrell
Racing Hometown: E. Peoria, IL

Year	Rank	Starts	Poles	1	2	3	4	5	6–10	Laps	Laps Led	Races Led	Miles	$
1963	156	1	0	0	0	0	0	0	0	4	0	0	10	0
Lifetime		1	0	0	0	0	0	0	0	4	0	0	10	$0

Dave Terrell

David Terrell
B: 2/21/1931
Racing Hometown: Newton, PA

Year	Rank	Starts	Poles	1	2	3	4	5	6–10	Laps	Laps Led	Races Led	Miles	$
1952	43	5	0	0	0	0	0	1	2	477	0	0	306	475
1954	12	30	0	0	0	0	0	0	8	3,876	0	0	2,608	2,225
1955	12	25	0	0	0	2	0	1	7	3,199	9	1	2,452	3,655
1956	121	5	0	0	0	0	0	0	1	363	0	0	235	260
1957	NR	2	0	0	0	0	0	0	1	290	0	0	290	750
1958	NR	1	0	0	0	0	0	0	0	113	0	0	57	50
Lifetime		68	0	0	0	2	0	2	19	8,318	9	1	5,947	$7,415

Kevin Terris

Kevin Terris
B: 10/27/1944
Racing Hometown: Hermosa Beach, CA

Year	Rank	Starts	Poles	1	2	3	4	5	6–10	Laps	Laps Led	Races Led	Miles	$
1970	72	2	0	0	0	0	0	0	0	169	0	0	443	1,875
1971	NR	4	0	0	0	0	0	0	2	519	0	0	1,361	5,965
1972	60	3	0	0	0	0	0	0	1	454	0	0	1,168	4,945
1982	107	1	0	0	0	0	0	0	0	12	0	0	31	525
1984	NR	1	0	0	0	0	0	0	0	78	0	0	204	1,275
Lifetime		11	0	0	0	0	0	0	3	1,232	0	0	3,207	$14,585

George Tet

Real Name: Tetsuo Fuchigami
B: 4/1/1923
Racing Hometown: Ozone Park, NY

Year	Rank	Starts	Poles	1	2	3	4	5	6–10	Laps	Laps Led	Races Led	Miles	$
1960	121	1	0	0	0	0	0	0	0	171	0	0	257	200
1961	185	2	0	0	0	0	0	0	0	60	0	0	150	250
Lifetime		3	0	0	0	0	0	0	0	231	0	0	407	$450

Ash Tharrett

Ashton Tharrett
Racing Hometown: Rochester, NY

Year	Rank	Starts	Poles	1	2	3	4	5	6–10	Laps	Laps Led	Races Led	Miles	$
1954	179T	1	0	0	0	0	0	0	0	153	0	0	77	0
Lifetime		1	0	0	0	0	0	0	0	153	0	0	77	$0

Rod Therrian

Roderick Therrian
Racing Hometown: Atlanta, GA

Year	Rank	Starts	Poles	1	2	3	4	5	6–10	Laps	Laps Led	Races Led	Miles	$
1951	N/A	1	0	0	0	0	0	0	0		0	0		25
Lifetime		1	0	0	0	0	0	0	0		0	0		$25

Year	Rank	Starts	Poles	Finish 1	2	3	4	5	6–10	Laps	Laps Led	Races Led	Miles	$

Jim Thirkettle

James Thirkettle
B: 3/9/1945
Racing Hometown: Sylmar, CA

Year	Rank	Starts	Poles	1	2	3	4	5	6–10	Laps	Laps Led	Races Led	Miles	$
1975	107T	1	0	0	0	0	0	0	0	50	0	0	125	750
1976	85	2	0	0	0	0	0	0	0	133	0	0	334	1,730
1977	66	2	0	0	0	0	0	0	0	154	0	0	403	2,265
1978	48	3	0	0	0	0	0	0	2	393	1	1	1,006	7,850
1979	79T	1	0	0	0	0	0	0	1	117	0	0	307	2,450
Lifetime		9	0	0	0	0	0	0	3	847	1	1	2,175	$15,045

Donald Thomas

Donald Thomas
B: 7/10/1932   D: 12/16/1977
Racing Hometown: Olivia, NC

Year	Rank	Starts	Poles	1	2	3	4	5	6–10	Laps	Laps Led	Races Led	Miles	$
1950	39	2	0	0	0	0	0	0	2	141	0	0	71	300
1951	20	17	0	0	0	1	0	3	4	479	0	0	563	2,385
1952	9	21	1	1	1	1	1	1	9	2,623	9	1	1,928	4,477
1953	9	17	0	0	0	0	0	0	4	1,034	0	0	1,119	1,765
1954	31	9	0	0	1	0	1	1	1	1,175	53	1	689	1,700
1955	38	10	0	0	0	0	2	0	2	1,320	0	0	855	1,240
1956	110	3	0	0	0	0	0	0	1	165	0	0	114	200
Lifetime		79	1	1	2	2	4	5	23	6,937	62	2	5,338	$12,067

Hank Thomas

Henry C. Thomas
Racing Hometown: Winston-Salem, NC

Year	Rank	Starts	Poles	1	2	3	4	5	6–10	Laps	Laps Led	Races Led	Miles	$
1963	126T	1	0	0	0	0	0	0	0	44	0	0	11	125
1966	42	14	0	0	0	1	0	2	4	3,114	0	0	1,482	3,630
Lifetime		15	0	0	0	1	0	2	4	3,158	0	0	1,493	$3,755

Herb Thomas

Herbert Watson Thomas
B: 4/6/1923
Racing Hometown: Olivia, NC

Year	Rank	Starts	Poles	1	2	3	4	5	6–10	Laps	Laps Led	Races Led	Miles	$
1949	25	4	0	0	0	0	0	1	0	197	0	0	99	225
1950	11	13	0	1	0	2	1	0	2	719	176	2	438	2,645
1951	1	36	4	7	1	3	4	1	2	2,159	954	10	1,686	20,850
1952	2	32	10	8	7	3	0	1	3	5,134	**1,509**	**16**	3,475	18,965
1953	1	37	12	12	8	3	3	1	4	**4,292**	**1,420**	**23**	**3,107**	28,910
1954	2	34	8	12	4	1	2	0	8	5,605	**1,366**	**18**	3,998	30,975
1955	5	23	2	3	3	3	3	2	1	3,248	250	7	2,707	18,024
1956	3	48	2	5	2	4	7	4	14	7,854	522	8	5,062	19,352
1957	148	2	0	0	0	0	0	0	0	146	0	0	123	25
1962	97	1	0	0	0	0	0	0	0	377	0	0	236	200
Lifetime		230	38	48 10th	25	19	20	10	34	29,731	6,197	84	20,930	$139,944

Hildrey Thomas

Hildrey M. Thomas
Racing Hometown: Chocowinity, NC

Year	Rank	Starts	Poles	1	2	3	4	5	6–10	Laps	Laps Led	Races Led	Miles	$
1953	108T	1	0	0	0	0	0	0	0		0	0		25
Lifetime		1	0	0	0	0	0	0	0		0	0		$25

Jabe Thomas

Cerry Ezra Thomas
B: 5/12/1930
Racing Hometown: Christiansburg, VA

Year	Rank	Starts	Poles	1	2	3	4	5	6–10	Laps	Laps Led	Races Led	Miles	$
1965	52	10	0	0	0	0	0	0	1	2,161	0	0	1,764	4,250
1966	47	13	0	0	0	0	0	0	0	1,559	0	0	1,373	3,580
1967	51	20	0	0	0	0	0	0	3	2,408	0	0	1,847	7,055
1968	8	48	0	0	0	0	0	1	14	11,194	0	0	7,362	21,166
1969	8	51	0	0	0	0	0	0	12	12,025	0	0	9,868	44,989
1970	7	46	0	0	0	0	0	0	23	10,928	0	0	9,510	42,958
1971	6	43	0	0	0	0	1	1	13	11,360	0	0	9,816	48,241
1972	12	28	0	0	0	0	0	0	4	7,132	0	0	8,207	43,438
1973	11	25	0	0	0	0	0	0	1	7,205	0	0	7,910	42,955
1974	42	10	0	0	0	0	0	0	1	1,504	0	0	1,006	7,835
1975	22	21	0	0	0	0	0	0	2	5,822	0	0	5,661	22,390
1976	40	6	0	0	0	0	0	0	0	1,944	0	0	1,291	6,530
1978	105T	1	0	0	0	0	0	0	0	1	0	0	1	480
Lifetime		322	0	0	0	0	1	2	74	75,243	0	0	65,616	$295,867

Year	Rank	Starts	Poles	Finish						Laps	Laps Led	Races Led	Miles	$
				1	2	3	4	5	6–10					

Larry Thomas

Larry Thomas
B: 4/13/1936   D: 1/25/1965   *Killed in highway crash @ Tifton, GA.*
Racing Hometown: Thomasville, NC

Year	Rank	Starts	Poles	1	2	3	4	5	6–10	Laps	Laps Led	Races Led	Miles	$
1961	43	14	0	0	0	0	0	0	4	2,830	0	0	1,256	2,065
1962	17	37	0	0	0	0	2	1	9	7,268	0	0	4,889	9,486
1963	22	32	0	0	0	2	1	3	7	6,991	0	0	4,209	8,945
1964	8	43	0	0	1	3	2	3	18	10,025	0	0	6,957	21,226
Lifetime		126	0	0	1	5	5	7	38	27,114	0	0	17,311	$41,722

Lou Thomas

Louis Thomas
Racing Hometown: Linthicum Heights, MD

Year	Rank	Starts	Poles	1	2	3	4	5	6–10	Laps	Laps Led	Races Led	Miles	$
1953	155	1	0	0	0	0	0	0	0		0	0		35
Lifetime		1	0	0	0	0	0	0	0		0	0		$35

Ronnie Thomas

Ronald Thomas
B: 3/8/1955
Racing Hometown: Christiansburg, VA

Year	Rank	Starts	Poles	1	2	3	4	5	6–10	Laps	Laps Led	Races Led	Miles	$
1977	52	4	0	0	0	0	0	0	0	821	0	0	715	4,590
1978	18	27	0	0	0	0	0	0	2	7,287	0	0	7,769	75,815
1979	17	30	0	0	0	0	0	0	3	6,928	1	1	7,840	100,079
1980	14	30	0	0	0	0	0	0	4	7,522	0	0	9,081	94,730
1981	26	23	0	0	0	0	0	0	0	5,756	0	0	5,928	53,605
1982	30	18	0	0	0	0	0	0	0	3,243	0	0	3,288	26,720
1983	22	26	0	0	0	0	0	0	0	7,141	1	1	7,705	47,190
1984	30	21	0	0	0	0	0	0	0	4,976	2	1	5,761	79,325
1985	39	7	0	0	0	0	0	0	0	1,510	0	0	1,157	10,505
1986	42	6	0	0	0	0	0	0	0	973	0	0	1,547	25,215
1987	60	4	0	0	0	0	0	0	0	874	0	0	694	6,320
1989	73	1	0	0	0	0	0	0	0	196	0	0	392	3,925
Lifetime		197	0	0	0	0	0	0	9	47,227	4	3	51,878	$528,019

Ted Thomas

Theodore Thomas

Year	Rank	Starts	Poles	1	2	3	4	5	6–10	Laps	Laps Led	Races Led	Miles	$
1989	90	1	0	0	0	0	0	0	0	55	0	0	134	1,975
Lifetime		1	0	0	0	0	0	0	0	55	0	0	134	$1,975

Jack B. Thomason *See* Perk Brown

Bob Thompson

Robert Thompson
Racing Hometown: Buena Park, CA

Year	Rank	Starts	Poles	1	2	3	4	5	6–10	Laps	Laps Led	Races Led	Miles	$
1965	122	1	0	0	0	0	0	0	0	26	0	0	70	500
Lifetime		1	0	0	0	0	0	0	0	26	0	0	70	$500

Chet Thompson

Chester Thompson
Racing Hometown: Oakland, CA

Year	Rank	Starts	Poles	1	2	3	4	5	6–10	Laps	Laps Led	Races Led	Miles	$
1955	NR	1	0	0	0	0	0	0	0	199	0	0	199	40
1956	203T	1	0	0	0	0	0	0	0	94	0	0	94	50
Lifetime		2	0	0	0	0	0	0	0	293	0	0	293	$90

Chuck Thompson

Charles H. Thompson
Racing Hometown: Holly Hill, FL

Year	Rank	Starts	Poles	1	2	3	4	5	6–10	Laps	Laps Led	Races Led	Miles	$
1957	136T	1	0	0	0	0	0	0	0	47	0	0	75	100
Lifetime		1	0	0	0	0	0	0	0	47	0	0	75	$100

Frank Thompson

Frank Thompson
Racing Hometown: Shewsbury, PA

Year	Rank	Starts	Poles	1	2	3	4	5	6–10	Laps	Laps Led	Races Led	Miles	$
1958	101	3	0	0	0	0	0	0	0	285	0	0	161	150
Lifetime		3	0	0	0	0	0	0	0	285	0	0	161	$150

Fred Thompson

Fred Thompson
Racing Hometown: Birmingham, AL

Year	Rank	Starts	Poles	1	2	3	4	5	6–10	Laps	Laps Led	Races Led	Miles	$
1951	N/A	1	0	0	0	0	0	0	0		0	0		25

Year	Rank	Starts	Poles	Finish						Laps	Laps Led	Races Led	Miles	$
				1	2	3	4	5	6–10					

Fred Thompson *continued*

Year	Rank	Starts	Poles	1	2	3	4	5	6–10	Laps	Laps Led	Races Led	Miles	$
1963	114T	1	0	0	0	0	0	0	1	186	0	0	93	175
Lifetime		2	0	0	0	0	0	0	1	186	0	0	93	$200

Gerald Thompson

Gerald Thompson
Racing Hometown: Clawson, MI

Year	Rank	Starts	Poles	1	2	3	4	5	6–10	Laps	Laps Led	Races Led	Miles	$
1973	91	1	0	0	0	0	0	0	0	162	0	0	424	1,195
Lifetime		1	0	0	0	0	0	0	0	162	0	0	424	$1,195

Jim Thompson

James Thompson
Racing Hometown: Huntington, WV

Year	Rank	Starts	Poles	1	2	3	4	5	6–10	Laps	Laps Led	Races Led	Miles	$
1955	163	2	0	0	0	0	0	0	0	357	0	0	340	200
Lifetime		2	0	0	0	0	0	0	0	357	0	0	340	$200

Jimmy Thompson

James Thompson
B: 2/1/1924   D: 9/26/1964
Racing Hometown: Monroe, NC

Year	Rank	Starts	Poles	1	2	3	4	5	6–10	Laps	Laps Led	Races Led	Miles	$
1949	36	2	0	0	0	0	0	0	2		0	0		175
1950	29	4	0	0	0	0	0	0	3	522	0	0	510	525
1951	N/A	3	0	0	0	0	0	0	0	236	0	0	295	25
1952	38	1	0	0	0	0	0	0	0	383	0	0	479	300
1954	153	1	0	0	0	0	0	0	0	4	0	0	6	75
1955	65	6	0	0	0	0	0	0	1	883	0	0	739	650
1957	46	2	0	0	0	0	0	0	0	352	0	0	489	325
1958	23	7	0	0	0	0	1	0	1	923	0	0	609	3,275
1959	29	5	0	0	0	0	0	0	1	1,002	0	0	1,145	1,580
1960	43	9	0	0	0	0	0	0	0	1,944	0	0	2,288	1,940
1961	121	3	0	0	0	0	0	0	0	267	0	0	301	450
1962	43	3	0	0	0	0	0	0	0	847	0	0	1,271	1,650
Lifetime		46	0	0	0	0	1	0	8	7,363	0	0	8,131	$10,970

Johnny Thompson

John Thompson
B: 9/9/1922
Racing Hometown: Jacksonville, FL

Year	Rank	Starts	Poles	1	2	3	4	5	6–10	Laps	Laps Led	Races Led	Miles	$
1951	N/A	2	0	0	0	0	0	0	0		0	0		50
1952	136	3	0	0	0	0	0	0	0		0	0		50
Lifetime		5	0	0	0	0	0	0	0		0	0		$100

Mark Thompson

Mark Thompson
B: 7/9/1951
Racing Hometown: Cartersville, GA

Year	Rank	Starts	Poles	1	2	3	4	5	6–10	Laps	Laps Led	Races Led	Miles	$
1992	90T	1	0	0	0	0	0	0	0	8	0	0	20	4,370
Lifetime		1	0	0	0	0	0	0	0	8	0	0	20	$4,370

Ray Thompson

Raymond Thompson
Racing Hometown: Orlando, FL

Year	Rank	Starts	Poles	1	2	3	4	5	6–10	Laps	Laps Led	Races Led	Miles	$
1951	N/A	1	0	0	0	0	0	0	0		0	0		25
1956	255	2	0	0	0	0	0	0	0	12	0	0	12	50
Lifetime		3	0	0	0	0	0	0	0	12	0	0	12	$75

Roscoe Thompson

Roscoe A. Thompson
B: 7/5/1922
Racing Hometown: Forrest Park, GA

Year	Rank	Starts	Poles	1	2	3	4	5	6–10	Laps	Laps Led	Races Led	Miles	$
1950	97	2	0	0	0	0	0	0	0	69	0	0	218	50
1951	N/A	3	0	0	0	0	0	0	0	64	0	0	64	75
1952	170	7	0	0	0	0	0	0	0	332	11	1	228	240
1953	82	2	0	0	0	0	0	0	0	0	0	0	0	50
1958	90	1	0	0	0	0	0	0	0	44	0	0	44	75
1959	96	2	0	0	0	0	0	0	0	96	0	0	138	100
1960	58	2	0	0	0	0	0	0	0	402	0	0	603	710
1961	40	6	0	0	0	0	0	0	2	721	0	0	1,341	2,535
1962	54	4	0	0	0	0	0	0	0	305	0	0	495	1,605
Lifetime		29	0	0	0	0	0	0	2	2,033	11	1	3,130	$5,440

Year	Rank	Starts	Poles			Finish				Laps	Laps Led	Races Led	Miles	$
				1	2	3	4	5	6–10					

Sam Thompson

Samuel Thompson
Racing Hometown: Pittsburgh, PA

Year	Rank	Starts	Poles	1	2	3	4	5	6–10	Laps	Laps Led	Races Led	Miles	$
1951	N/A	1	0	0	0	0	0	0	0	52	0	0	26	25
Lifetime		1	0	0	0	0	0	0	0	52	0	0	26	$25

Speedy Thompson

Alfred B. Thompson
B: 4/3/1926   D: 4/2/1972   *Died of heart attack while competing @ Metrolina Speedway in Charlotte, NC.*
Racing Hometown: Monroe, NC

Year	Rank	Starts	Poles	1	2	3	4	5	6–10	Laps	Laps Led	Races Led	Miles	$
1950	NR	1	0	0	0	0	0	0	0	0	0	0	0	0
1951	75	3	0	0	0	0	0	1	0	39	0	0	29	325
1952	37	2	0	0	0	0	0	0	0	409	0	0	511	305
1953	11	7	0	2	2	1	0	0	2	1,257	99	4	1,229	6,547
1954	23	7	0	0	0	0	1	0	2	949	0	0	942	1,165
1955	15	15	0	2	1	0	0	0	2	1,918	222	2	1,835	7,090
1956	2	42	6	8	5	5	4	2	5	6,957	**2,023**	**23**	4,646	27,169
1957	3	38	4	2	4	3	4	3	6	6,301	648	8	3,903	26,841
1958	3	38	7	4	2	7	3	3	5	6,808	230	7	4,437	17,295
1959	3	29	1	0	1	0	2	2	4	4,785	228	3	3,436	6,816
1960	25	9	0	2	0	0	1	1	1	1,646	217	2	2,129	18,035
1961	63	3	0	0	0	0	0	0	0	440	0	0	660	1,100
1962	41	3	0	0	0	0	0	0	1	443	0	0	850	1,400
1971	NR	1	0	0	0	0	0	0	0	376	0	0	564	1,800
Lifetime		198	18	20	15	16	15	12	28	32,328	3,667	49	25,170	$115,888

Tommy Thompson

Howard W. Thompson
B: 4/22/1922
Racing Hometown: Louisville, KY

Year	Rank	Starts	Poles	1	2	3	4	5	6–10	Laps	Laps Led	Races Led	Miles	$
1950	79	3	0	0	0	0	0	0	0	272	0	0	439	75
1951	19	5	0	1	0	0	0	0	1	398	58	1	435	5,510
1952	44	5	0	0	0	0	0	0	1	553	20	1	399	525
1953	41	3	0	0	0	1	0	0	0	39	0	0	160	865
1954	205	1	0	0	0	0	0	0	0	15	0	0	61	0
1955	205	1	0	0	0	0	0	0	0	41	0	0	56	50
1956	278	1	0	0	0	0	0	0	0	0	0	0	0	0
1959	40	3	0	0	0	0	0	0	0	367	0	0	422	510
Lifetime		22	0	1	0	1	0	0	2	1,685	78	2	1,973	$7,535

Gene Thonesen

Gene Thonesen
B: 12/1/1953   D: 8/4/1993   *Killed on tractor.*
Racing Hometown: Readley, CA

Year	Rank	Starts	Poles	1	2	3	4	5	6–10	Laps	Laps Led	Races Led	Miles	$
1981	83	1	0	0	0	0	0	0	0	110	0	0	288	2,125
Lifetime		1	0	0	0	0	0	0	0	110	0	0	288	$2,125

Bill Thorp

William Thorp
Racing Hometown: Gardena, CA

Year	Rank	Starts	Poles	1	2	3	4	5	6–10	Laps	Laps Led	Races Led	Miles	$
1958	104	1	0	0	0	0	0	0	0	154	0	0	405	110
Lifetime		1	0	0	0	0	0	0	0	154	0	0	405	$110

Marv Thorpe

Marvin Thorpe

Year	Rank	Starts	Poles	1	2	3	4	5	6–10	Laps	Laps Led	Races Led	Miles	$
1958	NR	1	0	0	0	0	0	0	0	67	0	0	22	100
Lifetime		1	0	0	0	0	0	0	0	67	0	0	22	$100

Ruben Thrash

Ruben Thrash
Racing Hometown: Inglewood, CA

Year	Rank	Starts	Poles	1	2	3	4	5	6–10	Laps	Laps Led	Races Led	Miles	$
1958	122	2	0	0	0	0	0	0	0	133	0	0	202	200
Lifetime		2	0	0	0	0	0	0	0	133	0	0	202	$200

Ray Throckmorton

Raymond Throckmorton
Racing Hometown: Richmond, VA

Year	Rank	Starts	Poles	1	2	3	4	5	6–10	Laps	Laps Led	Races Led	Miles	$
1951	N/A	1	0	0	0	0	0	0	0		0	0		50
Lifetime		1	0	0	0	0	0	0	0		0	0		$50

Year	Rank	Starts	Poles	Finish						Laps	Laps Led	Races Led	Miles	$
				1	2	3	4	5	6–10	Laps	Led	Led	Miles	$

Bill Thurber

William Thurber
Racing Hometown: Palm Beach, FL

Year	Rank	Starts	Poles	1	2	3	4	5	6–10	Laps	Laps Led	Races Led	Miles	$
1956	184T	1	0	0	0	0	0	0	0	173	0	0	87	75
Lifetime		1	0	0	0	0	0	0	0	173	0	0	87	$75

Billy Tibbett

William Tibbett
Racing Hometown: Natick, MA

Year	Rank	Starts	Poles	1	2	3	4	5	6–10	Laps	Laps Led	Races Led	Miles	$
1951	N/A	2	0	0	0	0	0	0	0	318	0	0	398	75
Lifetime		2	0	0	0	0	0	0	0	318	0	0	398	$75

Al Tibbetts

Al Tibbetts
Racing Hometown: Newportville, PA

Year	Rank	Starts	Poles	1	2	3	4	5	6–10	Laps	Laps Led	Races Led	Miles	$
1950	NR	1	0	0	0	0	0	0	0	48	0	0	48	0
Lifetime		1	0	0	0	0	0	0	0	48	0	0	48	$0

Charles Tidwell

Charles Tidwell
Racing Hometown: Macon, GA

Year	Rank	Starts	Poles	1	2	3	4	5	6–10	Laps	Laps Led	Races Led	Miles	$
1950	NR	2	0	0	0	0	0	0	0	300	0	0	375	100
Lifetime		2	0	0	0	0	0	0	0	300	0	0	375	$100

Travis Tiller

Travis Branton Tiller
B: 5/15/1937
Racing Hometown: Triangle, VA

Year	Rank	Starts	Poles	1	2	3	4	5	6–10	Laps	Laps Led	Races Led	Miles	$
1974	34	14	0	0	0	0	0	0	0	2,446	0	0	2,565	11,410
1975	36	10	0	0	0	0	0	0	0	1,958	0	0	2,178	7,780
1976	37	9	0	0	0	0	0	0	0	2,012	0	0	1,787	6,640
1977	61	3	0	0	0	0	0	0	0	250	0	0	183	1,615
1979	60	4	0	0	0	0	0	0	0	218	0	0	336	5,065
1980	65	4	0	0	0	0	0	0	0	830	0	0	733	3,050
1981	100	1	0	0	0	0	0	0	0	111	0	0	169	850
1982	51	4	0	0	0	0	0	0	0	557	0	0	1,107	6,395
1983	73	2	0	0	0	0	0	0	0	338	0	0	463	5,060
Lifetime		51	0	0	0	0	0	0	0	8,720	0	0	9,521	$47,865

Don Tilley

William Donald Tilley
Racing Hometown: Huntersville, NC

Year	Rank	Starts	Poles	1	2	3	4	5	6–10	Laps	Laps Led	Races Led	Miles	$
1964	105	2	0	0	0	0	0	0	0	275	0	0	164	250
1965	76	2	0	0	0	0	0	0	0	119	0	0	298	1,240
1966	118	2	0	0	0	0	0	0	6–10	63	0	0	56	505
Lifetime		6	0	0	0	0	0	0	0	457	0	0	517	$1,995

Hank Tillman

Harvey Tillman
Racing Hometown: Palm Beach, FL

Year	Rank	Starts	Poles	1	2	3	4	5	6–10	Laps	Laps Led	Races Led	Miles	$
1952	120T	1	0	0	0	0	0	0	0	160	0	0	80	25
1961	147	1	0	0	0	0	0	0	0	146	0	0	219	300
Lifetime		2	0	0	0	0	0	0	0	306	0	0	299	$325

Herb Tillman

Herbert Tillman
B: 1/8/1929
Racing Hometown: Miami, FL

Year	Rank	Starts	Poles	1	2	3	4	5	6–10	Laps	Laps Led	Races Led	Miles	$
1953	133	2	0	0	0	0	0	0	0	122	0	0	126	50
1960	35	9	0	0	0	0	0	0	0	1,705	0	0	2,244	2,695
1961	72	5	0	0	0	0	0	0	0	609	0	0	587	1,000
1962	118	1	0	0	0	0	0	0	0	194	0	0	291	500
Lifetime		17	0	0	0	0	0	0	0	2,630	0	0	3,248	$4,245

Cliff Timberman

Clifford Timberman
Racing Hometown: Charlotte, NC

Year	Rank	Starts	Poles	1	2	3	4	5	6–10	Laps	Laps Led	Races Led	Miles	$
1959	NR	1	0	0	0	0	0	0	0	2	0	0	1	0
Lifetime		1	0	0	0	0	0	0	0	2	0	0	1	$0

Year	Rank	Starts	Poles	Finish						Laps	Laps Led	Races Led	Miles	$
				1	2	3	4	5	6–10					

Leonard Tippett

Leonard Tippett
Racing Hometown: Greenville, SC

Year	Rank	Starts	Poles	1	2	3	4	5	6–10	Laps	Laps Led	Races Led	Miles	$
1951	N/A	8	0	0	1	0	0	0	1	359	19	1	270	850
1952	57	5	0	0	0	0	0	0	0	221	0	0	134	150
Lifetime		13	0	0	1	0	0	0	1	580	19	1	403	$1,000

Randy Tissot

Randall Tissot
B: 3/30/1944
Racing Hometown: Hollywood, FL

Year	Rank	Starts	Poles	1	2	3	4	5	6–10	Laps	Laps Led	Races Led	Miles	$
1973	44	3	0	0	0	0	0	0	0	816	0	0	1,384	4,245
1974	70	3	0	0	0	0	0	0	0	473	8	1	839	3,750
1975	51	7	0	0	0	0	0	0	0	1,121	0	0	1,657	10,030
Lifetime		13	0	0	0	0	0	0	0	2,410	8	1	3,880	$18,025

Jerry Titus

Jerry Titus
B: 10/24/1928   D: 8/5/1970   *Died of injuries suffered @ Elkhart Lake 7/20/70.*
Racing Hometown: Tarzana, CA

Year	Rank	Starts	Poles	1	2	3	4	5	6–10	Laps	Laps Led	Races Led	Miles	$
1968	106	1	0	0	0	0	0	0	0	5	0	0	14	500
Lifetime		1	0	0	0	0	0	0	0	5	0	0	14	$500

Toby Tobias

Richard Tobias
B: 2/12/1932   D: 6/23/1978   *Killed @ Flemington, NJ.*
Racing Hometown: Lebanon, PA

Year	Rank	Starts	Poles	1	2	3	4	5	6–10	Laps	Laps Led	Races Led	Miles	$
1973	121	1	0	0	0	0	0	0	0	50	0	0	50	680
Lifetime		1	0	0	0	0	0	0	0	50	0	0	50	$680

Don Tomberlin

Donald Tomberlin
Racing Hometown: Warner Robins, GA

Year	Rank	Starts	Poles	1	2	3	4	5	6–10	Laps	Laps Led	Races Led	Miles	$
1968	NR	1	0	0	0	0	0	0	0	181	0	0	91	100
1969	68	2	0	0	0	0	0	0	0	215	0	0	233	1,025
Lifetime		3	0	0	0	0	0	0	0	396	0	0	323	$1,125

Chuck Tombs

Charles Tombs
Racing Hometown: Jeffersonville, IN

Year	Rank	Starts	Poles	1	2	3	4	5	6–10	Laps	Laps Led	Races Led	Miles	$
1959	100	1	0	0	0	0	0	0	0	134	0	0	67	0
1960	102	20	0	0	0	0	0	0	0	227	0	0	114	100
Lifetime		3	0	0	0	0	0	0	0	361	0	0	181	$100

Red Tomlinson

Norman Tomlinson
Racing Hometown: Edgely, PA

Year	Rank	Starts	Poles	1	2	3	4	5	6–10	Laps	Laps Led	Races Led	Miles	$
1952	128	2	0	0	0	0	0	0	0	311	0	0	311	60
Lifetime		2	0	0	0	0	0	0	0	311	0	0	311	$60

T. A. Toomes

T. A. Toomes
B: 1930
Racing Hometown: Asheboro, NC

Year	Rank	Starts	Poles	1	2	3	4	5	6–10	Laps	Laps Led	Races Led	Miles	$
1957	34	11	0	0	0	0	0	0	1	1,920	0	0	1,040	1,450
Lifetime		11	0	0	0	0	0	0	1	1,920	0	0	1,040	$1,450

Warren Tope

Warren Tope
B: 4/24/1947   D: 7/5/1975   *Killed in practice for a street race.*
Racing Hometown: Troy, MI

Year	Rank	Starts	Poles	1	2	3	4	5	6–10	Laps	Laps Led	Races Led	Miles	$
1975	114T	2	0	0	0	0	0	0	0	305	0	0	467	3,170
Lifetime		2	0	0	0	0	0	0	0	305	0	0	467	$3,170

Pete Torres

Peter Torres
B: 4/17/1944
Racing Hometown: Alhambra, CA

Year	Rank	Starts	Poles	1	2	3	4	5	6–10	Laps	Laps Led	Races Led	Miles	$
1971	NR	1	0	0	0	0	0	0	0	19	0	0	50	645
1975	73T	2	0	0	0	0	0	0	0	162	0	0	424	2,035
Lifetime		3	0	0	0	0	0	0	0	181	0	0	474	$2,680

Year	Rank	Starts	Poles	Finish 1	2	3	4	5	6–10	Laps	Laps Led	Races Led	Miles	$

John Torrese

John Torrese
Racing Hometown: Ira, NY

Year	Rank	Starts	Poles	1	2	3	4	5	6–10	Laps	Laps Led	Races Led	Miles	$
1953	NR	1	0	0	0	0	0	0	0		0	0		25
Lifetime		1	0	0	0	0	0	0	0		0	0		$25

Pete Toth

Peter Toth
Racing Hometown: Toledo, OH

Year	Rank	Starts	Poles	1	2	3	4	5	6–10	Laps	Laps Led	Races Led	Miles	$
1952	140T	1	0	0	0	0	0	0	0	125	0	0	63	25
Lifetime		1	0	0	0	0	0	0	0	125	0	0	63	$25

Sal Tovella

Salvatore Tovella
B: 8/14/1928
Racing Hometown: Chicago, IL

Year	Rank	Starts	Poles	1	2	3	4	5	6–10	Laps	Laps Led	Races Led	Miles	$
1956	221	1	0	0	0	0	0	0	0	142	0	0	71	100
1960	107	2	0	0	0	0	0	0	0	43	0	0	108	275
1961	58	4	0	0	0	0	0	0	0	393	0	0	808	850
1962	105	2	0	0	0	0	0	0	0	77	0	0	193	450
1963	44	3	0	0	0	0	0	0	0	346	0	0	888	1,300
1964	73	2	0	0	0	0	0	0	0	167	0	0	418	850
1981	—	0												780
Lifetime		14	0	0	0	0	0	0	0	1,168	0	0	2,484	$4,605

Ward Towers

Ward Towers
Racing Hometown: Corinth, NY

Year	Rank	Starts	Poles	1	2	3	4	5	6–10	Laps	Laps Led	Races Led	Miles	$
1958	97	1	0	0	0	0	0	0	0	34	0	0	139	90
Lifetime		1	0	0	0	0	0	0	0	34	0	0	139	$90

Chuck Townsen

Charles Townsen
Racing Hometown: Hawthorne, CA

Year	Rank	Starts	Poles	1	2	3	4	5	6–10	Laps	Laps Led	Races Led	Miles	$
1958	115	1	0	0	0	0	0	0	0	152	0	0	400	110
Lifetime		1	0	0	0	0	0	0	0	152	0	0	400	$110

Roy Trantham

Roy Musten Trantham
B: 10/2/1941
Racing Hometown: Asheville, NC

Year	Rank	Starts	Poles	1	2	3	4	5	6–10	Laps	Laps Led	Races Led	Miles	$
1968	60	5	0	0	0	0	0	0	1	968	0	0	671	2,285
Lifetime		5	0	0	0	0	0	0	1	968	0	0	671	$2,285

Frank Travers

Frank Travers

Year	Rank	Starts	Poles	1	2	3	4	5	6–10	Laps	Laps Led	Races Led	Miles	$
1951	N/A	1	0	0	0	0	0	0	0		0	0		0
Lifetime		1	0	0	0	0	0	0	0		0	0		$0

Tom Travis

Tom Travis (Slow Poke)
Racing Hometown: Lexington, KY

Year	Rank	Starts	Poles	1	2	3	4	5	6–10	Laps	Laps Led	Races Led	Miles	$
1953	170	1	0	0	0	0	0	0	0	33	0	0	135	25
Lifetime		1	0	0	0	0	0	0	0	33	0	0	135	$25

Hank Trice

Hank Trice

Year	Rank	Starts	Poles	1	2	3	4	5	6–10	Laps	Laps Led	Races Led	Miles	$
1956	NR	1	0	0	0	0	0	0	0	73	0	0	37	50
Lifetime		1	0	0	0	0	0	0	0	73	0	0	37	$50

Dick Trickle

Richard Trickle
B: 10/27/1941
Racing Hometown: Wisconsin Rapids, WI

Year	Rank	Starts	Poles	1	2	3	4	5	6–10	Laps	Laps Led	Races Led	Miles	$
1970	NR	2	0	0	0	0	0	0	0	176	0	0	440	1,415
1973	81	1	0	0	0	0	0	1	0	327	2	1	491	3,385
1974	47	3	0	0	0	0	0	0	3	1,201	0	0	1,568	10,828
1975	113	1	0	0	0	0	0	0	0	3	0	0	8	1,705
1976	105T	1	0	0	0	0	0	0	0	142	0	0	213	1,225
1977	98T	1	0	0	0	0	0	0	0	141	0	0	212	1,100
1978	108	1	0	0	0	0	0	0	0	24	0	0	36	910
1984	87	1	0	0	0	0	0	0	0	53	0	0	133	7,500

Year	Rank	Starts	Poles	Finish						Laps	Laps Led	Races Led	Miles	$
				1	2	3	4	5	6–10					

Dick Trickle *continued*

Year	Rank	Starts	Poles	1	2	3	4	5	6–10	Laps	Laps Led	Races Led	Miles	$
1985	55	3	0	0	0	0	0	0	1	452	0	0	778	8,650
1986	55	2	0	0	0	0	0	0	0	676	0	0	975	19,175
1989	15	28	0	0	0	3	1	2	3	8,504	80	8	10,075	343,728
1990	22	29	1	0	0	1	0	1	2	8,311	82	4	9,827	350,990
1991	35	14	0	0	0	0	0	0	1	3,650	0	0	4,274	129,125
1992	20	29	0	0	0	0	0	3	6	8,259	5	2	9,883	429,521
1993	30	26	0	0	0	0	0	1	1	7,003	3	1	8,376	240,165
1994	34	25	0	0	0	0	0	0	1	6,423	1	1	7,107	244,806
1995	25	31	0	0	0	0	0	0	1	8,941	5	1	11,094	694,920
1996	36	26	0	0	0	0	0	0	1	6,694	2	1	8,352	404,927
Lifetime		224	1	0	0	4	1	8	20	60,980	180	19	73,840	$2,894,075

Herb Trimble

Herbert Trimble
Racing Hometown: Middletown, OH

Year	Rank	Starts	Poles	1	2	3	4	5	6–10	Laps	Laps Led	Races Led	Miles	$
1951	N/A	2	0	0	0	0	0	0	1	198	0	0	248	50
Lifetime		2	0	0	0	0	0	0	1	198	0	0	248	$50

Charles Triplett

Charles Triplett
Racing Hometown: N. Wilkesboro, NC

Year	Rank	Starts	Poles	1	2	3	4	5	6–10	Laps	Laps Led	Races Led	Miles	$
1966	116	1	0	0	0	0	0	0	0	85	0	0	43	100
Lifetime		1	0	0	0	0	0	0	0	85	0	0	43	$100

E. J. Trivette

E. J. Trivette
B: 6/6/1936
Racing Hometown: Deep Gap, NC

Year	Rank	Starts	Poles	1	2	3	4	5	6–10	Laps	Laps Led	Races Led	Miles	$
1959	NR	4	0	0	0	0	0	0	0	534	0	0	285	175
1960	62	9	0	0	0	0	0	0	0	1,000	0	0	532	940
1961	80	6	0	0	0	0	0	0	1	667	0	0	360	700
1962	135	1	0	0	0	0	0	0	0	29	0	0	15	100
1963	51	11	0	0	0	0	0	0	2	1,996	0	0	1,368	1,965
1964	38	26	0	0	0	0	0	0	3	2,969	0	0	1,903	5,495
1965	15	39	0	0	0	0	0	0	7	7,485	0	0	4,935	13,248
1966	84	3	0	0	0	0	0	0	0	187	0	0	279	1,445
1967	55	7	0	0	0	0	0	0	1	1,418	0	0	1,155	2,360
1968	36	13	0	0	0	0	0	0	0	2,684	0	0	2,746	8,295
1969	11	49	0	0	0	0	0	0	15	11,110	0	0	9,046	35,896
1970	62	4	0	0	0	0	0	0	0	188	0	0	347	2,840
1971	60	5	0	0	0	0	0	0	0	914	0	0	759	1,895
Lifetime		177	0	0	0	0	0	0	29	31,181	0	0	23,728	$75,354

Maynard Troyer

Maynard Ray Troyer
B: 11/22/1938
Racing Hometown: Spencerport, NY

Year	Rank	Starts	Poles	1	2	3	4	5	6–10	Laps	Laps Led	Races Led	Miles	$
1971	38	13	0	0	0	0	1	0	2	1,617	0	0	2,884	13,115
1973	98	1	0	0	0	0	0	0	0	150	0	0	375	1,825
Lifetime		14	0	0	0	0	1	0	2	1,767	0	0	3,259	$14,940

Russ Truelove

Russell Truelove
Racing Hometown: Waterbury, CT

Year	Rank	Starts	Poles	1	2	3	4	5	6–10	Laps	Laps Led	Races Led	Miles	$
1953	86T	1	0	0	0	0	0	0	1		0	0		75
1955	50	6	0	0	0	0	0	0	2	738	0	0	689	585
1956	60	5	0	0	0	0	0	0	2	521	0	0	476	450
1957	189	1	0	0	0	0	0	0	0		0	0		0
Lifetime		13	0	0	0	0	0	0	5	1,259	0	0	1,165	$1,110

Jimmy Trull

James Trull
B: 1953
Racing Hometown: Ft. Mill, SC

Year	Rank	Starts	Poles	1	2	3	4	5	6–10	Laps	Laps Led	Races Led	Miles	$
1966	137	1	0	0	0	0	0	0	0	247	0	0	124	247
Lifetime		1	0	0	0	0	0	0	0	247	0	0	124	$247

Year	Rank	Starts	Poles	Finish						Laps	Laps Led	Races Led	Miles	$
				1	2	3	4	5	6–10					

Donald Tucker

Donald Tucker
Racing Hometown: Greensboro, NC

Year	Rank	Starts	Poles	1	2	3	4	5	6–10	Laps	Laps Led	Races Led	Miles	$
1965	31	9	0	0	0	0	1	0	2	1,597	0	0	1,703	5,830
Lifetime		9	0	0	0	0	1	0	2	1,597	0	0	1,703	$5,830

Reino Tulonen

Reino Tulonen
B: 8/20/1924
Racing Hometown: Fitchburg, MA

Year	Rank	Starts	Poles	1	2	3	4	5	6–10	Laps	Laps Led	Races Led	Miles	$
1951	74	4	0	0	0	0	0	1	0	353	0	0	441	400
Lifetime		4	0	0	0	0	0	1	0	353	0	0	441	$400

Dick Turcott

Richard Turcott
Racing Hometown: Brewerton, NY

Year	Rank	Starts	Poles	1	2	3	4	5	6–10	Laps	Laps Led	Races Led	Miles	$
1952	140T	1	0	0	0	0	0	0	0	163	0	0	82	25
Lifetime		1	0	0	0	0	0	0	0	163	0	0	82	$25

Rod Turcott

Rod Turcott
Racing Hometown: Brewerton, NY

Year	Rank	Starts	Poles	1	2	3	4	5	6–10	Laps	Laps Led	Races Led	Miles	$
1952	138	1	0	0	0	0	0	0	0	167	0	0	84	25
Lifetime		1	0	0	0	0	0	0	0	167	0	0	84	$25

Curtis Turner

Curtis Morton Turner (Pops)
B: 4/12/1924   D: 10/4/1970   *Killed in private plane crash with Clarence King.*
Racing Hometown: Roanoke, VA

Year	Rank	Starts	Poles	1	2	3	4	5	6–10	Laps	Laps Led	Races Led	Miles	$
1949	6	6	1	1	0	0	0	0	3	564	78	2	382	2,675
1950	5	16	4	4	1	1	1	0	0	**1,626**	**1,110**	**12**	1,390	8,190
1951	NR	12	0	3	0	0	0	0	2	1,164	513	6	948	3,980
1952	50	7	0	0	0	0	0	1	0	500	12	1	320	290
1953	10	19	3	1	0	1	1	0	2	1,396	191	4	1,370	4,347
1954	9	10	1	1	1	2	1	2	1	1,678	277	3	1,497	10,120
1955	34	9	0	0	1	1	2	0	0	928	14	1	832	2,605
1956	20	13	0	1	3	0	0	0	1	1,967	287	3	1,431	14,541
1957	22	10	1	0	2	0	0	0	2	1,397	109	4	1,304	4,830
1958	20	17	1	3	2	0	1	2	2	3,068	827	6	2,190	10,029
1959	24	10	1	2	1	0	1	0	0	1,293	438	5	1,175	3,845
1960	36	9	1	0	0	0	0	0	1	1,090	106	2	1,694	3,220
1961	NR	8	0	0	1	0	0	0	1	1,182	162	6	1,257	6,090
1965	39	7	0	1	0	1	0	1	0	1,360	256	2	1,288	18,175
1966	24	21	2	0	1	1	3	0	1	3,697	385	11	4,120	16,920
1967	71	4	2	0	0	0	0	0	0	241	6	1	524	7,875
1968	47	6	0	0	0	0	1	0	3	1,448	0	0	1,542	5,850
Lifetime		184	17	17	13	7	11	6	19	24,599	4,771	69	23,264	$122,155

Danny Turner

Daniel Turner
Racing Hometown: Atlanta, GA

Year	Rank	Starts	Poles	1	2	3	4	5	6–10	Laps	Laps Led	Races Led	Miles	$
1969	66	3	0	0	0	0	0	0	0	285	0	0	150	1,040
Lifetime		3	0	0	0	0	0	0	0	285	0	0	150	$1,040

E. J. Turner

E. J. Turner
Racing Hometown: Glenolden, PA

Year	Rank	Starts	Poles	1	2	3	4	5	6–10	Laps	Laps Led	Races Led	Miles	$
1954	182	1	0	0	0	0	0	0	0	199	0	0	199	50
1955	172	1	0	0	0	0	0	0	0	194	0	0	194	50
Lifetime		2	0	0	0	0	0	0	0	393	0	0	393	$100

Bill Tuten

William Tuten
Racing Hometown: Hialeah, FL

Year	Rank	Starts	Poles	1	2	3	4	5	6–10	Laps	Laps Led	Races Led	Miles	$
1954	NR	1	0	0	0	0	0	0	0	179	0	0	90	25
Lifetime		1	0	0	0	0	0	0	0	179	0	0	90	$25

Jack Tykarski

Jack Tykarski

Year	Rank	Starts	Poles	1	2	3	4	5	6–10	Laps	Laps Led	Races Led	Miles	$
1956	109	1	0	0	0	0	0	0	0	250	0	0	250	225
Lifetime		1	0	0	0	0	0	0	0	250	0	0	250	$225

Year	Rank	Starts	Poles	Finish 1	2	3	4	5	6–10	Laps	Laps Led	Races Led	Miles	$

Carl Tyler

Carl Tyler
B: 1927   D: 1/6/1993
Racing Hometown: Bradford, PA

Year	Rank	Starts	Poles	1	2	3	4	5	6–10	Laps	Laps Led	Races Led	Miles	$
1958	70	10	0	0	0	0	0	0	0	1,016	0	0	843	745
1959	99	2	0	0	0	0	0	0	0	63	0	0	158	150
Lifetime		12	0	0	0	0	0	0	0	1,079	0	0	1,001	$895

Cliff Tyler

Cliff Tyler Jr.
Deceased
Racing Hometown: Cotchogue, NY

Year	Rank	Starts	Poles	1	2	3	4	5	6–10	Laps	Laps Led	Races Led	Miles	$
1970	73	4	0	0	0	0	0	0	0	455	0	0	393	1,315
Lifetime		4	0	0	0	0	0	0	0	455	0	0	393	$1,315

Paul Tyler

Paul John Tyler II
B: 2/10/1942
Racing Hometown: Palo Alto, CA

Year	Rank	Starts	Poles	1	2	3	4	5	6–10	Laps	Laps Led	Races Led	Miles	$
1971	47	10	0	0	0	0	0	0	0	1,521	0	0	1,680	6,635
1972	53	4	0	0	0	0	0	0	1	1,125	0	0	1,312	4,200
1973	67	6	0	0	0	0	0	0	0	702	0	0	954	6,575
Lifetime		20	0	0	0	0	0	0	1	3,348	0	0	3,947	$17,410

Roy Tyner

William Leroy Tyner
B: 1/13/1937   D: 2/23/1989   *Shot in truck in Conover, NC; truck set afire.*
Racing Hometown: Red Springs, NC

Year	Rank	Starts	Poles	1	2	3	4	5	6–10	Laps	Laps Led	Races Led	Miles	$
1957	33	10	0	0	0	0	0	0	2	1,705	0	0	1,099	1,055
1958	59	22	0	0	0	0	0	1	2	3,148	0	0	1,951	2,550
1959	33	28	0	0	1	0	3	3	7	5,234	0	0	3,405	5,425
1960	52	23	0	0	0	0	1	0	4	2,076	0	0	1,808	2,930
1961	57	10	0	0	0	0	0	0	1	1,480	0	0	1,354	1,560
1963	85	8	0	0	0	0	0	0	0	381	0	0	193	1,345
1964	16	46	0	0	0	0	0	0	17	7,327	0	0	4,641	11,488
1965	36	28	0	0	0	0	1	0	5	3,448	0	0	2,171	6,696
1966	41	26	0	0	0	0	0	0	4	3,511	0	0	1,790	4,435
1967	43	27	0	0	0	0	0	0	1	2,966	0	0	2,300	8,290
1968	10	48	0	0	0	0	2	2	10	8,789	0	0	5,857	20,247
1969	31	21	0	0	0	0	0	0	1	3,285	0	0	3,118	12,317
1970	42	14	0	0	0	0	0	0	3	1,890	0	0	1,197	5,565
Lifetime		311	0	0	1	0	7	6	57	45,240	0	0	30,884	$83,903

Bob Tyrell

Robert Tyrell
Racing Hometown: Los Angeles, CA

Year	Rank	Starts	Poles	1	2	3	4	5	6–10	Laps	Laps Led	Races Led	Miles	$
1954	106	1	0	0	0	0	0	0	0	450	0	0	225	100
1959	NR	1	0	0	0	0	0	0	0	406	0	0	162	120
Lifetime		2	0	0	0	0	0	0	0	856	0	0	387	$220

Ed Tyson

Edward Tyson
Racing Hometown: Langhorne, PA

Year	Rank	Starts	Poles	1	2	3	4	5	6–10	Laps	Laps Led	Races Led	Miles	$
1949	74	1	0	0	0	0	0	0	0	169	0	0	169	50
Lifetime		1	0	0	0	0	0	0	0	169	0	0	169	$50

D. K. Ulrich

Donald Keith Ulrich
B: 4/10/1944
Racing Hometown: Woodbury, NJ

Year	Rank	Starts	Poles	1	2	3	4	5	6–10	Laps	Laps Led	Races Led	Miles	$
1971	53	12	0	0	0	0	0	0	0	1,526	0	0	1,064	3,955
1972	64	4	0	0	0	0	0	0	0	1,001	0	0	1,041	2,695
1973	36	11	0	0	0	0	0	0	0	2,006	0	0	2,125	8,695
1974	32	15	0	0	0	0	0	0	0	3,194	0	0	3,606	12,305
1975	27	16	0	0	0	0	0	0	1	3,448	0	0	4,093	16,525
1976	14	30	0	0	0	0	0	0	2	8,489	0	0	9,932	69,435
1977	15	30	0	0	0	0	0	0	0	6,735	0	0	7,648	69,677
1978	22	22	0	0	0	0	0	0	3	6,175	1	1	7,425	54,550
1979	12	31	0	0	0	0	0	0	5	8,995	0	0	10,043	113,458
1980	38	11	0	0	0	0	0	0	1	1,734	0	0	1,898	23,085
1981	32	15	0	0	0	0	1	0	0	4,504	0	0	4,507	38,095
1982	24	25	0	0	0	0	0	0	1	7,102	0	0	7,587	78,130

Year	Rank	Starts	Poles	Finish						Laps	Laps Led	Races Led	Miles	$
				1	2	3	4	5	6–10	Laps	Led	Led	Miles	$

D. K. Ulrich *continued*

1983	24	22	0	0	0	0	0	0	2	6,983	0	0	7,875	85,245
1984	42	9	0	0	0	0	0	0	0	2,565	0	0	2,513	31,040
1985	NR	1	0	0	0	0	0	0	0	286	0	0	286	1,350
1986	37	10	0	0	0	0	0	0	0	2,159	0	0	2,554	47,795
1987	40	7	0	0	0	0	0	0	0	1,876	0	0	1,844	30,915
1990	91T	1	0	0	0	0	0	0	0	185	0	0	139	4,265
1992	90T	1	0	0	0	0	0	0	0	21	0	0	21	4,165
Lifetime		273	0	0	0	0	1	0	15	68,984	1	1	76,199	$695,380

Al Unser

Alfred Unser
B: 5/29/1939
Racing Hometown: Albuquerque, NM

1968	NR	2	0	0	0	0	1	0	1	382	1	1	991	7,800
1969	NR	1	0	0	0	0	1	0	0	183	0	0	494	3,825
1986	106	2	0	0	0	0	0	0	0	171	0	0	436	4,275
Lifetime		5	0	0	0	0	2	0	1	736	1	1	1,921	$15,900

Al Unser Jr.

Alfred Unser Jr. (Little Al)
B: 4/19/1962
Racing Hometown: Albuquerque, NM

1993	81T	1	0	0	0	0	0	0	0	157	0	0	393	23,005
Lifetime		1	0	0	0	0	0	0	0	157	0	0	393	$23,005

Bobby Unser

Robert William Unser
B: 2/20/1934
Racing Hometown: Albuquerque, NM

1969	NR	2	0	0	0	0	1	0	0	106	2	2	265	1,900
1972	NR	1	0	0	0	0	0	0	0	8	0	0	12	603
1973	NR	1	0	0	0	0	1	0	0	186	0	0	487	4,520
Lifetime		4	0	0	0	0	2	0	0	300	2	2	764	$7,023

Red Untiedt

Red Untiedt
Racing Hometown: Davenport, IA

1953	NR	1	0	0	0	0	0	0	0		0	0		25
Lifetime		1	0	0	0	0	0	0	0		0	0		$25

Tom Usry

Thomas R. Usry
B: 2/9/1937
Racing Hometown: Sanford, NC

1970	NR	1	0	0	0	0	0	0	0	226	0	0	82	255
Lifetime		1	0	0	0	0	0	0	0	226	0	0	82	$255

Dub Utsman

Dub Utsman
Racing Hometown: Bluff City, TN

1961	179	1	0	0	0	0	0	0	0	200	0	0	100	125
Lifetime		1	0	0	0	0	0	0	0	200	0	0	100	$125

John A. Utsman

John A. Utsman
B: 12/7/1939
Racing Hometown: Bluff City, TN

1973	64	3	0	0	0	0	0	0	1	775	0	0	780	2,965
1976	56	4	0	0	0	0	0	0	0	1,276	0	0	1,859	8,565
1978	59	4	0	0	0	0	0	0	0	612	0	0	1,026	7,740
1979	111T	1	0	0	0	0	0	0	0	101	0	0	253	2,850
1980	76	2	0	0	0	0	0	0	0	613	0	0	620	4,035
Lifetime		14	0	0	0	0	0	0	1	3,377	0	0	4,537	$26,155

Layman Utsman

Layman Utsman
Racing Hometown: Bluff City, TN

1959	NR	2	0	0	0	0	0	0	0	235	0	0	131	50

Year	Rank	Starts	Poles	Finish						Laps	Laps Led	Races Led	Miles	$
				1	2	3	4	5	6–10					

Layman Utsman *continued*

Year	Rank	Starts	Poles	1	2	3	4	5	6–10	Laps	Laps Led	Races Led	Miles	$
1961	180	1	0	0	0	0	0	0	0	35	0	0	18	100
Lifetime		3	0	0	0	0	0	0	0	270	0	0	149	$150

Sherman Utsman

Sherman Utsman
Racing Hometown: Bluff City, TN

Year	Rank	Starts	Poles	1	2	3	4	5	6–10	Laps	Laps Led	Races Led	Miles	$
1956	82	5	0	0	0	0	0	0	1	948	0	0	801	475
1961	102	1	0	0	0	0	0	0	1	481	0	0	241	450
1962	32	12	0	0	0	0	0	1	3	3,293	0	0	2,314	3,580
1963	78	3	0	0	0	0	0	0	3	582	0	0	204	555
Lifetime		21	0	0	0	0	0	1	8	5,304	0	0	3,559	$5,060

Pete Vail

Peter Vail
Racing Hometown: Ossining, NY

Year	Rank	Starts	Poles	1	2	3	4	5	6–10	Laps	Laps Led	Races Led	Miles	$
1952	156	2	0	0	0	0	0	0	0	152	0	0	76	50
Lifetime		2	0	0	0	0	0	0	0	152	0	0	76	$50

Joe Valente

Joseph Valente
Racing Hometown: Berkeley, CA

Year	Rank	Starts	Poles	1	2	3	4	5	6–10	Laps	Laps Led	Races Led	Miles	$
1954	54	4	0	0	0	0	0	0	1	1,066	0	0	650	275
Lifetime		4	0	0	0	0	0	0	1	1,066	0	0	650	$275

Sarel van der Merwe

Sarel van der Merwe
B: 12/5/1946
Racing Hometown: Port Elizabeth, South Africa

Year	Rank	Starts	Poles	1	2	3	4	5	6–10	Laps	Laps Led	Races Led	Miles	$
1988	—	0												1,400
1990	78T	1	0	0	0	0	0	0	0	77	0	0	187	12,070
Lifetime		1	0	0	0	0	0	0	0	77	0	0	187	$13,470

Carl Van Horn

Carl Van Horn
Racing Hometown: Belvedere, NJ

Year	Rank	Starts	Poles	1	2	3	4	5	6–10	Laps	Laps Led	Races Led	Miles	$
1975	94	1	0	0	0	0	0	0	0	110	0	0	275	1,355
Lifetime		1	0	0	0	0	0	0	0	110	0	0	275	$1,355

Eddie Van Horn

Edward Van Horn
Racing Hometown: Clifton, NJ

Year	Rank	Starts	Poles	1	2	3	4	5	6–10	Laps	Laps Led	Races Led	Miles	$
1952	NR	3	0	0	0	0	0	0	1	501	0	0	383	110
1953	140T	1	0	0	0	0	0	0	0		0	0		25
1954	121	2	0	0	0	0	0	0	0	197	0	0	111	25
Lifetime		6	0	0	0	0	0	0	1	698	0	0	494	$160

J. C. Van Landingham

J. C. Van Landingham
Racing Hometown: Deland, FL

Year	Rank	Starts	Poles	1	2	3	4	5	6–10	Laps	Laps Led	Races Led	Miles	$
1950	50	1	0	0	0	0	0	1	0	48	0	0	200	450
Lifetime		1	0	0	0	0	0	1	0	48	0	0	200	$450

Van Van Wey

Van Van Wey
Racing Hometown: W. Terre Haute, IN

Year	Rank	Starts	Poles	1	2	3	4	5	6–10	Laps	Laps Led	Races Led	Miles	$
1954	48	3	0	0	0	0	0	0	0	629	0	0	801	495
1955	200	1	0	0	0	0	0	0	0	247	0	0	340	60
Lifetime		4	0	0	0	0	0	0	0	876	0	0	1,141	$555

Bill Vanderhoff

William Vanderhoff
Racing Hometown: Roseland, NJ

Year	Rank	Starts	Poles	1	2	3	4	5	6–10	Laps	Laps Led	Races Led	Miles	$
1967	110T	1	0	0	0	0	0	0	0	114	0	0	57	100
1968	53	11	0	0	0	0	0	0	0	939	0	0	440	2,050
Lifetime		12	0	0	0	0	0	0	0	1,053	0	0	497	$2,150

Year	Rank	Starts	Poles			Finish				Laps	Laps Led	Races Led	Miles	$
				1	2	3	4	5	6–10					

Jim Vandiver

James Enoch Vandiver
B: 12/13/1939
Racing Hometown: Huntersville, NC

Year	Rank	Starts	Poles	1	2	3	4	5	6–10	Laps	Laps Led	Races Led	Miles	$
1968	124	1	0	0	0	0	0	0	0	5	0	0	2	100
1969	96	3	0	0	1	0	0	0	1	726	102	1	833	13,925
1970	45	14	0	0	0	0	0	0	5	2,634	6	1	3,671	16,080
1971	48	7	0	0	0	0	0	1	3	1,423	0	0	2,566	13,575
1972	31	16	0	0	0	2	0	0	1	2,871	6	1	3,462	28,533
1973	31	10	0	0	0	0	0	0	4	2,431	0	0	3,834	18,586
1974	40	7	0	0	0	0	0	0	1	1,061	1	1	1,996	15,909
1975	30	13	0	0	0	0	1	0	3	2,929	1	1	3,625	24,200
1976	86T	1	0	0	0	0	0	0	0	176	0	0	468	3,735
1977	90	1	0	0	0	0	0	0	0	137	0	0	343	3,520
1978	80	2	0	0	0	0	0	0	0	362	0	0	562	3,530
1979	61	4	0	0	0	0	0	0	0	716	1	1	1,069	8,015
1980	52	4	0	0	0	0	0	0	1	610	0	0	1,136	13,185
1983	88	2	0	0	0	0	0	0	0	448	0	0	674	4,810
Lifetime		85	0	0	1	2	1	1	19	16,529	117	6	24,241	$166,528

Keith VanHoughten

Keith VanHoughten

Year	Rank	Starts	Poles	1	2	3	4	5	6–10	Laps	Laps Led	Races Led	Miles	$
1991	NR	1	0	0	0	0	0	0	0	13	0	0	13	3,475
Lifetime		1	0	0	0	0	0	0	0	13	0	0	13	$3,475

Bud Vaughn

Bud Vaughn
Racing Hometown: Inglewood, CA

Year	Rank	Starts	Poles	1	2	3	4	5	6–10	Laps	Laps Led	Races Led	Miles	$
1957	117	2	0	0	0	0	0	0	0	265	0	0	133	145
1965	NR	4	0	0	0	0	0	0	1	164	0	0	72	840
Lifetime		6	0	0	0	0	0	0	1	429	0	0	205	$985

Jimmy Vaughn

James Dotson Vaughn
B: 3/20/1942
Racing Hometown: Greenville, SC

Year	Rank	Starts	Poles	1	2	3	4	5	6–10	Laps	Laps Led	Races Led	Miles	$
1965	NR	4	0	0	0	0	0	0	0	135	0	0	68	420
1969	NR	1	0	0	0	0	0	0	1	159	0	0	423	2,000
1971	NR	3	0	0	0	0	0	0	0	575	0	0	294	1,015
Lifetime		8	0	0	0	0	0	0	1	869	0	0	784	$3,435

Robert Vaughn

Robert Vaughn
Racing Hometown: Jackson, NJ

Year	Rank	Starts	Poles	1	2	3	4	5	6–10	Laps	Laps Led	Races Led	Miles	$
1965	73	2	0	0	0	0	0	0	0	5	0	0	13	1,160
Lifetime		2	0	0	0	0	0	0	0	5	0	0	13	$1,160

Billy Vee

William Vee
Racing Hometown: Rochester, NY

Year	Rank	Starts	Poles	1	2	3	4	5	6–10	Laps	Laps Led	Races Led	Miles	$
1954	NR	1	0	0	0	0	0	0	0	168	0	0	84	25
Lifetime		1	0	0	0	0	0	0	0	168	0	0	84	$25

Bill Venturini

William Venturini
B: 2/14/1953
Racing Hometown: Chicago, IL

Year	Rank	Starts	Poles	1	2	3	4	5	6–10	Laps	Laps Led	Races Led	Miles	$
1989	100	1	0	0	0	0	0	0	0	80	0	0	160	2,975
1990	45	4	0	0	0	0	0	0	0	702	0	0	1,647	25,270
1991	74T	2	0	0	0	0	0	0	0	71	0	0	146	10,125
1993	—	0												1,000
Lifetime		7	0	0	0	0	0	0	0	853	0	0	1,952	$39,370

Dick Vermillion

Richard Vermillion
Racing Hometown: Corbin, KY

Year	Rank	Starts	Poles	1	2	3	4	5	6–10	Laps	Laps Led	Races Led	Miles	$
1954	130	1	0	0	0	0	0	0	0	139	0	0	70	25
Lifetime		1	0	0	0	0	0	0	0	139	0	0	70	$25

Year	Rank	Starts	Poles	Finish 1	2	3	4	5	6–10	Laps	Laps Led	Races Led	Miles	$

Don Vershure

Donald Vershure
Racing Hometown: Atlanta, GA

Year	Rank	Starts	Poles	1	2	3	4	5	6–10	Laps	Laps Led	Races Led	Miles	$
1953	157	3	0	0	0	0	0	0	0	86	0	0	66	75
Lifetime		3	0	0	0	0	0	0	0	86	0	0	66	$75

Bill Vesler

William Vesler
Racing Hometown: Chicago, IL

Year	Rank	Starts	Poles	1	2	3	4	5	6–10	Laps	Laps Led	Races Led	Miles	$
1956	256	1	0	0	0	0	0	0	0	50	0	0	25	41
Lifetime		1	0	0	0	0	0	0	0	50	0	0	25	$41

Lou Volk

Louis Volk
B: 12/2/1910
Racing Hometown: Paterson, NJ

Year	Rank	Starts	Poles	1	2	3	4	5	6–10	Laps	Laps Led	Races Led	Miles	$
1949	41	1	0	0	0	0	0	0	1	182	0	0	182	125
1951	N/A	1	0	0	0	0	0	0	0		0	0		25
Lifetime		2	0	0	0	0	0	0	1	182	0	0	182	$150

Eli Vukovich

Eli Vukovich
Racing Hometown: Fresno, CA

Year	Rank	Starts	Poles	1	2	3	4	5	6–10	Laps	Laps Led	Races Led	Miles	$
1954	NR	1	0	0	0	0	0	0	0	262	0	0	131	25
Lifetime		1	0	0	0	0	0	0	0	262	0	0	131	$25

Bobby Waddell

Robert Waddell
Racing Hometown: N. Wilkesboro, NC

Year	Rank	Starts	Poles	1	2	3	4	5	6–10	Laps	Laps Led	Races Led	Miles	$
1955	55	7	0	0	0	0	0	0	0	992	0	0	942	385
1956	91	8	0	0	0	0	0	0	0	490	0	0	299	335
1957	175T	1	0	0	0	0	0	0	0	39	0	0	20	50
1959	88	7	0	0	0	0	0	0	0	512	0	0	262	360
1960	NR	1	0	0	0	0	0	0	0	168	0	0	84	50
1961	55	7	0	0	0	0	0	0	2	951	0	0	864	1,025
1962	91	6	0	0	0	0	0	0	0	303	0	0	161	470
Lifetime		37	0	0	0	0	0	0	2	3,455	0	0	2,633	$2,675

Billy Wade

Billy Drew Wade
B: 2/28/1930 D: 1/5/1965 *Killed in tire test @ Daytona.*
Racing Hometown: Houston, TX

Year	Rank	Starts	Poles	1	2	3	4	5	6–10	Laps	Laps Led	Races Led	Miles	$
1962	46	4	0	0	0	0	0	0	2	1,054	0	0	938	1,350
1963	16	31	0	0	1	0	2	1	10	6,008	21	2	4,989	15,204
1964	4	35	5	4	0	4	3	1	13	7,627	954	14	6,724	36,095
Lifetime		70	5	4	1	4	5	2	25	14,689	975	16	12,651	$52,649

Jack Wade

Jack Wade
Racing Hometown: Charlottesville, VA

Year	Rank	Starts	Poles	1	2	3	4	5	6–10	Laps	Laps Led	Races Led	Miles	$
1951	N/A	2	0	0	0	0	0	0	0		0	0		50
Lifetime		2	0	0	0	0	0	0	0		0	0		$50

Pat Wade

Patrick Wade

Year	Rank	Starts	Poles	1	2	3	4	5	6–10	Laps	Laps Led	Races Led	Miles	$
1951	N/A	1	0	0	0	0	0	0	0		0	0		25
Lifetime		1	0	0	0	0	0	0	0		0	0		$25

Ken Wagner

Kenneth W. Wagner
B: 9/19/1917
Racing Hometown: Pennington, NJ

Year	Rank	Starts	Poles	1	2	3	4	5	6–10	Laps	Laps Led	Races Led	Miles	$
1949	50	3	1	0	0	0	0	0	0	412	0	0	206	100
1950	72	3	0	0	0	0	0	0	1	274	0	0	313	250
1956	170	3	0	0	0	0	0	0	0	112	0	0	64	60
Lifetime		9	1	0	0	0	0	0	1	798	0	0	583	$410

Al Wagoner

Al Wagoner
Racing Hometown: Winston-Salem, NC

Year	Rank	Starts	Poles	1	2	3	4	5	6–10	Laps	Laps Led	Races Led	Miles	$
1949	37T	1	0	0	0	0	0	0	1	178	0	0	89	75
Lifetime		1	0	0	0	0	0	0	1	178	0	0	89	$75

Year	Rank	Starts	Poles	Finish						Laps	Laps Led	Races Led	Miles	$
				1	2	3	4	5	6–10					

Chuck Wahl

Chuck Wahl
B: 12/20/1950
Racing Hometown: Burbank, CA

Year	Rank	Starts	Poles	1	2	3	4	5	6–10	Laps	Laps Led	Races Led	Miles	$
1973	123	1	0	0	0	0	0	0	0	7	0	0	18	630
1974	74	2	0	0	0	0	0	0	1	275	0	0	702	2,870
1975	56	3	0	0	0	0	0	0	1	299	0	0	780	4,020
1976	71	2	0	0	0	0	0	0	0	182	3	1	477	2,705
1977	70	2	0	0	0	0	0	0	0	155	0	0	406	2,420
1978	79	2	0	0	0	0	0	0	0	102	0	0	262	1,520
1980	NR	1	0	0	0	0	0	0	0	88	0	0	231	1,005
Lifetime		13	0	0	0	0	0	0	2	1,108	3	1	2,876	$15,170

Frank Waite

Frank Waite
Racing Hometown: Tucker, GA

Year	Rank	Starts	Poles	1	2	3	4	5	6–10	Laps	Laps Led	Races Led	Miles	$
1963	81	4	0	0	0	0	0	0	0	617	0	0	309	425
Lifetime		4	0	0	0	0	0	0	0	617	0	0	309	$425

Augie Walackas

August Walackas
Racing Hometown: Brockton, MA

Year	Rank	Starts	Poles	1	2	3	4	5	6–10	Laps	Laps Led	Races Led	Miles	$
1950	NR	1	0	0	0	0	0	0	0		0	0		0
1951	53	4	0	0	0	1	0	0	2		0	0		525
Lifetime		5	0	0	0	1	0	0	2		0	0		$525

Bob Walden

Robert Walden
Racing Hometown: High Point, NC

Year	Rank	Starts	Poles	1	2	3	4	5	6–10	Laps	Laps Led	Races Led	Miles	$
1953	46	4	0	0	0	0	0	0	2	325	0	0	180	250
1958	56	14	0	0	0	0	1	0	8	2,104	0	0	1,167	1,810
Lifetime		18	0	0	0	0	1	0	10	2,429	0	0	1,347	$2,060

Lennie Waldo

Lennie Frank Waldo
B: 2/3/1944
Racing Hometown: Columbus, OH

Year	Rank	Starts	Poles	1	2	3	4	5	6–10	Laps	Laps Led	Races Led	Miles	$
1968	59	4	0	0	0	0	0	0	0	671	0	0	1,091	3,620
Lifetime		4	0	0	0	0	0	0	0	671	0	0	1,091	$3,620

Sam Waldrop

Samuel Waldrop
Racing Hometown: Charlotte, NC

Year	Rank	Starts	Poles	1	2	3	4	5	6–10	Laps	Laps Led	Races Led	Miles	$
1968	116	1	0	0	0	0	0	0	0	171	0	0	86	130
Lifetime		1	0	0	0	0	0	0	0	171	0	0	86	$130

Robert Wales

Robert E. Wales (Paddlefoot)
Racing Hometown: Pleasant Grove, AL

Year	Rank	Starts	Poles	1	2	3	4	5	6–10	Laps	Laps Led	Races Led	Miles	$
1972	118	2	0	0	0	0	0	0	0	14	0	0	37	1,510
Lifetime		2	0	0	0	0	0	0	0	14	0	0	37	$1,510

Bill Walker

William Walker
Racing Hometown: Springfield, MA

Year	Rank	Starts	Poles	1	2	3	4	5	6–10	Laps	Laps Led	Races Led	Miles	$
1956	83	2	0	0	0	0	0	0	1	418	0	0	328	600
1957	54	3	0	0	0	1	0	0	1	355	0	0	371	950
1958	NR	1	0	0	0	0	0	0	0	160	0	0	53	85
Lifetime		6	0	0	0	1	0	0	2	933	0	0	752	$1,635

Don Walker

Donald Walker
Racing Hometown: Palmer, WA

Year	Rank	Starts	Poles	1	2	3	4	5	6–10	Laps	Laps Led	Races Led	Miles	$
1964	98	1	0	0	0	0	0	0	0	106	0	0	286	525
1965	126	1	0	0	0	0	0	0	0	14	0	0	38	500
1966	71	1	0	0	0	0	0	0	0	154	0	0	416	590
Lifetime		3	0	0	0	0	0	0	0	274	0	0	740	$1,615

Jimmy Walker

James Walker

Year	Rank	Starts	Poles	1	2	3	4	5	6–10	Laps	Laps Led	Races Led	Miles	$
1982	60	3	0	0	0	0	0	0	0	131	0	0	130	2,320
1983	89	2	0	0	0	0	0	0	0	289	0	0	179	1,505

Year	Rank	Starts	Poles	1	2	3	4	5	6-10	Laps	Laps Led	Races Led	Miles	$

Jimmy Walker *continued*

Year	Rank	Starts	Poles	1	2	3	4	5	6-10	Laps	Laps Led	Races Led	Miles	$
1985	83	1	0	0	0	0	0	0	0	180	0	0	180	1,350
Lifetime		6	0	0	0	0	0	0	0	600	0	0	489	$5,175

John Walker

John Walker

Year	Rank	Starts	Poles	1	2	3	4	5	6-10	Laps	Laps Led	Races Led	Miles	$
1958	NR	1	0	0	0	0	0	0	1	135	0	0	45	155
Lifetime		1	0	0	0	0	0	0	1	135	0	0	45	$155

Mitch Walker

Mitchell Walker

Year	Rank	Starts	Poles	1	2	3	4	5	6-10	Laps	Laps Led	Races Led	Miles	$
1964	NR	1	0	0	0	0	0	0	0	174	0	0	87	130
Lifetime		1	0	0	0	0	0	0	0	174	0	0	87	$130

Murrace Walker

Murrace Walker
Racing Hometown: Whiteville, NC

Year	Rank	Starts	Poles	1	2	3	4	5	6-10	Laps	Laps Led	Races Led	Miles	$
1950	111	1	0	0	0	0	0	0	0	358	0	0	448	0
1951	N/A	1	0	0	0	0	0	0	0	104	0	0	130	0
Lifetime		2	0	0	0	0	0	0	0	462	0	0	578	$0

Bryant Wallace

Hugh Bryant Wallace
Racing Hometown: Concord, NC

Year	Rank	Starts	Poles	1	2	3	4	5	6-10	Laps	Laps Led	Races Led	Miles	$
1961	46	2	0	0	0	0	0	0	0	81	0	0	40	100
1966	113	1	0	0	0	0	0	0	0	39	0	0	20	100
1968	NR	1	0	0	0	0	0	0	0	118	0	0	59	100
Lifetime		4	0	0	0	0	0	0	0	238	0	0	118	$300

Cotton Wallace

Carl Wallace
Racing Hometown: Atlanta, GA

Year	Rank	Starts	Poles	1	2	3	4	5	6-10	Laps	Laps Led	Races Led	Miles	$
1965	NR	1	0	0	0	0	0	0	0	5	0	0	8	500
Lifetime		1	0	0	0	0	0	0	0	5	0	0	8	$500

Kenny Wallace

Kenneth Wallace
B: 8/23/1963
Racing Hometown: St. Louis, MO

Year	Rank	Starts	Poles	1	2	3	4	5	6-10	Laps	Laps Led	Races Led	Miles	$
1990	81T	1	0	0	0	0	0	0	0	315	0	0	197	6,050
1991	44	5	0	0	0	0	0	0	0	1,544	1	1	1,823	58,325
1993	23	30	0	0	0	0	0	0	3	8,806	1	1	10,551	330,325
1994	40	12	0	0	0	0	1	0	2	4,426	4	3	4,686	235,005
1995	42	11	0	0	0	0	0	0	0	3,127	0	0	4,070	151,700
1996	28	30	0	0	0	0	0	0	2	8,415	7	2	9,896	457,665
Lifetime		89	0	0	0	0	1	0	7	26,633	13	7	31,223	$1,239,070

Mike Wallace

Michael Wallace
B: 3/10/1959
Racing Hometown: St. Louis, MO

Year	Rank	Starts	Poles	1	2	3	4	5	6-10	Laps	Laps Led	Races Led	Miles	$
1991	62	2	0	0	0	0	0	0	0	315	0	0	351	7,000
1992	50	3	0	0	0	0	0	0	0	1,042	0	0	1,347	20,215
1993	46	4	0	0	0	0	0	0	0	1,287	0	0	1,819	30,125
1994	33	22	0	0	0	0	0	1	0	6,672	13	1	8,629	265,115
1995	34	26	0	0	0	0	0	0	1	6,819	1	1	8,807	428,006
1996	41	11	0	0	0	0	0	0	0	2,876	3	1	3,625	169,082
Lifetime		68	0	0	0	0	0	1	1	19,011	17	3	24,577	$919,543

Rusty Wallace

Russell William Wallace
B: 8/14/1956
Racing Hometown: St. Louis, MO

Year	Rank	Starts	Poles	1	2	3	4	5	6-10	Laps	Laps Led	Races Led	Miles	$
1980	57	2	0	0	1	0	0	0	0	653	0	0	987	22,860
1981	64	4	0	0	0	0	0	0	1	838	0	0	1,431	12,895
1982	65	3	0	0	0	0	0	0	0	418	0	0	669	7,655
1983	—	0												1,100
1984	14	30	0	0	0	0	1	1	2	8,868	11	7	10,024	201,739
1985	19	28	0	0	0	0	0	2	6	7,271	28	1	8,376	233,670
1986	6	29	0	2	0	0	2	0	12	8,486	427	8	10,416	557,354

Year	Rank	Starts	Poles	Finish						Laps	Laps Led	Races Led	Miles	$
				1	2	3	4	5	6–10	Laps	Led	Led	Miles	$

Rusty Wallace *continued*

Year	Rank	Starts	Poles	1	2	3	4	5	6–10	Laps	Laps Led	Races Led	Miles	$
1987	5	29	1	2	3	2	1	1	7	8,323	450	15	9,668	690,652
1988	2	29	2	6	5	4	2	2	4	9,222	908	18	11,180	1,411,567
1989	1	29	4	6	4	0	2	1	7	9,104	2,021	**23**	10,781	2,237,950
1990	6	29	2	2	3	2	0	2	7	8,459	1,137	16	10,073	954,129
1991	10	29	2	2	0	3	2	2	5	8,316	524	14	10,147	502,073
1992	13	29	1	1	2	1	1	0	7	8,759	673	11	10,450	657,925
1993	2	30	3	10	4	2	1	2	2	9,641	**2,860**	20	11,231	1,702,154
1994	3	31	2	8	3	1	4	1	3	9,281	**2,142**	19	10,730	1,959,072
1995	5	31	0	2	4	6	2	1	4	9,497	1,066	17	11,563	1,642,837
1996	7	31	0	5	1	0	1	1	10	8,383	965	13	10,159	1,665,315
Lifetime		393	17	46	30	21	19	16	77	115,519	13,212	182	137,883	$14,460,947
											8th			4th

Walter Wallace

Walter Wallace
Racing Hometown: Nashville, TN

Year	Rank	Starts	Poles	1	2	3	4	5	6–10	Laps	Laps Led	Races Led	Miles	$
1966	95	1	0	0	0	0	0	0	0	379	0	0	190	300
1967	125	1	0	0	0	0	0	0	0	11	0	0	6	100
1976	76	2	0	0	0	0	0	0	0	437	0	0	260	775
Lifetime		4	0	0	0	0	0	0	0	827	0	0	455	$1,175

Edgar Wallen

Edgar Wallen
Racing Hometown: Richmond, VA

Year	Rank	Starts	Poles	1	2	3	4	5	6–10	Laps	Laps Led	Races Led	Miles	$
1966	90	3	0	0	0	0	0	0	0	524	0	0	238	360
Lifetime		3	0	0	0	0	0	0	0	524	0	0	238	$360

Guy Waller

Guy Waller (Crash)
B: 2/9/1919
Racing Hometown: Atlanta, GA

Year	Rank	Starts	Poles	1	2	3	4	5	6–10	Laps	Laps Led	Races Led	Miles	$
1951	N/A	1	0	0	0	0	0	0	0	52	0	0	39	25
Lifetime		1	0	0	0	0	0	0	0	52	0	0	39	$25

Claude Wallington

Claude Wallington

Year	Rank	Starts	Poles	1	2	3	4	5	6–10	Laps	Laps Led	Races Led	Miles	$
1951	82	2	0	0	0	0	0	0	1		0	0		225
Lifetime		2	0	0	0	0	0	0	1		0	0		$225

Bob Walters

Robert William Walters
Racing Hometown: Salisbury, NC

Year	Rank	Starts	Poles	1	2	3	4	5	6–10	Laps	Laps Led	Races Led	Miles	$
1951	N/A	6	0	0	0	0	0	0	0	151	0	0	124	125
Lifetime		6	0	0	0	0	0	0	0	151	0	0	124	$125

Dan Walters

Daniel Walters
Racing Hometown: Griffen, IN

Year	Rank	Starts	Poles	1	2	3	4	5	6–10	Laps	Laps Led	Races Led	Miles	$
1953	NR	1	0	0	0	0	0	0	0	15	0	0	61	0
Lifetime		1	0	0	0	0	0	0	0	15	0	0	61	$0

Dick Walters

Richard Walters

Year	Rank	Starts	Poles	1	2	3	4	5	6–10	Laps	Laps Led	Races Led	Miles	$
1955	177	1	0	0	0	0	0	0	0	78	0	0	78	100
1957	NR	3	0	0	0	0	0	0	1	499	0	0	327	290
1958	99	4	0	0	0	0	0	0	0	305	0	0	129	290
Lifetime		8	0	0	0	0	0	0	1	882	0	0	534	$680

Lucky Walters

Lucky Walters

Year	Rank	Starts	Poles	1	2	3	4	5	6–10	Laps	Laps Led	Races Led	Miles	$
1954	NR	1	0	0	0	0	0	0	0	18	0	0	27	0
Lifetime		1	0	0	0	0	0	0	0	18	0	0	27	$0

Nook Walters

H. H. Walters
D: 1991
Racing Hometown: Niles, OH

Year	Rank	Starts	Poles	1	2	3	4	5	6–10	Laps	Laps Led	Races Led	Miles	$
1951	N/A	2	0	0	0	0	0	0	0		0	0		50
1952	120T	1	0	0	0	0	0	0	0	171	0	0	86	25

Year	Rank	Starts	Poles	Finish 1	2	3	4	5	6–10	Laps	Laps Led	Races Led	Miles	$

Nook Walters *continued*

Year	Rank	Starts	Poles	1	2	3	4	5	6–10	Laps	Laps Led	Races Led	Miles	$
1960	NR	1	0	0	0	0	1	0	0	179	0	0	90	275
Lifetime		4	0	0	0	0	1	0	0	350	0	0	175	$350

Sonny Walters

K. Sonny Walters
Racing Hometown: Syracuse, NY

Year	Rank	Starts	Poles	1	2	3	4	5	6–10	Laps	Laps Led	Races Led	Miles	$
1954	NR	1	0	0	0	0	0	0	0	134	0	0	67	0
1956	245	1	0	0	0	0	0	0	0	20	0	0	20	50
Lifetime		2	0	0	0	0	0	0	0	154	0	0	87	$50

Salt Walther

David Walther
B: 11/22/1947
Racing Hometown: Dayton, OH

Year	Rank	Starts	Poles	1	2	3	4	5	6–10	Laps	Laps Led	Races Led	Miles	$
1975	NR	2	0	0	0	0	0	0	0	240	0	0	506	2,330
1976	NR	1	0	0	0	0	0	0	0	187	0	0	468	5,880
1977	NR	1	0	0	0	0	0	0	0	114	0	0	285	2,725
Lifetime		4	0	0	0	0	0	0	0	541	0	0	1,259	$10,935

Chuck Walton

Chuck Walton

Year	Rank	Starts	Poles	1	2	3	4	5	6–10	Laps	Laps Led	Races Led	Miles	$
1985	95T	1	0	0	0	0	0	0	0	5	0	0	5	875
Lifetime		1	0	0	0	0	0	0	0	5	0	0	5	$875

Paul Walton

Paul Walton
Racing Hometown: High Point, NC

Year	Rank	Starts	Poles	1	2	3	4	5	6–10	Laps	Laps Led	Races Led	Miles	$
1958	NR	1	0	0	0	0	0	0	0	144	0	0	36	130
1959	NR	1	0	0	0	0	0	0	0	112	0	0	70	60
Lifetime		2	0	0	0	0	0	0	0	256	0	0	106	$190

Darrell Waltrip

Darrell Waltrip
B: 2/5/1947
Racing Hometown: Franklin, TN

Year	Rank	Starts	Poles	1	2	3	4	5	6–10	Laps	Laps Led	Races Led	Miles	$
1972	56	5	0	0	0	1	0	0	2	1,211	7	1	1,653	8,615
1973	28	19	0	0	1	0	0	0	4	3,783	50	3	5,352	42,466
1974	19	16	1	0	1	3	2	1	4	4,649	103	5	6,013	67,775
1975	7	28	2	2	2	2	3	2	3	7,240	562	13	7,425	160,192
1976	8	30	3	1	3	4	1	1	2	7,780	534	10	8,088	204,193
1977	4	30	3	6	4	3	1	2	8	9,301	948	23	10,589	324,814
1978	3	30	2	6	6	4	1	2	1	9,445	2,171	26	10,541	413,908
1979	2	31	5	7	4	5	1	2	3	**9,994**	**2,128**	**26**	**11,768**	557,012
1980	5	31	5	5	3	2	6	0	1	9,015	2,023	**28**	9,763	405,711
1981	1	31	11	12	6	3	0	0	4	9,575	**2,517**	27	10,974	799,134
1982	1	30	7	12	1	3	0	1	3	**9,455**	**3,027**	27	10,597	923,151
1983	2	30	7	6	8	4	2	2	3	9,403	**2,363**	22	10,546	865,185
1984	5	30	4	7	2	3	1	0	7	9,464	**2,030**	22	10,440	731,023
1985	1	28	4	3	6	6	2	1	3	8,932	969	21	**10,910**	1,318,375
1986	2	29	1	3	2	4	6	6	1	8,327	573	21	9,946	1,099,735
1987	4	29	0	1	1	1	2	1	10	8,996	311	14	**11,034**	511,768
1988	7	29	2	2	1	1	2	4	4	9,065	520	18	10,786	731,659
1989	4	29	0	6	2	2	2	2	4	**9,333**	758	17	10,984	1,312,479
1990	20	23	0	0	1	1	2	1	7	8,138	297	9	9,190	520,420
1991	8	29	0	2	2	1	0	0	12	9,229	203	12	10,900	604,854
1992	9	29	1	3	2	3	0	2	3	8,706	513	14	10,248	876,492
1993	13	30	0	0	0	2	1	1	6	9,194	151	9	10,817	746,646
1994	9	31	0	0	0	2	2	0	9	**9,905**	60	8	12,026	854,280
1995	19	31	1	0	0	1	3	0	4	8,222	168	8	9,581	850,632
1996	29	31	0	0	0	0	0	0	2	7,766	2	2	8,971	740,185
Lifetime		689	59	84	58	61	40	31	110	206,128	22,988	386	239,141	$15,674,704
		5th	4th	4th						3rd	6th	3rd		3rd

Michael Waltrip

Michael Waltrip
B: 4/30/1963
Racing Hometown: Owensboro, KY

Year	Rank	Starts	Poles	1	2	3	4	5	6–10	Laps	Laps Led	Races Led	Miles	$
1985	57	5	0	0	0	0	0	0	0	1,013	0	0	1,583	9,540
1986	19	28	0	0	0	0	0	0	0	7,952	6	4	9,295	108,767

Year	Rank	Starts	Poles	Finish						Laps	Laps Led	Races Led	Miles	$
				1	2	3	4	5	6–10	Laps	Led	Led	Miles	$

Michael Waltrip *continued*

Year	Rank	Starts	Poles	1	2	3	4	5	6–10	Laps	Laps Led	Races Led	Miles	$
1987	20	29	0	0	0	0	0	0	1	7,790	1	1	8,848	205,370
1988	18	29	0	0	1	0	0	0	2	7,734	6	2	10,041	240,400
1989	18	29	0	0	0	0	0	0	5	8,372	9	4	10,111	249,233
1990	16	29	0	0	0	1	2	2	5	8,226	17	4	10,124	395,507
1991	15	29	2	0	0	1	0	3	8	8,394	292	11	9,757	440,812
1992	23	29	0	0	0	0	1	0	1	8,474	3	1	10,184	410,545
1993	17	30	0	0	0	0	0	0	5	9,379	40	6	11,146	529,923
1994	12	31	0	0	0	1	0	1	7	9,508	8	5	11,666	720,426
1995	12	31	0	0	0	1	0	1	6	9,222	45	12	11,399	898,338
1996	14	31	0	0	0	0	0	1	10	9,279	18	5	11,165	1,182,811
Lifetime		330	2	0	1	4	3	8	50	95,343	445	55	115,320	$5,391,672

Blackie Wangerin

Ervin Wangerin
B: 4/4/1935
Racing Hometown: Bloomington, MN

Year	Rank	Starts	Poles	1	2	3	4	5	6–10	Laps	Laps Led	Races Led	Miles	$
1971	NR	1	0	0	0	0	0	0	0	16	0	0	40	0
1976	—	0												400
1977	NR	1	0	0	0	0	0	0	0	260	0	0	396	885
1978	37	10	0	0	0	0	0	0	0	1,342	0	0	2,522	13,515
1979	35	7	0	0	0	0	0	0	0	894	0	0	1,750	14,535
1980	63	3	0	0	0	0	0	0	0	548	0	0	808	6,920
1981	104	1	0	0	0	0	0	0	0	17	0	0	43	2,750
1982	95	1	0	0	0	0	0	0	0	73	0	0	183	2,000
1983	80	2	0	0	0	0	0	0	0	48	0	0	62	5,910
1984	NR	1	0	0	0	0	0	0	0	0	0	0	0	4,210
1986	—	0												1,100
1987	—	0												1,800
1988	—	0												2,000
1990	—	0												1,150
1991	—	0												1,750
Lifetime		27	0	0	0	0	0	0	0	3,198	0	0	5,803	$58,925

Bill Ward

William Ward
B: 8/8/1930
Racing Hometown: Anniston, AL

Year	Rank	Starts	Poles	1	2	3	4	5	6–10	Laps	Laps Led	Races Led	Miles	$
1969	NR	1	0	0	0	0	0	0	0	149	0	0	396	1,550
1971	72	2	0	0	0	0	0	0	0	281	0	0	747	2,865
1972	119	1	0	0	0	0	0	0	0	10	0	0	27	770
1973	87	2	0	0	0	0	0	0	0	188	0	0	500	2,275
1975	100T	1	0	0	0	0	0	0	0	145	0	0	386	1,320
Lifetime		7	0	0	0	0	0	0	0	773	0	0	2,056	$8,780

Glen Ward

Glen Ward
B: 10/2/1946
Racing Hometown: Ashland, OR

Year	Rank	Starts	Poles	1	2	3	4	5	6–10	Laps	Laps Led	Races Led	Miles	$
1980	105	1	0	0	0	0	0	0	0	77	0	0	193	875
Lifetime		1	0	0	0	0	0	0	0	77	0	0	193	$875

James Ward

James Ward
Racing Hometown: Atlanta, GA

Year	Rank	Starts	Poles	1	2	3	4	5	6–10	Laps	Laps Led	Races Led	Miles	$
1951	N/A	1	0	0	0	0	0	0	0	55	0	0	41	25
Lifetime		1	0	0	0	0	0	0	0	55	0	0	41	$25

Rodger Ward

Rodger Ward
B: 1/10/1921
Racing Hometown: Los Angeles, CA

Year	Rank	Starts	Poles	1	2	3	4	5	6–10	Laps	Laps Led	Races Led	Miles	$
1963	NR	2	0	0	0	0	0	0	0	251	0	0	386	325
1964	NR	1	0	0	0	0	0	0	0	24	0	0	65	525
Lifetime		3	0	0	0	0	0	0	0	275	0	0	450	$850

Jimmy Warden

James Warden
Racing Hometown: Bluff City, TN

Year	Rank	Starts	Poles	1	2	3	4	5	6–10	Laps	Laps Led	Races Led	Miles	$
1951	N/A	1	0	0	0	0	0	0	0	314	0	0	393	50
Lifetime		1	0	0	0	0	0	0	0	314	0	0	393	$50

Year	Rank	Starts	Poles	Finish 1	2	3	4	5	6–10	Laps	Laps Led	Races Led	Miles	$

Rick Ware

Richard Ware
Racing Hometown: Highpoint, NC

Year	Rank	Starts	Poles	1	2	3	4	5	6–10	Laps	Laps Led	Races Led	Miles	$
1990	97	1	0	0	0	0	0	0	0	42	0	0	102	2,295
Lifetime		1	0	0	0	0	0	0	0	42	0	0	102	$2,295

Daniel Warlick

Daniel Warlick
Racing Hometown: Shelby, NC

Year	Rank	Starts	Poles	1	2	3	4	5	6–10	Laps	Laps Led	Races Led	Miles	$
1965	NR	2	0	0	0	0	0	0	1	432	0	0	168	250
Lifetime		2	0	0	0	0	0	0	1	432	0	0	168	$250

Ken Warmington

Kenneth Warmington
Racing Hometown: Buffalo, NY

Year	Rank	Starts	Poles	1	2	3	4	5	6–10	Laps	Laps Led	Races Led	Miles	$
1950	90	3	0	0	0	0	0	0	0	177	0	0	89	25
Lifetime		3	0	0	0	0	0	0	0	177	0	0	89	$25

David Warren

David Warren
Racing Hometown: Cleveland, NC

Year	Rank	Starts	Poles	1	2	3	4	5	6–10	Laps	Laps Led	Races Led	Miles	$
1965	110T	1	0	0	0	0	0	0	0	32	0	0	16	100
Lifetime		1	0	0	0	0	0	0	0	32	0	0	16	$100

Frank Warren

Frank Warren
B: 9/8/1937
Racing Hometown: Augusta, GA

Year	Rank	Starts	Poles	1	2	3	4	5	6–10	Laps	Laps Led	Races Led	Miles	$
1963	101	2	0	0	0	0	0	0	1	373	0	0	187	260
1964	68	2	0	0	0	0	0	0	0	266	0	0	446	735
1965	46	4	0	0	0	0	0	0	1	769	0	0	1,088	2,880
1966	31	11	0	0	0	0	0	0	1	1,989	0	0	2,803	6,740
1967	24	12	0	0	0	0	0	0	1	1,805	0	0	2,668	9,185
1968	42	10	0	0	0	0	0	0	1	1,643	0	0	1,900	5,365
1969	29	23	0	0	0	0	0	0	1	3,343	0	0	3,892	15,677
1970	10	46	0	0	0	0	0	0	2	7,709	71	1	7,763	35,161
1971	8	47	0	0	0	0	0	1	9	8,984	0	0	8,599	40,072
1972	11	30	0	0	0	0	0	0	2	7,091	0	0	8,404	45,048
1973	16	26	0	0	0	0	0	0	0	6,713	0	0	7,171	36,551
1974	13	29	0	0	0	0	0	1	1	7,342	0	0	8,993	55,779
1975	12	27	0	0	0	0	0	0	0	7,758	0	0	9,123	55,671
1976	16	30	0	0	0	0	0	0	3	8,063	0	0	9,898	67,732
1977	16	29	0	0	0	0	0	0	1	6,466	1	1	8,107	67,945
1978	14	30	0	0	0	0	0	0	0	8,481	0	0	9,827	68,173
1979	16	31	0	0	0	0	0	0	3	8,477	0	0	10,046	94,539
1980	40	7	0	0	0	0	0	0	0	1,591	0	0	2,561	19,450
Lifetime		396	0	0	0	0	0	2	27	88,863	72	2	103,475	$626,963

Gayle Warren

Gayle Warren
Racing Hometown: Marion, VA

Year	Rank	Starts	Poles	1	2	3	4	5	6–10	Laps	Laps Led	Races Led	Miles	$
1950	22	10	0	0	0	0	0	1	1	429	10	1	356	600
1951	N/A	3	0	0	0	0	0	0	0	370	0	0	463	150
1953	83	2	0	0	0	0	0	0	0	327	0	0	348	150
Lifetime		15	0	0	0	0	0	1	1	1,126	10	1	1,166	$900

Jerome Warren

Jerome Warren
Racing Hometown: Charlotte, NC

Year	Rank	Starts	Poles	1	2	3	4	5	6–10	Laps	Laps Led	Races Led	Miles	$
1963	113	5	0	0	0	0	0	0	0	171	0	0	89	435
Lifetime		5	0	0	0	0	0	0	0	171	0	0	89	$435

Wayne Watercutter

Wayne Watercutter
B: 10/22/1944
Racing Hometown: Sidney, OH

Year	Rank	Starts	Poles	1	2	3	4	5	6–10	Laps	Laps Led	Races Led	Miles	$
1979	NR	3	0	0	0	0	0	0	0	681	0	0	722	2,380
1980	70	2	0	0	0	0	0	0	0	378	0	0	756	3,425
Lifetime		5	0	0	0	0	0	0	0	1,059	0	0	1,478	$5,805

Year	Rank	Starts	Poles	Finish 1	2	3	4	5	6–10	Laps	Laps Led	Races Led	Miles	$

Don Waterman
Donald Waterman
B: 4/15/1950
Racing Hometown: Portland, OR

Year	Rank	Starts	Poles	1	2	3	4	5	6–10	Laps	Laps Led	Races Led	Miles	$
1980	74	2	0	0	0	0	0	0	0	250	0	0	633	3,555
1981	51	3	0	0	0	0	0	0	1	301	1	1	789	8,570
1982	63	2	0	0	0	0	0	0	0	156	1	1	409	3,805
1983	63	2	0	0	0	0	0	0	0	189	0	0	495	3,355
Lifetime		9	0	0	0	0	0	0	1	896	2	2	2,325	$19,285

Richard Waters
Richard Waters

Year	Rank	Starts	Poles	1	2	3	4	5	6–10	Laps	Laps Led	Races Led	Miles	$
1978	NR	1	0	0	0	0	0	0	0	13	0	0	8	265
Lifetime		1	0	0	0	0	0	0	0	13	0	0	8	$265

Al Watkins
Al Watkins
Racing Hometown: Gardendale, AL

Year	Rank	Starts	Poles	1	2	3	4	5	6–10	Laps	Laps Led	Races Led	Miles	$
1954	NR	1	0	0	0	0	0	0	0	159	0	0	80	25
1955	74	3	0	0	0	0	0	0	0	491	0	0	386	300
1956	28	14	0	0	0	0	0	0	4	2,065	0	0	1,380	1,185
Lifetime		18	0	0	0	0	0	0	4	2,715	0	0	1,845	$1,510

Jim Watkins
James Watkins
Racing Hometown: Detroit, MI

Year	Rank	Starts	Poles	1	2	3	4	5	6–10	Laps	Laps Led	Races Led	Miles	$
1956	NR	3	0	0	0	0	0	0	0	156	0	0	69	300
Lifetime		3	0	0	0	0	0	0	0	156	0	0	69	$300

Bobby Watson
Robert Lee Watson
B: 4/22/1936
Racing Hometown: Prestonburg, KY

Year	Rank	Starts	Poles	1	2	3	4	5	6–10	Laps	Laps Led	Races Led	Miles	$
1970	101	1	0	0	0	0	0	0	0	11	0	0	6	430
Lifetime		1	0	0	0	0	0	0	0	11	0	0	6	$430

Dave Watson
David Watson
B: 11/7/1945
Racing Hometown: Milton, WI

Year	Rank	Starts	Poles	1	2	3	4	5	6–10	Laps	Laps Led	Races Led	Miles	$
1978	NR	1	0	0	0	0	0	0	0	316	0	0	481	1,600
1979	44	4	0	0	0	0	0	0	1	1,092	7	2	1,161	7,170
Lifetime		5	0	0	0	0	0	0	1	1,408	7	2	1,642	$8,770

Dick Watson
Richard Watson
Racing Hometown: Clinton, CT

Year	Rank	Starts	Poles	1	2	3	4	5	6–10	Laps	Laps Led	Races Led	Miles	$
1969	91	1	0	0	0	0	0	0	0	171	0	0	107	370
Lifetime		1	0	0	0	0	0	0	0	171	0	0	107	$370

Jimmy Watson
James Watson

Year	Rank	Starts	Poles	1	2	3	4	5	6–10	Laps	Laps Led	Races Led	Miles	$
1970	NR	1	0	0	0	0	0	0	0	451	0	0	247	505
1971	NR	1	0	0	0	0	0	0	0	29	0	0	16	350
Lifetime		2	0	0	0	0	0	0	0	480	0	0	263	$855

Blackie Watt
William O Watt
B: 12/6/1933
Racing Hometown: New Alexandria, PA

Year	Rank	Starts	Poles	1	2	3	4	5	6–10	Laps	Laps Led	Races Led	Miles	$
1966	30	20	0	0	0	0	0	0	9	4,067	0	0	3,003	7,050
1967	67	4	0	0	0	0	0	0	0	330	0	0	540	2,235
Lifetime		24	0	0	0	0	0	0	9	4,397	0	0	3,543	$9,285

Art Watts
Arthur Watts
Racing Hometown: Portland, OR

Year	Rank	Starts	Poles	1	2	3	4	5	6–10	Laps	Laps Led	Races Led	Miles	$
1954	58	4	0	0	0	0	0	0	0	848	0	0	797	240
1956	71	6	0	0	0	0	0	0	2	935	0	0	552	525
1957	52	5	5	1	0	1	0	0	1	689	100	1	377	1,755

Year	Rank	Starts	Poles	Finish 1	2	3	4	5	6–10	Laps	Laps Led	Races Led	Miles	$

Art Watts *continued*

Year	Rank	Starts	Poles	1	2	3	4	5	6–10	Laps	Laps Led	Races Led	Miles	$
1958	76	1	0	0	0	0	0	0	0	165	0	0	434	140
1960	82	1	0	0	0	0	0	0	1	168	0	0	235	525
1961	NR	1	0	0	0	0	0	0	0	85	0	0	119	100
1963	71	1	0	0	0	0	0	0	0	171	0	0	462	475
Lifetime		19	5	1	0	1	0	0	4	3,061	100	1	2,975	$3,760

Bobby Wawak

Robert L. Wawak
B: 9/4/1939
Racing Hometown: Villa Park, IL

Year	Rank	Starts	Poles	1	2	3	4	5	6–10	Laps	Laps Led	Races Led	Miles	$
1965	117	1	0	0	0	0	0	0	0	46	0	0	63	560
1967	31	14	0	0	0	0	0	0	3	2,225	0	0	2,320	8,070
1969	80	1	0	0	0	0	0	0	0	74	0	0	148	657
1971	76	2	0	0	0	0	0	0	0	615	0	0	891	2,665
1976	22	19	0	0	0	0	0	0	9	4,888	0	0	6,231	31,415
1977	45	8	0	0	0	0	0	0	0	1,633	0	0	2,407	13,455
1978	38	8	0	0	0	0	0	0	0	1,512	0	0	1,273	5,870
1979	46	4	0	0	0	0	0	0	0	740	0	0	855	7,295
1980	25	19	0	0	0	0	0	0	1	4,065	0	0	4,224	21,080
1981	31	14	0	0	0	0	0	0	1	2,734	0	0	3,485	23,460
1982	31	10	0	0	0	0	0	0	0	2,489	2	1	3,981	23,660
1983	36	9	0	0	0	0	0	0	0	2,167	0	0	3,262	20,780
1984	47	4	0	0	0	0	0	0	0	874	0	0	1,433	9,625
1985	32	14	0	0	0	0	0	0	0	3,157	0	0	4,452	42,165
1986	43	6	0	0	0	0	0	0	0	1,270	0	0	1,734	12,155
1987	39	8	0	0	0	0	0	0	0	1,648	0	0	2,343	24,955
Lifetime		141	0	0	0	0	0	0	14	30,137	2	1	39,103	$247,867

Bob Weatherly

Robert Weatherly
Racing Hometown: Timmonsville, SC

Year	Rank	Starts	Poles	1	2	3	4	5	6–10	Laps	Laps Led	Races Led	Miles	$
1953	NR	1	0	0	0	0	0	0	0	289	0	0	397	140
Lifetime		1	0	0	0	0	0	0	0	289	0	0	397	$140

Joe Weatherly

Joe Herbert Weatherly Jr.
B: 5/29/1922   D: 1/19/1964   *Killed @ Riverside, CA.*
Racing Hometown: Norfolk, VA

Year	Rank	Starts	Poles	1	2	3	4	5	6–10	Laps	Laps Led	Races Led	Miles	$
1952	51	1	0	0	0	0	0	0	0	376	0	0	470	150
1954	102	1	0	0	0	0	0	0	1	196	0	0	98	200
1955	47	6	0	0	0	0	1	0	3	994	140	1	873	2,575
1956	16	17	1	0	1	1	3	1	6	2,745	20	1	1,997	5,251
1957	50	14	0	0	1	3	0	1	2	2,059	3	1	1,350	5,340
1958	28	15	1	1	1	0	2	1	2	2,692	104	3	2,120	6,330
1959	18	17	0	0	2	0	1	3	4	2,776	189	7	2,105	9,816
1960	20	24	0	3	2	0	2	0	4	4,294	246	6	3,804	20,124
1961	4	25	4	9	3	0	1	1	4	5,790	809	18	5,329	47,079
1962	1	52	7	9	12	10	3	5	6	**12,431**	1,014	17	**8,001**	70,743
1963	1	53	6	3	5	5	5	2	15	11,343	878	12	**8,407**	74,624
1964	48	5	0	0	1	0	1	0	1	768	84	1	916	5,290
Lifetime		230	19	25	28	19	19	14	48	46,464	3,487	67	35,470	$247,522

Marshall Weatherly

Marshall Weatherly
Racing Hometown: Charlotte, NC

Year	Rank	Starts	Poles	1	2	3	4	5	6–10	Laps	Laps Led	Races Led	Miles	$
1951	N/A	4	0	0	0	0	0	0	0		0	0		100
Lifetime		4	0	0	0	0	0	0	0		0	0		$100

Frank Weathers

Frank Weathers
Racing Hometown: Maiden, NC

Year	Rank	Starts	Poles	1	2	3	4	5	6–10	Laps	Laps Led	Races Led	Miles	$
1964	122	2	0	0	0	0	0	0	0	53	0	0	22	500
1965	86	5	0	0	0	0	0	0	1	620	0	0	314	640
Lifetime		7	0	0	0	0	0	0	1	673	0	0	336	$1,140

Louis Weathersbee

Louis Weathersbee
Racing Hometown: N. Charleston, SC

Year	Rank	Starts	Poles	1	2	3	4	5	6–10	Laps	Laps Led	Races Led	Miles	$
1964	77	4	0	0	0	0	0	0	0	385	0	0	314	610
Lifetime		4	0	0	0	0	0	0	0	385	0	0	314	$610

Year	Rank	Starts	Poles	Finish 1	2	3	4	5	6–10	Laps	Laps Led	Races Led	Miles	$

Al Weaver

Al Weaver

Year	Rank	Starts	Poles	1	2	3	4	5	6–10	Laps	Laps Led	Races Led	Miles	$
1950	NR	1	0	0	0	0	0	0	0	119	0	0	60	0
Lifetime		1	0	0	0	0	0	0	0	119	0	0	60	$0

Chuck Webb

Chuck Webb
Racing Hometown: Sacramento, CA

Year	Rank	Starts	Poles	1	2	3	4	5	6–10	Laps	Laps Led	Races Led	Miles	$
1959	101	1	0	0	0	0	0	0	0	63	0	0	63	100
1961	119	2	0	0	0	0	0	0	1	120	0	0	129	200
Lifetime		3	0	0	0	0	0	0	1	183	0	0	192	$300

Al Weber

Al Weber
Racing Hometown: Akron, OH

Year	Rank	Starts	Poles	1	2	3	4	5	6–10	Laps	Laps Led	Races Led	Miles	$
1955	119	2	0	0	0	0	0	0	1	201	0	0	101	150
Lifetime		2	0	0	0	0	0	0	1	201	0	0	101	$150

Ewell Weddle

Ewell H. Weddle
Racing Hometown: Winston-Salem, NC

Year	Rank	Starts	Poles	1	2	3	4	5	6–10	Laps	Laps Led	Races Led	Miles	$
1950	38	3	0	0	0	1	0	0	0	158	0	0	79	600
1951	44	7	0	0	0	0	0	0	2	743	0	0	799	435
1952	15	3	0	0	0	0	0	0	0	465	0	0	316	125
1953	55	4	0	0	0	0	0	0	1	0	0	0	0	125
Lifetime		17	0	0	0	1	0	0	3	1,366	0	0	1,194	$1,175

F. Weichman

F. Weichman

Year	Rank	Starts	Poles	1	2	3	4	5	6–10	Laps	Laps Led	Races Led	Miles	$
1950	120T	1	0	0	0	0	0	0	0		0	0		0
Lifetime		1	0	0	0	0	0	0	0		0	0		$0

Charles Weidler

Charles Weidler
Racing Hometown: Williamsport, PA

Year	Rank	Starts	Poles	1	2	3	4	5	6–10	Laps	Laps Led	Races Led	Miles	$
1952	76	5	0	0	0	0	0	0	0	639	0	0	549	125
1953	164	2	0	0	0	0	0	0	0	9	0	0	37	25
Lifetime		7	0	0	0	0	0	0	0	648	0	0	586	$150

Ernie Weidler

Ernest Weidler

Year	Rank	Starts	Poles	1	2	3	4	5	6–10	Laps	Laps Led	Races Led	Miles	$
1953	NR	1	0	0	0	0	0	0	0		0	0		25
Lifetime		1	0	0	0	0	0	0	0		0	0		$25

Bill Weiman

William Weiman

Year	Rank	Starts	Poles	1	2	3	4	5	6–10	Laps	Laps Led	Races Led	Miles	$
1954	NR	1	0	0	0	0	0	0	0	20	0	0	10	0
Lifetime		1	0	0	0	0	0	0	0	20	0	0	10	$0

Danny Weinberg

Daniel Weinberg
Racing Hometown: Downey, CA

Year	Rank	Starts	Poles	1	2	3	4	5	6–10	Laps	Laps Led	Races Led	Miles	$
1951	30	6	0	1	0	0	0	1	1	297	1	1	149	1,500
1958	102	1	0	0	0	1	0	0	0	99	0	0	99	425
1959	NR	1	0	0	0	1	0	0	0	100	0	0	100	425
1960	90	3	0	0	0	0	0	1	0	216	0	0	231	525
1961	73	4	1	0	0	2	0	0	1	446	0	0	453	1,185
1963	144	1	0	0	0	0	0	0	0	27	0	0	73	300
1964	131	1	0	0	0	0	0	0	0	9	0	0	24	500
Lifetime		17	1	1	0	4	0	2	2	1,194	1	1	1,129	$4,860

Robert Weisemeyer

Robert L. Weisemeyer
Racing Hometown: Hepzibah, GA

Year	Rank	Starts	Poles	1	2	3	4	5	6–10	Laps	Laps Led	Races Led	Miles	$
1952	191T	1	0	0	0	0	0	0	0	9	0	0	9	25
Lifetime		1	0	0	0	0	0	0	0	9	0	0	9	$25

Bob Welborn

Robert Joe Welborn
B: 5/5/1928
Racing Hometown: Denton, NC

Year	Rank	Starts	Poles	1	2	3	4	5	6–10	Laps	Laps Led	Races Led	Miles	$
1952	81	3	0	0	0	0	0	0	0	324	0	0	195	90

Year	Rank	Starts	Poles	Finish 1	2	3	4	5	6–10	Laps	Laps Led	Races Led	Miles	$

Bob Welborn *continued*

Year	Rank	Starts	Poles	1	2	3	4	5	6–10	Laps	Laps Led	Races Led	Miles	$
1953	24	11	0	0	0	0	1	1	4	617	0	0	466	1,210
1954	51	12	0	0	0	1	0	0	2	1,251	0	0	794	1,125
1955	4	32	1	0	1	4	4	3	13	5,291	31	1	3,638	10,147
1956	84	6	0	0	0	0	0	0	2	974	0	0	474	650
1957	NR	4	0	1	0	0	0	2	0	1,152	457	2	968	5,050
1958	149	18	1	5	3	2	0	0	5	3,770	579	7	2,190	13,270
1959	17	29	5	3	1	3	3	0	3	3,895	176	7	2,364	9,370
1960	16	15	0	0	1	0	2	3	4	2,809	94	2	2,533	6,194
1961	14	14	0	0	1	2	0	0	4	2,996	104	4	3,424	13,487
1962	15	25	0	0	1	0	2	2	7	5,654	0	0	4,558	10,347
1963	40	11	0	0	1	2	1	0	0	2,221	0	0	1,741	4,830
1964	78	3	0	0	0	0	0	2	0	506	125	1	286	805
Lifetime		183	7	9	9	14	13	13	44	31,460	1,566	24	23,630	$76,575

Don Welch

Donald Welch
Racing Hometown: Rochester, NY

Year	Rank	Starts	Poles	1	2	3	4	5	6–10	Laps	Laps Led	Races Led	Miles	$
1954	126T	1	0	0	0	0	0	0	0	175	0	0	88	25
Lifetime		1	0	0	0	0	0	0	0	175	0	0	88	$25

Doug Wells

Douglas Wells
Racing Hometown: Fort Valley, GA

Year	Rank	Starts	Poles	1	2	3	4	5	6–10	Laps	Laps Led	Races Led	Miles	$
1953	175	1	0	0	0	0	0	0	0	13	0	0	53	0
Lifetime		1	0	0	0	0	0	0	0	13	0	0	53	$0

Tommy Wells

Thomas Wells
Racing Hometown: Guntersville, AL

Year	Rank	Starts	Poles	1	2	3	4	5	6–10	Laps	Laps Led	Races Led	Miles	$
1951	N/A	3	0	0	0	0	0	0	0	81	0	0	41	75
1961	98	4	0	0	0	0	0	1	0	727	0	0	507	750
Lifetime		7	0	0	0	0	0	1	0	808	0	0	547	$825

Phil Wendt

Philip Wendt
Racing Hometown: Irvington, AL

Year	Rank	Starts	Poles	1	2	3	4	5	6–10	Laps	Laps Led	Races Led	Miles	$
1968	69	3	0	0	0	0	0	0	0	418	0	0	445	1,980
Lifetime		3	0	0	0	0	0	0	0	418	0	0	445	$1,980

Paul Wensink

Harold Paul Wensink
B: 11/5/1929
Racing Hometown: Deshler, OH

Year	Rank	Starts	Poles	1	2	3	4	5	6–10	Laps	Laps Led	Races Led	Miles	$
1952	114T	1	0	0	0	0	0	0	0	127	0	0	64	25
Lifetime		1	0	0	0	0	0	0	0	127	0	0	64	$25

Pee Wee Wentz

James Elmo Wentz
B: 5/26/1941
Racing Hometown: Danville, VA

Year	Rank	Starts	Poles	1	2	3	4	5	6–10	Laps	Laps Led	Races Led	Miles	$
1971	NR	1	0	0	0	0	0	0	0	100	0	0	46	300
1973	78	2	0	0	0	0	0	0	0	594	0	0	498	1,315
1974	73	3	0	0	0	0	0	0	1	540	0	0	624	3,705
Lifetime		6	0	0	0	0	0	0	1	1,234	0	0	1,168	$5,320

Jim Wesley

James Wesley

Year	Rank	Starts	Poles	1	2	3	4	5	6–10	Laps	Laps Led	Races Led	Miles	$
1950	120T	1	0	0	0	0	0	0	0		0	0		0
Lifetime		1	0	0	0	0	0	0	0		0	0		$0

Bill West

William West
Racing Hometown: Downey, CA

Year	Rank	Starts	Poles	1	2	3	4	5	6–10	Laps	Laps Led	Races Led	Miles	$
1954	65	3	0	0	0	0	0	0	1	888	0	0	557	250
1955	52	3	0	0	0	1	0	0	1	374	0	0	374	910
1956	113	2	0	0	0	0	0	0	0	291	0	0	405	150
Lifetime		8	0	0	0	1	0	0	2	1,553	0	0	1,336	$1,310

Year	Rank	Starts	Poles	Finish						Laps	Laps Led	Races Led	Miles	$
				1	2	3	4	5	6–10					

George West
George West
Racing Hometown: St. Paul, VA

Year	Rank	Starts	Poles	1	2	3	4	5	6–10	Laps	Laps Led	Races Led	Miles	$
1957	185	1	0	0	0	0	0	0	0		0	0		0
Lifetime		1	0	0	0	0	0	0	0		0	0		$0

Vernon West
Vernon West

Year	Rank	Starts	Poles	1	2	3	4	5	6–10	Laps	Laps Led	Races Led	Miles	$
1958	NR	1	0	0	0	0	0	0	0	1	0	0	0.333	50
Lifetime		1	0	0	0	0	0	0	0	1	0	0	0.333	$50

Ed Westveer
Edward Westveer
Racing Hometown: Detroit, MI

Year	Rank	Starts	Poles	1	2	3	4	5	6–10	Laps	Laps Led	Races Led	Miles	$
1952	182	1	0	0	0	0	0	0	0	45	0	0	45	25
Lifetime		1	0	0	0	0	0	0	0	45	0	0	45	$25

Dick Whalen
Richard Whalen
B: 4/7/1935
Racing Hometown: San Jose, CA

Year	Rank	Starts	Poles	1	2	3	4	5	6–10	Laps	Laps Led	Races Led	Miles	$
1979	96T	1	0	0	0	0	0	0	0	81	0	0	212	950
Lifetime		1	0	0	0	0	0	0	0	81	0	0	212	$950

Buster Whaley
Buster Whaley
Racing Hometown: Sylacauga, AL

Year	Rank	Starts	Poles	1	2	3	4	5	6–10	Laps	Laps Led	Races Led	Miles	$
1954	119T	1	0	0	0	0	0	0	0	171	0	0	86	25
Lifetime		1	0	0	0	0	0	0	0	171	0	0	86	$25

Doug Wheeler
Stephen Douglas Wheeler

Year	Rank	Starts	Poles	1	2	3	4	5	6–10	Laps	Laps Led	Races Led	Miles	$
1983	58	2	0	0	0	0	0	0	0	203	0	0	532	4,625
Lifetime		2	0	0	0	0	0	0	0	203	0	0	532	$4,625

Legs Whitcomb
David Whitcomb
B: 8/25/1931
Racing Hometown: Valparaiso, IN

Year	Rank	Starts	Poles	1	2	3	4	5	6–10	Laps	Laps Led	Races Led	Miles	$
1954	NR	1	0	0	0	0	0	0	0	97	0	0	49	0
Lifetime		1	0	0	0	0	0	0	0	97	0	0	49	$0

Al White
Al White *Real Name*: Al Gristermacher
Racing Hometown: Buffalo, NY

Year	Rank	Starts	Poles	1	2	3	4	5	6–10	Laps	Laps Led	Races Led	Miles	$
1956	220	2	0	0	0	0	0	0	0	330	0	0	165	200
1957	107	3	0	0	0	0	0	0	1	161	0	0	200	200
1958	31	9	0	0	0	0	0	0	1	1,483	0	0	1,030	920
1959	49	5	0	0	0	0	0	0	0	826	0	0	644	575
1960	NR	2	0	0	0	0	0	0	1	643	0	0	322	450
1962	123	1	0	0	0	0	0	0	0	233	0	0	117	125
1963	154	1	0	0	0	0	0	0	0	211	0	0	106	150
1964	64	7	0	0	0	0	0	0	3	1,484	0	0	655	1,030
1965	NR	4	0	0	0	0	0	0	1	348	0	0	262	545
1966	99	2	0	0	0	0	0	0	0	449	0	0	142	230
Lifetime		36	0	0	0	0	0	0	7	6,168	0	0	3,643	$4,425

Bob White
Robert White

Year	Rank	Starts	Poles	1	2	3	4	5	6–10	Laps	Laps Led	Races Led	Miles	$
1951	N/A	1	0	0	0	0	0	0	0		0	0		0
Lifetime		1	0	0	0	0	0	0	0		0	0		$0

Dave White
David White
Racing Hometown: Silver Spring, MD

Year	Rank	Starts	Poles	1	2	3	4	5	6–10	Laps	Laps Led	Races Led	Miles	$
1958	74	2	0	0	0	0	0	0	1	205	0	0	266	150
1959	NR	5	0	0	0	0	0	0	1	1,253	0	0	533	660
Lifetime		7	0	0	0	0	0	0	2	1,458	0	0	799	$810

Don White
Donald White
Racing Hometown: Lockport, NY

Year	Rank	Starts	Poles	1	2	3	4	5	6–10	Laps	Laps Led	Races Led	Miles	$
1950	76	2	0	0	0	0	0	0	0	182	0	0	91	75
Lifetime		2	0	0	0	0	0	0	0	182	0	0	91	$75

Year	Rank	Starts	Poles	Finish 1	2	3	4	5	6–10	Laps	Laps Led	Races Led	Miles	$

Don White

Donald White
B: 6/24/1926
Racing Hometown: Keokuk, IA

Year	Rank	Starts	Poles	1	2	3	4	5	6–10	Laps	Laps Led	Races Led	Miles	$
1954	90	1	0	0	0	0	0	0	0	38	0	0	156	90
1955	79	3	0	0	2	1	0	0	0	296	0	0	198	1,750
1964	NR	1	0	0	0	0	0	0	0	176	0	0	475	825
1966	NR	8	0	0	1	2	0	0	2	1,961	8	1	3,199	19,670
1967	NR	6	0	0	0	0	1	0	2	997	0	0	1,691	8,410
1968	NR	2	0	0	0	0	0	0	1	585	0	0	738	2,105
1969	NR	1	0	0	0	0	0	0	0	41	0	0	111	835
1970	NR	1	0	0	0	0	0	0	0	16	0	0	42	880
1972	NR	1	0	0	0	0	0	0	0	114	0	0	285	1,745
Lifetime		24	0	0	3	3	1	0	5	4,224	8	1	6,895	$36,310

Gene White

Gene White
B: 5/12/1931   D: 4/15/1986
Racing Hometown: Marietta, GA

Year	Rank	Starts	Poles	1	2	3	4	5	6–10	Laps	Laps Led	Races Led	Miles	$
1956	277	1	0	0	0	0	0	0	0		0	0		0
1958	27	9	0	0	0	0	0	0	2	1,641	0	0	1,295	1,400
1959	95	9	0	0	0	0	0	0	2	1,457	0	0	1,319	2,060
1960	104	3	0	0	0	0	0	0	0	321	0	0	652	400
1961	138	1	0	0	0	0	0	0	0	147	0	0	221	300
Lifetime		23	0	0	0	0	0	0	4	3,566	0	0	3,487	$4,160

Herschel White

Herschel White
B: 1917   D: 10/18/1996
Racing Hometown: Speedway City, IN

Year	Rank	Starts	Poles	1	2	3	4	5	6–10	Laps	Laps Led	Races Led	Miles	$
1952	NR	1	0	0	0	0	0	0	1	283	0	0	142	75
Lifetime		1	0	0	0	0	0	0	1	283	0	0	142	$75

J. C. White

John C. White
Racing Hometown: Hildebran, NC

Year	Rank	Starts	Poles	1	2	3	4	5	6–10	Laps	Laps Led	Races Led	Miles	$
1951	28	4	0	0	0	0	0	0	0	128	0	0	128	125
1952	104T	1	0	0	0	0	0	0	0	164	0	0	103	25
Lifetime		5	0	0	0	0	0	0	0	292	0	0	231	$150

Jack White

Jack White
Racing Hometown: Lockport, NY

Year	Rank	Starts	Poles	1	2	3	4	5	6–10	Laps	Laps Led	Races Led	Miles	$
1949	18	1	0	1	0	0	0	0	0	200	66	1	100	1,580
1950	25	7	0	0	0	0	0	1	1	712	0	0	850	525
1951	N/A	4	0	0	0	0	0	0	0	158	0	0	158	85
Lifetime		12	0	1	0	0	0	1	1	1,070	66	1	1,108	$2,110

Jesse White

Jesse White
Racing Hometown: Hickory, NC

Year	Rank	Starts	Poles	1	2	3	4	5	6–10	Laps	Laps Led	Races Led	Miles	$
1951	195T	1	0	0	0	0	0	0	0		0	0		25
Lifetime		1	0	0	0	0	0	0	0		0	0		$25

Ken White

Kenneth White

Year	Rank	Starts	Poles	1	2	3	4	5	6–10	Laps	Laps Led	Races Led	Miles	$
1965	NR	1	0	0	0	0	0	0	0	0	0	0	0	400
Lifetime		1	0	0	0	0	0	0	0	0	0	0	0	$400

Pap White

John C. White
B: 6/26/1922
Racing Hometown: High Point, NC

Year	Rank	Starts	Poles	1	2	3	4	5	6–10	Laps	Laps Led	Races Led	Miles	$
1950	65	1	0	0	0	0	0	0	0		0	0		25
1951	62	1	0	0	0	0	0	0	1	383	0	0	479	400
Lifetime		2	0	0	0	0	0	0	1	383	0	0	479	$425

Rex White

Rex Allen White
B: 8/17/1929
Racing Hometown: Spartanburg, SC

Year	Rank	Starts	Poles	1	2	3	4	5	6–10	Laps	Laps Led	Races Led	Miles	$
1956	11	24	1	0	0	2	0	1	11	4,240	0	0	2,978	5,334

Year	Rank	Starts	Poles	Finish 1	2	3	4	5	6–10	Laps	Laps Led	Races Led	Miles	$

Rex White *continued*

Year	Rank	Starts	Poles	1	2	3	4	5	6–10	Laps	Laps Led	Races Led	Miles	$
1957	21	9	1	0	1	0	3	0	2	1,585	193	2	1,144	3,870
1958	7	22	7	2	4	6	0	1	4	3,848	471	7	2,122	12,233
1959	10	23	5	5	2	2	1	1	2	4,744	827	9	3,039	12,360
1960	1	40	3	6	6	7	4	2	10	**8,921**	541	**11**	**6,916**	57,525
1961	2	47	7	7	8	8	2	4	9	**10,307**	1,224	15	**7,542**	56,395
1962	5	37	9	8	3	3	1	3	5	7,683	1,129	15	5,760	36,246
1963	9	25	3	0	3	2	0	0	9	5,595	171	6	5,490	27,241
1964	28	6	0	0	0	1	0	1	1	1,444	27	1	1,683	12,310
Lifetime		233	36	28	27	31	11	13	53	48,367	4,583	66	36,674	$223,514

Richard White

Richard White
B: 12/17/1946
Racing Hometown: Escondido, CA

Year	Rank	Starts	Poles	1	2	3	4	5	6–10	Laps	Laps Led	Races Led	Miles	$
1973	63	2	0	0	0	0	0	0	2	329	0	0	862	3,370
1974	108	1	0	0	0	0	0	0	0	139	0	0	364	1,200
1975	84T	1	0	0	0	0	0	0	0	117	0	0	307	1,285
1977	73	2	0	0	0	0	0	0	0	251	0	0	637	2,375
1978	55	3	0	0	0	0	0	0	0	346	2	1	884	4,550
1979	54	3	0	0	0	0	0	0	0	234	0	0	599	4,070
Lifetime		12	0	0	0	0	0	0	2	1,416	2	1	3,652	$16,850

Bill Whitley

William L. Whitley
Racing Hometown: Winston-Salem, NC

Year	Rank	Starts	Poles	1	2	3	4	5	6–10	Laps	Laps Led	Races Led	Miles	$
1960	123	1	0	0	0	0	0	0	0	6	0	0	2	145
1961	NR	1	0	0	0	0	0	0	0	39	0	0	10	50
1962	NR	1	0	0	0	0	0	0	0	171	0	0	43	370
1963	NR	2	0	0	0	0	0	0	0	5	0	0	2	100
1964	96	6	0	0	0	0	0	0	0	455	0	0	195	700
Lifetime		11	0	0	0	0	0	0	0	676	0	0	251	$1,365

Bob Whitlow

Robert Whitlow
Racing Hometown: Pontiac, MI

Year	Rank	Starts	Poles	1	2	3	4	5	6–10	Laps	Laps Led	Races Led	Miles	$
1973	92	1	0	0	0	0	0	0	0	204	0	0	408	980
1974	NR	1	0	0	0	0	0	0	0	183	0	0	366	1,055
Lifetime		2	0	0	0	0	0	0	0	387	0	0	774	$2,035

Jim Whitman

James Whitman
B: 1/19/1937
Racing Hometown: Paramus, NJ

Year	Rank	Starts	Poles	1	2	3	4	5	6–10	Laps	Laps Led	Races Led	Miles	$
1960	53	5	0	0	0	0	0	0	0	567	0	0	1,055	1,450
Lifetime		5	0	0	0	0	0	0	0	567	0	0	1,055	$1,450

Russ Whitman

Russell Whitman

Year	Rank	Starts	Poles	1	2	3	4	5	6–10	Laps	Laps Led	Races Led	Miles	$
1959	NR	1	0	0	0	0	0	0	0	27	0	0	7	50
Lifetime		1	0	0	0	0	0	0	0	27	0	0	7	$50

Bob Whitmire

Robert Whitmire
Racing Hometown: Ft. Lauderdale, FL

Year	Rank	Starts	Poles	1	2	3	4	5	6–10	Laps	Laps Led	Races Led	Miles	$
1957	149	1	0	0	0	0	0	0	0	153	0	0	77	100
Lifetime		1	0	0	0	0	0	0	0	153	0	0	77	$100

Jim Whitt

James Whitt
Racing Hometown: El Cajon, CA

Year	Rank	Starts	Poles	1	2	3	4	5	6–10	Laps	Laps Led	Races Led	Miles	$
1972	57	3	0	0	0	0	0	0	0	607	0	0	1,303	3,485
1973	95	2	0	0	0	0	0	0	0	124	0	0	325	1,780
Lifetime		5	0	0	0	0	0	0	0	731	0	0	1,628	$5,265

Bill Whittington

William Whittington
B: 9/11/1949
Racing Hometown: Ft. Lauderdale, FL

Year	Rank	Starts	Poles	1	2	3	4	5	6–10	Laps	Laps Led	Races Led	Miles	$
1980	102T	2	0	0	0	0	0	0	1	183	0	0	472	7,385
Lifetime		2	0	0	0	0	0	0	1	183	0	0	472	$7,385

Year	Rank	Starts	Poles	1	2	3	4	5	6–10	Laps	Laps Led	Races Led	Miles	$

Don Whittington

Donald Whittington
B: 1/23/1946
Racing Hometown: Lubbock, TX

Year	Rank	Starts	Poles	1	2	3	4	5	6–10	Laps	Laps Led	Races Led	Miles	$
1980	46	7	0	0	0	0	0	0	1	659	0	0	1,512	18,885
1981	54	3	0	0	0	0	0	0	0	346	0	0	883	13,685
Lifetime		10	0	0	0	0	0	0	1	1,005	0	0	2,395	$32,570

Reb Wickersham

Charles Allmond Wickersham
B: 1/11/1934
Racing Hometown: Long Boat Key, FL

Year	Rank	Starts	Poles	1	2	3	4	5	6–10	Laps	Laps Led	Races Led	Miles	$
1960	70	7	0	0	0	0	0	0	0	1,119	0	0	1,948	2,575
1961	79	8	0	0	0	0	0	0	1	1,343	0	0	1,199	1,345
1962	134	1	0	0	0	0	0	0	0	133	0	0	67	0
1963	33	14	0	0	0	0	0	0	1	3,501	0	0	2,577	3,800
1964	53	4	0	0	0	0	0	0	0	330	0	0	639	1,675
1965	45	7	0	0	0	0	0	0	2	906	0	0	1,198	4,410
Lifetime		41	0	0	0	0	0	0	4	7,332	0	0	7,627	$13,805

Bill Widenhouse

William Widenhouse
B: 6/17/1929
Racing Hometown: Midland, NC

Year	Rank	Starts	Poles	1	2	3	4	5	6–10	Laps	Laps Led	Races Led	Miles	$
1950	140	1	0	0	0	0	0	0	0	350	0	0	438	0
1951	55	4	0	0	0	0	0	0	0	371	0	0	464	225
1952	100	2	0	0	0	0	0	0	0	181	0	0	105	50
1953	NR	1	0	0	0	0	0	0	0	234	0	0	322	110
1954	37	6	0	0	0	0	0	0	0	987	0	0	999	425
1955	26	5	0	0	0	0	0	1	2	799	2	1	780	1,065
1956	100	6	0	0	0	0	0	1	0	511	0	0	411	460
1963	63	5	0	0	0	0	0	0	1	575	0	0	535	850
1964	NR	1	0	0	0	0	0	0	0	153	0	0	77	90
Lifetime		31	0	0	0	0	0	2	3	4,161	2	1	4,129	$3,275

Dink Widenhouse

David Widenhouse
B: 1/1/1932
Racing Hometown: Concord, NC

Year	Rank	Starts	Poles	1	2	3	4	5	6–10	Laps	Laps Led	Races Led	Miles	$
1954	61	6	0	0	0	0	1	0	1	620	0	0	401	625
1955	24	15	1	0	0	0	0	0	6	1,743	0	0	1,185	1,660
1956	70	7	0	0	0	0	1	0	2	734	0	0	535	940
Lifetime		28	1	0	0	0	2	0	9	3,097	0	0	2,121	$3,225

Earl Wilcox

Earl Wilcox
Racing Hometown: Asheville, NC

Year	Rank	Starts	Poles	1	2	3	4	5	6–10	Laps	Laps Led	Races Led	Miles	$
1961	182	1	0	0	0	0	0	0	0	81	0	0	41	0
Lifetime		1	0	0	0	0	0	0	0	81	0	0	41	$0

Harold Wilcox

Harold Wilcox
Racing Hometown: Bangor, ME

Year	Rank	Starts	Poles	1	2	3	4	5	6–10	Laps	Laps Led	Races Led	Miles	$
1961	123	1	0	0	0	0	0	0	0	112	0	0	28	150
Lifetime		1	0	0	0	0	0	0	0	112	0	0	28	$150

Carl Wilkerson

Carl Wilkerson
Racing Hometown: Youngstown, OH

Year	Rank	Starts	Poles	1	2	3	4	5	6–10	Laps	Laps Led	Races Led	Miles	$
1950	NR	1	0	0	0	0	0	0	0	72	0	0	36	0
Lifetime		1	0	0	0	0	0	0	0	72	0	0	36	$0

Felix Wilkes

Felix Wilkes
Racing Hometown: Annendale, NJ

Year	Rank	Starts	Poles	1	2	3	4	5	6–10	Laps	Laps Led	Races Led	Miles	$
1949	NR	3	0	0	0	0	0	0	0	38	0	0	38	0
1950	NR	1	0	0	0	0	0	0	0		0	0		0
1951	N/A	2	0	0	0	0	0	0	0	18	0	0	14	10
1952	189	1	0	0	0	0	0	0	0	141	0	0	141	35
Lifetime		7	0	0	0	0	0	0	0	197	0	0	193	$45

Year	Rank	Starts	Poles	Finish 1	2	3	4	5	6–10	Laps	Laps Led	Races Led	Miles	$

Keith Wilkinson

Keith Wilkinson
Racing Hometown: Sacramento, CA

Year	Rank	Starts	Poles	1	2	3	4	5	6–10	Laps	Laps Led	Races Led	Miles	$
1961	158T	1	0	0	0	0	0	0	0	74	0	0	74	50
Lifetime		1	0	0	0	0	0	0	0	74	0	0	74	$50

Bill Williams

William Williams
Racing Hometown: Oakland, CA

Year	Rank	Starts	Poles	1	2	3	4	5	6–10	Laps	Laps Led	Races Led	Miles	$
1954	NR	1	0	0	0	0	0	0	0	113	0	0	57	0
1955	221	1	0	0	0	0	0	0	0	195	0	0	195	40
Lifetime		2	0	0	0	0	0	0	0	308	0	0	252	$40

Bob Williams

Robert Williams
B: 6/1/1937
Racing Hometown: Jackson, MS

Year	Rank	Starts	Poles	1	2	3	4	5	6–10	Laps	Laps Led	Races Led	Miles	$
1971	NR	2	0	0	0	0	0	0	0	475	0	0	283	835
Lifetime		2	0	0	0	0	0	0	0	475	0	0	283	$835

Buster Williams

Buster Williams
Racing Hometown: Philadelphia, PA

Year	Rank	Starts	Poles	1	2	3	4	5	6–10	Laps	Laps Led	Races Led	Miles	$
1950	NR	1	0	0	0	0	0	0	0		0	0		0
Lifetime		1	0	0	0	0	0	0	0		0	0		$0

Chet Williams

Chester Williams
Racing Hometown: Detroit, MI

Year	Rank	Starts	Poles	1	2	3	4	5	6–10	Laps	Laps Led	Races Led	Miles	$
1953	94	2	0	0	0	0	0	0	0	374	0	0	429	135
Lifetime		2	0	0	0	0	0	0	0	374	0	0	429	$135

Chub Williams

Chub Williams

Year	Rank	Starts	Poles	1	2	3	4	5	6–10	Laps	Laps Led	Races Led	Miles	$
1956	179	1	0	0	0	0	0	0	0	225	0	0	113	75
Lifetime		1	0	0	0	0	0	0	0	225	0	0	113	$75

Dale Williams

Dale Williams
Racing Hometown: North Wilkesboro, NC

Year	Rank	Starts	Poles	1	2	3	4	5	6–10	Laps	Laps Led	Races Led	Miles	$
1951	N/A	1	0	0	0	0	0	0	1		0	0		100
Lifetime		1	0	0	0	0	0	0	1		0	0		$100

Jack Williams

Jack Williams

Year	Rank	Starts	Poles	1	2	3	4	5	6–10	Laps	Laps Led	Races Led	Miles	$
1956	NR	1	0	0	0	0	0	0	0	94	0	0	59	50
Lifetime		1	0	0	0	0	0	0	0	94	0	0	59	$50

Raymond Williams

Raymond M. Williams
B: 4/15/1939
Racing Hometown: Chapel Hill, NC

Year	Rank	Starts	Poles	1	2	3	4	5	6–10	Laps	Laps Led	Races Led	Miles	$
1970	31	21	0	0	0	0	0	0	0	3,641	0	0	3,844	12,535
1971	31	20	0	0	0	0	0	0	0	2,822	0	0	4,071	14,585
1972	14	28	0	0	0	0	0	0	5	6,759	0	0	8,079	37,000
1973	25	22	0	0	0	0	0	0	3	4,684	0	0	5,220	23,063
1977	113T	1	0	0	0	0	0	0	0	0	0	0	0	490
1978	93T	1	0	0	0	0	0	0	0	74	0	0	185	1,290
Lifetime		93	0	0	0	0	0	0	8	17,980	0	0	21,398	$88,963

Rodney Williams

Rodney Williams
Racing Hometown: Chesnee, SC

Year	Rank	Starts	Poles	1	2	3	4	5	6–10	Laps	Laps Led	Races Led	Miles	$
1964	121	2	0	0	0	0	0	0	0	115	0	0	68	550
Lifetime		2	0	0	0	0	0	0	0	115	0	0	68	$550

Tom Williams

Thomas Williams
Racing Hometown: Schertz, TX

Year	Rank	Starts	Poles	1	2	3	4	5	6–10	Laps	Laps Led	Races Led	Miles	$
1975	NR	2	0	0	0	0	0	0	0	235	0	0	609	2,815

Year	Rank	Starts	Poles	Finish						Laps	Laps Led	Races Led	Miles	$
				1	2	3	4	5	6–10					

Tom Williams *continued*

Year	Rank	Starts	Poles	1	2	3	4	5	6–10	Laps	Laps Led	Races Led	Miles	$
1976	113	1	0	0	0	0	0	0	0	41	0	0	103	1,615
Lifetime		3	0	0	0	0	0	0	0	276	0	0	711	$4,430

Charles Williamson

Charles Williamson
Racing Hometown: Roanoke, VA

Year	Rank	Starts	Poles	1	2	3	4	5	6–10	Laps	Laps Led	Races Led	Miles	$
1961	161T	1	0	0	0	0	0	0	0	107	0	0	27	30
Lifetime		1	0	0	0	0	0	0	0	107	0	0	27	$30

Mooney Williamson

Mooney Williamson
Racing Hometown: Norfolk, VA

Year	Rank	Starts	Poles	1	2	3	4	5	6–10	Laps	Laps Led	Races Led	Miles	$
1952	201	1	0	0	0	0	0	0	0		0	0		0
Lifetime		1	0	0	0	0	0	0	0		0	0		$0

Tim Williamson

Timothy Williamson
B: 1/13/1956   D: 1/12/1980   *Killed @ Riverside, CA, in Grand American race.*
Racing Hometown: Seaside, CA

Year	Rank	Starts	Poles	1	2	3	4	5	6–10	Laps	Laps Led	Races Led	Miles	$
1979	53	3	0	0	0	0	0	0	1	340	0	0	868	5,580
Lifetime		3	0	0	0	0	0	0	1	340	0	0	868	$5,580

Andy Wilson

Andrew Wilson

Year	Rank	Starts	Poles	1	2	3	4	5	6–10	Laps	Laps Led	Races Led	Miles	$
1956	239T	1	0	0	0	0	0	0	0	59	0	0	30	50
Lifetime		1	0	0	0	0	0	0	0	59	0	0	30	$50

Baldy Wilson

C. L. Wilson
Racing Hometown: Roanoke, VA

Year	Rank	Starts	Poles	1	2	3	4	5	6–10	Laps	Laps Led	Races Led	Miles	$
1950	78	1	0	0	0	0	0	0	0	127	0	0	127	75
Lifetime		1	0	0	0	0	0	0	0	127	0	0	127	$75

Bob Wilson

Robert Wilson
Racing Hometown: Toledo, OH

Year	Rank	Starts	Poles	1	2	3	4	5	6–10	Laps	Laps Led	Races Led	Miles	$
1950	116T	1	0	0	0	0	0	0	0	150	0	0	75	0
Lifetime		1	0	0	0	0	0	0	0	150	0	0	75	$0

Buzz Wilson

Buzz Wilson
Racing Hometown: Parkton, MD

Year	Rank	Starts	Poles	1	2	3	4	5	6–10	Laps	Laps Led	Races Led	Miles	$
1957	109	1	0	0	0	0	0	0	0	114	0	0	114	75
1958	134	4	0	0	0	0	0	0	0	386	0	0	189	250
Lifetime		5	0	0	0	0	0	0	0	500	0	0	303	$325

Denny Wilson

Dennis Wilson

Year	Rank	Starts	Poles	1	2	3	4	5	6–10	Laps	Laps Led	Races Led	Miles	$
1992	89	1	0	0	0	0	0	0	0	9	0	0	22	3,450
Lifetime		1	0	0	0	0	0	0	0	9	0	0	22	$3,450

Doug Wilson

Douglas Wilson
Racing Hometown: Greensboro, NC

Year	Rank	Starts	Poles	1	2	3	4	5	6–10	Laps	Laps Led	Races Led	Miles	$
1964	88	4	0	0	0	0	0	0	0	1,086	0	0	523	750
Lifetime		4	0	0	0	0	0	0	0	1,086	0	0	523	$750

Elmer Wilson

Elmer Wilson
Racing Hometown: Toledo, OH

Year	Rank	Starts	Poles	1	2	3	4	5	6–10	Laps	Laps Led	Races Led	Miles	$
1950	71	4	0	0	0	0	0	0	0	497	0	0	519	200
1951	N/A	3	0	0	0	0	0	0	0	80	0	0	80	25
Lifetime		7	0	0	0	0	0	0	0	577	0	0	599	$225

Fritz Wilson

Fred Wilson
Racing Hometown: Denver, CO

Year	Rank	Starts	Poles	1	2	3	4	5	6–10	Laps	Laps Led	Races Led	Miles	$
1959	63	7	0		0	1	0	0	0	1	651	4	1	460	880

Year	Rank	Starts	Poles	Finish 1	2	3	4	5	6–10	Laps	Laps Led	Races Led	Miles	$

Fritz Wilson *continued*

Year	Rank	Starts	Poles	1	2	3	4	5	6–10	Laps	Laps Led	Races Led	Miles	$
1960	68	4	0	0	0	0	2	0	0	284	0	0	367	925
1965	NR	1	0	0	0	0	0	0	0	84	0	0	227	550
Lifetime		12	0	0	1	0	2	0	1	1,019	4	1	1,054	$2,355

Gus Wilson

Gus Wilson
Racing Hometown: Baltimore, MD

Year	Rank	Starts	Poles	1	2	3	4	5	6–10	Laps	Laps Led	Races Led	Miles	$
1957	162	2	0	0	0	0	0	0	0	260	0	0	130	150
1958	124	3	0	0	0	0	0	0	0	359	0	0	163	175
1959	NR	1	0	0	0	0	0	0	0	100	0	0	50	50
Lifetime		6	0	0	0	0	0	0	0	719	0	0	343	$375

Jim Wilson

James Wilson
Racing Hometown: Springfield, Ont., Canada

Year	Rank	Starts	Poles	1	2	3	4	5	6–10	Laps	Laps Led	Races Led	Miles	$
1955	174	1	0	0	0	0	0	0	0	37	0	0	152	50
1956	183	2	0	0	0	0	0	0	0	180	0	0	90	50
Lifetime		3	0	0	0	0	0	0	0	217	0	0	242	$100

Paul Wilson

Paul Wilson

Year	Rank	Starts	Poles	1	2	3	4	5	6–10	Laps	Laps Led	Races Led	Miles	$
1958	NR	1	0	0	0	0	0	0	0	58	0	0	19	60
Lifetime		1	0	0	0	0	0	0	0	58	0	0	19	$60

Rick Wilson

Richard Wilson
B: 1/31/1953
Racing Hometown: Bartow, FL

Year	Rank	Starts	Poles	1	2	3	4	5	6–10	Laps	Laps Led	Races Led	Miles	$
1980	68	3	0	0	0	0	0	0	0	262	0	0	595	5,510
1981	41	8	0	0	0	0	0	0	0	989	7	2	1,713	16,335
1982	34	8	0	0	0	0	0	0	2	1,404	0	0	2,612	33,230
1983	98T	1	0	0	0	0	0	0	0	55	0	0	146	3,285
1985	74	2	0	0	0	0	0	0	0	432	0	0	784	4,460
1986	28	17	0	0	0	0	0	0	4	3,265	7	1	5,309	88,820
1987	28	19	0	0	0	0	0	0	1	3,530	20	1	5,575	65,935
1988	21	28	1	0	1	0	1	0	3	6,870	152	4	8,703	209,925
1989	17	29	0	0	0	0	1	1	5	8,004	29	5	9,990	312,402
1990	23	29	0	0	0	0	0	1	2	8,036	0	0	9,305	242,067
1991	26	29	0	0	0	0	0	0	0	7,966	10	1	9,694	241,375
1992	73	1	0	0	0	0	0	0	0	195	0	0	488	24,045
1993	28	29	0	0	0	0	0	0	1	8,117	1	1	10,330	299,725
Lifetime		203	1	0	1	0	2	2	18	49,125	226	15	65,244	$1,547,114

Woodie Wilson

Woodrow Wilson
B: 8/8/1925 D: 1994
Racing Hometown: Mobile, AL

Year	Rank	Starts	Poles	1	2	3	4	5	6–10	Laps	Laps Led	Races Led	Miles	$
1949	NR	1	0	0	0	0	0	0	0		0	0		25
1955	NR	1	0	0	0	0	0	0	0	18	0	0	27	50
1961	41	5	0	0	0	0	0	0	1	828	0	0	1,324	2,625
1962	78	3	0	0	0	0	0	0	1	70	0	0	144	750
Lifetime		10	0	0	0	0	0	0	2	916	0	0	1,495	$3,450

George Wiltshire

George Wiltshire
B: 5/10/1947
Racing Hometown: Corona, NY

Year	Rank	Starts	Poles	1	2	3	4	5	6–10	Laps	Laps Led	Races Led	Miles	$
1971	NR	1	0	0	0	0	0	0	0	2	0	0	1	100
1975	107T	1	0	0	0	0	0	0	0	15	0	0	38	630
Lifetime		2	0	0	0	0	0	0	0	17	0	0	38	$730

Jerry Wimbish

Jerry Wimbish
Racing Hometown: Atlanta, GA

Year	Rank	Starts	Poles	1	2	3	4	5	6–10	Laps	Laps Led	Races Led	Miles	$
1950	62T	1	0	0	0	0	0	0	1		0	0		100
1951	N/A	2	0	0	0	0	0	0	1	51	0	0	51	75
1952	71	4	0	0	0	0	0	1	0	222	0	0	113	395
1953	69T	1	0	0	0	0	0	1	0		0	0		200

Year	Rank	Starts	Poles	Finish						Laps	Laps Led	Races Led	Miles	$
				1	2	3	4	5	6–10					

Jerry Wimbish *continued*

Year	Rank	Starts	Poles	1	2	3	4	5	6–10	Laps	Laps Led	Races Led	Miles	$
1954	NR	1	0	0	0	0	0	0	0	92	0	0	92	25
Lifetime		9	0	0	0	0	0	2	2	365	0	0	256	$795

Bill Wimble

William Wimble
B: 1/11/1932
Racing Hometown: Lisbon, N Y

Year	Rank	Starts	Poles	1	2	3	4	5	6–10	Laps	Laps Led	Races Led	Miles	$
1958	114	2	0	0	0	0	0	0	0	241	0	0	121	100
1962	48	2	0	0	0	0	0	0	0	231	0	0	578	675
Lifetime		4	0	0	0	0	0	0	0	472	0	0	698	$775

Doug Wimpy

Douglas Wimpy
Racing Hometown: Mobile, AL

Year	Rank	Starts	Poles	1	2	3	4	5	6–10	Laps	Laps Led	Races Led	Miles	$
1951	N/A	1	0	0	0	0	0	0	0		0	0		25
Lifetime		1	0	0	0	0	0	0	0		0	0		$25

Andy Winfree

Andrew Winfree
Racing Hometown: Greensboro, NC

Year	Rank	Starts	Poles	1	2	3	4	5	6–10	Laps	Laps Led	Races Led	Miles	$
1953	23	7	0	0	0	0	0	0	3	277	0	0	277	440
1954	NR	3	0	0	0	0	0	0	1	301	0	0	216	175
Lifetime		10	0	0	0	0	0	0	4	578	0	0	493	$615

John Winger

John Winger
Racing Hometown: California

Year	Rank	Starts	Poles	1	2	3	4	5	6–10	Laps	Laps Led	Races Led	Miles	$
1968	107	3	0	0	0	0	0	0	0	381	0	0	94	320
Lifetime		3	0	0	0	0	0	0	0	381	0	0	94	$320

Dorus Wisecraver

Dorus Wisecraver
B: 1936
Racing Hometown: Zanesville, OH

Year	Rank	Starts	Poles	1	2	3	4	5	6–10	Laps	Laps Led	Races Led	Miles	$
1967	NR	2	0	0	0	0	0	0	0	219	0	0	548	2,325
Lifetime		2	0	0	0	0	0	0	0	219	0	0	548	$2,325

Roland Wlodyka

Roland Wlodyka
B: 10/15/1938
Racing Hometown: Boston, MA

Year	Rank	Starts	Poles	1	2	3	4	5	6–10	Laps	Laps Led	Races Led	Miles	$
1977	63	5	0	0	0	0	0	0	0	501	0	0	1,100	5,520
1978	44	6	0	0	0	0	0	0	0	1,172	0	0	1,707	9,910
Lifetime		11	0	0	0	0	0	0	0	1,673	0	0	2,807	$15,430

Johnny Wohlfiel

John Wohlfiel
Racing Hometown: Drayton Plains, MI

Year	Rank	Starts	Poles	1	2	3	4	5	6–10	Laps	Laps Led	Races Led	Miles	$
1951	N/A	1	0	0	0	0	0	0	0	27	0	0	27	0
Lifetime		1	0	0	0	0	0	0	0	27	0	0	27	$0

Johnny Wolford

John Wolford
Racing Hometown: Circleville, OH

Year	Rank	Starts	Poles	1	2	3	4	5	6–10	Laps	Laps Led	Races Led	Miles	$
1960	NR	1	0	0	0	0	0	0	0	5	0	0	8	200
Lifetime		1	0	0	0	0	0	0	0	5	0	0	8	$200

Bob Wood

Robert Wood
Racing Hometown: Portland, OR

Year	Rank	Starts	Poles	1	2	3	4	5	6–10	Laps	Laps Led	Races Led	Miles	$
1957	NR	1	0	0	0	0	0	0	0	18	0	0	9	100
Lifetime		1	0	0	0	0	0	0	0	18	0	0	9	$100

Gifford Wood

Gifford Wood
Racing Hometown: Collinsville, VA

Year	Rank	Starts	Poles	1	2	3	4	5	6–10	Laps	Laps Led	Races Led	Miles	$
1953	NR	2	0	0	0	0	0	0	0	136	0	0	68	50
1954	144	1	0	0	0	0	0	0	0	152	0	0	76	25
Lifetime		3	0	0	0	0	0	0	0	288	0	0	144	$75

Year	Rank	Starts	Poles	Finish 1	2	3	4	5	6–10	Laps	Laps Led	Races Led	Miles	$

Glen Wood
Glen Wood
B: 7/18/1925
Racing Hometown: Stuart, VA

Year	Rank	Starts	Poles	1	2	3	4	5	6–10	Laps	Laps Led	Races Led	Miles	$
1953	64	2	0	0	0	0	0	0	0	274	0	0	274	125
1954	215T	1	0	0	0	0	0	0	0	33	0	0	17	0
1955	242T	1	0	0	0	0	0	0	0	55	0	0	28	0
1956	246T	2	0	0	0	0	0	0	0	177	0	0	89	50
1957	74	6	0	0	0	0	0	0	1	1,062	0	0	847	1,670
1958	NR	10	3	0	1	0	0	0	6	2,348	360	4	1,331	3,120
1959	57	20	3	0	5	1	1	2	4	4,186	98	2	2,292	6,875
1960	103	9	4	3	0	2	0	1	1	2,206	**766**	5	973	5,260
1961	65	6	1	0	2	1	0	0	0	1,101	138	1	445	2,000
1963	73	3	2	1	0	1	0	0	0	571	268	2	143	1,070
1964	100	2	1	0	0	1	0	0	0	305	5	1	76	530
Lifetime		62	14	4	8	6	1	3	12	12,318	1,635	15	6,513	$20,700

Rich Woodland Jr.
Richard Woodland Jr.
B: 8/5/1970
Racing Hometown: Templeton, CA

Year	Rank	Starts	Poles	1	2	3	4	5	6–10	Laps	Laps Led	Races Led	Miles	$
1993	85T	1	0	0	0	0	0	0	0	114	0	0	114	6,030
1996	63T	1	0	0	0	0	0	0	0	68	0	0	171	10,095
Lifetime		2	0	0	0	0	0	0	0	182	0	0	285	$16,125

Cliff Woodson
Clifford Woodson

Year	Rank	Starts	Poles	1	2	3	4	5	6–10	Laps	Laps Led	Races Led	Miles	$
1951	N/A	1	0	0	0	0	0	0	0	1	0	0	1	10
Lifetime		1	0	0	0	0	0	0	0	1	0	0	1	$10

Buzz Woodward
Benton H. Woodward
B: 1937
Racing Hometown: Coatesville, PA

Year	Rank	Starts	Poles	1	2	3	4	5	6–10	Laps	Laps Led	Races Led	Miles	$
1956	172	1	0	0	0	0	0	0	0	120	0	0	120	50
1957	NR	1	0	0	0	0	0	0	1	87	0	0	87	165
1958	40	9	0	0	0	0	0	0	2	1,508	0	0	1,028	1,195
1959	NR	1	0	0	0	0	0	1	0	191	0	0	96	225
1961	NR	1	0	0	0	0	0	0	1	456	0	0	114	400
Lifetime		13	0	0	0	0	0	1	4	2,362	0	0	1,445	$2,035

Wayne Woodward
Wayne Woodward
B: 8/26/1934   D: 1994
Racing Hometown: Ringgold, GA

Year	Rank	Starts	Poles	1	2	3	4	5	6–10	Laps	Laps Led	Races Led	Miles	$
1966	67	7	0	0	0	0	0	0	0	1,194	0	0	876	1,930
Lifetime		7	0	0	0	0	0	0	0	1,194	0	0	876	$1,930

Bill Woolkin
William Woolkin

Year	Rank	Starts	Poles	1	2	3	4	5	6–10	Laps	Laps Led	Races Led	Miles	$
1959	NR	1	0	0	0	0	0	0	0	109	0	0	27	70
Lifetime		1	0	0	0	0	0	0	0	109	0	0	27	$70

Satch Worley
Donald A. Worley Jr.
B: 6/2/1948
Racing Hometown: Rocky Mount, VA

Year	Rank	Starts	Poles	1	2	3	4	5	6–10	Laps	Laps Led	Races Led	Miles	$
1974	110	1	0	0	0	0	0	0	1	431	0	0	226	1,300
1978	50	4	0	0	0	0	0	0	1	1,298	0	0	1,589	6,205
1985	—	0												3,700
Lifetime		5	0	0	0	0	0	0	2	1,729	0	0	1,816	$11,205

Bruce Worrell
Bruce Worrell
Racing Hometown: Lakewood, CA

Year	Rank	Starts	Poles	1	2	3	4	5	6–10	Laps	Laps Led	Races Led	Miles	$
1960	72	3	0	0	0	0	0	0	2	333	0	0	394	650
1961	85	4	0	0	0	0	0	0	2	391	0	0	379	540
1963	153	1	0	0	0	0	0	0	0	1	0	0	3	200
1964	72	1	0	0	0	0	0	0	0	161	0	0	435	575
1965	128	1	0	0	0	0	0	0	0	1	0	0	3	500
1966	128	1	0	0	0	0	0	0	0	15	0	0	41	500

Year	Rank	Starts	Poles			Finish				Laps	Laps Led	Races Led	Miles	$
				1	2	3	4	5	6–10					

Bruce Worrell *continued*

Year	Rank	Starts	Poles	1	2	3	4	5	6–10	Laps	Laps Led	Races Led	Miles	$
1967	56	1	0	0	0	0	0	0	1	174	0	0	470	1,650
Lifetime		12	0	0	0	0	0	0	5	1,076	0	0	1,723	$4,615

Whitey Worton

Whitey Worton

| 1951 | N/A | 1 | 0 | 0 | 0 | 0 | 0 | 0 | 0 | | 0 | 0 | | 25 |
| **Lifetime** | | 1 | 0 | 0 | 0 | 0 | 0 | 0 | 0 | | 0 | 0 | | $25 |

Cecil Wray

Cecil Wray
Racing Hometown: Middletown, OH

| 1958 | 105 | 1 | 0 | 0 | 0 | 0 | 0 | 0 | 0 | 34 | 0 | 0 | 139 | 75 |
| **Lifetime** | | 1 | 0 | 0 | 0 | 0 | 0 | 0 | 0 | 34 | 0 | 0 | 139 | $75 |

Cliff Wright

Clifford Wright

| 1955 | 222 | 1 | 0 | 0 | 0 | 0 | 0 | 0 | 0 | 178 | 0 | 0 | 178 | 40 |
| **Lifetime** | | 1 | 0 | 0 | 0 | 0 | 0 | 0 | 0 | 178 | 0 | 0 | 178 | $40 |

Gary Wright

Gary Wright
B: 1959
Racing Hometown: Hooks, TX

| 1991 | 80T | 1 | 0 | 0 | 0 | 0 | 0 | 0 | 0 | 63 | 0 | 0 | 158 | 3,750 |
| **Lifetime** | | 1 | 0 | 0 | 0 | 0 | 0 | 0 | 0 | 63 | 0 | 0 | 158 | $3,750 |

Harold Wright

Harold Wright
Racing Hometown: Syracuse, NY

| 1952 | 120T | 1 | 0 | 0 | 0 | 0 | 0 | 0 | 0 | 162 | 0 | 0 | 81 | 25 |
| **Lifetime** | | 1 | 0 | 0 | 0 | 0 | 0 | 0 | 0 | 162 | 0 | 0 | 81 | $25 |

Jim Wright

James Wright
Racing Hometown: Richmond, VA

| 1967 | 121 | 1 | 0 | 0 | 0 | 0 | 0 | 0 | 0 | 9 | 0 | 0 | 5 | 125 |
| **Lifetime** | | 1 | 0 | 0 | 0 | 0 | 0 | 0 | 0 | 9 | 0 | 0 | 5 | $125 |

John Wright

John C. Wright
B: 2/14/1923
Racing Hometown: Ransomville, NY

| 1949 | 33 | 1 | 0 | 0 | 0 | 0 | 0 | 0 | 1 | 179 | 0 | 0 | 90 | 100 |
| **Lifetime** | | 1 | 0 | 0 | 0 | 0 | 0 | 0 | 1 | 179 | 0 | 0 | 90 | $100 |

L. W. Wright

L. W. Wright
Racing Hometown: Nashville, TN

| 1982 | NR | 1 | 0 | 0 | 0 | 0 | 0 | 0 | 0 | 13 | 0 | 0 | 35 | 1,545 |
| **Lifetime** | | 1 | 0 | 0 | 0 | 0 | 0 | 0 | 0 | 13 | 0 | 0 | 35 | $1,545 |

Millard Wright

Millard Wright
Racing Hometown: Montclair, NJ

1955	132	2	0	0	0	0	0	0	0	225	0	0	113	110
1956	NR	1	0	0	0	0	0	0	0	178	0	0	89	50
Lifetime		3	0	0	0	0	0	0	0	403	0	0	202	$160

Ted Wright

Theodore Wright
Racing Hometown: Greensburg, PA

| 1954 | NR | 1 | 0 | 0 | 0 | 0 | 0 | 0 | 0 | 132 | 0 | 0 | 66 | 25 |
| **Lifetime** | | 1 | 0 | 0 | 0 | 0 | 0 | 0 | 0 | 132 | 0 | 0 | 66 | $25 |

Bailey Wynkoop

Bailey Wynkoop
Racing Hometown: Falls Church, VA

| 1958 | 127 | 2 | 0 | 0 | 0 | 0 | 0 | 0 | 0 | 153 | 0 | 0 | 59 | 170 |
| **Lifetime** | | 2 | 0 | 0 | 0 | 0 | 0 | 0 | 0 | 153 | 0 | 0 | 59 | $170 |

Year	Rank	Starts	Poles	Finish						Laps	Laps Led	Races Led	Miles	$
				1	2	3	4	5	6–10					

Johnny Wynn

John Wynn (Jack)
B: 10/14/1931
Racing Hometown: Grand Rapids, MI

Year	Rank	Starts	Poles	1	2	3	4	5	6–10	Laps	Laps Led	Races Led	Miles	$
1966	38	21	0	0	0	0	0	0	5	3,245	0	0	2,224	4,650
Lifetime		21	0	0	0	0	0	0	5	3,245	0	0	2,224	$4,650

Eddie Yarboro

Edward James Yarboro
B: 7/7/1938
Racing Hometown: Elkin, NC

Year	Rank	Starts	Poles	1	2	3	4	5	6–10	Laps	Laps Led	Races Led	Miles	$
1966	102	3	0	0	0	0	0	0	1	457	0	0	184	165
1967	51	9	0	0	0	0	0	0	3	1,680	0	0	820	1,745
1968	49	6	0	0	0	0	0	0	0	2,109	0	0	1,347	2,255
1970	NR	1	0	0	0	0	0	0	1	338	0	0	201	800
1971	50	7	0	0	0	0	0	0	0	1,624	0	0	1,310	3,685
1972	50	6	0	0	0	0	0	0	0	1,728	0	0	1,336	3,435
1973	128	1	0	0	0	0	0	0	0	4	0	0	11	610
Lifetime		33	0	0	0	0	0	0	5	7,940	0	0	5,209	$12,695

Cale Yarborough

William Caleb Yarborough
B: 3/27/1939
Racing Hometown: Timmonsville, SC

Year	Rank	Starts	Poles	1	2	3	4	5	6–10	Laps	Laps Led	Races Led	Miles	$
1957	159	1	0	0	0	0	0	0	0	31	0	0	43	100
1959	110	1	0	0	0	0	0	0	0	219	0	0	301	150
1960	132	1	0	0	0	0	0	0	0	114	0	0	57	85
1961	NR	1	0	0	0	0	0	0	0	135	0	0	186	200
1962	50	8	0	0	0	0	0	0	1	727	0	0	1,046	2,725
1963	25	18	0	0	0	0	0	3	4	4,519	0	0	3,298	5,550
1964	19	24	0	0	0	0	0	2	7	4,990	10	1	4,121	10,378
1965	10	46	0	1	3	1	5	3	8	7,734	166	8	5,396	26,587
1966	18	14	0	0	2	0	1	0	4	3,831	252	4	3,944	28,130
1967	20	16	4	2	3	1	1	0	1	3,728	908	9	3,668	57,312
1968	17	21	4	6	2	1	0	3	0	5,661	1,215	16	5,747	138,052
1969	23	19	6	2	2	1	2	0	1	4,341	946	16	5,482	75,065
1970	34	19	5	3	4	3	0	1	2	5,034	906	14	6,237	117,600
1971	NR	4	0	0	0	0	0	0	1	564	13	1	961	3,844
1972	51	5	0	0	0	0	0	1	3	1,196	9	1	1,968	11,667
1973	2	28	5	4	6	4	1	1	3	9,314	**3,167**	**21**	9,737	267,513
1974	2	30	3	10	4	5	1	1	1	**9,398**	**3,630**	**26**	**11,058**	363,782
1975	9	27	3	3	3	3	3	1	0	7,353	2,542	20	8,100	214,691
1976	1	30	2	9	6	3	2	2	1	**9,269**	**3,791**	**28**	**10,547**	453,405
1977	1	30	3	9	6	4	3	3	2	**9,747**	**3,218**	**28**	**11,382**	561,642
1978	1	30	8	10	6	1	5	1	1	**9,758**	**3,587**	**28**	**11,366**	623,506
1979	4	31	1	4	2	6	4	3	3	9,677	1,323	22	11,192	440,129
1980	2	31	14	6	4	4	4	1	3	9,440	**2,810**	**28**	11,015	567,891
1981	24	18	2	2	1	2	0	1	4	4,922	769	13	7,134	150,840
1982	27	16	2	3	2	1	2	0	0	3,439	379	12	5,642	231,590
1983	28	16	3	4	0	0	0	0	4	3,783	608	13	5,975	265,035
1984	22	16	4	3	1	3	1	2	0	4,387	736	12	7,140	403,853
1985	26	16	0	2	2	2	0	0	1	3,450	664	11	5,669	310,465
1986	29	16	1	0	0	2	0	0	3	3,467	110	4	5,828	137,010
1987	29	16	0	0	0	0	1	1	2	2,671	11	2	4,519	111,025
1988	38	10	0	0	0	0	0	0	3	1,653	6	2	3,169	66,065
Lifetime		559	70	83	59	47	36	30	63	144,552	31,776	340	171,927	$5,645,887
			3rd	**5th**							**2nd**	**5th**	**10th**	

J. C. Yarborough

Julian C. Yarborough
Racing Hometown: Timmonsville, SC

Year	Rank	Starts	Poles	1	2	3	4	5	6–10	Laps	Laps Led	Races Led	Miles	$
1969	79	2	0	0	0	0	0	0	0	318	0	0	159	415
Lifetime		2	0	0	0	0	0	0	0	318	0	0	159	$415

Eldon Yarbrough

Eldon Yarbrough
Racing Hometown: Jacksonville, FL

Year	Rank	Starts	Poles	1	2	3	4	5	6–10	Laps	Laps Led	Races Led	Miles	$
1966	NR	1	0	0	0	0	0	0	0	74	0	0	111	500
1967	118	1	0	0	0	0	0	0	0	46	0	0	69	580
1969	NR	1	0	0	0	0	0	1	0	194	0	0	97	325
Lifetime		3	0	0	0	0	0	1	0	314	0	0	277	$1,405

Year	Rank	Starts	Poles	1	2	3	4	5	6–10	Laps	Laps Led	Races Led	Miles	$

LeeRoy Yarbrough

Lonnie LeeRoy Yarbrough
B: 9/17/1938   D: 12/7/1984   *Died in mental institution.*
Racing Hometown: Jacksonville, FL

Year	Rank	Starts	Poles	1	2	3	4	5	6–10	Laps	Laps Led	Races Led	Miles	$
1960	137	1	0	0	0	0	0	0	0	60	0	0	90	225
1962	36	12	0	0	0	0	0	1	0	1,478	0	0	1,730	3,485
1963	26	14	1	0	0	0	0	1	4	2,564	8	1	2,433	6,680
1964	15	34	0	2	3	2	3	1	4	5,896	200	5	4,477	16,630
1965	37	14	0	0	0	0	1	1	1	1,747	42	2	1,748	5,905
1966	26	9	2	1	0	0	1	0	2	1,545	364	5	2,546	23,980
1967	37	15	0	1	0	2	0	0	1	2,647	34	4	2,894	15,575
1968	16	26	6	2	3	6	1	3	1	6,423	1,300	14	5,897	87,920
1969	16	30	0	7	2	0	6	1	5	8,190	1,155	17	8,717	193,211
1970	43	19	1	1	1	4	2	0	3	4,250	284	12	5,438	61,980
1971	73	6	0	0	0	0	1	0	2	1,144	26	2	1,779	9,260
1972	34	18	0	0	0	1	2	2	4	4,174	8	4	4,866	40,920
Lifetime		198	10	14	9	15	17	10	27	40,118	3,421	66	42,613	$465,771

Jack Yardley

Jack Yardley
Racing Hometown: Haddonfield, NJ

Year	Rank	Starts	Poles	1	2	3	4	5	6–10	Laps	Laps Led	Races Led	Miles	$
1950	NR	1	0	0	0	0	0	0	0	89	0	0	111	0
Lifetime		1	0	0	0	0	0	0	0	89	0	0	111	$0

Doug Yates

Alfred Doug Yates
B: 1/5/1925
Racing Hometown: Chapel Hill, NC

Year	Rank	Starts	Poles	1	2	3	4	5	6–10	Laps	Laps Led	Races Led	Miles	$
1952	198	1	0	0	0	0	0	0	0	0	0	0	0	25
1956	178	2	0	0	0	0	0	0	0	86	0	0	90	150
1958	175	1	0	0	0	0	0	0	0	16	0	0	66	25
1960	21	24	1	0	0	2	1	0	5	4,030	39	1	3,262	5,205
1961	27	32	0	0	0	0	0	2	8	5,058	0	0	2,992	5,370
1962	67	7	0	0	0	0	0	0	2	883	0	0	510	1,090
1964	45	15	1	0	1	0	0	2	4	2,573	9	1	1,172	3,340
1965	88	4	0	0	0	0	0	0	1	271	13	1	150	550
Lifetime		86	2	0	1	2	1	4	20	12,917	61	3	8,241	$15,755

Cliff Yiskis

Clifford Yiskis
Racing Hometown: Cupertino, CA

Year	Rank	Starts	Poles	1	2	3	4	5	6–10	Laps	Laps Led	Races Led	Miles	$
1957	110	1	0	0	0	0	1	0	0	140	0	0	88	365
Lifetime		1	0	0	0	0	1	0	0	140	0	0	88	$365

Shorty York

Aaron Ransom York
B: 1/13/1924   D: 12/24/1970   *Suicide.*
Racing Hometown: Mocksville, NC

Year	Rank	Starts	Poles	1	2	3	4	5	6–10	Laps	Laps Led	Races Led	Miles	$
1950	96	1	0	0	0	0	0	0	0	358	0	0	448	0
1951	57	5	0	0	1	0	0	0	0	363	0	0	454	725
1956	102	1	0	0	0	0	0	0	0	336	0	0	462	130
1957	155	2	0	0	0	0	0	0	0	188	0	0	163	350
1959	NR	1	0	0	0	0	0	0	0	185	0	0	46	120
1960	95	2	0	0	0	0	0	0	0	434	0	0	412	325
Lifetime		12	0	0	1	0	0	0	0	1,864	0	0	1,985	$1,650

Ernie Yorton

Ernest Yorton
Racing Hometown: Fairport, NY

Year	Rank	Starts	Poles	1	2	3	4	5	6–10	Laps	Laps Led	Races Led	Miles	$
1951	N/A	1	0	0	0	0	0	0	1		0	0		100
Lifetime		1	0	0	0	0	0	0	1		0	0		$100

Buddy Young

Nicholas C. Young
B: 1/13/1943
Racing Hometown: Fairfax, VA

Year	Rank	Starts	Poles	1	2	3	4	5	6–10	Laps	Laps Led	Races Led	Miles	$
1969	35	21	0	0	0	0	0	1	5	4,510	0	0	3,873	15,542
1970	59	2	0	0	0	0	0	0	1	501	0	0	569	1,980
Lifetime		23	0	0	0	0	0	1	6	5,011	0	0	4,442	$17,402

Year	Rank	Starts	Poles	Finish						Laps	Laps Led	Races Led	Miles	$
				1	2	3	4	5	6–10					

Clay Young

Clay Young
B: 6/9/1947
Racing Hometown: Smyrna, GA

Year	Rank	Starts	Poles	1	2	3	4	5	6–10	Laps	Laps Led	Races Led	Miles	$
1980	NR	1	0	0	0	0	0	0	0	265	0	0	403	1,150
1986	97	1	0	0	0	0	0	0	0	90	0	0	236	1,400
1992	90T	1	0	0	0	0	0	0	0	40	0	0	106	7,890
1993	70	2	0	0	0	0	0	0	0	60	0	0	143	14,370
Lifetime		5	0	0	0	0	0	0	0	455	0	0	889	$24,810

Ernie Young

Ernest Young
Racing Hometown: Lakewood, CA

Year	Rank	Starts	Poles	1	2	3	4	5	6–10	Laps	Laps Led	Races Led	Miles	$
1954	138	3	0	0	0	0	0	0	0	739	0	0	459	65
1955	NR	3	0	0	0	0	0	0	1	311	0	0	249	150
1956	85	5	0	0	0	0	0	0	0	419	0	0	443	330
1957	102	2	0	0	0	0	1	0	0	153	0	0	97	375
1958	81	1	0	0	0	0	0	0	0	165	0	0	434	130
Lifetime		14	0	0	0	0	1	0	1	1,787	0	0	1,680	$1,050

Leslie Young

Leslie Young *Real Name*: Ray Elston
Racing Hometown: Wilkes-Barre, PA

Year	Rank	Starts	Poles	1	2	3	4	5	6–10	Laps	Laps Led	Races Led	Miles	$
1954	NR	1	0	0	0	0	0	0	0	5	0	0	5	0
1955	236	1	0	0	0	0	0	0	0	21	0	0	21	25
Lifetime		2	0	0	0	0	0	0	0	26	0	0	26	$25

Steve Young

Steve Young
Racing Hometown: Charlotte, NC

Year	Rank	Starts	Poles	1	2	3	4	5	6–10	Laps	Laps Led	Races Led	Miles	$
1964	74	9	0	0	0	0	0	0	1	991	0	0	513	1,375
Lifetime		9	0	0	0	0	0	0	1	991	0	0	513	$1,375

Johnny Yountz

John Yountz
Racing Hometown: Liberty, NC

Year	Rank	Starts	Poles	1	2	3	4	5	6–10	Laps	Laps Led	Races Led	Miles	$
1951	N/A	1	0	0	0	0	0	0	0	361	0	0	451	50
Lifetime		1	0	0	0	0	0	0	0	361	0	0	451	$50

Pete Yow

Pete Yow
Racing Hometown: Sanford, NC

Year	Rank	Starts	Poles	1	2	3	4	5	6–10	Laps	Laps Led	Races Led	Miles	$
1956	54	11	0	0	0	0	0	0	2	1,221	0	0	680	700
Lifetime		11	0	0	0	0	0	0	2	1,221	0	0	680	$700

Smokey Yunick

Henry Yunick
B: 5/25/1923
Racing Hometown: Daytona Beach, FL

Year	Rank	Starts	Poles	1	2	3	4	5	6–10	Laps	Laps Led	Races Led	Miles	$
1952	147T	1	0	0	0	0	0	0	0	7	0	0	4	25
Lifetime		1	0	0	0	0	0	0	0	7	0	0	4	$25

Johnny Zeke

John Zeke
B: 11/20/1920
Racing Hometown: Levittown, NY

Year	Rank	Starts	Poles	1	2	3	4	5	6–10	Laps	Laps Led	Races Led	Miles	$
1953	159	2	0	0	0	0	0	0	0	84	0	0	84	65
1954	213	1	0	0	0	0	0	0	0	6	0	0	3	10
1956	297T	1	0	0	0	0	0	0	0	49	0	0	25	0
Lifetime		4	0	0	0	0	0	0	0	139	0	0	112	$75

Emanuel Zervakis

Emanuel Zervakis (Manny)
B: 1/23/1930
Racing Hometown: Richmond, VA

Year	Rank	Starts	Poles	1	2	3	4	5	6–10	Laps	Laps Led	Races Led	Miles	$
1956	81	6	0	0	0	0	0	0	0	772	0	0	827	475
1957	140	5	0	0	0	0	0	0	0	1,032	0	0	739	675
1958	161	6	0	0	0	0	0	0	0	457	0	0	378	465
1960	8	14	1	0	0	1	1	0	8	3,382	0	0	3,457	12,124
1961	3	38	1	2	1	3	5	8	9	9,198	386	2	6,664	27,281

Year	Rank	Starts	Poles	Finish 1	2	3	4	5	6–10	Laps	Laps Led	Races Led	Miles	$

Emanuel Zervakis *continued*

Year	Rank	Starts	Poles	1	2	3	4	5	6–10	Laps	Laps Led	Races Led	Miles	$
1962	27	11	0	0	0	0	0	0	2	2,151	5	1	2,357	4,545
1963	54	3	0	0	0	0	0	0	0	436	0	0	586	1,400
Lifetime		83	2	2	1	4	6	8	19	17,428	391	3	15,007	$46,965

Dennis Zimmerman

Dennis Zimmerman (Denny)
B: 12/14/1940
Racing Hometown: Glastonburg, CT

Year	Rank	Starts	Poles	1	2	3	4	5	6–10	Laps	Laps Led	Races Led	Miles	$
1964	111	1	0	0	0	0	0	0	0	209	0	0	78	100
Lifetime		1	0	0	0	0	0	0	0	209	0	0	78	$100

Dick Zimmerman

Richard C. Zimmerman
B: 12/17/1918
Racing Hometown: Milwaukee, WI

Year	Rank	Starts	Poles	1	2	3	4	5	6–10	Laps	Laps Led	Races Led	Miles	$
1949	57	1	0	0	0	0	0	0	0	178	0	0	178	50
1954	149	2	0	0	0	0	0	0	0	350	0	0	236	40
1955	147	2	0	0	0	0	0	0	0	222	0	0	150	25
Lifetime		5	0	0	0	0	0	0	0	750	0	0	563	$115

Earl Zindahl

Earl Zindahl

Year	Rank	Starts	Poles	1	2	3	4	5	6–10	Laps	Laps Led	Races Led	Miles	$
1952	NR	1	0	0	0	0	0	0	0	88	0	0	44	25
Lifetime		1	0	0	0	0	0	0	0	88	0	0	44	$25

Jack Zink

John Smith Zink Jr.
B: 1929
Racing Hometown: Tulsa, OK

Year	Rank	Starts	Poles	1	2	3	4	5	6–10	Laps	Laps Led	Races Led	Miles	$
1956	195T	1	0	0	0	0	0	0	0	10	0	0	5	100
Lifetime		1	0	0	0	0	0	0	0	10	0	0	5	$100

Pat Zocano

Pat Zocano
Racing Hometown: Detroit, MI

Year	Rank	Starts	Poles	1	2	3	4	5	6–10	Laps	Laps Led	Races Led	Miles	$
1956	263	1	0	0	0	0	0	0	0		0	0		60
Lifetime		1	0	0	0	0	0	0	0		0	0		$60

Ralph Zrimsek

Ralph Zrimsek
B: 1/30/1918
Racing Hometown: Canonsburg, PA

Year	Rank	Starts	Poles	1	2	3	4	5	6–10	Laps	Laps Led	Races Led	Miles	$
1949	NR	1	0	0	0	0	0	0	0	59	0	0	30	0
Lifetime		1	0	0	0	0	0	0	0	59	0	0	30	$0

PART 4
THE OWNERS

Year	Driver	Starts	Poles	Finish						Laps	Laps Led	Races Led	Miles	$
				1	2	3	4	5	6–10					
Petty Enterprises														
1971	Buddy Baker	18	1	1	5	5	0	1	3	4,614	693	14	7,513	112,145
"	Richard Petty	46	9	21	8	7	2	0	3	13,739	4,932	41	12,870	351,071
"	**Total**	**47**	**10**	**22**	**13**	**12**	**2**	**1**	**6**	**18,353**	**5,625**[1]	**44**[1]	**20,383**	**463,216**
1972	Buddy Baker	10	0	1	0	2	0	0	1	1,838	146	8	3,365	54,975
"	Richard Petty	31	3	8	9	5	2	1	3	10,282	2,038	30	11,996	339,405
"	**Total**	**31**	**3**	**9**	**9**	**7**	**2**	**1**	**4**	**12,120**	**2,184**	**31**	**15,360**	**394,380**
Lifetime		1635	150	266	223	178	113	91	324	471,974	59,633	714	460,740	$12,068,812
		1st	**1st**	**1st**						**1st**	**1st**	**1st**	**1st**	**6th**

Key

STARTS	Number of starts that year; owners are only credited with one start per race, regardless of how many drivers competed in a particular race for that owner
POLES	Number of poles that year
FINISH	
1	Number of first place finishes that year
2	Number of second place finishes that year
3	Number of third place finishes that year
4	Number of fourth place finishes that year
5	Number of fifth place finishes that year
6–10	Number of sixth through tenth place finishes that year
LAPS	Number of laps completed that year
LAPS LED	Number of laps led that year
RACES LED	Number of races led that year; owners with more than one driver leading in the same race are only credited with one race led
MILES	Number of miles driven that year
$	Winnings for that year

Yearly Leaders. Statistics that appear in boldface indicate the owner led all others that year in a particular statistical category. Petty Enterprises, for example, drove more laps than any other team in 1971 with 18,353.

All-Time Yearly Leaders. Indicated by the small number "1" that appears next to the statistic. Petty Enterprises, for example, has a one next to their races led total of 44 in 1971. This means that no other team has ever led more races in a single season.

Lifetime Leaders. Indicated by the figure that appears beneath the line showing the owner's lifetime totals. Petty Enterprises has a "1st" shown beneath their 1st place finishes total. This indicates that Petty Enterprises has won more races than any other owner.

*Please note that the above record is incomplete and shown here for example purposes only.

Owner	Starts	Poles	Finish						Laps	Laps Led	Races Led	Miles	$
			1	2	3	4	5	6–10					

Owners with more than one entry

Ray DeWitt

Owner	Starts	Poles	1	2	3	4	5	6–10	Laps	Laps Led	Races Led	Miles	$
Ray DeWitt	23	0	0	0	0	0	0	0	5,771	2	2	8,120	266,990
Ulrich-DeWitt	87	0	0	0	0	0	3	9	26,857	25	11	31,964	1,108,646
Lifetime	110	0	0	0	0	0	3	9	32,628	27	13	40,084	$1,375,636

Leo Jackson

Owner	Starts	Poles	1	2	3	4	5	6–10	Laps	Laps Led	Races Led	Miles	$
Leo Jackson	207	3	9	8	8	9	10	31	59,985	2,980	66	73,878	5,552,412
L. Jackson & A. Petree	31	0	0	0	0	1	1	1	8,588	110	7	10,324	732,735
Lifetime	238	3	9	8	8	10	11	32	68,573	3,090	73	84,202	$6,285,147

Butch Mock

Owner	Starts	Poles	1	2	3	4	5	6–10	Laps	Laps Led	Races Led	Miles	$
Butch Mock	119	0	0	0	1	1	3	12	31,437	132	12	39,122	2,198,365
B. Rahilly & B. Mock	350	6	4	4	8	14	5	73	99,455	1,566	70	117,679	3,735,613
Lifetime	469	6	4	4	9	15	8	85	130,892	1,698	82	156,801	$5,933,978

Mark Smith

Owner	Starts	Poles	1	2	3	4	5	6–10	Laps	Laps Led	Races Led	Miles	$
Mark Smith	26	0	0	0	0	0	0	2	5,260	18	1	8,352	343,102
G. Bradshaw & M. Smith	111	3	0	0	0	0	0	7	30,168	20	7	39,138	1,136,256
Lifetime	137	3	0	0	0	0	0	9	35,428	38	8	47,490	$1,479,358

D. K. Ulrich

Owner	Starts	Poles	1	2	3	4	5	6–10	Laps	Laps Led	Races Led	Miles	$
D. K. Ulrich	457	1	0	0	0	1	0	31	123,608	117	16	143,927	2.235,990
Ulrich-DeWitt	87	0	0	0	0	0	3	9	26,857	25	11	31,964	1,108,646
Lifetime	544	1	0	0	0	1	3	40	150,465	142	27	175,891	$3,344,636

Year	Driver	Starts	Poles	Finish 1	2	3	4	5	6–10	Laps	Laps Led	Races Led	Miles	$

Ed Ackerman

Year	Driver	Starts	Poles	1	2	3	4	5	6–10	Laps	Laps Led	Races Led	Miles	$
1966	Rene Charland	5	0	0	0	1	0	0	0	452	0	0	185	1,590
"	Gil Hearne	1	0	0	0	0	0	0	0	90	0	0	45	100
"	**Total**	6	0	0	0	1	0	0	0	542	0	0	230	1,690
Lifetime		6	0	0	0	1	0	0	0	542	0	0	230	$1,690

Bill Adams

Year	Driver	Starts	Poles	1	2	3	4	5	6–10	Laps	Laps Led	Races Led	Miles	$
1953	Bill Adams	2	0	0	0	0	0	0	1	36	0	0	148	250
"	Mike Klapak	2	0	0	0	0	0	0	2	0	0	0	0	250
"	**Total**	4	0	0	0	0	0	0	3	36	0	0	148	500
Lifetime		4	0	0	0	0	0	0	3	36	0	0	148	$500

Bob Adams

Year	Driver	Starts	Poles	1	2	3	4	5	6–10	Laps	Laps Led	Races Led	Miles	$
1963	Elmo Langley	2	0	0	0	0	0	0	0	681	0	0	605	750
"	Larry Manning	22	0	0	0	0	1	0	8	5,147	0	0	2,965	4,855
"	**Total**	24	0	0	0	0	1	0	8	5,828	0	0	3,570	5,605
1964	Larry Manning	4	0	0	0	0	0	0	3	933	0	0	414	760
"	Roy Mayne	10	0	0	0	0	0	1	1	2,150	0	0	1,378	3,375
"	**Total**	14	0	0	0	0	0	1	4	3,083	0	0	1,793	4,135
1966	Larry Manning	9	0	0	0	0	1	0	0	1,810	0	0	981	2,330
1967	Melvin Bradley	3	0	0	0	0	0	0	1	549	0	0	321	525
"	Bill Dennis	3	0	0	0	0	0	0	0	1,012	0	0	1,160	2,335
"	Larry Manning	3	0	0	0	0	0	0	0	162	0	0	127	1,125
"	Don Tarr	1	0	0	0	0	0	0	0	404	0	0	202	360
"	**Total**	10	0	0	0	0	0	0	1	2,127	0	0	1,809	4,345
Lifetime		57	0	0	0	0	2	1	13	12,848	0	0	8,153	$16,415

Weldon Adams

Year	Driver	Starts	Poles	1	2	3	4	5	6–10	Laps	Laps Led	Races Led	Miles	$
1950	Weldon Adams	1	0	0	0	0	0	0	1		0	0		175
1952	Weldon Adams	4	0	0	0	0	0	0	2	532	0	0	355	250
1953	Weldon Adams	1	0	0	0	0	0	0	0	217	0	0	298	110
Lifetime		6	0	0	0	0	0	0	3	749	0	0	653	$535

Herb Adcox

Year	Driver	Starts	Poles	1	2	3	4	5	6–10	Laps	Laps Led	Races Led	Miles	$
1974	Grant Adcox	4	0	0	0	0	0	0	0	979	8	1	1,375	6,240
1975	Grant Adcox	10	0	0	0	0	0	0	1	1,519	0	0	2,530	15,985
1976	Grant Adcox	11	0	0	0	0	0	0	2	3,126	0	0	4,643	26,115
1977	Grant Adcox	6	0	0	0	0	0	0	0	776	0	0	1,482	8,750
1978	Grant Adcox	14	0	0	0	0	0	1	2	3,072	0	0	4,586	36,350
1979	Grant Adcox	6	0	0	0	0	0	0	0	1,132	5	1	2,104	15,290
1983	Grant Adcox	1	0	0	0	0	0	0	0	1	0	0	3	1,790
1984	Grant Adcox	1	0	0	0	0	0	0	0	1	0	0	3	1,800
"	Connie Saylor	1	0	0	0	0	0	0	0	186	0	0	465	6,900
"	**Total**	2	0	0	0	0	0	0	0	187	0	0	468	8,700
1985	Grant Adcox	2	0	0	0	0	0	0	0	169	0	0	426	4,590
1986	Grant Adcox	1	0	0	0	0	0	0	0	154	0	0	385	3,395
"	Ken Ragan	1	0	0	0	0	0	0	0	184	0	0	460	11,870
"	**Total**	2	0	0	0	0	0	0	0	338	0	0	845	15,265
1987	Grant Adcox	0												1,700
1989	Grant Adcox	3	0	0	0	0	0	0	0	541	0	0	1,188	11,815
Lifetime		61	0	0	0	0	0	1	5	11,840	13	2	19,650	$152,590

Akins-Sutton Motorsports (Brad Akins and Bob Sutton, co-owners)

Year	Driver	Starts	Poles	1	2	3	4	5	6–10	Laps	Laps Led	Races Led	Miles	$
1993	Bobby Hamilton	2	0	0	0	0	0	0	1	694	0	0	993	21,715
Lifetime		2	0	0	0	0	0	0	1	694	0	0	993	$21,715

Will Albright

Year	Driver	Starts	Poles	1	2	3	4	5	6–10	Laps	Laps Led	Races Led	Miles	$
1950	Will Albright	1	0	0	0	0	0	0	0	43	0	0	179	50
Lifetime		1	0	0	0	0	0	0	0	43	0	0	179	$50

Claude Alexander

Year	Driver	Starts	Poles	1	2	3	4	5	6–10	Laps	Laps Led	Races Led	Miles	$
1951	Ed Samples	4	0	0	0	0	0	0	2	15	0	0	11	285
1952	Ed Samples	8	0	0	1	1	0	0	2	614	0	0	370	1,535

Year	Driver	Starts	Poles	Finish 1	2	3	4	5	6–10	Laps	Laps Led	Races Led	Miles	$

Claude Alexander *continued*

Year	Driver	Starts	Poles	1	2	3	4	5	6–10	Laps	Laps Led	Races Led	Miles	$
1954	Ed Samples	1	0	0	0	0	0	0	0	36	0	0	148	40
Lifetime		13	0	0	1	1	0	0	4	665	0	0	529	$1,860

Chester Alford

Year	Driver	Starts	Poles	1	2	3	4	5	6–10	Laps	Laps Led	Races Led	Miles	$
1950	Russ Lee	1	0	0	0	0	0	0	0	38	0	0	158	25
Lifetime		1	0	0	0	0	0	0	0	38	0	0	158	$25

Jack Alger

Year	Driver	Starts	Poles	1	2	3	4	5	6–10	Laps	Laps Led	Races Led	Miles	$
1964	Dave James	1	0	0	0	0	0	0	0	79	0	0	213	500
Lifetime		1	0	0	0	0	0	0	0	79	0	0	213	$500

Ken Allen

Year	Driver	Starts	Poles	1	2	3	4	5	6–10	Laps	Laps Led	Races Led	Miles	$
1986	Ron Shephard	1	0	0	0	0	0	0	0	282	0	0	153	3,145
1987	Eddie Bierschwale	1	0	0	0	0	0	0	0	192	0	0	262	2,760
"	Jesse Samples Jr.	2	0	0	0	0	0	0	0	164	0	0	106	4,610
"	**Total**	3	0	0	0	0	0	0	0	356	0	0	368	7,370
1988	Rodney Combs	1	0	0	0	0	0	0	0	220	0	0	335	1,760
"	Connie Saylor	1	0	0	0	0	0	0	0	464	0	0	464	2,565
"	Donnie Allison	0												1,800
"	**Total**	2		0	0	0	0	0	0	684	0	0	799	6,125
1989	Jim Bown	1	0	0	0	0	0	0	0	195	0	0	198	1,900
"	Rodney Combs	3	0	0	0	0	0	0	0	696	0	0	794	6,135
"	Charlie Glotzbach	0												1,700
"	**Total**	4	0	0	0	0	0	0	0	891	0	0	992	9,735
1990	Charlie Glotzbach	0												1,200
1991	Gary Balough	0												2,600
"	Dick Trickle	4	0	0	0	0	0	0	0	714	0	0	433	14,235
"	**Total**	4	0	0	0	0	0	0	0	714	0	0	433	16,835
Lifetime		14	0	0	0	0	0	0	0	2,927	0	0	2,745	$44,410

Loy Allen Sr.

Year	Driver	Starts	Poles	1	2	3	4	5	6–10	Laps	Laps Led	Races Led	Miles	$
1993	Loy Allen Jr.	3	0	0	0	0	0	0	0	350	0	0	893	21,960
Lifetime		3	0	0	0	0	0	0	0	350	0	0	893	$21,960

Bobby Allison

Year	Driver	Starts	Poles	1	2	3	4	5	6–10	Laps	Laps Led	Races Led	Miles	$
1965	Bobby Allison	4	0	0	0	0	0	0	2	528	0	0	1,007	3,350
1966	Bobby Allison	21	4	3	0	2	0	2	3	4,496	714	6	2,708	11,115
1967	Bobby Allison	27	1	3	2	2	2	2	4	5,642	1,077	14	3,125	12,285
"	Donnie Allison	8	0	0	1	0	1	1	0	1,185	157	1	555	2,320
"	Paul Lewis	1	0	0	0	0	0	0	0	5	0	0	3	150
"	Sam McQuagg	1	0	0	0	0	0	0	0	63	0	0	32	125
"	**Total**	36	1	3	3	2	3	3	4	6,895	1,234	15	3,715	14,880
1968	Bobby Allison	22	0	1	2	3	3	1	2	5,113	42	3	3,425	21,260
"	Paul Lewis	4	0	0	0	0	0	1	0	584	0	0	571	3,100
"	G. C. Spencer	1	0	0	0	0	0	0	0	86	0	0	129	575
"	**Total**	27	0	1	2	3	3	2	2	5,783	42	3	4,125	24,935
1969	Bobby Allison	2	0	0	0	0	0	0	1	423	0	0	212	790
"	Red Farmer	1	0	0	0	0	0	0	0	101	0	0	51	100
"	**Total**	3	0	0	0	0	0	0	1	524	0	0	262	890
1970	Bobby Allison	21	2	2	8	4	2	0	2	6,115	841	9	2,883	26,330
"	Dave Marcis	1	0	0	0	0	0	0	1	195	0	0	293	795
"	**Total**	22	2	2	8	4	2	0	3	6,310	841	9	3,176	27,125
1971	Bobby Allison	18	3	2	1	0	3	1	3	4,130	621	9	4,062	38,605
1973	Bobby Allison	27	6	2	2	6	4	1	1	8,072	870	20	8,646	161,818
1974	Bobby Allison	20	3	1	3	5	1	2	0	5,598	712	15	6,288	111,875
"	Neil Bonnett	1	0	0	0	0	0	0	0	46	0	0	122	1,110
"	**Total**	20	3	1	3	5	1	2	0	5,644	712	15	6,411	112,985
1975	Neil Bonnett	2	0	0	0	0	0	0	0	474	12	1	483	2,705
1977	Bobby Allison	30	0	0	1	0	2	2	10	7,024	102	9	7,822	94,575
1985	Bobby Allison	13	0	0	0	0	1	0	1	3,153	51	4	3,790	33,915
1990	Mike Alexander	7	0	0	0	0	0	0	0	2,392	0	0	2,325	41,080
"	Jeff Purvis	1	0	0	0	0	0	0	0	247	0	0	130	3,300
"	Hut Stricklin	21	0	0	0	0	0	0	2	5,591	1	1	7,226	143,909
"	**Total**	29	0	0	0	0	0	0	2	8,230	1	1	9,681	188,289

Year	Driver	Starts	Poles	Finish 1	2	3	4	5	6–10	Laps	Laps Led	Races Led	Miles	$

Bobby Allison *continued*

Year	Driver	Starts	Poles	1	2	3	4	5	6–10	Laps	Laps Led	Races Led	Miles	$
1991	Hut Stricklin	29	0	0	1	0	2	0	4	8,813	69	7	10,433	346,030
1992	Jeff Purvis	4	0	0	0	0	0	0	0	1,080	0	0	745	34,920
"	Jimmy Spencer	4	0	0	0	0	2	1	0	1,463	0	0	1,810	103,905
"	Hut Stricklin	21	0	0	0	0	0	0	4	5,577	60	2	7,224	262,935
"	**Total**	29	0	0	0	0	2	1	4	8,120	60	2	9,778	401,760
1993	Jimmy Spencer	30	0	0	1	2	2	0	5	8,848	64	4	10,823	686,026
1994	Chuck Bown	13	1	0	0	0	0	0	1	3,714	0	0	4,176	225,260
"	Derrike Cope	12	0	0	0	0	0	0	2	3,889	4	1	3,799	178,140
"	Tim Steele	5	0	0	0	0	0	0	0	391	0	0	807	65,000
"	**Total**	30	1	0	0	0	0	0	3	7,994	4	1	8,782	468,400
1995	Derrike Cope	31	0	0	1	0	0	1	6	9,335	70	4	11,039	683,075
1996	Derrike Cope	29	0	0	0	0	0	0	3	7,329	28	2	8,831	674,081
Lifetime		430	20	14	23	24	25	15	57	111,702	5,495	112	115,574	$3,974,559

Dave Alonzo

Year	Driver	Starts	Poles	1	2	3	4	5	6–10	Laps	Laps Led	Races Led	Miles	$
1969	Dave Alonzo	2	0	0	0	0	0	0	0	486	0	0	504	1,555
1970	Dave Alonzo	2	0	0	0	0	0	0	0	160	0	0	420	2,260
Lifetime		4	0	0	0	0	0	0	0	646	0	0	924	$3,815

George Alsobrook

Year	Driver	Starts	Poles	1	2	3	4	5	6–10	Laps	Laps Led	Races Led	Miles	$
1962	George Alsobrook	1	0	0	0	0	0	0	0	32	0	0	16	100
Lifetime		1	0	0	0	0	0	0	0	32	0	0	16	$100

George Althiede

Year	Driver	Starts	Poles	1	2	3	4	5	6–10	Laps	Laps Led	Races Led	Miles	$
1971	George Althiede	5	0	0	0	0	0	0	0	840	0	0	1,857	4,620
1972	George Althiede	11	0	0	0	0	0	0	0	1,578	0	0	2,760	10,405
"	J. D. McDuffie	1	0	0	0	0	0	0	0	318	0	0	434	1,515
"	G. C. Spencer	1	0	0	0	0	0	0	0	95	0	0	143	785
"	**Total**	13	0	0	0	0	0	0	0	1,991	0	0	3,337	12,705
Lifetime		18	0	0	0	0	0	0	0	2,831	0	0	5,194	$17,325

Bernard Alvarez

Year	Driver	Starts	Poles	1	2	3	4	5	6–10	Laps	Laps Led	Races Led	Miles	$
1964	Bernard Alvarez	7	0	0	0	0	0	0	0	162	0	0	127	650
"	Buddy Baker	6	0	0	0	0	0	0	1	604	0	0	471	1,750
"	Rene Charland	1	0	0	0	0	0	0	0	9	0	0	2	100
"	Larry Thomas	2	0	0	0	0	0	0	1	365	0	0	659	1,375
"	**Total**	16	0	0	0	0	0	0	2	1,140	0	0	1,259	3,875
1966	Ned Jarrett	8	0	0	0	1	0	0	0	1,257	0	0	918	4,170
Lifetime		24	0	0	0	1	0	0	2	2,397	0	0	2,177	$8,045

Pancho Alvarez

Year	Driver	Starts	Poles	1	2	3	4	5	6–10	Laps	Laps Led	Races Led	Miles	$
1952	Pancho Alvarez	1	0	0	0	0	0	0	0		0	0		25
Lifetime		1	0	0	0	0	0	0	0		0	0		$25

Carmen Amica

Year	Driver	Starts	Poles	1	2	3	4	5	6–10	Laps	Laps Led	Races Led	Miles	$
1954	Bill Amick	1	0	0	0	0	0	0	0	124	0	0	62	0
"	Laird Bruner	19	0	0	0	0	0	1	4	2,485	0	0	1,915	1,330
"	Curtis Turner	1	0	0	0	1	0	0	0	198	0	0	99	450
"	**Total**	21	0	0	0	1	0	1	4	2,807	0	0	2,076	1,780
Lifetime		21	0	0	0	1	0	1	4	2,807	0	0	2,076	$1,780

Bill Amick

Year	Driver	Starts	Poles	1	2	3	4	5	6–10	Laps	Laps Led	Races Led	Miles	$
1957	Bill Amick	15	2	1	3	3	0	0	3	2,718	12	2	1,744	6,870
Lifetime		15	2	1	3	3	0	0	3	2,718	12	2	1,744	$6,870

Bill Andersen

Year	Driver	Starts	Poles	1	2	3	4	5	6–10	Laps	Laps Led	Races Led	Miles	$
1970	Glenn Francis	1	0	0	0	0	0	0	0	95	0	0	249	805
1971	Glenn Francis	1	0	0	0	0	0	0	0	27	0	0	71	1,015
Lifetime		2	0	0	0	0	0	0	0	122	0	0	320	$1,820

Year	Driver	Starts	Poles	Finish 1	2	3	4	5	6–10	Laps	Laps Led	Races Led	Miles	$

Carl Anderson

Year	Driver	Starts	Poles	1	2	3	4	5	6–10	Laps	Laps Led	Races Led	Miles	$
1985	Craig Spetman	1	0	0	0	0	0	0	0	188	0	0	188	1,150
Lifetime		1	0	0	0	0	0	0	0	188	0	0	188	$1,150

Eddie Anderson

1951	Eddie Anderson	5	0	0	0	0	0	0	0	8	0	0	6	110
Lifetime		5	0	0	0	0	0	0	0	8	0	0	6	$110

Jack Anderson

1963	Jack Anderson	3	0	0	0	0	0	0	0	532	0	0	231	475
1964	Jack Anderson	22	0	0	0	0	0	0	3	2,855	0	0	2,424	6,035
"	Buddy Baker	1	0	0	0	0	0	0	0	69	0	0	35	250
"	Don Branson	4	0	0	0	0	0	0	0	163	0	0	72	350
"	Jim Cook	2	0	0	0	0	0	0	0	4	0	0	10	825
"	Ronnie Croy	1	0	0	0	0	0	0	0	11	0	0	6	150
"	Frank Graham	3	0	0	0	0	0	0	0	410	0	0	206	820
"	Mark Hurley	3	0	0	0	0	0	0	0	104	0	0	27	350
"	Larry Manning	1	0	0	0	0	0	0	0	38	0	0	24	150
"	Roy Mayne	1	0	0	0	0	0	0	0	1	0	0	2	400
"	Larry Thomas	1	0	0	0	0	0	0	1	190	0	0	95	240
"	**Total**	34	0	0	0	0	0	0	4	3,845	0	0	2,900	9,570
Lifetime		37	0	0	0	0	0	0	4	4,377	0	0	3,131	$10,045

M. C. Anderson

1976	Sam Sommers	5	0	0	0	0	0	0	1	1,000	0	0	1,534	8,930
1977	Sam Sommers	22	1	0	0	0	1	1	6	5,387	28	3	6,845	53,975
1978	Buddy Baker	19	1	0	1	1	1	1	4	4,319	354	10	6,594	111,765
1979	Benny Parsons	31	1	2	2	2	5	5	5	9,335	736	12	10,574	264,930
1980	Benny Parsons	31	2	3	3	2	4	4	5	8,676	659	19	10,035	411,519
"	Marty Robbins	1	0	0	0	0	0	0	0	171	0	0	257	1,000
"	**Total**	31	2	3	3	2	4	4	5	8,847	659	19	10,291	412,519
1981	Cale Yarborough	18	2	2	1	2	0	1	4	4,922	769	13	7,134	150,090
1982	Cale Yarborough	16	2	3	2	1	2	0	0	3,439	379	12	5,642	231,590
Lifetime		142	9	10	9	8	13	12	25	37,249	2,925	69	48,613	$1,233,799

Don Angel

1958	Don Angel	3	0	0	0	0	0	0	0	401	0	0	241	210
"	Tiny Lund	12	0	0	0	1	1	0	3	2,439	0	0	1,145	1,890
"	Eddie Pagan	1	0	0	0	0	0	0	0	77	0	0	19	45
"	Jim Paschal	1	0	0	0	0	0	0	1	193	0	0	97	165
"	**Total**	16	0	0	0	1	1	0	4	3,110	0	0	1,502	2,310
1959	Don Angel	2	0	0	0	0	0	0	0	167	0	0	100	100
"	Marvin Panch	1	0	0	0	0	0	0	0	37	0	0	19	50
"	Speedy Thompson	1	0	0	0	0	0	0	0	190	0	0	48	100
"	**Total**	4	0	0	0	0	0	0	0	394	0	0	166	250
1960	Tommy Herbert	2	0	0	0	0	0	0	0	155	0	0	388	250
Lifetime		22	0	0	0	1	1	0	4	3,659	0	0	2,056	$2,810

Bob Apperson

1949	Bob Apperson	2	0	0	0	0	0	0	0	191	0	0	96	100
1950	Bob Apperson	7	0	0	0	0	0	0	0	573	0	0	631	200
1952	Bob Apperson	1	0	0	0	0	0	0	0		0	0		25
Lifetime		10	0	0	0	0	0	0	0	764	0	0	726	$325

Sam Arakalian

1977	Vince Giamformaggio	1	0	0	0	0	0	0	0	93	0	0	233	850
1978	Vince Giamformaggio	1	0	0	0	0	0	0	0	41	0	0	107	805
Lifetime		2	0	0	0	0	0	0	0	134	0	0	340	$1,655

Sam Arena

1954	Bill Bade	2	0	0	0	0	0	0	1	688	0	0	344	150
1957	Bill Bade	2	0	0	0	0	0	0	0	194	0	0	97	90
1959	Bob Rose	3	0	0	0	0	0	0	0	182	0	0	441	150
Lifetime		7	0	0	0	0	0	0	1	1,064	0	0	882	$390

Year	Driver	Starts	Poles	Finish 1	2	3	4	5	6–10	Laps	Laps Led	Races Led	Miles	$

Frank Arford

Year	Driver	Starts	Poles	1	2	3	4	5	6–10	Laps	Laps Led	Races Led	Miles	$
1952	Dick Passwater	6	0	0	0	0	0	1	2	1,366	0	0	1,085	945
1953	Frank Arford	4	0	0	0	0	0	0	0	255	0	0	261	100
"	Dick Passwater	13	0	1	0	0	3	2	4	643	3	1	644	3,925
"	Slick Smith	1	0	0	0	0	0	0	0		0	0		40
"	**Total**	14	0	1	0	0	3	2	4	898	3	1	905	4,065
Lifetime		20	0	1	0	0	3	3	6	2,264	3	1	1,990	$5,010

Ted Armstrong

Year	Driver	Starts	Poles	1	2	3	4	5	6–10	Laps	Laps Led	Races Led	Miles	$
1978	Gary Johnson	1	0	0	0	0	0	0	0	3	0	0	8	500
Lifetime		1	0	0	0	0	0	0	0	3	0	0	8	$500

Ben Arnold

Year	Driver	Starts	Poles	1	2	3	4	5	6–10	Laps	Laps Led	Races Led	Miles	$
1967	Red Farmer	2	0	0	0	0	0	0	0	58	0	0	145	1,000
1970	Ben Arnold	28	0	0	0	0	0	0	3	6,772	0	0	6,720	25,605
"	Alton Jones	1	0	0	0	0	0	0	0	155	0	0	412	1,485
"	**Total**	28	0	0	0	0	0	0	3	6,927	0	0	7,132	27,090
1971	Ben Arnold	17	0	0	0	0	0	0	3	4,097	0	0	6,122	17,701
1972	Ben Arnold	26	0	0	0	0	0	0	7	6,976	0	0	8,935	44,547
1973	Ben Arnold	1	0	0	0	0	0	0	0	9	0	0	24	885
Lifetime		74	0	0	0	0	0	0	13	18,067	0	0	22,358	$91,223

Alan Aroneck

Year	Driver	Starts	Poles	1	2	3	4	5	6–10	Laps	Laps Led	Races Led	Miles	$
1989	Jerry O'Neil	4	0	0	0	0	0	0	0	1,026	0	0	1,255	10,865
1990	Jerry O'Neil	3	0	0	0	0	0	0	0	349	0	0	806	26,605
1992	Jerry O'Neil	6	0	0	0	0	0	0	0	958	0	0	1,644	32,370
"	D. K. Ulrich	1	0	0	0	0	0	0	0	21	0	0	21	4,165
"	**Total**	6	0	0	0	0	0	0	0	979	0	0	1,665	36,535
1993	Jerry O'Neil	1	0	0	0	0	0	0	0	9	0	0	10	9,250
Lifetime		14	0	0	0	0	0	0	0	2,363	0	0	3,735	$83,255

Buddy Arrington

Year	Driver	Starts	Poles	1	2	3	4	5	6–10	Laps	Laps Led	Races Led	Miles	$
1964	Buddy Arrington	27	0	0	0	0	0	2	7	5,172	0	0	2,504	5,315
"	Raymond Carter	1	0	0	0	0	0	0	0	37	0	0	12	100
"	**Total**	28	0	0	0	0	0	2	7	5,209	0	0	2,516	5,415
1965	Buddy Arrington	29	0	0	0	1	1	4	3	4,784	0	0	2,810	10,100
"	Darrell Bryant	1	0	0	0	0	0	0	0	1	0	0	1	100
"	Raymond Carter	9	0	0	0	0	0	0	2	638	0	0	617	2,145
"	Billy DeCoster	1	0	0	0	0	0	0	0	252	0	0	378	700
"	Pee Wee Ellwanger	4	0	0	0	0	0	0	0	345	0	0	173	575
"	**Total**	30	0	0	0	1	1	4	5	6,020	0	0	3,978	13,620
1966	Buddy Arrington	18	0	0	0	0	0	0	3	2,456	0	0	2,133	7,050
"	Darrell Bryant	1	0	0	0	0	0	0	0	17	0	0	26	445
"	E. J. Trivette	1	0	0	0	0	0	0	0	2	0	0	3	525
"	**Total**	19	0	0	0	0	0	0	3	2,475	0	0	2,161	8,020
1967	Buddy Arrington	15	0	0	0	0	0	1	4	2,972	0	0	2,635	7,820
"	Larry Hess	1	0	0	0	0	0	0	0	53	0	0	80	800
"	Larry Manning	1	0	0	0	0	0	0	0	4	0	0	2	275
"	Don Schissler	1	0	0	0	0	0	0	0	140	0	0	70	275
"	**Total**	17	0	0	0	0	0	1	4	3,169	0	0	2,787	9,170
1968	Buddy Arrington	1	0	0	0	0	0	0	0	186	0	0	465	2,350
1969	Buddy Arrington	16	0	0	0	0	0	2	4	3,758	0	0	3,557	12,975
1970	Buddy Arrington	19	0	0	0	0	0	0	2	2,855	0	0	3,638	16,845
"	Larry Manning	1	0	0	0	0	0	0	0	83	0	0	52	755
"	**Total**	20	0	0	0	0	0	0	2	2,938	0	0	3,690	17,600
1971	Buddy Arrington	1	0	0	0	0	0	0	0	472	0	0	248	650
1972	Buddy Arrington	20	0	0	0	0	0	1	9	5,503	0	0	7,008	29,050
"	Ed Negre	1	0	0	0	0	0	0	0	167	0	0	104	425
"	**Total**	20	0	0	0	0	0	1	9	5,670	0	0	7,112	29,475
1973	Buddy Arrington	26	0	0	0	0	0	1	3	7,476	0	0	7,876	40,877
1974	Buddy Arrington	16	0	0	0	0	0	0	4	4,781	0	0	4,797	22,085
"	Joey Arrington	2	0	0	0	0	0	0	0	342	0	0	214	985
"	Larry Manning	1	0	0	0	0	0	0	0	1	0	0	1	580
"	John Martin	1	0	0	0	0	0	0	0	16	0	0	40	1,045
"	Joe Millikan	1	0	0	0	0	0	0	0	456	0	0	464	1,150
"	Pee Wee Wentz	1	0	0	0	0	0	0	1	342	0	0	467	2,500
"	Satch Worley	1	0	0	0	0	0	0	1	431	0	0	226	1,300
"	**Total**	23	0	0	0	0	0	0	6	6,369	0	0	6,209	29,645

Year	Driver	Starts	Poles	Finish 1	2	3	4	5	6–10	Laps	Laps Led	Races Led	Miles	$

Buddy Arrington *continued*

Year	Driver	Starts	Poles	1	2	3	4	5	6–10	Laps	Laps Led	Races Led	Miles	$
1975	Buddy Arrington	25	0	0	0	0	0	0	3	7,786	0	0	8,170	45,893
"	Joey Arrington	2	0	0	0	0	0	0	0	91	0	0	87	1,060
"	**Total**	25	0	0	0	0	0	0	3	7,877	0	0	8,256	46,953
1976	Buddy Arrington	25	0	0	0	0	0	0	3	6,256	0	0	6,737	56,647
1977	Buddy Arrington	28	0	0	0	0	0	0	5	8,601	0	0	10,037	88,887
1978	Buddy Arrington	30	0	0	0	0	0	1	6	9,580	0	0	10,739	112,960
"	Joey Arrington	2	0	0	0	0	0	0	0	326	0	0	509	1,990
"	Ed Negre	1	0	0	0	0	0	0	0	3	0	0	2	405
"	**Total**	30	0	0	0	0	0	1	6	9,909	0	0	11,250	115,355
1979	Buddy Arrington	31	0	0	0	1	0	0	6	8,452	2	1	10,333	131,833
"	Joey Arrington	1	0	0	0	0	0	0	0	42	0	0	42	650
"	Earl Brooks	1	0	0	0	0	0	0	0	79	0	0	49	405
"	**Total**	31	0	0	0	1	0	0	6	8,573	2	1	10,425	132,888
1980	Buddy Arrington	31	0	0	0	0	0	0	7	8,765	0	0	9,936	120,355
"	Eddie Dickerson	2	0	0	0	0	0	0	0	787	0	0	632	1,590
"	Dick May	1	0	0	0	0	0	0	0	4	0	0	2	380
"	**Total**	31	0	0	0	0	0	0	7	9,556	0	0	10,570	122,325
1981	Buddy Arrington	31	0	0	0	0	0	0	7	8,344	0	0	9,443	130,833
1982	Buddy Arrington	30	0	0	0	0	0	0	8	9,336	6	4	10,840	178,159
"	Randy Becker	1	0	0	0	0	0	0	0	31	0	0	81	575
"	**Total**	30	0	0	0	0	0	0	8	9,367	6	4	10,922	178,734
1983	Buddy Arrington	30	0	0	0	0	0	0	2	8,933	1	1	10,009	138,429
1984	Buddy Arrington	25	0	0	0	0	0	0	0	7,256	0	0	8,253	126,317
1985	Buddy Arrington	26	0	0	0	0	0	0	1	7,809	1	1	9,644	153,222
"	Phil Good	1	0	0	0	0	0	0	0	362	0	0	196	1,470
"	Morgan Shepherd	1	0	0	0	0	0	0	0	190	0	0	475	15,300
"	**Total**	28	0	0	0	0	0	0	1	8,361	1	1	10,315	169,992
1986	Buddy Arrington	26	0	0	0	0	0	0	0	8,152	4	1	9,457	186,588
"	Clark Dwyer	0												1,800
"	**Total**	26		0	0	0	0	0	0	8,152	4	1	9,457	188,388
1987	Buddy Arrington	18	0	0	0	0	0	0	0	4,865	0	0	6,322	111,305
"	Eddie Bierschwale	7	0	0	0	0	0	0	0	1,901	0	0	1,989	43,635
"	Chet Fillip	2	0	0	0	0	0	0	0	275	0	0	728	12,190
"	**Total**	27	0	0	0	0	0	0	0	7,041	0	0	9,039	167,130
1988	Buddy Arrington	4	0	0	0	0	0	0	0	760	0	0	1,549	22,165
"	Ron Esau	2	0	0	0	0	0	0	0	231	0	0	594	9,335
"	Jimmy Hensley	1	0	0	0	0	0	0	0	290	0	0	153	4,245
"	Dale Jarrett	1	0	0	0	0	0	0	0	27	0	0	41	4,200
"	Rick Jeffrey	2	0	0	0	0	0	0	0	652	0	0	952	11,310
"	Ken Schrader	1	0	0	0	0	0	0	0	395	0	0	214	4,610
"	Brad Teague	4	0	0	0	0	0	0	0	1,389	0	0	1,322	18,925
"	**Total**	15	0	0	0	0	0	0	0	3,744	0	0	4,823	74,790
1989	Brad Teague	1	0	0	0	0	0	0	0	488	0	0	260	2,480
Lifetime		584	0	0	0	2	1	12	91	156,200	14	8	170,395	$1,909,945

Bruce Atchley

Year	Driver	Starts	Poles	1	2	3	4	5	6–10	Laps	Laps Led	Races Led	Miles	$
1952	Bruce Atchley	6	0	0	0	0	0	0	0	307	0	0	187	200
"	Dick Rathmann	1	0	0	0	0	0	0	0	48	0	0	48	25
"	**Total**	7	0	0	0	0	0	0	0	355	0	0	235	225
Lifetime		7	0	0	0	0	0	0	0	355	0	0	235	$225

H. W. Atkinson

Year	Driver	Starts	Poles	1	2	3	4	5	6–10	Laps	Laps Led	Races Led	Miles	$
1956	W. H. Atkinson	1	0	0	0	0	0	0	0		0	0		0
Lifetime		1	0	0	0	0	0	0	0		0	0		$0

Roger Attard

Year	Driver	Starts	Poles	1	2	3	4	5	6–10	Laps	Laps Led	Races Led	Miles	$
1952	Roger Attard	1	0	0	0	0	0	0	0	25	0	0	25	0
Lifetime		1	0	0	0	0	0	0	0	25	0	0	25	$0

George Augustine

Year	Driver	Starts	Poles	1	2	3	4	5	6–10	Laps	Laps Led	Races Led	Miles	$
1958	Axel Anderson	3	0	0	0	0	0	0	0	203	0	0	178	155
Lifetime		3	0	0	0	0	0	0	0	203	0	0	178	$155

Year	Driver	Starts	Poles	Finish 1	2	3	4	5	6–10	Laps	Laps Led	Races Led	Miles	$

L. D. Austin

Year	Driver	Starts	Poles	1	2	3	4	5	6–10	Laps	Laps Led	Races Led	Miles	$
1957	L. D. Austin	40	0	0	0	0	0	1	12	6,920	0	0	4,132	6,485
1958	L. D. Austin	45	0	0	0	0	0	0	10	6,585	0	0	3,739	6,111
1959	L. D. Austin	29	0	0	0	0	0	0	10	5,073	0	0	2,632	3,816
1960	L. D. Austin	26	0	0	0	0	0	1	9	4,820	0	0	3,995	4,825
"	Buck Baker	1	0	0	0	0	0	0	1	189	0	0	47	175
"	Rex White	1	0	0	0	0	0	0	1	182	0	0	46	140
"	**Total**	28	0	0	0	0	0	1	11	5,191	0	0	4,088	5,140
1961	L. D. Austin	20	0	0	0	0	0	0	8	4,802	0	0	3,402	4,530
1962	L. D. Austin	1	0	0	0	0	0	0	0	53	0	0	27	0
Lifetime		163	0	0	0	0	0	2	51	28,624	0	0	18,020	$26,082

George Avery

Year	Driver	Starts	Poles	1	2	3	4	5	6–10	Laps	Laps Led	Races Led	Miles	$
1975	A. J. Reno	1	0	0	0	0	0	0	0	170	0	0	452	1,670
Lifetime		1	0	0	0	0	0	0	0	170	0	0	452	$1,670

Jimmy Ayers

Year	Driver	Starts	Poles	1	2	3	4	5	6–10	Laps	Laps Led	Races Led	Miles	$
1950	Jimmy Ayers	1	0	0	0	0	0	0	0		0	0		0
1951	Jimmy Ayers	7	0	0	0	0	0	0	5	225	0	0	281	500
1952	Jimmy Ayers	3	0	0	0	0	0	0	0	179	0	0	90	85
1953	Jimmy Ayers	4	0	0	0	0	0	0	2		0	0		175
1954	Jimmy Ayers	2	0	0	0	0	0	0	0	219	0	0	178	75
1955	Jimmy Ayers	2	0	0	0	0	0	0	1	277	0	0	292	350
Lifetime		19	0	0	0	0	0	0	8	900	0	0	840	$1,185

B & L Motors

Year	Driver	Starts	Poles	1	2	3	4	5	6–10	Laps	Laps Led	Races Led	Miles	$
1955	Buck Baker	1	0	0	0	0	0	0	1	93	0	0	93	100
"	Fred Johnson	2	0	0	0	0	0	0	0	258	0	0	345	460
"	Junior Johnson	33	2	5	0	2	1	3	6	4,297	790	7	2,954	13,028
"	Gwyn Staley	1	0	0	0	0	0	0	0	3	0	0	5	150
"	**Total**	34	2	5	0	2	1	3	7	4,651	790	7	3,397	13,738
Lifetime		34	2	5	0	2	1	3	7	4,651	790	7	3,397	$13,738

Hugh Babb

Year	Driver	Starts	Poles	1	2	3	4	5	6–10	Laps	Laps Led	Races Led	Miles	$
1956	Billy Myers	2	0	0	0	1	0	0	1	390	0	0	176	575
1957	Buck Baker	15	2	4	3	2	1	2	3	2,825	487	6	1,506	10,025
"	Johnny Beauchamp	1	0	0	1	0	0	0	0	39	160	0	160	2,450
"	Clyde Palmer	1	0	0	0	1	0	0	0	149	0	0	75	470
"	Tom Pistone	2	0	0	0	1	0	0	0	588	0	0	294	1,260
"	Frankie Schneider	2	0	0	0	0	1	0	0	194	0	0	97	355
"	Jack Smith	15	0	1	1	1	1	1	5	2,534	115	1	1,345	3,855
"	Speedy Thompson	15	1	0	2	3	0	2	2	2,347	55	2	1,280	4,540
"	Rex White	2	0	0	0	0	0	0	1	24	0	0	12	300
"	**Total**	16	3	5	7	8	3	5	11	8,700	817	8	4,769	23,255
Lifetime		18	3	5	7	9	3	5	12	9,090	817	8	4,945	$23,830

Dick Bahre

Year	Driver	Starts	Poles	1	2	3	4	5	6–10	Laps	Laps Led	Races Led	Miles	$
1981	Geoff Bodine	2	0	0	0	0	0	0	0	267	0	0	567	6,390
"	Charlie Glotzbach	1	0	0	0	0	0	0	0	218	0	0	327	1,275
"	**Total**	3	0	0	0	0	0	0	0	485	0	0	894	7,665
1982	Geoff Bodine	1	0	0	0	0	0	0	0	3	0	0	8	3,450
1983	Elliott Forbes-Robinson	1	0	0	0	0	0	0	0	36	0	0	90	5,550
1984	Gene Coyle	2	0	0	0	0	0	0	0	619	0	0	895	4,840
"	Don Hume	1	0	0	0	0	0	0	0	299	0	0	455	1,595
"	Sterling Marlin	1	0	0	0	0	0	0	0	1	0	0	1	1,085
"	Connie Saylor	2	0	0	0	0	0	0	0	262	0	0	378	2,935
"	Morgan Shepherd	4	0	0	0	0	0	0	0	689	0	0	965	7,450
"	**Total**	10	0	0	0	0	0	0	0	1,870	0	0	2,694	17,905
1985	Eldon Dotson	1	0	0	0	0	0	0	0	10	0	0	25	1,675
"	Jim Hull	1	0	0	0	0	0	0	0	68	0	0	136	1,570
"	Dick May	1	0	0	0	0	0	0	0	368	0	0	230	985
"	Morgan Shepherd	1	0	0	0	0	0	0	0	61	0	0	62	1,150
"	Michael Waltrip	5	0	0	0	0	0	0	0	1,013	0	0	1,583	9,540
"	**Total**	9	0	0	0	0	0	0	0	1,520	0	0	2,036	14,920
1986	Michael Waltrip	28	0	0	0	0	0	0	0	7,952	6	4	9,295	84,660

Year	Driver	Starts	Poles	Finish 1	2	3	4	5	6–10	Laps	Laps Led	Races Led	Miles	$

Dick Bahre *continued*

Year	Driver	Starts	Poles	1	2	3	4	5	6–10	Laps	Laps Led	Races Led	Miles	$
1988	Dave Mader III	1	0	0	0	0	0	0	0	271	0	0	144	1,565
1989	Dave Mader III	1	0	0	0	0	0	0	0	480	0	0	488	2,675
1990	Dave Mader III	1	0	0	0	0	0	0	0	323	0	0	492	4,525
1992	Denny Wilson	1	0	0	0	0	0	0	0	9	0	0	22	3,450
1993	Johnny Chapman	1	0	0	0	0	0	0	0	368	0	0	374	9,126
Lifetime		57	0	0	0	0	0	0	0	13,317	6	4	16,537	$155,491

Dick Bailey

Year	Driver	Starts	Poles	1	2	3	4	5	6–10	Laps	Laps Led	Races Led	Miles	$
1958	Dick Bailey	1	0	0	0	0	0	0	0	33	0	0	135	75
Lifetime		1	0	0	0	0	0	0	0	33	0	0	135	$75

H. B. Bailey

Year	Driver	Starts	Poles	1	2	3	4	5	6–10	Laps	Laps Led	Races Led	Miles	$
1962	H. B. Bailey	1	0	0	0	0	0	0	0	101	0	0	152	300
1963	H. B. Bailey	2	0	0	0	0	0	0	0	226	0	0	565	775
1964	H. B. Bailey	1	0	0	0	0	0	0	0	135	0	0	186	500
"	Ronnie Chumley	2	0	0	0	0	0	0	0	59	0	0	148	850
"	**Total**	3	0	0	0	0	0	0	0	194	0	0	333	1,350
1965	H. B. Bailey	5	0	0	0	0	0	1	2	810	0	0	1,338	5,000
1966	H. B. Bailey	4	0	0	0	0	0	0	0	450	0	0	671	2,745
"	Ronnie Chumley	2	0	0	0	0	0	0	0	42	0	0	105	1,130
"	**Total**	5	0	0	0	0	0	0	0	492	0	0	776	3,875
1967	H. B. Bailey	3	0	0	0	0	0	0	0	322	0	0	676	3,850
1968	H. B. Bailey	2	0	0	0	0	0	0	0	187	0	0	264	1,250
1969	H. B. Bailey	6	0	0	0	0	0	0	1	638	0	0	1,303	5,880
1970	H. B. Bailey	1	0	0	0	0	0	0	0	180	0	0	246	995
1971	H. B. Bailey	3	0	0	0	0	0	0	0	540	11	1	246	890
"	Frank Warren	1	0	0	0	0	0	1	0	289	0	0	145	650
"	**Total**	4	0	0	0	0	0	1	0	829	11	1	391	1,540
1973	H. B. Bailey	2	0	0	0	0	0	0	0	243	0	0	483	1,935
1975	H. B. Bailey	1	0	0	0	0	0	0	0	1	0	0	1	1,330
1979	H. B. Bailey	4	0	0	0	0	0	0	0	738	0	0	1,175	5,835
1981	H. B. Bailey	4	0	0	0	0	0	0	0	605	0	0	989	7,465
1982	H. B. Bailey	6	0	0	0	0	0	0	0	1,016	0	0	1,612	9,455
"	Dick May	1	0	0	0	0	0	0	0	260	0	0	396	2,430
"	**Total**	7	0	0	0	0	0	0	0	1,276	0	0	2,008	11,885
1983	H. B. Bailey	2	0	0	0	0	0	0	0	684	0	0	1,033	4,110
1984	H. B. Bailey	2	0	0	0	0	0	0	0	529	0	0	770	5,640
1985	H. B. Bailey	2	0	0	0	0	0	0	0	206	0	0	299	3,065
1986	H. B. Bailey	4	0	0	0	0	0	0	0	918	1	1	1,289	9,225
1987	H. B. Bailey	5	0	0	0	0	0	0	0	1,150	0	0	1,691	12,885
1988	H. B. Bailey	7	0	0	0	0	0	0	0	1,180	0	0	1,788	15,775
1989	H. B. Bailey	2	0	0	0	0	0	0	0	487	0	0	787	9,595
1990	H. B. Bailey	3	0	0	0	0	0	0	0	421	0	0	608	9,615
1991	H. B. Bailey	3	0	0	0	0	0	0	0	545	0	0	981	13,095
1992	H. B. Bailey	1	0	0	0	0	0	0	0	8	0	0	16	7,755
1993	H. B. Bailey	2	0	0	0	0	0	0	0	238	0	0	442	12,750
Lifetime		83	0	0	0	0	0	2	3	13,208	12	2	20,400	$156,775

Gary Baird

Year	Driver	Starts	Poles	1	2	3	4	5	6–10	Laps	Laps Led	Races Led	Miles	$
1971	E. J. Trivette	5	0	0	0	0	0	0	0	914	0	0	759	1,895
Lifetime		5	0	0	0	0	0	0	0	914	0	0	759	$1,895

R. L. Baird

Year	Driver	Starts	Poles	1	2	3	4	5	6–10	Laps	Laps Led	Races Led	Miles	$
1960	Bud Parnell	4	0	0	0	0	0	0	1	407	0	0	204	280
Lifetime		4	0	0	0	0	0	0	1	407	0	0	204	$280

Buck Baity

Year	Driver	Starts	Poles	1	2	3	4	5	6–10	Laps	Laps Led	Races Led	Miles	$
1951	Buck Baity	1	0	0	0	0	0	0	0	248	0	0	310	0
Lifetime		1	0	0	0	0	0	0	0	248	0	0	310	$0

Bill Baker

Year	Driver	Starts	Poles	1	2	3	4	5	6–10	Laps	Laps Led	Races Led	Miles	$
1977	Bill Baker	2	0	0	0	0	0	0	0	142	0	0	372	2,540

Year	Driver	Starts	Poles	Finish						Laps	Laps Led	Races Led	Miles	$
				1	2	3	4	5	6–10					

Bill Baker *continued*

Year	Driver	Starts	Poles	1	2	3	4	5	6–10	Laps	Laps Led	Races Led	Miles	$
1978	Bill Baker	1	0	0	0	0	0	0	0	20	0	0	52	550
Lifetime		3	0	0	0	0	0	0	0	162	0	0	424	$3,090

Buck Baker

Year	Driver	Starts	Poles	1	2	3	4	5	6–10	Laps	Laps Led	Races Led	Miles	$
1950	Buck Baker	4	1	0	0	0	0	0	2	213	10	1	286	400
1951	Buck Baker	8	0	0	0	1	0	1	1	338	0	0	407	1,000
1952	Buck Baker	2	0	0	0	0	0	0	0	49	0	0	38	25
1954	Tim Flock	2	1	0	1	0	0	0	1	389	180	1	195	750
1955	Buck Baker	10	0	1	0	1	0	3	4	1,927	40	2	1,764	5,075
"	Banks Simpson	1	0	0	0	0	0	0	0	172	0	0	258	95
"	**Total**	11	0	1	0	1	0	3	4	2,099	40	2	2,022	5,170
1957	Buck Baker	25	4	6	4	2	4	2	5	5,233	371	9	3,338	30,764
"	Fireball Roberts	1	0	0	0	0	0	0	0	482	0	0	241	350
"	**Total**	25	4	6	4	2	4	2	5	5,715	371	9	3,579	31,089
1958	Buck Baker	44	3	3	10	4	2	4	12	7,827	364	8	4,726	25,841
"	Possum Jones	1	0	0	0	0	0	0	1	246	0	0	246	575
"	Tiny Lund	1	1	0	0	0	0	0	0	46	14	1	41	0
"	Jack Smith	1	0	0	0	0	0	1	0	155	0	0	97	225
"	G. C. Spencer	1	0	0	0	0	0	0	0	343	0	0	472	315
"	Gwyn Staley	1	0	0	0	0	0	1	0	38	0	0	156	700
"	**Total**	44	4	3	10	4	2	6	13	8,655	378	9	5,738	27,656
1959	Buck Baker	22	3	0	1	4	1	4	2	2,778	182	4	1,636	6,241
"	Buddy Baker	6	0	0	0	0	0	0	3	781	0	0	391	680
"	Tiny Lund	3	0	0	0	0	0	0	1	227	0	0	414	350
"	Fireball Roberts	1	0	0	0	0	0	0	1	148	0	0	148	525
"	Shorty Rollins	1	0	0	0	0	0	0	0	15	0	0	8	50
"	**Total**	23	3	0	1	4	1	4	7	3,949	182	4	2,596	7,796
1960	Buck Baker	35	2	1	1	3	1	8	8	6,718	37	2	5,306	18,324
"	Buddy Baker	2	0	0	0	0	0	0	0	170	0	0	204	200
"	**Total**	36	2	1	1	3	1	8	8	6,888	37	2	5,510	18,524
1961	Buck Baker	42	1	1	1	3	4	2	4	7,195	114	3	5,226	13,697
"	Buddy Baker	13	0	0	0	0	0	1	2	2,311	0	0	2,405	4,915
"	Herb Tillman	2	0	0	0	0	0	0	0	91	0	0	137	550
"	**Total**	43	1	1	1	3	4	3	6	9,597	114	3	7,768	19,162
1962	Buck Baker	36	0	0	1	3	2	0	7	6,444	18	2	4,641	11,662
"	Buddy Baker	31	0	0	0	1	2	2	5	5,454	0	0	4,139	7,578
"	Thomas Cox	1	0	0	0	0	0	0	0	11	0	0	17	250
"	Darel Dieringer	1	0	0	0	0	0	0	0	36	0	0	18	85
"	Junior Johnson	1	0	0	0	0	0	0	0	8	0	0	4	50
"	**Total**	44	0	0	1	4	4	2	12	11,953	18	2	8,818	19,625
1963	Buck Baker	45	0	1	3	6	2	5	12	9,082	63	2	5,112	17,141
"	Buddy Baker	3	0	0	0	0	1	0	0	574	0	0	434	1,095
"	Ronnie Bristow	2	0	0	0	0	0	0	0	112	0	0	48	485
"	Neil Castles	28	0	0	0	0	1	1	6	4,093	0	0	2,330	5,590
"	Curtis Crider	1	0	0	0	0	0	0	1	171	0	0	86	175
"	Fred Harb	1	0	0	0	0	0	0	0	94	0	0	85	100
"	**Total**	47	0	1	3	6	4	6	19	14,126	63	2	8,093	24,586
1964	Buck Baker	3	0	0	1	0	0	0	0	509	0	0	255	805
"	Buddy Baker	1	0	0	0	0	0	0	1	127	0	0	381	1,050
"	Neil Castles	58	0	0	0	0	0	1	23	8,336	0	0	4,158	13,335
"	Bob Gray	1	0	0	0	0	0	0	0	2	0	0	3	400
"	Jimmy Helms	17	0	0	0	0	0	0	1	532	0	0	299	4,040
"	Bill McMahan	1	0	0	0	0	0	0	0	348	0	0	174	270
"	Steve Young	9	0	0	0	0	0	0	1	991	0	0	513	1,375
"	**Total**	59	0	0	1	0	0	1	26	10,845	0	0	5,783	21,275
1965	Buck Baker	31	0	0	2	0	0	1	9	5,266	0	0	4,173	21,580
"	Buddy Baker	38	0	0	2	4	2	4	4	6,710	0	0	5,280	24,865
"	Darrell Bryant	1	0	0	0	0	0	0	0	57	0	0	57	555
"	Neil Castles	49	0	0	0	1	1	4	22	9,409	0	0	6,225	16,155
"	Goldie Parsons	1	0	0	0	0	0	0	0	242	0	0	81	100
"	Ken White	1	0	0	0	0	0	0	0	0	0	0	0	400
"	**Total**	52	0	0	4	5	3	9	35	**21,684**	0	0	**15,815**	63,655
1966	Buck Baker	36	0	0	3	0	2	2	7	6,725	0	0	4,882	14,900
"	Buddy Baker	10	0	0	0	0	0	0	1	1,819	0	0	1,505	4,105
"	Neil Castles	40	0	0	1	1	3	2	10	8,804	0	0	6,118	18,935
"	Paul Connors	2	0	0	0	0	0	0	1	630	0	0	642	2,720
"	Doug Cooper	1	0	0	0	0	0	0	0	167	0	0	84	150

Year	Driver	Starts	Poles	Finish						Laps	Laps Led	Races Led	Miles	$
				1	2	3	4	5	6–10					

Buck Baker *continued*

Year	Driver	Starts	Poles	1	2	3	4	5	6–10	Laps	Laps Led	Races Led	Miles	$
"	Darel Dieringer	2	0	0	0	0	0	0	0	277	0	0	139	200
"	Ray Hill	6	0	0	0	0	0	0	3	1,430	0	0	604	1,045
"	Max Ledbetter	1	0	0	0	0	0	0	0	140	0	0	70	110
"	Eddie MacDonald	2	0	0	0	0	0	0	1	348	0	0	510	1,525
"	**Total**	45	0	0	4	1	5	4	23	**20,340**	0	0	**14,552**	43,690
1967	Buck Baker	20	0	0	0	0	0	0	5	4,544	0	0	3,156	7,730
"	Buddy Baker	3	0	0	0	0	0	0	0	257	0	0	83	330
"	Neil Castles	3	0	0	0	0	0	1	0	417	0	0	191	540
"	Doug Cooper	8	0	0	0	0	0	0	1	1,569	0	0	1,088	2,625
"	J. T. Putney	1	0	0	0	0	0	0	0	307	0	0	307	710
"	Ken Rice	3	0	0	0	0	0	0	0	22	0	0	8	200
"	Al Tasnady	1	0	0	0	0	0	0	0	89	0	0	89	275
"	**Total**	35	0	0	0	0	0	1	6	7,205	0	0	4,922	12,410
1968	Serge Adams	1	0	0	0	0	0	0	0	109	0	0	55	100
"	Buck Baker	16	0	0	0	0	0	1	2	2,645	0	0	1,545	3,455
"	Neil Castles	1	0	0	0	0	0	0	0	4	0	0	6	430
"	George England	1	0	0	0	0	0	0	0	235	0	0	118	275
"	Bobby Mausgrover	3	0	0	0	0	0	0	0	247	0	0	103	630
"	Ken Meisenhelder	1	0	0	0	0	0	0	0	103	0	0	93	100
"	Dub Simpson	3	0	0	0	0	0	1	0	721	0	0	589	1,350
"	Sam Waldrop	1	0	0	0	0	0	0	0	171	0	0	86	130
"	**Total**	22	0	0	0	0	0	2	2	4,235	0	0	2,592	6,470
1969	Buck Baker	1	0	0	0	0	0	0	0	108	0	0	287	1,300
1971	Buck Baker	6	0	0	0	0	1	0	1	1,775	0	0	835	2,345
1982	Randy Baker	1	0	0	0	0	0	0	0	347	0	0	353	1,300
"	J. R. Charbonneau	1	0	0	0	0	0	0	0	118	0	0	118	650
"	Tom Hessert	1	0	0	0	0	0	0	0	8	0	0	20	950
"	**Total**	3	0	0	0	0	0	0	0	473	0	0	491	2,900
1984	Randy Baker	3	0	0	0	0	0	0	0	553	0	0	826	6,400
1985	Randy Baker	1	0	0	0	0	0	0	0	453	0	0	453	2,025
1986	Randy Baker	2	0	0	0	0	0	0	0	328	0	0	499	2,790
1987	Randy Baker	2	0	0	0	0	0	0	0	653	0	0	986	8,060
"	Patrick Latimer	1	0	0	0	0	0	0	0	38	0	0	39	1,250
"	**Total**	3	0	0	0	0	0	0	0	691	0	0	1,025	9,310
1988	Randy Baker	1	0	0	0	0	0	0	0	135	0	0	184	2,055
1991	Randy Baker	2	0	0	0	0	0	0	0	689	0	0	941	8,055
1992	Randy Baker	1	0	0	0	0	0	0	0	459	0	0	467	8,700
Lifetime		525	16	13	31	34	29	52	171	133,944	1,393	35	94,721	$349,188

Jimmy Baker

Year	Driver	Starts	Poles	1	2	3	4	5	6–10	Laps	Laps Led	Races Led	Miles	$
1962	Roscoe Thompson	3	0	0	0	0	0	0	0	293	0	0	477	1,280
"	LeeRoy Yarbrough	2	0	0	0	0	0	0	0	79	0	0	119	500
"	**Total**	5	0	0	0	0	0	0	0	372	0	0	595	1,780
1963	LeeRoy Yarbrough	1	0	0	0	0	0	0	0	114	0	0	57	50
Lifetime		6	0	0	0	0	0	0	0	486	0	0	652	$1,830

W. E. Baker

Year	Driver	Starts	Poles	1	2	3	4	5	6–10	Laps	Laps Led	Races Led	Miles	$
1952	W. E. Baker Jr.	1	0	0	0	0	0	0	0	368	0	0	460	90
Lifetime		1	0	0	0	0	0	0	0	368	0	0	460	$90

Baker-Schiff Racing (Buddy Baker and Danny Schiff, co-owners)

Year	Driver	Starts	Poles	1	2	3	4	5	6–10	Laps	Laps Led	Races Led	Miles	$
1985	Buddy Baker	28	0	0	0	0	2	0	5	6,296	4	2	8,250	235,480
1986	Buddy Baker	17	0	0	0	1	2	3	0	3,964	45	5	6,465	138,600
"	Al Unser	1	0	0	0	0	0	0	0	61	0	0	148	1,915
"	**Total**	18	0	0	0	1	2	3	0	4,025	45	5	6,613	140,515
1987	Buddy Baker	20	0	0	1	1	1	0	7	4,509	91	7	7,163	255,320
"	Irv Hoerr	1	0	0	0	0	0	0	0	114	0	0	299	1,705
"	**Total**	21	0	0	1	1	1	0	7	4,623	91	7	7,462	257,025
1988	Buddy Baker	17	0	0	0	0	0	0	7	4,445	42	7	6,481	184,200
"	Rick Mast	2	0	0	0	0	0	0	0	512	2	1	527	9,190
"	Greg Sacks	7	0	0	0	0	0	0	1	2,349	1	1	2,079	51,079
"	Morgan Shepherd	3	0	0	0	0	0	1	0	1	661	6	1	990	36,770
"	**Total**	29	0	0	0	0	0	1	0	9	7,967	51	10	10,076	281,239
1989	Joe Ruttman	1	0	0	0	0	0	0	1	74	0	0	186	11,350
"	Greg Sacks	10	0	0	0	0	0	0	2	3,053	108	3	3,470	87,090

Year	Driver	Starts	Poles	Finish 1	2	3	4	5	6–10	Laps	Laps Led	Races Led	Miles	$

Baker-Schiff Racing *continued*

Year	Driver	Starts	Poles	1	2	3	4	5	6–10	Laps	Laps Led	Races Led	Miles	$
"	Jimmy Spencer	17	0	0	0	0	0	0	3	3,544	0	0	4,558	121,065
"	**Total**	28	0	0	0	0	0	0	6	6,671	108	3	8,215	219,505
Lifetime		124	0	0	1	2	6	3	27	29,582	299	27	40,615	$1,133,764

Ivan Baldwin

Year	Driver	Starts	Poles	1	2	3	4	5	6–10	Laps	Laps Led	Races Led	Miles	$
1971	Ivan Baldwin	2	0	0	0	0	0	0	0	174	0	0	435	2,665
1980	Bill Osborne	1	0	0	0	0	0	0	0	20	0	0	52	500
Lifetime		3	0	0	0	0	0	0	0	194	0	0	488	$3,165

Rick Baldwin

Year	Driver	Starts	Poles	1	2	3	4	5	6–10	Laps	Laps Led	Races Led	Miles	$
1982	Rick Baldwin	1	0	0	0	0	0	0	0	323	0	0	485	6,065
1983	Rick Baldwin	4	0	0	0	0	0	0	0	811	0	0	1,204	13,155
1985	Rick Baldwin	1	0	0	0	0	0	0	0	142	0	0	284	1,550
Lifetime		6	0	0	0	0	0	0	0	1,276	0	0	1,972	$20,770

Roger Baldwin

Year	Driver	Starts	Poles	1	2	3	4	5	6–10	Laps	Laps Led	Races Led	Miles	$
1957	Roger Baldwin	2	0	0	0	0	0	0	0	337	0	0	337	200
Lifetime		2	0	0	0	0	0	0	0	337	0	0	337	$200

Ralph Ball

Year	Driver	Starts	Poles	1	2	3	4	5	6–10	Laps	Laps Led	Races Led	Miles	$
1985	Connie Saylor	5	0	0	0	0	0	0	0	456	0	0	871	8,915
1986	Tom Bigelow	1	0	0	0	0	0	0	0	58	0	0	88	985
"	Connie Saylor	1	0	0	0	0	0	0	0	114	0	0	303	2,575
"	Brad Teague	3	0	0	0	0	0	0	0	419	0	0	321	3,860
"	**Total**	5	0	0	0	0	0	0	0	591	0	0	713	7,420
1987	Joe Ruttman	1	0	0	0	0	0	0	0	27	0	0	72	3,125
"	Brad Teague	2	0	0	0	0	0	0	0	51	0	0	82	3,455
"	**Total**	3	0	0	0	0	0	0	0	78	0	0	153	6,580
1988	Dale Jarrett	1	0	0	0	0	0	0	0	164	0	0	250	2,175
"	Connie Saylor	1	0	0	0	0	0	0	0	32	0	0	80	9,645
"	**Total**	2	0	0	0	0	0	0	0	196	0	0	330	11,820
1991	Brad Teague	1	0	0	0	0	0	0	0	322	0	0	483	4,175
1992	Brad Teague	1	0	0	0	0	0	0	0	147	0	0	368	5,200
1993	Brad Teague	1	0	0	0	0	0	0	0	13	0	0	18	5,010
Lifetime		18	0	0	0	0	0	0	0	1,803	0	0	2,935	$49,120

Walter Ballard

Year	Driver	Starts	Poles	1	2	3	4	5	6–10	Laps	Laps Led	Races Led	Miles	$
1966	Walter Ballard	1	0	0	0	0	0	0	0	234	0	0	322	525
1971	Walter Ballard	41	0	0	0	1	1	1	8	9,419	0	0	8,035	30,974
1972	Walter Ballard	30	0	0	0	0	0	0	7	8,293	0	0	9,578	58,880
1973	Walter Ballard	28	0	0	0	0	0	0	4	8,048	5	1	8,626	53,875
"	Dick May	1	0	0	0	0	0	0	0	139	0	0	370	1,530
"	**Total**	28	0	0	0	0	0	0	4	8,187	5	1	8,995	55,405
1974	Walter Ballard	26	0	0	0	0	0	1	5	6,788	2	1	7,166	53,394
"	Kenny Brightbill	1	0	0	0	0	0	0	1	187	0	0	468	2,125
"	**Total**	27	0	0	0	0	0	1	6	6,975	2	1	7,633	55,519
1975	Walter Ballard	27	0	0	0	0	0	0	3	7,148	16	2	7,503	52,746
"	Bill Champion	1	0	0	0	0	0	0	0	41	0	0	22	1,055
"	Carl Van Horn	1	0	0	0	0	0	0	0	110	0	0	275	1,355
"	Salt Walther	1	0	0	0	0	0	0	0	52	0	0	130	1,325
"	**Total**	30	0	0	0	0	0	0	3	7,351	16	2	7,931	56,481
1976	Walter Ballard	8	0	0	0	0	0	0	3	2,906	0	0	2,217	10,470
"	Terry Bivins	10	0	0	0	0	0	0	3	3,295	0	0	2,955	21,495
"	Dale Earnhardt	1	0	0	0	0	0	0	0	156	0	0	234	1,725
"	Bruce Hill	2	0	0	0	0	0	0	1	459	0	0	676	5,670
"	Tighe Scott	6	0	0	0	0	0	0	1	697	0	0	1,703	15,520
"	**Total**	26	0	0	0	0	0	0	8	7,513	0	0	7,785	54,880
1977	Walter Ballard	2	0	0	0	0	0	0	0	527	0	0	616	4,700
"	Tighe Scott	25	0	0	0	0	0	1	0	5,936	0	0	7,196	63,225
"	**Total**	26	0	0	0	0	0	1	0	6,463	0	0	7,813	67,925
1978	Tighe Scott	29	0	0	0	0	0	0	7	6,626	3	1	8,223	87,912
1979	Bruce Hill	7	0	0	0	0	0	0	0	1,352	0	0	2,693	17,265

Year	Driver	Starts	Poles	Finish 1	2	3	4	5	6–10	Laps	Laps Led	Races Led	Miles	$

Walter Ballard *continued*

"	Tighe Scott	17	0	0	0	0	1	0	6	3,834	0	0	5,684	87,300
"	**Total**	19	0	0	0	0	1	0	6	5,186	0	0	8,377	104,565
1980	Bruce Hill	6	0	0	0	0	0	0	0	418	0	0	808	7,540
"	Tighe Scott	10	0	0	0	0	0	1	1	1,066	4	1	1,968	21,925
"	**Total**	10	0	0	0	0	0	1	1	1,484	4	1	2,776	29,465
Lifetime		267	0	0	0	1	2	4	50	67,731	30	6	77,467	$602,531

Jack Balmer

1971	Joe Dean Huss	3	0	0	0	0	0	0	0	1,242	0	0	671	1,435
Lifetime		3	0	0	0	0	0	0	0	1,242	0	0	671	$1,435

Steve Balogh

1992	Mike Potter	10	0	0	0	0	0	0	0	1,862	0	0	3,151	67,035
1993	Mike Potter	0												2,800
Lifetime		10	0	0	0	0	0	0	0	1,862	0	0	3,151	$69,835

Patricia Bandyul

1992	Jeff Fuller	1	0	0	0	0	0	0	0	386	0	0	290	4,000
Lifetime		1	0	0	0	0	0	0	0	386	0	0	290	$4,000

Jim Bangsberry

1966	Bunkie Blackburn	1	0	0	0	0	0	0	0	53	0	0	53	550
"	T. L. Blakely	1	0	0	0	0	0	0	0	10	0	0	25	0
"	**Total**	2	0	0	0	0	0	0	0	63	0	0	78	550
Lifetime		2	0	0	0	0	0	0	0	63	0	0	78	$550

Phil Barkdoll

1989	Phil Barkdoll	4	0	0	0	0	0	0	0	658	2	1	1,702	29,050
1990	Phil Barkdoll	3	0	0	0	0	0	0	0	202	0	0	524	24,160
"	Phil Parsons	1	0	0	0	0	0	0	0	101	0	0	269	4,600
"	**Total**	4	0	0	0	0	0	0	0	303	0	0	793	28,760
1991	Phil Barkdoll	4	0	0	0	0	0	0	0	646	0	0	1,674	41,655
1992	Phil Barkdoll	2	0	0	0	0	0	0	0	354	0	0	885	33,255
1993	Stanley Smith	0												2,100
1994	Phil Barkdoll	0												1,850
1995	Phil Barkdoll	0												2,450
1996	Tracy Leslie	0												3,672
Lifetime		14	0	0	0	0	0	0	0	1,961	2	1	5,054	$142,792

M. C. Barlow

1955	Ed Bergin	1	0	0	0	0	0	0	0	302	0	0	415	160
Lifetime		1	0	0	0	0	0	0	0	302	0	0	415	$160

Malcomb Barlow

1956	Gene Bergin	2	0	0	0	0	0	0	0	384	0	0	500	310
Lifetime		2	0	0	0	0	0	0	0	384	0	0	500	$310

James Barnes

1952	Bill Pruitt	1	0	0	0	0	0	0	0	169	0	0	169	25
Lifetime		1	0	0	0	0	0	0	0	169	0	0	169	$25

Dean Barnicle

1971	Kevin Terris	3	0	0	0	0	0	0	2	369	0	0	962	4,365
1972	Kevin Terris	3	0	0	0	0	0	0	1	454	0	0	1,168	4,945
"	Jim Whitt	2	0	0	0	0	0	0	0	429	0	0	858	1,565
"	**Total**	5	0	0	0	0	0	0	1	883	0	0	2,026	6,510
1973	Richard White	2	0	0	0	0	0	0	2	329	0	0	862	3,370
1974	Richard White	1	0	0	0	0	0	0	0	139	0	0	364	1,200
Lifetime		11	0	0	0	0	0	0	5	1,720	0	0	4,214	$15,445

Year	Driver	Starts	Poles	Finish 1	2	3	4	5	6–10	Laps	Laps Led	Races Led	Miles	$

Bob Barron

Year	Driver	Starts	Poles	1	2	3	4	5	6–10	Laps	Laps Led	Races Led	Miles	$
1960	Bob Barron	1	0	0	0	0	0	0	0	186	0	0	279	900
"	Jimmy Pardue	5	0	0	0	0	0	0	1	589	0	0	486	805
"	**Total**	6	0	0	0	0	0	0	1	775	0	0	765	1,705
1961	Bob Barron	30	0	0	0	0	0	0	4	4,848	0	0	2,792	3,685
"	Bobby Waddell	1	0	0	0	0	0	0	0	22	0	0	30	220
"	**Total**	31	0	0	0	0	0	0	4	4,870	0	0	2,822	3,905
1962	Bobby Waddell	1	0	0	0	0	0	0	0	161	0	0	81	50
Lifetime		38	0	0	0	0	0	0	5	5,806	0	0	3,667	$5,660

Chester Barron

Year	Driver	Starts	Poles	1	2	3	4	5	6–10	Laps	Laps Led	Races Led	Miles	$
1956	Chester Barron	2	0	0	0	0	0	0	1	207	0	0	152	150
1958	Chester Barron	1	0	0	0	0	0	0	0	49	0	0	49	75
1959	Chester Barron	3	0	0	0	0	0	0	1	271	0	0	175	275
"	Joe Johnson	1	0	0	0	0	0	0	0	58	0	0	80	150
"	Ken Rush	2	0	0	0	0	0	0	0	650	0	0	280	200
"	**Total**	6	0	0	0	0	0	0	1	979	0	0	534	625
Lifetime		9	0	0	0	0	0	0	2	1,235	0	0	735	$850

Bud Barry

Year	Driver	Starts	Poles	1	2	3	4	5	6–10	Laps	Laps Led	Races Led	Miles	$
1952	Leo Caldwell	1	0	0	0	0	0	0	0		0	0		50
Lifetime		1	0	0	0	0	0	0	0		0	0		$50

H. B. Bassett

Year	Driver	Starts	Poles	1	2	3	4	5	6–10	Laps	Laps Led	Races Led	Miles	$
1957	Jim Cook	2	0	0	0	0	0	0	0	133	0	0	67	80
Lifetime		2	0	0	0	0	0	0	0	133	0	0	67	$80

Lorrin Bates

Year	Driver	Starts	Poles	1	2	3	4	5	6–10	Laps	Laps Led	Races Led	Miles	$
1957	Jim Blomgren	1	0	0	0	0	0	0	0	53	0	0	133	110
Lifetime		1	0	0	0	0	0	0	0	53	0	0	133	$110

Robert Bates

Year	Driver	Starts	Poles	1	2	3	4	5	6–10	Laps	Laps Led	Races Led	Miles	$
1971	Tommy Andrews	2	0	0	0	0	0	0	0	251	0	0	79	450
Lifetime		2	0	0	0	0	0	0	0	251	0	0	79	$450

Doug Bawel

Year	Driver	Starts	Poles	1	2	3	4	5	6–10	Laps	Laps Led	Races Led	Miles	$
1994*	Greg Sacks	31	1	0	0	0	0	0	3	8,266	38	7	10,041	411,728
"	P. J. Jones	1	0	0	0	0	0	0	0	67	0	0	164	6,085
"	**Total**	31	1	0	0	0	0	0	3	8,333	38	7	10,201	417,813
1995*	Bobby Hillin Jr.	18	0	0	0	0	0	0	1	4,410	1	1	6,351	244,270
"	Davey Jones	7	0	0	0	0	0	0	0	1,680	0	0	2,359	109,925
"	**Total**	25	0	0	0	0	0	0	1	6,090	1	1	8,710	354,195
1996	Bobby Hillin Jr.	25	0	0	0	0	0	0	0	6,673	4	1	8,608	395,224
Lifetime		81	1	0	0	0	0	0	4	21,096	43	9	27,519	$1,167,232

*Co-owned with D. K. Ulrich 1994–October 1995.

Raymond Beadle

Year	Driver	Starts	Poles	1	2	3	4	5	6–10	Laps	Laps Led	Races Led	Miles	$
1983	Tim Richmond	30	4	1	1	4	1	3	5	7,176	590	15	8,218	262,139
1984	Tim Richmond	30	0	1	3	0	0	2	5	8,225	58	7	9,416	345,848
1985	Tim Richmond	28	0	0	1	1	1	0	10	8,199	377	12	9,489	290,284
"	Sammy Swindell	1	0	0	0	0	0	0	0	242	0	0	368	1,175
"	**Total**	28	0	0	1	1	1	0	10	8,441	377	12	9,857	291,459
1986	Rusty Wallace	29	0	2	0	0	2	0	12	8,486	427	8	10,416	557,354
1987	Rusty Wallace	29	1	2	3	2	1	1	7	8,323	450	15	9,668	690,652
1988	Rusty Wallace	29	2	6	5	4	2	2	4	9,222	908	18	11,180	1,411,567
1989	Rusty Wallace	29	4	6	4	0	2	1	7	9,104	2,021	23	10,781	2,237,950
1990	Rusty Wallace	29	2	2	3	2	0	2	7	8,459	1,137	16	10,073	954,129
Lifetime		233	13	20	20	13	9	11	57	67,436	5,968	114	79,608	$6,751,098

Robert Beadle

Year	Driver	Starts	Poles	1	2	3	4	5	6–10	Laps	Laps Led	Races Led	Miles	$
1980	Roy Smith	2	0	0	0	0	0	0	0	109	3	1	277	2,075
1981	Roy Smith	3	0	0	0	0	0	0	1	178	0	0	466	8,695
Lifetime		5	0	0	0	0	0	0	1	287	3	1	744	$10,770

Year	Driver	Starts	Poles	Finish 1	2	3	4	5	6–10	Laps	Laps Led	Races Led	Miles	$

Wayne Beahr

Year	Driver	Starts	Poles	1	2	3	4	5	6–10	Laps	Laps Led	Races Led	Miles	$
1983	Dick May	3	0	0	0	0	0	0	0	765	0	0	888	4,370
"	Joe Millikan	1	0	0	0	0	0	0	0	384	0	0	240	1,075
"	Morgan Shepherd	1	0	0	0	0	0	0	0	50	0	0	27	850
"	**Total**	5	0	0	0	0	0	0	0	1,199	0	0	1,155	6,295
1984	Dick May	3	0	0	0	0	0	0	0	1,274	0	0	1,282	5,325
1985	Dick May	1	0	0	0	0	0	0	0	297	0	0	406	1,840
"	J. D. McDuffie	1	0	0	0	0	0	0	0	203	0	0	203	3,565
"	Morgan Shepherd	1	0	0	0	0	0	0	0	123	0	0	123	1,075
"	**Total**	3	0	0	0	0	0	0	0	623	0	0	732	6,480
1986	Joe Fields	1	0	0	0	0	0	0	0	0	0	0	0	875
"	Roy Lee Hendrick	1	0	0	0	0	0	0	0	91	0	0	91	875
"	Joe Millikan	2	0	0	0	0	0	0	0	59	0	0	56	1,950
"	**Total**	4	0	0	0	0	0	0	0	150	0	0	147	3,700
1987	Curtis Markham	1	0	0	0	0	0	0	0	29	0	0	29	1,175
Lifetime		16	0	0	0	0	0	0	0	3,275	0	0	3,345	$22,975

Herman Beam

Year	Driver	Starts	Poles	1	2	3	4	5	6–10	Laps	Laps Led	Races Led	Miles	$
1957	Herman Beam	1	0	0	0	0	0	0	0		0	0		50
1958	Herman Beam	20	0	0	0	0	0	0	1	3,651	0	0	2,251	2,599
1959	Herman Beam	30	0	0	0	0	0	1	11	6,034	0	0	4,011	6,380
1960	Herman Beam	26	0	0	0	0	1	0	5	5,348	0	0	4,730	5,916
1961	Herman Beam	41	0	0	0	0	1	0	13	8,827	0	0	6,403	9,392
1962	Herman Beam	51	0	0	0	0	0	0	18	11,217	0	0	7,140	12,751
1963	Herman Beam	25	0	0	0	0	0	0	6	5,061	0	0	3,476	5,255
"	Ned Jarrett	1	0	0	0	0	0	1	0	195	0	0	98	275
"	Larry Thomas	1	0	0	0	0	0	0	0	373	0	0	560	1,000
"	Cale Yarborough	14	0	0	0	0	0	3	4	3,926	0	0	2,389	4,100
"	**Total**	41	0	0	0	0	0	4	10	9,555	0	0	6,521	10,630
1964	H. B. Bailey	1	0	0	0	0	0	0	0	6	0	0	9	400
"	Larry Frank	1	0	0	0	0	0	0	0	12	0	0	11	0
"	Tiny Lund	1	0	0	0	0	0	1	0	196	0	0	98	275
"	Larry Thomas	10	0	0	1	1	2	1	4	3,712	0	0	2,189	7,350
"	Cale Yarborough	17	0	0	0	0	0	2	4	3,194	10	1	2,591	5,515
"	**Total**	30	0	0	1	1	2	4	8	7,120	10	1	4,897	13,540
1965	Rene Charland	1	0	0	0	0	0	0	0	18	0	0	18	550
"	J. T. Putney	28	0	0	1	3	4	2	10	6,614	0	0	4,984	16,155
"	Cale Yarborough	1	0	0	0	0	0	0	0	12	0	0	6	100
"	**Total**	28	0	0	1	3	4	2	10	6,644	0	0	5,008	16,805
1966	Gil Hearne	1	0	0	0	0	0	0	0	229	0	0	115	100
Lifetime		269	0	0	2	4	8	11	76	58,625	10	1	41,076	$77,983

Fred Bear

Year	Driver	Starts	Poles	1	2	3	4	5	6–10	Laps	Laps Led	Races Led	Miles	$
1969	Buddy Young	21	0	0	0	0	0	1	5	4,510	0	0	3,873	15,422
Lifetime		21	0	0	0	0	0	1	5	4,510	0	0	3,873	$15,422

Dick Beaty

Year	Driver	Starts	Poles	1	2	3	4	5	6–10	Laps	Laps Led	Races Led	Miles	$
1957	Bill Amick	1	0	0	0	0	0	0	1	189	0	0	95	210
"	Dick Beaty	20	0	0	0	0	0	1	6	3,202	0	0	2,061	3,648
"	Fireball Roberts	1	0	0	0	0	0	1	0	195	0	0	98	270
"	Speedy Thompson	1	0	0	0	0	0	0	0	144	0	0	72	100
"	**Total**	23	0	0	0	0	0	2	7	3,730	0	0	2,325	4,228
1958	Dick Beaty	2	0	0	0	0	0	0	0	448	0	0	224	150
"	Junior Johnson	1	0	0	0	0	0	0	1	148	0	0	37	215
"	Joe Weatherly	1	0	0	0	0	0	0	0	144	0	0	36	120
"	**Total**	4	0	0	0	0	0	0	1	740	0	0	297	485
Lifetime		27	0	0	0	0	0	2	8	4,470	0	0	2,622	$4,713

Joe Beccue

Year	Driver	Starts	Poles	1	2	3	4	5	6–10	Laps	Laps Led	Races Led	Miles	$
1951	Harvey Riley	7	0	0	0	0	0	1	1	238	0	0	164	525
Lifetime		7	0	0	0	0	0	1	1	238	0	0	164	$525

Gary Bechtel

Year	Driver	Starts	Poles	1	2	3	4	5	6–10	Laps	Laps Led	Races Led	Miles	$
1990	Bobby Hamilton	1	0	0	0	0	0	0	0	102	0	0	153	4,540

Year	Driver	Starts	Poles	Finish 1	2	3	4	5	6–10	Laps	Laps Led	Races Led	Miles	$

Gary Bechtel *continued*

Year	Driver	Starts	Poles	1	2	3	4	5	6–10	Laps	Laps Led	Races Led	Miles	$
"	Phil Parsons	3	0	0	0	0	0	0	0	586	0	0	959	14,755
"	**Total**	4	0	0	0	0	0	0	0	688	0	0	1,112	19,295
1992	John Krebs	2	0	0	0	0	0	0	0	380	0	0	489	12,990
1993	Steve Grissom	1	0	0	0	0	0	0	0	260	0	0	260	6,485
"	Andy Hillenburg	1	0	0	0	0	0	0	0	242	0	0	363	4,365
"	John Krebs	2	0	0	0	0	0	0	0	154	0	0	386	13,955
"	**Total**	4	0	0	0	0	0	0	0	656	0	0	1,009	24,805
1994	Steve Grissom	27	0	0	0	0	0	0	3	7,966	1	1	9,740	300,915
"	John Krebs	1	0	0	0	0	0	0	0	18	1	1	45	8,100
"	**Total**	27	0	0	0	0	0	0	3	7,984	2	2	9,785	309,015
1995	Steve Grissom	29	0	0	0	0	0	1	3	8,279	17	2	10,299	509,047
1996	Jeff Green	2	0	0	0	0	0	0	0	722	0	0	738	30,040
"	Steve Grissom	13	0	0	0	0	0	1	1	3,169	12	1	4,302	308,183
"	Butch Leitzinger	1	0	0	0	0	0	0	0	90	0	0	221	22,705
"	Chad Little	4	0	0	0	0	0	0	0	889	0	0	785	84,525
"	Robert Pressley	3	0	0	0	0	0	0	0	854	0	0	1,017	55,650
"	Greg Sacks	6	0	0	0	0	0	0	0	1,059	3	1	2,142	161,425
"	**Total**	29	0	0	0	0	0	1	1	6,783	15	2	9,205	662,528
Lifetime		95	0	0	0	0	0	2	7	24,770	34	6	31,900	$1,537,680

Bob Beck

Year	Driver	Starts	Poles	1	2	3	4	5	6–10	Laps	Laps Led	Races Led	Miles	$
1955	Bob Beck	2	0	0	0	0	0	0	0	223	0	0	144	75
Lifetime		2	0	0	0	0	0	0	0	223	0	0	144	$75

Tom Beck

Year	Driver	Starts	Poles	1	2	3	4	5	6–10	Laps	Laps Led	Races Led	Miles	$
1983	Lennie Pond	3	0	0	0	0	0	0	1	405	3	1	913	19,490
Lifetime		3	0	0	0	0	0	0	1	405	3	1	913	$19,490

Randy Becker

Year	Driver	Starts	Poles	1	2	3	4	5	6–10	Laps	Laps Led	Races Led	Miles	$
1983	Randy Becker	1	0	0	0	0	0	0	0	116	0	0	304	1,950
Lifetime		1	0	0	0	0	0	0	0	116	0	0	304	$1,950

Allen Beebe

Year	Driver	Starts	Poles	1	2	3	4	5	6–10	Laps	Laps Led	Races Led	Miles	$
1989	Troy Beebe	1	0	0	0	0	0	0	0	72	0	0	181	2,605
1990	Troy Beebe	2	0	0	0	0	0	0	0	333	0	0	439	6,560
Lifetime		3	0	0	0	0	0	0	0	405	0	0	621	$9,165

Jack Beebe

Year	Driver	Starts	Poles	1	2	3	4	5	6–10	Laps	Laps Led	Races Led	Miles	$
1978	Satch Worley	4	0	0	0	0	0	0	1	1,298	0	0	1,589	6,205
1979	Geoff Bodine	3	0	0	0	0	0	0	0	443	6	1	631	4,820
"	Harry Gant	22	1	0	0	0	0	0	4	5,927	29	4	6,770	40,560
"	**Total**	25	1	0	0	0	0	0	4	6,370	35	5	7,401	45,380
1980	Harry Gant	28	0	0	3	2	2	2	3	7,584	262	9	7,840	166,470
1981	Ron Bouchard	22	1	1	0	0	1	3	7	6,155	12	2	6,978	152,855
"	Harry Gant	4	0	0	1	0	0	0	1	1,329	112	2	1,587	46,920
"	**Total**	26	1	1	1	0	1	3	8	7,484	124	4	8,565	199,775
1982	Ron Bouchard	30	1	0	0	2	1	0	12	8,048	1	1	8,543	375,759
1983	Ron Bouchard	28	1	0	0	0	1	0	6	7,187	22	4	8,315	159,173
1984	Ron Bouchard	30	0	0	1	2	1	1	6	9,200	111	8	10,504	246,510
1985	Ron Bouchard	28	0	0	1	1	2	1	7	7,723	77	5	8,961	240,304
1986	Morgan Shepherd	12	0	1	0	0	2	0	3	2,782	130	6	4,776	129,915
Lifetime		211	4	2	6	7	10	7	50	57,676	762	42	66,494	$1,569,491

B. S. Beeson

Year	Driver	Starts	Poles	1	2	3	4	5	6–10	Laps	Laps Led	Races Led	Miles	$
1950	Shorty York	1	0	0	0	0	0	0	0	358	0	0	448	0
Lifetime		1	0	0	0	0	0	0	0	358	0	0	448	$0

Dick Behling

Year	Driver	Starts	Poles	1	2	3	4	5	6–10	Laps	Laps Led	Races Led	Miles	$
1968	Marty Robbins	1	0	0	0	0	0	0	0	312	0	0	468	1,525
Lifetime		1	0	0	0	0	0	0	0	312	0	0	468	$1,525

Year	Driver	Starts	Poles	Finish 1	2	3	4	5	6–10	Laps	Laps Led	Races Led	Miles	$

Torsten Behn

Year	Driver	Starts	Poles	1	2	3	4	5	6–10	Laps	Laps Led	Races Led	Miles	$
1981	Rick O'Dell	1	0	0	0	0	0	0	0	86	0	0	225	2,145
Lifetime		1	0	0	0	0	0	0	0	86	0	0	225	$2,145

John Belgard

Year	Driver	Starts	Poles	1	2	3	4	5	6–10	Laps	Laps Led	Races Led	Miles	$
1949	John Belgard	1	0	0	0	0	0	0	0		0	0		0
Lifetime		1	0	0	0	0	0	0	0		0	0		$0

Charles Bell

Year	Driver	Starts	Poles	1	2	3	4	5	6–10	Laps	Laps Led	Races Led	Miles	$
1967	Jack McCoy	1	0	0	0	0	0	0	0	88	0	0	238	575
1968	Jack McCoy	1	0	0	0	0	0	0	0	118	0	0	319	725
Lifetime		2	0	0	0	0	0	0	0	206	0	0	556	$1,300

Ron Benfield

Year	Driver	Starts	Poles	1	2	3	4	5	6–10	Laps	Laps Led	Races Led	Miles	$
1981	Johnny Rutherford	12	0	0	0	0	0	1	1	2,432	5	1	3,793	38,095
"	Morgan Shepherd	3	0	0	0	0	0	0	0	391	43	2	429	2,405
"	Rusty Wallace	2	0	0	0	0	0	0	0	351	0	0	697	4,245
"	**Total**	15	0	0	0	0	0	1	1	3,174	48	3	4,918	44,745
1982	Morgan Shepherd	29	2	0	0	1	1	4	7	7,708	211	12	8,620	166,030
1983	Joe Ruttman	30	2	0	0	1	3	0	6	7,887	397	10	8,817	223,809
1984	L. D. Ottinger	2	0	0	0	0	0	0	0	695	0	0	714	7,650
"	Joe Ruttman	25	1	0	0	0	0	0	7	6,233	54	3	7,504	133,620
"	Morgan Shepherd	3	0	0	0	0	0	0	1	926	1	1	1,285	17,300
"	**Total**	30	1	0	0	0	0	0	8	7,854	55	4	9,503	158,570
1985	Trevor Boys	6	0	0	0	0	0	0	0	542	0	0	695	21,980
Lifetime		110	5	0	0	2	4	5	22	27,165	711	29	32,554	$615,134

Arnold Bennett

Year	Driver	Starts	Poles	1	2	3	4	5	6–10	Laps	Laps Led	Races Led	Miles	$
1970	Arnold Bennett	1	0	0	0	0	0	0	0	1	0	0	3	0
Lifetime		1	0	0	0	0	0	0	0	1	0	0	3	$0

Mike Bennett

Year	Driver	Starts	Poles	1	2	3	4	5	6–10	Laps	Laps Led	Races Led	Miles	$
1973	Bill Ward	2	0	0	0	0	0	0	0	188	0	0	500	2,275
Lifetime		2	0	0	0	0	0	0	0	188	0	0	500	$2,275

Bill Benson

Year	Driver	Starts	Poles	1	2	3	4	5	6–10	Laps	Laps Led	Races Led	Miles	$
1958	Bill Benson	2	0	0	0	0	0	0	0	111	0	0	70	110
Lifetime		2	0	0	0	0	0	0	0	111	0	0	70	$110

Tiny Benson

Year	Driver	Starts	Poles	1	2	3	4	5	6–10	Laps	Laps Led	Races Led	Miles	$
1958	Tiny Benson	4	0	0	0	0	0	0	2	445	0	0	182	450
1959	Tiny Benson	2	0	0	0	0	0	0	2	298	0	0	205	350
Lifetime		6	0	0	0	0	0	0	4	743	0	0	387	$800

Clarence Benton

Year	Driver	Starts	Poles	1	2	3	4	5	6–10	Laps	Laps Led	Races Led	Miles	$
1949	Clarence Benton	1	0	0	0	0	0	0	0		0	0		0
Lifetime		1	0	0	0	0	0	0	0		0	0		$0

Millie Bernard

Year	Driver	Starts	Poles	1	2	3	4	5	6–10	Laps	Laps Led	Races Led	Miles	$
1953	Ned Jarrett	1	0	0	0	0	0	0	0		0	0		25
1954	Ned Jarrett	2	0	0	0	0	0	0	0	273	0	0	151	25
1955	Ned Jarrett	2	0	0	0	0	0	0	0	333	0	0	447	260
Lifetime		5	0	0	0	0	0	0	0	606	0	0	598	$310

Kenny Bernstein

Year	Driver	Starts	Poles	1	2	3	4	5	6–10	Laps	Laps Led	Races Led	Miles	$
1986	Joe Ruttman	29	0	0	2	0	0	3	9	7,732	55	5	8,707	259,263
1987	Morgan Shepherd	29	1	0	1	1	1	4	4	6,410	164	7	7,975	317,034
1988	Ricky Rudd	29	2	1	3	1	1	0	5	8,867	695	16	10,428	410,954
1989	Ricky Rudd	29	0	1	0	2	3	1	8	9,326	247	7	11,075	533,624
1990	Brett Bodine	29	1	1	0	2	2	0	4	9,097	216	7	10,878	442,681
1991	Brett Bodine	29	1	0	1	0	1	0	4	7,873	163	3	9,048	376,220

Year	Driver	Starts	Poles	Finish						Laps	Laps Led	Races Led	Miles	$
				1	2	3	4	5	6–10					

Kenny Bernstein *continued*

1992	Brett Bodine	29	1	0	0	1	1	0	11	8,581	237	11	10,021	495,224
1993	Brett Bodine	29	2	0	1	0	0	2	6	8,120	102	7	9,382	582,014
"	Dick Trickle	1	0	0	0	0	0	0	0	407	0	0	407	12,755
"	**Total**	30	2	0	1	0	0	2	6	8,527	102	7	9,789	594,769
1994	Brett Bodine	31	0	0	1	0	0	0	5	8,931	55	6	10,772	801,944
1995	Steve Kinser	5	0	0	0	0	0	0	0	958	0	0	948	105,224
"	Hut Stricklin	24	1	0	0	0	1	1	3	5,513	45	4	7,311	486,065
"	**Total**	29	1	0	0	0	1	1	3	6,471	45	4	8,258	591,289
Lifetime		293	9	3	9	7	10	11	59	81,815	1,979	73	96,951	$4,823,002

Joe Berreschick

1954	Danny Letner	4	1	1	0	1	0	0	1	1,058	142	2	674	1,975
Lifetime		4	1	1	0	1	0	0	1	1,058	142	2	674	$1,975

Max Berrier

1955	Max Berrier	2	0	0	0	0	0	0	0	232	0	0	116	100
1959	Max Berrier	2	0	0	0	0	0	0	0	214	0	0	64	110
Lifetime		4	0	0	0	0	0	0	0	446	0	0	180	$210

Fred Bethune

1952	Fred Bethune	2	0	0	0	0	0	0	1	377	0	0	293	125
Lifetime		2	0	0	0	0	0	0	1	377	0	0	293	$125

Larry Bettinger

1951	Bill Norton	3	0	1	0	1	0	0	1	200	19	1	100	1,675
Lifetime		3	0	1	0	1	0	0	1	200	19	1	100	$1,675

Rich Bickle

1989	Rich Bickle	2	0	0	0	0	0	0	0	355	0	0	540	4,185
1990	Rich Bickle	1	0	0	0	0	0	0	0	195	0	0	488	19,120
Lifetime		3	0	0	0	0	0	0	0	550	0	0	1,027	$23,305

Don Biederman

1967	Don Biederman	1	0	0	0	0	0	0	0	19	0	0	48	100
Lifetime		1	0	0	0	0	0	0	0	19	0	0	48	$100

Don Bierschwale

1971	Jimmy Finger	1	0	0	0	0	0	0	0	18	0	0	36	530
1972	Jimmy Finger	2	0	0	0	0	0	0	0	214	0	0	535	3,830
"	Clarence Lovell	12	0	0	0	0	0	0	0	2,202	0	0	3,586	10,770
"	**Total**	14	0	0	0	0	0	0	0	2,416	0	0	4,121	14,600
1973	Dick Brooks	1	0	0	0	0	0	0	1	351	0	0	479	2,880
"	Clarence Lovell	4	0	0	0	0	1	0	1	661	0	0	1,162	9,175
"	Johnny Rutherford	1	0	0	0	0	0	0	0	471	0	0	479	1,325
"	Ed Sczech	4	0	0	0	0	0	0	0	558	0	0	1,137	4,270
"	**Total**	10	0	0	0	0	1	0	2	2,041	0	0	3,258	17,650
1974	Iggy Katona	1	0	0	0	0	0	0	0	181	0	0	481	1,675
"	Johnny Rutherford	2	0	0	0	0	0	0	0	123	2	1	308	4,415
"	**Total**	3	0	0	0	0	0	0	0	304	2	1	789	6,090
1979	Jimmy Finger	3	0	0	0	0	0	0	0	152	0	0	398	5,020
1980	Jimmy Finger	1	0	0	0	0	0	0	0	181	0	0	362	2,200
1983	Eddie Bierschwale	3	0	0	0	0	0	0	0	524	0	0	888	3,665
1984	Eddie Bierschwale	2	0	0	0	0	0	0	0	317	0	0	583	3,495
1988	Eddie Bierschwale	20	0	0	0	0	0	0	0	4,106	0	0	6,117	59,355
1989	Eddie Bierschwale	14	0	0	0	0	0	0	1	3,740	2	1	4,752	67,910
1990	Eddie Bierschwale	2	0	0	0	0	0	0	0	474	0	0	787	8,415
1991	Eddie Bierschwale	3	0	0	0	0	0	0	0	621	0	0	1,174	41,785
1992	Eddie Bierschwale	4	0	0	0	0	0	0	0	628	0	0	1,092	25,995
"	A. J. Foyt	1	0	0	0	0	0	0	0	195	0	0	488	23,055
"	**Total**	5	0	0	0	0	0	0	0	823	0	0	1,580	49,050
Lifetime		81	0	0	0	0	1	0	3	15,717	4	2	24,842	$279,765

Year	Driver	Starts	Poles	Finish 1	2	3	4	5	6–10	Laps	Laps Led	Races Led	Miles	$

George Bignotti

Year	Driver	Starts	Poles	1	2	3	4	5	6–10	Laps	Laps Led	Races Led	Miles	$
1954	Jim Graham	2	0	0	0	0	0	0	1	530	0	0	385	400
Lifetime		2	0	0	0	0	0	0	1	530	0	0	385	$400

Bob Bilby

Year	Driver	Starts	Poles	1	2	3	4	5	6–10	Laps	Laps Led	Races Led	Miles	$
1989	Mike Miller	1	0	0	0	0	0	0	0	137	0	0	274	3,075
"	Phil Parsons	1	0	0	0	0	0	0	0	394	0	0	246	2,245
"	**Total**	2	0	0	0	0	0	0	0	531	0	0	520	5,320
Lifetime		2	0	0	0	0	0	0	0	531	0	0	520	$5,320

Fred Bince

Year	Driver	Starts	Poles	1	2	3	4	5	6–10	Laps	Laps Led	Races Led	Miles	$
1951	Fred Lee	3	0	0	0	0	0	0	1		0	0		175
1954	Sam Lamm	2	0	0	0	0	0	0	0	426	0	0	326	50
1956	Bob Stanclift	1	0	0	0	0	0	0	0	72	0	0	180	40
Lifetime		6	0	0	0	0	0	0	1	498	0	0	506	$265

Art Binkley

Year	Driver	Starts	Poles	1	2	3	4	5	6–10	Laps	Laps Led	Races Led	Miles	$
1956	Art Binkley	1	0	0	0	0	0	0	0	349	0	0	175	150
1957	Art Binkley	3	0	0	0	0	0	0	0	690	0	0	495	390
Lifetime		4	0	0	0	0	0	0	0	1,039	0	0	669	$540

Martin Birrane

Year	Driver	Starts	Poles	1	2	3	4	5	6–10	Laps	Laps Led	Races Led	Miles	$
1991	Bobby Hillin Jr.	2	0	0	0	0	0	0	0	554	10	1	836	10,975
"	John Paul Jr.	2	0	0	0	0	0	0	0	167	0	0	411	8,460
"	**Total**	4	0	0	0	0	0	0	0	721	10	1	1,247	19,435
1992	Bobby Hillin Jr.	11	0	0	0	0	0	0	0	2,100	0	0	4,031	92,550
Lifetime		15	0	0	0	0	0	0	0	2,821	10	1	5,279	$111,985

Bishop Brothers

Year	Driver	Starts	Poles	1	2	3	4	5	6–10	Laps	Laps Led	Races Led	Miles	$
1949	Jack Smith	1	0	0	0	0	0	0	0		0	0		50
1950	Billy Carden	1	0	0	0	0	0	0	0	30	0	0	125	25
"	Jack Smith	2	0	0	1	0	0	0	0	31	45	1	129	625
"	**Total**	2	0	0	1	0	0	0	0	61	45	1	254	650
1951	Billy Carden	1	0	0	0	0	0	0	0	377	0	0	471	300
"	Jack Smith	1	0	0	0	0	0	0	0		0	0		25
"	**Total**	2	0	0	0	0	0	0	0	377	0	0	471	325
1952	Billy Carden	2	0	0	0	0	0	0	0	186	0	0	93	50
"	Roscoe Thompson	2	0	0	0	0	0	0	0	236	0	0	135	85
"	**Total**	4	0	0	0	0	0	0	0	422	0	0	228	135
1955	Billy Carden	11	0	0	0	0	2	0	1	1,440	0	0	992	1,205
1957	Tiny Lund	1	0	0	0	0	0	0	1	486	0	0	243	450
1958	Billy Carden	4	0	0	0	0	0	0	1	349	0	0	224	350
Lifetime		25	0	0	1	0	2	0	3	3,135	45	1	2,411	$3,165

Gordon Bishop

Year	Driver	Starts	Poles	1	2	3	4	5	6–10	Laps	Laps Led	Races Led	Miles	$
1952	Gordon Bishop	2	0	0	0	0	0	0	0		0	0		25
Lifetime		2	0	0	0	0	0	0	0		0	0		$25

Bobby Black

Year	Driver	Starts	Poles	1	2	3	4	5	6–10	Laps	Laps Led	Races Led	Miles	$
1974	Bobby Ore	1	0	0	0	0	0	0	0	297	0	0	177	440
Lifetime		1	0	0	0	0	0	0	0	297	0	0	177	$440

Gene Black

Year	Driver	Starts	Poles	1	2	3	4	5	6–10	Laps	Laps Led	Races Led	Miles	$
1965	Gene Black	18	0	0	0	0	0	0	4	4,167	0	0	3,011	6,080
"	Darel Dieringer	1	0	0	0	0	0	0	0	420	0	0	210	330
"	J. T. Putney	2	0	0	0	0	0	0	1	224	0	0	112	300
"	**Total**	21	0	0	0	0	0	0	5	4,811	0	0	3,333	6,710
1966	Buddy Baker	1	0	0	0	0	0	0	0	317	0	0	198	225
1966	Gene Black	12	0	0	0	0	0	0	2	1,713	0	0	1,216	3,765
"	Bunkie Blackburn	1	0	0	0	0	0	0	0	1	0	0	2	580
"	Earl Brooks	8	0	0	0	0	0	0	1	1,677	0	0	1,060	2,595
"	Doug Cooper	1	0	0	0	0	0	0	0	25	0	0	63	0
"	Henley Gray	2	0	0	0	0	1	0	0	679	0	0	636	1,265

Year	Driver	Starts	Poles	1	2	3	4	5	6–10	Laps	Laps Led	Races Led	Miles	$

Gene Black *continued*

Year	Driver	Starts	Poles	1	2	3	4	5	6–10	Laps	Laps Led	Races Led	Miles	$
"	Don Israel	1	0	0	0	0	0	0	1	188	0	0	94	150
"	Elmo Langley	1	0	0	0	1	0	0	0	192	0	0	96	400
"	Bud Moore	1	0	0	0	0	0	0	0	35	0	0	18	100
"	Bill Seifert	1	0	0	0	0	0	0	0	63	0	0	32	100
"	Buster Sexton	1	0	0	0	0	0	0	0	183	0	0	92	100
"	**Total**	28	0	0	0	1	1	0	4	5,073	0	0	3,504	9,280
1967	Earl Brooks	13	0	0	0	0	0	0	3	1,655	0	0	844	2,245
"	Bob Cooper	1	0	0	0	0	0	0	0	24	0	0	33	565
"	Jackie Fox	2	0	0	0	0	0	0	0	57	0	0	23	0
"	Jimmy Helms	1	0	0	0	0	0	0	1	177	0	0	89	150
"	**Total**	17	0	0	0	0	0	0	4	1,913	0	0	989	2,960
1968	Gene Black	7	0	0	0	0	0	0	0	762	0	0	336	805
"	Earl Brooks	1	0	0	0	0	0	0	0	89	0	0	223	1,085
"	Bill Seifert	1	0	0	0	0	0	0	0	53	0	0	18	100
"	Bryant Wallace	1	0	0	0	0	0	0	0	118	0	0	59	100
"	**Total**	10	0	0	0	0	0	0	0	1,022	0	0	635	2,090
Lifetime		76	0	0	0	1	1	0	13	12,819	0	0	8,461	$21,040

John Black

Year	Driver	Starts	Poles	1	2	3	4	5	6–10	Laps	Laps Led	Races Led	Miles	$
1964	Henley Gray	1	0	0	0	0	0	0	0	126	0	0	63	100
"	John Sears	6	0	0	0	0	0	0	3	1,200	0	0	581	1,130
"	**Total**	7	0	0	0	0	0	0	3	1,326	0	0	644	1,230
Lifetime		7	0	0	0	0	0	0	3	1,326	0	0	644	$1,230

M. J. Black

Year	Driver	Starts	Poles	1	2	3	4	5	6–10	Laps	Laps Led	Races Led	Miles	$
1960	Curtis Crider	1	0	0	0	0	0	0	0	45	0	0	41	50
"	Jimmy Pardue	2	0	0	0	0	0	0	1	478	0	0	548	530
"	E. J. Trivette	9	0	0	0	0	0	0	0	1,000	0	0	532	940
"	**Total**	12	0	0	0	0	0	0	1	1,523	0	0	1,121	1,520
1961	George Green	7	0	0	0	0	0	0	2	1,130	0	0	613	685
"	Jimmy Pardue	2	0	0	0	0	0	0	0	238	0	0	119	200
"	E. J. Trivette	4	0	0	0	0	0	0	0	476	0	0	209	470
"	Bobby Waddell	1	0	0	0	0	0	0	0	3	0	0	5	50
"	**Total**	14	0	0	0	0	0	0	2	1,847	0	0	945	1,405
Lifetime		26	0	0	0	0	0	0	3	3,370	0	0	2,066	$2,925

Melvin Black

Year	Driver	Starts	Poles	1	2	3	4	5	6–10	Laps	Laps Led	Races Led	Miles	$
1961	Charlie Glotzbach	4	0	0	0	0	0	0	0	344	0	0	653	755
Lifetime		4	0	0	0	0	0	0	0	344	0	0	653	$755

Sonny Black

Year	Driver	Starts	Poles	1	2	3	4	5	6–10	Laps	Laps Led	Races Led	Miles	$
1951	Sonny Black	4	0	0	0	0	0	0	2	73	0	0	91	175
1955	Sonny Black	1	0	0	0	0	0	0	0	181	0	0	91	50
Lifetime		5	0	0	0	0	0	0	2	254	0	0	182	$225

A. J. Blackwelder

Year	Driver	Starts	Poles	1	2	3	4	5	6–10	Laps	Laps Led	Races Led	Miles	$
1959	Bunk Moore	1	0	0	0	0	0	0	0	24	0	0	24	0
"	Shorty Rollins	1	0	0	0	0	0	0	0	90	0	0	225	300
"	**Total**	2	0	0	0	0	0	0	0	114	0	0	249	300
1960	Carl Burris	2	0	0	0	0	0	0	0	81	0	0	151	200
Lifetime		4	0	0	0	0	0	0	0	195	0	0	400	$500

Clay Blackwell

Year	Driver	Starts	Poles	1	2	3	4	5	6–10	Laps	Laps Led	Races Led	Miles	$
1975	Bill Champion	1	0	0	0	0	0	0	0	144	0	0	197	1,340
"	Johnny Ray	4	0	0	0	0	0	0	0	247	0	0	577	3,435
"	**Total**	5	0	0	0	0	0	0	0	391	0	0	774	4,775
1976	Johnny Ray	1	0	0	0	0	0	0	0	111	0	0	278	2,270
Lifetime		6	0	0	0	0	0	0	0	502	0	0	1,052	$7,045

Bill Blair

Year	Driver	Starts	Poles	1	2	3	4	5	6–10	Laps	Laps Led	Races Led	Miles	$
1950	Bill Blair	1	0	0	0	0	0	1	0	0	0	0	0	300
1951	Bill Blair	14	0	0	0	1	2	0	2	616	0	0	656	2,725

Year	Driver	Starts	Poles	Finish						Laps	Laps Led	Races Led	Miles	$
				1	2	3	4	5	6–10					

Bill Blair *continued*

Year	Driver	Starts	Poles	1	2	3	4	5	6–10	Laps	Laps Led	Races Led	Miles	$
1953	Bill Blair	21	0	1	0	2	0	3	2	1,043	51	2	1,100	3,995
1954	Bill Blair	16	0	0	0	0	0	2	8	2,426	7	1	1,679	2,300
1955	Bill Blair	3	0	0	0	0	0	0	0	645	0	0	629	190
"	Jim Paschal	1	0	0	0	0	0	0	0	83	0	0	83	50
"	**Total**	4	0	0	0	0	0	0	0	728	0	0	712	240
1956	Bill Blair	2	0	0	0	0	0	0	1	360	0	0	341	500
1958	Bill Blair	1	0	0	0	0	0	0	0	104	0	0	94	125
Lifetime		59	0	1	0	3	2	6	13	5,277	58	3	4,581	$10,185

David Blair

Year	Driver	Starts	Poles	1	2	3	4	5	6–10	Laps	Laps Led	Races Led	Miles	$
1996	Todd Bodine	3	0	0	0	0	0	0	0	1,092	1	1	1,293	32,800
"	Elton Sawyer	8	0	0	0	0	0	0	0	2,121	0	0	2,833	115,603
"	**Total**	11	0	0	0	0	0	0	0	3,213	1	1	4,125	148,403
Lifetime		11	0	0	0	0	0	0	0	3,213	1	1	4,125	$148,403

Joe Blair

Year	Driver	Starts	Poles	1	2	3	4	5	6–10	Laps	Laps Led	Races Led	Miles	$
1954	Ray Duhigg	1	0	0	0	0	0	0	0	43	0	0	65	0
"	Jimmie Lewallen	10	0	0	2	0	0	1	2	1,602	0	0	1,031	2,400
"	**Total**	11	0	0	2	0	0	1	2	1,645	0	0	1,095	2,400
1955	Perk Brown	2	0	0	0	0	0	0	1	275	0	0	138	150
"	Richard Brownlee	7	0	0	0	0	0	0	0	681	0	0	359	315
"	Jimmie Lewallen	9	0	0	0	0	0	2	3	1,041	0	0	592	1,325
"	**Total**	18	0	0	0	0	0	2	4	1,997	0	0	1,088	1,790
1956	Bill Blair	5	0	0	0	0	0	0	2	353	0	0	280	280
"	Fred Harb	1	0	0	0	0	0	0	0	31	0	0	16	50
"	**Total**	6	0	0	0	0	0	0	2	384	0	0	295	330
Lifetime		35	0	0	2	0	0	3	8	4,026	0	0	2,478	$4,520

Cy Blalock

Year	Driver	Starts	Poles	1	2	3	4	5	6–10	Laps	Laps Led	Races Led	Miles	$
1951	Pug Blalock	2	0	0	0	0	0	0	1		0	0		75
Lifetime		2	0	0	0	0	0	0	1		0	0		$75

Leonard Blanchard

Year	Driver	Starts	Poles	1	2	3	4	5	6–10	Laps	Laps Led	Races Led	Miles	$
1970	Leonard Blanchard	2	0	0	0	0	0	0	0	92	0	0	230	1,135
1971	Leonard Blanchard	1	0	0	0	0	0	0	0	46	0	0	115	255
Lifetime		3	0	0	0	0	0	0	0	138	0	0	345	$1,390

Vernon Blank

Year	Driver	Starts	Poles	1	2	3	4	5	6–10	Laps	Laps Led	Races Led	Miles	$
1972	H. B. Bailey	3	0	0	0	0	0	1	0	687	6	1	1,151	6,245
"	Dick Brooks	1	0	0	0	0	0	0	0	21	0	0	29	575
"	Fred Drake	1	0	0	0	0	0	0	0	93	0	0	140	345
"	**Total**	5	0	0	0	0	0	1	0	801	6	1	1,320	7,165
Lifetime		5	0	0	0	0	0	1	0	801	6	1	1,320	$7,165

Erwin Blatt

Year	Driver	Starts	Poles	1	2	3	4	5	6–10	Laps	Laps Led	Races Led	Miles	$
1952	Erwin Blatt	1	0	0	0	0	0	0	0	337	0	0	421	60
Lifetime		1	0	0	0	0	0	0	0	337	0	0	421	$60

Brett Bodine

Year	Driver	Starts	Poles	1	2	3	4	5	6–10	Laps	Laps Led	Races Led	Miles	$
1996	Brett Bodine	30	0	0	0	0	0	0	1	8,732	3	2	10,718	767,716
Lifetime		30	0	0	0	0	0	0	1	8,732	3	2	10,718	$767,716

Geoff Bodine

Year	Driver	Starts	Poles	1	2	3	4	5	6–10	Laps	Laps Led	Races Led	Miles	$
1993	Geoff Bodine	7	0	0	0	0	0	0	1	1,974	32	1	1,830	124,730
"	Jimmy Hensley	12	0	0	0	0	0	0	1	3,240	1	1	4,399	223,330
"	Tommy Kendall	2	0	0	0	0	0	0	0	158	0	0	392	32,190
"	**Total**	21	0	0	0	0	0	0	2	5,372	33	2	6,622	380,250
1994	Geoff Bodine	31	5	3	1	1	1	1	3	8,150	1,744	20	9,771	1,287,626
1995	Geoff Bodine	31	0	0	0	0	0	1	3	9,257	13	4	11,571	1,011,090

Year	Driver	Starts	Poles	Finish 1	2	3	4	5	6–10	Laps	Laps Led	Races Led	Miles	$

Geoff Bodine *continued*

Year	Driver	Starts	Poles	1	2	3	4	5	6–10	Laps	Laps Led	Races Led	Miles	$
1996	Geoff Bodine	31	0	1	0	1	0	0	4	8,918	90	7	11,067	1,031,762
Lifetime		114	5	4	1	2	1	2	12	31,697	1,880	33	39,031	$3,710,728

Buzzy Boehman

Year	Driver	Starts	Poles	1	2	3	4	5	6–10	Laps	Laps Led	Races Led	Miles	$
1949	Buck Baker	1	0	0	0	0	0	0	0		0	0		0
Lifetime		1	0	0	0	0	0	0	0		0	0		$0

Tommy Boger

Year	Driver	Starts	Poles	1	2	3	4	5	6–10	Laps	Laps Led	Races Led	Miles	$
1953	Tommy Boger	1	0	0	0	0	0	0	0	32	0	0	131	25
Lifetime		1	0	0	0	0	0	0	0	32	0	0	131	$25

Fred Boggs

Year	Driver	Starts	Poles	1	2	3	4	5	6–10	Laps	Laps Led	Races Led	Miles	$
1957	Fred Boggs	1	0	0	0	0	0	0	0		0	0		25
Lifetime		1	0	0	0	0	0	0	0		0	0		$25

R. L. Boggs

Year	Driver	Starts	Poles	1	2	3	4	5	6–10	Laps	Laps Led	Races Led	Miles	$
1971	David Ray Boggs	7	0	0	0	0	0	0	2	1,985	0	0	1,711	4,969
1972	David Ray Boggs	23	0	0	0	0	0	0	0	3,664	0	0	4,708	18,575
"	Bill Shirey	1	0	0	0	0	0	0	0	212	0	0	424	765
"	**Total**	24	0	0	0	0	0	0	0	3,876	0	0	5,132	19,340
Lifetime		31	0	0	0	0	0	0	2	5,861	0	0	6,843	$24,309

Pete Boland

Year	Driver	Starts	Poles	1	2	3	4	5	6–10	Laps	Laps Led	Races Led	Miles	$
1961	Pete Boland	1	0	0	0	0	0	0	0	32	0	0	80	0
"	Tiny Lund	2	0	0	0	0	0	0	0	279	0	0	140	170
"	**Total**	3	0	0	0	0	0	0	0	311	0	0	220	170
Lifetime		3	0	0	0	0	0	0	0	311	0	0	220	$170

Aubrey Boles

Year	Driver	Starts	Poles	1	2	3	4	5	6–10	Laps	Laps Led	Races Led	Miles	$
1959	Aubrey Boles	4	0	0	0	0	0	0	1	796	0	0	398	300
1960	Aubrey Boles	1	0	0	0	0	0	0	0	97	0	0	49	50
Lifetime		5	0	0	0	0	0	0	1	893	0	0	447	$350

Lee Roy "Toy" Bolton

Year	Driver	Starts	Poles	1	2	3	4	5	6–10	Laps	Laps Led	Races Led	Miles	$
1962	Bob Cooper	2	0	0	0	0	0	0	0	205	0	0	103	180
"	Stick Elliott	20	0	0	0	0	0	0	2	2,687	0	0	1,806	3,528
"	**Total**	21	0	0	0	0	0	0	2	2,892	0	0	1,908	3,708
1963	Stick Elliott	23	0	0	0	0	0	0	7	3,560	0	0	2,418	4,310
"	Cale Yarborough	1	0	0	0	0	0	0	0	336	0	0	504	500
"	**Total**	24	0	0	0	0	0	0	7	3,896	0	0	2,922	4,810
1964	Toy Bolton	1	0	0	0	0	0	0	0	48	0	0	24	0
"	Stick Elliott	6	0	0	0	0	0	0	0	210	0	0	243	1,050
"	**Total**	7	0	0	0	0	0	0	0	258	0	0	267	1,050
1965	Darel Dieringer	1	0	0	0	0	0	0	0	24	0	0	8	0
"	Stick Elliott	15	0	0	1	0	1	0	1	2,082	0	0	1,562	5,235
"	Jim Paschal	3	0	0	0	0	0	0	0	454	0	0	657	2,160
"	Ned Setzer	7	0	0	0	0	0	0	3	792	0	0	796	4,695
"	**Total**	24	0	0	1	0	1	0	4	3,352	0	0	3,023	12,090
1966	Toy Bolton	3	0	0	0	0	0	0	2	455	0	0	217	880
"	Bob Cooper	1	0	0	0	0	0	0	1	259	0	0	130	300
"	Joel Davis	8	0	0	0	0	0	0	0	1,222	0	0	569	1,225
"	Darel Dieringer	1	0	0	0	0	0	0	1	293	0	0	147	425
"	Stick Elliott	19	0	0	0	0	1	0	2	3,285	0	0	2,716	7,335
"	J. T. Putney	1	0	0	0	0	0	0	0	150	0	0	405	570
"	Ned Setzer	2	0	0	0	0	0	0	0	147	0	0	368	1,200
"	Jimmy Trull	1	0	0	0	0	0	0	0	247	0	0	124	247
"	Curtis Turner	5	1	0	0	0	1	0	1	1,056	80	1	577	2,270
"	**Total**	30	1	0	0	0	2	0	7	7,114	80	1	5,252	14,452
1967	Buddy Baker	1	0	0	0	0	1	0	0	191	0	0	96	300
"	Joel Davis	1	0	0	0	0	0	0	0	129	0	0	65	100

Year	Driver	Starts	Poles	Finish						Laps	Laps Led	Races Led	Miles	$
				1	2	3	4	5	6–10					

Leroy "Toy" Bolton *continued*

Year	Driver	Starts	Poles	1	2	3	4	5	6–10	Laps	Laps Led	Races Led	Miles	$
"	Stick Elliott	1	0	0	0	0	0	0	0	370	0	0	555	1,650
"	**Total**	3	0	0	0	0	1	0	0	690	0	0	715	2,050
Lifetime		109	1	0	1	0	4	0	20	18,202	80	1	14,087	$38,160

Les Bomar

Year	Driver	Starts	Poles	1	2	3	4	5	6–10	Laps	Laps Led	Races Led	Miles	$
1951	Les Bomar	4	0	0	0	0	0	0	0	0	0	0	0	100
Lifetime		4	0	0	0	0	0	0	0	0	0	0	0	$100

Tony Bonadies

Year	Driver	Starts	Poles	1	2	3	4	5	6–10	Laps	Laps Led	Races Led	Miles	$
1952	Tony Bonadies	1	0	0	0	0	0	0	0	350	0	0	438	325
Lifetime		1	0	0	0	0	0	0	0	350	0	0	438	$325

Eddie Bond

Year	Driver	Starts	Poles	1	2	3	4	5	6–10	Laps	Laps Led	Races Led	Miles	$
1973	Eddie Bond	6	0	0	0	0	0	0	0	1,407	0	0	2,287	6,901
"	Frank Warren	1	0	0	0	0	0	0	0	167	0	0	89	415
"	**Total**	7	0	0	0	0	0	0	0	1,574	0	0	2,376	7,316
Lifetime		7	0	0	0	0	0	0	0	1,574	0	0	2,376	$7,316

Bob Bondurant

Year	Driver	Starts	Poles	1	2	3	4	5	6–10	Laps	Laps Led	Races Led	Miles	$
1981	Bob Bondurant	1	0	0	0	0	0	0	0	93	0	0	244	1,130
Lifetime		1	0	0	0	0	0	0	0	93	0	0	244	$1,130

Neil Bonnett

Year	Driver	Starts	Poles	1	2	3	4	5	6–10	Laps	Laps Led	Races Led	Miles	$
1976	Neil Bonnett	14	0	0	0	0	0	1	3	2,377	1	1	3,323	32,275
Lifetime		14	0	0	0	0	0	1	3	2,377	1	1	3,323	$32,275

Joe Booher

Year	Driver	Starts	Poles	1	2	3	4	5	6–10	Laps	Laps Led	Races Led	Miles	$
1980	Joe Booher	1	0	0	0	0	0	0	0	81	0	0	123	880
1985	Joe Booher	2	0	0	0	0	0	0	0	358	0	0	801	3,685
1987	Joe Booher	0												2,000
1988	Joe Booher	1	0	0	0	0	0	0	0	272	0	0	272	3,295
1990	Joe Booher	0												1,000
Lifetime		4	0	0	0	0	0	0	0	711	0	0	1,196	$10,860

Kay Borland

Year	Driver	Starts	Poles	1	2	3	4	5	6–10	Laps	Laps Led	Races Led	Miles	$
1975	John Harkins	1	0	0	0	0	0	0	0	382	0	0	382	800
Lifetime		1	0	0	0	0	0	0	0	382	0	0	382	$800

John Borneman

Year	Driver	Starts	Poles	1	2	3	4	5	6–10	Laps	Laps Led	Races Led	Miles	$
1977	John Borneman	1	0	0	0	0	0	0	0	150	0	0	375	1,200
1978	John Borneman	3	0	0	0	0	0	0	0	305	0	0	777	3,320
1979	John Borneman	1	0	0	0	0	0	0	0	79	0	0	207	1,305
"	Jim Robinson	1	0	0	0	0	0	0	0	17	0	0	45	755
"	**Total**	2	0	0	0	0	0	0	0	96	0	0	252	2,060
1980	John Borneman	2	0	0	0	0	0	0	0	84	0	0	220	1,250
1981	John Borneman	1	0	0	0	0	0	0	0	116	0	0	304	3,140
Lifetime		9	0	0	0	0	0	0	0	751	0	0	1,928	$10,970

R. L. Bowling

Year	Driver	Starts	Poles	1	2	3	4	5	6–10	Laps	Laps Led	Races Led	Miles	$
1953	Curtis Turner	1	0	0	0	0	0	0	1	38	0	0	156	300
Lifetime		1	0	0	0	0	0	0	1	38	0	0	156	$300

Bill Bowman

Year	Driver	Starts	Poles	1	2	3	4	5	6–10	Laps	Laps Led	Races Led	Miles	$
1955	Bill Bowman	3	0	0	0	0	0	0	2	675	0	0	610	610
1956	Bill Bowman	1	0	0	0	0	0	0	1	181	0	0	91	100
1957	Bill Bowman	4	0	0	0	0	0	0	1	817	0	0	463	510
Lifetime		8	0	0	0	0	0	0	4	1,673	0	0	1,163	$1,220

Year	Driver	Starts	Poles	1	2	3	4	5	6–10	Laps	Laps Led	Races Led	Miles	$

Oscar Bowman

Year	Driver	Starts	Poles	1	2	3	4	5	6–10	Laps	Laps Led	Races Led	Miles	$
1965	Rod Eulenfeld	1	0	0	0	0	0	0	0		0	0		100
Lifetime		1	0	0	0	0	0	0	0		0	0		$100

Dick Bown

Year	Driver	Starts	Poles	1	2	3	4	5	6–10	Laps	Laps Led	Races Led	Miles	$
1965	Dick Bown	1	0	0	0	0	0	0	0	47	0	0	127	525
1972	Chuck Bown	3	0	0	0	0	0	0	0	391	0	0	1,005	3,710
1973	Chuck Bown	1	0	0	0	0	0	0	1	145	0	0	380	1,275
1974	Chuck Bown	3	0	0	0	0	0	0	0	114	0	0	297	2,070
1975	Chuck Bown	5	0	0	0	0	0	0	0	415	0	0	634	5,160
1981	Jim Bown	2	0	0	0	0	0	0	0	48	0	0	126	1,415
"	Chuck Bown	2	0	0	0	0	0	0	0	513	0	0	683	2,775
"	**Total**	4	0	0	0	0	0	0	0	561	0	0	809	4,190
1982	Jim Bown	2	0	0	0	0	0	0	1	204	0	0	534	4,490
1988	Jim Bown	2	0	0	0	0	0	0	0	86	0	0	122	3,325
1989	Jim Bown	3	0	0	0	0	0	0	0	469	0	0	587	6,200
Lifetime		24	0	0	0	0	0	0	2	2,432	0	0	4,495	$30,945

Jack Bowsher

Year	Driver	Starts	Poles	1	2	3	4	5	6–10	Laps	Laps Led	Races Led	Miles	$
1966	Jack Bowsher	2	0	0	0	0	0	0	0	775	0	0	932	1,710
1967	Jack Bowsher	2	0	0	0	0	0	0	0	207	11	1	302	1,705
1969	A. J. Foyt	4	1	0	1	0	2	0	0	522	63	2	1,254	17,375
1970	A. J. Foyt	3	0	1	0	0	0	0	0	298	35	1	768	21,210
Lifetime		11	1	1	1	0	2	0	0	1,802	109	4	3,256	$42,000

James Boyd

Year	Driver	Starts	Poles	1	2	3	4	5	6–10	Laps	Laps Led	Races Led	Miles	$
1974	George Behlman	1	0	0	0	0	0	0	0	25	0	0	66	695
Lifetime		1	0	0	0	0	0	0	0	25	0	0	66	$695

Jim Boyd

Year	Driver	Starts	Poles	1	2	3	4	5	6–10	Laps	Laps Led	Races Led	Miles	$
1975	Jim Boyd	2	0	0	0	0	0	0	0	203	0	0	524	2,335
Lifetime		2	0	0	0	0	0	0	0	203	0	0	524	$2,335

Ray Boynton

Year	Driver	Starts	Poles	1	2	3	4	5	6–10	Laps	Laps Led	Races Led	Miles	$
1960	Dick Dixon	2	0	0	0	0	0	0	0	181	0	0	453	250
Lifetime		2	0	0	0	0	0	0	0	181	0	0	453	$250

Buddie Boys

Year	Driver	Starts	Poles	1	2	3	4	5	6–10	Laps	Laps Led	Races Led	Miles	$
1984	Buddie Boys	1	0	0	0	0	0	0	0	178	0	0	181	1,055
1985	Trevor Boys	1	0	0	0	0	0	0	0	14	0	0	37	925
1986	Buddie Boys	2	0	0	0	0	0	0	0	91	0	0	168	2,480
1988	Trevor Boys	1	0	0	0	0	0	0	0	306	0	0	306	2,875
Lifetime		5	0	0	0	0	0	0	0	589	0	0	692	$7,335

Trevor Boys

Year	Driver	Starts	Poles	1	2	3	4	5	6–10	Laps	Laps Led	Races Led	Miles	$
1982	Trevor Boys	1	0	0	0	0	0	0	0	105	0	0	275	1,200
Lifetime		1	0	0	0	0	0	0	0	105	0	0	275	$1,200

Gordon Bracken

Year	Driver	Starts	Poles	1	2	3	4	5	6–10	Laps	Laps Led	Races Led	Miles	$
1953	Gordon Bracken	6	0	0	0	0	0	0	1	221	0	0	221	215
Lifetime		6	0	0	0	0	0	0	1	221	0	0	221	$215

Charles Bradberry

Year	Driver	Starts	Poles	1	2	3	4	5	6–10	Laps	Laps Led	Races Led	Miles	$
1995	Gary Bradberry	2	0	0	0	0	0	0	0	32	0	0	61	14,295
Lifetime		2	0	0	0	0	0	0	0	32	0	0	61	$14,295

Melvin Bradley

Year	Driver	Starts	Poles	1	2	3	4	5	6–10	Laps	Laps Led	Races Led	Miles	$
1962	Melvin Bradley	3	0	0	0	0	1	0	1	1,007	0	0	445	990
"	Tommy Irwin	11	0	0	1	0	1	0	4	1,867	0	0	855	2,300

Year	Driver	Starts	Poles	Finish 1	2	3	4	5	6–10	Laps	Laps Led	Races Led	Miles	$

Melvin Bradley *continued*

Year	Driver	Starts	Poles	1	2	3	4	5	6–10	Laps	Laps Led	Races Led	Miles	$
"	Doug Yates	2	0	0	0	0	0	0	0	106	0	0	159	525
"	**Total**	16	0	0	1	0	2	0	5	2,980	0	0	1,459	3,815
Lifetime		16	0	0	1	0	2	0	5	2,980	0	0	1,459	$3,815

George Bradshaw & Mark Smith

Year	Driver	Starts	Poles	1	2	3	4	5	6–10	Laps	Laps Led	Races Led	Miles	$
1989	Ron Esau	1	0	0	0	0	0	0	0	117	0	0	311	3,460
1990	Mike Chase	1	0	0	0	0	0	0	0	198	0	0	396	4,925
"	Bobby Hamilton	2	0	0	0	0	0	0	0	305	0	0	458	8,525
"	Stanley Smith	1	0	0	0	0	0	0	0	54	0	0	144	4,285
"	Hut Stricklin	1	0	0	0	0	0	0	0	84	0	0	128	3,330
"	**Total**	5	0	0	0	0	0	0	0	641	0	0	1,126	21,065
1991	Bobby Hamilton	28	0	0	0	0	0	0	4	8,304	7	3	10,187	259,105
1992	Bobby Hamilton	29	0	0	0	0	0	0	2	8,998	0	0	10,736	367,065
1993	Loy Allen Jr.	2	0	0	0	0	0	0	0	528	0	0	644	12,735
"	Bobby Hamilton	8	0	0	0	0	0	0	0	2,134	0	0	2,452	84,710
"	Greg Sacks	18	0	0	0	0	0	0	1	4,931	1	1	6,732	157,750
"	Dorsey Schroeder	2	0	0	0	0	0	0	0	69	0	0	174	13,615
"	**Total**	29	0	0	0	0	0	0	1	7,662	1	1	10,002	268,810
1994	Loy Allen Jr.	19	3	0	0	0	0	0	0	4,446	12	3	6,776	216,751
Lifetime		111	3	0	0	0	0	0	7	30,168	20	7	39,138	$1,136,256

Les Brand

Year	Driver	Starts	Poles	1	2	3	4	5	6–10	Laps	Laps Led	Races Led	Miles	$
1954	Dick Zimmerman	2	0	0	0	0	0	0	0	350	0	0	236	40
1955	Dick Zimmerman	1	0	0	0	0	0	0	0	77	0	0	77	0
Lifetime		3	0	0	0	0	0	0	0	427	0	0	313	$40

Bruce Brantley

Year	Driver	Starts	Poles	1	2	3	4	5	6–10	Laps	Laps Led	Races Led	Miles	$
1963	Bruce Brantley	4	0	0	0	0	0	0	1	231	0	0	146	840
Lifetime		4	0	0	0	0	0	0	1	231	0	0	146	$840

Darin Brassfield

Year	Driver	Starts	Poles	1	2	3	4	5	6–10	Laps	Laps Led	Races Led	Miles	$
1989	Darin Brassfield	3	0	0	0	0	0	0	0	275	0	0	486	10,852
Lifetime		3	0	0	0	0	0	0	0	275	0	0	486	$10,852

J. D. Braswell

Year	Driver	Starts	Poles	1	2	3	4	5	6–10	Laps	Laps Led	Races Led	Miles	$
1960	Don O'Dell	1	0	0	0	0	0	0	0	90	0	0	135	200
1961	Red Hollingsworth	1	0	0	0	0	0	0	0	2	0	0	3	200
"	Tiny Lund	3	0	0	0	0	0	0	1	682	0	0	638	950
"	Don O'Dell	2	0	0	0	0	0	0	1	48	0	0	120	340
"	Fireball Roberts	1	0	1	0	0	0	0	0	178	178	1	249	2,000
"	**Total**	7	0	1	0	0	0	0	2	910	178	1	1,010	3,490
Lifetime		8	0	1	0	0	0	0	2	1,000	178	1	1,145	$3,690

Dan Bray

Year	Driver	Starts	Poles	1	2	3	4	5	6–10	Laps	Laps Led	Races Led	Miles	$
1974	Jim Hurtubise	1	0	0	0	0	0	0	0	112	0	0	280	3,600
Lifetime		1	0	0	0	0	0	0	0	112	0	0	280	$3,600

Jim Bray

Year	Driver	Starts	Poles	1	2	3	4	5	6–10	Laps	Laps Led	Races Led	Miles	$
1963	Jim Bray	1	0	0	0	0	0	0	0	171	0	0	43	100
1974	Jim Bray	4	0	0	0	0	0	0	0	388	0	0	395	2,880
Lifetime		5	0	0	0	0	0	0	0	559	0	0	438	$2,980

E. J. Brewer

Year	Driver	Starts	Poles	1	2	3	4	5	6–10	Laps	Laps Led	Races Led	Miles	$
1958	E. J. Brewer	4	0	0	0	0	0	0	1	249	0	0	153	240
"	Cecil Grubbs	1	0	0	0	0	0	0	0	79	0	0	49	50
"	**Total**	5	0	0	0	0	0	0	1	328	0	0	202	290
Lifetime		5	0	0	0	0	0	0	1	328	0	0	202	$290

Fred Bridgers

Year	Driver	Starts	Poles	1	2	3	4	5	6–10	Laps	Laps Led	Races Led	Miles	$
1952	Weldon Adams	2	0	0	0	0	0	0	0	176	0	0	182	25
Lifetime		2	0	0	0	0	0	0	0	176	0	0	182	$25

Year	Driver	Starts	Poles	Finish 1	2	3	4	5	6–10	Laps	Laps Led	Races Led	Miles	$

Johnny Bridgers

Year	Driver	Starts	Poles	1	2	3	4	5	6–10	Laps	Laps Led	Races Led	Miles	$
1952	Johnny Bridgers	1	0	0	0	0	0	0	0	244	0	0	305	0
1953	Johnny Bridgers	1	0	0	0	0	0	0	0	279	0	0	384	120
Lifetime		2	0	0	0	0	0	0	0	523	0	0	689	$120

Harley J. Briggs

Year	Driver	Starts	Poles	1	2	3	4	5	6–10	Laps	Laps Led	Races Led	Miles	$
1951	Andy Pierce	1	0	0	0	0	0	0	0		0	0		25
Lifetime		1	0	0	0	0	0	0	0		0	0		$25

Ralph Briggs

Year	Driver	Starts	Poles	1	2	3	4	5	6–10	Laps	Laps Led	Races Led	Miles	$
1956	Fred Bince	1	0	0	0	0	0	0	0	3	0	0	8	30
Lifetime		1	0	0	0	0	0	0	0	3	0	0	8	$30

Mason Bright

Year	Driver	Starts	Poles	1	2	3	4	5	6–10	Laps	Laps Led	Races Led	Miles	$
1953	Mason Bright	1	0	0	0	0	0	0	0	33	0	0	135	25
1954	Mason Bright	2	0	0	0	0	0	0	0	200	0	0	226	50
Lifetime		3	0	0	0	0	0	0	0	233	0	0	361	$75

Bob Bristol

Year	Driver	Starts	Poles	1	2	3	4	5	6–10	Laps	Laps Led	Races Led	Miles	$
1964	Walt Price	1	0	0	0	0	0	0	0	43	0	0	116	500
1965	Joe Clark	1	0	0	0	0	0	0	0	41	0	0	111	500
1966	Joe Clark	1	0	0	0	0	0	0	0	4	0	0	11	500
1967	Bruce Worrell	1	0	0	0	0	0	0	1	174	0	0	470	1,650
1968	Harold Hardesty	1	0	0	0	0	0	0	0	67	0	0	181	575
1969	Harold Hardesty	1	0	0	0	0	0	0	1	163	0	0	440	1,250
Lifetime		6	0	0	0	0	0	0	2	492	0	0	1,328	$4,975

Manley Britt

Year	Driver	Starts	Poles	1	2	3	4	5	6–10	Laps	Laps Led	Races Led	Miles	$
1958	George Dunn	10	1	0	1	0	1	1	3	1,747	10	1	939	1,880
"	Larry Frank	3	0	0	0	0	0	0	1	315	0	0	257	435
"	**Total**	13	1	0	1	0	1	1	4	2,062	10	1	1,197	2,315
1959	George Dunn	1	0	0	0	0	0	0	0	145	0	0	48	130
"	Phillip Jones	1	0	0	0	0	0	0	0	150	0	0	38	50
"	Earl Moss	2	0	0	0	0	0	0	1	279	0	0	140	140
"	Ken Rush	5	0	0	1	0	0	0	1	680	0	0	743	1,220
"	Bill Taylor	1	0	0	0	0	0	0	0	439	0	0	220	125
"	Gene White	1	0	0	0	0	0	0	0	155	0	0	78	0
"	**Total**	11	0	0	1	0	0	0	2	1,848	0	0	1,265	1,665
Lifetime		24	1	0	2	0	1	1	6	3,910	10	1	2,462	$3,980

Michael Brockman

Year	Driver	Starts	Poles	1	2	3	4	5	6–10	Laps	Laps Led	Races Led	Miles	$
1975	Jimmy Insolo	1	0	0	0	0	0	0	0	31	0	0	47	825
1976	Terry Bivins	1	0	0	0	0	0	0	1	194	0	0	485	3,540
"	Hershel McGriff	1	0	0	0	0	0	0	0	71	0	0	186	790
"	Rusty Sanders	1	0	0	0	0	0	0	0	29	0	0	76	815
"	**Total**	3	0	0	0	0	0	0	1	294	0	0	747	5,145
1977	Jimmy Insolo	1	0	0	0	0	0	0	0	4	0	0	10	590
Lifetime		5	0	0	0	0	0	0	1	329	0	0	804	$6,560

H. J. Brooking

Year	Driver	Starts	Poles	1	2	3	4	5	6–10	Laps	Laps Led	Races Led	Miles	$
1972	Bill Dennis	4	0	0	0	1	0	0	0	1,020	2	1	858	3,964
1973	Bill Dennis	4	0	0	0	0	0	0	2	1,430	0	0	1,114	4,225
Lifetime		8	0	0	0	1	0	0	2	2,450	2	1	1,972	$8,189

Brooks Brothers

Year	Driver	Starts	Poles	1	2	3	4	5	6–10	Laps	Laps Led	Races Led	Miles	$
1955	Ed Cole Jr.	5	0	0	0	0	0	0	0	580	0	0	359	210
"	Gene Simpson	13	0	0	0	0	0	0	4	1,396	0	0	974	960
"	**Total**	18	0	0	0	0	0	0	4	1,976	0	0	1,333	1,170
1956	Ed Cole Jr.	1	0	0	0	0	0	0	0	115	0	0	86	50
Lifetime		19	0	0	0	0	0	0	4	2,091	0	0	1,419	$1,220

Year	Driver	Starts	Poles	Finish 1	2	3	4	5	6–10	Laps	Laps Led	Races Led	Miles	$

Brooks Motors

Year	Driver	Starts	Poles	1	2	3	4	5	6–10	Laps	Laps Led	Races Led	Miles	$
1949	Chuck Mahoney	1	0	0	0	0	0	0	0		0	0		0
1950	Chuck Mahoney	11	1	0	1	1	0	1	3	705	18	1	638	2,550
"	Jack White	1	0	0	0	0	0	0	0	41	0	0	171	50
"	**Total**	12	1	0	1	1	0	1	3	746	18	1	809	2,600
Lifetime		13	1	0	1	1	0	1	3	746	18	1	809	$2,600

Dick Brooks

Year	Driver	Starts	Poles	1	2	3	4	5	6–10	Laps	Laps Led	Races Led	Miles	$
1969	Dick Brooks	28	0	0	0	1	0	2	9	5,741	2	1	6,255	28,187
1970	Dick Brooks	32	0	0	2	5	4	4	3	6,787	194	6	6,910	52,364
"	Pete Hamilton	1	0	0	0	1	0	0	0	299	0	0	118	600
"	**Total**	33	0	0	2	6	4	4	3	7,086	194	6	7,028	52,964
1971	Marv Acton	11	0	0	0	0	0	0	0	1,421	0	0	2,399	8,620
"	Dick Brooks	1	0	0	0	0	0	0	0	279	0	0	153	495
"	Bill Dennis	1	0	0	0	0	0	0	0	328	0	0	175	545
"	Kevin Terris	1	0	0	0	0	0	0	0	150	0	0	399	1,600
"	**Total**	14	0	0	0	0	0	0	0	2,178	0	0	3,126	11,260
1972	Johnny Halford	5	0	0	0	0	0	0	1	1,032	0	0	1,574	4,710
1973	Dick Brooks	2	0	0	0	0	0	0	1	532	1	1	565	3,644
1974	Dick Brooks	16	0	0	0	0	0	0	3	2,951	1	1	4,097	22,760
1994	Bobby Hamilton*	11	0	0	0	0	0	0	0	3,573	19	1	3,529	171,550
1995	Rich Bickle	8	0	0	0	0	0	0	0	1,995	2	1	2,400	148,250
"	Shane Hall	1	0	0	0	0	0	0	0	205	0	0	208	13,975
"	Andy Hillenburg	1	0	0	0	0	0	0	0	157	0	0	393	17,230
"	Randy LaJoie	1	0	0	0	0	0	0	0	96	0	0	255	16,175
"	Butch Leitzinger	1	0	0	0	0	0	0	0	90	0	0	221	17,060
"	Greg Sacks	10	0	0	0	0	0	0	0	2,795	0	0	3,137	179,730
"	**Total**	22	0	0	0	0	0	0	0	5,338	2	1	6,614	392,420
Lifetime		131	0	0	2	7	4	6	17	28,431	219	11	32,788	$687,495

*Became co-owner with Felix Sabates on Aug. 13, 1994.

Earl Brooks

Year	Driver	Starts	Poles	1	2	3	4	5	6–10	Laps	Laps Led	Races Led	Miles	$
1962	Earl Brooks	5	0	0	0	0	0	0	3	831	0	0	394	595
1968	Earl Brooks	19	0	0	0	0	0	0	3	2,513	0	0	1,207	3,220
"	Clyde Lynn	1	0	0	0	0	0	0	0	235	0	0	353	1,425
"	**Total**	20	0	0	0	0	0	0	3	2,748	0	0	1,560	4,645
1969	Earl Brooks	42	0	0	0	0	0	1	5	7,300	0	0	5,760	30,533
1970	Earl Brooks	20	0	0	0	0	0	0	1	1,750	0	0	1,851	9,545
"	Dave Marcis	6	0	0	0	0	0	0	1	1,531	0	0	781	2,190
"	Wendell Scott	2	0	0	0	0	0	0	0	233	0	0	205	860
"	**Total**	27	0	0	0	0	0	0	2	3,514	0	0	2,838	12,595
1971	Earl Brooks	29	0	0	0	0	1	0	2	5,328	0	0	5,100	20,540
"	Bill Hollar	11	0	0	0	0	0	0	1	2,095	0	0	1,602	4,275
"	Ed Negre	1	0	0	0	0	0	0	0	243	0	0	152	460
"	**Total**	32	0	0	0	0	1	0	3	7,666	0	0	6,854	25,275
1972	Earl Brooks	6	0	0	0	0	0	0	0	609	0	0	593	3,215
1973	Earl Brooks	9	0	0	0	0	0	0	0	2,267	0	0	1,396	4,880
"	Dick May	1	0	0	0	0	0	0	0	61	0	0	36	250
"	**Total**	9	0	0	0	0	0	0	0	2,328	0	0	1,433	5,130
Lifetime		141	0	0	0	0	1	1	16	24,996	0	0	19,431	$81,988

Elmer Brooks

Year	Driver	Starts	Poles	1	2	3	4	5	6–10	Laps	Laps Led	Races Led	Miles	$
1954	Bill Blair	2	0	0	0	0	0	0	0	334	0	0	167	25
"	Tim Flock	1	0	0	0	0	0	0	1	243	0	0	243	250
"	Charlie Micney	1	0	0	0	0	0	0	1	184	0	0	92	100
"	Slick Smith	1	0	0	0	0	0	0	0	38	0	0	19	25
"	Gober Sosebee	1	0	0	0	0	0	0	1	153	0	0	230	300
"	Curtis Turner	4	1	1	1	0	0	0	0	886	277	3	842	7,320
"	**Total**	10	1	1	1	0	0	0	3	1,838	277	3	1,592	8,020
Lifetime		10	1	1	1	0	0	0	3	1,838	277	3	1,592	$8,020

Gary Brooks

Year	Driver	Starts	Poles	1	2	3	4	5	6–10	Laps	Laps Led	Races Led	Miles	$
1991	Gary Brooks	1	0	0	0	0	0	0	0	11	0	0	11	3,425
Lifetime		1	0	0	0	0	0	0	0	11	0	0	11	$3,425

Allan Brown

Year	Driver	Starts	Poles	1	2	3	4	5	6–10	Laps	Laps Led	Races Led	Miles	$
1971	Robert Brown	5	0	0	0	0	0	0	0	462	0	0	335	1,335

Year	Driver	Starts	Poles	Finish 1	2	3	4	5	6–10	Laps	Laps Led	Races Led	Miles	$

Allan Brown *continued*

Year	Driver	Starts	Poles	1	2	3	4	5	6–10	Laps	Laps Led	Races Led	Miles	$
1972	Robert Brown	2	0	0	0	0	0	0	0	324	0	0	175	710
1973	Robert Brown	2	0	0	0	0	0	0	0	353	0	0	210	590
Lifetime		9	0	0	0	0	0	0	0	1,139	0	0	721	$2,635

Cannonball Brown

Year	Driver	Starts	Poles	1	2	3	4	5	6–10	Laps	Laps Led	Races Led	Miles	$
1958	Cannonball Brown	2	0	0	0	0	0	0	0	104	0	0	99	50
Lifetime		2	0	0	0	0	0	0	0	104	0	0	99	$50

Ed Brown

Year	Driver	Starts	Poles	1	2	3	4	5	6–10	Laps	Laps Led	Races Led	Miles	$
1955	Ed Brown	2	0	0	0	0	0	0	0	299	0	0	299	150
1956	Ed Brown	1	0	0	0	0	0	0	0	72	0	0	180	55
1957	Ed Brown	1	0	0	0	0	0	0	0	52	0	0	130	115
1961	Ed Brown	1	0	0	0	0	0	0	0	74	0	0	74	50
Lifetime		5	0	0	0	0	0	0	0	497	0	0	683	$370

James Brown

Year	Driver	Starts	Poles	1	2	3	4	5	6–10	Laps	Laps Led	Races Led	Miles	$
1968	Don Biederman	1	0	0	0	0	0	0	0	123	0	0	308	1,110
"	Bob Moore	1	0	0	0	0	0	0	1	227	0	0	114	200
"	**Total**	2	0	0	0	0	0	0	1	350	0	0	421	1,310
Lifetime		2	0	0	0	0	0	0	1	350	0	0	421	$1,310

Jerry Brown

Year	Driver	Starts	Poles	1	2	3	4	5	6–10	Laps	Laps Led	Races Led	Miles	$
1973	Richard Brown	12	0	0	0	0	0	0	0	911	0	0	582	6,915
"	Ed Negre	1	0	0	0	0	0	0	0	183	0	0	275	1,338
"	**Total**	13	0	0	0	0	0	0	0	1,094	0	0	857	8,253
1974	Richard Brown	1	0	0	0	0	0	0	0	51	0	0	51	595
1975	Richard Brown	4	0	0	0	0	0	0	0	365	0	0	218	1,660
1976	Richard Brown	3	0	0	0	0	0	0	0	591	0	0	340	1,310
Lifetime		21	0	0	0	0	0	0	0	2,101	0	0	1,465	$11,818

Len Brown

Year	Driver	Starts	Poles	1	2	3	4	5	6–10	Laps	Laps Led	Races Led	Miles	$
1949	Len Brown	1	0	0	0	0	0	0	0	158	0	0	158	25
Lifetime		1	0	0	0	0	0	0	0	158	0	0	158	$25

Richard Brown

Year	Driver	Starts	Poles	1	2	3	4	5	6–10	Laps	Laps Led	Races Led	Miles	$
1970	Butch Hirst	1	0	0	0	0	0	0	0	224	0	0	336	1,499
"	Roy Mayne	1	0	0	0	0	0	0	0	420	0	0	427	795
"	Bugs Stevens	3	0	0	0	0	0	0	1	458	0	0	682	6,145
"	Don Tarr	1	0	0	0	0	0	0	1	157	0	0	393	2,050
"	**Total**	6	0	0	0	0	0	0	2	1,259	0	0	1,838	10,489
Lifetime		6	0	0	0	0	0	0	2	1,259	0	0	1,838	$10,489

Robert Brown

Year	Driver	Starts	Poles	1	2	3	4	5	6–10	Laps	Laps Led	Races Led	Miles	$
1970	Buck Baker	1	0	0	0	0	0	0	0	267	0	0	267	610
Lifetime		1	0	0	0	0	0	0	0	267	0	0	267	$610

Frank Bruner

Year	Driver	Starts	Poles	1	2	3	4	5	6–10	Laps	Laps Led	Races Led	Miles	$
1956	Robert Slensby	1	0	0	0	0	0	0	0	117	0	0	59	100
Lifetime		1	0	0	0	0	0	0	0	117	0	0	59	$100

James Bryan

Year	Driver	Starts	Poles	1	2	3	4	5	6–10	Laps	Laps Led	Races Led	Miles	$
1960	Bobby Johns	7	0	0	0	0	0	0	2	915	0	0	566	1,765
Lifetime		7	0	0	0	0	0	0	2	915	0	0	566	$1,765

Darrell Bryant

Year	Driver	Starts	Poles	1	2	3	4	5	6–10	Laps	Laps Led	Races Led	Miles	$
1987	Kirk Bryant	1	0	0	0	0	0	0	0	205	0	0	208	1,415
Lifetime		1	0	0	0	0	0	0	0	205	0	0	208	$1,415

Year	Driver	Starts	Poles	Finish 1	2	3	4	5	6–10	Laps	Laps Led	Races Led	Miles	$

James Bryant

Year	Driver	Starts	Poles	1	2	3	4	5	6–10	Laps	Laps Led	Races Led	Miles	$
1973	L. D. Ottinger	3	0	0	1	0	0	0	1	813	0	0	955	7,452
Lifetime		3	0	0	1	0	0	0	1	813	0	0	955	$7,452

Herschel Buchanan

Year	Driver	Starts	Poles	1	2	3	4	5	6–10	Laps	Laps Led	Races Led	Miles	$
1950	Herschel Buchanan	2	0	0	0	0	0	0	1	3	0	0	13	200
1951	Herschel Buchanan	1	0	0	0	0	0	0	0		0	0		0
1952	Herschel Buchanan	4	0	0	0	1	0	2	1	1,116	0	0	975	1,850
1953	Herschel Buchanan	14	0	0	0	1	2	1	2	506	0	0	456	2,050
1954	Herschel Buchanan	1	0	0	0	0	0	1	0	160	0	0	240	500
Lifetime		22	0	0	0	2	2	4	4	1,785	0	0	1,683	$4,600

Roy Buckner

Year	Driver	Starts	Poles	1	2	3	4	5	6–10	Laps	Laps Led	Races Led	Miles	$
1968	Charles Burnett	2	0	0	0	0	0	0	0	215	0	0	469	1,765
"	Red Farmer	7	0	0	0	0	1	0	0	928	1	1	849	4,810
"	Bob Moore	3	0	0	0	0	0	0	0	806	0	0	943	2,545
"	Don Tomberlin	1	0	0	0	0	0	0	0	181	0	0	91	100
"	**Total**	10	0	0	0	0	1	0	0	2,130	1	1	2,352	9,220
1969	Don Tomberlin	2	0	0	0	0	0	0	0	215	0	0	233	1,025
Lifetime		12	0	0	0	0	1	0	0	2,345	1	1	2,584	$10,245

Jack Buemer

Year	Driver	Starts	Poles	1	2	3	4	5	6–10	Laps	Laps Led	Races Led	Miles	$
1954	Ed Normi	1	0	0	0	0	0	0	0	39	0	0	39	40
Lifetime		1	0	0	0	0	0	0	0	39	0	0	39	$40

Julian Buesink

Year	Driver	Starts	Poles	1	2	3	4	5	6–10	Laps	Laps Led	Races Led	Miles	$
1949	Lloyd Moore	1	0	0	0	0	0	0	1	186	0	0	93	150
"	Bill Rexford	3	0	0	0	1	0	1	0	370	0	0	274	625
"	**Total**	3	0	0	0	1	0	1	1	556	0	0	367	775
1950	George Hartley	8	0	0	0	0	0	0	2	371	0	0	464	850
"	Lloyd Moore	16	0	1	2	3	1	0	3	1,358	57	2	1,046	5,235
"	Jim Paschal	1	0	0	0	0	0	0	0	307	0	0	384	0
"	Bill Rexford	17	0	1	0	1	2	1	6	1,302	98	2	1,146	5,800
"	**Total**	17	0	2	2	4	3	1	11	**3,338**	155	4	**3,040**	11,885
1951	Julian Buesink	1	0	0	0	0	0	0	0	0	0	0	0	0
"	Don Eggert	5	0	0	0	0	0	0	2	0	0	0	0	250
"	Harold Kite	2	0	0	0	0	0	0	1	384	0	0	480	800
"	Jimmie Lewallen	1	0	0	0	0	0	0	1	0	0	0	0	150
"	Lloyd Moore	22	0	0	0	1	0	3	4	322	0	0	332	2,600
"	Jim Paschal	13	0	0	0	1	3	0	2	414	33	1	404	2,275
"	Bill Rexford	5	1	0	0	0	0	0	1	115	0	0	58	325
"	Dean Sprague	1	0	0	0	0	0	0	0	46	0	0	35	25
"	Walt Sprague	5	0	0	0	0	0	0	2	0	0	0	0	360
"	Ted Swaim	1	0	0	0	0	0	0	0	0	0	0	0	25
"	**Total**	31	1	0	0	2	3	3	13	1,281	33	1	1,308	6,810
1952	Lloyd Moore	8	0	0	1	0	1	0	2	1,457	0	0	1,084	2,193
"	Jim Paschal	6	0	0	0	0	0	0	4	582	0	0	338	515
"	Bill Rexford	1	0	0	0	0	0	0	0	131	0	0	66	25
"	**Total**	15	0	0	1	0	1	0	6	2,170	0	0	1,487	2,733
1953	Bill Rexford	2	0	0	0	0	0	1	1	173	0	0	173	350
1955	Lloyd Moore	2	0	0	0	0	0	0	0	439	0	0	567	235
"	Tommy Thompson	1	0	0	0	0	0	0	0	41	0	0	56	50
"	**Total**	2	0	0	0	0	0	0	0	480	0	0	624	285
1956	Bob Duell	6	0	0	0	0	0	1	0	642	0	0	443	670
1957	Bob Duell	5	0	0	0	0	0	0	0	503	0	0	476	260
1958	Bob Duell	7	1	0	1	1	0	1	3	1,273	0	0	969	2,415
1959	Buddy Baker	1	0	0	0	0	0	0	0	64	0	0	88	150
"	Bob Duell	4	0	0	0	0	0	0	0	672	0	0	578	650
"	**Total**	4	0	0	0	0	0	0	0	736	0	0	666	800
1960	Bob Duell	6	0	0	0	0	0	0	1	422	0	0	531	935
1961	Tom Dill	3	0	0	0	0	0	0	0	273	0	0	631	630
"	Cale Yarborough	1	0	0	0	0	0	0	0	135	0	0	186	200
"	**Total**	4	0	0	0	0	0	0	0	408	0	0	816	830
1962	Cale Yarborough	4	0	0	0	0	0	0	1	336	0	0	520	1,340
1963	Cale Yarborough	2	0	0	0	0	0	0	0	248	0	0	383	675
Lifetime		108	2	2	4	8	7	8	37	12,566	188	5	11,803	$30,763

Year	Driver	Starts	Poles	Finish 1	2	3	4	5	6–10	Laps	Laps Led	Races Led	Miles	$

A. L. Bumgarner

Year	Driver	Starts	Poles	1	2	3	4	5	6–10	Laps	Laps Led	Races Led	Miles	$
1956	Fonty Flock	1	0	0	0	0	0	0	1	97	0	0	97	200
"	Junior Johnson	8	1	0	0	0	0	0	0	381	17	1	233	200
"	Tiny Lund	2	0	0	0	0	0	0	0	631	0	0	316	150
"	Jack Smith	1	0	0	0	0	0	0	1	127	0	0	95	100
"	**Total**	12	1	0	0	0	0	0	2	1,236	17	1	741	650
1957	Junior Johnson	1	0	0	0	0	0	0	0	102	0	0	64	50
"	Tiny Lund	20	3	0	0	2	0	0	7	3,129	209	2	1,938	4,049
"	**Total**	21	3	0	0	2	0	0	7	3,231	209	2	2,002	4,099
1958	Jerry Draper	1	0	0	0	0	0	0	0	10	0	0	5	50
"	Tiny Lund	1	0	0	0	0	0	0	0	27	0	0	27	0
"	Jimmy Massey	7	1	0	0	0	0	0	1	1,006	0	0	607	870
"	Banjo Matthews	1	0	0	0	0	0	0	0	54	0	0	14	115
"	Jimmy Thompson	3	0	0	0	0	0	0	0	85	0	0	172	200
"	**Total**	13	1	0	0	0	0	0	1	1,182	0	0	825	1,235
Lifetime		46	5	0	0	2	0	0	10	5,649	226	3	3,568	$5,984

Bob Bunselmeyer

Year	Driver	Starts	Poles	1	2	3	4	5	6–10	Laps	Laps Led	Races Led	Miles	$
1956	Walt Schubert	4	0	0	0	0	0	0	1	413	0	0	324	375
Lifetime		4	0	0	0	0	0	0	1	413	0	0	324	$375

Clarence Burbank

Year	Driver	Starts	Poles	1	2	3	4	5	6–10	Laps	Laps Led	Races Led	Miles	$
1951	Tommy Melvin	1	0	0	0	0	0	0	0	367	0	0	459	50
Lifetime		1	0	0	0	0	0	0	0	367	0	0	459	$50

Bob Burcham

Year	Driver	Starts	Poles	1	2	3	4	5	6–10	Laps	Laps Led	Races Led	Miles	$
1969	Bob Burcham	1	0	0	0	0	0	0	0	2	0	0	5	900
Lifetime		1	0	0	0	0	0	0	0	2	0	0	5	$900

Paul Burchard

Year	Driver	Starts	Poles	1	2	3	4	5	6–10	Laps	Laps Led	Races Led	Miles	$
1972	Carl Adams	2	0	0	0	0	0	0	1	320	0	0	818	3,170
Lifetime		2	0	0	0	0	0	0	1	320	0	0	818	$3,170

Roy Burdick

Year	Driver	Starts	Poles	1	2	3	4	5	6–10	Laps	Laps Led	Races Led	Miles	$
1959	Johnny Beauchamp	4	0	1	1	0	0	0	0	430	130	2	741	8,625
"	Bob Burdick	6	2	0	1	0	0	0	3	912	25	1	1,000	10,050
"	**Total**	10	2	1	2	0	0	0	3	1,342	155	3	1,741	18,675
1960	Bob Burdick	2	0	0	0	0	0	0	1	71	0	0	178	850
"	Bud Burdick	2	0	0	0	0	0	0	1	236	0	0	590	750
"	Jerry Roedell	1	0	0	0	0	0	0	0	168	0	0	252	200
"	Herb Shannon	1	0	0	0	0	0	0	0	184	0	0	276	350
"	Jimmy Thompson	1	0	0	0	0	0	0	0	303	0	0	455	300
"	**Total**	6	0	0	0	0	0	0	2	962	0	0	1,750	2,450
1961	Bob Burdick	5	0	1	0	0	1	0	1	1,086	44	2	1,798	18,750
1962	Bob Burdick	2	0	0	0	0	0	0	1	95	0	0	238	625
Lifetime		23	2	2	2	0	1	0	7	3,485	199	5	5,527	$40,500

Harold Burke

Year	Driver	Starts	Poles	1	2	3	4	5	6–10	Laps	Laps Led	Races Led	Miles	$
1986	Gary Fedewa	4	0	0	0	0	0	0	0	819	0	0	1,229	7,230
1987	Gary Fedewa	1	0	0	0	0	0	0	0	355	0	0	355	1,650
Lifetime		5	0	0	0	0	0	0	0	1,174	0	0	1,584	$8,880

Frank Burnett

Year	Driver	Starts	Poles	1	2	3	4	5	6–10	Laps	Laps Led	Races Led	Miles	$
1967	Frank Burnett	1	0	0	0	0	0	0	0	60	0	0	162	500
Lifetime		1	0	0	0	0	0	0	0	60	0	0	162	$500

Geoff Burney

Year	Driver	Starts	Poles	1	2	3	4	5	6–10	Laps	Laps Led	Races Led	Miles	$
1991	Scott Gaylord	1	0	0	0	0	0	0	0	61	0	0	154	3,625
1996	Scott Gaylord	1	0	0	0	0	0	0	0	67	0	0	169	10,095
Lifetime		2	0	0	0	0	0	0	0	128	0	0	323	$13,720

Year	Driver	Starts	Poles	Finish						Laps	Laps Led	Races Led	Miles	$
				1	2	3	4	5	6–10					

Elmer Buxton

Year	Driver	Starts	Poles	1	2	3	4	5	6–10	Laps	Laps Led	Races Led	Miles	$
1968	Dexter Gainey	2	0	0	0	0	0	0	0	142	0	0	92	650
"	Bobby Mausgrover	1	0	0	0	0	0	0	0	51	0	0	70	605
"	Tony Tantarelli	1	0	0	0	0	0	0	0	74	0	0	111	650
"	Jabe Thomas	1	0	0	0	0	0	0	0	53	0	0	80	580
"	Lennie Waldo	4	0	0	0	0	0	0	0	671	0	0	1,091	3,620
"	**Total**	9	0	0	0	0	0	0	0	991	0	0	1,443	6,105
Lifetime		9	0	0	0	0	0	0	0	991	0	0	1,443	$6,105

Terry Byers

Year	Driver	Starts	Poles	1	2	3	4	5	6–10	Laps	Laps Led	Races Led	Miles	$
1989	Terry Byers	3	0	0	0	0	0	0	0	773	0	0	1,554	15,400
1990	Terry Byers	2	0	0	0	0	0	0	0	41	0	0	63	7,525
1995	Terry Byers	0												2,700
Lifetime		5	0	0	0	0	0	0	0	814	0	0	1,616	$25,625

C & M Motorsports (Buster Masten and Bobby Elder, co-owners)

Year	Driver	Starts	Poles	1	2	3	4	5	6–10	Laps	Laps Led	Races Led	Miles	$
1986	Eddie Bierschwale	3	0	0	0	0	0	0	0	463	0	0	467	3,710
"	Trevor Boys	3	0	0	0	0	0	0	0	903	0	0	1,164	6,075
"	Doug Heveron	1	0	0	0	0	0	0	0	185	0	0	492	4,940
"	Morgan Shepherd	1	0	0	0	0	0	0	0	381	0	0	200	1,525
"	**Total**	8	0	0	0	0	0	0	0	1,932	0	0	2,323	16,250
Lifetime		8	0	0	0	0	0	0	0	1,932	0	0	2,323	$16,250

Scotty Cain

Year	Driver	Starts	Poles	1	2	3	4	5	6–10	Laps	Laps Led	Races Led	Miles	$
1956	Scotty Cain	2	0	0	0	0	0	0	2	224	0	0	340	535
1957	Scotty Cain	11	0	0	0	0	3	0	4	1,151	0	0	782	2,005
1958	Scotty Cain	1	0	0	0	0	0	0	1	176	0	0	463	275
1959	Scotty Cain	2	0	0	1	0	0	0	0	467	0	0	247	700
1960	Scotty Cain	4	0	0	1	1	0	0	0	351	19	1	324	1,225
"	Rex White	1	0	0	0	0	0	0	1	162	0	0	227	500
"	**Total**	4	0	0	1	1	0	0	1	513	19	1	550	1,725
1961	Scotty Cain	4	0	0	0	0	0	0	1	218	0	0	335	705
1963	Scotty Cain	2	0	0	0	0	0	0	0	229	0	0	618	575
Lifetime		26	0	0	2	1	3	0	9	2,978	19	1	3,335	$6,520

Jim Calder

Year	Driver	Starts	Poles	1	2	3	4	5	6–10	Laps	Laps Led	Races Led	Miles	$
1970	Frank James	2	0	0	0	0	0	0	0	257	0	0	673	1,915
1971	Frank James	3	0	0	0	0	0	0	1	409	0	0	1,050	3,890
"	Mike James	1	0	0	0	0	0	0	0	1	0	0	3	615
"	**Total**	3	0	0	0	0	0	0	1	410	0	0	1,053	4,505
1972	Frank James	2	0	0	0	0	0	0	1	259	0	0	679	2,195
Lifetime		7	0	0	0	0	0	0	2	926	0	0	2,405	$8,615

Cliff Caldwell

Year	Driver	Starts	Poles	1	2	3	4	5	6–10	Laps	Laps Led	Races Led	Miles	$
1951	Fred Bince	2	0	0	0	0	0	0	0	98	0	0	49	50
Lifetime		2	0	0	0	0	0	0	0	98	0	0	49	$50

Hal Callentine

Year	Driver	Starts	Poles	1	2	3	4	5	6–10	Laps	Laps Led	Races Led	Miles	$
1979	Hal Callentine	2	0	0	0	0	0	0	0	279	0	0	708	4,065
Lifetime		2	0	0	0	0	0	0	0	279	0	0	708	$4,065

John Callis

Year	Driver	Starts	Poles	1	2	3	4	5	6–10	Laps	Laps Led	Races Led	Miles	$
1980	John Callis	2	0	0	0	0	0	0	0	464	0	0	472	1,500
1982	John Callis	3	0	0	0	0	0	0	0	352	0	0	507	2,675
1983	John Callis	2	0	0	0	0	0	0	0	525	0	0	671	2,775
Lifetime		7	0	0	0	0	0	0	0	1,341	0	0	1,649	$6,950

Bill Caltrider

Year	Driver	Starts	Poles	1	2	3	4	5	6–10	Laps	Laps Led	Races Led	Miles	$
1951	Dave Anderson	1	0	0	0	0	0	0	0	335	0	0	419	50
"	Jack Goodwin	2	0	0	0	0	0	0	1	617	0	0	712	700
"	**Total**	2	0	0	0	0	0	0	1	952	0	0	1,130	750

Year	Driver	Starts	Poles	Finish						Laps	Laps Led	Races Led	Miles	$
				1	2	3	4	5	6–10	Laps	Led	Led	Miles	$

Bill Caltrider *continued*

Year	Driver	Starts	Poles	1	2	3	4	5	6–10	Laps	Laps Led	Races Led	Miles	$
1952	Ted Chamberlain	2	0	0	0	0	0	0	1	350	0	0	350	125
"	Iggy Katona	3	0	0	0	0	0	0	1	887	0	0	835	400
"	**Total**	5	0	0	0	0	0	0	2	1,237	0	0	1,185	525
Lifetime		7	0	0	0	0	0	0	3	2,189	0	0	2,316	$1,275

J. W. Campbell

Year	Driver	Starts	Poles	1	2	3	4	5	6–10	Laps	Laps Led	Races Led	Miles	$
1955	Russ Truelove	6	0	0	0	0	0	0	2	738	0	0	689	585
Lifetime		6	0	0	0	0	0	0	2	738	0	0	689	$585

S. T. Campbell

Year	Driver	Starts	Poles	1	2	3	4	5	6–10	Laps	Laps Led	Races Led	Miles	$
1957	Joe Lee Johnson	2	0	0	0	0	0	0	0	63	0	0	95	175
1958	Joe Lee Johnson	5	0	0	0	0	0	1	1	843	0	0	587	835
1959	Joe Lee Johnson	1	0	0	0	0	0	0	1	147	0	0	49	170
Lifetime		8	0	0	0	0	0	1	2	1,053	0	0	731	$1,180

W. E. Campbell

Year	Driver	Starts	Poles	1	2	3	4	5	6–10	Laps	Laps Led	Races Led	Miles	$
1955	Bud Palmer	1	0	0	0	0	0	0	0	36	0	0	148	35
1956	Bud Palmer	1	0	0	0	0	0	0	0		0	0		0
Lifetime		2	0	0	0	0	0	0	0	36	0	0	148	$35

Earle Canavan

Year	Driver	Starts	Poles	1	2	3	4	5	6–10	Laps	Laps Led	Races Led	Miles	$
1971	Earle Canavan	5	0	0	0	0	0	0	0	375	0	0	483	2,530
1972	Earle Canavan	7	0	0	0	0	0	0	0	777	0	0	1,027	5,858
1973	Earle Canavan	5	0	0	0	0	0	0	0	1,223	0	0	1,674	4,980
1974	Earle Canavan	6	0	0	0	0	0	0	0	1,477	0	0	2,106	6,915
1975	Earle Canavan	12	0	0	0	0	0	0	0	1,601	0	0	1,861	9,725
1976	Earle Canavan	7	0	0	0	0	0	0	0	1,687	0	0	1,609	6,035
1977	Earle Canavan	5	0	0	0	0	0	0	0	646	0	0	783	4,390
1978	Earle Canavan	9	0	0	0	0	0	0	0	2,111	0	0	2,451	8,865
1979	Earle Canavan	7	0	0	0	0	0	0	0	698	0	0	1,032	6,675
1982	Earle Canavan	2	0	0	0	0	0	0	0	76	0	0	108	2,380
1985	Earle Canavan	1	0	0	0	0	0	0	0	53	0	0	53	875
1986	Earle Canavan	1	0	0	0	0	0	0	0	165	0	0	168	1,475
Lifetime		67	0	0	0	0	0	0	0	10,889	0	0	13,356	$60,703

Bob Cancro

Year	Driver	Starts	Poles	1	2	3	4	5	6–10	Laps	Laps Led	Races Led	Miles	$
1954	Ted Rambo	5	0	0	0	0	0	0	1	296	0	0	260	200
Lifetime		5	0	0	0	0	0	0	1	296	0	0	260	$200

Ted Cannady

Year	Driver	Starts	Poles	1	2	3	4	5	6–10	Laps	Laps Led	Races Led	Miles	$
1955	Ted Cannady	8	0	0	0	0	0	0	0	634	0	0	616	400
1956	Ted Cannady	6	0	0	0	0	0	0	0	814	0	0	484	260
Lifetime		14	0	0	0	0	0	0	0	1,448	0	0	1,100	$660

Ron Caragias

Year	Driver	Starts	Poles	1	2	3	4	5	6–10	Laps	Laps Led	Races Led	Miles	$
1987	Doug French	1	0	0	0	0	0	0	0	75	0	0	41	895
Lifetime		1	0	0	0	0	0	0	0	75	0	0	41	$895

Jack Carney

Year	Driver	Starts	Poles	1	2	3	4	5	6–10	Laps	Laps Led	Races Led	Miles	$
1993	Mike Wallace	1	0	0	0	0	0	0	0	326	0	0	496	10,600
Lifetime		1	0	0	0	0	0	0	0	326	0	0	496	$10,600

Bob Carpenter

Year	Driver	Starts	Poles	1	2	3	4	5	6–10	Laps	Laps Led	Races Led	Miles	$
1951	Bob Carpenter	1	0	0	0	0	0	0	0	0	0	0	0	25
"	Fred Steinbroner	6	0	0	0	0	1	1	1	198	0	0	99	675
"	**Total**	6	0	0	0	0	1	1	1	198	0	0	99	700
Lifetime		6	0	0	0	0	1	1	1	198	0	0	99	$700

Year	Driver	Starts	Poles	Finish 1	2	3	4	5	6–10	Laps	Laps Led	Races Led	Miles	$

Ken Carpenter

Year	Driver	Starts	Poles	1	2	3	4	5	6–10	Laps	Laps Led	Races Led	Miles	$
1966	Max Ledbetter	8	0	0	0	0	0	0	1	1,612	0	0	812	1,000
"	L. D. Ottinger	1	0	0	0	0	0	0	0	32	0	0	16	0
"	J. T. Putney	1	0	0	0	0	0	0	0	419	0	0	210	300
"	**Total**	10	0	0	0	0	0	0	1	2,063	0	0	1,037	1,300
1967	Max Ledbetter	8	0	0	0	0	0	0	3	1,634	0	0	751	1,525
"	Harold Stockton	6	0	0	0	0	0	0	0	626	0	0	287	705
"	**Total**	14	0	0	0	0	0	0	3	2,260	0	0	1,039	2,230
Lifetime		24	0	0	0	0	0	0	4	4,323	0	0	2,076	$3,530

Leslie Carr

Year	Driver	Starts	Poles	1	2	3	4	5	6–10	Laps	Laps Led	Races Led	Miles	$
1956	Buzz Auckland	1	0	0	0	0	0	0	0	43	0	0	43	0
Lifetime		1	0	0	0	0	0	0	0	43	0	0	43	$0

Dick Carter

Year	Driver	Starts	Poles	1	2	3	4	5	6–10	Laps	Laps Led	Races Led	Miles	$
1954	Dick Carter	3	0	0	0	0	0	0	0	376	0	0	265	65
Lifetime		3	0	0	0	0	0	0	0	376	0	0	265	$65

Travis Carter

Year	Driver	Starts	Poles	1	2	3	4	5	6–10	Laps	Laps Led	Races Led	Miles	$
1989	Rick Mast	13	0	0	0	0	0	0	1	4,160	14	2	4,439	128,102
1990	Rick Mast	6	0	0	0	0	0	0	1	1,400	0	0	1,667	26,625
"	Butch Miller	23	0	0	0	0	0	0	1	6,891	4	4	8,648	151,941
"	**Total**	29	0	0	0	0	0	0	2	8,291	4	4	10,316	178,566
1991	Jimmy Spencer	29	0	0	0	1	0	0	5	7,627	330	6	8,581	283,620
1992	Jimmy Spencer	7	0	0	0	0	0	0	0	1,853	1	1	2,107	76,055
1994	Hut Stricklin	29	0	0	0	0	0	0	1	8,562	26	2	10,585	333,495
1995	Jimmy Spencer	29	0	0	0	0	0	0	4	8,682	4	2	10,484	506,860
1996	Jimmy Spencer	31	0	0	0	0	1	1	7	9,339	156	7	11,238	1,090,876
Lifetime		167	0	0	0	1	1	1	20	48,514	535	24	57,749	$2,597,574

Neil Castles

Year	Driver	Starts	Poles	1	2	3	4	5	6–10	Laps	Laps Led	Races Led	Miles	$
1957	Neil Castles	4	0	0	0	0	0	0	0	441	0	0	333	375
1958	Neil Castles	11	0	0	0	0	0	0	0	1,568	0	0	874	570
1959	Erwin Carpenter	1	0	0	0	0	0	0	0	299	0	0	150	75
"	Neil Castles	2	0	0	0	0	0	0	0	299	0	0	150	110
"	**Total**	3	0	0	0	0	0	0	0	598	0	0	299	185
1960	Neil Castles	18	0	0	0	0	0	0	5	2,293	0	0	1,162	2,125
1962	Neil Castles	6	0	0	0	0	0	0	0	313	0	0	123	395
1967	Fats Caruso	1	0	0	0	0	0	0	0	96	0	0	32	100
"	Neil Castles	25	0	0	0	0	1	1	10	5,364	0	0	4,107	15,033
"	Jim Conway	1	0	0	0	0	0	0	0	215	0	0	108	100
"	Elmer Gilliam	3	0	0	0	0	0	0	0	9	0	0	6	325
"	Walter Wallace	1	0	0	0	0	0	0	0	11	0	0	6	100
"	**Total**	26	0	0	0	0	1	1	10	5,695	0	0	4,258	15,658
1968	Buck Baker	1	0	0	0	0	0	0	0	30	0	0	15	125
"	Neil Castles	42	0	0	0	1	1	1	11	8,926	0	0	5,312	18,377
"	Ray Hill	1	0	0	0	0	0	0	0	1	0	0	1	100
"	Dub Simpson	1	0	0	0	0	0	0	0	0	0	0	0	500
"	**Total**	44	0	0	0	1	1	1	11	8,957	0	0	5,328	19,102
1969	Neil Castles	49	0	0	2	1	4	6	16	12,406	29	1	9,920	52,282
"	Bill Champion	1	0	0	0	0	0	0	0	3	0	0	2	250
"	Ed Negre	3	0	0	0	0	0	0	0	24	0	0	22	875
"	Dub Simpson	1	0	0	0	0	0	0	0	243	0	0	243	775
"	Les Snow	1	0	0	0	0	0	0	0	2	0	0	5	925
"	**Total**	50	0	0	2	1	4	6	16	12,678	29	1	10,192	55,107
1970	Bobby Allison	1	0	0	0	0	0	0	0	152	0	0	55	255
"	Buddy Baker	1	0	0	0	0	0	0	0	7	0	0	3	225
"	Neil Castles	46	0	0	1	4	3	4	12	9,952	31	2	8,938	48,896
"	Roy Tyner	1	0	0	0	0	0	0	0	26	0	0	53	645
"	**Total**	46	0	0	1	4	3	4	12	10,137	31	2	9,050	50,021
1971	Buddy Baker	1	0	0	1	0	0	0	0	200	34	1	300	2,980
"	Neil Castles	36	0	0	0	0	1	0	9	6,830	10	1	5,446	21,790
"	Bill Champion	1	0	0	0	0	0	0	0	141	0	0	353	740
"	Frog Fagan	1	0	0	0	0	0	0	0	1	0	0	0	100

Year	Driver	Starts	Poles	1	2	3	4	5	6–10	Laps	Laps Led	Races Led	Miles	$

Neil Castles *continued*

Year	Driver	Starts	Poles	1	2	3	4	5	6–10	Laps	Laps Led	Races Led	Miles	$
"	Ed Hessert	1	0	0	0	0	0	0	0	94	0	0	34	100
"	Bobby Mausgrover	11	0	0	0	0	0	0	0	1,379	0	0	1,465	6,140
"	**Total**	38	0	0	1	0	1	0	9	8,645	44	2	7,598	31,850
1972	Neil Castles	21	0	0	0	0	0	0	1	4,075	0	0	3,936	18,895
"	Ed Hessert	1	0	0	0	0	0	0	0	107	0	0	268	1,170
"	Dave Marcis	1	0	0	0	0	0	0	1	382	0	0	239	650
"	**Total**	23	0	0	0	0	0	0	2	4,564	0	0	4,442	20,805
1973	Neil Castles	8	0	0	0	0	0	0	0	869	0	0	803	7,074
1974	Neil Castles	13	0	0	0	0	0	0	0	1,401	0	0	1,282	11,699
1975	Neil Castles	5	0	0	0	0	0	0	0	224	0	0	300	4,510
"	Harry Gant	1	0	0	0	0	0	0	0	306	0	0	459	1,130
"	**Total**	6	0	0	0	0	0	0	0	530	0	0	759	5,640
1976	Neil Castles	1	0	0	0	0	0	0	0	22	0	0	22	505
Lifetime		297	0	0	4	6	10	12	65	58,711	104	5	46,524	$221,111

John Cave

Year	Driver	Starts	Poles	1	2	3	4	5	6–10	Laps	Laps Led	Races Led	Miles	$
1995	Pancho Carter	1	0	0	0	0	0	0	0	180	0	0	450	8,475
Lifetime		1	0	0	0	0	0	0	0	180	0	0	450	$8,475

Ted Chamberlain

Year	Driver	Starts	Poles	1	2	3	4	5	6–10	Laps	Laps Led	Races Led	Miles	$
1949	Ted Chamberlain	2	0	0	0	0	0	0	0	148	0	0	74	100
1950	Ted Chamberlain	5	0	0	0	0	0	0	2	541	0	0	539	225
1951	Ted Chamberlain	2	0	0	0	0	0	0	1		0	0		125
1952	Ted Chamberlain	16	0	0	0	0	0	0	5	2,703	0	0	1,831	1,177
1953	Ted Chamberlain	9	0	0	0	0	0	0	3	572	0	0	442	500
1954	Ted Chamberlain	10	0	0	0	0	0	0	1	1,596	0	0	1,423	475
"	Slick Smith	1	0	0	0	0	0	0	0	114	0	0	86	25
"	**Total**	11	0	0	0	0	0	0	1	1,710	0	0	1,509	500
1957	Ted Chamberlain	5	0	0	0	0	0	0	1	903	0	0	738	550
1958	Ted Chamberlain	9	0	0	0	0	0	0	1	809	0	0	403	680
1959	Ted Chamberlain	1	0	0	0	0	0	0	0	68	0	0	17	50
Lifetime		60	0	0	0	0	0	0	14	7,454	0	0	5,552	$3,907

Bill Champion

Year	Driver	Starts	Poles	1	2	3	4	5	6–10	Laps	Laps Led	Races Led	Miles	$
1951	Bill Champion	1	0	0	0	0	0	0	1		0	0		50
1956	Bill Champion	2	0	0	0	0	0	0	1	277	0	0	139	200
1957	Neil Castles	1	0	0	0	0	0	0	0	51	0	0	26	100
"	Bill Champion	5	0	0	0	0	0	0	0	859	0	0	419	535
"	**Total**	6	0	0	0	0	0	0	0	910	0	0	445	635
1965	Neil Castles	1	0	0	0	0	0	0	0	173	0	0	238	595
1966	Bill Champion	9	0	0	0	0	0	0	0	1,120	0	0	1,220	3,735
1967	Bill Champion	11	0	0	0	0	0	0	0	1,889	0	0	2,027	6,205
"	Dick Johnson	3	0	0	0	0	0	0	0	428	0	0	206	330
"	**Total**	14	0	0	0	0	0	0	0	2,317	0	0	2,233	6,535
1968	Earl Brooks	1	0	0	0	0	0	0	0	23	0	0	23	555
"	Bill Champion	18	0	0	0	0	0	0	2	3,505	0	0	3,547	10,170
"	Elmo Langley	1	0	0	0	0	0	0	1	239	0	0	96	175
"	**Total**	19	0	0	0	0	0	0	3	3,767	0	0	3,666	10,900
1969	Don Biederman	2	0	0	0	0	0	0	0	338	0	0	483	1,445
"	Bill Champion	48	0	0	0	0	0	1	9	10,579	0	0	9,253	33,406
"	John Kennedy	1	0	0	0	0	0	0	0	1	0	0	1	345
"	John Kenney	1	0	0	0	0	0	0	0	4	0	0	6	1,050
"	Elmo Langley	1	0	0	0	0	0	0	0	304	0	0	309	930
"	Phil Montague	1	0	0	0	0	0	0	0	8	0	0	12	230
"	Jabe Thomas	1	0	0	0	0	0	0	0	56	0	0	56	410
"	**Total**	48	0	0	0	0	0	1	9	11,290	0	0	10,119	37,816
1970	Bill Champion	38	0	0	0	0	0	0	6	7,493	0	0	6,864	30,943
1971	Bill Champion	43	0	0	0	0	0	3	11	10,336	0	0	9,259	41,779
1972	Dick Brooks	1	0	0	0	0	0	0	0	232	0	0	464	930
"	Bill Champion	29	0	0	0	0	0	0	4	7,044	0	0	8,121	42,242
"	**Total**	29	0	0	0	0	0	0	4	7,276	0	0	8,585	43,172
1973	Bill Champion	26	0	0	0	0	0	0	1	5,103	0	0	6,364	32,138
1974	Bill Champion	18	0	0	0	0	0	0	0	2,324	0	0	2,262	13,480

Year	Driver	Starts	Poles	Finish 1	2	3	4	5	6–10	Laps	Laps Led	Races Led	Miles	$

Bill Champion *continued*

Year	Driver	Starts	Poles	1	2	3	4	5	6–10	Laps	Laps Led	Races Led	Miles	$
"	Randy Hutchison	1	0	0	0	0	0	0	0	66	0	0	35	730
"	**Total**	19	0	0	0	0	0	0	0	2,390	0	0	2,297	14,210
1975	Walter Ballard	1	0	0	0	0	0	0	0	89	0	0	48	640
"	Bill Champion	10	0	0	0	0	0	0	0	2,504	0	0	2,557	9,475
"	Tommy Gale	4	0	0	0	0	0	0	0	502	0	0	897	4,345
"	Elmo Langley	1	0	0	0	0	0	0	1	393	0	0	234	835
"	Ed Negre	1	0	0	0	0	0	0	0	338	0	0	177	625
"	Ricky Rudd	4	0	0	0	0	0	0	1	1,025	0	0	886	4,345
"	**Total**	21	0	0	0	0	0	0	2	4,851	0	0	4,800	20,265
1976	Terry Bivins	1	0	0	0	0	0	0	0	192	0	0	384	2,875
"	Earl Brooks	1	0	0	0	0	0	0	0	250	0	0	250	1,065
"	Bill Champion	3	0	0	0	0	0	0	0	530	0	0	317	2,575
"	Bill Elliott	4	0	0	0	0	0	0	0	628	0	0	812	6,765
"	Tommy Ellis	1	0	0	0	0	0	0	0	429	0	0	429	1,335
"	Bruce Jacobi	1	0	0	0	0	0	0	0	59	0	0	81	1,670
"	Clyde Lynn	1	0	0	0	0	0	0	0	123	0	0	66	735
"	Johnny Ray	1	0	0	0	0	0	0	0	34	0	0	89	735
"	**Total**	13	0	0	0	0	0	0	0	2,245	0	0	2,427	17,755
1977	Dean Dalton	1	0	0	0	0	0	0	0	391	0	0	398	1,100
"	Dick May	1	0	0	0	0	0	0	0	169	0	0	231	1,400
"	Raymond Williams	1	0	0	0	0	0	0	0	0	0	0	0	490
"	**Total**	3	0	0	0	0	0	0	0	560	0	0	629	2,990
1978	Jimmy Means	1	0	0	0	0	0	0	0	151	0	0	402	1,685
1979	Billy Smith	1	0	0	0	0	0	0	0	179	0	0	245	1,575
Lifetime		294	0	0	0	0	0	4	38	60,438	0	0	59,929	$266,978

Ralph Chaney

Year	Driver	Starts	Poles	1	2	3	4	5	6–10	Laps	Laps Led	Races Led	Miles	$
1950	Jim Paschal	1	0	0	0	0	0	0	1	188	0	0	94	75
1951	John Barker	3	0	0	0	0	0	0	0	40	0	0	30	75
"	Tommy Moon	1	0	0	0	0	0	0	0		0	0		25
"	Doug Wimpy	1	0	0	0	0	0	0	0		0	0		25
"	**Total**	5	0	0	0	0	0	0	0	40	0	0	30	125
Lifetime		6	0	0	0	0	0	0	1	228	0	0	124	$200

Ed Chann

Year	Driver	Starts	Poles	1	2	3	4	5	6–10	Laps	Laps Led	Races Led	Miles	$
1957	Lyle Matlock	1	0	0	0	0	0	0	0	47	0	0	24	0
Lifetime		1	0	0	0	0	0	0	0	47	0	0	24	$0

Chapman Racing

Year	Driver	Starts	Poles	1	2	3	4	5	6–10	Laps	Laps Led	Races Led	Miles	$
1982	Bob Slawinski	1	0	0	0	0	0	0	0	56	0	0	149	1,745
Lifetime		1	0	0	0	0	0	0	0	56	0	0	149	$1,745

Bob Chapman

Year	Driver	Starts	Poles	1	2	3	4	5	6–10	Laps	Laps Led	Races Led	Miles	$
1960	Bill Lutz	2	0	0	0	0	0	0	0	88	0	0	220	250
Lifetime		2	0	0	0	0	0	0	0	88	0	0	220	$250

Charlie Chapman

Year	Driver	Starts	Poles	1	2	3	4	5	6–10	Laps	Laps Led	Races Led	Miles	$
1960	Charlie Chapman	1	0	0	0	0	0	0	0	152	0	0	213	400
"	Jim Cook	1	0	0	0	0	0	0	0	343	0	0	515	400
"	Eddie Gray	1	0	0	0	0	0	0	0	36	0	0	90	0
"	Clem Proctor	1	0	0	0	0	0	0	0	338	0	0	465	500
"	Bob Ross	1	0	0	0	0	0	0	0	1	0	0	1	50
"	**Total**	5	0	0	0	0	0	0	0	870	0	0	1,284	1,350
1961	Charlie Chapman	6	0	0	0	0	0	0	0	702	0	0	515	610
"	Elmo Henderson	1	0	0	0	0	0	0	0	184	0	0	460	200
"	**Total**	7	0	0	0	0	0	0	0	886	0	0	975	810
Lifetime		12	0	0	0	0	0	0	0	1,756	0	0	2,257	$2,160

Hank Chapman

Year	Driver	Starts	Poles	1	2	3	4	5	6–10	Laps	Laps Led	Races Led	Miles	$
1957	Hank Chapman	1	0	0	0	0	0	0	0		0	0		25
Lifetime		1	0	0	0	0	0	0	0		0	0		$25

Year	Driver	Starts	Poles	Finish 1	2	3	4	5	6–10	Laps	Laps Led	Races Led	Miles	$

Walt Chapman

Year	Driver	Starts	Poles	1	2	3	4	5	6–10	Laps	Laps Led	Races Led	Miles	$
1951	John McGinley	6	0	0	1	0	1	0	0	224	0	0	224	1,175
"	Dick Rathmann	14	0	0	3	1	0	0	2	231	0	0	131	3,075
"	**Total**	15	0	0	4	1	1	0	2	455	0	0	355	4,250
1952	Frank Mundy	1	0	0	0	0	0	0	0	225	0	0	225	50
"	Dick Rathmann	24	1	5	1	4	0	4	0	3,300	701	10	2,319	11,153
"	Jack Smith	1	0	0	0	0	0	0	1	98	0	0	98	150
"	**Total**	25	1	5	1	4	0	4	1	3,623	701	10	2,642	11,353
1953	Dick Rathmann	33	1	5	12	1	2	1	3	2,545	542	8	2,002	20,195
1954	Russ Hepler	6	0	0	0	0	1	0	0	691	0	0	510	525
"	John McGinley	1	0	0	0	0	0	0	0	36	0	0	50	75
"	**Total**	7	0	0	0	0	1	0	0	727	0	0	559	600
1955	Herb Thomas	1	0	0	0	0	0	0	0	22	0	0	90	0
Lifetime		81	2	10	17	6	4	5	6	7,372	1,243	18	5,649	$36,398

Jack Chatenay

Year	Driver	Starts	Poles	1	2	3	4	5	6–10	Laps	Laps Led	Races Led	Miles	$
1957	Marvin Porter	2	0	0	0	0	0	0	1	307	0	0	154	245
1959	Bob Keefe	1	0	0	0	0	0	1	0	459	0	0	184	500
"	Owen Loggins	1	0	0	0	0	0	0	0	57	0	0	57	100
"	**Total**	2	0	0	0	0	0	1	0	516	0	0	241	600
1960	Owen Loggins	1	0	0	0	0	0	0	0	126	0	0	176	100
"	Marshall Sargent	1	0	0	0	0	0	0	0	1	0	0	1	25
"	**Total**	2	0	0	0	0	0	0	0	127	0	0	177	125
1961	Dick Carter	1	0	0	0	0	0	0	0	119	0	0	167	100
Lifetime		7	0	0	0	0	0	1	1	1,069	0	0	738	$1,070

J. L. Cheatham

Year	Driver	Starts	Poles	1	2	3	4	5	6–10	Laps	Laps Led	Races Led	Miles	$
1961	Johnny Allen	2	0	0	0	0	0	0	0	265	0	0	229	400
"	Friday Hassler	3	0	0	0	0	0	0	1	549	0	0	821	1,625
"	Elmo Langley	2	0	0	0	0	0	0	0	349	0	0	524	660
"	Tiny Lund	1	0	0	0	0	0	0	0	234	0	0	351	550
"	Dave Mader	2	0	0	0	0	0	0	0	114	0	0	57	75
"	Bill Morgan	1	0	0	0	0	0	0	0	237	0	0	119	225
"	**Total**	9	0	0	0	0	0	0	1	1,748	0	0	2,099	3,535
Lifetime		9	0	0	0	0	0	0	1	1,748	0	0	2,099	$3,535

Tom Cherry

Year	Driver	Starts	Poles	1	2	3	4	5	6–10	Laps	Laps Led	Races Led	Miles	$
1953	Tom Cherry	1	0	0	0	0	0	0	1	38	0	0	156	180
Lifetime		1	0	0	0	0	0	0	1	38	0	0	156	$180

Marshall Chesrown

Year	Driver	Starts	Poles	1	2	3	4	5	6–10	Laps	Laps Led	Races Led	Miles	$
1992	Rick Carelli	2	0	0	0	0	0	0	0	58	0	0	145	9,005
1993	Rick Carelli	3	0	0	0	0	0	0	0	499	0	0	671	19,650
1994	Rick Carelli	4	0	0	0	0	0	0	0	958	0	0	1,165	31,975
Lifetime		9	0	0	0	0	0	0	0	1,515	0	0	1,980	$60,630

David Chester

Year	Driver	Starts	Poles	1	2	3	4	5	6–10	Laps	Laps Led	Races Led	Miles	$
1949	Billy Carden	1	0	0	0	0	0	0	0		0	0		50
Lifetime		1	0	0	0	0	0	0	0		0	0		$50

Leon Chester

Year	Driver	Starts	Poles	1	2	3	4	5	6–10	Laps	Laps Led	Races Led	Miles	$
1949	Gober Sosebee	3	1	0	1	0	0	0	1	170	34	1	170	1,225
Lifetime		3	1	0	1	0	0	0	1	170	34	1	170	$1,225

Ted Chester

Year	Driver	Starts	Poles	1	2	3	4	5	6–10	Laps	Laps Led	Races Led	Miles	$
1950	Gober Sosebee	1	0	0	0	0	0	0	0	21	0	0	88	25
1951	Bob Flock	16	1	1	2	0	1	0	4	1,028	133	5	927	3,555
"	Fonty Flock	1	0	1	0	0	0	0	0	200	118	1	125	1,000
"	Tim Flock	29	6	7	4	3	3	1	2	2,408	817	11	1,773	13,545
"	Frank Mundy	1	0	1	0	0	0	0	0	200	114	1	100	1,000
"	**Total**	31	7	10	6	3	4	1	6	**3,836**	1,182	16	**2,925**	19,100
1952	Bob Flock	2	0	1	0	0	0	0	0	538	1	1	523	1,060
"	Tim Flock	33	4	8	5	2	7	0	3	5,345	1,469	16	3,564	22,890

Year	Driver	Starts	Poles	Finish						Laps	Laps Led	Races Led	Miles	$
				1	2	3	4	5	6–10					

Ted Chester *continued*

"	Frank Mundy	3	0	0	0	0	0	0	2	125	0	0	144	200
"	Jack Smith	1	0	0	0	0	0	0	0	387	0	0	484	420
"	Roscoe Thompson	1	0	0	0	0	0	0	0	0	0	0	0	25
"	**Total**	33	4	9	5	2	7	0	5	**6,395**	1,470	**17**	**4,714**	24,595
1953	Tim Flock	26	3	1	1	2	3	4	7	1,990	289	8	1,774	8,282
1956	Jack Smith	7	0	0	0	0	0	0	4	1,582	49	1	1,353	1,100
1957	Jack Smith	1	0	0	0	0	0	0	0	97	0	0	49	50
Lifetime		99	14	20	12	7	14	5	22	13,921	2,990	42	10,902	$53,152

Lloyd Chick

1960	Dave Hirschfield	2	0	0	0	0	0	0	0	50	0	0	125	100
Lifetime		2	0	0	0	0	0	0	0	50	0	0	125	$100

Kennie Childers

1978	Harry Gant	4	0	0	0	0	0	0	1	872	45	1	1,227	12,175
1979	Neil Bonnett	1	0	0	0	0	0	0	0	352	0	0	481	2,300
"	Harry Gant	3	0	0	0	0	0	0	1	299	0	0	597	5,875
"	Jack Ingram	4	0	0	0	0	0	0	0	532	0	0	661	4,240
"	Butch Lindley	1	0	0	0	0	0	0	0	82	0	0	43	570
"	Lennie Pond	8	0	0	0	0	0	0	2	1,287	12	1	1,935	16,350
"	Buck Simmons	2	0	0	0	0	0	0	0	438	0	0	787	3,025
"	**Total**	19	0	0	0	0	0	0	3	2,990	12	1	4,504	32,360
1980	Donnie Allison	13	1	0	0	1	0	1	2	2,639	196	5	3,355	34,585
"	Lennie Pond	1	0	0	0	0	0	0	0	12	0	0	18	1,220
"	Buck Simmons	6	0	0	0	0	0	0	0	1,333	0	0	1,308	7,145
"	**Total**	20	1	0	0	1	0	1	2	3,984	196	5	4,680	42,950
1981	Donnie Allison	3	0	0	0	0	0	0	0	493	0	0	886	14,320
"	Buddy Baker	1	0	0	0	0	0	0	0	43	0	0	23	610
"	Harry Gant	3	0	0	0	0	1	1	0	1,124	204	1	646	10,780
"	David Pearson	1	1	0	0	0	0	0	0	57	41	1	57	2,675
"	Tim Richmond	8	0	0	0	0	0	0	2	1,888	0	0	2,488	15,430
"	**Total**	16	1	0	0	0	1	1	2	3,605	245	2	4,100	43,815
Lifetime		59	2	0	0	1	1	2	8	11,451	498	9	14,512	$131,300

Richard Childress

1969	Richard Childress	1	0	0	0	0	0	0	0	80	0	0	213	1,175
1976	Richard Childress	30	0	0	0	0	0	0	11	8,147	0	0	9,779	85,780
1977	Richard Childress	30	0	0	0	0	0	0	11	7,973	27	4	9,411	97,012
1978	Richard Childress	30	0	0	0	1	0	0	11	8,946	52	4	10,060	108,702
1979	Richard Childress	31	0	0	0	0	0	1	10	9,109	13	2	10,442	132,922
1980	Richard Childress	31	0	0	0	0	0	0	10	8,693	21	6	10,692	157,420
1981	Richard Childress	20	0	0	0	0	1	0	0	5,213	16	3	6,455	70,665
"	Dale Earnhardt	11	0	0	0	0	2	0	4	3,082	18	2	3,426	69,905
"	**Total**	31	0	0	0	0	3	0	4	8,295	34	5	9,881	140,570
1982	Ricky Rudd	30	2	0	2	0	3	1	7	7,753	140	8	8,680	217,140
1983	Ricky Rudd	30	4	2	1	1	1	2	7	8,581	871	13	9,907	275,400
1984	Dale Earnhardt	30	0	2	4	2	0	4	10	9,584	446	16	10,850	634,671
1985	Dale Earnhardt	28	1	4	0	0	4	2	6	8,231	1,237	17	9,149	546,596
1986	Dale Earnhardt	29	1	5	5	3	1	2	7	9,212	2,127	26	11,164	1,768,880
1987	Dale Earnhardt	29	1	11	5	1	2	2	3	9,043	**3,358**	**27**	10,898	2,069,243
1988	Rodney Combs	1	0	0	0	0	0	0	0	4	0	0	4	1,500
"	Dale Earnhardt	29	0	3	2	3	3	2	6	9,561	1,808	20	11,314	1,214,089
"	**Total**	29	0	3	2	3	3	2	6	9,565	**1,808**	20	11,318	1,215,589
1989	Dale Earnhardt	29	1	5	3	5	1	0	5	9,112	**2,735**	22	10,796	1,432,230
1990	Dale Earnhardt	29	4	9	3	3	1	2	5	9,162	**2,438**	22	10,955	3,308,056
1991	Dale Earnhardt	29	0	4	3	4	1	2	7	9,541	1,125	20	11,435	2,416,685
"	Dave Marcis	1	0	0	0	0	0	0	0	479	0	0	487	7,050
"	**Total**	29	0	4	3	4	1	2	7	10,020	1,125	20	11,922	2,423,735
1992	Dale Earnhardt	29	1	1	2	2	1	0	9	8,694	487	10	10,198	915,463
1993	Neil Bonnett	2	0	0	0	0	0	0	0	134	0	0	353	14,515
"	Dale Earnhardt	30	2	6	5	3	3	0	4	9,787	1,475	21	11,808	3,353,789
"	**Total**	30	2	6	5	3	3	0	4	9,921	1,475	**21**	12,161	3,368,304
1994	Dale Earnhardt	31	2	4	7	6	1	2	5	9,546	1,013	**23**	11,409	3,400,733
1995	Dale Earnhardt	31	3	5	6	5	1	2	4	9,625	1,583	24	11,714	3,154,241
1996	Dale Earnhardt	31	2	2	3	3	4	1	4	9,530	614	18	11,523	2,285,926

Year	Driver	Starts	Poles	Finish 1	2	3	4	5	6–10	Laps	Laps Led	Races Led	Miles	$

Richard Childress *continued*

Year	Driver	Starts	Poles	1	2	3	4	5	6–10	Laps	Laps Led	Races Led	Miles	$
"	Mike Skinner	5	0	0	0	0	0	0	0	1,459	10	1	1,742	65,850
"	**Total**	31	2	2	3	3	4	1	4	10,989	624	19	13,265	2,351,776
Lifetime		628	24	63	51	42	30	25	146	190,281	21,614	309	224,864	$27,805,638
		8th		**5th**						**6th**	**5th**	**5th**	**6th**	**3rd**

John Childs

Year	Driver	Starts	Poles	1	2	3	4	5	6–10	Laps	Laps Led	Races Led	Miles	$
1981	Rusty Wallace	2	0	0	0	0	0	0	1	487	0	0	734	8,650
1982	Rusty Wallace	3	0	0	0	0	0	0	0	418	0	0	669	7,655
1983	Rusty Wallace	0												$1,100
Lifetime		5	0	0	0	0	0	0	1	905	0	0	1,402	$17,405

Chet Chiorso

Year	Driver	Starts	Poles	1	2	3	4	5	6–10	Laps	Laps Led	Races Led	Miles	$
1954	Sam Hawks	2	0	0	0	0	0	0	0	447	0	0	325	65
"	Marvin Panch	1	0	0	0	0	0	0	1	186	0	0	93	100
"	Cliff Roberts	1	0	0	0	0	0	0	0	194	0	0	97	25
"	**Total**	4	0	0	0	0	0	0	1	827	0	0	515	190
Lifetime		4	0	0	0	0	0	0	1	827	0	0	515	$190

Keith Christensen

Year	Driver	Starts	Poles	1	2	3	4	5	6–10	Laps	Laps Led	Races Led	Miles	$
1971	Paul Tyler	1	0	0	0	0	0	0	0	11	0	0	5	300
Lifetime		1	0	0	0	0	0	0	0	11	0	0	5	$300

Frank Christian

Year	Driver	Starts	Poles	1	2	3	4	5	6–10	Laps	Laps Led	Races Led	Miles	$
1949	Frank Christian	1	0	0	0	0	0	0	1		0	0		175
"	Sara Christian	5	0	0	0	0	0	1	1	606	0	0	417	735
"	Bob Flock	4	0	2	1	0	0	0	0	690	22	3	545	4,870
"	Joe Littlejohn	1	0	0	0	0	1	0	0	40	0	0	166	300
"	Buckshot Morris	2	0	0	0	0	0	0	0		0	0		0
"	Curtis Turner	2	1	0	0	0	0	0	2	364	18	1	182	100
"	**Total**	7	1	2	1	0	1	1	4	**1,700**	40	**4**	1,310	6,180
1950	Sara Christian	1	0	0	0	0	0	0	0		0	0		50
"	Bob Flock	4	0	0	1	0	0	0	2	595	5	1	781	1,155
"	Fonty Flock	5	2	1	0	0	1	0	0	875	369	4	863	2,045
"	Tim Flock	1	0	0	0	0	0	0	0		0	0		0
"	**Total**	8	2	1	1	0	1	0	2	1,470	374	5	1,644	3,250
1951	Billy Carden	1	0	0	0	0	0	0	0		0	0		25
"	Fonty Flock	33	14	7	2	4	5	1	2	2,588	1,950	20	1,943	14,200
"	Slick Smith	1	0	0	0	0	0	0	0	379	0	0	474	240
"	**Total**	34	14	7	2	4	5	1	2	2,967	**1,950**	**20**	2,417	14,465
1952	Herschel Buchanan	1	0	0	0	0	1	0	0	186	0	0	93	350
"	Fonty Flock	28	7	2	6	2	2	2	2	3,743	984	10	2,685	18,987
"	Slick Smith	5	0	0	0	0	0	0	3	613	0	0	516	725
"	Gober Sosebee	1	0	0	0	0	0	0	0		39	1		25
"	Roscoe Thompson	2	0	0	0	0	0	0	0	83	11	1	77	80
"	**Total**	29	7	2	6	2	3	2	5	4,625	1,034	12	3,371	20,167
1953	Fonty Flock	33	3	4	5	4	3	1	0	1,999	581	10	1,626	17,756
"	Slick Smith	21	1	0	0	0	0	0	9	592	4	1	755	1,740
"	Curtis Turner	3	1	1	0	1	0	0	0	459	100	1	594	2,525
"	**Total**	35	5	5	5	5	3	1	9	3,050	685	11	2,974	22,021
1954	Bill Amick	4	0	0	0	0	0	0	0	510	9	1	555	250
"	Fonty Flock	3	0	0	1	0	0	0	0	545	15	1	273	700
"	Dick Garlington	1	0	0	0	0	0	0	0	11	0	0	11	0
"	Pop McGinnis	1	0	0	0	0	0	0	1	123	0	0	92	150
"	Hershel McGriff	21	4	4	3	5	0	1	4	3,688	122	6	2,453	13,145
"	Dick Rathmann	1	0	0	0	0	0	0	0	148	0	0	74	25
"	Slick Smith	3	0	0	0	0	1	0	1	321	0	0	358	750
"	Curtis Turner	5	0	0	0	1	1	2	1	594	0	0	556	2,050
"	**Total**	29	4	4	4	6	2	3	7	5,940	146	8	4,372	17,070
1955	Buck Baker	1	0	0	1	0	0	0	0	200	0	0	100	650
"	Fonty Flock	8	0	1	0	1	0	2	0	680	66	1	584	2,485
"	Banjo Matthews	2	0	0	0	0	0	0	2	386	0	0	193	500
"	Buddy Shuman	1	0	0	0	0	0	0	1	193	0	0	97	100
"	Slick Smith	3	0	0	0	0	0	0	2	424	0	0	434	525

Year	Driver	Starts	Poles	Finish 1	2	3	4	5	6–10	Laps	Laps Led	Races Led	Miles	$

Frank Christian *continued*

Year	Driver	Starts	Poles	1	2	3	4	5	6–10	Laps	Laps Led	Races Led	Miles	$
"	Speedy Thompson	2	0	0	0	0	0	0	0	134	0	0	67	125
"	**Total**	17	0	1	1	1	0	2	5	2,017	66	1	1,475	4,385
Lifetime		159	33	22	20	18	15	10	34	21,769	4,295	61	17,562	$87,538

R. B. Chumley

Year	Driver	Starts	Poles	1	2	3	4	5	6–10	Laps	Laps Led	Races Led	Miles	$
1971	Ronnie Chumley	2	0	0	0	0	0	0	0	291	0	0	378	990
Lifetime		2	0	0	0	0	0	0	0	291	0	0	378	$990

Bill Church

Year	Driver	Starts	Poles	1	2	3	4	5	6–10	Laps	Laps Led	Races Led	Miles	$
1962	E. J. Trivette	1	0	0	0	0	0	0	0	29	0	0	15	100
1966	E. J. Trivette	1	0	0	0	0	0	0	0	2	0	0	1	300
"	Wayne Woodward	1	0	0	0	0	0	0	0	258	0	0	387	640
"	**Total**	2	0	0	0	0	0	0	0	260	0	0	388	940
Lifetime		3	0	0	0	0	0	0	0	289	0	0	403	$1,040

William Church

Year	Driver	Starts	Poles	1	2	3	4	5	6–10	Laps	Laps Led	Races Led	Miles	$
1963	E. J. Trivette	4	0	0	0	0	0	0	2	846	0	0	418	555
"	Billy Wade	1	0	0	0	0	0	0	0	10	0	0	3	95
"	**Total**	5	0	0	0	0	0	0	2	856	0	0	420	650
Lifetime		5	0	0	0	0	0	0	2	856	0	0	420	$650

Jerry Churchill

Year	Driver	Starts	Poles	1	2	3	4	5	6–10	Laps	Laps Led	Races Led	Miles	$
1971	Jerry Churchill	6	0	0	0	0	0	0	0	664	0	0	299	1,815
1984	Jerry Churchill	1	0	0	0	0	0	0	0	118	0	0	118	3,120
Lifetime		7	0	0	0	0	0	0	0	782	0	0	417	$4,935

Cicci-Welliver Racing (Frank Cicci and Scott Welliver, co-owners)

Year	Driver	Starts	Poles	1	2	3	4	5	6–10	Laps	Laps Led	Races Led	Miles	$
1990	Tommy Riggins	4	0	0	0	0	0	0	0	469	0	0	952	12,140
1991	Jim Derhaag	1	0	0	0	0	0	0	0	88	0	0	214	5,120
1994	Mike McLaughlin	2	0	0	0	0	0	0	0	386	0	0	529	17,975
Lifetime		7	0	0	0	0	0	0	0	943	0	0	1,695	$35,235

Raul Cilloniz

Year	Driver	Starts	Poles	1	2	3	4	5	6–10	Laps	Laps Led	Races Led	Miles	$
1959	Raul Cilloniz	2	0	0	0	0	0	0	0	229	0	0	573	550
Lifetime		2	0	0	0	0	0	0	0	229	0	0	573	$550

Al Clark

Year	Driver	Starts	Poles	1	2	3	4	5	6–10	Laps	Laps Led	Races Led	Miles	$
1976	Gary Johnson	1	0	0	0	0	0	0	0	72	0	0	189	840
1977	Gary Johnson	2	0	0	0	0	0	0	0	126	0	0	330	2,445
Lifetime		3	0	0	0	0	0	0	0	198	0	0	519	$3,285

Bob Clark

Year	Driver	Starts	Poles	1	2	3	4	5	6–10	Laps	Laps Led	Races Led	Miles	$
1987	Brad Teague	2	0	0	0	0	0	0	0	648	17	1	979	8,135
1988	Donnie Allison	1	0	0	0	0	0	0	0	114	0	0	228	3,000
"	Lee Faulk	3	0	0	0	0	0	0	0	841	0	0	858	9,320
"	Butch Miller	2	0	0	0	0	0	0	0	790	18	1	497	5,905
"	Johnny Rutherford	1	0	0	0	0	0	0	0	155	0	0	155	3,775
"	Joe Ruttman	9	0	0	0	0	0	0	1	1,657	0	0	3,127	41,630
"	Jim Sauter	4	0	0	0	0	0	0	0	1,376	6	1	1,643	14,280
"	Brad Teague	8	0	0	0	0	0	0	0	1,959	0	0	2,230	29,155
"	**Total**	27	0	0	0	0	0	0	1	6,892	24	2	8,737	107,065
1989	Jim Sauter	8	0	0	0	0	0	0	1	2,076	0	0	2,400	31,480
Lifetime		37	0	0	0	0	0	0	2	9,616	41	3	12,117	$146,680

Fred Clark

Year	Driver	Starts	Poles	1	2	3	4	5	6–10	Laps	Laps Led	Races Led	Miles	$
1961	Friday Hassler	3	0	0	0	0	0	0	0	275	0	0	635	450
"	J. C. Hendrix	1	0	0	0	0	0	0	1	254	0	0	381	875
"	Elmo Langley	1	0	0	0	0	0	0	0	341	0	0	469	500
"	Tiny Lund	3	0	0	0	0	0	0	1	1,065	0	0	1,184	3,225
"	Bob Welborn	1	0	0	0	0	0	0	0	112	0	0	56	150

Year	Driver	Starts	Poles	Finish 1	2	3	4	5	6–10	Laps	Laps Led	Races Led	Miles	$

Fred Clark *continued*

Year	Driver	Starts	Poles	1	2	3	4	5	6–10	Laps	Laps Led	Races Led	Miles	$
"	Gene White	1	0	0	0	0	0	0	0	147	0	0	221	300
"	**Total**	10	0	0	0	0	0	0	2	2,194	0	0	2,944	5,500
1962	J. C. Hendrix	1	0	0	0	0	0	0	0	379	0	0	237	250
"	Tiny Lund	6	0	0	0	0	0	0	0	1,748	8	1	1,765	1,870
"	Johnny Sudderth	2	0	0	0	0	0	0	0	256	0	0	384	575
"	**Total**	9	0	0	0	0	0	0	0	2,383	8	1	2,386	2,695
1963	Bunkie Blackburn	1	0	0	0	0	0	0	0	194	0	0	291	450
"	Johnny Sudderth	1	0	0	0	0	0	0	0	16	0	0	24	250
"	**Total**	2	0	0	0	0	0	0	0	210	0	0	315	700
Lifetime		21	0	0	0	0	0	0	2	4,787	8	1	5,645	$8,895

Paul Clark

Year	Driver	Starts	Poles	1	2	3	4	5	6–10	Laps	Laps Led	Races Led	Miles	$
1963	Paul Clark	4	0	0	0	0	0	0	0	470	0	0	370	875
Lifetime		4	0	0	0	0	0	0	0	470	0	0	370	$875

Sherman Clark

Year	Driver	Starts	Poles	1	2	3	4	5	6–10	Laps	Laps Led	Races Led	Miles	$
1955	Sherman Clark	2	0	0	0	0	1	0	0	214	0	0	214	380
1956	Sherman Clark	5	0	0	0	0	0	0	2	405	0	0	428	425
1957	Sherman Clark	1	0	0	0	0	0	0	0	54	0	0	135	115
Lifetime		8	0	0	0	0	1	0	2	673	0	0	777	$920

Allan J. Clarke

Year	Driver	Starts	Poles	1	2	3	4	5	6–10	Laps	Laps Led	Races Led	Miles	$
1973	Earl Ross	3	0	0	0	0	0	0	0	335	0	0	797	4,005
1974	Earl Ross	6	0	0	1	0	0	1	0	1,429	6	1	2,428	22,865
Lifetime		9	0	0	1	0	0	1	0	1,764	6	1	3,225	$26,870

Harry Clary

Year	Driver	Starts	Poles	1	2	3	4	5	6–10	Laps	Laps Led	Races Led	Miles	$
1978	Bruce Hill	14	0	0	0	0	0	0	2	2,805	0	0	3,796	25,870
Lifetime		14	0	0	0	0	0	0	2	2,805	0	0	3,796	$25,870

Edgar Clay

Year	Driver	Starts	Poles	1	2	3	4	5	6–10	Laps	Laps Led	Races Led	Miles	$
1955	Bud Harless	4	0	0	0	0	0	0	1	324	0	0	294	210
Lifetime		4	0	0	0	0	0	0	1	324	0	0	294	$210

Paul Clayton

Year	Driver	Starts	Poles	1	2	3	4	5	6–10	Laps	Laps Led	Races Led	Miles	$
1963	Bunkie Blackburn	1	0	0	0	0	0	0	0	339	0	0	466	800
"	Floyd Powell	4	0	0	0	0	0	0	1	389	0	0	529	1,040
"	**Total**	5	0	0	0	0	0	0	1	728	0	0	995	1,840
1964	Ralph Earnhardt	1	0	0	0	0	0	0	0	5	0	0	8	675
"	Cotton Farmer	2	0	0	0	0	0	0	0	289	0	0	136	260
"	Elmo Henderson	7	0	0	0	0	0	1	2	655	0	0	344	1,650
"	G. C. Spencer	4	0	0	0	0	0	1	1	604	0	0	337	1,025
"	LeeRoy Yarbrough	1	0	0	0	0	0	0	0	69	0	0	43	150
"	**Total**	15	0	0	0	0	0	2	3	1,622	0	0	868	3,760
Lifetime		20	0	0	0	0	0	2	4	2,350	0	0	1,862	$5,600

June Cleveland

Year	Driver	Starts	Poles	1	2	3	4	5	6–10	Laps	Laps Led	Races Led	Miles	$
1953	June Cleveland	1	0	0	0	0	0	0	0		0	0		25
Lifetime		1	0	0	0	0	0	0	0		0	0		$25

Dub Clewis

Year	Driver	Starts	Poles	1	2	3	4	5	6–10	Laps	Laps Led	Races Led	Miles	$
1968	Richard Brickhouse	7	0	0	0	0	1	0	1	1,571	0	0	1,977	7,190
1969	Richard Brickhouse	16	0	0	0	0	0	1	4	2,388	0	0	2,875	13,822
"	Joe Hines Jr.	1	0	0	0	0	0	0	0	38	0	0	76	800
"	Bill Shirey	2	0	0	0	0	0	0	0	336	0	0	168	450
"	**Total**	19	0	0	0	0	0	1	4	2,762	0	0	3,119	15,072
Lifetime		26	0	0	0	0	1	1	5	4,333	0	0	5,096	$22,262

Ebart Clifton

Year	Driver	Starts	Poles	1	2	3	4	5	6–10	Laps	Laps Led	Races Led	Miles	$
1960	Jimmy Pardue	25	0	0	0	0	0	1	8	3,937	0	0	2,670	4,275
Lifetime		25	0	0	0	0	0	1	8	3,937	0	0	2,670	$4,275

Year	Driver	Starts	Poles	Finish 1	2	3	4	5	6–10	Laps	Laps Led	Races Led	Miles	$

Ernie Cline

Year	Driver	Starts	Poles	1	2	3	4	5	6–10	Laps	Laps Led	Races Led	Miles	$
1980	Ernie Cline	1	0	0	0	0	0	0	0	74	0	0	75	610
Lifetime		1	0	0	0	0	0	0	0	74	0	0	75	$610

Gene Cline

Year	Driver	Starts	Poles	1	2	3	4	5	6–10	Laps	Laps Led	Races Led	Miles	$
1965	Henley Gray	38	0	0	0	0	0	1	6	5,291	0	0	3,225	8,320
"	Jimmy Helms	2	0	0	0	0	0	0	0	435	0	0	435	885
"	E. J. Trivette	1	0	0	0	0	0	0	0	72	0	0	36	275
"	**Total**	41	0	0	0	0	0	1	6	5,798	0	0	3,695	9,480
1966	Gene Cline	13	0	0	0	0	0	0	2	2,125	0	0	1,451	3,945
"	Henley Gray	3	0	0	0	0	0	0	0	548	0	0	274	250
"	Jeff Hawkins	1	0	0	0	0	0	0	1	168	0	0	84	150
"	Jim Hunter	1	0	0	0	0	0	0	0	8	0	0	4	0
"	Bill Seifert	2	0	0	0	0	0	0	1	578	0	0	312	365
"	E. J. Trivette	1	0	0	0	0	0	0	0	183	0	0	275	620
"	**Total**	21	0	0	0	0	0	0	4	3,610	0	0	2,400	5,330
Lifetime		62	0	0	0	0	0	1	10	9,408	0	0	6,096	$14,810

Ken Cline

Year	Driver	Starts	Poles	1	2	3	4	5	6–10	Laps	Laps Led	Races Led	Miles	$
1968	David Mote	7	0	0	0	0	0	0	0	396	0	0	376	1,150
Lifetime		7	0	0	0	0	0	0	0	396	0	0	376	$1,150

Bill Clinton

Year	Driver	Starts	Poles	1	2	3	4	5	6–10	Laps	Laps Led	Races Led	Miles	$
1960	Dick Getty	2	0	0	0	0	0	0	0	198	0	0	254	385
1961	Bill Clinton	3	0	0	0	0	0	0	0	183	0	0	102	145
"	Eddie Pagan	4	0	0	0	0	0	1	3	492	0	0	523	985
"	**Total**	4	0	0	0	0	0	1	3	675	0	0	625	1,130
1963	Bill Clinton	2	0	0	0	0	0	0	0	247	0	0	667	725
1964	Bill Clinton	1	0	0	0	0	0	0	0	150	0	0	405	525
1965	Scotty Cain	1	0	0	0	0	0	0	1	172	0	0	464	1,175
1966	Scotty Cain	1	0	0	0	0	0	0	0	20	0	0	54	525
1967	Scotty Cain	1	0	0	0	0	0	0	1	171	0	0	462	1,400
"	Carl Carday	1	0	0	0	0	0	0	0	0	0	0	0	500
"	**Total**	1	0	0	0	0	0	0	1	171	0	0	462	1,900
1968	Scotty Cain	1	0	0	0	0	0	0	1	167	0	0	451	1,150
1969	Scotty Cain	1	0	0	0	0	0	0	1	170	0	0	459	1,450
1970	Scotty Cain	2	0	0	0	0	0	0	0	60	0	0	157	1,495
Lifetime		16	0	0	0	0	0	1	7	2,030	0	0	3,998	$10,460

Derick Close

Year	Driver	Starts	Poles	1	2	3	4	5	6–10	Laps	Laps Led	Races Led	Miles	$
1989	Jack Pennington	2	0	0	0	0	0	0	0	580	0	0	743	4,475
1990	Jack Pennington	14	0	0	0	0	0	0	0	3,450	7	2	5,902	93,660
1991	Rich Bickle	3	0	0	0	0	0	0	0	1,118	0	0	1,404	13,425
"	Greg Sacks	10	0	0	0	0	0	0	0	2,081	0	0	3,111	46,765
"	**Total**	13	0	0	0	0	0	0	0	3,199	0	0	4,515	60,190
1992	Buddy Baker	3	0	0	0	0	0	0	0	547	0	0	1,227	49,400
Lifetime		32	0	0	0	0	0	0	0	7,776	7	2	12,387	$207,725

Dick Clothier

Year	Driver	Starts	Poles	1	2	3	4	5	6–10	Laps	Laps Led	Races Led	Miles	$
1950	Dick Clothier	5	0	0	0	0	0	0	2	194	0	0	115	300
Lifetime		5	0	0	0	0	0	0	2	194	0	0	115	$300

Millard Clothier

Year	Driver	Starts	Poles	1	2	3	4	5	6–10	Laps	Laps Led	Races Led	Miles	$
1949	Jim Roper	1	0	0	0	0	0	0	0		0	0		50
Lifetime		1	0	0	0	0	0	0	0		0	0		$50

George Clugston

Year	Driver	Starts	Poles	1	2	3	4	5	6–10	Laps	Laps Led	Races Led	Miles	$
1954	George Seeger	1	0	0	0	0	0	0	0	183	0	0	92	0
Lifetime		1	0	0	0	0	0	0	0	183	0	0	92	$0

Tommy Coates

Year	Driver	Starts	Poles	1	2	3	4	5	6–10	Laps	Laps Led	Races Led	Miles	$
1950	Tommy Coates	1	0	0	0	0	0	0	0		0	0		50
Lifetime		1	0	0	0	0	0	0	0		0	0		$50

Year	Driver	Starts	Poles	Finish 1	2	3	4	5	6–10	Laps	Laps Led	Races Led	Miles	$

Talmadge Cochrane

Year	Driver	Starts	Poles	1	2	3	4	5	6–10	Laps	Laps Led	Races Led	Miles	$
1958	Benny Rakestraw	4	0	0	0	0	0	0	0	567	0	0	290	250
1959	Benny Rakestraw	7	0	0	0	0	1	0	0	1,144	0	0	774	1,165
"	Wilbur Rakestraw	1	0	0	0	0	0	0	0	87	0	0	218	300
"	**Total**	7	0	0	0	0	1	0	0	1,231	0	0	991	1,465
1960	Wilbur Rakestraw	12	0	0	0	0	0	0	1	1,862	0	0	2,038	2,695
Lifetime		23	0	0	0	0	1	0	1	3,660	0	0	3,318	$4,410

Ed Cole

Year	Driver	Starts	Poles	1	2	3	4	5	6–10	Laps	Laps Led	Races Led	Miles	$
1956	Ed Cole	1	0	0	0	0	0	0	0	145	0	0	91	50
Lifetime		1	0	0	0	0	0	0	0	145	0	0	91	$50

Neil Cole

Year	Driver	Starts	Poles	1	2	3	4	5	6–10	Laps	Laps Led	Races Led	Miles	$
1952	Neil Cole	5	0	0	0	0	0	0	2	591	0	0	361	375
Lifetime		5	0	0	0	0	0	0	2	591	0	0	361	$375

R. H. Coleman

Year	Driver	Starts	Poles	1	2	3	4	5	6–10	Laps	Laps Led	Races Led	Miles	$
1956	Joseph Hatcher	1	0	0	0	0	0	0	0	172	0	0	86	100
Lifetime		1	0	0	0	0	0	0	0	172	0	0	86	$100

Frank Coletto

Year	Driver	Starts	Poles	1	2	3	4	5	6–10	Laps	Laps Led	Races Led	Miles	$
1975	Bill Osborne	1	0	0	0	0	0	0	0	67	0	0	176	795
"	Pete Torres	2	0	0	0	0	0	0	0	162	0	0	424	2,035
"	**Total**	2	0	0	0	0	0	0	0	229	0	0	600	2,830
1976	Sam Beler	1	0	0	0	0	0	0	0	15	0	0	39	585
Lifetime		3	0	0	0	0	0	0	0	244	0	0	639	$3,415

Harold Collins

Year	Driver	Starts	Poles	1	2	3	4	5	6–10	Laps	Laps Led	Races Led	Miles	$
1967	Ken Spikes	7	0	0	0	0	0	0	0	316	0	0	394	2,920
"	Roy Tyner	2	0	0	0	0	0	0	0	185	0	0	272	1,235
"	**Total**	9	0	0	0	0	0	0	0	501	0	0	666	4,155
Lifetime		9	0	0	0	0	0	0	0	501	0	0	666	$4,155

Marion Collins

Year	Driver	Starts	Poles	1	2	3	4	5	6–10	Laps	Laps Led	Races Led	Miles	$
1990	Gary Collins	1	0	0	0	0	0	0	0	280	0	0	280	3,125
1991	Gary Collins	1	0	0	0	0	0	0	0	61	0	0	61	3,250
Lifetime		2	0	0	0	0	0	0	0	341	0	0	341	$6,375

Dan Colone

Year	Driver	Starts	Poles	1	2	3	4	5	6–10	Laps	Laps Led	Races Led	Miles	$
1965	Dick Dixon	8	0	0	0	2	1	2	2	2,029	0	0	733	2,215
Lifetime		8	0	0	0	2	1	2	2	2,029	0	0	733	$2,215

Bob Colvin

Year	Driver	Starts	Poles	1	2	3	4	5	6–10	Laps	Laps Led	Races Led	Miles	$
1954	Carl Burris	1	0	0	0	0	0	0	0	150	0	0	75	0
"	Dave Terrell	1	0	0	0	0	0	0	0	18	0	0	27	100
"	**Total**	2	0	0	0	0	0	0	0	168	0	0	102	100
Lifetime		2	0	0	0	0	0	0	0	168	0	0	102	$100

Leland Colvin

Year	Driver	Starts	Poles	1	2	3	4	5	6–10	Laps	Laps Led	Races Led	Miles	$
1950	Jimmy Thompson	4	0	0	0	0	0	0	3	522	0	0	510	450
1951	Weldon Adams	3	0	0	0	0	0	0	0	104	0	0	130	50
"	Leland Colvin	4	0	0	0	0	0	0	1		0	0		150
"	Jim Delaney	1	0	0	0	0	0	0	0		0	0		25
"	Jimmy Thompson	3	0	0	0	0	0	0	0	236	0	0	295	25
"	Speedy Thompson	2	0	0	0	0	0	0	0	39	0	0	29	75
"	**Total**	11	0	0	0	0	0	0	1	379	0	0	454	325
1953	Fireball Roberts	1	0	0	0	0	0	0	0	198	41	1	272	340
1954	Fireball Roberts	5	0	0	0	0	0	0	2	811	0	0	975	1,055
1955	Bill Champion	1	0	0	0	0	0	0	0	346	0	0	476	195
1956	Bill Brown	1	0	0	0	0	0	0	0	235	0	0	323	250
"	Doug Yates	1	0	0	0	0	0	0	0	54	0	0	74	50
"	**Total**	1	0	0	0	0	0	0	0	289	0	0	397	300

Year	Driver	Starts	Poles	Finish 1	2	3	4	5	6–10	Laps	Laps Led	Races Led	Miles	$

Leland Colvin *continued*

Year	Driver	Starts	Poles	1	2	3	4	5	6–10	Laps	Laps Led	Races Led	Miles	$
1958	J. V. Hamby	2	0	0	0	0	0	0	1	237	0	0	119	200
1963	Stan Parker	1	0	0	0	0	0	0	0	59	0	0	18	0
"	H. G. Rosier	1	0	0	0	0	0	0	0	66	0	0	91	500
"	Bill Widenhouse	4	0	0	0	0	0	0	0	461	0	0	432	675
"	**Total**	6	0	0	0	0	0	0	0	586	0	0	540	1,175
1964	Weldon Adams	1	0	0	0	0	0	0	0	2	0	0	6	525
"	Leland Colvin	1	0	0	0	0	0	0	0	118	0	0	59	100
"	Bill Widenhouse	1	0	0	0	0	0	0	0	153	0	0	77	90
"	**Total**	3	0	0	0	0	0	0	0	273	0	0	142	715
Lifetime		34	0	0	0	0	0	0	7	3,641	41	1	3,885	$4,755

R. L. Combs

Year	Driver	Starts	Poles	1	2	3	4	5	6–10	Laps	Laps Led	Races Led	Miles	$
1957	R. L. Combs	3	0	0	0	0	0	0	0	123	0	0	62	210
1958	R. L. Combs	9	0	0	0	0	0	0	1	1,062	0	0	473	785
1959	R. L. Combs	9	0	0	0	0	0	0	1	1,478	0	0	665	735
Lifetime		21	0	0	0	0	0	0	2	2,663	0	0	1,200	$1,730

Vincent Comella

Year	Driver	Starts	Poles	1	2	3	4	5	6–10	Laps	Laps Led	Races Led	Miles	$
1954	John Kieper	1	0	0	0	0	0	0	0	420	0	0	210	25
Lifetime		1	0	0	0	0	0	0	0	420	0	0	210	$25

Lucky Compton

Year	Driver	Starts	Poles	1	2	3	4	5	6–10	Laps	Laps Led	Races Led	Miles	$
1988	Ralph Jones	1	0	0	0	0	0	0	0	190	0	0	475	10,595
"	David Sosebee	2	0	0	0	0	0	0	0	289	0	0	499	4,960
"	**Total**	3	0	0	0	0	0	0	0	479	0	0	974	15,555
1989	Lee Raymond	1	0	0	0	0	0	0	0	189	0	0	473	13,530
"	Ronnie Thomas	1	0	0	0	0	0	0	0	196	0	0	392	3,925
"	**Total**	2	0	0	0	0	0	0	0	385	0	0	865	17,455
Lifetime		5	0	0	0	0	0	0	0	864	0	0	1,839	$33,010

Gene Comstock

Year	Driver	Starts	Poles	1	2	3	4	5	6–10	Laps	Laps Led	Races Led	Miles	$
1950	Gene Comstock	1	0	0	0	0	0	0	0	355	0	0	444	0
1951	Gene Comstock	3	0	0	0	0	0	0	0		0	0		75
1952	Gene Comstock	8	0	0	0	0	1	0	2	1,496	0	0	1,185	785
1953	Gene Comstock	13	0	0	0	0	0	0	3	756	0	0	895	990
"	Arden Mounts	10	0	0	0	0	0	0	1	792	0	0	759	395
"	**Total**	15	0	0	0	0	0	0	4	1,548	0	0	1,653	1,120
1954	Gene Comstock	1	0	0	0	0	0	0	0	334	0	0	459	400
"	Arden Mounts	11	0	0	0	0	0	0	1	1,552	0	0	1,287	850
"	Dick Rathmann	1	0	0	0	0	0	0	0	115	0	0	86	25
"	**Total**	12	0	0	0	0	0	0	1	2,001	0	0	1,832	1,275
1955	Bill Blair	1	0	0	0	0	0	0	0	43	0	0	22	25
"	Gene Comstock	2	0	0	0	0	0	0	0	239	0	0	380	250
"	Arden Mounts	3	0	0	0	0	0	0	2	411	0	0	328	385
"	**Total**	5	0	0	0	0	0	0	2	693	0	0	730	660
Lifetime		44	0	0	0	0	1	0	9	6,093	0	0	5,844	$4,180

Coz Concilla

Year	Driver	Starts	Poles	1	2	3	4	5	6–10	Laps	Laps Led	Races Led	Miles	$
1951	Ben Gregory	1	0	0	0	0	0	0	0		0	0		50
1955	Danny Letner	3	0	1	0	1	0	0	0	523	34	1	423	1,755
1956	Danny Letner	1	0	0	0	0	0	0	0	75	0	0	188	110
1963	Bob Perry	3	0	0	0	0	0	0	0	381	0	0	551	775
"	Bruce Worrell	1	0	0	0	0	0	0	0	1	0	0	3	200
"	**Total**	4	0	0	0	0	0	0	0	382	0	0	553	975
1964	Bruce Worrell	1	0	0	0	0	0	0	0	161	0	0	435	575
1965	Ed Brown	1	0	0	0	0	0	0	0	151	0	0	408	605
1967	Jim Cook	1	0	0	0	0	0	0	0	92	0	0	248	530
1968	Jim Cook	1	0	0	0	0	0	0	0	162	0	0	437	1,000
1969	Ray Johnstone	1	0	0	0	0	0	0	0	163	0	0	440	1,225
1970	Jerry Oliver	2	0	0	0	0	0	0	1	268	0	0	702	2,175
1971	Jerry Oliver	2	0	0	0	0	0	1	0	192	0	0	503	2,970
1972	Ray Johnstone	1	0	0	0	0	0	0	0	62	0	0	162	725
"	Jerry Oliver	1	0	0	0	0	0	0	0	122	0	0	320	1,100
"	**Total**	2	0	0	0	0	0	0	0	184	0	0	482	1,825
Lifetime		20	0	1	0	1	0	1	1	2,353	34	1	4,819	$13,795

Year	Driver	Starts	Poles	Finish 1	2	3	4	5	6–10	Laps	Laps Led	Races Led	Miles	$

Ernie Conn

Year	Driver	Starts	Poles	1	2	3	4	5	6–10	Laps	Laps Led	Races Led	Miles	$
1969	Jack McCoy	2	0	0	0	0	0	0	1	257	0	0	533	2,750
1970	Jack McCoy	2	0	0	0	0	0	0	1	207	0	0	542	2,740
1971	Jack McCoy	3	0	0	0	0	0	0	0	443	0	0	1,138	4,315
1972	Jack McCoy	3	0	0	0	0	0	0	0	228	0	0	575	4,070
1973	Jack McCoy	3	0	0	0	0	0	1	2	797	0	0	1,106	5,270
1974	Jack McCoy	3	0	0	0	0	0	0	0	175	4	1	453	3,390
1975	Ivan Baldwin	2	0	0	0	0	0	0	0	9	0	0	24	1,040
Lifetime		18	0	0	0	0	0	1	4	2,116	4	1	4,370	$23,575

Lee Connell

Year	Driver	Starts	Poles	1	2	3	4	5	6–10	Laps	Laps Led	Races Led	Miles	$
1951	Lee Connell	1	0	0	0	0	0	0	0	58	0	0	73	0
Lifetime		1	0	0	0	0	0	0	0	58	0	0	73	$0

James Cook

Year	Driver	Starts	Poles	1	2	3	4	5	6–10	Laps	Laps Led	Races Led	Miles	$
1968	Wayne Smith	1	0	0	0	0	0	0	0	106	0	0	42	100
Lifetime		1	0	0	0	0	0	0	0	106	0	0	42	$100

Bob Cooper

Year	Driver	Starts	Poles	1	2	3	4	5	6–10	Laps	Laps Led	Races Led	Miles	$
1962	Bob Cooper	11	0	0	0	0	0	0	1	1,439	0	0	780	1,120
1963	Bob Cooper	9	0	0	0	0	0	0	1	1,559	0	0	1,889	3,115
"	Doug Cooper	2	0	0	0	1	0	0	0	154	0	0	139	750
"	**Total**	11	0	0	0	1	0	0	1	1,713	0	0	2,027	3,865
1964	Bob Cooper	7	0	0	0	0	0	0	0	186	0	0	200	2,065
"	Doug Cooper	38	0	0	0	1	2	1	7	5,492	0	0	3,835	9,945
"	Jim Dimeo	3	0	0	0	0	0	0	1	368	0	0	136	385
"	Jimmy Helms	1	0	0	0	0	0	0	1	218	0	0	87	140
"	Pop McGinnis	1	0	0	0	0	0	0	0	238	0	0	104	200
"	**Total**	40	0	0	0	1	2	1	9	6,502	0	0	4,362	12,735
1965	Barry Brooks	4	0	0	0	0	0	0	0	131	0	0	76	1,450
"	Bob Cooper	4	0	0	0	0	0	0	1	697	0	0	252	600
"	Doug Cooper	28	0	0	0	0	1	0	8	4,959	0	0	3,575	11,670
"	Darel Dieringer	1	0	0	0	0	0	0	0	4	0	0	2	100
"	Roy Mayne	2	0	0	0	0	0	0	0	20	0	0	50	1,250
"	Sam McQuagg	1	0	0	0	0	0	0	0	249	0	0	374	545
"	Daniel Warlick	1	0	0	0	0	0	0	0	51	0	0	26	0
"	**Total**	34	0	0	0	0	1	0	9	6,111	0	0	4,354	15,615
1966	Bob Cooper	1	0	0	0	0	0	0	0	375	0	0	188	200
"	Doug Cooper	17	0	0	0	1	1	1	1	2,969	0	0	1,929	4,625
"	Paul Goldsmith	3	0	0	1	0	0	1	0	497	16	1	224	975
"	**Total**	21	0	0	1	1	1	2	1	3,841	16	1	2,341	5,800
1967	Bob Cooper	6	0	0	0	0	0	0	2	1,171	0	0	710	1,780
"	Doug Cooper	13	0	0	0	0	0	2	2	1,782	0	0	1,003	3,040
"	**Total**	19	0	0	0	0	0	2	4	2,953	0	0	1,713	4,820
1968	Bob Cooper	14	0	0	0	0	0	0	1	2,170	0	0	1,415	4,540
"	Walson Gardner	2	0	0	0	0	0	0	0	128	0	0	64	350
"	**Total**	16	0	0	0	0	0	0	1	2,298	0	0	1,480	4,890
1969	Bob Cooper	1	0	0	0	0	0	0	0	55	0	0	83	675
Lifetime		153	0	0	1	3	4	5	26	24,912	16	1	17,139	$49,520

Edward Cooper

Year	Driver	Starts	Poles	1	2	3	4	5	6–10	Laps	Laps Led	Races Led	Miles	$
1985	Edward Cooper	1	0	0	0	0	0	0	0	7	0	0	14	1,375
1990	Edward Cooper	2	0	0	0	0	0	0	0	94	0	0	188	8,225
Lifetime		3	0	0	0	0	0	0	0	101	0	0	202	$9,600

W. T. Coppedge

Year	Driver	Starts	Poles	1	2	3	4	5	6–10	Laps	Laps Led	Races Led	Miles	$
1960	Larry Frank	1	0	0	0	0	0	0	1	118	0	0	59	130
"	Tommy Irwin	1	0	0	0	0	0	0	1	196	0	0	98	175
"	Junior Johnson	1	0	0	0	0	0	0	0	113	0	0	57	110
"	Tom Pistone	17	0	0	0	1	0	1	4	3,385	183	4	2,868	4,930
"	**Total**	20	0	0	0	1	0	1	6	3,812	183	4	3,081	5,345
Lifetime		20	0	0	0	1	0	1	6	3,812	183	4	3,081	$5,345

Jim B. Copperheat

Year	Driver	Starts	Poles	1	2	3	4	5	6–10	Laps	Laps Led	Races Led	Miles	$
1952	Bill Rexford	1	0	0	0	0	0	0	0	82	0	0	82	25
Lifetime		1	0	0	0	0	0	0	0	82	0	0	82	$25

Year	Driver	Starts	Poles	Finish 1	2	3	4	5	6–10	Laps	Laps Led	Races Led	Miles	$

Ken Corman

Year	Driver	Starts	Poles	1	2	3	4	5	6–10	Laps	Laps Led	Races Led	Miles	$
1958	Johnny Mackison	8	0	0	0	1	0	1	1	897	0	0	585	965
Lifetime		8	0	0	0	1	0	1	1	897	0	0	585	$965

Fred Correa

Year	Driver	Starts	Poles	1	2	3	4	5	6–10	Laps	Laps Led	Races Led	Miles	$
1982	John Krebs	2	0	0	0	0	0	0	0	127	0	0	333	1,750
Lifetime		2	0	0	0	0	0	0	0	127	0	0	333	$1,750

Ron Cory

Year	Driver	Starts	Poles	1	2	3	4	5	6–10	Laps	Laps Led	Races Led	Miles	$
1965	Jack Anderson	2	0	0	0	0	0	0	0	18	0	0	45	1,220
Lifetime		2	0	0	0	0	0	0	0	18	0	0	45	$1,220

Luther Costales

Year	Driver	Starts	Poles	1	2	3	4	5	6–10	Laps	Laps Led	Races Led	Miles	$
1962	Harlan Richardson	1	0	0	0	0	0	0	0	17	0	0	43	50
"	Billy Wade	1	0	0	0	0	0	0	0	182	0	0	455	425
"	**Total**	2	0	0	0	0	0	0	0	199	0	0	498	475
Lifetime		2	0	0	0	0	0	0	0	199	0	0	498	$475

Howard Coulter

Year	Driver	Starts	Poles	1	2	3	4	5	6–10	Laps	Laps Led	Races Led	Miles	$
1957	Russ Hepler	4	1	0	0	0	0	0	0	365	0	0	206	345
Lifetime		4	1	0	0	0	0	0	0	365	0	0	206	$345

Bobby Courtwright

Year	Driver	Starts	Poles	1	2	3	4	5	6–10	Laps	Laps Led	Races Led	Miles	$
1952	Bobby Courtwright	3	0	0	0	0	0	1	0	244	0	0	128	250
1954	Bobby Courtwright	1	0	0	0	0	0	0	0	107	0	0	107	25
Lifetime		4	0	0	0	0	0	1	0	351	0	0	235	$275

A. J. Cox

Year	Driver	Starts	Poles	1	2	3	4	5	6–10	Laps	Laps Led	Races Led	Miles	$
1971	A. J. Cox	1	0	0	0	0	0	0	0	82	0	0	82	615
1972	A. J. Cox	1	0	0	0	0	0	0	0	2	0	0	3	325
"	Jim Vandiver	1	0	0	0	0	0	0	0	299	0	0	299	875
"	**Total**	2	0	0	0	0	0	0	0	301	0	0	302	1,200
Lifetime		3	0	0	0	0	0	0	0	383	0	0	384	$1,815

Doug Cox

Year	Driver	Starts	Poles	1	2	3	4	5	6–10	Laps	Laps Led	Races Led	Miles	$
1955	Doug Cox	1	0	0	0	0	0	0	0	181	0	0	91	50
1958	Doug Cox	14	0	0	1	0	1	1	6	2,479	0	0	1,592	3,404
1959	Doug Cox	4	0	0	0	0	0	0	2	532	0	0	266	380
1961	Doug Cox	5	0	0	0	0	0	0	0	367	0	0	190	510
Lifetime		24	0	0	1	0	1	1	8	3,559	0	0	2,138	$4,344

Marion C. Cox

Year	Driver	Starts	Poles	1	2	3	4	5	6–10	Laps	Laps Led	Races Led	Miles	$
1955	Roy Bentley	1	0	0	0	0	0	0	0	317	0	0	436	60
1956	Roy Bentley	3	0	0	0	0	0	0	0	329	0	0	292	200
Lifetime		4	0	0	0	0	0	0	0	646	0	0	728	$260

Owen Cox

Year	Driver	Starts	Poles	1	2	3	4	5	6–10	Laps	Laps Led	Races Led	Miles	$
1955	Pop McGinnis	2	0	0	0	0	0	0	0	201	0	0	116	100
Lifetime		2	0	0	0	0	0	0	0	201	0	0	116	$100

Paul Cox

Year	Driver	Starts	Poles	1	2	3	4	5	6–10	Laps	Laps Led	Races Led	Miles	$
1950	Marshall Teague	3	0	0	0	0	0	0	0	240	0	0	329	50
Lifetime		3	0	0	0	0	0	0	0	240	0	0	329	$50

Cozze Brothers

Year	Driver	Starts	Poles	1	2	3	4	5	6–10	Laps	Laps Led	Races Led	Miles	$
1967	Ray Hill	1	0	0	0	0	0	0	0	91	0	0	46	275
"	Bob Pickell	3	0	0	0	0	0	0	0	467	0	0	304	1,600
"	Gary Sain	4	0	0	0	0	0	0	1	399	0	0	271	2,335
"	**Total**	8	0	0	0	0	0	0	1	957	0	0	620	4,210
Lifetime		8	0	0	0	0	0	0	1	957	0	0	620	$4,210

Year	Driver	Starts	Poles	Finish						Laps	Laps Led	Races Led	Miles	$
				1	2	3	4	5	6–10					

Paul Craig Jr.

Year	Driver	Starts	Poles	1	2	3	4	5	6–10	Laps	Laps Led	Races Led	Miles	$
1958	Cecil Wray	1	0	0	0	0	0	0	0	34	0	0	139	75
Lifetime		1	0	0	0	0	0	0	0	34	0	0	139	$75

Tom Craigen

Year	Driver	Starts	Poles	1	2	3	4	5	6–10	Laps	Laps Led	Races Led	Miles	$
1993	Dirk Stephens	2	0	0	0	0	0	0	0	96	0	0	205	12,880
Lifetime		2	0	0	0	0	0	0	0	96	0	0	205	$12,880

Gerald Craker

Year	Driver	Starts	Poles	1	2	3	4	5	6–10	Laps	Laps Led	Races Led	Miles	$
1974	Don Hall	1	0	0	0	0	0	0	0	102	0	0	255	1,100
1976	Chuck Bown	5	0	0	0	0	0	0	0	568	3	1	1,192	5,480
1977	Chuck Bown	3	0	0	0	0	0	0	0	180	0	0	468	7,270
1978	Jimmy Insolo	2	0	0	0	0	0	0	1	147	5	2	385	5,025
1979	Jimmy Insolo	3	0	0	0	0	0	0	0	192	0	0	499	6,905
1981	Hershel McGriff	3	0	0	0	0	0	0	0	80	1	1	210	2,170
Lifetime		17	0	0	0	0	0	0	1	1,269	9	4	3,009	$27,950

Bill Cramer

Year	Driver	Starts	Poles	1	2	3	4	5	6–10	Laps	Laps Led	Races Led	Miles	$
1951	George Seeger	1	0	0	0	1	0	0	0	199	0	0	100	400
Lifetime		1	0	0	0	1	0	0	0	199	0	0	100	$400

Gil Cramer

Year	Driver	Starts	Poles	1	2	3	4	5	6–10	Laps	Laps Led	Races Led	Miles	$
1973	Bobby Mausgrover	1	0	0	0	0	0	0	0	58	0	0	87	915
Lifetime		1	0	0	0	0	0	0	0	58	0	0	87	$915

Pappy Crane

Year	Driver	Starts	Poles	1	2	3	4	5	6–10	Laps	Laps Led	Races Led	Miles	$
1957	Joe Caspolich	1	0	0	0	0	0	0	0	66	0	0	91	200
1958	Bill Corley	1	0	0	0	0	0	0	0	7	0	0	29	0
1960	Pappy Crane	1	0	0	0	0	0	0	1	181	0	0	91	140
Lifetime		3	0	0	0	0	0	0	1	254	0	0	210	$340

Crawford Brothers (Jimmy and Peter Crawford, co-owners)

Year	Driver	Starts	Poles	1	2	3	4	5	6–10	Laps	Laps Led	Races Led	Miles	$
1966	Bunkie Blackburn	2	0	0	0	0	0	0	0	81	0	0	151	860
"	Tommy Bostick	1	0	0	0	0	0	0	0	42	0	0	42	500
"	**Total**	3	0	0	0	0	0	0	0	123	0	0	193	1,360
1970	Jimmy Crawford	3	0	0	0	0	0	0	0	292	0	0	526	1,795
"	E. J. Trivette	1	0	0	0	0	0	0	0	68	0	0	37	395
"	**Total**	4	0	0	0	0	0	0	0	360	0	0	563	2,190
1971	Jimmy Crawford	3	0	0	0	0	0	0	0	110	0	0	284	1,575
1972	Donnie Allison	1	0	0	0	0	0	0	0	61	19	1	162	2,090
"	Jimmy Crawford	1	0	0	0	0	0	0	0	181	0	0	481	1,695
"	Gordon Johncock	2	0	0	0	0	0	0	0	226	0	0	430	1,384
"	**Total**	4	0	0	0	0	0	0	0	468	19	1	1,074	5,169
1973	Dick Brooks	2	0	1	0	0	0	0	0	295	24	2	785	22,620
"	Jimmy Crawford	4	0	0	0	0	0	0	0	1,053	0	0	1,228	4,059
"	Pete Hamilton	1	0	0	0	0	0	0	0	38	0	0	57	905
"	**Total**	7	0	1	0	0	0	0	0	1,386	24	2	2,070	27,584
1974	Jimmy Crawford	4	0	0	0	0	0	0	0	559	0	0	903	5,965
Lifetime		25	0	1	0	0	0	0	0	3,006	43	3	5,085	$43,843

Spook Crawford

Year	Driver	Starts	Poles	1	2	3	4	5	6–10	Laps	Laps Led	Races Led	Miles	$
1955	Johnny Allen	1	0	0	0	0	0	0	0	169	0	0	254	195
1956	Johnny Allen	32	0	0	0	0	0	2	9	4,888	0	0	3,349	4,559
"	Spook Crawford	1	0	0	0	0	0	0	0	13	0	0	7	50
"	**Total**	32	0	0	0	0	0	2	9	4,901	0	0	3,356	4,609
1957	Johnny Allen	42	1	0	0	1	1	2	13	6,033	0	0	3,876	9,815
"	Spook Crawford	1	0	0	0	0	0	0	0	34	0	0	78	125
"	**Total**	42	1	0	0	1	1	2	13	6,067	0	0	3,954	9,940
1958	Johnny Allen	18	0	0	0	1	0	1	3	2,214	0	0	1,206	1,950
"	Neil Castles	1	0	0	0	0	0	0	0	141	0	0	88	50
"	Spook Crawford	1	0	0	0	0	0	0	0	152	0	0	76	85
"	Shorty Rollins	2	0	0	0	0	0	1	0	327	0	0	181	275
"	Roy Tyner	20	0	0	0	0	0	0	2	2,865	0	0	1,810	2,215

Year	Driver	Starts	Poles	Finish 1	2	3	4	5	6–10	Laps	Laps Led	Races Led	Miles	$

Spook Crawford *continued*

Year	Driver	Starts	Poles	1	2	3	4	5	6–10	Laps	Laps Led	Races Led	Miles	$
"	Vernon West	1	0	0	0	0	0	0	0	1	0	0	0	50
"	**Total**	35	0	0	0	1	0	2	5	5,700	0	0	3,362	4,625
1959	Tiny Lund	4	0	0	0	0	0	0	0	1,059	0	0	723	430
"	Jimmy Pardue	1	0	0	0	0	0	0	0	131	0	0	44	50
"	**Total**	5	0	0	0	0	0	0	0	1,190	0	0	766	480
1960	L. D. Austin	1	0	0	0	0	0	0	0	2	0	0	1	60
"	Buddy Baker	4	0	0	0	0	0	0	0	576	0	0	751	720
"	Bunkie Blackburn	20	0	0	0	0	0	1	3	2,789	0	0	2,110	3,600
"	Spook Crawford	3	0	0	0	0	0	0	1	439	0	0	212	320
"	Curtis Crider	2	0	0	0	0	0	0	0	417	0	0	626	650
"	Tiny Lund	1	0	0	0	0	0	0	1	187	0	0	94	140
"	Bob Reuther	1	0	0	0	0	0	0	0	285	0	0	143	140
"	G. C. Spencer	1	0	0	0	0	0	0	0	301	0	0	414	200
"	**Total**	27	0	0	0	0	0	1	5	4,996	0	0	4,349	5,830
1961	Curtis Crider	1	0	0	0	0	0	0	0	35	0	0	18	50
"	Paul Parks	2	0	0	0	0	0	0	0	208	0	0	520	200
"	Johnny Sudderth	1	0	0	0	0	0	0	0	22	0	0	33	200
"	**Total**	4	0	0	0	0	0	0	0	265	0	0	571	450
Lifetime		146	1	0	0	2	1	7	32	23,288	0	0	16,611	$26,129

Charlie Cregar

Year	Driver	Starts	Poles	1	2	3	4	5	6–10	Laps	Laps Led	Races Led	Miles	$
1956	Charlie Cregar	2	0	0	0	0	0	0	0	74	0	0	37	0
1957	Charlie Cregar	3	0	0	0	0	0	0	3	356	0	0	178	500
1958	Charlie Cregar	1	0	0	0	0	0	0	0	127	0	0	127	100
Lifetime		6	0	0	0	0	0	0	3	557	0	0	342	$600

J. C. Crews

Year	Driver	Starts	Poles	1	2	3	4	5	6–10	Laps	Laps Led	Races Led	Miles	$
1971	H. B. Bailey	1	0	0	0	0	0	0	0	117	0	0	234	600
"	Bobby Brack	5	0	0	0	0	0	0	0	946	0	0	1,610	4,608
"	Rod Eulenfeld	1	0	0	0	0	0	0	0	293	0	0	446	1,135
"	**Total**	7	0	0	0	0	0	0	0	1,356	0	0	2,290	6,343
1972	H. B. Bailey	2	0	0	0	0	0	0	0	480	0	0	502	1,765
"	Bobby Mausgrover	2	0	0	0	0	0	0	0	334	0	0	549	1,545
"	Dick May	4	0	0	0	0	0	0	0	636	0	0	1,067	3,330
"	Bill Ward	1	0	0	0	0	0	0	0	10	0	0	27	770
"	**Total**	9	0	0	0	0	0	0	0	1,460	0	0	2,146	7,410
1973	Johnny Barnes	8	0	0	0	0	0	0	0	1,416	0	0	2,174	8,585
"	Bobby Mausgrover	1	0	0	0	0	0	0	0	9	0	0	24	560
"	**Total**	8	0	0	0	0	0	0	0	1,425	0	0	2,198	9,145
1974	Johnny Barnes	1	0	0	0	0	0	0	0	1	0	0	3	750
Lifetime		25	0	0	0	0	0	0	0	4,242	0	0	6,636	$23,648

Curtis Crider

Year	Driver	Starts	Poles	1	2	3	4	5	6–10	Laps	Laps Led	Races Led	Miles	$
1960	Curtis Crider	20	0	0	0	0	0	0	2	3,413	0	0	2,279	2,820
"	Richard Riley	1	0	0	0	0	0	0	0	143	0	0	215	200
"	**Total**	21	0	0	0	0	0	0	2	3,556	0	0	2,494	3,020
1961	Bob Barron	1	0	0	0	0	0	0	1	157	0	0	79	140
"	Pete Boland	1	0	0	0	0	0	0	0	185	0	0	46	110
"	Curtis Crider	40	0	0	0	0	0	1	1	5,847	0	0	4,169	7,370
"	David Ezell	1	0	0	0	0	0	0	0	87	0	0	44	50
"	Homer Galloway	1	0	0	0	0	0	0	0	127	0	0	42	110
"	Ed Livingston	10	0	0	0	0	0	0	0	1,477	0	0	2,201	1,945
"	Bob Presnell	1	0	0	0	0	0	0	0	1	0	0	0	50
"	Charles Williamson	1	0	0	0	0	0	0	0	107	0	0	27	30
"	**Total**	42	0	0	0	0	0	1	2	7,988	0	0	6,607	9,805
1962	Frank Brantley	1	0	0	0	0	0	0	0	164	0	0	82	85
"	Earl Brooks	1	0	0	0	0	0	0	0	2	0	0	1	150
"	Curtis Crider	52	0	0	0	1	1	1	15	10,051	0	0	6,431	12,016
"	John Hardy	1	0	0	0	0	0	0	0	435	0	0	218	125
"	Runt Harris	2	0	0	0	0	0	0	0	130	0	0	51	100
"	Glenn Killian	1	0	0	0	0	0	0	0	3	0	0	1	50
"	Ed Livingston	2	0	0	0	0	0	0	0	320	0	0	160	175
"	H. G. Rosier	1	0	0	0	0	0	0	0	119	0	0	60	65
"	Jerry Smith	1	0	0	0	0	0	0	0	109	0	0	36	60
"	**Total**	52	0	0	0	1	1	1	15	11,333	0	0	7,039	12,826
1963	Curtis Crider	43	0	0	0	1	0	1	11	7,618	0	0	4,653	10,499

Year	Driver	Starts	Poles	Finish						Laps	Laps Led	Races Led	Miles	$
				1	2	3	4	5	6–10					

Curtis Crider *continued*

Year	Driver	Starts	Poles	1	2	3	4	5	6–10	Laps	Laps Led	Races Led	Miles	$
"	Chuck Huckabee	3	0	0	0	0	0	0	1	171	0	0	86	450
"	Jerome Warren	1	0	0	0	0	0	0	0	25	0	0	13	100
"	**Total**	45	0	0	0	1	0	1	12	7,719	0	0	4,727	11,049
1964	Buddy Baker	2	0	0	0	0	0	0	0	56	0	0	33	235
"	Pete Boland	3	0	0	0	0	0	0	0	7	0	0	6	200
"	Rodney Bottinger	2	0	0	0	0	0	0	0	9	0	0	5	200
"	Darrell Bryant	4	0	0	0	0	0	0	1	365	0	0	177	450
"	Bob Cooper	5	0	0	0	0	0	0	0	292	0	0	183	1,420
"	Joe Cote	4	0	0	0	0	0	0	0	23	0	0	12	350
"	Curtis Crider	58	0	0	0	1	1	5	23	11,411	0	0	7,786	21,671
"	Wally Dallenbach	1	0	0	0	0	0	0	0	142	0	0	71	110
"	Stick Elliott	1	0	0	0	0	0	0	0	1	0	0	2	400
"	J. V. Hamby	5	0	0	0	0	0	0	1	484	0	0	173	735
"	Chuck Huckabee	9	0	0	0	0	0	0	0	788	0	0	306	830
"	Ed Livingston	1	0	0	0	0	0	0	0	2	0	0	3	500
"	Gene Lovelace	1	0	0	0	0	0	0	0	125	0	0	50	130
"	Roy Mayne	2	0	0	0	0	0	0	0	43	0	0	66	930
"	Frank Tanner	1	0	0	0	0	0	0	0	2	0	0	1	100
"	**Total**	58	0	0	0	1	1	5	25	13,750	0	0	8,873	28,261
1965	Curtis Crider	1	0	0	0	0	1	0	0	238	0	0	119	600
"	Darel Dieringer	1	0	0	0	0	0	0	0	119	0	0	107	100
"	**Total**	2	0	0	0	0	1	0	0	357	0	0	226	700
Lifetime		221	0	0	0	3	3	8	56	44,798	0	0	29,990	$65,661

Will Cronkrite

Year	Driver	Starts	Poles	1	2	3	4	5	6–10	Laps	Laps Led	Races Led	Miles	$
1978	Dale Earnhardt	4	0	0	0	0	0	0	1	1,032	0	0	1,872	13,245
"	Baxter Price	1	0	0	0	0	0	0	0	179	0	0	269	1,165
"	**Total**	5	0	0	0	0	0	0	1	1,211	0	0	2,140	14,410
1979	Ferrel Harris	1	0	0	0	0	0	0	0	2	0	0	3	1,260
"	Jim Hurlbert	1	0	0	0	0	0	0	0	150	0	0	300	1,400
"	Jerry Jolly	1	0	0	0	0	0	0	0	99	0	0	263	2,440
"	**Total**	3	0	0	0	0	0	0	0	251	0	0	566	5,100
1982	Elliott Forbes-Robinson	2	0	0	0	0	0	0	0	174	0	0	447	7,985
"	John McFadden	1	0	0	0	0	0	0	0	368	0	0	196	655
"	**Total**	3	0	0	0	0	0	0	0	542	0	0	643	8,640
1983	Rick Baldwin	1	0	0	0	0	0	0	0	7	0	0	19	1,985
"	Jimmy Walker	1	0	0	0	0	0	0	0	50	0	0	30	705
"	**Total**	2	0	0	0	0	0	0	0	57	0	0	48	2,690
Lifetime		13	0	0	0	0	0	0	1	2,061	0	0	3,398	$30,840

Don Culpepper

Year	Driver	Starts	Poles	1	2	3	4	5	6–10	Laps	Laps Led	Races Led	Miles	$
1967	Earl Brooks	20	0	0	0	0	0	0	5	3,503	24	1	2,558	6,140
"	Tiny Lund	3	0	0	0	0	0	0	0	981	0	0	536	690
"	Curley Mills	3	0	0	0	0	0	0	1	226	0	0	106	350
"	Roy Tyner	1	0	0	0	0	0	0	0	260	0	0	390	1,200
"	**Total**	27	0	0	0	0	0	0	6	4,970	24	1	3,590	8,380
1968	Ben Arnold	9	0	0	0	0	0	0	0	1,129	0	0	845	1,960
"	Earl Brooks	2	0	0	0	0	0	0	0	529	0	0	252	400
"	Tiny Lund	2	0	0	0	0	0	0	1	287	0	0	144	440
"	Stan Meserve	1	0	0	0	0	0	0	0	346	0	0	216	275
"	James Sears	1	0	0	0	0	0	0	0	92	0	0	92	710
"	Roy Tyner	17	0	0	0	0	0	1	4	2,835	0	0	2,255	7,735
"	**Total**	32	0	0	0	0	0	1	5	5,218	0	0	3,804	11,520
Lifetime		59	0	0	0	0	0	1	11	10,188	24	1	7,394	$19,900

Red Culpepper

Year	Driver	Starts	Poles	1	2	3	4	5	6–10	Laps	Laps Led	Races Led	Miles	$
1969	Ben Arnold	45	0	0	0	0	0	0	7	9,858	0	0	7,933	24,712
"	Tommy Gale	1	0	0	0	0	0	0	0	46	0	0	115	290
"	**Total**	46	0	0	0	0	0	0	7	9,904	0	0	8,048	25,002
Lifetime		46	0	0	0	0	0	0	7	9,904	0	0	8,048	$25,002

Clayton Cunningham

Year	Driver	Starts	Poles	1	2	3	4	5	6–10	Laps	Laps Led	Races Led	Miles	$
1994	Ken Bouchard	1	0	0	0	0	0	0	0	280	0	0	426	675
1995	Ken Bouchard	0												2,100
Lifetime		1	0	0	0	0	0	0	0	280	0	0	426	$2,775

Year	Driver	Starts	Poles	Finish 1	2	3	4	5	6–10	Laps	Laps Led	Races Led	Miles	$

H. B. Cunningham

Year	Driver	Starts	Poles	1	2	3	4	5	6–10	Laps	Laps Led	Races Led	Miles	$
1967	Coo Coo Marlin	3	0	0	0	0	0	0	0	158	0	0	155	755
1969	Coo Coo Marlin	7	0	0	0	0	0	0	2	993	0	0	1,285	5,680
1970	Coo Coo Marlin	13	0	0	0	0	0	0	4	2,531	0	0	3,825	14,799
1971	Coo Coo Marlin	12	0	0	0	0	0	0	0	1,495	0	0	2,334	9,135
"	Wendell Scott	1	0	0	0	0	0	0	0	64	0	0	96	714
"	Jabe Thomas	1	0	0	0	0	0	0	0	292	0	0	438	1,230
"	**Total**	14	0	0	0	0	0	0	0	1,851	0	0	2,868	11,079
1972	Coo Coo Marlin	20	0	0	0	1	1	0	3	4,092	31	5	5,383	28,924
1973	Coo Coo Marlin	21	0	0	0	1	0	0	7	5,454	16	3	5,937	29,997
1974	Coo Coo Marlin	23	0	0	0	0	1	0	4	5,623	28	7	6,261	41,944
1975	Coo Coo Marlin	23	0	0	0	1	0	3	7	5,199	25	5	6,400	60,013
1976	Charlie Glotzbach	1	0	0	0	0	0	0	0	121	0	0	182	1,535
"	Coo Coo Marlin	12	0	0	0	0	0	0	6	3,074	0	0	4,309	39,485
"	Sterling Marlin	1	0	0	0	0	0	0	0	55	0	0	33	565
"	Walter Wallace	2	0	0	0	0	0	0	0	437	0	0	260	775
"	**Total**	14	0	0	0	0	0	0	6	3,687	0	0	4,784	42,360
1977	Coo Coo Marlin	11	0	0	0	0	1	0	4	2,930	1	1	4,210	42,450
1978	Coo Coo Marlin	9	0	0	0	0	0	0	2	1,518	4	2	2,372	19,415
"	Sterling Marlin	2	0	0	0	0	0	0	1	591	0	0	708	10,320
"	**Total**	11	0	0	0	0	0	0	3	2,109	4	2	3,080	29,735
1979	Coo Coo Marlin	7	0	0	0	0	0	0	2	907	0	0	1,989	27,540
"	Sterling Marlin	1	0	0	0	0	0	0	0	341	11	1	203	505
"	Jimmy Means	1	0	0	0	0	0	0	0	1	0	0	2	855
"	**Total**	9	0	0	0	0	0	0	2	1,249	11	1	2,194	28,900
1980	Coo Coo Marlin	3	0	0	0	0	0	0	0	377	0	0	978	8,400
"	Sterling Marlin	2	0	0	0	0	0	0	1	332	0	0	692	18,750
"	**Total**	5	0	0	0	0	0	0	1	709	0	0	1,670	27,150
Lifetime		174	0	0	0	3	3	3	43	36,585	116	24	48,051	$363,786

J. B. Cunningham

Year	Driver	Starts	Poles	1	2	3	4	5	6–10	Laps	Laps Led	Races Led	Miles	$
1955	Tommy Ringstaff	3	0	0	0	0	0	0	1	225	0	0	199	125
Lifetime		3	0	0	0	0	0	0	1	225	0	0	199	$125

Pepper Cunningham

Year	Driver	Starts	Poles	1	2	3	4	5	6–10	Laps	Laps Led	Races Led	Miles	$
1949	Pepper Cunningham	1	0	0	0	0	0	0	0	134	0	0	134	0
1950	Pepper Cunningham	2	0	0	0	0	0	0	2	130	0	0	130	300
1951	Pepper Cunningham	4	0	0	0	0	0	0	0		0	0		85
1953	Pepper Cunningham	1	0	0	0	0	0	0	0		0	0		50
Lifetime		8	0	0	0	0	0	0	2	264	0	0	264	$435

Mike Curb

Year	Driver	Starts	Poles	1	2	3	4	5	6–10	Laps	Laps Led	Races Led	Miles	$
1984	Richard Petty	30	0	2	0	0	2	1	8	8,835	275	8	9,917	257,932
1985	Richard Petty	28	0	0	0	1	0	0	12	7,767	105	7	8,858	306,142
"	Tom Sneva	1	0	0	0	0	0	0	0	138	0	0	210	2,655
"	**Total**	28	0	0	0	1	0	0	12	7,905	105	7	9,068	308,797
1986	Ron Bouchard	17	0	0	0	0	0	0	2	3,654	1	1	5,093	106,835
"	Dale Jarrett	1	0	0	0	0	0	0	0	69	0	0	37	990
"	**Total**	18	0	0	0	0	0	0	2	3,723	1	1	5,129	107,825
1987	Ed Pimm	3	0	0	0	0	0	0	0	243	1	1	595	6,810
1988	Brad Noffsinger	17	0	0	0	0	0	0	0	3,555	1	1	5,513	50,645
"	Ed Pimm	2	0	0	0	0	0	0	0	502	0	0	794	13,350
"	**Total**	19	0	0	0	0	0	0	0	4,057	1	1	6,307	63,995
Lifetime		98	0	2	0	1	2	1	22	24,763	383	18	31,016	$745,359

Dick Curry

Year	Driver	Starts	Poles	1	2	3	4	5	6–10	Laps	Laps Led	Races Led	Miles	$
1953	Dick Allwine	1	0	0	0	0	0	0	0	198	0	0	272	105
Lifetime		1	0	0	0	0	0	0	0	198	0	0	272	$105

Jim Cushman

Year	Driver	Starts	Poles	1	2	3	4	5	6–10	Laps	Laps Led	Races Led	Miles	$
1956	Jim Cushman	1	0	0	0	0	0	0	0		0	0		50
Lifetime		1	0	0	0	0	0	0	0		0	0		$50

Doug Cutler

Year	Driver	Starts	Poles	1	2	3	4	5	6–10	Laps	Laps Led	Races Led	Miles	$
1968	Bob Senneker	1	0	0	0	0	0	0	0	182	0	0	455	3,200
Lifetime		1	0	0	0	0	0	0	0	182	0	0	455	$3,200

Year	Driver	Starts	Poles	Finish						Laps	Laps Led	Races Led	Miles	$
				1	2	3	4	5	6–10	Laps	Led	Led	Miles	$

Clyde Dagit

Year	Driver	Starts	Poles	1	2	3	4	5	6–10	Laps	Laps Led	Races Led	Miles	$
1974	Clyde Dagit	1	0	0	0	0	0	0	0	183	0	0	366	1,020
1975	Clyde Dagit	1	0	0	0	0	0	0	0	418	0	0	425	1,400
Lifetime		2	0	0	0	0	0	0	0	601	0	0	791	$2,420

Dean Dalton

Year	Driver	Starts	Poles	1	2	3	4	5	6–10	Laps	Laps Led	Races Led	Miles	$
1971	Dean Dalton	19	0	0	0	0	0	0	1	3,487	0	0	4,311	13,690
"	Bill Dennis	1	0	0	0	0	0	0	0	434	0	0	228	675
"	Ed Negre	1	0	0	0	0	0	0	0	106	0	0	56	435
"	**Total**	21	0	0	0	0	0	0	1	4,027	0	0	4,596	14,800
1972	Dean Dalton	29	0	0	0	0	0	0	4	7,533	0	0	9,068	42,299
1973	Dean Dalton	25	0	0	0	0	0	0	2	5,751	0	0	6,687	40,269
1974	Dean Dalton	12	0	0	0	0	0	0	0	2,073	6	1	2,102	11,575
"	Henley Gray	1	0	0	0	0	0	0	0	332	0	0	198	550
"	Jackie Rogers	1	0	0	0	0	0	0	0	9	0	0	5	515
"	**Total**	14	0	0	0	0	0	0	0	2,414	6	1	2,305	12,640
1975	Walter Ballard	1	0	0	0	0	0	0	0	187	0	0	468	1,425
"	Dean Dalton	14	0	0	0	0	0	0	3	3,777	0	0	4,177	17,960
"	Ed Negre	2	0	0	0	0	0	0	0	528	0	0	407	2,030
"	**Total**	17	0	0	0	0	0	0	3	4,492	0	0	5,052	21,415
1976	Dean Dalton	6	0	0	0	0	0	0	0	1,433	0	0	1,853	7,245
"	Jack Donohue	3	0	0	0	0	0	0	0	888	0	0	896	2,680
"	Cecil Gordon	1	0	0	0	0	0	0	0	385	0	0	229	565
"	Ed Negre	1	0	0	0	0	0	0	0	16	0	0	40	825
"	D. K. Ulrich	1	0	0	0	0	0	0	0	378	0	0	567	2,965
"	Frank Warren	1	0	0	0	0	0	0	0	320	0	0	320	1,700
"	**Total**	13	0	0	0	0	0	0	0	3,420	0	0	3,753	15,980
1977	Dean Dalton	5	0	0	0	0	0	0	0	417	0	0	488	2,685
Lifetime		124	0	0	0	0	0	0	10	28,054	6	1	31,949	$150,088

Carl Dane

Year	Driver	Starts	Poles	1	2	3	4	5	6–10	Laps	Laps Led	Races Led	Miles	$
1954	George Seeger	1	0	0	0	0	0	1	0	486	0	0	243	350
1956	Chuck Stevenson	1	0	1	0	0	0	0	0	80	54	1	200	1,570
1959	Danny Weinberg	1	0	0	0	1	0	0	0	100	0	0	100	425
1960	Danny Weinberg	3	0	0	0	0	0	1	0	216	0	0	231	525
1963	Joe Ruttman	1	0	0	0	0	0	0	1	176	0	0	475	850
"	Danny Weinberg	1	0	0	0	0	0	0	0	27	0	0	73	300
"	**Total**	1	0	0	0	0	0	0	1	203	0	0	548	1,150
1964	Danny Weinberg	1	0	0	0	0	0	0	0	9	0	0	24	500
1967	Marvin Porter	1	0	0	0	0	0	0	0	15	0	0	41	500
Lifetime		9	0	1	0	1	0	2	1	1,109	54	1	1,387	$5,020

Jim Dane

Year	Driver	Starts	Poles	1	2	3	4	5	6–10	Laps	Laps Led	Races Led	Miles	$
1955	Bill West	2	0	0	0	1	0	0	1	350	0	0	350	910
1956	Bill West	1	0	0	0	0	0	0	0	76	0	0	190	110
Lifetime		3	0	0	0	1	0	0	1	426	0	0	540	$1,020

Lloyd Dane

Year	Driver	Starts	Poles	1	2	3	4	5	6–10	Laps	Laps Led	Races Led	Miles	$
1951	Lloyd Dane	7	0	0	0	1	1	0	1	447	0	0	421	1,025
1954	Lloyd Dane	4	0	0	1	0	0	2	1	1,268	180	1	756	1,600
1955	Lloyd Dane	3	0	0	0	1	0	0	0	303	5	1	204	505
1956	Lloyd Dane	10	0	2	0	1	2	0	4	1,706	91	2	1,257	4,370
1957	Lloyd Dane	10	1	1	5	1	0	0	3	1,296	1	1	863	4,985
1958	Lloyd Dane	5	0	0	1	0	0	0	1	1,084	0	0	1,198	2,490
1959	Lloyd Dane	2	0	0	1	0	0	0	1	578	0	0	286	1,100
1960	Lloyd Dane	3	0	0	0	1	0	1	0	323	89	1	375	950
1961	Lloyd Dane	4	0	1	0	0	0	0	1	396	0	0	443	1,390
1963	Lloyd Dane	1	0	0	0	0	0	0	0	8	0	0	22	300
Lifetime		49	1	4	8	5	3	3	12	7,409	366	6	5,824	$18,715

Ronnie Daniel

Year	Driver	Starts	Poles	1	2	3	4	5	6–10	Laps	Laps Led	Races Led	Miles	$
1971	Ronnie Daniel	1	0	0	0	0	0	0	0	16	0	0	6	200
1972	Ronnie Daniel	2	0	0	0	0	0	0	0	490	0	0	471	1,360
1973	Ronnie Daniel	5	0	0	0	0	0	0	0	1,148	0	0	624	2,480
Lifetime		8	0	0	0	0	0	0	0	1,654	0	0	1,101	$4,040

Year	Driver	Starts	Poles	Finish 1	2	3	4	5	6–10	Laps	Laps Led	Races Led	Miles	$

Tom Daniels

Year	Driver	Starts	Poles	1	2	3	4	5	6–10	Laps	Laps Led	Races Led	Miles	$
1960	Tommy Irwin	1	0	0	0	0	0	0	0	300	0	0	450	260
"	Possum Jones	12	0	0	3	1	0	0	1	2,303	0	0	1,691	6,055
"	**Total**	13	0	0	3	1	0	0	1	2,603	0	0	2,141	6,315
1961	Tommy Irwin	23	0	0	2	0	1	0	5	3,187	166	1	2,552	6,450
Lifetime		36	0	0	5	1	1	0	6	5,790	166	1	4,693	$12,765

Jim Danielson

Year	Driver	Starts	Poles	1	2	3	4	5	6–10	Laps	Laps Led	Races Led	Miles	$
1972	Jim Danielson	2	0	0	0	0	0	0	0	282	0	0	717	3,140
Lifetime		2	0	0	0	0	0	0	0	282	0	0	717	$3,140

B. J. Dantone

Year	Driver	Starts	Poles	1	2	3	4	5	6–10	Laps	Laps Led	Races Led	Miles	$
1951	Red Byron	4	0	0	0	0	1	0	1	609	0	0	701	925
"	Bill Miller	4	0	0	0	0	0	0	2		0	0		275
"	Jack Smith	1	0	0	0	0	0	0	0	123	0	0	123	0
"	**Total**	8	0	0	0	0	1	0	3	732	0	0	824	1,200
1952	Bill Miller	4	0	0	0	0	0	0	0	547	0	0	562	125
Lifetime		12	0	0	0	0	1	0	3	1,279	0	0	1,386	$1,325

Bay Darnell

Year	Driver	Starts	Poles	1	2	3	4	5	6–10	Laps	Laps Led	Races Led	Miles	$
1967	Bay Darnell	1	0	0	0	0	0	0	0	123	0	0	185	600
1983	Tom Sneva	2	0	0	0	0	0	0	1	274	0	0	648	29,740
Lifetime		3	0	0	0	0	0	0	1	397	0	0	832	$30,340

Mason Darnell

Year	Driver	Starts	Poles	1	2	3	4	5	6–10	Laps	Laps Led	Races Led	Miles	$
1953	Keith Hamner	2	0	0	0	0	0	0	1	33	0	0	135	75
Lifetime		2	0	0	0	0	0	0	1	33	0	0	135	$75

Gene Darragh

Year	Driver	Starts	Poles	1	2	3	4	5	6–10	Laps	Laps Led	Races Led	Miles	$
1952	Gene Darragh	3	0	0	0	0	0	0	0	237	0	0	228	60
1953	Gene Darragh	1	0	0	0	0	0	0	0		0	0		0
Lifetime		4	0	0	0	0	0	0	0	237	0	0	228	$60

Anthony Davella

Year	Driver	Starts	Poles	1	2	3	4	5	6–10	Laps	Laps Led	Races Led	Miles	$
1949	Johnny Rogers	1	0	0	0	0	0	0	0		0	0		0
Lifetime		1	0	0	0	0	0	0	0		0	0		$0

Davis Brothers

Year	Driver	Starts	Poles	1	2	3	4	5	6–10	Laps	Laps Led	Races Led	Miles	$
1949	Bob Flock	1	1	0	0	0	0	0	0	38	5	1	29	0
1950	Slick Smith	1	0	0	0	0	0	0	0	4	0	0	17	25
1959	Billy Carden	2	0	0	0	0	0	0	1	233	0	0	443	265
Lifetime		4	1	0	0	0	0	0	1	275	5	1	488	$290

Bill Davis

Year	Driver	Starts	Poles	1	2	3	4	5	6–10	Laps	Laps Led	Races Led	Miles	$
1993	Bobby Labonte	30	1	0	0	0	0	0	6	9,295	33	7	10,937	395,660
1994	Bobby Labonte	31	0	0	0	0	0	1	1	8,541	3	2	10,456	550,305
1995	Ward Burton	9	0	1	0	0	1	1	1	3,173	130	3	3,201	300,325
"	Wally Dallenbach Jr.	1	0	0	1	0	0	0	0	90	21	1	221	54,140
"	Jimmy Hensley	5	0	0	0	0	0	0	0	741	0	0	1,705	129,595
"	Randy LaJoie	13	0	0	0	0	0	0	0	3,510	0	0	4,235	265,770
"	**Total**	28	0	1	1	0	1	1	1	7,514	151	4	9,362	749,830
1996	Ward Burton	27	1	0	0	0	0	0	4	6,544	54	4	8,845	873,619
Lifetime		116	2	1	1	0	1	2	12	31,894	241	17	39,600	$2,569,414

Buster Davis

Year	Driver	Starts	Poles	1	2	3	4	5	6–10	Laps	Laps Led	Races Led	Miles	$
1970	Bobby Mausgrover	3	0	0	0	0	0	0	0	103	0	0	179	2,710
"	Raymond Williams	1	0	0	0	0	0	0	0	14	0	0	14	460
"	**Total**	4	0	0	0	0	0	0	0	117	0	0	193	3,170
1971	Freddy Fryar	2	0	0	0	0	0	0	0	238	0	0	595	2,010
"	Bobby Mausgrover	1	0	0	0	0	0	0	0	39	0	0	98	0
"	Ed Negre	1	0	0	0	0	0	0	0	354	0	0	531	1,525
"	**Total**	4	0	0	0	0	0	0	0	631	0	0	1,224	3,535

Year	Driver	Starts	Poles	Finish 1	2	3	4	5	6–10	Laps	Laps Led	Races Led	Miles	$

Buster Davis *continued*

Year	Driver	Starts	Poles	1	2	3	4	5	6–10	Laps	Laps Led	Races Led	Miles	$
1972	Dick May	1	0	0	0	0	0	0	0	178	0	0	356	790
1973	Johnny Benson, Sr.	1	0	0	0	0	0	0	0	185	0	0	370	850
"	Tony Bettenhausen Jr.	1	0	0	0	0	0	0	0	9	0	0	14	900
"	Bob Davis	1	0	0	0	0	0	0	0	93	0	0	247	1,140
"	Frank Warren	1	0	0	0	0	0	0	0	78	0	0	107	680
"	**Total**	4	0	0	0	0	0	0	0	365	0	0	737	3,570
1974	Johnny Ray	2	0	0	0	0	0	0	0	252	0	0	670	2,435
Lifetime		15	0	0	0	0	0	0	0	1,543	0	0	3,180	$13,500

George Davis

Year	Driver	Starts	Poles	1	2	3	4	5	6–10	Laps	Laps Led	Races Led	Miles	$
1967	Bobby Allison	1	0	0	0	0	1	0	0	290	0	0	145	575
"	George Davis	21	0	0	0	0	0	1	5	3,342	0	0	1,866	4,360
"	**Total**	22	0	0	0	0	1	1	5	3,632	0	0	2,011	4,935
1968	George Davis	6	0	0	0	0	0	0	1	576	0	0	362	1,915
Lifetime		28	0	0	0	0	1	1	6	4,208	0	0	2,373	$6,850

Gus Davis

Year	Driver	Starts	Poles	1	2	3	4	5	6–10	Laps	Laps Led	Races Led	Miles	$
1954	Allen Adkins	2	0	0	0	1	1	0	0	545	0	0	397	1,150
1956	Allen Adkins	2	0	0	0	0	0	1	0	215	0	0	332	495
Lifetime		4	0	0	0	1	1	1	0	760	0	0	729	$1,645

Jeff Davis

Year	Driver	Starts	Poles	1	2	3	4	5	6–10	Laps	Laps Led	Races Led	Miles	$
1992	Jeff Davis	1	0	0	0	0	0	0	0	299	0	0	299	4,785
1993	Jeff Davis	1	0	0	0	0	0	0	0	46	0	0	116	6,560
Lifetime		2	0	0	0	0	0	0	0	345	0	0	415	$11,345

Jerry Davis

Year	Driver	Starts	Poles	1	2	3	4	5	6–10	Laps	Laps Led	Races Led	Miles	$
1974	Bill Osborne	1	0	0	0	0	0	0	0	96	0	0	240	900
1975	Bill Osborne	1	0	0	0	0	0	0	0	125	0	0	328	1,435
Lifetime		2	0	0	0	0	0	0	0	221	0	0	568	$2,335

Jim Davis

Year	Driver	Starts	Poles	1	2	3	4	5	6–10	Laps	Laps Led	Races Led	Miles	$
1950	Fireball Roberts	1	0	0	0	0	0	0	0	8	0	0	33	25
Lifetime		1	0	0	0	0	0	0	0	8	0	0	33	$25

Joel Davis

Year	Driver	Starts	Poles	1	2	3	4	5	6–10	Laps	Laps Led	Races Led	Miles	$
1963	Curtis Crider	1	0	0	0	0	0	0	0	90	0	0	45	75
"	Joel Davis	3	0	0	0	0	0	0	0	280	0	0	140	245
"	**Total**	4	0	0	0	0	0	0	0	370	0	0	185	320
Lifetime		4	0	0	0	0	0	0	0	370	0	0	185	$320

Keith Davis

Year	Driver	Starts	Poles	1	2	3	4	5	6–10	Laps	Laps Led	Races Led	Miles	$
1979	Keith Davis	2	0	0	0	0	0	0	0	45	0	0	103	2,310
Lifetime		2	0	0	0	0	0	0	0	45	0	0	103	$2,310

Morris Davis

Year	Driver	Starts	Poles	1	2	3	4	5	6–10	Laps	Laps Led	Races Led	Miles	$
1970	Gary DuPuis	1	0	0	0	0	0	0	0	78	0	0	195	735
"	Rod Eulenfeld	1	0	0	0	0	0	0	0	80	0	0	44	390
"	Butch Hirst	4	0	0	0	0	0	0	0	439	0	0	1,062	3,915
"	**Total**	6	0	0	0	0	0	0	0	597	0	0	1,301	5,040
1974	Dan Daughtry	8	0	0	0	0	0	0	1	772	6	2	1,321	12,413
1975	Dan Daughtry	2	0	0	0	0	0	0	0	9	0	0	23	2,530
"	Darel Dieringer	3	0	0	0	0	0	0	2	550	2	1	1,069	7,515
"	**Total**	5	0	0	0	0	0	0	2	559	2	1	1,093	10,045
1977	Jim Hurtubise	1	0	0	0	0	0	0	0	0	0	0	0	535
Lifetime		20	0	0	0	0	0	0	3	1,928	8	3	3,714	$28,033

Ralph Davis

Year	Driver	Starts	Poles	1	2	3	4	5	6–10	Laps	Laps Led	Races Led	Miles	$
1971	Dick May	3	0	0	0	0	0	0	0	441	0	0	857	2,495
Lifetime		3	0	0	0	0	0	0	0	441	0	0	857	$2,495

Year	Driver	Starts	Poles	Finish 1	2	3	4	5	6–10	Laps	Laps Led	Races Led	Miles	$

Robert Davis (See Gerald Duke & Robert Davis)

Hanley Dawson

Year	Driver	Starts	Poles	1	2	3	4	5	6–10	Laps	Laps Led	Races Led	Miles	$
1960	Johnny Allen	10	0	0	1	0	0	1	3	1,820	0	0	2,501	14,035
Lifetime		10	0	0	1	0	0	1	3	1,820	0	0	2,501	$14,035

Russ Dawson

Year	Driver	Starts	Poles	1	2	3	4	5	6–10	Laps	Laps Led	Races Led	Miles	$
1969	Benny Parsons	4	0	0	0	1	0	1	1	568	0	0	1,259	7,650
Lifetime		4	0	0	0	1	0	1	1	568	0	0	1,259	$7,650

Charles Dean

Year	Driver	Starts	Poles	1	2	3	4	5	6–10	Laps	Laps Led	Races Led	Miles	$
1977	Peter Knab	3	0	0	0	0	0	0	0	507	0	0	1,017	6,865
"	Lella Lombardi	1	0	0	0	0	0	0	0	103	0	0	258	785
"	**Total**	4	0	0	0	0	0	0	0	610	0	0	1,274	7,650
1978	Bill Green	1	0	0	0	0	0	0	0	0	0	0	0	400
"	Jerry Jolly	3	0	0	0	0	0	0	0	307	0	0	652	5,740
"	**Total**	4	0	0	0	0	0	0	0	307	0	0	652	6,140
1979	Bill Green	1	0	0	0	0	0	0	0	76	2	1	152	980
"	Glenn Jarrett	1	0	0	0	0	0	0	0	166	0	0	249	1,630
"	**Total**	2	0	0	0	0	0	0	0	242	2	1	401	2,610
Lifetime		10	0	0	0	0	0	0	0	1,159	2	1	2,327	$16,400

Donald Dean

Year	Driver	Starts	Poles	1	2	3	4	5	6–10	Laps	Laps Led	Races Led	Miles	$
1977	Harry Goularte	1	0	0	0	0	0	0	0	81	0	0	212	900
Lifetime		1	0	0	0	0	0	0	0	81	0	0	212	$900

Larry DeBeau

Year	Driver	Starts	Poles	1	2	3	4	5	6–10	Laps	Laps Led	Races Led	Miles	$
1966	Cy Fairchild	1	0	0	0	0	0	0	0	18	0	0	45	0
"	Tiny Lund	1	0	0	0	0	0	0	0	267	0	0	267	725
"	**Total**	2	0	0	0	0	0	0	0	285	0	0	312	725
Lifetime		2	0	0	0	0	0	0	0	285	0	0	312	$725

J. R. DeLotto

Year	Driver	Starts	Poles	1	2	3	4	5	6–10	Laps	Laps Led	Races Led	Miles	$
1976	D. K. Ulrich	28	0	0	0	0	0	0	2	7,943	0	0	8,918	63,685
1977	D. K. Ulrich	30	0	0	0	0	0	0	0	6,735	0	0	7,648	69,677
Lifetime		58	0	0	0	0	0	0	2	14,678	0	0	16,566	$133,362

J. A. Delvecchio

Year	Driver	Starts	Poles	1	2	3	4	5	6–10	Laps	Laps Led	Races Led	Miles	$
1973	John Soares Jr.	2	0	0	0	0	0	0	0	122	0	0	320	1,980
Lifetime		2	0	0	0	0	0	0	0	122	0	0	320	$1,980

Matt DeMatthews

Year	Driver	Starts	Poles	1	2	3	4	5	6–10	Laps	Laps Led	Races Led	Miles	$
1960	Johnny Dollar	2	0	0	0	0	0	0	0	8	0	0	17	200
"	Ed Markstellar	2	0	0	0	0	0	0	0	34	0	0	58	325
"	Johnny Wolford	1	0	0	0	0	0	0	0	5	0	0	8	200
"	**Total**	4	0	0	0	0	0	0	0	47	0	0	83	725
1961	Ed Markstellar	4	0	0	0	0	0	0	0	616	0	0	991	700
"	Sammy Packard	1	0	0	0	0	0	0	1	444	0	0	111	275
"	Roy Tyner	2	0	0	0	0	0	0	0	158	0	0	245	600
"	**Total**	7	0	0	0	0	0	0	1	1,218	0	0	1,347	1,575
1962	Matthew DeMatthews	1	0	0	0	0	0	0	0	2	0	0	3	400
"	John Dodd Jr.	2	0	0	0	0	0	0	0	78	0	0	127	625
"	Sammy Packard	1	0	0	0	0	0	0	0	45	0	0	23	110
"	G. C. Spencer	3	0	0	0	0	0	0	0	95	0	0	187	650
"	Woodie Wilson	2	0	0	0	0	0	0	0	31	0	0	47	525
"	**Total**	9	0	0	0	0	0	0	0	251	0	0	387	2,310
1963	Bob Hurt	1	0	0	0	0	0	0	0	144	0	0	48	75
Lifetime		21	0	0	0	0	0	0	1	1,660	0	0	1,865	$4,685

Pete DePaolo

Year	Driver	Starts	Poles	1	2	3	4	5	6–10	Laps	Laps Led	Races Led	Miles	$
1955	Buck Baker	7	1	1	1	1	0	1	3	1,142	337	2	884	3,410

Year	Driver	Starts	Poles	Finish 1	2	3	4	5	6–10	Laps	Laps Led	Races Led	Miles	$

Pete DePaolo *continued*

Year	Driver	Starts	Poles	1	2	3	4	5	6–10	Laps	Laps Led	Races Led	Miles	$
"	Johnny Mantz	1	0	0	0	0	0	0	0	46	0	0	69	60
"	Marvin Panch	4	0	0	1	0	0	0	0	535	0	0	520	1,600
"	Chuck Stevenson	1	0	0	0	0	0	0	0	43	0	0	65	60
"	Speedy Thompson	2	0	1	0	0	0	0	0	270	158	1	370	2,900
"	Joe Weatherly	1	0	0	0	0	0	0	0	29	0	0	44	60
"	**Total**	7	1	2	2	1	0	1	3	2,065	495	3	1,951	8,090
1956	Bill Amick	13	0	0	1	3	1	2	3	2,446	10	2	1,631	5,381
"	Billy Carden	5	0	0	0	0	0	0	2	622	0	0	310	550
"	Ralph Earnhardt	1	1	0	1	0	0	0	0	250	15	1	100	625
"	Bob Flock	1	0	0	0	0	0	0	0	52	0	0	52	50
"	Fonty Flock	1	0	0	0	0	0	0	1	194	0	0	78	150
"	Junior Johnson	2	0	0	0	0	0	0	0	211	43	1	88	200
"	Ralph Moody	35	5	4	5	2	1	1	8	5,258	312	6	3,506	15,493
"	Marvin Panch	1	0	0	0	1	0	0	0	359	43	1	494	3,370
"	Fireball Roberts	33	3	5	1	2	7	2	5	5,695	470	10	3,789	14,742
"	Jack Smith	1	0	0	0	0	0	0	0	109	0	0	55	100
"	Speedy Thompson	1	0	0	0	0	0	1	0	193	67	1	97	310
"	Curtis Turner	2	0	0	0	0	0	0	0	320	0	0	236	200
"	Joe Weatherly	2	0	0	1	0	0	0	1	594	20	1	297	1,175
"	**Total**	37	9	9	9	8	9	6	20	16,303	980	17	10,731	42,346
1957	Allen Adkins	1	0	0	0	0	0	0	1	158	0	0	99	250
"	Bill Amick	3	0	0	0	1	0	0	0	199	0	0	100	480
"	Ralph Earnhardt	1	0	0	0	0	0	0	0	164	0	0	82	100
"	Paul Goldsmith	6	0	1	1	0	1	0	1	782	41	1	455	2,095
"	Ralph Moody	9	0	1	0	2	2	0	0	1,014	100	1	548	2,830
"	Marvin Panch	18	4	3	1	3	3	1	1	2,496	349	8	1,539	7,375
"	Jim Reed	1	0	0	0	0	0	0	0	0	0	0	0	0
"	Fireball Roberts	17	3	5	4	0	1	1	2	2,795	744	10	1,649	8,905
"	Curtis Turner	5	1	0	2	0	0	0	1	617	2	1	370	3,045
"	Joe Weatherly	4	0	0	0	0	0	0	1	248	0	0	143	525
"	**Total**	18	8	10	8	6	7	2	7	8,473	**1,236**	**13**	4,983	25,605
Lifetime		62	18	21	19	15	16	9	30	26,841	2,711	33	17,665	$76,041

Ernie Derr

Year	Driver	Starts	Poles	1	2	3	4	5	6–10	Laps	Laps Led	Races Led	Miles	$
1953	Ernie Derr	1	0	0	0	0	0	0	0		0	0		25
Lifetime		1	0	0	0	0	0	0	0		0	0		$25

Bob Derrington

Year	Driver	Starts	Poles	1	2	3	4	5	6–10	Laps	Laps Led	Races Led	Miles	$
1964	Bob Derrington	18	0	0	0	0	0	0	2	1,897	1	1	1,819	3,580
1965	Bob Derrington	51	0	0	0	1	0	2	16	10,374	0	0	6,777	14,580
1966	Bob Derrington	7	0	0	0	0	0	0	0	868	0	0	1,040	2,465
"	Larry Manning	2	0	0	0	0	0	0	0	581	0	0	569	1,480
"	Bunk Moore	1	0	0	0	0	0	0	0	101	0	0	51	100
"	**Total**	10	0	0	0	0	0	0	0	1,550	0	0	1,660	4,045
Lifetime		79	0	0	0	1	0	2	18	13,821	1	1	10,256	$22,205

L. G. DeWitt

Year	Driver	Starts	Poles	1	2	3	4	5	6–10	Laps	Laps Led	Races Led	Miles	$
1965	John Sears	2	0	0	0	0	0	0	1	281	0	0	94	650
1966	John Sears	46	0	0	1	1	4	5	19	9,981	109	2	6,632	25,192
1967	Henley Gray	1	0	0	0	0	0	0	0	266	0	0	399	1,175
"	Elmo Langley	2	0	0	0	1	0	1	0	491	0	0	246	975
"	James Sears	1	0	0	0	0	0	0	0	72	0	0	72	505
"	John Sears	41	1	0	1	3	3	2	16	10,031	59	4	7,468	28,937
"	**Total**	44	1	0	1	4	3	3	16	10,860	59	4	8,184	31,592
1968	John Sears	49	0	0	0	1	1	3	19	11,077	0	0	7,861	29,179
1969	Jim Hurtubise	1	0	0	0	0	0	0	0	63	0	0	168	1,125
"	John Sears	51	0	0	1	3	7	6	10	11,617	18	3	8,911	51,556
"	LeeRoy Yarbrough	1	0	0	0	0	0	1	0	196	2	1	294	675
"	**Total**	52	0	0	1	3	7	7	10	11,876	20	4	9,373	53,356
1970	Benny Parsons	43	1	0	1	2	4	5	10	8,929	164	6	8,137	57,332
"	James Sears	1	0	0	0	0	0	0	1	448	0	0	456	1,390
"	John Sears	1	0	0	0	0	0	0	0	40	0	0	20	200
"	Buddy Young	2	0	0	0	0	0	0	1	501	0	0	569	1,980
"	**Total**	44	1	0	1	2	4	5	12	9,918	164	6	9,182	60,902
1971	Ray Hendrick	1	0	0	0	0	0	0	0	295	0	0	300	665

Year	Driver	Starts	Poles	Finish						Laps	Laps Led	Races Led	Miles	$
				1	2	3	4	5	6–10					

L. G. DeWitt *continued*

Year	Driver	Starts	Poles	1	2	3	4	5	6–10	Laps	Laps Led	Races Led	Miles	$
"	Benny Parsons	35	0	1	2	5	1	4	5	7,981	144	4	7,633	55,896
"	**Total**	35	0	1	2	5	1	4	5	8,276	144	4	7,933	56,561
1972	Benny Parsons	31	0	0	1	0	8	1	9	7,922	19	2	9,463	102,043
1973	Benny Parsons	28	0	1	3	3	3	5	6	9,311	374	8	10,047	182,321
1974	Jan Opperman	1	0	0	0	0	0	0	1	188	0	0	470	1,850
"	Benny Parsons	30	0	0	2	2	5	2	3	8,120	87	11	8,865	185,080
"	**Total**	30	0	0	2	2	5	2	4	8,308	87	11	9,335	186,930
1975	Benny Parsons	30	3	1	3	3	3	1	6	8,198	496	16	8,454	214,354
1976	David Hobbs	1	0	0	0	0	0	0	0	68	2	1	170	1,900
"	Benny Parsons	30	2	2	2	7	2	5	5	8,679	455	15	10,403	270,043
"	Earl Ross	1	0	0	0	0	0	0	0	28	0	0	70	2,025
"	**Total**	30	2	2	2	7	2	5	5	8,775	457	15	**10,643**	273,968
1977	Benny Parsons	30	3	4	3	10	0	3	2	9,410	1,399	25	10,755	359,341
1978	Bill Elliott	1	0	0	0	0	0	0	0	80	0	0	122	630
"	Benny Parsons	30	2	3	3	6	2	1	6	9,609	824	21	10,832	329,993
"	**Total**	30	2	3	3	6	2	1	6	9,689	824	21	10,953	330,623
1979	Joe Millikan	31	1	0	1	1	0	3	15	9,122	188	8	10,509	229,713
1980	Joe Millikan	9	0	0	0	0	1	1	3	2,172	4	2	1,893	59,240
Lifetime		521	13	12	24	48	44	49	138	135,176	4,344	128	131,313	$2,195,965

Ray DeWitt (See also Ulrich-DeWitt)

Year	Driver	Starts	Poles	1	2	3	4	5	6–10	Laps	Laps Led	Races Led	Miles	$
1990	Ted Musgrave	4	0	0	0	0	0	0	0	786	0	0	1,019	17,190
1994	Tim Fedewa	1	0	0	0	0	0	0	0	487	0	0	487	8,565
"	Jimmy Hensley	15	0	0	0	0	0	0	0	3,460	2	2	5,142	188,115
"	Butch Miller	2	0	0	0	0	0	0	0	842	0	0	982	17,335
"	**Total**	18	0	0	0	0	0	0	0	4,789	2	2	6,611	214,015
1995	Ben Hess	1	0	0	0	0	0	0	0	196	0	0	490	35,785
Lifetime		23	0	0	0	0	0	0	0	5,771	2	2	8,120	$266,990

Clarence DeZalia

Year	Driver	Starts	Poles	1	2	3	4	5	6–10	Laps	Laps Led	Races Led	Miles	$
1955	Woody Arrington	1	0	0	0	0	0	0	0	4	0	0	4	0
"	Ed Cole Jr.	4	0	0	0	0	0	0	0	479	0	0	250	335
"	Clarence DeZalia	5	0	0	0	0	0	0	0	691	0	0	610	200
"	**Total**	9	0	0	0	0	0	0	0	1,174	0	0	864	535
1956	Ed Cole Jr.	10	0	0	0	0	0	0	1	1,226	0	0	835	850
1957	Ed Cole Jr.	1	0	0	0	0	0	0	0	163	0	0	82	100
"	Clarence DeZalia	25	0	0	0	0	0	0	6	4,059	0	0	2,119	3,308
"	**Total**	26	0	0	0	0	0	0	6	4,222	0	0	2,200	3,408
1958	Clarence DeZalia	27	0	0	0	0	0	0	6	4,073	0	0	2,412	3,004
1959	Clarence DeZalia	1	0	0	0	0	0	0	0	136	0	0	45	60
Lifetime		73	0	0	0	0	0	0	13	10,831	0	0	6,356	$7,857

Eduardo Dibos

Year	Driver	Starts	Poles	1	2	3	4	5	6–10	Laps	Laps Led	Races Led	Miles	$
1959	Eduardo Dibos	3	0	0	0	0	0	2	0	181	0	0	453	1,050
Lifetime		3	0	0	0	0	0	2	0	181	0	0	453	$1,050

William Dickenson

Year	Driver	Starts	Poles	1	2	3	4	5	6–10	Laps	Laps Led	Races Led	Miles	$
1957	Dean Layfield	1	0	0	0	0	1	0	0	97	0	0	97	295
1958	Dean Layfield	7	0	0	0	0	0	0	0	522	0	0	433	370
Lifetime		8	0	0	0	0	1	0	0	619	0	0	530	$665

R. L. Diestler

Year	Driver	Starts	Poles	1	2	3	4	5	6–10	Laps	Laps Led	Races Led	Miles	$
1967	Gordon Johncock	4	0	0	0	0	0	0	0	160	0	0	391	2,350
"	John Martin	1	0	0	0	0	0	0	0	44	0	0	66	500
"	**Total**	4	0	0	0	0	0	0	0	204	0	0	457	2,850
Lifetime		4	0	0	0	0	0	0	0	204	0	0	457	$2,850

DiGard (Jim Gardner, Bill Gardner, and Mike DiProspero, co-owners)

Year	Driver	Starts	Poles	1	2	3	4	5	6–10	Laps	Laps Led	Races Led	Miles	$
1973	Donnie Allison	14	0	0	1	1	0	0	3	2,904	44	3	3,690	41,246
1974	Donnie Allison	21	2	0	1	1	2	2	4	5,101	182	10	5,761	60,315
1975	Donnie Allison	10	2	0	0	1	0	1	2	1,935	9	3	2,652	35,495
"	Johnny Rutherford	1	0	0	0	0	0	0	0	51	0	0	128	2,075

Year	Driver	Starts	Poles	Finish						Laps	Laps Led	Races Led	Miles	$
				1	2	3	4	5	6–10					

DiGard *continued*

Year	Driver	Starts	Poles	1	2	3	4	5	6–10	Laps	Laps Led	Races Led	Miles	$
"	Darrell Waltrip	11	0	1	0	2	0	0	1	2,760	271	5	2,354	61,842
"	**Total**	21	2	1	0	3	0	1	3	4,746	280	8	5,134	99,412
1976	Darrell Waltrip	30	3	1	3	4	1	1	2	7,780	534	10	8,088	204,193
1977	Darrell Waltrip	30	3	6	4	3	1	2	8	9,301	948	23	10,589	324,814
1978	Darrell Waltrip	30	2	6	6	4	1	2	1	9,445	2,171	26	10,541	413,908
1979	Darrell Waltrip	30	5	7	4	5	1	2	2	9,794	**2,066**	**25**	11,268	554,297
1980	Darrell Waltrip	30	5	5	3	2	5	0	1	8,815	1,956	27	9,363	399,661
"	Don Whittington	1	0	0	0	0	0	0	1	117	0	0	307	2,300
"	**Total**	30	5	5	3	2	5	0	2	8,932	1,956	27	9,670	401,961
1981	Ricky Rudd	31	3	0	3	4	3	4	3	8,942	443	12	9,879	395,685
1982	Bobby Allison	30	1	8	2	1	2	1	6	9,184	2,423	24	10,860	795,078
1983	Bobby Allison	30	0	6	5	6	1	0	7	10,038	1,755	25	11,526	883,010
"	Jimmy Insolo	1	0	0	0	0	0	0	0	1	0	0	3	840
"	**Total**	30	0	6	5	6	1	0	7	10,039	1,755	**25**	11,528	883,850
1984	Bobby Allison	30	0	2	1	2	4	4	5	9,051	1,160	23	10,545	641,049
1985	Bobby Allison	15	0	0	0	3	2	1	3	4,503	371	10	5,546	217,690
"	Ken Ragan	1	0	0	0	0	0	0	0	224	0	0	336	1,475
"	Greg Sacks	14	0	1	0	0	0	0	2	3,501	34	2	4,195	162,381
"	Dick Trickle	1	0	0	0	0	0	0	1	199	0	0	398	5,850
"	**Total**	28	0	1	0	3	2	1	6	8,427	405	12	10,475	387,396
1986	Trevor Boys	1	0	0	0	0	0	0	0	111	0	0	113	1,175
"	Willy T. Ribbs	3	0	0	0	0	0	0	0	516	0	0	540	3,520
"	Greg Sacks	8	0	0	0	0	0	0	1	1,181	0	0	1,743	54,810
"	Jeff Swindell	1	0	0	0	0	0	0	0	227	0	0	345	1,160
"	**Total**	13	0	0	0	0	0	0	1	2,035	0	0	2,741	60,665
1987	Rodney Combs	3	0	0	0	0	0	0	0	621	0	0	786	19,065
Lifetime		371	26	43	33	39	23	20	53	106,302	14,367	228	121,553	$5,282,934
				10th							**9th**	**8th**		

A. G. Dillard

Year	Driver	Starts	Poles	1	2	3	4	5	6–10	Laps	Laps Led	Races Led	Miles	$
1994	Ward Burton	26	1	0	1	0	0	0	1	5,230	74	5	6,180	304,700
1995	Gary Bradberry	2	0	0	0	0	0	0	0	572	0	0	742	19,280
"	Ward Burton	20	0	0	0	0	0	0	2	4,571	43	1	6,687	334,330
"	Jimmy Hensley	2	0	0	0	0	0	0	0	501	0	0	407	13,780
"	Greg Sacks	3	0	0	0	0	0	0	0	874	0	0	727	34,240
"	**Total**	27	0	0	0	0	0	0	2	6,518	43	1	8,563	401,630
Lifetime		53	1	0	1	0	0	0	3	11,748	117	6	14,743	$706,330

Ray Dillon

Year	Driver	Starts	Poles	1	2	3	4	5	6–10	Laps	Laps Led	Races Led	Miles	$
1981	Mark Martin	5	2	0	0	1	0	0	1	1,478	76	2	829	13,950
"	Morgan Shepherd	1	0	0	0	0	0	0	0	20	0	0	40	1,120
"	**Total**	6	2	0	0	1	0	0	1	1,498	76	2	869	15,070
Lifetime		6	2	0	0	1	0	0	1	1,498	76	2	869	$15,070

C. H. Dingler

Year	Driver	Starts	Poles	1	2	3	4	5	6–10	Laps	Laps Led	Races Led	Miles	$
1951	C. H. Dingler	3	0	0	0	0	0	0	0		0	0		100
1952	C. H. Dingler	1	0	0	0	0	0	0	0	160	0	0	80	35
1953	C. H. Dingler	4	0	0	0	0	0	0	2	119	0	0	60	200
1954	C. H. Dingler	3	0	0	0	0	0	0	1	383	0	0	348	175
1955	C. H. Dingler	1	0	0	0	0	0	0	0	8	0	0	4	0
1956	C. H. Dingler	3	0	0	0	0	0	0	0	181	0	0	239	200
Lifetime		15	0	0	0	0	0	0	3	851	0	0	730	$710

Dingman Brothers (Billy and Richie Dingman, co-owners)

Year	Driver	Starts	Poles	1	2	3	4	5	6–10	Laps	Laps Led	Races Led	Miles	$
1986	Tommy Riggins	1	0	0	0	0	0	0	0	89	0	0	216	3,525
"	Al Unser	1	0	0	0	0	0	0	0	110	0	0	288	2,360
"	**Total**	2	0	0	0	0	0	0	0	199	0	0	504	5,885
1987	Greg Sacks	16	0	0	0	0	0	0	0	2,705	1	1	4,254	44,815
1988	Greg Sacks	8	0	0	0	0	0	0	2	1,194	0	0	2,420	44,500
1989	Mickey Gibbs	2	0	0	0	0	0	0	0	505	0	0	969	6,535
"	Jim Sauter	1	0	0	0	0	0	0	0	5	0	0	13	2,715
"	**Total**	3	0	0	0	0	0	0	0	510	0	0	981	9,250
Lifetime		29	0	0	0	0	0	0	2	4,608	1	1	8,159	$104,450

Year	Driver	Starts	Poles	Finish 1	2	3	4	5	6–10	Laps	Laps Led	Races Led	Miles	$

Dave Dion

Year	Driver	Starts	Poles	1	2	3	4	5	6–10	Laps	Laps Led	Races Led	Miles	$
1978	Dave Dion	4	0	0	0	0	0	0	0	335	0	0	314	2,285
1979	Dave Dion	1	0	0	0	0	0	0	0	380	0	0	206	675
1980	Dave Dion	4	0	0	0	0	0	0	1	1,075	0	0	1,171	5,015
1981	Dave Dion	1	0	0	0	0	0	0	0	143	0	0	78	615
1983	Dave Dion	1	0	0	0	0	0	0	0	50	0	0	27	700
Lifetime		11	0	0	0	0	0	0	1	1,983	0	0	1,795	$9,290

Sam DiRusso

Year	Driver	Starts	Poles	1	2	3	4	5	6–10	Laps	Laps Led	Races Led	Miles	$
1953	Sam DiRusso	2	0	0	0	0	0	0	1	213	0	0	225	75
Lifetime		2	0	0	0	0	0	0	1	213	0	0	225	$75

John Ditz

Year	Driver	Starts	Poles	1	2	3	4	5	6–10	Laps	Laps Led	Races Led	Miles	$
1954	Arden Mounts	1	0	0	0	0	0	0	0	40	0	0	30	25
"	Dick Rathmann	28	4	2	5	7	6	1	3	4,524	621	10	3,094	14,314
"	Donald Thomas	6	0	0	1	0	1	0	1	772	53	1	469	1,350
"	**Total**	30	4	2	6	7	7	1	4	5,336	674	11	3,593	15,689
1955	Dick Rathmann	17	3	0	2	2	3	0	1	1,985	176	5	1,172	4,203
Lifetime		47	7	2	8	9	10	1	5	7,321	850	16	4,765	$19,892

J. I. Divers

Year	Driver	Starts	Poles	1	2	3	4	5	6–10	Laps	Laps Led	Races Led	Miles	$
1961	Wes Morgan	3	0	0	0	0	0	0	1	493	0	0	573	405
"	Bill Morton	1	0	0	0	0	0	0	0	182	0	0	46	125
"	**Total**	4	0	0	0	0	0	0	1	675	0	0	618	530
Lifetime		4	0	0	0	0	0	0	1	675	0	0	618	$530

Robert Dixon

Year	Driver	Starts	Poles	1	2	3	4	5	6–10	Laps	Laps Led	Races Led	Miles	$
1949	Raymond Lewis	1	0	0	0	0	0	0	1	194	0	0	97	75
Lifetime		1	0	0	0	0	0	0	1	194	0	0	97	$75

Thee Dixon

Year	Driver	Starts	Poles	1	2	3	4	5	6–10	Laps	Laps Led	Races Led	Miles	$
1990	Mike Skinner	1	0	0	0	0	0	0	0	230	0	0	234	2,825
"	Mike Potter	0												1,500
"	**Total**	1	0	0	0	0	0	0	0	230	0	0	234	4,325
1991	Brian Ross	0												2,600
"	Mike Skinner	2	0	0	0	0	0	0	0	350	0	0	362	8,505
"	**Total**	2	0	0	0	0	0	0	0	350	0	0	362	11,105
1992	Bob Schacht	1	0	0	0	0	0	0	0	245	0	0	368	5,725
"	Mike Skinner	2	0	0	0	0	0	0	0	929	0	0	945	13,450
"	**Total**	3	0	0	0	0	0	0	0	1,174	0	0	1,312	19,175
1993	Ken Bouchard	3	0	0	0	0	0	0	0	503	0	0	849	25,785
"	Jim Sauter	1	0	0	0	0	0	0	0	265	0	0	398	4,380
"	Dorsey Schroeder	0												2,700
"	**Total**	4	0	0	0	0	0	0	0	768	0	0	1,246	32,865
Lifetime		10	0	0	0	0	0	0	0	2,522	0	0	3,154	$67,470

John Dodd Sr.

Year	Driver	Starts	Poles	1	2	3	4	5	6–10	Laps	Laps Led	Races Led	Miles	$
1954	John Dodd Jr.	1	0	0	0	0	0	0	1	161	0	0	81	150
"	John Dodd,Sr.	1	0	0	0	0	0	0	1	240	0	0	240	300
"	**Total**	2	0	0	0	0	0	0	2	401	0	0	321	450
1955	John Dodd Jr.	13	0	0	0	0	0	1	6	1,653	0	0	915	1,695
"	John Dodd,Sr.	2	0	0	0	0	0	0	0	292	0	0	160	100
"	Elmo Langley	1	0	0	0	0	0	0	0	174	0	0	87	50
"	**Total**	13	0	0	0	0	0	1	6	2,119	0	0	1,162	1,845
1956	John Dodd Jr.	4	0	0	0	0	0	0	1	372	0	0	180	100
"	John Dodd,Sr.	1	0	0	0	0	0	0	0	28	0	0	14	0
"	**Total**	5	0	0	0	0	0	0	1	400	0	0	194	100
1957	John Dodd Jr.	1	0	0	0	0	0	0	0	67	0	0	34	25
"	John Dodd,Sr.	1	0	0	0	0	0	0	1	189	0	0	95	140
"	**Total**	2	0	0	0	0	0	0	1	256	0	0	128	165
1958	John Dodd,Sr.	1	0	0	0	0	0	0	0	290	0	0	290	150
1959	John Dodd,Sr.	3	0	0	0	0	0	0	1	704	0	0	352	540
"	Ralph Moody	1	0	0	0	0	0	0	1	197	0	0	99	200
"	**Total**	4	0	0	0	0	0	0	2	901	0	0	451	740

Year	Driver	Starts	Poles	Finish						Laps	Laps Led	Races Led	Miles	$
				1	2	3	4	5	6–10					

John Dodd Sr. *continued*

Year	Driver	Starts	Poles	1	2	3	4	5	6–10	Laps	Laps Led	Races Led	Miles	$
1960	John Dodd Jr.	2	0	0	0	0	0	0	0	51	0	0	54	50
Lifetime		29	0	0	0	0	0	1	12	4,418	0	0	2,599	$3,500

Frank Dodge

Year	Driver	Starts	Poles	1	2	3	4	5	6–10	Laps	Laps Led	Races Led	Miles	$
1953	Eddie Skinner	3	0	0	0	0	0	0	1		0	0		175
1954	Bill Amick	1	0	0	1	0	0	0	0	250	0	0	250	1,500
"	Bill Blair	1	0	0	0	0	0	0	0	93	0	0	47	0
"	Laird Bruner	3	0	0	0	0	0	1	0	370	0	0	195	325
"	Blackie Pitt	1	0	0	0	0	0	0	0	119	0	0	60	25
"	Eddie Skinner	15	0	0	0	0	0	0	1	2,044	0	0	1,659	1,017
"	**Total**	21	0	0	1	0	0	1	1	2,876	0	0	2,210	2,867
1955	Eddie Skinner	38	0	0	0	0	0	4	11	5,473	0	0	3,629	4,737
1956	Eddie Skinner	4	0	0	0	0	0	0	0	335	0	0	150	100
Lifetime		66	0	0	1	0	0	5	13	8,684	0	0	5,989	$7,879

Johnny Dodson

Year	Driver	Starts	Poles	1	2	3	4	5	6–10	Laps	Laps Led	Races Led	Miles	$
1956	Johnny Dodson	9	0	0	0	0	0	0	3	1,587	0	0	1,213	1,250
1957	Johnny Dodson	1	0	0	0	0	0	0	0	141	0	0	71	100
Lifetime		10	0	0	0	0	0	0	3	1,728	0	0	1,284	$1,350

Doe & Associates

Year	Driver	Starts	Poles	1	2	3	4	5	6–10	Laps	Laps Led	Races Led	Miles	$
1988	Jay Sommers	1	0	0	0	0	0	0	0	280	0	0	280	1,510
Lifetime		1	0	0	0	0	0	0	0	280	0	0	280	$1,510

Jack Doering

Year	Driver	Starts	Poles	1	2	3	4	5	6–10	Laps	Laps Led	Races Led	Miles	$
1966	Jack Goodwin	1	0	0	0	0	0	0	0	35	0	0	88	100
1974	Dick Trickle	1	0	0	0	0	0	0	1	389	0	0	584	3,825
Lifetime		2	0	0	0	0	0	0	1	424	0	0	671	$3,925

Junie Donlavey

Year	Driver	Starts	Poles	1	2	3	4	5	6–10	Laps	Laps Led	Races Led	Miles	$
1950	Runt Harris	1	0	0	0	0	0	0	0	41	0	0	21	0
1952	Joe Weatherly	1	0	0	0	0	0	0	0	376	0	0	470	150
1957	Runt Harris	1	0	0	0	0	0	0	0	50	0	0	69	100
"	Emanuel Zervakis	3	0	0	0	0	0	0	0	892	0	0	669	525
"	**Total**	4	0	0	0	0	0	0	0	942	0	0	737	625
1958	Emanuel Zervakis	6	0	0	0	0	0	0	0	457	0	0	378	465
1959	Runt Harris	1	0	0	0	0	0	1	0	193	0	0	97	250
1960	Runt Harris	3	0	0	0	0	0	0	0	391	0	0	233	350
"	Tiny Lund	1	0	0	0	0	0	0	0	52	0	0	78	250
"	Speedy Thompson	3	0	0	0	0	0	0	0	589	0	0	870	1,450
"	**Total**	7	0	0	0	0	0	0	0	1,032	0	0	1,181	2,050
1961	Johnny Roberts	1	0	0	0	0	0	0	0	113	0	0	57	75
1965	Sonny Hutchins	10	0	0	0	0	0	1	1	2,272	0	0	1,332	3,585
1966	Sonny Hutchins	4	0	0	0	0	0	0	0	222	0	0	318	2,190
1967	Sonny Hutchins	7	0	0	0	0	0	0	2	998	0	0	1,711	6,385
1968	Sonny Hutchins	4	0	0	0	0	0	0	0	420	0	0	528	2,810
1969	Sonny Hutchins	8	0	0	2	0	0	0	0	1,694	0	0	1,640	9,565
1970	Bill Dennis	3	0	0	0	0	0	0	0	385	0	0	521	2,460
"	Sonny Hutchins	2	0	0	0	0	0	1	0	722	0	0	612	2,575
"	LeeRoy Yarbrough	1	0	0	0	0	0	0	0	22	0	0	33	320
"	**Total**	6	0	0	0	0	0	1	0	1,129	0	0	1,166	5,355
1971	Bill Dennis	26	1	0	0	1	1	2	6	5,349	47	2	6,574	28,200
1972	Max Berrier	1	0	0	0	0	0	0	0	349	0	0	218	740
"	Dick Brooks	4	0	0	0	0	0	0	1	334	0	0	785	5,885
"	Richard Brown	1	0	0	0	0	0	0	0	48	0	0	72	663
"	Bill Dennis	2	0	0	0	0	0	1	0	570	0	0	475	3,520
"	Butch Hartman	1	0	0	0	0	0	1	0	326	0	0	489	3,570
"	Jimmy Hensley	2	0	0	0	0	0	1	0	548	0	0	288	1,900
"	Ron Hutcherson	1	0	0	0	0	0	0	0	29	0	0	29	550
"	Bobby Isaac	1	0	0	0	0	0	0	0	19	0	0	10	250
"	Fred Lorenzen	1	0	0	0	0	1	0	0	197	0	0	296	1,475
"	Jackie Oliver	7	0	0	0	0	1	0	0	1,034	0	0	1,486	11,575
"	David Pearson	1	0	0	0	0	0	0	0	86	1	1	47	680

Junie Donlavey *continued*

Year	Driver	Starts	Poles	1	2	3	4	5	6–10	Laps	Laps Led	Races Led	Miles	$
"	Johnny Rutherford	1	0	0	0	0	0	0	0	224	0	0	448	1,280
"	Ramo Stott	2	0	0	1	1	0	0	0	674	3	1	986	14,390
"	LeeRoy Yarbrough	2	0	0	0	0	0	1	0	334	2	1	506	5,495
"	**Total**	24	0	0	1	1	2	4	1	4,772	6	3	6,135	51,973
1973	Dick Brooks	8	0	0	0	0	0	1	4	2,073	0	0	2,625	16,425
"	Yvon DuHamel	1	0	0	0	0	0	0	1	381	0	0	238	800
"	Harry Gant	1	0	0	0	0	0	0	0	307	0	0	461	2,260
"	Charlie Glotzbach	1	0	0	0	0	0	0	1	483	0	0	491	2,625
"	Ray Hendrick	2	0	0	0	0	0	0	0	613	0	0	324	1,950
"	Jimmy Hensley	1	0	0	0	0	0	0	1	485	0	0	255	1,550
"	Bud Moore	1	0	0	0	0	0	0	0	174	0	0	238	1,225
"	Richie Panch	4	0	0	0	0	0	0	0	510	0	0	654	4,510
"	Eddie Pettyjohn	2	0	0	0	0	0	0	1	491	0	0	491	2,145
"	Jody Ridley	2	0	0	0	0	0	1	0	396	0	0	683	6,175
"	Ramo Stott	2	0	0	0	0	0	0	1	202	0	0	506	5,650
"	**Total**	22	0	0	0	0	0	2	9	6,115	0	0	6,966	45,315
1974	Bill Dennis	3	0	0	0	0	0	0	2	1,118	0	0	1,147	7,775
"	George Follmer	1	0	0	0	0	0	0	0	50	0	0	125	1,500
"	Harry Gant	1	0	0	0	0	0	0	1	387	0	0	242	1,055
"	Charlie Glotzbach	11	0	0	0	0	3	0	1	2,731	116	4	2,852	24,047
"	Jimmy Hensley	1	0	0	0	0	0	0	1	489	0	0	257	1,650
"	Bobby Isaac	1	0	0	0	0	0	0	0	59	0	0	81	1,115
"	Richie Panch	1	0	0	0	0	0	0	0	96	0	0	51	795
"	Eddie Pettyjohn	2	0	0	0	0	0	0	0	297	1	1	297	2,885
"	Paul Radford	1	0	0	0	0	0	0	0	20	0	0	11	750
"	Jody Ridley	2	0	0	0	0	0	0	0	163	0	0	205	2,935
"	**Total**	24	0	0	0	0	3	0	5	5,410	117	5	5,267	44,507
1975	Kenny Brightbill	1	0	0	0	0	0	0	1	480	0	0	480	2,000
"	Dick Brooks	25	0	0	1	2	3	0	9	7,344	60	4	8,052	93,001
"	Dick May	1	0	0	0	0	0	0	0	8	0	0	8	505
"	Jody Ridley	2	0	0	0	0	0	0	0	410	0	0	624	3,000
"	Earl Ross	1	0	0	0	0	0	0	0	372	0	0	558	2,965
"	**Total**	25	0	0	1	2	3	0	10	8,614	60	4	9,723	101,471
1976	Buck Baker	1	0	0	0	0	0	0	1	360	0	0	492	3,670
"	Dick Brooks	26	0	0	0	1	1	1	15	7,479	16	2	8,511	110,680
"	Gene Felton	1	0	0	0	0	0	0	0	308	0	0	469	1,635
"	Dick Trickle	1	0	0	0	0	0	0	0	142	0	0	213	1,225
"	**Total**	26	0	0	0	1	1	1	16	8,289	16	2	9,685	117,210
1977	Christine Beckers	1	0	0	0	0	0	0	0	33	0	0	83	695
"	Dick Brooks	27	0	0	1	0	1	5	13	7,833	8	2	9,117	147,629
"	**Total**	27	0	0	1	0	1	5	13	7,866	8	2	9,200	148,324
1978	Dick Brooks	27	0	0	0	0	1	4	12	8,124	24	2	9,326	132,350
1979	Jody Ridley	3	0	0	0	0	0	1	1	787	0	0	1,403	11,245
"	Ricky Rudd	28	0	0	0	2	0	2	13	8,836	22	4	9,917	150,898
"	**Total**	28	0	0	0	2	0	3	14	9,623	22	4	11,320	162,143
1980	Jody Ridley	31	0	0	0	0	0	2	16	9,579	2	2	10,976	204,883
1981	Jody Ridley	30	0	1	0	0	1	1	15	8,528	28	6	10,077	263,315
1982	Jody Ridley	30	0	0	0	0	0	0	10	7,983	4	4	8,789	308,664
1983	Dick Brooks	30	0	0	0	0	0	2	4	7,866	108	6	8,872	180,556
1984	Dick Brooks	30	0	0	0	1	0	0	4	8,157	185	3	9,320	192,407
1985	Ken Schrader	28	0	0	0	0	0	0	3	7,786	4	1	9,356	211,523
1986	Ken Schrader	29	0	0	0	0	0	0	4	8,047	2	2	9,697	235,904
1987	Ken Schrader	29	1	0	0	0	0	1	9	8,162	154	10	9,900	375,918
1988	Jimmy Means	1	0	0	0	0	0	0	0	394	0	0	246	3,650
"	Benny Parsons	27	0	0	0	0	0	0	1	7,420	82	3	8,744	210,755
"	**Total**	28	0	0	0	0	0	0	1	7,814	82	3	8,991	214,405
1989	Stan Barrett	4	0	0	0	0	0	0	0	391	0	0	613	11,500
"	Chad Little	8	0	0	0	0	0	0	0	1,936	0	0	2,594	44,690
"	Lennie Pond	1	0	0	0	0	0	0	0	394	0	0	296	3,475
"	**Total**	13	0	0	0	0	0	0	0	2,721	0	0	3,502	59,665
1990	Buddy Baker	8	0	0	0	0	0	0	0	1,326	1	1	2,353	40,085
"	Charlie Glotzbach	1	0	0	0	0	0	0	0	394	0	0	296	3,100
"	Ernie Irvan	3	0	0	0	0	0	0	0	983	0	0	1,191	37,605
"	**Total**	12	0	0	0	0	0	0	0	2,703	1	1	3,840	80,790
1991	Wally Dallenbach Jr.	11	0	0	0	0	0	0	0	2,070	0	0	3,244	54,020
"	Robby Gordon	2	0	0	0	0	0	0	0	584	0	0	781	27,265
"	Steve Perry	1	0	0	0	0	0	0	0	244	0	0	244	4,150
"	**Total**	14	0	0	0	0	0	0	0	2,898	0	0	4,269	85,435

Year	Driver	Starts	Poles	Finish						Laps	Laps Led	Races Led	Miles	$
				1	2	3	4	5	6–10	Laps	Led	Led	Miles	$

Junie Donlavey *continued*

Year	Driver	Starts	Poles	1	2	3	4	5	6–10	Laps	Laps Led	Races Led	Miles	$
1992	Todd Bodine	1	0	0	0	0	0	0	0	16	0	0	39	3,485
"	Pancho Carter	1	0	0	0	0	0	0	0	297	0	0	446	3,735
"	Charlie Glotzbach	7	0	0	0	0	0	0	0	1,528	0	0	2,564	48,060
"	Bobby Hillin Jr.	1	0	0	0	0	0	0	0	235	0	0	358	4,350
"	Dorsey Schroeder	1	0	0	0	0	0	0	0	196	0	0	490	25,750
"	Hut Stricklin	4	0	0	0	0	0	0	0	1,734	0	0	1,266	18,810
"	Kerry Teague	1	0	0	0	0	0	0	0	15	0	0	20	3,790
"	**Total**	16	0	0	0	0	0	0	0	4,021	0	0	5,183	107,980
1993	Bobby Hillin Jr.	30	0	0	0	0	0	0	0	8,343	3	1	9,768	263,540
1994	Bobby Hillin Jr.	3	0	0	0	0	0	0	0	1,044	0	0	1,251	48,455
"	Mike Wallace	22	0	0	0	0	0	1	0	6,672	13	1	8,629	265,115
"	**Total**	25	0	0	0	0	0	1	0	7,716	13	1	9,880	313,570
1995	Mike Wallace	26	0	0	0	0	0	0	1	6,819	1	1	8,807	428,006
1996	Dick Trickle	17	0	0	0	0	0	0	0	4,336	2	1	5,440	404,927
"	Mike Wallace	10	0	0	0	0	0	0	0	2,677	3	1	3,227	169,082
"	**Total**	27	0	0	0	0	0	0	0	7,013	5	2	8,667	574,009
Lifetime		717	2	1	5	8	13	31	156	190,207	892	67	223,723	$4,965,568
		5th								7th		7th		

Jack Donohue

Year	Driver	Starts	Poles	1	2	3	4	5	6–10	Laps	Laps Led	Races Led	Miles	$
1974	Jack Donohue	1	0	0	0	0	0	0	0	95	0	0	95	645
Lifetime		1	0	0	0	0	0	0	0	95	0	0	95	$645

Glen Dorrity

Year	Driver	Starts	Poles	1	2	3	4	5	6–10	Laps	Laps Led	Races Led	Miles	$
1968	Paul Dorrity	1	0	0	0	0	0	0	0	28	0	0	76	500
1969	Paul Dorrity	1	0	0	0	0	0	0	0	129	0	0	348	850
1970	Paul Dorrity	1	0	0	0	0	0	0	0	0	0	0	0	615
1971	Paul Dorrity	2	0	0	0	0	0	0	0	74	0	0	194	1,685
1972	Paul Dorrity	2	0	0	0	0	0	0	0	208	0	0	545	1,860
Lifetime		7	0	0	0	0	0	0	0	439	0	0	1,163	$5,510

Larry Dorsey

Year	Driver	Starts	Poles	1	2	3	4	5	6–10	Laps	Laps Led	Races Led	Miles	$
1954	Chuck Meekins	3	0	0	0	0	0	0	1	719	0	0	479	300
1955	Chuck Meekins	2	0	0	0	0	1	0	0	241	0	0	143	350
Lifetime		5	0	0	0	0	1	0	1	960	0	0	622	$650

Dan Dostinich

Year	Driver	Starts	Poles	1	2	3	4	5	6–10	Laps	Laps Led	Races Led	Miles	$
1967	Charles Prickett	1	0	0	0	0	0	0	1	162	0	0	437	1,000
"	Clyde Prickett	1	0	0	0	0	0	0	0	104	0	0	281	610
"	**Total**	1	0	0	0	0	0	0	1	266	0	0	718	1,610
1968	Clyde Prickett	1	0	0	0	0	0	0	0	140	0	0	378	700
1969	Jim Cook	1	0	0	0	0	0	0	0	3	0	0	8	750
Lifetime		3	0	0	0	0	0	0	1	409	0	0	1,104	$3,060

R. W. Douglass

Year	Driver	Starts	Poles	1	2	3	4	5	6–10	Laps	Laps Led	Races Led	Miles	$
1953	Red Douglass	1	0	0	0	0	0	0	0	33	0	0	135	25
Lifetime		1	0	0	0	0	0	0	0	33	0	0	135	$25

Fred Dove

Year	Driver	Starts	Poles	1	2	3	4	5	6–10	Laps	Laps Led	Races Led	Miles	$
1952	Fred Dove	7	0	0	0	0	0	0	2	779	0	0	587	340
1953	Fred Dove	19	0	0	0	0	0	0	4	734	0	0	687	975
1954	Fred Dove	10	0	0	0	0	0	0	2	1,245	0	0	770	525
"	Fred Starr	1	0	0	0	0	0	0	0	163	0	0	82	25
"	**Total**	10	0	0	0	0	0	0	2	1,408	0	0	852	550
1955	Fred Dove	6	0	0	0	1	0	0	2	790	0	0	396	725
Lifetime		42	0	0	0	1	0	0	10	3,711	0	0	2,521	$2,590

Russ Draime

Year	Driver	Starts	Poles	1	2	3	4	5	6–10	Laps	Laps Led	Races Led	Miles	$
1979	John Anderson	4	0	0	0	0	0	1	0	1,263	1	1	1,757	11,210
Lifetime		4	0	0	0	0	0	1	0	1,263	1	1	1,757	$11,210

Year	Driver	Starts	Poles	Finish						Laps	Laps Led	Races Led	Miles	$
				1	2	3	4	5	6–10					

Gary Drake

Year	Driver	Starts	Poles	1	2	3	4	5	6–10	Laps	Laps Led	Races Led	Miles	$
1954	Lee Petty	1	0	0	0	0	1	0	0	196	0	0	98	350
"	Blackie Pitt	26	0	0	0	0	0	0	6	3,612	0	0	2,448	1,900
"	**Total**	27	0	0	0	0	1	0	6	3,808	0	0	2,546	2,250
1955	Blackie Pitt	1	0	0	0	0	0	0	1	189	0	0	95	200
Lifetime		28	0	0	0	0	1	0	7	3,997	0	0	2,640	$2,450

Jerry Draper

Year	Driver	Starts	Poles	1	2	3	4	5	6–10	Laps	Laps Led	Races Led	Miles	$
1959	Jerry Draper	6	0	0	0	0	0	0	3	1,049	0	0	503	640
"	Roy Tyner	1	0	0	0	0	0	0	0	141	0	0	141	250
"	Bob Welborn	1	0	0	0	0	1	0	0	199	0	0	100	250
"	**Total**	8	0	0	0	0	1	0	3	1,389	0	0	743	1,140
Lifetime		8	0	0	0	0	1	0	3	1,389	0	0	743	$1,140

Larry Drover

Year	Driver	Starts	Poles	1	2	3	4	5	6–10	Laps	Laps Led	Races Led	Miles	$
1969	Larry Bock	1	0	0	0	0	0	0	0	85	0	0	226	1,225
Lifetime		1	0	0	0	0	0	0	0	85	0	0	226	$1,225

Philip Duffie

Year	Driver	Starts	Poles	1	2	3	4	5	6–10	Laps	Laps Led	Races Led	Miles	$
1982	Philip Duffie	5	0	0	0	0	0	0	0	1,166	0	0	2,273	13,755
1983	Philip Duffie	4	0	0	0	0	0	0	0	750	0	0	1,168	6,480
1988	Philip Duffie	1	0	0	0	0	0	0	0	332	0	0	454	2,540
1990	Philip Duffie	2	0	0	0	0	0	0	0	191	0	0	419	8,030
Lifetime		12	0	0	0	0	0	0	0	2,439	0	0	4,314	$30,805

Gerald Duke & Robert Davis

Year	Driver	Starts	Poles	1	2	3	4	5	6–10	Laps	Laps Led	Races Led	Miles	$
1959	Gerald Duke	1	0	0	0	0	0	0	0	249	0	0	125	125
"	Possum Jones	1	0	0	0	0	0	0	0	74	0	0	102	295
"	Jack Smith	1	0	0	0	0	1	0	0	196	0	0	98	275
"	Speedy Thompson	1	0	0	0	0	0	0	0	75	0	0	38	0
"	**Total**	4	0	0	0	0	1	0	0	594	0	0	362	695
1960	Gerald Duke	11	0	0	0	0	1	0	6	2,062	0	0	2,017	5,930
"	Charley Griffith	2	0	0	0	0	0	0	0	22	0	0	55	100
"	Elmo Langley	1	0	0	0	0	0	0	0	25	0	0	34	220
"	**Total**	14	0	0	0	0	1	0	6	2,109	0	0	2,106	6,250
1961	Gerald Duke	1	0	0	0	0	0	0	0	39	0	0	20	50
Lifetime		19	0	0	0	0	2	0	6	2,742	0	0	2,487	$6,995

J. R. Dunberry

Year	Driver	Starts	Poles	1	2	3	4	5	6–10	Laps	Laps Led	Races Led	Miles	$
1953	Buddy Shuman	1	0	0	0	0	0	0	0	4	0	0	16	0
Lifetime		1	0	0	0	0	0	0	0	4	0	0	16	$0

Glenn Dunnaway

Year	Driver	Starts	Poles	1	2	3	4	5	6–10	Laps	Laps Led	Races Led	Miles	$
1949	Glenn Dunnaway	5	0	0	0	1	0	0	2	394	1	1	197	810
1950	Glenn Dunnaway	7	0	0	1	0	1	0	1	866	0	0	731	1,275
1951	Glenn Dunnaway	3	0	0	0	0	0	0	2	0	0	0	0	200
Lifetime		15	0	0	1	1	1	0	5	1,260	1	1	928	$2,285

Roy Dutton

Year	Driver	Starts	Poles	1	2	3	4	5	6–10	Laps	Laps Led	Races Led	Miles	$
1967	Henley Gray	2	0	0	0	0	0	0	0	302	0	0	448	1,545
"	E. J. Trivette	6	0	0	0	0	0	0	1	1,289	0	0	961	1,810
"	**Total**	8	0	0	0	0	0	0	1	1,591	0	0	1,409	3,355
Lifetime		8	0	0	0	0	0	0	1	1,591	0	0	1,409	$3,355

Duane Duvall

Year	Driver	Starts	Poles	1	2	3	4	5	6–10	Laps	Laps Led	Races Led	Miles	$
1953	Red Duvall	1	0	0	0	0	0	0	0	37	0	0	152	75
Lifetime		1	0	0	0	0	0	0	0	37	0	0	152	$75

Carson Dyer

Year	Driver	Starts	Poles	1	2	3	4	5	6–10	Laps	Laps Led	Races Led	Miles	$
1951	Carson Dyer	1	0	0	0	0	0	0	0		0	0		25
Lifetime		1	0	0	0	0	0	0	0		0	0		$25

Year	Driver	Starts	Poles	Finish 1	2	3	4	5	6–10	Laps	Laps Led	Races Led	Miles	$

Ralph Dyer

Year	Driver	Starts	Poles	1	2	3	4	5	6–10	Laps	Laps Led	Races Led	Miles	$
1953	Ralph Dyer	6	0	0	0	0	0	0	3	480	0	0	384	600
Lifetime		6	0	0	0	0	0	0	3	480	0	0	384	$600

Dick Eagan

Year	Driver	Starts	Poles	1	2	3	4	5	6–10	Laps	Laps Led	Races Led	Miles	$
1950	Dick Eagan	1	0	0	0	0	0	0	0		0	0		0
1951	Dick Eagan	3	0	0	0	1	0	0	1		0	0		625
1952	Dick Eagan	2	0	0	0	0	0	0	1		0	0		100
Lifetime		6	0	0	0	1	0	0	2		0	0		$725

Harvey Eakin

Year	Driver	Starts	Poles	1	2	3	4	5	6–10	Laps	Laps Led	Races Led	Miles	$
1954	Harvey Eakin	6	0	0	0	0	0	0	0	711	0	0	885	400
1955	Harvey Eakin	3	0	0	0	0	0	0	0	307	0	0	416	210
1956	Harvey Eakin	2	0	0	0	0	0	0	0	278	0	0	278	100
1957	Harvey Eakin	5	0	0	0	0	0	0	0	763	0	0	575	375
Lifetime		16	0	0	0	0	0	0	0	2,059	0	0	2,154	$1,085

John Eanes

Year	Driver	Starts	Poles	1	2	3	4	5	6–10	Laps	Laps Led	Races Led	Miles	$
1950	Pee Wee Martin	1	0	0	0	0	0	0	0	344	0	0	430	100
"	Curtis Turner	15	4	4	1	1	1	0	0	1,580	1,110	12	1,198	8,140
"	**Total**	15	4	4	1	1	1	0	0	1,924	**1,110**	**12**	1,628	8,240
1951	Curtis Turner	8	0	2	0	0	0	0	1	1,014	409	5	836	2,680
1952	Jimmie Lewallen	2	0	0	0	0	0	0	0	100	0	0	82	25
"	Jim Paschal	2	0	0	0	0	0	0	2	261	0	0	187	200
"	Curtis Turner	7	0	0	0	0	0	1	0	500	12	1	320	290
"	**Total**	11	0	0	0	0	0	1	2	861	12	1	589	515
1953	Jimmie Lewallen	3	0	0	0	0	0	0	2	0	0	0	0	190
"	Curtis Turner	15	2	0	0	0	1	0	1	899	91	3	621	1,597
"	**Total**	18	2	0	0	0	1	0	3	899	91	3	621	1,787
1954	Dick Garlington	1	0	0	0	0	0	0	0	35	0	0	144	25
Lifetime		53	6	6	1	1	2	1	6	4,733	1,622	21	3,817	$13,247

Dale Earnhardt

Year	Driver	Starts	Poles	1	2	3	4	5	6–10	Laps	Laps Led	Races Led	Miles	$
1996	Jeff Green	2	0	0	0	0	0	0	0	91	0	0	228	16,835
Lifetime		2	0	0	0	0	0	0	0	91	0	0	228	$16,835

Sonny Easley

Year	Driver	Starts	Poles	1	2	3	4	5	6–10	Laps	Laps Led	Races Led	Miles	$
1977	Sonny Easley	2	0	0	0	0	0	0	1	245	0	0	624	3,200
Lifetime		2	0	0	0	0	0	0	1	245	0	0	624	$3,200

John Edgett

Year	Driver	Starts	Poles	1	2	3	4	5	6–10	Laps	Laps Led	Races Led	Miles	$
1981	Gary Kershaw	1	0	0	0	0	0	0	0	117	0	0	307	1,800
1982	Roy Smith	3	0	0	0	0	0	0	2	394	0	0	1,009	26,770
1983	Roy Smith	1	0	0	0	0	0	0	0	36	0	0	94	2,025
Lifetime		5	0	0	0	0	0	0	2	547	0	0	1,410	$30,595

Bill Edwards

Year	Driver	Starts	Poles	1	2	3	4	5	6–10	Laps	Laps Led	Races Led	Miles	$
1990	Larry Pearson	1	0	0	0	0	0	0	0	2	0	0	3	4,520
Lifetime		1	0	0	0	0	0	0	0	2	0	0	3	$4,520

Jimmy Edwards

Year	Driver	Starts	Poles	1	2	3	4	5	6–10	Laps	Laps Led	Races Led	Miles	$
1978	Glenn Jarrett	1	0	0	0	0	0	0	0	317	0	0	476	2,940
1979	Richard Brickhouse	1	0	0	0	0	0	0	0	15	0	0	23	870
Lifetime		2	0	0	0	0	0	0	0	332	0	0	498	$3,810

Jonathan Lee Edwards

Year	Driver	Starts	Poles	1	2	3	4	5	6–10	Laps	Laps Led	Races Led	Miles	$
1985	Jonathan Lee Edwards	2	0	0	0	0	0	0	0	633	0	0	640	3,220
1986	Jonathan Lee Edwards	4	0	0	0	0	0	0	0	1,114	0	0	1,405	8,030
1987	Jonathan Lee Edwards	2	0	0	0	0	0	0	0	226	0	0	309	3,055
Lifetime		8	0	0	0	0	0	0	0	1,973	0	0	2,355	$14,305

Year	Driver	Starts	Poles	1	2	3	4	5	6–10	Laps	Laps Led	Races Led	Miles	$
						Finish								

Fred Elder

1967	Ray Elder	1	0	0	0	0	0	0	0	23	0	0	62	500
1968	Ray Elder	1	0	0	0	0	0	0	0	37	0	0	100	500
1969	Ray Elder	4	0	0	0	0	0	0	4	642	0	0	1,523	7,200
1970	Ray Elder	4	0	0	0	0	0	0	1	441	0	0	1,127	4,570
1971	Ray Elder	4	0	1	1	0	0	0	1	564	70	2	1,439	30,595
1972	Ray Elder	3	0	1	0	0	1	1	0	493	50	2	1,268	23,165
1973	Ray Elder	3	0	0	0	1	0	0	0	381	0	0	977	9,225
1974	Ray Elder	2	0	0	0	0	0	0	0	37	0	0	94	1,435
1975	Ray Elder	3	0	0	0	0	1	0	0	368	1	1	956	8,020
1976	Ray Elder	2	0	0	0	0	2	0	0	254	0	0	665	11,715
Lifetime		27	0	2	1	1	4	1	6	3,240	121	5	8,211	$96,925

Ronnie Elder

1973	Lennie Pond	23	0	0	0	0	1	0	8	5,850	4	2	5,472	25,610
1974	Lennie Pond	22	0	0	0	0	1	4	6	6,684	17	6	7,191	55,990
1975	Lennie Pond	22	0	0	3	0	1	2	3	5,859	275	8	6,361	59,265
1976	Lennie Pond	30	0	0	2	0	4	4	9	8,182	217	10	10,055	159,701
1977	Lennie Pond	14	0	0	0	0	2	2	2	3,154	5	3	3,713	49,440
Lifetime		111	0	0	5	0	9	12	28	29,729	518	29	32,791	$350,006

Hoss Ellington

1968	Hoss Ellington	3	0	0	0	0	0	0	0	494	0	0	703	2,395
1969	Hoss Ellington	15	0	0	0	0	0	0	4	2,988	0	0	4,136	16,552
1970	Hoss Ellington	3	0	0	0	0	0	0	0	728	0	0	875	3,133
1972	Fred Lorenzen	7	0	0	0	0	2	0	1	1,604	4	1	2,537	18,030
"	John Sears	1	0	0	0	0	0	1	0	388	0	0	243	950
"	Cale Yarborough	3	0	0	0	0	0	0	2	812	9	1	1,106	4,857
"	**Total**	11	0	0	0	0	2	1	3	2,804	13	2	3,886	23,837
1973	Charlie Glotzbach	4	0	0	0	0	0	0	0	565	11	2	816	3,826
"	Gordon Johncock	6	0	0	0	0	1	0	0	1,307	0	0	1,802	10,600
"	Ramo Stott	1	0	0	0	0	0	0	0	46	1	1	122	740
"	**Total**	11	0	0	0	0	1	0	0	1,918	12	3	2,740	15,166
1974	A. J. Foyt	2	0	0	0	0	1	0	0	369	64	2	753	7,905
"	Charlie Glotzbach	3	0	0	0	0	1	0	0	851	10	1	1,098	10,125
"	Bobby Isaac	7	0	0	0	0	0	0	3	1,070	9	3	1,527	9,300
"	Sam McQuagg	3	0	0	0	0	0	0	2	698	1	1	1,221	6,100
"	**Total**	14	0	0	0	0	2	0	5	2,988	84	7	4,598	33,430
1975	Donnie Allison	2	0	0	0	1	0	0	0	306	23	1	679	10,100
"	A. J. Foyt	7	0	0	0	0	0	1	0	1,420	186	5	2,462	17,155
"	Charlie Glotzbach	1	0	0	0	0	0	0	1	395	0	0	593	5,355
"	Bobby Isaac	1	0	0	0	0	0	0	0	113	0	0	115	600
"	Gordon Johncock	1	0	0	0	0	0	0	0	47	0	0	125	1,230
"	**Total**	12	0	0	0	1	0	1	1	2,281	209	6	3,973	34,440
1976	Donnie Allison	9	0	1	0	1	0	0	3	2,178	104	4	3,254	48,445
"	A. J. Foyt	5	1	0	0	0	1	0	0	581	79	3	1,335	15,610
"	**Total**	13	1	1	0	1	1	0	3	2,759	183	7	4,589	64,055
1977	Donnie Allison	17	3	2	2	1	4	0	1	4,133	1,163	13	5,910	146,435
1978	Donnie Allison	14	0	1	2	2	1	1	0	3,232	209	12	5,300	123,530
1979	Donnie Allison	20	1	0	2	1	2	2	3	4,841	293	9	6,345	144,770
"	Neil Bonnett	1	0	0	0	0	0	0	0	9	0	0	9	1,035
"	**Total**	20	1	0	2	1	2	2	3	4,850	293	9	6,354	145,805
1980	Donnie Allison	3	0	0	0	0	0	1	1	894	35	2	1,303	44,285
"	David Pearson	9	1	1	2	1	0	0	1	1,787	172	7	3,252	94,330
"	**Total**	12	1	1	2	1	0	1	2	2,681	207	9	4,556	138,615
1981	Buddy Baker	15	0	0	1	0	2	3	3	3,519	110	9	5,788	113,735
"	David Pearson	1	0	0	0	0	0	0	1	365	0	0	499	4,850
"	**Total**	15	0	0	1	0	2	3	4	3,884	110	9	6,287	118,585
1982	Donnie Allison	1	0	0	0	0	0	0	0	36	0	0	55	745
"	Buddy Baker	7	1	0	0	0	0	1	1	1,491	18	6	2,511	68,605
"	Benny Parsons	2	0	0	0	0	0	0	0	149	1	1	231	2,430
"	Kyle Petty	6	0	0	0	0	0	0	0	974	0	0	1,745	12,105
"	**Total**	16	1	0	0	0	0	1	1	2,650	19	7	4,542	83,885
1983	Lake Speed	18	0	0	0	1	1	0	3	4,933	22	2	6,928	78,220
1984	Lake Speed	17	0	0	0	1	0	1	5	4,372	122	5	6,245	90,705
1985	Davey Allison	3	0	0	0	0	0	0	1	539	0	0	1,025	10,615
"	Pancho Carter	1	0	0	0	0	0	0	0	336	0	0	459	2,755
"	David Pearson	8	0	0	0	0	0	0	1	1,215	2	1	2,270	38,090
"	Rick Wilson	1	0	0	0	0	0	0	0	321	0	0	489	1,945
"	**Total**	12	0	0	0	0	0	0	2	2,411	2	1	4,242	53,405

Year	Driver	Starts	Poles	Finish 1	2	3	4	5	6–10	Laps	Laps Led	Races Led	Miles	$

Hoss Ellington *continued*

Year	Driver	Starts	Poles	1	2	3	4	5	6–10	Laps	Laps Led	Races Led	Miles	$
1986	Sterling Marlin	10	0	0	1	0	1	0	2	1,738	21	3	3,225	113,070
1987	Brett Bodine	14	0	0	0	0	0	0	0	2,908	20	3	4,485	51,145
"	Ron Bouchard	5	0	0	0	0	0	0	1	917	0	0	1,446	24,105
"	**Total**	19	0	0	0	0	0	0	1	3,825	20	3	5,931	75,250
1988	Dale Jarrett	8	0	0	0	0	0	0	0	1,004	1	1	2,363	44,655
Lifetime		260	7	5	10	9	17	11	40	56,673	2,690	99	87,384	$1,405,168

Bill Elliott

Year	Driver	Starts	Poles	1	2	3	4	5	6–10	Laps	Laps Led	Races Led	Miles	$
1995	Bill Elliott*	31	2	0	0	0	2	2	7	8,995	123	8	11,073	996,816
1996	Bill Elliott*	24	0	0	0	0	0	0	6	7,439	108	7	8,641	716,506
"	Bobby Hillin Jr.	1	0	0	0	0	0	0	0	491	0	0	262	25,735
"	Dorsey Schroeder	1	0	0	0	0	0	0	0	90	1	1	221	22,745
"	**Total**	26	0	0	0	0	0	0	6	8,020	109	8	9,123	764,986
Lifetime		57	2	0	0	0	2	2	13	17,015	232	16	20,196	$1,761,802

*Co-owned with Charles Hardy through first half of 1996.

Brent Elliott

Year	Driver	Starts	Poles	1	2	3	4	5	6–10	Laps	Laps Led	Races Led	Miles	$
1984	Brent Elliott	1	0	0	0	0	0	0	0	203	0	0	127	835
1985	Brent Elliott	3	0	0	0	0	0	0	0	837	0	0	469	3,210
1986	Brent Elliott	1	0	0	0	0	0	0	0	325	0	0	203	950
Lifetime		5	0	0	0	0	0	0	0	1,365	0	0	799	$4,995

Buddy Elliott

Year	Driver	Starts	Poles	1	2	3	4	5	6–10	Laps	Laps Led	Races Led	Miles	$
1949	Tim Flock	5	0	0	1	0	0	1	1	347	0	0	415	1,510
1950	Tim Flock	5	0	0	0	0	1	0	1	778	0	0	843	1,225
"	Frank Mundy	1	0	0	0	0	0	0	0	5	0	0	21	25
"	**Total**	5	0	0	0	0	1	0	1	783	0	0	864	1,250
Lifetime		10	0	0	1	0	1	1	2	1,130	0	0	1,278	$2,760

George Elliott

Year	Driver	Starts	Poles	1	2	3	4	5	6–10	Laps	Laps Led	Races Led	Miles	$
1966	Don Tilley	1	0	0	0	0	0	0	0	48	0	0	48	505
1971	Harry Gailey	1	0	0	0	0	0	0	0	141	0	0	375	990
1973	Charles Barrett	4	0	0	0	0	0	0	1	726	9	1	1,298	5,610
"	Jody Ridley	1	0	0	0	0	0	0	0	294	0	0	299	945
"	**Total**	5	0	0	0	0	0	0	1	1,020	9	1	1,597	6,555
1974	A. J. Reno	1	0	0	0	0	0	0	0	15	0	0	40	760
1976	Bill Elliott	4	0	0	0	0	0	0	0	419	0	0	640	4,870
"	David Hobbs	1	0	0	0	0	0	0	0	187	0	0	374	1,130
"	Al Holbert	1	0	0	0	0	0	0	0	7	0	0	11	855
"	**Total**	6	0	0	0	0	0	0	0	613	0	0	1,025	6,855
1977	Bill Elliott	10	0	0	0	0	0	0	2	2,082	0	0	3,319	20,075
1978	Bill Elliott	9	0	0	0	0	0	0	5	2,198	0	0	3,978	41,585
1979	Bill Elliott	10	0	0	1	0	0	0	3	2,061	8	3	3,763	49,605
1980	Bill Elliott	11	0	0	0	0	0	0	4	2,106	4	4	4,076	42,545
1981	Bill Elliott	13	1	0	0	0	1	0	6	2,777	33	3	4,444	68,570
Lifetime		67	1	0	1	0	1	0	21	13,061	54	11	22,664	$238,045

Bill Ellis

Year	Driver	Starts	Poles	1	2	3	4	5	6–10	Laps	Laps Led	Races Led	Miles	$
1969	Richard Brickhouse	6	0	0	0	0	0	0	3	1,000	1	1	1,148	6,395
"	Sam McQuagg	3	0	0	0	0	0	0	2	1,056	0	0	845	2,625
"	Ramo Stott	1	0	0	0	1	0	0	0	188	4	1	500	7,050
"	**Total**	10	0	0	0	1	0	0	5	2,244	5	2	2,493	16,070
1970	Richard Brickhouse	2	0	0	0	0	0	1	1	247	0	0	618	3,625
"	Freddy Fryar	1	0	0	0	0	0	0	1	182	0	0	484	3,000
"	**Total**	3	0	0	0	0	0	1	2	429	0	0	1,102	6,625
1971	Jim Paschal	1	0	0	0	0	0	0	0	386	0	0	579	2,050
"	Pedro Rodriguez	1	0	0	0	0	0	0	0	16	0	0	40	0
"	**Total**	2	0	0	0	0	0	0	0	402	0	0	619	2,050
Lifetime		15	0	0	0	1	0	1	7	3,075	5	2	4,214	$24,745

Tommy Ellis

Year	Driver	Starts	Poles	1	2	3	4	5	6–10	Laps	Laps Led	Races Led	Miles	$
1981	Tommy Ellis	4	0	0	0	0	1	0	0	651	2	2	767	13,475

Year	Driver	Starts	Poles	1	2	3	4	5	6–10	Laps	Laps Led	Races Led	Miles	$

Tommy Ellis *continued*

Year	Driver	Starts	Poles	1	2	3	4	5	6–10	Laps	Laps Led	Races Led	Miles	$
1982	Tommy Ellis	2	0	0	0	0	0	0	0	642	0	0	348	3,720
Lifetime		6	0	0	0	0	1	0	0	1,293	2	2	1,115	$17,195

Ray Elston

Year	Driver	Starts	Poles	1	2	3	4	5	6–10	Laps	Laps Led	Races Led	Miles	$
1955	Leslie Young	1	0	0	0	0	0	0	0	21	0	0	21	25
Lifetime		1	0	0	0	0	0	0	0	21	0	0	21	$25

Jack Ely

Year	Driver	Starts	Poles	1	2	3	4	5	6–10	Laps	Laps Led	Races Led	Miles	$
1989	Jack Ely	1	0	0	0	0	0	0	0	204	0	0	204	1,800
Lifetime		1	0	0	0	0	0	0	0	204	0	0	204	$1,800

Adel Emerson

Year	Driver	Starts	Poles	1	2	3	4	5	6–10	Laps	Laps Led	Races Led	Miles	$
1990	Jack Sellers	1	0	0	0	0	0	0	0	41	0	0	103	3,225
1992	Jack Sellers	1	0	0	0	0	0	0	0	48	0	0	121	4,725
Lifetime		2	0	0	0	0	0	0	0	89	0	0	224	$7,950

Ernestine Emerson

Year	Driver	Starts	Poles	1	2	3	4	5	6–10	Laps	Laps Led	Races Led	Miles	$
1977	Jim Hurtubise	1	0	0	0	0	0	0	0	154	0	0	385	2,065
1978	Harry Gant	1	0	0	0	0	0	0	0	1	0	0	3	1,975
Lifetime		2	0	0	0	0	0	0	0	155	0	0	388	$4,040

Bob England

Year	Driver	Starts	Poles	1	2	3	4	5	6–10	Laps	Laps Led	Races Led	Miles	$
1969	Bob England	1	0	0	0	0	0	0	0	1	0	0	3	750
1970	Bob England	2	0	0	0	0	0	0	0	126	0	0	330	1,740
1971	Bob England	4	0	0	0	0	0	0	0	477	0	0	1,160	4,105
Lifetime		7	0	0	0	0	0	0	0	604	0	0	1,493	$6,595

Erick Erickson

Year	Driver	Starts	Poles	1	2	3	4	5	6–10	Laps	Laps Led	Races Led	Miles	$
1951	Erick Erickson	3	0	0	0	1	0	0	0		0	0		550
1954	Erick Erickson	5	0	0	0	0	0	1	1	921	0	0	952	1,115
1955	Erick Erickson	2	0	0	0	0	0	0	0	74	0	0	74	30
1956	Erick Erickson	5	0	0	0	0	0	0	1	736	0	0	639	365
Lifetime		15	0	0	0	1	0	1	2	1,731	0	0	1,665	$2,060

Ray Erickson

Year	Driver	Starts	Poles	1	2	3	4	5	6–10	Laps	Laps Led	Races Led	Miles	$
1954	Dick Rathmann	1	0	1	0	0	0	0	0	250	108	1	125	1,000
Lifetime		1	0	1	0	0	0	0	0	250	108	1	125	$1,000

Ron Esau

Year	Driver	Starts	Poles	1	2	3	4	5	6–10	Laps	Laps Led	Races Led	Miles	$
1976	Ron Esau	2	0	0	0	0	0	0	0	160	0	0	419	2,310
Lifetime		2	0	0	0	0	0	0	0	160	0	0	419	$2,310

Clay Esteridge

Year	Driver	Starts	Poles	1	2	3	4	5	6–10	Laps	Laps Led	Races Led	Miles	$
1965	Lionel Johnson	8	0	0	0	0	0	0	2	1,663	0	0	1,338	3,165
"	Wendell Scott	1	0	0	0	0	0	0	1	320	0	0	440	900
"	**Total**	9	0	0	0	0	0	0	3	1,983	0	0	1,778	4,065
1966	Lionel Johnson	5	0	0	0	0	0	0	0	328	0	0	274	1,895
Lifetime		14	0	0	0	0	0	0	3	2,311	0	0	2,051	$5,960

Tootle Estes

Year	Driver	Starts	Poles	1	2	3	4	5	6–10	Laps	Laps Led	Races Led	Miles	$
1958	Herb Estes	10	0	0	0	0	0	0	3	2,010	0	0	1,562	1,895
"	Tiny Lund	2	0	0	0	0	0	0	0	152	0	0	99	185
"	**Total**	12	0	0	0	0	0	0	3	2,162	0	0	1,661	2,080
Lifetime		12	0	0	0	0	0	0	3	2,162	0	0	1,661	$2,080

Jack Etheridge

Year	Driver	Starts	Poles	1	2	3	4	5	6–10	Laps	Laps Led	Races Led	Miles	$
1949	Jack Etheridge	1	0	0	0	0	0	0	1		0	0		75
1967	Jack Etheridge	3	0	0	0	0	0	0	0	160	0	0	84	645

Bill France Sr.
© *International Speedway Corporation (ISC)/NASCAR*

Tiny Lund
© *ISC/NASCAR*

Joe Weatherly
© *Daytona International Speedway*

Glenn "Fireball" Roberts
© *ISC/NASCAR*

Herb Thomas
© ISC/NASCAR

Curtis Turner
© ISC/NASCAR

Bobby Isaac and David Pearson
© ISC/NASCAR

Bud Moore, Buck Baker, and Jack Smith
© ISC/NASCAR

Ned Jarrett and Marvin Panch
© ISC/NASCAR

Bob, Tim, and Fonty Flock
© ISC/NASCAR

David Pearson
© ISC/NASCAR

Ralph Moody and Fred Lorenzen
© ISC/NASCAR

Wendell Scott
© ISC/NASCAR

Cale Yarborough and Junior Johnson
© ISC/NASCAR

Tim Richmond
© ISC/NASCAR

Lee, Kyle, and Richard Petty
© ISC/NASCAR

Richard Petty, Bud Moore, and Buddy Baker
© ISC/NASCAR

Dale Earnhardt and Neil Bonnett
© ISC/NASCAR

Bobby Allison

Benny Parsons

Davey Allison

Alan Kulwicki

Bill Elliott

Ricky Rudd

Mark Martin

Rusty Wallace

Harry Gant

A.J. Foyt

Richard Petty

Dale Jarrett

Darrell Waltrip

Sterling Marlin

Ernie Irvan

Jeff Gordon

Dale Earnhardt

Year	Driver	Starts	Poles	Finish 1	2	3	4	5	6–10	Laps	Laps Led	Races Led	Miles	$

Jack Etheridge *continued*

Year	Driver	Starts	Poles	1	2	3	4	5	6–10	Laps	Laps Led	Races Led	Miles	$
1969	Jack Etheridge	1	0	0	0	0	0	0	0	7	0	0	4	100
Lifetime		5	0	0	0	0	0	0	1	167	0	0	88	$820

Ernest Eury

Year	Driver	Starts	Poles	1	2	3	4	5	6–10	Laps	Laps Led	Races Led	Miles	$
1966	Buddy Baker	3	0	0	0	0	0	0	1	772	0	0	457	770
"	Jimmy Helms	1	0	0	0	0	0	0	0	6	0	0	2	100
"	**Total**	4	0	0	0	0	0	0	1	778	0	0	458	870
1971	Ernest Eury	1	0	0	0	0	0	0	0	1	0	0	1	200
Lifetime		5	0	0	0	0	0	0	1	779	0	0	459	$1,070

Gene Evans

Year	Driver	Starts	Poles	1	2	3	4	5	6–10	Laps	Laps Led	Races Led	Miles	$
1974	Johnny Barnes	1	0	0	0	0	0	0	0	116	0	0	158	700
Lifetime		1	0	0	0	0	0	0	0	116	0	0	158	$700

Dave Everett

Year	Driver	Starts	Poles	1	2	3	4	5	6–10	Laps	Laps Led	Races Led	Miles	$
1956	Herb Estes	1	0	0	0	0	0	0	0	178	0	0	89	100
"	Wayne Fielden	2	0	0	0	0	0	0	1	361	0	0	181	200
"	Ken Milligan	3	0	0	0	0	0	0	0	255	0	0	175	200
"	**Total**	6	0	0	0	0	0	0	1	794	0	0	444	500
Lifetime		6	0	0	0	0	0	0	1	794	0	0	444	$500

Don Every

Year	Driver	Starts	Poles	1	2	3	4	5	6–10	Laps	Laps Led	Races Led	Miles	$
1959	Joe Eubanks	12	0	0	1	0	0	1	5	1,253	0	0	910	1,810
"	Cotton Owens	5	0	0	0	1	0	0	2	940	0	0	375	915
"	**Total**	17	0	0	1	1	0	1	7	2,193	0	0	1,285	2,725
1960	Joe Eubanks	7	0	0	0	0	0	1	1	822	0	0	687	1,310
1961	Joe Eubanks	2	0	0	0	0	0	0	0	448	0	0	672	1,475
Lifetime		26	0	0	1	1	0	2	8	3,463	0	0	2,644	$5,510

Freddie Farmer

Year	Driver	Starts	Poles	1	2	3	4	5	6–10	Laps	Laps Led	Races Led	Miles	$
1951	Freddie Farmer	4	0	0	0	0	0	0	0	447	0	0	540	150
Lifetime		4	0	0	0	0	0	0	0	447	0	0	540	$150

Dudley Farrell

Year	Driver	Starts	Poles	1	2	3	4	5	6–10	Laps	Laps Led	Races Led	Miles	$
1961	Nelson Stacy	15	0	1	0	1	2	0	4	3,024	144	4	3,281	26,760
Lifetime		15	0	1	0	1	2	0	4	3,024	144	4	3,281	$26,760

Bart Faucett

Year	Driver	Starts	Poles	1	2	3	4	5	6–10	Laps	Laps Led	Races Led	Miles	$
1961	Ralph Earnhardt	1	0	0	0	0	0	0	0	62	0	0	93	250
"	Woodie Wilson	5	0	0	0	0	0	0	1	828	0	0	1,324	2,625
"	**Total**	5	0	0	0	0	0	0	1	890	0	0	1,417	2,875
1962	Stick Elliott	1	0	0	0	0	0	0	0	341	0	0	512	350
"	Woodie Wilson	1	0	0	0	0	0	0	1	39	0	0	98	225
"	**Total**	2	0	0	0	0	0	0	1	380	0	0	609	575
Lifetime		7	0	0	0	0	0	0	2	1,270	0	0	2,026	$3,450

Doc Faustina

Year	Driver	Starts	Poles	1	2	3	4	5	6–10	Laps	Laps Led	Races Led	Miles	$
1971	Earl Brooks	2	0	0	0	0	0	0	0	450	0	0	662	2,095
"	Richard Childress	1	0	0	0	0	0	0	0	180	0	0	180	645
"	Doc Faustina	3	0	0	0	0	0	0	0	402	0	0	864	2,745
"	Dave Marcis	2	0	0	0	0	0	0	0	146	0	0	360	1,555
"	Dick May	1	0	0	0	0	0	0	0	268	0	0	402	590
"	Jim Vandiver	1	0	0	0	0	0	0	0	10	0	0	15	640
"	**Total**	10	0	0	0	0	0	0	0	1,456	0	0	2,484	8,270
1972	Doc Faustina	5	0	0	0	0	0	0	0	607	0	0	1,161	3,635
"	Mel Larson	1	0	0	0	0	0	0	0	209	0	0	418	760
"	J. D. McDuffie	1	0	0	0	0	0	0	0	3	0	0	2	275
"	**Total**	7	0	0	0	0	0	0	0	819	0	0	1,581	4,670
1973	Charlie Blanton	1	0	0	0	0	0	0	0	351	0	0	527	1,825
"	Wendell Scott	1	0	0	0	0	0	0	0	305	0	0	458	1,800
"	Dick Simon	2	0	0	0	0	0	0	1	264	0	0	689	3,700
"	**Total**	4	0	0	0	0	0	0	1	920	0	0	1,673	7,325

Year	Driver	Starts	Poles	Finish						Laps	Laps Led	Races Led	Miles	$
				1	2	3	4	5	6–10					

Doc Faustina *continued*

Year	Driver	Starts	Poles	1	2	3	4	5	6–10	Laps	Laps Led	Races Led	Miles	$
1974	Charlie Blanton	1	0	0	0	0	0	0	0	231	0	0	235	720
"	Earl Brooks	1	0	0	0	0	0	0	0	1	0	0	1	1,100
"	Neil Castles	1	0	0	0	0	0	0	0	21	0	0	21	780
"	Harry Gant	2	0	0	0	0	0	0	0	403	0	0	605	3,729
"	John Martin	3	0	0	0	0	0	0	0	267	0	0	599	3,420
"	Dick Simon	1	0	0	0	0	0	0	0	96	0	0	240	3,410
"	**Total**	9	0	0	0	0	0	0	0	1,019	0	0	1,701	13,159
1975	Neil Castles	2	0	0	0	0	0	0	0	354	0	0	213	1,055
"	Doc Faustina	1	0	0	0	0	0	0	0	116	0	0	290	880
"	**Total**	3	0	0	0	0	0	0	0	470	0	0	503	1,935
1976	Bruce Blodgett	1	0	0	0	0	0	0	0	447	0	0	235	800
"	Neil Castles	1	0	0	0	0	0	0	0	125	0	0	78	425
"	Doc Faustina	1	0	0	0	0	0	0	0	378	0	0	378	735
"	James Hylton	1	0	0	0	0	0	0	0	171	0	0	174	655
"	**Total**	4	0	0	0	0	0	0	0	1,121	0	0	865	2,615
Lifetime		37	0	0	0	0	0	0	1	5,805	0	0	8,806	$37,974

G. A. Faver

Year	Driver	Starts	Poles	1	2	3	4	5	6–10	Laps	Laps Led	Races Led	Miles	$
1953	Lou Faver	1	0	0	0	0	0	0	0	12	0	0	12	25
Lifetime		1	0	0	0	0	0	0	0	12	0	0	12	$25

Martin Fay

Year	Driver	Starts	Poles	1	2	3	4	5	6–10	Laps	Laps Led	Races Led	Miles	$
1970	Pat Fay	1	0	0	0	0	0	0	0	24	0	0	63	655
Lifetime		1	0	0	0	0	0	0	0	24	0	0	63	$655

Ross Ferguson

Year	Driver	Starts	Poles	1	2	3	4	5	6–10	Laps	Laps Led	Races Led	Miles	$
1971	Dick Brooks	3	0	0	0	0	0	0	0	250	0	0	212	1,821
Lifetime		3	0	0	0	0	0	0	0	250	0	0	212	$1,821

Ed Ferree

Year	Driver	Starts	Poles	1	2	3	4	5	6–10	Laps	Laps Led	Races Led	Miles	$
1992	Ed Ferree	1	0	0	0	0	0	0	0	50	0	0	123	4,035
1993	Ed Ferree	2	0	0	0	0	0	0	0	511	0	0	571	12,865
Lifetime		3	0	0	0	0	0	0	0	561	0	0	694	$16,900

Lynda Ferreri

Year	Driver	Starts	Poles	1	2	3	4	5	6–10	Laps	Laps Led	Races Led	Miles	$
1976	Janet Guthrie	5	0	0	0	0	0	0	0	1,183	0	0	2,015	8,179
1977	Janet Guthrie	19	0	0	0	0	0	0	4	5,031	5	1	6,182	38,045
1978	Janet Guthrie	7	0	0	0	0	0	0	1	1,147	0	0	2,406	18,120
Lifetime		31	0	0	0	0	0	0	5	7,361	5	1	10,603	$64,344

Jim Fiebelkorn

Year	Driver	Starts	Poles	1	2	3	4	5	6–10	Laps	Laps Led	Races Led	Miles	$
1951	Jim Fiebelkorn	15	0	0	1	0	0	0	3	624	0	0	463	1,200
Lifetime		15	0	0	1	0	0	0	3	624	0	0	463	$1,200

Joe Fields

Year	Driver	Starts	Poles	1	2	3	4	5	6–10	Laps	Laps Led	Races Led	Miles	$
1981	Joe Fields	6	0	0	0	0	0	0	0	1,681	0	0	1,160	7,750
1982	Joe Fields	3	0	0	0	0	0	0	0	738	0	0	397	2,610
1983	Joe Fields	3	0	0	0	0	0	0	0	1,064	0	0	787	4,315
1984	Joe Fields	2	0	0	0	0	0	0	0	661	0	0	661	1,915
Lifetime		14	0	0	0	0	0	0	0	4,144	0	0	3,005	$16,590

Wade Fields

Year	Driver	Starts	Poles	1	2	3	4	5	6–10	Laps	Laps Led	Races Led	Miles	$
1951	Wade Fields	1	0	0	0	0	0	0	0		0	0		25
Lifetime		1	0	0	0	0	0	0	0		0	0		$25

Lou Figaro

Year	Driver	Starts	Poles	1	2	3	4	5	6–10	Laps	Laps Led	Races Led	Miles	$
1954	Lou Figaro	3	0	0	0	0	0	0	2	461	0	0	403	425
Lifetime		3	0	0	0	0	0	0	2	461	0	0	403	$425

Year	Driver	Starts	Poles	Finish						Laps	Laps Led	Races Led	Miles	$
				1	2	3	4	5	6–10					

Corey Fillip

Year	Driver	Starts	Poles	1	2	3	4	5	6–10	Laps	Laps Led	Races Led	Miles	$
1987	Buddy Arrington	2	0	0	0	0	0	0	0	881	0	0	470	3,995
"	Eddie Bierschwale	1	0	0	0	0	0	0	0	392	0	0	245	1,430
"	Chet Fillip	4	0	0	0	0	0	0	0	620	0	0	896	23,375
"	Slick Johnson	1	0	0	0	0	0	0	0	11	0	0	7	1,125
"	Mike Potter	4	0	0	0	0	0	0	0	920	0	0	766	5,955
"	**Total**	12	0	0	0	0	0	0	0	2,824	0	0	2,384	35,880
Lifetime		12	0	0	0	0	0	0	0	2,824	0	0	2,384	$35,880

James Finch

Year	Driver	Starts	Poles	1	2	3	4	5	6–10	Laps	Laps Led	Races Led	Miles	$
1990	Jeff Purvis	4	0	0	0	0	0	0	0	653	0	0	617	11,070
1991	Jeff Purvis	6	0	0	0	0	0	0	0	888	0	0	1,486	46,205
1992	Jeff Purvis	2	0	0	0	0	0	0	0	338	0	0	535	10,625
1993	Jeff Purvis	3	0	0	0	0	0	0	0	378	0	0	980	27,175
1994	Jeff Purvis	6	0	0	0	0	0	0	0	942	0	0	1,981	70,040
1995	Jeff Purvis	6	0	0	0	0	0	0	0	631	0	0	1,441	86,505
1996	Jeff Purvis	4	0	0	0	0	0	0	0	532	0	0	1,364	91,127
Lifetime		31	0	0	0	0	0	0	0	4,362	0	0	8,405	$342,747

John Findlay

Year	Driver	Starts	Poles	1	2	3	4	5	6–10	Laps	Laps Led	Races Led	Miles	$
1958	John Findlay	1	0	0	0	0	0	1	0	189	0	0	95	225
1959	John Findlay	1	0	0	0	0	0	0	0	116	0	0	58	50
Lifetime		2	0	0	0	0	0	1	0	305	0	0	153	$275

Wallace Finney

Year	Driver	Starts	Poles	1	2	3	4	5	6–10	Laps	Laps Led	Races Led	Miles	$
1971	Phil Finney	1	0	0	0	0	0	0	0	357	0	0	193	400
1972	Phil Finney	1	0	0	0	0	0	0	0	321	0	0	174	450
1973	Phil Finney	1	0	0	0	0	0	0	0	55	0	0	146	910
1974	Phil Finney	1	0	0	0	0	0	0	0	100	0	0	266	1,010
1977	Phil Finney	1	0	0	0	0	0	0	0	148	0	0	225	1,145
1980	Phil Finney	2	0	0	0	0	0	0	0	188	0	0	476	3,850
Lifetime		7	0	0	0	0	0	0	0	1,169	0	0	1,481	$7,765

Bob Fish

Year	Driver	Starts	Poles	1	2	3	4	5	6–10	Laps	Laps Led	Races Led	Miles	$
1955	Fireball Roberts	2	1	0	0	0	0	0	0	69	4	1	201	140
1956	Tommy Thompson	1	0	0	0	0	0	0	0		0	0		0
1958	Fireball Roberts	1	0	0	0	0	0	0	1	37	0	0	152	250
Lifetime		4	1	0	0	0	0	0	1	106	4	1	353	$390

Lonnie Fish

Year	Driver	Starts	Poles	1	2	3	4	5	6–10	Laps	Laps Led	Races Led	Miles	$
1956	Larry Frank	1	0	0	0	0	0	0	0	77	0	0	39	50
1957	Larry Frank	4	0	0	0	0	0	0	0	1,113	0	0	935	995
"	Don Gray	3	0	0	0	0	0	0	0	549	0	0	604	325
"	George Green	11	0	0	0	0	0	0	2	1,779	0	0	928	1,435
"	Shep Langdon	2	0	0	0	0	0	0	0	268	0	0	268	0
"	George West	1	0	0	0	0	0	0	0		0	0		0
"	**Total**	15	0	0	0	0	0	0	2	3,709	0	0	2,734	2,755
1958	Tiny Lund	1	0	0	0	1	0	0	0	149	0	0	50	380
Lifetime		17	0	0	0	1	0	0	2	3,935	0	0	2,822	$3,185

Bob Fisher

Year	Driver	Starts	Poles	1	2	3	4	5	6–10	Laps	Laps Led	Races Led	Miles	$
1992	Ron Hornaday Jr.	2	0	0	0	0	0	0	0	373	0	0	482	11,290
Lifetime		2	0	0	0	0	0	0	0	373	0	0	482	$11,290

Bobby Fisher

Year	Driver	Starts	Poles	1	2	3	4	5	6–10	Laps	Laps Led	Races Led	Miles	$
1978	Bobby Fisher	2	0	0	0	0	0	0	0	33	0	0	22	1,410
1979	Bobby Fisher	1	0	0	0	0	0	0	0	136	0	0	204	1,465
Lifetime		3	0	0	0	0	0	0	0	169	0	0	226	$2,875

Jack Fisher

Year	Driver	Starts	Poles	1	2	3	4	5	6–10	Laps	Laps Led	Races Led	Miles	$
1952	Jack Fisher	1	0	0	0	0	0	0	0	95	0	0	95	25

Year	Driver	Starts	Poles	Finish						Laps	Laps Led	Races Led	Miles	$
				1	2	3	4	5	6–10					

Jack Fisher *continued*

Year	Driver	Starts	Poles	1	2	3	4	5	6–10	Laps	Laps Led	Races Led	Miles	$
"	Dick Stacey	1	0	0	0	0	0	0	0	175	0	0	175	25
"	**Total**	1	0	0	0	0	0	0	0	270	0	0	270	50
Lifetime		1	0	0	0	0	0	0	0	270	0	0	270	$50

Joe Fisher

Year	Driver	Starts	Poles	1	2	3	4	5	6–10	Laps	Laps Led	Races Led	Miles	$
1954	Art Watts	1	0	0	0	0	0	0	0	284	0	0	142	25
Lifetime		1	0	0	0	0	0	0	0	284	0	0	142	$25

Ken Fisher

Year	Driver	Starts	Poles	1	2	3	4	5	6–10	Laps	Laps Led	Races Led	Miles	$
1955	Ken Fisher	9	0	0	0	0	0	0	1	453	0	0	292	175
Lifetime		9	0	0	0	0	0	0	1	453	0	0	292	$175

J. M. Fitzgibbons

Year	Driver	Starts	Poles	1	2	3	4	5	6–10	Laps	Laps Led	Races Led	Miles	$
1955	Bill Blair	5	0	0	0	0	0	0	0	427	0	0	262	175
"	Sonny Hutchins	1	0	0	0	0	0	0	0	15	0	0	8	0
"	Blackie Pitt	7	0	0	0	0	0	0	2	806	0	0	443	660
"	Millard Wright	1	0	0	0	0	0	0	0	43	0	0	22	50
"	**Total**	14	0	0	0	0	0	0	2	1,291	0	0	734	885
1956	Red Farmer	3	0	0	0	0	0	0	0	324	0	0	162	125
"	Bobby Johns	1	0	0	0	0	0	0	1	349	0	0	480	700
"	**Total**	4	0	0	0	0	0	0	1	673	0	0	642	825
Lifetime		18	0	0	0	0	0	0	3	1,964	0	0	1,376	$1,710

Tommy Fleming

Year	Driver	Starts	Poles	1	2	3	4	5	6–10	Laps	Laps Led	Races Led	Miles	$
1969	Bobby Fleming	1	0	0	0	0	0	0	0	146	0	0	388	1,400
Lifetime		1	0	0	0	0	0	0	0	146	0	0	388	$1,400

Ray Fletcher

Year	Driver	Starts	Poles	1	2	3	4	5	6–10	Laps	Laps Led	Races Led	Miles	$
1955	Van Van Wey	1	0	0	0	0	0	0	0	247	0	0	340	60
Lifetime		1	0	0	0	0	0	0	0	247	0	0	340	$60

Sam Fletcher

Year	Driver	Starts	Poles	1	2	3	4	5	6–10	Laps	Laps Led	Races Led	Miles	$
1965	Johnny Allen	2	0	0	0	0	0	0	0	120	0	0	300	1,235
"	Bunkie Blackburn	2	0	0	0	0	0	0	0	155	0	0	220	925
"	Iggy Katona	1	0	0	0	0	0	0	1	251	0	0	377	850
"	Nelson Stacy	1	0	0	0	0	0	0	0	83	0	0	208	480
"	Curtis Turner	1	0	0	0	0	0	0	0	51	0	0	70	545
"	**Total**	7	0	0	0	0	0	0	1	660	0	0	1,174	4,035
Lifetime		7	0	0	0	0	0	0	1	660	0	0	1,174	$4,035

Ruby Flock

Year	Driver	Starts	Poles	1	2	3	4	5	6–10	Laps	Laps Led	Races Led	Miles	$
1949	Sara Christian	1	0	0	0	0	0	0	0	0	0	0	0	25
Lifetime		1	0	0	0	0	0	0	0	0	0	0	0	$25

Tim Flock

Year	Driver	Starts	Poles	1	2	3	4	5	6–10	Laps	Laps Led	Races Led	Miles	$
1958	Tim Flock	1	0	0	0	0	0	0	0	66	25	1	66	310
Lifetime		1	0	0	0	0	0	0	0	66	25	1	66	$310

City of Florence, S.C. (The city of Florence, S.C., bought the 1959 Daytona 500 winning car for Joe Caspolich to run in the Southern 500 at Darlington.)

Year	Driver	Starts	Poles	1	2	3	4	5	6–10	Laps	Laps Led	Races Led	Miles	$
1959	Joe Caspolich	1	0	0	0	0	0	0	0	342	0	0	470	470
Lifetime		1	0	0	0	0	0	0	0	342	0	0	470	$470

Jimmy Florian

Year	Driver	Starts	Poles	1	2	3	4	5	6–10	Laps	Laps Led	Races Led	Miles	$
	Jimmy Florian	10	1	1	0	1	1	0	3	1,060	40	1	850	2,610
	y Florian	9	0	0	0	0	2	0	3	0	0	0	0	1,100
	ian	6	0	0	0	0	0	0	2	283	0	0	188	175
	an	1	0	0	0	0	0	0	0	34	0	0	139	25
		26	1	1	0	1	3	0	8	1,377	40	1	1,178	$3,910

Year	Driver	Starts	Poles	Finish 1	2	3	4	5	6–10	Laps	Laps Led	Races Led	Miles	$

Bill Flowers

Year	Driver	Starts	Poles	1	2	3	4	5	6–10	Laps	Laps Led	Races Led	Miles	$
1970	Morgan Shepherd	3	0	0	0	0	0	0	0	522	0	0	241	965
Lifetime		3	0	0	0	0	0	0	0	522	0	0	241	$965

Larry Flynn

Year	Driver	Starts	Poles	1	2	3	4	5	6–10	Laps	Laps Led	Races Led	Miles	$
1959	Larry Flynn	4	0	0	0	0	0	0	0	206	0	0	283	275
Lifetime		4	0	0	0	0	0	0	0	206	0	0	283	$275

Sam Fogle

Year	Driver	Starts	Poles	1	2	3	4	5	6–10	Laps	Laps Led	Races Led	Miles	$
1965	Doug Cooper	1	0	0	0	0	0	0	0	124	0	0	62	110
1965	Curtis Crider	1	0	0	0	0	0	0	1	157	0	0	141	225
"	Darel Dieringer	3	0	0	0	0	0	0	0	129	0	0	65	320
"	Bob Grossman	1	0	0	0	0	0	0	0	13	0	0	30	175
"	Elmo Henderson	1	0	0	0	0	0	0	0	101	0	0	51	130
"	Harvey Jones	1	0	0	0	0	0	1	0	195	0	0	98	275
"	Possum Jones	1	0	0	0	0	0	0	0	0	0	0	0	100
"	Bud Moore	1	0	0	0	0	0	0	1	376	0	0	141	225
"	J. T. Putney	1	0	0	0	0	0	0	1	233	0	0	47	175
"	Ned Setzer	1	0	0	0	0	0	0	0	70	0	0	63	110
"	Sam Smith	1	0	0	0	0	0	0	0	108	0	0	54	110
"	Cale Yarborough	11	0	0	0	0	0	0	5	1,593	3	1	736	2,105
"	LeeRoy Yarbrough	3	0	0	0	0	0	0	0	234	0	0	109	120
"	**Total**	27	0	0	0	0	0	1	8	3,333	3	1	1,595	4,180
Lifetime		27	0	0	0	0	0	1	8	3,333	3	1	1,595	$4,180

Dick Foley

Year	Driver	Starts	Poles	1	2	3	4	5	6–10	Laps	Laps Led	Races Led	Miles	$
1957	Dick Foley	1	0	0	0	0	0	0	0	0	0	0	0	0
1958	Dick Foley	1	0	0	0	0	0	0	0	34	0	0	139	75
1959	Dick Foley	3	0	0	0	0	0	0	0	226	0	0	565	250
1960	Dick Foley	2	0	0	0	0	0	0	0	69	0	0	173	325
Lifetime		7	0	0	0	0	0	0	0	329	0	0	877	$650

Clint Folsom

Year	Driver	Starts	Poles	1	2	3	4	5	6–10	Laps	Laps Led	Races Led	Miles	$
1991	Dave Mader III	2	0	0	0	0	0	0	0	515	0	0	753	10,210
1992	Stan Fox	2	0	0	0	0	0	0	0	146	0	0	359	11,750
Lifetime		4	0	0	0	0	0	0	0	661	0	0	1,112	$21,960

Henry Ford

Year	Driver	Starts	Poles	1	2	3	4	5	6–10	Laps	Laps Led	Races Led	Miles	$
1955	Buck Baker	5	0	0	0	1	1	1	0	715	8	1	358	1,160
"	Henry Ford	4	0	0	0	0	0	0	0	408	0	0	259	165
"	Junior Johnson	1	0	0	0	0	0	0	0	75	0	0	75	50
"	**Total**	10	0	0	0	1	1	1	0	1,198	8	1	692	1,375
Lifetime		10	0	0	0	1	1	1	0	1,198	8	1	692	$1,375

John Foster

Year	Driver	Starts	Poles	1	2	3	4	5	6–10	Laps	Laps Led	Races Led	Miles	$
1956	Doug Cox	3	1	0	0	0	0	1	1	511	0	0	231	460
"	Tim Flock	4	2	0	0	0	0	0	0	670	73	3	637	740
"	**Total**	7	3	0	0	0	0	1	1	1,181	73	3	868	1,200
1957	Doug Cox	3	0	0	0	0	0	1	0	230	0	0	176	460
Lifetime		10	3	0	0	0	0	2	1	1,411	73	3	1,044	$1,660

Earl Foushee

Year	Driver	Starts	Poles	1	2	3	4	5	6–10	Laps	Laps Led	Races Led	Miles	$
1953	Earl Foushee	1	0	0	0	0	0	0	0	256	0	0	256	50
Lifetime		1	0	0	0	0	0	0	0	256	0	0	256	$50

James Fowler

Year	Driver	Starts	Poles	1	2	3	4	5	6–10	Laps	Laps Led	Races Led	Miles	$
1983	Ed Baugess	1	0	0	0	0	0	0	0	13	0	0	8	725
Lifetime		1	0	0	0	0	0	0	0	13	0	0	8	$725

Jim Fowler

Year	Driver	Starts	Poles	1	2	3	4	5	6–10	Laps	Laps Led	Races Led	Miles	$
1953	Cotton Hodges	1	0	0	0	0	0	0	0	32	0	0	131	25
Lifetime		1	0	0	0	0	0	0	0	32	0	0	131	$?

Year	Driver	Starts	Poles	Finish 1	2	3	4	5	6–10	Laps	Laps Led	Races Led	Miles	$

Bobby Fox

Year	Driver	Starts	Poles	1	2	3	4	5	6–10	Laps	Laps Led	Races Led	Miles	$
1984	Bobby Fox	1	0	0	0	0	0	0	0	352	0	0	358	1,495
Lifetime		1	0	0	0	0	0	0	0	352	0	0	358	$1,495

Leon Fox

Year	Driver	Starts	Poles	1	2	3	4	5	6–10	Laps	Laps Led	Races Led	Miles	$
1974	Leon Fox	1	0	0	0	0	0	0	0	113	0	0	296	1,210
Lifetime		1	0	0	0	0	0	0	0	113	0	0	296	$1,210

Ray Fox

Year	Driver	Starts	Poles	1	2	3	4	5	6–10	Laps	Laps Led	Races Led	Miles	$
1962	Darel Dieringer	1	1	0	0	0	0	0	0	3	0	0	8	50
"	Junior Johnson	6	1	1	1	0	0	0	0	1,347	332	4	1,297	22,385
"	David Pearson	7	0	0	0	0	0	0	5	1,284	278	3	2,028	10,390
"	**Total**	14	2	1	1	0	0	0	5	2,634	610	7	3,333	32,825
1963	Buck Baker	1	0	0	0	0	0	0	0	67	0	0	101	450
"	Junior Johnson	32	9	7	2	2	0	1	1	5,526	2,396	21	4,332	66,051
"	Jim Paschal	2	0	0	0	0	0	0	0	231	8	1	408	1,300
"	G. C. Spencer	2	0	0	0	0	0	0	0	133	21	1	333	1,700
"	**Total**	32	9	7	2	2	0	1	1	5,957	2,425	22	5,172	69,501
1964	Buck Baker	22	0	2	1	3	2	3	2	4,940	138	4	4,022	36,691
"	Buddy Baker	2	0	0	0	0	0	0	0	10	0	0	4	200
"	Junior Johnson	11	0	1	1	0	3	0	2	2,284	16	2	2,148	8,940
"	Bobby Schuyler	1	0	0	0	0	0	0	0	3	0	0	1	100
"	LeeRoy Yarbrough	11	0	0	1	0	1	1	1	2,175	8	1	2,586	7,935
"	**Total**	36	0	3	3	3	6	4	5	9,412	162	6	8,761	53,866
1965	Bunkie Blackburn	2	0	0	0	0	0	0	0	129	0	0	200	1,130
"	LeeRoy Yarbrough	6	0	0	0	0	0	1	0	860	42	2	1,313	4,745
"	**Total**	6	0	0	0	0	0	1	0	989	42	2	1,513	5,875
1966	Buddy Baker	6	0	0	1	0	0	0	1	1,155	106	3	1,625	13,930
"	Earl Balmer	2	0	1	0	0	0	0	0	61	1	1	153	2,045
"	Bunkie Blackburn	1	0	0	0	0	1	0	0	283	0	0	389	2,225
"	**Total**	9	0	1	1	0	1	0	1	1,499	107	4	2,167	18,200
1967	Buddy Baker	11	0	1	1	1	1	0	1	2,403	480	8	3,349	44,445
"	Robert Ireland	2	0	0	0	0	0	0	1	165	0	0	413	1,265
"	**Total**	12	0	1	1	1	1	0	2	2,568	480	8	3,762	45,710
1968	Buddy Baker	37	4	1	4	6	3	2	2	7,890	564	12	5,568	55,448
1969	Buddy Baker	6	2	0	0	0	1	1	0	911	191	4	1,097	13,440
"	Neil Castles	2	0	0	0	0	0	0	0	255	0	0	370	2,085
"	Charlie Glotzbach	1	0	0	0	0	0	0	0	46	4	1	115	740
"	Paul Goldsmith	1	0	0	0	0	0	0	0	40	0	0	20	465
"	Don Tarr	6	0	0	0	0	0	0	3	1,160	6	1	2,121	10,485
"	Jim Vandiver	2	0	0	1	0	0	0	0	252	102	1	596	13,225
"	**Total**	14	2	0	1	0	1	1	3	2,664	303	6	4,318	40,440
1970	Fred Lorenzen	4	1	0	0	1	0	0	0	656	3	1	1,031	9,295
"	Jim Vandiver	3	0	0	0	0	0	0	1	324	0	0	555	2,640
"	**Total**	7	1	0	0	1	0	0	1	980	3	1	1,585	11,935
1971	Cale Yarborough	3	0	0	0	0	0	0	1	355	13	1	648	2,790
1972	Cale Yarborough	1	0	0	0	0	0	0	1	188	0	0	470	4,660
1974	Wally Dallenbach	1	0	0	0	0	0	0	0	125	0	0	188	1,395
Lifetime		172	18	14	13	13	12	9	22	35,261	4,709	69	37,485	$342,645

A. J. Foyt

Year	Driver	Starts	Poles	1	2	3	4	5	6–10	Laps	Laps Led	Races Led	Miles	$
1977	A. J. Foyt	6	1	0	0	0	0	1	2	1,058	20	3	2,165	29,200
1978	A. J. Foyt	2	0	0	0	1	0	0	0	255	0	0	667	24,875
"	Ron Hutcherson	3	0	0	0	0	1	0	0	388	0	0	870	24,720
"	**Total**	3	0	0	0	1	1	0	0	643	0	0	1,538	49,595
1979	A. J. Foyt	2	0	0	0	1	0	0	1	356	7	2	890	41,690
1980	A. J. Foyt	1	0	0	0	0	0	0	0	69	0	0	173	3,575
"	Don Whittington	1	0	0	0	0	0	0	0	61	0	0	93	830
"	**Total**	2	0	0	0	0	0	0	0	130	0	0	265	4,405
1981	A. J. Foyt	3	0	0	0	0	0	0	1	530	0	0	1,007	9,210
1982	A. J. Foyt	2	0	0	0	0	0	0	0	162	0	0	388	9,405
1983	A. J. Foyt	3	0	0	0	0	0	0	0	406	0	0	890	22,935
	A. J. Foyt	3	0	0	0	0	0	0	0	224	0	0	418	8,830
		7	0	0	0	0	0	1	0	966	2	2	1,781	29,750
		5	0	0	0	0	0	0	0	640	1	1	1,220	24,135
		5	0	0	0	0	0	0	0	738	2	2	1,249	13,205

Year	Driver	Starts	Poles	1	2	3	4	5	6–10	Laps	Laps Led	Races Led	Miles	$

A. J. Foyt *continued*

Year	Driver	Starts	Poles	1	2	3	4	5	6–10	Laps	Laps Led	Races Led	Miles	$
1988	A. J. Foyt	7	0	0	0	0	0	0	0	920	9	3	1,992	29,660
1989	A. J. Foyt	7	0	0	0	0	0	0	0	860	6	2	1,869	31,995
"	Tracy Leslie	2	0	0	0	0	0	0	0	557	0	0	934	8,800
"	**Total**	9	0	0	0	0	0	0	0	1,417	6	2	2,803	40,795
1990	A. J. Foyt	3	0	0	0	0	0	0	0	301	4	1	782	26,725
1991	Mike Chase	3	0	0	0	0	0	0	0	446	0	0	1,066	15,400
1994	A. J. Foyt	1	0	0	0	0	0	0	0	156	0	0	390	29,000
Lifetime		64	1	0	0	2	1	2	4	9,093	51	16	18,847	$383,940

Bill France

Year	Driver	Starts	Poles	1	2	3	4	5	6–10	Laps	Laps Led	Races Led	Miles	$
1950*	Johnny Mantz	1	0	1	0	0	0	0	0	400	351	1	439	10,710
1969	Tiny Lund	1	0	0	0	0	0	0	1	152	28	1	404	1,675
Lifetime		2	0	1	0	0	0	0	1	552	379	2	843	$12,385

*Co-owned with Hubert Westmoreland.

Trent Francis

Year	Driver	Starts	Poles	1	2	3	4	5	6–10	Laps	Laps Led	Races Led	Miles	$
1976	Glenn Francis	1	0	0	0	0	0	0	0	125	0	0	313	1,065
1977	Glenn Francis	1	0	0	0	0	0	0	0	9	0	0	24	640
1980	Glenn Francis	1	0	0	0	0	0	0	0	91	0	0	228	1,025
1982	Glenn Francis	1	0	0	0	0	0	0	0	113	0	0	296	1,650
1983	Glenn Francis	2	0	0	0	0	0	0	0	179	0	0	469	2,775
1984	Glenn Francis	1	0	0	0	0	0	0	0	91	0	0	238	1,475
1985	Glenn Francis	1	0	0	0	0	0	0	0	84	0	0	220	1,665
Lifetime		8	0	0	0	0	0	0	0	692	0	0	1,787	$10,295

Larry Frank

Year	Driver	Starts	Poles	1	2	3	4	5	6–10	Laps	Laps Led	Races Led	Miles	$
1958	Larry Frank	7	0	0	0	1	0	0	2	1,713	0	0	904	1,880
1959	Larry Frank	14	0	0	1	0	1	2	5	3,210	39	1	2,602	5,918
1960	Larry Frank	1	0	0	0	0	0	0	0	85	0	0	53	75
1964	Larry Frank	6	0	0	0	0	0	0	1	1,052	0	0	1,469	4,680
1965	Larry Frank	9	0	0	0	0	1	0	0	1,009	33	1	1,200	5,080
Lifetime		37	0	0	1	1	2	2	8	7,069	72	2	6,228	$17,633

Walt Frank

Year	Driver	Starts	Poles	1	2	3	4	5	6–10	Laps	Laps Led	Races Led	Miles	$
1949	Budd Olsen	1	0	0	0	0	0	0	0	180	0	0	180	75
Lifetime		1	0	0	0	0	0	0	0	180	0	0	180	$75

Warren Fraser

Year	Driver	Starts	Poles	1	2	3	4	5	6–10	Laps	Laps Led	Races Led	Miles	$
1951	Dick Rathmann	1	0	0	0	0	0	0	1	0	0	0	0	150
"	George Seeger	1	0	0	0	0	0	0	1	0	0	0	0	50
"	Danny Weinberg	1	0	0	0	0	0	0	0	0	0	0	0	25
"	**Total**	3	0	0	0	0	0	0	2	0	0	0	0	225
Lifetime		3	0	0	0	0	0	0	2	0	0	0	0	$225

Joe Frasson

Year	Driver	Starts	Poles	1	2	3	4	5	6–10	Laps	Laps Led	Races Led	Miles	$
1970	Joe Frasson	19	0	0	0	0	0	0	2	4,358	0	0	5,995	19,477
1971	Joe Frasson	17	0	0	0	0	0	1	3	3,752	0	0	5,698	20,975
1972	George Follmer	1	0	0	0	0	0	0	0	4	0	0	10	1,440
"	Joe Frasson	16	0	0	0	1	0	0	3	3,013	9	2	4,638	21,645
"	**Total**	17	0	0	0	1	0	0	3	3,017	9	2	4,648	23,085
1973	Joe Frasson	14	0	0	0	1	1	0	2	2,732	1	1	4,379	25,884
1974	Joe Frasson	14	0	0	0	0	0	0	3	2,141	13	3	3,671	22,629
1975	Joe Frasson	9	0	0	0	0	0	0	1	1,352	1	1	2,018	11,975
1976	Buck Baker	1	0	0	0	0	0	0	0	32	0	0	80	830
"	Joe Frasson	9	0	0	0	0	0	0	1	863	1	1	1,510	13,565
"	Harry Gant	1	0	0	0	0	0	0	1	387	0	0	581	5,430
"	**Total**	11	0	0	0	0	0	0	2	1,282	1	1	2,170	19,825
1977	Joe Frasson	1	0	0	0	0	0	0	0	126	0	0	335	2,050
"	Dick Trickle	1	0	0	0	0	0	0	0	141	0	0	212	1,100
"	**Total**	2	0	0	0	0	0	0	0	267	0	0	547	3,150

Year	Driver	Starts	Poles	Finish 1	2	3	4	5	6–10	Laps	Laps Led	Races Led	Miles	$

Joe Frasson *continued*

Year	Driver	Starts	Poles	1	2	3	4	5	6–10	Laps	Laps Led	Races Led	Miles	$
1978	Joe Frasson	5	0	0	0	0	0	0	0	1,436	0	0	1,878	9,210
Lifetime		108	0	0	0	2	1	1	16	20,337	25	8	31,004	$156,210

Fred Frazier

Year	Driver	Starts	Poles	1	2	3	4	5	6–10	Laps	Laps Led	Races Led	Miles	$
1956	Lee Petty	1	0	0	0	0	0	0	0	340	0	0	468	175
"	Glen Wood	1	0	0	0	0	0	0	0	67	0	0	34	50
"	**Total**	2	0	0	0	0	0	0	0	407	0	0	501	225
Lifetime		2	0	0	0	0	0	0	0	407	0	0	501	$225

Joe Frazier

Year	Driver	Starts	Poles	1	2	3	4	5	6–10	Laps	Laps Led	Races Led	Miles	$
1957	George Parrish	5	0	0	0	0	0	0	0	483	0	0	472	525
1958	George Parrish	1	0	0	0	0	0	0	0	7	0	0	2	50
Lifetime		6	0	0	0	0	0	0	0	490	0	0	474	$575

Ray Frederick

Year	Driver	Starts	Poles	1	2	3	4	5	6–10	Laps	Laps Led	Races Led	Miles	$
1974	Jackie Rogers	21	0	0	0	0	0	0	6	4,546	1	1	6,672	31,702
1975	Jackie Rogers	1	0	0	0	0	0	0	0	370	0	0	555	2,815
Lifetime		22	0	0	0	0	0	0	6	4,916	1	1	7,227	$34,517

Eric Freedlander

Year	Driver	Starts	Poles	1	2	3	4	5	6–10	Laps	Laps Led	Races Led	Miles	$
1985	Tommy Ellis	14	0	0	0	0	0	0	1	2,853	0	0	3,505	27,695
1986	Tommy Ellis	24	0	0	0	0	0	0	3	6,559	50	5	7,334	78,310
1987	Tommy Ellis	4	0	0	0	0	0	0	0	564	0	0	661	17,735
"	Dale Jarrett	24	0	0	0	0	0	0	2	4,788	0	0	5,680	143,305
"	**Total**	28	0	0	0	0	0	0	2	5,352	0	0	6,341	161,040
Lifetime		66	0	0	0	0	0	0	6	14,764	50	5	17,180	$267,045

Bob Freeman

Year	Driver	Starts	Poles	1	2	3	4	5	6–10	Laps	Laps Led	Races Led	Miles	$
1970	John Kenney	11	0	0	0	0	0	0	0	1,385	0	0	675	4,115
"	Roy Mayne	1	0	0	0	0	0	0	0	405	0	0	222	465
"	**Total**	12	0	0	0	0	0	0	0	1,790	0	0	897	4,580
Lifetime		12	0	0	0	0	0	0	0	1,790	0	0	897	$4,580

Dick Freeman

Year	Driver	Starts	Poles	1	2	3	4	5	6–10	Laps	Laps Led	Races Led	Miles	$
1954	Dick Freeman	1	0	0	0	0	0	0	0	20	0	0	10	0
1959	Dick Freeman	3	0	0	0	0	0	0	0	695	0	0	800	475
1960	Dick Freeman	2	0	0	0	0	0	0	0	41	0	0	103	250
"	Cotton Owens	1	0	0	0	0	0	0	0	137	0	0	86	60
"	George Tet	1	0	0	0	0	0	0	0	171	0	0	257	200
"	**Total**	4	0	0	0	0	0	0	0	349	0	0	445	510
Lifetime		8	0	0	0	0	0	0	0	1,064	0	0	1,254	$985

Charles French

Year	Driver	Starts	Poles	1	2	3	4	5	6–10	Laps	Laps Led	Races Led	Miles	$
1959	Ken Johnson	4	0	0	0	0	0	0	1	408	0	0	366	370
1960	Ken Johnson	4	0	0	0	0	0	0	0	317	0	0	721	460
1961	Jim Hendrickson	1	0	0	0	0	0	0	0	37	0	0	93	75
"	Ken Johnson	2	0	0	0	0	0	0	0	36	0	0	90	250
"	**Total**	3	0	0	0	0	0	0	0	73	0	0	183	325
Lifetime		11	0	0	0	0	0	0	1	798	0	0	1,269	$1,155

Don Freymiller

Year	Driver	Starts	Poles	1	2	3	4	5	6–10	Laps	Laps Led	Races Led	Miles	$
1990	Mike Chase	2	0	0	0	0	0	0	0	142	4	1	251	6,575
1991	Mike Chase	2	0	0	0	0	0	0	0	358	0	0	439	7,300
Lifetime		4	0	0	0	0	0	0	0	500	4	1	690	$13,875

Tom Friedkin

Year	Driver	Starts	Poles	1	2	3	4	5	6–10	Laps	Laps Led	Races Led	Miles	$
1965	Jerry Grant	3	0	0	0	0	0	0	1	327	0	0	851	2,150
"	Jim Paschal	4	0	0	0	0	1	0	0	1,057	9	1	870	2,475
		7	0	0	0	0	1	0	1	1,384	9	1	1,721	4,625

Year	Driver	Starts	Poles	Finish 1	2	3	4	5	6–10	Laps	Laps Led	Races Led	Miles	$

Tom Friedkin *continued*

Year	Driver	Starts	Poles	1	2	3	4	5	6–10	Laps	Laps Led	Races Led	Miles	$
1966	Jerry Grant	3	0	0	0	0	0	1	0	433	1	1	854	3,180
"	Marvin Panch	1	0	0	0	0	0	0	1	154	0	0	385	1,475
"	Jim Paschal	16	2	2	0	1	1	1	4	4,430	743	6	4,975	30,145
"	**Total**	17	2	2	0	1	1	2	5	5,017	744	6	6,214	34,800
1967	Jerry Grant	4	0	0	0	0	0	1	0	312	0	0	727	5,520
"	Jim Paschal	45	1	4	5	5	3	3	5	9,402	1,074	16	7,228	60,123
"	**Total**	46	1	4	5	5	3	4	5	9,714	1,074	16	7,955	65,643
1968	Bobby Allison	5	2	0	1	0	2	1	0	1,489	201	3	1,374	7,795
"	Charlie Glotzbach	2	0	0	0	0	0	0	0	242	0	0	308	1,375
"	Paul Goldsmith	1	0	0	0	0	0	0	0	63	0	0	32	275
"	Jerry Grant	7	0	0	0	0	0	0	1	971	1	1	1,312	5,665
"	Ray Hendrick	4	0	0	0	0	0	1	3	1,295	7	1	627	1,470
"	James Hylton	1	0	0	0	0	0	0	0	134	0	0	184	640
"	Norm Nelson	1	0	0	0	0	0	0	0	87	0	0	235	720
"	Jim Paschal	1	0	0	0	0	0	0	0	171	0	0	91	275
"	Curtis Turner	6	0	0	0	0	1	0	3	1,448	0	0	1,542	5,850
"	**Total**	23	2	0	1	0	3	2	7	5,900	209	5	5,706	24,065
1969	Bobby Allison	2	0	1	0	0	0	0	0	452	94	2	226	1,275
Lifetime		95	5	7	6	6	8	8	18	22,467	2,130	30	21,822	$130,408

Bernard Friedland

Year	Driver	Starts	Poles	1	2	3	4	5	6–10	Laps	Laps Led	Races Led	Miles	$
1958	Ben Benz	4	0	0	0	0	0	0	2	831	0	0	408	400
1959	Ben Benz	5	0	0	0	0	0	0	2	665	0	0	740	625
Lifetime		9	0	0	0	0	0	0	4	1,496	0	0	1,148	$1,025

Ken Friez

Year	Driver	Starts	Poles	1	2	3	4	5	6–10	Laps	Laps Led	Races Led	Miles	$
1974	David Sisco	1	0	0	0	0	0	0	0	315	0	0	473	2,793
1975	Darel Dieringer	1	0	0	0	0	0	0	0	373	0	0	560	3,015
"	Hershel McGriff	2	0	0	0	0	0	0	0	63	0	0	158	2,200
"	**Total**	3	0	0	0	0	0	0	0	436	0	0	717	5,215
Lifetime		4	0	0	0	0	0	0	0	751	0	0	1,190	$8,008

Ted Fritz

Year	Driver	Starts	Poles	1	2	3	4	5	6–10	Laps	Laps Led	Races Led	Miles	$
1975	Ted Fritz	1	0	0	0	0	0	0	0	10	0	0	26	620
Lifetime		1	0	0	0	0	0	0	0	10	0	0	26	$620

Herb Fry

Year	Driver	Starts	Poles	1	2	3	4	5	6–10	Laps	Laps Led	Races Led	Miles	$
1952	Herb Fry	1	0	0	0	0	0	0	0	366	0	0	458	95
Lifetime		1	0	0	0	0	0	0	0	366	0	0	458	$95

Irving Frye

Year	Driver	Starts	Poles	1	2	3	4	5	6–10	Laps	Laps Led	Races Led	Miles	$
1952	Pop McGinnis	1	0	0	0	0	0	0	1	180	0	0	90	125
1953	Pop McGinnis	13	0	0	0	0	0	2	3	775	13	1	664	975
1954	Pop McGinnis	3	0	0	0	0	0	0	0	413	4	1	526	165
Lifetime		17	0	0	0	0	0	2	4	1,368	17	2	1,280	$1,265

Tetsuo Fuchigami (George Tet)

Year	Driver	Starts	Poles	1	2	3	4	5	6–10	Laps	Laps Led	Races Led	Miles	$
1961	George Tet	2	0	0	0	0	0	0	0	60	0	0	150	250
Lifetime		2	0	0	0	0	0	0	0	60	0	0	150	$250

Harold Furr

Year	Driver	Starts	Poles	1	2	3	4	5	6–10	Laps	Laps Led	Races Led	Miles	$
1971	Richard Brown	5	0	0	0	0	0	0	0	779	0	0	823	3,910
"	Dub Simpson	2	0	0	0	0	0	0	0	109	0	0	220	1,305
"	**Total**	7	0	0	0	0	0	0	0	888	0	0	1,043	5,215
1972	Buck Baker	4	0	0	0	0	0	0	0	503	0	0	507	2,320
Lifetime		11	0	0	0	0	0	0	0	1,391	0	0	1,550	$7,535

Harry Gailey

Year	Driver	Starts	Poles	1	2	3	4	5	6–10	Laps	Laps Led	Races Led	Miles	$
1971	Ernie Shaw	1	0	0	0	0	0	0	1	469	0	0	257	575
Lifetime		1	0	0	0	0	0	0	1	469	0	0	257	$575

Year	Driver	Starts	Poles	Finish 1	2	3	4	5	6–10	Laps	Laps Led	Races Led	Miles	$

Bill Galearisi

Year	Driver	Starts	Poles	1	2	3	4	5	6–10	Laps	Laps Led	Races Led	Miles	$
1954	Bill Galdarisi	1	0	0	0	0	0	0	0	445	0	0	223	100
Lifetime		1	0	0	0	0	0	0	0	445	0	0	223	$100

Dale Gallagher

Year	Driver	Starts	Poles	1	2	3	4	5	6–10	Laps	Laps Led	Races Led	Miles	$
1949	Dick Zimmerman	1	0	0	0	0	0	0	0	178	0	0	178	50
Lifetime		1	0	0	0	0	0	0	0	178	0	0	178	$50

Dennis Gallion

Year	Driver	Starts	Poles	1	2	3	4	5	6–10	Laps	Laps Led	Races Led	Miles	$
1970	Dick Brooks	2	0	0	0	0	0	0	0	34	0	0	86	1,390
"	John Sears	4	0	0	0	0	0	0	0	623	0	0	1,361	4,635
"	**Total**	6	0	0	0	0	0	0	0	657	0	0	1,447	6,025
Lifetime		6	0	0	0	0	0	0	0	657	0	0	1,447	$6,025

George Gallup

Year	Driver	Starts	Poles	1	2	3	4	5	6–10	Laps	Laps Led	Races Led	Miles	$
1952	George Gallup	4	0	0	0	0	0	0	1	441	13	1	356	175
1953	George Gallup	1	0	0	0	0	0	0	0	36	0	0	148	50
Lifetime		5	0	0	0	0	0	0	1	477	13	1	504	$225

Richard Gallup

Year	Driver	Starts	Poles	1	2	3	4	5	6–10	Laps	Laps Led	Races Led	Miles	$
1956	Ken Love	1	0	0	0	0	0	0	0	134	0	0	184	50
1957	Ken Love	1	0	0	0	0	0	0	0		0	0		60
Lifetime		2	0	0	0	0	0	0	0	134	0	0	184	$110

Frank Galpin

Year	Driver	Starts	Poles	1	2	3	4	5	6–10	Laps	Laps Led	Races Led	Miles	$
1960	Ron Hornaday	3	0	0	0	0	1	0	0	283	0	0	328	610
1961	Ron Hornaday	4	0	0	0	0	0	1	0	283	0	0	219	325
1963	Ron Hornaday	2	0	0	0	0	0	0	1	316	0	0	853	1,600
Lifetime		9	0	0	0	0	1	1	1	882	0	0	1,400	$2,535

Johnny Gardner

Year	Driver	Starts	Poles	1	2	3	4	5	6–10	Laps	Laps Led	Races Led	Miles	$
1958	Johnny Gardner	14	0	0	0	0	0	0	0	1,510	0	0	894	780
Lifetime		14	0	0	0	0	0	0	0	1,510	0	0	894	$780

Slick Gardner

Year	Driver	Starts	Poles	1	2	3	4	5	6–10	Laps	Laps Led	Races Led	Miles	$
1973	Slick Gardner	1	0	0	0	0	0	0	0	9	0	0	24	990
Lifetime		1	0	0	0	0	0	0	0	9	0	0	24	$990

Walson Gardner

Year	Driver	Starts	Poles	1	2	3	4	5	6–10	Laps	Laps Led	Races Led	Miles	$
1967	Walson Gardner	1	0	0	0	0	0	0	0	47	0	0	24	150
1968	Walson Gardner	12	0	0	0	0	0	0	2	3,418	0	0	2,139	3,925
"	Elmo Langley	1	0	0	0	0	0	0	1	187	0	0	94	200
"	**Total**	13	0	0	0	0	0	0	3	3,605	0	0	2,233	4,125
1969	Walson Gardner	7	0	0	0	0	0	0	0	1,299	0	0	650	2,115
Lifetime		21	0	0	0	0	0	0	3	4,951	0	0	2,907	$6,390

Tom Garn

Year	Driver	Starts	Poles	1	2	3	4	5	6–10	Laps	Laps Led	Races Led	Miles	$
1971	Richard Childress	11	0	0	0	0	0	0	0	1,214	0	0	826	3,210
"	Wendell Scott	1	0	0	0	0	0	0	0	153	0	0	407	1,115
"	**Total**	12	0	0	0	0	0	0	0	1,367	0	0	1,233	4,325
1972	Richard Childress	14	0	0	0	0	0	0	0	1,502	0	0	1,294	6,365
1973	Richard Childress	25	0	0	0	0	1	0	1	6,918	1	1	7,456	37,880
1974	Richard Childress	29	0	0	0	0	0	0	3	5,138	0	0	6,484	50,249
"	Ronnie Childress	1	0	0	0	0	0	0	0	43	0	0	27	325
"	**Total**	29	0	0	0	0	0	0	3	5,181	0	0	6,510	50,574
1975	Richard Childress	30	0	0	0	0	1	1	13	9,433	3	2	10,925	96,780
Lifetime		110	0	0	0	0	2	1	17	24,401	4	3	27,418	$195,924

Chick Garno

Year	Driver	Starts	Poles	1	2	3	4	5	6–10	Laps	Laps Led	Races Led	Miles	$
1956	Bud Geiselman	1	0	0	0	0	0	0	0	112	0	0	112	50
Lifetime		1	0	0	0	0	0	0	0	112	0	0	112	$50

Year	Driver	Starts	Poles	1	2	3	4	5	6–10	Laps	Laps Led	Races Led	Miles	$

Charles Gattalia

Year	Driver	Starts	Poles	1	2	3	4	5	6–10	Laps	Laps Led	Races Led	Miles	$
1951	Charles Gattalia	2	0	0	0	0	0	0	0		0	0		100
1952	Charles Gattalia	8	0	0	0	0	0	0	3	810	0	0	565	485
Lifetime		10	0	0	0	0	0	0	3	810	0	0	565	$585

Ron Gautsche

Year	Driver	Starts	Poles	1	2	3	4	5	6–10	Laps	Laps Led	Races Led	Miles	$
1971	Ron Gautsche	3	0	0	0	0	0	0	0	176	0	0	460	2,935
1972	Ron Gautsche	2	0	0	0	0	0	0	0	215	0	0	544	2,735
Lifetime		5	0	0	0	0	0	0	0	391	0	0	1,004	$5,670

Jack Gaynor

Year	Driver	Starts	Poles	1	2	3	4	5	6–10	Laps	Laps Led	Races Led	Miles	$
1951	Lou Figaro	11	1	1	0	0	2	0	1	431	200	1	331	2,150
"	Jack Gaynor	1	0	0	0	0	0	0	0		0	0		25
"	**Total**	11	1	1	0	0	2	0	1	431	200	1	331	2,175
Lifetime		11	1	1	0	0	2	0	1	431	200	1	331	$2,175

Bill Gazaway

Year	Driver	Starts	Poles	1	2	3	4	5	6–10	Laps	Laps Led	Races Led	Miles	$
1960	Joe Caspolich	2	0	0	0	0	0	0	0	526	0	0	762	1,425
"	Bill Gazaway	1	0	0	0	0	0	0	0	1	0	0	2	200
"	Tiny Lund	4	0	0	0	0	0	0	0	586	0	0	945	650
"	**Total**	7	0	0	0	0	0	0	0	1,113	0	0	1,709	2,275
Lifetime		7	0	0	0	0	0	0	0	1,113	0	0	1,709	$2,275

Robert Gee

Year	Driver	Starts	Poles	1	2	3	4	5	6–10	Laps	Laps Led	Races Led	Miles	$
1978	Ferrel Harris	10	0	0	0	0	0	0	3	2,079	0	0	3,152	21,245
"	Skip Manning	1	0	0	0	0	0	0	0	59	0	0	89	1,525
"	**Total**	11	0	0	0	0	0	0	3	2,138	0	0	3,240	22,770
Lifetime		11	0	0	0	0	0	0	3	2,138	0	0	3,240	$22,770

Frank Geiselman

Year	Driver	Starts	Poles	1	2	3	4	5	6–10	Laps	Laps Led	Races Led	Miles	$
1955	Bud Geiselman	1	0	0	0	0	0	0	0	164	0	0	82	50
Lifetime		1	0	0	0	0	0	0	0	164	0	0	82	$50

Romeo Gelsi

Year	Driver	Starts	Poles	1	2	3	4	5	6–10	Laps	Laps Led	Races Led	Miles	$
1957	Al Tasnady	1	0	0	0	0	0	0	0		0	0		0
Lifetime		1	0	0	0	0	0	0	0		0	0		$0

Eldon George

Year	Driver	Starts	Poles	1	2	3	4	5	6–10	Laps	Laps Led	Races Led	Miles	$
1995	Doug George	2	0	0	0	0	0	0	0	251	0	0	362	18,610
Lifetime		2	0	0	0	0	0	0	0	251	0	0	362	$18,610

Jay George

Year	Driver	Starts	Poles	1	2	3	4	5	6–10	Laps	Laps Led	Races Led	Miles	$
1959	Jack Austin	1	0	0	0	0	0	0	0	54	0	0	54	75
1960	Brownie Brown	1	0	0	0	0	0	0	0	12	0	0	17	0
"	Bill Cook	1	0	0	0	0	0	0	0	137	0	0	192	200
"	**Total**	1	0	0	0	0	0	0	0	149	0	0	209	200
Lifetime		2	0	0	0	0	0	0	0	203	0	0	263	$275

Benny Georgeson

Year	Driver	Starts	Poles	1	2	3	4	5	6–10	Laps	Laps Led	Races Led	Miles	$
1949	Benny Georgeson	1	0	0	0	0	0	0	0		0	0		0
Lifetime		1	0	0	0	0	0	0	0		0	0		$0

Gerhart Racing (Bobby and Billy Gerhart, co-owners)

Year	Driver	Starts	Poles	1	2	3	4	5	6–10	Laps	Laps Led	Races Led	Miles	$
1984	Bobby Gerhart	4	0	0	0	0	0	0	0	655	0	0	813	7,585
1985	Bobby Gerhart	5	0	0	0	0	0	0	0	1,166	0	0	1,503	7,400
1986	Bobby Gerhart	4	0	0	0	0	0	0	0	575	0	0	1,178	6,535
1987	Bobby Gerhart	2	0	0	0	0	0	0	0	169	0	0	423	3,665
1988	Bobby Gerhart	2	0	0	0	0	0	0	0	377	0	0	943	5,050
1989	Bobby Gerhart	1	0	0	0	0	0	0	0	193	0	0	483	4,575
1990	Bobby Gerhart	1	0	0	0	0	0	0	0	151	0	0	151	4,550

Year	Driver	Starts	Poles	Finish						Laps	Laps Led	Races Led	Miles	$
				1	2	3	4	5	6–10					

Gerhart Racing *continued*

Year	Driver	Starts	Poles	1	2	3	4	5	6–10	Laps	Laps Led	Races Led	Miles	$
1992	Bobby Gerhart	3	0	0	0	0	0	0	0	350	0	0	904	15,810
Lifetime		22	0	0	0	0	0	0	0	3,636	0	0	6,396	$55,170

Whitey Gerkin

Year	Driver	Starts	Poles	1	2	3	4	5	6–10	Laps	Laps Led	Races Led	Miles	$
1967	Whitey Gerkin	2	0	0	0	0	0	0	0	407	2	1	408	1,410
Lifetime		2	0	0	0	0	0	0	0	407	2	1	408	$1,410

James Gess

Year	Driver	Starts	Poles	1	2	3	4	5	6–10	Laps	Laps Led	Races Led	Miles	$
1955	Charlie Cregar	2	0	0	0	0	0	0	0	47	0	0	60	0
Lifetime		2	0	0	0	0	0	0	0	47	0	0	60	$0

Dick Getty

Year	Driver	Starts	Poles	1	2	3	4	5	6–10	Laps	Laps Led	Races Led	Miles	$
1956	Dick Getty	3	0	0	0	0	0	0	0	186	0	0	217	90
1957	Dick Getty	10	0	0	0	0	0	3	5	1,174	0	0	786	1,890
1959	Dick Getty	2	0	0	0	0	0	0	0	138	0	0	59	175
1961	Dick Getty	3	0	0	0	0	0	0	0	175	0	0	142	200
1962	Dick Getty	5	0	0	0	0	0	0	2	525	0	0	213	675
"	Eddie Pagan	1	0	0	0	0	0	0	0	354	0	0	177	250
"	**Total**	6	0	0	0	0	0	0	2	879	0	0	390	925
1963	Eddie Pagan	1	0	0	0	0	0	0	0	137	0	0	370	325
Lifetime		25	0	0	0	0	0	3	7	2,689	0	0	1,963	$3,605

Richard Giachetti

Year	Driver	Starts	Poles	1	2	3	4	5	6–10	Laps	Laps Led	Races Led	Miles	$
1968	Jack Ingram	1	0	0	0	0	0	0	0	25	0	0	13	0
"	Blaine Kauffman	2	0	0	0	0	0	0	0	710	0	0	480	750
"	Don Wingier	3	0	0	0	0	0	0	0	381	0	0	94	320
"	**Total**	6	0	0	0	0	0	0	0	1,116	0	0	586	1,070
1969	Bob Ashbrook	2	0	0	0	0	0	0	0	200	0	0	399	1,587
"	George Ashbrook	1	0	0	0	0	0	0	0	262	0	0	262	540
"	Lennie Pond	1	0	0	0	0	0	0	0	73	0	0	74	650
"	Dub Simpson	3	0	0	0	0	0	0	0	277	0	0	638	2,425
"	**Total**	7	0	0	0	0	0	0	0	812	0	0	1,372	5,202
1970	Bob Ashbrook	1	0	0	0	0	0	0	0	44	0	0	110	220
"	Frog Fagan	2	0	0	0	0	0	0	0	179	0	0	466	1,925
"	Harold Smith	1	0	0	0	0	0	0	0	30	0	0	60	635
"	**Total**	4	0	0	0	0	0	0	0	253	0	0	636	2,780
1971	Red Farmer	3	0	0	0	0	0	0	1	213	0	0	533	2,835
"	Tommy Gale	1	0	0	0	0	0	0	0	185	0	0	377	1,045
"	David Pearson	1	0	0	1	3	0	0	0	275	1	1	100	1,500
"	James Sears	1	0	0	0	0	0	0	0	9	0	0	9	545
"	**Total**	6	0	0	1	0	0	0	1	682	1	1	1,019	5,925
1972	Larry Dickson	1	0	0	0	0	0	0	0	103	0	0	258	1,535
"	Bill Seifert	1	0	0	0	0	0	0	0	1	0	0	2	705
"	**Total**	2	0	0	0	0	0	0	0	104	0	0	260	2,240
197	Larry Dickson	0												310
Lifetime		25	0	0	1	0	0	0	1	2,967	1	1	3,873	$17,527

Don Gibbs

Year	Driver	Starts	Poles	1	2	3	4	5	6–10	Laps	Laps Led	Races Led	Miles	$
1988	Mickey Gibbs	5	0	0	0	0	0	0	0	636	2	1	1,134	14,750
1989	Mickey Gibbs	1	0	0	0	0	0	0	0	37	0	0	56	1,935
1990	Mickey Gibbs	9	0	0	0	0	0	0	0	1,837	1	1	2,541	38,665
Lifetime		15	0	0	0	0	0	0	0	2,510	3	2	3,731	$55,350

Joe Gibbs

Year	Driver	Starts	Poles	1	2	3	4	5	6–10	Laps	Laps Led	Races Led	Miles	$
1992	Dale Jarrett	29	0	0	1	1	0	0	6	8,586	99	5	10,295	418,648
1993	Dale Jarrett	30	0	1	1	4	5	2	5	9,149	263	15	11,335	1,242,394
1994	Dale Jarrett	30	0	1	0	0	2	1	5	8,410	55	8	10,441	893,754
1995	Bobby Labonte	31	2	3	3	0	0	1	7	9,019	278	14	10,974	1,413,682
1996	Bobby Labonte	31	4	1	1	0	1	2	9	8,916	337	13	10,570	1,475,196
Lifetime		151	6	6	6	5	8	6	32	44,080	1,032	55	53,616	$5,443,674

Year	Driver	Starts	Poles	1	2	3	4	5	6–10	Laps	Laps Led	Races Led	Miles	$

Shorty Gibbs

Year	Driver	Starts	Poles	1	2	3	4	5	6–10	Laps	Laps Led	Races Led	Miles	$
1952	Shorty Gibbs	2	0	0	0	0	0	0	0	87	0	0	53	50
Lifetime		2	0	0	0	0	0	0	0	87	0	0	53	$50

Bo Gibson

Year	Driver	Starts	Poles	1	2	3	4	5	6–10	Laps	Laps Led	Races Led	Miles	$
1987	Mark Gibson	1	0	0	0	0	0	0	0	204	0	0	204	1,300
1989	Mark Gibson	1	0	0	0	0	0	0	0	100	0	0	250	2,880
Lifetime		2	0	0	0	0	0	0	0	304	0	0	454	$4,180

Ed Gibson

Year	Driver	Starts	Poles	1	2	3	4	5	6–10	Laps	Laps Led	Races Led	Miles	$
1975	Charlie Glotzbach	1	0	0	0	0	0	0	0	59	1	1	89	1,035
"	Bobby Isaac	3	0	0	0	0	0	0	1	740	0	0	727	4,135
"	**Total**	4	0	0	0	0	0	0	1	799	1	1	815	5,170
Lifetime		4	0	0	0	0	0	0	1	799	1	1	815	$5,170

Kyle Gibson

Year	Driver	Starts	Poles	1	2	3	4	5	6–10	Laps	Laps Led	Races Led	Miles	$
1966	Johnny Steele	2	0	0	0	0	0	0	0	325	0	0	523	900
1967	Johnny Steele	1	0	0	0	0	0	0	0	13	0	0	35	500
1968	Johnny Steele	1	0	0	0	0	0	0	0	33	0	0	89	500
Lifetime		4	0	0	0	0	0	0	0	371	0	0	648	$1,900

Tom Gifford

Year	Driver	Starts	Poles	1	2	3	4	5	6–10	Laps	Laps Led	Races Led	Miles	$
1952	Tom Gifford	3	0	0	0	0	0	0	0	53	0	0	27	50
Lifetime		3	0	0	0	0	0	0	0	53	0	0	27	$50

Boyce Gillette

Year	Driver	Starts	Poles	1	2	3	4	5	6–10	Laps	Laps Led	Races Led	Miles	$
1952	Al Funderburk	1	0	0	0	0	0	0	1		0	0		50
Lifetime		1	0	0	0	0	0	0	1		0	0		$50

Emory Gilliam

Year	Driver	Starts	Poles	1	2	3	4	5	6–10	Laps	Laps Led	Races Led	Miles	$
1965	Jack Goodwin	1	0	0	0	0	0	0	0	0	0	0	0	0
"	Elmo Langley	2	0	0	0	0	0	0	0	186	0	0	86	200
"	Tom Pistone	12	1	0	0	0	1	0	1	709	0	0	481	2,995
"	Bert Robbins	3	0	0	0	0	0	0	1	290	0	0	146	1,040
"	**Total**	18	1	0	0	0	1	0	2	1,185	0	0	713	4,235
1966	Buddy Baker	5	1	0	0	0	0	0	0	497	36	1	236	425
"	Jack Ingram	1	0	0	0	0	0	0	0	14	0	0	5	100
"	Roy Mayne	3	0	0	0	0	0	0	1	290	0	0	468	835
"	**Total**	9	1	0	0	0	0	0	1	801	36	1	708	1,360
1967	Neil Castles	5	0	0	0	0	1	0	1	841	0	0	987	4,660
"	Armond Holley	1	0	0	0	0	0	0	0	31	0	0	47	775
"	Paul Lewis	4	0	0	0	0	0	1	2	644	0	0	307	690
"	Bud Moore	1	0	0	0	0	0	0	0	33	0	0	17	100
"	Bill Vanderhoff	1	0	0	0	0	0	0	0	114	0	0	57	100
"	**Total**	12	0	0	0	0	1	1	3	1,663	0	0	1,414	6,325
Lifetime		39	2	0	0	0	2	1	6	3,649	36	1	2,836	$11,920

Butch Gilliland

Year	Driver	Starts	Poles	1	2	3	4	5	6–10	Laps	Laps Led	Races Led	Miles	$
1990	Butch Gilliland	1	0	0	0	0	0	0	0	71	0	0	179	4,200
1991	Butch Gilliland	1	0	0	0	0	0	0	0	299	0	0	299	3,750
1992	Butch Gilliland	2	0	0	0	0	0	0	0	347	0	0	431	10,990
1993	Butch Gilliland	1	0	0	0	0	0	0	0	71	0	0	179	6,765
1994	Butch Gilliland	1	0	0	0	0	0	0	0	72	0	0	181	7,755
1995	Butch Gilliland	1	0	0	0	0	0	0	0	19	0	0	48	9,760
Lifetime		7	0	0	0	0	0	0	0	879	0	0	1,317	$43,220

Bob Gilreath

Year	Driver	Starts	Poles	1	2	3	4	5	6–10	Laps	Laps Led	Races Led	Miles	$
1967	Frog Fagan	5	0	0	0	0	0	0	0	309	0	0	210	600
Lifetime		5	0	0	0	0	0	0	0	309	0	0	210	$600

Year	Driver	Starts	Poles	Finish 1	2	3	4	5	6–10	Laps	Laps Led	Races Led	Miles	$

John Glazebrook

Year	Driver	Starts	Poles	1	2	3	4	5	6–10	Laps	Laps Led	Races Led	Miles	$
1968	Larry Manning	4	0	0	0	0	0	0	0	367	0	0	181	600
Lifetime		4	0	0	0	0	0	0	0	367	0	0	181	$600

Fred Goad

Year	Driver	Starts	Poles	1	2	3	4	5	6–10	Laps	Laps Led	Races Led	Miles	$
1965	Joe Adams	2	0	0	0	0	0	0	1	244	0	0	99	450
"	Fred Goad	2	0	0	0	0	0	0	0	9	0	0	11	515
"	Wendell Scott	1	0	0	0	0	0	0	0	179	0	0	269	950
"	**Total**	5	0	0	0	0	0	0	1	432	0	0	378	1,915
Lifetime		5	0	0	0	0	0	0	1	432	0	0	378	$1,915

Tom Goff

Year	Driver	Starts	Poles	1	2	3	4	5	6–10	Laps	Laps Led	Races Led	Miles	$
1974	Dick Skillen	3	0	0	0	0	0	0	0	908	0	0	1,137	3,740
1975	Dick Skillen	5	0	0	0	0	0	0	0	1,052	0	0	1,333	4,865
1976	Dick Skillen	5	0	0	0	0	0	0	0	810	0	0	1,716	8,250
1977	Dick Skillen	1	0	0	0	0	0	0	0	38	0	0	101	1,830
1982	Richard Brickhouse	2	0	0	0	0	0	0	0	557	0	0	673	2,610
"	Dick Skillen	0												550
"	**Total**	2	0	0	0	0	0	0	0	557	0	0	673	3,160
1983	Dick Skillen	1	0	0	0	0	0	0	0	1	0	0	3	2,050
1985	Dick Skillen	1	0	0	0	0	0	0	0	167	0	0	444	5,720
1986	Dick Skillen	0												1,800
Lifetime		18	0	0	0	0	0	0	0	3,533	0	0	5,407	$31,415

John Golabek

Year	Driver	Starts	Poles	1	2	3	4	5	6–10	Laps	Laps Led	Races Led	Miles	$
1951	Neil Cole	5	1	1	1	0	0	1	0	399	45	1	200	2,050
1952	Neil Cole	9	0	0	0	1	0	0	4	1,166	0	0	653	1,025
1953	Neil Cole	1	0	0	0	0	0	0	0		0	0		25
"	Ronnie Kohler	3	0	0	0	0	0	1	0		0	0		350
"	**Total**	4	0	0	0	0	0	1	0		0	0		375
Lifetime		18	1	1	1	1	0	2	4	1,565	45	1	853	$3,450

Tubby Gonzales

Year	Driver	Starts	Poles	1	2	3	4	5	6–10	Laps	Laps Led	Races Led	Miles	$
1961	Darel Dieringer	1	0	0	0	0	0	0	0	45	0	0	62	300
"	Tubby Gonzales	5	0	0	0	0	1	0	0	598	0	0	889	1,300
"	Fred Lorenzen	1	0	0	0	0	1	0	0	198	0	0	495	3,825
"	**Total**	7	0	0	0	0	2	0	0	841	0	0	1,446	5,425
1962	Tubby Gonzales	4	0	0	0	0	0	0	0	422	0	0	629	1,050
1963	Sal Tovella	3	0	0	0	0	0	0	0	346	0	0	888	1,300
Lifetime		14	0	0	0	0	2	0	0	1,609	0	0	2,964	$7,775

James Good

Year	Driver	Starts	Poles	1	2	3	4	5	6–10	Laps	Laps Led	Races Led	Miles	$
1970	Dick Gulstrand	2	0	0	0	0	0	1	1	309	0	0	810	3,890
1971	Dick Gulstrand	2	0	0	0	0	0	0	0	251	0	0	637	2,775
Lifetime		4	0	0	0	0	0	1	1	560	0	0	1,446	$6,665

Phil Good

Year	Driver	Starts	Poles	1	2	3	4	5	6–10	Laps	Laps Led	Races Led	Miles	$
1984	Phil Good	1	0	0	0	0	0	0	0	331	0	0	331	1,065
1985	Phil Good	3	0	0	0	0	0	0	0	977	0	0	1,135	5,400
1986	Phil Good	2	0	0	0	0	0	0	0	439	0	0	254	2,825
1987	Phil Good	1	0	0	0	0	0	0	0	10	0	0	24	1,435
Lifetime		7	0	0	0	0	0	0	0	1,757	0	0	1,744	$10,725

Dick Goode

Year	Driver	Starts	Poles	1	2	3	4	5	6–10	Laps	Laps Led	Races Led	Miles	$
1963	Dick Goode	2	0	0	0	0	0	0	1	107	0	0	268	700
Lifetime		2	0	0	0	0	0	0	1	107	0	0	268	$700

J. O. Goode

Year	Driver	Starts	Poles	1	2	3	4	5	6–10	Laps	Laps Led	Races Led	Miles	$
1951	Jimmie Lewallen	3	0	0	0	0	0	0	1	111	0	0	111	150
1952	Ray Duhigg	8	0	0	0	1	0	0	3	1,458	0	0	1,270	1,825
"	Jimmie Lewallen	6	0	0	0	0	0	0	1	510	0	0	258	300
"	Bob Welborn	2	0	0	0	0	0	0	0	187	0	0	127	65
"	**Total**	16	0	0	0	1	0	0	4	2,155	0	0	1,655	2,190

Year	Driver	Starts	Poles	1	2	3	4	5	6–10	Laps	Laps Led	Races Led	Miles	$

J. O. Goode *continued*

Year	Driver	Starts	Poles	1	2	3	4	5	6–10	Laps	Laps Led	Races Led	Miles	$
1953	Ray Duhigg	1	0	0	0	0	0	0	1		0	0		100
"	Bob Welborn	8	0	0	0	0	1	1	2	617	0	0	466	935
"	**Total**	9	0	0	0	0	1	1	3	617	0	0	466	1,035
1954	Ray Duhigg	6	0	0	0	0	1	1	3	1,036	0	0	684	1,325
"	Jimmie Lewallen	2	0	0	0	0	0	0	1	190	0	0	114	125
"	**Total**	8	0	0	0	0	1	1	4	1,226	0	0	798	1,450
1955	Ray Duhigg	1	0	0	0	1	0	0	0	39	0	0	160	1,000
Lifetime		37	0	0	0	2	2	2	12	4,148	0	0	3,189	$5,825

Cecil Gordon

Year	Driver	Starts	Poles	1	2	3	4	5	6–10	Laps	Laps Led	Races Led	Miles	$
1970	Bill Dennis	1	0	0	0	0	0	0	0	158	0	0	420	1,140
"	Cecil Gordon	44	0	0	0	0	1	1	9	8,424	0	0	6,872	32,713
"	Lee Gordon	6	0	0	0	0	0	0	0	729	0	0	346	1,745
"	Henley Gray	1	0	0	0	0	0	0	0	24	0	0	9	220
"	Dave Marcis	2	0	0	0	0	0	1	0	420	0	0	158	665
"	Jim Vandiver	1	0	0	0	0	0	0	0	281	0	0	111	240
"	**Total**	45	0	0	0	0	1	2	9	10,036	0	0	7,916	36,723
1971	Cecil Gordon	46	0	0	0	2	2	2	15	12,468	0	0	12,034	69,080
1972	Cecil Gordon	31	0	0	0	0	1	3	12	9,033	3	2	10,421	73,126
1973	Cecil Gordon	28	0	0	0	1	1	6	10	8,995	5	3	9,988	102,120
1974	Cecil Gordon	30	0	0	0	0	1	0	9	7,396	2	2	9,079	66,166
1975	Cecil Gordon	30	0	0	1	1	2	3	9	8,577	6	2	9,683	101,467
1976	Cecil Gordon	28	0	0	0	0	0	0	5	6,637	7	3	7,980	70,660
1977	Cecil Gordon	30	0	0	0	0	0	0	2	8,133	0	0	9,604	86,312
1978	Cecil Gordon	25	0	0	0	0	0	0	1	6,647	0	0	7,113	53,350
"	Junior Miller	1	0	0	0	0	0	0	0	376	0	0	235	1,480
"	**Total**	26	0	0	0	0	0	0	1	7,023	0	0	7,348	54,830
1979	Cecil Gordon	26	0	0	0	0	0	0	0	6,907	0	0	7,707	64,165
"	D. K. Ulrich	1	0	0	0	0	0	0	0	383	0	0	228	1,135
"	**Total**	27	0	0	0	0	0	0	0	7,290	0	0	7,936	65,300
1980	Cecil Gordon	26	0	0	0	0	0	0	3	7,353	0	0	8,512	79,880
"	Lake Speed	1	0	0	0	0	0	0	0	79	0	0	207	1,305
"	**Total**	27	0	0	0	0	0	0	3	7,432	0	0	8,719	81,185
1981	Cecil Gordon	18	0	0	0	0	0	0	0	4,470	0	0	5,830	50,650
"	Jimmy Hensley	1	0	0	0	0	0	0	1	487	0	0	256	4,650
"	Lennie Pond	1	0	0	0	0	0	0	0	388	0	0	582	8,100
"	Morgan Shepherd	7	0	0	0	0	0	0	2	2,155	104	1	2,278	28,925
"	Steve Spencer	1	0	0	0	0	0	0	0	400	0	0	238	1,890
"	**Total**	28	0	0	0	0	0	0	3	7,900	104	1	9,185	94,215
1982	John Anderson	1	0	0	0	0	0	0	0	305	0	0	458	6,100
"	Tony Bettenhausen Jr.	1	0	0	0	0	0	0	0	139	0	0	278	3,215
"	Tommy Ellis	0												950
"	Cecil Gordon	4	0	0	0	0	0	0	0	1,125	0	0	1,445	13,920
"	Dick May	1	0	0	0	0	0	0	0	193	0	0	386	4,445
"	J. D. McDuffie	1	0	0	0	0	0	0	0	422	0	0	222	2,655
"	Lennie Pond	10	0	0	0	0	0	0	1	1,425	1	1	1,820	30,175
"	Ronnie Thomas	2	0	0	0	0	0	0	0	344	0	0	542	5,690
"	**Total**	20	0	0	0	0	0	0	1	3,953	1	1	5,150	67,150
1983	Lowell Cowell	0												0
"	Cecil Gordon	8	0	0	0	0	0	0	0	1,831	0	0	3,021	17,790
"	Jim Vandiver	2	0	0	0	0	0	0	0	448	0	0	674	4,810
"	**Total**	10	0	0	0	0	0	0	0	2,279	0	0	3,695	22,600
Lifetime		406	0	0	1	4	8	16	79	107,152	128	14	118,738	$990,934

Harry Goularte

Year	Driver	Starts	Poles	1	2	3	4	5	6–10	Laps	Laps Led	Races Led	Miles	$
1978	Harry Goularte	2	0	0	0	0	0	0	0	185	0	0	473	1,930
1979	Harry Goularte	1	0	0	0	0	0	0	0	82	0	0	215	1,460
1984	Harry Goularte	2	0	0	0	0	0	0	0	172	0	0	451	3,490
1987	Harry Goularte	2	0	0	0	0	0	0	0	171	0	0	448	4,770
Lifetime		7	0	0	0	0	0	0	0	610	0	0	1,587	$11,650

Mel Gould

Year	Driver	Starts	Poles	1	2	3	4	5	6–10	Laps	Laps Led	Races Led	Miles	$
1954	Bill Tanner	1	0	0	0	0	0	0	0	4	0	0	4	0
Lifetime		1	0	0	0	0	0	0	0	4	0	0	4	$0

Year	Driver	Starts	Poles	Finish 1	2	3	4	5	6–10	Laps	Laps Led	Races Led	Miles	$

Johnny Gouveia

Year	Driver	Starts	Poles	1	2	3	4	5	6–10	Laps	Laps Led	Races Led	Miles	$
1952	Johnny Gouveia	1	0	0	0	0	0	0	0	61	0	0	76	0
1955	Johnny Gouveia	4	0	0	0	0	0	0	1	614	0	0	307	260
Lifetime		5	0	0	0	0	0	0	1	675	0	0	383	$260

Matt Gowan

Year	Driver	Starts	Poles	1	2	3	4	5	6–10	Laps	Laps Led	Races Led	Miles	$
1953	Matt Gowan	2	0	0	0	0	0	0	0	250	0	0	344	110
"	Stewart McDonald	1	0	0	0	0	0	0	0	271	0	0	271	50
"	Larry Schultz	1	0	0	0	0	0	0	0	0	0	0	0	40
"	**Total**	4	0	0	0	0	0	0	0	521	0	0	615	200
1954	Matt Gowan	1	0	0	0	0	0	0	0	53	0	0	53	25
Lifetime		5	0	0	0	0	0	0	0	574	0	0	668	$225

Ed Grady

Year	Driver	Starts	Poles	1	2	3	4	5	6–10	Laps	Laps Led	Races Led	Miles	$
1965	Bobby Allison	4	0	0	0	0	0	0	1	271	0	0	317	1,430
Lifetime		4	0	0	0	0	0	0	1	271	0	0	317	$1,430

C. J. Grana

Year	Driver	Starts	Poles	1	2	3	4	5	6–10	Laps	Laps Led	Races Led	Miles	$
1969	Ron Grana	1	0	0	0	0	0	0	0	162	0	0	324	1,275
1970	Ron Grana	3	0	0	0	0	0	0	1	243	0	0	546	2,165
1971	Ron Grana	1	0	0	0	0	0	0	0	187	0	0	381	920
1972	Ron Grana	1	0	0	0	0	0	0	0	31	0	0	62	690
Lifetime		6	0	0	0	0	0	0	1	623	0	0	1,313	$5,050

Danny Graves

Year	Driver	Starts	Poles	1	2	3	4	5	6–10	Laps	Laps Led	Races Led	Miles	$
1957	Danny Graves	7	1	1	0	1	0	1	1	787	1	1	473	1,895
1958	Danny Graves	2	0	0	0	0	0	0	0	90	0	0	198	125
Lifetime		9	1	1	0	1	0	1	1	877	1	1	671	$2,020

Bill Gray

Year	Driver	Starts	Poles	1	2	3	4	5	6–10	Laps	Laps Led	Races Led	Miles	$
1976	Jimmy Means	19	0	0	0	0	0	0	0	4,336	1	1	5,117	20,945
1977	Jimmy Means	25	0	0	0	0	0	0	6	5,972	0	0	6,658	51,630
Lifetime		44	0	0	0	0	0	0	6	10,308	1	1	11,775	$72,575

Eddie Gray

Year	Driver	Starts	Poles	1	2	3	4	5	6–10	Laps	Laps Led	Races Led	Miles	$
1957	Eddie Gray	2	0	0	0	0	0	0	1	206	0	0	153	350
1958	Eddie Gray	3	0	1	0	0	0	0	0	437	43	1	807	3,375
1961	Eddie Gray	4	1	2	1	0	0	0	0	509	75	1	532	3,485
Lifetime		9	1	3	1	0	0	0	1	1,152	118	2	1,491	$7,210

Henley Gray

Year	Driver	Starts	Poles	1	2	3	4	5	6–10	Laps	Laps Led	Races Led	Miles	$
1966	Henley Gray	40	0	0	0	0	0	3	14	9,492	0	0	6,493	20,386
"	Ned Jarrett	2	0	0	0	0	0	0	1	512	0	0	618	2,575
"	Coo Coo Marlin	1	0	0	0	0	0	0	1	375	0	0	188	375
"	G. C. Spencer	1	0	0	0	0	0	1	0	193	0	0	97	275
"	**Total**	44	0	0	0	0	0	4	16	10,572	0	0	7,395	23,611
1967	Red Farmer	2	0	0	0	0	0	0	0	552	7	1	604	1,925
"	Henley Gray	40	0	0	0	0	0	0	10	7,296	0	0	5,012	13,267
"	**Total**	42	0	0	0	0	0	0	10	7,848	7	1	5,616	15,192
1968	Doug Cooper	1	0	0	0	0	0	0	0	206	0	0	103	275
"	Frog Fagan	11	0	0	0	0	0	0	1	1,805	0	0	1,340	3,430
"	Cecil Gordon	5	0	0	0	0	0	0	0	717	0	0	384	670
"	Henley Gray	30	0	0	0	0	0	0	6	6,072	0	0	4,580	12,566
"	Jeff Hawkins	1	0	0	0	0	0	0	0	107	0	0	54	100
"	Paul Dean Holt	4	0	0	0	0	0	0	0	504	0	0	288	535
"	Wendell Scott	1	0	0	0	0	0	0	0	115	0	0	173	650
"	E. J. Trivette	2	0	0	0	0	0	0	0	613	0	0	322	475
"	**Total**	35	0	0	0	0	0	0	7	10,139	0	0	7,242	18,701
1969	Henley Gray	46	0	0	0	0	0	0	5	8,632	0	0	6,843	26,775
1970	Lee Gordon	1	0	0	0	0	0	0	0	26	0	0	9	25
"	Henley Gray	32	0	0	0	0	0	0	2	5,816	0	0	4,799	21,256
"	**Total**	33	0	0	0	0	0	0	2	5,842	0	0	4,808	21,281
1971	Henley Gray	38	0	0	0	0	0	0	4	7,565	0	0	7,442	31,464

Year	Driver	Starts	Poles	1	2	3	4	5	6–10	Laps	Laps Led	Races Led	Miles	$

Henley Gray *continued*

Year	Driver	Starts	Poles	1	2	3	4	5	6–10	Laps	Laps Led	Races Led	Miles	$
1972	Henley Gray	26	0	0	0	0	0	0	2	5,983	0	0	7,199	37,566
"	Charlie Roberts	2	0	0	0	0	0	0	0	226	0	0	484	2,740
"	**Total**	26	0	0	0	0	0	0	2	6,209	0	0	7,683	40,306
1973	Henley Gray	24	0	0	0	0	0	0	4	7,517	0	0	7,608	34,467
"	Jabe Thomas	1	0	0	0	0	0	0	0	315	0	0	430	1,605
"	**Total**	25	0	0	0	0	0	0	4	7,832	0	0	8,038	36,072
1974	Bob Burcham	7	0	0	0	0	0	0	1	1,730	2	1	2,632	8,653
"	Dean Dalton	2	0	0	0	0	0	0	0	341	0	0	201	910
"	Henley Gray	4	0	0	0	0	0	0	1	1,010	0	0	996	4,635
"	Dick May	1	0	0	0	0	0	0	0	176	0	0	461	1,825
"	**Total**	14	0	0	0	0	0	0	2	3,257	2	1	4,289	16,023
1975	Bob Burcham	2	0	0	0	0	0	0	0	549	0	0	829	2,920
"	Henley Gray	7	0	0	0	0	0	0	1	1,497	2	1	1,824	7,060
"	Dick May	1	0	0	0	0	0	0	0	139	0	0	348	1,085
"	Jabe Thomas	1	0	0	0	0	0	0	0	177	0	0	471	1,910
"	**Total**	11	0	0	0	0	0	0	1	2,362	2	1	3,472	12,975
1976	Bill Dennis	1	0	0	0	0	0	0	0	313	0	0	470	1,385
"	Tommy Gale	1	0	0	0	0	0	0	0	70	0	0	175	990
"	Cecil Gordon	1	0	0	0	0	0	0	0	365	0	0	548	2,605
"	Henley Gray	15	0	0	0	0	0	0	0	2,992	0	0	3,598	15,195
"	Ed Negre	2	0	0	0	0	0	0	0	78	0	0	203	1,960
"	Frank Warren	1	0	0	0	0	0	0	0	434	0	0	441	835
"	**Total**	21	0	0	0	0	0	0	0	4,252	0	0	5,435	22,970
1977	Bob Burcham	2	0	0	0	0	0	0	1	408	0	0	808	13,825
"	Dale Earnhardt	1	0	0	0	0	0	0	0	25	0	0	38	1,375
"	Henley Gray	12	0	0	0	0	0	0	0	2,658	0	0	2,391	15,900
"	Dave Marcis	1	0	0	0	0	0	0	0	382	0	0	239	1,600
"	Dick May	6	0	0	0	0	0	0	0	2,084	0	0	1,558	8,595
"	Bobby Wawak	1	0	0	0	0	0	0	0	319	0	0	436	2,465
"	**Total**	23	0	0	0	0	0	0	1	5,876	0	0	5,469	43,760
1978	Joey Arrington	1	0	0	0	0	0	0	0	364	0	0	197	800
"	Joe Booher	1	0	0	0	0	0	0	0	178	0	0	445	1,775
"	Bob Burcham	1	0	0	0	0	0	0	0	243	0	0	332	2,790
"	Bill Dennis	1	0	0	0	0	0	0	0	66	0	0	99	1,560
"	Woody Fisher	3	0	0	0	0	0	0	0	383	0	0	510	4,250
"	Elmo Langley	2	0	0	0	0	0	0	0	93	0	0	94	1,600
"	Dick May	18	0	0	0	0	0	0	0	4,185	0	0	4,803	31,035
"	**Total**	26	0	0	0	0	0	0	0	5,512	0	0	6,482	43,810
1979	Bob Burcham	2	0	0	0	0	0	0	0	356	0	0	826	6,565
"	Bill Dennis	2	0	0	0	0	0	0	0	387	0	0	777	12,645
"	Joe Fields	1	0	0	0	0	0	0	0	379	0	0	205	1,385
"	Vince Giamformaggio	2	0	0	0	0	0	0	0	139	0	0	361	4,295
"	Cecil Gordon	2	0	0	0	0	0	0	0	512	0	0	456	3,015
"	Steve Gray	1	0	0	0	0	0	0	0	1	0	0	3	1,305
"	Billy Hagan	1	0	0	0	0	0	0	0	185	0	0	370	3,280
"	Glenn Jarrett	1	0	0	0	0	0	0	0	164	0	0	167	1,115
"	Dick May	9	0	0	0	0	0	0	0	2,329	0	0	2,136	14,305
"	Lennie Pond	5	0	0	0	0	0	0	0	1,286	0	0	1,512	11,895
"	Steve Spencer	2	0	0	0	0	0	0	0	556	0	0	331	2,270
"	**Total**	28	0	0	0	0	0	0	0	6,294	0	0	7,143	62,075
1980	John Anderson	8	0	0	0	0	0	0	0	1,499	0	0	2,097	21,585
"	Bill Dennis	0													1,200
"	Vince Giamformaggio	1	0	0	0	0	0	0	0	109	0	0	286	2,260
"	Cecil Gordon	1	0	0	0	0	0	0	0	166	0	0	253	1,860
"	Steve Gray	1	0	0	0	0	0	0	0	35	0	0	35	450
"	James Hylton	1	0	0	0	0	0	0	0	312	0	0	468	3,425
"	Dick May	6	0	0	0	0	0	0	1	1,443	0	0	2,148	18,260
"	J. D. McDuffie	1	0	0	0	0	0	0	0	150	0	0	375	4,290
"	Steve Spencer	3	0	0	0	0	0	0	0	599	0	0	344	2,050
"	John Utsman	1	0	0	0	0	0	0	0	464	0	0	247	1,340
"	**Total**	22	0	0	0	0	0	0	1	4,777	0	0	6,252	56,720
1981	Bill Dennis	1	0	0	0	0	0	0	0	327	0	0	491	3,200
"	Cecil Gordon	1	0	0	0	0	0	0	0	189	0	0	378	905
"	Dick May	3	0	0	0	0	0	0	0	274	0	0	712	4,960
"	Ronnie Sanders	1	0	0	0	0	0	0	0	191	0	0	478	7,635
"	**Total**	6	0	0	0	0	0	0	0	981	0	0	2,058	16,700
1982	John Anderson	3	0	0	0	0	0	0	0	320	0	0	650	5,755
"	Buddy Baker	1	0	0	0	0	0	0	0	51	0	0	27	820

Year	Driver	Starts	Poles	Finish 1	2	3	4	5	6–10	Laps	Laps Led	Races Led	Miles	$

Henley Gray *continued*

Year	Driver	Starts	Poles	1	2	3	4	5	6–10	Laps	Laps Led	Races Led	Miles	$
"	Charlie Baker	3	0	0	0	0	0	0	0	444	0	0	1,025	5,235
"	Dennis DeVea	1	0	0	0	0	0	0	0	185	1	1	370	1,670
"	Steve Gray	1	0	0	0	0	0	0	0	103	0	0	258	1,250
"	Dick May	2	0	0	0	0	0	0	0	404	0	0	560	4,680
"	Benny Parsons	1	0	0	0	0	0	0	0	100	0	0	250	1,730
"	**Total**	12	0	0	0	0	0	0	0	1,607	1	1	3,139	21,140
1983	John Anderson	1	0	0	0	0	0	0	0	317	0	0	476	1,350
"	Bobby Gerhart	2	0	0	0	0	0	0	0	69	0	0	173	2,550
"	Steve Gray	3	0	0	0	0	0	0	0	853	0	0	853	3,525
"	Billie Harvey	1	0	0	0	0	0	0	0	1	0	0	3	1,730
"	J. D. McDuffie	1	0	0	0	0	0	0	0	177	0	0	269	1,030
"	Ronnie Sanders	0												950
"	**Total**	7	0	0	0	0	0	0	0	1,417	0	0	1,773	11,135
1984	Steve Gray	1	0	0	0	0	0	0	0	178	0	0	445	1,675
1985	Steve Gray	1	0	0	0	0	0	0	0	151	0	0	378	1,970
"	Slick Johnson	1	0	0	0	0	0	0	0	175	0	0	438	11,210
"	Charles Poalillo	1	0	0	0	0	0	0	0	22	0	0	55	1,395
"	Bobby Wawak	1	0	0	0	0	0	0	0	175	0	0	466	3,210
"	**Total**	3	0	0	0	0	0	0	0	523	0	0	1,336	17,785
1986	Donnie Allison	1	0	0	0	0	0	0	0	131	0	0	179	1,840
"	Eddie Bierschwale	5	0	0	0	0	0	0	0	610	0	0	1,296	18,195
"	Slick Johnson	0												1,100
"	**Total**	6	0	0	0	0	0	0	0	741	0	0	1,475	21,135
1987	Donnie Allison	0												1,050
"	Chuck Schroedel	1	0	0	0	0	0	0	0	8	0	0	19	1,375
"	**Total**	1	0	0	0	0	0	0	0	8	0	0	19	2,425
1988	Ronnie Sanders	0												1,300
1989	Bill Ingram	1	0	0	0	0	0	0	0	181	0	0	481	3,875
"	Ronnie Sanders	1	0	0	0	0	0	0	0	184	0	0	460	12,570
"	**Total**	2	0	0	0	0	0	0	0	365	0	0	941	16,445
1992	Mark Thompson	1	0	0	0	0	0	0	0	8	0	0	20	4,370
1993	Mike Potter	1	0	0	0	0	0	0	0	232	0	0	236	9,275
"	Clay Young	2	0	0	0	0	0	0	0	60	0	0	143	14,370
"	**Total**	3	0	0	0	0	0	0	0	292	0	0	379	23,645
1995	Ronnie Sanders	0												2,650
Lifetime		476	0	0	0	0	0	4	55	103,089	12	4	105,194	$612,140

Chuck Green

Year	Driver	Starts	Poles	1	2	3	4	5	6–10	Laps	Laps Led	Races Led	Miles	$
1957	Eddie Gray	3	0	0	0	0	0	1	0	319	0	0	268	405
Lifetime		3	0	0	0	0	0	1	0	319	0	0	268	$405

George Green

Year	Driver	Starts	Poles	1	2	3	4	5	6–10	Laps	Laps Led	Races Led	Miles	$
1958	George Green	7	0	0	0	0	0	0	0	650	0	0	278	380
Lifetime		7	0	0	0	0	0	0	0	650	0	0	278	$380

Bobby Greene

Year	Driver	Starts	Poles	1	2	3	4	5	6–10	Laps	Laps Led	Races Led	Miles	$
1949	Bobby Greene	2	0	0	0	0	0	0	0	148	0	0	74	50
Lifetime		2	0	0	0	0	0	0	0	148	0	0	74	$50

Oda Greene

Year	Driver	Starts	Poles	1	2	3	4	5	6–10	Laps	Laps Led	Races Led	Miles	$
1952	Oda Greene	1	0	0	0	0	0	0	0	134	0	0	67	25
Lifetime		1	0	0	0	0	0	0	0	134	0	0	67	$25

Allan Grice

Year	Driver	Starts	Poles	1	2	3	4	5	6–10	Laps	Laps Led	Races Led	Miles	$
1987	Allan Grice	1	0	0	0	0	0	0	0	161	0	0	242	1,700
1989	Allan Grice	1	0	0	0	0	0	0	0	294	0	0	441	1,900
Lifetime		2	0	0	0	0	0	0	0	455	0	0	683	$3,600

Griffin Motors (Bob, Johnny, and T. C. Griffin, co-owners)

Year	Driver	Starts	Poles	1	2	3	4	5	6–10	Laps	Laps Led	Races Led	Miles	$
1950	Buck Baker	5	0	0	1	1	0	0	1	374	0	0	319	1,745
1951	Buck Baker	3	0	0	0	0	0	2	0		0	0		800

Year	Driver	Starts	Poles	Finish						Laps	Laps Led	Races Led	Miles	$
				1	2	3	4	5	6–10					

Griffin Motors *continued*

Year	Driver	Starts	Poles	1	2	3	4	5	6–10	Laps	Laps Led	Races Led	Miles	$
"	Gene Darragh	1	0	0	0	0	0	0	0	309	0	0	386	50
"	**Total**	4	0	0	0	0	0	2	0	309	0	0	386	850
1952	Buck Baker	1	0	0	0	0	0	0	0		0	0		25
1953	Buck Baker	30	4	4	2	3	4	3	7	1,582	564	9	1,398	17,892
1954	Buck Baker	19	1	2	6	3	2	1	2	3,085	336	6	2,217	13,668
"	Ray Duhigg	2	0	0	0	0	0	0	0	80	0	0	40	50
"	Jim Paschal	5	1	1	0	1	0	1	0	704	193	1	407	1,800
"	Bob Welborn	1	0	0	0	1	0	0	0	196	0	0	98	450
"	**Total**	27	2	3	6	5	2	2	2	4,065	529	7	2,761	15,968
1955	Buck Baker	18	1	1	4	3	3	0	2	2,628	423	4	1,583	9,376
"	Buddy Shuman	1	0	0	0	0	0	0	1	186	0	0	93	250
"	Speedy Thompson	5	0	0	1	0	0	0	0	743	0	0	900	1,955
"	**Total**	24	1	1	5	3	3	0	3	3,557	423	4	2,576	11,581
Lifetime		91	7	8	14	12	9	7	13	9,887	1,516	20	7,441	$48,061

Charles Griffin

Year	Driver	Starts	Poles	1	2	3	4	5	6–10	Laps	Laps Led	Races Led	Miles	$
1960	Johnny Miller	2	0	0	0	0	0	0	0	207	0	0	307	500
Lifetime		2	0	0	0	0	0	0	0	207	0	0	307	$500

PeeWee Griffin

Year	Driver	Starts	Poles	1	2	3	4	5	6–10	Laps	Laps Led	Races Led	Miles	$
1978	Donnie Allison	3	0	0	0	0	0	0	1	644	0	0	829	3,380
Lifetime		3	0	0	0	0	0	0	1	644	0	0	829	$3,380

Charley Griffith

Year	Driver	Starts	Poles	1	2	3	4	5	6–10	Laps	Laps Led	Races Led	Miles	$
1959	Freddy Fryar	1	0	0	0	0	0	0	0	53	0	0	27	0
"	Charley Griffith	6	0	0	0	1	0	0	2	438	0	0	697	4,955
"	**Total**	7	0	0	0	1	0	0	2	491	0	0	724	4,955
Lifetime		7	0	0	0	1	0	0	2	491	0	0	724	$4,955

Pat Grogan

Year	Driver	Starts	Poles	1	2	3	4	5	6–10	Laps	Laps Led	Races Led	Miles	$
1956	Pat Grogan	1	0	0	0	0	0	0	0	202	0	0	278	50
Lifetime		1	0	0	0	0	0	0	0	202	0	0	278	$50

Heyward Grooms

Year	Driver	Starts	Poles	1	2	3	4	5	6–10	Laps	Laps Led	Races Led	Miles	$
1981	Delma Cowart	1	0	0	0	0	0	0	0	315	0	0	479	1,940
1982	Delma Cowart	5	0	0	0	0	0	0	0	775	0	0	1,466	11,855
Lifetime		6	0	0	0	0	0	0	0	1,090	0	0	1,946	$13,795

Bill Groves

Year	Driver	Starts	Poles	1	2	3	4	5	6–10	Laps	Laps Led	Races Led	Miles	$
1965	Gene Davis	1	0	0	0	0	0	1	0	177	0	0	478	1,850
Lifetime		1	0	0	0	0	0	1	0	177	0	0	478	$1,850

Johnny Grubb

Year	Driver	Starts	Poles	1	2	3	4	5	6–10	Laps	Laps Led	Races Led	Miles	$
1950	Johnny Grubb	3	0	0	0	0	0	0	1	162	0	0	81	225
1951	Johnny Grubb	1	0	0	0	0	0	0	0	0	0	0	0	25
Lifetime		4	0	0	0	0	0	0	1	162	0	0	81	$250

Sally Guide

Year	Driver	Starts	Poles	1	2	3	4	5	6–10	Laps	Laps Led	Races Led	Miles	$
1952	Joe Guide Jr.	2	0	0	0	0	0	0	0	200	0	0	250	0
1953	Joe Guide Jr.	2	0	0	0	0	0	0	0	147	0	0	300	150
1954	Joe Guide Jr.	2	0	0	0	0	0	0	1	160	0	0	331	75
1955	Joe Guide Jr.	2	0	0	0	0	0	0	0	275	0	0	413	360
1956	Joe Guide Jr.	1	0	0	0	0	0	0	0	141	0	0	212	200
Lifetime		9	0	0	0	0	0	0	0	923	0	0	1,505	$785

William Gundaker

Year	Driver	Starts	Poles	1	2	3	4	5	6–10	Laps	Laps Led	Races Led	Miles	$
1951	Bud Farrell	4	0	0	0	0	0	0	1	373	0	0	466	325
"	Tom Jerris	1	0	0	0	0	0	1	0		0	0		250
"	**Total**	5	0	0	0	0	0	1	1	373	0	0	466	575

Year	Driver	Starts	Poles	Finish						Laps	Laps Led	Races Led	Miles	$
				1	2	3	4	5	6–10					

William Gundaker *continued*

Year	Driver	Starts	Poles	1	2	3	4	5	6–10	Laps	Laps Led	Races Led	Miles	$
1952	Bud Farrell	6	0	0	0	0	0	0	2	881	0	0	621	325
Lifetime		11	0	0	0	0	0	1	3	1,254	0	0	1,087	$900

Gerry Gunderman

Year	Driver	Starts	Poles	1	2	3	4	5	6–10	Laps	Laps Led	Races Led	Miles	$
1986	Mark Martin	5	0	0	0	0	0	0	0	1,342	0	0	1,955	20,515
Lifetime		5	0	0	0	0	0	0	0	1,342	0	0	1,955	$20,515

Don Guy

Year	Driver	Starts	Poles	1	2	3	4	5	6–10	Laps	Laps Led	Races Led	Miles	$
1979	Robert Tartaglia	1	0	0	0	0	0	0	0	47	0	0	123	825
1980	Steve Pfeifer	1	0	0	0	0	0	0	0	82	0	0	215	905
Lifetime		2	0	0	0	0	0	0	0	129	0	0	338	$1,730

John Gwinn

Year	Driver	Starts	Poles	1	2	3	4	5	6–10	Laps	Laps Led	Races Led	Miles	$
1976	Bobby Wawak	19	0	0	0	0	0	0	9	4,888	0	0	6,231	30,415
1977	Ron Hutcherson	4	0	0	0	0	0	0	1	1,019	0	0	1,862	21,685
"	Bobby Wawak	3	0	0	0	0	0	0	0	202	0	0	332	5,770
"	**Total**	7	0	0	0	0	0	0	1	1,221	0	0	2,194	27,455
Lifetime		26	0	0	0	0	0	0	10	6,109	0	0	8,426	$57,870

C. B. Gwynn

Year	Driver	Starts	Poles	1	2	3	4	5	6–10	Laps	Laps Led	Races Led	Miles	$
1969	C. B. Gwynn	1	0	0	0	0	0	0	0	73	0	0	194	1,150
Lifetime		1	0	0	0	0	0	0	0	73	0	0	194	$1,150

Ted Haak

Year	Driver	Starts	Poles	1	2	3	4	5	6–10	Laps	Laps Led	Races Led	Miles	$
1960	Al Self	2	0	0	0	0	0	0	1	227	0	0	290	550
Lifetime		2	0	0	0	0	0	0	1	227	0	0	290	$550

Bob Haas

Year	Driver	Starts	Poles	1	2	3	4	5	6–10	Laps	Laps Led	Races Led	Miles	$
1982	Ernie Cline	1	0	0	0	0	0	0	0	154	0	0	157	900
Lifetime		1	0	0	0	0	0	0	0	154	0	0	157	$900

Billy Hagan

Year	Driver	Starts	Poles	1	2	3	4	5	6–10	Laps	Laps Led	Races Led	Miles	$
1969	Billy Hagan	1	0	0	0	0	0	0	1	155	0	0	412	1,750
1975	Billy Hagan	1	0	0	0	0	0	0	0	175	0	0	466	1,770
"	Skip Manning	5	0	0	0	0	0	0	0	995	0	0	1,794	9,705
"	**Total**	6	0	0	0	0	0	0	0	1,170	0	0	2,260	11,475
1976	Skip Manning	25	0	0	0	0	0	0	4	6,446	0	0	7,806	58,952
1977	Skip Manning	28	0	0	0	1	0	0	7	7,533	13	1	8,355	111,317
1978	Terry Labonte	5	0	0	0	0	1	0	2	1,849	0	0	1,879	21,395
"	Mel Larson	1	0	0	0	0	0	0	0	31	0	0	62	1,175
"	Skip Manning	15	0	0	0	0	1	0	3	4,043	0	0	4,928	51,145
"	Dick May	2	0	0	0	0	0	0	1	956	0	0	964	6,780
"	**Total**	23	0	0	0	0	2	0	6	6,879	0	0	7,833	80,495
1979	Terry Labonte	31	0	0	0	1	0	1	11	8,766	8	4	9,886	134,653
1980	Terry Labonte	31	0	1	0	1	1	3	10	8,760	46	6	9,951	222,502
1981	Terry Labonte	31	2	0	1	3	2	2	9	9,074	114	14	10,530	348,703
1982	Terry Labonte	30	2	0	6	2	6	3	4	8,900	263	17	10,259	398,635
1983	Terry Labonte	30	3	1	0	0	4	6	9	8,498	434	13	9,774	388,419
1984	Terry Labonte	30	2	2	6	6	2	1	7	9,886	880	26	11,236	767,716
"	Joe Millikan	1	0	0	0	0	0	0	0	53	0	0	139	900
"	**Total**	30	2	2	6	6	2	1	7	9,939	880	**26**	11,375	768,816
1985	Terry Labonte	28	4	1	2	3	1	1	9	7,973	563	14	9,603	694,510
1986	Terry Labonte	29	1	1	2	2	0	0	5	8,284	565	10	9,588	522,235
1987	Sterling Marlin	29	0	0	0	1	2	1	4	8,356	68	6	10,304	306,412
1988	Sterling Marlin	29	0	0	1	1	0	4	7	8,798	332	13	10,383	521,464
1989	Sterling Marlin	29	0	0	1	1	0	2	9	8,840	42	6	10,578	473,267
1990	Sterling Marlin	29	0	0	0	1	1	3	5	8,310	71	6	10,139	369,167
1991	Terry Labonte	29	1	0	0	0	0	1	6	7,989	52	2	9,615	348,898
1992	Terry Labonte	29	0	0	1	0	2	1	12	8,912	43	4	10,612	600,381
1993	John Andretti	4	0	0	0	0	0	0	0	874	0	0	895	24,915
"	Terry Labonte	30	0	0	0	0	0	0	10	8,866	55	3	10,641	531,717
"	**Total**	30	0	0	0	0	0	0	10	9,740	55	3	11,536	556,632

Year	Driver	Starts	Poles	Finish						Laps	Laps Led	Races Led	Miles	$
				1	2	3	4	5	6–10					

Billy Hagan *continued*

Year	Driver	Starts	Poles	1	2	3	4	5	6–10	Laps	Laps Led	Races Led	Miles	$
1994	John Andretti	18	0	0	0	0	0	0	0	3,786	1	1	5,130	275,520
"	Randy MacDonald	1	0	0	0	0	0	0	0	466	0	0	474	8,200
"	**Total**	19	0	0	0	0	0	0	0	4,252	1	1	5,604	283,720
Lifetime		546	15	6	20	23	23	29	135	157,574	3,550	146	186,404 **9th**	$7,202,403

Budd Hagelin

Year	Driver	Starts	Poles	1	2	3	4	5	6–10	Laps	Laps Led	Races Led	Miles	$
1976	Budd Hagelin	1	0	0	0	0	0	0	0	409	0	0	409	1,040
Lifetime		1	0	0	0	0	0	0	0	409	0	0	409	$1,040

Ed Hale

Year	Driver	Starts	Poles	1	2	3	4	5	6–10	Laps	Laps Led	Races Led	Miles	$
1980	Ed Hale	1	0	0	0	0	0	0	0	37	0	0	97	1,200
Lifetime		1	0	0	0	0	0	0	0	37	0	0	97	$1,200

D. G. Hall

Year	Driver	Starts	Poles	1	2	3	4	5	6–10	Laps	Laps Led	Races Led	Miles	$
1950	June Cleveland	2	0	0	0	0	0	0	0	130	0	0	251	50
1951	June Cleveland	1	0	0	0	0	0	0	0	0	0	0	0	25
Lifetime		3	0	0	0	0	0	0	0	130	0	0	251	$75

Roy Hallquist

Year	Driver	Starts	Poles	1	2	3	4	5	6–10	Laps	Laps Led	Races Led	Miles	$
1963	Roy Hallquist	1	0	0	0	0	0	0	0	34	0	0	97	130
1966	Roy Hallquist	4	0	0	0	0	2	0	0	547	0	0	335	895
1968	Roy Hallquist	1	0	0	0	0	0	0	0	51	0	0	51	250
1969	Roy Hallquist	3	0	0	0	0	0	0	0	260	0	0	259	1,070
Lifetime		9	0	0	0	0	2	0	0	892	0	0	741	$2,345

Joel Halpern

Year	Driver	Starts	Poles	1	2	3	4	5	6–10	Laps	Laps Led	Races Led	Miles	$
1980	Donnie Allison	1	0	0	0	0	0	0	0	127	0	0	338	2,125
"	Chuck Bown	4	0	0	0	0	0	0	0	496	0	0	904	4,270
"	Darrell Waltrip	1	0	0	0	0	1	0	0	200	67	1	400	6,050
"	**Total**	6	0	0	0	0	1	0	0	823	67	1	1,642	12,445
1981	David Pearson	4	0	0	0	0	0	0	1	887	7	2	1,320	9,625
Lifetime		10	0	0	0	0	1	0	1	1,710	74	3	2,962	$22,070

Jeff Halverson

Year	Driver	Starts	Poles	1	2	3	4	5	6–10	Laps	Laps Led	Races Led	Miles	$
1979	Jeff Halverson	1	0	0	0	0	0	0	0	1	0	0	1	490
1983	Dick May	1	0	0	0	0	0	0	0	34	0	0	85	1,350
1984	Johnny Coy Jr.	1	0	0	0	0	0	0	0	416	0	0	416	1,090
Lifetime		3	0	0	0	0	0	0	0	451	0	0	502	$2,930

Roger Hamby

Year	Driver	Starts	Poles	1	2	3	4	5	6–10	Laps	Laps Led	Races Led	Miles	$
1977	Roger Hamby	2	0	0	0	0	0	0	0	614	0	0	605	2,275
1978	Roger Hamby	26	0	0	0	0	0	0	2	7,181	0	0	7,688	41,565
1979	Bill Elliott	4	0	0	0	0	0	0	1	1,630	0	0	1,059	8,610
"	Roger Hamby	12	0	0	0	0	0	0	0	2,974	0	0	2,736	21,660
"	Skip Manning	2	0	0	0	0	0	0	0	182	0	0	326	5,880
"	Steve Pfeifer	2	0	0	0	0	0	0	0	360	0	0	544	3,595
"	Jim Vandiver	1	0	0	0	0	0	0	0	240	0	0	328	1,800
"	**Total**	21	0	0	0	0	0	0	1	5,386	0	0	4,992	41,545
1980	Bill Elliott	1	0	0	0	0	0	0	0	466	0	0	248	1,460
"	Roger Hamby	25	0	0	0	0	0	0	0	6,777	0	0	7,588	51,534
"	Glenn Jarrett	1	0	0	0	0	0	0	0	195	0	0	488	3,850
"	Don Whittington	1	0	0	0	0	0	0	0	187	0	0	468	9,510
"	**Total**	28	0	0	0	0	0	0	0	7,625	0	0	8,792	66,354
1981	John Anderson	2	0	0	0	0	0	0	0	542	0	0	711	6,835
"	Lowell Cowell	4	0	0	0	0	0	0	0	812	0	0	1,220	8,055
"	Harry Gant	1	0	0	0	0	0	0	0	114	0	0	299	3,120
"	Roger Hamby	1	0	0	0	0	0	0	0	72	0	0	144	2,450
"	Tommy Houston	7	0	0	0	0	0	0	0	2,219	0	0	1,902	20,760
"	Glenn Jarrett	3	0	0	0	0	0	0	0	679	0	0	864	12,650
"	Steve Pfeifer	1	0	0	0	0	0	0	0	92	0	0	241	3,080
"	Mike Potter	6	0	0	0	0	0	0	0	1,051	0	0	1,351	14,500

Year	Driver	Starts	Poles	1	2	3	4	5	6–10	Laps	Laps Led	Races Led	Miles	$

Roger Hamby *continued*

Year	Driver	Starts	Poles	1	2	3	4	5	6–10	Laps	Laps Led	Races Led	Miles	$
"	Lake Speed	1	0	0	0	0	0	0	0	115	0	0	301	3,345
"	Steve Spencer	2	0	0	0	0	0	0	0	638	0	0	508	3,915
"	**Total**	27	0	0	0	0	0	0	0	6,334	0	0	7,541	78,710
1982	Lowell Cowell	5	0	0	0	0	0	0	0	862	0	0	2,210	26,215
"	Mike Potter	2	0	0	0	0	0	0	0	322	0	0	645	3,535
"	Lake Speed	29	0	0	0	0	0	0	5	5,827	0	0	6,848	113,007
"	**Total**	30	0	0	0	0	0	0	5	7,011	0	0	9,703	142,757
1983	Clark Dwyer	5	0	0	0	0	0	0	1	851	0	0	1,412	14,570
"	Sterling Marlin	30	0	0	0	0	0	0	1	8,053	0	0	9,166	148,253
"	**Total**	30	0	0	0	0	0	0	2	8,904	0	0	10,578	162,823
1984	Clark Dwyer	21	0	0	0	0	0	0	0	5,396	1	1	6,647	94,665
"	Sterling Marlin	1	0	0	0	0	0	0	0	197	0	0	493	15,150
"	Morgan Shepherd	6	0	0	0	0	0	0	0	1,658	0	0	1,412	19,035
"	Lake Speed	2	0	0	0	0	0	0	0	442	0	0	508	7,615
"	**Total**	28	0	0	0	0	0	0	0	7,693	1	1	9,059	136,465
1985	Bosco Lowe	1	0	0	0	0	0	0	0	171	0	0	455	6,825
"	Phil Parsons	14	0	0	0	0	0	0	1	4,491	0	0	3,471	55,065
"	Lennie Pond	7	0	0	0	0	0	0	0	1,271	3	2	2,759	38,595
"	Ken Ragan	6	0	0	0	0	0	0	0	1,135	0	0	1,919	34,520
"	**Total**	27	0	0	0	0	0	0	1	7,068	3	2	8,604	135,005
1986	Eddie Bierschwale	9	0	0	0	0	0	0	0	3,399	0	0	3,076	41,960
"	Pancho Carter	6	0	0	0	0	0	0	0	751	3	2	1,809	33,805
"	Doug Heveron	10	0	0	0	0	0	0	0	1,854	0	0	2,440	62,285
"	Jim Hull	1	0	0	0	0	0	0	0	191	0	0	382	5,390
"	Phil Parsons	2	0	0	0	0	0	0	0	245	0	0	241	7,870
"	**Total**	28	0	0	0	0	0	0	0	6,440	3	2	7,948	151,310
1987	Jim Bown	2	0	0	0	0	0	0	0	264	0	0	668	8,850
"	Trevor Boys	4	0	0	0	0	0	0	0	822	4	1	1,199	21,065
"	Larry Caudill	1	0	0	0	0	0	0	0	470	0	0	470	4,725
"	Rodney Combs	1	0	0	0	0	0	0	0	43	0	0	65	4,490
"	Slick Johnson	7	0	0	0	0	0	0	0	2,102	3	2	1,832	36,505
"	Mark Martin	1	0	0	0	0	0	0	0	68	0	0	102	3,550
"	Larry Pollard	4	0	0	0	0	0	0	0	1,415	0	0	1,324	19,130
"	David Sosebee	3	0	0	0	0	0	0	0	570	0	0	1,013	25,030
"	Jeff Swindell	1	0	0	0	0	0	0	0	102	0	0	271	5,230
"	Brad Teague	1	0	0	0	0	0	0	0	216	0	0	115	3,455
"	**Total**	25	0	0	0	0	0	0	0	6,072	7	3	7,059	132,030
1988	Steve Moore	3	0	0	0	0	0	0	0	726	0	0	1,069	18,790
"	Lennie Pond	1	0	0	0	0	0	0	0	383	0	0	208	2,375
"	**Total**	4	0	0	0	0	0	0	0	1,109	0	0	1,276	21,165
Lifetime		276	0	0	0	0	0	0	11	71,437	14	8	83,846	$1,112,004

Hubert Hamilton

Year	Driver	Starts	Poles	1	2	3	4	5	6–10	Laps	Laps Led	Races Led	Miles	$
1951	Jimmie Lewallen	6	0	0	0	2	0	2	2		0	0		1,775
1952	Ray Duhigg	1	0	0	0	0	0	0	0		0	0		25
Lifetime		7	0	0	0	2	0	2	2		0	0		$1,800

Roger Hamilton

Year	Driver	Starts	Poles	1	2	3	4	5	6–10	Laps	Laps Led	Races Led	Miles	$
1996	Ed Berrier	1	0	0	0	0	0	0	0	57	0	0	78	9,895
Lifetime		1	0	0	0	0	0	0	0	57	0	0	78	$9,895

Margo Hamm

Year	Driver	Starts	Poles	1	2	3	4	5	6–10	Laps	Laps Led	Races Led	Miles	$
1968	Stan Meserve	29	0	0	0	0	0	0	1	3,769	0	0	2,459	7,100
Lifetime		29	0	0	0	0	0	0	1	3,769	0	0	2,459	$7,100

Richard Hammond

Year	Driver	Starts	Poles	1	2	3	4	5	6–10	Laps	Laps Led	Races Led	Miles	$
1972	Jim Hurtubise	1	0	0	0	0	0	0	0	100	0	0	250	1,700
Lifetime		1	0	0	0	0	0	0	0	100	0	0	250	$1,700

Greg Hamson

Year	Driver	Starts	Poles	1	2	3	4	5	6–10	Laps	Laps Led	Races Led	Miles	$
1976	John Hamson	1	0	0	0	0	0	0	0	26	0	0	68	790
Lifetime		1	0	0	0	0	0	0	0	26	0	0	68	$790

Year	Driver	Starts	Poles	1	2	3	4	5	6–10	Laps	Laps Led	Races Led	Miles	$

Mack Hanbury

Year	Driver	Starts	Poles	1	2	3	4	5	6–10	Laps	Laps Led	Races Led	Miles	$
1955	Mack Hanbury	8	0	0	0	0	0	0	2	807	0	0	584	575
Lifetime		8	0	0	0	0	0	0	2	807	0	0	584	$575

Mark Handley

Year	Driver	Starts	Poles	1	2	3	4	5	6–10	Laps	Laps Led	Races Led	Miles	$
1954	Kenneth Bridge	1	0	0	0	0	0	0	0	5	0	0	5	0
Lifetime		1	0	0	0	0	0	0	0	5	0	0	5	$0

Hiram Handy

Year	Driver	Starts	Poles	1	2	3	4	5	6–10	Laps	Laps Led	Races Led	Miles	$
1975	Jeff Handy	1	0	0	0	0	0	0	0	174	0	0	463	1,820
"	Elmo Langley	1	0	0	0	0	0	0	0	310	0	0	472	1,500
"	Dick May	4	0	0	0	0	0	0	1	1,248	0	0	1,449	6,575
"	**Total**	6	0	0	0	0	0	0	1	1,732	0	0	2,384	9,895
1976	Buck Baker	5	0	0	0	0	0	0	0	1,284	0	0	1,655	6,920
"	Earl Brooks	2	0	0	0	0	0	0	0	667	0	0	662	2,170
"	Jeff Handy	1	0	0	0	0	0	0	0	3	0	0	2	370
"	Dick May	3	0	0	0	0	0	0	0	818	0	0	1,003	4,790
"	J. D. McDuffie	1	0	0	0	0	0	0	0	389	0	0	396	735
"	**Total**	12	0	0	0	0	0	0	0	3,161	0	0	3,718	14,985
1977	Earl Brooks	5	0	0	0	0	0	0	0	1,129	0	0	867	2,645
1978	Jim Hurtubise	0												700
Lifetime		23	0	0	0	0	0	0	1	6,022	0	0	6,969	$28,225

Chuck Hansen

Year	Driver	Starts	Poles	1	2	3	4	5	6–10	Laps	Laps Led	Races Led	Miles	$
1957	Chuck Hansen	7	0	0	0	0	0	0	0	990	0	0	734	510
1958	Chuck Hansen	7	0	0	0	0	0	0	1	1,011	0	0	659	580
Lifetime		14	0	0	0	0	0	0	1	2,001	0	0	1,393	$1,090

Jerry Hansen

Year	Driver	Starts	Poles	1	2	3	4	5	6–10	Laps	Laps Led	Races Led	Miles	$
1974	Jerry Hansen	3	0	0	0	0	0	0	0	221	0	0	543	3,230
1977	Steve Stolarek	1	0	0	0	0	0	0	0	21	0	0	21	490
Lifetime		4	0	0	0	0	0	0	0	242	0	0	564	$3,720

Walt Hansgen

Year	Driver	Starts	Poles	1	2	3	4	5	6–10	Laps	Laps Led	Races Led	Miles	$
1964	Walt Hansgen	2	0	0	0	2	0	0	0	113	0	0	286	1,100
1965	Walt Hansgen	1	0	0	0	0	0	0	1	58	0	0	133	355
Lifetime		3	0	0	0	2	0	0	1	171	0	0	420	$1,455

Fred Harb

Year	Driver	Starts	Poles	1	2	3	4	5	6–10	Laps	Laps Led	Races Led	Miles	$
1955	Fred Harb	1	0	0	0	0	0	0	0	183	0	0	92	75
1956	Fred Harb	2	0	0	0	0	0	0	0	200	0	0	85	50
1957	Fred Harb	3	0	0	0	0	0	0	0	322	0	0	161	360
"	Billy Myers	1	0	0	0	0	0	0	0	160	0	0	80	100
"	Shorty York	1	0	0	0	0	0	0	0	109	0	0	55	50
"	**Total**	5	0	0	0	0	0	0	0	591	0	0	296	510
1958	Fred Harb	25	0	0	0	1	2	1	3	3,651	0	0	1,840	3,315
1959	Fred Harb	17	0	0	0	1	0	1	3	2,324	0	0	1,094	1,625
1960	Buddy Baker	2	0	0	0	0	0	0	0	302	0	0	189	160
"	Fred Harb	18	0	0	0	0	0	2	4	2,701	0	0	1,233	2,305
"	Harvey Hege	1	0	0	0	0	0	0	0	62	0	0	31	100
"	Shorty York	2	0	0	0	0	0	0	0	434	0	0	412	325
"	**Total**	21	0	0	0	0	0	2	4	3,499	0	0	1,865	2,890
1961	Buddy Baker	1	0	0	0	0	0	0	0	59	0	0	30	50
"	Fred Harb	26	0	0	0	0	1	0	6	3,898	0	0	1,987	3,320
"	Harvey Hege	1	0	0	0	0	0	0	0	166	0	0	42	100
"	**Total**	26	0	0	0	0	1	0	6	4,123	0	0	2,058	3,470
1962	Fred Harb	20	0	0	0	0	0	0	3	2,703	0	0	1,160	2,220
"	Joe Weatherly	1	0	0	0	0	1	0	0	197	0	0	66	290
"	**Total**	21	0	0	0	0	1	0	3	2,900	0	0	1,225	2,510
1963	Bunkie Blackburn	1	0	0	0	0	0	0	0	161	0	0	242	325
"	Ralph Earnhardt	1	0	0	0	0	0	0	0	88	0	0	121	570
"	Fred Harb	11	0	0	1	0	0	0	5	2,104	0	0	793	2,040
"	Floyd Powell	1	0	0	0	0	0	0	1	154	0	0	139	275
"	Joe Weatherly	2	0	0	0	0	2	0	0	394	0	0	197	1,000

Year	Driver	Starts	Poles	Finish 1	2	3	4	5	6–10	Laps	Laps Led	Races Led	Miles	$

Fred Harb *continued*

Year	Driver	Starts	Poles	1	2	3	4	5	6–10	Laps	Laps Led	Races Led	Miles	$
"	Bob Welborn	3	0	0	0	1	0	0	0	845	0	0	446	875
"	**Total**	19	0	0	1	1	2	0	6	3,746	0	0	1,937	5,085
1964	Fred Harb	1	0	0	0	0	0	0	1	188	0	0	47	180
Lifetime		138	0	0	1	3	6	4	26	21,405	0	0	10,539	$19,710

Bud Harbaugh

Year	Driver	Starts	Poles	1	2	3	4	5	6–10	Laps	Laps Led	Races Led	Miles	$
1956	Gene Simpson	1	0	0	0	0	0	0	0		0	0		100
Lifetime		1	0	0	0	0	0	0	0		0	0		$100

Tom Harbison

Year	Driver	Starts	Poles	1	2	3	4	5	6–10	Laps	Laps Led	Races Led	Miles	$
1956	Allen Adkins	2	0	0	0	0	0	0	2	304	0	0	245	400
"	Danny Letner	4	0	0	0	0	0	0	0	510	0	0	518	300
"	Marvin Panch	19	1	1	2	4	2	0	3	2,939	107	5	2,008	8,150
"	**Total**	23	1	1	2	4	2	0	5	3,753	107	5	2,771	8,850
1957	Jim Delaney	1	0	0	0	0	0	0	0	0	0	0	0	75
"	Danny Letner	1	0	0	0	0	0	0	0	22	0	0	55	65
"	Mickey McGreevey	1	0	0	0	0	0	0	0	55	0	0	138	135
"	**Total**	2	0	0	0	0	0	0	0	77	0	0	193	275
Lifetime		25	1	1	2	4	2	0	5	3,830	107	5	2,963	$9,125

Jack Harden

Year	Driver	Starts	Poles	1	2	3	4	5	6–10	Laps	Laps Led	Races Led	Miles	$
1967	Jack Harden	1	0	0	0	0	0	0	0	11	0	0	10	0
"	Bobby Mausgrover	1	0	0	0	0	0	0	1	273	0	0	137	200
"	**Total**	2	0	0	0	0	0	0	1	284	0	0	146	200
Lifetime		2	0	0	0	0	0	0	1	284	0	0	146	$200

J. E. Hardie

Year	Driver	Starts	Poles	1	2	3	4	5	6–10	Laps	Laps Led	Races Led	Miles	$
1951	J. E. Hardie	1	0	0	0	0	0	0	0	339	0	0	424	50
1952	J. E. Hardie	2	0	0	0	0	0	0	0	69	0	0	86	25
Lifetime		3	0	0	0	0	0	0	0	408	0	0	510	$75

Charles Hardy

Year	Driver	Starts	Poles	1	2	3	4	5	6–10	Laps	Laps Led	Races Led	Miles	$
1994	Jimmy Hensley	1	0	0	0	0	0	0	0	325	2	1	495	10,950
"	Bobby Hillin Jr.	4	0	0	0	0	0	0	0	689	2	1	1,292	60,315
"	Kenny Wallace	1	0	0	0	0	0	0	1	188	0	0	500	13,370
"	**Total**	6	0	0	0	0	0	0	1	1,202	4	2	2,287	84,635
1995	Bill Elliott*	31	2	0	0	0	2	2	7	8,995	123	8	11,073	996,816
1996	Todd Bodine	4	0	0	0	0	0	0	1	1,104	0	0	1,708	92,945
"	Bill Elliott*	11	0	0	0	0	0	0	3	3,311	100	4	3,568	310,306
"	Tommy Kendall	1	0	0	0	0	0	0	0	73	4	1	184	20,730
"	**Total**	16	0	0	0	0	0	0	4	4,488	104	5	5,460	423,981
Lifetime		53	2	0	0	0	2	2	12	14,685	231	15	18,820	$1,505,432

*Co-owned with Bill Elliott through the first half of 1996.

Fred Harless

Year	Driver	Starts	Poles	1	2	3	4	5	6–10	Laps	Laps Led	Races Led	Miles	$
1953	Bud Harless	1	0	0	0	0	0	0	0	168	0	0	84	25
1954	Bud Harless	4	0	0	0	0	0	0	0	353	0	0	283	50
1963	Bud Harless	5	0	0	0	0	0	0	1	1,508	0	0	958	1,550
1964	Bud Harless	7	0	0	0	0	0	0	0	1,371	0	0	709	1,830
1965	Bud Harless	1	0	0	0	0	0	0	0	222	0	0	305	605
Lifetime		18	0	0	0	0	0	0	1	3,622	0	0	2,339	$4,060

Robert Harper

Year	Driver	Starts	Poles	1	2	3	4	5	6–10	Laps	Laps Led	Races Led	Miles	$
1966	Donnie Allison	2	0	0	0	0	0	0	1	664	0	0	757	2,180
1967	Donnie Allison	5	0	0	0	0	0	0	1	1,282	0	0	1,397	5,255
"	Armond Holley	4	0	0	0	0	0	0	0	347	0	0	404	2,000
"	**Total**	9	0	0	0	0	0	0	1	1,629	0	0	1,801	7,255
Lifetime		11	0	0	0	0	0	0	2	2,293	0	0	2,558	$9,435

Red Harrelson

Year	Driver	Starts	Poles	1	2	3	4	5	6–10	Laps	Laps Led	Races Led	Miles	$
1952	Lamar Crabtree	1	0	0	0	0	0	0	0	254	0	0	318	0

Year	Driver	Starts	Poles	Finish 1	2	3	4	5	6–10	Laps	Laps Led	Races Led	Miles	$

Red Harrelson *continued*

Year	Driver	Starts	Poles	1	2	3	4	5	6–10	Laps	Laps Led	Races Led	Miles	$
"	Bucky Sager	1	0	0	0	0	0	0	0	142	0	0	178	0
"	**Total**	1	0	0	0	0	0	0	0	396	0	0	495	0
Lifetime		1	0	0	0	0	0	0	0	396	0	0	495	$0

Robert Harrington

Year	Driver	Starts	Poles	1	2	3	4	5	6–10	Laps	Laps Led	Races Led	Miles	$
1984	Rodney Combs	1	0	0	0	0	0	0	0	192	0	0	384	1,750
"	Elliott Forbes-Robinson	5	0	0	0	0	0	0	0	895	0	0	1,513	11,335
"	Morgan Shepherd	1	0	0	0	0	0	0	0	397	0	0	215	1,735
"	**Total**	7	0	0	0	0	0	0	0	1,484	0	0	2,112	14,820
1986	Rodney Combs	5	0	0	0	0	0	0	0	909	4	1	1,767	12,180
Lifetime		12	0	0	0	0	0	0	0	2,393	4	1	3,880	$27,000

Ferrel Harris

Year	Driver	Starts	Poles	1	2	3	4	5	6–10	Laps	Laps Led	Races Led	Miles	$
1975	Ferrel Harris	10	0	0	0	0	0	0	0	2,357	0	0	3,854	16,165
"	Hershel McGriff	1	0	0	0	0	0	0	0	310	4	1	465	3,360
"	**Total**	11	0	0	0	0	0	0	0	2,667	4	1	4,319	19,525
1976	Ferrel Harris	2	0	0	0	0	0	0	0	217	0	0	565	2,950
"	Skip Manning	1	0	0	0	0	0	0	0	107	0	0	268	1,835
"	**Total**	3	0	0	0	0	0	0	0	324	0	0	833	4,785
1977	Elliott Forbes-Robinson	1	0	0	0	0	0	0	0	44	0	0	110	2,025
1980	Ferrel Harris	1	0	0	0	0	0	0	0	342	0	0	467	2,675
"	Dick May	1	0	0	0	0	0	0	0	323	0	0	485	3,700
"	**Total**	2	0	0	0	0	0	0	0	665	0	0	952	6,375
Lifetime		17	0	0	0	0	0	0	0	3,700	4	1	6,213	$32,710

Bill Harrison

Year	Driver	Starts	Poles	1	2	3	4	5	6–10	Laps	Laps Led	Races Led	Miles	$
1951	Bill Harrison	1	0	0	0	0	0	0	0	133	0	0	100	25
Lifetime		1	0	0	0	0	0	0	0	133	0	0	100	$25

Donald Harrison

Year	Driver	Starts	Poles	1	2	3	4	5	6–10	Laps	Laps Led	Races Led	Miles	$
1962	Gerald Duke	4	0	0	0	0	0	0	0	607	0	0	754	800
"	Cale Yarborough	3	0	0	0	0	0	0	0	179	0	0	208	1,010
"	**Total**	7	0	0	0	0	0	0	0	786	0	0	962	1,810
1963	LeeRoy Yarbrough	1	0	0	0	0	0	0	0	19	0	0	26	630
Lifetime		8	0	0	0	0	0	0	0	805	0	0	988	$2,440

Joe Harrison

Year	Driver	Starts	Poles	1	2	3	4	5	6–10	Laps	Laps Led	Races Led	Miles	$
1950	Joe Harrison	1	0	0	0	0	0	0	0	3	0	0	13	25
Lifetime		1	0	0	0	0	0	0	0	3	0	0	13	$25

W. M. Harrison

Year	Driver	Starts	Poles	1	2	3	4	5	6–10	Laps	Laps Led	Races Led	Miles	$
1963	Bubba Farr	2	0	0	0	0	0	0	0	34	0	0	85	550
"	LeeRoy Yarbrough	1	0	0	0	0	0	0	0	130	0	0	179	420
"	**Total**	3	0	0	0	0	0	0	0	164	0	0	264	970
Lifetime		3	0	0	0	0	0	0	0	164	0	0	264	$970

George Harrivel

Year	Driver	Starts	Poles	1	2	3	4	5	6–10	Laps	Laps Led	Races Led	Miles	$
1976	John Haver	1	0	0	0	0	0	0	0	49	0	0	98	780
Lifetime		1	0	0	0	0	0	0	0	49	0	0	98	$780

Bud Hartje

Year	Driver	Starts	Poles	1	2	3	4	5	6–10	Laps	Laps Led	Races Led	Miles	$
1966	James Hylton	41	1	0	4	6	7	3	12	10,804	155	3	8,498	38,723
1967	James Hylton	46	1	0	3	3	12	8	13	11,526	109	5	8,534	49,732
Lifetime		87	2	0	7	9	19	11	25	22,330	264	8	17,032	$88,455

George Hartley

Year	Driver	Starts	Poles	1	2	3	4	5	6–10	Laps	Laps Led	Races Led	Miles	$
1951	Bill Rexford	1	0	0	0	0	0	0	0	143	0	0	179	0
Lifetime		1	0	0	0	0	0	0	0	143	0	0	179	$0

Year	Driver	Starts	Poles	Finish						Laps	Laps Led	Races Led	Miles	$
				1	2	3	4	5	6–10	Laps	Led	Led	Miles	$

Butch Hartman

Year	Driver	Starts	Poles	1	2	3	4	5	6–10	Laps	Laps Led	Races Led	Miles	$
1966	Butch Hartman	1	0	0	0	0	0	0	0	307	0	0	461	875
1968	Butch Hartman	5	0	0	0	0	0	0	2	1,458	10	2	2,278	6,455
1977	Butch Hartman	11	0	0	0	0	0	0	2	2,005	0	0	3,690	18,615
1978	Butch Hartman	1	0	0	0	0	0	0	0	121	0	0	184	640
1979	Butch Hartman	1	0	0	0	0	0	0	0	351	0	0	479	2,225
Lifetime		19	0	0	0	0	0	0	4	4,242	10	2	7,092	$28,810

Billie Harvey

Year	Driver	Starts	Poles	1	2	3	4	5	6–10	Laps	Laps Led	Races Led	Miles	$
1977	Billy McGinnis	1	0	0	0	0	0	0	0	264	0	0	402	1,570
1978	Billy McGinnis	1	0	0	0	0	0	0	0	221	0	0	336	875
1979	Gary Balough	3	0	0	0	0	0	0	0	216	0	0	540	6,015
"	Dick May	1	0	0	0	0	0	0	0	0	0	0	0	1,050
"	**Total**	4	0	0	0	0	0	0	0	216	0	0	540	7,065
1980	Gary Balough	1	0	0	0	0	0	0	0	16	0	0	24	610
"	Billie Harvey	4	0	0	0	0	0	0	0	805	0	0	1,691	7,995
"	**Total**	5	0	0	0	0	0	0	0	821	0	0	1,715	8,605
1981	Billie Harvey	2	0	0	0	0	0	0	0	60	0	0	150	3,915
1982	Billie Harvey	1	0	0	0	0	0	0	0	6	0	0	15	3,875
Lifetime		14	0	0	0	0	0	0	0	1,588	0	0	3,158	$25,905

Friday Hassler

Year	Driver	Starts	Poles	1	2	3	4	5	6–10	Laps	Laps Led	Races Led	Miles	$
1969	Friday Hassler	17	0	0	0	0	0	0	6	4,145	3	1	4,434	17,275
"	John Sears	1	0	0	0	0	0	0	0	3	0	0	5	725
"	**Total**	18	0	0	0	0	0	0	6	4,148	3	1	4,439	18,000
1970	Friday Hassler	26	0	0	0	0	0	1	5	5,439	56	1	6,518	27,535
1971	Friday Hassler	29	2	0	1	2	0	1	9	5,650	68	3	7,130	37,305
1972	Friday Hassler	1	0	0	0	0	0	0	1	137	0	0	359	2,225
Lifetime		74	2	0	1	2	0	2	21	15,374	127	5	18,445	$85,065

Ed Hastings

Year	Driver	Starts	Poles	1	2	3	4	5	6–10	Laps	Laps Led	Races Led	Miles	$
1949	Ray Erickson	4	0	0	1	1	0	0	1	713	0	0	357	1,300
1950	Ray Erickson	2	0	0	0	0	0	0	0	137	31	1	131	50
1951	Ray Erickson	2	0	0	0	0	0	0	0	120	0	0	90	45
"	Dale Williams	1	0	0	0	0	0	0	1		0	0		100
"	**Total**	3	0	0	0	0	0	0	1	120	0	0	90	145
1956	Danny Letner	1	0	0	0	0	0	0	0		0	0		0
Lifetime		10	0	0	1	1	0	0	2	970	31	1	578	$1,495

Bob Havenmann

Year	Driver	Starts	Poles	1	2	3	4	5	6–10	Laps	Laps Led	Races Led	Miles	$
1954	Bob Havenmann	2	0	0	0	0	0	0	1	694	0	0	347	275
1955	Bob Havenmann	3	0	0	0	0	0	0	2	506	0	0	410	400
1956	Bob Havenmann	2	0	0	0	0	0	0	0	291	0	0	201	90
1957	Bob Havenmann	1	0	0	0	0	0	0	0	117	0	0	73	100
1958	Bob Havenmann	1	0	0	0	0	0	0	0	91	0	0	91	100
Lifetime		9	0	0	0	0	0	0	3	1,699	0	0	1,122	$965

John Haver

Year	Driver	Starts	Poles	1	2	3	4	5	6–10	Laps	Laps Led	Races Led	Miles	$
1979	John Haver	1	0	0	0	0	0	0	0	36	0	0	72	950
Lifetime		1	0	0	0	0	0	0	0	36	0	0	72	$950

Butch Hawkersmith

Year	Driver	Starts	Poles	1	2	3	4	5	6–10	Laps	Laps Led	Races Led	Miles	$
1973	Alton Jones	5	0	0	0	0	0	0	1	686	0	0	807	4,195
1974	Alton Jones	5	0	0	0	0	0	1	1	1,163	0	0	1,095	4,745
1975	Alton Jones	2	0	0	0	0	0	0	1	790	0	0	471	1,935
Lifetime		12	0	0	0	0	0	1	3	2,639	0	0	2,373	$10,875

Bobby Hawkins

Year	Driver	Starts	Poles	1	2	3	4	5	6–10	Laps	Laps Led	Races Led	Miles	$
1981	Dick Brooks	2	0	0	0	0	0	0	0	702	0	0	877	3,175
"	Jack Ingram	5	0	0	0	0	0	0	1	822	0	0	1,285	9,965
"	**Total**	7	0	0	0	0	0	0	1	1,524	0	0	2,162	13,140
1982	Dick Brooks	4	0	0	0	0	0	0	0	278	0	0	330	7,955
"	David Pearson	6	2	0	0	1	0	1	0	1,019	7	2	1,721	47,945
"	**Total**	10	2	0	0	1	0	1	0	1,297	7	2	2,051	55,900

Year	Driver	Starts	Poles	Finish 1	2	3	4	5	6–10	Laps	Laps Led	Races Led	Miles	$

Bobby Hawkins *continued*

Year	Driver	Starts	Poles	1	2	3	4	5	6–10	Laps	Laps Led	Races Led	Miles	$
1983	David Pearson	10	0	0	0	1	0	0	3	1,643	18	1	3,094	59,720
1984	David Pearson	11	0	0	0	0	0	0	3	1,630	10	3	2,949	54,125
1985	Butch Lindley	1	0	0	0	0	0	0	0	352	0	0	191	1,365
"	Morgan Shepherd	4	0	0	0	0	0	1	1	820	0	0	1,099	18,575
"	**Total**	5	0	0	0	0	0	1	1	1,172	0	0	1,290	19,940
Lifetime		43	2	0	0	2	0	2	8	7,266	35	6	11,545	$202,825

Joe Hawkins

Year	Driver	Starts	Poles	1	2	3	4	5	6–10	Laps	Laps Led	Races Led	Miles	$
1952	Billy Myers	1	0	0	0	0	0	0	0	220	0	0	220	50
"	Buddy Shuman	1	0	0	0	0	0	0	0	376	0	0	470	100
"	**Total**	2	0	0	0	0	0	0	0	596	0	0	690	150
Lifetime		2	0	0	0	0	0	0	0	596	0	0	690	$150

Tom Hawkins

Year	Driver	Starts	Poles	1	2	3	4	5	6–10	Laps	Laps Led	Races Led	Miles	$
1962	Sal Tovella	2	0	0	0	0	0	0	0	77	0	0	193	450
Lifetime		2	0	0	0	0	0	0	0	77	0	0	193	$450

Ed Hawks

Year	Driver	Starts	Poles	1	2	3	4	5	6–10	Laps	Laps Led	Races Led	Miles	$
1974	Walter Ballard	1	0	0	0	0	0	0	0	32	0	0	80	645
"	Johnny Barnes	2	0	0	0	0	0	0	0	18	0	0	10	1,065
"	Bobby Fleming	1	0	0	0	0	0	0	0	341	0	0	182	525
"	Ernie Shaw	4	0	0	0	0	0	0	0	842	0	0	538	2,280
"	**Total**	8	0	0	0	0	0	0	0	1,233	0	0	809	4,515
Lifetime		8	0	0	0	0	0	0	0	1,233	0	0	809	$4,515

Johnny Hayes

Year	Driver	Starts	Poles	1	2	3	4	5	6–10	Laps	Laps Led	Races Led	Miles	$
1982	Benny Parsons	6	0	0	0	0	0	3	2	1,803	2	1	2,645	29,165
1983	Benny Parsons	16	0	0	2	1	0	1	1	2,847	116	7	5,285	119,760
"	Phil Parsons	5	0	0	0	0	0	0	0	887	0	0	1,696	23,850
"	**Total**	16	0	0	2	1	0	1	1	3,734	116	7	6,981	143,610
1984	Benny Parsons	14	2	1	1	0	1	4	3	2,877	407	6	5,451	211,665
"	Phil Parsons	22	0	0	0	0	0	0	3	6,286	4	1	7,762	86,925
"	**Total**	23	2	1	1	0	1	4	6	9,163	411	6	13,213	298,590
Lifetime		45	2	1	3	1	1	8	9	14,700	529	14	22,839	$471,365

Frank Hayworth

Year	Driver	Starts	Poles	1	2	3	4	5	6–10	Laps	Laps Led	Races Led	Miles	$
1956	Bill Blair	2	0	0	0	0	0	0	1	562	0	0	544	225
"	Jim Paschal	36	1	1	8	2	3	1	7	5,404	110	4	3,488	13,844
"	**Total**	38	1	1	8	2	3	1	8	5,966	110	4	4,032	14,069
1957	Max Berrier	2	0	0	0	0	0	0	0	0	0	0	0	50
"	Jim Paschal	6	0	0	0	1	1	0	2	822	0	0	636	1,605
"	Ken Rush	13	0	0	0	0	0	0	4	1,878	0	0	1,203	1,505
"	**Total**	21	0	0	0	1	1	0	6	2,700	0	0	1,839	3,160
1959	Curtis Turner	1	0	0	0	0	0	0	0	159	0	0	80	75
Lifetime		60	1	1	8	3	4	1	14	8,825	110	4	5,951	$17,304

Pete Hazelwood

Year	Driver	Starts	Poles	1	2	3	4	5	6–10	Laps	Laps Led	Races Led	Miles	$
1969	Pete Hazelwood	16	0	0	0	0	0	0	1	2,367	0	0	1,163	4,390
"	Paul Dean Holt	1	0	0	0	0	0	0	0	16	0	0	8	210
"	**Total**	16	0	0	0	0	0	0	1	2,383	0	0	1,171	4,600
1970	Pete Hazelwood	3	0	0	0	0	0	0	0	51	0	0	26	620
Lifetime		19	0	0	0	0	0	0	1	2,434	0	0	1,197	$5,220

Allen Heath

Year	Driver	Starts	Poles	1	2	3	4	5	6–10	Laps	Laps Led	Races Led	Miles	$
1951	Allen Heath	3	0	0	0	0	0	0	0		0	0		75
1954	Allen Heath	1	0	0	0	0	0	0	0	52	0	0	26	0
Lifetime		4	0	0	0	0	0	0	0	52	0	0	26	$75

Charles Heckert

Year	Driver	Starts	Poles	1	2	3	4	5	6–10	Laps	Laps Led	Races Led	Miles	$
1972	Sonny Easley	1	0	0	0	0	0	0	0	35	0	0	92	670
Lifetime		1	0	0	0	0	0	0	0	35	0	0	92	$670

Year	Driver	Starts	Poles	Finish						Laps	Laps Led	Races Led	Miles	$
				1	2	3	4	5	6–10					

Larry Hedrick

Year	Driver	Starts	Poles	1	2	3	4	5	6–10	Laps	Laps Led	Races Led	Miles	$
1990	Larry Pearson	4	0	0	0	0	0	0	0	1,676	0	0	1,750	17,865
1991	Larry Pearson	11	0	0	0	0	0	0	0	1,543	0	0	2,662	56,570
1992	Dave Marcis	7	0	0	0	0	0	0	0	2,077	0	0	1,697	43,060
"	Greg Sacks	20	0	0	0	0	0	0	0	4,926	6	1	6,502	178,120
"	Hut Stricklin	2	0	0	0	0	0	0	0	312	0	0	313	13,670
"	**Total**	29	0	0	0	0	0	0	0	7,315	6	1	8,511	234,850
1993	Phil Parsons	25	0	0	0	0	0	0	1	6,003	0	0	7,541	281,000
"	Dick Trickle	5	0	0	0	0	0	1	1	1,741	3	1	1,958	61,790
"	**Total**	30	0	0	0	0	0	1	2	7,744	3	1	9,499	342,790
1994	Joe Nemechek	29	0	0	0	1	0	0	2	7,951	22	2	9,486	389,565
1995	Ricky Craven	31	0	0	0	0	0	0	4	8,711	6	4	11,086	597,054
1996	Ricky Craven	31	2	0	0	2	0	1	2	8,561	136	9	10,229	941,959
Lifetime		165	2	0	0	3	0	2	10	43,501	173	17	53,223	$2,580,653

Harvey Hege

Year	Driver	Starts	Poles	1	2	3	4	5	6–10	Laps	Laps Led	Races Led	Miles	$
1958	Harvey Hege	13	0	0	0	0	0	0	2	1,498	0	0	786	1,200
"	Shep Langdon	2	0	0	0	0	0	0	0	586	0	0	293	300
"	**Total**	15	0	0	0	0	0	0	2	2,084	0	0	1,079	1,500
1959	Neil Castles	2	0	0	0	0	0	0	0	363	0	0	182	150
"	Fred Harb	2	0	0	0	0	0	0	1	365	0	0	183	250
"	Harvey Hege	10	0	0	0	0	0	0	3	1,485	0	0	765	955
"	Shorty York	1	0	0	0	0	0	0	0	185	0	0	46	120
"	**Total**	15	0	0	0	0	0	0	4	2,398	0	0	1,176	1,475
Lifetime		30	0	0	0	0	0	0	6	4,482	0	0	2,254	$2,975

Greg Heller

Year	Driver	Starts	Poles	1	2	3	4	5	6–10	Laps	Laps Led	Races Led	Miles	$
1977	Greg Heller	1	0	0	0	0	0	0	0	110	0	0	275	680
1978	Greg Heller	1	0	0	0	0	0	0	0	250	0	0	250	575
"	Bobby Wawak	1	0	0	0	0	0	0	0	65	0	0	163	850
"	**Total**	2	0	0	0	0	0	0	0	315	0	0	413	1,425
Lifetime		3	0	0	0	0	0	0	0	425	0	0	688	$2,105

Buddy Helms

Year	Driver	Starts	Poles	1	2	3	4	5	6–10	Laps	Laps Led	Races Led	Miles	$
1949	Buddy Helms	1	0	0	0	0	0	0	1		0	0		75
"	Slick Smith	3	0	0	0	0	0	0	0	277	0	0	139	150
"	**Total**	4	0	0	0	0	0	0	1	277	0	0	139	225
1950	Buddy Helms	3	0	0	0	0	0	0	0	36	0	0	18	0
1951	Buddy Helms	1	0	0	0	0	0	0	0	132	0	0	99	25
Lifetime		8	0	0	0	0	0	0	1	445	0	0	256	$250

Bill Hemby

Year	Driver	Starts	Poles	1	2	3	4	5	6–10	Laps	Laps Led	Races Led	Miles	$
1969	Bill Ward	1	0	0	0	0	0	0	0	149	0	0	396	1,550
Lifetime		1	0	0	0	0	0	0	0	149	0	0	396	$1,550

Charlie Henderson

Year	Driver	Starts	Poles	1	2	3	4	5	6–10	Laps	Laps Led	Races Led	Miles	$
1982	Brad Teague	9	0	0	0	0	0	0	0	3,052	0	0	2,611	14,750
1983	Ronnie Hopkins Jr.	13	0	0	0	0	0	0	0	2,563	0	0	3,101	26,445
1984	Morgan Shepherd	2	0	0	0	0	0	0	0	667	0	0	353	1,700
Lifetime		24	0	0	0	0	0	0	0	6,282	0	0	6,065	$42,895

Elmo Henderson

Year	Driver	Starts	Poles	1	2	3	4	5	6–10	Laps	Laps Led	Races Led	Miles	$
1959	Elmo Henderson	2	0	0	0	0	0	0	0	176	0	0	102	200
1961	Joe Weatherly	1	0	0	0	0	0	0	0	189	0	0	76	70
Lifetime		3	0	0	0	0	0	0	0	365	0	0	178	$270

Harvey Henderson

Year	Driver	Starts	Poles	1	2	3	4	5	6–10	Laps	Laps Led	Races Led	Miles	$
1952	Harvey Henderson	1	0	0	0	0	0	0	0		0	0		25
1955	Harvey Henderson	17	0	0	0	0	0	1	5	2,284	0	0	1,344	1,810
1956	Harvey Henderson	16	0	0	0	0	0	0	3	2,361	0	0	1,537	1,210
1957	Harvey Henderson	1	0	0	0	0	0	0	0	172	0	0	86	100
1958	Harvey Henderson	2	0	0	0	0	0	0	0	160	0	0	58	125
Lifetime		37	0	0	0	0	0	1	8	4,977	0	0	3,026	$3,270

Ray Henderson

Year	Driver	Starts	Poles	1	2	3	4	5	6–10	Laps	Laps Led	Races Led	Miles	$
1954	Rick Henderson	3	0	0	0	0	0	0	0	609	0	0	404	65
Lifetime		3	0	0	0	0	0	0	0	609	0	0	404	$65

Rick Hendrick

Year	Driver	Starts	Poles	1	2	3	4	5	6–10	Laps	Laps Led	Races Led	Miles	$
1984	Geoff Bodine	30	3	3	0	1	2	1	7	8,848	686	12	10,064	413,748
1985	Geoff Bodine	28	3	0	3	3	2	2	4	8,719	692	18	10,711	565,868
"	Dick Brooks	1	0	0	0	0	0	0	1	393	0	0	590	9,000
"	**Total**	28	3	0	3	3	2	2	5	9,112	692	18	11,301	574,868
1986	Brett Bodine	1	0	0	0	0	0	0	0	394	0	0	591	10,100
"	Geoff Bodine	29	8	2	2	5	1	0	5	7,791	1,676	25	9,359	795,111
"	Tim Richmond	29	8	7	4	0	1	1	4	8,544	1,006	21	10,526	973,830
"	**Total**	29	16	9	6	5	2	1	9	**16,729**	**2,682**	**28**	**20,476**	1,779,041
1987	Geoff Bodine	29	2	0	1	1	0	1	7	7,638	342	13	8,753	449,816
"	Jim Fitzgerald	1	0	0	0	0	0	0	0	93	0	0	244	1,675
"	Rick Hendrick	1	0	0	0	0	0	0	0	75	0	0	197	1,150
"	Jimmy Means	1	0	0	0	0	0	0	0	20	0	0	30	5,960
"	Benny Parsons	29	0	0	3	0	1	2	3	6,975	87	9	8,864	566,484
"	Tim Richmond	8	1	2	0	0	1	0	1	1,199	161	6	2,858	151,850
"	Darrell Waltrip	29	0	1	1	1	2	1	10	8,996	311	14	11,034	511,768
"	**Total**	29	3	3	5	2	4	4	21	**24,996**	901	**27**	**31,979**	1,688,703
1988	Geoff Bodine	29	3	1	1	4	1	3	6	8,995	464	15	10,559	570,643
"	Rick Hendrick	1	0	0	0	0	0	0	0	94	0	0	246	2,550
"	Rob Moroso	1	0	0	0	0	0	0	0	331	0	0	497	4,500
"	Ken Schrader	28	2	1	1	0	1	1	13	8,720	151	13	10,819	626,934
"	Darrell Waltrip	29	2	2	1	1	2	4	4	9,065	520	18	10,786	731,659
"	**Total**	29	7	4	3	5	4	8	23	**27,205**	1,135	**23**	**32,906**	1,936,286
1989	Geoff Bodine	29	3	1	1	3	3	1	2	9,051	511	14	10,533	619,494
"	Bobby Hamilton	1	0	0	0	0	0	0	0	215	5	1	215	3,075
"	Tommy Kendall	1	0	0	0	0	0	0	0	79	1	1	192	3,015
"	Kyle Petty	1	0	0	0	0	0	0	0	392	0	0	588	6,000
"	Ken Schrader	29	4	1	1	3	4	1	4	8,675	364	17	10,780	1,037,941
"	Darrell Waltrip	29	0	6	2	2	2	2	4	9,333	758	17	10,984	1,312,479
"	**Total**	29	7	8	4	8	9	4	10	**27,745**	1,639	**27**	**33,292**	3,604,573
1990	Stan Barrett	1	0	0	0	0	0	0	0	74	0	0	186	3,850
"	Jimmy Horton	2	0	0	0	0	0	0	0	342	0	0	885	30,475
"	Ricky Rudd	29	2	1	0	3	2	2	7	8,664	180	7	10,392	573,650
"	Greg Sacks	16	1	0	2	0	0	0	2	3,790	107	4	5,401	190,348
"	Ken Schrader	29	3	0	2	2	1	2	7	8,649	242	12	9,948	769,934
"	Hut Stricklin	2	0	0	0	0	0	0	0	272	0	0	587	20,960
"	Sarel van der Merwe	1	0	0	0	0	0	0	0	77	0	0	187	12,070
"	Darrell Waltrip	23	0	0	1	1	2	1	7	8,138	297	9	9,190	520,420
"	**Total**	29	6	1	5	6	5	5	23	**30,006**[1]	826	**25**	**36,777**[1]	2,121,707
1991	Ricky Rudd	29	1	1	3	0	2	3	8	9,561	425	13	11,427	1,093,765
"	Ken Schrader	29	0	2	2	2	1	3	8	8,331	440	16	9,841	772,434
"	**Total**	29	1	3	5	2	3	6	16	17,892	865	21	21,268	1,866,199
1992	Jeff Gordon	1	0	0	0	0	0	0	0	164	0	0	250	6,285
"	Ricky Rudd	29	1	1	0	2	3	3	9	8,968	331	9	10,269	793,903
"	Ken Schrader	29	1	0	0	2	1	1	7	8,425	83	5	9,815	639,679
"	**Total**	29	2	1	0	4	4	4	16	17,557	414	13	20,334	1,439,867
1993	Jeff Gordon	30	1	0	2	1	1	3	4	8,390	230	14	10,066	765,168
"	Ricky Rudd	30	0	1	1	1	3	3	5	8,635	136	7	10,265	752,562
"	Ken Schrader	30	6	0	2	2	3	2	6	8,877	286	14	10,994	952,748
"	Al Unser Jr.	1	0	0	0	0	0	0	0	157	0	0	393	23,005
"	**Total**	30	7	1	5	4	7	8	15	**26,059**	652	**21**	**31,717**	2,493,483
1994	Jeff Gordon	31	1	2	1	1	2	1	7	9,277	446	17	11,548	1,799,523
"	Terry Labonte	31	0	3	1	1	0	1	8	9,149	487	8	11,313	1,150,921
"	Ken Schrader	31	0	0	1	2	4	2	9	9,704	222	9	11,740	1,211,062
"	**Total**	31	1	5	3	4	6	4	24	**28,130**	1,155	**23**	**34,601**	4,161,506
1995	Jeff Gordon	31	8	7	4	5	0	1	6	9,405	2,600	29	11,608	4,347,343
"	Terry Labonte	31	1	3	4	2	3	2	3	9,076	438	11	11,376	1,558,659
"	Ken Schrader	31	1	0	0	1	1	0	8	8,550	238	9	10,166	886,566
"	**Total**	31	10	10	8	8	4	3	17	**27,031**	3,276	**30**	**33,150**	6,792,568
1996	Jeff Gordon	31	5	10	3	4	2	2	3	8,972	2,314	25	10,517	3,428,485
"	Terry Labonte	31	4	2	7	5	1	6	3	9,443	973	22	11,522	4,030,648
"	Ken Schrader	31	0	0	0	1	1	1	7	9,408	45	7	11,499	1,089,603
"	Jack Sprague	2	0	0	0	0	0	0	0	333	2	1	345	22,720
"	**Total**	31	9	12	10	10	4	9	13	**28,156**	3,334	**31**	**33,883**	8,571,456[1]
Lifetime		384	75	60	57	62	56	59	199	289,466	18,257	299	351,748	$37,444,005
			5th	**7th**							**3rd**	**6th**	**6th**	**2nd**	**1st**

Year	Driver	Starts	Poles	Finish						Laps	Laps Led	Races Led	Miles	$
				1	2	3	4	5	6–10					

R. G. Henschel

Year	Driver	Starts	Poles	1	2	3	4	5	6–10	Laps	Laps Led	Races Led	Miles	$
1961	Robert Roeber	2	0	0	0	0	0	0	0	208	0	0	520	315
Lifetime		2	0	0	0	0	0	0	0	208	0	0	520	$315

Casper Hensley

Year	Driver	Starts	Poles	1	2	3	4	5	6–10	Laps	Laps Led	Races Led	Miles	$
1964	Bunkie Blackburn	12	0	0	0	0	1	0	3	2,294	0	0	2,327	5,780
"	Bill McMahan	19	0	0	0	0	0	1	3	3,786	0	0	2,723	6,935
"	**Total**	21	0	0	0	0	1	1	6	6,080	0	0	5,050	12,715
1965	Bunkie Blackburn	2	0	0	0	0	0	0	1	87	0	0	218	1,365
"	Jim Hunter	1	0	0	0	0	1	0	0	191	0	0	96	300
"	Bill McMahan	1	0	0	0	0	0	0	0		0	0		100
"	**Total**	4	0	0	0	0	1	0	1	278	0	0	313	1,765
1967	Jim Hunter	3	1	0	0	1	0	0	0	382	0	0	191	720
"	Joe Ed Neubert	3	0	0	0	0	0	0	1	254	0	0	127	465
"	**Total**	3	1	0	0	1	0	0	1	636	0	0	318	1,185
Lifetime		28	1	0	0	1	2	1	8	6,994	0	0	5,681	$15,665

Bernie Hentges

Year	Driver	Starts	Poles	1	2	3	4	5	6–10	Laps	Laps Led	Races Led	Miles	$
1959	Bernie Hentges	2	0	0	0	0	0	0	0	176	0	0	440	210
Lifetime		2	0	0	0	0	0	0	0	176	0	0	440	$210

Ray Herlocker

Year	Driver	Starts	Poles	1	2	3	4	5	6–10	Laps	Laps Led	Races Led	Miles	$
1962	Harold Carmac	2	0	0	0	0	0	0	1	172	0	0	86	525
"	Thomas Cox	33	0	0	0	0	1	1	15	6,344	0	0	4,020	6,635
"	Ray Hughes	6	0	0	0	0	0	0	2	1,289	0	0	536	965
"	**Total**	40	0	0	0	0	1	1	18	7,805	0	0	4,642	8,125
1963	Ray Hughes	1	0	0	0	0	0	0	0	183	0	0	46	110
Lifetime		41	0	0	0	0	1	1	18	7,988	0	0	4,687	$8,235

John Hernandez

Year	Driver	Starts	Poles	1	2	3	4	5	6–10	Laps	Laps Led	Races Led	Miles	$
1955	Marvin Panch	2	0	0	1	0	1	0	0	346	0	0	346	1,300
Lifetime		2	0	0	1	0	1	0	0	346	0	0	346	$1,300

Skimp Hersey

Year	Driver	Starts	Poles	1	2	3	4	5	6–10	Laps	Laps Led	Races Led	Miles	$
1949	Skimp Hersey	1	0	0	0	0	0	0	0		0	0		25
Lifetime		1	0	0	0	0	0	0	0		0	0		$25

Homer Hess

Year	Driver	Starts	Poles	1	2	3	4	5	6–10	Laps	Laps Led	Races Led	Miles	$
1988	Ben Hess	1	0	0	0	0	0	0	0	472	0	0	472	3,370
1989	Ben Hess	9	0	0	0	0	0	0	0	3,194	0	0	3,818	48,490
Lifetime		10	0	0	0	0	0	0	0	3,666	0	0	4,290	$51,860

Larry Hess

Year	Driver	Starts	Poles	1	2	3	4	5	6–10	Laps	Laps Led	Races Led	Miles	$
1965	Larry Hess	10	0	0	0	0	0	0	3	2,347	0	0	3,543	8,295
"	Jim Tatum	1	0	0	0	0	0	0	0	103	0	0	34	100
"	**Total**	11	0	0	0	0	0	0	3	2,450	0	0	3,577	8,395
1966	Larry Hess	13	0	0	0	0	0	0	0	1,830	0	0	2,160	5,290
1967	Larry Hess	1	0	0	0	0	0	0	0	5	0	0	3	100
1968	Larry Hess	1	0	0	0	0	0	0	0	0	0	0	0	460
Lifetime		26	0	0	0	0	0	0	3	4,285	0	0	5,740	$14,245

Ed Hessert

Year	Driver	Starts	Poles	1	2	3	4	5	6–10	Laps	Laps Led	Races Led	Miles	$
1969	Ed Hessert	14	0	0	0	0	0	0	4	2,535	1	1	3,251	16,820
1970	Ed Hessert	1	0	0	0	0	0	0	0	45	0	0	113	255
1971	Ed Hessert	1	0	0	0	0	0	0	0	14	0	0	21	315
Lifetime		16	0	0	0	0	0	0	4	2,594	1	1	3,385	$17,390

Doug Heveron

Year	Driver	Starts	Poles	1	2	3	4	5	6–10	Laps	Laps Led	Races Led	Miles	$
1984	Doug Heveron	14	0	0	0	0	0	0	0	2,960	7	1	4,320	36,145
1985	Doug Heveron	1	0	0	0	0	0	0	0	44	0	0	110	8,460
Lifetime		15	0	0	0	0	0	0	0	3,004	7	1	4,430	$44,605

Year	Driver	Starts	Poles	Finish 1	2	3	4	5	6–10	Laps	Laps Led	Races Led	Miles	$

George Hicks

Year	Driver	Starts	Poles	1	2	3	4	5	6–10	Laps	Laps Led	Races Led	Miles	$
1951	George Seeger	1	0	0	0	0	0	0	0		0	0		25
Lifetime		1	0	0	0	0	0	0	0		0	0		$25

Gilbert Hildebrant

Year	Driver	Starts	Poles	1	2	3	4	5	6–10	Laps	Laps Led	Races Led	Miles	$
1970	Paul Connors	1	0	0	0	0	0	0	0	134	0	0	183	890
Lifetime		1	0	0	0	0	0	0	0	134	0	0	183	$890

Elton Hildreth

Year	Driver	Starts	Poles	1	2	3	4	5	6–10	Laps	Laps Led	Races Led	Miles	$
1952	Elton Hildreth	6	0	0	0	0	0	0	1	815	0	0	608	375
1953	Elton Hildreth	25	0	0	0	0	1	0	4	821	0	0	785	1,997
1954	Elton Hildreth	14	0	0	0	0	0	0	2	1,519	0	0	1,420	1,152
1955	Boyce Hildreth	1	0	0	0	0	0	0	0	5	0	0	3	0
"	Elton Hildreth	3	0	0	0	0	0	0	0	130	0	0	79	100
"	**Total**	4	0	0	0	0	0	0	0	135	0	0	82	100
1956	Elton Hildreth	1	0	0	0	0	0	0	0	122	0	0	122	75
1957	Elton Hildreth	2	0	0	0	0	0	0	0	153	0	0	153	150
Lifetime		52	0	0	0	0	1	0	7	3,565	0	0	3,170	$3,849

Bruce Hill

Year	Driver	Starts	Poles	1	2	3	4	5	6–10	Laps	Laps Led	Races Led	Miles	$
1974	Bruce Hill	1	0	0	0	0	0	0	0	189	0	0	473	1,575
1975	Bruce Hill	26	0	0	0	0	0	3	8	7,088	2	2	7,868	79,428
1976	Bruce Hill	20	0	0	0	0	0	0	3	3,010	3	1	4,462	38,035
1977	Bruce Hill	16	0	0	0	0	0	0	4	2,883	4	1	4,290	25,035
1981	Bruce Hill	6	0	0	0	0	0	0	0	551	0	0	960	9,045
Lifetime		69	0	0	0	0	0	3	15	13,721	9	4	18,053	$153,118

Charlie Hill

Year	Driver	Starts	Poles	1	2	3	4	5	6–10	Laps	Laps Led	Races Led	Miles	$
1952	Charlie Hill	1	0	0	0	0	0	0	0	217	0	0	217	50
Lifetime		1	0	0	0	0	0	0	0	217	0	0	217	$50

Dave Hill

Year	Driver	Starts	Poles	1	2	3	4	5	6–10	Laps	Laps Led	Races Led	Miles	$
1977	Ray Elder	1	0	0	0	0	0	0	0	14	0	0	37	625
"	Gary Matthews	1	0	0	0	0	0	0	0	91	0	0	238	1,225
"	**Total**	2	0	0	0	0	0	0	0	105	0	0	275	1,850
1978	Ray Elder	3	0	0	0	0	0	0	1	108	0	0	283	5,305
Lifetime		5	0	0	0	0	0	0	1	213	0	0	558	$7,155

Bobby Hillin Sr.

Year	Driver	Starts	Poles	1	2	3	4	5	6–10	Laps	Laps Led	Races Led	Miles	$
1982	Bobby Hillin Jr.	5	0	0	0	0	0	0	0	917	0	0	1,515	9,830
1983	Bobby Hillin Jr.	6	0	0	0	0	0	0	0	1,546	0	0	2,068	17,740
Lifetime		11	0	0	0	0	0	0	0	2,463	0	0	3,583	$27,570

Jimmy Hindman

Year	Driver	Starts	Poles	1	2	3	4	5	6–10	Laps	Laps Led	Races Led	Miles	$
1979	Jimmy Hindman	1	0	0	0	0	0	0	0	2	0	0	1	350
Lifetime		1	0	0	0	0	0	0	0	2	0	0	1	$350

Joe Hines

Year	Driver	Starts	Poles	1	2	3	4	5	6–10	Laps	Laps Led	Races Led	Miles	$
1970	Joe Hines Jr.	1	0	0	0	0	0	0	0	43	0	0	108	245
1971	Joe Hines Jr.	1	0	0	0	0	0	0	0	1	0	0	3	0
Lifetime		2	0	0	0	0	0	0	0	44	0	0	110	$245

John Hines

Year	Driver	Starts	Poles	1	2	3	4	5	6–10	Laps	Laps Led	Races Led	Miles	$
1960	Fireball Roberts	9	6	2	0	0	0	0	1	1,338	578	9	2,072	19,895
Lifetime		9	6	2	0	0	0	0	1	1,338	578	9	2,072	$19,895

Jane Hinnant

Year	Driver	Starts	Poles	1	2	3	4	5	6–10	Laps	Laps Led	Races Led	Miles	$
1951	Wade Fields	1	0	0	0	0	0	0	0	268	0	0	335	50
Lifetime		1	0	0	0	0	0	0	0	268	0	0	335	$50

Year	Driver	Starts	Poles	Finish 1	2	3	4	5	6–10	Laps	Laps Led	Races Led	Miles	$

Edgar Hinton

Year	Driver	Starts	Poles	1	2	3	4	5	6–10	Laps	Laps Led	Races Led	Miles	$
1962	Red Foote	4	0	0	0	0	0	0	0	939	0	0	1,367	1,600
"	Ernie Gahan	3	0	0	0	0	0	0	1	284	0	0	604	725
"	**Total**	7	0	0	0	0	0	0	1	1,223	0	0	1,971	2,325
1963	Red Foote	3	0	0	0	0	0	0	0	316	0	0	625	950
1964	Nathan Boutwell	2	0	0	0	0	0	0	0	217	0	0	543	1,100
Lifetime		12	0	0	0	0	0	0	1	1,756	0	0	3,138	$4,375

Rocky Hinton

Year	Driver	Starts	Poles	1	2	3	4	5	6–10	Laps	Laps Led	Races Led	Miles	$
1968	Pete Hamilton	10	0	0	1	0	0	2	1	2,064	14	1	1,346	3,800
"	David Pearson	1	0	0	0	0	0	0	0	300	0	0	150	0
"	G. C. Spencer	2	0	0	0	0	0	0	1	516	0	0	502	1,200
"	Roy Trentham	5	0	0	0	0	0	0	1	968	0	0	671	2,285
"	**Total**	18	0	0	1	0	0	2	3	3,848	14	1	2,669	7,285
Lifetime		18	0	0	1	0	0	2	3	3,848	14	1	2,669	$7,285

Rudy Hires

Year	Driver	Starts	Poles	1	2	3	4	5	6–10	Laps	Laps Led	Races Led	Miles	$
1951	Rudy Hires	1	0	0	0	0	0	0	0	82	0	0	103	0
1952	Rudy Hires	1	0	0	0	0	0	0	0	267	0	0	334	50
Lifetime		2	0	0	0	0	0	0	0	349	0	0	436	$50

Tom Hixon

Year	Driver	Starts	Poles	1	2	3	4	5	6–10	Laps	Laps Led	Races Led	Miles	$
1966	George England	1	0	0	0	0	0	0	0	293	0	0	440	745
1967	George England	5	0	0	0	0	0	0	1	748	0	0	780	3,050
"	George Hixon	1	0	0	0	0	0	0	0	187	0	0	94	120
"	**Total**	6	0	0	0	0	0	0	1	935	0	0	874	3,170
Lifetime		7	0	0	0	0	0	0	1	1,228	0	0	1,313	$3,915

Chuck Hobbs

Year	Driver	Starts	Poles	1	2	3	4	5	6–10	Laps	Laps Led	Races Led	Miles	$
1957	Chuck Hobbs	1	0	0	0	0	0	0	0		0	0		25
Lifetime		1	0	0	0	0	0	0	0		0	0		$25

Gene Hobby

Year	Driver	Starts	Poles	1	2	3	4	5	6–10	Laps	Laps Led	Races Led	Miles	$
1965	Buddy Baker	1	0	0	0	0	0	0	0	16	0	0	8	100
"	Darrell Bryant	1	0	0	0	0	0	0	0	44	0	0	11	100
"	Gene Hobby	15	0	0	0	0	1	0	1	1,979	0	0	971	2,560
"	Joe Holder	2	0	0	0	0	0	0	0	135	0	0	47	200
"	J. T. Putney	1	0	0	0	0	0	0	0	1	0	0	1	100
"	LeeRoy Yarbrough	1	0	0	0	0	0	0	0	25	0	0	13	100
"	**Total**	21	0	0	0	0	1	0	1	2,200	0	0	1,050	3,160
1966	Gene Hobby	2	0	0	0	0	0	0	0	34	0	0	12	0
Lifetime		23	0	0	0	0	1	0	1	2,234	0	0	1,063	$3,160

John Hodges

Year	Driver	Starts	Poles	1	2	3	4	5	6–10	Laps	Laps Led	Races Led	Miles	$
1971	Gordon Birkett	2	0	0	0	0	0	0	0	263	0	0	123	635
Lifetime		2	0	0	0	0	0	0	0	263	0	0	123	$635

Rudy Hoerr

Year	Driver	Starts	Poles	1	2	3	4	5	6–10	Laps	Laps Led	Races Led	Miles	$
1966	Billy Foster	1	0	0	0	0	0	0	1	181	0	0	489	1,275
1968	Al Unser	1	0	0	0	0	0	0	1	182	0	0	491	1,550
Lifetime		2	0	0	0	0	0	0	2	363	0	0	980	$2,825

Al Holbert

Year	Driver	Starts	Poles	1	2	3	4	5	6–10	Laps	Laps Led	Races Led	Miles	$
1979	Al Holbert	6	0	0	0	0	0	0	1	938	5	1	1,620	14,170
Lifetime		6	0	0	0	0	0	0	1	938	5	1	1,620	$14,170

Don Holcomb

Year	Driver	Starts	Poles	1	2	3	4	5	6–10	Laps	Laps Led	Races Led	Miles	$
1956	Allen Adkins	1	0	0	0	0	0	0	0	315	0	0	433	50
"	Al Watkins	12	0	0	0	0	0	0	4	1,812	0	0	1,254	1,035
"	**Total**	13	0	0	0	0	0	0	4	2,127	0	0	1,687	1,085
Lifetime		13	0	0	0	0	0	0	4	2,127	0	0	1,687	$1,085

Year	Driver	Starts	Poles	Finish						Laps	Laps Led	Races Led	Miles	$
				1	2	3	4	5	6–10					

Grimes Holcomb

Year	Driver	Starts	Poles	1	2	3	4	5	6–10	Laps	Laps Led	Races Led	Miles	$
1982	Jerry Bowman	1	0	0	0	0	0	0	0	53	0	0	81	765
1983	Jerry Bowman	5	0	0	0	0	0	0	0	1,183	0	0	1,553	8,610
1984	Jerry Bowman	5	0	0	0	0	0	0	0	834	0	0	1,000	8,115
1985	Jerry Bowman	5	0	0	0	0	0	0	0	1,326	0	0	1,628	8,665
1986	Jerry Bowman	2	0	0	0	0	0	0	0	255	0	0	255	2,125
1987	Jerry Bowman	1	0	0	0	0	0	0	0	161	0	0	161	1,450
Lifetime		19	0	0	0	0	0	0	0	3,812	0	0	4,678	$29,730

Jerry Holden

Year	Driver	Starts	Poles	1	2	3	4	5	6–10	Laps	Laps Led	Races Led	Miles	$
1985	Don Hume	1	0	0	0	0	0	0	0	63	0	0	158	1,370
1986	Jerry Holden	1	0	0	0	0	0	0	0	100	0	0	100	1,200
1987	Jerry Holden	1	0	0	0	0	0	0	0	8	0	0	8	1,250
Lifetime		3	0	0	0	0	0	0	0	171	0	0	266	$3,820

Bill Hollar

Year	Driver	Starts	Poles	1	2	3	4	5	6–10	Laps	Laps Led	Races Led	Miles	$
1970	Bill Hollar	3	0	0	0	0	0	0	1	792	0	0	414	970
1972	Henley Gray	1	0	0	0	0	0	0	0	57	0	0	58	565
"	Bill Hollar	1	0	0	0	0	0	0	0	64	0	0	128	705
"	**Total**	2	0	0	0	0	0	0	0	121	0	0	186	1,270
1973	Dean Dalton	1	0	0	0	0	0	0	0	138	0	0	138	700
"	Bill Hollar	1	0	0	0	0	0	0	0	419	0	0	419	1,060
"	Dick May	2	0	0	0	0	0	0	0	137	0	0	160	1,825
"	**Total**	4	0	0	0	0	0	0	0	694	0	0	717	3,585
1975	Bill Hollar	3	0	0	0	0	0	0	0	1,107	0	0	777	1,865
1976	Walter Ballard	2	0	0	0	0	0	0	0	382	0	0	586	2,750
"	Bill Hollar	1	0	0	0	0	0	0	0	2	0	0	5	540
"	**Total**	3	0	0	0	0	0	0	0	384	0	0	591	3,290
1978	Cecil Gordon	1	0	0	0	0	0	0	0	126	0	0	79	465
"	Bill Hollar	3	0	0	0	0	0	0	0	90	0	0	62	1,360
"	**Total**	4	0	0	0	0	0	0	0	216	0	0	140	1,825
1979	Bill Hollar	5	0	0	0	0	0	0	0	552	0	0	381	2,545
"	Dick May	2	0	0	0	0	0	0	0	354	0	0	390	1,615
"	**Total**	7	0	0	0	0	0	0	0	906	0	0	771	4,160
1980	Bill Hollar	1	0	0	0	0	0	0	0	281	0	0	152	600
"	Dick May	6	0	0	0	0	0	0	0	1,847	0	0	1,363	4,880
"	D. K. Ulrich	1	0	0	0	0	0	0	0	2	0	0	2	510
"	**Total**	8	0	0	0	0	0	0	0	2,130	0	0	1,518	5,990
Lifetime		34	0	0	0	0	0	0	1	6,350	0	0	5,114	$22,955

Red Hollingsworth

Year	Driver	Starts	Poles	1	2	3	4	5	6–10	Laps	Laps Led	Races Led	Miles	$
1960	Charlie Glotzbach	2	0	0	0	0	0	0	0	266	0	0	399	400
1961	Red Hollingsworth	2	0	0	0	0	0	0	0	68	0	0	170	250
Lifetime		4	0	0	0	0	0	0	0	334	0	0	569	$650

Bee Gee Holloway

Year	Driver	Starts	Poles	1	2	3	4	5	6–10	Laps	Laps Led	Races Led	Miles	$
1961	Johnny Allen	14	1	0	0	1	0	1	5	2,530	3	1	2,566	7,533
"	Ned Jarrett	44	4	1	4	8	4	6	11	9,686	606	9	7,121	40,897
"	**Total**	45	5	1	4	9	4	7	16	**12,216**	609	10	**9,686**	48,430
1962	Johnny Allen	2	0	0	0	0	0	1	0	222	0	0	555	750
"	Ned Jarrett	51	4	6	2	3	3	5	15	11,100	866	11	7,160	43,014
"	Bob Welborn	1	0	0	0	0	0	0	0	213	0	0	320	750
"	**Total**	51	4	6	2	3	3	6	15	11,535	866	11	8,034	44,514
1963	Ned Jarrett	2	0	0	0	0	0	0	0	280	0	0	122	200
Lifetime		98	9	7	6	12	7	13	31	24,031	1,475	21	17,842	$93,144

Jack Holloway

Year	Driver	Starts	Poles	1	2	3	4	5	6–10	Laps	Laps Led	Races Led	Miles	$
1952	Jack Holloway	1	0	0	0	0	0	0	0	12	0	0	6	25
Lifetime		1	0	0	0	0	0	0	0	12	0	0	6	$25

Lynn Holloway

Year	Driver	Starts	Poles	1	2	3	4	5	6–10	Laps	Laps Led	Races Led	Miles	$
1960	Tom Pistone	2	0	0	0	0	0	0	1	484	0	0	726	900
1961	Tiny Lund	1	0	0	0	0	0	0	0	323	0	0	444	650
"	Tom Pistone	4	0	0	0	0	0	0	3	576	0	0	1,081	2,050

Year	Driver	Starts	Poles	1	2	3	4	5	6–10	Laps	Laps Led	Races Led	Miles	$

Lynn Holloway *continued*

Year	Driver	Starts	Poles	1	2	3	4	5	6–10	Laps	Laps Led	Races Led	Miles	$
"	Fireball Roberts	1	0	0	0	0	0	0	0	144	0	0	72	0
"	Ken Rush	5	0	0	0	0	0	1	1	1,254	0	0	899	2,200
"	**Total**	11	0	0	0	0	0	1	4	2,297	0	0	2,496	4,900
1962	Ralph Earnhardt	1	0	0	0	0	0	0	0	94	0	0	47	50
"	Fred Harb	1	0	0	0	0	0	0	0	60	0	0	30	0
"	**Total**	2	0	0	0	0	0	0	0	154	0	0	77	50
Lifetime		15	0	0	0	0	0	1	5	2,935	0	0	3,299	$5,850

Holman-Moody (John Holman and Ralph Moody, co-owners)

Year	Driver	Starts	Poles	1	2	3	4	5	6–10	Laps	Laps Led	Races Led	Miles	$
1957	Bill Amick	2	0	0	0	0	0	0	0	258	0	0	129	150
"	Curtis Turner	3	0	0	0	0	0	0	1	434	56	2	458	675
"	Joe Weatherly	10	0	0	1	3	0	1	1	1,811	3	1	1,207	4,815
"	**Total**	12	0	0	1	3	0	1	2	2,503	59	2	1,795	5,640
1958	Possum Jones	1	0	0	0	0	0	0	0	169	0	0	85	125
"	Curtis Turner	13	1	3	2	0	1	2	2	2,547	827	6	1,837	9,579
"	Joe Weatherly	11	1	1	1	0	1	1	1	1,909	104	3	1,690	4,935
"	**Total**	17	2	4	3	0	2	3	3	4,625	931	8	3,612	14,693
1959	Joe Weatherly	1	0	0	0	0	0	0	0	54	0	0	74	210
1960	Johnny Beauchamp	2	0	0	0	0	0	0	0	102	0	0	89	60
"	Curtis Turner	6	1	0	0	0	0	0	1	817	106	2	1,341	2,770
"	Joe Weatherly	17	0	3	1	0	1	0	2	3,194	246	6	3,150	16,970
"	**Total**	19	1	3	1	0	1	0	3	4,113	352	8	4,581	19,800
1961	Fred Lorenzen	14	4	3	1	0	0	1	0	2,459	781	10	2,545	26,570
1962	Dan Gurney	2	0	0	0	0	1	0	0	174	0	0	435	700
"	Fred Lorenzen	17	3	1	2	4	1	2	1	4,129	452	8	4,230	45,050
"	Nelson Stacy	15	0	3	1	0	0	1	2	3,484	371	4	3,171	42,515
"	Speedy Thompson	2	0	0	0	0	0	0	0	185	0	0	463	500
"	**Total**	18	3	4	3	4	2	3	3	7,972	823	9	8,298	88,765
1963	Larry Frank	2	0	0	0	0	1	0	0	235	5	1	588	1,800
"	Dan Gurney	3	0	1	0	0	0	2	0	424	120	1	1,097	18,250
"	Fred Lorenzen	25	9	6	8	3	0	4	1	6,895	2,411	19	5,878	121,678
"	Tiny Lund	5	0	0	0	0	0	0	3	1,299	2	1	1,561	4,375
"	Dave MacDonald	1	0	0	0	0	0	0	0	176	0	0	475	675
"	Ken Miles	1	0	0	0	0	0	0	0	139	0	0	375	710
"	Jimmy Pardue	1	0	0	0	0	0	0	0	384	0	0	576	1,050
"	Fireball Roberts	15	0	4	1	0	3	1	2	3,817	662	9	3,895	60,820
"	Nelson Stacy	12	0	0	0	1	2	1	5	2,816	76	2	3,179	20,025
"	**Total**	29	9	11	9	4	6	8	11	16,185	**3,276**	22	**17,625**	229,383
1964	Bay Darnell	1	0	0	0	0	0	0	0	205	0	0	308	625
"	Larry Frank	3	0	0	0	0	0	0	2	347	0	0	758	2,475
"	Skip Hudson	1	0	0	0	0	0	0	1	178	0	0	481	1,075
"	Bobby Johns	5	0	0	0	0	0	0	1	1,150	0	0	1,193	2,250
"	Junior Johnson	1	1	0	0	0	0	0	0	8	2	1	3	100
"	Fred Lorenzen	16	7	8	1	0	1	0	0	4,426	2,375	11	4,181	73,860
"	Dave MacDonald	1	0	0	1	0	0	0	0	138	0	0	414	6,745
"	Bobby Marshman	2	0	0	0	0	0	0	1	56	0	0	140	925
"	Marvin Panch	1	0	0	0	0	1	0	0	44	0	0	125	350
"	Benny Parsons	1	0	0	0	0	0	0	0	258	0	0	129	250
"	Fireball Roberts	9	0	1	2	1	0	1	1	1,702	17	2	2,013	28,345
"	Johnny Rutherford	1	0	0	0	0	0	0	1	156	0	0	390	1,350
"	Bob Welborn	3	0	0	0	0	0	2	0	506	125	1	286	805
"	Don White	1	0	0	0	0	0	0	0	176	0	0	475	825
"	Cale Yarborough	5	0	0	0	0	0	0	3	1,681	0	0	1,382	3,140
"	**Total**	24	8	9	4	1	2	3	10	11,031	2,519	14	12,278	123,120
1965	A. J. Foyt	1	0	0	0	0	0	0	1	169	12	1	456	1,035
"	Dick Hutcherson	52	9	9	9	8	4	2	5	11,610	2,065	23	8,131	57,851
"	Bobby Johns	8	0	0	2	2	0	1	0	1,612	35	5	1,914	22,630
"	Fred Lorenzen	17	6	4	1	0	0	0	1	3,677	981	12	3,998	80,615
"	Pedro Rodriguez	1	0	0	0	0	0	1	0	391	0	0	587	3,425
"	**Total**	52	15	13	12	10	4	4	7	17,459	3,093	**35**	15,086	165,556
1966	Dick Hutcherson	7	1	1	0	2	0	2	0	1,423	147	3	1,667	13,420
"	Fred Lorenzen	10	2	2	1	0	1	2	0	2,927	758	6	3,216	36,675
"	**Total**	13	3	3	1	2	1	4	0	4,350	905	8	4,883	50,095
1967	Bobby Allison	2	1	2	0	0	0	0	0	1,000	426	2	750	19,550
"	Mario Andretti	6	0	1	0	0	0	0	2	867	137	3	1,757	52,165
"	Jimmy Clark	1	0	0	0	0	0	0	0	144	0	0	144	665
"	Dick Hutcherson	1	0	0	0	0	1	0	0	490	3	1	245	900

Year	Driver	Starts	Poles	Finish 1	2	3	4	5	6–10	Laps	Laps Led	Races Led	Miles	$

Holman-Moody *continued*

Year	Driver	Starts	Poles	1	2	3	4	5	6–10	Laps	Laps Led	Races Led	Miles	$
"	Fred Lorenzen	5	0	1	1	0	0	0	0	895	23	4	1,411	19,125
"	David Pearson	12	2	0	4	2	1	0	0	3,572	327	7	3,908	56,391
"	Swede Savage	3	0	0	0	0	0	0	2	1,091	0	0	571	1,275
"	**Total**	18	3	4	5	2	2	0	4	8,059	916	11	8,786	150,071
1968	Bobby Allison	2	0	1	1	0	0	0	0	700	317	2	367	3,900
"	Donnie Allison	1	0	0	0	0	0	0	0	48	0	0	120	1,000
"	Mario Andretti	3	0	0	0	0	0	0	0	297	20	2	751	2,845
"	A. J. Foyt	1	0	0	0	0	0	0	1	325	0	0	488	1,600
"	Frank Gardner	1	0	0	0	0	0	0	0	1	0	0	1	515
"	David Pearson	47	12	16	12	4	2	2	2	12,797	3,950	37	9,418	133,065
"	**Total**	47	12	17	13	4	2	2	3	**14,168**	**4,287**	**38**	**11,144**	142,925
1969	Mario Andretti	1	0	0	0	0	0	0	0	132	7	1	356	925
"	Parnelli Jones	1	0	0	0	0	0	0	0	22	0	0	59	770
"	David Pearson	51	14	11	18	9	2	2	2	14,270	3,018	39	11,369	229,760
"	**Total**	51	14	11	18	9	2	2	2	14,424	3,025	**40**	11,784	231,455
1970	David Pearson	18	2	1	2	2	3	0	2	3,835	580	11	5,618	85,968
1971	Bobby Allison	22	5	8	5	3	2	0	1	6,838	2,622	20	7,771	213,211
"	A. J. Foyt	1	0	0	0	0	0	0	0	33	0	0	83	655
"	David Pearson	9	2	2	3	0	2	0	0	2,228	251	9	2,104	24,425
"	Rolf Stommelen	1	0	0	0	0	0	0	0	53	0	0	141	790
"	**Total**	31	7	10	8	3	4	0	1	9,152	2,873	29	10,098	239,081
1973	Bobby Unser	1	0	0	0	0	1	0	0	186	0	0	487	4,520
Lifetime		366	83	93	81	44	32	31	50	120,575	24,420	245	118,694	$1,577,798
			4th	4th								4th	7th	

C. C. Holt

Year	Driver	Starts	Poles	1	2	3	4	5	6–10	Laps	Laps Led	Races Led	Miles	$
1975	Paul Dean Holt	2	0	0	0	0	0	0	0	120	0	0	72	685
Lifetime		2	0	0	0	0	0	0	0	120	0	0	72	$685

Dennis Holt

Year	Driver	Starts	Poles	1	2	3	4	5	6–10	Laps	Laps Led	Races Led	Miles	$
1967	Bill Ervin	1	0	0	0	0	0	0	0	135	0	0	68	120
"	Paul Dean Holt	23	0	0	0	0	0	0	1	2,921	0	0	1,840	4,230
"	Don Tarr	1	0	0	0	0	0	0	0	170	0	0	234	680
"	**Total**	25	0	0	0	0	0	0	1	3,226	0	0	2,141	5,030
1968	Paul Dean Holt	34	0	0	0	0	0	0	0	5,306	0	0	3,184	6,810
1969	Don Biederman	1	0	0	0	0	0	0	0	45	0	0	113	245
"	Paul Dean Holt	10	0	0	0	0	0	0	0	1,072	0	0	803	3,287
"	Wendell Scott	1	0	0	0	0	0	0	0	187	0	0	281	1,100
"	James Sears	1	0	0	0	0	0	0	0	247	0	0	247	725
"	J. C. Yarborough	2	0	0	0	0	0	0	0	318	0	0	159	415
"	**Total**	15	0	0	0	0	0	0	0	1,869	0	0	1,602	5,772
Lifetime		74	0	0	0	0	0	0	1	10,401	0	0	6,927	$17,612

Gus Holzmueller

Year	Driver	Starts	Poles	1	2	3	4	5	6–10	Laps	Laps Led	Races Led	Miles	$
1955	Ray Chaike	1	0	0	0	0	0	0	0	37	0	0	152	50
1956	Ray Chaike	1	0	0	0	0	0	0	0	0	0	0	0	100
"	Tiny Lund	19	0	0	0	0	1	0	7	3,357	0	0	2,151	2,661
"	**Total**	20	0	0	0	0	1	0	7	3,357	0	0	2,151	2,761
1957	Mel Larson	1	0	0	0	0	0	0	1	186	0	0	93	200
"	Tiny Lund	2	0	0	0	0	1	0	0	323	0	0	226	395
"	Jimmy Thompson	1	0	0	0	0	0	0	0	24	0	0	38	100
"	**Total**	3	0	0	0	0	1	0	1	533	0	0	357	695
Lifetime		24	0	0	0	0	2	0	8	3,927	0	0	2,660	$3,506

Hooker Hood

Year	Driver	Starts	Poles	1	2	3	4	5	6–10	Laps	Laps Led	Races Led	Miles	$
1954	Hooker Hood	2	0	0	0	0	0	0	0	248	0	0	244	75
1955	Hooker Hood	3	0	0	0	0	0	0	0	256	0	0	420	175
Lifetime		5	0	0	0	0	0	0	0	504	0	0	665	$250

Jeff Hooker

Year	Driver	Starts	Poles	1	2	3	4	5	6–10	Laps	Laps Led	Races Led	Miles	$
1985	Jeff Hooker	1	0	0	0	0	0	0	0	11	0	0	15	1,100
Lifetime		1	0	0	0	0	0	0	0	11	0	0	15	$1,100

Year	Driver	Starts	Poles	Finish 1	2	3	4	5	6–10	Laps	Laps Led	Races Led	Miles	$

Randy Hope

Year	Driver	Starts	Poles	1	2	3	4	5	6–10	Laps	Laps Led	Races Led	Miles	$
1988	Patty Moise	2	0	0	0	0	0	0	0	241	0	0	596	4,870
1989	Patty Moise	2	0	0	0	0	0	0	0	33	0	0	88	6,180
1990	Kenny Wallace	1	0	0	0	0	0	0	0	315	0	0	197	2,550
Lifetime		5	0	0	0	0	0	0	0	589	0	0	881	$13,600

Ronnie Hopkins

Year	Driver	Starts	Poles	1	2	3	4	5	6–10	Laps	Laps Led	Races Led	Miles	$
1971	Earl Brooks	1	0	0	0	0	0	0	1	481	0	0	253	775
"	Tiny Lund	6	0	2	2	0	1	0	1	2,111	250	5	1,009	9,525
"	**Total**	7	0	2	2	0	1	0	2	2,592	250	5	1,261	10,300
Lifetime		7	0	2	2	0	1	0	2	2,592	250	5	1,261	$10,300

Gene Horne

Year	Driver	Starts	Poles	1	2	3	4	5	6–10	Laps	Laps Led	Races Led	Miles	$
1949	Fonty Flock	1	0	0	0	0	0	0	0		0	0		25
1953	Obie Chupp	1	0	0	0	0	0	0	0	36	0	0	148	50
Lifetime		2	0	0	0	0	0	0	0	36	0	0	148	$75

Joe Horner

Year	Driver	Starts	Poles	1	2	3	4	5	6–10	Laps	Laps Led	Races Led	Miles	$
1992	Jimmy Horton	9	0	0	0	0	0	0	0	2,166	0	0	2,874	50,125
1993	Jimmy Horton	13	0	0	0	0	0	0	0	2,198	0	0	3,632	115,105
Lifetime		22	0	0	0	0	0	0	0	4,364	0	0	6,506	$165,230

Pappy Hough

Year	Driver	Starts	Poles	1	2	3	4	5	6–10	Laps	Laps Led	Races Led	Miles	$
1950	Lee Hough	2	0	0	0	0	0	0	0	60	0	0	30	0
"	Pappy Hough	5	0	0	0	0	0	0	2	296	0	0	215	300
"	**Total**	5	0	0	0	0	0	0	2	356	0	0	245	300
1951	Pappy Hough	9	0	0	0	0	0	1	3	0	0	0	0	950
1952	Pappy Hough	4	0	0	0	0	0	0	1	565	0	0	393	250
1955	Pappy Hough	3	0	0	0	0	0	0	0	422	0	0	256	160
Lifetime		21	0	0	0	0	0	1	6	1,343	0	0	894	$1,660

Jack Housby

Year	Driver	Starts	Poles	1	2	3	4	5	6–10	Laps	Laps Led	Races Led	Miles	$
1972	Pete Hamilton	5	0	0	0	0	0	1	0	1,044	8	2	1,630	8,005
"	Ramo Stott	2	0	0	0	0	0	0	1	201	0	0	503	3,740
"	**Total**	7	0	0	0	0	0	1	1	1,090	8	2	1,823	10,835
1973	Pete Hamilton	1	0	0	0	0	0	0	0	33	0	0	83	2,000
"	Ramo Stott	1	0	0	0	0	0	0	1	240	0	0	480	2,050
"	**Total**	2	0	0	0	0	0	0	1	273	0	0	563	4,050
1979	Kevin Housby	1	0	0	0	0	0	0	0	149	0	0	396	3,190
1980	Kevin Housby	3	0	0	0	0	0	0	0	524	0	0	1,006	6,165
Lifetime		13	0	0	0	0	0	1	2	2,191	8	2	4,097	$25,150

Bill House

Year	Driver	Starts	Poles	1	2	3	4	5	6–10	Laps	Laps Led	Races Led	Miles	$
1953	Don Oldenberg	2	0	0	0	0	0	1	0	223	0	0	245	275
Lifetime		2	0	0	0	0	0	1	0	223	0	0	245	$275

Don House

Year	Driver	Starts	Poles	1	2	3	4	5	6–10	Laps	Laps Led	Races Led	Miles	$
1961	Joe Kelly	2	0	0	0	0	0	0	0	200	0	0	500	300
1962	Wally Dallenbach	2	0	0	0	0	0	0	1	92	0	0	230	650
1963	Joe Kelly	1	0	0	0	0	0	0	0	120	0	0	60	85
1964	Don Hume	2	0	0	0	0	0	0	0	18	0	0	26	900
1965	Billy DeCoster	1	0	0	0	0	0	0	0	0	0	0	0	100
"	Don Hume	1	0	0	0	0	0	0	0	146	0	0	219	950
"	**Total**	2	0	0	0	0	0	0	0	146	0	0	219	1,050
Lifetime		9	0	0	0	0	0	0	1	576	0	0	1,035	$2,985

Stan Hover

Year	Driver	Starts	Poles	1	2	3	4	5	6–10	Laps	Laps Led	Races Led	Miles	$
1992	Dave Blaney	1	0	0	0	0	0	0	0	371	0	0	377	4,500
1994	Jimmy Horton	1	0	0	0	0	0	0	0	199	0	0	498	33,485
"	Joe Ruttman	1	0	0	0	0	0	0	0	328	0	0	492	5,690
"	**Total**	2	0	0	0	0	0	0	0	527	0	0	990	39,175
1995	Joe Ruttman	1	0	0	0	0	0	0	0	200	0	0	500	40,135

Year	Driver	Starts	Poles	Finish						Laps	Laps Led	Races Led	Miles	$
				1	2	3	4	5	6–10					

Stan Hover *continued*

Year	Driver	Starts	Poles	1	2	3	4	5	6–10	Laps	Laps Led	Races Led	Miles	$
1996	Joe Ruttman	0												3,522
Lifetime		4	0	0	0	0	0	0	0	1,098	0	0	1,867	$87,332

Hubert Howard

Year	Driver	Starts	Poles	1	2	3	4	5	6–10	Laps	Laps Led	Races Led	Miles	$
1966	Jeff Hawkins	1	0	0	0	0	0	1	0	192	0	0	96	275
"	Calvin Kelly	2	0	0	0	0	0	0	0	41	0	0	103	1,120
"	**Total**	3	0	0	0	0	0	1	0	233	0	0	199	1,395
Lifetime		3	0	0	0	0	0	1	0	233	0	0	199	$1,395

Phil Howard

Year	Driver	Starts	Poles	1	2	3	4	5	6–10	Laps	Laps Led	Races Led	Miles	$
1978	Dave Watson	1	0	0	0	0	0	0	0	316	0	0	481	1,600
1979	Dave Watson	4	0	0	0	0	0	0	1	1,092	7	2	1,161	7,170
1980	John Anderson	2	0	0	0	0	0	0	0	536	0	0	817	9,885
"	Rick Wilson	3	0	0	0	0	0	0	0	262	0	0	595	5,510
"	**Total**	5	0	0	0	0	0	0	0	798	0	0	1,411	15,395
Lifetime		10	0	0	0	0	0	0	1	2,206	7	2	3,053	$24,165

Richard Howard

Year	Driver	Starts	Poles	1	2	3	4	5	6–10	Laps	Laps Led	Races Led	Miles	$
1970	Fred Lorenzen	2	0	0	0	0	0	0	0	300	47	1	404	2,295
1971*	Charlie Glotzbach	14	4	1	2	0	3	1	0	3,897	805	10	3,931	34,055
"	LeeRoy Yarbrough	1	0	0	0	0	0	0	0	120	0	0	180	865
"	**Total**	14	4	1	2	0	3	1	0	4,017	805	10	4,111	34,920
1972*	Bobby Allison	31	12	10	12	2	1	0	2	10,063	4,398	30	11,801	348,939
"	Jim Paschal	1	0	0	0	0	0	0	0	338	0	0	507	1,825
"	Wendell Scott	1	0	0	0	0	0	0	0	283	0	0	425	1,710
"	**Total**	31	12	10	12	2	1	0	2	10,684	**4,398**	30	12,732	352,474
1973*	Billy Scott	1	0	0	0	0	0	0	0	340	0	0	510	1,850
"	Dick Trickle	1	0	0	0	0	1	0	327	2	1	491	3,385	
"	Cale Yarborough	28	5	4	6	4	1	1	3	9,314	3,167	21	9,737	267,513
"	**Total**	28	5	4	6	4	1	2	3	9,981	**3,169**	**21**	**10,737**	272,748
1974*	Billy Scott	1	0	0	0	0	0	0	0	262	0	0	393	1,625
"	Cale Yarborough	15	2	6	3	1	0	1	1	5,061	1,791	12	5,787	169,810
"	**Total**	15	2	6	3	1	0	1	1	5,323	1,791	12	6,180	171,435
1975	Donnie Allison	2	0	0	0	0	0	0	1	578	1	1	640	3,485
1976	Bobby Isaac	2	0	0	0	0	0	0	1	512	0	0	540	4,190
1981	Elliott Forbes-Robinson	10	0	0	0	0	0	0	3	1,923	0	0	3,364	26,480
Lifetime		104	23	21	23	7	5	4	11	33,318	10,211	75	38,707	$868,027
											10th			

*Co-owned with Junior Johnson from May 1971–July 1974.

Roz Howard

Year	Driver	Starts	Poles	1	2	3	4	5	6–10	Laps	Laps Led	Races Led	Miles	$
1956	Roz Howard	1	0	0	0	0	0	0	0	343	0	0	472	250
1958	Roz Howard	2	0	0	0	0	0	0	1	300	0	0	150	215
1960	Roz Howard	3	0	0	0	0	0	0	2	676	0	0	535	1,490
Lifetime		6	0	0	0	0	0	0	3	1,319	0	0	1,157	$1,955

Ed Huegele

Year	Driver	Starts	Poles	1	2	3	4	5	6–10	Laps	Laps Led	Races Led	Miles	$
1952	Jim Millard	1	0	0	0	0	0	0	1	0	0	0	0	100
Lifetime		1	0	0	0	0	0	0	1	0	0	0	0	$100

Ross Huggins

Year	Driver	Starts	Poles	1	2	3	4	5	6–10	Laps	Laps Led	Races Led	Miles	$
1969	Earle Canavan	1	0	0	0	0	0	0	0	62	0	0	165	1,100
Lifetime		1	0	0	0	0	0	0	0	62	0	0	165	$1,100

Harry Huhn

Year	Driver	Starts	Poles	1	2	3	4	5	6–10	Laps	Laps Led	Races Led	Miles	$
1960	Arnold Gardner	4	0	0	0	0	0	0	0	614	0	0	904	575
Lifetime		4	0	0	0	0	0	0	0	614	0	0	904	$575

Lloyd Hulette

Year	Driver	Starts	Poles	1	2	3	4	5	6–10	Laps	Laps Led	Races Led	Miles	$
1953	Lloyd Hulette	1	0	0	0	0	0	0	0	328	0	0	451	250
Lifetime		1	0	0	0	0	0	0	0	328	0	0	451	$250

Year	Driver	Starts	Poles	Finish						Laps	Laps Led	Races Led	Miles	$
				1	2	3	4	5	6–10					

Don Hume

Year	Driver	Starts	Poles	1	2	3	4	5	6–10	Laps	Laps Led	Races Led	Miles	$
1965	Don Hume	3	0	0	0	0	0	0	0	494	0	0	697	1,770
Lifetime		3	0	0	0	0	0	0	0	494	0	0	697	$1,770

Barney Humphries

Year	Driver	Starts	Poles	1	2	3	4	5	6–10	Laps	Laps Led	Races Led	Miles	$
1964	Gene Hobby	18	0	0	0	0	0	0	3	4,013	0	0	1,804	2,795
Lifetime		18	0	0	0	0	0	0	3	4,013	0	0	1,804	$2,795

Willie Humphries

Year	Driver	Starts	Poles	1	2	3	4	5	6–10	Laps	Laps Led	Races Led	Miles	$
1972	Red Farmer	5	0	0	0	0	1	0	0	474	0	0	1,101	9,575
1973	Red Farmer	3	0	0	0	0	0	0	0	247	0	0	647	4,235
1974	Red Farmer	2	0	0	0	0	0	0	0	329	0	0	875	2,860
1975	Bob Burcham	1	0	0	0	0	0	0	0	184	0	0	460	4,320
"	Red Farmer	2	0	0	0	0	0	0	0	44	0	0	117	2,245
"	**Total**	3	0	0	0	0	0	0	0	228	0	0	577	6,565
Lifetime		13	0	0	0	0	1	0	0	1,278	0	0	3,200	$23,235

T. C. Hunt

Year	Driver	Starts	Poles	1	2	3	4	5	6–10	Laps	Laps Led	Races Led	Miles	$
1969	T. C. Hunt	1	0	0	0	0	0	0	0	53	0	0	141	1,050
1971	Bob Williams	1	0	0	0	0	0	0	0	178	0	0	98	390
Lifetime		2	0	0	0	0	0	0	0	231	0	0	239	$1,440

Lester Hunter

Year	Driver	Starts	Poles	1	2	3	4	5	6–10	Laps	Laps Led	Races Led	Miles	$
1965	Buddy Arrington	1	0	0	0	0	0	0	1	253	0	0	380	800
"	Doug Cooper	1	0	0	0	0	0	0	0	198	0	0	272	600
"	Jeff Hawkins	6	0	0	0	0	0	0	0	322	0	0	261	2,160
"	Harold Painter	1	0	0	0	0	0	0	0	0	0	0	0	100
"	Cale Yarborough	1	0	0	0	0	0	0	0	193	0	0	290	550
"	**Total**	10	0	0	0	0	0	0	1	966	0	0	1,202	4,210
Lifetime		10	0	0	0	0	0	0	1	966	0	0	1,202	$4,210

Tom Hunter

Year	Driver	Starts	Poles	1	2	3	4	5	6–10	Laps	Laps Led	Races Led	Miles	$
1965	Roy Mayne	12	0	0	0	0	1	0	4	2,443	0	0	2,399	7,810
1966	Roy Mayne	15	0	0	0	0	0	1	3	3,762	0	0	3,583	9,555
1967	Larry Manning	1	0	0	0	0	0	0	0	102	0	0	153	875
"	Roy Mayne	12	0	0	0	0	0	0	1	1,658	0	0	2,028	7,635
"	**Total**	13	0	0	0	0	0	0	1	1,760	0	0	2,181	8,510
1968	Max Ledbetter	1	0	0	0	0	0	0	0	134	0	0	67	100
"	Larry Manning	8	0	0	0	0	0	0	0	1,784	0	0	2,088	6,395
"	Roy Mayne	1	0	0	0	0	0	0	0	77	0	0	116	775
"	**Total**	10	0	0	0	0	0	0	0	1,995	0	0	2,271	7,270
1969	Max Ledbetter	1	0	0	0	0	0	0	0	91	0	0	46	260
"	Roy Mayne	8	0	0	0	0	0	0	0	2,161	0	0	2,112	6,715
"	**Total**	9	0	0	0	0	0	0	0	2,252	0	0	2,158	6,975
1970	Roy Mayne	12	0	0	0	0	0	0	3	2,717	0	0	3,736	13,460
1971	Earl Brooks	1	0	0	0	0	0	0	0	264	0	0	396	585
"	Roy Mayne	10	0	0	0	0	0	0	0	1,598	0	0	2,225	8,205
"	**Total**	11	0	0	0	0	0	0	0	1,862	0	0	2,621	8,790
1972	Roy Mayne	2	0	0	0	0	0	0	0	94	0	0	244	1,620
Lifetime		84	0	0	0	0	1	1	11	16,885	0	0	19,192	$63,990

Walt Hunter

Year	Driver	Starts	Poles	1	2	3	4	5	6–10	Laps	Laps Led	Races Led	Miles	$
1964	Ken Anderson	2	0	0	0	0	0	0	0	488	0	0	283	250
"	J. T. Putney	17	0	0	0	1	0	0	5	4,226	0	0	3,370	7,295
"	**Total**	19	0	0	0	1	0	0	5	4,714	0	0	3,653	7,545
Lifetime		19	0	0	0	1	0	0	5	4,714	0	0	3,653	$7,545

Jim Hurlbert

Year	Driver	Starts	Poles	1	2	3	4	5	6–10	Laps	Laps Led	Races Led	Miles	$
1982	Jim Hurlbert	1	0	0	0	0	0	0	0	1	0	0	3	1,430
Lifetime		1	0	0	0	0	0	0	0	1	0	0	3	$1,430

Mark Hurley

Year	Driver	Starts	Poles	1	2	3	4	5	6–10	Laps	Laps Led	Races Led	Miles	$
1963	Darel Dieringer	1	0	0	0	0	0	0	1	291	0	0	97	240

Year	Driver	Starts	Poles	Finish 1	2	3	4	5	6–10	Laps	Laps Led	Races Led	Miles	$
Mark Hurley *continued*														
"	Mark Hurley	2	0	0	0	0	1	0	0	272	0	0	76	400
"	Billy Wade	1	0	0	0	0	0	0	0	1	0	0	0	55
"	**Total**	4	0	0	0	0	1	0	1	564	0	0	173	695
1964	Mark Hurley	1	0	0	0	0	0	0	0	11	0	0	17	625
Lifetime		5	0	0	0	0	1	0	1	575	0	0	189	$1,320
George Hutchens														
1952	Bill Blair	19	1	1	3	4	2	0	3	2,427	120	4	1,920	7,899
"	Jimmie Lewallen	1	0	0	0	0	1	0	0	78	0	0	98	350
"	Bobby Myers	1	0	0	0	0	0	0	0	145	0	0	181	0
"	Jim Paschal	3	0	0	0	0	0	0	0	242	0	0	200	50
"	Dick Rathmann	1	0	0	0	0	0	0	0	85	0	0	85	45
"	**Total**	21	1	1	3	4	3	0	3	2,977	120	4	2,484	8,344
1953	Cotton Owens	1	0	0	0	0	0	0	0	274	0	0	274	50
"	Jim Paschal	19	1	1	0	1	2	2	3	887	73	1	926	5,186
"	**Total**	20	1	1	0	1	2	2	3	1,161	73	1	1,200	5,236
1954	Ray Duhigg	1	0	0	0	0	0	0	0	122	0	0	61	0
"	Jimmie Lewallen	5	0	0	0	0	0	2	2	844	0	0	552	1,150
"	Cotton Owens	1	0	0	0	0	0	0	1	183	0	0	92	100
"	Jim Paschal	6	0	0	0	0	1	0	2	660	0	0	519	700
"	Bob Welborn	3	0	0	0	0	0	0	1	207	0	0	118	325
"	**Total**	16	0	0	0	0	1	2	6	2,016	0	0	1,341	2,275
1955	Jim Paschal	1	0	0	0	0	0	0	0	7	0	0	4	0
Lifetime		58	2	2	3	5	6	4	12	6,161	193	5	5,029	$15,855
Dick Hutcherson														
1964	Dick Hutcherson	4	2	0	1	0	0	1	0	592	75	2	362	1,585
Lifetime		4	2	0	1	0	0	1	0	592	75	2	362	$1,585
James Hylton														
1968	James Hylton	39	0	0	1	4	8	3	11	9,731	15	3	7,004	31,728
1969	James Hylton	50	0	0	4	9	8	5	12	12,929	162	12	10,581	113,166
1970	James Hylton	45	1	1	4	2	8	7	17	12,492	199	8	10,673	76,711
1971	James Hylton	46	1	0	2	3	5	4	23	12,785	105	5	12,718	90,282
1972	James Hylton	31	0	1	0	0	5	3	14	9,672	111	4	11,431	126,705
"	Cale Yarborough	1	0	0	0	0	0	1	0	196	0	0	392	2,150
"	**Total**	31	0	1	0	0	5	4	14	9,868	111	4	11,823	128,855
1973	Wayne Andrews	1	0	0	0	0	0	0	0	5	0	0	8	1,005
"	James Hylton	28	0	0	0	0	1	0	10	9,324	1	1	10,044	85,512
"	**Total**	28	0	0	0	0	1	0	10	9,329	1	1	10,051	86,517
1974	James Hylton	29	0	0	0	0	0	1	7	6,774	29	6	7,969	61,385
1975	James Hylton	30	0	0	0	0	1	1	14	**9,650**	11	4	**11,032**	113,642
1976	James Hylton	29	0	0	0	0	1	1	3	7,954	14	4	9,157	78,050
1977	James Hylton	30	0	0	0	0	0	0	11	8,375	3	1	9,591	108,392
1978	Walter Ballard	0	0	0	0	0	0	0	0	0	0	0	0	505
"	Al Holbert	12	0	0	0	0	0	0	3	2,479	0	0	3,919	30,885
"	James Hylton	18	0	0	0	0	0	0	4	5,773	16	2	5,016	46,915
"	**Total**	28	0	0	0	0	0	0	7	8,252	16	2	8,935	78,305
1979	James Hylton	30	0	0	0	0	0	0	5	8,658	11	4	9,603	98,333
1980	James Hylton	30	0	0	0	0	0	0	4	8,920	26	1	10,079	105,805
1981	Harry Gant	1	0	0	0	0	0	0	1	493	1	1	263	4,270
"	James Hylton	28	0	0	0	0	0	0	0	7,051	12	2	8,509	87,305
"	Kirk Shelmerdine	1	0	0	0	0	0	0	0	2	0	0	4	950
"	**Total**	29	0	0	0	0	0	0	1	7,546	13	3	8,775	92,525
1982	Tommy Gale	1	0	0	0	0	0	0	0	351	0	0	527	5,020
"	James Hylton	13	0	0	0	0	0	0	0	4,208	0	0	4,332	50,630
"	Slick Johnson	7	0	0	0	0	0	0	1	1,943	1	1	1,793	23,775
"	Joe Millikan	1	0	0	0	0	0	0	0	343	0	0	469	6,095
"	Lennie Pond	3	0	0	0	0	0	0	1	1,065	0	0	1,373	15,540
"	D. K. Ulrich	3	0	0	0	0	0	0	0	393	0	0	1,007	11,550
"	**Total**	28	0	0	0	0	0	0	2	8,303	1	1	9,499	112,610
1983	Trevor Boys	23	0	0	0	0	0	0	1	5,907	3	2	6,896	87,555
"	James Hylton	2	0	0	0	0	0	0	0	556	0	0	662	12,105
"	Lennie Pond	4	0	0	0	0	0	0	0	1,189	0	0	1,094	13,900
"	**Total**	28	0	0	0	0	0	0	1	7,652	3	2	8,651	113,560
1984	Trevor Boys	30	0	0	0	0	0	0	1	8,719	20	3	9,970	165,376

Year	Driver	Starts	Poles	Finish 1	2	3	4	5	6–10	Laps	Laps Led	Races Led	Miles	$

James Hylton *continued*

Year	Driver	Starts	Poles	1	2	3	4	5	6–10	Laps	Laps Led	Races Led	Miles	$
1985	Trevor Boys	13	0	0	0	0	0	0	0	3,117	3	1	3,668	53,420
"	Ron Esau	1	0	0	0	0	0	0	0	10	0	0	26	2,925
"	Don Hume	6	0	0	0	0	0	0	0	1,994	0	0	1,749	20,860
"	James Hylton	1	0	0	0	0	0	0	0	201	0	0	201	3,945
"	Lennie Pond	5	0	0	0	0	0	0	0	1,560	0	0	1,561	32,045
"	Greg Sacks	3	0	0	0	0	0	0	0	348	0	0	748	11,350
"	**Total**	28	0	0	0	0	0	0	0	7,230	3	1	7,953	124,545
1986	Eddie Bierschwale	1	0	0	0	0	0	0	0	2	0	0	1	2,515
"	Trevor Boys	1	0	0	0	0	0	0	0	17	0	0	11	3,035
"	Johnny Coy Jr.	2	0	0	0	0	0	0	0	591	0	0	593	9,200
"	Jerry Cranmer	5	0	0	0	0	0	0	0	1,727	0	0	1,771	23,510
"	Ron Esau	2	0	0	0	0	0	0	0	168	0	0	440	8,475
"	James Hylton	4	0	0	0	0	0	0	0	544	0	0	576	22,090
"	Morgan Shepherd	1	0	0	0	0	0	0	0	394	0	0	246	3,880
"	Wayne Slark	1	0	0	0	0	0	0	0	96	0	0	98	4,055
"	Ronnie Thomas	3	0	0	0	0	0	0	0	451	0	0	1,092	20,925
"	**Total**	20	0	0	0	0	0	0	0	3,990	0	0	4,828	97,685
1987	Jerry Holden	1	0	0	0	0	0	0	0	133	0	0	354	2,850
"	James Hylton	2	0	0	0	0	0	0	0	93	0	0	99	2,550
"	Steve Moore	0													1,150
"	Tony Spanos	1	0	0	0	0	0	0	0	386	0	0	203	1,555
"	**Total**	4	0	0	0	0	0	0	0	612	0	0	656	8,105
1989	Trevor Boys	1	0	0	0	0	0	0	0	118	2	1	295	3,775
"	Bill Flowers	1	0	0	0	0	0	0	0	2	0	0	2	1,800
"	James Hylton	2	0	0	0	0	0	0	0	38	0	0	43	3,775
"	**Total**	4	0	0	0	0	0	0	0	158	2	1	340	9,350
1990	Freddie Crawford	1	0	0	0	0	0	0	0	6	0	0	6	2,775
"	Ben Hess	1	0	0	0	0	0	0	0	169	0	0	338	4,275
"	James Hylton	1	0	0	0	0	0	0	0	202	0	0	202	2,800
"	**Total**	3	0	0	0	0	0	0	0	377	0	0	546	9,850
1991	James Hylton	4	0	0	0	0	0	0	0	87	0	0	113	14,190
1992	James Hylton	8	0	0	0	0	0	0	0	611	0	0	1,100	37,910
1993	Trevor Boys	1	0	0	0	0	0	0	0	38	1	1	95	6,510
"	James Hylton	2	0	0	0	0	0	0	0	86	0	0	109	17,295
"	**Total**	3	0	0	0	0	0	0	0	124	1	1	204	23,805
1995	James Hylton	0													3,950
Lifetime		**634**	**2**	**2**	**11**	**18**	**37**	**26**	**143**	**171,126**	**746**	**67**	**181,853**	**$1,984,632**
		7th								**8th**		**10th**		

Thomas Hynes

Year	Driver	Starts	Poles	1	2	3	4	5	6–10	Laps	Laps Led	Races Led	Miles	$
1971	Harry Schilling	3	0	0	0	0	0	0	0	222	0	0	561	3,395
1972	Harry Schilling	3	0	0	0	0	0	0	0	587	0	0	923	2,399
Lifetime		**6**	**0**	**0**	**0**	**0**	**0**	**0**	**0**	**809**	**0**	**0**	**1,484**	**$5,794**

Jimmy Ingalls

Year	Driver	Starts	Poles	1	2	3	4	5	6–10	Laps	Laps Led	Races Led	Miles	$
1983	Jimmy Ingalls	2	0	0	0	0	0	0	0	901	0	0	901	3,080
Lifetime		**2**	**0**	**0**	**0**	**0**	**0**	**0**	**0**	**901**	**0**	**0**	**901**	**$3,080**

Paul Ingle

Year	Driver	Starts	Poles	1	2	3	4	5	6–10	Laps	Laps Led	Races Led	Miles	$
1985	Tommy Houston	1	0	0	0	0	0	0	0	47	0	0	64	1,645
1986	Eddie Bierschwale	1	0	0	0	0	0	0	0	374	1	1	561	2,000
"	Jim Sauter	1	0	0	0	0	0	0	0	26	0	0	69	2,400
"	**Total**	2	0	0	0	0	0	0	0	400	1	1	630	4,400
Lifetime		**3**	**0**	**0**	**0**	**0**	**0**	**0**	**0**	**447**	**1**	**1**	**694**	**$6,045**

Jim Ingram

Year	Driver	Starts	Poles	1	2	3	4	5	6–10	Laps	Laps Led	Races Led	Miles	$
1980	Jim Ingram	1	0	0	0	0	0	0	0	437	0	0	437	1,435
Lifetime		**1**	**0**	**0**	**0**	**0**	**0**	**0**	**0**	**437**	**0**	**0**	**437**	**$1,435**

Tommy Ingram

Year	Driver	Starts	Poles	1	2	3	4	5	6–10	Laps	Laps Led	Races Led	Miles	$
1967	Jack Ingram	4	0	0	1	0	0	0	0	506	0	0	218	1,165
"	Tommy Ingram	2	0	0	0	0	0	0	0	58	0	0	73	1,060
"	**Total**	6	0	0	1	0	0	0	0	564	0	0	291	2,225
Lifetime		**6**	**0**	**0**	**1**	**0**	**0**	**0**	**0**	**564**	**0**	**0**	**291**	**$2,225**

Year	Driver	Starts	Poles	Finish						Laps	Laps Led	Races Led	Miles	$
				1	2	3	4	5	6–10					

Doug Innes

Year	Driver	Starts	Poles	1	2	3	4	5	6–10	Laps	Laps Led	Races Led	Miles	$
1994	Butch Leitzinger	1	0	0	0	0	0	0	0	81	0	0	198	6,330
Lifetime		1	0	0	0	0	0	0	0	81	0	0	198	$6,330

Jimmy Insolo

Year	Driver	Starts	Poles	1	2	3	4	5	6–10	Laps	Laps Led	Races Led	Miles	$
1977	Jimmy Insolo	1	0	0	0	0	1	0	0	93	0	0	244	3,900
Lifetime		1	0	0	0	0	1	0	0	93	0	0	244	$3,900

John Irvan

Year	Driver	Starts	Poles	1	2	3	4	5	6–10	Laps	Laps Led	Races Led	Miles	$
1976	Jim Danielson	1	0	0	0	0	0	0	0	39	0	0	102	890
Lifetime		1	0	0	0	0	0	0	0	39	0	0	102	$890

Tommy Irwin

Year	Driver	Starts	Poles	1	2	3	4	5	6–10	Laps	Laps Led	Races Led	Miles	$
1958	Tommy Irwin	5	0	0	0	1	1	0	1	1,255	0	0	689	1,280
1959	Tommy Irwin	25	1	0	1	2	3	4	6	4,410	174	2	2,847	9,190
"	Tiny Lund	1	0	0	0	0	0	0	1	147	0	0	49	170
"	**Total**	25	1	0	1	2	3	4	7	4,557	174	2	2,896	9,360
1960	Tommy Irwin	13	1	0	0	0	3	1	6	2,104	0	0	1,064	2,370
1961	Tommy Irwin	1	0	0	0	0	0	0	0	97	0	0	49	70
Lifetime		44	2	0	1	3	7	5	14	8,013	174	2	4,698	$13,080

Gene Isenhour

Year	Driver	Starts	Poles	1	2	3	4	5	6–10	Laps	Laps Led	Races Led	Miles	$
1991	Gary Balough	1	0	0	0	0	0	0	0	42	0	0	63	3,110
1992	Rich Bickle	3	0	0	0	0	0	0	0	816	0	0	881	13,370
1993	Rich Bickle	5	0	0	0	0	0	0	0	842	1	1	1,356	36,305
1994	Rich Bickle	1	0	0	0	0	0	0	0	106	0	0	212	11,165
Lifetime		10	0	0	0	0	0	0	0	1,806	1	1	2,512	$63,950

Earl Ivey

Year	Driver	Starts	Poles	1	2	3	4	5	6–10	Laps	Laps Led	Races Led	Miles	$
1967	Joel Davis	5	0	0	0	0	0	0	2	759	0	0	709	1,725
Lifetime		5	0	0	0	0	0	0	2	759	0	0	709	$1,725

Wayne Jacks

Year	Driver	Starts	Poles	1	2	3	4	5	6–10	Laps	Laps Led	Races Led	Miles	$
1993	Wayne Jacks	1	0	0	0	0	0	0	0	48	0	0	48	5,980
Lifetime		1	0	0	0	0	0	0	0	48	0	0	48	$5,980

Beryl Jackson

Year	Driver	Starts	Poles	1	2	3	4	5	6–10	Laps	Laps Led	Races Led	Miles	$
1952	Hershel McGriff	2	0	0	0	0	0	0	1	283	0	0	261	325
1954	Hershel McGriff	2	1	0	0	0	0	0	0	166	0	0	216	105
"	Marvin Panch	9	1	0	2	1	0	0	3	1,914	17	1	1,686	4,430
"	**Total**	10	2	0	2	1	0	0	3	2,080	17	1	1,902	4,535
1955	Ed Negre	1	0	0	0	0	0	0	1	239	0	0	239	200
1956	Harold Hardesty	3	0	0	0	0	0	1	0	780	0	0	687	730
1971	Hershel McGriff	2	0	0	0	0	0	0	0	234	3	1	613	2,085
1972	Hershel McGriff	4	0	0	0	0	0	2	1	727	3	1	1,728	12,290
1973	Hershel McGriff	3	0	0	0	0	0	1	1	426	0	0	1,093	8,690
Lifetime		25	2	0	2	1	0	4	7	4,769	23	3	6,521	$28,855

Lacy Jackson

Year	Driver	Starts	Poles	1	2	3	4	5	6–10	Laps	Laps Led	Races Led	Miles	$
1953	Lacy Jackson	1	0	0	0	0	0	0	0	288	0	0	396	130
Lifetime		1	0	0	0	0	0	0	0	288	0	0	396	$130

Larry Jackson

Year	Driver	Starts	Poles	1	2	3	4	5	6–10	Laps	Laps Led	Races Led	Miles	$
1971	Tommy Gale	8	0	0	0	0	0	0	1	1,431	0	0	2,591	7,680
Lifetime		8	0	0	0	0	0	0	1	1,431	0	0	2,591	$7,680

Leo Jackson

Year	Driver	Starts	Poles	1	2	3	4	5	6–10	Laps	Laps Led	Races Led	Miles	$
1989	Harry Gant	29	0	1	3	1	2	2	5	8,627	440	11	10,293	639,792
1990	Harry Gant	28	0	1	0	1	1	3	3	7,441	53	9	9,669	522,519
"	Phil Parsons	1	0	0	0	0	0	0	0	342	0	0	182	9,080
"	**Total**	29	0	1	0	1	1	3	3	7,783	53	9	9,851	531,599

Year	Driver	Starts	Poles	Finish						Laps	Laps Led	Races Led	Miles	$
				1	2	3	4	5	6–10					

Leo Jackson *continued*

Year	Driver	Starts	Poles	1	2	3	4	5	6–10	Laps	Laps Led	Races Led	Miles	$
1991	Harry Gant	29	1	5	2	3	4	1	2	9,428	**1,684**	17	11,124	1,194,033
1992	Harry Gant	29	0	2	3	2	0	3	5	9,197	407	15	11,220	1,122,776
1993	Harry Gant	30	1	0	0	1	2	1	8	8,843	265	8	10,867	772,832
1994	Harry Gant	30	1	0	0	0	0	0	7	7,329	94	3	9,570	556,020
"	Robert Pressley	3	0	0	0	0	0	0	0	587	0	0	947	39,485
"	**Total**	30	1	0	0	0	0	0	7	7,916	94	3	10,517	595,505
1995	Robert Pressley	31	0	0	0	0	0	0	1	8,191	37	3	10,006	695,875
Lifetime		207	3	9	8	8	9	10	31	59,985	2,980	66	73,878	$5,552,412

Leo Jackson & Andy Petree

Year	Driver	Starts	Poles	1	2	3	4	5	6–10	Laps	Laps Led	Races Led	Miles	$
1996	Todd Bodine	3	0	0	0	0	0	0	0	1,014	0	0	1,183	73,780
"	Robert Pressley	27	0	0	0	0	1	1	1	7,094	110	7	8,661	634,815
"	Greg Sacks	1	0	0	0	0	0	0	0	480	0	0	480	24,140
"	**Total**	31	0	0	0	0	1	1	1	8,588	110	7	10,324	732,735
Lifetime		31	0	0	0	0	1	1	1	8,588	110	7	10,324	$732,735

Richard Jackson

Year	Driver	Starts	Poles	1	2	3	4	5	6–10	Laps	Laps Led	Races Led	Miles	$
1985	Benny Parsons	14	0	0	0	0	0	1	5	2,230	8	3	4,279	94,450
"	Phil Parsons	14	0	0	0	0	0	0	3	2,187	1	1	4,131	49,995
"	**Total**	14	0	0	0	0	0	1	8	4,417	9	4	8,410	144,445
1986	Benny Parsons	16	1	0	0	0	0	2	2	2,620	13	7	5,098	176,985
"	Phil Parsons	15	0	0	0	0	0	1	4	3,159	1	1	5,909	77,160
"	**Total**	16	1	0	0	0	0	3	6	5,779	14	7	11,008	254,145
1987	Phil Parsons	29	0	0	0	0	1	0	6	8,216	18	2	9,672	180,261
"	Tom Sneva	1	0	0	0	0	0	0	0	182	0	0	455	11,135
"	**Total**	29	0	0	0	0	1	0	6	8,398	18	2	10,127	191,396
1988	Phil Parsons	29	0	1	1	2	1	1	9	8,494	108	10	10,287	532,043
1989	Phil Parsons	28	0	0	0	1	0	1	1	7,341	39	4	9,072	285,012
1990	Irv Hoerr	2	0	0	0	0	0	0	2	164	3	1	405	14,775
"	Terry Labonte	29	0	0	1	0	3	0	5	8,518	9	3	10,143	450,230
"	**Total**	29	0	0	1	0	3	0	7	8,682	12	4	10,548	465,005
1991	Rick Mast	29	0	0	0	0	1	0	2	8,861	32	3	10,650	344,020
1992	Irv Hoerr	1	0	0	0	0	0	0	0	42	0	0	106	4,725
"	Rick Mast	29	1	0	0	0	0	0	1	8,123	0	0	9,985	350,740
"	**Total**	29	1	0	0	0	0	0	1	8,165	0	0	10,090	355,465
1993	Rick Mast	30	0	0	0	0	0	1	4	8,488	32	4	9,802	568,095
1994	Rick Mast	31	1	0	1	3	0	0	6	8,756	166	8	10,753	733,361
1995	Rick Mast	31	1	0	0	0	0	0	3	8,560	143	3	10,599	749,550
1996	Rick Mast	31	0	0	0	0	1	0	4	8,972	1	1	10,936	924,559
Lifetime		326	4	1	3	6	7	7	57	94,913	574	50	122,284	$5,547,096

Al Jacobs

Year	Driver	Starts	Poles	1	2	3	4	5	6–10	Laps	Laps Led	Races Led	Miles	$
1951	Al Jacobs	3	0	0	0	0	0	0	0		0	0		100
Lifetime		3	0	0	0	0	0	0	0		0	0		$100

Skip Jaehne

Year	Driver	Starts	Poles	1	2	3	4	5	6–10	Laps	Laps Led	Races Led	Miles	$
1987	Hut Stricklin	3	0	0	0	0	0	0	0	912	0	0	1,009	6,085
Lifetime		3	0	0	0	0	0	0	0	912	0	0	1,009	$6,085

Rocco Janette

Year	Driver	Starts	Poles	1	2	3	4	5	6–10	Laps	Laps Led	Races Led	Miles	$
1949	Jack O'Brien	2	0	0	0	0	0	0	0	115	0	0	58	0
Lifetime		2	0	0	0	0	0	0	0	115	0	0	58	$0

Jack Janos

Year	Driver	Starts	Poles	1	2	3	4	5	6–10	Laps	Laps Led	Races Led	Miles	$
1970	Paul Feldner	2	0	0	0	0	0	0	1	214	0	0	535	1,490
Lifetime		2	0	0	0	0	0	0	1	214	0	0	535	$1,490

Michael Jarema

Year	Driver	Starts	Poles	1	2	3	4	5	6–10	Laps	Laps Led	Races Led	Miles	$
1953	Mike Magill	3	0	0	0	0	0	0	0	244	0	0	336	235
Lifetime		3	0	0	0	0	0	0	0	244	0	0	336	$235

Year	Driver	Starts	Poles	Finish						Laps	Laps Led	Races Led	Miles	$
				1	2	3	4	5	6–10	Laps	Led	Led	Miles	$

Ned Jarrett

Year	Driver	Starts	Poles	1	2	3	4	5	6–10	Laps	Laps Led	Races Led	Miles	$
1953	Ned Jarrett	1	0	0	0	0	0	0	0	8	0	0	11	100
1955	Ned Jarrett	1	0	0	0	0	0	0	0	70	0	0	44	0
1956	Ned Jarrett	2	0	0	0	0	0	0	0	244	0	0	140	60
1957	Ned Jarrett	1	0	0	0	0	0	0	0	7	0	0	4	50
1959	Ned Jarrett	16	0	2	0	1	0	0	3	2,729	0	0	1,389	3,335
1960	Ned Jarrett	40	5	5	3	4	4	4	6	7,399	382	11	5,479	25,438
1961	Ned Jarrett	2	0	0	0	0	0	0	0	127	0	0	64	110
Lifetime		63	5	7	3	5	4	4	9	10,584	382	11	7,130	$29,093

Walt Jarrod

Year	Driver	Starts	Poles	1	2	3	4	5	6–10	Laps	Laps Led	Races Led	Miles	$
1951	Fred Moore	1	0	0	0	0	0	0	0	112	0	0	140	0
Lifetime		1	0	0	0	0	0	0	0	112	0	0	140	$0

George Jefferson

Year	Driver	Starts	Poles	1	2	3	4	5	6–10	Laps	Laps Led	Races Led	Miles	$
1973	Harry Jefferson	1	0	0	0	0	0	0	0	37	0	0	97	1,015
1974	Harry Jefferson	4	0	0	0	0	0	0	1	457	0	0	775	6,083
1975	Harry Jefferson	5	0	0	0	0	0	0	2	1,036	0	0	1,787	11,395
1976	Harry Jefferson	1	0	0	0	0	0	0	0	14	0	0	37	535
1977	Harry Jefferson	1	0	0	0	0	0	0	0	195	0	0	488	1,600
1978	Hershel McGriff	1	0	0	0	0	0	0	1	118	0	0	309	2,850
1982	Derrike Cope	1	0	0	0	0	0	0	0	42	0	0	110	625
1984	Derrike Cope	3	0	0	0	0	0	0	0	370	0	0	631	6,500
1985	Derrike Cope	2	0	0	0	0	0	0	0	206	0	0	540	7,100
1986	Chad Little	2	0	0	0	0	0	0	0	145	0	0	380	6,065
1987	Chad Little	2	0	0	0	0	0	0	0	211	0	0	553	8,810
Lifetime		23	0	0	0	0	0	0	4	2,831	0	0	5,705	$52,578

Doreen Jeffrey

Year	Driver	Starts	Poles	1	2	3	4	5	6–10	Laps	Laps Led	Races Led	Miles	$
1988	Rick Jeffrey	2	0	0	0	0	0	0	0	326	0	0	815	14,225
1990	Rick Jeffrey	1	0	0	0	0	0	0	0	467	0	0	475	5,300
Lifetime		3	0	0	0	0	0	0	0	793	0	0	1,290	$19,525

W. S. Jenkins

Year	Driver	Starts	Poles	1	2	3	4	5	6–10	Laps	Laps Led	Races Led	Miles	$
1964	Bobby Keck	2	0	0	0	0	0	0	0	420	0	0	511	950
"	Doug Wilson	4	0	0	0	0	0	0	0	1,086	0	0	523	750
"	**Total**	6	0	0	0	0	0	0	0	1,506	0	0	1,034	1,700
1966	Hank Thomas	13	0	0	0	1	0	2	3	2,926	0	0	1,435	3,465
Lifetime		19	0	0	0	1	0	2	3	4,432	0	0	2,469	$5,165

Joe Jernigan

Year	Driver	Starts	Poles	1	2	3	4	5	6–10	Laps	Laps Led	Races Led	Miles	$
1950	Joe Jernigan	2	0	0	0	0	0	0	0	166	0	0	296	100
1951	Joe Jernigan	2	0	0	0	0	0	0	0		0	0		25
Lifetime		4	0	0	0	0	0	0	0	166	0	0	296	$125

Paul Jett

Year	Driver	Starts	Poles	1	2	3	4	5	6–10	Laps	Laps Led	Races Led	Miles	$
1972	Paul Jett	2	0	0	0	0	0	0	1	391	0	0	895	2,495
Lifetime		2	0	0	0	0	0	0	1	391	0	0	895	$2,495

Shorty Johns

Year	Driver	Starts	Poles	1	2	3	4	5	6–10	Laps	Laps Led	Races Led	Miles	$
1956	Bobby Johns	8	0	0	0	0	0	0	2	1,188	0	0	611	750
1957	Bobby Johns	1	0	0	0	0	0	0	0	335	0	0	461	225
1958	Bobby Johns	3	0	0	0	0	1	0	0	894	0	0	835	1,625
"	Joe Lee Johnson	1	0	0	0	0	0	0	1	146	0	0	146	375
"	**Total**	4	0	0	0	0	1	0	1	1,040	0	0	981	2,000
1959	Bobby Johns	8	1	0	0	1	0	0	1	1,911	129	2	1,440	5,951
1960	Bobby Johns	2	0	0	0	0	0	1	0	665	49	1	333	445
1961	Bobby Johns	13	0	0	0	0	1	0	2	2,217	3	1	2,856	4,570
1962	Bobby Johns	13	0	1	0	1	0	0	1	2,745	614	8	2,976	14,535
1963	Bobby Johns	12	0	0	0	1	0	2	3	2,433	84	3	3,383	15,515
1964	Bobby Johns	6	0	0	0	0	0	0	1	629	0	0	625	2,950
1965	Jim Bray	2	0	0	0	0	0	0	0	6	0	0	15	1,190

Year	Driver	Starts	Poles	Finish 1	2	3	4	5	6–10	Laps	Laps Led	Races Led	Miles	$

Shorty Johns *continued*

Year	Driver	Starts	Poles	1	2	3	4	5	6–10	Laps	Laps Led	Races Led	Miles	$
"	Bobby Johns	5	0	0	0	0	0	0	0	1,084	2	1	1,027	2,300
"	**Total**	7	0	0	0	0	0	0	0	1,090	2	1	1,042	3,490
1966	Bobby Johns	11	0	0	0	0	0	0	1	1,419	0	0	1,236	5,245
"	Bub Strickler	1	0	0	0	0	0	0	0	25	0	0	63	0
"	**Total**	12	0	0	0	0	0	0	1	1,444	0	0	1,299	5,245
1967	Bobby Johns	11	0	0	0	0	0	0	0	1,279	0	0	1,301	6,405
1968	Bobby Johns	7	0	0	0	0	0	0	0	750	0	0	1,108	5,010
1969	Bobby Johns	8	0	0	0	0	0	0	0	1,075	0	0	1,185	5,875
Lifetime		112	1	1	0	3	2	3	12	18,801	881	16	19,600	$72,966

Amos Johnson

Year	Driver	Starts	Poles	1	2	3	4	5	6–10	Laps	Laps Led	Races Led	Miles	$
1969	Amos Johnson	1	0	0	0	0	0	0	0	147	0	0	391	1,450
Lifetime		1	0	0	0	0	0	0	0	147	0	0	391	$1,450

Berendt Johnson

Year	Driver	Starts	Poles	1	2	3	4	5	6–10	Laps	Laps Led	Races Led	Miles	$
1994	Billy Standridge	8	0	0	0	0	0	0	0	1,260	0	0	1,706	58,605
1995	Billy Standridge	2	0	0	0	0	0	0	0	594	0	0	859	22,595
Lifetime		10	0	0	0	0	0	0	0	1,854	0	0	2,565	$81,200

Charles Johnson

Year	Driver	Starts	Poles	1	2	3	4	5	6–10	Laps	Laps Led	Races Led	Miles	$
1966	Gene Petro	1	0	0	0	0	0	0	0	35	0	0	88	100
Lifetime		1	0	0	0	0	0	0	0	35	0	0	88	$100

Dick Johnson (California)

Year	Driver	Starts	Poles	1	2	3	4	5	6–10	Laps	Laps Led	Races Led	Miles	$
1967	Dick Johnson	19	0	0	0	0	0	0	0	2,203	0	0	1,433	4,240
1968	Earl Brooks	1	0	0	0	0	0	0	0	189	0	0	284	715
"	Dick Johnson	11	0	0	0	0	0	0	0	2,187	0	0	2,040	5,920
"	**Total**	12	0	0	0	0	0	0	0	2,376	0	0	2,324	6,635
1969	Dick Johnson	22	0	0	0	0	0	0	4	3,803	0	0	2,910	11,477
Lifetime		53	0	0	0	0	0	0	4	8,382	0	0	6,667	$22,352

Dick Johnson (Australia)

Year	Driver	Starts	Poles	1	2	3	4	5	6–10	Laps	Laps Led	Races Led	Miles	$
1989	Dick Johnson	4	0	0	0	0	0	0	0	497	0	0	1,269	11,515
1990	Dick Johnson	3	0	0	0	0	0	0	0	166	0	0	300	8,950
"	Jim Sauter	1	0	0	0	0	0	0	0	199	0	0	498	3,925
"	**Total**	4	0	0	0	0	0	0	0	365	0	0	798	12,875
Lifetime		8	0	0	0	0	0	0	0	862	0	0	2,067	$24,390

Floyd Johnson

Year	Driver	Starts	Poles	1	2	3	4	5	6–10	Laps	Laps Led	Races Led	Miles	$
1956	Len Fraker	1	0	0	0	0	0	0	0	10	0	0	25	30
1957	Jim Cook	1	0	0	0	0	0	0	0	51	0	0	128	85
1959	Jim Cook	1	0	0	0	0	0	0	0	270	0	0	108	175
1960	Jim Cook	2	1	1	0	0	0	0	0	217	0	0	264	1,200
1961	Jim Cook	4	0	0	0	0	1	0	1	314	0	0	421	925
1963	Jim Cook	1	0	0	0	0	0	0	0	143	0	0	386	325
1964	Jim Cook	1	0	0	0	0	0	0	0	170	0	0	459	575
1965	Jim Cook	1	0	0	0	0	0	0	0	36	0	0	97	550
1966	Jim Cook	1	0	0	0	0	0	0	0	14	0	0	38	500
Lifetime		13	1	1	0	0	1	0	1	1,225	0	0	1,925	$4,365

Fred Johnson

Year	Driver	Starts	Poles	1	2	3	4	5	6–10	Laps	Laps Led	Races Led	Miles	$
1949	Fred Johnson	2	0	0	0	0	0	0	0		0	0		0
1950	Fred Johnson	2	0	0	0	0	0	0	1	244	0	0	197	125
Lifetime		4	0	0	0	0	0	0	1	244	0	0	197	$125

J. D. "Junior" Johnson

Year	Driver	Starts	Poles	1	2	3	4	5	6–10	Laps	Laps Led	Races Led	Miles	$
1979	Slick Johnson	2	0	0	0	0	0	0	1	791	0	0	965	4,300
1980	Slick Johnson	18	0	0	0	0	0	0	5	4,724	7	2	4,731	35,460
1981	Slick Johnson	3	0	0	0	0	0	0	0	501	0	0	602	2,725
Lifetime		23	0	0	0	0	0	0	6	6,016	7	2	6,297	$42,485

Year	Driver	Starts	Poles	Finish						Laps	Laps Led	Races Led	Miles	$
				1	2	3	4	5	6–10					

Joe Lee Johnson

Year	Driver	Starts	Poles	1	2	3	4	5	6–10	Laps	Laps Led	Races Led	Miles	$
1959	Joe Lee Johnson	10	0	1	0	0	1	1	2	2,538	0	0	1,879	6,487
1960	Charley Griffith	1	0	0	0	0	0	0	0	132	0	0	198	200
"	Joe Lee Johnson	3	0	0	0	1	0	0	0	505	0	0	386	870
"	**Total**	4	0	0	0	1	0	0	0	637	0	0	584	1,070
1961	Johnny Allen	5	0	0	0	1	0	0	3	1,464	0	0	1,325	4,120
"	Joe Lee Johnson	9	0	0	0	0	0	0	3	1,276	0	0	1,461	2,615
"	Herb Tillman	3	0	0	0	0	0	0	0	518	0	0	450	450
"	Bob Welborn	2	0	0	0	0	0	0	0	117	0	0	59	160
"	**Total**	19	0	0	0	1	0	0	6	3,375	0	0	3,295	7,345
1962	Charley Griffith	2	0	0	0	0	0	0	0	92	0	0	230	525
"	Joe Lee Johnson	3	0	0	0	0	0	0	0	379	0	0	190	190
"	**Total**	5	0	0	0	0	0	0	0	471	0	0	420	715
Lifetime		38	0	1	0	2	1	1	8	7,021	0	0	6,176	$15,617

Junior Johnson (See also Richard Howard)

Year	Driver	Starts	Poles	1	2	3	4	5	6–10	Laps	Laps Led	Races Led	Miles	$
1953	Junior Johnson	1	0	0	0	0	0	0	0	222	0	0	305	110
1966	Darel Dieringer	2	0	0	1	0	0	0	0	798	5	1	965	8,575
"	A. J. Foyt	1	0	0	0	0	0	0	0	45	0	0	122	575
"	Bobby Isaac	7	0	0	0	1	0	0	1	794	10	1	945	4,065
"	Gordon Johncock	2	0	0	0	0	1	0	0	709	9	1	876	3,470
"	Junior Johnson	7	3	0	0	0	0	1	0	1,813	467	6	1,160	3,610
"	Fred Lorenzen	1	0	0	0	0	0	0	0	139	24	1	209	630
"	Curtis Turner	3	0	0	0	1	0	0	0	662	154	3	607	1,100
"	**Total**	19	3	0	1	2	1	1	1	4,960	669	12	4,883	22,025
1967	Darel Dieringer	16	6	1	3	3	0	1	1	3,952	730	10	4,223	32,400
"	Lloyd Ruby	1	0	0	0	0	0	0	0	96	0	0	259	565
"	LeeRoy Yarbrough	3	0	0	0	1	0	0	0	825	3	1	665	2,705
"	**Total**	20	6	1	3	4	0	1	1	4,873	733	11	5,147	35,670
1968	LeeRoy Yarbrough	20	6	2	3	5	1	2	0	5,554	1,300	14	5,475	86,795
1969	LeeRoy Yarbrough	28	0	7	2	0	6	0	5	7,678	1,153	16	8,265	192,311
1970	Donnie Allison	1	0	0	0	1	0	0	0	399	5	1	249	1,975
"	Fred Lorenzen	1	0	0	0	0	0	0	0	209	0	0	285	1,020
"	David Pearson	1	0	0	0	0	1	0	0	375	0	0	197	1,525
"	LeeRoy Yarbrough	17	1	1	1	4	2	0	3	4,126	232	11	5,352	60,960
"	**Total**	20	1	1	1	5	3	0	3	5,109	237	12	6,084	65,480
1971*	Charlie Glotzbach	14	4	1	2	0	3	1	0	3,897	805	10	3,931	34,055
"	LeeRoy Yarbrough	5	0	0	0	0	1	0	2	898	26	2	1,404	8,180
"	**Total**	18	4	1	2	0	3	1	2	4,795	831	12	5,335	41,370
1972*	Bobby Allison	31	12	10	12	2	1	0	2	10,063	4,398	30	11,801	348,939
"	Jim Paschal	1	0	0	0	0	0	0	0	338	0	0	507	1,825
"	Wendell Scott	1	0	0	0	0	0	0	0	283	0	0	425	1,710
"	**Total**	31	12	10	12	2	1	0	2	10,684	**4,398**	30	12,732	352,474
1973*	Billy Scott	1	0	0	0	0	0	0	0	340	0	0	510	1,850
"	Dick Trickle	1	0	0	0	0	0	1	0	327	2	1	491	3,385
"	Cale Yarborough	28	5	4	6	4	1	1	3	9,314	3,167	21	9,737	267,513
"	**Total**	28	5	4	6	4	1	2	3	**9,981**	**3,169**	**21**	**10,737**	272,748
1974*	Earl Ross	15	0	1	0	1	1	0	5	4,431	121	5	5,216	58,334
"	Johnny Rutherford	1	0	0	0	0	0	0	0	202	1	1	303	749
"	Cale Yarborough	30	3	10	4	5	1	1	1	9,398	3,630	20	11,058	363,782
"	**Total**	30	3	11	4	6	2	1	6	14,031	3,752	26	16,577	422,865
1975	Cale Yarborough	27	3	3	3	3	3	1	0	7,353	2,542	20	8,100	214,691
1976	Cale Yarborough	30	2	9	6	3	2	2	1	**9,269**	**3,791**	**28**	10,547	453,405
1977	Cale Yarborough	30	3	9	6	4	3	3	2	**9,747**	**3,218**	**28**	**11,382**	561,642
1978	Cale Yarborough	30	8	10	6	1	5	1	1	9,758	**3,587**	**28**	11,366	623,506
1979	Cale Yarborough	31	1	4	2	6	4	3	3	9,677	1,323	22	11,192	440,129
1980	Cale Yarborough	31	14	6	4	4	4	1	3	9,440	2,810	**28**	11,015	432,325
1981	Richard Childress	1	0	0	0	0	0	0	0	5	0	0	13	460
"	Darrell Waltrip	31	11	12	6	3	0	0	4	9,575	2,517	27	10,974	799,134
"	**Total**	31	11	12	6	3	0	0	4	9,580	**2,517**	**27**	10,987	799,594
1982	J. D. McDuffie	1	0	0	0	0	0	0	0	111	1	1	291	3,540
"	Darrell Waltrip	30	7	12	1	3	0	1	3	9,455	3,027	27	10,597	923,151
"	**Total**	30	7	12	1	3	0	1	3	9,566	**3,028**	**27**	10,888	926,691
1983	Darrell Waltrip	30	7	6	8	4	2	2	3	9,403	**2,363**	22	10,546	865,185
1984	Neil Bonnett	30	1	0	2	0	2	3	7	9,126	641	11	10,460	282,533
"	Darrell Waltrip	30	4	7	2	3	1	0	7	9,464	2,030	22	10,440	731,023
"	**Total**	30	5	7	4	3	3	3	14	**18,590**	**2,671**	25	**20,900**	1,013,566
1985	Neil Bonnett	28	1	2	2	3	1	3	7	8,675	618	15	10,350	530,145

Year	Driver	Starts	Poles	Finish 1	2	3	4	5	6–10	Laps	Laps Led	Races Led	Miles	$

Junior Johnson *continued*

Year	Driver	Starts	Poles	1	2	3	4	5	6–10	Laps	Laps Led	Races Led	Miles	$
"	Darrell Waltrip	28	4	3	6	6	2	1	3	8,932	969	21	10,910	1,318,375
"	**Total**	28	5	5	8	9	3	4	10	**17,607**	1,587	**26**	**21,259**	1,848,520
1986	Davey Allison	1	0	0	0	0	0	0	1	188	13	1	500	17,820
"	Neil Bonnett	28	0	1	1	1	1	2	6	7,691	323	16	8,990	485,930
"	Darrell Waltrip	29	1	3	2	4	6	6	1	8,327	573	21	9,946	1,099,735
"	**Total**	29	1	4	3	5	7	8	8	16,206	909	26	19,436	1,603,485
1987	Terry Labonte	29	4	1	2	2	5	3	9	8,609	592	16	10,157	805,054
1988	Terry Labonte	29	1	1	2	3	4	1	7	9,206	207	17	11,032	950,781
1989	Terry Labonte	29	0	2	2	1	1	3	2	8,306	104	10	9,771	703,806
1990	Geoff Bodine	29	2	3	3	2	3	0	8	8,852	976	21	10,646	1,131,222
1991	Geoff Bodine	27	2	1	2	1	1	1	6	7,997	152	12	9,589	625,256
"	Tommy Ellis	2	0	0	0	0	0	0	0	887	0	0	1,085	13,250
"	Sterling Marlin	29	2	0	2	1	1	3	9	9,205	201	8	11,207	633,690
"	**Total**	29	4	1	4	2	2	4	15	**18,089**	353	17	**21,881**	1,272,196
1992	Bill Elliott	29	2	5	2	3	1	3	3	9,115	1,273	18	11,124	1,692,381
"	Sterling Marlin	29	5	0	3	0	1	2	7	8,462	218	8	10,286	649,048
"	Hut Stricklin	1	0	0	0	0	0	0	0	305	0	0	458	3,800
"	**Total**	29	7	5	5	3	2	5	10	**17,882**	**1,491**	21	**21,868**	2,345,229
1993	Bill Elliott	30	2	0	1	2	2	1	9	9,329	14	4	11,335	955,859
"	Hut Stricklin	30	0	0	0	0	1	0	1	8,356	98	3	10,211	494,600
"	**Total**	30	2	0	1	2	3	1	10	17,685	112	7	21,546	1,450,459
1994	Bill Elliott	31	1	1	1	3	0	1	6	9,172	62	8	11,380	951,679
"	Jeff Green	1	0	0	0	0	0	0	0	321	0	0	489	8,815
"	Tommy Kendall	1	0	0	0	0	0	0	0	88	0	0	216	9,435
"	Jimmy Spencer	29	1	2	0	0	1	0	1	6,904	47	6	8,732	479,235
"	**Total**	31	2	3	1	3	1	1	7	16,485	109	11	20,816	1,449,164
1995	Loy Allen Jr.	4	0	0	0	0	0	0	0	1,271	0	0	1,572	103,155
"	Brett Bodine	31	0	0	0	0	0	0	2	9,159	6	1	11,084	893,029
"	Jimmy Horton	1	0	0	0	0	0	0	0	192	0	0	480	16,550
"	Greg Sacks	1	0	0	0	0	0	0	0	160	0	0	400	22,620
"	Elton Sawyer	20	0	0	0	0	0	0	0	4,573	0	0	6,185	416,490
"	**Total**	31	0	0	0	0	0	0	2	15,355	6	1	19,721	1,451,844
Lifetime		838	129	140	111	94	76	55	145	324,552	50,538	582	380,596	$22,834,342
		4th	**3rd**	**2nd**						**2nd**	**2nd**	**2nd**	**3rd**	**2nd**

*Co-owned with Richard Howard from May 1971–July 1974.

Lou Johnson

Year	Driver	Starts	Poles	1	2	3	4	5	6–10	Laps	Laps Led	Races Led	Miles	$
1953	Lou Johnson	1	0	0	0	0	0	0	0	0	0	0	0	25
Lifetime		1	0	0	0	0	0	0	0	0	0	0	0	$25

Norm Johnson

Year	Driver	Starts	Poles	1	2	3	4	5	6–10	Laps	Laps Led	Races Led	Miles	$
1953	Hank Ribet	1	0	0	0	0	0	0	0	68	0	0	34	25
"	Hank Rivet	1	0	0	0	0	0	0	0	32	0	0	131	25
"	**Total**	2	0	0	0	0	0	0	0	100	0	0	165	50
Lifetime		2	0	0	0	0	0	0	0	100	0	0	165	$50

Raeford Johnson

Year	Driver	Starts	Poles	1	2	3	4	5	6–10	Laps	Laps Led	Races Led	Miles	$
1960	Doug Yates	24	1	0	0	2	1	0	5	4,030	39	1	3,262	5,205
1961	Doug Yates	32	0	0	0	0	0	2	8	5,058	0	0	2,992	5,370
1962	Doug Yates	5	0	0	0	0	0	0	2	777	0	0	351	565
Lifetime		61	1	0	0	2	1	2	15	9,865	39	1	6,604	$11,140

Rush Johnson

Year	Driver	Starts	Poles	1	2	3	4	5	6–10	Laps	Laps Led	Races Led	Miles	$
1974	Jerry Schild	5	0	0	0	0	0	0	1	1,142	0	0	1,750	8,396
Lifetime		5	0	0	0	0	0	0	1	1,142	0	0	1,750	$8,396

Stoney Johnson

Year	Driver	Starts	Poles	1	2	3	4	5	6–10	Laps	Laps Led	Races Led	Miles	$
1962	Herb Thomas	1	0	0	0	0	0	0	0	377	0	0	236	200
Lifetime		1	0	0	0	0	0	0	0	377	0	0	236	$200

Ray Johnstone

Year	Driver	Starts	Poles	1	2	3	4	5	6–10	Laps	Laps Led	Races Led	Miles	$
1970	Ray Johnstone	1	0	0	0	0	0	0	0	26	0	0	68	660
1971	Ray Johnstone	3	0	0	0	0	0	0	0	211	0	0	541	3,405
Lifetime		4	0	0	0	0	0	0	0	237	0	0	609	$4,065

Year	Driver	Starts	Poles	Finish 1	2	3	4	5	6–10	Laps	Laps Led	Races Led	Miles	$

Carl Joiner

Year	Driver	Starts	Poles	1	2	3	4	5	6–10	Laps	Laps Led	Races Led	Miles	$
1975	Carl Joiner	1	0	0	0	0	0	0	0	87	0	0	228	895
1976	Carl Joiner	2	0	0	0	0	0	0	0	227	0	0	581	2,155
1977	Carl Joiner	1	0	0	0	0	0	0	0	10	0	0	26	740
Lifetime		4	0	0	0	0	0	0	0	324	0	0	836	$3,790

Jerry Jolly

Year	Driver	Starts	Poles	1	2	3	4	5	6–10	Laps	Laps Led	Races Led	Miles	$
1984	Jerry Jolly	1	0	0	0	0	0	0	0	10	0	0	26	715
Lifetime		1	0	0	0	0	0	0	0	10	0	0	26	$715

B. J. Jones

Year	Driver	Starts	Poles	1	2	3	4	5	6–10	Laps	Laps Led	Races Led	Miles	$
1956	Jack Smith	2	0	0	0	0	0	0	0	61	0	0	31	0
1959	George Alsobrook	3	0	0	0	0	0	0	0	794	0	0	581	825
"	Wilbur Rakestraw	1	0	0	0	0	0	0	0	181	0	0	453	250
"	**Total**	4	0	0	0	0	0	0	0	975	0	0	1,034	1,075
1961	George Alsobrook	7	0	0	0	0	0	0	1	875	0	0	641	1,575
"	Wilbur Rakestraw	5	0	0	0	0	0	0	1	360	0	0	306	635
"	**Total**	12	0	0	0	0	0	0	2	1,235	0	0	947	2,210
Lifetime		18	0	0	0	0	0	0	2	2,271	0	0	2,011	$3,285

Bobby Jones

Year	Driver	Starts	Poles	1	2	3	4	5	6–10	Laps	Laps Led	Races Led	Miles	$
1990	Rick Mast	4	0	0	0	0	0	0	0	1,116	0	0	1,328	15,775
"	Rick Ware	1	0	0	0	0	0	0	0	42	0	0	102	2,295
"	**Total**	5	0	0	0	0	0	0	0	1,158	0	0	1,430	18,070
Lifetime		5	0	0	0	0	0	0	0	1,158	0	0	1,430	$18,070

James Jones

Year	Driver	Starts	Poles	1	2	3	4	5	6–10	Laps	Laps Led	Races Led	Miles	$
1956	James Jones	1	0	0	0	0	0	0	0	169	0	0	85	100
1958	James Jones	1	0	0	0	0	0	0	0	212	0	0	212	100
Lifetime		2	0	0	0	0	0	0	0	381	0	0	297	$200

Joe Jones

Year	Driver	Starts	Poles	1	2	3	4	5	6–10	Laps	Laps Led	Races Led	Miles	$
1956	Sonny Black	1	0	0	0	0	0	0	0	79	0	0	79	50
"	Wilbur Rakestraw	1	0	0	0	0	0	0	0	29	0	0	15	100
"	Jack Smith	1	0	0	0	0	0	0	0	92	0	0	46	50
"	**Total**	3	0	0	0	0	0	0	0	200	0	0	140	200
1958	Wilbur Rakestraw	8	0	0	0	0	1	0	1	1,534	0	0	1,347	1,490
1959	George Alsobrook	1	0	0	0	0	0	0	1	142	0	0	142	325
"	Wilbur Rakestraw	1	0	0	0	0	0	0	1	145	0	0	145	475
"	**Total**	1	0	0	0	0	0	0	2	287	0	0	287	800
1961	George Green	2	0	0	0	0	1	0	0	424	0	0	212	400
"	Joe Jones	8	0	0	0	0	0	0	0	893	0	0	637	1,015
"	**Total**	10	0	0	0	0	1	0	0	1,317	0	0	849	1,415
1962	Joe Jones	2	0	0	0	0	0	0	0	250	0	0	125	100
Lifetime		24	0	0	0	0	2	0	3	3,588	0	0	2,747	$4,005

Possum Jones

Year	Driver	Starts	Poles	1	2	3	4	5	6–10	Laps	Laps Led	Races Led	Miles	$
1963	Possum Jones	5	0	0	0	0	0	0	1	576	0	0	251	1,080
"	Jim McGuirk	1	0	0	0	0	0	0	0	142	0	0	355	650
"	Joe Weatherly	1	0	0	0	0	0	0	1	191	0	0	96	175
"	**Total**	7	0	0	0	0	0	0	2	909	0	0	702	1,905
1964	Possum Jones	1	0	0	0	0	0	0	0	156	0	0	78	130
"	Joe Penland	1	0	0	0	0	0	0	0	4	0	0	12	525
"	**Total**	2	0	0	0	0	0	0	0	160	0	0	90	655
Lifetime		9	0	0	0	0	0	0	2	1,069	0	0	792	$2,560

Preston Jones

Year	Driver	Starts	Poles	1	2	3	4	5	6–10	Laps	Laps Led	Races Led	Miles	$
1951	Oliver Dial	2	0	0	0	0	0	0	0	355	0	0	444	100
Lifetime		2	0	0	0	0	0	0	0	355	0	0	444	$100

R. J. Jones

Year	Driver	Starts	Poles	1	2	3	4	5	6–10	Laps	Laps Led	Races Led	Miles	$
1961	George Alsobrook	1	0	0	0	0	0	0	0	63	0	0	95	250
Lifetime		1	0	0	0	0	0	0	0	63	0	0	95	$250

Year	Driver	Starts	Poles	Finish 1	2	3	4	5	6–10	Laps	Laps Led	Races Led	Miles	$

Ralph Jones

Year	Driver	Starts	Poles	1	2	3	4	5	6–10	Laps	Laps Led	Races Led	Miles	$
1977	Ralph Jones	4	0	0	0	0	0	0	0	871	0	0	645	3,395
1978	Ralph Jones	7	0	0	0	0	0	0	0	1,871	0	0	1,856	6,305
1979	Ralph Jones	6	0	0	0	0	0	0	0	729	0	0	1,171	12,785
Lifetime		17	0	0	0	0	0	0	0	3,471	0	0	3,673	$22,485

Melvin Joseph

Year	Driver	Starts	Poles	1	2	3	4	5	6–10	Laps	Laps Led	Races Led	Miles	$
1971	Bobby Allison	2	1	1	1	0	0	0	0	748	339	2	289	2,500
Lifetime		2	1	1	1	0	0	0	0	748	339	2	289	$2,500

Dick Joslin

Year	Driver	Starts	Poles	1	2	3	4	5	6–10	Laps	Laps Led	Races Led	Miles	$
1959	Dick Joslin	4	0	0	0	0	0	0	0	338	0	0	793	485
1960	Jim Reed	1	0	0	0	0	0	0	0	35	0	0	53	200
Lifetime		5	0	0	0	0	0	0	0	373	0	0	846	$685

Stuart Joyce

Year	Driver	Starts	Poles	1	2	3	4	5	6–10	Laps	Laps Led	Races Led	Miles	$
1952	Stuart Joyce	1	0	0	0	0	0	0	1	229	0	0	229	200
"	Leon Meadows	1	0	0	0	0	0	0	0	67	0	0	67	25
"	**Total**	1	0	0	0	0	0	0	1	296	0	0	296	225
Lifetime		1	0	0	0	0	0	0	1	296	0	0	296	$225

C. M. Julian

Year	Driver	Starts	Poles	1	2	3	4	5	6–10	Laps	Laps Led	Races Led	Miles	$
1957	Don Bailey	1	0	0	0	0	0	0	0	62	0	0	62	75
"	Tiny Lund	1	0	0	0	0	0	0	0	148	0	0	93	100
"	**Total**	2	0	0	0	0	0	0	0	210	0	0	155	175
Lifetime		2	0	0	0	0	0	0	0	210	0	0	155	$175

J. L. Justice

Year	Driver	Starts	Poles	1	2	3	4	5	6–10	Laps	Laps Led	Races Led	Miles	$
1953	J. L. Justice	3	0	0	0	0	0	0	0	226	0	0	307	145
Lifetime		3	0	0	0	0	0	0	0	226	0	0	307	$145

Hoss Kagle

Year	Driver	Starts	Poles	1	2	3	4	5	6–10	Laps	Laps Led	Races Led	Miles	$
1956	Hoss Kagle	1	0	0	0	0	0	0	0	135	0	0	135	100
"	Reds Kagle	2	0	0	0	0	0	0	0	202	0	0	85	60
"	**Total**	3	0	0	0	0	0	0	0	337	0	0	220	160
1957	Reds Kagle	1	0	0	0	0	0	0	0	23	0	0	12	25
1958	Reds Kagle	11	0	0	0	0	0	2	5	1,479	0	0	715	1,550
1959	Reds Kagle	4	0	0	0	0	1	0	0	627	0	0	340	525
Lifetime		19	0	0	0	0	1	2	5	2,466	0	0	1,286	$2,260

Iggy Katona

Year	Driver	Starts	Poles	1	2	3	4	5	6–10	Laps	Laps Led	Races Led	Miles	$
1951	Iggy Katona	5	0	0	0	0	0	0	0	559	0	0	643	150
1952	Iggy Katona	2	0	0	0	0	0	0	1	180	0	0	90	125
1966	Iggy Katona	1	0	0	0	0	0	0	0	286	0	0	429	715
Lifetime		8	0	0	0	0	0	0	1	1,025	0	0	1,162	$990

Bobby Keck

Year	Driver	Starts	Poles	1	2	3	4	5	6–10	Laps	Laps Led	Races Led	Miles	$
1956	Bobby Keck	15	0	0	0	0	0	0	3	2,236	0	0	1,308	1,250
1957	Bobby Keck	16	0	0	0	0	0	0	2	2,144	0	0	1,419	1,525
"	Speedy Thompson	1	0	0	0	0	0	0	0	99	0	0	50	125
"	**Total**	17	0	0	0	0	0	0	2	2,243	0	0	1,468	1,650
1958	Bobby Keck	30	0	0	0	0	0	0	7	4,345	0	0	2,219	2,885
1959	Bobby Keck	18	0	0	0	0	0	0	0	2,484	0	0	1,152	1,270
Lifetime		80	0	0	0	0	0	0	12	11,308	0	0	6,147	$7,055

Joe Keistler

Year	Driver	Starts	Poles	1	2	3	4	5	6–10	Laps	Laps Led	Races Led	Miles	$
1965	Don Tilley	2	0	0	0	0	0	0	0	119	0	0	298	1,240
"	Frank Weathers	5	0	0	0	0	0	0	1	620	0	0	314	640
"	**Total**	7	0	0	0	0	0	0	1	739	0	0	612	1,880
Lifetime		7	0	0	0	0	0	0	1	739	0	0	612	$1,880

Year	Driver	Starts	Poles	Finish						Laps	Laps Led	Races Led	Miles	$
				1	2	3	4	5	6–10					

Al Keller

Year	Driver	Starts	Poles	1	2	3	4	5	6–10	Laps	Laps Led	Races Led	Miles	$
1956	Al Keller	4	0	0	1	0	0	0	1	446	0	0	247	1,300
Lifetime		4	0	0	1	0	0	0	1	446	0	0	247	$1,300

Pete Kelley

Year	Driver	Starts	Poles	1	2	3	4	5	6–10	Laps	Laps Led	Races Led	Miles	$
1952	Pete Kelly	1	0	0	0	0	0	0	0	162	0	0	203	0
Lifetime		1	0	0	0	0	0	0	0	162	0	0	203	$0

Fran Kelly

Year	Driver	Starts	Poles	1	2	3	4	5	6–10	Laps	Laps Led	Races Led	Miles	$
1970	Dick Trickle	2	0	0	0	0	0	0	0	176	0	0	440	1,415
Lifetime		2	0	0	0	0	0	0	0	176	0	0	440	$1,415

James Kelly

Year	Driver	Starts	Poles	1	2	3	4	5	6–10	Laps	Laps Led	Races Led	Miles	$
1963	Sonny Fogle	8	0	0	0	0	0	0	0	779	0	0	382	600
"	Billy Oswald	1	0	0	0	0	0	0	0	61	0	0	31	60
"	**Total**	9	0	0	0	0	0	0	0	840	0	0	412	660
Lifetime		9	0	0	0	0	0	0	0	840	0	0	412	$660

Pete Kelly

Year	Driver	Starts	Poles	1	2	3	4	5	6–10	Laps	Laps Led	Races Led	Miles	$
1959	Pete Kelly	2	0	0	0	0	0	0	0	44	0	0	95	150
Lifetime		2	0	0	0	0	0	0	0	44	0	0	95	$150

Ray Kelly

Year	Driver	Starts	Poles	1	2	3	4	5	6–10	Laps	Laps Led	Races Led	Miles	$
1986	Ray Kelly	1	0	0	0	0	0	0	0	36	0	0	94	850
Lifetime		1	0	0	0	0	0	0	0	36	0	0	94	$850

Mike Kempton

Year	Driver	Starts	Poles	1	2	3	4	5	6–10	Laps	Laps Led	Races Led	Miles	$
1977	Terry Bivins	1	0	0	0	0	0	0	0	154	0	0	210	880
"	Mike Kempton	2	0	0	0	0	0	0	0	336	0	0	450	2,555
"	**Total**	3	0	0	0	0	0	0	0	490	0	0	660	3,435
1979	Henry Jones	3	0	0	0	0	0	0	0	77	0	0	43	1,160
"	Mike Kempton	2	0	0	0	0	0	0	0	499	0	0	487	1,605
"	**Total**	5	0	0	0	0	0	0	0	576	0	0	530	2,765
1980	Henry Jones	3	0	0	0	0	0	0	0	198	0	0	405	3,175
1983	Mike Kempton	0												2,550
Lifetime		11	0	0	0	0	0	0	0	1,264	0	0	1,595	$11,925

Dave Kennedy

Year	Driver	Starts	Poles	1	2	3	4	5	6–10	Laps	Laps Led	Races Led	Miles	$
1952	Ray Chase	1	0	0	0	0	0	0	0	173	0	0	173	25
"	Ed Westveer	1	0	0	0	0	0	0	0	45	0	0	45	25
"	**Total**	1	0	0	0	0	0	0	0	218	0	0	218	50
Lifetime		1	0	0	0	0	0	0	0	218	0	0	218	$50

John Kennedy

Year	Driver	Starts	Poles	1	2	3	4	5	6–10	Laps	Laps Led	Races Led	Miles	$
1969	John Kennedy	8	0	0	0	0	0	0	0	1,084	0	0	1,675	6,462
1977	Jim Hurtubise	1	0	0	0	0	0	0	0	12	0	0	12	460
"	John Kennedy	1	0	0	0	0	0	0	0	66	0	0	132	880
"	**Total**	2	0	0	0	0	0	0	0	78	0	0	144	1,340
1978	John Kennedy	4	0	0	0	0	0	0	0	296	0	0	350	2,900
1979	John Kennedy	5	0	0	0	0	0	0	0	600	0	0	942	4,515
"	Dick May	1	0	0	0	0	0	0	0	4	0	0	6	600
"	Ronnie Thomas	1	0	0	0	0	0	0	0	379	0	0	569	5,490
"	**Total**	7	0	0	0	0	0	0	0	983	0	0	1,517	10,605
Lifetime		21	0	0	0	0	0	0	0	2,441	0	0	3,685	$21,307

Ted Kennedy

Year	Driver	Starts	Poles	1	2	3	4	5	6–10	Laps	Laps Led	Races Led	Miles	$
1990	Ted Kennedy	1	0	0	0	0	0	0	0	11	0	0	28	3,225
Lifetime		1	0	0	0	0	0	0	0	11	0	0	28	$3,225

Year	Driver	Starts	Poles	Finish 1	2	3	4	5	6–10	Laps	Laps Led	Races Led	Miles	$

Dave Kent

Year	Driver	Starts	Poles	1	2	3	4	5	6–10	Laps	Laps Led	Races Led	Miles	$
1963	John Hoffman	1	0	0	0	0	0	0	0	51	0	0	13	100
"	Mark Hurley	1	0	0	0	0	0	0	0	396	0	0	198	235
"	Tiny Lund	7	0	0	0	0	0	0	3	1,342	1	1	680	1,300
"	**Total**	9	0	0	0	0	0	0	3	1,789	1	1	890	1,635
1964	Jack Anderson	4	0	0	0	0	1	0	0	920	0	0	407	825
"	Mark Hurley	5	0	0	0	0	0	0	1	967	0	0	460	795
"	Tiny Lund	7	0	0	0	1	0	0	1	1,417	0	0	1,382	2,420
"	**Total**	16	0	0	0	1	1	0	2	3,304	0	0	2,249	4,040
Lifetime		25	0	0	0	1	1	0	5	5,093	1	1	3,139	$5,675

Joe Kersey

Year	Driver	Starts	Poles	1	2	3	4	5	6–10	Laps	Laps Led	Races Led	Miles	$
1953	Buck Mason	1	0	0	0	0	0	0	0		0	0		50
Lifetime		1	0	0	0	0	0	0	0		0	0		$50

John Keselowski

Year	Driver	Starts	Poles	1	2	3	4	5	6–10	Laps	Laps Led	Races Led	Miles	$
1969	Homer Newland	2	0	0	0	0	0	0	0	179	0	0	393	1,875
1970	Ron Keselowski	17	0	0	0	0	0	0	1	2,339	9	1	2,842	11,985
"	Dave Marcis	1	0	0	0	0	0	0	0	255	0	0	348	1,145
"	**Total**	18	0	0	0	0	0	0	1	2,594	9	1	3,191	13,130
1971	Rene Charland	1	0	0	0	0	0	0	0	33	0	0	12	100
"	Ron Keselowski	1	0	0	0	0	0	0	0	0	0	0	0	200
"	Bennis Listman	1	0	0	0	0	0	0	0	6	0	0	1	100
"	Dick Poling	2	0	0	0	0	0	0	0	228	0	0	340	915
"	Bill Shirey	1	0	0	0	0	0	0	0	118	0	0	64	325
"	**Total**	6	0	0	0	0	0	0	0	385	0	0	417	1,640
1974	Bob Whitlow	1	0	0	0	0	0	0	0	183	0	0	366	1,055
Lifetime		27	0	0	0	0	0	0	1	3,341	9	1	4,367	$17,700

Jerry Keyes

Year	Driver	Starts	Poles	1	2	3	4	5	6–10	Laps	Laps Led	Races Led	Miles	$
1954	Jerry Keyes	1	0	0	0	0	0	0	0	338	0	0	169	25
Lifetime		1	0	0	0	0	0	0	0	338	0	0	169	$25

Carl Kiekhaefer

Year	Driver	Starts	Poles	1	2	3	4	5	6–10	Laps	Laps Led	Races Led	Miles	$
1955	Bob Flock	1	0	0	0	0	0	1	0	195	0	0	293	650
"	Fonty Flock	20	5	2	5	1	0	0	2	2,608	364	6	1,885	10,615
"	Tim Flock	38	19	18	5	4	1	3	1	6,011	3,495	33	4,477	37,330
"	Norm Nelson	2	1	1	0	0	0	0	0	273	106	1	354	1,420
"	Speedy Thompson	2	0	1	0	0	0	0	1	357	64	1	198	1,300
"	**Total**	39	25	22	10	5	1	4	4	**9,444**	**4,029**	**35**	**7,207**	51,315
1956	Buck Baker	44	12	14	7	3	3	2	6	7,779	1,401	23	5,088	33,102
"	Fonty Flock	4	2	1	0	0	0	0	1	221	150	2	155	1,350
"	Tim Flock	8	3	3	1	2	0	0	1	1,033	314	4	786	8,410
"	Junior Johnson	1	0	0	1	0	0	0	0	133	0	0	100	700
"	Frank Mundy	9	1	0	1	1	0	1	2	1,589	0	0	1,479	3,585
"	Charlie Scott	1	0	0	0	0	0	0	0	0	0	0	0	75
"	Jack Smith	3	0	1	0	0	0	0	0	698	185	1	336	2,475
"	Herb Thomas	18	2	3	2	2	2	1	3	2,829	222	5	1,695	7,860
"	Speedy Thompson	39	6	8	5	5	4	1	5	6,655	1,956	22	4,476	26,809
"	**Total**	51	26[1]	30[1]	17	13	9	5	18	**20,937**	**4,228**	**40**	**14,115**	84,366
Lifetime		90	51	52	27	18	10	9	22	30,381	8,257	75	21,322	$135,681
			7th	8th										

John Kieper

Year	Driver	Starts	Poles	1	2	3	4	5	6–10	Laps	Laps Led	Races Led	Miles	$
1955	John Kieper	2	0	0	1	0	0	0	0	323	89	1	323	1,500
1956	John Kieper	8	3	1	1	1	1	0	3	1,479	67	2	917	3,250
1957	John Kieper	1	0	0	0	0	0	0	0	6	0	0	3	50
1975	John Kieper	2	0	0	0	0	0	0	0	191	0	0	490	2,110
1976	John Kieper	1	0	0	0	0	0	0	0	62	0	0	155	710
1977	John Kieper	1	0	0	0	0	0	0	0	50	0	0	125	740
"	Don Noel	1	0	0	0	0	0	0	0	0	0	0	0	500
"	**Total**	2	0	0	0	0	0	0	0	50	0	0	125	1,240
1980	Hershel McGriff	1	0	0	0	0	0	0	0	158	0	0	395	1,500

Year	Driver	Starts	Poles	Finish 1	2	3	4	5	6–10	Laps	Laps Led	Races Led	Miles	$

John Kieper *continued*

Year	Driver	Starts	Poles	1	2	3	4	5	6–10	Laps	Laps Led	Races Led	Miles	$
1983	Jim Bown	1	0	0	0	0	0	0	0	37	0	0	97	1,025
1984	Jim Bown	2	0	0	0	0	0	0	0	132	4	1	346	2,330
1985	Jim Bown	2	0	0	0	0	0	0	0	185	0	0	485	4,860
1986	Jim Bown	1	0	0	0	0	0	0	0	81	0	0	212	1,175
Lifetime		23	3	1	2	1	1	0	3	2,704	160	4	3,548	$19,750

C. L. Kilpatrick

Year	Driver	Starts	Poles	1	2	3	4	5	6–10	Laps	Laps Led	Races Led	Miles	$
1963	Jack Deniston	1	0	0	0	0	0	0	0	187	0	0	47	135
"	Roy Mayne	19	0	0	0	0	0	1	3	3,854	0	0	1,940	3,065
"	**Total**	20	0	0	0	0	0	1	3	4,041	0	0	1,987	3,200
1964	Roy Mayne	1	0	0	0	0	0	0	0	13	0	0	12	0
Lifetime		21	0	0	0	0	0	1	3	4,054	0	0	1,999	$3,200

Frank Kiltzer

Year	Driver	Starts	Poles	1	2	3	4	5	6–10	Laps	Laps Led	Races Led	Miles	$
1960	Pat Moore	1	0	0	0	0	0	0	0	72	0	0	36	50
"	Sal Tovella	2	0	0	0	0	0	0	0	43	0	0	108	275
"	**Total**	3	0	0	0	0	0	0	0	115	0	0	144	325
Lifetime		3	0	0	0	0	0	0	0	115	0	0	144	$325

Guy Kimball

Year	Driver	Starts	Poles	1	2	3	4	5	6–10	Laps	Laps Led	Races Led	Miles	$
1961	Danny Letner	1	0	0	0	1	0	0	0	175	0	0	245	750
"	Danny Weinberg	4	1	0	0	2	0	0	1	446	0	0	453	1,185
"	**Total**	4	1	0	0	3	0	0	1	621	0	0	698	1,935
Lifetime		4	1	0	0	3	0	0	1	621	0	0	698	$1,935

Bill Kimmel

Year	Driver	Starts	Poles	1	2	3	4	5	6–10	Laps	Laps Led	Races Led	Miles	$
1970	Bill Kimmel	1	0	0	0	0	0	0	0	41	0	0	103	220
Lifetime		1	0	0	0	0	0	0	0	41	0	0	103	$220

A. J. King

Year	Driver	Starts	Poles	1	2	3	4	5	6–10	Laps	Laps Led	Races Led	Miles	$
1967	Bobby Isaac	1	0	0	0	0	0	0	0	76	0	0	38	250
"	Paul Lewis	8	0	0	0	0	0	1	3	2,013	4	1	2,135	6,710
"	Bud Moore	5	0	0	0	0	0	2	1	1,318	0	0	1,664	7,100
"	**Total**	14	0	0	0	0	0	3	4	3,407	4	1	3,837	14,060
1968	Pete Hamilton	6	0	0	0	0	0	0	2	1,491	28	2	1,246	4,439
"	Sam McQuagg	2	0	0	0	0	0	0	0	295	0	0	270	795
"	Bud Moore	9	0	0	0	0	0	0	5	1,907	24	1	1,806	6,965
"	**Total**	17	0	0	0	0	0	0	7	3,693	52	3	3,321	12,199
1969	Pete Hamilton	2	0	0	0	0	0	0	1	92	14	1	230	2,210
1975	Tiny Lund	1	0	0	0	0	0	0	0	6	0	0	16	620
Lifetime		34	0	0	0	0	0	3	12	7,198	70	5	7,404	$29,089

Brownie King

Year	Driver	Starts	Poles	1	2	3	4	5	6–10	Laps	Laps Led	Races Led	Miles	$
1956	Brownie King	15	0	0	0	0	0	0	0	1,994	0	0	1,322	925
1959	Brownie King	1	0	0	0	0	0	0	0	84	0	0	42	75
Lifetime		16	0	0	0	0	0	0	0	2,078	0	0	1,364	$1,000

Bub King

Year	Driver	Starts	Poles	1	2	3	4	5	6–10	Laps	Laps Led	Races Led	Miles	$
1951	Bub King	9	0	0	0	0	0	0	2	247	0	0	260	450
1952	Bub King	10	0	0	0	1	1	0	3	1,743	0	0	1,419	2,335
1953	Bub King	13	0	0	0	0	0	0	5	1,029	0	0	1,013	750
Lifetime		32	0	0	0	1	1	0	10	3,019	0	0	2,692	$3,535

Pat Kirkwood

Year	Driver	Starts	Poles	1	2	3	4	5	6–10	Laps	Laps Led	Races Led	Miles	$
1949	Pat Kirkwood	1	0	0	0	0	0	0	0		0	0		0
1952	Pat Kirkwood	4	1	0	0	1	0	1	0	764	0	0	972	1,215
Lifetime		5	1	0	0	1	0	1	0	764	0	0	972	$1,215

Year	Driver	Starts	Poles	Finish 1	2	3	4	5	6–10	Laps	Laps Led	Races Led	Miles	$

Ike Kiser

Year	Driver	Starts	Poles	1	2	3	4	5	6–10	Laps	Laps Led	Races Led	Miles	$
1955	Dick Beaty	1	0	0	0	0	0	0	0	184	0	0	253	50
"	Jimmy Thompson	2	0	0	0	0	0	0	1	254	0	0	127	300
"	Speedy Thompson	1	0	0	0	0	0	0	0	88	0	0	88	50
"	**Total**	4	0	0	0	0	0	0	1	526	0	0	468	400
1956	Dick Beaty	15	0	0	0	0	0	0	3	1,513	0	0	1,091	910
Lifetime		19	0	0	0	0	0	0	4	2,039	0	0	1,559	$1,310

Bob Kitchell

Year	Driver	Starts	Poles	1	2	3	4	5	6–10	Laps	Laps Led	Races Led	Miles	$
1963	Lloyd Dane	1	0	0	0	0	0	0	0	131	0	0	354	250
1964	Lloyd Dane	1	0	0	0	0	0	0	0	154	0	0	416	525
Lifetime		2	0	0	0	0	0	0	0	285	0	0	770	$775

Harold Kite

Year	Driver	Starts	Poles	1	2	3	4	5	6–10	Laps	Laps Led	Races Led	Miles	$
1950	Tim Flock	2	1	1	0	0	1	0	0	339	190	2	289	2,000
"	Harold Kite	3	0	1	0	0	0	0	0	382	38	1	618	1,550
"	**Total**	5	1	2	0	0	1	0	0	721	228	3	907	3,550
Lifetime		5	1	2	0	0	1	0	0	721	228	3	907	$3,550

Mike Klapak

Year	Driver	Starts	Poles	1	2	3	4	5	6–10	Laps	Laps Led	Races Led	Miles	$
1950	Mike Klapak	4	0	0	0	0	0	0	0	158	0	0	79	50
Lifetime		4	0	0	0	0	0	0	0	158	0	0	79	$50

Julian Kline

Year	Driver	Starts	Poles	1	2	3	4	5	6–10	Laps	Laps Led	Races Led	Miles	$
1968	Rod Eulenfeld	2	0	0	0	0	0	0	0	229	0	0	464	2,150
Lifetime		2	0	0	0	0	0	0	0	229	0	0	464	$2,150

Sam Knox

Year	Driver	Starts	Poles	1	2	3	4	5	6–10	Laps	Laps Led	Races Led	Miles	$
1951	Billy Carden	8	2	0	0	1	1	0	3	142	58	1	142	1,185
"	Tim Flock	1	1	0	1	0	0	0	0	0	27	1	0	1,000
"	Gober Sosebee	3	1	0	1	0	0	0	0	104	7	1	104	625
"	**Total**	11	4	0	2	1	1	0	3	246	92	3	246	2,810
1952	Gober Sosebee	4	0	1	0	0	0	0	1	451	176	2	360	1,125
"	Speedy Thompson	1	0	0	0	0	0	0	0	383	0	0	479	280
"	**Total**	5	0	1	0	0	0	0	1	834	176	2	839	1,405
1954	Stan Kross	2	0	0	0	0	0	0	0	82	0	0	44	0
Lifetime		18	4	1	2	1	1	0	4	1,162	268	5	1,129	$4,215

Robert Koehler

Year	Driver	Starts	Poles	1	2	3	4	5	6–10	Laps	Laps Led	Races Led	Miles	$
1971	Hershel McGriff	1	0	0	0	0	0	0	0	163	1	1	408	1,775
Lifetime		1	0	0	0	0	0	0	0	163	1	1	408	$1,775

Ronnie Kohler

Year	Driver	Starts	Poles	1	2	3	4	5	6–10	Laps	Laps Led	Races Led	Miles	$
1952	Ronnie Kohler	2	0	0	0	0	0	1	0	253	0	0	127	225
1953	Ronnie Kohler	1	0	0	0	0	0	0	0		0	0		75
Lifetime		3	0	0	0	0	0	1	0	253	0	0	127	$300

Phil Kord

Year	Driver	Starts	Poles	1	2	3	4	5	6–10	Laps	Laps Led	Races Led	Miles	$
1975	Ron Esau	1	0	0	0	0	0	0	0	96	0	0	252	1,125
1983	Bob Kennedy	1	0	0	0	0	0	0	0	89	0	0	233	1,990
Lifetime		2	0	0	0	0	0	0	0	185	0	0	485	$3,115

Joe Kosiske

Year	Driver	Starts	Poles	1	2	3	4	5	6–10	Laps	Laps Led	Races Led	Miles	$
1960	Bob Kosiski	2	0	0	0	0	0	0	0	163	0	0	408	250
Lifetime		2	0	0	0	0	0	0	0	163	0	0	408	$250

John Koszeln

Year	Driver	Starts	Poles	1	2	3	4	5	6–10	Laps	Laps Led	Races Led	Miles	$
1960	Ernie Gahan	2	0	0	0	0	0	0	0	818	0	0	759	625
1961	Ernie Gahan	5	0	0	0	0	0	0	1	707	0	0	348	750
Lifetime		7	0	0	0	0	0	0	1	1,525	0	0	1,107	$1,375

Year	Driver	Starts	Poles	Finish						Laps	Laps Led	Races Led	Miles	$
				1	2	3	4	5	6–10	Laps	Led	Led	Miles	$

Kranefuss-Haas Racing (Michael Kranefuss and Carl Haas, co-owners)

Year	Driver	Starts	Poles	1	2	3	4	5	6–10	Laps	Laps Led	Races Led	Miles	$
1994	Geoff Brabham	1	0	0	0	0	0	0	0	127	0	0	318	27,400
"	Robby Gordon	1	0	0	0	0	0	0	0	69	0	0	138	7,965
"	**Total**	2	0	0	0	0	0	0	0	196	0	0	456	35,365
1995	John Andretti	31	1	0	0	0	1	0	4	8,412	77	9	10,178	593,542
1996	John Andretti	22	0	0	0	0	0	1	1	4,832	31	4	7,099	561,471
"	Jeremy Mayfield	7	0	0	0	0	0	0	0	1,952	0	0	1,564	128,990
"	**Total**	29	0	0	0	0	0	1	1	6,784	31	4	8,663	690,461
Lifetime		62	1	0	0	0	1	1	5	15,392	108	13	19,297	$1,319,368

Dick Kranzler

Year	Driver	Starts	Poles	1	2	3	4	5	6–10	Laps	Laps Led	Races Led	Miles	$
1970	Dick Kranzler	1	0	0	0	0	0	0	0	148	0	0	388	1,100
1971	Dick Kranzler	3	0	0	0	0	0	0	0	215	0	0	562	3,105
1972	Dick Kranzler	3	0	0	0	0	0	0	0	391	0	0	1,008	3,635
1973	Dick Kranzler	1	0	0	0	0	0	0	0	108	0	0	283	890
1979	Dick Kranzler	1	0	0	0	0	0	0	0	23	0	0	60	700
Lifetime		9	0	0	0	0	0	0	0	885	0	0	2,301	$9,430

Nord Krauskopf

Year	Driver	Starts	Poles	1	2	3	4	5	6–10	Laps	Laps Led	Races Led	Miles	$
1966	Earl Balmer	7	0	0	0	0	0	1	0	1,327	3	1	1,944	5,890
"	Gordon Johncock	3	0	0	0	0	0	0	1	430	12	1	797	2,015
"	**Total**	10	0	0	0	0	0	1	1	1,757	15	2	2,741	7,905
1967	Bobby Allison	2	0	0	0	0	0	0	0	597	0	0	896	2,375
"	Charlie Glotzbach	9	0	0	0	0	3	0	2	1,783	4	1	2,461	14,870
"	Bobby Isaac	11	0	0	1	0	0	2	2	2,549	65	3	3,889	24,225
"	Sam McQuagg	1	0	0	0	0	0	0	0	57	1	1	143	535
"	**Total**	11	0	0	1	0	3	2	4	4,986	70	4	7,388	42,005
1968	Bobby Isaac	49	3	3	9	7	4	4	9	12,947	1,384	20	9,160	60,342
"	Sam McQuagg	3	0	0	0	0	0	0	2	750	5	1	1,296	4,165
"	**Total**	49	3	3	9	7	4	4	11	13,697	1,389	21	10,456	64,507
1969	Bobby Isaac	50	20	17	3	5	3	1	4	12,308	**5,072**	38	9,329	92,074
1970	Bobby Isaac	47	13	11	9	5	4	3	6	12,726	3,188	35	11,251	199,600
1971	Bobby Isaac	25	5	4	4	2	4	2	1	6,856	1,753	17	7,602	106,526
"	Dave Marcis	1	0	0	0	0	0	0	1	181	38	1	481	6,025
"	**Total**	26	5	4	4	2	4	2	2	7,037	1,791	18	8,083	112,551
1972	Buddy Baker	7	1	1	1	2	1	0	0	2,803	448	6	2,665	48,165
"	Bobby Isaac	24	8	1	3	5	0	1	0	5,326	1,314	18	6,458	133,007
"	**Total**	31	9	2	4	7	1	1	0	8,129	1,762	24	9,123	181,172
1973	Buddy Baker	27	4	2	4	6	4	0	4	8,369	975	14	8,908	190,531
1974	Buddy Baker	3	0	0	0	2	0	0	0	780	45	1	1,276	14,775
"	Ray Hendrick	1	0	0	0	0	0	0	0	179	0	0	94	620
"	Bobby Isaac	1	0	0	0	0	0	0	0	81	0	0	122	1,372
"	Dave Marcis	2	0	0	0	0	0	0	0	268	0	0	326	2,087
"	**Total**	6	0	0	0	2	0	0	0	1,308	45	1	1,817	18,854
1975	Dave Marcis	30	4	1	1	5	6	3	2	8,324	458	17	9,789	240,646
1976	Dave Marcis	30	7	3	0	1	2	3	7	8,355	893	20	9,733	218,250
1977	Neil Bonnett	11	3	0	0	0	1	1	2	2,864	47	4	3,130	53,450
Lifetime		328	68	43	35	40	32	21	43	89,860	15,705	198	91,748	$1,421,545
			6th	**10th**								**8th**	**9th**		

Art Krebs

Year	Driver	Starts	Poles	1	2	3	4	5	6–10	Laps	Laps Led	Races Led	Miles	$
1956	Jim Cook	2	0	0	0	0	0	0	0	121	0	0	226	65
1959	Jim Blomgren	1	0	0	0	0	0	0	0	49	0	0	49	50
1960	Bruce Worrell	3	0	0	0	0	0	0	2	333	0	0	394	650
Lifetime		6	0	0	0	0	0	0	2	503	0	0	669	$765

John Krebs

Year	Driver	Starts	Poles	1	2	3	4	5	6–10	Laps	Laps Led	Races Led	Miles	$
1983	John Krebs	1	0	0	0	0	0	0	0	60	0	0	157	1,100
1984	John Krebs	2	0	0	0	0	0	0	0	54	0	0	141	1,790
1985	John Krebs	1	0	0	0	0	0	0	0	73	0	0	191	2,250
1986	John Krebs	2	0	0	0	0	0	0	0	94	0	0	246	2,075
1987	John Krebs	1	0	0	0	0	0	0	0	80	0	0	210	1,125
1988	John Krebs	1	0	0	0	0	0	0	0	92	0	0	241	1,600
1989	John Krebs	1	0	0	0	0	0	0	0	65	0	0	164	3,000
1990	John Krebs	2	0	0	0	0	0	0	0	366	0	0	477	8,435

Year	Driver	Starts	Poles	Finish						Laps	Laps Led	Races Led	Miles	$
				1	2	3	4	5	6–10					

John Krebs *continued*

Year	Driver	Starts	Poles	1	2	3	4	5	6–10	Laps	Laps Led	Races Led	Miles	$
1991	John Krebs	1	0	0	0	0	0	0	0	57	1	1	144	3,525
Lifetime		12	0	0	0	0	0	0	0	941	1	1	1,971	$24,900

Jeff Krogh

Year	Driver	Starts	Poles	1	2	3	4	5	6–10	Laps	Laps Led	Races Led	Miles	$
1996	Jeff Krogh	2	0	0	0	0	0	0	0	222	0	0	330	19,680
Lifetime		2	0	0	0	0	0	0	0	222	0	0	330	$19,680

Carl Krueger

Year	Driver	Starts	Poles	1	2	3	4	5	6–10	Laps	Laps Led	Races Led	Miles	$
1955	Lloyd Dane	1	0	0	0	0	0	0	0	0	0	0	0	25
"	Carl Krueger	7	0	0	0	0	0	1	1	955	0	0	534	585
"	Lee Petty	1	0	0	0	0	0	0	0	116	0	0	116	50
"	Mario Rossi	1	0	0	0	0	0	0	1	223	0	0	223	200
"	**Total**	9	0	0	0	0	0	1	2	1,294	0	0	873	860
Lifetime		9	0	0	0	0	0	1	2	1,294	0	0	873	$860

Alan Kulwicki

Year	Driver	Starts	Poles	1	2	3	4	5	6–10	Laps	Laps Led	Races Led	Miles	$
1986	Alan Kulwicki	9	0	0	0	0	0	0	1	3,368	7	2	3,445	31,980
1987	Alan Kulwicki	29	3	0	1	0	1	1	6	7,758	102	8	9,119	369,889
1988	Alan Kulwicki	29	4	1	2	1	1	2	2	8,149	134	8	9,317	448,547
1989	Alan Kulwicki	29	6	0	4	0	0	1	4	8,324	564	14	9,560	501,295
1990	Alan Kulwicki	29	1	1	1	1	1	1	8	8,635	400	10	10,655	550,936
1991	Alan Kulwicki	29	4	1	0	1	1	1	7	8,507	233	9	10,145	595,614
1992	Alan Kulwicki	29	6	2	3	2	2	2	6	8,991	1,235	20	10,852	2,322,561
1993	Alan Kulwicki	5	0	0	0	1	1	0	1	1,588	4	2	1,995	165,470
Lifetime		188	24	5	11	6	7	8	35	55,320	2,679	73	65,088	$4,986,292

Gerald Kulwicki

Year	Driver	Starts	Poles	1	2	3	4	5	6–10	Laps	Laps Led	Races Led	Miles	$
1993	Jimmy Hensley	3	0	0	0	0	0	0	1	1,081	0	0	1,009	53,640
Lifetime		3	0	0	0	0	0	0	1	1,081	0	0	1,009	$53,640

La Belle Motors

Year	Driver	Starts	Poles	1	2	3	4	5	6–10	Laps	Laps Led	Races Led	Miles	$
1949	Dick Linder	3	0	0	1	0	0	0	0	416	0	0	289	775
1950	Russell Bennett	1	0	0	0	0	0	0	0	0	0	0	0	50
"	Dick Linder	1	0	0	0	0	0	0	0	161	0	0	81	50
"	**Total**	2	0	0	0	0	0	0	0	161	0	0	81	100
Lifetime		5	0	0	1	0	0	0	0	577	0	0	370	$875

Terry Labonte

Year	Driver	Starts	Poles	1	2	3	4	5	6–10	Laps	Laps Led	Races Led	Miles	$
1991	Irv Hoerr	3	0	0	0	0	0	0	0	243	0	0	608	11,125
"	Bobby Labonte	2	0	0	0	0	0	0	0	128	0	0	168	8,350
"	**Total**	5	0	0	0	0	0	0	0	371	0	0	776	19,475
Lifetime		5	0	0	0	0	0	0	0	371	0	0	776	$19,475

Chip Lain

Year	Driver	Starts	Poles	1	2	3	4	5	6–10	Laps	Laps Led	Races Led	Miles	$
1984	Connie Saylor	4	0	0	0	0	0	0	0	595	1	1	948	5,510
Lifetime		4	0	0	0	0	0	0	0	595	1	1	948	$5,510

Lancaster Brothers

Year	Driver	Starts	Poles	1	2	3	4	5	6–10	Laps	Laps Led	Races Led	Miles	$
1955	Joe Eubanks	7	0	0	0	0	0	0	1	655	0	0	516	285
"	Cotton Owens	2	0	0	0	0	0	1	1	549	0	0	584	900
"	**Total**	9	0	0	0	0	0	1	2	1,204	0	0	1,100	1,185
1956	Cotton Owens	2	0	0	0	0	0	0	1	299	0	0	158	100
Lifetime		11	0	0	0	0	0	1	3	1,503	0	0	1,259	$1,285

Shep Langdon

Year	Driver	Starts	Poles	1	2	3	4	5	6–10	Laps	Laps Led	Races Led	Miles	$
1958	Shep Langdon	15	0	0	0	0	0	0	1	2,441	0	0	1,306	1,180
1959	L. D. Austin	1	0	0	0	0	0	0	0	180	0	0	90	60
"	Shep Langdon	21	0	0	0	0	0	0	6	3,976	0	0	2,259	3,466
"	**Total**	22	0	0	0	0	0	0	6	4,156	0	0	2,349	3,526

Year	Driver	Starts	Poles	Finish 1	2	3	4	5	6–10	Laps	Laps Led	Races Led	Miles	$

Shep Langdon *continued*

Year	Driver	Starts	Poles	1	2	3	4	5	6–10	Laps	Laps Led	Races Led	Miles	$
1960	Shep Langdon	4	0	0	0	0	0	0	1	588	0	0	756	635
Lifetime		41	0	0	0	0	0	0	8	7,185	0	0	4,411	$5,341

Elmo Langley

Year	Driver	Starts	Poles	1	2	3	4	5	6–10	Laps	Laps Led	Races Led	Miles	$
1954	Elmo Langley	2	0	0	0	0	0	0	0	340	0	0	466	450
1955	Elmo Langley	3	0	0	0	0	0	0	1	344	0	0	283	300
1956	Elmo Langley	1	0	0	0	0	0	0	0	338	0	0	465	140
1957	Elmo Langley	1	0	0	0	0	0	0	0	189	0	0	95	150
1958	Elmo Langley	7	0	0	0	0	0	1	2	1,116	0	0	759	895
1962	Elmo Langley	3	0	0	0	0	0	0	0	505	0	0	673	820
1965	Buddy Arrington	1	0	0	0	0	0	0	0	237	0	0	356	700
"	Buddy Baker	2	0	0	0	0	0	0	0	51	0	0	10	200
"	Darel Dieringer	1	0	0	0	0	0	0	1	282	0	0	94	150
"	Elmer Gilliam	1	0	0	0	0	0	0	0	1	0	0	1	100
"	Hop Holmes	1	0	0	0	0	0	0	0	71	0	0	36	100
"	Jack Ingram	1	0	0	0	0	0	0	0	4	0	0	2	100
"	Elmo Langley	32	0	0	0	2	1	0	6	5,512	19	1	3,729	10,695
"	Bud Moore	1	0	0	0	0	0	0	0	23	0	0	12	100
"	Bert Robbins	2	0	0	0	0	0	0	1	189	0	0	95	200
"	Daniel Warlick	1	0	0	0	0	0	0	1	381	0	0	143	250
"	**Total**	39	0	0	0	2	1	0	9	6,751	19	1	4,476	12,595
1966	Elmo Langley	1	0	0	0	0	0	0	0	14	0	0	7	0
1968	Elmo Langley	41	0	0	0	1	1	4	18	9,475	0	0	6,593	23,627
"	Bill Seifert	3	0	0	0	0	0	0	0	310	0	0	455	1,525
"	**Total**	44	0	0	0	1	1	4	18	9,785	0	0	7,048	25,152
1969	Larry Hess	1	0	0	0	0	0	0	0	122	0	0	183	1,325
"	Elmo Langley	51	0	0	0	1	6	6	15	12,227	40	1	9,503	72,162
"	Clyde Lynn	1	0	0	0	0	0	0	0	40	0	0	41	645
"	J. D. McDuffie	1	0	0	0	0	0	0	0	277	0	0	416	1,175
"	Dub Simpson	3	0	0	0	0	0	0	0	81	0	0	76	940
"	**Total**	52	0	0	0	1	6	6	15	12,747	40	1	10,218	76,247
1970	Elmo Langley	46	0	0	0	1	0	0	17	10,225	0	0	9,081	44,493
"	John Sears	2	0	0	0	0	0	0	0	242	0	0	138	1,085
"	Bill Seifert	1	0	0	0	0	0	0	0	1	0	0	1	430
"	**Total**	47	0	0	0	1	0	0	17	10,468	0	0	9,219	46,008
1971	Earl Brooks	1	0	0	0	0	0	0	0	67	0	0	35	350
"	Elmo Langley	40	0	0	3	1	3	2	10	9,569	48	1	9,448	53,562
"	Clyde Lynn	1	0	0	0	0	0	0	0	15	0	0	9	365
"	Dick May	4	0	0	0	0	0	0	0	176	0	0	114	900
"	**Total**	44	0	0	3	1	3	2	10	9,827	48	1	9,607	55,177
1972	Elmo Langley	30	0	0	0	0	0	1	8	8,150	0	0	9,459	59,644
"	Dick May	1	0	0	0	0	0	0	1	141	0	0	369	1,525
"	**Total**	31	0	0	0	0	0	1	9	8,291	0	0	9,829	61,169
1973	Elmo Langley	27	0	0	0	0	0	0	4	8,016	0	0	8,377	49,892
1974	Tony Bettenhausen Jr.	1	0	0	0	0	0	0	0	144	0	0	360	1,225
"	Elmo Langley	22	0	0	0	0	0	0	3	5,420	0	0	5,403	23,142
"	Dave Marcis	1	0	0	0	0	0	0	0	183	0	0	458	1,525
"	Dick May	1	0	0	0	0	0	0	0	174	0	0	463	1,485
"	**Total**	25	0	0	0	0	0	0	3	5,921	0	0	6,683	27,377
1975	Bill Champion	1	0	0	0	0	0	0	0	1	0	0	1	530
"	Tommy Gale	1	0	0	0	0	0	0	0	83	0	0	208	2,625
"	Elmo Langley	27	0	0	0	0	0	2	4	7,898	0	0	9,178	65,265
"	**Total**	29	0	0	0	0	0	2	4	7,982	0	0	9,386	68,420
1976	Dick Brooks	1	0	0	0	0	0	0	0	45	0	0	27	565
"	Tommy Gale	11	0	0	0	0	0	0	0	2,135	0	0	3,027	18,335
"	Elmo Langley	7	0	0	0	0	0	0	1	2,451	0	0	1,368	7,515
"	Skip Manning	1	0	0	0	0	0	0	0	360	0	0	225	750
"	Ed Negre	1	0	0	0	0	0	0	0	238	0	0	125	880
"	**Total**	21	0	0	0	0	0	0	1	5,229	0	0	4,771	28,045
1977	Dick Brooks	2	0	0	0	0	0	0	0	358	0	0	394	3,745
"	Dean Dalton	1	0	0	0	0	0	0	0	113	0	0	60	695
"	Tommy Gale	18	0	0	0	0	0	0	0	4,402	0	0	6,071	39,865
"	Henley Gray	1	0	0	0	0	0	0	0	376	0	0	235	1,480
"	Elmo Langley	4	0	0	0	0	0	0	0	1,093	0	0	582	4,380
"	**Total**	26	0	0	0	0	0	0	0	6,342	0	0	7,343	50,165
1978	Dick Brooks	3	0	0	0	0	0	0	0	565	0	0	697	5,240
"	Tommy Gale	25	0	0	0	0	0	0	0	6,727	0	0	8,482	60,065

Year	Driver	Starts	Poles	1	2	3	4	5	6–10	Laps	Laps Led	Races Led	Miles	$

Elmo Langley *continued*

Year	Driver	Starts	Poles	1	2	3	4	5	6–10	Laps	Laps Led	Races Led	Miles	$
"	Elmo Langley	1	0	0	0	0	0	0	0	389	0	0	232	1,165
"	**Total**	29	0	0	0	0	0	0	0	7,681	0	0	9,411	66,470
1979	Tommy Gale	27	0	0	0	0	0	0	1	7,054	0	0	8,092	73,029
"	Elmo Langley	2	0	0	0	0	0	0	0	461	0	0	248	2,410
"	**Total**	29	0	0	0	0	0	0	1	7,515	0	0	8,339	75,439
1980	Tommy Gale	28	0	0	0	0	0	0	0	7,411	0	0	8,425	80,874
1981	Tommy Gale	26	0	0	0	0	0	0	0	7,728	2	1	8,973	105,438
1982	Tommy Gale	25	0	0	0	0	0	0	0	7,215	1	1	8,081	96,465
"	Mark Stahl	1	0	0	0	0	0	0	0	24	0	0	63	1,550
"	**Total**	26	0	0	0	0	0	0	0	7,239	1	1	8,144	98,015
1983	Tommy Gale	25	0	0	0	0	0	0	1	5,845	0	0	7,327	82,950
"	D. K. Ulrich	2	0	0	0	0	0	0	0	588	0	0	520	5,070
"	**Total**	27	0	0	0	0	0	0	1	6,433	0	0	7,848	88,020
1984	Clark Dwyer	1	0	0	0	0	0	0	0	473	0	0	473	3,815
"	Tommy Gale	16	0	0	0	0	0	0	0	4,248	0	0	5,268	69,385
"	Jimmy Hensley	4	0	0	0	0	0	0	0	1,484	0	0	793	12,895
"	Gary Mayeda	1	0	0	0	0	0	0	0	21	0	0	55	2,215
"	Joe Millikan	1	0	0	0	0	0	0	0	459	0	0	467	4,745
"	Ken Schrader	5	0	0	0	0	0	0	0	1,508	0	0	1,632	16,425
"	**Total**	28	0	0	0	0	0	0	0	8,193	0	0	8,688	109,480
1985	Clark Dwyer	28	0	0	0	0	0	0	0	7,205	0	0	8,550	128,710
1986	Brian Baker	1	0	0	0	0	0	0	0	252	0	0	252	3,985
1986	Rick Baldwin	2	0	0	0	0	0	0	0	393	0	0	260	6,905
"	Eddie Bierschwale	5	0	0	0	0	0	0	0	710	0	0	1,582	28,730
"	Pancho Carter	3	0	0	0	0	0	0	0	672	0	0	880	22,550
"	Tommy Gale	1	0	0	0	0	0	0	0	175	0	0	466	5,845
"	Jimmy Hensley	3	0	0	0	0	0	0	0	1,194	0	0	634	11,755
"	Doug Heveron	1	0	0	0	0	0	0	0	391	0	0	212	4,760
"	Rick McCray	1	0	0	0	0	0	0	0	90	0	0	236	4,060
"	Mike Potter	1	0	0	0	0	0	0	0	375	0	0	381	3,990
"	Connie Saylor	5	0	0	0	0	0	0	0	1,270	0	0	1,979	28,995
"	Morgan Shepherd	1	0	0	0	0	0	0	0	22	0	0	12	2,940
"	**Total**	24	0	0	0	0	0	0	0	5,544	0	0	6,894	124,515
1987	Trevor Boys	4	0	0	0	0	0	0	0	1,101	1	1	961	17,415
"	Rodney Combs	10	0	0	0	0	0	0	0	2,088	0	0	3,559	56,435
"	Jerry Cranmer	5	0	0	0	0	0	0	0	1,914	0	0	1,278	20,660
"	Curtis Markham	3	0	0	0	0	0	0	0	675	0	0	650	11,445
"	Rick McCray	1	0	0	0	0	0	0	0	88	0	0	231	3,200
"	Connie Saylor	4	0	0	0	0	0	0	0	440	0	0	789	26,390
"	**Total**	27	0	0	0	0	0	0	0	6,306	1	1	7,467	135,545
Lifetime		675	0	0	3	6	11	16	95	165,712	111	6	172,443	$1,519,493
			6th								**9th**			

Jerry Lankford

Year	Driver	Starts	Poles	1	2	3	4	5	6–10	Laps	Laps Led	Races Led	Miles	$
1973	Sonny Easley	2	0	0	0	0	0	0	0	144	0	0	377	2,015
1974	Sonny Easley	3	0	0	0	0	0	0	1	415	0	0	1,074	4,800
1975	Sonny Easley	3	0	0	0	0	0	0	0	136	2	1	355	2,405
1976	Sonny Easley	7	0	0	0	0	0	0	2	1,861	0	0	2,137	11,290
"	Larry Phillips	1	0	0	0	0	0	0	0	188	0	0	470	1,990
"	**Total**	7	0	0	0	0	0	0	2	2,049	0	0	2,607	13,280
1977	Sonny Easley	1	0	0	0	0	0	1	0	115	0	0	301	6,290
Lifetime		16	0	0	0	0	0	1	3	2,859	2	1	4,714	$28,790

Russell Large

Year	Driver	Starts	Poles	1	2	3	4	5	6–10	Laps	Laps Led	Races Led	Miles	$
1974	Jimmy Hensley	1	0	0	0	0	0	0	0	179	9	1	94	610
"	L. D. Ottinger	4	0	0	0	0	0	0	0	290	0	0	395	4,985
"	**Total**	5	0	0	0	0	0	0	0	469	9	1	489	5,595
Lifetime		5	0	0	0	0	0	0	0	469	9	1	489	$5,595

Curtis Larimer

Year	Driver	Starts	Poles	1	2	3	4	5	6–10	Laps	Laps Led	Races Led	Miles	$
1965	Neil Castles	1	0	0	0	0	0	0	0	186	0	0	93	260
"	Darel Dieringer	1	0	0	0	0	0	0	0	430	0	0	215	450
"	Paul Lewis	4	0	0	0	0	0	1	1	1,102	0	0	848	1,175
"	Bill Morton	5	0	0	0	0	0	0	0	601	0	0	832	2,590
"	**Total**	11	0	0	0	0	0	1	1	2,319	0	0	1,988	4,475

Year	Driver	Starts	Poles	Finish 1	2	3	4	5	6–10	Laps	Laps Led	Races Led	Miles	$

Curtis Larimer *continued*

Year	Driver	Starts	Poles	1	2	3	4	5	6–10	Laps	Laps Led	Races Led	Miles	$
1966	Don Tilley	1	0	0	0	0	0	0	0	15	0	0	8	0
Lifetime		12	0	0	0	0	0	1	1	2,334	0	0	1,996	$4,475

Mel Larson

Year	Driver	Starts	Poles	1	2	3	4	5	6–10	Laps	Laps Led	Races Led	Miles	$
1955	Mel Larson	2	0	0	0	0	0	0	1	230	0	0	135	150
1956	Mel Larson	6	0	0	0	0	0	0	1	504	0	0	471	385
1957	Mel Larson	9	1	0	0	0	0	1	3	1,058	0	0	587	935
1958	Mel Larson	4	0	0	0	0	0	0	1	546	0	0	412	280
1959	Mel Larson	2	0	0	0	0	0	0	2	529	0	0	258	350
1960	Mel Larson	4	1	0	1	0	0	0	1	465	19	2	835	1,325
1975	Mel Larson	1	0	0	0	0	0	0	0	36	0	0	72	665
Lifetime		28	2	0	1	0	0	1	9	3,368	19	2	2,770	$4,090

Stan Lasky

Year	Driver	Starts	Poles	1	2	3	4	5	6–10	Laps	Laps Led	Races Led	Miles	$
1978	Paul Fess	1	0	0	0	0	0	0	0	75	0	0	188	835
1979	Paul Fess	2	0	0	0	0	0	0	0	232	0	0	532	4,860
Lifetime		3	0	0	0	0	0	0	0	307	0	0	719	$5,695

Fred Lauria

Year	Driver	Starts	Poles	1	2	3	4	5	6–10	Laps	Laps Led	Races Led	Miles	$
1959	Bob Price	2	0	0	0	0	0	0	0	427	0	0	176	225
1960	Bob Price	3	0	0	0	0	0	0	0	258	0	0	314	445
1961	Bob Price	2	0	0	0	0	0	0	1	204	0	0	150	180
Lifetime		7	0	0	0	0	0	0	1	889	0	0	639	$850

Tony Lavati

Year	Driver	Starts	Poles	1	2	3	4	5	6–10	Laps	Laps Led	Races Led	Miles	$
1961	David Pearson	2	0	0	0	0	0	0	0	223	0	0	558	275
Lifetime		2	0	0	0	0	0	0	0	223	0	0	558	$275

Coleman Lawrence

Year	Driver	Starts	Poles	1	2	3	4	5	6–10	Laps	Laps Led	Races Led	Miles	$
1951	Coleman Lawrence	6	0	0	0	0	0	0	2	130	0	0	130	250
1952	Coleman Lawrence	8	0	0	0	0	0	0	3	1,326	0	0	1,045	375
1953	Coleman Lawrence	8	0	0	0	0	0	0	1	263	0	0	263	250
Lifetime		22	0	0	0	0	0	0	6	1,719	0	0	1,438	$875

Ed Lawrence

Year	Driver	Starts	Poles	1	2	3	4	5	6–10	Laps	Laps Led	Races Led	Miles	$
1949	Fonty Flock	4	0	0	0	1	1	0	0	304	85	1	153	750
1950	Fonty Flock	2	0	0	0	0	0	0	1	76	0	0	214	150
"	Pee Wee Martin	1	0	0	0	0	0	0	0		12	1		50
"	**Total**	3	0	0	0	0	0	0	1	76	12	1	214	200
Lifetime		7	0	0	0	1	1	0	1	380	97	2	367	$950

Jack Lawrence

Year	Driver	Starts	Poles	1	2	3	4	5	6–10	Laps	Laps Led	Races Led	Miles	$
1953	Jack Lawrence	2	0	0	0	0	0	0	0	101	0	0	51	50
Lifetime		2	0	0	0	0	0	0	0	101	0	0	51	$50

Mike Laws

Year	Driver	Starts	Poles	1	2	3	4	5	6–10	Laps	Laps Led	Races Led	Miles	$
1986	Mike Laws	2	0	0	0	0	0	0	0	422	0	0	698	3,095
Lifetime		2	0	0	0	0	0	0	0	422	0	0	698	$3,095

Lawson & Netti

Year	Driver	Starts	Poles	1	2	3	4	5	6–10	Laps	Laps Led	Races Led	Miles	$
1956	Judge Rider	1	0	0	0	0	0	0	0	258	0	0	355	50
"	Jack Tykarski	1	0	0	0	0	0	0	0	250	0	0	250	225
"	Ken Wagner	3	0	0	0	0	0	0	0	112	0	0	64	60
"	**Total**	5	0	0	0	0	0	0	0	620	0	0	669	335
Lifetime		5	0	0	0	0	0	0	0	620	0	0	669	$335

Harry Leake

Year	Driver	Starts	Poles	1	2	3	4	5	6–10	Laps	Laps Led	Races Led	Miles	$
1961	Harry Leake	15	0	0	0	0	0	0	7	2,375	0	0	1,107	2,000

Year	Driver	Starts	Poles	Finish 1	2	3	4	5	6–10	Laps	Laps Led	Races Led	Miles	$

Harry Leake *continued*

Year	Driver	Starts	Poles	1	2	3	4	5	6–10	Laps	Laps Led	Races Led	Miles	$
"	E. J. Trivette	1	0	0	0	0	0	0	0	56	0	0	84	100
"	**Total**	16	0	0	0	0	0	0	7	2,431	0	0	1,191	2,100
1962	Harry Leake	1	0	0	0	0	0	0	0	98	0	0	49	50
Lifetime		17	0	0	0	0	0	0	7	2,529	0	0	1,240	$2,150

Tom Lechlider

Year	Driver	Starts	Poles	1	2	3	4	5	6–10	Laps	Laps Led	Races Led	Miles	$
1952	Thomas Lechlider	1	0	0	0	0	0	0	0		0	0		25
Lifetime		1	0	0	0	0	0	0	0		0	0		$25

Bill Ledbetter

Year	Driver	Starts	Poles	1	2	3	4	5	6–10	Laps	Laps Led	Races Led	Miles	$
1951	Bill Ledbetter	3	0	0	0	0	0	0	1		0	0		250
Lifetime		3	0	0	0	0	0	0	1		0	0		$250

Bobby Lee

Year	Driver	Starts	Poles	1	2	3	4	5	6–10	Laps	Laps Led	Races Led	Miles	$
1958	Bobby Lee	5	0	0	0	0	0	0	0	532	0	0	568	285
Lifetime		5	0	0	0	0	0	0	0	532	0	0	568	$285

Jack Lee

Year	Driver	Starts	Poles	1	2	3	4	5	6–10	Laps	Laps Led	Races Led	Miles	$
1983	Ron Esau	2	0	0	0	0	0	0	0	70	0	0	183	1,575
1984	Ron Esau	2	0	0	0	0	0	0	0	170	0	0	445	2,660
Lifetime		4	0	0	0	0	0	0	0	240	0	0	629	$4,235

Jim Lee

Year	Driver	Starts	Poles	1	2	3	4	5	6–10	Laps	Laps Led	Races Led	Miles	$
1974	Jim Lee	1	0	0	0	0	0	0	0	21	0	0	55	650
1982	Jim Lee	2	0	0	0	0	0	0	0	125	0	0	328	1,760
Lifetime		3	0	0	0	0	0	0	0	146	0	0	383	$2,410

Ted Lee

Year	Driver	Starts	Poles	1	2	3	4	5	6–10	Laps	Laps Led	Races Led	Miles	$
1953	Ted Lee	4	0	0	0	0	0	0	0	294	0	0	387	125
1954	Ted Lee	2	0	0	0	0	0	0	0	492	0	0	328	65
Lifetime		6	0	0	0	0	0	0	0	786	0	0	715	$190

Warren Lee

Year	Driver	Starts	Poles	1	2	3	4	5	6–10	Laps	Laps Led	Races Led	Miles	$
1956	Possum Jones	1	0	0	0	0	0	0	0	336	0	0	462	110
Lifetime		1	0	0	0	0	0	0	0	336	0	0	462	$110

Bob Lehman

Year	Driver	Starts	Poles	1	2	3	4	5	6–10	Laps	Laps Led	Races Led	Miles	$
1977	Don Graham	1	0	0	0	0	0	0	0	118	0	0	295	1,000
1978	Don Graham	1	0	0	0	0	0	0	0	75	0	0	197	875
1979	Don Graham	1	0	0	0	0	0	0	0	100	0	0	262	1,495
Lifetime		3	0	0	0	0	0	0	0	293	0	0	754	$3,370

Larry LeMay

Year	Driver	Starts	Poles	1	2	3	4	5	6–10	Laps	Laps Led	Races Led	Miles	$
1977	Larry LeMay	1	0	0	0	0	0	0	0	252	0	0	158	360
Lifetime		1	0	0	0	0	0	0	0	252	0	0	158	$360

Bill Leonard

Year	Driver	Starts	Poles	1	2	3	4	5	6–10	Laps	Laps Led	Races Led	Miles	$
1984	Tommie Crozier	1	0	0	0	0	0	0	0	277	0	0	277	990
1985	Tommie Crozier	3	0	0	0	0	0	0	0	516	0	0	560	4,895
1986	Tommie Crozier	2	0	0	0	0	0	0	0	354	0	0	359	2,475
1989	Tommie Crozier	2	0	0	0	0	0	0	0	112	0	0	136	4,600
Lifetime		8	0	0	0	0	0	0	0	1,259	0	0	1,332	$12,960

Damon Leonard

Year	Driver	Starts	Poles	1	2	3	4	5	6–10	Laps	Laps Led	Races Led	Miles	$
1960	Harold Smith	2	0	0	0	0	0	0	0	105	0	0	263	200
Lifetime		2	0	0	0	0	0	0	0	105	0	0	263	$200

Year	Driver	Starts	Poles	Finish						Laps	Laps Led	Races Led	Miles	$
				1	2	3	4	5	6–10					

Roscoe Leonard

Year	Driver	Starts	Poles	1	2	3	4	5	6–10	Laps	Laps Led	Races Led	Miles	$
1969	Bobby Brewer	1	0	0	0	0	0	0	0	9	0	0	24	975
Lifetime		1	0	0	0	0	0	0	0	9	0	0	24	$975

Bert Letner

Year	Driver	Starts	Poles	1	2	3	4	5	6–10	Laps	Laps Led	Races Led	Miles	$
1951	Fuzzy Anderson	3	0	0	0	0	0	0	0		0	0		100
"	Danny Letner	5	0	0	0	0	0	0	2	153	0	0	153	225
"	**Total**	5	0	0	0	0	0	0	2	153	0	0	153	325
1954	Bill West	3	0	0	0	0	0	0	1	888	0	0	557	250
Lifetime		8	0	0	0	0	0	0	3	1,041	0	0	710	$575

Jimmie Lewallen

Year	Driver	Starts	Poles	1	2	3	4	5	6–10	Laps	Laps Led	Races Led	Miles	$
1949	Jimmie Lewallen	1	0	0	0	0	0	0	0		0	0		25
Lifetime		1	0	0	0	0	0	0	0		0	0		$25

Paul Lewis

Year	Driver	Starts	Poles	1	2	3	4	5	6–10	Laps	Laps Led	Races Led	Miles	$
1962	Tiny Lund	2	0	0	0	0	0	0	0	294	0	0	147	185
1963	Paul Lewis	1	0	0	0	0	0	0	0	2	0	0	3	500
1965	Paul Lewis	20	1	0	0	0	1	1	9	4,852	0	0	4,209	11,472
1966	Buddy Arrington	1	0	0	0	0	0	0	0	463	0	0	463	805
"	Paul Lewis	20	0	1	1	6	1	0	5	5,952	67	2	4,434	17,157
"	**Total**	21	0	1	1	6	1	0	5	6,415	67	2	4,897	17,962
1967	Paul Lewis	1	0	0	1	0	0	0	0	297	0	0	149	1,170
Lifetime		45	1	1	2	6	2	1	14	11,860	67	2	9,405	$31,289

Raymond Lewis

Year	Driver	Starts	Poles	1	2	3	4	5	6–10	Laps	Laps Led	Races Led	Miles	$
1949	Otis Martin	2	0	0	0	0	0	0	0	66	0	0	33	50
1950	Otis Martin	1	0	0	0	0	0	0	1	47	0	0	196	175
Lifetime		3	0	0	0	0	0	0	1	113	0	0	229	$225

Al Liberty

Year	Driver	Starts	Poles	1	2	3	4	5	6–10	Laps	Laps Led	Races Led	Miles	$
1955	Bill Tanner	5	0	0	0	0	0	0	1	423	0	0	443	475
1956	Bill Tanner	2	0	0	0	0	0	0	0	230	0	0	230	75
Lifetime		7	0	0	0	0	0	0	1	653	0	0	673	$550

Ralph Liguori

Year	Driver	Starts	Poles	1	2	3	4	5	6–10	Laps	Laps Led	Races Led	Miles	$
1952	Ralph Liguori	3	0	0	0	0	1	0	0	680	0	0	646	475
1953	Ralph Liguori	5	0	0	0	0	0	0	1	149	0	0	93	295
1954	Dick Kable	1	0	0	0	0	0	0	0	168	0	0	84	0
"	Ralph Liguori	21	0	0	0	1	0	1	8	3,072	0	0	2,253	2,820
"	**Total**	22	0	0	0	1	0	1	8	3,240	0	0	2,337	2,820
1955	Ralph Liguori	10	0	0	0	0	0	0	5	865	0	0	660	950
1956	Ralph Liguori	12	0	0	0	0	0	0	3	776	0	0	502	860
Lifetime		52	0	0	0	1	1	1	17	5,710	0	0	4,237	$5,400

Betty Lilly

Year	Driver	Starts	Poles	1	2	3	4	5	6–10	Laps	Laps Led	Races Led	Miles	$
1965	Sam McQuagg	10	0	0	0	1	0	1	2	1,728	31	1	2,132	8,985
1966	Bobby Allison	11	0	0	0	2	1	0	2	2,450	0	0	2,658	9,350
"	Darel Dieringer	1	0	0	0	0	0	0	0	0	0	0	0	100
"	Ned Jarrett	1	0	0	0	0	0	0	0	386	0	0	193	905
"	Tiny Lund	3	0	0	0	0	0	0	1	442	0	0	785	2,470
"	Curtis Turner	1	0	0	0	0	0	0	0	19	0	0	29	645
"	**Total**	17	0	0	0	2	1	0	3	3,297	0	0	3,664	13,470
1967	Jack Harden	9	0	0	0	0	0	0	0	1,382	0	0	1,948	4,450
"	Bobby Mausgrover	3	0	0	0	0	0	0	0	337	0	0	312	1,600
"	**Total**	12	0	0	0	0	0	0	0	1,719	0	0	2,260	6,050
Lifetime		39	0	0	0	3	1	1	5	6,744	31	1	8,056	$28,505

Butch Lindley

Year	Driver	Starts	Poles	1	2	3	4	5	6–10	Laps	Laps Led	Races Led	Miles	$
1981	Bobby Allison	1	0	0	0	0	0	0	0	276	0	0	150	5,415

Year	Driver	Starts	Poles	Finish 1	2	3	4	5	6–10	Laps	Laps Led	Races Led	Miles	$

Butch Lindley *continued*

Year	Driver	Starts	Poles	1	2	3	4	5	6–10	Laps	Laps Led	Races Led	Miles	$
"	Butch Lindley	3	0	0	0	0	0	0	0	559	28	2	323	2,375
"	**Total**	4	0	0	0	0	0	0	0	835	28	2	472	7,790
Lifetime		4	0	0	0	0	0	0	0	835	28	2	472	$7,790

John Lindsay

Year	Driver	Starts	Poles	1	2	3	4	5	6–10	Laps	Laps Led	Races Led	Miles	$
1955	John Lindsay	6	0	0	0	0	0	0	3	853	0	0	630	575
1956	John Lindsay	5	0	0	0	0	0	0	1	715	0	0	585	425
1958	John Lindsay	3	0	0	0	0	0	0	1	476	0	0	262	310
Lifetime		14	0	0	0	0	0	0	5	2,044	0	0	1,476	$1,310

Jim Lineberger

Year	Driver	Starts	Poles	1	2	3	4	5	6–10	Laps	Laps Led	Races Led	Miles	$
1969	Jim Lineberger	1	0	0	0	0	0	0	0	131	0	0	197	925
"	Jim Vandiver	1	0	0	0	0	0	0	1	474	0	0	237	700
"	**Total**	2	0	0	0	0	0	0	1	605	0	0	434	1,625
Lifetime		2	0	0	0	0	0	0	1	605	0	0	434	$1,625

Al Lingons

Year	Driver	Starts	Poles	1	2	3	4	5	6–10	Laps	Laps Led	Races Led	Miles	$
1955	Mickey McGreevey	1	0	0	0	0	0	0	0	232	0	0	232	150
Lifetime		1	0	0	0	0	0	0	0	232	0	0	232	$150

Mike Link

Year	Driver	Starts	Poles	1	2	3	4	5	6–10	Laps	Laps Led	Races Led	Miles	$
1974	Terry Link	2	0	0	0	0	0	0	0	146	0	0	388	2,185
1975	Terry Link	1	0	0	0	0	0	0	0	6	0	0	16	595
Lifetime		3	0	0	0	0	0	0	0	152	0	0	404	$2,780

Robert Link

Year	Driver	Starts	Poles	1	2	3	4	5	6–10	Laps	Laps Led	Races Led	Miles	$
1968	Robert Link	1	0	0	0	0	0	0	0	14	0	0	38	500
1969	Robert Link	1	0	0	0	0	0	0	0	62	0	0	167	775
Lifetime		2	0	0	0	0	0	0	0	76	0	0	205	$1,275

Jim Linke

Year	Driver	Starts	Poles	1	2	3	4	5	6–10	Laps	Laps Led	Races Led	Miles	$
1958	Tiny Lund	1	0	0	0	0	0	0	0	285	0	0	392	230
Lifetime		1	0	0	0	0	0	0	0	285	0	0	392	$230

Bob Lipseia

Year	Driver	Starts	Poles	1	2	3	4	5	6–10	Laps	Laps Led	Races Led	Miles	$
1990	Hershel McGriff	1	0	0	0	0	0	0	0	2	0	0	5	3,225
1991	Hershel McGriff	2	0	0	0	0	0	0	0	361	0	0	454	7,475
Lifetime		3	0	0	0	0	0	0	0	363	0	0	459	$10,700

Charles Little

Year	Driver	Starts	Poles	1	2	3	4	5	6–10	Laps	Laps Led	Races Led	Miles	$
1973	Randy Tissot	3	0	0	0	0	0	0	0	816	0	0	1,384	4,245
1974	Randy Tissot	3	0	0	0	0	0	0	0	473	8	1	839	3,750
1975	Randy Tissot	7	0	0	0	0	0	0	0	1,121	0	0	1,657	10,030
Lifetime		13	0	0	0	0	0	0	0	2,410	8	1	3,880	$18,025

Chuck Little

Year	Driver	Starts	Poles	1	2	3	4	5	6–10	Laps	Laps Led	Races Led	Miles	$
1975	Chuck Little	1	0	0	0	0	0	0	0	35	0	0	92	875
1990	Chad Little	17	0	0	0	0	0	0	0	4,513	0	0	6,102	76,690
1991	Chad Little	28	0	0	0	0	0	0	1	7,784	21	3	9,528	184,190
Lifetime		46	0	0	0	0	0	0	1	12,332	21	3	15,721	$261,755

Joe Littlejohn

Year	Driver	Starts	Poles	1	2	3	4	5	6–10	Laps	Laps Led	Races Led	Miles	$
1950	Joe Littlejohn	1	1	0	0	0	0	0	0	7	0	0	29	25
Lifetime		1	1	0	0	0	0	0	0	7	0	0	29	$25

Virgil Livengood

Year	Driver	Starts	Poles	1	2	3	4	5	6–10	Laps	Laps Led	Races Led	Miles	$
1953	Virgil Livengood	3	0	0	0	0	0	0	1	7	0	0	4	100
1954	Virgil Livengood	1	0	0	0	0	0	0	0	35	0	0	144	25
Lifetime		4	0	0	0	0	0	0	1	42	0	0	147	$125

Year	Driver	Starts	Poles	Finish 1	2	3	4	5	6–10	Laps	Laps Led	Races Led	Miles	$

Dub Livingston

Year	Driver	Starts	Poles	1	2	3	4	5	6–10	Laps	Laps Led	Races Led	Miles	$
1953	Dub Livingston	6	0	0	0	0	0	0	1	309	0	0	252	225
Lifetime		6	0	0	0	0	0	0	1	309	0	0	252	$225

Ed Livingston

Year	Driver	Starts	Poles	1	2	3	4	5	6–10	Laps	Laps Led	Races Led	Miles	$
1962	Ed Livingston	11	0	0	0	0	0	0	0	1,438	0	0	1,986	2,765
1963	Thomas Cox	1	0	0	0	0	0	0	0	2	0	0	3	250
"	Frank Graham	3	0	0	0	0	0	0	0	99	0	0	245	1,050
"	Ed Livingston	8	0	0	0	0	0	0	1	965	0	0	462	850
"	Tiny Lund	1	0	0	0	0	0	0	0	71	0	0	36	85
"	**Total**	13	0	0	0	0	0	0	1	1,137	0	0	745	2,235
1964	Ed Livingston	3	0	0	0	0	1	0	0	211	0	0	113	875
"	Mitch Walker	1	0	0	0	0	0	0	0	174	0	0	87	130
"	**Total**	4	0	0	0	0	1	0	0	385	0	0	200	1,005
Lifetime		28	0	0	0	0	1	0	1	2,960	0	0	2,931	$6,005

Les Loeser

Year	Driver	Starts	Poles	1	2	3	4	5	6–10	Laps	Laps Led	Races Led	Miles	$
1970	Les Loeser	1	0	0	0	0	0	0	0	38	0	0	100	830
Lifetime		1	0	0	0	0	0	0	0	38	0	0	100	$830

Bondy Long

Year	Driver	Starts	Poles	1	2	3	4	5	6–10	Laps	Laps Led	Races Led	Miles	$
1963	Larry Frank	5	0	0	0	1	0	0	0	1,108	0	0	843	2,050
"	Bobby Isaac	26	0	0	0	1	0	2	4	4,932	30	1	4,214	7,935
"	**Total**	31	0	0	0	2	0	2	4	6,040	30	1	5,057	9,985
1964	James Hylton	3	0	0	0	0	0	0	0	47	0	0	72	350
"	Ned Jarrett	55	8	14	7	5	7	5	4	12,693	3,071	27	8,139	68,650
"	Marvin Panch	1	0	0	0	0	0	0	0	3	0	0	7	0
"	Joe Schlesser	2	0	0	0	0	0	0	1	231	0	0	578	1,350
"	**Total**	56	8	14	7	5	7	5	5	12,974	3,071	27	8,796	70,350
1965	Ned Jarrett	53	9	13	12	10	4	2	3	13,326	2,244	29	9,021	93,025
1966	Mario Andretti	1	0	0	0	0	0	0	0	154	0	0	416	580
"	Dick Hutcherson	7	1	2	0	0	1	0	1	1,729	253	4	1,375	9,065
"	Ned Jarrett	9	0	0	0	1	1	1	2	1,933	167	3	2,111	8,825
"	**Total**	15	1	2	0	1	2	1	3	3,816	420	7	3,902	18,470
1967	Dick Hutcherson	32	9	2	9	7	2	1	3	8,403	1,452	20	7,033	84,085
1968	Bobby Allison	8	0	0	0	1	1	0	0	1,479	130	5	2,255	17,435
"	A. J. Foyt	1	0	0	0	0	0	0	0	64	0	0	160	475
"	Bud Moore	7	0	0	1	0	1	0	2	1,492	27	1	1,413	5,360
"	Swede Savage	2	0	0	0	1	0	0	0	841	0	0	592	2,635
"	**Total**	18	0	0	1	2	2	0	2	3,876	157	6	4,419	25,905
Lifetime		205	27	31	29	27	17	11	20	48,435	7,374	89	38,227	$301,820

Newman Long

Year	Driver	Starts	Poles	1	2	3	4	5	6–10	Laps	Laps Led	Races Led	Miles	$
1968	Leonard Brock	3	0	0	0	0	0	0	0	17	0	0	8	175
"	Bill Ervin	4	0	0	0	0	0	0	0	636	0	0	318	600
"	Paul Dean Holt	1	0	0	0	0	0	0	0	52	0	0	26	100
"	**Total**	8	0	0	0	0	0	0	0	705	0	0	352	875
1969	Bill Ervin	1	0	0	0	0	0	0	0	161	0	0	81	100
Lifetime		9	0	0	0	0	0	0	0	866	0	0	433	$975

Sterling Long

Year	Driver	Starts	Poles	1	2	3	4	5	6–10	Laps	Laps Led	Races Led	Miles	$
1949	Sterling Long	2	0	0	0	0	0	0	1		0	0		150
1950	Sterling Long	1	0	0	0	0	0	0	0		0	0		0
Lifetime		3	0	0	0	0	0	0	1		0	0		$150

William Long

Year	Driver	Starts	Poles	1	2	3	4	5	6–10	Laps	Laps Led	Races Led	Miles	$
1957	Lucky Long	1	0	0	0	0	0	0	0	24	0	0	12	0
1960	Dick Smith	1	0	0	0	0	0	0	1	170	0	0	238	550
Lifetime		2	0	0	0	0	0	0	1	194	0	0	250	$550

Fred Lorenzen

Year	Driver	Starts	Poles	1	2	3	4	5	6–10	Laps	Laps Led	Races Led	Miles	$
1956	Fred Lorenzen	7	0	0	0	0	0	0	0	778	0	0	420	235
1960	Fred Lorenzen	9	0	0	0	2	0	1	2	1,898	93	1	2,262	8,886
Lifetime		16	0	0	0	2	0	1	2	2,676	93	1	2,682	$9,121

Year	Driver	Starts	Poles	Finish 1	2	3	4	5	6–10	Laps	Laps Led	Races Led	Miles	$

S. J. Lorenzo

Year	Driver	Starts	Poles	1	2	3	4	5	6–10	Laps	Laps Led	Races Led	Miles	$
1952	Clyde Pittinger	1	0	0	0	0	0	0	0	375	0	0	469	90
Lifetime		1	0	0	0	0	0	0	0	375	0	0	469	$90

Russ Lou

Year	Driver	Starts	Poles	1	2	3	4	5	6–10	Laps	Laps Led	Races Led	Miles	$
1951	Shorty York	5	0	0	1	0	0	0	0	363	0	0	454	725
Lifetime		5	0	0	1	0	0	0	0	363	0	0	454	$725

Ken Love

Year	Driver	Starts	Poles	1	2	3	4	5	6–10	Laps	Laps Led	Races Led	Miles	$
1956	Ken Love	1	0	0	0	0	0	0	0	144	0	0	144	100
1958	Ken Love	3	0	0	0	0	0	0	0	125	0	0	156	135
Lifetime		4	0	0	0	0	0	0	0	269	0	0	300	$235

Mike Lovern

Year	Driver	Starts	Poles	1	2	3	4	5	6–10	Laps	Laps Led	Races Led	Miles	$
1982	Tim Richmond	1	0	0	0	0	0	0	0	112	0	0	114	6,670
Lifetime		1	0	0	0	0	0	0	0	112	0	0	114	$6,670

Fred Lovette

Year	Driver	Starts	Poles	1	2	3	4	5	6–10	Laps	Laps Led	Races Led	Miles	$
1961	Brian Naylor	1	0	0	0	0	0	0	0	1	0	0	3	0
1962	Johnny Allen	12	1	1	0	0	3	0	1	2,529	284	3	1,849	5,175
Lifetime		13	1	1	0	0	3	0	1	2,530	284	3	1,852	$5,175

Rex Lovette

Year	Driver	Starts	Poles	1	2	3	4	5	6–10	Laps	Laps Led	Races Led	Miles	$
1961	Bobby Isaac	1	0	0	0	0	0	0	0	2	0	0	3	50
"	Junior Johnson	40	9	7	2	2	3	1	6	6,949	2,352	20	5,127	28,016
"	Fireball Roberts	4	0	0	0	0	0	1	0	620	51	1	372	745
"	Curtis Turner	1	0	0	0	0	0	0	1	233	3	1	93	130
"	**Total**	41	9	7	2	2	3	2	7	7,804	**2,406**	**20**	5,595	28,941
1962	Johnny Allen	1	0	0	0	0	0	0	0	380	4	1	570	590
"	Junior Johnson	11	1	0	0	2	1	1	0	1,630	150	6	1,089	3,960
"	Fireball Roberts	1	0	0	0	0	0	1	0	163	0	0	82	450
"	**Total**	12	1	0	0	2	1	2	0	2,173	154	7	1,741	5,000
1965	Bobby Isaac	1	1	0	1	0	0	0	0	299	172	1	100	600
"	Junior Johnson	36	10	13	2	1	2	0	1	7,144	3,998	30	5,040	62,216
"	Curtis Turner	2	0	0	0	0	0	0	0	101	0	0	47	250
"	**Total**	37	11	13	3	1	2	0	1	7,544	**4,170**	31	5,187	63,066
1966	Bobby Isaac	1	0	0	1	0	0	0	0	300	11	1	150	850
Lifetime		91	21	20	6	5	6	4	8	17,821	6,741	59	12,673	$97,857

James Lowery

Year	Driver	Starts	Poles	1	2	3	4	5	6–10	Laps	Laps Led	Races Led	Miles	$
1958	Bill Morton	8	0	0	0	0	0	0	0	1,370	0	0	917	1,045
Lifetime		8	0	0	0	0	0	0	0	1,370	0	0	917	$1,045

Roger Lubinski

Year	Driver	Starts	Poles	1	2	3	4	5	6–10	Laps	Laps Led	Races Led	Miles	$
1971	Ron Keselowski	19	0	0	0	0	0	0	6	3,046	0	0	4,248	17,480
"	J. D. McDuffie	1	0	0	0	0	0	0	0	441	0	0	448	1,015
"	Frank Warren	1	0	0	0	0	0	0	0	25	0	0	13	625
"	**Total**	21	0	0	0	0	0	0	6	3,512	0	0	4,709	19,120
1972	Ron Keselowski	22	0	0	0	0	0	1	2	3,398	0	0	4,976	22,175
1973	Ron Keselowski	5	0	0	0	0	0	1	0	733	0	0	1,293	6,060
1974	Jim Hurtubise	1	0	0	0	0	0	0	0	232	0	0	353	1,600
"	Ron Keselowski	4	0	0	0	0	0	0	0	456	0	0	797	5,160
"	**Total**	5	0	0	0	0	0	0	0	688	0	0	1,150	6,760
1975	Jim Vandiver	1	0	0	0	0	0	0	0	3	0	0	8	1,350
Lifetime		54	0	0	0	0	0	2	8	8,334	0	0	12,136	$55,465

Harold Lucas

Year	Driver	Starts	Poles	1	2	3	4	5	6–10	Laps	Laps Led	Races Led	Miles	$
1951	Oda Greene	6	0	0	0	1	0	1	1	173	0	0	173	850
"	Harold Lucas	1	0	0	0	0	0	0	0	0	0	0	0	25
"	**Total**	6	0	0	0	1	0	1	1	173	0	0	173	875
Lifetime		6	0	0	0	1	0	1	1	173	0	0	173	$875

Year	Driver	Starts	Poles	Finish						Laps	Laps Led	Races Led	Miles	$
				1	2	3	4	5	6–10					

Tom Lucas

Year	Driver	Starts	Poles	1	2	3	4	5	6–10	Laps	Laps Led	Races Led	Miles	$
1952	Mooney Williamson	1	0	0	0	0	0	0	0	0	0	0	0	0
Lifetime		1	0	0	0	0	0	0	0	0	0	0	0	$0

Tiny Lund

Year	Driver	Starts	Poles	1	2	3	4	5	6–10	Laps	Laps Led	Races Led	Miles	$
1959	Tiny Lund	18	0	0	2	0	3	0	3	3,374	0	0	1,771	3,941
"	Bunk Moore	2	0	0	0	0	0	0	0	522	0	0	261	150
"	Tom Pistone	1	0	0	0	0	0	0	1	192	0	0	48	175
"	Rex White	1	0	0	0	0	0	0	0	27	0	0	11	50
"	**Total**	22	0	0	2	0	3	0	4	4,115	0	0	2,091	4,316
1960	Tiny Lund	1	0	0	0	0	0	0	0	54	0	0	27	50
"	Bunk Moore	1	0	0	0	0	0	0	0	66	0	0	33	0
"	**Total**	2	0	0	0	0	0	0	0	120	0	0	60	50
1971	Ben Arnold	1	0	0	0	0	0	0	0	33	0	0	50	790
"	Tiny Lund	4	0	0	0	0	0	0	0	754	0	0	1,047	3,130
"	**Total**	5	0	0	0	0	0	0	0	787	0	0	1,097	3,920
Lifetime		29	0	0	2	0	3	0	4	5,022	0	0	3,248	$8,286

Milt Lunda

Year	Driver	Starts	Poles	1	2	3	4	5	6–10	Laps	Laps Led	Races Led	Miles	$
1969	Dave Marcis	36	0	0	0	1	2	0	7	6,919	22	3	6,840	32,243
Lifetime		36	0	0	0	1	2	0	7	6,919	22	3	6,840	$32,243

Leon Lundy

Year	Driver	Starts	Poles	1	2	3	4	5	6–10	Laps	Laps Led	Races Led	Miles	$
1954	Leon Lundy	1	0	0	0	0	0	0	0	192	0	0	192	50
1955	Leon Lundy	1	0	0	0	0	0	0	0	193	0	0	193	150
Lifetime		2	0	0	0	0	0	0	0	385	0	0	385	$200

Frank Luptow

Year	Driver	Starts	Poles	1	2	3	4	5	6–10	Laps	Laps Led	Races Led	Miles	$
1950	Frank Luptow	1	0	0	0	0	0	0	0	43	0	0	179	50
1951	Frank Luptow	4	0	0	0	0	0	1	0	161	0	0	125	250
Lifetime		5	0	0	0	0	0	1	0	204	0	0	305	$300

Norman Lynch

Year	Driver	Starts	Poles	1	2	3	4	5	6–10	Laps	Laps Led	Races Led	Miles	$
1952	Norman Lynch	1	0	0	0	0	0	0	0	130	0	0	130	25
Lifetime		1	0	0	0	0	0	0	0	130	0	0	130	$25

Sandy Lynch

Year	Driver	Starts	Poles	1	2	3	4	5	6–10	Laps	Laps Led	Races Led	Miles	$
1951	Sandy Lynch	2	0	0	0	0	0	0	0	215	0	0	269	25
Lifetime		2	0	0	0	0	0	0	0	215	0	0	269	$25

Clyde Lynn

Year	Driver	Starts	Poles	1	2	3	4	5	6–10	Laps	Laps Led	Races Led	Miles	$
1965	Clyde Lynn	24	0	0	0	0	0	0	9	4,522	0	0	2,067	4,520
"	J. T. Putney	1	0	0	0	0	0	0	0	7	0	0	16	175
"	**Total**	25	0	0	0	0	0	0	9	4,529	0	0	2,083	4,695
1966	Clyde Lynn	38	0	0	1	0	0	0	13	8,527	0	0	5,152	12,132
1967	Clyde Lynn	44	0	0	0	0	2	3	17	9,556	0	0	6,551	17,699
1968	Earl Brooks	5	0	0	0	0	0	0	1	1,321	0	0	917	2,100
"	Bosco Lowe	1	0	0	0	0	0	0	0	38	0	0	19	0
"	Clyde Lynn	48	0	0	0	0	1	1	23	11,778	0	0	8,545	27,801
"	Bill Seifert	1	0	0	0	0	0	0	1	456	0	0	244	400
"	**Total**	48	0	0	0	0	1	1	25	13,593	0	0	9,724	30,301
1969	Clyde Lynn	2	0	0	0	0	0	0	1	648	0	0	345	1,270
1970	Clyde Lynn	1	0	0	0	0	0	0	1	386	0	0	241	625
1971	Elmo Langley	3	0	0	0	0	0	1	1	840	0	0	431	1,840
"	Clyde Lynn	2	0	0	0	0	0	0	0	493	0	0	261	715
"	**Total**	5	0	0	0	0	0	1	1	1,333	0	0	693	2,555
1973	Ed Negre	5	0	0	0	0	0	0	0	1,148	0	0	1,120	4,935
"	Bobby Poole	1	0	0	0	0	0	0	0	2	0	0	1	250
"	**Total**	5	0	0	0	0	0	0	0	1,150	0	0	1,121	5,185
Lifetime		168	0	0	1	0	3	5	67	39,722	0	0	25,910	$74,462

Year	Driver	Starts	Poles	Finish						Laps	Laps Led	Races Led	Miles	$
				1	2	3	4	5	6–10	Laps	Led	Led	Miles	$

Johnny Mackison

Year	Driver	Starts	Poles	1	2	3	4	5	6–10	Laps	Laps Led	Races Led	Miles	$
1957	Johnny Mackison	5	0	0	0	0	0	1	1	769	0	0	693	1,330
1958	Johnny Mackison	3	0	0	0	0	0	0	0	526	0	0	489	290
"	Frank Thompson	1	0	0	0	0	0	0	0	5	0	0	21	0
"	**Total**	4	0	0	0	0	0	0	0	531	0	0	510	290
Lifetime		9	0	0	0	0	0	1	1	1,300	0	0	1,202	$1,620

Dave Mader

Year	Driver	Starts	Poles	1	2	3	4	5	6–10	Laps	Laps Led	Races Led	Miles	$
1961	Dave Mader	3	0	0	0	0	0	0	0	473	0	0	657	555
Lifetime		3	0	0	0	0	0	0	0	473	0	0	657	$555

Jocko Maggiacomo

Year	Driver	Starts	Poles	1	2	3	4	5	6–10	Laps	Laps Led	Races Led	Miles	$
1977	Jocko Maggiacomo	3	0	0	0	0	0	0	0	467	0	0	806	2,080
1978	Jocko Maggiacomo	1	0	0	0	0	0	0	0	45	0	0	113	815
1979	Jocko Maggiacomo	1	0	0	0	0	0	0	0	172	0	0	430	1,105
1980	Jocko Maggiacomo	2	0	0	0	0	0	0	0	280	0	0	283	2,325
1981	Jocko Maggiacomo	1	0	0	0	0	0	0	0	189	0	0	189	540
1982	Jocko Maggiacomo	4	0	0	0	0	0	0	0	411	0	0	546	3,525
Lifetime		12	0	0	0	0	0	0	0	1,564	0	0	2,367	$10,390

Jim Makar

Year	Driver	Starts	Poles	1	2	3	4	5	6–10	Laps	Laps Led	Races Led	Miles	$
1977	Kenny Brightbill	2	0	0	0	0	0	0	0	206	0	0	497	1,950
"	Jody Ridley	1	0	0	0	0	0	0	0	316	0	0	481	2,080
"	Morgan Shepherd	3	0	0	0	0	0	0	1	1,114	0	0	1,433	7,465
"	**Total**	6	0	0	0	0	0	0	1	1,636	0	0	2,411	11,495
1978	Kenny Brightbill	1	0	0	0	0	0	0	0	177	0	0	443	1,130
"	Morgan Shepherd	2	0	0	0	0	0	0	0	397	0	0	604	8,115
"	**Total**	3	0	0	0	0	0	0	0	574	0	0	1,046	9,245
Lifetime		9	0	0	0	0	0	0	1	2,210	0	0	3,457	$20,740

George Mallinger

Year	Driver	Starts	Poles	1	2	3	4	5	6–10	Laps	Laps Led	Races Led	Miles	$
1957	Ed Fiola	2	0	0	0	0	0	0	0	127	0	0	127	75
Lifetime		2	0	0	0	0	0	0	0	127	0	0	127	$75

Nelson Malloch

Year	Driver	Starts	Poles	1	2	3	4	5	6–10	Laps	Laps Led	Races Led	Miles	$
1979	Dick Brooks	27	0	0	0	1	0	0	7	6,307	16	1	7,422	61,985
"	Elmo Langley	1	0	0	0	0	0	0	0	5	0	0	5	600
"	**Total**	28	0	0	0	1	0	0	7	6,312	16	1	7,427	62,585
1980	Dick Brooks	16	0	0	0	0	0	2	1	3,236	6	1	4,066	51,765
"	Ricky Rudd	7	0	0	0	0	0	0	1	1,089	0	0	1,897	18,745
"	Lake Speed	7	0	0	0	0	0	0	2	1,993	0	0	2,301	38,560
"	**Total**	30	0	0	0	0	0	2	4	6,318	6	1	8,264	109,070
1981	Bruce Hill	2	0	0	0	0	0	0	0	329	0	0	554	6,440
1991	Buddy Baker	1	0	0	0	0	0	0	0	35	0	0	88	18,800
Lifetime		61	0	0	0	1	0	2	11	12,994	22	2	16,332	$196,895

Joe Mangini

Year	Driver	Starts	Poles	1	2	3	4	5	6–10	Laps	Laps Led	Races Led	Miles	$
1951	Woody Brown	3	0	0	0	1	0	1	0	14	0	0	7	1,225
1952	Bill Davis	1	0	0	0	0	0	0	1		0	0		75
1954	Woody Brown	4	0	0	0	0	0	0	0	991	0	0	613	175
"	Joe Valente	4	0	0	0	0	0	0	1	1,066	0	0	650	275
"	**Total**	4	0	0	0	0	0	0	1	2,057	0	0	1,263	450
Lifetime		8	0	0	0	1	0	1	2	2,071	0	0	1,270	$1,750

Lou Mangini

Year	Driver	Starts	Poles	1	2	3	4	5	6–10	Laps	Laps Led	Races Led	Miles	$
1951	Robert Caswell	3	0	0	1	0	0	0	0	247	0	0	154	1,300
1954	Robert Caswell	3	0	0	0	0	0	0	1	751	0	0	498	225
1955	Ed Normi	1	0	0	0	0	0	0	0	237	0	0	237	250
Lifetime		7	0	0	1	0	0	0	1	1,235	0	0	889	$1,775

Carl Manis

Year	Driver	Starts	Poles	1	2	3	4	5	6–10	Laps	Laps Led	Races Led	Miles	$
1969	Bill Kimmel	2	0	0	0	0	0	0	0	39	0	0	98	1,100
Lifetime		2	0	0	0	0	0	0	0	39	0	0	98	$1,100

Year	Driver	Starts	Poles	Finish 1	2	3	4	5	6–10	Laps	Laps Led	Races Led	Miles	$

Jesse Mann

Year	Driver	Starts	Poles	1	2	3	4	5	6–10	Laps	Laps Led	Races Led	Miles	$
1953	Roy Bentley	1	0	0	0	0	0	0	0	220	0	0	220	25
Lifetime		1	0	0	0	0	0	0	0	220	0	0	220	$25

Larry Mann

Year	Driver	Starts	Poles	1	2	3	4	5	6–10	Laps	Laps Led	Races Led	Miles	$
1952	Larry Mann	6	0	0	0	0	0	0	0	767	0	0	632	135
Lifetime		6	0	0	0	0	0	0	0	767	0	0	632	$135

Pete Mann

Year	Driver	Starts	Poles	1	2	3	4	5	6–10	Laps	Laps Led	Races Led	Miles	$
1953	Jimmie Lewallen	1	0	0	0	0	0	0	0	340	0	0	468	350
Lifetime		1	0	0	0	0	0	0	0	340	0	0	468	$350

Larry Manning

Year	Driver	Starts	Poles	1	2	3	4	5	6–10	Laps	Laps Led	Races Led	Miles	$
1965	Red Foote	3	0	0	0	0	0	0	0	181	0	0	88	420
"	Larry Manning	10	0	0	0	0	0	0	1	1,683	0	0	1,062	2,465
"	**Total**	13	0	0	0	0	0	0	1	1,864	0	0	1,150	2,885
1967	Larry Manning	1	0	0	0	0	0	0	0	362	0	0	226	300
Lifetime		14	0	0	0	0	0	0	1	2,226	0	0	1,376	$3,185

Johnny Mantz

Year	Driver	Starts	Poles	1	2	3	4	5	6–10	Laps	Laps Led	Races Led	Miles	$
1951	Freddie Farmer	1	0	0	0	0	0	0	1		0	0		100
"	Johnny Mantz	6	0	0	1	1	0	0	2	332	28	1	354	1,975
"	George Seeger	1	0	0	0	0	0	0	0		0	0		50
"	**Total**	8	0	0	1	1	0	0	3	332	28	1	354	2,125
Lifetime		8	0	0	1	1	0	0	3	332	28	1	354	$2,125

Oscar Maples

Year	Driver	Starts	Poles	1	2	3	4	5	6–10	Laps	Laps Led	Races Led	Miles	$
1956	Jim Blomgren	1	0	0	0	0	0	0	0	141	0	0	141	75
"	George Seeger	1	0	0	0	0	0	0	1	78	0	0	195	350
"	**Total**	2	0	0	0	0	0	0	1	219	0	0	336	425
1957	Parnelli Jones	10	1	1	0	0	0	0	2	743	1	1	582	1,625
"	George Seeger	6	0	0	1	3	1	0	0	764	19	1	520	2,740
"	**Total**	10	1	1	1	3	1	0	2	1,507	20	2	1,103	4,365
Lifetime		12	1	1	1	3	1	0	3	1,726	20	2	1,439	$4,790

Dave Marcis

Year	Driver	Starts	Poles	1	2	3	4	5	6–10	Laps	Laps Led	Races Led	Miles	$
1970	Dave Marcis	35	0	0	0	3	0	3	6	6,435	14	1	6,425	35,881
1971	Dave Marcis	23	2	0	1	1	4	1	4	5,382	293	7	5,073	25,170
"	Bill Seifert	1	0	0	0	0	0	0	0	177	0	0	471	1,950
"	**Total**	24	2	0	1	1	4	1	4	5,559	293	7	5,544	27,120
1972	Ray Hendrick	1	0	0	0	0	0	0	0	311	0	0	163	625
"	Dave Marcis	18	0	0	0	2	1	2	2	4,689	4	2	5,102	33,721
"	Roger McCluskey	1	0	0	0	0	0	0	0	241	0	0	362	1,586
"	Ken Rush	1	0	0	0	0	0	0	0	149	0	0	224	1,625
"	Bill Seifert	1	0	0	0	0	0	0	0	3	0	0	6	1,180
"	**Total**	22	0	0	0	2	1	2	2	5,393	4	2	5,856	38,737
1973	Dave Marcis	14	0	0	0	0	1	0	2	3,094	0	0	3,290	16,705
1974	Dave Marcis	26	0	0	0	0	2	4	11	7,880	1	1	8,736	77,740
"	Dick Trickle	2	0	0	0	0	0	0	2	812	0	0	985	7,003
"	**Total**	28	0	0	0	0	2	4	13	8,692	1	1	9,721	84,743
1975	John Martin	1	0	0	0	0	0	0	0	53	0	0	133	850
"	Dick May	1	0	0	0	0	0	0	0	184	0	0	460	1,505
"	Ed Negre	3	0	0	0	0	0	0	0	585	0	0	951	5,120
"	**Total**	5	0	0	0	0	0	0	0	822	0	0	1,543	7,475
1977	Dave Marcis	2	0	0	0	0	0	0	0	755	2	1	400	5,640
1979	Dave Marcis	25	0	0	0	0	0	1	5	6,842	20	4	7,634	56,434
1980	Dave Marcis	31	0	0	0	1	2	1	10	9,012	94	14	9,790	150,165
1981	Dave Marcis	31	1	0	0	2	1	1	5	8,004	178	15	9,255	162,213
1982	Dave Marcis	30	1	1	0	0	0	0	12	8,370	56	10	9,642	249,027
1983	Dave Marcis	30	0	0	0	0	0	0	7	7,771	24	6	9,171	306,355
1984	Mike Alexander	18	0	0	0	0	0	0	1	4,469	0	0	5,227	83,865
"	Lennie Pond	7	0	0	0	0	0	0	2	2,609	0	0	2,237	31,610
"	**Total**	25	0	0	0	0	0	0	3	7,078	0	0	7,463	115,475

Year	Driver	Starts	Poles	Finish						Laps	Laps Led	Races Led	Miles	$
				1	2	3	4	5	6–10					

Dave Marcis *continued*

Year	Driver	Starts	Poles	1	2	3	4	5	6–10	Laps	Laps Led	Races Led	Miles	$
1985	Dave Marcis	28	0	0	0	0	0	0	5	7,319	30	4	8,729	173,467
1986	Dave Marcis	28	0	0	0	0	0	1	3	6,921	63	11	7,928	210,636
1987	Dave Marcis	29	0	0	0	2	0	0	5	6,880	84	9	8,749	256,354
1988	Dave Marcis	29	0	0	0	0	0	0	2	8,178	62	7	9,545	212,485
1989	Dave Marcis	27	0	0	0	0	0	0	1	7,866	16	5	9,984	196,161
1990	Dave Marcis	28	0	0	0	0	0	0	0	8,766	8	4	10,261	234,154
1991	Dave Marcis	26	0	0	0	0	0	0	1	6,792	3	3	8,686	212,710
1992	Dave Marcis	22	0	0	0	0	0	0	0	4,662	0	0	6,780	174,985
"	Jim Sauter	7	0	0	0	0	0	0	0	2,604	0	0	2,081	43,265
"	**Total**	29	0	0	0	0	0	0	0	7,266	0	0	8,862	218,250
1993	Dave Marcis	23	0	0	0	0	0	0	0	6,233	14	3	7,818	202,305
1994	Dave Marcis	23	0	0	0	0	0	0	1	5,914	17	4	7,762	261,650
1995	Dave Marcis	28	0	0	0	0	0	0	0	7,319	3	2	9,225	337,853
1996	Dave Marcis	27	0	0	0	0	0	0	0	7,202	20	8	8,698	435,177
"	Jim Sauter	0												3,472
"	**Total**	27	0	0	0	0	0	0	0	7,202	20	8	8,698	438,649
Lifetime		627	3	1	2	11	11	14	87	164,483	1,006	121	191,980	$4,210,644
		9th								**10th**		**8th**		

John Marcum

Year	Driver	Starts	Poles	1	2	3	4	5	6–10	Laps	Laps Led	Races Led	Miles	$
1951	Mike Klapak	1	0	0	0	0	0	0	1	0	0	0	0	100
"	Dick Linder	1	0	0	0	0	0	0	0	0	0	0	0	50
"	**Total**	2	0	0	0	0	0	0	1	0	0	0	0	150
Lifetime		2	0	0	0	0	0	0	1	0	0	0	0	$150

Wally Marks

Year	Driver	Starts	Poles	1	2	3	4	5	6–10	Laps	Laps Led	Races Led	Miles	$
1949	Wally Campbell	1	0	0	0	0	0	0	0	166	0	0	166	25
1950	Wally Campbell	2	1	0	0	0	0	0	0	309	0	0	386	175
1951	Red Byron	1	0	0	0	0	0	0	0		0	0		50
"	Wally Campbell	5	0	0	0	0	0	0	0	21	0	0	11	85
"	Jack Smith	1	0	0	0	0	0	0	0	323	0	0	404	50
"	**Total**	7	0	0	0	0	0	0	0	344	0	0	414	185
Lifetime		10	1	0	0	0	0	0	0	819	0	0	967	$385

Jack Marlin

Year	Driver	Starts	Poles	1	2	3	4	5	6–10	Laps	Laps Led	Races Led	Miles	$
1968	Jack Marlin	1	0	0	0	0	0	0	1	237	0	0	119	300
Lifetime		1	0	0	0	0	0	0	1	237	0	0	119	$300

Gene Marmor

Year	Driver	Starts	Poles	1	2	3	4	5	6–10	Laps	Laps Led	Races Led	Miles	$
1960	Gene Marmor	1	0	0	0	0	0	0	0	184	0	0	460	200
Lifetime		1	0	0	0	0	0	0	0	184	0	0	460	$200

Gene Marquardt

Year	Driver	Starts	Poles	1	2	3	4	5	6–10	Laps	Laps Led	Races Led	Miles	$
1975	Dick Bown	1	0	0	0	0	0	0	0	17	0	0	45	775
Lifetime		1	0	0	0	0	0	0	0	17	0	0	45	$775

Terry Marra

Year	Driver	Starts	Poles	1	2	3	4	5	6–10	Laps	Laps Led	Races Led	Miles	$
1983	Bob Senneker	5	0	0	0	0	0	0	0	1,317	0	0	2,186	11,335
Lifetime		5	0	0	0	0	0	0	0	1,317	0	0	2,186	$11,335

Ken Marriott

Year	Driver	Starts	Poles	1	2	3	4	5	6–10	Laps	Laps Led	Races Led	Miles	$
1950	Ken Marriott	1	0	0	0	0	0	0	0		0	0		0
1959	Ken Marriott	1	0	0	0	0	0	0	0	1	0	0	3	100
Lifetime		2	0	0	0	0	0	0	0	1	0	0	3	$100

John Marsh

Year	Driver	Starts	Poles	1	2	3	4	5	6–10	Laps	Laps Led	Races Led	Miles	$
1965	Jesse Samples Jr.	1	0	0	0	0	0	0	0	198	0	0	297	495
Lifetime		1	0	0	0	0	0	0	0	198	0	0	297	$495

Year	Driver	Starts	Poles	Finish 1	2	3	4	5	6–10	Laps	Laps Led	Races Led	Miles	$

Sam Marshall

Year	Driver	Starts	Poles	1	2	3	4	5	6–10	Laps	Laps Led	Races Led	Miles	$
1949	Sam Marshall	1	0	0	0	0	0	0	0		0	0		0
Lifetime		1	0	0	0	0	0	0	0		0	0		$0

Otis Martin

Year	Driver	Starts	Poles	1	2	3	4	5	6–10	Laps	Laps Led	Races Led	Miles	$
1952	Otis Martin	4	0	0	0	0	0	0	1	483	0	0	474	225
1953	Otis Martin	7	0	0	0	0	0	0	2	519	0	0	608	585
1954	Otis Martin	3	0	0	0	0	0	0	0	414	0	0	637	225
Lifetime		14	0	0	0	0	0	0	3	1,416	0	0	1,720	$1,035

Walter Martinson

Year	Driver	Starts	Poles	1	2	3	4	5	6–10	Laps	Laps Led	Races Led	Miles	$
1952	Bud Kohler	1	0	0	0	0	0	0	0	140	0	0	140	25
Lifetime		1	0	0	0	0	0	0	0	140	0	0	140	$25

Fil Martocci

Year	Driver	Starts	Poles	1	2	3	4	5	6–10	Laps	Laps Led	Races Led	Miles	$
1993	Jeff Burton	1	0	0	0	0	0	0	0	86	0	0	91	9,550
1994	Kenny Wallace	1	0	0	0	0	0	0	0	198	0	0	396	9,825
1995	Kenny Wallace	11	0	0	0	0	0	0	0	3,127	0	0	4,070	151,700
1996	Kenny Wallace	30	0	0	0	0	0	0	2	8,415	7	2	9,896	457,665
Lifetime		43	0	0	0	0	0	0	2	11,826	7	2	14,454	$628,740

Hammer Mason

Year	Driver	Starts	Poles	1	2	3	4	5	6–10	Laps	Laps Led	Races Led	Miles	$
1972	Dave Marcis	1	0	0	0	0	0	0	0	90	0	0	180	735
Lifetime		1	0	0	0	0	0	0	0	90	0	0	180	$735

James Mason

Year	Driver	Starts	Poles	1	2	3	4	5	6–10	Laps	Laps Led	Races Led	Miles	$
1971	Jackie Oliver	1	0	0	0	0	0	0	0	117	0	0	234	605
"	Cale Yarborough	1	0	0	0	0	0	0	0	209	0	0	314	1,054
"	**Total**	2	0	0	0	0	0	0	0	326	0	0	548	1,659
Lifetime		2	0	0	0	0	0	0	0	326	0	0	548	$1,659

John Masoni

Year	Driver	Starts	Poles	1	2	3	4	5	6–10	Laps	Laps Led	Races Led	Miles	$
1960	Junior Johnson	28	1	3	2	4	1	3	4	4,636	320	7	3,568	38,410
1961	Junior Johnson	1	1	0	1	0	0	0	0	67	12	1	101	525
"	Marvin Panch	2	1	0	0	0	0	0	2	546	44	1	792	4,085
"	Jim Paschal	2	0	0	1	0	0	0	0	69	0	0	173	800
"	David Pearson	7	1	3	0	1	0	0	0	1,548	247	5	2,179	47,790
"	**Total**	12	3	3	2	1	0	0	2	2,230	303	7	3,244	53,200
Lifetime		40	4	6	4	5	1	3	6	6,866	623	14	6,811	$91,610

Banjo Matthews

Year	Driver	Starts	Poles	1	2	3	4	5	6–10	Laps	Laps Led	Races Led	Miles	$
1957	Banjo Matthews	4	0	0	0	1	0	0	0	713	56	1	404	755
1959	Banjo Matthews	3	0	0	0	0	0	0	0	517	55	1	414	1,990
1960	Banjo Matthews	12	0	0	0	0	0	0	4	1,894	9	1	2,815	15,617
"	Speedy Thompson	2	0	0	0	0	0	0	1	67	0	0	168	350
"	**Total**	13	0	0	0	0	0	0	5	1,961	9	1	2,983	15,967
1961	Banjo Matthews	13	0	0	0	0	1	0	2	1,817	197	6	2,884	5,510
1962	Banjo Matthews	5	2	0	1	0	0	0	1	532	145	3	1,098	11,375
"	Fireball Roberts	7	2	1	1	0	2	0	1	2,022	450	6	1,875	18,475
"	**Total**	9	4	1	2	0	2	0	2	2,554	595	8	2,973	29,850
1963	Fireball Roberts	5	2	0	1	0	1	0	1	826	30	3	1,575	12,240
1964	A. J. Foyt	4	0	0	0	0	1	0	0	564	2	1	1,194	2,550
"	Junior Johnson	17	4	2	1	4	0	0	1	4,006	1,098	12	2,323	17,935
"	**Total**	21	4	2	1	4	1	0	1	4,570	1,100	13	3,517	20,485
1965	Cale Yarborough	8	0	0	2	0	0	0	0	1,800	142	5	1,798	12,385
1966	A. J. Foyt	1	0	0	0	0	0	0	0	12	0	0	18	580
"	Ned Jarrett	1	0	0	0	1	0	0	0	496	0	0	496	4,700
"	Cale Yarborough	6	0	0	2	0	0	0	2	1,348	210	2	1,954	23,025
"	**Total**	8	0	0	2	1	0	0	2	1,856	210	2	2,468	28,305
1967	A. J. Foyt	7	0	0	1	0	1	0	0	1,060	57	5	1,534	8,035
"	Bosco Lowe	2	0	0	0	0	0	0	1	333	0	0	143	340
"	**Total**	9	0	0	1	0	1	0	1	1,393	57	5	1,678	8,375

Year	Driver	Starts	Poles	1	2	3	4	5	6–10	Laps	Laps Led	Races Led	Miles	$

Banjo Matthews *continued*

Year	Driver	Starts	Poles	1	2	3	4	5	6–10	Laps	Laps Led	Races Led	Miles	$
1968	Donnie Allison	12	1	1	1	3	0	0	3	3,781	284	6	3,987	49,815
"	A. J. Foyt	2	0	0	0	0	0	0	0	183	0	0	458	2,900
"	Bosco Lowe	1	0	0	0	0	0	0	0	220	0	0	117	225
"	**Total**	15	1	1	1	3	0	0	3	4,184	284	6	4,561	52,940
1969	Donnie Allison	16	2	1	2	4	1	2	1	3,893	400	10	5,106	78,055
"	Pete Hamilton	1	0	0	0	0	0	1	0	329	0	0	494	3,225
"	Swede Savage	1	0	0	0	0	0	0	1	485	0	0	243	875
"	**Total**	18	2	1	2	4	1	3	2	4,707	400	10	5,842	82,155
1970	Donnie Allison	18	0	3	0	1	3	2	2	4,853	692	9	5,424	94,106
"	Cale Yarborough	1	0	0	0	0	0	0	0	250	0	0	342	1,200
"	LeeRoy Yarbrough	1	1	0	0	0	0	0	0	102	52	1	54	700
"	**Total**	20	1	3	0	1	3	2	2	5,205	744	10	5,819	96,006
1971	Donnie Allison	2	0	0	0	0	0	0	1	220	11	2	550	1,750
"	A. J. Foyt	2	0	0	0	0	0	0	0	323	0	0	417	1,569
"	**Total**	4	0	0	0	0	0	0	1	543	11	2	967	3,319
1972	Bobby Isaac	2	0	0	0	0	0	0	0	291	12	2	404	1,839
1973	A. J. Foyt	3	0	0	0	0	1	0	0	467	0	0	943	8,555
1974	A. J. Foyt	2	0	0	0	0	0	1	0	243	6	1	608	9,205
"	Bobby Isaac	2	0	0	1	0	0	0	1	697	2	1	761	10,855
"	**Total**	3	0	0	1	0	0	1	1	940	8	2	1,368	20,060
Lifetime		158	14	8	13	14	11	6	23	34,344	3,910	77	40,599	$400,736

Billy Matthews

Year	Driver	Starts	Poles	1	2	3	4	5	6–10	Laps	Laps Led	Races Led	Miles	$
1980	Dick Brooks	3	0	0	0	0	0	0	2	742	0	0	1,040	8,935
1981	Dick Brooks	3	0	0	0	0	0	0	0	695	1	1	1,188	11,670
1982	Sterling Marlin	1	0	0	0	0	0	0	0	256	0	0	384	3,615
"	Joe Millikan	1	0	0	0	0	0	0	0	277	0	0	282	1,020
"	**Total**	2	0	0	0	0	0	0	0	533	0	0	666	4,635
1983	Lennie Pond	2	0	0	0	0	0	0	1	501	0	0	518	3,985
1984	Dick Trickle	1	0	0	0	0	0	0	0	53	0	0	133	7,500
1985	Dick Trickle	2	0	0	0	0	0	0	0	253	0	0	380	2,800
1986	Dick Trickle	2	0	0	0	0	0	0	0	676	0	0	975	19,175
Lifetime		15	0	0	0	0	0	0	3	3,453	1	1	4,899	$58,700

Gary Matthews

Year	Driver	Starts	Poles	1	2	3	4	5	6–10	Laps	Laps Led	Races Led	Miles	$
1974	Gary Matthews	1	0	0	0	0	0	0	0	37	0	0	97	725
1975	Gary Matthews	2	0	0	0	0	0	0	1	298	0	0	781	3,795
Lifetime		3	0	0	0	0	0	0	1	335	0	0	878	$4,520

Van Matthews

Year	Driver	Starts	Poles	1	2	3	4	5	6–10	Laps	Laps Led	Races Led	Miles	$
1955	Boyce Hildreth	1	0	0	0	0	0	0	0	41	0	0	21	50
Lifetime		1	0	0	0	0	0	0	0	41	0	0	21	$50

Nace Mattingly

Year	Driver	Starts	Poles	1	2	3	4	5	6–10	Laps	Laps Led	Races Led	Miles	$
1955	Nace Mattingly	3	0	0	0	0	0	1	0	696	0	0	653	700
1956	Nace Mattingly	3	0	0	0	0	0	1	0	311	0	0	219	410
1957	Nace Mattingly	4	0	0	0	0	0	0	0	658	0	0	614	400
1958	Thomas Aiken	1	0	0	0	0	0	0	0	93	0	0	93	110
"	Nace Mattingly	4	0	0	0	0	0	0	1	325	0	0	145	285
"	**Total**	5	0	0	0	0	0	0	1	418	0	0	238	395
1960	Nace Mattingly	2	0	0	0	0	0	0	1	361	0	0	181	285
Lifetime		17	0	0	0	0	0	2	2	2,444	0	0	1,906	$2,190

Bobby Mausgrover

Year	Driver	Starts	Poles	1	2	3	4	5	6–10	Laps	Laps Led	Races Led	Miles	$
1972	Bobby Mausgrover	4	0	0	0	0	0	0	0	321	0	0	665	3,555
1973	Bobby Mausgrover	2	0	0	0	0	0	0	0	611	0	0	888	2,035
Lifetime		6	0	0	0	0	0	0	0	932	0	0	1,553	$5,590

Joe May

Year	Driver	Starts	Poles	1	2	3	4	5	6–10	Laps	Laps Led	Races Led	Miles	$
1980	Bob Riley	1	0	0	0	0	0	0	0	55	0	0	55	460

Year	Driver	Starts	Poles	Finish						Laps	Laps Led	Races Led	Miles	$
				1	2	3	4	5	6–10					

Joe May *continued*

Year	Driver	Starts	Poles	1	2	3	4	5	6–10	Laps	Laps Led	Races Led	Miles	$
1981	Bob Riley	3	0	0	0	0	0	0	0	139	0	0	265	1,975
Lifetime		4	0	0	0	0	0	0	0	194	0	0	320	$2,435

Carl Mays

Year	Driver	Starts	Poles	1	2	3	4	5	6–10	Laps	Laps Led	Races Led	Miles	$
1952	June Cleveland	5	0	0	0	0	1	0	1	655	0	0	517	510
"	Buddy Shuman	1	0	0	0	0	0	0	0	72	0	0	72	25
"	**Total**	6	0	0	0	0	1	0	1	727	0	0	589	535
Lifetime		6	0	0	0	0	1	0	1	727	0	0	589	$535

Harold Mays

Year	Driver	Starts	Poles	1	2	3	4	5	6–10	Laps	Laps Led	Races Led	Miles	$
1950	Weldon Adams	3	0	0	0	1	0	1	0	560	0	0	555	950
1951	Weldon Adams	8	0	0	0	0	0	0	2	142	0	0	107	375
"	Wade Fields	4	0	0	0	0	0	0	0		0	0		100
"	**Total**	10	0	0	0	0	0	0	2	142	0	0	107	475
1952	Lucky Mays	1	0	0	0	0	0	0	0	1	0	0	1	60
1965	Harold Kite	1	0	0	0	0	0	0	0	1	0	0	2	410
1966	Joel Davis	11	0	0	0	0	1	0	2	1,750	0	0	1,109	2,685
1967	Johnny Allen	2	0	0	0	0	0	0	0	137	0	0	170	1,565
"	Blackie Watt	1	0	0	0	0	0	0	0	283	0	0	425	845
"	Eldon Yarbrough	1	0	0	0	0	0	0	0	46	0	0	69	580
"	**Total**	4	0	0	0	0	0	0	0	466	0	0	664	2,990
Lifetime		30	0	0	0	1	1	1	4	2,920	0	0	2,437	$7,570

Lloyd McBee

Year	Driver	Starts	Poles	1	2	3	4	5	6–10	Laps	Laps Led	Races Led	Miles	$
1977	Paul Dean Holt	1	0	0	0	0	0	0	0	47	0	0	28	275
Lifetime		1	0	0	0	0	0	0	0	47	0	0	28	$275

Harold McCann

Year	Driver	Starts	Poles	1	2	3	4	5	6–10	Laps	Laps Led	Races Led	Miles	$
1961	Buzz McCann	1	0	0	0	0	0	0	0	1	0	0	3	0
Lifetime		1	0	0	0	0	0	0	0	1	0	0	3	$0

Buck McCardell

Year	Driver	Starts	Poles	1	2	3	4	5	6–10	Laps	Laps Led	Races Led	Miles	$
1952	Buck McCardell	2	0	0	0	0	0	0	0	49	0	0	49	35
Lifetime		2	0	0	0	0	0	0	0	49	0	0	49	$35

John McCarthy

Year	Driver	Starts	Poles	1	2	3	4	5	6–10	Laps	Laps Led	Races Led	Miles	$
1966	Johnny Wynn	21	0	0	0	0	0	0	5	3,245	0	0	2,224	4,650
1971	Charlie Glotzbach	4	0	0	0	0	0	0	3	796	0	0	728	3,780
Lifetime		25	0	0	0	0	0	0	8	4,041	0	0	2,952	$8,430

Jimmy McClain

Year	Driver	Starts	Poles	1	2	3	4	5	6–10	Laps	Laps Led	Races Led	Miles	$
1971	Jim Hurtubise	3	0	0	0	0	0	0	1	290	0	0	682	4,100
"	Pedro Rodriguez	1	0	0	0	0	0	0	0	18	0	0	45	1,175
"	Bill Ward	2	0	0	0	0	0	0	0	281	0	0	747	2,865
"	**Total**	6	0	0	0	0	0	0	1	589	0	0	1,474	8,140
Lifetime		6	0	0	0	0	0	0	1	589	0	0	1,474	$8,140

Al McCline

Year	Driver	Starts	Poles	1	2	3	4	5	6–10	Laps	Laps Led	Races Led	Miles	$
1964	Joe Clark	5	0	0	0	0	0	0	0	246	0	0	138	1,750
Lifetime		5	0	0	0	0	0	0	0	246	0	0	138	$1,750

Michael McCluney

Year	Driver	Starts	Poles	1	2	3	4	5	6–10	Laps	Laps Led	Races Led	Miles	$
1978	Steve Pfeifer	1	0	0	0	0	0	0	0	98	0	0	245	955
1979	Steve Pfeifer	1	0	0	0	0	0	0	0	8	0	0	21	625
Lifetime		2	0	0	0	0	0	0	0	106	0	0	266	$1,580

Lanty McClung

Year	Driver	Starts	Poles	1	2	3	4	5	6–10	Laps	Laps Led	Races Led	Miles	$
1965	Darel Dieringer	5	0	0	0	1	0	0	1	1,155	0	0	525	1,070

Year	Driver	Starts	Poles	Finish 1	2	3	4	5	6–10	Laps	Laps Led	Races Led	Miles	$

Lanty McClung *continued*

Year	Driver	Starts	Poles	1	2	3	4	5	6–10	Laps	Laps Led	Races Led	Miles	$
"	Bub Strickler	8	0	0	0	0	0	0	2	1,488	0	0	1,699	4,375
"	**Total**	13	0	0	0	1	0	0	3	2,643	0	0	2,224	5,445
Lifetime		13	0	0	0	1	0	0	3	2,643	0	0	2,224	$5,445

A. L. McClure

Year	Driver	Starts	Poles	1	2	3	4	5	6–10	Laps	Laps Led	Races Led	Miles	$
1960	Don Noel	3	0	0	0	0	0	1	0	240	0	0	309	725
Lifetime		3	0	0	0	0	0	1	0	240	0	0	309	$725

Alfred McClure

Year	Driver	Starts	Poles	1	2	3	4	5	6–10	Laps	Laps Led	Races Led	Miles	$
1977	Dick May	4	0	0	0	0	0	0	0	1,329	0	0	1,917	8,340
1978	Dick May	5	0	0	0	0	0	0	1	1,201	0	0	2,174	18,055
1979	Ron Hutcherson	1	0	0	0	0	0	0	0	0	0	0	0	1,165
"	Dick May	2	0	0	0	0	0	0	0	425	0	0	741	5,160
"	**Total**	3	0	0	0	0	0	0	0	425	0	0	741	6,325
1980	Janet Guthrie	1	0	0	0	0	0	0	0	134	0	0	335	1,140
"	Dick May	0	0	0	0	0	0	0	0	425	0	0	741	1,040
"	**Total**	3	0	0	0	0	0	0	0	425	0	0	741	2,180
Lifetime		13	0	0	0	0	0	0	1	3,089	0	0	5,166	$34,900

Jeff McClure

Year	Driver	Starts	Poles	1	2	3	4	5	6–10	Laps	Laps Led	Races Led	Miles	$
1992	Jeff McClure	1	0	0	0	0	0	0	0	173	0	0	346	5,990
Lifetime		1	0	0	0	0	0	0	0	173	0	0	346	$5,990

Larry McClure

Year	Driver	Starts	Poles	1	2	3	4	5	6–10	Laps	Laps Led	Races Led	Miles	$
1983	Mark Martin	6	0	0	0	0	0	0	1	1,313	0	0	2,466	17,040
"	Connie Saylor	1	0	0	0	0	0	0	0	22	0	0	59	1,985
"	**Total**	7	0	0	0	0	0	0	1	1,335	0	0	2,524	19,025
1984	Tommy Ellis	20	0	0	0	0	0	0	1	5,010	1	1	5,356	44,315
"	Lennie Pond	4	0	0	0	0	0	0	0	972	0	0	1,101	21,590
"	Joe Ruttman	3	0	0	0	0	0	0	1	394	1	1	645	5,525
"	**Total**	27	0	0	0	0	0	0	2	6,376	2	2	7,101	71,430
1985	Joe Ruttman	16	0	0	0	0	0	1	3	3,378	5	1	4,599	81,425
1986	Lake Speed	1	0	0	0	0	0	0	0	397	6	1	596	6,400
"	Rick Wilson	17	0	0	0	0	0	0	4	3,265	7	1	5,309	88,820
"	**Total**	18	0	0	0	0	0	0	4	3,662	13	2	5,904	95,220
1987	A. J. Foyt	1	0	0	0	0	0	0	0	10	0	0	25	7,870
"	Rick Wilson	19	0	0	0	0	0	0	1	3,530	20	1	5,575	65,935
"	**Total**	19	0	0	0	0	0	0	1	3,540	20	1	5,600	73,805
1988	Rick Wilson	28	1	0	1	0	1	0	3	6,870	152	4	8,703	209,925
1989	Rick Wilson	29	0	0	0	0	1	1	5	8,004	29	5	9,990	312,402
1990	Ernie Irvan	26	3	1	2	1	1	1	7	8,008	280	10	9,221	497,675
"	Phil Parsons	3	0	0	0	0	0	0	0	881	0	0	862	39,350
"	**Total**	29	3	1	2	1	1	1	7	8,889	280	10	10,084	537,025
1991	Ernie Irvan	29	1	2	3	0	4	2	8	8,720	584	16	10,465	1,079,017
1992	Ernie Irvan	29	3	3	2	1	2	1	2	8,561	477	17	10,279	996,885
1993	Jimmy Hensley	2	0	0	0	0	0	0	0	550	0	0	711	31,895
"	Ernie Irvan	21	2	1	3	2	0	1	1	5,066	226	12	6,931	628,485
"	Joe Nemechek	2	0	0	0	0	0	0	0	811	0	0	982	32,280
"	Jeff Purvis	5	0	0	0	0	0	0	0	2,113	3	2	1,761	81,370
"	**Total**	30	2	1	3	2	0	1	1	8,540	229	14	10,385	774,030
1994	Sterling Marlin	31	1	1	1	1	0	2	6	9,184	144	11	10,841	1,140,683
1995	Sterling Marlin	31	1	3	2	0	3	1	13	9,728	472	12	11,936	2,253,502
1996	Sterling Marlin	31	0	2	0	1	1	1	5	8,877	331	10	10,582	1,588,425
Lifetime		354	12	13	14	6	13	11	61	95,664	2,738	105	118,993	$8,965,699
														10th

John McConnell

Year	Driver	Starts	Poles	1	2	3	4	5	6–10	Laps	Laps Led	Races Led	Miles	$
1970	Tiny Lund	5	0	0	0	0	2	0	0	819	7	2	1,540	11,365
1971	Tiny Lund	5	0	0	1	0	0	0	2	918	8	2	1,199	6,310
Lifetime		10	0	0	1	0	2	0	2	1,737	15	4	2,738	$17,675

Johnny McCoy

Year	Driver	Starts	Poles	1	2	3	4	5	6–10	Laps	Laps Led	Races Led	Miles	$
1956	Ray Thompson	1	0	0	0	0	0	0	0		0	0		50
Lifetime		1	0	0	0	0	0	0	0		0	0		$50

Year	Driver	Starts	Poles	1	2	3	4	5	6–10	Laps	Laps Led	Races Led	Miles	$

Rick McCray

Year	Driver	Starts	Poles	1	2	3	4	5	6–10	Laps	Laps Led	Races Led	Miles	$
1978	Rick McCray	3	0	0	0	0	0	0	0	220	0	0	575	4,585
1979	Rick McCray	1	0	0	0	0	0	0	0	31	0	0	81	750
1980	Rick McCray	3	0	0	0	0	0	0	0	238	0	0	601	3,415
1981	Rick McCray	1	0	0	0	0	0	0	0	66	0	0	173	1,655
1982	Rick McCray	2	0	0	0	0	0	0	0	151	0	0	396	3,355
1983	Rick McCray	4	0	0	0	0	0	0	0	760	0	0	629	3,710
1984	Rick McCray	1	0	0	0	0	0	0	0	45	0	0	118	1,045
1985	Rick McCray	2	0	0	0	0	0	0	0	47	0	0	123	1,665
1986	Rick McCray	1	0	0	0	0	0	0	0	33	0	0	86	850
1987	Rick McCray	1	0	0	0	0	0	0	0	63	0	0	165	3,100
1988	Rick McCray	1	0	0	0	0	0	0	0	46	0	0	121	1,140
1989	Rick McCray	1	0	0	0	0	0	0	0	72	0	0	181	3,200
Lifetime		21	0	0	0	0	0	0	0	1,772	0	0	3,249	$28,470

Dave McCredy

Year	Driver	Starts	Poles	1	2	3	4	5	6–10	Laps	Laps Led	Races Led	Miles	$
1962	Bill Wimble	2	0	0	0	0	0	0	0	231	0	0	578	675
Lifetime		2	0	0	0	0	0	0	0	231	0	0	578	$675

Sam McCuthen

Year	Driver	Starts	Poles	1	2	3	4	5	6–10	Laps	Laps Led	Races Led	Miles	$
1955	Bill Widenhouse	5	0	0	0	0	0	1	2	799	2	1	780	1,065
1956	Ray Hendrick	1	0	0	0	0	0	0	0	14	0	0	7	50
"	Phillip Jones	1	0	0	0	0	0	0	0	70	0	0	35	0
"	Jimmie Lewallen	1	0	0	0	0	0	0	0	93	0	0	58	0
"	Doug Yates	1	0	0	0	0	0	0	0	32	0	0	16	100
"	**Total**	4	0	0	0	0	0	0	0	209	0	0	116	150
Lifetime		9	0	0	0	0	0	1	2	1,008	2	1	897	$1,215

Bob McDonald

Year	Driver	Starts	Poles	1	2	3	4	5	6–10	Laps	Laps Led	Races Led	Miles	$
1965	Dick Gulstrand	1	0	0	0	0	0	0	0	151	0	0	408	615
Lifetime		1	0	0	0	0	0	0	0	151	0	0	408	$615

J. L. McDonald

Year	Driver	Starts	Poles	1	2	3	4	5	6–10	Laps	Laps Led	Races Led	Miles	$
1950	Alton Haddock	1	0	0	0	0	0	0	0	41	0	0	171	25
Lifetime		1	0	0	0	0	0	0	0	41	0	0	171	$25

Roy McDonald

Year	Driver	Starts	Poles	1	2	3	4	5	6–10	Laps	Laps Led	Races Led	Miles	$
1960	Burrhead Nantz	3	0	0	0	0	0	0	0	66	0	0	133	300
"	Bob Roberts	1	0	0	0	0	0	0	0	10	0	0	5	50
"	Roy Tyner	4	0	0	0	0	0	0	0	389	0	0	416	475
"	**Total**	8	0	0	0	0	0	0	0	465	0	0	554	825
Lifetime		8	0	0	0	0	0	0	0	465	0	0	554	$825

J. D. McDuffie

Year	Driver	Starts	Poles	1	2	3	4	5	6–10	Laps	Laps Led	Races Led	Miles	$
1963	Larry Manning	1	0	0	0	0	0	0	0	11	0	0	15	500
"	J. D. McDuffie	12	0	0	0	0	0	0	3	1,918	0	0	765	1,620
"	**Total**	13	0	0	0	0	0	0	3	1,929	0	0	781	2,120
1966	J. D. McDuffie	36	0	0	0	0	0	1	8	7,166	0	0	4,255	8,545
1967	J. D. McDuffie	1	0	0	0	0	0	0	0	137	0	0	69	150
1968	J. D. McDuffie	32	0	0	0	0	0	0	9	5,587	0	0	3,020	8,355
1969	J. D. McDuffie	45	0	0	0	0	0	0	12	9,156	0	0	6,898	27,156
1970	Rodney Bruce	1	0	0	0	0	0	0	0	261	0	0	103	225
"	J. D. McDuffie	35	0	0	0	0	0	1	9	8,431	0	0	6,241	24,150
"	Tom Usry	1	0	0	0	0	0	0	0	226	0	0	82	255
"	**Total**	35	0	0	0	0	0	1	9	8,918	0	0	6,426	24,630
1971	J. D. McDuffie	40	0	0	0	1	0	1	6	8,724	5	1	8,386	32,801
1972	J. D. McDuffie	24	0	0	0	0	0	0	1	5,444	0	0	6,410	33,743
1973	J. D. McDuffie	27	0	0	0	0	0	3	7	7,388	11	2	8,129	56,140
1974	J. D. McDuffie	30	0	0	0	0	0	0	7	8,283	1	1	9,518	59,535
1975	Henley Gray	2	0	0	0	0	0	0	0	682	0	0	648	2,990
"	Dick May	1	0	0	0	0	0	0	0	66	0	0	36	855
"	Glenn McDuffie	1	0	0	0	0	0	0	0	431	0	0	438	1,130
"	J. D. McDuffie	26	0	0	0	0	0	1	5	5,832	0	0	7,054	50,937
"	**Total**	29	0	0	0	0	0	1	5	7,011	0	0	8,177	55,912
1976	Larry Esau	1	0	0	0	0	0	0	0	169	0	0	443	1,745

Year	Driver	Starts	Poles	Finish						Laps	Laps Led	Races Led	Miles	$
				1	2	3	4	5	6–10					

J. D. McDuffie *continued*

Year	Driver	Starts	Poles	1	2	3	4	5	6–10	Laps	Laps Led	Races Led	Miles	$
"	Glenn McDuffie	1	0	0	0	0	0	0	0	205	0	0	208	730
"	J. D. McDuffie	29	0	0	0	0	0	1	7	7,565	0	0	9,268	81,505
"	**Total**	29	0	0	0	0	0	1	7	7,939	0	0	9,920	83,980
1977	J. D. McDuffie	30	0	0	0	0	0	0	4	8,252	1	1	9,688	85,227
1978	J. D. McDuffie	30	1	0	0	0	0	1	5	7,300	15	4	8,715	86,857
1979	J. D. McDuffie	31	0	0	0	0	0	1	6	8,014	116	3	9,634	113,478
1980	J. D. McDuffie	29	0	0	0	0	0	0	3	5,749	0	0	6,814	75,312
"	Jeff McDuffie	3	0	0	0	0	0	0	0	1,138	0	0	869	2,725
"	**Total**	29	0	0	0	0	0	0	3	6,887	0	0	7,683	78,037
1981	J. D. McDuffie	28	0	0	0	0	0	0	1	7,110	8	2	8,871	105,499
1982	J. D. McDuffie	28	0	0	0	0	0	0	1	6,162	0	0	7,338	106,549
"	Jeff McDuffie	1	0	0	0	0	0	0	0	377	0	0	236	1,005
"	**Total**	28	0	0	0	0	0	0	1	6,539	0	0	7,574	107,554
1983	J. D. McDuffie	24	0	0	0	0	0	0	0	5,713	0	0	6,255	74,095
1984	J. D. McDuffie	16	0	0	0	0	0	0	0	4,064	0	0	3,422	54,170
1985	J. D. McDuffie	22	0	0	0	0	0	0	0	4,464	0	0	5,328	81,400
"	Jeff McDuffie	1	0	0	0	0	0	0	0	445	0	0	445	1,875
"	**Total**	22	0	0	0	0	0	0	0	4,909	0	0	5,773	83,275
1986	J. D. McDuffie	8	0	0	0	0	0	0	0	2,227	0	0	2,315	51,600
1987	Charlie Baker	1	0	0	0	0	0	0	0	147	0	0	224	1,350
"	J. D. McDuffie	13	0	0	0	0	0	0	0	2,389	0	0	2,865	26,615
"	**Total**	14	0	0	0	0	0	0	0	2,536	0	0	3,089	27,965
1988	J. D. McDuffie	2	0	0	0	0	0	0	0	516	1	1	573	3,750
1989	J. D. McDuffie	7	0	0	0	0	0	0	0	1,381	0	0	1,847	27,745
1990	Dave Marcis	1	0	0	0	0	0	0	0	140	0	0	350	8,570
"	J. D. McDuffie	8	0	0	0	0	0	0	0	1,301	0	0	1,657	27,570
"	**Total**	9	0	0	0	0	0	0	0	1,441	0	0	2,007	36,140
1991	J. D. McDuffie	5	0	0	0	0	0	0	0	732	0	0	1,142	20,495
Lifetime		624	1	0	0	1	0	10	94	145,303	158	15	150,576	$1,348,954
		10th												

Paul McDuffie

Year	Driver	Starts	Poles	1	2	3	4	5	6–10	Laps	Laps Led	Races Led	Miles	$
1960	Joe Lee Johnson	7	0	1	0	0	1	1	0	1,404	48	1	1,231	29,708
Lifetime		7	0	1	0	0	1	1	0	1,404	48	1	1,231	$29,708

Robert McEntyre

Year	Driver	Starts	Poles	1	2	3	4	5	6–10	Laps	Laps Led	Races Led	Miles	$
1983	Jody Ridley	10	0	0	0	0	0	0	3	1,963	0	0	3,494	45,710
1984	Jody Ridley	14	0	0	0	0	0	0	3	2,891	4	2	4,810	64,135
Lifetime		24	0	0	0	0	0	0	6	4,854	4	2	8,304	$109,845

John McFadden

Year	Driver	Starts	Poles	1	2	3	4	5	6–10	Laps	Laps Led	Races Led	Miles	$
1983	John McFadden	3	0	0	0	0	0	0	0	289	0	0	181	2,260
1989	John McFadden	2	0	0	0	0	0	0	0	213	0	0	291	5,279
Lifetime		5	0	0	0	0	0	0	0	502	0	0	472	$7,539

Charlie McGee

Year	Driver	Starts	Poles	1	2	3	4	5	6–10	Laps	Laps Led	Races Led	Miles	$
1971	David Sisco	4	0	0	0	0	0	0	0	853	0	0	1,019	3,625
1972	David Sisco	12	0	0	0	0	0	0	2	2,067	0	0	3,269	14,490
"	Jabe Thomas	1	0	0	0	0	0	0	0	94	0	0	141	814
"	**Total**	13	0	0	0	0	0	0	2	2,161	0	0	3,410	15,304
1973	David Sisco	23	0	0	0	0	1	1	4	6,552	12	2	7,140	36,205
Lifetime		40	0	0	0	0	1	1	6	9,566	12	2	11,569	$55,134

John McGinley

Year	Driver	Starts	Poles	1	2	3	4	5	6–10	Laps	Laps Led	Races Led	Miles	$
1954	John McGinley	3	0	0	0	0	0	0	1	399	0	0	200	275
1955	John McGinley	1	0	0	0	0	0	0	0	157	0	0	79	60
Lifetime		4	0	0	0	0	0	0	1	556	0	0	278	$335

Robert McGrath

Year	Driver	Starts	Poles	1	2	3	4	5	6–10	Laps	Laps Led	Races Led	Miles	$
1952	Bill Holland	1	0	0	0	0	0	0	0	123	0	0	123	25
Lifetime		1	0	0	0	0	0	0	0	123	0	0	123	$25

Year	Driver	Starts	Poles	Finish 1	2	3	4	5	6–10	Laps	Laps Led	Races Led	Miles	$

Hershel McGriff

Year	Driver	Starts	Poles	1	2	3	4	5	6–10	Laps	Laps Led	Races Led	Miles	$
1950	Hershel McGriff	1	0	0	0	0	0	0	1	374	0	0	468	500
1951	Hershel McGriff	2	0	0	0	0	0	0	0	73	0	0	73	25
1953	Hershel McGriff	2	0	0	0	0	0	0	0	274	101	1	274	125
1976	Hershel McGriff	1	0	0	0	0	0	0	0	108	0	0	270	865
1977	Hershel McGriff	2	0	0	0	0	0	0	1	120	0	0	314	3,240
1978	Hershel McGriff	1	0	0	0	0	0	0	0	90	0	0	236	1,640
Lifetime		9	0	0	0	0	0	0	2	1,039	101	1	1,635	$6,395

R. B. McIntosh

Year	Driver	Starts	Poles	1	2	3	4	5	6–10	Laps	Laps Led	Races Led	Miles	$
1949	Bill Blair	3	0	0	0	0	0	1	1	40	145	1	166	425
"	Bill Harrison	1	0	0	0	0	0	0	0		0			25
"	Jim Roper	1	0	1	0	0	0	0	0	197	47	1	148	2,000
"	**Total**	3	0	1	0	0	0	1	1	237	**192**	1	314	2,450
1950	Bill Harrison	2	0	0	0	0	0	0	0	38	0	0	29	0
Lifetime		5	0	1	0	0	0	1	1	275	192	1	342	$2,450

Stewart McKinney

Year	Driver	Starts	Poles	1	2	3	4	5	6–10	Laps	Laps Led	Races Led	Miles	$
1963	Larry Frank	2	0	0	0	0	0	0	0	573	0	0	610	750
"	Tommy Irwin	6	0	0	0	1	0	0	3	1,330	0	0	1,046	2,415
"	Fred Lorenzen	3	0	0	0	0	0	0	1	431	0	0	167	380
"	Tiny Lund	1	0	0	0	0	0	0	0	384	0	0	576	1,150
"	**Total**	12	0	0	0	1	0	0	4	2,718	0	0	2,399	4,695
Lifetime		12	0	0	0	1	0	0	4	2,718	0	0	2,399	$4,695

Sumner McKnight

Year	Driver	Starts	Poles	1	2	3	4	5	6–10	Laps	Laps Led	Races Led	Miles	$
1977	Sumner McKnight	1	0	0	0	0	0	0	0	15	0	0	39	650
1983	Sumner McKnight	2	0	0	0	0	0	0	0	204	0	0	534	5,275
1984	Sumner McKnight	2	0	0	0	0	0	0	0	192	0	0	503	5,140
1985	Sumner McKnight	1	0	0	0	0	0	0	0	91	0	0	238	3,985
Lifetime		6	0	0	0	0	0	0	0	502	0	0	1,315	$15,050

Jim McLain

Year	Driver	Starts	Poles	1	2	3	4	5	6–10	Laps	Laps Led	Races Led	Miles	$
1955	Jim McLain	1	0	0	0	0	0	0	0	82	0	0	123	50
Lifetime		1	0	0	0	0	0	0	0	82	0	0	123	$50

Sam McMahon

Year	Driver	Starts	Poles	1	2	3	4	5	6–10	Laps	Laps Led	Races Led	Miles	$
1991	Mickey Gibbs	15	0	0	0	0	0	0	0	4,078	0	0	5,308	98,260
"	Jimmy Hensley	4	0	0	0	0	0	0	1	1,708	0	0	1,491	32,125
"	Dorsey Schroeder	1	0	0	0	0	0	0	0	90	3	1	219	6,840
"	Dick Trickle	6	0	0	0	0	0	0	1	1,574	0	0	2,106	41,655
"	Kenny Wallace	3	0	0	0	0	0	0	0	668	0	0	748	11,425
"	**Total**	29	0	0	0	0	0	0	2	8,118	3	1	9,871	190,305
Lifetime		29	0	0	0	0	0	0	2	8,118	3	1	9,871	$190,305

Allen McMillion

Year	Driver	Starts	Poles	1	2	3	4	5	6–10	Laps	Laps Led	Races Led	Miles	$
1962	Bunkie Blackburn	2	0	0	0	0	1	0	0	519	0	0	779	2,775
"	Worth McMillion	4	0	0	0	0	0	0	0	1,105	0	0	517	675
"	LeeRoy Yarbrough	1	0	0	0	0	0	0	0	259	0	0	356	400
"	**Total**	7	0	0	0	0	1	0	0	1,883	0	0	1,652	3,850
1963	Worth McMillion	15	0	0	0	0	0	0	4	4,177	0	0	2,412	3,145
"	Joe Weatherly	1	0	0	0	0	0	0	0	48	0	0	18	380
"	**Total**	16	0	0	0	0	0	0	4	4,225	0	0	2,430	3,525
1964	Worth McMillion	18	0	0	0	0	0	0	6	4,681	0	0	2,756	4,710
1965	Earl Brooks	1	0	0	0	0	0	0	0	0	0	0	0	100
"	Allen McMillion	1	0	0	0	0	0	0	0	236	0	0	79	110
"	Worth McMillion	10	0	0	0	0	0	0	2	2,290	0	0	1,289	2,120
"	G. T. Nolan	8	0	0	0	0	0	0	1	1,018	0	0	563	1,165
"	**Total**	19	0	0	0	0	0	0	3	3,544	0	0	1,930	3,495
1966	Allen McMillion	1	0	0	0	0	0	0	0	250	0	0	125	150
"	Worth McMillion	9	0	0	0	0	0	0	3	2,311	0	0	1,282	2,440
"	G. T. Nolan	3	0	0	0	0	0	0	0	486	0	0	199	305
"	**Total**	9	0	0	0	0	0	0	3	3,047	0	0	1,606	2,895
1967	Worth McMillion	2	0	0	0	0	0	0	2	497	0	0	249	775

Year	Driver	Starts	Poles	Finish						Laps	Laps Led	Races Led	Miles	$
				1	2	3	4	5	6–10					

Allen McMillion *continued*

Year	Driver	Starts	Poles	1	2	3	4	5	6–10	Laps	Laps Led	Races Led	Miles	$
"	G. T. Nolan	1	0	0	0	0	0	0	0	144	0	0	130	100
"	**Total**	3	0	0	0	0	0	0	2	641	0	0	378	875
1968	Worth McMillion	3	0	0	0	0	0	1	0	772	0	0	474	875
"	G. T. Nolan	1	0	0	0	0	0	0	0	123	0	0	62	110
"	**Total**	4	0	0	0	0	0	1	0	895	0	0	535	985
Lifetime		76	0	0	0	0	1	1	18	18,916	0	0	11,287	$20,335

Ralph McNabb

Year	Driver	Starts	Poles	1	2	3	4	5	6–10	Laps	Laps Led	Races Led	Miles	$
1971	Richard Brown	8	0	0	0	0	0	0	2	1,675	0	0	2,258	7,830
"	Bill Chevalier	1	0	0	0	0	0	0	1	188	0	0	282	620
"	Junior Fields	1	0	0	0	0	0	0	0	31	0	0	31	570
"	Charlie Glotzbach	2	0	0	0	0	0	0	0	42	0	0	36	1,045
"	Pete Hamilton	2	0	0	0	0	0	0	0	118	5	1	37	200
"	J. D. McDuffie	1	0	0	0	0	0	0	0	2	0	0	3	645
"	Ed Negre	4	0	0	0	0	0	0	1	1,004	0	0	788	2,708
"	Speedy Thompson	1	0	0	0	0	0	0	0	376	0	0	564	1,800
"	**Total**	20	0	0	0	0	0	0	4	3,436	5	1	3,998	15,418
1972	Richard Brown	15	0	0	0	0	0	1	0	3,355	0	0	4,118	19,570
1974	Marv Acton	1	0	0	0	0	0	0	0	66	0	0	41	365
Lifetime		36	0	0	0	0	0	1	4	6,857	5	1	8,157	$35,353

Jim McNeil

Year	Driver	Starts	Poles	1	2	3	4	5	6–10	Laps	Laps Led	Races Led	Miles	$
1960	Clyde Mitchell	1	0	0	0	0	0	0	1	88	0	0	88	140
"	John Potter	1	0	0	0	0	0	0	0	47	0	0	47	50
"	**Total**	2	0	0	0	0	0	0	1	135	0	0	135	190
Lifetime		2	0	0	0	0	0	0	1	135	0	0	135	$190

Sam McQuagg

Year	Driver	Starts	Poles	1	2	3	4	5	6–10	Laps	Laps Led	Races Led	Miles	$
1962	Sam McQuagg	1	0	0	0	0	0	0	0	51	0	0	26	120
Lifetime		1	0	0	0	0	0	0	0	51	0	0	26	$120

E. A. McQuaig

Year	Driver	Starts	Poles	1	2	3	4	5	6–10	Laps	Laps Led	Races Led	Miles	$
1963	Charley Griffith	1	0	0	0	0	0	0	0	182	0	0	91	60
"	Fred Thompson	1	0	0	0	0	0	0	1	186	0	0	93	175
"	Bob Welborn	2	0	0	0	0	0	0	0	282	0	0	446	675
"	LeeRoy Yarbrough	5	0	0	0	0	0	0	2	947	0	0	1,457	2,940
"	**Total**	9	0	0	0	0	0	0	3	1,597	0	0	2,087	3,850
1964	LeeRoy Yarbrough	1	0	0	0	0	0	0	0	23	0	0	12	50
Lifetime		10	0	0	0	0	0	0	3	1,620	0	0	2,098	$3,900

John McVitty

Year	Driver	Starts	Poles	1	2	3	4	5	6–10	Laps	Laps Led	Races Led	Miles	$
1955	John McVitty	7	0	0	0	0	0	0	2	951	0	0	559	550
1956	John McVitty	4	0	0	0	0	0	0	1	431	0	0	228	250
Lifetime		11	0	0	0	0	0	0	3	1,382	0	0	787	$800

Charles Meacham

Year	Driver	Starts	Poles	1	2	3	4	5	6–10	Laps	Laps Led	Races Led	Miles	$
1990	Bill Meacham	1	0	0	0	0	0	0	0	87	0	0	65	2,425
1991	Bill Meacham	2	0	0	0	0	0	0	0	146	0	0	159	6,535
Lifetime		3	0	0	0	0	0	0	0	233	0	0	225	$8,960

Jimmy Means

Year	Driver	Starts	Poles	1	2	3	4	5	6–10	Laps	Laps Led	Races Led	Miles	$
1978	Jimmy Means	26	0	0	0	0	0	0	2	6,932	0	0	7,590	60,040
1979	Jimmy Means	26	0	0	0	0	0	0	1	5,430	0	0	6,315	54,705
1980	Jimmy Means	27	0	0	0	0	0	0	0	7,649	0	0	8,872	104,778
1981	Charlie Chamblee	1	0	0	0	0	0	0	0	10	0	0	6	830
"	Cecil Gordon	1	0	0	0	0	0	0	0	8	0	0	5	550
"	Jimmy Means	29	0	0	0	0	0	0	2	8,320	0	0	8,903	101,878
"	Baxter Price	1	0	0	0	0	0	0	0	1	0	0	2	900
"	**Total**	29	0	0	0	0	0	0	2	8,339	0	0	8,916	104,158
1982	Jimmy Means	30	0	0	0	0	0	0	2	8,837	2	1	10,273	154,160
1983	Jimmy Means	28	0	0	0	0	0	0	3	8,269	2	1	8,974	132,915

Year	Driver	Starts	Poles	Finish						Laps	Laps Led	Races Led	Miles	$
				1	2	3	4	5	6–10					

Jimmy Means *continued*

Year	Driver	Starts	Poles	1	2	3	4	5	6–10	Laps	Laps Led	Races Led	Miles	$
"	Lennie Pond	1	0	0	0	0	0	0	0	193	0	0	386	4,155
"	**Total**	29	0	0	0	0	0	0	3	8,462	2	1	9,360	137,070
1984	Dale Jarrett	1	0	0	0	0	0	0	0	155	0	0	388	4,955
"	Sterling Marlin	1	0	0	0	0	0	0	0	116	0	0	69	2,800
"	Jimmy Means	22	0	0	0	0	0	0	0	7,044	0	0	7,482	105,105
"	Morgan Shepherd	1	0	0	0	0	0	0	0	105	0	0	279	4,655
"	Roy Smith	1	0	0	0	0	0	0	0	70	0	0	183	2,475
"	Bobby Wawak	1	0	0	0	0	0	0	0	180	0	0	450	4,025
"	**Total**	27	0	0	0	0	0	0	0	7,670	0	0	8,851	124,015
1985	Jimmy Means	28	0	0	0	0	0	0	0	6,774	0	0	7,512	132,140
1986	Jimmy Means	26	0	0	0	0	0	0	0	6,472	5	3	8,102	157,940
1987	Jimmy Means	27	0	0	0	0	0	0	1	6,319	21	1	7,252	148,095
1988	Jimmy Means	26	0	0	0	0	0	0	0	4,778	12	4	6,343	135,640
1989	Mickey Gibbs	1	0	0	0	0	0	0	0	76	0	0	190	9,940
"	Jimmy Means	22	0	0	0	0	0	0	0	4,868	4	1	6,288	65,005
"	**Total**	23	0	0	0	0	0	0	0	4,944	4	1	6,478	74,945
1990	Jimmy Means	27	0	0	0	0	0	0	0	7,419	0	0	8,650	135,165
1991	Bobby Hillin Jr.	2	0	0	0	0	0	0	0	564	0	0	675	8,650
"	Jimmy Means	20	0	0	0	0	0	0	0	4,425	3	3	6,580	111,210
"	Mike Wallace	2	0	0	0	0	0	0	0	315	0	0	351	7,000
"	**Total**	24	0	0	0	0	0	0	0	5,304	3	3	7,606	126,860
1992	Scott Gaylord	1	0	0	0	0	0	0	0	124	0	0	124	4,265
"	Tommy Kendall	1	0	0	0	0	0	0	0	74	0	0	186	6,755
"	John McFadden	5	0	0	0	0	0	0	0	37	0	0	53	21,810
"	Jimmy Means	22	0	0	0	0	0	0	0	4,370	0	0	5,165	133,160
"	Scott Sharp	1	0	0	0	0	0	0	0	51	0	0	125	7,155
"	Graham Taylor	2	0	0	0	0	0	0	0	17	0	0	17	8,595
"	Brad Teague	1	0	0	0	0	0	0	0	456	0	0	243	7,080
"	**Total**	26	0	0	0	0	0	0	0	5,129	0	0	5,913	188,820
1993	Scott Gaylord	1	0	0	0	0	0	0	0	75	0	0	184	5,935
"	Jimmy Hensley	3	0	0	0	0	0	0	0	680	0	0	657	35,410
"	Jimmy Means	18	0	0	0	0	0	0	0	4,765	2	2	5,644	148,205
"	Mike Potter	1	0	0	0	0	0	0	0	4	0	0	5	5,440
"	Mike Skinner	1	0	0	0	0	0	0	0	145	0	0	198	5,180
"	Graham Taylor	1	0	0	0	0	0	0	0	3	0	0	8	6,210
"	Mike Wallace	1	0	0	0	0	0	0	0	323	0	0	485	4,745
"	**Total**	23	0	0	0	0	0	0	0	5,995	2	2	7,180	211,125
1994	Gary Bradberry	1	0	0	0	0	0	0	0	276	0	0	420	6,600
"	Bob Keselowski	1	0	0	0	0	0	0	0	17	0	0	43	7,150
"	Kirk Shelmerdine	1	0	0	0	0	0	0	0	179	0	0	476	11,265
"	Mike Skinner	1	0	0	0	0	0	0	0	469	0	0	477	9,550
"	Brad Teague	8	0	0	0	0	0	0	0	1,959	0	0	2,094	62,790
"	**Total**	12	0	0	0	0	0	0	0	2,900	0	0	3,510	97,355
1995	Gary Bradberry	0												2,500
"	Randy Macdonald	0												2,400
"	**Total**	0												4,900
Lifetime		436	0	0	0	0	0	0	11	109,353	51	16	128,723	$2,152,211

Bill Meazel

Year	Driver	Starts	Poles	1	2	3	4	5	6–10	Laps	Laps Led	Races Led	Miles	$
1979	Bill Meazel	1	0	0	0	0	0	0	0	46	0	0	92	1,000
Lifetime		1	0	0	0	0	0	0	0	46	0	0	92	$1,000

Chuck Meekins

Year	Driver	Starts	Poles	1	2	3	4	5	6–10	Laps	Laps Led	Races Led	Miles	$
1951	Chuck Meekins	4	0	0	1	0	0	0	0	200	0	0	100	675
Lifetime		4	0	0	1	0	0	0	0	200	0	0	100	$675

Doug Meeks

Year	Driver	Starts	Poles	1	2	3	4	5	6–10	Laps	Laps Led	Races Led	Miles	$
1952	Donald Thomas	11	0	0	0	0	1	1	5	874	0	0	587	1,285
1953	Earl Moss	1	0	0	0	0	0	0	0	190	0	0	190	25
"	Donald Thomas	9	0	0	0	0	0	0	0	32	0	0	16	225
"	**Total**	10	0	0	0	0	0	0	0	222	0	0	206	250
Lifetime		21	0	0	0	0	1	1	5	1,096	0	0	793	$1,535

Jack Meeks

Year	Driver	Starts	Poles	1	2	3	4	5	6–10	Laps	Laps Led	Races Led	Miles	$
1961	Tim Flock	1	0	0	0	0	0	0	0	184	0	0	460	200

Year	Driver	Starts	Poles	Finish 1	2	3	4	5	6–10	Laps	Laps Led	Races Led	Miles	$

Jack Meeks *continued*

Year	Driver	Starts	Poles	1	2	3	4	5	6–10	Laps	Laps Led	Races Led	Miles	$
"	Bob Pronger	1	0	0	0	0	0	0	0	37	0	0	93	85
"	Sal Tovella	1	0	0	0	0	0	0	0	31	0	0	47	250
"	**Total**	3	0	0	0	0	0	0	0	252	0	0	599	535
Lifetime		3	0	0	0	0	0	0	0	252	0	0	599	$535

Ken Meisenhelder

Year	Driver	Starts	Poles	1	2	3	4	5	6–10	Laps	Laps Led	Races Led	Miles	$
1969	Ken Meisenhelder	16	0	0	0	0	0	0	0	1,832	0	0	1,305	5,630
1970	Ken Meisenhelder	18	0	0	0	0	0	0	2	2,569	0	0	1,448	6,030
1971	Ken Meisenhelder	14	0	0	0	0	0	0	1	2,150	0	0	1,522	5,170
Lifetime		48	0	0	0	0	0	0	3	6,551	0	0	4,275	$16,830

Harry Melling

Year	Driver	Starts	Poles	1	2	3	4	5	6–10	Laps	Laps Led	Races Led	Miles	$
1982	Bill Elliott	21	1	0	3	3	1	1	1	5,540	151	9	7,886	201,030
1983	Bill Elliott	30	0	1	4	1	3	3	10	9,536	173	15	11,272	514,030
1984	Bill Elliott	30	4	3	1	4	4	1	11	9,848	570	17	11,385	680,344
1985	Bill Elliott	28	11	11	2	0	2	1	2	8,724	**1,920**	19	10,727	2,433,187
1986	Bill Elliott	29	4	2	0	2	1	3	8	8,549	511	15	10,591	1,049,142
1987	Bill Elliott	29	8	6	3	1	5	1	4	8,902	1,399	22	10,422	1,599,210
1988	Bill Elliott	29	6	6	2	2	4	1	7	9,647	1,598	20	11,521	1,554,639
1989	Bill Elliott	29	2	3	0	1	3	1	6	9,037	380	11	10,834	849,370
1990	Bill Elliott	29	2	1	4	1	5	1	4	9,349	1,182	13	11,087	1,090,730
1991	Bill Elliott	29	2	1	2	1	0	2	6	9,030	211	6	10,826	705,605
1992	Chad Little	13	0	0	0	0	0	0	1	3,262	0	0	4,799	79,995
"	Dave Mader III	5	0	0	0	0	0	0	0	1,387	7	1	1,389	69,635
"	Phil Parsons	2	0	0	0	0	0	0	1	567	0	0	872	58,475
"	Dorsey Schroeder	1	0	0	0	0	0	0	0	176	0	0	268	10,385
"	**Total**	21	0	0	0	0	0	0	2	5,392	7	1	7,327	218,490
1993	P. J. Jones	6	0	0	0	0	0	0	1	710	0	0	1,447	53,370
"	Chad Little	2	0	0	0	0	0	0	0	461	0	0	890	34,865
"	Greg Sacks	1	0	0	0	0	0	0	0	320	0	0	487	10,305
"	**Total**	9	0	0	0	0	0	0	1	1,491	0	0	2,824	98,540
1994	Rich Bickle	10	0	0	0	0	0	0	0	1,837	0	0	3,260	100,845
"	P. J. Jones	0												10,000
"	Phil Parsons	3	0	0	0	0	0	0	0	757	0	0	922	21,415
"	Joe Ruttman	1	0	0	0	0	0	0	0	199	0	0	498	34,005
"	**Total**	14	0	0	0	0	0	0	0	2,793	0	0	4,679	166,265
1995	Lake Speed	31	0	0	0	0	0	0	2	9,073	17	1	11,196	529,435
1996	Lake Speed	31	0	0	0	0	0	0	2	8,493	10	3	10,027	817,175
Lifetime		389	40	34	21	16	28	15	66	115,404	8,129	152	142,602	$12,507,192
			9th											**9th**

Johnny Mello

Year	Driver	Starts	Poles	1	2	3	4	5	6–10	Laps	Laps Led	Races Led	Miles	$
1960	Johnny Mello	1	0	0	0	0	0	0	0	22	0	0	31	0
"	Art Watts	1	0	0	0	0	0	0	1	168	0	0	235	525
"	**Total**	1	0	0	0	0	0	0	1	190	0	0	266	525
Lifetime		1	0	0	0	0	0	0	1	190	0	0	266	$525

Major Melton

Year	Driver	Starts	Poles	1	2	3	4	5	6–10	Laps	Laps Led	Races Led	Miles	$
1963	Nace Mattingly	1	0	0	0	0	0	0	1	288	0	0	108	240
"	Major Melton	17	0	0	0	0	0	0	0	2,780	0	0	1,287	1,910
"	Joe Weatherly	1	0	0	0	0	0	0	0	98	0	0	49	330
"	**Total**	19	0	0	0	0	0	0	1	3,166	0	0	1,444	2,480
Lifetime		19	0	0	0	0	0	0	1	3,166	0	0	1,444	$2,480

Jack Mercer

Year	Driver	Starts	Poles	1	2	3	4	5	6–10	Laps	Laps Led	Races Led	Miles	$
1969	Ben Arnold	1	0	0	0	0	0	0	0	135	0	0	359	1,375
1972	Les Covey	7	0	0	0	0	0	0	0	1,347	0	0	1,540	4,865
Lifetime		8	0	0	0	0	0	0	0	1,482	0	0	1,899	$6,240

Joe Merola

Year	Driver	Starts	Poles	1	2	3	4	5	6–10	Laps	Laps Led	Races Led	Miles	$
1951	Joe Merola	4	0	0	0	0	0	0	1	472	0	0	522	175
Lifetime		4	0	0	0	0	0	0	1	472	0	0	522	$175

Year	Driver	Starts	Poles	Finish						Laps	Laps Led	Races Led	Miles	$
				1	2	3	4	5	6–10					

Dick Meyer

1953	Dick Meyer	1	0	0	0	0	1	0	0	355	0	0	488	1,000
Lifetime		1	0	0	0	0	1	0	0	355	0	0	488	$1,000

William Meyer

1957	Peck Peckham	9	0	0	0	0	0	0	0	880	0	0	626	825
Lifetime		9	0	0	0	0	0	0	0	880	0	0	626	$825

Dick Midgley

1974	Hershel McGriff	1	0	0	0	0	0	0	0	1	0	0	3	750
"	Ross Surgenor	2	0	0	0	0	0	0	0	134	0	0	351	2,095
"	**Total**	2	0	0	0	0	0	0	0	135	0	0	354	2,845
1975	Hershel McGriff	2	0	0	0	0	0	0	1	279	0	0	731	3,170
1976	Roy Smith	3	0	0	0	0	0	0	0	225	0	0	569	4,285
1977	Elliott Forbes-Robinson	2	0	0	0	0	0	0	0	527	0	0	606	1,550
"	Roy Smith	3	0	0	0	0	0	0	0	205	0	0	532	5,365
"	**Total**	5	0	0	0	0	0	0	0	732	0	0	1,138	6,915
1978	Roy Smith	1	0	0	0	0	0	0	1	115	0	0	301	2,300
1980	Hershel McGriff	1	0	0	0	0	0	0	0	67	0	0	176	825
1986	George Follmer	2	0	0	0	0	0	0	0	130	0	0	324	3,885
1987	George Follmer	2	0	0	0	0	0	0	0	122	8	1	320	2,880
1989	Terry Fisher	1	0	0	0	0	0	0	0	72	0	0	181	2,825
"	Roy Smith	1	0	0	0	0	0	0	0	40	0	0	40	4,445
"	**Total**	2	0	0	0	0	0	0	0	112	0	0	221	7,270
1990	Terry Fisher	1	0	0	0	0	0	0	0	74	0	0	186	4,575
1991	R. K. Smith	1	0	0	0	0	0	0	0	2	0	0	5	3,475
1992	R. K. Smith	1	0	0	0	0	0	0	0	70	0	0	176	4,880
1993	Terry Fisher	1	0	0	0	0	0	0	0	132	0	0	132	6,040
1995	Terry Fisher	1	0	0	0	0	0	0	0	57	0	0	144	9,760
Lifetime		25	0	0	0	0	0	0	2	2,252	8	1	4,777	$63,105

Joe Mihalic

1977	Joe Mihalic	8	0	0	0	0	0	0	0	1,550	0	0	2,137	8,275
Lifetime		8	0	0	0	0	0	0	0	1,550	0	0	2,137	$8,275

Jim Miles

1996	Randy Baker	1	0	0	0	0	0	0	0	51	0	0	78	12,550
Lifetime		1	0	0	0	0	0	0	0	51	0	0	78	$12,550

Vel Miletich

1956	Parnelli Jones	3	0	0	1	0	0	0	0	591	0	0	564	1,705
1958	Parnelli Jones	3	2	1	0	0	0	0	0	587	148	2	954	1,010
1959	Eddie Gray	2	0	1	0	0	0	0	0	317	1	1	187	870
"	Parnelli Jones	2	0	1	0	0	0	0	0	560	1	1	268	1,905
"	**Total**	2	0	2	0	0	0	0	0	877	2	2	455	2,775
1960	Parnelli Jones	3	0	0	0	0	0	0	1	204	25	1	371	465
"	Marvin Porter	3	0	1	0	0	0	0	0	223	61	2	295	2,100
"	Joe Weatherly	1	0	0	1	0	0	0	0	179	0	0	251	1,250
"	**Total**	5	0	1	1	0	0	0	1	606	86	2	916	3,815
1963	Marvin Porter	2	0	0	0	0	0	0	1	202	0	0	545	1,100
1964	Marvin Porter	1	0	0	0	0	0	0	1	179	0	0	483	1,150
Lifetime		16	2	4	2	0	0	0	2	3,042	236	6	3,917	$11,555

Les Milfield

1955	Lloyd Dane	1	0	0	0	0	0	0	1	242	0	0	242	250
Lifetime		1	0	0	0	0	0	0	1	242	0	0	242	$250

A. L. Miller

1951	Tommy Thompson	1	0	0	0	0	0	0	0	148	0	0	185	0
Lifetime		1	0	0	0	0	0	0	0	148	0	0	185	$0

Year	Driver	Starts	Poles	Finish 1	2	3	4	5	6–10	Laps	Laps Led	Races Led	Miles	$

Carl Miller

Year	Driver	Starts	Poles	1	2	3	4	5	6–10	Laps	Laps Led	Races Led	Miles	$
1969	Paul Connors	1	0	0	0	0	0	0	0	31	0	0	78	635
"	Billy Taylor	2	0	0	0	0	0	0	0	65	0	0	163	1,140
"	**Total**	3	0	0	0	0	0	0	0	96	0	0	240	1,775
Lifetime		3	0	0	0	0	0	0	0	96	0	0	240	$1,775

Garland Miller

Year	Driver	Starts	Poles	1	2	3	4	5	6–10	Laps	Laps Led	Races Led	Miles	$
1967	Neil Castles	3	0	0	0	0	0	0	1	518	0	0	464	1,050
"	Max Ledbetter	2	0	0	0	0	0	0	1	760	0	0	420	800
"	Roy Mayne	1	0	0	0	0	0	0	0	217	3	1	87	120
"	**Total**	6	0	0	0	0	0	0	2	1,495	3	1	970	1,970
Lifetime		6	0	0	0	0	0	0	2	1,495	3	1	970	$1,970

George Miller

Year	Driver	Starts	Poles	1	2	3	4	5	6–10	Laps	Laps Led	Races Led	Miles	$
1953	Al Keller	4	0	0	0	0	0	0	0	73	0	0	37	115
"	Steve McGrath	2	0	0	0	0	0	0	0	0	0	0	0	50
"	**Total**	6	0	0	0	0	0	0	0	73	0	0	37	165
1954	Junior Johnson	1	0	0	0	0	0	1	0	194	0	0	97	300
"	Al Keller	12	1	1	2	0	2	0	3	1,761	350	4	1,272	4,135
"	Jimmie Lewallen	1	0	0	0	0	0	0	0	153	0	0	230	200
"	Ralph Liguori	2	0	0	0	0	0	0	2	389	0	0	195	350
"	**Total**	16	1	1	2	0	2	1	5	2,497	350	4	1,793	4,985
1955	Jack Choquette	4	0	0	1	0	0	0	0	469	0	0	371	825
Lifetime		26	1	1	3	0	2	1	5	3,039	350	4	2,201	$5,975

Harold Miller

Year	Driver	Starts	Poles	1	2	3	4	5	6–10	Laps	Laps Led	Races Led	Miles	$
1975	Harold Miller	5	0	0	0	0	0	0	0	455	0	0	980	4,520
"	Ed Negre	1	0	0	0	0	0	0	0	128	0	0	175	1,290
"	**Total**	6	0	0	0	0	0	0	0	583	0	0	1,155	5,810
1976	Bob Burcham	4	0	0	0	0	0	0	0	569	0	0	969	5,485
"	Dick May	1	0	0	0	0	0	0	0	60	0	0	91	825
"	Harold Miller	3	0	0	0	0	0	0	0	499	0	0	1,184	4,885
"	**Total**	8	0	0	0	0	0	0	0	1,128	0	0	2,244	11,195
1977	Terry Bivins	1	0	0	0	0	0	0	0	290	0	0	396	1,700
"	Billy McGinnis	0												725
"	Harold Miller	6	0	0	0	0	0	0	0	1,267	0	0	2,276	8,480
"	**Total**	7	0	0	0	0	0	0	0	1,557	0	0	2,672	10,905
1978	Earl Ross	0												500
Lifetime		21	0	0	0	0	0	0	0	3,268	0	0	6,072	$28,410

John Miller

Year	Driver	Starts	Poles	1	2	3	4	5	6–10	Laps	Laps Led	Races Led	Miles	$
1967	Tom Raley	1	0	0	0	0	0	0	0	30	0	0	75	100
Lifetime		1	0	0	0	0	0	0	0	30	0	0	75	$100

Junior Miller

Year	Driver	Starts	Poles	1	2	3	4	5	6–10	Laps	Laps Led	Races Led	Miles	$
1976	Jim Hurtubise	1	0	0	0	0	0	0	0	180	0	0	450	3,975
"	Junior Miller	2	0	0	0	0	0	0	0	744	0	0	465	1,325
"	Gary Myers	11	0	0	0	0	0	0	0	2,493	0	0	2,453	9,230
"	Ernie Shaw	1	0	0	0	0	0	0	0	372	0	0	202	700
"	Jerry Sisco	3	0	0	0	0	0	0	0	781	0	0	797	3,070
"	**Total**	18	0	0	0	0	0	0	0	4,570	0	0	4,367	18,300
1977	Jim Hurtubise	1	0	0	0	0	0	0	0	69	0	0	173	2,050
"	Elmo Langley	1	0	0	0	0	0	0	0	119	0	0	119	540
"	Junior Miller	5	0	0	0	0	0	0	0	1,028	0	0	648	2,475
"	**Total**	7	0	0	0	0	0	0	0	1,216	0	0	940	5,065
1978	Ferrel Harris	1	0	0	0	0	0	0	0	453	0	0	238	650
"	Junior Miller	1	0	0	0	0	0	0	0	122	0	0	124	630
"	**Total**	2	0	0	0	0	0	0	0	575	0	0	362	1,280
1979	Dave Dion	1	0	0	0	0	0	0	0	148	0	0	78	590
"	Ernie Shaw	1	0	0	0	0	0	0	0	368	0	0	230	625
"	**Total**	2	0	0	0	0	0	0	0	516	0	0	308	1,215
1980	Tommy Houston	2	0	0	0	0	0	0	0	686	10	1	690	3,310
"	Junior Miller	11	0	0	0	0	0	0	0	2,654	0	0	1,945	15,260
"	**Total**	13	0	0	0	0	0	0	0	3,340	10	1	2,635	18,570
1981	Tommy Gale	1	0	0	0	0	0	0	0	381	0	0	207	2,035

Year	Driver	Starts	Poles	Finish 1	2	3	4	5	6–10	Laps	Laps Led	Races Led	Miles	$

Junior Miller *continued*

Year	Driver	Starts	Poles	1	2	3	4	5	6–10	Laps	Laps Led	Races Led	Miles	$
"	Dick May	1	0	0	0	0	0	0	0	267	0	0	406	2,805
"	Junior Miller	2	0	0	0	0	0	0	0	276	0	0	190	3,130
"	Jody Ridley	1	0	0	0	0	0	0	0	443	0	0	451	4,290
"	**Total**	5	0	0	0	0	0	0	0	1,367	0	0	1,253	12,260
Lifetime		47	0	0	0	0	0	0	0	11,584	10	1	9,865	$56,690

Larry Miller

Year	Driver	Starts	Poles	1	2	3	4	5	6–10	Laps	Laps Led	Races Led	Miles	$
1967	Larry Miller	15	0	0	0	0	0	0	1	1,558	0	0	704	2,075
Lifetime		15	0	0	0	0	0	0	1	1,558	0	0	704	$2,075

Lew Miller

Year	Driver	Starts	Poles	1	2	3	4	5	6–10	Laps	Laps Led	Races Led	Miles	$
1995	Ernie Cope	1	0	0	0	0	0	0	0	19	0	0	19	8,605
Lifetime		1	0	0	0	0	0	0	0	19	0	0	19	$8,605

Mike Miller

Year	Driver	Starts	Poles	1	2	3	4	5	6–10	Laps	Laps Led	Races Led	Miles	$
1980	Mike Miller	2	0	0	0	0	0	0	0	176	0	0	267	2,145
Lifetime		2	0	0	0	0	0	0	0	176	0	0	267	$2,145

Scott Miller

Year	Driver	Starts	Poles	1	2	3	4	5	6–10	Laps	Laps Led	Races Led	Miles	$
1983	Scott Miller	2	0	0	0	0	0	0	0	173	0	0	453	2,400
1984	Scott Miller	2	0	0	0	0	0	0	0	98	0	0	257	1,815
Lifetime		4	0	0	0	0	0	0	0	271	0	0	710	$4,215

J. Marvin Mills

Year	Driver	Starts	Poles	1	2	3	4	5	6–10	Laps	Laps Led	Races Led	Miles	$
1972	John Sears	27	0	0	0	0	0	1	5	7,494	0	0	8,752	50,364
1973	Ed Negre	3	0	0	0	0	0	0	0	1,046	0	0	1,316	4,990
"	John Sears	17	0	0	0	0	0	0	0	3,568	0	0	3,332	16,890
"	Jim Vandiver	1	0	0	0	0	0	0	0	88	0	0	234	1,290
"	**Total**	21	0	0	0	0	0	0	0	4,702	0	0	4,882	23,170
Lifetime		48	0	0	0	0	0	1	5	12,196	0	0	13,634	$73,534

Chris Milovich

Year	Driver	Starts	Poles	1	2	3	4	5	6–10	Laps	Laps Led	Races Led	Miles	$
1954	Ben Gregory	2	0	0	0	0	1	0	0	524	0	0	376	400
1955	Ben Gregory	1	0	0	0	0	0	0	1	96	0	0	96	200
Lifetime		3	0	0	0	0	1	0	1	620	0	0	472	$600

Clyde Minter

Year	Driver	Starts	Poles	1	2	3	4	5	6–10	Laps	Laps Led	Races Led	Miles	$
1949	Clyde Minter	1	0	0	0	0	1	0	0	199	0	0	100	300
1950	Clyde Minter	8	0	0	0	1	0	2	0	665	0	0	546	1,155
1951	Bill Lawrence	1	0	0	0	0	0	0	0		0	0		25
"	Clyde Minter	3	0	0	0	0	0	0	0	59	0	0	44	50
"	**Total**	4	0	0	0	0	0	0	0	59	0	0	44	75
1952	Clyde Minter	1	0	0	0	0	0	0	1	175	0	0	88	125
1953	Clyde Minter	6	0	0	0	0	0	0	2	591	0	0	519	305
1954	Billy Minter	2	0	0	0	0	0	0	0	241	0	0	136	50
Lifetime		22	0	0	0	1	1	2	3	1,930	0	0	1,432	$2,010

Pat Mintey

Year	Driver	Starts	Poles	1	2	3	4	5	6–10	Laps	Laps Led	Races Led	Miles	$
1981	Pat Mintey	1	0	0	0	0	0	0	0	40	0	0	105	850
1983	Pat Mintey	2	0	0	0	0	0	0	0	76	0	0	199	1,875
Lifetime		3	0	0	0	0	0	0	0	116	0	0	304	$2,725

Turkey Minton

Year	Driver	Starts	Poles	1	2	3	4	5	6–10	Laps	Laps Led	Races Led	Miles	$
1967	Tiny Lund	2	0	0	0	0	0	0	0	163	0	0	151	680
"	Tom Pistone	8	0	0	0	1	0	0	3	1,177	0	0	614	2,150
"	Curtis Turner	1	0	0	0	0	0	0	0	82	0	0	123	800
"	**Total**	11	0	0	0	1	0	0	3	1,422	0	0	888	3,630
1968	Tom Pistone	2	0	0	0	0	1	0	0	350	35	1	180	525
Lifetime		13	0	0	0	1	1	0	3	1,772	35	1	1,068	$4,155

Year	Driver	Starts	Poles	Finish 1	2	3	4	5	6–10	Laps	Laps Led	Races Led	Miles	$

Tom Mitchell

Year	Driver	Starts	Poles	1	2	3	4	5	6–10	Laps	Laps Led	Races Led	Miles	$
1985	Chet Fillip	1	0	0	0	0	0	0	0	308	0	0	469	1,425
1986	Chet Fillip	17	0	0	0	0	0	0	0	3,276	0	0	4,550	36,110
Lifetime		18	0	0	0	0	0	0	0	3,584	0	0	5,019	$37,535

Charles Mobley

Year	Driver	Starts	Poles	1	2	3	4	5	6–10	Laps	Laps Led	Races Led	Miles	$
1949	Ethel Mobley	2	0	0	0	0	0	0	0		0	0		50
Lifetime		2	0	0	0	0	0	0	0		0	0		$50

Butch Mock (See also Bob Rahilly & Butch Mock)

Year	Driver	Starts	Poles	1	2	3	4	5	6–10	Laps	Laps Led	Races Led	Miles	$
1992	Dick Trickle	1	0	0	0	0	0	1	0	200	0	0	500	78,800
1993	Todd Bodine	10	0	0	0	0	0	0	0	2,393	0	0	2,310	63,245
"	Phil Parsons	1	0	0	0	0	0	0	1	328	3	1	499	11,725
"	Dick Trickle	18	0	0	0	0	0	0	0	4,381	0	0	5,557	156,600
"	**Total**	29	0	0	0	0	0	0	1	7,102	3	1	8,366	231,570
1994	Todd Bodine	30	0	0	0	1	0	1	5	8,475	60	5	10,478	504,316
1995	Todd Bodine	28	0	0	0	0	1	0	2	6,684	19	2	9,058	664,620
1996	Morgan Shepherd	31	0	0	0	0	0	1	4	8,976	50	4	10,720	719,059
Lifetime		119	0	0	0	1	1	3	12	31,437	132	12	39,122	$2,198,365

Larry Mollicone

Year	Driver	Starts	Poles	1	2	3	4	5	6–10	Laps	Laps Led	Races Led	Miles	$
1974	Bill Osborne	1	0	0	0	0	0	0	0	68	0	0	178	975
Lifetime		1	0	0	0	0	0	0	0	68	0	0	178	$975

Bill Monaghan

Year	Driver	Starts	Poles	1	2	3	4	5	6–10	Laps	Laps Led	Races Led	Miles	$
1976	Terry Ryan	5	0	0	0	0	0	1	2	603	1	1	1,516	24,640
1977	Terry Bivins	2	0	0	0	0	0	0	1	549	0	0	679	5,700
"	Dave Marcis	1	0	0	0	0	0	0	0	148	0	0	225	700
"	Terry Ryan	7	0	0	0	0	0	0	1	1,142	0	0	2,240	12,405
"	**Total**	9	0	0	0	0	0	0	2	1,839	0	0	3,144	18,805
Lifetime		14	0	0	0	0	0	1	4	2,442	1	1	4,660	$43,445

Chris Monoleos

Year	Driver	Starts	Poles	1	2	3	4	5	6–10	Laps	Laps Led	Races Led	Miles	$
1977	Bill Osborne	1	0	0	0	0	0	0	0	188	0	0	470	1,350
1979	Chris Monoleos	1	0	0	0	0	0	0	0	2	0	0	5	550
Lifetime		2	0	0	0	0	0	0	0	190	0	0	475	$1,900

Dean Monroe

Year	Driver	Starts	Poles	1	2	3	4	5	6–10	Laps	Laps Led	Races Led	Miles	$
1996	Stacy Compton	2	0	0	0	0	0	0	0	756	0	0	397	18,115
Lifetime		2	0	0	0	0	0	0	0	756	0	0	397	$18,115

Jack Montrangelo

Year	Driver	Starts	Poles	1	2	3	4	5	6–10	Laps	Laps Led	Races Led	Miles	$
1956	Jack Montgangelo	1	0	0	0	0	0	0	0	206	0	0	206	100
Lifetime		1	0	0	0	0	0	0	0	206	0	0	206	$100

Tommy Moon

Year	Driver	Starts	Poles	1	2	3	4	5	6–10	Laps	Laps Led	Races Led	Miles	$
1951	Tommy Moon	1	0	0	0	0	0	0	1		0	0		200
Lifetime		1	0	0	0	0	0	0	1		0	0		$200

Bill Moore

Year	Driver	Starts	Poles	1	2	3	4	5	6–10	Laps	Laps Led	Races Led	Miles	$
1956	Bill Moore	6	0	0	0	0	0	0	2	633	0	0	574	485
Lifetime		6	0	0	0	0	0	0	2	633	0	0	574	$485

Bob Moore

Year	Driver	Starts	Poles	1	2	3	4	5	6–10	Laps	Laps Led	Races Led	Miles	$
1950	Bob Moore	1	0	0	0	0	0	0	0	0	0	0	0	0
"	Bob Moore	1	0	0	0	0	0	0	0	0	0	0	0	0
"	**Total**	2	0	0	0	0	0	0	0	0	0	0	0	0
1951	Bob Moore	1	0	0	0	0	0	0	0	0	0	0	0	0

Year	Driver	Starts	Poles	Finish 1	2	3	4	5	6–10	Laps	Laps Led	Races Led	Miles	$

Bob Moore *continued*

Year	Driver	Starts	Poles	1	2	3	4	5	6–10	Laps	Laps Led	Races Led	Miles	$
1952	Bob Moore	5	0	0	0	1	0	0	2	524	0	0	270	575
Lifetime		8	0	0	0	1	0	0	2	524	0	0	270	$575

Bud Moore

Year	Driver	Starts	Poles	1	2	3	4	5	6–10	Laps	Laps Led	Races Led	Miles	$
1950	Joe Eubanks	1	0	0	0	0	0	0	0	359	0	0	449	0
1961	Tommy Irwin	1	0	0	0	0	0	0	0	361	0	0	542	500
"	Cotton Owens	1	0	0	0	0	0	0	0	11	0	0	17	60
"	Fireball Roberts	2	0	0	1	0	0	1	0	537	108	1	499	2,790
"	Joe Weatherly	23	4	8	3	0	1	1	4	5,401	569	16	5,153	46,209
"	Bob Welborn	2	0	0	0	1	0	0	1	747	51	1	641	3,860
"	**Total**	23	4	8	4	1	1	2	5	7,057	728	16	6,851	53,419
1962	David Pearson	1	0	0	0	0	0	0	0	261	0	0	392	750
"	Joe Weatherly	51	7	9	12	10	2	5	6	12,234	1,014	17	7,935	70,453
"	**Total**	51	7	9	12	10	2	5	6	12,495	1,014	17	8,326	71,203
1963	Joe Weatherly	34	6	3	4	4	2	2	9	8,321	878	12	7,185	67,039
1964	Darel Dieringer	15	1	1	0	1	1	0	5	3,439	211	3	2,583	11,120
"	Bobby Johns	1	0	0	0	0	0	0	0	27	0	0	41	500
"	Johnny Rutherford	2	0	0	0	0	0	0	0	124	0	0	310	825
"	Billy Wade	32	5	4	0	3	3	1	12	7,142	954	14	6,139	32,125
"	Joe Weatherly	2	0	0	1	0	0	0	0	336	84	1	357	2,000
"	Rex White	5	0	0	0	1	0	1	1	1,427	27	1	1,632	11,735
"	**Total**	33	6	5	1	5	4	2	18	12,495	1,276	16	11,062	58,305
1965	Earl Balmer	9	0	0	1	0	1	0	2	1,320	32	6	2,174	19,045
"	Darel Dieringer	13	2	1	4	1	1	0	1	3,014	737	10	3,493	45,154
"	**Total**	14	2	1	5	1	2	0	3	4,334	769	11	5,667	64,199
1966	Darel Dieringer	14	0	2	2	0	0	0	1	2,858	332	6	2,981	40,785
1967	Bobby Allison	4	0	0	0	0	0	0	1	657	0	0	791	2,420
"	Dan Gurney	1	0	0	0	0	0	0	0	143	36	1	386	990
"	Gordon Johncock	2	0	0	0	0	0	1	0	525	1	1	539	2,595
"	Sam McQuagg	6	0	0	0	0	0	1	0	1,021	2	1	1,608	6,365
"	Cale Yarborough	1	0	0	0	0	0	0	0	196	0	0	98	375
"	LeeRoy Yarbrough	6	0	0	0	1	0	0	1	1,306	11	1	1,503	8,145
"	**Total**	17	0	0	0	1	0	2	2	3,848	50	4	4,925	20,890
1968	Tiny Lund	13	0	0	0	0	1	2	4	3,574	1	1	3,878	15,795
"	Cale Yarborough	1	0	0	0	0	0	0	0	164	0	0	88	250
"	**Total**	14	0	0	0	0	1	2	4	3,738	1	1	3,966	16,045
1969	Don Schissler	1	0	0	0	0	0	0	0	0	0	0	0	850
1972	Donnie Allison	6	0	0	0	0	0	0	1	702	5	2	1,228	5,886
"	Dick Brooks	1	0	0	0	0	0	0	0	119	1	1	121	580
"	David Pearson	2	0	0	0	0	1	0	0	439	3	1	791	7,860
"	LeeRoy Yarbrough	1	0	0	0	0	0	0	0	145	1	1	198	630
"	**Total**	10	0	0	0	0	1	0	1	1,405	10	5	2,339	14,956
1973	Bobby Isaac	19	0	0	2	1	2	0	1	4,177	62	7	4,536	84,550
"	Darrell Waltrip	5	0	0	0	0	0	0	1	818	0	0	945	14,691
"	**Total**	24	0	0	2	1	2	0	2	4,995	62	7	5,482	99,241
1974	Buddy Baker	16	2	0	4	3	1	1	1	3,566	336	12	4,615	136,250
"	George Follmer	11	0	0	0	0	1	2	2	3,029	26	1	3,604	50,180
"	**Total**	27	2	0	4	3	2	3	3	6,595	362	13	8,219	186,430
1975	Buddy Baker	23	3	4	2	4	1	1	1	6,281	788	18	8,113	236,351
1976	Buddy Baker	30	2	1	3	1	4	7	0	7,335	1,028	15	8,610	239,922
1977	Buddy Baker	30	0	0	1	1	4	3	11	8,084	52	7	9,876	224,847
1978	Bobby Allison	30	1	5	3	4	0	2	8	9,283	1,043	19	10,539	411,517
1979	Bobby Allison	31	3	5	7	2	4	0	4	9,885	1,854	24	11,237	428,801
1980	Bobby Allison	31	2	4	2	4	1	1	6	8,244	948	18	9,027	378,970
1981	Benny Parsons	31	0	3	0	3	0	4	2	6,709	537	10	7,515	311,093
1982	Dale Earnhardt	30	1	1	1	3	2	0	5	7,208	1,062	18	7,787	400,880
1983	Dale Earnhardt	30	0	2	3	0	3	1	5	7,701	1,027	19	8,946	465,203
1984	Ricky Rudd	30	4	1	1	3	1	1	9	9,271	566	8	10,584	497,779
1985	Ricky Rudd	28	0	1	2	1	5	4	6	8,475	329	6	10,281	512,441
1986	Ricky Rudd	29	1	2	4	2	3	0	6	8,120	525	7	10,193	671,548
1987	Ricky Rudd	29	0	2	2	4	1	1	3	8,206	505	12	9,891	653,508
1988	Brett Bodine	29	0	0	0	1	1	0	3	7,789	200	5	9,155	433,658
1989	Brett Bodine	29	0	0	0	0	0	1	5	8,202	2	2	10,354	281,274
1990	Morgan Shepherd	29	0	1	2	2	0	2	9	8,794	202	8	10,575	666,915
1991	Morgan Shepherd	29	0	0	0	2	2	0	10	9,021	86	5	10,479	445,470
1992	Geoff Bodine	29	0	2	0	2	2	1	4	8,222	474	5	9,780	716,583

Year	Driver	Starts	Poles	Finish 1	2	3	4	5	6–10	Laps	Laps Led	Races Led	Miles	$

Bud Moore *continued*

Year	Driver	Starts	Poles	1	2	3	4	5	6–10	Laps	Laps Led	Races Led	Miles	$
1993	Geoff Bodine	23	1	1	0	1	0	0	6	6,522	70	10	8,367	659,032
"	Lake Speed	7	0	0	0	0	0	0	0	2,544	0	0	2,503	109,825
"	**Total**	30	1	1	0	1	0	0	6	9,066	70	10	10,871	768,857
1994	Lake Speed	31	0	0	0	1	1	2	5	9,111	39	5	11,291	845,963
1995	Dick Trickle	31	0	0	0	0	0	0	1	8,941	5	1	11,094	694,920
1996	Wally Dallenbach Jr.	30	0	0	0	1	0	0	2	8,191	0	0	10,417	837,001
Lifetime		912	45	63	67	68	52	49	165	250,639	16,824	330	284,063	$12,653,864
		2nd	**8th**	**5th**							**4th**	**7th**	**4th**	**5th**	**7th**

Doug Moore

Year	Driver	Starts	Poles	1	2	3	4	5	6–10	Laps	Laps Led	Races Led	Miles	$
1964	Doug Moore	8	0	0	0	0	0	0	0	1,085	0	0	574	1,900
1965	Doug Moore	5	0	0	0	0	0	0	0	664	0	0	452	1,160
Lifetime		13	0	0	0	0	0	0	0	1,749	0	0	1,027	$3,060

Fred Moore

Year	Driver	Starts	Poles	1	2	3	4	5	6–10	Laps	Laps Led	Races Led	Miles	$
1953	Fred Moore	1	0	0	0	0	0	0	0		0	0		25
Lifetime		1	0	0	0	0	0	0	0		0	0		$25

Howard Moore

Year	Driver	Starts	Poles	1	2	3	4	5	6–10	Laps	Laps Led	Races Led	Miles	$
1956	Pat Kirkwood	1	0	0	0	0	0	0	1	347	0	0	477	550
Lifetime		1	0	0	0	0	0	0	1	347	0	0	477	$550

Stanley Moore

Year	Driver	Starts	Poles	1	2	3	4	5	6–10	Laps	Laps Led	Races Led	Miles	$
1951	Bobby Booth	3	0	0	0	0	0	0	0	156	0	0	169	25
Lifetime		3	0	0	0	0	0	0	0	156	0	0	169	$25

Steve Moore

Year	Driver	Starts	Poles	1	2	3	4	5	6–10	Laps	Laps Led	Races Led	Miles	$
1978	Steve Moore	1	0	0	0	0	0	0	0	150	0	0	399	1,590
1979	Steve Moore	1	0	0	0	0	0	0	0	170	0	0	452	2,415
1980	Ferrel Harris	1	0	0	0	0	0	0	0	17	0	0	45	1,350
"	Steve Moore	4	0	0	0	0	0	0	0	735	0	0	1,469	9,040
"	**Total**	5	0	0	0	0	0	0	0	752	0	0	1,514	10,390
1981	Steve Moore	0												3,155
1982	Steve Moore	4	0	0	0	0	0	0	0	456	4	1	727	7,975
1983	Steve Moore	2	0	0	0	0	0	0	0	316	0	0	714	5,215
1984	Steve Moore	2	0	0	0	0	0	0	0	237	0	0	622	6,245
Lifetime		15	0	0	0	0	0	0	0	2,081	4	1	4,428	$36,985

Rocky Moran

Year	Driver	Starts	Poles	1	2	3	4	5	6–10	Laps	Laps Led	Races Led	Miles	$
1978	Rocky Moran	3	0	0	0	0	0	0	0	289	0	0	735	3,195
Lifetime		3	0	0	0	0	0	0	0	289	0	0	735	$3,195

Bill Morehart

Year	Driver	Starts	Poles	1	2	3	4	5	6–10	Laps	Laps Led	Races Led	Miles	$
1983	Jim Bown	1	0	0	0	0	0	0	0	81	0	0	212	1,100
Lifetime		1	0	0	0	0	0	0	0	81	0	0	212	$1,100

Beau Morgan

Year	Driver	Starts	Poles	1	2	3	4	5	6–10	Laps	Laps Led	Races Led	Miles	$
1958	Tim Flock	1	0	0	0	0	0	0	0	98	0	0	98	100
"	Fireball Roberts	1	0	0	0	1	0	0	0	100	0	0	100	400
"	Joe Weatherly	1	0	0	0	0	1	0	0	149	0	0	149	650
"	**Total**	2	0	0	0	1	1	0	0	347	0	0	347	1,150
1959	L. D. Austin	1	0	0	0	0	0	0	0	469	0	0	235	180
"	Johnny Beauchamp	1	0	0	1	0	0	0	0	495	0	0	248	1,625
"	Tim Flock	2	0	0	0	0	0	0	1	223	0	0	558	850
"	Speedy Thompson	2	0	0	0	0	0	0	0	334	0	0	185	170
"	Rex White	2	0	0	0	0	0	0	0	301	0	0	168	175
"	**Total**	8	0	0	1	0	0	0	1	1,822	0	0	1,393	3,000
1960	Tim Flock	1	0	0	0	0	0	0	1	213	0	0	293	700
"	Johnny Sudderth	3	0	0	0	0	0	0	0	351	0	0	676	515

Year	Driver	Starts	Poles	Finish						Laps	Laps Led	Races Led	Miles	$
				1	2	3	4	5	6–10	Laps	Led	Led	Miles	$

Beau Morgan *continued*

"	Roscoe Thompson	2	0	0	0	0	0	0	0	402	0	0	603	710
"	Curtis Turner	1	0	0	0	0	0	0	0	185	0	0	278	350
"	**Total**	7	0	0	0	0	0	0	1	1,151	0	0	1,849	2,275
1961	Johnny Allen	1	0	0	0	0	0	0	0	249	0	0	374	650
"	Jim Bennett	2	0	0	0	0	0	0	0	170	0	0	351	500
"	Tim Flock	6	0	0	0	0	0	0	3	1,043	0	0	938	1,405
"	Jesse James Taylor	1	0	0	0	0	0	0	0	10	0	0	15	250
"	Speedy Thompson	2	0	0	0	0	0	0	0	188	0	0	282	275
"	**Total**	10	0	0	0	0	0	0	3	1,660	0	0	1,959	3,080
Lifetime		27	0	0	1	1	1	0	5	4,980	0	0	5,547	$9,505

Sonny Morgan

1957	Sonny Morgan	1	0	0	0	0	0	0	0		0	0		25
Lifetime		1	0	0	0	0	0	0	0		0	0		$25

Wayne Morgan

1978	Wayne Morgan	2	0	0	0	0	0	0	0	19	0	0	12	785
Lifetime		2	0	0	0	0	0	0	0	19	0	0	12	$785

Wes Morgan

1960	Wes Morgan	2	0	0	0	0	0	0	0	277	0	0	378	350
Lifetime		2	0	0	0	0	0	0	0	277	0	0	378	$350

Dick Moroso

1988	Rob Moroso	1	0	0	0	0	0	0	0	142	0	0	89	1,250
1989	Rob Moroso	2	0	0	0	0	0	0	0	583	0	0	671	4,725
1990	Steve Grissom	1	0	0	0	0	0	0	0	322	0	0	490	4,275
"	Jimmy Hensley	2	0	0	0	0	0	0	0	692	0	0	820	17,475
"	Chad Little	1	0	0	0	0	0	0	0	309	0	0	309	450
"	Rob Moroso	25	0	0	0	0	0	0	1	5,666	9	3	6,900	162,002
"	**Total**	29	0	0	0	0	0	0	1	6,989	9	3	8,518	184,202
1991	Buddy Baker	5	0	0	0	0	0	0	0	810	0	0	1,870	39,260
"	Kim Campbell	1	0	0	0	0	0	0	0	64	0	0	155	3,725
"	Ricky Craven	1	0	0	0	0	0	0	0	221	0	0	225	3,750
"	Bobby Hillin Jr.	10	0	0	0	0	0	0	1	3,713	0	0	4,113	111,285
"	Sammy Swindell	1	0	0	0	0	0	0	0	28	0	0	70	16,500
"	**Total**	16	0	0	0	0	0	0	1	4,836	0	0	6,433	174,520
1992	Joe Ruttman	1	0	0	0	0	0	0	0	213	0	0	320	5,250
"	Jimmy Spencer	1	0	0	0	0	0	0	0	487	0	0	260	6,125
"	Mike Wallace	1	0	0	0	0	0	0	0	251	0	0	382	7,980
"	**Total**	3	0	0	0	0	0	0	0	951	0	0	961	19,355
1993	Bobby Hamilton	5	0	0	0	0	0	0	0	1,161	0	0	1,833	36,315
"	Joe Ruttman	5	0	0	0	0	0	1	0	1,133	0	0	1,597	70,700
"	**Total**	10	0	0	0	0	0	1	0	2,294	0	0	3,430	107,015
1994	Buddy Baker	0												1,850
"	Jimmy Hensley	1	0	0	0	0	0	0	0	76	0	0	114	4,455
"	Bobby Hillin Jr.	2	0	0	0	0	0	0	0	274	0	0	628	16,570
"	Randy LaJoie	2	0	0	0	0	0	0	0	692	0	0	906	21,990
"	**Total**	5	0	0	0	0	0	0	0	1,042	0	0	1,647	44,865
1995	Bobby Hillin Jr.	0												2,750
Lifetime		66	0	0	0	0	0	1	2	16,837	9	3	21,750	$538,632

B. B. Morris

1956	Larry Flynn	2	0	0	0	0	0	0	0	402	0	0	395	250
Lifetime		2	0	0	0	0	0	0	0	402	0	0	395	$250

Bob Morris

1984	Jeff Hooker	4	0	0	0	0	0	0	0	980	0	0	861	4,495
1985	Rick Baldwin	1	0	0	0	0	0	0	0	316	0	0	481	1,485
1986	Ken Ragan	1	0	0	0	0	0	0	0	5	0	0	8	1,500
Lifetime		6	0	0	0	0	0	0	0	1,301	0	0	1,349	$7,480

Year	Driver	Starts	Poles	Finish						Laps	Laps Led	Races Led	Miles	$
				1	2	3	4	5	6–10					

Buckshot Morris

Year	Driver	Starts	Poles	1	2	3	4	5	6–10	Laps	Laps Led	Races Led	Miles	$
1952	Billy Carden	1	0	0	0	0	0	0	0		0	0		0
"	Jim Paschal	4	0	0	0	0	1	0	0	620	0	0	384	450
"	**Total**	5	0	0	0	0	1	0	0	620	0	0	384	450
1953	Speedy Thompson	6	0	2	2	1	0	0	1	906	99	4	746	5,400
1954	Jim Paschal	1	0	0	0	0	0	0	0	180	0	0	90	25
"	Speedy Thompson	7	0	0	0	0	1	0	2	949	0	0	942	1,165
"	Joe Weatherly	1	0	0	0	0	0	0	1	196	0	0	98	200
"	**Total**	9	0	0	0	0	1	0	3	1,325	0	0	1,130	1,390
Lifetime		20	0	2	2	1	2	0	4	2,851	99	4	2,260	$7,240

Bill Morton

Year	Driver	Starts	Poles	1	2	3	4	5	6–10	Laps	Laps Led	Races Led	Miles	$
1957	Bill Morton	5	0	0	0	0	0	0	4	653	0	0	365	600
1959	Bill Morton	3	0	0	0	0	0	0	0	398	0	0	218	100
1961	Bill Morton	5	0	0	0	0	0	0	3	1,697	0	0	886	1,490
1962	Bill Morton	3	0	0	0	0	0	0	2	784	0	0	392	615
Lifetime		16	0	0	0	0	0	0	9	3,532	0	0	1,861	$2,805

Ray Moss

Year	Driver	Starts	Poles	1	2	3	4	5	6–10	Laps	Laps Led	Races Led	Miles	$
1987	Ronnie Sanders	1	0	0	0	0	0	0	0	195	0	0	488	13,930
Lifetime		1	0	0	0	0	0	0	0	195	0	0	488	$13,930

Arden Mounts

Year	Driver	Starts	Poles	1	2	3	4	5	6–10	Laps	Laps Led	Races Led	Miles	$
1955	Arden Mounts	8	0	0	0	0	0	0	2	1,133	0	0	714	640
"	Herb Thomas	1	0	0	0	0	0	0	0	105	0	0	66	25
"	**Total**	9	0	0	0	0	0	0	2	1,238	0	0	780	665
1956	Arden Mounts	3	0	0	0	0	0	0	0	545	0	0	381	210
Lifetime		12	0	0	0	0	0	0	2	1,783	0	0	1,160	$875

Billy Moyer

Year	Driver	Starts	Poles	1	2	3	4	5	6–10	Laps	Laps Led	Races Led	Miles	$
1975	Terry Bivins	2	0	0	0	0	0	0	1	562	0	0	758	2,735
"	George Follmer	1	0	0	0	0	0	0	0	67	0	0	168	1,650
"	Jimmy Hensley	2	0	0	0	0	0	0	1	534	0	0	280	1,860
"	Don Hoffman	1	0	0	0	0	0	0	0	178	0	0	445	1,650
"	**Total**	6	0	0	0	0	0	0	2	1,341	0	0	1,651	7,895
1976	Terry Bivins	6	0	0	0	0	0	1	1	1,556	6	1	1,992	16,160
"	Jimmy Hensley	2	0	0	0	0	0	0	1	474	0	0	249	2,150
"	Bruce Jacobi	2	0	0	0	0	0	0	0	562	0	0	708	1,715
"	**Total**	10	0	0	0	0	0	1	2	2,592	6	1	2,949	20,025
1977	Jimmy Hensley	2	0	0	0	0	0	0	1	812	0	0	426	2,680
Lifetime		18	0	0	0	0	0	1	5	4,745	6	1	5,026	$30,600

Dailey Moyer

Year	Driver	Starts	Poles	1	2	3	4	5	6–10	Laps	Laps Led	Races Led	Miles	$
1949	Ken Marriott	1	0	0	0	0	0	0	0	169	0	0	169	50
"	Ken Wagner	3	1	0	0	0	0	0	0	412	0	0	206	100
"	Jack White	1	0	1	0	0	0	0	0	200	66	1	100	1,500
"	**Total**	5	1	1	0	0	0	0	0	781	66	1	475	1,650
1950	Ken Wagner	3	0	0	0	0	0	0	1	274	0	0	313	250
"	Jack White	2	0	0	0	0	0	1	1	190	0	0	143	450
"	**Total**	5	0	0	0	0	0	1	2	464	0	0	455	700
Lifetime		10	1	1	0	0	0	1	2	1,245	66	1	930	$2,350

Mueller Brothers (Tom and Jerry Mueller, co-owners)

Year	Driver	Starts	Poles	1	2	3	4	5	6–10	Laps	Laps Led	Races Led	Miles	$
1983	Dean Roper	2	0	0	0	0	0	0	0	364	0	0	937	16,485
1984	Dean Roper	3	0	0	0	0	0	0	0	500	0	0	1,274	19,150
1985	Jim Sauter	3	0	0	0	0	0	0	0	565	0	0	1,107	15,465
1986	Jim Sauter	2	0	0	0	0	0	0	0	335	0	0	739	14,875
1987	Jim Sauter	3	0	0	0	0	0	0	1	781	0	0	1,364	28,665
1988	Jim Sauter	5	0	0	0	0	0	0	0	1,037	0	0	1,553	23,810
"	Michael Waltrip	1	0	0	0	0	0	0	0	197	0	0	493	14,065
"	**Total**	6	0	0	0	0	0	0	0	1,234	0	0	2,046	37,875
1989	Rodney Combs	5	0	0	0	0	0	0	0	610	0	0	836	20,560
1990	Rodney Combs	5	0	0	0	0	0	0	0	988	0	0	1,407	24,415
1991	Jim Sauter	6	0	0	0	0	0	0	0	1,012	0	0	1,843	44,895

Year	Driver	Starts	Poles	Finish 1	2	3	4	5	6–10	Laps	Laps Led	Races Led	Miles	$

Mueller Brothers *continued*

Year	Driver	Starts	Poles	1	2	3	4	5	6–10	Laps	Laps Led	Races Led	Miles	$
1992	Jim Sauter	2	0	0	0	0	0	0	0	225	0	0	353	15,730
1993	Jim Sauter	2	0	0	0	0	0	0	0	307	0	0	714	39,385
1994	Jim Sauter	0												6,200
Lifetime		39	0	0	0	0	0	0	1	6,921	0	0	12,619	$283,700

A. T. Mulherin

Year	Driver	Starts	Poles	1	2	3	4	5	6–10	Laps	Laps Led	Races Led	Miles	$
1966	Rock Harn	1	0	0	0	0	0	0	0	33	0	0	83	0
Lifetime		1	0	0	0	0	0	0	0	33	0	0	83	$0

Jerry Mullins

Year	Driver	Starts	Poles	1	2	3	4	5	6–10	Laps	Laps Led	Races Led	Miles	$
1964	Junior Spencer	3	0	0	0	0	0	0	0	1,172	0	0	558	670
1965	Junior Spencer	20	0	0	0	0	0	1	6	3,822	0	0	2,767	8,430
"	Jabe Thomas	1	0	0	0	0	0	0	0	242	0	0	363	515
"	**Total**	21	0	0	0	0	0	1	6	4,064	0	0	3,130	8,945
Lifetime		24	0	0	0	0	0	1	6	5,236	0	0	3,688	$9,615

Penny Mullis

Year	Driver	Starts	Poles	1	2	3	4	5	6–10	Laps	Laps Led	Races Led	Miles	$
1949	Buck Baker	1	0	0	0	0	0	0	0		0	0		50
Lifetime		1	0	0	0	0	0	0	0		0	0		$50

Richard Mummert

Year	Driver	Starts	Poles	1	2	3	4	5	6–10	Laps	Laps Led	Races Led	Miles	$
1973	Carl Adams	2	0	0	0	0	0	0	0	290	0	0	760	2,030
1974	Carl Adams	4	0	0	0	0	0	0	0	667	0	0	1,413	5,100
"	Elmo Langley	1	0	0	0	0	0	0	0	169	0	0	450	1,435
"	**Total**	5	0	0	0	0	0	0	0	836	0	0	1,862	6,535
1975	Carl Adams	20	0	0	0	0	0	0	4	5,332	0	0	5,827	25,220
Lifetime		27	0	0	0	0	0	0	4	6,458	0	0	8,449	$40,320

Ralph Murphy

Year	Driver	Starts	Poles	1	2	3	4	5	6–10	Laps	Laps Led	Races Led	Miles	$
1967	Bill Ervin	17	0	0	0	0	0	0	0	1,669	0	0	858	1,885
"	Paul Dean Holt	1	0	0	0	0	0	0	0	244	0	0	122	100
"	Ed Negre	1	0	0	0	0	0	0	0	8	0	0	11	555
"	**Total**	19	0	0	0	0	0	0	0	1,921	0	0	991	2,540
1968	Bill Ervin	1	0	0	0	0	0	0	0	149	0	0	75	100
1973	Buck Baker	1	0	0	0	0	0	0	0	357	0	0	363	670
Lifetime		21	0	0	0	0	0	0	0	2,427	0	0	1,429	$3,310

Billy Myers

Year	Driver	Starts	Poles	1	2	3	4	5	6–10	Laps	Laps Led	Races Led	Miles	$
1957	Billy Myers	10	0	0	0	0	1	0	4	1,668	0	0	1,114	2,380
1958	Billy Myers	2	0	0	0	0	0	0	0	28	0	0	115	50
Lifetime		12	0	0	0	0	1	0	4	1,696	0	0	1,229	$2,430

Dean Myers

Year	Driver	Starts	Poles	1	2	3	4	5	6–10	Laps	Laps Led	Races Led	Miles	$
1994	Dick Trickle	25	0	0	0	0	0	0	1	6,423	1	1	7,107	244,806
1995	Ed Berrier	1	0	0	0	0	0	0	0	358	0	0	489	15,460
"	Chuck Bown	8	0	0	0	0	0	0	0	1,673	0	0	2,815	87,795
"	Mike Chase	0												2,100
"	Jimmy Hensley	2	0	0	0	0	0	0	0	270	0	0	322	17,650
"	Michael Ritch	1	0	0	0	0	0	0	0	226	0	0	226	12,655
"	Greg Sacks	6	0	0	0	0	0	0	0	853	0	0	1,369	87,130
"	**Total**	18	0	0	0	0	0	0	0	3,380	0	0	5,221	222,790
Lifetime		43	0	0	0	0	0	0	1	9,803	1	1	12,328	$467,596

Gary Myers

Year	Driver	Starts	Poles	1	2	3	4	5	6–10	Laps	Laps Led	Races Led	Miles	$
1976	Gary Myers	4	0	0	0	0	0	0	0	584	0	0	346	2,200
1977	Gary Myers	10	0	0	0	0	0	0	0	2,648	0	0	2,691	10,975
"	Randy Myers	1	0	0	0	0	0	0	0	377	0	0	383	1,000
"	**Total**	11	0	0	0	0	0	0	0	3,025	0	0	3,074	11,975
1978	Gary Myers	19	0	0	0	0	0	0	0	5,524	0	0	6,134	21,290
Lifetime		34	0	0	0	0	0	0	0	9,133	0	0	9,554	$35,465

Year	Driver	Starts	Poles	Finish						Laps	Laps Led	Races Led	Miles	$
				1	2	3	4	5	6–10	Laps	Led	Led	Miles	$

Monty Myers

1972	Donnie Allison	2	0	0	0	0	0	1	0	472	11	1	883	4,825
Lifetime		2	0	0	0	0	0	1	0	472	11	1	883	$4,825

Kenny Myler

1965	Sam McQuagg	2	0	0	0	0	0	0	1	384	0	0	155	350
"	Cale Yarborough	18	0	1	1	0	5	3	2	3,545	18	1	1,935	8,737
"	**Total**	20	0	1	1	0	5	3	3	3,929	18	1	2,090	9,087
1966	Cale Yarborough	1	0	0	0	0	0	0	1	291	0	0	146	390
Lifetime		21	0	1	1	0	5	3	4	4,220	18	1	2,236	$9,477

David Nagle

1971	Maynard Troyer	13	0	0	0	0	1	0	2	1,617	0	0	2,884	13,115
1973	Maynard Troyer	1	0	0	0	0	0	0	0	150	0	0	375	1,825
Lifetime		14	0	0	0	0	1	0	2	1,767	0	0	3,259	$14,940

Joe Nagle

1950	Joe Nagle	1	0	0	0	0	0	0	1		0	0		75
"	John Schelesky	1	0	0	0	0	0	0	0		0	0		25
"	**Total**	2	0	0	0	0	0	0	1		0	0		100
Lifetime		2	0	0	0	0	0	0	1		0	0		$100

Nash Motor Co.

1950	Frank Mundy	2	0	0	0	0	0	0	0		0	0		0
"	Slick Smith	2	0	0	0	0	0	0	0	31	0	0	16	0
"	Bill Snowden	3	0	0	0	0	0	0	1	338	0	0	423	100
"	**Total**	7	0	0	0	0	0	0	1	369	0	0	438	100
1951	Curtis Turner	4	0	1	0	0	0	0	1	150	104	1	113	1,300
Lifetime		11	0	1	0	0	0	0	2	519	104	1	551	$1,400

Harry Neal

1966	Bill Seifert	1	0	0	0	0	0	0	0	1	0	0	1	125
"	Blackie Watt	20	0	0	0	0	0	0	9	4,067	0	0	3,003	7,050
"	**Total**	21	0	0	0	0	0	0	9	4,068	0	0	3,004	7,175
Lifetime		21	0	0	0	0	0	0	9	4,068	0	0	3,004	$7,175

Hal Needham

1981	Stan Barrett	10	0	0	0	0	0	0	1	1,559	4	2	3,265	28,540
"	Harry Gant	22	3	0	6	1	3	0	3	6,022	852	16	7,458	214,957
"	**Total**	25	3	0	6	1	3	0	4	7,581	856	16	10,723	243,497
1982	Harry Gant	30	1	2	2	3	1	1	7	8,454	420	17	9,641	337,582
1983	Harry Gant	30	0	1	1	3	1	4	6	9,024	60	10	10,193	414,353
1984	Harry Gant	30	3	3	6	0	5	1	8	9,899	1,186	19	11,395	673,060
1985	Harry Gant	28	3	3	5	3	1	2	5	8,806	1,270	20	10,177	804,287
1986	Harry Gant	29	2	0	3	1	3	2	4	7,965	646	17	9,565	583,024
1987	Harry Gant	29	1	0	0	0	0	0	4	6,497	71	3	7,921	197,645
1988	Harry Gant	24	0	0	0	0	0	0	3	5,896	343	8	6,867	173,325
"	Morgan Shepherd	5	0	0	1	0	0	0	1	951	110	1	1,587	57,570
"	**Total**	29	0	0	1	0	0	0	4	6,847	453	9	8,455	230,895
Lifetime		230	13	9	24	11	14	10	42	65,073	4,962	111	78,069	$3,484,343

Ed Negre

1957	Ed Negre	6	0	0	0	0	0	1	2	519	0	0	307	825
1967	Ed Negre	12	0	0	0	0	0	0	0	985	0	0	643	2,250
1968	Ed Negre	24	0	0	0	0	0	0	1	2,930	0	0	1,487	5,085
1969	Ed Negre	13	0	0	0	0	0	0	1	2,310	0	0	1,786	6,000
1970	Joe Frasson	2	0	0	0	0	0	0	0	508	0	0	235	695
"	Henley Gray	1	0	0	0	0	0	0	0	294	0	0	441	1,654
"	Ed Negre	31	0	0	0	0	0	0	1	3,336	0	0	2,700	14,580
"	**Total**	34	0	0	0	0	0	0	1	4,138	0	0	3,376	16,929
1971	Ed Negre	34	0	0	0	0	0	0	1	6,549	0	0	5,969	23,685
1972	Ed Negre	25	0	0	0	0	0	0	0	5,588	0	0	6,597	30,358
1973	Ed Negre	15	0	0	0	0	0	1	1	3,853	0	0	4,469	22,972
1974	Ed Negre	25	0	0	0	0	0	0	0	5,152	0	0	6,044	23,917

Year	Driver	Starts	Poles	Finish 1	2	3	4	5	6–10	Laps	Laps Led	Races Led	Miles	$

Ed Negre *continued*

Year	Driver	Starts	Poles	1	2	3	4	5	6–10	Laps	Laps Led	Races Led	Miles	$
"	D. K. Ulrich	1	0	0	0	0	0	0	0	46	0	0	92	955
"	**Total**	26	0	0	0	0	0	0	0	5,198	0	0	6,136	24,872
1975	Dean Dalton	2	0	0	0	0	0	0	0	23	0	0	59	2,405
"	Dale Earnhardt	1	0	0	0	0	0	0	0	355	0	0	533	2,425
"	Dick May	1	0	0	0	0	0	0	0	43	0	0	43	1,000
"	Ed Negre	21	0	0	0	0	0	0	4	5,428	2	1	5,555	36,174
"	**Total**	25	0	0	0	0	0	0	4	5,849	2	1	6,190	42,004
1976	Walter Ballard	1	0	0	0	0	0	0	0	28	0	0	70	550
"	Gary Matthews	1	0	0	0	0	0	0	0	138	0	0	362	1,395
"	Ed Negre	24	0	0	0	0	0	0	2	5,821	0	0	6,853	47,254
"	**Total**	25	0	0	0	0	0	0	2	5,987	0	0	7,284	49,199
1977	Ed Negre	23	0	0	0	0	0	0	0	5,446	0	0	5,923	41,625
1978	Ferrel Harris	1	0	0	0	0	0	0	0	3	0	0	3	490
"	Dick May	1	0	0	0	0	0	0	0	379	0	0	205	1,370
"	Ed Negre	20	0	0	0	0	0	0	1	4,823	0	0	4,949	28,740
"	**Total**	20	0	0	0	0	0	0	1	5,205	0	0	5,157	30,600
1979	Ed Negre	3	0	0	0	0	0	0	0	849	0	0	1,387	11,215
Lifetime		285	0	0	0	0	0	2	14	55,406	2	1	56,711	$307,619

Norman Negre

Year	Driver	Starts	Poles	1	2	3	4	5	6–10	Laps	Laps Led	Races Led	Miles	$
1980	Cecil Gordon	1	0	0	0	0	0	0	0	10	0	0	14	1,110
"	Dick May	1	0	0	0	0	0	0	0	178	0	0	473	3,550
"	**Total**	2	0	0	0	0	0	0	0	188	0	0	487	4,660
1981	Dick May	1	0	0	0	0	0	0	0	353	0	0	482	2,875
"	Jimmy Means	1	0	0	0	0	0	0	0	327	0	0	491	3,750
"	**Total**	2	0	0	0	0	0	0	0	680	0	0	973	6,625
1982	Dick Brooks	1	0	0	0	0	0	0	0	239	0	0	359	1,515
Lifetime		5	0	0	0	0	0	0	0	1,107	0	0	1,818	$12,800

Jon Nelson

Year	Driver	Starts	Poles	1	2	3	4	5	6–10	Laps	Laps Led	Races Led	Miles	$
1973	Eddie Yarboro	1	0	0	0	0	0	0	0	4	0	0	11	610
Lifetime		1	0	0	0	0	0	0	0	4	0	0	11	$610

Norm Nelson

Year	Driver	Starts	Poles	1	2	3	4	5	6–10	Laps	Laps Led	Races Led	Miles	$
1964	Jim Hurtubise	1	0	0	0	0	0	0	0	77	2	1	116	585
1966	Jim Hurtubise	6	0	1	1	0	0	1	2	1,215	158	4	2,434	25,010
"	Norm Nelson	1	0	0	0	0	0	0	1	176	0	0	475	1,000
"	**Total**	6	0	1	1	0	0	1	3	1,391	158	4	2,909	26,010
1967	Jim Hurtubise	2	0	0	0	0	0	0	1	196	0	0	490	2,600
"	Norm Nelson	1	0	0	0	1	0	0	0	183	0	0	494	5,250
"	**Total**	3	0	0	0	1	0	0	1	379	0	0	984	7,850
1969	Roger McCluskey	1	0	0	0	0	0	0	0	100	0	0	270	825
1970	Roger McCluskey	1	0	0	1	0	0	0	0	193	2	1	506	9,000
Lifetime		12	0	1	2	1	0	1	4	2,140	162	6	4,784	$44,270

Joe Nemechek

Year	Driver	Starts	Poles	1	2	3	4	5	6–10	Laps	Laps Led	Races Led	Miles	$
1993	Joe Nemechek	3	0	0	0	0	0	0	0	303	0	0	534	24,300
1995	Joe Nemechek	29	0	0	0	0	1	0	3	8,504	1	1	10,223	428,925
1996	Robby Gordon	1	0	0	0	0	0	0	0	206	0	0	309	4,800
"	Joe Nemechek	29	0	0	0	0	0	0	2	8,110	2	1	9,710	666,247
"	**Total**	30	0	0	0	0	0	0	2	8,316	2	1	10,019	671,047
Lifetime		62	0	0	0	0	1	0	5	17,123	3	2	20,776	$1,124,272

Al Neves

Year	Driver	Starts	Poles	1	2	3	4	5	6–10	Laps	Laps Led	Races Led	Miles	$
1954	Al Neves	2	0	0	0	0	0	0	0	455	0	0	333	65
"	Clyde Palmer	2	0	0	0	0	1	0	1	526	0	0	263	450
"	**Total**	3	0	0	0	0	1	0	1	981	0	0	596	515
Lifetime		3	0	0	0	0	1	0	1	981	0	0	596	$515

Paul Newkirk

Year	Driver	Starts	Poles	1	2	3	4	5	6–10	Laps	Laps Led	Races Led	Miles	$
1952	Paul Newkirk	1	0	0	0	0	0	0	0	27	0	0	27	0
Lifetime		1	0	0	0	0	0	0	0	27	0	0	27	$0

Year	Driver	Starts	Poles	Finish						Laps	Laps Led	Races Led	Miles	$
				1	2	3	4	5	6–10					

O. L. Newsom

Year	Driver	Starts	Poles	1	2	3	4	5	6–10	Laps	Laps Led	Races Led	Miles	$
1972	Rick Newsom	1	0	0	0	0	0	0	0	231	0	0	462	800
1973	Rick Newsom	12	0	0	0	0	0	0	0	3,209	0	0	2,551	8,530
1974	Bob Burcham	1	0	0	0	0	0	0	0	313	0	0	170	760
"	Rick Newsom	2	0	0	0	0	0	0	0	535	0	0	507	1,425
"	**Total**	3	0	0	0	0	0	0	0	848	0	0	676	2,185
1975	Rick Newsom	10	0	0	0	0	0	0	0	1,672	0	0	1,695	9,780
1976	Rick Newsom	7	0	0	0	0	0	0	0	1,604	0	0	1,392	5,520
1977	Rick Newsom	7	0	0	0	0	0	0	0	1,240	0	0	888	3,260
1979	Rick Newsom	4	0	0	0	0	0	0	0	484	0	0	1,236	5,530
1980	Rick Newsom	6	0	0	0	0	0	0	0	1,179	0	0	790	3,830
1981	Cecil Gordon	1	0	0	0	0	0	0	0	296	0	0	296	650
"	Rick Newsom	9	0	0	0	0	0	0	0	1,676	0	0	1,741	8,625
"	**Total**	10	0	0	0	0	0	0	0	1,972	0	0	2,037	9,275
1982	Rick Newsom	8	0	0	0	0	0	0	0	1,143	0	0	1,931	12,390
1983	Rick Newsom	1	0	0	0	0	0	0	0	199	0	0	202	1,675
1984	Rick Newsom	1	0	0	0	0	0	0	0	242	0	0	246	2,835
1985	Rick Newsom	6	0	0	0	0	0	0	0	834	0	0	1,105	12,840
1986	Rick Newsom	3	0	0	0	0	0	0	0	358	0	0	447	4,185
Lifetime		79	0	0	0	0	0	0	0	15,215	0	0	15,659	$82,635

Ray Nichels

Year	Driver	Starts	Poles	1	2	3	4	5	6–10	Laps	Laps Led	Races Led	Miles	$
1957	Banjo Matthews	1	1	0	0	0	0	0	0		0	0		100
"	Cotton Owens	16	1	1	1	0	0	1	2	2,139	179	3	1,688	12,684
"	**Total**	16	2	1	1	0	0	1	2	2,139	179	3	1,688	12,784
1961	Darel Dieringer	2	0	0	0	0	0	1	0	230	0	0	575	600
"	Paul Goldsmith	2	0	0	0	1	0	0	1	239	0	0	598	6,050
"	**Total**	3	0	0	0	1	0	1	1	469	0	0	1,173	6,650
1962	Paul Goldsmith	1	0	0	0	0	0	0	1	218	0	0	327	1,375
"	Junior Johnson	1	0	0	0	0	0	0	0	7	0	0	10	200
"	LeeRoy Yarbrough	2	0	0	0	0	0	0	0	420	0	0	664	1,600
"	**Total**	4	0	0	0	0	0	0	1	645	0	0	1,001	3,175
1963	A. J. Foyt	3	0	0	1	1	0	0	0	368	8	2	957	7,520
"	Paul Goldsmith	6	1	0	1	0	0	0	0	545	22	3	1,058	4,170
"	Jim McGuirk	2	0	0	0	0	0	0	0	70	0	0	175	550
"	David Pearson	1	0	0	0	0	0	0	0	255	0	0	383	550
"	Pedro Rodriguez	1	0	0	0	0	0	0	0	54	0	0	135	400
"	Len Sutton	4	0	0	0	0	0	0	0	274	0	0	570	1,175
"	**Total**	7	1	0	2	1	0	0	0	1,566	30	3	3,277	14,365
1964	A. J. Foyt	2	0	1	0	0	0	0	0	287	14	1	591	13,400
"	Paul Goldsmith	14	2	0	0	3	0	0	1	2,281	319	8	2,903	20,835
"	Bobby Isaac	13	0	1	2	0	0	0	2	2,125	134	6	2,895	25,103
"	Troy Ruttman	1	0	0	0	0	0	0	1	177	0	0	478	850
"	**Total**	16	2	2	2	3	0	0	4	4,870	467	10	6,867	60,188
1965	Bobby Isaac	3	0	0	0	0	0	0	0	400	11	1	372	1,260
1966	Larry Frank	2	0	0	0	0	0	0	2	232	0	0	580	1,575
"	Paul Goldsmith	18	1	3	2	2	1	1	0	4,600	436	9	5,159	53,634
"	Sam McQuagg	16	0	1	0	1	0	2	3	3,575	175	3	3,906	29,530
"	Don White	8	0	0	1	2	0	0	2	1,961	8	1	3,199	19,670
"	**Total**	18	1	4	3	5	1	3	7	10,368	619	11	12,843	104,409
1967	Paul Goldsmith	21	0	0	2	3	1	1	1	4,851	398	7	5,409	38,732
"	Don White	6	0	0	0	0	1	0	2	997	0	0	1,691	8,410
"	**Total**	22	0	0	2	3	2	1	3	5,848	398	7	7,100	47,142
1968	Paul Goldsmith	14	0	0	1	0	0	1	2	2,730	304	8	3,473	24,040
"	Don White	2	0	0	0	0	0	0	1	585	0	0	738	2,105
"	**Total**	15	0	0	1	0	0	1	3	3,315	304	8	4,211	26,145
1969	Richard Brickhouse	2	0	1	0	0	0	0	0	241	33	1	606	25,420
"	Charlie Glotzbach	4	1	0	0	0	1	0	1	1,001	80	1	1,419	8,640
"	Paul Goldsmith	10	0	0	0	3	1	0	1	1,959	20	4	2,950	22,385
"	Don White	1	0	0	0	0	0	0	0	41	0	0	111	835
"	**Total**	16	1	1	0	3	2	0	2	3,242	133	6	5,086	57,280
1970	Charlie Glotzbach	17	4	2	0	3	2	0	1	3,177	417	16	5,161	50,274
"	Don White	1	0	0	0	0	0	0	0	16	0	0	42	880
"	**Total**	18	4	2	0	3	2	0	1	3,193	417	16	5,203	51,154
1971	Fred Lorenzen	14	1	0	1	0	2	4	2	3,229	152	6	5,038	45,100
"	Dave Marcis	2	0	0	0	0	0	1	0	507	0	0	713	4,507
"	David Pearson	7	0	0	0	0	0	1	1	495	0	0	915	6,085
"	**Total**	18	1	0	1	0	2	5	3	4,231	152	6	6,666	55,692
1972	Bobby Unser	1	0	0	0	0	0	0	0	8	0	0	12	603
"	Don White	1	0	0	0	0	0	0	0	114	0	0	285	1,745

Year	Driver	Starts	Poles	Finish 1	2	3	4	5	6–10	Laps	Laps Led	Races Led	Miles	$

Ray Nichels *continued*

Year	Driver	Starts	Poles	1	2	3	4	5	6–10	Laps	Laps Led	Races Led	Miles	$
"	LeeRoy Yarbrough	0												215
"	**Total**	2	0	0	0	0	0	0	0	122	0	0	297	2,563
Lifetime		158	12	10	12	19	9	12	27	40,408	2,710	71	55,783	$442,807

Wayne Niedecken

Year	Driver	Starts	Poles	1	2	3	4	5	6–10	Laps	Laps Led	Races Led	Miles	$
1953	Wayne Niedecken	1	0	0	0	0	0	0	0		0	0		25
Lifetime		1	0	0	0	0	0	0	0		0	0		$25

Dick Niles

Year	Driver	Starts	Poles	1	2	3	4	5	6–10	Laps	Laps Led	Races Led	Miles	$
1963	Bill Amick	1	0	0	0	0	0	0	1	142	0	0	383	1,000
1964	Bill Amick	1	0	0	0	0	1	0	0	181	0	0	489	2,470
1965	Bill Amick	1	0	0	0	0	0	0	0	95	0	0	257	620
Lifetime		3	0	0	0	0	1	0	1	418	0	0	1,129	$4,090

Louis Nissen

Year	Driver	Starts	Poles	1	2	3	4	5	6–10	Laps	Laps Led	Races Led	Miles	$
1973	Jim Danielson	1	0	0	0	0	0	0	1	176	0	0	461	1,520
1974	Jim Danielson	1	0	0	0	0	0	0	0	178	0	0	466	1,425
Lifetime		2	0	0	0	0	0	0	1	354	0	0	927	$2,945

O. L. Nixon

Year	Driver	Starts	Poles	1	2	3	4	5	6–10	Laps	Laps Led	Races Led	Miles	$
1970	Jim Vandiver	9	0	0	0	0	0	0	4	1,744	6	1	2,849	12,745
1971	Stick Elliott	2	0	0	0	0	0	0	0	598	0	0	687	1,818
"	Jim Vandiver	6	0	0	0	0	0	1	3	1,413	0	0	2,551	12,910
"	**Total**	8	0	0	0	0	0	1	3	2,011	0	0	3,238	14,728
1972	Jim Vandiver	14	0	0	0	2	0	0	1	2,506	6	1	3,128	27,408
1973	Jim Vandiver	9	0	0	0	0	0	0	4	2,343	0	0	3,600	17,296
1974	Jim Vandiver	7	0	0	0	0	0	0	1	1,061	1	1	1,996	15,409
1978	Sam Sommers	2	0	0	0	0	0	0	0	512	0	0	748	3,190
"	Jim Vandiver	2	0	0	0	0	0	0	0	362	0	0	562	3,530
"	**Total**	4	0	0	0	0	0	0	0	874	0	0	1,310	6,720
1979	Jim Vandiver	3	0	0	0	0	0	0	0	476	1	1	741	6,215
1980	Jim Vandiver	4	0	0	0	0	0	0	1	610	0	0	1,136	13,185
Lifetime		58	0	0	0	2	0	1	14	11,625	14	4	18,000	$113,706

Charles Noble

Year	Driver	Starts	Poles	1	2	3	4	5	6–10	Laps	Laps Led	Races Led	Miles	$
1976	Gary Matthews	1	0	0	0	0	0	0	0	71	0	0	186	1,015
Lifetime		1	0	0	0	0	0	0	0	71	0	0	186	$1,015

Stan Noble

Year	Driver	Starts	Poles	1	2	3	4	5	6–10	Laps	Laps Led	Races Led	Miles	$
1951	Stan Noble	3	0	0	0	0	0	0	0		0	0		75
"	Lloyd Porter	3	0	0	0	0	0	0	0		0	0		75
"	**Total**	6	0	0	0	0	0	0	0		0	0		150
Lifetime		6	0	0	0	0	0	0	0		0	0		$150

Don Noel

Year	Driver	Starts	Poles	1	2	3	4	5	6–10	Laps	Laps Led	Races Led	Miles	$
1967	Don Noel	1	0	0	0	0	0	0	0	131	0	0	354	625
1970	Don Noel	2	0	0	0	0	0	0	0	38	0	0	100	1,450
1971	Don Noel	2	0	0	0	0	0	0	0	137	0	0	354	2,145
1978	Don Noel	2	0	0	0	0	0	0	0	180	0	0	453	1,765
1979	Don Noel	1	0	0	0	0	0	0	0	15	0	0	39	700
Lifetime		8	0	0	0	0	0	0	0	501	0	0	1,300	$6,685

Noel-Lewin

Year	Driver	Starts	Poles	1	2	3	4	5	6–10	Laps	Laps Led	Races Led	Miles	$
1971	Don Noel	1	0	0	0	0	0	0	0	27	0	0	71	1,090
Lifetime		1	0	0	0	0	0	0	0	27	0	0	71	$1,090

Whitey Norman

Year	Driver	Starts	Poles	1	2	3	4	5	6–10	Laps	Laps Led	Races Led	Miles	$
1956	Whitey Norman	1	0	0	0	0	0	0	1	150	0	0	94	100
1957	Bill Massey	1	0	0	0	0	0	0	0	86	0	0	43	100
"	Bobby Myers	1	0	0	0	0	0	0	0	26	0	0	13	75

Year	Driver	Starts	Poles	1	2	3	4	5	6–10	Laps	Laps Led	Races Led	Miles	$

Whitey Norman *continued*

Year	Driver	Starts	Poles	1	2	3	4	5	6–10	Laps	Laps Led	Races Led	Miles	$
"	Whitey Norman	13	0	0	1	0	0	0	3	2,437	0	0	1,614	3,990
"	Speedy Thompson	1	0	0	0	0	0	0	0	101	0	0	51	100
"	**Total**	15	0	0	1	0	0	0	3	2,650	0	0	1,720	4,265
1958	Whitey Norman	9	0	0	0	0	2	0	1	1,348	0	0	752	1,635
1959	Whitey Norman	6	0	0	0	0	0	0	0	899	0	0	403	445
Lifetime		31	0	0	1	0	2	0	5	5,047	0	0	2,969	$6,445

J. M. Norris

Year	Driver	Starts	Poles	1	2	3	4	5	6–10	Laps	Laps Led	Races Led	Miles	$
1979	Bub Strickler	1	0	0	0	0	0	0	0	67	0	0	68	550
1980	Baxter Price	1	0	0	0	0	0	0	0	125	0	0	250	740
"	Bub Strickler	4	0	0	0	0	0	0	0	832	0	0	534	2,275
"	**Total**	5	0	0	0	0	0	0	0	957	0	0	784	3,015
Lifetime		6	0	0	0	0	0	0	0	1,024	0	0	852	$3,565

Jim Norris

Year	Driver	Starts	Poles	1	2	3	4	5	6–10	Laps	Laps Led	Races Led	Miles	$
1978	Joe Mihalic	6	0	0	0	0	0	0	0	1,216	0	0	1,537	6,030
"	Bobby Wawak	1	0	0	0	0	0	0	0	214	0	0	218	675
"	**Total**	7	0	0	0	0	0	0	0	1,430	0	0	1,755	6,705
1979	Wayne Broome	2	0	0	0	0	0	0	0	125	0	0	318	2,140
Lifetime		9	0	0	0	0	0	0	0	1,555	0	0	2,073	$8,845

Jack Norton

Year	Driver	Starts	Poles	1	2	3	4	5	6–10	Laps	Laps Led	Races Led	Miles	$
1961	Jack Norton	4	0	0	0	0	0	0	1	352	0	0	418	590
1963	Jack Norton	1	0	0	0	0	0	0	0	140	0	0	378	325
Lifetime		5	0	0	0	0	0	0	1	492	0	0	796	$915

James Norton

Year	Driver	Starts	Poles	1	2	3	4	5	6–10	Laps	Laps Led	Races Led	Miles	$
1960	James Norton	5	0	0	0	0	0	0	1	814	0	0	352	540
Lifetime		5	0	0	0	0	0	0	1	814	0	0	352	$540

Paul Nunn

Year	Driver	Starts	Poles	1	2	3	4	5	6–10	Laps	Laps Led	Races Led	Miles	$
1952	Clyde Minter	1	0	0	0	0	0	0	0	21	0	0	26	0
1953	Fred Dove	1	0	0	0	0	0	0	0	8	0	0	33	0
Lifetime		2	0	0	0	0	0	0	0	29	0	0	59	$0

Don Nuzum

Year	Driver	Starts	Poles	1	2	3	4	5	6–10	Laps	Laps Led	Races Led	Miles	$
1972	Johnny Anderson	4	0	0	0	0	0	0	0	385	0	0	969	4,600
1973	Johnny Anderson	2	0	0	0	3	0	0	0	186	0	0	487	1,840
1974	Johnny Anderson	2	0	0	0	0	0	0	0	154	0	0	403	2,130
Lifetime		8	0	0	0	0	0	0	0	725	0	0	1,860	$8,570

Homer O'Dell

Year	Driver	Starts	Poles	1	2	3	4	5	6–10	Laps	Laps Led	Races Led	Miles	$
1966	Neil Castles	1	0	0	0	0	0	0	0	20	0	0	8	100
"	Jimmy Helms	1	0	0	0	0	0	0	0	183	0	0	92	225
"	Hugh Lanphear	12	0	0	0	0	0	0	1	618	0	0	339	2,270
"	Clyde Lynn	1	0	0	0	0	0	0	1	440	0	0	220	400
"	Jack Soper	1	0	0	0	0	0	0	0	25	0	0	5	0
"	Billy Stiles	1	0	0	0	0	0	0	0	4	0	0	1	0
"	**Total**	17	0	0	0	0	0	0	2	1,290	0	0	665	2,995
Lifetime		17	0	0	0	0	0	0	2	1,290	0	0	665	$2,995

Joseph O'Neal

Year	Driver	Starts	Poles	1	2	3	4	5	6–10	Laps	Laps Led	Races Led	Miles	$
1989	Norm Benning	3	0	0	0	0	0	0	0	653	0	0	880	6,875
1993	Norm Benning	1	0	0	0	0	0	0	0	1	0	0	1	5,410
Lifetime		4	0	0	0	0	0	0	0	654	0	0	881	$12,285

Jerry O'Neil

Year	Driver	Starts	Poles	1	2	3	4	5	6–10	Laps	Laps Led	Races Led	Miles	$
1993	Jerry O'Neil	1	0	0	0	0	0	0	0	311	0	0	467	4,450
Lifetime		1	0	0	0	0	0	0	0	311	0	0	467	$4,450

Year	Driver	Starts	Poles	Finish						Laps	Laps Led	Races Led	Miles	$
				1	2	3	4	5	6–10	Laps	Led	Led	Miles	$

Phil Oates

Year	Driver	Starts	Poles	1	2	3	4	5	6–10	Laps	Led	Led	Miles	$
1951	Joe Eubanks	12	0	0	1	2	0	0	0	490	7	1	513	3,415
1952	Joe Eubanks	18	0	0	0	1	1	2	5	2,552	0	0	1,992	3,605
1953	Joe Eubanks	24	1	0	1	2	4	0	8	718	82	2	588	5,254
1954	Joe Eubanks	33	0	0	1	2	5	3	13	5,167	0	0	3,542	8,559
1955	Joe Eubanks	7	0	0	0	0	0	0	3	952	0	0	971	1,450
Lifetime		94	1	0	3	7	10	5	29	9,879	89	3	7,605	$22,283

Mike Ober

Year	Driver	Starts	Poles	1	2	3	4	5	6–10	Laps	Led	Led	Miles	$
1969	Dick Bown	1	0	0	0	0	0	0	0	160	0	0	432	1,230
1970	Dick Bown	6	0	0	0	0	0	0	1	836	0	0	1,187	4,275
1971	Dick Bown	4	0	0	0	0	0	0	0	414	0	0	941	4,500
1972	Dick Bown	3	0	0	0	0	0	0	0	459	0	0	1,181	4,465
1973	Dick Bown	2	0	0	0	0	0	0	0	196	0	0	514	1,860
"	Chuck Bown	1	0	0	0	0	0	0	0	59	0	0	155	1,030
"	**Total**	2	0	0	0	0	0	0	0	255	0	0	668	2,890
1974	Dick Bown	2	0	0	0	0	0	0	0	68	0	0	178	1,655
Lifetime		18	0	0	0	0	0	0	1	2,192	0	0	4,587	$19,015

Dan Obrist

Year	Driver	Starts	Poles	1	2	3	4	5	6–10	Laps	Led	Led	Miles	$
1995	Dan Obrist	1	0	0	0	0	0	0	0	7	0	0	18	9,760
Lifetime		1	0	0	0	0	0	0	0	7	0	0	18	$9,760

Tony Oddo

Year	Driver	Starts	Poles	1	2	3	4	5	6–10	Laps	Led	Led	Miles	$
1972	Mike James	2	0	0	0	0	0	0	0	180	0	0	450	2,620
1973	Mike James	1	0	0	0	0	0	0	0	129	0	0	338	1,065
Lifetime		3	0	0	0	0	0	0	0	309	0	0	788	$3,685

Larry Odo

Year	Driver	Starts	Poles	1	2	3	4	5	6–10	Laps	Led	Led	Miles	$
1956	Larry Odo	1	0	0	0	0	0	0	0	361	0	0	181	150
1959	Larry Odo	1	0	0	0	0	0	0	0	3	0	0	8	100
Lifetime		2	0	0	0	0	0	0	0	364	0	0	188	$250

Jack Ogden

Year	Driver	Starts	Poles	1	2	3	4	5	6–10	Laps	Led	Led	Miles	$
1979	Randy Ogden	3	0	0	0	0	0	0	0	473	0	0	737	2,465
1980	Donnie Allison	1	0	0	0	0	0	0	0	134	0	0	201	1,645
"	Randy Ogden	3	0	0	0	0	0	0	0	135	0	0	267	2,385
"	**Total**	4	0	0	0	0	0	0	0	269	0	0	468	4,030
1981	Randy Ogden	4	0	0	0	0	0	0	0	577	0	0	762	3,905
1982	Donnie Allison	3	0	0	0	0	0	0	0	608	0	0	840	9,330
Lifetime		14	0	0	0	0	0	0	0	1,927	0	0	2,808	$19,730

Don Oldenberg

Year	Driver	Starts	Poles	1	2	3	4	5	6–10	Laps	Led	Led	Miles	$
1951	Don Oldenberg	3	0	0	0	0	0	1	1		0	0		375
1954	Don Oldenberg	6	0	0	0	0	0	0	3	806	0	0	715	900
1955	Don Oldenberg	2	0	0	0	0	0	0	2	260	0	0	178	350
1956	Don Oldenberg	2	0	0	0	0	0	0	0	395	0	0	204	150
Lifetime		13	0	0	0	0	0	1	6	1,461	0	0	1,097	$1,775

Charles Oldham

Year	Driver	Starts	Poles	1	2	3	4	5	6–10	Laps	Led	Led	Miles	$
1956	Charles Oldham	1	0	0	0	0	0	0	0		0	0		25
Lifetime		1	0	0	0	0	0	0	0		0	0		$25

Don Oliver

Year	Driver	Starts	Poles	1	2	3	4	5	6–10	Laps	Led	Led	Miles	$
1954	Ben Gregory	2	0	0	0	0	1	0	0	708	0	0	354	425
"	Dick Rathmann	1	0	0	0	1	0	0	0	249	0	0	249	900
"	Eli Vukovich	1	0	0	0	0	0	0	0	262	0	0	131	25
"	**Total**	4	0	0	0	1	1	0	0	1,219	0	0	734	1,350
1955	Dick Rathmann	1	0	0	0	0	0	0	0	197	0	0	197	40
Lifetime		5	0	0	0	1	1	0	0	1,416	0	0	931	$1,390

Year	Driver	Starts	Poles	Finish						Laps	Laps Led	Races Led	Miles	$
				1	2	3	4	5	6–10					

Budd Olsen

Year	Driver	Starts	Poles	1	2	3	4	5	6–10	Laps	Laps Led	Races Led	Miles	$
1961	Budd Olsen	1	0	0	0	0	0	0	0	168	0	0	42	175
Lifetime		1	0	0	0	0	0	0	0	168	0	0	42	$175

Herb Onash

Year	Driver	Starts	Poles	1	2	3	4	5	6–10	Laps	Laps Led	Races Led	Miles	$
1964	Sal Tovella	2	0	0	0	0	0	0	0	167	0	0	418	850
Lifetime		2	0	0	0	0	0	0	0	167	0	0	418	$850

Phil Orr

Year	Driver	Starts	Poles	1	2	3	4	5	6–10	Laps	Laps Led	Races Led	Miles	$
1957	Phil Orr	1	0	0	0	0	0	0	0		0	0		110
1958	Phil Orr	1	0	0	0	0	0	0	0	31	0	0	127	50
Lifetime		2	0	0	0	0	0	0	0	31	0	0	127	$160

Bill Osborne

Year	Driver	Starts	Poles	1	2	3	4	5	6–10	Laps	Laps Led	Races Led	Miles	$
1980	Bill Osborne	1	0	0	0	0	0	0	0	22	0	0	22	575
1985	Bill Osborne	2	0	0	0	0	0	0	0	198	0	0	519	3,605
1986	Bill Osborne	1	0	0	0	0	0	0	0	38	0	0	100	850
Lifetime		4	0	0	0	0	0	0	0	258	0	0	641	$5,030

George Osborne

Year	Driver	Starts	Poles	1	2	3	4	5	6–10	Laps	Laps Led	Races Led	Miles	$
1953	George Osborne	2	0	0	0	0	0	0	0	477	0	0	528	300
1954	George Osborne	1	0	0	0	0	0	0	0	16	0	0	66	0
Lifetime		3	0	0	0	0	0	0	0	493	0	0	594	$300

Lewis Osborne

Year	Driver	Starts	Poles	1	2	3	4	5	6–10	Laps	Laps Led	Races Led	Miles	$
1962	Bruce Brantley	1	0	0	0	0	0	0	0	139	0	0	209	275
"	George Dunn	1	0	0	0	0	1	0	0	108	0	0	27	305
"	Bubba Farr	1	0	0	0	0	0	0	0	22	0	0	11	75
"	T. C. Hunt	1	0	0	0	0	0	0	0	196	0	0	270	400
"	Harry Leake	2	0	0	0	0	0	0	1	225	0	0	56	225
"	Paul Lewis	4	0	0	0	0	0	0	0	741	0	0	830	1,225
"	Tom Pistone	1	0	0	0	0	0	0	0	2	0	0	5	250
"	LeeRoy Yarbrough	6	0	0	0	0	0	0	0	529	0	0	496	710
"	**Total**	15	0	0	0	0	1	0	1	1,962	0	0	1,903	3,465
1963	Possum Jones	2	0	0	0	0	0	0	0	341	0	0	511	800
"	Cale Yarborough	1	0	0	0	0	0	0	0	9	0	0	23	250
"	**Total**	3	0	0	0	0	0	0	0	350	0	0	534	1,050
Lifetime		18	0	0	0	0	1	0	1	2,312	0	0	2,437	$4,515

Ray Osborne

Year	Driver	Starts	Poles	1	2	3	4	5	6–10	Laps	Laps Led	Races Led	Miles	$
1963	LeeRoy Yarbrough	1	0	0	0	0	0	0	0	20	0	0	30	600
1964	Johnny Allen	1	0	0	0	0	0	0	1	179	0	0	90	150
"	Jack Anderson	3	0	0	0	0	0	0	0	491	0	0	348	1,100
"	Buddy Baker	1	0	0	0	0	0	0	0	43	0	0	39	100
"	Rodney Bottinger	1	0	0	0	0	0	0	0	8	0	0	4	100
"	Jim Cook	1	0	0	0	0	0	0	0	222	0	0	111	150
"	Joe Weatherly	1	0	0	0	0	0	0	1	175	0	0	88	340
"	Bill Whitley	6	0	0	0	0	0	0	0	455	0	0	195	700
"	Reb Wickersham	1	0	0	0	0	0	0	0	186	0	0	279	400
"	Rodney Williams	2	0	0	0	0	0	0	0	115	0	0	68	550
"	Cale Yarborough	1	0	0	0	0	0	0	0	74	0	0	111	540
"	**Total**	18	0	0	0	0	0	0	2	1,948	0	0	1,331	4,130
Lifetime		19	0	0	0	0	0	0	2	1,968	0	0	1,361	$4,730

Bob Osiecki

Year	Driver	Starts	Poles	1	2	3	4	5	6–10	Laps	Laps Led	Races Led	Miles	$
1951	Jim Delaney	6	0	0	0	0	0	1	1	494	0	0	468	350
1952	Charlie Causey	1	0	0	0	0	0	0	0	7	0	0	7	25
1956	Jack Choquette	1	0	0	0	0	0	0	0		0	0		0
1957	Everett Brashear	1	0	0	0	0	0	0	0		0	0		25
"	Don Oldenberg	1	0	0	0	0	0	0	0		0	0		100
"	**Total**	1	0	0	0	0	0	0	0		0	0		125
1962	Darel Dieringer	7	0	0	0	0	0	1	1	1,878	17	1	1,861	2,890
"	Ralph Earnhardt	2	0	0	0	0	0	0	1	517	0	0	776	1,675

Year	Driver	Starts	Poles	Finish 1	2	3	4	5	6–10	Laps	Laps Led	Races Led	Miles	$

Bob Osiecki *continued*

Year	Driver	Starts	Poles	1	2	3	4	5	6–10	Laps	Laps Led	Races Led	Miles	$
"	Marvin Panch	2	0	0	0	0	0	0	0	23	0	0	58	450
"	Gary Sain	5	0	0	0	0	0	0	0	986	0	0	533	700
"	Jimmy Thompson	2	0	0	0	0	0	0	0	483	0	0	725	1,175
"	Herb Tillman	1	0	0	0	0	0	0	0	194	0	0	291	500
"	**Total**	16	0	0	0	0	0	1	2	4,081	17	1	4,243	7,390
Lifetime		25	0	0	0	0	0	2	3	4,582	17	1	4,717	$7,890

Rod Osterlund

Year	Driver	Starts	Poles	1	2	3	4	5	6–10	Laps	Laps Led	Races Led	Miles	$
1977	Marv Acton	2	0	0	0	0	0	0	0	359	0	0	202	945
"	Dave Marcis	2	0	0	0	0	0	0	0	324	0	0	620	2,510
"	Dick May	1	0	0	0	0	0	0	0	247	0	0	376	740
"	Jimmy Means	1	0	0	0	0	0	0	0	38	0	0	101	875
"	Sam Sommers	1	0	0	0	0	0	0	0	377	0	0	236	650
"	Roland Wlodyka	5	0	0	0	0	0	0	0	501	0	0	1,100	5,520
"	**Total**	11	0	0	0	0	0	0	0	1,846	0	0	2,635	11,240
1978	Dale Earnhardt	1	0	0	0	0	1	0	0	327	0	0	498	7,500
"	Jimmy Insolo	1	0	0	0	0	0	0	1	198	0	0	495	5,640
"	Dave Marcis	30	0	0	1	3	8	2	10	9,672	115	12	10,992	205,871
"	Roland Wlodyka	6	0	0	0	0	0	0	0	1,172	0	0	1,707	9,910
"	**Total**	30	0	0	1	3	9	2	11	**11,369**	115	12	**13,691**	228,921
1979	Dale Earnhardt	27	4	1	1	3	4	2	6	8,340	604	16	9,357	274,810
"	David Pearson	4	1	1	1	0	1	0	1	1,250	91	2	1,664	64,865
"	**Total**	31	5	2	2	3	5	2	7	9,590	695	18	11,021	339,675
1980	Dale Earnhardt	31	0	5	3	4	3	4	5	9,615	1,185	25	11,136	671,991
"	Dan Gurney	1	0	0	0	0	0	0	0	79	0	0	207	1,105
"	Janet Guthrie	1	0	0	0	0	0	0	0	193	0	0	483	13,925
"	**Total**	31	0	5	3	4	3	4	5	9,887	1,185	25	11,825	687,021
1981	Dale Earnhardt	16	0	0	2	3	0	2	3	4,282	272	7	5,494	249,767
1989	Hut Stricklin	27	0	0	0	0	1	0	3	7,557	3	1	9,285	152,504
1990	Jim Bown	3	0	0	0	0	0	0	0	837	0	0	874	11,655
"	Jimmy Spencer	26	0	0	0	0	0	0	2	7,576	10	5	8,929	219,775
"	**Total**	29	0	0	0	0	0	0	2	8,413	10	5	9,803	213,430
Lifetime		175	5	7	8	13	18	10	31	52,944	2,280	68	63,755	$1,900,558

Nelson Oswald

Year	Driver	Starts	Poles	1	2	3	4	5	6–10	Laps	Laps Led	Races Led	Miles	$
1978	Nelson Oswald	6	0	0	0	0	0	0	0	1,103	0	0	781	3,530
1979	Dick May	1	0	0	0	0	0	0	0	113	0	0	226	1,100
"	Nelson Oswald	6	0	0	0	0	0	0	0	842	0	0	1,000	3,610
"	Bill Seifert	1	0	0	0	0	0	0	0	32	0	0	64	960
"	**Total**	8	0	0	0	0	0	0	0	987	0	0	1,290	5,670
1980	Cecil Gordon	1	0	0	0	0	0	0	0	335	0	0	200	450
"	Dick May	2	0	0	0	0	0	0	0	508	0	0	524	2,315
"	Nelson Oswald	2	0	0	0	0	0	0	0	184	0	0	374	2,520
"	**Total**	5	0	0	0	0	0	0	0	1,027	0	0	1,097	5,285
Lifetime		19	0	0	0	0	0	0	0	3,117	0	0	3,168	$14,485

Barry Owen

Year	Driver	Starts	Poles	1	2	3	4	5	6–10	Laps	Laps Led	Races Led	Miles	$
1992	Mike Wallace	2	0	0	0	0	0	0	0	791	0	0	965	12,235
1993	Mike Wallace	2	0	0	0	0	0	0	0	638	0	0	838	14,800
1996	Mike Wallace	1	0	0	0	0	0	0	0	199	0	0	398	16,665
Lifetime		5	0	0	0	0	0	0	0	1,628	0	0	2,201	$43,700

Cotton Owens

Year	Driver	Starts	Poles	1	2	3	4	5	6–10	Laps	Laps Led	Races Led	Miles	$
1950	Cotton Owens	3	0	0	0	0	0	0	1	511	23	1	727	1,100
1951	Cotton Owens	5	0	0	0	0	0	1	2	370	0	0	463	725
1959	Cotton Owens	6	1	1	1	0	0	0	0	1,211	114	3	929	2,125
1960	Bobby Johns	4	0	1	0	0	2	0	0	1,173	366	3	1,269	20,040
"	Cotton Owens	13	3	1	3	1	0	0	0	1,984	185	7	2,276	14,005
"	**Total**	16	3	2	3	1	2	0	0	3,157	551	9	3,545	34,045
1961	Ralph Earnhardt	7	0	0	1	1	0	0	3	1,602	90	3	2,429	10,195
"	Cotton Owens	16	3	4	3	1	2	1	0	2,683	58	5	2,108	11,890
"	Marvin Panch	1	0	0	0	0	0	0	1	262	0	0	393	875
"	Fireball Roberts	1	0	0	0	0	1	0	0	496	2	1	248	850
"	**Total**	25	3	4	4	2	3	1	4	5,043	150	9	5,177	23,810

Cotton Owens *continued*

Year	Driver	Starts	Poles	Finish 1	2	3	4	5	6–10	Laps	Laps Led	Races Led	Miles	$
1962	Junior Johnson	4	0	0	1	0	0	0	1	671	166	1	824	7,345
"	Cotton Owens	16	1	0	2	2	2	1	1	2,000	36	2	1,515	5,905
"	David Pearson	3	0	0	0	0	1	0	1	1,055	2	1	1,076	4,435
"	**Total**	22	1	0	3	2	3	1	3	3,726	204	4	3,414	17,685
1963	Cotton Owens	1	0	0	0	0	0	0	1	170	0	0	85	175
"	David Pearson	40	2	0	3	2	5	3	6	8,442	178	6	6,120	24,436
"	G. C. Spencer	1	0	0	0	0	0	0	0	210	0	0	289	500
"	Billy Wade	29	0	0	1	0	2	1	10	5,997	21	2	4,986	13,705
"	Bob Welborn	1	0	0	0	0	0	0	0	253	0	0	380	450
"	**Total**	42	2	0	4	2	7	4	17	15,072	199	8	11,859	39,266
1964	Earl Balmer	10	0	0	0	0	1	1	2	2,771	1	1	2,052	5,795
"	Bobby Isaac	3	0	0	1	0	1	0	0	727	0	0	309	1,200
"	Cotton Owens	2	0	1	1	0	0	0	0	466	54	1	299	3,400
"	Jim Paschal	9	0	0	0	0	1	2	4	2,305	0	0	1,941	7,115
"	David Pearson	61	12	8	8	4	7	2	13	13,225	2,256	31	8,906	45,542
"	Larry Thomas	2	0	0	0	0	0	0	0	403	0	0	579	1,200
"	Billy Wade	3	0	0	0	1	0	0	1	485	0	0	585	3,970
"	**Total**	62	12	9	10	5	10	5	20	20,382	2,311	33	14,672	68,222
1965	David Pearson	14	1	2	2	2	1	1	3	3,242	744	8	1,803	8,925
1966	Mario Andretti	1	0	0	0	0	0	0	0	78	0	0	195	395
"	Bobby Isaac	1	0	0	0	0	0	0	0	293	0	0	293	615
"	David Pearson	42	7	15	5	5	1	0	7	10,781	3,174	25	8,409	78,194
"	**Total**	42	7	15	5	5	1	0	7	11,152	**3,174**	25	8,897	79,204
1967	Bobby Allison	9	0	1	2	3	1	0	1	1,971	51	5	1,981	16,130
"	Buddy Baker	4	0	0	0	1	0	0	0	589	0	0	375	1,350
"	Darel Dieringer	3	0	0	0	0	0	0	0	585	35	1	683	2,310
"	Ray Hendrick	1	0	0	0	0	0	0	0	107	0	0	54	175
"	Sam McQuagg	6	0	0	0	0	2	0	0	1,053	8	1	695	2,845
"	David Pearson	10	0	2	0	1	1	0	2	2,066	340	6	2,032	16,995
"	6th place owner point money (not assigned to any driver)													2,145
"	**Total**	32	0	3	2	5	4	0	3	6,371	434	13	5,819	41,950
1968	Buddy Baker	1	0	0	0	0	0	0	0	59	0	0	159	575
"	Charlie Glotzbach	19	3	1	3	1	4	0	2	4,336	291	5	4,336	41,251
"	Al Unser	1	0	0	0	0	1	0	0	200	0	0	500	6,250
"	**Total**	21	3	1	3	1	5	0	2	4,595	291	5	4,995	48,076
1969	Buddy Baker	12	1	0	2	4	0	1	2	3,266	579	10	4,113	50,085
"	Charlie Glotzbach	6	0	0	2	0	0	1	0	1,443	82	5	1,924	24,550
"	James Hylton	2	0	0	0	0	0	1	0	611	0	0	355	1,250
"	**Total**	20	1	0	4	4	0	3	2	5,320	661	15	6,391	75,885
1970	Buddy Baker	17	1	1	2	0	1	2	2	3,604	485	11	5,871	63,553
"	Sam Posey	1	0	0	0	0	0	0	0	82	0	0	215	900
"	**Total**	18	1	1	2	0	1	2	2	3,686	485	11	6,086	64,453
1971	Pete Hamilton	20	2	1	0	5	4	1	1	4,407	219	13	6,853	60,140
1972	Charlie Glotzbach	3	0	0	1	1	0	0	0	709	0	0	1,150	26,175
1973	Dick Brooks	1	0	0	0	1	0	0	0	197	0	0	493	9,800
"	Peter Gregg	1	0	0	0	0	0	0	0	34	0	0	51	775
"	**Total**	2	0	0	0	1	0	0	0	231	0	0	544	10,575
Lifetime		353	37	39	44	36	41	19	67	89,185	9,560	157	83,325	$602,361
												10th		

Ken Pace

Year	Driver	Starts	Poles	Finish 1	2	3	4	5	6–10	Laps	Laps Led	Races Led	Miles	$
1954	Fred Dove	2	0	0	0	0	0	0	0	183	0	0	99	0
"	Clyde Minter	11	0	0	0	0	0	0	6	1,638	0	0	855	850
"	Ken Pace	2	0	0	0	0	0	0	0	258	0	0	144	25
"	**Total**	11	0	0	0	0	0	0	6	2,079	0	0	1,097	875
1955	Fred Dove	1	0	0	0	0	0	0	0	40	0	0	20	25
"	Clyde Minter	1	0	0	0	0	0	0	1	178	0	0	89	100
"	Ken Pace	2	0	0	0	0	0	0	0	160	0	0	80	25
"	**Total**	2	0	0	0	0	0	0	1	378	0	0	189	150
Lifetime		13	0	0	0	0	0	0	7	2,457	0	0	1,286	$1,025

Eddie Pagan

Year	Driver	Starts	Poles	Finish 1	2	3	4	5	6–10	Laps	Laps Led	Races Led	Miles	$
1954	Eddie Pagan	2	0	0	0	0	0	0	0	682	0	0	453	140
"	Marian Pagan	1	0	0	0	0	0	0	0	261	0	0	131	25
"	**Total**	3	0	0	0	0	0	0	0	943	0	0	583	165
1955	Eddie Pagan	1	0	0	0	0	0	0	0	62	0	0	62	20

Year	Driver	Starts	Poles	Finish 1	2	3	4	5	6–10	Laps	Laps Led	Races Led	Miles	$

Eddie Pagan *continued*

Year	Driver	Starts	Poles	1	2	3	4	5	6–10	Laps	Laps Led	Races Led	Miles	$
1956	Eddie Pagan	8	2	1	1	0	0	2	0	1,366	31	2	1,037	3,095
1957	Eddie Pagan	15	2	3	3	3	1	1	0	2,611	3	3	1,802	7,274
1958	Eddie Pagan	23	2	0	2	1	1	7	6	3,701	57	2	2,444	7,142
Lifetime		50	6	4	6	4	2	10	6	8,683	91	7	5,927	$17,696

Lennie Page

Year	Driver	Starts	Poles	1	2	3	4	5	6–10	Laps	Laps Led	Races Led	Miles	$
1957	Lennie Page	4	0	0	0	0	0	0	1	396	0	0	332	410
1958	Lennie Page	8	0	0	0	0	0	0	2	901	0	0	355	760
1959	Lennie Page	2	0	0	0	0	0	0	1	251	0	0	143	280
1960	Lennie Page	5	0	0	0	0	0	0	2	774	0	0	616	1,050
Lifetime		19	0	0	0	0	0	0	6	2,322	0	0	1,446	$2,500

Norm Palmer

Year	Driver	Starts	Poles	1	2	3	4	5	6–10	Laps	Laps Led	Races Led	Miles	$
1977	Norm Palmer	3	0	0	0	0	0	0	1	239	0	0	620	4,560
1978	Norm Palmer	2	0	0	0	0	0	0	0	119	0	0	312	2,100
1979	Norm Palmer	1	0	0	0	0	0	0	1	91	0	0	238	2,500
1985	Norm Palmer	1	0	0	0	0	0	0	0	22	0	0	58	745
Lifetime		7	0	0	0	0	0	0	2	471	0	0	1,227	$9,905

Robert Palmer

Year	Driver	Starts	Poles	1	2	3	4	5	6–10	Laps	Laps Led	Races Led	Miles	$
1983	Randy Becker	1	0	0	0	0	0	0	0	23	0	0	60	1,700
Lifetime		1	0	0	0	0	0	0	0	23	0	0	60	$1,700

Walt Palozi

Year	Driver	Starts	Poles	1	2	3	4	5	6–10	Laps	Laps Led	Races Led	Miles	$
1954	Ernie Young	3	0	0	0	0	0	0	0	739	0	0	459	65
1955	Ernie Young	3	0	0	0	0	0	0	1	311	0	0	249	150
1956	Ernie Young	5	0	0	0	0	0	0	0	419	0	0	443	330
1957	Don Johns	2	0	0	0	0	0	0	1	255	0	0	128	200
"	Ernie Young	2	0	0	0	0	1	0	0	153	0	0	97	375
"	**Total**	4	0	0	0	0	1	0	1	408	0	0	224	575
1959	Bob Hogle	2	0	0	0	0	0	0	0	429	0	0	184	165
1960	Kuzie Kuzmanich	1	0	0	0	0	0	0	1	93	0	0	93	250
Lifetime		18	0	0	0	0	1	0	3	2,399	0	0	1,650	$1,535

Bettie Panch

Year	Driver	Starts	Poles	1	2	3	4	5	6–10	Laps	Laps Led	Races Led	Miles	$
1975	Richie Panch	14	0	0	0	0	0	1	3	2,276	8	3	3,132	32,535
Lifetime		14	0	0	0	0	0	1	3	2,276	8	3	3,132	$32,535

Marvin Panch

Year	Driver	Starts	Poles	1	2	3	4	5	6–10	Laps	Laps Led	Races Led	Miles	$
1951	Sam Hawks	3	0	0	0	0	1	0	0	0	0	0	0	800
"	Marvin Panch	3	0	0	1	0	0	0	1	0	0	0	0	950
"	**Total**	3	0	0	1	0	1	0	1	0	0	0	0	1,750
1953	Marvin Panch	2	0	0	0	0	0	0	0	275	0	0	378	160
1955	Marvin Panch	1	0	0	0	0	0	0	0	70	15	1	35	25
1957	Marvin Panch	20	0	2	2	3	3	0	4	3,595	91	3	2,306	13,022
Lifetime		26	0	2	3	3	4	0	5	3,940	106	4	2,719	$14,957

Chester Papienski

Year	Driver	Starts	Poles	1	2	3	4	5	6–10	Laps	Laps Led	Races Led	Miles	$
1974	Eddie Bradshaw	1	0	0	0	0	0	0	1	123	0	0	322	1,375
1975	Eddie Bradshaw	1	0	0	0	0	0	0	0	63	0	0	165	820
1976	Eddie Bradshaw	2	0	0	0	0	0	0	0	224	0	0	587	2,685
1977	Eddie Bradshaw	2	0	0	0	0	0	0	1	152	0	0	394	2,920
1978	Eddie Bradshaw	1	0	0	0	0	0	0	0	15	0	0	39	600
"	Jack Simpson	1	0	0	0	0	0	0	0	74	0	0	194	1,105
"	**Total**	1	0	0	0	0	0	0	0	89	0	0	233	1,705
Lifetime		7	0	0	0	0	0	0	2	651	0	0	1,701	$9,505

Roger Paquette

Year	Driver	Starts	Poles	1	2	3	4	5	6–10	Laps	Laps Led	Races Led	Miles	$
1972	Jimmy Insolo	1	0	0	0	0	0	0	0	130	0	0	341	835
1973	Jimmy Insolo	2	0	0	0	0	1	1	0	335	0	0	878	6,295

Year	Driver	Starts	Poles	Finish						Laps	Laps Led	Races Led	Miles	$
				1	2	3	4	5	6–10					

Roger Paquette *continued*

Year	Driver	Starts	Poles	1	2	3	4	5	6–10	Laps	Laps Led	Races Led	Miles	$
1974	Jimmy Insolo	3	0	0	0	0	0	0	0	338	1	1	867	3,360
1975	Jimmy Insolo	3	0	0	0	0	0	0	1	265	18	1	671	4,815
1976	Jimmy Insolo	3	0	0	0	1	0	0	1	454	0	0	1,169	12,105
Lifetime		12	0	0	0	1	1	1	2	1,522	19	2	3,925	$27,410

Jimmy Pardue

Year	Driver	Starts	Poles	1	2	3	4	5	6–10	Laps	Laps Led	Races Led	Miles	$
1955	Jimmy Pardue	1	0	0	0	0	0	0	0	10	0	0	5	0
"	Bobby Waddell	6	0	0	0	0	0	0	0	805	0	0	849	325
"	**Total**	7	0	0	0	0	0	0	0	815	0	0	854	325
1956	Bobby Waddell	3	0	0	0	0	0	0	0	67	0	0	29	0
1959	Jimmy Pardue	6	0	0	0	0	0	0	1	526	0	0	264	465
1961	Jimmy Pardue	40	0	0	0	0	1	2	13	7,310	0	0	5,439	10,362
1962	Jimmy Pardue	29	0	1	1	1	1	1	11	7,274	200	3	4,855	12,066
1963	Jimmy Pardue	2	0	0	0	0	2	0	0	395	0	0	158	575
Lifetime		87	0	1	1	1	4	3	25	16,387	200	3	11,599	$23,793

J. C. Parker

Year	Driver	Starts	Poles	1	2	3	4	5	6–10	Laps	Laps Led	Races Led	Miles	$
1962	Charley Griffith	1	0	0	0	0	0	0	0	137	0	0	69	100
"	Friday Hassler	2	0	0	0	0	0	0	0	257	0	0	321	300
"	Ned Jarrett	1	0	0	0	0	0	0	1	196	0	0	49	430
"	Nero Steptoe	1	0	0	0	0	0	0	0	78	0	0	39	150
"	Bob Welborn	19	0	0	1	0	2	2	4	4,669	0	0	3,001	7,347
"	**Total**	22	0	0	1	0	2	2	5	5,337	0	0	3,479	8,327
1963	Buddy Baker	2	0	0	0	0	0	0	0	289	0	0	209	395
"	Joe Jones	1	0	0	0	0	0	0	0	186	0	0	47	130
"	Jimmy Pardue	1	0	0	0	0	0	0	1	193	0	0	48	160
"	Hank Thomas	1	0	0	0	0	0	0	0	44	0	0	11	125
"	Larry Thomas	3	0	0	0	0	0	0	0	632	0	0	315	570
"	**Total**	8	0	0	0	0	0	0	1	1,344	0	0	630	1,380
1964	Buddy Baker	18	0	0	0	1	1	1	2	2,197	0	0	1,088	3,600
Lifetime		48	0	0	1	1	3	3	8	8,878	0	0	5,197	$13,307

Ron Parker

Year	Driver	Starts	Poles	1	2	3	4	5	6–10	Laps	Laps Led	Races Led	Miles	$
1990	Tracy Leslie	1	0	0	0	0	0	0	0	67	0	0	68	2,650
Lifetime		1	0	0	0	0	0	0	0	67	0	0	68	$2,650

Chuck Parkko

Year	Driver	Starts	Poles	1	2	3	4	5	6–10	Laps	Laps Led	Races Led	Miles	$
1961	Don Noel	4	0	0	2	0	0	1	0	493	0	0	518	1,705
1964	Dick Mitchell	1	0	0	0	0	0	0	0	152	0	0	410	525
Lifetime		5	0	0	2	0	0	1	0	645	0	0	928	$2,230

Paul Parks

Year	Driver	Starts	Poles	1	2	3	4	5	6–10	Laps	Laps Led	Races Led	Miles	$
1960	Paul Parks	3	0	0	0	0	0	0	0	273	0	0	537	250
Lifetime		3	0	0	0	0	0	0	0	273	0	0	537	$250

Raymond Parks

Year	Driver	Starts	Poles	1	2	3	4	5	6–10	Laps	Laps Led	Races Led	Miles	$
1949	Red Byron	6	1	2	0	2	0	0	0	633	103	2	582	5,800
"	Bob Flock	1	0	0	0	0	0	0	0		0	0		0
"	Roy Hall	1	0	0	0	0	0	0	1	196	0	0	98	150
"	**Total**	6	1	2	0	2	0	0	1	829	103	2	680	5,950
1950	Red Byron	4	1	0	1	1	1	0	0	634	85	3	835	3,325
1955	Curtis Turner	4	0	0	0	1	2	0	0	554	0	0	437	1,625
Lifetime		14	2	2	1	4	3	0	1	2,017	188	5	1,951	$10,900

Stan Parnell

Year	Driver	Starts	Poles	1	2	3	4	5	6–10	Laps	Laps Led	Races Led	Miles	$
1952	Possum Jones	1	0	0	0	0	0	0	0	193	0	0	241	0
Lifetime		1	0	0	0	0	0	0	0	193	0	0	241	$0

George Parrish

Year	Driver	Starts	Poles	1	2	3	4	5	6–10	Laps	Laps Led	Races Led	Miles	$
1955	George Parrish	12	0	0	0	0	0	0	1	1,057	0	0	606	740
Lifetime		12	0	0	0	0	0	0	1	1,057	0	0	606	$740

Year	Driver	Starts	Poles	Finish						Laps	Laps Led	Races Led	Miles	$
				1	2	3	4	5	6–10					

Harry Parry

Year	Driver	Starts	Poles	1	2	3	4	5	6–10	Laps	Laps Led	Races Led	Miles	$
1955	Ray Platte	1	0	0	0	0	0	0	0	339	0	0	466	100
Lifetime		1	0	0	0	0	0	0	0	339	0	0	466	$100

Jim Parsley

Year	Driver	Starts	Poles	1	2	3	4	5	6–10	Laps	Laps Led	Races Led	Miles	$
1958	Jim Parsley	7	0	0	0	0	0	0	4	1,338	0	0	617	950
1959	Jim Parsley	1	0	0	0	0	0	0	1	177	0	0	89	150
Lifetime		8	0	0	0	0	0	0	5	1,515	0	0	706	$1,100

Benny Parsons

Year	Driver	Starts	Poles	1	2	3	4	5	6–10	Laps	Laps Led	Races Led	Miles	$
1970	Benny Parsons	2	0	0	0	0	0	0	1	235	0	0	588	2,070
Lifetime		2	0	0	0	0	0	0	1	235	0	0	588	$2,070

Jim Paschal

Year	Driver	Starts	Poles	1	2	3	4	5	6–10	Laps	Laps Led	Races Led	Miles	$
1949	Jim Paschal	1	0	0	0	0	0	0	0		0	0		0
1953	Jim Paschal	1	0	0	0	0	0	0	0		0	0		25
1957	Jim Paschal	11	0	0	1	0	1	1	2	1,320	0	0	696	1,800
"	Shorty York	1	0	0	0	0	0	0	0	79	0	0	109	300
"	**Total**	12	0	0	1	0	1	1	2	1,399	0	0	805	2,100
1958	Jim Paschal	2	0	0	0	0	0	0	0	321	0	0	441	260
Lifetime		16	0	0	1	0	1	1	2	1,720	0	0	1,246	$2,385

Dick Passwater

Year	Driver	Starts	Poles	1	2	3	4	5	6–10	Laps	Laps Led	Races Led	Miles	$
1953	Dick Passwater	1	0	0	0	0	0	0	1	350	0	0	481	630
Lifetime		1	0	0	0	0	0	0	1	350	0	0	481	$630

Jim Patrick

Year	Driver	Starts	Poles	1	2	3	4	5	6–10	Laps	Laps Led	Races Led	Miles	$
1979	Darrell Busham	1	0	0	0	0	0	0	0	101	0	0	60	385
Lifetime		1	0	0	0	0	0	0	0	101	0	0	60	$385

Dana Patten

Year	Driver	Starts	Poles	1	2	3	4	5	6–10	Laps	Laps Led	Races Led	Miles	$
1988	Dana Patten	4	0	0	0	0	0	0	0	1,059	0	0	1,446	9,595
Lifetime		4	0	0	0	0	0	0	0	1,059	0	0	1,446	$9,595

Otis Patton

Year	Driver	Starts	Poles	1	2	3	4	5	6–10	Laps	Laps Led	Races Led	Miles	$
1969	Bill Massuch	1	0	0	0	0	0	0	0	157	0	0	314	1,075
Lifetime		1	0	0	0	0	0	0	0	157	0	0	314	$1,075

Donny Paul

Year	Driver	Starts	Poles	1	2	3	4	5	6–10	Laps	Laps Led	Races Led	Miles	$
1984	Donny Paul	1	0	0	0	0	0	0	0	1	0	0	2	2,755
1985	Donny Paul	1	0	0	0	0	0	0	0	156	0	0	234	2,620
1986	Donny Paul													2,450
1987	Donny Paul	1	0	0	0	0	0	0	0	104	0	0	208	4,015
Lifetime		3	0	0	0	0	0	0	0	261	0	0	444	$11,840

Bill Payne

Year	Driver	Starts	Poles	1	2	3	4	5	6–10	Laps	Laps Led	Races Led	Miles	$
1954	Charles Pemberton	2	0	0	0	0	0	0	1	525	0	0	381	200
Lifetime		2	0	0	0	0	0	0	1	525	0	0	381	$200

Curtis Payne

Year	Driver	Starts	Poles	1	2	3	4	5	6–10	Laps	Laps Led	Races Led	Miles	$
1979	John Rezek	4	0	0	0	0	0	0	0	584	0	0	1,012	5,035
Lifetime		4	0	0	0	0	0	0	0	584	0	0	1,012	$5,035

David Pearson

Year	Driver	Starts	Poles	1	2	3	4	5	6–10	Laps	Laps Led	Races Led	Miles	$
1960	David Pearson	22	1	0	1	0	1	1	4	3,885	0	0	3,768	5,030
1961	David Pearson	10	0	0	0	1	1	1	1	1,316	0	0	713	1,515
1985	David Pearson	4	0	0	0	0	0	0	0	203	0	0	372	7,535
1986	David Pearson	2	0	0	0	0	0	0	1	337	0	0	605	8,405
"	Larry Pearson	2	0	0	0	0	0	0	0	358	0	0	566	14,310
"	**Total**	4	0	0	0	0	0	0	1	695	0	0	1,171	22,715
1987	Larry Pearson	4	0	0	0	0	0	0	1	1,162	1	1	1,435	18,555

Year	Driver	Starts	Poles	Finish						Laps	Laps Led	Races Led	Miles	$
				1	2	3	4	5	6–10	Laps	Led	Led	Miles	$

David Pearson *continued*

Year	Driver	Starts	Poles	1	2	3	4	5	6–10	Laps	Laps Led	Races Led	Miles	$
1988	Larry Pearson	2	0	0	0	0	0	0	0	281	0	0	427	3,705
1989	Larry Pearson	29	0	0	0	0	0	0	2	7,993	5	2	9,735	156,060
1990	Larry Pearson	4	0	0	0	0	0	0	0	1,193	0	0	1,468	41,920
Lifetime		79	1	0	1	1	2	2	9	16,728	6	3	19,089	$257,035

Del Pearson

Year	Driver	Starts	Poles	1	2	3	4	5	6–10	Laps	Laps Led	Races Led	Miles	$
1951	Ted Chamberlain	1	0	0	0	0	0	0	0	340	0	0	425	50
"	Dell Pearson	8	0	0	1	0	0	0	2	310	0	0	310	900
"	**Total**	9	0	0	1	0	0	0	2	650	0	0	735	950
Lifetime		9	0	0	1	0	0	0	2	650	0	0	735	$950

Hugh Pcarson

Year	Driver	Starts	Poles	1	2	3	4	5	6–10	Laps	Laps Led	Races Led	Miles	$
1974	Hugh Pearson	2	0	0	0	0	0	0	0	116	0	0	302	1,385
1975	Hugh Pearson	2	0	0	0	0	0	0	0	218	0	0	553	2,550
1976	Hugh Pearson	2	0	0	0	0	0	0	0	115	0	0	301	1,930
1977	Hugh Pearson	1	0	0	0	0	0	0	1	114	0	0	299	2,490
Lifetime		7	0	0	0	0	0	0	1	563	0	0	1,454	$8,355

Peck Peckham

Year	Driver	Starts	Poles	1	2	3	4	5	6–10	Laps	Laps Led	Races Led	Miles	$
1958	Peck Peckham	11	0	0	0	0	0	0	0	1,263	0	0	834	835
Lifetime		11	0	0	0	0	0	0	0	1,263	0	0	834	$835

Nestor Peles

Year	Driver	Starts	Poles	1	2	3	4	5	6–10	Laps	Laps Led	Races Led	Miles	$
1977	Nestor Peles	2	0	0	0	0	0	0	0	209	0	0	473	1,330
1978	Nestor Peles	3	0	0	0	0	0	0	0	979	0	0	1,249	3,280
1979	Nestor Peles	1	0	0	0	0	0	0	0	465	0	0	465	1,765
"	Steve Peles	2	0	0	0	0	0	0	0	641	0	0	922	2,180
"	**Total**	3	0	0	0	0	0	0	0	1,106	0	0	1,387	3,945
1980	Nestor Peles	1	0	0	0	0	0	0	0	207	0	0	207	600
"	Steve Peles	0												935
"	**Total**	1	0	0	0	0	0	0		207	0	0	207	1,535
Lifetime		9	0	0	0	0	0	0	0	2,501	0	0	3,316	$10,090

John Pemberton

Year	Driver	Starts	Poles	1	2	3	4	5	6–10	Laps	Laps Led	Races Led	Miles	$
1970	Lee Roy Carrigg	9	0	0	0	0	0	0	0	1,002	0	0	1,021	4,130
1971	Butch Hirst	1	0	0	0	0	0	0	0	2	0	0	5	0
Lifetime		10	0	0	0	0	0	0	0	1,004	0	0	1,026	$4,130

Bob Penrod

Year	Driver	Starts	Poles	1	2	3	4	5	6–10	Laps	Laps Led	Races Led	Miles	$
1984	Bob Penrod	1	0	0	0	0	0	0	0	55	0	0	84	955
Lifetime		1	0	0	0	0	0	0	0	55	0	0	84	$955

Roger Penske

Year	Driver	Starts	Poles	1	2	3	4	5	6–10	Laps	Laps Led	Races Led	Miles	$
1972	Donnie Allison	1	0	0	0	1	0	0	0	150	0	0	393	4,025
"	Mark Donohue	4	0	0	0	0	0	0	0	390	0	0	669	5,580
"	Dave Marcis	7	0	0	0	0	0	0	3	1,547	0	0	2,001	9,906
"	**Total**	12	0	0	0	1	0	0	3	2,087	0	0	3,064	19,511
1973	Mark Donohue	2	0	1	0	0	0	0	0	393	138	1	803	16,120
"	Dave Marcis	9	0	0	0	0	0	1	1	1,811	0	0	2,159	13,548
"	**Total**	11	0	1	0	0	0	1	1	2,204	138	1	2,962	29,668
1974	Bobby Allison	7	0	1	0	0	1	3	0	1,925	188	5	2,866	33,935
"	Gary Bettenhausen	5	0	0	0	0	1	0	2	986	35	1	2,100	12,750
"	George Follmer	1	1	0	0	0	0	0	0	7	1	1	18	1,000
"	Dave Marcis	1	0	0	0	0	0	0	1	327	11	1	447	2,025
"	**Total**	14	1	1	0	0	2	3	3	3,245	235	8	5,431	49,710
1975	Bobby Allison	19	3	3	3	1	2	1	0	4,268	578	14	6,226	126,735
1976	Bobby Allison	30	3	0	2	6	5	2	4	8,735	360	18	10,203	230,170
"	Neil Bonnett	0	1	0	0	0	0	0	0	0	0	0	0	0
"	**Total**	30	4	0	2	6	5	2	4	8,735	360	18	10,203	230,170
1977	Dave Marcis	12	0	0	0	0	4	1	2	2,777	90	6	4,015	62,155
1980	Rusty Wallace	2	0	0	1	0	0	0	0	653	0	0	987	22,860

Year	Driver	Starts	Poles	Finish 1	2	3	4	5	6–10	Laps	Laps Led	Races Led	Miles	$

Roger Penske *continued*

Year	Driver	Starts	Poles	1	2	3	4	5	6–10	Laps	Laps Led	Races Led	Miles	$
1991	Rusty Wallace	29	2	2	0	3	2	2	5	8,316	524	14	10,147	502,073
1992	Rusty Wallace	29	1	1	2	1	1	0	7	8,759	673	11	10,450	657,925
1993	Rusty Wallace	30	3	10	4	2	1	2	2	9,641	**2,860**	20	11,231	1,702,154
1994	Rusty Wallace	31	2	8	3	1	4	1	3	9,281	**2,142**	19	10,730	1,959,072
1995	Rusty Wallace	31	0	2	4	6	2	1	4	9,497	1,066	17	11,563	1,642,837
1996	Rusty Wallace	31	0	5	1	0	1	1	10	8,383	964	13	10,159	1,665,315
Lifetime		281	16	33	20	21	24	15	44	77,846	9,630	141	97,168	$8,670,185

Richard Peralta

Year	Driver	Starts	Poles	1	2	3	4	5	6–10	Laps	Laps Led	Races Led	Miles	$
1974	Buck Peralta	1	0	0	0	0	0	0	0	121	0	0	317	1,250
Lifetime		1	0	0	0	0	0	0	0	121	0	0	317	$1,250

Bob Perry

Year	Driver	Starts	Poles	1	2	3	4	5	6–10	Laps	Laps Led	Races Led	Miles	$
1959	Bob Perry	3	0	0	0	0	0	0	1	509	0	0	317	500
1960	Bob Perry	3	0	0	0	0	0	0	1	256	0	0	314	475
1961	Bob Perry	4	0	0	0	0	0	1	2	424	0	0	452	840
Lifetime		10	0	0	0	0	0	1	4	1,189	0	0	1,083	$1,815

J. E. Peters

Year	Driver	Starts	Poles	1	2	3	4	5	6–10	Laps	Laps Led	Races Led	Miles	$
1952	Gibb Orr	2	0	0	0	0	0	0	0	197	0	0	120	25
Lifetime		2	0	0	0	0	0	0	0	197	0	0	120	$25

Natz Peters

Year	Driver	Starts	Poles	1	2	3	4	5	6–10	Laps	Laps Led	Races Led	Miles	$
1983	Natz Peters	1	0	0	0	0	0	0	0	103	0	0	103	800
1984	Natz Peters	0												1,700
Lifetime		1	0	0	0	0	0	0	0	103	0	0	103	$2,500

Joan Petre

Year	Driver	Starts	Poles	1	2	3	4	5	6–10	Laps	Laps Led	Races Led	Miles	$
1966	Buddy Arrington	4	0	0	0	0	0	0	0	339	0	0	284	955
"	Buddy Baker	14	0	0	0	0	0	0	3	1,499	0	0	757	1,660
"	Earl Brooks	1	0	0	0	0	0	0	0	92	0	0	138	875
"	Al DeAngelo	1	0	0	0	0	0	0	0	23	0	0	5	0
"	Pee Wee Ellwanger	1	0	0	0	0	0	0	0	127	0	0	64	250
"	Ernest Eury	4	0	0	0	0	0	0	1	481	0	0	243	495
"	Buzz Gregory	2	0	0	0	0	0	0	0	563	0	0	282	500
"	Jimmy Helms	1	0	0	0	0	0	0	0	1	0	0	1	450
"	Bub Strickler	1	0	0	0	0	0	0	0	57	0	0	29	0
"	Walter Wallace	1	0	0	0	0	0	0	0	379	0	0	190	300
"	**Total**	27	0	0	0	0	0	0	4	3,561	0	0	1,990	5,485
1967	Curley Mills	1	0	0	0	0	0	0	1	274	0	0	137	230
Lifetime		28	0	0	0	0	0	0	5	3,835	0	0	2,127	$5,715

Andy Petree (See Leo Jackson & Andy Petree)

Terry Petris

Year	Driver	Starts	Poles	1	2	3	4	5	6–10	Laps	Laps Led	Races Led	Miles	$
1985	Dale Perry	1	0	0	0	0	0	0	0	57	0	0	149	880
1986	Terry Petris	2	0	0	0	0	0	0	0	149	0	0	390	3,110
1988	Terry Petris	1	0	0	0	0	0	0	0	52	0	0	136	1,150
Lifetime		4	0	0	0	0	0	0	0	258	0	0	676	$5,140

Paul Pettitt

Year	Driver	Starts	Poles	1	2	3	4	5	6–10	Laps	Laps Led	Races Led	Miles	$
1952	Paul Pettitt	3	0	0	0	0	0	0	0	198	0	0	116	60
1954	Paul Pettitt	2	0	0	0	0	0	1	0	166	0	0	149	325
1955	Paul Pettitt	2	0	0	0	0	0	0	0	50	0	0	25	100
Lifetime		7	0	0	0	0	0	1	0	414	0	0	290	$485

Petty Enterprises

Year	Driver	Starts	Poles	1	2	3	4	5	6–10	Laps	Laps Led	Races Led	Miles	$
1949	Lee Petty	6	0	1	2	0	0	0	2	890	1	1	565	3,855
1950	Lee Petty	17	0	1	1	2	3	2	4	1,558	43	1	1,407	7,120

Petty Enterprises *continued*

Year	Driver	Starts	Poles	1	2	3	4	5	6–10	Laps	Laps Led	Races Led	Miles	$
1951	Lee Petty	32	0	1	4	2	1	3	8	1,248	99	1	1,168	8,240
"	Pap White	1	0	0	0	0	0	0	1	383	0	0	479	400
"	**Total**	32	0	1	4	2	1	3	9	1,631	99	1	1,646	8,640
1952	Lee Petty	32	0	3	6	5	5	2	6	5,094	193	7	3,439	16,876
1953	Jimmie Lewallen	1	0	0	1	0	0	0	0	198	0	0	99	700
"	Lee Petty	36	0	5	4	10	4	3	6	3,021	209	6	2,201	18,447
"	**Total**	36	0	5	5	10	4	3	6	3,219	209	6	2,300	19,147
1954	Lee Petty	33	3	7	5	5	3	3	8	5,707	681	12	3,962	20,777
"	Bob Welborn	3	0	0	0	0	0	0	1	534	0	0	286	250
"	**Total**	33	3	7	5	5	3	3	9	**6,241**	681	12	4,248	21,027
1955	Lee Petty	41	1	6	4	5	4	1	10	6,212	769	6	4,307	18,870
1956	Lee Petty	46	1	2	1	6	2	6	11	7,167	252	6	4,486	15,163
1957	Johnny Dodson	1	0	0	0	0	0	0	0	244	0	0	244	425
"	Ralph Earnhardt	8	0	0	0	0	0	0	3	1,301	0	0	682	1,050
"	Tiny Lund	5	0	0	0	0	0	1	1	335	0	0	259	710
"	Bill Lutz	1	0	0	0	0	0	0	1		0	0		600
"	Bobby Myers	1	0	0	0	0	0	0	0	27	1	1	37	260
"	Lee Petty	41	3	4	4	3	3	6	13	7,466	449	11	4,595	18,326
"	**Total**	43	3	4	4	3	3	7	18	**9,373**	450	11	**5,818**	21,371
1958	Jim Linke	2	0	0	0	0	0	0	0	219	0	0	219	100
"	Lee Petty	50	4	7	5	4	9	3	15	9,173	439	14	5,671	26,565
"	Richard Petty	9	0	0	0	0	0	0	1	977	0	0	410	760
"	Jim Reed	1	0	0	0	0	0	0	0	207	0	0	285	315
"	Jimmy Thompson	1	0	0	0	0	1	0	0	198	0	0	99	575
"	Joe Weatherly	1	0	0	0	0	0	0	1	489	0	0	245	575
"	Bob Welborn	1	0	0	0	0	0	0	1	341	0	0	171	565
"	**Total**	50	4	7	5	4	10	3	18	**11,604**	439	**14**	7,098	29,445
1959	Lee Petty	42	2	11	5	7	4	0	8	8,278	1,011	11	4,977	49,220
"	Richard Petty	21	0	0	1	3	1	1	3	3,648	7	1	2,419	8,111
"	**Total**	42	2	11	6	10	5	1	11	**11,926**	**1,018**	12	7,396	57,331
1960	Bobby Johns	1	0	0	0	1	0	0	0	394	0	0	591	6,975
"	Jim Paschal	8	0	0	0	2	1	0	4	2,559	11	1	2,427	13,595
"	Lee Petty	39	3	5	7	2	6	1	9	7,518	515	10	5,389	31,823
"	Maurice Petty	2	0	0	0	0	0	0	2	375	0	0	142	290
"	Richard Petty	40	2	3	6	3	3	1	14	8,189	447	6	6,015	41,873
"	**Total**	41	5	8	13	8	10	2	29	**19,035**	973	**13**	**14,564**	94,016
1961	Darel Dieringer	1	0	0	0	0	0	0	1	263	0	0	395	1,375
"	Art Malone	1	0	0	0	0	0	0	1	484	0	0	242	500
"	Marvin Panch	1	0	0	0	0	0	0	0	94	0	0	129	200
"	Jim Paschal	1	0	0	0	0	0	0	0	25	0	0	13	100
"	Lee Petty	3	1	1	0	1	0	0	0	433	126	2	291	1,260
"	Maurice Petty	9	0	0	0	1	1	0	2	1,207	0	0	611	1,460
"	Richard Petty	42	2	2	4	4	5	3	5	7,866	703	7	5,392	25,239
"	**Total**	43	3	3	4	6	6	3	9	10,372	829	9	7,072	30,134
1962	Bunkie Blackburn	6	0	0	0	0	0	0	2	1,424	0	0	1,713	2,740
"	Jim Paschal	9	0	3	1	0	0	1	3	3,486	767	5	2,617	15,580
"	Lee Petty	1	0	0	0	0	0	1	0	499	0	0	250	750
"	Maurice Petty	5	0	0	0	0	1	1	1	800	0	0	443	965
"	Richard Petty	52	4	8	9	8	5	2	7	11,544	1,396	19	7,558	60,764
"	Speedy Thompson	1	0	0	0	0	0	0	1	258	0	0	387	900
"	**Total**	53	4	11	10	8	6	5	14	**18,011**	**2,163**	**21**	**12,966**	81,699
1963	Jim Hurtubise	3	0	0	0	0	0	0	0	441	0	0	813	975
"	Bob James	4	0	0	0	0	0	0	0	589	0	0	876	1,750
"	Jimmy Massey	2	0	0	0	0	0	0	0	78	0	0	49	250
"	Jim Paschal	29	1	5	3	5	2	0	3	6,652	392	11	4,176	19,579
"	Lee Petty	3	0	0	0	0	1	0	1	291	0	0	179	600
"	Maurice Petty	4	0	0	0	0	0	1	1	654	0	0	238	575
"	Richard Petty	54	8	14	9	2	4	1	9	12,183	2,316	29	7,873	55,964
"	Joe Weatherly	1	0	0	0	0	1	0	0	296	0	0	99	500
"	Bob Welborn	4	0	0	1	1	1	0	0	837	0	0	464	2,330
"	**Total**	55	9	19	13	8	9	2	14	**22,021**	2,708	**33**	14,766	82,253
1964	Buck Baker	6	0	0	1	0	1	1	1	1,462	21	1	1,605	5,825
"	Jim Paschal	13	0	1	3	1	1	1	1	3,725	155	4	3,590	53,001
"	Lee Petty	2	0	0	0	0	0	0	0	28	0	0	30	250
"	Maurice Petty	6	0	0	0	0	1	1	3	1,130	0	0	587	1,540
"	Richard Petty	61	9	9	14	12	0	2	6	14,041	3,534	33	9,480	114,772
"	**Total**	62	9	10	18	13	3	5	11	**20,386**	**3,710**	**35**	**15,292**	175,388
1965	Jim Paschal	3	0	0	0	1	1	1	0	892	90	2	683	2,700
"	Richard Petty	14	7	4	4	2	0	0	0	3,697	1,169	8	1,693	16,450

Year	Driver	Starts	Poles	1	2	3	4	5	6–10	Laps	Laps Led	Races Led	Miles	$

Petty Enterprises *continued*

Year	Driver	Starts	Poles	1	2	3	4	5	6–10	Laps	Laps Led	Races Led	Miles	$
"	LeeRoy Yarbrough	1	0	0	0	0	0	0	0	81	0	0	41	150
"	**Total**	17	7	4	4	3	1	1	0	4,670	1,259	10	2,416	19,300
1966	Darel Dieringer	1	0	0	0	0	0	0	0	52	0	0	52	545
"	Paul Lewis	1	0	0	0	0	0	0	0	308	0	0	308	670
"	Marvin Panch	4	0	1	0	0	1	0	1	1,187	113	2	1,736	30,765
"	Jim Paschal	1	0	0	0	0	0	0	0	281	0	0	141	325
"	Richard Petty	39	16	8	9	3	0	0	2	8,737	2,924	26	6,458	94,666
"	**Total**	41	16	9	9	3	1	0	3	10,565	3,037	**26**	8,694	126,971
1967	Tiny Lund	4	0	0	0	0	1	2	0	879	1	1	1,556	11,525
"	Richard Petty	48	19	27	7	2	1	1	2	12,739	5,537	41	9,387	150,197
"	G. C. Spencer	3	0	0	0	1	0	1	0	743	0	0	1,042	10,105
"	**Total**	49	19	27	7	3	2	4	2	**14,361**	**5,538**	**42**	**11,985**	171,827
1968	Richard Petty	49	12	16	6	5	2	2	4	12,254	4,242	35	8,907	99,535
1969	Richard Petty	50	6	10	9	9	0	3	7	12,589	2,778	32	10,520	129,906
1970	Dan Gurney	1	1	0	0	0	0	0	1	180	0	0	472	2,400
"	Pete Hamilton	15	1	3	1	2	0	3	2	3,770	338	9	6,092	130,806
"	Jim Paschal	1	0	0	0	0	0	0	0	325	11	1	488	1,800
"	Richard Petty	38	9	16	5	0	0	4	4	10,136	4,791	30	9,611	148,624
"	**Total**	39	11	19	6	2	0	7	7	14,411	**5,140**	36	**16,663**	283,630
1971	Buddy Baker	18	1	1	5	5	0	1	3	4,614	693	14	7,513	112,145
"	Richard Petty	46	9	21	8	7	2	0	3	13,739	4,932	41	12,870	351,071
"	**Total**	47	10	22	13	12	2	1	6	**18,353**	**5,625**[1]	**44**[1]	**20,383**	463,216
1972	Buddy Baker	10	0	1	0	2	0	0	1	1,838	146	8	3,365	54,975
"	Richard Petty	31	3	8	9	5	2	1	3	10,282	2,038	30	11,996	339,405
"	**Total**	31	3	9	9	7	2	1	4	**12,120**	2,184	**31**	**15,360**	394,380
1973	Richard Petty	28	3	6	6	1	2	0	2	8,644	1,815	16	9,286	234,389
1974	Hershel McGriff	4	0	0	0	0	0	0	1	558	0	0	1,196	7,635
"	Richard Petty	30	7	10	8	4	0	0	1	9,097	3,100	24	10,830	432,020
"	**Total**	30	7	10	8	4	0	0	2	**9,655**	**3,100**	**24**	**12,025**	439,655
1975	Richard Petty	30	3	13	5	3	0	0	3	9,082	**3,158**	**26**	10,846	481,751
1976	Richard Petty	30	1	3	9	3	4	0	3	8,941	1,269	23	10,345	374,806
1977	Richard Petty	30	5	5	6	6	2	1	3	8,840	1,403	24	10,418	406,608
1978	Richard Petty	30	0	0	3	3	3	2	6	8,904	419	15	10,162	242,273
1979	Kyle Petty	5	0	0	0	0	0	0	1	1,069	0	0	2,111	10,810
"	Richard Petty	31	1	5	7	2	4	5	4	9,367	1,150	16	10,933	561,934
"	**Total**	31	1	5	7	2	4	5	5	**10,436**	1,150	16	**13,044**	572,744
1980	Kyle Petty	14	0	0	0	0	0	0	6	3,306	0	0	4,525	36,350
"	Richard Petty	31	0	2	4	3	2	4	4	9,314	713	23	10,147	397,318
"	**Total**	31	0	2	4	3	2	4	10	**12,620**	713	23	**14,672**	433,668
1981	Kyle Petty	31	0	0	0	0	0	1	9	7,402	20	3	8,483	100,725
"	Richard Petty	31	0	3	1	4	3	1	4	7,276	546	21	8,602	396,072
"	**Total**	31	0	3	1	4	3	2	13	**14,678**	566	21	**17,085**	496,797
1982	Kyle Petty	23	0	0	1	0	1	0	2	5,440	13	3	5,975	114,180
"	Richard Petty	30	0	0	5	2	1	1	7	7,834	355	18	9,024	465,793
"	**Total**	30	0	0	6	2	2	1	9	**13,274**	368	19	**14,999**	579,973
1983	Kyle Petty	30	0	0	0	0	0	0	2	8,345	13	5	9,436	163,848
"	Richard Petty	30	0	3	1	1	1	3	12	9,439	279	16	10,696	508,884
"	**Total**	30	0	3	1	1	1	3	14	**17,784**	292	17	**20,132**	672,732
1984	Kyle Petty	30	0	0	0	0	0	1	5	8,400	2	1	9,302	329,920
1985	Dick Brooks	3	0	0	0	0	0	0	0	683	0	0	982	20,340
"	Morgan Shepherd	1	0	0	0	0	0	0	0	345	0	0	471	3,415
"	**Total**	4	0	0	0	0	0	0	0	1,028	0	0	1,453	23,755
1986	Richard Petty	28	0	0	1	2	1	0	7	7,516	153	7	8,764	439,762
1987	Richard Petty	29	0	0	1	3	2	3	5	8,306	38	8	9,985	445,227
1988	Richard Petty	29	0	0	0	1	0	0	4	6,207	11	3	7,619	190,155
1989	Richard Petty	25	0	0	0	0	0	0	0	5,567	9	1	7,927	133,050
1990	Richard Petty	29	0	0	0	0	0	0	1	7,438	5	1	9,063	169,465
1991	Richard Petty	29	0	0	0	0	0	0	1	8,341	1	1	9,644	268,035
1992	Richard Petty	29	0	0	0	0	0	0	0	7,977	5	1	9,624	348,870
1993	Jimmy Hensley	1	0	0	0	0	0	0	0	292	0	0	153	5,875
"	Rick Wilson	29	0	0	0	0	0	0	1	8,117	1	1	10,330	299,725
"	**Total**	30	0	0	0	0	0	0	1	8,409	1	1	10,483	305,600
1994	John Andretti	11	0	0	0	0	0	0	0	3,722	40	3	3,790	116,400
"	Wally Dallenbach Jr.	14	0	0	0	0	1	0	2	3,568	1	1	5,323	241,492
"	**Total**	25	0	0	0	0	1	0	2	7,290	41	4	9,113	357,892
1995	Bobby Hamilton	31	0	0	1	0	2	1	6	9,421	131	7	11,555	804,505
1996	Bobby Hamilton	31	2	1	0	1	0	1	8	9,153	648	11	10,896	1,151,235
Lifetime		1635	150	266	223	178	113	91	324	471,974	59,638	719	460,740	$12,274,247
		1st	1st	1st							1st	1st	1st	6th

609

Year	Driver	Starts	Poles	Finish 1	2	3	4	5	6–10	Laps	Laps Led	Races Led	Miles	$

J. H. Petty

Year	Driver	Starts	Poles	1	2	3	4	5	6–10	Laps	Laps Led	Races Led	Miles	$
1952	Ray Duhigg	9	0	0	0	1	1	1	3	1,365	0	0	759	1,425
"	Jimmie Lewallen	2	0	0	0	0	0	0	2	377	0	0	213	275
"	Julian Petty	1	0	0	0	0	0	0	1	193	0	0	97	125
"	Bob Welborn	1	0	0	0	0	0	0	0	137	0	0	69	25
"	**Total**	12	0	0	0	1	1	1	6	2,072	0	0	1,136	1,850
1953	Ray Duhigg	10	0	0	0	2	2	0	3	489	0	0	411	2,625
"	Bob Welborn	1	0	0	0	0	0	0	0		0	0		25
"	**Total**	11	0	0	0	2	2	0	3	489	0	0	411	2,650
1954	Bob Welborn	2	0	0	0	0	0	0	0	61	0	0	157	50
1955	Junior Johnson	1	0	0	1	0	0	0	0	197	0	0	99	700
"	Jimmie Lewallen	1	0	0	0	0	0	0	0	60	0	0	60	0
"	Ralph Liguori	1	0	0	0	0	0	0	1	189	0	0	284	350
"	Marvin Panch	3	0	0	0	0	1	0	0	646	0	0	753	1,050
"	Jim Paschal	3	0	0	0	1	0	0	1	535	0	0	287	650
"	Julian Petty	2	0	0	0	0	0	0	0	5	0	0	3	75
"	Bob Welborn	19	0	0	0	2	4	3	7	2,924	0	0	1,800	7,047
"	**Total**	29	0	0	1	3	5	3	9	4,556	0	0	3,284	9,872
1956	Jimmy Massey	1	0	0	0	0	0	0	0	389	0	0	195	300
"	Gwyn Staley	1	0	0	0	0	0	0	1	389	0	0	195	350
"	**Total**	1	0	0	0	0	0	0	1	778	0	0	389	650
1957	Gwyn Staley	12	2	3	1	0	2	1	2	2,206	196	4	1,273	8,680
1958	Possum Jones	5	0	0	0	0	0	0	0	879	0	0	660	545
"	Tiny Lund	3	1	0	0	0	0	1	0	399	0	0	199	385
"	Banjo Matthews	1	0	0	0	0	0	0	0	19	0	0	10	50
"	Jim Paschal	3	1	1	0	0	1	0	1	591	150	1	381	1,245
"	Ken Rush	10	1	0	0	0	0	0	3	1,625	0	0	828	1,640
"	Gwyn Staley	3	0	0	1	0	2	0	0	298	0	0	99	1,030
"	Roy Tyner	1	0	0	0	0	0	1	0	157	0	0	98	225
"	Joe Weatherly	1	0	0	0	0	0	0	0	1	0	0	1	50
"	Bob Welborn	17	1	5	3	2	0	0	4	3,429	579	7	2,019	12,705
"	Rex White	16	6	2	4	5	0	1	2	2,565	353	6	1,176	9,408
"	**Total**	32	10	8	8	7	3	3	10	9,963	**1,082**	13	5,472	27,283
1959	Tiny Lund	1	0	0	0	0	0	0	0	30	0	0	15	50
"	Jim Paschal	4	0	0	2	0	0	1	0	758	0	0	337	1,440
"	Ermon Rush	1	0	0	0	0	0	0	0	188	0	0	47	140
"	Ken Rush	2	0	0	0	0	0	0	0	159	0	0	86	100
"	Joe Weatherly	1	0	0	0	0	0	0	1	188	4	1	94	140
"	Bob Welborn	1	1	1	0	0	0	0	0	150	117	1	50	600
"	**Total**	9	1	1	2	0	0	1	1	1,473	121	2	628	2,470
1961	Jim Paschal	20	1	2	3	1	2	3	4	5,370	203	3	3,480	17,200
1962	Jim Paschal	1	0	0	0	0	0	0	1	198	55	1	99	150
"	David Pearson	1	0	0	0	0	0	0	0	90	0	0	56	0
"	Bob Welborn	4	0	0	0	0	0	0	3	771	0	0	1,235	1,975
"	**Total**	6	0	0	0	0	0	0	4	1,059	55	1	1,390	2,125
Lifetime		134	14	14	15	14	15	12	40	28,027	1,657	23	17,620	$72,830

Marvin K. Petty

Year	Driver	Starts	Poles	1	2	3	4	5	6–10	Laps	Laps Led	Races Led	Miles	$
1979	Freddy Smith	2	0	0	0	0	0	0	0	765	0	0	936	2,950
Lifetime		2	0	0	0	0	0	0	0	765	0	0	936	$2,950

Maurice Petty

Year	Driver	Starts	Poles	1	2	3	4	5	6–10	Laps	Laps Led	Races Led	Miles	$
1993	Ritchie Petty	3	0	0	0	0	0	0	0	364	0	0	950	22,990
1994	Ritchie Petty	1	0	0	0	0	0	0	0	73	0	0	183	10,455
1995	Ritchie Petty	0												2,050
Lifetime		4	0	0	0	0	0	0	0	437	0	0	1,133	$35,495

Steve Pfeifer

Year	Driver	Starts	Poles	1	2	3	4	5	6–10	Laps	Laps Led	Races Led	Miles	$
1980	Steve Pfeifer	1	0	0	0	0	0	0	0	75	0	0	197	900
1981	Steve Pfeifer	1	0	0	0	0	0	0	0	83	0	0	217	1,055
Lifetime		2	0	0	0	0	0	0	0	158	0	0	414	$1,955

Bob Phillippi

Year	Driver	Starts	Poles	1	2	3	4	5	6–10	Laps	Laps Led	Races Led	Miles	$
1951	Marvin Burke	1	0	1	0	0	0	0	0	250	156	1	156	1,875
Lifetime		1	0	1	0	0	0	0	0	250	156	1	156	$1,875

Year	Driver	Starts	Poles	Finish 1	2	3	4	5	6–10	Laps	Laps Led	Races Led	Miles	$

Howard Phillippi

Year	Driver	Starts	Poles	1	2	3	4	5	6–10	Laps	Laps Led	Races Led	Miles	$
1956	Howard Phillippi	4	0	0	0	0	0	0	0	501	0	0	398	125
1957	Howard Phillippi	3	0	0	0	0	0	0	1	334	0	0	167	200
1958	Howard Phillippi	2	0	0	0	0	0	0	1	190	0	0	55	320
Lifetime		9	0	0	0	0	0	0	2	1,025	0	0	620	$645

Joe Phipps

Year	Driver	Starts	Poles	1	2	3	4	5	6–10	Laps	Laps Led	Races Led	Miles	$
1970	Joe Phipps	7	0	0	0	0	0	0	0	1,506	0	0	1,583	4,090
"	Lennie Pond	1	0	0	0	0	0	0	0	88	0	0	134	1,020
"	**Total**	8	0	0	0	0	0	0	0	1,594	0	0	1,716	5,110
1971	Joe Phipps	2	0	0	0	0	0	0	0	73	0	0	53	920
1972	Buck Baker	1	0	0	0	0	0	0	0	157	0	0	214	935
"	Walter Ballard	1	0	0	0	0	0	0	0	167	0	0	170	865
"	Roy Mayne	1	0	0	0	0	0	0	0	1	0	0	3	720
"	**Total**	3	0	0	0	0	0	0	0	325	0	0	387	2,520
Lifetime		13	0	0	0	0	0	0	0	1,992	0	0	2,156	$8,550

Andy Pierce

Year	Driver	Starts	Poles	1	2	3	4	5	6–10	Laps	Laps Led	Races Led	Miles	$
1951	Andy Pierce	2	1	0	0	0	0	0	0	98	0	0	49	50
Lifetime		2	1	0	0	0	0	0	0	98	0	0	49	$50

Steve Pierce

Year	Driver	Starts	Poles	1	2	3	4	5	6–10	Laps	Laps Led	Races Led	Miles	$
1955	Possum Jones	1	0	0	0	0	0	0	0	276	0	0	380	60
1958	Speedy Thompson	1	0	0	0	0	0	0	0	344	6	1	473	310
1959	Richard Riley	2	0	0	0	0	0	0	1	240	0	0	120	250
"	Speedy Thompson	13	1	0	1	0	1	1	2	2,038	226	2	1,600	2,365
"	**Total**	15	1	0	1	0	1	1	3	2,278	226	2	1,720	2,615
Lifetime		17	1	0	1	0	1	1	3	2,898	232	3	2,573	$2,985

Tom Pistone

Year	Driver	Starts	Poles	1	2	3	4	5	6–10	Laps	Laps Led	Races Led	Miles	$
1955	Tom Pistone	1	0	0	0	0	0	0	0	28	0	0	18	0
1956	Tom Pistone	1	0	0	0	0	0	0	0	199	0	0	80	0
1966	Tom Pistone	27	4	0	3	1	0	2	0	3,825	385	8	2,088	7,625
"	Wendell Scott	1	0	0	0	0	0	0	0	119	0	0	119	540
"	**Total**	28	4	0	3	1	0	2	0	3,944	385	8	2,207	8,165
1967	Tom Pistone	1	0	0	0	0	0	0	1	278	0	0	139	345
1970	Bunkie Blackburn	1	0	0	0	0	0	0	0	35	0	0	36	620
"	Richard Brickhouse	3	0	0	0	0	0	0	0	162	2	1	285	3,300
"	Jim Hurtubise	2	0	0	0	0	0	0	1	211	0	0	528	2,575
"	**Total**	6	0	0	0	0	0	0	1	408	2	1	848	6,495
1971	Vic Elford	1	0	0	0	0	0	0	0	46	0	0	115	220
"	Don Tarr	2	0	0	0	0	0	0	1	199	0	0	526	2,935
"	**Total**	3	0	0	0	0	0	0	1	245	0	0	641	3,155
1982	Tighe Scott	1	0	0	0	0	0	0	0	81	0	0	203	5,050
Lifetime		41	4	0	3	1	0	2	3	5,183	387	9	4,135	$23,210

Brownie Pitt

Year	Driver	Starts	Poles	1	2	3	4	5	6–10	Laps	Laps Led	Races Led	Miles	$
1955	Jimmie Lewallen	1	0	0	0	0	0	0	0	14	0	0	57	0
"	Blackie Pitt	12	0	0	0	0	0	0	4	1,537	0	0	1,207	975
"	**Total**	13	0	0	0	0	0	0	4	1,551	0	0	1,265	975
1956	Blackie Pitt	24	0	0	0	0	0	0	4	2,279	0	0	1,448	1,295
1958	Blackie Pitt	7	0	0	0	0	0	0	1	361	0	0	217	315
Lifetime		44	0	0	0	0	0	0	9	4,191	0	0	2,930	$2,585

Chuck Pittinger

Year	Driver	Starts	Poles	1	2	3	4	5	6–10	Laps	Laps Led	Races Led	Miles	$
1981	Chuck Pittinger	1	0	0	0	0	0	0	0	80	0	0	210	1,155
Lifetime		1	0	0	0	0	0	0	0	80	0	0	210	$1,155

Hoyt Platt

Year	Driver	Starts	Poles	1	2	3	4	5	6–10	Laps	Laps Led	Races Led	Miles	$
1957	Dick Hoffman	1	0	0	0	0	0	0	0	50	0	0	125	60
Lifetime		1	0	0	0	0	0	0	0	50	0	0	125	$60

Year	Driver	Starts	Poles	Finish 1	2	3	4	5	6–10	Laps	Laps Led	Races Led	Miles	$

B. A. Pless

Year	Driver	Starts	Poles	1	2	3	4	5	6–10	Laps	Laps Led	Races Led	Miles	$
1952	Buck Baker	10	2	1	0	0	2	0	2	1,113	139	3	751	2,235
"	Buddy Shuman	6	0	1	1	0	0	0	1	816	65	2	589	3,777
"	Jimmy Thompson	1	0	0	0	0	0	0	0	383	0	0	479	300
"	**Total**	17	2	2	1	0	2	0	3	2,312	204	5	1,819	6,312
1953	Buddy Shuman	2	0	0	0	0	0	0	0	338	0	0	465	380
Lifetime		19	2	2	1	0	2	0	3	2,650	204	5	2,283	$6,692

Greg Pollex

Year	Driver	Starts	Poles	1	2	3	4	5	6–10	Laps	Laps Led	Races Led	Miles	$
1993	Chad Little	1	0	0	0	0	0	0	0	314	0	0	471	6,275
1994	Chad Little	1	0	0	0	0	0	0	0	196	1	1	490	30,805
1995	Chad Little	2	0	0	0	0	0	0	0	195	0	0	508	22,775
1996	Chad Little	5	0	0	0	0	0	0	0	927	0	0	1,611	80,227
Lifetime		9	0	0	0	0	0	0	0	1,632	1	1	3,080	$140,082

Lennie Pond

Year	Driver	Starts	Poles	1	2	3	4	5	6–10	Laps	Laps Led	Races Led	Miles	$
1981	Lennie Pond	9	0	0	0	0	0	0	0	2,145	0	0	2,262	13,625
Lifetime		9	0	0	0	0	0	0	0	2,145	0	0	2,262	$13,625

Elmer Pooler

Year	Driver	Starts	Poles	1	2	3	4	5	6–10	Laps	Laps Led	Races Led	Miles	$
1952	George Fleming	1	0	0	0	0	0	0	0		0	0		0
"	Donald Thomas	5	0	0	0	0	0	0	3	999	0	0	816	460
"	**Total**	6	0	0	0	0	0	0	3	999	0	0	816	460
1953	George Fleming	1	0	0	0	0	0	0	0	33	0	0	135	25
Lifetime		7	0	0	0	0	0	0	3	1,032	0	0	951	$485

Bill Poor

Year	Driver	Starts	Poles	1	2	3	4	5	6–10	Laps	Laps Led	Races Led	Miles	$
1956	Bill Poor	1	0	0	0	0	0	0	0	364	0	0	182	200
1957	Bill Poor	2	0	0	0	0	0	0	0	167	0	0	84	160
1958	Darel Dieringer	1	0	0	0	0	0	0	0	114	0	0	57	85
"	Bill Poor	23	0	0	0	0	0	1	6	3,544	0	0	1,779	2,835
"	Richard Spittle	1	0	0	0	0	0	0	0	125	0	0	63	50
"	**Total**	25	0	0	0	0	0	1	6	3,783	0	0	1,898	2,970
1959	Bill Poor	4	0	0	0	0	0	0	0	484	0	0	219	190
Lifetime		32	0	0	0	0	0	1	6	4,798	0	0	2,382	$3,520

Claude Porter

Year	Driver	Starts	Poles	1	2	3	4	5	6–10	Laps	Laps Led	Races Led	Miles	$
1955	Doug Cox	1	0	0	0	0	0	0	0	225	0	0	309	150
Lifetime		1	0	0	0	0	0	0	0	225	0	0	309	$150

H. C. Porter

Year	Driver	Starts	Poles	1	2	3	4	5	6–10	Laps	Laps Led	Races Led	Miles	$
1976	Buck Baker	1	0	0	0	0	0	0	0	301	0	0	452	1,235
Lifetime		1	0	0	0	0	0	0	0	301	0	0	452	$1,235

James Porter

Year	Driver	Starts	Poles	1	2	3	4	5	6–10	Laps	Laps Led	Races Led	Miles	$
1992	Randy Porter	2	0	0	0	0	0	0	0	502	0	0	962	12,475
Lifetime		2	0	0	0	0	0	0	0	502	0	0	962	$12,475

Marvin Porter

Year	Driver	Starts	Poles	1	2	3	4	5	6–10	Laps	Laps Led	Races Led	Miles	$
1957	Marvin Porter	2	0	1	1	0	0	0	0	216	1	1	158	1,350
1958	Marvin Porter	1	0	0	0	0	0	0	1	196	0	0	49	175
1959	Marvin Porter	7	0	0	0	1	1	0	2	1,696	0	0	706	1,940
Lifetime		10	0	1	1	1	1	0	3	2,108	1	1	913	$3,465

Nick Porter

Year	Driver	Starts	Poles	1	2	3	4	5	6–10	Laps	Laps Led	Races Led	Miles	$
1957	Don Porter	6	0	0	0	0	0	0	4	722	0	0	456	810
Lifetime		6	0	0	0	0	0	0	4	722	0	0	456	$810

Bob Potter

Year	Driver	Starts	Poles	1	2	3	4	5	6–10	Laps	Laps Led	Races Led	Miles	$
1959	Bob Potter	2	0	0	0	0	0	0	0	46	0	0	115	150

Year	Driver	Starts	Poles	Finish 1	2	3	4	5	6–10	Laps	Laps Led	Races Led	Miles	$

Bob Potter *continued*

Year	Driver	Starts	Poles	1	2	3	4	5	6–10	Laps	Laps Led	Races Led	Miles	$
1960	Bob Potter	3	0	0	0	0	0	0	1	708	0	0	822	640
Lifetime		5	0	0	0	0	0	0	1	754	0	0	937	$790

Jess Potter

Year	Driver	Starts	Poles	1	2	3	4	5	6–10	Laps	Laps Led	Races Led	Miles	$
1957	George Green	4	0	0	0	0	1	0	0	582	0	0	404	555
"	Brownie King	36	0	0	0	0	0	1	15	5,756	0	0	3,464	5,589
"	**Total**	36	0	0	0	0	1	1	15	6,338	0	0	3,867	6,144
1958	George Green	5	0	0	0	0	0	0	0	654	0	0	286	275
"	Brownie King	24	0	0	0	0	0	0	5	3,926	0	0	2,153	3,205
"	**Total**	25	0	0	0	0	0	0	5	4,580	0	0	2,439	3,480
1959	George Green	18	0	0	0	0	0	0	5	3,337	0	0	1,966	2,385
"	Bob Hundley	1	0	0	0	0	0	0	0	141	0	0	71	100
"	Brownie King	17	0	0	0	0	0	1	4	3,163	0	0	1,861	1,800
"	Richard Riley	1	0	0	0	0	0	0	0	149	0	0	75	0
"	Layman Utsman	2	0	0	0	0	0	0	0	235	0	0	131	50
"	**Total**	28	0	0	0	0	0	1	9	7,025	0	0	4,103	4,335
1960	Buddy Baker	7	0	0	0	0	0	0	1	1,101	0	0	738	665
"	George Green	3	0	0	0	0	0	0	0	237	0	0	327	360
"	Brownie King	3	0	0	0	0	0	0	1	410	0	0	647	465
"	Paul Lewis	22	0	0	0	0	0	0	4	3,690	0	0	2,562	3,535
"	Richard Riley	3	0	0	0	0	0	0	1	466	0	0	348	400
"	**Total**	30	0	0	0	0	0	0	7	5,904	0	0	4,621	5,425
1961	George Green	2	0	0	0	0	0	0	0	372	0	0	361	550
"	Paul Lewis	18	0	0	0	0	0	0	5	3,036	0	0	2,476	3,675
"	**Total**	20	0	0	0	0	0	0	5	3,408	0	0	2,837	4,225
1962	George Green	46	0	0	0	0	0	1	14	9,279	0	0	5,896	9,221
1963	George Green	3	0	0	0	0	0	0	2	569	0	0	198	425
"	Bill Morton	1	0	0	0	0	0	0	0	115	0	0	58	125
"	E. J. Trivette	7	0	0	0	0	0	0	0	1,150	0	0	950	1,410
"	**Total**	11	0	0	0	0	0	0	2	1,834	0	0	1,206	1,960
1964	Jack Anderson	1	0	0	0	0	0	0	0	118	0	0	177	400
"	Paul Lewis	1	0	0	0	0	0	0	0	27	0	0	17	150
"	E. J. Trivette	26	0	0	0	0	0	0	3	2,969	0	0	1,903	5,495
"	**Total**	28	0	0	0	0	0	0	3	3,114	0	0	2,097	6,045
1965	E. J. Trivette	38	0	0	0	0	0	0	7	7,413	0	0	4,899	12,973
Lifetime		262	0	0	0	0	1	3	67	48,895	0	0	31,966	$53,808

Mike Potter

Year	Driver	Starts	Poles	1	2	3	4	5	6–10	Laps	Laps Led	Races Led	Miles	$
1979	Mike Potter	4	0	0	0	0	0	0	0	1,021	0	0	835	3,165
1980	Mike Potter	3	0	0	0	0	0	0	0	450	0	0	535	2,370
1983	Lowell Cowell	1	0	0	0	0	0	0	0	93	0	0	247	3,335
"	Mike Potter	5	0	0	0	0	0	0	0	587	0	0	1,268	8,750
"	**Total**	6	0	0	0	0	0	0	0	680	0	0	1,515	12,085
1984	Lowell Cowell	0												1,550
1988	Mike Potter	1	0	0	0	0	0	0	0	44	0	0	110	3,000
Lifetime		14	0	0	0	0	0	0	0	2,195	0	0	2,994	$22,170

George Poulos

Year	Driver	Starts	Poles	1	2	3	4	5	6–10	Laps	Laps Led	Races Led	Miles	$
1967	Jimmy Helms	1	0	0	0	0	0	0	0	430	0	0	215	490
"	George Poulos	23	0	0	0	0	0	0	1	2,872	0	0	1,457	3,040
"	**Total**	24	0	0	0	0	0	0	1	3,302	0	0	1,672	3,530
Lifetime		24	0	0	0	0	0	0	1	3,302	0	0	1,672	$3,530

Floyd Powell

Year	Driver	Starts	Poles	1	2	3	4	5	6–10	Laps	Laps Led	Races Led	Miles	$
1962	Joe Penland	3	0	0	0	0	0	0	0	379	0	0	190	235
"	Floyd Powell	1	0	0	0	0	0	0	0	142	0	0	71	110
"	**Total**	4	0	0	0	0	0	0	0	521	0	0	261	345
Lifetime		4	0	0	0	0	0	0	0	521	0	0	261	$345

Tex Powell

Year	Driver	Starts	Poles	1	2	3	4	5	6–10	Laps	Laps Led	Races Led	Miles	$
1990	Chuck Bown	3	0	0	0	0	0	0	0	951	0	0	1,280	10,150

Year	Driver	Starts	Poles	Finish 1	2	3	4	5	6–10	Laps	Laps Led	Races Led	Miles	$

Tex Powell *continued*

Year	Driver	Starts	Poles	1	2	3	4	5	6–10	Laps	Laps Led	Races Led	Miles	$
"	Tracy Leslie	2	0	0	0	0	0	0	0	249	0	0	436	9,090
"	**Total**	5	0	0	0	0	0	0	0	1,200	0	0	1,716	19,240
1995	Pancho Carter	0												1,000
"	Jim Sauter	0												2,400
"	**Total**	0												3,400
Lifetime		5	0	0	0	0	0	0	0	1,200	0	0	1,716	$22,640

Baxter Price

Year	Driver	Starts	Poles	1	2	3	4	5	6–10	Laps	Laps Led	Races Led	Miles	$
1973	Baxter Price	1	0	0	0	0	0	0	0	3	0	0	2	325
1975	Baxter Price	3	0	0	0	0	0	0	0	331	0	0	548	1,685
1976	Walter Ballard	3	0	0	0	0	0	0	0	852	0	0	669	2,210
"	Baxter Price	6	0	0	0	0	0	0	0	1,680	0	0	1,432	3,730
"	**Total**	9	0	0	0	0	0	0	0	2,532	0	0	2,102	5,940
1977	Walter Ballard	1	0	0	0	0	0	0	0	225	0	0	122	475
"	Earl Brooks	1	0	0	0	0	0	0	0	131	0	0	82	400
"	Elmo Langley	1	0	0	0	0	0	0	0	182	0	0	108	325
"	Larry LeMay	1	0	0	0	0	0	0	0	36	0	0	19	350
"	Baxter Price	12	0	0	0	0	0	0	0	2,566	0	0	2,706	10,890
"	Tighe Scott	1	0	0	0	0	0	0	0	198	0	0	270	845
"	**Total**	17	0	0	0	0	0	0	0	3,338	0	0	3,308	13,285
1978	Baxter Price	23	0	0	0	0	0	0	0	7,164	0	0	7,342	33,630
1979	Baxter Price	24	0	0	0	0	0	0	0	6,791	0	0	6,665	44,405
"	Roy Smith	1	0	0	0	0	0	0	0	193	0	0	483	2,690
"	**Total**	25	0	0	0	0	0	0	0	6,984	0	0	7,147	47,095
1980	Charlie Chamblee	1	0	0	0	0	0	0	0	298	0	0	454	2,825
"	Jimmy Means	1	0	0	0	0	0	0	0	35	0	0	18	850
"	Baxter Price	17	0	0	0	0	0	0	0	4,765	0	0	4,679	25,885
"	Roy Smith	1	0	0	0	0	0	0	0	114	0	0	299	1,970
"	Joel Stowe	2	0	0	0	0	0	0	0	835	0	0	694	4,685
"	**Total**	22	0	0	0	0	0	0	0	6,047	0	0	6,144	36,215
1981	Tommy Gale	1	0	0	0	0	0	0	0	25	0	0	66	675
"	Cecil Gordon	1	0	0	0	0	0	0	0	296	0	0	185	800
"	Baxter Price	1	0	0	0	0	0	0	0	16	0	0	9	3,100
"	Ronnie Thomas	1	0	0	0	0	0	0	0	75	0	0	200	1,805
"	D. K. Ulrich	2	0	0	0	0	0	0	0	673	0	0	371	1,370
"	**Total**	6	0	0	0	0	0	0	0	1,085	0	0	830	7,750
1982	Ferrel Harris	1	0	0	0	0	0	0	0	146	0	0	388	2,625
"	Jimmy Hensley	1	0	0	0	0	0	0	0	104	0	0	56	735
"	Slick Johnson	10	0	0	0	0	0	0	0	1,883	2	1	2,437	15,415
"	Joel Stowe	1	0	0	0	0	0	0	0	57	0	0	36	705
"	**Total**	13	0	0	0	0	0	0	0	2,190	2	1	2,917	19,480
Lifetime		119	0	0	0	0	0	0	0	29,674	2	1	30,339	$165,405

Carl Price

Year	Driver	Starts	Poles	1	2	3	4	5	6–10	Laps	Laps Led	Races Led	Miles	$
1973	Tiny Lund	5	0	0	0	0	0	0	0	388	0	0	409	4,420
Lifetime		5	0	0	0	0	0	0	0	388	0	0	409	$4,420

Chester Price

Year	Driver	Starts	Poles	1	2	3	4	5	6–10	Laps	Laps Led	Races Led	Miles	$
1954	Bud Diamond	2	0	0	0	0	0	0	0	277	0	0	139	25
Lifetime		2	0	0	0	0	0	0	0	277	0	0	139	$25

Norris Price

Year	Driver	Starts	Poles	1	2	3	4	5	6–10	Laps	Laps Led	Races Led	Miles	$
1977	Steve Moore	1	0	0	0	0	0	0	0	139	0	0	370	2,165
Lifetime		1	0	0	0	0	0	0	0	139	0	0	370	$2,165

Walt Price

Year	Driver	Starts	Poles	1	2	3	4	5	6–10	Laps	Laps Led	Races Led	Miles	$
1974	Walt Price	2	0	0	0	0	0	0	0	136	0	0	349	1,800
Lifetime		2	0	0	0	0	0	0	0	136	0	0	349	$1,800

Cotton Priddy

Year	Driver	Starts	Poles	1	2	3	4	5	6–10	Laps	Laps Led	Races Led	Miles	$
1953	Cotton Priddy	2	0	0	0	0	0	0	0	35	0	0	144	75
1956	Cotton Priddy	1	0	0	0	0	0	0	0	38	0	0	57	50
Lifetime		3	0	0	0	0	0	0	0	73	0	0	201	$125

Year	Driver	Starts	Poles	Finish						Laps	Laps Led	Races Led	Miles	$
				1	2	3	4	5	6–10	Laps	Led	Led	Miles	$

Talmadge Prince

Year	Driver	Starts	Poles	1	2	3	4	5	6–10	Laps	Laps Led	Races Led	Miles	$
1970	Tab Prince	1	0	0	0	0	0	0	0	18	0	0	45	0
Lifetime		1	0	0	0	0	0	0	0	18	0	0	45	$0

Clem Proctor

Year	Driver	Starts	Poles	1	2	3	4	5	6–10	Laps	Laps Led	Races Led	Miles	$
1963	Clem Proctor	2	0	0	0	0	0	0	0	260	0	0	702	850
1964	Jim Blomgren	1	0	0	0	0	0	0	0	94	0	0	254	500
"	Clem Proctor	1	0	0	0	0	0	0	0	15	0	0	41	500
"	**Total**	1	0	0	0	0	0	0	0	109	0	0	294	1,000
1965	Bob Bondurant	1	0	0	0	0	0	0	0	47	0	0	127	520
1966	Clem Proctor	1	0	0	0	0	0	0	0	114	0	0	308	600
Lifetime		5	0	0	0	0	0	0	0	530	0	0	1,431	$2,970

Bob Pronger

Year	Driver	Starts	Poles	1	2	3	4	5	6–10	Laps	Laps Led	Races Led	Miles	$
1951	Bob Pronger	1	0	0	0	0	0	0	0	332	0	0	415	50
1952	Bob Pronger	1	0	0	0	0	0	0	0	140	0	0	175	0
1953	Bob Pronger	1	1	0	0	0	0	0	0	5	0	0	21	0
"	Speedy Thompson	1	0	0	0	0	0	0	1	351	0	0	483	750
"	**Total**	2	1	0	0	0	0	0	1	356	0	0	503	750
1958	Bob Pronger	2	0	0	0	0	0	0	0	16	0	0	66	25
1959	Bob Pronger	2	0	0	0	0	0	0	0	156	0	0	390	125
Lifetime		8	1	0	0	0	0	0	1	1,000	0	0	1,549	$950

Oren Prosser

Year	Driver	Starts	Poles	1	2	3	4	5	6–10	Laps	Laps Led	Races Led	Miles	$
1963	Oren Prosser	1	0	0	0	0	0	0	0	95	0	0	257	200
Lifetime		1	0	0	0	0	0	0	0	95	0	0	257	$200

Warren Prout

Year	Driver	Starts	Poles	1	2	3	4	5	6–10	Laps	Laps Led	Races Led	Miles	$
1971	Randy Hutchison	6	0	0	0	0	0	0	1	1,233	0	0	556	2,010
Lifetime		6	0	0	0	0	0	0	1	1,233	0	0	556	$2,010

Don Pruitt

Year	Driver	Starts	Poles	1	2	3	4	5	6–10	Laps	Laps Led	Races Led	Miles	$
1974	Don Pruitt	1	0	0	0	0	0	0	0	28	0	0	73	670
Lifetime		1	0	0	0	0	0	0	0	28	0	0	73	$670

Sherral Pruitt

Year	Driver	Starts	Poles	1	2	3	4	5	6–10	Laps	Laps Led	Races Led	Miles	$
1968	Neil Castles	1	0	0	0	1	0	0	0	152	0	0	137	700
"	Charlie Glotzbach	1	0	0	0	0	0	1	0	293	0	0	147	475
"	Paul Dean Holt	1	0	0	0	0	0	0	0	1	0	0	1	275
"	James Hylton	1	0	0	0	0	0	0	1	193	0	0	97	240
"	Ervin Pruitt	5	0	0	0	0	0	0	1	1,376	0	0	766	1,930
"	Roy Tyner	2	0	0	0	0	0	0	0	383	0	0	505	1,275
"	Frank Warren	1	0	0	0	0	0	0	0	144	0	0	198	700
"	**Total**	12	0	0	0	1	0	1	2	2,542	0	0	1,849	5,595
1969	Johnny Halford	8	0	0	0	0	0	0	0	1,881	0	0	1,494	4,200
"	Bobby Mausgrover	13	0	0	0	0	0	0	0	1,192	0	0	1,082	5,305
"	Roy Mayne	1	0	0	0	0	0	0	0	9	0	0	23	725
"	Ervin Pruitt	4	0	0	0	0	0	0	1	565	0	0	371	850
"	**Total**	26	0	0	0	0	0	0	1	3,647	0	0	2,969	11,080
1970	Johnny Halford	25	0	0	0	0	0	0	0	3,619	16	1	4,057	15,654
Lifetime		63	0	0	0	1	0	1	3	9,808	16	1	8,875	$32,329

Delbert Puro

Year	Driver	Starts	Poles	1	2	3	4	5	6–10	Laps	Laps Led	Races Led	Miles	$
1975	Bobby Isaac	1	0	0	0	0	0	0	0	40	0	0	60	855
"	Dick Trickle	1	0	0	0	0	0	0	0	3	0	0	8	1,705
"	**Total**	2	0	0	0	0	0	0	0	43	0	0	68	2,560
1976	Richie Panch	1	0	0	0	0	0	0	0	252	0	0	384	1,035
1978	Dick Trickle	1	0	0	0	0	0	0	0	24	0	0	36	910
Lifetime		4	0	0	0	0	0	0	0	319	0	0	487	$4,505

Smokey Purser

Year	Driver	Starts	Poles	1	2	3	4	5	6–10	Laps	Laps Led	Races Led	Miles	$
1952	Smokey Purser	1	0	0	0	0	0	0	0		0	0		0
Lifetime		1	0	0	0	0	0	0	0		0	0		$0

Year	Driver	Starts	Poles	Finish						Laps	Laps Led	Races Led	Miles	$
				1	2	3	4	5	6–10	Laps	Led	Led	Miles	$

Matt Puskarich

Year	Driver	Starts	Poles	1	2	3	4	5	6–10	Laps	Laps Led	Races Led	Miles	$
1975	Don Puskarich	3	0	0	0	0	0	0	0	184	0	0	480	3,060
1976	Don Puskarich	3	0	0	0	0	0	0	0	343	0	0	876	3,770
1977	Don Puskarich	2	0	0	0	0	0	0	0	51	0	0	134	1,520
1978	Don Puskarich	1	0	0	0	0	0	0	0	36	0	0	94	700
1979	Don Puskarich	1	0	0	0	0	0	0	0	47	0	0	123	855
1980	Don Puskarich	3	0	0	0	0	0	0	0	201	0	0	526	3,835
1981	Don Puskarich	3	0	0	0	0	0	0	0	211	0	0	553	4,770
1982	Don Puskarich	1	0	0	0	0	0	0	0	87	0	0	228	1,870
1983	Stephen Wheeler	2	0	0	0	0	0	0	0	203	0	0	532	4,625
Lifetime		19	0	0	0	0	0	0	0	1,363	0	0	3,546	$25,005

J. T. Putney

Year	Driver	Starts	Poles	1	2	3	4	5	6–10	Laps	Laps Led	Races Led	Miles	$
1966	J. T. Putney	36	0	0	1	2	1	0	5	7,261	32	2	5,842	17,783
1967	J. T. Putney	28	0	0	0	1	0	0	9	5,743	0	0	4,510	14,977
Lifetime		64	0	0	1	3	1	0	14	13,004	32	2	10,352	$32,760

Dave Quate

Year	Driver	Starts	Poles	1	2	3	4	5	6–10	Laps	Laps Led	Races Led	Miles	$
1953	Ray Duhigg	1	0	0	0	0	0	0	0		0	0		40
"	Jimmie Lewallen	4	0	0	0	1	0	1	0		0	0		700
"	Jim Paschal	4	0	0	0	0	0	0	0	292	0	0	292	360
"	**Total**	9	0	0	0	1	0	1	0	292	0	0	292	1,100
1954	Billy Irvin	3	0	0	0	0	0	0	0	344	0	0	234	50
"	Bob Welborn	2	0	0	0	0	0	0	0	93	0	0	55	25
"	**Total**	5	0	0	0	0	0	0	0	437	0	0	289	75
Lifetime		14	0	0	0	1	0	1	0	729	0	0	581	$1,175

Danny Queen

Year	Driver	Starts	Poles	1	2	3	4	5	6–10	Laps	Laps Led	Races Led	Miles	$
1977	Charlie Blanton	0												600
1978	Charlie Blanton	1	0	0	0	0	0	0	0	52	0	0	53	590
1979	Melvin Revis	1	0	0	0	0	0	0	0	76	0	0	41	410
1980	Melvin Revis	1	0	0	0	0	0	0	0	23	0	0	31	1,115
Lifetime		3	0	0	0	0	0	0	0	151	0	0	125	$2,715

Grady Quinn

Year	Driver	Starts	Poles	1	2	3	4	5	6–10	Laps	Laps Led	Races Led	Miles	$
1952	Joie Ray	1	0	0	0	0	0	0	0		0	0		0
Lifetime		1	0	0	0	0	0	0	0		0	0		$0

The Racing Club

Year	Driver	Starts	Poles	1	2	3	4	5	6–10	Laps	Laps Led	Races Led	Miles	$
1955	Ted Cannady	1	0	0	0	0	0	0	0	178	0	0	89	50
"	Billy Carden	1	0	0	0	0	0	0	0	94	0	0	94	75
"	Harold Kite	2	0	0	0	0	0	0	0	279	0	0	387	110
"	Speedy Thompson	1	0	0	0	0	0	0	0	85	0	0	43	50
"	Bob Welborn	3	0	0	0	0	0	0	2	464	0	0	232	250
"	**Total**	8	0	0	0	0	0	0	2	1,100	0	0	844	535
Lifetime		8	0	0	0	0	0	0	2	1,100	0	0	844	$535

Billy Rafter

Year	Driver	Starts	Poles	1	2	3	4	5	6–10	Laps	Laps Led	Races Led	Miles	$
1956	Billy Rafter	9	0	0	0	0	0	0	1	1,140	0	0	623	975
1957	Ed Jackson	1	0	0	0	0	0	0	0	72	0	0	72	110
"	Billy Rafter	2	0	0	0	0	0	0	0	102	0	0	52	100
"	**Total**	2	0	0	0	0	0	0	0	174	0	0	124	210
1958	Billy Rafter	19	0	0	0	0	0	1	7	3,160	0	0	1,529	2,490
Lifetime		30	0	0	0	0	0	1	8	4,474	0	0	2,276	$3,675

Marvin Ragan

Year	Driver	Starts	Poles	1	2	3	4	5	6–10	Laps	Laps Led	Races Led	Miles	$
1983	Ken Ragan	8	0	0	0	0	0	0	0	1,984	0	0	3,526	27,905
1984	Ken Ragan	10	0	0	0	0	0	0	0	1,839	1	1	3,467	37,045
1986	Ken Ragan	5	0	0	0	0	0	0	0	1,095	1	1	2,036	20,520
1987	Eddie Bierschwale	3	0	0	0	0	0	0	0	535	0	0	1,018	7,715
"	Ken Ragan	6	0	0	0	0	0	0	0	1,259	0	0	2,354	30,575
"	**Total**	9	0	0	0	0	0	0	0	1,794	0	0	3,372	38,290
1988	Ken Ragan	5	0	0	0	0	0	0	0	731	0	0	1,426	15,755
1989	Ken Ragan	3	0	0	0	0	0	0	0	550	0	0	922	7,295

Year	Driver	Starts	Poles	Finish						Laps	Laps Led	Races Led	Miles	$
				1	2	3	4	5	6–10					

Marvin Ragan *continued*

Year	Driver	Starts	Poles	1	2	3	4	5	6–10	Laps	Laps Led	Races Led	Miles	$
1990	Ken Ragan	4	0	0	0	0	0	0	0	398	0	0	745	23,020
Lifetime		44	0	0	0	0	0	0	0	8,391	2	2	15,495	$169,830

Bob Rahilly & Butch Mock

Year	Driver	Starts	Poles	1	2	3	4	5	6–10	Laps	Laps Led	Races Led	Miles	$
1978	Butch Mock	2	0	0	0	0	0	0	0	564	0	0	853	2,390
1979	Bobby Brack	1	0	0	0	0	0	0	0	70	1	1	105	930
"	Bill Elswick	3	0	0	0	0	0	0	0	1,112	0	0	842	3,400
"	Butch Mock	1	0	0	0	0	0	0	0	38	0	0	95	3,035
"	**Total**	5	0	0	0	0	0	0	0	1,220	1	1	1,042	7,365
1980	John Anderson	7	0	0	0	0	0	0	1	1,958	0	0	1,562	11,585
"	Chuck Bown	1	0	0	0	0	0	0	0	364	0	0	497	3,725
"	Bill Elswick	11	0	0	0	0	0	0	0	2,708	0	0	2,354	15,000
"	Harry Gant	3	0	0	0	0	0	0	2	402	1	1	934	10,680
"	Joe Millikan	3	0	0	0	0	0	0	1	624	1	1	1,043	5,525
"	Kyle Petty	1	0	0	0	0	0	0	0	416	0	0	416	775
"	Lennie Pond	2	0	0	0	0	0	0	1	438	0	0	856	19,195
"	**Total**	27	0	0	0	0	0	0	5	6,910	2	2	7,661	66,485
1981	Gary Balough	10	0	0	0	0	0	0	1	2,267	1	1	3,232	34,430
"	Bill Elswick	3	0	0	0	0	0	0	0	662	0	0	1,345	20,100
"	Dick May	1	0	0	0	0	0	0	0	184	0	0	368	3,520
"	Joe Millikan	12	0	0	0	0	0	0	5	3,017	15	4	3,578	63,675
"	Tim Richmond	1	0	0	0	0	0	0	0	413	0	0	246	3,450
"	**Total**	25	0	0	0	0	0	0	6	6,543	16	5	8,769	125,175
1982	Gary Balough	5	0	0	0	0	0	0	1	1,359	0	0	1,608	35,735
"	Jimmy Insolo	1	0	0	0	0	0	0	0	89	0	0	233	2,470
"	Joe Ruttman	23	0	0	0	0	2	2	2	6,023	30	4	6,585	113,954
"	**Total**	29	0	0	0	0	2	2	3	7,471	30	4	8,426	152,159
1983	Neil Bonnett	30	4	2	1	2	5	0	7	9,418	650	15	10,451	453,586
1984	Dave Marcis	30	0	0	0	0	3	0	6	9,383	30	5	10,387	330,766
1985	Lake Speed	28	0	0	1	0	1	0	12	8,308	8	4	9,937	300,326
1986	Jody Ridley	12	0	0	0	0	0	0	1	3,183	0	0	4,055	84,380
"	Jim Sauter	4	0	0	0	0	0	0	0	769	2	1	1,509	28,535
"	Morgan Shepherd	11	0	0	0	1	0	0	1	2,598	227	7	2,659	90,418
"	Lake Speed	4	0	0	0	0	0	0	2	1,382	4	1	1,676	51,400
"	**Total**	29	0	0	0	1	0	0	4	7,932	233	9	9,898	254,733
1987	Neil Bonnett	26	0	0	0	4	1	0	10	7,834	120	10	9,072	401,541
"	Joe Ruttman	3	0	0	0	0	0	0	2	936	0	0	1,308	25,280
"	**Total**	29	0	0	0	4	1	0	12	8,770	120	10	10,380	426,821
1988	Neil Bonnett	27	0	2	0	0	1	0	4	8,017	324	7	9,131	440,139
"	Morgan Shepherd	3	1	0	0	0	0	0	1	319	4	1	757	27,685
"	**Total**	28	1	2	0	0	1	0	5	8,336	328	8	9,888	467,824
1989	Morgan Shepherd	29	1	0	2	0	1	2	8	7,590	137	6	9,908	544,255
1990	Rick Wilson	29	0	0	0	0	0	1	2	8,036	0	0	9,305	242,067
1991	Joe Ruttman	29	0	0	0	1	0	0	3	8,974	11	1	10,774	361,661
Lifetime		350	6	4	4	8	14	5	73	99,455	1,566	70	117,679	$3,735,613

A. C. Rakestraw

Year	Driver	Starts	Poles	1	2	3	4	5	6–10	Laps	Laps Led	Races Led	Miles	$
1967	Dick Johnson	1	0	0	0	0	0	0	0	5	0	0	8	500
"	Don Schissler	1	0	0	0	0	0	0	0	36	0	0	54	740
"	G. C. Spencer	1	0	0	0	0	0	0	1	311	0	0	467	1,125
"	E. J. Trivette	1	0	0	0	0	0	0	0	129	0	0	194	550
"	Eddie Yarboro	1	0	0	0	0	0	0	0	362	0	0	226	250
"	**Total**	5	0	0	0	0	0	0	1	843	0	0	948	3,165
Lifetime		5	0	0	0	0	0	0	1	843	0	0	948	$3,165

Ansel Rakestraw

Year	Driver	Starts	Poles	1	2	3	4	5	6–10	Laps	Laps Led	Races Led	Miles	$
1956	Bobby Myers	2	0	0	0	0	0	0	1	104	0	0	52	200
"	Benny Rakestraw	1	0	0	0	0	0	0	1	156	0	0	78	100
"	**Total**	3	0	0	0	0	0	0	2	260	0	0	130	300
1957	Ansel Rakestraw	2	0	0	0	0	0	0	0	276	0	0	138	200
Lifetime		5	0	0	0	0	0	0	2	536	0	0	268	$500

Tyre Rakestraw

Year	Driver	Starts	Poles	1	2	3	4	5	6–10	Laps	Laps Led	Races Led	Miles	$
1953	Tyre Rakestraw	1	0	0	0	0	0	0	0	308	0	0	424	160
Lifetime		1	0	0	0	0	0	0	0	308	0	0	424	$160

Year	Driver	Starts	Poles	Finish 1	2	3	4	5	6–10	Laps	Laps Led	Races Led	Miles	$

Tom Raley

Year	Driver	Starts	Poles	1	2	3	4	5	6–10	Laps	Laps Led	Races Led	Miles	$
1967	Tom Raley	8	0	0	0	0	0	0	0	602	0	0	288	825
"	Don Tarr	1	0	0	0	0	0	0	0	47	0	0	71	540
"	**Total**	9	0	0	0	0	0	0	0	649	0	0	359	1,365
Lifetime		9	0	0	0	0	0	0	0	649	0	0	359	$1,365

Robert Ramey

Year	Driver	Starts	Poles	1	2	3	4	5	6–10	Laps	Laps Led	Races Led	Miles	$
1960	Buzz McCann	1	0	0	0	0	0	0	0	8	0	0	20	0
"	Jimmy Thompson	1	0	0	0	0	0	0	0	397	0	0	199	125
"	**Total**	2	0	0	0	0	0	0	0	405	0	0	219	125
Lifetime		2	0	0	0	0	0	0	0	405	0	0	219	$125

Nick Rampling

Year	Driver	Starts	Poles	1	2	3	4	5	6–10	Laps	Laps Led	Races Led	Miles	$
1964	Jim Bray	4	0	0	0	0	0	0	0	167	0	0	452	1,875
1966	Nick Rampling	1	0	0	0	0	0	0	0	27	0	0	68	0
Lifetime		5	0	0	0	0	0	0	0	194	0	0	520	$1,875

Darvin Randahl

Year	Driver	Starts	Poles	1	2	3	4	5	6–10	Laps	Laps Led	Races Led	Miles	$
1956	Darvin Randahl	7	0	0	0	0	0	0	1	492	0	0	301	710
Lifetime		7	0	0	0	0	0	0	1	492	0	0	301	$710

Maurice Randall

Year	Driver	Starts	Poles	1	2	3	4	5	6–10	Laps	Laps Led	Races Led	Miles	$
1984	Maurice Randall	1	0	0	0	0	0	0	0	50	0	0	30	1,010
1985	Maurice Randall	3	0	0	0	0	0	0	0	104	0	0	107	3,450
Lifetime		4	0	0	0	0	0	0	0	154	0	0	137	$4,460

H. B. Ranier

Year	Driver	Starts	Poles	1	2	3	4	5	6–10	Laps	Laps Led	Races Led	Miles	$
1952	Johnny Patterson	5	0	0	1	0	0	1	0	1,054	0	0	879	3,350
1953	Johnny Patterson	11	0	0	0	0	0	1	1	534	0	0	410	645
1954	Bud Harless	1	0	0	0	0	0	0	0	129	0	0	81	25
"	Johnny Patterson	4	0	0	0	0	1	0	0	582	0	0	759	1,240
"	**Total**	5	0	0	0	0	1	0	0	711	0	0	840	1,265
1956	Johnny Patterson	1	0	0	0	0	0	0	0	343	0	0	472	225
1967	Buddy Baker	1	0	0	0	0	0	0	0	465	0	0	233	525
"	Gary Bettenhausen	3	0	0	0	0	0	0	1	124	0	0	310	1,680
"	**Total**	4	0	0	0	0	0	0	1	589	0	0	543	2,205
1968	Andy Hampton	1	0	0	0	0	0	0	1	193	0	0	483	2,525
1969	Vic Elford	2	0	0	0	0	0	0	0	236	0	0	590	2,950
"	Andy Hampton	2	0	0	0	0	0	0	1	197	0	0	493	2,500
"	**Total**	2	0	0	0	0	0	0	1	433	0	0	1,083	5,450
1970	Bobby Watson	1	0	0	0	0	0	0	0	11	0	0	6	430
Lifetime		30	0	0	1	0	1	2	4	3,868	0	0	4,714	$16,095

Harry Ranier

Year	Driver	Starts	Poles	1	2	3	4	5	6–10	Laps	Laps Led	Races Led	Miles	$
1976	Jim Vandiver	1	0	0	0	0	0	0	0	176	0	0	468	3,735
1977	Jim Vandiver	1	0	0	0	0	0	0	0	137	0	0	343	3,520
1978	Lennie Pond	28	5	1	2	2	1	5	8	8,443	319	12	9,412	181,096
1979	Buddy Baker	26	7	3	2	3	3	1	3	6,107	1,083	20	7,421	342,148
1980	Buddy Baker	19	6	2	2	4	2	0	2	5,042	671	15	6,952	275,200
1981	Bobby Allison	30	2	5	7	4	3	2	5	9,822	1,182	23	11,459	529,250
1982	Buddy Baker	15	0	0	1	0	0	2	6	4,130	85	6	4,855	184,250
"	Benny Parsons	14	3	0	0	4	3	0	1	3,579	250	6	4,188	218,942
"	Joe Ruttman	1	0	0	0	0	0	0	0	20	0	0	52	8,525
"	**Total**	30	3	0	1	4	3	2	7	7,729	335	12	9,096	411,717
1983	Cale Yarborough	16	3	4	0	0	0	0	4	3,783	608	13	5,975	265,035
1984	Cale Yarborough	16	4	3	1	3	1	2	0	4,387	736	12	7,140	403,853
1985	Cale Yarborough	16	0	2	2	2	0	0	1	3,450	664	11	5,669	310,465
1986	Cale Yarborough	16	1	0	0	2	0	0	3	3,467	110	4	5,828	137,010
1987	Davey Allison	22	5	2	3	0	0	4	1	5,511	710	11	8,518	361,060
1988	Davey Allison	29	3	2	2	3	2	3	4	8,333	611	14	9,740	844,532
1996	Elton Sawyer	1	0	0	0	0	0	0	0	327	0	0	498	14,015
Lifetime		251	39	24	22	27	15	19	38	66,714	7,029	147	88,518	$4,082,636
			10th											

Year	Driver	Starts	Poles	1	2	3	4	5	6–10	Laps	Laps Led	Races Led	Miles	$

Jim Rathmann

Year	Driver	Starts	Poles	1	2	3	4	5	6–10	Laps	Laps Led	Races Led	Miles	$
1950	Jim Rathmann	1	0	0	0	0	0	0	0	46	0	0	192	50
1958	Banjo Matthews	1	0	0	0	0	0	0	0	17	0	0	70	25
Lifetime		2	0	0	0	0	0	0	0	63	0	0	262	$75

Johnny Ray

Year	Driver	Starts	Poles	1	2	3	4	5	6–10	Laps	Laps Led	Races Led	Miles	$
1976	Bob Burcham	1	0	0	0	0	0	0	0	52	0	0	138	980
"	Dale Earnhardt	1	0	0	0	0	0	0	0	260	0	0	396	1,360
"	Johnny Rutherford	2	0	0	0	0	0	0	0	347	0	0	660	2,745
"	**Total**	4	0	0	0	0	0	0	0	659	0	0	1,194	5,085
1977	Johnny Rutherford	2	0	0	0	0	0	0	0	79	0	0	149	2,285
1978	Chuck Bown	4	0	0	0	0	0	0	0	539	0	0	732	3,585
Lifetime		10	0	0	0	0	0	0	0	1,277	0	0	2,074	$10,955

Warren Razore

Year	Driver	Starts	Poles	1	2	3	4	5	6–10	Laps	Laps Led	Races Led	Miles	$
1986	Derrike Cope	5	0	0	0	0	0	0	1	1,101	0	0	1,349	8,025
1987	Roy Smith	2	0	0	0	0	0	0	0	29	0	0	76	2,325
1988	Roy Smith	2	0	0	0	0	0	0	0	303	1	1	441	4,550
1989	Roy Smith	1	0	0	0	0	0	0	0	46	0	0	116	3,375
Lifetime		10	0	0	0	0	0	0	1	1,479	1	1	1,982	$18,275

Rebel Racing

Year	Driver	Starts	Poles	1	2	3	4	5	6–10	Laps	Laps Led	Races Led	Miles	$
1962	Ray Hendrick	2	0	0	0	0	0	0	0	714	0	0	357	275
1963	Ray Hendrick	2	0	0	0	0	0	1	1	573	0	0	238	625
Lifetime		4	0	0	0	0	0	1	1	1,287	0	0	595	$900

John Rebhan

Year	Driver	Starts	Poles	1	2	3	4	5	6–10	Laps	Laps Led	Races Led	Miles	$
1980	John Anderson	3	0	0	0	0	0	0	1	289	0	0	612	5,100
"	Kenny Hemphill	5	0	0	0	0	0	0	1	884	4	1	1,493	8,970
"	**Total**	8	0	0	0	0	0	0	2	1,173	4	1	2,106	14,070
1981	Donnie Allison	3	0	0	0	0	0	1	0	813	2	1	1,196	13,425
"	John Anderson	0												815
"	**Total**	3	0	0	0	0	0	1	0	813	2	1	1,196	14,240
Lifetime		11	0	0	0	0	0	1	2	1,986	6	2	3,302	$28,310

Red Star Garage

Year	Driver	Starts	Poles	1	2	3	4	5	6–10	Laps	Laps Led	Races Led	Miles	$
1950	Tim Flock	3	0	0	0	0	0	0	2	286	0	0	143	175
"	Johnny Mantz	2	0	0	0	0	0	0	1		0	0		100
"	Frank Mundy	1	0	0	0	0	0	0	1	135	0	0	135	200
"	**Total**	6	0	0	0	0	0	0	4	421	0	0	278	475
Lifetime		6	0	0	0	0	0	0	4	421	0	0	278	$475

James Reed

Year	Driver	Starts	Poles	1	2	3	4	5	6–10	Laps	Laps Led	Races Led	Miles	$
1990	Mark Reed	1	0	0	0	0	0	0	0	269	0	0	269	3,100
1991	Mark Reed	1	0	0	0	0	0	0	0	177	0	0	177	3,375
Lifetime		2	0	0	0	0	0	0	0	446	0	0	446	$6,475

Jim Reed

Year	Driver	Starts	Poles	1	2	3	4	5	6–10	Laps	Laps Led	Races Led	Miles	$
1951	Jim Reed	4	0	0	1	0	0	0	0	199	58	1	100	675
1952	Jim Reed	7	0	0	0	0	0	1	2	597	0	0	336	475
1953	Jim Reed	1	0	0	0	0	0	0	0	0	0	0	0	25
1954	Charles McDuffie	2	0	0	0	0	0	0	0	150	0	0	75	0
"	Jim Reed	9	0	0	0	0	0	2	1	1,083	0	0	815	965
"	**Total**	9	0	0	0	0	0	2	1	1,233	0	0	890	965
1955	Jim Reed	14	0	0	1	0	1	2	0	1,691	32	1	1,265	2,710
1956	Jim Reed	11	2	0	1	1	2	1	0	1,505	286	3	1,514	4,830
1957	Jim Reed	5	0	0	0	1	1	0	1	892	11	2	980	3,408
1958	Jim Reed	16	2	4	0	5	1	0	2	3,486	692	4	2,189	9,329
1959	Jim Reed	14	1	3	0	1	1	2	2	2,512	289	5	2,071	23,534
1960	Jim Reed	7	0	0	0	1	0	0	0	1,140	28	1	1,618	2,040
1961	Jim Reed	8	0	0	2	0	0	1	1	1,735	32	1	1,717	3,350
Lifetime		96	5	7	5	9	6	9	9	14,990	1,428	18	12,680	$51,341

Year	Driver	Starts	Poles	Finish 1	2	3	4	5	6–10	Laps	Laps Led	Races Led	Miles	$

Norris Reed

Year	Driver	Starts	Poles	1	2	3	4	5	6–10	Laps	Laps Led	Races Led	Miles	$
1971	Gary Myers	1	0	0	0	0	0	0	1	474	0	0	216	500
1972	David Ray Boggs	1	0	0	0	0	0	0	0	304	0	0	456	1,194
"	Paul Tyler	4	0	0	0	0	0	0	1	1,125	0	0	1,312	4,200
"	**Total**	5	0	0	0	0	0	0	1	1,429	0	0	1,768	5,394
1973	Toby Tobias	1	0	0	0	0	0	0	0	50	0	0	50	680
"	Paul Tyler	5	0	0	0	0	0	0	0	597	0	0	847	5,335
"	**Total**	6	0	0	0	0	0	0	0	647	0	0	897	6,015
1974	Kenny Brightbill	1	0	0	0	0	0	0	1	476	0	0	476	1,825
"	Ramo Stott	6	0	0	0	1	0	0	3	1,414	0	0	2,481	21,955
"	**Total**	7	0	0	0	1	0	0	4	1,890	0	0	2,957	23,780
1975	Bobby Isaac	1	0	0	0	0	0	0	0	208	0	0	312	1,105
"	Johnny Rutherford	3	0	0	0	0	0	0	0	138	0	0	209	2,850
"	Ramo Stott	2	0	0	0	0	0	1	0	259	0	0	657	13,030
"	**Total**	6	0	0	0	0	0	1	0	605	0	0	1,179	16,985
1976	Ramo Stott	1	1	0	0	0	0	0	0	113	0	0	283	6,830
1977	Ron Hutcherson	1	0	0	0	0	0	0	0	85	0	0	213	4,525
Lifetime		27	1	0	0	1	0	1	6	5,243	0	0	7,511	$64,029

Bo Reeder

Year	Driver	Starts	Poles	1	2	3	4	5	6–10	Laps	Laps Led	Races Led	Miles	$
1967	Bo Reeder	1	0	0	0	0	0	0	0	159	0	0	429	700
1968	Bo Reeder	1	0	0	0	0	0	0	0	4	0	0	11	500
1982	Mark Martin	29	0	0	0	0	0	2	6	7,338	4	3	8,208	142,710
1983	Tommy Gale	2	0	0	0	0	0	0	0	305	0	0	282	3,775
"	Dick May	1	0	0	0	0	0	0	0	301	0	0	411	1,670
"	Rick Newsom	5	0	0	0	0	0	0	0	1,898	0	0	1,496	13,220
"	Mike Potter	6	0	0	0	0	0	0	0	1,329	0	0	1,054	12,325
"	Jim Sauter	1	0	0	0	0	0	0	0	321	0	0	482	4,145
"	D. K. Ulrich	4	0	0	0	0	0	0	0	772	0	0	1,228	11,570
"	**Total**	19	0	0	0	0	0	0	0	4,926	0	0	4,953	46,705
Lifetime		50	0	0	0	0	0	2	6	12,427	4	3	13,601	$190,615

Nat Reeder

Year	Driver	Starts	Poles	1	2	3	4	5	6–10	Laps	Laps Led	Races Led	Miles	$
1965	Nat Reeder	1	0	0	0	0	0	0	0	100	0	0	270	625
Lifetime		1	0	0	0	0	0	0	0	100	0	0	270	$625

Tom Reet

Year	Driver	Starts	Poles	1	2	3	4	5	6–10	Laps	Laps Led	Races Led	Miles	$
1988	Bob Schacht	1	0	0	0	0	0	0	0	138	0	0	104	1,650
Lifetime		1	0	0	0	0	0	0	0	138	0	0	104	$1,650

Bobby Reeves

Year	Driver	Starts	Poles	1	2	3	4	5	6–10	Laps	Laps Led	Races Led	Miles	$
1971	Charlie Roberts	13	0	0	0	0	0	0	2	1,942	0	0	2,656	9,145
"	Frank Warren	1	0	0	0	0	0	0	1	464	0	0	247	800
"	**Total**	14	0	0	0	0	0	0	3	2,406	0	0	2,903	9,945
1978	Raymond Williams	1	0	0	0	0	0	0	0	74	0	0	185	1,290
Lifetime		15	0	0	0	0	0	0	3	2,480	0	0	3,088	$11,235

Curtis Reid

Year	Driver	Starts	Poles	1	2	3	4	5	6–10	Laps	Laps Led	Races Led	Miles	$
1956	Eddie Skinner	1	0	0	0	0	0	0	0		0	0		50
Lifetime		1	0	0	0	0	0	0	0		0	0		$50

E. C. Reid

Year	Driver	Starts	Poles	1	2	3	4	5	6–10	Laps	Laps Led	Races Led	Miles	$
1968	Bob Burcham	2	0	0	0	0	0	0	0	366	0	0	183	515
"	Don Tarr	1	0	0	0	0	0	0	0	242	0	0	363	1,685
"	E. J. Trivette	11	0	0	0	0	0	0	0	2,071	0	0	2,424	7,820
"	**Total**	13	0	0	0	0	0	0	0	2,679	0	0	2,970	10,020
1969	Wayne Gillette	16	0	0	0	0	0	0	0	887	0	0	981	6,127
"	Henley Gray	1	0	0	0	0	0	0	0	34	0	0	51	1,135
"	J. D. McDuffie	1	0	0	0	0	0	0	0	6	0	0	15	600
"	Don Patton	1	0	0	0	0	0	0	0	441	0	0	242	500
"	J. C. Spradley	1	0	0	0	0	0	0	0	203	0	0	279	1,075
"	E. J. Trivette	47	0	0	0	0	0	0	14	10,649	0	0	8,811	35,121
"	Danny Turner	3	0	0	0	0	0	0	0	285	0	0	150	1,040
"	Frank Warren	5	0	0	0	0	0	0	0	961	0	0	1,272	4,725

Year	Driver	Starts	Poles	1	2	3	4	5	6–10	Laps	Laps Led	Races Led	Miles	$

E. C. Reid *continued*

Year	Driver	Starts	Poles	1	2	3	4	5	6–10	Laps	Laps Led	Races Led	Miles	$
"	Dick Watson	1	0	0	0	0	0	0	0	171	0	0	107	370
"	**Total**	47	0	0	0	0	0	0	14	13,637	0	0	11,908	50,693
1970	E. J. Trivette	2	0	0	0	0	0	0	0	47	0	0	116	1,235
Lifetime		62	0	0	0	0	0	0	14	16,363	0	0	14,993	$61,948

Lee Reitzel

Year	Driver	Starts	Poles	1	2	3	4	5	6–10	Laps	Laps Led	Races Led	Miles	$
1961	Darel Dieringer	1	0	0	0	0	0	0	0	1	0	0	1	50
"	Lee Reitzel	17	0	0	0	0	0	0	3	2,566	0	0	2,039	2,910
"	**Total**	18	0	0	0	0	0	0	3	2,567	0	0	2,039	2,960
1962	Lee Reitzel	8	0	0	0	0	0	0	1	1,056	0	0	863	1,205
1963	Bobby Keck	1	0	0	0	0	0	0	0	26	0	0	13	100
"	Lee Reitzel	4	0	0	0	0	0	0	0	496	0	0	275	875
"	**Total**	5	0	0	0	0	0	0	0	522	0	0	288	975
Lifetime		31	0	0	0	0	0	0	4	4,145	0	0	3,190	$5,140

B. E. Renfro

Year	Driver	Starts	Poles	1	2	3	4	5	6–10	Laps	Laps Led	Races Led	Miles	$
1949	B. E. Renfro	2	0	0	0	0	0	0	0		0	0		25
Lifetime		2	0	0	0	0	0	0	0		0	0		$25

Marc Reno

Year	Driver	Starts	Poles	1	2	3	4	5	6–10	Laps	Laps Led	Races Led	Miles	$
1987	Ernie Irvan	2	0	0	0	0	0	0	1	367	1	1	517	9,875
"	Patty Moise	1	0	0	0	0	0	0	0	53	0	0	129	1,690
"	**Total**	3	0	0	0	0	0	0	1	420	1	1	646	11,565
1989	Joe Ruttman	1	0	0	0	0	0	0	0	309	0	0	309	4,430
1990	Ron Esau	1	0	0	0	0	0	0	0	383	0	0	287	3,050
"	Tommy Kendall	3	0	0	0	0	0	0	1	613	4	1	820	14,120
"	**Total**	4	0	0	0	0	0	0	1	996	4	1	1,107	17,170
Lifetime		8	0	0	0	0	0	0	2	1,725	5	2	2,061	$33,165

Tom Reymonds

Year	Driver	Starts	Poles	1	2	3	4	5	6–10	Laps	Laps Led	Races Led	Miles	$
1975	Gene Riniker	1	0	0	0	0	0	0	1	138	0	0	362	1,735
Lifetime		1	0	0	0	0	0	0	1	138	0	0	362	$1,735

Mamie Reynolds

Year	Driver	Starts	Poles	1	2	3	4	5	6–10	Laps	Laps Led	Races Led	Miles	$
1962	Darel Dieringer	5	0	0	0	0	0	0	1	1,262	0	0	1,099	1,975
"	Fred Lorenzen	2	0	1	0	0	0	0	0	306	19	1	142	1,050
"	**Total**	7	0	1	0	0	0	0	1	1,568	19	1	1,242	3,025
1963	Darel Dieringer	1	0	0	0	0	0	1	0	197	0	0	99	275
"	Ed Livingston	12	0	0	0	0	0	0	0	2,329	0	0	2,734	3,980
"	**Total**	13	0	0	0	0	0	1	0	2,526	0	0	2,833	4,255
Lifetime		20	0	1	0	0	0	1	1	4,094	19	1	4,074	$7,280

Tom Reynolds

Year	Driver	Starts	Poles	1	2	3	4	5	6–10	Laps	Laps Led	Races Led	Miles	$
1974	Don Reynolds	2	0	0	0	0	0	0	1	303	0	0	772	2,600
1975	Don Reynolds	1	0	0	0	0	0	0	0	110	0	0	288	1,230
Lifetime		3	0	0	0	0	0	0	1	413	0	0	1,060	$3,830

Frank Rhoads

Year	Driver	Starts	Poles	1	2	3	4	5	6–10	Laps	Laps Led	Races Led	Miles	$
1962	Red Farmer	2	0	0	0	0	0	0	0	72	0	0	180	535
Lifetime		2	0	0	0	0	0	0	0	72	0	0	180	$535

Harold Rhodes

Year	Driver	Starts	Poles	1	2	3	4	5	6–10	Laps	Laps Led	Races Led	Miles	$
1965	Joe Penland	3	0	0	0	0	0	0	0	112	0	0	60	1,260
"	Frank Warren	4	0	0	0	0	0	0	1	769	0	0	1,088	2,880
"	**Total**	7	0	0	0	0	0	0	1	881	0	0	1,148	4,140
1966	Frank Warren	11	0	0	0	0	0	0	1	1,989	0	0	2,803	6,740
1967	Frank Warren	12	0	0	0	0	0	0	1	1,805	0	0	2,668	9,185
1968	Frank Warren	5	0	0	0	0	0	0	1	1,256	0	0	1,632	4,265
Lifetime		35	0	0	0	0	0	0	4	5,931	0	0	8,251	$24,330

Year	Driver	Starts	Poles	Finish						Laps	Laps Led	Races Led	Miles	$
				1	2	3	4	5	6–10	Laps	Led	Led	Miles	$

Sam Rice

Year	Driver	Starts	Poles	1	2	3	4	5	6–10	Laps	Laps Led	Races Led	Miles	$
1949	Bill Blair	3	0	0	0	0	0	2	1	573	180	1	385	575
"	Jimmie Lewallen	2	0	0	0	0	0	0	0	0	0	0	0	0
"	Frank Mundy	3	0	0	0	1	1	0	0	236	0	0	362	1,160
"	Sam Rice	2	0	0	0	0	2	0	0	192	0	0	96	680
"	**Total**	7	0	0	0	1	3	2	1	1,001	180	1	843	2,415
1950	Bill Blair	15	0	1	2	0	0	1	2	1,550	218	3	1,253	4,100
"	Jimmie Lewallen	2	0	0	0	0	0	0	0	330	0	0	413	25
"	Fireball Roberts	7	1	1	2	1	0	0	1	1,009	60	3	911	6,750
"	**Total**	16	1	2	4	1	0	1	3	2,889	278	6	2,576	10,875
1951	Jim Paschal	1	0	0	0	0	0	0	1		0	0		100
"	Fireball Roberts	6	0	0	0	0	0	0	1	238	0	0	154	175
"	**Total**	6	0	0	0	0	0	0	2	238	0	0	154	275
1957	Bill Blair	1	0	0	0	0	0	0	0	63	0	0	87	100
"	Wally Gore	1	0	0	0	0	0	0	0	203	0	0	81	110
"	Jimmie Lewallen	7	0	0	0	0	0	0	0	895	0	0	865	1,030
"	Tiny Lund	2	0	0	0	1	0	0	0	309	0	0	169	450
"	Billy Myers	1	0	0	0	0	1	0	0	196	0	0	98	280
"	Jim Paschal	2	0	0	0	0	0	0	0	534	0	0	331	365
"	Ken Rush	3	1	0	0	1	0	0	1	388	0	0	194	540
"	**Total**	16	1	0	0	2	1	0	1	2,588	0	0	1,825	2,875
1958	Ken Rush	1	0	0	0	0	0	0	0	0	0	0	0	0
1959	Jim Paschal	1	0	0	0	0	0	0	0	371	0	0	186	80
Lifetime		47	2	2	4	4	4	3	7	7,087	458	7	5,583	$16,520

E. B. Rich

Year	Driver	Starts	Poles	1	2	3	4	5	6–10	Laps	Laps Led	Races Led	Miles	$
1964	Bobby Keck	8	0	0	0	0	1	1	3	1,717	0	0	896	1,900
Lifetime		8	0	0	0	0	1	1	3	1,717	0	0	896	$1,900

Hank Richardson

Year	Driver	Starts	Poles	1	2	3	4	5	6–10	Laps	Laps Led	Races Led	Miles	$
1972	Tiny Lund	4	0	0	0	0	0	0	0	638	0	0	704	2,345
Lifetime		4	0	0	0	0	0	0	0	638	0	0	704	$2,345

Harlan Richardson

Year	Driver	Starts	Poles	1	2	3	4	5	6–10	Laps	Laps Led	Races Led	Miles	$
1959	Harlan Richardson	10	0	0	0	0	0	0	2	1,893	0	0	948	1,120
Lifetime		10	0	0	0	0	0	0	2	1,893	0	0	948	$1,120

Larry Richardson

Year	Driver	Starts	Poles	1	2	3	4	5	6–10	Laps	Laps Led	Races Led	Miles	$
1974	Larry Richardson	1	0	0	0	0	0	0	0	36	0	0	90	670
Lifetime		1	0	0	0	0	0	0	0	36	0	0	90	$670

J. B. Richter

Year	Driver	Starts	Poles	1	2	3	4	5	6–10	Laps	Laps Led	Races Led	Miles	$
1953	Russell Armentrout	2	0	0	0	0	0	0	0	60	0	0	60	50
Lifetime		2	0	0	0	0	0	0	0	60	0	0	60	$50

Chuck Rider

Year	Driver	Starts	Poles	1	2	3	4	5	6–10	Laps	Laps Led	Races Led	Miles	$
1987	Michael Waltrip	29	0	0	0	0	0	0	1	7,790	1	1	8,848	179,010
1988	Michael Waltrip	28	0	0	1	0	0	0	2	7,537	6	2	9,548	226,335
1989	Michael Waltrip	29	0	0	0	0	0	0	5	8,372	9	4	10,112	249,233
1990	Michael Waltrip	29	0	0	0	1	2	2	5	8,226	17	4	10,124	395,507
1991	Michael Waltrip	29	2	0	0	1	0	3	8	8,394	292	11	9,757	440,812
1992	Michael Waltrip	29	0	0	0	0	1	0	1	8,474	3	1	10,184	410,545
1993	Michael Waltrip	30	0	0	0	0	0	0	5	9,379	40	6	11,146	529,923
1994	Michael Waltrip	31	0	0	0	1	0	1	7	9,508	8	5	11,666	720,426
1995	Michael Waltrip	31	0	0	0	1	0	1	6	9,222	45	12	11,399	898,338
1996	Johnny Benson Jr.	30	1	0	0	0	0	1	5	8,507	105	4	10,483	947,080
Lifetime		295	3	0	1	4	3	8	45	85,409	526	50	103,267	$4,997,209

W. J. Ridgeway

Year	Driver	Starts	Poles	1	2	3	4	5	6–10	Laps	Laps Led	Races Led	Miles	$
1959	Johnny Allen	1	0	0	0	1	0	0	0	99	0	0	248	1,925
"	Speedy Thompson	2	0	0	0	0	0	1	0	830	2	1	706	1,465
"	Curtis Turner	1	0	0	0	0	1	0	0	150	0	0	150	950

Year	Driver	Starts	Poles	Finish 1	2	3	4	5	6–10	Laps	Laps Led	Races Led	Miles	$

W. J. Ridgeway *continued*

Year	Driver	Starts	Poles	1	2	3	4	5	6–10	Laps	Laps Led	Races Led	Miles	$
"	Bob Welborn	2	1	1	0	0	0	0	0	115	42	2	288	1,125
"	**Total**	6	1	1	0	1	1	1	0	1,194	44	3	1,391	5,465
1960	Joe Lee Johnson	5	0	0	0	0	0	0	0	289	0	0	248	575
"	Marvin Panch	8	0	0	0	0	0	0	1	1,265	0	0	1,911	2,875
"	Curtis Turner	1	0	0	0	0	0	0	0	10	0	0	5	50
"	Bob Welborn	2	0	0	1	0	0	0	0	199	76	1	100	575
"	**Total**	16	0	0	1	0	0	0	1	1,763	76	1	2,263	4,075
1961	Darel Dieringer	1	0	0	0	0	0	0	0	231	0	0	347	250
"	J. C. Hendrix	1	0	0	0	0	0	0	0	202	0	0	303	300
"	**Total**	2	0	0	0	0	0	0	0	433	0	0	650	550
Lifetime		24	1	1	1	1	1	1	1	3,390	120	4	4,304	$10,090

Bob Riley

Year	Driver	Starts	Poles	1	2	3	4	5	6–10	Laps	Laps Led	Races Led	Miles	$
1983	Bob Riley	3	0	0	0	0	0	0	0	329	0	0	491	3,530
1985	Bob Riley	1	0	0	0	0	0	0	0	449	0	0	449	2,100
Lifetime		4	0	0	0	0	0	0	0	778	0	0	940	$5,630

Richard Riley

Year	Driver	Starts	Poles	1	2	3	4	5	6–10	Laps	Laps Led	Races Led	Miles	$
1959	Curtis Crider	2	0	0	0	0	0	0	0	244	0	0	122	135
"	Bunk Moore	5	0	0	0	0	0	0	0	312	0	0	153	280
"	Richard Riley	3	0	0	0	0	0	0	0	466	0	0	233	210
"	**Total**	10	0	0	0	0	0	0	0	1,022	0	0	508	625
Lifetime		10	0	0	0	0	0	0	0	1,022	0	0	508	$625

Laurent Rioux

Year	Driver	Starts	Poles	1	2	3	4	5	6–10	Laps	Laps Led	Races Led	Miles	$
1983	Laurent Rioux	2	0	0	0	0	0	0	0	884	0	0	674	4,565
1984	Laurent Rioux	1	0	0	0	0	0	0	0	424	0	0	431	5,745
Lifetime		3	0	0	0	0	0	0	0	1,308	0	0	1,105	$10,310

Pat Rissi

Year	Driver	Starts	Poles	1	2	3	4	5	6–10	Laps	Laps Led	Races Led	Miles	$
1991	Andy Belmont	1	0	0	0	0	0	0	0	11	0	0	11	3,450
1992	Andy Belmont	8	0	0	0	0	0	0	0	784	0	0	1,548	39,820
Lifetime		9	0	0	0	0	0	0	0	795	0	0	1,559	$43,270

Marty Robbins

Year	Driver	Starts	Poles	1	2	3	4	5	6–10	Laps	Laps Led	Races Led	Miles	$
1970	Marty Robbins	1	0	0	0	0	0	0	0	105	0	0	158	1,160
1971	Marty Robbins	5	0	0	0	0	0	0	1	1,295	0	0	1,984	7,152
1972	Marty Robbins	5	0	0	0	0	0	0	2	1,096	0	0	1,864	7,950
1973	Marty Robbins	4	0	0	0	0	0	0	1	334	1	1	829	5,395
1974	Marty Robbins	4	0	0	0	0	0	1	1	550	0	0	1,343	5,734
1975	Marty Robbins	2	0	0	0	0	0	0	0	65	2	1	172	3,160
1977	Elmo Langley	1	0	0	0	0	0	0	0	1	0	0	2	610
"	Marty Robbins	2	0	0	0	0	0	0	0	229	0	0	482	2,590
"	**Total**	3	0	0	0	0	0	0	0	230	0	0	484	3,200
1978	Marty Robbins	1	0	0	0	0	0	0	0	171	0	0	455	2,240
1979	Marty Robbins	3	0	0	0	0	0	0	0	235	0	0	520	3,120
1980	Marty Robbins	2	0	0	0	0	0	0	0	227	0	0	604	4,235
1982	Marty Robbins	2	0	0	0	0	0	0	0	134	0	0	248	2,055
Lifetime		32	0	0	0	0	0	0	1	5	4,442	3	2	8,660	$45,401

Charlie Roberts

Year	Driver	Starts	Poles	1	2	3	4	5	6–10	Laps	Laps Led	Races Led	Miles	$
1970	Charlie Roberts	3	0	0	0	0	0	0	0	95	0	0	149	1,470
1971	Johnny Barnes	1	0	0	0	0	0	0	0	23	0	0	61	615
"	Bill Champion	1	0	0	0	0	0	0	0	41	0	0	103	1,250
"	Roy Mulligan	1	0	0	0	0	0	0	0	83	0	0	221	1,450
"	Charlie Roberts	5	0	0	0	0	0	0	0	785	0	0	960	2,135
"	Frank Warren	1	0	0	0	0	0	0	0	26	0	0	36	570
"	**Total**	9	0	0	0	0	0	0	0	958	0	0	1,380	6,020
1972	Charlie Roberts	24	0	0	0	0	0	0	1	6,211	0	0	7,244	29,748
"	Robert Wales	2	0	0	0	0	0	0	0	14	0	0	37	1,510
"	**Total**	25	0	0	0	0	0	0	1	6,225	0	0	7,281	31,258

Year	Driver	Starts	Poles	Finish 1	2	3	4	5	6–10	Laps	Laps Led	Races Led	Miles	$

Charlie Roberts *continued*

Year	Driver	Starts	Poles	1	2	3	4	5	6–10	Laps	Laps Led	Races Led	Miles	$
1973	Charlie Roberts	24	0	0	0	0	0	0	0	7,017	0	0	6,848	32,469
1974	Neil Bonnett	1	0	0	0	0	0	0	0	51	0	0	136	1,450
"	Charlie Roberts	3	0	0	0	0	0	0	0	226	0	0	471	3,940
"	**Total**	4	0	0	0	0	0	0	0	277	0	0	606	5,390
Lifetime		65	0	0	0	0	0	0	1	14,572	0	0	16,264	$76,607

Fireball Roberts

Year	Driver	Starts	Poles	1	2	3	4	5	6–10	Laps	Laps Led	Races Led	Miles	$
1957	Marvin Panch	1	0	0	0	0	0	0	0	473	0	0	237	210
"	Fireball Roberts	22	1	3	2	1	0	2	4	3,285	363	6	2,080	8,929
"	**Total**	23	1	3	2	1	0	2	4	3,758	363	6	2,317	9,139
Lifetime		23	1	3	2	1	0	2	4	3,758	363	6	2,317	$9,139

Johnny Roberts

Year	Driver	Starts	Poles	1	2	3	4	5	6–10	Laps	Laps Led	Races Led	Miles	$
1953	Johnny Roberts	2	0	0	0	0	0	0	0	33	0	0	135	50
1954	Johnny Roberts	2	0	0	0	0	0	0	0	160	0	0	159	25
1955	Johnny Roberts	4	0	0	0	0	0	0	1	600	0	0	406	250
1956	Johnny Roberts	4	0	0	0	0	0	0	0	461	0	0	215	210
Lifetime		12	0	0	0	0	0	0	1	1,254	0	0	916	$535

Neil Roberts

Year	Driver	Starts	Poles	1	2	3	4	5	6–10	Laps	Laps Led	Races Led	Miles	$
1953	Neil Roberts	1	0	0	0	0	0	0	0	335	0	0	461	300
Lifetime		1	0	0	0	0	0	0	0	335	0	0	461	$300

Paul Roberts

Year	Driver	Starts	Poles	1	2	3	4	5	6–10	Laps	Laps Led	Races Led	Miles	$
1950	Curtis Turner	1	0	0	0	0	0	0	0	46	0	0	192	50
Lifetime		1	0	0	0	0	0	0	0	46	0	0	192	$50

Don Robertson

Year	Driver	Starts	Poles	1	2	3	4	5	6–10	Laps	Laps Led	Races Led	Miles	$
1967	Sam McQuagg	1	0	0	0	0	0	0	0	50	0	0	31	175
"	Jabe Thomas	19	0	0	0	0	0	0	2	2,139	0	0	1,713	6,855
"	**Total**	20	0	0	0	0	0	0	2	2,189	0	0	1,744	7,030
1968	Earl Brooks	10	0	0	0	0	0	0	1	1,416	0	0	1,064	3,280
"	Frog Fagan	1	0	0	0	0	0	0	0	3	0	0	3	250
"	Jabe Thomas	47	0	0	0	0	0	1	14	11,141	0	0	7,283	20,586
"	**Total**	47	0	0	0	0	0	1	15	12,560	0	0	8,350	24,116
1969	Earl Brooks	2	0	0	0	0	0	0	0	363	0	0	182	370
"	James Cox	8	0	0	0	0	0	0	0	606	0	0	299	1,935
"	Paul Dean Holt	3	0	0	0	0	0	0	0	320	0	0	205	733
"	Wendell Scott	1	0	0	0	0	0	0	0	10	0	0	25	605
"	Jabe Thomas	50	0	0	0	0	0	0	12	11,969	0	0	9,812	44,579
"	**Total**	51	0	0	0	0	0	0	12	13,268	0	0	10,523	48,222
1970	Bobby Allison	3	0	0	1	0	0	0	1	921	0	0	525	5,060
"	Earl Brooks	1	0	0	0	0	0	0	0	29	0	0	40	815
"	James Cox	6	0	0	0	0	0	0	0	314	0	0	208	2,200
"	Charlie Glotzbach	2	0	0	0	0	0	0	0	219	0	0	97	475
"	Ed Hessert	1	0	0	0	0	0	0	0	60	0	0	90	240
"	James Hylton	2	0	0	0	0	0	0	0	220	0	0	550	1,490
"	Richard Petty	2	0	2	0	0	0	0	0	400	216	2	200	2,500
"	Wendell Scott	11	0	0	0	0	0	0	0	1,876	0	0	1,929	6,615
"	Jabe Thomas	46	0	0	0	0	0	0	23	10,928	0	0	9,510	42,958
"	**Total**	46	0	2	1	0	0	0	24	**14,967**	216	2	13,149	62,353
1971	Neil Castles	1	0	0	0	0	0	0	0	2	0	0	3	315
"	James Cox	5	0	0	0	0	0	0	0	531	0	0	327	1,650
"	Pedro Rodriguez	1	0	0	0	0	0	0	0	194	0	0	485	1,975
"	Fritz Schultz	1	0	0	0	0	0	0	0	45	0	0	113	205
"	Bill Seifert	1	0	0	0	0	0	0	0	9	0	0	5	240
"	Jabe Thomas	41	0	0	0	0	1	1	13	10,729	0	0	9,166	46,556
"	**Total**	44	0	0	0	0	1	1	13	11,510	0	0	10,099	50,941
1972	James Cox	2	0	0	0	0	0	0	0	527	0	0	323	1,220
"	Bill Dennis	5	0	0	0	0	0	0	0	737	0	0	916	3,465
"	Vic Elford	1	0	0	0	0	0	0	1	182	0	0	455	3,445
"	Henley Gray	1	0	0	0	0	0	0	0	81	0	0	51	330
"	Ed Hessert	1	0	0	0	0	0	0	0	50	0	0	75	335

Year	Driver	Starts	Poles	Finish 1	2	3	4	5	6–10	Laps	Laps Led	Races Led	Miles	$

Don Robertson *continued*

Year	Driver	Starts	Poles	1	2	3	4	5	6–10	Laps	Laps Led	Races Led	Miles	$
"	Mel Larson	3	0	0	0	0	0	0	0	400	0	0	918	2,870
"	Roy Mayne	1	0	0	0	0	0	0	0	267	0	0	272	650
"	Jabe Thomas	27	0	0	0	0	0	0	4	7,038	0	0	8,066	42,624
"	**Total**	27	0	0	0	0	0	0	5	9,282	0	0	11,074	54,939
1973	Mel Larson	7	0	0	0	0	0	0	0	1,967	0	0	1,666	5,370
"	Roy Mayne	3	0	0	0	0	0	0	1	658	0	0	1,091	5,470
"	Jabe Thomas	23	0	0	0	0	0	0	1	6,553	0	0	7,300	31,768
"	**Total**	25	0	0	0	0	0	0	2	9,178	0	0	10,057	42,608
1974	Roy Mayne	11	0	0	0	0	0	0	0	1,681	0	0	2,856	14,895
"	Richie Panch	1	0	0	0	0	0	0	0	56	0	0	33	535
"	Jabe Thomas	10	0	0	0	0	0	0	1	1,504	0	0	1,006	7,835
"	**Total**	22	0	0	0	0	0	0	1	3,241	0	0	3,896	23,265
1975	Earl Brooks	7	0	0	0	0	0	0	0	1,229	0	0	1,376	4,900
"	Charlie Griffin	2	0	0	0	0	0	0	0	82	0	0	52	720
"	Jabe Thomas	20	0	0	0	0	0	0	2	5,645	0	0	5,191	19,720
"	**Total**	21	0	0	0	0	0	0	2	6,956	0	0	6,618	25,340
1976	Earl Brooks	1	0	0	0	0	0	0	0	313	0	0	428	1,990
"	Larry LeMay	2	0	0	0	0	0	0	0	460	0	0	280	975
"	Dick May	13	0	0	0	0	0	0	0	3,504	0	0	3,980	21,725
"	Jabe Thomas	6	0	0	0	0	0	0	0	1,944	0	0	1,291	6,530
"	D. K. Ulrich	1	0	0	0	0	0	0	0	168	0	0	447	2,785
"	**Total**	21	0	0	0	0	0	0	0	6,389	0	0	6,425	34,005
1977	Terry Bivins	4	0	0	0	0	0	0	0	1,009	0	0	909	6,640
"	Dean Dalton	1	0	0	0	0	0	0	0	179	0	0	358	1,775
"	Ferrel Harris	11	0	0	0	0	0	0	0	2,979	0	0	2,560	19,365
"	Dick May	1	0	0	0	0	0	0	0	148	0	0	394	3,165
"	Ronnie Thomas	4	0	0	0	0	0	0	0	821	0	0	715	4,590
"	**Total**	21	0	0	0	0	0	0	0	5,136	0	0	4,936	35,535
1978	Jabe Thomas	1	0	0	0	0	0	0	0	1	0	0	1	480
"	Ronnie Thomas	27	0	0	0	0	0	0	2	7,287	0	0	7,769	72,255
"	**Total**	27	0	0	0	0	0	0	2	7,288	0	0	7,770	72,735
1979	Ronnie Thomas	29	0	0	0	0	0	0	3	6,549	1	1	7,272	94,589
1980	Ronnie Thomas	30	0	0	0	0	0	0	4	7,522	0	0	9,081	94,730
Lifetime		431	0	2	1	0	1	2	85	116,035	217	3	110,994	$670,408

H. R. Robertson

Year	Driver	Starts	Poles	1	2	3	4	5	6–10	Laps	Laps Led	Races Led	Miles	$
1952	Buck McCardell	1	0	0	0	0	0	0	0		0	0		25
Lifetime		1	0	0	0	0	0	0	0		0	0		$25

Charles Robinson

Year	Driver	Starts	Poles	1	2	3	4	5	6–10	Laps	Laps Led	Races Led	Miles	$
1963	Ned Jarrett	50	4	8	7	5	7	4	7	11,370	1,897	18	7,719	45,369
1964	Ned Jarrett	4	1	1	0	0	0	1	1	632	233	3	646	3,275
"	Jimmy Pardue	47	2	0	2	4	4	4	9	9,163	237	5	6,158	39,678
"	Larry Thomas	3	0	0	0	1	0	1	0	671	0	0	519	1,325
"	**Total**	54	3	1	2	5	4	6	10	10,466	470	8	7,323	44,278
Lifetime		104	7	9	9	10	11	10	17	21,836	2,367	26	15,042	$89,647

Lefty Robinson

Year	Driver	Starts	Poles	1	2	3	4	5	6–10	Laps	Laps Led	Races Led	Miles	$
1975	Larry Esau	1	0	0	0	0	0	0	0	135	0	0	354	1,535
Lifetime		1	0	0	0	0	0	0	0	135	0	0	354	$1,535

Robbie Robinson

Year	Driver	Starts	Poles	1	2	3	4	5	6–10	Laps	Laps Led	Races Led	Miles	$
1952	Robbie Robinson	4	0	0	0	0	0	0	0	300	0	0	160	75
Lifetime		4	0	0	0	0	0	0	0	300	0	0	160	$75

Truett Rodgers

Year	Driver	Starts	Poles	1	2	3	4	5	6–10	Laps	Laps Led	Races Led	Miles	$
1966	Roy Tyner	24	0	0	0	0	0	0	4	3,241	0	0	1,604	3,735
1967	Earl Brooks	1	0	0	0	0	0	0	0	215	0	0	134	225
"	Ken Spikes	2	0	0	0	0	0	0	0	305	0	0	423	1,325
"	Roy Tyner	24	0	0	0	0	0	0	1	2,521	0	0	1,638	5,855
"	**Total**	27	0	0	0	0	0	0	1	3,041	0	0	2,195	7,405
1968	Bill Vanderhoff	1	0	0	0	0	0	0	0	151	0	0	76	100
Lifetime		52	0	0	0	0	0	0	5	6,433	0	0	3,875	$11,240

Year	Driver	Starts	Poles	1	2	3	4	5	6–10	Laps	Laps Led	Races Led	Miles	$

Don Rogalla

Year	Driver	Starts	Poles	1	2	3	4	5	6–10	Laps	Laps Led	Races Led	Miles	$
1949	Al Bonnell	2	1	0	0	0	0	0	1	183	0	0	183	150
"	Don Rogala	1	0	0	0	0	0	0	1	167	0	0	84	50
"	**Total**	2	1	0	0	0	0	0	2	350	0	0	267	200
1950	Dick Linder	11	5	3	1	1	0	0	2	1,144	460	5	847	5,175
1951	Dan Daniels	2	0	0	0	0	0	0	0		0	0		50
"	Dick Linder	9	0	0	0	0	0	0	2	21	0	0	11	325
"	**Total**	9	0	0	0	0	0	0	2	21	0	0	11	375
Lifetime		22	6	3	1	1	0	0	6	1,515	460	5	1,124	$5,750

Bob Rogers

Year	Driver	Starts	Poles	1	2	3	4	5	6–10	Laps	Laps Led	Races Led	Miles	$
1980	Don Sprouse	4	0	0	0	0	0	0	0	1,312	0	0	745	2,880
1981	Mike Alexander	19	0	0	0	0	0	0	3	4,340	4	1	4,886	33,305
"	Tim Richmond	7	0	0	0	0	0	0	1	2,227	24	2	2,438	15,240
"	Don Sprouse	2	0	0	0	0	0	0	0	570	0	0	663	6,850
"	**Total**	28	0	0	0	0	0	0	4	7,137	28	3	7,987	55,395
1982	Donnie Allison	5	0	0	0	0	0	0	3	1,174	1	1	1,646	28,105
"	Neil Bonnett	3	0	0	0	0	0	1	1	1,214	0	0	710	9,530
"	Mark Martin	1	0	0	0	0	0	0	0	111	0	0	113	2,440
"	Tom Sneva	3	0	0	0	0	0	0	0	520	0	0	840	15,585
"	**Total**	12	0	0	0	0	0	1	4	3,019	1	1	3,309	55,660
Lifetime		44	0	0	0	0	0	1	8	11,468	29	4	12,040	$113,935

John Rogers

Year	Driver	Starts	Poles	1	2	3	4	5	6–10	Laps	Laps Led	Races Led	Miles	$
1962	John Rogers	1	0	0	0	0	0	0	0	35	0	0	88	50
1963	John Rogers	2	0	0	0	0	0	0	0	109	0	0	273	625
Lifetime		3	0	0	0	0	0	0	0	144	0	0	360	$675

George Rogge

Year	Driver	Starts	Poles	1	2	3	4	5	6–10	Laps	Laps Led	Races Led	Miles	$
1954	George Rogge	1	0	0	0	0	0	0	0	64	0	0	64	40
Lifetime		1	0	0	0	0	0	0	0	64	0	0	64	$40

R. C. Rollings

Year	Driver	Starts	Poles	1	2	3	4	5	6–10	Laps	Laps Led	Races Led	Miles	$
1955	Jimmy Roland	1	0	0	0	0	0	0	0	137	0	0	188	50
Lifetime		1	0	0	0	0	0	0	0	137	0	0	188	$50

Shorty Rollins

Year	Driver	Starts	Poles	1	2	3	4	5	6–10	Laps	Laps Led	Races Led	Miles	$
1958	Shorty Rollins	26	0	1	1	3	5	1	9	4,853	87	4	2,984	12,954
"	Jack Smith	1	0	0	0	0	0	0	0	171	0	0	86	0
"	**Total**	27	0	1	1	3	5	1	9	5,024	87	4	3,070	12,954
1959	Shorty Rollins	8	0	0	0	0	0	0	4	1,286	0	0	890	1,150
"	Fritz Wilson	4	0	0	0	0	0	0	1	263	0	0	156	180
"	**Total**	12	0	0	0	0	0	0	5	1,549	0	0	1,046	1,330
1960	Larry Frank	3	0	0	0	0	0	0	1	991	11	1	994	1,335
"	Shorty Rollins	4	0	0	0	0	0	0	1	952	0	0	1,480	2,120
"	**Total**	7	0	0	0	0	0	0	2	1,943	11	1	2,473	3,455
Lifetime		46	0	1	1	3	5	1	16	8,516	98	5	6,589	$17,739

Paul Romine

Year	Driver	Starts	Poles	1	2	3	4	5	6–10	Laps	Laps Led	Races Led	Miles	$
1990	Pancho Carter	1	0	0	0	0	0	0	0	298	0	0	454	3,040
Lifetime		1	0	0	0	0	0	0	0	298	0	0	454	$3,040

Slim Rominger

Year	Driver	Starts	Poles	1	2	3	4	5	6–10	Laps	Laps Led	Races Led	Miles	$
1953	Slim Rominger	1	0	0	0	0	0	0	0	84	0	0	53	25
1957	Darel Dieringer	1	0	0	0	0	0	0	1	279	0	0	279	450
"	Paul Goldsmith	1	0	0	0	0	0	0	1	55	0	0	138	225
"	**Total**	2	0	0	0	0	0	0	2	334	0	0	417	675
1958	Paul Goldsmith	1	0	0	0	0	0	0	1	139	0	0	46	140
Lifetime		4	0	0	0	0	0	0	3	557	0	0	515	$840

Ron Ronacher

Year	Driver	Starts	Poles	1	2	3	4	5	6–10	Laps	Laps Led	Races Led	Miles	$
1970	Dick May	16	0	0	0	0	0	0	0	1,028	0	0	689	5,195

Year	Driver	Starts	Poles	Finish 1	2	3	4	5	6–10	Laps	Laps Led	Races Led	Miles	$

Ron Ronacher *continued*

Year	Driver	Starts	Poles	1	2	3	4	5	6–10	Laps	Laps Led	Races Led	Miles	$
1971	Elmo Langley	3	0	0	0	0	0	1	1	890	0	0	610	1,635
"	Dick May	13	0	0	0	0	0	0	1	1,206	0	0	709	4,385
"	**Total**	16	0	0	0	0	0	1	2	2,096	0	0	1,319	6,020
Lifetime		32	0	0	0	0	0	1	2	3,124	0	0	2,008	$11,215

Bruce Root

Year	Driver	Starts	Poles	1	2	3	4	5	6–10	Laps	Laps Led	Races Led	Miles	$
1952	Speedy Thompson	1	0	0	0	0	0	0	0	26	0	0	33	25
Lifetime		1	0	0	0	0	0	0	0	26	0	0	33	$25

Charles Roscoe

Year	Driver	Starts	Poles	1	2	3	4	5	6–10	Laps	Laps Led	Races Led	Miles	$
1951	Bill Stammer	3	0	0	0	0	0	0	2		0	0		175
Lifetime		3	0	0	0	0	0	0	2		0	0		$175

Bob Rose

Year	Driver	Starts	Poles	1	2	3	4	5	6–10	Laps	Laps Led	Races Led	Miles	$
1961	Sal Tovella	3	0	0	0	0	0	0	0	362	0	0	761	600
Lifetime		3	0	0	0	0	0	0	0	362	0	0	761	$600

Mauri Rose

Year	Driver	Starts	Poles	1	2	3	4	5	6–10	Laps	Laps Led	Races Led	Miles	$
1956	Bob Flock	3	0	0	0	0	0	1	0	390	0	0	345	435
"	Tim Flock	7	0	0	0	0	1	1	2	964	0	0	768	2,219
"	Speedy Thompson	2	0	0	0	0	0	0	0	109	0	0	74	50
"	Dink Widenhouse	1	0	0	0	0	0	0	0	64	0	0	32	0
"	**Total**	10	0	0	0	0	1	2	2	1,527	0	0	1,218	2,704
Lifetime		10	0	0	0	0	1	2	2	1,527	0	0	1,218	$2,704

Sam Rose

Year	Driver	Starts	Poles	1	2	3	4	5	6–10	Laps	Laps Led	Races Led	Miles	$
1968	Sam Rose	1	0	0	0	0	0	0	0	92	0	0	248	630
1969	Sam Rose	1	0	0	0	0	0	0	0	65	0	0	176	775
1970	Sam Rose	1	0	0	0	0	0	0	0	157	0	0	411	1,175
Lifetime		3	0	0	0	0	0	0	0	314	0	0	835	$2,580

Jim Rosenblum

Year	Driver	Starts	Poles	1	2	3	4	5	6–10	Laps	Laps Led	Races Led	Miles	$
1983	Jocko Maggiacomo	3	0	0	0	0	0	0	0	312	0	0	722	4,990
1984	Jocko Maggiacomo	0												1,650
1986	Jocko Maggiacomo	2	0	0	0	0	0	0	0	14	0	0	35	2,695
1987	Jocko Maggiacomo	3	0	0	0	0	0	0	0	233	0	0	582	4,885
1988	Jocko Maggiacomo	3	0	0	0	0	0	0	0	125	0	0	320	6,455
1989	Eddie Bierschwale	1	0	0	0	0	0	0	0	83	0	0	208	2,575
"	Oma Kimbrough	1	0	0	0	0	0	0	0	64	0	0	155	2,135
"	Randy LaJoie	1	0	0	0	0	0	0	0	178	0	0	445	2,725
"	**Total**	3	0	0	0	0	0	0	0	325	0	0	808	7,435
1990	Oma Kimbrough	1	0	0	0	0	0	0	0	40	0	0	97	2,240
"	Randy LaJoie	2	0	0	0	0	0	0	0	177	0	0	438	6,675
"	**Total**	3	0	0	0	0	0	0	0	217	0	0	535	8,915
1991	Gary Balough	1	0	0	0	0	0	0	0	2	0	0	5	3,300
"	Oma Kimbrough	1	0	0	0	0	0	0	0	80	0	0	194	3,620
"	Randy LaJoie	1	0	0	0	0	0	0	0	154	0	0	385	4,250
"	**Total**	3	0	0	0	0	0	0	0	236	0	0	584	11,170
1992	Gary Balough	1	0	0	0	0	0	0	0	131	0	0	197	5,100
"	Bob Schacht	2	0	0	0	0	0	0	0	107	0	0	265	8,075
"	**Total**	3	0	0	0	0	0	0	0	238	0	0	462	13,175
1993	Kerry Teague	2	0	0	0	0	0	0	0	223	0	0	558	17,350
Lifetime		25	0	0	0	0	0	0	0	1,923	0	0	4,604	$78,720

Bob Rosenthal

Year	Driver	Starts	Poles	1	2	3	4	5	6–10	Laps	Laps Led	Races Led	Miles	$
1966	Bunkie Blackburn	2	0	0	0	0	0	0	0	65	4	1	163	1,070
Lifetime		2	0	0	0	0	0	0	0	65	4	1	163	$1,070

H. G. Rosier

Year	Driver	Starts	Poles	1	2	3	4	5	6–10	Laps	Laps Led	Races Led	Miles	$
1962	H. G. Rosier	4	0	0	0	0	0	0	1	653	0	0	748	1,440

Year	Driver	Starts	Poles	Finish						Laps	Laps Led	Races Led	Miles	$
				1	2	3	4	5	6–10					

H. G. Rosier *continued*

Year	Driver	Starts	Poles	1	2	3	4	5	6–10	Laps	Laps Led	Races Led	Miles	$
1963	H. G. Rosier	2	0	0	0	0	1	0	0	162	0	0	81	350
Lifetime		6	0	0	0	0	1	0	1	815	0	0	829	$1,790

Bob Ross

Year	Driver	Starts	Poles	1	2	3	4	5	6–10	Laps	Laps Led	Races Led	Miles	$
1957	Bob Ross	3	0	0	0	0	0	0	3	396	0	0	314	720
1959	Bob Ross	1	0	0	0	0	1	0	0	482	0	0	193	600
1960	Bob Ross	2	0	0	0	0	0	0	0	104	0	0	116	200
Lifetime		6	0	0	0	0	1	0	3	982	0	0	623	$1,520

Brian Ross

Year	Driver	Starts	Poles	1	2	3	4	5	6–10	Laps	Laps Led	Races Led	Miles	$
1991	Brian Ross	1	0	0	0	0	0	0	0	37	0	0	37	3,475
Lifetime		1	0	0	0	0	0	0	0	37	0	0	37	$3,475

Mario Rossi

Year	Driver	Starts	Poles	1	2	3	4	5	6–10	Laps	Laps Led	Races Led	Miles	$
1958	Mario Rossi	2	0	0	0	0	0	0	0	501	0	0	475	220
1968	Darel Dieringer	18	1	0	1	0	3	1	3	4,409	159	2	4,972	28,215
1969	Bobby Allison	23	1	4	3	1	2	2	1	5,570	1,157	13	6,145	67,418
"	Darel Dieringer	1	0	0	0	0	0	0	0	119	0	0	60	250
"	**Total**	24	1	4	3	1	2	2	1	5,689	1,157	13	6,204	65,365
1970	Bobby Allison	21	3	1	6	4	2	0	2	5,264	405	13	7,700	118,100
1971	Dick Brooks	15	0	0	1	5	0	3	3	3,936	16	5	4,408	30,420
Lifetime		80	5	5	11	10	7	6	9	19,799	1,737	33	23,759	$242,320

John Rostek

Year	Driver	Starts	Poles	1	2	3	4	5	6–10	Laps	Laps Led	Races Led	Miles	$
1960	John Rostek	5	1	1	0	1	0	0	1	658	65	2	688	2,060
Lifetime		5	1	1	0	1	0	0	1	658	65	2	688	$2,060

Dr. Gil Roth

Year	Driver	Starts	Poles	1	2	3	4	5	6–10	Laps	Laps Led	Races Led	Miles	$
1982	Gil Roth	1	0	0	0	0	0	0	0	91	0	0	91	615
Lifetime		1	0	0	0	0	0	0	0	91	0	0	91	$615

Roulo Brothers (Gary and Rusty Roulo, co-owners)

Year	Driver	Starts	Poles	1	2	3	4	5	6–10	Laps	Laps Led	Races Led	Miles	$
1993	Chuck Bown	1	0	0	0	0	0	0	0	306	0	0	306	6,610
"	Scott Lagasse	1	0	0	0	0	0	0	0	90	0	0	221	7,800
"	Jim Sauter	1	0	0	0	0	0	0	0	197	0	0	394	8,195
"	Dick Trickle	2	0	0	0	0	0	0	0	474	0	0	454	13,920
"	**Total**	5	0	0	0	0	0	0	0	1,067	0	0	1,375	36,525
1994	Rich Bickle	1	0	0	0	0	0	0	0	144	0	0	144	6,515
"	Scott Lagasse	1	0	0	0	0	0	0	0	65	0	0	159	6,055
"	**Total**	2	0	0	0	0	0	0	0	209	0	0	303	12,570
Lifetime		7	0	0	0	0	0	0	0	1,276	0	0	1,678	$49,095

Larry Rouse

Year	Driver	Starts	Poles	1	2	3	4	5	6–10	Laps	Laps Led	Races Led	Miles	$
1991	Robert Sprague	1	0	0	0	0	0	0	0	54	1	1	136	3,500
Lifetime		1	0	0	0	0	0	0	0	54	1	1	136	$3,500

Jack Roush

Year	Driver	Starts	Poles	1	2	3	4	5	6–10	Laps	Laps Led	Races Led	Miles	$
1988	Mark Martin	29	1	0	1	0	2	0	7	7,615	123	5	9,193	223,630
1989	Mark Martin	29	6	1	5	6	1	1	4	9,010	480	16	10,716	1,016,850
1990	Mark Martin	29	3	3	5	4	2	2	7	9,636	451	15	11,487	1,302,958
1991	Mark Martin	29	5	1	1	5	4	3	3	8,927	663	15	10,810	1,039,991
1992	Wally Dallenbach Jr.	29	0	0	0	0	0	1	0	8,118	0	0	9,714	220,245
"	Mark Martin	29	1	2	5	2	1	0	7	8,954	533	17	10,670	1,000,571
"	**Total**	29	1	2	5	2	1	1	7	17,072	533	17	20,383	1,220,816
1993	Wally Dallenbach Jr.	30	0	0	1	0	0	0	3	8,411	3	2	10,056	474,340
"	Mark Martin	30	5	5	3	1	1	2	7	9,381	1,353	20	11,106	1,657,662
"	**Total**	30	5	5	4	1	1	2	10	17,792	1,356	**21**	21,162	2,132,002
1994	Mark Martin	31	1	2	4	2	4	3	5	9,549	733	18	11,403	1,678,906
"	Ted Musgrave	31	3	0	0	0	0	1	7	9,237	50	4	10,817	669,687
"	**Total**	31	4	2	4	2	4	4	12	18,786	783	21	22,220	2,348,593
1995	Mark Martin	31	4	4	1	4	1	3	9	9,393	740	14	11,427	1,893,519

Year	Driver	Starts	Poles	Finish 1	2	3	4	5	6–10	Laps	Laps Led	Races Led	Miles	$

Jack Roush *continued*

	Driver	Starts	Poles	1	2	3	4	5	6–10	Laps	Laps Led	Races Led	Miles	$
"	Ted Musgrave	31	1	0	2	2	2	1	6	9,580	43	6	11,822	1,147,445
"	**Total**	31	5	4	3	6	3	4	15	18,973	783	18	23,249	3,040,964
1996	Jeff Burton	30	1	0	0	1	3	2	6	8,592	210	7	10,551	961,512
"	Mark Martin	31	4	0	4	5	3	2	9	9,064	702	16	11,066	1,887,396
"	Ted Musgrave	31	1	0	0	1	1	0	5	9,352	5	3	11,388	884,303
"	**Total**	31	6	0	4	7	7	4	20	27,008	917	20	33,005	3,733,211
Lifetime		268	36	18	32	33	25	21	85	134,819	6,089	148	162,224	$16,059,015
														4th

Marvin Rowley

Year	Driver	Starts	Poles	1	2	3	4	5	6–10	Laps	Laps Led	Races Led	Miles	$
1970	Jimmy Insolo	2	0	0	0	0	0	0	0	137	0	0	359	1,635
1971	Jimmy Insolo	3	0	0	0	0	0	0	0	349	0	0	892	3,790
Lifetime		5	0	0	0	0	0	0	0	486	0	0	1,251	$5,425

Al Rudd

Year	Driver	Starts	Poles	1	2	3	4	5	6–10	Laps	Laps Led	Races Led	Miles	$
1976	Ricky Rudd	4	0	0	0	0	0	0	1	876	0	0	1,527	7,525
1977	Ricky Rudd	25	0	0	0	0	1	0	9	6,233	13	3	7,509	75,905
1978	James Hylton	1	0	0	0	0	0	0	0	1	0	0	3	1,130
"	Ricky Rudd	13	0	0	0	0	0	0	4	2,535	16	5	4,334	50,630
"	**Total**	13	0	0	0	0	0	0	4	2,536	16	5	4,337	51,760
1979	Lennie Pond	2	0	0	0	0	0	0	0	470	2	1	417	2,975
"	Al Rudd Jr.	1	0	0	0	0	0	0	0	39	0	0	78	740
"	Darrell Waltrip	1	0	0	0	0	0	0	1	200	62	1	500	2,715
"	**Total**	4	0	0	0	0	0	0	1	709	64	2	995	6,430
1980	Ricky Rudd	3	0	0	0	0	1	0	1	839	1	1	1,314	23,515
Lifetime		49	0	0	0	0	2	0	16	11,193	94	11	15,682	$165,135

Ricky Rudd

Year	Driver	Starts	Poles	1	2	3	4	5	6–10	Laps	Laps Led	Races Led	Miles	$
1994	Ricky Rudd	31	1	1	0	0	3	2	9	9,728	192	10	12,046	1,079,441
1995	Ricky Rudd	31	2	1	0	1	4	4	6	8,813	368	11	10,834	1,337,703
1996	Ricky Rudd	31	0	1	2	1	1	0	11	9,281	151	12	11,400	1,503,025
Lifetime		93	3	3	2	2	8	6	26	27,822	711	33	34,280	$3,920,169

James Rudolph

Year	Driver	Starts	Poles	1	2	3	4	5	6–10	Laps	Laps Led	Races Led	Miles	$
1987	Charlie Rudolph	4	0	0	0	0	0	0	0	924	0	0	1,583	9,995
Lifetime		4	0	0	0	0	0	0	0	924	0	0	1,583	$9,995

Carl Rupert

Year	Driver	Starts	Poles	1	2	3	4	5	6–10	Laps	Laps Led	Races Led	Miles	$
1955	Tiny Lund	1	0	0	0	0	0	0	0	65	0	0	98	60
1959	Tom Pistone	21	0	2	2	4	2	2	5	3,710	181	7	2,918	11,290
"	Curtis Turner	2	0	0	0	0	0	0	0	187	19	1	111	195
"	**Total**	23	0	2	2	4	2	2	5	3,897	200	8	3,029	11,485
1960	Fred Lorenzen	1	0	0	0	0	0	0	0	188	0	0	259	250
"	Tom Pistone	2	0	0	0	0	0	0	1	268	0	0	134	180
"	**Total**	3	0	0	0	0	0	0	1	456	0	0	393	430
Lifetime		27	0	2	2	4	2	2	6	4,418	200	8	3,519	$11,975

James Rush

Year	Driver	Starts	Poles	1	2	3	4	5	6–10	Laps	Laps Led	Races Led	Miles	$
1971	Dave Marcis	1	0	0	0	0	0	1	0	244	0	0	61	325
"	Junior Spencer	1	0	0	0	0	0	0	0	112	0	0	51	310
"	Bob Williams	1	0	0	0	0	0	0	0	297	0	0	186	445
"	**Total**	3	0	0	0	0	0	1	0	653	0	0	298	1,080
Lifetime		3	0	0	0	0	0	1	0	653	0	0	298	$1,080

Jim Rush

Year	Driver	Starts	Poles	1	2	3	4	5	6–10	Laps	Laps Led	Races Led	Miles	$
1955	Chuck Meekins	1	0	0	0	0	0	0	0	226	0	0	226	100
1956	Chuck Meekins	3	0	0	0	0	0	0	2	412	0	0	431	465
"	Lou Sherman	1	0	0	0	1	0	0	0	199	0	0	100	500
"	**Total**	4	0	0	0	1	0	0	2	611	0	0	530	965
1957	Ben Eyerly	1	0	0	0	0	0	0	0	41	0	0	21	50
"	Danny Letner	3	0	0	0	0	0	0	1	388	0	0	227	335

Year	Driver	Starts	Poles	Finish 1	2	3	4	5	6–10	Laps	Laps Led	Races Led	Miles	$

James Rush *continued*

"	Chuck Meekins	4	0	0	0	1	1	0	0	323	0	0	264	855
"	**Total**	6	0	0	0	1	1	0	1	752	0	0	511	1,240
1959	Bob Ross	1	0	0	0	0	1	0	0	100	0	0	100	335
Lifetime		12	0	0	0	2	2	0	3	1,689	0	0	1,367	$2,640

Jack Russell

1962	Jim Cushman	4	0	0	0	0	0	0	1	782	0	0	883	850
1963	Jim Cushman	2	0	0	0	0	0	0	0	211	0	0	528	625
Lifetime		6	0	0	0	0	0	0	1	993	0	0	1,411	$1,475

Jim Russell

| 1957 | Jim Russell | 1 | 0 | 0 | 0 | 0 | 0 | 0 | 0 | | | 0 | 0 | 0 |
| **Lifetime** | | 1 | 0 | 0 | 0 | 0 | 0 | 0 | 0 | | | 0 | 0 | $0 |

S. G. Russell

| 1956 | David Ezell | 1 | 0 | 0 | 0 | 0 | 0 | 0 | 0 | | | 0 | 0 | 50 |
| **Lifetime** | | 1 | 0 | 0 | 0 | 0 | 0 | 0 | 0 | | | 0 | 0 | $50 |

Troy Ruttman

| 1964 | Joe Ruttman | 1 | 0 | 0 | 0 | 0 | 0 | 0 | 0 | 46 | 0 | 0 | 124 | 500 |
| **Lifetime** | | 1 | 0 | 0 | 0 | 0 | 0 | 0 | 0 | 46 | 0 | 0 | 124 | $500 |

Felix Sabates

1989	Kyle Petty	18	0	0	0	0	1	0	4	4,815	16	1	6,757	111,022
1990	Kyle Petty	29	2	1	0	0	1	0	12	8,795	852	12	10,496	746,326
1991	Bobby Hillin Jr.	8	0	0	0	0	0	0	0	1,321	0	0	2,727	103,005
"	Tommy Kendall	1	0	0	0	0	0	0	0	74	12	1	186	12,450
"	Kyle Petty	18	2	1	1	0	0	0	2	6,631	553	7	6,556	413,727
"	Kenny Wallace	2	0	0	0	0	0	0	0	876	1	1	1,075	28,900
"	**Total**	29	2	1	1	0	0	0	2	8,902	566	9	10,545	558,082
1992	Kyle Petty	29	3	2	0	4	3	0	8	9,059	970	8	10,940	1,107,063
1993	Kyle Petty	30	1	1	1	2	2	3	6	9,259	526	13	11,186	914,662
"	Kenny Wallace	30	0	0	0	0	0	0	3	8,806	1	1	10,551	330,325
"	**Total**	30	1	1	1	2	2	3	9	18,065	527	14	21,737	1,244,987
1994	Bobby Hamilton*	30	0	0	0	0	0	0	1	8,337	24	4	10,220	514,520
"	Kyle Petty	31	0	0	0	0	1	1	5	9,085	7	2	11,104	818,832
"	**Total**	31	0	0	0	0	1	1	6	17,422	31	6	21,324	1,333,352
1995	Kyle Petty	30	0	1	0	0	0	0	4	8,127	311	4	10,077	698,875
1996	Robby Gordon	2	0	0	0	0	0	0	0	138	0	0	138	18,565
"	Kyle Petty	28	0	0	0	0	0	0	2	8,081	72	5	9,682	689,041
"	Greg Sacks	2	0	0	0	0	0	0	0	657	0	0	993	21,190
"	Jim Sauter	2	0	0	0	0	0	0	0	633	0	0	631	51,172
"	**Total**	31	0	0	0	0	0	0	2	9,509	72	5	11,443	779,968
Lifetime		236	8	6	2	6	8	4	47	84,694	3,345	59	103,319	$6,579,675

*Co-owned with Dick Brooks from August 13, 1994–December 31, 1994.

Greg Sacks

1983	Greg Sacks	5	0	0	0	0	0	0	0	638	0	0	1,202	8,060
1984	Greg Sacks	29	0	0	0	0	0	0	1	6,348	0	0	7,781	75,184
1985	Cecil Gordon	1	0	0	0	0	0	0	0	7	0	0	4	2,640
"	Greg Sacks	3	0	0	0	0	0	0	2	1,006	2	1	1,482	60,410
"	**Total**	4	0	0	0	0	0	0	2	1,013	2	1	1,486	63,050
1991	Greg Sacks	1	0	0	0	0	0	0	0	20	0	0	50	27,450
Lifetime		39	0	0	0	0	0	0	3	8,019	2	1	10,519	$173,744

Sadler Brothers (Earl and Check Sadler, co-owners)

1984	Sterling Marlin	11	0	0	0	0	0	0	2	2,423	0	0	3,420	35,320
1985	Mike Alexander	4	0	0	0	0	0	0	0	1,081	0	0	1,197	9,290
"	Sterling Marlin	7	0	0	0	0	0	0	0	1,102	1	1	2,019	29,805
"	**Total**	11	0	0	0	0	0	0	0	2,183	1	1	3,217	39,095
1986	Davey Allison	4	0	0	0	0	0	0	0	1,247	0	0	867	8,070
1988	Trevor Boys	1	0	0	0	0	0	0	0	199	0	0	498	15,085

Year	Driver	Starts	Poles	Finish 1	2	3	4	5	6–10	Laps	Laps Led	Races Led	Miles	$

Sadler Brothers *continued*

Year	Driver	Starts	Poles	1	2	3	4	5	6–10	Laps	Laps Led	Races Led	Miles	$
1991	Eddie Bierschwale	2	0	0	0	0	0	0	0	491	0	0	953	9,740
"	Rick Jeffrey	0												2,700
"	Kerry Teague	1	0	0	0	0	0	0	0	124	0	0	186	9,125
"	**Total**	3	0	0	0	0	0	0	0	615	0	0	1,139	21,565
1992	Bob Schacht	4	0	0	0	0	0	0	0	566	2	1	1,018	36,160
1993	Jeremy Mayfield	1	0	0	0	0	0	0	0	324	0	0	486	4,830
1994	Jeff Green	2	0	0	0	0	0	0	0	396	0	0	253	11,455
"	Jeremy Mayfield	4	0	0	0	0	0	0	0	1,083	0	0	1,315	48,255
"	**Total**	6	0	0	0	0	0	0	0	1,479	0	0	1,568	59,710
1995	Doug Heveron	0												2,550
1996	Chuck Bown	3	0	0	0	0	0	0	0	338	0	0	723	38,867
"	Gary Bradberry	9	0	0	0	0	0	0	0	2,212	0	0	2,827	155,785
"	**Total**	12	0	0	0	0	0	0	0	2,550	0	0	3,550	194,652
Lifetime		53	0	0	0	0	0	0	2	11,586	3	2	15,762	$417,037

Darryl Sage

Year	Driver	Starts	Poles	1	2	3	4	5	6–10	Laps	Laps Led	Races Led	Miles	$
1982	Darryl Sage	5	0	0	0	0	0	0	0	1,572	0	0	1,148	4,970
1983	Darryl Sage	3	0	0	0	0	0	0	0	638	0	0	675	3,610
Lifetime		8	0	0	0	0	0	0	0	2,210	0	0	1,823	$8,580

Hank Salat

Year	Driver	Starts	Poles	1	2	3	4	5	6–10	Laps	Laps Led	Races Led	Miles	$
1951	Red Duvall	1	0	0	0	1	0	0	0		0	0		500
1952	Red Duvall	4	0	0	0	0	0	0	2	538	0	0	372	275
"	Don Oldenberg	1	0	0	0	0	0	0	0		0	0		25
"	**Total**	4	0	0	0	0	0	0	2	538	0	0	372	300
1955	Jim Ord	2	0	0	0	0	0	0	1	217	0	0	192	225
Lifetime		7	0	0	0	1	0	0	3	755	0	0	564	$1,025

Patsy Salmon

Year	Driver	Starts	Poles	1	2	3	4	5	6–10	Laps	Laps Led	Races Led	Miles	$
1986	Charlie Baker	1	0	0	0	0	0	0	0	457	0	0	465	2,500
1987	Charlie Baker	1	0	0	0	0	0	0	0	463	0	0	471	6,565
"	Mike Potter	1	0	0	0	0	0	0	0	291	0	0	443	2,945
"	**Total**	2	0	0	0	0	0	0	0	754	0	0	914	9,510
1988	Charlie Baker	1	0	0	0	0	0	0	0	136	0	0	138	3,190
1989	Charlie Baker	3	0	0	0	0	0	0	0	255	0	0	611	16,370
1990	Charlie Baker	2	0	0	0	0	0	0	0	84	0	0	85	5,325
Lifetime		9	0	0	0	0	0	0	0	1,686	0	0	2,214	$36,895

Tony Sampo

Year	Driver	Starts	Poles	1	2	3	4	5	6–10	Laps	Laps Led	Races Led	Miles	$
1951	George Seeger	2	0	0	0	0	0	0	0	373	0	0	465	175
"	Danny Weinberg	3	0	1	0	0	0	1	0	200	1	1	100	1,325
"	**Total**	5	0	1	0	0	0	1	0	573	1	1	565	1,500
Lifetime		5	0	1	0	0	0	1	0	573	1	1	565	$1,500

Roscoe Sanders

Year	Driver	Starts	Poles	1	2	3	4	5	6–10	Laps	Laps Led	Races Led	Miles	$
1963	Bob James	6	0	0	0	0	0	0	0	825	0	0	1,192	1,625
1964	Bunkie Blackburn	2	0	0	0	0	0	0	0	1	0	0	3	850
"	Roy Gemberling	1	0	0	0	0	0	0	0	34	0	0	85	100
"	LeeRoy Yarbrough	1	0	0	0	0	0	0	0	482	0	0	241	450
"	**Total**	4	0	0	0	0	0	0	0	517	0	0	329	1,400
Lifetime		10	0	0	0	0	0	0	0	1,342	0	0	1,521	$3,025

Irv Sanderson

Year	Driver	Starts	Poles	1	2	3	4	5	6–10	Laps	Laps Led	Races Led	Miles	$
1981	Dean Combs	2	0	0	0	0	0	0	0	183	0	0	149	1,155
1982	Dean Combs	5	0	0	0	0	0	0	0	639	0	0	1,100	7,940
1983	Dean Combs	5	0	0	0	0	0	0	1	1,296	0	0	1,995	12,275
1984	Dean Combs	12	0	0	0	0	0	0	0	2,399	0	0	3,152	22,385
Lifetime		24	0	0	0	0	0	0	1	4,517	0	0	6,396	$43,755

Irwin Sandlin

Year	Driver	Starts	Poles	1	2	3	4	5	6–10	Laps	Laps Led	Races Led	Miles	$
1965	Sam Stanley	1	0	0	0	0	0	0	1	172	0	0	464	1,050
Lifetime		1	0	0	0	0	0	0	1	172	0	0	464	$1,050

Year	Driver	Starts	Poles	Finish						Laps	Laps Led	Races Led	Miles	$
				1	2	3	4	5	6–10					

Bobby Sands

Year	Driver	Starts	Poles	1	2	3	4	5	6–10	Laps	Laps Led	Races Led	Miles	$
1980	Bobby Sands	1	0	0	0	0	0	0	0	2	0	0	1	450
Lifetime		1	0	0	0	0	0	0	0	2	0	0	1	$450

Marshall Sargent

Year	Driver	Starts	Poles	1	2	3	4	5	6–10	Laps	Laps Led	Races Led	Miles	$
1961	Marshall Sargent	3	0	0	0	0	0	0	0	369	0	0	690	450
Lifetime		3	0	0	0	0	0	0	0	369	0	0	690	$450

James Satcher

Year	Driver	Starts	Poles	1	2	3	4	5	6–10	Laps	Laps Led	Races Led	Miles	$
1956	Buck Baker	3	0	0	0	0	1	1	1	526	0	0	276	875
"	Joe Eubanks	26	2	0	0	3	0	4	6	3,398	107	2	2,529	5,584
"	**Total**	29	2	0	0	3	1	5	7	3,924	107	2	2,805	6,459
1957	Joe Eubanks	1	0	0	0	0	0	0	1	180	0	0	90	100
"	Cotton Owens	1	0	0	0	0	0	0	1	161	0	0	81	100
"	**Total**	2	0	0	0	0	0	0	2	341	0	0	171	200
Lifetime		31	2	0	0	3	1	5	9	4,265	107	2	2,976	$6,659

Curtis Satterfield

Year	Driver	Starts	Poles	1	2	3	4	5	6–10	Laps	Laps Led	Races Led	Miles	$
1966	Joel Davis	2	0	0	0	0	0	0	0	5	0	0	12	975
"	Johnny Rutherford	2	0	0	0	0	0	0	0	150	0	0	375	1,210
"	Bub Strickler	1	0	0	0	0	0	0	0	148	0	0	148	585
"	Eldon Yarbrough	1	0	0	0	0	0	0	0	74	0	0	111	500
"	**Total**	6	0	0	0	0	0	0	0	377	0	0	646	3,270
Lifetime		6	0	0	0	0	0	0	0	377	0	0	646	$3,270

Don Satterfield

Year	Driver	Starts	Poles	1	2	3	4	5	6–10	Laps	Laps Led	Races Led	Miles	$
1978	Johnny Halford	1	0	0	0	0	0	0	0	84	0	0	85	610
1979	Joe Booher	0												1,250
"	Bruce Jacobi	0												1,050
"	Slick Johnson	2	0	0	0	0	0	0	0	248	0	0	170	1,060
"	Dick May	2	0	0	0	0	0	0	0	14	0	0	13	865
"	**Total**	4	0	0	0	0	0	0	0	262	0	0	183	4,225
1981	Bruce Jacobi	1	0	0	0	0	0	0	0	117	0	0	293	955
"	Don Satterfield	1	0	0	0	0	0	0	0	1	0	0	1	450
"	Joel Stowe	1	0	0	0	0	0	0	0	14	0	0	7	540
"	**Total**	3	0	0	0	0	0	0	0	132	0	0	301	1,945
1983	Joe Millikan	0												400
Lifetime		8	0	0	0	0	0	0	0	478	0	0	569	$7,180

Leon Satterfield

Year	Driver	Starts	Poles	1	2	3	4	5	6–10	Laps	Laps Led	Races Led	Miles	$
1983	Joe Booher	1	0	0	0	0	0	0	0	2	0	0	3	935
"	Slick Johnson	9	0	0	0	0	0	0	0	1,933	0	0	2,097	12,270
"	Don Satterfield	3	0	0	0	0	0	0	0	645	0	0	359	2,555
"	**Total**	13	0	0	0	0	0	0	0	2,580	0	0	2,458	15,760
1984	Slick Johnson	1	0	0	0	0	0	0	0	70	0	0	96	1,495
Lifetime		14	0	0	0	0	0	0	0	2,650	0	0	2,554	$17,255

Sandy Satullo

Year	Driver	Starts	Poles	1	2	3	4	5	6–10	Laps	Laps Led	Races Led	Miles	$
1979	Sandy Satullo	2	0	0	0	0	0	0	0	210	0	0	429	2,360
1981	John Anderson	1	0	0	0	0	0	0	0	41	0	0	62	965
"	Sandy Satullo	1	0	0	0	0	0	0	0	68	0	0	181	1,500
"	**Total**	2	0	0	0	0	0	0	0	109	0	0	242	2,465
Lifetime		4	0	0	0	0	0	0	0	319	0	0	671	$4,825

Joe Savatier

Year	Driver	Starts	Poles	1	2	3	4	5	6–10	Laps	Laps Led	Races Led	Miles	$
1954	Tony Nelson	2	0	0	0	0	0	0	0	520	0	0	378	125
Lifetime		2	0	0	0	0	0	0	0	520	0	0	378	$125

Ed Saverance

Year	Driver	Starts	Poles	1	2	3	4	5	6–10	Laps	Laps Led	Races Led	Miles	$
1951	Fireball Roberts	2	0	0	1	0	0	1	0	587	0	0	584	1,510
1952	Fireball Roberts	6	0	0	0	0	0	0	1	390	15	1	383	175
1953	Fireball Roberts	1	0	0	0	0	0	0	0	154	0	0	154	25
Lifetime		9	0	0	1	0	0	1	1	1,131	15	1	1,120	$1,710

Year	Driver	Starts	Poles	Finish 1	2	3	4	5	6–10	Laps	Laps Led	Races Led	Miles	$

John Savoca

Year	Driver	Starts	Poles	1	2	3	4	5	6–10	Laps	Laps Led	Races Led	Miles	$
1970	Harry Shipe	2	0	0	0	0	0	0	0	45	0	0	65	450
Lifetime		2	0	0	0	0	0	0	0	45	0	0	65	$450

Lucky Sawyer

Year	Driver	Starts	Poles	1	2	3	4	5	6–10	Laps	Laps Led	Races Led	Miles	$
1953	Lucky Sawyer	4	0	0	0	0	0	0	0	27	0	0	96	75
Lifetime		4	0	0	0	0	0	0	0	27	0	0	96	$75

Bob Schacht

Year	Driver	Starts	Poles	1	2	3	4	5	6–10	Laps	Laps Led	Races Led	Miles	$
1981	Bob Schacht	2	0	0	0	0	0	0	0	241	0	0	263	1,290
1982	Bob Schacht	3	0	0	0	0	0	0	0	576	0	0	318	2,880
1989	Bob Schacht	1	0	0	0	0	0	0	0	463	0	0	471	2,700
1993	Bob Schacht	1	0	0	0	0	0	0	0	20	0	0	20	13,240
1994	Bob Schacht	1	0	0	0	0	0	0	0	11	0	0	28	7,560
Lifetime		8	0	0	0	0	0	0	0	1,311	0	0	1,099	$27,670

Norman Schihl

Year	Driver	Starts	Poles	1	2	3	4	5	6–10	Laps	Laps Led	Races Led	Miles	$
1956	Norman Schihl	1	0	0	0	0	0	0	0	349	0	0	175	150
Lifetime		1	0	0	0	0	0	0	0	349	0	0	175	$150

Robin Schildnecht

Year	Driver	Starts	Poles	1	2	3	4	5	6–10	Laps	Laps Led	Races Led	Miles	$
1977	Robin Schildnecht	2	0	0	0	0	0	0	0	581	0	0	344	2,075
Lifetime		2	0	0	0	0	0	0	0	581	0	0	344	$2,075

Harry Schilling

Year	Driver	Starts	Poles	1	2	3	4	5	6–10	Laps	Laps Led	Races Led	Miles	$
1974	Harry Schilling	1	0	0	0	0	0	0	0	65	0	0	170	1,005
Lifetime		1	0	0	0	0	0	0	0	65	0	0	170	$1,005

Allan Schlauer

Year	Driver	Starts	Poles	1	2	3	4	5	6–10	Laps	Laps Led	Races Led	Miles	$
1969	Larry Baumel	6	0	0	0	0	0	0	0	964	0	0	682	2,760
1970	Larry Baumel	23	1	0	0	0	0	0	1	2,731	0	0	3,697	16,620
1971	Larry Baumel	16	0	0	0	0	0	0	1	2,245	0	0	2,998	10,910
Lifetime		45	1	0	0	0	0	0	2	5,940	0	0	7,376	$30,290

Al Schmidhamer

Year	Driver	Starts	Poles	1	2	3	4	5	6–10	Laps	Laps Led	Races Led	Miles	$
1957	Art Watts	4	4	1	0	1	0	0	1	502	100	1	283	1,620
Lifetime		4	4	1	0	1	0	0	1	502	100	1	283	$1,620

Lee Schmidt

Year	Driver	Starts	Poles	1	2	3	4	5	6–10	Laps	Laps Led	Races Led	Miles	$
1949	Lee Schmidt	1	0	0	0	0	0	0	0	171	0	0	171	50
1950	Lee Schmidt	1	0	0	0	0	0	0	0	40	0	0	167	25
Lifetime		2	0	0	0	0	0	0	0	211	0	0	338	$75

Bill Schmitt

Year	Driver	Starts	Poles	1	2	3	4	5	6–10	Laps	Laps Led	Races Led	Miles	$
1975	Bill Schmitt	3	0	0	0	0	0	0	1	293	0	0	764	3,970
1976	Bill Schmitt	2	0	0	0	0	0	0	1	318	0	0	816	3,360
1977	Bill Schmitt	3	0	0	0	0	0	0	0	144	0	0	375	3,285
1978	Bill Schmitt	3	0	0	0	0	0	0	1	304	0	0	773	8,430
1979	Bill Schmitt	3	0	0	0	0	1	0	0	325	0	0	828	11,695
1980	Bill Schmitt	4	0	0	0	0	0	1	0	579	0	0	1,473	21,610
1981	Bill Schmitt	3	0	0	0	0	0	0	0	257	1	1	673	6,610
1982	Bill Schmitt	2	0	0	0	0	0	0	0	186	0	0	487	2,210
1983	Bill Schmitt	2	0	0	0	0	0	0	1	107	0	0	280	4,520
1984	Bill Schmitt	2	0	0	0	0	0	0	0	125	0	0	328	5,270
1985	Bill Schmitt	2	0	0	0	0	0	0	0	157	0	0	411	5,640
1986	Bill Schmitt	2	0	0	0	0	0	0	0	207	0	0	542	7,840
1987	Bill Schmitt	2	0	0	0	0	0	0	0	99	0	0	259	2,500
1988	Bill Schmitt	2	0	0	0	0	0	0	0	252	0	0	406	6,245
1989	Bill Schmitt	2	0	0	0	0	0	0	0	380	0	0	491	7,920
1990	Bill Schmitt	2	0	0	0	0	0	0	0	384	0	0	496	11,525
1991	Bill Schmitt	2	0	0	0	0	0	0	0	210	0	0	322	10,605
1992	Bill Schmitt	2	0	0	0	0	0	0	0	282	0	0	393	13,095

Year	Driver	Starts	Poles	Finish						Laps	Laps Led	Races Led	Miles	$
				1	2	3	4	5	6–10					

Bill Schmitt *continued*

1993	Bill Schmitt	1	0	0	0	0	0	0	0	71	0	0	179	6,815
Lifetime		44	0	0	0	0	1	1	4	4,680	1	1	10,299	$143,145

Frankie Schneider

1957	Frankie Schneider	4	0	0	0	0	0	0	1	917	0	0	613	765
1958	Frankie Schneider	6	0	1	1	0	3	0	0	1,186	106	1	487	1,920
Lifetime		10	0	1	1	0	3	0	1	2,103	106	1	1,100	$2,685

Brittan Schnell

1996	Ed Berrier	0												1,500
"	Dick Trickle	1	0	0	0	0	0	0	0	9	0	0	23	36,552
"	**Total**	1	0	0	0	0	0	0	0	9	0	0	23	38,052
Lifetime		1	0	0	0	0	0	0	0	9	0	0	23	$38,052

Lloyd Schoenheit

1952	Jim Mayes	1	0	0	0	0	0	0	0	0	0	0	0	25
Lifetime		1	0	0	0	0	0	0	0	0	0	0	0	$25

Terry Schoonover

1984	Terry Schoonover	2	0	0	0	0	0	0	0	543	0	0	614	2,585
Lifetime		2	0	0	0	0	0	0	0	543	0	0	614	$2,585

Ken Schrader

1995	David Green	0												10,000
"	Jeff Purvis	1	0	0	0	0	0	0	0	320	0	0	487	7,370
"	**Total**	1	0	0	0	0	0	0	0	320	0	0	487	17,370
Lifetime		1	0	0	0	0	0	0	0	320	0	0	487	$17,370

Ken Schroeder

1949	Ken Schroeder	1	0	0	0	0	0	0	0	168	0	0	168	50
Lifetime		1	0	0	0	0	0	0	0	168	0	0	168	$50

Robert Schultz

1969	George Bauer	2	0	0	0	0	0	0	0	203	0	0	508	2,410
Lifetime		2	0	0	0	0	0	0	0	203	0	0	508	$2,410

Volney Schulze

1955	Volney Schulze	6	0	0	0	0	0	0	1	674	0	0	456	300
1957	Volney Schulze	3	0	0	0	0	0	0	1	530	0	0	380	340
1958	Volney Schulze	7	0	0	0	0	0	0	0	725	0	0	370	490
Lifetime		16	0	0	0	0	0	0	2	1,929	0	0	1,205	$1,130

Charlie Schwam

1955	Billy Carden	1	0	0	0	0	0	0	0	55	0	0	83	60
"	Curtis Turner	5	0	0	1	0	0	0	0	374	14	1	395	980
"	Joe Weatherly	5	0	0	0	0	1	0	3	965	140	1	830	2,515
"	**Total**	7	0	0	1	0	1	0	3	1,394	154	1	1,307	3,555
1956	Billy Carden	3	0	0	0	0	0	0	0	632	0	0	755	350
"	Curtis Turner	11	0	1	3	0	0	0	1	1,647	287	3	1,196	14,095
"	Joe Weatherly	13	1	0	0	1	2	1	4	1,784	0	0	1,534	3,310
"	**Total**	15	1	1	3	1	2	1	5	4,063	287	3	3,485	17,755
Lifetime		22	1	1	4	1	3	1	8	5,457	441	4	4,792	$21,310

Max Schwimer

1955	Jack Farris	1	0	0	0	0	0	0	0	30	0	0	123	25
Lifetime		1	0	0	0	0	0	0	0	30	0	0	123	$25

Year	Driver	Starts	Poles	Finish 1	2	3	4	5	6–10	Laps	Laps Led	Races Led	Miles	$

Andrew Scott

Year	Driver	Starts	Poles	1	2	3	4	5	6–10	Laps	Laps Led	Races Led	Miles	$
1987	Trevor Boys	1	0	0	0	0	0	0	0	198	0	0	495	2,965
Lifetime		1	0	0	0	0	0	0	0	198	0	0	495	$2,965

Lyle Scott

Year	Driver	Starts	Poles	1	2	3	4	5	6–10	Laps	Laps Led	Races Led	Miles	$
1956	Lyle Scott	1	0	0	0	0	0	0	0		0	0		60
Lifetime		1	0	0	0	0	0	0	0		0	0		$60

Wendell Scott

Year	Driver	Starts	Poles	1	2	3	4	5	6–10	Laps	Laps Led	Races Led	Miles	$
1961	Wendell Scott	23	0	0	0	0	0	0	5	4,364	0	0	2,217	3,240
1962	Earl Brooks	1	0	0	0	0	0	0	0	3	0	0	1	0
"	Wendell Scott	41	1	0	0	2	1	1	15	8,542	0	0	4,211	7,133
"	**Total**	41	1	0	0	2	1	1	15	8,545	0	0	4,212	7,133
1963	Earl Brooks	3	0	0	0	0	0	1	0	783	0	0	354	725
"	Wendell Scott	47	0	0	0	0	0	1	14	9,459	0	0	6,165	10,966
"	**Total**	47	0	0	0	0	0	2	14	10,242	0	0	6,519	11,691
1964	Earl Brooks	28	0	0	0	0	0	0	8	3,988	0	0	1,834	3,925
"	Wendell Scott	56	0	1	0	0	6	1	17	10,752	27	1	6,466	16,495
"	**Total**	56	0	1	0	0	6	1	25	14,740	27	1	8,300	20,420
1965	Wendell Scott	50	0	0	0	0	2	2	16	9,260	0	0	5,742	16,789
1966	Wendell Scott	43	0	0	0	1	1	1	14	9,530	0	0	6,597	22,062
1967	Wendell Scott	43	0	0	0	0	0	0	11	8,737	0	0	6,217	18,230
1968	Wendell Scott	45	0	0	0	0	0	0	10	9,428	0	0	6,611	18,573
1969	Wendell Scott	48	0	0	0	0	0	0	11	11,362	0	0	8,414	44,391
1970	Wendell Scott	28	0	0	0	0	0	0	9	6,167	0	0	4,815	21,043
1971	Wendell Scott	34	0	0	0	0	0	0	4	7,323	0	0	6,184	19,477
1972	Wendell Scott	5	0	0	0	0	0	0	0	1,480	0	0	1,502	3,885
1973	Wendell Scott	2	0	0	0	0	0	0	0	327	0	0	457	1,730
Lifetime		465	1	1	0	3	10	7	134	101,505	27	1	67,787	$208,634

Arley Scranton

Year	Driver	Starts	Poles	1	2	3	4	5	6–10	Laps	Laps Led	Races Led	Miles	$
1954	Jim Cook	1	0	0	0	0	0	0	1	226	0	0	113	100
"	Arley Scranton	1	0	0	0	0	0	0	0	413	0	0	207	25
"	**Total**	2	0	0	0	0	0	0	1	639	0	0	320	125
1956	Arley Scranton	1	0	0	0	0	0	0	0	9	0	0	23	20
1957	Arley Scranton	1	0	0	0	0	0	0	0	25	0	0	25	25
1958	Arley Scranton	2	0	0	0	0	0	0	0	17	0	0	17	100
1959	Arley Scranton	2	0	0	0	0	0	0	0	361	0	0	158	100
1961	Arley Scranton	1	0	0	0	0	0	0	0	3	0	0	8	0
1966	Arley Scranton	1	0	0	0	0	0	0	0	3	0	0	8	500
Lifetime		10	0	0	0	0	0	0	1	1,057	0	0	557	$870

Rick Scribner

Year	Driver	Starts	Poles	1	2	3	4	5	6–10	Laps	Laps Led	Races Led	Miles	$
1992	Rick Scribner	2	0	0	0	0	0	0	0	75	0	0	178	9,025
Lifetime		2	0	0	0	0	0	0	0	75	0	0	178	$9,025

John Sears

Year	Driver	Starts	Poles	1	2	3	4	5	6–10	Laps	Laps Led	Races Led	Miles	$
1970	Neil Castles	1	0	0	0	0	0	0	0	345	0	0	216	850
"	John Sears	33	1	0	0	0	3	1	3	6,872	10	1	6,420	26,755
"	**Total**	34	1	0	0	0	3	1	3	7,217	10	1	6,635	27,605
1971	John Sears	37	0	0	0	0	0	0	3	7,512	0	0	6,815	26,735
Lifetime		71	1	0	0	0	3	1	6	14,729	10	1	13,450	$54,340

Frank Secrist

Year	Driver	Starts	Poles	1	2	3	4	5	6–10	Laps	Laps Led	Races Led	Miles	$
1960	Frank Secrist	1	0	0	0	0	0	0	0	60	0	0	60	75
Lifetime		1	0	0	0	0	0	0	0	60	0	0	60	$75

George Seeger

Year	Driver	Starts	Poles	1	2	3	4	5	6–10	Laps	Laps Led	Races Led	Miles	$
1951	George Seeger	3	0	0	0	0	0	0	1	133	0	0	133	135
Lifetime		3	0	0	0	0	0	0	1	133	0	0	133	$135

Year	Driver	Starts	Poles	Finish 1	2	3	4	5	6–10	Laps	Laps Led	Races Led	Miles	$

Bill Seifert

Year	Driver	Starts	Poles	1	2	3	4	5	6–10	Laps	Laps Led	Races Led	Miles	$
1966	Blaine Kauffman	1	0	0	0	0	0	0	0	33	0	0	83	0
"	Bill Latham	2	0	0	0	0	0	0	0	160	0	0	54	200
"	Clyde Lynn	1	0	0	0	0	0	0	0	417	0	0	417	690
"	Tex McCullough	1	0	0	0	0	0	0	0	5	0	0	5	535
"	J. T. Putney	1	0	0	0	0	0	0	0	6	0	0	3	0
"	Bill Seifert	11	0	0	0	0	0	0	3	2,680	0	0	1,362	3,240
"	Jim Tatum	4	0	0	0	0	0	0	0	351	0	0	174	445
"	Cale Yarborough	1	0	0	0	0	0	0	0	121	0	0	48	100
"	**Total**	22	0	0	0	0	0	0	3	3,773	0	0	2,145	5,210
1967	Don Biederman	1	0	0	0	0	0	0	0	247	0	0	340	900
"	Bill Seifert	41	0	0	0	0	0	0	12	8,171	0	0	5,133	11,910
"	Buster Sexton	1	0	0	0	0	0	0	0	15	0	0	8	100
"	**Total**	43	0	0	0	0	0	0	12	8,433	0	0	5,480	12,910
1968	Earl Brooks	1	0	0	0	0	0	0	0	427	0	0	427	890
"	Niles Gage	1	0	0	0	0	0	0	0	274	0	0	91	155
"	Cecil Gordon	4	0	0	0	0	0	0	0	427	0	0	377	1,625
"	Elmo Langley	3	0	0	0	0	0	0	1	595	0	0	661	1,830
"	Bill Seifert	39	0	0	0	0	0	1	7	7,214	0	0	5,148	16,378
"	**Total**	43	0	0	0	0	0	1	8	8,937	0	0	6,705	20,878
1969	Cecil Gordon	49	0	0	0	0	0	1	7	10,159	0	0	8,679	27,237
"	Lee Gordon	1	0	0	0	0	0	0	0	160	0	0	80	100
"	Bill Seifert	50	0	0	0	0	1	0	14	9,728	0	0	7,475	44,361
"	**Total**	51	0	0	0	0	1	1	21	**20,047**	0	0	**16,234**	71,698
1970	Elmo Langley	1	0	0	0	0	0	0	1	447	0	0	238	700
"	Bill Seifert	38	0	0	0	0	0	1	3	5,188	0	0	5,196	25,217
"	Raymond Williams	20	0	0	0	0	0	0	0	3,627	0	0	3,830	12,075
"	**Total**	43	0	0	0	0	0	1	4	9,262	0	0	9,264	37,992
1971	Bill Seifert	35	0	0	0	0	0	0	4	6,366	0	0	6,675	31,030
"	Dub Simpson	1	0	0	0	0	0	0	0	11	0	0	29	1,100
"	Raymond Williams	7	0	0	0	0	0	0	0	458	0	0	601	5,035
"	LeeRoy Yarbrough	1	0	0	0	0	0	0	0	246	0	0	374	1,080
"	**Total**	37	0	0	0	0	0	0	4	7,081	0	0	7,679	38,245
1972	Dick Brooks	2	0	0	0	0	0	0	0	214	2	1	303	2,546
"	Vic Parsons	1	0	0	0	0	0	0	1	380	0	0	238	800
"	Bill Seifert	4	0	0	0	0	0	0	1	468	0	0	644	5,405
"	Ramo Stott	1	0	0	0	0	0	0	0	238	0	0	476	1,525
"	Raymond Williams	1	0	0	0	0	0	0	0	422	0	0	429	1,300
"	LeeRoy Yarbrough	15	0	0	0	1	2	1	4	3,695	5	2	4,161	34,580
"	**Total**	24	0	0	0	1	2	1	6	5,417	7	3	6,251	46,156
1973	Vic Parsons	16	0	0	0	0	0	0	6	3,205	0	0	3,539	16,795
Lifetime		279	0	0	0	1	3	4	64	66,155	7	3	57,298	$249,884

Al Self

Year	Driver	Starts	Poles	1	2	3	4	5	6–10	Laps	Laps Led	Races Led	Miles	$
1963	Al Self	1	0	0	0	0	0	0	0	1	0	0	3	200
1964	Al Self	1	0	0	0	0	0	0	0	9	0	0	24	500
1965	Al Self	1	0	0	0	0	0	0	0	49	0	0	132	500
Lifetime		3	0	0	0	0	0	0	0	59	0	0	159	$1,200

David Lee Sellers

Year	Driver	Starts	Poles	1	2	3	4	5	6–10	Laps	Laps Led	Races Led	Miles	$
1976	Jimmy Lee Capps	4	0	0	0	0	0	0	1	505	0	0	1,229	6,950
1977	Jimmy Lee Capps	3	0	0	0	0	0	0	0	815	0	0	1,097	4,800
1978	Jimmy Lee Capps	3	0	0	0	0	0	0	0	586	0	0	701	3,880
Lifetime		10	0	0	0	0	0	0	1	1,906	0	0	3,027	$15,630

Mack Sellers

Year	Driver	Starts	Poles	1	2	3	4	5	6–10	Laps	Laps Led	Races Led	Miles	$
1969	George Davis	1	0	0	0	0	0	0	0	24	0	0	24	400
"	Roy Mayne	4	0	0	0	0	0	0	0	685	0	0	653	2,660
"	Dick Poling	8	0	0	0	0	0	0	0	895	0	0	942	3,575
"	Mark Sellers	3	0	0	0	0	0	0	0	164	0	0	82	450
"	Buster Sexton	1	0	0	0	0	0	0	0	9	0	0	5	0
"	**Total**	17	0	0	0	0	0	0	0	1,777	0	0	1,706	7,085
1970	Bobby Boyles	1	0	0	0	0	0	0	0	3	0	0	1	200
"	John Jennings	6	0	0	0	0	0	0	0	610	0	0	281	1,515
"	Roy Tyner	1	0	0	0	0	0	0	1	188	0	0	94	260
"	**Total**	8	0	0	0	0	0	0	1	801	0	0	376	1,975
Lifetime		25	0	0	0	0	0	0	1	2,578	0	0	2,082	$9,060

Year	Driver	Starts	Poles	Finish 1	2	3	4	5	6–10	Laps	Laps Led	Races Led	Miles	$

Frank Sessoms

1969	Frank Sessoms	1	0	0	0	0	0	0	0	128	0	0	340	1,325
1971	Frank Sessoms	2	0	0	0	0	0	0	2	852	0	0	496	1,180
Lifetime		3	0	0	0	0	0	0	2	980	0	0	837	$2,505

Red Sharp

1966	Friday Hassler	9	0	0	0	0	0	1	2	2,431	0	0	1,797	4,290
1967	Friday Hassler	21	0	0	0	0	1	2	6	4,309	12	1	3,091	10,270
1968	Friday Hassler	20	0	0	0	0	2	1	5	5,012	0	0	4,245	12,000
1969	Friday Hassler	1	0	0	0	0	0	0	1	462	0	0	231	725
Lifetime		51	0	0	0	0	3	4	14	12,214	12	1	9,363	$27,285

Ernie Shaw

1969	Ernie Shaw	1	0	0	0	0	0	0	0	149	0	0	396	1,500
1971	Ernie Shaw	1	0	0	0	0	0	0	0	109	0	0	55	200
Lifetime		2	0	0	0	0	0	0	0	258	0	0	451	$1,700

Graham Shaw

1964	Tiny Lund	4	0	0	0	0	0	0	1	339	14	1	668	1,650
"	Graham Shaw	2	0	0	0	0	0	0	0	127	0	0	379	1,000
"	Total	6	0	0	0	0	0	0	1	466	14	1	1,047	2,650
Lifetime		6	0	0	0	0	0	0	1	466	14	1	1,047	$2,650

Kenny Shaw

| 1995 | Ken Pedersen | 1 | 0 | 0 | 0 | 0 | 0 | 0 | 0 | 25 | 0 | 0 | 63 | 9,760 |
| Lifetime | | 1 | 0 | 0 | 0 | 0 | 0 | 0 | 0 | 25 | 0 | 0 | 63 | $9,760 |

Reid Shaw

1965	Boyd Adams	1	0	0	0	0	0	0	0	15	0	0	8	100
"	Buren Skeen	8	0	0	0	0	0	1	2	1,319	0	0	676	2,875
"	Total	9	0	0	0	0	0	1	2	1,334	0	0	684	2,975
1966	Johnny Allen	3	0	0	0	0	0	0	0	598	0	0	633	1,585
"	Darel Dieringer	4	0	1	0	0	1	0	0	540	178	1	262	1,900
"	Bryant Wallace	1	0	0	0	0	0	0	0	39	0	0	20	100
"	Cale Yarborough	1	0	0	0	0	0	0	1	195	0	0	49	265
"	Total	9	0	1	0	0	1	0	1	1,372	178	1	963	3,850
1971	Wayne Andrews	5	0	0	0	0	0	1	2	1,372	0	0	600	1,780
Lifetime		23	0	1	0	0	1	2	5	4,078	178	1	2,248	$8,605

Fred Sheibert

| 1956 | Bill Widenhouse | 1 | 0 | 0 | 0 | 0 | 0 | 0 | 0 | | 0 | 0 | | 0 |
| Lifetime | | 1 | 0 | 0 | 0 | 0 | 0 | 0 | 0 | | 0 | 0 | | $0 |

Bill Sheldon

| 1951 | Ray Chase | 6 | 0 | 0 | 0 | 0 | 0 | 0 | 0 | 354 | 0 | 0 | 399 | 100 |
| Lifetime | | 6 | 0 | 0 | 0 | 0 | 0 | 0 | 0 | 354 | 0 | 0 | 399 | $100 |

R. G. Shelton

1951	Bob Flock	1	0	0	0	0	0	0	1		0	0		50
"	Billy Myers	5	0	0	0	1	0	0	0	113	23	1	113	625
"	Total	5	0	0	0	1	0	0	1	113	23	1	113	675
1952	Perk Brown	18	1	0	0	2	0	0	3	2,160	0	0	1,370	1,610
"	Jimmie Lewallen	6	0	0	0	0	0	0	2	980	0	0	755	430
"	Leon Sales	2	0	0	0	0	0	0	0	0	0	0	0	25
"	Total	24	1	0	0	2	0	0	5	3,140	0	0	2,124	2,065
1953	Perk Brown	2	0	0	0	0	0	0	0	14	0	0	57	25
"	Jimmie Lewallen	10	0	0	0	1	0	2	2	370	0	0	225	1,125
"	Total	12	0	0	0	1	0	2	2	384	0	0	282	1,150
1954	Perk Brown	2	0	0	0	0	0	0	0	174	0	0	126	50
Lifetime		43	1	0	0	4	0	2	8	3,811	23	1	2,645	$3,940

Ralph Shelton

| 1964 | Eddie Gray | 1 | 0 | 0 | 0 | 0 | 0 | 0 | 0 | 174 | 0 | 0 | 470 | 650 |

Year	Driver	Starts	Poles	Finish 1	2	3	4	5	6–10	Laps	Laps Led	Races Led	Miles	$

Ralph Shelton *continued*

Year	Driver	Starts	Poles	1	2	3	4	5	6–10	Laps	Laps Led	Races Led	Miles	$
1965	Eddie Gray	1	0	0	0	0	0	0	1	176	0	0	475	1,300
1966	Eddie Gray	1	0	0	0	0	0	0	0	43	0	0	116	500
Lifetime		3	0	0	0	0	0	0	1	393	0	0	1,061	$2,450

Ron Shephard

Year	Driver	Starts	Poles	1	2	3	4	5	6–10	Laps	Laps Led	Races Led	Miles	$
1987	Ron Shephard	2	0	0	0	0	0	0	0	198	0	0	462	3,745
Lifetime		2	0	0	0	0	0	0	0	198	0	0	462	$3,745

Morgan Shepherd

Year	Driver	Starts	Poles	1	2	3	4	5	6–10	Laps	Laps Led	Races Led	Miles	$
1988	Morgan Shepherd	9	0	0	0	0	0	0	0	1,770	0	0	2,000	20,605
Lifetime		9	0	0	0	0	0	0	0	1,770	0	0	2,000	$20,605

Bill Shirey

Year	Driver	Starts	Poles	1	2	3	4	5	6–10	Laps	Laps Led	Races Led	Miles	$
1969	Bill Shirey	1	0	0	0	0	0	0	0	82	0	0	164	865
1970	Bill Shirey	29	0	0	0	0	0	0	1	3,691	0	0	2,542	12,390
1971	Bill Shirey	26	0	0	0	0	0	0	2	3,549	0	0	2,510	8,835
"	Jabe Thomas	1	0	0	0	0	0	0	0	339	0	0	212	455
"	**Total**	27	0	0	0	0	0	0	2	3,888	0	0	2,722	9,290
1972	Bill Shirey	12	0	0	0	0	0	0	0	1,600	0	0	1,527	7,305
Lifetime		69	0	0	0	0	0	0	3	9,261	0	0	6,955	$29,850

Monroe Shook

Year	Driver	Starts	Poles	1	2	3	4	5	6–10	Laps	Laps Led	Races Led	Miles	$
1958	Johnny Allen	1	0	0	0	0	0	0	0	56	0	0	56	0
"	Bob Bolheimer	1	0	0	0	0	0	0	0	15	0	0	21	100
"	Jerry Draper	1	0	0	0	0	0	0	0	107	0	0	54	0
"	Doug Yates	1	0	0	0	0	0	0	0	16	0	0	66	25
"	**Total**	4	0	0	0	0	0	0	0	194	0	0	196	125
1960	Emanuel Zervakis	14	1	0	0	1	1	0	8	3,382	0	0	3,457	9,675
1961	Tommy Irwin	1	0	0	0	0	0	0	0	103	0	0	93	150
"	Emanuel Zervakis	38	1	2	1	3	5	8	9	9,198	386	2	6,664	20,800
"	**Total**	39	1	2	1	3	5	8	9	9,301	386	2	6,757	20,950
1962	Johnny Allen	5	0	0	0	0	0	0	2	963	0	0	427	715
"	Tommy Irwin	8	0	0	0	0	0	0	3	991	10	1	595	1,175
"	**Total**	13	0	0	0	0	0	0	5	1,954	10	1	1,022	1,890
Lifetime		70	2	2	1	4	6	8	22	14,831	396	3	11,432	$32,640

Barney Shore

Year	Driver	Starts	Poles	1	2	3	4	5	6–10	Laps	Laps Led	Races Led	Miles	$
1958	Barney Shore	12	0	0	0	0	0	1	2	1,741	0	0	835	1,320
1959	Barney Shore	6	0	0	0	0	0	0	2	628	0	0	212	425
1960	Barney Shore	1	0	0	0	0	0	0	0	93	0	0	47	50
Lifetime		19	0	0	0	0	0	1	4	2,462	0	0	1,094	$1,795

Buddy Shuman

Year	Driver	Starts	Poles	1	2	3	4	5	6–10	Laps	Laps Led	Races Led	Miles	$
1952	Buddy Shuman	7	0	0	0	0	0	1	3	521	0	0	282	685
"	Bill Widenhouse	1	0	0	0	0	0	0	0	19	0	0	24	25
"	**Total**	8	0	0	0	0	0	1	3	540	0	0	306	710
1953	Buddy Shuman	2	0	0	0	0	0	0	0		0	0		50
Lifetime		10	0	0	0	0	0	1	3	540	0	0	306	$760

Larry Shurter

Year	Driver	Starts	Poles	1	2	3	4	5	6–10	Laps	Laps Led	Races Led	Miles	$
1950	Larry Shurter	1	0	0	0	0	0	0	0	37	0	0	154	25
1952	Al Conroy	1	0	0	0	0	0	0	0	308	0	0	385	150
"	Larry Shurter	4	0	0	0	0	0	0	0	138	0	0	107	125
"	**Total**	5	0	0	0	0	0	0	0	446	0	0	492	275
Lifetime		6	0	0	0	0	0	0	0	483	0	0	646	$300

Lou Sidoit

Year	Driver	Starts	Poles	1	2	3	4	5	6–10	Laps	Laps Led	Races Led	Miles	$
1963	Johnny Allen	2	0	0	0	0	0	0	1	150	0	0	375	700
"	LeeRoy Yarbrough	2	0	0	0	0	0	1	0	904	0	0	452	1,150
"	**Total**	4	0	0	0	0	0	1	1	1,054	0	0	827	1,850
Lifetime		4	0	0	0	0	0	1	1	1,054	0	0	827	$1,850

Year	Driver	Starts	Poles	Finish 1	2	3	4	5	6–10	Laps	Laps Led	Races Led	Miles	$

Ted Sidwell

Year	Driver	Starts	Poles	1	2	3	4	5	6–10	Laps	Laps Led	Races Led	Miles	$
1967	Dorus Wisecraver	2	0	0	0	0	0	0	0	219	0	0	548	2,325
Lifetime		2	0	0	0	0	0	0	0	219	0	0	548	$2,325

Gary Sigman

Year	Driver	Starts	Poles	1	2	3	4	5	6–10	Laps	Laps Led	Races Led	Miles	$
1969	Joe Frasson	1	0	0	0	0	0	0	0	3	0	0	8	825
1970	Kevin Terris	2	0	0	0	0	0	0	0	169	0	0	443	1,875
1972	Bill Butts	2	0	0	0	0	0	0	0	313	0	0	798	3,060
Lifetime		5	0	0	0	0	0	0	0	485	0	0	1,249	$5,760

Leo Sigman

Year	Driver	Starts	Poles	1	2	3	4	5	6–10	Laps	Laps Led	Races Led	Miles	$
1951	John Barker	4	0	0	0	0	0	0	0	431	0	0	496	100
"	Leo Sigman	2	0	0	0	0	0	0	0	0	0	0	0	50
"	**Total**	4	0	0	0	0	0	0	0	431	0	0	496	150
Lifetime		4	0	0	0	0	0	0	0	431	0	0	496	$150

Elmer Simko

Year	Driver	Starts	Poles	1	2	3	4	5	6–10	Laps	Laps Led	Races Led	Miles	$
1982	David Simko	2	0	0	0	0	0	0	0	100	0	0	203	3,200
1983	David Simko	1	0	0	0	0	0	0	0	154	0	0	234	3,815
1984	David Simko	1	0	0	0	0	0	0	0	189	0	0	378	4,000
1986	David Simko	1	0	0	0	0	0	0	0	170	0	0	340	1,625
1987	David Simko	4	0	0	0	0	0	0	0	850	0	0	1,211	9,330
1988	David Simko	1	0	0	0	0	0	0	0	9	0	0	18	2,450
Lifetime		10	0	0	0	0	0	0	0	1,472	0	0	2,384	$24,420

Banks Simpson

Year	Driver	Starts	Poles	1	2	3	4	5	6–10	Laps	Laps Led	Races Led	Miles	$
1955	Bunk Moore	2	0	0	0	0	0	0	0	199	0	0	100	50
"	Banks Simpson	6	0	0	0	0	0	0	0	931	0	0	1,119	775
"	**Total**	8	0	0	0	0	0	0	0	1,130	0	0	1,218	825
Lifetime		8	0	0	0	0	0	0	0	1,130	0	0	1,218	$825

Gene Simpson

Year	Driver	Starts	Poles	1	2	3	4	5	6–10	Laps	Laps Led	Races Led	Miles	$
1955	Gene Simpson	9	0	0	0	0	0	1	2	1,271	0	0	1,027	925
Lifetime		9	0	0	0	0	0	1	2	1,271	0	0	1,027	$925

Sims Brothers

Year	Driver	Starts	Poles	1	2	3	4	5	6–10	Laps	Laps Led	Races Led	Miles	$
1984	Mike Alexander	1	0	0	0	0	0	0	0	187	0	0	468	10,955
1985	Mike Alexander	7	0	0	0	0	0	0	0	1,255	0	0	2,212	34,475
Lifetime		8	0	0	0	0	0	0	0	1,442	0	0	2,680	$45,430

Harry Sims

Year	Driver	Starts	Poles	1	2	3	4	5	6–10	Laps	Laps Led	Races Led	Miles	$
1960	Eddie Gray	3	0	0	0	0	0	0	1	243	0	0	305	580
Lifetime		3	0	0	0	0	0	0	1	243	0	0	305	$580

David Sisco

Year	Driver	Starts	Poles	1	2	3	4	5	6–10	Laps	Laps Led	Races Led	Miles	$
1974	David Sisco	27	0	0	0	1	1	0	7	7,168	43	4	8,539	53,055
"	Jerry Sisco	1	0	0	0	0	0	0	0	142	0	0	85	295
"	**Total**	27	0	0	0	1	1	0	7	7,310	43	4	8,624	53,350
1975	David Sisco	28	0	0	0	1	0	1	5	7,572	37	4	8,455	62,186
1976	Billy McGinnis	1	0	0	0	0	0	0	0	15	0	0	23	805
"	David Sisco	27	0	0	0	0	0	0	7	7,077	6	3	8,049	62,622
"	**Total**	28	0	0	0	0	0	0	7	7,092	6	3	8,072	63,427
1977	Ed Negre	1	0	0	0	0	0	0	0	77	0	0	117	1,040
"	David Sisco	10	0	0	0	0	0	0	0	2,030	0	0	2,186	14,520
"	**Total**	11	0	0	0	0	0	0	0	2,107	0	0	2,303	15,560
Lifetime		94	0	0	0	2	1	1	19	24,081	86	11	27,454	$194,523

Eddie Skinner

Year	Driver	Starts	Poles	1	2	3	4	5	6–10	Laps	Laps Led	Races Led	Miles	$
1957	Eddie Skinner	4	0	0	0	0	0	0	0	833	0	0	534	605
1958	Eddie Skinner	5	0	0	0	0	0	0	0	750	0	0	440	420
Lifetime		9	0	0	0	0	0	0	0	1,583	0	0	973	$1,025

Year	Driver	Starts	Poles	Finish 1	2	3	4	5	6–10	Laps	Laps Led	Races Led	Miles	$

Frank Skinner

Year	Driver	Starts	Poles	1	2	3	4	5	6–10	Laps	Laps Led	Races Led	Miles	$
1960	Whitey Gerkin	2	0	0	0	0	0	0	0	233	0	0	583	400
"	Tiny Lund	1	0	0	0	0	0	0	1	375	0	0	563	1,350
"	Gene Marmor	3	0	0	0	0	0	0	1	548	0	0	376	575
"	**Total**	5	0	0	0	0	0	0	2	1,156	0	0	1,521	2,325
Lifetime		5	0	0	0	0	0	0	2	1,156	0	0	1,521	$2,325

William Slate

Year	Driver	Starts	Poles	1	2	3	4	5	6–10	Laps	Laps Led	Races Led	Miles	$
1996	Hermie Sadler	1	0	0	0	0	0	0	0	349	0	0	349	13,055
Lifetime		1	0	0	0	0	0	0	0	349	0	0	349	$13,055

Barney Smith

Year	Driver	Starts	Poles	1	2	3	4	5	6–10	Laps	Laps Led	Races Led	Miles	$
1951	Barney Smith	2	0	0	0	0	0	0	0		0	0		75
1952	Barney Smith	3	0	0	0	0	0	0	2	647	0	0	324	285
Lifetime		5	0	0	0	0	0	0	2	647	0	0	324	$360

Bob Smith

Year	Driver	Starts	Poles	1	2	3	4	5	6–10	Laps	Laps Led	Races Led	Miles	$
1957	Jim Blomgren	3	0	0	0	0	0	1	0	303	0	0	187	410
1959	John Potter	2	0	0	0	0	0	0	2	549	0	0	277	550
1960	Jim Blomgren	3	0	0	0	0	0	0	2	288	0	0	332	400
1961	Jim Blomgren	4	0	0	0	0	1	0	1	401	0	0	406	590
"	Bruce Worrell	4	0	0	0	0	0	0	2	391	0	0	379	540
"	**Total**	4	0	0	0	0	1	0	3	792	0	0	785	1,130
Lifetime		12	0	0	0	0	1	1	7	1,932	0	0	1,581	$2,490

Don Smith

Year	Driver	Starts	Poles	1	2	3	4	5	6–10	Laps	Laps Led	Races Led	Miles	$
1970	Mel Larson	1	0	0	0	0	0	0	1	133	0	0	348	1,115
Lifetime		1	0	0	0	0	0	0	1	133	0	0	348	$1,115

Douglas Smith

Year	Driver	Starts	Poles	1	2	3	4	5	6–10	Laps	Laps Led	Races Led	Miles	$
1989	Ron Esau	1	0	0	0	0	0	0	0	194	0	0	194	2,960
"	Joe Ruttman	3	0	0	0	0	0	0	0	743	0	0	923	7,710
"	**Total**	4	0	0	0	0	0	0	0	937	0	0	1,117	10,670
Lifetime		4	0	0	0	0	0	0	0	937	0	0	1,117	$10,670

F. W. Smith

Year	Driver	Starts	Poles	1	2	3	4	5	6–10	Laps	Laps Led	Races Led	Miles	$
1954	Bill Smith	2	0	0	0	0	0	0	1	373	0	0	228	240
Lifetime		2	0	0	0	0	0	0	1	373	0	0	228	$240

Frank Smith

Year	Driver	Starts	Poles	1	2	3	4	5	6–10	Laps	Laps Led	Races Led	Miles	$
1949	Archie Smith	2	0	0	0	0	0	0	2	161	0	0	81	225
"	Frank Smith	2	0	0	0	0	0	0	0		0	0		50
"	**Total**	3	0	0	0	0	0	0	2	161	0	0	81	275
Lifetime		3	0	0	0	0	0	0	2	161	0	0	81	$275

Gary Smith

Year	Driver	Starts	Poles	1	2	3	4	5	6–10	Laps	Laps Led	Races Led	Miles	$
1982	Hershel McGriff	2	0	0	0	0	0	0	0	115	0	0	301	1,545
1983	Hershel McGriff	2	0	0	0	0	0	0	1	191	0	0	500	5,650
1984	Hershel McGriff	2	0	0	0	0	0	0	1	149	1	1	390	3,815
1985	Hershel McGriff	2	0	0	0	0	0	0	0	178	0	0	466	2,835
1986	Hershel McGriff	2	0	0	0	0	0	0	0	170	0	0	445	4,080
1987	Hershel McGriff	2	0	0	0	0	0	0	0	101	0	0	265	7,530
1988	Hershel McGriff	3	0	0	0	0	0	0	0	316	0	0	524	5,960
1989	Hershel McGriff	1	0	0	0	0	0	0	0	74	0	0	186	5,075
Lifetime		16	0	0	0	0	0	0	2	1,294	1	1	3,079	$36,490

George Smith

Year	Driver	Starts	Poles	1	2	3	4	5	6–10	Laps	Laps Led	Races Led	Miles	$
1987	Eddie Bierschwale	2	0	0	0	0	0	0	0	540	0	0	548	3,250
"	Jimmy Horton	2	0	0	0	0	0	0	0	256	0	0	640	4,405
"	**Total**	4	0	0	0	0	0	0	0	796	0	0	1,188	7,655
1988	Jimmy Horton	8	0	0	0	0	0	0	0	2,007	0	0	2,894	23,575

Year	Driver	Starts	Poles	Finish 1	2	3	4	5	6–10	Laps	Laps Led	Races Led	Miles	$

George Smith *continued*

Year	Driver	Starts	Poles	1	2	3	4	5	6–10	Laps	Laps Led	Races Led	Miles	$
1989	Jimmy Horton	5	0	0	0	0	0	0	0	955	0	0	1,391	19,232
1990	Jimmy Horton	6	0	0	0	0	0	0	0	1,599	0	0	2,175	35,875
1991	Jimmy Horton	0												2,400
Lifetime		23	0	0	0	0	0	0	0	5,357	0	0	7,648	$88,737

Gerald Smith

Year	Driver	Starts	Poles	1	2	3	4	5	6–10	Laps	Laps Led	Races Led	Miles	$
1990	Brent Keading	1	0	0	0	0	0	0	0	304	0	0	304	3,230
Lifetime		1	0	0	0	0	0	0	0	304	0	0	304	$3,230

Gordon Smith

Year	Driver	Starts	Poles	1	2	3	4	5	6–10	Laps	Laps Led	Races Led	Miles	$
1955	Gordon Smith	14	0	0	0	0	0	0	2	1,495	0	0	821	925
Lifetime		14	0	0	0	0	0	0	2	1,495	0	0	821	$925

Harley Smith

Year	Driver	Starts	Poles	1	2	3	4	5	6–10	Laps	Laps Led	Races Led	Miles	$
1971	Larry Smith	4	0	0	0	0	0	0	1	896	0	0	1,699	5,058
1972	Larry Smith	23	0	0	0	0	0	0	7	4,320	0	0	5,831	24,215
1973	Larry Smith	11	0	0	0	0	0	0	1	2,103	0	0	3,562	14,090
Lifetime		38	0	0	0	0	0	0	9	7,319	0	0	11,092	$43,363

Helen Rae Smith

Year	Driver	Starts	Poles	1	2	3	4	5	6–10	Laps	Laps Led	Races Led	Miles	$
1984	Phil Barkdoll	2	0	0	0	0	0	0	0	212	0	0	564	5,075
"	Joe Ruttman	1	0	0	0	0	0	0	0	8	0	0	12	1,005
"	Morgan Shepard	1	0	0	0	0	0	0	0	196	0	0	392	2,250
"	**Total**	2	0	0	0	0	0	0	0	416	0	0	968	8,330
1985	Phil Barkdoll	2	0	0	0	0	0	0	0	200	0	0	532	5,525
"	Sterling Marlin	1	0	0	0	0	0	0	0	219	0	0	329	1,350
"	Ed Sanger	1	0	0	0	0	0	0	0	358	0	0	224	910
"	Morgan Shepherd	8	0	0	0	0	0	0	0	1,412	1	1	1,829	16,470
"	**Total**	11	0	0	0	0	0	0	0	2,189	1	1	2,914	24,255
1986	Phil Barkdoll	2	0	0	0	0	0	0	0	249	3	2	662	6,045
"	Dave Marcis	1	0	0	0	0	0	0	0	395	0	0	593	9,825
"	**Total**	3	0	0	0	0	0	0	0	644	3	2	1,255	15,870
1987	Phil Barkdoll	1	0	0	0	0	0	0	0	27	0	0	72	6,000
1988	Phil Barkdoll	3	0	0	0	0	0	0	0	465	0	0	1,220	22,145
"	Joe Ruttman	2	0	0	0	0	0	0	0	171	0	0	224	3,275
"	**Total**	5	0	0	0	0	0	0	0	636	0	0	1,444	20,420
Lifetime		24	0	0	0	0	0	0	0	3,912	4	3	6,653	$74,875

Jack Smith

Year	Driver	Starts	Poles	1	2	3	4	5	6–10	Laps	Laps Led	Races Led	Miles	$
1951	Jack Smith	3	0	0	1	1	0	0	0	34	0	0	26	1,125
1954	Jack Smith	6	0	0	0	0	0	0	1	381	0	0	423	500
1957	Jack Smith	23	2	3	0	1	2	6	3	3,958	314	8	2,575	10,657
1958	Johnny Allen	2	0	0	0	0	0	0	1	108	0	0	127	180
"	Jack Smith	35	4	2	5	2	3	2	6	5,030	381	7	3,304	12,004
"	**Total**	35	4	2	5	2	3	2	7	5,138	381	7	3,431	12,184
1959	Jack Smith	20	3	4	1	2	1	0	3	3,398	222	7	2,637	13,015
1960	Buck Baker	1	0	1	0	0	0	0	0	364	175	1	501	19,900
"	Jack Smith	13	4	3	1	2	0	1	0	2,198	514	10	2,570	24,721
"	**Total**	14	4	4	1	2	0	1	0	2,562	689	11	3,071	44,621
1961	Larry Frank	2	0	0	0	0	0	0	0	485	0	0	667	880
"	Bobby Johns	1	1	0	0	0	0	0	0	457	49	1	229	440
"	Jack Smith	25	0	2	2	4	1	1	4	4,695	278	4	4,098	21,410
"	Bob Welborn	5	0	0	1	1	0	0	2	1,305	52	2	1,542	6,555
"	Rex White	1	0	0	0	0	0	0	1	345	0	0	474	925
"	**Total**	28	1	2	3	5	1	1	7	7,287	379	5	7,009	30,210
1962	Buck Baker	1	0	0	0	0	0	0	1	263	0	0	395	1,125
"	Art Malone	1	0	0	0	0	0	0	1	95	0	0	238	600
"	Jack Smith	51	7	5	6	5	8	3	8	10,781	894	9	7,110	34,748
"	**Total**	51	7	5	6	5	8	3	10	11,139	894	9	7,742	36,473
1963	Stick Elliott	5	0	0	0	0	0	0	0	1,133	0	0	1,347	1,925
"	Jack Smith	29	2	0	0	0	1	3	7	5,300	25	2	3,625	8,885
"	G. C. Spencer	6	0	0	0	0	0	0	1	1,098	8	1	919	2,530
"	**Total**	32	2	0	0	0	1	3	8	7,531	33	3	5,891	13,340

Year	Driver	Starts	Poles	Finish						Laps	Laps Led	Races Led	Miles	$
				1	2	3	4	5	6–10					

Jack Smith *continued*

Year	Driver	Starts	Poles	1	2	3	4	5	6–10	Laps	Laps Led	Races Led	Miles	$
1964	Jack Smith	4	1	0	1	1	0	0	0	459	20	1	240	1,575
Lifetime		216	24	20	18	19	16	16	39	41,887	2,932	51	33,044	$163,700

Jimmy Smith

Year	Driver	Starts	Poles	1	2	3	4	5	6–10	Laps	Laps Led	Races Led	Miles	$
1994	P. J. Jones	1	0	0	0	0	0	0	0	303	0	0	303	6,960
Lifetime		1	0	0	0	0	0	0	0	303	0	0	303	$6,960

Louise Smith

Year	Driver	Starts	Poles	1	2	3	4	5	6–10	Laps	Laps Led	Races Led	Miles	$
1949	Louise Smith	3	0	0	0	0	0	0	0	175	0	0	175	75
1950	Louise Smith	5	0	0	0	0	0	0	0	84	0	0	84	25
1951	Buck Clardy	1	0	0	0	0	0	0	0	0	0	0	0	25
1952	E. C. Ramsey	5	0	0	0	0	0	0	0	679	0	0	619	160
"	Louise Smith	3	0	0	0	0	0	0	0	118	0	0	101	85
"	J. O. Staton	6	0	0	0	0	0	0	1	310	0	0	164	250
"	**Total**	11	0	0	0	0	0	0	1	1,107	0	0	884	495
Lifetime		20	0	0	0	0	0	0	1	1,366	0	0	1,143	$620

Mark Smith (See also George Bradshaw and Mark Smith)

Year	Driver	Starts	Poles	1	2	3	4	5	6–10	Laps	Laps Led	Races Led	Miles	$
1995	Loy Allen Jr.	7	0	0	0	0	0	0	1	1,436	18	1	2,609	72,515
"	Phil Parsons	2	0	0	0	0	0	0	0	36	0	0	81	41,450
"	**Total**	9	0	0	0	0	0	0	1	1,472	18	1	2,690	113,965
1996	Loy Allen Jr.	9	0	0	0	0	0	0	0	1,439	0	0	2,772	130,667
"	Dick Trickle	8	0	0	0	0	0	0	1	2,349	0	0	2,889	98,470
"	**Total**	17	0	0	0	0	0	0	1	3,788	0	0	5,661	229,137
Lifetime		26	0	0	0	0	0	0	2	5,260	18	1	8,352	$343,102

Perry Smith

Year	Driver	Starts	Poles	1	2	3	4	5	6–10	Laps	Laps Led	Races Led	Miles	$
1951	Mike Klapak	1	0	0	0	0	0	0	0		0	0		0
"	Frank Mundy	25	4	2	2	1	2	1	3	674	331	4	479	6,060
"	Bill Rexford	1	0	0	0	0	0	0	0		0	0		25
"	Perry Smith	1	0	0	0	0	1	0	0		0	0		300
"	**Total**	27	4	2	2	1	3	1	3	674	331	4	479	6,385
1952	Al Keller	2	0	0	0	0	0	0	0		0	0		75
"	Jack Smith	2	1	0	0	0	0	0	0	216	186	1	123	100
"	**Total**	4	1	0	0	0	0	0	0	216	186	1	123	175
Lifetime		31	5	2	2	1	3	1	3	890	517	5	602	$6,560

Ralph Smith

Year	Driver	Starts	Poles	1	2	3	4	5	6–10	Laps	Laps Led	Races Led	Miles	$
1962	Bill Champion	1	0	0	0	0	0	0	0	15	0	0	21	400
"	Harold Fryar	1	0	0	0	0	0	0	0	187	0	0	62	110
"	Theodore Hunt	5	0	0	0	0	0	0	2	561	0	0	273	690
"	Harry Leake	2	0	0	0	0	0	0	0	346	0	0	173	250
"	Bill Smith	1	0	0	0	0	0	0	0	60	0	0	30	200
"	Ralph Smith	2	0	0	0	0	0	0	0	684	0	0	342	300
"	G. C. Spencer	2	0	0	0	0	0	0	0	567	0	0	851	750
"	LeeRoy Yarbrough	1	0	0	0	0	0	1	0	191	0	0	96	275
"	**Total**	15	0	0	0	0	0	1	2	2,611	0	0	1,847	2,975
1963	Theodore Hunt	1	0	0	0	0	0	0	0	184	0	0	92	65
Lifetime		16	0	0	0	0	0	1	2	2,795	0	0	1,939	$3,040

Robert Smith

Year	Driver	Starts	Poles	1	2	3	4	5	6–10	Laps	Laps Led	Races Led	Miles	$
1962	Ralph Earnhardt	11	0	0	0	1	0	1	3	1,183	0	0	910	2,020
1963	Bunkie Blackburn	2	0	0	0	0	0	0	0	158	0	0	79	250
"	Thomas Cox	1	0	0	0	0	0	0	0	6	0	0	9	450
"	G. C. Spencer	1	0	0	0	0	0	0	1	177	0	0	89	200
"	**Total**	4	0	0	0	0	0	0	1	341	0	0	177	900
Lifetime		15	0	0	0	1	0	1	4	1,524	0	0	1,086	$2,920

Rollin Smith

Year	Driver	Starts	Poles	1	2	3	4	5	6–10	Laps	Laps Led	Races Led	Miles	$
1952	Rollin Smith	1	0	0	0	0	0	0	0	385	0	0	481	350
Lifetime		1	0	0	0	0	0	0	0	385	0	0	481	$350

Year	Driver	Starts	Poles	Finish 1	2	3	4	5	6–10	Laps	Laps Led	Races Led	Miles	$

Ron Smith

Year	Driver	Starts	Poles	1	2	3	4	5	6–10	Laps	Laps Led	Races Led	Miles	$
1967	Don Stives	3	0	0	0	0	0	0	1	188	0	0	49	510
Lifetime		3	0	0	0	0	0	0	1	188	0	0	49	$510

Ronald Smith

Year	Driver	Starts	Poles	1	2	3	4	5	6–10	Laps	Laps Led	Races Led	Miles	$
1965	Bud Vaughn	4	0	0	0	0	0	0	1	164	0	0	72	840
"	Robert Vaughn	2	0	0	0	0	0	0	0	5	0	0	13	1,160
"	**Total**	6	0	0	0	0	0	0	1	169	0	0	85	2,000
Lifetime		6	0	0	0	0	0	0	1	169	0	0	85	$2,000

Scott Smith

Year	Driver	Starts	Poles	1	2	3	4	5	6–10	Laps	Laps Led	Races Led	Miles	$
1980	Don Whittington	1	0	0	0	0	0	0	0	87	0	0	119	1,275
1981	Don Whittington	3	0	0	0	0	0	0	0	346	0	0	883	13,685
Lifetime		4	0	0	0	0	0	0	0	433	0	0	1,002	$14,960

Slick Smith

Year	Driver	Starts	Poles	1	2	3	4	5	6–10	Laps	Laps Led	Races Led	Miles	$
1949	Slick Smith	1	0	0	0	0	0	0	1		0	0		125
1953	Slick Smith	1	0	0	0	0	0	0	1		0	0		125
1954	Buck Baker	1	0	0	0	0	0	0	0	231	0	0	231	100
Lifetime		3	0	0	0	0	0	0	2	231	0	0	231	$350

Stanley Smith

Year	Driver	Starts	Poles	1	2	3	4	5	6–10	Laps	Laps Led	Races Led	Miles	$
1991	Stanley Smith	12	0	0	0	0	0	0	0	1,932	12	1	3,201	56,915
1992	Stanley Smith	14	0	0	0	0	0	0	0	2,685	0	0	4,009	89,650
1993	Stanley Smith	1	0	0	0	0	0	0	0	68	0	0	181	9,790
Lifetime		27	0	0	0	0	0	0	0	4,685	12	1	7,390	$156,355

Walt Smith

Year	Driver	Starts	Poles	1	2	3	4	5	6–10	Laps	Laps Led	Races Led	Miles	$
1954	Erick Erickson	1	0	0	0	0	0	0	1	477	0	0	239	250
Lifetime		1	0	0	0	0	0	0	1	477	0	0	239	$250

Wayne Smith

Year	Driver	Starts	Poles	1	2	3	4	5	6–10	Laps	Laps Led	Races Led	Miles	$
1965	J. T. Putney	3	0	0	0	0	0	0	0	34	0	0	17	310
"	Wayne Smith	25	0	0	0	0	0	0	2	3,744	0	0	2,475	6,790
"	**Total**	28	0	0	0	0	0	0	2	3,778	0	0	2,492	7,100
1966	Wayne Smith	23	0	0	0	0	0	0	1	4,108	0	0	3,655	9,930
1967	Wayne Smith	27	0	0	0	0	0	0	2	4,364	0	0	3,629	10,025
"	Blackie Watt	1	0	0	0	0	0	0	0	2	0	0	3	540
"	**Total**	27	0	0	0	0	0	0	2	4,366	0	0	3,632	10,565
1968	Wayne Smith	17	0	0	0	0	0	0	1	2,350	0	0	1,977	7,135
1969	Earl Brooks	1	0	0	0	0	0	0	0	183	0	0	252	900
"	Cecil Gordon	1	0	0	0	0	0	0	0	349	0	0	218	475
"	Wayne Smith	16	0	0	0	0	0	0	2	2,692	0	0	2,961	10,610
"	**Total**	18	0	0	0	0	0	0	2	3,224	0	0	3,431	11,985
1970	Dave Marcis	1	0	0	0	0	0	0	0	3	0	0	1	200
"	Wayne Smith	8	0	0	0	0	0	0	0	593	0	0	813	4,505
"	**Total**	9	0	0	0	0	0	0	0	596	0	0	814	4,705
1971	Wayne Smith	2	0	0	0	0	0	0	0	67	0	0	39	660
1972	Wayne Smith	3	0	0	0	0	0	0	1	270	0	0	624	3,445
Lifetime		127	0	0	0	0	0	0	9	18,759	0	0	16,665	$55,525

Parker Snead

Year	Driver	Starts	Poles	1	2	3	4	5	6–10	Laps	Laps Led	Races Led	Miles	$
1963	Johnny Allen	1	0	0	0	0	0	0	0	134	0	0	201	350
"	Ted Hairfield	2	0	0	0	0	0	0	0	50	0	0	125	675
"	**Total**	3	0	0	0	0	0	0	0	184	0	0	326	1,025
Lifetime		3	0	0	0	0	0	0	0	184	0	0	326	$1,025

Snellman Brothers

Year	Driver	Starts	Poles	1	2	3	4	5	6–10	Laps	Laps Led	Races Led	Miles	$
1985	Randy LaJoie	1	0	0	0	0	0	0	0	319	0	0	486	8,325
1986	Randy LaJoie	1	0	0	0	0	0	0	0	144	0	0	360	3,315

Year	Driver	Starts	Poles	Finish						Laps	Laps Led	Races Led	Miles	$
				1	2	3	4	5	6–10					

Snellman Brothers *continued*

Year	Driver	Starts	Poles	1	2	3	4	5	6–10	Laps	Laps Led	Races Led	Miles	$
"	Morgan Shepherd	1	0	0	0	0	0	0	0	181	0	0	453	15,465
"	**Total**	2	0	0	0	0	0	0	0	325	0	0	813	18,780
Lifetime		3	0	0	0	0	0	0	0	644	0	0	1,298	$27,105

Grant Sniffen

Year	Driver	Starts	Poles	1	2	3	4	5	6–10	Laps	Laps Led	Races Led	Miles	$
1951	Dick Meyer	6	0	0	1	0	0	2	1		82	1		1,550
Lifetime		6	0	0	1	0	0	2	1		82	1		$1,550

Les Snow

Year	Driver	Starts	Poles	1	2	3	4	5	6–10	Laps	Laps Led	Races Led	Miles	$
1951	Les Snow	2	0	0	0	0	0	0	1	222	0	0	222	375
Lifetime		2	0	0	0	0	0	0	1	222	0	0	222	$375

Bill Snowden

Year	Driver	Starts	Poles	1	2	3	4	5	6–10	Laps	Laps Led	Races Led	Miles	$
1949	Bill Snowden	3	0	0	0	0	0	0	2	182	0	0	91	460
1950	Bill Snowden	1	0	0	0	0	0	1	0	194	0	0	146	200
1951	Bill Snowden	12	0	0	0	0	2	1	6	383	0	0	479	2,640
1952	Banjo Matthews	3	0	0	0	0	0	1	0	667	0	0	628	1,000
"	Fireball Roberts	1	0	0	0	0	0	0	0	53	0	0	53	24
"	Bill Snowden	4	0	0	0	0	0	0	1	384	0	0	237	290
"	**Total**	7	0	0	0	0	0	1	1	1,104	0	0	918	1,314
Lifetime		23	0	0	0	0	2	3	9	1,863	0	0	1,634	$4,614

Don Snyder

Year	Driver	Starts	Poles	1	2	3	4	5	6–10	Laps	Laps Led	Races Led	Miles	$
1965	Donald Tucker	9	0	0	0	0	1	0	2	1,597	0	0	1,703	5,830
Lifetime		9	0	0	0	0	1	0	2	1,597	0	0	1,703	$5,830

John Soares

Year	Driver	Starts	Poles	1	2	3	4	5	6–10	Laps	Laps Led	Races Led	Miles	$
1951	John Soares	2	0	0	0	0	0	0	0		0	0		50
Lifetime		2	0	0	0	0	0	0	0		0	0		$50

John Soares Jr.

Year	Driver	Starts	Poles	1	2	3	4	5	6–10	Laps	Laps Led	Races Led	Miles	$
1970	John Soares Jr.	1	0	0	0	0	1	0	0	141	0	0	369	3,415
1971	John Soares Jr.	4	0	0	0	0	0	0	1	764	0	0	1,280	4,855
1972	John Soares Jr.	3	0	0	0	0	0	0	0	337	0	0	861	4,315
1975	John Soares Jr.	1	0	0	0	0	0	0	0	18	0	0	47	670
1985	John Soares Jr.	1	0	0	0	0	0	0	0	87	0	0	228	1,875
Lifetime		10	0	0	0	0	1	0	1	1,347	0	0	2,785	$15,130

Rol Soderin

Year	Driver	Starts	Poles	1	2	3	4	5	6–10	Laps	Laps Led	Races Led	Miles	$
1957	Elgin Holmes	1	0	0	0	0	0	0	0	14	0	0	35	35
Lifetime		1	0	0	0	0	0	0	0	14	0	0	35	$35

Lyle Sokoll

Year	Driver	Starts	Poles	1	2	3	4	5	6–10	Laps	Laps Led	Races Led	Miles	$
1957	George Bumgardner	1	0	0	0	0	0	0	0	111	0	0	111	100
1958	Bill Wimble	2	0	0	0	0	0	0	0	241	0	0	121	100
Lifetime		3	0	0	0	0	0	0	0	352	0	0	232	$200

Gober Sosebee

Year	Driver	Starts	Poles	1	2	3	4	5	6–10	Laps	Laps Led	Races Led	Miles	$
1950	Gober Sosebee	1	0	0	0	0	0	0	0	364	4	1	455	290
1951	Gober Sosebee	7	0	0	2	0	0	1	1	613	0	0	607	2,085
1952	Gober Sosebee	4	0	0	0	0	0	3	0	293	0	0	196	975
1953	Gober Sosebee	17	0	0	1	1	0	0	7	943	73	1	928	2,722
1954	Gober Sosebee	17	1	1	0	1	1	1	2	1,817	170	2	1,147	2,850
1955	Gober Sosebee	6	0	0	0	0	2	2	0	344	0	0	218	775
1958	Bill Poor	1	0	0	0	0	0	0	0	336	0	0	168	280
"	Gober Sosebee	5	1	0	0	0	0	0	3	692	0	0	476	695
"	**Total**	6	1	0	0	0	0	0	3	1,028	0	0	644	975
1959	Gober Sosebee	1	0	0	0	0	0	0	0	44	0	0	110	100
1979	David Sosebee	3	0	0	0	0	0	0	0	547	0	0	892	2,910

Year	Driver	Starts	Poles	Finish 1	2	3	4	5	6–10	Laps	Laps Led	Races Led	Miles	$

Gober Sosebee *continued*

Year	Driver	Starts	Poles	1	2	3	4	5	6–10	Laps	Laps Led	Races Led	Miles	$
1986	David Sosebee	2	0	0	0	0	0	0	0	267	0	0	404	2,310
Lifetime		64	2	1	3	2	3	5	13	6,260	247	4	5,600	$15,992

Jim Southard

1984	Jim Southard	4	0	0	0	0	0	0	0	1,113	0	0	1,653	6,965
1985	Jim Southard	1	0	0	0	0	0	0	0	431	0	0	438	1,970
Lifetime		5	0	0	0	0	0	0	0	1,544	0	0	2,091	$8,935

George Sparks

1960	Gene White	2	0	0	0	0	0	0	0	187	0	0	468	200
Lifetime		2	0	0	0	0	0	0	0	187	0	0	468	$200

Ralph Sparks

1963	Gary Sain	7	0	0	0	0	0	0	1	994	0	0	523	700
Lifetime		7	0	0	0	0	0	0	1	994	0	0	523	$700

Huck Spaulding

1957	Huck Spaulding	8	0	0	0	0	0	0	3	1,006	0	0	659	1,130
1958	Huck Spaulding	1	0	0	0	0	0	0	0	0	0	0	0	50
Lifetime		9	0	0	0	0	0	0	3	1,006	0	0	659	$1,180

Paul Spaulding

1957	Fireball Roberts	1	0	0	0	1	0	0	0	134	0	0	201	1,375
1958	Junior Johnson	26	0	6	2	3	1	0	3	4,096	317	9	2,760	13,544
"	Lloyd Ragon	2	0	0	0	0	0	0	1	34	0	0	139	230
"	**Total**	28	0	6	2	3	1	0	4	4,130	317	9	2,900	13,774
1959	Ned Jarrett	1	0	0	1	0	0	0	0	200	0	0	100	525
"	Junior Johnson	26	1	5	1	3	2	2	1	4,109	164	5	2,608	9,400
"	Glen Wood	1	0	0	0	0	0	0	1	195	0	0	49	165
"	**Total**	28	1	5	2	3	2	2	2	4,504	164	5	2,757	10,090
1960	Junior Johnson	2	1	0	0	0	0	0	0	98	0	0	49	50
Lifetime		59	2	11	4	7	3	2	6	8,866	481	14	5,907	$25,289

Wayne Spears

1987	Tommy Kendall	1	0	0	0	0	0	0	0	26	0	0	68	950
1988	Tommy Kendall	1	0	0	0	0	0	0	0	94	1	1	246	3,400
1989	Bill Sedgwick	1	0	0	0	0	0	0	0	170	0	0	170	3,525
1990	Bill Sedgwick	3	0	0	0	0	0	0	0	730	0	0	653	11,355
1991	Bill Sedgwick	3	0	0	0	0	0	0	0	848	0	0	740	15,150
1992	Bill Sedgwick	2	0	0	0	0	0	0	0	373	0	0	485	16,365
1993	Ron Hornaday Jr.	1	0	0	0	0	0	0	0	307	0	0	307	6,660
"	Bill Sedgwick	1	0	0	0	0	0	0	0	73	0	0	184	8,140
"	**Total**	2	0	0	0	0	0	0	0	380	0	0	491	14,800
1994	Ron Hornaday Jr.	2	0	0	0	0	0	0	0	350	1	1	431	13,710
Lifetime		15	0	0	0	0	0	0	0	2,971	2	2	3,284	$79,255

Lake Speed

1980	Lake Speed	11	0	0	0	0	0	0	3	1,947	2	1	3,763	32,080
1981	Elmo Langley	1	0	0	0	0	0	0	0	6	0	0	6	575
"	Lake Speed	25	0	0	0	0	0	0	6	6,517	14	2	7,181	92,345
"	**Total**	26	0	0	0	0	0	0	6	6,523	14	2	7,187	92,920
1982	Lake Speed	1	0	0	0	0	0	0	0	3	0	0	8	5,450
1987	Lake Speed	13	0	0	0	1	0	0	4	2,591	1	1	4,433	110,810
1988	Lake Speed	29	0	1	1	0	1	1	3	7,005	368	6	8,534	260,500
1989	Eddie Bierschwale	1	0	0	0	0	0	0	0	6	0	0	15	4,260
"	Rodney Combs	1	0	0	0	0	0	0	0	351	0	0	479	6,895
"	Joe Ruttman	3	0	0	0	0	0	0	0	379	0	0	757	16,650
"	Lake Speed	24	0	0	0	0	0	1	4	7,028	11	4	8,245	201,977
"	**Total**	29	0	0	0	0	0	1	4	7,764	11	4	9,496	229,782
1990	Tommy Ellis	1	0	0	0	0	0	0	0	285	0	0	285	3,050

Year	Driver	Starts	Poles	1	2	3	4	5	6–10	Laps	Laps Led	Races Led	Miles	$

Lake Speed *continued*

Year	Driver	Starts	Poles	1	2	3	4	5	6–10	Laps	Laps Led	Races Led	Miles	$
"	Phil Parsons	1	0	0	0	0	0	0	0	330	0	0	495	4,225
"	Lake Speed	6	0	0	0	0	0	0	0	835	3	1	1,753	75,537
"	**Total**	8	0	0	0	0	0	0	0	1,450	3	1	2,533	82,812
1992	Lake Speed	9	0	0	0	0	0	0	0	2,248	0	0	3,200	52,645
1993	Lake Speed	11	0	0	0	0	0	0	0	2,536	0	0	3,858	115,355
Lifetime		137	0	1	1	1	1	2	20	32,067	399	15	43,011	$982,354

Tom Spell

Year	Driver	Starts	Poles	1	2	3	4	5	6–10	Laps	Laps Led	Races Led	Miles	$
1964	Ralph Earnhardt	10	0	0	0	0	1	0	0	1,102	0	0	1,047	2,615
"	Possum Jones	4	0	0	0	0	0	0	0	375	0	0	149	610
"	Cale Yarborough	1	0	0	0	0	0	0	0	41	0	0	37	100
"	**Total**	15	0	0	0	0	1	0	0	1,518	0	0	1,233	3,325
1965	Cale Yarborough	1	0	0	0	0	0	0	0	22	0	0	20	100
Lifetime		16	0	0	0	0	1	0	0	1,540	0	0	1,253	$3,425

G. C. Spencer

Year	Driver	Starts	Poles	1	2	3	4	5	6–10	Laps	Laps Led	Races Led	Miles	$
1959	G. C. Spencer	28	0	0	0	0	1	0	4	4,552	0	0	2,574	3,386
1960	G. C. Spencer	25	0	0	0	0	1	1	4	4,606	0	0	3,409	3,710
1961	G. C. Spencer	31	0	0	0	0	3	0	15	6,221	0	0	3,824	7,363
1962	G. C. Spencer	37	0	0	0	0	2	4	7	6,638	0	0	3,753	6,860
1963	G. C. Spencer	18	0	0	1	1	1	1	4	2,467	0	0	1,021	5,484
1964	Elmo Henderson	1	0	0	0	0	0	0	0	6	0	0	18	525
"	Doug Moore	16	0	0	0	0	0	0	6	2,809	0	0	1,296	3,275
"	G. C. Spencer	14	0	0	0	1	0	2	1	2,934	0	0	2,309	7,640
"	**Total**	31	0	0	0	1	0	2	7	5,749	0	0	3,622	11,440
1965	G. C. Spencer	46	1	0	3	4	3	4	11	9,063	90	5	6,480	29,675
1966	G. C. Spencer	19	0	0	3	0	0	2	3	4,508	2	1	4,155	26,447
1967	Ed Negre	1	0	0	0	0	0	0	0	446	0	0	446	1,000
"	Wendell Scott	1	0	0	0	0	0	0	0	182	0	0	273	950
"	G. C. Spencer	25	0	0	0	2	0	1	4	3,893	0	0	2,648	8,995
"	**Total**	27	0	0	0	2	0	1	4	4,521	0	0	3,367	10,945
1968	Wendell Scott	1	0	0	0	0	0	0	0	436	0	0	218	425
"	G. C. Spencer	23	0	0	0	0	1	0	4	3,778	0	0	2,645	8,335
"	**Total**	23	0	0	0	0	1	0	4	4,214	0	0	2,863	8,760
1969	J. D. McDuffie	1	0	0	0	0	0	0	0	380	0	0	238	525
"	Ed Negre	13	0	0	0	0	0	0	3	2,198	0	0	1,622	6,870
"	Wendell Scott	1	0	0	0	0	0	0	0	297	0	0	446	1,355
"	G. C. Spencer	26	0	0	0	0	2	2	4	4,823	0	0	3,982	21,675
"	E. J. Trivette	2	0	0	0	0	0	0	1	461	0	0	235	775
"	Frank Warren	1	0	0	0	0	0	0	0	73	0	0	146	840
"	**Total**	35	0	0	0	0	2	2	8	8,232	0	0	6,668	32,040
1970	James Cox	1	0	0	0	0	0	0	0	4	0	0	2	555
"	G. C. Spencer	20	0	0	0	0	2	1	6	4,618	0	0	4,091	17,915
"	**Total**	21	0	0	0	0	2	1	6	4,622	0	0	4,093	18,470
1971	Earl Brooks	1	0	0	0	0	0	0	0	67	0	0	102	1,015
"	Neil Castles	1	0	0	0	0	0	0	0	114	0	0	171	834
"	Ed Negre	2	0	0	0	0	0	0	0	103	0	0	52	925
"	G. C. Spencer	16	0	0	0	0	0	2	4	3,116	12	1	2,754	11,030
"	**Total**	20	0	0	0	0	0	2	4	3,400	12	1	3,079	13,804
1972	G. C. Spencer	9	0	0	0	0	0	0	1	1,397	0	0	1,469	7,255
1973	G. C. Spencer	10	0	0	0	0	0	0	1	1,459	0	0	2,036	12,013
"	John Utsman	3	0	0	0	0	0	0	1	775	0	0	780	2,965
"	**Total**	13	0	0	0	0	0	0	2	2,234	0	0	2,816	14,978
1974	G. C. Spencer	10	0	0	0	0	0	0	1	1,205	3	1	1,721	12,985
1975	G. C. Spencer	9	0	0	0	0	0	0	1	906	11	1	1,663	14,945
1976	Henley Gray	1	0	0	0	0	0	0	0	1	0	0	1	585
"	Dick May	1	0	0	0	0	0	0	0	213	0	0	291	1,395
"	G. C. Spencer	4	0	0	0	0	0	0	0	501	0	0	941	4,965
"	John Utsman	4	0	0	0	0	0	0	0	1,276	0	0	1,859	8,185
"	**Total**	10	0	0	0	0	0	0	0	1,991	0	0	3,091	15,130
1977	Henley Gray	1	0	0	0	0	0	0	0	15	0	0	40	1,230
"	G. C. Spencer	8	0	0	0	0	0	0	1	1,817	0	0	2,908	15,755
"	**Total**	9	0	0	0	0	0	0	1	1,832	0	0	2,948	16,985
1978	Claude Ballot-Lena	4	0	0	0	0	0	0	0	460	0	0	1,186	7,770
"	Connie Saylor	3	0	0	0	0	0	0	1	820	0	0	1,237	9,115
"	**Total**	7	0	0	0	0	0	0	1	1,280	0	0	2,423	16,885

Year	Driver	Starts	Poles	Finish 1	2	3	4	5	6–10	Laps	Laps Led	Races Led	Miles	$

G. C. Spencer *continued*

Year	Driver	Starts	Poles	1	2	3	4	5	6–10	Laps	Laps Led	Races Led	Miles	$
1979	Claude Ballot-Lena	2	0	0	0	0	0	0	0	251	0	0	463	3,020
"	Connie Saylor	2	0	0	0	0	0	0	0	262	0	0	565	5,130
"	**Total**	4	0	0	0	0	0	0	0	513	0	0	1,028	8,150
1980	Gary Baker	1	0	0	0	0	0	0	0	145	0	0	386	3,440
"	Connie Saylor	5	0	0	0	0	0	0	0	1,171	5	2	1,729	10,285
"	**Total**	6	0	0	0	0	0	0	0	1,316	5	2	2,115	13,725
1981	Connie Saylor	7	0	0	0	0	0	0	0	1,267	0	0	2,139	18,715
1982	Connie Saylor	7	0	0	0	0	0	0	0	1,450	3	1	1,704	18,025
1983	Connie Saylor	0												1,200
Lifetime		452	1	0	7	8	16	20	88	84,184	126	12	72,047	$336,162

Speedy Spiers

Year	Driver	Starts	Poles	1	2	3	4	5	6–10	Laps	Laps Led	Races Led	Miles	$
1964	Larry Frank	1	0	0	0	0	0	0	0	35	0	0	18	100
Lifetime		1	0	0	0	0	0	0	0	35	0	0	18	$100

Ken Spikes

Year	Driver	Starts	Poles	1	2	3	4	5	6–10	Laps	Laps Led	Races Led	Miles	$
1964	Ken Spikes	6	0	0	0	0	0	0	1	1,018	0	0	1,570	3,100
"	Reb Wickersham	2	0	0	0	0	0	0	0	134	0	0	335	825
"	**Total**	8	0	0	0	0	0	0	1	1,152	0	0	1,905	3,925
1970	Roy Mayne	2	0	0	0	0	0	0	0	189	0	0	380	2,190
"	J. D. McDuffie	1	0	0	0	0	0	0	0	30	0	0	46	755
"	Ken Spikes	1	0	0	0	0	0	0	0	116	0	0	309	890
"	Jimmy Watson	1	0	0	0	0	0	0	0	451	0	0	247	505
"	**Total**	5	0	0	0	0	0	0	0	786	0	0	981	4,340
1971	Dub Simpson	1	0	0	0	0	0	0	0	48	0	0	120	255
"	Jimmy Watson	1	0	0	0	0	0	0	0	29	0	0	16	350
"	**Total**	2	0	0	0	0	0	0	0	77	0	0	136	605
Lifetime		15	0	0	0	0	0	0	1	2,015	0	0	3,022	$8,870

Ron Spohn

Year	Driver	Starts	Poles	1	2	3	4	5	6–10	Laps	Laps Led	Races Led	Miles	$
1979	Dick May	1	0	0	0	0	0	0	0	148	0	0	202	1,450
1980	Bruce Jacobi	1	0	0	0	0	0	0	0	189	0	0	378	985
"	Ralph Jones	2	0	0	0	0	0	0	0	547	0	0	780	3,495
"	**Total**	3	0	0	0	0	0	0	0	736	0	0	1,158	4,480
1983	Joe Booher	0												500
"	Glenn Jarrett	1	0	0	0	0	0	0	0	24	0	0	60	1,200
"	**Total**	1	0	0	0	0	0	0	0	24	0	0	60	1,700
1984	Ralph Jones	0												2,350
1985	Doug Heveron	1	0	0	0	0	0	0	0	194	0	0	485	2,555
"	Slick Johnson	5	0	0	0	0	0	0	0	1,433	0	0	1,890	13,785
"	Dean Roper	0												3,550
"	**Total**	6	0	0	0	0	0	0	0	1,627	0	0	2,375	19,890
1986	Connie Saylor	1	0	0	0	0	0	0	0	376	0	0	564	2,200
Lifetime		12	0	0	0	0	0	0	0	2,911	0	0	4,359	$32,070

Jim Stacy

Year	Driver	Starts	Poles	1	2	3	4	5	6–10	Laps	Laps Led	Races Led	Miles	$
1977	Neil Bonnett	12	3	2	0	1	0	0	2	3,029	446	7	3,260	69,075
"	Tom Sneva	1	0	0	0	0	0	0	0	194	0	0	291	1,150
"	**Total**	12	3	2	0	1	0	0	2	3,223	446	7	3,551	70,225
1978	Neil Bonnett	30	3	0	1	1	2	3	5	6,278	316	6	6,761	162,742
"	Ferrel Harris	2	0	0	0	0	0	0	2	380	0	0	980	17,250
"	**Total**	30	3	0	1	1	2	3	7	6,658	316	6	7,740	179,992
1979	Neil Bonnett	2	0	0	0	0	0	0	0	86	12	1	216	5,525
1980	Sterling Marlin	2	0	0	0	0	0	0	0	566	0	0	824	6,725
"	Joe Ruttman	1	0	0	0	0	0	0	0	29	0	0	73	1,055
"	**Total**	3	0	0	0	0	0	0	0	595	0	0	897	7,780
1981	Dale Earnhardt	4	0	0	0	0	0	0	1	770	10	3	1,142	34,300
"	Joe Ruttman	17	0	0	1	0	0	1	5	4,194	106	7	5,588	137,275
"	Bob Senneker	1	0	0	0	0	0	0	0	256	0	0	384	1,975
"	**Total**	19	0	0	1	0	0	1	6	5,220	116	10	7,115	173,550
1982	Rodney Combs	1	0	0	0	0	0	0	1	325	5	1	495	2,900
"	Robin McCall	2	0	0	0	0	0	0	0	154	0	0	308	2,395
"	Tim Richmond	25	1	2	2	0	1	2	5	6,722	321	13	8,132	175,160
"	Joe Ruttman	5	0	0	0	1	0	0	0	1,311	148	2	1,396	69,155

Year	Driver	Starts	Poles	Finish						Laps	Laps Led	Races Led	Miles	$
				1	2	3	4	5	6–10					

Jim Stacy *continued*

"	Jim Sauter	3	0	0	0	0	0	0	1	511	5	1	961	23,270
"	**Total**	30	1	2	2	1	1	2	7	9,023	479	16	11,292	272,880
1983	Rodney Combs	1	0	0	0	0	0	0	0	320	0	0	480	1,725
"	Mark Martin	7	0	0	0	1	0	0	1	2,123	1	1	2,279	75,240
"	Morgan Shepherd	23	0	0	1	1	1	0	10	6,251	5	4	7,582	285,476
"	**Total**	30	0	0	1	2	1	0	11	8,694	6	5	10,341	362,441
Lifetime		126	7	4	5	5	4	6	33	33,499	1,375	45	41,152	$1,072,393

Mark Stahl

1981	Mark Stahl	1	0	0	0	0	0	0	0	109	0	0	286	1,080
1982	Mark Stahl	1	0	0	0	0	0	0	0	85	0	0	223	2,690
1983	Mark Stahl	2	0	0	0	0	0	0	0	622	0	0	363	1,970
1984	Mark Stahl	3	0	0	0	0	0	0	0	842	0	0	892	6,985
1985	Mark Stahl	1	0	0	0	0	0	0	0	375	0	0	563	6,750
1986	Mark Stahl	3	0	0	0	0	0	0	0	719	0	0	889	7,290
1987	Mark Stahl	9	0	0	0	0	0	0	0	1,635	0	0	2,643	30,250
1988	Mark Stahl	1	0	0	0	0	0	0	0	233	0	0	237	2,815
1989	Mark Stahl	1	0	0	0	0	0	0	0	176	0	0	468	7,285
1990	Mark Stahl	5	0	0	0	0	0	0	0	1,268	0	0	1,890	19,770
1991	Mark Stahl	2	0	0	0	0	0	0	0	30	0	0	35	12,755
Lifetime		29	0	0	0	0	0	0	0	6,094	0	0	8,489	$99,640

Bill Stammer

1951	Bill Stammer	1	0	0	0	0	0	0	0		0	0		25
1954	Bill Stammer	2	0	0	0	0	0	0	0	631	0	0	316	75
1955	Bill Stammer	2	0	0	0	0	0	0	2	338	0	0	338	400
1956	Bill Stammer	2	0	0	0	0	0	0	0	131	0	0	241	140
Lifetime		7	0	0	0	0	0	0	2	1,100	0	0	894	$640

Dick Stanley

1960	Jim Whitman	5	0	0	0	0	0	0	0	567	0	0	1,055	1,450
Lifetime		5	0	0	0	0	0	0	0	567	0	0	1,055	$1,450

George Stark

1976	John Dineen	1	0	0	0	0	0	0	0	73	0	0	191	1,040
1977	John Dineen	1	0	0	0	0	0	0	0	89	0	0	233	1,400
Lifetime		2	0	0	0	0	0	0	0	162	0	0	424	$2,440

John Stark

1988	Larry Moyer	1	0	0	0	0	0	0	0	148	0	0	370	4,255
Lifetime		1	0	0	0	0	0	0	0	148	0	0	370	$4,255

Ralph Stark

1960	Bobby Johns	1	0	0	0	0	0	0	0	57	0	0	29	50
"	Herb Tillman	9	0	0	0	0	0	0	0	1,705	0	0	2,244	2,695
"	**Total**	10	0	0	0	0	0	0	0	1,762	0	0	2,273	2,745
1961	Bobby Allison	4	0	0	0	0	0	0	0	359	0	0	751	650
Lifetime		14	0	0	0	0	0	0	0	2,121	0	0	3,023	$3,395

Flo Starr

1969	Wilbur Pickett	1	0	0	0	0	0	0	0	92	0	0	245	1,250
Lifetime		1	0	0	0	0	0	0	0	92	0	0	245	$1,250

Stan Starr Jr.

1969	Stan Starr Jr.	1	0	0	0	0	0	0	0	82	0	0	218	1,200
Lifetime		1	0	0	0	0	0	0	0	82	0	0	218	$1,200

Stavola Brothers (Bill and Mickey Stavola, co-owners)

1983	Bobby Hillin Jr.	6	0	0	0	0	0	0	0	1,245	0	0	2,131	14,085
1984	Bobby Hillin Jr.	16	0	0	0	0	0	0	0	3,452	0	0	5,655	45,020

Year	Driver	Starts	Poles	Finish						Laps	Laps Led	Races Led	Miles	$
				1	2	3	4	5	6–10	Laps	Led	Led	Miles	$

Stavola Brothers *continued*

Year	Driver	Starts	Poles	1	2	3	4	5	6–10	Laps	Laps Led	Races Led	Miles	$
1985	Bobby Hillin Jr.	28	0	0	0	0	0	0	5	8,636	2	2	10,204	145,070
1986	Bobby Allison	29	0	1	2	1	1	1	9	8,391	127	11	9,928	503,095
"	Bobby Hillin Jr.	29	0	1	0	1	2	0	10	8,121	25	4	9,978	448,452
"	**Total**	29	0	2	2	2	3	1	19	16,512	152	13	19,906	951,547
1987	Bobby Allison	29	1	1	1	0	1	1	9	7,962	331	10	9,599	515,894
"	Bobby Hillin Jr.	29	0	0	0	0	0	1	3	6,889	1	1	8,559	346,735
"	**Total**	29	1	1	1	0	1	2	12	14,851	332	11	18,159	862,629
1988	Mike Alexander	16	0	0	0	1	0	1	4	4,677	51	5	6,004	191,620
"	Bobby Allison	13	0	1	1	0	0	1	3	4,303	104	4	4,762	409,925
"	Bobby Hillin Jr.	29	0	0	0	1	0	0	6	9,383	70	4	11,179	330,217
"	**Total**	29	0	1	1	2	0	2	13	18,363	225	12	21,945	931,132
1989	Mike Alexander	1	0	0	0	0	0	0	0	188	0	0	470	16,275
"	Bobby Hillin Jr.	28	0	0	0	0	0	1	6	8,377	26	4	10,296	283,181
"	Dick Trickle	28	0	0	0	3	1	2	3	8,504	80	8	10,075	343,728
"	**Total**	29	0	0	0	3	1	3	9	17,069	106	11	20,841	643,184
1990	Bobby Hillin Jr.	29	0	0	0	0	0	1	3	8,281	60	5	10,086	339,366
1991	Rick Wilson	29	0	0	0	0	0	0	0	7,966	10	1	9,694	241,375
1992	Dick Trickle	28	0	0	0	0	0	2	6	8,059	5	2	9,383	350,721
"	Rick Wilson	1	0	0	0	0	0	0	0	195	0	0	488	24,045
"	**Total**	29	0	0	0	0	0	2	6	8,254	5	2	9,870	374,766
1993	Sterling Marlin	30	0	0	1	0	0	0	7	9,153	341	6	11,221	628,835
1994	Jeff Burton	30	0	0	0	0	2	0	1	7,752	122	4	10,225	594,700
1995	Jeff Burton	29	0	0	0	0	0	1	1	8,050	4	2	10,193	628,270
1996	Hut Stricklin	31	0	0	1	0	0	0	0	8,620	163	3	10,632	631,055
Lifetime		373	1	4	6	7	7	12	76	138,204	1,522	72	170,762	$7,031,034

Johnny Steele

Year	Driver	Starts	Poles	1	2	3	4	5	6–10	Laps	Laps Led	Races Led	Miles	$
1965	Johnny Steele	1	0	0	0	0	0	0	0	16	0	0	43	500
1967	Johnny Steele	4	0	0	0	0	0	0	0	389	0	0	219	400
1969	Johnny Steele	1	0	0	0	0	0	0	0	3	0	0	8	750
1971	Johnny Steele	1	0	0	0	0	0	0	0	79	0	0	198	1,375
Lifetime		7	0	0	0	0	0	0	0	487	0	0	467	$3,025

Happy Steigel

Year	Driver	Starts	Poles	1	2	3	4	5	6–10	Laps	Laps Led	Races Led	Miles	$
1959	Charlie Cregar	3	0	0	0	0	0	0	0	496	0	0	725	560
"	Jim McGuirk	4	0	0	0	0	0	0	0	314	0	0	590	275
"	**Total**	7	0	0	0	0	0	0	0	810	0	0	1,315	835
1960	Dick Joslin	3	0	0	0	0	0	0	0	302	0	0	755	535
"	Elmo Langley	1	0	0	0	0	0	0	0	24	0	0	36	200
"	Steve McGrath	1	0	0	0	0	0	0	0	188	0	0	259	200
"	**Total**	5	0	0	0	0	0	0	0	514	0	0	1,050	935
1961	Elmo Langley	3	0	0	0	0	0	0	0	453	0	0	900	550
1962	Ralph Earnhardt	3	0	0	0	0	0	0	0	228	0	0	427	800
Lifetime		18	0	0	0	0	0	0	0	2,005	0	0	3,691	$3,120

Fred Steinbroner

Year	Driver	Starts	Poles	1	2	3	4	5	6–10	Laps	Laps Led	Races Led	Miles	$
1955	Fred Steinbroner	1	0	0	0	0	0	0	0	84	0	0	84	80
1956	Fred Steinbroner	1	0	0	0	0	0	0	0	72	0	0	180	40
Lifetime		2	0	0	0	0	0	0	0	156	0	0	264	$120

Lyle Stelter

Year	Driver	Starts	Poles	1	2	3	4	5	6–10	Laps	Laps Led	Races Led	Miles	$
1960	Lyle Stelter	2	0	0	0	0	0	0	0	130	0	0	164	160
1961	Larry Frank	1	0	0	0	0	0	0	0	10	0	0	15	225
1963	Elmo Langley	1	0	0	0	0	0	0	0	314	0	0	471	400
"	Lyle Stelter	2	0	0	0	0	0	0	0	304	0	0	85	175
"	LeeRoy Yarbrough	3	1	0	0	0	0	0	2	430	8	1	232	390
"	**Total**	6	1	0	0	0	0	0	2	1,048	8	1	788	965
1964	Tiny Lund	5	0	0	0	0	0	0	3	768	0	0	423	1,685
1965	Tiny Lund	27	0	1	1	1	3	1	7	3,871	209	2	2,702	10,100
1966	Fats Caruso	1	0	0	0	0	0	0	0	167	0	0	56	130
"	Paul Connors	1	0	0	0	0	0	0	0	38	0	0	95	100
"	Paul Dean Holt	4	0	0	0	0	0	0	0	213	0	0	87	475
"	Tiny Lund	26	1	1	2	1	0	1	4	3,564	654	6	2,490	8,685
"	Harold Smith	2	0	0	0	0	1	0	0	627	0	0	848	3,270

Year	Driver	Starts	Poles	Finish						Laps	Laps Led	Races Led	Miles	$
				1	2	3	4	5	6–10					

Lyle Stelter *continued*

Year	Driver	Starts	Poles	1	2	3	4	5	6–10	Laps	Laps Led	Races Led	Miles	$
"	Lyle Stelter	2	0	0	0	0	0	0	0	38	0	0	35	0
"	**Total**	33	1	1	2	1	1	1	4	4,647	654	6	3,611	12,660
1967	Tiny Lund	10	0	0	0	0	0	1	1	1,564	35	2	1,008	3,210
1968	Serge Adams	1	0	0	0	0	0	0	0	24	0	0	33	535
"	Tommy Gale	1	0	0	0	0	0	0	0	172	0	0	172	760
"	Jim Hurtubise	3	0	0	0	0	0	0	1	495	0	0	895	2,365
"	Tiny Lund	2	0	0	0	1	0	1	0	686	0	0	360	1,550
"	Tom Pistone	2	0	0	0	0	0	0	1	354	0	0	153	300
"	Harold Smith	1	0	0	0	0	0	0	0	244	0	0	366	1,850
"	LeeRoy Yarbrough	6	0	0	0	1	0	1	1	869	0	0	422	1,125
"	**Total**	16	0	0	0	2	0	2	3	2,844	0	0	2,400	8,485
1969	Gerald Chamberlain	2	0	0	0	0	0	0	1	324	0	0	453	2,225
"	Ed Hessert	2	0	0	0	0	0	0	0	100	0	0	50	870
"	Eldon Yarbrough	1	0	0	0	0	0	1	0	194	0	0	97	325
"	LeeRoy Yarbrough	1	0	0	0	0	0	0	0	316	0	0	158	225
"	**Total**	6	0	0	0	0	0	1	1	934	0	0	758	3,645
Lifetime		106	2	2	3	4	4	6	21	15,816	906	11	11,870	$41,135

I. D. Stenstrom

Year	Driver	Starts	Poles	1	2	3	4	5	6–10	Laps	Laps Led	Races Led	Miles	$
1951	Bob Johnson	1	0	0	0	0	0	0	0	214	0	0	268	0
Lifetime		1	0	0	0	0	0	0	0	214	0	0	268	$0

Jim Stephens

Year	Driver	Starts	Poles	1	2	3	4	5	6–10	Laps	Laps Led	Races Led	Miles	$
1956	Don Carr	5	0	0	0	0	0	0	0	499	0	0	364	210
"	Tim Flock	1	0	0	0	0	1	0	0	197	0	0	99	365
"	Junior Johnson	1	0	0	0	0	0	0	0	64	0	0	64	50
"	Pat Kirkwood	2	0	0	0	1	0	0	0	368	0	0	451	1,475
"	Ed Kretz	1	0	0	0	0	0	0	0	0	0	0	0	0
"	Jimmie Lewallen	1	0	0	0	0	0	0	0	15	0	0	15	0
"	Cotton Owens	6	0	0	0	0	0	1	2	827	0	0	505	770
"	**Total**	10	0	0	0	1	1	1	2	1,970	0	0	1,498	2,870
1958	Joe Eubanks	7	0	1	0	0	1	0	1	956	38	2	737	2,055
"	Cotton Owens	27	2	1	4	2	1	0	9	3,559	241	5	2,124	6,479
"	**Total**	28	2	2	4	2	2	0	10	4,515	279	6	2,861	8,534
1959	Fireball Roberts	5	3	1	0	0	0	0	2	609	147	3	997	10,180
1960	Bobby Johns	4	0	0	2	0	1	0	0	491	23	2	1,029	11,565
1961	Fireball Roberts	13	6	1	3	2	1	1	1	3,100	639	9	3,593	36,365
1962	Fireball Roberts	11	7	2	2	0	0	0	2	2,127	510	6	2,111	47,227
1963	Bunkie Blackburn	2	0	0	0	0	0	0	1	57	0	0	143	700
Lifetime		73	18	6	11	5	5	2	18	12,869	1,598	26	12,232	$117,441

Glenn Steurer

Year	Driver	Starts	Poles	1	2	3	4	5	6–10	Laps	Laps Led	Races Led	Miles	$
1985	Glenn Steurer	2	0	0	0	0	0	0	0	211	0	0	553	6,850
1986	Glenn Steurer	2	0	0	0	0	0	0	1	210	0	0	550	10,755
1987	Glenn Steurer	1	0	0	0	0	0	0	0	19	0	0	50	925
Lifetime		5	0	0	0	0	0	0	1	440	0	0	1,153	$18,530

Cliff Stewart

Year	Driver	Starts	Poles	1	2	3	4	5	6–10	Laps	Laps Led	Races Led	Miles	$
1962	Thomas Cox	6	0	0	0	0	0	1	2	1,370	0	0	605	1,970
"	Bill Foster	5	0	0	0	0	0	0	1	1,230	0	0	740	800
"	Tiny Lund	2	0	0	0	0	0	0	0	445	0	0	668	825
"	Jim Paschal	29	0	1	3	3	3	2	3	4,627	34	3	3,153	11,618
"	Ken Rush	1	0	0	0	0	0	0	0	463	0	0	232	150
"	Bob Welborn	1	0	0	0	0	0	0	0	1	0	0	3	275
"	**Total**	43	0	1	3	3	3	3	6	8,136	34	3	5,399	15,638
1963	Buddy Baker	3	0	0	0	0	0	0	1	615	0	0	456	1,175
"	Curtis Crider	1	0	0	0	0	0	0	0	93	0	0	31	65
"	Bill Foster	10	0	0	0	0	0	0	2	1,628	0	0	1,049	1,410
"	Fred Harb	4	0	0	0	0	1	0	0	365	0	0	175	580
"	Jimmy Pardue	3	0	0	0	0	0	0	1	579	0	0	528	825
"	Jim Paschal	1	0	0	0	0	0	0	0	32	0	0	8	100
"	Larry Thomas	1	0	0	0	0	0	0	0	157	0	0	236	300
"	Joe Weatherly	10	0	0	1	1	0	0	3	1,308	0	0	471	3,800

Year	Driver	Starts	Poles	Finish 1	2	3	4	5	6–10	Laps	Laps Led	Races Led	Miles	$

Cliff Stewart *continued*

Year	Driver	Starts	Poles	1	2	3	4	5	6–10	Laps	Laps Led	Races Led	Miles	$
"	Bob Welborn	1	0	0	0	0	0	0	0	4	0	0	6	500
"	**Total**	34	0	0	1	1	1	0	7	4,781	0	0	2,959	8,755
1964	Doug Cooper	1	0	0	0	0	0	0	0	57	0	0	29	50
"	Fred Harb	2	0	0	0	0	0	1	0	362	0	0	91	375
"	Jimmy Pardue	2	0	0	0	0	0	0	1	138	0	0	399	1,850
"	Ken Rush	8	0	0	0	0	1	0	1	768	0	0	398	1,640
"	G. C. Spencer	2	0	0	0	0	0	0	0	63	0	0	158	825
"	Reb Wickersham	1	0	0	0	0	0	0	0	10	0	0	25	450
"	**Total**	16	0	0	0	0	1	1	2	1,398	0	0	1,098	5,190
1965	Fred Harb	5	0	0	0	0	0	1	1	766	0	0	291	840
"	T. C. Hunt	1	0	0	0	0	0	0	0	214	0	0	321	550
"	G. C. Spencer	1	0	0	0	0	0	0	0	29	0	0	26	100
"	**Total**	7	0	0	0	0	0	1	1	1,009	0	0	638	1,490
1971	Jim Paschal	5	0	0	0	2	0	0	1	1,360	50	2	574	2,165
1976	Darrell Bryant	8	0	0	0	0	0	0	1	1,678	0	0	2,105	11,775
1981	Joe Millikan	11	0	0	0	1	0	2	2	3,718	0	0	3,692	76,795
"	Morgan Shepherd	18	1	1	0	0	2	0	5	4,875	371	3	5,172	138,023
"	**Total**	29	1	1	0	1	2	2	7	8,593	371	3	8,864	214,818
1982	Geoff Bodine	24	2	0	0	1	2	1	6	6,515	118	6	7,932	244,300
"	Joe Millikan	6	0	0	0	0	0	0	2	1,788	5	1	1,702	55,210
"	**Total**	30	2	0	0	1	2	1	8	8,303	123	7	9,634	299,510
1983	Donnie Allison	2	0	0	0	0	0	0	0	138	0	0	339	6,375
"	Geoff Bodine	28	1	0	1	0	2	2	4	7,042	490	13	7,328	209,611
"	**Total**	30	1	0	1	0	2	2	4	7,180	490	13	7,666	215,986
1984	Rusty Wallace	30	0	0	0	0	1	1	2	8,868	11	7	10,024	201,739
1985	Rusty Wallace	28	0	0	0	0	0	2	6	7,271	28	1	8,376	233,670
1986	Kirk Bryant	4	0	0	0	0	0	0	0	842	0	0	978	26,335
Lifetime		264	4	2	5	8	12	13	45	59,419	1,107	36	58,315	$1,237,071

Pete Stewart

Year	Driver	Starts	Poles	1	2	3	4	5	6–10	Laps	Laps Led	Races Led	Miles	$
1954	Pete Stewart	1	0	0	0	0	0	0	0	77	0	0	39	0
1963	Perk Brown	1	0	0	0	0	0	0	1	192	0	0	48	165
"	Ralph Earnhardt	1	0	0	0	0	0	0	0	59	0	0	89	450
"	Bobby Keck	7	0	0	0	0	0	0	2	883	0	0	429	1,330
"	Jimmy Pardue	44	1	1	0	1	2	1	10	7,885	74	3	5,914	17,574
"	Pete Stewart	2	0	0	0	0	0	0	0	78	0	0	109	150
"	Joe Weatherly	1	0	0	0	0	0	0	0	23	0	0	9	250
"	**Total**	47	1	1	0	1	2	1	13	9,120	74	3	6,598	19,919
1964	Pete Stewart	1	0	0	0	0	0	0	0	1	0	0	2	600
Lifetime		49	1	1	0	1	2	1	13	9,198	74	3	6,638	$20,519

Ernie Stierly

Year	Driver	Starts	Poles	1	2	3	4	5	6–10	Laps	Laps Led	Races Led	Miles	$
1976	Ernie Stierly	1	0	0	0	0	0	0	0	21	0	0	55	765
1977	Ernie Stierly	2	0	0	0	0	0	0	0	137	0	0	352	1,805
1978	Ernie Stierly	2	0	0	0	0	0	0	0	141	0	0	369	2,520
Lifetime		5	0	0	0	0	0	0	0	299	0	0	777	$5,090

Paul Stockwell

Year	Driver	Starts	Poles	1	2	3	4	5	6–10	Laps	Laps Led	Races Led	Miles	$
1971	Bob Kauf	2	0	0	0	0	0	0	0	64	0	0	168	1,675
1972	Bob Kauf	2	0	0	0	0	0	0	0	178	0	0	445	2,500
1973	Bob Kauf	1	0	0	0	0	0	0	0	9	0	0	24	1,015
Lifetime		5	0	0	0	0	0	0	0	251	0	0	637	$5,190

Fred Stoke

Year	Driver	Starts	Poles	1	2	3	4	5	6–10	Laps	Laps Led	Races Led	Miles	$
1984	Ruben Garcia	2	0	0	0	0	0	0	0	121	0	0	317	1,885
1985	Blair Aiken	2	0	0	0	0	0	0	0	135	0	0	354	2,020
"	Ruben Garcia	2	0	0	0	0	0	0	0	196	0	0	514	6,525
"	**Total**	2	0	0	0	0	0	0	0	331	0	0	867	8,545
1986	Ruben Garcia	2	0	0	0	0	0	0	0	169	0	0	443	4,530
"	Ted Kennedy	2	0	0	0	0	0	0	0	172	0	0	451	3,255
"	**Total**	2	0	0	0	0	0	0	0	341	0	0	893	7,785
1987	Derrike Cope	11	0	0	0	0	0	0	0	1,631	0	0	1,977	30,750
"	Ruben Garcia	2	0	0	0	0	0	0	0	116	0	0	304	4,180
"	**Total**	12	0	0	0	0	0	0	0	1,747	0	0	2,281	34,930

Year	Driver	Starts	Poles	Finish						Laps	Laps Led	Races Led	Miles	$
				1	2	3	4	5	6–10					

Fred Stoke *continued*

Year	Driver	Starts	Poles	1	2	3	4	5	6–10	Laps	Laps Led	Races Led	Miles	$
1988	Ruben Garcia	1	0	0	0	0	0	0	0	27	0	0	71	3,380
"	Chad Little	4	0	0	0	0	0	0	0	1,089	3	1	1,435	14,225
"	**Total**	4	0	0	0	0	0	0	0	1,116	3	1	1,505	17,605
1989	Bill Cooper	1	0	0	0	0	0	0	0	61	0	0	154	2,360
Lifetime		23	0	0	0	0	0	0	0	3,717	3	1	6,018	$73,110

Gene Stokes

Year	Driver	Starts	Poles	1	2	3	4	5	6–10	Laps	Laps Led	Races Led	Miles	$
1961	Gene Stokes	2	0	0	0	0	0	0	0	96	0	0	144	250
1962	Frank Sessoms	2	0	0	0	0	0	0	0	319	0	0	160	185
Lifetime		4	0	0	0	0	0	0	0	415	0	0	304	$435

Mike Stolarcyk

Year	Driver	Starts	Poles	1	2	3	4	5	6–10	Laps	Laps Led	Races Led	Miles	$
1985	Mike Stolarcyk	1	0	0	0	0	0	0	0	116	0	0	290	1,615
Lifetime		1	0	0	0	0	0	0	0	116	0	0	290	$1,615

Charlie Stone

Year	Driver	Starts	Poles	1	2	3	4	5	6–10	Laps	Laps Led	Races Led	Miles	$
1958	Charlie Stone	1	0	0	0	0	0	0	0	35	0	0	144	100
Lifetime		1	0	0	0	0	0	0	0	35	0	0	144	$100

Ramo Stott

Year	Driver	Starts	Poles	1	2	3	4	5	6–10	Laps	Laps Led	Races Led	Miles	$
1967	Ramo Stott	3	0	0	0	0	0	0	1	588	0	0	1,082	3,335
1969	Ramo Stott	2	0	0	0	0	0	0	1	187	0	0	468	1,735
1970	Ramo Stott	3	0	0	0	0	0	0	3	424	2	1	1,089	4,875
1971	Ramo Stott	3	0	0	0	0	0	0	1	476	0	0	1,075	3,715
Lifetime		11	0	0	0	0	0	0	6	1,675	2	1	3,713	$13,660

Ron Stotten

Year	Driver	Starts	Poles	1	2	3	4	5	6–10	Laps	Laps Led	Races Led	Miles	$
1966	Don Biederman	14	0	0	0	0	0	0	0	2,169	0	0	1,285	2,215
1967	Don Biederman	20	0	0	0	0	0	0	1	2,413	0	0	1,844	4,935
"	Wendell Scott	1	0	0	0	0	0	0	0	298	0	0	149	330
"	**Total**	21	0	0	0	0	0	0	1	2,711	0	0	1,993	5,265
1968	Don Biederman	1	0	0	0	0	0	0	0	129	0	0	65	100
Lifetime		36	0	0	0	0	0	0	1	5,009	0	0	3,343	$7,580

Al Straub

Year	Driver	Starts	Poles	1	2	3	4	5	6–10	Laps	Laps Led	Races Led	Miles	$
1969	Doug Easton	1	0	0	0	0	0	0	0	0	0	0	0	875
"	Al Straub	1	0	0	0	0	0	0	0	9	0	0	24	950
"	**Total**	1	0	0	0	0	0	0	0	9	0	0	24	1,825
1971	Al Straub	1	0	0	0	0	0	0	0	48	0	0	22	300
Lifetime		2	0	0	0	0	0	0	0	57	0	0	46	$2,125

John Strauser

Year	Driver	Starts	Poles	1	2	3	4	5	6–10	Laps	Laps Led	Races Led	Miles	$
1992	Hershel McGriff	1	0	0	0	0	0	0	0	19	0	0	48	4,725
1993	Mike Chase	1	0	0	0	0	0	0	0	87	0	0	87	6,015
"	Hershel McGriff	1	0	0	0	0	0	0	0	27	0	0	68	6,560
"	**Total**	2	0	0	0	0	0	0	0	114	0	0	155	12,575
1994	Mike Chase	3	0	0	0	0	0	0	0	463	0	0	706	36,090
1995	Wally Dallenbach Jr.	1	0	0	0	0	0	0	0	41	0	0	103	9,760
"	Ron Hornaday Jr.	1	0	0	0	0	0	0	0	307	0	0	307	9,660
"	**Total**	2	0	0	0	0	0	0	0	348	0	0	410	19,420
Lifetime		8	0	0	0	0	0	0	0	944	0	0	1,319	$72,810

Frank Strickland

Year	Driver	Starts	Poles	1	2	3	4	5	6–10	Laps	Laps Led	Races Led	Miles	$
1958	Fireball Roberts	8	0	6	1	0	0	0	0	2,354	877	7	1,946	31,569
Lifetime		8	0	6	1	0	0	0	0	2,354	877	7	1,946	$31,569

Bub Strickler

Year	Driver	Starts	Poles	1	2	3	4	5	6–10	Laps	Laps Led	Races Led	Miles	$
1966	Bob Derrington	2	0	0	0	0	0	0	0	38	0	0	95	1,110
1970	Bub Strickler	1	0	0	0	0	0	0	0	316	0	0	198	455

Year	Driver	Starts	Poles	Finish 1	2	3	4	5	6–10	Laps	Laps Led	Races Led	Miles	$

Bub Strickler *continued*

Year	Driver	Starts	Poles	1	2	3	4	5	6–10	Laps	Laps Led	Races Led	Miles	$
"	Jim Vandiver	1	0	0	0	0	0	0	0	285	0	0	156	455
"	**Total**	2	0	0	0	0	0	0	0	601	0	0	354	910
1971	Bub Strickler	1	0	0	0	0	0	0	0	1	0	0	3	1,000
1980	Bub Strickler	1	0	0	0	0	0	0	0	367	0	0	199	1,705
Lifetime		6	0	0	0	0	0	0	0	1,007	0	0	650	$4,725

Doug Stringer

Year	Driver	Starts	Poles	1	2	3	4	5	6–10	Laps	Laps Led	Races Led	Miles	$
1992	Bob Schacht	2	0	0	0	0	0	0	0	445	0	0	670	8,855
1993	Bob Schacht	2	0	0	0	0	0	0	0	252	0	0	345	12,725
Lifetime		4	0	0	0	0	0	0	0	697	0	0	1,015	$21,580

W. S. Strong

Year	Driver	Starts	Poles	1	2	3	4	5	6–10	Laps	Laps Led	Races Led	Miles	$
1969	Dub Simpson	11	0	0	0	0	0	0	0	2,187	0	0	1,974	8,350
1970	Dave Marcis	1	0	0	0	0	0	0	0	70	0	0	35	235
"	Dub Simpson	6	0	0	0	0	0	0	1	1,155	0	0	1,111	4,510
"	**Total**	7	0	0	0	0	0	0	1	1,225	0	0	1,146	4,745
1971	Dub Simpson	7	0	0	0	0	0	0	0	453	0	0	284	2,740
1972	Dub Simpson	5	0	0	0	0	0	0	0	563	0	0	637	3,525
"	Jim Vandiver	1	0	0	0	0	0	0	0	66	0	0	35	250
"	**Total**	6	0	0	0	0	0	0	0	629	0	0	672	3,775
1973	Richard Brown	1	0	0	0	0	0	0	0	349	0	0	189	425
"	Vic Parsons	1	0	0	0	0	0	0	0	108	0	0	108	540
"	**Total**	2	0	0	0	0	0	0	0	457	0	0	297	965
1974	Jack Donohue	1	0	0	0	0	0	0	0	238	0	0	142	375
"	Bobby Fleming	1	0	0	0	0	0	0	0	53	0	0	28	500
"	Jerry Hufflin	2	0	0	0	0	0	0	0	262	0	0	155	900
"	Dick Simpson	1	0	0	0	0	0	0	0	157	0	0	94	340
"	**Total**	5	0	0	0	0	0	0	0	710	0	0	419	2,115
Lifetime		38	0	0	0	0	0	0	1	5,661	0	0	4,792	$22,690

Bill Stroppe

Year	Driver	Starts	Poles	1	2	3	4	5	6–10	Laps	Laps Led	Races Led	Miles	$
1955	Johnny Mantz	1	0	0	0	0	0	0	1	102	0	0	102	185
1956	Fonty Flock	1	0	0	0	0	0	0	0	117	0	0	161	80
"	Tim Flock	1	0	1	0	0	0	0	0	63	17	1	258	2,950
"	Bob Korf	1	0	0	0	0	0	0	1		0	0		400
"	Johnny Mantz	1	0	0	0	1	0	0	0	79	0	0	198	1,130
"	Billy Myers	40	1	2	6	2	1	1	8	5,880	103	4	4,055	15,255
"	Bobby Myers	4	0	0	0	0	0	0	0	263	0	0	355	200
"	Jim Paschal	2	0	0	0	0	1	0	1	650	102	2	784	2,800
"	**Total**	42	1	3	6	3	2	1	10	7,052	222	7	5,811	22,815
1957	Fonty Flock	1	0	0	0	1	0	0	0		0	0		1,500
"	Tim Flock	1	0	0	0	0	0	0	0		0	0		135
"	Billy Myers	16	0	0	0	0	2	0	1	1,899	201	1	1,149	2,875
"	Jim Paschal	15	0	0	0	1	1	2	4	2,236	0	0	1,197	2,650
"	**Total**	17	0	0	0	2	3	2	5	4,135	201	1	2,346	7,160
1958	Tim Flock	1	0	0	0	0	0	0	0	3	0	0	12	0
1962	Troy Ruttman	1	0	0	0	0	0	1	0	218	0	0	327	1,750
1963	Chuck Daigh	1	0	0	0	0	0	0	0	37	0	0	93	75
"	Darel Dieringer	14	0	1	0	1	2	1	6	4,011	84	3	4,791	28,320
"	Larry Frank	2	0	0	0	0	0	0	0	476	0	0	695	850
"	Whitey Gerkin	1	0	0	0	0	0	0	0	23	0	0	58	75
"	Junior Johnson	1	0	0	0	0	0	1	0	145	0	0	392	1,300
"	Parnelli Jones	4	0	0	0	0	0	0	1	444	39	1	993	2,000
"	Troy Ruttman	5	0	0	0	1	0	0	2	796	0	0	1,699	6,430
"	G. C. Spencer	3	0	0	0	0	0	0	2	803	1	1	1,354	3,100
"	Rodger Ward	2	0	0	0	0	0	0	0	251	0	0	386	325
"	**Total**	16	0	1	0	2	2	2	11	6,986	124	5	10,458	42,475
1964	Johnny Allen	2	0	0	0	0	0	0	0	239	0	0	299	925
"	Chuck Daigh	1	0	0	0	0	0	0	0	62	0	0	167	500
"	Darel Dieringer	11	0	0	0	0	1	2	2	2,166	27	2	2,753	9,515
"	Parnelli Jones	4	0	0	0	0	0	0	1	202	9	1	502	2,110
"	Dave MacDonald	4	0	0	0	0	0	0	2	523	0	0	1,185	2,450
"	Jim McElreath	3	0	0	0	0	0	0	0	336	0	0	667	1,350
"	Rodger Ward	1	0	0	0	0	0	0	0	24	0	0	65	525

Year	Driver	Starts	Poles	Finish 1	2	3	4	5	6–10	Laps	Laps Led	Races Led	Miles	$

Bill Stroppe *continued*

Year	Driver	Starts	Poles	1	2	3	4	5	6–10	Laps	Laps Led	Races Led	Miles	$
"	Joe Weatherly	1	0	0	0	0	1	0	0	137	0	0	411	2,650
"	**Total**	12	0	0	0	0	2	2	5	3,689	36	3	6,048	20,025
1965	Parnelli Jones	1	0	0	0	0	0	0	0	37	36	1	100	980
1967	Curtis Turner	1	0	0	0	0	0	0	0	15	0	0	41	550
1968	Parnelli Jones	1	0	0	0	1	0	0	0	186	49	1	502	5,600
Lifetime		93	1	4	6	8	9	8	32	22,423	668	18	25,746	$101,540

D. Wayne Strout

Year	Driver	Starts	Poles	1	2	3	4	5	6–10	Laps	Laps Led	Races Led	Miles	$
1987	D. Wayne Strout	1	0	0	0	0	0	0	0	381	0	0	381	1,700
Lifetime		1	0	0	0	0	0	0	0	381	0	0	381	$1,700

M. J. Sullivan

Year	Driver	Starts	Poles	1	2	3	4	5	6–10	Laps	Laps Led	Races Led	Miles	$
1987	Ken Bouchard	1	0	0	0	0	0	0	0	158	0	0	316	2,075
Lifetime		1	0	0	0	0	0	0	0	158	0	0	316	$2,075

Lem Svajian

Year	Driver	Starts	Poles	1	2	3	4	5	6–10	Laps	Laps Led	Races Led	Miles	$
1956	Tommy Herbert	1	0	0	0	0	0	0	0		0	0		0
1957	Lem Svajian	1	0	0	0	0	0	0	0		0	0		50
Lifetime		2	0	0	0	0	0	0	0		0	0		$50

Dale Swanson

Year	Driver	Starts	Poles	1	2	3	4	5	6–10	Laps	Laps Led	Races Led	Miles	$
1960	Johnny Beauchamp	9	0	1	1	0	0	1	2	2,567	1	1	2,441	15,431
1961	Johnny Beauchamp	1	0	0	0	0	0	0	0	37	0	0	93	75
Lifetime		10	0	1	1	0	0	1	2	2,604	1	1	2,533	$15,506

Glenn Sweet

Year	Driver	Starts	Poles	1	2	3	4	5	6–10	Laps	Laps Led	Races Led	Miles	$
1965	Danny Byrd	4	0	0	0	0	0	1	0	294	0	0	210	1,075
"	Tom Pistone	21	0	0	1	0	0	2	3	2,625	0	0	1,425	6,955
"	**Total**	24	0	0	1	0	0	3	3	2,919	0	0	1,635	8,030
1966	Tom Pistone	1	0	0	0	0	0	0	0	265	0	0	133	150
Lifetime		25	0	0	1	0	0	3	3	3,184	0	0	1,767	$8,180

Ken Swihart

Year	Driver	Starts	Poles	1	2	3	4	5	6–10	Laps	Laps Led	Races Led	Miles	$
1951	Ed Benedict	5	0	0	0	0	0	0	1	445	0	0	538	275
1952	Ed Benedict	3	0	0	0	0	0	1	1	511	0	0	305	325
"	Chuck Mahoney	1	0	0	0	0	0	0	0		0	0		25
"	Bucky Sager	9	0	0	0	0	1	0	2	1,403	0	0	891	710
"	Johnny Thompson	1	0	0	0	0	0	0	0		0	0		25
"	**Total**	13	0	0	0	0	1	1	3	1,914	0	0	1,195	1,085
1953	Ed Benedict	1	0	0	0	0	0	0	1	189	0	0	95	125
Lifetime		19	0	0	0	0	1	1	5	2,548	0	0	1,827	$1,485

Robert Switzer

Year	Driver	Starts	Poles	1	2	3	4	5	6–10	Laps	Laps Led	Races Led	Miles	$
1977	Joe Ruttman	1	0	0	0	0	0	0	0	196	0	0	490	2,035
1980	Robert Switzer	0												725
Lifetime		1	0	0	0	0	0	0	0	196	0	0	490	$2,760

G. T. Tallas

Year	Driver	Starts	Poles	1	2	3	4	5	6–10	Laps	Laps Led	Races Led	Miles	$
1970	G. T. Tallas	2	0	0	0	0	0	0	0	139	0	0	364	1,585
1971	G. T. Tallas	2	0	0	0	0	0	0	0	189	0	0	491	2,490
1972	G. T. Tallas	1	0	0	0	0	0	0	0	88	0	0	220	1,620
1975	G. T. Tallas	1	0	0	0	0	0	0	0	28	0	0	73	1,170
Lifetime		6	0	0	0	0	0	0	0	444	0	0	1,149	$6,865

Frank Tanner

Year	Driver	Starts	Poles	1	2	3	4	5	6–10	Laps	Laps Led	Races Led	Miles	$
1964	Frank Tanner	3	0	0	0	0	0	0	0	7	0	0	6	200
Lifetime		3	0	0	0	0	0	0	0	7	0	0	6	$200

Year	Driver	Starts	Poles	Finish 1	2	3	4	5	6–10	Laps	Laps Led	Races Led	Miles	$

Dr. Don Tarr

Year	Driver	Starts	Poles	1	2	3	4	5	6–10	Laps	Laps Led	Races Led	Miles	$
1968	Don Tarr	11	0	0	0	0	0	0	0	1,699	0	0	2,052	5,825
"	Frank Warren	4	0	0	0	0	0	0	0	243	0	0	70	400
"	**Total**	15	0	0	0	0	0	0	0	1,942	0	0	2,122	6,225
1969	Earl Brooks	3	0	0	0	0	0	0	0	560	0	0	566	2,045
"	J. D. McDuffie	2	0	0	0	0	0	0	0	354	0	0	347	1,405
"	Ed Negre	2	0	0	0	0	0	0	0	24	0	0	47	1,870
"	Dick Poling	4	0	0	0	0	0	0	0	410	0	0	688	1,892
"	Don Tarr	6	0	0	0	0	0	0	0	594	0	0	1,001	3,465
"	Frank Warren	9	0	0	0	0	0	0	1	1,166	0	0	795	2,570
"	**Total**	26	0	0	0	0	0	0	1	3,108	0	0	3,444	13,247
1970	James Sears	1	0	0	0	0	0	0	1	193	0	0	97	275
"	Don Tarr	16	0	0	0	0	0	0	4	2,314	5	1	3,023	14,542
"	**Total**	17	0	0	0	0	0	0	5	2,507	5	1	3,119	14,817
1971	G. C. Spencer	1	0	0	0	0	0	0	0	209	0	0	115	415
"	Don Tarr	2	0	0	0	0	0	0	0	297	0	0	245	1,060
"	**Total**	3	0	0	0	0	0	0	0	506	0	0	359	1,475
1972	J. D. McDuffie	1	0	0	0	0	0	1	0	466	0	0	248	1,300
Lifetime		62	0	0	0	0	0	1	6	8,529	5	1	9,293	$37,064

Robert Tartaglia

Year	Driver	Starts	Poles	1	2	3	4	5	6–10	Laps	Laps Led	Races Led	Miles	$
1981	Robert Tartaglia	1	0	0	0	0	0	0	0	4	0	0	10	500
Lifetime		1	0	0	0	0	0	0	0	4	0	0	10	$500

Al Tasnady

Year	Driver	Starts	Poles	1	2	3	4	5	6–10	Laps	Laps Led	Races Led	Miles	$
1960	Al Tasnady	1	0	0	0	0	0	0	0	172	0	0	86	110
Lifetime		1	0	0	0	0	0	0	0	172	0	0	86	$110

Acey Taylor

Year	Driver	Starts	Poles	1	2	3	4	5	6–10	Laps	Laps Led	Races Led	Miles	$
1963	Curtis Crider	1	0	0	0	0	0	0	0	205	0	0	282	450
"	Ralph Earnhardt	3	0	0	0	0	0	0	0	344	0	0	557	975
"	**Total**	4	0	0	0	0	0	0	0	549	0	0	839	1,425
Lifetime		4	0	0	0	0	0	0	0	549	0	0	839	$1,425

Jesse James Taylor

Year	Driver	Starts	Poles	1	2	3	4	5	6–10	Laps	Laps Led	Races Led	Miles	$
1950	Jesse James Taylor	1	0	0	0	0	0	0	0	329	0	0	411	0
1951	Jesse James Taylor	10	0	0	1	0	0	0	2	519	104	3	566	3,750
1956	Jesse James Taylor	3	0	0	0	0	0	0	0	269	0	0	186	250
1958	Jesse James Taylor	1	0	0	0	0	0	0	0	95	0	0	131	100
Lifetime		15	0	0	1	0	0	0	2	1,212	104	3	1,294	$4,100

T. W. Taylor

Year	Driver	Starts	Poles	1	2	3	4	5	6–10	Laps	Laps Led	Races Led	Miles	$
1993	T. W. Taylor	3	0	0	0	0	0	0	0	280	1	1	391	21,605
1994	Derrike Cope	2	0	0	0	0	0	0	0	356	0	0	890	35,110
"	Randy LaJoie	1	0	0	0	0	0	0	0	318	0	0	484	8,575
"	Curtis Markham	1	0	0	0	0	0	0	0	32	0	0	49	8,325
"	Jeremy Mayfield	4	0	0	0	0	0	0	0	1,046	0	0	1,694	40,145
"	Jeff Purvis	1	0	0	0	0	0	0	0	139	0	0	278	8,715
"	**Total**	9	0	0	0	0	0	0	0	1,891	0	0	3,394	100,870
1995	T. W. Taylor	0												2,700
Lifetime		12	0	0	0	0	0	0	0	2,171	1	1	3,785	$125,175

W. O. Taylor

Year	Driver	Starts	Poles	1	2	3	4	5	6–10	Laps	Laps Led	Races Led	Miles	$
1949	Tommy Coates	1	0	0	0	0	0	0	0	167	0	0	167	50
"	Al Keller	1	0	0	0	0	0	0	1	185	0	0	185	200
"	**Total**	1	0	0	0	0	0	0	1	352	0	0	352	250
1950	Al Keller	1	0	0	0	0	0	0	0	44	0	0	183	50
1955	Larry Flynn	1	0	0	0	0	0	1	0	359	0	0	494	1,175
Lifetime		3	0	0	0	0	0	1	1	755	0	0	1,029	$1,475

Kerry Teague

Year	Driver	Starts	Poles	1	2	3	4	5	6–10	Laps	Laps Led	Races Led	Miles	$
1992	Kerry Teague	1	0	0	0	0	0	0	0	122	0	0	305	22,445
Lifetime		1	0	0	0	0	0	0	0	122	0	0	305	$22,445

Year	Driver	Starts	Poles	Finish						Laps	Laps Led	Races Led	Miles	$
				1	2	3	4	5	6–10					

Marshall Teague

Year	Driver	Starts	Poles	1	2	3	4	5	6–10	Laps	Laps Led	Races Led	Miles	$
1951	Marshall Teague	15	1	5	0	2	0	0	2	1,611	789	8	1,417	7,410
"	Herb Thomas	2	1	1	0	0	0	0	0	200	1	1	100	1,025
"	**Total**	17	2	6	0	2	0	0	2	1,811	790	9	1,517	8,435
1952	Pepper Cunningham	1	0	0	0	0	0	0	0		0	0		25
"	Mike Klapak	1	0	0	0	0	0	0	0		0	0		0
"	Marshall Teague	4	1	2	0	0	0	0	0	317	236	2	299	2,550
"	Herb Thomas	2	0	0	2	0	0	0	0	237	1	1	252	1,700
"	**Total**	4	1	2	2	0	0	0	0	554	237	2	551	4,275
Lifetime		21	3	8	2	2	0	0	2	2,365	1,027	11	2,068	$12,710

Steve Temme

Year	Driver	Starts	Poles	1	2	3	4	5	6–10	Laps	Laps Led	Races Led	Miles	$
1977	Ron McGee	1	0	0	0	0	0	0	0	103	0	0	258	950
Lifetime		1	0	0	0	0	0	0	0	103	0	0	258	$950

Dave Terrell

Year	Driver	Starts	Poles	1	2	3	4	5	6–10	Laps	Laps Led	Races Led	Miles	$
1952	Dave Terrell	5	0	0	0	0	0	1	2	477	0	0	306	475
1954	Dave Terrell	29	0	0	0	0	0	0	8	3,858	0	0	2,581	1,750
1955	Dick Rathmann	1	0	0	0	0	0	0	0	76	0	0	76	25
"	Dave Terrell	25	0	0	0	2	0	1	7	3,199	9	1	2,452	3,655
"	**Total**	26	0	0	0	2	0	1	7	3,275	9	1	2,528	3,680
1956	Dave Terrell	5	0	0	0	0	0	0	1	363	0	0	235	260
1957	Dave Terrell	2	0	0	0	0	0	0	1	290	0	0	290	750
1958	Dave Terrell	1	0	0	0	0	0	0	0	113	0	0	57	50
Lifetime		68	0	0	0	2	0	2	19	8,376	9	1	5,996	$6,965

Kevin Terris

Year	Driver	Starts	Poles	1	2	3	4	5	6–10	Laps	Laps Led	Races Led	Miles	$
1982	Kevin Terris	1	0	0	0	0	0	0	0	12	0	0	31	525
1984	Kevin Terris	1	0	0	0	0	0	0	0	78	0	0	204	1,275
Lifetime		2	0	0	0	0	0	0	0	90	0	0	236	$1,800

Bill Terry

Year	Driver	Starts	Poles	1	2	3	4	5	6–10	Laps	Laps Led	Races Led	Miles	$
1982	Bob Jarvis	1	0	0	0	0	0	0	0	145	0	0	86	595
"	Bosco Lowe	1	0	0	0	0	0	0	0	381	0	0	572	3,900
"	**Total**	2	0	0	0	0	0	0	0	526	0	0	658	4,495
1983	Tommy Ellis	1	0	0	0	0	0	0	0	386	0	0	579	4,350
"	Butch Lindley	1	0	0	0	0	0	0	0	122	0	0	64	1,050
"	Bosco Lowe	1	0	0	0	0	0	0	0	36	0	0	90	5,350
"	**Total**	3	0	0	0	0	0	0	0	544	0	0	733	10,750
1985	Alan Kulwicki	5	0	0	0	0	0	0	0	1,843	0	0	1,991	10,290
1986	Alan Kulwicki	14	0	0	0	0	1	0	2	4,504	7	4	5,157	51,470
Lifetime		24	0	0	0	0	1	0	2	7,417	7	4	8,539	$77,005

Jim Testa

Year	Driver	Starts	Poles	1	2	3	4	5	6–10	Laps	Laps Led	Races Led	Miles	$
1979	Chuck Bown	7	0	0	0	0	0	0	2	1,388	0	0	2,143	31,380
1980	Chuck Bown	1	0	0	0	0	0	0	0	50	0	0	125	3,350
"	John Greenwood	2	0	0	0	0	0	0	0	174	0	0	411	2,730
"	Lennie Pond	13	0	0	0	1	1	0	4	2,790	68	6	3,248	36,365
"	**Total**	16	0	0	0	1	1	0	4	3,014	68	6	3,784	42,445
1981	Lennie Pond	2	0	0	0	0	0	0	0	550	0	0	602	7,320
1984	Lennie Pond	1	0	0	0	0	0	0	0	9	0	0	12	1,000
1988	Derrike Cope	26	0	0	0	0	0	0	0	4,772	0	0	6,535	132,835
1989	Derrike Cope	3	0	0	0	0	0	0	0	451	0	0	632	5,440
Lifetime		55	0	0	0	1	1	0	6	10,184	68	6	13,707	$220,420

George Tet (See Tetsuo Fuchigami)

Marvin Thaxton

Year	Driver	Starts	Poles	1	2	3	4	5	6–10	Laps	Laps Led	Races Led	Miles	$
1982	Glenn Jarrett	1	0	0	0	0	0	0	0	35	0	0	53	735
Lifetime		1	0	0	0	0	0	0	0	35	0	0	53	$735

Dave Thomas

Year	Driver	Starts	Poles	1	2	3	4	5	6–10	Laps	Laps Led	Races Led	Miles	$
1994	Pancho Carter	1	0	0	0	0	0	0	0	322	0	0	490	9,130
Lifetime		1	0	0	0	0	0	0	0	322	0	0	490	$9,130

Year	Driver	Starts	Poles	Finish 1	2	3	4	5	6–10	Laps	Laps Led	Races Led	Miles	$

Herb Thomas

Year	Driver	Starts	Poles	1	2	3	4	5	6–10	Laps	Laps Led	Races Led	Miles	$
1949	Herb Thomas	4	0	0	0	0	0	1	0	197	0	0	99	225
1950	Donald Thomas	2	0	0	0	0	0	0	2	141	0	0	71	250
"	Herb Thomas	13	0	1	0	2	1	0	2	719	176	2	438	2,645
"	**Total**	13	0	1	0	2	1	0	4	860	176	2	509	2,895
1951	Donald Thomas	17	0	0	0	1	0	3	4	479	0	0	563	2,385
"	Herb Thomas	31	3	5	1	3	4	1	2	1,719	774	8	1,456	18,800
"	**Total**	33	3	5	1	4	4	4	6	2,198	774	8	2,020	21,185
1952	Donald Thomas	4	1	1	1	1	0	0	0	605	9	1	453	2,255
"	Herb Thomas	30	10	8	5	3	0	1	3	4,897	1,508	15	3,223	17,265
"	Smokey Yunick	1	0	0	0	0	0	0	0	7	0	0	4	25
"	**Total**	30	11	9	6	4	0	1	3	5,509	**1,517**	15	3,679	19,545
1953	Jim Reed	2	0	0	0	0	1	0	0	260	0	0	358	610
"	Donald Thomas	8	0	0	0	0	0	0	4	1,002	0	0	1,103	1,540
"	Herb Thomas	37	11	12	8	3	3	1	4	4,292	1,420	23	3,107	28,910
"	**Total**	37	11	12	8	3	4	1	8	**5,554**	**1,420**	**23**	**4,567**	31,060
1954	Donald Thomas	3	0	0	0	0	0	1	0	403	0	0	220	350
"	Herb Thomas	33	8	12	4	1	2	0	8	5,664	1,358	19	3,998	30,975
"	**Total**	34	8	12	4	1	2	1	8	1,358	**1,358**	**19**	4,218	31,325
1955	Fonty Flock	2	0	0	0	0	0	0	0	85	0	0	43	0
"	Donald Thomas	10	0	0	0	0	2	0	2	1,320	0	0	855	1,240
"	Herb Thomas	21	2	3	3	3	3	2	1	3,121	250	7	2,551	17,999
"	Speedy Thompson	1	0	0	0	0	0	0	0	145	0	0	73	50
"	**Total**	26	2	3	3	3	5	2	3	4,671	250	7	3,522	19,289
1956	Donald Thomas	1	0	0	0	0	0	0	0		0	0		75
"	Herb Thomas	26	1	1	0	1	5	3	9	4,481	299	2	3,095	11,492
"	**Total**	27	1	1	0	1	5	3	9	4,481	299	2	3,095	11,567
1957	Fonty Flock	1	0	0	0	0	0	0	0	18	0	0	25	100
"	Paul Goldsmith	1	0	0	0	0	0	0	0	83	0	0	33	50
"	Marvin Panch	3	0	1	0	0	0	0	0	326	9	1	320	3,700
"	Herb Thomas	2	0	0	0	0	0	0	0	146	0	0	123	25
"	**Total**	7	0	1	0	0	0	0	0	573	9	1	501	3,875
Lifetime		211	36	44	22	18	21	13	41	30,110	5,803	77	22,209	$140,966
				9th										

Jabe Thomas

Year	Driver	Starts	Poles	1	2	3	4	5	6–10	Laps	Laps Led	Races Led	Miles	$
1965	Ned Jarrett	1	0	0	1	0	0	0	0	199	0	0	100	600
"	Bud Moore	1	0	0	0	0	0	0	0	9	0	0	12	520
"	Junior Spencer	1	0	0	0	0	0	0	0	240	0	0	360	510
"	Jabe Thomas	9	0	0	0	0	0	0	1	1,919	0	0	1,401	3,735
"	**Total**	12	0	0	1	0	0	0	1	2,367	0	0	1,873	5,365
1966	Buddy Baker	1	0	0	0	0	0	0	0	149	0	0	75	120
"	Doug Cooper	1	0	0	0	0	0	0	0	16	0	0	22	460
"	Wendell Scott	1	0	0	0	0	0	0	0	144	0	0	198	450
"	Jabe Thomas	13	0	0	0	0	0	0	0	1,559	0	0	1,373	3,480
"	**Total**	16	0	0	0	0	0	0	0	1,868	0	0	1,667	4,510
1967	Jabe Thomas	1	0	0	0	0	0	0	1	269	0	0	135	200
Lifetime		29	0	0	1	0	0	0	2	4,504	0	0	3,675	$10,075

James Thomas

Year	Driver	Starts	Poles	1	2	3	4	5	6–10	Laps	Laps Led	Races Led	Miles	$
1964	Andy Buffington	1	0	0	0	0	0	0	1	173	0	0	87	175
"	Sam McQuagg	5	0	0	0	0	0	0	0	653	0	0	842	1,700
"	**Total**	6	0	0	0	0	0	0	1	826	0	0	929	1,875
1965	Sam McQuagg	1	0	0	0	0	0	0	0	97	0	0	262	575
1974	Mike James	1	0	0	0	0	0	0	0	103	0	0	270	995
Lifetime		8	0	0	0	0	0	0	1	1,026	0	0	1,460	$3,445

Ronnie Thomas

Year	Driver	Starts	Poles	1	2	3	4	5	6–10	Laps	Laps Led	Races Led	Miles	$
1981	Joe Booher	1	0	0	0	0	0	0	0	4	0	0	11	1,700
"	Dick May	1	0	0	0	0	0	0	1	183	0	0	487	8,745
"	Ronnie Thomas	21	0	0	0	0	0	0	0	5,544	0	0	5,523	50,725
"	**Total**	23	0	0	0	0	0	0	1	5,731	0	0	6,021	61,170
1982	Ronnie Thomas	16	0	0	0	0	0	0	0	2,899	0	0	2,746	21,030
1983	Ronnie Thomas	26	0	0	0	0	0	0	0	7,141	1	1	7,705	47,190
1984	Buddy Arrington	1	0	0	0	0	0	0	0	67	0	0	42	2,485
"	Ronnie Thomas	21	0	0	0	0	0	0	0	4,976	2	1	5,761	79,325
"	**Total**	22	0	0	0	0	0	0	0	5,043	2	1	5,803	81,810
1985	Ronnie Thomas	7	0	0	0	0	0	0	0	1,510	0	0	1,157	10,505

Year	Driver	Starts	Poles	Finish						Laps	Laps Led	Races Led	Miles	$
				1	2	3	4	5	6–10					

Ronnie Thomas *continued*

Year	Driver	Starts	Poles	1	2	3	4	5	6–10	Laps	Laps Led	Races Led	Miles	$
1986	Ronnie Thomas	3	0	0	0	0	0	0	0	522	0	0	455	4,290
1987	Ronnie Thomas	4	0	0	0	0	0	0	0	874	0	0	694	6,320
Lifetime		101	0	0	0	0	0	0	1	23,720	3	2	24,580	$232,315

Bruce Thompson

Year	Driver	Starts	Poles	1	2	3	4	5	6–10	Laps	Laps Led	Races Led	Miles	$
1949	Jimmy Thompson	2	0	0	0	0	0	0	2		0	0		175
1950	Speedy Thompson	1	0	0	0	0	0	0	0		0	0		0
1959	Richard Riley	4	0	0	0	0	0	0	1	578	0	0	340	450
"	Jimmy Thompson	3	0	0	0	0	0	0	0	511	0	0	621	625
"	Speedy Thompson	7	0	0	0	0	1	0	2	1,153	0	0	577	840
"	**Total**	14	0	0	0	0	1	0	3	2,242	0	0	1,537	1,915
1960	Bunk Moore	1	0	0	0	0	0	0	0	147	0	0	74	85
"	Speedy Thompson	1	0	0	0	0	0	1	0	193	0	0	97	250
"	**Total**	2	0	0	0	0	0	1	0	340	0	0	170	335
Lifetime		19	0	0	0	0	1	1	5	2,582	0	0	1,707	$2,425

Jimmy Thompson

Year	Driver	Starts	Poles	1	2	3	4	5	6–10	Laps	Laps Led	Races Led	Miles	$
1957	Jimmy Thompson	1	0	0	0	0	0	0	0	328	0	0	451	225
Lifetime		1	0	0	0	0	0	0	0	328	0	0	451	$225

Maurice Thompson

Year	Driver	Starts	Poles	1	2	3	4	5	6–10	Laps	Laps Led	Races Led	Miles	$
1955	Jim McLain	1	0	0	0	0	0	0	0	36	0	0	148	35
Lifetime		1	0	0	0	0	0	0	0	36	0	0	148	$35

Speedy Thompson

Year	Driver	Starts	Poles	1	2	3	4	5	6–10	Laps	Laps Led	Races Led	Miles	$
1957	Speedy Thompson	20	3	2	2	0	4	1	4	3,610	593	6	2,452	21,976
1958	Jimmy Thompson	1	0	0	0	0	0	0	1	483	0	0	242	375
"	Speedy Thompson	36	7	4	2	7	2	3	5	6,106	224	6	3,471	17,295
"	**Total**	37	7	4	2	7	2	3	6	6,589	224	6	3,713	17,670
Lifetime		57	10	6	4	7	6	4	10	10,119	817	12	6,165	$39,646

Tommy Thompson

Year	Driver	Starts	Poles	1	2	3	4	5	6–10	Laps	Laps Led	Races Led	Miles	$
1950	Tommy Thompson	3	0	0	0	0	0	0	0	272	0	0	439	75
1951	Tommy Thompson	4	0	1	0	0	0	0	1	250	58	1	250	5,510
1952	Tommy Thompson	4	0	0	0	0	0	0	1	297	20	1	271	500
1953	Tommy Thompson	2	0	0	0	1	0	0	0	39	0	0	160	840
1954	Tommy Thompson	1	0	0	0	0	0	0	0	15	0	0	61	0
1959	Earl Balmer	2	0	0	0	0	0	0	0	436	0	0	423	250
"	Andy Hampton	1	0	0	0	0	0	0	0	76	0	0	38	50
"	Tommy Thompson	3	0	0	0	0	0	0	0	367	0	0	422	510
"	Chuck Tombs	1	0	0	0	0	0	0	0	134	0	0	67	0
"	**Total**	7	0	0	0	0	0	0	0	1,013	0	0	950	810
Lifetime		21	0	1	0	1	0	0	2	1,886	78	2	2,132	$7,735

Gene Thonesen

Year	Driver	Starts	Poles	1	2	3	4	5	6–10	Laps	Laps Led	Races Led	Miles	$
1981	Gene Thonesen	1	0	0	0	0	0	0	0	110	0	0	288	2,125
Lifetime		1	0	0	0	0	0	0	0	110	0	0	288	$2,125

Dean Thorne

Year	Driver	Starts	Poles	1	2	3	4	5	6–10	Laps	Laps Led	Races Led	Miles	$
1957	Carl Joiner	1	0	0	0	0	0	0	0	18	0	0	9	100
1961	Carl Joiner	1	0	0	0	0	0	0	0	125	0	0	175	100
1963	Carl Joiner	1	0	0	0	0	0	0	0	143	0	0	386	375
1966	Carl Joiner	1	0	0	0	0	0	0	0	41	0	0	111	500
1970	Carl Joiner	1	0	0	0	0	0	0	0	23	0	0	60	800
1971	Carl Joiner	3	0	0	0	0	0	0	1	385	0	0	987	4,250
1972	Carl Joiner	2	0	0	0	0	0	1	0	283	0	0	741	3,420
1973	Carl Joiner	1	0	0	0	0	0	0	0	46	0	0	121	1,015
Lifetime		11	0	0	0	0	0	1	1	1,064	0	0	2,590	$10,560

Year	Driver	Starts	Poles	Finish						Laps	Laps Led	Races Led	Miles	$
				1	2	3	4	5	6–10					

Jon Thorne

Year	Driver	Starts	Poles	1	2	3	4	5	6–10	Laps	Laps Led	Races Led	Miles	$
1966	LeeRoy Yarbrough	9	2	1	0	0	1	0	2	1,545	364	5	2,546	23,980
1967	Donnie Allison	7	0	0	0	0	1	0	2	1,869	1	1	2,585	8,815
"	LeeRoy Yarbrough	5	0	1	0	0	0	0	0	457	20	2	696	4,540
"	**Total**	12	0	1	0	0	1	0	2	2,326	21	3	3,281	13,355
1968	Earl Balmer	1	0	0	0	0	0	0	0	59	0	0	89	1,075
"	Jim Hurtubise	3	0	0	0	0	0	0	0	487	0	0	626	2,125
"	Tom Pistone	3	0	0	0	1	0	1	0	827	8	1	414	1,425
"	**Total**	7	0	0	0	1	0	1	0	1,373	8	1	1,128	4,625
Lifetime		28	2	2	0	1	2	1	4	5,244	393	9	6,955	$41,960

Roy Thornley

Year	Driver	Starts	Poles	1	2	3	4	5	6–10	Laps	Laps Led	Races Led	Miles	$
1974	Richie Panch	26	0	0	0	1	0	1	5	6,105	1	1	6,787	51,383
Lifetime		26	0	0	0	1	0	1	5	6,105	1	1	6,787	$51,383

Leroy Throop

Year	Driver	Starts	Poles	1	2	3	4	5	6–10	Laps	Laps Led	Races Led	Miles	$
1986	Butch Miller	3	0	0	0	0	0	0	0	799	0	0	891	5,085
1987	Butch Miller	2	0	0	0	0	0	0	0	215	0	0	307	3,145
1989	Butch Miller	8	0	0	0	0	0	0	0	1,113	0	0	1,178	19,695
Lifetime		13	0	0	0	0	0	0	0	2,127	0	0	2,376	$27,925

Ken Thurlby

Year	Driver	Starts	Poles	1	2	3	4	5	6–10	Laps	Laps Led	Races Led	Miles	$
1975	John Banks	3	0	0	0	0	0	0	0	478	0	0	816	2,760
Lifetime		3	0	0	0	0	0	0	0	478	0	0	816	$2,760

Billy Tibbett

Year	Driver	Starts	Poles	1	2	3	4	5	6–10	Laps	Laps Led	Races Led	Miles	$
1951	Billy Tibbett	2	0	0	0	0	0	0	0	318	0	0	398	75
Lifetime		2	0	0	0	0	0	0	0	318	0	0	398	$75

L. W. Tickle

Year	Driver	Starts	Poles	1	2	3	4	5	6–10	Laps	Laps Led	Races Led	Miles	$
1952	Al Fleming	1	0	0	0	0	0	0	0	336	0	0	420	210
Lifetime		1	0	0	0	0	0	0	0	336	0	0	420	$210

Willie Tierney

Year	Driver	Starts	Poles	1	2	3	4	5	6–10	Laps	Laps Led	Races Led	Miles	$
1991	Jerry Hill	2	0	0	0	0	0	0	0	52	0	0	52	6,975
1992	Jerry Hill	4	0	0	0	0	0	0	0	520	0	0	554	17,705
"	T. W. Taylor	1	0	0	0	0	0	0	0	138	0	0	367	6,045
"	**Total**	5	0	0	0	0	0	0	0	658	0	0	921	23,750
1993	Jerry Hill	2	0	0	0	0	0	0	0	353	0	0	359	13,885
1994	Jerry Hill	0												5,600
Lifetime		9	0	0	0	0	0	0	0	1,063	0	0	1,332	$50,210

Adelmo Tiezzi

Year	Driver	Starts	Poles	1	2	3	4	5	6–10	Laps	Laps Led	Races Led	Miles	$
1956	Benny DeRosier	4	0	0	0	0	0	0	0	236	0	0	236	200
Lifetime		4	0	0	0	0	0	0	0	236	0	0	236	$200

Travis Tiller

Year	Driver	Starts	Poles	1	2	3	4	5	6–10	Laps	Laps Led	Races Led	Miles	$
1974	Travis Tiller	14	0	0	0	0	0	0	0	2,446	0	0	2,565	11,410
1975	Travis Tiller	10	0	0	0	0	0	0	0	1,958	0	0	2,178	7,780
1976	Travis Tiller	9	0	0	0	0	0	0	0	2,012	0	0	1,787	6,640
1977	Travis Tiller	3	0	0	0	0	0	0	0	250	0	0	183	1,615
1979	Travis Tiller	4	0	0	0	0	0	0	0	218	0	0	336	5,065
1980	Travis Tiller	3	0	0	0	0	0	0	0	507	0	0	561	2,280
1981	Travis Tiller	1	0	0	0	0	0	0	0	111	0	0	169	850
1982	Travis Tiller	4	0	0	0	0	0	0	0	557	0	0	1,107	6,395
1983	Travis Tiller	2	0	0	0	0	0	0	0	338	0	0	463	5,060
Lifetime		50	0	0	0	0	0	0	0	8,397	0	0	9,349	$47,095

Leonard Tippett

Year	Driver	Starts	Poles	1	2	3	4	5	6–10	Laps	Laps Led	Races Led	Miles	$
1951	Herb Thomas	1	0	0	0	0	0	0	0	40	0	0	30	25

Year	Driver	Starts	Poles	Finish						Laps	Laps Led	Races Led	Miles	$
				1	2	3	4	5	6–10	Laps	Led	Led	Miles	$

Leonard Tippett *continued*

Year	Driver	Starts	Poles	1	2	3	4	5	6–10	Laps	Laps Led	Races Led	Miles	$
"	Leonard Tippett	8	0	0	1	0	0	0	1	359	19	1	270	850
"	**Total**	9	0	0	1	0	0	0	1	399	19	1	300	875
1952	Leonard Tippett	5	0	0	0	0	0	0	0	221	0	0	134	150
Lifetime		14	0	0	1	0	0	0	1	620	19	1	433	$1,025

T. A. Toomes

Year	Driver	Starts	Poles	1	2	3	4	5	6–10	Laps	Laps Led	Races Led	Miles	$
1957	Johnny Dodson	1	0	0	0	0	0	0	0	19	0	0	12	50
"	Billy Rafter	2	0	0	0	0	0	0	1	148	0	0	252	340
"	T. A. Toomes	11	0	0	0	0	0	0	1	1,920	0	0	1,040	1,450
"	**Total**	14	0	0	0	0	0	0	2	2,087	0	0	1,303	1,840
Lifetime		14	0	0	0	0	0	0	2	2,087	0	0	1,303	$1,840

Warren Tope

Year	Driver	Starts	Poles	1	2	3	4	5	6–10	Laps	Laps Led	Races Led	Miles	$
1975	Warren Tope	2	0	0	0	0	0	0	0	305	0	0	467	3,170
Lifetime		2	0	0	0	0	0	0	0	305	0	0	467	$3,170

Ward Towers

Year	Driver	Starts	Poles	1	2	3	4	5	6–10	Laps	Laps Led	Races Led	Miles	$
1958	Ward Towers	1	0	0	0	0	0	0	0	34	0	0	139	90
Lifetime		1	0	0	0	0	0	0	0	34	0	0	139	$90

Frank Townsend

Year	Driver	Starts	Poles	1	2	3	4	5	6–10	Laps	Laps Led	Races Led	Miles	$
1969	Marty Kinerk	1	0	0	0	0	0	0	0	40	0	0	108	755
Lifetime		1	0	0	0	0	0	0	0	40	0	0	108	$755

Tom Travis

Year	Driver	Starts	Poles	1	2	3	4	5	6–10	Laps	Laps Led	Races Led	Miles	$
1953	Tom Travis	1	0	0	0	0	0	0	0	33	0	0	135	25
Lifetime		1	0	0	0	0	0	0	0	33	0	0	135	$25

Herb Trimble

Year	Driver	Starts	Poles	1	2	3	4	5	6–10	Laps	Laps Led	Races Led	Miles	$
1951	Herb Trimble	2	0	0	0	0	0	0	1	198	0	0	248	50
Lifetime		2	0	0	0	0	0	0	1	198	0	0	248	$50

E. J. Trivette

Year	Driver	Starts	Poles	1	2	3	4	5	6–10	Laps	Laps Led	Races Led	Miles	$
1959	E. J. Trivette	4	0	0	0	0	0	0	0	534	0	0	285	175
Lifetime		4	0	0	0	0	0	0	0	534	0	0	285	$175

Randy Trogdon

Year	Driver	Starts	Poles	1	2	3	4	5	6–10	Laps	Laps Led	Races Led	Miles	$
1991	Andy Hillenburg	2	0	0	0	0	0	0	0	320	0	0	484	7,520
Lifetime		2	0	0	0	0	0	0	0	320	0	0	484	$7,520

Bob Tullius

Year	Driver	Starts	Poles	1	2	3	4	5	6–10	Laps	Laps Led	Races Led	Miles	$
1989	Jim Sauter	8	0	0	0	0	0	0	1	1,893	8	1	2,704	30,237
1990	Jimmy Horton	1	0	0	0	0	0	0	0	323	0	0	485	3,525
"	Jim Sauter	0												2,300
"	**Total**	1	0	0	0	0	0	0	0	323	0	0	485	5,825
Lifetime		9	0	0	0	0	0	0	1	2,216	8	1	3,188	$36,062

Reino Tulonen

Year	Driver	Starts	Poles	1	2	3	4	5	6–10	Laps	Laps Led	Races Led	Miles	$
1951	Reino Tulonen	3	0	0	0	0	0	1	0	353	0	0	441	375
Lifetime		3	0	0	0	0	0	1	0	353	0	0	441	$375

Curtis Turner

Year	Driver	Starts	Poles	1	2	3	4	5	6–10	Laps	Laps Led	Races Led	Miles	$
1949	Curtis Turner	3	0	0	0	0	0	0	1		0	0		125
Lifetime		3	0	0	0	0	0	0	1		0	0		$125

Year	Driver	Starts	Poles	Finish						Laps	Laps Led	Races Led	Miles	$
				1	2	3	4	5	6–10					

George Turner

Year	Driver	Starts	Poles	1	2	3	4	5	6–10	Laps	Laps Led	Races Led	Miles	$
1968	Willie Crane	1	0	0	0	0	0	0	0	300	0	0	450	875
Lifetime		1	0	0	0	0	0	0	0	300	0	0	450	$875

James Turner

Year	Driver	Starts	Poles	1	2	3	4	5	6–10	Laps	Laps Led	Races Led	Miles	$
1961	Darel Dieringer	1	0	0	0	0	0	0	0	238	0	0	357	575
"	Roscoe Thompson	6	0	0	0	0	0	0	2	721	0	0	1,341	2,535
"	**Total**	7	0	0	0	0	0	0	2	959	0	0	1,698	3,110
1962	Billy Wade	3	0	0	0	0	0	0	2	872	0	0	483	925
Lifetime		10	0	0	0	0	0	0	4	1,831	0	0	2,181	$4,035

Tamara Turner

Year	Driver	Starts	Poles	1	2	3	4	5	6–10	Laps	Laps Led	Races Led	Miles	$
1996	Larry Gunselman	1	0	0	0	0	0	0	0	70	0	0	176	10,200
Lifetime		1	0	0	0	0	0	0	0	70	0	0	176	$10,200

Carl Tyler

Year	Driver	Starts	Poles	1	2	3	4	5	6–10	Laps	Laps Led	Races Led	Miles	$
1958	Carl Tyler	10	0	0	0	0	0	0	0	1,016	0	0	843	745
1959	Carl Tyler	2	0	0	0	0	0	0	0	63	0	0	158	150
Lifetime		12	0	0	0	0	0	0	0	1,079	0	0	1,001	$895

Paul Tyler

Year	Driver	Starts	Poles	1	2	3	4	5	6–10	Laps	Laps Led	Races Led	Miles	$
1971	Paul Tyler	9	0	0	0	0	0	0	0	1,510	0	0	1,675	6,335
Lifetime		9	0	0	0	0	0	0	0	1,510	0	0	1,675	$6,335

Roy Tyner

Year	Driver	Starts	Poles	1	2	3	4	5	6–10	Laps	Laps Led	Races Led	Miles	$
1957	Roy Tyner	10	0	0	0	0	0	0	2	1,705	0	0	1,099	1,055
1958	Roy Tyner	1	0	0	0	0	0	0	0	126	0	0	42	110
1959	Johnny Allen	1	0	0	0	0	0	0	0	57	0	0	57	50
"	Cotton Owens	1	0	0	0	0	0	0	1	290	0	0	145	450
"	Roy Tyner	27	0	0	1	0	3	3	7	5,093	0	0	3,264	5,175
"	**Total**	29	0	0	1	0	3	3	8	5,440	0	0	3,466	5,675
1960	Jim Austin	2	0	0	0	0	0	0	0	199	0	0	124	310
"	Roy Tyner	15	0	0	0	0	1	0	2	1,156	0	0	747	1,815
"	**Total**	17	0	0	0	0	1	0	2	1,355	0	0	870	2,125
1961	Roy Tyner	8	0	0	0	0	0	0	1	1,322	0	0	1,109	960
1963	Roy Tyner	8	0	0	0	0	0	0	0	381	0	0	193	1,345
1964	Roy Tyner	46	0	0	0	0	0	0	17	7,327	0	0	4,641	11,488
1965	Darel Dieringer	4	0	0	0	0	0	0	2	658	0	0	346	710
"	Walson Gardner	2	0	0	0	0	0	0	0	61	0	0	31	200
"	J. T. Putney	3	0	0	0	0	0	0	2	701	0	0	430	1,315
"	Roy Tyner	28	0	0	0	0	1	0	5	3,448	0	0	2,171	6,696
"	**Total**	33	0	0	0	0	1	0	9	4,868	0	0	2,977	8,921
1966	Roy Tyner	2	0	0	0	0	0	0	0	270	0	0	186	600
1968	Ben Arnold	1	0	0	0	0	0	0	0	284	0	0	391	825
"	Jack Ingram	1	0	0	0	0	0	0	1	481	0	0	241	700
"	Glenn Luce	1	0	0	0	0	0	0	0	223	0	0	74	125
"	Stan Meserve	1	0	0	0	0	0	0	0	168	0	0	84	100
"	Wendell Scott	1	0	0	0	0	0	0	0	252	0	0	347	850
"	Roy Tyner	29	0	0	0	0	2	1	6	5,571	0	0	3,098	11,237
"	Bill Vanderhoff	10	0	0	0	0	0	0	0	788	0	0	364	1,950
"	**Total**	39	0	0	0	0	2	1	7	7,767	0	0	4,597	15,787
1969	Earl Brooks	1	0	0	0	0	0	0	0	313	0	0	318	945
"	Worth McMillion	1	0	0	0	0	0	0	0	328	0	0	164	480
"	Sherral Pruitt	1	0	0	0	0	0	0	0	10	0	0	5	100
"	Roy Tyner	21	0	0	0	0	0	0	1	3,285	0	0	3,118	12,317
"	**Total**	23	0	0	0	0	0	0	1	3,936	0	0	3,605	13,842
1970	Roy Tyner	12	0	0	0	0	0	0	2	1,676	0	0	1,050	4,660
Lifetime		228	0	0	1	0	7	4	49	36,173	0	0	23,835	$66,568

Lynton Tyson

Year	Driver	Starts	Poles	1	2	3	4	5	6–10	Laps	Laps Led	Races Led	Miles	$
1959	Buck Baker	13	1	1	1	2	0	0	3	3,278	1	1	1,970	4,820
"	Buddy Baker	5	0	0	0	0	1	0	1	794	0	0	397	875
"	Banjo Matthews	1	0	0	0	0	0	0	0	137	0	0	69	0

Year	Driver	Starts	Poles	Finish 1	2	3	4	5	6–10	Laps	Laps Led	Races Led	Miles	$

Lynton Tyson *continued*

Year	Driver	Starts	Poles	1	2	3	4	5	6–10	Laps	Laps Led	Races Led	Miles	$
"	Jim Paschal	1	0	0	0	0	0	0	1	356	0	0	490	1,460
"	Fireball Roberts	1	0	0	0	0	0	0	0	303	0	0	152	75
"	**Total**	13	1	1	1	2	1	0	5	4,868	1	1	3,076	7,230
1960	Larry Frank	3	0	0	0	0	0	0	0	405	0	0	786	400
Lifetime		16	1	1	1	2	1	0	5	5,273	1	1	3,863	$7,630

D. K. Ulrich (See also Ulrich-DeWitt)

Year	Driver	Starts	Poles	1	2	3	4	5	6–10	Laps	Laps Led	Races Led	Miles	$
1971	Dick May	1	0	0	0	0	0	0	0	436	0	0	436	855
"	Roy Mayne	1	0	0	0	0	0	0	1	320	0	0	437	2,050
"	D. K. Ulrich	12	0	0	0	0	0	0	0	1,526	0	0	1,064	3,955
"	**Total**	14	0	0	0	0	0	0	1	2,282	0	0	1,937	6,860
1972	D. K. Ulrich	4	0	0	0	0	0	0	0	1,001	0	0	1,041	2,695
1973	D. K. Ulrich	11	0	0	0	0	0	0	0	2,006	0	0	2,125	8,695
"	Frank Warren	3	0	0	0	0	0	0	0	828	0	0	467	1,705
"	**Total**	14	0	0	0	0	0	0	0	2,834	0	0	2,591	10,400
1974	Tony Bettenhausen Jr.	1	0	0	0	0	0	0	0	443	0	0	451	1,300
"	Ed Negre	1	0	0	0	0	0	0	0	150	0	0	300	1,025
"	D. K. Ulrich	14	0	0	0	0	0	0	0	3,148	0	0	3,514	11,350
"	**Total**	16	0	0	0	0	0	0	0	3,741	0	0	4,264	13,675
1975	Randy Bethea	1	0	0	0	0	0	0	0	251	0	0	377	1,055
"	D. K. Ulrich	16	0	0	0	0	0	0	1	3,448	0	0	4,093	16,525
"	**Total**	17	0	0	0	0	0	0	1	3,699	0	0	4,469	17,580
1978	D. K. Ulrich	22	0	0	0	0	0	0	3	6,175	1	1	7,425	54,550
1979	Al Elmore	1	0	0	0	0	0	0	0	389	0	0	232	1,265
"	D. K. Ulrich	30	0	0	0	0	0	0	5	8,612	0	0	9,815	112,323
"	**Total**	31	0	0	0	0	0	0	5	9,001	0	0	10,046	113,588
1980	Mike Alexander	1	0	0	0	0	0	0	1	409	0	0	244	3,130
"	Stan Barrett	3	0	0	0	0	0	0	1	987	0	0	1,454	13,760
"	Joe Booher	1	0	0	0	0	0	0	0	376	0	0	204	2,350
"	Harry Dinwiddie	1	0	0	0	0	0	0	0	173	0	0	460	5,250
"	Tommy Gale	1	0	0	0	0	0	0	0	194	0	0	388	3,405
"	Sterling Marlin	1	0	0	0	0	0	0	1	413	0	0	246	4,335
"	Dick May	2	0	0	0	0	0	0	1	962	0	0	741	6,625
"	J. D. McDuffie	1	0	0	0	0	0	0	0	145	0	0	218	2,800
"	Lennie Pond	1	0	0	0	0	0	0	0	156	0	0	390	5,385
"	Tim Richmond	5	0	0	0	0	0	0	0	1,359	0	0	1,650	14,925
"	Ricky Rudd	3	0	0	0	0	0	0	0	791	6	1	939	8,025
"	Dick Skillen	1	0	0	0	0	0	0	0	76	0	0	202	2,785
"	D. K. Ulrich	10	0	0	0	0	0	0	1	1,732	0	0	1,896	22,575
"	Bill Whittington	2	0	0	0	0	0	0	1	183	0	0	472	7,385
"	**Total**	31	0	0	0	0	0	0	6	7,956	6	1	9,502	102,735
1981	Rick Baldwin	1	0	0	0	0	0	0	0	149	0	0	298	1,550
"	Joe Booher	3	0	0	0	0	0	0	0	577	0	0	1,249	3,295
"	Chuck Bown	1	0	0	0	0	0	0	0	118	0	0	177	1,950
"	Elliott Forbes-Robinson	1	0	0	0	0	0	0	0	246	0	0	131	870
"	Tommy Gale	2	0	0	0	0	0	0	0	881	0	0	681	2,370
"	Cecil Gordon	2	0	0	0	0	0	0	0	326	0	0	177	1,220
"	Terry Herman	2	0	0	0	0	0	0	0	238	0	0	631	7,035
"	Kevin Housby	1	0	0	0	0	0	0	0	53	0	0	133	2,480
"	Don Hume	1	0	0	0	0	0	0	0	101	0	0	103	590
"	Slick Johnson	1	0	0	0	0	0	0	0	110	0	0	150	1,425
"	Rick Knoop	1	0	0	0	0	0	0	0	197	0	0	394	3,405
"	Al Loquasto	1	0	0	0	0	0	0	0	184	0	0	460	2,345
"	Sterling Marlin	1	0	0	0	0	0	0	0	244	0	0	145	730
"	Dick May	2	0	0	0	0	0	0	0	582	0	0	718	3,375
"	Bob McElee	2	0	0	0	0	0	0	1	803	0	0	460	5,450
"	Tim Richmond	13	0	0	0	0	0	0	3	3,738	0	0	3,903	50,555
"	Ronnie Thomas	1	0	0	0	0	0	0	0	137	0	0	206	1,075
"	D. K. Ulrich	13	0	0	0	0	1	0	0	3,831	0	0	4,136	36,725
"	**Total**	31	0	0	0	0	1	0	4	12,515	0	0	14,152	126,445
1982	Stan Barrett	1	0	0	0	0	0	0	0	65	0	0	163	5,585
"	Randy Becker	1	0	0	0	0	0	0	0	85	0	0	223	1,065
"	Joe Booher	2	0	0	0	0	0	0	0	371	0	0	832	3,300
"	Jimmy Hensley	2	0	0	0	0	0	0	1	687	0	0	361	2,470
"	Terry Herman	1	0	0	0	0	0	0	0	113	0	0	296	4,220
"	Tommy Houston	1	0	0	0	0	0	0	0	238	0	0	129	875
"	Bob Jarvis	1	0	0	0	0	0	0	0	47	0	0	118	2,300

Year	Driver	Starts	Poles	Finish						Laps	Laps Led	Races Led	Miles	$
				1	2	3	4	5	6–10					

D. K. Ulrich *continued*

Year	Driver	Starts	Poles	1	2	3	4	5	6–10	Laps	Laps Led	Races Led	Miles	$
"	Al Loquasto	5	0	0	0	0	0	0	0	519	0	0	1,228	14,090
"	Dick May	4	0	0	0	0	0	0	0	1,073	0	0	1,180	5,255
"	D. K. Ulrich	22	0	0	0	0	0	0	1	6,709	0	0	6,580	66,580
"	**Total**	30	0	0	0	0	0	0	2	9,907	0	0	11,108	105,740
1983	Al Elmore	4	0	0	0	0	0	0	0	1,151	0	0	1,384	13,155
"	Tommy Gale	1	0	0	0	0	0	0	0	390	0	0	205	1,580
"	Mark Martin	2	0	0	0	0	0	0	0	415	0	0	382	5,745
"	Jim Sauter	4	0	0	0	0	0	0	0	1,093	0	0	1,349	22,765
"	Connie Saylor	1	0	0	0	0	0	0	0	153	0	0	383	4,875
"	D. K. Ulrich	16	0	0	0	0	0	0	2	5,623	0	0	6,126	68,595
"	**Total**	28	0	0	0	0	0	0	2	8,825	0	0	9,828	116,715
1984	Clark Dwyer	4	0	0	0	0	0	0	0	1,156	0	0	938	15,855
"	Doug Heveron	2	0	0	0	0	0	0	0	593	0	0	544	7,285
"	Jimmy Ingalls	3	0	0	0	0	0	0	0	491	0	0	597	8,865
"	Jim Sauter	3	0	0	0	0	0	0	0	737	0	0	1,152	18,015
"	Connie Saylor	1	0	0	0	0	0	0	0	150	0	0	375	4,330
"	Morgan Shepherd	2	0	0	0	0	0	0	0	496	0	0	577	5,545
"	D. K. Ulrich	9	0	0	0	0	0	0	0	2,565	0	0	2,513	31,040
"	**Total**	24	0	0	0	0	0	0	0	6,188	0	0	6,696	90,935
1985	Eddie Bierschwale	26	0	0	0	0	0	0	0	6,559	0	0	7,752	109,625
"	D. K. Ulrich	1	0	0	0	0	0	0	0	286	0	0	286	1,350
"	**Total**	26	0	0	0	0	0	0	0	6,845	0	0	8,038	110,975
1986	Joe Booher	2	0	0	0	0	0	0	0	556	0	0	556	8,930
"	Trevor Boys	9	0	0	0	0	0	0	0	2,179	2	1	2,214	54,360
"	Rick Knoop	1	0	0	0	0	0	0	0	88	0	0	214	6,995
"	Richard Petty	1	0	0	0	0	0	0	0	123	0	0	185	5,465
"	Jim Sauter	1	0	0	0	0	0	0	0	155	0	0	388	6,210
"	D. K. Ulrich	10	0	0	0	0	0	0	0	2,159	0	0	2,554	47,795
"	**Total**	24	0	0	0	0	0	0	0	5,260	2	1	6,109	129,755
1987	Bobby Baker	1	0	0	0	0	0	0	0	380	0	0	238	3,500
"	Trevor Boys	1	0	0	0	0	0	0	0	191	0	0	478	16,795
"	Ron Esau	1	0	0	0	0	0	0	0	90	0	0	236	4,165
"	Ernie Irvan	3	0	0	0	0	0	0	0	974	0	0	794	13,175
"	Rick Knoop	3	0	0	0	0	0	0	0	686	0	0	1,025	17,375
"	Connie Saylor	6	0	0	0	0	0	0	0	1,335	0	0	1,987	33,065
"	D. K. Ulrich	7	0	0	0	0	0	0	0	1,876	0	0	1,844	30,915
"	**Total**	22	0	0	0	0	0	0	0	5,532	0	0	6,600	118,990
1988	Ernie Irvan	25	0	0	0	0	0	0	0	7,337	1	1	8,845	96,370
1989	Ernie Irvan	29	0	0	0	0	0	0	4	8,286	69	4	9,961	155,329
1990	Troy Beebe	2	0	0	0	0	0	0	0	251	0	0	562	13,115
"	Eddie Bierschwale	1	0	0	0	0	0	0	0	191	0	0	478	20,125
"	Jim Bown	1	0	0	0	0	0	0	0	73	0	0	184	6,675
"	Charlie Glotzbach	2	0	0	0	0	0	0	0	257	0	0	353	12,255
"	Rick Mast	10	0	0	0	0	0	0	0	2,819	0	0	2,749	66,795
"	Jerry O'Neil	1	0	0	0	0	0	0	0	74	0	0	180	2,975
"	Jim Sauter	1	0	0	0	0	0	0	0	203	0	0	203	4,900
"	D. K. Ulrich	1	0	0	0	0	0	0	0	185	0	0	139	4,265
"	**Total**	19	0	0	0	0	0	0	0	4,053	0	0	4,847	131,105
1994*	P. J. Jones	1	0	0	0	0	0	0	0	67	0	0	164	6,085
"	Greg Sacks	31	1	0	0	0	0	0	3	8,266	38	8	10,041	411,728
"	**Total**	31	1	0	0	0	0	0	3	8,333	38	8	10,205	417,813
1995*	Bobby Hillin Jr.	12	0	0	0	0	0	0	0	2,158	0	0	3,904	203,810
"	Davy Jones	7	0	0	0	0	0	0	0	1,680	0	0	2,359	109,925
"	**Total**	19	0	0	0	0	0	0	0	3,838	0	0	6,263	313,735
Lifetime		457	1	0	0	0	1	0	31	123,608	117	16	143,927	$2,235,990

*Co-owned with Doug Bawel.

Ulrich-DeWitt (D. K. Ulrich and Ray DeWitt, co-owners)

Year	Driver	Starts	Poles	1	2	3	4	5	6–10	Laps	Laps Led	Races Led	Miles	$
1991	Ted Musgrave	29	0	0	0	0	0	0	0	9,074	6	5	10,579	200,910
1992	Ted Musgrave	29	0	0	0	0	0	1	6	9,253	11	3	10,988	449,121
1993	Ted Musgrave	29	0	0	0	0	0	2	3	8,530	8	3	10,397	458,615
Lifetime		87	0	0	0	0	0	3	9	26,857	25	11	31,964	$1,108,646

Ray Underwood

Year	Driver	Starts	Poles	1	2	3	4	5	6–10	Laps	Laps Led	Races Led	Miles	$
1965	Reb Wickersham	7	0	0	0	0	0	0	2	906	0	0	1,198	4,410
Lifetime		7	0	0	0	0	0	0	2	906	0	0	1,198	$4,410

Year	Driver	Starts	Poles	Finish 1	2	3	4	5	6–10	Laps	Laps Led	Races Led	Miles	$

Sherman Utsman

Year	Driver	Starts	Poles	1	2	3	4	5	6–10	Laps	Laps Led	Races Led	Miles	$
1962	Sherman Utsman	12	0	0	0	0	0	1	3	3,293	0	0	2,314	3,580
1963	Sherman Utsman	3	0	0	0	0	0	0	3	582	0	0	204	555
1964	Joe Weatherly	1	0	0	0	0	0	0	0	120	0	0	60	300
Lifetime		16	0	0	0	0	0	1	6	3,995	0	0	2,578	$4,435

Walt Valerie

Year	Driver	Starts	Poles	1	2	3	4	5	6–10	Laps	Laps Led	Races Led	Miles	$
1970	Tommy Gale	5	0	0	0	0	0	0	1	391	0	0	659	3,135
Lifetime		5	0	0	0	0	0	0	1	391	0	0	659	$3,135

J. C. Van Landingham

Year	Driver	Starts	Poles	1	2	3	4	5	6–10	Laps	Laps Led	Races Led	Miles	$
1950	J. C. Van Landingham	1	0	0	0	0	0	1	0	48	0	0	200	450
1955	Dick Joslin	1	0	0	0	0	0	0	1	38	0	0	156	425
Lifetime		2	0	0	0	0	0	1	1	86	0	0	356	$875

Gordon Van Liew

Year	Driver	Starts	Poles	1	2	3	4	5	6–10	Laps	Laps Led	Races Led	Miles	$
1972	Ronnie Chumley	1	0	0	0	0	0	0	0	200	0	0	400	645
1973	Tony Bettenhausen Jr.	4	0	0	0	0	0	0	0	854	0	0	1,305	4,115
1974	Tony Bettenhausen Jr.	25	0	0	0	0	0	0	1	4,961	0	0	5,340	36,470
Lifetime		30	0	0	0	0	0	0	1	6,015	0	0	7,045	$41,230

Van Van Wey

Year	Driver	Starts	Poles	1	2	3	4	5	6–10	Laps	Laps Led	Races Led	Miles	$
1954	Van Van Wey	3	0	0	0	0	0	0	0	629	0	0	801	495
Lifetime		3	0	0	0	0	0	0	0	629	0	0	801	$495

Charles Vance

Year	Driver	Starts	Poles	1	2	3	4	5	6–10	Laps	Laps Led	Races Led	Miles	$
1954	John Soares	9	0	1	0	1	0	0	2	1,947	0	0	1,374	3,045
1955	Allen Adkins	1	0	0	0	0	0	0	0	233	0	0	233	150
"	John Soares	1	0	0	0	0	0	0	0	86	0	0	86	25
"	**Total**	2	0	0	0	0	0	0	0	319	0	0	319	175
Lifetime		11	0	1	0	1	0	0	2	2,266	0	0	1,693	$3,220

J. R. VanCurren

Year	Driver	Starts	Poles	1	2	3	4	5	6–10	Laps	Laps Led	Races Led	Miles	$
1967	Cliff Garner	1	0	0	0	0	0	0	0	25	0	0	68	500
Lifetime		1	0	0	0	0	0	0	0	25	0	0	68	$500

Jim Vandiver

Year	Driver	Starts	Poles	1	2	3	4	5	6–10	Laps	Laps Led	Races Led	Miles	$
1975	Jim Vandiver	12	0	0	0	0	1	0	3	2,926	1	1	3,617	22,200
Lifetime		12	0	0	0	0	1	0	3	2,926	1	1	3,617	$22,200

Tom Vandiver

Year	Driver	Starts	Poles	1	2	3	4	5	6–10	Laps	Laps Led	Races Led	Miles	$
1968	Jim Vandiver	1	0	0	0	0	0	0	0	5	0	0	2	100
Lifetime		1	0	0	0	0	0	0	0	5	0	0	2	$100

Jenny VanHouten

Year	Driver	Starts	Poles	1	2	3	4	5	6–10	Laps	Laps Led	Races Led	Miles	$
1991	Keith VanHoughten	1	0	0	0	0	0	0	0	13	0	0	13	3,475
Lifetime		1	0	0	0	0	0	0	0	13	0	0	13	$3,475

Frank Vasko

Year	Driver	Starts	Poles	1	2	3	4	5	6–10	Laps	Laps Led	Races Led	Miles	$
1972	Tommy Gale	6	0	0	0	0	0	0	0	1,144	0	0	1,959	7,477
1973	Tommy Gale	5	0	0	0	0	0	0	0	451	0	0	982	5,680
Lifetime		11	0	0	0	0	0	0	0	1,595	0	0	2,941	$13,157

David Vaughn

Year	Driver	Starts	Poles	1	2	3	4	5	6–10	Laps	Laps Led	Races Led	Miles	$
1957	Keith Olson	1	0	0	0	0	0	0	0	17	0	0	9	100
Lifetime		1	0	0	0	0	0	0	0	17	0	0	9	$100

Jimmy Vaughn

Year	Driver	Starts	Poles	1	2	3	4	5	6–10	Laps	Laps Led	Races Led	Miles	$
1969	Jimmy Vaughn	1	0	0	0	0	0	0	1	159	0	0	423	2,000

Year	Driver	Starts	Poles	Finish 1	2	3	4	5	6–10	Laps	Laps Led	Races Led	Miles	$

Jimmy Vaughn *continued*

Year	Driver	Starts	Poles	1	2	3	4	5	6–10	Laps	Laps Led	Races Led	Miles	$
1971	Jimmy Vaughn	3	0	0	0	0	0	0	0	575	0	0	294	1,015
Lifetime		4	0	0	0	0	0	0	1	734	0	0	717	$3,015

Charles Venable

Year	Driver	Starts	Poles	1	2	3	4	5	6–10	Laps	Laps Led	Races Led	Miles	$
1950	Roscoe Thompson	1	0	0	0	0	0	0	0	45	0	0	188	50
Lifetime		1	0	0	0	0	0	0	0	45	0	0	188	$50

Jim Venable

Year	Driver	Starts	Poles	1	2	3	4	5	6–10	Laps	Laps Led	Races Led	Miles	$
1994	Gary Collins	1	0	0	0	0	0	0	0	43	0	0	108	7,100
Lifetime		1	0	0	0	0	0	0	0	43	0	0	108	$7,100

Bill Venturini

Year	Driver	Starts	Poles	1	2	3	4	5	6–10	Laps	Laps Led	Races Led	Miles	$
1989	Bill Venturini	1	0	0	0	0	0	0	0	80	0	0	160	2,975
1990	Bill Venturini	4	0	0	0	0	0	0	0	702	0	0	1,647	25,270
1991	Bill Venturini	2	0	0	0	0	0	0	0	71	0	0	146	10,125
1993	Bill Venturini	0												1,000
Lifetime		7	0	0	0	0	0	0	0	853	0	0	1,952	$39,370

Tom Vernon

Year	Driver	Starts	Poles	1	2	3	4	5	6–10	Laps	Laps Led	Races Led	Miles	$
1959	Marvin Panch	3	0	0	0	0	0	0	0	603	0	0	841	1,000
"	Glen Wood	1	0	0	0	0	0	1	0	288	0	0	144	400
"	**Total**	4	0	0	0	0	0	1	0	891	0	0	985	1,400
1960	Marvin Panch	3	0	0	0	0	0	0	0	217	22	1	411	350
Lifetime		7	0	0	0	0	0	1	0	1,108	22	1	1,396	$1,750

Lou Viglione

Year	Driver	Starts	Poles	1	2	3	4	5	6–10	Laps	Laps Led	Races Led	Miles	$
1974	Joe Mihalic	5	0	0	0	0	0	0	1	1,725	0	0	1,570	7,595
1975	Joe Mihalic	10	0	0	0	0	0	0	1	1,939	0	0	2,694	13,385
"	Jackie Rogers	7	0	0	0	0	0	0	1	543	2	1	1,191	8,185
"	**Total**	14	0	0	0	0	0	0	2	2,482	2	1	3,885	21,570
1976	Joe Mihalic	9	0	0	0	0	0	0	0	2,171	0	0	3,129	12,925
"	Jackie Rogers	11	0	0	0	0	0	0	3	2,439	3	2	3,874	21,215
"	David Sisco	1	0	0	0	0	0	0	0	34	0	0	52	815
"	**Total**	16	0	0	0	0	0	0	3	4,644	3	2	7,055	34,955
1977	Ramo Stott	5	0	0	0	0	0	0	0	688	0	0	1,438	10,170
Lifetime		40	0	0	0	0	0	0	6	9,539	5	3	13,948	$74,290

Chris Virtue

Year	Driver	Starts	Poles	1	2	3	4	5	6–10	Laps	Laps Led	Races Led	Miles	$
1994	Danny Sullivan	1	0	0	0	0	0	0	0	152	0	0	380	22,750
Lifetime		1	0	0	0	0	0	0	0	152	0	0	380	$22,750

Opal Voight

Year	Driver	Starts	Poles	1	2	3	4	5	6–10	Laps	Laps Led	Races Led	Miles	$
1975	Bruce Jacobi	15	0	0	0	0	0	0	3	3,863	0	0	5,767	29,040
1977	Jim Raptis	3	0	0	0	0	0	0	0	116	0	0	252	2,530
Lifetime		18	0	0	0	0	0	0	3	3,979	0	0	6,019	$31,570

Bobby Waddell

Year	Driver	Starts	Poles	1	2	3	4	5	6–10	Laps	Laps Led	Races Led	Miles	$
1959	Bobby Waddell	7	0	0	0	0	0	0	0	512	0	0	262	360
1960	Bobby Waddell	1	0	0	0	0	0	0	0	168	0	0	84	50
1961	Bobby Waddell	4	0	0	0	0	0	0	2	565	0	0	288	455
1962	George Fox	1	0	0	0	0	0	0	0	3	0	0	2	50
"	Bobby Waddell	5	0	0	0	0	0	0	0	142	0	0	80	420
"	**Total**	5	0	0	0	0	0	0	0	145	0	0	82	470
Lifetime		17	0	0	0	0	0	0	2	1,390	0	0	717	$1,335

Weldon Wagner

Year	Driver	Starts	Poles	1	2	3	4	5	6–10	Laps	Laps Led	Races Led	Miles	$
1960	Darrell Dake	2	0	0	0	0	0	0	1	235	0	0	588	575
1961	Darrell Dake	2	0	0	0	0	0	0	0	54	0	0	135	200
Lifetime		4	0	0	0	0	0	0	1	289	0	0	723	$775

Year	Driver	Starts	Poles	Finish						Laps	Laps Led	Races Led	Miles	$
				1	2	3	4	5	6–10					

Al Wagoner

Year	Driver	Starts	Poles	1	2	3	4	5	6–10	Laps	Laps Led	Races Led	Miles	$
1949	Bill Snowden	1	0	0	0	0	0	1	0		0	0		200
"	Al Wagoner	1	0	0	0	0	0	0	1	178	0	0	89	75
"	**Total**	2	0	0	0	0	0	1	1	178	0	0	89	275
Lifetime		2	0	0	0	0	0	1	1	178	0	0	89	$275

DuWayne Wahl

Year	Driver	Starts	Poles	1	2	3	4	5	6–10	Laps	Laps Led	Races Led	Miles	$
1973	Chuck Wahl	1	0	0	0	0	0	0	0	7	0	0	18	630
1974	Jack Simpson	1	0	0	0	0	0	0	0	105	0	0	275	875
"	Chuck Wahl	2	0	0	0	0	0	0	1	275	0	0	702	2,870
"	**Total**	2	0	0	0	0	0	0	1	380	0	0	977	3,745
1975	Chuck Wahl	3	0	0	0	0	0	0	1	299	0	0	780	4,020
1976	Chuck Wahl	2	0	0	0	0	0	0	0	182	3	1	477	2,705
1977	Chuck Wahl	2	0	0	0	0	0	0	0	155	0	0	406	2,420
1978	Chuck Wahl	2	0	0	0	0	0	0	0	102	0	0	262	1,520
1980	Chuck Wahl	1	0	0	0	0	0	0	0	88	0	0	231	1,005
Lifetime		13	0	0	0	0	0	0	2	1,213	3	1	3,151	$16,045

Russell Wainscott

Year	Driver	Starts	Poles	1	2	3	4	5	6–10	Laps	Laps Led	Races Led	Miles	$
1956	Joy Fair	1	0	0	0	0	0	0	0		0	0		0
Lifetime		1	0	0	0	0	0	0	0		0	0		$0

Frank Waite

Year	Driver	Starts	Poles	1	2	3	4	5	6–10	Laps	Laps Led	Races Led	Miles	$
1963	James Norton	1	0	0	0	0	0	0	0	84	0	0	126	275
"	Frank Waite	4	0	0	0	0	0	0	0	617	0	0	309	425
"	**Total**	5	0	0	0	0	0	0	0	701	0	0	435	700
Lifetime		5	0	0	0	0	0	0	0	701	0	0	435	$700

Bob Walden

Year	Driver	Starts	Poles	1	2	3	4	5	6–10	Laps	Laps Led	Races Led	Miles	$
1958	Johnny Allen	1	0	0	0	0	0	0	0	235	0	0	94	110
"	Shep Langdon	1	0	0	0	0	0	0	0	193	0	0	48	165
"	Eddie Pagan	1	0	0	0	0	0	0	1	143	0	0	48	185
"	Bob Walden	14	0	0	0	0	1	0	8	2,104	0	0	1,167	1,810
"	Paul Walton	1	0	0	0	0	0	0	0	144	0	0	36	130
"	**Total**	18	0	0	0	0	1	0	9	2,819	0	0	1,392	2,400
Lifetime		18	0	0	0	0	1	0	9	2,819	0	0	1,392	$2,400

Monty Walden

Year	Driver	Starts	Poles	1	2	3	4	5	6–10	Laps	Laps Led	Races Led	Miles	$
1960	Pappy Crane	1	0	0	0	0	0	0	0	89	0	0	223	200
Lifetime		1	0	0	0	0	0	0	0	89	0	0	223	$200

W. R. Waldron

Year	Driver	Starts	Poles	1	2	3	4	5	6–10	Laps	Laps Led	Races Led	Miles	$
1956	Buck Hall	1	0	0	0	0	0	0	0	11	0	0	10	25
"	George Mantooth	1	0	0	0	0	0	0	0	43	0	0	22	0
"	Bunk Moore	1	0	0	0	0	0	0	0	20	0	0	15	0
"	Bill Widenhouse	1	0	0	0	0	0	0	0	49	0	0	25	0
"	**Total**	4	0	0	0	0	0	0	0	123	0	0	71	25
Lifetime		4	0	0	0	0	0	0	0	123	0	0	71	$25

David Walker

Year	Driver	Starts	Poles	1	2	3	4	5	6–10	Laps	Laps Led	Races Led	Miles	$
1964	Buck Baker	3	0	0	0	0	0	0	0	352	0	0	198	460
"	Buddy Baker	1	0	0	0	0	0	0	0	64	0	0	160	725
"	Tiny Lund	5	0	0	0	1	0	0	1	831	0	0	1,092	2,900
"	Marshall Sargent	1	0	0	0	0	0	0	1	77	0	0	39	150
"	LeeRoy Yarbrough	2	0	0	0	0	0	0	0	81	0	0	125	750
"	**Total**	11	0	0	0	1	0	0	2	1,405	0	0	1,612	4,985
Lifetime		11	0	0	0	1	0	0	2	1,405	0	0	1,612	$4,985

Jimmy Walker

Year	Driver	Starts	Poles	1	2	3	4	5	6–10	Laps	Laps Led	Races Led	Miles	$
1982	Jimmy Walker	3	0	0	0	0	0	0	0	131	0	0	130	2,320
1983	Jimmy Walker	1	0	0	0	0	0	0	0	239	0	0	149	800

Year	Driver	Starts	Poles	Finish 1	2	3	4	5	6–10	Laps	Laps Led	Races Led	Miles	$

Jimmy Walker *continued*

Year	Driver	Starts	Poles	1	2	3	4	5	6–10	Laps	Laps Led	Races Led	Miles	$
1984	Mike Potter	1	0	0	0	0	0	0	0	9	0	0	9	710
1985	Mike Potter	6	0	0	0	0	0	0	0	1,434	0	0	1,721	10,855
"	Jimmy Walker	1	0	0	0	0	0	0	0	180	0	0	180	1,350
"	**Total**	7	0	0	0	0	0	0	0	1,614	0	0	1,901	12,205
1986	Mike Potter	2	0	0	0	0	0	0	0	95	0	0	95	1,900
Lifetime		14	0	0	0	0	0	0	0	2,088	0	0	2,284	$17,935

Murrace Walker

Year	Driver	Starts	Poles	1	2	3	4	5	6–10	Laps	Laps Led	Races Led	Miles	$
1951	Murrace Walker	1	0	0	0	0	0	0	0	104	0	0	130	0
Lifetime		1	0	0	0	0	0	0	0	104	0	0	130	$0

B. R. Waller

Year	Driver	Starts	Poles	1	2	3	4	5	6–10	Laps	Laps Led	Races Led	Miles	$
1951	Frank Gise	2	0	0	0	0	0	0	1	215	0	0	269	100
Lifetime		2	0	0	0	0	0	0	1	215	0	0	269	$100

Dick Walters

Year	Driver	Starts	Poles	1	2	3	4	5	6–10	Laps	Laps Led	Races Led	Miles	$
1957	Dick Walters	3	0	0	0	0	0	0	1	499	0	0	327	290
1958	Dick Walters	4	0	0	0	0	0	0	0	305	0	0	129	290
Lifetime		7	0	0	0	0	0	0	1	804	0	0	456	$580

Harvey Walters

Year	Driver	Starts	Poles	1	2	3	4	5	6–10	Laps	Laps Led	Races Led	Miles	$
1956	Buddy Krebs	1	0	0	0	0	0	0	0		0	0		0
"	Jim Wilson	2	0	0	0	0	0	0	0	180	0	0	90	50
"	**Total**	2	0	0	0	0	0	0	0	180	0	0	90	50
Lifetime		2	0	0	0	0	0	0	0	180	0	0	90	$50

Nook Walters

Year	Driver	Starts	Poles	1	2	3	4	5	6–10	Laps	Laps Led	Races Led	Miles	$
1960	Nook Walters	1	0	0	0	0	1	0	0	179	0	0	90	275
Lifetime		1	0	0	0	0	1	0	0	179	0	0	90	$275

Ratus Walters

Year	Driver	Starts	Poles	1	2	3	4	5	6–10	Laps	Laps Led	Races Led	Miles	$
1958	Reds Kagle	1	0	0	0	0	0	0	0	49	0	0	67	100
"	Elmo Langley	2	0	0	0	0	0	0	0	124	0	0	115	195
"	**Total**	3	0	0	0	0	0	0	0	173	0	0	182	295
1959	Elmo Langley	13	0	0	0	1	0	0	1	1,694	0	0	1,314	2,280
"	Pedro Rodriguez	1	0	0	0	0	0	0	1	144	0	0	144	300
"	**Total**	13	0	0	0	1	0	0	2	1,838	0	0	1,458	2,580
1960	Elmo Langley	4	0	0	0	0	0	0	0	358	0	0	437	500
"	Bill Morgan	1	0	0	0	0	0	0	1	183	0	0	92	130
"	**Total**	5	0	0	0	0	0	0	1	541	0	0	529	630
1961	Hoss Kagle	1	0	0	0	0	0	0	0	2	0	0	1	125
"	Reds Kagle	3	0	0	0	0	0	0	1	720	0	0	963	1,495
"	Bill Morgan	3	0	0	0	0	0	0	1	692	0	0	756	1,225
"	Jimmy Thompson	1	0	0	0	0	0	0	0	113	0	0	170	200
"	**Total**	7	0	0	0	0	0	0	2	1,527	0	0	1,889	3,045
1962	George Alsobrook	4	0	0	0	0	0	0	1	374	0	0	707	825
"	Larry Frank	19	0	1	0	0	0	1	6	3,566	85	1	3,506	32,987
"	Elmo Langley	3	0	0	0	0	0	0	0	269	0	0	413	975
"	Ralph Moody	1	0	0	0	0	0	0	0	1	0	0	1	75
"	Jim Reed	4	0	0	0	0	0	1	0	919	0	0	781	1,030
"	**Total**	23	0	1	0	0	0	2	7	5,129	85	1	5,407	35,892
1963	Johnny Allen	5	0	0	0	0	0	0	0	459	0	0	375	1,275
"	Elmo Langley	1	0	0	0	0	0	0	0	8	0	0	4	100
"	Jim Reed	1	0	0	0	0	0	0	0	29	0	0	15	50
"	**Total**	7	0	0	0	0	0	0	0	496	0	0	393	1,425
1964	Elmo Langley	1	0	0	0	0	0	0	0	119	0	0	107	100
Lifetime		59	0	1	0	1	0	2	12	9,823	85	1	9,965	$43,967

Salt Walther

Year	Driver	Starts	Poles	1	2	3	4	5	6–10	Laps	Laps Led	Races Led	Miles	$
1975	Salt Walther	1	0	0	0	0	0	0	0	188	0	0	376	1,005

Year	Driver	Starts	Poles	Finish 1	2	3	4	5	6–10	Laps	Laps Led	Races Led	Miles	$

Salt Walther *continued*

Year	Driver	Starts	Poles	1	2	3	4	5	6–10	Laps	Laps Led	Races Led	Miles	$
1976	Salt Walther	1	0	0	0	0	0	0	0	187	0	0	468	5,880
1977	Salt Walther	1	0	0	0	0	0	0	0	114	0	0	285	2,725
Lifetime		3	0	0	0	0	0	0	0	489	0	0	1,129	$9,610

Paul Walton

Year	Driver	Starts	Poles	1	2	3	4	5	6–10	Laps	Laps Led	Races Led	Miles	$
1959	Ken Rush	1	0	0	0	0	1	0	0	246	0	0	98	250
"	Paul Walton	1	0	0	0	0	0	0	0	112	0	0	70	60
"	**Total**	2	0	0	0	0	1	0	0	358	0	0	168	310
Lifetime		2	0	0	0	0	1	0	0	358	0	0	168	$310

Darrell Waltrip

Year	Driver	Starts	Poles	1	2	3	4	5	6–10	Laps	Laps Led	Races Led	Miles	$
1972	Darrell Waltrip	5	0	0	0	1	0	0	2	1,211	7	1	1,653	8,615
1973	Darrell Waltrip	14	0	0	1	0	0	0	3	2,965	50	3	4,406	27,775
1974	Darrell Waltrip	16	1	0	1	3	2	1	4	4,649	103	5	6,013	67,775
1975	Darrell Waltrip	17	2	1	2	0	3	2	2	4,480	291	8	5,071	98,350
1991	Darrell Waltrip	29	0	2	2	1	0	0	12	9,229	203	12	10,900	604,854
1992	Darrell Waltrip	29	1	3	2	3	0	2	3	8,706	513	14	10,248	876,492
1993	Darrell Waltrip	30	0	0	0	2	1	1	6	9,194	151	9	10,817	746,646
1994	Darrell Waltrip	31	0	0	0	2	2	0	9	9,905	60	8	12,026	835,680
1995	Darrell Waltrip	31	1	0	0	1	3	0	4	8,222	168	8	9,581	850,632
1996	Darrell Waltrip	31	0	0	0	0	0	0	2	7,766	2	2	8,971	740,185
Lifetime		233	5	6	8	13	11	6	47	66,327	1,548	70	79,688	$4,857,004

Blackie Wangerin

Year	Driver	Starts	Poles	1	2	3	4	5	6–10	Laps	Laps Led	Races Led	Miles	$
1971	Blackie Wangerin	1	0	0	0	0	0	0	0	16	0	0	40	0
1976	Blackie Wangerin	0												400
1977	Blackie Wangerin	1	0	0	0	0	0	0	0	260	0	0	396	885
1978	Skip Manning	1	0	0	0	0	0	0	0	308	0	0	469	1,050
"	Blackie Wangerin	10	0	0	0	0	0	0	0	1,342	0	0	2,522	13,515
"	**Total**	11	0	0	0	0	0	0	0	1,650	0	0	2,991	14,565
1979	Blackie Wangerin	7	0	0	0	0	0	0	0	894	0	0	1,750	14,535
1980	Blackie Wangerin	3	0	0	0	0	0	0	0	548	0	0	808	6,920
1981	Blackie Wangerin	1	0	0	0	0	0	0	0	17	0	0	43	2,750
1982	Blackie Wangerin	1	0	0	0	0	0	0	0	73	0	0	183	2,000
1983	Blackie Wangerin	2	0	0	0	0	0	0	0	48	0	0	62	5,910
1984	Blackie Wangerin	1	0	0	0	0	0	0	0	0	0	0	0	4,210
1986	Blackie Wangerin	0												1,100
1987	Blackie Wangerin	0												1,800
1988	Blackie Wangerin	0												2,000
1990	Blackie Wangerin	0												1,150
1991	Blackie Wangerin	0												1,750
Lifetime		28	0	0	0	0	0	0	0	3,506	0	0	6,272	$59,975

Bill Ward

Year	Driver	Starts	Poles	1	2	3	4	5	6–10	Laps	Laps Led	Races Led	Miles	$
1975	Bill Ward	1	0	0	0	0	0	0	0	145	0	0	386	1,320
Lifetime		1	0	0	0	0	0	0	0	145	0	0	386	$1,320

Glen Ward

Year	Driver	Starts	Poles	1	2	3	4	5	6–10	Laps	Laps Led	Races Led	Miles	$
1980	Glen Ward	1	0	0	0	0	0	0	0	77	0	0	193	875
Lifetime		1	0	0	0	0	0	0	0	77	0	0	193	$875

Warner Brothers

Year	Driver	Starts	Poles	1	2	3	4	5	6–10	Laps	Laps Led	Races Led	Miles	$
1961	Brian Naylor	1	0	0	0	0	0	0	0	85	0	0	213	200
"	Frank Secrist	2	0	0	0	0	0	0	0	150	0	0	214	350
"	**Total**	3	0	0	0	0	0	0	0	235	0	0	427	550
Lifetime		3	0	0	0	0	0	0	0	235	0	0	427	$550

David Warren

Year	Driver	Starts	Poles	1	2	3	4	5	6–10	Laps	Laps Led	Races Led	Miles	$
1963	Tiny Lund	1	0	0	0	0	0	0	0	18	0	0	5	75
1964	Bob Cooper	1	0	0	0	0	0	0	1	305	0	0	419	1,025

Year	Driver	Starts	Poles	1	2	3	4	5	6–10	Laps	Laps Led	Races Led	Miles	$

David Warren *continued*

Year	Driver	Starts	Poles	1	2	3	4	5	6–10	Laps	Laps Led	Races Led	Miles	$
"	Pete Stewart	6	0	0	0	0	0	0	0	1,242	0	0	877	1,765
"	Don Tilley	2	0	0	0	0	0	0	0	275	0	0	164	250
"	**Total**	9	0	0	0	0	0	0	1	1,822	0	0	1,461	3,040
1965	Curtis Crider	1	0	0	0	0	0	0	0	390	0	0	195	375
"	Jimmy Helms	35	0	0	0	0	0	0	4	5,248	0	0	3,478	8,140
"	J. T. Putney	1	0	0	0	0	0	0	0	118	0	0	74	175
"	Pete Stewart	2	0	0	0	0	0	0	0	2	0	0	5	1,165
"	David Warren	1	0	0	0	0	0	0	0	32	0	0	16	100
"	**Total**	40	0	0	0	0	0	0	4	5,790	0	0	3,768	9,955
1966	Jimmy Helms	25	0	0	0	0	0	0	0	2,823	0	0	2,528	5,030
"	Marty Robbins	1	0	0	0	0	0	0	0	48	0	0	24	100
"	**Total**	26	0	0	0	0	0	0	0	2,871	0	0	2,552	5,130
Lifetime		76	0	0	0	0	0	0	5	10,501	0	0	7,785	$18,200

Frank Warren

Year	Driver	Starts	Poles	1	2	3	4	5	6–10	Laps	Laps Led	Races Led	Miles	$
1969	Frank Warren	8	0	0	0	0	0	0	0	1,143	0	0	1,679	7,322
1970	Frank Warren	46	0	0	0	0	0	0	2	7,709	71	1	7,763	35,161
1971	Dick Poling	1	0	0	0	0	0	0	0	21	0	0	53	0
"	Frank Warren	43	0	0	0	0	0	0	8	8,180	0	0	8,159	37,427
"	**Total**	43	0	0	0	0	0	0	8	8,201	0	0	8,211	37,427
1972	Richard Childress	1	0	0	0	0	0	0	0	179	0	0	358	880
"	Frank Warren	30	0	0	0	0	0	0	2	7,091	0	0	8,404	45,048
"	**Total**	30	0	0	0	0	0	0	2	7,270	0	0	8,762	45,928
1973	David Ray Boggs	1	0	0	0	0	0	0	0	116	0	0	158	1,235
"	Jabe Thomas	1	0	0	0	0	0	0	0	337	0	0	180	700
"	Paul Tyler	1	0	0	0	0	0	0	0	105	0	0	107	1,240
"	Frank Warren	21	0	0	0	0	0	0	0	5,640	0	0	6,508	33,751
"	**Total**	24	0	0	0	0	0	0	0	6,198	0	0	6,953	36,926
1974	Frank Warren	29	0	0	0	0	0	1	1	7,342	0	0	8,993	55,779
1975	Ed Negre	1	0	0	0	0	0	0	0	184	0	0	460	4,390
"	Frank Warren	27	0	0	0	0	0	0	0	7,758	0	0	9,123	55,671
"	**Total**	28	0	0	0	0	0	0	0	7,942	0	0	9,583	60,061
1976	Frank Warren	28	0	0	0	0	0	0	3	7,309	0	0	9,289	65,197
1977	Frank Warren	29	0	0	0	0	0	0	1	6,466	1	1	8,107	67,945
1978	Frank Warren	30	0	0	0	0	0	0	0	8,481	0	0	9,827	68,173
1979	Frank Warren	31	0	0	0	0	0	0	3	8,477	0	0	10,046	94,539
1980	Joey Arrington	1	0	0	0	0	0	0	0	368	0	0	199	2,030
"	Joe Booher	2	0	0	0	0	0	0	0	161	0	0	412	3,430
"	Jim Hurlbert	1	0	0	0	0	0	0	0	33	0	0	83	2,950
"	Dick May	2	0	0	0	0	0	0	0	502	0	0	624	3,235
"	Junior Miller	5	0	0	0	0	0	0	0	1,194	0	0	1,194	8,160
"	Marty Robbins	1	0	0	0	0	0	0	0	131	0	0	328	2,285
"	Travis Tiller	1	0	0	0	0	0	0	0	323	0	0	172	770
"	Frank Warren	7	0	0	0	0	0	0	0	1,591	0	0	2,561	19,450
"	**Total**	20	0	0	0	0	0	0	0	4,303	0	0	5,574	42,310
Lifetime		346	0	0	0	0	0	1	20	80,841	72	2	94,787	$616,768

Gayle Warren

Year	Driver	Starts	Poles	1	2	3	4	5	6–10	Laps	Laps Led	Races Led	Miles	$
1953	Gayle Warren	2	0	0	0	0	0	0	0	327	0	0	348	150
Lifetime		2	0	0	0	0	0	0	0	327	0	0	348	$150

Jerome Warren

Year	Driver	Starts	Poles	1	2	3	4	5	6–10	Laps	Laps Led	Races Led	Miles	$
1963	Curtis Crider	1	0	0	0	0	0	0	0	397	0	0	199	150
"	Jerome Warren	4	0	0	0	0	0	0	0	146	0	0	77	335
"	**Total**	5	0	0	0	0	0	0	0	543	0	0	275	485
Lifetime		5	0	0	0	0	0	0	0	543	0	0	275	$485

Don Waterman

Year	Driver	Starts	Poles	1	2	3	4	5	6–10	Laps	Laps Led	Races Led	Miles	$
1980	Don Waterman	2	0	0	0	0	0	0	0	250	0	0	633	3,555
1981	Don Waterman	3	0	0	0	0	0	0	1	301	1	1	789	8,570
1982	Don Waterman	2	0	0	0	0	0	0	0	156	1	1	409	3,805
1983	Don Waterman	2	0	0	0	0	0	0	0	189	0	0	495	3,355
Lifetime		9	0	0	0	0	0	0	1	896	2	2	2,325	$19,285

Year	Driver	Starts	Poles	Finish 1	2	3	4	5	6–10	Laps	Laps Led	Races Led	Miles	$

H. L. Waters

Year	Driver	Starts	Poles	1	2	3	4	5	6–10	Laps	Laps Led	Races Led	Miles	$
1983	Delma Cowart	4	0	0	0	0	0	0	0	643	0	0	1,141	7,750
1984	Delma Cowart	2	0	0	0	0	0	0	0	533	0	0	803	4,170
1985	Delma Cowart	2	0	0	0	0	0	0	0	71	0	0	183	9,930
1986	Delma Cowart	3	0	0	0	0	0	0	0	403	0	0	977	7,595
"	Doug Heveron	1	0	0	0	0	0	0	0	106	1	1	265	2,045
"	**Total**	4	0	0	0	0	0	0	0	509	1	1	1,242	9,640
1987	Delma Cowart	1	0	0	0	0	0	0	0	180	0	0	479	4,640
1989	Delma Cowart	0												1,400
1990	Delma Cowart	0												1,500
"	Jim Sauter	1	0	0	0	0	0	0	0	310	0	0	472	3,050
"	**Total**	1	0	0	0	0	0	0	0	310	0	0	472	4,550
1991	Delma Cowart	0												1,750
1992	Delma Cowart	3	0	0	0	0	0	0	0	498	0	0	950	33,470
1993	Delma Cowart	0												2,300
1994	Delma Cowart	0												2,300
1995	Delma Cowart	0												2,150
"	Brad Teague	0												1,000
"	**Total**	0												3,150
1996	Delma Cowart	0												3,440
Lifetime		17	0	0	0	0	0	0	0	2,744	1	1	5,268	$88,490

Richard Waters

Year	Driver	Starts	Poles	1	2	3	4	5	6–10	Laps	Laps Led	Races Led	Miles	$
1978	Richard Waters	1	0	0	0	0	0	0	0	13	0	0	8	265
Lifetime		1	0	0	0	0	0	0	0	13	0	0	8	$265

J. B. Watkins

Year	Driver	Starts	Poles	1	2	3	4	5	6–10	Laps	Laps Led	Races Led	Miles	$
1951	Earl Moss	4	0	0	0	0	0	0	1	479	0	0	515	285
Lifetime		4	0	0	0	0	0	0	1	479	0	0	515	$285

W. H. Watson

Year	Driver	Starts	Poles	1	2	3	4	5	6–10	Laps	Laps Led	Races Led	Miles	$
1959	Joe Eubanks	1	0	0	0	0	0	0	0	26	0	0	36	190
"	Cotton Owens	25	1	0	3	1	2	4	6	4,292	95	1	2,948	14,190
"	Speedy Thompson	1	0	0	0	0	0	0	0	29	0	0	26	50
"	**Total**	27	1	0	3	1	2	4	6	4,347	95	1	3,010	14,430
1960	Elmo Henderson	6	0	0	0	0	0	0	0	870	0	0	1,083	1,375
Lifetime		33	1	0	3	1	2	4	6	5,217	95	1	4,093	$15,805

J. M. Wattenbarger

Year	Driver	Starts	Poles	1	2	3	4	5	6–10	Laps	Laps Led	Races Led	Miles	$
1957	Frank Secrist	1	0	0	0	0	0	0	0	24	0	0	60	45
Lifetime		1	0	0	0	0	0	0	0	24	0	0	60	$45

Ken Watter

Year	Driver	Starts	Poles	1	2	3	4	5	6–10	Laps	Laps Led	Races Led	Miles	$
1968	Phil Wendt	3	0	0	0	0	0	0	0	418	0	0	445	1,980
Lifetime		3	0	0	0	0	0	0	0	418	0	0	445	$1,980

Art Watts

Year	Driver	Starts	Poles	1	2	3	4	5	6–10	Laps	Laps Led	Races Led	Miles	$
1961	Art Watts	1	0	0	0	0	0	0	0	85	0	0	119	100
Lifetime		1	0	0	0	0	0	0	0	85	0	0	119	$100

Bobby Wawak

Year	Driver	Starts	Poles	1	2	3	4	5	6–10	Laps	Laps Led	Races Led	Miles	$
1967	Bobby Wawak	14	0	0	0	0	0	0	3	2,225	0	0	2,320	8,070
1969	Bobby Wawak	1	0	0	0	0	0	0	0	74	0	0	148	657
1971	Bobby Wawak	2	0	0	0	0	0	0	0	615	0	0	891	2,665
1977	Bobby Wawak	4	0	0	0	0	0	0	0	1,112	0	0	1,639	5,195
1978	Joe Booher	2	0	0	0	0	0	0	0	417	0	0	324	1,430
"	Tommy Gale	1	0	0	0	0	0	0	0	253	0	0	385	700
"	Dick May	2	0	0	0	0	0	0	0	500	0	0	475	1,495
"	Bobby Wawak	6	0	0	0	0	0	0	0	1,233	0	0	893	4,335
"	**Total**	11	0	0	0	0	0	0	0	2,403	0	0	2,077	7,960
1979	Bobby Wawak	4	0	0	0	0	0	0	0	740	0	0	855	6,785
1980	Joe Booher	2	0	0	0	0	0	0	0	655	0	0	934	9,270
"	Stuart Huffman	1	0	0	0	0	0	0	0	340	0	0	181	510

Year	Driver	Starts	Poles	Finish						Laps	Laps Led	Races Led	Miles	$
				1	2	3	4	5	6–10					

Bobby Wawak *continued*

Year	Driver	Starts	Poles	1	2	3	4	5	6–10	Laps	Laps Led	Races Led	Miles	$
"	Henry Jones	1	0	0	0	0	0	0	0	178	0	0	445	1,550
"	Bob Riley	1	0	0	0	0	0	0	0	141	0	0	353	1,165
"	Bobby Wawak	19	0	0	0	0	0	0	1	4,065	0	0	4,224	21,080
"	**Total**	24	0	0	0	0	0	0	1	5,379	0	0	6,137	33,575
1981	Cecil Gordon	1	0	0	0	0	0	0	0	2	0	0	1	455
"	Henry Jones	1	0	0	0	0	0	0	0	363	0	0	197	765
"	Bobby Wawak	14	0	0	0	0	0	0	1	2,734	0	0	3,485	23,460
"	**Total**	16	0	0	0	0	0	0	1	3,099	0	0	3,683	24,680
1982	Bobby Wawak	10	0	0	0	0	0	0	0	2,489	2	1	3,981	23,660
1983	Ralph Jones	0												1,250
"	Bobby Wawak	9	0	0	0	0	0	0	0	2,167	0	0	3,262	20,780
"	**Total**	9	0	0	0	0	0	0	0	2,167	0	0	3,262	22,030
1984	Bob Riley	1	0	0	0	0	0	0	0	179	0	0	448	1,735
"	Bobby Wawak	3	0	0	0	0	0	0	0	694	0	0	983	5,600
"	**Total**	4	0	0	0	0	0	0	0	873	0	0	1,431	7,335
1985	Bobby Wawak	13	0	0	0	0	0	0	0	2,982	0	0	3,987	38,955
"	Rick Wilson	1	0	0	0	0	0	0	0	111	0	0	295	2,515
"	**Total**	14	0	0	0	0	0	0	0	3,093	0	0	4,282	41,470
1986	Jack Ely	2	0	0	0	0	0	0	0	329	0	0	823	5,145
"	Jim Fitzgerald	1	0	0	0	0	0	0	0	28	0	0	73	925
"	Bobby Wawak	6	0	0	0	0	0	0	0	1,270	0	0	1,734	12,155
"	**Total**	9	0	0	0	0	0	0	0	1,627	0	0	2,630	18,225
1987	Bobby Wawak	8	0	0	0	0	0	0	0	1,648	0	0	2,343	24,955
1988	Randy LaJoie	1	0	0	0	0	0	0	0	89	0	0	89	1,460
1989	Randy LaJoie	0												2,450
1990	Mike Potter	3	0	0	0	0	0	0	0	463	0	0	652	9,775
Lifetime		134	0	0	0	0	0	0	5	28,096	2	1	36,419	$240,947

Bob Weatherly

Year	Driver	Starts	Poles	1	2	3	4	5	6–10	Laps	Laps Led	Races Led	Miles	$
1953	Bob Weatherly	1	0	0	0	0	0	0	0	289	0	0	397	140
1957	Cale Yarborough	1	0	0	0	0	0	0	0	31	0	0	43	100
1959	Cale Yarborough	1	0	0	0	0	0	0	0	219	0	0	301	150
1960	Cale Yarborough	1	0	0	0	0	0	0	0	114	0	0	57	85
Lifetime		4	0	0	0	0	0	0	0	653	0	0	798	$475

Louis Weathersbee

Year	Driver	Starts	Poles	1	2	3	4	5	6–10	Laps	Laps Led	Races Led	Miles	$
1964	Louis Weathersbee	4	0	0	0	0	0	0	0	385	0	0	314	610
Lifetime		4	0	0	0	0	0	0	0	385	0	0	314	$610

Louie Weathersby

Year	Driver	Starts	Poles	1	2	3	4	5	6–10	Laps	Laps Led	Races Led	Miles	$
1964	Bobby Isaac	3	0	0	0	0	0	0	0	311	0	0	155	430
"	Bud Moore	2	0	0	0	0	0	0	0	206	0	0	227	600
"	LeeRoy Yarbrough	17	0	2	2	2	2	0	3	2,970	192	4	1,422	5,755
"	Doug Yates	1	0	0	0	0	0	1	0	249	0	0	125	450
"	**Total**	23	0	2	2	2	2	1	3	3,736	192	4	1,929	7,235
1965	Bud Moore	11	1	0	1	1	1	0	3	1,279	93	2	639	2,590
Lifetime		34	1	2	3	3	3	1	6	5,015	285	6	2,568	$9,825

Gary Weaver

Year	Driver	Starts	Poles	1	2	3	4	5	6–10	Laps	Laps Led	Races Led	Miles	$
1965	Bernard Alvarez	2	0	0	0	0	0	0	0	9	0	0	7	600
"	Rene Charland	1	0	0	0	0	0	0	0	8	0	0	12	455
"	Darel Dieringer	3	0	0	0	0	1	0	0	429	0	0	253	1,205
"	Tiny Lund	3	0	0	0	0	1	0	2	1,353	0	0	724	1,650
"	Cale Yarborough	6	0	0	0	1	0	0	1	569	3	1	612	2,610
"	LeeRoy Yarbrough	3	0	0	0	0	1	0	1	547	0	0	274	790
"	**Total**	18	0	0	0	1	3	0	4	2,915	3	1	1,881	7,310
1966	Paul Bumhaver	1	0	0	0	0	0	0	0	291	0	0	146	200
"	Tiny Lund	1	0	0	0	0	0	0	0	33	0	0	83	0
"	Jim Paschal	1	0	0	0	0	1	0	0	297	16	1	149	515
"	**Total**	3	0	0	0	0	1	0	0	621	16	1	377	715
Lifetime		21	0	0	0	1	4	0	4	3,536	19	2	2,258	$8,025

J. C. Weaver

Year	Driver	Starts	Poles	1	2	3	4	5	6–10	Laps	Laps Led	Races Led	Miles	$
1987	Dave Pletcher	2	0	0	0	0	0	0	0	210	0	0	548	4,915

Year	Driver	Starts	Poles		Finish					Laps	Laps Led	Races Led	Miles	$
				1	2	3	4	5	6–10					

J. C. Weaver *continued*

Year	Driver	Starts	Poles	1	2	3	4	5	6–10	Laps	Laps Led	Races Led	Miles	$
1988	Dave Pletcher	1	0	0	0	0	0	0	0	464	0	0	472	2,015
Lifetime		3	0	0	0	0	0	0	0	674	0	0	1,020	$6,930

William P. Webb

Year	Driver	Starts	Poles	1	2	3	4	5	6–10	Laps	Laps Led	Races Led	Miles	$
1955	Bob Dawson	1	0	0	0	0	0	0	0	37	0	0	152	50
Lifetime		1	0	0	0	0	0	0	0	37	0	0	152	$50

Ewell Weddle

Year	Driver	Starts	Poles	1	2	3	4	5	6–10	Laps	Laps Led	Races Led	Miles	$
1950	Ewell Weddle	3	0	0	0	1	0	0	0	158	0	0	79	600
1951	Ewell Weddle	1	0	0	0	0	0	0	0	0	0	0	0	25
1952	Ewell Weddle	3	0	0	0	0	0	0	0	465	0	0	316	125
1953	Ewell Weddle	4	0	0	0	0	0	0	1	0	0	0	0	125
Lifetime		11	0	0	0	1	0	0	1	623	0	0	395	$875

Larry Wehrs

Year	Driver	Starts	Poles	1	2	3	4	5	6–10	Laps	Laps Led	Races Led	Miles	$
1968	Dave Marcis	10	0	0	0	0	0	0	2	3,240	0	0	3,179	8,199
1969	Don Biederman	1	0	0	0	0	0	0	1	183	0	0	92	270
"	Cecil Gordon	1	0	0	0	0	0	0	0	237	0	0	119	395
"	Henley Gray	1	0	0	0	0	0	0	0	288	0	0	432	1,425
"	Dave Marcis	1	0	0	0	0	0	0	1	180	0	0	90	140
"	**Total**	4	0	0	0	0	0	0	2	888	0	0	732	2,230
Lifetime		14	0	0	0	0	0	0	4	4,128	0	0	3,911	$10,429

Curly Weida

Year	Driver	Starts	Poles	1	2	3	4	5	6–10	Laps	Laps Led	Races Led	Miles	$
1955	Royce Haggerty	1	0	0	0	0	0	0	0	228	0	0	228	100
1956	Royce Haggerty	6	1	1	0	0	0	0	1	1,017	72	2	610	1,720
1957	Royce Haggerty	2	0	0	0	0	0	0	1	172	0	0	86	185
Lifetime		9	1	1	0	0	0	0	1	1,417	72	2	924	$2,005

Charles Weidler

Year	Driver	Starts	Poles	1	2	3	4	5	6–10	Laps	Laps Led	Races Led	Miles	$
1953	Charles Weidler	2	0	0	0	0	0	0	0	9	0	0	37	25
Lifetime		2	0	0	0	0	0	0	0	9	0	0	37	$25

Danny Weinberg

Year	Driver	Starts	Poles	1	2	3	4	5	6–10	Laps	Laps Led	Races Led	Miles	$
1951	Danny Weinberg	2	0	0	0	0	0	0	1	97	0	0	49	150
Lifetime		2	0	0	0	0	0	0	1	97	0	0	49	$150

Bob Welborn

Year	Driver	Starts	Poles	1	2	3	4	5	6–10	Laps	Laps Led	Races Led	Miles	$
1955	Bob Welborn	10	1	0	1	2	0	0	4	1,903	31	1	1,606	2,850
1956	Jimmie Lewallen	3	0	0	0	0	0	0	0	91	0	0	66	100
"	Jimmy Massey	1	0	0	0	0	0	0	1	96	0	0	86	100
"	Jim Paschal	4	0	0	0	0	0	1	2	572	0	0	271	560
"	Bob Welborn	6	0	0	0	0	0	0	2	974	0	0	474	650
"	Rex White	24	1	0	0	2	0	1	11	4,240	0	0	2,978	5,334
"	**Total**	27	1	0	0	2	0	2	16	5,973	0	0	3,875	6,744
1957	Possum Jones	6	0	0	0	0	0	0	4	1,443	0	0	1,395	2,375
"	Tiny Lund	1	0	0	0	0	0	1	0	192	0	0	96	245
"	Gwyn Staley	1	0	0	0	0	0	0	0	243	0	0	243	400
"	Curtis Turner	1	0	0	0	0	0	0	0		0			50
"	Bob Welborn	4	0	1	0	0	0	2	0	1,152	457	2	968	5,050
"	Rex White	7	1	0	1	0	3	0	1	1,561	193	2	1,132	3,570
"	**Total**	10	1	1	1	0	3	3	5	4,591	650	3	3,833	11,690
1958	Darel Dieringer	1	0	0	0	0	0	0	0	11	0	0	45	25
"	Possum Jones	3	1	0	0	0	0	1	1	394	28	1	172	445
"	Tiny Lund	1	0	0	0	0	0	0	0	9	0	0	37	0
"	**Total**	4	1	0	0	0	0	1	1	414	28	1	254	470
1959	Bob Welborn	25	3	1	1	3	2	0	3	3,431	17	4	1,927	7,395
1960	Junior Johnson	1	0	0	0	0	0	0	0	2	0	0	1	75
"	Jim Paschal	2	0	0	0	0	0	0	0	193	0	0	287	370
"	Bob Welborn	12	0	0	0	0	2	3	4	2,483	18	1	2,402	5,494
"	**Total**	14	0	0	0	0	2	3	4	2,678	18	1	2,689	5,939

Year	Driver	Starts	Poles	Finish						Laps	Laps Led	Races Led	Miles	$
				1	2	3	4	5	6–10	Laps	Led	Led	Miles	$

Bob Welborn *continued*

Year	Driver	Starts	Poles	1	2	3	4	5	6–10	Laps	Laps Led	Races Led	Miles	$
1961	Bob Welborn	4	0	0	0	0	0	0	1	715	1	1	1,128	1,390
Lifetime		94	7	2	3	7	7	9	34	19,705	745	11	15,312	$36,478

O. C. Welch

Year	Driver	Starts	Poles	1	2	3	4	5	6–10	Laps	Laps Led	Races Led	Miles	$
1989	Mike Potter	1	0	0	0	0	0	0	0	137	0	0	187	2,455
Lifetime		1	0	0	0	0	0	0	0	137	0	0	187	$2,455

Chuck Wellings

Year	Driver	Starts	Poles	1	2	3	4	5	6–10	Laps	Laps Led	Races Led	Miles	$
1989	Joe Ruttman	1	0	0	0	0	0	0	0	199	0	0	498	24,505
1990	Joe Ruttman	1	0	0	0	0	0	0	0	196	0	0	490	22,950
Lifetime		2	0	0	0	0	0	0	0	395	0	0	988	$47,455

Marvin Welty

Year	Driver	Starts	Poles	1	2	3	4	5	6–10	Laps	Laps Led	Races Led	Miles	$
1972	Dick Brooks	4	0	0	0	0	0	0	0	175	0	0	376	2,695
Lifetime		4	0	0	0	0	0	0	0	175	0	0	376	$2,695

Jerry Wentz

Year	Driver	Starts	Poles	1	2	3	4	5	6–10	Laps	Laps Led	Races Led	Miles	$
1971	Pee Wee Wentz	1	0	0	0	0	0	0	0	100	0	0	46	300
1974	Pee Wee Wentz	2	0	0	0	0	0	0	0	198	0	0	157	1,205
Lifetime		3	0	0	0	0	0	0	0	298	0	0	202	$1,505

Carl S. Wesson

Year	Driver	Starts	Poles	1	2	3	4	5	6–10	Laps	Laps Led	Races Led	Miles	$
1955	Bo Fields	3	0	0	0	0	0	0	0	347	0	0	292	100
Lifetime		3	0	0	0	0	0	0	0	347	0	0	292	$100

Hubert Westmoreland

Year	Driver	Starts	Poles	1	2	3	4	5	6–10	Laps	Laps Led	Races Led	Miles	$
1949	Glenn Dunnaway	1	0	0	0	0	0	0	0	200	0	0	150	0
"	Curtis Turner	1	0	1	0	0	0	0	0	200	60	1	200	2,250
"	**Total**	2	0	1	0	0	0	0	0	400	60	1	350	2,250
1950	Tim Flock	1	0	0	0	0	1	0	0		0	0		400
"	Johnny Mantz	1	0	1	0	0	0	0	0	400	351	1	500	10,710
"	Jim Paschal	1	0	0	0	0	0	0	0		0	0		0
"	Leon Sales	2	0	1	0	0	0	0	0	227	18	1	139	1,000
"	Ted Swaim	1	0	0	1	0	0	0	0	200	0	0	100	600
"	**Total**	5	0	2	1	0	1	0	0	827	369	2	739	12,310
1951	Bill Blair	3	0	0	1	0	0	0	1	199	0	0	100	725
"	Bill Holland	4	0	0	0	0	1	0	0	144	0	0	111	360
"	Billy Myers	2	0	0	0	0	0	0	0	496	0	0	589	200
"	Leon Sales	3	0	0	0	0	0	0	2	384	0	0	480	825
"	Jack Smith	1	0	0	0	0	0	0	0		0	0		25
"	Herb Thomas	1	0	1	0	0	0	0	0	200	179	1	100	1,000
"	Johnny Yountz	1	0	0	0	0	0	0	0	361	0	0	451	50
"	**Total**	12	0	1	1	0	1	0	3	1,784	179	1	1,831	3,185
1955	Tim Flock	1	0	0	0	1	0	0	0	197	0	0	99	450
"	Phillip Jones	2	0	0	0	0	0	0	0	204	0	0	102	50
"	Jimmy Massey	11	0	0	0	1	1	2	4	1,906	0	0	1,721	3,510
"	Billy Myers	2	0	0	0	0	0	0	1	512	0	0	555	215
"	Gwyn Staley	23	1	0	1	2	2	2	7	3,193	33	1	2,231	6,397
"	**Total**	24	1	0	1	4	3	4	12	6,012	33	1	4,708	10,622
1956	Jimmy Massey	5	0	0	0	0	1	2	0	655	0	0	436	1,145
"	Gwyn Staley	20	0	0	0	0	2	3	7	2,925	0	0	2,113	4,709
"	**Total**	23	0	0	0	0	3	5	7	3,580	0	0	2,549	5,854
1957	Billy Carden	2	0	0	0	0	0	0	2	483	0	0	680	1,575
"	Frankie Schneider	4	1	0	1	0	1	0	2	670	37	1	537	3,095
"	**Total**	6	1	0	1	0	1	0	4	1,153	37	1	1,218	4,670
1958	Frankie Schneider	1	0	0	0	0	0	0	0	29	0	0	119	50
1963	Curtis Crider	1	0	0	0	0	0	0	1	285	0	0	107	175
"	Bobby Keck	1	0	0	0	0	0	0	0	26	0	0	16	100
"	Jimmy Massey	13	0	0	0	0	1	0	7	3,101	0	0	1,384	2,620
"	**Total**	15	0	0	0	0	1	0	8	3,412	0	0	1,507	2,895
1964	Jimmy Massey	1	0	0	0	0	0	0	0	0	0	0	0	0
Lifetime		89	2	4	4	4	10	9	34	17,197	678	6	13,021	$39,836

Year	Driver	Starts	Poles	Finish 1	2	3	4	5	6–10	Laps	Laps Led	Races Led	Miles	$

LeRoy Weyher

Year	Driver	Starts	Poles	1	2	3	4	5	6–10	Laps	Laps Led	Races Led	Miles	$
1954	Jim Cook	2	0	0	0	0	0	0	0	460	0	0	322	65
"	Howard Phillippi	2	0	0	0	0	0	0	0	264	0	0	232	40
"	**Total**	2	0	0	0	0	0	0	0	724	0	0	554	105
1955	Jim Cook	1	0	0	0	0	0	0	0	110	0	0	110	40
Lifetime		3	0	0	0	0	0	0	0	834	0	0	664	$145

Dick Whalen

Year	Driver	Starts	Poles	1	2	3	4	5	6–10	Laps	Laps Led	Races Led	Miles	$
1979	Dick Whalen	1	0	0	0	0	0	0	0	81	0	0	212	950
Lifetime		1	0	0	0	0	0	0	0	81	0	0	212	$950

Fred Wheat

Year	Driver	Starts	Poles	1	2	3	4	5	6–10	Laps	Laps Led	Races Led	Miles	$
1960	T. C. Hunt	3	0	0	0	0	0	0	0	353	0	0	497	600
"	Joe Weatherly	3	0	0	0	0	0	0	2	478	0	0	142	515
"	**Total**	6	0	0	0	0	0	0	2	831	0	0	639	1,115
1961	T. C. Hunt	7	0	0	0	0	0	0	0	940	0	0	1,445	2,750
1962	T. C. Hunt	1	0	0	0	0	0	0	0	6	0	0	9	200
Lifetime		14	0	0	0	0	0	0	2	1,777	0	0	2,093	$4,065

Al Wheatley

Year	Driver	Starts	Poles	1	2	3	4	5	6–10	Laps	Laps Led	Races Led	Miles	$
1950	Jim Paschal	3	0	0	1	0	0	0	0	174	0	0	94	600
1951	Billy Carden	1	0	0	0	0	0	0	0	0	0	0	0	25
"	Bill Holluck	1	0	0	0	0	0	0	0	0	0	0	0	25
"	Jim Paschal	2	0	0	0	0	0	0	0	353	0	0	441	75
"	Ewell Weddle	3	0	0	0	0	0	0	2	743	0	0	799	375
"	**Total**	6	0	0	0	0	0	0	2	1,096	0	0	1,240	500
1952	Buck Baker	1	0	0	0	0	0	0	1	388	0	0	485	500
1953	Buck Baker	2	0	0	0	0	0	0	1	37	0	0	152	225
"	Ralph Liguori	3	0	0	0	0	0	0	0	190	0	0	190	75
"	**Total**	5	0	0	0	0	0	0	1	227	0	0	342	300
1955	Ralph Liguori	1	0	0	0	0	0	0	0	348	0	0	479	400
1956	Ralph Liguori	1	0	0	0	0	0	0	0	189	0	0	76	50
Lifetime		17	0	0	1	0	0	0	4	2,422	0	0	2,714	$2,350

Johnny Wheeler

Year	Driver	Starts	Poles	1	2	3	4	5	6–10	Laps	Laps Led	Races Led	Miles	$
1971	Ken Rush	1	0	0	0	0	0	0	0	117	0	0	29	240
Lifetime		1	0	0	0	0	0	0	0	117	0	0	29	$240

Ed Whitaker

Year	Driver	Starts	Poles	1	2	3	4	5	6–10	Laps	Laps Led	Races Led	Miles	$
1978	John Utsman	4	0	0	0	0	0	0	0	612	0	0	1,026	7,040
1979	John Utsman	1	0	0	0	3	0	0	0	101	0	0	253	2,850
1980	John Utsman	1	0	0	0	0	0	0	0	149	0	0	373	2,695
Lifetime		6	0	0	0	0	0	0	0	862	0	0	1,651	$12,585

Bob Whitcomb

Year	Driver	Starts	Poles	1	2	3	4	5	6–10	Laps	Laps Led	Races Led	Miles	$
1988	Ken Bouchard	24	0	0	0	0	0	0	1	7,281	4	1	8,480	109,410
1989	Ken Bouchard	4	0	0	0	0	0	0	0	911	0	0	1,373	33,930
"	Derrike Cope	20	0	0	0	0	0	0	4	4,931	5	3	6,231	120,190
"	**Total**	24	0	0	0	0	0	0	4	5,842	5	3	7,604	154,120
1990	Derrike Cope	29	0	2	0	0	0	0	4	7,961	109	6	9,654	569,451
1991	Derrike Cope	28	0	0	0	0	1	0	1	6,784	0	0	8,448	419,380
1992	Derrike Cope	29	0	0	0	0	0	0	3	8,483	0	0	10,174	277,215
Lifetime		134	0	2	0	0	1	0	13	36,351	118	10	44,360	$1,529,576

Al White

Year	Driver	Starts	Poles	1	2	3	4	5	6–10	Laps	Laps Led	Races Led	Miles	$
1956	Al White	2	0	0	0	0	0	0	0	330	0	0	165	200
1957	Al White	3	0	0	0	0	0	0	1	161	0	0	200	200
1958	Al White	9	0	0	0	0	0	0	1	1,483	0	0	1,030	920
1959	Al White	5	0	0	0	0	0	0	0	826	0	0	644	575
1960	Al White	2	0	0	0	0	0	0	1	643	0	0	322	450
1962	Al White	1	0	0	0	0	0	0	0	233	0	0	117	125
1963	Al White	1	0	0	0	0	0	0	0	211	0	0	106	150
1964	Al White	7	0	0	0	0	0	0	3	1,484	0	0	655	1,030

Year	Driver	Starts	Poles	1	2	3	4	5	6–10	Laps	Laps Led	Races Led	Miles	$

Al White *continued*

Year	Driver	Starts	Poles	1	2	3	4	5	6–10	Laps	Laps Led	Races Led	Miles	$
1965	Al White	4	0	0	0	0	0	0	1	348	0	0	262	545
1966	Al White	2	0	0	0	0	0	0	0	449	0	0	142	230
Lifetime		36	0	0	0	0	0	0	7	6,168	0	0	3,643	$4,425

Bill White

Year	Driver	Starts	Poles	1	2	3	4	5	6–10	Laps	Laps Led	Races Led	Miles	$
1957	Russ Truelove	1	0	0	0	0	0	0	0		0	0		0
Lifetime		1	0	0	0	0	0	0	0		0	0		$0

Billy White

Year	Driver	Starts	Poles	1	2	3	4	5	6–10	Laps	Laps Led	Races Led	Miles	$
1991	Gary Wright	1	0	0	0	0	0	0	0	63	0	0	158	3,750
Lifetime		1	0	0	0	0	0	0	0	63	0	0	158	$3,750

Bob White

Year	Driver	Starts	Poles	1	2	3	4	5	6–10	Laps	Laps Led	Races Led	Miles	$
1956	Russ Truelove	5	0	0	0	0	0	0	2	521	0	0	476	450
Lifetime		5	0	0	0	0	0	0	2	521	0	0	476	$450

Dave White

Year	Driver	Starts	Poles	1	2	3	4	5	6–10	Laps	Laps Led	Races Led	Miles	$
1959	Dave White	5	0	0	0	0	0	0	1	1,253	0	0	533	660
Lifetime		5	0	0	0	0	0	0	1	1,253	0	0	533	$660

Dr. Bradford "Doc" White

Year	Driver	Starts	Poles	1	2	3	4	5	6–10	Laps	Laps Led	Races Led	Miles	$
1958	Dick Joslin	1	0	0	0	0	0	0	0	6	0	0	25	0
1959	Jimmy Thompson	1	0	0	0	0	0	0	1	346	0	0	476	805
"	Speedy Thompson	1	0	0	0	0	0	0	0	94	0	0	235	375
"	Curtis Turner	6	1	2	1	0	0	0	0	797	419	4	834	2,625
"	Joe Weatherly	12	0	0	2	0	0	2	2	2,099	178	4	1,291	6,820
"	**Total**	19	1	2	3	0	0	2	3	3,336	597	8	2,836	10,625
1960	Joe Caspolich	2	0	0	0	0	0	0	0	227	0	0	568	315
"	Possum Jones	1	0	0	0	0	0	0	0	291	0	0	437	275
"	Elmo Langley	5	0	0	0	0	0	0	0	827	0	0	687	720
"	Jimmy Thompson	6	0	0	0	0	0	0	0	1,087	0	0	1,400	1,190
"	Joe Weatherly	1	0	0	0	0	0	0	0	49	0	0	25	50
"	**Total**	15	0	0	0	0	0	0	0	2,481	0	0	3,115	2,550
1961	Elmo Langley	9	0	0	0	0	0	1	4	1,683	0	0	1,120	1,820
"	Joe Weatherly	1	0	1	0	0	0	0	0	200	40	1	100	800
"	**Total**	9	0	1	0	0	0	1	4	1,883	40	1	1,220	2,620
Lifetime		44	1	3	3	0	0	3	7	7,706	637	9	7,195	$15,795

Don White

Year	Driver	Starts	Poles	1	2	3	4	5	6–10	Laps	Laps Led	Races Led	Miles	$
1954	Don White	1	0	0	0	0	0	0	0	38	0	0	156	90
1955	Don White	3	0	0	2	1	0	0	0	296	0	0	198	1,750
Lifetime		4	0	0	2	1	0	0	0	334	0	0	354	$1,840

Gene White

Year	Driver	Starts	Poles	1	2	3	4	5	6–10	Laps	Laps Led	Races Led	Miles	$
1958	Billy Carden	1	0	0	0	0	0	0	0	141	0	0	71	0
"	Jack Smith	1	0	0	0	0	0	0	0	338	0	0	169	305
"	Gene White	9	0	0	0	0	0	0	2	1,641	0	0	1,295	1,400
"	**Total**	11	0	0	0	0	0	0	2	2,120	0	0	1,535	1,705
1959	Gene White	7	0	0	0	0	0	0	2	1,210	0	0	1,012	1,360
Lifetime		18	0	0	0	0	0	0	4	3,330	0	0	2,546	$3,065

Herschel White

Year	Driver	Starts	Poles	1	2	3	4	5	6–10	Laps	Laps Led	Races Led	Miles	$
1957	Pat Kirkwood	1	0	0	0	0	0	0	0		0	0		50
Lifetime		1	0	0	0	0	0	0	0		0	0		$50

Jack White

Year	Driver	Starts	Poles	1	2	3	4	5	6–10	Laps	Laps Led	Races Led	Miles	$
1974	Bob Burcham	12	0	0	0	0	1	0	3	2,776	0	0	3,604	18,510
Lifetime		12	0	0	0	0	1	0	3	2,776	0	0	3,604	$18,510

Year	Driver	Starts	Poles	Finish						Laps	Laps Led	Races Led	Miles	$
				1	2	3	4	5	6–10					

Jim White

1951	Bill Majot	3	0	0	0	0	0	0	0	233	0	0	233	75
1961	Harlan Richardson	4	0	0	0	0	0	0	0	284	0	0	640	525
Lifetime		7	0	0	0	0	0	0	0	517	0	0	873	$600

Mike White

1975	Richard White	1	0	0	0	0	0	0	0	117	0	0	307	1,285
1977	Richard White	2	0	0	0	0	0	0	0	251	0	0	637	2,375
1978	Richard White	3	0	0	0	0	0	0	0	346	2	1	884	4,550
1979	Richard White	3	0	0	0	0	0	0	0	234	0	0	599	4,070
Lifetime		9	0	0	0	0	0	0	0	948	2	1	2,426	$12,280

Rex White

1958	Rex White	6	1	0	0	1	0	0	2	1,283	118	1	946	2,825
1959	Ken Rush	1	0	0	0	0	0	0	0	177	0	0	89	75
"	Rex White	20	5	5	2	2	1	1	2	4,416	826	9	2,860	12,135
"	**Total**	21	5	5	2	2	1	1	2	4,593	826	9	2,949	12,210
1960	Rex White	37	3	6	6	7	4	2	8	8,405	541	11	6,557	56,800
1961	Rex White	46	7	7	8	8	2	4	8	9,962	1,224	15	7,067	55,470
1962	Tommy Irwin	1	0	0	0	0	0	0	0	124	0	0	186	300
"	Rex White	37	9	8	3	3	1	3	5	7,683	1,129	15	5,760	32,246
"	**Total**	37	9	8	3	3	1	3	5	7,807	1,129	15	5,946	32,546
1963	Rex White	25	3	0	3	2	0	0	9	5,595	171	6	5,490	27,241
1964	Rex White	1	0	0	0	0	0	0	0	17	0	0	51	575
Lifetime		173	28	26	22	23	8	10	34	37,662	4,009	57	29,006	$187,667

Jim Whitehead

1966	Dave James	1	0	0	0	0	0	0	0	4	0	0	11	500
1968	Dave James	1	0	0	0	0	0	0	1	171	0	0	462	1,250
1969	Dave James	1	0	0	0	0	0	0	0	5	0	0	14	850
Lifetime		3	0	0	0	0	0	0	1	180	0	0	486	$2,600

Paul Whiteman

1954	Junior Johnson	3	1	0	0	0	0	0	0	341	0	0	292	250
"	Al Keller	1	0	1	0	0	0	0	0	50	28	1	100	1,000
"	Gwyn Staley	2	0	0	0	0	0	0	1	357	0	0	480	670
"	**Total**	6	1	1	0	0	0	0	1	748	28	1	871	1,920
1955	Junior Johnson	1	0	0	0	0	0	0	0	51	0	0	26	25
Lifetime		7	1	1	0	0	0	0	1	799	28	1	897	$1,945

John Whitford

1956	Buck Baker	1	0	0	0	0	0	0	1	190	0	0	95	100
"	Bill Champion	12	0	0	0	0	0	0	3	2,020	0	0	1,487	1,370
"	Bunk Moore	1	0	0	0	0	0	0	1	394	0	0	197	400
"	Joe Weatherly	2	0	0	0	0	1	0	1	367	0	0	167	450
"	**Total**	14	0	0	0	0	1	0	6	2,971	0	0	1,946	2,320
1957	Bill Champion	5	0	0	0	0	0	0	1	804	0	0	748	590
"	Darel Dieringer	7	0	0	0	0	0	0	2	983	0	0	570	760
"	Phillip Jones	1	0	0	0	0	0	0	0	262	0	0	262	225
"	**Total**	10	0	0	0	0	0	0	3	2,049	0	0	1,580	1,575
1958	Jimmy Massey	1	0	0	0	0	0	0	1	458	0	0	458	500
"	Marvin Panch	11	2	0	1	1	1	2	0	1,833	157	3	1,576	3,805
"	Curtis Turner	2	0	0	0	0	0	0	0	414	0	0	305	275
"	**Total**	13	2	0	1	1	1	2	1	2,705	157	3	2,339	4,580
Lifetime		37	2	0	1	1	2	2	10	7,725	157	3	5,865	$8,475

Ken Whitney

1949	Jack Russell	2	0	0	0	0	0	0	1	178	0	0	89	75
1952	Jim Fiebelkorn	1	0	0	0	0	0	0	0	35	0	0	35	0
1955	Bill Blair	1	0	0	0	0	0	0	0	6	0	0	25	0
Lifetime		4	0	0	0	0	0	0	1	219	0	0	149	$75

Year	Driver	Starts	Poles	Finish 1	2	3	4	5	6–10	Laps	Laps Led	Races Led	Miles	$

Basil Whittaker

Year	Driver	Starts	Poles	1	2	3	4	5	6–10	Laps	Laps Led	Races Led	Miles	$
1965	Bud Harless	4	0	0	0	0	0	0	0	627	0	0	316	1,460
Lifetime		4	0	0	0	0	0	0	0	627	0	0	316	$1,460

Don Whittington

Year	Driver	Starts	Poles	1	2	3	4	5	6–10	Laps	Laps Led	Races Led	Miles	$
1980	Don Whittington	2	0	0	0	0	0	0	0	196	0	0	497	3,970
Lifetime		2	0	0	0	0	0	0	0	196	0	0	497	$3,970

Reb Wickersham

Year	Driver	Starts	Poles	1	2	3	4	5	6–10	Laps	Laps Led	Races Led	Miles	$
1960	Reb Wickersham	7	0	0	0	0	0	0	0	1,119	0	0	1,948	2,575
1961	Bryant Wallace	2	0	0	0	0	0	0	0	81	0	0	40	100
"	Reb Wickersham	8	0	0	0	0	0	0	1	1,343	0	0	1,199	1,345
"	**Total**	10	0	0	0	0	0	0	1	1,424	0	0	1,239	1,445
1962	Jerry Burnett	1	0	0	0	0	0	0	0	143	0	0	57	75
"	Reb Wickersham	1	0	0	0	0	0	0	0	133	0	0	67	0
"	**Total**	2	0	0	0	0	0	0	0	276	0	0	124	75
1963	Jimmy Pardue	1	0	0	0	0	0	0	1	283	0	0	71	175
"	Reb Wickersham	14	0	0	0	0	0	0	1	3,501	0	0	2,577	3,800
"	**Total**	15	0	0	0	0	0	0	2	3,784	0	0	2,647	3,975
Lifetime		34	0	0	0	0	0	0	3	6,603	0	0	5,958	$8,070

Bill Widenhouse

Year	Driver	Starts	Poles	1	2	3	4	5	6–10	Laps	Laps Led	Races Led	Miles	$
1951	Bill Widenhouse	3	0	0	0	0	0	0	0		0	0		75
1954	Bill Widenhouse	6	0	0	0	0	0	0	0	987	0	0	999	425
1963	Bill Widenhouse	1	0	0	0	0	0	0	1	114	0	0	103	175
Lifetime		10	0	0	0	0	0	0	1	1,101	0	0	1,101	$675

Dink Widenhouse

Year	Driver	Starts	Poles	1	2	3	4	5	6–10	Laps	Laps Led	Races Led	Miles	$
1954	Dink Widenhouse	5	0	0	0	0	1	0	1	541	0	0	361	625
1955	Dink Widenhouse	15	1	0	0	0	0	0	6	1,743	0	0	1,185	1,660
1956	Dink Widenhouse	6	0	0	0	0	1	0	2	670	0	0	503	940
Lifetime		26	1	0	0	0	2	0	9	2,954	0	0	2,050	$3,225

Felix Wilkes

Year	Driver	Starts	Poles	1	2	3	4	5	6–10	Laps	Laps Led	Races Led	Miles	$
1949	Felix Wilkes	3	0	0	0	0	0	0	0	38	0	0	38	0
1950	Felix Wilkes	1	0	0	0	0	0	0	0		0	0		0
1951	Felix Wilkes	2	0	0	0	0	0	0	0	18	0	0	14	10
1952	Felix Wilkes	1	0	0	0	0	0	0	0	141	0	0	141	35
Lifetime		7	0	0	0	0	0	0	0	197	0	0	193	$45

Thurman Wilkes

Year	Driver	Starts	Poles	1	2	3	4	5	6–10	Laps	Laps Led	Races Led	Miles	$
1962	Jim Bennett	5	0	0	0	0	0	1	1	402	0	0	341	950
Lifetime		5	0	0	0	0	0	1	1	402	0	0	341	$950

Chet Williams

Year	Driver	Starts	Poles	1	2	3	4	5	6–10	Laps	Laps Led	Races Led	Miles	$
1953	Chet Williams	2	0	0	0	0	0	0	0	374	0	0	429	135
Lifetime		2	0	0	0	0	0	0	0	374	0	0	429	$135

Lois Williams

Year	Driver	Starts	Poles	1	2	3	4	5	6–10	Laps	Laps Led	Races Led	Miles	$
1981	Jim Robinson	3	0	0	0	0	0	0	2	264	0	0	692	9,505
1982	Jim Robinson	2	0	0	0	0	0	0	0	150	0	0	393	2,220
1983	Jim Robinson	2	0	0	0	0	0	0	0	204	0	0	534	6,075
1984	Jim Robinson	2	0	0	0	0	0	0	0	189	0	0	495	7,560
1985	Jim Robinson	2	0	0	0	0	0	0	0	209	0	0	548	10,820
1986	Jim Robinson	2	0	0	0	0	0	0	0	192	0	0	503	9,300
1987	Jim Robinson	2	0	0	0	0	0	0	0	157	0	0	411	5,685
Lifetime		15	0	0	0	0	0	0	2	1,365	0	0	3,576	$51,165

Raymond Williams

Year	Driver	Starts	Poles	1	2	3	4	5	6–10	Laps	Laps Led	Races Led	Miles	$
1971	J. D. McDuffie	1	0	0	0	0	0	0	0	222	0	0	333	1,117

Year	Driver	Starts	Poles	Finish 1	2	3	4	5	6–10	Laps	Laps Led	Races Led	Miles	$

Raymond Williams *continued*

Year	Driver	Starts	Poles	1	2	3	4	5	6–10	Laps	Laps Led	Races Led	Miles	$
"	Raymond Williams	13	0	0	0	0	0	0	0	2,364	0	0	3,470	9,550
"	**Total**	14	0	0	0	0	0	0	0	2,586	0	0	3,803	10,667
1972	Raymond Williams	27	0	0	0	0	0	0	5	6,337	0	0	7,649	30,965
1973	Raymond Williams	22	0	0	0	0	0	0	3	4,684	0	0	5,220	23,063
Lifetime		63	0	0	0	0	0	0	8	13,607	0	0	16,672	$64,695

Tom Williams

Year	Driver	Starts	Poles	1	2	3	4	5	6–10	Laps	Laps Led	Races Led	Miles	$
1975	Grant Adcox	1	0	0	0	0	0	0	0	101	0	0	269	995
"	Walter Ballard	1	0	0	0	0	0	0	0	94	0	0	235	885
"	Tom Williams	2	0	0	0	0	0	0	0	235	0	0	609	2,815
"	**Total**	4	0	0	0	0	0	0	0	430	0	0	1,112	4,695
1976	Tom Williams	1	0	0	0	0	0	0	0	41	0	0	103	1,615
Lifetime		5	0	0	0	0	0	0	0	471	0	0	1,215	$6,310

Wildcat Williams

Year	Driver	Starts	Poles	1	2	3	4	5	6–10	Laps	Laps Led	Races Led	Miles	$
1962	Bunkie Blackburn	1	0	0	0	0	0	0	0	23	0	0	35	200
"	Art Brady	2	0	0	0	0	0	0	0	179	0	0	448	450
"	T. C. Hunt	2	0	0	0	0	0	0	0	157	0	0	63	50
"	Jimmy Thompson	1	0	0	0	0	0	0	0	364	0	0	546	475
"	Cale Yarborough	1	0	0	0	0	0	0	0	212	0	0	318	375
"	**Total**	7	0	0	0	0	0	0	0	935	0	0	1,409	1,550
1963	Cotton Hodges	1	0	0	0	0	0	0	0	9	0	0	5	50
"	Al Terell	1	0	0	0	0	0	0	0	4	0	0	10	0
"	**Total**	2	0	0	0	0	0	0	0	13	0	0	15	50
Lifetime		9	0	0	0	0	0	0	0	948	0	0	1,423	$1,600

Tim Williamson

Year	Driver	Starts	Poles	1	2	3	4	5	6–10	Laps	Laps Led	Races Led	Miles	$
1979	Tim Williamson	3	0	0	0	0	0	0	1	340	0	0	868	5,580
Lifetime		3	0	0	0	0	0	0	1	340	0	0	868	$5,580

Bobby Wilson

Year	Driver	Starts	Poles	1	2	3	4	5	6–10	Laps	Laps Led	Races Led	Miles	$
1981	Rick Wilson	8	0	0	0	0	0	0	0	989	7	2	1,713	16,335
1982	Rick Wilson	8	0	0	0	0	0	0	2	1,404	0	0	2,612	33,230
1983	Rick Wilson	1	0	0	0	0	0	0	0	55	0	0	146	3,285
Lifetime		17	0	0	0	0	0	0	2	2,448	7	2	4,472	$52,850

C. D. Wilson

Year	Driver	Starts	Poles	1	2	3	4	5	6–10	Laps	Laps Led	Races Led	Miles	$
1952	Tommy Moon	5	1	0	1	0	0	1	1	403	0	0	386	1,110
1953	Tommy Moon	1	0	0	0	0	0	0	0	5	0	0	21	0
Lifetime		6	1	0	1	0	0	1	1	408	0	0	407	$1,110

E. C. Wilson

Year	Driver	Starts	Poles	1	2	3	4	5	6–10	Laps	Laps Led	Races Led	Miles	$
1959	Fireball Roberts	1	0	0	0	0	0	0	0	385	0	0	193	85
"	Joe Weatherly	2	0	0	0	0	1	1	0	239	7	2	598	2,125
"	**Total**	3	0	0	0	0	1	1	0	624	7	2	790	2,210
1960	Charley Griffith	2	0	0	0	0	0	0	0	445	0	0	668	1,000
"	Friday Hassler	2	0	0	0	0	0	0	0	251	0	0	377	425
"	Tommy Irwin	1	0	0	0	0	0	0	0	59	0	0	30	0
"	JoeLee Johnson	7	0	0	1	0	0	1	2	1,255	0	0	787	2,235
"	Roy Tyner	4	0	0	0	0	0	0	2	531	0	0	645	640
"	**Total**	16	0	0	1	0	0	1	4	2,541	0	0	2,506	4,300
Lifetime		19	0	0	1	0	1	2	4	3,165	7	2	3,296	$6,510

Fritz Wilson

Year	Driver	Starts	Poles	1	2	3	4	5	6–10	Laps	Laps Led	Races Led	Miles	$
1959	Fritz Wilson	3	0	0	1	0	0	0	0	388	4	1	304	700
1960	Fritz Wilson	4	0	0	0	0	2	0	0	284	0	0	367	925
1965	Fritz Wilson	1	0	0	0	0	0	0	0	84	0	0	227	550
Lifetime		8	0	0	1	0	2	0	0	756	4	1	898	$2,175

Gus Wilson

Year	Driver	Starts	Poles	1	2	3	4	5	6–10	Laps	Laps Led	Races Led	Miles	$
1958	Gus Wilson	3	0	0	0	0	0	0	0	359	0	0	163	175

Year	Driver	Starts	Poles	Finish 1	2	3	4	5	6–10	Laps	Laps Led	Races Led	Miles	$

Gus Wilson *continued*

Year	Driver	Starts	Poles	1	2	3	4	5	6–10	Laps	Laps Led	Races Led	Miles	$
1959	Gus Wilson	1	0	0	0	0	0	0	0	100	0	0	50	50
Lifetime		4	0	0	0	0	0	0	0	459	0	0	213	$225

Jim Wilson

Year	Driver	Starts	Poles	1	2	3	4	5	6–10	Laps	Laps Led	Races Led	Miles	$
1993	Jay Hedgecock	1	0	0	0	0	0	0	0	372	0	0	233	4,780
1994	Jay Hedgecock	2	0	0	0	0	0	0	0	537	0	0	287	9,475
1996	Randy MacDonald	3	0	0	0	0	0	0	0	680	0	0	1,285	31,610
"	Billy Standridge	3	0	0	0	0	0	0	0	789	0	0	1,123	27,780
"	**Total**	6	0	0	0	0	0	0	0	1,469	0	0	2,408	59,390
Lifetime		9	0	0	0	0	0	0	0	2,378	0	0	2,927	$73,645

Woodie Wilson

Year	Driver	Starts	Poles	1	2	3	4	5	6–10	Laps	Laps Led	Races Led	Miles	$
1949	Woodie Wilson	1	0	0	0	0	0	0	0		0	0		25
Lifetime		1	0	0	0	0	0	0	0		0	0		$25

George Wiltshire

Year	Driver	Starts	Poles	1	2	3	4	5	6–10	Laps	Laps Led	Races Led	Miles	$
1971	George Wiltshire	1	0	0	0	0	0	0	0	2	0	0	0	100
1975	George Wiltshire	1	0	0	0	0	0	0	0	15	0	0	38	630
Lifetime		2	0	0	0	0	0	0	0	17	0	0	38	$730

Jerry Wimbish

Year	Driver	Starts	Poles	1	2	3	4	5	6–10	Laps	Laps Led	Races Led	Miles	$
1950	Jerry Wimbish	1	0	0	0	0	0	0	1		0	0		100
1951	Jerry Wimbish	2	0	0	0	0	0	0	1	51	0	0	51	75
1952	Jerry Wimbish	4	0	0	0	0	0	1	0	222	0	0	113	395
1953	Jerry Wimbish	1	0	0	0	0	0	1	0	0	0	0	0	200
1954	Jerry Wimbish	1	0	0	0	0	0	0	0	92	0	0	92	25
Lifetime		9	0	0	0	0	0	2	2	365	0	0	256	$795

Andy Winfree

Year	Driver	Starts	Poles	1	2	3	4	5	6–10	Laps	Laps Led	Races Led	Miles	$
1953	Andy Winfree	7	0	0	0	0	0	0	3	277	0	0	277	440
1954	Andy Winfree	3	0	0	0	0	0	0	1	301	0	0	216	175
Lifetime		10	0	0	0	0	0	0	4	578	0	0	493	$615

Tom Winkle

Year	Driver	Starts	Poles	1	2	3	4	5	6–10	Laps	Laps Led	Races Led	Miles	$
1986	J. D. McDuffie	12	0	0	0	0	0	0	0	2,523	1	1	2,768	54,515
1987	Steve Christman	20	0	0	0	0	0	0	0	4,404	0	0	5,100	54,965
"	J. D. McDuffie	4	0	0	0	0	0	0	0	1,070	0	0	1,195	18,940
"	**Total**	22	0	0	0	0	0	0	0	5,474	0	0	6,294	73,905
1988	Rodney Combs	17	0	0	0	0	0	0	0	3,469	0	0	4,568	50,890
"	Tommy Ellis	2	0	0	0	0	0	0	0	178	0	0	267	3,125
"	Joe Ruttman	1	0	0	0	0	0	0	0	71	0	0	71	1,550
"	Morgan Shepherd	3	1	0	0	0	0	0	1	900	7	2	743	27,145
"	**Total**	23	1	0	0	0	0	0	1	4,618	7	2	5,649	82,710
1989	Mickey Gibbs	3	0	0	0	0	0	0	0	745	0	0	712	8,630
"	Greg Sacks	9	0	0	0	0	0	0	0	1,742	2	1	2,061	23,550
"	**Total**	12	0	0	0	0	0	0	0	2,487	2	1	2,773	32,180
Lifetime		69	1	0	0	0	0	0	1	15,102	10	4	17,483	$243,310

Hans Winter

Year	Driver	Starts	Poles	1	2	3	4	5	6–10	Laps	Laps Led	Races Led	Miles	$
1950	Al Gross	1	0	0	0	0	1	0	0	48	0	0	200	550
Lifetime		1	0	0	0	0	1	0	0	48	0	0	200	$550

Wiss Brothers

Year	Driver	Starts	Poles	1	2	3	4	5	6–10	Laps	Laps Led	Races Led	Miles	$
1951	Jack Reynolds	2	0	0	0	0	0	0	1		0	0		175
1952	Jack Reynolds	5	0	0	0	0	1	0	1	577	0	0	332	525
Lifetime		7	0	0	0	0	1	0	2	577	0	0	332	$700

Wood Brothers (Glen, Leonard, Delano, Clay, Eddie, and Len Wood, co-owners)

Year	Driver	Starts	Poles	1	2	3	4	5	6–10	Laps	Laps Led	Races Led	Miles	$
1953	Glen Wood	2	0	0	0	0	0	0	0	274	0	0	274	125
1955	Glen Wood	1	0	0	0	0	0	0	0	55	0	0	28	0

Year	Driver	Starts	Poles	Finish						Laps	Laps Led	Races Led	Miles	$
				1	2	3	4	5	6–10					

Wood Brothers *continued*

Year	Driver	Starts	Poles	1	2	3	4	5	6–10	Laps	Laps Led	Races Led	Miles	$
1956	Glen Wood	1	0	0	0	0	0	0	0	110	0	0	55	0
1957	Jimmy Massey	2	0	0	1	0	0	0	1	652	7	1	345	2,115
"	Glen Wood	6	0	0	0	0	0	0	1	1,062	0	0	847	1,670
"	**Total**	7	0	0	1	0	0	0	2	1,714	7	1	1,192	3,785
1958	Jimmy Massey	1	0	0	0	0	0	1	0	148	0	0	49	255
"	Curtis Turner	1	0	0	0	0	0	0	0	26	0	0	7	125
"	Glen Wood	10	3	0	1	0	0	0	6	2,348	360	4	1,331	3,120
"	**Total**	12	3	0	1	0	0	1	6	2,522	360	4	1,387	3,500
1959	Johnny Beauchamp	1	0	0	0	0	0	0	0	132	0	0	132	190
"	Larry Frank	1	0	0	0	0	0	0	0	90	0	0	45	50
"	Junior Johnson	2	0	0	0	0	1	0	0	324	0	0	137	275
"	Joe Weatherly	1	0	0	0	0	0	0	1	196	0	0	49	200
"	Glen Wood	18	3	0	5	1	1	1	3	3,703	98	2	2,100	6,310
"	**Total**	22	3	0	5	1	2	1	4	4,445	98	2	2,463	7,025
1960	Fred Harb	2	0	0	0	0	0	0	1	568	0	0	235	475
"	Junior Johnson	2	1	0	0	0	1	0	0	247	0	0	124	345
"	Jimmy Massey	3	0	0	1	1	0	0	0	835	26	1	368	2,085
"	Speedy Thompson	3	0	2	0	0	1	0	0	797	217	2	996	15,985
"	Curtis Turner	1	0	0	0	0	0	0	0	78	0	0	70	50
"	Joe Weatherly	2	0	0	0	0	1	0	0	394	0	0	237	585
"	Bob Welborn	1	0	0	0	0	0	0	0	127	0	0	32	125
"	Glen Wood	9	4	3	0	2	0	1	1	2,206	766	5	973	5,260
"	**Total**	15	5	5	1	3	3	1	2	5,252	**1,009**	7	3,033	24,910
1961	Banjo Matthews	1	0	0	0	0	0	0	0	202	0	0	126	100
"	Speedy Thompson	1	0	0	0	0	0	0	0	252	0	0	378	825
"	Curtis Turner	7	0	0	1	0	0	0	0	949	148	4	1,164	5,960
"	Glen Wood	6	1	0	2	1	0	0	0	1,101	138	1	445	2,000
"	**Total**	15	1	0	3	1	0	0	0	2,504	286	5	2,113	8,885
1962	Marvin Panch	14	0	0	2	3	0	1	3	3,552	156	3	3,667	26,221
1963	Tommy Irwin	1	0	0	0	0	0	1	0	198	0	0	59	240
"	Fred Lorenzen	1	0	0	0	0	0	0	0	158	8	1	427	530
"	Tiny Lund	7	0	1	1	1	1	1	1	1,979	124	3	2,024	42,412
"	Dave MacDonald	1	0	0	1	0	0	0	0	147	92	1	397	4,655
"	Marvin Panch	12	3	1	2	5	1	0	3	3,510	291	6	3,742	39,102
"	Glen Wood	3	2	1	0	1	0	0	0	571	268	2	143	1,070
"	**Total**	24	5	3	4	7	2	2	4	6,563	783	13	6,792	88,009
1964	Dan Gurney	4	0	1	0	0	0	0	1	433	142	1	1,103	14,770
"	Marvin Panch	29	5	3	7	3	3	1	3	6,452	648	10	4,899	34,486
"	Nelson Stacy	1	0	0	0	0	0	0	0	5	0	0	7	500
"	Glen Wood	2	1	0	0	1	0	0	0	305	5	1	76	530
"	**Total**	33	6	4	7	4	3	1	4	7,195	795	12	6,084	50,286
1965	A. J. Foyt	3	0	1	0	0	0	0	1	516	149	2	934	11,005
"	Dan Gurney	1	0	1	0	0	0	0	0	185	126	1	500	13,625
"	Marvin Panch	20	5	4	1	4	1	2	2	4,743	856	12	4,716	64,027
"	Curtis Turner	4	0	1	0	1	0	1	0	1,208	256	2	1,171	17,380
"	**Total**	20	5	7	1	5	1	3	3	6,652	1,387	14	7,320	106,037
1966	A. J. Foyt	2	0	0	0	0	0	0	0	84	0	0	210	1,235
"	Dan Gurney	1	0	1	0	0	0	0	0	185	148	1	500	18,445
"	Marvin Panch	6	0	0	0	0	1	0	0	1,231	70	3	1,531	4,400
"	Curtis Turner	6	0	0	1	0	1	0	0	1,275	80	4	1,830	6,790
"	Cale Yarborough	5	0	0	0	0	1	0	0	1,876	42	2	1,748	4,350
"	**Total**	13	0	1	1	0	3	0	0	4,651	340	8	5,818	35,220
1967	Earl Balmer	1	0	0	0	0	0	0	0	102	0	0	140	625
"	Parnelli Jones	1	0	1	0	0	0	0	0	185	126	1	500	18,720
"	Cale Yarborough	15	4	2	3	1	1	0	1	3,532	908	9	3,570	56,937
"	**Total**	17	4	3	3	1	1	0	1	3,819	1,034	10	4,209	76,282
1968	Dan Gurney	1	1	1	0	0	0	0	0	186	124	1	502	21,250
"	Cale Yarborough	20	4	6	2	1	0	3	0	5,497	1,215	16	5,659	137,802
"	**Total**	20	5	7	2	1	0	3	0	5,683	1,339	17	6,161	159,052
1969	Dan Gurney	1	0	0	0	0	0	0	0	66	0	0	178	980
"	Swede Savage	2	0	0	0	0	0	1	0	173	0	0	433	2,970
"	Cale Yarborough	19	6	2	2	1	2	0	1	4,341	946	16	5,482	75,065
"	**Total**	20	6	2	2	1	2	1	1	4,580	946	16	6,093	79,015
1970	Parnelli Jones	1	0	0	0	0	0	0	0	168	88	1	440	1,275
"	Cale Yarborough	18	5	3	4	3	0	1	2	4,784	906	14	5,896	116,400
"	**Total**	19	5	3	4	3	0	1	2	4,952	994	15	6,336	117,675
1971	Donnie Allison	11	5	1	1	1	2	2	1	2,797	795	6	3,777	68,245
"	A. J. Foyt	4	4	2	1	1	0	0	0	778	392	4	1,624	86,350
"	**Total**	15	9	3	2	2	2	2	1	3,575	1,187	10	5,402	154,595

Year	Driver	Starts	Poles	Finish						Laps	Laps Led	Races Led	Miles	$
				1	2	3	4	5	6–10					

Wood Brothers *continued*

Year	Driver	Starts	Poles	1	2	3	4	5	6–10	Laps	Laps Led	Races Led	Miles	$
1972	A. J. Foyt	6	3	2	2	0	1	0	0	1,417	344	6	2,778	101,340
"	David Pearson	14	4	6	1	3	1	0	1	4,377	1,567	14	5,755	137,540
"	**Total**	19	7	8	3	3	2	0	1	5,794	1,911	19	8,533	238,880
1973	David Pearson	18	8	11	2	1	0	0	0	5,338	2,658	16	7,182	228,408
1974	David Pearson	19	11	7	5	2	1	0	0	4,630	1,168	18	7,746	252,819
1975	David Pearson	21	7	3	6	2	2	0	1	5,653	1,323	18	8,579	192,141
1976	David Pearson	22	8	10	3	2	1	0	2	6,194	1,213	19	9,048	346,890
1977	David Pearson	22	5	2	7	2	2	3	0	5,694	868	17	8,180	221,272
1978	David Pearson	22	7	4	2	1	1	3	0	5,375	757	13	7,602	198,775
1979	Neil Bonnett	17	4	3	0	0	1	0	2	3,766	557	13	5,426	142,375
"	David Pearson	5	1	0	1	0	0	0	0	1,021	173	4	1,564	22,815
"	**Total**	22	5	3	1	0	1	0	2	4,787	730	17	6,990	165,190
1980	Neil Bonnett	22	0	2	4	1	1	2	3	5,173	331	14	7,503	231,854
1981	Neil Bonnett	22	1	3	1	0	3	0	1	4,917	1,549	16	6,365	181,670
1982	Neil Bonnett	22	0	1	0	2	1	2	2	5,516	412	12	7,193	148,667
1983	Buddy Baker	21	1	1	1	2	0	1	7	5,111	174	7	6,816	216,355
1984	Buddy Baker	21	1	0	1	2	0	1	8	6,213	84	2	7,447	151,635
"	Bobby Rahal	1	0	0	0	0	0	0	0	44	0	0	115	875
"	**Total**	22	1	0	1	2	0	1	8	6,257	84	2	7,562	152,510
1985	Kyle Petty	28	0	0	1	1	1	4	5	8,796	75	6	10,377	296,367
1986	Kyle Petty	29	0	1	0	1	0	2	10	8,546	17	6	10,338	403,242
1987	Kyle Petty	29	0	1	1	4	0	0	8	8,523	103	7	10,399	544,347
1988	Kyle Petty	29	0	0	0	0	0	2	6	8,883	67	3	10,514	377,092
1989	Neil Bonnett	26	0	0	0	0	0	0	11	7,795	23	6	9,488	271,628
"	Tommy Ellis	3	0	0	0	0	0	0	0	996	0	0	885	15,385
"	**Total**	29	0	0	0	0	0	0	11	8,791	23	6	10,373	287,013
1990	Neil Bonnett	5	0	0	0	0	0	0	0	1,179	0	0	1,635	62,600
"	Dale Jarrett	24	0	0	0	0	1	0	6	6,801	73	4	7,699	214,495
"	**Total**	29	0	0	0	0	1	0	6	7,980	73	4	9,334	277,095
1991	Dale Jarrett	29	0	1	0	0	0	2	5	7,767	47	7	9,438	444,256
"	Morgan Shepherd	1	0	0	0	0	0	0	0	276	0	0	145	9,450
"	**Total**	29	0	1	0	0	0	2	5	8,043	47	7	9,583	453,706
1992	Morgan Shepherd	29	0	0	2	0	0	1	8	9,093	60	3	10,839	634,222
1993	Morgan Shepherd	30	0	1	1	0	1	0	12	9,442	92	9	11,406	782,523
1994	Morgan Shepherd	31	0	0	2	2	1	4	7	9,788	80	10	11,950	1,119,038
1995	Morgan Shepherd	31	0	0	1	1	1	1	6	9,275	31	8	11,547	862,041
1996	Michael Waltrip	31	0	0	0	0	0	1	10	9,279	18	5	11,165	1,182,811
Lifetime		898	118	97	83	61	39	45	154	244,976	24,585	399	295,548	$10,935,550
		3rd	**2nd**	**3rd**						**5th**	**3rd**	**3rd**	**4th**	**8th**

Gifford Wood

Year	Driver	Starts	Poles	1	2	3	4	5	6–10	Laps	Laps Led	Races Led	Miles	$
1953	Gifford Wood	2	0	0	0	0	0	0	0	136	0	0	68	50
1954	Gifford Wood	1	0	0	0	0	0	0	0	152	0	0	76	25
Lifetime		3	0	0	0	0	0	0	0	288	0	0	144	$75

Henry Woodfield

Year	Driver	Starts	Poles	1	2	3	4	5	6–10	Laps	Laps Led	Races Led	Miles	$
1963	Elmo Langley	7	0	0	0	0	0	1	1	1,193	0	0	433	920
1964	Elmo Langley	13	0	0	0	0	0	0	5	2,620	0	0	1,551	3,805
"	Bert Robbins	2	0	0	0	0	0	1	0	918	0	0	401	600
"	**Total**	13	0	0	0	0	0	1	5	3,538	0	0	1,952	4,405
1966	Elmo Langley	45	1	2	1	0	4	4	8	9,255	308	5	6,269	22,055
1967	Elmo Langley	43	0	0	1	2	2	3	14	9,161	0	0	6,536	22,923
"	Dub Simpson	1	0	0	0	0	0	0	0	89	0	0	134	865
"	**Total**	43	0	0	1	2	2	3	14	9,250	0	0	6,669	23,788
1968	Elmo Langley	2	0	0	0	0	0	0	1	653	0	0	342	845
Lifetime		110	1	2	2	2	6	9	29	23,889	308	5	15,665	$52,013

Richard Woodland

Year	Driver	Starts	Poles	1	2	3	4	5	6–10	Laps	Laps Led	Races Led	Miles	$
1993	Rich Woodland Jr.	1	0	0	0	0	0	0	0	114	0	0	114	6,030
1996	Rich Woodland Jr.	1	0	0	0	0	0	0	0	68	0	0	171	10,095
Lifetime		2	0	0	0	0	0	0	0	182	0	0	285	$16,125

Ernest Woods

Year	Driver	Starts	Poles	1	2	3	4	5	6–10	Laps	Laps Led	Races Led	Miles	$
1953	Emory Lewis	2	0	0	0	0	0	0	1	387	0	0	364	255
"	Tommy Thompson	1	0	0	0	0	0	0	0		0	0		25
"	**Total**	3	0	0	0	0	0	0	1	387	0	0	364	280

Year	Driver	Starts	Poles	Finish						Laps	Laps Led	Races Led	Miles	$
				1	2	3	4	5	6–10					

Ernest Woods *continued*

Year	Driver	Starts	Poles	1	2	3	4	5	6–10	Laps	Laps Led	Races Led	Miles	$
1954	Buck Baker	14	6	2	1	3	1	2	3	2,410	432	8	1,445	5,600
"	Ray Duhigg	1	0	0	0	0	0	0	0	2	0	0	1	0
"	Bob Flock	2	0	0	0	0	0	0	0	167	0	0	84	25
"	Tim Flock	1	0	0	0	0	0	0	0	39	0	0	160	0
"	Emory Lewis	5	0	0	0	0	0	0	2	422	0	0	378	475
"	Joel Million	9	0	0	0	0	0	0	1	1,298	0	0	1,324	875
"	Jim Paschal	14	1	0	0	0	0	1	4	1,886	0	0	1,419	2,060
"	**Total**	26	7	2	1	3	1	3	10	6,224	432	8	**4,810**	9,035
1955	Fred Harb	1	0	0	0	0	0	0	0	93	0	0	93	60
"	Jimmie Lewallen	22	1	0	2	0	4	0	5	2,913	0	0	2,249	5,115
"	Joel Million	8	0	0	1	0	1	0	4	973	0	0	624	1,685
"	Jim Paschal	31	2	3	3	2	2	1	7	4,126	306	7	2,849	9,886
"	Dick Rathmann	1	0	0	0	0	0	0	0	38	0	0	156	100
"	**Total**	36	3	3	6	2	7	1	16	8,143	306	7	5,971	16,846
1956	Jimmie Lewallen	4	0	0	0	0	1	0	0	370	0	0	198	1,000
"	Ralph Liguori	2	0	0	0	0	0	0	0	390	0	0	503	300
"	Banjo Matthews	1	0	0	0	0	0	0	0	149	0	0	224	200
"	Joel Million	2	0	0	0	0	0	0	0	175	0	0	88	50
"	Blackie Pitt	2	0	0	0	0	0	0	1	291	0	0	173	200
"	**Total**	8	0	0	0	0	1	0	1	1,375	0	0	1,185	1,750
1957	Jim Linke	2	0	0	0	0	0	0	1	213	0	0	179	300
Lifetime		75	10	5	7	5	9	4	29	16,342	738	15	12,508	$28,211

Buzz Woodward

Year	Driver	Starts	Poles	1	2	3	4	5	6–10	Laps	Laps Led	Races Led	Miles	$
1958	Buzz Woodward	9	0	0	0	0	0	0	2	1,508	0	0	1,028	1,195
1959	Buzz Woodward	1	0	0	0	0	0	1	0	191	0	0	96	225
1961	Buzz Woodward	1	0	0	0	0	0	0	1	456	0	0	114	400
Lifetime		11	0	0	0	0	0	1	3	2,155	0	0	1,238	$1,820

Wayne Woodward

Year	Driver	Starts	Poles	1	2	3	4	5	6–10	Laps	Laps Led	Races Led	Miles	$
1966	Wayne Woodward	6	0	0	0	0	0	0	0	936	0	0	489	1,290
Lifetime		6	0	0	0	0	0	0	0	936	·0	0	489	$1,290

Bruce Worrell

Year	Driver	Starts	Poles	1	2	3	4	5	6–10	Laps	Laps Led	Races Led	Miles	$
1965	Bruce Worrell	1	0	0	0	0	0	0	0	1	0	0	3	500
Lifetime		1	0	0	0	0	0	0	0	1	0	0	3	$500

Dick Wright

Year	Driver	Starts	Poles	1	2	3	4	5	6–10	Laps	Laps Led	Races Led	Miles	$
1960	Larry Frank	1	0	0	0	0	0	0	0	8	0	0	7	50
"	Jimmy Thompson	1	0	0	0	0	0	0	0	157	0	0	236	325
"	**Total**	2	0	0	0	0	0	0	0	165	0	0	243	375
1961	Larry Frank	5	0	0	0	0	0	0	1	483	0	0	904	1,275
Lifetime		7	0	0	0	0	0	0	1	648	0	0	1,146	$1,650

Earl Wright

Year	Driver	Starts	Poles	1	2	3	4	5	6–10	Laps	Laps Led	Races Led	Miles	$
1955	Dick Allwine	1	0	0	0	0	0	0	0	202	0	0	278	50
"	Russ Graham	5	0	0	0	0	0	0	0	735	0	0	702	375
"	**Total**	5	0	0	0	0	0	0	0	937	0	0	980	425
1956	Dick Allwine	2	0	0	0	0	0	0	0	294	0	0	294	200
"	Russ Graham	1	0	0	0	0	0	0	0	26	0	0	36	50
"	**Total**	3	0	0	0	0	0	0	0	320	0	0	330	250
Lifetime		8	0	0	0	0	0	0	0	1,257	0	0	1,309	$675

James Wright

Year	Driver	Starts	Poles	1	2	3	4	5	6–10	Laps	Laps Led	Races Led	Miles	$
1969	Ben Arnold	1	0	0	0	0	0	0	0	105	0	0	107	665
"	Bill Dennis	2	0	0	0	0	0	0	0	222	0	0	180	1,240
"	**Total**	3	0	0	0	0	0	0	0	327	0	0	287	1,905
1970	Ben Arnold	1	0	0	0	0	0	0	0	66	0	0	26	200
"	Bill Dennis	21	0	0	0	0	0	0	5	3,471	0	0	2,807	12,070
"	**Total**	22	0	0	0	0	0	0	5	3,537	0	0	2,833	12,270
Lifetime		25	0	0	0	0	0	0	5	3,864	0	0	3,120	$14,175

Year	Driver	Starts	Poles	Finish 1	2	3	4	5	6–10	Laps	Laps Led	Races Led	Miles	$

Jim Wright

Year	Driver	Starts	Poles	1	2	3	4	5	6–10	Laps	Laps Led	Races Led	Miles	$
1967	Jim Wright	1	0	0	0	0	0	0	0	9	0	0	5	125
1969	Bill Dennis	1	0	0	0	0	0	0	0	54	0	0	29	415
Lifetime		2	0	0	0	0	0	0	0	63	0	0	34	$540

L. W. Wright

Year	Driver	Starts	Poles	1	2	3	4	5	6–10	Laps	Laps Led	Races Led	Miles	$
1982	L. W. Wright	1	0	0	0	0	0	0	0	13	0	0	35	1,545
Lifetime		1	0	0	0	0	0	0	0	13	0	0	35	$1,545

Millard Wright

Year	Driver	Starts	Poles	1	2	3	4	5	6–10	Laps	Laps Led	Races Led	Miles	$
1954	Tommie Elliott	3	0	0	0	0	0	0	3	546	0	0	273	400
"	Ronnie Kohler	2	0	0	0	0	0	0	1	368	0	0	276	150
"	**Total**	5	0	0	0	0	0	0	4	914	0	0	549	550
1955	Millard Wright	1	0	0	0	0	0	0	0	182	0	0	91	60
1956	Millard Wright	1	0	0	0	0	0	0	0	178	0	0	89	50
Lifetime		7	0	0	0	0	0	0	4	1,274	0	0	729	$660

R. H. Yandell

Year	Driver	Starts	Poles	1	2	3	4	5	6–10	Laps	Laps Led	Races Led	Miles	$
1951	Buddy Shuman	7	0	0	0	1	0	0	6	391	0	0	489	2,200
Lifetime		7	0	0	0	1	0	0	6	391	0	0	489	$2,200

Eddie Yarboro

Year	Driver	Starts	Poles	1	2	3	4	5	6–10	Laps	Laps Led	Races Led	Miles	$
1966	Eddie Yarboro	3	0	0	0	0	0	0	1	457	0	0	184	165
1967	Eddie Yarboro	8	0	0	0	0	0	0	3	1,318	0	0	594	1,495
1968	Eddie Yarboro	6	0	0	0	0	0	0	0	2,109	0	0	1,347	2,255
1970	Eddie Yarboro	1	0	0	0	0	0	0	1	338	0	0	201	800
1971	Wendell Scott	1	0	0	0	0	0	0	0	251	0	0	132	425
"	Eddie Yarboro	7	0	0	0	0	0	0	0	1,624	0	0	1,310	3,685
"	**Total**	8	0	0	0	0	0	0	0	1,875	0	0	1,442	4,110
1972	Eddie Yarboro	6	0	0	0	0	0	0	0	1,728	0	0	1,336	3,435
Lifetime		32	0	0	0	0	0	0	5	7,825	0	0	5,104	$12,260

Cale Yarborough

Year	Driver	Starts	Poles	1	2	3	4	5	6–10	Laps	Laps Led	Races Led	Miles	$
1987	Cale Yarborough	16	0	0	0	0	1	1	2	2,671	11	2	4,519	111,025
1988	Dale Jarrett	19	0	0	0	0	0	0	1	5,361	4	1	5,507	59,610
"	Cale Yarborough	10	0	0	0	0	0	0	3	1,653	6	2	3,169	66,065
"	**Total**	29	0	0	0	0	0	0	4	7,014	10	3	8,676	125,675
1989	Dale Jarrett	29	0	0	0	0	0	2	3	7,798	99	3	9,178	232,317
1990	Dick Trickle	29	1	0	0	1	0	1	2	8,311	82	4	9,827	293,490
1991	Chuck Bown	1	0	0	0	0	0	0	0	391	0	0	244	5,225
"	Randy LaJoie	3	0	0	0	0	0	0	0	926	0	0	1,062	19,625
"	Dorsey Schroeder	1	0	0	0	0	0	0	0	2	0	0	3	5,105
"	Lake Speed	20	0	0	0	0	0	0	0	4,513	0	0	5,052	149,300
"	Dick Trickle	4	0	0	0	0	0	0	0	1,362	0	0	1,736	61,235
"	**Total**	29	0	0	0	0	0	0	0	7,194	0	0	8,096	240,490
1992	Jimmy Hensley	22	0	0	0	0	0	0	4	6,804	22	3	8,491	247,660
"	Bobby Hillin Jr.	1	0	0	0	0	0	0	0	393	0	0	246	5,260
"	Chad Little	6	0	0	0	0	0	0	0	1,852	0	0	1,909	55,810
"	**Total**	29	0	0	0	0	0	0	4	9,049	22	3	10,645	308,730
1993	Derrike Cope	30	0	0	0	0	0	0	1	8,406	38	3	9,965	402,515
1994	Derrike Cope	16	0	0	0	0	0	0	0	4,261	7	1	5,028	185,816
"	Jeremy Mayfield	12	0	0	0	0	0	0	0	3,452	0	0	4,304	137,865
"	**Total**	28	0	0	0	0	0	0	0	7,713	7	1	9,332	323,681
1995	Jeremy Mayfield	27	0	0	0	0	0	0	1	7,943	79	3	10,440	436,805
1996	John Andretti	8	0	0	0	0	0	1	0	3,018	1	1	2,813	117,030
"	Jeremy Mayfield	23	1	0	0	0	1	1	0	5,862	20	4	7,844	463,763
"	**Total**	31	1	0	0	0	1	2	0	8,880	21	5	10,657	580,793
Lifetime		277	2	0	0	1	2	6	17	74,979	369	27	91,337	$3,055,521

Doug Yates

Year	Driver	Starts	Poles	1	2	3	4	5	6–10	Laps	Laps Led	Races Led	Miles	$
1952	Doug Yates	1	0	0	0	0	0	0	0		0	0		25
1964	Doug Yates	14	1	0	1	0	0	1	4	2,324	9	1	1,047	2,890
1965	Doug Yates	4	0	0	0	0	0	0	1	271	13	1	150	550
Lifetime		19	1	0	1	0	0	1	5	2,595	22	2	1,197	$3,465

Year	Driver	Starts	Poles	Finish						Laps	Laps Led	Races Led	Miles	$
				1	2	3	4	5	6–10	Laps	Led	Led	Miles	$

Robert Yates

Year	Driver	Starts	Poles	1	2	3	4	5	6–10	Laps	Laps Led	Races Led	Miles	$
1989	Davey Allison	29	1	2	1	0	2	2	6	8,287	241	13	10,111	640,956
1990	Davey Allison	29	0	2	0	1	0	2	5	9,154	222	8	10,816	640,684
1991	Davey Allison	29	3	5	4	2	1	0	4	8,770	1,528	**23**	10,610	1,712,924
1992	Davey Allison	29	2	5	1	1	5	3	2	8,976	1,377	18	10,998	1,955,628
1993	Davey Allison	16	0	1	1	2	1	1	2	5,061	276	9	6,214	513,585
"	Robby Gordon	1	0	0	0	0	0	0	0	55	0	0	146	17,665
"	Ernie Irvan	8	2	2	1	1	0	1	1	3,119	886	6	3,206	584,483
"	Lake Speed	3	0	0	0	0	0	0	1	772	2	1	856	60,620
"	**Total**	28	2	3	2	3	1	2	4	9,007	1,164	16	10,422	1,176,353
1994	Ernie Irvan	20	5	3	6	2	0	2	2	5,357	1,781	17	7,643	1,311,522
"	Kenny Wallace	10	0	0	0	0	1	0	1	4,040	4	3	3,790	211,810
"	**Total**	30	5	3	6	2	1	2	3	9,397	1,785	20	11,433	1,523,332
1995	Ernie Irvan	3	0	0	0	0	0	0	2	924	142	2	945	54,875
"	Dale Jarrett	31	1	1	1	2	1	4	5	8,671	324	8	10,417	1,363,158
"	**Total**	31	1	1	1	2	1	4	7	9,595	466	9	11,362	1,418,033
1996	Ernie Irvan	31	1	2	2	0	6	2	4	8,618	370	15	10,220	1,683,313
"	Dale Jarrett	31	2	4	7	4	2	0	4	9,307	755	20	11,180	2,985,418
"	**Total**	31	3	6	9	4	8	2	8	17,925	1,125	25	21,400	4,668,731
Lifetime		236	17	27	24	15	19	17	39	81,111	7,908	132	97,152	$13,736,641
														5th

Howard York

Year	Driver	Starts	Poles	1	2	3	4	5	6–10	Laps	Laps Led	Races Led	Miles	$
1965	Bob Connor	1	0	0	0	0	0	0	0	115	0	0	311	580
Lifetime		1	0	0	0	0	0	0	0	115	0	0	311	$580

Clay Young

Year	Driver	Starts	Poles	1	2	3	4	5	6–10	Laps	Laps Led	Races Led	Miles	$
1986	Clay Young	1	0	0	0	0	0	0	0	90	0	0	236	1,400
1992	Clay Young	1	0	0	0	0	0	0	0	40	0	0	106	5,690
Lifetime		2	0	0	0	0	0	0	0	130	0	0	342	$7,090

Kaylan Young

Year	Driver	Starts	Poles	1	2	3	4	5	6–10	Laps	Laps Led	Races Led	Miles	$
1992	Mike Chase	1	0	0	0	0	0	0	0	69	0	0	174	6,330
Lifetime		1	0	0	0	0	0	0	0	69	0	0	174	$6,330

Wade Younts

Year	Driver	Starts	Poles	1	2	3	4	5	6–10	Laps	Laps Led	Races Led	Miles	$
1961	Larry Thomas	12	0	0	0	0	0	0	4	2,547	0	0	1,185	1,900
1962	Larry Thomas	37	0	0	0	0	2	1	9	7,268	0	0	4,889	9,486
1963	Larry Thomas	27	0	0	0	2	1	3	7	5,829	0	0	3,099	7,075
"	Joe Weatherly	2	0	0	0	0	0	0	2	664	0	0	284	1,150
"	**Total**	28	0	0	0	2	1	3	9	6,493	0	0	3,383	8,225
1964	Darrell Bryant	1	0	0	0	0	0	0	0	1	0	0	1	275
"	Major Melton	3	0	0	0	0	0	0	1	737	0	0	648	1,100
"	Larry Thomas	21	0	0	0	1	0	1	11	3,819	0	0	2,062	7,886
"	**Total**	25	0	0	0	1	0	1	12	4,557	0	0	2,711	9,261
Lifetime		102	0	0	0	3	3	5	34	20,865	0	0	12,168	$28,872

Pete Yow

Year	Driver	Starts	Poles	1	2	3	4	5	6–10	Laps	Laps Led	Races Led	Miles	$
1956	Pete Yow	11	0	0	0	0	0	0	2	1,221	0	0	680	700
Lifetime		11	0	0	0	0	0	0	2	1,221	0	0	680	$700

Smokey Yunick

Year	Driver	Starts	Poles	1	2	3	4	5	6–10	Laps	Laps Led	Races Led	Miles	$
1956	Tim Flock	1	0	0	0	1	0	0	0	149	41	1	149	725
"	Paul Goldsmith	9	0	1	0	0	2	1	2	2,292	182	1	2,090	8,569
"	Herb Thomas	3	1	1	0	1	0	0	1	301	1	1	151	1,775
"	**Total**	13	1	2	0	2	2	1	3	2,742	224	3	2,390	11,069
1957	Paul Goldsmith	17	4	3	3	1	0	0	3	2,839	547	9	1,869	10,909
"	Ralph Moody	1	0	0	0	0	0	0	0	25	0	0	13	75
"	Curtis Turner	1	0	0	0	0	0	0	0	346	51	1	476	1,060
"	**Total**	18	4	3	3	1	0	0	3	3,210	598	9	2,358	12,044
1958	Paul Goldsmith	1	1	1	0	0	0	0	0	39	39	1	160	4,550
"	Cotton Owens	1	0	0	0	0	0	0	0	126	0	0	63	0
"	**Total**	2	1	1	0	0	0	0	0	165	39	1	223	4,550
1961	Marvin Panch	5	0	1	1	0	1	0	0	615	13	1	1,262	24,005

Year	Driver	Starts	Poles	Finish						Laps	Laps Led	Races Led	Miles	$
				1	2	3	4	5	6–10					

Smokey Yunick *continued*

Year	Driver	Starts	Poles	1	2	3	4	5	6–10	Laps	Laps Led	Races Led	Miles	$
1963	Buck Baker	1	0	0	0	0	0	0	1	356	0	0	490	1,025
"	A. J. Foyt	2	0	0	0	0	0	0	0	271	56	1	552	1,330
"	Bobby Isaac	1	0	0	0	0	0	0	0	57	0	0	86	425
"	Banjo Matthews	1	0	0	0	0	0	0	0	358	0	0	537	700
"	Johnny Rutherford	2	0	1	0	0	0	0	1	236	6	1	590	2,350
"	**Total**	7	0	1	0	0	0	0	2	1,278	62	2	2,254	5,830
1966	Bobby Allison	1	0	0	0	0	0	0	0	3	0	0	5	630
"	Mario Andretti	2	0	0	0	0	0	0	0	68	1	1	170	1,165
"	Curtis Turner	6	1	0	0	0	1	0	0	685	71	3	1,078	6,115
"	**Total**	9	1	0	0	0	1	0	0	756	72	4	1,252	7,910
1967	Curtis Turner	2	2	0	0	0	0	0	0	144	6	1	360	6,525
1969	Charlie Glotzbach	1	0	0	0	0	1	0	0	333	5	1	500	3,585
"	Joe Leonard	1	0	0	0	0	0	0	0	47	0	0	118	720
"	Swede Savage	1	0	0	0	0	0	0	0	266	0	0	399	1,275
"	Bobby Unser	2	0	0	0	0	1	0	0	106	2	2	265	1,900
"	**Total**	5	0	0	0	0	2	0	0	752	7	3	1,281	7,480
Lifetime		61	9	8	4	3	6	1	8	9,662	1,021	24	11,403	$79,413

Zanworth Racing

Year	Driver	Starts	Poles	1	2	3	4	5	6–10	Laps	Laps Led	Races Led	Miles	$
1986	Mike Skinner	3	0	0	0	0	0	0	0	807	0	0	635	4,255
Lifetime		3	0	0	0	0	0	0	0	807	0	0	635	$4,255

Emanuel Zervakis

Year	Driver	Starts	Poles	1	2	3	4	5	6–10	Laps	Laps Led	Races Led	Miles	$
1956	Emanuel Zervakis	6	0	0	0	0	0	0	0	772	0	0	827	475
1957	Emanuel Zervakis	2	0	0	0	0	0	0	0	140	0	0	70	150
1962	Emanuel Zervakis	11	0	0	0	0	0	0	2	2,151	5	1	2,357	4,545
1963	Emanuel Zervakis	3	0	0	0	0	0	0	0	436	0	0	586	1,400
1974	Sonny Hutchins	1	0	0	0	0	0	0	0	150	79	1	79	590
1981	Geoff Bodine	3	0	0	0	0	0	0	1	678	14	2	821	8,610
1982	Butch Lindley	4	0	0	1	0	0	0	0	1,020	165	2	547	16,695
1983	Butch Lindley	1	0	0	0	0	0	0	0	396	7	1	215	2,485
"	Mark Martin	1	0	0	0	0	0	0	0	279	0	0	419	1,640
"	Morgan Shepherd	1	0	0	0	0	0	0	0	8	0	0	4	1,000
"	**Total**	3	0	0	0	0	0	0	0	683	7	1	637	5,125
1984	Sam Ard	1	0	0	0	0	0	0	0	1	0	0	1	1,100
"	Dale Jarrett	2	0	0	0	0	0	0	0	641	0	0	410	2,350
"	**Total**	3	0	0	0	0	0	0	0	642	0	0	411	3,450
Lifetime		36	0	0	1	0	0	0	3	6,672	270	7	6,335	$41,040

John Zink

Year	Driver	Starts	Poles	1	2	3	4	5	6–10	Laps	Laps Led	Races Led	Miles	$
1956	Jack Zink Jr.	1	0	0	0	0	0	0	0	10	0	0	5	100
1957	Darel Dieringer	1	0	0	0	0	0	0	0	9	0	0	37	0
Lifetime		2	0	0	0	0	0	0	0	19	0	0	42	$100

PART 5
THE TRACKS

Alabama

Chisholm Speedway
Montgomery, AL
Half-mile Dirt Track

Half-mile dirt oval built circa 1951. Only NASCAR Winston Cup (then Grand National) race staged on 9/9/56 (won by Buck Baker) before a sparse crowd of 2,000. Promoters lost money on the event and the track closed shortly thereafter.

Winston Cup Victories
Buck Baker   1

Winston Cup Poles
Tim Flock   1

Winston Cup Money
Buck Baker $950

Most Cars Started
21—September 9, 1956

Narrowest Margin of Victory
N/A

Race Record
60.893 MPH—September 9, 1956

Most Race Leaders
4—September 9, 1956

Most Cars Running at Finish
15—September 9, 1956

1956 Grand National Race No. 45
September 9, 1956 Average Speed: 60.893

Driver	Owner	Car #	Make	Laps	Winnings
1. Buck Baker	Carl Kiekhaefer	87	56 Chrys	200	950
2. Ralph Moody	Pete DePaolo	12	56 Ford	200	675
3. Marvin Panch	Tom Harbison	98	56 Ford	199	475
4. Fireball Roberts	Pete DePaolo	22	56 Ford	195	365
5. Johnny Allen	Spook Crawford	264	56 Plym	194	320

Dixie Speedway
Birmingham, AL
Quarter-mile Paved Track

(aka Midfield Speedway) Quarter-mile paved oval built in 1958. Located in Birmingham suburb of Midfield. Only NASCAR Winston Cup (then Grand National) race staged on 8/3/60 (won by Ned Jarrett). The 50-mile event saw three Petty racers (Lee, Richard, and Maurice) all finish in the top 10; Richard was second, Lee third, and Maurice eighth. Track continued weekly operation until 1974.

Winston Cup Victories
Ned Jarrett   1

Winston Cup Poles
Ned Jarrett   1

Winston Cup Money
Ned Jarrett $770

Most Cars Started
16—August 3, 1960

Narrowest Margin of Victory
2 laps-plus—August 3, 1960

Race Record
54.463 MPH—August 3, 1960

Most Race Leaders
1—August 3, 1960

Most Cars Running at Finish
11—August 3, 1960

1960 Grand National Race No. 28
August 3, 1960 Average Speed: 54.463

Driver	Owner	Car #	Make	Laps	Winnings
1. Ned Jarrett	Ned Jarrett	11	60 Ford	200	770
2. Richard Petty	Petty Enterprises	43	60 Plym	198	535
3. Lee Petty	Petty Enterprises	42	60 Plym	196	485
4. Joe Lee Johnson	Paul McDuffie	89	60 Chev	195	365
5. Johnny Beauchamp	Dale Swanson	73	60 Chev	192	245

Fairgrounds Raceway
Birmingham, AL
Half-mile Dirt Track

(aka Birmingham Int'l Raceway; Birmingham Int'l Speedway; Birmingham Super Speedway; Birmingham Super Raceway) Originally built as 1-mile horse track circa 1906. The half-mile dirt track was built circa 1933. First NASCAR Winston Cup (then Grand National) race 9/7/58 (Fireball Roberts won). Final Grand National event took place on 6/8/68 (won by Richard Petty). Track is still in operation and is now measured at .625-miles.

Winston Cup Starts

Buck Baker	5
Ned Jarrett	5
Richard Petty	5
Wendell Scott	5

Winston Cup Victories

Ned Jarrett	3

Winston Cup Poles

Jim Paschal	2
David Pearson	2

Winston Cup Money

Richard Petty	$3,800

Most Cars Started
21—November 4, 1962

Fewest Cars Started
13—June 4, 1961

Narrowest Margin of Victory
1 car length—June 10, 1967

Slowest Race
56.364 MPH—June 6, 1965
Birmingham 200

Race Record
89.153 MPH—June 8, 1968

Most Cautions
N/A

Most Race Leaders
N/A

Most Cars Running at Finish
16—November 4, 1962

1958 Grand National Race No. 43
September 7, 1958 Average Speed: 60.678

Driver	Owner	Car #	Make	Laps	Winnings
1. Fireball Roberts	Frank Strickland	22	57 Chev	200	800
2. Buck Baker	Buck Baker	87	57 Chev	200	525
3. Lee Petty	Petty Enterprises	42	57 Olds	199	450
4. Joe Eubanks	Jim Stephens	6	57 Pont	194	325
5. Tiny Lund	J. H. Petty	48	57 Chev	194	225

1961 Grand National Race No. 26
June 4, 1961 Average Speed: 61.068

Driver	Owner	Car #	Make	Laps	Winnings
1. Ned Jarrett	Bee Gee Holloway	11	61 Chev	200	800
2. Jim Paschal	J. H. Petty	14	61 Pont	198	525
3. Jack Smith	Jack Smith	46	61 Pont	198	375
4. Rex White	Rex White	4	60 Chev	197	375
5. Tommy Wells		39	60 Chev	192	250

1963 Grand National Race No. 1
November 4, 1962 Average Speed: 68.350

Driver	Owner	Car #	Make	Laps	Winnings
1. Jim Paschal	Petty Enterprises	41	62 Plym	200	1,000
2. Richard Petty	Petty Enterprises	43	62 Plym	199	600
3. Buck Baker	Buck Baker	87	62 Chrys	196	400
4. Jimmy Pardue	Jimmy Pardue	54	62 Pont	196	300
5. Darel Dieringer	Mamie Reynolds	26	62 Ford	197	275

1963 Grand National Race No. 27
June 9, 1963 Average Speed: 68.195

Driver	Owner	Car #	Make	Laps	Winnings
1. Richard Petty	Petty Enterprises	41	63 Plym	200	1,000
2. Junior Johnson	Ray Fox	3	63 Chev	200	600
3. Buck Baker	Buck Baker	87	63 Pont	198	400
4. Ned Jarrett	Charles Robinson	11	63 Ford	196	300
5. Jack Smith	Jack Smith	47	63 Plym	195	275

1964 Grand National Race No. 32
June 21, 1964 Average Speed: 67.643

Driver	Owner	Car #	Make	Laps	Winnings
1. Ned Jarrett	Bondy Long	11	64 Ford	200	1,150
2. Richard Petty	Petty Enterprises	43	64 Plym	199	600
3. Billy Wade	Bud Moore	1	64 Merc	198	450
4. David Pearson	Cotton Owens	6	64 Dodg	198	300
5. Buck Baker	Ray Fox	3	64 Dodg	194	275

1965 Grand National Race No. 24 Birmingham 200
June 6, 1965 Average Speed: 56.364

Driver	Owner	Car #	Make	Laps	Winnings
1. Ned Jarrett	Bondy Long	11	65 Ford	108	1,000
2. Dick Hutcherson	Holman-Moody	29	65 Ford	108	600
3. G. C. Spencer	G. C. Spencer	49	64 Ford	108	400
4. Tom Pistone	Emory Gilliam	00	64 Ford	108	300
5. Junior Spencer	Jerry Mullins	17	64 Ford	107	275

1967 Grand National Race No. 24
June 10, 1967 Average Speed: 88.999

Driver	Owner	Car #	Make	Laps	Winnings
1. Bobby Allison	Cotton Owens	6	67 Dodg	160	1,000
2. Jim Paschal	Tom Friedkin	14	67 Plym	160	600
3. Richard Petty	Petty Enterprises	43	67 Plym	160	400
4. James Hylton	Bud Hartje	48	65 Dodg	158	300
5. Friday Hassler	Red Sharp	39	66 Chev	157	275

1968 Grand National Race No. 22
June 8, 1968 Average Speed: 89.153

Driver	Owner	Car #	Make	Laps	Winnings
1. Richard Petty	Petty Enterprises	43	68 Plym	160	1,200
2. Bobby Isaac	Nord Krauskopf	71	67 Dodg	160	600
3. James Hylton	James Hylton	48	67 Dodg	158	400
4. Friday Hassler	Red Sharp	39	66 Chev	157	300
5. Bobby Allison	Bobby Allison	2	66 Chev	157	275

Huntsville Speedway
Huntsville, AL
Quarter-mile Paved Track

(aka Huntsville Motor Speedway; Huntsville Int'l Speedway; Huntsville Int'l Raceway) Quarter-mile paved track built circa 1961. Only NASCAR Winston Cup (then Grand National) race held on 8/8/62 (won by Richard Petty). Track still active today.

Winston Cup Victories
Richard Petty   1

Winston Cup Poles
Richard Petty   1

Winston Cup Money
Richard Petty $580

Most Cars Started
16—August 8, 1962

Narrowest Margin of Victory
1 lap-plus—August 8, 1962

Race Record
54.644 MPH—August 8, 1962

Most Race Leaders
1—August 8, 1962

Most Cars Running at Finish
13—August 8, 1962

1962 Grand National Race No. 39
August 8, 1962 Average Speed: 54.644

Driver	Owner	Car #	Make	Laps	Winnings
1. Richard Petty	Petty Enterprises	43	62 Plym	200	580
2. Bob Welborn	J. C. Parker	49	62 Pont	199	475
3. Jim Paschal	Cliff Stewart	2	62 Pont	198	400
4. Buck Baker	Buck Baker	87	62 Chrys	198	325
5. Ned Jarrett	Bee Gee Holloway	11	62 Chev	198	450

Lakeview Speedway
Mobile, AL
.75-mile Dirt Track

(aka Lake View Estates) 0.75-mile dirt oval built in 1948. First NASCAR Winston Cup (then Grand National) race run on 4/8/51 (Tim Flock won) and was promoted by Fonty Flock. Track also held '51 season finale on 11/25/51 (won by Frank Mundy in a Studebaker). Track closed circa 1953.

Winston Cup Starts
Sonny Black   2
Bud Erb   2
Bob Flock   2
Tim Flock   2
Fonty Flock   2
Lee Petty   2
Gene Tapia   2
Herb Thomas   2

Winston Cup Victories
Tim Flock   1
Frank Mundy   1

Winston Cup Poles
Frank Mundy   1

Winston Cup Money
Tim Flock $1,600

Most Cars Started
24—April 8, 1951

Fewest Cars Started
23—November 25, 1951

Narrowest Margin of Victory
Half-lap—April 8, 1951

Slowest Race
50.260 MPH—April 8, 1951

Race Record
50.260 MPH—April 8, 1951

Most Race Leaders
2—April 8, 1951

Most Cars Running at Finish
15—April 8, 1951

1951 Grand National Race No. 3
April 8, 1951 Average Speed: 50.260

Driver	Owner	Car #	Make	Laps	Winnings
1. Tim Flock	Ted Chester	91	51 Olds	150	1,000
2. Fonty Flock	Frank Christian	14	50 Olds	150	600
3. Herb Thomas	Herb Thomas	92	50 Plym	149	400
4. Bill Osborne		9	50 Olds	148	300
5. Donald Thomas	Herb Thomas	93	50 Plym	—	250

1951 Grand National Race No. 41
November 25, 1951

Driver	Owner	Car #	Make	Laps	Winnings
1. Frank Mundy	Perry Smith	23	51 Stud	150	1,000
2. Tim Flock	Ted Chester	91	51 Huds	149	600
3. Red Duvall	Hank Salat	87	51 Pack	—	500
4. Fonty Flock	Frank Christian	14	51 Olds	—	400
5. Don Oldenberg	Don Oldenberg	142	51 Pack	—	300

Montgomery Motor Speedway
Montgomery, AL
Half-mile Dirt Track

(aka Montgomery Int'l Raceway) Half-mile paved oval built in 1955. First NASCAR Winston Cup (then Grand National) race staged on 4/17/55 (Tim Flock won). Last race run on 12/8/68 (Bobby Allison won). Bobby Allison was promoter in late '60s. Track still in operation.

Winston Cup Starts
Buck Baker   5

Winston Cup Victories
Tim Flock   2

Winston Cup Poles
Richard Petty   3

Winston Cup Money
Richard Petty $2,400

Most Cars Started
30—November 26, 1967

Fewest Cars Started
14—July 29, 1956

Narrowest Margin of Victory
4 feet—December 8, 1968

Slowest Race
60.872 MPH—April 17, 1955

Race Record
73.200 MPH—December 8, 1968
Alabama 200

Most Cautions
4—November 26, 1967

Most Race Leaders
3—April 17, 1955
3—December 8, 1968 Alabama 200

Most Cars Running at Finish
18—September 11, 1955

1955 Grand National Race No. 9
April 17, 1955 Average Speed: 60.872

Driver	Owner	Car #	Make	Laps	Winnings
1. Tim Flock	Carl Kiekhaefer	300	55 Chrys	200	1,000
2. Joel Million	Ernest Woods	88	55 Olds	196	650
3. Fonty Flock	Frank Christian	14	55 Chev	196	450
4. Curtis Turner	Raymond Parks	99	55 Olds	192	350
5. Herb Thomas	Herb Thomas	92	55 Chev	190	300

1955 Grand National Race No. 36
September 11, 1955 Average Speed: 63.773

Driver	Owner	Car #	Make	Laps	Winnings
1. Tim Flock	Carl Kiekhaefer	300	55 Chrys	200	1,100
2. Herb Thomas	Herb Thomas	92	55 Chev	199	700
3. Bob Welborn	Bob Welborn	49	55 Chev	197	475
4. Lee Petty	Petty Enterprises	42	55 Dodg	196	365
5. Buck Baker	Buck Baker	89	55 Buick	195	310

1956 Grand National Race No. 35
July 29, 1956 Average Speed: 67.252

Driver	Owner	Car #	Make	Laps	Winnings
1. Marvin Panch	Tom Harbison	98	56 Ford	200	950
2. Buck Baker	Carl Kiekhaefer	300	56 Chrys	199	675
3. Bill Amick	Pete DePaolo	97	56 Ford	197	475
4. Speedy Thompson	Carl Kiekhaefer	500	56 Dodg	197	365
5. Lee Petty	Petty Enterprises	42	56 Dodg	195	320

1967 Grand National Race No. 27
June 27, 1967 Average Speed: 72.435

Driver	Owner	Car #	Make	Laps	Winnings
1. Jim Paschal	Tom Friedkin	14	67 Plym	200	1,000
2. Richard Petty	Petty Enterprises	43	67 Plym	200	600
3. Bobby Allison	Cotton Owens	6	67 Dodg	198	400
4. James Hylton	Bud Hartje	48	65 Dodg	196	300
5. Elmo Langley	Henry Woodfield	64	66 Ford	193	275

1968 Grand National Race No. 2
November 26, 1967 Average Speed: 70.644

Driver	Owner	Car #	Make	Laps	Winnings
1. Richard Petty	Petty Enterprises	43	67 Plym	200	1,200
2. Bobby Allison	Holman-Moody	11	67 Ford	200	600
3. Bobby Isaac	Nord Krauskopf	37	67 Dodg	196	400
4. Tom Pistone	Turkey Minton	74	67 Chev	196	300
5. Paul Lewis	Bobby Allison	2	65 Chev	195	275

1969 Grand National Race No. 2 Alabama 200
December 8, 1968 Average Speed: 73.200

Driver	Owner	Car #	Make	Laps	Winnings
1. Bobby Allison	Tom Friedkin	14	68 Plym	200	1,000
2. Richard Petty	Petty Enterprises	43	68 Plym	200	600
3. James Hylton	James Hylton	48	68 Dodg	195	400
4. Bobby Isaac	Nord Krauskopf	71	68 Dodg	193	300
5. Neil Castles	Neil Castles	06	67 Plym	188	275

Talladega Superspeedway
Eastaboga, AL
2.66-mile Superspeedway

(aka Alabama Int'l Motor Speedway) 2.66-mile tri-oval opened in September, 1969 with inaugural Talladega 500 on 9/14/69 (Richard Brickhouse won). Turns are banked 33 degrees. Patterned after the Daytona Int'l Speedway. Inaugural event hit by driver's boycott, citing dangerous conditions and tires that would tear apart after only a few laps. Regarded as fastest closed circuit in the country. Track was the site of the all-time Winston Cup qualifying record (212.809 MPH, Bill Elliott, 4/30/87) and the fastest 500-mile stock car race (186.288 MPH), won by Bill Elliott on May 5, 1985.

Winston Cup Starts
Dave Marcis   52

Winston Cup Victories
Dale Earnhardt   7

Winston Cup Poles
Bill Elliott   8

Winston Cup Money
Dale Earnhardt $1,371,315

Most Cars Started
60—May 6, 1973 Winston 500

Fewest Cars Started
36—September 14, 1969 Talladega 500

Narrowest Margin of Victory
0.005 seconds—July 25, 1993
DieHard 500

Slowest Race
130.220 MPH—May 5, 1974
Winston 500

Race Record
186.288 MPH—May 5, 1985
Winston 500

Most Cautions
9—May 7, 1972 Winston 500
9—May 4, 1986 Winston 500
9—July 27, 1986 Talladega 500
9—May 3, 1987 Winston 500

Most Race Leaders
26—July 27, 1986 Talladega 500

Most Cars Running at Finish
39—April 30, 1995 Winston Select 500

1969 Grand National Race No. 44 Talladega 500
September 14, 1969 Average Speed: 153.778

Driver	Owner	Car #	Make	Laps	Winnings
1. Richard Brickhouse	Ray Nichels	99	69 Dodg	188	24,550
2. Jim Vandiver	Ray Fox	3	69 Dodg	188	12,400
3. Ramo Stott	Bill Ellis	14	69 Dodg	188	7,050
4. Bobby Isaac	Nord Krauskopf	71	69 Dodg	187	4,725
5. Dick Brooks	Dick Brooks	32	69 Plym	180	3,300

1970 Grand National Race No. 10 Alabama 500
April 12, 1970 Average Speed: 152.321

Driver	Owner	Car #	Make	Laps	Winnings
1. Pete Hamilton	Petty Enterprises	40	70 Plym	188	26,650
2. Bobby Isaac	Nord Krauskopf	71	69 Dodg	188	12,500
3. David Pearson	Holman-Moody	17	69 Ford	187	8,675
4. Benny Parsons	L. G. DeWitt	72	69 Ford	187	5,825
5. Cale Yarborough	Wood Brothers	21	69 Merc	183	4,425

1970 Grand National Race No. 35 Talladega 500
August 23, 1970 Average Speed: 158.517

Driver	Owner	Car #	Make	Laps	Winnings
1. Pete Hamilton	Petty Enterprises	40	70 Plym	188	23,165
2. Bobby Isaac	Nord Krauskopf	71	69 Dodg	188	11,490
3. Charlie Glotzbach	Ray Nichels	99	69 Dodg	187	7,380
4. David Pearson	Holman-Moody	17	69 Ford	184	5,540
5. Buddy Baker	Cotton Owens	6	69 Dodg	184	3,915

1971 Winston Cup GN Race No. 18 Winston 500
May 16, 1971 Average Speed: 147.419

Driver	Owner	Car #	Make	Laps	Winnings
1. Donnie Allison	Wood Brothers	21	69 Merc	188	31,140
2. Bobby Allison	Holman-Moody	12	69 Merc	188	19,225
3. Buddy Baker	Petty Enterprises	11	71 Dodg	188	9,825
4. Pete Hamilton	Cotton Owens	6	71 Plym	187	5,825
5. Fred Lorenzen	Ray Nichels	99	71 Plym	187	3,950

1971 Winston Cup GN Race No. 37 Talladega 500
August 22, 1971 Average Speed: 145.945

Driver	Owner	Car #	Make	Laps	Winnings
1. Bobby Allison	Holman-Moody	12	69 Merc	188	19,565
2. Richard Petty	Petty Enterprises	43	71 Plym	188	10,040
3. Pete Hamilton	Cotton Owens	6	71 Plym	187	6,265
4. Fred Lorenzen	Ray Nichels	99	71 Plym	184	4,290
5. James Hylton	James Hylton	48	69 Merc	183	4,340

1972 Winston Cup GN Race No. 11 Winston 500
May 7, 1972 Average Speed: 134.400

Driver	Owner	Car #	Make	Laps	Winnings
1. David Pearson	Wood Brothers	21	71 Merc	188	23,745
2. Bobby Isaac	Nord Krauskopf	71	72 Dodg	188	15,895
3. Buddy Baker	Petty Enterprises	11	72 Dodg	188	9,995
4. Fred Lorenzen	Hoss Ellington	28	72 Ford	188	6,095
5. Richard Petty	Petty Enterprises	43	72 Dodg	187	6,970

1972 Winston Cup GN Race No. 21 Talladega 500
August 6, 1972 Average Speed: 148.728

Driver	Owner	Car #	Make	Laps	Winnings
1. James Hylton	James Hylton	48	71 Merc	188	24,865
2. Ramo Stott	Junie Donlavey	90	72 Ford	188	9,440
3. Bobby Allison	Richard Howard	12	72 Chev	183	9,465
4. Red Farmer	Willie Humphries	97	72 Ford	180	4,540
5. Buddy Arrington	Buddy Arrington	67	70 Dodg	179	3,615

1973 Winston Cup GN Race No. 10 Winston 500
May 6, 1973 Average Speed: 131.956

Driver	Owner	Car #	Make	Laps	Winnings
1. David Pearson	Wood Brothers	21	71 Merc	188	26,345
2. Donnie Allison	DiGard	08	72 Chev	187	11,445
3. Benny Parsons	L. G. DeWitt	72	72 Chev	187	8,935
4. Clarence Lovell	Don Bierschwale	61	73 Chev	185	5,870
5. Cecil Gordon	Cecil Gordon	24	73 Chev	184	4,495

1973 Winston Cup GN Race No. 20 Talladega 500
August 12, 1973 Average Speed: 145.454

Driver	Owner	Car #	Make	Laps	Winnings
1. Dick Brooks	Crawford Brothers	22	72 Plym	188	20,815
2. Buddy Baker	Nord Krauskopf	71	73 Dodg	188	14,590
3. David Pearson	Wood Brothers	21	71 Merc	188	9,540
4. James Hylton	James Hylton	48	71 Merc	186	5,590
5. David Sisco	Charlie McGee	05	72 Chev	186	4,665

1974 Winston Cup GN Race No. 10 Winston 500
May 5, 1974 Average Speed: 130.220

Driver	Owner	Car #	Make	Laps	Winnings
1. David Pearson	Wood Brothers	21	73 Merc	188	20,785
2. Benny Parsons	L. G. DeWitt	72	74 Chev	188	15,015
3. Richard Petty	Petty Enterprises	43	74 Dodg	188	11,245
4. Charlie Glotzbach	Junie Donlavey	90	72 Ford	188	6,490
5. Lennie Pond	Ronnie Elder	54	74 Chev	187	4,640

Talladega Superspeedway *continued*

1974 Winston Cup GN Race No. 21 Talladega 500
August 11, 1974 Average Speed: 148.637

Driver	Owner	Car #	Make	Laps	Winnings
1. Richard Petty	Petty Enterprises	43	74 Dodg	188	24,465
2. David Pearson	Wood Brothers	21	73 Merc	188	12,890
3. Bobby Allison	Bobby Allison	12	74 Chev	187	7,140
4. Cale Yarborough	Junior Johnson	11	74 Chev	186	8,285
5. Benny Parsons	L. G. DeWitt	72	74 Chev	186	7,465

1975 Winston Cup GN Race No. 10 Winston 500
May 4, 1975 Average Speed: 144.948

Driver	Owner	Car #	Make	Laps	Winnings
1. Buddy Baker	Bud Moore	15	75 Ford	188	28,725
2. David Pearson	Wood Brothers	21	73 Merc	188	14,600
3. Dick Brooks	Junie Donlavey	90	73 Ford	188	9,750
4. Darrell Waltrip	Darrell Waltrip	17	75 Chev	182	9,825
5. Coo Coo Marlin	H. B. Cunningham	14	75 Chev	182	6,800

1975 Winston Cup GN Race No. 19 Talladega 500
August 17, 1975 Average Speed: 130.892

Driver	Owner	Car #	Make	Laps	Winnings
1. Buddy Baker	Bud Moore	15	75 Ford	188	26,390
2. Richard Petty	Petty Enterprises	43	74 Dodg	188	17,295
3. Donnie Allison	Hoss Ellington	28	75 Chev	187	9,295
4. Dave Marcis	Nord Krauskopf	71	74 Dodg	186	9,620
5. Coo Coo Marlin	H. B. Cunningham	14	75 Chev	186	5,220

1976 Winston Cup GN Race No. 10 Winston 500
May 2, 1976 Average Speed: 169.887

Driver	Owner	Car #	Make	Laps	Winnings
1. Buddy Baker	Bud Moore	15	Ford	188	32,735
2. Cale Yarborough	Junior Johnson	11	Chev	188	19,670
3. Bobby Allison	Roger Penske	2	Merc	187	14,960
4. Richard Petty	Petty Enterprises	43	Dodg	186	13,805
5. Terry Ryan	Bill Monaghan	81	Chev	184	6,335

1976 Winston Cup GN Race No. 19 Talladega 500
August 8, 1976 Average Speed: 157.547

Driver	Owner	Car #	Make	Laps	Winnings
1. Dave Marcis	Nord Krauskopf	71	Dodg	188	26,110
2. Buddy Baker	Bud Moore	15	Ford	188	20,865
3. Dick Brooks	Junie Donlavey	90	Ford	187	11,945
4. James Hylton	James Hylton	48	Chev	186	8,260
5. Lennie Pond	Ronnie Elder	54	Chev	182	6,750

1977 Winston Cup GN Race No. 10 Winston 500
May 1, 1977 Average Speed: 164.877

Driver	Owner	Car #	Make	Laps	Winnings
1. Darrell Waltrip	DiGard	88	Chev	188	26,875
2. Cale Yarborough	Junior Johnson	11	Chev	188	23,310
3. Benny Parsons	L. G. DeWitt	72	Chev	188	16,500
4. Donnie Allison	Hoss Ellington	1	Chev	188	12,100
5. Dave Marcis	Roger Penske	2	Merc	188	10,250

1977 Winston Cup GN Race No. 19 Talladega 500
August 7, 1977 Average Speed: 162.524

Driver	Owner	Car #	Make	Laps	Winnings
1. Donnie Allison	Hoss Ellington	1	Chev	188	26,375
2. Cale Yarborough	Junior Johnson	11	Chev	188	18,300
3. Skip Manning	Billy Hagan	92	Chev	188	14,700
4. Ricky Rudd	Al Rudd	22	Chev	186	8,000
5. Lennie Pond	Ronnie Elder	54	Chev	186	8,050

1978 Winston Cup GN Race No. 10 Winston 500
May 14, 1978 Average Speed: 155.699

Driver	Owner	Car #	Make	Laps	Winnings
1. Cale Yarborough	Junior Johnson	11	Olds	188	34,300
2. Buddy Baker	M. C. Anderson	27	Olds	188	21,900
3. A. J. Foyt	A. J. Foyt	51	Buick	187	12,200
4. Skip Manning	Billy Hagan	92	Buick	187	11,350
5. Grant Adcox	Herb Adcox	41	Chev	186	7,650

1978 Winston Cup GN Race No. 19 Talladega 500
August 6, 1978 Average Speed: 174.700

Driver	Owner	Car #	Make	Laps	Winnings
1. Lennie Pond	Harry Ranier	54	Olds	188	26,025
2. Donnie Allison	Hoss Ellington	1	Olds	188	16,250
3. Benny Parsons	L. G. DeWitt	72	Olds	188	15,350
4. Cale Yarborough	Junior Johnson	11	Olds	188	17,850
5. David Pearson	Wood Brothers	21	Merc	187	6,400

1979 Winston Cup GN Race No. 10 Winston 500
May 6, 1979 Average Speed: 154.770

Driver	Owner	Car #	Make	Laps	Winnings
1. Bobby Allison	Bud Moore	15	Ford	188	33,750
2. Darrell Waltrip	DiGard	88	Olds	187	25,025
3. Buddy Arrington	Buddy Arrington	67	Dodg	186	18,120
4. Richard Petty	Petty Enterprises	43	Olds	185	13,100
5. Joe Millikan	L. G. DeWitt	72	Olds	185	11,900

1979 Winston Cup GN Race No. 20 Talladega 500
August 5, 1979 Average Speed: 161.229

Driver	Owner	Car #	Make	Laps	Winnings
1. Darrell Waltrip	DiGard	88	Olds	188	32,325
2. David Pearson	Rod Osterlund	2	Olds	188	20,925
3. Ricky Rudd	Junie Donlavey	90	Merc	186	13,920
4. Richard Petty	Petty Enterprises	43	Olds	186	11,475
5. Jody Ridley	Junie Donlavey	77	Merc	186	6,025

1980 Winston Cup GN Race No. 10 Winston 500
May 4, 1980 Average Speed: 170.481

Driver	Owner	Car #	Make	Laps	Winnings
1. Buddy Baker	Harry Ranier	28	Olds	188	32,150
2. Dale Earnhardt	Rod Osterlund	2	Olds	188	28,700
3. David Pearson	Hoss Ellington	1	Olds	188	23,150
4. Lennie Pond	Jim Testa	68	Olds	187	10,500
5. Tighe Scott	Walter Ballard	30	Olds	186	9,200

1980 Winston Cup GN Race No. 20 Talladega 500
August 3, 1980 Average Speed: 166.894

Driver	Owner	Car #	Make	Laps	Winnings
1. Neil Bonnett	Wood Brothers	21	Merc	188	35,675
2. Cale Yarborough	Junior Johnson	11	Olds	188	20,625
3. Dale Earnhardt	Rod Osterlund	2	Olds	188	16,975
4. Benny Parsons	M. C. Anderson	27	Olds	188	12,125
5. Harry Gant	Jack Beebe	47	Olds	188	9,550

1981 Winston Cup GN Race No. 10 Winston 500
May 3, 1981 Average Speed: 149.376

Driver	Owner	Car #	Make	Laps	Winnings
1. Bobby Allison	Harry Ranier	28	Buick	188	41,500
2. Buddy Baker	Hoss Ellington	1	Buick	188	34,450
3. Darrell Waltrip	Junior Johnson	11	Buick	188	20,325
4. Ricky Rudd	DiGard	88	Olds	188	18,750
5. Donnie Allison	John Rebhan	77	Olds	187	10,050

Talladega Superspeedway *continued*

1981 Winston Cup GN Race No. 20 Talladega 500
August 2, 1981 Average Speed: 156.737

Driver	Owner	Car #	Make	Laps	Winnings
1. Ron Bouchard	Jack Beebe	47	Buick	188	38,905
2. Darrell Waltrip	Junior Johnson	11	Buick	188	23,000
3. Terry Labonte	Billy Hagan	44	Buick	188	18,500
4. Harry Gant	Hal Needham	33	Buick	188	10,000
5. Bobby Allison	Harry Ranier	28	Buick	188	17,825

1982 Winston Cup GN Race No. 9 Winston 500
May 2, 1982 Average Speed: 156.697

Driver	Owner	Car #	Make	Laps	Winnings
1. Darrell Waltrip	Junior Johnson	11	Buick	188	44,250
2. Terry Labonte	Billy Hagan	44	Buick	188	29,230
3. Benny Parsons	Harry Ranier	28	Pont	188	33,565
4. Kyle Petty	Petty Enterprises	42	Pont	188	17,095
5. Morgan Shepherd	Ron Benfield	98	Buick	188	11,100

1982 Winston Cup GN Race No. 19 Talladega 500
August 1, 1982 Average Speed: 168.157

Driver	Owner	Car #	Make	Laps	Winnings
1. Darrell Waltrip	Junior Johnson	11	Buick	188	58,770
2. Buddy Baker	Harry Ranier	28	Pont	188	34,350
3. Richard Petty	Petty Enterprises	43	Pont	188	26,975
4. Cale Yarborough	M. C. Anderson	27	Buick	188	11,625
5. Terry Labonte	Billy Hagan	44	Buick	188	13,095

1983 Winston Cup GN Race No. 8 Winston 500
May 1, 1983 Average Speed: 153.936

Driver	Owner	Car #	Make	Laps	Winnings
1. Richard Petty	Petty Enterprises	43	Pont	188	46,650
2. Benny Parsons	Johnny Hayes	55	Buick	188	24,575
3. Lake Speed	Hoss Ellington	1	Chev	188	18,975
4. Harry Gant	Hal Needham	33	Buick	188	22,425
5. Bill Elliott	Harry Melling	9	Ford	188	15,905

1983 Winston Cup GN Race No. 19 Talladega 500
July 31, 1983 Average Speed: 170.611

Driver	Owner	Car #	Make	Laps	Winnings
1. Dale Earnhardt	Bud Moore	15	Ford	188	46,950
2. Darrell Waltrip	Junior Johnson	11	Chev	188	32,965
3. Tim Richmond	Raymond Beadle	27	Pont	188	20,680
4. Richard Petty	Petty Enterprises	43	Pont	188	17,475
5. Harry Gant	Hal Needham	33	Buick	188	17,650

1984 Winston Cup GN Race No. 9 Winston 500
May 6, 1984 Average Speed: 172.988

Driver	Owner	Car #	Make	Laps	Winnings
1. Cale Yarborough	Harry Ranier	28	Chev	188	42,300
2. Harry Gant	Hal Needham	33	Chev	188	31,780
3. Buddy Baker	Wood Brothers	21	Ford	188	22,250
4. Bobby Allison	DiGard	22	Buick	188	31,250
5. Benny Parsons	Johnny Hayes	55	Chev	188	19,650

1984 Winston Cup GN Race No. 19 Talladega 500
July 29, 1984 Average Speed: 155.485

Driver	Owner	Car #	Make	Laps	Winnings
1. Dale Earnhardt	Richard Childress	3	Chev	188	47,100
2. Buddy Baker	Wood Brothers	21	Ford	188	28,225
3. Terry Labonte	Billy Hagan	44	Chev	188	22,455
4. Bobby Allison	DiGard	22	Buick	188	24,350
5. Cale Yarborough	Harry Ranier	28	Chev	188	15,350

1985 Winston Cup GN Race No. 9 Winston 500
May 5, 1985 Average Speed: 186.288

Driver	Owner	Car #	Make	Laps	Winnings
1. Bill Elliott	Harry Melling	9	Ford	188	60,500
2. Kyle Petty	Wood Brothers	7	Ford	188	34,905
3. Cale Yarborough	Harry Ranier	28	Ford	188	37,750
4. Bobby Allison	DiGard	22	Buick	187	23,075
5. Ricky Rudd	Bud Moore	15	Ford	187	21,025

1985 Winston Cup GN Race No. 17 Talladega 500
July 28, 1985 Average Speed: 148.772

Driver	Owner	Car #	Make	Laps	Winnings
1. Cale Yarborough	Harry Ranier	28	Ford	188	48,655
2. Neil Bonnett	Junior Johnson	12	Chev	188	34,250
3. Ron Bouchard	Jack Beebe	47	Buick	188	23,205
4. Bill Elliott	Harry Melling	9	Ford	188	29,475
5. A. J. Foyt	A. J. Foyt	14	Olds	187	11,625

1986 Winston Cup Race No. 9 Winston 500
May 4, 1986 Average Speed: 157.698

Driver	Owner	Car #	Make	Laps	Winnings
1. Bobby Allison	Stavola Brothers	22	Buick	188	77,905
2. Dale Earnhardt	Richard Childress	3	Chev	188	53,900
3. Buddy Baker	Buddy Baker & Danny Schiff	88	Olds	188	27,600
4. Bobby Hillin Jr.	Stavola Brothers	8	Buick	188	21,470
5. Phil Parsons	Richard Jackson	66	Olds	188	15,525

1986 Winston Cup Race No. 17 Talladega 500
July 27, 1986 Average Speed: 151.522

Driver	Owner	Car #	Make	Laps	Winnings
1. Bobby Hillin Jr.	Stavola Brothers	8	Buick	188	60,055
2. Tim Richmond	Rick Hendrick	25	Chev	188	34,345
3. Ricky Rudd	Bud Moore	15	Ford	188	29,255
4. Sterling Marlin	Hoss Ellington	1	Chev	188	15,750
5. Benny Parsons	Richard Jackson	55	Olds	188	12,815

1987 Winston Cup Race No. 9 Winston 500
May 3, 1987 Average Speed: 154.228

Driver	Owner	Car #	Make	Laps	Winnings
1. Davey Allison	Harry Ranier	28	Ford	178	71,250
2. Terry Labonte	Junior Johnson	11	Chev	178	47,060
3. Kyle Petty	Wood Brothers	21	Ford	178	30,915
4. Dale Earnhardt	Richard Childress	3	Chev	178	31,350
5. Bobby Hillin Jr.	Stavola Brothers	8	Buick	178	25,055

1987 Winston Cup Race No. 17 Talladega 500
July 26, 1987 Average Speed: 171.293

Driver	Owner	Car #	Make	Laps	Winnings
1. Bill Elliott	Harry Melling	9	Ford	188	70,920
2. Davey Allison	Harry Ranier	28	Ford	188	39,115
3. Dale Earnhardt	Richard Childress	3	Chev	188	35,050
4. Darrell Waltrip	Rick Hendrick	17	Chev	188	19,120
5. Cale Yarborough	Cale Yarborough	29	Olds	188	13,465

1988 Winston Cup Race No. 9 Winston 500
May 1, 1988 Average Speed: 156.547

Driver	Owner	Car #	Make	Laps	Winnings
1. Phil Parsons	Richard Jackson	55	Olds	188	86,850
2. Bobby Allison	Stavola Brothers	12	Buick	188	50,060
3. Geoff Bodine	Rick Hendrick	5	Chev	188	37,560
4. Terry Labonte	Junior Johnson	11	Chev	188	28,425
5. Ken Schrader	Rick Hendrick	25	Chev	188	27,165

Talladega Superspeedway *continued*

1988 Winston Cup Race No. 17 Talladega DieHard 500
July 31, 1988 Average Speed: 154.505

Driver	Owner	Car #	Make	Laps	Winnings
1. Ken Schrader	Rick Hendrick	25	Chev	188	67,920
2. Geoff Bodine	Rick Hendrick	5	Chev	188	39,915
3. Dale Earnhardt	Richard Childress	3	Chev	188	37,775
4. Rick Wilson	Larry McClure	4	Olds	188	20,075
5. Rusty Wallace	Raymond Beadle	27	Pont	188	23,215

1989 Winston Cup Race No. 17 Talladega DieHard 500
July 30, 1989 Average Speed: 157.354

Driver	Owner	Car #	Make	Laps	Winnings
1. Terry Labonte	Junior Johnson	11	Ford	188	73,920
2. Darrell Waltrip	Rick Hendrick	17	Chev	188	47,965
3. Mark Martin	Jack Roush	6	Ford	188	37,950
4. Ken Schrader	Rick Hendrick	25	Chev	188	28,400
5. Rick Wilson	Larry McClure	4	Olds	188	20,200

1990 Winston Cup Series Race No. 17 DieHard 500
July 29, 1990 Average Speed: 174.430

Driver	Owner	Car #	Make	Laps	Winnings
1. Dale Earnhardt	Richard Childress	3	Chev	188	152,975
2. Bill Elliott	Harry Melling	9	Ford	188	48,390
3. Sterling Marlin	Billy Hagan	94	Olds	188	34,050
4. Alan Kulwicki	Alan Kulwicki	7	Ford	188	24,750
5. Ricky Rudd	Rick Hendrick	5	Chev	188	22,050

1991 Winston Cup Series Race No. 17 DieHard 500
July 28, 1991 Average Speed: 147.383

Driver	Owner	Car #	Make	Laps	Winnings
1. Dale Earnhardt	Richard Childress	3	Chev	188	88,670
2. Bill Elliott	Harry Melling	9	Ford	188	51,185
3. Mark Martin	Jack Roush	6	Ford	188	46,390
4. Ricky Rudd	Rick Hendrick	5	Chev	188	29,400
5. Sterling Marlin	Junior Johnson	22	Ford	188	27,075

1992 Winston Cup Race No. 17 DieHard 500
July 26, 1992 Average Speed: 176.309

Driver	Owner	Car #	Make	Laps	Winnings
1. Ernie Irvan	Larry McClure	4	Chev	188	81,815
2. Sterling Marlin	Junior Johnson	22	Ford	188	54,760
3. Davey Allison	Robert Yates	28	Ford	188	42,845
4. Ricky Rudd	Rick Hendrick	5	Chev	187	32,195
5. Bill Elliott	Junior Johnson	11	Ford	187	27,965

1993 Winston Cup Series Race No. 18 DieHard 500
July 25, 1993 Average Speed: 153.858

Driver	Owner	Car #	Make	Laps	Winnings
1. Dale Earnhardt	Richard Childress	3	Chev	188	87,315
2. Ernie Irvan	Larry McClure	4	Chev	188	53,210
3. Mark Martin	Jack Roush	6	Ford	188	40,495
4. Kyle Petty	Felix Sabates	42	Pont	188	31,395
5. Dale Jarrett	Joe Gibbs	18	Chev	188	30,390

1994 Winston Cup Series Race No. 18 DieHard 500
July 24, 1994 Average Speed: 163.217

Driver	Owner	Car #	Make	Laps	Winnings
1. Jimmy Spencer	Junior Johnson	27	Ford	188	81,450
2. Bill Elliott	Junior Johnson	11	Ford	188	52,445
3. Ernie Irvan	Robert Yates	28	Ford	188	47,130
4. Ken Schrader	Rick Hendrick	25	Chev	188	33,530
5. Sterling Marlin	Larry McClure	4	Chev	188	32,675

1989 Winston Cup Race No. 9 Winston 500
May 7, 1989 Average Speed: 155.869

Driver	Owner	Car #	Make	Laps	Winnings
1. Davey Allison	Robert Yates	28	Ford	188	98,675
2. Terry Labonte	Junior Johnson	11	Ford	188	51,275
3. Mark Martin	Jack Roush	6	Ford	188	39,850
4. Morgan Shepherd	Bob Rahilly & Butch Mock	75	Pont	188	34,250
5. Darrell Waltrip	Rick Hendrick	17	Chev	188	28,900

1990 Winston Cup Series Race No. 9 Winston 500
May 6, 1990 Average Speed: 159.571

Driver	Owner	Car #	Make	Laps	Winnings
1. Dale Earnhardt	Richard Childress	3	Chev	188	98,975
2. Greg Sacks	Rick Hendrick	18	Chev	188	46,900
3. Mark Martin	Jack Roush	6	Ford	188	39,050
4. Ernie Irvan	Larry McClure	4	Olds	188	30,150
5. Michael Waltrip	Chuck Rider	30	Pont	188	26,425

1991 Winston Cup Series Race No. 9 Winston 500
May 6, 1991 Average Speed: 165.620

Driver	Owner	Car #	Make	Laps	Winnings
1. Harry Gant	Leo Jackson	33	Olds	188	81,950
2. Darrell Waltrip	Darrell Waltrip	17	Chev	188	47,400
3. Dale Earnhardt	Richard Childress	3	Chev	188	56,100
4. Sterling Marlin	Junior Johnson	22	Ford	188	25,450
5. Michael Waltrip	Chuck Rider	30	Pont	188	25,800

1992 Winston Cup Race No. 9 Winston 500
May 3, 1992 Average Speed: 167.609

Driver	Owner	Car #	Make	Laps	Winnings
1. Davey Allison	Robert Yates	28	Ford	188	189,325
2. Bill Elliott	Junior Johnson	11	Ford	188	56,225
3. Dale Earnhardt	Richard Childress	3	Chev	188	46,970
4. Sterling Marlin	Junior Johnson	22	Ford	188	45,470
5. Ernie Irvan	Larry McClure	4	Chev	188	35,840

1993 Winston Cup Series Race No. 9 Winston 500
May 2, 1993 Average Speed: 155.412

Driver	Owner	Car #	Make	Laps	Winnings
1. Ernie Irvan	Larry McClure	4	Chev	188	85,875
2. Jimmy Spencer	Bobby Allison	12	Ford	188	56,850
3. Dale Jarrett	Joe Gibbs	18	Chev	188	44,870
4. Dale Earnhardt	Richard Childress	3	Chev	188	39,870
5. Joe Ruttman	Dick Moroso	20	Ford	188	25,765

1994 Winston Cup Series Race No. 9 Winston Select 500
May 1, 1994 Average Speed: 157.478

Driver	Owner	Car #	Make	Laps	Winnings
1. Dale Earnhardt	Richard Childress	3	Chev	188	94,865
2. Ernie Irvan	Robert Yates	28	Ford	188	67,990
3. Michael Waltrip	Chuck Rider	30	Pont	188	50,995
4. Jimmy Spencer	Junior Johnson	27	Ford	188	32,570
5. Ken Schrader	Rick Hendrick	25	Chev	188	33,540

1995 Winston Cup Series Race No. 9 Winston Select 500
April 30, 1995 Average Speed: 178.902

Driver	Owner	Car #	Make	Laps	Winnings
1. Mark Martin	Jack Roush	6	Ford	188	98,565
2. Jeff Gordon	Rick Hendrick	24	Chev	188	165,315
3. Morgan Shepherd	Wood Brothers	21	Ford	188	62,145
4. Darrell Waltrip	Darrell Waltrip	17	Chev	188	43,095
5. Bobby Labonte	Joe Gibbs	18	Chev	188	40,115

Talladega Superspeedway *continued*

1995 Winston Cup Series Race No. 18 DieHard 500
July 23, 1995 Average Speed: 173.188

Driver	Owner	Car #	Make	Laps	Winnings
1. Sterling Marlin	Larry McClure	4	Chev	188	219,425
2. Dale Jarrett	Robert Yates	28	Ford	188	65,895
3. Dale Earnhardt	Richard Childress	3	Chev	188	57,105
4. Morgan Shepherd	Wood Brothers	21	Ford	188	40,805
5. Bill Elliott	Bill Elliott	94	Ford	188	32,325

1996 Winston Cup Series Race No. 9 Winston Select 500
April 28, 1996 Average Speed: 149.999

Driver	Owner	Car #	Make	Laps	Winnings
1. Sterling Marlin	Larry McClure	4	Chev	188	109,845
2. Dale Jarrett	Robert Yates	88	Ford	188	64,145
3. Dale Earnhardt	Richard Childress	3	Chev	188	64,620
4. Terry Labonte	Rick Hendrick	5	Chev	188	60,570
5. Michael Waltrip	Wood Brothers	21	Ford	188	44,490

1996 Winston Cup Series Race No. 18 DieHard 500
July 28, 1996 Average Speed: 133.387

Driver	Owner	Car #	Make	Laps	Winnings
1. Jeff Gordon	Rick Hendrick	24	Chev	129	272,550
2. Dale Jarrett	Robert Yates	88	Ford	129	55,070
3. Mark Martin	Jack Roush	6	Ford	129	53,980
4. Ernie Irvan	Robert Yates	28	Ford	129	44,455
5. Jimmy Spencer	Travis Carter	23	Ford	129	50,025

Arizona

Arizona State Fairgrounds
Phoenix, AZ
1-mile Dirt Track

(aka Phoenix Fairgrounds) Originally built as 1-mile dirt oval in 1910. First NASCAR Winston Cup (then Grand National) race staged on 4/29/51 (won by Marshall Teague). Final Grand National race run on 4/3/60 (John Rostek won). Track closed in 1963. Re-opened as 1/8-mile dirt oval in 1985.

Winston Cup Starts

Lloyd Dane — 4

Winston Cup Victories

Buck Baker	1
Tim Flock	1
John Rostek	1
Marshall Teague	1

Winston Cup Poles

Bill Amick	1
Fonty Flock	1
Mel Larson	1
Joe Weatherly	1

Winston Cup Money

Tim Flock — $2,160

Most Cars Started

30—April 22, 1951
30—January 22, 1956

Fewest Cars Started

19—April 3, 1960
Copper Cup Championship

Narrowest Margin of Victory

1/4-mile—April 22, 1951

Slowest Race

60.153 MPH—April 22, 1951

Race Record

71.899 MPH—April 3, 1960
Copper Cup Championship

Most Race Leaders

4—April 3, 1960
Copper Cup Championship

Most Cars Running at Finish

21—May 8, 1955

1951 Grand National Race No. 6
April 22, 1951 Average Speed: 60.153

Driver	Owner	Car #	Make	Laps	Winnings
1. Marshall Teague	Marshall Teague	6	51 Huds	150	1,100
2. Erick Erickson		1	48 Pont	150	750
3. Tim Flock	Ted Chester	91	51 Olds	—	450
4. Fonty Flock	Frank Christian	14	50 Olds	—	300
5. Dick Meyer	Grant Sniffen	9	50 Merc	—	200

1955 Grand National Race No. 13
May 8, 1955 Average Speed: 71.485

Driver	Owner	Car #	Make	Laps	Winnings
1. Tim Flock	Carl Kiekhaefer	301	55 Chrys	100	1,000
2. Marvin Panch	John Hernandez	98	55 Merc	99	650
3. Clyde Palmer		47	55 Merc	98	450
4. Bill Amick		3	55 Dodg	97	350
5. Allen Adkins		7	54 Dodg	97	300

1956 Grand National Race No. 5
January 22, 1956 Average Speed: 64.408

Driver	Owner	Car #	Make	Laps	Winnings
1. Buck Baker	Carl Kiekhaefer	301	55 Chrys	150	1,500
2. Frank Mundy	Carl Kiekhaefer	30	55 Chrys	150	970
3. Tim Flock	Carl Kiekhaefer	300	55 Chrys	150	710
4. Marvin Panch	Tom Harbison	98	56 Ford	149	560
5. Lee Petty	Petty Enterprises	42	56 Dodg	149	415

1960 Grand National Race No. 8 Copper Cup Championship
April 3, 1960 Average Speed: 71.899

Driver	Owner	Car #	Make	Laps	Winnings
1. John Rostek	John Rostek	19	58 Ford	100	800
2. Mel Larson	Mel Larson	35	60 Pont	100	525
3. Scotty Cain	Scotty Cain	4	59 Ford	97	375
4. Fritz Wilson	Fritz Wilson	48	58 Ford	95	275
5. Lloyd Dane	Lloyd Dane	44	59 Ford	95	250

Phoenix Int'l Raceway
Phoenix, AZ
1-mile Superspeedway

1-mile paved oval opened in 1964 with USAC IndyCar race. A. J. Foyt won first event. First NASCAR Winston Cup race 11/6/88 (Alan Kulwicki won). Track hosts a variety of NASCAR, USAC, and Indy Racing League events.

Winston Cup Starts
15 drivers tied with 9

Winston Cup Victories
Davey Allison   2

Winston Cup Poles
Geoff Bodine   2
Bill Elliott   2
Rusty Wallace   2

Winston Cup Money
Mark Martin $298,165

Most Cars Started
44—October 29, 1995 Dura-Lube 500
44—October 27, 1996 Dura-Lube 500

Fewest Cars Started
42—November 1, 1992 Pyroil 500

Narrowest Margin of Victory
0.170 seconds October 31, 1993
Slick 50 500

Slowest Race
90.457 MPH—November 6, 1988
Checker 500

Race Record
109.709 MPH—October 27, 1996
Dura-Lube 500

Most Cautions
10—November 3, 1991 Pyroil 500

Most Race Leaders
13—November 3, 1991 Pyroil 500

Most Cars Running at Finish
34—October 30, 1994 Slick 50 500
34—October 29, 1995 Dura-Lube 500

1988 Winston Cup Race No. 28 Checker 500
November 6, 1988 Average Speed: 90.457

Driver	Owner	Car #	Make	Laps	Winnings
1. Alan Kulwicki	Alan Kulwicki	7	Ford	312	54,100
2. Terry Labonte	Junior Johnson	11	Chev	312	31,075
3. Davey Allison	Harry Ranier	28	Ford	312	24,275
4. Bill Elliott	Harry Melling	9	Ford	312	19,475
5. Rusty Wallace	Raymond Beadle	27	Pont	312	20,400

1989 Winston Cup Race No. 28 Autoworks 500
November 5, 1989 Average Speed: 105.683

Driver	Owner	Car #	Make	Laps	Winnings
1. Bill Elliott	Harry Melling	9	Ford	312	57,900
2. Terry Labonte	Junior Johnson	11	Ford	312	34,275
3. Mark Martin	Jack Roush	6	Ford	312	23,725
4. Darrell Waltrip	Rick Hendrick	17	Chev	312	20,290
5. Dale Jarrett	Cale Yarborough	29	Pont	312	22,112

1990 Winston Cup Series Race No. 28 Checker 500
November 4, 1990 Average Speed: 96.786

Driver	Owner	Car #	Make	Laps	Winnings
1. Dale Earnhardt	Richard Childress	3	Chev	312	72,100
2. Ken Schrader	Rick Hendrick	25	Chev	312	32,900
3. Morgan Shepherd	Bud Moore	15	Ford	312	23,357
4. Darrell Waltrip	Rick Hendrick	17	Chev	312	21,500
5. Bill Elliott	Harry Melling	9	Ford	312	19,775

1991 Winston Cup Series Race No. 28 Pyroil 500
November 3, 1991 Average Speed: 95.746

Driver	Owner	Car #	Make	Laps	Winnings
1. Davey Allison	Robert Yates	28	Ford	312	78,500
2. Darrell Waltrip	Darrell Waltrip	17	Chev	312	37,225
3. Sterling Marlin	Junior Johnson	22	Ford	312	25,000
4. Alan Kulwicki	Alan Kulwicki	7	Ford	312	22,600
5. Rusty Wallace	Roger Penske	2	Pont	312	16,475

1992 Winston Cup Race No. 28 Pyroil 500
November 1, 1992 Average Speed: 103.885

Driver	Owner	Car #	Make	Laps	Winnings
1. Davey Allison	Robert Yates	28	Ford	312	65,285
2. Mark Martin	Jack Roush	6	Ford	312	40,555
3. Darrell Waltrip	Darrell Waltrip	17	Chev	312	32,130
4. Alan Kulwicki	Alan Kulwicki	7	Ford	312	25,730
5. Jimmy Spencer	Bobby Allison	12	Ford	312	22,105

1993 Winston Cup Series Race No. 29 Slick 50 500
October 31, 1993 Average Speed: 100.375

Driver	Owner	Car #	Make	Laps	Winnings
1. Mark Martin	Jack Roush	6	Ford	312	67,035
2. Ernie Irvan	Robert Yates	28	Ford	312	44,155
3. Kyle Petty	Felix Sabates	42	Pont	312	28,430
4. Dale Earnhardt	Richard Childress	3	Chev	312	29,980
5. Bill Elliott	Junior Johnson	11	Ford	312	31,655

1994 Winston Cup Series Race No. 30 Slick 50 500
October 30, 1994 Average Speed: 107.463

Driver	Owner	Car #	Make	Laps	Winnings
1. Terry Labonte	Rick Hendrick	5	Chev	312	67,885
2. Mark Martin	Jack Roush	6	Ford	312	46,155
3. Sterling Marlin	Larry McClure	4	Chev	312	40,330
4. Jeff Gordon	Rick Hendrick	24	Chev	311	26,780
5. Ted Musgrave	Jack Roush	16	Ford	311	25,405

1995 Winston Cup Series Race No. 30 Dura-Lube 500
October 29, 1995 Average Speed: 102.128

Driver	Owner	Car #	Make	Laps	Winnings
1. Ricky Rudd	Ricky Rudd	10	Ford	312	78,260
2. Derrike Cope	Bobby Allison	12	Ford	312	52,205
3. Dale Earnhardt	Richard Childress	3	Chev	312	49,105
4. Rusty Wallace	Roger Penske	2	Ford	312	36,118
5. Jeff Gordon	Rick Hendrick	24	Chev	312	33,580

1996 Winston Cup Series Race No. 30 Dura-Lube 500
October 27, 1996 Average Speed: 109.709

Driver	Owner	Car #	Make	Laps	Winnings
1. Bobby Hamilton	Petty Enterprises	43	Pont	312	95,550
2. Mark Martin	Jack Roush	6	Ford	312	59,795
3. Terry Labonte	Rick Hendrick	5	Chev	312	61,590
4. Ted Musgrave	Jack Roush	16	Ford	312	35,153
5. Jeff Gordon	Rick Hendrick	24	Chev	312	45,065

Tucson Rodeo Grounds
Tucson, AZ
Half-mile Dirt Track

Half-mile dirt track opened in November, 1939. Only NASCAR Winston Cup (then Grand National) race run on 5/15/55 (won by Danny Letner). Automobile racing was discontinued shortly after the conclusion of the NASCAR event.

Winston Cup Victories
Danny Letner   1

Winston Cup Poles
Bill Amick   1

Winston Cup Money
Danny Letner $1,000

Most Cars Started
19—May 15, 1955

Narrowest Margin of Victory
1 lap plus—May 15, 1955

Race Record
51.428 MPH—May 15, 1955

Most Race Leaders
5—May 15, 1955

Most Cars Running at Finish
12—May 15, 1955

1955 Grand National Race No. 14
May 15, 1955 Average Speed: 51.428

Driver	Owner	Car #	Make	Laps	Winnings
1. Danny Letner	Coz Concilla	6	54 Olds	200	1,000
2. Allen Adkins		7	54 Dodg	199	650
3. Lloyd Dane	Lloyd Dane	33	53 Huds	198	450
4. Chuck Meekins	Larry Dorsey	65	52 Olds	196	350
5. Bill Amick		3	55 Dodg	194	300

Arkansas

Memphis-Arkansas Speedway
LeHi, Arkansas
1.5-mile Dirt Track

1.5-mile high-banked dirt track opened with NASCAR Winston Cup (then Grand National) race on 10/10/54 (won by Buck Baker; Junior Johnson won the pole in a Cadillac). Final NASCAR race was held on 7/14/57 (won by Marvin Panch). Track was extremely dangerous and was the site of two NASCAR fatalities in 1956 (Clint McHugh and Thomas "Cotton" Priddy). Track was closed when major highways were built in the area, blocking all access to the track. It never re-opened following the completion of the highway project.

Winston Cup Starts
Buck Baker 5
Lee Petty 5

Winston Cup Victories
Buck Baker 1
Fonty Flock 1
Ralph Moody 1
Marvin Panch 1
Speedy Thompson 1

Winston Cup Poles
Fonty Flock 2

Winston Cup Money
Marvin Panch $5,350

Most Cars Started
52—October 10, 1954 Mid-South 250

Fewest Cars Started
28—July 14, 1957

Narrowest Margin of Victory
4.000 seconds June 10, 1956

Slowest Race
67.167 MPH—July 14, 1957

Race Record
89.892 MPH—August 14, 1955 Mid-South 250

Most Cautions
5—June 10, 1956

Most Race Leaders
4—June 10, 1956
4—July 14, 1957

Most Cars Running at Finish
28—October 10, 1954 Mid-South 250

1954 Grand National Race No. 35 Mid-South 250
October 10, 1954 Average Speed: 89.013

Driver	Owner	Car #	Make	Laps	Winnings
1. Buck Baker	Griffin Motors	87	54 Olds	167	2,750
2. Dick Rathmann	John Ditz	3	54 Huds	162	1,150
3. Lee Petty	Petty Enterprises	42	54 Chrys	161	850
4. Herb Thomas	Herb Thomas	92	54 Huds	161	700
5. Herschel Buchanan	Herschel Buchanan	4	54 Huds	160	500

1955 Grand National Race No. 33 Mid-South 250
August 14, 1955 Average Speed: 89.892

Driver	Owner	Car #	Make	Laps	Winnings
1. Fonty Flock	Carl Kiekhaefer	301	55 Chrys	167	2,950
2. Speedy Thompson	Griffin Motors	87	54 Olds	167	1,675
3. Tim Flock	Carl Kiekhaefer	300	55 Chrys	165	1,175
4. Jim Paschal	Ernest Woods	78	55 Olds	163	815
5. Buck Baker	Buck Baker	89	55 Buick	161	685

1955 Grand National Race No. 40
October 9, 1955 Average Speed: 83.948

Driver	Owner	Car #	Make	Laps	Winnings
1. Speedy Thompson	Pete DePaolo	297	55 Ford	200	2,900
2. Marvin Panch	Pete DePaolo	98	55 Ford	200	1,450
3. Jimmy Massey	Hubert Westmoreland	04	55 Chev	196	1,000
4. Tim Flock	Carl Kiekhaefer	300	55 Chrys	195	850
5. Bob Flock	Carl Kiekhaefer	308	55 Chrys	195	650

1956 Grand National Race No. 25
June 10, 1956 Average Speed: 74.313

Driver	Owner	Car #	Make	Laps	Winnings
1. Ralph Moody	Pete DePaolo	12	56 Ford	167	4,100
2. Jim Paschal	Frank Hayworth	75	56 Merc	167	2,100
3. Pat Kirkwood	Jim Stephens	286	56 Pont	165	1,325
4. Tim Flock	Mauri Rose	11	56 Chev	164	950
5. Joe Eubanks	James Satcher	82	56 Ford	163	650

1957 Grand National Race No. 30
July 14, 1957 Average Speed: 67.167

Driver	Owner	Car #	Make	Laps	Winnings
1. Marvin Panch	Herb Thomas	92	57 Pont	134	3,500
2. Bill Amick	Bill Amick	97	57 Ford	134	2,075
3. Fireball Roberts	Paul Spaulding	11	57 Ford	134	1,375
4. Buck Baker	Buck Baker	87	57 Chev	132	950
5. Bob Welborn	Bob Welborn	49	57 Chev	131	750

California

Ascot Stadium
Los Angeles, CA
.4-mile Dirt Track

(aka Bill McKay's Los Angeles Speedway; Ascot Park; Ascot Speedway) Half-mile dirt oval built in May 1957. Final race run in 1990. First Winston Cup race staged on 6/8/57 (won by Eddie Pagan). Final Winston Cup race run on 5/27/61 (won by Eddie Cray). Track closed in 1990. Now the site of an industrial park.

Winston Cup Starts

Scotty Cain	3
Jim Cook	3
Lloyd Dane	3
Dick Getty	3
Eddie Gray	3
Eddie Pagan	3

Winston Cup Victories

Eddie Gray	1
Parnelli Jones	1
Eddie Pagan	1

Winston Cup Poles

Eddie Pagan	1
Jim Reed	1
Danny Weinberg	1

Winston Cup Money

Parnelli Jones $1,855

Most Cars Started

33—May 30, 1959

Fewest Cars Started

22—May 27, 1961

Narrowest Margin of Victory

N/A

Slowest Race

50.982 MPH—May 30, 1959

Race Record

68.833 MPH—May 27, 1961

Most Race Leaders

N/A

Most Cars Running at Finish

17—May 30, 1959

1957 Grand National Race No. 22
June 8, 1957

Driver	Owner	Car #	Make	Laps	Winnings
1. Eddie Pagan	Eddie Pagan	45	57 Ford	150	800
2. Lloyd Dane	Lloyd Dane	44	57 Ford	149	550
3. Chuck Meekins	Jim Rush	1	57 Chev	148	400
4. George Seeger	Oscar Maples	12	57 Ford	148	305
5. Eddie Gray	Chuck Green	18	56 Chev	147	270

1959 Grand National Race No. 17
May 30, 1959 Average Speed: 50.982

Driver	Owner	Car #	Make	Laps	Winnings
1. Parnelli Jones	Vel Miletich	97	59 Ford	487	1,805
2. Lloyd Dane	Lloyd Dane	44	57 Ford	487	900
3. Marvin Porter	Marvin Porter	12	57 Ford	485	700
4. Bob Ross	Bob Ross	34	57 Chev	482	600
5. Bob Keefe	Jack Chatenay	11	58 Plym	459	500

1961 Grand National Race No. 23
May 27, 1961 Average Speed: 68.833

Driver	Owner	Car #	Make	Laps	Winnings
1. Eddie Gray	Eddie Gray	98	61 Ford	200	850
2. Don Noel	Chuck Parkko	7	61 Ford	199	500
3. Danny Weinberg	Guy Kimball	76	61 Ford	196	370
4. Jim Blomgren	Bob Smith	10	60 Ford	196	305
5. Ron Hornaday	Frank Galpin	2	60 Ford	196	250

Bay Meadows Race Track
San Mateo, CA
1-mile Dirt Track

(aka Bay Meadows Race Course) 1-mile dirt track opened in November of 1950. First Winston Cup race staged on 8/22/54 (Hershel McGriff won). Last Winston Cup race run on 8/19/56 (Eddie Pagan won). Still a famous horse track.

Winston Cup Starts

Buck Baker	3
Jim Cook	3
Lloyd Dane	3
Chuck Meekins	3
Eddie Pagan	3
Bill West	3

Winston Cup Victories

Tim Flock	1
Hershel McGriff	1
Eddie Pagan	1

Winston Cup Poles

Hershel McGriff	1
Eddie Pagan	1

Winston Cup Money
Hershel McGriff $2,425

Most Cars Started
41—August 22, 1954

Fewest Cars Started
34—July 31, 1955

Narrowest Margin of Victory
N/A

Slowest Race
64.710 MPH—August 22, 1954

Race Record
68.571 MPH—July 31, 1955

Most Race Leaders
3—July 31, 1955

Most Cars Running at Finish
32—August 22, 1954

1954 Grand National Race No. 29
August 22, 1954 Average Speed: 64.710

Driver	Owner	Car #	Make	Laps	Winnings
1. Hershel McGriff	Frank Christian	14	54 Olds	250	2,425
2. Bill Amick	Frank Dodge	28	53 Olds	250	1,500
3. Dick Rathmann	Don Oliver	12	53 Olds	249	900
4. Allen Adkins	Gus Davis	68	54 Dodg	249	700
5. Lee Petty	Petty Enterprises	42	54 Chrys	247	500

1955 Grand National Race No. 30
July 31, 1955 Average Speed: 68.571

Driver	Owner	Car #	Make	Laps	Winnings
1. Tim Flock	Carl Kiekhaefer	300	55 Chrys	252	2,050
2. John Kieper	John Kieper	11	55 Olds	251	1,450
3. Danny Letner	Coz Concilla	6	54 Olds	249	700
4. Marvin Panch	John Hernandez	98	55 Merc	247	650
5. Buck Baker	Buck Baker	89	55 Buick	247	550

1956 Grand National Race No. 39
August 19, 1956 Average Speed: 68.161

Driver	Owner	Car #	Make	Laps	Winnings
1. Eddie Pagan	Eddie Pagan	45	56 Ford	241	1,475
2. Parnelli Jones	Vel Miletich	11	56 Ford	241	1,575
3. Chuck Meekins		56	56 Chev	239	1,100
4. Lloyd Dane	Lloyd Dane	225	56 Merc	239	750
5. Scotty Cain		21	56 Ford	239	550

California State Fairgrounds
Sacramento, CA
1-mile Dirt Track

(aka Sacramento Fairgrounds) Originally built as horse track in 1906. 1-mile dirt track (September 1946-October 1970). First NASCAR Winston Cup (then Grand National) race staged on 7/8/56 (Lloyd Dane won). Last Grand National race run on 9/10/61 (won by Eddie Gray). Track closed after October 1970 event. Now a shopping center.

Winston Cup Starts
Jim Blomgren	6
Jim Cook	6

Winston Cup Victories
Eddie Gray	2

Winston Cup Poles
Bill Amick	1
Jim Cook	1
Danny Graves	1
Parnelli Jones	1
Eddie Pagan	1

Winston Cup Money
Eddie Gray	$2,325

Most Cars Started
32—September 10, 1961

Fewest Cars Started
21—July 8, 1956

Narrowest Margin of Victory
N/A

Slowest Race
54.753 MPH—September 13, 1959

Race Record
74.074 MPH—July 8, 1956

Most Race Leaders
4—July 8, 1956

Most Cars Running at Finish
20—September 10, 1961

1956 Grand National Race No. 32
July 8, 1956 Average Speed: 74.074

Driver	Owner	Car #	Make	Laps	Winnings
1. Lloyd Dane	Lloyd Dane	225	56 Merc	100	1,100
2. Chuck Meekins		56	56 Chev	100	700
3. John Kieper	John Kieper	88	56 Olds	100	475
4. Gordon Haines		77	56 Dodg	100	365
5. Clyde Palmer		1	56 Dodg	99	310

1957 Grand National Race No. 43
September 8, 1957 Average Speed: 68.663

Driver	Owner	Car #	Make	Laps	Winnings
1. Danny Graves	Danny Graves	81	57 Chev	100	800
2. Marvin Porter	Marvin Porter	12	57 Ford	100	550
3. Eddie Pagan	Eddie Pagan	45	57 Ford	100	450
4. Chuck Meekins		1	57 Chev	100	325
5. Dick Getty	Dick Getty	00	56 Chev	100	325

1958 Grand National Race No. 44
September 7, 1958 Average Speed: 65.550

Driver	Owner	Car #	Make	Laps	Winnings
1. Parnelli Jones	Vel Miletich	97	56 Ford	100	700
2. Bob Ross		43	56 Merc	100	500
3. Danny Weinberg		8	57 Ford	99	425
4. Jim Cook		5	57 Ford	98	335
5. Harold Hardesty		22N	56 Ford	98	300

1959 Grand National Race No. 39
September 13, 1959 Average Speed: 54.753

Driver	Owner	Car #	Make	Laps	Winnings
1. Eddie Gray	Vel Miletich	1	59 Ford	100	700
2. Scotty Cain	Scotty Cain	3	59 Ford	100	500
3. Danny Weinberg	Carl Dane	16	58 Merc	100	425
4. Bob Ross	Jim Rush	34	57 Chev	100	335
5. Lucky Long		10	57 Chev	97	300

1960 Grand National Race No. 37
September 11, 1960 Average Speed: 70.629

Driver	Owner	Car #	Make	Laps	Winnings
1. Jim Cook	Floyd Johnson	0	60 Dodg	100	1,100
2. Scotty Cain	Scotty Cain	4	59 Ford	100	700
3. Lloyd Dane	Lloyd Dane	44	59 Ford	99	500
4. Ron Hornaday	Frank Galpin	2	60 Ford	96	400
5. Danny Weinberg	Carl Dane	16	60 Ford	95	300

1961 Grand National Race No. 45
September 10, 1961

Driver	Owner	Car #	Make	Laps	Winnings
1. Eddie Gray	Eddie Gray	98	61 Ford	100	1,300
2. Bob Ross		6	61 Olds	99	800
3. Danny Weinberg	Guy Kimball	76	61 Ford	99	500
4. Frank Secrist		36	60 Ford	99	400
5. Don Noel	Chuck Parkko	7	61 Ford	98	300

Capital Speedway
Sacramento, CA
Half-mile Dirt Track

(aka West Capital Speedway; West Capital Raceway) Quarter-mile dirt track built in 1947. Half-mile dirt track oval 1954–72. Only NASCAR Winston Cup (then Grand National) race held on 6/22/57 (Bill Amick won). Track closed in 1980.

Winston Cup Victories
Bill Amick   1

Winston Cup Poles
Art Watts   1

Winston Cup Money
Bill Amick $900

Most Cars Started
31—June 22, 1957

Narrowest Margin of Victory
1lap plus—June 22, 1957

Race Record
59.580 MPH—June 22, 1957

Most Race Leaders
1—June 22, 1957

Most Cars Running at Finish
17—June 22, 1957

1957 Grand National Race No. 25
June 22, 1957 Average Speed: 59.580

Driver	Owner	Car #	Make	Laps	Winnings
1. Bill Amick	Bill Amick	97	57 Ford	199	900
2. Lloyd Dane	Lloyd Dane	44	57 Ford	198	600
3. George Seeger	Oscar Maples	12	57 Ford	197	475
4. Scotty Cain	Scotty Cain	14	56 Merc	196	365
5. Danny Graves	Danny Graves	81	57 Chev	196	320

Carrell Speedway
Gardena, CA
Half-mile Dirt Track

(aka Gardena Bowl) Half-mile dirt oval built in 1940. Half-mile dirt oval opened in 1948. Closed circa 1954. First NASCAR Winston Cup (then Grand National) race run on 4/8/51 (Marshall Teague won). Final race staged on 5/30/54 (won by John Soares). Track closed in early '50s to make room for Artesia Boulevard.

Winston Cup Starts
Fred Bince   4
Lloyd Dane   4
Erick Erickson   4
Chuck Meekins   4
George Seeger   4

Winston Cup Victories
Lou Figaro   1
Bill Norton   1
John Soares   1
Marshall Teague   1

Winston Cup Poles
Lou Figaro   1
Fonty Flock   1
Danny Letner   1
Andy Pierce   1

Winston Cup Money
John Soares $1,525

Most Cars Started
32—May 30, 1954

Fewest Cars Started
20—April 8, 1951

Narrowest Margin of Victory
100 yards—June 30,1951

Slowest Race
53.438 MPH—May 30, 1954

Race Record
61.047 MPH—April 8, 1951

Most Cautions
1—April 8, 1951
1—June 30, 1951

Most Race Leaders
4—November 11, 1951

Most Cars Running at Finish
21—May 30, 1954

1951 Grand National Race No. 4
April 8, 1951 Average Speed: 61.047

Driver	Owner	Car #	Make	Laps	Winnings
1. Marshall Teague	Marshall Teague	6	51 Huds	200	1,000
2. Johnny Mantz	Johnny Mantz	98	51 Nash	200	700
3. George Seeger	Bill Cramer	2	49 Plym	199	400
4. Fred Steinbroner	Bob Carpenter	16	48 Ford	198	300
5. Erick Erickson		1	48 Pont	195	250

1951 Grand National Race No. 13
June 30, 1951

Driver	Owner	Car #	Make	Laps	Winnings
1. Lou Figaro	Jack Gaynor	33	51 Huds	200	1,000
2. Chuck Meekins	Chuck Meekins	7	49 Plym	200	600
3. Lloyd Dane	Lloyd Dane	22	51 Ford	—	400
4. Fred Bince		11	48 Pont	—	300
5. Fred Steinbroner	Bob Carpenter	16	50 Ford	—	250

1951 Grand National Race No. 40
November 11, 1951

Driver	Owner	Car #	Make	Laps	Winnings
1. Bill Norton	Larry Bettinger	48	51 Merc	200	1,000
2. Dick Meyer	Grant Sniffen	9	50 Merc	—	600
3. Erick Erickson	Erick Erickson	25	51 KAI	—	500
4. Lou Figaro	Jack Gaynor	33	51 Huds	—	400
5. Danny Weinberg	Tony Sampo	2	51 Stud	—	300

1954 Grand National Race No. 16
May 30, 1954 Average Speed: 53.438

Driver	Owner	Car #	Make	Laps	Winnings
1. John Soares	Charles Vance	4	54 Dodg	496	1,500
2. Lloyd Dane	Lloyd Dane	33	53 Huds	495	800
3. Danny Letner	Joe Berreschick	39	52 Huds	490	600
4. Ben Gregory	Don Oliver	12	53 Olds	486	400
5. George Seeger	Carl Dane	73	54 Ford	486	350

Marchbanks Speedway
Hanford, CA
1.4-mile Paved Track

(aka Hanford Motor Speedway) California's first high-banked paved superspeedway to be run under NASCAR sanction. 1.4-mile track opened in June 1960. Half-mile oval originally built in 1951. First Grand National event was staged on 10/28/51 (won by Danny Weinberg). Fireball Roberts won the first race on the the high-banked superspeedway and led every lap (3/12/61). He remains the only driver to lead from start to finish on a long-distance superspeedway event. Track also had a road course that was closed circa 1965. Additionally, .333-mile and .75-mile tracks held motor racing events. Complex torn down in 1984.

Winston Cup Starts
Lloyd Dane   3
Danny Weinberg 3

Winston Cup Victories
Marvin Porter   1
Fireball Roberts 1
Danny Weinberg   1

Winston Cup Poles
Bob Ross   1
Frank Secrist 1

Winston Cup Money
Marvin Porter $2,100

Most Cars Started
36—March 12, 1961

Fewest Cars Started
33—June 12, 1960 California 250

Narrowest Margin of Victory
46 seconds June 12, 1960 California 250

Slowest Race
88.032 MPH—June 12, 1960 California 250

Race Record
95.621 MPH—March 12, 1961

Most Race Leaders
5—June 12, 1960 California 250

Most Cars Running at Finish
18—March 12, 1961

1951 Grand National Race No. 37
October 28, 1951

Driver	Owner	Car #	Make	Laps	Winnings
1. Danny Weinberg	Tony Sampo	2	51 Stud	200	1,000
2. Marvin Panch	Marvin Panch	56	50 Merc	—	600
3. Bill Norton	Larry Bettinger	48	50 Merc	—	500
4. Lloyd Dane	Lloyd Dane	22	51 Ford	—	400
5. Woody Brown	Joe Mangini	88	50 Olds	—	300

1960 Grand National Race No. 20 California 250
June 12, 1960 Average Speed: 88.032

Driver	Owner	Car #	Make	Laps	Winnings
1. Marvin Porter	Vel Miletich	98	59 Ford	179	2,000
2. Joe Weatherly	Vel Miletich	97	60 Ford	179	1,250
3. John Rostek	John Rostek	19	60 Ford	175	750
4. Fritz Wilson	Fritz Wilson	48	58 Ford	173	600
5. Don Noel	A. L. McClure	7	59 Ford	172	575

1961 Grand National Race No. 8
March 12, 1961 Average Speed: 95.621

Driver	Owner	Car #	Make	Laps	Winnings
1. Fireball Roberts	J. D. Braswell	75	61 Pont	178	2,000
2. Eddie Gray	Eddie Gray	98	61 Ford	176	1,250
3. Danny Letner	Guy Kimball	76	61 Ford	175	750
4. Tubby Gonzales	Tubby Gonzales	80	61 Ford	168	600
5. Eddie Pagan	Bill Clinton	45	61 Ford	168	575

Merced Fairgrounds Speedway
Merced, CA
Half-mile Dirt Track

.2-mile dirt oval built circa 1946. Half-mile dirt track built for NASCAR Winston Cup (then Grand National) race run on 6/3/56 (won by Herb Thomas). Current configuration is a quarter-mile dirt oval.

Winston Cup Victories
Herb Thomas 1

Winston Cup Poles
Herb Thomas 1

Winston Cup Money
Herb Thomas $910

Most Cars Started
28—June 3, 1956

Narrowest Margin of Victory
N/A

Race Record
47.325 MPH—June 3, 1956

Most Race Leaders
N/A

Most Cars Running at Finish
17—June 3, 1956

1956 Grand National Race No. 24
June 3, 1956 Average Speed: 47.325

Driver	Owner	Car #	Make	Laps	Winnings
1. Herb Thomas	Carl Kiekhaefer	300B	56 Chrys	200	910
2. Harold Hardesty		52	56 Chev	200	650
3. Jim Graham		30	56 Plym	200	495
4. Lloyd Dane	Lloyd Dane	225	56 Merc	198	375
5. Eddie Pagan	Eddie Pagan	45	56 Ford	197	310

Oakland Stadium
Oakland, CA
Half-mile Paved and Dirt Track

(aka Oakland Speedway) 1-mile high-banked dirt oval built in 1931. Scene of 500-mile races in 1930s. Half-mile flat oval built inside big track. A .625-mile track that utilized high-banked turns, sloping upwards to 45 degrees, was built in 1946. First NASCAR Winston Cup (then Grand National) race held on 10/14/51 (won by Marvin Burke). Final NASCAR race run on 8/1/54 (Danny Letner won). The 1954 events used dirt turns and paved straightaways.

Winston Cup Starts

Woody Brown	3
Robert Caswell	3
Lloyd Dane	3
Sam Hawks	3
Marvin Panch	3
John Soares	3

Winston Cup Victories

Marvin Burke	1
Danny Letner	1
Dick Rathmann	1

Winston Cup Poles

Fonty Flock	1
Hershel McGriff	1
Marvin Panch	1

Winston Cup Money

Marvin Burke $1,875

Most Cars Started
32—August 1, 1954

Fewest Cars Started
26—March 28, 1954

Narrowest Margin of Victory
2 car lengths—August 1, 1954

Slowest Race
50.692 MPH—March 28, 1954

Race Record
78.748 MPH—October 14, 1951

Most Race Leaders
N/A

Most Cars Running at Finish
18—March 28, 1954
18—August 1, 1954

1951 Grand National Race No. 35
October 14, 1951 Average Speed: 78.748

Driver	Owner	Car #	Make	Laps	Winnings
1. Marvin Burke	Bob Phillippi	18	50 Merc	250	1,875
2. Robert Caswell	Lou Mangini	84	50 Plym	247	1,250
3. Woody Brown	Joe Mangini	88	50 Olds	—	900
4. Sam Hawks	Marvin Panch	55	50 Plym	—	750
5. Dick Meyer	Grant Sniffen	9	50 Merc	—	500

1954 Grand National Race No. 6
March 28, 1954 Average Speed: 50.692

Driver	Owner	Car #	Make	Laps	Winnings
1. Dick Rathmann	Ray Erickson	3	52 Huds	250	1,000
2. Marvin Panch	Beryl Jackson	98	54 Dodg	249	650
3. John Soares	Charles Vance	4	54 Dodg	247	450
4. Clyde Palmer	Al Neves	1	51 Merc	238	350
5. Lloyd Dane	Lloyd Dane	18	50 Olds	234	300

1954 Grand National Race No. 27
August 1, 1954 Average Speed: 53.045

Driver	Owner	Car #	Make	Laps	Winnings
1. Danny Letner	Joe Berreschick	3	52 Huds	297	1,000
2. Marvin Panch	Beryl Jackson	98	54 Dodg	297	650
3. Allen Adkins	Gus Davis	68	54 Dodg	296	450
4. Ben Gregory	Chris Milovich	6	54 Olds	296	350
5. Lloyd Dane	Lloyd Dane	33	53 Huds	295	300

Ontario Motor Speedway
Ontario, CA
2.5-mile Paved Track

2.5-mile rectangular shaped track opened in 1970 with USAC IndyCar race. First NASCAR Winston Cup Grand National race staged on 2/28/71 (the 1,000th NASCAR Winston Cup race to be run); won by A. J. Foyt. Final NASCAR event staged on 11/15/80 (Benny Parsons won). The track, then regarded as the premier motorsports facility in America, was purchased by Chevron Oil Co. and leveled in 1981.

Winston Cup Starts
Bobby Allison	9
Cecil Gordon	9
James Hylton	9
J. D. McDuffie	9
Benny Parsons	9
Richard Petty	9

Winston Cup Victories
Bobby Allison	2
A. J. Foyt	2
Benny Parsons	2

Winston Cup Poles
Cale Yarborough 3

Winston Cup Money
Bobby Allison $99,655

Most Cars Started
51—February 28, 1971
Miller High Life 500
51—March 5, 1972 Miller High Life 500

Fewest Cars Started
37—November 18, 1979
Los Angeles Times 500

Narrowest Margin of Victory
2 car lengths—November 20, 1977
Los Angeles Times 500

Slowest Race
127.082 MPH—March 5, 1972
Miller High Life 500

Race Record
140.712 MPH—November 23, 1975
Los Angeles Times 500

Most Cautions
6—November 18, 1979
Los Angeles Times 500
6—November 15, 1980
Los Angeles Times 500

Most Race Leaders
11—November 20, 1977
Los Angeles Times 500

Most Cars Running at Finish
33—March 5, 1972 Miller High Life 500

1971 Winston Cup GN Race No. 5 Miller High Life 500
February 28, 1971 Average Speed: 134.168

Driver	Owner	Car #	Make	Laps	Winnings
1. A. J. Foyt	Wood Brothers	21	69 Merc	200	51,850
2. Buddy Baker	Petty Enterprises	11	71 Dodg	200	15,325
3. Richard Petty	Petty Enterprises	43	71 Plym	200	12,825
4. Bobby Isaac	Nord Krauskopf	71	71 Dodg	199	9,325
5. Dick Brooks	Mario Rossi	22	70 Dodg	198	5,025

1972 Winston Cup GN Race No. 4 Miller High Life 500
March 5, 1972 Average Speed: 127.082

Driver	Owner	Car #	Make	Laps	Winnings
1. A. J. Foyt	Wood Brothers	21	71 Merc	200	31,695
2. Bobby Allison	R. Howard & J. Johnson	12	72 Chev	200	16,945
3. Buddy Baker	Petty Enterprises	11	72 Dodg	200	11,670
4. Richard Petty	Petty Enterprises	43	72 Plym	199	9,970
5. Ray Elder	Fred Elder	96	72 Dodg	194	5,845

1974 Winston Cup GN Race No. 30 Los Angeles Times 500
November 24, 1974 Average Speed: 134.963

Driver	Owner	Car #	Make	Laps	Winnings
1. Bobby Allison	Roger Penske	12	74 Mata	200	15,125
2. David Pearson	Wood Brothers	21	73 Merc	200	9,925
3. Cale Yarborough	Junior Johnson	11	74 Chev	200	10,125
4. A. J. Foyt	Hoss Ellington	28	74 Chev	199	5,725
5. Buddy Baker	Bud Moore	15	73 Ford	197	6,825

1975 Winston Cup GN Race No. 30 Los Angeles Times 500
November 23, 1975 Average Speed: 140.712

Driver	Owner	Car #	Make	Laps	Winnings
1. Buddy Baker	Bud Moore	15	75 Ford	200	35,300
2. David Pearson	Wood Brothers	21	73 Merc	200	14,300
3. Dave Marcis	Nord Krauskopf	71	74 Dodg	200	12,000
4. Cale Yarborough	Junior Johnson	11	75 Chev	199	8,825
5. Bobby Allison	Roger Penske	16	75 Mata	199	4,925

1976 Winston Cup GN Race No. 30 Los Angeles Times 500
November 21, 1976 Average Speed: 137.101

Driver	Owner	Car #	Make	Laps	Winnings
1. David Pearson	Wood Brothers	21	Merc	200	27,715
2. Lennie Pond	Ronnie Elder	54	Chev	199	14,690
3. Benny Parsons	L. G. DeWitt	72	Chev	198	11,670
4. Dick Brooks	Junie Donlavey	90	Ford	198	7,810
5. James Hylton	James Hylton	48	Chev	196	6,250

1977 Winston Cup GN Race No. 30 Los Angeles Times 500
November 20, 1977 Average Speed: 128.296

Driver	Owner	Car #	Make	Laps	Winnings
1. Neil Bonnett	Jim Stacy	5	Dodg	200	22,510
2. Richard Petty	Petty Enterprises	43	Dodg	200	17,535
3. Cale Yarborough	Junior Johnson	11	Chev	200	14,285
4. Buddy Baker	Bud Moore	15	Ford	200	9,385
5. David Pearson	Wood Brothers	21	Merc	199	5,285

1978 Winston Cup GN Race No. 30 Los Angeles Times 500
November 19, 1978 Average Speed: 137.783

Driver	Owner	Car #	Make	Laps	Winnings
1. Bobby Allison	Bud Moore	15	Ford	200	24,025
2. Cale Yarborough	Junior Johnson	11	Olds	200	19,700
3. Donnie Allison	Hoss Ellington	1	Chev	200	12,925
4. Buddy Baker	M. C. Anderson	27	Chev	199	8,600
5. Darrell Waltrip	DiGard	88	Chev	199	9,200

1979 Winston Cup GN Race No. 31 Los Angeles Times 500
November 18, 1979 Average Speed: 132.822

Driver	Owner	Car #	Make	Laps	Winnings
1. Benny Parsons	M. C. Anderson	27	Chev	200	27,050
2. Bobby Allison	Bud Moore	15	Ford	200	17,350
3. Cale Yarborough	Junior Johnson	11	Olds	200	18,000
4. Buddy Baker	Harry Ranier	28	Chev	200	7,000
5. Richard Petty	Petty Enterprises	43	Chev	200	9,025

1980 Winston Cup GN Race No. 31 Los Angeles Times 500
November 15, 1980 Average Speed: 129.441

Driver	Owner	Car #	Make	Laps	Winnings
1. Benny Parsons	M. C. Anderson	27	Chev	200	24,835
2. Neil Bonnett	Wood Brothers	21	Merc	200	13,335
3. Cale Yarborough	Junior Johnson	11	Chev	200	17,035
4. Bobby Allison	Bud Moore	15	Ford	200	10,985
5. Dale Earnhardt	Rod Osterlund	2	Chev	200	10,835

Redwood Speedway
Eureka, CA
.625-mile Dirt Track

(aka Redwood Acres Speedway; Redwood Acres Raceway; Redwood Acres Fairgrounds; Eureka Speedway) Alternate configurations: .375-mile dirt track (1947–1987); .375-mile paved track (1988–present); .625-mile dirt oval (1956–1957). First NASCAR Winston Cup (then Grand National) race staged on 5/30/56 (Herb Thomas won). Final Grand National race staged on 5/30/57 (Lloyd Dane won). Track is still in operation.

Winston Cup Starts

Lloyd Dane	2
Harold Hardesty	2
Bob Havenmann	2
Ed Negre	2
Don Porter	2

Winston Cup Victories

Lloyd Dane	1
Herb Thomas	1

Winston Cup Poles

Parnelli Jones	1
John Kieper	1

Winston Cup Money

Lloyd Dane	$1,375

Most Cars Started
25—May 30, 1956

Fewest Cars Started
15—May 30, 1957

Narrowest Margin of Victory
1 lap plus—May 30, 1956

Slowest Race
38.814 MPH—May 30, 1956

Race Record
55.957 MPH—May 30, 1957

Most Race Leaders
N/A

Most Cars Running at Finish
16—May 30, 1956

1956 Grand National Race No. 22
May 30, 1956 Average Speed: 38.814

Driver	Owner	Car #	Make	Laps	Winnings
1. Herb Thomas	Carl Kiekhaefer	300B	56 Chrys	125	1,000
2. Gordon Haines		77	56 Dodg	124	700
3. Lloyd Dane	Lloyd Dane	225	56 Merc	124	475
4. Bob Keefe		14	56 Ford	124	365
5. Jim Cook		9	56 Pont	123	310

1957 Grand National Race No. 19
May 30, 1957 Average Speed: 55.957

Driver	Owner	Car #	Make	Laps	Winnings
1. Lloyd Dane	Lloyd Dane	44	57 Ford	153	900
2. George Seeger	Oscar Maples	12	57 Ford	147	650
3. Eddie Pagan	Eddie Pagan	45	57 Ford	146	475
4. Cliff Yiskis		25	56 Ford	140	365
5. Ed Negre	Ed Negre	98	55 Olds	139	310

Riverside Int'l Raceway
Riverside, CA
2.631-mile Paved Road Course

Road course with four different length built in 1957. Closed in 1988. First NASCAR Winston Cup (then Grand National) race staged on 6/1/58 (won by Eddie Gray). Final NASCAR event staged on 6/12/88 (won by Rusty Wallace). Track sold and turned into shopping complex.

Winston Cup Starts
Richard Petty   45

Winston Cup Victories
Bobby Allison   6

Winston Cup Poles
Darrell Waltrip   9

Winston Cup Money
Bobby Allison $390,350

Most Cars Started
46—June 1, 1958 Crown America 500

Fewest Cars Started
27—May 21, 1961

Narrowest Margin of Victory
0.240 seconds November 22, 1981
Winston Western 500

Slowest Race
79.481 MPH—June 1, 1958 Crown America 500

Race Record
107.820 MPH—January 14, 1979 Winston Western 500

Most Cautions
7—November 22, 1981
Winston Western 500
7—November 16, 1986
Winston Western 500
7—June 12, 1988 Budweiser 400

Most Race Leaders
9—January 18, 1976
Winston Western 500
9—January 11, 1981
Winston Western 500
9—November 22, 1981
Winston Western 500
9—June 12, 1988 Budweiser 400

Most Cars Running at Finish
31—June 12, 1988 Budweiser 400

1958 Grand National Race No. 21 Crown America 500
June 1, 1958 Average Speed: 79.481

Driver	Owner	Car #	Make	Laps	Winnings
1. Eddie Gray	Eddie Gray	98	57 Ford	190	3,225
2. Lloyd Dane	Lloyd Dane	44	58 Ford	190	1,850
3. Jack Smith	Jack Smith	47	58 Pont	186	1,375
4. Lee Petty	Petty Enterprises	42	57 Olds	184	1,100
5. Bob Keefe		15	56 Ford	181	725

1961 Grand National Race No. 22
May 21, 1961 Average Speed: 82.512

Driver	Owner	Car #	Make	Laps	Winnings
1. Lloyd Dane	Lloyd Dane	44	61 Chev	39	825
2. Don Noel	Chuck Parkko	7	61 Ford	39	505
3. Dick Smith		18	60 Ford	38	350
4. Jim Cook	Floyd Johnson	0	60 Dodg	38	290
5. Bob Perry	Bob Perry	84	59 Ford	38	250

1963 Grand National Race No. 4 Riverside 500
January 20, 1963 Average Speed: 84.965

Driver	Owner	Car #	Make	Laps	Winnings
1. Dan Gurney	Holman-Moody	28	63 Ford	185	14,400
2. A. J. Foyt	Ray Nichels	02	63 Pont	185	6,570
3. Troy Ruttman	Bill Stroppe	14	63 Merc	184	3,980
4. Fireball Roberts	Banjo Matthews	22	63 Pont	184	2,630
5. Bobby Johns	Shorty Johns	7	63 Pont	182	1,750

1963 Grand National Race No. 55 Golden State 400
November 3, 1963 Average Speed: 91.465

Driver	Owner	Car #	Make	Laps	Winnings
1. Darel Dieringer	Bill Stroppe	16	63 Merc	148	7,875
2. Dave MacDonald	Wood Brothers	21	63 Ford	147	4,655
3. Marvin Panch	Wood Brothers	121	63 Ford	147	2,860
4. Fireball Roberts	Holman-Moody	22	63 Ford	147	1,775
5. Junior Johnson	Bill Stroppe	26	63 Merc	145	1,300

1964 Grand National Race No. 5 Motor Trend 500
January 19, 1964 Average Speed: 91.245

Driver	Owner	Car #	Make	Laps	Winnings
1. Dan Gurney	Wood Brothers	121	64 Ford	185	12,870
2. Marvin Panch	Wood Brothers	21	64 Ford	184	6,650
3. Fireball Roberts	Holman-Moody	22	64 Ford	183	3,900
4. Bill Amick	Dick Niles	9W	63 Merc	181	2,470
5. Ned Jarrett	Bondy Long	11	64 Ford	180	1,750

1965 Grand National Race No. 1 Motor Trend 500
January 17, 1965 Average Speed: 87.708

Driver	Owner	Car #	Make	Laps	Winnings
1. Dan Gurney	Wood Brothers	121	65 Ford	185	13,625
2. Junior Johnson	Rex Lovette	27	65 Ford	185	7,310
3. Marvin Panch	Wood Brothers	21	65 Ford	184	4,075
4. Darel Dieringer		06	65 Ford	181	2,625
5. Gene Davis	Bill Groves	5	64 Merc	177	1,850

1966 Grand National Race No. 2 Motor Trend 500
January 23, 1966 Average Speed: 97.952

Driver	Owner	Car #	Make	Laps	Winnings
1. Dan Gurney	Wood Brothers	121	66 Ford	185	18,445
2. David Pearson	Cotton Owens	6	65 Dodg	185	8,395
3. Paul Goldsmith	Ray Nichels	99	65 Plym	183	5,055
4. Curtis Turner	Wood Brothers	41	66 Ford	183	3,445
5. Dick Hutcherson	Holman-Moody	29	66 Ford	182	2,120

1967 Grand National Race No. 2 Motor Trend 500
January 22 & 29, 1967 Average Speed: 91.080

Driver	Owner	Car #	Make	Laps	Winnings
1. Parnelli Jones	Wood Brothers	115	67 Ford	185	18,720
2. Paul Goldsmith	Ray Nichels	99	66 Plym	183	8,600
3. Norm Nelson	Norm Nelson	11	67 Plym	183	5,250
4. Don White	Ray Nichels	31	66 Dodg	183	3,325
5. James Hylton	Bud Hartje	48	65 Dodg	178	2,175

1968 Grand National Race No. 3 Motor Trend 500
January 21, 1968 Average Speed: 100.598

Driver	Owner	Car #	Make	Laps	Winnings
1. Dan Gurney	Wood Brothers	121	68 Ford	186	21,250
2. David Pearson	Holman-Moody	17	68 Ford	186	9,600
3. Parnelli Jones	Bill Stroppe	115	68 Ford	186	5,600
4. Bobby Allison	Bondy Long	29	68 Ford	185	3,250
5. Cale Yarborough	Wood Brothers	21	68 Ford	184	2,225

1969 Grand National Race No. 3 Motor Trend 500
February 1, 1969 Average Speed: 105.498

Driver	Owner	Car #	Make	Laps	Winnings
1. Richard Petty	Petty Enterprises	43	69 Ford	186	19,650
2. A. J. Foyt	Jack Bowsher	1	69 Ford	186	10,200
3. David Pearson	Holman-Moody	17	69 Ford	184	6,775
4. Al Unser		41	69 Dodg	183	3,825
5. James Hylton	James Hylton	48	67 Dodg	177	2,450

Riverside Int'l Raceway *continued*

1970 Grand National Race No. 1 Motor Trend 500
January 18, 1970 Average Speed: 97.450

Driver	Owner	Car #	Make	Laps	Winnings
1. A. J. Foyt	Jack Bowsher	11	70 Ford	193	19,700
2. Roger McCluskey	Norm Nelson	1	70 Plym	193	9,000
3. LeeRoy Yarbrough	Junior Johnson	98	70 Ford	193	6,275
4. Donnie Allison	Banjo Matthews	27	70 Ford	190	4,475
5. Richard Petty	Petty Enterprises	43	70 Plym	186	3,000

1971 Winston Cup GN Race No. 1 Motor Trend 500
January 10, 1971 Average Speed: 100.783

Driver	Owner	Car #	Make	Laps	Winnings
1. Ray Elder	Fred Elder	96	70 Dodg	191	18,715
2. Bobby Allison	Bobby Allison	12	70 Dodg	191	9,215
3. Benny Parsons	L. G. DeWitt	72	69 Ford	189	6,390
4. Bobby Isaac	Nord Krauskopf	71	71 Dodg	189	4,540
5. James Hylton	James Hylton	48	70 Ford	185	2,915

1972 Winston Cup GN Race No. 1 Winston Western 500
January 23, 1972 Average Speed: 104.016

Driver	Owner	Car #	Make	Laps	Winnings
1. Richard Petty	Petty Enterprises	43	72 Plym	149	18,170
2. Bobby Allison	R. Howard & J. Johnson	12	72 Chev	149	10,720
3. Bobby Isaac	Nord Krauskopf	71	71 Dodg	146	7,845
4. Ray Elder	Fred Elder	96	72 Dodg	146	4,945
5. Hershel McGriff	Beryl Jackson	04	70 Plym	145	3,120

1973 Winston Cup GN Race No. 1 Winston Western 500
January 21, 1973 Average Speed: 104.055

Driver	Owner	Car #	Make	Laps	Winnings
1. Mark Donohue	Roger Penske	16	73 Mata	191	15,170
2. Bobby Allison	Bobby Allison	12	73 Chev	190	10,770
3. Ray Elder	Fred Elder	96	72 Dodg	189	6,120
4. Bobby Unser	Holman-Moody	41	72 Ford	186	4,520
5. Jimmy Insolo	Roger Paquette	38	72 Chev	184	3,070

1974 Winston Cup GN Race No. 1 Winston Western 500
January 20 & 26, 1974 Average Speed: 101.140

Driver	Owner	Car #	Make	Laps	Winnings
1. Cale Yarborough	R. Howard & J. Johnson	11	74 Chev	191	19,325
2. Richard Petty	Petty Enterprises	43	74 Dodg	191	12,825
3. David Pearson	Wood Brothers	21	71 Merc	191	8,525
4. Benny Parsons	L. G. DeWitt	72	74 Chev	188	8,825
5. Bobby Allison	Bobby Allison	12	74 Chev	188	6,975

1975 Winston Cup GN Race No. 1 Winston Western 500
January 19, 1975 Average Speed: 98.627

Driver	Owner	Car #	Make	Laps	Winnings
1. Bobby Allison	Roger Penske	16	75 Mata	191	14,735
2. David Pearson	Wood Brothers	21	73 Merc	191	11,135
3. Cecil Gordon	Cecil Gordon	24	75 Chev	184	8,535
4. Dave Marcis	Nord Krauskopf	71	74 Dodg	183	8,235
5. Elmo Langley	Elmo Langley	64	72 Ford	178	4,535

1976 Winston Cup GN Race No. 1 Winston Western 500
January 18, 1976 Average Speed: 99.180

Driver	Owner	Car #	Make	Laps	Winnings
1. David Pearson	Wood Brothers	21	Merc	191	17,295
2. Cale Yarborough	Junior Johnson	11	Chev	191	14,920
3. Jimmy Insolo	Roger Paquette	38	Chev	191	8,620
4. Ray Elder	Fred Elder	96	Dodg	160	6,745
5. Benny Parsons	L. G. DeWitt	72	Chev	189	4,445

1970 Grand National Race No. 20 Falstaff 400
June 14, 1970 Average Speed: 101.120

Driver	Owner	Car #	Make	Laps	Winnings
1. Richard Petty	Petty Enterprises	43	70 Plym	153	18,840
2. Bobby Allison	Mario Rossi	22	69 Dodg	152	9,365
3. James Hylton	James Hylton	48	69 Ford	144	5,340
4. John Soares Jr.	John Soares	08	70 Plym	141	3,415
5. Dick Gulstrand	James Good	44	68 Chev	139	2,540

1971 Winston Cup GN Race No. 24 Winston Golden State 400
June 20, 1971 Average Speed: 93.427

Driver	Owner	Car #	Make	Laps	Winnings
1. Bobby Allison	Bobby Allison	12	70 Dodg	153	14,395
2. Ray Elder	Fred Elder	96	71 Dodg	153	7,695
3. Cecil Gordon	Cecil Gordon	24	69 Merc	147	4,595
4. James Hylton	James Hylton	48	70 Ford	146	2,870
5. Jerry Oliver	Coz Cancilla	6	70 Dodg	145	1,945

1972 Winston Cup GN Race No. 15 Golden State 400
June 18, 1972 Average Speed: 98.761

Driver	Owner	Car #	Make	Laps	Winnings
1. Ray Elder	Fred Elder	96	71 Dodg	153	12,375
2. Benny Parsons	L. G. DeWitt	72	71 Merc	152	6,850
3. Donnie Allison	Roger Penske	16	72 Mata	150	4,025
4. James Hylton	James Hylton	48	70 Ford	149	3,300
5. Carl Joiner	Dean Thorne	26	72 Chev	148	2,150

1973 Winston Cup GN Race No. 15 Tuborg 400
June 17, 1973 Average Speed: 100.215

Driver	Owner	Car #	Make	Laps	Winnings
1. Bobby Allison	Bobby Allison	12	73 Chev	153	12,750
2. Richard Petty	Petty Enterprises	43	73 Dodg	153	10,275
3. Benny Parsons	L. G. DeWitt	72	72 Chev	152	5,325
4. Jimmy Insolo	Roger Paquette	38	72 Chev	151	3,225
5. Cecil Gordon	Cecil Gordon	24	72 Chev	149	2,650

1974 Winston Cup GN Race No. 14 Tuborg 400
June 9, 1974 Average Speed: 102.489

Driver	Owner	Car #	Make	Laps	Winnings
1. Cale Yarborough	R. Howard & J. Johnson	11	74 Chev	138	17,925
2. Bobby Allison	Bobby Allison	12	74 Chev	138	11,400
3. Benny Parsons	L. G. DeWitt	72	72 Chev	136	8,800
4. Cecil Gordon	Cecil Gordon	24	72 Chev	134	3,550
5. Frank Warren	Frank Warren	79	74 Dodg	130	2,850

1975 Winston Cup GN Race No. 14 Tuborg 400
June 8, 1975 Average Speed: 101.028

Driver	Owner	Car #	Make	Laps	Winnings
1. Richard Petty	Petty Enterprises	43	74 Dodg	153	18,135
2. Bobby Allison	Roger Penske	16	75 Mata	153	10,410
3. Benny Parsons	L. G. DeWitt	72	75 Chev	152	8,510
4. Ray Elder	Fred Elder	96	74 Dodg	152	4,185
5. Dave Marcis	Nord Krauskopf	71	74 Dodg	148	6,135

1976 Winston Cup GN Race No. 14 Riverside 400
June 13, 1976 Average Speed: 106.279

Driver	Owner	Car #	Make	Laps	Winnings
1. David Pearson	Wood Brothers	21	Merc	95	15,150
2. Bobby Allison	Roger Penske	2	Merc	95	10,695
3. Benny Parsons	L. G. DeWitt	72	Chev	94	7,550
4. Ray Elder	Fred Elder	96	Dodg	94	4,970
5. Buddy Baker	Bud Moore	15	Ford	94	5,540

Riverside Int'l Raceway *continued*

1977 Winston Cup GN Race No. 1 Winston Western 500
January 16, 1977 Average Speed: 107.038

Driver	Owner	Car #	Make	Laps	Winnings
1. David Pearson	Wood Brothers	21	Merc	119	15,400
2. Cale Yarborough	Junior Johnson	11	Chev	119	16,220
3. Richard Petty	Petty Enterprises	43	Dodg	118	11,095
4. Dave Marcis	Roger Penske	2	Chev	116	8,645
5. Sonny Easley	Jerry Lankford	67	Ford	115	6,290

1977 Winston Cup GN Race No. 14 NAPA 400
June 12, 1977 Average Speed: 105.021

Driver	Owner	Car #	Make	Laps	Winnings
1. Richard Petty	Petty Enterprises	43	Dodg	95	18,255
2. David Pearson	Wood Brothers	21	Merc	95	10,400
3. Cale Yarborough	Junior Johnson	11	Chev	95	10,475
4. Jimmy Insolo	Jimmy Insolo	51	Ford	93	3,900
5. Buddy Baker	Bud Moore	15	Ford	93	6,400

1978 Winston Cup GN Race No. 1 Winston Western 500
January 22, 1978 Average Speed: 102.269

Driver	Owner	Car #	Make	Laps	Winnings
1. Cale Yarborough	Junior Johnson	11	Olds	119	20,850
2. Benny Parsons	L. G. DeWitt	72	Chev	119	14,800
3. David Pearson	Wood Brothers	21	Merc	119	9,850
4. Neil Bonnett	Jim Stacy	5	Dodg	119	8,800
5. Dave Marcis	Rod Osterlund	2	Chev	118	4,050

1978 Winston Cup GN Race No. 14 NAPA 400
June 11, 1978 Average Speed: 104.311

Driver	Owner	Car #	Make	Laps	Winnings
1. Benny Parsons	L. G. DeWitt	72	Chev	95	22,750
2. Richard Petty	Petty Enterprises	43	Dodg	95	14,200
3. Bobby Allison	Bud Moore	15	Ford	95	10,050
4. Dave Marcis	Rod Osterlund	2	Chev	95	5,850
5. Cale Yarborough	Junior Johnson	11	Olds	94	8,400

1979 Winston Cup GN Race No. 1 Winston Western 500
January 14, 1979 Average Speed: 107.820

Driver	Owner	Car #	Make	Laps	Winnings
1. Darrell Waltrip	DiGard	88	Chev	119	21,150
2. David Pearson	Wood Brothers	21	Merc	119	14,200
3. Cale Yarborough	Junior Johnson	11	Olds	119	12,675
4. Bill Schmitt	Bill Schmitt	73	Olds	118	8,000
5. Donnie Allison	Hoss Ellington	1	Chev	118	7,550

1979 Winston Cup GN Race No. 15 NAPA Riverside 400
June 10, 1979 Average Speed: 103.732

Driver	Owner	Car #	Make	Laps	Winnings
1. Bobby Allison	Bud Moore	15	Ford	95	22,700
2. Darrell Waltrip	DiGard	88	Chev	95	14,875
3. Richard Petty	Petty Enterprises	43	Chev	95	10,350
4. Cale Yarborough	Junior Johnson	11	Chev	95	11,800
5. Benny Parsons	M. C. Anderson	27	Chev	94	6,800

1980 Winston Cup GN Race No. 1 Winston Western 500
January 13 & 19, 1980 Average Speed: 94.974

Driver	Owner	Car #	Make	Laps	Winnings
1. Darrell Waltrip	DiGard	88	Chev	119	24,700
2. Dale Earnhardt	Rod Osterlund	2	Chev	119	19,400
3. Richard Petty	Petty Enterprises	43	Chev	119	15,100
4. Joe Millikan	L. G. DeWitt	72	Chev	119	10,200
5. Bill Schmitt	Bill Schmitt	73	Olds	119	7,455

1980 Winston Cup GN Race No. 15 Warner W. Hodgdon 400
June 8, 1980 Average Speed: 101.846

Driver	Owner	Car #	Make	Laps	Winnings
1. Darrell Waltrip	DiGard	88	Chev	95	22,100
2. Neil Bonnett	Wood Brothers	21	Merc	95	10,950
3. Benny Parsons	M. C. Anderson	27	Chev	95	10,950
4. Cale Yarborough	Junior Johnson	11	Chev	95	9,650
5. Dale Earnhardt	Rod Osterlund	2	Chev	95	9,100

1981 Winston Cup GN Race No. 1 Winston Western 500
January 11, 1981 Average Speed: 95.263

Driver	Owner	Car #	Make	Laps	Winnings
1. Bobby Allison	Harry Ranier	28	Chev	119	24,600
2. Terry Labonte	Billy Hagan	44	Chev	119	19,600
3. Dale Earnhardt	Rod Osterlund	2	Pont	119	16,325
4. Richard Childress	Richard Childress	3	Chev	119	8,510
5. Richard Petty	Petty Enterprises	42	Chev	119	4,250

1981 Winston Cup GN Race No. 15 Warner W. Hodgdon 400
June 14, 1981 Average Speed: 93.597

Driver	Owner	Car #	Make	Laps	Winnings
1. Darrell Waltrip	Junior Johnson	11	Buick	95	23,650
2. Dale Earnhardt	Rod Osterlund	2	Pont	95	18,725
3. Richard Petty	Petty Enterprises	43	Buick	95	12,200
4. Neil Bonnett	Wood Brothers	21	Ford	95	4,650
5. Ricky Rudd	DiGard	88	Buick	95	8,900

1981 Winston Cup GN Race No. 31 Winston Western 500
November 22, 1981 Average Speed: 95.288

Driver	Owner	Car #	Make	Laps	Winnings
1. Bobby Allison	Harry Ranier	28	Buick	119	24,300
2. Joe Ruttman	Jim Stacy	2	Buick	119	17,675
3. Terry Labonte	Billy Hagan	44	Buick	119	16,450
4. Dale Earnhardt	Richard Childress	3	Pont	119	10,560
5. Joe Millikan	Cliff Stewart	5	Pont	119	9,125

1982 Winston Cup GN Race No. 14 Budweiser 400
June 13, 1982 Average Speed: 103.000

Driver	Owner	Car #	Make	Laps	Winnings
1. Tim Richmond	Jim Stacy	2	Buick	95	21,530
2. Terry Labonte	Billy Hagan	44	Buick	95	17,930
3. Geoff Bodine	Cliff Stewart	50	Pont	95	14,670
4. Dale Earnhardt	Bud Moore	15	Ford	95	11,935
5. Neil Bonnett	Wood Brothers	21	Ford	95	3,485

1982 Winston Cup GN Race No. 30 Winston Western 500
November 21, 1982 Average Speed: 99.823

Driver	Owner	Car #	Make	Laps	Winnings
1. Tim Richmond	Jim Stacy	2	Buick	119	24,730
2. Ricky Rudd	Richard Childress	3	Pont	119	16,980
3. Darrell Waltrip	Junior Johnson	11	Buick	119	21,150
4. Neil Bonnett	Wood Brothers	21	Ford	119	6,100
5. Mark Martin	Bo Reeder	02	Buick	118	7,760

1983 Winston Cup GN Race No. 13 Budweiser 400
June 5, 1983 Average Speed: 88.063

Driver	Owner	Car #	Make	Laps	Winnings
1. Ricky Rudd	Richard Childress	3	Chev	95	24,530
2. Bill Elliott	Harry Melling	9	Ford	95	14,655
3. Harry Gant	Hal Needham	33	Buick	95	14,775
4. Dale Earnhardt	Bud Moore	15	Ford	95	11,475
5. Dick Brooks	Junie Donlavey	90	Ford	95	6,760

Riverside Int'l Raceway *continued*

1983 Winston Cup GN Race No. 30 Winston Western 500
November 20, 1983 Average Speed: 95.859

Driver	Owner	Car #	Make	Laps	Winnings
1. Bill Elliott	Harry Melling	9	Ford	119	26,380
2. Benny Parsons	Johnny Hayes	55	Chev	119	13,225
3. Neil Bonnett	Bob Rahilly & Butch Mock	75	Chev	119	18,375
4. Dale Earnhardt	Bud Moore	15	Ford	119	13,725
5. Tim Richmond	Raymond Beadle	27	Pont	119	8,930

1984 Winston Cup GN Race No. 30 Winston Western 500
November 18, 1984 Average Speed: 98.448

Driver	Owner	Car #	Make	Laps	Winnings
1. Geoff Bodine	Rick Hendrick	5	Chev	119	31,900
2. Tim Richmond	Raymond Beadle	27	Pont	119	21,325
3. Terry Labonte	Billy Hagan	44	Chev	119	17,255
4. Bill Elliott	Harry Melling	9	Ford	119	13,500
5. Benny Parsons	Johnny Hayes	55	Chev	119	8,450

1985 Winston Cup GN Race No. 28 Winston Western 500
November 17, 1985 Average Speed: 105.065

Driver	Owner	Car #	Make	Laps	Winnings
1. Ricky Rudd	Bud Moore	15	Ford	119	37,875
2. Terry Labonte	Billy Hagan	44	Chev	119	38,375
3. Neil Bonnett	Junior Johnson	12	Chev	119	18,550
4. Harry Gant	Hal Needham	33	Chev	119	16,225
5. Dale Earnhardt	Richard Childress	3	Chev	119	13,175

1986 Winston Cup Race No. 29 Winston Western 500
November 16, 1986 Average Speed: 101.246

Driver	Owner	Car #	Make	Laps	Winnings
1. Tim Richmond	Rick Hendrick	25	Chev	119	50,955
2. Dale Earnhardt	Richard Childress	3	Chev	119	26,750
3. Geoff Bodine	Rick Hendrick	5	Chev	119	20,175
4. Darrell Waltrip	Junior Johnson	11	Chev	119	22,350
5. Joe Ruttman	Kenny Bernstein	26	Buick	119	11,945

1987 Winston Cup Race No. 28 Winston Western 500
November 8, 1987 Average Speed: 98.035

Driver	Owner	Car #	Make	Laps	Winnings
1. Rusty Wallace	Raymond Beadle	27	Pont	119	47,725
2. Benny Parsons	Rick Hendrick	35	Chev	119	28,700
3. Kyle Petty	Wood Brothers	21	Ford	119	21,125
4. Richard Petty	Petty Enterprises	43	Pont	119	13,780
5. Bobby Allison	Stavola Brothers	22	Buick	119	14,575

1984 Winston Cup GN Race No. 13 Budweiser 400
June 3, 1984 Average Speed: 102.910

Driver	Owner	Car #	Make	Laps	Winnings
1. Terry Labonte	Billy Hagan	44	Chev	95	31,955
2. Neil Bonnett	Junior Johnson	12	Chev	95	15,670
3. Bobby Allison	DiGard	22	Buick	95	18,850
4. Geoff Bodine	Rick Hendrick	5	Chev	95	11,600
5. Dale Earnhardt	Richard Childress	3	Chev	95	10,950

1985 Winston Cup GN Race No. 12 Budweiser 400
June 2, 1985 Average Speed: 104.276

Driver	Owner	Car #	Make	Laps	Winnings
1. Terry Labonte	Billy Hagan	44	Chev	95	39,200
2. Harry Gant	Hal Needham	33	Chev	95	23,450
3. Bobby Allison	DiGard	22	Buick	95	15,900
4. Ricky Rudd	Bud Moore	15	Ford	95	11,825
5. Kyle Petty	Wood Brothers	7	Ford	95	9,330

1986 Winston Cup Race No. 12 Budweiser 400
June 1, 1986 Average Speed: 105.083

Driver	Owner	Car #	Make	Laps	Winnings
1. Darrell Waltrip	Junior Johnson	11	Chev	95	49,000
2. Tim Richmond	Rick Hendrick	25	Chev	95	22,155
3. Ricky Rudd	Bud Moore	15	Ford	95	18,650
4. Rusty Wallace	Raymond Beadle	27	Pont	95	12,775
5. Dale Earnhardt	Richard Childress	3	Chev	95	14,125

1987 Winston Cup Race No. 13 Budweiser 400
June 21, 1987 Average Speed: 102.183

Driver	Owner	Car #	Make	Laps	Winnings
1. Tim Richmond	Rick Hendrick	25	Chev	95	36,450
2. Ricky Rudd	Bud Moore	15	Ford	95	28,450
3. Neil Bonnett	Bob Rahilly & Butch Mock	75	Pont	95	17,005
4. Terry Labonte	Junior Johnson	11	Chev	95	19,125
5. Bill Elliott	Harry Melling	9	Ford	95	13,850

1988 Winston Cup Race No. 12 Budweiser 400
June 12, 1988 Average Speed: 88.341

Driver	Owner	Car #	Make	Laps	Winnings
1. Rusty Wallace	Raymond Beadle	27	Pont	95	49,100
2. Terry Labonte	Junior Johnson	11	Chev	95	26,175
3. Ricky Rudd	Kenny Bernstein	26	Buick	95	20,950
4. Dale Earnhardt	Richard Childress	3	Chev	95	18,600
5. Phil Parsons	Richard Jackson	55	Olds	95	10,725

Santa Clara Fairgrounds
San Jose, CA
Half-mile Dirt Track

(aka San Jose Fairgrounds) Half-mile dirt oval built in 1948. Only NASCAR Winston Cup (then Grand National) race staged on 9/15/57 (won by Marvin Porter). Half-mile track closed in 1990. A .333-mile track opened in 1991.

Winston Cup Victories
Marvin Porter   1

Winston Cup Poles
Lloyd Dane   1

Winston Cup Money
Marvin Porter $800

Most Cars Started
22—September 15, 1957

Narrowest Margin of Victory
None, red flag—September 15, 1957

Most Race Leaders
N/A

Most Cars Running at Finish
5—September 15, 1957

1957 Grand National Race No. 44
September 15, 1957

Driver	Owner	Car #	Make	Laps	Winnings
1. Marvin Porter	Marvin Porter	12	57 Ford	116	800
2. Eddie Pagan	Eddie Pagan	45	57 Ford	116	550
3. Lloyd Dane	Lloyd Dane	44	57 Ford	115	450
4. Ernie Young	Walt Palozi	8	57 Pont	113	350
5. Jim Blomgren	Bob Smith	5	57 Ford	112	310

Sears Point Int'l Raceway
Sonoma, CA
2.52-mile Paved Road Course

1.7- and 2.52-mile road course built in 1968. First NASCAR Winston Cup race staged on 6/11/89 (Ricky Rudd won).

Winston Cup Starts
15 drivers tied with 8

Winston Cup Victories
Ernie Irvan 2
Rusty Wallace 2

Winston Cup Poles
Ricky Rudd 4

Winston Cup Money
Rusty Wallace $272,970

Most Cars Started
44—June 10, 1990
Banquet Frozen Foods 300
44—May 5, 1996
Save Mart Supermarkets 300K

Fewest Cars Started
42—June 11, 1989
Banquet Frozen Foods 300

Narrowest Margin of Victory
0.320 seconds May 7, 1993
Save Mart Supermarkets 300K

Slowest Race
69.245 MPH—June 10, 1990
Banquet Frozen Foods 300

Race Record
81.413 MPH—June 7, 1992
Save Mart Supermarkets 300K

Most Cautions
9—June 10, 1990 Banquet Frozen Foods 300

Most Race Leaders
8—June 7, 1992
Save Mart Supermarkets 300K

Most Cars Running at Finish
42—May 5, 1996
Save Mart Supermarkets 300K

1989 Winston Cup Race No. 12 Banquet Frozen Foods 300
June 11, 1989 Average Speed: 76.088

Driver	Owner	Car #	Make	Laps	Winnings
1. Ricky Rudd	Kenny Bernstein	26	Buick	74	62,350
2. Rusty Wallace	Raymond Beadle	27	Pont	74	39,225
3. Bill Elliott	Harry Melling	9	Ford	74	28,375
4. Dale Earnhardt	Richard Childress	3	Chev	74	20,350
5. Lake Speed	Lake Speed	83	Olds	74	18,507

1990 Winston Cup Series Race No. 12 Banquet Frozen Foods 300
June 10, 1990 Average Speed: 69.245

Driver	Owner	Car #	Make	Laps	Winnings
1. Rusty Wallace	Raymond Beadle	27	Pont	74	69,100
2. Mark Martin	Jack Roush	6	Ford	74	34,000
3. Ricky Rudd	Rick Hendrick	5	Chev	74	28,675
4. Geoff Bodine	Junior Johnson	11	Ford	74	20,650
5. Bobby Hillin Jr.	Stavola Brothers	8	Buick	74	17,007

1991 Winston Cup Series Race No. 12 Banquet Frozen Foods 300
June 9, 1991 Average Speed: 72.970

Driver	Owner	Car #	Make	Laps	Winnings
1. Davey Allison	Robert Yates	28	Ford	74	61,950
2. Ricky Rudd	Rick Hendrick	5	Chev	74	41,975
3. Rusty Wallace	Roger Penske	2	Pont	74	34,975
4. Ernie Irvan	Larry McClure	4	Chev	74	20,350
5. Ken Schrader	Rick Hendrick	25	Chev	74	17,225

1992 Winston Cup Race No. 12 Save Mart Supermarkets 300K
June 7, 1992 Average Speed: 81.413

Driver	Owner	Car #	Make	Laps	Winnings
1. Ernie Irvan	Larry McClure	4	Chev	74	61,810
2. Terry Labonte	Billy Hagan	94	Olds	74	36,685
3. Mark Martin	Jack Roush	6	Ford	74	28,185
4. Ricky Rudd	Rick Hendrick	5	Chev	74	25,710
5. Bill Elliott	Junior Johnson	11	Ford	74	32,585

1993 Winston Cup Series Race No. 10 Save Mart Supermarkets 300K
May 16, 1993 Average Speed: 77.013

Driver	Owner	Car #	Make	Laps	Winnings
1. Geoff Bodine	Bud Moore	15	Ford	74	66,510
2. Ernie Irvan	Larry McClure	4	Chev	74	41,190
3. Ricky Rudd	Rick Hendrick	5	Chev	74	29,590
4. Ken Schrader	Rick Hendrick	25	Chev	74	22,415
5. Kyle Petty	Felix Sabates	42	Pont	74	22,715

1994 Winston Cup Series Race No. 10 Save Mart Supermarkets 300K
May 15, 1994 Average Speed: 77.458

Driver	Owner	Car #	Make	Laps	Winnings
1. Ernie Irvan	Robert Yates	28	Ford	74	78,810
2. Geoff Bodine	Geoff Bodine	7	Ford	74	45,640
3. Dale Earnhardt	Richard Childress	3	Chev	74	37,825
4. Wally Dallenbach Jr.	Petty Enterprises	43	Pont	74	24,920
5. Rusty Wallace	Roger Penske	2	Ford	74	25,970

1995 Winston Cup Series Race No. 10 Save Mart Supermarkets 300K
May 7, 1993 Average Speed: 70.681

Driver	Owner	Car #	Make	Laps	Winnings
1. Dale Earnhardt	Richard Childress	3	Chev	74	74,860
2. Mark Martin	Jack Roush	6	Ford	74	68,915
3. Jeff Gordon	Rick Hendrick	24	Chev	74	41,625
4. Ricky Rudd	Ricky Rudd	10	Ford	74	39,870
5. Terry Labonte	Rick Hendrick	5	Chev	74	35,020

1996 Winston Cup Series Race No. 10 Save Mart Supermarkets 300K
May 5, 1996 Average Speed: 77.673

Driver	Owner	Car #	Make	Laps	Winnings
1. Rusty Wallace	Roger Penske	2	Ford	74	58,395
2. Mark Martin	Jack Roush	6	Ford	74	58,640
3. Wally Dallenbach Jr.	Bud Moore	15	Ford	74	50,850
4. Dale Earnhardt	Richard Childress	3	Chev	74	39,160
5. Terry Labonte	Rick Hendrick	5	Chev	74	41,995

Willow Springs Int'l Raceway
Lancaster, CA
2.5-mile Oiled Dirt Road Course

(aka Willow Springs Speedway; Kern County Speedway) 2-mile oiled dirt road course built in 1953. First NASCAR Winston Cup (then Grand National) race run on 11/20/55 (won by Chuck Stevenson), and was a part of 1956 season schedule. Final NASCAR race run on 11/11/56 (Marvin Panch won), and the race was counted as 1957 season opener. Track is still in operation.

Winston Cup Starts
15 drivers tied with 2

Winston Cup Victories
Marvin Panch   1
Chuck Stevenson   1

Winston Cup Poles
Marvin Panch   1
Jim Reed   1

Winston Cup Money
Marvin Panch $2,680

Most Cars Started
37—November 20, 1955

Fewest Cars Started
34—November 11, 1956

Narrowest Margin of Victory
500 feet—November 20, 1955

Slowest Race
66.512 MPH—November 20, 1955

Race Record
78.648 MPH—November 11, 1956

Most Cautions
Both races ran caution-free

Most Race Leaders
2—November 20, 1955
2—November 11, 1956

Most Cars Running at Finish
32—November 20, 1955

1956 Grand National Race No. 3
November 20, 1955 Average Speed: 66.512

Driver	Owner	Car #	Make	Laps	Winnings
1. Chuck Stevenson	Carl Dane	22	56 Ford	80	1,570
2. Marvin Panch	Tom Harbison	98	56 Ford	80	1,130
3. Johnny Mantz	Bill Stroppe	15	56 Merc	79	1,130
4. Jim Reed	Jim Reed	7	56 Chev	79	580
5. Allen Adkins	Gus Davis	2	55 Dodg	78	445

1957 Grand National Race No. 1
November 11, 1956 Average Speed: 78.648

Driver	Owner	Car #	Make	Laps	Winnings
1. Marvin Panch	Pete DePaolo	98	56 Ford	60	1,550
2. Fireball Roberts	Pete DePaolo	22	56 Ford	60	1,000
3. George Seeger	Oscar Maples	12	56 Ford	60	755
4. Jim Paschal	Frank Hayworth	75	56 Merc	59	570
5. Eddie Pagan	Eddie Pagan	45	56 Ford	50	430

Connecticut

Thompson Int'l Speedway
Thompson, CT
Half-mile Paved Track

(aka Thompson Speedway; New Thompson Speedway) .625-mile paved track built in 1940. Originally listed as half-mile track, currently measured as .542-mile oval. Also included a road course (1952–1970s), a quarter-mile Midget oval, and a drag strip. First NASCAR Winston Cup (then Grand National) race staged on 10/12/51 (won by Neil Cole). Final big NASCAR race run on 7/12/70 (Bobby Isaac won). Track is still in operation.

Winston Cup Starts
16 drivers tied with 2

Winston Cup Victories
Neil Cole 1
Bobby Isaac 1
David Pearson 1

Winston Cup Poles
Neil Cole 1
Bobby Isaac 1
David Pearson 1

Winston Cup Money
Bobby Isaac $2,500

Most Cars Started
38—October 12, 1951

Fewest Cars Started
30—July 9, 1970
Thompson Speedway 200

Narrowest Margin of Victory
N/A

Slowest Race
80.296 MPH—July 9, 1970
Thompson Speedway 200

Race Record
89.498 MPH—July 10, 1969
Thompson Speedway 200

Most Cautions
2—July 10, 1969
Thompson Speedway 200

Most Race Leaders
4—October 12, 1951

Most Cars Running at Finish
19—July 9, 1970
Thompson Speedway 200

1951 Grand National Race No. 32
October 12, 1951

Driver	Owner	Car #	Make	Laps	Winnings
1. Neil Cole	John Golabek	52	50 Olds	200	1,000
2. Jim Reed	Jim Reed	67	51 Ford	199	600
3. Dick Eagan	Dick Eagan		50 Plym	—	500
4. Billy Carden	Sam Knox	8	50 Olds	—	400
5. Reino Tulonen	Reino Tulonen	32	51 HEN	—	300

1969 Grand National Race No. 30 Thompson Speedway 200
July 10, 1969 Average Speed: 89.498

Driver	Owner	Car #	Make	Laps	Winnings
1. David Pearson	Holman-Moody	17	69 Ford	200	2,200
2. James Hylton	James Hylton	48	69 Dodg	199	1,500
3. John Sears	L. G. DeWitt	4	68 Ford	199	1,000
4. G. C. Spencer	G. C. Spencer	49	68 Plym	197	900
5. Richard Brickhouse	Dub Clewis	03	67 Plym	193	800

1970 Grand National Race No. 26 Thompson Speedway 200
July 9, 1970 Average Speed: 80.296

Driver	Owner	Car #	Make	Laps	Winnings
1. Bobby Isaac	Nord Krauskopf	71	69 Dodg	200	2,500
2. Richard Petty	Petty Enterprises	43	70 Plym	200	1,800
3. Benny Parsons	L. G. DeWitt	72	69 Ford	198	1,100
4. Dick Brooks	Dick Brooks	32	69 Plym	198	900
5. Neil Castles	Neil Castles	06	69 Dodg	198	800

Delaware

Dover Downs Int'l Speedway
Dover, DE
1-mile Paved Track

1-mile paved track built in 1969. First NASCAR Winston Cup (then Grand National) race staged on 7/6/69 (won by Richard Petty). Elevated horse track sits inside NASCAR oval. First superspeedway to offer air-conditioned general seating.

Winston Cup Starts
Dave Marcis 47
Darrell Waltrip 47

Winston Cup Victories
Bobby Allison 7
Richard Petty 7

Winston Cup Poles
David Pearson 6

Winston Cup Money
Dale Earnhardt $871,525

Most Cars Started
42—June 4, 1995 Miller Genuine Draft 500
42—June 2, 1996 Miller 500

Fewest Cars Started
31—May 20, 1979 Mason-Dixon 500

Narrowest Margin of Victory
0.220 seconds June 4, 1995
Miller Genuine Draft 500

Slowest Race
100.334 MPH—September 19, 1993
SplitFire Spark Plug 500

Race Record
125.945 MPH—September 16, 1990
Peak AntiFreeze 500

Most Cautions
16—September 19, 1993
SplitFire Spark Plug 500

Most Race Leaders
12—June 6, 1993 Budweiser 500
12—September 18, 1994
SplitFire Spark Plug 500
12—September 15, 1996 MBNA 500

Most Cars Running at Finish
35—June 4, 1995
Miller Genuine Draft 500

1969 Grand National Race No. 29 Mason-Dixon 300
July 6, 1969 Average Speed: 115.772

Driver	Owner	Car #	Make	Laps	Winnings
1. Richard Petty	Petty Enterprises	43	69 Ford	300	4,725
2. Sonny Hutchins	Junie Donlavey	90	67 Ford	294	2,050
3. James Hylton	James Hylton	48	69 Dodg	294	1,275
4. John Sears	L. G. DeWitt	4	69 Ford	293	825
5. Elmo Langley	Elmo Langley	84	68 Ford	287	725

1970 Grand National Race No. 41 Mason-Dixon 300
September 20, 1970 Average Speed: 112.103

Driver	Owner	Car #	Make	Laps	Winnings
1. Richard Petty	Petty Enterprises	43	70 Plym	300	6,195
2. Bobby Allison	Mario Rossi	22	69 Dodg	300	3,095
3. Charlie Glotzbach	Ray Nichels	99	69 Dodg	299	2,170
4. David Pearson	Holman-Moody	17	70 Ford	296	1,885
5. Benny Parsons	L. G. DeWitt	72	69 Ford	296	1,280

1971 Winston Cup GN Race No. 22 Mason-Dixon 500
June 6, 1971 Average Speed: 123.119

Driver	Owner	Car #	Make	Laps	Winnings
1. Bobby Allison	Holman-Moody	12	71 Ford	500	15,720
2. Fred Lorenzen	Ray Nichels	99	71 Plym	499	9,045
3. Richard Petty	Petty Enterprises	43	71 Plym	498	5,020
4. Bobby Isaac	Nord Krauskopf	71	71 Dodg	496	3,495
5. G. C. Spencer	G. C. Spencer	49	69 Plym	486	2,020

1971 Winston Cup GN Race No. 43 Delaware 500
October 17, 1971 Average Speed: 123.254

Driver	Owner	Car #	Make	Laps	Winnings
1. Richard Petty	Petty Enterprises	43	71 Plym	500	14,570
2. Charlie Glotzbach	R. Howard & J. Johnson	98	71 Chev	499	7,945
3. Bobby Isaac	Nord Krauskopf	71	71 Dodg	499	4,970
4. Bobby Allison	Holman-Moody	12	69 Merc	498	2,695
5. Bill Dennis	Junie Donlavey	90	69 Merc	483	1,595

1972 Winston Cup GN Race No. 13 Mason-Dixon 500
June 4, 1972 Average Speed: 118.019

Driver	Owner	Car #	Make	Laps	Winnings
1. Bobby Allison	R. Howard & J. Johnson	12	72 Chev	500	14,625
2. Richard Petty	Petty Enterprises	43	72 Dodg	499	10,375
3. LeeRoy Yarbrough	Bill Seifert	45	72 Merc	486	4,850
4. Jackie Oliver	Junie Donlavey	90	71 Ford	486	3,550
5. John Sears	J Marvin Mills	4	70 Plym	484	2,750

1972 Winston Cup GN Race No. 26 Delaware 500
September 17, 1972 Average Speed: 120.506

Driver	Owner	Car #	Make	Laps	Winnings
1. David Pearson	Wood Brothers	21	71 Merc	500	13,250
2. Richard Petty	Petty Enterprises	43	72 Plym	497	10,600
3. Ramo Stott	Junie Donlavey	90	71 Ford	486	4,950
4. James Hylton	James Hylton	48	71 Ford	478	3,550
5. Cecil Gordon	Cecil Gordon	24	71 Merc	477	2,885

1973 Winston Cup GN Race No. 13 Mason-Dixon 500
June 3, 1973 Average Speed: 119.745

Driver	Owner	Car #	Make	Laps	Winnings
1. David Pearson	Wood Brothers	21	71 Merc	500	14,025
2. Cale Yarborough	R. Howard & J. Johnson	11	73 Chev	500	10,700
3. Bobby Allison	Bobby Allison	12	73 Chev	497	6,775
4. Richard Petty	Petty Enterprises	43	73 Dodg	492	5,475
5. Cecil Gordon	Cecil Gordon	24	72 Chev	490	2,750

1973 Winston Cup GN Race No. 24 Delaware 500
September 16, 1973 Average Speed: 112.852

Driver	Owner	Car #	Make	Laps	Winnings
1. David Pearson	Wood Brothers	21	71 Merc	500	16,325
2. Bobby Allison	Bobby Allison	12	73 Chev	500	10,125
3. Buddy Baker	Nord Krauskopf	71	73 Dodg	500	7,050
4. Benny Parsons	L. G. DeWitt	72	73 Chev	493	4,175
5. J. D. McDuffie	J. D. McDuffie	70	72 Chev	484	3,275

Dover Downs Int'l Speedway *continued*

1974 Winston Cup GN Race No. 12 Mason-Dixon 500
May 19, 1974 Average Speed: 115.057

Driver	Owner	Car #	Make	Laps	Winnings
1. Cale Yarborough	R. Howard & J. Johnson	11	74 Chev	500	18,300
2. David Pearson	Wood Brothers	21	73 Merc	500	8,900
3. Richard Petty	Petty Enterprises	43	74 Dodg	498	8,250
4. Benny Parsons	L. G. DeWitt	72	74 Chev	492	7,150
5. George Follmer	Bud Moore	15	73 Ford	492	5,850

1974 Winston Cup GN Race No. 25 Delaware 500
September 15, 1974 Average Speed: 113.640

Driver	Owner	Car #	Make	Laps	Winnings
1. Richard Petty	Petty Enterprises	43	74 Dodg	500	18,175
2. Buddy Baker	Bud Moore	15	73 Ford	497	11,425
3. Earl Ross	Junior Johnson	52	74 Chev	491	5,750
4. Benny Parsons	L. G. DeWitt	72	74 Chev	488	7,250
5. Dave Marcis	Dave Marcis	2	73 Dodg	486	3,275

1975 Winston Cup GN Race No. 12 Mason-Dixon 500
May 18 & 19, 1975 Average Speed: 100.820

Driver	Owner	Car #	Make	Laps	Winnings
1. David Pearson	Wood Brothers	21	73 Merc	500	15,425
2. Cecil Gordon	Cecil Gordon	24	75 Chev	493	10,400
3. Richard Petty	Petty Enterprises	43	74 Dodg	490	10,050
4. James Hylton	James Hylton	48	74 Chev	487	6,950
5. David Sisco	David Sisco	05	75 Chev	486	3,725

1975 Winston Cup GN Race No. 22 Delaware 500
September 14, 1975 Average Speed: 111.372

Driver	Owner	Car #	Make	Laps	Winnings
1. Richard Petty	Petty Enterprises	43	74 Dodg	500	18,250
2. Dick Brooks	Junie Donlavey	90	73 Ford	500	10,425
3. Benny Parsons	L. G. DeWitt	72	75 Chev	170	8,975
4. Cale Yarborough	Junior Johnson	11	75 Chev	497	7,050
5. Bruce Hill	Bruce Hill	47	75 Chev	496	3,725

1976 Winston Cup GN Race No. 12 Mason-Dixon 500
May 16, 1976 Average Speed: 115.436

Driver	Owner	Car #	Make	Laps	Winnings
1. Benny Parsons	L. G. DeWitt	72	Chev	500	18,890
2. David Pearson	Wood Brothers	21	Merc	500	11,190
3. Dave Marcis	Nord Krauskopf	71	Dodg	499	9,620
4. Bobby Allison	Roger Penske	2	Merc	497	7,360
5. Buddy Baker	Bud Moore	15	Ford	495	6,525

1976 Winston Cup GN Race No. 24 Delaware 500
September 19, 1976 Average Speed: 115.740

Driver	Owner	Car #	Make	Laps	Winnings
1. Cale Yarborough	Junior Johnson	11	Chev	500	18,075
2. Richard Petty	Petty Enterprises	43	Dodg	500	14,990
3. David Pearson	Wood Brothers	21	Merc	498	7,620
4. Bobby Allison	Roger Penske	2	Merc	496	7,285
5. Buddy Baker	Bud Moore	15	Ford	493	6,525

1977 Winston Cup GN Race No. 12 Mason-Dixon 500
May 15, 1977 Average Speed: 123.327

Driver	Owner	Car #	Make	Laps	Winnings
1. Cale Yarborough	Junior Johnson	11	Chev	500	17,175
2. David Pearson	Wood Brothers	21	Merc	500	9,600
3. Richard Petty	Petty Enterprises	43	Dodg	499	9,830
4. Darrell Waltrip	DiGard	88	Chev	496	7,870
5. Dick Brooks	Junie Donlavey	90	Ford	496	5,250

1977 Winston Cup GN Race No. 24 Delaware 500
September 18, 1977 Average Speed: 114.708

Driver	Owner	Car #	Make	Laps	Winnings
1. Benny Parsons	L. G. DeWitt	72	Chev	500	15,675
2. David Pearson	Wood Brothers	21	Merc	500	9,600
3. Cale Yarborough	Junior Johnson	11	Chev	499	10,925
4. Donnie Allison	Hoss Ellington	1	Chev	498	3,900
5. Darrell Waltrip	DiGard	88	Chev	497	6,400

1978 Winston Cup GN Race No. 11 Mason-Dixon 500
May 21, 1978 Average Speed: 114.664

Driver	Owner	Car #	Make	Laps	Winnings
1. David Pearson	Wood Brothers	21	Merc	500	16,600
2. Cale Yarborough	Junior Johnson	11	Olds	500	15,100
3. Lennie Pond	Harry Ranier	54	Chev	499	8,200
4. Benny Parsons	L. G. DeWitt	72	Chev	498	8,000
5. Neil Bonnett	Jim Stacy	5	Dodg	497	6,500

1978 Winston Cup GN Race No. 24 Delaware 500
September 17, 1978 Average Speed: 119.323

Driver	Owner	Car #	Make	Laps	Winnings
1. Bobby Allison	Bud Moore	15	Ford	500	19,500
2. Cale Yarborough	Junior Johnson	11	Olds	500	15,100
3. Buddy Baker	M. C. Anderson	27	Chev	499	8,700
4. David Pearson	Wood Brothers	21	Merc	498	4,600
5. Darrell Waltrip	DiGard	88	Chev	497	7,000

1979 Winston Cup GN Race No. 12 Mason-Dixon 500
May 20, 1979 Average Speed: 111.269

Driver	Owner	Car #	Make	Laps	Winnings
1. Neil Bonnett	Wood Brothers	21	Merc	500	17,750
2. Cale Yarborough	Junior Johnson	11	Chev	500	14,800
3. Buddy Baker	Harry Ranier	28	Chev	498	10,650
4. Bobby Allison	Bud Moore	15	Ford	498	8,100
5. Dale Earnhardt	Rod Osterlund	2	Chev	497	7,750

1979 Winston Cup GN Race No. 25 CRC Chemicals 500
September 16, 1979 Average Speed: 114.366

Driver	Owner	Car #	Make	Laps	Winnings
1. Richard Petty	Petty Enterprises	43	Chev	500	21,650
2. Donnie Allison	Hoss Ellington	1	Chev	500	11,350
3. Cale Yarborough	Junior Johnson	11	Chev	500	11,250
4. Buddy Baker	Harry Ranier	28	Chev	499	4,700
5. Joe Millikan	L. G. DeWitt	72	Chev	499	7,500

1980 Winston Cup GN Race No. 12 Mason-Dixon 500
May 18, 1980 Average Speed: 113.866

Driver	Owner	Car #	Make	Laps	Winnings
1. Bobby Allison	Bud Moore	15	Ford	500	21,900
2. Richard Petty	Petty Enterprises	43	Chev	500	16,775
3. Buddy Baker	Harry Ranier	28	Chev	497	7,800
4. Harry Gant	Jack Beebe	47	Chev	495	7,530
5. Terry Labonte	Billy Hagan	44	Chev	494	6,255

1980 Winston Cup GN Race No. 25 CRC Chemicals 500
September 14, 1980 Average Speed: 116.024

Driver	Owner	Car #	Make	Laps	Winnings
1. Darrell Waltrip	DiGard	88	Chev	500	22,900
2. Harry Gant	Jack Beebe	47	Chev	500	12,930
3. Buddy Baker	Harry Ranier	28	Chev	500	8,150
4. Cale Yarborough	Junior Johnson	11	Chev	499	10,700
5. Benny Parsons	M. C. Anderson	27	Chev	499	8,425

Dover Downs Int'l Speedway *continued*

1981 Winston Cup GN Race No. 12 Mason-Dixon 500
May 17, 1981 Average Speed: 116.595

Driver	Owner	Car #	Make	Laps	Winnings
1. Jody Ridley	Junie Donlavey	90	Ford	500	22,560
2. Bobby Allison	Harry Ranier	28	Buick	500	16,725
3. Dale Earnhardt	Rod Osterlund	2	Pont	499	15,125
4. D. K. Ulrich	D. K. Ulrich	99	Buick	491	7,160
5. Ricky Rudd	DiGard	88	Buick	490	9,450

1981 Winston Cup GN Race No. 25 CRC Chemicals 500
September 20, 1981 Average Speed: 119.561

Driver	Owner	Car #	Make	Laps	Winnings
1. Neil Bonnett	Wood Brothers	21	Ford	500	19,000
2. Darrell Waltrip	Junior Johnson	11	Buick	499	16,025
3. Bobby Allison	Harry Ranier	28	Buick	499	13,000
4. Ron Bouchard	Jack Beebe	47	Buick	495	9,060
5. Ricky Rudd	DiGard	88	Chev	495	11,375

1982 Winston Cup GN Race No. 11 Mason-Dixon 500
May 16, 1982 Average Speed: 120.136

Driver	Owner	Car #	Make	Laps	Winnings
1. Bobby Allison	DiGard	88	Chev	500	25,350
2. Dave Marcis	Dave Marcis	71	Chev	497	14,605
3. Dale Earnhardt	Bud Moore	15	Ford	497	15,700
4. Terry Labonte	Billy Hagan	44	Chev	496	8,305
5. Mark Martin	Bo Reeder	02	Buick	496	7,710

1982 Winston Cup GN Race No. 24 CRC Chemicals 500
September 19, 1982 Average Speed: 107.642

Driver	Owner	Car #	Make	Laps	Winnings
1. Darrell Waltrip	Junior Johnson	11	Buick	500	29,600
2. Kyle Petty	Petty Enterprises	42	Pont	500	11,500
3. Bill Elliott	Harry Melling	9	Ford	500	8,400
4. Geoff Bodine	Cliff Stewart	50	Pont	500	12,650
5. Benny Parsons	Johnny Hayes	55	Buick	496	4,150

1983 Winston Cup GN Race No. 10 Mason-Dixon 500
May 15, 1983 Average Speed: 114.847

Driver	Owner	Car #	Make	Laps	Winnings
1. Bobby Allison	DiGard	22	Buick	500	28,500
2. Darrell Waltrip	Junior Johnson	11	Chev	500	20,425
3. Joe Ruttman	Ron Benfield	98	Buick	499	13,565
4. Bill Elliott	Harry Melling	9	Ford	498	8,655
5. Buddy Baker	Wood Brothers	21	Ford	497	4,550

1983 Winston Cup GN Race No. 24 Budweiser 500
September 18, 1983 Average Speed: 116.077

Driver	Owner	Car #	Make	Laps	Winnings
1. Bobby Allison	DiGard	22	Buick	500	30,985
2. Geoff Bodine	Cliff Stewart	88	Pont	500	16,190
3. Tim Richmond	Raymond Beadle	27	Pont	500	11,565
4. Terry Labonte	Billy Hagan	44	Chev	499	10,470
5. Darrell Waltrip	Junior Johnson	11	Chev	499	14,335

1984 Winston Cup GN Race No. 11 Budweiser 500
May 20, 1984 Average Speed: 118.717

Driver	Owner	Car #	Make	Laps	Winnings
1. Richard Petty	Mike Curb	43	Pont	500	28,105
2. Tim Richmond	Raymond Beadle	27	Pont	500	19,220
3. Terry Labonte	Billy Hagan	44	Chev	500	13,075
4. Bill Elliott	Harry Melling	9	Ford	500	13,250
5. Dale Earnhardt	Richard Childress	3	Chev	499	11,600

1984 Winston Cup GN Race No. 24 Delaware 500
September 16, 1984 Average Speed: 111.856

Driver	Owner	Car #	Make	Laps	Winnings
1. Harry Gant	Hal Needham	33	Chev	500	40,005
2. Terry Labonte	Billy Hagan	44	Chev	500	17,870
3. Ricky Rudd	Bud Moore	15	Ford	498	17,200
4. Dave Marcis	Bob Rahilly & Butch Mock	75	Pont	497	15,020
5. Dale Earnhardt	Richard Childress	3	Chev	497	11,710

1985 Winston Cup GN Race No. 10 Budweiser 500
May 19, 1985 Average Speed: 123.094

Driver	Owner	Car #	Make	Laps	Winnings
1. Bill Elliott	Harry Melling	9	Ford	500	44,500
2. Harry Gant	Hal Needham	33	Chev	499	29,950
3. Kyle Petty	Wood Brothers	7	Ford	499	19,055
4. Ricky Rudd	Bud Moore	15	Ford	498	15,375
5. Darrell Waltrip	Junior Johnson	11	Chev	497	15,975

1985 Winston Cup GN Race No. 22 Delaware 500
September 15, 1985 Average Speed: 120.538

Driver	Owner	Car #	Make	Laps	Winnings
1. Harry Gant	Hal Needham	33	Chev	501	44,950
2. Darrell Waltrip	Junior Johnson	11	Chev	500	29,750
3. Ricky Rudd	Bud Moore	15	Ford	499	31,450
4. Bobby Allison	Bobby Allison	22	Ford	496	9,975
5. Neil Bonnett	Junior Johnson	12	Chev	496	14,275

1986 Winston Cup Race No. 10 Budweiser 500
May 18, 1986 Average Speed: 115.009

Driver	Owner	Car #	Make	Laps	Winnings
1. Geoff Bodine	Rick Hendrick	5	Chev	500	51,700
2. Bobby Allison	Stavola Brothers	22	Buick	500	29,150
3. Dale Earnhardt	Richard Childress	3	Chev	499	24,900
4. Ricky Rudd	Bud Moore	15	Ford	498	18,875
5. Darrell Waltrip	Junior Johnson	11	Chev	498	18,975

1986 Winston Cup Race No. 23 Delaware 500
September 14, 1986 Average Speed: 114.329

Driver	Owner	Car #	Make	Laps	Winnings
1. Ricky Rudd	Bud Moore	15	Ford	500	51,500
2. Neil Bonnett	Junior Johnson	12	Chev	500	30,800
3. Kyle Petty	Wood Brothers	7	Ford	500	22,850
4. Buddy Baker	Buddy Baker & Danny Schiff	88	Olds	499	8,975
5. Dave Marcis	Dave Marcis	71	Chev	498	12,830

1987 Winston Cup Race No. 11 Budweiser 500
May 31, 1987 Average Speed: 112.958

Driver	Owner	Car #	Make	Laps	Winnings
1. Davey Allison	Harry Ranier	28	Ford	500	46,600
2. Bill Elliott	Harry Melling	9	Ford	500	35,575
3. Terry Labonte	Junior Johnson	11	Chev	499	25,575
4. Dale Earnhardt	Richard Childress	3	Chev	498	20,775
5. Benny Parsons	Rick Hendrick	35	Chev	498	18,025

1987 Winston Cup Race No. 23 Delaware 500
September 20, 1987 Average Speed: 124.706

Driver	Owner	Car #	Make	Laps	Winnings
1. Ricky Rudd	Bud Moore	15	Ford	500	54,550
2. Davey Allison	Harry Ranier	28	Ford	500	25,875
3. Neil Bonnett	Bob Rahilly & Butch Mock	75	Pont	500	21,335
4. Bill Elliott	Harry Melling	9	Ford	500	19,375
5. Sterling Marlin	Billy Hagan	44	Olds	500	17,620

Dover Downs Int'l Speedway *continued*

1988 Winston Cup Race No. 11 Budweiser 500
June 5, 1988 Average Speed: 118.726

Driver	Owner	Car #	Make	Laps	Winnings
1. Bill Elliott	Harry Melling	9	Ford	500	53,000
2. Morgan Shepherd	Hal Needham	33	Chev	500	29,300
3. Rusty Wallace	Raymond Beadle	27	Pont	500	26,350
4. Lake Speed	Lake Speed	83	Olds	499	13,550
5. Davey Allison	Harry Ranier	28	Ford	499	20,150

1988 Winston Cup Race No. 23 Delaware 500
September 18, 1988 Average Speed: 109.349

Driver	Owner	Car #	Make	Laps	Winnings
1. Bill Elliott	Harry Melling	9	Ford	500	56,400
2. Dale Earnhardt	Richard Childress	3	Chev	500	37,450
3. Rusty Wallace	Raymond Beadle	27	Pont	500	26,200
4. Davey Allison	Harry Ranier	28	Ford	500	21,600
5. Geoff Bodine	Rick Hendrick	5	Chev	500	16,250

1989 Winston Cup Race No. 11 Budweiser 500
June 4, 1989 Average Speed: 121.670

Driver	Owner	Car #	Make	Laps	Winnings
1. Dale Earnhardt	Richard Childress	3	Chev	500	59,350
2. Mark Martin	Jack Roush	6	Ford	500	38,950
3. Ken Schrader	Rick Hendrick	25	Chev	500	36,525
4. Terry Labonte	Junior Johnson	11	Ford	500	18,425
5. Rusty Wallace	Raymond Beadle	27	Pont	500	20,975

1989 Winston Cup Race No. 23 Peak Performance 500
September 17, 1989 Average Speed: 122.909

Driver	Owner	Car #	Make	Laps	Winnings
1. Dale Earnhardt	Richard Childress	3	Chev	500	59,950
2. Mark Martin	Jack Roush	6	Ford	500	35,540
3. Ken Schrader	Rick Hendrick	25	Chev	500	25,875
4. Bill Elliott	Harry Melling	9	Ford	499	23,125
5. Ricky Rudd	Kenny Bernstein	26	Buick	498	18,375

1990 Winston Cup Series Race No. 11
June 3, 1990 Average Speed: 123.960

Driver	Owner	Car #	Make	Laps	Winnings
1. Derrike Cope	Bob Whitcomb	10	Chev	500	55,050
2. Ken Schrader	Rick Hendrick	25	Chev	500	34,575
3. Dick Trickle	Cale Yarborough	66	Pont	500	29,125
4. Mark Martin	Jack Roush	6	Ford	500	23,575
5. Sterling Marlin	Billy Hagan	94	Olds	500	16,325

1990 Winston Cup Series Race No. 23 Peak AntiFreeze 500
September 16, 1990 Average Speed: 125.945

Driver	Owner	Car #	Make	Laps	Winnings
1. Bill Elliott	Harry Melling	9	Ford	500	83,100
2. Mark Martin	Jack Roush	6	Ford	500	35,325
3. Dale Earnhardt	Richard Childress	3	Chev	500	29,375
4. Harry Gant	Leo Jackson	33	Olds	499	19,425
5. Michael Waltrip	Chuck Rider	30	Pont	499	16,825

1991 Winston Cup Series Race No. 11 Budweiser 500
June 2, 1991 Average Speed: 120.152

Driver	Owner	Car #	Make	Laps	Winnings
1. Ken Schrader	Rick Hendrick	25	Chev	500	64,800
2. Dale Earnhardt	Richard Childress	3	Chev	500	44,275
3. Harry Gant	Leo Jackson	33	Olds	500	28,800
4. Ernie Irvan	Larry McClure	4	Chev	500	21,750
5. Mark Martin	Jack Roush	6	Ford	500	23,325

1991 Winston Cup Series Race No. 23 Peak AntiFreeze 500
September 15, 1991 Average Speed: 110.179

Driver	Owner	Car #	Make	Laps	Winnings
1. Harry Gant	Leo Jackson	33	Olds	500	67,100
2. Geoff Bodine	Junior Johnson	11	Ford	499	42,225
3. Morgan Shepherd	Bud Moore	15	Ford	499	31,250
4. Hut Stricklin	Bobby Allison	12	Buick	499	20,350
5. Michael Waltrip	Chuck Rider	30	Pont	498	17,625

1992 Winston Cup Race No. 11 Budweiser 500
May 31, 1992 Average Speed: 109.456

Driver	Owner	Car #	Make	Laps	Winnings
1. Harry Gant	Leo Jackson	33	Olds	500	65,145
2. Dale Earnhardt	Richard Childress	3	Chev	500	43,720
3. Rusty Wallace	Roger Penske	2	Pont	499	25,795
4. Ernie Irvan	Larry McClure	4	Chev	499	29,445
5. Darrell Waltrip	Darrell Waltrip	17	Chev	499	25,140

1992 Winston Cup Race No. 23 Peak AntiFreeze 500
September 20, 1992 Average Speed: 115.289

Driver	Owner	Car #	Make	Laps	Winnings
1. Ricky Rudd	Rick Hendrick	5	Chev	500	64,965
2. Bill Elliott	Junior Johnson	11	Ford	500	51,260
3. Kyle Petty	Felix Sabates	42	Pont	500	27,310
4. Davey Allison	Robert Yates	28	Ford	499	29,410
5. Morgan Shepherd	Wood Brothers	21	Ford	498	21,980

1993 Winston Cup Series Race No. 12 Budweiser 500
June 6, 1993 Average Speed: 105.600

Driver	Owner	Car #	Make	Laps	Winnings
1. Dale Earnhardt	Richard Childress	3	Chev	500	68,030
2. Dale Jarrett	Joe Gibbs	18	Chev	500	42,435
3. Davey Allison	Robert Yates	28	Ford	500	38,240
4. Mark Martin	Jack Roush	6	Ford	500	28,100
5. Ken Schrader	Rick Hendrick	25	Chev	500	25,330

1993 Winston Cup Series Race No. 24 SplitFire Spark Plug 500
September 19, 1993 Average Speed: 100.334

Driver	Owner	Car #	Make	Laps	Winnings
1. Rusty Wallace	Roger Penske	2	Pont	500	77,645
2. Ken Schrader	Rick Hendrick	25	Chev	500	53,115
3. Darrell Waltrip	Darrell Waltrip	17	Chev	500	38,410
4. Dale Jarrett	Joe Gibbs	18	Chev	500	31,035
5. Harry Gant	Leo Jackson	33	Chev	500	27,830

1994 Winston Cup Series Race No. 12 Budweiser 500
June 6, 1994 Average Speed: 102.529

Driver	Owner	Car #	Make	Laps	Winnings
1. Rusty Wallace	Roger Penske	2	Ford	500	70,605
2. Ernie Irvan	Robert Yates	28	Ford	500	54,830
3. Ken Schrader	Rick Hendrick	25	Chev	500	35,605
4. Mark Martin	Jack Roush	6	Ford	500	29,765
5. Jeff Gordon	Rick Hendrick	24	Chev	500	33,570

1994 Winston Cup Series Race No. 25 SplitFire Spark Plug 500
September 18, 1994 Average Speed: 112.556

Driver	Owner	Car #	Make	Laps	Winnings
1. Rusty Wallace	Roger Penske	2	Ford	500	55,055
2. Dale Earnhardt	Richard Childress	3	Chev	500	47,980
3. Darrell Waltrip	Darrell Waltrip	17	Chev	500	36,705
4. Ken Schrader	Rick Hendrick	25	Chev	500	32,965
5. Geoff Bodine	Geoff Bodine	7	Ford	500	31,520

Dover Downs Int'l Speedway *continued*

1995 Winston Cup Series Race No. 12 Miller Genuine Draft 500
June 4, 1995 Average Speed: 119.880

Driver	Owner	Car #	Make	Laps	Winnings
1. Kyle Petty	Felix Sabates	42	Pont	500	77,655
2. Bobby Labonte	Joe Gibbs	18	Chev	500	61,555
3. Ted Musgrave	Jack Roush	16	Ford	500	43,305
4. Hut Stricklin	Kenny Bernstein	26	Ford	500	35,615
5. Dale Earnhardt	Richard Childress	3	Chev	500	45,545

1995 Winston Cup Series Race No. 25 MBNA 500
September 17, 1995 Average Speed: 124.740

Driver	Owner	Car #	Make	Laps	Winnings
1. Jeff Gordon	Rick Hendrick	24	Chev	500	74,655
2. Bobby Hamilton	Petty Enterprises	43	Pont	500	62,505
3. Rusty Wallace	Roger Penske	2	Ford	500	46,905
4. Joe Nemechek	Joe Nemechek	87	Chev	500	34,465
5. Dale Earnhardt	Richard Childress	3	Chev	500	40,970

1996 Winston Cup Series Race No. 12 Miller 500
June 2, 1996 Average Speed: 122.741

Driver	Owner	Car #	Make	Laps	Winnings
1. Jeff Gordon	Rick Hendrick	24	Chev	500	138,730
2. Terry Labonte	Rick Hendrick	5	Chev	500	57,480
3. Dale Earnhardt	Richard Childress	3	Chev	500	60,080
4. Ernie Irvan	Robert Yates	28	Ford	500	42,440
5. Bobby Labonte	Joe Gibbs	18	Chev	499	42,295

1996 Winston Cup Series Race No. 25 MBNA 500
September 15, 1996 Average Speed: 105.646

Driver	Owner	Car #	Make	Laps	Winnings
1. Jeff Gordon	Rick Hendrick	24	Chev	500	153,630
2. Rusty Wallace	Roger Penske	2	Ford	500	54,580
3. Dale Jarrett	Robert Yates	88	Ford	500	40,880
4. Bobby Labonte	Joe Gibbs	18	Chev	500	50,390
5. Mark Martin	Jack Roush	6	Ford	500	48,820

Florida

Beach & Road Course
Daytona Beach, FL
4.17-mile Beach & Road Course

4.1-mile sand and paved course, utilizing highway A-1-A and the beachfront at south tip of Daytona Beach in Ponce Inlet. First Beach-Road course built in 1936 (near Daytona Beach Shores), and later moved south due to beachfront development. First NASCAR Winston Cup (then Strictly Stock) race staged on 7/10/49 (won by Red Byron). Final auto racing event staged on 2/23/58 (won by Paul Goldsmith). Track continued to present annual motorcycle races through 1960. Concrete blocks that held the South Turn grandstand are still in the ground today. The South Turn is still recognizable today, and Brewster's Restaurant is currently located at the old North Turn.

Winston Cup Starts
Buck Baker   10
Tim Flock   10
Curtis Turner   10

Winston Cup Victories
Tim Flock   2
Marshall Teague   2

Winston Cup Poles
Tim Flock   3

Winston Cup Money
Tim Flock $9,360

Most Cars Started
76—February 26, 1956

Fewest Cars Started
28—July 10, 1949

Narrowest Margin of Victory
5 car lengths—February 23, 1958

Slowest Race
80.883 MPH—July 10, 1949

Race Record
101.541 MPH—February 17, 1957

Most Cautions
2—February 26, 1956

Most Race Leaders
2—July 10, 1949
2—February 5, 1950
2—February 11, 1951
2—February 10, 1952
2—February 15, 1953
2—February 21, 1954
2—February 26, 1956
2—February 17, 1957

Most Cars Running at Finish
47—February 21, 1954

1949 Strictly Stock Race No. 2
July 10, 1949 Average Speed: 80.883

Driver	Owner	Car #	Make	Laps	Winnings
1. Red Byron	Raymond Parks	22	49 Olds	40	2,000
2. Tim Flock	Buddy Elliott	90	49 Olds	40	1,000
3. Frank Mundy	Sam Rice	5	49 Olds	40	500
4. Joe Littlejohn	Frank Christian	7	49 Olds	40	300
5. Bill Blair	R. B. McIntosh	44	49 Linc	40	200

1950 Grand National Race No. 1
February 5, 1950 Average Speed: 89.894

Driver	Owner	Car #	Make	Laps	Winnings
1. Harold Kite	Harold Kite	21	49 Linc	48	1,500
2. Red Byron	Raymond Parks	22	50 Olds	48	1,000
3. Lloyd Moore	Julian Buesink	59	49 Linc	48	600
4. Al Gross	Hans Winter	88	50 Olds	48	550
5. J. C. Van Landingham	J. C. Van Landingham	35	50 Buick	48	450

1951 Grand National Race No. 1
February 11, 1951 Average Speed: 82.328

Driver	Owner	Car #	Make	Laps	Winnings
1. Marshall Teague	Marshall Teague	6	51 Huds	39	1,500
2. Tim Flock	Sam Knox	91	50 Linc	—	1,000
3. Fonty Flock	Frank Christian	14	50 Olds	—	600
4. Bill Blair	Bill Blair	41.5	49 Olds	—	550
5. Buck Baker	Griffin Motors	87	50 Olds	—	450

1952 Grand National Race No. 2
February 10, 1952 Average Speed: 85.612

Driver	Owner	Car #	Make	Laps	Winnings
1. Marshall Teague	Marshall Teague	6	52 Huds	37	1,500
2. Herb Thomas	Marshall Teague	92	52 Huds	37	1,000
3. Pat Kirkwood	Pat Kirkwood	99	51 Chrys	37	600
4. Fonty Flock	Frank Christian	14	51 Olds	—	550
5. Gober Sosebee	Gober Sosebee	51	51 Olds	—	450

1953 Grand National Race No. 2
February 15, 1953 Average Speed: 89.789

Driver	Owner	Car #	Make	Laps	Winnings
1. Bill Blair	Bill Blair	2	53 Olds	39	1,500
2. Fonty Flock	Frank Christian	14	53 Olds	39	1,000
3. Tommy Thompson	Tommy Thompson	40	53 Linc	39	800
4. Herb Thomas	Herb Thomas	92	53 Huds	39	600
5. Tim Flock	Ted Chester	91	52 Huds	39	500

1954 Grand National Race No. 2
February 21, 1954 Average Speed: 89.108

Driver	Owner	Car #	Make	Laps	Winnings
1. Lee Petty	Petty Enterprises	42	54 Chrys	39	1,700
2. Buck Baker	Griffin Motors	87	53 Olds	39	1,325
3. Curtis Turner	Frank Christian	14	54 Olds	39	900
4. Dick Rathmann	John Ditz	3	54 Huds	38	625
5. Bill Blair	Bill Blair	2	54 Olds	38	475

1955 Grand National Race No. 4
February 27, 1955 Average Speed: 91.999

Driver	Owner	Car #	Make	Laps	Winnings
1. Tim Flock	Carl Kiekhaefer	300	55 Chrys	39	2,350
2. Lee Petty	Petty Enterprises	42	55 Chrys	39	1,600
3. Ray Duhigg	J. O. Goode	24	55 Buick	39	1,000
4. Curtis Turner	Raymond Parks	99	55 Olds	39	800
5. Fonty Flock	Frank Christian	14	55 Olds	39	625

1956 Grand National Race No. 6
February 26, 1956 Average Speed: 90.657

Driver	Owner	Car #	Make	Laps	Winnings
1. Tim Flock	Carl Kiekhaefer	300A	56 Chrys	37	4,025
2. Billy Myers	Bill Stroppe	14W	56 Merc	37	2,375
3. Ralph Moody	Pete DePaolo	12	56 Ford	37	1,450
4. Jimmie Lewallen	Ernest Woods	88	56 Olds	—	900
5. Jim Reed	Jim Reed	7	56 Chev	—	700

Beach & Road Course *continued*

1957 Grand National Race No. 4
February 17, 1957 Average Speed: 101.541

Driver	Owner	Car #	Make	Laps	Winnings
1. Cotton Owens	Ray Nichels	6	57 Pont	39	4,250
2. Johnny Beauchamp	Hugh Babb	50	57 Chev	39	2,450
3. Fonty Flock	Bill Stroppe	18	57 Merc	—	1,500
4. Buck Baker	Hugh Babb	87	57 Chev	—	900
5. Marvin Panch	Pete DePaolo	98	57 Ford	—	700

1958 Grand National Race No. 2
February 23, 1958 Average Speed: 101.113

Driver	Owner	Car #	Make	Laps	Winnings
1. Paul Goldsmith	Smokey Yunick	3	58 Pont	39	4,550
2. Curtis Turner	Holman-Moody	26	58 Ford	39	2,600
3. Jack Smith	Jack Smith	47	57 Pont	39	1,575
4. Joe Weatherly	Holman-Moody	12	58 Ford	39	900
5. Gwyn Staley	Buck Baker	187	57 Chev	38	700

Daytona Int'l Speedway
Daytona Beach, FL
2.5-mile Superspeedway

2.5-mile high-banked speedway opened in February 1959, and was the first ultra-fast speedway in NASCAR circuit. First race staged on 2/20/59 (Convertible race won by Shorty Rollins). The first Daytona 500 (originally named the International Sweepstakes 500) was won by Lee Petty on 2/22/59. The road course is set in the infield, site of the 24 Hours of Daytona. Track is banked 31 degrees. When asked why the degree of banking was set at 31, founder Bill France said, "Because they couldn't lay asphalt any steeper." Just prior to opening, driver Jimmy Thompson offered his assessment of the new facility, "There have been other tracks that separated the men from the boys. This is the track that will separate the brave from the weak after the boys are gone."

Winston Cup Starts
Richard Petty   74

Winston Cup Victories
Richard Petty   10

Winston Cup Poles
Cale Yarborough   13

Winston Cup Money
Dale Earnhardt $2,119,261

Most Cars Started
68—February 14, 1960 Daytona 500

Fewest Cars Started
21—February 12, 1965
(40-lap race)

Narrowest Margin of Victory
0.008 seconds July 2, 1994 Pepsi 400

Slowest Race
111.076 MPH—February 12, 1965
(40-lap race)

Race Record
183.295 MPH—February 19, 1970

Most Cautions
12—July 1, 1989 Pepsi 400

Most Race Leaders
16—February 17, 1974 Daytona 500

Most Cars Running at Finish
38—February 14, 1960 Daytona 500
38—July 1, 1995 Pepsi 400
38—July 6, 1996 Pepsi 400

1959 Grand National Race No. 2
February 20, 1959 Average Speed: 143.198

Driver	Owner	Car #	Make	Laps	Winnings
1. Bob Welborn	W. J. Ridgeway	49	59 Chev	40	800
2. Fritz Wilson	Fritz Wilson	64	59 Ford	40	525
3. Tom Pistone	Carl Rupert	59	59 Ford	40	350
4. Joe Weatherly	E. C. Wilson	48	59 Chev	40	250
5. Eduardo Dibos	Eduardo Dibos	37	59 Ford	39	225

1959 Grand National Race No. 3 Daytona 500
February 22, 1959 Average Speed: 135.521

Driver	Owner	Car #	Make	Laps	Winnings
1. Lee Petty	Petty Enterprises	42	59 Olds	200	19,050
2. Johnny Beauchamp	Roy Burdick Gar	73	59 Ford	200	7,650
3. Charley Griffith	Charley Griffith	18	57 Pont	199	4,600
4. Cotton Owens	W. H. Watson	6	58 Pont	199	2,525
5. Joe Weatherly	E. C. Wilson	48	59 Chev	199	1,875

1959 Grand National Race No. 26 Firecracker 250
July 4, 1959 Average Speed: 140.581

Driver	Owner	Car #	Make	Laps	Winnings
1. Fireball Roberts	Jim Stephens	3	59 Pont	100	7,050
2. Joe Weatherly	Doc White	12	59 Ford	100	4,625
3. Johnny Allen	W. J. Ridgeway	22	59 Chev	99	1,925
4. Jack Smith	Jack Smith	47	59 Chev	99	1,175
5. Eduardo Dibos	Eduardo Dibos	37	59 Ford	98	725

1960 Grand National Race No. 3
February 12, 1960 Average Speed: 137.614

Driver	Owner	Car #	Make	Laps	Winnings
1. Fireball Roberts	John Hines	22	60 Pont	40	1,000
2. Cotton Owens	Cotton Owens	6	60 Pont	40	600
3. Fred Lorenzen	Fred Lorenzen	28	60 Ford	40	400
4. Joe Weatherly	Holman-Moody	12	60 Ford	40	300
5. Junior Johnson	John Masoni	27	59 Chev	40	275

1960 Grand National Race No. 4
February 12, 1960 Average Speed: 146.520

Driver	Owner	Car #	Make	Laps	Winnings
1. Jack Smith	Jack Smith	47	60 Pont	40	1,000
2. Bobby Johns	Jim Stephens	3	59 Ford	40	600
3. Jim Reed	Jim Reed	7	60 Chev	40	400
4. Rex White	Rex White	4	60 Chev	40	300
5. Bob Welborn	Bob Welborn	49	60 Chev	40	275

1960 Grand National Race No. 5 Daytona 500
February 14, 1960

Driver	Owner	Car #	Make	Laps	Winnings
1. Junior Johnson	John Masoni	27	59 Chev	200	19,600
2. Bobby Johns	Jim Stephens	3	59 Pont	200	8,600
3. Richard Petty	Petty Enterprises	43	60 Plym	200	6,450
4. Lee Petty	Petty Enterprises	42	60 Plym	200	3,650
5. Johnny Allen	Hanley Dawson	69	60 Chev	199	3,300

1960 Grand National Race No. 23 Firecracker 250
July 4, 1960 Average Speed: 146.842

Driver	Owner	Car #	Make	Laps	Winnings
1. Jack Smith	Jack Smith	47	60 Pont	100	11,500
2. Cotton Owens	Cotton Owens	6	60 Pont	100	5,100
3. Fred Lorenzen	Fred Lorenzen	28	60 Ford	99	2,600
4. Lee Petty	Petty Enterprises	42	60 Plym	99	1,525
5. Bunkie Blackburn	Spook Crawford	64	60 Ford	98	1,150

1961 Grand National Race No. 3
February 24, 1961 Average Speed: 129.711

Driver	Owner	Car #	Make	Laps	Winnings
1. Fireball Roberts	Jim Stephens	22	61 Pont	39	1,000
2. Jim Paschal	John Masoni	3	61 Pont	39	600
3. Jack Smith	Jack Smith	47	61 Pont	39	400
4. Buck Baker	Buck Baker	87	61 Chrys	39	300
5. Ned Jarrett	Bee Gee Holloway	11	61 Chev	39	275

1961 Grand National Race No. 4
February 24, 1961 Average Speed: 152.671

Driver	Owner	Car #	Make	Laps	Winnings
1. Joe Weatherly	Bud Moore	8	61 Pont	40	1,000
2. Marvin Panch	Smokey Yunick	20	60 Pont	40	600
3. Cotton Owens	Cotton Owens	6	61 Pont	40	400
4. Banjo Matthews	Banjo Matthews	94	61 Ford	39	300
5. Darel Dieringer	Ray Nichels	32	61 Pont	39	275

1961 Grand National Race No. 5 Daytona 500
February 26, 1961 Average Speed: 149.601

Driver	Owner	Car #	Make	Laps	Winnings
1. Marvin Panch	Smokey Yunick	20	60 Pont	200	21,050
2. Joe Weatherly	Bud Moore	8	61 Pont	200	9,150
3. Paul Goldsmith	Ray Nichels	31	61 Pont	200	5,900
4. Fred Lorenzen	Tubby Gonzales	80	61 Ford	198	3,825
5. Cotton Owens	Cotton Owens	6	61 Pont	198	2,975

Daytona Int'l Speedway *continued*

1961 Grand National Race No. 32 Firecracker 250
July 4, 1961 Average Speed: 154.294

Driver	Owner	Car #	Make	Laps	Winnings
1. David Pearson	John Masoni	3	Pont	100	8,450
2. Fred Lorenzen	Holman-Moody	28	61 Ford	100	4,275
3. Jack Smith	Jack Smith	46	61 Pont	99	2,700
4. Marvin Panch	Smokey Yunick	20	60 Pont	99	1,525
5. Fireball Roberts	Jim Stephens	22	61 Pont	98	1,525

1962 Grand National Race No. 3
February 16, 1962 Average Speed: 156.999

Driver	Owner	Car #	Make	Laps	Winnings
1. Fireball Roberts	Jim Stephens	22	62 Pont	40	1,000
2. Jack Smith	Jack Smith	47	62 Pont	40	600
3. Cotton Owens	Cotton Owens	6	62 Pont	40	400
4. Dan Gurney	Holman-Moody	0	62 Ford	40	300
5. Junior Johnson	Rex Lovette	27	62 Pont	40	300

1962 Grand National Race No. 4
February 16, 1962 Average Speed: 145.395

Driver	Owner	Car #	Make	Laps	Winnings
1. Joe Weatherly	Bud Moore	8	62 Pont	40	1,000
2. Nelson Stacy	Holman-Moody	29	62 Ford	40	600
3. Rex White	Rex White	4	62 Chev	40	400
4. Richard Petty	Petty Enterprises	43	62 Plym	39	300
5. Johnny Allen	Bee Gee Holloway	7	62 Chev	39	300

1962 Grand National Race No. 5 Daytona 500
February 18, 1962 Average Speed: 152.529

Driver	Owner	Car #	Make	Laps	Winnings
1. Fireball Roberts	Jim Stephens	22	62 Pont	200	24,190
2. Richard Petty	Petty Enterprises	43	62 Plym	200	10,250
3. Joe Weatherly	Bud Moore	8	62 Pont	199	7,100
4. Jack Smith	Jack Smith	47	62 Pont	199	4,025
5. Fred Lorenzen	Holman-Moody	28	62 Ford	199	2,975

1962 Grand National Race No. 29 Firecracker 250
July 4, 1962 Average Speed: 153.688

Driver	Owner	Car #	Make	Laps	Winnings
1. Fireball Roberts	Banjo Matthews	22	62 Pont	100	9,850
2. Junior Johnson	Cotton Owens	6	62 Pont	100	5,450
3. Marvin Panch	Wood Brothers	21	62 Ford	98	3,400
4. Jack Smith	Jack Smith	47	62 Pont	98	1,675
5. Jimmy Pardue	Jimmy Pardue	54	62 Pont	97	1,225

1963 Grand National Race No. 5
February 22, 1963 Average Speed: 164.083

Driver	Owner	Car #	Make	Laps	Winnings
1. Junior Johnson	Ray Fox	3	63 Chev	40	1,100
2. Paul Goldsmith	Ray Nichels	01	63 Pont	40	600
3. A. J. Foyt	Ray Nichels	02	63 Pont	40	400
4. Larry Frank	Holman-Moody	06	63 Ford	40	300
5. Dan Gurney	Dan Gurney	0	63 Ford	40	300

1963 Grand National Race No. 6
February 22, 1963 Average Speed: 162.969

Driver	Owner	Car #	Make	Laps	Winnings
1. Johnny Rutherford	Smokey Yunick	13	63 Chev	40	1,100
2. Rex White	Rex White	4	63 Chev	40	600
3. Fred Lorenzen	Holman-Moody	28	63 Ford	40	400
4. Ned Jarrett	Charles Robinson	11	63 Ford	40	300
5. Nelson Stacy	Holman-Moody	29	63 Ford	40	300

1963 Grand National Race No. 7 Daytona 500
February 24, 1963 Average Speed: 151.566

Driver	Owner	Car #	Make	Laps	Winnings
1. Tiny Lund	Wood Brothers	21	63 Ford	200	24,550
2. Fred Lorenzen	Holman-Moody	28	63 Ford	200	15,450
3. Ned Jarrett	Charles Robinson	11	63 Ford	200	8,700
4. Nelson Stacy	Holman-Moody	29	63 Ford	199	8,275
5. Dan Gurney	Holman-Moody	0	63 Ford	199	3,550

1963 Grand National Race No. 29 Firecracker 400
July 4, 1963 Average Speed: 150.927

Driver	Owner	Car #	Make	Laps	Winnings
1. Fireball Roberts	Holman-Moody	22	63 Ford	160	12,100
2. Fred Lorenzen	Holman-Moody	28	63 Ford	160	8,015
3. Marvin Panch	Wood Brothers	21	63 Ford	160	5,310
4. Darel Dieringer	Bill Stroppe	16	63 Merc	158	3,175
5. Ned Jarrett	Charles Robinson	11	63 Ford	156	1,900

1964 Grand National Race No. 6
February 21, 1964 Average Speed: 170.777

Driver	Owner	Car #	Make	Laps	Winnings
1. Junior Johnson	Ray Fox	3	64 Dodg	40	1,100
2. Buck Baker	Petty Enterprises	41	64 Plym	40	600
3. David Pearson	Cotton Owens	6	64 Dodg	40	400
4. Marvin Panch	Wood Brothers	21	64 Ford	40	300
5. Darel Dieringer	Bill Stroppe	16	64 Merc	40	300

1964 Grand National Race No. 7
February 21, 1964 Average Speed: 169.811

Driver	Owner	Car #	Make	Laps	Winnings
1. Bobby Isaac	Ray Nichels	26	64 Dodg	40	1,100
2. Jimmy Pardue	Charles Robinson	54	64 Plym	40	600
3. Richard Petty	Petty Enterprises	43	64 Plym	40	400
4. A. J. Foyt	Banjo Matthews	00	64 Ford	40	300
5. Jim Paschal	Cotton Owens	5	64 Dodg	40	300

1964 Grand National Race No. 8 Daytona 500
February 23, 1964 Average Speed: 154.334

Driver	Owner	Car #	Make	Laps	Winnings
1. Richard Petty	Petty Enterprises	43	64 Plym	200	33,300
2. Jimmy Pardue	Charles Robinson	54	64 Plym	199	11,600
3. Paul Goldsmith	Ray Nichels	25	64 Plym	198	8,600
4. Marvin Panch	Wood Brothers	21	64 Ford	198	4,350
5. Jim Paschal	Cotton Owens	5	64 Dodg	197	3,700

1964 Grand National Race No. 35 Firecracker 400
July 4, 1964 Average Speed: 151.451

Driver	Owner	Car #	Make	Laps	Winnings
1. A. J. Foyt	Ray Nichels	47	64 Dodg	160	13,000
2. Bobby Isaac	Ray Nichels	26	64 Dodg	160	8,895
3. Jimmy Pardue	Charles Robinson	54	64 Plym	160	5,430
4. Buck Baker	Ray Fox	3	64 Dodg	158	3,475
5. Jim Paschal	Petty Enterprises	41	64 Plym	158	2,200

1965 Grand National Race No. 2
February 12, 1965 Average Speed: 165.669

Driver	Owner	Car #	Make	Laps	Winnings
1. Darel Dieringer	Bud Moore	16	64 Merc	40	1,100
2. Ned Jarrett	Bondy Long	11	65 Ford	40	600
3. Bobby Johns	Holman-Moody	7	65 Ford	40	400
4. Larry Frank	Larry Frank	76	64 Ford	39	300
5. H. B. Bailey	H. B. Bailey	04	64 Pont	39	300

Daytona Int'l Speedway *continued*

1965 Grand National Race No. 3
February 12, 1965 Average Speed: 111.076

Driver	Owner	Car #	Make	Laps	Winnings
1. Junior Johnson	Rex Lovette	27	65 Ford	40	1,100
2. Fred Lorenzen	Holman-Moody	28	65 Ford	40	600
3. Marvin Panch	Wood Brothers	21	65 Ford	40	400
4. Donald Tucker	Don Snyder	74	63 Ford	38	300
5. Sam McQuagg	Betty Lilly	24	65 Ford	38	300

1965 Grand National Race No. 4 Daytona 500
February 14, 1965 Average Speed: 141.539

Driver	Owner	Car #	Make	Laps	Winnings
1. Fred Lorenzen	Holman-Moody	28	65 Ford	133	27,100
2. Darel Dieringer	Bud Moore	16	64 Merc	132	12,900
3. Bobby Johns	Holman-Moody	7	65 Ford	132	7,850
4. Earl Balmer	Bud Moore	15	64 Merc	132	4,350
5. Ned Jarrett	Bondy Long	11	65 Ford	132	3,750

1965 Grand National Race No. 29 Firecracker 400
July 4, 1965 Average Speed: 150.046

Driver	Owner	Car #	Make	Laps	Winnings
1. A. J. Foyt	Wood Brothers	41	65 Ford	160	8,500
2. Buddy Baker	Buck Baker	86	65 Plym	160	5,400
3. G. C. Spencer	G. C. Spencer	49	64 Ford	158	4,200
4. J. T. Putney	Herman Beam	19	65 Chev	153	2,525
5. Neil Castles	Buck Baker	88	64 Dodg	152	1,725

1966 Grand National Race No. 3
February 25, 1966 Average Speed: 160.427

Driver	Owner	Car #	Make	Laps	Winnings
1. Paul Goldsmith	Ray Nichels	99	65 Plym	40	1,100
2. Richard Petty	Petty Enterprises	43	66 Plym	40	600
3. Don White	Ray Nichels	07	65 Dodg	40	400
4. Marvin Panch	Wood Brothers	21	66 Ford	40	300
5. Fred Lorenzen	Holman-Moody	28	66 Ford	40	300

1966 Grand National Race No. 4
February 25, 1966 Average Speed: 153.191

Driver	Owner	Car #	Make	Laps	Winnings
1. Earl Balmer	Ray Fox	3	65 Dodg	40	1,000
2. Jim Hurtubise	Norm Nelson	56	65 Plym	40	600
3. Dick Hutcherson	Holman-Moody	29	66 Ford	40	400
4. LeeRoy Yarbrough	Jon Thorne	12	66 Dodg	40	300
5. Ned Jarrett	Bondy Long	11	66 Ford	40	500

1966 Grand National Race No. 5 Daytona 500
February 27, 1966 Average Speed: 160.627

Driver	Owner	Car #	Make	Laps	Winnings
1. Richard Petty	Petty Enterprises	43	66 Plym	198	28,150
2. Cale Yarborough	Banjo Matthews	27	66 Ford	197	12,800
3. David Pearson	Cotton Owens	6	66 Dodg	196	7,950
4. Fred Lorenzen	Holman-Moody	28	66 Ford	196	4,250
5. Sam McQuagg	Ray Nichels	98	66 Dodg	195	3,600

1966 Grand National Race No. 28 Firecracker 400
July 4, 1966 Average Speed: 153.613

Driver	Owner	Car #	Make	Laps	Winnings
1. Sam McQuagg	Ray Nichels	98	66 Dodg	160	13,600
2. Darel Dieringer	Bud Moore	16	66 Merc	160	8,870
3. Jim Paschal	Tom Friedkin	14	66 Plym	159	5,985
4. Curtis Turner	Smokey Yunick	13	66 Chev	159	3,100
5. Jim Hurtubise	Norm Nelson	56	66 Plym	158	1,550

1967 Grand National Race No. 3
February 24, 1967 Average Speed: 163.934

Driver	Owner	Car #	Make	Laps	Winnings
1. LeeRoy Yarbrough	Jon Thorne	12	67 Dodg	40	1,350
2. A. J. Foyt	Banjo Matthews	27	67 Ford	40	650
3. Paul Goldsmith	Ray Nichels	99	67 Plym	40	400
4. Buddy Baker	Ray Fox	3	67 Dodg	40	400
5. Tiny Lund	Petty Enterprises	42	66 Plym	39	300

1967 Grand National Race No. 4
February 24, 1967 Average Speed: 174.587

Driver	Owner	Car #	Make	Laps	Winnings
1. Fred Lorenzen	Holman-Moody	28	67 Ford	40	1,350
2. Darel Dieringer	Junior Johnson	26	67 Ford	40	650
3. Cale Yarborough	Wood Brothers	21	67 Ford	40	400
4. Dick Hutcherson	Bondy Long	29	67 Ford	40	300
5. Richard Petty	Petty Enterprises	43	67 Plym	40	300

1967 Grand National Race No. 5 Daytona 500
February 26, 1967 Average Speed: 146.926

Driver	Owner	Car #	Make	Laps	Winnings
1. Mario Andretti	Holman-Moody	11	67 Ford	200	48,900
2. Fred Lorenzen	Holman-Moody	28	67 Ford	200	15,950
3. James Hylton	Bud Hartje	48	65 Dodg	199	10,925
4. Tiny Lund	Petty Enterprises	42	66 Plym	198	6,675
5. Jerry Grant	Tom Friedkin	40	67 Plym	197	4,725

1967 Grand National Race No. 28 Firecracker 400
July 4, 1967 Average Speed: 143.583

Driver	Owner	Car #	Make	Laps	Winnings
1. Cale Yarborough	Wood Brothers	21	67 Ford	160	15,725
2. Dick Hutcherson	Bondy Long	29	67 Ford	160	8,395
3. Darel Dieringer	Junior Johnson	26	67 Ford	160	5,905
4. David Pearson	Holman-Moody	17	67 Ford	160	3,525
5. Bobby Isaac	Nord Krauskopf	71	67 Dodg	159	1,950

1968 Grand National Race No. 4 Daytona 500
February 25, 1968 Average Speed: 143.251

Driver	Owner	Car #	Make	Laps	Winnings
1. Cale Yarborough	Wood Brothers	21	68 Merc	200	47,250
2. LeeRoy Yarbrough	Junior Johnson	26	68 Merc	200	17,525
3. Bobby Allison	Bondy Long	29	68 Ford	200	10,150
4. Al Unser	Cotton Owens	6	68 Dodg	200	6,250
5. David Pearson	Holman-Moody	17	68 Ford	199	4,750

1968 Grand National Race No. 25 Firecracker 400
July 4, 1968 Average Speed: 167.247

Driver	Owner	Car #	Make	Laps	Winnings
1. Cale Yarborough	Wood Brothers	21	68 Merc	160	15,400
2. LeeRoy Yarbrough	Junior Johnson	98	68 Merc	158	8,545
3. David Pearson	Holman-Moody	17	68 Ford	157	5,730
4. Darel Dieringer	Mario Rossi	22	68 Plym	157	2,975
5. Tiny Lund	Bud Moore	16	68 Merc	157	1,875

1969 Grand National Race No. 4
February 20, 1969 Average Speed: 152.181

Driver	Owner	Car #	Make	Laps	Winnings
1. David Pearson	Holman-Moody	17	69 Ford	50	1,200
2. Cale Yarborough	Wood Brothers	21	69 Merc	50	800
3. Donnie Allison	Banjo Matthews	27	69 Ford	50	550
4. A. J. Foyt	Jack Bowsher	11	69 Ford	49	500
5. Benny Parsons	Russ Dawson	88	69 Ford	49	450

Daytona Int'l Speedway *continued*

1969 Grand National Race No. 5
February 20, 1969 Average Speed: 151.668

Driver	Owner	Car #	Make	Laps	Winnings
1. Bobby Isaac	Nord Krauskopf	71	69 Dodg	50	1,200
2. Charlie Glotzbach	Cotton Owens	6	69 Dodg	50	800
3. Paul Goldsmith	Ray Nichels	99	69 Dodg	50	550
4. Bobby Unser	Smokey Yunick	13	69 Ford	50	500
5. Swede Savage	Wood Brothers	41	68 Merc	50	450

1969 Grand National Race No. 6 Daytona 500
February 23, 1969 Average Speed: 157.950

Driver	Owner	Car #	Make	Laps	Winnings
1. LeeRoy Yarbrough	Junior Johnson	98	69 Ford	200	38,950
2. Charlie Glotzbach	Cotton Owens	6	69 Dodg	200	18,425
3. Donnie Allison	Banjo Matthews	27	69 Ford	199	13,275
4. A. J. Foyt	Jack Bowsher	11	69 Ford	199	5,800
5. Buddy Baker	Ray Fox	3	69 Dodg	198	10,050

1969 Grand National Race No. 28 Firecracker 400
July 4, 1969 Average Speed: 160.875

Driver	Owner	Car #	Make	Laps	Winnings
1. LeeRoy Yarbrough	Junior Johnson	98	69 Ford	160	22,175
2. Buddy Baker	Cotton Owens	6	69 Dodg	160	11,195
3. Donnie Allison	Banjo Matthews	27	69 Ford	159	6,905
4. David Pearson	Holman-Moody	17	69 Ford	156	4,050
5. Richard Petty	Petty Enterprises	43	69 Ford	156	1,950

1970 Grand National Race No. 2
February 19, 1970 Average Speed: 183.295

Driver	Owner	Car #	Make	Laps	Winnings
1. Cale Yarborough	Wood Brothers	21	69 Merc	50	1,300
2. Bobby Isaac	Nord Krauskopf	71	69 Dodg	50	800
3. LeeRoy Yarbrough	Junior Johnson	98	69 Ford	50	550
4. Donnie Allison	Banjo Matthews	27	69 Ford	50	500
5. Pete Hamilton	Petty Enterprises	40	70 Plym	50	450

1970 Grand National Race No. 3
February 19, 1970 Average Speed: 147.734

Driver	Owner	Car #	Make	Laps	Winnings
1. Charlie Glotzbach	Ray Nichels	99	69 Dodg	50	1,300
2. Buddy Baker	Cotton Owens	6	69 Dodg	50	800
3. Bobby Allison	Mario Rossi	22	69 Dodg	50	550
4. Tiny Lund	John McConnell	55	69 Dodg	49	500
5. Richard Brickhouse	Bill Ellis	14	70 Plym	49	450

1970 Grand National Race No. 4 Daytona 500
February 22, 1970 Average Speed: 149.601

Driver	Owner	Car #	Make	Laps	Winnings
1. Pete Hamilton	Petty Enterprises	40	70 Plym	200	44,850
2. David Pearson	Holman-Moody	17	69 Ford	200	17,650
3. Bobby Allison	Mario Rossi	22	69 Dodg	199	9,950
4. Charlie Glotzbach	Ray Nichels	99	69 Dodg	199	5,850
5. Bobby Isaac	Nord Krauskopf	71	69 Dodg	198	4,450

1970 Grand National Race No. 24 Firecracker 400
July 4, 1970 Average Speed: 162.235

Driver	Owner	Car #	Make	Laps	Winnings
1. Donnie Allison	Banjo Matthews	27	69 Ford	160	21,025
2. Buddy Baker	Cotton Owens	6	69 Dodg	160	10,795
3. Bobby Allison	Mario Rossi	22	69 Dodg	160	7,005
4. Charlie Glotzbach	Ray Nichels	99	69 Dodg	159	3,825
5. Dick Brooks	Dick Brooks	32	70 Plym	158	2,500

1971 Winston Cup GN Race No. 2
February 11, 1971 Average Speed: 175.029

Driver	Owner	Car #	Make	Laps	Winnings
1. Pete Hamilton	Cotton Owens	6	71 Plym	50	1,300
2. A. J. Foyt	Wood Brothers	21	69 Merc	50	800
3. Richard Petty	Petty Enterprises	43	71 Plym	50	550
4. LeeRoy Yarbrough	Junior Johnson	98	69 Merc	50	500
5. Fred Lorenzen	Ray Nichels	99	71 Plym	50	450

1971 Winston Cup GN Race No. 3
February 11, 1971 Average Speed: 168.728

Driver	Owner	Car #	Make	Laps	Winnings
1. David Pearson	Holman-Moody	17	69 Merc	50	1,200
2. Buddy Baker	Petty Enterprises	11	71 Dodg	50	800
3. Dick Brooks	Mario Rossi	22	69 Dodg	50	550
4. Bill Dennis	Junie Donlavey	90	69 Merc	50	500
5. Benny Parsons	L. G. DeWitt	72	69 Ford	50	450

1971 Winston Cup GN Race No. 4 Daytona 500
February 14, 1971 Average Speed: 144.462

Driver	Owner	Car #	Make	Laps	Winnings
1. Richard Petty	Petty Enterprises	43	71 Plym	200	45,450
2. Buddy Baker	Petty Enterprises	11	71 Dodg	200	16,100
3. A. J. Foyt	Wood Brothers	21	69 Merc	200	14,500
4. David Pearson	Holman-Moody	17	69 Merc	199	4,225
5. Fred Lorenzen	Ray Nichels	99	71 Plym	199	3,825

1971 Winston Cup GN Race No. 27 Firecracker 400
July 4, 1971 Average Speed: 161.947

Driver	Owner	Car #	Make	Laps	Winnings
1. Bobby Isaac	Nord Krauskopf	71	71 Dodg	160	16,450
2. Richard Petty	Petty Enterprises	43	71 Plym	160	8,825
3. Buddy Baker	Petty Enterprises	11	71 Dodg	160	6,325
4. Pete Hamilton	Cotton Owens	6	71 Plym	160	3,275
5. Donnie Allison	Wood Brothers	21	69 Merc	160	2,200

1972 Winston Cup GN Race No. 2 Daytona 500
February 20, 1972 Average Speed: 161.550

Driver	Owner	Car #	Make	Laps	Winnings
1. A. J. Foyt	Wood Brothers	21	71 Merc	200	45,400
2. Charlie Glotzbach	Cotton Owens	6	71 Dodg	199	16,250
3. Jim Vandiver	O. L. Nixon	31	70 Dodg	194	10,475
4. Benny Parsons	L. G. DeWitt	72	70 Merc	194	7,150
5. James Hylton	James Hylton	48	71 Ford	191	5,925

1972 Winston Cup GN Race No. 17 Firecracker 400
July 4, 1972 Average Speed: 160.821

Driver	Owner	Car #	Make	Laps	Winnings
1. David Pearson	Wood Brothers	21	71 Merc	160	15,650
2. Richard Petty	Petty Enterprises	43	72 Dodg	160	11,725
3. Bobby Allison	R. Howard & J. Johnson	12	72 Chev	160	8,925
4. Coo Coo Marlin	H. B. Cunningham	14	72 Chev	157	4,275
5. James Hylton	James Hylton	48	70 Ford	157	3,600

1973 Winston Cup GN Race No. 2 Daytona 500
February 18, 1973 Average Speed: 157.205

Driver	Owner	Car #	Make	Laps	Winnings
1. Richard Petty	Petty Enterprises	43	73 Dodg	200	36,100
2. Bobby Isaac	Bud Moore	15	73 Ford	198	17,300
3. Dick Brooks	Cotton Owens	6	73 Dodg	197	9,800
4. A. J. Foyt	Banjo Matthews	50	73 Chev	196	7,020
5. Hershel McGriff	Beryl Jackson	04	72 Plym	195	6,025

Daytona Int'l Speedway *continued*

1973 Winston Cup GN Race No. 17 Firecracker 400
July 4, 1973 Average Speed: 158.468

Driver	Owner	Car #	Make	Laps	Winnings
1. David Pearson	Wood Brothers	21	71 Merc	160	16,100
2. Richard Petty	Petty Enterprises	43	73 Dodg	160	11,875
3. Buddy Baker	Nord Krauskopf	71	73 Dodg	156	9,375
4. Gordon Johncock	Hoss Ellington	28	73 Chev	156	4,350
5. Benny Parsons	L. G. DeWitt	72	73 Chev	156	4,200

1974 Winston Cup GN Race No. 16 Firecracker 400
July 4, 1974 Average Speed: 138.310

Driver	Owner	Car #	Make	Laps	Winnings
1. David Pearson	Wood Brothers	21	73 Merc	160	17,350
2. Richard Petty	Petty Enterprises	43	74 Dodg	160	12,825
3. Cale Yarborough	Junior Johnson	11	74 Chev	160	12,187
3. Buddy Baker	Bud Moore	15	73 Ford	160	12,237
5. Bobby Allison	Roger Penske	16	74 Mata	159	4,100

1975 Winston Cup GN Race No. 16 Firecracker 400
July 4, 1975 Average Speed: 158.381

Driver	Owner	Car #	Make	Laps	Winnings
1. Richard Petty	Petty Enterprises	43	74 Dodg	160	19,935
2. Buddy Baker	Bud Moore	15	75 Ford	160	15,635
3. Dave Marcis	Nord Krauskopf	71	74 Dodg	159	11,635
4. Darrell Waltrip	Darrell Waltrip	17	75 Chev	159	8,810
5. Donnie Allison	DiGard	88	75 Chev	158	5,810

1976 Winston Cup GN Race No. 16 Firecracker 400
July 4, 1976 Average Speed: 160.966

Driver	Owner	Car #	Make	Laps	Winnings
1. Cale Yarborough	Junior Johnson	11	Chev	160	22,215
2. David Pearson	Wood Brothers	21	Merc	160	13,615
3. Bobby Allison	Roger Penske	2	Merc	160	13,245
4. A. J. Foyt	Hoss Ellington	28	Chev	159	7,440
5. Dave Marcis	Nord Krauskopf	71	Dodg	157	7,810

1977 Winston Cup GN Race No. 16 Firecracker 400
July 4, 1977 Average Speed: 142.716

Driver	Owner	Car #	Make	Laps	Winnings
1. Richard Petty	Petty Enterprises	43	Dodg	160	23,075
2. Darrell Waltrip	DiGard	88	Chev	160	16,350
3. Benny Parsons	L. G. DeWitt	72	Chev	160	12,300
4. David Pearson	Wood Brothers	21	Merc	160	6,900
5. A. J. Foyt	A. J. Foyt	51	Chev	160	4,700

1978 Winston Cup GN Race No. 16 Firecracker 400
July 4, 1978 Average Speed: 154.340

Driver	Owner	Car #	Make	Laps	Winnings
1. David Pearson	Wood Brothers	21	Merc	160	18,450
2. Cale Yarborough	Junior Johnson	11	Olds	160	18,350
3. Darrell Waltrip	DiGard	88	Chev	159	13,550
4. Richard Petty	Petty Enterprises	43	Dodg	159	10,800
5. Lennie Pond	Harry Ranier	54	Chev	158	7,350

1979 Winston Cup GN Race No. 17 Firecracker 400
July 4, 1979 Average Speed: 172.890

Driver	Owner	Car #	Make	Laps	Winnings
1. Neil Bonnett	Wood Brothers	21	Merc	160	21,705
2. Benny Parsons	M. C. Anderson	27	Olds	160	16,875
3. Dale Earnhardt	Rod Osterlund	2	Olds	160	14,980
4. Darrell Waltrip	DiGard	88	Olds	159	12,280
5. Richard Petty	Petty Enterprises	43	Olds	158	9,480

1974 Winston Cup GN Race No. 2 Daytona 500
February 17, 1974 Average Speed: 140.894

Driver	Owner	Car #	Make	Laps	Winnings
1. Richard Petty	Petty Enterprises	43	74 Dodg	200	39,650
2. Cale Yarborough	R. Howard & J. Johnson	11	74 Chev	200	21,250
3. Ramo Stott	Norris Reed	83	74 Chev	200	11,390
4. Coo Coo Marlin	H. B. Cunningham	14	73 Chev	200	8,350
5. A. J. Foyt	Banjo Matthews	50	74 Chev	199	8,465

1975 Winston Cup GN Race No. 2 Daytona 500
February 16, 1975 Average Speed: 153.649

Driver	Owner	Car #	Make	Laps	Winnings
1. Benny Parsons	L. G. DeWitt	72	75 Chev	200	43,905
2. Bobby Allison	Roger Penske	16	75 Mata	199	26,700
3. Cale Yarborough	Junior Johnson	11	75 Chev	198	21,850
4. David Pearson	Wood Brothers	21	73 Merc	198	18,150
5. Ramo Stott	Norris Reed	83	75 Chev	197	11,650

1976 Winston Cup GN Race No. 2 Daytona 500
February 15, 1976 Average Speed: 152.181

Driver	Owner	Car #	Make	Laps	Winnings
1. David Pearson	Wood Brothers	21	Merc	200	46,800
2. Richard Petty	Petty Enterprises	43	Dodg	199	35,750
3. Benny Parsons	L. G. DeWitt	72	Chev	199	23,680
4. Lennie Pond	Ronnie Elder	54	Chev	198	16,890
5. Neil Bonnett	Neil Bonnett	12	Chev	197	14,000

1977 Winston Cup GN Race No. 2 Daytona 500
February 20, 1977 Average Speed: 153.218

Driver	Owner	Car #	Make	Laps	Winnings
1. Cale Yarborough	Junior Johnson	11	Chev	200	63,700
2. Buddy Baker	Bud Moore	15	Ford	199	28,075
2. Benny Parsons	L. G. DeWitt	72	Chev	200	38,825
4. Coo Coo Marlin	H. B. Cunningham	14	Chev	198	17,825
5. Dick Brooks	Junie Donlavey	90	Ford	198	18,100

1978 Winston Cup GN Race No. 2 Daytona 500
February 19, 1978 Average Speed: 159.730

Driver	Owner	Car #	Make	Laps	Winnings
1. Bobby Allison	Bud Moore	15	Ford	200	56,300
2. Cale Yarborough	Junior Johnson	11	Olds	200	41,900
3. Benny Parsons	L. G. DeWitt	72	Olds	199	31,865
4. Ron Hutcherson	A. J. Foyt	53	Buick	199	22,250
5. Dick Brooks	Junie Donlavey	90	Merc	198	19,925

1979 Winston Cup GN Race No. 2 Daytona 500
February 18, 1979 Average Speed: 143.977

Driver	Owner	Car #	Make	Laps	Winnings
1. Richard Petty	Petty Enterprises	43	Olds	200	73,900
2. Darrell Waltrip	DiGard	88	Olds	200	59,350
3. A. J. Foyt	A. J. Foyt	51	Olds	200	38,550
4. Donnie Allison	Hoss Ellington	1	Olds	199	39,600
5. Cale Yarborough	Junior Johnson	11	Olds	199	34,525

1980 Winston Cup GN Race No. 2 Daytona 500
February 17,1980 Average Speed: 177.602

Driver	Owner	Car #	Make	Laps	Winnings
1. Buddy Baker	Harry Ranier	28	Olds	200	102,175
2. Bobby Allison	Bud Moore	15	Ford	200	54,450
3. Neil Bonnett	Wood Brothers	21	Merc	199	51,100
4. Dale Earnhardt	Rod Osterlund	2	Olds	199	36,350
5. Benny Parsons	M. C. Anderson	27	Olds	197	32,375

Daytona Int'l Speedway *continued*

1980 Winston Cup GN Race No. 17 Firecracker 400
July 4, 1980 Average Speed: 173.473

Driver	Owner	Car #	Make	Laps	Winnings
1. Bobby Allison	Bud Moore	15	Ford	160	24,805
2. David Pearson	Hoss Ellington	1	Olds	160	14,230
3. Dale Earnhardt	Rod Osterlund	2	Chev	160	16,580
4. Buddy Baker	Harry Ranier	28	Olds	160	8,880
5. Richard Petty	Petty Enterprises	43	Olds	160	12,130

1981 Winston Cup GN Race No. 17 Firecracker 400
July 4, 1981 Average Speed: 142.588

Driver	Owner	Car #	Make	Laps	Winnings
1. Cale Yarborough	M. C. Anderson	27	Buick	160	24,625
2. Harry Gant	Hal Needham	33	Buick	160	15,350
3. Richard Petty	Petty Enterprises	43	Buick	160	17,200
4. Buddy Baker	Hoss Ellington	1	Olds	160	8,765
5. Johnny Rutherford	Ron Benfield	98	Pont	160	7,075

1982 Winston Cup GN Race No. 16 Firecracker 400
July 4, 1982 Average Speed: 163.099

Driver	Owner	Car #	Make	Laps	Winnings
1. Bobby Allison	DiGard	88	Buick	160	42,100
2. Bill Elliott	Harry Melling	9	Ford	160	21,800
3. Ron Bouchard	Jack Beebe	47	Buick	160	22,500
4. Morgan Shepherd	Ron Benfield	98	Buick	160	13,030
5. David Pearson	Bobby Hawkins	03	Buick	160	8,190

1983 Winston Cup GN Race No. 16 Firecracker 400
July 4, 1983 Average Speed: 167.442

Driver	Owner	Car #	Make	Laps	Winnings
1. Buddy Baker	Wood Brothers	21	Ford	160	32,950
2. Morgan Shepherd	Jim Stacy	2	Buick	160	27,175
3. David Pearson	Bobby Hawkins	16	Chev	160	13,275
4. Ron Bouchard	Jack Beebe	47	Buick	160	13,380
5. Terry Labonte	Billy Hagan	44	Chev	160	13,545

1984 Winston Cup GN Race No. 16 Pepsi Firecracker 400
July 4, 1984 Average Speed: 171.204

Driver	Owner	Car #	Make	Laps	Winnings
1. Richard Petty	Mike Curb	43	Pont	160	43,755
2. Harry Gant	Hal Needham	33	Chev	160	25,570
3. Cale Yarborough	Harry Ranier	28	Chev	160	23,640
4. Bobby Allison	DiGard	22	Buick	160	21,850
5. Benny Parsons	Johnny Hayes	55	Chev	160	10,450

1985 Winston Cup GN Race No. 15 Pepsi Firecracker 400
July 4, 1985 Average Speed: 158.730

Driver	Owner	Car #	Make	Laps	Winnings
1. Greg Sacks	DiGard	10	Chev	160	45,350
2. Bill Elliott	Harry Melling	9	Ford	160	41,900
3. Darrell Waltrip	Junior Johnson	11	Chev	160	26,100
4. Ron Bouchard	Jack Beebe	47	Buick	160	16,730
5. Kyle Petty	Wood Brothers	7	Ford	160	15,570

1986 Winston Cup Race No. 15 Pepsi Firecracker 400
July 4, 1986 Average Speed: 131.916

Driver	Owner	Car #	Make	Laps	Winnings
1. Tim Richmond	Rick Hendrick	25	Chev	160	58,655
2. Sterling Marlin	Hoss Ellington	1	Chev	160	37,700
3. Bobby Hillin Jr.	Stavola Brothers	8	Buick	160	24,545
4. Darrell Waltrip	Junior Johnson	11	Chev	160	24,750
5. Kyle Petty	Wood Brothers	7	Ford	160	19,725

1981 Winston Cup GN Race No. 2 Daytona 500
February 15, 1981 Average Speed: 169.651

Driver	Owner	Car #	Make	Laps	Winnings
1. Richard Petty	Petty Enterprises	43	Buick	200	90,575
2. Bobby Allison	Harry Ranier	28	Pont	200	84,050
3. Ricky Rudd	DiGard	88	Olds	200	53,115
4. Buddy Baker	Hoss Ellington	1	Olds	200	35,740
5. Dale Earnhardt	Rod Osterlund	2	Pont	200	37,365

1982 Winston Cup GN Race No. 1 Daytona 500
February 14, 1982 Average Speed: 153.991

Driver	Owner	Car #	Make	Laps	Winnings
1. Bobby Allison	DiGard	88	Buick	200	120,630
2. Cale Yarborough	M. C. Anderson	27	Buick	200	70,725
3. Joe Ruttman	Jim Stacy	2	Buick	200	54,820
4. Terry Labonte	Billy Hagan	44	Buick	199	51,975
5. Bill Elliott	Harry Melling	9	Ford	198	36,125

1983 Winston Cup GN Race No. 1 Daytona 500
February 20, 1983 Average Speed: 155.979

Driver	Owner	Car #	Make	Laps	Winnings
1. Cale Yarborough	Harry Ranier	28	Pont	200	119,600
2. Bill Elliott	Harry Melling	9	Ford	200	66,425
3. Buddy Baker	Wood Brothers	21	Ford	200	59,650
4. Joe Ruttman	Ron Benfield	98	Chev	200	55,980
5. Dick Brooks	Junie Donlavey	90	Ford	199	44,545

1984 Winston Cup GN Race No. 1 Daytona 500
February 19, 1984 Average Speed: 150.994

Driver	Owner	Car #	Make	Laps	Winnings
1. Cale Yarborough	Harry Ranier	28	Chev	200	160,300
2. Dale Earnhardt	Richard Childress	3	Chev	200	81,825
3. Darrell Waltrip	Junior Johnson	11	Chev	200	68,650
4. Neil Bonnett	Junior Johnson	12	Chev	200	50,000
5. Bill Elliott	Harry Melling	9	Ford	200	58,700

1985 Winston Cup GN Race No. 1 Daytona 500
February 17, 1985 Average Speed: 172.265

Driver	Owner	Car #	Make	Laps	Winnings
1. Bill Elliott	Harry Melling	9	Ford	200	185,500
2. Lake Speed	Bob Rahilly & Butch Mock	75	Pont	200	85,705
3. Darrell Waltrip	Junior Johnson	11	Chev	199	79,350
4. Buddy Baker	Buddy Baker & Danny Schiff	88	Olds	199	53,075
5. Ricky Rudd	Bud Moore	15	Ford	199	52,900

1986 Winston Cup Race No. 1 Daytona 500
February 16, 1986 Average Speed: 148.124

Driver	Owner	Car #	Make	Laps	Winnings
1. Geoff Bodine	Rick Hendrick	5	Chev	200	192,715
2. Terry Labonte	Billy Hagan	44	Olds	200	103,240
3. Darrell Waltrip	Junior Johnson	11	Chev	200	80,515
4. Bobby Hillin Jr.	Stavola Brothers	8	Chev	200	58,975
5. Benny Parsons	Richard Jackson	55	Olds	199	47,415

1987 Winston Cup Race No. 1 Daytona 500
February 15, 1987 Average Speed: 176.263

Driver	Owner	Car #	Make	Laps	Winnings
1. Bill Elliott	Harry Melling	9	Ford	200	204,150
2. Benny Parsons	Rick Hendrick	35	Chev	200	122,420
3. Richard Petty	Petty Enterprises	43	Pont	200	76,040
4. Buddy Baker	Buddy Baker & Danny Schiff	88	Olds	200	74,450
5. Dale Earnhardt	Richard Childress	3	Chev	200	64,925

Daytona Int'l Speedway *continued*

1987 Winston Cup Race No. 15 Pepsi Firecracker 400
July 4, 1987 Average Speed: 161.074

Driver	Owner	Car #	Make	Laps	Winnings
1. Bobby Allison	Stavola Brothers	22	Buick	160	57,375
2. Buddy Baker	Buddy Baker & Danny Schiff	88	Olds	160	30,800
3. Dave Marcis	Dave Marcis	71	Chev	160	27,805
4. Darrell Waltrip	Rick Hendrick	17	Chev	160	17,470
5. Morgan Shepherd	Kenny Bernstein	26	Buick	160	17,130

1988 Winston Cup Race No. 15 Pepsi Firecracker 400
July 2, 1988 Average Speed: 163.302

Driver	Owner	Car #	Make	Laps	Winnings
1. Bill Elliott	Harry Melling	9	Ford	160	63,500
2. Rick Wilson	Larry McClure	4	Olds	160	45,825
3. Phil Parsons	Richard Jackson	55	Olds	160	22,250
4. Dale Earnhardt	Richard Childress	3	Chev	160	22,825
5. Darrell Waltrip	Rick Hendrick	17	Chev	160	25,430

1989 Winston Cup Race No. 15 Pepsi 400
July 1, 1989 Average Speed: 132.207

Driver	Owner	Car #	Make	Laps	Winnings
1. Davey Allison	Robert Yates	28	Ford	160	65,000
2. Morgan Shepherd	Bob Rahilly & Butch Mock	75	Pont	160	39,975
3. Phil Parsons	Richard Jackson	55	Olds	160	27,700
4. Bill Elliott	Harry Melling	9	Ford	160	27,750
5. Alan Kulwicki	Alan Kulwicki	7	Ford	160	19,855

1990 Winston Cup Series Race No. 15 Pepsi 400
July 7, 1990 Average Speed: 160.000

Driver	Owner	Car #	Make	Laps	Winnings
1. Dale Earnhardt	Richard Childress	3	Chev	160	72,850
2. Alan Kulwicki	Alan Kulwicki	7	Ford	160	38,700
3. Ken Schrader	Rick Hendrick	25	Chev	160	31,400
4. Terry Labonte	Richard Jackson	1	Olds	160	23,450
5. Sterling Marlin	Billy Hagan	94	Olds	160	21,250

1991 Winston Cup Series Race No. 15 Pepsi 400
July 6, 1991 Average Speed: 159.116

Driver	Owner	Car #	Make	Laps	Winnings
1. Bill Elliott	Harry Melling	9	Ford	160	75,000
2. Geoff Bodine	Junior Johnson	11	Ford	160	48,325
3. Davey Allison	Robert Yates	28	Ford	160	36,950
4. Ken Schrader	Rick Hendrick	25	Chev	160	27,450
5. Ernie Irvan	Larry McClure	4	Chev	160	36,525

1992 Winston Cup Race No. 15 Pepsi 400
July 4, 1992 Average Speed: 170.457

Driver	Owner	Car #	Make	Laps	Winnings
1. Ernie Irvan	Larry McClure	4	Chev	160	86,300
2. Sterling Marlin	Junior Johnson	22	Ford	160	50,025
3. Dale Jarrett	Joe Gibbs	18	Chev	160	37,200
4. Geoff Bodine	Bud Moore	15	Ford	160	26,075
5. Bill Elliott	Junior Johnson	11	Ford	160	26,500

1993 Winston Cup Series Race No. 15 Pepsi 400
July 3, 1993 Average Speed: 151.755

Driver	Owner	Car #	Make	Laps	Winnings
1. Dale Earnhardt	Richard Childress	3	Chev	160	75,940
2. Sterling Marlin	Stavola Brothers	8	Ford	160	46,000
3. Ken Schrader	Rick Hendrick	25	Chev	160	37,125
4. Ricky Rudd	Rick Hendrick	5	Chev	160	28,250
5. Jeff Gordon	Rick Hendrick	24	Chev	160	24,625

1988 Winston Cup Race No. 1 Daytona 500
February 14, 1988 Average Speed: 137.531

Driver	Owner	Car #	Make	Laps	Winnings
1. Bobby Allison	Stavola Brothers	12	Buick	200	202,940
2. Davey Allison	Harry Ranier	28	Ford	200	113,760
3. Phil Parsons	Richard Jackson	55	Olds	200	81,625
4. Neil Bonnett	Bob Rahilly & Butch Mock	75	Pont	200	67,290
5. Terry Labonte	Junior Johnson	11	Chev	200	62,415

1989 Winston Cup Race No. 1 Daytona 500
February 19, 1989 Average Speed: 148.466

Driver	Owner	Car #	Make	Laps	Winnings
1. Darrell Waltrip	Rick Hendrick	17	Chev	200	184,900
2. Ken Schrader	Rick Hendrick	25	Chev	200	182,700
3. Dale Earnhardt	Richard Childress	3	Chev	200	95,550
4. Geoff Bodine	Rick Hendrick	5	Chev	200	79,250
5. Phil Parsons	Richard Jackson	55	Olds	200	70,325

1990 Winston Cup Series Race No. 1 Daytona 500
February 18, 1990 Average Speed: 165.761

Driver	Owner	Car #	Make	Laps	Winnings
1. Derrike Cope	Bob Whitcomb	10	Chev	200	188,150
2. Terry Labonte	Richard Jackson	1	Olds	200	117,800
3. Bill Elliott	Harry Melling	9	Ford	200	114,100
4. Ricky Rudd	Rick Hendrick	5	Chev	200	77,050
5. Dale Earnhardt	Richard Childress	3	Chev	200	109,325

1991 Winston Cup Series Race No. 1 Daytona 500
February 19, 1991 Average Speed: 148.148

Driver	Owner	Car #	Make	Laps	Winnings
1. Ernie Irvan	Larry McClure	4	Chev	200	233,000
2. Sterling Marlin	Junior Johnson	22	Ford	200	133,925
3. Joe Ruttman	Bob Rahilly & Butch Mock	75	Olds	200	111,450
4. Rick Mast	Richard Jackson	1	Olds	200	100,900
5. Dale Earnhardt	Richard Childress	3	Chev	200	113,850

1992 Winston Cup Race No. 1 Daytona 500
February 16, 1992 Average Speed: 160.256

Driver	Owner	Car #	Make	Laps	Winnings
1. Davey Allison	Robert Yates	28	Ford	200	244,050
2. Morgan Shepherd	Wood Brothers	21	Ford	200	161,300
3. Geoff Bodine	Bud Moore	15	Ford	200	116,250
4. Alan Kulwicki	Alan Kulwicki	7	Ford	200	87,500
5. Dick Trickle	Butch Mock	75	Olds	200	78,800

1993 Winston Cup Series Race No. 1 Daytona 500
February 14, 1993 Average Speed: 154.972

Driver	Owner	Car #	Make	Laps	Winnings
1. Dale Jarrett	Joe Gibbs	18	Chev	200	238,200
2. Dale Earnhardt	Richard Childress	3	Chev	200	181,825
3. Geoff Bodine	Bud Moore	15	Ford	200	141,450
4. Hut Stricklin	Junior Johnson	27	Ford	200	95,950
5. Jeff Gordon	Rick Hendrick	24	Chev	200	111,150

1994 Winston Cup Series Race No. 1 Daytona 500
February 20, 1994 Average Speed: 156.931

Driver	Owner	Car #	Make	Laps	Winnings
1. Sterling Marlin	Larry McClure	4	Chev	200	253,275
2. Ernie Irvan	Robert Yates	28	Ford	200	190,750
3. Terry Labonte	Rick Hendrick	5	Chev	200	138,475
4. Jeff Gordon	Rick Hendrick	24	Chev	200	112,525
5. Morgan Shepherd	Wood Brothers	21	Ford	200	92,805

Daytona Int'l Speedway *continued*

1994 Winston Cup Series Race No. 15 Pepsi 400
July 2, 1994 Average Speed: 155.558

Driver	Owner	Car #	Make	Laps	Winnings
1. Jimmy Spencer	Junior Johnson	27	Ford	160	75,880
2. Ernie Irvan	Robert Yates	28	Ford	160	50,275
3. Dale Earnhardt	Richard Childress	3	Chev	160	50,050
4. Mark Martin	Jack Roush	6	Ford	160	36,575
5. Ken Schrader	Rick Hendrick	25	Chev	160	30,150

1995 Winston Cup Series Race No. 1 Daytona 500
February 19, 1995 Average Speed: 141.710

Driver	Owner	Car #	Make	Laps	Winnings
1. Sterling Marlin	Larry McClure	4	Chev	200	300,460
2. Dale Earnhardt	Richard Childress	3	Chev	200	212,250
3. Mark Martin	Jack Roush	6	Ford	200	153,700
4. Ted Musgrave	Jack Roush	16	Ford	200	111,200
5. Dale Jarrett	Robert Yates	28	Ford	200	119,855

1995 Winston Cup Series Race No. 15 Pepsi 400
July 1, 1995 Average Speed: 166.976

Driver	Owner	Car #	Make	Laps	Winnings
1. Jeff Gordon	Rick Hendrick	24	Chev	160	96,580
2. Sterling Marlin	Larry McClure	4	Chev	160	63,450
3. Dale Earnhardt	Richard Childress	3	Chev	160	66,200
4. Mark Martin	Jack Roush	6	Ford	160	43,225
5. Ted Musgrave	Jack Roush	16	Ford	160	39,075

1996 Winston Cup Series Race No. 1 Daytona 500
February 18, 1996 Average Speed: 154.308

Driver	Owner	Car #	Make	Laps	Winnings
1. Dale Jarrett	Robert Yates	88	Ford	200	360,775
2. Dale Earnhardt	Richard Childress	3	Chev	200	215,065
3. Ken Schrader	Rick Hendrick	25	Chev	200	169,547
4. Mark Martin	Jack Roush	6	Ford	200	118,840
5. Jeff Burton	Jack Roush	99	Ford	200	91,702

1996 Winston Cup Series Race No. 15 Pepsi 400
July 6, 1996 Average Speed: 161.602

Driver	Owner	Car #	Make	Laps	Winnings
1. Sterling Marlin	Larry McClure	4	Chev	117	106,565
2. Terry Labonte	Rick Hendrick	5	Chev	117	63,335
3. Jeff Gordon	Rick Hendrick	24	Chev	117	63,735
4. Dale Earnhardt	Richard Childress	3	Chev	117	97,960
5. Ernie Irvan	Robert Yates	28	Ford	117	44,210

Five Flags Speedway
Pensacola, FL
Half-mile Dirt Track

Half-mile dirt oval opened in May 1953. Only NASCAR Winston Cup (then Grand National) event run on 6/14/53 (won by Herb Thomas).
Track is currently the site of the Snowball Derby.

Winston Cup Victories
Herb Thomas   1

Winston Cup Money
Herb Thomas $1,000

Most Cars Started
18—June 14, 1953

Narrowest Margin of Victory
N/A

Race Record
63.316 MPH—June 14, 1953

Most Race Leaders
N/A

Most Cars Running at Finish
N/A

1953 Grand National Race No. 15
June 14, 1953 Average Speed: 63.316

Driver	Owner	Car #	Make	Laps	Winnings
1. Herb Thomas	Herb Thomas	92	53 Huds	140	1,000
2. Dick Rathmann	Walt Chapman	120	53 Huds	—	900
3. Lee Petty	Petty Enterprises	42	53 Dodg	—	450
4. Buck Baker	Griffin Motors	87	53 Olds	—	350
5. Tim Flock	Ted Chester	91	53 Huds	—	200

Golden Gate Speedway
Tampa, FL
.333-mile Dirt Track

Located on the Northeast side of town. The .333 mile track opened in May of 1962. Only NASCAR Winston Cup (then Grand National) race
staged on 11/11/62 (won by Richard Petty). Track closed in 1978 and re-opened in 1981. Closed for good in 1984.

Winston Cup Victories
Richard Petty   1

Winston Cup Poles
Rex White   1

Winston Cup Money
Richard Petty $780

Most Cars Started
24—November 11, 1962

Narrowest Margin of Victory
1 car length—November 11, 1962

Race Record
57.167 MPH—November 11, 1962

Most Cautions
2—November 11, 1962

Most Race Leaders
3—November 11, 1962

Most Cars Running at Finish
18—November 11, 1962

1963 Grand National Race No. 2
November 11, 1962 Average Speed: 57.167

Driver	Owner	Car #	Make	Laps	Winnings
1. Richard Petty	Petty Enterprises	43	62 Plym	200	780
2. Jim Paschal	Petty Enterprises	41	62 Plym	200	490
3. Joe Weatherly	Bud Moore	8	62 Pont	200	580
4. Jimmy Pardue	Jimmy Pardue	54	62 Pont	199	275
5. Tommy Irwin	Wood Brothers	21	62 Ford	198	240

Jacksonville Speedway Park
Jacksonville, FL
Half-mile Dirt Track

(aka Speedway Park) Half-mile dirt track opened in March 1947. First NASCAR Winston Cup (then Grand National) race held on 11/4/51 (won by Herb Thomas). Final big NASCAR race was staged on 12/1/63 (won by Wendell Scott, the only win by an African-American driver in the history of big-league NASCAR racing), and was included on 1964 championship season schedule. Track closed in 1973.

Winston Cup Starts
Buck Baker 5
Lee Petty 5

Winston Cup Victories
Lee Petty 2
Herb Thomas 2

Winston Cup Poles
Junior Johnson 1
Dick Rathmann 1
Jack Smith 1
Marshall Teague 1
Herb Thomas 1
Curtis Turner 1

Winston Cup Money
Herb Thomas $3,150

Most Cars Started
29—March 6, 1952

Fewest Cars Started
19—February 13, 1955

Narrowest Margin of Victory
N/A

Slowest Race
53.412 MPH—November 4, 1951

Race Record
69.031 MPH—February 13, 1955

Most Cautions
5—December 1, 1963

Most Race Leaders
4—November 20, 1960
4—December 1, 1963

Most Cars Running at Finish
N/A

1951 Grand National Race No. 38
November 4, 1951 Average Speed: 53.412

Driver	Owner	Car #	Make	Laps	Winnings
1. Herb Thomas	Marshall Teague	6	51 Huds	200	1,000
2. Jack Smith	Jack Smith	44	51 Huds	—	600
3. Fonty Flock	Frank Christian	14	51 Olds	—	500
4. Bill Snowden	Bill Snowden	16	51 Ford	—	400
5. Frank Mundy	Perry Smith	23	51 Stud	—	300

1952 Grand National Race No. 3
March 6, 1952 Average Speed: 55.197

Driver	Owner	Car #	Make	Laps	Winnings
1. Marshall Teague	Marshall Teague	6	52 Huds	200	1,000
2. Herb Thomas	Marshall Teague	4	52 Huds	200	700
3. Frankie Schneider		88	51 Olds	200	450
4. Tim Flock	Ted Chester	91	51 Huds	—	350
5. Tommy Moon	C. D. Wilson	157	51 Huds	—	200

1954 Grand National Race No. 3
March 7, 1954 Average Speed: 56.461

Driver	Owner	Car #	Make	Laps	Winnings
1. Herb Thomas	Herb Thomas	92	53 Huds	200	1,000
2. Fonty Flock	Frank Christian	14	53 Huds	198	650
3. Lee Petty	Petty Enterprises	42	54 Dodg	197	450
4. Joe Eubanks	Phil Oates	82	51 Huds	197	350
5. Buck Baker	Griffin Motors	87	53 Olds	194	300

1955 Grand National Race No. 3
February 13, 1955 Average Speed: 69.031

Driver	Owner	Car #	Make	Laps	Winnings
1. Lee Petty	Petty Enterprises	42	54 Chrys	200	1,000
2. Dick Rathmann	John Ditz	3	54 Huds	200	650
3. Herb Thomas	Herb Thomas	92	54 Huds	200	450
4. Buck Baker	Griffin Motors	87	54 Olds	194	350
5. Junior Johnson	B & L Motors	55	55 Olds	191	300

1961 Grand National Race No. 2
November 20, 1960 Average Speed: 64.400

Driver	Owner	Car #	Make	Laps	Winnings
1. Lee Petty	Petty Enterprises	42	60 Plym	200	800
2. Tommy Irwin	Tom Daniels	2	60 Chev	199	525
3. Rex White	Rex White	4	59 Chev	198	475
4. Richard Petty	Petty Enterprises	43	60 Plym	197	275
5. Doug Yates	Raeford Johnson	23	59 Plym	194	250

1964 Grand National Race No. 3
December 1, 1963 Average Speed: 58.252

Driver	Owner	Car #	Make	Laps	Winnings
1. Wendell Scott	Wendell Scott	34	62 Chev	202	1,000
2. Buck Baker	Buck Baker	87	63 Pont	200	600
3. Jack Smith	Jack Smith	47	63 Plym	199	400
4. Ed Livingston	Ed Livingston	68	62 Ford	195	300
5. Richard Petty	Petty Enterprises	42	63 Plym	193	275

Palm Beach Speedway
West Palm Beach, FL
Half-mile Dirt Track

(aka West Palm Beach Speedway; West Palm Beach Fairgrounds; South Florida Fairgrounds Speedway; Palm Beach County Fairgrounds; Southland Speedway) Half-mile dirt oval built in 1949. First NASCAR Winston Cup (then Grand National) race staged on 1/20/52 (won by Tim Flock). Final race staged on 3/4/56 (won by Billy Myers). Track paved in 1955, and torn down in 1984.

Winston Cup Starts Lee Petty 7	**Winston Cup Money** Herb Thomas $5,150	**Narrowest Margin of Victory** 3 car lengths—February 6, 1955	**Most Cautions** 2—January 20, 1952
Winston Cup Victories Herb Thomas 4	**Most Cars Started** 30—March 4, 1956	**Slowest Race** 56.013 MPH—February 6, 1955	**Most Race Leaders** 4—February 7, 1954
Winston Cup Poles Dick Rathmann 3	**Fewest Cars Started** 16—February 6, 1955	**Race Record** 68.990 MPH—March 4, 1956	**Most Cars Running at Finish** 19—March 4, 1956

1952 Grand National Race No. 1
January 20, 1952

Driver	Owner	Car #	Make	Laps	Winnings
1. Tim Flock	Ted Chester	91	51 Huds	200	1,025
2. Lee Petty	Petty Enterprises	42	51 Plym	—	700
3. Fonty Flock	Frank Christian	14	51 Olds	—	450
4. Frankie Schneider		88	51 Olds	—	360
5. Buddy Shuman	Buddy Shuman	17	51 Ford	—	210

1952 Grand National Race No. 34
November 30, 1952 Average Speed: 58.008

Driver	Owner	Car #	Make	Laps	Winnings
1. Herb Thomas	Herb Thomas	92	52 Huds	200	1,000
2. Fonty Flock	Frank Christian	14	52 Olds	198	700
3. Perk Brown	R. G. Shelton	22	52 Huds	196	450
4. Lee Petty	Petty Enterprises	42	51 Plym	194	350
5. Marion Edwards			50 Dodg	183	200

1953 Grand National Race No. 1
February 1, 1953 Average Speed: 60.220

Driver	Owner	Car #	Make	Laps	Winnings
1. Lee Petty	Petty Enterprises	42	53 Dodg	200	1,000
2. Jimmie Lewallen	Petty Enterprises	41	52 Plym	198	700
3. Tim Flock	Ted Chester	91	52 Huds	197	450
4. Herschel Buchanan	Herschel Buchanan	1	52 Nash	192	350
5. Don Oldenberg	Bill House	86	53 Linc	186	200

1954 Grand National Race No. 1
February 7, 1954 Average Speed: 58.938

Driver	Owner	Car #	Make	Laps	Winnings
1. Herb Thomas	Herb Thomas	92	53 Huds	200	1,600
2. Buck Baker	Griffin Motors	87	53 Olds	198	1,050
3. Lee Petty	Petty Enterprises	42	54 Dodg	198	750
4. Jim Paschal	George Hutchens	80	54 Dodg	196	350
5. Ray Duhigg	J. O. Goode	24	50 Plym	190	300

1955 Grand National Race No. 2
February 6, 1955 Average Speed: 56.013

Driver	Owner	Car #	Make	Laps	Winnings
1. Herb Thomas	Herb Thomas	92	54 Huds	200	1,000
2. Jack Choquette	George Miller	23	54 Huds	200	650
3. Buck Baker	Griffin Motors	87	54 Olds	200	450
4. Dick Rathmann	John Ditz	3	54 Huds	200	350
5. Lee Petty	Petty Enterprises	42	54 Chrys	196	300

1956 Grand National Race No. 4
December 11, 1955 Average Speed: 65.009

Driver	Owner	Car #	Make	Laps	Winnings
1. Herb Thomas	Herb Thomas	92	56 Chev	199	1,100
2. Al Keller	Al Keller	64	56 Chev	198	700
3. Billy Myers	Hugh Babb	46	55 Chev	197	475
4. Buck Baker	James Satcher	87	56 Ford	195	365
5. Lee Petty	Petty Enterprises	42	56 Dodg	193	310

1956 Grand National Race No. 7
March 4, 1956 Average Speed: 68.990

Driver	Owner	Car #	Make	Laps	Winnings
1. Billy Myers	Bill Stroppe	14W	56 Merc	199	900
2. Buck Baker	Carl Kiekhaefer	500B	56 Dodg	199	600
3. Herb Thomas	Smokey Yunick	92	56 Chev	195	425
4. Joe Weatherly	Charlie Schwam	9	56 Ford	191	335
5. Fireball Roberts	Pete DePaolo	22	56 Ford	191	290

Titusville-Cocoa Speedway
Titusville, FL
1.6-mile Paved Road Course

1.6-mile road course utilizing runways at airport. Only Winston Cup (then Grand National) race staged on 12/30/56 (counted toward 1957 season and won by Fireball Roberts). Last race run in July 1958.

Winston Cup Victories
Fireball Roberts   1

Winston Cup Poles
Paul Goldsmith   1

Winston Cup Money
Fireball Roberts $850

Most Cars Started
15—December 30, 1956

Narrowest Margin of Victory
N/A

Race Record
69.106 MPH—December 30, 1956

Most Race Leaders
2—December 30, 1956

Most Cars Running at Finish
12—December 30, 1956

1957 Grand National Race No. 3
December 30, 1956 Average Speed: 69.106

Driver	Owner	Car #	Make	Laps	Winnings
1. Fireball Roberts	Pete DePaolo	22	56 Ford	56	850
2. Curtis Turner	Pete DePaolo	C22	56 Ford	56	625
3. Marvin Panch	Pete DePaolo	98	56 Ford	56	450
4. Ralph Moody	Pete DePaolo	12	56 Ford	56	350
5. Doug Cox	John Foster	86	56 Ford	55	310

Georgia

Atlanta Motor Speedway
Hampton, GA
1.522-mile Superspeedway

(aka Atlanta Int'l Raceway) 1.522-mile banked oval opened in 1960. Originally measured as 1.5-mile oval. First NASCAR Winston Cup (then Grand National) race staged on 7/31/60 (won by Fireball Roberts). Track scheduled to open in 1959, but construction delays and bad weather forced postponement until summer of 1960.

Winston Cup Starts
Richard Petty   65

Winston Cup Victories
Dale Earnhardt   8

Winston Cup Poles
Buddy Baker   7

Winston Cup Money
Dale Earnhardt $1,308,670

Most Cars Started
46—March 26, 1961 Atlanta 500
46—June 10, 1962 Atlanta 500
46—March 17, 1963 Atlanta 500

Fewest Cars Started
35—June 7, 1964 Dixie 400

Narrowest Margin of Victory
half car length—November 4, 1971
Dixie 500

Slowest Race
101.983 MPH—June 10, 1962
Atlanta 500

Race Record
163.633 MPH—November 12, 1995
NAPA 500

Most Cautions
11—March 31, 1968 Atlanta 500
11—August 4, 1968 Dixie 500
11—November 14, 1993 Hooters 500

Most Race Leaders
15—November 20, 1988
Atlanta Journal 500

Most Cars Running at Finish
36—November 12, 1995 NAPA 500

1960 Grand National Race No. 27 Dixie 300
July 31, 1960 Average Speed: 112.652

Driver	Owner	Car #	Make	Laps	Winnings
1. Fireball Roberts	John Hines	22	60 Pont	200	10,130
2. Cotton Owens	Cotton Owens	6	60 Pont	200	5,215
3. Jack Smith	Jack Smith	47	60 Pont	200	3,090
4. Bobby Johns	Jim Stephens	3	60 Pont	199	1,865
5. Fred Lorenzen	Fred Lorenzen	28	60 Ford	199	1,565

1960 Grand National Race No. 44 Atlanta 500
October 30, 1960 Average Speed: 108.408

Driver	Owner	Car #	Make	Laps	Winnings
1. Bobby Johns	Cotton Owens	5	60 Pont	334	15,975
2. Johnny Allen	Hanley Dawson	69	60 Chev	333	7,475
3. Jim Paschal	Petty Enterprises	44	60 Plym	333	4,425
4. Speedy Thompson	Wood Brothers	21	60 Ford	330	2,475
5. Rex White	Rex White	4	60 Chev	330	1,850

1961 Grand National Race No. 9 Atlanta 500
March 26, 1961 Average Speed: 124.172

Driver	Owner	Car #	Make	Laps	Winnings
1. Bob Burdick	Roy Burdick Gar	53	61 Pont	334	15,775
2. Rex White	Rex White	4	61 Chev	334	8,850
3. Ralph Earnhardt	Cotton Owens	6	61 Pont	334	4,850
4. Nelson Stacy	Dudley Farrell	29	61 Ford	333	2,475
5. Ned Jarrett	Bee Gee Holloway	11	61 Chev	332	1,775

1961 Grand National Race No. 33 Festival 250
July 9, 1961 Average Speed: 118.067

Driver	Owner	Car #	Make	Laps	Winnings
1. Fred Lorenzen	Holman-Moody	28	61 Ford	167	7,085
2. Bob Welborn	Jack Smith	47	61 Pont	166	3,580
3. Richard Petty	Petty Enterprises	43	61 Plym	164	2,275
4. Emanuel Zervakis	Monroe Shook	85	61 Chev	163	1,475
5. Jack Smith	Jack Smith	46	61 Pont	161	1,310

1961 Grand National Race No. 46 Dixie 400
September 17, 1961 Average Speed: 125.384

Driver	Owner	Car #	Make	Laps	Winnings
1. David Pearson	John Masoni	3	61 Pont	267	9,330
2. Junior Johnson	Rex Lovette	27	61 Pont	267	4,795
3. Fireball Roberts	Jim Stephens	22	61 Pont	267	3,165
4. Jack Smith	Jack Smith	47	61 Pont	264	2,250
5. Richard Petty	Petty Enterprises	43	61 Plym	264	1,625

1962 Grand National Race No. 24 Atlanta 500
June 10, 1962 Average Speed: 101.983

Driver	Owner	Car #	Make	Laps	Winnings
1. Fred Lorenzen	Holman-Moody	28	62 Ford	219	15,555
2. Banjo Matthews	Banjo Matthews	02	62 Pont	219	9,490
3. Bobby Johns	Shorty Johns	72	62 Pont	218	5,220
4. Fireball Roberts	Banjo Matthews	22	62 Pont	218	2,525
5. Troy Ruttman	Bill Stroppe	98	62 Merc	218	1,750

1962 Grand National Race No. 53 Dixie 400
October 28, 1962 Average Speed: 124.740

Driver	Owner	Car #	Make	Laps	Winnings
1. Rex White	Rex White	4	62 Chev	267	10,315
2. Joe Weatherly	Bud Moore	8	62 Pont	267	5,270
3. Marvin Panch	Wood Brothers	21	62 Ford	267	3,535
4. Richard Petty	Petty Enterprises	43	62 Plym	266	2,415
5. Fred Lorenzen	Holman-Moody	28	62 Ford	266	2,000

1963 Grand National Race No. 11 Atlanta 500
March 17, 1963 Average Speed: 130.582

Driver	Owner	Car #	Make	Laps	Winnings
1. Fred Lorenzen	Holman-Moody	28	63 Ford	334	16,855
2. Fireball Roberts	Banjo Matthews	22	63 Pont	333	8,655
3. Bobby Johns	Shorty Johns	7	63 Pont	333	5,700
4. Joe Weatherly	Bud Moore	8	63 Pont	333	3,790
5. Tiny Lund	Wood Brothers	21	63 Ford	331	1,875

Atlanta Motor Speedway *continued*

1963 Grand National Race No. 28 Dixie 400
June 30, 1963 Average Speed: 121.139

Driver	Owner	Car #	Make	Laps	Winnings
1. Junior Johnson	Ray Fox	3	63 Chev	267	12,445
2. Fred Lorenzen	Holman-Moody	28	63 Ford	267	6,190
3. Marvin Panch	Wood Brothers	21	63 Ford	267	3,370
4. Darel Dieringer	Bill Stroppe	26	63 Merc	266	2,245
5. Joe Weatherly	Bud Moore	8	63 Pont	266	2,050

1964 Grand National Race No. 28 Dixie 400
June 7, 1964 Average Speed: 112.535

Driver	Owner	Car #	Make	Laps	Winnings
1. Ned Jarrett	Bondy Long	11	64 Ford	267	11,500
2. Richard Petty	Petty Enterprises	43	64 Plym	267	5,790
3. Paul Goldsmith	Ray Nichels	25	64 Plym	266	3,530
4. Darel Dieringer	Bill Stroppe	16	64 Merc	266	2,425
5. Rex White	Bud Moore	4	64 Merc	266	2,025

1965 Grand National Race No. 25 Dixie 400
June 13, 1965 Average Speed: 110.120

Driver	Owner	Car #	Make	Laps	Winnings
1. Marvin Panch	Wood Brothers	21	65 Ford	267	12,300
2. Darel Dieringer	Bud Moore	16	64 Merc	267	6,770
3. Ned Jarrett	Bondy Long	11	65 Ford	267	3,730
4. Junior Johnson	Rex Lovette	26	65 Ford	265	2,975
5. Buddy Baker	Buck Baker	88	64 Dodg	263	1,675

1966 Grand National Race No. 37 Dixie 400
August 7, 1966 Average Speed: 130.244

Driver	Owner	Car #	Make	Laps	Winnings
1. Richard Petty	Petty Enterprises	43	66 Plym	267	13,525
2. Buddy Baker	Ray Fox	3	66 Dodg	267	8,345
3. Sam McQuagg	Ray Nichels	98	66 Dodg	260	3,505
4. James Hylton	Bud Hartje	48	65 Dodg	259	3,000
5. Jerry Grant	Tom Friedkin	04	65 Plym	255	1,925

1967 Grand National Race No. 36 Dixie 500
August 6, 1967 Average Speed: 132.286

Driver	Owner	Car #	Make	Laps	Winnings
1. Dick Hutcherson	Bondy Long	29	67 Ford	334	16,500
2. Paul Goldsmith	Ray Nichels	99	67 Plym	334	7,900
3. LeeRoy Yarbrough	Bud Moore	16	67 Merc	331	4,725
4. Donnie Allison	Jon Thorne	12	67 Ford	323	2,550
5. Bud Moore	A. J. King	53	67 Dodg	323	1,925

1968 Grand National Race No. 33 Dixie 500
August 4, 1968 Average Speed: 127.068

Driver	Owner	Car #	Make	Laps	Winnings
1. LeeRoy Yarbrough	Junior Johnson	98	68 Merc	334	17,260
2. Bobby Isaac	Nord Krauskopf	71	68 Dodg	334	8,440
3. Donnie Allison	Banjo Matthews	27	68 Ford	334	5,925
4. David Pearson	Holman-Moody	17	68 Ford	334	3,005
5. Richard Petty	Petty Enterprises	43	68 Plym	333	2,535

1969 Grand National Race No. 36 Dixie 500
August 10, 1969 Average Speed: 133.001

Driver	Owner	Car #	Make	Laps	Winnings
1. LeeRoy Yarbrough	Junior Johnson	98	69 Ford	334	18,620
2. David Pearson	Holman-Moody	17	69 Ford	334	9,750
3. Richard Petty	Petty Enterprises	43	69 Ford	334	6,100
4. Charlie Glotzbach	Smokey Yunick	13	69 Ford	333	3,585
5. Donnie Allison	Banjo Matthews	27	69 Ford	333	2,775

1964 Grand National Race No. 13 Atlanta 500
April 5, 1964 Average Speed: 134.137

Driver	Owner	Car #	Make	Laps	Winnings
1. Fred Lorenzen	Holman-Moody	28	64 Ford	334	18,000
2. Bobby Isaac	Ray Nichels	26	64 Dodg	332	8,065
3. Ned Jarrett	Bondy Long	11	64 Ford	331	4,500
4. Junior Johnson	Ray Fox	3	64 Dodg	330	2,925
5. Buck Baker	Petty Enterprises	41	64 Plym	327	1,850

1965 Grand National Race No. 9 Atlanta 500
April 11, 1965 Average Speed: 129.410

Driver	Owner	Car #	Make	Laps	Winnings
1. Marvin Panch	Wood Brothers	21	65 Ford	334	18,420
2. Bobby Johns	Holman-Moody	7	65 Ford	334	7,995
3. Ned Jarrett	Bondy Long	11	65 Ford	330	4,700
4. Dick Hutcherson	Holman-Moody	29	65 Ford	327	2,775
5. Buddy Baker	Buck Baker	88	64 Dodg	325	1,850

1966 Grand National Race No. 8 Atlanta 500
March 27, 1966 Average Speed: 131.247

Driver	Owner	Car #	Make	Laps	Winnings
1. Jim Hurtubise	Norm Nelson	56	66 Plym	334	17,920
2. Fred Lorenzen	Holman-Moody	28	66 Ford	333	8,290
3. Dick Hutcherson	Holman-Moody	29	66 Ford	333	4,825
4. Paul Goldsmith	Ray Nichels	99	66 Plym	331	2,750
5. Jim Paschal	Tom Friedkin	14	66 Plym	330	1,925

1967 Grand National Race No. 10 Atlanta 500
April 2, 1967 Average Speed: 131.238

Driver	Owner	Car #	Make	Laps	Winnings
1. Cale Yarborough	Wood Brothers	21	67 Ford	334	21,035
2. Dick Hutcherson	Bondy Long	29	67 Ford	333	8,600
3. Buddy Baker	Ray Fox	3	67 Dodg	332	4,900
4. Charlie Glotzbach	Nord Krauskopf	37	65 Dodg	327	2,750
5. Bobby Isaac	Nord Krauskopf	71	67 Dodg	326	1,875

1968 Grand National Race No. 7 Atlanta 500
March 31, 1968 Average Speed: 125.564

Driver	Owner	Car #	Make	Laps	Winnings
1. Cale Yarborough	Wood Brothers	21	68 Merc	334	20,680
2. LeeRoy Yarbrough	Junior Johnson	26	68 Merc	334	9,360
3. Donnie Allison	Banjo Matthews	27	68 Ford	333	5,415
4. Charlie Glotzbach	Cotton Owens	6	68 Dodg	332	3,225
5. Darel Dieringer	Mario Rossi	2	68 Plym	332	2,300

1969 Grand National Race No. 10 Atlanta 500
March 30, 1969 Average Speed: 132.191

Driver	Owner	Car #	Make	Laps	Winnings
1. Cale Yarborough	Wood Brothers	21	69 Merc	334	21,590
2. David Pearson	Holman-Moody	17	69 Ford	334	10,630
3. Paul Goldsmith	Ray Nichels	99	69 Dodg	332	6,225
4. Bobby Allison	Mario Rossi	22	69 Dodg	331	4,100
5. Pete Hamilton	Banjo Matthews	27	69 Ford	329	3,225

1970 Grand National Race No. 8 Atlanta 500
March 29, 1970 Average Speed: 139.554

Driver	Owner	Car #	Make	Laps	Winnings
1. Bobby Allison	Mario Rossi	22	69 Dodg	328	21,825
2. Cale Yarborough	Wood Brothers	21	69 Merc	328	11,375
3. Pete Hamilton	Petty Enterprises	40	70 Plym	326	6,550
4. LeeRoy Yarbrough	Junior Johnson	98	69 Ford	325	4,300
5. Richard Petty	Petty Enterprises	43	70 Plym	321	3,375

Atlanta Motor Speedway *continued*

1970 Grand National Race No. 31 Dixie 500
August 2, 1970 Average Speed: 142.712

Driver	Owner	Car #	Make	Laps	Winnings
1. Richard Petty	Petty Enterprises	43	70 Plym	328	19,600
2. Cale Yarborough	Wood Brothers	21	69 Merc	327	11,525
3. LeeRoy Yarbrough	Junior Johnson	98	69 Merc	326	7,200
4. Buddy Baker	Cotton Owens	6	69 Dodg	326	3,775
5. Donnie Allison	Banjo Matthews	27	69 Ford	325	2,800

1971 Winston Cup GN Race No. 10 Atlanta 500
April 4, 1971 Average Speed: 131.375

Driver	Owner	Car #	Make	Laps	Winnings
1. A. J. Foyt	Wood Brothers	21	69 Merc	328	19,200
2. Richard Petty	Petty Enterprises	43	71 Plym	328	10,700
3. Pete Hamilton	Cotton Owens	6	71 Plym	327	6,975
4. David Pearson	Holman-Moody	17	70 Ford	327	4,490
5. Bobby Isaac	Nord Krauskopf	71	71 Dodg	327	3,500

1971 Winston Cup GN Race No. 33 Dixie 500
August 1, 1971 Average Speed: 129.061

Driver	Owner	Car #	Make	Laps	Winnings
1. Richard Petty	Petty Enterprises	43	71 Plym	328	20,220
2. Bobby Allison	Holman-Moody	12	69 Merc	328	9,530
3. Benny Parsons	L. G. DeWitt	72	69 Merc	319	6,225
4. Charlie Glotzbach	R. Howard & J. Johnson	3	71 Chev	318	4,525
5. Friday Hassler	Friday Hassler	39	70 Chev	317	3,375

1972 Winston Cup GN Race No. 6 Atlanta 500
March 26, 1972 Average Speed: 128.214

Driver	Owner	Car #	Make	Laps	Winnings
1. Bobby Allison	R. Howard & J. Johnson	12	72 Chev	328	21,605
2. A. J. Foyt	Wood Brothers	21	71 Merc	328	10,600
3. Bobby Isaac	Nord Krauskopf	71	72 Dodg	328	10,380
4. David Pearson	Bud Moore	15	72 Ford	327	4,800
5. Donnie Allison	Monty Myers	27	72 Chev	327	3,530

1972 Winston Cup GN Race No. 20 Dixie 500
July 23, 1972 Average Speed: 131.295

Driver	Owner	Car #	Make	Laps	Winnings
1. Bobby Allison	R. Howard & J. Johnson	12	72 Chev	328	17,955
2. Richard Petty	Petty Enterprises	43	72 Dodg	328	11,005
3. David Pearson	Wood Brothers	21	71 Merc	325	6,380
4. Benny Parsons	L. G. DeWitt	72	71 Merc	323	5,230
5. LeeRoy Yarbrough	Junie Donlavey	90	71 Ford	322	4,230

1973 Winston Cup GN Race No. 6 Atlanta 500
April 1, 1973 Average Speed: 139.351

Driver	Owner	Car #	Make	Laps	Winnings
1. David Pearson	Wood Brothers	21	71 Merc	328	16,625
2. Bobby Isaac	Bud Moore	15	72 Ford	326	11,325
3. Benny Parsons	L. G. DeWitt	72	72 Chev	323	6,700
4. Buddy Baker	Nord Krauskopf	71	73 Dodg	322	6,525
5. Cale Yarborough	R. Howard & J. Johnson	11	73 Chev	321	6,575

1973 Winston Cup GN Race No. 19 Dixie 500
July 22, 1973 Average Speed: 130.211

Driver	Owner	Car #	Make	Laps	Winnings
1. David Pearson	Wood Brothers	21	71 Merc	328	16,650
2. Cale Yarborough	R. Howard & J. Johnson	11	73 Chev	327	10,625
3. Donnie Allison	DiGard	88	73 Chev	323	6,075
4. Joe Frasson	Joe Frasson	18	73 Dodg	321	4,800
5. Jody Ridley	Junie Donlavey	90	71 Merc	319	4,535

1974 Winston Cup GN Race No. 6 Atlanta 500
March 24, 1974 Average Speed: 136.910

Driver	Owner	Car #	Make	Laps	Winnings
1. Cale Yarborough	R. Howard & J. Johnson	11	74 Chev	328	18,650
2. David Pearson	Wood Brothers	21	73 Merc	328	9,950
3. Buddy Baker	Nord Krauskopf	71	74 Dodg	327	6,650
4. George Follmer	Bud Moore	15	72 Ford	327	7,300
5. Donnie Allison	DiGard	88	74 Chev	326	4,150

1974 Winston Cup GN Race No. 19 Dixie 500
July 28, 1974 Average Speed: 131.651

Driver	Owner	Car #	Make	Laps	Winnings
1. Richard Petty	Petty Enterprises	43	74 Dodg	328	19,350
2. David Pearson	Wood Brothers	21	73 Merc	328	9,225
3. Buddy Baker	Bud Moore	15	73 Ford	327	9,425
4. Darrell Waltrip	Darrell Waltrip	95	74 Chev	324	5,800
5. Lennie Pond	Ronnie Elder	54	74 Chev	319	4,425

1975 Winston Cup GN Race No. 6 Atlanta 500
March 23, 1975 Average Speed: 133.496

Driver	Owner	Car #	Make	Laps	Winnings
1. Richard Petty	Petty Enterprises	43	74 Dodg	328	19,500
2. Buddy Baker	Bud Moore	15	75 Ford	328	13,025
3. David Pearson	Wood Brothers	21	73 Merc	327	8,025
4. Dick Brooks	Junie Donlavey	90	73 Ford	324	5,525
5. Darrell Waltrip	Darrell Waltrip	17	75 Chev	323	6,525

1975 Winston Cup GN Race No. 29 Dixie 500
November 9, 1975 Average Speed: 130.990

Driver	Owner	Car #	Make	Laps	Winnings
1. Buddy Baker	Bud Moore	15	75 Ford	328	18,550
2. Dave Marcis	Nord Krauskopf	71	74 Dodg	328	13,375
3. Richard Petty	Petty Enterprises	43	74 Dodg	328	10,725
4. David Pearson	Wood Brothers	21	73 Merc	327	6,150
5. Cale Yarborough	Junior Johnson	11	75 Chev	327	7,600

1976 Winston Cup GN Race No. 6 Atlanta 500
March 21, 1976 Average Speed: 128.904

Driver	Owner	Car #	Make	Laps	Winnings
1. David Pearson	Wood Brothers	21	Merc	328	16,750
2. Benny Parsons	L. G. DeWitt	72	Chev	328	13,375
3. Cale Yarborough	Junior Johnson	11	Chev	327	17,855
4. Lennie Pond	Ronnie Elder	54	Chev	326	5,870
5. Darrell Waltrip	DiGard	88	Chev	325	7,360

1976 Winston Cup GN Race No. 29 Dixie 500
November 7, 1976 Average Speed: 127.396

Driver	Owner	Car #	Make	Laps	Winnings
1. Dave Marcis	Nord Krauskopf	71	Dodg	328	20,165
2. David Pearson	Wood Brothers	21	Merc	328	11,765
3. Donnie Allison	Hoss Ellington	1	Chev	328	7,790
4. Cale Yarborough	Junior Johnson	11	Chev	328	8,670
5. Buddy Baker	Bud Moore	15	Ford	327	8,985

1977 Winston Cup GN Race No. 5 Atlanta 500
March 20, 1977 Average Speed: 144.093

Driver	Owner	Car #	Make	Laps	Winnings
1. Richard Petty	Petty Enterprises	43	Dodg	328	22,550
2. David Pearson	Wood Brothers	21	Merc	328	12,850
3. Cale Yarborough	Junior Johnson	11	Chev	327	13,025
4. Donnie Allison	Hoss Ellington	1	Chev	327	6,000
5. Buddy Baker	Bud Moore	15	Ford	326	7,650

Atlanta Motor Speedway *continued*

1977 Winston Cup GN Race No. 29 Dixie 500
November 6, 1977 Average Speed: 110.052

Driver	Owner	Car #	Make	Laps	Winnings
1. Darrell Waltrip	DiGard	88	Chev	268	20,425
2. David Pearson	Wood Brothers	21	Merc	268	11,500
3. Benny Parsons	L. G. DeWitt	72	Chev	268	11,250
4. Donnie Allison	Hoss Ellington	1	Chev	268	18,250
5. Cale Yarborough	Junior Johnson	11	Chev	268	9,450

1978 Winston Cup GN Race No. 29 Dixie 500
November 5, 1978 Average Speed: 124.312

Driver	Owner	Car #	Make	Laps	Winnings
1. Donnie Allison	Hoss Ellington	1	Chev	328	19,850
2. Richard Petty	Petty Enterprises	43	.Chev	328	14,750
3. Dave Marcis	Rod Osterlund	2	Chev	328	9,750
4. Dale Earnhardt	Rod Osterlund	98	Chev	327	7,500
5. Benny Parsons	L. G. DeWitt	72	Olds	327	9,000

1979 Winston Cup GN Race No. 30 Dixie 500
November 4, 1979 Average Speed: 140.120

Driver	Owner	Car #	Make	Laps	Winnings
1. Neil Bonnett	Wood Brothers	21	Merc	328	20,050
2. Dale Earnhardt	Rod Osterlund	2	Chev	328	16,700
3. Cale Yarborough	Junior Johnson	11	Olds	328	23,150
4. Bobby Allison	Bud Moore	15	Ford	328	10,200
5. Darrell Waltrip	DiGard	88	Chev	327	9,100

1980 Winston Cup GN Race No. 30 Atlanta Journal 500
November 2, 1980 Average Speed: 131.190

Driver	Owner	Car #	Make	Laps	Winnings
1. Cale Yarborough	Junior Johnson	11	Chev	328	31,600
2. Neil Bonnett	Wood Brothers	21	Merc	328	12,600
3. Dale Earnhardt	Rod Osterlund	2	Chev	327	14,700
4. Buddy Baker	Harry Ranier	28	Buick	327	7,050
5. Terry Labonte	Billy Hagan	44	Chev	327	9,850

1981 Winston Cup GN Race No. 30 Atlanta Journal 500
November 8, 1981 Average Speed: 130.391

Driver	Owner	Car #	Make	Laps	Winnings
1. Neil Bonnett	Wood Brothers	21	Ford	328	31,500
2. Darrell Waltrip	Junior Johnson	11	Buick	328	17,350
3. Cale Yarborough	M. C. Anderson	27	Buick	328	8,800
4. Bobby Allison	Harry Ranier	28	Buick	328	12,090
5. Jody Ridley	Junie Donlavey	90	Ford	328	11,700

1982 Winston Cup GN Race No. 29 Atlanta Journal 500
November 7, 1982 Average Speed: 130.884

Driver	Owner	Car #	Make	Laps	Winnings
1. Bobby Allison	DiGard	88	Buick	328	45,500
2. Harry Gant	Hal Needham	33	Buick	328	19,230
3. Darrell Waltrip	Junior Johnson	11	Buick	328	19,700
4. Tim Richmond	Jim Stacy	2	Buick	328	9,895
5. Joe Ruttman	Bob Rahilly & Butch Mock	75	Buick	327	8,775

1983 Winston Cup GN Race No. 29 Atlanta Journal 500
November 6, 1983 Average Speed: 137.643

Driver	Owner	Car #	Make	Laps	Winnings
1. Neil Bonnett	Bob Rahilly & Butch Mock	75	Chev	328	36,975
2. Buddy Baker	Wood Brothers	21	Ford	328	15,800
3. Bobby Allison	DiGard	22	Buick	328	31,025
4. Terry Labonte	Billy Hagan	44	Chev	327	12,955
5. Richard Petty	Petty Enterprises	43	Pont	326	12,100

1978 Winston Cup GN Race No. 5 Atlanta 500
March 19, 1978 Average Speed: 142.520

Driver	Owner	Car #	Make	Laps	Winnings
1. Bobby Allison	Bud Moore	15	Ford	328	33,050
2. Dave Marcis	Rod Osterlund	2	Chev	327	16,925
3. Donnie Allison	Hoss Ellington	1	Chev	327	11,000
4. Cale Yarborough	Junior Johnson	11	Olds	327	23,600
5. Lennie Pond	Harry Ranier	54	Chev	327	5,950

1979 Winston Cup GN Race No. 5 Atlanta 500
March 18, 1979 Average Speed: 135.136

Driver	Owner	Car #	Make	Laps	Winnings
1. Buddy Baker	Harry Ranier	28	Olds	328	35,975
2. Bobby Allison	Bud Moore	15	Ford	328	32,875
3. Darrell Waltrip	DiGard	88	Chev	328	15,400
4. Cale Yarborough	Junior Johnson	11	Olds	327	11,725
5. Benny Parsons	M. C. Anderson	27	Chev	327	5,775

1980 Winston Cup GN Race No. 5 Atlanta 500
March 16, 1980 Average Speed: 134.808

Driver	Owner	Car #	Make	Laps	Winnings
1. Dale Earnhardt	Rod Osterlund	2	Chev	328	36,200
2. Rusty Wallace	Roger Penske	16	Chev	328	14,250
3. Bobby Allison	Bud Moore	15	Ford	328	16,250
4. Dave Marcis	Dave Marcis	71	Olds	327	13,600
5. Dick Brooks	Nelson Malloch	7	Chev	325	9,490

1981 Winston Cup GN Race No. 5 Coca-Cola 500
March 15, 1981 Average Speed: 133.619

Driver	Owner	Car #	Make	Laps	Winnings
1. Cale Yarborough	M. C. Anderson	27	Buick	328	28,950
2. Harry Gant	Jack Beebe	47	Buick	328	32,705
3. Dale Earnhardt	Rod Osterlund	2	Pont	327	19,400
4. Bobby Allison	Harry Ranier	28	Pont	327	14,415
5. Benny Parsons	Bud Moore	15	Ford	326	11,975

1982 Winston Cup GN Race No. 4 Coca-Cola 500
March 21, 1982 Average Speed: 124.824

Driver	Owner	Car #	Make	Laps	Winnings
1. Darrell Waltrip	Junior Johnson	11	Buick	287	49,615
2. Richard Petty	Petty Enterprises	43	Pont	287	37,725
3. Cale Yarborough	M. C. Anderson	27	Buick	287	16,250
4. Benny Parsons	Harry Ranier	28	Pont	287	19,345
5. Harry Gant	Hal Needham	33	Buick	286	12,890

1983 Winston Cup GN Race No. 4 Coca-Cola 500
March 27, 1983 Average Speed: 124.055

Driver	Owner	Car #	Make	Laps	Winnings
1. Cale Yarborough	Harry Ranier	28	Chev	328	33,300
2. Neil Bonnett	Bob Rahilly & Butch Mock	75	Chev	328	34,530
3. Buddy Baker	Wood Brothers	21	Ford	328	12,125
4. Joe Ruttman	Ron Benfield	98	Buick	328	13,620
5. Richard Petty	Petty Enterprises	43	Pont	328	12,650

1984 Winston Cup GN Race No. 4 Coca-Cola 500
March 18, 1984 Average Speed: 144.945

Driver	Owner	Car #	Make	Laps	Winnings
1. Benny Parsons	Johnny Hayes	55	Chev	328	51,110
2. Dale Earnhardt	Richard Childress	3	Chev	328	26,935
3. Cale Yarborough	Harry Ranier	28	Chev	328	12,550
4. Richard Petty	Mike Curb	43	Pont	327	8,650
5. Bobby Allison	DiGard	22	Buick	326	18,050

Atlanta Motor Speedway *continued*

1984 Winston Cup GN Race No. 29 Atlanta Journal 500
November 11, 1984 Average Speed: 134.610

Driver	Owner	Car #	Make	Laps	Winnings
1. Dale Earnhardt	Richard Childress	3	Chev	328	40,610
2. Bill Elliott	Harry Melling	9	Ford	328	28,085
3. Ricky Rudd	Bud Moore	15	Ford	328	19,350
4. Benny Parsons	Johnny Hayes	55	Chev	328	7,000
5. Bobby Allison	DiGard	22	Buick	327	16,850

1985 Winston Cup GN Race No. 27 Atlanta Journal 500
November 3, 1985 Average Speed: 139.597

Driver	Owner	Car #	Make	Laps	Winnings
1. Bill Elliott	Harry Melling	9	Ford	328	57,650
2. Cale Yarborough	Harry Ranier	28	Ford	328	29,600
3. Darrell Waltrip	Junior Johnson	11	Chev	328	21,125
4. Dale Earnhardt	Richard Childress	3	Chev	328	15,300
5. Morgan Shepherd	Bobby Hawkins	16	Chev	327	7,150

1986 Winston Cup Race No. 28 Atlanta Journal 500
November 2, 1986 Average Speed: 152.523

Driver	Owner	Car #	Make	Laps	Winnings
1. Dale Earnhardt	Richard Childress	3	Chev	328	67,950
2. Richard Petty	Petty Enterprises	43	Pont	327	26,130
3. Bill Elliott	Harry Melling	9	Ford	327	26,450
4. Tim Richmond	Rick Hendrick	25	Chev	327	12,845
5. Buddy Baker	Buddy Baker & Danny Schiff	88	Olds	327	7,725

1987 Winston Cup Race No. 29 Atlanta Journal 500
November 22, 1987 Average Speed: 139.047

Driver	Owner	Car #	Make	Laps	Winnings
1. Bill Elliott	Harry Melling	9	Ford	328	74,200
2. Dale Earnhardt	Richard Childress	3	Chev	328	35,350
3. Ricky Rudd	Bud Moore	15	Ford	328	22,585
4. Bobby Allison	Stavola Brothers	22	Buick	328	16,725
5. Davey Allison	Harry Ranier	28	Ford	327	9,985

1988 Winston Cup Race No. 29 Atlanta Journal 500
November 20, 1988 Average Speed: 129.024

Driver	Owner	Car #	Make	Laps	Winnings
1. Rusty Wallace	Raymond Beadle	27	Pont	328	87,575
2. Davey Allison	Harry Ranier	28	Ford	328	35,625
3. Mike Alexander	Stavola Brothers	12	Buick	328	23,610
4. Ricky Rudd	Kenny Bernstein	26	Buick	328	14,725
5. Darrell Waltrip	Rick Hendrick	17	Chev	328	16,525

1989 Winston Cup Race No. 29 Atlanta Journal 500
November 19, 1989 Average Speed: 140.229

Driver	Owner	Car #	Make	Laps	Winnings
1. Dale Earnhardt	Richard Childress	3	Chev	328	81,700
2. Geoff Bodine	Rick Hendrick	5	Chev	328	33,625
3. Sterling Marlin	Billy Hagan	94	Olds	328	25,275
4. Ken Schrader	Rick Hendrick	25	Chev	328	18,875
5. Darrell Waltrip	Rick Hendrick	17	Chev	327	18,800

1990 Winston Cup Series Race No. 29 Atlanta Journal 500
November 18, 1990 Average Speed: 140.911

Driver	Owner	Car #	Make	Laps	Winnings
1. Morgan Shepherd	Bud Moore	15	Ford	328	62,250
2. Geoff Bodine	Junior Johnson	11	Ford	328	40,850
3. Dale Earnhardt	Richard Childress	3	Chev	328	26,700
4. Dale Jarrett	Wood Brothers	21	Ford	328	17,225
5. Darrell Waltrip	Rick Hendrick	17	Chev	327	22,300

1985 Winston Cup GN Race No. 4 Coca-Cola 500
March 17, 1985 Average Speed: 140.273

Driver	Owner	Car #	Make	Laps	Winnings
1. Bill Elliott	Harry Melling	9	Ford	328	59,800
2. Geoff Bodine	Rick Hendrick	5	Chev	328	29,800
3. Neil Bonnett	Junior Johnson	12	Chev	328	23,700
4. Ricky Rudd	Bud Moore	15	Ford	327	15,825
5. Bobby Allison	DiGard	22	Buick	327	15,000

1986 Winston Cup Race No. 4 Motorcraft 500
March 16, 1986 Average Speed: 132.126

Driver	Owner	Car #	Make	Laps	Winnings
1. Morgan Shepherd	Jack Beebe	47	Buick	328	62,350
2. Dale Earnhardt	Richard Childress	3	Chev	328	51,300
3. Terry Labonte	Billy Hagan	44	Olds	328	22,150
4. Darrell Waltrip	Junior Johnson	11	Chev	328	24,075
5. Bill Elliott	Harry Melling	9	Ford	328	18,250

1987 Winston Cup Race No. 4 Motorcraft Quality Parts 500
March 15, 1987 Average Speed: 133.689

Driver	Owner	Car #	Make	Laps	Winnings
1. Ricky Rudd	Bud Moore	15	Ford	328	62,400
2. Benny Parsons	Rick Hendrick	35	Chev	328	36,125
3. Rusty Wallace	Raymond Beadle	27	Pont	328	25,950
4. Terry Labonte	Junior Johnson	11	Chev	328	20,825
5. Davey Allison	Harry Ranier	28	Ford	327	18,550

1988 Winston Cup Race No. 4 Motorcraft Quality Parts 500
March 20, 1988 Average Speed: 137.588

Driver	Owner	Car #	Make	Laps	Winnings
1. Dale Earnhardt	Richard Childress	3	Chev	328	67,950
2. Rusty Wallace	Raymond Beadle	27	Pont	328	37,875
3. Darrell Waltrip	Rick Hendrick	17	Chev	327	26,150
4. Terry Labonte	Junior Johnson	11	Chev	327	19,575
5. Kyle Petty	Wood Brothers	21	Ford	327	18,750

1989 Winston Cup Race No. 3 Motorcraft Quality Parts 500
March 19, 1989 Average Speed: 139.684

Driver	Owner	Car #	Make	Laps	Winnings
1. Darrell Waltrip	Rick Hendrick	17	Chev	328	63,500
2. Dale Earnhardt	Richard Childress	3	Chev	328	39,675
3. Dick Trickle	Stavola Brothers	84	Buick	328	30,250
4. Kyle Petty	Felix Sabates	42	Pont	327	13,250
5. Sterling Marlin	Billy Hagan	94	Olds	326	22,500

1990 Winston Cup Series Race No. 4 Motorcraft Quality Parts 500
March 18, 1990 Average Speed: 156.849

Driver	Owner	Car #	Make	Laps	Winnings
1. Dale Earnhardt	Richard Childress	3	Chev	328	85,000
2. Morgan Shepherd	Bud Moore	15	Ford	328	36,000
3. Ernie Irvan	Larry McClure	4	Olds	328	31,957
4. Ken Schrader	Rick Hendrick	25	Chev	328	22,900
5. Mark Martin	Jack Roush	6	Ford	328	20,850

1991 Winston Cup Series Race No. 4 Motorcraft Quality Parts 500
March 18, 1991 Average Speed: 140.470

Driver	Owner	Car #	Make	Laps	Winnings
1. Ken Schrader	Rick Hendrick	25	Chev	328	69,250
2. Bill Elliott	Harry Melling	9	Ford	328	47,675
3. Dale Earnhardt	Richard Childress	3	Chev	328	37,000
4. Morgan Shepherd	Bud Moore	15	Ford	328	23,600
5. Michael Waltrip	Chuck Rider	30	Pont	328	21,400

Atlanta Motor Speedway *continued*

1991 Winston Cup Series Race No. 29 Hardee's 500
November 17, 1991 Average Speed: 137.968

Driver	Owner	Car #	Make	Laps	Winnings
1. Mark Martin	Jack Roush	6	Ford	328	88,950
2. Ernie Irvan	Larry McClure	4	Chev	328	39,025
3. Bill Elliott	Harry Melling	9	Ford	328	36,950
4. Harry Gant	Leo Jackson	33	Olds	328	21,250
5. Dale Earnhardt	Richard Childress	3	Chev	328	27,825

1992 Winston Cup Race No. 29 Hooters 500
November 15, 1992 Average Speed: 133.322

Driver	Owner	Car #	Make	Laps	Winnings
1. Bill Elliott	Junior Johnson	11	Ford	328	93,600
2. Alan Kulwicki	Alan Kulwicki	7	Ford	328	56,000
3. Geoff Bodine	Bud Moore	15	Ford	328	32,400
4. Jimmy Spencer	Bobby Allison	12	Ford	328	27,000
5. Terry Labonte	Billy Hagan	94	Chev	328	22,235

1993 Winston Cup Series Race No. 30 Hooters 500
November 14, 1993 Average Speed: 125.221

Driver	Owner	Car #	Make	Laps	Winnings
1. Rusty Wallace	Roger Penske	2	Pont	328	93,100
2. Ricky Rudd	Rick Hendrick	5	Chev	328	57,225
3. Darrell Waltrip	Darrell Waltrip	17	Chev	328	40,175
4. Bill Elliott	Junior Johnson	11	Ford	328	34,250
5. Dick Trickle	Larry Hedrick	41	Chev	328	24,300

1994 Winston Cup Series Race No. 31 Hooters 500
November 13, 1994 Average Speed: 148.982

Driver	Owner	Car #	Make	Laps	Winnings
1. Mark Martin	Jack Roush	6	Ford	328	104,200
2. Dale Earnhardt	Richard Childress	3	Chev	328	55,950
3. Todd Bodine	Butch Mock	75	Ford	328	44,000
4. Lake Speed	Bud Moore	15	Ford	328	32,000
5. Mike Wallace	Junie Donlavey	90	Ford	328	23,800

1995 Winston Cup Series Race No. 31 NAPA 500
November 12, 1995 Average Speed: 163.633

Driver	Owner	Car #	Make	Laps	Winnings
1. Dale Earnhardt	Richard Childress	3	Chev	328	141,850
2. Sterling Marlin	Larry McClure	4	Chev	328	58,250
3. Rusty Wallace	Roger Penske	2	Ford	328	40,300
4. Bill Elliott	Bill Elliott	94	Ford	328	29,700
5. Ward Burton	Bill Davis	22	Pont	328	30,000

1992 Winston Cup Race No. 4 Motorcraft Quality Parts 500
March 15, 1992 Average Speed: 147.746

Driver	Owner	Car #	Make	Laps	Winnings
1. Bill Elliott	Junior Johnson	11	Ford	328	71,000
2. Harry Gant	Leo Jackson	33	Olds	328	45,875
3. Dale Earnhardt	Richard Childress	3	Chev	328	36,850
4. Davey Allison	Robert Yates	28	Ford	328	32,550
5. Dick Trickle	Stavola Brothers	8	Ford	328	28,125

1993 Winston Cup Series Race No. 4 Motorcraft Quality Parts 500
March 20, 1993 Average Speed: 150.442

Driver	Owner	Car #	Make	Laps	Winnings
1. Morgan Shepherd	Wood Brothers	21	Ford	328	70,350
2. Ernie Irvan	Larry McClure	4	Chev	328	45,950
3. Rusty Wallace	Roger Penske	2	Pont	328	41,550
4. Jeff Gordon	Rick Hendrick	24	Chev	327	32,000
5. Ricky Rudd	Rick Hendrick	5	Chev	327	26,550

1994 Winston Cup Series Race No. 4 Motorcraft Quality Parts 500
March 13, 1994 Average Speed: 146.136

Driver	Owner	Car #	Make	Laps	Winnings
1. Ernie Irvan	Robert Yates	28	Ford	328	86,100
2. Morgan Shepherd	Wood Brothers	21	Ford	328	48,300
3. Darrell Waltrip	Darrell Waltrip	17	Chev	328	39,450
4. Jeff Burton	Stavola Brothers	8	Ford	328	32,600
5. Mark Martin	Jack Roush	6	Ford	327	30,300

1995 Winston Cup Series Race No. 4 Purolator 500
March 12, 1995 Average Speed: 150.115

Driver	Owner	Car #	Make	Laps	Winnings
1. Jeff Gordon	Rick Hendrick	24	Chev	328	104,950
2. Bobby Labonte	Joe Gibbs	18	Chev	328	50,000
3. Terry Labonte	Rick Hendrick	5	Chev	328	44,150
4. Dale Earnhardt	Richard Childress	3	Chev	328	52,950
5. Dale Jarrett	Robert Yates	28	Ford	327	33,725

1996 Winston Cup Series Race No. 4 Purolator 500
March 10, 1996 Average Speed: 161.298

Driver	Owner	Car #	Make	Laps	Winnings
1. Dale Earnhardt	Richard Childress	3	Chev	328	91,050
2. Terry Labonte	Rick Hendrick	5	Chev	328	60,500
3. Jeff Gordon	Rick Hendrick	24	Chev	328	61,600
4. Ernie Irvan	Robert Yates	28	Ford	328	40,400
5. Jeremy Mayfield	Cale Yarborough	98	Ford	328	32,100

1996 Winston Cup Series Race No. 31 NAPA 500
November 10, 1996 Average Speed: 134.661

Driver	Owner	Car #	Make	Laps	Winnings
1. Bobby Labonte	Joe Gibbs	18	Chev	328	274,900
2. Dale Jarrett	Robert Yates	88	Ford	328	59,500
3. Jeff Gordon	Rick Hendrick	24	Chev	328	71,600
4. Dale Earnhardt	Richard Childress	3	Chev	328	47,400
5. Terry Labonte	Rick Hendrick	5	Chev	328	48,800

Augusta Int'l Raceway
Augusta, GA
3-mile Paved Road Course

3-mile road course opened in 1963. Only NASCAR Winston Cup (then Grand National) race staged on 11/10/63 (won by Fireball Roberts—his 33rd and final Winston Cup victory; race counted in the 1964 championship season). Track was abandoned and left to decay after first and only event.

Winston Cup Victories
Fireball Roberts   1

Winston Cup Money
Fireball Roberts $13,190

Narrowest Margin of Victory
1 lap and 28 seconds—November 17, 1963

Most Race Leaders
5—November 17, 1963

Winston Cup Poles
Fred Lorenzen   1

Most Cars Started
36—November 17, 1963

Race Record
86.320 MPH—November 17, 1963

Most Cars Running at Finish
16—November 17, 1963

1964 Grand National Race No. 2
November 17, 1963 Average Speed: 86.320

Driver	Owner	Car #	Make	Laps	Winnings
1. Fireball Roberts	Holman-Moody	22	63 Ford	139	13,190
2. Dave MacDonald	Holman-Moody	29	63 Ford	138	6,745
3. Billy Wade	Cotton Owens	5	63 Dodg	137	3,730
4. Joe Weatherly	Bill Stroppe	26	63 Merc	137	2,650
5. Ned Jarrett	Charles Robinson	11	63 Ford	132	1,675

Augusta Int'l Speedway
Augusta, GA
Half-mile Dirt Track

(aka Augusta Speedway; New Augusta Speedway) Half-mile dirt oval built in 1961. First NASCAR Winston Cup (then Grand National) race staged on 6/19/62 (won by Joe Weatherly). Track paved in 1964. Final NASCAR race staged on 10/19/69 (won by Bobby Isaac). Track closed in 1970.

Winston Cup Starts
Richard Petty	11
Wendell Scott	11

Winston Cup Victories
Bobby Isaac	2
David Pearson	2
Richard Petty	2
Joe Weatherly	2

Winston Cup Poles
Bobby Isaac	3

Winston Cup Money
Richard Petty	$7,785

Most Cars Started
30—November 1, 1964 Jaycee 300
30—November 14, 1965 Georgia Cracker 300

Fewest Cars Started
15—April 4, 1963

Narrowest Margin of Victory
2.750 seconds August 15, 1965

Slowest Race
55.104 MPH—July 17, 1962

Race Record
78.740 MPH—October 19, 1969

Most Cautions
6—November 1, 1964 Jaycee 300

Most Race Leaders
4—November 1, 1964 Jaycee 300
4—November 14, 1965 Georgia Cracker 300

Most Cars Running at Finish
21—November 14, 1965 Georgia Cracker 300

1962 Grand National Race No. 26
June 19, 1962 Average Speed: 59.850

	Driver	Owner	Car #	Make	Laps	Winnings
1.	Joe Weatherly	Bud Moore	8	61 Pont	200	1,000
2.	Ned Jarrett	Bee Gee Holloway	11	62 Chev	199	800
3.	Richard Petty	Petty Enterprises	43	62 Plym	198	400
4.	Jim Paschal	Cliff Stewart	2	62 Pont	193	300
5.	G. C. Spencer	G. C. Spencer	48	60 Chev	193	275

1962 Grand National Race No. 33
July 17, 1962 Average Speed: 55.104

	Driver	Owner	Car #	Make	Laps	Winnings
1.	Joe Weatherly	Bud Moore	8	61 Pont	200	1,000
2.	Richard Petty	Petty Enterprises	43	62 Plym	200	600
3.	Buck Baker	Buck Baker	87	62 Chrys	198	400
4.	Buddy Baker	Buck Baker	86	61 Chrys	196	300
5.	Bob Welborn	J. C. Parker	49	62 Pont	195	275

1962 Grand National Race No. 49
September 13, 1962 Average Speed: 60.759

	Driver	Owner	Car #	Make	Laps	Winnings
1.	Fred Lorenzen	Mamie Reynolds	26	62 Ford	200	1,000
2.	Richard Petty	Petty Enterprises	41	62 Plym	200	600
3.	Joe Weatherly	Bud Moore	8	62 Pont	197	400
4.	Ned Jarrett	Bee Gee Holloway	11	62 Chev	190	500
5.	Wendell Scott	Wendell Scott	34	61 Chev	190	275

1963 Grand National Race No. 14
April 4, 1963 Average Speed: 60.089

	Driver	Owner	Car #	Make	Laps	Winnings
1.	Ned Jarrett	Charles Robinson	11	63 Ford	112	1,000
2.	Richard Petty	Petty Enterprises	43	62 Plym	112	600
3.	Curtis Crider	Curtis Crider	62	62 Merc	110	400
4.	H. G. Rosier	H. G. Rosier	5	61 Pont	108	300
5.	Buck Baker	Buck Baker	87	62 Chrys	106	275

1964 Grand National Race No. 61 Jaycee 300
November 1, 1964 Average Speed: 68.641

	Driver	Owner	Car #	Make	Laps	Winnings
1.	Darel Dieringer	Bud Moore	16	64 Merc	300	1,750
2.	Bobby Isaac	Cotton Owens	5	64 Dodg	300	800
3.	Larry Thomas	Charles Robinson	36	64 Plym	298	600
4.	Doug Cooper	Bob Cooper	60	64 Ford	283	500
4.	Billy Wade	Bud Moore	1	64 Merc	293	525

1965 Grand National Race No. 40
August 15, 1965 Average Speed: 71.499

	Driver	Owner	Car #	Make	Laps	Winnings
1.	Dick Hutcherson	Holman-Moody	29	65 Ford	200	1,000
2.	David Pearson	Cotton Owens	6	65 Dodg	200	600
3.	Ned Jarrett	Bondy Long	11	65 Ford	200	400
4.	LeeRoy Yarbrough	Gary Weaver	10	64 Ford	199	300
5.	G. C. Spencer	G. C. Spencer	49	64 Ford	196	375

1966 Grand National Race No. 1 Georgia Cracker 300
November 14, 1965 Average Speed: 73.569

	Driver	Owner	Car #	Make	Laps	Winnings
1.	Richard Petty	Petty Enterprises	42	65 Plym	300	1,700
2.	Bobby Isaac	Rex Lovette	26	65 Ford	300	850
3.	Ned Jarrett	Bondy Long	11	65 Ford	300	820
4.	Jim Paschal	Gary Weaver	10	64 Ford	297	515
5.	Roy Mayne	Tom Hunter	46	65 Chev	296	490

1967 Grand National Race No. 1 Augusta 300
November 13, 1966 Average Speed: 71.809

	Driver	Owner	Car #	Make	Laps	Winnings
1.	Richard Petty	Petty Enterprises	43	66 Plym	300	1,735
2.	Paul Lewis	Paul Lewis	1	65 Plym	297	1,170
3.	David Pearson	Cotton Owens	6	66 Dodg	297	1,050
4.	James Hylton	Bud Hartje	48	65 Dodg	296	645
5.	Tiny Lund	Lyle Stelter	55	64 Ford	289	605

1968 Grand National Race No. 13 Dixie 250
May 3, 1968 Average Speed: 73.099

	Driver	Owner	Car #	Make	Laps	Winnings
1.	Bobby Isaac	Nord Krauskopf	71	67 Dodg	250	1,100
2.	Buddy Baker	Ray Fox	3	67 Dodg	249	700
3.	Tom Pistone	Jon Thorne	12	68 Merc	249	600
4.	James Hylton	James Hylton	48	67 Dodg	244	500
5.	Buck Baker	Buck Baker	87	67 Olds	239	425

1968 Grand National Race No. 46 Augusta 200
October 5, 1968 Average Speed: 75.821

	Driver	Owner	Car #	Make	Laps	Winnings
1.	David Pearson	Holman-Moody	17	68 Ford	200	1,000
2.	Bobby Allison	Tom Friedkin	14	68 Plym	200	600
3.	Richard Petty	Petty Enterprises	43	68 Plym	200	600
4.	Bobby Isaac	Nord Krauskopf	71	68 Dodg	199	300
5.	John Sears	L. G. DeWitt	4	67 Ford	194	275

Augusta Int'l Speedway *continued*

1969 Grand National Race No. 8 Cracker 200
March 16, 1969 Average Speed: 77.586

Driver	Owner	Car #	Make	Laps	Winnings
1. David Pearson	Holman-Moody	17	69 Ford	200	1,200
2. Richard Petty	Petty Enterprises	43	69 Ford	200	600
3. Bobby Isaac	Nord Krauskopf	71	69 Dodg	200	400
4. James Hylton	James Hylton	48	67 Dodg	196	350
5. John Sears	L. G. DeWitt	4	67 Ford	195	325

1969 Grand National Race No. 50
October 19, 1969 Average Speed: 78.740

Driver	Owner	Car #	Make	Laps	Winnings
1. Bobby Isaac	Nord Krauskopf	71	69 Dodg	200	1,000
2. Richard Petty	Petty Enterprises	43	69 Ford	200	600
3. David Pearson	Holman-Moody	17	69 Ford	199	600
4. LeeRoy Yarbrough	Junior Johnson	98	69 Ford	198	350
5. Elmo Langley	Elmo Langley	64	68 Ford	195	325

Central City Speedway
Macon, GA
Half-mile Dirt Track

(aka Central City Park Speedway; Macon Speedway; Macon Fairgrounds Speedway; Georgia State Fairgrounds) Originally built in 1920s as 1-mile dirt track. Half-mile dirt track built in 1947. First NASCAR Winston Cup (then Grand National) race staged on 9/9/51 (won by Herb Thomas). Final Grand National race run on 9/12/54 (won by Hershel McGriff). Track operated until May 1956.

Winston Cup Starts

Joe Eubanks	7
Jim Paschal	7
Lee Petty	7
Herb Thomas	7

Winston Cup Victories

Herb Thomas	2

Winston Cup Poles

Joe Eubanks	1
Bob Flock	1
Tim Flock	1
Fonty Flock	1
Dick Rathmann	1
Jack Smith	1

Winston Cup Money

Herb Thomas	$3,980

Most Cars Started
28—April 27, 1952

Fewest Cars Started
20—September 13, 1953

Narrowest Margin of Victory
N/A

Slowest Race
48.404 MPH—September 7, 1952

Race Record
56.417 MPH—April 26, 1953

Most Race Leaders
5—September 13, 1953

Most Cars Running at Finish
20—April 27, 1952

1951 Grand National Race No. 26
September 8, 1951 Average Speed: 53.222

Driver	Owner	Car #	Make	Laps	Winnings
1. Herb Thomas	Herb Thomas	92	51 Plym	200	1,000
2. Gober Sosebee	Gober Sosebee	51	51 Olds	198	600
3. Jim Paschal	Julian Buesink	60	50 Ford	—	500
4. Fonty Flock	Frank Christian	14	51 Olds	—	400
5. Donald Thomas	Herb Thomas	93	51 Plym	—	300

1952 Grand National Race No. 8
April 27, 1952 Average Speed: 53.853

Driver	Owner	Car #	Make	Laps	Winnings
1. Herb Thomas	Herb Thomas	92	52 Huds	198	1,270
2. Fonty Flock	Frank Christian	14	51 Olds	198	800
3. Ed Samples	Claude Alexander	9	51 Olds	198	600
4. Buck Baker	B. A. Pless	89	52 Huds	197	500
5. Gober Sosebee	Gober Sosebee	51	50 Olds	195	300

1952 Grand National Race No. 26
September 7, 1952 Average Speed: 48.404

Driver	Owner	Car #	Make	Laps	Winnings
1. Lee Petty	Petty Enterprises	42	51 Plym	300	1,260
2. Herb Thomas	Herb Thomas	92	52 Huds	300	810
3. Tim Flock	Ted Chester	91	52 Huds	298	630
4. Joe Eubanks	Phil Oates	82	52 Huds	295	500
5. Herschel Buchanan	Herschel Buchanan	1	52 Nash	289	300

1953 Grand National Race No. 7
April 26, 1953 Average Speed: 56.417

Driver	Owner	Car #	Make	Laps	Winnings
1. Dick Rathmann	Walt Chapman	120	52 Huds	200	1,000
2. Herb Thomas	Herb Thomas	92	53 Huds	—	700
3. Jimmie Lewallen	Dave Quate	43	53 Olds	—	450
4. Fonty Flock	Frank Christian	14	53 Olds	—	350
5. Dick Passwater	Frank Arford	78	53 Olds	—	200

1953 Grand National Race No. 31
September 13, 1953 Average Speed: 55.172

Driver	Owner	Car #	Make	Laps	Winnings
1. Speedy Thompson	Buckshot Morris	12	53 Olds	200	1,000
2. Lee Petty	Petty Enterprises	42	53 Dodg	—	700
3. Gober Sosebee	Gober Sosebee	51	53 Olds	—	450
4. Joe Eubanks	Phil Oates	82	53 Huds	—	350
5. Tim Flock	Ted Chester	91	53 Huds	—	200

1954 Grand National Race No. 9
April 25, 1954 Average Speed: 55.410

Driver	Owner	Car #	Make	Laps	Winnings
1. Gober Sosebee	Gober Sosebee	51	54 Olds	200	1,000
2. Dick Rathmann	John Ditz	3	54 Huds	200	650
3. Jim Paschal	Griffin Motors	87	53 Olds	199	450
4. Al Keller	George Miller	23	54 Huds	199	350
5. Curtis Turner	Frank Christian	14	53 Olds	199	300

1954 Grand National Race No. 32
September 12, 1954 Average Speed: 50.536

Driver	Owner	Car #	Make	Laps	Winnings
1. Hershel McGriff	Frank Christian	14	51 Olds	200	1,000
2. Tim Flock	Buck Baker	89	53 Olds	200	650
3. Lee Petty	Petty Enterprises	42	54 Chrys	200	450
4. Joe Eubanks	Phil Oates	82	51 Huds	199	350
5. Ralph Liguori	Ralph Liguori	6	54 Dodg	197	300

Columbus Speedway
Columbus, GA
Half-mile Dirt Track

Half-mile dirt track built circa 1949. Only NASCAR Winston Cup (then Grand National) event staged on 6/10/51 (won by Tim Flock). Track closed in late '50s.

Winston Cup Victories
Tim Flock   1

Winston Cup Money
Tim Flock $1,000

Narrowest Margin of Victory
N/A

Most Race Leaders
1—June 10, 1951

Winston Cup Poles
Gober Sosebee   1

Most Cars Started
31—June 10, 1951

Most Cautions
4—June 10, 1951

Most Cars Running at Finish
N/A

1951 Grand National Race No. 10
June 10, 1951

Driver	Owner	Car #	Make	Laps	Winnings
1. Tim Flock	Ted Chester	91	51 Olds	200	1,000
2. Gober Sosebee	Sam Knox	51	50 Cad	—	600
3. Herb Thomas	Herb Thomas	92	50 Plym	—	400
4. Jim Paschal	Julian Buesink	60	50 Ford	—	300
5. Lee Petty	Petty Enterprises	42	49 Plym	—	250

Hayloft Speedway
Augusta, GA
Half-mile Dirt Track

(aka Augusta Speedway; Gordon Park Speedway) Opened in March 1948. Only NASCAR Winston Cup (then Grand National) race staged on 6/1/52 (won by Gober Sosebee). Track closed in 1955. Dirt track was built on grounds in 1980s.

Winston Cup Victories
Gober Sosebee   1

Winston Cup Money
Gober Sosebee $1,000

Narrowest Margin of Victory
22 seconds June 1, 1952

Most Cars Running at Finish
10—June 1, 1952

Winston Cup Poles
Tommy Moon   1

Most Cars Started
14—June 1, 1952

Most Race Leaders
N/A

1952 Grand National Race No. 13
June 1, 1952

Driver	Owner	Car #	Make	Laps	Winnings
1. Gober Sosebee	Sam Knox	51	52 Chrys	154	1,000
2. Tommy Moon	C. D. Wilson	57	52 Huds	154	700
3. David Ezell			52 Huds	153	450
4. June Cleveland	Carl Mays	17	51 Chrys	150	350
5. Jerry Wimbish	Jerry Wimbish		50 Olds	150	300

Jeffco Speedway
Jefferson, GA
Half-mile Paved Track

(aka Peach State Speedway; Georgia Int'l Speedway) Half-mile paved oval opened in July 1967. First NASCAR Winston Cup (then Grand National) race staged on 11/3/68 (won by Cale Yarborough). Only other NASCAR event staged on 11/2/69 (won by Bobby Isaac). Track is still in operation.

Winston Cup Starts
18 drivers tied with 2

Winston Cup Victories
Bobby Isaac   1
Cale Yarborough   1

Winston Cup Poles
David Pearson   2

Winston Cup Money
Bobby Isaac $1,500

Most Cars Started
29—November 3, 1968 Peach State 200

Fewest Cars Started
27—November 2, 1969 Jeffco 200

Narrowest Margin of Victory
Half lap—November 3, 1968

Slowest Race
77.737 MPH—November 3, 1968
Peach State 200

Race Record
85.106 MPH—November 2, 1969
Jeffco 200

Most Cautions
N/A

Most Race Leaders
3—November 3, 1968 Peach State 200

Most Cars Running at Finish
21—November 3, 1968 Peach State 200
21—November 2, 1969 Jeffco 200

1968 Grand National Race No. 49 Peach State 200
November 3, 1968 Average Speed: 77.737

Driver	Owner	Car #	Make	Laps	Winnings
1. Cale Yarborough	Wood Brothers	21	68 Merc	200	1,000
2. Richard Petty	Petty Enterprises	43	68 Plym	200	800
3. David Pearson	Holman-Moody	17	68 Ford	199	400
4. James Hylton	James Hylton	48	68 Dodg	199	300
5. LeeRoy Yarbrough	Lyle Stelter	56	67 Merc	197	275

1969 Grand National Race No. 52 Jeffco 200
November 2, 1969 Average Speed: 85.106

Driver	Owner	Car #	Make	Laps	Winnings
1. Bobby Isaac	Nord Krauskopf	71	69 Dodg	200	1,350
2. David Pearson	Holman-Moody	17	69 Ford	200	950
3. Richard Petty	Petty Enterprises	43	69 Ford	198	500
4. LeeRoy Yarbrough	Junior Johnson	98	69 Ford	196	350
5. Neil Castles	Neil Castles	06	69 Dodg	191	325

Lakewood Speedway
Atlanta, GA
1-mile Dirt Track

(aka Lakewood Park; Lakewood Fairgrounds) Originally built in 1915. First auto race was run in 1917. Held AM Indy Car races in '40s and '50s. Sam Nunis ran two Strictly Stock races (not sanctioned by NASCAR) in 1949. Tim Flock and June Cleveland won, and both were mistakenly given credit for Winston Cup victories. First NASCAR Winston Cup (then Grand National) race staged on 11/11/51 (won by Tim Flock). Final Grand National race run on 6/14/59 (won by Lee Petty after successfully protesting Richard Petty's apparent first Winston Cup victory). Track closed following completion of Atlanta Int'l Raceway. Re-opened for selected shows (NASCAR Grand American, Sprint Cars, Dirt Late Models). Final event held on Labor Day 1979.

Winston Cup Starts
Lee Petty   11

Winston Cup Victories
Buck Baker   2
Herb Thomas   2

Winston Cup Poles
Tim Flock   3

Winston Cup Money
Lee Petty $5,860

Most Cars Started
40—October 26, 1958
40—June 14, 1959

Fewest Cars Started
17—July 12, 1953

Narrowest Margin of Victory
1 car length—March 21, 1954

Slowest Race
58.499 MPH—June 14, 1959

Race Record
79.016 MPH—April 13, 1958

Most Cautions
N/A

Most Race Leaders
4—April 20, 1952
4—November 16, 1952
4—November 1, 1953

Most Cars Running at Finish
21—October 26, 1958
21—June 14, 1959

1951 Grand National Race No. 39
November 11, 1951 Average Speed: 59.960

Driver	Owner	Car #	Make	Laps	Winnings
1. Tim Flock	Ted Chester	91	51 Huds	100	1,000
2. Bob Flock	Ted Chester	7	51 Olds	—	600
3. Jack Smith	Jack Smith	44X	51 Huds	—	500
4. Frank Mundy	Perry Smith	23	51 Stud	—	400
5. Gober Sosebee	Gober Sosebee	51	51 Olds	—	300

1952 Grand National Race No. 7
April 20, 1952 Average Speed: 66.877

Driver	Owner	Car #	Make	Laps	Winnings
1. Bill Blair	George Hutchens	2	52 Olds	100	1,000
2. Ed Samples	Claude Alexander	9	51 Olds	100	700
3. Lee Petty	Petty Enterprises	42	51 Plym	100	450
4. Buck Baker	B. A. Pless	89	52 Huds	99	350
5. Ed Benedict	Ken Swihart	118	52 Huds	98	200

1952 Grand National Race No. 33
November 16, 1952 Average Speed: 64.853

Driver	Owner	Car #	Make	Laps	Winnings
1. Donald Thomas	Herb Thomas	9	52 Huds	100	1,080
2. Lee Petty	Petty Enterprises	42	51 Plym	100	700
3. Joe Eubanks	Phil Oates	82	52 Huds	100	450
4. Tim Flock	Ted Chester	91	52 Huds	99	385
5. Gober Sosebee	Gober Sosebee	51	52 Chrys	98	200

1953 Grand National Race No. 22
July 12, 1953 Average Speed: 70.685

Driver	Owner	Car #	Make	Laps	Winnings
1. Herb Thomas	Herb Thomas	92	53 Huds	100	1,000
2. Dick Rathmann	Walt Chapman	120	53 Huds	—	700
3. Lee Petty	Petty Enterprises	42	53 Dodg	—	450
4. Joe Eubanks	Phil Oates	82	52 Huds	—	350
5. Jerry Wimbish	Jerry Wimbish		52 Huds	—	200

1953 Grand National Race No. 37
November 1, 1953 Average Speed: 63.180

Driver	Owner	Car #	Make	Laps	Winnings
1. Buck Baker	Griffin Motors	87	53 Olds	100	1,000
2. Fonty Flock	Frank Christian	14	53 Huds	—	700
3. Lee Petty	Petty Enterprises	42	53 Dodg	—	450
4. Jim Paschal	George Hutchens	80	53 Dodg	—	350
5. Jimmie Lewallen	R. G. Shelton	22	53 Olds	—	200

1954 Grand National Race No. 4
March 21, 1954 Average Speed: 60.494

Driver	Owner	Car #	Make	Laps	Winnings
1. Herb Thomas	Herb Thomas	92	53 Huds	100	1,000
2. Buck Baker	Griffin Motors	87	53 Olds	100	650
3. Dick Rathmann	John Ditz	3	54 Huds	100	450
4. Gober Sosebee	Gober Sosebee	51	54 Olds	99	350
5. Fonty Flock		99	53 Huds	99	300

1956 Grand National Race No. 9
March 25, 1956 Average Speed: 70.643

Driver	Owner	Car #	Make	Laps	Winnings
1. Buck Baker	Carl Kiekhaefer	300c	56 Chrys	100	1,400
2. Speedy Thompson	Carl Kiekhaefer	500	56 Dodg	100	800
3. Herb Thomas	Herb Thomas	92	56 Chev	99	550
4. Jimmy Massey	Hubert Westmoreland	2	56 Chev	99	365
5. Lee Petty	Petty Enterprises	42	56 Dodg	99	310

1958 Grand National Race No. 10
April 13, 1958 Average Speed: 79.016

Driver	Owner	Car #	Make	Laps	Winnings
1. Curtis Turner	Holman-Moody	26	58 Ford	100	1,540
2. Joe Weatherly	Holman-Moody	12	58 Ford	100	545
3. Fireball Roberts	Beau Morgan	494	57 Ford	100	400
4. Marvin Panch	John Whitford	98	57 Ford	100	250
5. Joe Lee Johnson	S. T. Campbell	310	57 Chev	99	225

1958 Grand National Race No. 51
October 26, 1958 Average Speed: 69.570

Driver	Owner	Car #	Make	Laps	Winnings
1. Junior Johnson	Paul Spaulding	11	57 Ford	150	1,925
2. Fireball Roberts	Frank Strickland	22	57 Chev	150	1,200
3. Lee Petty	Petty Enterprises	2	57 Olds	150	950
4. Joe Weatherly	Beau Morgan	45	58 Ford	149	650
5. Charlie Micney		29	57 Chev	148	550

1959 Grand National Race No. 6
March 22, 1959 Average Speed: 75.172

Driver	Owner	Car #	Make	Laps	Winnings
1. Johnny Beauchamp	Roy Burdick Gar	73	59 Ford	100	800
2. Buck Baker	Buck Baker	87	59 Chev	99	525
3. Tom Pistone	Carl Rupert	59	59 Ford	97	350
4. Speedy Thompson	Steve Pierce	1	57 Chev	96	250
5. Joe Eubanks	Don Every	82	58 Ford	95	225

Lakewood Speedway *continued*

1959 Grand National Race No. 20
June 14, 1959 Average Speed: 58.499

Driver	Owner	Car #	Make	Laps	Winnings
1. Lee Petty	Petty Enterprises	42	59 Plym	150	2,200
2. Richard Petty	Petty Enterprises	43	57 Olds	150	1,400
3. Buck Baker	Buck Baker	87	59 Chev	150	1,025
4. Curtis Turner	W. J. Ridgeway	22	59 Chev	150	950
5. Tom Pistone	Carl Rupert	59	59 Ford	148	625

Middle Georgia Raceway
Macon, GA
Half-mile Paved Track

(aka Macon Raceway; Peach State Fairgrounds) Half-mile track built in 1966 on site of former Central City Speedway. Re-measured as .5479-mile paved oval. First NASCAR Winston Cup (then Grand National) race staged on 5/10/66 (won by Richard Petty). Final race staged on 11/7/71 (won by Bobby Allison). A fully operative moonshine still was found beneath the track shortly before 1968 season opener. The entrance to the still was through a ticket booth. A 35-foot ladder led to a trap door. Authorities found a 125-foot tunnel leading to the still. "This is one of the most cleverly run moonshine operations I have ever seen," said one federal agent. Promoter was arrested, but later acquitted. The race went on as scheduled.

Winston Cup Starts
Wendell Scott   9

Winston Cup Victories
Richard Petty   4

Winston Cup Poles
David Pearson   3
Richard Petty   3

Winston Cup Money
Richard Petty $13,765

Most Cars Started
32—November 7, 1971 Georgia 500

Fewest Cars Started
15—May 10, 1966
     Speedy Morelock 200

Narrowest Margin of Victory
5 car lengths—November 9, 1969
     Georgia 500

Slowest Race
73.717 MPH—June 1, 1969 Macon 300

Race Record
85.121 MPH—November 17, 1968

Most Cautions
10—November 9, 1969 Georgia 500

Most Race Leaders
4—November 17, 1968
4—November 12, 1967
     Middle Georgia 500
4—November 9, 1969 Georgia 500
4—November 8, 1970 Georgia 500
4—November 7, 1971 Georgia 500

Most Cars Running at Finish
17—November 8, 1970 Georgia 500

1966 Grand National Race No. 17 Speedy Morelock 200
May 10, 1966 Average Speed: 82.023

Driver	Owner	Car #	Make	Laps	Winnings
1. Richard Petty	Petty Enterprises	43	66 Plym	200	1,000
2. Tom Pistone	Tom Pistone	59	64 Ford	200	600
3. Bobby Allison	Betty Lilly	24	66 Ford	197	400
4. James Hylton	Bud Hartje	48	65 Dodg	193	300
5. Neil Castles	Buck Baker	86	66 Plym	184	275

1967 Grand National Race No. 22 Macon 300
June 6, 1967 Average Speed: 80.321

Driver	Owner	Car #	Make	Laps	Winnings
1. Richard Petty	Petty Enterprises	43	67 Plym	300	1,400
2. James Hylton	Bud Hartje	48	65 Dodg	295	1,000
3. Elmo Langley	L. G. DeWitt	4	66 Ford	292	700
4. Bobby Allison	George Davis	07	67 Chev	290	575
5. Doug Cooper	Bob Cooper	02	66 Chev	286	425

1968 Grand National Race No. 1 Middle Georgia 500
November 12, 1967 Average Speed: 81.001

Driver	Owner	Car #	Make	Laps	Winnings
1. Bobby Allison	Holman-Moody	11	67 Ford	500	3,300
2. Richard Petty	Petty Enterprises	43	67 Plym	499	2,040
3. Tiny Lund	Lyle Stelter	55	66 Ford	491	1,275
4. Red Farmer	Roy Buckner	97	67 Ford	476	900
5. Dub Simpson	Buck Baker	88	67 Olds	470	800

1968 Grand National Race No. 20 Macon 300
June 2, 1968 Average Speed: 79.342

Driver	Owner	Car #	Make	Laps	Winnings
1. David Pearson	Holman-Moody	17	68 Ford	300	1,400
2. Bobby Isaac	Nord Krauskopf	71	67 Dodg	300	1,000
3. Richard Petty	Petty Enterprises	43	68 Plym	300	900
4. James Hylton	James Hylton	48	67 Dodg	297	575
5. Tiny Lund	Bud Moore	16	68 Merc	292	425

1969 Grand National Race No. 1
November 17, 1968 Average Speed: 85.121

Driver	Owner	Car #	Make	Laps	Winnings
1. Richard Petty	Petty Enterprises	43	68 Plym	500	3,500
2. David Pearson	Holman-Moody	17	68 Ford	500	2,345
3. James Hylton	James Hylton	48	68 Dodg	490	1,375
4. Elmo Langley	Elmo Langley	64	66 Ford	476	925
5. John Sears	L. G. DeWitt	4	66 Ford	466	825

1969 Grand National Race No. 22 Macon 300
June 1, 1969 Average Speed: 73.717

Driver	Owner	Car #	Make	Laps	Winnings
1. Bobby Isaac	Nord Krauskopf	71	69 Dodg	300	2,500
2. David Pearson	Holman-Moody	17	69 Ford	300	1,700
3. Richard Petty	Petty Enterprises	43	69 Ford	299	1,000
4. John Sears	L. G. DeWitt	4	67 Ford	295	750
5. Neil Castles	Neil Castles	06	67 Plym	295	600

1969 Grand National Race No. 53 Georgia 500
November 9, 1969 Average Speed: 81.079

Driver	Owner	Car #	Make	Laps	Winnings
1. Bobby Allison	Mario Rossi	22	69 Dodg	500	3,050
2. David Pearson	Holman-Moody	17	69 Ford	500	2,025
3. Bobby Isaac	Nord Krauskopf	71	69 Dodg	500	1,300
4. John Sears	L. G. DeWitt	4	67 Ford	482	775
5. Bill Champion	Bill Champion	10	68 Ford	471	675

1970 Grand National Race No. 46 Georgia 500
November 8, 1970 Average Speed: 83.284

Driver	Owner	Car #	Make	Laps	Winnings
1. Richard Petty	Petty Enterprises	43	70 Plym	500	3,275
2. Bobby Isaac	Nord Krauskopf	71	70 Dodg	500	1,800
3. Dick Brooks	Dick Brooks	32	69 Plym	498	1,150
4. Bobby Allison	Bobby Allison	22	69 Dodg	497	925
5. John Sears	John Sears	4	69 Dodg	487	700

1971 Winston Cup GN Race No. 45 Georgia 500
November 7, 1971 Average Speed: 80.859

Driver	Owner	Car #	Make	Laps	Winnings
1. Bobby Allison	Holman-Moody	12	71 Ford	500	3,275
2. Tiny Lund	Ronnie Hopkins	55	70 Chev	499	2,000
3. Friday Hassler	Friday Hassler	39	70 Chev	490	1,200
4. Neil Castles	Neil Castles	06	70 Dodg	486	800
5. Bill Champion	Bill Champion	10	71 Ford	483	700

Oglethorpe Speedway
Savannah, GA
Half-mile Dirt Track

Half-mile dirt track opened in May 1951. First NASCAR Winston Cup (then Grand National) race staged on 3/28/54 (won by Al Keller). Final race staged on 3/6/55 (won by Lee Petty). The track still conducts weekly NASCAR racing.

Winston Cup Starts

Buck Baker	2
Jimmie Lewallen	2
Jim Paschal	2
Eddie Skinner	2
Gober Sosebee	2
Dave Terrell	2
Herb Thomas	2

Winston Cup Victories

Al Keller	1
Lee Petty	1

Winston Cup Poles

Dick Rathmann	1
Herb Thomas	1

Winston Cup Money

Al Keller	$1,000
Lee Petty	$1,000

Most Cars Started
21—March 28, 1954

Fewest Cars Started
18—March 6, 1955

Narrowest Margin of Victory
2 laps plus—March 28, 1954

Slowest Race
59.820 MPH—March 28, 1954

Race Record
60.150 MPH—March 6, 1955

Most Race Leaders
2—March 28, 1954
2—March 6, 1955

Most Cars Running at Finish
12—March 6, 1955

1954 Grand National Race No. 5
March 28, 1954 Average Speed: 59.820

Driver	Owner	Car #	Make	Laps	Winnings
1. Al Keller	George Miller	23	54 Huds	200	1,000
2. Buck Baker	Griffin Motors	87	53 Olds	198	650
3. Gober Sosebee	Gober Sosebee	51	54 Olds	194	450
4. Donald Thomas	John Ditz	3	54 Huds	189	350
5. Joe Eubanks	Phil Oates	82	51 Huds	188	300

1955 Grand National Race No. 5
March 6, 1955 Average Speed: 60.150

Driver	Owner	Car #	Make	Laps	Winnings
1. Lee Petty	Petty Enterprises	42	54 Chrys	200	1,000
2. Don White	Don White	1	55 Olds	196	650
3. Dick Rathmann	John Ditz	3	54 Huds	194	450
4. Herb Thomas	Herb Thomas	92	54 Huds	192	350
5. Eddie Skinner	Frank Dodge	28	53 Olds	185	300

Savannah Speedway
Savannah, GA
Half-mile Paved Track

(aka New Savannah Speedway) Half-mile dirt track built in 1962. First NASCAR Winston Cup (then Grand National) race staged on 3/17/62 (won by Jack Smith). LeeRoy Yarbrough won his first Grand National race here on 5/1/64. Track paved in 1969. Final Grand National race run on 3/15/70 (won by Richard Petty). Track closed in 1981.

Winston Cup Starts
Richard Petty   10

Winston Cup Victories
Richard Petty   3

Winston Cup Poles
Richard Petty   3

Winston Cup Money
Richard Petty $5,785

Most Cars Started
29—October 17, 1969

Fewest Cars Started
12—May 1, 1964 Savannah 200
12—October 9, 1964

Narrowest Margin of Victory
N/A

Slowest Race
58.775 MPH—March 17, 1962
St. Patrick's Day 200

Race Record
82.418 MPH—March 15, 1970
Savannah 200

Most Cautions
3—March 17, 1962 St. Patrick's Day 200
3—December 29, 1963 Sunshine 200

Most Race Leaders
4—March 17, 1962 St. Patrick's Day 200
4—April 28, 1967

Most Cars Running at Finish
23—October 17, 1969

1962 Grand National Race No. 8 St. Patrick's Day 200
March 17, 1962 Average Speed: 58.775

Driver	Owner	Car #	Make	Laps	Winnings
1. Jack Smith	Jack Smith	47	61 Pont	200	1,000
2. Cotton Owens	Cotton Owens	6	60 Pont	200	600
3. Joe Weatherly	Bud Moore	8	61 Pont	198	400
4. Curtis Crider	Curtis Crider	62	61 Merc	190	300
5. Rex White	Rex White	4	61 Chev	183	275

1962 Grand National Race No. 34
July 20, 1962 Average Speed: 67.239

Driver	Owner	Car #	Make	Laps	Winnings
1. Joe Weatherly	Bud Moore	8	61 Pont	200	1,000
2. Tommy Irwin	Melvin Bradley	27	62 Chev	200	600
3. Richard Petty	Petty Enterprises	43	62 Plym	200	400
4. Bob Welborn	J. C. Parker	49	62 Pont	199	300
5. Jim Paschal	Cliff Stewart	2	62 Pont	198	275

1963 Grand National Race No. 31
July 10, 1963 Average Speed: 59.622

Driver	Owner	Car #	Make	Laps	Winnings
1. Ned Jarrett	Charles Robinson	11	63 Ford	200	1,000
2. David Pearson	Cotton Owens	6	63 Dodg	200	600
3. Jimmy Pardue	Pete Stewart	57	62 Pont	199	400
4. Jack Smith	Jack Smith	48	63 Plym	199	300
5. Cale Yarborough	Herman Beam	19	62 Ford	198	275

1964 Grand National Race No. 4 Sunshine 200
December 29, 1963 Average Speed: 68.143

Driver	Owner	Car #	Make	Laps	Winnings
1. Richard Petty	Petty Enterprises	43	63 Plym	200	1,000
2. Jack Smith	Jack Smith	47	63 Plym	199	600
3. Tiny Lund	Dave Kent	32	63 Ford	196	400
4. Maurice Petty	Petty Enterprises	42	63 Plym	195	300
5. Curtis Crider	Curtis Crider	62	63 Ford	194	275

1964 Grand National Race No. 20 Savannah 200
May 1, 1964 Average Speed: 70.326

Driver	Owner	Car #	Make	Laps	Winnings
1. LeeRoy Yarbrough	Louie Weathersby	45	63 Plym	200	1,000
2. Marvin Panch	Wood Brothers	21	64 Ford	199	600
3. Richard Petty	Petty Enterprises	43	64 Plym	197	400
4. Buddy Baker	J. C. Parker	87	63 Dodg	197	300
5. Cale Yarborough	Herman Beam	19	64 Ford	185	275

1964 Grand National Race No. 57
October 9, 1964 Average Speed: 68.663

Driver	Owner	Car #	Make	Laps	Winnings
1. Ned Jarrett	Bondy Long	11	64 Ford	200	1,000
2. Richard Petty	Petty Enterprises	43	64 Plym	199	600
3. David Pearson	Cotton Owens	6	64 Dodg	198	400
4. Jack Anderson	Dave Kent	32	64 Ford	193	300
5. Wendell Scott	Wendell Scott	34	63 Ford	192	275

1967 Grand National Race No. 15
April 28, 1967 Average Speed: 66.802

Driver	Owner	Car #	Make	Laps	Winnings
1. Bobby Allison	Bobby Allison	2	65 Chev	200	1,000
2. Richard Petty	Petty Enterprises	43	67 Plym	200	600
3. Jim Paschal	Tom Friedkin	14	67 Plym	198	400
4. Elmo Langley	Henry Woodfield	64	66 Ford	194	300
5. Clyde Lynn	Clyde Lynn	20	66 Ford	194	275

1967 Grand National Race No. 39
August 25, 1967 Average Speed: 65.041

Driver	Owner	Car #	Make	Laps	Winnings
1. Richard Petty	Petty Enterprises	43	67 Plym	200	1,000
2. Elmo Langley	Henry Woodfield	64	66 Ford	195	600
3. Tom Pistone	Turkey Minton	74	67 Chev	194	400
4. Neil Castles	Neil Castles	91	65 Plym	190	300
5. George Davis	George Davis	07	66 Chev	186	275

1969 Grand National Race No. 49
October 17, 1969 Average Speed: 78.482

Driver	Owner	Car #	Make	Laps	Winnings
1. Bobby Isaac	Nord Krauskopf	71	69 Dodg	200	1,000
2. Richard Petty	Petty Enterprises	43	69 Ford	200	600
3. David Pearson	Holman-Moody	17	69 Ford	200	600
4. LeeRoy Yarbrough	Junior Johnson	98	69 Ford	198	350
5. Elmo Langley	Elmo Langley	64	68 Ford	194	325

1970 Grand National Race No. 7 Savannah 200
March 15, 1970 Average Speed: 82.418

Driver	Owner	Car #	Make	Laps	Winnings
1. Richard Petty	Petty Enterprises	43	70 Plym	200	1,000
2. Bobby Isaac	Nord Krauskopf	71	69 Dodg	199	600
3. James Hylton	James Hylton	48	69 Ford	196	400
4. Benny Parsons	L. G. DeWitt	72	69 Ford	195	350
5. Dave Marcis	Dave Marcis	30	69 Dodg	195	325

Valdosta 75 Speedway
Valdosta, GA
Half-mile Dirt Track

(aka I-75 Speedway; Valdosta Speedway) Half-mile dirt track built in April 1962. First NASCAR Winston Cup (then Grand National) race staged on 8/25/62 (won by Ned Jarrett). Final race staged on 6/25/65 (won by Cale Yarborough, his first Grand National victory). Track closed in 1966.

Winston Cup Starts
Ned Jarrett   3
Wendell Scott   3

Winston Cup Victories
Buck Baker   1
Ned Jarrett   1
Cale Yarborough 1

Winston Cup Poles
Dick Hutcherson 1
Ned Jarrett   1
Richard Petty   1

Winston Cup Money
Ned Jarrett $1,410

Most Cars Started
23—June 23, 1964

Fewest Cars Started
13—August 25, 1962

Narrowest Margin of Victory
15.000 seconds June 23, 1964

Slowest Race
58.862 MPH—June 27, 1965

Race Record
61.454 MPH—August 25, 1962

Most Race Leaders
3—June 23, 1964
3—June 27, 1965

Most Cars Running at Finish
13—June 23, 1964

1962 Grand National Race No. 44
August 25, 1962 Average Speed: 61.454

Driver	Owner	Car #	Make	Laps	Winnings
1. Ned Jarrett	Bee Gee Holloway	11	62 Chev	200	1,200
2. Richard Petty	Petty Enterprises	43	62 Plym	199	600
3. Joe Weatherly	Bud Moore	8	61 Pont	197	400
4. G. C. Spencer	G. C. Spencer	48	62 Chev	191	300
5. LeeRoy Yarbrough	Ralph Smith	179	62 Chev	191	275

1964 Grand National Race No. 33
June 23, 1964 Average Speed: 61.328

Driver	Owner	Car #	Make	Laps	Winnings
1. Buck Baker	Ray Fox	3	64 Dodg	200	1,000
2. LeeRoy Yarbrough	Louie Weathersby	45	63 Plym	200	600
3. Tiny Lund	David Walker	89	64 Plym	196	400
4. Wendell Scott	Wendell Scott	34	63 Ford	195	300
5. Curtis Crider	Curtis Crider	02	63 Merc	193	275

1965 Grand National Race No. 28
June 27, 1965 Average Speed: 58.862

Driver	Owner	Car #	Make	Laps	Winnings
1. Cale Yarborough	Kenny Myler	06	64 Ford	200	1,000
2. J. T. Putney	Herman Beam	19	64 Ford	197	600
3. G. C. Spencer	G. C. Spencer	49	64 Ford	196	400
4. Stick Elliott	Toy Bolton	18	65 Chev	196	300
5. Harvey Jones	Sam Fogle	31	63 Ford	195	275

Illinois

Santa Fe Speedway
Willow Springs, IL
Half-mile Dirt Track

Half-mile dirt track opened in May 1953. Only NASCAR Winston Cup (then Grand National) race run on 7/10/54 (won by Dick Rathmann). Track still active in 1990s.

Winston Cup Victories
Dick Rathmann   1

Winston Cup Poles
Buck Baker   1

Winston Cup Money
Dick Rathmann $1,000

Most Cars Started
23—July 10, 1954

Narrowest Margin of Victory
3/4 lap—July 10, 1954

Race Record
72.216 MPH—July 10, 1954

Most Race Leaders
2—July 10, 1954

Most Cars Running at Finish
16—July 10, 1954

1954 Grand National Race No. 24
July 10, 1954 Average Speed: 72.216

Driver	Owner	Car #	Make	Laps	Winnings
1. Dick Rathmann	John Ditz	3	54 Huds	200	1,000
2. Herb Thomas	Herb Thomas	92	54 Huds	200	650
3. Hershel McGriff	Frank Christian	14	51 Olds	200	450
4. Lee Petty	Petty Enterprises	42	54 Chrys	199	350
5. Buck Baker	Ernest Woods	88	54 Olds	197	300

Soldier Field
Chicago, IL
Half-mile Paved Track

Famous football stadium built in 1926. Quarter-mile cinder oval built inside stadium in 1935. Half-mile paved track ran from 1956-67. A .375-mile track followed in 1968. Track torn out in 1970 following protests by hippies who objected to city financing of auto racing. Only NASCAR Winston Cup (then Grand National) race staged on 7/21/56 (won by Fireball Roberts).

Winston Cup Victories
Fireball Roberts   1

Winston Cup Poles
Billy Myers   1

Winston Cup Money
Fireball Roberts $850

Most Cars Started
25—July 21, 1956

Narrowest Margin of Victory
N/A

Race Record
61.037 MPH—July 21, 1956

Most Race Leaders
N/A

Most Cars Running at Finish
15—July 21, 1956

1956 Grand National Race No. 33
July 21, 1956 Average Speed: 61.037

Driver	Owner	Car #	Make	Laps	Winnings
1. Fireball Roberts	Pete DePaolo	22	56 Ford	200	850
2. Jim Paschal	Frank Hayworth	75	56 Merc	200	625
3. Ralph Moody	Pete DePaolo	12	56 Ford	200	450
4. Speedy Thompson	Carl Kiekhaefer	500	56 Dodg	200	350
5. Frank Mundy	Carl Kiekhaefer	500B	56 Dodg	200	310

Indiana

Indianapolis Motor Speedway
Speedway, IN
2.5-mile Superspeedway

Since 1911, the scene of the Greatest Spectacle in Racing, the Indianapolis 500. 2.5-mile rectangular shaped track was built in 1909 with 3.2-million bricks, hence the nickname "Brickyard". Track was built by the Carl Fisher group. Eddie Rickenbacker was president during Depression years. Following the Second World War, Anton Hulman purchased track. First NASCAR Winston Cup race staged on 8/6/94 (won by Jeff Gordon).

Winston Cup Starts
31 drivers tied with 3

Winston Cup Victories
Dale Earnhardt 1
Jeff Gordon 1
Dale Jarrett 1

Winston Cup Poles
Jeff Gordon 2

Winston Cup Money
Jeff Gordon $1,049,791

Most Cars Started
43—August 6, 1994 Brickyard 400

Fewest Cars Started
40—August 3, 1996 Brickyard 400

Narrowest Margin of Victory
0.370 seconds August 5, 1995 Brickyard 400

Slowest Race
131.977 MPH—August 6, 1994 Brickyard 400

Race Record
155.206 MPH—August 5, 1995 Brickyard 400

Most Cautions
6—August 6, 1994 Brickyard 400

Most Race Leaders
13—August 6, 1994 Brickyard 400
13—August 3, 1996 Brickyard 400

Most Cars Running at Finish
36—August 6, 1994 Brickyard 400
36—August 5, 1995 Brickyard 400

1994 Winston Cup Series Race No. 19 Brickyard 400
August 6, 1994 Average Speed: 131.977

Driver	Owner	Car #	Make	Laps	Winnings
1. Jeff Gordon	Rick Hendrick	24	Chev	160	613,000
2. Brett Bodine	Kenny Bernstein	26	Ford	160	203,575
3. Bill Elliott	Junior Johnson	11	Ford	160	164,850
4. Rusty Wallace	Roger Penske	2	Ford	160	140,600
5. Dale Earnhardt	Richard Childress	3	Chev	160	121,625

1995 Winston Cup Series Race No. 19 Brickyard 400
August 5, 1995 Average Speed: 155.206

Driver	Owner	Car #	Make	Laps	Winnings
1. Dale Earnhardt	Richard Childress	3	Chev	160	565,600
2. Rusty Wallace	Roger Penske	2	Ford	160	250,500
3. Dale Jarrett	Robert Yates	28	Ford	160	203,200
4. Bill Elliott	Bill Elliott	94	Ford	160	233,450
5. Mark Martin	Jack Roush	6	Ford	160	144,850

1996 Winston Cup Series Race No. 19 Brickyard 400
August 3, 1996 Average Speed: 139.508

Driver	Owner	Car #	Make	Laps	Winnings
1. Dale Jarrett	Robert Yates	88	Ford	160	564,035
2. Ernie Irvan	Robert Yates	28	Ford	160	267,285
3. Terry Labonte	Rick Hendrick	5	Chev	160	209,535
4. Mark Martin	Jack Roush	6	Ford	160	195,235
5. Morgan Shepherd	Butch Mock	75	Ford	160	140,135

Playland Park Speedway
South Bend, IN
Half-mile Dirt Track

Half-mile dirt track built in 1919. Only NASCAR Winston Cup (then Grand National) race staged on 7/20/52 (won by Tim Flock). Track closed circa 1956.

Winston Cup Victories
Tim Flock   1

Winston Cup Poles
Herb Thomas   1

Winston Cup Money
Tim Flock $1,000

Most Cars Started
19—July 20, 1952

Narrowest Margin of Victory
N/A

Race Record
41.889 MPH—July 20, 1952

Most Race Leaders
2—July 20, 1952

Most Cars Running at Finish
8—July 20, 1952

1952 Grand National Race No. 22
July 20, 1952 Average Speed: 41.889

Driver	Owner	Car #	Make	Laps	Winnings
1. Tim Flock	Ted Chester	91	51 Huds	200	1,000
2. Lee Petty	Petty Enterprises	42	52 Chrys	200	700
3. Bub King	Bub King	55	52 Huds	189	450
4. Herschel Buchanan	Frank Christian	4	51 Olds	186	350
5. Dick Passwater	Frank Arford	77	52 DES	184	200

Winchester Speedway
Winchester, IN
Half-mile Oiled Dirt Track

(aka Funk's Speedway; Funk's Lake; Funk's Motor Speedway) Half-mile dirt track built by Frank Funk in a cornfield in 1914. High-banks were added in 1929. Only Winston Cup (then Grand National) race run on 10/15/50 (won by Lloyd Moore). Track paved in 1951. Still active today, hosting a variety of open wheel and stock car events.

Winston Cup Victories
Lloyd Moore   1

Winston Cup Poles
Dick Linder   1

Winston Cup Money
Lloyd Moore $1,000

Most Cars Started
13—October 15, 1950

Narrowest Margin of Victory
N/A

Race Record
63.875 MPH—October 15, 1950

Most Race Leaders
3—October 15, 1950

Most Cars Running at Finish
N/A

1950 Grand National Race No. 18
October 15, 1950 Average Speed: 63.875

Driver	Owner	Car #	Make	Laps	Winnings
1. Lloyd Moore	Julian Buesink	59	50 Merc	200	1,000
2. Bucky Sager		101	49 Plym	—	625
3. Bill Rexford	Julian Buesink	60	49 Ford	—	400
4. Chuck James			46 Ford	—	300
5. Ray Duhigg		10	50 Plym	—	225

Iowa

Davenport Speedway
Davenport, IA
Half-mile Dirt Track

Half-mile dirt oval opened in August 1920. Only NASCAR Winston Cup (then Grand National) race run on 8/2/53 (won by Herb Thomas).
Track still active today.

Winston Cup Victories		**Winston Cup Money**		**Narrowest Margin of Victory**	**Most Race Leaders**
Herb Thomas	1	Herb Thomas	$1,000	N/A	N/A

Winston Cup Poles		**Most Cars Started**	**Race Record**	**Most Cars Running at Finish**
Buck Baker	1	14—August 2, 1953	62.500 MPH—August 2, 1953	N/A

1953 Grand National Race No. 25
August 2, 1953 Average Speed: 62.500

Driver	Owner	Car #	Make	Laps	Winnings
1. Herb Thomas	Herb Thomas	92	53 Huds	200	1,000
2. Buck Baker	Griffin Motors	87	53 Olds	—	700
3. Lee Petty	Petty Enterprises	42	53 Dodg	—	450
4. Dick Rathmann	Walt Chapman	120	53 Huds	—	350
5. Fonty Flock	Frank Christian	14	53 Huds	—	200

Kentucky

Corbin Speedway
Corbin, KY
Half-mile Dirt Track

Half-mile dirt track opened circa 1953. Only NASCAR Winston Cup (then Grand National) race staged on 8/29/54 (won by Lee Petty). Track closed in early 1960s.

Winston Cup Victories
Lee Petty   1

Winston Cup Money
Lee Petty $1,000

Narrowest Margin of Victory
N/A

Most Race Leaders
N/A

Winston Cup Poles
Jim Paschal   1

Most Cars Started
21—August 29, 1954

Race Record
63.080 MPH—August 29, 1954

Most Cars Running at Finish
13—August 29, 1954

1954 Grand National Race No. 30
August 29, 1954 Average Speed: 63.080

Driver	Owner	Car #	Make	Laps	Winnings
1. Lee Petty	Petty Enterprises	42	54 Chrys	200	1,000
2. Hershel McGriff	Frank Christian	14	52 Olds	200	650
3. Buck Baker	Griffin Motors	87	53 Olds	198	450
4. Herb Thomas	Herb Thomas	92	54 Huds	195	350
5. Donald Thomas	Herb Thomas	9	53 Huds	191	300

Louisiana

Louisiana Fairgrounds
Shreveport, LA
Half-mile Dirt Track

(aka Louisiana Speedway; Louisiana State Fair Speedway) Originally built as 1-mile horse track in 1905. Autos first raced at facility in 1910. The legendary Barney Oldfield won first race. Half-mile dirt oval built circa 1931. Only NASCAR Winston Cup (then Grand National) race staged on 6/7/53 (won by Lee Petty). Track closed in 1980.

Winston Cup Victories		**Winston Cup Money**		**Narrowest Margin of Victory**	**Most Race Leaders**
Lee Petty	1	Lee Petty	$1,000	N/A	N/A
Winston Cup Poles		**Most Cars Started**		**Race Record**	**Most Cars Running at Finish**
Herb Thomas	1	19—June 7, 1953		53.199 MPH—June 7, 1953	N/A

1953 Grand National Race No. 14
June 7, 1953 Average Speed: 53.199

	Driver	Owner	Car #	Make	Laps	Winnings
1.	Lee Petty	Petty Enterprises	42	53 Dodg	200	1,000
2.	Dick Rathmann	Walt Chapman	120	53 Huds	—	700
3.	Herb Thomas	Herb Thomas	92	53 Huds	—	650
4.	Tim Flock	Ted Chester	91	52 Huds	—	350
5.	Buck Baker	Griffin Motors	87	53 Olds	—	200

Maine

Oxford Plains Speedway
Oxford, ME
.333-mile Paved Track

Half-mile dirt oval opened in May 1950. Track reconfigured to .333-mile paved oval in June 1960. First NASCAR Winston Cup (then Grand National) race staged on 7/12/66 (won by Bobby Allison, his first of 85 career victories). Final Grand National race held on 7/9/68 (won by Richard Petty). Track still active today.

Winston Cup Starts
Many drivers tied with3

Winston Cup Victories
Bobby Allison   2

Winston Cup Poles
Bobby Allison   1
Buddy Baker   1
James Hylton   1

Winston Cup Money
Bobby Allison $2,575

Most Cars Started
30—July 11, 1967 Maine 300

Fewest Cars Started
27—July 12, 1966
27—July 9, 1968 Maine 300

Narrowest Margin of Victory
12 seconds July 9, 1968 Maine 300

Slowest Race
56.782 MPH—July 12, 1966

Race Record
63.717 MPH—July 9, 1968 Maine 300

Most Cautions
4—July 12, 1966

Most Race Leaders
4—July 11, 1967 Maine 300

Most Cars Running at Finish
15—July 9, 1968 Maine 300

1966 Grand National Race No. 31
July 12, 1966 Average Speed: 56.782

Driver	Owner	Car #	Make	Laps	Winnings
1. Bobby Allison	Bobby Allison	2	65 Chev	300	1,100
2. Tiny Lund	Lyle Stelter	55	64 Ford	299	675
3. Richard Petty	Petty Enterprises	43	66 Plym	299	450
4. Neil Castles	Buck Baker	87	66 Olds	297	325
5. James Hylton	Bud Hartje	48	65 Dodg	297	315

1967 Grand National Race No. 30 Maine 300
July 11, 1967 Average Speed: 61.697

Driver	Owner	Car #	Make	Laps	Winnings
1. Bobby Allison	Bobby Allison	2	65 Chev	300	1,150
2. Richard Petty	Petty Enterprises	43	67 Plym	299	700
3. Jim Paschal	Tom Friedkin	14	67 Plym	297	450
4. James Hylton	Bud Hartje	48	65 Dodg	297	325
5. Neil Castles	Neil Castles	06	65 Dodg	294	315

1968 Grand National Race No. 27 Maine 300
July 9, 1968 Average Speed: 63.717

Driver	Owner	Car #	Make	Laps	Winnings
1. Richard Petty	Petty Enterprises	43	68 Plym	300	1,350
2. David Pearson	Holman-Moody	17	68 Ford	300	700
3. Buddy Baker	Ray Fox	3	67 Dodg	297	450
4. Bobby Allison	Bobby Allison	2	66 Chev	297	325
5. Bobby Isaac	Nord Krauskopf	71	67 Dodg	292	315

Maryland

Beltsville Speedway
Beltsville, MD
Half-mile Paved Track

(aka Baltimore-Washington Speedway) Half-mile paved oval opened in July 1965. First NASCAR Winston Cup (then Grand National) race staged on 8/25/65 (won by Ned Jarrett). Final race held on 5/15/70 (won by Bobby Isaac). Nearby residents, who built homes in the area long after the track was built, complained about noise, prompting track officials to apply mufflers to all race cars in the early '70s. Track closed in 1979.

Winston Cup Starts
Elmo Langley 10
Wendell Scott 10

Winston Cup Victories
Bobby Isaac 3

Winston Cup Poles
Richard Petty 5

Winston Cup Money
Bobby Isaac $7,120

Most Cars Started
31—June 15, 1966 Beltsville 200

Fewest Cars Started
16—May 19, 1967 Beltsville 200

Narrowest Margin of Victory
2 feet—June 15, 1966
Beltsville 200

Slowest Race
68.899 MPH—August 24, 1966
Maryland 200

Race Record
77.253 MPH—July 15, 1969
Maryland 300

Most Cautions
3—May 19, 1967 Beltsville 200
3—May 16, 1969 Beltsville 300

Most Race Leaders
4—July 15, 1969 Maryland 300
4—May 15, 1970 Beltsville 300

Most Cars Running at Finish
15—June 15, 1966 Beltsville 200

1965 Grand National Race No. 43
August 25, 1965 Average Speed: 74.165

Driver	Owner	Car #	Make	Laps	Winnings
1. Ned Jarrett	Bondy Long	11	65 Ford	200	1,000
2. Tiny Lund	Lyle Stelter	55	64 Ford	198	600
3. Darel Dieringer	Lanty McClung	37	64 Ford	198	400
4. Dick Dixon	Dan Colone	8	63 Ford	197	300
5. Wendell Scott	Wendell Scott	34	63 Ford	191	275

1966 Grand National Race No. 26 Beltsville 200
June 15, 1966 Average Speed: 73.409

Driver	Owner	Car #	Make	Laps	Winnings
1. Tiny Lund	Lyle Stelter	55	64 Ford	200	1,000
2. James Hylton	Bud Hartje	48	65 Dodg	200	600
3. Hank Thomas	W. S. Jenkins	92	64 Ford	195	400
4. John Sears	L. G. DeWitt	4	64 Ford	195	300
5. G. C. Spencer	Henley Gray	97	66 Ford	193	275

1966 Grand National Race No. 40 Maryland 200
August 24, 1966 Average Speed: 68.899

Driver	Owner	Car #	Make	Laps	Winnings
1. Bobby Allison	Bobby Allison	2	65 Chev	200	1,000
2. Elmo Langley	Henry Woodfield	64	64 Ford	199	600
3. James Hylton	Bud Hartje	48	65 Dodg	196	400
4. Buck Baker	Buck Baker	87	66 Olds	195	300
5. Tiny Lund	Lyle Stelter	55	64 Ford	194	275

1967 Grand National Race No. 18 Beltsville 200
May 19, 1967 Average Speed: 71.036

Driver	Owner	Car #	Make	Laps	Winnings
1. Jim Paschal	Tom Friedkin	14	67 Plym	200	1,000
2. Richard Petty	Petty Enterprises	43	67 Plym	200	600
3. Bobby Allison	Cotton Owens	6	67 Dodg	200	400
4. Donnie Allison	Bobby Allison	2	65 Chev	198	300
5. Paul Lewis	Emory Gilliam	00	65 Dodg	195	275

1967 Grand National Race No. 43 Maryland 300
September 15, 1967 Average Speed: 76.563

Driver	Owner	Car #	Make	Laps	Winnings
1. Richard Petty	Petty Enterprises	43	67 Plym	300	1,400
2. Bobby Allison	Bobby Allison	2	65 Chev	298	1,000
3. Jim Paschal	Tom Friedkin	14	67 Plym	298	700
4. James Hylton	Bud Hartje	48	65 Dodg	292	575
5. John Sears	L. G. DeWitt	4	66 Ford	286	425

1968 Grand National Race No. 16 Beltsville 300
May 17, 1968 Average Speed: 74.844

Driver	Owner	Car #	Make	Laps	Winnings
1. David Pearson	Holman-Moody	17	68 Ford	300	1,400
2. Bobby Isaac	Nord Krauskopf	71	67 Dodg	299	1,000
3. Buddy Baker	Ray Fox	3	67 Dodg	297	700
4. James Hylton	James Hylton	48	67 Dodg	297	575
5. John Sears	L. G. DeWitt	4	67 Ford	285	425

1968 Grand National Race No. 42 Maryland 300
September 13, 1968 Average Speed: 71.033

Driver	Owner	Car #	Make	Laps	Winnings
1. Bobby Isaac	Nord Krauskopf	71	67 Dodg	300	1,400
2. Bobby Allison	Bobby Allison	2	66 Chev	298	1,000
3. Richard Petty	Petty Enterprises	43	68 Plym	294	700
4. G. C. Spencer	G. C. Spencer	49	67 Plym	294	750
5. Roy Tyner	Roy Tyner	9	67 Pont	285	425

1969 Grand National Race No. 19 Beltsville 300
May 16, 1969 Average Speed: 73.059

Driver	Owner	Car #	Make	Laps	Winnings
1. Bobby Isaac	Nord Krauskopf	71	69 Dodg	300	2,500
2. Neil Castles	Neil Castles	06	67 Plym	298	1,500
3. John Sears	L. G. DeWitt	4	67 Ford	295	1,000
4. Elmo Langley	Elmo Langley	64	68 Ford	295	750
5. James Hylton	James Hylton	48	69 Dodg	292	600

Beltsville Speedway *continued*

1969 Grand National Race No. 32 Maryland 300
July 15, 1969 Average Speed: 77.253

Driver	Owner	Car #	Make	Laps	Winnings
1. Richard Petty	Petty Enterprises	43	69 Ford	300	2,500
2. David Pearson	Holman-Moody	17	69 Ford	300	1,700
3. James Hylton	James Hylton	48	69 Dodg	299	1,000
4. Neil Castles	Neil Castles	06	67 Plym	296	750
5. John Sears	L. G. DeWitt	4	68 Ford	294	600

1970 Grand National Race No. 14 Beltsville 300
May 15, 1970 Average Speed: 76.370

Driver	Owner	Car #	Make	Laps	Winnings
1. Bobby Isaac	Nord Krauskopf	71	70 Dodg	300	1,900
2. James Hylton	James Hylton	48	69 Ford	299	1,300
3. Bobby Allison	Bobby Allison	22	69 Dodg	298	900
4. Neil Castles	Neil Castles	06	69 Dodg	297	600
5. Dave Marcis	Dave Marcis	30	69 Dodg	294	475

Massachusetts

Norwood Arena
Norwood, MA
Quarter-mile Asphalt

Quarter-mile paved oval opened in June 1948. Only NASCAR Winston Cup (then Grand National) event run on 6/17/61 (won by Emanuel Zervakis). Track closed in 1972 and is now the site of an industrial park.

Winston Cup Victories
Emanuel Zervakis   1

Winston Cup Poles
Rex White   1

Winston Cup Money
Emanuel Zervakis $2,250

Most Cars Started
18—June 17, 1961 Yankee 500

Narrowest Margin of Victory
1/4 lap—June 17, 1961

Race Record
53.827 MPH—June 17, 1961 Yankee 500

Most Cautions
1—June 17, 1961 Yankee 500

Most Race Leaders
3—June 17, 1961 Yankee 500

Most Cars Running at Finish
11—June 17, 1961 Yankee 500

1961 Grand National Race No. 29 Yankee 500
June 17, 1961 Average Speed: 53.827

Driver	Owner	Car #	Make	Laps	Winnings
1. Emanuel Zervakis	Monroe Shook	85	60 Chev	500	2,250
2. Rex White	Rex White	4	60 Chev	500	1,000
3. Ned Jarrett	Bee Gee Holloway	11	61 Chev	491	800
4. Buck Baker	Buck Baker	86	61 Chrys	476	700
5. Jim Reed	Jim Reed	7	61 Chev	473	600

Michigan

Grand River Speedrome
Grand Rapids, MI
Half-mile Dirt Track

(aka Comstock Park; West Michigan State Fair; Kent County Fairgrounds; Comstock Park Fairgrounds; Grand River Speedway) Original track built in 1903, a 1.125-mile dirt oval. Quarter mile and half-mile dirt track built in 1950. First NASCAR Winston Cup (then Grand National) race staged on 7/1/51 (won by Marshall Teague). The only other big NASCAR race was run on 7/11/54 (won by Lee Petty). Track closed in 1966 to make way for US 131 Expressway.

Winston Cup Starts

Ray Duhigg	2
Lee Petty	2
Dick Rathmann	2
Donald Thomas	2
Herb Thomas	2

Winston Cup Victories

Lee Petty	1
Marshall Teague	1

Winston Cup Poles

Tim Flock	1
Herb Thomas	1

Winston Cup Money

Lee Petty	$1,200

Most Cars Started

25—July 11, 1954

Fewest Cars Started

22—July 1, 1951

Narrowest Margin of Victory

N/A

Slowest Race

52.090 MPH—July 11, 1954

Race Record

52.090 MPH—July 11, 1954

Most Race Leaders

3—July 11, 1954

Most Cars Running at Finish

15—July 11, 1954

1951 Grand National Race No. 14
July 1, 1951

Driver	Owner	Car #	Make	Laps	Winnings
1. Marshall Teague	Marshall Teague	6	51 Huds	200	1,000
2. Dick Rathmann	Walt Chapman	120	51 Huds	—	600
3. Fonty Flock	Frank Christian	14	50 Olds	—	400
4. Tim Flock	Ted Chester	91	51 Olds	—	300
5. Lloyd Moore	Julian Buesink	59	51 Ford	—	250

1954 Grand National Race No. 25
July 11, 1954 Average Speed: 52.090

Driver	Owner	Car #	Make	Laps	Winnings
1. Lee Petty	Petty Enterprises	42	54 Chrys	200	1,000
2. Buck Baker	Ernest Woods	88	54 Olds	196	650
3. Dick Rathmann	John Ditz	3	54 Huds	196	450
4. Ray Duhigg	J. O. Goode	24	51 Plym	193	350
5. Jim Reed	Jim Reed	7	54 Huds	192	300

Michigan Int'l Speedway
Brooklyn, MI
2.04-mile Paved Track

2-mile oval opened in October 1968 with USAC IndyCar race. First NASCAR Winston Cup (then Grand National) event staged on 6/15/69 (won by Cale Yarborough). Built by Larry LoPatin (rhymes with Go Skatin'), who operated the track under American Raceways corporate umbrella. Roger Penske bought track in 1973.

Winston Cup Starts
Dave Marcis   54

Winston Cup Victories
David Pearson   9

Winston Cup Poles
David Pearson   10

Winston Cup Money
Bill Elliott $889,680

Most Cars Started
44—August 17, 1969 Yankee 600

Fewest Cars Started
36—June 16, 1974 Motor State 400
36—August 25, 1974 Yankee 400
36—June 15, 1975 Motor State 400
36—August 24, 1975
    Champion Spark Plug 400
36—June 20, 1976 Cam 2 Motor Oil 400
36—August 22, 1976
    Champion Spark Plug 400
36—June 19, 1977 Cam 2 Motor Oil 400
36—August 22, 1977
    Champion Spark Plug 400
36—June 18, 1978 Gabriel 400
36—August 20, 1978
    Champion Spark Plug 400
36—June 17, 1979 Gabriel 400
36—August 19, 1979
    Champion Spark Plug 400
36—August 16, 1981
    Champion Spark Plug 400

Narrowest Margin of Victory
10 inches—August 18, 1991
    Champion Spark Plug 400

Slowest Race
107.583 MPH—August 24, 1975
    Champion Spark Plug 400

Race Record
166.033 MPH—June 23, 1996
    Miller Genuine Draft 400

Most Cautions
9—August 16, 1981
    Champion Spark Plug 400

Most Race Leaders
15—June 20, 1982 Gabriel 400

Most Cars Running at Finish
34—August 20, 1989
    Champion Spark Plug 400

1969 Grand National Race No. 24 Motor State 500
June 15, 1969 Average Speed: 139.254

Driver	Owner	Car #	Make	Laps	Winnings
1. Cale Yarborough	Wood Brothers	21	69 Merc	250	17,625
2. David Pearson	Holman-Moody	17	69 Ford	250	10,100
3. Richard Petty	Petty Enterprises	43	69 Ford	250	5,875
4. LeeRoy Yarbrough	Junior Johnson	98	69 Merc	249	4,100
5. Charlie Glotzbach	Cotton Owens	6	69 Dodg	249	3,150

1969 Grand National Race No. 37 Yankee 600
August 17, 1969 Average Speed: 115.508

Driver	Owner	Car #	Make	Laps	Winnings
1. David Pearson	Holman-Moody	17	69 Ford	165	21,950
2. Buddy Baker	Cotton Owens	6	69 Dodg	165	10,880
3. Richard Petty	Petty Enterprises	43	69 Ford	165	7,020
4. Cale Yarborough	Wood Brothers	21	69 Merc	165	3,675
5. Bobby Allison	Mario Rossi	22	69 Dodg	165	2,775

1970 Grand National Race No. 19 Motor State 400
June 7, 1970 Average Speed: 138.302

Driver	Owner	Car #	Make	Laps	Winnings
1. Cale Yarborough	Wood Brothers	21	69 Merc	200	14,675
2. Pete Hamilton	Petty Enterprises	40	70 Plym	200	7,120
3. David Pearson	Holman-Moody	17	69 Ford	200	4,980
4. LeeRoy Yarbrough	Junior Johnson	98	69 Ford	200	2,800
5. Bobby Isaac	Nord Krauskopf	71	69 Dodg	199	2,025

1970 Grand National Race No. 34 Yankee 400
August 16, 1970 Average Speed: 147.571

Driver	Owner	Car #	Make	Laps	Winnings
1. Charlie Glotzbach	Ray Nichels	99	69 Dodg	197	14,275
2. Bobby Allison	Mario Rossi	22	69 Dodg	197	6,845
3. Dick Brooks	Dick Brooks	32	70 Plym	196	4,430
4. Bobby Isaac	Nord Krauskopf	71	69 Dodg	196	2,800
5. Pete Hamilton	Petty Enterprises	40	70 Plym	196	1,975

1971 Winston Cup GN Race No. 23 Motor State 400
June 13, 1971 Average Speed: 149.567

Driver	Owner	Car #	Make	Laps	Winnings
1. Bobby Allison	Holman-Moody	12	69 Merc	197	14,945
2. Bobby Isaac	Nord Krauskopf	71	71 Dodg	197	7,620
3. Pete Hamilton	Cotton Owens	6	71 Plym	197	4,920
4. Donnie Allison	Wood Brothers	21	69 Merc	197	2,945
5. Buddy Baker	Petty Enterprises	11	71 Dodg	195	1,945

1971 Winston Cup GN Race No. 36 Yankee 400
August 15, 1971 Average Speed: 149.862

Driver	Owner	Car #	Make	Laps	Winnings
1. Bobby Allison	Holman-Moody	12	69 Merc	197	15,395
2. Richard Petty	Petty Enterprises	43	71 Plym	197	7,870
3. Buddy Baker	Petty Enterprises	11	71 Dodg	196	4,700
4. Maynard Troyer	David Nagle	60	69 Merc	193	2,870
5. Joe Frasson	Joe Frasson	18	70 Dodg	192	2,020

1972 Winston Cup GN Race No. 14 Motor State 400
June 11, 1972 Average Speed: 146.639

Driver	Owner	Car #	Make	Laps	Winnings
1. David Pearson	Wood Brothers	21	71 Merc	200	12,935
2. Bobby Allison	R. Howard & J. Johnson	12	72 Chev	200	8,980
3. Richard Petty	Petty Enterprises	43	72 Dodg	200	6,925
4. James Hylton	James Hylton	48	70 Ford	195	3,350
5. Ron Keselowski	Roger Lubinski	88	70 Dodg	194	2,150

1972 Winston Cup GN Race No. 22 Yankee 400
August 20, 1972 Average Speed: 134.416

Driver	Owner	Car #	Make	Laps	Winnings
1. David Pearson	Wood Brothers	21	71 Merc	200	13,385
2. Bobby Allison	R. Howard & J. Johnson	12	72 Chev	200	9,230
3. Bobby Isaac	Nord Krauskopf	71	72 Dodg	199	6,525
4. Richard Petty	Petty Enterprises	43	72 Dodg	199	5,475
5. Cale Yarborough	James Hylton	98	71 Merc	196	2,150

Michigan Int'l Speedway *continued*

1973 Winston Cup GN Race No. 16 Motor State 400
June 24, 1973 Average Speed: 153.485

Driver	Owner	Car #	Make	Laps	Winnings
1. David Pearson	Wood Brothers	21	71 Merc	200	12,710
2. Buddy Baker	Nord Krauskopf	71	73 Dodg	200	9,055
3. Richard Petty	Petty Enterprises	43	73 Dodg	199	6,800
4. Bobby Allison	Bobby Allison	12	73 Chev	199	4,575
5. Ron Keselowski	Roger Lubinski	99	71 Dodg	197	2,000

1974 Winston Cup GN Race No. 22 Yankee 400
August 25, 1974 Average Speed: 133.045

Driver	Owner	Car #	Make	Laps	Winnings
1. David Pearson	Wood Brothers	21	73 Merc	200	15,765
2. Richard Petty	Petty Enterprises	43	74 Dodg	200	11,155
3. Cale Yarborough	Junior Johnson	11	74 Chev	200	7,700
4. Buddy Baker	Bud Moore	15	73 Ford	199	6,000
5. Bobby Allison	Roger Penske	12	74 Mata	198	2,050

1975 Winston Cup GN Race No. 20 Champion Spark Plug 400
August 24, 1975 Average Speed: 107.583

Driver	Owner	Car #	Make	Laps	Winnings
1. Richard Petty	Petty Enterprises	43	74 Dodg	200	18,140
2. David Pearson	Wood Brothers	21	73 Merc	200	10,735
3. Cale Yarborough	Junior Johnson	11	75 Chev	200	9,385
4. Bobby Allison	Roger Penske	16	75 Mata	200	4,060
5. Dave Marcis	Nord Krauskopf	71	74 Dodg	199	6,310

1976 Winston Cup GN Race No. 20 Champion Spark Plug 400
August 22, 1976 Average Speed: 140.078

Driver	Owner	Car #	Make	Laps	Winnings
1. David Pearson	Wood Brothers	21	Merc	200	16,700
2. Cale Yarborough	Junior Johnson	11	Chev	200	13,705
3. Richard Petty	Petty Enterprises	43	Dodg	200	10,985
4. Bobby Allison	Roger Penske	2	Merc	200	7,375
5. Dave Marcis	Nord Krauskopf	71	Dodg	199	6,565

1977 Winston Cup GN Race No. 20 Champion Spark Plug 400
August 22, 1977 Average Speed: 137.944

Driver	Owner	Car #	Make	Laps	Winnings
1. Darrell Waltrip	DiGard	88	Chev	200	16,820
2. David Pearson	Wood Brothers	21	Merc	200	10,300
3. Benny Parsons	L. G. DeWitt	72	Chev	200	9,350
4. Sam Sommers	M. C. Anderson	27	Chev	200	4,900
5. Cale Yarborough	Junior Johnson	11	Chev	200	8,100

1978 Winston Cup GN Race No. 20 Champion Spark Plug 400
August 20, 1978 Average Speed: 129.566

Driver	Owner	Car #	Make	Laps	Winnings
1. David Pearson	Wood Brothers	21	Merc	200	16,025
2. Cale Yarborough	Junior Johnson	11	Olds	200	14,275
3. Darrell Waltrip	DiGard	88	Chev	200	10,950
4. Dave Marcis	Rod Osterlund	2	Chev	200	6,500
5. Bobby Allison	Bud Moore	15	Ford	198	7,550

1979 Winston Cup GN Race No. 21 Champion Spark Plug 400
August 19, 1979 Average Speed: 130.376

Driver	Owner	Car #	Make	Laps	Winnings
1. Richard Petty	Petty Enterprises	43	Chev	200	21,100
2. Buddy Baker	Harry Ranier	28	Chev	200	12,425
3. Benny Parsons	M. C. Anderson	27	Chev	200	12,820
4. David Pearson	Rod Osterlund	2	Chev	199	10,215
5. John Anderson	Russ Draime	08	Chev	199	4,355

1974 Winston Cup GN Race No. 15 Motor State 400
June 16, 1974 Average Speed: 127.098

Driver	Owner	Car #	Make	Laps	Winnings
1. Richard Petty	Petty Enterprises	43	74 Dodg	180	17,190
2. Earl Ross	Allan J. Clarke	52	74 Chev	180	7,930
3. David Pearson	Wood Brothers	21	74 Merc	180	3,475
4. Gary Bettenhausen	Roger Penske	16	74 Mata	178	2,400
5. Marty Robbins	Marty Robbins	42	74 Dodg	178	2,050

1975 Winston Cup GN Race No. 15 Motor State 400
June 15, 1975 Average Speed: 131.398

Driver	Owner	Car #	Make	Laps	Winnings
1. David Pearson	Wood Brothers	21	73 Merc	200	14,405
2. Richard Petty	Petty Enterprises	43	74 Dodg	200	13,130
3. Dave Marcis	Nord Krauskopf	71	74 Dodg	199	9,205
4. Cale Yarborough	Junior Johnson	11	75 Chev	199	7,180
5. Darrell Waltrip	Darrell Waltrip	17	75 Chev	199	5,530

1976 Winston Cup GN Race No. 15 Cam 2 Motor Oil 400
June 20, 1976 Average Speed: 141.148

Driver	Owner	Car #	Make	Laps	Winnings
1. David Pearson	Wood Brothers	21	Merc	200	15,845
2. Cale Yarborough	Junior Johnson	11	Chev	200	11,845
3. Bobby Allison	Roger Penske	2	Merc	200	9,275
4. Richard Petty	Petty Enterprises	43	Dodg	200	9,065
5. Buddy Baker	Bud Moore	15	Ford	199	6,630

1977 Winston Cup GN Race No. 15 Cam 2 Motor Oil 400
June 19, 1977 Average Speed: 135.033

Driver	Owner	Car #	Make	Laps	Winnings
1. Cale Yarborough	Junior Johnson	11	Chev	200	20,625
2. Richard Petty	Petty Enterprises	43	Dodg	200	14,425
3. Benny Parsons	L. G. DeWitt	72	Chev	200	10,700
4. Dave Marcis	Roger Penske	2	Chev	199	4,750
5. David Pearson	Wood Brothers	21	Merc	199	4,550

1978 Winston Cup GN Race No. 15 Gabriel 400
June 18, 1978 Average Speed: 149.563

Driver	Owner	Car #	Make	Laps	Winnings
1. Cale Yarborough	Junior Johnson	11	Olds	200	21,555
2. David Pearson	Wood Brothers	21	Merc	200	12,580
3. Benny Parsons	L. G. DeWitt	72	Olds	200	10,880
4. Dave Marcis	Rod Osterlund	2	Chev	200	6,830
5. Donnie Allison	Hoss Ellington	1	Chev	199	4,080

1979 Winston Cup GN Race No. 16 Gabriel 400
June 17, 1979 Average Speed: 135.798

Driver	Owner	Car #	Make	Laps	Winnings
1. Buddy Baker	Harry Ranier	28	Chev	200	16,870
2. Donnie Allison	Hoss Ellington	1	Chev	200	12,970
3. Cale Yarborough	Junior Johnson	11	Olds	200	12,620
4. Neil Bonnett	Wood Brothers	21	Merc	200	7,410
5. Richard Petty	Petty Enterprises	43	Chev	200	8,325

1980 Winston Cup GN Race No. 16 Gabriel 400
June 15, 1980 Average Speed: 131.808

Driver	Owner	Car #	Make	Laps	Winnings
1. Benny Parsons	M. C. Anderson	27	Chev	200	24,800
2. Cale Yarborough	Junior Johnson	11	Chev	200	16,300
3. Buddy Baker	Harry Ranier	28	Chev	200	9,300
4. Neil Bonnett	Wood Brothers	21	Merc	200	6,325
5. Richard Petty	Petty Enterprises	43	Chev	199	13,075

Michigan Int'l Speedway *continued*

1980 Winston Cup GN Race No. 21 Champion Spark Plug 400
August 17, 1980 Average Speed: 145.352

Driver	Owner	Car #	Make	Laps	Winnings
1. Cale Yarborough	Junior Johnson	11	Chev	200	19,700
2. Neil Bonnett	Wood Brothers	21	Merc	200	12,875
3. Donnie Allison	Kennie Childers	12	Chev	200	9,050
4. Darrell Waltrip	Joel Halpern	02	Chev	200	6,050
5. Richard Petty	Petty Enterprises	43	Chev	200	11,075

1981 Winston Cup GN Race No. 21 Champion Spark Plug 400
August 16, 1981 Average Speed: 123.457

Driver	Owner	Car #	Make	Laps	Winnings
1. Richard Petty	Petty Enterprises	43	Buick	200	23,750
2. Darrell Waltrip	Junior Johnson	11	Buick	200	17,525
3. Ricky Rudd	DiGard	88	Chev	200	15,150
4. Harry Gant	Hal Needham	33	Pont	200	6,000
5. Buddy Baker	Hoss Ellington	1	Buick	200	5,175

1982 Winston Cup GN Race No. 20 Champion Spark Plug 400
August 22, 1982 Average Speed: 136.454

Driver	Owner	Car #	Make	Laps	Winnings
1. Bobby Allison	DiGard	88	Buick	200	26,900
2. Richard Petty	Petty Enterprises	43	Pont	200	20,505
3. Harry Gant	Hal Needham	33	Buick	200	13,255
4. Geoff Bodine	Cliff Stewart	50	Pont	200	15,200
5. Benny Parsons	Johnny Hayes	55	Buick	200	6,725

1983 Winston Cup GN Race No. 20 Champion Spark Plug 400
August 21, 1983 Average Speed: 147.511

Driver	Owner	Car #	Make	Laps	Winnings
1. Cale Yarborough	Harry Ranier	28	Chev	200	26,100
2. Darrell Waltrip	Junior Johnson	11	Chev	200	23,775
3. Bill Elliott	Harry Melling	9	Ford	200	17,205
4. Terry Labonte	Billy Hagan	44	Chev	200	13,245
5. Tim Richmond	Raymond Beadle	27	Pont	200	10,205

1984 Winston Cup GN Race No. 20 Champion Spark Plug 400
August 12, 1984 Average Speed: 153.863

Driver	Owner	Car #	Make	Laps	Winnings
1. Darrell Waltrip	Junior Johnson	11	Chev	200	40,800
2. Terry Labonte	Billy Hagan	44	Chev	200	26,030
3. Bill Elliott	Harry Melling	9	Ford	200	22,150
4. Harry Gant	Hal Needham	33	Chev	200	12,920
5. Cale Yarborough	Harry Ranier	28	Chev	200	8,100

1985 Winston Cup GN Race No. 18 Champion Spark Plug 400
August 11, 1985 Average Speed: 137.430

Driver	Owner	Car #	Make	Laps	Winnings
1. Bill Elliott	Harry Melling	9	Ford	200	57,600
2. Darrell Waltrip	Junior Johnson	11	Chev	200	29,050
3. Harry Gant	Hal Needham	33	Chev	200	23,100
4. Kyle Petty	Wood Brothers	7	Ford	200	13,780
5. Benny Parsons	Richard Jackson	55	Chev	199	8,575

1986 Winston Cup Race No. 19 Champion Spark Plug 400
August 17, 1986 Average Speed: 135.376

Driver	Owner	Car #	Make	Laps	Winnings
1. Bill Elliott	Harry Melling	9	Ford	200	55,950
2. Tim Richmond	Rick Hendrick	25	Chev	200	27,980
3. Darrell Waltrip	Junior Johnson	11	Chev	200	27,275
4. Geoff Bodine	Rick Hendrick	5	Chev	200	17,225
5. Dale Earnhardt	Richard Childress	3	Chev	199	18,750

1981 Winston Cup GN Race No. 16 Gabriel 400
June 21, 1981 Average Speed: 130.589

Driver	Owner	Car #	Make	Laps	Winnings
1. Bobby Allison	Harry Ranier	28	Buick	200	24,075
2. Harry Gant	Hal Needham	33	Pont	200	10,825
3. Benny Parsons	Bud Moore	15	Ford	200	14,325
4. Jody Ridley	Junie Donlavey	90	Ford	200	10,005
5. Dale Earnhardt	Rod Osterlund	2	Pont	200	11,925

1982 Winston Cup GN Race No. 15 Gabriel 400
June 20, 1982 Average Speed: 118.101

Driver	Owner	Car #	Make	Laps	Winnings
1. Cale Yarborough	M. C. Anderson	27	Buick	200	24,700
2. Darrell Waltrip	Junior Johnson	11	Buick	200	25,650
3. Bill Elliott	Harry Melling	9	Ford	200	12,500
4. Bobby Allison	DiGard	88	Buick	200	16,100
5. Ricky Rudd	Richard Childress	3	Pont	200	11,530

1983 Winston Cup GN Race No. 15 Gabriel 400
June 19, 1983 Average Speed: 138.728

Driver	Owner	Car #	Make	Laps	Winnings
1. Cale Yarborough	Harry Ranier	28	Chev	200	24,170
2. Bobby Allison	DiGard	22	Buick	200	23,800
3. Tim Richmond	Raymond Beadle	27	Pont	200	16,310
4. Darrell Waltrip	Junior Johnson	11	Chev	200	19,825
5. Terry Labonte	Billy Hagan	44	Chev	200	16,595

1984 Winston Cup GN Race No. 15 Miller High Life 400
June 17, 1984 Average Speed: 134.705

Driver	Owner	Car #	Make	Laps	Winnings
1. Bill Elliott	Harry Melling	9	Ford	200	41,600
2. Dale Earnhardt	Richard Childress	3	Chev	200	28,175
3. Darrell Waltrip	Junior Johnson	11	Chev	200	24,350
4. Harry Gant	Hal Needham	33	Chev	200	15,605
5. Lake Speed	Hoss Ellington	1	Chev	200	9,850

1985 Winston Cup GN Race No. 14 Miller 400
June 16, 1985 Average Speed: 144.724

Driver	Owner	Car #	Make	Laps	Winnings
1. Bill Elliott	Harry Melling	9	Ford	200	48,600
2. Darrell Waltrip	Junior Johnson	11	Chev	200	32,100
3. Cale Yarborough	Harry Ranier	28	Ford	200	16,900
4. Tim Richmond	Raymond Beadle	27	Pont	200	15,630
5. Dale Earnhardt	Richard Childress	3	Chev	200	17,925

1986 Winston Cup Race No. 14 Miller American 400
June 15, 1986 Average Speed: 138.851

Driver	Owner	Car #	Make	Laps	Winnings
1. Bill Elliott	Harry Melling	9	Ford	200	56,900
2. Harry Gant	Hal Needham	33	Chev	200	37,400
3. Geoff Bodine	Rick Hendrick	5	Chev	200	25,600
4. Buddy Baker	Buddy Baker & Danny Schiff	88	Olds	200	11,825
5. Darrell Waltrip	Junior Johnson	11	Chev	200	21,625

1987 Winston Cup Race No. 14 Miller American 400
June 28, 1987 Average Speed: 148.454

Driver	Owner	Car #	Make	Laps	Winnings
1. Dale Earnhardt	Richard Childress	3	Chev	200	60,250
2. Davey Allison	Harry Ranier	28	Ford	200	27,575
3. Kyle Petty	Wood Brothers	21	Ford	200	26,025
4. Tim Richmond	Rick Hendrick	25	Chev	200	13,175
5. Rusty Wallace	Raymond Beadle	27	Pont	200	25,150

Michigan Int'l Speedway *continued*

1987 Winston Cup Race No. 19 Champion Spark Plug 400
August 16, 1987 Average Speed: 138.648

Driver	Owner	Car #	Make	Laps	Winnings
1. Bill Elliott	Harry Melling	9	Ford	200	52,875
2. Dale Earnhardt	Richard Childress	3	Chev	200	34,325
3. Morgan Shepherd	Kenny Bernstein	26	Buick	200	20,505
4. Rusty Wallace	Raymond Beadle	27	Pont	200	20,650
5. Davey Allison	Harry Ranier	28	Ford	200	13,500

1988 Winston Cup Race No. 19 Champion Spark Plug 400
August 21, 1988 Average Speed: 156.863

Driver	Owner	Car #	Make	Laps	Winnings
1. Davey Allison	Harry Ranier	28	Ford	200	60,475
2. Rusty Wallace	Raymond Beadle	27	Pont	200	37,250
3. Bill Elliott	Harry Melling	9	Ford	200	31,775
4. Morgan Shepherd	Buddy Baker & Danny Schiff	88	Olds	200	19,600
5. Lake Speed	Lake Speed	83	Olds	200	14,650

1989 Winston Cup Race No. 19 Champion Spark Plug 400
August 20, 1989 Average Speed: 157.704

Driver	Owner	Car #	Make	Laps	Winnings
1. Rusty Wallace	Raymond Beadle	27	Pont	200	67,900
2. Morgan Shepherd	Bob Rahilly & Butch Mock	75	Pont	200	38,975
3. Harry Gant	Leo Jackson	33	Olds	200	28,425
4. Hut Stricklin	Rod Osterlund	57	Pont	200	20,232
5. Geoff Bodine	Rick Hendrick	5	Chev	200	23,750

1990 Winston Cup Series Race No. 19 Champion Spark Plug 400
August 19, 1990 Average Speed: 138.822

Driver	Owner	Car #	Make	Laps	Winnings
1. Mark Martin	Jack Roush	6	Ford	200	71,200
2. Greg Sacks	Rick Hendrick	17	Chev	200	41,600
3. Rusty Wallace	Raymond Beadle	27	Pont	200	33,900
4. Bill Elliott	Harry Melling	9	Ford	200	27,000
5. Ricky Rudd	Rick Hendrick	5	Chev	200	20,607

1991 Winston Cup Series Race No. 19 Champion Spark Plug 400
August 18, 1991 Average Speed: 142.972

Driver	Owner	Car #	Make	Laps	Winnings
1. Dale Jarrett	Wood Brothers	21	Ford	200	74,150
2. Davey Allison	Robert Yates	28	Ford	200	47,700
3. Rusty Wallace	Roger Penske	2	Pont	200	23,600
4. Mark Martin	Jack Roush	6	Ford	200	30,050
5. Bill Elliott	Harry Melling	9	Ford	200	26,600

1992 Winston Cup Race No. 19 Champion Spark Plug 400
August 16, 1992 Average Speed: 146.056

Driver	Owner	Car #	Make	Laps	Winnings
1. Harry Gant	Leo Jackson	33	Olds	200	71,545
2. Darrell Waltrip	Darrell Waltrip	17	Chev	200	45,670
3. Bill Elliott	Junior Johnson	11	Ford	200	45,820
4. Ernie Irvan	Larry McClure	4	Chev	200	28,920
5. Davey Allison	Robert Yates	28	Ford	200	29,265

1993 Winston Cup Series Race No. 20 Champion Spark Plug 400
August 15, 1993 Average Speed: 144.564

Driver	Owner	Car #	Make	Laps	Winnings
1. Mark Martin	Jack Roush	6	Ford	200	76,645
2. Morgan Shepherd	Wood Brothers	21	Ford	200	47,320
3. Jeff Gordon	Rick Hendrick	24	Chev	200	34,745
4. Dale Jarrett	Joe Gibbs	18	Chev	200	29,045
5. Ted Musgrave	Ray DeWitt	55	Ford	200	27,990

1988 Winston Cup Race No. 14 Miller High Life 400
June 26, 1988 Average Speed: 153.551

Driver	Owner	Car #	Make	Laps	Winnings
1. Rusty Wallace	Raymond Beadle	27	Pont	200	64,100
2. Bill Elliott	Harry Melling	9	Ford	200	42,875
3. Terry Labonte	Junior Johnson	11	Chev	200	28,075
4. Dale Earnhardt	Richard Childress	3	Chev	200	26,175
5. Geoff Bodine	Rick Hendrick	5	Chev	200	20,325

1989 Winston Cup Race No. 14 Miller High Life 400
June 25, 1989 Average Speed: 139.023

Driver	Owner	Car #	Make	Laps	Winnings
1. Bill Elliott	Harry Melling	9	Ford	200	71,450
2. Rusty Wallace	Raymond Beadle	27	Pont	200	53,025
3. Darrell Waltrip	Rick Hendrick	17	Chev	200	31,600
4. Ricky Rudd	Kenny Bernstein	26	Buick	200	24,575
5. Brett Bodine	Bud Moore	15	Ford	200	22,025

1990 Winston Cup Series Race No. 14 Miller Genuine Draft 400
June 24, 1990 Average Speed: 150.219

Driver	Owner	Car #	Make	Laps	Winnings
1. Dale Earnhardt	Richard Childress	3	Chev	200	72,950
2. Ernie Irvan	Larry McClure	4	Chev	200	41,000
3. Geoff Bodine	Junior Johnson	11	Ford	200	33,375
4. Mark Martin	Jack Roush	6	Ford	200	25,400
5. Harry Gant	Leo Jackson	33	Olds	200	23,425

1991 Winston Cup Series Race No. 14 Miller Genuine Draft 400
June 23, 1991 Average Speed: 160.912

Driver	Owner	Car #	Make	Laps	Winnings
1. Davey Allison	Robert Yates	28	Ford	200	90,650
2. Hut Stricklin	Bobby Allison	12	Buick	200	41,925
3. Mark Martin	Jack Roush	6	Ford	200	37,650
4. Dale Earnhardt	Richard Childress	3	Chev	200	30,950
5. Ernie Irvan	Larry McClure	4	Chev	200	24,725

1992 Winston Cup Race No. 14 Miller Genuine Draft 400
June 21, 1992 Average Speed: 152.672

Driver	Owner	Car #	Make	Laps	Winnings
1. Davey Allison	Robert Yates	28	Ford	200	150,665
2. Darrell Waltrip	Darrell Waltrip	17	Chev	200	47,840
3. Alan Kulwicki	Alan Kulwicki	7	Ford	200	38,215
4. Kyle Petty	Felix Sabates	42	Pont	200	25,265
5. Ricky Rudd	Rick Hendrick	5	Chev	200	25,760

1993 Winston Cup Series Race No. 14 Miller Genuine Draft 400
June 20, 1993 Average Speed: 148.484

Driver	Owner	Car #	Make	Laps	Winnings
1. Ricky Rudd	Rick Hendrick	5	Chev	200	77,890
2. Jeff Gordon	Rick Hendrick	24	Chev	200	44,915
3. Ernie Irvan	Larry McClure	4	Chev	200	41,240
4. Dale Jarrett	Joe Gibbs	18	Chev	200	29,590
5. Rusty Wallace	Roger Penske	2	Pont	200	26,160

1994 Winston Cup Series Race No. 14 Miller Genuine Draft 400
June 19, 1994 Average Speed: 125.022

Driver	Owner	Car #	Make	Laps	Winnings
1. Rusty Wallace	Roger Penske	2	Ford	200	66,980
2. Dale Earnhardt	Richard Childress	3	Chev	200	55,905
3. Mark Martin	Jack Roush	6	Ford	200	42,330
4. Ricky Rudd	Ricky Rudd	10	Ford	200	31,430
5. Morgan Shepherd	Wood Brothers	21	Ford	200	31,025

Michigan Int'l Speedway *continued*

1994 Winston Cup Series Race No. 21 GM Goodwrench Dealers 400
August 21, 1994 Average Speed: 139.914

Driver	Owner	Car #	Make	Laps	Winnings
1. Geoff Bodine	Geoff Bodine	7	Ford	200	89,595
2. Mark Martin	Jack Roush	6	Ford	200	50,320
3. Rick Mast	Richard Jackson	1	Ford	200	38,320
4. Rusty Wallace	Roger Penske	2	Ford	200	34,070
5. Bobby Labonte	Bill Davis	22	Pont	200	28,415

1995 Winston Cup Series Race No. 14 Miller Genuine Draft 400
June 18, 1995 Average Speed: 134.141

Driver	Owner	Car #	Make	Laps	Winnings
1. Bobby Labonte	Joe Gibbs	18	Chev	200	84,080
2. Jeff Gordon	Rick Hendrick	24	Chev	200	72,530
3. Rusty Wallace	Roger Penske	2	Ford	200	44,780
4. John Andretti	Michael Kranefuss & Carl Haas	37	Ford	200	31,375
5. Morgan Shepherd	Wood Brothers	21	Ford	200	36,075

1995 Winston Cup Series Race No. 21 GM Goodwrench Dealers 400
August 20, 1995 Average Speed: 157.739

Driver	Owner	Car #	Make	Laps	Winnings
1. Bobby Labonte	Joe Gibbs	18	Chev	200	97,445
2. Terry Labonte	Rick Hendrick	5	Chev	200	52,695
3. Jeff Gordon	Rick Hendrick	24	Chev	200	46,420
4. Sterling Marlin	Larry McClure	4	Chev	200	38,170
5. Rusty Wallace	Roger Penske	2	Ford	200	37,690

1996 Winston Cup Series Race No. 14 Miller Genuine Draft 400
June 23, 1996 Average Speed: 166.033

Driver	Owner	Car #	Make	Laps	Winnings
1. Rusty Wallace	Roger Penske	2	Ford	200	71,380
2. Terry Labonte	Rick Hendrick	5	Chev	200	59,730
3. Sterling Marlin	Larry McClure	4	Chev	200	55,930
4. Jimmy Spencer	Travis Carter	23	Ford	200	43,775
5. Ernie Irvan	Robert Yates	28	Ford	200	40,525

1996 Winston Cup Series Race No. 21 GM Goodwrench Dealers 400
August 18, 1996 Average Speed: 139.792

Driver	Owner	Car #	Make	Laps	Winnings
1. Dale Jarrett	Robert Yates	88	Ford	200	83,195
2. Mark Martin	Jack Roush	6	Ford	200	79,170
3. Terry Labonte	Rick Hendrick	5	Chev	200	57,120
4. Ernie Irvan	Robert Yates	28	Ford	200	43,770
5. Jeff Gordon	Rick Hendrick	24	Chev	200	44,040

Michigan State Fairgrounds
Detroit, MI
1-mile Dirt Track

1-mile dirt oval built in 1899. Automobiles ran there in early 1900s. First NASCAR Winston Cup (then Grand National) race held on 8/12/51 (won by Tommy Thompson). The event was titled Motor City 250 in honor of Detroit's 250th anniversary. The only other Grand National event was staged on 6/29/52 (won by Tim Flock). The track is now the site of parking lots for the fairgrounds.

Winston Cup Starts
17 drivers tied with 2

Winston Cup Victories
Tim Flock 1
Tommy Thompson 1

Winston Cup Poles
Dick Rathmann 1
Marshall Teague 1

Winston Cup Money
Tim Flock $5,175

Most Cars Started
59—August 12, 1951 Motor City 250

Fewest Cars Started
47—June 29, 1952 Motor City 250

Narrowest Margin of Victory
N/A

Slowest Race
57.588 MPH—August 12, 1951
Motor City 250

Race Record
59.908 MPH—June 29, 1952
Motor City 250

Most Cautions
N/A

Most Race Leaders
6—August 12, 1951 Motor City 250

Most Cars Running at Finish
N/A

1951 Grand National Race No. 20 Motor City 250
August 12, 1951 Average Speed: 57.588

Driver	Owner	Car #	Make	Laps	Winnings
1. Tommy Thompson	Tommy Thompson	40	51 Chrys	250	5,000
2. Joe Eubanks	Phil Oates	82	50 Olds	250	2,000
3. Johnny Mantz	Johnny Mantz	98	51 Nash	244	1,000
4. Red Byron	B. J. Dantone	83	50 Ford	241	600
5. Paul Newkirk		43	51 Nash	241	500

1952 Grand National Race No. 17 Motor City 250
June 29, 1952 Average Speed: 59.908

Driver	Owner	Car #	Make	Laps	Winnings
1. Tim Flock	Ted Chester	91	51 Huds	250	5,050
2. Buddy Shuman	B. A. Pless	89	52 Huds	250	2,225
3. Herb Thomas	Herb Thomas	92	51 Huds	249	1,000
4. Bill Blair	George Hutchens	2	52 Olds	249	600
5. Pat Kirkwood	Pat Kirkwood	99	51 Chrys	246	500

Monroe Speedway
Monroe, MI
Half-mile Dirt Track

(aka Fairgrounds Speedway) Half-mile dirt track opened in July 1949. Only NASCAR Winston Cup (then Grand National) race held on 7/6/52 (won by Tim Flock). The track was later shortened to a quarter-mile and then closed circa 1954.

Winston Cup Victories
Tim Flock 1

Winston Cup Poles
Tim Flock 1

Winston Cup Money
Tim Flock $1,000

Most Cars Started
15—July 6, 1952

Narrowest Margin of Victory
N/A

Race Record
44.499 MPH—July 6, 1952

Most Race Leaders
N/A

Most Cars Running at Finish
9—July 6, 1952

1952 Grand National Race No. 20
July 6, 1952 Average Speed: 44.499

Driver	Owner	Car #	Make	Laps	Winnings
1. Tim Flock	Ted Chester	91	51 Huds	200	1,000
2. Herb Thomas	Herb Thomas	92	52 Huds	200	700
3. Lee Petty	Petty Enterprises	42	52 Plym	199	450
4. Fonty Flock	Frank Christian	14	52 Olds	194	350
5. Ray Duhigg	J. H. Petty	44	51 Plym	193	200

Nebraska

Lincoln City Fairgrounds
North Platte, NE
Half-mile Dirt Track

(aka Lincoln County Raceway; North Platte Speedway) Half-mile dirt track built circa 1951. Only NASCAR Winston Cup (then Grand National) race staged on 7/26/53 (won by Dick Rathmann). Track still active today.

Winston Cup Victories
Dick Rathmann   1

Winston Cup Poles
Herb Thomas   1

Winston Cup Money
Dick Rathmann $1,000

Most Cars Started
18—July 26, 1953

Narrowest Margin of Victory
6 feet—July 26, 1953

Race Record
54.380 MPH—July 26, 1953

Most Race Leaders
2—July 26, 1953

Most Cars Running at Finish
N/A

1953 Grand National Race No. 24
July 26, 1953 Average Speed: 54.380

Driver	Owner	Car #	Make	Laps	Winnings
1. Dick Rathmann	Walt Chapman	120	53 Huds	200	1,000
2. Herb Thomas	Herb Thomas	92	53 Huds	200	700
3. Lee Petty	Petty Enterprises	42	53 Dodg	—	450
4. Buck Baker	Griffin Motors	87	53 Olds	—	350
5. Marvin Copple			49 Olds	—	200

Nevada

Las Vegas Park Speedway
Las Vegas, NV
1-mile Dirt Track

Originally the 1-mile Las Vegas Jockey Club horse track. The track only hosted three races, one of which was a NASCAR Winston Cup (then Grand National) event on 10/16/55 (won by Norm Nelson). Other events were an AM IndyCar Championship event (1954) and a USAC Late Model race (1959). Now the site of the Las Vegas Hilton.

Winston Cup Victories
Norm Nelson   1

Winston Cup Poles
Norm Nelson   1

Winston Cup Money
Norm Nelson $1,325

Most Cars Started
27—October 16, 1955

Narrowest Margin of Victory
2 laps plus—October 16, 1955

Race Record
44.449 MPH—October 16, 1955

Most Race Leaders
2—October 16, 1955

Most Cars Running at Finish
13—October 16, 1955

1955 Grand National Race No. 43
October 16, 1955 Average Speed: 44.449

Driver	Owner	Car #	Make	Laps	Winnings
1. Norm Nelson	Carl Kiekhaefer	299	55 Chrys	111	1,325
2. Bill Hyde		96	53 Olds	109	820
3. Bill West	Jim Dane	33	53 Huds	107	560
4. Sherman Clark	Sherman Clark	34	55 Chev	104	340
5. Jim Murray		46	55 Buick	102	270

New Hampshire

New Hampshire Int'l Speedway
Loudon, NH
1.058-mile Superspeedway

1.063-mile paved oval opened in July 1990. First NASCAR Winston Cup event was staged on 7/11/93 (won by Rusty Wallace); the event was also Davey Allison's final race—he was mortally injured in a helicopter crash the following day). Track is located on the site of the former Bryar Motorsports Park, which opened in early 1960s.

Winston Cup Starts
27 drivers tied with 4

Winston Cup Victories
Jeff Gordon	1
Ernie Irvan	1
Ricky Rudd	1
Rusty Wallace	1

Winston Cup Poles
Mark Martin   2

Winston Cup Money
Jeff Gordon $237,425

Most Cars Started
42—July 10, 1994 Slick 50 300

Fewest Cars Started
40—July 11, 1993 Slick 50 300
40—July 14, 1996 Slick 50 300

Narrowest Margin of Victory
0.690 seconds July 10, 1994
      Slick 50 300

Slowest Race
87.599 MPH—July 10, 1994 Slick 50 300

Race Record
107.029 MPH—July 9, 1995 Slick 50 300

Most Cautions
17—July 10, 1994 Slick 50 300

Most Race Leaders
15—July 14, 1996 Slick 50 300

Most Cars Running at Finish
33—July 9, 1995 Slick 50 300
33—July 14, 1996 Slick 50 300

1993 Winston Cup Series Race No. 16 Slick 50 300
July 11, 1993 Average Speed: 105.947

Driver	Owner	Car #	Make	Laps	Winnings
1. Rusty Wallace	Roger Penske	2	Pont	300	77,500
2. Mark Martin	Jack Roush	6	Ford	300	74,800
3. Davey Allison	Robert Yates	28	Ford	300	44,725
4. Dale Jarrett	Joe Gibbs	18	Chev	300	33,850
5. Ricky Rudd	Rick Hendrick	5	Chev	300	25,375

1994 Winston Cup Series Race No. 16 Slick 50 300
July 10, 1994 Average Speed: 87.599

Driver	Owner	Car #	Make	Laps	Winnings
1. Ricky Rudd	Ricky Rudd	10	Ford	300	91,875
2. Dale Earnhardt	Richard Childress	3	Chev	300	68,000
3. Rusty Wallace	Roger Penske	2	Ford	300	38,975
4. Mark Martin	Jack Roush	6	Ford	300	33,625
5. Todd Bodine	Butch Mock	75	Ford	300	21,850

1995 Winston Cup Series Race No. 16 Slick 50 300
July 9, 1995 Average Speed: 107.029

Driver	Owner	Car #	Make	Laps	Winnings
1. Jeff Gordon	Rick Hendrick	24	Chev	300	160,300
2. Morgan Shepherd	Wood Brothers	21	Ford	300	61,500
3. Mark Martin	Jack Roush	6	Ford	300	54,650
4. Terry Labonte	Rick Hendrick	5	Chev	300	37,925
5. Ricky Rudd	Ricky Rudd	10	Ford	300	35,125

1996 Winston Cup Series Race No. 16 Slick 50 300
July 14, 1996 Average Speed: 98.930

Driver	Owner	Car #	Make	Laps	Winnings
1. Ernie Irvan	Robert Yates	28	Ford	300	112,625
2. Dale Jarrett	Robert Yates	88	Ford	300	59,725
3. Ricky Rudd	Ricky Rudd	10	Ford	300	49,825
4. Jeff Burton	Jack Roush	99	Ford	300	31,600
5. Robert Pressley	Leo Jackson & Andy Petree	33	Chev	300	34,825

New Jersey

Linden Airport
Linden, NJ
2-mile Paved Road Course

2-mile road course utilizing runways at airport. Site of first NASCAR Winston Cup (then Grand National) road race on 6/13/54 (won by Al Keller in a Jaguar). For this special NASCAR event, foreign cars were permitted to compete. Track was originally a 2.2-mile course opened in August of 1949. Track was never again used for auto racing sometime after 1955.

Winston Cup Victories
Al Keller   1

Most Cars Started
43—June 13, 1954

Race Record
77.569 MPH—June 13, 1954

Most Race Leaders
3—June 13, 1954

Winston Cup Poles
Buck Baker   1

Narrowest Margin of Victory
N/A

Most Cautions
4—June 13, 1954

Most Cars Running at Finish
N/A

Winston Cup Money
Al Keller $1,000

1954 Grand National Race No. 18
June 13, 1954 Average Speed: 77.569

Driver	Owner	Car #	Make	Laps	Winnings
1. Al Keller	Paul Whiteman	4	JAG	50	1,000
2. Joe Eubanks	Phil Oates	82	51 Huds	50	650
3. Buck Baker	Ernest Woods	88	54 Olds	49	500
4. Bob Grossman		32	JAG	49	400
5. Harry LaVois		7-A	JAG	49	275

Morristown Speedway
Morristown, NJ
Half-mile Dirt Track

(aka Soranno Park; Morristown Raceway) Half-mile dirt track opened in June 1950. First NASCAR Winston Cup (then Grand National) race staged on 8/24/51 (won by Tim Flock). Final NASCAR race run on 7/15/55 (also won by Tim Flock). Track closed in October 1955.

Winston Cup Starts		**Winston Cup Money**		**Narrowest Margin of Victory**		**Most Cautions**
Lee Petty	5	Lee Petty	$3,000	N/A		N/A

Winston Cup Victories		**Most Cars Started**	**Slowest Race**	**Most Race Leaders**
Tim Flock	2	44—August 24, 1951	58.092 MPH—July 15, 1955	3—July 11, 1952

Winston Cup Poles		**Fewest Cars Started**	**Race Record**	**Most Cars Running at Finish**
Tim Flock	2	23—July 10, 1953	69.417 MPH July 10, 1953	20 July 30, 1954
Herb Thomas	2			20—July 15, 1955

1951 Grand National Race No. 22
August 24, 1951

Driver	Owner	Car #	Make	Laps	Winnings
1. Tim Flock	Ted Chester	91	51 Olds	200	1,000
2. Lee Petty	Petty Enterprises	42	51 Plym	—	700
3. Ronnie Kohler			51 Plym	—	450
4. John DuBoise			50 Plym	—	350
5. Jim Delaney	Bob Osiecki	21	50 Ford	—	200

1952 Grand National Race No. 21
July 11, 1952 Average Speed: 59.661

Driver	Owner	Car #	Make	Laps	Winnings
1. Lee Petty	Petty Enterprises	42	51 Plym	200	1,000
2. Tim Flock	Ted Chester	91	51 Huds	200	700
3. Neil Cole	John Golabek	52	50 Plym	196	450
4. Ralph Liguori	Ralph Liguori	00	51 Huds	196	350
5. Ronnie Kohler	Ronnie Kohler		50 Plym	192	200

1953 Grand National Race No. 21
July 10, 1953 Average Speed: 69.417

Driver	Owner	Car #	Make	Laps	Winnings
1. Dick Rathmann	Walt Chapman	120	53 Huds	200	1,000
2. Herb Thomas	Herb Thomas	92	53 Huds	199	700
3. Lee Petty	Petty Enterprises	42	53 Dodg	198	450
4. Jim Paschal	George Hutchens	80	53 Dodg	—	350
5. Ronnie Kohler	John Golabek	53	50 Plym	—	200

1954 Grand National Race No. 26
July 30, 1954 Average Speed: 58.968

Driver	Owner	Car #	Make	Laps	Winnings
1. Buck Baker	Ernest Woods	88	54 Olds	200	1,000
2. Herb Thomas	Herb Thomas	92	54 Huds	199	650
3. Hershel McGriff	Frank Christian	14	53 Olds	199	450
4. Dick Rathmann	John Ditz	3	54 Huds	196	350
5. Jimmie Lewallen	Joe Blair	5	54 Merc	195	300

1955 Grand National Race No. 27 July 15, 1955 Average Speed: 58.092

Driver	Owner	Car #	Make	Laps	Winnings
1. Tim Flock	Carl Kiekhaefer	300	55 Chrys	200	900
2. Lee Petty	Petty Enterprises	42	55 Chrys	198	600
3. Dave Terrell	Dave Terrell	98	54 Olds	197	425
4. Junior Johnson	B & L Motors	55	54 Olds	196	335
5. Jim Reed	Jim Reed	7	55 Chev	195	290

Old Bridge Stadium
Old Bridge, NJ
Half-mile Paved Track

Half-mile paved oval opened in August 1953. First NASCAR Winston Cup (then Grand National) event staged on 8/17/56 (won by Ralph Moody). Final NASCAR Grand National event run on 7/9/65 (won by Junior Johnson). Track closed in 1968.

Winston Cup Starts
Lee Petty   5

Winston Cup Victories
Junior Johnson   1
Ralph Moody   1
Lee Petty   1
Jim Reed   1
Fireball Roberts   1
Billy Wade   1

Winston Cup Poles
Jim Reed   2

Winston Cup Money
Jim Reed $1,775

Most Cars Started
27—April 27, 1958

Fewest Cars Started
20—July 19, 1963
20—July 9, 1965 Old Bridge 200

Narrowest Margin of Victory
6 car lengths—July 19, 1963

Slowest Race
65.170 MPH—August 17, 1956

Race Record
73.891 MPH—July 10, 1964
 Fireball Roberts 200

Most Cautions
4—July 19, 1963

Most Race Leaders
3—August 16, 1957
3—July 10, 1964 Fireball Roberts 200
3—July 9, 1965 Old Bridge 200

Most Cars Running at Finish
16—August 16, 1957

1956 Grand National Race No. 38
August 17, 1956 Average Speed: 65.170

Driver	Owner	Car #	Make	Laps	Winnings
1. Ralph Moody	Pete DePaolo	12	56 Ford	200	650
2. Jim Reed	Jim Reed	7	56 Chev	200	525
3. Billy Myers	Bill Stroppe	4	56 Merc	199	400
4. Fireball Roberts	Pete DePaolo	22	56 Ford	199	320
5. Jim Paschal	Frank Hayworth	75	56 Merc	197	290

1957 Grand National Race No. 38
August 16, 1957 Average Speed: 65.813

Driver	Owner	Car #	Make	Laps	Winnings
1. Lee Petty	Petty Enterprises	42	57 Olds	200	1,000
2. Rex White	Bob Welborn	44	57 Chev	200	625
3. Jim Reed	Jim Reed	7	57 Ford	200	400
4. Marvin Panch	Marvin Panch	98	57 Ford	200	295
5. Jack Smith	Jack Smith	47	57 Chev	199	255

1958 Grand National Race No. 14
April 27, 1958 Average Speed: 68.438

Driver	Owner	Car #	Make	Laps	Winnings
1. Jim Reed	Jim Reed	7	57 Ford	187	800
2. Eddie Pagan	Eddie Pagan	45	57 Ford	186	525
3. Rex White	J. H. Petty	44	57 Chev	185	350
4. Frankie Schneider	Frankie Schneider	62	57 Chev	184	250
5. Elmo Langley	Elmo Langley	8	56 Chev	184	225

1963 Grand National Race No. 35
July 19, 1963 Average Speed: 73.022

Driver	Owner	Car #	Make	Laps	Winnings
1. Fireball Roberts	Holman-Moody	22	63 Ford	200	1,000
2. Rex White	Rex White	4	63 Merc	200	600
3. Fred Lorenzen	Holman-Moody	28	63 Ford	199	400
4. Ned Jarrett	Charles Robinson	11	63 Ford	199	300
5. Bobby Isaac	Bondy Long	99	63 Ford	196	275

1964 Grand National Race No. 37 Fireball Roberts 200
July 10, 1964 Average Speed: 73.891

Driver	Owner	Car #	Make	Laps	Winnings
1. Billy Wade	Bud Moore	1	63 Merc	200	1,000
2. Ned Jarrett	Bondy Long	11	64 Ford	199	600
3. Richard Petty	Petty Enterprises	43	64 Plym	198	400
4. Jimmy Pardue	Charles Robinson	54	64 Plym	195	300
5. David Pearson	Cotton Owens	6	64 Dodg	193	275

1965 Grand National Race No. 31 Old Bridge 200
July 9, 1965 Average Speed: 72.087

Driver	Owner	Car #	Make	Laps	Winnings
1. Junior Johnson	Rex Lovette	26	65 Ford	200	1,000
2. Dick Hutcherson	Holman-Moody	29	65 Ford	199	600
3. Marvin Panch	Wood Brothers	21	65 Ford	199	400
4. Darel Dieringer	Bud Moore	16	64 Merc	198	300
5. Ned Jarrett	Bondy Long	11	65 Ford	198	275

Trenton Speedway
Trenton, NJ
1-Mile Paved Track

(aka New Jersey State Fairgrounds; Trenton Int'l Speedway) Half-mile dirt track originally built in 1900. 1-mile dirt track opened in May 1946. Track paved in 1957. A 500-mile NASCAR Winston Cup (then Grand National) race was staged on 5/30/58 (won by Fireball Roberts). Track was lengthened to 1.5 miles in the shape of a peanut in 1969. Final Winston Cup race run on 7/16/72 (won by Bobby Allison). Another Winston Cup event was scheduled in 1973 but was rained out after qualifying trials had determined the field. The event was never rescheduled.

Winston Cup Starts
Elmo Langley   8

Winston Cup Victories
Richard Petty   3

Winston Cup Poles
Bobby Isaac   3

Winston Cup Money
Richard Petty $22,755

Most Cars Started
40—July 18, 1971 Northern 300

Fewest Cars Started
18—May 17, 1959

Narrowest Margin of Victory
1.400 seconds July 16, 1972
Northern 300

Slowest Race
84.522 MPH—May 30, 1958
Northern 500

Race Record
121.008 MPH—July 13, 1969
Northern 300

Most Cautions
5—July 14, 1968 Northern 300
5—July 16, 1972 Northern 300

Most Race Leaders
6—July 12, 1970 Schaefer 300

Most Cars Running at Finish
22—July 12, 1970 Schaefer 300
22—July 18, 1971 Northern 300
22—July 16, 1972 Northern 300

1958 Grand National Race No. 20 Northern 500
May 30, 1958 Average Speed: 84.522

	Driver	Owner	Car #	Make	Laps	Winnings
1.	Fireball Roberts	Frank Strickland	22	57 Chev	500	6,500
2.	Junior Johnson	Paul Spaulding	11	57 Ford	498	3,160
3.	Lee Petty	Petty Enterprises	42	57 Olds	492	2,125
4.	Jim Reed	Jim Reed	7	57 Ford	489	1,510
5.	Eddie Pagan	Eddie Pagan	45	57 Ford	488	1,225

1959 Grand National Race No. 14
May 17, 1959

	Driver	Owner	Car #	Make	Laps	Winnings
1.	Tom Pistone	Carl Rupert	59	59 Ford	150	1,450
2.	Cotton Owens	W. H. Watson	6	58 Pont	150	750
3.	Lee Petty	Petty Enterprises	42	59 Plym	149	575
4.	Jim Reed	Jim Reed	7	59 Chev	148	375
5.	Tommy Irwin	Tommy Irwin	36	59 Ford	147	350

1967 Grand National Race No. 29 Northern 300
July 9, 1967 Average Speed: 95.208

	Driver	Owner	Car #	Make	Laps	Winnings
1.	Richard Petty	Petty Enterprises	43	67 Plym	300	4,350
2.	Darel Dieringer	Junior Johnson	26	67 Ford	300	1,965
3.	Jim Paschal	Tom Friedkin	14	67 Plym	297	1,310
4.	Paul Goldsmith	Ray Nichels	99	67 Plym	293	700
5.	Elmo Langley	Henry Woodfield	64	66 Ford	288	625

1968 Grand National Race No. 29 Northern 300
July 14, 1968 Average Speed: 89.079

	Driver	Owner	Car #	Make	Laps	Winnings
1.	LeeRoy Yarbrough	Junior Johnson	98	68 Ford	300	2,900
2.	David Pearson	Holman-Moody	17	68 Ford	299	1,475
3.	Bobby Allison	Bobby Allison	2	66 Chev	299	1,025
4.	Charlie Glotzbach	Cotton Owens	6	68 Dodg	297	675
5.	Pete Hamilton	Rocky Hinton	5	68 Ford	294	625

1969 Grand National Race No. 31 Northern 300
July 13, 1969 Average Speed: 121.008

	Driver	Owner	Car #	Make	Laps	Winnings
1.	David Pearson	Holman-Moody	17	69 Ford	200	5,300
2.	Bobby Allison	Mario Rossi	22	69 Dodg	199	2,050
3.	Bobby Isaac	Nord Krauskopf	71	69 Dodg	199	1,350
4.	James Hylton	James Hylton	48	69 Dodg	198	725
5.	LeeRoy Yarbrough	L. G. DeWitt	14	69 Ford	196	675

1970 Grand National Race No. 27 Schaefer 300
July 12, 1970 Average Speed: 120.724

	Driver	Owner	Car #	Make	Laps	Winnings
1.	Richard Petty	Petty Enterprises	43	70 Plym	200	6,730
2.	Bobby Allison	Mario Rossi	22	69 Dodg	200	2,470
3.	Charlie Glotzbach	Ray Nichels	99	69 Dodg	200	1,720
4.	Dick Brooks	Dick Brooks	32	70 Plym	198	1,320
5.	James Hylton	James Hylton	48	69 Ford	196	1,045

1971 Winston Cup GN Race No. 31 Northern 300
July 18, 1971 Average Speed: 120.347

	Driver	Owner	Car #	Make	Laps	Winnings
1.	Richard Petty	Petty Enterprises	43	71 Plym	200	6,760
2.	Buddy Baker	Neil Castles	06	70 Dodg	200	2,980
3.	Bobby Allison	Holman-Moody	12	71 Ford	199	2,055
4.	Dave Marcis	Dave Marcis	2	69 Dodg	198	1,370
5.	Pete Hamilton	Cotton Owens	6	71 Plym	198	1,075

1972 Winston Cup GN Race No. 19 Northern 300
July 16, 1972 Average Speed: 114.030

	Driver	Owner	Car #	Make	Laps	Winnings
1.	Bobby Allison	Richard Howard	12	72 Chev	200	7,900
2.	Bobby Isaac	Nord Krauskopf	71	72 Dodg	200	4,825
3.	Richard Petty	Petty Enterprises	43	72 Plym	199	3,800
4.	Fred Lorenzen	Junie Donlavey	90	71 Ford	197	1,475
5.	Cecil Gordon	Cecil Gordon	24	71 Merc	194	1,325

Wall Stadium
Belmar, NJ
.333-Mile Paved Track

.333-mile paved track opened in May 1950. Only NASCAR Winston Cup (the Grand National) event staged on 7/26/58 (won by Jim Reed).
Track is still in operation.

Winston Cup Victories
Jim Reed   1

Winston Cup Poles
Rex White   1

Winston Cup Money
Jim Reed $800

Most Cars Started
19—July 26, 1958

Narrowest Margin of Victory
1 car length—July 26, 1958

Race Record
65.395 MPH—July 26, 1958

Most Cautions
1—July 26, 1958

Most Race Leaders
1—July 26, 1958

Most Cars Running at Finish
14—July 26, 1958

1958 Grand National Race No. 34
July 26, 1958 Average Speed: 65.395

Driver	Owner	Car #	Make	Laps	Winnings
1. Jim Reed	Jim Reed	7	57 Ford	300	800
2. Rex White	J. H. Petty	44	57 Chev	300	525
3. Buck Baker	Buck Baker	87	57 Chev	300	350
4. Lee Petty	Petty Enterprises	42	57 Olds	300	250
5. Jack Smith	Jack Smith	47	57 Chev	291	225

New York

Airborne Speedway
Plattsburg, NY
Half-mile Dirt Track

(aka Plattsburg Speedway) Half-mile dirt track built in 1954. Only NASCAR Winston Cup (then Grand National) event staged on 6/19/55 (won by Lee Petty). Track was paved in 1961 and is still in operation.

Winston Cup Victories
Lee Petty   1

Winston Cup Poles
Lee Petty   1

Winston Cup Money
Lee Petty $1,000

Most Cars Started
16—June 19, 1955

Narrowest Margin of Victory
1 lap plus—June 19, 1955

Race Record
59.074 MPH—June 19, 1955

Most Race Leaders
2—June 19, 1955

Most Cars Running at Finish
10—June 19, 1955

1955 Grand National Race No. 22
June 19, 1955 Average Speed: 59.074

Driver	Owner	Car #	Make	Laps	Winnings
1. Lee Petty	Petty Enterprises	42	55 Chrys	200	1,000
2. Buck Baker	Griffin Motors	87	54 Olds	199	650
3. Tim Flock	Hubert Westmoreland	2	55 Chev	197	450
4. Bob Welborn	J. H. Petty	44	55 Chev	194	350
5. Carl Krueger	Carl Krueger	302	55 Chrys	190	300

Albany-Saratoga Speedway
Malta, NY
.362-mile Paved Track

(aka Malta Speedway) .362-mile paved oval opened in May 1965, built by Joe Lesik. First NASCAR Winston Cup (then Grand National) race staged on 7/7/70 (won by Richard Petty). Only other Winston Cup Grand National event run on 7/14/71 (also won by Richard Petty). Track closed in 1975, but one final event was conducted in 1991.

Winston Cup Starts
20 drivers tied with 2

Winston Cup Victories
Richard Petty 2

Winston Cup Poles
Bobby Isaac 1
Richard Petty 1

Winston Cup Money
Richard Petty $3,000

Most Cars Started
34—July 14, 1971 Albany-Saratoga 250

Fewest Cars Started
28—July 7, 1970 Albany-Saratoga 250

Narrowest Margin of Victory
1 lap plus—July 7, 1970

Slowest Race
66.748 MPH—July 14, 1971
Albany-Saratoga 250

Race Record
68.589 MPH—July 7, 1970
Albany-Saratoga 250

Most Cautions
2—July 14, 1971 Albany-Saratoga 250

Most Race Leaders
4—July 14, 1971 Albany-Saratoga 250

Most Cars Running at Finish
18—July 7, 1970 Albany-Saratoga 250

1970 Grand National Race No. 25 Albany-Saratoga 250
July 7, 1970 Average Speed: 68.589

Driver	Owner	Car #	Make	Laps	Winnings
1. Richard Petty	Petty Enterprises	43	70 Plym	250	1,500
2. Bobby Allison	Bobby Allison	22	69 Dodg	249	900
3. Dave Marcis	Dave Marcis	30	69 Dodg	246	500
4. Neil Castles	Neil Castles	06	69 Dodg	243	350
5. G. C. Spencer	G. C. Spencer	49	69 Plym	240	325

1971 Winston Cup GN Race No. 29 Albany-Saratoga 250
July 14, 1971 Average Speed: 66.748

Driver	Owner	Car #	Make	Laps	Winnings
1. Richard Petty	Petty Enterprises	43	71 Plym	250	1,500
2. Dave Marcis	Dave Marcis	2	69 Dodg	248	900
3. J. D. McDuffie	J. D. McDuffie	70	69 Merc	244	500
4. James Hylton	James Hylton	48	71 Ford	243	350
5. Elmo Langley	Ron Ronacher	67	69 Ford	242	325

Altamont-Schenectady Fairgrounds
Altamont, NY
Half-mile Dirt Track

(aka Altamont Speedway; Tri-County Fairgrounds; Albany-Schenectady Fairgrounds) Half-mile dirt oval opened in July 1932. First NASCAR Winston Cup (then Grand National) race staged on 8/1/51 (won by Fonty Flock). Last NASCAR race held on 7/29/55 (won by Junior Johnson). Track closed shortly after the final Grand National event.

Winston Cup Starts
Pappy Hough 2
Lee Petty 2
Jim Reed 2

Winston Cup Victories
Fonty Flock 1
Junior Johnson 1

Winston Cup Poles
Tim Flock 1
Fonty Flock 1

Winston Cup Money
Fonty Flock $1,000

Most Cars Started
25—July 29, 1955

Fewest Cars Started
21—August 1, 1951

Narrowest Margin of Victory
N/A

Most Race Leaders
3—July 29, 1955

Most Cars Running at Finish
16—July 29, 1955

1951 Grand National Race No. 19
August 1, 1951

Driver	Owner	Car #	Make	Laps	Winnings
1. Fonty Flock	Frank Christian	14	51 Olds	200	1,000
2. Herb Thomas	Herb Thomas	92	51 Plym	—	600
3. Lee Petty	Petty Enterprises	42	51 Plym	—	400
4. Perry Smith	Perry Smith	23	51 Stud	—	300
5. Jerry Morese		227	51 Ford	—	250

1955 Grand National Race No. 28
July 29, 1955

Driver	Owner	Car #	Make	Laps	Winnings
1. Junior Johnson	B & L Motors	55	55 Olds	177	900
2. Jim Paschal	Ernest Woods	78	55 Olds	176	600
3. Lee Petty	Petty Enterprises	42	55 Chrys	172	525
4. Jimmie Lewallen	Ernest Woods	88	55 Olds	170	335
5. Gene Simpson	Gene Simpson	40	55 Buick	170	200

Bridgehampton Race Circuit
Bridgehampton, NY
2.85-mile Paved Road Course

(aka Bridgehampton Raceway) 2.85-mile road course located on eastern reaches of Long Island, opened in September 1957. First NASCAR Winston Cup (then Grand National) race held on 8/2/58 (won by Jack Smith). Richard Petty's first career win on a road course came here on 7/21/63. Final Grand National run on 7/10/66 (won by David Pearson). Track is still in operation.

Winston Cup Starts
Buck Baker 4

Winston Cup Victories
David Pearson 1
Richard Petty 1
Jack Smith 1
Billy Wade 1

Winston Cup Poles
Richard Petty 2

Winston Cup Money
David Pearson $2,075

Most Cars Started
28—July 10, 1966

Fewest Cars Started
17—August 2, 1958
17—July 21, 1963

Narrowest Margin of Victory
12.000 seconds August 2, 1958

Slowest Race
80.696 MPH—August 2, 1958

Race Record
87.707 MPH—July 12, 1964

Most Race Leaders
4—July 12, 1964

Most Cars Running at Finish
20—July 10, 1966

1958 Grand National Race No. 35
August 2, 1958 Average Speed: 80.696

Driver	Owner	Car #	Make	Laps	Winnings
1. Jack Smith	Jack Smith	47	57 Chev	35	800
2. Cotton Owens	Jim Stephens	3	58 Pont	35	525
3. Jim Reed	Jim Reed	7	57 Ford	35	350
4. Junior Johnson	Paul Spaulding	11	57 Ford	35	250
5. Buck Baker	Buck Baker	87	57 Chev	35	225

1963 Grand National Race No. 36
July 21, 1963 Average Speed: 86.047

Driver	Owner	Car #	Make	Laps	Winnings
1. Richard Petty	Petty Enterprises	43	63 Plym	35	1,000
2. Fred Lorenzen	Holman-Moody	28	63 Ford	35	600
3. Marvin Panch	Wood Brothers	21	63 Ford	35	400
4. David Pearson	Cotton Owens	6	63 Dodg	35	300
5. Fireball Roberts	Holman-Moody	22	63 Ford	35	275

1964 Grand National Race No. 38
July 12, 1964 Average Speed: 87.707

Driver	Owner	Car #	Make	Laps	Winnings
1. Billy Wade	Bud Moore	1	64 Merc	50	1,225
2. Buck Baker	Ray Fox	3	64 Dodg	50	675
3. Walt Hansgen	Walt Hansgen	46	64 Ford	48	500
4. Marvin Panch	Holman-Moody	06	64 Ford	44	350
5. Curtis Crider	Curtis Crider	02	63 Merc	42	350

1966 Grand National Race No. 30
July 10, 1966 Average Speed: 86.949

Driver	Owner	Car #	Make	Laps	Winnings
1. David Pearson	Cotton Owens	6	65 Dodg	52	1,375
2. James Hylton	Bud Hartje	48	65 Dodg	52	775
3. Marvin Panch		22	64 Ford	51	570
4. Roy Hallquist	Roy Hallquist	144	64 Ford	51	350
5. Elmo Langley	Henry Woodfield	64	64 Ford	51	350

Buffalo Civic Stadium
Buffalo, NY
Quarter-mile Paved Track

(aka Jopp Stadium; War Memorial Stadium) Quarter-mile cinder track opened for auto racing in May 1940. Track paved in August 1940. Only NASCAR Winston Cup (then Grand National) event staged on 7/19/58 (won by Jim Reed). The stadium is where Buffalo Bills played football in their early AFL days.

Winston Cup Victories
Jim Reed 1

Winston Cup Poles
Rex White 1

Winston Cup Money
Jim Reed $605

Most Cars Started
19—July 19, 1958

Narrowest Margin of Victory
N/A

Race Record
46.972 MPH—July 19, 1958

Most Race Leaders
2—July 19, 1958

Most Cars Running at Finish
17—July 19, 1958

1958 Grand National Race No. 32
July 19, 1958 Average Speed: 46.972

Driver	Owner	Car #	Make	Laps	Winnings
1. Jim Reed	Jim Reed	7	57 Ford	100	605
2. Cotton Owens	Jim Stephens	6	57 Pont	100	450
3. Johnny Mackison	Ken Corman	23	57 Merc	100	320
4. Shorty Rollins	Shorty Rollins	99	58 Ford	99	275
5. Rex White	J. H. Petty	44	57 Chev	99	250

Fonda Speedway
Fonda, NY
Half-mile Paved Track

(aka Montgomery County Fairgrounds; Fonda-Fultonville Speedway) A half-mile dirt oval that opened circa 1926 and closed in 1939. Re-opened in 1948 and closed again later that same year. Refurbished and opened a third time in May 1953. First NASCAR Winston Cup (then Grand National) race staged on 6/18/55 (won by Junior Johnson). Final Grand National event run on 7/11/68 (won by Richard Petty). Track is still in operation.

Winston Cup Starts
Buck Baker   4

Winston Cup Victories
Richard Petty   2

Winston Cup Poles
Richard Petty   2

Winston Cup Money
Richard Petty $3,025

Most Cars Started
31—July 14,1966

Fewest Cars Started
19—June 18, 1955

Narrowest Margin of Victory
N/A

Slowest Race
58.413 MPH—June 18, 1955

Race Record
65.826 MPH—July 13, 1967

Most Cautions
5—July 13, 1967

Most Race Leaders
4—July 14,1966

Most Cars Running at Finish
15—July 14,1966
15—July 13, 1967

1955 Grand National Race No. 21
June 18, 1955 Average Speed: 58.413

Driver	Owner	Car #	Make	Laps	Winnings
1. Junior Johnson	B & L Motors	55	55 Olds	200	1,000
2. Tim Flock	Carl Kiekhaefer	300	55 Chrys	199	650
3. Lee Petty	Petty Enterprises	42	55 Chrys	191	450
4. Buck Baker	Griffin Motors	87	54 Olds	188	350
5. Bob Welborn	J. H. Petty	44	55 Chev	188	300

1966 Grand National Race No. 32
July 14,1966 Average Speed: 61.010

Driver	Owner	Car #	Make	Laps	Winnings
1. David Pearson	Cotton Owens	6	65 Dodg	200	1,100
2. Richard Petty	Petty Enterprises	43	66 Plym	200	675
3. Rene Charland	Ed Ackerman	03	64 Ford	199	450
4. Roy Hallquist	Roy Hallquist	144	64 Ford	196	300
5. Buck Baker	Buck Baker	87	66 Olds	193	275

1967 Grand National Race No. 31
July 13, 1967 Average Speed: 65.826

Driver	Owner	Car #	Make	Laps	Winnings
1. Richard Petty	Petty Enterprises	43	67 Plym	200	1,150
2. Bobby Allison	Bobby Allison	2	65 Chev	199	700
3. G. C. Spencer	G. C. Spencer	49	66 Plym	197	450
4. John Sears	L. G. DeWitt	4	66 Ford	196	300
5. James Hylton	Bud Hartje	48	65 Dodg	196	275

1968 Grand National Race No. 28 Fonda 200
July 11, 1968 Average Speed: 64.935

Driver	Owner	Car #	Make	Laps	Winnings
1. Richard Petty	Petty Enterprises	43	68 Plym	200	1,200
2. Buddy Baker	Ray Fox	3	68 Dodg	200	600
3. Bobby Allison	Bobby Allison	2	66 Chev	200	400
4. Bobby Isaac	Nord Krauskopf	71	67 Dodg	197	300
5. David Pearson	Holman-Moody	17	68 Ford	196	275

Hamburg Speedway
Hamburg, NY
Half-mile Dirt Track

(aka Erie County Fairgrounds) A half-mile dirt oval that opened circa 1929 for automobile racing. The original horse track was built in the 1840s. First NASCAR Winston Cup (then Strictly Stock) race held on 9/18/49 (won by Jack White; the fifth Winston Cup race ever run). Only other big NASCAR event held on 8/27/50 (won by Dick Linder). Track is still in operation.

Winston Cup Starts
Ted Chamberlain   2
Chuck Mahoney   2
Bill Rexford   2
Frankie Schneider   2
Jack White   2

Winston Cup Victories
Dick Linder   1
Jack White   1

Winston Cup Poles
Dick Linder   1

Winston Cup Money
Jack White $1,800

Most Cars Started
33—August 27, 1950

Fewest Cars Started
16—September 18, 1949

Narrowest Margin of Victory
20 yards—August 27, 1950

Slowest Race
50.747 MPH—August 27, 1950

Race Record
50.747 MPH—August 27, 1950

Most Cautions
N/A

Most Race Leaders
3—August 27, 1950

Most Cars Running at Finish
N/A

1949 Strictly Stock Race No. 5
September 18, 1949

Driver	Owner	Car #	Make	Laps	Winnings
1. Jack White	Dailey Moyer	25	49 Linc	200	1,500
2. Ray Erickson	Ed Hastings	5	49 Merc	200	750
3. Billy Rafter			49 Ford	—	400
4. Mike Eagan			49 Merc	—	300
5. Bill Rexford	Julian Buesink	59	49 Ford	—	175

1950 Grand National Race No. 12
August 27, 1950 Average Speed: 50.747

Driver	Owner	Car #	Make	Laps	Winnings
1. Dick Linder	Don Rogalla	25	50 Olds	200	1,500
2. Fireball Roberts	Sam Rice	11	49 Olds	200	750
3. Curtis Turner	John Eanes	41	50 Olds	199	500
4. Lloyd Moore	Julian Buesink	59	50 Linc	—	400
5. Jack White	Dailey Moyer		50 Merc	—	300

Islip Speedway
Islip, NY
.2-mile Paved Track

*.2-mile paved oval opened in August 1947. First NASCAR Winston Cup (then Grand National) race was held on 7/15/64 (won by Billy Wade).
Final big NASCAR event staged on 7/15/71 (won by Richard Petty). The track was the scene of the World Figure 8 Championships that frequently
aired on ABC's Wide World of Sports. Final event run on 9/8/84. The property is now the site of a cookie factory.*

Winston Cup Starts
Neil Castles	6
Wendell Scott	6

Winston Cup Victories
Bobby Allison	2
Richard Petty	2

Winston Cup Poles
Richard Petty	2

Winston Cup Money
Richard Petty	$3,650

Most Cars Started
33—July 15, 1971 Islip 250

Fewest Cars Started
22—July 15, 1964
22—July 14, 1965

Narrowest Margin of Victory
6 car lengths—July 7, 1968

Slowest Race
42.428 MPH—July 15, 1967 Islip 300

Race Record
49.925 MPH—July 15, 1971 Islip 250

Most Cautions
5—July 15, 1967 Islip 300

Most Race Leaders
4—July 15, 1967 Islip 300
4—July 7, 1968 Islip 300

Most Cars Running at Finish
14—July 7, 1968 Islip 300

1964 Grand National Race No. 39
July 15, 1964 Average Speed: 46.252

Driver	Owner	Car #	Make	Laps	Winnings
1. Billy Wade	Bud Moore	1	64 Merc	300	1,000
2. Ned Jarrett	Bondy Long	11	64 Ford	299	600
3. Richard Petty	Petty Enterprises	41	64 Plym	295	400
4. Jimmy Pardue	Charles Robinson	54	64 Plym	283	300
5. Bob Welborn	Holman-Moody	06	64 Ford	273	275

1965 Grand National Race No. 32
July 14, 1965 Average Speed: 43.838

Driver	Owner	Car #	Make	Laps	Winnings
1. Marvin Panch	Wood Brothers	21	65 Ford	250	1,000
2. Dick Hutcherson	Holman-Moody	29	65 Ford	249	600
3. Ned Jarrett	Bondy Long	11	65 Ford	246	400
4. Cale Yarborough	Kenny Myler	06	64 Ford	245	300
5. Dick Dixon	Dan Colone	8	64 Ford	242	275

1966 Grand National Race No. 33
July 16, 1966 Average Speed: 47.285

Driver	Owner	Car #	Make	Laps	Winnings
1. Bobby Allison	Bobby Allison	2	65 Chev	300	1,100
2. James Hylton	Bud Hartje	48	65 Dodg	298	675
3. Ned Jarrett	Bernard Alvarez	11	64 Ford	297	650
4. David Pearson	Cotton Owens	6	65 Dodg	295	300
5. Elmo Langley	Henry Woodfield	64	64 Ford	290	275

1967 Grand National Race No. 32 Islip 300
July 15, 1967 Average Speed: 42.428

Driver	Owner	Car #	Make	Laps	Winnings
1. Richard Petty	Petty Enterprises	43	67 Plym	300	1,150
2. James Hylton	Bud Hartje	48	65 Dodg	297	800
3. G. C. Spencer	G. C. Spencer	49	66 Plym	297	500
4. John Sears	L. G. DeWitt	4	66 Ford	295	300
5. Jim Paschal	Tom Friedkin	14	67 Plym	294	275

1968 Grand National Race No. 26 Islip 300
July 7, 1968 Average Speed: 48.561

Driver	Owner	Car #	Make	Laps	Winnings
1. Bobby Allison	Bobby Allison	2	66 Chev	300	1,000
2. David Pearson	Holman-Moody	17	68 Ford	300	600
3. Buddy Baker	Ray Fox	3	68 Dodg	299	400
4. Richard Petty	Petty Enterprises	43	68 Plym	298	500
5. James Hylton	James Hylton	48	67 Dodg	294	275

1971 Winston Cup GN Race No. 30 Islip 250
July 15, 1971 Average Speed: 49.925

Driver	Owner	Car #	Make	Laps	Winnings
1. Richard Petty	Petty Enterprises	43	71 Plym	230	1,500
2. Friday Hassler	Friday Hassler	39	70 Chev	228	900
3. Elmo Langley	Elmo Langley	67	69 Merc	224	500
4. Bobby Allison	Holman-Moody	12	69 Merc	223	350
5. G. C. Spencer	G. C. Spencer	49	69 Plym	222	325

Monroe County Fairgrounds
Rochester, NY
Half-mile Dirt Track

Half-mile dirt track built circa 1948. First NASCAR Winston Cup (then Grand National) event staged on 7/2/50 (won by Curtis Turner). Final NASCAR event held on 7/25/58 (won by Cotton Owens). Track closed circa 1962 and was briefly re-opened in 1981.

Winston Cup Starts
Lee Petty — 8

Winston Cup Victories
Tim Flock — 2
Lee Petty — 2

Winston Cup Poles
Buck Baker — 1
Fonty Flock — 1
Jim Paschal — 1
Herb Thomas — 1
Curtis Turner — 1
Rex White — 1

Winston Cup Money
Lee Petty — $3,500

Most Cars Started
32—June 25, 1954

Fewest Cars Started
18—July 3, 1953

Narrowest Margin of Victory
10 car lengths—July 3, 1953

Slowest Race
50.614 MPH—July 2, 1950

Race Record
59.990 MPH—July 25, 1958

Most Cautions
N/A

Most Race Leaders
3—August 15, 1952
3—July 25, 1958

Most Cars Running at Finish
24—June 25, 1954

1950 Grand National Race No. 8
July 2, 1950 Average Speed: 50.614

	Driver	Owner	Car #	Make	Laps	Winnings
1.	Curtis Turner	John Eanes	41	50 Olds	200	1,500
2.	Bill Blair	Sam Rice	2	50 Merc	197	600
3.	Lee Petty	Petty Enterprises	42	50 Plym	197	400
4.	Jimmy Florian	Jimmy Florian	27	50 Ford	192	300
5.	Bill Rexford	Julian Buesink	80	50 Olds	192	225

1951 Grand National Race No. 18
July 31, 1951

	Driver	Owner	Car #	Make	Laps	Winnings
1.	Lee Petty	Petty Enterprises	42	51 Plym	200	1,000
2.	Charles Gattalia			51 Ford	—	600
3.	Ronnie Kohler			51 Plym	—	400
4.	Don Bailey		54	51 Stud	—	300
5.	Pappy Hough	Pappy Hough	81	51 Ford	—	250

1952 Grand National Race No. 23
August 15, 1952

	Driver	Owner	Car #	Make	Laps	Winnings
1.	Tim Flock	Ted Chester	91	52 Huds	176	1,000
2.	Herb Thomas	Herb Thomas	92	52 Huds	176	700
3.	Dick Rathmann	Walt Chapman	120	52 Huds	174	450
4.	Lee Petty	Petty Enterprises	42	52 Plym	174	350
5.	Jim Reed	Jim Reed	47	51 Ford	173	200

1953 Grand National Race No. 19
July 3, 1953 Average Speed: 56.939

	Driver	Owner	Car #	Make	Laps	Winnings
1.	Herb Thomas	Herb Thomas	92	53 Huds	200	1,000
2.	Dick Rathmann	Walt Chapman	120	53 Huds	200	700
3.	Lee Petty	Petty Enterprises	42	53 Dodg	200	450
4.	Tim Flock	Ted Chester	91	53 Huds	199	350
5.	Bill Rexford	Julian Buesink	60	53 Chev	—	200

1954 Grand National Race No. 20
June 25, 1954 Average Speed: 52.455

	Driver	Owner	Car #	Make	Laps	Winnings
1.	Lee Petty	Petty Enterprises	42	54 Chrys	200	1,000
2.	Herb Thomas	Herb Thomas	92	54 Huds	200	650
3.	Dick Rathmann	John Ditz	3	54 Huds	199	450
4.	Buck Baker	Griffin Motors	87	53 Olds	198	350
5.	Hershel McGriff	Frank Christian	14	54 Olds	198	300

1955 Grand National Race No. 20
June 17, 1955 Average Speed: 57.170

	Driver	Owner	Car #	Make	Laps	Winnings
1.	Tim Flock	Carl Kiekhaefer	300	55 Chrys	200	1,000
2.	Fonty Flock	Carl Kiekhaefer	301	55 Chrys	199	650
3.	Bob Welborn	J. H. Petty	44	55 Chev	196	450
4.	Jimmie Lewallen	Ernest Woods	88	55 Olds	194	350
5.	Harvey Henderson	Harvey Henderson	121	53 Huds	191	300

1956 Grand National Race No. 27
June 22, 1956 Average Speed: 57.288

	Driver	Owner	Car #	Make	Laps	Winnings
1.	Speedy Thompson	Carl Kiekhaefer	300c	56 Chrys	200	850
2.	Jim Paschal	Frank Hayworth	75	56 Merc	199	625
3.	Herb Thomas	Carl Kiekhaefer	500B	56 Dodg	199	450
4.	Buck Baker	Carl Kiekhaefer	300	56 Chrys	197	350
5.	Bob Duell	Julian Buesink	95	56 Ford	192	310

1958 Grand National Race No. 33
July 25, 1958 Average Speed: 59.990

	Driver	Owner	Car #	Make	Laps	Winnings
1.	Cotton Owens	Jim Stephens	6	57 Pont	200	800
2.	Buck Baker	Buck Baker	87	57 Chev	198	525
3.	Speedy Thompson	Speedy Thompson	46	57 Chev	198	350
4.	Lee Petty	Petty Enterprises	42	57 Olds	197	250
5.	Bob Duell	Julian Buesink	95	57 Ford	195	225

Montgomery Air Base
Montgomery, NY
2-mile Paved Track

(aka Stewart Air Force Base) 1.85-mile concrete road course opened for first race in August 1956. Track was laid out on runways in a triangular fashion with "kinks" or chicanes in each of the three corners to incorporate quick left- and right-hand turns. Only NASCAR Winston Cup (then Grand National) race run on 7/17/60 (won by Rex White). NASCAR course did not include chicanes, and drivers frequently ran into the dirt beyond the course boundaries in order to set up a more favorable angle into each flat corner. The NASCAR course measured 2 miles. Final motor racing event held on track in August 1960.

Winston Cup Victories
Rex White — 1

Winston Cup Poles
John Rostek — 1

Winston Cup Money
Rex White — $2,970

Most Cars Started
19—July 17, 1960 Empire State 200

Narrowest Margin of Victory
1 lap plus—July 17, 1960
Empire State 200

Race Record
88.626 MPH—July 17, 1960
Empire State 200

Most Cautions
1—July 17, 1960 Empire State 200

Most Race Leaders
4—July 17, 1960 Empire State 200

Most Cars Running at Finish
14—July 17, 1960 Empire State 200

1960 Grand National Race No. 25 Empire State 200
July 17, 1960 Average Speed: 88.626

	Driver	Owner	Car #	Make	Laps	Winnings
1.	Rex White	Rex White	4	60 Chev	100	2,970
2.	Richard Petty	Petty Enterprises	43	60 Plym	99	1,600
3.	Lee Petty	Petty Enterprises	42	60 Plym	97	1,200
4.	Ned Jarrett	Ned Jarrett	11	60 Ford	96	725
5.	Buck Baker	Buck Baker	87	60 Chev	96	625

New York State Fairgrounds
Syracuse, NY
1.0-mile Dirt Track

1-mile dirt track originally built as a horse track in 1880. Its premier auto racing event was staged in September 1909. First NASCAR Winston Cup (then Grand National) race held on 7/30/55 (won by Tim Flock). Final big NASCAR event held on 9/5/57 (won by Gwyn Staley). Track is now home of the Syracuse Nationals. In 1911, Lee Oldfield crashed through a fence and plunged into the crowd. Eleven spectators were killed in one of America's worst racing accidents. Early AAA champion and Indianapolis 500 winner Jimmy Murphy was also killed here in 1924.

Winston Cup Starts
Lee Petty — 3
Jim Reed — 3

Winston Cup Victories
Buck Baker — 1
Tim Flock — 1
Gwyn Staley — 1

Winston Cup Poles
Buck Baker — 1
Tim Flock — 1
Gwyn Staley — 1

Winston Cup Money
Buck Baker — $2,000

Most Cars Started
24—May 30, 1956
24—September 5, 1957

Fewest Cars Started
22—July 30, 1955

Narrowest Margin of Victory
N/A

Slowest Race
76.522 MPH—July 30, 1955

Race Record
86.179 MPH—May 30, 1956

Most Cautions
N/A

Most Race Leaders
2—May 30, 1956
2—September 5, 1957

Most Cars Running at Finish
18—July 30, 1955

1955 Grand National Race No. 29
July 30, 1955 Average Speed: 76.522

Driver	Owner	Car #	Make	Laps	Winnings
1. Tim Flock	Carl Kiekhaefer	300	55 Chrys	100	950
2. Jimmie Lewallen	Ernest Woods	88	55 Olds	100	650
3. Lee Petty	Petty Enterprises	42	55 Chrys	99	525
4. Bob Welborn	J. H. Petty	44	55 Chev	98	385
5. Jim Paschal	Ernest Woods	78	55 Olds	98	290

1956 Grand National Race No. 23
May 30, 1956 Average Speed: 86.179

Driver	Owner	Car #	Make	Laps	Winnings
1. Buck Baker	Carl Kiekhaefer	300	56 Chrys	150	1,900
2. Jim Paschal	Frank Hayworth	75	56 Merc	147	1,300
3. Jim Reed	Jim Reed	7	56 Chev	146	950
4. Lee Petty	Petty Enterprises	42	56 Dodg	145	700
5. Gwyn Staley	Hubert Westmoreland	2	56 Chev	145	535

1957 Grand National Race No. 41
September 5, 1957 Average Speed: 80.591

	Driver	Owner	Car #	Make	Laps	Winnings
1.	Gwyn Staley	J. H. Petty	38	57 Chev	100	1,000
2.	Lee Petty	Petty Enterprises	42	57 Olds	99	625
3.	Bill Walker		150	57 Ford	99	400
4.	Dean Layfield	William Dickenson	916	56 Ford	97	295
5.	Fireball Roberts	Fireball Roberts	22	57 Ford	95	255

Shangri-La Speedway
Oswego, NY
Half-mile Paved Track

(aka Tioga Speedway) Half-mile paved oval opened in July 1946. Only NASCAR Winston Cup (then Grand National) race staged on 7/4/52 (won by Tim Flock). Track is still in operation.

Winston Cup Victories		**Winston Cup Money**		**Narrowest Margin of Victory**		**Most Race Leaders**
Tim Flock	1	Tim Flock	$1,000	N/A		N/A

Winston Cup Poles		**Most Cars Started**	**Race Record**	**Most Cars Running at Finish**
Tim Flock	1	26—July 4, 1952	56.603 MPH—July 4, 1952	16—July 4, 1952

1952 Grand National Race No. 19
July 4, 1952 Average Speed: 56.603

	Driver	Owner	Car #	Make	Laps	Winnings
1.	Tim Flock	Ted Chester	91	51 Huds	200	1,000
2.	Herb Thomas	Herb Thomas	92	52 Huds	200	700
3.	Dick Rathmann	Walt Chapman	120	51 Huds	199	450
4.	Bucky Sager	Ken Swihart	118	51 Huds	199	350
5.	Lee Petty	Petty Enterprises	42	50 Plym	198	200

State Line Speedway
Busti, NY
.333-Mile Dirt Track

.333-mile paved oval opened in July 1956. Only NASCAR Winston Cup (then Grand National) race staged on 7/16/58 (won by rookie Shorty Rollins). Track is still in operation and should not be confused with the other track in Busti, named Satan's Bowl-O-Death.

Winston Cup Victories		**Winston Cup Money**		**Narrowest Margin of Victory**		**Most Race Leaders**
Shorty Rollins	1	Shorty Rollins	$600	N/A		N/A

Winston Cup Poles		**Most Cars Started**	**Race Record**	**Most Cars Running at Finish**
Lee Petty	1	23—July 16, 1958	47.110 MPH—July 16, 1958	14—July 16, 1958

1958 Grand National Race No. 30
July 16, 1958 Average Speed: 47.110

	Driver	Owner	Car #	Make	Laps	Winnings
1.	Shorty Rollins	Shorty Rollins	99	58 Ford	150	600
2.	Bob Duell	Julian Buesink	95	57 Ford	150	470
3.	Ken Johnson		36	56 Ford	149	375
4.	Emory Mahon		8	57 Chev	149	270
5.	John Seeley		16	57 Ford	143	245

Vernon Fairgrounds
Vernon, NY
Half-mile Dirt Track

Half-mile dirt oval opened in 1949. First Winston Cup (then Grand National) race held on 6/18/50 (won by Bill Blair). Only other Grand National ran on 10/1/50 (won by Dick Linder). Track closed circa 1951. It is currently a training track for the Vernon Downs horse track.

Winston Cup Starts

Dick Linder	2
Chuck Mahoney	2
Lloyd Moore	2
Lee Petty	2
Bill Rexford	2
Herb Thomas	2

Winston Cup Victories

Bill Blair	1
Dick Linder	1

Winston Cup Poles

Dick Linder	1
Chuck Mahoney	1

Winston Cup Money

Bill Blair	$1,255

Most Cars Started
29—October 1, 1950

Fewest Cars Started
23—June 18, 1950

Narrowest Margin of Victory
5 car lengths—October 1, 1950

Most Race Leaders
3—June 18, 1950

Most Cars Running at Finish
N/A

1950 Grand National Race No. 6
June 18, 1950

Driver	Owner	Car #	Make	Laps	Winnings
1. Bill Blair	Sam Rice	2	50 Merc	200	1,255
2. Lloyd Moore	Julian Buesink	59	50 Ford	—	680
3. Chuck Mahoney	Brooks Motors	77	50 Merc	—	490
4. Dick Burns		18	50 Merc	—	300
5. Lee Petty	Petty Enterprises	42	49 Plym	—	225

1950 Grand National Race No. 16
October 1, 1950

Driver	Owner	Car #	Make	Laps	Winnings
1. Dick Linder	Don Rogalla	25	50 Olds	200	1,025
2. Ted Swaim	Hubert Westmoreland	38	50 Plym	200	600
3. Lloyd Moore	Julian Buesink	59	50 Merc	198	400
4. Tim Flock	Buddy Elliott	9	50 Olds	198	300
5. Jack Reynolds			50 Plym	—	225

Watkins Glen International
Watkins Glen, NY
2.428-mile Road Course

2.3-mile road course opened on 9/15/56. Track was built following the destruction of the 6.6-mile street and road course through the Watkins Glen village in 1952. First NASCAR Winston Cup (then Grand National) race held on 8/4/57 (won by Buck Baker). Site of United States Formula One Grand Prix from 1960–81. 2.428-mile course played host to return of the Winston Cup Series on 8/10/86 (won by Tim Richmond).

Winston Cup Starts

Geoff Bodine	11
Dale Earnhardt	11
Terry Labonte	11
Ricky Rudd	11
Ken Schrader	11
Morgan Shepherd	11
Rusty Wallace	11
Michael Waltrip	11

Winston Cup Victories

Mark Martin	3

Winston Cup Poles

Dale Earnhardt	3
Mark Martin	3

Winston Cup Money

Mark Martin	$507,285

Most Cars Started

40—August 10, 1987
The Budweiser at the Glen
40—August 14, 1988
The Budweiser at the Glen
40—August 13, 1989
The Budweiser at the Glen
40—August 12, 1990
The Budweiser at the Glen
40—August 11, 1991
The Budweiser at the Glen
40—August 14, 1994
The Budweiser at the Glen
40—August 13, 1995
The Budweiser at the Glen

Fewest Cars Started

19—July 18, 1965

Narrowest Margin of Victory

0.440 seconds August 11, 1996
The Budweiser at the Glen

Slowest Race

74.096 MPH—August 14, 1988
The Budweiser at the Glen

Race Record

103.030 MPH—August 13, 1995
The Budweiser at the Glen

Most Cautions

8—August 14, 1988
The Budweiser at the Glen

Most Race Leaders

10—August 14, 1988
The Budweiser at the Glen

Most Cars Running at Finish

35—August 14, 1994
The Budweiser at the Glen
35—August 11, 1996
The Budweiser at the Glen

1957 Grand National Race No. 35
August 4, 1957 Average Speed: 83.064

	Driver	Owner	Car #	Make	Laps	Winnings
1.	Buck Baker	Buck Baker	87	57 Chev	44	1,000
2.	Fireball Roberts	Fireball Roberts	22	57 Ford	44	625
3.	Tiny Lund	A. L. Bumgarner	55	57 Pont	44	400
4.	Frankie Schneider	Hubert Westmoreland	2	57 Chev	43	295
5.	Johnny Allen	Spook Crawford	64	57 Plym	43	255

1964 Grand National Race No. 40
July 19, 1964 Average Speed: 97.988

	Driver	Owner	Car #	Make	Laps	Winnings
1.	Billy Wade	Bud Moore	1	64 Merc	66	1,400
2.	LeeRoy Yarbrough	Ray Fox	03	64 Dodg	66	800
3.	Walt Hansgen	Walt Hansgen	46	64 Chev	65	600
4.	Buck Baker	Ray Fox	3	64 Dodg	65	500
5.	Bob Welborn	Holman-Moody	06	64 Ford	64	400

1965 Grand National Race No. 33
July 18, 1965 Average Speed: 98.182

	Driver	Owner	Car #	Make	Laps	Winnings
1.	Marvin Panch	Wood Brothers	21	65 Ford	66	1,425
2.	Ned Jarrett	Bondy Long	11	65 Ford	66	650
3.	Buddy Baker	Buck Baker	88	64 Dodg	64	490
4.	Cale Yarborough	Kenny Myler	06	64 Ford	63	415
5.	Tiny Lund	Lyle Stelter	55	64 Ford	58	385

1986 Winston Cup Race No. 18 The Budweiser at the Glen
August 10, 1986 Average Speed: 90.463

	Driver	Owner	Car #	Make	Laps	Winnings
1.	Tim Richmond	Rick Hendrick	25	Chev	90	50,955
2.	Darrell Waltrip	Junior Johnson	11	Chev	90	32,450
3.	Dale Earnhardt	Richard Childress	3	Chev	90	25,250
4.	Bill Elliott	Harry Melling	9	Ford	90	20,350
5.	Neil Bonnett	Junior Johnson	12	Chev	90	18,575

1987 Winston Cup Race No. 18 The Budweiser at the Glen
August 10, 1987 Average Speed: 90.682

	Driver	Owner	Car #	Make	Laps	Winnings
1.	Rusty Wallace	Raymond Beadle	27	Pont	90	52,925
2.	Terry Labonte	Junior Johnson	11	Chev	90	35,850
3.	Dave Marcis	Dave Marcis	71	Chev	90	23,880
4.	Ricky Rudd	Bud Moore	15	Ford	90	20,135
5.	Benny Parsons	Rick Hendrick	35	Chev	90	19,655

1988 Winston Cup Race No. 18 The Budweiser at the Glen
August 14, 1988 Average Speed: 74.096

	Driver	Owner	Car #	Make	Laps	Winnings
1.	Ricky Rudd	Kenny Bernstein	26	Buick	90	49,625
2.	Rusty Wallace	Raymond Beadle	27	Pont	90	33,900
3.	Bill Elliott	Harry Melling	9	Ford	90	26,640
4.	Phil Parsons	Richard Jackson	55	Olds	90	16,540
5.	Mike Alexander	Stavola Brothers	12	Buick	90	19,295

1989 Winston Cup Race No. 18 The Budweiser at the Glen
August 13, 1989 Average Speed: 87.242

	Driver	Owner	Car #	Make	Laps	Winnings
1.	Rusty Wallace	Raymond Beadle	27	Pont	90	56,400
2.	Mark Martin	Jack Roush	6	Ford	90	32,550
3.	Dale Earnhardt	Richard Childress	3	Chev	90	38,140
4.	Davey Allison	Robert Yates	28	Ford	90	21,005
5.	Bobby Hillin Jr.	Stavola Brothers	8	Buick	90	16,690

1990 Winston Cup Series Race No. 18 Budweiser at the Glen
August 12, 1990 Average Speed: 92.452

	Driver	Owner	Car #	Make	Laps	Winnings
1.	Ricky Rudd	Rick Hendrick	5	Chev	90	55,000
2.	Geoff Bodine	Junior Johnson	11	Ford	90	33,900
3.	Brett Bodine	Kenny Bernstein	26	Buick	90	22,490
4.	Michael Waltrip	Chuck Rider	30	Pont	90	16,980
5.	Mark Martin	Jack Roush	6	Ford	90	20,790

Watkins Glen International *continued*

1991 Winston Cup Series Race No. 18 The Budweiser at the Glen
August 11, 1991 Average Speed: 98.977

Driver	Owner	Car #	Make	Laps	Winnings
1. Ernie Irvan	Larry McClure	4	Chev	90	64,850
2. Ricky Rudd	Rick Hendrick	5	Chev	90	37,325
3. Mark Martin	Jack Roush	6	Ford	90	31,440
4. Rusty Wallace	Roger Penske	2	Pont	90	16,680
5. Dale Jarrett	Wood Brothers	21	Ford	90	18,565

1992 Winston Cup Race No. 18 The Budweiser at the Glen
August 9, 1992 Average Speed: 88.980

Driver	Owner	Car #	Make	Laps	Winnings
1. Kyle Petty	Felix Sabates	42	Pont	51	50,895
2. Morgan Shepherd	Wood Brothers	21	Ford	51	48,545
3. Ernie Irvan	Larry McClure	4	Chev	51	35,060
4. Mark Martin	Jack Roush	6	Ford	51	28,325
5. Wally Dallenbach Jr.	Jack Roush	16	Ford	51	13,480

1993 Winston Cup Series Race No. 19 The Budweiser at the Glen
August 8, 1993 Average Speed: 84.771

Driver	Owner	Car #	Make	Laps	Winnings
1. Mark Martin	Jack Roush	6	Ford	90	166,110
2. Wally Dallenbach Jr.	Jack Roush	16	Ford	90	37,045
3. Jimmy Spencer	Bobby Allison	12	Ford	90	31,135
4. Bill Elliott	Junior Johnson	11	Ford	90	28,075
5. Ken Schrader	Rick Hendrick	25	Chev	90	24,655

1994 Winston Cup Series Race No. 20 The Budweiser at the Glen
August 14, 1994 Average Speed: 93.752

Driver	Owner	Car #	Make	Laps	Winnings
1. Mark Martin	Jack Roush	6	Ford	90	85,100
2. Ernie Irvan	Robert Yates	28	Ford	90	42,015
3. Dale Earnhardt	Richard Childress	3	Chev	90	39,605
4. Ken Schrader	Rick Hendrick	25	Chev	90	26,245
5. Ricky Rudd	Ricky Rudd	10	Ford	90	20,875

1995 Winston Cup Series Race No. 20 The Budweiser at the Glen
August 13, 1995 Average Speed: 103.030

Driver	Owner	Car #	Make	Laps	Winnings
1. Mark Martin	Jack Roush	6	Ford	90	95,290
2. Wally Dallenbach Jr.	Bill Davis	22	Pont	90	54,140
3. Jeff Gordon	Rick Hendrick	24	Chev	90	42,205
4. Ricky Rudd	Ricky Rudd	10	Ford	90	34,320
5. Terry Labonte	Rick Hendrick	5	Chev	90	36,325

1996 Winston Cup Series Race No. 20 The Budweiser at the Glen
August 11, 1996 Average Speed: 92.334

Driver	Owner	Car #	Make	Laps	Winnings
1. Geoff Bodine	Geoff Bodine	7	Ford	90	88,740
2. Terry Labonte	Rick Hendrick	5	Chev	90	51,390
3. Mark Martin	Jack Roush	6	Ford	90	44,755
4. Jeff Gordon	Rick Hendrick	24	Chev	90	44,370
5. Bobby Labonte	Joe Gibbs	18	Chev	90	35,465

North Carolina

Asheville-Weaverville Speedway
Weaverville, NC
Half-mile Dirt Track

(aka Skyline Speedway) Half-mile dirt oval opened in May 1950. First NASCAR Winston Cup (then Grand National) race staged on 7/29/51 (won by Fonty Flock). Track was paved in 1958. This was often referred to as the fastest half-mile track in the nation. Final Grand National event held on 8/24/69 (won by Bobby Isaac). The track was the scene of a riot during a Grand National event held on 8/13/61 when the race was shortened from 500 to 258 laps. Spectators held drivers and crewmen hostage, and teams were held captive inside the speedway for nearly four hours. Law enforcement officials could not disperse crowd, and the riot fizzled out near dark with no serious injuries reported. Track closed in 1970. Last activity on track was slow-pitch soft-ball.

Winston Cup Starts
Buck Baker   23

Winston Cup Victories
Rex White   5

Winston Cup Poles
Junior Johnson   4
Rex White   4

Winston Cup Money
Richard Petty $16,135

Most Cars Started
41—August 16, 1959
    Western North Carolina 500

Fewest Cars Started
15—March 5, 1961

Narrowest Margin of Victory
70 feet—September 8, 1957

Slowest Race
56.435 MPH—July 1, 1956

Race Record
83.360 MPH—March 5, 1967
    Fireball 300

Most Cautions
10—November 5, 1967
    Western North Carolina 500

Most Race Leaders
6—August 14, 1960
    Western North Carolina 500

Most Cars Running at Finish
28—August 13, 1961
    Western North Carolina 500

1951 Grand National Race No. 17
July 29, 1951

Driver	Owner	Car #	Make	Laps	Winnings
1. Fonty Flock	Frank Christian	14	51 Olds	200	1,000
2. Gober Sosebee	Gober Sosebee	51	50 Olds	—	600
3. Herb Thomas	Herb Thomas	92	50 Plym	—	400
4. Frank Mundy	Perry Smith	23	51 Stud	—	300
5. Speedy Thompson			51 Stud	—	250

1952 Grand National Race No. 24
August 17, 1952 Average Speed: 57.288

Driver	Owner	Car #	Make	Laps	Winnings
1. Bob Flock	Ted Chester	7	51 Huds	200	1,000
2. Tim Flock	Ted Chester	91	52 Huds	198	700
3. Herb Thomas	Herb Thomas	92	52 Huds	195	450
4. Gene Comstock	Gene Comstock	8	52 Huds	192	350
5. Herschel Buchanan	Herschel Buchanan	1	52 Nash	189	200

1953 Grand National Race No. 27
August 16, 1953 Average Speed: 62.434

Driver	Owner	Car #	Make	Laps	Winnings
1. Fonty Flock	Frank Christian	14	53 Huds	200	1,000
2. Herb Thomas	Herb Thomas	92	53 Huds	—	700
3. Bill Blair	Bill Blair	2	53 Olds	—	450
4. Buck Baker	Griffin Motors	87	53 Olds	—	350
5. Jimmie Lewallen	R. G. Shelton	22	52 Olds	—	200

1954 Grand National Race No. 23
July 4, 1954 Average Speed: 61.318

Driver	Owner	Car #	Make	Laps	Winnings
1. Herb Thomas	Herb Thomas	92	54 Huds	200	1,000
2. Jimmie Lewallen	Joe Blair	5	54 Merc	199	650
3. Dick Rathmann	John Ditz	3	54 Huds	199	450
4. Lee Petty	Gary Drake	100	54 Olds	196	350
5. Gober Sosebee	Gober Sosebee	51	54 Olds	193	300

1955 Grand National Race No. 26
July 10, 1955 Average Speed: 62.739

Driver	Owner	Car #	Make	Laps	Winnings
1. Tim Flock	Carl Kiekhaefer	300	55 Chrys	200	1,000
2. Fonty Flock	Carl Kiekhaefer	301	55 Chrys	199	700
3. Jim Paschal	Ernest Woods	78	55 Olds	198	475
4. Donald Thomas	Herb Thomas	9	54 Huds	189	365
5. Eddie Skinner	Frank Dodge	28	53 Olds	180	310

1956 Grand National Race No. 29
July 1, 1956 Average Speed: 56.435

Driver	Owner	Car #	Make	Laps	Winnings
1. Lee Petty	Petty Enterprises	42	56 Dodg	200	850
2. Jim Paschal	Frank Hayworth	75	56 Merc	200	625
3. Joe Eubanks	James Satcher	82	56 Ford	197	450
4. Gwyn Staley	Hubert Westmoreland	2	56 Chev	194	350
5. Herb Thomas	Carl Kiekhaefer	300B	56 Chrys	193	310

1957 Grand National Race No. 8
March 31, 1957 Average Speed: 65.693

Driver	Owner	Car #	Make	Laps	Winnings
1. Buck Baker	Hugh Babb	87	57 Chev	200	850
2. Speedy Thompson	Hugh Babb	46	57 Chev	199	625
3. Jim Paschal	Bill Stroppe	17	57 Merc	198	350
4. Jack Smith	Hugh Babb	47	57 Chev	189	300
5. Dick Beaty	Dick Beaty	34	56 Ford	188	310

1957 Grand National Race No. 42
September 8, 1957 Average Speed: 67.950

Driver	Owner	Car #	Make	Laps	Winnings
1. Lee Petty	Petty Enterprises	42	57 Olds	200	1,000
2. Buck Baker	Buck Baker	87	57 Chev	200	625
3. Bill Amick	Bill Amick	97	57 Ford	200	400
4. Rex White	Bob Welborn	44	57 Chev	200	295
5. Jack Smith	Jack Smith	47	57 Chev	199	255

Asheville-Weaverville Speedway *continued*

1958 Grand National Race No. 27
June 29, 1958 Average Speed: 73.892

Driver	Owner	Car #	Make	Laps	Winnings
1. Rex White	J. H. Petty	44	57 Chev	200	800
2. Buck Baker	Buck Baker	87	57 Chev	199	525
3. Speedy Thompson	Speedy Thompson	46	57 Chev	196	350
4. Jim Paschal	J. H. Petty	4	57 Chev	196	250
5. Eddie Pagan	Eddie Pagan	45	57 Ford	196	225

1958 Grand National Race No. 38 Western North Carolina 500
August 17, 1958 Average Speed: 66.780

Driver	Owner	Car #	Make	Laps	Winnings
1. Fireball Roberts	Frank Strickland	22	57 Chev	500	2,650
2. Bob Welborn	J. H. Petty	49	57 Chev	499	1,800
3. Lee Petty	Petty Enterprises	42	57 Olds	497	1,250
4. Speedy Thompson	Speedy Thompson	46	57 Chev	494	925
5. Buck Baker	Buck Baker	87	57 Chev	493	775

1959 Grand National Race No. 25
June 28, 1959 Average Speed: 72.934

Driver	Owner	Car #	Make	Laps	Winnings
1. Rex White	Rex White	4	59 Chev	200	900
2. Lee Petty	Petty Enterprises	42	59 Plym	200	525
3. Junior Johnson	Paul Spaulding	11	57 Ford	196	350
4. Roy Tyner	Roy Tyner	9	57 Chev	194	250
5. Herman Beam	Herman Beam	19	57 Chev	190	225

1959 Grand National Race No. 32 Western North Carolina 500
August 16, 1959 Average Speed: 71.833

Driver	Owner	Car #	Make	Laps	Winnings
1. Bob Welborn	Bob Welborn	49	59 Chev	500	3,200
2. Lee Petty	Petty Enterprises	42	59 Plym	497	2,025
3. Jack Smith	Jack Smith	47	59 Chev	493	1,325
4. Joe Lee Johnson	Joe Lee Johnson	77	57 Chev	489	975
5. Rex White	Rex White	4	59 Chev	489	800

1959 Grand National Race No. 42
October 11, 1959 Average Speed: 76.433

Driver	Owner	Car #	Make	Laps	Winnings
1. Lee Petty	Petty Enterprises	42	59 Plym	200	900
2. Glen Wood	Wood Brothers	16	58 Ford	200	525
3. Jack Smith	Jack Smith	47	59 Chev	199	375
4. Rex White	Rex White	4	59 Chev	199	275
5. Richard Petty	Petty Enterprises	43	59 Plym	198	250

1960 Grand National Race No. 15
April 24, 1960 Average Speed: 63.368

Driver	Owner	Car #	Make	Laps	Winnings
1. Lee Petty	Petty Enterprises	42	60 Plym	167	900
2. Joe Lee Johnson	E. C. Wilson	78	60 Chev	166	625
3. Ned Jarrett	Ned Jarrett	11	60 Ford	164	375
4. Bob Welborn	Bob Welborn	49	60 Chev	158	275
5. G. C. Spencer	Weldon Wagner	48	58 Chev	157	250

1960 Grand National Race No. 30 Western North Carolina 500
August 14, 1960 Average Speed: 65.024

Driver	Owner	Car #	Make	Laps	Winnings
1. Rex White	Rex White	4	60 Chev	500	3,650
2. Possum Jones	Tom Daniels	2	60 Chev	496	2,225
3. Emanuel Zervakis	Monroe Shook	85	60 Chev	492	1,525
4. Bobby Johns	Cotton Owens	5	60 Pont	479	975
5. Jack Smith	Jack Smith	47	60 Pont	479	800

1961 Grand National Race No. 7
March 5, 1961 Average Speed: 72.492

Driver	Owner	Car #	Make	Laps	Winnings
1. Rex White	Rex White	4	61 Chev	200	900
2. Cotton Owens	Cotton Owens	5	60 Pont	200	525
3. Ned Jarrett	Bee Gee Holloway	11	60 Ford	200	375
4. Richard Petty	Petty Enterprises	43	60 Plym	196	275
5. Emanuel Zervakis	Monroe Shook	85	61 Chev	194	250

1961 Grand National Race No. 39 Western North Carolina 500
August 13, 1961 Average Speed: 65.704

Driver	Owner	Car #	Make	Laps	Winnings
1. Junior Johnson	Rex Lovette	27	60 Pont	258	2,000
2. Joe Weatherly	Bud Moore	8	61 Pont	255	1,400
3. Rex White	Rex White	4	61 Chev	254	1,100
4. Ned Jarrett	Bee Gee Holloway	11	61 Chev	254	850
5. Emanuel Zervakis	Monroe Shook	85	61 Chev	254	750

1962 Grand National Race No. 2
November 12, 1961 Average Speed: 68.467

Driver	Owner	Car #	Make	Laps	Winnings
1. Rex White	Rex White	4	61 Chev	200	800
2. Buck Baker	Buck Baker	86	61 Chrys	200	525
3. Joe Weatherly	Bud Moore	8	61 Pont	200	375
4. Jack Smith	Jack Smith	46	61 Pont	200	275
5. Ned Jarrett	Bee Gee Holloway	11	61 Chev	200	350

1962 Grand National Race No. 7
March 4, 1962 Average Speed: 75.471

Driver	Owner	Car #	Make	Laps	Winnings
1. Joe Weatherly	Bud Moore	8	61 Pont	200	1,000
2. Jim Paschal	Cliff Stewart	2	62 Pont	197	600
3. Buddy Baker	Buck Baker	87	61 Chrys	197	400
4. Maurice Petty	Petty Enterprises	41	62 Plym	192	300
5. Jack Smith	Jack Smith	47	61 Pont	191	275

1962 Grand National Race No. 40 Western North Carolina 500
August 12, 1962 Average Speed: 77.492

Driver	Owner	Car #	Make	Laps	Winnings
1. Jim Paschal	Petty Enterprises	42	62 Plym	500	2,350
2. Joe Weatherly	Bud Moore	8	62 Pont	497	1,625
3. Rex White	Rex White	4	62 Chev	495	1,150
4. Ned Jarrett	Bee Gee Holloway	11	62 Chev	494	1,150
5. Jack Smith	Jack Smith	47	62 Pont	488	800

1963 Grand National Race No. 9
March 3, 1963 Average Speed: 76.664

Driver	Owner	Car #	Make	Laps	Winnings
1. Richard Petty	Petty Enterprises	43	63 Plym	200	1,000
2. Buck Baker	Buck Baker	87	62 Chrys	200	600
3. Junior Johnson	Ray Fox	3	63 Chev	200	400
4. Joe Weatherly	Fred Harb	17	62 Pont	200	500
5. Ned Jarrett	Herman Beam	19	62 Ford	195	275

1963 Grand National Race No. 41 Western North Carolina 500
August 11, 1963 Average Speed: 77.673

Driver	Owner	Car #	Make	Laps	Winnings
1. Fred Lorenzen	Holman-Moody	28	63 Ford	500	2,550
2. Richard Petty	Petty Enterprises	43	63 Plym	499	1,425
3. Jim Paschal	Petty Enterprises	42	63 Plym	498	1,150
4. David Pearson	Cotton Owens	6	63 Dodg	494	950
5. Billy Wade	Cotton Owens	5	63 Dodg	493	800

Asheville-Weaverville Speedway *continued*

1964 Grand National Race No. 14
April 11, 1964 Average Speed: 81.669

Driver	Owner	Car #	Make	Laps	Winnings
1. Marvin Panch	Wood Brothers	21	64 Ford	200	1,150
2. Junior Johnson	Ray Fox	3	64 Dodg	199	700
3. Billy Wade	Bud Moore	1	64 Merc	199	450
4. David Pearson	Cotton Owens	6	64 Dodg	198	300
5. Jimmy Pardue	Charles Robinson	54	64 Plym	198	275

1964 Grand National Race No. 45 Western North Carolina 500
August 9, 1964 Average Speed: 77.600

Driver	Owner	Car #	Make	Laps	Winnings
1. Ned Jarrett	Bondy Long	11	64 Ford	500	2,550
2. David Pearson	Cotton Owens	6	64 Dodg	500	1,400
3. Junior Johnson	Banjo Matthews	27	64 Ford	496	1,100
4. Darel Dieringer	Bud Moore	16	64 Merc	494	875
5. Buck Baker	Ray Fox	3	64 Dodg	485	750

1965 Grand National Race No. 6
February 28, 1965 Average Speed: 75.678

Driver	Owner	Car #	Make	Laps	Winnings
1. Ned Jarrett	Bondy Long	11	65 Ford	200	1,150
2. Dick Hutcherson	Holman-Moody	29	65 Ford	200	700
3. Cale Yarborough	Gary Weaver	10	64 Ford	197	450
4. G. C. Spencer	G. C. Spencer	49	64 Ford	196	300
5. Danny Byrd	Glenn Sweet	08	64 Ford	195	275

1965 Grand National Race No. 37 Western North Carolina 500
August 8, 1965 Average Speed: 74.343

Driver	Owner	Car #	Make	Laps	Winnings
1. Richard Petty	Petty Enterprises	43	65 Plym	500	3,200
2. Ned Jarrett	Bondy Long	11	65 Ford	498	1,650
3. Dick Hutcherson	Holman-Moody	29	65 Ford	495	1,200
4. Buddy Baker	Buck Baker	88	64 Dodg	488	900
5. Cale Yarborough	Kenny Myler	06	64 Ford	487	800

1966 Grand National Race No. 25 Fireball 300
June 12, 1966 Average Speed: 81.423

Driver	Owner	Car #	Make	Laps	Winnings
1. Richard Petty	Petty Enterprises	43	66 Plym	300	1,400
2. David Pearson	Cotton Owens	6	66 Dodg	300	1,000
3. Paul Lewis	Paul Lewis	1	65 Plym	298	700
4. Buck Baker	Buck Baker	87	66 Olds	290	575
5. John Sears	L. G. DeWitt	4	64 Ford	289	425

1966 Grand National Race No. 39 Western North Carolina 500
August 21, 1966 Average Speed: 76.700

Driver	Owner	Car #	Make	Laps	Winnings
1. Darel Dieringer	Bud Moore	16	66 Merc	500	3,150
2. G. C. Spencer	G. C. Spencer	49	65 Plym	492	1,750
3. James Hylton	Bud Hartje	48	65 Dodg	486	1,250
4. John Sears	L. G. DeWitt	4	64 Ford	478	900
5. Friday Hassler	Red Sharp	09	66 Chev	470	800

1967 Grand National Race No. 6 Fireball 300
March 5, 1967 Average Speed: 83.360

Driver	Owner	Car #	Make	Laps	Winnings
1. Richard Petty	Petty Enterprises	43	67 Plym	300	1,800
2. Darel Dieringer	Junior Johnson	26	67 Ford	298	1,050
3. Bobby Allison	Bobby Allison	2	66 Chev	297	700
4. David Pearson	Cotton Owens	6	66 Dodg	295	775
5. John Sears	L. G. DeWitt	4	66 Ford	289	425

1967 Grand National Race No. 49 Western North Carolina 500
November 5, 1967 Average Speed: 76.291

Driver	Owner	Car #	Make	Laps	Winnings
1. Bobby Allison	Holman-Moody	11	67 Ford	500	3,250
2. Richard Petty	Petty Enterprises	43	67 Plym	500	2,300
3. David Pearson	Holman-Moody	17	67 Ford	500	1,500
4. Dick Hutcherson	Holman-Moody	66	67 Ford	490	900
5. Friday Hassler	Red Sharp	39	66 Chev	471	800

1968 Grand National Race No. 14 Fireball 300
May 5, 1968 Average Speed: 75.167

Driver	Owner	Car #	Make	Laps	Winnings
1. David Pearson	Holman-Moody	17	68 Ford	300	1,400
2. Bobby Isaac	Nord Krauskopf	71	67 Dodg	298	1,000
3. Richard Petty	Petty Enterprises	43	68 Plym	297	900
4. James Hylton	James Hylton	48	67 Dodg	295	575
5. Elmo Langley	Elmo Langley	64	66 Ford	291	425

1968 Grand National Race No. 36 Western North Carolina 500
August 18, 1968 Average Speed: 73.686

Driver	Owner	Car #	Make	Laps	Winnings
1. David Pearson	Holman-Moody	17	68 Ford	500	2,150
2. Bobby Isaac	Nord Krauskopf	71	67 Dodg	497	1,270
3. Neil Castles	Neil Castles	06	67 Plym	472	1,050
4. Roy Tyner	Roy Tyner	9	67 Pont	467	850
5. Bill Seifert	Bill Seifert	45	68 Ford	457	750

1969 Grand National Race No. 17 Fireball 300
May 4, 1969 Average Speed: 72.581

Driver	Owner	Car #	Make	Laps	Winnings
1. Bobby Isaac	Nord Krauskopf	71	68 Dodg	300	2,050
2. James Hylton	James Hylton	48	68 Dodg	299	1,275
3. John Sears	L. G. DeWitt	4	67 Ford	298	1,000
4. Neil Castles	Neil Castles	06	67 Plym	297	625
5. Earl Brooks	Earl Brooks	26	67 Ford	284	475

1969 Grand National Race No. 40 Western North Carolina 500
August 24, 1969 Average Speed: 80.450

Driver	Owner	Car #	Make	Laps	Winnings
1. Bobby Isaac	Nord Krauskopf	71	69 Dodg	500	2,800
2. David Pearson	Holman-Moody	17	69 Ford	496	1,725
3. Dick Brooks	Dick Brooks	32	69 Plym	487	1,050
4. Elmo Langley	Elmo Langley	64	68 Ford	481	850
5. James Hylton	James Hylton	48	68 Dodg	467	750

Bowman-Gray Stadium
Winston-Salem, NC
Quarter-mile Paved Track

Quarter-mile paved oval opened in June 1947. First NASCAR Winston Cup (then Grand National) race staged on 5/24/58 (won by Bob Welborn). Final Winston Cup Grand National race staged on 8/6/71 (won by Bobby Allison in a Mustang). Richard Petty's 100th career Winston Cup victory came on this track on 8/22/69 while driving a Ford. The track still hosts weekly racing.

Winston Cup Starts
Richard Petty   26

Winston Cup Victories
Rex White   6

Winston Cup Poles
Richard Petty   8

Winston Cup Money
Richard Petty $10,855

Most Cars Started
29—August 6, 1971 Myers Brothers Memorial

Fewest Cars Started
15—April 18, 1960

Narrowest Margin of Victory
6 inches—June 16, 1962
Myers Brothers Memorial

Slowest Race
39.258 MPH—August 22, 1958

Race Record
51.527 MPH—August 28, 1970
Myers Brothers Memorial

Most Cautions
6—August 6, 1971
Myers Brothers Memorial

Most Race Leaders
3—August 22, 1958
3—July 13, 1963
3—August 27, 1966
  Myers Brothers Memorial
3—March 27, 1967

Most Cars Running at Finish
20—August 22, 1958
20—August 21, 1959

1958 Grand National Race No. 19
May 24, 1958 Average Speed: 40.407

Driver	Owner	Car #	Make	Laps	Winnings
1. Bob Welborn	J. H. Petty	49	57 Chev	150	600
2. Rex White	J. H. Petty	44	57 Chev	150	475
3. Jim Reed	Jim Reed	7	57 Ford	150	355
4. Fred Harb	Fred Harb	17	57 Merc	149	275
5. Barney Shore	Barney Shore	97	57 Chev	148	230

1958 Grand National Race No. 39
August 22, 1958 Average Speed: 39.258

Driver	Owner	Car #	Make	Laps	Winnings
1. Lee Petty	Petty Enterprises	42	57 Olds	200	765
2. Shorty Rollins	Shorty Rollins	99	58 Ford	200	550
3. Jim Reed	Jim Reed	7	57 Ford	200	495
4. Fred Harb	Fred Harb	17	57 Merc	199	295
5. Buck Baker	Buck Baker	87	57 Chev	199	250

1959 Grand National Race No. 8
March 30, 1959 Average Speed: 43.562

Driver	Owner	Car #	Make	Laps	Winnings
1. Jim Reed	Jim Reed	7	57 Ford	200	550
2. Lee Petty	Petty Enterprises	43	57 Olds	200	480
3. Rex White	Rex White	4	59 Chev	200	350
4. Bob Welborn	Bob Welborn	49	59 Chev	198	270
5. Buck Baker	Buck Baker	89	59 Chev	197	230

1959 Grand National Race No. 24
June 27, 1959 Average Speed: 41.228

Driver	Owner	Car #	Make	Laps	Winnings
1. Rex White	Rex White	4	59 Chev	200	675
2. Ken Rush	Manley Britt	14	57 Ford	200	480
3. Bob Welborn	Bob Welborn	49	57 Chev	199	375
4. Junior Johnson	Paul Spaulding	11	57 Ford	198	270
5. Jim Reed	Jim Reed	7	59 Chev	196	235

1959 Grand National Race No. 33
August 21, 1959 Average Speed: 44.085

Driver	Owner	Car #	Make	Laps	Winnings
1. Rex White	Rex White	4	59 Chev	200	1,125
2. Glen Wood	Wood Brothers	16	58 Ford	200	690
3. Lee Petty	Petty Enterprises	42	59 Plym	198	595
4. Bob Welborn	Bob Welborn	49	59 Chev	197	425
5. Jim Reed	Jim Reed	7	57 Ford	196	290

1960 Grand National Race No. 13
April 18, 1960 Average Speed: 43.082

Driver	Owner	Car #	Make	Laps	Winnings
1. Glen Wood	Wood Brothers	16	58 Ford	200	600
2. Rex White	Rex White	4	60 Chev	200	475
3. Jimmy Massey	Wood Brothers	21	59 Ford	199	400
4. Richard Petty	Petty Enterprises	43	60 Plym	199	305
5. Ned Jarrett	Ned Jarrett	11	60 Ford	196	245

1960 Grand National Race No. 22
June 26, 1960 Average Speed: 45.872

Driver	Owner	Car #	Make	Laps	Winnings
1. Glen Wood	Wood Brothers	16	58 Ford	200	1,125
2. Lee Petty	Petty Enterprises	42	60 Plym	200	595
3. Rex White	Rex White	4	59 Chev	198	415
4. Richard Petty	Petty Enterprises	43	60 Plym	197	250
5. Ned Jarrett	Ned Jarrett	11	60 Ford	195	255

1960 Grand National Race No. 34
August 23, 1960 Average Speed: 44.389

Driver	Owner	Car #	Make	Laps	Winnings
1. Glen Wood	Wood Brothers	16	58 Ford	200	770
2. Lee Petty	Petty Enterprises	42	60 Plym	199	635
3. Junior Johnson	John Masoni	27	59 Chev	199	365
4. Rex White	Rex White	4	59 Chev	199	260
5. Buck Baker	Buck Baker	87	60 Chev	198	245

1961 Grand National Race No. 12
April 3, 1961 Average Speed: 45.500

Driver	Owner	Car #	Make	Laps	Winnings
1. Rex White	Rex White	4	60 Chev	150	700
2. Glen Wood	Wood Brothers	21	61 Ford	150	500
3. Richard Petty	Petty Enterprises	43	60 Plym	147	375
4. Fred Harb	Fred Harb	17	59 Ford	147	305
5. Ned Jarrett	Bee Gee Holloway	11	61 Chev	147	245

1961 Grand National Race No. 28 Myers Brothers Memorial
June 10, 1961 Average Speed: 42.714

Driver	Owner	Car #	Make	Laps	Winnings
1. Rex White	Rex White	4	60 Chev	200	900
2. Jim Reed	Jim Reed	7	61 Chev	200	525
3. Junior Johnson	Rex Lovette	27	60 Pont	199	375
4. Emanuel Zervakis	Monroe Shook	85	60 Chev	198	275
5. Richard Petty	Petty Enterprises	43	60 Plym	198	250

Bowman-Gray Stadium *continued*

1961 Grand National Race No. 38
August 9, 1961 Average Speed: 42.452

Driver	Owner	Car #	Make	Laps	Winnings
1. Rex White	Rex White	4	60 Chev	150	665
2. Glen Wood	Wood Brothers	21	61 Ford	150	500
3. Ned Jarrett	Bee Gee Holloway	11	61 Chev	150	370
4. Emanuel Zervakis	Monroe Shook	85	60 Chev	149	305
5. Richard Petty	Petty Enterprises	43	61 Plym	149	225

1962 Grand National Race No. 16
April 23, 1962 Average Speed: 43.392

Driver	Owner	Car #	Make	Laps	Winnings
1. Rex White	Rex White	4	62 Chev	108	565
2. Jack Smith	Jack Smith	47	61 Pont	108	475
3. Joe Weatherly	Bud Moore	8	62 Pont	108	370
4. George Dunn	Lewis Osborne	97	62 Chev	108	305
5. Richard Petty	Petty Enterprises	43	61 Plym	107	225

1962 Grand National Race No. 25 Myers Brothers Memorial
June 16, 1962 Average Speed: 45.466

Driver	Owner	Car #	Make	Laps	Winnings
1. Johnny Allen	Fred Lovette	58	61 Pont	200	580
2. Rex White	Rex White	4	62 Chev	200	500
3. Richard Petty	Petty Enterprises	43	62 Plym	196	375
4. Larry Thomas	Wade Younts	36	62 Dodg	195	305
5. Joe Weatherly	Bud Moore	8	61 Pont	194	275

1962 Grand National Race No. 42 International 200
August 18, 1962 Average Speed: 46.875

Driver	Owner	Car #	Make	Laps	Winnings
1. Richard Petty	Petty Enterprises	43	62 Plym	200	600
2. Jack Smith	Jack Smith	47	61 Pont	199	450
3. Joe Weatherly	Bud Moore	8	61 Pont	199	400
4. Jimmy Pardue	Jimmy Pardue	54	62 Pont	199	290
5. G. C. Spencer	G. C. Spencer	48	62 Chev	196	250

1963 Grand National Race No. 18
April 15, 1963 Average Speed: 46.814

Driver	Owner	Car #	Make	Laps	Winnings
1. Jim Paschal	Petty Enterprises	43	62 Plym	200	575
2. Fred Harb	Fred Harb	12	62 Pont	198	465
3. Larry Thomas	Wade Younts	36	62 Dodg	195	370
4. Buck Baker	Buck Baker	87	62 Chrys	195	290
5. Ned Jarrett	Charles Robinson	11	63 Ford	194	275

1963 Grand National Race No. 33
July 13, 1963 Average Speed: 44.390

Driver	Owner	Car #	Make	Laps	Winnings
1. Glen Wood	Wood Brothers	21	63 Ford	200	575
2. Ned Jarrett	Charles Robinson	11	63 Ford	200	480
3. Buck Baker	Buck Baker	87	63 Pont	198	350
4. Lee Petty	Petty Enterprises	41	63 Plym	197	300
5. Jack Smith	Jack Smith	48	63 Plym	195	240

1963 Grand National Race No. 43 International 200
August 16, 1963 Average Speed: 46.320

Driver	Owner	Car #	Make	Laps	Winnings
1. Junior Johnson	Ray Fox	3	63 Plym	200	580
2. Richard Petty	Petty Enterprises	43	63 Plym	199	500
3. Glen Wood	Wood Brothers	21	63 Ford	198	370
4. David Pearson	Cotton Owens	6	63 Dodg	196	275
5. Ned Jarrett	Charles Robinson	11	63 Ford	196	225

1964 Grand National Race No. 12
March 30, 1964 Average Speed: 47.796

Driver	Owner	Car #	Make	Laps	Winnings
1. Marvin Panch	Wood Brothers	21	64 Ford	200	820
2. Ned Jarrett	Bondy Long	11	64 Ford	200	530
3. Richard Petty	Petty Enterprises	43	64 Plym	199	425
4. Jim Paschal	Cotton Owens	5	64 Dodg	198	325
5. David Pearson	Cotton Owens	6	64 Dodg	197	290

1964 Grand National Race No. 49 Myers Brothers Memorial
August 22, 1964 Average Speed: 46.192

Driver	Owner	Car #	Make	Laps	Winnings
1. Junior Johnson	Banjo Matthews	27	64 Ford	250	1,000
2. Richard Petty	Petty Enterprises	43	64 Plym	249	600
3. Ned Jarrett	Bondy Long	11	64 Ford	249	400
4. David Pearson	Cotton Owens	6	64 Dodg	245	300
5. Fred Harb	Cliff Stewart	2	63 Pont	240	275

1965 Grand National Race No. 17
May 15, 1965 Average Speed: 47.911

Driver	Owner	Car #	Make	Laps	Winnings
1. Junior Johnson	Rex Lovette	26	65 Ford	200	850
2. Ned Jarrett	Bondy Long	11	65 Ford	198	550
3. Dick Hutcherson	Holman-Moody	29	65 Ford	196	430
4. G. C. Spencer	G. C. Spencer	49	64 Ford	193	330
5. Buren Skeen	Reid Shaw	23	64 Ford	193	285

1965 Grand National Race No. 44 Myers Brothers Memorial
August 28, 1965 Average Speed: 46.632

Driver	Owner	Car #	Make	Laps	Winnings
1. Junior Johnson	Rex Lovette	26	65 Ford	250	1,000
2. Richard Petty	Petty Enterprises	43	65 Plym	246	800
3. Dick Hutcherson	Holman-Moody	29	65 Ford	245	400
4. Ned Jarrett	Bondy Long	11	65 Ford	243	300
5. Cale Yarborough	Kenny Myler	06	64 Ford	240	275

1966 Grand National Race No. 12
April, 11, 1966 Average Speed: 51.341

Driver	Owner	Car #	Make	Laps	Winnings
1. David Pearson	Cotton Owens	6	64 Dodg	200	850
2. Tom Pistone	Tom Pistone	59	64 Ford	200	550
3. Richard Petty	Petty Enterprises	43	65 Plym	198	425
4. Bobby Allison	Betty Lilly	24	66 Ford	198	330
5. Elmo Langley	Henry Woodfield	64	64 Ford	197	305

1966 Grand National Race No. 41 Myers Brothers Memorial
August 27, 1966 Average Speed: 45.928

Driver	Owner	Car #	Make	Laps	Winnings
1. David Pearson	Cotton Owens	6	65 Dodg	250	1,000
2. Richard Petty	Petty Enterprises	42	66 Plym	250	600
3. James Hylton	Bud Hartje	48	65 Dodg	246	400
4. John Sears	L. G. DeWitt	4	64 Ford	246	300
5. Tom Pistone	Tom Pistone	59	64 Ford	240	275

1967 Grand National Race No. 9
March 27, 1967 Average Speed: 49.248

Driver	Owner	Car #	Make	Laps	Winnings
1. Bobby Allison	Bobby Allison	2	65 Chev	200	820
2. Richard Petty	Petty Enterprises	43	67 Plym	198	550
3. John Sears	L. G. DeWitt	4	66 Ford	196	430
4. Clyde Lynn	Clyde Lynn	20	66 Ford	195	320
5. James Hylton	Bud Hartje	48	65 Dodg	192	300

Bowman-Gray Stadium *continued*

1967 Grand National Race No. 37 Myers Brothers Memorial
August 12, 1967 Average Speed: 50.893

Driver	Owner	Car #	Make	Laps	Winnings
1. Richard Petty	Petty Enterprises	43	67 Plym	250	100
2. Jim Paschal	Tom Friedkin	14	67 Plym	247	600
3. Bobby Allison	Bobby Allison	2	65 Chev	247	400
4. John Sears	L. G. DeWitt	4	66 Ford	245	300
5. James Hylton	Bud Hartje	48	65 Dodg	243	275

1968 Grand National Race No. 35 Myers Brothers Memorial
August 10, 1968 Average Speed: 42.940

Driver	Owner	Car #	Make	Laps	Winnings
1. David Pearson	Holman-Moody	17	68 Ford	250	1,000
2. Richard Petty	Petty Enterprises	43	68 Plym	250	850
3. Bobby Isaac	Nord Krauskopf	71	67 Dodg	246	400
4. James Hylton	James Hylton	48	68 Dodg	244	300
5. Elmo Langley	Elmo Langley	64	66 Ford	244	275

1969 Grand National Race No. 39 Myers Brothers Stock Car Spectacle
August 22, 1969 Average Speed: 47.458

Driver	Owner	Car #	Make	Laps	Winnings
1. Richard Petty	Petty Enterprises	43	69 Ford	250	1,000
2. Bobby Isaac	Nord Krauskopf	71	69 Dodg	250	600
3. David Pearson	Holman-Moody	17	69 Ford	250	600
4. Elmo Langley	Elmo Langley	64	68 Ford	248	350
5. James Hylton	James Hylton	48	68 Dodg	246	325

1970 Grand National Race No. 36 Myers Brothers Memorial
August 28, 1970 Average Speed: 51.527

Driver	Owner	Car #	Make	Laps	Winnings
1. Richard Petty	Petty Enterprises	43	70 Plym	250	1,000
2. Bobby Allison	Bobby Allison	22	69 Dodg	250	600
3. Bobby Isaac	Nord Krauskopf	71	70 Dodg	247	400
4. James Hylton	James Hylton	48	69 Ford	246	350
5. Benny Parsons	L. G. DeWitt	72	69 Ford	243	325

1971 Winston Cup GN Race No. 34 Myers Brothers Memorial
August 6, 1971 Average Speed: 44.792

Driver	Owner	Car #	Make	Laps	Winnings
1. Bobby Allison	Melvin Joseph	49	70 Ford	250	1,000
2. Richard Petty	Petty Enterprises	43	70 Plym	250	600
3. Jim Paschal	Cliff Stewart	14	70 Mata	249	400
4. Buck Baker	Buck Baker	87	71 Pont	247	350
5. Dave Marcis	James Rush	11	69 Chev	244	325

Champion Speedway
Fayetteville, NC
.333-mile Paved Track

.333-mile paved oval built by Harold Brasington and opened in May 1953. First NASCAR Winston Cup (then Grand National) race staged on 11/3/57 (won by Rex White; race was included in the 1958 championship season). Final Grand National race run on 11/9/58 (won by Bob Welborn; race was included in the 1959 championship season). Track closed in 1959.

Winston Cup Starts

L. D. Austin	4
Buck Baker	4
Clarence DeZalia	4
Fred Harb	4
Brownie King	4
Lee Petty	4
Rex White	4

Winston Cup Victories
Bob Welborn   2

Winston Cup Poles
Lee Petty   2

Winston Cup Money
Bob Welborn $1,365

Most Cars Started
29—April 5, 1958

Fewest Cars Started
22—November 3, 1957

Narrowest Margin of Victory
1 car length—March 15, 1958

Slowest Race
50.229 MPH—April 5, 1958

Race Record
59.170 MPH—November 3, 1957

Most Cautions
2—April 5, 1958

Most Race Leaders
3—November 3, 1957
3—March 15, 1958
3—April 5, 1958

Most Cars Running at Finish
20—November 9, 1958

1958 Grand National Race No. 1
November 3, 1957 Average Speed: 59.170

Driver	Owner	Car #	Make	Laps	Winnings
1. Rex White	J. H. Petty	44	57 Chev	150	630
2. Lee Petty	Petty Enterprises	42	57 Olds	150	500
3. Tiny Lund	Lonnie Fish	76	57 Chev	149	380
4. Gwyn Staley	J. H. Petty	38	57 Chev	148	310
5. Jimmy Massey	Wood Brothers	21	56 Ford	148	255

1958 Grand National Race No. 4
March 15, 1958 Average Speed: 56.141

Driver	Owner	Car #	Make	Laps	Winnings
1. Curtis Turner	Holman-Moody	21	57 Ford	150	600
2. Gwyn Staley	J. H. Petty	38	57 Chev	150	470
3. Buck Baker	Buck Baker	87	57 Chev	150	350
4. Frankie Schneider	Frankie Schneider	62	57 Chev	150	275
5. Fred Harb	Fred Harb	17	57 Merc	—	225

1958 Grand National Race No. 7
April 5, 1958 Average Speed: 50.229

Driver	Owner	Car #	Make	Laps	Winnings
1. Bob Welborn	J. H. Petty	38	57 Chev	150	600
2. Frankie Schneider	Frankie Schneider	62	57 Chev	150	470
3. Speedy Thompson	Speedy Thompson	46	57 Chev	150	350
4. Curtis Turner	Holman-Moody	126	58 Ford	150	275
5. Eddie Pagan	Eddie Pagan	45	57 Ford	149	225

1959 Grand National Race No. 1
November 9, 1958 Average Speed: 56.001

Driver	Owner	Car #	Make	Laps	Winnings
1. Bob Welborn	J. H. Petty	46	57 Chev	150	600
2. Glen Wood	Wood Brothers	21	58 Ford	150	475
3. Buck Baker	Buck Baker	86	58 Chev	150	350
4. Roy Tyner	Roy Tyner	49	57 Chev	149	250
5. Junior Johnson	Paul Spaulding	11	57 Ford	148	215

Charlotte Speedway
Charlotte, NC
.75-mile Dirt Track

.75-mile dirt track built by Harvey and Pat Charles and opened in June 1948. The track was the site of the inaugural NASCAR Winston Cup (then Strictly Stock) championship race on 6/19/49 (won by Jim Roper). Final Grand National race staged on 10/17/56 (won by Buck Baker), and the track was closed soon thereafter.

Winston Cup Starts		**Winston Cup Money**		**Narrowest Margin of Victory**	**Most Cautions**
Lee Petty	11	Tim Flock	$4,235	1/2 car length—November 20, 1955	N/A
Herb Thomas	11				

Winston Cup Victories — Buck Baker 3 · **Most Cars Started** 40—April 1, 1951 · **Slowest Race** N/A · **Most Race Leaders** 6—April 5, 1953

Winston Cup Poles — Fonty Flock 3 · **Fewest Cars Started** 24—June 15, 1952 · **Race Record** 72.268 MPH—October 17, 1956 · **Most Cars Running at Finish** N/A

1949 Strictly Stock Race No. 1
June 19, 1949

Driver	Owner	Car #	Make	Laps	Winnings
1. Jim Roper	R. B. McIntosh	34	49 Linc	197	2,000
2. Fonty Flock		47	49 Huds	—	1,000
3. Red Byron	Raymond Parks	22	49 Olds	—	500
4. Sam Rice	Sam Rice	2	49 Olds	—	300
5. Tim Flock	Buddy Elliott	90	49 Olds	—	200

1950 Grand National Race No. 2
April 2, 1950

Driver	Owner	Car #	Make	Laps	Winnings
1. Tim Flock	Harold Kite	21	49 Linc	200	1,500
2. Bob Flock	Frank Christian	7	49 Olds	200	750
3. Clyde Minter	Clyde Minter	19	50 Merc	197	500
4. Red Byron	Raymond Parks	22	50 Olds	196	300
5. Bill Snowden	Bill Snowden		49 Buick	194	200

1950 Grand National Race No. 9
July 23, 1950

Driver	Owner	Car #	Make	Laps	Winnings
1. Curtis Turner	John Eanes	41	50 Olds	200	1,500
2. Chuck Mahoney	Brooks Motors	77	50 Merc	—	600
3. Herb Thomas	Herb Thomas	92	50 Plym	—	400
4. Jimmie Lewallen			50 Merc	—	300
5. Dick Burns		18	50 Olds	—	225

1951 Grand National Race No. 2
April 1, 1951 Average Speed: 70.545

Driver	Owner	Car #	Make	Laps	Winnings
1. Curtis Turner	Nash Motor Co.	41	51 Nash	150	1,000
2. Lee Petty	Petty Enterprises	42	49 Plym	150	700
3. Marshall Teague	Marshall Teague	6	51 Huds	148	450
4. Herb Thomas	Herb Thomas	92	50 Plym	145	350
5. Frank Luptow	Frank Luptow	88	50 Olds	143	200

1951 Grand National Race No. 28
September 23, 1951

Driver	Owner	Car #	Make	Laps	Winnings
1. Herb Thomas	Herb Thomas	92	51 Huds	200	1,000
2. Shorty York	Russ Lou	90	50 Plym	—	600
3. Donald Thomas	Herb Thomas	93	50 Plym	—	500
4. Bill Blair	Bill Blair	2	51 Ford	—	400
5. Jimmie Lewallen	Hubert Hamilton	0	51 Plym	—	300

1952 Grand National Race No. 16
June 15, 1952 Average Speed: 64.820

Driver	Owner	Car #	Make	Laps	Winnings
1. Herb Thomas	Herb Thomas	92	52 Huds	150	1,000
2. Tim Flock	Ted Chester	91	51 Huds	150	700
3. Bill Blair	George Hutchens	2	52 Olds	149	450
4. Lee Petty	Petty Enterprises	42	51 Plym	146	350
5. Dick Rathmann	Walt Chapman	120	51 Huds	145	200

1953 Grand National Race No. 5
April 5, 1953

Driver	Owner	Car #	Make	Laps	Winnings
1. Dick Passwater	Frank Arford	78	53 Olds	150	1,000
2. Gober Sosebee	Gober Sosebee	51	53 Olds	150	700
3. Herschel Buchanan	Herschel Buchanan	1	52 Nash	150	450
4. Tim Flock	Ted Chester	91	53 Huds	150	350
5. Pop McGinnis	Irving Frye	13	52 Huds	149	200

1954 Grand National Race No. 15
May 30, 1954 Average Speed: 49.805

Driver	Owner	Car #	Make	Laps	Winnings
1. Buck Baker	Griffin Motors	87	53 Olds	133	1,000
2. Lee Petty	Petty Enterprises	42	54 Chrys	133	650
3. Joe Eubanks	Phil Oates	82	51 Huds	132	450
4. Russ Hepler	Walt Chapman	120	53 Huds	128	350
5. Bill Blair	Bill Blair	2	53 Huds	126	300

1955 Grand National Race No. 11
May 1, 1955 Average Speed: 52.630

Driver	Owner	Car #	Make	Laps	Winnings
1. Buck Baker	Buck Baker	89	55 Buick	133	1,000
2. Tim Flock	Carl Kiekhaefer	300	55 Chrys	133	650
3. Dave Terrell	Dave Terrell	98	55 Olds	131	450
4. Gober Sosebee	Gober Sosebee	51	55 Olds	127	350
5. Bob Welborn	J. H. Petty	44	55 Chev	127	300

1956 Grand National Race No. 2
November 20, 1955 Average Speed: 61.825

Driver	Owner	Car #	Make	Laps	Winnings
1. Fonty Flock	Carl Kiekhaefer	301	55 Chrys	134	1,100
2. Tim Flock	Carl Kiekhaefer	300	55 Chrys	134	700
3. Lee Petty	Petty Enterprises	42	56 Dodg	134	475
4. Joe Weatherly	Charlie Schwam	9	56 Ford	133	365
5. Buck Baker	James Satcher	87	56 Ford	133	310

Charlotte Speedway *continued*

1956 Grand National Race No. 20
May 27, 1956 Average Speed: 64.866

Driver	Owner	Car #	Make	Laps	Winnings
1. Speedy Thompson	Carl Kiekhaefer	300c	56 Chrys	133	1,100
2. Junior Johnson	Carl Kiekhaefer	502	56 Dodg	133	700
3. Buck Baker	Carl Kiekhaefer	300	56 Chrys	132	475
4. Jim Paschal	Frank Hayworth	75	56 Merc	131	465
5. Lee Petty	Petty Enterprises	42	56 Dodg	131	310

1956 Grand National Race No. 52
October 17, 1956 Average Speed: 72.268

Driver	Owner	Car #	Make	Laps	Winnings
1. Buck Baker	Carl Kiekhaefer	300B	56 Chrys	133	950
2. Ralph Moody	Pete DePaolo	12	56 Ford	133	675
3. Marvin Panch	Tom Harbison	98	56 Ford	132	475
4. Jim Paschal	Frank Hayworth	75	56 Merc	132	365
5. Bill Amick	Pete DePaolo	97	56 Ford	130	320

Charlotte Motor Speedway
Harrisburg, NC
1.5-mile Superspeedway

1.5-mile paved tri-oval opened in June 1960. First World 600 staged on 6/19/60 (won by Joe Lee Johnson). Curtis Turner and Bruton Smith, the original builders, were ousted in 1961 following bankruptcy as the project greatly exceeded the original cost estimates. Promoter Richard Howard subsequently elevated the facility to one of America's hottest properties before Smith regained control in 1975. Permanent lights were erected in 1992, and the track is currently the site of the annual All-Star race.

Winston Cup Starts
Richard Petty   64

Winston Cup Victories
Bobby Allison   6
Darrell Waltrip   6

Winston Cup Poles
David Pearson   14

Winston Cup Money
Dale Earnhardt $1,445,928

Most Cars Started
60—June 19, 1960 World 600

Fewest Cars Started
19—May 21, 1961
19—May 21, 1961

Narrowest Margin of Victory
1/2 car length—May 25, 1980
World 600

Slowest Race
104.207 MPH—May 26, 1968 World 600

Race Record
156.324 MPH—October 20, 1968
National 500

Most Cautions
14—May 25, 1980 World 600

Most Race Leaders
18 May 29, 1988 Coca Cola 600

Most Cars Running at Finish
36—October 10, 1993 Mello Yello 500

1960 Grand National Race No. 21 World 600
June 19, 1960 Average Speed: 107.735

Driver	Owner	Car #	Make	Laps	Winnings
1. Joe Lee Johnson	Paul McDuffie	89	60 Chev	400	27,150
2. Johnny Beauchamp	Dale Swanson	73	60 Chev	396	9,110
3. Bobby Johns	Petty Enterprises	46	60 Plym	394	6,975
4. Gerald Duke	Gerald Duke & Robert Davis	92	59 Ford	388	3,675
5. Buck Baker	Buck Baker	87	60 Chev	386	3,075

1960 Grand National Race No. 42 National 400
October 16, 1960 Average Speed: 112.905

Driver	Owner	Car #	Make	Laps	Winnings
1. Speedy Thompson	Wood Brothers	21	60 Ford	267	12,710
2. Richard Petty	Petty Enterprises	43	60 Plym	266	5,550
3. Ned Jarrett	Ned Jarrett	11	60 Ford	266	3,275
4. Bobby Johns	Cotton Owens	5	60 Pont	265	2,880
5. Junior Johnson	John Masoni	27	60 Pont	265	1,855

1961 Grand National Race No. 20
May 21, 1961 Average Speed: 133.554

Driver	Owner	Car #	Make	Laps	Winnings
1. Richard Petty	Petty Enterprises	43	61 Plym	67	800
2. Ralph Earnhardt	Cotton Owens	6	61 Pont	67	525
3. Bob Welborn	Jack Smith	47	61 Pont	67	375
4. Bobby Johns	Shorty Johns	72	61 Ford	67	275
5. Fred Lorenzen	Holman-Moody	28	61 Ford	67	250

1961 Grand National Race No. 21
May 21, 1961 Average Speed: 115.591

Driver	Owner	Car #	Make	Laps	Winnings
1. Joe Weatherly	Bud Moore	8	61 Pont	67	800
2. Junior Johnson	John Masoni	3	61 Pont	67	525
3. Jack Smith	Jack Smith	46	61 Pont	66	375
4. Nelson Stacy	Dudley Farrell	29	61 Ford	66	275
5. Marvin Porter		44	60 Plym	66	250

1961 Grand National Race No. 24 World 600
May 28, 1961 Average Speed: 111.633

Driver	Owner	Car #	Make	Laps	Winnings
1. David Pearson	John Masoni	3	61 Pont	400	24,280
2. Fireball Roberts	Jim Stephens	22	61 Pont	398	9,320
3. Rex White	Rex White	4	61 Chev	397	7,070
4. Ned Jarrett	Bee Gee Holloway	11	61 Chev	397	4,475
5. Jim Paschal	J. H. Petty	14	61 Pont	394	3,150

1961 Grand National Race No. 49 National 400
October 15, 1961 Average Speed: 119.950

Driver	Owner	Car #	Make	Laps	Winnings
1. Joe Weatherly	Bud Moore	8	61 Pont	267	9,510
2. Richard Petty	Petty Enterprises	43	61 Plym	267	4,870
3. Bob Welborn	Bud Moore	18	61 Pont	267	3,275
4. Cotton Owens	Cotton Owens	6	61 Pont	266	2,275
5. Rex White	Rex White	4	61 Chev	264	1,800

1962 Grand National Race No. 23 World 600
May 27, 1962 Average Speed: 125.552

Driver	Owner	Car #	Make	Laps	Winnings
1. Nelson Stacy	Holman-Moody	29	62 Ford	400	25,505
2. Joe Weatherly	Bud Moore	8	62 Pont	400	11,105
3. Fred Lorenzen	Holman-Moody	0	62 Ford	399	6,870
4. Richard Petty	Petty Enterprises	43	62 Plym	397	5,400
5. Larry Frank	Ratus Walters	66	62 Ford	395	3,475

1962 Grand National Race No. 52 National 400
October 14, 1962 Average Speed: 132.085

Driver	Owner	Car #	Make	Laps	Winnings
1. Junior Johnson	Ray Fox	3	62 Pont	267	11,355
2. Fireball Roberts	Jim Stephens	22	62 Pont	265	5,420
3. Fred Lorenzen	Holman-Moody	28	62 Ford	264	3,230
5. Joe Weatherly	Bud Moore	8	62 Pont	261	1,725

1963 Grand National Race No. 26 World 600
June 2, 1963 Average Speed: 132.417

Driver	Owner	Car #	Make	Laps	Winnings
1. Fred Lorenzen	Holman-Moody	28	63 Ford	400	27,780
2. Junior Johnson	Ray Fox	3	63 Chev	400	17,460
3. Rex White	Rex White	4	63 Chev	398	8,310
4. Joe Weatherly	Bud Moore	8	63 Pont	397	6,275
5. David Pearson	Cotton Owens	6	63 Dodg	396	4,425

1963 Grand National Race No. 52 National 400
October 13, 1963 Average Speed: 132.105

Driver	Owner	Car #	Make	Laps	Winnings
1. Junior Johnson	Ray Fox	3	63 Chev	267	11,720
2. Fred Lorenzen	Holman-Moody	28	63 Ford	267	6,215
3. Marvin Panch	Wood Brothers	21	63 Ford	267	3,596
4. Fireball Roberts	Holman-Moody	22	63 Ford	263	2,225
5. Joe Weatherly	Bud Moore	8	63 Merc	261	2,075

Charlotte Motor Speedway *continued*

1964 Grand National Race No. 25 World 600
May 24, 1964 Average Speed: 125.772

Driver	Owner	Car #	Make	Laps	Winnings
1. Jim Paschal	Petty Enterprises	41	64 Plym	400	24,785
2. Richard Petty	Petty Enterprises	43	64 Plym	396	10,455
3. Rex White	Bud Moore	4	64 Merc	393	8,095
4. Fred Lorenzen	Holman-Moody	28	64 Ford	393	6,425
5. Billy Wade	Bud Moore	1	64 Merc	390	4,050

1964 Grand National Race No. 59 National 400
October 18, 1964 Average Speed: 134.475

Driver	Owner	Car #	Make	Laps	Winnings
1. Fred Lorenzen	Holman-Moody	28	64 Ford	267	11,185
2. Jim Paschal	Petty Enterprises	41	64 Plym	266	5,725
3. Richard Petty	Petty Enterprises	43	64 Plym	265	4,245
4. Ned Jarrett	Bondy Long	11	64 Ford	265	2,375
5. LeeRoy Yarbrough	Ray Fox	03	64 Dodg	264	1,650

1965 Grand National Race No. 19 World 600
May 23, 1965 Average Speed: 121.722

Driver	Owner	Car #	Make	Laps	Winnings
1. Fred Lorenzen	Holman-Moody	28	65 Ford	400	27,270
2. Earl Balmer	Bud Moore	15	64 Merc	400	10,900
3. Dick Hutcherson	Holman-Moody	29	65 Ford	397	6,895
4. Buddy Baker	Buck Baker	88	64 Dodg	392	4,250
5. Pedro Rodriguez	Holman-Moody	51	65 Ford	391	3,425

1965 Grand National Race No. 52 National 400
October 17, 1965 Average Speed: 119.117

Driver	Owner	Car #	Make	Laps	Winnings
1. Fred Lorenzen	Holman-Moody	28	65 Ford	267	9,920
2. Dick Hutcherson	Holman-Moody	29	65 Ford	267	5,225
3. Curtis Turner	Wood Brothers	47	65 Ford	267	3,340
4. Ned Jarrett	Bondy Long	11	65 Ford	266	2,390
5. LeeRoy Yarbrough	Ray Fox	3	65 Chev	265	1,630

1966 Grand National Race No. 20 World 600
May 22, 1966 Average Speed: 135.042

Driver	Owner	Car #	Make	Laps	Winnings
1. Marvin Panch	Petty Enterprises	42	65 Plym	400	26,060
2. G. C. Spencer	G. C. Spencer	49	65 Plym	398	10,980
3. Don White	Ray Nichels	31	66 Dodg	394	7,045
4. James Hylton	Bud Hartje	48	65 Dodg	391	4,325
5. Neil Castles	Buck Baker	87	66 Olds	371	3,440

1966 Grand National Race No. 48 National 500
October 16, 1966 Average Speed: 130.576

Driver	Owner	Car #	Make	Laps	Winnings
1. LeeRoy Yarbrough	Jon Thorne	12	66 Dodg	334	17,455
2. Darel Dieringer	Junior Johnson	15	66 Ford	334	7,670
3. Paul Goldsmith	Ray Nichels	99	66 Plym	334	4,205
4. Gordon Johncock	Junior Johnson	26	66 Ford	334	2,865
5. Earl Balmer	Nord Krauskopf	71	66 Dodg	332	1,975

1967 Grand National Race No. 20 World 600
May 28, 1967 Average Speed: 135.832

Driver	Owner	Car #	Make	Laps	Winnings
1. Jim Paschal	Tom Friedkin	14	67 Plym	400	28,450
2. David Pearson	Holman-Moody	17	67 Ford	400	12,530
3. Bobby Allison	Cotton Owens	6	67 Dodg	400	7,670
4. Richard Petty	Petty Enterprises	43	67 Plym	397	4,875
5. Tiny Lund	Petty Enterprises	42	67 Plym	396	4,000

1967 Grand National Race No. 47 National 500
October 15, 1967 Average Speed: 130.317

Driver	Owner	Car #	Make	Laps	Winnings
1. Buddy Baker	Ray Fox	3	67 Dodg	334	18,950
2. Bobby Isaac	Nord Krauskopf	71	67 Dodg	333	9,480
3. Dick Hutcherson	Bondy Long	29	67 Ford	332	5,860
4. Charlie Glotzbach	Nord Krauskopf	72	65 Dodg	329	4,250
5. G. C. Spencer	Petty Enterprises	42	67 Plym	328	3,375

1968 Grand National Race No. 18 World 600
May 26, 1968 Average Speed: 104.207

Driver	Owner	Car #	Make	Laps	Winnings
1. Buddy Baker	Ray Fox	3	68 Dodg	255	27,780
2. Donnie Allison	Banjo Matthews	27	68 Ford	255	12,975
3. LeeRoy Yarbrough	Junior Johnson	98	68 Merc	254	9,290
4. David Pearson	Holman-Moody	17	68 Ford	254	6,300
5. Bobby Isaac	Nord Krauskopf	71	68 Dodg	253	5,475

1968 Grand National Race No. 47 National 500
October 20, 1968 Average Speed: 156.324

Driver	Owner	Car #	Make	Laps	Winnings
1. Charlie Glotzbach	Cotton Owens	6	68 Dodg	334	19,280
2. Paul Goldsmith	Ray Nichels	99	68 Dodg	334	9,505
3. David Pearson	Holman-Moody	17	68 Ford	334	6,800
4. Bobby Allison	Tom Friedkin	14	68 Plym	332	4,195
5. Cale Yarborough	Wood Brothers	21	68 Merc	332	3,335

1969 Grand National Race No. 21 World 600
May 25, 1969 Average Speed: 134.361

Driver	Owner	Car #	Make	Laps	Winnings
1. LeeRoy Yarbrough	Junior Johnson	98	69 Merc	400	29,325
2. Donnie Allison	Banjo Matthews	27	69 Ford	398	14,755
3. James Hylton	James Hylton	48	69 Dodg	382	9,670
4. G. C. Spencer	G. C. Spencer	49	67 Plym	381	6,300
5. Bobby Isaac	Nord Krauskopf	71	69 Dodg	374	5,375

1969 Grand National Race No. 48 National 500
October 12, 1969 Average Speed: 131.271

Driver	Owner	Car #	Make	Laps	Winnings
1. Donnie Allison	Banjo Matthews	27	69 Ford	334	20,280
2. Bobby Allison	Mario Rossi	22	69 Dodg	334	10,465
3. Buddy Baker	Cotton Owens	6	69 Dodg	334	6,550
4. Charlie Glotzbach	Ray Nichels	99	69 Dodg	334	4,025
5. David Pearson	Holman-Moody	17	69 Ford	332	3,800

1970 Grand National Race No. 16 World 600
May 24, 1970 Average Speed: 129.680

Driver	Owner	Car #	Make	Laps	Winnings
1. Donnie Allison	Banjo Matthews	27	69 Ford	400	39,750
2. Cale Yarborough	Wood Brothers	21	69 Merc	398	17,080
3. Benny Parsons	L. G. DeWitt	72	69 Ford	396	11,445
4. Tiny Lund	John McConnell	55	69 Dodg	395	7,575
5. James Hylton	James Hylton	48	69 Ford	395	6,200

1970 Grand National Race No. 44 National 500
October 11, 1970 Average Speed: 123.246

Driver	Owner	Car #	Make	Laps	Winnings
1. LeeRoy Yarbrough	Junior Johnson	98	69 Merc	334	23,700
2. Bobby Allison	Mario Rossi	22	69 Dodg	334	10,950
3. Fred Lorenzen	Ray Fox	3	69 Dodg	333	6,400
4. Benny Parsons	L. G. DeWitt	72	69 Ford	329	3,955
5. Bobby Isaac	Nord Krauskopf	71	69 Dodg	323	3,330

Charlotte Motor Speedway *continued*

1971 Winston Cup GN Race No. 21 World 600
May 30, 1971 Average Speed: 140.422

Driver	Owner	Car #	Make	Laps	Winnings
1. Bobby Allison	Holman-Moody	12	69 Merc	400	28,400
2. Donnie Allison	Wood Brothers	21	69 Merc	400	14,900
3. Pete Hamilton	Cotton Owens	6	71 Plym	399	10,425
4. Richard Petty	Petty Enterprises	43	71 Plym	398	7,175
5. Fred Lorenzen	Ray Nichels	99	71 Plym	395	5,600

1971 Winston Cup GN Race No. 42 National 500
October 10, 1971 Average Speed: 126.140

Driver	Owner	Car #	Make	Laps	Winnings
1. Bobby Allison	Holman-Moody	12	69 Merc	238	18,450
2. Bobby Isaac	Nord Krauskopf	71	71 Dodg	238	10,525
3. Donnie Allison	Wood Brothers	21	69 Merc	238	6,050
4. Richard Petty	Petty Enterprises	43	71 Plym	238	4,025
5. Charlie Glotzbach	R. Howard & J. Johnson	3	71 Chev	238	2,975

1972 Winston Cup GN Race No. 12 World 600
May 28, 1972 Average Speed: 142.255

Driver	Owner	Car #	Make	Laps	Winnings
1. Buddy Baker	Petty Enterprises	11	72 Dodg	400	22,075
2. Bobby Allison	R. Howard & J. Johnson	12	72 Chev	400	18,950
3. Charlie Glotzbach	Cotton Owens	6	72 Dodg	395	9,625
4. Benny Parsons	L. G. DeWitt	72	71 Merc	391	7,350
5. LeeRoy Yarbrough	Bill Seifert	45	71 Merc	382	6,325

1972 Winston Cup GN Race No. 29 National 500
October 8, 1972 Average Speed: 133.234

Driver	Owner	Car #	Make	Laps	Winnings
1. Bobby Allison	R. Howard & J. Johnson	12	72 Chev	334	21,450
2. Buddy Baker	Nord Krauskopf	71	72 Dodg	334	12,400
3. David Pearson	Wood Brothers	21	71 Merc	332	6,815
4. A. J. Foyt	Wood Brothers	41	71 Merc	332	4,090
5. Butch Hartman	Junie Donlavey	90	72 Ford	326	3,570

1973 Winston Cup GN Race No. 12 World 600
May 27, 1973 Average Speed: 134.890

Driver	Owner	Car #	Make	Laps	Winnings
1. Buddy Baker	Nord Krauskopf	71	73 Dodg	400	27,200
2. David Pearson	Wood Brothers	21	71 Merc	400	14,850
3. Cale Yarborough	R. Howard & J. Johnson	11	73 Chev	399	11,700
4. Bobby Isaac	Bud Moore	15	73 Ford	397	10,200
5. Benny Parsons	L. G. DeWitt	72	73 Chev	393	6,715

1973 Winston Cup GN Race No. 27 National 500
October 7, 1973 Average Speed: 145.240

Driver	Owner	Car #	Make	Laps	Winnings
1. Cale Yarborough	R. Howard & J. Johnson	11	73 Chev	334	45,425
2. Richard Petty	Petty Enterprises	43	73 Dodg	334	17,275
3. Bobby Allison	Bobby Allison	12	73 Chev	331	8,815
4. Benny Parsons	L. G. DeWitt	72	73 Chev	330	4,630
5. Dick Trickle	Richard Howard	1	73 Chev	327	3,385

1974 Winston Cup GN Race No. 13 World 600
May 26, 1974 Average Speed: 135.720

Driver	Owner	Car #	Make	Laps	Winnings
1. David Pearson	Wood Brothers	21	73 Merc	400	26,400
2. Richard Petty	Petty Enterprises	43	74 Dodg	400	21,200
3. Bobby Allison	Bobby Allison	12	74 Chev	395	12,975
4. Darrell Waltrip	Darrell Waltrip	95	74 Chev	395	7,875
5. Earl Ross	Allan J. Clarke	52	74 Chev	392	5,930

1974 Winston Cup GN Race No. 28 National 500
October 6, 1974 Average Speed: 119.912

Driver	Owner	Car #	Make	Laps	Winnings
1. David Pearson	Wood Brothers	21	73 Merc	334	22,575
2. Richard Petty	Petty Enterprises	43	74 Dodg	334	13,475
3. Darrell Waltrip	Darrell Waltrip	95	72 Chev	334	8,765
4. Donnie Allison	DiGard	88	74 Chev	334	6,055
5. Bobby Allison	Roger Penske	12	74 Mata	333	5,935

1975 Winston Cup GN Race No. 13 World 600
May 25, 1975 Average Speed: 145.327

Driver	Owner	Car #	Make	Laps	Winnings
1. Richard Petty	Petty Enterprises	43	74 Dodg	400	30,290
2. Cale Yarborough	Junior Johnson	1	75 Chev	399	16,915
3. David Pearson	Wood Brothers	21	73 Merc	396	10,790
4. Darrell Waltrip	Darrell Waltrip	17	75 Chev	395	10,265
5. Buddy Baker	Bud Moore	15	75 Ford	395	9,640

1975 Winston Cup GN Race No. 25 National 500
October 5, 1975 Average Speed: 132.209

Driver	Owner	Car #	Make	Laps	Winnings
1. Richard Petty	Petty Enterprises	43	74 Dodg	334	30,970
2. David Pearson	Wood Brothers	21	73 Merc	334	23,445
3. Buddy Baker	Bud Moore	15	75 Ford	334	12,450
4. Benny Parsons	L. G. DeWitt	72	75 Chev	330	9,370
5. Cecil Gordon	Cecil Gordon	24	75 Chev	324	5,955

1976 Winston Cup GN Race No. 13 World 600
May 30, 1976 Average Speed: 137.352

Driver	Owner	Car #	Make	Laps	Winnings
1. David Pearson	Wood Brothers	21	Merc	400	49,990
2. Richard Petty	Petty Enterprises	43	Dodg	400	22,465
3. Cale Yarborough	Junior Johnson	11	Chev	399	19,220
4. Bobby Allison	Roger Penske	2	Merc	397	12,555
5. Benny Parsons	L. G. DeWitt	72	Chev	396	10,750

1976 Winston Cup GN Race No. 27 National 500
October 10, 1976 Average Speed: 141.226

Driver	Owner	Car #	Make	Laps	Winnings
1. Donnie Allison	Hoss Ellington	1	Chev	334	22,435
2. Cale Yarborough	Junior Johnson	11	Chev	334	22,955
3. Bobby Allison	Roger Penske	2	Merc	334	17,069
4. Buddy Baker	Bud Moore	15	Ford	334	17,710
5. Benny Parsons	L. G. DeWitt	72	Chev	333	9,279

1977 Winston Cup GN Race No. 13 World 600
May 29, 1977 Average Speed: 137.676

Driver	Owner	Car #	Make	Laps	Winnings
1. Richard Petty	Petty Enterprises	43	Dodg	400	69,550
2. David Pearson	Wood Brothers	21	Merc	400	38,535
3. Benny Parsons	L. G. DeWitt	72	Chev	398	16,735
4. Lennie Pond	Ronnie Elder	54	Chev	397	12,850
5. Buddy Baker	Bud Moore	15	Ford	397	12,240

1977 Winston Cup GN Race No. 27 NAPA National 500
October 9, 1977 Average Speed: 142.780

Driver	Owner	Car #	Make	Laps	Winnings
1. Benny Parsons	L. G. DeWitt	72	Chev	334	41,075
2. Cale Yarborough	Junior Johnson	11	Chev	333	25,900
3. David Pearson	Wood Brothers	21	Merc	333	22,500
4. Buddy Baker	Bud Moore	15	Ford	333	12,100
5. Darrell Waltrip	DiGard	88	Chev	333	10,250

Charlotte Motor Speedway *continued*

1978 Winston Cup GN Race No. 12 World 600
May 28, 1978 Average Speed: 138.355

Driver	Owner	Car #	Make	Laps	Winnings
1. Darrell Waltrip	DiGard	88	Chev	400	48,608
2. Donnie Allison	Hoss Ellington	1	Chev	400	27,000
3. Bobby Allison	Bud Moore	15	Ford	400	19,695
4. Cale Yarborough	Junior Johnson	11	Olds	400	31,133
5. David Pearson	Wood Brothers	21	Merc	400	28,135

1979 Winston Cup GN Race No. 13 World 600
May 27, 1979 Average Speed: 136.674

Driver	Owner	Car #	Make	Laps	Winnings
1. Darrell Waltrip	DiGard	88	Chev	400	55,400
2. Richard Petty	Petty Enterprises	43	Chev	400	35,650
3. Dale Earnhardt	Rod Osterlund	2	Chev	400	27,100
4. Cale Yarborough	Junior Johnson	11	Olds	398	18,225
5. Benny Parsons	M. C. Anderson	27	Chev	398	13,570

1980 Winston Cup GN Race No. 13 World 600
May 25, 1980 Average Speed: 119.265

Driver	Owner	Car #	Make	Laps	Winnings
1. Benny Parsons	M. C. Anderson	27	Chev	400	44,850
2. Darrell Waltrip	DiGard	88	Chev	400	38,700
3. Terry Labonte	Billy Hagan	44	Chev	398	22,660
4. Richard Petty	Petty Enterprises	43	Chev	397	19,550
5. Neil Bonnett	Wood Brothers	21	Merc	397	11,250

1981 Winston Cup GN Race No. 13 World 600
May 24, 1981 Average Speed: 129.326

Driver	Owner	Car #	Make	Laps	Winnings
1. Bobby Allison	Harry Ranier	28	Buick	400	60,200
2. Harry Gant	Hal Needham	33	Chev	400	28,600
3. Cale Yarborough	M. C. Anderson	27	Buick	398	22,425
4. Ricky Rudd	DiGard	88	Buick	397	18,975
5. Kyle Petty	Petty Enterprises	42	Buick	396	13,080

1982 Winston Cup GN Race No. 12 World 600
May 30, 1982 Average Speed: 130.058

Driver	Owner	Car #	Make	Laps	Winnings
1. Neil Bonnett	Wood Brothers	21	Ford	400	50,650
2. Bill Elliott	Harry Melling	9	Ford	400	35,625
3. Bobby Allison	DiGard	88	Buick	399	29,525
4. Cale Yarborough	M. C. Anderson	27	Buick	398	15,850
5. Buddy Baker	Hoss Ellington	1	Buick	398	17,440

1983 Winston Cup GN Race No. 12 World 600
May 29, 1983 Average Speed: 140.707

Driver	Owner	Car #	Make	Laps	Winnings
1. Neil Bonnett	Bob Rahilly & Butch Mock	75	Chev	400	50,405
2. Richard Petty	Petty Enterprises	43	Pont	400	31,450
3. Bobby Allison	DiGard	22	Buick	400	61,925
4. Darrell Waltrip	Junior Johnson	11	Chev	399	23,425
5. Dale Earnhardt	Bud Moore	15	Ford	399	28,700

1984 Winston Cup GN Race No. 12 World 600
May 27, 1984 Average Speed: 129.233

Driver	Owner	Car #	Make	Laps	Winnings
1. Bobby Allison	DiGard	22	Buick	400	88,500
2. Dale Earnhardt	Richard Childress	3	Chev	400	49,625
3. Ron Bouchard	Jack Beebe	47	Buick	399	24,430
4. Harry Gant	Hal Needham	33	Chev	399	42,005
5. Geoff Bodine	Rick Hendrick	5	Chev	399	20,500

1978 Winston Cup GN Race No. 27 NAPA National 500
October 8, 1978 Average Speed: 141.826

Driver	Owner	Car #	Make	Laps	Winnings
1. Bobby Allison	Bud Moore	15	Ford	334	40,000
2. Darrell Waltrip	DiGard	88	Chev	334	23,575
3. Dave Marcis	Rod Osterlund	2	Chev	334	20,050
4. Donnie Allison	Hoss Ellington	1	Chev	334	16,775
5. David Pearson	Wood Brothers	21	Merc	333	23,750

1979 Winston Cup GN Race No. 27 NAPA National 500
October 7, 1979 Average Speed: 134.266

Driver	Owner	Car #	Make	Laps	Winnings
1. Cale Yarborough	Junior Johnson	11	Chev	334	39,000
2. Bobby Allison	Bud Moore	15	Ford	333	27,475
3. Darrell Waltrip	DiGard	88	Chev	332	23,100
4. Richard Petty	Petty Enterprises	43	Chev	332	15,375
5. Donnie Allison	Hoss Ellington	1	Chev	331	7,700

1980 Winston Cup GN Race No. 28 National 500
October 5, 1980 Average Speed: 135.243

Driver	Owner	Car #	Make	Laps	Winnings
1. Dale Earnhardt	Rod Osterlund	2	Chev	334	49,050
2. Cale Yarborough	Junior Johnson	11	Chev	334	30,200
3. Buddy Baker	Harry Ranier	28	Buick	334	21,850
4. Ricky Rudd	Al Rudd	22	Chev	334	15,350
5. Donnie Allison	Kennie Childers	12	Chev	333	8,400

1981 Winston Cup GN Race No. 28 National 500
October 11, 1981 Average Speed: 117.483

Driver	Owner	Car #	Make	Laps	Winnings
1. Darrell Waltrip	Junior Johnson	11	Buick	334	51,600
2. Bobby Allison	Harry Ranier	28	Chev	334	27,400
3. Ricky Rudd	DiGard	88	Chev	334	29,925
4. Tommy Ellis	Tommy Ellis	55	Chev	333	11,400
5. Ron Bouchard	Jack Beebe	47	Buick	332	12,180

1982 Winston Cup GN Race No. 26 National 500
October 10, 1982 Average Speed: 137.208

Driver	Owner	Car #	Make	Laps	Winnings
1. Harry Gant	Hal Needham	33	Buick	334	47,740
2. Bill Elliott	Harry Melling	9	Ford	334	33,040
3. David Pearson	Bobby Hawkins	03	Buick	333	13,915
4. Joe Ruttman	Bob Rahilly & Butch Mock	75	Buick	331	14,010
5. Benny Parsons	Johnny Hayes	55	Buick	331	8,765

1983 Winston Cup GN Race No. 27 Miller High Life 500
October 9, 1983 Average Speed: 139.998

Driver	Owner	Car #	Make	Laps	Winnings
1. Richard Petty	Petty Enterprises	43	Pont	334	40,400
2. Darrell Waltrip	Junior Johnson	11	Chev	334	34,850
3. Benny Parsons	Johnny Hayes	55	Chev	334	43,775
4. Terry Labonte	Billy Hagan	44	Chev	334	16,230
5. Tim Richmond	Raymond Beadle	27	Pont	334	35,195

1984 Winston Cup GN Race No. 26 Miller High Life 500
October 7, 1984 Average Speed: 148.861

Driver	Owner	Car #	Make	Laps	Winnings
1. Bill Elliott	Harry Melling	9	Ford	334	52,633
2. Benny Parsons	Johnny Hayes	55	Chev	334	68,475
3. Cale Yarborough	Harry Ranier	28	Chev	334	23,258
4. Harry Gant	Hal Needham	33	Chev	334	34,938
5. Terry Labonte	Billy Hagan	44	Chev	333	19,228

Charlotte Motor Speedway *continued*

1985 Winston Cup GN Race No. 11 Coca-Cola World 600
May 26, 1985 Average Speed: 141.807

Driver	Owner	Car #	Make	Laps	Winnings
1. Darrell Waltrip	Junior Johnson	11	Chev	400	90,733
2. Harry Gant	Hal Needham	33	Chev	400	49,300
3. Bobby Allison	DiGard	22	Buick	400	30,900
4. Dale Earnhardt	Richard Childress	3	Chev	399	49,238
5. Terry Labonte	Billy Hagan	44	Chev	398	24,000

1985 Winston Cup GN Race No. 25 Miller High Life 500
October 6, 1985 Average Speed: 136.761

Driver	Owner	Car #	Make	Laps	Winnings
1. Cale Yarborough	Harry Ranier	28	Ford	334	51,600
2. Bill Elliott	Harry Melling	9	Ford	334	65,400
3. Geoff Bodine	Rick Hendrick	5	Chev	334	33,625
4. Darrell Waltrip	Junior Johnson	11	Chev	333	23,450
5. Joe Ruttman	Larry McClure	4	Chev	333	12,400

1986 Winston Cup Race No. 11 Coca-Cola 600
May 25, 1986 Average Speed: 140.406

Driver	Owner	Car #	Make	Laps	Winnings
1. Dale Earnhardt	Richard Childress	3	Chev	400	98,150
2. Tim Richmond	Rick Hendrick	25	Chev	400	64,355
3. Cale Yarborough	Harry Ranier	28	Ford	400	34,375
4. Harry Gant	Hal Needham	33	Chev	400	35,630
5. Darrell Waltrip	Junior Johnson	11	Chev	400	27,250

1986 Winston Cup Race No. 26 Oakwood Homes 500
October 5, 1986 Average Speed: 132.403

Driver	Owner	Car #	Make	Laps	Winnings
1. Dale Earnhardt	Richard Childress	3	Chev	334	82,050
2. Harry Gant	Hal Needham	33	Chev	334	54,100
3. Neil Bonnett	Junior Johnson	12	Chev	333	33,125
4. Ricky Rudd	Bud Moore	15	Ford	333	25,700
5. Buddy Baker	Buddy Baker & Danny Schiff	88	Olds	333	15,200

1987 Winston Cup Race No. 10 Coca-Cola 600
May 24, 1987 Average Speed: 131.483

Driver	Owner	Car #	Make	Laps	Winnings
1. Kyle Petty	Wood Brothers	21	Ford	400	89,405
2. Morgan Shepherd	Kenny Bernstein	26	Buick	399	49,070
3. Lake Speed	Lake Speed	83	Olds	399	27,625
4. Richard Petty	Petty Enterprises	43	Pont	398	24,925
5. Darrell Waltrip	Rick Hendrick	17	Chev	398	16,900

1987 Winston Cup Race No. 26 Oakwood Homes 500
October 11, 1987 Average Speed: 128.443

Driver	Owner	Car #	Make	Laps	Winnings
1. Bill Elliott	Harry Melling	9	Ford	334	74,040
2. Bobby Allison	Stavola Brothers	22	Buick	334	67,765
3. Sterling Marlin	Billy Hagan	44	Olds	334	34,770
4. Terry Labonte	Junior Johnson	11	Chev	333	30,240
5. Richard Petty	Petty Enterprises	43	Pont	333	31,860

1988 Winston Cup Race No. 10 Coca-Cola 600
May 29, 1988 Average Speed: 124.460

Driver	Owner	Car #	Make	Laps	Winnings
1. Darrell Waltrip	Rick Hendrick	17	Chev	400	104,250
2. Rusty Wallace	Raymond Beadle	27	Pont	400	56,425
3. Alan Kulwicki	Alan Kulwicki	7	Ford	400	38,100
4. Brett Bodine	Bud Moore	15	Ford	400	49,305
5. Davey Allison	Harry Ranier	28	Ford	400	62,050

1988 Winston Cup Race No. 25 Oakwood Homes 500
October 9, 1988 Average Speed: 130.677

Driver	Owner	Car #	Make	Laps	Winnings
1. Rusty Wallace	Raymond Beadle	27	Pont	334	84,300
2. Darrell Waltrip	Rick Hendrick	17	Chev	334	54,525
3. Brett Bodine	Bud Moore	15	Ford	334	43,350
4. Bill Elliott	Harry Melling	9	Ford	334	35,900
5. Sterling Marlin	Billy Hagan	44	Olds	334	28,200

1989 Winston Cup Race No. 10 Coca-Cola 600
May 28, 1989 Average Speed: 144.077

Driver	Owner	Car #	Make	Laps	Winnings
1. Darrell Waltrip	Rick Hendrick	17	Chev	400	126,400
2. Sterling Marlin	Billy Hagan	94	Olds	400	61,675
3. Ken Schrader	Rick Hendrick	25	Chev	400	44,275
4. Geoff Bodine	Rick Hendrick	5	Chev	399	30,950
5. Bill Elliott	Harry Melling	9	Ford	399	32,305

1989 Winston Cup Race No. 25 All Pro Auto Parts 500
October 8, 1989 Average Speed: 149.863

Driver	Owner	Car #	Make	Laps	Winnings
1. Ken Schrader	Rick Hendrick	25	Chev	334	91,700
2. Harry Gant	Leo Jackson	33	Olds	334	50,375
3. Mark Martin	Jack Roush	6	Ford	334	55,075
4. Bill Elliott	Harry Melling	9	Ford	334	75,650
5. Davey Allison	Robert Yates	28	Ford	334	27,990

1990 Winston Cup Series Race No. 10 Coca-Cola 600
May 27, 1990 Average Speed: 137.650

Driver	Owner	Car #	Make	Laps	Winnings
1. Rusty Wallace	Raymond Beadle	27	Pont	400	151,000
2. Bill Elliott	Harry Melling	9	Ford	400	67,450
3. Mark Martin	Jack Roush	6	Ford	400	51,700
4. Michael Waltrip	Chuck Rider	30	Pont	400	32,600
5. Ernie Irvan	Larry McClure	4	Olds	400	28,350

1990 Winston Cup Series Race No. 26 Mello Yello 500
October 7, 1990 Average Speed: 137.428

Driver	Owner	Car #	Make	Laps	Winnings
1. Davey Allison	Robert Yates	28	Ford	334	90,650
2. Morgan Shepherd	Bud Moore	15	Ford	334	51,800
3. Michael Waltrip	Chuck Rider	30	Pont	334	38,100
4. Kyle Petty	Felix Sabates	42	Pont	334	30,450
5. Alan Kulwicki	Alan Kulwicki	7	Ford	334	24,757

1991 Winston Cup Series Race No. 10 Coca-Cola 600
May 26, 1991 Average Speed: 138.951

Driver	Owner	Car #	Make	Laps	Winnings
1. Davey Allison	Robert Yates	28	Ford	400	137,100
2. Ken Schrader	Rick Hendrick	25	Chev	400	84,850
3. Dale Earnhardt	Richard Childress	3	Chev	400	53,650
4. Harry Gant	Leo Jackson	33	Olds	400	37,700
5. Dale Jarrett	Wood Brothers	21	Ford	400	27,400

1991 Winston Cup Series Race No. 26 Mello Yello 500
October 6, 1991 Average Speed: 138.984

Driver	Owner	Car #	Make	Laps	Winnings
1. Geoff Bodine	Junior Johnson	11	Ford	334	92,200
2. Davey Allison	Robert Yates	28	Ford	334	69,350
3. Alan Kulwicki	Alan Kulwicki	7	Ford	333	47,250
4. Harry Gant	Leo Jackson	33	Olds	333	31,350
5. Sterling Marlin	Junior Johnson	22	Ford	331	25,100

Charlotte Motor Speedway *continued*

1992 Winston Cup Race No. 10 Coca-Cola 600
May 24, 1992 Average Speed: 132.980

Driver	Owner	Car #	Make	Laps	Winnings
1. Dale Earnhardt	Richard Childress	3	Chev	400	125,100
2. Ernie Irvan	Larry McClure	4	Chev	400	67,275
3. Kyle Petty	Felix Sabates	42	Pont	400	60,900
4. Davey Allison	Robert Yates	28	Ford	400	45,750
5. Harry Gant	Leo Jackson	33	Olds	400	35,800

1992 Winston Cup Race No. 26 Mello Yello 500
October 11, 1992 Average Speed: 153.537

Driver	Owner	Car #	Make	Laps	Winnings
1. Mark Martin	Jack Roush	6	Ford	334	101,500
2. Alan Kulwicki	Alan Kulwicki	7	Ford	334	89,000
3. Kyle Petty	Felix Sabates	42	Pont	334	68,600
4. Jimmy Spencer	Bobby Allison	12	Ford	334	41,200
5. Ricky Rudd	Rick Hendrick	5	Chev	334	35,550

1993 Winston Cup Series Race No. 11 Coca-Cola 600
May 30, 1993 Average Speed: 145.504

Driver	Owner	Car #	Make	Laps	Winnings
1. Dale Earnhardt	Richard Childress	3	Chev	400	156,650
2. Jeff Gordon	Rick Hendrick	24	Chev	400	79,050
3. Dale Jarrett	Joe Gibbs	18	Chev	400	73,100
4. Ken Schrader	Rick Hendrick	25	Chev	400	91,550
5. Ernie Irvan	Larry McClure	4	Chev	400	46,600

1993 Winston Cup Series Race No. 27 Mello Yello 500
October 10, 1993 Average Speed: 154.537

Driver	Owner	Car #	Make	Laps	Winnings
1. Ernie Irvan	Robert Yates	28	Ford	334	147,450
2. Mark Martin	Jack Roush	6	Ford	334	67,900
3. Dale Earnhardt	Richard Childress	3	Chev	334	56,900
4. Rusty Wallace	Roger Penske	2	Pont	334	42,950
5. Jeff Gordon	Rick Hendrick	24	Chev	334	56,875

1994 Winston Cup Series Race No. 11 Coca-Cola 600
May 29, 1994 Average Speed: 139.445

Driver	Owner	Car #	Make	Laps	Winnings
1. Jeff Gordon	Rick Hendrick	24	Chev	400	196,500
2. Rusty Wallace	Roger Penske	2	Ford	400	88,075
3. Geoff Bodine	Geoff Bodine	7	Ford	400	75,500
4. Dale Jarrett	Joe Gibbs	18	Chev	400	54,600
5. Ernie Irvan	Robert Yates	28	Ford	400	47,800

1994 Winston Cup Series Race No. 28 Mello Yello 500
October 10, 1994 Average Speed: 145.922

Driver	Owner	Car #	Make	Laps	Winnings
1. Dale Jarrett	Joe Gibbs	18	Chev	334	106,800
2. Morgan Shepherd	Wood Brothers	21	Ford	334	71,900
3. Dale Earnhardt	Richard Childress	3	Chev	334	66,000
4. Ken Schrader	Rick Hendrick	25	Chev	334	47,800
5. Lake Speed	Bud Moore	15	Ford	334	42,925

1995 Winston Cup Series Race No. 11 Coca-Cola 600
May 28, 1995 Average Speed: 151.952

Driver	Owner	Car #	Make	Laps	Winnings
1. Bobby Labonte	Joe Gibbs	18	Chev	400	163,850
2. Terry Labonte	Rick Hendrick	5	Chev	400	93,050
3. Michael Waltrip	Chuck Rider	30	Pont	400	70,650
4. Sterling Marlin	Larry McClure	4	Chev	399	62,700
5. Ricky Rudd	Ricky Rudd	10	Ford	399	49,000

1995 Winston Cup Series Race No. 28 UAW - GM Quality 500
October 8, 1995 Average Speed: 145.358

Driver	Owner	Car #	Make	Laps	Winnings
1. Mark Martin	Jack Roush	6	Ford	334	105,650
2. Dale Earnhardt	Richard Childress	3	Chev	334	86,800
3. Terry Labonte	Rick Hendrick	5	Chev	334	73,750
4. Ricky Rudd	Ricky Rudd	10	Ford	334	90,200
5. Dale Jarrett	Robert Yates	28	Ford	334	51,400

1996 Winston Cup Series Race No. 11 Coca-Cola 600
May 26, 1996 Average Speed: 147.581

Driver	Owner	Car #	Make	Laps	Winnings
1. Dale Jarrett	Robert Yates	88	Ford	400	165,250
2. Dale Earnhardt	Richard Childress	3	Chev	400	97,000
3. Terry Labonte	Rick Hendrick	5	Chev	400	75,300
4. Jeff Gordon	Rick Hendrick	24	Chev	400	118,200
5. Ken Schrader	Rick Hendrick	25	Chev	399	46,350

1996 Winston Cup Series Race No. 28 UAW - GM Quality 500
October 6, 1996 Average Speed: 143.143

Driver	Owner	Car #	Make	Laps	Winnings
1. Terry Labonte	Rick Hendrick	5	Chev	334	133,950
2. Mark Martin	Jack Roush	6	Ford	334	85,100
3. Dale Jarrett	Robert Yates	88	Ford	334	58,300
4. Sterling Marlin	Larry McClure	4	Chev	334	60,100
5. Ricky Craven	Larry Hedrick	41	Chev	334	63,400

Cleveland County Fairgrounds
Shelby, NC
Half-mile Dirt Track

(aka Shelby Fairgrounds; Shelby Motor Speedway) Half-mile dirt oval built in 1924. First Winston Cup (then Grand National) race held on 7/17/56 (won by Speedy Thompson). Final Grand National race run on 8/5/65 (won by Ned Jarrett). Track was leased by team owner Carl Kiekhaefer in 1956 and inserted late in the championship season in order to give his drivers (Baker and Thompson) an additional chance to cut into point leader Herb Thomas's (who had quit Kiekhaefer's team in mid-season) lead. In the race run on 10/23/56, Thompson hooked Thomas on the straightaway, sending him into the retaining wall. Thomas was critically injured. Essentially, Thomas's career ended, and he lost the 1956 championship to Baker (who ended up winning the race). The track has been the scene of recent demolition derbies during the fair in October.

Winston Cup Starts
Buck Baker   5

Winston Cup Victories
Buck Baker   2
Ned Jarrett   2

Winston Cup Poles
Buck Baker   1
Doug Cox   1
Dick Hutcherson 1
Tiny Lund   1
Ralph Moody   1
David Pearson   1

Winston Cup Money
Buck Baker $2,395

Most Cars Started
26—October 23, 1956

Fewest Cars Started
14—August 5, 1965

Narrowest Margin of Victory
2 car lengths—October 23, 1956

Slowest Race
53.699 MPH—July 27, 1956
53.699 MPH—September 21, 1957

Race Record
64.748 MPH—August 5, 1965

Most Cautions
4—September 21, 1957

Most Race Leaders
4—May 4, 1957
4—September 21, 1957

Most Cars Running at Finish
15—October 23, 1956

1956 Grand National Race No. 34
July 27, 1956 Average Speed: 53.699

Driver	Owner	Car #	Make	Laps	Winnings
1. Speedy Thompson	Carl Kiekhaefer	500	56 Dodg	201	950
2. Ralph Moody	Pete DePaolo	12	58 Ford	201	675
3. Billy Myers	Bill Stroppe	14	56 Merc	200	475
4. Fireball Roberts	Pete DePaolo	22	56 Ford	200	365
5. Buck Baker	Carl Kiekhaefer	500B	56 Dodg	197	320

1956 Grand National Race No. 53
October 23, 1956 Average Speed: 54.054

Driver	Owner	Car #	Make	Laps	Winnings
1. Buck Baker	Carl Kiekhaefer	300B	56 Chrys	200	850
2. Bill Amick	Pete DePaolo	97	56 Ford	200	625
3. Marvin Panch	Tom Harbison	98	56 Ford	200	450
4. Speedy Thompson	Carl Kiekhaefer	500B	56 Dodg	197	350
5. Joe Eubanks	James Satcher	82	56 Ford	191	310

1957 Grand National Race No. 15
May 4, 1957 Average Speed: 54.861

Driver	Owner	Car #	Make	Laps	Winnings
1. Fireball Roberts	Pete DePaolo	22	57 Ford	200	700
2. Paul Goldsmith	Smokey Yunick	3	57 Ford	200	525
3. Marvin Panch	Pete DePaolo	98	57 Ford	200	400
4. Jim Paschal	Bill Stroppe	17	57 Merc	197	330
5. Jack Smith	Hugh Babb	47	57 Chev	196	270

1957 Grand National Race No. 47
September 21, 1957 Average Speed: 53.699

Driver	Owner	Car #	Make	Laps	Winnings
1. Buck Baker	Buck Baker	87	57 Chev	200	900
2. Marvin Panch	Marvin Panch	98	57 Ford	200	575
3. Bill Amick	Bill Amick	97	57 Ford	198	375
4. Gwyn Staley	J. H. Petty	38	57 Chev	198	280
5. Lee Petty	Petty Enterprises	42	57 Olds	195	245

1965 Grand National Race No. 20
May 27, 1965 Average Speed: 63.909

Driver	Owner	Car #	Make	Laps	Winnings
1. Ned Jarrett	Bondy Long	11	65 Ford	200	1,000
2. Bud Moore	Louie Weathersby	45	65 Plym	178	600
3. Dick Hutcherson	Holman-Moody	29	65 Ford	175	400
4. Doug Cooper	Bob Cooper	60	64 Ford	175	300
5. Bob Derrington	Bob Derrington	68	63 Ford	172	275

1965 Grand National Race No. 36
August 5, 1965 Average Speed: 64.748

Driver	Owner	Car #	Make	Laps	Winnings
1. Ned Jarrett	Bondy Long	11	65 Ford	200	1,000
2. Richard Petty	Petty Enterprises	43	64 Plym	196	600
3. Dick Hutcherson	Holman-Moody	29	65 Ford	189	400
4. Neil Castles	Buck Baker	89	65 Olds	185	300
5. David Pearson	Cotton Owens	6	65 Dodg	184	275

Concord Speedway
Concord, NC
Half-mile Dirt Track

(aka Concord Int'l Speedway; New Concord Speedway) Half-mile dirt track opened in 1955. First NASCAR Winston Cup (then Grand National) race held on 5/6/56 (won by Speedy Thompson). Final Grand National race run on 6/11/64 (won by Richard Petty). Track closed in 1978, and later re-opened for NDRA Dirt Late Model race in 1979.

Winston Cup Starts
Cotton Owens   9
Jack Smith   9

Winston Cup Victories
Jack Smith   3

Winston Cup Poles
Speedy Thompson 2
Joe Weatherly   2

Winston Cup Money
Jack Smith $3,945

Most Cars Started
34—October 25, 1959
Lee Kirby Memorial

Fewest Cars Started
19—March 8, 1959
19—June 11, 1964

Narrowest Margin of Victory
3 car lengths—March 2, 1958

Slowest Race
53.161 MPH—February 25, 1962

Race Record
66.352 MPH—June 11, 1964

Most Cautions
5—October 13, 1957

Most Race Leaders
4—October 13, 1957
4—November 10, 1963 Textile 250

Most Cars Running at Finish
21—October 13, 1957

1956 Grand National Race No. 14
May 6, 1956 Average Speed: 61.633

Driver	Owner	Car #	Make	Laps	Winnings
1. Speedy Thompson	Carl Kiekhaefer	300c	56 Chrys	200	1,100
2. Buck Baker	Carl Kiekhaefer	300	56 Chrys	200	700
3. Herb Thomas	Carl Kiekhaefer	300B	56 Chrys	198	475
4. Tim Flock	Jim Stephens	285	56 Pont	197	365
5. Rex White	Bob Welborn	X	56 Chev	195	310

1957 Grand National Race No. 2
December 2, 1956 Average Speed: 55.883

Driver	Owner	Car #	Make	Laps	Winnings
1. Marvin Panch	Pete DePaolo	98	56 Ford	200	650
2. Paul Goldsmith	Smokey Yunick	3	56 Chev	200	525
3. Bill Amick	Pete DePaolo	97	56 Ford	199	400
4. Tiny Lund	Gus Holzmueller	16	56 Chev	194	320
5. Lee Petty	Petty Enterprises	42	56 Dodg	193	290

1957 Grand National Race No. 5
March 3, 1957 Average Speed: 59.860

Driver	Owner	Car #	Make	Laps	Winnings
1. Jack Smith	Hugh Babb	47	57 Chev	200	650
2. Buck Baker	Hugh Babb	87	57 Chev	200	525
3. Speedy Thompson	Hugh Babb	46	57 Chev	200	400
4. Fireball Roberts	Pete DePaolo	22	57 Ford	200	320
5. Mel Larson	Mel Larson	55	56 Ford	189	290

1957 Grand National Race No. 51
October 13, 1957 Average Speed: 59.553

Driver	Owner	Car #	Make	Laps	Winnings
1. Fireball Roberts	Fireball Roberts	22	57 Ford	200	900
2. Lee Petty	Petty Enterprises	42	57 Olds	200	575
3. Ken Rush	Sam Rice	26	57 Ford	197	375
4. Marvin Panch	Marvin Panch	98	57 Ford	193	280
5. Jack Smith	Jack Smith	47	57 Chev	192	245

1958 Grand National Race No. 3
March 2, 1958 Average Speed: 58.555

Driver	Owner	Car #	Make	Laps	Winnings
1. Lee Petty	Petty Enterprises	42	57 Olds	200	800
2. Curtis Turner	Holman-Moody	21	58 Ford	200	525
3. Speedy Thompson	Speedy Thompson	46	57 Chev	200	350
4. Gwyn Staley	J. H. Petty	38	57 Chev	—	250
5. Eddie Pagan	Eddie Pagan	45	57 Ford	—	225

1959 Grand National Race No. 5
March 8, 1959 Average Speed: 59.239

Driver	Owner	Car #	Make	Laps	Winnings
1. Curtis Turner	Doc White	41	59 Ford	200	800
2. Cotton Owens	W. H. Watson	6	58 Pont	199	525
3. Lee Petty	Petty Enterprises	42	57 Olds	198	350
4. Junior Johnson	Paul Spaulding	11	57 Ford	196	250
5. Speedy Thompson	Steve Pierce	1	57 Chev	196	225

1959 Grand National Race No. 44 Lee Kirby Memorial
October 25, 1959 Average Speed: 54.005

Driver	Owner	Car #	Make	Laps	Winnings
1. Jack Smith	Jack Smith	47	59 Chev	300	1,500
2. Lee Petty	Petty Enterprises	42	59 Plym	299	1,000
3. Buck Baker	Lynton Tyson	87	59 Chev	293	700
4. Buddy Baker	Lynton Tyson	88	59 Chev	291	500
5. Glen Wood	Tom Vernon	98	59 Ford	288	400

1962 Grand National Race No. 1
November 5, 1961 Average Speed: 59.405

Driver	Owner	Car #	Make	Laps	Winnings
1. Jack Smith	Jack Smith	46	61 Pont	200	800
2. Joe Weatherly	Bud Moore	8	61 Pont	200	525
3. Cotton Owens	Cotton Owens	6	61 Pont	198	375
4. Rex White	Rex White	4	61 Chev	198	275
5. Ned Jarrett	Bee Gee Holloway	11	61 Chev	196	350

1962 Grand National Race No. 6
February 25, 1962 Average Speed: 53.161

Driver	Owner	Car #	Make	Laps	Winnings
1. Joe Weatherly	Bud Moore	8	61 Pont	78	500
2. Richard Petty	Petty Enterprises	43	62 Plym	78	300
3. Ralph Earnhardt	Robert Smith	75	61 Pont	77	200
4. Jack Smith	Jack Smith	47	61 Pont	77	150
5. Buddy Baker	Buck Baker	87	61 Chrys	77	138

1962 Grand National Race No. 20
May 6, 1962 Average Speed: 57.052

Driver	Owner	Car #	Make	Laps	Winnings
1. Joe Weatherly	Bud Moore	8	61 Pont	200	1,000
2. Cotton Owens	Cotton Owens	6	60 Pont	200	600
3. Wendell Scott	Wendell Scott	34	61 Chev	192	400
4. Jack Smith	Jack Smith	47	61 Pont	191	300
5. Maurice Petty	Petty Enterprises	41	62 Plym	188	275

Concord Speedway *continued*

1964 Grand National Race No. 1 Textile 250
November 10, 1963 Average Speed: 56.897

Driver	Owner	Car #	Make	Laps	Winnings
1. Ned Jarrett	Charles Robinson	11	63 Ford	250	1,350
2. Joe Weatherly	Bud Moore	8	63 Pont	250	1,000
3. Richard Petty	Petty Enterprises	42	63 Plym	248	650
4. David Pearson	Cotton Owens	5	63 Dodg	241	500
5. Maurice Petty	Petty Enterprises	41	63 Plym	241	400

1964 Grand National Race No. 29
June 11, 1964 Average Speed: 66.352

Driver	Owner	Car #	Make	Laps	Winnings
1. Richard Petty	Petty Enterprises	43	64 Plym	200	1,000
2. David Pearson	Cotton Owens	6	64 Dodg	200	600
3. Ned Jarrett	Bondy Long	11	64 Ford	198	400
4. Wendell Scott	Wendell Scott	34	63 Ford	191	300
5. Curtis Crider	Curtis Crider	02	63 Merc	185	275

Dog Track Speedway
Moyock, NC
Quarter-mile Dirt Track

(aka Dogtrack Raceway; Moyock Speedway) Quarter-mile dirt oval opened in August 1960. First NASCAR Winston Cup (then Grand National) race staged on 9/11/62 (won by Ned Jarrett). Track paved in 1964 and enlarged to .333-mile oval. Final Grand National event held on 5/29/66 (won by David Pearson).

Winston Cup Starts
Wendell Scott   7

Winston Cup Victories
Ned Jarrett   4

Winston Cup Poles
Ned Jarrett   2
Richard Petty   2

Winston Cup Money
Ned Jarrett $4,631

Most Cars Started
25—November 7, 1965 Tidewater 300
25—May 29, 1966

Fewest Cars Started
14—July 11, 1963

Narrowest Margin of Victory
N/A

Slowest Race
43.000 MPH—September 24, 1963

Race Record
63.965 MPH—August 13, 1964
Moyock 300

Most Cautions
N/A

Most Race Leaders
3—November 7, 1965 Tidewater 300

Most Cars Running at Finish
15—November 7, 1965 Tidewater 300

1962 Grand National Race No. 48
September 11, 1962 Average Speed: 43.078

	Driver	Owner	Car #	Make	Laps	Winnings
1.	Ned Jarrett	Bee Gee Holloway	11	62 Chev	250	775
2.	Joe Weatherly	Bud Moore	8	61 Pont	249	500
3.	Curtis Crider	Curtis Crider	62	62 Merc	240	380
4.	Melvin Bradley	Melvin Bradley	27	62 Chev	235	290
5.	George Green	Jess Potter	1	60 Chev	228	245

1963 Grand National Race No. 32
July 11, 1963 Average Speed: 45.464

	Driver	Owner	Car #	Make	Laps	Winnings
1.	Jimmy Pardue	Pete Stewart	54	63 Ford	250	550
2.	Ned Jarrett	Charles Robinson	11	63 Ford	250	500
3.	Buck Baker	Buck Baker	87	63 Pont	246	365
4.	Mark Hurley	Mark Hurley	61	63 Ford	241	300
5.	Neil Castles	Buck Baker	86	62 Chrys	236	255

1963 Grand National Race No. 49
September 24, 1963 Average Speed: 43.000

	Driver	Owner	Car #	Make	Laps	Winnings
1.	Ned Jarrett	Charles Robinson	11	63 Ford	300	645
2.	Joe Weatherly	Bud Moore	8	63 Merc	300	680
3.	David Pearson	Cotton Owens	5	63 Dodg	291	375
4.	Richard Petty	Petty Enterprises	42	63 Plym	290	300
5.	Fred Lorenzen	Holman-Moody	28	63 Ford	289	250

1964 Grand National Race No. 46 Moyock 300
August 13, 1964 Average Speed: 63.965

	Driver	Owner	Car #	Make	Laps	Winnings
1.	Ned Jarrett	Bondy Long	11	64 Ford	300	1,000
2.	David Pearson	Cotton Owens	6	64 Dodg	299	600
3.	Richard Petty	Petty Enterprises	43	64 Plym	296	400
4.	Bunkie Blackburn	Casper Hensley	82	64 Pont	294	300
5.	Bill McMahan	Casper Hensley	42	63 Pont	286	275

1965 Grand National Race No. 42 Moyock 300
August 24, 1965 Average Speed: 63.047

	Driver	Owner	Car #	Make	Laps	Winnings
1.	Dick Hutcherson	Holman-Moody	29	65 Ford	300	1,000
2.	Ned Jarrett	Bondy Long	11	65 Ford	300	600
3.	Richard Petty	Petty Enterprises	43	65 Plym	300	600
4.	Tiny Lund	Lyle Stelter	55	64 Ford	298	300
5.	Sonny Hutchins	Junie Donlavey	90	64 Ford	297	275

1965 Grand National Race No. 55 Tidewater 300
November 7, 1965 Average Speed: 63.773

	Driver	Owner	Car #	Make	Laps	Winnings
1.	Ned Jarrett	Bondy Long	11	65 Ford	300	1,111
2.	Bobby Isaac	Rex Lovette	26	65 Ford	299	600
3.	Buddy Baker	Buck Baker	87	65 Chev	297	400
4.	Jim Paschal	Petty Enterprises	42	65 Plym	297	300
5.	Tom Pistone	Glenn Sweet	59	64 Ford	295	275

1966 Grand National Race No. 21
May 29, 1966 Average Speed: 61.913

	Driver	Owner	Car #	Make	Laps	Winnings
1.	David Pearson	Cotton Owens	6	64 Dodg	301	1,000
2.	Tiny Lund	Lyle Stelter	55	64 Ford	300	600
3.	James Hylton	Bud Hartje	48	65 Dodg	298	400
4.	John Sears	L. G. DeWitt	4	64 Ford	294	300
5.	Wendell Scott	Wendell Scott	34	65 Ford	291	275

Forsyth County Fairgrounds
Winston-Salem, NC
Half-mile Dirt Track

(aka Winston-Salem Fairgrounds; Dixie Classic Fairgrounds) Half-mile dirt oval built circa 1929. First NASCAR Winston Cup (then Grand National) race staged on 5/29/55 (won by Lee Petty). Only other NASCAR race was run on 8/7/55 (won by Lee Petty). Final auto racing event was held in October 1963.

Winston Cup Starts
13 drivers tied with 2

Winston Cup Victories
Lee Petty 2

Winston Cup Poles
Tim Flock 1
Fonty Flock 1

Winston Cup Money
Lee Petty $2,100

Most Cars Started
23—May 29, 1955

Fewest Cars Started
22—August 7, 1955

Narrowest Margin of Victory
6 car lengths—August 2, 1955

Slowest Race
50.111 MPH—August 7, 1955

Race Record
50.583 MPH—May 29, 1955

Most Cautions
8—May 29, 1955

Most Race Leaders
3—May 29, 1955

Most Cars Running at Finish
12—May 29, 1955
12—August 7, 1955

1955 Grand National Race No. 18
May 29, 1955 Average Speed: 50.583

Driver	Owner	Car #	Make	Laps	Winnings
1. Lee Petty	Petty Enterprises	42	54 Chrys	200	1,000
2. Jim Paschal	Ernest Woods	78	55 Olds	200	650
3. Fred Dove	Fred Dove	71	55 Olds	197	450
4. Dick Rathmann	John Ditz	3	55 Chrys	193	350
5. John Dodd Jr.	John Dodd, Sr.	171	55 Dodg	190	300

1955 Grand National Race No. 32
August 7, 1955 Average Speed: 50.111

Driver	Owner	Car #	Make	Laps	Winnings
1. Lee Petty	Petty Enterprises	42	55 Dodg	200	1,100
2. Jim Paschal	Ernest Woods	78	55 Olds	200	700
3. Buck Baker	Buck Baker	89	55 Buick	199	475
4. Billy Carden	Bishop Brothers	8	55 Buick	198	365
5. Eddie Skinner	Frank Dodge	28	53 Olds	189	310

Gastonia Fairgrounds
Gastonia, NC
.333-Mile Dirt Track

(aka Spindle City Fairgrounds; Gaston Speedway; Lowell Fairgrounds) .333-mile dirt oval built circa 1953. Only NASCAR Winston Cup (then Grand National) race staged on 9/12/58 (won by Buck Baker). Track closed in late 1980s.

Winston Cup Victories
Buck Baker 1

Winston Cup Poles
Tiny Lund 1

Winston Cup Money
Buck Baker $800

Most Cars Started
19—September 12, 1958

Narrowest Margin of Victory
N/A

Race Record
47.856 MPH—September 12, 1958

Most Race Leaders
N/A

Most Cars Running at Finish
14—September 12, 1958

1958 Grand National Race No. 45
September 12, 1958 Average Speed: 47.856

Driver	Owner	Car #	Make	Laps	Winnings
1. Buck Baker	Buck Baker	87	57 Chev	200	800
2. Lee Petty	Petty Enterprises	42	57 Olds	200	525
3. Bob Welborn	J. H. Petty	49	57 Chev	200	350
4. Whitey Norman	Whitey Norman	41	57 Chev	196	250
5. Speedy Thompson	Speedy Thompson	46	57 Chev	193	225

Greensboro Agricultural Fairgrounds
Greensboro, NC
.333-mile Dirt Track

(aka Central Carolina Fairgrounds; Greensboro Fairgrounds) Track originally built circa 1926. A .333-mile track opened in June 1953. Grandstands burned down on 5/1/55, and bleachers were rebuilt later that year. First NASCAR Winston Cup (then Grand National) race staged on 4/28/57 (won by Paul Goldsmith). Final race staged on 5/11/58 (won by Bob Welborn). Track closed in 1957.

Winston Cup Starts
L. D. Austin	3
Buck Baker	3
Brownie King	3
Lee Petty	3
Jack Smith	3
Speedy Thompson	3

Winston Cup Victories
Buck Baker	1
Paul Goldsmith	1
Bob Welborn	1

Winston Cup Poles
Buck Baker	1
Ken Rush	1
Bob Welborn	1

Winston Cup Money
Buck Baker	$1,520

Most Cars Started
31—October 27, 1957

Fewest Cars Started
19—April 28, 1957

Narrowest Margin of Victory
5 seconds April 28, 1957

Slowest Race
38.927 MPH—October 27, 1957

Race Record
49.905 MPH—April 28, 1957

Most Cautions
4—April 28, 1957

Most Race Leaders
2—April 28, 1957
2—October 27, 1957
2—May 11, 1958

Most Cars Running at Finish
N/A

1957 Grand National Race No. 13
April 28, 1957 Average Speed: 49.905

	Driver	Owner	Car #	Make	Laps	Winnings
1.	Paul Goldsmith	Smokey Yunick	3	57 Ford	250	700
2.	Jack Smith	Hugh Babb	47	57 Chev	250	525
3.	Buck Baker	Hugh Babb	87	57 Chev	249	400
4.	Ralph Moody	Pete DePaolo	12	57 Ford	248	430
5.	Fireball Roberts	Pete DePaolo	22	57 Ford	247	270

1957 Grand National Race No. 53
October 27, 1957 Average Speed: 38.927

	Driver	Owner	Car #	Make	Laps	Winnings
1.	Buck Baker	Buck Baker	87	57 Chev	250	900
2.	Speedy Thompson	Speedy Thompson	46	57 Chev	—	575
3.	Joe Weatherly	Holman-Moody	12	57 Ford	—	375
4.	Jack Smith	Jack Smith	47	57 Chev	—	280
5.	Lee Petty	Petty Enterprises	42	57 Olds	—	245

1958 Grand National Race No. 16
May 11, 1958 Average Speed: 45.628

	Driver	Owner	Car #	Make	Laps	Winnings
1.	Bob Welborn	J. H. Petty	44	57 Chev	150	600
2.	Lee Petty	Petty Enterprises	42	57 Olds	149	500
3.	Junior Johnson	Paul Spaulding	11	57 Ford	148	355
4.	Speedy Thompson	Speedy Thompson	46	57 Chev	147	260
5.	Doug Cox	Doug Cox	30	57 Ford	147	240

Harnett Speedway
Spring Lake, NC
Half-mile Dirt Track

Half-mile dirt track built in 1952. One Winston Cup (then Grand National) race run on 3/8/53 (won by Herb Thomas). Track closed circa 1970.

Winston Cup Victories
Herb Thomas	1

Winston Cup Poles
Herb Thomas	1

Winston Cup Money
Herb Thomas	$1,000

Most Cars Started
32—March 8, 1953

Narrowest Margin of Victory
3 laps plus—March 8, 1953

Race Record
48.826 MPH—March 8, 1953

Most Race Leaders
1—March 8, 1953

Most Cars Running at Finish
N/A

1953 Grand National Race No. 3
March 8, 1953 Average Speed: 48.826

	Driver	Owner	Car #	Make	Laps	Winnings
1.	Herb Thomas	Herb Thomas	92	53 Huds	200	1,000
2.	Dick Rathmann	Walt Chapman	120	53 Huds	197	700
3.	Lee Petty	Petty Enterprises	42	53 Dodg	—	450
4.	Dick Passwater	Frank Arford	78	53 Olds	—	350
5.	Herschel Buchanan	Herschel Buchanan	1	53 Nash	—	200

Harris Speedway
Harris, NC
.333-mile Paved Track

(aka Tri-City Motor Speedway; Harris Motor Speedway) .3-mile paved track built in 1964. First NASCAR Winston Cup (then Grand National) race staged on 5/5/56 (won by Speedy Thompson). Final NASCAR event held on 5/30/65 (won by Ned Jarrett). Track is still in operation.

Winston Cup Starts
Buddy Arrington	2
Neil Castles	2
Doug Cooper	2
Ned Jarrett	2
Larry Manning	2
J. T. Putney	2
Wendell Scott	2
Roy Tyner	2

Winston Cup Victories
Ned Jarrett	1
Richard Petty	1

Winston Cup Poles
Paul Lewis	1
Billy Wade	1

Winston Cup Money
Ned Jarrett	$1,600

Most Cars Started
22—May 30, 1965

Fewest Cars Started
21—October 25, 1964

Narrowest Margin of Victory
1 lap plus—October 25, 1964

Slowest Race
56.851 MPH—May 30, 1965

Race Record
59.009 MPH—October 25, 1964

Most Cautions
3—October 25, 1964

Most Race Leaders
3—October 25, 1964

Most Cars Running at Finish
12—October 25, 1964

1964 Grand National Race No. 60
October 25, 1964 Average Speed: 59.009

Driver	Owner	Car #	Make	Laps	Winnings
1. Richard Petty	Petty Enterprises	41	64 Plym	334	1,000
2. Ned Jarrett	Bondy Long	11	64 Ford	333	600
3. Curtis Crider	Curtis Crider	02	63 Merc	325	400
4. Bobby Isaac	Cotton Owens	5	64 Dodg	324	300
5. Larry Thomas	Wade Younts	36	63 Dodg	321	275

1965 Grand National Race No. 22
May 30, 1965 Average Speed: 56.851

Driver	Owner	Car #	Make	Laps	Winnings
1. Ned Jarrett	Bondy Long	11	65 Ford	334	1,000
2. G. C. Spencer	G. C. Spencer	49	64 Ford	330	600
3. Dick Dixon	Dan Colone	8	63 Ford	326	400
4. Dick Hutcherson	Holman-Moody	29	65 Ford	325	300
5. J. T. Putney	Herman Beam	19	65 Chev	317	275

Hickory Speedway
Hickory, NC
Half-mile Dirt Track

(aka Hickory Motor Speedway) Dirt track built in 1951. Originally measured at half-mile. Later re-measured at .4-mile and today listed as .362-mile. First NASCAR Winston Cup (then Grand National) race staged on 5/16/53 (won by Tim Flock). Track paved in 1967. First Grand National race run on pavement was 9/8/67 (won by Richard Petty, his 5th of his record-setting 10 straight wins). Final Winston Cup Grand National race run on 8/28/71 (won by Tiny Lund in a Camaro). The track still hosts a variety of NASCAR weekly and special events.

Winston Cup Starts
Buck Baker   24

Winston Cup Victories
Junior Johnson   7

Winston Cup Poles
Junior Johnson   6

Winston Cup Money
Richard Petty $14,975

Most Cars Started
33—September 8, 1967
Buddy Shuman Memorial

Fewest Cars Started
12—August 29, 1953

Narrowest Margin of Victory
1 car length—June 28, 1958

Slowest Race
56.962 MPH—November 13, 1955

Race Record
82.872 MPH—June 19, 1954

Most Cautions
6—May 7, 1955
6—May 12, 1956
6—April 3, 1966 Hickory 250
6—September 8, 1967
Buddy Shuman Memorial

Most Race Leaders
6—July 20, 1957
6—April 9, 1967 Hickory 250

Most Cars Running at Finish
23—June 28, 1958

1953 Grand National Race No. 10
May 16, 1953

Driver	Owner	Car #	Make	Laps	Winnings
1. Tim Flock	Ted Chester	91	53 Huds	200	1,000
2. Joe Eubanks	Phil Oates	82	52 Huds	—	700
3. Ray Duhigg	J. H. Petty	44	52 Plym	—	450
4. Dick Passwater	Frank Arford	78	53 Olds	—	350
5. Dick Rathmann	Walt Chapman	120	53 Huds	—	200

1953 Grand National Race No. 29
August 29, 1953

Driver	Owner	Car #	Make	Laps	Winnings
1. Fonty Flock	Frank Christian	14	53 Huds	200	1,000
2. Herb Thomas	Herb Thomas	92	53 Huds	—	700
3. Joe Eubanks	Phil Oates	82	52 Huds	—	450
4. Lee Petty	Petty Enterprises	42	53 Dodg	—	350
5. Jimmie Lewallen		22	52 Plym	—	200

1954 Grand National Race No. 19
June 19, 1954 Average Speed: 82.872

Driver	Owner	Car #	Make	Laps	Winnings
1. Herb Thomas	Herb Thomas	92	54 Huds	200	1,000
2. Lee Petty	Petty Enterprises	42	54 Chrys	200	650
3. Buck Baker	Ernest Woods	88	54 Olds	198	450
4. Dick Rathmann	John Ditz	3	54 Huds	198	350
5. Junior Johnson	George Miller	23	54 Huds	194	300

1955 Grand National Race No. 12
May 7, 1955 Average Speed: 58.823

Driver	Owner	Car #	Make	Laps	Winnings
1. Junior Johnson	B & L Motors	55	55 Olds	200	1,000
2. Tim Flock	Carl Kiekhaefer	300	55 Chrys	200	650
3. Jim Paschal	Ernest Woods	78	55 Olds	200	450
4. Lee Petty	Petty Enterprises	42	55 Chrys	198	350
5. Jimmie Lewallen	Joe Blair	5	54 Merc	196	300

1956 Grand National Race No. 1
November 13, 1955 Average Speed: 56.962

Driver	Owner	Car #	Make	Laps	Winnings
1. Tim Flock	Carl Kiekhaefer	301	55 Chrys	200	1,150
2. Curtis Turner	Charlie Schwam	99	56 Ford	200	720
3. Lee Petty	Petty Enterprises	42	56 Dodg	200	505
4. Dink Widenhouse	Dink Widenhouse	B 29	56 Ford	199	365
5. Jim Paschal	Bob Welborn	44	55 Chev	199	360

1956 Grand National Race No. 16
May 12, 1956 Average Speed: 59.442

Driver	Owner	Car #	Make	Laps	Winnings
1. Speedy Thompson	Carl Kiekhaefer	300c	56 Chrys	200	1,100
2. Billy Myers	Bill Stroppe	14	56 Merc	200	700
3. Buck Baker	Carl Kiekhaefer	500B	56 Dodg	200	475
4. Herb Thomas	Carl Kiekhaefer	502	56 Dodg	200	365
5. Gwyn Staley	Hubert Westmoreland	2	56 Chev	200	310

1956 Grand National Race No. 55 Buddy Shuman Memorial
November 11, 1956 Average Speed: 66.420

Driver	Owner	Car #	Make	Laps	Winnings
1. Speedy Thompson	Carl Kiekhaefer	300	56 Chrys	250	850
2. Ralph Earnhardt	Pete DePaolo	22	56 Ford	250	625
3. Buck Baker	Carl Kiekhaefer	300B	56 Chrys	249	450
4. Ralph Moody	Pete DePaolo	12	56 Ford	249	350
5. Doug Cox	John Foster	86	56 Ford	247	310

1957 Grand National Race No. 32
July 20, 1957 Average Speed: 58.737

Driver	Owner	Car #	Make	Laps	Winnings
1. Jack Smith	Jack Smith	47	57 Chev	250	1,000
2. Lee Petty	Petty Enterprises	42	57 Olds	250	625
3. Joe Weatherly	Holman-Moody	12	57 Ford	250	400
4. Gwyn Staley	J. H. Petty	38	57 Chev	250	280
5. Fireball Roberts	Fireball Roberts	22	57 Ford	250	245

1958 Grand National Race No. 26
June 28, 1958 Average Speed: 62.413

Driver	Owner	Car #	Make	Laps	Winnings
1. Lee Petty	Petty Enterprises	42	57 Olds	250	800
2. Junior Johnson	Paul Spaulding	11	57 Ford	250	525
3. Speedy Thompson	Speedy Thompson	46	57 Chev	250	350
4. Jack Smith	Jack Smith	47	57 Chev	248	250
5. Shorty Rollins	Shorty Rollins	99	58 Ford	247	225

1959 Grand National Race No. 12
May 2, 1959 Average Speed: 62.165

Driver	Owner	Car #	Make	Laps	Winnings
1. Junior Johnson	Paul Spaulding	11	57 Ford	250	800
2. Joe Weatherly	Doc White	41	59 Ford	248	525
3. Lee Petty	Petty Enterprises	42	57 Olds	247	350
4. Ken Rush	Paul Walton	40	57 Chev	246	250
5. Cotton Owens	W. H. Watson	6	58 Pont	246	225

Hickory Speedway *continued*

1959 Grand National Race No. 37
September 11, 1959 Average Speed: 63.380

Driver	Owner	Car #	Make	Laps	Winnings
1. Lee Petty	Petty Enterprises	42	59 Plym	250	900
2. Buck Baker	Lynton Tyson	88	59 Chev	249	525
3. Rex White	Rex White	4	59 Chev	248	375
4. Junior Johnson	Wood Brothers	21	58 Ford	248	275
5. Brownie King	Jess Potter	31	57 Chev	243	250

1960 Grand National Race No. 11
April 15, 1960 Average Speed: 66.347

Driver	Owner	Car #	Make	Laps	Winnings
1. Joe Weatherly	Holman-Moody	12	60 Ford	250	800
2. Ned Jarrett	Ned Jarrett	11	60 Ford	250	525
3. Richard Petty	Petty Enterprises	43	60 Plym	249	375
4. Bob Welborn	Bob Welborn	49	60 Chev	247	275
5. Tom Pistone	W. T. Coppedge	59	60 Chev	246	250

1960 Grand National Race No. 36 Buddy Shuman Memorial
September 9, 1960 Average Speed: 69.998

Driver	Owner	Car #	Make	Laps	Winnings
1. Junior Johnson	John Masoni	27	60 Chev	250	800
2. Possum Jones	Tom Daniels	2	60 Chev	249	525
3. Rex White	Rex White	4	59 Chev	246	375
4. David Pearson	David Pearson	67	59 Chev	246	275
5. Ned Jarrett	Ned Jarrett	11	60 Ford	241	250

1961 Grand National Race No. 16
April 22, 1961 Average Speed: 66.654

Driver	Owner	Car #	Make	Laps	Winnings
1. Junior Johnson	Rex Lovette	27	61 Pont	250	950
2. Buck Baker	Buck Baker	86	62 Chrys	250	625
3. Rex White	Rex White	4	60 Chev	245	525
4. G. C. Spencer	G. C. Spencer	48	60 Chev	245	275
5. Jimmy Pardue	Jimmy Pardue	54	59 Chev	242	250

1961 Grand National Race No. 43 Buddy Shuman Memorial
September 8, 1961 Average Speed: 67.529

Driver	Owner	Car #	Make	Laps	Winnings
1. Rex White	Rex White	4	61 Chev	250	900
2. Jack Smith	Jack Smith	47	61 Pont	249	525
3. Buck Baker	Buck Baker	86	61 Chrys	249	375
4. Cotton Owens	Cotton Owens	6	60 Pont	248	275
5. Emanuel Zervakis	Monroe Shook	85	60 Chev	246	250

1962 Grand National Race No. 19 Hickory 250
May 5, 1962 Average Speed: 71.216

Driver	Owner	Car #	Make	Laps	Winnings
1. Jack Smith	Jack Smith	47	61 Pont	250	1,000
2. Rex White	Rex White	4	62 Chev	248	600
3. Joe Weatherly	Bud Moore	8	61 Pont	246	400
4. Jim Paschal	Cliff Stewart	2	62 Pont	240	300
5. Ralph Earnhardt	Robert Smith	75	61 Pont	237	275

1962 Grand National Race No. 46 Buddy Shuman Memorial
September 7, 1962 Average Speed: 70.574

Driver	Owner	Car #	Make	Laps	Winnings
1. Rex White	Rex White	4	62 Chev	250	1,000
2. Jimmy Pardue	Jimmy Pardue	54	62 Pont	241	600
3. Buck Baker	Buck Baker	87	62 Chrys	240	400
4. Larry Thomas	Wade Younts	36	62 Dodg	240	300
5. Joe Weatherly	Bud Moore	8	61 Pont	239	275

1963 Grand National Race No. 12 Hickory 250
March 24, 1963 Average Speed: 67.950

Driver	Owner	Car #	Make	Laps	Winnings
1. Junior Johnson	Ray Fox	3	63 Chev	250	1,150
2. Richard Petty	Petty Enterprises	43	63 Plym	249	700
3. Ned Jarrett	Charles Robinson	11	63 Ford	248	450
4. Jim Paschal	Petty Enterprises	41	62 Plym	246	300
5. Roy Mayne	C. L. Kilpatrick	33	62 Chev	237	275

1963 Grand National Race No. 46 Buddy Shuman Memorial
September 6, 1963 Average Speed: 62.926

Driver	Owner	Car #	Make	Laps	Winnings
1. Junior Johnson	Ray Fox	3	63 Chev	250	1,775
2. G. C. Spencer	G. C. Spencer	03	62 Chev	246	700
3. Bob Welborn	Fred Harb	17	62 Pont	237	450
4. Jimmy Massey	Hubert Westmoreland	96	61 Chev	232	300
5. Larry Thomas	Wade Younts	36	62 Dodg	232	275

1964 Grand National Race No. 23 Hickory 250
May 16, 1964 Average Speed: 69.364

Driver	Owner	Car #	Make	Laps	Winnings
1. Ned Jarrett	Bondy Long	11	64 Ford	250	1,150
2. David Pearson	Cotton Owens	6	64 Dodg	249	600
3. Richard Petty	Petty Enterprises	43	64 Plym	249	400
4. LeeRoy Yarbrough	Louie Weathersby	45	63 Plym	248	300
5. Buddy Baker	J. C. Parker	87	63 Dodg	244	275

1964 Grand National Race No. 52 Buddy Shuman Memorial
September 11, 1964 Average Speed: 67.797

Driver	Owner	Car #	Make	Laps	Winnings
1. David Pearson	Cotton Owens	6	64 Dodg	250	2,035
2. Larry Thomas	Herman Beam	19	64 Ford	247	600
3. Buck Baker	Ray Fox	3	64 Dodg	246	400
4. Jimmy Pardue	Charles Robinson	54	64 Plym	246	300
5. Richard Petty	Petty Enterprises	43	64 Plym	238	275

1965 Grand National Race No. 18 Hickory 250
May 16, 1965 Average Speed: 72.130

Driver	Owner	Car #	Make	Laps	Winnings
1. Junior Johnson	Rex Lovette	26	65 Ford	250	1,000
2. Ned Jarrett	Bondy Long	11	65 Ford	250	600
3. G. C. Spencer	G. C. Spencer	49	64 Ford	245	400
4. Paul Lewis	Paul Lewis	27	64 Ford	241	300
5. Buddy Baker	Buck Baker	87	65 Olds	240	275

1965 Grand National Race No. 46 Buddy Shuman Memorial
September 10, 1965 Average Speed: 74.365

Driver	Owner	Car #	Make	Laps	Winnings
1. Richard Petty	Petty Enterprises	43	65 Plym	250	1,200
2. David Pearson	Cotton Owens	6	65 Dodg	250	600
3. Ned Jarrett	Bondy Long	11	65 Ford	248	400
4. Junior Johnson	Rex Lovette	26	65 Ford	248	300
5. J. T. Putney	Herman Beam	19	65 Chev	246	275

1966 Grand National Race No. 9 Hickory 250
April 3, 1966 Average Speed: 68.428

Driver	Owner	Car #	Make	Laps	Winnings
1. David Pearson	Cotton Owens	6	64 Dodg	250	1,000
2. Curtis Turner	Wood Brothers	41	66 Ford	250	600
3. Bobby Isaac	Junior Johnson	26	66 Ford	248	400
4. Ned Jarrett	Bondy Long	11	66 Ford	248	500
5. Paul Goldsmith	Bob Cooper	02	65 Plym	247	275

Hickory Speedway *continued*

1966 Grand National Race No. 43 Buddy Shuman Memorial
September 9, 1966 Average Speed: 76.923

Driver	Owner	Car #	Make	Laps	Winnings
1. David Pearson	Cotton Owens	6	65 Dodg	250	1,000
2. Richard Petty	Petty Enterprises	42	66 Plym	249	600
3. Paul Lewis	Paul Lewis	1	65 Plym	248	400
4. James Hylton	Bud Hartje	48	65 Dodg	242	300
5. Hank Thomas	W. S. Jenkins	92	64 Ford	240	275

1967 Grand National Race No. 12 Hickory 250
April 9, 1967 Average Speed: 69.699

Driver	Owner	Car #	Make	Laps	Winnings
1. Richard Petty	Petty Enterprises	43	67 Plym	250	1,000
2. Dick Hutcherson	Bondy Long	29	67 Ford	248	600
3. James Hylton	Bud Hartje	48	65 Dodg	247	400
4. Jim Paschal	Tom Friedkin	14	65 Plym	246	300
5. Bobby Allison	Bobby Allison	2	65 Chev	245	275

1967 Grand National Race No. 41 Buddy Shuman Memorial
September 8, 1967 Average Speed: 71.414

Driver	Owner	Car #	Make	Laps	Winnings
1. Richard Petty	Petty Enterprises	43	67 Plym	250	1,500
2. Jack Ingram	Tommy Ingram	81	66 Chev	249	600
3. Jim Paschal	Tom Friedkin	14	67 Plym	248	400
4. James Hylton	Bud Hartje	48	65 Dodg	245	300
5. Elmo Langley	Henry Woodfield	64	66 Ford	244	275

1968 Grand National Race No. 8
April 7, 1968 Average Speed: 79.435

Driver	Owner	Car #	Make	Laps	Winnings
1. Richard Petty	Petty Enterprises	43	67 Plym	250	1,200
2. David Pearson	Holman-Moody	17	68 Ford	250	600
3. Bobby Isaac	Nord Krauskopf	71	67 Dodg	250	400
4. Friday Hassler	Red Sharp	39	66 Chev	246	300
5. James Hylton	James Hylton	48	67 Dodg	244	275

1968 Grand National Race No. 40 Buddy Shuman Memorial
September 6, 1968 Average Speed: 80.357

Driver	Owner	Car #	Make	Laps	Winnings
1. David Pearson	Holman-Moody	17	68 Ford	250	1,000
2. Bobby Isaac	Nord Krauskopf	71	67 Dodg	250	600
3. Buddy Baker	Ray Fox	3	68 Dodg	249	400
4. Richard Petty	Petty Enterprises	43	68 Plym	244	500
5. Elmo Langley	Elmo Langley	64	66 Ford	244	275

1969 Grand National Race No. 12 Hickory 250
April 6, 1969 Average Speed: 79.086

Driver	Owner	Car #	Make	Laps	Winnings
1. Bobby Isaac	Nord Krauskopf	71	69 Dodg	250	1,700
2. Richard Petty	Petty Enterprises	43	69 Ford	248	1,300
3. David Pearson	Holman-Moody	17	69 Ford	245	1,100
4. Dave Marcis	Milt Lunda	30	69 Dodg	244	700
5. G. C. Spencer	G. C. Spencer	49	67 Plym	243	600

1969 Grand National Race No. 42 Buddy Shuman Memorial
September 5, 1969 Average Speed: 80.519

Driver	Owner	Car #	Make	Laps	Winnings
1. Bobby Isaac	Nord Krauskopf	71	69 Dodg	250	1,700
2. Neil Castles	Neil Castles	06	69 Dodg	249	1,200
3. Richard Petty	Petty Enterprises	43	69 Ford	247	900
4. John Sears	L. G. DeWitt	4	69 Ford	246	700
5. Buddy Young	Fred Bear	31	67 Chev	245	600

1970 Grand National Race No. 21 Hickory 276
June 20, 1970 Average Speed: 68.011

Driver	Owner	Car #	Make	Laps	Winnings
1. Bobby Isaac	Nord Krauskopf	71	69 Dodg	276	2,200
2. Dick Brooks	Dick Brooks	32	69 Plym	274	1,500
3. Dave Marcis	Dave Marcis	30	69 Dodg	272	1,000
4. G. C. Spencer	G. C. Spencer	49	69 Plym	269	700
5. Bill Seifert	Bill Seifert	45	69 Ford	268	600

1970 Grand National Race No. 39 Buddy Shuman Memorial
September 11, 1970 Average Speed: 73.365

Driver	Owner	Car #	Make	Laps	Winnings
1. Bobby Isaac	Nord Krauskopf	71	70 Dodg	276	2,200
2. Richard Petty	Petty Enterprises	43	70 Plym	276	1,500
3. Bobby Allison	Bobby Allison	22	69 Dodg	276	1,000
4. Dick Brooks	Dick Brooks	32	69 Plym	273	700
5. James Hylton	James Hylton	48	69 Ford	273	600

1971 Winston Cup GN Race No. 8 Hickory 276
March 21, 1971 Average Speed: 67.700

Driver	Owner	Car #	Make	Laps	Winnings
1. Richard Petty	Petty Enterprises	43	71 Plym	276	2,200
2. David Pearson	Richard Giachetti	44	71 Ford	275	1,500
3. Benny Parsons	L. G. DeWitt	72	70 Ford	273	1,000
4. James Hylton	James Hylton	48	70 Ford	273	700
5. Elmo Langley	Elmo Langley	64	69 Merc	273	600

1971 Winston Cup GN Race No. 39 Buddy Shuman Memorial
August 28, 1971 Average Speed: 72.937

Driver	Owner	Car #	Make	Laps	Winnings
1. Tiny Lund	Ronnie Hopkins	55	69 Chev	276	1,500
2. Elmo Langley	Elmo Langley	64	71 Ford	276	900
3. Richard Petty	Petty Enterprises	43	71 Plym	276	500
4. Bobby Allison	Bobby Allison	12	70 Dodg	276	350
5. Wayne Andrews	Reid Shaw	15	71 Ford	274	325

Jacksonville Speedway
Jacksonville, NC
Half-mile Dirt Track

(aka Onslow Speedway) Half-mile dirt track built in 1952. First NASCAR Winston Cup (then Grand National) race run on 6/30/57 (won by Buck Baker). Final NASCAR Winston Cup (then Grand National) race staged on 11/8/64 (won by Ned Jarrett, the season finale in 1964). Track closed shortly thereafter.

Winston Cup Starts
Buck Baker 2
Tiny Lund 2

Winston Cup Victories
Buck Baker 1
Ned Jarrett 1

Winston Cup Poles
Lee Petty 1
Doug Yates 1

Winston Cup Money
Buck Baker $1,050

Most Cars Started
25—November 8, 1964

Fewest Cars Started
19—June 30, 1957

Narrowest Margin of Victory
1 lap plus—November 8, 1964

Slowest Race
55.342 MPH—June 30, 1957

Race Record
57.535 MPH—November 8, 1964

Most Cautions
4—November 8, 1964

Most Race Leaders
4—November 8, 1964

Most Cars Running at Finish
12—November 8, 1964

1957 Grand National Race No. 27
June 30, 1957 Average Speed: 55.342

Driver	Owner	Car #	Make	Laps	Winnings
1. Buck Baker	Buck Baker	87	57 Chev	200	1,000
2. Jim Paschal	Jim Paschal	17	57 Merc	197	575
3. Tiny Lund	Sam Rice	80	57 Pont	191	400
4. George Green	Jess Potter	33	56 Chev	187	295
5. Jack Smith	Jack Smith	47	57 Chev	179	255

1964 Grand National Race No. 62
November 8, 1964 Average Speed: 57.535

Driver	Owner	Car #	Make	Laps	Winnings
1. Ned Jarrett	Bondy Long	11	64 Ford	200	1,000
2. Richard Petty	Petty Enterprises	43	64 Plym	199	600
3. G. C. Spencer	G. C. Spencer	49	64 Ford	196	400
4. Doug Cooper	Bob Cooper	60	64 Ford	195	300
5. Larry Thomas	Charles Robinson	36	64 Plym	190	275

McCormick Field
Asheville, NC
Quarter-mile Paved Track

Quarter-mile paved oval built circa 1949. Track was laid around a baseball diamond where the minor league baseball team the Asheville Tourists played. Only NASCAR Winston Cup (then Grand National) race staged on 7/12/58 (won by Jim Paschal). Lee Petty crashed into the dugout in preliminary event to Grand National. Races were discontinued in 1959.

Winston Cup Victories
Jim Paschal 1

Winston Cup Poles
Jim Paschal 1

Winston Cup Money
Jim Paschal $570

Most Cars Started
15—July 12, 1958

Narrowest Margin of Victory
1 car length—July 12, 1958

Race Record
46.440 MPH—July 12, 1958

Most Race Leaders
1—July 12, 1958

Most Cars Running at Finish
12—July 12, 1958

1958 Grand National Race No. 29
July 12, 1958 Average Speed: 46.440

Driver	Owner	Car #	Make	Laps	Winnings
1. Jim Paschal	J. H. Petty	49	57 Chev	150	570
2. Cotton Owens	Jim Stephens	6	57 Pont	150	465
3. Rex White	J. H. Petty	44	57 Chev	150	340
4. Lee Petty	Petty Enterprises	42	57 Olds	149	265
5. Jack Smith	Jack Smith	47	57 Chev	148	235

New Asheville Speedway
Asheville, NC
.4-mile Paved Track

(aka Asheville Speedway; New Asheville Motor Speedway; Asheville Motor Speedway) .333-mile paved oval built in 1961 and originally measured at .4-mile oval. First NASCAR Winston Cup (then Grand National) race run on 7/13/62 (won by Jack Smith). Final Winston Cup Grand National race held on 5/12/71 (won by Richard Petty). Track is still in operation.

Winston Cup Starts

Richard Petty	7
Wendell Scott	7

Winston Cup Victories

Ned Jarrett	2
Richard Petty	2

Winston Cup Poles

Richard Petty	5

Winston Cup Money

Richard Petty	$4,800

Most Cars Started

23—May 31, 1968 Asheville 300

Fewest Cars Started

17—May 21, 1971 Asheville 300

Narrowest Margin of Victory

N/A

Slowest Race

63.080 MPH—June 2, 1967 Asheville 300

Race Record

78.294 MPH—July 13, 1962

Most Race Leaders

4—July 14, 1963
4—June 2, 1967 Asheville 300

Most Cars Running at Finish

14—July 13, 1962
14—May 31, 1968 Asheville 300

1962 Grand National Race No. 31
July 13, 1962 Average Speed: 78.294

Driver	Owner	Car #	Make	Laps	Winnings
1. Jack Smith	Jack Smith	47	61 Pont	250	1,000
2. Joe Weatherly	Bud Moore	8	61 Pont	249	600
3. Richard Petty	Petty Enterprises	43	62 Plym	248	400
4. Buck Baker	Buck Baker	87	62 Chrys	244	300
5. Ned Jarrett	Bee Gee Holloway	11	62 Chev	241	475

1963 Grand National Race No. 34
July 14, 1963 Average Speed: 63.384

Driver	Owner	Car #	Make	Laps	Winnings
1. Ned Jarrett	Charles Robinson	11	63 Ford	300	1,000
2. Richard Petty	Petty Enterprises	43	63 Plym	300	600
3. David Pearson	Cotton Owens	6	63 Dodg	297	400
4. Joe Weatherly	Petty Enterprises	41	63 Plym	296	500
5. Buck Baker	Buck Baker	87	63 Pont	291	275

1964 Grand National Race No. 27
May 31, 1964 Average Speed: 66.538

Driver	Owner	Car #	Make	Laps	Winnings
1. Ned Jarrett	Bondy Long	11	64 Ford	300	1,000
2. Richard Petty	Petty Enterprises	43	674 Plym	298	600
3. Marvin Panch	Wood Brothers	21	64 Ford	297	400
4. David Pearson	Cotton Owens	6	64 Dodg	293	300
5. Cale Yarborough	Herman Beam	19	64 Ford	293	275

1965 Grand National Race No. 21
May 29, 1965 Average Speed: 66.293

Driver	Owner	Car #	Make	Laps	Winnings
1. Junior Johnson	Rex Lovette	26	65 Ford	300	1,000
2. Ned Jarrett	Bondy Long	11	65 Ford	296	600
3. Dick Dixon	Dan Colone	8	63 Ford	284	400
4. J. T. Putney	Herman Beam	19	65 Chev	283	300
5. Neil Castles	Buck Baker	39	65 Olds	278	275

1966 Grand National Race No. 22 Asheville 300
June 2, 1966 Average Speed: 64.917

Driver	Owner	Car #	Make	Laps	Winnings
1. David Pearson	Cotton Owens	6	64 Dodg	300	1,000
2. J. T. Putney	J. T. Putney	19	66 Chev	299	600
3. John Sears	L. G. DeWitt	4	64 Ford	286	400
4. James Hylton	Bud Hartje	48	65 Dodg	285	300
5. Hank Thomas	W. S. Jenkins	92	64 Ford	284	275

1967 Grand National Race No. 21 Asheville 300
June 2, 1967 Average Speed: 63.080

Driver	Owner	Car #	Make	Laps	Winnings
1. Jim Paschal	Tom Friedkin	14	67 Plym	300	1,000
2. Donnie Allison	Bobby Allison	2	66 Chev	300	600
3. Richard Petty	Petty Enterprises	43	67 Plym	298	400
4. James Hylton	Bud Hartje	48	65 Dodg	297	300
5. Buddy Arrington	Buddy Arrington	67	65 Dodg	281	275

1968 Grand National Race No. 19 Asheville 300
May 31, 1968 Average Speed: 65.741

Driver	Owner	Car #	Make	Laps	Winnings
1. Richard Petty	Petty Enterprises	43	68 Plym	300	1,200
2. Buddy Baker	Ray Fox	3	67 Dodg	299	600
3. Bobby Isaac	Nord Krauskopf	71	67 Dodg	296	400
4. James Hylton	James Hylton	48	67 Dodg	292	300
5. Elmo Langley	Elmo Langley	64	66 Ford	288	275

1971 Winston Cup GN Race No. 19 Asheville 300
May 21, 1971 Average Speed: 71.231

Driver	Owner	Car #	Make	Laps	Winnings
1. Richard Petty	Petty Enterprises	43	71 Plym	300	1,500
2. Elmo Langley	Elmo Langley	64	69 Merc	296	900
3. Cecil Gordon	Cecil Gordon	24	69 Merc	284	500
4. Jabe Thomas	Don Robertson	25	69 Plym	281	350
5. Bill Champion	Bill Champion	10	69 Ford	259	325

North Carolina Motor Speedway
Rockingham, NC
1.017-mile Superspeedway

1-mile track built in 1965. Harold Brasington was consultant in track layout. First NASCAR Winston Cup (then Grand National) race run on 10/31/65 (won by Curtis Turner). Victory was the first and final win for Turner after being re-instated by NASCAR following his "lifetime" suspension for Teamster Union involvement in 1961. David Pearson also scored his 100th career victory here on 3/5/78.

Winston Cup Starts
Dave Marcis 57

Winston Cup Victories
Richard Petty 11

Winston Cup Poles
David Pearson 5
Kyle Petty 5
Cale Yarborough 5

Winston Cup Money
Kyle Petty $914,672

Most Cars Started
44—March 13, 1966 Peach Blossom 500
44—October 30, 1966 American 500
44—June 18, 1967 Carolina 500
44—October 29, 1967 American 500
44—June 16, 1968 Carolina 500
44—October 27, 1968 American 500

Fewest Cars Started
31—March 2, 1975 Carolina 500

Narrowest Margin of Victory
8 inches—March 3, 1985
Carolina 500

Slowest Race
97.860 MPH—March 13, 1977
Carolina 500

Race Record
130.748 MPH—October 25, 1992
AC Delco 500

Most Cautions
14—March 1, 1981 Carolina 500
14—October 22, 1989 AC Delco 500

Most Race Leaders
13—October 22, 1978 American 500

Most Cars Running at Finish
35—February 27, 1994
GM Goodwrench 500

1965 Grand National Race No. 54 American 500
October 31, 1965 Average Speed: 101.942

Driver	Owner	Car #	Make	Laps	Winnings
1. Curtis Turner	Wood Brothers	41	65 Ford	500	13,090
2. Cale Yarborough	Banjo Matthews	27	65 Ford	500	6,450
3. Marvin Panch	Wood Brothers	21	65 Ford	498	4,010
4. G. C. Spencer	G. C. Spencer	49	64 Ford	490	2,450
5. Jim Paschal	Petty Enterprises	42	65 Plym	486	2,000

1966 Grand National Race No. 6 Peach Blossom 500
March 13, 1966 Average Speed: 100.027

Driver	Owner	Car #	Make	Laps	Winnings
1. Paul Goldsmith	Ray Nichels	99	66 Plym	500	14,340
2. Cale Yarborough	Banjo Matthews	27	66 Ford	500	7,875
3. Bobby Allison	Betty Lilly	24	65 Ford	488	4,250
4. Harold Smith	Lyle Stelter	55	64 Ford	480	2,675
5. John Sears	L. G. DeWitt	04	64 Ford	478	1,750

1966 Grand National Race No. 49 American 500
October 30, 1966 Average Speed: 104.348

Driver	Owner	Car #	Make	Laps	Winnings
1. Fred Lorenzen	Holman-Moody	28	66 Ford	500	14,550
2. Don White	Ray Nichels	31	66 Dodg	496	7,350
3. Ned Jarrett	Banjo Matthews	11	66 Ford	496	4,700
4. Cale Yarborough	Wood Brothers	21	66 Ford	494	2,250
5. Junior Johnson	Junior Johnson	47	66 Ford	494	1,475

1967 Grand National Race No. 25 Carolina 500
June 18, 1967 Average Speed: 104.682

Driver	Owner	Car #	Make	Laps	Winnings
1. Richard Petty	Petty Enterprises	43	67 Plym	500	16,175
2. Buddy Baker	Ray Fox	3	67 Dodg	499	9,700
3. Dick Hutcherson	Bondy Long	29	67 Ford	498	5,200
4. Cale Yarborough	Wood Brothers	21	67 Ford	496	2,650
5. Darel Dieringer	Junior Johnson	26	67 Ford	494	1,875

1967 Grand National Race No. 48 American 500
October 29, 1967 Average Speed: 98.420

Driver	Owner	Car #	Make	Laps	Winnings
1. Bobby Allison	Holman-Moody	11	67 Ford	500	16,300
2. David Pearson	Holman-Moody	17	67 Ford	499	10,150
3. Paul Goldsmith	Ray Nichels	99	67 Plym	499	5,250
4. A. J. Foyt	Banjo Matthews	27	67 Ford	498	2,800
5. Gordon Johncock	Bud Moore	16	67 Merc	497	1,875

1968 Grand National Race No. 23 Carolina 500
June 16, 1968 Average Speed: 99.338

Driver	Owner	Car #	Make	Laps	Winnings
1. Donnie Allison	Banjo Matthews	27	68 Ford	500	16,675
2. Bobby Allison	Bobby Allison	2	66 Chev	498	9,650
3. James Hylton	James Hylton	48	67 Dodg	494	5,150
4. Richard Brickhouse	Dub Clewis	03	67 Plym	470	2,650
5. Roy Tyner	Don Culpepper	76	66 Ford	469	1,850

1968 Grand National Race No. 48 American 500
October 27, 1968 Average Speed: 105.060

Driver	Owner	Car #	Make	Laps	Winnings
1. Richard Petty	Petty Enterprises	43	68 Plym	500	17,075
2. David Pearson	Holman-Moody	17	68 Ford	500	9,775
3. LeeRoy Yarbrough	Junior Johnson	98	68 Ford	498	5,225
4. Tiny Lund	Bud Moore	16	68 Merc	497	2,800
5. Bobby Allison	Tom Friedkin	14	68 Plym	496	1,850

1969 Grand National Race No. 7 Carolina 500
March 9, 1969 Average Speed: 102.569

Driver	Owner	Car #	Make	Laps	Winnings
1. David Pearson	Holman-Moody	17	69 Ford	500	16,150
2. Bobby Allison	Mario Rossi	22	69 Dodg	500	9,500
3. Cale Yarborough	Wood Brothers	21	69 Merc	498	4,975
4. Paul Goldsmith	Ray Nichels	99	69 Dodg	497	2,700
5. Richard Petty	Petty Enterprises	43	69 Ford	492	1,850

1969 Grand National Race No. 51 American 500
October 26, 1969 Average Speed: 111.938

Driver	Owner	Car #	Make	Laps	Winnings
1. LeeRoy Yarbrough	Junior Johnson	98	69 Ford	492	17,600
2. David Pearson	Holman-Moody	17	69 Ford	491	10,725
3. Buddy Baker	Cotton Owens	6	69 Dodg	485	5,350
4. Dave Marcis	Milt Lunda	30	69 Dodg	472	2,850
5. John Sears	L. G. DeWitt	4	69 Ford	465	2,070

1970 Grand National Race No. 6 Carolina 500
March 8, 1970 Average Speed: 116.117

Driver	Owner	Car #	Make	Laps	Winnings
1. Richard Petty	Petty Enterprises	43	70 Plym	492	16,715
2. Cale Yarborough	Wood Brothers	21	70 Merc	489	9,890
3. Dick Brooks	Dick Brooks	32	70 Plym	484	5,265
4. Bobby Allison	Mario Rossi	22	69 Dodg	483	3,315
5. Pete Hamilton	Petty Enterprises	40	70 Plym	475	2,090

North Carolina Motor Speedway *continued*

1970 Grand National Race No. 47 American 500
November 15, 1970 Average Speed: 117.811

Driver	Owner	Car #	Make	Laps	Winnings
1. Cale Yarborough	Wood Brothers	21	69 Merc	492	20,445
2. David Pearson	Holman-Moody	17	69 Ford	492	11,170
3. Bobby Allison	Mario Rossi	22	69 Dodg	489	6,195
4. Donnie Allison	Banjo Matthews	27	69 Ford	486	3,045
5. Buddy Baker	Cotton Owens	6	69 Dodg	485	2,190

1971 Winston Cup GN Race No. 44 American 500
October 24, 1971 Average Speed: 113.405

Driver	Owner	Car #	Make	Laps	Winnings
1. Richard Petty	Petty Enterprises	43	71 Plym	492	17,120
2. Buddy Baker	Petty Enterprises	11	71 Dodg	492	9,745
3. Bobby Allison	Holman-Moody	12	71 Merc	488	6,320
4. Pete Hamilton	Cotton Owens	6	71 Plym	487	4,195
5. Bobby Isaac	Nord Krauskopf	71	71 Dodg	483	3,920

1972 Winston Cup GN Race No. 30 American 500
October 22, 1972 Average Speed: 118.275

Driver	Owner	Car #	Make	Laps	Winnings
1. Bobby Allison	R. Howard & J. Johnson	12	72 Chev	492	19,400
2. Richard Petty	Petty Enterprises	43	72 Plym	490	12,050
3. Buddy Baker	Nord Krauskopf	71	72 Dodg	489	8,425
4. David Pearson	Wood Brothers	21	71 Merc	488	5,400
5. Pete Hamilton	Jack Housby	9	72 Plym	486	3,850

1973 Winston Cup GN Race No. 28 American 500
October 21, 1973 Average Speed: 117.749

Driver	Owner	Car #	Make	Laps	Winnings
1. David Pearson	Wood Brothers	21	71 Merc	492	16,795
2. Buddy Baker	Nord Krauskopf	71	73 Dodg	491	11,050
3. Cale Yarborough	R. Howard & J. Johnson	11	73 Chev	491	7,925
4. Bobby Allison	Bobby Allison	12	73 Chev	488	6,525
5. Dave Marcis	Roger Penske	2	73 Mata	484	4,175

1974 Winston Cup GN Race No. 29 American 500
October 20, 1974 Average Speed: 118.493

Driver	Owner	Car #	Make	Laps	Winnings
1. David Pearson	Wood Brothers	21	73 Merc	492	16,350
2. Cale Yarborough	Junior Johnson	11	74 Chev	492	11,925
3. Richard Petty	Petty Enterprises	43	74 Dodg	490	9,725
4. Bobby Allison	Roger Penske	12	74 Mata	487	4,600
5. Darrell Waltrip	Darrell Waltrip	95	72 Chev	487	4,200

1975 Winston Cup GN Race No. 27 American 500
October 19, 1975 Average Speed: 120.129

Driver	Owner	Car #	Make	Laps	Winnings
1. Cale Yarborough	Junior Johnson	11	75 Chev	492	19,930
2. Bobby Allison	Roger Penske	16	75 Mata	492	10,355
3. Dave Marcis	Nord Krauskopf	71	74 Dodg	491	11,505
4. Lennie Pond	Ronnie Elder	54	75 Chev	488	5,580
5. A. J. Foyt	Hoss Ellington	28	75 Chev	487	4,530

1976 Winston Cup GN Race No. 28 American 500
October 24, 1976 Average Speed: 117.718

Driver	Owner	Car #	Make	Laps	Winnings
1. Richard Petty	Petty Enterprises	43	Dodg	492	20,395
2. Lennie Pond	Ronnie Elder	54	Chev	491	12,870
3. Darrell Waltrip	DiGard	88	Chev	489	10,075
4. Bobby Allison	Roger Penske	2	Merc	489	7,965
5. Cale Yarborough	Junior Johnson	11	Chev	488	7,255

1971 Winston Cup GN Race No. 7 Carolina 500
March 14, 1971 Average Speed: 118.696

Driver	Owner	Car #	Make	Laps	Winnings
1. Richard Petty	Petty Enterprises	43	71 Plym	492	17,315
2. Bobby Isaac	Nord Krauskopf	71	71 Dodg	492	11,240
3. Buddy Baker	Petty Enterprises	11	71 Dodg	492	5,065
4. Fred Lorenzen	Ray Nichels	99	71 Plym	488	3,815
5. Dick Brooks	Mario Rossi	22	69 Dodg	488	1,875

1972 Winston Cup GN Race No. 5 Carolina 500
March 12, 1972 Average Speed: 113.895

Driver	Owner	Car #	Make	Laps	Winnings
1. Bobby Isaac	Nord Krauskopf	71	72 Dodg	492	17,250
2. Richard Petty	Petty Enterprises	43	72 Plym	491	11,825
3. Jim Vandiver	O. L. Nixon	31	70 Dodg	491	5,550
4. LeeRoy Yarbrough	Bill Seifert	45	71 Ford	477	6,250
5. Dave Marcis	Dave Marcis	2	70 Dodg	477	3,300

1973 Winston Cup GN Race No. 4 Carolina 500
March 18, 1973 Average Speed: 118.649

Driver	Owner	Car #	Make	Laps	Winnings
1. David Pearson	Wood Brothers	21	71 Merc	492	15,475
2. Cale Yarborough	R. Howard & J. Johnson	11	73 Chev	492	10,125
3. Buddy Baker	Nord Krauskopf	71	73 Dodg	491	7,325
4. Bobby Allison	Bobby Allison	12	73 Chev	490	6,000
5. Dick Brooks	Junie Donlavey	90	72 Ford	486	3,600

1974 Winston Cup GN Race No. 4 Carolina 500
March 3, 1974 Average Speed: 121.622

Driver	Owner	Car #	Make	Laps	Winnings
1. Richard Petty	Petty Enterprises	43	74 Dodg	492	18,025
2. Cale Yarborough	R. Howard & J. Johnson	11	74 Chev	491	11,600
3. Bobby Allison	Bobby Allison	12	74 Chev	486	8,400
4. Charlie Glotzbach	Hoss Ellington	28	74 Chev	483	4,125
5. George Follmer	Bud Moore	15	73 Ford	483	6,475

1975 Winston Cup GN Race No. 4 Carolina 500
March 2, 1975 Average Speed: 117.588

Driver	Owner	Car #	Make	Laps	Winnings
1. Cale Yarborough	Junior Johnson	11	75 Chev	492	17,200
2. David Pearson	Wood Brothers	21	73 Merc	492	10,815
3. Richard Petty	Petty Enterprises	43	74 Dodg	483	10,925
4. Dick Brooks	Junie Donlavey	90	73 Ford	478	5,200
5. Bruce Hill	Bruce Hill	47	75 Chev	465	3,950

1976 Winston Cup GN Race No. 3 Carolina 500
February 29, 1976 Average Speed: 113.665

Driver	Owner	Car #	Make	Laps	Winnings
1. Richard Petty	Petty Enterprises	43	Dodg	492	19,915
2. Darrell Waltrip	DiGard	88	Chev	490	14,055
3. Cale Yarborough	Junior Johnson	11	Chev	490	10,665
4. Buddy Baker	Bud Moore	15	Ford	487	8,250
5. Benny Parsons	L. G. DeWitt	72	Chev	477	7,190

1977 Winston Cup GN Race No. 4 Carolina 500
March 13, 1977 Average Speed: 97.860

Driver	Owner	Car #	Make	Laps	Winnings
1. Richard Petty	Petty Enterprises	43	Dodg	492	18,594
2. Darrell Waltrip	DiGard	88	Chev	492	14,170
3. Donnie Allison	Hoss Ellington	1	Chev	491	8,520
4. Buddy Baker	Bud Moore	15	Ford	491	7,770
5. Neil Bonnett	Nord Krauskopf	71	Dodg	488	7,070

North Carolina Motor Speedway *continued*

1977 Winston Cup GN Race No. 28 American 500
October 23, 1977 Average Speed: 113.584

Driver	Owner	Car #	Make	Laps	Winnings
1. Donnie Allison	Hoss Ellington	1	Chev	492	17,135
2. Richard Petty	Petty Enterprises	43	Dodg	492	14,350
3. Darrell Waltrip	DiGard	88	Chev	492	10,800
4. Cale Yarborough	Junior Johnson	11	Chev	490	9,550
5. Dick Brooks	Junie Donlavey	90	Ford	489	6,250

1978 Winston Cup GN Race No. 28 American 500
October 22, 1978 Average Speed: 117.288

Driver	Owner	Car #	Make	Laps	Winnings
1. Cale Yarborough	Junior Johnson	11	Olds	492	23,360
2. Bobby Allison	Bud Moore	15	Ford	490	14,650
3. Darrell Waltrip	DiGard	88	Chev	488	11,400
4. Benny Parsons	L. G. DeWitt	72	Chev	486	8,500
5. Dick Brooks	Junie Donlavey	90	Ford	486	6,330

1979 Winston Cup GN Race No. 29 American 500
October 21, 1979 Average Speed: 108.356

Driver	Owner	Car #	Make	Laps	Winnings
1. Richard Petty	Petty Enterprises	43	Chev	492	20,960
2. Benny Parsons	M. C. Anderson	27	Chev	492	15,950
3. Cale Yarborough	Junior Johnson	11	Chev	492	11,800
4. Donnie Allison	Hoss Ellington	1	Chev	490	5,000
5. Dale Earnhardt	Rod Osterlund	2	Chev	488	8,300

1980 Winston Cup GN Race No. 29 American 500
October 19, 1980 Average Speed: 114.159

Driver	Owner	Car #	Make	Laps	Winnings
1. Cale Yarborough	Junior Johnson	11	Chev	492	20,160
2. Harry Gant	Jack Beebe	47	Chev	492	14,030
3. Darrell Waltrip	DiGard	88	Chev	490	12,700
4. Terry Labonte	Billy Hagan	44	Chev	487	9,400
5. Jody Ridley	Junie Donlavey	90	Ford	486	7,030

1981 Winston Cup GN Race No. 29 American 500
November 1, 1981 Average Speed: 107.399

Driver	Owner	Car #	Make	Laps	Winnings
1. Darrell Waltrip	Junior Johnson	11	Buick	492	23,410
2. Bobby Allison	Harry Ranier	28	Buick	492	17,100
3. Harry Gant	Hal Needham	33	Pont	492	10,150
4. Richard Petty	Petty Enterprises	43	Buick	492	10,400
5. Joe Ruttman	Jim Stacy	2	Pont	492	9,700

1982 Winston Cup GN Race No. 28 Warner W. Hodgdon American 500
October 31, 1982 Average Speed: 115.122

Driver	Owner	Car #	Make	Laps	Winnings
1. Darrell Waltrip	Junior Johnson	11	Buick	492	26,610
2. Bobby Allison	DiGard	88	Chev	492	20,100
3. Neil Bonnett	Wood Brothers	21	Ford	492	8,100
4. Terry Labonte	Billy Hagan	44	Buick	491	8,480
5. Morgan Shepherd	Ron Benfield	98	Buick	491	7,455

1983 Winston Cup GN Race No. 28 Warner W. Hodgdon American 500
October 30, 1983 Average Speed: 119.324

Driver	Owner	Car #	Make	Laps	Winnings
1. Terry Labonte	Billy Hagan	44	Chev	492	25,505
2. Tim Richmond	Raymond Beadle	27	Pont	492	18,490
3. Ricky Rudd	Richard Childress	3	Chev	491	11,370
4. Neil Bonnett	Bob Rahilly & Butch Mock	75	Chev	490	13,410
5. Darrell Waltrip	Junior Johnson	11	Chev	489	14,335

1978 Winston Cup GN Race No. 4 Carolina 500
March 5, 1978 Average Speed: 116.681

Driver	Owner	Car #	Make	Laps	Winnings
1. David Pearson	Wood Brothers	21	Merc	492	16,665
2. Bobby Allison	Bud Moore	15	Ford	492	14,570
3. Benny Parsons	L. G. DeWitt	72	Chev	492	11,220
4. Richard Petty	Petty Enterprises	43	Dodg	490	8,470
5. Lennie Pond	Harry Ranier	54	Chev	489	3,920

1979 Winston Cup GN Race No. 3 Carolina 500
March 4, 1979 Average Speed: 122.727

Driver	Owner	Car #	Make	Laps	Winnings
1. Bobby Allison	Bud Moore	15	Ford	492	21,555
2. Joe Millikan	L. G. DeWitt	72	Chev	491	15,670
3. Dick Brooks	Nelson Malloch	05	Olds	487	8,220
4. Tighe Scott	Walter Ballard	30	Buick	485	7,520
5. Richard Childress	Richard Childress	3	Chev	484	6,320

1980 Winston Cup GN Race No. 4 Carolina 500
March 9, 1980 Average Speed: 108.735

Driver	Owner	Car #	Make	Laps	Winnings
1. Cale Yarborough	Junior Johnson	11	Olds	492	19,280
2. Richard Petty	Petty Enterprises	43	Chev	492	18,720
3. Dale Earnhardt	Rod Osterlund	2	Chev	491	14,420
4. Darrell Waltrip	DiGard	88	Chev	491	11,270
5. Donnie Allison	Hoss Ellington	1	Chev	491	6,750

1981 Winston Cup GN Race No. 4 Carolina 500
March 1, 1981 Average Speed: 114.594

Driver	Owner	Car #	Make	Laps	Winnings
1. Darrell Waltrip	Junior Johnson	11	Buick	492	21,655
2. Cale Yarborough	M. C. Anderson	27	Buick	492	12,370
3. Richard Petty	Petty Enterprises	43	Buick	492	14,370
4. Neil Bonnett	Wood Brothers	21	Ford	492	6,920
5. Buddy Baker	Hoss Ellington	1	Olds	491	3,895

1982 Winston Cup GN Race No. 5 Warner W. Hodgdon Carolina 500
March 28, 1982 Average Speed: 108.992

Driver	Owner	Car #	Make	Laps	Winnings
1. Cale Yarborough	M. C. Anderson	27	Buick	492	17,360
2. Terry Labonte	Billy Hagan	44	Chev	491	13,705
3. Benny Parsons	Harry Ranier	28	Pont	491	17,300
4. Bobby Allison	DiGard	88	Chev	491	10,825
5. Morgan Shepherd	Ron Benfield	98	Buick	489	4,825

1983 Winston Cup GN Race No. 3 Warner W. Hodgdon Carolina 500
March 13, 1983 Average Speed: 113.055

Driver	Owner	Car #	Make	Laps	Winnings
1. Richard Petty	Petty Enterprises	43	Pont	492	24,150
2. Bill Elliott	Harry Melling	9	Ford	492	14,990
3. Darrell Waltrip	Junior Johnson	11	Chev	492	17,760
4. Lake Speed	Hoss Ellington	1	Chev	489	5,110
5. Harry Gant	Hal Needham	33	Buick	489	12,335

1984 Winston Cup GN Race No. 3 Warner W. Hodgdon Carolina 500
March 4, 1984 Average Speed: 122.931

Driver	Owner	Car #	Make	Laps	Winnings
1. Bobby Allison	DiGard	22	Buick	492	33,150
2. Terry Labonte	Billy Hagan	44	Chev	492	17,830
3. Lake Speed	Hoss Ellington	1	Chev	492	13,015
4. Richard Petty	Mike Curb	43	Pont	491	5,545
5. Buddy Baker	Wood Brothers	21	Ford	488	6,875

North Carolina Motor Speedway *continued*

1984 Winston Cup GN Race No. 28 Warner W. Hodgdon American 500
October 21, 1984 Average Speed: 112.617

Driver	Owner	Car #	Make	Laps	Winnings
1. Bill Elliott	Harry Melling	9	Ford	492	30,400
2. Harry Gant	Hal Needham	33	Chev	492	20,230
3. Terry Labonte	Billy Hagan	44	Chev	492	13,115
4. Darrell Waltrip	Junior Johnson	11	Chev	492	13,845
5. Bobby Allison	DiGard	22	Buick	491	15,625

1985 Winston Cup GN Race No. 26 Nationwise 500
October 20, 1985 Average Speed: 118.344

Driver	Owner	Car #	Make	Laps	Winnings
1. Darrell Waltrip	Junior Johnson	11	Chev	492	40,900
2. Ron Bouchard	Jack Beebe	47	Buick	492	21,055
3. Harry Gant	Hal Needham	33	Chev	492	20,900
4. Bill Elliott	Harry Melling	9	Ford	492	15,675
5. Geoff Bodine	Rick Hendrick	5	Chev	492	14,400

1986 Winston Cup Race No. 27 Nationwise 500
October 19, 1986 Average Speed: 126.381

Driver	Owner	Car #	Make	Laps	Winnings
1. Neil Bonnett	Junior Johnson	12	Chev	492	47,000
2. Ricky Rudd	Bud Moore	15	Ford	492	26,550
3. Darrell Waltrip	Junior Johnson	11	Chev	492	23,650
4. Harry Gant	Hal Needham	33	Chev	492	16,525
5. Buddy Baker	Buddy Baker & Danny Schiff	88	Olds	492	8,575

1987 Winston Cup Race No. 27 AC Delco 500
October 25, 1987 Average Speed: 118.258

Driver	Owner	Car #	Make	Laps	Winnings
1. Bill Elliott	Harry Melling	9	Ford	492	50,025
2. Dale Earnhardt	Richard Childress	3	Chev	492	38,915
3. Darrell Waltrip	Rick Hendrick	17	Chev	492	16,690
4. Terry Labonte	Junior Johnson	11	Chev	492	19,315
5. Morgan Shepherd	Kenny Bernstein	26	Buick	492	16,160

1988 Winston Cup Race No. 27 AC Delco 500
October 23, 1988 Average Speed: 111.557

Driver	Owner	Car #	Make	Laps	Winnings
1. Rusty Wallace	Raymond Beadle	27	Pont	492	52,150
2. Ricky Rudd	Kenny Bernstein	26	Buick	492	26,985
3. Terry Labonte	Junior Johnson	11	Chev	492	25,095
4. Bill Elliott	Harry Melling	9	Ford	491	23,480
5. Dale Earnhardt	Richard Childress	3	Chev	491	27,965

1989 Winston Cup Race No. 27 AC Delco 500
October 22, 1989 Average Speed: 114.079

Driver	Owner	Car #	Make	Laps	Winnings
1. Mark Martin	Jack Roush	6	Ford	492	52,800
2. Rusty Wallace	Raymond Beadle	27	Pont	492	33,675
3. Darrell Waltrip	Rick Hendrick	17	Chev	492	32,225
4. Ken Schrader	Rick Hendrick	25	Chev	491	16,725
5. Dick Trickle	Stavola Brothers	84	Buick	491	15,250

1990 Winston Cup Series Race No. 27 AC Delco 500
October 21, 1990 Average Speed: 126.452

Driver	Owner	Car #	Make	Laps	Winnings
1. Alan Kulwicki	Alan Kulwicki	7	Ford	492	53,300
2. Bill Elliott	Harry Melling	9	Ford	492	40,775
3. Harry Gant	Leo Jackson	33	Olds	492	23,575
4. Geoff Bodine	Junior Johnson	11	Ford	492	23,625
5. Ken Schrader	Rick Hendrick	25	Chev	492	26,025

1985 Winston Cup GN Race No. 3 Carolina 500
March 3, 1985 Average Speed: 114.953

Driver	Owner	Car #	Make	Laps	Winnings
1. Neil Bonnett	Junior Johnson	12	Chev	492	35,505
2. Harry Gant	Hal Needham	33	Chev	492	26,330
3. Terry Labonte	Billy Hagan	44	Chev	492	23,310
4. Lake Speed	Bob Rahilly & Butch Mock	75	Pont	492	11,360
5. Kyle Petty	Wood Brothers	7	Ford	491	10,520

1986 Winston Cup Race No. 3 Goodwrench 500
March 2, 1986 Average Speed: 120.488

Driver	Owner	Car #	Make	Laps	Winnings
1. Terry Labonte	Billy Hagan	44	Olds	492	44,550
2. Harry Gant	Hal Needham	33	Chev	492	28,110
3. Richard Petty	Petty Enterprises	43	Pont	492	15,970
4. Morgan Shepherd	Jack Beebe	47	Buick	491	9,255
5. Darrell Waltrip	Junior Johnson	11	Chev	491	18,615

1987 Winston Cup Race No. 2 Goodwrench 500
March 1, 1987 Average Speed: 117.556

Driver	Owner	Car #	Make	Laps	Winnings
1. Dale Earnhardt	Richard Childress	3	Chev	492	53,900
2. Ricky Rudd	Bud Moore	15	Ford	492	28,135
3. Neil Bonnett	Bob Rahilly & Butch Mock	75	Pont	492	17,875
4. Bill Elliott	Harry Melling	9	Ford	492	17,405
5. Morgan Shepherd	Kenny Bernstein	26	Buick	491	12,010

1988 Winston Cup Race No. 3 Goodwrench 500
March 6, 1988 Average Speed: 120.159

Driver	Owner	Car #	Make	Laps	Winnings
1. Neil Bonnett	Bob Rahilly & Butch Mock	75	Pont	492	45,800
2. Lake Speed	Lake Speed	83	Olds	492	22,310
3. Sterling Marlin	Billy Hagan	44	Olds	492	19,195
4. Alan Kulwicki	Alan Kulwicki	7	Ford	492	14,330
5. Dale Earnhardt	Richard Childress	3	Chev	492	19,865

1989 Winston Cup Race No. 2 Goodwrench 500
March 5, 1989 Average Speed: 115.122

Driver	Owner	Car #	Make	Laps	Winnings
1. Rusty Wallace	Raymond Beadle	27	Pont	492	72,100
2. Alan Kulwicki	Alan Kulwicki	7	Ford	492	29,600
3. Dale Earnhardt	Richard Childress	3	Chev	492	24,200
4. Geoff Bodine	Rick Hendrick	5	Chev	492	17,975
5. Mark Martin	Jack Roush	6	Ford	492	15,963

1990 Winston Cup Series Race No. 3 GM Goodwrench 500
March 4, 1990 Average Speed: 122.864

Driver	Owner	Car #	Make	Laps	Winnings
1. Kyle Petty	Felix Sabates	42	Pont	492	284,450
2. Geoff Bodine	Junior Johnson	11	Ford	492	31,825
3. Ken Schrader	Rick Hendrick	25	Chev	491	24,575
4. Sterling Marlin	Billy Hagan	94	Olds	490	17,725
5. Rusty Wallace	Raymond Beadle	27	Pont	490	21,625

1991 Winston Cup Series Race No. 3 GM Goodwrench 500
March 3, 1991 Average Speed: 124.083

Driver	Owner	Car #	Make	Laps	Winnings
1. Kyle Petty	Felix Sabates	42	Pont	492	131,450
2. Ken Schrader	Rick Hendrick	25	Chev	492	34,575
3. Harry Gant	Leo Jackson	33	Olds	491	23,950
4. Ricky Rudd	Rick Hendrick	5	Chev	491	20,250
5. Bill Elliott	Harry Melling	9	Ford	491	21,275

North Carolina Motor Speedway *continued*

1991 Winston Cup Series Race No. 27 AC Delco 500
October 20, 1991 Average Speed: 127.292

Driver	Owner	Car #	Make	Laps	Winnings
1. Davey Allison	Robert Yates	28	Ford	492	66,050
2. Harry Gant	Leo Jackson	33	Olds	492	34,675
3. Mark Martin	Jack Roush	6	Ford	492	29,350
4. Geoff Bodine	Junior Johnson	11	Ford	492	26,450
5. Ken Schrader	Rick Hendrick	25	Chev	491	17,325

1992 Winston Cup Race No. 2 GM Goodwrench 500
March 1, 1992 Average Speed: 126.125

Driver	Owner	Car #	Make	Laps	Winnings
1. Bill Elliott	Junior Johnson	11	Ford	492	57,800
2. Davey Allison	Robert Yates	28	Ford	492	48,875
3. Harry Gant	Leo Jackson	33	Olds	492	31,600
4. Michael Waltrip	Chuck Rider	30	Pont	491	18,650
5. Ken Schrader	Rick Hendrick	25	Chev	491	21,650

1992 Winston Cup Race No. 27 AC Delco 500
October 25, 1992 Average Speed: 130.748

Driver	Owner	Car #	Make	Laps	Winnings
1. Kyle Petty	Felix Sabates	42	Pont	492	153,100
2. Ernie Irvan	Larry McClure	4	Chev	492	31,225
3. Ricky Rudd	Rick Hendrick	5	Chev	491	31,225
4. Bill Elliott	Junior Johnson	11	Ford	491	26,200
5. Sterling Marlin	Junior Johnson	22	Ford	491	20,075

1993 Winston Cup Series Race No. 2 GM Goodwrench 500
February 28, 1993 Average Speed: 124.486

Driver	Owner	Car #	Make	Laps	Winnings
1. Rusty Wallace	Roger Penske	2	Pont	492	42,735
2. Dale Earnhardt	Richard Childress	3	Chev	492	47,585
3. Ernie Irvan	Larry McClure	4	Chev	492	33,785
4. Alan Kulwicki	Alan Kulwicki	7	Ford	492	28,085
5. Mark Martin	Jack Roush	6	Ford	492	29,160

1993 Winston Cup Series Race No. 28 AC Delco 500
October 24, 1993 Average Speed: 114.036

Driver	Owner	Car #	Make	Laps	Winnings
1. Rusty Wallace	Roger Penske	2	Pont	492	52,850
2. Dale Earnhardt	Richard Childress	3	Chev	492	49,550
3. Bill Elliott	Junior Johnson	11	Ford	492	35,675
4. Harry Gant	Leo Jackson	33	Chev	492	29,225
5. Mark Martin	Jack Roush	6	Ford	491	33,150

1994 Winston Cup Series Race No. 2 GM Goodwrench 500
February 27, 1994 Average Speed: 125.239

Driver	Owner	Car #	Make	Laps	Winnings
1. Rusty Wallace	Roger Penske	2	Ford	492	52,885
2. Sterling Marlin	Larry McClure	4	Chev	492	48,935
3. Rick Mast	Richard Jackson	1	Ford	492	31,085
4. Mark Martin	Jack Roush	6	Ford	491	28,986
5. Ernie Irvan	Robert Yates	28	Ford	491	26,410

1994 Winston Cup Series Race No. 29 AC Delco 500
October 23, 1994 Average Speed: 126.408

Driver	Owner	Car #	Make	Laps	Winnings
1. Dale Earnhardt	Richard Childress	3	Chev	492	60,600
2. Rick Mast	Richard Jackson	1	Ford	492	45,425
3. Morgan Shepherd	Wood Brothers	21	Ford	492	32,100
4. Ricky Rudd	Ricky Rudd	10	Ford	492	28,076
5. Terry Labonte	Rick Hendrick	5	Chev	492	28,750

1995 Winston Cup Series Race No. 2 GM Goodwrench 500
February 26, 1995 Average Speed: 125.305

Driver	Owner	Car #	Make	Laps	Winnings
1. Jeff Gordon	Rick Hendrick	24	Chev	492	167,600
2. Bobby Labonte	Joe Gibbs	18	Chev	492	61,350
3. Dale Earnhardt	Richard Childress	3	Chev	492	40,740
4. Ricky Rudd	Ricky Rudd	10	Ford	492	33,480
5. Dale Jarrett	Robert Yates	28	Ford	491	34,075

1995 Winston Cup Series Race No. 29 AC Delco 500
October 22, 1995 Average Speed: 114.778

Driver	Owner	Car #	Make	Laps	Winnings
1. Ward Burton	Bill Davis	22	Pont	393	70,250
2. Rusty Wallace	Roger Penske	2	Ford	393	50,050
3. Mark Martin	Jack Roush	6	Ford	393	44,850
4. Terry Labonte	Rick Hendrick	5	Chev	393	34,925
5. Jeff Burton	Stavola Brothers	8	Ford	393	40,325

1996 Winston Cup Series Race No. 2 Goodwrench Service 400
February 25, 1996 Average Speed: 113.959

Driver	Owner	Car #	Make	Laps	Winnings
1. Dale Earnhardt	Richard Childress	3	Chev	393	83,840
2. Dale Jarrett	Robert Yates	88	Ford	393	48,960
3. Ricky Craven	Larry Hedrick	41	Chev	393	47,760
4. Ricky Rudd	Ricky Rudd	10	Ford	393	35,810
5. Steve Grissom	Gary Bechtel	29	Chev	393	31,475

1996 Winston Cup Series Race No. 29 AC Delco 400
October 20, 1996 Average Speed: 122.320

Driver	Owner	Car #	Make	Laps	Winnings
1. Ricky Rudd	Ricky Rudd	10	Ford	393	90,025
2. Dale Jarrett	Robert Yates	88	Ford	393	62,125
3. Terry Labonte	Rick Hendrick	5	Chev	393	46,725
4. Ernie Irvan	Robert Yates	28	Ford	393	35,950
5. Jeff Burton	Jack Roush	99	Ford	393	25,675

North Carolina State Fairgrounds
Raleigh, NC
Half-mile Dirt Track

(aka Raleigh Speedway; State Fair Speedway) Originally a 1-mile dirt track built circa 1926. Half-mile dirt track built in 1940 and re-opened in October 1946. First NASCAR Winston Cup (then Grand National) race staged on 5/28/55 (won by Junior Johnson). Final Grand National race run on 9/30/70 (won by Richard Petty). Track hosted the final Winston Cup (then Grand National) race on a dirt track. Petty won in a Plymouth owned by Don Robertson. Track closed after 1970 Grand National event.

Winston Cup Starts
14 drivers tied with 2

Winston Cup Victories

Junior Johnson	1
David Pearson	1
Richard Petty	1

Winston Cup Poles

Tim Flock	1
Bobby Isaac	1
John Sears	1

Winston Cup Money
Richard Petty $1,600

Most Cars Started
27—May 28, 1955

Fewest Cars Started
23—Sept . 30, 1970 Home State 200

Narrowest Margin of Victory
1 lap plus—May 28, 1955

Slowest Race
50.522 MPH—May 28, 1955

Race Record
68.376 MPH—Sept . 30, 1970
Home State 200

Most Cautions
6—May 28, 1955

Most Race Leaders
3—Sept . 30, 1970 Home State 200

Most Cars Running at Finish
18—May 28, 1955

1955 Grand National Race No. 17
May 28, 1955 Average Speed: 50.522

Driver	Owner	Car #	Make	Laps	Winnings
1. Junior Johnson	B & L Motors	55	55 Olds	172	1,350
2. Fonty Flock	Carl Kiekhaefer	301	55 Chrys	171	875
3. Buck Baker	Griffin Motors	87	54 Olds	171	550
4. Lee Petty	Petty Enterprises	42	55 Chrys	170	400
5. Gwyn Staley	Hubert Westmoreland	2	55 Chev	167	315

1969 Grand National Race No. 27 North State 200
June 26, 1969 Average Speed: 65.418

Driver	Owner	Car #	Make	Laps	Winnings
1. David Pearson	Holman-Moody	17	69 Ford	200	1,200
2. Richard Petty	Petty Enterprises	43	69 Ford	197	600
3. James Hylton	James Hylton	48	67 Dodg	189	400
4. John Sears	L. G. DeWitt	4	67 Ford	184	350
5. Elmo Langley	Elmo Langley	64	68 Ford	183	325

1970 Grand National Race No. 42 Home State 200 Sept . 30, 1970
Average Speed: 68.376

Driver	Owner	Car #	Make	Laps	Winnings
1. Richard Petty	Don Robertson	43	69 Plym	200	1,000
2. Neil Castles	Neil Castles	06	69 Dodg	198	600
3. Bobby Isaac	Nord Krauskopf	71	69 Dodg	195	400
4. James Hylton	James Hylton	48	70 Ford	193	350
5. Cecil Gordon	Cecil Gordon	97	68 Ford	186	325

North Wilkesboro Speedway
North Wilkesboro, NC
.625-mile Short Track

.625-mile dirt track opened in May 1947. First NASCAR Winston Cup (then Strictly Stock) race held on 10/16/49 (won by Bob Flock). Event was the finale for the 1949 season. Track paved in 1957, and the Winston Cup race staged here on 9/29/96 was likely the last race ever run here. The track was purchased by Bruton Smith and Bob Bahre, and annual events have been shifted to the new Texas Motor Speedway and New Hampshire Int'l Speedway for the 1997 season. It is uncertain what the future holds for this track.

Winston Cup Starts
Richard Petty   66

Winston Cup Victories
Richard Petty   15

Winston Cup Poles
Darrell Waltrip   9

Winston Cup Money
Dale Earnhardt $853,685

Most Cars Started
38—April 29, 1951

Fewest Cars Started
20—April 7, 1957

Narrowest Margin of Victory
3 feet—April 3, 1955

Slowest Race
53.364 MPH—October 16, 1949

Race Record
107.360 MPH—October 5, 1992
Tyson/Holly Farms 400

Most Cautions
17—April 21, 1991 First Union 400

Most Race Leaders
13—October 1, 1995
Tyson/Holly Farms 400

Most Cars Running at Finish
37—September 29, 1996
Tyson/Holly Farms 400

1949 Strictly Stock Race No. 8
October 16, 1949 Average Speed: 53.364

Driver	Owner	Car #	Make	Laps	Winnings
1. Bob Flock	Frank Christian	7	49 Olds	200	1,500
2. Lee Petty	Petty Enterprises	42	49 Plym	200	750
3. Fonty Flock	Ed Lawrence	47	47 Buick	199	400
4. Clyde Minter	Clyde Minter	19	47 Ford	199	300
5. Herb Thomas	Herb Thomas	92	49 Ford	197	175

1950 Grand National Race No. 15
September 24, 1950

Driver	Owner	Car #	Make	Laps	Winnings
1. Leon Sales	Hubert Westmoreland	98	50 Plym	200	1,000
2. Jack Smith	Bishop Brothers		50 Plym	—	600
3. Ewell Weddle	Ewell Weddle	78	49 Linc	—	400
4. Herb Thomas	Herb Thomas	92	50 Plym	—	300
5. Gayle Warren		44	50 Plym	—	225

1951 Grand National Race No. 7
April 29, 1951

Driver	Owner	Car #	Make	Laps	Winnings
1. Fonty Flock	Frank Christian	14	50 Olds	150	1,000
2. Tim Flock	Ted Chester	91	51 Olds	—	600
3. Lee Petty	Petty Enterprises	42	49 Plym	—	400
4. Bill Holland	Hubert Westmoreland	98	50 Plym	—	300
5. Donald Thomas	Herb Thomas	93	50 Plym	—	250

1951 Grand National Race No. 36
October 21, 1951 Average Speed: 67.791

Driver	Owner	Car #	Make	Laps	Winnings
1. Fonty Flock	Ted Chester	7	51 Olds	200	1,000
2. Lee Petty	Petty Enterprises	42	51 Plym	—	600
3. Joe Eubanks	Phil Oates	82	50 Olds	—	500
4. Tim Flock	Ted Chester	91	51 Olds	—	400
5. Cotton Owens	Cotton Owens	71	51 Stud	—	300

1952 Grand National Race No. 4
March 30, 1952 Average Speed: 58.597

Driver	Owner	Car #	Make	Laps	Winnings
1. Herb Thomas	Herb Thomas	92	52 Huds	200	1,000
2. Fonty Flock	Frank Christian	14	51 Olds	199	700
3. Bill Blair	George Hutchens	2	52 Olds	—	450
4. Donald Thomas	Doug Meeks	72	51 Ford	—	350
5. Dave Terrell	Dave Terrell	126	51 Plym	—	200

1952 Grand National Race No. 32
October 26, 1952 Average Speed: 67.044

Driver	Owner	Car #	Make	Laps	Winnings
1. Herb Thomas	Herb Thomas	9	52 Huds	200	1,000
2. Fonty Flock	Frank Christian	14	52 Olds	200	700
3. Donald Thomas	Herb Thomas	92	52 Huds	200	450
4. Tim Flock	Ted Chester	91	51 Huds	199	350
5. Dick Rathmann	Walt Chapman	120	52 Huds	194	200

1953 Grand National Race No. 4
March 29, 1953 Average Speed: 71.907

Driver	Owner	Car #	Make	Laps	Winnings
1. Herb Thomas	Herb Thomas	92	53 Huds	200	1,000
2. Dick Rathmann	Walt Chapman	120	53 Huds	200	700
3. Fonty Flock	Frank Christian	14	53 Olds	—	450
4. Lee Petty	Petty Enterprises	42	53 Dodg	—	350
5. Jimmie Lewallen	Dave Quate	43	53 Dodg	—	200

1953 Grand National Race No. 35
October 11, 1953 Average Speed: 71.202

Driver	Owner	Car #	Make	Laps	Winnings
1. Speedy Thompson	Buckshot Morris	12	53 Olds	160	1,000
2. Fonty Flock	Frank Christian	14	53 Huds	158	700
3. Ray Duhigg	J. H. Petty	44	52 Plym	156	450
4. Bob Welborn	J. O. Goode	24	51 Plym	156	350
5. Lee Petty	Petty Enterprises	42	53 Dodg	155	200

1954 Grand National Race No. 7
April 4, 1954 Average Speed: 68.545

Driver	Owner	Car #	Make	Laps	Winnings
1. Dick Rathmann	John Ditz	3	54 Huds	160	1,000
2. Herb Thomas	Herb Thomas	92	54 Huds	160	650
3. Joe Eubanks	Phil Oates	82	51 Huds	160	450
4. Curtis Turner	Frank Christian	14	52 Olds	158	350
5. Lee Petty	Petty Enterprises	42	54 Dodg	156	300

1954 Grand National Race No. 37
October 24, 1954 Average Speed: 65.175

Driver	Owner	Car #	Make	Laps	Winnings
1. Hershel McGriff	Frank Christian	14	54 Olds	157	1,000
2. Buck Baker	Griffin Motors	87	54 Olds	157	650
3. Herb Thomas	Herb Thomas	92	54 Huds	157	450
4. Slick Smith	Frank Christian	143	51 Olds	156	350
5. Dick Rathmann	John Ditz	3	54 Huds	156	300

North Wilkesboro Speedway *continued*

1955 Grand National Race No. 8
April 3, 1955 Average Speed: 73.126

Driver	Owner	Car #	Make	Laps	Winnings
1. Buck Baker	Griffin Motors	87	54 Olds	160	1,000
2. Dick Rathmann	John Ditz	3	54 Huds	160	650
3. Curtis Turner	Raymond Parks	99	55 Olds	156	450
4. Lee Petty	Petty Enterprises	42	55 Chrys	155	350
5. Eddie Skinner	Frank Dodge	28	53 Olds	154	300

1955 Grand National Race No. 44
October 23, 1955 Average Speed: 72.347

Driver	Owner	Car #	Make	Laps	Winnings
1. Buck Baker	Pete DePaolo	87	56 Ford	160	1,100
2. Lee Petty	Petty Enterprises	42	55 Dodg	160	700
3. Gwyn Staley	Hubert Westmoreland	2	55 Chev	159	475
4. Joe Weatherly	Charlie Schwam	9	56 Ford	159	365
5. Tim Flock	Carl Kiekhaefer	300	55 Chrys	159	310

1956 Grand National Race No. 10
April 8, 1956 Average Speed: 71.034

Driver	Owner	Car #	Make	Laps	Winnings
1. Tim Flock	Carl Kiekhaefer	300A	56 Chrys	160	1,100
2. Billy Myers	Bill Stroppe	14	56 Merc	160	700
3. Jim Paschal	Frank Hayworth	75	56 Merc	160	475
4. Herb Thomas	Herb Thomas	92	56 Chev	160	365
5. Ralph Moody	Pete DePaolo	12	56 Ford	159	310

1957 Grand National Race No. 9
April 7, 1957 Average Speed: 75.015

Driver	Owner	Car #	Make	Laps	Winnings
1. Fireball Roberts	Pete DePaolo	22	57 Ford	160	850
2. Paul Goldsmith	Pete DePaolo	97	57 Ford	160	625
3. Ralph Moody	Pete DePaolo	12	57 Ford	160	450
4. Marvin Panch	Pete DePaolo	98	57 Ford	159	350
5. Buck Baker	Hugh Babb	87	57 Chev	149	310

1957 Grand National Race No. 52
October 20, 1957 Average Speed: 69.902

Driver	Owner	Car #	Make	Laps	Winnings
1. Jack Smith	Jack Smith	47	57 Chev	160	900
2. Lee Petty	Petty Enterprises	42	57 Olds	160	575
3. Banjo Matthews	Banjo Matthews	84	57 Ford	160	375
4. Speedy Thompson	Speedy Thompson	46	57 Chev	160	280
5. Cotton Owens	Ray Nichels	6	57 Pont	160	245

1958 Grand National Race No. 18
May 18 , 1958 Average Speed: 78.636

Driver	Owner	Car #	Make	Laps	Winnings
1. Junior Johnson	Paul Spaulding	11	57 Ford	160	800
2. Jack Smith	Jack Smith	47	57 Chev	160	525
3. Rex White	J. H. Petty	44	57 Chev	160	350
4. Buck Baker	Buck Baker	87	57 Chev	159	250
5. Eddie Pagan	Eddie Pagan	45	57 Ford	157	225

1958 Grand National Race No. 50
October 19, 1958 Average Speed: 84.906

Driver	Owner	Car #	Make	Laps	Winnings
1. Junior Johnson	Paul Spaulding	11	57 Ford	160	800
2. Glen Wood	Wood Brothers	21	58 Ford	159	525
3. Speedy Thompson	Speedy Thompson	46	57 Chev	158	350
4. Cotton Owens	Jim Stephens	3	58 Pont	158	250
5. Jack Smith	Buck Baker	86	57 Chev	155	225

1959 Grand National Race No. 10
April 5, 1959 Average Speed: 71.985

Driver	Owner	Car #	Make	Laps	Winnings
1. Lee Petty	Petty Enterprises	43	57 Olds	160	800
2. Jack Smith	Jack Smith	47	59 Chev	160	525
3. Cotton Owens	W. H. Watson	6	58 Pont	159	350
4. Tiny Lund	Tiny Lund	5	57 Chev	159	250
5. Fred Harb	Fred Harb	17	57 Merc	154	225

1959 Grand National Race No. 43
October 18, 1959 Average Speed: 74.829

Driver	Owner	Car #	Make	Laps	Winnings
1. Lee Petty	Petty Enterprises	42	59 Plym	160	900
2. Rex White	Rex White	4	59 Chev	160	525
3. Richard Petty	Petty Enterprises	43	59 Plym	160	375
4. Tom Pistone	Carl Rupert	49	59 Ford	159	275
5. Junior Johnson	Paul Spaulding	11	59 Dodg	159	250

1960 Grand National Race No. 7
March 27, 1960 Average Speed: 66.347

Driver	Owner	Car #	Make	Laps	Winnings
1. Lee Petty	Petty Enterprises	42	60 Plym	160	900
2. Rex White	Rex White	4	59 Chev	160	525
3. Glen Wood	Wood Brothers	21	59 Ford	160	375
4. Ned Jarrett	Ned Jarrett	11	60 Ford	160	275
5. Junior Johnson	John Masoni	27	59 Chev	160	250

1960 Grand National Race No. 41 Wilkes 200
October 2, 1960 Average Speed: 77.444

Driver	Owner	Car #	Make	Laps	Winnings
1. Rex White	Rex White	4	60 Chev	320	2,200
2. Junior Johnson	John Masoni	27	60 Chev	320	1,225
3. Possum Jones	Tom Daniels	2	60 Chev	320	800
4. Joe Weatherly	Wood Brothers	16	58 Ford	318	525
5. Buck Baker	Buck Baker	87	60 Chev	314	375

1961 Grand National Race No. 14
April 16, 1961 Average Speed: 83.248

Driver	Owner	Car #	Make	Laps	Winnings
1. Rex White	Rex White	4	61 Chev	400	2,455
2. Tommy Irwin	Tom Daniels	2	60 Chev	398	1,175
3. Richard Petty	Petty Enterprises	43	61 Plym	396	900
4. Fireball Roberts	Jim Stephens	22	60 Pont	390	575
5. Johnny Allen	Bee Gee Holloway	69	61 Chev	387	575

1961 Grand National Race No. 48 Wilkes 200
October 1, 1961 Average Speed: 84.675

Driver	Owner	Car #	Make	Laps	Winnings
1. Rex White	Rex White	4	61 Chev	320	3,105
2. Fireball Roberts	Bud Moore	18	61 Pont	319	1,125
3. Richard Petty	Petty Enterprises	42	61 Plym	316	850
4. Junior Johnson	Rex Lovette	27	61 Pont	315	1,265
5. Ned Jarrett	Bee Gee Holloway	11	61 Chev	315	575

1962 Grand National Race No. 12 Gwyn Staley 400
April 15, 1962 Average Speed: 84.737

Driver	Owner	Car #	Make	Laps	Winnings
1. Richard Petty	Petty Enterprises	43	62 Plym	400	2,725
2. Fred Lorenzen	Holman-Moody	28	62 Ford	400	1,450
3. Junior Johnson	Rex Lovette	27	61 Pont	399	1,110
4. Fireball Roberts	Banjo Matthews	22	62 Pont	398	850
5. Darel Dieringer	Bob Osiecki	90	62 Dodg	396	675

North Wilkesboro Speedway *continued*

1962 Grand National Race No. 51 Wilkes 320
September 30, 1962 Average Speed: 86.186

Driver	Owner	Car #	Make	Laps	Winnings
1. Richard Petty	Petty Enterprises	43	62 Plym	320	2,560
2. Marvin Panch	Wood Brothers	21	62 Ford	320	1,400
3. Joe Weatherly	Bud Moore	8	62 Pont	320	875
4. Junior Johnson	Rex Lovette	27	62 Pont	319	765
5. Jim Paschal	Petty Enterprises	41	62 Plym	319	650

1963 Grand National Race No. 20 Gwyn Staley 400
April 28, 1963 Average Speed: 83.301

Driver	Owner	Car #	Make	Laps	Winnings
1. Richard Petty	Petty Enterprises	43	63 Plym	257	3,575
2. Fred Lorenzen	Holman-Moody	28	63 Ford	256	2,575
3. Tiny Lund	Wood Brothers	21	63 Ford	256	1,300
4. Jim Paschal	Petty Enterprises	41	63 Plym	254	825
5. Buck Baker	Buck Baker	87	63 Pont	254	700

1963 Grand National Race No. 50 Wilkes 250
September 29, 1963 Average Speed: 89.428

Driver	Owner	Car #	Make	Laps	Winnings
1. Marvin Panch	Wood Brothers	21	63 Ford	400	3,225
2. Fred Lorenzen	Holman-Moody	28	62 Ford	400	2,050
3. Nelson Stacy	Holman-Moody	29	63 Ford	398	1,450
4. Fireball Roberts	Holman-Moody	22	63 Ford	397	1,225
5. Ned Jarrett	Charles Robinson	11	63 Ford	397	625

1964 Grand National Race No. 18 Gwyn Staley 400
April 19, 1964 Average Speed: 81.930

Driver	Owner	Car #	Make	Laps	Winnings
1. Fred Lorenzen	Holman-Moody	28	64 Ford	400	3,950
2. Ned Jarrett	Bondy Long	11	64 Ford	400	1,900
3. Marvin Panch	Wood Brothers	21	64 Ford	399	1,250
4. Junior Johnson	Ray Fox	3	64 Dodg	395	850
5. Darel Dieringer	Bill Stroppe	16	64 Merc	395	625

1964 Grand National Race No. 58 Wilkes 400
October 11, 1964 Average Speed: 91.398

Driver	Owner	Car #	Make	Laps	Winnings
1. Marvin Panch	Wood Brothers	21	64 Ford	400	3,225
2. Fred Lorenzen	Holman-Moody	28	64 Ford	400	2,150
3. Darel Dieringer	Bud Moore	16	64 Merc	397	1,225
4. Billy Wade	Bud Moore	1	64 Merc	394	850
5. Buck Baker	Ray Fox	3	64 Dodg	390	625

1965 Grand National Race No. 11 Gwyn Staley 400
April 18, 1965 Average Speed: 95.047

Driver	Owner	Car #	Make	Laps	Winnings
1. Junior Johnson	Rex Lovette	26	65 Ford	400	4,900
2. Bobby Johns	Holman-Moody	7	65 Ford	400	2,125
3. Ned Jarrett	Bondy Long	11	65 Ford	399	1,300
4. Dick Hutcherson	Holman-Moody	29	65 Ford	393	850
5. Marvin Panch	Wood Brothers	21	65 Ford	389	675

1965 Grand National Race No. 51 Wilkes 400
October 3, 1965 Average Speed: 88.801

Driver	Owner	Car #	Make	Laps	Winnings
1. Junior Johnson	Rex Lovette	26	65 Ford	400	4,475
2. Cale Yarborough	Banjo Matthews	27	65 Ford	398	2,125
3. Ned Jarrett	Bondy Long	11	65 Ford	398	1,275
4. David Pearson	Cotton Owens	6	65 Dodg	397	825
5. Curtis Turner	Wood Brothers	47	65 Ford	396	675

1966 Grand National Race No. 13 Gwyn Staley 400
April 17, 1966 Average Speed: 89.045

Driver	Owner	Car #	Make	Laps	Winnings
1. Jim Paschal	Tom Friedkin	14	66 Plym	400	4,950
2. G. C. Spencer	G. C. Spencer	49	65 Plym	394	2,225
3. David Pearson	Cotton Owens	6	66 Dodg	382	1,350
4. Wendell Scott	Wendell Scott	34	65 Ford	378	825
5. Henley Gray	Henley Gray	97	66 Ford	375	625

1966 Grand National Race No. 47 Wilkes 400
October 2, 1966 Average Speed: 89.012

Driver	Owner	Car #	Make	Laps	Winnings
1. Dick Hutcherson	Bondy Long	29	66 Ford	400	4,325
2. David Pearson	Cotton Owens	6	66 Dodg	400	2,225
3. Paul Lewis	Paul Lewis	1	65 Plym	400	1,325
4. Jim Paschal	Tom Friedkin	14	66 Plym	397	800
5. James Hylton	Bud Hartje	48	65 Dodg	395	625

1967 Grand National Race No. 13 Gwyn Staley 400
April 16, 1967 Average Speed: 93.594

Driver	Owner	Car #	Make	Laps	Winnings
1. Darel Dieringer	Junior Johnson	26	67 Ford	400	5,150
2. Cale Yarborough	Wood Brothers	21	67 Ford	399	2,275
3. Dick Hutcherson	Bondy Long	29	67 Ford	396	1,325
4. Jim Paschal	Tom Friedkin	14	67 Plym	396	825
5. Paul Lewis	A. J. King	1	67 Dodg	392	625

1967 Grand National Race No. 46 Wilkes 400
October 1, 1967 Average Speed: 94.837

Driver	Owner	Car #	Make	Laps	Winnings
1. Richard Petty	Petty Enterprises	43	67 Plym	400	4,725
2. Dick Hutcherson	Bondy Long	29	67 Ford	398	2,400
3. LeeRoy Yarbrough	Junior Johnson	26	67 Ford	398	1,300
4. Bobby Allison	Bobby Allison	2	65 Chev	398	1,125
5. Jim Paschal	Tom Friedkin	14	67 Plym	398	650

1968 Grand National Race No. 11 Gwyn Staley 400
April 21, 1968 Average Speed: 90.425

Driver	Owner	Car #	Make	Laps	Winnings
1. David Pearson	Holman-Moody	17	68 Ford	400	5,100
2. Buddy Baker	Ray Fox	3	68 Dodg	399	2,275
3. Bobby Isaac	Nord Krauskopf	71	67 Dodg	399	1,325
4. Darel Dieringer	Mario Rossi	22	68 Plym	396	825
5. LeeRoy Yarbrough	Junior Johnson	98	68 Ford	391	750

1968 Grand National Race No. 45 Wilkes 400
September 29, 1968 Average Speed: 94.103

Driver	Owner	Car #	Make	Laps	Winnings
1. Richard Petty	Petty Enterprises	43	68 Plym	400	5,975
2. David Pearson	Holman-Moody	17	68 Ford	399	2,500
3. LeeRoy Yarbrough	Junior Johnson	98	68 Merc	399	1,450
4. Bobby Allison	Tom Friedkin	14	68 Plym	397	1,150
5. Cale Yarborough	Wood Brothers	21	68 Merc	395	625

1969 Grand National Race No. 15 Gwyn Staley 400
April 20, 1969 Average Speed: 95.268

Driver	Owner	Car #	Make	Laps	Winnings
1. Bobby Allison	Mario Rossi	22	69 Dodg	400	5,125
2. LeeRoy Yarbrough	Junior Johnson	98	69 Merc	400	3,750
3. David Pearson	Holman-Moody	17	69 Ford	400	2,100
4. Buddy Baker	Ray Fox	3	69 Dodg	400	1,150
5. James Hylton	Cotton Owens	6	69 Dodg	398	775

North Wilkesboro Speedway *continued*

1969 Grand National Race No. 47 Wilkes 400
October 5, 1969 Average Speed: 93.429

Driver	Owner	Car #	Make	Laps	Winnings
1. David Pearson	Holman-Moody	17	69 Ford	400	5,750
2. Richard Petty	Petty Enterprises	43	69 Ford	400	3,000
3. Bobby Isaac	Nord Krauskopf	71	69 Dodg	399	2,075
4. LeeRoy Yarbrough	Junior Johnson	98	69 Ford	397	1,125
5. Buddy Baker	Cotton Owens	6	69 Dodg	396	875

1970 Grand National Race No. 43 Wilkes 400
October 4, 1970 Average Speed: 90.162

Driver	Owner	Car #	Make	Laps	Winnings
1. Bobby Isaac	Nord Krauskopf	71	70 Dodg	400	5,825
2. Richard Petty	Petty Enterprises	43	70 Plym	400	2,850
3. Donnie Allison	Junior Johnson	98	70 Ford	399	1,975
4. Bobby Allison	Mario Rossi	22	70 Dodg	395	1,250
5. James Hylton	James Hylton	48	70 Ford	393	900

1971 Winston Cup GN Race No. 47 Wilkes 400
November 21, 1971 Average Speed: 96.174

Driver	Owner	Car #	Make	Laps	Winnings
1. Tiny Lund	Ronnie Hopkins	55	70 Chev	400	3,875
2. Charlie Glotzbach	R. Howard & J. Johnson	3	71 Chev	400	3,525
3. Richard Petty	Petty Enterprises	43	70 Plym	400	1,650
4. Dave Marcis	Dave Marcis	2	69 Dodg	398	1,175
5. Benny Parsons	L. G. DeWitt	72	71 Ford	394	1,000

1972 Winston Cup GN Race No. 28 Wilkes 400
October 1, 1972 Average Speed: 95.816

Driver	Owner	Car #	Make	Laps	Winnings
1. Richard Petty	Petty Enterprises	43	72 Plym	400	7,200
2. Bobby Allison	R. Howard & J. Johnson	12	72 Chev	400	4,550
3. Buddy Baker	Nord Krauskopf	71	72 Dodg	396	3,950
4. Benny Parsons	L. G. DeWitt	72	71 Merc	392	1,475
5. John Sears	Hoss Ellington	28	72 Chev	388	950

1973 Winston Cup GN Race No. 25 Wilkes 400
September 23, 1973 Average Speed: 95.198

Driver	Owner	Car #	Make	Laps	Winnings
1. Bobby Allison	Bobby Allison	12	73 Chev	400	7,425
2. Richard Petty	Petty Enterprises	43	73 Dodg	400	4,800
3. Cale Yarborough	R. Howard & J. Johnson	11	73 Chev	400	3,475
4. Buddy Baker	Nord Krauskopf	71	73 Dodg	399	2,930
5. Benny Parsons	L. G. DeWitt	72	73 Chev	395	1,200

1974 Winston Cup GN Race No. 26 Wilkes 400
September 22, 1974 Average Speed: 80.782

Driver	Owner	Car #	Make	Laps	Winnings
1. Cale Yarborough	Junior Johnson	11	74 Chev	400	9,275
2. Richard Petty	Petty Enterprises	43	74 Dodg	400	6,300
3. Buddy Baker	Bud Moore	15	73 Ford	399	4,625
4. Earl Ross	Junior Johnson	52	74 Chev	394	1,700
5. Dave Marcis	Dave Marcis	2	73 Dodg	393	1,600

1975 Winston Cup GN Race No. 23 Wilkes 400
September 21, 1975 Average Speed: 88.986

Driver	Owner	Car #	Make	Laps	Winnings
1. Richard Petty	Petty Enterprises	43	74 Dodg	400	9,960
2. Cale Yarborough	Junior Johnson	11	75 Chev	400	5,960
3. Darrell Waltrip	DiGard	88	75 Chev	396	4,535
4. Buddy Baker	Bud Moore	15	75 Ford	394	4,060
5. Lennie Pond	Ronnie Elder	54	75 Chev	394	1,810

1970 Grand National Race No. 11 Gwyn Staley 400
April 18, 1970 Average Speed: 94.246

Driver	Owner	Car #	Make	Laps	Winnings
1. Richard Petty	Petty Enterprises	43	70 Plym	400	6,025
2. Bobby Isaac	Nord Krauskopf	71	69 Dodg	399	3,725
3. LeeRoy Yarbrough	Junior Johnson	98	70 Ford	399	2,350
4. James Hylton	James Hylton	48	69 Ford	396	1,500
5. Dick Brooks	Dick Brooks	32	69 Plym	394	1,250

1971 Winston Cup GN Race No. 14 Gwyn Staley 400
April 18, 1971 Average Speed: 98.479

Driver	Owner	Car #	Make	Laps	Winnings
1. Richard Petty	Petty Enterprises	43	71 Plym	400	4,545
2. David Pearson	Holman-Moody	17	70 Ford	399	2,570
3. Dick Brooks	Mario Rossi	22	70 Dodg	396	1,745
4. Benny Parsons	L. G. DeWitt	72	71 Ford	394	1,145
5. Bobby Allison	Bobby Allison	12	71 Dodg	394	895

1972 Winston Cup GN Race No. 9 Gwyn Staley 400
April 23, 1972 Average Speed: 86.381

Driver	Owner	Car #	Make	Laps	Winnings
1. Richard Petty	Petty Enterprises	43	72 Plym	400	6,600
2. Bobby Allison	R. Howard & J. Johnson	12	72 Chev	400	4,375
3. Bobby Isaac	Nord Krauskopf	71	72 Dodg	400	3,950
4. James Hylton	James Hylton	48	70 Ford	392	1,550
5. Benny Parsons	L. G. DeWitt	72	70 Merc	392	1,200

1973 Winston Cup GN Race No. 7 Gwyn Staley 400
April 8, 1973 Average Speed: 97.224

Driver	Owner	Car #	Make	Laps	Winnings
1. Richard Petty	Petty Enterprises	43	73 Dodg	400	6,230
2. Benny Parsons	L. G. DeWitt	72	72 Chev	396	2,805
3. Buddy Baker	Nord Krauskopf	71	72 Dodg	394	3,380
4. Bobby Allison	Bobby Allison	12	73 Chev	394	3,205
5. Cecil Gordon	Cecil Gordon	24	72 Chev	394	1,205

1974 Winston Cup GN Race No. 8 Gwyn Staley 400
April 21, 1974 Average Speed: 96.200

Driver	Owner	Car #	Make	Laps	Winnings
1. Richard Petty	Petty Enterprises	43	74 Dodg	400	8,250
2. Cale Yarborough	R. Howard & J. Johnson	11	74 Chev	398	5,550
3. Bobby Allison	Bobby Allison	12	74 Chev	396	4,725
4. Benny Parsons	L. G. DeWitt	72	74 Chev	392	3,400
5. Lennie Pond	Ronnie Elder	54	74 Chev	392	1,150

1975 Winston Cup GN Race No. 7 Gwyn Staley 400
April 6, 1975 Average Speed: 90.009

Driver	Owner	Car #	Make	Laps	Winnings
1. Richard Petty	Petty Enterprises	43	74 Dodg	400	8,675
2. Cale Yarborough	Junior Johnson	11	75 Chev	397	5,825
3. Buddy Baker	Bud Moore	15	75 Ford	394	4,975
4. Dave Marcis	Nord Krauskopf	71	74 Dodg	394	4,025
5. Lennie Pond	Ronnie Elder	54	75 Chev	393	1,850

1976 Winston Cup GN Race No. 7 Gwyn Staley 400
April 4, 1976 Average Speed: 96.858

Driver	Owner	Car #	Make	Laps	Winnings
1. Cale Yarborough	Junior Johnson	11	Chev	400	11,125
2. Richard Petty	Petty Enterprises	43	Dodg	399	8,125
3. Bobby Allison	Roger Penske	2	Merc	397	5,575
4. Benny Parsons	L. G. DeWitt	72	Chev	397	4,370
5. J. D. McDuffie	J. D. McDuffie	70	Chev	393	2,100

North Wilkesboro Speedway *continued*

1976 Winston Cup GN Race No. 26 Wilkes 400
October 3, 1976 Average Speed: 96.380

Driver	Owner	Car #	Make	Laps	Winnings
1. Cale Yarborough	Junior Johnson	11	Chev	400	11,885
2. Benny Parsons	L. G. DeWitt	72	Chev	399	6,975
3. Richard Petty	Petty Enterprises	43	Dodg	399	6,705
4. Buddy Baker	Bud Moore	15	Ford	399	4,370
5. Lennie Pond	Ronnie Elder	54	Chev	395	2,925

1977 Winston Cup GN Race No. 26 Wilkes 400
October 2, 1977 Average Speed: 86.713

Driver	Owner	Car #	Make	Laps	Winnings
1. Darrell Waltrip	DiGard	88	Chev	400	12,500
2. Cale Yarborough	Junior Johnson	11	Chev	400	8,775
3. Neil Bonnett	Jim Stacy	5	Dodg	399	5,700
4. Bobby Allison	Bobby Allison	12	Mata	397	3,225
5. Benny Parsons	L. G. DeWitt	72	Chev	396	3,875

1978 Winston Cup GN Race No. 26 Wilkes 400
October 1, 1978 Average Speed: 97.847

Driver	Owner	Car #	Make	Laps	Winnings
1. Cale Yarborough	Junior Johnson	11	Olds	400	14,000
2. Darrell Waltrip	DiGard	88	Chev	400	13,450
3. Bobby Allison	Bud Moore	15	Ford	399	6,075
4. Richard Petty	Petty Enterprises	43	Chev	397	4,875
5. Neil Bonnett	Jim Stacy	5	Chev	397	4,400

1979 Winston Cup GN Race No. 28 Holly Farms 400
October 14, 1979 Average Speed: 91.454

Driver	Owner	Car #	Make	Laps	Winnings
1. Benny Parsons	M. C. Anderson	27	Chev	400	12,225
2. Bobby Allison	Bud Moore	15	Ford	400	8,200
3. Richard Petty	Petty Enterprises	43	Chev	399	6,500
4. Dale Earnhardt	Rod Osterlund	2	Chev	398	10,425
5. Ricky Rudd	Junie Donlavey	90	Ford	398	3,325

1980 Winston Cup GN Race No. 26 Holly Farms 400
September 21, 1980 Average Speed: 75.510

Driver	Owner	Car #	Make	Laps	Winnings
1. Bobby Allison	Bud Moore	15	Ford	400	17,725
2. Darrell Waltrip	DiGard	88	Chev	400	11,175
3. Dave Marcis	Dave Marcis	71	Chev	400	6,685
4. Harry Gant	Jack Beebe	47	Chev	399	5,235
5. Dale Earnhardt	Rod Osterlund	2	Chev	399	6,925

1981 Winston Cup GN Race No. 27 Holly Farms 400
October 4, 1981 Average Speed: 93.091

Driver	Owner	Car #	Make	Laps	Winnings
1. Darrell Waltrip	Junior Johnson	11	Buick	400	23,725
2. Bobby Allison	Harry Ranier	28	Buick	399	12,725
3. Joe Millikan	Cliff Stewart	5	Pont	399	9,600
4. Dale Earnhardt	Richard Childress	3	Pont	399	7,270
5. Ron Bouchard	Jack Beebe	47	Buick	398	5,145

1982 Winston Cup GN Race No. 25 Holly Farms 400
October 3, 1982 Average Speed: 98.071

Driver	Owner	Car #	Make	Laps	Winnings
1. Darrell Waltrip	Junior Johnson	11	Buick	400	32,775
2. Harry Gant	Hal Needham	33	Buick	400	11,985
3. Terry Labonte	Billy Hagan	44	Chev	399	8,395
4. Richard Petty	Petty Enterprises	43	Pont	399	11,125
5. Geoff Bodine	Cliff Stewart	50	Pont	399	9,775

1977 Winston Cup GN Race No. 6 Gwyn Staley 400
March 27, 1977 Average Speed: 88.950

Driver	Owner	Car #	Make	Laps	Winnings
1. Cale Yarborough	Junior Johnson	11	Chev	400	14,600
2. Richard Petty	Petty Enterprises	43	Dodg	400	8,025
3. Benny Parsons	L. G. DeWitt	72	Chev	400	6,175
4. Buddy Baker	Bud Moore	15	Ford	399	4,400
5. Bobby Allison	Bobby Allison	12	Mata	398	2,125

1978 Winston Cup GN Race No. 8 Gwyn Staley 400
April 16, 1978 Average Speed: 92.345

Driver	Owner	Car #	Make	Laps	Winnings
1. Darrell Waltrip	DiGard	88	Chev	400	13,075
2. Richard Petty	Petty Enterprises	43	Dodg	400	7,950
3. Benny Parsons	L. G. DeWitt	72	Chev	399	9,300
4. Lennie Pond	Harry Ranier	54	Chev	399	3,175
5. Dave Marcis	Rod Osterlund	2	Chev	398	1,675

1979 Winston Cup GN Race No. 6 Northwestern Bank 400
March 25, 1979 Average Speed: 88.400

Driver	Owner	Car #	Make	Laps	Winnings
1. Bobby Allison	Bud Moore	15	Ford	400	13,750
2. Richard Petty	Petty Enterprises	43	Chev	400	8,300
3. Benny Parsons	M. C. Anderson	27	Chev	400	8,600
4. Dale Earnhardt	Rod Osterlund	2	Chev	400	4,275
5. Darrell Waltrip	DiGard	88	Chev	399	4,575

1980 Winston Cup GN Race No. 8 Northwestern Bank 400
April 20, 1980 Average Speed: 95.501

Driver	Owner	Car #	Make	Laps	Winnings
1. Richard Petty	Petty Enterprises	43	Chev	400	18,925
2. Harry Gant	Jack Beebe	47	Chev	399	9,160
3. Bobby Allison	Bud Moore	15	Ford	399	13,675
4. Cale Yarborough	Junior Johnson	11	Chev	397	8,475
5. Benny Parsons	M. C. Anderson	27	Chev	397	5,925

1981 Winston Cup GN Race No. 7 Northwestern Bank 400
April 5, 1981 Average Speed: 85.381

Driver	Owner	Car #	Make	Laps	Winnings
1. Richard Petty	Petty Enterprises	43	Buick	400	18,850
2. Bobby Allison	Harry Ranier	28	Pont	400	12,350
3. Darrell Waltrip	Junior Johnson	11	Buick	400	9,875
4. Dave Marcis	Dave Marcis	71	Chev	400	10,470
5. Harry Gant	Kennie Childers	12	Olds	400	2,550

1982 Winston Cup GN Race No. 7 Northwestern Bank 400
April 18, 1982 Average Speed: 97.646

Driver	Owner	Car #	Make	Laps	Winnings
1. Darrell Waltrip	Junior Johnson	11	Buick	400	32,300
2. Terry Labonte	Billy Hagan	44	Chev	400	13,835
3. Dale Earnhardt	Bud Moore	15	Ford	400	12,425
4. Benny Parsons	Harry Ranier	28	Pont	400	11,525
5. Richard Petty	Petty Enterprises	43	Pont	399	10,000

1983 Winston Cup GN Race No. 6 Northwestern Bank 400
April 17, 1983 Average Speed: 91.436

Driver	Owner	Car #	Make	Laps	Winnings
1. Darrell Waltrip	Junior Johnson	11	Chev	400	28,075
2. Bobby Allison	DiGard	22	Buick	400	16,975
3. Harry Gant	Hal Needham	33	Buick	400	12,885
4. Neil Bonnett	Bob Rahilly & Butch Mock	75	Chev	400	10,995
5. Geoff Bodine	Cliff Stewart	88	Pont	400	7,070

North Wilkesboro Speedway *continued*

1983 Winston Cup GN Race No. 26 Holly Farms 400
October 2, 1983 Average Speed: 100.716

Driver	Owner	Car #	Make	Laps	Winnings
1. Darrell Waltrip	Junior Johnson	11	Chev	400	34,800
2. Dale Earnhardt	Bud Moore	15	Ford	400	15,500
3. Bobby Allison	DiGard	22	Buick	400	12,855
4. Bill Elliott	Harry Melling	9	Ford	400	6,345
5. Terry Labonte	Billy Hagan	44	Chev	399	5,820

1984 Winston Cup GN Race No. 27 Holly Farms 400
October 14, 1984 Average Speed: 90.525

Driver	Owner	Car #	Make	Laps	Winnings
1. Darrell Waltrip	Junior Johnson	11	Chev	400	38,900
2. Harry Gant	Hal Needham	33	Chev	400	15,230
3. Bobby Allison	DiGard	22	Buick	400	17,000
4. Neil Bonnett	Junior Johnson	12	Chev	400	6,630
5. Rusty Wallace	Cliff Stewart	88	Pont	400	7,510

1985 Winston Cup GN Race No. 24 Holly Farms 400
September 29, 1985 Average Speed: 95.077

Driver	Owner	Car #	Make	Laps	Winnings
1. Harry Gant	Hal Needham	33	Chev	400	32,025
2. Geoff Bodine	Rick Hendrick	5	Chev	400	25,000
3. Terry Labonte	Billy Hagan	44	Chev	400	15,860
4. Dale Earnhardt	Richard Childress	3	Chev	400	10,960
5. Ricky Rudd	Bud Moore	15	Ford	399	9,500

1986 Winston Cup Race No. 25 Holly Farms 400
September 28, 1986 Average Speed: 95.612

Driver	Owner	Car #	Make	Laps	Winnings
1. Darrell Waltrip	Junior Johnson	11	Chev	400	38,100
2. Geoff Bodine	Rick Hendrick	5	Chev	400	20,700
3. Richard Petty	Petty Enterprises	43	Pont	400	12,105
4. Rusty Wallace	Raymond Beadle	27	Pont	400	10,500
5. Harry Gant	Hal Needham	33	Chev	400	11,800

1987 Winston Cup Race No. 25 Holly Farms 400
October 4, 1987 Average Speed: 96.051

Driver	Owner	Car #	Make	Laps	Winnings
1. Terry Labonte	Junior Johnson	11	Chev	400	45,575
2. Dale Earnhardt	Richard Childress	3	Chev	400	26,950
3. Bill Elliott	Harry Melling	9	Ford	399	25,450
4. Morgan Shepherd	Kenny Bernstein	26	Buick	398	11,205
5. Geoff Bodine	Rick Hendrick	5	Chev	398	11,975

1988 Winston Cup Race No. 26 Holly Farms 400
October 16, 1988 Average Speed: 94.192

Driver	Owner	Car #	Make	Laps	Winnings
1. Rusty Wallace	Raymond Beadle	27	Pont	400	47,000
2. Phil Parsons	Richard Jackson	55	Olds	400	22,900
3. Geoff Bodine	Rick Hendrick	5	Chev	400	16,750
4. Terry Labonte	Junior Johnson	11	Chev	400	12,825
5. Bill Elliott	Harry Melling	9	Ford	400	21,625

1989 Winston Cup Race No. 26 Holly Farms 400
October 15, 1989 Average Speed: 90.289

Driver	Owner	Car #	Make	Laps	Winnings
1. Geoff Bodine	Rick Hendrick	5	Chev	400	47,800
2. Mark Martin	Jack Roush	6	Ford	400	28,075
3. Terry Labonte	Junior Johnson	11	Ford	400	18,300
4. Harry Gant	Leo Jackson	33	Olds	400	12,775
5. Morgan Shepherd	Bob Rahilly & Butch Mock	75	Pont	400	15,200

1984 Winston Cup GN Race No. 6 Northwestern Bank 400
April 8, 1984 Average Speed: 97.830

Driver	Owner	Car #	Make	Laps	Winnings
1. Tim Richmond	Raymond Beadle	27	Pont	400	24,780
2. Harry Gant	Hal Needham	33	Chev	400	16,455
3. Ricky Rudd	Bud Moore	15	Ford	400	22,190
4. Terry Labonte	Billy Hagan	44	Chev	400	7,355
5. Kyle Petty	Petty Enterprises	7	Ford	400	11,220

1985 Winston Cup GN Race No. 7 Northwestern Bank 400
April 21, 1985 Average Speed: 93.818

Driver	Owner	Car #	Make	Laps	Winnings
1. Neil Bonnett	Junior Johnson	12	Chev	400	30,025
2. Darrell Waltrip	Junior Johnson	11	Chev	400	27,500
3. Bobby Allison	DiGard	22	Buick	400	12,965
4. Ricky Rudd	Bud Moore	15	Ford	400	9,870
5. Geoff Bodine	Rick Hendrick	5	Chev	400	11,955

1986 Winston Cup Race No. 7 First Union 400
April 20, 1986 Average Speed: 88.408

Driver	Owner	Car #	Make	Laps	Winnings
1. Dale Earnhardt	Richard Childress	3	Chev	400	38,550
2. Ricky Rudd	Bud Moore	15	Ford	400	20,075
3. Geoff Bodine	Rick Hendrick	5	Chev	400	17,415
4. Darrell Waltrip	Junior Johnson	11	Chev	400	13,750
5. Joe Ruttman	Kenny Bernstein	26	Buick	400	4,415

1987 Winston Cup Race No. 6 First Union 400
April 5, 1987 Average Speed: 94.103

Driver	Owner	Car #	Make	Laps	Winnings
1. Dale Earnhardt	Richard Childress	3	Chev	400	44,675
2. Kyle Petty	Wood Brothers	21	Ford	400	20,055
3. Neil Bonnett	Bob Rahilly & Butch Mock	75	Pont	400	14,470
4. Alan Kulwicki	Alan Kulwicki	7	Ford	400	12,935
5. Ricky Rudd	Bud Moore	15	Ford	399	14,890

1988 Winston Cup Race No. 7 First Union 400
April 17, 1988 Average Speed: 99.075

Driver	Owner	Car #	Make	Laps	Winnings
1. Terry Labonte	Junior Johnson	11	Chev	400	48,050
2. Ricky Rudd	Kenny Bernstein	26	Buick	400	21,025
3. Dale Earnhardt	Richard Childress	3	Chev	400	22,115
4. Rusty Wallace	Raymond Beadle	27	Pont	400	14,650
5. Kyle Petty	Wood Brothers	21	Ford	400	12,965

1989 Winston Cup Race No. 7 First Union 400
April 16, 1989 Average Speed: 89.937

Driver	Owner	Car #	Make	Laps	Winnings
1. Dale Earnhardt	Richard Childress	3	Chev	400	51,225
2. Alan Kulwicki	Alan Kulwicki	7	Ford	400	25,575
3. Mark Martin	Jack Roush	6	Ford	400	19,425
4. Dick Trickle	Stavola Brothers	84	Buick	400	13,800
5. Terry Labonte	Junior Johnson	11	Ford	400	14,025

1990 Winston Cup Series Race No. 7 First Union 400
April 22, 1990 Average Speed: 83.908

Driver	Owner	Car #	Make	Laps	Winnings
1. Brett Bodine	Kenny Bernstein	26	Buick	400	50,682
2. Darrell Waltrip	Rick Hendrick	17	Chev	400	31,625
3. Dale Earnhardt	Richard Childress	3	Chev	400	21,775
4. Ricky Rudd	Rick Hendrick	5	Chev	400	12,775
5. Morgan Shepherd	Bud Moore	15	Ford	400	12,100

North Wilkesboro Speedway *continued*

1990 Winston Cup Series Race No. 25 Tyson/Holly Farms 400
September 30, 1990 Average Speed: 93.818

Driver	Owner	Car #	Make	Laps	Winnings
1. Mark Martin	Jack Roush	6	Ford	400	52,875
2. Dale Earnhardt	Richard Childress	3	Chev	400	32,075
3. Brett Bodine	Kenny Bernstein	26	Buick	400	18,750
4. Bill Elliott	Harry Melling	9	Ford	400	16,775
5. Ken Schrader	Rick Hendrick	25	Chev	400	15,325

1991 Winston Cup Series Race No. 7 First Union 400
April 21, 1991 Average Speed: 79.604

Driver	Owner	Car #	Make	Laps	Winnings
1. Darrell Waltrip	Darrell Waltrip	17	Chev	400	53,800
2. Dale Earnhardt	Richard Childress	3	Chev	400	35,225
3. Jimmy Spencer	Travis Carter	98	Chev	400	20,350
4. Morgan Shepherd	Bud Moore	15	Ford	400	16,450
5. Ken Schrader	Rick Hendrick	25	Chev	400	14,725

1991 Winston Cup Series Race No. 25 Tyson/Holly Farms 400
September 29, 1991 Average Speed: 94.113

Driver	Owner	Car #	Make	Laps	Winnings
1. Dale Earnhardt	Richard Childress	3	Chev	400	69,350
2. Harry Gant	Leo Jackson	33	Olds	400	40,575
3. Morgan Shepherd	Bud Moore	15	Ford	400	25,375
4. Davey Allison	Robert Yates	28	Ford	400	19,600
5. Mark Martin	Jack Roush	6	Ford	400	18,875

1992 Winston Cup Race No. 7 First Union 400
April 12, 1992 Average Speed: 90.653

Driver	Owner	Car #	Make	Laps	Winnings
1. Davey Allison	Robert Yates	28	Ford	400	51,740
2. Rusty Wallace	Roger Penske	2	Pont	400	29,140
3. Ricky Rudd	Rick Hendrick	5	Chev	400	23,465
4. Geoff Bodine	Bud Moore	15	Ford	400	22,665
5. Harry Gant	Leo Jackson	33	Olds	400	19,590

1992 Winston Cup Race No. 25 Tyson/Holly Farms 400
October 5, 1992 Average Speed: 107.360

Driver	Owner	Car #	Make	Laps	Winnings
1. Geoff Bodine	Bud Moore	15	Ford	400	71,625
2. Mark Martin	Jack Roush	6	Ford	400	36,475
3. Kyle Petty	Felix Sabates	42	Pont	399	20,325
4. Rusty Wallace	Roger Penske	2	Pont	399	18,600
5. Sterling Marlin	Junior Johnson	22	Ford	399	20,000

1993 Winston Cup Series Race No. 7 First Union 400
April 18, 1993 Average Speed: 92.602

Driver	Owner	Car #	Make	Laps	Winnings
1. Rusty Wallace	Roger Penske	2	Pont	400	43,535
2. Kyle Petty	Felix Sabates	42	Pont	400	29,210
3. Ken Schrader	Rick Hendrick	25	Chev	400	40,235
4. Davey Allison	Robert Yates	28	Ford	400	28,285
5. Darrell Waltrip	Darrell Waltrip	17	Chev	400	25,935

1993 Winston Cup Series Race No. 26 Tyson/Holly Farms 400
October 3, 1993 Average Speed: 96.920

Driver	Owner	Car #	Make	Laps	Winnings
1. Rusty Wallace	Roger Penske	2	Pont	400	46,260
2. Dale Earnhardt	Richard Childress	3	Chev	400	46,285
3. Ernie Irvan	Robert Yates	28	Ford	400	39,435
4. Kyle Petty	Felix Sabates	42	Pont	400	20,085
5. Ricky Rudd	Rick Hendrick	5	Chev	399	21,235

1994 Winston Cup Series Race No. 7 First Union 400
April 17, 1994 Average Speed: 95.816

Driver	Owner	Car #	Make	Laps	Winnings
1. Terry Labonte	Rick Hendrick	5	Chev	400	61,640
2. Rusty Wallace	Roger Penske	2	Ford	400	42,215
3. Ernie Irvan	Robert Yates	28	Ford	400	41,565
4. Kyle Petty	Felix Sabates	42	Pont	400	32,165
5. Dale Earnhardt	Richard Childress	3	Chev	400	26,740

1994 Winston Cup Series Race No. 27 Tyson/Holly Farms 400
October 2, 1994 Average Speed: 98.522

Driver	Owner	Car #	Make	Laps	Winnings
1. Geoff Bodine	Geoff Bodine	7	Ford	400	61,440
2. Terry Labonte	Rick Hendrick	5	Chev	399	39,365
3. Rick Mast	Richard Jackson	1	Ford	399	32,590
4. Rusty Wallace	Roger Penske	2	Ford	399	23,590
5. Mark Martin	Jack Roush	6	Ford	398	24,090

1995 Winston Cup Series Race No. 7 First Union 400
April 9, 1995 Average Speed: 102.424

Driver	Owner	Car #	Make	Laps	Winnings
1. Dale Earnhardt	Richard Childress	3	Chev	400	77,400
2. Jeff Gordon	Rick Hendrick	24	Chev	400	61,625
3. Mark Martin	Jack Roush	6	Ford	400	40,250
4. Rusty Wallace	Roger Penske	2	Ford	400	29,630
5. Steve Grissom	Gary Bechtel	29	Chev	400	20,655

1995 Winston Cup Series Race No. 27 Tyson/Holly Farms 400
October 1, 1995 Average Speed: 102.998

Driver	Owner	Car #	Make	Laps	Winnings
1. Mark Martin	Jack Roush	6	Ford	400	71,590
2. Rusty Wallace	Roger Penske	2	Ford	400	38,915
3. Jeff Gordon	Rick Hendrick	24	Chev	400	33,065
4. Terry Labonte	Rick Hendrick	5	Chev	400	28,595
5. Ricky Rudd	Ricky Rudd	10	Ford	400	31,640

1996 Winston Cup Series Race No. 7 First Union 400
April 14, 1996 Average Speed: 96.370

Driver	Owner	Car #	Make	Laps	Winnings
1. Terry Labonte	Rick Hendrick	5	Chev	400	229,025
2. Jeff Gordon	Rick Hendrick	24	Chev	400	52,750
3. Dale Earnhardt	Richard Childress	3	Chev	400	38,525
4. Robert Pressley	Leo Jackson & Andy Petree	33	Chev	400	35,305
5. Sterling Marlin	Larry McClure	4	Chev	400	31,855

1996 Winston Cup Series Race No. 27 Tyson/Holly Farms 400
September 29, 1996 Average Speed: 96.837

Driver	Owner	Car #	Make	Laps	Winnings
1. Jeff Gordon	Rick Hendrick	24	Chev	400	91,350
2. Dale Earnhardt	Richard Childress	3	Chev	400	51,940
3. Dale Jarrett	Robert Yates	88	Ford	400	35,790
4. Jeff Burton	Jack Roush	99	Ford	400	27,570
5. Terry Labonte	Rick Hendrick	5	Chev	400	31,115

Occoneechee Speedway
Hillsboro, NC
1-mile Dirt Track

(aka Orange Speedway in Hillsborough, NC) Track opened in June of 1948. First NASCAR Winston Cup (then Strictly Stock) race held on 8/7/49 (won by Bob Flock, the third big league NASCAR race ever staged). Originally measured at 1-mile, the track was re-measured at 0.9-mile in 1956. Final Grand National race held on 9/15/68 (won by Richard Petty). The superspeedway at Talladega assumed its race date in 1969.

Winston Cup Starts
Buck Baker   22

Winston Cup Victories
Buck Baker   3
Lee Petty   3
Richard Petty   3

Winston Cup Poles
Richard Petty   4
Joe Weatherly   4

Winston Cup Money
Buck Baker $8,660

Most Cars Started
33—April 15, 1951
33—September 28, 1958

Fewest Cars Started
18—March 23, 1958
18—September 18, 1960

Narrowest Margin of Victory
1 car length—April 18, 1954

Slowest Race
70.465 MPH—October 30, 1955

Race Record
90.663 MPH—March 14, 1965

Most Cautions
4—September 30, 1956
4—September 28, 1958

Most Race Leaders
4—September 28, 1958

Most Cars Running at Finish
21—April 18, 1954
21—May 13, 1956

1949 Strictly Stock Race No. 3
August 7, 1949 Average Speed: 76.800

Driver	Owner	Car #	Make	Laps	Winnings
1. Bob Flock	Frank Christian	7	48 Olds	200	2,000
2. Gober Sosebee	Leon Chester	50	49 Olds	—	1,000
3. Glenn Dunnaway	Glenn Dunnaway	55	49 Olds	—	500
4. Fonty Flock	Ed Lawrence	47	47 Buick	—	300
5. Bill Snowden	Al Wagoner	3	49 Chev	—	200

1950 Grand National Race No. 10
August 13, 1950

Driver	Owner	Car #	Make	Laps	Winnings
1. Fireball Roberts	Sam Rice	71	49 Olds	100	1,125
2. Curtis Turner	John Eanes	41	50 Olds	100	775
3. Dick Linder	Don Rogalla	25	50 Olds	—	400
4. Bill Rexford	Julian Buesink	80	50 Olds	—	300
5. Clyde Minter	Clyde Minter	19	50 Merc	—	225

1950 Grand National Race No. 19
October 29, 1950

Driver	Owner	Car #	Make	Laps	Winnings
1. Lee Petty	Petty Enterprises	42	49 Plym	175	1,500
2. Buck Baker	Griffin Motors	87	50 Olds	—	1,000
3. Weldon Adams	Harold Mays	72	50 Plym	—	500
4. Tim Flock	Hubert Westmoreland	98	50 Plym	—	400
5. Bill Blair	Bill Blair	41.5	50 Olds	—	300

1951 Grand National Race No. 5
April 15, 1951 Average Speed: 80.889

Driver	Owner	Car #	Make	Laps	Winnings
1. Fonty Flock	Frank Christian	14	50 Olds	95	1,300
2. Frank Mundy	Perry Smith	23	51 Stud	95	800
3. Bill Blair	Bill Blair	41.5	50 Olds	—	600
4. Tim Flock	Ted Chester	91	51 Olds	—	500
5. Neil Cole	John Golabek	52	50 Olds	—	300

1951 Grand National Race No. 31
October 7, 1951 Average Speed: 72.454

Driver	Owner	Car #	Make	Laps	Winnings
1. Herb Thomas	Herb Thomas	92	51 Huds	150	1,000
2. Leonard Tippett	Leonard Tippett	99	51 Huds	149	600
3. Joe Eubanks	Phil Oates	82	50 Olds	148	500
4. Jim Paschal	Julian Buesink	60	50 Ford	147	400
5. Lee Petty	Petty Enterprises	42	51 Plym	147	300

1952 Grand National Race No. 15
June 8, 1952 Average Speed: 81.008

Driver	Owner	Car #	Make	Laps	Winnings
1. Tim Flock	Ted Chester	91	51 Huds	100	1,000
2. Fonty Flock	Frank Christian	14	52 Olds	100	700
3. Dick Rathmann	Walt Chapman	120	51 Huds	100	450
4. Bill Blair	George Hutchens	2	52 Olds	98	350
5. Jimmie Lewallen			52 Ford	97	200

1952 Grand National Race No. 30
October 12, 1952 Average Speed: 73.489

Driver	Owner	Car #	Make	Laps	Winnings
1. Fonty Flock	Frank Christian	14	52 Olds	150	1,200
2. Donald Thomas	Herb Thomas	9	52 Huds	150	700
3. Bill Blair	George Hutchens	2	52 Olds	150	500
4. Tim Flock	Ted Chester	91	52 Huds	149	450
5. Lee Petty	Petty Enterprises	42	51 Plym	147	400

1953 Grand National Race No. 26
August 9, 1953 Average Speed: 75.125

Driver	Owner	Car #	Make	Laps	Winnings
1. Curtis Turner	Frank Christian	41	53 Olds	100	1,000
2. Herb Thomas	Herb Thomas	92	53 Huds	100	700
3. Lee Petty	Petty Enterprises	42	53 Dodg	99	450
4. Joe Eubanks	Phil Oates	82	52 Huds	—	350
5. Bill Blair	Bill Blair	2	53 Olds	—	200

1954 Grand National Race No. 8
April 18, 1954 Average Speed: 77.386

Driver	Owner	Car #	Make	Laps	Winnings
1. Herb Thomas	Herb Thomas	92	54 Huds	100	1,000
2. Donald Thomas	John Ditz	31	53 Huds	100	650
3. Buck Baker	Ernest Woods	88	54 Olds	100	450
4. Dick Rathmann	John Ditz	3	54 Huds	100	350
5. Curtis Turner	Frank Christian	14	54 Olds	99	300

1955 Grand National Race No. 7
March 27, 1955 Average Speed: 82.304

Driver	Owner	Car #	Make	Laps	Winnings
1. Jim Paschal	Ernest Woods	78	55 Olds	100	1,000
2. Buck Baker	Griffin Motors	87	54 Olds	100	650
3. Don White	Don White	1	55 Olds	100	450
4. Joel Million	Ernest Woods	88	55 Olds	99	350
5. Fonty Flock	Frank Christian	14	55 Chev	99	300

Occoneechee Speedway *continued*

1955 Grand National Race No. 45
October 30, 1955 Average Speed: 70.465

Driver	Owner	Car #	Make	Laps	Winnings
1. Tim Flock	Carl Kiekhaefer	301	55 Chrys	100	1,100
2. Curtis Turner	Charlie Schwam	99	56 Ford	100	700
3. Buck Baker	Pete DePaolo	87	56 Ford	100	475
4. Herb Thomas	Herb Thomas	92	55 Chev	100	365
5. Dave Terrell	Dave Terrell	198	55 Olds	100	310

1956 Grand National Race No. 17
May 13, 1956 Average Speed: 83.720

Driver	Owner	Car #	Make	Laps	Winnings
1. Buck Baker	Carl Kiekhaefer	300	56 Chrys	100	1,100
2. Speedy Thompson	Carl Kiekhaefer	300c	56 Chrys	100	700
3. Lee Petty	Petty Enterprises	42	56 Dodg	100	475
4. Fireball Roberts	Pete DePaolo	22	56 Ford	100	365
5. Cotton Owens	Jim Stephens	286	56 Pont	99	310

1956 Grand National Race No. 50
September 30, 1956 Average Speed: 72.734

Driver	Owner	Car #	Make	Laps	Winnings
1. Fireball Roberts	Pete DePaolo	22	56 Ford	110	950
2. Buck Baker	Carl Kiekhaefer	300B	56 Chrys	110	675
3. Speedy Thompson	Carl Kiekhaefer	300	56 Chrys	108	475
4. Herb Thomas	Herb Thomas	92	56 Chev	108	365
5. Bunk Moore		35	56 Ford	107	320

1957 Grand National Race No. 7
March 24, 1957 Average Speed: 82.233

Driver	Owner	Car #	Make	Laps	Winnings
1. Buck Baker	Hugh Babb	87	57 Chev	110	650
2. Speedy Thompson	Hugh Babb	46	57 Chev	110	525
3. Jack Smith	Hugh Babb	47	57 Chev	109	400
4. Paul Goldsmith	Pete DePaolo	99	57 Ford	109	320
5. Lee Petty	Petty Enterprises	42	57 Olds	107	290

1958 Grand National Race No. 6
March 23, 1958 Average Speed: 78.502

Driver	Owner	Car #	Make	Laps	Winnings
1. Buck Baker	Buck Baker	87	57 Chev	110	800
2. Marvin Panch	John Whitford	98	57 Ford	110	525
3. Speedy Thompson	Speedy Thompson	46	57 Chev	110	350
4. Lee Petty	Petty Enterprises	42	57 Olds	110	250
5. Curtis Turner	Holman-Moody	21	57 Ford	108	225

1958 Grand National Race No. 47
September 28, 1958 Average Speed: 72.439

Driver	Owner	Car #	Make	Laps	Winnings
1. Joe Eubanks	Jim Stephens	6	57 Pont	110	800
2. Doug Cox	Doug Cox	30	57 Ford	110	525
3. Buck Baker	Buck Baker	87	57 Chev	109	350
4. Tommy Irwin	Tommy Irwin	16	57 Ford	109	250
5. Lee Petty	Petty Enterprises	42	57 Olds	108	225

1959 Grand National Race No. 4
March 1, 1959 Average Speed: 81.612

Driver	Owner	Car #	Make	Laps	Winnings
1. Curtis Turner	Doc White	41	59 Ford	110	800
2. Tom Pistone	Carl Rupert	59	59 Ford	110	525
3. Bob Welborn	Bob Welborn	49	59 Chev	109	350
4. Lee Petty	Petty Enterprises	42	57 Olds	109	250
5. Buck Baker	Buck Baker	88	59 Chev	109	225

1959 Grand National Race No. 40
September 20, 1959 Average Speed: 77.868

Driver	Owner	Car #	Make	Laps	Winnings
1. Lee Petty	Petty Enterprises	42	59 Plym	110	900
2. Cotton Owens	Cotton Owens	6	59 Ford	109	525
3. Richard Petty	Petty Enterprises	43	59 Plym	100	375
4. Larry Frank	Larry Frank	76	57 Chev	100	250
5. Roy Tyner	Roy Tyner	9	57 Chev	100	250

1960 Grand National Race No. 18
May 29, 1960 Average Speed: 83.583

Driver	Owner	Car #	Make	Laps	Winnings
1. Lee Petty	Petty Enterprises	42	60 Plym	110	900
2. Ned Jarrett	Ned Jarrett	11	60 Ford	108	525
3. Jack Smith	Jack Smith	47	60 Pont	108	375
4. Tommy Irwin	Tommy Irwin	36	59 Ford	107	275
5. Buck Baker	Buck Baker	87	60 Chev	107	250

1960 Grand National Race No. 39
September 18, 1960 Average Speed: 80.161

Driver	Owner	Car #	Make	Laps	Winnings
1. Richard Petty	Petty Enterprises	43	60 Plym	110	800
2. Ned Jarrett	Ned Jarrett	11	60 Ford	109	525
3. Rex White	Rex White	4	59 Chev	106	375
4. Herman Beam	Herman Beam	19	60 Ford	103	275
5. Jimmy Pardue	Ebart Clifton	54	59 Dodg	103	250

1961 Grand National Race No. 11
April 2, 1961 Average Speed: 84.695

Driver	Owner	Car #	Make	Laps	Winnings
1. Cotton Owens	Cotton Owens	6	60 Pont	110	800
2. Richard Petty	Petty Enterprises	42	60 Plym	110	525
3. Buck Baker	Buck Baker	86	61 Chrys	110	375
4. Junior Johnson	Rex Lovette	27	60 Pont	109	275
5. Rex White	Rex White	4	60 Chev	109	350

1961 Grand National Race No. 52
October 29, 1961 Average Speed: 85.249

Driver	Owner	Car #	Make	Laps	Winnings
1. Joe Weatherly	Bud Moore	8	61 Pont	165	1,150
2. Rex White	Rex White	4	61 Chev	164	850
3. Ned Jarrett	Bee Gee Holloway	11	61 Chev	163	475
4. Maurice Petty	Petty Enterprises	42	61 Plym	155	375
5. Fireball Roberts	Rex Lovette	22	61 Pont	154	325

1962 Grand National Race No. 9
March 18, 1962 Average Speed: 86.948

Driver	Owner	Car #	Make	Laps	Winnings
1. Rex White	Rex White	4	61 Chev	110	1,000
2. Richard Petty	Petty Enterprises	43	62 Plym	110	600
3. Jim Paschal	Cliff Stewart	2	62 Pont	110	400
4. Jack Smith	Jack Smith	47	61 Pont	110	300
5. Buddy Baker	Buck Baker	87	61 Chrys	109	275

1963 Grand National Race No. 10
March 10, 1963 Average Speed: 83.129

Driver	Owner	Car #	Make	Laps	Winnings
1. Junior Johnson	Ray Fox	3	63 Chev	165	1,550
2. Jim Paschal	Petty Enterprises	41	62 Plym	165	1,100
3. Richard Petty	Petty Enterprises	43	63 Plym	165	750
4. Ned Jarrett	Charles Robinson	11	63 Ford	161	575
5. Jimmy Pardue	Pete Stewart	54	62 Pont	157	425

Occoneechee Speedway *continued*

1963 Grand National Race No. 54
October 27, 1963 Average Speed: 85.559

Driver	Owner	Car #	Make	Laps	Winnings
1. Joe Weatherly	Bud Moore	8	63 Pont	167	1,600
2. Bob Welborn	Petty Enterprises	41	63 Plym	166	1,000
3. Doug Cooper	Bob Cooper	02	62 Pont	154	700
4. Buck Baker	Buck Baker	87	63 Pont	152	550
5. Curtis Crider	Curtis Crider	62	63 Merc	149	425

1964 Grand National Race No. 55
September 20, 1964 Average Speed: 86.725

Driver	Owner	Car #	Make	Laps	Winnings
1. Ned Jarrett	Bondy Long	11	64 Ford	167	1,550
2. Cotton Owens	Cotton Owens	5	64 Dodg	166	1,000
3. Larry Thomas	Herman Beam	19	64 Ford	162	750
4. Wendell Scott	Wendell Scott	34	63 Ford	156	575
5. Buddy Arrington	Buddy Arrington	78	63 Dodg	153	425

1965 Grand National Race No. 53
October 24, 1965 Average Speed: 87.462

Driver	Owner	Car #	Make	Laps	Winnings
1. Dick Hutcherson	Holman-Moody	47	65 Ford	112	1,000
2. Tom Pistone	Glenn Sweet	59	64 Ford	109	600
3. Jim Paschal	Petty Enterprises	43	64 Plym	109	400
4. Cale Yarborough	Kenny Myler	06	64 Ford	106	300
5. Paul Lewis	Curtis Larimer	56	64 Ford	105	275

1967 Grand National Race No. 44 Hillsborough 150
September 17, 1967 Average Speed: 81.574

Driver	Owner	Car #	Make	Laps	Winnings
1. Richard Petty	Petty Enterprises	43	67 Plym	167	1,500
2. Dick Hutcherson	Bondy Long	29	67 Ford	167	1,050
3. Buddy Baker	Cotton Owens	6	67 Dodg	165	700
4. James Hylton	Bud Hartje	48	65 Dodg	164	575
5. G. C. Spencer	G. C. Spencer	49	67 Plym	164	425

1964 Grand National Race No. 15 Joe Weatherly Memorial 150
April 12, 1964 Average Speed: 83.319

Driver	Owner	Car #	Make	Laps	Winnings
1. David Pearson	Cotton Owens	6	64 Dodg	167	1,400
2. Dick Hutcherson	Dick Hutcherson	1	64 Ford	164	1,100
3. Larry Thomas	Wade Younts	36	62 Dodg	160	700
4. Ralph Earnhardt	Tom Spell	31	63 Ford	160	575
5. Bobby Keck	E. B. Rich	23	63 Ford	155	425

1965 Grand National Race No. 8
March 14, 1965 Average Speed: 90.663

Driver	Owner	Car #	Make	Laps	Winnings
1. Ned Jarrett	Bondy Long	11	65 Ford	167	1,400
2. Junior Johnson	Rex Lovette	26	65 Ford	166	1,000
3. Bud Moore	Louie Weathersby	45	64 Plym	162	700
4. Elmo Langley	Elmo Langley	64	64 Ford	161	575
5. Buddy Arrington	Buddy Arrington	67	64 Dodg	160	425

1966 Grand National Race No. 45 Joe Weatherly Memorial 150
September 18, 1966 Average Speed: 90.603

Driver	Owner	Car #	Make	Laps	Winnings
1. Dick Hutcherson	Bondy Long	29	66 Ford	167	1,400
2. David Pearson	Cotton Owens	6	65 Dodg	167	1,000
3. Paul Lewis	Paul Lewis	1	65 Plym	165	700
4. James Hylton	Bud Hartje	48	65 Dodg	163	575
5. John Sears	L. G. DeWitt	4	64 Ford	163	425

1968 Grand National Race No. 43 Hillsborough 150
September 15, 1968 Average Speed: 87.681

Driver	Owner	Car #	Make	Laps	Winnings
1. Richard Petty	Petty Enterprises	43	68 Plym	167	1,600
2. James Hylton	James Hylton	48	67 Dodg	160	1,000
3. Neil Castles	Sherral Pruitt	57	67 Dodg	152	700
4. John Sears	L. G. DeWitt	4	66 Ford	150	575
5. Worth McMillion	Allen McMillion	83	67 Pont	145	425

Raleigh Speedway
Raleigh, NC
1-mile Paved Track

(aka Southland Speedway; Dixie Speedway) Modern 1-mile high-banked paved oval was North Carolina's first superspeedway. Opened to AAA IndyCar championship event in 1952. First NASCAR Winston Cup (then Grand National) race staged on 5/30/53 (won by Fonty Flock). During the inaugural NASCAR 300-mile event, Tim Flock gave up second place in order to remove a monkey (Jocko Flocko) from his car when the animal broke loose from his seat. Flock had the monkey riding with him as promotional gimmick in 1953. Lights erected in 1955, the first superspeedway race held at night was held on 8/20/55 (won by Herb Thomas). Final Grand National race held on 7/4/58 (won by Fireball Roberts). Track lost its July 4 date when Daytona Int'l Speedway opened in 1959 and never re-opened.

Winston Cup Starts

Buck Baker	7
Jim Paschal	7
Lee Petty	7
Speedy Thompson	7

Winston Cup Victories

Fonty Flock	2
Fireball Roberts	2
Herb Thomas	2

Winston Cup Poles

Tim Flock	1
Fonty Flock	1
Cotton Owens	1
Lee Petty	1
Frankie Schneider	1
Slick Smith	1
Herb Thomas	1

Winston Cup Money

Fireball Roberts $7,275

Most Cars Started
55—July 4, 1958 Raleigh 250

Fewest Cars Started
29—August 20, 1955

Narrowest Margin of Victory
6 car lengths—September 30, 1955

Slowest Race
70.629 MPH—May 30, 1953 Raleigh 300

Race Record
79.822 MPH—July 4, 1956 Raleigh 250

Most Cautions
8—July 4, 1958 Raleigh 250

Most Race Leaders
7—July 4, 1958 Raleigh 250

Most Cars Running at Finish
41—July 4, 1957 Raleigh 250

1953 Grand National Race No. 13 Raleigh 300
May 30, 1953 Average Speed: 70.629

Driver	Owner	Car #	Make	Laps	Winnings
1. Fonty Flock	Frank Christian	14	53 Huds	300	3,500
2. Speedy Thompson	Buckshot Morris	12	53 Olds	298	1,800
3. Tim Flock	Ted Chester	91	53 Huds	297	1,200
4. Herb Thomas	Herb Thomas	92	53 Huds	296	1,000
5. Dick Passwater	Frank Arford	78	53 Olds	296	800

1954 Grand National Race No. 14 Raleigh 250
May 29, 1954 Average Speed: 73.909

Driver	Owner	Car #	Make	Laps	Winnings
1. Herb Thomas	Herb Thomas	92	54 Huds	250	2,250
2. Dick Rathmann	John Ditz	3	54 Huds	248	1,175
3. Hershel McGriff	Frank Christian	14	54 Olds	246	800
4. Lee Petty	Petty Enterprises	42	54 Dodg	244	700
5. Jimmie Lewallen	George Hutchens	80	54 Merc	241	600

1955 Grand National Race No. 34
August 20, 1955 Average Speed: 76.400

Driver	Owner	Car #	Make	Laps	Winnings
1. Herb Thomas	Herb Thomas	92	55 Buick	100	1,500
2. Tim Flock	Carl Kiekhaefer	300	55 Chrys	100	1,000
3. Bob Welborn	J. H. Petty	44	55 Chev	100	600
4. Jimmie Lewallen	Ernest Woods	88	55 Olds	100	500
5. Gwyn Staley	Hubert Westmoreland	2	55 Chev	99	400

1955 Grand National Race No. 38
September 30, 1955 Average Speed: 73.289

Driver	Owner	Car #	Make	Laps	Winnings
1. Fonty Flock	Carl Kiekhaefer	301	55 Chrys	100	1,100
2. Herb Thomas	Herb Thomas	92	55 Chev	100	700
3. Tim Flock	Carl Kiekhaefer	300	55 Chrys	100	475
4. Donald Thomas	Herb Thomas	91	55 Buick	100	365
5. Bill Widenhouse	Sam McCuthen	25	55 Chev	100	310

1956 Grand National Race No. 30 Raleigh 250
July 4, 1956 Average Speed: 79.822

Driver	Owner	Car #	Make	Laps	Winnings
1. Fireball Roberts	Pete DePaolo	22	56 Ford	250	3,000
2. Speedy Thompson	Carl Kiekhaefer	500	56 Dodg	248	2,000
3. Frank Mundy	Carl Kiekhaefer	502	56 Dodg	247	1,275
4. Herb Thomas	Herb Thomas	92	56 Chev	246	925
5. Tim Flock	Mauri Rose	11	56 Chev	243	750

1957 Grand National Race No. 28 Raleigh 250
July 4, 1957 Average Speed: 75.693

Driver	Owner	Car #	Make	Laps	Winnings
1. Paul Goldsmith	Smokey Yunick	3	57 Ford	250	4,000
2. Frankie Schneider	Hubert Westmoreland	44	57 Chev	250	2,475
3. Joe Weatherly	Holman-Moody	12	57 Ford	249	1,575
4. Speedy Thompson	Speedy Thompson	46	57 Chev	249	1,050
5. Bob Welborn	Bob Welborn	49	57 Chev	248	850

1958 Grand National Race No. 28 Raleigh 250
July 4, 1958 Average Speed: 73.691

Driver	Owner	Car #	Make	Laps	Winnings
1. Fireball Roberts	Frank Strickland	22	57 Chev	250	3,800
2. Buck Baker	Buck Baker	87	57 Chev	249	2,325
3. Rex White	J. H. Petty	44	57 Chev	248	1,575
4. Shorty Rollins	Shorty Rollins	99	58 Ford	248	1,075
5. Speedy Thompson	Speedy Thompson	46	57 Chev	248	850

Salisbury Superspeedway
Salisbury, NC
.625-Mile Dirt Track

A superspeedway in name only. Track, built in 1958, was measured at .625-paved oval. Track opened with Winston Cup (then Grand National) race on 10/5/58 (won by Lee Petty). Track closed in 1961.

Winston Cup Victories
Lee Petty   1

Winston Cup Money
Lee Petty $800

Narrowest Margin of Victory
N/A

Most Race Leaders
N/A

Winston Cup Poles
Gober Sosebee   1

Most Cars Started
30—October 5, 1958

Race Record
58.271 MPH—October 5, 1958

Most Cars Running at Finish
25—October 5, 1958

1958 Grand National Race No. 48
October 5, 1958 Average Speed: 58.271

Driver	Owner	Car #	Make	Laps	Winnings
1. Lee Petty	Petty Enterprises	42	57 Olds	160	800
2. Buck Baker	Buck Baker	87	57 Chev	160	525
3. Cotton Owens	Jim Stephens	3	58 Pont	157	350
4. George Dunn	Manley Britt	14	57 Merc	157	250
5. Roy Tyner	J. H. Petty	49	57 Chev	157	225

Southern States Fairgrounds
Charlotte, NC
Half-mile Dirt Track

(aka Charlotte Fairgrounds) Half-mile dirt track built circa 1926. First NASCAR Winston Cup (then Grand National) race staged on 8/13/54 (won by Lee Petty). Final Grand National race was held on 11/6/60 (won by Richard Petty, who won his first career race here on 2/28/60). Track closed to auto racing with the construction of Charlotte Motor Speedway in 1960.

Winston Cup Starts
Buck Baker   17
Lee Petty   17

Winston Cup Victories
Lee Petty   3

Winston Cup Poles
Lee Petty   4

Winston Cup Money
Lee Petty $6,110

Most Cars Started
35—July 26, 1959

Fewest Cars Started
15—August 5, 1955

Narrowest Margin of Victory
20 yards—May 22, 1959

Slowest Race
48.806 MPH—August 5, 1955

Race Record
59.435 MPH—November 6, 1960

Most Cautions
9—July 26, 1959

Most Race Leaders
4—July 12, 1957
4—September 5, 1958
4—May 22, 1959
4—November 8, 1959

Most Cars Running at Finish
17—July 26, 1959

1954 Grand National Race No. 28
August 13, 1954 Average Speed: 51.362

Driver	Owner	Car #	Make	Laps	Winnings
1. Lee Petty	Petty Enterprises	42	54 Chrys	200	1,000
2. Dick Rathmann	John Ditz	3	54 Huds	198	650
3. Bob Welborn	Griffin Motors	87	53 Olds	196	450
4. Dink Widenhouse	Dink Widenhouse	B-29	53 Olds	196	350
5. Buck Baker	Ernest Woods	88	54 Olds	192	300

1954 Grand National Race No. 33
September 24, 1954 Average Speed: 53.167

Driver	Owner	Car #	Make	Laps	Winnings
1. Hershel McGriff	Frank Christian	14	54 Olds	200	1,000
2. Lee Petty	Petty Enterprises	42	54 Chrys	199	650
3. Buck Baker	Griffin Motors	87	54 Olds	199	450
4. Dick Rathmann	John Ditz	3	54 Huds	196	350
5. Joe Eubanks	Phil Oates	82	51 Huds	195	300

1955 Grand National Race No. 23
June 24, 1955 Average Speed: 51.289

Driver	Owner	Car #	Make	Laps	Winnings
1. Tim Flock	Carl Kiekhaefer	301	55 Chrys	200	1,000
2. Buck Baker	Griffin Motors	87	54 Olds	198	650
3. Gwyn Staley	Hubert Westmoreland	2	55 Chev	198	450
4. Bob Welborn	J. H. Petty	44	55 Chev	198	350
5. Junior Johnson	B & L Motors	55	55 Olds	194	300

1955 Grand National Race No. 31
August 5, 1955 Average Speed: 48.806

Driver	Owner	Car #	Make	Laps	Winnings
1. Jim Paschal	Ernest Woods	78	55 Olds	200	1,100
2. Gwyn Staley	Hubert Westmoreland	2	55 Chev	198	700
3. Buck Baker	Henry Ford	303	55 Chrys	198	475
4. Bob Welborn	J. H. Petty	44	55 Chev	195	365
5. Tim Flock	Carl Kiekhaefer	300	55 Chrys	192	310

1956 Grand National Race No. 26
June 15, 1956 Average Speed: 56.022

Driver	Owner	Car #	Make	Laps	Winnings
1. Speedy Thompson	Carl Kiekhaefer	300c	56 Chrys	200	650
2. Curtis Turner	Charlie Schwam	99	56 Ford	195	525
3. Lee Petty	Petty Enterprises	42	56 Dodg	195	400
4. Fireball Roberts	Pete DePaolo	22	56 Ford	193	320
5. Buck Baker	Carl Kiekhaefer	300	56 Chrys	189	290

1956 Grand National Race No. 46
September 12, 1956 Average Speed: 52.847

Driver	Owner	Car #	Make	Laps	Winnings
1. Ralph Moody	Pete DePaolo	12	56 Ford	200	850
2. Billy Myers	Bill Stroppe	4	56 Merc	200	625
3. Joe Eubanks	James Satcher	82	56 Ford	200	450
4. Marvin Panch	Tom Harbison	98	56 Ford	199	350
5. Herb Thomas	Herb Thomas	92	56 Chev	196	310

1957 Grand National Race No. 11
April 19, 1957 Average Speed: 52.083

Driver	Owner	Car #	Make	Laps	Winnings
1. Fireball Roberts	Pete DePaolo	22	57 Ford	200	700
2. Marvin Panch	Pete DePaolo	98	57 Ford	200	595
3. Buck Baker	Hugh Babb	87	57 Chev	200	400
4. Lee Petty	Petty Enterprises	42	57 Olds	191	300
5. Jim Paschal	Bill Stroppe	17	57 Merc	190	270

1957 Grand National Race No. 29
July 12, 1957 Average Speed: 56.302

Driver	Owner	Car #	Make	Laps	Winnings
1. Marvin Panch	Marvin Panch	98	57 Ford	200	700
2. Buck Baker	Buck Baker	87	57 Chev	200	525
3. Lee Petty	Petty Enterprises	42	57 Olds	200	400
4. Speedy Thompson	Speedy Thompson	46	57 Chev	199	330
5. Fireball Roberts	Dick Beaty	34	56 Ford	195	270

1957 Grand National Race No. 48
October 5, 1957 Average Speed: 51.583

Driver	Owner	Car #	Make	Laps	Winnings
1. Lee Petty	Petty Enterprises	42	57 Olds	200	900
2. Fireball Roberts	Fireball Roberts	22	57 Ford	200	575
3. Eddie Pagan	Eddie Pagan	45	57 Ford	199	375
4. Buck Baker	Buck Baker	87	57 Chev	195	280
5. Tiny Lund	Bob Welborn	48	57 Chev	192	245

1958 Grand National Race No. 11
April 18, 1958 Average Speed: 53.254

Driver	Owner	Car #	Make	Laps	Winnings
1. Curtis Turner	Holman-Moody	26	58 Ford	200	800
2. Jack Smith	Jack Smith	47	57 Chev	199	525
3. Johnny Allen	Spook Crawford	64	57 Plym	196	350
4. Lee Petty	Petty Enterprises	42	57 Olds	196	250
5. Joe Weatherly	Holman-Moody	12	58 Ford	195	225

Southern States Fairgrounds *continued*

1958 Grand National Race No. 42
September 5, 1958 Average Speed: 52.280

Driver	Owner	Car #	Make	Laps	Winnings
1. Buck Baker	Buck Baker	87	57 Chev	200	800
2. Speedy Thompson	Speedy Thompson	46	57 Chev	199	525
3. Shorty Rollins	Shorty Rollins	99	58 Ford	191	350
4. Bob Walden	Bob Walden	52	57 Ford	183	250
5. Bill Poor	Bill Poor	711	56 Chev	179	225

1959 Grand National Race No. 15
May 22, 1959 Average Speed: 55.300

Driver	Owner	Car #	Make	Laps	Winnings
1. Lee Petty	Petty Enterprises	42	57 Olds	200	800
2. Tiny Lund	Tiny Lund	5	57 Chev	200	525
3. Cotton Owens	Don Every	82	58 Ford	200	350
4. Speedy Thompson	Bruce Thompson	2	57 Chev	200	250
5. Buck Baker	Buck Baker	87	59 Chev	199	225

1959 Grand National Race No. 28
July 26, 1959 Average Speed: 49.553

Driver	Owner	Car #	Make	Laps	Winnings
1. Jack Smith	Jack Smith	47	59 Chev	200	900
2. Bob Welborn	Bob Welborn	49	57 Chev	200	525
3. Buck Baker	Lynton Tyson	87	59 Chev	200	350
4. Cotton Owens	W. H. Watson	6	58 Pont	200	250
5. Larry Frank	Larry Frank	76	57 Chev	200	225

1959 Grand National Race No. 30
August 2, 1959 Average Speed: 52.794

Driver	Owner	Car #	Make	Laps	Winnings
1. Ned Jarrett	Ned Jarrett	11	57 Ford	200	800
2. Jim Paschal	J. H. Petty	48	57 Chev	199	525
3. Bob Welborn	Bob Welborn	49	59 Chev	199	350
4. Tommy Irwin	Tommy Irwin	36	57 Ford	193	250
5. Larry Frank	Larry Frank	76	57 Chev	190	225

1960 Grand National Race No. 1
November 8, 1959 Average Speed: 52.409

Driver	Owner	Car #	Make	Laps	Winnings
1. Jack Smith	Jack Smith	47	59 Chev	200	800
2. Bob Welborn	W. J. Ridgeway	22	59 Chev	199	525
3. Buck Baker	Buck Baker	87	59 Chev	198	375
4. Roy Tyner	Roy Tyner	9	57 Chev	196	275
5. Speedy Thompson	Bruce Thompson	2	57 Chev	193	250

1960 Grand National Race No. 6
February 28, 1960 Average Speed: 53.404

Driver	Owner	Car #	Make	Laps	Winnings
1. Richard Petty	Petty Enterprises	43	59 Plym	200	800
2. Rex White	Rex White	4	59 Chev	200	525
3. Doug Yates	Raeford Johnson	23	59 Plym	199	375
4. Junior Johnson	Wood Brothers	21	59 Ford	198	275
5. Joe Eubanks	Don Every	82	59 Chev	193	250

1961 Grand National Race No. 1
November 6, 1960 Average Speed: 59.435

Driver	Owner	Car #	Make	Laps	Winnings
1. Joe Weatherly	Doc White	16	58 Ford	200	800
2. Rex White	Rex White	4	59 Chev	200	525
3. Lee Petty	Petty Enterprises	42	60 Plym	196	375
4. Buck Baker	Buck Baker	87	60 Chev	194	275
5. David Pearson	David Pearson	67	59 Chev	190	250

Starlite Speedway
Monroe, NC
Half-mile Dirt Track

Half-mile dirt track built circa 1962. Only NASCAR Winston Cup (then Grand National) race staged on 5/13/66 (won by Darel Dieringer). No factory backed teams were permitted to compete in race. James Sears was killed here in August 1973 after striking an opening in the guard rail, an event which ultimately led to the track's closure.

Winston Cup Victories
Darel Dieringer   1

Winston Cup Poles
James Hylton   1

Winston Cup Money
Darel Dieringer $1,000

Most Cars Started
25—May 13, 1966

Narrowest Margin of Victory
8 laps plus—May 13, 1966

Race Record
60.140 MPH—May 13, 1966

Most Cautions
3—May 13, 1966

Most Race Leaders
4—May 13, 1966

Most Cars Running at Finish
7—May 13, 1966

1966 Grand National Race No. 18
May 13, 1966 Average Speed: 60.140

Driver	Owner	Car #	Make	Laps	Winnings
1. Darel Dieringer	Reid Shaw	0	64 Ford	250	1,000
2. Clyde Lynn	Clyde Lynn	20	64 Ford	242	600
3. Wendell Scott	Wendell Scott	34	65 Ford	238	400
4. Neil Castles	Buck Baker	86	65 Plym	237	300
5. Henley Gray	Henley Gray	97	66 Ford	230	275

Tar Heel Speedway
Randleman, NC
Quarter-mile Dirt Track

(aka Kings Kountry Motor Speedway) Quarter-mile paved track opened in May 1957; built by Harold Brasington. First NASCAR Winston Cup (then Grand National) race staged on 11/22/62 (won by Jim Paschal; race was included in 1963 championship season). Final Grand National race run on 10/5/63 (won by Richard Petty). Track closed circa 1967, but may have run a special event in 1975.

Winston Cup Starts
Curtis Crider   3
Ned Jarrett   3
Jimmy Pardue   3
Jim Paschal   3
Richard Petty   3
Wendell Scott   3
Larry Thomas   3
Joe Weatherly   3

Winston Cup Victories
Jim Paschal   2

Winston Cup Poles
Ned Jarrett   1
Fred Lorenzen   1
Glen Wood   1

Winston Cup Money
Joe Weatherly $1,995

Most Cars Started
24—November 22, 1962 Turkey Day 200

Fewest Cars Started
15—May 5, 1963

Narrowest Margin of Victory
4 car lengths—October 5, 1963

Slowest Race
46.001 MPH—October 5, 1963

Race Record
48.605 MPH—May 5, 1963

Most Race Leaders
2—November 22, 1962 Turkey Day 200
2—May 5, 1963
2—October 5, 1963

Most Cars Running at Finish
16—November 22, 1962 Turkey Day 200

1963 Grand National Race No. 3 Turkey Day 200
November 22, 1962 Average Speed: 47.544

Driver	Owner	Car #	Make	Laps	Winnings
1. Jim Paschal	Petty Enterprises	41	62 Plym	200	575
2. Joe Weatherly	Bud Moore	8	62 Pont	198	650
3. Tommy Irwin	Stewart McKinney	44	62 Ford	197	350
4. David Pearson	Cotton Owens	6	62 Dodg	197	290
5. Maurice Petty	Petty Enterprises	42	62 Plym	196	225

1963 Grand National Race No. 22
May 5, 1963 Average Speed: 48.605

Driver	Owner	Car #	Make	Laps	Winnings
1. Jim Paschal	Petty Enterprises	43	62 Plym	200	570
2. Joe Weatherly	Cliff Stewart	2	62 Pont	196	675
3. Ned Jarrett	Charles Robinson	11	63 Ford	196	400
4. Jimmy Pardue	Pete Stewart	57	62 Pont	195	290
5. Larry Thomas	Wade Younts	36	62 Dodg	195	240

1963 Grand National Race No. 51
October 5, 1963 Average Speed: 46.001

Driver	Owner	Car #	Make	Laps	Winnings
1. Richard Petty	Petty Enterprises	43	63 Plym	200	580
2. Joe Weatherly	Bud Moore	8	63 Merc	200	670
3. Bob Welborn	Petty Enterprises	42	63 Plym	199	380
4. Darel Dieringer		14	63 Ford	196	290
5. Fred Lorenzen	Holman-Moody	28	63 Ford	194	275

Tri-City Speedway
High Point, NC
Half-mile Dirt Track

(aka High Point Motor Speedway) Originally a 1-mile track built in 1940. Half-mile track built sometime in the early '50s. First NASCAR Winston Cup (then Grand National) race staged on 6/26/53 (won by Herb Thomas). Only other Grand National race staged on 11/7/54 (won by Lee Petty; race was the 1955 season opener). Track closed in late '50s or early '60s.

Winston Cup Starts
12 drivers tied with 2

Winston Cup Victories
Lee Petty   1
Herb Thomas   1

Winston Cup Poles
Herb Thomas   2

Winston Cup Money
Herb Thomas $1,450

Most Cars Started
23—June 26, 1953

Fewest Cars Started
21—November 7, 1954

Narrowest Margin of Victory
1/2 lap—November 7, 1954

Slowest Race
58.186 MPH—June 26, 1953

Race Record
62.882 MPH—November 7, 1954

Most Race Leaders
N/A

Most Cars Running at Finish
N/A

1953 Grand National Race No. 17
June 26, 1953 Average Speed: 58.186

Driver	Owner	Car #	Make	Laps	Winnings
1. Herb Thomas	Herb Thomas	92	53 Huds	200	1,000
2. Dick Rathmann	Walt Chapman	120	53 Huds	—	700
3. Joe Eubanks	Phil Oates	82	52 Huds	—	450
4. Buck Baker	Griffin Motors	87	53 Olds	—	350
5. Lee Petty	Petty Enterprises	42	53 Dodg	—	200

1955 Grand National Race No. 1
November 7, 1954 Average Speed: 62.882

Driver	Owner	Car #	Make	Laps	Winnings
1. Lee Petty	Petty Enterprises	42	54 Chrys	200	1,000
2. Buck Baker	Frank Christian	14	54 Olds	200	650
3. Herb Thomas	Herb Thomas	92	54 Huds	199	450
4. Gober Sosebee	Gober Sosebee	51	54 Olds	196	350
5. Jimmie Lewallen	Joe Blair	5	54 Merc	196	300

Wilson Speedway
Wilson, NC
Half-mile Dirt Track

(aka Wilson Fairgrounds; Wilson County Speedway; Legion Speedway) Half-mile dirt track built in 1934. First NASCAR Winston Cup (then Grand National) race staged on 9/30/51 (won by Fonty Flock). Final Grand National race held on 4/17/60 (won by Joe Weatherly). Track operated weekly and special events until it closed sometime in 1989.

Winston Cup Starts
Buck Baker   12

Winston Cup Victories
Herb Thomas   3

Winston Cup Poles
Herb Thomas   3

Winston Cup Money
Buck Baker $4,895

Most Cars Started
32—March 18, 1956

Fewest Cars Started
16—May 9, 1954

Narrowest Margin of Victory
1 foot—November 18, 1956

Slowest Race
35.398 MPH—September 28, 1952

Race Record
58.065 MPH—June 20, 1959

Most Race Leaders
4—March 29, 1959

Most Cars Running at Finish
18—March 18, 1956

1951 Grand National Race No. 30
September 30, 1951

Driver	Owner	Car #	Make	Laps	Winnings
1. Fonty Flock	Frank Christian	14	51 Olds	200	1,000
2. Bob Flock	Ted Chester	7	51 Olds	—	600
3. Jimmie Lewallen	Hubert Hamilton	0	51 Plym	—	500
4. Jim Paschal	Julian Buesink	60	50 Ford	—	400
5. Bill Snowden	Bill Snowden	16	51 Ford	—	300

1952 Grand National Race No. 29
September 28, 1952   Average Speed: 35.398

Driver	Owner	Car #	Make	Laps	Winnings
1. Herb Thomas	Herb Thomas	92	52 Huds	200	1,000
2. Lee Petty	Petty Enterprises	42	51 Plym	199	700
3. Bill Blair	George Hutchens	2	52 Olds	199	450
4. Jim Paschal	Buckshot Morris	12	52 Olds	199	350
5. Dick Rathmann	Walt Chapman	120	52 Huds	198	200

1953 Grand National Race No. 18
June 28, 1953   Average Speed: 53.803

Driver	Owner	Car #	Make	Laps	Winnings
1. Fonty Flock	Frank Christian	14	53 Huds	200	1,000
2. Dick Rathmann	Walt Chapman	120	53 Huds	—	700
3. Herb Thomas	Herb Thomas	92	53 Huds	—	450
4. Joe Eubanks	Phil Oates	82	52 Huds	—	350
5. Buck Baker	Griffin Motors	87	53 Olds	—	200

1953 Grand National Race No. 34
October 4, 1953   Average Speed: 56.022

Driver	Owner	Car #	Make	Laps	Winnings
1. Herb Thomas	Herb Thomas	92	53 Huds	200	1,000
2. Speedy Thompson	Buckshot Morris	12	53 Olds	—	700
3. Fonty Flock	Frank Christian	14	53 Huds	—	450
4. Lee Petty	Petty Enterprises	42	53 Dodg	—	350
5. Ralph Liguori		45	51 Plym	—	200

1954 Grand National Race No. 11
May 9, 1954   Average Speed: 52.279

Driver	Owner	Car #	Make	Laps	Winnings
1. Buck Baker	Ernest Woods	88	54 Olds	200	1,000
2. Al Keller	George Miller	23	54 Huds	199	650
3. Ralph Liguori	Ralph Liguori	6	53 Dodg	199	450
4. Lee Petty	Petty Enterprises	42	54 Dodg	197	350
5. Jim Paschal	Griffin Motors	87	53 Olds	196	300

1956 Grand National Race No. 8
March 18, 1956   Average Speed: 46.287

Driver	Owner	Car #	Make	Laps	Winnings
1. Herb Thomas	Smokey Yunick	92	56 Chev	106	1,100
2. Buck Baker	Carl Kiekhaefer	500B	56 Dodg	106	700
3. Tim Flock	Carl Kiekhaefer	300B	56 Chrys	106	475
4. Jim Paschal	Frank Hayworth	75	56 Merc	105	365
5. Bill Widenhouse		68	56 Ford	105	310

1956 Grand National Race No. 56
November 18, 1956   Average Speed: 50.597

Driver	Owner	Car #	Make	Laps	Winnings
1. Buck Baker	Carl Kiekhaefer	300B	56 Chrys	200	950
2. Joe Weatherly	Pete DePaolo	112	56 Ford	200	675
3. Speedy Thompson	Carl Kiekhaefer	300	56 Chrys	200	475
4. Fireball Roberts	Pete DePaolo	22	56 Ford	200	365
5. Bill Amick	Pete DePaolo	97	56 Ford	199	320

1957 Grand National Race No. 6
March 17, 1957   Average Speed: 55.079

Driver	Owner	Car #	Make	Laps	Winnings
1. Ralph Moody	Pete DePaolo	12	57 Ford	200	850
2. Buck Baker	Hugh Babb	87	57 Chev	198	625
3. Speedy Thompson	Hugh Babb	46	57 Chev	196	450
4. Lee Petty	Petty Enterprises	42	57 Olds	195	350
5. Tiny Lund	Petty Enterprises	188	57 Olds	195	310

1958 Grand National Race No. 5
March 16, 1958   Average Speed: 48.459

Driver	Owner	Car #	Make	Laps	Winnings
1. Lee Petty	Petty Enterprises	42	57 Olds	200	800
2. Buck Baker	Buck Baker	87	57 Chev	196	525
3. Marvin Panch	John Whitford	98	57 Ford	193	350
4. Jack Smith	Jack Smith	47	57 Chev	192	250
5. Reds Kagle	Hoss Kagle	88	57 Chev	191	225

1959 Grand National Race No. 7
March 29, 1959   Average Speed: 50.300

Driver	Owner	Car #	Make	Laps	Winnings
1. Junior Johnson	Paul Spaulding	11	57 Ford	200	800
2. Curtis Turner	Doc White	41	59 Ford	200	525
3. Richard Petty	Petty Enterprises	43	57 Olds	198	350
4. Lee Petty	Petty Enterprises	42	57 Olds	196	250
5. Tom Pistone	Carl Rupert	59	59 Ford	196	225

Wilson Speedway *continued*

1959 Grand National Race No. 22
June 20, 1959 Average Speed: 58.065

Driver	Owner	Car #	Make	Laps	Winnings
1. Junior Johnson	Paul Spaulding	11	57 Ford	200	800
2. Tom Pistone	Carl Rupert	59	59 Ford	200	525
3. Glen Wood	Wood Brothers	21	58 Ford	196	350
4. Lee Petty	Petty Enterprises	42	57 Olds	194	250
5. Buck Baker	Buck Baker	87	59 Chev	194	225

1960 Grand National Race No. 12
April 17, 1960 Average Speed: 55.113

Driver	Owner	Car #	Make	Laps	Winnings
1. Joe Weatherly	Holman-Moody	12	60 Ford	200	1,275
2. Lee Petty	Petty Enterprises	42	60 Plym	199	750
3. Tom Pistone	W. T. Coppedge	59	60 Chev	199	525
4. Rex White	Rex White	4	50 Chev	198	275
5. Buck Baker	Buck Baker	87	60 Chev	198	250

Ohio

Bainbridge Fairgrounds
Bainbridge, OH
1-mile Dirt Track

1-mile dirt track opened in June 1946. Half-mile dirt track utilized for only one NASCAR Winston Cup (then Grand National) race on 7/8/51 (won by Fonty Flock). Auto races were discontinued after 1951, and the track became the Grandview Race Track for horse racing in 1950s.

Winston Cup Victories
Fonty Flock   1

Winston Cup Poles
Fonty Flock   1

Winston Cup Money
Fonty Flock $1,000

Most Cars Started
34—July 8, 1951

Narrowest Margin of Victory
N/A

Race Record
65.753 MPH—July 8, 1951

Most Race Leaders
1—July 8, 1951

Most Cars Running at Finish
N/A

1951 Grand National Race No. 15
July 8, 1951 Average Speed: 65.753

Driver	Owner	Car #	Make	Laps	Winnings
1. Fonty Flock	Frank Christian	14	50 Olds	100	1,000
2. Dick Rathmann	Walt Chapman	120	51 Huds	—	600
3. Frank Mundy	Perry Smith	23	51 Stud	—	400
4. Jimmy Florian	Jimmy Florian	27	51 Ford	—	300
5. Oda Greene	Harold Lucas	22	51 Huds	—	250

Canfield Fairgrounds
Canfield, OH
Half-mile Dirt Track

(aka Canfield Motor Speedway; Mahoning County Fairgrounds) Half-mile dirt oval built circa 1929. First NASCAR Winston Cup (then Grand National) race staged on 5/30/50 (won by Bill Rexford, his only Grand National win came in his championship season). Event was named "Poor Man's 500"—and was run on the same day as the Indianapolis 500. Final NASCAR race held on 5/30/52 (won by Herb Thomas). Track closed in 1973.

Winston Cup Starts

Tim Flock	3
Lloyd Moore	3
Lee Petty	3
Bill Rexford	3

Winston Cup Victories

Bill Rexford	1
Marshall Teague	1
Herb Thomas	1

Winston Cup Poles

Jimmy Florian	1
Dick Rathmann	1
Bill Rexford	1

Winston Cup Money

Bill Rexford	$1,525

Most Cars Started

38—May 30, 1951 Poor Man's 500

Fewest Cars Started

29—May 30, 1950 Poor Man's 500

Narrowest Margin of Victory

4 feet—May 30, 1952
Poor Man's 500

Slowest Race

48.057 MPH—May 30, 1952
Poor Man's 500

Race Record

49.308 MPH—May 30, 1951
Poor Man's 500

Most Cautions

4—May 30, 1952 Poor Man's 500

Most Race Leaders

2—May 30, 1950 Poor Man's 500
2—May 30, 1952 Poor Man's 500

Most Cars Running at Finish

N/A

1950 Grand National Race No. 5 Poor Man's 500
May 30, 1950

Driver	Owner	Car #	Make	Laps	Winnings
1. Bill Rexford	Julian Buesink	60	50 Olds	200	1,400
2. Glenn Dunnaway	Glenn Dunnaway	49	49 Plym	198	750
3. Lloyd Moore	Julian Buesink	59	50 Ford	198	500
4. Lee Petty	Petty Enterprises	42	49 Plym	195	400
5. Bill Blair	Sam Rice	22	50 Merc	195	300

1951 Grand National Race No. 9 Poor Man's 500
May 30, 1951 Average Speed: 49.308

Driver	Owner	Car #	Make	Laps	Winnings
1. Marshall Teague	Marshall Teague	6	51 Huds	200	1,000
2. Tim Flock	Ted Chester	91	51 Olds	197	600
3. Fonty Flock	Frank Christian	14	50 Olds	—	400
4. Herb Thomas	Herb Thomas	92	50 Plym	—	300
5. Lee Petty	Petty Enterprises	42	49 Plym	—	250

1952 Grand National Race No. 12 Poor Man's 500
May 30, 1952 Average Speed: 48.057

Driver	Owner	Car #	Make	Laps	Winnings
1. Herb Thomas	Herb Thomas	92	52 Huds	200	1,000
2. Bill Blair	George Hutchens	2	52 Olds	200	700
3. Bob Moore	Bob Moore	78	51 Olds	199	450
4. Tim Flock	Ted Chester	91	51 Huds	196	350
5. Curtis Turner	John Eanes	41	51 Huds	189	200

Dayton Speedway
Dayton, OH
Half-mile Paved Track

(aka Greater Dayton Speedway) Half-mile high-banked dirt oval opened in 1939. First NASCAR Winston Cup (then Grand National) race staged on 6/25/50 (won by Jimmy Florian, the first driver to win a Grand National event in a Ford). Final Grand National race run on 5/18/52 (won by Dick Rathmann). Track closed in 1982 and is now a landfill.

Winston Cup Starts
Lloyd Moore 6
Lee Petty 6

Winston Cup Victories
Dick Rathmann 2

Winston Cup Poles
Fonty Flock 3

Winston Cup Money
Dick Rathmann $3,125

Most Cars Started
31—September 23, 1951

Fewest Cars Started
15—May 18, 1952

Narrowest Margin of Victory
5.000 seconds September 21, 1952

Slowest Race
61.643 MPH—September 21, 1952

Race Record
65.526 MPH—May 18, 1952

Most Cautions
N/A

Most Race Leaders
4—June 25, 1950

Most Cars Running at Finish
21—September 21, 1952

1950 Grand National Race No. 7
June 25, 1950 Average Speed: 63.351

Driver	Owner	Car #	Make	Laps	Winnings
1. Jimmy Florian	Jimmy Florian	27	50 Ford	200	1,160
2. Dick Linder	Don Rogalla	25	50 Olds	—	625
3. Buck Barr			50 Ford	—	400
4. Curtis Turner	John Eanes	41	50 Olds	—	620
5. Art Lamey		9	49 Plym	—	225

1950 Grand National Race No. 11
August 20, 1950

Driver	Owner	Car #	Make	Laps	Winnings
1. Dick Linder	Don Rogalla	25	50 Olds	195	1,125
2. Red Harvey			49 Olds	—	600
3. Herb Thomas	Herb Thomas	92	50 Plym	—	400
4. Lee Petty	Petty Enterprises	42	49 Plym	—	300
5. Art Lamey			49 Plym	—	225

1951 Grand National Race No. 12
June 24, 1951

Driver	Owner	Car #	Make	Laps	Winnings
1. Curtis Turner	John Eanes	41	51 Olds	200	1,000
2. Dick Rathmann	Walt Chapman	120	51 Huds	200	600
3. Tim Flock	Ted Chester	91	51 Olds	—	400
4. Fonty Flock	Frank Christian	14	51 Olds	—	300
5. Lloyd Moore	Julian Buesink	59	51 Ford	—	250

1951 Grand National Race No. 29
September 23, 1951

Driver	Owner	Car #	Make	Laps	Winnings
1. Fonty Flock	Frank Christian	14	51 Olds	200	1,000
2. Neil Cole	John Golabek	52	50 Olds	199	600
3. Lloyd Moore	Julian Buesink	59	51 Ford	—	500
4. Lee Petty	Petty Enterprises	42	51 Plym	—	400
5. Harvey Riley	Joe Beccue	66	51 Huds	—	300

1952 Grand National Race No. 11
May 18, 1952 Average Speed: 65.526

Driver	Owner	Car #	Make	Laps	Winnings
1. Dick Rathmann	Walt Chapman	120	51 Huds	200	1,000
2. Lloyd Moore	Julian Buesink	59	51 Ford	199	700
3. Tim Flock	Ted Chester	91	51 Huds	195	450
4. Lee Petty	Petty Enterprises	42	51 Plym	195	350
5. Donald Thomas	Doug Meeks	72	51 Ford	192	200

1952 Grand National Race No. 28
September 21, 1952 Average Speed: 61.643

Driver	Owner	Car #	Make	Laps	Winnings
1. Dick Rathmann	Walt Chapman	120	51 Huds	300	1,500
2. Lee Petty	Petty Enterprises	42	51 Plym	300	1,000
3. Ray Duhigg	J. O. Goode	24	50 Plym	297	700
4. Lloyd Moore	Julian Buesink	59	51 Ford	295	600
5. Herb Thomas	Herb Thomas	92	52 Huds	293	350

Ft. Miami Speedway
Toledo, OH
Half-mile Dirt Track

1-mile dirt track built in October 1902. Half-mile dirt track opened in September 1941. Closed during war, re-opened in July of 1947. First NASCAR Winston Cup (then Grand National) race staged on 8/19/51 (won by Tim Flock). Final Grand National race run 6/1/52 (also won by Tim Flock). Half-mile track closed in 1956. A .375-mile track operated in 1957 and 1958.

Winston Cup Starts
Ray Duhigg	2
Joe Eubanks	2
Tim Flock	2
Fonty Flock	2
Bob Moore	2
Lee Petty	2
Dick Rathmann	2
Herb Thomas	2

Winston Cup Victories
Tim Flock   2

Winston Cup Poles
Fonty Flock   2

Winston Cup Money
Tim Flock $2,000

Most Cars Started
33—August 19, 1951

Fewest Cars Started
24—June 1, 1952

Narrowest Margin of Victory
N/A

Slowest Race
47.175 MPH—June 1, 1952

Race Record
50.847 MPH—August 19, 1951

Most Cautions
N/A

Most Race Leaders
3—August 19, 1951

Most Cars Running at Finish
N/A

1951 Grand National Race No. 21
August 19, 1951 Average Speed: 50.847

Driver	Owner	Car #	Make	Laps	Winnings
1. Tim Flock	Ted Chester	91	51 Olds	200	1,000
2. Dell Pearson	Del Pearson	88	51 Plym	—	600
3. Oda Greene	Harold Lucas	22	51 Huds	—	400
4. Lou Figaro	Jack Gaynor	33	51 Huds	—	300
5. Herb Thomas	Herb Thomas	92	51 Plym	—	250

1952 Grand National Race No. 14
June 1, 1952 Average Speed: 47.175

Driver	Owner	Car #	Make	Laps	Winnings
1. Tim Flock	Ted Chester	91	51 Huds	200	1,000
2. Dick Rathmann	Walt Chapman	120	51 Huds	200	700
3. Lee Petty	Petty Enterprises	42	51 Plym	194	450
4. Ray Duhigg	J. H. Petty	44	51 Plym	193	350
5. Fonty Flock	Frank Christian	14	50 Olds	175	200

Powell Motor Speedway
Columbus, OH
Half-mile Dirt Track

(aka Powell Speedway) Half-mile dirt track originally built in 1939. Re-opened after the war in June 1946. Only NASCAR Winston Cup (then Grand National) race staged on 5/24/53 (won by Herb Thomas). Half-mile track closed in 1959. Smaller tracks were built on site and ran until 1965.

Winston Cup Victories
Herb Thomas   1

Winston Cup Poles
Fonty Flock   1

Winston Cup Money
Herb Thomas $1,000

Most Cars Started
27—May 24, 1953

Narrowest Margin of Victory
3 car lengths—May 24, 1953

Race Record
56.127 MPH—May 24, 1953

Most Race Leaders
N/A

Most Cars Running at Finish
15—May 24, 1953

1953 Grand National Race No. 12
May 24, 1953 Average Speed: 56.127

Driver	Owner	Car #	Make	Laps	Winnings
1. Herb Thomas	Herb Thomas	92	53 Huds	200	1,000
2. Dick Rathmann	Walt Chapman	120	53 Huds	200	700
3. Buck Baker	Griffin Motors	87	53 Olds	198	450
4. Curtis Turner	John Eanes	41	53 Olds	198	350
5. Pop McGinnis	Irving Frye	13	53 Huds	193	200

Oklahoma

Oklahoma State Fairgrounds
Oklahoma City, OK
Half-mile Dirt Track

(aka State Fair Speedway) Half-mile dirt track opened in 1954. Only Winston Cup (then Grand National) race held on 8/3/56 (won by Jim Paschal). Track still in operation.

Winston Cup Victories
Jim Paschal   1

Winston Cup Poles
Speedy Thompson   1

Winston Cup Money
Jim Paschal $850

Most Cars Started
12—August 3, 1956

Narrowest Margin of Victory
1/4 lap—August 3, 1956

Race Record
60.100 MPH—August 3, 1956

Most Race Leaders
3—August 3, 1956

Most Cars Running at Finish
7—August 3, 1956

1956 Grand National Race No. 36
August 3, 1956 Average Speed: 60.100

Driver	Owner	Car #	Make	Laps	Winnings
1. Jim Paschal	Frank Hayworth	75	56 Merc	200	850
2. Ralph Moody	Pete DePaolo	12	56 Ford	200	625
3. Fireball Roberts	Pete DePaolo	22	56 Ford	198	450
4. Herb Thomas	Herb Thomas	92	56 Chev	196	350
5. Lee Petty	Petty Enterprises	42	56 Dodg	193	310

Oregon

Portland Speedway
Portland, OR
Half-mile Paved Track

(aka Union Avenue Speedway; Rankin Speedway; City of Roses Speedway; Portland Drive-In Speedway; Rose City Speedway) .625-mile dirt track built in 1924 and paved in 1951. Shortened to half-mile in 1952. First NASCAR Winston Cup (then Grand National) race staged on 5/27/56 (won by Herb Thomas). Final Grand National race run on 7/14/57 (won by Eddie Pagan). The infield was the parking lot for a drive-in theater, with the screen just off the backstretch. Track is still in operation and currently hosts a variety of NASCAR events.

Winston Cup Starts
Harold Beal	7
Lloyd Dane	7
Art Watts	7

Winston Cup Victories
Eddie Pagan	2

Winston Cup Poles
Art Watts	3

Winston Cup Money
Eddie Pagan	$3,665

Most Cars Started
23—May 26, 1957

Fewest Cars Started
16—April 28, 1957

Narrowest Margin of Victory
N/A

Slowest Race
62.586 MPH—June 24, 1956

Race Record
64.754 MPH—April 28, 1957

Most Race Leaders
4—May 27, 1956

Most Cars Running at Finish
17—May 27, 1956
17—August 26, 1956

1956 Grand National Race No. 21
May 27, 1956 Average Speed: 63.815

Driver	Owner	Car #	Make	Laps	Winnings
1. Herb Thomas	Carl Kiekhaefer	300B	56 Chrys	150	1,000
2. John Kieper	John Kieper	98	55 Olds	150	700
3. Clyde Palmer		1C	56 Dodg	150	475
4. Ed Negre		88	56 Olds	149	365
5. Curley Barker		11	56 Chev	148	310

1956 Grand National Race No. 28
June 24, 1956 Average Speed: 62.586

Driver	Owner	Car #	Make	Laps	Winnings
1. John Kieper	John Kieper	98	55 Olds	200	950
2. Clyde Palmer		1C	56 Dodg	200	665
3. Lou Sherman	Jim Rush	56	56 Merc	199	500
4. Harold Beal		50	56 Ford	199	395
5. Ed Negre		6	54 Olds	199	310

1956 Grand National Race No. 43
August 26, 1956 Average Speed: 63.429

Driver	Owner	Car #	Make	Laps	Winnings
1. Royce Haggerty	Curly Weida	15N	56 Dodg	246	1,200
2. Clyde Palmer		1	56 Ford	246	730
3. Curley Barker		11	56 Chev	246	500
4. Chuck Meekins		56	56 Chev	245	400
5. Eddie Pagan	Eddie Pagan	45	56 Ford	244	350

1956 Grand National Race No. 48
September 23, 1956

Driver	Owner	Car #	Make	Laps	Winnings
1. Lloyd Dane	Lloyd Dane	1	56 Ford	250	1,020
2. Eddie Pagan	Eddie Pagan	45	56 Ford	249	650
3. Curley Barker		11N	56 Chev	249	450
4. John Kieper	John Kieper	57	56 Chev	248	370
5. Harold Hardesty	Beryl Jackson	80N	56 Olds	247	330

1957 Grand National Race No. 14
April 28, 1957 Average Speed: 64.754

Driver	Owner	Car #	Make	Laps	Winnings
1. Art Watts	Al Schmidhamer	22N	56 Ford	100	940
2. Eddie Pagan	Eddie Pagan	45	57 Ford	100	635
3. George Seeger	Oscar Maples	12	57 Ford	100	480
4. Chuck Meekins	Jim Rush	1	57 Chev	99	340
5. Jack McCoy		22	56 Ford	99	270

1957 Grand National Race No. 18
May 26, 1957 Average Speed: 64.732

Driver	Owner	Car #	Make	Laps	Winnings
1. Eddie Pagan	Eddie Pagan	45	57 Ford	150	930
2. Lloyd Dane	Lloyd Dane	44	57 Ford	150	600
3. Clyde Palmer	Hugh Babb	82	57 Chev	149	470
4. Scotty Cain	Scotty Cain	44	56 Merc	147	345
5. Dick Getty	Dick Getty	00	56 Chev	146	270

1957 Grand National Race No. 31
July 14, 1957 Average Speed: 64.539

Driver	Owner	Car #	Make	Laps	Winnings
1. Eddie Pagan	Eddie Pagan	45	57 Ford	200	1,000
2. Lloyd Dane	Lloyd Dane	44	57 Ford	198	625
3. Danny Graves	Danny Graves	81	57 Chev	198	400
4. Scotty Cain	Scotty Cain	14	56 Merc	197	295
5. Dick Getty	Dick Getty	00	56 Chev	194	255

Pennsylvania

Bloomsburg Fairgrounds
Bloomsburg, PA
Half-mile Dirt Track

Built on Columbia County Fairgrounds circa 1927. Only NASCAR Winston Cup (then Grand National) race staged on 10/3/53 (won by Herb Thomas). Track closed in mid-1980s.

Winston Cup Victories
Herb Thomas 1

Winston Cup Poles
Jim Paschal 1

Winston Cup Money
Herb Thomas $1,000

Most Cars Started
21—October 3, 1953

Narrowest Margin of Victory
N/A

Most Race Leaders
N/A

Most Cars Running at Finish
N/A

1953 Grand National Race No. 33
October 3, 1953

	Driver	Owner	Car #	Make	Laps	Winnings
1.	Herb Thomas	Herb Thomas	92	53 Huds	200	1,000
2.	Dick Rathmann	Walt Chapman	120	53 Huds	—	700
3.	Buck Baker	Griffin Motors	87	53 Olds	—	450
4.	Elton Hildreth	Elton Hildreth	167	53 Nash	—	350
5.	Bob Welborn	J. O. Goode	24	51 Plym	—	200

Heidelberg Raceway
Pittsburgh, PA
Quarter-mile Dirt Track

(aka Heidelberg Speedway; Heidelberg Stadium) Half-mile and quarter-mile tracks opened in May 1948. First NASCAR Winston Cup (then Grand National) race staged on 10/2/49 (won by Lee Petty, his first of 54 Grand National victories). Last Grand National race run 7/10/60 (won by Lee Petty). Track paved in 1966. Final event run 10/7/73.

Winston Cup Starts
Lee Petty 4

Winston Cup Victories
Lee Petty 2

Winston Cup Poles
Dick Bailey 1
Al Bonnell 1
Fonty Flock 1
Lee Petty 1

Winston Cup Money
Lee Petty $2,775

Most Cars Started
42—July 15, 1951

Fewest Cars Started
17—July 10, 1960

Narrowest Margin of Victory
N/A

Slowest Race
45.000 MPH—July 21, 1959

Race Record
67.450 MPH—July 10, 1960

Most Cautions
N/A

Most Race Leaders
4—July 21, 1959

Most Cars Running at Finish
14—July 10, 1960

1949 Strictly Stock Race No. 7
October 2, 1949 Average Speed: 57.458

	Driver	Owner	Car #	Make	Laps	Winnings
1.	Lee Petty	Petty Enterprises	42	49 Plym	200	1,500
2.	Dick Linder	La Belle Motors	8	KAI	195	750
3.	Bill Rexford	Julian Buesink	4	49 Ford	193	400
4.	Sam Rice	Sam Rice	2	49 Chev	192	300
5.	Sara Christian	Frank Christian	1	49 Ford	190	175

1951 Grand National Race No. 16
July 15, 1951

	Driver	Owner	Car #	Make	Laps	Winnings
1.	Herb Thomas	Hubert Westmoreland	2	51 Olds	200	1,000
2.	Jim Fiebelkorn	Jim Fiebelkorn	10	51 Merc	199	600
3.	Augie Walackas			51 Merc	—	400
4.	Bud Farrell			51 Plym	—	300
5.	Tom Jerris	William Gundaker		51 Buick	—	250

1959 Grand National Race No. 27
July 21, 1959 Average Speed: 45.000

	Driver	Owner	Car #	Make	Laps	Winnings
1.	Jim Reed	Jim Reed	7	59 Chev	200	900
2.	Rex White	Rex White	4	59 Chev	200	525
3.	Lee Petty	Petty Enterprises	42	59 Plym	197	350
4.	Marvin Porter	Marvin Porter	12	57 Ford	195	250
5.	Cotton Owens	W. H. Watson	6	59 Pont	193	225

1960 Grand National Race No. 24
July 10, 1960 Average Speed: 67.450

	Driver	Owner	Car #	Make	Laps	Winnings
1.	Lee Petty	Petty Enterprises	42	60 Plym	188	900
2.	Richard Petty	Petty Enterprises	43	60 Plym	185	525
3.	Rex White	Rex White	4	59 Chev	184	375
4.	Nook Walters	Nook Walters	1	59 Chev	179	275
5.	L. D. Austin	L. D. Austin	74	58 Chev	174	250

Langhorne Speedway
Langhorne, PA
1-mile Dirt Track

1-mile circular track opened in May 1926. First named Philadelphia Speedway. Closed on 5/10/92. Re-opened after the war in June 1946. First NASCAR Winston Cup (then Grand National) race staged on 9/11/49 (won by Curtis Turner). Sara Christian, the first woman to compete at top level NASCAR racing, finished 6th in the field of 45 and was invited to share Victory Lane ceremonies with Turner. Final Grand National race run on 9/15/57 (won by Gwyn Staley). The track was commonly referred to as the "Track that ate the heroes" due to its danger. Track paved in 1965 and hosted USAC IndyCar races. Final event was 10/17/71. Now a shopping center.

Winston Cup Starts
Lee Petty   17

Winston Cup Victories
Dick Rathmann   3
Herb Thomas   3

Winston Cup Poles
Herb Thomas   4

Winston Cup Money
Lee Petty $11,515

Most Cars Started
63—September 26, 1954

Fewest Cars Started
24—May 2, 1954

Narrowest Margin of Victory
N/A

Slowest Race
64.434 MPH—June 21, 1953

Race Record
85.850 MPH—April 14, 1957

Most Cautions
9—September 23, 1956

Most Race Leaders
5—April 16, 1950
5—September 14, 1952
5—September 23, 1956

Most Cars Running at Finish
35—September 26, 1954

1949 Strictly Stock Race No. 4
September 11, 1949 Average Speed: 69.403

Driver	Owner	Car #	Make	Laps	Winnings
1. Curtis Turner	Hubert Westmoreland	41	49 Olds	200	2,250
2. Bob Flock	Frank Christian	7	49 Olds	200	1,000
3. Red Byron	Raymond Parks	22	49 Olds	199	800
4. Frank Mundy	Sam Rice	44	49 Cad	196	500
5. Bill Blair	Sam Rice	46	49 Cad	196	350

1950 Grand National Race No. 3
April 16, 1950 Average Speed: 69.399

Driver	Owner	Car #	Make	Laps	Winnings
1. Curtis Turner	John Eanes	41	50 Olds	150	1,500
2. Lloyd Moore	Julian Buesink	59	49 Linc	149	1,000
3. Jimmy Florian	Jimmy Florian	27	50 Ford	144	700
4. Tim Flock	Harold Kite	21	49 Linc	139	500
5. Lee Petty	Petty Enterprises	42	49 Plym	139	300

1950 Grand National Race No. 14
September 17, 1950 Average Speed: 72.801

Driver	Owner	Car #	Make	Laps	Winnings
1. Fonty Flock	Frank Christian	47	50 Olds	200	1,500
2. Bill Blair	Sam Rice	2	49 Olds	200	1,000
3. Fireball Roberts	Sam Rice	82	50 Olds	—	700
4. Lee Petty	Petty Enterprises	42	49 Plym	—	400
5. Neil Cole			49 Ford	—	300

1951 Grand National Race No. 27
September 15, 1951 Average Speed: 71.043

Driver	Owner	Car #	Make	Laps	Winnings
1. Herb Thomas	Herb Thomas	92	51 Huds	150	1,275
2. Fonty Flock	Frank Christian	14	51 Olds	150	800
3. Dick Rathmann	Walt Chapman	21	51 Huds	—	600
4. John McGinley	Walt Chapman	120	51 Huds	—	500
5. Tim Flock	Ted Chester	91	51 Olds	—	300

1952 Grand National Race No. 9
May 4, 1952 Average Speed: 67.669

Driver	Owner	Car #	Make	Laps	Winnings
1. Dick Rathmann	Walt Chapman	120	52 Huds	150	1,275
2. Tim Flock	Ted Chester	91	51 Huds	145	810
3. Lee Petty	Petty Enterprises	42	51 Plym	140	600
4. Jack Reynolds		421	50 Plym	140	500
5. Fonty Flock	Frank Christian	14	51 Olds	139	310

1952 Grand National Race No. 27
September 14, 1952 Average Speed: 72.463

Driver	Owner	Car #	Make	Laps	Winnings
1. Lee Petty	Petty Enterprises	42	51 Plym	250	2,500
2. Bill Blair	George Hutchens	2	52 Olds	250	1,250
3. Herschel Buchanan	Herschel Buchanan	1	52 Nash	248	750
4. Tim Flock	Ted Chester	91	52 Huds	247	500
5. Dick Rathmann	Walt Chapman	120	52 Huds	246	450

1953 Grand National Race No. 8
May 3, 1953 Average Speed: 72.743

Driver	Owner	Car #	Make	Laps	Winnings
1. Buck Baker	Griffin Motors	87	53 Olds	150	1,525
2. Lee Petty	Petty Enterprises	42	53 Dodg	150	1,000
3. Fonty Flock	Frank Christian	14	53 Olds	—	800
4. Herschel Buchanan	Herschel Buchanan	1	52 Nash	—	600
5. Tim Flock	Ted Chester	91	53 Huds	—	500

1953 Grand National Race No. 16
June 21, 1953 Average Speed: 64.434

Driver	Owner	Car #	Make	Laps	Winnings
1. Dick Rathmann	Walt Chapman	120	53 Huds	200	2,500
2. Lee Petty	Petty Enterprises	42	53 Dodg	196	1,500
3. Jim Paschal	George Hutchens	80	53 Dodg	191	900
4. Herb Thomas	Herb Thomas	92	53 Huds	188	700
5. Bill Blair	Bill Blair	2	53 Olds	187	500

1953 Grand National Race No. 32
September 20, 1953 Average Speed: 67.046

Driver	Owner	Car #	Make	Laps	Winnings
1. Dick Rathmann	Walt Chapman	120	53 Huds	250	2,500
2. Herb Thomas	Herb Thomas	92	53 Huds	249	1,250
3. Speedy Thompson	Buckshot Morris	46	53 Olds	248	750
4. Jim Reed	Herb Thomas	9	52 Huds	—	500
5. Jim Paschal	George Hutchens	80	53 Dodg	—	450

1954 Grand National Race No. 10
May 2, 1954 Average Speed: 74.883

Driver	Owner	Car #	Make	Laps	Winnings
1. Herb Thomas	Herb Thomas	92	54 Huds	150	1,685
2. Al Keller	George Miller	23	54 Huds	149	810
3. Dick Rathmann	John Ditz	3	54 Huds	149	610
4. Joe Eubanks	Phil Oates	82	51 Huds	133	510
5. Paul Pettit	Paul Pettitt	45	53 Huds	132	325

Langhorne Speedway *continued*

1954 Grand National Race No. 34
September 26, 1954 Average Speed: 71.186

Driver	Owner	Car #	Make	Laps	Winnings
1. Herb Thomas	Herb Thomas	92	54 Huds	250	2,450
2. Lee Petty	Petty Enterprises	42	54 Chrys	250	1,150
3. Hershel McGriff	Frank Christian	14	54 Olds	250	850
4. Buck Baker	Griffin Motors	87	54 Olds	245	625
5. Erick Erickson	Erick Erickson	23	54 Buick	245	600

1955 Grand National Race No. 10
April 24, 1955 Average Speed: 72.893

Driver	Owner	Car #	Make	Laps	Winnings
1. Tim Flock	Carl Kiekhaefer	300	55 Chrys	124	1,430
2. Buck Baker	Griffin Motors	87	54 Olds	124	860
3. Junior Johnson	B & L Motors	55	55 Olds	124	600
4. Dick Rathmann	John Ditz	3	54 Huds	124	515
5. Herb Thomas	Herb Thomas	92	55 Buick	122	350

1955 Grand National Race No. 37
September 18, 1955 Average Speed: 77.888

Driver	Owner	Car #	Make	Laps	Winnings
1. Tim Flock	Carl Kiekhaefer	300	55 Chrys	250	2,250
2. Herb Thomas	Herb Thomas	92	55 Chev	249	1,525
3. Fonty Flock	Carl Kiekhaefer	301	55 Chrys	246	950
4. Marvin Panch	J. H. Petty	44	5 Chev	245	750
5. Jimmy Massey	Hubert Westmoreland	04	55 Chev	244	600

1956 Grand National Race No. 11
April 22, 1956 Average Speed: 75.928

Driver	Owner	Car #	Make	Laps	Winnings
1. Buck Baker	Carl Kiekhaefer	87	56 Chrys	150	1,750
2. Herb Thomas	Carl Kiekhaefer	92	56 Chrys	149	1,000
3. Tim Flock	Smokey Yunick	3	56 Chev	149	725
4. Lee Petty	Petty Enterprises	42	56 Dodg	149	530
5. Jimmy Massey	Hubert Westmoreland	2	56 Chev	146	345

1956 Grand National Race No. 47
September 23, 1956 Average Speed: 70.615

Driver	Owner	Car #	Make	Laps	Winnings
1. Paul Goldsmith	Smokey Yunick	3	56 Chev	300	4,150
2. Lee Petty	Petty Enterprises	42	56 Dodg	293	1,800
3. Speedy Thompson	Carl Kiekhaefer	67	56 Dodg	292	1,175
4. Jim Paschal	Bill Stroppe	26	56 Merc	292	950
5. Herb Thomas	Herb Thomas	92	56 Chev	290	700

1957 Grand National Race No. 10
April 14, 1957 Average Speed: 85.850

Driver	Owner	Car #	Make	Laps	Winnings
1. Fireball Roberts	Pete DePaolo	22	57 Ford	150	1,890
2. Paul Goldsmith	Smokey Yunick	3	57 Ford	150	1,125
3. Speedy Thompson	Hugh Babb	46	57 Chev	147	750
4. Billy Myers	Bill Stroppe	14	57 Merc	146	540
5. Buck Baker	Hugh Babb	87	57 Chev	145	345

1957 Grand National Race No. 45
September 15, 1957 Average Speed: 72.759

Driver	Owner	Car #	Make	Laps	Winnings
1. Gwyn Staley	J. H. Petty	38	57 Chev	300	4,500
2. Whitey Norman	Whitey Norman	0	57 Ford	298	2,350
3. Johnny Allen	Spook Crawford	64	57 Plym	295	1,700
4. Rex White	Bob Welborn	44	57 Chev	295	1,135
5. Buck Baker	Buck Baker	87	57 Chev	295	960

Lincoln Speedway
Abbottstown, PA (New Oxford, PA)
Half-mile Dirt Track

Half-mile dirt track built in 1951. First Winston Cup (then Grand National) race run on 6/10/55 (won by Junior Johnson). Final Grand National race run on 9/14/65 (won by Dick Hutcherson). Track still in operation.

Winston Cup Starts
Buck Baker   6

Winston Cup Victories
Buck Baker   2

Winston Cup Poles
Junior Johnson   1
Tiny Lund   1
Marvin Panch   1
David Pearson   1
Richard Petty   1
Ken Rush   1
Speedy Thompson   1

Winston Cup Money
Buck Baker $2,900

Most Cars Started
32—August 10, 1957

Fewest Cars Started
17—May 25, 1956

Narrowest Margin of Victory
1 car length—May 25, 1956

Slowest Race
65.371 MPH—June 10, 1955

Race Record
82.607 MPH—September 14, 1965
Pennsylvania 200 Classic

Most Cautions
N/A

Most Race Leaders
3—June 10, 1955
3—May 25, 1956

Most Cars Running at Finish
20—May 30, 1957

1955 Grand National Race No. 19
June 10, 1955 Average Speed: 65.371

Driver	Owner	Car #	Make	Laps	Winnings
1. Junior Johnson	B & L Motors	55	55 Olds	200	1,000
2. Tim Flock	Carl Kiekhaefer	300	55 Chrys	198	650
3. Buck Baker	Griffin Motors	87	54 Olds	197	450
4. Jim Reed	Jim Reed	7	55 Chev	195	350
5. Nace Mattingly	Nace Mattingly	54	55 Ford	190	300

1956 Grand National Race No. 19
May 25, 1956 Average Speed: 69.619

Driver	Owner	Car #	Make	Laps	Winnings
1. Buck Baker	Carl Kiekhaefer	500B	56 Dodg	200	1,100
2. Jim Paschal	Frank Hayworth	75	56 Merc	200	700
3. Lee Petty	Petty Enterprises	42	56 Dodg	200	475
4. Herb Thomas	Carl Kiekhaefer	502	56 Dodg	195	365
5. Nace Mattingly	Nace Mattingly	54	56 Ford	185	310

1957 Grand National Race No. 20
May 30, 1957 Average Speed: 76.126

Driver	Owner	Car #	Make	Laps	Winnings
1. Buck Baker	Hugh Babb	87	57 Chev	200	700
2. Fireball Roberts	Pete DePaolo	22	57 Ford	200	525
3. Paul Goldsmith	Smokey Yunick	3	57 Ford	200	400
4. Marvin Panch	Pete DePaolo	98	57 Ford	200	330
5. Speedy Thompson	Hugh Babb	46	57 Chev	200	270

1957 Grand National Race No. 37
August 10, 1957 Average Speed: 77.569

Driver	Owner	Car #	Make	Laps	Winnings
1. Marvin Panch	Marvin Panch	98	57 Ford	200	1,000
2. Speedy Thompson	Speedy Thompson	46	57 Chev	200	625
3. Tiny Lund	A. L. Bumgarner	55	57 Pont	198	400
4. Johnny Allen	Spook Crawford	64	57 Plym	191	295
5. Johnny Mackison	Johnny Mackison	104	57 Ford	188	255

1958 Grand National Race No. 25
June 25, 1958 Average Speed: 69.726

Driver	Owner	Car #	Make	Laps	Winnings
1. Lee Petty	Petty Enterprises	42	57 Olds	200	800
2. Buck Baker	Buck Baker	87	57 Chev	200	525
3. Bob Welborn	J. H. Petty	49	57 Chev	199	350
4. Shorty Rollins	Shorty Rollins	99	58 Ford	196	250
5. Reds Kagle	Hoss Kagle	88	57 Chev	194	225

1964 Grand National Race No. 41 Pennsylvania 200 Classic
July 21, 1964 Average Speed: 82.568

Driver	Owner	Car #	Make	Laps	Winnings
1. David Pearson	Cotton Owens	6	64 Dodg	200	1,000
2. Richard Petty	Petty Enterprises	41	64 Plym	200	600
3. Jimmy Pardue	Charles Robinson	54	64 Plym	194	400
4. Wendell Scott	Wendell Scott	34	63 Ford	193	300
5. Doug Yates	Doug Yates	72	64 Plym	192	275

1965 Grand National Race No. 47 Pennsylvania 200 Classic
September 14, 1965 Average Speed: 82.607

Driver	Owner	Car #	Make	Laps	Winnings
1. Dick Hutcherson	Holman-Moody	29	65 Ford	200	1,000
2. G. C. Spencer	G. C. Spencer	49	64 Ford	192	600
3. David Pearson	Cotton Owens	6	65 Dodg	190	400
4. Ned Jarrett	Bondy Long	11	65 Ford	190	300
5. Buddy Baker	Buck Baker	86	64 Dodg	189	275

New Bradford Speedway
Bradford, PA
.333-mile Dirt Track

.333-mile dirt oval built in 1958. Staged first Winston Cup (then Grand National) race on 6/12/58 (won by Junior Johnson). Track now measured at a quarter-mile.

Winston Cup Victories
Junior Johnson   1

Winston Cup Poles
Bob Duell   1

Winston Cup Money
Junior Johnson $550

Most Cars Started
21—June 12, 1958

Narrowest Margin of Victory
N/A

Race Record
59.840 MPH—June 12, 1958

Most Race Leaders
N/A

Most Cars Running at Finish
14—June 12, 1958

1958 Grand National Race No. 23
June 12, 1958 Average Speed: 59.840

Driver	Owner	Car #	Make	Laps	Winnings
1. Junior Johnson	Paul Spaulding	11	57 Ford	150	550
2. Lee Petty	Petty Enterprises	42	57 Olds	150	450
3. Bob Duell	Julian Buesink	95	57 Ford	148	325
4. Jack Smith	Jack Smith	47	57 Chev	148	250
5. Billy Rafter	Billy Rafter	57	57 Ford	147	215

Pine Grove Speedway
Shippenville, PA
Half-mile Dirt Track

Half-mile dirt track built in 1950. Only NASCAR Winston Cup (then Grand National) race staged on 10/14/51 (won by Tim Flock). Track conducted races in sporadic manner until it closed in 1960s.

Winston Cup Victories
Tim Flock   1

Winston Cup Money
Tim Flock $1,000

Most Cars Started
20—October 14, 1951

Narrowest Margin of Victory
N/A

Most Race Leaders
N/A

Most Cars Running at Finish
N/A

1951 Grand National Race No. 33
October 14, 1951

Driver	Owner	Car #	Make	Laps	Winnings
1. Tim Flock	Ted Chester	91	51 Olds	200	1,000
2. John McGinley	Walt Chapman	120	51 Huds	—	600
3. Billy Carden	Sam Knox	8	50 Olds	—	500
4. Jimmy Florian	Jimmy Florian		50 Olds	—	400
5. Lloyd Moore	Julian Buesink	59	51 Ford	—	300

Pocono Int'l Raceway
Long Pond, PA
2.5-mile Paved Track

Proposed in 1960, but not constructed until 1969. First track was .75-mile oval. Road courses were also built. 2.5-mile triangular speedway opened with USAC IndyCar race on 7/3/71. First Winston Cup Grand National race staged on 8/4/74 (won by Richard Petty). Track has three straightaways of different lengths and three corners, each with a different radius and banking.

Winston Cup Starts
Darrell Waltrip 37

Winston Cup Victories
Bill Elliott 4
Tim Richmond 4
Darrell Waltrip 4

Winston Cup Poles
Ken Schrader 5

Winston Cup Money
Dale Earnhardt $699,025

Most Cars Started
42—June 12, 1994
UAW-GM Teamwork 500
42—July 17, 1994
Miller Genuine Draft 500
42—June 11, 1995
UAW-GM Teamwork 500

Fewest Cars Started
35—August 4, 1974 Purolator 500
35—August 3, 1975 Purolator 500
35—July 31, 1977 Coca-Cola 500
35—July 26, 1981 Mountain Dew 500

Narrowest Margin of Victory
0.050 seconds July 20, 1986
Summer 500

Slowest Race
111.179 MPH—August 3, 1975
Purolator 500

Race Record
144.892 MPH—July 21, 1996
Miller Genuine Draft 500

Most Cautions
13—June 17, 1990
Miller Genuine Draft 500

Most Race Leaders
16—June 17, 1990
Miller Genuine Draft 500

Most Cars Running at Finish
35—June 11, 1995
UAW-GM Teamwork 500

1974 Winston Cup GN Race No. 20 Purolator 500
August 4, 1974 Average Speed: 115.593

Driver	Owner	Car #	Make	Laps	Winnings
1. Richard Petty	Petty Enterprises	43	74 Dodg	192	17,000
2. Buddy Baker	Bud Moore	15	73 Ford	192	10,650
3. Cale Yarborough	Junior Johnson	11	74 Chev	192	7,350
4. David Pearson	Wood Brothers	21	73 Merc	192	3,750
5. Benny Parsons	L. G. DeWitt	72	74 Chev	190	6,100

1975 Winston Cup GN Race No. 18 Purolator 500
August 3, 1975 Average Speed: 111.179

Driver	Owner	Car #	Make	Laps	Winnings
1. David Pearson	Wood Brothers	21	73 Merc	200	15,725
2. Richard Petty	Petty Enterprises	43	74 Dodg	200	13,000
3. Buddy Baker	Bud Moore	15	73 Ford	200	9,200
4. Benny Parsons	L. G. DeWitt	72	75 Chev	200	6,725
5. Richard Childress	Tom Garn	96	75 Chev	196	3,525

1976 Winston Cup GN Race No. 18 Purolator 500
August 1, 1976 Average Speed: 115.875

Driver	Owner	Car #	Make	Laps	Winnings
1. Richard Petty	Petty Enterprises	43	Dodg	200	20,640
2. Buddy Baker	Bud Moore	15	Ford	200	13,465
3. Benny Parsons	L. G. DeWitt	72	Chev	200	9,790
4. David Pearson	Wood Brothers	21	Merc	200	5,060
5. Lennie Pond	Ronnie Elder	54	Chev	198	5,400

1977 Winston Cup GN Race No. 18 Coca-Cola 500
July 31, 1977 Average Speed: 128.379

Driver	Owner	Car #	Make	Laps	Winnings
1. Benny Parsons	L. G. DeWitt	72	Chev	200	15,475
2. Richard Petty	Petty Enterprises	43	Dodg	200	12,200
3. Darrell Waltrip	DiGard	88	Chev	200	9,825
4. Bobby Allison	Bobby Allison	12	Mata	200	6,150
5. Dick Brooks	Junie Donlavey	90	Ford	198	5,200

1978 Winston Cup GN Race No. 18 Coca-Cola 500
July 30, 1978 Average Speed: 142.540

Driver	Owner	Car #	Make	Laps	Winnings
1. Darrell Waltrip	DiGard	88	Chev	200	20,890
2. David Pearson	Wood Brothers	21	Merc	200	11,165
3. Bobby Allison	Bud Moore	15	Ford	199	10,965
4. Dave Marcis	Rod Osterlund	2	Chev	197	6,665
5. Buddy Baker	M. C. Anderson	27	Chev	197	5,615

1979 Winston Cup GN Race No. 19 Coca-Cola 500
July 30, 1979 Average Speed: 115.207

Driver	Owner	Car #	Make	Laps	Winnings
1. Cale Yarborough	Junior Johnson	11	Chev	200	21,465
2. Richard Petty	Petty Enterprises	43	Chev	200	15,465
3. Buddy Baker	Harry Ranier	28	Chev	200	8,490
4. Benny Parsons	M. C. Anderson	27	Chev	200	7,765
5. Ricky Rudd	Junie Donlavey	90	Merc	200	6,215

1980 Winston Cup GN Race No. 19 Coca-Cola 500
July 27, 1980 Average Speed: 124.395

Driver	Owner	Car #	Make	Laps	Winnings
1. Neil Bonnett	Wood Brothers	21	Merc	200	19,915
2. Buddy Baker	Harry Ranier	28	Buick	200	12,590
3. Cale Yarborough	Junior Johnson	11	Chev	200	13,640
4. Dale Earnhardt	Rod Osterlund	2	Chev	200	11,415
5. Harry Gant	Jack Beebe	47	Chev	200	7,545

1981 Winston Cup GN Race No. 19 Mountain Dew 500
July 26, 1981 Average Speed: 119.111

Driver	Owner	Car #	Make	Laps	Winnings
1. Darrell Waltrip	Junior Johnson	11	Buick	200	23,640
2. Richard Petty	Petty Enterprises	43	Buick	200	18,915
3. Benny Parsons	Bud Moore	15	Ford	200	13,515
4. Harry Gant	Hal Needham	33	Pont	200	4,990
5. Cale Yarborough	M. C. Anderson	27	Buick	200	4,290

1982 Winston Cup GN Race No. 13 Van Scoy Diamond Mine 500
June 6, 1982 Average Speed: 113.579

Driver	Owner	Car #	Make	Laps	Winnings
1. Bobby Allison	DiGard	88	Buick	200	25,500
2. Tim Richmond	Jim Stacy	2	Buick	200	15,430
3. Benny Parsons	Harry Ranier	28	Pont	199	17,375
4. Harry Gant	Hal Needham	33	Buick	199	10,180
5. Terry Labonte	Billy Hagan	44	Chev	199	8,735

1982 Winston Cup GN Race No. 18 Mountain Dew 500
July 25, 1982 Average Speed: 115.496

Driver	Owner	Car #	Make	Laps	Winnings
1. Bobby Allison	DiGard	88	Buick	200	24,200
2. Richard Petty	Petty Enterprises	43	Pont	200	21,500
3. Terry Labonte	Billy Hagan	44	Buick	200	12,755
4. Ron Bouchard	Jack Beebe	47	Buick	200	14,100
5. Buddy Baker	Harry Ranier	28	Pont	200	13,850

Pocono Int'l Raceway *continued*

1983 Winston Cup GN Race No. 14 Van Scoy Diamond Mine 500
June 12, 1983 Average Speed: 128.636

Driver	Owner	Car #	Make	Laps	Winnings
1. Bobby Allison	DiGard	22	Buick	200	31,100
2. Darrell Waltrip	Junior Johnson	11	Chev	200	25,950
3. Richard Petty	Petty Enterprises	43	Pont	200	17,225
4. Tim Richmond	Raymond Beadle	27	Pont	199	10,580
5. Benny Parsons	Johnny Hayes	55	Buick	199	7,100

1983 Winston Cup GN Race No. 18 Like Cola 500
July 24, 1983 Average Speed: 114.818

Driver	Owner	Car #	Make	Laps	Winnings
1. Tim Richmond	Raymond Beadle	27	Pont	200	27,430
2. Darrell Waltrip	Junior Johnson	11	Chev	200	23,375
3. Bobby Allison	DiGard	22	Buick	200	21,950
4. Neil Bonnett	Bob Rahilly & Butch Mock	75	Chev	200	16,525
5. Harry Gant	Hal Needham	33	Buick	200	14,700

1984 Winston Cup GN Race No. 14 Van Scoy Diamond Mine 500
June 10, 1984 Average Speed: 138.164

Driver	Owner	Car #	Make	Laps	Winnings
1. Cale Yarborough	Harry Ranier	28	Chev	200	30,850
2. Harry Gant	Hal Needham	33	Chev	200	21,980
3. Terry Labonte	Billy Hagan	44	Chev	200	17,295
4. Bill Elliott	Harry Melling	9	Ford	200	16,150
5. Tim Richmond	Raymond Beadle	27	Pont	200	14,900

1984 Winston Cup GN Race No. 18 Like Cola 500
July 22, 1984 Average Speed: 121.351

Driver	Owner	Car #	Make	Laps	Winnings
1. Harry Gant	Hal Needham	33	Chev	200	34,605
2. Cale Yarborough	Harry Ranier	28	Chev	200	17,275
3. Bill Elliott	Harry Melling	9	Ford	200	24,250
4. Terry Labonte	Billy Hagan	44	Chev	200	13,695
5. Benny Parsons	Johnny Hayes	55	Chev	200	8,450

1985 Winston Cup GN Race No. 13 Van Scoy Diamond Mine 500
June 9, 1985 Average Speed: 138.974

Driver	Owner	Car #	Make	Laps	Winnings
1. Bill Elliott	Harry Melling	9	Ford	200	44,525
2. Harry Gant	Hal Needham	33	Chev	200	27,675
3. Darrell Waltrip	Junior Johnson	11	Chev	200	23,100
4. Geoff Bodine	Rick Hendrick	5	Chev	200	28,325
5. Neil Bonnett	Junior Johnson	12	Chev	199	15,525

1985 Winston Cup GN Race No. 16 Summer 500
July 21, 1985 Average Speed: 134.008

Driver	Owner	Car #	Make	Laps	Winnings
1. Bill Elliott	Harry Melling	9	Ford	200	41,750
2. Neil Bonnett	Junior Johnson	12	Chev	200	38,450
3. Darrell Waltrip	Junior Johnson	11	Chev	200	25,375
4. Geoff Bodine	Rick Hendrick	5	Chev	200	18,325
5. Harry Gant	Hal Needham	33	Chev	200	17,425

1986 Winston Cup Race No. 13 Miller High Life 500
June 8, 1986 Average Speed: 113.279

Driver	Owner	Car #	Make	Laps	Winnings
1. Tim Richmond	Rick Hendrick	25	Chev	200	46,705
2. Dale Earnhardt	Richard Childress	3	Chev	200	29,750
3. Cale Yarborough	Harry Ranier	28	Ford	200	15,450
4. Ricky Rudd	Bud Moore	15	Ford	200	18,375
5. Bill Elliott	Harry Melling	9	Ford	200	19,725

1986 Winston Cup Race No. 16 Summer 500
July 20, 1986 Average Speed: 124.218

Driver	Owner	Car #	Make	Laps	Winnings
1. Tim Richmond	Rick Hendrick	25	Chev	150	46,805
2. Ricky Rudd	Bud Moore	15	Ford	150	29,500
3. Geoff Bodine	Rick Hendrick	5	Chev	150	22,350
4. Darrell Waltrip	Junior Johnson	11	Chev	150	23,825
5. Bobby Allison	Stavola Brothers	22	Buick	150	17,525

1987 Winston Cup Race No. 12 Miller High Life 500
June 14, 1987 Average Speed: 122.166

Driver	Owner	Car #	Make	Laps	Winnings
1. Tim Richmond	Rick Hendrick	25	Chev	200	40,325
2. Bill Elliott	Harry Melling	9	Ford	200	30,600
3. Kyle Petty	Wood Brothers	21	Ford	200	24,575
4. Cale Yarborough	Cale Yarborough	29	Olds	200	11,505
5. Dale Earnhardt	Richard Childress	3	Chev	200	22,400

1987 Winston Cup Race No. 16 Summer 500
July 19, 1987 Average Speed: 121.745

Driver	Owner	Car #	Make	Laps	Winnings
1. Dale Earnhardt	Richard Childress	3	Chev	200	55,875
2. Alan Kulwicki	Alan Kulwicki	7	Ford	200	32,880
3. Buddy Baker	Buddy Baker & Danny Schiff	88	Olds	200	18,100
4. Benny Parsons	Rick Hendrick	35	Chev	200	21,445
5. Davey Allison	Harry Ranier	28	Ford	200	11,650

1988 Winston Cup Race No. 13 Miller High Life 500
June 19, 1988 Average Speed: 126.147

Driver	Owner	Car #	Make	Laps	Winnings
1. Geoff Bodine	Rick Hendrick	5	Chev	200	51,200
2. Michael Waltrip	Chuck Rider	30	Pont	200	31,100
3. Rusty Wallace	Raymond Beadle	27	Pont	200	26,500
4. Mark Martin	Jack Roush	6	Ford	200	15,080
5. Davey Allison	Harry Ranier	28	Ford	200	20,925

1988 Winston Cup Race No. 16 AC Spark Plug 500
July 24, 1988 Average Speed: 122.866

Driver	Owner	Car #	Make	Laps	Winnings
1. Bill Elliott	Harry Melling	9	Ford	200	53,200
2. Ken Schrader	Rick Hendrick	25	Chev	200	30,725
3. Davey Allison	Harry Ranier	28	Ford	200	26,275
4. Geoff Bodine	Rick Hendrick	5	Chev	200	17,775
5. Darrell Waltrip	Rick Hendrick	17	Chev	200	17,925

1989 Winston Cup Race No. 13 Miller High Life 500
June 18, 1989 Average Speed: 131.320

Driver	Owner	Car #	Make	Laps	Winnings
1. Terry Labonte	Junior Johnson	11	Ford	200	54,807
2. Harry Gant	Leo Jackson	33	Olds	200	33,875
3. Dale Earnhardt	Richard Childress	3	Chev	200	29,250
4. Ken Schrader	Rick Hendrick	25	Chev	200	20,600
5. Morgan Shepherd	Bob Rahilly & Butch Mock	75	Pont	200	21,850

1989 Winston Cup Race No. 16 AC Spark Plug 500
July 23, 1989 Average Speed: 117.847

Driver	Owner	Car #	Make	Laps	Winnings
1. Bill Elliott	Harry Melling	9	Ford	200	58,400
2. Rusty Wallace	Raymond Beadle	27	Pont	200	46,875
3. Mark Martin	Jack Roush	6	Ford	200	26,300
4. Darrell Waltrip	Rick Hendrick	17	Chev	200	23,850
5. Harry Gant	Leo Jackson	33	Olds	200	20,350

Pocono Int'l Raceway *continued*

1990 Winston Cup Series Race No. 13 Miller Genuine Draft 500
June 17, 1990 Average Speed: 120.600

Driver	Owner	Car #	Make	Laps	Winnings
1. Harry Gant	Leo Jackson	33	Olds	200	54,350
2. Rusty Wallace	Raymond Beadle	27	Pont	200	37,307
3. Geoff Bodine	Junior Johnson	11	Ford	200	30,750
4. Brett Bodine	Kenny Bernstein	26	Buick	200	19,850
5. Davey Allison	Robert Yates	28	Ford	200	20,700

1990 Winston Cup Series Race No. 16 AC Spark Plug 500
July 22, 1990 Average Speed: 124.070

Driver	Owner	Car #	Make	Laps	Winnings
1. Geoff Bodine	Junior Johnson	11	Ford	200	58,500
2. Bill Elliott	Harry Melling	9	Ford	200	33,650
3. Rusty Wallace	Raymond Beadle	27	Pont	200	30,000
4. Dale Earnhardt	Richard Childress	3	Chev	200	22,800
5. Davey Allison	Robert Yates	28	Ford	200	25,950

1991 Winston Cup Series Race No. 13 Champion Spark Plug 500
June 16, 1991 Average Speed: 122.666

Driver	Owner	Car #	Make	Laps	Winnings
1. Darrell Waltrip	Darrell Waltrip	17	Chev	200	60,650
2. Dale Earnhardt	Richard Childress	3	Chev	200	43,775
3. Mark Martin	Jack Roush	6	Ford	200	38,875
4. Harry Gant	Leo Jackson	33	Olds	200	22,600
5. Geoff Bodine	Junior Johnson	97	Ford	200	15,125

1991 Winston Cup Series Race No. 16 Miller Genuine Draft 500
July 21, 1991 Average Speed: 115.459

Driver	Owner	Car #	Make	Laps	Winnings
1. Rusty Wallace	Roger Penske	2	Pont	179	34,100
2. Mark Martin	Jack Roush	6	Ford	179	41,475
3. Geoff Bodine	Junior Johnson	11	Ford	179	32,350
4. Hut Stricklin	Bobby Allison	12	Buick	179	21,750
5. Sterling Marlin	Junior Johnson	22	Ford	179	14,100

1992 Winston Cup Race No. 13 Champion Spark Plug 500
June 14, 1992 Average Speed: 144.023

Driver	Owner	Car #	Make	Laps	Winnings
1. Alan Kulwicki	Alan Kulwicki	7	Ford	200	74,255
2. Mark Martin	Jack Roush	6	Ford	200	39,480
3. Bill Elliott	Junior Johnson	11	Ford	200	32,355
4. Ken Schrader	Rick Hendrick	25	Chev	200	32,980
5. Davey Allison	Robert Yates	28	Ford	200	27,175

1992 Winston Cup Race No. 16 Miller Genuine Draft 500
July 19, 1992 Average Speed: 134.058

Driver	Owner	Car #	Make	Laps	Winnings
1. Darrell Waltrip	Darrell Waltrip	17	Chev	200	63,445
2. Harry Gant	Leo Jackson	33	Olds	200	40,520
3. Alan Kulwicki	Alan Kulwicki	7	Ford	200	42,095
4. Ricky Rudd	Rick Hendrick	5	Chev	200	24,695
5. Ted Musgrave	D K. Ulrich & Ray DeWitt	55	Ford	200	22,365

1993 Winston Cup Series Race No. 13 Champion Spark Plug 500
June 13, 1993 Average Speed: 138.005

Driver	Owner	Car #	Make	Laps	Winnings
1. Kyle Petty	Felix Sabates	42	Pont	200	44,960
2. Ken Schrader	Rick Hendrick	25	Chev	200	58,435
3. Harry Gant	Leo Jackson	33	Chev	200	38,335
4. Jimmy Spencer	Bobby Allison	12	Ford	200	31,410
5. Ted Musgrave	Ray DeWitt	55	Ford	200	24,040

1993 Winston Cup Series Race No. 17 Miller Genuine Draft 500
July 18, 1993 Average Speed: 133.343

Driver	Owner	Car #	Make	Laps	Winnings
1. Dale Earnhardt	Richard Childress	3	Chev	200	66,795
2. Rusty Wallace	Roger Penske	2	Pont	200	35,145
3. Bill Elliott	Junior Johnson	11	Ford	200	39,720
4. Morgan Shepherd	Wood Brothers	21	Ford	200	26,345
5. Brett Bodine	Kenny Bernstein	26	Ford	200	25,940

1994 Winston Cup Series Race No. 13 UAW-GM Teamwork 500
June 12, 1994 Average Speed: 128.801

Driver	Owner	Car #	Make	Laps	Winnings
1. Rusty Wallace	Roger Penske	2	Ford	200	84,525
2. Dale Earnhardt	Richard Childress	3	Chev	200	46,425
3. Ken Schrader	Rick Hendrick	25	Chev	200	33,400
4. Morgan Shepherd	Wood Brothers	21	Ford	200	24,900
5. Mark Martin	Jack Roush	6	Ford	200	30,400

1994 Winston Cup Series Race No. 17 Miller Genuine Draft 500
July 17, 1994 Average Speed: 136.075

Driver	Owner	Car #	Make	Laps	Winnings
1. Geoff Bodine	Geoff Bodine	7	Ford	200	103,270
2. Ward Burton	A. G. Dillard	31	Chev	200	39,720
3. Joe Nemechek	Larry Hedrick	41	Chev	200	29,790
4. Jeff Burton	Stavola Brothers	8	Ford	200	29,640
5. Morgan Shepherd	Wood Brothers	21	Ford	200	30,635

1995 Winston Cup Series Race No. 13 UAW-GM Teamwork 500
June 11, 1995 Average Speed: 137.720

Driver	Owner	Car #	Make	Laps	Winnings
1. Terry Labonte	Rick Hendrick	5	Chev	200	71,175
2. Ted Musgrave	Jack Roush	16	Ford	200	50,525
3. Ken Schrader	Rick Hendrick	25	Chev	200	45,550
4. Sterling Marlin	Larry McClure	4	Chev	200	35,250
5. Hut Stricklin	Kenny Bernstein	26	Ford	200	30,900

1995 Winston Cup Series Race No. 17 Miller Genuine Draft 500
July 16, 1995 Average Speed: 134.038

Driver	Owner	Car #	Make	Laps	Winnings
1. Dale Jarrett	Robert Yates	28	Ford	200	72,970
2. Jeff Gordon	Rick Hendrick	24	Chev	200	48,520
3. Ricky Rudd	Ricky Rudd	10	Ford	200	41,010
4. Ted Musgrave	Jack Roush	16	Ford	200	32,135
5. Bill Elliott	Bill Elliott	94	Ford	200	32,780

1996 Winston Cup Series Race No. 13 UAW-GM Teamwork 500
June 16, 1996 Average Speed: 139.104

Driver	Owner	Car #	Make	Laps	Winnings
1. Jeff Gordon	Rick Hendrick	24	Chev	200	96,980
2. Ricky Rudd	Ricky Rudd	10	Ford	200	52,900
3. Geoff Bodine	Geoff Bodine	7	Ford	200	54,700
4. Mark Martin	Jack Roush	6	Ford	200	38,975
5. Bobby Hamilton	Petty Enterprises	43	Pont	200	31,875

1996 Winston Cup Series Race No. 17 Miller Genuine Draft 500
July 21, 1996 Average Speed: 144.892

Driver	Owner	Car #	Make	Laps	Winnings
1. Rusty Wallace	Roger Penske	2	Ford	200	59,165
2. Ricky Rudd	Ricky Rudd	10	Ford	200	56,615
3. Dale Jarrett	Robert Yates	88	Ford	200	35,705
4. Ernie Irvan	Robert Yates	28	Ford	200	44,590
5. Johnny Benson Jr.	Chuck Rider	30	Pont	200	36,400

Reading Fairgrounds
Reading, PA
Half-mile Dirt Track

One of the most famous tracks in the East. Built in 1924, the first race was run on 9/20/24. Ralph Hankinson was the first promoter. Sam Nunis operated track from 1946–1954. First NASCAR Winston Cup (then Grand National) race staged on 6/15/58 (won by Junior Johnson). Only other Grand National race run 4/26/59 (also won by Johnson). Final event run in June of 1979. Now the site of an art mall.

Winston Cup Starts
9 drivers tied with   2

Winston Cup Victories
Junior Johnson   2

Winston Cup Poles
Speedy Thompson   1

Winston Cup Money
Junior Johnson $1,600

Most Cars Started
30—June 15, 1958

Fewest Cars Started
25—April 26, 1959

Narrowest Margin of Victory
10 car lengths—June 15, 1954

Slowest Race
53.011 MPH—April 26, 1959

Race Record
53.763 MPH—June 15, 1958

Most Cautions
N/A

Most Race Leaders
4—June 15, 1958

Most Cars Running at Finish
19—June 15, 1958

1958 Grand National Race No. 24
June 15, 1958 Average Speed: 53.763

Driver	Owner	Car #	Make	Laps	Winnings
1. Junior Johnson	Paul Spaulding	11	57 Ford	200	800
2. Eddie Pagan	Eddie Pagan	45	57 Ford	200	525
3. Buck Baker	Buck Baker	87	57 Chev	199	350
4. Lee Petty	Petty Enterprises	42	57 Olds	199	250
5. Speedy Thompson	Speedy Thompson	46	57 Chev	198	225

1959 Grand National Race No. 11
April 26, 1959 Average Speed: 53.011

Driver	Owner	Car #	Make	Laps	Winnings
1. Junior Johnson	Paul Spaulding	11	57 Ford	200	800
2. Speedy Thompson	Steve Pierce	1	57 Chev	196	525
3. Tom Pistone	Carl Rupert	59	59 Ford	196	350
4. Tommy Irwin	Tommy Irwin	36	59 Ford	192	250
5. Buzz Woodward	Buzz Woodward	90	57 Ford	191	225

Sharon Speedway
Sharon, PA
Half-mile Dirt Track

(actually located in Hartford, OH; named for nearest big city) Half-mile dirt track opened in 1929. Only NASCAR Winston Cup (then Grand National) race staged on 5/24/54 (won by Lee Petty). Track paved in 1971 and subsequently went back to dirt in 1981. Still in operation.

Winston Cup Victories
Lee Petty   1

Winston Cup Poles
Dick Rathmann   1

Winston Cup Money
Lee Petty $1,000

Most Cars Started
22—May 23, 1954

Narrowest Margin of Victory
1 lap plus—May 23, 1954

Most Race Leaders
3—May 23, 1954

Most Cars Running at Finish
13—May 23, 1954

1954 Grand National Race No. 13
May 23, 1954

Driver	Owner	Car #	Make	Laps	Winnings
1. Lee Petty	Petty Enterprises	42	54 Chrys	160	1,000
2. Buck Baker	Griffin Motors	87	53 Olds	159	650
3. Dick Rathmann	John Ditz	3	54 Huds	157	450
4. Joe Eubanks	Phil Oates	82	51 Huds	154	350
5. Laird Bruner	Carmen Amica	21	53 Olds	153	300

Williams Grove Speedway
Mechanicsburg, PA
Half-mile Dirt Track

Half-mile dirt track opened in May 1939; built by Roy Richwine. Only NASCAR Winston Cup (then Grand National) race staged on 6/17/54 (won by Herb Thomas). Track still in operation.

Winston Cup Victories
Herb Thomas   1

Winston Cup Poles
Dick Rathmann   1

Winston Cup Money
Herb Thomas $1,000

Most Cars Started
41—June 27, 1954

Narrowest Margin of Victory
4 car lengths—June 27, 1954

Race Record
51.085 MPH—June 27, 1954

Most Race Leaders
2—June 27, 1954

Most Cars Running at Finish
27—June 27, 1954

1954 Grand National Race No. 21
June 27, 1954 Average Speed: 51.085

Driver	Owner	Car #	Make	Laps	Winnings
1. Herb Thomas	Herb Thomas	92	54 Huds	200	1,000
2. Dick Rathmann	John Ditz	3	54 Huds	200	650
3. Hershel McGriff	Frank Christian	14	54 Olds	199	450
4. Joe Eubanks	Phil Oates	82	51 Huds	199	350
5. Jimmie Lewallen	George Hutchens	80	54 Merc	197	300

South Carolina

Coastal Speedway
Myrtle Beach, SC
Half-mile Dirt Track

Half-mile dirt track originally built as horse track circa 1940s. Opened to auto racing in 1950s. First NASCAR Winston Cup (then Grand National) race staged on 8/25/56 (won by Fireball Roberts). Only other Grand National race run 8/26/57 (won by Gwyn Staley). Now the site of a bank across the street from the Convention Center.

Winston Cup Starts
Johnny Allen	2
Buck Baker	2
Lee Petty	2
Fireball Roberts	2
Speedy Thompson	2

Winston Cup Victories
Fireball Roberts	1
Gwyn Staley	1

Winston Cup Poles
Johnny Allen	1
Ralph Moody	1

Winston Cup Money
Fireball Roberts	$1,350

Most Cars Started
20—August 25, 1956

Fewest Cars Started
15—August 26, 1957

Narrowest Margin of Victory
N/A

Slowest Race
50.576 MPH—August 25, 1956

Race Record
50.782 MPH—August 26, 1957

Most Race Leaders
N/A

Most Cars Running at Finish
10—August 25, 1956
10—August 26, 1957

1956 Grand National Race No. 42
August 25, 1956 Average Speed: 50.576

Driver	Owner	Car #	Make	Laps	Winnings
1. Fireball Roberts	Pete DePaolo	22	56 Ford	200	950
2. Billy Myers	Bill Stroppe	4	56 Merc	200	675
3. Jim Paschal	Frank Hayworth	75	56 Merc	199	475
4. Buck Baker	Carl Kiekhaefer	300	56 Chrys	196	365
5. Speedy Thompson	Carl Kiekhaefer	501	56 Dodg	196	320

1957 Grand National Race No. 39
August 26, 1957 Average Speed: 50.782

Driver	Owner	Car #	Make	Laps	Winnings
1. Gwyn Staley	J. H. Petty	38	57 Chev	200	1,000
2. Eddie Pagan	Eddie Pagan	45	57 Ford	199	625
3. Fireball Roberts	Fireball Roberts	22	57 Ford	198	400
4. Buck Baker	Buck Baker	87	57 Chev	183	295
5. L. D. Austin	L. D. Austin	74	56 Chev	180	255

Columbia Speedway
Columbia, SC
Half-mile Paved Track

Half-mile dirt track originally built in 1932. First NASCAR Winston Cup (then Grand National) race staged on 6/16/51 (won by Frank Mundy in a Studebaker). Track paved in 1971. Final Grand National race run on 8/27/71 (won by Richard Petty). Track closed in 1977.

Winston Cup Starts
Buck Baker   28

Winston Cup Victories
Richard Petty   7

Winston Cup Poles
Richard Petty   7

Winston Cup Money
Richard Petty $15,025

Most Cars Started
34—June 16, 1951

Fewest Cars Started
13—August 29, 1959

Narrowest Margin of Victory
1/2 car length—August 8, 1968
Sandlapper 200

Slowest Race
48.264 MPH—August 29, 1959

Race Record
76.514 MPH—April 8, 1971 Sandlapper
200

Most Cautions
13—May 2, 1963

Most Race Leaders
5—April 16, 1964 Columbia 200
5—August 21, 1964 Sandlapper 200
5—April 3, 1969 Columbia 200

Most Cars Running at Finish
20—August 18, 1966

1951 Grand National Race No. 11
June 16, 1951 Average Speed: 50.683

Driver	Owner	Car #	Make	Laps	Winnings
1. Frank Mundy	Perry Smith	23	51 Stud	200	1,000
2. Bill Blair	Hubert Westmoreland	98	50 Plym	199	600
3. Marshall Teague	Marshall Teague	6	51 Huds	—	400
4. Herb Thomas	Herb Thomas	92	50 Plym	—	300
5. Buck Baker	Buck Baker	87	50 Plym	—	250

1951 Grand National Race No. 25
September 7, 1951

Driver	Owner	Car #	Make	Laps	Winnings
1. Tim Flock	Ted Chester	91	51 Olds	200	1,000
2. Fireball Roberts	Ed Saverance	11	51 Ford	200	600
3. Jimmie Lewallen	Hubert Hamilton	0	51 Plym	—	500
4. Bob Flock	Ted Chester	7	51 Olds	—	400
5. Buck Baker	Griffin Motors	87	51 Olds	—	300

1952 Grand National Race No. 6
April 12, 1952 Average Speed: 53.460

Driver	Owner	Car #	Make	Laps	Winnings
1. Buck Baker	B. A. Pless	89	52 Huds	200	1,000
2. Lee Petty	Petty Enterprises	42	51 Plym	200	700
3. Dick Rathmann	Walt Chapman	120	51 Huds	—	450
4. Frankie Schneider		88	51 Olds	—	350
5. Joe Eubanks	Phil Oates	82	50 Olds	—	200

1953 Grand National Race No. 9
May 9, 1953 Average Speed: 53.707

Driver	Owner	Car #	Make	Laps	Winnings
1. Buck Baker	Griffin Motors	87	53 Olds	200	1,000
2. Tim Flock	Ted Chester	91	53 Huds	—	700
3. Jimmie Lewallen	R. G. Shelton	32	51 Huds	—	450
4. Ray Duhigg	J. H. Petty	44	52 Plym	—	350
5. Lee Petty	Petty Enterprises	42	53 Dodg	—	200

1954 Grand National Race No. 17
June 6, 1954 Average Speed: 56.719

Driver	Owner	Car #	Make	Laps	Winnings
1. Curtis Turner	Elmer Brooks	44	52 Olds	200	1,000
2. Hershel McGriff	Frank Christian	14	54 Olds	198	650
3. Dick Rathmann	John Ditz	3	54 Huds	197	450
4. Speedy Thompson	Buckshot Morris	12	53 Olds	197	350
5. Lee Petty	Petty Enterprises	42	54 Chrys	195	300

1955 Grand National Race No. 6
March 26, 1955

Driver	Owner	Car #	Make	Laps	Winnings
1. Fonty Flock	Frank Christian	14	55 Chev	200	1,000
2. Don White	Don White	1	55 Olds	—	650
3. Dick Rathmann	John Ditz	3	54 Huds	—	450
4. Buck Baker	Griffin Motors	87	54 Olds	—	350
5. Tim Flock	Carl Kiekhaefer	300	55 Chrys	—	300

1955 Grand National Race No. 25
July 9, 1955 Average Speed: 55.469

Driver	Owner	Car #	Make	Laps	Winnings
1. Jim Paschal	Ernest Woods	78	54 Olds	200	1,000
2. Jimmie Lewallen	Ernest Woods	88	55 Olds	200	700
3. Tim Flock	Carl Kiekhaefer	300	55 Chrys	200	475
4. Billy Carden	Bishop Brothers	8	55 Buick	197	365
5. Buck Baker	Henry Ford	303	55 Chrys	195	310

1955 Grand National Race No. 41
October 15, 1955 Average Speed: 55.393

Driver	Owner	Car #	Make	Laps	Winnings
1. Tim Flock	Carl Kiekhaefer	300	55 Chrys	200	1,100
2. Buck Baker	Pete DePaolo	87	56 Ford	200	700
3. Herb Thomas	Herb Thomas	92	55 Chev	197	475
4. Gwyn Staley	Hubert Westmoreland	2	55 Chev	194	365
5. Jimmy Massey	Hubert Westmoreland	04	55 Chev	194	310

1956 Grand National Race No. 13
May 5, 1956 Average Speed: 54.545

Driver	Owner	Car #	Make	Laps	Winnings
1. Speedy Thompson	Carl Kiekhaefer	500	56 Dodg	200	1,100
2. Buck Baker	Carl Kiekhaefer	500b	56 Dodg	198	700
3. Joe Weatherly	Charlie Schwam	9	56 Ford	196	475
4. Tiny Lund	Gus Holzmueller	37	56 Pont	192	365
5. Bob Flock	Mauri Rose	49	56 Chev	191	310

1956 Grand National Race No. 49
September 29, 1956 Average Speed: 61.193

Driver	Owner	Car #	Make	Laps	Winnings
1. Buck Baker	Carl Kiekhaefer	500B	56 Dodg	200	950
2. Ralph Moody	Pete DePaolo	12	56 Ford	200	675
3. Speedy Thompson	Carl Kiekhaefer	500	56 Dodg	200	475
4. Fireball Roberts	Pete DePaolo	22	56 Ford	200	360
5. Billy Myers	Bill Stroppe	4	56 Merc	198	320

Columbia Speedway *continued*

1957 Grand National Race No. 24
June 20, 1957 Average Speed: 58.045

Driver	Owner	Car #	Make	Laps	Winnings
1. Jack Smith	Jack Smith	47	57 Chev	200	1,000
2. Buck Baker	Buck Baker	87	57 Chev	200	625
3. Marvin Panch	Marvin Panch	98	57 Ford	200	400
4. Jim Paschal	Jim Paschal	17	57 Merc	199	295
5. Speedy Thompson	Speedy Thompson	46	57 Chev	199	255

1957 Grand National Race No. 46
September 19, 1957 Average Speed: 60.514

Driver	Owner	Car #	Make	Laps	Winnings
1. Buck Baker	Buck Baker	87	57 Chev	200	900
2. Gwyn Staley	J. H. Petty	38	57 Chev	199	575
3. Bill Amick	Bill Amick	97	57 Ford	198	375
4. Billy Myers	Sam Rice	26	57 Ford	196	280
5. Brownie King	Jess Potter	32	57 Chev	194	245

1958 Grand National Race No. 8
April 10, 1958

Driver	Owner	Car #	Make	Laps	Winnings
1. Speedy Thompson	Speedy Thompson	46	57 Chev	200	800
2. Jack Smith	Jack Smith	47	57 Chev	200	525
3. Tiny Lund	Don Angel	37	56 Ford	199	350
4. Lee Petty	Petty Enterprises	42	57 Olds	199	250
5. Eddie Pagan	Eddie Pagan	45	57 Ford	198	225

1958 Grand National Race No. 22
June 5, 1958 Average Speed: 54.752

Driver	Owner	Car #	Make	Laps	Winnings
1. Junior Johnson	Paul Spaulding	11	57 Ford	200	800
2. George Dunn	Manley Britt	14	57 Merc	192	525
3. Fred Harb	Fred Harb	17	57 Merc	192	350
4. Wilbur Rakestraw	Joe Jones	999	57 Ford	190	250
5. Shorty Rollins	Spook Crawford	67	57 Plym	189	225

1958 Grand National Race No. 36
August 7, 1958 Average Speed: 54.820

Driver	Owner	Car #	Make	Laps	Winnings
1. Speedy Thompson	Speedy Thompson	46	57 Chev	200	800
2. Bob Welborn	J. H. Petty	49	57 Chev	200	525
3. Cotton Owens	Jim Stephens	6	57 Pont	195	350
4. Shorty Rollins	Shorty Rollins	99	58 Ford	193	250
5. George Dunn	Manley Britt	14	57 Merc	183	225

1959 Grand National Race No. 9
April 4, 1959 Average Speed: 57.343

Driver	Owner	Car #	Make	Laps	Winnings
1. Jack Smith	Jack Smith	47	59 Chev	200	900
2. Ned Jarrett	Paul Spaulding	11	57 Ford	200	525
3. Lee Petty	Petty Enterprises	42	57 Olds	191	350
4. Tiny Lund	Tiny Lund	5	57 Chev	190	250
5. Cotton Owens	W. H. Watson	6	58 Pont	186	225

1959 Grand National Race No. 21
June 18, 1959 Average Speed: 58.726

Driver	Owner	Car #	Make	Laps	Winnings
1. Lee Petty	Petty Enterprises	42	59 Plym	200	900
2. Tommy Irwin	Tommy Irwin	36	59 Ford	200	525
3. Buck Baker	Buck Baker	87	59 Chev	200	350
4. Benny Rakestraw	Talmadge Cochrane	20	57 Merc	196	250
5. Joe Weatherly	Doc White	41	59 Ford	196	225

1959 Grand National Race No. 35
August 29, 1959 Average Speed: 48.264

Driver	Owner	Car #	Make	Laps	Winnings
1. Lee Petty	Petty Enterprises	42	59 Plym	200	900
2. Tiny Lund	Tiny Lund	5	57 Chev	199	525
3. Fred Harb	Fred Harb	17	57 Ford	197	375
4. Roy Tyner	Roy Tyner	49	57 Chev	194	275
5. Glen Wood	Wood Brothers	21	58 Ford	193	250

1960 Grand National Race No. 2
November 26, 1959 Average Speed: 55.071

Driver	Owner	Car #	Make	Laps	Winnings
1. Ned Jarrett	Ned Jarrett	38	57 Ford	200	800
2. Jack Smith	Jack Smith	47	59 Chev	200	525
3. Joe Lee Johnson	Joe Lee Johnson	77	59 Chev	200	375
4. Lee Petty	Petty Enterprises	42	59 Plym	200	275
5. Bobby Johns	Shorty Johns	72	57 Chev	195	250

1960 Grand National Race No. 9
April 5, 1960 Average Speed: 50.697

Driver	Owner	Car #	Make	Laps	Winnings
1. Rex White	Rex White	4	60 Chev	200	800
2. Buck Baker	Buck Baker	87	60 Chev	199	525
3. Doug Yates	Raeford Johnson	23	59 Plym	199	375
4. Lee Petty	Petty Enterprises	42	60 Plym	199	375
5. Joe Lee Johnson	E. C. Wilson	78	59 Chev	197	350

1960 Grand National Race No. 32
August 18, 1960 Average Speed: 54.265

Driver	Owner	Car #	Make	Laps	Winnings
1. Rex White	Rex White	4	60 Chev	300	1,000
2. Richard Petty	Petty Enterprises	43	60 Plym	300	600
3. Buck Baker	Buck Baker	87	60 Chev	293	450
4. Ned Jarrett	Ned Jarrett	11	60 Ford	293	350
5. Tommy Irwin	Tommy Irwin	36	59 Ford	293	325

1961 Grand National Race No. 15
April 20, 1961 Average Speed: 51.940

Driver	Owner	Car #	Make	Laps	Winnings
1. Cotton Owens	Cotton Owens	6	60 Pont	200	950
2. Ned Jarrett	Bee Gee Holloway	11	61 Chev	199	625
3. Emanuel Zervakis	Monroe Shook	85	60 Chev	199	425
4. G. C. Spencer	G. C. Spencer	48	60 Chev	197	275
5. Rex White	Rex White	4	60 Chev	197	350

1961 Grand National Race No. 34
July 20, 1961 Average Speed: 62.198

Driver	Owner	Car #	Make	Laps	Winnings
1. Cotton Owens	Cotton Owens	6	60 Pont	200	950
2. Jim Paschal	J. H. Petty	14	61 Chev	200	625
3. Ned Jarrett	Bee Gee Holloway	11	61 Chev	200	425
4. Junior Johnson	Rex Lovette	27	60 Pont	198	275
5. Joe Weatherly	Bud Moore	8	61 Pont	198	250

1962 Grand National Race No. 11 Arclite 200
April 13, 1962 Average Speed: 56.710

Driver	Owner	Car #	Make	Laps	Winnings
1. Ned Jarrett	Bee Gee Holloway	11	62 Chev	200	1,200
2. Joe Weatherly	Bud Moore	8	61 Pont	200	600
3. Jack Smith	Jack Smith	47	61 Pont	198	400
4. Jim Paschal	Cliff Stewart	2	62 Pont	198	300
5. G. C. Spencer	G. C. Spencer	48	60 Chev	197	275

Columbia Speedway *continued*

1962 Grand National Race No. 30
July 7, 1962 Average Speed: 62.370

Driver	Owner	Car #	Make	Laps	Winnings
1. Rex White	Rex White	4	62 Chev	200	1,000
2. Joe Weatherly	Bud Moore	8	61 Pont	200	600
3. Jack Smith	Jack Smith	47	61 Pont	199	400
4. Cotton Owens	Cotton Owens	6	62 Pont	199	300
5. Ned Jarrett	Bee Gee Holloway	11	62 Chev	199	475

1963 Grand National Race No. 21
May 2, 1963 Average Speed: 51.650

Driver	Owner	Car #	Make	Laps	Winnings
1. Richard Petty	Petty Enterprises	41	63 Plym	200	1,000
2. Buck Baker	Buck Baker	87	63 Pont	200	600
3. Ned Jarrett	Charles Robinson	11	63 Ford	200	400
4. Buddy Baker	Buck Baker	7	62 Chrys	200	300
5. Jack Smith	Jack Smith	47	63 Plym	200	275

1963 Grand National Race No. 40 Sandlapper 200
August 8, 1963 Average Speed: 55.598

Driver	Owner	Car #	Make	Laps	Winnings
1. Richard Petty	Petty Enterprises	43	63 Plym	200	1,140
2. David Pearson	Cotton Owens	6	63 Dodg	200	600
3. Bobby Isaac	Bondy Long	99	63 Ford	200	400
4. Ned Jarrett	Charles Robinson	11	63 Ford	200	350
5. G. C. Spencer	G. C. Spencer	03	62 Chev	198	275

1964 Grand National Race No. 17 Columbia 200
April 16, 1964 Average Speed: 64.412

Driver	Owner	Car #	Make	Laps	Winnings
1. Ned Jarrett	Bondy Long	11	64 Ford	200	1,150
2. Marvin Panch	Wood Brothers	21	64 Ford	199	700
3. LeeRoy Yarbrough	Louie Weathersby	45	63 Plym	198	400
4. Billy Wade	Bud Moore	1	64 Merc	198	300
5. Dick Hutcherson	Dick Hutcherson	7	64 Ford	198	275

1964 Grand National Race No. 48 Sandlapper 200
August 21, 1964 Average Speed: 61.697

Driver	Owner	Car #	Make	Laps	Winnings
1. David Pearson	Cotton Owens	6	64 Dodg	200	1,000
2. Doug Yates	Doug Yates	72	63 Plym	198	600
3. Jimmy Pardue	Charles Robinson	54	64 Plym	196	400
4. Ned Jarrett	Bondy Long	11	64 Ford	193	300
5. Doug Cooper	Bob Cooper	60	63 Ford	186	275

1965 Grand National Race No. 13 Columbia 200
April 28, 1965 Average Speed: 55.591

Driver	Owner	Car #	Make	Laps	Winnings
1. Tiny Lund	Lyle Stelter	55	64 Ford	124	1,000
2. Ned Jarrett	Bondy Long	11	65 Ford	124	600
3. Neil Castles	Buck Baker	86	65 Plym	122	400
4. Darel Dieringer	Gary Weaver	10	65 Ford	121	300
5. Dick Hutcherson	Holman-Moody	29	65 Ford	120	275

1965 Grand National Race No. 41 Sandlapper 200
August 19, 1965 Average Speed: 57.361

Driver	Owner	Car #	Make	Laps	Winnings
1. David Pearson	Cotton Owens	6	65 Dodg	200	1,000
2. Richard Petty	Petty Enterprises	43	65 Plym	200	800
3. Dick Hutcherson	Holman-Moody	29	65 Ford	200	400
4. Tiny Lund	Lyle Stelter	55	64 Ford	198	300
5. Cale Yarborough	Kenny Myler	06	64 Ford	197	275

1966 Grand National Race No. 10
April 7, 1966 Average Speed: 65.574

Driver	Owner	Car #	Make	Laps	Winnings
1. David Pearson	Cotton Owens	6	64 Dodg	200	1,000
2. Paul Goldsmith	Bob Cooper	02	65 Plym	200	600
3. Tom Pistone	Tom Pistone	59	64 Ford	198	400
4. J. T. Putney	J. T. Putney	19	66 Chev	198	300
5. John Sears	L. G. DeWitt	04	64 Ford	195	275

1966 Grand National Race No. 38
August 18, 1966 Average Speed: 66.128

Driver	Owner	Car #	Make	Laps	Winnings
1. David Pearson	Cotton Owens	6	65 Dodg	200	1,000
2. Richard Petty	Petty Enterprises	42	66 Plym	200	600
3. Curtis Turner	Junior Johnson	26	66 Ford	200	400
4. James Hylton	Bud Hartje	48	65 Dodg	198	300
5. Dick Hutcherson	Holman-Moody	29	66 Ford	198	275

1967 Grand National Race No. 11 Sandlapper 200
April 6, 1967 Average Speed: 65.455

Driver	Owner	Car #	Make	Laps	Winnings
1. Richard Petty	Petty Enterprises	43	67 Plym	200	1,000
2. Jim Paschal	Tom Friedkin	14	67 Plym	199	600
3. Dick Hutcherson	Bondy Long	29	67 Ford	198	400
4. James Hylton	Bud Hartje	48	65 Dodg	197	300
5. Neil Castles	Buck Baker	88	66 Olds	193	275

1967 Grand National Race No. 38
August 17, 1967 Average Speed: 64.274

Driver	Owner	Car #	Make	Laps	Winnings
1. Richard Petty	Petty Enterprises	43	67 Plym	200	1,000
2. John Sears	L. G. DeWitt	4	66 Ford	199	600
3. Elmo Langley	Henry Woodfield	64	66 Ford	197	400
4. Bobby Allison	Bobby Allison	2	66 Chev	197	300
5. James Hylton	Bud Hartje	48	65 Dodg	196	275

1968 Grand National Race No. 10
April 18, 1968 Average Speed: 71.358

Driver	Owner	Car #	Make	Laps	Winnings
1. Bobby Isaac	Nord Krauskopf	37	67 Dodg	200	1,000
2. Charlie Glotzbach	Cotton Owens	6	67 Dodg	200	600
3. James Hylton	James Hylton	48	67 Dodg	200	400
4. Buddy Baker	Ray Fox	3	67 Dodg	199	300
5. Richard Petty	Petty Enterprises	43	68 Plym	198	475

1968 Grand National Race No. 34 Sandlapper 200
August 8, 1968 Average Speed: 67.039

Driver	Owner	Car #	Make	Laps	Winnings
1. David Pearson	Holman-Moody	17	68 Ford	200	1,000
2. Charlie Glotzbach	Cotton Owens	6	68 Dodg	200	600
3. LeeRoy Yarbrough	Lyle Stelter	56	67 Ford	199	400
4. Elmo Langley	Elmo Langley	64	66 Ford	198	300
5. Neil Castles	Neil Castles	06	67 Plym	197	275

1969 Grand National Race No. 11 Columbia 200
April 3, 1969 Average Speed: 68.558

Driver	Owner	Car #	Make	Laps	Winnings
1. Bobby Isaac	Nord Krauskopf	71	69 Dodg	200	1,000
2. David Pearson	Holman-Moody	17	69 Ford	200	800
3. Richard Petty	Petty Enterprises	43	69 Ford	199	400
4. James Hylton	James Hylton	48	67 Dodg	197	350
5. John Sears	L. G. DeWitt	4	67 Ford	197	325

Columbia Speedway *continued*

1969 Grand National Race No. 45 Sandlapper 200
September 18, 1969 Average Speed: 70.230

Driver	Owner	Car #	Make	Laps	Winnings
1. Bobby Isaac	Nord Krauskopf	71	69 Dodg	200	1,000
2. Richard Petty	Petty Enterprises	43	69 Ford	200	600
3. James Hylton	James Hylton	48	69 Dodg	196	400
4. John Sears	L. G. DeWitt	4	69 Ford	195	350
5. Eldon Yarbrough	Lyle Stelter	56	67 Ford	194	325

1970 Grand National Race No. 12 Columbia 200
April 30, 1970 Average Speed: 62.685

Driver	Owner	Car #	Make	Laps	Winnings
1. Richard Petty	Don Robertson	43	70 Plym	200	1,500
2. Bobby Allison	Bobby Allison	22	69 Dodg	199	900
3. Bobby Isaac	Nord Krauskopf	71	69 Dodg	197	500
4. Neil Castles	Neil Castles	06	69 Dodg	197	350
5. James Hylton	James Hylton	48	69 Ford	195	325

1970 Grand National Race No. 32 Sandlapper 200
August 6, 1970 Average Speed: 67.101

Driver	Owner	Car #	Make	Laps	Winnings
1. Bobby Isaac	Nord Krauskopf	71	70 Dodg	200	1,500
2. Richard Petty	Petty Enterprises	43	70 Plym	200	900
3. Bobby Allison	Bobby Allison	22	69 Dodg	199	500
4. John Sears	John Sears	4	69 Dodg	197	350
5. Neil Castles	Neil Castles	06	69 Dodg	196	325

1971 Winston Cup GN Race No. 11 Sandlapper 200
April 8, 1971 Average Speed: 76.514

Driver	Owner	Car #	Make	Laps	Winnings
1. Richard Petty	Petty Enterprises	43	71 Plym	200	1,700
2. Benny Parsons	L. G. DeWitt	72	69 Ford	200	1,200
3. Dick Brooks	Mario Rossi	22	70 Dodg	200	800
4. James Hylton	James Hylton	48	60 Ford	198	550
5. Elmo Langley	Clyde Lynn	20	70 Ford	198	425

1971 Winston Cup GN Race No. 38 Sandlapper 200
August 27, 1971 Average Speed: 64.831

Driver	Owner	Car #	Make	Laps	Winnings
1. Richard Petty	Petty Enterprises	43	70 Plym	200	1,500
2. Tiny Lund	Ronnie Hopkins	55	69 Chev	200	900
3. Jim Paschal	Cliff Stewart	14	70 Mata	200	500
4. James Hylton	James Hylton	48	70 Ford	197	350
5. Jabe Thomas	Don Robertson	25	70 Plym	196	325

Darlington Raceway
Darlington, SC
1.366-mile Superspeedway

Built in 1948–50 by Harold Brasington. First race was inaugural Southern 500 (9/4/50), won by Johnny Mantz. Original measurement was 1.25-mile egg-shaped oval. Configuration determined by location of minnow pond. Track upgraded and lengthened to 1.375-mile oval in 1953. Currently measured at 1.366-miles. AM and USAC IndyCars have also run on track on occasion from 1950–56.

Winston Cup Starts
Richard Petty   66

Winston Cup Victories
David Pearson   10

Winston Cup Poles
David Pearson   12

Winston Cup Money
Bill Elliott $1,818,075

Most Cars Started
82—September 3, 1951 Southern 500

Fewest Cars Started
24—May 10, 1952 (100-mile race)

Narrowest Margin of Victory
3 feet—April 4, 1982
CRC Chemicals Rebel 500

Slowest Race
74.512 MPH—September 1, 1952
Southern 500

Race Record
139.958 MPH—March 28, 1993
TranSouth 500

Most Cautions
15—March 26, 1995 TranSouth 400

Most Race Leaders
17—September 6, 1982 Southern 500

Most Cars Running at Finish
50—September 4, 1950 Southern 500

1950 Grand National Race No. 13 Southern 500
September 4, 1950 Average Speed: 75.250

Driver	Owner	Car #	Make	Laps	Winnings
1. Johnny Mantz	Johnny Mantz & Bill France	98	50 Plym	400	10,510
2. Fireball Roberts	Sam Rice	82	50 Olds	391	3,500
3. Red Byron	Raymond Parks	22	50 Cad	390	2,000
4. Bill Rexford	Julian Buesink	59	50 Olds	385	1,500
5. Chuck Mahoney	Brooks Motors	77	50 Merc	381	1,000

1951 Grand National Race No. 24 Southern 500
September 3, 1951 Average Speed: 76.906

Driver	Owner	Car #	Make	Laps	Winnings
1. Herb Thomas	Herb Thomas	92	51 Huds	400	8,800
2. Jesse James Taylor	Jesse James Taylor	31	51 Huds	399	2,800
3. Buddy Shuman	R. H. Yandell	17	51 Ford	391	1,500
4. Hershel McGriff		77	51 Olds	390	1,210
5. Fireball Roberts	Ed Saverance	11	51 Ford	387	910

1952 Grand National Race No. 10
May 10, 1952 Average Speed: 83.818

Driver	Owner	Car #	Make	Laps	Winnings
1. Dick Rathmann	Walt Chapman	120	51 Huds	80	1,000
2. Tim Flock	Ted Chester	91	51 Huds	80	700
3. Fonty Flock	Frank Christian	14	51 Olds	78	450
4. Jimmie Lewallen	George Hutchens	2	52 Olds	78	350
5. Joe Eubanks	Phil Oates	82	52 Huds	78	200

1952 Grand National Race No. 25 Southern 500
September 1, 1952 Average Speed: 74.512

Driver	Owner	Car #	Make	Laps	Winnings
1. Fonty Flock	Frank Christian	14	52 Olds	400	9,430
2. Johnny Patterson	H. B. Ranier	58	52 Huds	399	3,000
3. Herb Thomas	Herb Thomas	92	52 Huds	399	1,590
4. Bub King	Bub King	55	52 Huds	398	1,230
5. Banjo Matthews	Bill Snowden	16	52 Huds	393	950

1953 Grand National Race No. 30 Southern 500
September 7, 1953 Average Speed: 92.881

Driver	Owner	Car #	Make	Laps	Winnings
1. Buck Baker	Griffin Motors	87	53 Olds	364	6,285
2. Fonty Flock	Frank Christian	14	53 Huds	361	3,040
3. Curtis Turner	Frank Christian	44	53 Olds	359	1,500
4. Dick Meyer	Dick Meyer	49	53 Dodg	355	1,000
5. Herb Thomas	Herb Thomas	92	53 Huds	354	1,550

1954 Grand National Race No. 31
September 6, 1954 Average Speed: 95.026

Driver	Owner	Car #	Make	Laps	Winnings
1. Herb Thomas	Herb Thomas	92	54 Huds	364	6,830
2. Curtis Turner	Elmer Brooks	44	52 Olds	364	6,245
3. Marvin Panch	Beryl Jackson	98	54 Dodg	362	2,155
4. Johnny Patterson	H. B. Ranier	58	54 Merc	360	1,165
5. Jim Paschal	Ernest Woods	88	54 Olds	357	975

1955 Grand National Race No. 35 Southern 500
September 5, 1955 Average Speed: 92.281

Driver	Owner	Car #	Make	Laps	Winnings
1. Herb Thomas	Herb Thomas	92	55 Chev	366	7,480
2. Jim Reed	Jim Reed	7	55 Chev	365	1,550
3. Tim Flock	Carl Kiekhaefer	16	55 Chrys	363	2,500
4. Gwyn Staley	Hubert Westmoreland	2	55 Chev	359	1,300
5. Larry Flynn	W. O. Taylor	96	55 Ford	359	1,175

1956 Grand National Race No. 44 Southern 500
September 3, 1956 Average Speed: 95.167

Driver	Owner	Car #	Make	Laps	Winnings
1. Curtis Turner	Charlie Schwam	99	56 Ford	364	11,750
2. Speedy Thompson	Carl Kiekhaefer	57	56 Chrys	362	5,000
3. Marvin Panch	Pete DePaolo	8	56 Ford	359	3,370
4. Jim Reed	Jim Reed	7	56 Chev	350	1,850
5. Paul Goldsmith	Smokey Yunick	3	56 Chev	358	1,300

1957 Grand National Race No. 40 Southern 500
September 2, 1957 Average Speed: 100.094

Driver	Owner	Car #	Make	Laps	Winnings
1. Speedy Thompson	Speedy Thompson	46	57 Chev	364	13,590
2. Cotton Owens	Ray Nichels	6	57 Pont	361	6,100
3. Marvin Panch	Marvin Panch	98	57 Ford	360	3,745
4. Jim Reed	Jim Reed	7	57 Ford	356	2,155
5. Buck Baker	Buck Baker	87	57 Chev	356	1,650

1958 Grand National Race No. 41 Southern 500
September 1, 1958 Average Speed: 102.585

Driver	Owner	Car #	Make	Laps	Winnings
1. Fireball Roberts	Frank Strickland	22	57 Chev	364	13,220
2. Buck Baker	Buck Baker	87	57 Chev	359	5,750
3. Shorty Rollins	Shorty Rollins	99	58 Ford	359	3,815
4. Jimmy Thompson	Speedy Thompson	46	57 Chev	358	1,995
5. Marvin Panch	John Whitford	98	58 Ford	357	1,525

Darlington Raceway *continued*

1959 Grand National Race No. 36 Southern 500
September 7, 1959 Average Speed: 111.836

Driver	Owner	Car #	Make	Laps	Winnings
1. Jim Reed	Jim Reed	7	57 Chev	364	17,250
2. Bob Burdick	Roy Burdick Gar	73	59 Ford	362	7,760
3. Bobby Johns	Shorty Johns	72	57 Chev	362	4,760
4. Richard Petty	Petty Enterprises	43	59 Plym	361	2,830
5. Tommy Irwin	Tommy Irwin	36	59 Ford	358	2,010

1960 Grand National Race No. 16 Rebel 300
May 7 & 14, 1960 Average Speed: 102.640

Driver	Owner	Car #	Make	Laps	Winnings
1. Joe Weatherly	Holman-Moody	12	60 Ford	219	9,250
2. Richard Petty	Petty Enterprises	43	60 Plym	219	4,875
3. Rex White	Rex White	4	60 Chev	218	2,900
4. Lee Petty	Petty Enterprises	42	60 Plym	218	1,940
5. Buck Baker	Buck Baker	87	60 Chev	216	1,500

1960 Grand National Race No. 35 Southern 500
September 5, 1960 Average Speed: 105.901

Driver	Owner	Car #	Make	Laps	Winnings
1. Buck Baker	Jack Smith	47	60 Pont	364	19,900
2. Rex White	Rex White	4	60 Chev	364	9,780
3. Jim Paschal	Petty Enterprises	44	60 Plym	362	5,595
4. Emanuel Zervakis	Monroe Shook	85	60 Chev	362	3,125
5. Ned Jarrett	Ned Jarrett	11	60 Ford	362	2,000

1961 Grand National Race No. 19 Rebel 300
May 6, 1961 Average Speed: 119.520

Driver	Owner	Car #	Make	Laps	Winnings
1. Fred Lorenzen	Holman-Moody	28	61 Ford	219	8,420
2. Curtis Turner	Wood Brothers	21	61 Ford	219	4,600
3. Johnny Allen	Bee Gee Holloway	69	61 Chev	218	3,200
4. Bob Burdick	Roy Burdick Gar	53	61 Pont	218	2,400
5. Fireball Roberts	Bud Moore	22	61 Pont	218	1,665

1961 Grand National Race No. 42 Southern 500
September 4, 1961 Average Speed: 117.787

Driver	Owner	Car #	Make	Laps	Winnings
1. Nelson Stacy	Dudley Farrell	29	61 Ford	364	18,430
2. Fireball Roberts	Jim Stephens	22	61 Pont	364	10,670
3. David Pearson	John Masoni	3	Pont	363	5,060
4. Jim Paschal	J. H. Petty	44	61 Pont	359	2,625
5. Emanuel Zervakis	Monroe Shook	85	61 Chev	359	2,450

1962 Grand National Race No. 21 Rebel 300
May 12, 1962 Average Speed: 117.429

Driver	Owner	Car #	Make	Laps	Winnings
1. Nelson Stacy	Holman-Moody	29	62 Ford	219	7,900
2. Marvin Panch	Wood Brothers	21	62 Ford	219	4,890
3. Fred Lorenzen	Holman-Moody	28	62 Ford	218	3,400
4. Jack Smith	Jack Smith	47	62 Pont	217	2,270
5. Cotton Owens	Cotton Owens	6	62 Pont	216	1,765

1962 Grand National Race No. 45 Southern 500
September 3, 1962 Average Speed: 117.965

Driver	Owner	Car #	Make	Laps	Winnings
1. Larry Frank	Ratus Walters	66	62 Ford	364	21,730
2. Junior Johnson	Ray Fox	3	62 Pont	364	10,155
3. Marvin Panch	Wood Brothers	21	62 Ford	364	5,150
4. David Pearson	Cotton Owens	6	62 Pont	364	3,325
5. Richard Petty	Petty Enterprises	43	62 Plym	363	5,450

1963 Grand National Race No. 23 Rebel 300
May 11, 1963

Driver	Owner	Car #	Make	Laps	Winnings
1. Joe Weatherly	Bud Moore	8	63 Pont	220	11,100
2. Fireball Roberts	Holman-Moody	22	63 Ford	219	6,200
3. Richard Petty	Petty Enterprises	42	63 Plym	219	4,980
4. Tiny Lund	Wood Brothers	21	63 Ford	219	2,665
5. Bobby Johns	Shorty Johns	7	63 UNK	218	1,965

1963 Grand National Race No. 45 Southern 500
September 2, 1963 Average Speed: 129.784

Driver	Owner	Car #	Make	Laps	Winnings
1. Fireball Roberts	Holman-Moody	22	63 Ford	364	22,150
2. Marvin Panch	Wood Brothers	21	63 Ford	364	12,650
3. Fred Lorenzen	Holman-Moody	28	73 Ford	364	6,550
4. Nelson Stacy	Holman-Moody	29	63 Ford	363	3,500
5. Darel Dieringer	Bill Stroppe	26	63 Merc	360	2,625

1964 Grand National Race No. 21 Rebel 300
May 9, 1964 Average Speed: 130.013

Driver	Owner	Car #	Make	Laps	Winnings
1. Fred Lorenzen	Holman-Moody	28	64 Ford	219	10,265
2. Fireball Roberts	Holman-Moody	22	64 Ford	219	5,990
3. Junior Johnson	Banjo Matthews	27	64 Ford	218	4,510
4. Ned Jarrett	Bondy Long	11	64 Ford	216	2,995
5. Jimmy Pardue	Charles Robinson	54	64 Plym	215	2,170

1964 Grand National Race No. 51 Southern 500
September 7, 1964 Average Speed: 117.757

Driver	Owner	Car #	Make	Laps	Winnings
1. Buck Baker	Ray Fox	3	64 Dodg	364	21,230
2. Jim Paschal	Petty Enterprises	41	64 Plym	362	8,960
3. Richard Petty	Petty Enterprises	43	64 Plym	360	8,170
4. Ned Jarrett	Bondy Long	11	64 Ford	359	3,575
5. Jimmy Pardue	Charles Robinson	54	64 Plym	358	2,955

1965 Grand National Race No. 15 Rebel 300
May 8, 1965 Average Speed: 111.849

Driver	Owner	Car #	Make	Laps	Winnings
1. Junior Johnson	Rex Lovette	26	65 Ford	219	10,490
2. Darel Dieringer	Bud Moore	16	64 Merc	219	6,155
3. Ned Jarrett	Bondy Long	11	65 Ford	218	4,460
4. Dick Hutcherson	Holman-Moody	29	65 Ford	217	2,925
5. Bobby Johns	Holman-Moody	7	65 Ford	217	1,100

1965 Grand National Race No. 45 Southern 500
September 6, 1965 Average Speed: 115.878

Driver	Owner	Car #	Make	Laps	Winnings
1. Ned Jarrett	Bondy Long	11	65 Ford	364	21,060
2. Buck Baker	Buck Baker	86	65 Plym	350	9,170
3. Darel Dieringer	Bud Moore	16	64 Merc	345	7,200
4. Roy Mayne	Tom Hunter	46	65 Chev	345	3,225
5. Buddy Arrington	Buddy Arrington	67	64 Dodg	344	2,400

1966 Grand National Race No. 15 Rebel 400
April 30, 1966 Average Speed: 131.993

Driver	Owner	Car #	Make	Laps	Winnings
1. Richard Petty	Petty Enterprises	43	66 Plym	291	12,115
2. Paul Goldsmith	Ray Nichels	99	65 Plym	288	6,570
3. David Pearson	Cotton Owens	6	65 Dodg	288	4,145
4. Bunkie Blackburn	Ray Fox	3	65 Dodg	283	2,225
5. G. C. Spencer	G. C. Spencer	49	65 Plym	283	1,670

Darlington Raceway *continued*

1966 Grand National Race No. 42 Southern 500
September 5, 1966 Average Speed: 114.830

Driver	Owner	Car #	Make	Laps	Winnings
1. Darel Dieringer	Bud Moore	16	66 Merc	364	20,900
2. Richard Petty	Petty Enterprises	43	66 Plym	364	8,975
3. David Pearson	Cotton Owens	6	66 Dodg	361	4,700
4. Marvin Panch	Petty Enterprises	42	66 Plym	360	2,725
5. Fred Lorenzen	Holman-Moody	28	66 Ford	360	2,300

1967 Grand National Race No. 17 Rebel 300
May 13, 1967 Average Speed: 125.738

Driver	Owner	Car #	Make	Laps	Winnings
1. Richard Petty	Petty Enterprises	43	67 Plym	291	14,090
2. David Pearson	Holman-Moody	17	67 Ford	290	8,285
3. Dick Hutcherson	Bondy Long	29	67 Ford	285	5,005
4. Bobby Allison	Cotton Owens	6	67 Dodg	285	2,775
5. Sam McQuagg	Bud Moore	16	67 Merc	283	2,175

1967 Grand National Race No. 40 Southern 500
September 4, 1967 Average Speed: 130.423

Driver	Owner	Car #	Make	Laps	Winnings
1. Richard Petty	Petty Enterprises	43	67 Plym	364	26,900
2. David Pearson	Holman-Moody	17	67 Ford	359	10,825
3. G. C. Spencer	Petty Enterprises	42	67 Plym	359	6,175
4. Charlie Glotzbach	Nord Krauskopf	72	67 Dodg	356	3,325
5. Bud Moore	A. J. King	53	67 Dodg	355	2,725

1968 Grand National Race No. 15 Rebel 400
May 11, 1968 Average Speed: 132.699

Driver	Owner	Car #	Make	Laps	Winnings
1. David Pearson	Holman-Moody	17	68 Ford	291	13,700
2. Darel Dieringer	Mario Rossi	22	68 Plym	291	7,620
3. Richard Petty	Petty Enterprises	43	68 Plym	291	5,330
4. Buddy Baker	Ray Fox	3	67 Dodg	290	2,675
5. LeeRoy Yarbrough	Junior Johnson	26	68 Ford	287	2,225

1968 Grand National Race No. 39 Southern 500
September 2, 1968 Average Speed: 126.132

Driver	Owner	Car #	Make	Laps	Winnings
1. Cale Yarborough	Wood Brothers	21	68 Merc	364	25,415
2. David Pearson	Holman-Moody	17	68 Ford	364	10,850
3. Buddy Baker	Ray Fox	3	68 Dodg	362	6,200
4. Charlie Glotzbach	Cotton Owens	6	68 Dodg	360	3,800
5. Paul Goldsmith	Ray Nichels	99	68 Dodg	357	3,075

1969 Grand National Race No. 18 Rebel 400
May 10, 1969 Average Speed: 131.572

Driver	Owner	Car #	Make	Laps	Winnings
1. LeeRoy Yarbrough	Junior Johnson	98	69 Merc	291	14,700
2. Cale Yarborough	Wood Brothers	21	69 Merc	290	8,020
3. Paul Goldsmith	Ray Nichels	99	69 Dodg	288	5,005
4. Bobby Allison	Mario Rossi	22	69 Dodg	287	2,650
5. David Pearson	Holman-Moody	17	69 Ford	285	2,550

1969 Grand National Race No. 41 Southern 500
September 1, 1969 Average Speed: 105.612

Driver	Owner	Car #	Make	Laps	Winnings
1. LeeRoy Yarbrough	Junior Johnson	98	69 Ford	230	21,800
2. David Pearson	Holman-Moody	17	69 Ford	230	12,250
3. Buddy Baker	Cotton Owens	6	69 Dodg	230	6,700
4. Donnie Allison	Banjo Matthews	27	69 Ford	227	3,325
5. Bobby Allison	Mario Rossi	22	69 Dodg	225	2,750

1970 Grand National Race No. 13 Rebel 400
May 9, 1970 Average Speed: 129.668

Driver	Owner	Car #	Make	Laps	Winnings
1. David Pearson	Holman-Moody	17	69 Ford	291	15,650
2. Dick Brooks	Dick Brooks	32	70 Plym	288	8,170
3. Bobby Isaac	Nord Krauskopf	71	69 Dodg	284	5,580
4. James Hylton	James Hylton	48	69 Ford	282	3,350
5. Benny Parsons	L. G. DeWitt	72	69 Ford	279	2,600

1970 Grand National Race No. 38 Southern 500
September 7, 1970 Average Speed: 128.817

Driver	Owner	Car #	Make	Laps	Winnings
1. Buddy Baker	Cotton Owens	6	69 Dodg	367	27,450
2. Bobby Isaac	Nord Krauskopf	71	69 Dodg	366	11,825
3. Pete Hamilton	Petty Enterprises	40	70 Plym	364	7,000
4. David Pearson	Holman-Moody	17	69 Ford	363	6,175
5. Richard Petty	Petty Enterprises	43	70 Plym	362	3,100

1971 Winston Cup GN Race No. 16 Rebel 400
May 2, 1971 Average Speed: 130.678

Driver	Owner	Car #	Make	Laps	Winnings
1. Buddy Baker	Petty Enterprises	11	71 Dodg	293	16,065
2. Dick Brooks	Mario Rossi	22	70 Dodg	286	8,165
3. Dave Marcis	Dave Marcis	2	69 Dodg	286	5,540
4. Donnie Allison	Wood Brothers	21	71 Merc	283	4,090
5. Jim Vandiver	O. L. Nixon	31	70 Dodg	276	2,215

1971 Winston Cup GN Race No. 40 Southern 500
September 6, 1971 Average Speed: 131.398

Driver	Owner	Car #	Make	Laps	Winnings
1. Bobby Allison	Holman-Moody	12	69 Merc	367	22,450
2. Richard Petty	Petty Enterprises	43	71 Plym	366	10,050
3. Buddy Baker	Petty Enterprises	11	71 Dodg	363	6,575
4. Bobby Isaac	Nord Krauskopf	71	71 Dodg	361	4,625
5. Dave Marcis	Ray Nichels	99	71 Plym	355	3,600

1972 Winston Cup GN Race No. 8 Rebel 400
April 16, 1972 Average Speed: 124.406

Driver	Owner	Car #	Make	Laps	Winnings
1. David Pearson	Wood Brothers	21	71 Merc	293	16,850
2. Richard Petty	Petty Enterprises	43	72 Plym	292	10,375
3. Joe Frasson	Joe Frasson	18	71 Dodg	285	5,475
4. Benny Parsons	L. G. DeWitt	72	71 Merc	284	4,675
5. James Hylton	James Hylton	48	71 Ford	281	2,875

1972 Winston Cup GN Race No. 24 Southern 500
September 4, 1972 Average Speed: 128.124

Driver	Owner	Car #	Make	Laps	Winnings
1. Bobby Allison	R. Howard & J. Johnson	12	72 Chev	367	23,990
2. David Pearson	Wood Brothers	21	71 Merc	367	11,065
3. Richard Petty	Petty Enterprises	43	72 Dodg	360	8,990
4. Fred Lorenzen	Hoss Ellington	28	72 Chev	354	4,940
5. H. B. Bailey	Vernon Blank	66	71 Pont	351	4,630

1973 Winston Cup GN Race No. 8 Rebel 500
April 15, 1973 Average Speed: 122.655

Driver	Owner	Car #	Make	Laps	Winnings
1. David Pearson	Wood Brothers	21	71 Merc	367	16,335
2. Benny Parsons	L. G. DeWitt	72	72 Chev	354	8,885
3. Bobby Allison	Bobby Allison	12	73 Chev	349	7,585
4. Richard Childress	Tom Garn	96	73 Chev	346	4,035
5. J. D. McDuffie	J. D. McDuffie	70	72 Chev	344	3,685

Darlington Raceway *continued*

1973 Winston Cup GN Race No. 22 Southern 500
September 3, 1973 Average Speed: 134.033

Driver	Owner	Car #	Make	Laps	Winnings
1. Cale Yarborough	R. Howard & J. Johnson	11	73 Chev	367	23,140
2. David Pearson	Wood Brothers	21	71 Merc	367	12,130
3. Buddy Baker	Nord Krauskopf	71	73 Dodg	366	8,585
4. Richard Petty	Petty Enterprises	43	73 Dodg	361	7,510
5. Benny Parsons	L. G. DeWitt	72	73 Chev	360	4,685

1974 Winston Cup GN Race No. 23 Southern 500
September 2, 1974 Average Speed: 111.075

Driver	Owner	Car #	Make	Laps	Winnings
1. Cale Yarborough	Junior Johnson	11	74 Chev	367	28,000
2. Darrell Waltrip	Darrell Waltrip	95	74 Chev	366	11,000
3. David Sisco	David Sisco	05	74 Chev	365	7,575
4. Dave Marcis	Dave Marcis	2	73 Dodg	362	5,850
5. James Hylton	James Hylton	48	74 Chev	360	4,650

1975 Winston Cup GN Race No. 21 Southern 500
September 1, 1975 Average Speed: 116.825

Driver	Owner	Car #	Make	Laps	Winnings
1. Bobby Allison	Roger Penske	16	75 Mata	367	20,870
2. Richard Petty	Petty Enterprises	43	75 Dodg	367	16,395
3. David Sisco	David Sisco	05	75 Chev	358	9,120
4. Jim Vandiver	Jim Vandiver	31	74 Dodg	353	6,495
5. Bruce Hill	Bruce Hill	47	75 Chev	352	5,600

1976 Winston Cup GN Race No. 22 Southern 500
September 6, 1976 Average Speed: 120.534

Driver	Owner	Car #	Make	Laps	Winnings
1. David Pearson	Wood Brothers	21	Merc	367	16,155
2. Richard Petty	Petty Enterprises	43	Dodg	367	18,055
3. Darrell Waltrip	DiGard	88	Chev	367	13,135
4. Dave Marcis	Nord Krauskopf	71	Dodg	367	10,800
5. Lennie Pond	Ronnie Elder	54	Chev	365	8,315

1977 Winston Cup GN Race No. 22 Southern 500
September 5, 1977 Average Speed: 106.797

Driver	Owner	Car #	Make	Laps	Winnings
1. David Pearson	Wood Brothers	21	Merc	367	24,550
2. Donnie Allison	Hoss Ellington	1	Chev	367	14,285
3. Buddy Baker	Bud Moore	15	Ford	367	12,710
4. Richard Petty	Petty Enterprises	43	Dodg	365	10,360
5. Cale Yarborough	Junior Johnson	11	Chev	362	12,435

1978 Winston Cup GN Race No. 22 Southern 500
September 4, 1978 Average Speed: 116.828

Driver	Owner	Car #	Make	Laps	Winnings
1. Cale Yarborough	Junior Johnson	11	Olds	367	30,175
2. Darrell Waltrip	DiGard	88	Chev	367	18,450
3. Richard Petty	Petty Enterprises	43	Chev	366	13,175
4. Terry Labonte	Billy Hagan	92	Chev	356	9,850
5. Bobby Allison	Bud Moore	15	Ford	355	10,875

1979 Winston Cup GN Race No. 23 Southern 500
September 3, 1979 Average Speed: 126.259

Driver	Owner	Car #	Make	Laps	Winnings
1. David Pearson	Rod Osterlund	2	Chev	367	29,925
2. Bill Elliott	George Elliott	17	Merc	365	19,235
3. Terry Labonte	Billy Hagan	44	Chev	365	13,460
4. Buddy Baker	Harry Ranier	28	Chev	365	7,975
5. Benny Parsons	M. C. Anderson	27	Chev	364	8,915

1974 Winston Cup GN Race No. 7 Rebel 450
April 7, 1974 Average Speed: 117.543

Driver	Owner	Car #	Make	Laps	Winnings
1. David Pearson	Wood Brothers	21	73 Merc	330	16,575
2. Bobby Allison	Bobby Allison	12	74 Chev	330	11,725
3. Buddy Baker	Nord Krauskopf	71	74 Dodg	330	6,275
4. Donnie Allison	DiGard	88	74 Chev	329	4,825
5. Cale Yarborough	R. Howard & J. Johnson	11	74 Chev	328	6,025

1975 Winston Cup GN Race No. 8 Rebel 500
April 13, 1975 Average Speed: 117.597

Driver	Owner	Car #	Make	Laps	Winnings
1. Bobby Allison	Roger Penske	16	75 Mata	367	15,080
2. Darrell Waltrip	Darrell Waltrip	17	75 Chev	367	13,180
3. Donnie Allison	DiGard	88	75 Chev	367	8,080
4. Dave Marcis	Nord Krauskopf	71	74 Dodg	364	7,880
5. Coo Coo Marlin	H. B. Cunningham	14	75 Chev	357	4,580

1976 Winston Cup GN Race No. 8 Rebel 500
April 11, 1976 Average Speed: 122.973

Driver	Owner	Car #	Make	Laps	Winnings
1. David Pearson	Wood Brothers	21	Merc	367	17,570
2. Buddy Baker	Bud Moore	15	Ford	367	14,875
3. Benny Parsons	L. G. DeWitt	72	Chev	365	12,055
4. Lennie Pond	Ronnie Elder	54	Chev	363	6,015
5. Dave Marcis	Nord Krauskopf	71	Dodg	362	7,580

1977 Winston Cup GN Race No. 7 Rebel 500
April 3, 1977 Average Speed: 128.817

Driver	Owner	Car #	Make	Laps	Winnings
1. Darrell Waltrip	DiGard	88	Chev	367	19,270
2. Donnie Allison	Hoss Ellington	1	Chev	367	11,875
3. Richard Petty	Petty Enterprises	43	Dodg	367	11,600
4. David Pearson	Wood Brothers	21	Merc	367	6,600
5. Benny Parsons	L. G. DeWitt	72	Chev	365	7,720

1978 Winston Cup GN Race No. 7 Rebel 500
April 9, 1978 Average Speed: 127.544

Driver	Owner	Car #	Make	Laps	Winnings
1. Benny Parsons	L. G. DeWitt	72	Chev	367	21,700
2. Darrell Waltrip	DiGard	88	Chev	367	16,550
3. Lennie Pond	Harry Ranier	54	Olds	366	8,755
4. Dave Marcis	Rod Osterlund	2	Chev	365	5,700
5. Richard Petty	Petty Enterprises	43	Dodg	364	8,500

1979 Winston Cup GN Race No. 8 CRC Chemicals Rebel 500
April 8, 1979 Average Speed: 121.721

Driver	Owner	Car #	Make	Laps	Winnings
1. Darrell Waltrip	DiGard	88	Chev	367	23,400
2. Richard Petty	Petty Enterprises	43	Chev	367	16,100
3. Donnie Allison	Hoss Ellington	1	Chev	367	13,650
4. Benny Parsons	M. C. Anderson	27	Chev	365	5,700
5. Buddy Baker	Harry Ranier	28	Chev	365	8,500

1980 Winston Cup GN Race No. 7 CRC Chemicals Rebel 500
April 13, 1980 Average Speed: 112.397

Driver	Owner	Car #	Make	Laps	Winnings
1. David Pearson	Hoss Ellington	1	Chev	189	21,430
2. Benny Parsons	M. C. Anderson	27	Chev	189	19,475
3. Harry Gant	Jack Beebe	47	Chev	189	10,180
4. Darrell Waltrip	DiGard	88	Chev	188	10,500
5. Dick Brooks	Nelson Malloch	7	Chev	187	7,310

Darlington Raceway *continued*

1980 Winston Cup GN Race No. 23 Southern 500
September 1, 1980 Average Speed: 115.210

Driver	Owner	Car #	Make	Laps	Winnings
1. Terry Labonte	Billy Hagan	44	Chev	367	27,325
2. David Pearson	Hoss Ellington	1	Chev	367	15,540
3. Harry Gant	Jack Beebe	47	Chev	367	15,190
4. Benny Parsons	M. C. Anderson	27	Chev	367	14,625
5. Neil Bonnett	Wood Brothers	21	Merc	367	7,575

1981 Winston Cup GN Race No. 8 CRC Chemicals Rebel 500
April 12, 1981 Average Speed: 126.703

Driver	Owner	Car #	Make	Laps	Winnings
1. Darrell Waltrip	Junior Johnson	11	Buick	367	23,225
2. Harry Gant	Hal Needham	33	Pont	367	11,000
3. Dave Marcis	Dave Marcis	71	Chev	366	12,860
4. Bill Elliott	George Elliott	9	Ford	366	7,625
5. Benny Parsons	Bud Moore	15	Ford	366	10,750

1981 Winston Cup GN Race No. 23 Southern 500
September 7, 1981 Average Speed: 126.410

Driver	Owner	Car #	Make	Laps	Winnings
1. Neil Bonnett	Wood Brothers	21	Ford	367	33,375
2. Darrell Waltrip	Junior Johnson	11	Buick	367	19,365
3. Dave Marcis	Dave Marcis	71	Buick	367	14,330
4. Terry Labonte	Billy Hagan	44	Buick	367	13,225
5. Buddy Baker	Hoss Ellington	1	Buick	367	6,500

1982 Winston Cup GN Race No. 6 CRC Chemicals Rebel 500
April 4, 1982 Average Speed: 123.554

Driver	Owner	Car #	Make	Laps	Winnings
1. Dale Earnhardt	Bud Moore	15	Ford	367	31,450
2. Cale Yarborough	M. C. Anderson	27	Buick	367	12,550
3. Bill Elliott	Harry Melling	9	Ford	367	9,900
4. Benny Parsons	Harry Ranier	28	Pont	367	14,275
5. Tim Richmond	Jim Stacy	2	Buick	366	9,180

1982 Winston Cup GN Race No. 22 Southern 500
September 6, 1982 Average Speed: 115.224

Driver	Owner	Car #	Make	Laps	Winnings
1. Cale Yarborough	M. C. Anderson	27	Buick	367	34,300
2. Richard Petty	Petty Enterprises	43	Pont	367	26,165
3. Dale Earnhardt	Bud Moore	15	Ford	367	21,225
4. Bill Elliott	Harry Melling	9	Ford	367	13,925
5. Buddy Baker	Harry Ranier	28	Pont	365	16,140

1983 Winston Cup GN Race No. 5 TranSouth 500
April 10, 1983 Average Speed: 130.406

Driver	Owner	Car #	Make	Laps	Winnings
1. Harry Gant	Hal Needham	33	Buick	367	30,050
2. Darrell Waltrip	Junior Johnson	11	Chev	367	24,525
3. Mark Martin	Jim Stacy	2	Buick	367	17,530
4. Ricky Rudd	Richard Childress	3	Chev	366	9,905
5. Bill Elliott	Harry Melling	9	Ford	365	9,225

1983 Winston Cup GN Race No. 22 Southern 500
September 5, 1983 Average Speed: 123.343

Driver	Owner	Car #	Make	Laps	Winnings
1. Bobby Allison	DiGard	22	Buick	367	42,050
2. Bill Elliott	Harry Melling	9	Ford	367	19,045
3. Darrell Waltrip	Junior Johnson	11	Chev	367	23,475
4. Neil Bonnett	Bob Rahilly & Butch Mock	75	Chev	367	19,320
5. Terry Labonte	Billy Hagan	44	Chev	367	11,045

1984 Winston Cup GN Race No. 7 TranSouth 500
April 15, 1984 Average Speed: 119.925

Driver	Owner	Car #	Make	Laps	Winnings
1. Darrell Waltrip	Junior Johnson	11	Chev	367	39,450
2. Terry Labonte	Billy Hagan	44	Chev	367	22,180
3. Bill Elliott	Harry Melling	9	Ford	366	17,775
4. Cale Yarborough	Harry Ranier	28	Chev	366	6,850
5. Dale Earnhardt	Richard Childress	3	Chev	366	12,825

1984 Winston Cup GN Race No. 22 Southern 500
September 2, 1984 Average Speed: 128.270

Driver	Owner	Car #	Make	Laps	Winnings
1. Harry Gant	Hal Needham	33	Chev	367	46,180
2. Tim Richmond	Raymond Beadle	27	Pont	367	29,420
3. Buddy Baker	Wood Brothers	21	Ford	367	12,200
4. Rusty Wallace	Cliff Stewart	88	Pont	365	14,405
5. Ricky Rudd	Bud Moore	15	Ford	364	17,050

1985 Winston Cup GN Race No. 6 TranSouth 500
April 14, 1985 Average Speed: 126.295

Driver	Owner	Car #	Make	Laps	Winnings
1. Bill Elliott	Harry Melling	9	Ford	367	42,900
2. Darrell Waltrip	Junior Johnson	11	Chev	367	26,550
3. Tim Richmond	Raymond Beadle	27	Pont	367	15,860
4. Terry Labonte	Billy Hagan	44	Chev	366	17,105
5. Rusty Wallace	Cliff Stewart	2	Pont	365	11,800

1985 Winston Cup GN Race No. 20 Southern 500
September 1, 1985 Average Speed: 121.254

Driver	Owner	Car #	Make	Laps	Winnings
1. Bill Elliott	Harry Melling	9	Ford	367	1,053,725
2. Cale Yarborough	Harry Ranier	28	Ford	367	22,050
3. Geoff Bodine	Rick Hendrick	5	Chev	367	21,975
4. Neil Bonnett	Junior Johnson	12	Chev	366	17,425
5. Ron Bouchard	Jack Beebe	47	Buick	366	13,330

1986 Winston Cup Race No. 6 TranSouth 500
April 13, 1986 Average Speed: 128.994

Driver	Owner	Car #	Make	Laps	Winnings
1. Dale Earnhardt	Richard Childress	3	Chev	367	52,250
2. Darrell Waltrip	Junior Johnson	11	Chev	367	31,600
3. Bobby Allison	Stavola Brothers	22	Buick	366	13,355
4. Neil Bonnett	Junior Johnson	12	Chev	366	16,480
5. Tim Richmond	Rick Hendrick	25	Chev	364	7,305

1986 Winston Cup Race No. 21 Southern 500
August 31, 1986 Average Speed: 121.068

Driver	Owner	Car #	Make	Laps	Winnings
1. Tim Richmond	Rick Hendrick	25	Chev	367	60,005
2. Bobby Allison	Stavola Brothers	22	Buick	367	31,500
3. Bill Elliott	Harry Melling	9	Ford	367	25,625
4. Morgan Shepherd	Jack Beebe	47	Buick	367	11,125
5. Darrell Waltrip	Junior Johnson	11	Chev	367	21,055

1987 Winston Cup Race No. 5 TranSouth 500
March 29, 1987 Average Speed: 122.540

Driver	Owner	Car #	Make	Laps	Winnings
1. Dale Earnhardt	Richard Childress	3	Chev	367	52,985
2. Bill Elliott	Harry Melling	9	Ford	367	31,485
3. Richard Petty	Petty Enterprises	43	Pont	367	20,450
4. Sterling Marlin	Billy Hagan	44	Olds	367	17,105
5. Ken Schrader	Junie Donlavey	90	Ford	367	16,650

Darlington Raceway *continued*

1987 Winston Cup Race No. 21 Southern 500
September 6, 1987 Average Speed: 115.520

Driver	Owner	Car #	Make	Laps	Winnings
1. Dale Earnhardt	Richard Childress	3	Chev	202	64,650
2. Rusty Wallace	Raymond Beadle	27	Pont	202	33,695
3. Richard Petty	Petty Enterprises	43	Pont	202	22,530
4. Sterling Marlin	Billy Hagan	44	Olds	202	18,665
5. Terry Labonte	Junior Johnson	11	Chev	202	19,945

1988 Winston Cup Race No. 21 Southern 500
September 4, 1988 Average Speed: 128.297

Driver	Owner	Car #	Make	Laps	Winnings
1. Bill Elliott	Harry Melling	9	Ford	367	75,800
2. Rusty Wallace	Raymond Beadle	27	Pont	367	38,850
3. Dale Earnhardt	Richard Childress	3	Chev	367	31,375
4. Darrell Waltrip	Rick Hendrick	17	Chev	367	19,850
5. Sterling Marlin	Billy Hagan	44	Olds	367	21,130

1989 Winston Cup Race No. 21 Heinz Southern 500
September 3, 1989 Average Speed: 135.462

Driver	Owner	Car #	Make	Laps	Winnings
1. Dale Earnhardt	Richard Childress	3	Chev	367	71,150
2. Mark Martin	Jack Roush	6	Ford	367	37,550
3. Ricky Rudd	Kenny Bernstein	26	Buick	367	26,865
4. Rusty Wallace	Raymond Beadle	27	Pont	367	24,330
5. Ken Schrader	Rick Hendrick	25	Chev	367	20,390

1990 Winston Cup Series Race No. 21 Heinz Southern 500
September 2, 1990 Average Speed: 123.141

Driver	Owner	Car #	Make	Laps	Winnings
1. Dale Earnhardt	Richard Childress	3	Chev	367	210,350
2. Ernie Irvan	Larry McClure	4	Chev	367	35,900
3. Alan Kulwicki	Alan Kulwicki	7	Ford	367	23,340
4. Bill Elliott	Harry Melling	9	Ford	367	24,380
5. Harry Gant	Leo Jackson	33	Olds	367	21,340

1991 Winston Cup Series Race No. 21 Heinz Southern 500
September 1, 1991 Average Speed: 133.508

Driver	Owner	Car #	Make	Laps	Winnings
1. Harry Gant	Leo Jackson	33	Olds	367	179,450
2. Ernie Irvan	Larry McClure	4	Chev	367	40,525
3. Ken Schrader	Rick Hendrick	25	Chev	367	26,940
4. Derrike Cope	Bob Whitcomb	10	Chev	366	24,330
5. Terry Labonte	Billy Hagan	94	Olds	366	19,515

1992 Winston Cup Race No. 21 Mountain Dew Southern 500
September 6, 1992 Average Speed: 129.114

Driver	Owner	Car #	Make	Laps	Winnings
1. Darrell Waltrip	Darrell Waltrip	17	Chev	298	66,030
2. Mark Martin	Jack Roush	6	Ford	298	41,355
3. Bill Elliott	Junior Johnson	11	Ford	298	32,620
4. Brett Bodine	Kenny Bernstein	26	Ford	298	23,260
5. Davey Allison	Robert Yates	28	Ford	298	38,845

1993 Winston Cup Series Race No. 22 Mountain Dew Southern 500
September 5, 1993 Average Speed: 137.932

Driver	Owner	Car #	Make	Laps	Winnings
1. Mark Martin	Jack Roush	6	Ford	351	67,765
2. Brett Bodine	Kenny Bernstein	26	Ford	351	40,690
3. Rusty Wallace	Roger Penske	2	Pont	351	27,495
4. Dale Earnhardt	Richard Childress	3	Chev	351	31,090
5. Ernie Irvan	Robert Yates	28	Ford	350	28,395

1988 Winston Cup Race No. 5 TranSouth 500
March 27, 1988 Average Speed: 131.284

Driver	Owner	Car #	Make	Laps	Winnings
1. Lake Speed	Lake Speed	83	Olds	367	49,435
2. Alan Kulwicki	Alan Kulwicki	7	Ford	367	30,905
3. Davey Allison	Harry Ranier	28	Ford	367	26,095
4. Bill Elliott	Harry Melling	9	Ford	366	19,260
5. Sterling Marlin	Billy Hagan	44	Olds	366	14,800

1989 Winston Cup Race No. 5 TranSouth 500
April 2, 1989 Average Speed: 115.475

Driver	Owner	Car #	Make	Laps	Winnings
1. Harry Gant	Leo Jackson	33	Olds	367	59,935
2. Davey Allison	Robert Yates	28	Ford	367	35,435
3. Geoff Bodine	Rick Hendrick	5	Chev	367	25,345
4. Mark Martin	Jack Roush	6	Ford	367	18,810
5. Sterling Marlin	Billy Hagan	94	Olds	367	18,270

1990 Winston Cup Series Race No. 5 TranSouth 500
April 1, 1990 Average Speed: 124.073

Driver	Owner	Car #	Make	Laps	Winnings
1. Dale Earnhardt	Richard Childress	3	Chev	367	61,985
2. Mark Martin	Jack Roush	6	Ford	367	34,460
3. Davey Allison	Robert Yates	28	Ford	367	25,795
4. Geoff Bodine	Junior Johnson	11	Ford	367	28,110
5. Morgan Shepherd	Bud Moore	15	Ford	367	17,610

1991 Winston Cup Series Race No. 5 TranSouth 500
April 7, 1991 Average Speed: 135.594

Driver	Owner	Car #	Make	Laps	Winnings
1. Ricky Rudd	Rick Hendrick	5	Chev	367	62,185
2. Davey Allison	Robert Yates	28	Ford	367	38,860
3. Michael Waltrip	Chuck Rider	30	Pont	367	20,320
4. Mark Martin	Jack Roush	6	Ford	366	22,710
5. Rusty Wallace	Roger Penske	2	Pont	365	10,260

1992 Winston Cup Race No. 5 TranSouth 500
March 29, 1992 Average Speed: 139.364

Driver	Owner	Car #	Make	Laps	Winnings
1. Bill Elliott	Junior Johnson	11	Ford	367	64,290
2. Harry Gant	Leo Jackson	33	Olds	367	40,715
3. Mark Martin	Jack Roush	6	Ford	367	29,375
4. Davey Allison	Robert Yates	28	Ford	366	35,315
5. Ricky Rudd	Rick Hendrick	5	Chev	366	21,020

1993 Winston Cup Series Race No. 5 TranSouth 500
March 28, 1993 Average Speed: 139.958

Driver	Owner	Car #	Make	Laps	Winnings
1. Dale Earnhardt	Richard Childress	3	Chev	367	64,815
2. Mark Martin	Jack Roush	6	Ford	367	38,875
3. Dale Jarrett	Joe Gibbs	18	Chev	367	30,685
4. Ken Schrader	Rick Hendrick	25	Chev	367	23,125
5. Rusty Wallace	Roger Penske	2	Pont	366	20,400

1994 Winston Cup Series Race No. 5 TranSouth 500
March 27, 1994 Average Speed: 132.432

Driver	Owner	Car #	Make	Laps	Winnings
1. Dale Earnhardt	Richard Childress	3	Chev	293	70,190
2. Mark Martin	Jack Roush	6	Ford	293	42,835
3. Bill Elliott	Junior Johnson	11	Ford	293	35,285
4. Dale Jarrett	Joe Gibbs	18	Chev	293	27,550
5. Lake Speed	Bud Moore	15	Ford	293	26,300

Darlington Raceway *continued*

1994 Winston Cup Series Race No. 23 Mountain Dew Southern 500
September 4, 1994 Average Speed: 127.952

Driver	Owner	Car #	Make	Laps	Winnings
1. Bill Elliott	Junior Johnson	11	Ford	367	68,330
2. Dale Earnhardt	Richard Childress	3	Chev	367	45,030
3. Morgan Shepherd	Wood Brothers	21	Ford	367	32,730
4. Ricky Rudd	Ricky Rudd	10	Ford	367	24,715
5. Sterling Marlin	Larry McClure	4	Chev	367	26,870

1995 Winston Cup Series Race No. 5 TranSouth 400
March 26, 1995 Average Speed: 111.392

Driver	Owner	Car #	Make	Laps	Winnings
1. Sterling Marlin	Larry McClure	4	Chev	293	86,185
2. Dale Earnhardt	Richard Childress	3	Chev	293	54,355
3. Ted Musgrave	Jack Roush	16	Ford	293	43,565
4. Todd Bodine	Butch Mock	75	Ford	293	36,570
5. Derrike Cope	Bobby Allison	12	Ford	293	22,950

1995 Winston Cup Series Race No. 23 Mountain Dew Southern 500
September 3, 1995 Average Speed: 121.231

Driver	Owner	Car #	Make	Laps	Winnings
1. Jeff Gordon	Rick Hendrick	24	Chev	367	70,630
2. Dale Earnhardt	Richard Childress	3	Chev	367	62,155
3. Rusty Wallace	Roger Penske	2	Ford	367	40,580
4. Ward Burton	Bill Davis	22	Pont	367	39,090
5. Michael Waltrip	Chuck Rider	30	Pont	367	28,870

1996 Winston Cup Series Race No. 5 TranSouth 400
March 24, 1996 Average Speed: 124.792

Driver	Owner	Car #	Make	Laps	Winnings
1. Jeff Gordon	Rick Hendrick	24	Chev	293	97,310
2. Bobby Labonte	Joe Gibbs	18	Chev	293	57,550
3. Ricky Craven	Larry Hedrick	41	Chev	293	46,690
4. Rusty Wallace	Roger Penske	2	Ford	293	29,480
5. Terry Labonte	Rick Hendrick	5	Chev	293	34,325

1996 Winston Cup Series Race No. 23 Mountain Dew Southern 500
September 1, 1996 Average Speed: 135.757

Driver	Owner	Car #	Make	Laps	Winnings
1. Jeff Gordon	Rick Hendrick	24	Chev	367	99,630
2. Hut Stricklin	Stavola Brothers	8	Ford	367	52,405
3. Mark Martin	Jack Roush	6	Ford	367	45,430
4. Ken Schrader	Rick Hendrick	25	Chev	366	40,590
5. John Andretti	Michael Kranefuss & Carl Haas	37	Ford	366	32,120

Darlington Rebel 300 Races, 1957-59

1957 NASCAR Convertible Race No. 14 Rebel 300
May 12, 1957 Average Speed: 107.941

Driver	Owner	Car #	Make	Laps	Winnings
1. Fireball Roberts	Pete DePaolo	22	57 Ford	219	4,200
2. Tim Flock	Bill Stroppe	15	57 Merc	217	2,600
3. Bobby Myers	Bill Stroppe	4	57 Merc	216	1,850
4. Bob Welborn	Hugh Babb	49	57 Chev	216	1,150
5. Lee Petty	Petty Enterprises	42	57 Olds	213	825

1958 NASCAR Convertible Race No. 9 Rebel 300
May 10, 1958 Average Speed: 109.624

Driver	Owner	Car #	Make	Laps	Winnings
1. Curtis Turner	Holman-Moody	26	58 Ford	219	5,600
2. Joe Weatherly	Holman-Moody	12	58 Ford	219	2,800
3. Marvin Panch	Marvin Panch	98	58 Ford	218	1,950
4. Eddie Pagan	Eddie Pagan	45	58 Ford	218	1,150
5. Fireball Roberts	Frank Strickland	22	57 Chev	217	925

1959 NASCAR Convertible Race No. 8 Rebel 300
May 9, 1959 Average Speed: 115.817

Driver	Owner	Car #	Make	Laps	Winnings
1. Fireball Roberts	W. J. Ridgeway	22	59 Chev	219	6,550
2. Joe Weatherly	Doc White	12	59 Ford	219	3,950
3. Larry Frank	Larry Frank	76	57 Chev	217	2,350
4. Bob Burdick	Roy Burdick	73	59 Ford	217	1,375
5. Rex White	Rex White	40	59 Chev	216	1,150

Gamecock Speedway
Sumter, SC
Quarter-mile Dirt Track

(aka Sumter Rebel Speedway; Sumter Speedway; Rebel Speedway) Quarter-mile dirt track built circa 1955. Cale Yarborough began career here. Only NASCAR Winston Cup (then Grand National) race staged on 9/15/60 (won by Ned Jarrett). Track closed in 1984, re-opened in 1987, and closed again in 1993.

Winston Cup Victories
Ned Jarrett   1

Winston Cup Poles
David Pearson   1

Winston Cup Money
Ned Jarrett $770

Most Cars Started
13—September 15, 1960

Narrowest Margin of Victory
N/A

Race Record
41.208 MPH—September 15, 1960

Most Race Leaders
N/A

Most Cars Running at Finish
10—September 15, 1960

1960 Grand National Race No. 38
September 15, 1960 Average Speed: 41.208

Driver	Owner	Car #	Make	Laps	Winnings
1. Ned Jarrett	Ned Jarrett	11	60 Ford	200	770
2. David Pearson	David Pearson	67	59 Chev	200	535
3. Junior Johnson	John Masoni	27	60 Chev	199	385
4. G. C. Spencer	Weldon Wagner	48	58 Chev	195	270
5. Lee Petty	Petty Enterprises	42	60 Plym	195	325

Greenville-Pickens Speedway
Greenville, SC
Half-mile Paved Track

Half-mile dirt track built in 1940. First NASCAR Winston Cup (then Grand National) race staged on 8/25/51 (won by Bob Flock). Track paved in April 1970. The April 10, 1971, race was the first official Winston Cup point race to be televised live in its entirety on network television. Final Winston Cup Grand National race conducted on 6/26/71 (won by Richard Petty). Still an active track, hosting a variety of NASCAR events.

Winston Cup Starts
Richard Petty   20

Winston Cup Victories
Richard Petty   6

Winston Cup Poles
David Pearson   5

Winston Cup Money
Richard Petty $11,710

Most Cars Started
29—June 27, 1970 Greenville 200
29—June 26, 1971 Pickens 200

Fewest Cars Started
15—August 25, 1951

Narrowest Margin of Victory
1 car length—April 17, 1965

Slowest Race
51.480 MPH—June 13, 1959

Race Record
78.159 MPH—April 10, 1971
Greenville 200

Most Cautions
7—April 13, 1963

Most Race Leaders
5—April 13, 1963
5—April 8, 1969 Greenville 200

Most Cars Running at Finish
20—October 6, 1955

1951 Grand National Race No. 23
August 25, 1951

Driver	Owner	Car #	Make	Laps	Winnings
1. Bob Flock	Ted Chester	7	51 Olds	200	1,000
2. Tim Flock	Ted Chester	91	51 Olds	—	600
3. Buck Baker	Buck Baker	87	51 Plym	—	400
4. Fonty Flock	Frank Christian	14	51 Olds	—	300
5. Erick Erickson		1-X	51 Pont	—	250

1955 Grand National Race No. 39
October 6, 1955 Average Speed: 57.942

Driver	Owner	Car #	Make	Laps	Winnings
1. Tim Flock	Carl Kiekhaefer	300	55 Chrys	199	1,100
2. Junior Johnson	J. H. Petty	44	55 Chev	197	700
3. Bob Welborn	Bob Welborn	49	55 Chev	197	475
4. Jimmy Massey	Hubert Westmoreland	04	55 Chev	197	365
5. Buck Baker	Pete DePaolo	87	55 Ford	197	310

1956 Grand National Race No. 15
May 10, 1956 Average Speed: 60.362

Driver	Owner	Car #	Make	Laps	Winnings
1. Buck Baker	Carl Kiekhaefer	500B	56 Dodg	200	1,100
2. Curtis Turner	Charlie Schwam	99	56 Ford	199	700
3. Joe Eubanks	James Satcher	82	56 Ford	197	475
4. Gwyn Staley	Hubert Westmoreland	2	56 Chev	195	365
5. Joe Weatherly	Charlie Schwam	9	56 Ford	192	310

1958 Grand National Race No. 15
May 3, 1958 Average Speed: 62.295

Driver	Owner	Car #	Make	Laps	Winnings
1. Jack Smith	Jack Smith	47	57 Chev	200	800
2. Buck Baker	Buck Baker	87	57 Chev	199	525
3. Junior Johnson	Paul Spaulding	11	57 Ford	197	350
4. Doug Cox	Doug Cox	30	57 Ford	196	250
5. Eddie Pagan	Eddie Pagan	45	57 Ford	192	225

1959 Grand National Race No. 19
June 13, 1959 Average Speed: 51.480

Driver	Owner	Car #	Make	Laps	Winnings
1. Junior Johnson	Paul Spaulding	11	57 Ford	200	800
2. Roy Tyner	Roy Tyner	9	57 Chev	198	525
3. Lee Petty	Petty Enterprises	42	57 Olds	198	350
4. Tiny Lund	Tiny Lund	5	57 Chev	196	250
5. Tommy Irwin	Tommy Irwin	36	59 Ford	193	225

1959 Grand National Race No. 34
August 22, 1959 Average Speed: 58.055

Driver	Owner	Car #	Make	Laps	Winnings
1. Buck Baker	Lynton Tyson	88	59 Chev	200	800
2. Cotton Owens	W. H. Watson	6	58 Pont	200	525
3. Ned Jarrett	Ned Jarrett	11	57 Ford	200	375
4. Jack Smith	Gerald Duke & Robert Davis	92	59 Ford	196	275
5. Jim Paschal	J. H. Petty	48	57 Chev	190	250

1960 Grand National Race No. 14
April 23, 1960 Average Speed: 62.337

Driver	Owner	Car #	Make	Laps	Winnings
1. Ned Jarrett	Ned Jarrett	11	60 Ford	200	800
2. Lee Petty	Petty Enterprises	42	60 Plym	200	625
3. Richard Petty	Petty Enterprises	43	60 Plym	199	375
4. Tommy Irwin	Tommy Irwin	36	59 Ford	194	275
5. Bob Welborn	Bob Welborn	49	60 Chev	192	250

1961 Grand National Race No. 10
April 1, 1961 Average Speed: 52.189

Driver	Owner	Car #	Make	Laps	Winnings
1. Emanuel Zervakis	Monroe Shook	85	60 Chev	200	800
2. Richard Petty	Petty Enterprises	43	60 Plym	200	525
3. Rex White	Rex White	4	60 Chev	199	475
4. G. C. Spencer	G. C. Spencer	48	60 Chev	199	275
5. Buck Baker	Buck Baker	86	61 Chrys	196	250

1961 Grand National Race No. 27
June 8, 1961 Average Speed: 58.441

Driver	Owner	Car #	Make	Laps	Winnings
1. Jack Smith	Jack Smith	47	61 Pont	200	800
2. Ned Jarrett	Bee Gee Holloway	11	61 Chev	199	525
3. Emanuel Zervakis	Monroe Shook	85	61 Chev	198	375
4. Joe Weatherly	Bud Moore	8	61 Pont	198	275
5. Jim Paschal	J. H. Petty	14	61 Pont	196	250

1961 Grand National Race No. 51
October 28, 1961 Average Speed: 63.346

Driver	Owner	Car #	Make	Laps	Winnings
1. Junior Johnson	Rex Lovette	27	61 Pont	200	950
2. Joe Weatherly	Bud Moore	8	61 Pont	199	625
3. Rex White	Rex White	4	61 Chev	198	425
4. Richard Petty	Petty Enterprises	42	61 Plym	195	275
5. Curtis Crider	Curtis Crider	62	61 Merc	192	250

Greenville-Pickens Speedway *continued*

1962 Grand National Race No. 13
April 19, 1962 Average Speed: 57.480

Driver	Owner	Car #	Make	Laps	Winnings
1. Ned Jarrett	Bee Gee Holloway	11	62 Chev	200	1,200
2. Jim Paschal	Cliff Stewart	2	62 Pont	200	600
3. Joe Weatherly	Bud Moore	8	61 Pont	200	400
4. Wendell Scott	Wendell Scott	34	61 Chev	194	300
5. Jim Bennett	Thurman Wilkes	25	61 Ford	191	275

1962 Grand National Race No. 32
July 14, 1962 Average Speed: 62.219

Driver	Owner	Car #	Make	Laps	Winnings
1. Richard Petty	Petty Enterprises	43	62 Plym	200	1,000
2. Jack Smith	Jack Smith	47	61 Pont	197	600
3. Wendell Scott	Wendell Scott	34	61 Chev	194	400
4. Tommy Irwin	Melvin Bradley	27	62 Chev	194	300
5. Rex White	Rex White	4	62 Chev	192	275

1963 Grand National Race No. 16
April 13, 1963 Average Speed: 54.853

Driver	Owner	Car #	Make	Laps	Winnings
1. Buck Baker	Buck Baker	87	63 Pont	200	1,000
2. Ned Jarrett	Charles Robinson	11	63 Ford	200	600
3. G. C. Spencer	G. C. Spencer	03	62 Chev	200	400
4. Richard Petty	Petty Enterprises	41	62 Plym	199	300
5. David Pearson	Cotton Owens	6	63 Dodg	199	275

1963 Grand National Race No. 38
July 30, 1963 Average Speed: 62.456

Driver	Owner	Car #	Make	Laps	Winnings
1. Richard Petty	Petty Enterprises	41	63 Plym	200	1,000
2. Ned Jarrett	Charles Robinson	11	63 Ford	200	600
3. Buck Baker	Buck Baker	87	63 Pont	199	400
4. Fred Harb	Cliff Stewart	2	62 Pont	195	300
5. Bobby Isaac	Bondy Long	99	63 Ford	195	275

1964 Grand National Race No. 11
March 28, 1964 Average Speed: 57.554

Driver	Owner	Car #	Make	Laps	Winnings
1. David Pearson	Cotton Owens	6	64 Dodg	200	1,100
2. Ned Jarrett	Bondy Long	11	64 Ford	200	700
3. Marvin Panch	Wood Brothers	21	64 Ford	200	450
4. LeeRoy Yarbrough	Louie Weathersby	45	63 Plym	197	300
5. Tiny Lund	Herman Beam	19	63 Ford	196	275

1964 Grand National Race No. 26
May 30, 1964 Average Speed: 56.559

Driver	Owner	Car #	Make	Laps	Winnings
1. LeeRoy Yarbrough	Louie Weathersby	45	63 Plym	199	1,000
2. Richard Petty	Petty Enterprises	43	63 Plym	199	600
3. J. T. Putney	Walt Hunter	46	62 Chev	197	400
4. Bobby Keck	E. B. Rich	23	63 Ford	197	300
5. G. C. Spencer	Paul Clayton	75	62 Pont	193	275

1965 Grand National Race No. 10
April 17, 1965 Average Speed: 56.899

Driver	Owner	Car #	Make	Laps	Winnings
1. Dick Hutcherson	Holman-Moody	29	65 Ford	200	1,000
2. Ned Jarrett	Bondy Long	11	65 Ford	200	600
3. Buddy Baker	Buck Baker	86	64 Dodg	197	400
4. Bud Moore	Louie Weathersby	45	65 Plym	197	300
5. Fred Harb	Cliff Stewart	2	64 Pont	193	275

1965 Grand National Race No. 26
June 19, 1965 Average Speed: 55.274

Driver	Owner	Car #	Make	Laps	Winnings
1. Dick Hutcherson	Holman-Moody	29	65 Ford	200	1,000
2. Stick Elliott	Toy Bolton	18	65 Chev	197	600
3. J. T. Putney	Herman Beam	19	65 Chev	196	400
4. Roy Tyner	Roy Tyner	9	64 Chev	190	300
5. Buddy Arrington	Buddy Arrington	62	64 Dodg	188	275

1966 Grand National Race No. 11
April 9, 1966 Average Speed: 68.850

Driver	Owner	Car #	Make	Laps	Winnings
1. David Pearson	Cotton Owens	6	64 Dodg	200	1,000
2. Richard Petty	Petty Enterprises	43	65 Plym	199	600
3. Tiny Lund	Lyle Stelter	55	64 Ford	194	400
4. Neil Castles	Buck Baker	86	65 Plym	192	300
5. Jeff Hawkins	Hubert Howard	23	64 Ford	192	275

1966 Grand National Race No. 27
June 25, 1966 Average Speed: 66.286

Driver	Owner	Car #	Make	Laps	Winnings
1. David Pearson	Cotton Owens	6	64 Dodg	200	1,000
2. Tom Pistone	Tom Pistone	59	64 Ford	196	600
3. Elmo Langley	Gene Black	74	64 Ford	192	400
4. Stick Elliott	Toy Bolton	61	66 Chev	189	300
5. Henley Gray	Henley Gray	97	66 Ford	188	275

1967 Grand National Race No. 8
March 25, 1967 Average Speed: 61.824

Driver	Owner	Car #	Make	Laps	Winnings
1. David Pearson	Cotton Owens	6	66 Dodg	200	1,200
2. Jim Paschal	Tom Friedkin	14	65 Plym	197	600
3. John Sears	L. G. DeWitt	4	66 Ford	197	400
4. Buddy Baker	Toy Bolton	47	66 Chev	191	300
5. James Hylton	Bud Hartje	48	65 Dodg	190	275

1967 Grand National Race No. 26
June 24, 1967 Average Speed: 61.781

Driver	Owner	Car #	Make	Laps	Winnings
1. Richard Petty	Petty Enterprises	43	67 Plym	200	1,000
2. Dick Hutcherson	Bondy Long	29	67 Ford	200	600
3. Elmo Langley	Henry Woodfield	64	64 Ford	195	400
4. Clyde Lynn	Clyde Lynn	20	66 Ford	192	300
5. Doug Cooper	Bob Cooper	02	67 Chev	191	275

1968 Grand National Race No. 9
April 13, 1968 Average Speed: 63.347

Driver	Owner	Car #	Make	Laps	Winnings
1. Richard Petty	Petty Enterprises	43	68 Plym	200	1,200
2. Bobby Isaac	Nord Krauskopf	37	67 Dodg	197	600
3. Charlie Glotzbach	Cotton Owens	6	67 Dodg	197	400
4. Roy Tyner	Roy Tyner	9	67 Pont	195	300
5. Tiny Lund	Lyle Stelter	56	66 Ford	195	275

1968 Grand National Race No. 24
June 22, 1968 Average Speed: 64.609

Driver	Owner	Car #	Make	Laps	Winnings
1. Richard Petty	Petty Enterprises	43	68 Plym	200	1,200
2. David Pearson	Holman-Moody	17	68 Ford	200	600
3. John Sears	L. G. DeWitt	4	66 Ford	195	400
4. Clyde Lynn	Clyde Lynn	20	66 Ford	194	300
5. Jabe Thomas	Don Robertson	25	67 Ford	193	275

Greenville-Pickens Speedway *continued*

1969 Grand National Race No. 13 Greenville 200
April 8, 1969 Average Speed: 64.389

Driver	Owner	Car #	Make	Laps	Winnings
1. Bobby Isaac	Nord Krauskopf	71	69 Dodg	200	1,000
2. James Hylton	James Hylton	48	69 Dodg	199	600
3. David Pearson	Holman-Moody	17	69 Ford	198	600
4. Elmo Langley	Elmo Langley	64	68 Ford	197	350
5. Richard Petty	Petty Enterprises	43	69 Ford	197	325

1969 Grand National Race No. 26 Greenville 200
June 21, 1969 Average Speed: 61.813

Driver	Owner	Car #	Make	Laps	Winnings
1. Bobby Isaac	Nord Krauskopf	71	69 Dodg	200	1,000
2. David Pearson	Holman-Moody	17	69 Ford	200	800
3. Richard Petty	Petty Enterprises	43	69 Ford	200	400
4. James Hylton	James Hylton	48	68 Dodg	196	350
5. Neil Castles	Neil Castles	06	67 Plym	195	325

1970 Grand National Race No. 23 Greenville 200
June 27, 1970 Average Speed: 75.345

Driver	Owner	Car #	Make	Laps	Winnings
1. Bobby Isaac	Nord Krauskopf	71	70 Dodg	200	1,500
2. Bobby Allison	Bobby Allison	22	69 Dodg	200	900
3. Dick Brooks	Dick Brooks	32	69 Plym	198	400
4. James Hylton	James Hylton	48	69 Ford	197	350
5. Benny Parsons	L. G. DeWitt	72	69 Ford	196	325

1971 Winston Cup GN Race No. 12 Greenville 200
April 10, 1971 Average Speed: 78.159

Driver	Owner	Car #	Make	Laps	Winnings
1. Bobby Isaac	Nord Krauskopf	71	71 Dodg	200	1,430
2. David Pearson	Holman-Moody	17	70 Ford	198	1,030
3. Dick Brooks	Mario Rossi	22	70 Dodg	198	830
4. Dave Marcis	Dave Marcis	2	69 Dodg	198	780
5. Benny Parsons	L. G. DeWitt	72	70 Ford	198	755

1971 Winston Cup GN Race No. 26 Pickens 200
June 26, 1971 Average Speed: 74.297

Driver	Owner	Car #	Make	Laps	Winnings
1. Richard Petty	Petty Enterprises	43	71 Plym	200	1,500
2. Tiny Lund	John McConnell	55	70 Dodg	199	900
3. Bill Dennis	Junie Donlavey	90	69 Merc	199	500
4. Elmo Langley	Elmo Langley	64	71 Ford	197	350
5. Walter Ballard	Walter Ballard	30	71 Ford	197	325

Hartsville Speedway
Hartsville, SC
.333-mile Dirt Track

.333-mile dirt oval opened circa 1956. Only NASCAR Winston Cup (then Grand National) race staged on 6/23/61 (won by Buck Baker). Track closed circa 1962.

Winston Cup Victories
Buck Baker   1

Winston Cup Poles
Emanuel Zervakis   1

Winston Cup Money
Buck Baker $760

Most Cars Started
18—June 23, 1961

Narrowest Margin of Victory
1/2 lap—June 23, 1961

Race Record
46.234 MPH—June 23, 1961

Most Race Leaders
N/A

Most Cars Running at Finish
14—June 23, 1961

1961 Grand National Race No. 30
June 23, 1961 Average Speed: 46.234

	Driver	Owner	Car #	Make	Laps	Winnings
1.	Buck Baker	Buck Baker	86	61 Chrys	150	760
2.	Jack Smith	Jack Smith	47	61 Pont	150	520
3.	Rex White	Rex White	4	60 Chev	149	460
4.	David Pearson	David Pearson	67	60 Chev	148	265
5.	Junior Johnson	Rex Lovette	27	60 Pont	148	260

Lancaster Speedway
Lancaster, SC
Half-mile Dirt Track

Half-mile dirt track opened in 1954. First NASCAR Winston Cup (then Grand National) race staged on 6/1/57 (won by Paul Goldsmith). Only other Grand National race held on 7/30/57 (won by Speedy Thompson). This event has disappeared from all official NASCAR records and Thompson is listed as having 19 career Grand National wins instead of 20. Track still in operation.

Winston Cup Starts
13 drivers tied with 2

Winston Cup Victories
Paul Goldsmith   1
Speedy Thompson   1

Winston Cup Poles
Buck Baker   1
Speedy Thompson   1

Winston Cup Money
Speedy Thompson $1,270

Most Cars Started
19—July 30, 1957

Fewest Cars Started
17—June 1, 1957

Slowest Race
61.622 MPH—June 1, 1957

Narrowest Margin of Victory
N/A

Race Record
66.543 MPH—July 30, 1957

Most Race Leaders
N/A

Most Cars Running at Finish
15—June 1, 1957

1957 Grand National Race No. 21
June 1, 1957 Average Speed: 61.622

Driver	Owner	Car #	Make	Laps	Winnings
1. Paul Goldsmith	Smokey Yunick	3	57 Ford	200	700
2. Buck Baker	Hugh Babb	87	57 Chev	200	525
3. Lee Petty	Petty Enterprises	42	57 Olds	199	400
4. Marvin Panch	Pete DePaolo	98	57 Ford	198	330
5. Speedy Thompson	Hugh Babb	46	57 Chev	198	270

1957 Grand National Race No. 34
July 30, 1957 Average Speed: 66.543

Driver	Owner	Car #	Make	Laps	Winnings
1. Speedy Thompson	Speedy Thompson	46	57 Chev	200	1,000
2. Bill Amick	Bill Amick	97	57 Ford	200	625
3. Marvin Panch	Marvin Panch	98	57 Ford	197	400
4. Buck Baker	Buck Baker	87	57 Chev	194	295
5. Lee Petty	Petty Enterprises	42	57 Olds	192	255

Newberry Speedway
Newberry, SC
Half-mile Dirt Track

Half-mile dirt track opened in August 1952. Only NASCAR Winston Cup (then Grand National) race staged on 10/12/57 (Fireball Roberts won). Has the distinction of having the smallest crowd ever recorded at a top level NASCAR event (900 in attendance). Track shortened to quarter-mile circa 1961. Closed circa 1979.

Winston Cup Victories	**Winston Cup Money**	**Narrowest Margin of Victory**	**Most Race Leaders**
Fireball Roberts 1	Fireball Roberts $900	1 lap plus—October 12, 1957	4—October 12, 1957
Winston Cup Poles	**Most Cars Started**	**Race Record**	**Most Cars Running at Finish**
Jack Smith 1	23—October 12, 1957	50.398 MPH—October 12, 1957	17—October 12, 1957

1957 Grand National Race No. 50
October 12, 1957 Average Speed: 50.398

Driver	Owner	Car #	Make	Laps	Winnings
1. Fireball Roberts	Fireball Roberts	22	57 Ford	200	900
2. Buck Baker	Buck Baker	87	57 Chev	199	575
3. Jack Smith	Jack Smith	47	57 Chev	198	375
4. Marvin Panch	Marvin Panch	98	57 Ford	197	280
5. Gwyn Staley	J. H. Petty	38	57 Chev	194	245

Piedmont Interstate Fairgrounds
Spartanburg, SC
Half-mile Dirt Track

(aka Hub City Speedway) Half-mile dirt track opened in October 1937. First NASCAR Winston Cup (then Grand National) race staged on 7/4/53 (won by Lee Petty). Final Grand National race run on 6/4/66 (won by Elmo Langley, his first of two career victories). Closed circa 1986.

Winston Cup Starts
Buck Baker   14

Winston Cup Victories
Ned Jarrett   6

Winston Cup Poles
Dick Hutcherson   3
Cotton Owens   3

Winston Cup Money
Ned Jarrett $7,990

Most Cars Started
27—July 6, 1955
27—April 12, 1958

Fewest Cars Started
15—May 19, 1962

Narrowest Margin of Victory
60 feet (20 yards)—August 16, 1960

Slowest Race
46.287 MPH—June 29, 1957

Race Record
66.367 MPH—February 27, 1965

Most Cautions
6—July 6, 1955

Most Race Leaders
4—August 14, 1963
4—June 26, 1964

Most Cars Running at Finish
17—April 12, 1958

1953 Grand National Race No. 20
July 4, 1953 Average Speed: 56.934

Driver	Owner	Car #	Make	Laps	Winnings
1. Lee Petty	Petty Enterprises	42	53 Dodg	200	1,000
2. Buck Baker	Griffin Motors	87	53 Olds	—	700
3. Herb Thomas	Herb Thomas	92	53 Huds	—	450
4. Fonty Flock	Frank Christian	14	53 Huds	—	350
5. Johnny Patterson	H. B. Ranier	58	52 Huds	—	200

1954 Grand National Race No. 22
July 3, 1954 Average Speed: 59.181

Driver	Owner	Car #	Make	Laps	Winnings
1. Herb Thomas	Herb Thomas	92	54 Huds	200	1,000
2. Jimmie Lewallen	Joe Blair	5	54 Merc	199	650
3. Lee Petty	Petty Enterprises	42	54 Chrys	199	450
4. Buck Baker	Ernest Woods	88	54 Olds	196	350
5. Joe Eubanks	Phil Oates	82	52 Huds	194	300

1955 Grand National Race No. 24
July 6, 1955 Average Speed: 49.106

Driver	Owner	Car #	Make	Laps	Winnings
1. Tim Flock	Carl Kiekhaefer	300	55 Chrys	200	1,100
2. Fonty Flock	Carl Kiekhaefer	301	55 Chrys	200	650
3. Lee Petty	Petty Enterprises	42	55 Chrys	200	450
4. Buck Baker	Henry Ford	303	55 Chrys	198	350
5. Cotton Owens	Lancaster Brothers	70	55 Chev	195	300

1956 Grand National Race No. 31
July 7, 1956 Average Speed: 50.483

Driver	Owner	Car #	Make	Laps	Winnings
1. Lee Petty	Petty Enterprises	42	56 Dodg	200	850
2. Fireball Roberts	Pete DePaolo	22	56 Ford	200	625
3. Marvin Panch	Tom Harbison	99	56 Ford	198	450
4. Bill Amick	Pete DePaolo	66	56 Ford	189	350
5. Joe Eubanks	James Satcher	82	56 Ford	186	310

1956 Grand National Race No. 41
August 23, 1956 Average Speed: 54.372

Driver	Owner	Car #	Make	Laps	Winnings
1. Ralph Moody	Pete DePaolo	12	56 Ford	200	850
2. Jim Paschal	Frank Hayworth	75	56 Merc	198	625
3. Rex White	Bob Welborn	X	56 Chev	198	450
4. Herb Thomas	Herb Thomas	92	56 Chev	196	350
5. Speedy Thompson	Pete DePaolo	296	56 Ford	193	310

1957 Grand National Race No. 12
April 27, 1957 Average Speed: 55.130

Driver	Owner	Car #	Make	Laps	Winnings
1. Marvin Panch	Pete DePaolo	98	57 Ford	200	700
2. Fireball Roberts	Pete DePaolo	22	57 Ford	200	525
3. Ralph Moody	Pete DePaolo	12	57 Ford	200	500
4. Lee Petty	Petty Enterprises	42	57 Olds	199	330
5. Johnny Allen	Spook Crawford	64	57 Plym	191	320

1957 Grand National Race No. 26
June 29, 1957 Average Speed: 46.287

Driver	Owner	Car #	Make	Laps	Winnings
1. Lee Petty	Petty Enterprises	42	57 Olds	187	1,000
2. Bill Amick	Bill Amick	97	57 Ford	187	575
3. Buck Baker	Buck Baker	87	57 Chev	187	400
4. Speedy Thompson	Speedy Thompson	46	57 Chev	187	295
5. Jack Smith	Jack Smith	47	57 Chev	186	255

1958 Grand National Race No. 9
April 12, 1958 Average Speed: 56.613

Driver	Owner	Car #	Make	Laps	Winnings
1. Speedy Thompson	Speedy Thompson	46	57 Chev	200	800
2. Jack Smith	Jack Smith	47	57 Chev	200	525
3. Junior Johnson	Paul Spaulding	11	57 Ford	196	350
4. Eddie Pagan	Eddie Pagan	45	57 Ford	196	250
5. Possum Jones	Bob Welborn	2B	57 Chev	193	225

1959 Grand National Race No. 18
June 5, 1959 Average Speed: 55.547

Driver	Owner	Car #	Make	Laps	Winnings
1. Jack Smith	Jack Smith	47	59 Chev	200	1,000
2. Joe Eubanks	Don Every	82	58 Ford	199	525
3. Junior Johnson	Paul Spaulding	11	57 Ford	198	350
4. G. C. Spencer	G. C. Spencer	34	57 Chev	197	250
5. Roy Tyner	Roy Tyner	9	57 Chev	195	225

1960 Grand National Race No. 17
May 28, 1960 Average Speed: 51.843

Driver	Owner	Car #	Make	Laps	Winnings
1. Ned Jarrett	Ned Jarrett	11	60 Ford	200	800
2. Lee Petty	Petty Enterprises	42	60 Plym	200	625
3. Cotton Owens	Cotton Owens	5	60 Pont	199	375
4. Tommy Irwin	Tommy Irwin	36	59 Ford	198	275
5. David Pearson	David Pearson	67	59 Chev	198	250

Piedmont Interstate Fairgrounds *continued*

1960 Grand National Race No. 31
August 16, 1960 Average Speed: 59.681

Driver	Owner	Car #	Make	Laps	Winnings
1. Cotton Owens	Cotton Owens	5	60 Pont	200	800
2. Lee Petty	Petty Enterprises	42	60 Plym	200	625
3. Junior Johnson	John Masoni	27	60 Chev	198	375
4. Ned Jarrett	Ned Jarrett	11	60 Ford	198	275
5. Rex White	Rex White	4	60 Chev	198	250

1961 Grand National Race No. 6
March 4, 1961 Average Speed: 59.152

Driver	Owner	Car #	Make	Laps	Winnings
1. Cotton Owens	Cotton Owens	5	60 Pont	200	800
2. Richard Petty	Petty Enterprises	43	60 Plym	199	525
3. David Pearson	David Pearson	67	60 Chev	197	375
4. Jimmy Pardue	Jimmy Pardue	54	59 Chev	195	275
5. Doug Yates	Raeford Johnson	23	59 Plym	193	250

1961 Grand National Race No. 25
June 2, 1961 Average Speed: 55.495

Driver	Owner	Car #	Make	Laps	Winnings
1. Jim Paschal	J. H. Petty	14	61 Pont	200	800
2. Cotton Owens	Cotton Owens	6	60 Pont	198	525
3. Maurice Petty	Petty Enterprises	42	60 Plym	197	375
4. Herman Beam	Herman Beam	19	60 Ford	188	275
5. Ned Jarrett	Bee Gee Holloway	11	61 Chev	187	250

1962 Grand National Race No. 22
May 19, 1962 Average Speed: 60.080

Driver	Owner	Car #	Make	Laps	Winnings
1. Ned Jarrett	Bee Gee Holloway	11	62 Chev	200	1,200
2. Jim Paschal	Cliff Stewart	2	62 Pont	200	600
3. Richard Petty	Petty Enterprises	43	60 Plym	200	400
4. G. C. Spencer	G. C. Spencer	48	60 Chev	198	300
5. Joe Weatherly	Bud Moore	8	61 Pont	197	275

1962 Grand National Race No. 43
August 21, 1962 Average Speed: 59.870

Driver	Owner	Car #	Make	Laps	Winnings
1. Richard Petty	Petty Enterprises	43	62 Plym	200	1,000
2. Joe Weatherly	Bud Moore	8	61 Pont	200	600
3. Jack Smith	Jack Smith	47	61 Pont	197	400
4. Cotton Owens	Cotton Owens	6	60 Pont	197	300
5. G. C. Spencer	G. C. Spencer	48	62 Chev	195	275

1963 Grand National Race No. 8
March 2, 1963 Average Speed: 55.598

Driver	Owner	Car #	Make	Laps	Winnings
1. Richard Petty	Petty Enterprises	43	63 Plym	200	1,000
2. Ned Jarrett	Charles Robinson	11	63 Ford	199	600
3. Jim Paschal	Petty Enterprises	42	63 Plym	199	400
4. Joe Weatherly	Fred Harb	17	62 Pont	194	500
5. Wendell Scott	Wendell Scott	34	61 Chev	190	275

1963 Grand National Race No. 42
August 14, 1963 Average Speed: 52.424

Driver	Owner	Car #	Make	Laps	Winnings
1. Ned Jarrett	Charles Robinson	11	63 Ford	200	1,000
2. Richard Petty	Petty Enterprises	43	63 Plym	200	600
3. Buck Baker	Buck Baker	87	63 Pont	200	400
4. Billy Wade	Cotton Owens	5	63 Dodg	199	300
5. Cale Yarborough	Herman Beam	19	62 Ford	195	275

1964 Grand National Race No. 16
April 14, 1964 Average Speed: 58.852

Driver	Owner	Car #	Make	Laps	Winnings
1. Ned Jarrett	Bondy Long	11	64 Ford	200	1,150
2. Marvin Panch	Wood Brothers	21	64 Ford	200	700
3. David Pearson	Cotton Owens	6	64 Dodg	197	400
4. Ken Rush	Cliff Stewart	2	63 Pont	195	300
5. Elmo Henderson	Paul Clayton	75	62 Pont	191	275

1964 Grand National Race No. 34
June 26, 1964 Average Speed: 58.233

Driver	Owner	Car #	Make	Laps	Winnings
1. Richard Petty	Petty Enterprises	43	64 Plym	200	1,000
2. LeeRoy Yarbrough	Louie Weathersby	45	63 Plym	199	600
3. Doug Cooper	Bob Cooper	60	63 Ford	193	400
4. Wendell Scott	Wendell Scott	34	63 Ford	190	300
5. Ned Jarrett	Bondy Long	11	64 Ford	185	275

1965 Grand National Race No. 5
February 27, 1965 Average Speed: 66.367

Driver	Owner	Car #	Make	Laps	Winnings
1. Ned Jarrett	Bondy Long	11	65 Ford	200	1,150
2. G. C. Spencer	G. C. Spencer	49	64 Ford	178	700
3. Bob Derrington	Bob Derrington	68	64 Ford	177	450
4. Gene Hobby	Gene Hobby	99	64 Dodg	179	300
5. Dick Hutcherson	Holman-Moody	29	64 Ford	160	275

1965 Grand National Race No. 39
August 14, 1965 Average Speed: 56.926

Driver	Owner	Car #	Make	Laps	Winnings
1. Ned Jarrett	Bondy Long	11	65 Ford	200	1,000
2. Cale Yarborough	Kenny Myler	06	64 Ford	198	600
3. Elmo Langley	Elmo Langley	64	64 Ford	191	400
4. Wendell Scott	Wendell Scott	34	63 Ford	187	300
5. G. C. Spencer	G. C. Spencer	49	64 Ford	185	275

1966 Grand National Race No. 23
June 4, 1966 Average Speed: 60.050

Driver	Owner	Car #	Make	Laps	Winnings
1. Elmo Langley	Henry Woodfield	64	64 Ford	200	1,000
2. Neil Castles	Buck Baker	86	65 Dodg	196	600
3. Doug Cooper	Bob Cooper	02	65 Plym	195	400
4. Joel Davis	Harold Mays	77	64 Plym	190	300
5. J. D. McDuffie	J. D. McDuffie	70	64 Ford	189	275

Rambi Race Track
Myrtle Beach, SC
Half-mile Dirt Track

(aka Myrtle Beach Speedway; Rambi Raceway) Track built in 1958. Rambi stood for Racing Association of Myrtle Beach, Inc. Half-mile dirt track played to host first Winston Cup (then Grand National) race on 8/23/58 (won by Bob Welborn). Final Grand National race run on 6/24/65 (won by Dick Hutcherson). Track remains the only speedway in the world to host all three generations of Pettys (Lee, Richard, and Kyle) and never yielded a victory to any of them. Kyle drove in two weekly-dirt-track events in 1979. Track was paved in 1971. Promoters laid dirt over pavement in 1976, only to go back to pavement in 1977. Pavement torn up again in 1978, paved again in 1987. Track still in operation.

Winston Cup Starts
Ned Jarrett 8
Richard Petty 8

Winston Cup Victories
Ned Jarrett 3

Winston Cup Poles
Ned Jarrett 3

Winston Cup Money
Ned Jarrett $5,140

Most Cars Started
27—August 1, 1959

Fewest Cars Started
12—August 7, 1964

Narrowest Margin of Victory
N/A

Slowest Race
52.941 MPH—August 1, 1959

Race Record
64.171 MPH—July 21, 1962

Most Race Leaders
3—July 7, 1963 Speedorama 200
3—June 24, 1965

Most Cars Running at Finish
16—August 1, 1959

1958 Grand National Race No. 40
August 23, 1958 Average Speed: 60.443

Driver	Owner	Car #	Make	Laps	Winnings
1. Bob Welborn	J. H. Petty	49	57 Chev	200	800
2. Buck Baker	Buck Baker	87	57 Chev	200	525
3. Shorty Rollins	Shorty Rollins	99	58 Ford	200	350
4. Tiny Lund	Don Angel	37	56 Ford	198	250
5. Lee Petty	Petty Enterprises	42	57 Olds	197	225

1959 Grand National Race No. 29
August 1, 1959 Average Speed: 52.941

Driver	Owner	Car #	Make	Laps	Winnings
1. Ned Jarrett	Ned Jarrett	11	57 Ford	200	800
2. Jim Paschal	J. H. Petty	48	57 Chev	199	525
3. Tommy Irwin	Tommy Irwin	36	57 Ford	199	350
4. Glen Wood	Wood Brothers	21	58 Ford	198	250
5. Joe Weatherly	Doc White	41	59 Ford	197	225

1960 Grand National Race No. 26
July 23, 1960 Average Speed: 60.985

Driver	Owner	Car #	Make	Laps	Winnings
1. Buck Baker	Buck Baker	87	60 Chev	200	800
2. Lee Petty	Petty Enterprises	42	60 Plym	200	625
3. Rex White	Rex White	4	60 Chev	198	375
4. Junior Johnson	John Masoni	27	60 Chev	197	275
5. Richard Petty	Petty Enterprises	43	60 Plym	197	250

1961 Grand National Race No. 35
July 22, 1961 Average Speed: 57.655

Driver	Owner	Car #	Make	Laps	Winnings
1. Joe Weatherly	Bud Moore	8	61 Pont	200	950
2. Jim Paschal	J. H. Petty	14	61 Pont	200	625
3. Ned Jarrett	Bee Gee Holloway	11	61 Chev	199	425
4. George Green	Joe Jones	77	60 Ford	188	275
5. Emanuel Zervakis	Monroe Shook	85	61 Chev	185	250

1962 Grand National Race No. 14
April 21, 1962 Average Speed: 63.036

Driver	Owner	Car #	Make	Laps	Winnings
1. Jack Smith	Jack Smith	47	61 Pont	200	1,000
2. Richard Petty	Petty Enterprises	43	60 Plym	198	600
3. Ned Jarrett	Bee Gee Holloway	11	62 Chev	195	600
4. Thomas Cox	Ray Herlocker	60	60 Plym	188	300
5. Curtis Crider	Curtis Crider	62	61 Merc	183	275

1962 Grand National Race No. 35
July 21, 1962 Average Speed: 64.171

Driver	Owner	Car #	Make	Laps	Winnings
1. Ned Jarrett	Bee Gee Holloway	11	62 Chev	200	1,200
2. Joe Weatherly	Bud Moore	8	60 Pont	199	600
3. Jack Smith	Jack Smith	47	62 Pont	196	400
4. Buddy Baker	Buck Baker	86	61 Chrys	195	300
5. Bob Welborn	J. C. Parker	49	62 Pont	190	275

1963 Grand National Race No. 30 Speedorama 200
July 7, 1963 Average Speed: 60.996

Driver	Owner	Car #	Make	Laps	Winnings
1. Ned Jarrett	Charles Robinson	11	63 Ford	200	1,000
2. Buck Baker	Buck Baker	87	63 Pont	193	600
3. Joe Weatherly	Cliff Stewart	2	62 Pont	191	600
4. Neil Castles	Buck Baker	86	62 Chrys	190	300
5. Cale Yarborough	Herman Beam	19	62 Ford	185	275

1964 Grand National Race No. 44
August 7, 1964 Average Speed: 61.750

Driver	Owner	Car #	Make	Laps	Winnings
1. David Pearson	Cotton Owens	6	64 Dodg	200	1,000
2. Richard Petty	Petty Enterprises	43	64 Plym	199	600
3. LeeRoy Yarbrough	Louie Weathersby	45	63 Plym	195	400
4. Ned Jarrett	Bondy Long	11	64 Ford	192	300
5. Neil Castles	Buck Baker	88	62 Chrys	187	275

1965 Grand National Race No. 27
June 24, 1965 Average Speed: 59.701

Driver	Owner	Car #	Make	Laps	Winnings
1. Dick Hutcherson	Holman-Moody	29	65 Ford	200	1,000
2. Ned Jarrett	Bondy Long	11	65 Ford	200	600
3. Tiny Lund	Lyle Stelter	55	64 Ford	195	400
4. Cale Yarborough	Kenny Myler	06	64 Ford	193	300
5. G. C. Spencer	G. C. Spencer	49	64 Ford	183	275

South Dakota

Rapid Valley Speedway
Rapid City, SD
Half-mile Dirt Track

(aka Rapid Valley Race Track; Black Hills Speedway) Half-mile dirt track opened circa 1949. Only NASCAR Winston Cup (then Grand National) race staged on 7/22/53 (Herb Thomas won). Track still in operation.

Winston Cup Victories
Herb Thomas   1

Winston Cup Money
Herb Thomas $1,000

Narrowest Margin of Victory
N/A

Most Race Leaders
N/A

Winston Cup Poles
Herb Thomas   1

Most Cars Started
15—July 22, 1953

Race Record
57.270 MPH—July 22, 1953

Most Cars Running at Finish
N/A

1953 Grand National Race No. 23
July 22, 1953 Average Speed: 57.270

Driver	Owner	Car #	Make	Laps	Winnings
1. Herb Thomas	Herb Thomas	92	53 Huds	200	1,000
2. Dick Rathmann	Walt Chapman	120	53 Huds	—	700
3. Fonty Flock	Frank Christian	14	53 Huds	—	450
4. Lee Petty	Petty Enterprises	42	53 Dodg	—	350
5. Buck Baker	Griffin Motors	87	53 Olds	—	200

Tennessee

Boyd Speedway
Chattanooga, TN
.333-mile Paved Track

(aka Chattanooga Int'l Raceway; Chattanooga Raceway Park) Actually located just south of Georgia-Tennessee state line. A .333-mile dirt track that opened in 1952, and was paved in 1962. First NASCAR Winston Cup (then Grand National) race staged on 8/3/62 (won by Joe Weatherly). Final Grand National race run on 6/19/64 (won by David Pearson). Track still in operation.

Winston Cup Starts
Buddy Baker	2
Buck Baker	2
Curtis Crider	2
Ned Jarrett	2
Richard Petty	2
Wendell Scott	2
G. C. Spencer	2

Winston Cup Victories
David Pearson	1
Joe Weatherly	1

Winston Cup Poles
Richard Petty	2

Winston Cup Money
David Pearson	$1,000
Joe Weatherly	$1,000

Most Cars Started
21—August 3, 1962 Confederate 200

Fewest Cars Started
18—June 19, 1964 Confederate 300

Narrowest Margin of Victory
N/A

Slowest Race
70.051 MPH—June 19, 1964
Confederate 300

Race Record
71.145 MPH—August 3, 1962
Confederate 200

Most Race Leaders
3—August 3, 1962 Confederate 200

Most Cars Running at Finish
16—August 3, 1962 Confederate 200

1962 Grand National Race No. 37 Confederate 200
August 3, 1962 Average Speed: 71.145

Driver	Owner	Car #	Make	Laps	Winnings
1. Joe Weatherly	Bud Moore	8	61 Pont	200	1,000
2. Fireball Roberts	Jim Stephens	22	62 Pont	200	600
3. Jim Paschal	Cliff Stewart	2	62 Pont	197	400
4. Richard Petty	Petty Enterprises	42	62 Plym	197	300
5. Sherman Utsman	Sherman Utsman	61	62 Ford	196	275

1964 Grand National Race No. 31 Confederate 300
June 19, 1964 Average Speed: 70.051

Driver	Owner	Car #	Make	Laps	Winnings
1. David Pearson	Cotton Owens	6	64 Dodg	300	1,000
2. Richard Petty	Petty Enterprises	43	64 Plym	298	600
3. Buck Baker	Ray Fox	3	64 Dodg	293	400
4. Ned Jarrett	Bondy Long	11	64 Ford	290	300
5. G. C. Spencer	G. C. Spencer	49	64 Chev	289	275

Bristol Motor Speedway
Bristol, TN
.533-mile Paved Track

(aka Bristol Int'l Raceway; Bristol Int'l Speedway) Half-mile paved oval built in 1961. First NASCAR Winston Cup (then Grand National) race staged on 7/29/61 (won by Jack Smith with relief help from Johnny Allen). Track originally had a football field in the infield to attract NFL pre-season games. Track was re-designed in 1969, banking turns to 36 degrees, which are the steepest banks on the current Winston Cup schedule.

Winston Cup Starts
Richard Petty   60

Winston Cup Victories
Darrell Waltrip   12

Winston Cup Poles
Cale Yarborough   9

Winston Cup Money
Dale Earnhardt $889,836

Most Cars Started
44—July 29, 1962 Southeastern 500

Fewest Cars Started
23—March 16, 1975 Southeastern 500

Narrowest Margin of Victory
8 inches—April 8, 1980
Valleydale Meats 500

Slowest Race
61.826 MPH—July 25, 1965
Volunteer 500

Race Record
101.074 MPH—July 11, 1971
Volunteer 500

Most Cautions
20—April 9, 1989 Valleydale Meats 500

Most Race Leaders
16—April 9, 1989 Valleydale Meats 500

Most Cars Running at Finish
34—April 2, 1995 Food City 500
34—March 31, 1996 Food City 500
34—August 24, 1996 Goody's 500

1961 Grand National Race No. 36 Volunteer 500
July 30, 1961 Average Speed: 68.373

Driver	Owner	Car #	Make	Laps	Winnings
1. Jack Smith	Jack Smith	46	61 Pont	500	3,025
2. Fireball Roberts	Jim Stephens	22	61 Pont	498	1,325
3. Ned Jarrett	Bee Gee Holloway	11	61 Chev	495	1,125
4. Richard Petty	Petty Enterprises	43	61 Plym	493	800
5. Buddy Baker	Buck Baker	87	61 Chrys	492	750

1961 Grand National Race No. 50 Southeastern 500
October 22, 1961 Average Speed: 72.452

Driver	Owner	Car #	Make	Laps	Winnings
1. Joe Weatherly	Bud Moore	8	61 Pont	500	3,680
2. Rex White	Rex White	4	61 Chev	500	2,365
3. Nelson Stacy	Dudley Farrell	29	61 Ford	500	1,525
4. Jim Paschal	J. H. Petty	44	61 Pont	498	1,125
5. Emanuel Zervakis	Monroe Shook	85	61 Chev	495	950

1962 Grand National Race No. 17 Volunteer 500
April 29, 1962 Average Speed: 73.397

Driver	Owner	Car #	Make	Laps	Winnings
1. Bobby Johns	Shorty Johns	72	62 Pont	500	4,405
2. Fireball Roberts	Banjo Matthews	22	62 Pont	494	2,500
3. Jack Smith	Jack Smith	47	62 Pont	492	1,635
4. Ned Jarrett	Bee Gee Holloway	11	62 Chev	475	1,400
5. Thomas Cox	Ray Herlocker	60	60 Plym	470	850

1962 Grand National Race No. 36 Southeastern 500
July 29, 1962 Average Speed: 75.276

Driver	Owner	Car #	Make	Laps	Winnings
1. Jim Paschal	Petty Enterprises	42	62 Plym	500	3,930
2. Fred Lorenzen	Holman-Moody	20	62 Ford	500	2,370
3. Richard Petty	Petty Enterprises	43	62 Plym	500	1,540
4. Johnny Allen	Fred Lovette	46	62 Pont	498	1,270
5. Nelson Stacy	Holman-Moody	29	62 Ford	498	875

1963 Grand National Race No. 13 Southeastern 500
March 31, 1963 Average Speed: 76.910

Driver	Owner	Car #	Make	Laps	Winnings
1. Fireball Roberts	Holman-Moody	22	63 Ford	500	4,060
2. Fred Lorenzen	Holman-Moody	28	63 Ford	500	2,395
3. Junior Johnson	Ray Fox	3	63 Chev	497	1,725
4. Richard Petty	Petty Enterprises	43	63 Plym	495	1,225
5. LeeRoy Yarbrough	Lou Sidoit	69	62 Merc	490	975

1963 Grand National Race No. 37 Volunteer 500
July 28, 1963 Average Speed: 74.844

Driver	Owner	Car #	Make	Laps	Winnings
1. Fred Lorenzen	Holman-Moody	28	63 Ford	500	4,540
2. Richard Petty	Petty Enterprises	43	63 Plym	500	2,365
3. Jim Paschal	Petty Enterprises	42	63 Plym	499	1,825
4. Marvin Panch	Wood Brothers	21	63 Ford	492	1,225
5. David Pearson	Cotton Owens	6	63 Dodg	491	1,075

1964 Grand National Race No. 10 Southeastern 500
March 22, 1964 Average Speed: 72.196

Driver	Owner	Car #	Make	Laps	Winnings
1. Fred Lorenzen	Holman-Moody	28	64 Ford	500	4,300
2. Fireball Roberts	Holman-Moody	22	64 Ford	500	2,150
3. Paul Goldsmith	Ray Nichels	25	64 Plym	497	1,685
4. Buck Baker	Petty Enterprises	41	64 Plym	496	1,075
5. Marvin Panch	Wood Brothers	21	64 Ford	494	1,075

1964 Grand National Race No. 42 Volunteer 500
July 26, 1964 Average Speed: 78.044

Driver	Owner	Car #	Make	Laps	Winnings
1. Fred Lorenzen	Holman-Moody	28	64 Ford	500	4,185
2. Richard Petty	Petty Enterprises	43	64 Plym	499	2,730
3. Jim Paschal	Petty Enterprises	41	64 Plym	499	1,500
4. LeeRoy Yarbrough	Ray Fox	03	64 Dodg	489	1,260
5. Larry Thomas	Herman Beam	19	64 Ford	482	975

1965 Grand National Race No. 14 Southeastern 500
May 2, 1965 Average Speed: 74.937

Driver	Owner	Car #	Make	Laps	Winnings
1. Junior Johnson	Rex Lovette	26	65 Ford	500	4,550
2. Dick Hutcherson	Holman-Moody	29	65 Ford	500	2,460
3. Ned Jarrett	Bondy Long	11	65 Ford	500	1,730
4. Marvin Panch	Wood Brothers	21	65 Ford	487	1,375
5. Wendell Scott	Wendell Scott	34	63 Ford	468	1,035

1965 Grand National Race No. 34 Volunteer 500
July 25, 1965 Average Speed: 61.826

Driver	Owner	Car #	Make	Laps	Winnings
1. Ned Jarrett	Bondy Long	11	65 Ford	500	4,315
2. Dick Hutcherson	Holman-Moody	29	65 Ford	500	2,275
3. Sam McQuagg	Betty Lilly	24	65 Ford	494	1,650
4. Jim Paschal	Tom Friedkin	41	65 Chev	494	1,125
5. Buck Baker	Buck Baker	87	65 Chev	484	1,025

Bristol Motor Speedway *continued*

1966 Grand National Race No. 7 Southeastern 500
March 20, 1966 Average Speed: 69.952

Driver	Owner	Car #	Make	Laps	Winnings
1. Dick Hutcherson	Holman-Moody	29	66 Ford	500	4,150
2. Paul Lewis	Paul Lewis	1	65 Plym	496	1,825
3. James Hylton	Bud Hartje	48	65 Dodg	494	1,550
4. Elmo Langley	Henry Woodfield	64	64 Ford	492	1,125
5. Sam McQuagg	Ray Nichels	98	66 Dodg	489	1,000

1966 Grand National Race No. 34 Volunteer 500
July 24, 1966 Average Speed: 77.963

Driver	Owner	Car #	Make	Laps	Winnings
1. Paul Goldsmith	Ray Nichels	99	66 Plym	500	5,400
2. Richard Petty	Petty Enterprises	43	66 Plym	500	2,950
3. David Pearson	Cotton Owens	6	66 Dodg	496	2,150
4. Paul Lewis	Paul Lewis	1	65 Plym	492	1,200
5. Bobby Allison	Bobby Allison	2	65 Chev	490	1,060

1967 Grand National Race No. 7 Southeastern 500
March 19, 1967 Average Speed: 75.937

Driver	Owner	Car #	Make	Laps	Winnings
1. David Pearson	Cotton Owens	6	67 Dodg	500	5,290
2. Cale Yarborough	Wood Brothers	21	67 Ford	500	3,050
3. Darel Dieringer	Junior Johnson	26	67 Ford	497	2,700
4. Neil Castles	Emory Gilliam	00	65 Plym	485	1,400
5. Dick Hutcherson	Bondy Long	29	67 Ford	482	1,125

1967 Grand National Race No. 33 Volunteer 500
July 23, 1967 Average Speed: 78.705

Driver	Owner	Car #	Make	Laps	Winnings
1. Richard Petty	Petty Enterprises	43	67 Plym	500	6,050
2. Dick Hutcherson	Bondy Long	29	67 Ford	500	3,250
3. Darel Dieringer	Junior Johnson	26	67 Ford	498	2,300
4. Jim Paschal	Tom Friedkin	14	67 Plym	492	1,325
5. James Hylton	Bud Hartje	48	65 Dodg	486	1,100

1968 Grand National Race No. 5 Southeastern 500
March 17, 1968 Average Speed: 77.247

Driver	Owner	Car #	Make	Laps	Winnings
1. David Pearson	Holman-Moody	17	68 Ford	500	5,725
2. Richard Petty	Petty Enterprises	43	68 Plym	500	4,125
3. LeeRoy Yarbrough	Junior Johnson	26	68 Ford	499	2,100
4. Darel Dieringer	Mario Rossi	22	68 Plym	492	1,325
5. Bobby Isaac	Nord Krauskopf	71	67 Dodg	491	900

1968 Grand National Race No. 30 Volunteer 500
July 21, 1968 Average Speed: 76.310

Driver	Owner	Car #	Make	Laps	Winnings
1. David Pearson	Holman-Moody	17	68 Ford	500	5,175
2. Cale Yarborough	Wood Brothers	21	68 Merc	499	2,650
3. Swede Savage	Bondy Long	29	68 Ford	498	1,700
4. Bobby Isaac	Nord Krauskopf	71	67 Dodg	497	900
5. Friday Hassler	Red Sharp	39	66 Chev	488	800

1969 Grand National Race No. 9 Southeastern 500
March 23, 1969 Average Speed: 81.455

Driver	Owner	Car #	Make	Laps	Winnings
1. Bobby Allison	Mario Rossi	22	69 Dodg	500	5,025
2. LeeRoy Yarbrough	Junior Johnson	98	69 Ford	496	3,000
3. David Pearson	Holman-Moody	17	69 Ford	495	2,400
4. Cale Yarborough	Wood Brothers	21	69 Merc	494	1,275
5. Donnie Allison	Banjo Matthews	27	69 Ford	491	800

1969 Grand National Race No. 33 Volunteer 500
July 20, 1969 Average Speed: 79.737

Driver	Owner	Car #	Make	Laps	Winnings
1. David Pearson	Holman-Moody	17	69 Ford	500	5,525
2. Bobby Isaac	Nord Krauskopf	71	69 Dodg	497	3,150
3. Donnie Allison	Banjo Matthews	27	69 Ford	487	2,300
4. James Hylton	James Hylton	48	69 Dodg	477	1,500
5. Cecil Gordon	Bill Seifert	47	68 Ford	431	1,000

1970 Grand National Race No. 9 Southeastern 500
April 5, 1970 Average Speed: 87.543

Driver	Owner	Car #	Make	Laps	Winnings
1. Donnie Allison	Banjo Matthews	27	70 Ford	500	6,670
2. Bobby Allison	Don Robertson	22	69 Plym	497	3,820
3. Cale Yarborough	Wood Brothers	21	70 Merc	456	2,345
4. James Hylton	James Hylton	48	69 Ford	453	1,295
5. Dick Brooks	Dick Brooks	32	70 Plym	447	1,020

1970 Grand National Race No. 28 Volunteer 500
July 19, 1970 Average Speed: 84.880

Driver	Owner	Car #	Make	Laps	Winnings
1. Bobby Allison	Bobby Allison	22	69 Dodg	500	4,850
2. LeeRoy Yarbrough	Junior Johnson	98	69 Ford	498	2,850
3. Bobby Isaac	Nord Krauskopf	71	70 Dodg	491	2,075
4. G. C. Spencer	G. C. Spencer	49	69 Plym	479	1,385
5. Richard Petty	Petty Enterprises	43	70 Plym	464	1,050

1971 Winston Cup GN Race No. 9 Southeastern 500
March 28, 1971 Average Speed: 91.704

Driver	Owner	Car #	Make	Laps	Winnings
1. David Pearson	Holman-Moody	17	71 Ford	500	6,120
2. Richard Petty	Petty Enterprises	43	71 Plym	500	3,570
3. Dick Brooks	Mario Rossi	22	70 Dodg	489	2,245
4. Bobby Allison	Bobby Allison	12	71 Dodg	487	1,320
5. Benny Parsons	L. G. DeWitt	72	70 Ford	485	1,045

1971 Winston Cup GN Race No. 28 Volunteer 500
July 11, 1971 Average Speed: 101.074

Driver	Owner	Car #	Make	Laps	Winnings
1. Charlie Glotzbach	R. Howard & J. Johnson	3	71 Chev	500	5,675
2. Bobby Allison	Holman-Moody	12	70 Ford	497	3,450
3. Richard Petty	Petty Enterprises	43	71 Plym	494	2,575
4. Cecil Gordon	Cecil Gordon	24	69 Merc	477	1,200
5. James Hylton	James Hylton	48	70 Ford	473	1,025

1972 Winston Cup GN Race No. 7 Southeastern 500
April 9, 1972 Average Speed: 92.826

Driver	Owner	Car #	Make	Laps	Winnings
1. Bobby Allison	R. Howard & J. Johnson	12	72 Chev	500	8,325
2. Bobby Isaac	Nord Krauskopf	71	72 Dodg	496	5,350
3. Richard Petty	Petty Enterprises	43	72 Plym	491	4,225
4. LeeRoy Yarbrough	Bill Seifert	45	71 Ford	483	1,720
5. Cecil Gordon	Cecil Gordon	24	71 Merc	474	1,325

1972 Winston Cup GN Race No. 18 Volunteer 500
July 9, 1972 Average Speed: 92.735

Driver	Owner	Car #	Make	Laps	Winnings
1. Bobby Allison	R. Howard & J. Johnson	12	72 Chev	500	8,400
2. Richard Petty	Petty Enterprises	43	72 Plym	497	5,700
3. Dave Marcis	Dave Marcis	2	70 Dodg	489	2,775
4. Benny Parsons	L. G. DeWitt	72	71 Merc	477	1,750
5. J. D. McDuffie	Dr. Don Tarr	70	70 Dodg	466	1,300

Bristol Motor Speedway *continued*

1973 Winston Cup GN Race No. 5 Southeastern 500
March 25, 1973 Average Speed: 88.952

Driver	Owner	Car #	Make	Laps	Winnings
1. Cale Yarborough	R. Howard & J. Johnson	11	73 Chev	500	8,030
2. Richard Petty	Petty Enterprises	43	73 Dodg	498	5,305
3. Bobby Allison	Bobby Allison	12	73 Chev	495	3,855
4. Dave Marcis	Dave Marcis	2	73 Dodg	484	1,440
5. Benny Parsons	L. G. DeWitt	72	71 Merc	484	1,330

1973 Winston Cup GN Race No. 18 Volunteer 500
July 8, 1973 Average Speed: 91.342

Driver	Owner	Car #	Make	Laps	Winnings
1. Benny Parsons	L. G. DeWitt	72	73 Chev	500	6,800
2. L. D. Ottinger	James Bryant	45	73 Chev	493	4,060
3. Cecil Gordon	Cecil Gordon	24	73 Chev	492	2,875
4. Lennie Pond	Ronnie Elder	54	73 Chev	485	1,475
5. J. D. McDuffie	J. D. McDuffie	70	72 Chev	473	1,435

1974 Winston Cup GN Race No. 5 Southeastern 500
March 17, 1974 Average Speed: 64.533

Driver	Owner	Car #	Make	Laps	Winnings
1. Cale Yarborough	R. Howard & J. Johnson	11	74 Chev	500	8,655
2. Bobby Isaac	Banjo Matthews	27	74 Chev	499	4,030
3. Benny Parsons	L. G. DeWitt	72	74 Chev	498	4,905
4. Bobby Allison	Bobby Allison	12	74 Chev	497	3,355
5. Donnie Allison	DiGard	88	74 Chev	491	1,980

1974 Winston Cup GN Race No. 17 Volunteer 500
July 14, 1974 Average Speed: 75.430

Driver	Owner	Car #	Make	Laps	Winnings
1. Cale Yarborough	Junior Johnson	11	74 Chev	500	7,725
2. Buddy Baker	Bud Moore	15	73 Ford	500	5,525
3. Richard Petty	Petty Enterprises	43	74 Dodg	498	4,900
4. Charlie Glotzbach	Junie Donlavey	90	72 Ford	494	1,700
5. Bobby Allison	Bobby Allison	12	74 Chev	494	1,025

1975 Winston Cup GN Race No. 5 Southeastern 500
March 16, 1975 Average Speed: 97.053

Driver	Owner	Car #	Make	Laps	Winnings
1. Richard Petty	Petty Enterprises	43	74 Dodg	500	7,350
2. Benny Parsons	L. G. DeWitt	72	75 Chev	494	5,325
3. Buddy Baker	Bud Moore	15	75 Ford	493	5,500
4. Cecil Gordon	Cecil Gordon	24	75 Chev	486	2,300
5. James Hylton	James Hylton	48	74 Chev	482	1,900

1975 Winston Cup GN Race No. 28 Volunteer 500
November 2, 1975 Average Speed: 97.016

Driver	Owner	Car #	Make	Laps	Winnings
1. Richard Petty	Petty Enterprises	43	74 Dodg	500	7,560
2. Lennie Pond	Ronnie Elder	54	75 Chev	499	4,110
3. Darrell Waltrip	DiGard	88	75 Chev	498	4,355
4. Dave Marcis	Nord Krauskopf	71	74 Dodg	494	4,060
5. Benny Parsons	L. G. DeWitt	72	75 Chev	488	3,035

1976 Winston Cup GN Race No. 5 Southeastern 400
March 14, 1976 Average Speed: 87.377

Driver	Owner	Car #	Make	Laps	Winnings
1. Cale Yarborough	Junior Johnson	11	Chev	400	18,070
2. Darrell Waltrip	DiGard	88	Chev	399	7,910
3. Benny Parsons	L. G. DeWitt	72	Chev	398	5,330
4. Dave Marcis	Nord Krauskopf	71	Dodg	398	4,280
5. Bobby Allison	Roger Penske	2	Merc	395	3,950

1976 Winston Cup GN Race No. 21 Volunteer 400
August 29, 1976 Average Speed: 99.175

Driver	Owner	Car #	Make	Laps	Winnings
1. Cale Yarborough	Junior Johnson	11	Chev	400	10,025
2. Richard Petty	Petty Enterprises	43	Dodg	398	7,800
3. Darrell Waltrip	DiGard	88	Chev	398	5,700
4. Benny Parsons	L. G. DeWitt	72	Chev	395	4,320
5. Buddy Baker	Bud Moore	15	Ford	394	3,950

1977 Winston Cup GN Race No. 8 Southeastern 500
April 17, 1977 Average Speed: 100.989

Driver	Owner	Car #	Make	Laps	Winnings
1. Cale Yarborough	Junior Johnson	11	Chev	500	23,300
2. Dick Brooks	Junie Donlavey	90	Ford	493	7,750
3. Richard Petty	Petty Enterprises	43	Dodg	491	6,100
4. Neil Bonnett	Nord Krauskopf	71	Dodg	490	4,200
5. Benny Parsons	L. G. DeWitt	72	Chev	488	3,950

1977 Winston Cup GN Race No. 21 Volunteer 400
August 28, 1977 Average Speed: 79.726

Driver	Owner	Car #	Make	Laps	Winnings
1. Cale Yarborough	Junior Johnson	11	Chev	400	12,100
2. Darrell Waltrip	DiGard	88	Chev	400	7,200
3. Benny Parsons	L. G. DeWitt	72	Chev	399	5,670
4. Dick Brooks	Junie Donlavey	90	Ford	396	3,400
5. Tighe Scott	Walter Ballard	30	Chev	389	2,900

1978 Winston Cup GN Race No. 6 Southeastern 500
April 2, 1978 Average Speed: 92.401

Driver	Owner	Car #	Make	Laps	Winnings
1. Darrell Waltrip	DiGard	88	Chev	500	19,200
2. Benny Parsons	L. G. DeWitt	72	Chev	499	15,300
3. Dave Marcis	Rod Osterlund	2	Chev	497	45,100
4. Cale Yarborough	Junior Johnson	11	Olds	494	6,850
5. Lennie Pond	Harry Ranier	54	Chev	494	2,000

1978 Winston Cup GN Race No. 21 Volunteer 500
August 26, 1978 Average Speed: 88.628

Driver	Owner	Car #	Make	Laps	Winnings
1. Cale Yarborough	Junior Johnson	11	Olds	500	15,910
2. Benny Parsons	L. G. DeWitt	72	Olds	500	8,350
3. Darrell Waltrip	DiGard	88	Chev	499	7,100
4. Dick Brooks	Junie Donlavey	90	Ford	497	1,950
5. Richard Petty	Petty Enterprises	43	Chev	495	4,350

1979 Winston Cup GN Race No. 7 Southeastern 500
April 1, 1979 Average Speed: 91.033

Driver	Owner	Car #	Make	Laps	Winnings
1. Dale Earnhardt	Rod Osterlund	2	Chev	500	19,800
2. Bobby Allison	Bud Moore	15	Ford	500	11,150
3. Darrell Waltrip	DiGard	88	Chev	500	8,300
4. Richard Petty	Petty Enterprises	43	Olds	498	5,850
5. Benny Parsons	M. C. Anderson	27	Olds	497	3,150

1979 Winston Cup GN Race No. 22 Volunteer 500
August 25, 1979 Average Speed: 91.493

Driver	Owner	Car #	Make	Laps	Winnings
1. Darrell Waltrip	DiGard	88	Chev	500	13,510
2. Richard Petty	Petty Enterprises	43	Chev	500	10,100
3. Bobby Allison	Bud Moore	15	Ford	500	6,950
4. Benny Parsons	M. C. Anderson	27	Chev	499	4,900
5. Cale Yarborough	Junior Johnson	11	Chev	497	5,600

Bristol Motor Speedway *continued*

1980 Winston Cup GN Race No. 6 Valleydale Southeastern 500
March 30, 1980 Average Speed: 96.977

Driver	Owner	Car #	Make	Laps	Winnings
1. Dale Earnhardt	Rod Osterlund	2	Chev	500	20,625
2. Darrell Waltrip	DiGard	88	Chev	500	13,100
3. Bobby Allison	Bud Moore	15	Ford	500	9,400
4. Benny Parsons	M. C. Anderson	27	Chev	499	6,835
5. Cale Yarborough	Junior Johnson	11	Chev	498	7,100

1980 Winston Cup GN Race No. 22 Busch Volunteer 500
August 23, 1980 Average Speed: 86.973

Driver	Owner	Car #	Make	Laps	Winnings
1. Cale Yarborough	Junior Johnson	11	Chev	500	16,550
2. Dale Earnhardt	Rod Osterlund	2	Chev	500	11,450
3. Darrell Waltrip	DiGard	88	Chev	500	7,500
4. Richard Petty	Petty Enterprises	43	Chev	499	7,700
5. Benny Parsons	M. C. Anderson	27	Chev	499	5,450

1981 Winston Cup GN Race No. 6 Valleydale 500
March 29, 1981 Average Speed: 89.530

Driver	Owner	Car #	Make	Laps	Winnings
1. Darrell Waltrip	Junior Johnson	11	Buick	500	22,450
2. Ricky Rudd	DiGard	88	Olds	500	14,375
3. Bobby Allison	Harry Ranier	28	Pont	500	10,450
4. Morgan Shepherd	Cliff Stewart	5	Pont	500	4,600
5. Benny Parsons	Bud Moore	15	Ford	499	7,375

1981 Winston Cup GN Race No. 22 Busch 500
August 22, 1981 Average Speed: 84.723

Driver	Owner	Car #	Make	Laps	Winnings
1. Darrell Waltrip	Junior Johnson	11	Buick	500	18,800
2. Ricky Rudd	DiGard	88	Chev	499	12,375
3. Terry Labonte	Billy Hagan	44	Buick	498	8,800
4. Bobby Allison	Harry Ranier	28	Buick	497	7,075
5. Ron Bouchard	Jack Beebe	47	Buick	497	5,650

1982 Winston Cup GN Race No. 3 Valleydale 500
March 14, 1982 Average Speed: 94.025

Driver	Owner	Car #	Make	Laps	Winnings
1. Darrell Waltrip	Junior Johnson	11	Buick	500	26,520
2. Dale Earnhardt	Bud Moore	15	Ford	500	18,480
3. Morgan Shepherd	Ron Benfield	98	Buick	500	6,705
4. Terry Labonte	Billy Hagan	44	Chev	499	6,575
5. Bobby Allison	DiGard	88	Chev	498	7,680

1982 Winston Cup GN Race No. 21 Busch 500
August 28, 1982 Average Speed: 94.318

Driver	Owner	Car #	Make	Laps	Winnings
1. Darrell Waltrip	Junior Johnson	11	Buick	500	22,925
2. Bobby Allison	DiGard	88	Chev	500	16,325
3. Harry Gant	Hal Needham	33	Buick	500	7,395
4. Terry Labonte	Billy Hagan	44	Buick	499	6,495
5. Morgan Shepherd	Ron Benfield	98	Buick	499	5,150

1983 Winston Cup GN Race No. 11 Valleydale 500
May 21, 1983 Average Speed: 93.445

Driver	Owner	Car #	Make	Laps	Winnings
1. Darrell Waltrip	Junior Johnson	11	Chev	500	29,965
2. Bobby Allison	DiGard	22	Buick	500	16,955
3. Morgan Shepherd	Jim Stacy	2	Buick	499	13,260
4. Neil Bonnett	Bob Rahilly & Butch Mock	75	Chev	499	7,700
5. Richard Petty	Petty Enterprises	43	Pont	498	7,930

1983 Winston Cup GN Race No. 21 Busch 500
August 27, 1983 Average Speed: 89.430

Driver	Owner	Car #	Make	Laps	Winnings
1. Darrell Waltrip	Junior Johnson	11	Chev	419	30,400
2. Dale Earnhardt	Bud Moore	15	Ford	419	15,725
3. Bobby Allison	DiGard	22	Buick	419	13,360
4. Geoff Bodine	Cliff Stewart	88	Pont	418	7,370
5. Terry Labonte	Billy Hagan	44	Chev	418	5,770

1984 Winston Cup GN Race No. 5 Valleydale 500
April 1, 1984 Average Speed: 93.967

Driver	Owner	Car #	Make	Laps	Winnings
1. Darrell Waltrip	Junior Johnson	11	Chev	500	31,670
2. Terry Labonte	Billy Hagan	44	Chev	500	15,885
3. Ron Bouchard	Jack Beebe	47	Buick	500	11,010
4. Dave Marcis	Bob Rahilly & Butch Mock	75	Pont	499	10,630
5. Tim Richmond	Raymond Beadle	27	Pont	499	6,490

1984 Winston Cup GN Race No. 21 Busch 500
August 25, 1984 Average Speed: 85.365

Driver	Owner	Car #	Make	Laps	Winnings
1. Terry Labonte	Billy Hagan	44	Chev	500	28,480
2. Bobby Allison	DiGard	22	Buick	500	22,475
3. Dick Brooks	Junie Donlavey	90	Ford	498	11,930
4. Dave Marcis	Bob Rahilly & Butch Mock	75	Pont	494	11,300
5. Harry Gant	Hal Needham	33	Chev	494	6,910

1985 Winston Cup GN Race No. 5 Valleydale 500
April 6, 1985 Average Speed: 81.790

Driver	Owner	Car #	Make	Laps	Winnings
1. Dale Earnhardt	Richard Childress	3	Chev	500	31,525
2. Ricky Rudd	Bud Moore	15	Ford	500	18,050
3. Terry Labonte	Billy Hagan	44	Chev	498	16,625
4. Buddy Baker	Buddy Baker & Danny Schiff	88	Olds	498	4,470
5. Rusty Wallace	Cliff Stewart	2	Pont	497	8,230

1985 Winston Cup GN Race No. 19 Busch 500
August 24, 1985 Average Speed: 81.388

Driver	Owner	Car #	Make	Laps	Winnings
1. Dale Earnhardt	Richard Childress	3	Chev	500	34,675
2. Tim Richmond	Raymond Beadle	27	Pont	500	19,230
3. Neil Bonnett	Junior Johnson	12	Chev	500	13,900
4. Darrell Waltrip	Junior Johnson	11	Chev	500	12,500
5. Bill Elliott	Harry Melling	9	Ford	499	11,350

1986 Winston Cup Race No. 5 Valleydale 500
April 6, 1986 Average Speed: 89.747

Driver	Owner	Car #	Make	Laps	Winnings
1. Rusty Wallace	Raymond Beadle	27	Pont	500	34,780
2. Ricky Rudd	Bud Moore	15	Ford	500	20,125
3. Darrell Waltrip	Junior Johnson	11	Chev	500	17,825
4. Harry Gant	Hal Needham	33	Chev	499	11,770
5. Bill Elliott	Harry Melling	9	Ford	499	12,050

1986 Winston Cup Race No. 20 Busch 500
August 23, 1986 Average Speed: 86.934

Driver	Owner	Car #	Make	Laps	Winnings
1. Darrell Waltrip	Junior Johnson	11	Chev	500	41,725
2. Terry Labonte	Billy Hagan	44	Chev	500	21,350
3. Geoff Bodine	Rick Hendrick	5	Chev	499	17,025
4. Dale Earnhardt	Richard Childress	3	Chev	499	12,800
5. Harry Gant	Hal Needham	33	Chev	499	12,950

Bristol Motor Speedway *continued*

1987 Winston Cup Race No. 7 Valleydale Meats 500
April 12, 1987 Average Speed: 75.621

Driver	Owner	Car #	Make	Laps	Winnings
1. Dale Earnhardt	Richard Childress	3	Chev	500	43,850
2. Richard Petty	Petty Enterprises	43	Pont	500	21,030
3. Ricky Rudd	Bud Moore	15	Ford	500	17,175
4. Bill Elliott	Harry Melling	9	Ford	500	12,570
5. Alan Kulwicki	Alan Kulwicki	7	Ford	500	11,605

1987 Winston Cup Race No. 20 Busch 500
August 22, 1987 Average Speed: 90.373

Driver	Owner	Car #	Make	Laps	Winnings
1. Dale Earnhardt	Richard Childress	3	Chev	500	47,175
2. Rusty Wallace	Raymond Beadle	27	Pont	500	26,300
3. Ricky Rudd	Bud Moore	15	Ford	500	20,275
4. Terry Labonte	Junior Johnson	11	Chev	500	17,500
5. Richard Petty	Petty Enterprises	43	Pont	500	10,030

1988 Winston Cup Race No. 6 Valleydale Meats 500
April 10, 1988 Average Speed: 83.115

Driver	Owner	Car #	Make	Laps	Winnings
1. Bill Elliott	Harry Melling	9	Ford	500	45,750
2. Mark Martin	Jack Roush	6	Ford	500	21,250
3. Geoff Bodine	Rick Hendrick	5	Chev	500	17,425
4. Rusty Wallace	Raymond Beadle	27	Pont	499	14,370
5. Bobby Allison	Stavola Brothers	12	Buick	498	12,625

1988 Winston Cup Race No. 20 Busch 500
August 27, 1988 Average Speed: 78.775

Driver	Owner	Car #	Make	Laps	Winnings
1. Dale Earnhardt	Richard Childress	3	Chev	500	48,500
2. Bill Elliott	Harry Melling	9	Ford	500	29,150
3. Geoff Bodine	Rick Hendrick	5	Chev	499	17,475
4. Davey Allison	Harry Ranier	28	Ford	499	16,775
5. Alan Kulwicki	Alan Kulwicki	7	Ford	499	16,410

1989 Winston Cup Race No. 6 Valleydale Meats 500
April 9, 1989 Average Speed: 76.034

Driver	Owner	Car #	Make	Laps	Winnings
1. Rusty Wallace	Raymond Beadle	27	Pont	500	48,750
2. Darrell Waltrip	Rick Hendrick	17	Chev	500	28,900
3. Geoff Bodine	Rick Hendrick	5	Chev	500	21,950
4. Davey Allison	Robert Yates	28	Ford	500	17,802
5. Dick Trickle	Stavola Brothers	84	Buick	400	12,950

1989 Winston Cup Race No. 20 Busch 500
August 26, 1989 Average Speed: 85.554

Driver	Owner	Car #	Make	Laps	Winnings
1. Darrell Waltrip	Rick Hendrick	17	Chev	500	52,450
2. Alan Kulwicki	Alan Kulwicki	7	Ford	500	30,875
3. Ricky Rudd	Kenny Bernstein	26	Buick	500	19,200
4. Harry Gant	Leo Jackson	33	Olds	500	13,300
5. Terry Labonte	Junior Johnson	11	Ford	499	13,400

1990 Winston Cup Series Race No. 6 Valleydale Meats 500
April 8, 1990 Average Speed: 87.258

Driver	Owner	Car #	Make	Laps	Winnings
1. Davey Allison	Robert Yates	28	Ford	500	50,100
2. Mark Martin	Jack Roush	6	Ford	500	31,300
3. Ricky Rudd	Rick Hendrick	5	Chev	500	19,775
4. Terry Labonte	Richard Jackson	1	Olds	500	13,500
5. Rick Wilson	Bob Rahilly & Butch Mock	75	Pont	500	13,857

1990 Winston Cup Series Race No. 20 Busch 500
August 25, 1990 Average Speed: 91.782

Driver	Owner	Car #	Make	Laps	Winnings
1. Ernie Irvan	Larry McClure	4	Chev	500	49,600
2. Rusty Wallace	Raymond Beadle	27	Pont	500	32,850
3. Mark Martin	Jack Roush	6	Ford	500	22,830
4. Terry Labonte	Richard Jackson	1	Olds	500	14,150
5. Sterling Marlin	Billy Hagan	94	Olds	500	12,900

1991 Winston Cup Series Race No. 6 Valleydale Meats 500
April 14, 1991 Average Speed: 72.809

Driver	Owner	Car #	Make	Laps	Winnings
1. Rusty Wallace	Roger Penske	2	Pont	500	51,300
2. Ernie Irvan	Larry McClure	4	Chev	500	26,000
3. Davey Allison	Robert Yates	28	Ford	500	18,950
4. Mark Martin	Jack Roush	6	Ford	500	18,950
5. Ricky Rudd	Rick Hendrick	5	Chev	500	37,950

1991 Winston Cup Series Race No. 20 Bud 500
August 24, 1991 Average Speed: 82.028

Driver	Owner	Car #	Make	Laps	Winnings
1. Alan Kulwicki	Alan Kulwicki	7	Ford	500	61,400
2. Sterling Marlin	Junior Johnson	22	Ford	500	30,275
3. Ken Schrader	Rick Hendrick	25	Chev	500	22,950
4. Mark Martin	Jack Roush	6	Ford	499	19,700
5. Ricky Rudd	Rick Hendrick	5	Chev	499	16,450

1992 Winston Cup Race No. 6 Food City 500
April 5, 1992 Average Speed: 86.316

Driver	Owner	Car #	Make	Laps	Winnings
1. Alan Kulwicki	Alan Kulwicki	7	Ford	500	83,360
2. Dale Jarrett	Joe Gibbs	18	Chev	500	29,835
3. Ken Schrader	Rick Hendrick	25	Chev	500	29,410
4. Terry Labonte	Billy Hagan	94	Olds	499	20,010
5. Dick Trickle	Stavola Brothers	8	Ford	499	18,410

1992 Winston Cup Race No. 20 Bud 500
August 29, 1992 Average Speed: 91.198

Driver	Owner	Car #	Make	Laps	Winnings
1. Darrell Waltrip	Darrell Waltrip	17	Chev	500	73,050
2. Dale Earnhardt	Richard Childress	3	Chev	500	39,325
3. Ken Schrader	Rick Hendrick	25	Chev	500	28,350
4. Kyle Petty	Felix Sabates	42	Pont	500	18,000
5. Alan Kulwicki	Alan Kulwicki	7	Ford	499	19,800

1993 Winston Cup Series Race No. 6 Food City 500
April 4, 1993 Average Speed: 84.730

Driver	Owner	Car #	Make	Laps	Winnings
1. Rusty Wallace	Roger Penske	2	Pont	500	107,610
2. Dale Earnhardt	Richard Childress	3	Chev	500	47,760
3. Kyle Petty	Felix Sabates	42	Pont	500	31,485
4. Jimmy Spencer	Bobby Allison	12	Ford	500	26,050
5. Davey Allison	Robert Yates	28	Ford	500	25,180

1993 Winston Cup Series Race No. 21 Bud 500
August 28, 1993 Average Speed: 88.172

Driver	Owner	Car #	Make	Laps	Winnings
1. Mark Martin	Jack Roush	6	Ford	500	80,125
2. Rusty Wallace	Roger Penske	2	Pont	500	31,875
3. Dale Earnhardt	Richard Childress	3	Chev	500	32,325
4. Harry Gant	Leo Jackson	33	Chev	500	28,150
5. Rick Mast	Richard Jackson	1	Ford	500	22,000

Bristol Motor Speedway *continued*

1994 Winston Cup Series Race No. 6 Food City 500
April 10, 1994 Average Speed: 89.647

Driver	Owner	Car #	Make	Laps	Winnings
1. Dale Earnhardt	Richard Childress	3	Chev	500	72,570
2. Ken Schrader	Rick Hendrick	25	Chev	500	43,445
3. Lake Speed	Bud Moore	15	Ford	500	35,020
4. Geoff Bodine	Geoff Bodine	7	Ford	499	24,356
5. Michael Waltrip	Chuck Rider	30	Pont	497	20,135

1994 Winston Cup Series Race No. 22 Goody's 500
August 27, 1994 Average Speed: 91.363

Driver	Owner	Car #	Make	Laps	Winnings
1. Rusty Wallace	Roger Penske	2	Ford	500	53,015
2. Mark Martin	Jack Roush	6	Ford	500	35,915
3. Dale Earnhardt	Richard Childress	3	Chev	500	33,265
4. Darrell Waltrip	Darrell Waltrip	17	Chev	500	28,730
5. Bill Elliott	Junior Johnson	11	Ford	500	22,275

1995 Winston Cup Series Race No. 6 Food City 500
April 2, 1995 Average Speed: 92.011

Driver	Owner	Car #	Make	Laps	Winnings
1. Jeff Gordon	Rick Hendrick	24	Chev	500	67,645
2. Rusty Wallace	Roger Penske	2	Ford	500	42,045
3. Darrell Waltrip	Darrell Waltrip	17	Chev	500	35,845
4. Bobby Hamilton	Petty Enterprises	43	Pont	500	28,631
5. Ricky Rudd	Ricky Rudd	10	Ford	500	32,260

1995 Winston Cup Series Race No. 22 Goody's 500
August 26, 1995 Average Speed: 81.979

Driver	Owner	Car #	Make	Laps	Winnings
1. Terry Labonte	Rick Hendrick	5	Chev	500	66,940
2. Dale Earnhardt	Richard Childress	3	Chev	500	66,890
3. Dale Jarrett	Robert Yates	28	Ford	500	39,390
4. Darrell Waltrip	Darrell Waltrip	17	Chev	500	32,780
5. Mark Martin	Jack Roush	6	Ford	500	41,775

1996 Winston Cup Series Race No. 6 Food City 500
March 31, 1996 Average Speed: 91.308

Driver	Owner	Car #	Make	Laps	Winnings
1. Jeff Gordon	Rick Hendrick	24	Chev	342	93,765
2. Terry Labonte	Rick Hendrick	5	Chev	342	54,215
3. Mark Martin	Jack Roush	6	Ford	342	44,815
4. Dale Earnhardt	Richard Childress	3	Chev	342	35,351
5. Rusty Wallace	Roger Penske	2	Ford	342	29,895

1996 Winston Cup Series Race No. 22 Goody's 500
August 24, 1996 Average Speed: 91.267

Driver	Owner	Car #	Make	Laps	Winnings
1. Rusty Wallace	Roger Penske	2	Ford	500	77,090
2. Jeff Gordon	Rick Hendrick	24	Chev	500	54,590
3. Mark Martin	Jack Roush	6	Ford	500	46,490
4. Dale Jarrett	Robert Yates	88	Ford	500	32,980
5. Terry Labonte	Rick Hendrick	5	Chev	500	37,875

Kingsport Speedway
Kingsport, TN
.4-mile Paved Track

(aka MARCA Motorsports Community; Raceland Kingsport; Kingsport Motor Speedway; New Kingsport Speedway; Kingsport Int'l Speedway; Tri-Cities Speedway) .4-mile paved oval opened circa 1967. First NASCAR Winston Cup (then Grand National) race staged on 6/19/69 (won by Richard Petty). Re-measured in 1970 at .337-mile oval. Final Winston Cup Grand National race run 5/23/71 (won by Bobby Isaac). Pavement torn up in 1984. Still active today.

Winston Cup Starts
12 drivers tied with 3

Winston Cup Victories
Richard Petty 2

Winston Cup Poles
Bobby Isaac 2

Winston Cup Money
Richard Petty $2,790

Most Cars Started
25—May 23, 1971 Kingsport 300

Fewest Cars Started
22—June 26, 1970 Kingsport 100

Narrowest Margin of Victory
1 lap plus—June 19, 1969 Kingsport 250

Slowest Race
63.242 MPH—May 23, 1971 Kingsport 300

Race Record
73.619 MPH—June 19, 1969 Kingsport 250

Most Cautions
6—May 23, 1971 Kingsport 300

Most Race Leaders
3—June 19, 1969 Kingsport 250

Most Cars Running at Finish
13—June 19, 1969 Kingsport 250

1969 Grand National Race No. 25 Kingsport 250
June 19, 1969 Average Speed: 73.619

Driver	Owner	Car #	Make	Laps	Winnings
1. Richard Petty	Petty Enterprises	43	69 Ford	250	1,000
2. John Sears	L. G. DeWitt	4	68 Ford	249	600
3. David Pearson	Holman-Moody	17	69 Ford	248	600
4. Neil Castles	Neil Castles	06	67 Plym	247	350
5. G. C. Spencer	G. C. Spencer	49	67 Plym	246	325

1970 Grand National Race No. 22 Kingsport 100
June 26, 1970 Average Speed: 68.583

Driver	Owner	Car #	Make	Laps	Winnings
1. Richard Petty	Petty Enterprises	43	70 Plym	297	1,500
2. James Hylton	James Hylton	48	69 Ford	295	900
3. Dave Marcis	Dave Marcis	30	69 Dodg	293	500
4. Bobby Allison	Bobby Allison	22	69 Dodg	292	350
5. Neil Castles	Neil Castles	06	69 Dodg	292	325

1971 Winston Cup GN Race No. 20 Kingsport 300
May 23, 1971 Average Speed: 63.242

Driver	Owner	Car #	Make	Laps	Winnings
1. Bobby Isaac	Nord Krauskopf	71	71 Dodg	300	1,800
2. Elmo Langley	Elmo Langley	64	71 Ford	295	1,100
3. James Hylton	James Hylton	48	71 Ford	293	800
4. Cecil Gordon	Cecil Gordon	24	69 Merc	283	600
5. Bill Champion	Bill Champion	10	69 Ford	282	500

Nashville Speedway
Nashville, TN
Half-mile Paved Track

(aka Nashville Speedway USA; Nashville Motor Speedway; Nashville Int'l Speedway; Cumberland Park; Fairgrounds Speedway) Originally built in 1907 as a 1-mile horse track. Track paved and shortened to half-mile in 1958. First NASCAR Winston Cup (then Grand National) race staged on 8/10/58 (won by Joe Weatherly, his first of 25 career wins). Track renovated to .675-mile high-banked (35 degree turns) in 1970. Following several fatalities, turns were shaved down to 24 degrees. Final Winston Cup race run on 7/14/84 (Geoff Bodine won). The track is still active today, hosting a variety of NASCAR events and weekly Late Model Stock racing.

Winston Cup Starts
Richard Petty   39

Winston Cup Victories
Richard Petty   9

Winston Cup Poles
Richard Petty   7
Darrell Waltrip   7

Winston Cup Money
Darrell Waltrip $238,120

Most Cars Started
36—July 25, 1970 Nashville 420

Fewest Cars Started
12—May 24, 1959

Narrowest Margin of Victory
1/2 car length—July 26, 1969
Nashville 400

Slowest Race
56.455 MPH—August 6, 1961
Nashville 500

Race Record
98.419 MPH—May 12, 1973
Music City 420

Most Cautions
10—July 16, 1977 Nashville 420

Most Race Leaders
7—May 8, 1976 Music City USA 420
7—July 14, 1984 Pepsi 420

Most Cars Running at Finish
25—May 10, 1980 Music City USA 420

1958 Grand National Race No. 37
August 10, 1958 Average Speed: 59.269

Driver	Owner	Car #	Make	Laps	Winnings
1. Joe Weatherly	Holman-Moody	72	58 Ford	200	1,850
2. Bob Welborn	J. H. Petty	49	57 Chev	200	1,050
3. Larry Frank	Larry Frank	76	57 Chev	200	800
4. Jimmy Thompson	Petty Enterprises	2	57 Olds	198	575
5. Lee Petty	Petty Enterprises	42	57 Olds	197	475

1959 Grand National Race No. 16
May 24, 1959 Average Speed: 71.006

Driver	Owner	Car #	Make	Laps	Winnings
1. Rex White	Rex White	4	59 Chev	200	900
2. Junior Johnson	Paul Spaulding	11	57 Ford	200	525
3. Tommy Irwin	Tommy Irwin	36	59 Ford	199	350
4. Buck Baker	Buck Baker	87	59 Chev	198	250
5. Joe Lee Johnson	Joe Lee Johnson	77	57 Chev	198	225

1959 Grand National Race No. 31
August 9, 1959 Average Speed: 63.343

Driver	Owner	Car #	Make	Laps	Winnings
1. Joe Lee Johnson	Joe Lee Johnson	77	57 Chev	300	2,912
2. Larry Frank	Larry Frank	76	57 Chev	297	1,453
3. Elmo Langley	Ratus Walters	10	59 Buick	297	1,125
4. Lee Petty	Petty Enterprises	42	59 Plym	297	900
5. Tommy Irwin	Tommy Irwin	36	59 Ford	295	750

1960 Grand National Race No. 29
August 7, 1960 Average Speed: 56.966

Driver	Owner	Car #	Make	Laps	Winnings
1. Johnny Beauchamp	Dale Swanson	73	60 Chev	333	3,666
2. Rex White	Rex White	4	60 Chev	333	2,390
3. Buck Baker	Buck Baker	87	60 Chev	331	1,225
4. Lee Petty	Petty Enterprises	42	60 Plym	330	825
5. Joe Lee Johnson	Paul McDuffie	89	60 Chev	330	718

1961 Grand National Race No. 37 Nashville 500
August 6, 1961 Average Speed: 56.455

Driver	Owner	Car #	Make	Laps	Winnings
1. Jim Paschal	J. H. Petty	44	61 Pont	403	2,523
2. Ned Jarrett	Bee Gee Holloway	11	61 Chev	403	1,275
3. Johnny Allen	Joe Lee Johnson	14	61 Chev	401	975
4. Buck Baker	Buck Baker	86	61 Chrys	401	675
5. Emanuel Zervakis	Monroe Shook	85	61 Chev	397	575

1962 Grand National Race No. 38 Nashville 500
August 5, 1962 Average Speed: 64.469

Driver	Owner	Car #	Make	Laps	Winnings
1. Jim Paschal	Petty Enterprises	42	62 Plym	500	3,250
2. Richard Petty	Petty Enterprises	43	62 Pont	489	1,875
3. Buck Baker	Buck Baker	87	62 Chrys	493	1,350
4. Joe Weatherly	Bud Moore	8	62 Pont	489	800
5. Thomas Cox	Cliff Stewart	2	62 Pont	471	700

1963 Grand National Race No. 39 Nashville 400
August 4, 1963 Average Speed: 60.126

Driver	Owner	Car #	Make	Laps	Winnings
1. Jim Paschal	Petty Enterprises	42	63 Plym	350	2,500
2. Billy Wade	Cotton Owens	5	63 Dodg	349	1,350
3. Joe Weatherly	Bud Moore	8	63 Pont	349	1,025
4. Richard Petty	Petty Enterprises	43	63 Plym	348	675
5. Buck Baker	Buck Baker	87	63 Pont	348	475

1964 Grand National Race No. 30
June 14, 1964 Average Speed: 76.498

Driver	Owner	Car #	Make	Laps	Winnings
1. Richard Petty	Petty Enterprises	43	64 Plym	200	1,000
2. David Pearson	Cotton Owens	6	64 Dodg	199	600
3. Buck Baker	Ray Fox	3	64 Dodg	199	400
4. Jimmy Pardue	Charles Robinson	54	64 Plym	195	300
5. G. C. Spencer	G. C. Spencer	49	64 Chev	191	275

1964 Grand National Race No. 43
August 2, 1964 Average Speed: 73.208

Driver	Owner	Car #	Make	Laps	Winnings
1. Richard Petty	Petty Enterprises	43	64 Plym	400	2,150
2. Jim Paschal	Petty Enterprises	41	64 Plym	400	1,000
3. David Pearson	Cotton Owens	6	64 Dodg	399	800
4. Earl Balmer	Cotton Owens	5	64 Dodg	392	500
5. Ned Jarrett	Bondy Long	11	64 Ford	392	575

1965 Grand National Race No. 23
June 3, 1965 Average Speed: 71.386

Driver	Owner	Car #	Make	Laps	Winnings
1. Dick Hutcherson	Holman-Moody	29	65 Ford	200	1,000
2. Ned Jarrett	Jabe Thomas	25	64 Ford	199	600
3. J. T. Putney	Herman Beam	19	65 Chev	199	400
4. Wendell Scott	Wendell Scott	34	63 Ford	196	300
5. Henley Gray	Gene Cline	97	64 Ford	177	275

Nashville Speedway *continued*

1965 Grand National Race No. 35 Nashville 400
July 31, 1965 Average Speed: 72.383

Driver	Owner	Car #	Make	Laps	Winnings
1. Richard Petty	Petty Enterprises	43	65 Plym	400	2,350
2. Ned Jarrett	Bondy Long	11	65 Ford	394	1,100
3. Buddy Arrington	Buddy Arrington	67	64 Dodg	382	750
4. J. T. Putney	Herman Beam	19	65 Chev	381	500
5. G. C. Spencer	G. C. Spencer	49	64 Ford	374	475

1966 Grand National Race No. 36
July 30, 1966 Average Speed: 71.770

Driver	Owner	Car #	Make	Laps	Winnings
1. Richard Petty	Petty Enterprises	43	66 Plym	400	2,750
2. Buck Baker	Buck Baker	87	66 Olds	395	1,400
3. Bobby Allison	Bobby Allison	2	65 Chev	394	850
4. Henley Gray	Gene Black	74	66 Ford	383	500
5. John Sears	L. G. DeWitt	4	64 Ford	383	475

1967 Grand National Race No. 35 Nashville 400
July 29, 1967 Average Speed: 70.866

Driver	Owner	Car #	Make	Laps	Winnings
1. Richard Petty	Petty Enterprises	43	67 Plym	400	2,050
2. James Hylton	Bud Hartje	48	65 Dodg	395	1,500
3. John Sears	L. G. DeWitt	4	66 Ford	390	900
4. Sam McQuagg	Cotton Owens	6	67 Dodg	390	500
5. Clyde Lynn	Clyde Lynn	20	66 Ford	375	475

1968 Grand National Race No. 32 Nashville 400
July 27, 1968 Average Speed: 72.980

Driver	Owner	Car #	Make	Laps	Winnings
1. David Pearson	Holman-Moody	17	68 Ford	301	2,950
2. Richard Petty	Petty Enterprises	43	68 Plym	298	1,700
3. Bobby Allison	Bobby Allison	2	66 Chev	295	900
4. Bobby Isaac	Nord Krauskopf	71	67 Dodg	294	500
5. Charlie Glotzbach	Sherral Pruitt	57	67 Dodg	293	475

1969 Grand National Race No. 34 Nashville 400
July 26, 1969 Average Speed: 78.740

Driver	Owner	Car #	Make	Laps	Winnings
1. Richard Petty	Petty Enterprises	43	69 Ford	400	3,000
2. Bobby Isaac	Nord Krauskopf	71	69 Dodg	400	1,700
3. James Hylton	James Hylton	48	68 Dodg	387	950
4. John Sears	L. G. DeWitt	4	68 Ford	384	550
5. Neil Castles	Neil Castles	06	67 Plym	379	500

1970 Grand National Race No. 30 Nashville 420
July 25, 1970 Average Speed: 87.943

Driver	Owner	Car #	Make	Laps	Winnings
1. Bobby Isaac	Nord Krauskopf	71	69 Dodg	420	3,310
2. Bobby Allison	Bobby Allison	22	69 Dodg	418	1,910
3. Neil Castles	Neil Castles	06	69 Dodg	394	1,310
4. Cecil Gordon	Cecil Gordon	24	68 Ford	391	1,010
5. J. D. McDuffie	J. D. McDuffie	70	69 Merc	385	910

1971 Winston Cup GN Race No. 32 Nashville 420
July 24, 1971 Average Speed: 89.667

Driver	Owner	Car #	Make	Laps	Winnings
1. Richard Petty	Petty Enterprises	43	71 Plym	420	4,325
2. James Hylton	James Hylton	48	70 Ford	416	2,415
3. Benny Parsons	L. G. DeWitt	72	70 Merc	416	1,600
4. Earl Brooks	Earl Brooks	26	69 Ford	411	1,160
5. J. D. McDuffie	J. D. McDuffie	70	69 Merc	403	1,025

1972 Winston Cup GN Race No. 23 Nashville 420
August 27, 1972 Average Speed: 92.578

Driver	Owner	Car #	Make	Laps	Winnings
1. Bobby Allison	R. Howard & J. Johnson	12	72 Chev	420	6,925
2. Richard Petty	Petty Enterprises	43	72 Plym	420	5,010
3. Darrell Waltrip	Darrell Waltrip	95	71 Merc	404	2,040
4. Benny Parsons	L. G. DeWitt	72	71 Merc	400	1,630
5. Elmo Langley	Elmo Langley	64	71 Ford	387	1,400

1973 Winston Cup GN Race No. 11 Music City 420
May 12, 1973 Average Speed: 98.419

Driver	Owner	Car #	Make	Laps	Winnings
1. Cale Yarborough	R. Howard & J. Johnson	11	73 Chev	420	6,755
2. Benny Parsons	L. G. DeWitt	72	72 Chev	418	3,365
3. Buddy Baker	Nord Krauskopf	71	73 Dodg	415	3,680
4. Cecil Gordon	Cecil Gordon	24	72 Chev	413	1,710
5. Bobby Allison	Bobby Allison	12	73 Chev	411	2,755

1973 Winston Cup GN Race No. 21 Nashville 420
August 25, 1973 Average Speed: 89.310

Driver	Owner	Car #	Make	Laps	Winnings
1. Buddy Baker	Nord Krauskopf	71	73 Dodg	420	6,750
2. Richard Petty	Petty Enterprises	43	73 Dodg	416	4,960
3. Coo Coo Marlin	H. B. Cunningham	14	72 Chev	409	2,125
4. David Sisco	Charlie McGee	05	72 Chev	402	1,750
5. Ed Negre	Ed Negre	8	73 Dodg	399	1,570

1974 Winston Cup GN Race No. 11 Music City USA 420
May 11 & 12, 1974 Average Speed: 82.240

Driver	Owner	Car #	Make	Laps	Winnings
1. Richard Petty	Petty Enterprises	43	74 Dodg	420	7,900
2. Donnie Allison	DiGard	88	74 Chev	420	3,850
3. Darrell Waltrip	Darrell Waltrip	95	74 Chev	416	2,390
4. Bob Burcham	Jack White	57	74 Chev	415	1,370
5. Dave Marcis	Dave Marcis	2	73 Dodg	414	1,520

1974 Winston Cup GN Race No. 18 Nashville 420
July 20, 1974 Average Speed: 76.368

Driver	Owner	Car #	Make	Laps	Winnings
1. Cale Yarborough	Junior Johnson	11	74 Chev	420	8,025
2. Bobby Allison	Bobby Allison	12	74 Chev	420	3,675
3. Darrell Waltrip	Darrell Waltrip	95	74 Chev	416	2,855
4. David Sisco	David Sisco	05	74 Chev	416	1,675
5. Alton Jones	Butch Hawkersmith	68	72 Chev	415	1,230

1975 Winston Cup GN Race No. 11 Music City USA 420
May 10, 1975 Average Speed: 94.107

Driver	Owner	Car #	Make	Laps	Winnings
1. Darrell Waltrip	Darrell Waltrip	17	75 Chev	420	8,000
2. Benny Parsons	L. G. DeWitt	72	75 Chev	418	5,450
3. Coo Coo Marlin	H. B. Cunningham	14	75 Chev	409	2,700
4. Dave Marcis	Nord Krauskopf	71	74 Dodg	407	3,400
5. Cecil Gordon	Cecil Gordon	24	75 Chev	407	1,550

1975 Winston Cup GN Race No. 17 Nashville 420
July 20, 1975 Average Speed: 89.792

Driver	Owner	Car #	Make	Laps	Winnings
1. Cale Yarborough	Junior Johnson	11	75 Chev	420	7,735
2. Richard Petty	Petty Enterprises	43	74 Dodg	419	6,205
3. Dave Marcis	Nord Krauskopf	71	74 Dodg	418	4,560
4. Benny Parsons	L. G. DeWitt	72	75 Chev	412	3,185
5. Cecil Gordon	Cecil Gordon	24	75 Chev	407	1,585

Nashville Speedway *continued*

1976 Winston Cup GN Race No. 11 Music City USA 420
May 8, 1976 Average Speed: 84.512

Driver	Owner	Car #	Make	Laps	Winnings
1. Cale Yarborough	Junior Johnson	11	Chev	420	8,565
2. Richard Petty	Petty Enterprises	43	Dodg	420	6,965
3. Benny Parsons	L. G. DeWitt	72	Chev	420	4,645
4. Buddy Baker	Bud Moore	15	Ford	419	3,585
5. Bobby Allison	Roger Penske	2	Merc	417	3,465

1976 Winston Cup GN Race No. 17 Nashville 420
July 17, 1976 Average Speed: 86.908

Driver	Owner	Car #	Make	Laps	Winnings
1. Benny Parsons	L. G. DeWitt	72	Chev	420	8,315
2. Richard Petty	Petty Enterprises	43	Dodg	420	7,140
3. Darrell Waltrip	DiGard	88	Chev	420	4,395
4. Lennie Pond	Ronnie Elder	54	Chev	419	2,685
5. Cale Yarborough	Junior Johnson	11	Chev	418	3,615

1977 Winston Cup GN Race No. 11 Music City USA 420
May 7, 1977 Average Speed: 87.490

Driver	Owner	Car #	Make	Laps	Winnings
1. Benny Parsons	L. G. DeWitt	72	Chev	420	9,565
2. Cale Yarborough	Junior Johnson	11	Chev	420	7,965
3. Darrell Waltrip	DiGard	88	Chev	418	5,215
4. Dave Marcis	Roger Penske	2	Chev	417	3,565
5. Richard Petty	Petty Enterprises	43	Dodg	416	3,465

1977 Winston Cup GN Race No. 17 Nashville 420
July 16, 1977 Average Speed: 78.999

Driver	Owner	Car #	Make	Laps	Winnings
1. Darrell Waltrip	DiGard	88	Chev	420	9,415
2. Bobby Allison	Bobby Allison	12	Mata	419	5,540
3. Richard Petty	Petty Enterprises	43	Dodg	418	4,965
4. Cale Yarborough	Junior Johnson	11	Chev	417	4,965
5. Dick Brooks	Junie Donlavey	90	Ford	416	2,515

1978 Winston Cup GN Race No. 13 Music City USA 420
June 3, 1978 Average Speed: 87.541

Driver	Owner	Car #	Make	Laps	Winnings
1. Cale Yarborough	Junior Johnson	11	Olds	420	11,215
2. Lennie Pond	Harry Ranier	54	Chev	418	5,315
3. Richard Petty	Petty Enterprises	43	Dodg	416	5,265
4. Dave Marcis	Rod Osterlund	2	Chev	415	2,465
5. Neil Bonnett	Jim Stacy	5	Dodg	413	3,715

1978 Winston Cup GN Race No. 17 Nashville 420
July 15, 1978 Average Speed: 88.924

Driver	Owner	Car #	Make	Laps	Winnings
1. Cale Yarborough	Junior Johnson	11	Olds	420	11,240
2. Darrell Waltrip	DiGard	88	Chev	418	6,715
3. Richard Childress	Richard Childress	3	Olds	415	3,860
4. Dave Marcis	Rod Osterlund	2	Chev	414	2,690
5. J. D. McDuffie	J. D. McDuffie	70	Chev	413	2,445

1979 Winston Cup GN Race No. 11 Sun-Drop Music City USA 420
May 12, 1979 Average Speed: 88.652

Driver	Owner	Car #	Make	Laps	Winnings
1. Cale Yarborough	Junior Johnson	11	Olds	420	12,275
2. Richard Petty	Petty Enterprises	43	Chev	420	8,150
3. Bobby Allison	Bud Moore	15	Ford	419	6,450
4. Dale Earnhardt	Rod Osterlund	2	Chev	419	5,350
5. J. D. McDuffie	J. D. McDuffie	70	Chev	418	3,080

1979 Winston Cup GN Race No. 18 Busch Nashville 420
July 14, 1979 Average Speed: 92.227

Driver	Owner	Car #	Make	Laps	Winnings
1. Darrell Waltrip	DiGard	88	Chev	420	14,000
2. Cale Yarborough	Junior Johnson	11	Chev	419	8,700
3. Dale Earnhardt	Rod Osterlund	2	Chev	417	7,200
4. Benny Parsons	M. C. Anderson	27	Chev	417	3,650
5. Richard Petty	Petty Enterprises	43	Chev	406	4,280

1980 Winston Cup GN Race No. 11 Music City USA 420
May 10, 1980 Average Speed: 89.471

Driver	Owner	Car #	Make	Laps	Winnings
1. Richard Petty	Petty Enterprises	43	Chev	420	15,350
2. Benny Parsons	M. C. Anderson	27	Chev	420	10,310
3. Cale Yarborough	Junior Johnson	11	Chev	420	8,660
4. Darrell Waltrip	DiGard	88	Chev	419	5,750
5. Bobby Allison	Bud Moore	15	Ford	418	5,130

1980 Winston Cup GN Race No. 18 Busch Nashville 420
July 12, 1980 Average Speed: 93.821

Driver	Owner	Car #	Make	Laps	Winnings
1. Dale Earnhardt	Rod Osterlund	2	Chev	420	14,600
2. Cale Yarborough	Junior Johnson	11	Chev	420	10,160
3. Benny Parsons	M. C. Anderson	27	Chev	420	7,910
4. Darrell Waltrip	DiGard	88	Chev	419	5,750
5. Richard Petty	Petty Enterprises	43	Chev	416	6,630

1981 Winston Cup GN Race No. 11 Melling Tool 420
May 9, 1981 Average Speed: 89.756

Driver	Owner	Car #	Make	Laps	Winnings
1. Benny Parsons	Bud Moore	15	Ford	420	15,950
2. Darrell Waltrip	Junior Johnson	11	Buick	420	10,950
3. Bobby Allison	Harry Ranier	28	Pont	420	8,500
4. Richard Petty	Petty Enterprises	43	Buick	419	6,950
5. Ricky Rudd	DiGard	88	Buick	419	7,375

1981 Winston Cup GN Race No. 18 Busch Nashville 420
July 11, 1981 Average Speed: 90.052

Driver	Owner	Car #	Make	Laps	Winnings
1. Darrell Waltrip	Junior Johnson	11	Buick	420	15,700
2. Bobby Allison	Harry Ranier	28	Buick	420	10,975
3. Benny Parsons	Bud Moore	15	Ford	420	8,750
4. Ricky Rudd	DiGard	88	Chev	419	7,450
5. Terry Labonte	Billy Hagan	44	Buick	418	6,300

1982 Winston Cup GN Race No. 10 Cracker Barrel Country Store 420
May 8, 1982 Average Speed: 83.502

Driver	Owner	Car #	Make	Laps	Winnings
1. Darrell Waltrip	Junior Johnson	11	Buick	420	24,025
2. Terry Labonte	Billy Hagan	44	Chev	419	9,095
3. Ron Bouchard	Jack Beebe	47	Buick	418	10,110
4. Joe Ruttman	Bob Rahilly & Butch Mock	75	Buick	417	4,730
5. Neil Bonnett	Bob Rogers	37	Buick	417	4,235

1982 Winston Cup GN Race No. 17 Busch Nashville 420
July 10, 1982 Average Speed: 86.524

Driver	Owner	Car #	Make	Laps	Winnings
1. Darrell Waltrip	Junior Johnson	11	Buick	420	22,025
2. Terry Labonte	Billy Hagan	44	Chev	419	8,595
3. Harry Gant	Hal Needham	33	Buick	419	6,805
4. Ricky Rudd	Richard Childress	3	Pont	419	5,360
5. Tim Richmond	Jim Stacy	2	Buick	419	4,175

Nashville Speedway *continued*

1983 Winston Cup GN Race No. 9 Marty Robbins 420
May 7, 1983 Average Speed: 70.717

Driver	Owner	Car #	Make	Laps	Winnings
1. Darrell Waltrip	Junior Johnson	11	Chev	420	25,650
2. Bobby Allison	DiGard	22	Buick	419	13,650
3. Harry Gant	Hal Needham	33	Buick	419	11,285
4. Morgan Shepherd	Jim Stacy	2	Buick	418	9,000
5. Bill Elliott	Harry Melling	9	Ford	416	4,520

1983 Winston Cup GN Race No. 17 Busch Nashville 420
July 16, 1983 Average Speed: 85.726

Driver	Owner	Car #	Make	Laps	Winnings
1. Dale Earnhardt	Bud Moore	15	Ford	420	23,125
2. Darrell Waltrip	Junior Johnson	11	Chev	420	16,425
3. Tim Richmond	Raymond Beadle	27	Pont	419	8,030
4. Bobby Allison	DiGard	22	Buick	419	9,400
5. Ricky Rudd	Richard Childress	3	Chev	417	4,770

1984 Winston Cup GN Race No. 10 Coors 420
May 12, 1984 Average Speed: 85.702

Driver	Owner	Car #	Make	Laps	Winnings
1. Darrell Waltrip	Junior Johnson	11	Chev	420	29,300
2. Neil Bonnett	Junior Johnson	12	Chev	420	13,500
3. Geoff Bodine	Rick Hendrick	5	Chev	420	12,025
4. Ricky Rudd	Bud Moore	15	Ford	420	10,450
5. Ron Bouchard	Jack Beebe	47	Buick	420	6,785

1984 Winston Cup GN Race No. 17 Pepsi 420
July 14, 1984 Average Speed: 80.908

Driver	Owner	Car #	Make	Laps	Winnings
1. Geoff Bodine	Rick Hendrick	5	Chev	420	25,800
2. Darrell Waltrip	Junior Johnson	11	Chev	420	16,125
3. Dale Earnhardt	Richard Childress	3	Chev	419	10,775
4. Ron Bouchard	Jack Beebe	47	Buick	419	6,330
5. Bobby Allison	DiGard	22	Buick	419	13,450

Smoky Mountain Raceway
Maryville, TN
Half-mile Paved Track

(aka Smoky Mountain Race Park; Smoky Mountain Speedway) Half-mile dirt track opened circa 1965. First NASCAR Winston Cup (then Grand National) race staged on 8/13/65 (won by Dick Hutcherson). Track paved in 1968. Final Winston Cup Grand National race was 4/15/71 (won by Richard Petty). Track still active.

Winston Cup Starts
Henley Gray 12
Elmo Langley 12
Wendell Scott 12

Winston Cup Victories
Richard Petty 6

Winston Cup Poles
David Pearson 3

Winston Cup Money
Richard Petty $8,170

Most Cars Started
33—July 27, 1967 Smoky 200

Fewest Cars Started
20—June 8, 1967 East Tennessee 200

Narrowest Margin of Victory
1 car length—July 25, 1968
1 car length—July 27, 1969
1 car length—July 24, 1970

Slowest Race
65.455 MPH—August 13, 1965

Race Record
88.697 MPH—April 15, 1971 Maryville 200

Most Cautions
N/A

Most Race Leaders
3—July 28, 1966 Smoky 200
3—June 6, 1968
3—July 27, 1969 Smoky 200
3—July 24, 1970 East Tennessee 200
3—April 15, 1971 Maryville 200

Most Cars Running at Finish
21—July 28, 1966 Smoky 200
21—July 27, 1967 Smoky 200

1965 Grand National Race No. 38
August 13, 1965 Average Speed: 65.455

Driver	Owner	Car #	Make	Laps	Winnings
1. Dick Hutcherson	Holman-Moody	29	65 Ford	200	1,000
2. Buddy Baker	Buck Baker	88	64 Dodg	196	600
3. Richard Petty	Petty Enterprises	43	64 Plym	195	400
4. Jim Hunter	Casper Hensley	82	64 Pont	191	300
5. Paul Lewis	Paul Lewis	1	64 Ford	186	275

1966 Grand National Race No. 24 East Tennessee 200
June 9, 1966 Average Speed: 71.986

Driver	Owner	Car #	Make	Laps	Winnings
1. David Pearson	Cotton Owens	6	64 Dodg	200	1,000
2. Buck Baker	Buck Baker	87	66 Olds	198	600
3. Paul Lewis	Paul Lewis	1	65 Plym	198	400
4. Elmo Langley	Henry Woodfield	64	64 Ford	197	300
5. Doug Cooper	Bob Cooper	02	65 Plym	196	275

1966 Grand National Race No. 35 Smoky 200
July 28, 1966 Average Speed: 69.822

Driver	Owner	Car #	Make	Laps	Winnings
1. Paul Lewis	Paul Lewis	1	65 Plym	200	1,000
2. David Pearson	Cotton Owens	6	65 Dodg	200	600
3. J. T. Putney	J. T. Putney	19	66 Chev	199	400
4. Doug Cooper	Bob Cooper	02	65 Plym	195	300
5. Bobby Allison	Bobby Allison	2	65 Chev	194	275

1967 Grand National Race No. 23 East Tennessee 200
June 8, 1967 Average Speed: 72.919

Driver	Owner	Car #	Make	Laps	Winnings
1. Richard Petty	Petty Enterprises	43	67 Plym	200	1,000
2. Jim Paschal	Tom Friedkin	14	67 Plym	200	600
3. Dick Hutcherson	Bondy Long	29	67 Ford	200	400
4. Friday Hassler	Red Sharp	39	66 Chev	199	300
5. Elmo Langley	L. G. DeWitt	4	66 Ford	199	275

1967 Grand National Race No. 34 Smoky 200
July 27, 1967 Average Speed: 65.765

Driver	Owner	Car #	Make	Laps	Winnings
1. Dick Hutcherson	Bondy Long	29	67 Ford	200	1,050
2. Richard Petty	Petty Enterprises	43	67 Plym	200	600
3. Jim Hunter	Casper Hensley	85	65 Chev	199	400
4. James Hylton	Bud Hartje	48	65 Dodg	199	300
5. Bobby Allison	Bobby Allison	2	65 Chev	197	275

1968 Grand National Race No. 21
June 6, 1968 Average Speed: 76.743

Driver	Owner	Car #	Make	Laps	Winnings
1. Richard Petty	Petty Enterprises	43	68 Plym	200	1,200
2. Pete Hamilton	Rocky Hinton	5	68 Ford	199	600
3. James Hylton	James Hylton	48	67 Dodg	199	400
4. Curtis Turner	Tom Friedkin	14	68 Plym	195	300
5. John Sears	L. G. DeWitt	4	66 Ford	192	275

1968 Grand National Race No. 31 Smoky 200
July 25, 1968 Average Speed: 71.513

Driver	Owner	Car #	Make	Laps	Winnings
1. Richard Petty	Petty Enterprises	43	68 Plym	200	1,200
2. Bud Moore	Bondy Long	29	68 Ford	200	600
3. David Pearson	Holman-Moody	17	68 Ford	199	400
4. Buddy Baker	Ray Fox	3	68 Dodg	199	300
5. James Hylton	James Hylton	48	67 Dodg	197	275

1969 Grand National Race No. 23 Maryville 300
June 5, 1969 Average Speed: 81.706

Driver	Owner	Car #	Make	Laps	Winnings
1. Bobby Isaac	Nord Krauskopf	71	69 Dodg	300	1,400
2. David Pearson	Holman-Moody	17	69 Ford	294	1,250
3. James Hylton	James Hylton	48	69 Dodg	293	825
4. Neil Castles	Neil Castles	06	67 Plym	292	650
5. Elmo Langley	Elmo Langley	64	68 Ford	287	500

1969 Grand National Race No. 35 Smoky 200
July 27, 1969 Average Speed: 82.417

Driver	Owner	Car #	Make	Laps	Winnings
1. Richard Petty	Petty Enterprises	43	69 Ford	200	1,000
2. David Pearson	Holman-Moody	17	69 Ford	200	800
3. Neil Castles	Neil Castles	06	67 Plym	195	400
4. Elmo Langley	Elmo Langley	64	68 Ford	189	350
5. James Hylton	James Hylton	48	68 Dodg	189	325

1970 Grand National Race No. 17 Maryville 200
May 28, 1970 Average Speed: 82.558

Driver	Owner	Car #	Make	Laps	Winnings
1. Bobby Isaac	Nord Krauskopf	71	70 Dodg	200	1,500
2. James Hylton	James Hylton	48	69 Ford	199	900
3. Neil Castles	Neil Castles	06	69 Dodg	199	500
4. Dick Brooks	Dick Brooks	32	69 Plym	197	350
5. Dave Marcis	Dave Marcis	30	69 Dodg	195	325

Smoky Mountain Raceway *continued*

1970 Grand National Race No. 29 East Tennessee 200
July 24, 1970 Average Speed: 84.956

Driver	Owner	Car #	Make	Laps	Winnings
1. Richard Petty	Petty Enterprises	43	70 Plym	200	1,500
2. Bobby Isaac	Nord Krauskopf	71	69 Dodg	200	900
3. Dick Brooks	Dick Brooks	32	69 Plym	198	500
4. James Hylton	James Hylton	48	69 Ford	196	350
5. Friday Hassler	Friday Hassler	39	69 Chev	196	325

1971 Winston Cup GN Race No. 13 Maryville 200
April 15, 1971 Average Speed: 88.697

Driver	Owner	Car #	Make	Laps	Winnings
1. Richard Petty	Petty Enterprises	43	71 Plym	200	1,000
2. Benny Parsons	L. G. DeWitt	72	70 Ford	200	600
3. Friday Hassler	Friday Hassler	39	69 Chev	199	400
4. Elmo Langley	Elmo Langley	64	70 Ford	196	350
5. Dick Brooks	Mario Rossi	22	70 Dodg	196	325

Tennessee-Carolina Speedway
Newport, TN
Half-mile Dirt Track

(aka Newport Fairgrounds; Cocke County Fairgrounds) Half-mile dirt track opened in 1956. First NASCAR Winston Cup (then Grand National) race staged on 10/7/56 (won by Fireball Roberts). Only other Grand National race run 6/15/57 (also won by Roberts). Track closed in 1967.

Winston Cup Starts
11 drivers tied with 2

Winston Cup Victories
Fireball Roberts 2

Winston Cup Poles
Joe Eubanks 1
Speedy Thompson 1

Winston Cup Money
Fireball Roberts $1,850

Most Cars Started
22—October 7, 1956

Fewest Cars Started
17—June 15, 1957

Narrowest Margin of Victory
N/A

Slowest Race
60.687 MPH—June 15, 1957

Race Record
61.475 MPH—October 7, 1956

Most Race Leaders
N/A

Most Cars Running at Finish
14—October 7, 1956

1956 Grand National Race No. 51
October 7, 1956 Average Speed: 61.475

Driver	Owner	Car #	Make	Laps	Winnings
1. Fireball Roberts	Pete DePaolo	22	56 Ford	200	850
2. Buck Baker	Carl Kiekhaefer	300B	56 Chrys	200	625
3. Bill Amick	Pete DePaolo	97	56 Ford	199	450
4. Joe Weatherly	John Whitford	31	56 Ford	197	350
5. Herb Thomas	Herb Thomas	92	56 Chev	196	310

1957 Grand National Race No. 23
June 15, 1957 Average Speed: 60.687

Driver	Owner	Car #	Make	Laps	Winnings
1. Fireball Roberts	Fireball Roberts	22	57 Ford	200	1,000
2. Marvin Panch	Marvin Panch	98	57 Ford	200	625
3. Buck Baker	Buck Baker	87	57 Chev	200	400
4. Jack Smith	Jack Smith	47	57 Chev	199	295
5. Jim Paschal	Jim Paschal	17	57 Merc	190	255

Texas

Meyer Speedway
Houston, TX
Half-mile Paved Track

(aka Joseph F. Meyer Speedway) Half-mile paved oval opened in October 1959. Only NASCAR Winston Cup (then Grand National) race staged on 6/23/71 (won by Bobby Allison). Track closed in 1979.

Winston Cup Victories
Bobby Allison   1

Winston Cup Poles
Bobby Allison   1

Winston Cup Money
Bobby Allison $2,200

Most Cars Started
14—June 23, 1971 Space City 300

Narrowest Margin of Victory
2 laps plus—June 23, 1971
Space City 300

Race Record
73.489 MPH—June 23, 1971
Space City 300

Most Race Leaders
3—June 23, 1971 Space City 300

Most Cars Running at Finish
11—June 23, 1971 Space City 300

1971 Winston Cup GN Race No. 25 Space City 300
June 23, 1971 Average Speed: 73.489

Driver	Owner	Car #	Make	Laps	Winnings
1. Bobby Allison	Bobby Allison	12	70 Dodg	300	2,200
2. James Hylton	James Hylton	48	70 Ford	298	1,500
3. Walter Ballard	Walter Ballard	30	71 Ford	292	1,000
4. Elmo Langley	Elmo Langley	64	69 Merc	290	700
5. Frank Warren	H. B. Bailey	36	70 Pont	289	650

Texas World Speedway
College Station, TX
2-mile Paved Track

(aka Texas Int'l Speedway) Built in 1969 by Larry LoPatin. Part of the American Raceways complex. First NASCAR Winston Cup (then Grand National) race staged on 12/12/69 (won by Bobby Isaac, his first superspeedway victory). Final Winston Cup Grand National race staged on 6/7/81 (won by Benny Parsons, before a sparse crowd of 18,000). Track closed in 1989, and was purchased by Japanese businessmen in 1991. The grandstands were later declared unsafe and only a few minor sportscar events were staged thereafter.

Winston Cup Starts
Bobby Allison   8
Cecil Gordon   8
James Hylton   8
Benny Parsons   8
Richard Petty   8

Winston Cup Victories
Richard Petty   3

Winston Cup Poles
Buddy Baker   3

Winston Cup Money
Richard Petty $94,755

Most Cars Started
49—December 12, 1971 Texas 500

Fewest Cars Started
31—June 1, 1980 NASCAR 400

Narrowest Margin of Victory
1/2 car length—November 12, 1972
Texas 500

Slowest Race
132.475 MPH—June 7, 1981
Budweiser NASCAR 400

Race Record
159.046 MPH—June 1, 1980
NASCAR 400

Most Cautions
5—November 12, 1972 Texas 500
5—June 10, 1973 Alamo 500
5—June 7, 1981 Budweiser NASCAR 400

Most Race Leaders
9—June 7, 1981 Budweiser NASCAR 400

Most Cars Running at Finish
29—November 12, 1972 Texas 500

1969 Grand National Race No. 54 Texas 500
December 7, 1969 Average Speed: 144.277

Driver	Owner	Car #	Make	Laps	Winnings
1. Bobby Isaac	Nord Krauskopf	71	69 Dodg	250	15,640
2. Donnie Allison	Banjo Matthews	27	69 Ford	248	8,200
3. Benny Parsons	Russ Dawson	18	69 Ford	247	4,000
4. James Hylton	James Hylton	48	69 Dodg	239	3,700
5. Dick Brooks	Dick Brooks	32	69 Plym	237	3,350

1971 Winston Cup GN Race No. 48 Texas 500
December 12, 1971 Average Speed: 144.000

Driver	Owner	Car #	Make	Laps	Winnings
1. Richard Petty	Petty Enterprises	43	71 Plym	250	13,395
2. Buddy Baker	Petty Enterprises	11	71 Dodg	250	6,805
3. Bobby Allison	Holman-Moody	12	71 Merc	248	5,125
4. Pete Hamilton	Cotton Owens	6	71 Plym	245	3,865
5. Bill Dennis	Junie Donlavey	90	69 Merc	239	3,100

1972 Winston Cup GN Race No. 16 Lone Star 500
June 25, 1972 Average Speed: 144.185

Driver	Owner	Car #	Make	Laps	Winnings
1. Richard Petty	Petty Enterprises	43	72 Plym	250	16,245
2. Bobby Allison	R. Howard & J. Johnson	12	72 Chev	249	8,670
3. Coo Coo Marlin	H. B. Cunningham	14	72 Chev	244	5,045
4. Benny Parsons	L. G. DeWitt	72	71 Merc	244	4,355
5. Bobby Isaac	Nord Krauskopf	71	72 Dodg	244	5,400

1972 Winston Cup GN Race No. 31 Texas 500
November 12, 1972 Average Speed: 147.059

Driver	Owner	Car #	Make	Laps	Winnings
1. Buddy Baker	Nord Krauskopf	71	71 Dodg	250	14,920
2. A. J. Foyt	Wood Brothers	2	71 Merc	250	7,545
3. Richard Petty	Petty Enterprises	43	72 Dodg	250	8,220
4. Bobby Allison	R. Howard & J. Johnson	12	72 Chev	249	7,345
5. Hershel McGriff	Beryl Jackson	04	72 Plym	248	3,725

1973 Winston Cup GN Race No. 14 Alamo 500
June 10, 1973 Average Speed: 142.114

Driver	Owner	Car #	Make	Laps	Winnings
1. Richard Petty	Petty Enterprises	43	73 Dodg	250	17,820
2. Darrell Waltrip	Darrell Waltrip	95	71 Merc	248	7,720
3. Joe Frasson	Joe Frasson	18	73 Dodg	247	5,795
4. Cale Yarborough	R. Howard & J. Johnson	11	73 Chev	247	6,445
5. Cecil Gordon	Cecil Gordon	24	72 Chev	245	4,200

1979 Winston Cup GN Race No. 14 Texas 400
June 3, 1979 Average Speed: 156.216

Driver	Owner	Car #	Make	Laps	Winnings
1. Darrell Waltrip	DiGard	88	Chev	200	21,750
2. Bobby Allison	Bud Moore	15	Ford	199	14,600
3. Buddy Baker	Harry Ranier	28	Chev	199	13,950
4. Cale Yarborough	Junior Johnson	11	Chev	199	12,150
5. Terry Labonte	Billy Hagan	44	Chev	196	12,150

1980 Winston Cup GN Race No. 14 NASCAR 400
June 1, 1980 Average Speed: 159.046

Driver	Owner	Car #	Make	Laps	Winnings
1. Cale Yarborough	Junior Johnson	11	Chev	200	21,000
2. Richard Petty	Petty Enterprises	43	Chev	199	16,800
3. Bobby Allison	Bud Moore	15	Ford	199	13,500
4. Darrell Waltrip	DiGard	88	Chev	197	11,550
5. Terry Labonte	Billy Hagan	44	Chev	196	8,680

1981 Winston Cup GN Race No. 14 Budweiser NASCAR 400
June 7, 1981 Average Speed: 132.475

Driver	Owner	Car #	Make	Laps	Winnings
1. Benny Parsons	Bud Moore	15	Ford	200	22,750
2. Dale Earnhardt	Rod Osterlund	2	Pont	200	18,650
3. Bobby Allison	Harry Ranier	28	Buick	200	14,650
4. Richard Petty	Petty Enterprises	43	Buick	199	12,550
5. Dave Marcis	Dave Marcis	71	Buick	198	8,935

Virginia

Langley Field Speedway
Hampton, VA
.4-mile Paved Track

(aka Dude Ranch Speedway; Langley Field; Langley Speedway) .333-mile dirt oval opened circa 1949. Closed in 1953. .4-mile dirt oval re-opened in 1963. First NASCAR Winston Cup (then Grand National) race staged on 5/15/64 (won by Ned Jarrett). Track paved and re-measured at .395-mile in 1968. Final Winston Cup Grand National race was run 11/22/70 (won by Bobby Allison). Track active today.

Winston Cup Starts
Elmo Langley 9
Wendell Scott 9

Winston Cup Victories
David Pearson 3

Winston Cup Poles
David Pearson 3
Richard Petty 3

Winston Cup Money
David Pearson $4,920

Most Cars Started
30—November 22, 1970 Tidewater 300

Fewest Cars Started
16—May 20, 1967 Tidewater 250

Narrowest Margin of Victory
100 yards—May 18, 1970 Tidewater 250

Slowest Race
57.815 MPH—May 14, 1965
Tidewater 250

Race Record
75.789 MPH—May 17, 1969
Tidewater 375

Most Cautions
2—May 18, 1970 Tidewater 300
2—November 22, 1970 Tidewater 300

Most Race Leaders
3—May 20, 1967 Tidewater 250
3—May 18, 1968 Tidewater 250
3—May 18, 1970 Tidewater 300

Most Cars Running at Finish
20—November 22, 1970 Tidewater 300

1964 Grand National Race No. 22 Tidewater 250
May 15, 1964 Average Speed: 65.300

Driver	Owner	Car #	Make	Laps	Winnings
1. Ned Jarrett	Bondy Long	11	64 Ford	250	1,000
2. Marvin Panch	Wood Brothers	21	64 Ford	247	600
3. Buddy Baker	J. C. Parker	87	63 Dodg	242	400
4. Wendell Scott	Wendell Scott	34	63 Ford	240	300
5. Curtis Crider	Curtis Crider	02	63 Merc	234	275

1965 Grand National Race No. 16 Tidewater 250
May 14, 1965 Average Speed: 57.815

Driver	Owner	Car #	Make	Laps	Winnings
1. Ned Jarrett	Bondy Long	11	65 Ford	250	1,000
2. Dick Hutcherson	Holman-Moody	29	65 Ford	249	600
3. Elmo Langley	Elmo Langley	64	64 Ford	240	400
4. Buddy Arrington	Buddy Arrington	6	64 Dodg	237	300
5. Neil Castles	Buck Baker	86	65 Plym	233	275

1966 Grand National Race No. 16 Tidewater 250
May 7, 1966 Average Speed: 60.616

Driver	Owner	Car #	Make	Laps	Winnings
1. Richard Petty	Petty Enterprises	43	66 Plym	250	1,000
2. James Hylton	Bud Hartje	48	65 Dodg	250	600
3. Neil Castles	Buck Baker	86	66 Plym	246	400
4. Elmo Langley	Henry Woodfield	64	64 Ford	244	300
5. Tom Pistone	Tom Pistone	59	64 Ford	244	275

1967 Grand National Race No. 19 Tidewater 250
May 20, 1967 Average Speed: 66.704

Driver	Owner	Car #	Make	Laps	Winnings
1. Richard Petty	Petty Enterprises	43	67 Plym	250	1,000
2. Bobby Allison	Cotton Owens	6	67 Dodg	250	600
3. James Hylton	Bud Hartje	48	65 Dodg	246	400
4. Elmo Langley	Henry Woodfield	64	66 Ford	233	300
5. Donnie Allison	Bobby Allison	2	65 Chev	230	275

1968 Grand National Race No. 17 Tidewater 250
May 18, 1968 Average Speed: 71.457

Driver	Owner	Car #	Make	Laps	Winnings
1. David Pearson	Holman-Moody	17	68 Ford	250	1,000
2. Bobby Isaac	Nord Krauskopf	71	67 Dodg	250	600
3. Buddy Baker	Ray Fox	3	67 Dodg	249	400
4. James Hylton	James Hylton	48	67 Dodg	246	300
5. Pete Hamilton	Rocky Hinton	5	68 Ford	243	275

1968 Grand National Race No. 38 Crabber 250
August 24, 1968 Average Speed: 75.582

Driver	Owner	Car #	Make	Laps	Winnings
1. David Pearson	Holman-Moody	17	68 Ford	250	1,000
2. Richard Petty	Petty Enterprises	43	68 Plym	250	800
3. Bobby Isaac	Nord Krauskopf	71	67 Dodg	249	400
4. Bobby Allison	Bobby Allison	2	66 Chev	247	300
5. Ray Hendrick	Tom Friedkin	15	68 Plym	245	255

1969 Grand National Race No. 20 Tidewater 375
May 17, 1969 Average Speed: 75.789

Driver	Owner	Car #	Make	Laps	Winnings
1. David Pearson	Holman-Moody	17	69 Ford	375	2,700
2. James Hylton	James Hylton	48	69 Dodg	370	1,500
3. Dave Marcis	Milt Lunda	30	69 Dodg	369	1,000
4. Bobby Isaac	Nord Krauskopf	71	69 Dodg	368	750
5. Neil Castles	Neil Castles	06	Plym	366	600

1970 Grand National Race No. 15 Tidewater 300
May 18, 1970 Average Speed: 73.245

Driver	Owner	Car #	Make	Laps	Winnings
1. Bobby Isaac	Nord Krauskopf	71	70 Dodg	300	1,700
2. Bobby Allison	Bobby Allison	22	69 Dodg	298	1,035
3. Neil Castles	Neil Castles	06	69 Dodg	298	630
4. James Hylton	James Hylton	48	69 Ford	296	440
5. Benny Parsons	L. G. DeWitt	72	69 Ford	296	350

Langley Field Speedway *continued*

1970 Grand National Race No. 48 Tidewater 300
November 22, 1970 Average Speed: 69.584

Driver	Owner	Car #	Make	Laps	Winnings
1. Bobby Allison	Bobby Allison	22	70 Dodg	300	1,635
2. Benny Parsons	L. G. DeWitt	72	69 Ford	300	1,100
3. Pete Hamilton	Dick Brooks	32	69 Plym	299	600
4. John Sears	John Sears	4	69 Dodg	298	425
5. James Hylton	James Hylton	48	70 Ford	297	355

Martinsville Speedway
Martinsville, VA
.526-mile Paved Track

Half-mile dirt track opened in July 1947. First NASCAR Winston Cup (then Grand National) race staged on 9/25/49 (won by Red Byron). Track paved in mid-1955, between the spring and fall races. Track re-measured as .525-mile in 1970. Re-measured at .526-mile in late '80s.

Winston Cup Starts
Richard Petty   67

Winston Cup Victories
Richard Petty   15

Winston Cup Poles
Darrell Waltrip   8

Winston Cup Money
Darrell Waltrip $901,650

Most Cars Started
47—April 20, 1958 Virginia 500
47—September 27, 1959
Virginia Sweepstakes 500

Fewest Cars Started
15—September 25, 1949

Narrowest Margin of Victory
1 car length—September 25, 1960
Old Dominion 500

Slowest Race
42.862 MPH—April 6, 1952

Race Record
82.223 MPH—September 22, 1996
Goody's 500

Most Cautions
17—September 28, 1980
Old Dominion 500

Most Race Leaders
12—September 22, 1991 Goody's 500

Most Cars Running at Finish
33—April 23, 1993 Hanes 500

1949 Strictly Stock Race No. 6
September 25, 1949

Driver	Owner	Car #	Make	Laps	Winnings
1. Red Byron	Raymond Parks	22	49 Olds	200	1,500
2. Lee Petty	Petty Enterprises	42	49 Plym	197	750
3. Ray Erickson	Ed Hastings	5	49 Merc	197	400
4. Clyde Minter	Mitchell Motors	19	46 Ford	187	300
5. Bill Blair	Sam Rice	2	49 Chev	186	175

1950 Grand National Race No. 4
May 21, 1950

Driver	Owner	Car #	Make	Laps	Winnings
1. Curtis Turner	John Eanes	41	50 Olds	150	1,250
2. Jim Paschal	Al Wheatley	79	47 Ford	148	600
3. Lee Petty	Petty Enterprises	42	49 Plym	144	400
4. Glenn Dunnaway	Glenn Dunnaway	49	49 Plym	144	300
5. Clyde Minter	Clyde Minter	19	50 Merc	143	225

1950 Grand National Race No. 17
October 15, 1950

Driver	Owner	Car #	Make	Laps	Winnings
1. Herb Thomas	Herb Thomas	92	50 Plym	200	1,000
2. Lee Petty	Petty Enterprises	42	49 Plym	199	600
3. Buck Baker	Griffin Motors	87	40 Olds	198	400
4. Fonty Flock	Frank Christian	7	50 Olds	197	325
5. Weldon Adams	Harold Mays	52	50 Plym	193	225

1951 Grand National Race No. 8
May 6, 1951

Driver	Owner	Car #	Make	Laps	Winnings
1. Curtis Turner	John Eanes	41	50 Olds	200	1,000
2. Frank Mundy	Perry Smith	23	51 Stud	—	600
3. Tim Flock	Ted Chester	91	51 Olds	—	400
4. Herb Thomas	Herb Thomas	92	50 Plym	—	300
5. Fonty Flock	Frank Christian	14	50 Olds	—	250

1951 Grand National Race No. 34
October 14, 1951

Driver	Owner	Car #	Make	Laps	Winnings
1. Frank Mundy	Ted Chester	7	51 Olds	200	1,000
2. Lee Petty	Petty Enterprises	42	51 Plym	—	600
3. Billy Myers	R. G. Shelton	22	51 Huds	—	500
4. Bill Snowden	Bill Snowden	16	51 Ford	—	400
5. Jimmie Lewallen	Hubert Hamilton	0	51 Plym	—	300

1952 Grand National Race No. 5
April 6, 1952 Average Speed: 42.862

Driver	Owner	Car #	Make	Laps	Winnings
1. Dick Rathmann	Walt Chapman	120	51 Huds	200	1,000
2. Bill Blair	George Hutchens	2	52 Olds	200	700
3. Perk Brown	R. G. Shelton	22	51 Huds	199	450
4. Lee Petty	Petty Enterprises	42	51 Plym	199	350
5. Bobby Courtwright	Bobby Courtwright		50 Olds	197	200

1952 Grand National Race No. 31
October 19, 1952 Average Speed: 47.556

Driver	Owner	Car #	Make	Laps	Winnings
1. Herb Thomas	Herb Thomas	92	52 Huds	200	1,000
2. Fonty Flock	Frank Christian	14	52 Olds	200	700
3. Lee Petty	Petty Enterprises	42	52 Plym	199	450
4. Tim Flock	Ted Chester	91	52 Huds	195	350
5. Johnny Patterson	H. B. Ranier	58	52 Huds	194	200

1953 Grand National Race No. 11
May 17, 1953

Driver	Owner	Car #	Make	Laps	Winnings
1. Lee Petty	Petty Enterprises	42	53 Dodg	200	1,000
2. Herb Thomas	Herb Thomas	92	53 Huds	200	700
3. Dick Rathmann	Walt Chapman	120	53 Huds	—	450
4. Ray Duhigg	J. H. Petty	44	52 Plym	—	350
5. Ralph Liguori		46	53 Linc	—	200

1953 Grand National Race No. 36
October 18, 1953 Average Speed: 56.013

Driver	Owner	Car #	Make	Laps	Winnings
1. Jim Paschal	George Hutchens	80	53 Dodg	200	1,000
2. Lee Petty	Petty Enterprises	42	53 Dodg	200	700
3. Bill Blair	Bill Blair	2	53 Olds	199	450
4. Fonty Flock	Frank Christian	14	53 Huds	199	350
5. Carl Burris			51 Plym	194	200

1954 Grand National Race No. 12
May 16, 1954 Average Speed: 46.153

Driver	Owner	Car #	Make	Laps	Winnings
1. Jim Paschal	Griffin Motors	87	53 Olds	200	1,000
2. Lee Petty	Petty Enterprises	42	54 Chrys	199	650
3. Curtis Turner	Carmen Amica	21	53 Olds	198	450
4. Al Keller	George Miller	23	54 Huds	195	350
5. Laird Bruner	Frank Dodge	28	53 Olds	187	300

Martinsville Speedway *continued*

1954 Grand National Race No. 36
October 17, 1954 Average Speed: 44.547

Driver	Owner	Car #	Make	Laps	Winnings
1. Lee Petty	Petty Enterprises	42	Chrys	165	1,000
2. Hershel McGriff	Frank Christian	14	54 Olds	165	650
3. Buck Baker	Griffin Motors	87	54 Olds	163	450
4. Dick Rathmann	John Ditz	3	54 Huds	163	350
5. Jim Reed	Jim Reed	7	52 Huds	162	300

1955 Grand National Race No. 15
May 15, 1955 Average Speed: 52.554

Driver	Owner	Car #	Make	Laps	Winnings
1. Tim Flock	Carl Kiekhaefer	300	55 Chrys	200	1,000
2. Lee Petty	Petty Enterprises	42	55 Chrys	200	650
3. Junior Johnson	B & L Motors	55	55 Olds	198	450
4. Jimmie Lewallen	Ernest Woods	88	55 Olds	198	350
5. Bob Welborn	J. H. Petty	44	55 Chev	194	300

1955 Grand National Race No. 42
October 16, 1955

Driver	Owner	Car #	Make	Laps	Winnings
1. Speedy Thompson	Carl Kiekhaefer	30	55 Chrys	200	1,100
2. Bob Welborn	Bob Welborn	49	55 Chev	200	700
3. Jim Paschal	J. H. Petty	44	55 Chev	200	475
4. Herb Thomas	Herb Thomas	92	55 Chev	199	365
5. Jim Reed	Jim Reed	7	55 Chev	198	310

1956 Grand National Race No. 18 Virginia 500
May 20, 1956 Average Speed: 60.824

Driver	Owner	Car #	Make	Laps	Winnings
1. Buck Baker	Carl Kiekhaefer	502	56 Dodg	500	3,100
2. Speedy Thompson	Carl Kiekhaefer	500	56 Dodg	500	1,500
3. Lee Petty	Petty Enterprises	42	56 Dodg	497	1,025
4. Paul Goldsmith	Smokey Yunick	3	56 Chev	596	750
5. Gwyn Staley	Hubert Westmoreland	2	56 Chev	491	600

1956 Grand National Race No. 54 Mixed 400
October 28, 1956 Average Speed: 61.136

Driver	Owner	Car #	Make	Laps	Winnings
1. Jack Smith	Carl Kiekhaefer	5	56 Dodg	400	2,275
2. Marvin Panch	Tom Harbison	98	56 Ford	400	1,400
3. Bill Amick	Pete DePaolo	97	56 Ford	400	950
4. Speedy Thompson	Carl Kiekhaefer	300	56 Chrys	396	700
5. Fireball Roberts	Pete DePaolo	22	56 Ford	394	600

1957 Grand National Race No. 17 Virginia 500
May 19, 1957 Average Speed: 57.318

Driver	Owner	Car #	Make	Laps	Winnings
1. Buck Baker	Hugh Babb	87	57 Chev	441	3,170
2. Curtis Turner	Pete DePaolo	99	57 Ford	441	1,770
3. Tom Pistone	Hugh Babb	50	57 Chev	441	1,125
4. Billy Myers	Bill Stroppe	14	57 Merc	441	980
5. Lee Petty	Petty Enterprises	42	57 Olds	440	675

1957 Grand National Race No. 49 Sweepstakes 500
October 6, 1957 Average Speed: 63.025

Driver	Owner	Car #	Make	Laps	Winnings
1. Bob Welborn	Bob Welborn	49	57 Chev	500	3,100
2. Jimmy Massey	Wood Brothers	11	56 Ford	500	1,975
3. Lee Petty	Petty Enterprises	42	57 Olds	498	1,425
4. Rex White	Bob Welborn	44	57 Chev	497	1,150
5. Joe Weatherly	Holman-Moody	12	57 Ford	493	850

1958 Grand National Race No. 12 Virginia 500
April 20, 1958 Average Speed: 66.007

Driver	Owner	Car #	Make	Laps	Winnings
1. Bob Welborn	J. H. Petty	4	57 Chev	500	3,640
2. Rex White	J. H. Petty	44	57 Chev	500	1,675
3. Jim Reed	Jim Reed	7	57 Ford	500	1,125
4. Whitey Norman	Whitey Norman	41	57 Chev	495	800
5. Marvin Panch	John Whitford	98	57 Ford	494	675

1958 Grand National Race No. 49 Old Dominion 500
October 12, 1958 Average Speed: 64.344

Driver	Owner	Car #	Make	Laps	Winnings
1. Fireball Roberts	Frank Strickland	22	57 Chev	350	2,875
2. Speedy Thompson	Speedy Thompson	46	57 Chev	349	1,925
3. Rex White	Rex White	40	58 Chev	348	1,405
4. Bobby Johns	Shorty Johns	77	57 Chev	347	1,075
5. Buck Baker	Buck Baker	87	58 Chev	347	850

1959 Grand National Race No. 13 Virginia 500
May 3, 1959 Average Speed: 59.512

Driver	Owner	Car #	Make	Laps	Winnings
1. Lee Petty	Petty Enterprises	42	57 Olds	500	3,630
2. Johnny Beauchamp	Beau Morgan	76	57 Chev	495	1,625
3. Junior Johnson	Paul Spaulding	11	57 Ford	495	1,205
4. Tom Pistone	Carl Rupert	59	59 Ford	491	775
5. Roy Tyner	Roy Tyner	9	57 Chev	491	600

1959 Grand National Race No. 41 Virginia Sweepstakes 500
September 27, 1959 Average Speed: 60.500

Driver	Owner	Car #	Make	Laps	Winnings
1. Rex White	Rex White	4	59 Chev	500	3,250
2. Glen Wood	Wood Brothers	16	58 Ford	500	1,975
3. Jim Reed	Jim Reed	7	59 Chev	497	1,425
4. Tommy Irwin	Tommy Irwin	36	59 Ford	497	1,175
5. Speedy Thompson	W. J. Ridgeway	22	59 Chev	497	900

1960 Grand National Race No. 10 Virginia 500
April 10, 1960 Average Speed: 63.943

Driver	Owner	Car #	Make	Laps	Winnings
1. Richard Petty	Petty Enterprises	43	60 Plym	500	3,340
2. Jimmy Massey	Wood Brothers	21	58 Ford	500	1,535
3. Glen Wood	Wood Brothers	24	58 Ford	499	1,155
4. Rex White	Rex White	4	60 Chev	499	835
5. Bob Welborn	Bob Welborn	49	60 Chev	495	650

1960 Grand National Race No. 40 Old Dominion 500
September 25, 1960 Average Speed: 60.439

Driver	Owner	Car #	Make	Laps	Winnings
1. Rex White	Rex White	4	60 Chev	500	3,110
2. Joe Weatherly	Holman-Moody	12	60 Ford	500	1,790
3. Junior Johnson	John Masoni	27	59 Chev	499	975
4. Jim Paschal	Petty Enterprises	44	60 Plym	497	625
5. Buck Baker	Buck Baker	87	60 Chev	494	575

1961 Grand National Race No. 13 Virginia 500
April 9, 1961 Average Speed: 68.366

Driver	Owner	Car #	Make	Laps	Winnings
1. Fred Lorenzen	Holman-Moody	28	61 Ford	149	1,150
2. Rex White	Rex White	4	61 Ford	149	1,275
3. Glen Wood	Wood Brothers	21	61 Ford	147	500
4. Emanuel Zervakis	Monroe Shook	85	61 Chev	147	325
5. Ned Jarrett	Bee Gee Holloway	11	61 Chev	147	450

Martinsville Speedway *continued*

1961 Grand National Race No. 18 Virginia 500 Sweepstakes
April 30, 1961 Average Speed: 66.278

Driver	Owner	Car #	Make	Laps	Winnings
1. Junior Johnson	Rex Lovette	27	61 Pont	500	2,315
2. Emanuel Zervakis	Monroe Shook	85	61 Chev	496	1,200
3. Fireball Roberts	Jim Stephens	75	61 Pont	496	825
4. Tommy Irwin	Tom Daniels	2	60 Chev	491	625
5. Buck Baker	Buck Baker	86	61 Chrys	491	550

1961 Grand National Race No. 47 Old Dominion 500
September 24, 1961 Average Speed: 62.586

Driver	Owner	Car #	Make	Laps	Winnings
1. Joe Weatherly	Bud Moore	8	61 Pont	500	3,595
2. Rex White	Rex White	4	61 Pont	500	2,000
3. Junior Johnson	Rex Lovette	27	61 Pont	499	1,570
4. Fireball Roberts	Cotton Owens	6	61 Pont	496	850
5. Ken Rush	Lynn Holloway	59	61 Pont	494	750

1962 Grand National Race No. 15 Virginia 500
April 22, 1962 Average Speed: 66.425

Driver	Owner	Car #	Make	Laps	Winnings
1. Richard Petty	Petty Enterprises	43	62 Plym	500	3,400
2. Joe Weatherly	Bud Moore	8	62 Pont	500	1,625
3. Rex White	Rex White	4	62 Chev	499	1,210
4. Fred Lorenzen	Holman-Moody	28	61 Ford	499	860
5. Lee Petty	Petty Enterprises	41	62 Plym	499	750

1962 Grand National Race No. 50 Old Dominion 500
September 23, 1962 Average Speed: 66.874

Driver	Owner	Car #	Make	Laps	Winnings
1. Nelson Stacy	Holman-Moody	29	62 Ford	500	3,655
2. Richard Petty	Petty Enterprises	43	672 Plym	497	1,650
3. Ned Jarrett	Bee Gee Holloway	11	62 Chev	496	1,500
4. Jack Smith	Jack Smith	47	62 Pont	495	850
5. Joe Weatherly	Bud Moore	8	62 Pont	495	920

1963 Grand National Race No. 19 Virginia 500
April 21, 1963 Average Speed: 64.823

Driver	Owner	Car #	Make	Laps	Winnings
1. Richard Petty	Petty Enterprises	43	63 Plym	500	3,375
2. Tiny Lund	Wood Brothers	21	63 Ford	499	1,675
3. Darel Dieringer	Bill Stroppe	26	63 Merc	496	1,225
4. Ned Jarrett	Charles Robinson	11	63 Ford	495	875
5. Fred Lorenzen	Holman-Moody	28	63 Ford	494	1,150

1963 Grand National Race No. 48 Old Dominion 500
September 22, 1963 Average Speed: 67.486

Driver	Owner	Car #	Make	Laps	Winnings
1. Fred Lorenzen	Holman-Moody	28	63 Ford	500	3,800
2. Marvin Panch	Wood Brothers	21	63 Ford	499	1,675
3. Joe Weatherly	Bud Moore	8	63 Merc	497	1,475
4. David Pearson	Cotton Owens	6	63 Dodg	496	875
5. Richard Petty	Petty Enterprises	41	63 Plym	496	775

1964 Grand National Race No. 19 Virginia 500
April 26, 1964 Average Speed: 70.098

Driver	Owner	Car #	Make	Laps	Winnings
1. Fred Lorenzen	Holman-Moody	28	64 Ford	500	4,175
2. Marvin Panch	Wood Brothers	21	64 Ford	499	1,925
3. Junior Johnson	Banjo Matthews	00	64 Ford	497	1,250
4. Ned Jarrett	Bondy Long	11	64 Ford	495	850
5. Fireball Roberts	Holman-Moody	22	64 Ford	494	800

1964 Grand National Race No. 56 Old Dominion 500
September 27, 1964 Average Speed: 67.320

Driver	Owner	Car #	Make	Laps	Winnings
1. Fred Lorenzen	Holman-Moody	28	64 Ford	500	4,175
2. Richard Petty	Petty Enterprises	43	64 Plym	500	1,725
3. Junior Johnson	Banjo Matthews	27	64 Ford	500	1,250
4. Marvin Panch	Wood Brothers	21	64 Ford	499	850
5. Ned Jarrett	Bondy Long	11	64 Ford	497	775

1965 Grand National Race No. 12 Virginia 500
April 25, 1965 Average Speed: 66.765

Driver	Owner	Car #	Make	Laps	Winnings
1. Fred Lorenzen	Holman-Moody	28	65 Ford	500	4,350
2. Marvin Panch	Wood Brothers	21	65 Ford	500	2,075
3. Dick Hutcherson	Holman-Moody	29	65 Ford	494	1,250
4. Tiny Lund	Gary Weaver	10	64 Ford	487	775
5. Buddy Arrington	Buddy Arrington	67	64 Dodg	472	725

1965 Grand National Race No. 50 Old Dominion 500
September 26, 1965 Average Speed: 67.056

Driver	Owner	Car #	Make	Laps	Winnings
1. Junior Johnson	Rex Lovette	26	65 Ford	500	4,625
2. Richard Petty	Petty Enterprises	43	65 Plym	499	2,400
3. David Pearson	Cotton Owens	6	65 Dodg	497	1,250
4. Ned Jarrett	Bondy Long	11	65 Ford	495	775
5. Marvin Panch	Wood Brothers	21	65 Ford	495	725

1966 Grand National Race No. 14 Virginia 500
April 24, 1966 Average Speed: 69.156

Driver	Owner	Car #	Make	Laps	Winnings
1. Jim Paschal	Tom Friedkin	14	66 Plym	500	4,550
2. Paul Goldsmith	Ray Nichels	99	65 Plym	500	2,150
3. Richard Petty	Petty Enterprises	43	66 Plym	495	1,250
4. Elmo Langley	Henry Woodfield	64	64 Ford	488	775
5. G. C. Spencer	G. C. Spencer	49	65 Plym	486	725

1966 Grand National Race No. 46 Old Dominion 500
September 25, 1966 Average Speed: 69.177

Driver	Owner	Car #	Make	Laps	Winnings
1. Fred Lorenzen	Holman-Moody	28	66 Ford	500	4,350
2. Darel Dieringer	Bud Moore	16	66 Merc	495	2,100
3. Bobby Allison	Bobby Allison	2	65 Chev	494	1,425
4. Dick Hutcherson	Bondy Long	29	66 Ford	492	775
5. James Hylton	Bud Hartje	48	65 Dodg	490	725

1967 Grand National Race No. 14 Virginia 500
April 23, 1967 Average Speed: 67.446

Driver	Owner	Car #	Make	Laps	Winnings
1. Richard Petty	Petty Enterprises	43	67 Plym	500	4,450
2. Cale Yarborough	Wood Brothers	21	67 Ford	500	2,300
3. J. T. Putney	J. T. Putney	11	66 Chev	491	1,300
4. Dick Hutcherson	Bondy Long	99	67 Ford	488	925
5. Paul Goldsmith	Ray Nichels	99	67 Plym	488	725

1967 Grand National Race No. 45 Old Dominion 500
September 24, 1967 Average Speed: 69.605

Driver	Owner	Car #	Make	Laps	Winnings
1. Richard Petty	Petty Enterprises	43	67 Plym	500	4,400
2. Dick Hutcherson	Bondy Long	29	67 Ford	496	2,075
3. David Pearson	Holman-Moody	17	67 Ford	495	1,475
4. James Hylton	Bud Hartje	48	65 Ford	493	775
5. Jim Paschal	Tom Friedkin	14	67 Plym	493	800

Martinsville Speedway *continued*

1968 Grand National Race No. 12 Virginia 500
April 28, 1968 Average Speed: 66.686

Driver	Owner	Car #	Make	Laps	Winnings
1. Cale Yarborough	Wood Brothers	21	68 Merc	500	5,476
2. David Pearson	Holman-Moody	17	68 Ford	500	2,797
3. Donnie Allison	Banjo Matthews	27	68 Ford	498	1,245
4. LeeRoy Yarbrough	Junior Johnson	26	68 Ford	498	800
5. Tom Pistone	Jon Thorne	12	68 Ford	497	725

1968 Grand National Race No. 44 Old Dominion 500
September 22, 1968 Average Speed: 65.808

Driver	Owner	Car #	Make	Laps	Winnings
1. Richard Petty	Petty Enterprises	43	68 Plym	500	5,999
2. Cale Yarborough	Wood Brothers	21	68 Merc	497	2,700
3. LeeRoy Yarbrough	Junior Johnson	98	68 Ford	497	1,244
4. Bud Moore	Bondy Long	29	68 Ford	494	775
5. Bobby Isaac	Nord Krauskopf	71	67 Dodg	494	725

1969 Grand National Race No. 16 Virginia 500
April 27, 1969 Average Speed: 64.405

Driver	Owner	Car #	Make	Laps	Winnings
1. Richard Petty	Petty Enterprises	43	69 Ford	500	10,275
2. David Pearson	Holman-Moody	17	69 Ford	500	5,050
3. Bobby Allison	Mario Rossi	22	69 Dodg	500	2,840
4. LeeRoy Yarbrough	Junior Johnson	98	69 Merc	496	1,550
5. Buddy Arrington	Buddy Arrington	67	69 Dodg	496	1,075

1969 Grand National Race No. 46 Old Dominion 500
September 28, 1969 Average Speed: 63.127

Driver	Owner	Car #	Make	Laps	Winnings
1. Richard Petty	Petty Enterprises	43	69 Ford	500	10,085
2. David Pearson	Holman-Moody	17	69 Ford	500	5,190
3. Buddy Baker	Cotton Owens	6	69 Dodg	496	2,675
4. James Hylton	James Hylton	48	69 Dodg	496	2,525
5. Buddy Arrington	Buddy Arrington	67	69 Dodg	489	1,075

1970 Grand National Race No. 18 Virginia 500
May 31, 1970 Average Speed: 68.584

Driver	Owner	Car #	Make	Laps	Winnings
1. Bobby Isaac	Nord Krauskopf	71	69 Dodg	377	10,795
2. Bobby Allison	Bobby Allison	22	69 Dodg	377	5,140
3. Cale Yarborough	Wood Brothers	21	70 Merc	376	3,100
4. David Pearson	Junior Johnson	98	70 Ford	375	1,525
5. Dick Brooks	Dick Brooks	32	69 Plym	373	1,025

1970 Grand National Race No. 45 Old Dominion 500
October 18, 1970 Average Speed: 72.235

Driver	Owner	Car #	Make	Laps	Winnings
1. Richard Petty	Petty Enterprises	43	70 Plym	500	8,775
2. Bobby Allison	Mario Rossi	22	69 Dodg	499	6,175
3. Cale Yarborough	Wood Brothers	21	70 Merc	498	4,100
4. Bobby Isaac	Nord Krauskopf	71	70 Dodg	498	3,525
5. Donnie Allison	Banjo Matthews	27	69 Ford	497	2,125

1971 Winston Cup GN Race No. 15 Virginia 500
April 25, 1971 Average Speed: 77.707

Driver	Owner	Car #	Make	Laps	Winnings
1. Richard Petty	Petty Enterprises	43	71 Plym	500	5,075
2. David Pearson	Holman-Moody	17	71 Ford	500	2,550
3. Bobby Isaac	Nord Krauskopf	71	71 Dodg	492	2,350
4. Dave Marcis	Dave Marcis	2	69 Dodg	486	1,525
5. James Hylton	James Hylton	48	70 Ford	483	1,225

1971 Winston Cup GN Race No. 41 Old Dominion 500
September 26, 1971 Average Speed: 73.681

Driver	Owner	Car #	Make	Laps	Winnings
1. Bobby Isaac	Nord Krauskopf	71	71 Dodg	500	6,250
2. Bobby Allison	Holman-Moody	12	71 Ford	499	2,600
3. Richard Petty	Petty Enterprises	43	71 Plym	499	2,200
4. Charlie Glotzbach	R. Howard & J. Johnson	3	71 Chev	496	1,575
5. Donnie Allison	Wood Brothers	21	71 Merc	495	1,250

1972 Winston Cup GN Race No. 10 Virginia 500
April 30, 1972 Average Speed: 72.657

Driver	Owner	Car #	Make	Laps	Winnings
1. Richard Petty	Petty Enterprises	43	72 Plym	500	8,250
2. Bobby Allison	R. Howard & J. Johnson	12	72 Chev	493	5,800
3. Dave Marcis	Dave Marcis	2	72 Dodg	487	2,675
4. Cecil Gordon	Cecil Gordon	24	71 Merc	485	1,825
5. Richard Brown	Ralph McNabb	91	72 Chev	479	1,250

1972 Winston Cup GN Race No. 27 Old Dominion 500
September 24, 1972 Average Speed: 69.989

Driver	Owner	Car #	Make	Laps	Winnings
1. Richard Petty	Petty Enterprises	43	72 Plym	500	7,350
2. Bobby Allison	R. Howard & J. Johnson	12	72 Chev	500	10,600
3. David Pearson	Wood Brothers	21	71 Merc	498	2,775
4. Buddy Baker	Nord Krauskopf	71	70 Dodg	496	3,225
5. Jimmy Hensley	Junie Donlavey	90	71 Ford	493	1,400

1973 Winston Cup GN Race No. 9 Virginia 500
April 29, 1973 Average Speed: 70.251

Driver	Owner	Car #	Make	Laps	Winnings
1. David Pearson	Wood Brothers	21	71 Merc	500	11,250
2. Cale Yarborough	R. Howard & J. Johnson	11	73 Chev	500	11,500
3. Bobby Isaac	Bud Moore	15	73 Ford	495	4,500
4. Buddy Baker	Nord Krauskopf	71	72 Dodg	494	3,500
5. Cecil Gordon	Cecil Gordon	24	72 Chev	490	1,750

1973 Winston Cup GN Race No. 26 Old Dominion 500
September 30, 1973 Average Speed: 68.831

Driver	Owner	Car #	Make	Laps	Winnings
1. Richard Petty	Petty Enterprises	43	73 Dodg	480	11,750
2. Cale Yarborough	R. Howard & J. Johnson	11	73 Chev	479	12,500
3. Bobby Allison	Bobby Allison	12	73 Chev	476	4,500
4. Buddy Baker	Nord Krauskopf	71	73 Dodg	475	3,500
5. Jack McCoy	Ernie Conn	07	73 Dodg	469	1,750

1974 Winston Cup GN Race No. 9 Virginia 500
April 28, 1974 Average Speed: 70.427

Driver	Owner	Car #	Make	Laps	Winnings
1. Cale Yarborough	R. Howard & J. Johnson	11	74 Chev	500	20,000
2. Richard Petty	Petty Enterprises	43	74 Dodg	500	8,000
3. Bobby Allison	Bobby Allison	12	74 Chev	496	5,000
4. Benny Parsons	L. G. DeWitt	72	74 Chev	494	4,250
5. Lennie Pond	Ronnie Elder	54	74 Chev	491	1,750

1974 Winston Cup GN Race No. 27 Old Dominion 500
September 29, 1974 Average Speed: 66.232

Driver	Owner	Car #	Make	Laps	Winnings
1. Earl Ross	Junior Johnson	52	72 Chev	500	14,550
2. Buddy Baker	Bud Moore	15	74 Ford	499	10,000
3. Donnie Allison	DiGard	88	74 Chev	497	4,250
4. Dave Marcis	Dave Marcis	2	73 Dodg	497	3,375
5. Richie Panch	Roy Thornley	98	72 Chev	488	2,000

Martinsville Speedway *continued*

1975 Winston Cup GN Race No. 9 Virginia 500
April 27, 1975 Average Speed: 69.282

Driver	Owner	Car #	Make	Laps	Winnings
1. Richard Petty	Petty Enterprises	43	74 Dodg	500	20,000
2. Darrell Waltrip	Darrell Waltrip	17	75 Chev	500	8,700
3. Cale Yarborough	Junior Johnson	11	75 Chev	499	6,550
4. Bobby Allison	Roger Penske	16	75 Mata	496	4,000
5. Dave Marcis	Nord Krauskopf	71	74 Dodg	493	4,500

1975 Winston Cup GN Race No. 24 Old Dominion 500
September 28, 1975 Average Speed: 75.819

Driver	Owner	Car #	Make	Laps	Winnings
1. Dave Marcis	Nord Krauskopf	71	74 Dodg	500	14,500
2. Benny Parsons	L. G. DeWitt	72	75 Chev	500	8,550
3. Bobby Allison	Roger Penske	16	75 Mata	496	4,850
4. Richard Childress	Tom Garn	96	75 Chev	487	3,785
5. Richie Panch	Bettie Panch	98	75 Chev	487	2,885

1976 Winston Cup GN Race No. 9 Virginia 500
April 25, 1976 Average Speed: 71.759

Driver	Owner	Car #	Make	Laps	Winnings
1. Darrell Waltrip	DiGard	88	Chev	500	22,500
2. Cale Yarborough	Junior Johnson	11	Chev	499	10,450
3. David Pearson	Wood Brothers	21	Merc	498	6,080
4. Richard Petty	Petty Enterprises	43	Dodg	498	7,070
5. Dick Brooks	Junie Donlavey	90	Ford	493	2,950

1976 Winston Cup GN Race No. 25 Old Dominion 500
September 26,1976 Average Speed: 75.370

Driver	Owner	Car #	Make	Laps	Winnings
1. Cale Yarborough	Junior Johnson	11	Chev	340	22,700
2. Darrell Waltrip	DiGard	88	Chev	340	11,700
3. Buddy Baker	Bud Moore	15	Ford	338	7,130
4. Richard Petty	Petty Enterprises	43	Dodg	338	7,070
5. Benny Parsons	L. G. DeWitt	72	Chev	336	4,700

1977 Winston Cup GN Race No. 9 Virginia 500
April 24, 1977 Average Speed: 77.405

Driver	Owner	Car #	Make	Laps	Winnings
1. Cale Yarborough	Junior Johnson	11	Chev	384	21,600
2. Benny Parsons	L. G. DeWitt	72	Chev	384	12,200
3. Richard Petty	Petty Enterprises	43	Dodg	381	7,750
4. Lennie Pond	Ronnie Elder	54	Chev	381	5,700
5. David Pearson	Wood Brothers	21	Merc	380	2,900

1977 Winston Cup GN Race No. 25 Old Dominion 500
September 25, 1977 Average Speed: 73.447

Driver	Owner	Car #	Make	Laps	Winnings
1. Cale Yarborough	Junior Johnson	11	Chev	500	23,700
2. Benny Parsons	L. G. DeWitt	72	Chev	500	11,850
3. David Pearson	Wood Brothers	21	Merc	500	5,700
4. Richard Petty	Petty Enterprises	43	Dodg	499	5,850
5. Sam Sommers	M. C. Anderson	27	Chev	491	3,550

1978 Winston Cup GN Race No. 9 Virginia 500
April 23, 1978 Average Speed: 77.971

Driver	Owner	Car #	Make	Laps	Winnings
1. Darrell Waltrip	DiGard	88	Chev	500	22,700
2. Neil Bonnett	Jim Stacy	5	Dodg	497	11,450
3. Richard Petty	Petty Enterprises	43	Dodg	497	8,700
4. Dave Marcis	Rod Osterlund	2	Chev	489	4,000
5. Buddy Arrington	Buddy Arrington	67	Dodg	485	4,950

1978 Winston Cup GN Race No. 25 Old Dominion 500
September 24, 1978 Average Speed: 79.185

Driver	Owner	Car #	Make	Laps	Winnings
1. Cale Yarborough	Junior Johnson	11	Olds	500	24,950
2. Darrell Waltrip	DiGard	88	Chev	500	11,700
3. Benny Parsons	L. G. DeWitt	72	Chev	498	8,700
4. Neil Bonnett	Jim Stacy	5	Chev	498	6,700
5. Lennie Pond	Harry Ranier	54	Chev	497	6,950

1979 Winston Cup GN Race No. 9 Virginia 500
April 22, 1979 Average Speed: 76.562

Driver	Owner	Car #	Make	Laps	Winnings
1. Richard Petty	Petty Enterprises	43	Chev	500	23,400
2. Buddy Baker	Harry Ranier	28	Chev	500	14,700
3. Darrell Waltrip	DiGard	88	Chev	499	10,200
4. Bobby Allison	Bud Moore	15	Ford	498	7,100
5. Joe Millikan	L. G. DeWitt	72	Chev	497	6,550

1979 Winston Cup GN Race No. 26 Old Dominion 500
September 23, 1979 Average Speed: 75.119

Driver	Owner	Car #	Make	Laps	Winnings
1. Buddy Baker	Harry Ranier	28	Chev	500	19,900
2. Richard Petty	Petty Enterprises	43	Chev	500	12,550
3. Joe Millikan	L. G. DeWitt	72	Chev	499	9,650
4. Bobby Allison	Bud Moore	15	Ford	495	6,950
5. Dave Marcis	Dave Marcis	71	Chev	494	3,150

1980 Winston Cup GN Race No. 9 Virginia 500
April 27, 1980 Average Speed: 69.049

Driver	Owner	Car #	Make	Laps	Winnings
1. Darrell Waltrip	DiGard	88	Chev	500	26,850
2. Benny Parsons	M. C. Anderson	27	Chev	500	15,400
3. Richard Petty	Petty Enterprises	43	Chev	500	13,475
4. Cale Yarborough	Junior Johnson	11	Chev	500	8,750
5. Joe Millikan	L. G. DeWitt	72	Chev	496	6,800

1980 Winston Cup GN Race No. 27 Old Dominion 500
September 28, 1980 Average Speed: 69.654

Driver	Owner	Car #	Make	Laps	Winnings
1. Dale Earnhardt	Rod Osterlund	2	Chev	500	25,375
2. Buddy Baker	Harry Ranier	28	Chev	500	16,400
3. Cale Yarborough	Junior Johnson	11	Olds	500	11,975
4. Benny Parsons	M. C. Anderson	27	Chev	499	7,700
5. Dave Marcis	Dave Marcis	71	Chev	499	5,860

1981 Winston Cup GN Race No. 9 Virginia 500
April 26, 1981 Average Speed: 75.019

Driver	Owner	Car #	Make	Laps	Winnings
1. Morgan Shepherd	Cliff Stewart	5	Pont	500	24,525
2. Neil Bonnett	Wood Brothers	21	Ford	500	12,650
3. Ricky Rudd	DiGard	88	Buick	499	15,250
4. Harry Gant	Kennie Childers	12	Olds	497	7,700
5. Terry Labonte	Billy Hagan	44	Buick	497	7,725

1981 Winston Cup GN Race No. 26 Old Dominion 500
September 27, 1981 Average Speed: 70.089

Driver	Owner	Car #	Make	Laps	Winnings
1. Darrell Waltrip	Junior Johnson	11	Buick	500	29,275
2. Harry Gant	Hal Needham	33	Pont	500	18,570
3. Mark Martin	Ray Dillon	02	Pont	497	7,525
4. Neil Bonnett	Wood Brothers	21	Ford	497	4,500
5. Joe Millikan	Cliff Stewart	5	Pont	497	7,425

Martinsville Speedway *continued*

1982 Winston Cup GN Race No. 8 Virginia National Bank 500
April 25, 1982 Average Speed: 75.073

Driver	Owner	Car #	Make	Laps	Winnings
1. Harry Gant	Hal Needham	33	Buick	500	26,795
2. Butch Lindley	Emanuel Zervakis	01	Buick	499	14,250
3. Neil Bonnett	Wood Brothers	21	Ford	497	8,275
4. Ricky Rudd	Richard Childress	3	Pont	496	8,520
5. Darrell Waltrip	Junior Johnson	11	Buick	496	12,600

1982 Winston Cup GN Race No. 27 Old Dominion 500
October 17, 1982 Average Speed: 71.315

Driver	Owner	Car #	Make	Laps	Winnings
1. Darrell Waltrip	Junior Johnson	11	Buick	500	33,225
2. Ricky Rudd	Richard Childress	3	Pont	500	22,770
3. Richard Petty	Petty Enterprises	43	Pont	500	14,925
4. Terry Labonte	Billy Hagan	44	Chev	498	8,270
5. Joe Ruttman	Bob Rahilly & Butch Mock	75	Buick	498	6,500

1983 Winston Cup GN Race No. 7 Virginia National Bank 500
April 24, 1983 Average Speed: 66.460

Driver	Owner	Car #	Make	Laps	Winnings
1. Darrell Waltrip	Junior Johnson	11	Chev	500	35,225
2. Harry Gant	Hal Needham	33	Buick	500	20,200
3. Bobby Allison	DiGard	22	Buick	500	15,780
4. Joe Ruttman	Ron Benfield	98	Buick	500	8,870
5. Ricky Rudd	Richard Childress	3	Chev	500	9,670

1983 Winston Cup GN Race No. 25 Goody's 500
September 25, 1983 Average Speed: 76.134

Driver	Owner	Car #	Make	Laps	Winnings
1. Ricky Rudd	Richard Childress	3	Chev	500	31,395
2. Bobby Allison	DiGard	22	Buick	500	19,600
3. Darrell Waltrip	Junior Johnson	11	Chev	500	20,150
4. Dale Earnhardt	Bud Moore	15	Ford	499	11,200
5. Geoff Bodine	Cliff Stewart	88	Pont	499	7,670

1984 Winston Cup GN Race No. 8 Sovran Bank 500
April 29, 1984 Average Speed: 73.264

Driver	Owner	Car #	Make	Laps	Winnings
1. Geoff Bodine	Rick Hendrick	5	Chev	500	29,880
2. Ron Bouchard	Jack Beebe	47	Buick	500	18,905
3. Darrell Waltrip	Junior Johnson	11	Chev	500	17,450
4. Bobby Allison	DiGard	22	Buick	500	18,000
5. Neil Bonnett	Junior Johnson	12	Chev	499	4,900

1984 Winston Cup GN Race No. 25 Goody's 500
September 23, 1984 Average Speed: 75.532

Driver	Owner	Car #	Make	Laps	Winnings
1. Darrell Waltrip	Junior Johnson	11	Chev	500	38,300
2. Terry Labonte	Billy Hagan	44	Chev	499	19,905
3. Bill Elliott	Harry Melling	9	Ford	499	15,550
4. Harry Gant	Hal Needham	33	Chev	498	9,530
5. Neil Bonnett	Junior Johnson	12	Chev	498	8,960

1985 Winston Cup GN Race No. 8 Sovran Bank 500
April 28, 1985 Average Speed: 73.022

Driver	Owner	Car #	Make	Laps	Winnings
1. Harry Gant	Hal Needham	33	Chev	500	38,525
2. Ricky Rudd	Bud Moore	15	Ford	500	22,450
3. Geoff Bodine	Rick Hendrick	5	Chev	500	19,825
4. Bobby Allison	DiGard	22	Buick	500	12,050
5. Neil Bonnett	Junior Johnson	12	Chev	500	10,550

1985 Winston Cup GN Race No. 23 Goody's 500
September 22, 1985 Average Speed: 70.694

Driver	Owner	Car #	Make	Laps	Winnings
1. Dale Earnhardt	Richard Childress	3	Chev	500	37,725
2. Darrell Waltrip	Junior Johnson	11	Chev	500	24,650
3. Harry Gant	Hal Needham	33	Chev	499	18,225
4. Ricky Rudd	Bud Moore	15	Ford	499	12,350
5. Kyle Petty	Wood Brothers	7	Ford	498	8,430

1986 Winston Cup Race No. 8 Sovran Bank 500
April 27, 1986 Average Speed: 76.882

Driver	Owner	Car #	Make	Laps	Winnings
1. Ricky Rudd	Bud Moore	15	Ford	500	40,850
2. Joe Ruttman	Kenny Bernstein	26	Buick	499	17,325
3. Terry Labonte	Billy Hagan	44	Olds	496	17,125
4. Alan Kulwicki	Bill Terry	35	Ford	496	8,350
5. Kyle Petty	Wood Brothers	7	Ford	496	11,050

1986 Winston Cup Race No. 24 Goody's 500
September 21, 1986 Average Speed: 73.191

Driver	Owner	Car #	Make	Laps	Winnings
1. Rusty Wallace	Raymond Beadle	27	Pont	500	40,175
2. Geoff Bodine	Rick Hendrick	5	Chev	500	28,250
3. Harry Gant	Hal Needham	33	Chev	500	19,625
4. Darrell Waltrip	Junior Johnson	11	Chev	499	16,350
5. Joe Ruttman	Kenny Bernstein	26	Buick	499	9,730

1987 Winston Cup Race No. 8 Sovran Bank 500
April 26, 1987 Average Speed: 72.808

Driver	Owner	Car #	Make	Laps	Winnings
1. Dale Earnhardt	Richard Childress	3	Chev	500	50,850
2. Rusty Wallace	Raymond Beadle	27	Pont	500	27,325
3. Geoff Bodine	Rick Hendrick	5	Chev	500	20,750
4. Phil Parsons	Richard Jackson	55	Olds	500	10,275
5. Terry Labonte	Junior Johnson	11	Chev	498	16,425

1987 Winston Cup Race No. 24 Goody's 500
September 27, 1987 Average Speed: 76.410

Driver	Owner	Car #	Make	Laps	Winnings
1. Darrell Waltrip	Rick Hendrick	17	Chev	500	43,830
2. Dale Earnhardt	Richard Childress	3	Chev	500	29,875
3. Terry Labonte	Junior Johnson	11	Chev	500	23,950
4. Neil Bonnett	Bob Rahilly & Butch Mock	75	Pont	498	13,005
5. Morgan Shepherd	Kenny Bernstein	26	Buick	497	12,335

1988 Winston Cup Race No. 8 Pannill Sweatshirts 500
April 24, 1988 Average Speed: 74.740

Driver	Owner	Car #	Make	Laps	Winnings
1. Dale Earnhardt	Richard Childress	3	Chev	500	53,550
2. Sterling Marlin	Billy Hagan	44	Olds	500	29,975
3. Bobby Hillin Jr.	Stavola Brothers	8	Buick	499	20,775
4. Terry Labonte	Junior Johnson	11	Chev	498	14,550
5. Darrell Waltrip	Rick Hendrick	17	Chev	498	14,250

1988 Winston Cup Race No. 24 Goody's 500
September 25, 1988 Average Speed: 74.988

Driver	Owner	Car #	Make	Laps	Winnings
1. Darrell Waltrip	Rick Hendrick	17	Chev	500	48,750
2. Alan Kulwicki	Alan Kulwicki	7	Ford	500	28,225
3. Rusty Wallace	Raymond Beadle	27	Pont	500	26,825
4. Ken Schrader	Rick Hendrick	25	Chev	499	13,500
5. Geoff Bodine	Rick Hendrick	5	Chev	499	13,050

Martinsville Speedway *continued*

1989 Winston Cup Race No. 8 Pannill Sweatshirts 500
April 23, 1989 Average Speed: 79.025

Driver	Owner	Car #	Make	Laps	Winnings
1. Darrell Waltrip	Rick Hendrick	17	Chev	500	53,600
2. Dale Earnhardt	Richard Childress	3	Chev	500	34,525
3. Dick Trickle	Stavola Brothers	84	Buick	500	21,050
4. Rick Wilson	Larry McClure	4	Olds	499	15,975
5. Terry Labonte	Junior Johnson	11	Ford	499	15,575

1989 Winston Cup Race No. 24 Goody's 500
September 24, 1989 Average Speed: 76.571

Driver	Owner	Car #	Make	Laps	Winnings
1. Darrell Waltrip	Rick Hendrick	17	Chev	500	55,650
2. Harry Gant	Leo Jackson	33	Olds	500	33,802
3. Dick Trickle	Stavola Brothers	84	Buick	500	22,250
4. Rusty Wallace	Raymond Beadle	27	Pont	500	18,875
5. Dale Jarrett	Cale Yarborough	29	Pont	500	15,125

1990 Winston Cup Series Race No. 8 Hanes Activewear 500
April 29, 1990 Average Speed: 77.423

Driver	Owner	Car #	Make	Laps	Winnings
1. Geoff Bodine	Junior Johnson	11	Ford	500	95,950
2. Rusty Wallace	Raymond Beadle	27	Pont	500	36,800
3. Morgan Shepherd	Bud Moore	15	Ford	500	19,750
4. Darrell Waltrip	Rick Hendrick	17	Chev	500	19,600
5. Dale Earnhardt	Richard Childress	3	Chev	499	20,800

1990 Winston Cup Series Race No. 24 Goody's 500
September 23, 1990 Average Speed: 76.386

Driver	Owner	Car #	Make	Laps	Winnings
1. Geoff Bodine	Junior Johnson	11	Ford	500	53,850
2. Dale Earnhardt	Richard Childress	3	Chev	500	30,550
3. Mark Martin	Jack Roush	6	Ford	500	24,450
4. Brett Bodine	Kenny Bernstein	26	Buick	500	16,807
5. Harry Gant	Leo Jackson	33	Olds	500	18,100

1991 Winston Cup Series Race No. 8 Hanes 500
April 28, 1991 Average Speed: 75.139

Driver	Owner	Car #	Make	Laps	Winnings
1. Dale Earnhardt	Richard Childress	3	Chev	500	63,600
2. Kyle Petty	Felix Sabates	42	Pont	500	29,625
3. Darrell Waltrip	Darrell Waltrip	17	Chev	500	16,150
4. Brett Bodine	Kenny Bernstein	26	Buick	500	15,550
5. Harry Gant	Leo Jackson	33	Olds	499	17,625

1991 Winston Cup Series Race No. 24 Goody's 500
September 22, 1991 Average Speed: 74.535

Driver	Owner	Car #	Make	Laps	Winnings
1. Harry Gant	Leo Jackson	33	Olds	500	64,000
2. Brett Bodine	Kenny Bernstein	26	Buick	500	36,625
3. Dale Earnhardt	Richard Childress	3	Chev	500	30,350
4. Ernie Irvan	Larry McClure	4	Chev	500	19,300
5. Mark Martin	Jack Roush	6	Ford	500	24,575

1992 Winston Cup Race No. 8 Hanes 500
April 26, 1992 Average Speed: 78.086

Driver	Owner	Car #	Make	Laps	Winnings
1. Mark Martin	Jack Roush	6	Ford	500	59,300
2. Sterling Marlin	Junior Johnson	22	Ford	500	32,775
3. Darrell Waltrip	Darrell Waltrip	17	Chev	499	30,700
4. Terry Labonte	Billy Hagan	94	Olds	499	19,700
5. Harry Gant	Leo Jackson	33	Olds	498	22,875

1992 Winston Cup Race No. 24 Goody's 500
September 28, 1992 Average Speed: 75.424

Driver	Owner	Car #	Make	Laps	Winnings
1. Geoff Bodine	Bud Moore	15	Ford	500	60,550
2. Rusty Wallace	Roger Penske	2	Pont	500	39,400
3. Brett Bodine	Kenny Bernstein	26	Ford	500	29,125
4. Kyle Petty	Felix Sabates	42	Pont	500	22,000
5. Alan Kulwicki	Alan Kulwicki	7	Ford	500	23,330

1993 Winston Cup Series Race No. 8 Hanes 500
April 25, 1993 Average Speed: 79.078

Driver	Owner	Car #	Make	Laps	Winnings
1. Rusty Wallace	Roger Penske	2	Pont	500	45,175
2. Davey Allison	Robert Yates	28	Ford	500	49,725
3. Dale Jarrett	Joe Gibbs	18	Chev	500	30,350
4. Darrell Waltrip	Darrell Waltrip	17	Chev	500	28,800
5. Kyle Petty	Felix Sabates	42	Pont	499	21,050

1993 Winston Cup Series Race No. 25 Goody's 500
September 26, 1993 Average Speed: 74.102

Driver	Owner	Car #	Make	Laps	Winnings
1. Ernie Irvan	Robert Yates	28	Ford	500	75,300
2. Rusty Wallace	Roger Penske	2	Pont	500	31,875
3. Jimmy Spencer	Bobby Allison	12	Ford	500	31,000
4. Ricky Rudd	Rick Hendrick	5	Chev	500	25,250
5. Dale Jarrett	Joe Gibbs	18	Chev	499	22,675

1994 Winston Cup Series Race No. 8 Hanes 500
April 24, 1994 Average Speed: 76.700

Driver	Owner	Car #	Make	Laps	Winnings
1. Rusty Wallace	Roger Penske	2	Ford	500	173,675
2. Ernie Irvan	Robert Yates	28	Ford	500	41,750
3. Mark Martin	Jack Roush	6	Ford	500	33,425
4. Darrell Waltrip	Darrell Waltrip	17	Chev	500	23,050
5. Morgan Shepherd	Wood Brothers	21	Ford	500	23,875

1994 Winston Cup Series Race No. 26 Goody's 500
September 25, 1994 Average Speed: 77.139

Driver	Owner	Car #	Make	Laps	Winnings
1. Rusty Wallace	Roger Penske	2	Ford	500	69,125
2. Dale Earnhardt	Richard Childress	3	Chev	500	42,400
3. Bill Elliott	Junior Johnson	11	Ford	500	29,525
4. Kenny Wallace	Robert Yates	28	Ford	500	30,650
5. Dale Jarrett	Joe Gibbs	18	Chev	500	26,775

1995 Winston Cup Series Race No. 8 Hanes 500
April 23, 1995 Average Speed: 72.145

Driver	Owner	Car #	Make	Laps	Winnings
1. Rusty Wallace	Roger Penske	2	Ford	356	61,945
2. Ted Musgrave	Jack Roush	16	Ford	356	42,965
3. Jeff Gordon	Rick Hendrick	24	Chev	356	37,895
4. Darrell Waltrip	Darrell Waltrip	17	Chev	356	42,695
5. Mark Martin	Jack Roush	6	Ford	356	33,195

1995 Winston Cup Series Race No. 26 Goody's 500
September 24, 1995 Average Speed: 73.946

Driver	Owner	Car #	Make	Laps	Winnings
1. Dale Earnhardt	Richard Childress	3	Chev	500	78,150
2. Terry Labonte	Rick Hendrick	5	Chev	500	45,600
3. Rusty Wallace	Roger Penske	2	Ford	500	42,400
4. Bobby Hamilton	Petty Enterprises	43	Pont	500	24,450
5. Geoff Bodine	Geoff Bodine	7	Ford	500	32,100

Martinsville Speedway *continued*

1996 Winston Cup Series Race No. 8 Goody's 500
April 21, 1996 Average Speed: 81.410

Driver	Owner	Car #	Make	Laps	Winnings
1. Rusty Wallace	Roger Penske	2	Ford	500	59,245
2. Ernie Irvan	Robert Yates	28	Ford	500	57,395
3. Jeff Gordon	Rick Hendrick	24	Chev	500	57,495
4. Jeremy Mayfield	Cale Yarborough	98	Ford	500	32,545
5. Dale Earnhardt	Richard Childress	3	Chev	500	35,195

1996 Winston Cup Series Race No. 26 Hanes 500
September 22, 1996 Average Speed: 82.223

Driver	Owner	Car #	Make	Laps	Winnings
1. Jeff Gordon	Rick Hendrick	24	Chev	500	93,825
2. Terry Labonte	Rick Hendrick	5	Chev	500	56,175
3. Bobby Hamilton	Petty Enterprises	43	Pont	500	50,425
4. Rick Mast	Richard Jackson	1	Pont	500	36,125
5. John Andretti	Cale Yarborough	98	Ford	500	26,235

Norfolk Speedway
Norfolk, VA
.4-mile Dirt Track

Half-mile dirt track opened briefly in 1949. Re-opened in 1956. First NASCAR Winston Cup (then Grand National) race staged on 8/22/56 (won by Billy Myers). Final Grand National race run on 7/24/57 (won by Buck Baker). Track closed shortly after last NASCAR race.

Winston Cup Starts

Johnny Allen	2
Buck Baker	2
Bill Champion	2
Billy Myers	2
Jim Paschal	2
Lee Petty	2
Fireball Roberts	2
Joe Weatherly	2

Winston Cup Victories

Buck Baker	1
Billy Myers	1

Winston Cup Poles

Bill Amick	1
Ralph Moody	1

Winston Cup Money

Buck Baker	$1,250

Most Cars Started
23—July 24, 1957

Fewest Cars Started
14—August 22, 1956

Narrowest Margin of Victory
N/A

Slowest Race
47.987 MPH—July 24, 1957

Race Record
56.408 MPH—August 22, 1956

Most Race Leaders
N/A

Most Cars Running at Finish
14—July 24, 1957

1956 Grand National Race No. 40
August 22, 1956 Average Speed: 56.408

Driver	Owner	Car #	Make	Laps	Winnings
1. Billy Myers	Bill Stroppe	4	56 Merc	250	850
2. Jim Paschal	Frank Hayworth	75	56 Merc	249	625
3. Rex White	Bob Welborn	X	56 Chev	246	450
4. Buck Baker	Carl Kiekhaefer	501	56 Dodg	245	350
5. Johnny Allen	Spook Crawford	264	56 Plym	241	310

1957 Grand National Race No. 33
July 24, 1957 Average Speed: 47.987

Driver	Owner	Car #	Make	Laps	Winnings
1. Buck Baker	Buck Baker	87	57 Chev	250	900
2. Joe Weatherly	Holman-Moody	12	57 Ford	249	575
3. Jim Paschal	Frank Hayworth	75	56 Merc	249	375
4. Billy Myers	Billy Myers	14	57 Merc	248	280
5. Jack Smith	Jack Smith	47	57 Chev	245	245

Old Dominion Speedway
Manassas, VA
.375-Mile Paved Track

(aka Longview Speedway) .375-mile dirt track opened in September 1948. Track paved in 1952. Re-measured at .333-mile oval. First NASCAR Winston Cup (then Grand National) race staged on 4/25/58 (won by Frankie Schneider). Final Grand National race run on 7/7/66 (won by Elmo Langley). Track still in operation.

Winston Cup Starts
Elmo Langley   7

Winston Cup Victories
Ned Jarrett   2
Richard Petty   2

Winston Cup Poles
Ned Jarrett   3

Winston Cup Money
Ned Jarrett $4,275

Most Cars Started
30—September 17, 1965

Fewest Cars Started
16—May 18, 1963

Narrowest Margin of Victory
N/A

Slowest Race
67.590 MPH—April 25, 1958

Race Record
70.275 MPH—May 18, 1963

Most Cautions
2—July 7, 1966

Most Race Leaders
3—September 18, 1964
3—September 17, 1965
3—July 7, 1966

Most Cars Running at Finish
22—September 17, 1965

1958 Grand National Race No. 13
April 25, 1958 Average Speed: 67.590

Driver	Owner	Car #	Make	Laps	Winnings
1. Frankie Schneider	Frankie Schneider	62	57 Chev	150	600
2. Jack Smith	Jack Smith	47	57 Chev	150	475
3. Rex White	J. H. Petty	44	57 Chev	148	355
4. Lee Petty	Petty Enterprises	42	57 Olds	148	280
5. Johnny Allen	Spook Crawford	64	57 Plym	147	240

1963 Grand National Race No. 24
May 18, 1963 Average Speed: 70.275

Driver	Owner	Car #	Make	Laps	Winnings
1. Richard Petty	Petty Enterprises	41	63 Pont	300	1,000
2. Ned Jarrett	Charles Robinson	11	63 Ford	299	600
3. Jim Paschal	Petty Enterprises	43	63 Plym	298	400
4. Larry Thomas	Wade Younts	36	62 Dodg	292	300
5. Elmo Langley	Henry Woodfield	64	62 Ford	289	275

1964 Grand National Race No. 36 Old Dominion 400
July 8, 1964 Average Speed: 67.652

Driver	Owner	Car #	Make	Laps	Winnings
1. Ned Jarrett	Bondy Long	11	64 Ford	400	1,100
2. David Pearson	Cotton Owens	6	64 Dodg	399	625
3. Jimmy Pardue	Charles Robinson	54	64 Plym	388	450
4. Curtis Crider	Curtis Crider	02	63 Merc	371	350
5. Buddy Arrington	Buddy Arrington	78	63 Dodg	370	325

1964 Grand National Race No. 54
September 18, 1964 Average Speed: 68.842

Driver	Owner	Car #	Make	Laps	Winnings
1. Ned Jarrett	Bondy Long	11	64 Ford	500	1,500
2. David Pearson	Cotton Owens	6	64 Dodg	499	1,000
3. Richard Petty	Petty Enterprises	41	64 Plym	496	725
4. Larry Thomas	Herman Beam	19	64 Ford	480	600
5. Bert Robbins	Henry Woodfield	84	63 Ford	467	400

1965 Grand National Race No. 30
July 8, 1965 Average Speed: 68.165

Driver	Owner	Car #	Make	Laps	Winnings
1. Junior Johnson	Rex Lovette	26	65 Ford	400	1,100
2. Dick Hutcherson	Holman-Moody	29	65 Ford	400	625
3. Ned Jarrett	Bondy Long	11	65 Ford	398	450
4. Cale Yarborough	Kenny Myler	06	64 Ford	393	350
5. Dick Dixon	Dan Colone	8	63 Ford	388	325

1965 Grand National Race No. 48
September 17, 1965 Average Speed: 67.890

Driver	Owner	Car #	Make	Laps	Winnings
1. Richard Petty	Petty Enterprises	43	65 Plym	400	1,300
2. Ned Jarrett	Bondy Long	11	65 Ford	399	625
3. Buddy Baker	Buck Baker	86	64 Dodg	396	450
4. Tiny Lund	Lyle Stelter	55	64 Ford	396	350
5. Tom Pistone	Glenn Sweet	59	64 Ford	393	325

1966 Grand National Race No. 29
July 7, 1966 Average Speed: 68.079

Driver	Owner	Car #	Make	Laps	Winnings
1. Elmo Langley	Henry Woodfield	64	64 Ford	400	1,100
2. John Sears	L. G. DeWitt	4	64 Ford	393	625
3. James Hylton	Bud Hartje	48	65 Dodg	393	450
4. Larry Manning	Bob Adams	63	65 Plym	393	350
5. Buck Baker	Buck Baker	87	66 Olds	392	325

Princess Anne Speedway
Norfolk, VA
Half-mile Dirt Track

First opened as 1-mile dirt track in 1930s. Half-mile dirt track built in 1950. Only NASCAR Winston Cup (then Grand National) race staged on 8/23/53 (won by Herb Thomas). Closed in 1954. Sold for housing development in 1955. Now the site of a shopping center.

Winston Cup Victories
Herb Thomas   1

Winston Cup Poles
Curtis Turner   1

Winston Cup Money
Herb Thomas $1,000

Most Cars Started
19—August 23, 1953

Narrowest Margin of Victory
N/A

Race Record
51.040 MPH—August 23, 1953

Most Race Leaders
N/A

Most Cars Running at Finish
N/A

1953 Grand National Race No. 28
August 23, 1953 Average Speed: 51.040

Driver	Owner	Car #	Make	Laps	Winnings
1. Herb Thomas	Herb Thomas	92	53 Huds	200	1,000
2. Fonty Flock	Frank Christian	14	53 Huds	—	700
3. Lee Petty	Petty Enterprises	42	53 Dodg	—	450
4. Dick Rathmann	Walt Chapman	120	53 Huds	—	350
5. Jim Paschal	George Hutchens	80	53 Dodg	—	200

Richmond Int'l Raceway
Richmond, VA
.75-mile Paved Track

(aka Fairgrounds Speedway; Strawberry Hill; Atlantic Rural Exposition Fairgrounds; Virginia State Fairgrounds; Strawberry Hill Speedway; Richmond Fairgrounds) Half-mile dirt oval opened in October 1946. First NASCAR Winston Cup (then Grand National) race staged on 4/19/53 (Lee Petty won). Top drivers Tim and Fonty Flock boycotted event due to qualifying procedure. Track paved in 1968. Re-measured as .563-mile oval in 1970. Re-measured in 1971 as .542-mile oval. Track re-designed in 1988 as .75-mile D-shaped oval. Davey Allison won first race on big track (9/11/88).

Winston Cup Starts
Richard Petty   63

Winston Cup Victories
Richard Petty   13

Winston Cup Poles
Bobby Allison   8
Richard Petty   8

Winston Cup Money
Dale Earnhardt $912,190

Most Cars Started
40—March 3, 1996
  Pontiac Excitement 400
40—September 7, 1996
  Miller Genuine Draft 400

Fewest Cars Started
12—April 23, 1961

Narrowest Margin of Victory
18 inches—March 8, 1992
  Pontiac Excitement 400

Slowest Race
45.535 MPH—April 19, 1953

Race Record
107.000 MPH—March 7, 1993
  Pontiac Excitement 400

Most Cautions
14—February 21, 1988
  Pontiac Excitement 400
14—September 10, 1989
  Miller High Life 400

Most Race Leaders
12—September 7, 1986
  Wrangler Jeans Indigo 400

Most Cars Running at Finish
38—March 3, 1996
  Pontiac Excitement 400

1953 Grand National Race No. 6
April 19, 1953 Average Speed: 45.535

Driver	Owner	Car #	Make	Laps	Winnings
1. Lee Petty	Petty Enterprises	42	53 Dodg	200	1,000
2. Dick Rathmann	Walt Chapman	120	52 Huds	—	700
3. Buck Baker	Griffin Motors	87	53 Olds	—	450
4. Dick Passwater	Frank Arford	78	53 Olds	—	350
5. Bill Blair	Bill Blair	2	53 Olds	—	200

1955 Grand National Race No. 16
May 22, 1955 Average Speed: 54.298

Driver	Owner	Car #	Make	Laps	Winnings
1. Tim Flock	Carl Kiekhaefer	300	55 Chrys	200	1,000
2. Fonty Flock	Carl Kiekhaefer	301	55 Chrys	200	650
3. Lee Petty	Petty Enterprises	42	55 Chrys	200	450
4. Jim Paschal	Ernest Woods	78	55 Olds	199	350
5. Junior Johnson	B & L Motors	55	55 Olds	197	300

1956 Grand National Race No. 12
April 29, 1956 Average Speed: 56.232

Driver	Owner	Car #	Make	Laps	Winnings
1. Buck Baker	Carl Kiekhaefer	87	56 Dodg	200	1,100
2. Herb Thomas	Carl Kiekhaefer	92	56 Dodg	199	700
3. Speedy Thompson	Carl Kiekhaefer	300	56 Chrys	199	475
4. Billy Myers	Bill Stroppe	14	56 Merc	198	365
5. Jimmy Massey	Hubert Westmoreland	2	56 Chev	197	310

1957 Grand National Race No. 16
May 5, 1957 Average Speed: 62.445

Driver	Owner	Car #	Make	Laps	Winnings
1. Paul Goldsmith	Pete DePaolo	12	57 Ford	200	700
2. Fireball Roberts	Pete DePaolo	22	57 Ford	199	525
3. Marvin Panch	Pete DePaolo	98	57 Ford	199	400
4. Frankie Schneider	Hugh Babb	45	57 Chev	194	330
5. Jim Paschal	Bill Stroppe	17	57 Merc	188	270

1958 Grand National Race No. 46
September 14, 1958 Average Speed: 57.878

Driver	Owner	Car #	Make	Laps	Winnings
1. Speedy Thompson	Speedy Thompson	46	57 Chev	200	800
2. Lee Petty	Petty Enterprises	42	57 Olds	200	525
3. Tommy Irwin	Tommy Irwin	16	57 Ford	197	350
4. Buck Baker	Buck Baker	87	57 Chev	195	250
5. John Findlay	John Findlay	100	57 Chev	189	225

1959 Grand National Race No. 23
June 21, 1959 Average Speed: 56.881

Driver	Owner	Car #	Make	Laps	Winnings
1. Tom Pistone	Carl Rupert	59	59 Ford	200	900
2. Glen Wood	Wood Brothers	21	58 Ford	200	525
3. Buck Baker	Buck Baker	87	59 Chev	200	350
4. Bob Welborn	Jerry Draper	79	57 Chev	199	250
5. Cotton Owens	W. H. Watson	6	58 Pont	191	225

1959 Grand National Race No. 38
September 13, 1959 Average Speed: 60.382

Driver	Owner	Car #	Make	Laps	Winnings
1. Cotton Owens	Cotton Owens	6	59 Ford	200	800
2. Lee Petty	Petty Enterprises	42	59 Plym	200	625
3. Tom Pistone	Carl Rupert	59	59 Ford	198	375
4. Reds Kagle	Hoss Kagle	88	57 Chev	194	275
5. Runt Harris	Junie Donlavey	90	57 Chev	193	250

1960 Grand National Race No. 19
June 5, 1960 Average Speed: 62.251

Driver	Owner	Car #	Make	Laps	Winnings
1. Lee Petty	Petty Enterprises	42	60 Plym	200	900
2. Rex White	Rex White	4	59 Chev	200	525
3. Ned Jarrett	Ned Jarrett	11	60 Ford	199	375
4. Doug Yates	Raeford Johnson	23	59 Plym	198	275
5. Glen Wood	Wood Brothers	21	59 Ford	197	250

1960 Grand National Race No. 43
October 23, 1960 Average Speed: 63.739

Driver	Owner	Car #	Make	Laps	Winnings
1. Speedy Thompson	Wood Brothers	21	60 Ford	200	800
2. Junior Johnson	John Masoni	27	59 Chev	200	525
3. Ned Jarrett	Ned Jarrett	11	60 Ford	200	375
4. Richard Petty	Petty Enterprises	43	60 Plym	197	275
5. Fred Harb	Fred Harb	17	59 Ford	197	250

1961 Grand National Race No. 17
April 23, 1961 Average Speed: 62.456

Driver	Owner	Car #	Make	Laps	Winnings
1. Richard Petty	Petty Enterprises	43	60 Plym	200	950
2. Cotton Owens	Cotton Owens	6	60 Pont	199	625
3. Buck Baker	Buck Baker	86	61 Chrys	193	425
4. Ned Jarrett	Bee Gee Holloway	11	61 Chev	186	275
5. Elmo Langley	Doc White	61	59 Ford	186	250

Richmond Int'l Raceway *continued*

1961 Grand National Race No. 44
September 10, 1961 Average Speed: 61.677

Driver	Owner	Car #	Make	Laps	Winnings
1. Joe Weatherly	Bud Moore	8	61 Pont	250	1,350
2. Junior Johnson	Rex Lovette	27	60 Pont	250	850
3. Rex White	Rex White	4	61 Chev	249	750
4. Ned Jarrett	Bee Gee Holloway	11	61 Chev	249	450
5. Jim Paschal	J. H. Petty	44	61 Pont	248	300

1962 Grand National Race No. 10 Richmond 250
April 1, 1962 Average Speed: 51.363

Driver	Owner	Car #	Make	Laps	Winnings
1. Rex White	Rex White	4	61 Chev	180	1,850
2. Ned Jarrett	Bee Gee Holloway	11	62 Chev	179	1,300
3. Junior Johnson	Rex Lovette	27	61 Pont	178	800
4. Joe Weatherly	Bud Moore	8	61 Pont	168	600
5. Fireball Roberts	Rex Lovette	22	61 Pont	163	450

1962 Grand National Race No. 47 Capital City 300
September 9, 1962 Average Speed: 64.981

Driver	Owner	Car #	Make	Laps	Winnings
1. Joe Weatherly	Bud Moore	8	62 Pont	300	2,000
2. Jim Paschal	Petty Enterprises	41	62 Plym	299	1,350
3. Fred Lorenzen	Holman-Moody	26	62 Ford	296	950
4. Richard Petty	Petty Enterprises	42	62 Plym	296	675
5. Rex White	Rex White	4	62 Chev	294	510

1963 Grand National Race No. 15 Richmond 250
April 7, 1963 Average Speed: 58.624

Driver	Owner	Car #	Make	Laps	Winnings
1. Joe Weatherly	Bud Moore	8	63 Pont	250	2,400
2. Ned Jarrett	Charles Robinson	11	63 Ford	249	1,300
3. Rex White	Rex White	4	62 Chev	247	900
4. Billy Wade	Cotton Owens	5	63 Dodg	245	625
5. Junior Johnson	Ray Fox	3	63 Chev	242	450

1963 Grand National Race No. 47 Capital City 300
September 8, 1963 Average Speed: 66.339

Driver	Owner	Car #	Make	Laps	Winnings
1. Ned Jarrett	Charles Robinson	11	63 Ford	300	2,200
2. Rex White	Rex White	4	63 Merc	298	1,475
3. Larry Frank	Bondy Long	99	63 Ford	293	1,050
4. G. C. Spencer	G. C. Spencer	03	62 Chev	291	775
5. Fred Lorenzen	Holman-Moody	28	63 Ford	289	560

1964 Grand National Race No. 9 Richmond 250
March 8 &10, 1964 Average Speed: 60.233

Driver	Owner	Car #	Make	Laps	Winnings
1. David Pearson	Cotton Owens	6	64 Dodg	250	1,500
2. Richard Petty	Petty Enterprises	43	64 Plym	250	1,000
3. Billy Wade	Bud Moore	1	64 Merc	250	750
4. Junior Johnson	Ray Fox	3	64 Dodg	249	600
5. Doug Yates	Louie Weathersby	45	63 Plym	249	450

1964 Grand National Race No. 53 Capital City 300
September 14, 1964 Average Speed: 61.955

Driver	Owner	Car #	Make	Laps	Winnings
1. Cotton Owens	Cotton Owens	5	64 Dodg	300	2,400
2. David Pearson	Cotton Owens	6	64 Dodg	299	1,600
3. Richard Petty	Petty Enterprises	41	64 Plym	292	1,200
4. Larry Thomas	Herman Beam	19	64 Ford	289	900
5. Ned Jarrett	Bondy Long	11	64 Ford	280	710

1965 Grand National Race No. 7 Richmond 250
March 7, 1965 Average Speed: 61.416

Driver	Owner	Car #	Make	Laps	Winnings
1. Junior Johnson	Rex Lovette	26	65 Ford	250	2,200
2. Buck Baker	Buck Baker	88	64 Dodg	250	1,275
3. J. T. Putney	Herman Beam	19	65 Chev	242	900
4. Curtis Crider	Curtis Crider	02	64 Merc	238	600
5. Bob Derrington	Bob Derrington	68	63 Ford	237	450

1965 Grand National Race No. 49 Capital City 300
September 18, 1965 Average Speed: 60.983

Driver	Owner	Car #	Make	Laps	Winnings
1. David Pearson	Cotton Owens	6	65 Dodg	300	2,300
2. Darel Dieringer	Bud Moore	15	64 Merc	299	1,525
3. Junior Johnson	Rex Lovette	26	65 Ford	298	1,200
4. J. T. Putney	Herman Beam	19	65 Chev	298	875
5. Neil Castles	Buck Baker	89	65 Olds	278	710

1966 Grand National Race No. 19 Richmond 250
May 15, 1966 Average Speed: 66.539

Driver	Owner	Car #	Make	Laps	Winnings
1. David Pearson	Cotton Owens	6	64 Dodg	250	2,050
2. Richard Petty	Petty Enterprises	43	66 Plym	248	1,250
3. J. T. Putney	J. T. Putney	19	66 Chev	244	950
4. Darel Dieringer	Reid Shaw	0	64 Ford	242	700
5. Paul Goldsmith	Ray Nichels	99	65 Plym	241	550

1966 Grand National Race No. 44 Capital City 300
September 11, 1966 Average Speed: 62.886

Driver	Owner	Car #	Make	Laps	Winnings
1. David Pearson	Cotton Owens	6	66 Dodg	300	2,350
2. Buck Baker	Buck Baker	87	66 Olds	295	1,600
3. Paul Lewis	Paul Lewis	1	65 Plym	295	1,250
4. Curtis Turner	Toy Bolton	47	66 Chev	292	875
5. Elmo Langley	Henry Woodfield	64	64 Ford	286	710

1967 Grand National Race No. 16 Richmond 250
April 30, 1967 Average Speed: 65.982

Driver	Owner	Car #	Make	Laps	Winnings
1. Richard Petty	Petty Enterprises	43	67 Plym	250	2,150
2. Bobby Allison	Cotton Owens	6	67 Dodg	250	1,300
3. Dick Hutcherson	Bondy Long	29	67 Ford	247	950
4. James Hylton	Bud Hartje	48	65 Dodg	241	700
5. Clyde Lynn	Clyde Lynn	20	66 Ford	231	550

1967 Grand National Race No. 42 Capital City 300
September 10, 1967 Average Speed: 57.631

Driver	Owner	Car #	Make	Laps	Winnings
1. Richard Petty	Petty Enterprises	43	67 Plym	300	2,450
2. Dick Hutcherson	Bondy Long	29	67 Ford	300	1,540
3. Paul Goldsmith	Ray Nichels	99	67 Plym	299	1,210
4. Sam McQuagg	Cotton Owens	6	67 Dodg	289	875
5. James Hylton	Bud Hartje	48	65 Dodg	285	710

1968 Grand National Race No. 6 Richmond 250
March 24, 1968 Average Speed: 65.217

Driver	Owner	Car #	Make	Laps	Winnings
1. David Pearson	Holman-Moody	17	68 Ford	250	2,300
2. Charlie Glotzbach	Cotton Owens	6	67 Dodg	249	1,275
3. Elmo Langley	Elmo Langley	64	66 Ford	237	950
4. Neil Castles	Neil Castles	88	67 Olds	237	700
5. Clyde Lynn	Clyde Lynn	20	66 Ford	232	550

Richmond Int'l Raceway *continued*

1968 Grand National Race No. 41 Capital City 300
September 8, 1968 Average Speed: 85.659

Driver	Owner	Car #	Make	Laps	Winnings
1. Richard Petty	Petty Enterprises	43	68 Plym	300	2,400
2. David Pearson	Holman-Moody	17	68 Ford	300	1,490
3. Cale Yarborough	Wood Brothers	21	68 Merc	299	1,210
4. Bobby Allison	Bobby Allison	2	66 Chev	299	875
5. Buddy Baker	Ray Fox	3	68 Dodg	298	710

1969 Grand National Race No. 43 Capital City 250
September 7, 1969 Average Speed: 76.388

Driver	Owner	Car #	Make	Laps	Winnings
1. Bobby Allison	Mario Rossi	22	69 Dodg	462	5,000
2. Sonny Hutchins	Junie Donlavey	90	67 Ford	459	2,575
3. Bobby Isaac	Nord Krauskopf	71	69 Dodg	456	1,775
4. David Pearson	Holman-Moody	17	69 Ford	455	1,250
5. John Sears	L. G. DeWitt	4	69 Ford	454	925

1970 Grand National Race No. 40 Capital City 500
September 13, 1970 Average Speed: 81.476

Driver	Owner	Car #	Make	Laps	Winnings
1. Richard Petty	Petty Enterprises	43	70 Plym	500	4,675
2. Bobby Allison	Bobby Allison	22	69 Dodg	498	2,550
3. Donnie Allison	Banjo Matthews	27	70 Ford	497	1,800
4. Bobby Isaac	Nord Krauskopf	71	69 Dodg	496	1,175
5. Sonny Hutchins	Junie Donlavey	90	69 Ford	492	950

1971 Winston Cup GN Race No. 46 Capital City 500
November 14, 1971 Average Speed: 80.025

Driver	Owner	Car #	Make	Laps	Winnings
1. Richard Petty	Petty Enterprises	43	71 Plym	500	4,450
2. Bobby Allison	Holman-Moody	12	71 Ford	499	2,585
3. Pete Hamilton	Cotton Owens	6	71 Plym	490	1,750
4. Charlie Glotzbach	R. Howard & J. Johnson	98	71 Chev	487	1,175
5. Elmo Langley	Elmo Langley	64	71 Ford	480	965

1972 Winston Cup GN Race No. 25 Capital City 500
September 10, 1972 Average Speed: 75.899

Driver	Owner	Car #	Make	Laps	Winnings
1. Richard Petty	Petty Enterprises	43	72 Plym	500	6,775
2. Bobby Allison	R. Howard & J. Johnson	12	72 Chev	500	4,825
3. Bill Dennis	H. J. Brooking	17	72 Chev	492	2,100
4. James Hylton	James Hylton	48	71 Ford	482	1,650
5. Dave Marcis	Dave Marcis	2	72 Dodg	479	1,400

1973 Winston Cup GN Race No. 23 Capital City 500
September 9, 1973 Average Speed: 63.215

Driver	Owner	Car #	Make	Laps	Winnings
1. Richard Petty	Petty Enterprises	43	73 Dodg	500	6,775
2. Cale Yarborough	R. Howard & J. Johnson	11	73 Chev	498	4,425
3. Bobby Allison	Bobby Allison	12	73 Chev	497	4,150
4. Benny Parsons	L. G. DeWitt	72	73 Chev	492	1,750
5. Buddy Arrington	Buddy Arrington	67	72 Dodg	482	1,580

1974 Winston Cup GN Race No. 24 Capital City 500
September 8, 1974 Average Speed: 64.430

Driver	Owner	Car #	Make	Laps	Winnings
1. Richard Petty	Petty Enterprises	43	74 Dodg	500	8,740
2. Benny Parsons	L. G. DeWitt	72	74 Chev	500	6,010
3. Richie Panch	Roy Thornley	98	72 Chev	493	3,295
4. Charlie Glotzbach	Junie Donlavey	90	72 Ford	491	1,985
5. Walter Ballard	Walter Ballard	30	74 Chev	487	1,510

1969 Grand National Race No. 14 Richmond 500
April 13, 1969 Average Speed: 73.752

Driver	Owner	Car #	Make	Laps	Winnings
1. David Pearson	Holman-Moody	17	69 Ford	500	3,650
2. Richard Petty	Petty Enterprises	43	69 Ford	499	1,800
3. Elmo Langley	Elmo Langley	64	68 Ford	483	1,075
4. Bill Seifert	Bill Seifert	45	68 Ford	465	675

1970 Grand National Race No. 5 Richmond 500
March 1, 1970 Average Speed: 82.044

Driver	Owner	Car #	Make	Laps	Winnings
1. James Hylton	James Hylton	48	69 Ford	500	5,195
2. Richard Petty	Petty Enterprises	43	70 Plym	500	2,970
3. Elmo Langley	Elmo Langley	64	69 Ford	491	1,845
4. Bobby Isaac	Nord Krauskopf	71	69 Dodg	485	1,220
5. Neil Castles	Neil Castles	06	69 Dodg	482	945

1971 Winston Cup GN Race No. 6 Richmond 500
March 7, 1971 Average Speed: 79.836

Driver	Owner	Car #	Make	Laps	Winnings
1. Richard Petty	Petty Enterprises	43	70 Plym	500	4,425
2. Bobby Isaac	Nord Krauskopf	71	70 Dodg	498	2,850
3. Benny Parsons	L. G. DeWitt	72	69 Ford	492	1,525
4. Bobby Allison	Bobby Allison	12	69 Dodg	491	1,125
5. Dave Marcis	Dave Marcis	2	69 Dodg	490	1,075

1972 Winston Cup GN Race No. 3 Richmond 500
February 27, 1972 Average Speed: 76.258

Driver	Owner	Car #	Make	Laps	Winnings
1. Richard Petty	Petty Enterprises	43	72 Plym	500	5,300
2. Bobby Allison	R. Howard & J. Johnson	12	72 Chev	499	4,025
3. Bobby Isaac	Nord Krauskopf	71	72 Dodg	493	3,175
4. Dave Marcis	Dave Marcis	2	70 Dodg	488	1,575
5. Bill Dennis	Junie Donlavey	90	71 Ford	485	1,400

1973 Winston Cup GN Race No. 3 Richmond 500
February 25, 1973 Average Speed: 74.764

Driver	Owner	Car #	Make	Laps	Winnings
1. Richard Petty	Petty Enterprises	43	73 Dodg	500	6,350
2. Buddy Baker	Nord Krauskopf	71	71 Dodg	500	4,050
3. Cale Yarborough	R. Howard & J. Johnson	11	73 Chev	497	3,450
4. Bobby Isaac	Bud Moore	15	72 Ford	495	2,900
5. Dave Marcis	Dave Marcis	2	71 Dodg	491	1,150

1974 Winston Cup GN Race No. 3 Richmond 500
February 24, 1974 Average Speed: 80.095

Driver	Owner	Car #	Make	Laps	Winnings
1. Bobby Allison	Bobby Allison	12	74 Chev	500	8,330
2. Richard Petty	Petty Enterprises	43	74 Dodg	500	5,455
3. Cale Yarborough	R. Howard & J. Johnson	11	74 Chev	494	5,505
4. Lennie Pond	Ronnie Elder	54	74 Chev	492	1,730
5. Dave Marcis	Dave Marcis	2	73 Dodg	487	1,705

1975 Winston Cup GN Race No. 3 Richmond 500
February 23, 1975 Average Speed: 74.913

Driver	Owner	Car #	Make	Laps	Winnings
1. Richard Petty	Petty Enterprises	43	74 Dodg	500	8,265
2. Lennie Pond	Ronnie Elder	54	75 Chev	494	4,410
3. Benny Parsons	L. G. DeWitt	72	75 Chev	491	4,435
4. Dick Brooks	Junie Donlavey	90	73 Ford	489	2,010
5. Elmo Langley	Elmo Langley	64	73 Ford	476	1,435

Richmond Int'l Raceway *continued*

1975 Winston Cup GN Race No. 26 Capital City 500
October 12, 1975 Average Speed: 81.886

Driver	Owner	Car #	Make	Laps	Winnings
1. Darrell Waltrip	DiGard	88	75 Chev	500	7,835
2. Lennie Pond	Ronnie Elder	54	75 Chev	499	4,210
3. Dick Brooks	Junie Donlavey	90	73 Ford	494	3,295
4. Cecil Gordon	Cecil Gordon	24	75 Chev	484	2,285
5. J. D. McDuffie	J. D. McDuffie	70	75 Chev	483	1,785

1976 Winston Cup GN Race No. 23 Capital City 400
September 12, 1976 Average Speed: 77.993

Driver	Owner	Car #	Make	Laps	Winnings
1. Cale Yarborough	Junior Johnson	11	Chev	400	10,300
2. Bobby Allison	Roger Penske	2	Merc	400	7,250
3. Richard Petty	Petty Enterprises	43	Dodg	399	7,180
4. Darrell Waltrip	DiGard	88	Chev	399	4,770
5. Buddy Baker	Bud Moore	15	Ford	398	4,225

1977 Winston Cup GN Race No. 23 Capital City 400
September 11, 1977 Average Speed: 80.644

Driver	Owner	Car #	Make	Laps	Winnings
1. Neil Bonnett	Jim Stacy	5	Dodg	400	8,700
2. Richard Petty	Petty Enterprises	43	Dodg	400	7,775
3. Benny Parsons	L. G. DeWitt	72	Chev	400	6,800
4. Cale Yarborough	Junior Johnson	11	Chev	400	5,950
5. Lennie Pond	Ronnie Elder	54	Chev	400	3,340

1978 Winston Cup GN Race No. 23 Capital City 400
September 10, 1978 Average Speed: 79.568

Driver	Owner	Car #	Make	Laps	Winnings
1. Darrell Waltrip	DiGard	88	Chev	400	13,800
2. Bobby Allison	Bud Moore	15	Ford	400	8,800
3. Neil Bonnett	Jim Stacy	5	Chev	400	6,575
4. Cale Yarborough	Junior Johnson	11	Olds	399	6,450
5. Dick Brooks	Junie Donlavey	90	Ford	397	3,300

1979 Winston Cup GN Race No. 24 Capital City 400
September 9, 1979 Average Speed: 80.604

Driver	Owner	Car #	Make	Laps	Winnings
1. Bobby Allison	Bud Moore	15	Ford	400	15,400
2. Darrell Waltrip	DiGard	88	Chev	400	9,525
3. Ricky Rudd	Junie Donlavey	90	Ford	399	5,650
4. Dale Earnhardt	Rod Osterlund	2	Chev	399	7,250
5. Cale Yarborough	Junior Johnson	11	Olds	398	5,975

1980 Winston Cup GN Race No. 24 Capital City 400
September 7, 1980 Average Speed: 79.722

Driver	Owner	Car #	Make	Laps	Winnings
1. Bobby Allison	Bud Moore	15	Ford	400	17,175
2. Richard Petty	Petty Enterprises	43	Chev	400	13,350
3. Lennie Pond	Jim Testa	68	Chev	400	5,150
4. Dale Earnhardt	Rod Osterlund	2	Chev	399	7,575
5. Jody Ridley	Junie Donlavey	90	Ford	398	4,710

1981 Winston Cup GN Race No. 24 Wrangler Sanfor-Set 400
September 13, 1981 Average Speed: 69.998

Driver	Owner	Car #	Make	Laps	Winnings
1. Benny Parsons	Bud Moore	15	Ford	400	18,525
2. Harry Gant	Hal Needham	33	Pont	400	10,195
3. Darrell Waltrip	Junior Johnson	11	Buick	400	12,500
4. Terry Labonte	Billy Hagan	44	Buick	400	7,550
5. Bobby Allison	Harry Ranier	28	Buick	400	7,275

1976 Winston Cup GN Race No. 4 Richmond 400
March 7, 1976 Average Speed: 72.792

Driver	Owner	Car #	Make	Laps	Winnings
1. Dave Marcis	Nord Krauskopf	71	Dodg	400	9,300
2. Richard Petty	Petty Enterprises	43	Dodg	400	8,025
3. Bobby Allison	Roger Penske	2	Merc	399	6,230
4. Cale Yarborough	Junior Johnson	11	Chev	388	4,745
5. Terry Bivins	Billy Moyer	63	Chev	386	2,050

1977 Winston Cup GN Race No. 3 Richmond 400
February 27, 1977 Average Speed: 73.084

Driver	Owner	Car #	Make	Laps	Winnings
1. Cale Yarborough	Junior Johnson	11	Chev	245	12,100
2. Darrell Waltrip	DiGard	88	Chev	245	7,775
3. Benny Parsons	L. G. DeWitt	72	Chev	245	6,325
4. Dave Marcis	Roger Penske	2	Chev	244	4,700
5. Bobby Allison	Bobby Allison	12	Mata	244	2,000

1978 Winston Cup GN Race No. 3 Richmond 400
February 26, 1978 Average Speed: 80.304

Driver	Owner	Car #	Make	Laps	Winnings
1. Benny Parsons	L. G. DeWitt	72	Chev	400	13,200
2. Lennie Pond	Harry Ranier	54	Chev	400	6,050
3. Cale Yarborough	Junior Johnson	11	Olds	399	8,050
4. Darrell Waltrip	DiGard	88	Chev	399	5,250
5. Dick Brooks	Junie Donlavey	90	Ford	397	3,325

1979 Winston Cup GN Race No. 4 Richmond 400
March 11, 1979 Average Speed: 83.608

Driver	Owner	Car #	Make	Laps	Winnings
1. Cale Yarborough	Junior Johnson	11	Olds	400	16,275
2. Bobby Allison	Bud Moore	15	Ford	400	10,750
3. Darrell Waltrip	DiGard	88	Chev	399	6,925
4. Benny Parsons	M. C. Anderson	27	Chev	399	2,550
5. Richard Petty	Petty Enterprises	43	Chev	399	4,800

1980 Winston Cup GN Race No. 3 Richmond 400
February 24, 1980 Average Speed: 67.703

Driver	Owner	Car #	Make	Laps	Winnings
1. Darrell Waltrip	DiGard	88	Chev	400	17,800
2. Bobby Allison	Bud Moore	15	Ford	400	10,975
3. Richard Petty	Petty Enterprises	43	Chev	400	9,375
4. Dave Marcis	Dave Marcis	71	Chev	400	4,310
5. Dale Earnhardt	Rod Osterlund	2	Chev	398	6,550

1981 Winston Cup GN Race No. 3 Richmond 400
February 22, 1981 Average Speed: 76.570

Driver	Owner	Car #	Make	Laps	Winnings
1. Darrell Waltrip	Junior Johnson	11	Buick	400	18,800
2. Ricky Rudd	DiGard	88	Olds	400	13,400
3. Richard Petty	Petty Enterprises	43	Buick	399	9,775
4. Morgan Shepherd	Cliff Stewart	5	Pont	399	5,100
5. Benny Parsons	Bud Moore	15	Ford	399	7,050

1982 Winston Cup GN Race No. 2 Richmond 400
February 21, 1982 Average Speed: 72.914

Driver	Owner	Car #	Make	Laps	Winnings
1. Dave Marcis	Dave Marcis	71	Chev	250	19,145
2. Richard Petty	Petty Enterprises	43	Pont	250	16,325
3. Benny Parsons	Harry Ranier	28	Pont	250	15,475
4. Dale Earnhardt	Bud Moore	15	Ford	250	10,960
5. Terry Labonte	Billy Hagan	44	Chev	249	6,330

Richmond Int'l Raceway *continued*

1982 Winston Cup GN Race No. 23 Wrangler Sanfor-Set 400
September 12, 1982 Average Speed: 82.800

Driver	Owner	Car #	Make	Laps	Winnings
1. Bobby Allison	DiGard	88	Chev	400	25,750
2. Tim Richmond	Jim Stacy	2	Buick	400	13,795
3. Darrell Waltrip	Junior Johnson	11	Buick	399	15,525
4. Ricky Rudd	Richard Childress	3	Pont	399	7,930
5. Neil Bonnett	Wood Brothers	21	Ford	398	3,710

1983 Winston Cup GN Race No. 2 Richmond 400
February 27, 1983 Average Speed: 79.584

Driver	Owner	Car #	Make	Laps	Winnings
1. Bobby Allison	DiGard	22	Chev	400	23,725
2. Dale Earnhardt	Bud Moore	15	Ford	400	16,575
3. Neil Bonnett	Bob Rahilly & Butch Mock	75	Chev	400	9,975
4. Geoff Bodine	Cliff Stewart	88	Pont	399	8,445
5. Harry Gant	Hal Needham	33	Buick	399	11,260

1983 Winston Cup GN Race No. 23 Wrangler Sanfor-Set 400
September 11, 1983 Average Speed: 79.381

Driver	Owner	Car #	Make	Laps	Winnings
1. Bobby Allison	DiGard	22	Buick	400	39,925
2. Ricky Rudd	Richard Childress	3	Chev	400	19,025
3. Darrell Waltrip	Junior Johnson	11	Chev	399	24,010
4. Bill Elliott	Harry Melling	9	Ford	399	8,270
5. Terry Labonte	Billy Hagan	44	Chev	398	8,005

1984 Winston Cup GN Race No. 2 Miller High Life 400
February 26, 1984 Average Speed: 76.736

Driver	Owner	Car #	Make	Laps	Winnings
1. Ricky Rudd	Bud Moore	15	Ford	400	31,775
2. Darrell Waltrip	Junior Johnson	11	Chev	400	27,865
3. Terry Labonte	Billy Hagan	44	Chev	400	12,465
4. Bill Elliott	Harry Melling	9	Ford	399	11,000
5. Neil Bonnett	Junior Johnson	12	Chev	399	4,820

1984 Winston Cup GN Race No. 23 Wrangler Sanfor-Set 400
September 9, 1984 Average Speed: 74.780

Driver	Owner	Car #	Make	Laps	Winnings
1. Darrell Waltrip	Junior Johnson	11	Chev	400	46,550
2. Ricky Rudd	Bud Moore	15	Ford	400	22,325
3. Dale Earnhardt	Richard Childress	3	Chev	400	13,450
4. Geoff Bodine	Rick Hendrick	5	Chev	399	10,400
5. Richard Petty	Mike Curb	43	Pont	399	7,730

1985 Winston Cup GN Race No. 2 Miller High Life 400
February 24, 1985 Average Speed: 67.945

Driver	Owner	Car #	Make	Laps	Winnings
1. Dale Earnhardt	Richard Childress	3	Chev	400	33,625
2. Geoff Bodine	Rick Hendrick	5	Chev	400	22,165
3. Darrell Waltrip	Junior Johnson	11	Chev	400	21,110
4. Ron Bouchard	Jack Beebe	47	Buick	400	9,530
5. Harry Gant	Hal Needham	33	Chev	399	12,120

1985 Winston Cup GN Race No. 21 Wrangler Sanfor-Set 400
September 8, 1985 Average Speed: 72.508

Driver	Owner	Car #	Make	Laps	Winnings
1. Darrell Waltrip	Junior Johnson	11	Chev	400	35,300
2. Terry Labonte	Billy Hagan	44	Chev	400	23,850
3. Richard Petty	Mike Curb	43	Pont	400	14,625
4. Dale Earnhardt	Richard Childress	3	Chev	400	12,050
5. Ricky Rudd	Bud Moore	15	Ford	400	9,900

1986 Winston Cup Race No. 2 Miller High Life 400
February 23, 1986 Average Speed: 71.078

Driver	Owner	Car #	Make	Laps	Winnings
1. Kyle Petty	Wood Brothers	7	Ford	400	37,880
2. Joe Ruttman	Kenny Bernstein	26	Buick	400	16,215
3. Dale Earnhardt	Richard Childress	3	Chev	400	19,310
4. Bobby Allison	Stavola Brothers	22	Buick	399	6,275
5. Darrell Waltrip	Junior Johnson	11	Chev	398	14,295

1986 Winston Cup Race No. 22 Wrangler Jeans Indigo 400
September 7, 1986 Average Speed: 70.161

Driver	Owner	Car #	Make	Laps	Winnings
1. Tim Richmond	Rick Hendrick	25	Chev	400	35,005
2. Dale Earnhardt	Richard Childress	3	Chev	400	24,525
3. Morgan Shepherd	Bob Rahilly & Butch Mock	75	Pont	400	13,655
4. Richard Petty	Petty Enterprises	43	Pont	400	10,260
5. Neil Bonnett	Junior Johnson	12	Chev	400	12,075

1987 Winston Cup Race No. 3 Miller High Life 400
March 8, 1987 Average Speed: 81.520

Driver	Owner	Car #	Make	Laps	Winnings
1. Dale Earnhardt	Richard Childress	3	Chev	400	49,150
2. Geoff Bodine	Rick Hendrick	5	Chev	400	24,010
3. Rusty Wallace	Raymond Beadle	27	Pont	400	18,225
4. Bill Elliott	Harry Melling	9	Ford	400	14,285
5. Terry Labonte	Junior Johnson	11	Chev	400	13,590

1987 Winston Cup Race No. 22 Wrangler Jeans Indigo 400
September 13, 1987 Average Speed: 67.074

Driver	Owner	Car #	Make	Laps	Winnings
1. Dale Earnhardt	Richard Childress	3	Chev	400	44,950
2. Darrell Waltrip	Rick Hendrick	17	Chev	400	22,680
3. Ricky Rudd	Bud Moore	15	Ford	400	20,050
4. Bill Elliott	Harry Melling	9	Ford	400	14,675
5. Richard Petty	Petty Enterprises	43	Pont	399	10,180

1988 Winston Cup Race No. 2 Pontiac Excitement 400
February 21, 1988 Average Speed: 66.401

Driver	Owner	Car #	Make	Laps	Winnings
1. Neil Bonnett	Bob Rahilly & Butch Mock	75	Pont	400	45,900
2. Ricky Rudd	Kenny Bernstein	26	Buick	400	25,660
3. Richard Petty	Petty Enterprises	43	Pont	400	16,975
4. Darrell Waltrip	Rick Hendrick	17	Chev	400	14,185
5. Sterling Marlin	Billy Hagan	44	Olds	400	12,315

1988 Winston Cup Race No. 22 Miller High Life 400
September 11, 1988 Average Speed: 95.770

Driver	Owner	Car #	Make	Laps	Winnings
1. Davey Allison	Harry Ranier	28	Ford	400	57,800
2. Dale Earnhardt	Richard Childress	3	Chev	400	29,625
3. Terry Labonte	Junior Johnson	11	Chev	400	20,525
4. Mark Martin	Jack Roush	6	Ford	400	10,925
5. Alan Kulwicks	Alan Kulwicki	7	Ford	400	15,825

1989 Winston Cup Race No. 4 Pontiac Excitement 400
March 26, 1989 Average Speed: 89.619

Driver	Owner	Car #	Make	Laps	Winnings
1. Rusty Wallace	Raymond Beadle	27	Pont	400	63,025
2. Alan Kulwicki	Alan Kulwicki	7	Ford	400	28,625
3. Dale Earnhardt	Richard Childress	3	Chev	400	30,900
4. Ricky Rudd	Kenny Bernstein	26	Buick	400	13,600
5. Davey Allison	Robert Yates	28	Ford	399	17,607

Richmond Int'l Raceway *continued*

1989 Winston Cup Race No. 22 Miller High Life 400
September 10, 1989 Average Speed: 88.380

Driver	Owner	Car #	Make	Laps	Winnings
1. Rusty Wallace	Raymond Beadle	27	Pont	400	55,650
2. Dale Earnhardt	Richard Childress	3	Chev	400	31,475
3. Geoff Bodine	Rick Hendrick	5	Chev	400	21,750
4. Ricky Rudd	Kenny Bernstein	26	Buick	399	16,450
5. Harry Gant	Leo Jackson	33	Olds	399	15,175

1990 Winston Cup Series Race No. 2 Pontiac Excitement 400
February 25, 1990 Average Speed: 92.158

Driver	Owner	Car #	Make	Laps	Winnings
1. Mark Martin	Jack Roush	6	Ford	400	59,150
2. Dale Earnhardt	Richard Childress	3	Chev	400	42,600
3. Ricky Rudd	Rick Hendrick	5	Chev	400	25,050
4. Bill Elliott	Harry Melling	9	Ford	400	16,650
5. Dick Trickle	Cale Yarborough	66	Pont	400	14,325

1990 Winston Cup Series Race No. 22 Miller Genuine Draft 400
September 9, 1990 Average Speed: 95.567

Driver	Owner	Car #	Make	Laps	Winnings
1. Dale Earnhardt	Richard Childress	3	Chev	400	59,225
2. Mark Martin	Jack Roush	6	Ford	400	30,550
3. Darrell Waltrip	Rick Hendrick	17	Chev	400	25,107
4. Bill Elliott	Harry Melling	9	Ford	400	16,950
5. Rusty Wallace	Raymond Beadle	27	Pont	400	19,525

1991 Winston Cup Series Race No. 2 Pontiac Excitement 400
February 24, 1991 Average Speed: 105.937

Driver	Owner	Car #	Make	Laps	Winnings
1. Dale Earnhardt	Richard Childress	3	Chev	400	67,950
2. Ricky Rudd	Rick Hendrick	5	Chev	400	45,675
3. Harry Gant	Leo Jackson	33	Olds	400	25,500
4. Rusty Wallace	Roger Penske	2	Pont	400	13,050
5. Alan Kulwicki	Alan Kulwicki	7	Ford	400	19,025

1991 Winston Cup Series Race No. 22 Miller Genuine Draft 400
September 7, 1991 Average Speed: 101.361

Driver	Owner	Car #	Make	Laps	Winnings
1. Harry Gant	Leo Jackson	33	Olds	400	63,650
2. Davey Allison	Robert Yates	28	Ford	400	39,425
3. Rusty Wallace	Roger Penske	2	Pont	400	21,700
4. Ernie Irvan	Larry McClure	4	Chev	400	20,800
5. Ricky Rudd	Rick Hendrick	5	Chev	400	18,125

1992 Winston Cup Race No. 3 Pontiac Excitement 400
March 8, 1992 Average Speed: 104.378

Driver	Owner	Car #	Make	Laps	Winnings
1. Bill Elliott	Junior Johnson	11	Ford	400	272,700
2. Alan Kulwicki	Alan Kulwicki	7	Ford	400	36,525
3. Harry Gant	Leo Jackson	33	Olds	400	31,950
4. Davey Allison	Robert Yates	28	Ford	400	25,100
5. Darrell Waltrip	Darrell Waltrip	17	Chev	400	21,775

1992 Winston Cup Race No. 22 Miller Genuine Draft 400
September 12, 1992 Average Speed: 104.661

Driver	Owner	Car #	Make	Laps	Winnings
1. Rusty Wallace	Roger Penske	2	Pont	400	47,115
2. Mark Martin	Jack Roush	6	Ford	400	48,365
3. Darrell Waltrip	Darrell Waltrip	17	Chev	400	44,360
4. Dale Earnhardt	Richard Childress	3	Chev	400	29,655
5. Geoff Bodine	Bud Moore	15	Ford	400	19,980

1993 Winston Cup Series Race No. 3 Pontiac Excitement 400
March 7, 1993 Average Speed: 107.000

Driver	Owner	Car #	Make	Laps	Winnings
1. Davey Allison	Robert Yates	28	Ford	400	70,125
2. Rusty Wallace	Roger Penske	2	Pont	400	31,550
3. Alan Kulwicki	Alan Kulwicki	7	Ford	400	39,225
4. Dale Jarrett	Joe Gibbs	18	Chev	400	29,050
5. Kyle Petty	Felix Sabates	42	Pont	400	21,600

1993 Winston Cup Series Race No. 23 Miller Genuine Draft 400
September 11, 1993 Average Speed: 99.917

Driver	Owner	Car #	Make	Laps	Winnings
1. Rusty Wallace	Roger Penske	2	Pont	400	49,415
2. Bill Elliott	Junior Johnson	11	Ford	400	54,665
3. Dale Earnhardt	Richard Childress	3	Chev	400	35,780
4. Ricky Rudd	Rick Hendrick	5	Chev	400	26,505
5. Brett Bodine	Kenny Bernstein	26	Ford	400	21,580

1994 Winston Cup Series Race No. 3 Pontiac Excitement 400
March 4, 1994 Average Speed: 98.334

Driver	Owner	Car #	Make	Laps	Winnings
1. Ernie Irvan	Robert Yates	28	Ford	400	66,175
2. Rusty Wallace	Roger Penske	2	Ford	400	39,575
3. Jeff Gordon	Rick Hendrick	24	Chev	400	34,000
4. Dale Earnhardt	Richard Childress	3	Chev	400	29,550
5. Kyle Petty	Felix Sabates	42	Pont	400	26,500

1994 Winston Cup Series Race No. 24 Miller Genuine Draft 400
September 10, 1994 Average Speed: 104.156

Driver	Owner	Car #	Make	Laps	Winnings
1. Terry Labonte	Rick Hendrick	5	Chev	400	67,765
2. Jeff Gordon	Rick Hendrick	24	Chev	400	40,365
3. Dale Earnhardt	Richard Childress	3	Chev	400	38,830
4. Rusty Wallace	Roger Penske	2	Ford	400	30,780
5. Ricky Rudd	Ricky Rudd	10	Ford	400	26,705

1995 Winston Cup Series Race No. 3 Pontiac Excitement 400
March 5, 1995 Average Speed: 106.425

Driver	Owner	Car #	Make	Laps	Winnings
1. Terry Labonte	Rick Hendrick	5	Chev	400	82,950
2. Dale Earnhardt	Richard Childress	3	Chev	400	57,200
3. Rusty Wallace	Roger Penske	2	Ford	400	29,600
4. Ken Schrader	Rick Hendrick	25	Chev	400	31,100
5. Sterling Marlin	Larry McClure	4	Chev	400	34,400

1995 Winston Cup Series Race No. 24 Miller Genuine Draft 400
September 9, 1995 Average Speed: 104.459

Driver	Owner	Car #	Make	Laps	Winnings
1. Rusty Wallace	Roger Penske	2	Ford	400	64,515
2. Terry Labonte	Rick Hendrick	5	Chev	400	49,065
3. Dale Earnhardt	Richard Childress	3	Chev	400	54,005
4. Dale Jarrett	Robert Yates	28	Ford	400	40,605
5. Bobby Hamilton	Petty Enterprises	43	Pont	400	26,805

1996 Winston Cup Series Race No. 3 Pontiac Excitement 400
March 3, 1996 Average Speed: 102.750

Driver	Owner	Car #	Make	Laps	Winnings
1. Jeff Gordon	Rick Hendrick	24	Chev	400	92,400
2. Dale Jarrett	Robert Yates	88	Ford	400	44,225
3. Ted Musgrave	Jack Roush	16	Ford	400	42,200
4. Jeff Burton	Jack Roush	99	Ford	400	22,350
5. Mark Martin	Jack Roush	6	Ford	400	37,850

Richmond Int'l Raceway *continued*

1996 Winston Cup Series Race No. 24 Miller Genuine Draft 400
September 7, 1996 Average Speed: 105.469

Driver	Owner	Car #	Make	Laps	Winnings
1. Ernie Irvan	Robert Yates	28	Ford	400	86,665
2. Jeff Gordon	Rick Hendrick	24	Chev	400	59,640
3. Jeff Burton	Jack Roush	99	Ford	400	50,755
4. Dale Jarrett	Robert Yates	88	Ford	400	30,505
5. Terry Labonte	Rick Hendrick	5	Chev	400	37,155

South Boston Speedway
South Boston, VA
Quarter-mile Paved Track

Quarter-mile dirt oval opened in August 1957. First NASCAR Winston Cup (then Grand National) race staged on 8/20/60 (won by Junior Johnson). Re-measured as .375-mile oval in 1962 and again as .357-mile oval in 1970. Final Winston Cup Grand National race run on 5/9/71 (won by Benny Parsons, his first Winston Cup victory). Track still in operation, operating as .4-mile oval.

Winston Cup Starts
Richard Petty   10

Winston Cup Victories
Richard Petty   5

Winston Cup Poles
Bobby Isaac   2
Ned Jarrett   2
Richard Petty   2
Jack Smith   2

Winston Cup Money
Richard Petty $8,735

Most Cars Started
28—May 9, 1971 Halifax County 100

Fewest Cars Started
15—August 20, 1960

Narrowest Margin of Victory
5 car lengths—August 23, 1968

Narrowest Margin of Victory
8.000 seconds May 17, 1964

Slowest Race
48.348 MPH—August 27, 1961

Race Record
76.906 MPH—August 21, 1969
South Boston 100

Most Cautions
3—May 17, 1964

Most Race Leaders
4—October 20, 1963 South Boston 400
4—May 17, 1964

Most Cars Running at Finish
17—June 23, 1962

1960 Grand National Race No. 33
August 20, 1960 Average Speed: 50.732

Driver	Owner	Car #	Make	Laps	Winnings
1. Junior Johnson	John Masoni	27	59 Chev	150	810
2. Possum Jones	Tom Daniels	2	60 Chev	149	545
3. Rex White	Rex White	4	59 Chev	148	410
4. Buck Baker	Buck Baker	87	60 Chev	147	290
5. Fred Harb	Fred Harb	17	58 Ford	146	260

1961 Grand National Race No. 41
August 27, 1961 Average Speed: 48.348

Driver	Owner	Car #	Make	Laps	Winnings
1. Junior Johnson	Rex Lovette	27	60 Pont	200	800
2. Jim Reed	Jim Reed	7	61 Chev	199	525
3. Ned Jarrett	Bee Gee Holloway	11	61 Chev	197	375
4. Emanuel Zervakis	Monroe Shook	85	60 Chev	196	275
5. Rex White	Rex White	4	60 Chev	195	350

1962 Grand National Race No. 28
June 23, 1962 Average Speed: 72.540

Driver	Owner	Car #	Make	Laps	Winnings
1. Rex White	Rex White	4	62 Chev	267	1,000
2. Jack Smith	Jack Smith	47	61 Pont	267	600
3. Richard Petty	Petty Enterprises	43	62 Plym	267	400
4. Johnny Allen	Fred Lovette	58	61 Pont	265	300
5. Larry Thomas	Wade Younts	36	62 Dodg	262	275

1963 Grand National Race No. 17 South Boston 400
April 14, 1963 Average Speed: 75.229

Driver	Owner	Car #	Make	Laps	Winnings
1. Richard Petty	Petty Enterprises	43	63 Plym	400	1,500
2. Jim Paschal	Petty Enterprises	41	62 Plym	398	900
3. Ned Jarrett	Charles Robinson	11	63 Ford	394	700
4. Larry Manning	Bob Adams	09	62 Chev	374	550
5. Earl Brooks	Wendell Scott	134	61 Chev	369	450

1963 Grand National Race No. 53 South Boston 400
October 20, 1963 Average Speed: 76.325

Driver	Owner	Car #	Make	Laps	Winnings
1. Richard Petty	Petty Enterprises	41	63 Plym	400	1,550
2. David Pearson	Cotton Owens	6	63 Dodg	397	900
3. Joe Weatherly	Bud Moore	8	63 Pont	396	925
4. Bob Welborn	Petty Enterprises	42	63 Plym	394	550
5. Larry Thomas	Wade Younts	36	62 Dodg	388	450

1964 Grand National Race No. 24
May 17, 1964 Average Speed: 71.957

Driver	Owner	Car #	Make	Laps	Winnings
1. Richard Petty	Petty Enterprises	43	63 Plym	267	1,000
2. Marvin Panch	Wood Brothers	21	64 Ford	267	600
3. Ned Jarrett	Bondy Long	11	64 Ford	265	400
4. David Pearson	Cotton Owens	6	64 Dodg	260	300
5. Roy Mayne	Bob Adams	09	62 Chev	256	275

1968 Grand National Race No. 37
August 23, 1968 Average Speed: 75.916

Driver	Owner	Car #	Make	Laps	Winnings
1. Richard Petty	Petty Enterprises	43	68 Plym	267	1,200
2. David Pearson	Holman-Moody	17	68 Ford	267	600
3. Bobby Isaac	Nord Krauskopf	71	67 Dodg	267	400
4. Charlie Glotzbach	Cotton Owens	6	68 Dodg	265	300
5. Buddy Baker	Ray Fox	3	68 Dodg	264	255

1969 Grand National Race No. 38 South Boston 100
August 21, 1969 Average Speed: 76.906

Driver	Owner	Car #	Make	Laps	Winnings
1. Bobby Isaac	Nord Krauskopf	71	68 Dodg	267	1,000
2. David Pearson	Holman-Moody	17	69 Ford	267	800
3. Richard Petty	Petty Enterprises	43	69 Ford	266	400
4. James Hylton	James Hylton	48	68 Dodg	261	350
5. Elmo Langley	Elmo Langley	64	68 Ford	259	325

1970 Grand National Race No. 37 Halifax County 100
August 29, 1970 Average Speed: 73.060

Driver	Owner	Car #	Make	Laps	Winnings
1. Richard Petty	Petty Enterprises	43	70 Plym	281	1,500
2. Bobby Isaac	Nord Krauskopf	71	70 Dodg	281	900
3. Bobby Allison	Bobby Allison	22	69 Dodg	280	500
4. Benny Parsons	L. G. DeWitt	72	69 Ford	279	350
5. James Hylton	James Hylton	48	70 Ford	277	325

1971 Winston Cup GN Race No. 17 Halifax County 100
May 9, 1971 Average Speed: 72.271

Driver	Owner	Car #	Make	Laps	Winnings
1. Benny Parsons	L. G. DeWitt	72	70 Ford	281	1,500
2. Richard Petty	Petty Enterprises	43	71 Plym	280	900
3. James Hylton	James Hylton	48	71 Ford	277	500
4. Walter Ballard	Walter Ballard	30	71 Ford	273	350
5. Cecil Gordon	Cecil Gordon	24	69 Merc	273	325

Southside Speedway
Richmond, VA
Quarter-mile Paved Track

(aka Royall Speedway) .2-mile paved oval built in 1947. Lengthened to quarter-mile track in April 1950. First NASCAR Winston Cup (then Grand National) race staged on 8/18/61 (won by Junior Johnson). Re-measured at .333-mile in 1962. Final Grand National race run on 5/19/63 (won by Ned Jarett). Track still in operation.

Winston Cup Starts

Curtis Crider	4
Ned Jarrett	4
Jimmy Pardue	4
Richard Petty	4
Wendell Scott	4
Larry Thomas	4

Winston Cup Victories

Ned Jarrett	1
Junior Johnson	1
Jimmy Pardue	1
Jim Paschal	1

Winston Cup Poles

Rex White	2

Winston Cup Money

Ned Jarrett	$2,265

Most Cars Started
25—June 22, 1962

Fewest Cars Started
16—May 4, 1962

Narrowest Margin of Victory
N/A

Slowest Race
51.605 MPH—August 18, 1961

Race Record
67.747 MPH—May 4, 1962

Most Cautions
N/A

Most Race Leaders
3—June 22, 1962

Most Cars Running at Finish
19—June 22, 1962

1961 Grand National Race No. 40
August 18, 1961 Average Speed: 51.605

Driver	Owner	Car #	Make	Laps	Winnings
1. Junior Johnson	Rex Lovette	27	60 Pont	150	600
2. Ned Jarrett	Bee Gee Holloway	11	61 Chev	149	475
3. Emanuel Zervakis	Monroe Shook	85	61 Chev	149	380
4. Rex White	Rex White	4	60 Chev	148	425
5. Jimmy Pardue	Jimmy Pardue	54	60 Chev	148	225

1962 Grand National Race No. 18
May 4, 1962 Average Speed: 67.747

Driver	Owner	Car #	Make	Laps	Winnings
1. Jimmy Pardue	Jimmy Pardue	54	62 Pont	200	550
2. Jack Smith	Jack Smith	47	61 Pont	200	480
3. Richard Petty	Petty Enterprises	43	60 Plym	199	375
4. Joe Weatherly	Fred Harb	17	61 Ford	197	290
5. Jim Paschal	Cliff Stewart	2	62 Pont	196	275

1962 Grand National Race No. 27
June 22, 1962 Average Speed: 66.293

Driver	Owner	Car #	Make	Laps	Winnings
1. Jim Paschal	Cliff Stewart	2	62 Pont	300	1,010
2. Rex White	Rex White	4	62 Chev	299	650
3. Jimmy Pardue	Jimmy Pardue	54	62 Pont	298	400
4. Johnny Allen	Fred Lovette	58	61 Pont	297	300
5. Jim Reed	Ratus Walters	77	62 Pont	296	290

1963 Grand National Race No. 25
May 19, 1963 Average Speed: 65.052

Driver	Owner	Car #	Make	Laps	Winnings
1. Ned Jarrett	Charles Robinson	11	63 Ford	300	1,000
2. Richard Petty	Petty Enterprises	41	63 Plym	298	600
3. Larry Thomas	Wade Younts	36	62 Dodg	294	400
4. Jimmy Pardue	Pete Stewart	57	62 Pont	291	300
5. Ray Hendrick	Rebel Racing	35	61 Pont	288	275

Starkey Speedway
Roanoke, VA
Quarter-mile Paved Track

Quarter-mile paved oval opened in October 1950. First NASCAR Winston Cup (then Grand National) race staged on 5/15/58 (Jim Reed won). Last Grand National race staged on 8/23/64 (won by Junior Johnson). Track closed in 1966.

Winston Cup Starts

Curtis Crider	3
Fred Harb	3
Ned Jarrett	3
Jimmy Pardue	3
Richard Petty	3
Wendell Scott	3
Larry Thomas	3

Winston Cup Victories

Junior Johnson 2

Winston Cup Poles

Jim Reed	1
Jack Smith	1
Rex White	1
Glen Wood	1

Winston Cup Money

Junior Johnson $1,750

Most Cars Started

22—May 15, 1958
22—August 23, 1964

Fewest Cars Started

18—August 15, 1962

Narrowest Margin of Victory

N/A

Slowest Race

49.504 MPH—May 15, 1958

Race Record

51.165 MPH—August 15, 1962

Most Race Leaders

N/A

Most Cars Running at Finish

19—May 15, 1958

1958 Grand National Race No. 17
May 15, 1958 Average Speed: 49.504

Driver	Owner	Car #	Make	Laps	Winnings
1. Jim Reed	Jim Reed	7	57 Ford	150	550
2. Rex White	J. H. Petty	44	57 Chev	150	450
3. Eddie Pagan	Eddie Pagan	45	57 Ford	149	325
4. Frankie Schneider	Frankie Schneider	62	57 Chev	148	250
5. Curtis Turner	Holman-Moody	26	58 Ford	148	215

1961 Grand National Race No. 31
June 24, 1961 Average Speed: 49.907

Driver	Owner	Car #	Make	Laps	Winnings
1. Junior Johnson	Rex Lovette	27	60 Pont	150	900
2. Rex White	Rex White	4	60 Chev	149	725
3. Jim Paschal	J. H. Petty	14	61 Pont	149	475
4. Richard Petty	Petty Enterprises	43	61 Plym	147	295
5. Emanuel Zervakis	Monroe Shook	85	60 Chev	146	250

1962 Grand National Race No. 41
August 15, 1962 Average Speed: 51.165

Driver	Owner	Car #	Make	Laps	Winnings
1. Richard Petty	Petty Enterprises	42	62 Plym	200	550
2. Joe Weatherly	Bud Moore	8	62 Pont	200	480
3. Ned Jarrett	Bee Gee Holloway	11	62 Chev	200	575
4. Bob Welborn	J. C. Parker	49	62 Pont	200	325
5. Jack Smith	Jack Smith	47	62 Pont	200	245

1964 Grand National Race No. 50
August 23, 1964 Average Speed: 49.847

Driver	Owner	Car #	Make	Laps	Winnings
1. Junior Johnson	Banjo Matthews	27	64 Ford	200	850
2. Ned Jarrett	Bondy Long	11	64 Ford	199	530
3. Glen Wood	Wood Brothers	21	64 Ford	199	430
4. David Pearson	Cotton Owens	6	64 Dodg	199	350
5. Jimmy Pardue	Charles Robinson	54	64 Plym	199	300

Washington

Bremerton Raceway
Bremerton, WA
.9-mile Paved Road Course

(aka Kitsap County Airport; Sea Fair Races; Thunderbird Stadium) Originated as 1.25-mile dirt oval. Started using airport runways for races in 1950. Three different size road courses (.9-mile, 2-mile, and 4-mile) were used from 1955–57. Only NASCAR Winston Cup (then Grand National) race staged on 8/4/57 (won by Parnelli Jones on .9-mile track). Course discontinued in 1958.

Winston Cup Victories
Parnelli Jones   1

Winston Cup Money
Parnelli Jones $900

Narrowest Margin of Victory
N/A

Most Race Leaders
1—August 4, 1957

Winston Cup Poles
Art Watts   1

Most Cars Started
14—August 4, 1957

Race Record
38.959 MPH—August 4, 1957

Most Cars Running at Finish
12—August 4, 1957

1957 Grand National Race No. 36
August 4, 1957 Average Speed: 38.959

Driver	Owner	Car #	Make	Laps	Winnings
1. Parnelli Jones	Oscar Maples	11	57 Ford	80	900
2. Lloyd Dane	Lloyd Dane	44	57 Ford	80	610
3. Art Watts	Al Schmidhamer	22N	56 Ford	80	465
4. Eddie Pagan	Eddie Pagan	45	57 Ford	79	315
5. Bob Rauscher		21N	57 Ford	77	270

West Virginia

West Virginia Int'l Speedway
Huntington, WV
.4375-mile Paved Track

(aka Huntington Int'l Speedway; Int'l Raceway Park; Dick Clark's Int'l Raceway Park) Once owned by TV personality Dick Clark, the .375-mile paved track opened with NASCAR Winston Cup (then Grand National) race on 8/18/63 (Fred Lorenzen won). Re-measured as .4375-mile oval in 1964. Final Winston Cup Grand National race run on 8/8/71 (won by Richard Petty). Track closed in 1972.

Winston Cup Starts
Neil Castles 4
Richard Petty 4
Wendell Scott 4

Winston Cup Victories
Richard Petty 3

Winston Cup Poles
Bobby Allison 2

Winston Cup Money
Richard Petty $6,800

Most Cars Started
35—August 8, 1971 West Virginia 500

Fewest Cars Started
20—August 18, 1963 Mountaineer 300

Narrowest Margin of Victory
1 lap plus—August 18, 1963
Mountaineer 300

Slowest Race
59.340 MPH—August 18, 1963
Mountaineer 300

Race Record
83.805 MPH—August 8, 1971
West Virginia 500

Most Cautions
7—August 18, 1963 Mountaineer 300

Most Race Leaders
4—August 18, 1963 Mountaineer 300
4—August 16, 1964 Mountaineer 500

Most Cars Running at Finish
16—August 18, 1963 Mountaineer 300

1963 Grand National Race No. 44 Mountaineer 300
August 18, 1963 Average Speed: 59.340

Driver	Owner	Car #	Make	Laps	Winnings
1. Fred Lorenzen	Holman-Moody	28	63 Ford	300	1,600
2. Joe Weatherly	Bud Moore	8	63 Pont	299	1,225
3. Jim Paschal	Petty Enterprises	42	63 Plym	299	750
4. Ned Jarrett	Charles Robinson	11	63 Ford	297	600
5. Buck Baker	Buck Baker	87	63 Pont	296	450

1964 Grand National Race No. 47 Mountaineer 500
August 16, 1964 Average Speed: 70.488

Driver	Owner	Car #	Make	Laps	Winnings
1. Richard Petty	Petty Enterprises	43	64 Plym	500	2,550
2. Junior Johnson	Banjo Matthews	27	64 Ford	497	1,600
3. Ned Jarrett	Bondy Long	11	64 Ford	494	1,225
4. Jim Paschal	Petty Enterprises	41	64 Plym	494	1,000
5. Earl Balmer	Cotton Owens	5	64 Dodg	489	800

1970 Grand National Race No. 33 West Virginia 300
August 11, 1970 Average Speed: 78.358

Driver	Owner	Car #	Make	Laps	Winnings
1. Richard Petty	Petty Enterprises	43	70 Plym	300	1,700
2. James Hylton	James Hylton	48	70 Ford	292	1,100
3. Neil Castles	Neil Castles	06	69 Dodg	290	600
4. John Sears	John Sears	4	69 Dodg	290	480
5. Dave Marcis	Cecil Gordon	97	68 Ford	283	425

1971 Winston Cup GN Race No. 35 West Virginia 500
August 8, 1971 Average Speed: 83.805

Driver	Owner	Car #	Make	Laps	Winnings
1. Richard Petty	Petty Enterprises	43	71 Plym	500	2,300
2. Bobby Allison	Melvin Joseph	49	70 Ford	498	1,500
3. James Hylton	James Hylton	48	71 Ford	495	950
4. Tiny Lund	Ronnie Hopkins	55	70 Chev	493	750
5. Cecil Gordon	Cecil Gordon	24	69 Merc	482	650

Wisconsin

Road America
Elkhart Lake, WI
4.1-mile Road Course

4.0-mile road course opened in September 1955. Track was built after races through the street and village were discontinued. Only NASCAR Winston Cup (then Grand National) race staged on 8/12/56 (won by Tim Flock, his final Grand National victory). The NASCAR race was run in the rain. Old store-bought-type tires, then utilized in big-league NASCAR racing, had treaded grooves, so the race went on as scheduled. A second event was scheduled in 1957, but was canceled due to conflicting race dates with other NASCAR events. Today the site of IndyCar races and sportscar events.

Winston Cup Victories	**Winston Cup Money**	**Narrowest Margin of Victory**	**Most Race Leaders**
Tim Flock 1	Tim Flock $2,950	17 seconds August 12, 1956	4—August 12, 1956
Winston Cup Poles	**Most Cars Started**	**Race Record**	**Most Cars Running at Finish**
Frank Mundy 1	26—August 12, 1956	73.858 MPH—August 12, 1956	14—August 12, 1956

1956 Grand National Race No. 37
August 12, 1956 Average Speed: 73.858

Driver	Owner	Car #	Make	Laps	Winnings
1. Tim Flock	Bill Stroppe	15	56 Merc	63	2,950
2. Billy Myers	Bill Stroppe	14	56 Merc	63	1,900
3. Fireball Roberts	Pete DePaolo	22	56 Ford	63	1,275
4. Paul Goldsmith	Smokey Yunick	3	56 Chev	63	900
5. Joe Eubanks	James Satcher	56	56 Ford	63	675

Canada

Canadian National Exposition Speedway
Toronto, Canada
.333-Mile Paved Track

(aka CNE Stadium) Originally built as horse track in 1904, and converted to a .333-mile track circa 1952. Paved in mid-'50s. First NASCAR Winston Cup (then Grand National) race staged on 7/18/58 (won by Lee Petty). Site of Richard Petty's first Winston Cup (then Grand National) start. Lorne Greene, of Bonanza fame. served as public address announcer in 1950s. Track closed in 1966, but special events have been run into the '90s. Both the Toronto Blue Jays baseball team and Canadian football team, the Toronto Argonauts played in the stadium in later years until a new downtown sports facility was built.

Winston Cup Victories
Lee Petty   1

Winston Cup Poles
Rex White   1

Winston Cup Money
Lee Petty $575

Most Cars Started
19—July 18, 1958

Narrowest Margin of Victory
N/A

Race Record
43.184 MPH—July 18, 1958

Most Race Leaders
2—July 18, 1958

Most Cars Running at Finish
16—July 18, 1958

1958 Grand National Race No. 31
July 18, 1958 Average Speed: 43.184

Driver	Owner	Car #	Make	Laps	Winnings
1. Lee Petty	Petty Enterprises	42	57 Olds	100	575
2. Cotton Owens	Jim Stephens	6	57 Pont	100	480
3. Jim Reed	Jim Reed	7	57 Ford	100	305
4. Shorty Rollins	Shorty Rollins	99	58 Ford	100	275
5. Johnny Mackison	Ken Corman	23	57 Merc	99	220

Stamford Park
Niagara Falls, ONT
Half-mile Dirt Track

Originally a horse track built in 1950. Half-mile dirt track was the site of first NASCAR Winston Cup (then Grand National) race run outside the boundaries of the United States. Buddy Shuman won the 7/1/52 event. Closed after final auto race in July of 1953.

Winston Cup Victories
Buddy Shuman   1

Winston Cup Poles
Herb Thomas   1

Winston Cup Money
Buddy Shuman $1,000

Most Cars Started
17—July 1, 1952

Narrowest Margin of Victory
2 laps plus—July 1, 1952

Race Record
45.610 MPH—July 1, 1952

Most Cautions
3—July 1, 1952

Most Race Leaders
2—July 1, 1952

Most Cars Running at Finish
6—July 1, 1952

1952 Grand National Race No. 18
July 1, 1952 Average Speed: 45.610

Driver	Owner	Car #	Make	Laps	Winnings
1. Buddy Shuman	B. A. Pless	89	52 Huds	200	1,000
2. Herb Thomas	Herb Thomas	92	52 Huds	198	700
3. Ray Duhigg	J. H. Petty	44	51 Plym	193	450
4. Jack Reynolds	Wiss Brothers	421	51 Plym	183	350
5. Perk Brown			50 Ford	176	200

Index of Tracks

Smoky Mountain Speedway (TN) *see Smoky Mountain Raceway*, 892–93
Soldier Field (IL), 755
Soranno Park (NJ) *see Morristown Speedway*, 776
South Boston Speedway (VA), 917
South Florida Fairgrounds Speedway (FL) *see Palm Beach Speedway*, 735
Southern States Fairgrounds (NC), 836–37
Southland Speedway (FL) *see Palm Beach Speedway*, 735
Southland Speedway (NC) *see Raleigh Speedway*, 834
Southside Speedway (VA), 918
Speedway Park (FL) *see Jacksonville Speedway Park*, 734
Spindle City Fairgrounds (NC) *see Gastonia Fairgrounds*, 810
Stamford Park (Canada), 923
Starkey Speedway (VA), 919
Starlite Speedway (NC), 838
State Fair Speedway (NC) *see North Carolina State Fairgrounds*, 823
State Fair Speedway (OK) *see Oklahoma State Fairgrounds*, 846
State Line Speedway (NY), 787
Stewart Air Force Base (NY) *see Montgomery Air Base*, 786
Strawberry Hill (VA) *see Richmond International Raceway*, 910–16
Strawberry Hill Speedway (VA) *see Richmond International Raceway*, 910–16
Sumter Rebel Speedway (SC) *see Gamecock Speedway*, 870
Sumter Speedway (SC) *see Gamecock Speedway*, 870

Talladega Superspeedway (AL), 693–97
Tar Heel Speedway (NC), 838
Tennessee-Carolina Speedway (TN), 894
Texas International Speedway *see Texas World Speedway*, 896
Texas World Speedway, 896
Thompson International Speedway (CT), 717
Thompson Speedway (CT) *see Thompson International Speedway*, 717
Thunderbird Stadium (WA) *see Bremerton Raceway*, 920
Tioga Speedway (NY) *see Shangri-La Speedway*, 787
Titusville-Cocoa Speedway (FL), 736

Trenton International Speedway (NJ) *see Trenton Speedway*, 778
Trenton Speedway (NJ), 778
Tri-Cities Speedway (TN) *see Kingsport Speedway*, 887
Tri-City Motor Speedway (NC) *see Harris Speedway*, 812
Tri-City Speedway (NC), 839
Tri-County Fairgrounds (NY) *see Altamont-Schenectady Fairgrounds*, 781
Tucson Rodeo Grounds (AZ), 700

Union Avenue Speedway (OR) *see Portland Speedway*, 847

Valdosta Speedway (GA) *see Valdosta 75 Speedway*, 754
Valdosta 75 Speedway (GA), 754
Vernon Fairgrounds (NY), 788
Virginia State Fairgrounds *see Richmond International Raceway*, 910–16

Wall Stadium (NJ), 779
War Memorial Stadium (NY) *see Buffalo Civic Stadium*, 782
Watkins Glen International (NY), 789–90
West Capital Raceway (CA) *see Capital Speedway*, 705
West Capital Speedway (CA) *see Capital Speedway*, 705
West Michigan State Fair (MI) *see Grand River Speedrome*, 765
West Palm Beach Fairgrounds (FL) *see Palm Beach Speedway*, 735
West Palm Beach Speedway (FL) *see Palm Beach Speedway*, 735
West Virginia International Speedway, 921
Williams Grove Speedway (PA), 857
Willow Springs International Raceway (CA), 716
Willow Springs Speedway (CA) *see Willow Springs International Raceway*, 716
Wilson County Speedway (NC) *see Wilson Speedway*, 840–41
Wilson Fairgrounds (NC) *see Wilson Speedway*, 840–41
Wilson Speedway (NC), 840–41
Winchester Speedway (IN), 757
Winston-Salem Fairgrounds (NC) *see Forsyth County Fairgrounds*, 810

PART 6
THE RACES

Cum. No.	Yr. No.	Date	Site	Track Length	Surface	Miles	Race Winner	Make	Speed	Pole Winner	Make	Pole Speed
1951												
28	1	2/11/51	Daytona Beach, FL	4.1	B-R	159.9	Marshall Teague	Hudson	82.328	Tim Flock	Lincoln	102.200
29	2	4/1/51	Charlotte, NC	0.75	D	112.5	Curtis Turner	Nash	70.545	Fonty Flock	Olds	68.337
30	3	4/8/51	Mobile, AL	0.75	D	112.5	Tim Flock	Olds	50.260	No Time Trials	NTT	NTT
31	4	4/8/51	Gardena, CA	0.5	D	100	Marshall Teague	Hudson	61.047	Andy Pierce	Buick	62.959
32	5	4/15/51	Hillsboro, NC	1.0	D	95	Fonty Flock	Olds	80.889	Fonty Flock	Olds	88.278
33	6	4/29/51	Phoenix, AZ	1.0	D	150	Marshall Teague	Hudson	60.153	Fonty Flock	Olds	N/A
34	7	4/29/51	N. Wilkesboro, NC	0.625	D	93.75	Fonty Flock	Olds	None	Fonty Flock	Olds	72.184
35	8	5/6/51	Martinsville, VA	0.5	D	100	Curtis Turner	Olds	N/A	Tim Flock	Olds	55.062
36	9	5/30/51	Canfield, OH	0.5	D	100	Marshall Teague	Hudson	49.308	Bill Rexford	Olds	54.233
37	10	6/10/51	Columbus, GA	0.5	D	100	Tim Flock	Olds	N/A	Gober Sosebee	Cadillac	57.766
38	11	6/16/51	Columbia, SC	0.5	D	100	Frank Mundy	Studebaker	50.683	Frank Mundy	Studebaker	57.563
39	12	6/24/51	Dayton, OH	0.5	P	100	Curtis Turner	Olds	N/A	Tim Flock	Olds	70.838

Key

CUM. NO.	The cumulative number of all Winston Cup races ever run. For example, the number 28 besides the first race in 1951 indicates that race was the 28th Winston Cup race ever run. Counting through the end of the 1996 season, there have been a grand total of 1789 Winston Cup races
YR. NO.	The number of races run that year. For example, the 6 next to the April 29 race indicates that race was the 6th of the season
TRACK LENGTH	Track configuration when that race was run
SURFACE	The type of track surface
B-R	Beach and Road course
D	Dirt track
P	Paved track
MILES	Number of miles driven that race
MAKE	Car manufacturer
SPEED	Average speed
POLE SPEED	Pole winner's qualifying speed

Cum. No.	Yr. No.	Date	Site	Track Length	Surface	Miles	Race Winner	Make	Speed	Pole Winner	Make	Pole Speed

CHRONOLOGICAL LISTING OF RACES

1949

Cum. No.	Yr. No.	Date	Site	Track Length	Surface	Miles	Race Winner	Make	Speed	Pole Winner	Make	Pole Speed
1	1	6/19/49	Charlotte, NC	0.75	D	150	Jim Roper	Lincoln	N/A	Bob Flock	Hudson	67.958
2	2	7/10/49	Daytona Beach, FL	4.15	B-R	166	Red Byron	Olds	80.883	Gober Sosebee	Olds	N/A
3	3	8/7/49	Hillsboro, NC	1.0	D	200	Bob Flock	Olds	76.800	N/A	N/A	N/A
4	4	9/11/49	Langhorne, PA	1.0	D	200	Curtis Turner	Olds	69.403	Red Byron	Olds	77.482
5	5	9/18/49	Hamburg, NY	0.5	D	100	Jack White	Lincoln	N/A	N/A	N/A	N/A
6	6	9/25/49	Martinsville, VA	0.5	D	100	Red Byron	Olds	N/A	Curtis Turner	Olds	N/A
7	7	10/2/49	Heidelberg, PA	0.5	D	100	Lee Petty	Plymouth	57.458	Al Bonnell	Olds	61.475
8	8	10/16/49	N. Wilkesboro, NC	0.5	D	100	Bob Flock	Olds	53.364	Ken Wagner	Lincoln	57.563

1950

Cum. No.	Yr. No.	Date	Site	Track Length	Surface	Miles	Race Winner	Make	Speed	Pole Winner	Make	Pole Speed
9	1	2/5/50	Daytona Beach, FL	4.17	B-R	200.16	Harold Kite	Lincoln	89.894	Joe Littlejohn	Olds	98.840
10	2	4/3/50	Charlotte, NC	0.75	D	150	Tim Flock	Lincoln	N/A	Red Byron	Olds	67.839
11	3	4/16/50	Langhorne, PA	1.0	D	150	Curtis Turner	Olds	69.399	Tim Flock	Lincoln	N/A
12	4	5/21/50	Martinsville, VA	0.5	D	75	Curtis Turner	Olds	N/A	Buck Baker	Ford	54.216
13	5	5/30/50	Canfield, OH	0.5	D	100	Bill Rexford	Olds	N/A	Jimmy Florian	Ford	N/A
14	6	6/18/50	Vernon, NY	0.5	D	100	Bill Blair	Mercury	N/A	Chuck Mahoney	Mercury	N/A
15	7	6/25/50	Dayton, OH	0.5	D	100	Jimmy Florian	Ford	63.354	Dick Linder	Olds	66.543
16	8	7/2/50	Rochester, NY	0.5	D	100	Curtis Turner	Olds	50.614	Curtis Turner	Olds	54.974
17	9	7/23/50	Charlotte, NC	0.75	D	150	Curtis Turner	Olds	N/A	Curtis Turner	Olds	N/A
18	10	8/13/50	Hillsboro, NC	1.0	D	100	Fireball Roberts	Olds	N/A	Dick Linder	Olds	N/A
19	11	8/20/50	Dayton, OH	0.5	D	97.5	Dick Linder	Olds	None	Curtis Turner	Olds	N/A
20	12	8/27/50	Hamburg, NY	0.5	D	100	Dick Linder	Olds	50.747	Dick Linder	Olds	53.113
21	13	9/4/50	Darlington, SC	1.25	P	500	Johnny Mantz	Plymouth	75.250	Curtis Turner	Olds	82.034
22	14	9/17/50	Langhorne, PA	1.0	D	200	Fonty Flock	Olds	72.801	Wally Campbell	Olds	N/A
23	15	9/24/50	N. Wilkesboro, NC	0.625	D	125	Leon Sales	Plymouth	N/A	Fireball Roberts	Olds	73.266
24	16	10/1/50	Vernon, NY	0.5	D	100	Dick Linder	Olds	N/A	Dick Linder	Olds	N/A
25	17	10/15/50	Martinsville, VA	0.5	D	100	Herb Thomas	Plymouth	N/A	Fonty Flock	Olds	54.761
26	18	10/15/50	Winchester, IN	0.5	D	100	Lloyd Moore	Mercury	N/A	N/A	N/A	N/A
27	19	10/29/50	Hillsboro, NC	1.0	D	200	Lee Petty	Plymouth	N/A	Fonty Flock	Olds	85.898

1951

Cum. No.	Yr. No.	Date	Site	Track Length	Surface	Miles	Race Winner	Make	Speed	Pole Winner	Make	Pole Speed
28	1	2/11/51	Daytona Beach, FL	4.1	B-R	159.9	Marshall Teague	Hudson	82.328	Tim Flock	Lincoln	102.200
29	2	4/1/51	Charlotte, NC	0.75	D	112.5	Curtis Turner	Nash	70.545	Fonty Flock	Olds	68.337
30	3	4/8/51	Mobile, AL	0.75	D	112.5	Tim Flock	Olds	50.260	No Time Trials	NTT	NTT
31	4	4/8/51	Gardena, CA	0.5	D	100	Marshall Teague	Hudson	61.047	Andy Pierce	Buick	62.959
32	5	4/15/51	Hillsboro, NC	1.0	D	95	Fonty Flock	Olds	80.889	Fonty Flock	Olds	88.278
33	6	4/22/51	Phoenix, AZ	1.0	D	150	Marshall Teague	Hudson	60.153	Fonty Flock	Olds	N/A
34	7	4/29/51	N. Wilkesboro, NC	0.625	D	93.75	Fonty Flock	Olds	None	Fonty Flock	Olds	72.184
35	8	5/6/51	Martinsville, VA	0.5	D	100	Curtis Turner	Olds	N/A	Tim Flock	Olds	55.062
36	9	5/30/51	Canfield, OH	0.5	D	100	Marshall Teague	Hudson	49.308	Bill Rexford	Olds	54.233
37	10	6/10/51	Columbus, GA	0.5	D	100	Tim Flock	Olds	N/A	Gober Sosebee	Cadillac	57.766
38	11	6/16/51	Columbia, SC	0.5	D	100	Frank Mundy	Studebaker	50.683	Frank Mundy	Studebaker	57.563
39	12	6/24/51	Dayton, OH	0.5	P	100	Curtis Turner	Olds	N/A	Tim Flock	Olds	70.838
40	13	6/30/51	Gardena, CA	0.5	D	100	Lou Figaro	Hudson	N/A	Lou Figaro	Hudson	76.988
41	14	7/1/51	Grand Rapids, MI	0.5	D	100	Marshall Teague	Hudson	N/A	Tim Flock	Hudson	N/A
42	15	7/8/51	Bainbridge, OH	0.5	D	100	Fonty Flock	Olds	65.753	Fonty Flock	Olds	N/A
43	16	7/15/51	Heidelberg, PA	0.5	D	100	Herb Thomas	Olds	None	Fonty Flock	Olds	61.983
44	17	7/29/51	Weaverville, NC	0.5	D	100	Fonty Flock	Olds	N/A	Billy Carden	Olds	64.608
45	18	7/31/51	Rochester, NY	0.5	D	100	Lee Petty	Plymouth	N/A	Fonty Flock	Olds	N/A
46	19	8/1/51	Altamont, NY	0.5	D	100	Fonty Flock	Olds	N/A	N/A	N/A	N/A
47	20	8/12/51	Detroit, MI	1.0	D	250	Tommy Thompson	Chrysler	57.588	Marshall Teague	Hudson	69.131
48	21	8/19/51	Toledo, OH	0.5	D	100	Tim Flock	Olds	50.847	Fonty Flock	Olds	55.521
49	22	8/24/51	Morristown, NJ	0.5	D	100	Tim Flock	Olds	N/A	Tim Flock	Olds	58.670
50	23	8/25/51	Greenville, SC	0.5	D	100	Bob Flock	Olds	N/A	N/A	N/A	N/A
51	24	9/3/51	Darlington, SC	1.25	P	500	Herb Thomas	Hudson	76.906	Frank Mundy	Studebaker	84.173
52	25	9/7/51	Columbia, SC	0.5	D	100	Tim Flock	Olds	N/A	Tim Flock	Olds	58.843
53	26	9/8/51	Macon, GA	0.5	D	100	Herb Thomas	Olds	53.222	Bob Flock	Olds	N/A
54	27	9/15/51	Langhorne, PA	1.0	D	150	Herb Thomas	Hudson	71.043	Fonty Flock	Olds	81.773
55	28	9/23/51	Charlotte, NC	0.75	D	150	Herb Thomas	Hudson	N/A	Billy Carden	Olds	66.914
56	29	9/23/51	Dayton, OH	0.5	P	100	Fonty Flock	Olds	N/A	Fonty Flock	Olds	N/A

Cum. No.	Yr. No.	Date	Site	Track Length	Surface	Miles	Race Winner	Make	Speed	Pole Winner	Make	Pole Speed
57	30	9/30/51	Wilson, NC	0.5	D	100	Fonty Flock	Olds	N/A	Fonty Flock	Olds	N/A
58	31	10/7/51	Hillsboro, NC	1.0	D	150	Herb Thomas	Hudson	72.454	Herb Thomas	Hudson	79.628
59	32	10/12/51	Thompson, CT	0.5	P	100	Neil Cole	Olds	N/A	Neil Cole	Olds	59.269
60	33	10/14/51	Shippenville, PA	0.5	D	100	Tim Flock	Olds	N/A	N/A	N/A	N/A
61	34	10/14/51	Martinsville, VA	0.5	D	100	Frank Mundy	Olds	N/A	Herb Thomas	Hudson	56.109
62	35	10/14/51	Oakland, CA	0.625	D	250	Marvin Burke	Mercury	N/A	N/A	N/A	N/A
63	36	10/21/51	N. Wilkesboro, NC	0.625	D	125	Fonty Flock	Olds	67.791	Herb Thomas	Hudson	68.828
64	37	10/28/51	Hanford, CA	0.5	D	100	Danny Weinberg	Studebaker	N/A	N/A	N/A	N/A
65	38	11/4/51	Jacksonville, FL	0.5	D	100	Herb Thomas	Hudson	53.412	Herb Thomas	Hudson	64.818
66	39	11/11/51	Atlanta, GA	1.0	D	100	Tim Flock	Hudson	59.960	Frank Mundy	Studebaker	74.013
67	40	11/11/51	Gardena, CA	0.5	D	100	Bill Norton	Mercury	N/A	Fonty Flock	Olds	N/A
68	41	11/25/51	Mobile, AL	0.75	D	112.5	Frank Mundy	Studebaker	N/A	Frank Mundy	Studebaker	61.113

1952

Cum. No.	Yr. No.	Date	Site	Track Length	Surface	Miles	Race Winner	Make	Speed	Pole Winner	Make	Pole Speed
69	1	1/20/52	W. Palm Beach, FL	0.5	D	100	Tim Flock	Hudson	None	Tim Flock	Hudson	67.794
70	2	2/10/52	Daytona Beach, FL	4.1	B-R	151.7	Marshall Teague	Hudson	85.612	Pat Kirkwood	Chrysler	110.970
71	3	3/6/52	Jacksonville, FL	0.5	D	100	Marshall Teague	Hudson	55.197	Marshall Teague	Hudson	60.100
72	4	3/30/52	N. Wilkesboro, NC	0.625	D	125	Herb Thomas	Hudson	58.593	Herb Thomas	Hudson	75.075
73	5	4/6/52	Martinsville, VA	0.5	D	100	Dick Rathmann	Hudson	42.862	Buck Baker	Hudson	54.945
74	6	4/12/52	Columbia, SC	0.5	D	100	Buck Baker	Hudson	53.460	Buck Baker	Hudson	N/A
75	7	4/20/52	Atlanta, GA	1.0	D	100	Bill Blair	Olds	66.877	Tim Flock	Hudson	71.613
76	8	4/27/52	Macon, GA	0.5	D	99	Herb Thomas	Hudson	53.853	Jack Smith	Studebaker	54.429
77	9	5/4/52	Langhorne, PA	1.0	D	150	Dick Rathmann	Hudson	67.669	Herb Thomas	Hudson	76.045
78	10	5/10/52	Darlington, SC	1.25	P	100	Dick Rathmann	Hudson	83.818	No Time Trials	NTT	NTT
79	11	5/18/52	Dayton, OH	0.5	P	100	Dick Rathmann	Hudson	65.526	Fonty Flock	Olds	71.884
80	12	5/30/52	Canfield, OH	0.5	D	100	Herb Thomas	Hudson	48.057	Dick Rathmann	Hudson	58.102
81	13	6/1/52	Augusta, GA	0.5	D	100	Gober Sosebee	Chrysler	None	Tommy Moon	Hudson	51.561
82	14	6/1/52	Toledo, OH	0.5	D	100	Tim Flock	Hudson	47.175	Fonty Flock	Olds	57.034
83	15	6/8/52	Hillsboro, NC	1.0	D	100	Tim Flock	Hudson	81.008	Fonty Flock	Olds	91.977
84	16	6/15/52	Charlotte, NC	0.75	D	112.5	Herb Thomas	Hudson	64.820	Fonty Flock	Olds	70.038
85	17	6/29/52	Detroit, MI	1.0	D	250	Tim Flock	Hudson	59.908	Dick Rathmann	Hudson	70.230
86	18	7/1/52	Niagara Falls, ONT	0.5	D	100	Buddy Shuman	Hudson	45.620	Herb Thomas	Hudson	52.401
87	19	7/4/52	Owego, NY	0.5	D	100	Tim Flock	Hudson	56.603	Tim Flock	Hudson	67.669
88	20	7/6/52	Monroe, MI	0.5	D	100	Tim Flock	Hudson	44.499	Tim Flock	Hudson	57.600
89	21	7/11/52	Morristown, NJ	0.5	D	100	Lee Petty	Plymouth	59.661	Herb Thomas	Hudson	60.996
90	22	7/20/52	South Bend, IN	0.5	D	100	Tim Flock	Hudson	41.889	Herb Thomas	Hudson	58.120
91	23	8/15/52	Rochester, NY	0.5	D	88	Tim Flock	Hudson	None	No Time Trials	NTT	NTT
92	24	8/17/52	Weaverville, NC	0.5	D	100	Bob Flock	Hudson	57.288	Herb Thomas	Hudson	64.888
93	25	9/1/52	Darlington, SC	1.25	P	500	Fonty Flock	Olds	74.512	Fonty Flock	Olds	88.550
94	26	9/7/52	Macon, GA	0.5	D	150	Lee Petty	Plymouth	48.404	Fonty Flock	Olds	50.113
95	27	9/14/52	Langhorne, PA	1.0	D	250	Lee Petty	Plymouth	72.463	Herb Thomas	Hudson	85.287
96	28	9/21/52	Dayton, OH	0.5	P	150	Dick Rathmann	Hudson	61.643	Fonty Flock	Olds	72.741
97	29	9/28/52	Wilson, NC	0.5	D	100	Herb Thomas	Hudson	35.398	Herb Thomas	Hudson	55.883
98	30	10/12/52	Hillsboro, NC	1.0	D	150	Fonty Flock	Olds	73.489	Bill Blair	Olds	75.901
99	31	10/29/52	Martinsville, VA	0.5	D	100	Herb Thomas	Hudson	47.556	Perk Brown	Hudson	55.333
100	32	10/26/52	N. Wilkesboro, NC	0.625	D	125	Herb Thomas	Hudson	67.044	Herb Thomas	Hudson	76.013
101	33	11/16/52	Atlanta, GA	1.0	D	100	Donald Thomas	Hudson	64.853	Donald Thomas	Hudson	72.874
102	34	11/30/52	W. Palm Beach, FL	0.5	D	100	Herb Thomas	Hudson	58.008	Herb Thomas	Hudson	63.716

1953

Cum. No.	Yr. No.	Date	Site	Track Length	Surface	Miles	Race Winner	Make	Speed	Pole Winner	Make	Pole Speed
103	1	2/1/53	W. Palm Beach, FL	0.5	D	100	Lee Petty	Dodge	60.220	Dick Rathmann	Hudson	65.028
104	2	2/15/53	Daytona Beach, FL	4.1	B-R	159.9	Bill Blair	Olds	89.789	Bob Pronger	Olds	115.770
105	3	3/8/53	Spring Lake, NC	0.5	D	100	Herb Thomas	Hudson	48.826	Herb Thomas	Hudson	51.918
106	4	3/29/53	N. Wilkesboro, NC	0.625	D	125	Herb Thomas	Hudson	71.907	Herb Thomas	Hudson	78.108
107	5	4/5/53	Charlotte, NC	0.75	D	112.5	Dick Passwater	Olds	N/A	Tim Flock	Hudson	71.108
108	6	4/19/53	Richmond, VA	0.5	D	100	Lee Petty	Dodge	45.535	Buck Baker	Olds	48.465
109	7	4/26/53	Macon, GA	0.5	D	100	Dick Rathmann	Hudson	56.417	N/A	N/A	N/A
110	8	5/3/53	Langhorne, PA	1.0	D	150	Buck Baker	Olds	72.743	No Time Trials	NTT	NTT
111	9	5/9/53	Columbia, SC	0.5	D	100	Buck Baker	Olds	53.707	Herb Thomas	Hudson	58.670
112	10	5/9/53	Hickory, NC	0.5	D	100	Tim Flock	Hudson	N/A	N/A	N/A	N/A
113	11	5/17/53	Martinsville, VA	0.5	D	100	Lee Petty	Dodge	N/A	N/A	N/A	N/A
114	12	5/24/53	Columbus, OH	0.5	D	100	Herb Thomas	Hudson	56.127	Fonty Flock	Olds	59.288
115	13	5/30/53	Raleigh, NC	1.0	P	300	Fonty Flock	Hudson	70.629	Slick Smith	Olds	76.230

Cum. No.	Yr. No.	Date	Site	Track Length	Surface	Miles	Race Winner	Make	Speed	Pole Winner	Make	Pole Speed
116	14	6/7/53	Shreveport, LA	0.5	D	100	Lee Petty	Dodge	53.199	Herb Thomas	Hudson	58.727
117	15	6/14/53	Pensacola, FL	0.5	D	70	Herb Thomas	Hudson	63.316	Dick Rathmann	Hudson	67.039
118	16	6/21/53	Langhorne, PA	1.0	D	200	Dick Rathmann	Hudson	64.434	Lloyd Shaw	Jaguar	82.200
119	17	6/23/53	High Point, NC	0.5	D	100	Herb Thomas	Hudson	58.186	Herb Thomas	Hudson	66.152
120	18	6/28/53	Wilson, NC	0.5	D	100	Fonty Flock	Hudson	53.803	N/A	N/A	N/A
121	19	7/3/53	Rochester, NY	0.5	D	100	Herb Thomas	Hudson	56.939	No Time Trials	NTT	NTT
122	20	7/4/53	Spartanburg, SC	0.5	D	100	Lee Petty	Dodge	56.934	Buck Baker	Olds	58.027
123	21	7/10/53	Morristown, NJ	0.5	D	100	Dick Rathmann	Hudson	69.417	Herb Thomas	Hudson	61.016
124	22	7/12/53	Atlanta, GA	1.0	D	100	Herb Thomas	Hudson	70.685	Herb Thomas	Hudson	72.756
125	23	7/22/53	Rapid City, SD	0.5	D	100	Herb Thomas	Hudson	57.720	Herb Thomas	Hudson	55.727
126	24	7/26/53	N. Platte, NE	0.5	D	100	Dick Rathmann	Hudson	54.380	Herb Thomas	Hudson	54.397
127	25	8/2/53	Davenport, IA	0.5	D	100	Herb Thomas	Hudson	62.500	Buck Baker	Olds	54.397
128	26	8/9/53	Hillsboro, NC	1.0	D	100	Curtis Turner	Olds	75.125	Curtis Turner	Olds	89.078
129	27	8/16/53	Weaverville, NC	0.5	D	100	Fonty Flock	Hudson	62.434	Curtis Turner	Olds	N/A
130	28	8/23/53	Norfolk, VA	0.5	D	100	Herb Thomas	Hudson	51.040	Curtis Turner	Olds	54.200
131	29	8/29/53	Hickory, NC	0.5	D	100	Fonty Flock	Hudson	N/A	Tim Flock	Hudson	79.362
132	30	9/7/53	Darlington, SC	1.375	P	500.5	Buck Baker	Olds	92.881	Fonty Flock	Hudson	107.893
133	31	9/13/53	Macon, GA	0.5	D	100	Speedy Thompson	Olds	55.172	Joe Eubanks	Hudson	60.810
134	32	9/20/53	Langhorne, PA	1.0	D	250	Dick Rathmann	Hudson	67.046	Herb Thomas	Hudson	N/A
135	33	10/3/53	Bloomsburg, PA	0.5	D	100	Herb Thomas	Hudson	N/A	Jim Paschal	Dodge	55.953
136	34	10/4/53	Wilson, NC	0.5	D	100	Herb Thomas	Hudson	56.022	Herb Thomas	Hudson	56.962
137	35	10/11/53	N. Wilkesboro, NC	0.625	D	100	Speedy Thompson	Olds	71.202	Buck Baker	Olds	78.288
138	36	10/18/53	Martinsville, VA	0.5	D	100	Jim Paschal	Dodge	56.013	Fonty Flock	Hudson	58.958
139	37	11/1/53	Atlanta, GA	1.0	D	100	Buck Baker	Olds	63.180	Tim Flock	Hudson	73.580

1954

Cum. No.	Yr. No.	Date	Site	Track Length	Surface	Miles	Race Winner	Make	Speed	Pole Winner	Make	Pole Speed
140	1	2/7/54	W. Palm Beach, FL	0.5	D	100	Herb Thomas	Hudson	58.958	Dick Rathmann	Hudson	66.371
141	2	2/21/54	Daytona Beach, FL	4.1	B-R	159.9	Lee Petty	Chrysler	89.108	Lee Petty	Chrysler	123.410
142	3	3/7/54	Jacksonville, FL	0.5	D	100	Herb Thomas	Hudson	56.561	Curtis Turner	Olds	63.581
143	4	3/21/54	Atlanta, GA	1.0	D	100	Herb Thomas	Hudson	60.494	Herb Thomas	Hudson	73.514
144	5	3/28/54	Savannah, GA	0.5	D	100	Al Keller	Hudson	59.820	Herb Thomas	Hudson	63.202
145	6	3/28/54	Oakland, CA	0.5	D+P	125	Dick Rathmann	Hudson	50.692	Hershel McGriff	Olds	55.624
146	7	4/4/54	N. Wilkesboro, NC	0.625	D	100	Dick Rathmann	Hudson	68.545	Gober Sosebee	Olds	78.698
147	8	4/18/54	Hillsboro, NC	1.0	D	100	Herb Thomas	Hudson	77.386	Buck Baker	Olds	86.767
148	9	4/25/54	Macon, GA	0.5	D	100	Gober Sosebee	Olds	55.410	Dick Rathmann	Hudson	57.859
149	10	5/2/54	Langhorne, PA	1.0	D	150	Herb Thomas	Hudson	74.883	Lee Petty	Chrysler	87.217
150	11	5/9/54	Wilson, NC	0.5	D	100	Buck Baker	Olds	52.279	Jim Paschal	Olds	55.469
151	12	5/16/54	Martinsville, VA	0.5	D	100	Jim Paschal	Olds	46.153	No Time Trials	NTT	NTT
152	13	5/23/54	Sharon, PA	0.5	D	100	Lee Petty	Chrysler	None	Dick Rathmann	Hudson	62.090
153	14	5/29/54	Raleigh, NC	1.0	P	250	Herb Thomas	Hudson	73.909	Herb Thomas	Hudson	76.660
154	15	5/30/54	Charlotte, NC	0.75	D	99.75	Buck Baker	Olds	49.805	Al Keller	Hudson	68.947
155	16	5/30/54	Gardena, CA	0.5	D	248	John Soares	Dodge	53.438	Danny Letner	Hudson	62.849
156	17	6/6/54	Columbia, SC	0.5	D	100	Curtis Turner	Olds	56.719	Buck Baker	Olds	62.240
157	18	6/13/54	Linden, NJ	2.0	P	100	Al Keller	Jaguar	77.469	Buck Baker	Olds	80.536
158	19	6/19/54	Hickory, NC	0.5	D	100	Herb Thomas	Hudson	82.872	Herb Thomas	Hudson	81.669
159	20	6/25/54	Rochester, NY	0.5	D	100	Lee Petty	Chrysler	52.455	Herb Thomas	Hudson	60.422
160	21	6/27/54	Mechanicsburg, PA	0.5	D	100	Herb Thomas	Hudson	51.085	Dick Rathmann	Hudson	54.945
161	22	7/3/54	Spartanburg, SC	0.5	D	100	Herb Thomas	Hudson	59.181	Hershel McGriff	Olds	58.120
162	23	7/4/54	Weaverville, NC	0.5	D	100	Herb Thomas	Hudson	61.318	Herb Thomas	Hudson	67.771
163	24	7/10/54	Willow Springs, IL	0.5	D	100	Dick Rathmann	Hudson	72.216	Buck Baker	Olds	75.662
164	25	7/11/54	Grand Rapids, MI	0.5	D	100	Lee Petty	Chrysler	52.090	Herb Thomas	Hudson	59.055
165	26	7/30/54	Morristown, NJ	0.5	D	100	Buck Baker	Olds	58.968	Buck Baker	Olds	66.667
166	27	8/1/54	Oakland, CA	0.5	D+P	150	Danny Letner	Hudson	53.045	Marvin Panch	Dodge	55.248
167	28	8/13/54	Charlotte, NC	0.5	D	100	Lee Petty	Chrysler	51.362	Buck Baker	Olds	57.270
168	29	8/22/54	San Mateo, CA	1.0	D	250	Hershel McGriff	Olds	64.710	Hershel McGriff	Olds	75.566
169	30	8/29/54	Corbin, KY	0.5	D	100	Lee Petty	Chrysler	63.080	Jim Paschal	Olds	65.789
170	31	9/6/54	Darlington, SC	1.375	P	500.5	Herb Thomas	Hudson	95.026	Buck Baker	Olds	108.261
171	32	9/12/54	Macon, GA	0.5	D	100	Hershel McGriff	Olds	50.526	Tim Flock	Olds	56.907
172	33	9/24/54	Charlotte, NC	0.5	D	100	Hershel McGriff	Olds	53.167	Hershel McGriff	Olds	54.054
173	34	9/26/54	Langhorne, PA	1.0	D	250	Herb Thomas	Hudson	71.186	Herb Thomas	Hudson	89.418
174	35	10/10/54	LeHi, AR	1.5	D	250	Buck Baker	Olds	89.013	Junior Johnson	Cadillac	N/A
175	36	10/17/54	Martinsville, VA	0.5	D	82.5	Lee Petty	Chrysler	44.547	Lee Petty	Chrysler	53.191
176	37	10/24/54	N. Wilkesboro, NC	0.625	D	98.125	Hershel McGriff	Olds	65.175	Hershel McGriff	Olds	77.612

Cum. No.	Yr. No.	Date	Site	Track Length	Surface	Miles	Race Winner	Make	Speed	Pole Winner	Make	Pole Speed
1955												
177	1	11/7/54	High Point, NC	0.5	D	100	Lee Petty	Chrysler	62.882	Herb Thomas	Hudson	71.942
178	2	2/6/55	W. Palm Beach, FL	0.5	D	100	Herb Thomas	Hudson	56.013	Dick Rathmann	Hudson	65.454
179	3	2/13/55	Jacksonville, FL	0.5	D	100	Lee Petty	Chrysler	69.031	Dick Rathmann	Hudson	63.514
180	4	2/27/55	Daytona Beach, FL	4.1	B-R	159.9	Tim Flock	Chrysler	91.999	Tim Flock	Chrysler	130.293
181	5	3/6/55	Savannah, GA	0.5	D	100	Lee Petty	Chrysler	60.150	Dick Rathmann	Hudson	62.805
182	6	3/26/55	Columbia, SC	0.5	D	100	Fonty Flock	Chevy	None	Tim Flock	Chrysler	N/A
183	7	3/27/55	Hillsboro, NC	1.0	D	100	Jim Paschal	Olds	82.304	Tim Flock	Chrysler	91.696
184	8	4/3/55	N. Wilkesboro, NC	0.625	D	100	Buck Baker	Olds	73.126	Dink Widenhouse	Olds	77.720
185	9	4/17/55	Montgomery, AL	0.5	D	100	Tim Flock	Chrysler	60.872	Jim Paschal	Olds	64.290
186	10	4/24/55	Langhorne, PA	1.0	D	150	Tim Flock	Chrysler	72.893	Tim Flock	Chrysler	86.699
187	11	5/1/55	Charlotte, NC	0.75	D	99.75	Buck Baker	Buick	52.630	Herb Thomas	Buick	70.184
188	12	5/7/55	Hickory, NC	0.5	D	100	Junior Johnson	Olds	65.502	Tim Flock	Chrysler	67.748
189	13	5/8/55	Phoenix, AZ	1.0	D	100	Tim Flock	Chrysler	71.485	Bill Amick	Dodge	75.519
190	14	5/15/55	Tucson, AZ	0.5	D	100	Danny Letner	Olds	51.428	Bill Amick	Dodge	56.179
191	15	5/15/55	Martinsville, VA	0.5	D	100	Tim Flock	Chrysler	52.554	Jim Paschal	Olds	58.823
192	16	5/22/55	Richmond, VA	0.5	D	100	Tim Flock	Chrysler	54.298	No Time Trials	NTT	NTT
193	17	5/28/55	Raleigh, NC	0.5	D	100	Junior Johnson	Olds	50.522	Tim Flock	Chrysler	58.612
194	18	5/29/55	Winston Salem, NC	0.5	D	100	Lee Petty	Chrysler	50.583	Fonty Flock	Chrysler	56.710
195	19	6/10/55	New Oxford, PA	0.5	D	100	Junior Johnson	Olds	65.371	Junior Johnson	Olds	75.853
196	20	6/17/55	Rochester, NY	0.5	D	100	Tim Flock	Chrysler	57.710	Buck Baker	Chrysler	61.141
197	21	6/18/55	Fonda, NY	0.5	D	100	Junior Johnson	Olds	58.413	Fonty Flock	Chrysler	61.770
198	22	6/19/55	Plattsburg, NY	0.5	D	100	Lee Petty	Chrysler	59.074	Lee Petty	Chrysler	55.744
199	23	6/24/55	Charlotte, NC	0.5	D	100	Tim Flock	Chrysler	51.289	Tim Flock	Chrysler	57.915
200	24	7/6/55	Spartanburg, SC	0.5	D	100	Tim Flock	Chrysler	49.106	Tim Flock	Chrysler	58.517
201	25	7/9/55	Columbia, SC	0.5	D	100	Jim Paschal	Olds	55.469	Jimmie Lewallen	Olds	59.741
202	26	7/10/55	Weaverville, NC	0.5	D	100	Tim Flock	Chrysler	62.739	Tim Flock	Chrysler	69.310
203	27	7/15/55	Morristown, NJ	0.5	D	100	Tim Flock	Chrysler	58.092	Tim Flock	Chrysler	63.649
204	28	7/29/55	Altamont, NY	0.5	D	89	Junior Johnson	Olds	None	Tim Flock	Chrysler	56.603
205	29	7/30/55	Syracuse, NY	0.5	D	100	Tim Flock	Chrysler	76.522	Tim Flock	Chrysler	78.311
206	30	7/31/55	San Mateo, CA	1.0	D	252	Tim Flock	Chrysler	68.571	Fonty Flock	Chrysler	79.330
207	31	8/5/55	Charlotte, NC	0.5	D	100	Jim Paschal	Olds	48.806	Tim Flock	Chrysler	57.859
208	32	8/7/55	Winston-Salem, NC	0.5	D	100	Lee Petty	Dodge	50.111	Tim Flock	Chrysler	59.016
209	33	8/14/55	LeHi, AR	1.5	D	250	Fonty Flock	Chrysler	89.892	Fonty Flock	Chrysler	99.944
210	34	8/20/55	Raleigh, NC	1.0	P	100	Herb Thomas	Buick	76.400	Tim Flock	Chrysler	78.722
211	35	9/5/55	Darlington, SC	1.375	P	503.25	Herb Thomas	Chevy	92.281	Fireball Roberts	Buick	110.682
212	36	9/11/55	Montgomery, AL	0.5	D	100	Tim Flock	Chrysler	62.773	Tim Flock	Chrysler	68.728
213	37	9/18/55	Langhorne, PA	1.0	D	250	Tim Flock	Chrysler	77.888	Tim Flock	Chrysler	92.095
214	38	9/30/55	Raleigh, NC	1.0	P	100	Fonty Flock	Chrysler	73.289	Fonty Flock	Chrysler	82.098
215	39	10/6/55	Greenville, SC	0.5	D	100	Tim Flock	Chrysler	57.942	Bob Welborn	Chevy	58.027
216	40	10/9/55	LeHi, AR	1.5	D	300	Speedy Thompson	Ford	83.898	Fonty Flock	Chrysler	100.390
217	41	10/15/55	Columbia, SC	0.5	D	100	Tim Flock	Chrysler	55.393	Junior Johnson	Olds	61.728
218	42	10/16/55	Martinsville, VA	0.5	P	100	Speedy Thompson	Chrysler	59.210	No Time Trials	NTT	NTT
219	43	10/16/55	Las Vegas, NV	1.0	D	111	Norm Nelson	Chrysler	44.449	Norm Nelson	Chrysler	74.518
220	44	10/23/55	N. Wilkesboro, NC	0.625	D	100	Buck Baker	Ford	72.347	Buck Baker	Ford	79.815
221	45	10/30/55	Hillsboro, NC	1.0	D	100	Tim Flock	Chrysler	70.465	Tim Flock	Chrysler	81.673
1956												
222	1	11/13/55	Hickory, NC	0.4	D	80	Tim Flock	Chrysler	56.962	Tim Flock	Chrysler	N/A
223	2	11/20/55	Charlotte, NC	0.75	D	99.75	Fonty Flock	Chrysler	61.825	Fonty Flock	Chrysler	70.496
224	3	11/20/55	Lancaster, CA	0.5	D	200	Chuck Stevenson	Ford	66.512	Jim Reed	Chevy	76.556
225	4	12/11/55	W. Palm Beach, FL	0.5	D	100	Herb Thomas	Chevy	65.009	Fonty Flock	Chrysler	78.912
226	5	1/22/56	Phoenix, AZ	1.0	D	150	Buck Baker	Chrysler	64.408	Joe Weatherly	Ford	71.315
227	6	2/26/56	Daytona Beach, FL	4.1	B-R	151.7	Tim Flock	Chrysler	90.657	Tim Flock	Chrysler	135.747
228	7	3/4/56	W. Palm Beach, FL	0.5	D	100	Billy Myers	Mercury	68.990	Buck Baker	Dodge	81.081
229	8	3/18/56	Wilson, NC	0.5	D	53	Herb Thomas	Chevy	46.287	Herb Thomas	Chevy	57.157
230	9	3/25/56	Atlanta, GA	1.0	D	100	Buck Baker	Chrysler	70.643	Tim Flock	Chrysler	82.154
231	10	4/8/56	N. Wilkesboro, NC	0.625	D	100	Tim Flock	Chrysler	71.034	Junior Johnson	Pontiac	78.370
232	11	4/22/56	Langhorne, PA	1.0	D	150	Buck Baker	Chrysler	75.928	Buck Baker	Chrysler	104.590
233	12	4/29/56	Richmond, VA	0.5	D	100	Buck Baker	Dodge	56.232	Buck Baker	Dodge	67.091
234	13	5/5/56	Columbia, SC	0.5	D	100	Speedy Thompson	Dodge	54.545	Buck Baker	Dodge	63.224
235	14	5/6/56	Concord, NC	0.5	D	100	Speedy Thompson	Chrysler	61.633	Speedy Thompson	Chrysler	65.241
236	15	5/10/56	Greenville, SC	0.5	D	100	Buck Baker	Dodge	60.362	Rex White	Chevy	61.100

Cum. No.	Yr. No.	Date	Site	Track Length	Surface	Miles	Race Winner	Make	Speed	Pole Winner	Make	Pole Speed
237	16	5/12/56	Hickory, NC	0.4	D	80	Speedy Thompson	Chrysler	59.442	Speedy Thompson	Chrysler	67.447
238	17	5/13/56	Hillsboro, NC	0.9	D	90	Buck Baker	Chrysler	83.720	Buck Baker	Chrysler	89.305
239	18	5/20/56	Martinsville, VA	0.5	P	250	Buck Baker	Dodge	60.824	Buck Baker	Dodge	66.103
240	19	5/25/56	Abbottstown, PA	0.5	D	100	Buck Baker	Dodge	69.619	Speedy Thompson	Dodge	76.628
241	20	5/27/56	Charlotte, NC	0.75	D	99.75	Speedy Thompson	Chrysler	64.866	Speedy Thompson	Chrysler	76.966
242	21	5/27/56	Portland, OR	0.5	P	75	Herb Thomas	Chrysler	63.815	John Kieper	Olds	67.239
243	22	5/30/56	Eureka, CA	0.625	D	78.125	Herb Thomas	Chrysler	38.814	John Kieper	Olds	66.040
244	23	5/30/56	Syracuse, NY	1.0	D	150	Buck Baker	Chrysler	86.179	Buck Baker	Chrysler	83.975
245	24	6/3/56	Merced, CA	0.5	D	100	Herb Thomas	Chrysler	47.325	Herb Thomas	Chrysler	58.234
246	25	6/10/56	LeHi, AR	1.5	D	250	Ralph Moody	Ford	74.313	Buck Baker	Chrysler	98.504
247	26	6/15/56	Charlotte, NC	0.5	D	100	Speedy Thompson	Chrysler	56.022	Fireball Roberts	Ford	59.661
248	27	6/22/56	Rochester, NY	0.5	D	100	Speedy Thompson	Chrysler	57.288	Jim Paschal	Mercury	57.434
249	28	6/24/56	Portland, OR	0.5	P	100	John Kieper	Olds	62.586	Herb Thomas	Chrysler	65.934
250	29	7/1/56	Weaverville, NC	0.5	D	100	Lee Petty	Dodge	56.435	Fireball Roberts	Ford	72.260
251	30	7/4/56	Raleigh, NC	1.0	P	250	Fireball Roberts	Ford	79.822	Lee Petty	Dodge	82.587
252	31	7/7/56	Spartanburg, SC	0.5	D	100	Lee Petty	Dodge	50.483	Fireball Roberts	Ford	58.900
253	32	7/8/56	Sacramento, CA	1.0	D	100	Lloyd Dane	Mercury	74.074	Eddie Pagan	Ford	76.612
254	33	7/21/56	Chicago, IL	0.5	P	100	Fireball Roberts	Ford	61.037	Billy Myers	Mercury	N/A
255	34	7/17/56	Shelby, NC	0.5	D	101	Speedy Thompson	Dodge	53.699	Ralph Moody	Ford	55.658
256	35	7/29/56	Montgomery, AL	0.5	D	100	Marvin Panch	Ford	67.252	Marvin Panch	Ford	69.444
257	36	8/3/56	Oklahoma City, OK	0.5	D	100	Jim Paschal	Mercury	60.100	Speedy Thompson	Dodge	64.655
258	37	8/12/56	Elkhart Lake, WI	4.1	P	258.3	Tim Flock	Mercury	73.858	Frank Mundy	Dodge	N/A
259	38	8/17/56	Old Bridge, NJ	0.5	P	100	Ralph Moody	Ford	65.170	Jim Reed	Chevy	72.028
260	39	8/19/56	San Mateo, CA	1.0	D	241	Eddie Pagan	Ford	68.161	Eddie Pagan	Ford	81.614
261	40	8/22/56	Norfolk, VA	0.5	D	100	Billy Myers	Mercury	56.408	Ralph Moody	Ford	58.631
262	41	8/23/56	Spartanburg, SC	0.5	D	100	Ralph Moody	Ford	54.372	Ralph Moody	Ford	61.433
263	42	8/25/56	Myrtle Beach, SC	0.5	D	100	Fireball Roberts	Ford	50.576	Ralph Moody	Ford	58.346
264	43	8/26/56	Portland, OR	0.5	P	123	Royce Haggerty	Dodge	None	John Kieper	Olds	65.861
265	44	9/3/56	Darlington, SC	1.375	P	500.5	Curtis Turner	Ford	95.167	Speedy Thompson	Chrysler	118.683
266	45	9/9/56	Montgomery, AL	0.5	D	100	Buck Baker	Chrysler	60.893	Tim Flock	Ford	64.864
267	46	9/12/56	Charlotte, NC	0.5	D	100	Ralph Moody	Ford	52.847	Joe Eubanks	Ford	59.464
268	47	9/23/56	Langhorne, PA	1.0	D	300	Paul Goldsmith	Chevy	70.615	Buck Baker	Chrysler	93.628
269	48	9/23/56	Portland, OR	0.5	P	125	Lloyd Dane	Ford	None	Royce Haggerty	Dodge	N/A
270	49	9/29/56	Columbia, SC	0.5	D	100	Buck Baker	Dodge	61.193	Tim Flock	Ford	61.940
271	50	9/30/56	Hillsboro, NC	0.9	D	99	Fireball Roberts	Ford	72.734	Speedy Thompson	Chrysler	88.067
272	51	10/7/56	Newport, TN	0.5	D	100	Fireball Roberts	Ford	61.475	Joe Eubanks	Ford	65.597
273	52	10/14/56	Charlotte, NC	0.75	D	97.75	Buck Baker	Chrysler	72.268	Ralph Moody	Ford	75.041
274	53	10/23/56	Shelby, NC	0.5	D	100	Buck Baker	Chrysler	54.054	Doug Cox	Ford	58.479
275	54	10/28/56	Martinsville, VA	0.5	P	200	Jack Smith	Dodge	61.136	Buck Baker	Chrysler	67.643
276	55	11/11/56	Hickory, NC	0.4	D	100	Speedy Thompson	Chrysler	66.420	Ralph Earnhardt	Ford	68.278
277	56	11/18/56	Wilson, NC	0.5	D	100	Buck Baker	Chrysler	50.579	Buck Baker	Chrysler	60.160

1957

Cum. No.	Yr. No.	Date	Site	Track Length	Surface	Miles	Race Winner	Make	Speed	Pole Winner	Make	Pole Speed
278	1	11/11/56	Lancaster, CA	2.5	P	150	Marvin Panch	Ford	78.648	Marvin Panch	Ford	78.596
279	2	12/2/56	Concord, NC	0.5	D	100	Marvin Panch	Ford	55.883	Curtis Turner	Ford	62.586
280	3	12/30/56	Titusville, FL	1.6	P	89.6	Fireball Roberts	Ford	None	Paul Goldsmith	Chevy	69.106
281	4	2/17/57	Daytona Beach, FL	4.1	B-R	159.9	Cotton Owens	Pontiac	101.541	Banjo Matthews	Pontiac	134.382
282	5	3/3/57	Concord, NC	0.5	D	100	Jack Smith	Chevy	59.860	Mel Larson	Ford	62.225
283	6	3/17/57	Wilson, NC	0.5	D	100	Ralph Moody	Ford	55.079	Fireball Roberts	Ford	59.269
284	7	3/24/57	Hillsboro, NC	0.9	D	99	Buck Baker	Chevy	82.233	Fireball Roberts	Ford	87.828
285	8	3/31/57	Weaverville, NC	0.5	D	100	Buck Baker	Chevy	65.693	Marvin Panch	Ford	73.649
286	9	4/7/57	N. Wilkesboro, NC	0.625	D	100	Fireball Roberts	Ford	75.015	Fireball Roberts	Ford	81.521
287	10	4/14/57	Langhorne, PA	1.0	D	150	Fireball Roberts	Ford	85.850	Paul Goldsmith	Ford	93.701
288	11	4/19/57	Charlotte, NC	0.5	D	100	Fireball Roberts	Ford	52.083	Marvin Panch	Ford	60.060
289	12	4/27/57	Spartanburg, SC	0.5	D	100	Marvin Panch	Ford	55.130	Speedy Thompson	Chevy	61.538
290	13	4/28/57	Greensboro, NC	0.333	D	83.25	Paul Goldsmith	Ford	49.905	Buck Baker	Chevy	50.120
291	14	4/28/57	Portland, OR	0.5	P	50	Art Watts	Ford	64.754	Art Watts	Ford	65.813
292	15	5/4/57	Shelby, NC	0.5	D	100	Fireball Roberts	Ford	54.861	Tiny Lund	Pontiac	57.544
293	16	5/5/57	Richmond, VA	0.5	D	100	Paul Goldsmith	Ford	62.445	Russ Hepler	Pontiac	64.239
294	17	5/19/57	Martinsville, VA	0.5	P	221	Buck Baker	Chevy	57.318	Paul Goldsmith	Ford	65.693
295	18	5/26/57	Portland, OR	0.5	P	75	Eddie Pagan	Ford	64.732	Art Watts	Ford	66.347
296	19	5/30/57	Eureka, CA	0.625	D	96.625	Lloyd Dane	Ford	55.957	Parnelli Jones	Ford	63.920
297	20	5/30/57	New Oxford, PA	0.5	D	100	Buck Baker	Chevy	76.126	Marvin Panch	Ford	78.238

Cum. No.	Yr. No.	Date	Site	Track Length	Surface	Miles	Race Winner	Make	Speed	Pole Winner	Make	Pole Speed
298	21	6/1/57	Lancaster, SC	0.5	D	100	Paul Goldsmith	Ford	61.622	Buck Baker	Chevy	67.365
299	22	6/8/57	Los Angeles, CA	0.5	D	75	Eddie Pagan	Ford	None	Eddie Pagan	Ford	67.290
300	23	6/15/57	Newport, TN	0.5	D	100	Fireball Roberts	Ford	60.687	Speedy Thompson	Chevy	61.813
301	24	6/20/57	Columbia, SC	0.5	D	100	Jack Smith	Chevy	58.045	Buck Baker	Chevy	64.585
302	25	6/22/57	Sacramento, CA	0.5	D	100	Bill Amick	Ford	59.580	Art Watts	Ford	69.337
303	26	6/29/57	Spartanburg, SC	0.5	D	100	Lee Petty	Olds	46.287	Lee Petty	Olds	59.642
304	27	6/30/57	Jacksonville, NC	0.5	D	100	Buck Baker	Chevy	55.342	Lee Petty	Olds	61.328
305	28	7/4/57	Raleigh, NC	1.0	P	250	Paul Goldsmith	Ford	75.693	Frankie Schneider	Chevy	83.371
306	29	7/12/57	Charlotte, NC	0.5	D	100	Marvin Panch	Ford	56.302	Tiny Lund	Pontiac	60.913
307	30	7/14/57	LeHi, AR	1.5	D	200	Marvin Panch	Pontiac	67.167	Speedy Thompson	Chevy	98.991
308	31	7/14/57	Portland, OR	0.5	P	100	Eddie Pagan	Ford	64.539	Art Watts	Ford	66.396
309	32	7/20/57	Hickory, NC	0.5	D	100	Jack Smith	Chevy	58.737	Gwyn Staley	Chevy	66.085
310	33	7/24/57	Norfolk, VA	0.5	D	100	Buck Baker	Chevy	47.987	Bill Amick	Ford	56.338
311	34	7/30/57	Lancaster, SC	0.5	D	100	Speedy Thompson	Chevy	66.543	Speedy Thompson	Chevy	67.694
312	35	8/4/57	Watkins Glen, NY	2.3	P	101.2	Buck Baker	Chevy	83.064	Buck Baker	Chevy	87.071
313	36	8/4/57	Bremerton, WA	0.9	P	72	Parnelli Jones	Ford	38.959	Art Watts	Ford	62.657
314	37	8/10/57	New Oxford, PA	0.5	D	100	Marvin Panch	Ford	77.569	Tiny Lund	Pontiac	80.971
315	38	8/16/57	Old Bridge, NJ	0.5	P	100	Lee Petty	Olds	65.813	Rex White	Chevy	71.599
316	39	8/26/57	Myrtle Beach, SC	0.5	D	100	Gwyn Staley	Chevy	50.782	Johnny Allen	Plymouth	58.139
317	40	9/2/57	Darlington, SC	1.375	P	500.5	Speedy Thompson	Chevy	100.094	Cotton Owens	Pontiac	117.416
318	41	9/5/57	Syracuse, NY	1.0	D	100	Gwyn Staley	Chevy	80.591	Gwyn Staley	Chevy	83.045
319	42	9/8/57	Weaverville, NC	0.5	P	100	Lee Petty	Olds	67.950	Bill Amick	Ford	77.687
320	43	9/8/57	Sacramento, CA	1.0	D	100	Danny Graves	Chevy	68.663	Danny Graves	Chevy	78.007
321	44	9/15/57	San Jose, CA	0.5	D	58	Marvin Porter	Ford	None	No Time Trials	NTT	NTT
322	45	9/15/57	Langhorne, PA	1.0	D	300	Gwyn Staley	Chevy	72.759	Paul Goldsmith	Ford	92.072
323	46	9/19/57	Columbia, SC	0.5	D	100	Buck Baker	Chevy	60.514	Buck Baker	Chevy	63.649
324	47	9/21/57	Shelby, NC	0.5	D	100	Buck Baker	Chevy	53.699	Buck Baker	Chevy	58.177
325	48	10/5/57	Charlotte, NC	0.5	D	100	Lee Petty	Olds	51.583	Lee Petty	Olds	60.585
326	49	10/6/57	Martinsville, VA	0.5	P	250	Bob Welborn	Chevy	63.025	Eddie Pagan	Ford	65.837
327	50	10/12/57	Newberry, SC	0.5	D	100	Fireball Roberts	Ford	50.398	Jack Smith	Chevy	56.514
328	51	10/13/57	Concord, NC	0.5	D	100	Fireball Roberts	Ford	59.553	Jack Smith	Chevy	65.052
329	52	10/20/57	N. Wilkesboro, NC	0.625	P	100	Jack Smith	Chevy	69.902	Fireball Roberts	Ford	81.640
330	53	10/27/57	Greensboro, NC	0.333	D	83.25	Buck Baker	Chevy	38.927	Ken Rush	Ford	48.358

1958

Cum. No.	Yr. No.	Date	Site	Track Length	Surface	Miles	Race Winner	Make	Speed	Pole Winner	Make	Pole Speed
331	1	11/3/57	Fayetteville, NC	0.333	P	49.95	Rex White	Chevy	59.170	Jack Smith	Chevy	62.665
332	2	2/23/58	Daytona Beach, FL	4.1	B-R	159.9	Paul Goldsmith	Pontiac	101.113	Paul Goldsmith	Pontiac	140.570
333	3	3/2/58	Concord, NC	0.5	D	100	Lee Petty	Olds	58.555	Speedy Thompson	Chevy	N/A
334	4	3/15/58	Fayetteville, NC	0.333	P	49.95	Curtis Turner	Ford	56.141	Lee Petty	Olds	62.600
335	5	3/16/58	Wilson, NC	0.5	D	100	Lee Petty	Olds	48.459	Marvin Panch	Ford	58.901
336	6	3/23/58	Hillsboro, NC	0.9	D	99	Buck Baker	Chevy	78.502	Buck Baker	Chevy	83.076
337	7	4/5/58	Fayetteville, NC	0.333	P	49.95	Bob Welborn	Chevy	50.229	Lee Petty	Olds	60.576
338	8	4/10/58	Columbia, SC	0.5	D	100	Speedy Thompson	Chevy	None	Possum Jones	Chevy	66.201
339	9	4/12/58	Spartanburg, SC	0.5	D	100	Speedy Thompson	Chevy	56.613	Speedy Thompson	Chevy	61.412
340	10	4/13/58	Atlanta, GA	1.0	D	100	Curtis Turner	Ford	79.016	Joe Weatherly	Ford	81.577
341	11	4/18/58	Charlotte, NC	0.5	D	100	Curtis Turner	Ford	53.254	Curtis Turner	Ford	54.471
342	12	4/20/58	Martinsville, VA	0.5	P	250	Bob Welborn	Chevy	61.166	Buck Baker	Chevy	66.007
343	13	4/25/58	Manassas, VA	0.375	P	56.25	Frankie Schneider	Chevy	67.590	Eddie Pagan	Ford	69.018
344	14	4/27/58	Old Bridge, NJ	0.5	P	93.5	Jim Reed	Ford	68.438	Jim Reed	Ford	71.371
345	15	5/3/58	Greenville, SC	0.5	D	100	Jack Smith	Chevy	62.295	Jack Smith	Chevy	60.484
346	16	5/11/58	Greensboro, NC	0.333	D	49.95	Bob Welborn	Chevy	45.628	Bob Welborn	Chevy	46.250
347	17	5/15/58	Roanoke, VA	0.25	P	37.5	Jim Reed	Ford	49.504	Jim Reed	Ford	51.963
348	18	5/18/58	N. Wilkesboro, NC	0.625	P	100	Junior Johnson	Ford	78.636	Jack Smith	Chevy	82.056
349	19	5/24/58	Winston-Salem, NC	0.25	P	37.5	Bob Welborn	Chevy	40.407	Rex White	Chevy	46.851
350	20	5/30/58	Trenton, NJ	1.0	P	500	Fireball Roberts	Chevy	84.522	Marvin Panch	Ford	89.020
351	21	6/1/58	Riverside, CA	2.631	P	499.89	Eddie Gray	Ford	79.481	Danny Graves	Chevy	N/A
352	22	6/5/58	Columbia, SC	0.5	D	100	Junior Johnson	Ford	54.752	Buck Baker	Chevy	64.308
353	23	6/12/58	Bradford, PA	0.333	D	49.95	Junior Johnson	Ford	59.840	Bob Duell	Ford	65.831
354	24	6/15/58	Reading, PA	0.5	D	100	Junior Johnson	Ford	53.763	Speedy Thompson	Chevy	60.687
355	25	6/25/58	New Oxford, PA	0.5	D	100	Lee Petty	Olds	69.726	Ken Rush	Chevy	82.796
356	26	6/28/58	Hickory, NC	0.4	D	100	Lee Petty	Olds	62.413	Speedy Thompson	Chevy	68.768
357	27	6/29/58	Weaverville, NC	0.5	P	100	Rex White	Chevy	73.892	Rex White	Chevy	76.857
358	28	7/4/58	Raleigh, NC	1.0	P	250	Fireball Roberts	Chevy	73.691	Cotton Owens	Pontiac	83.896

Cum. No.	Yr. No.	Date	Site	Track Length	Surface	Miles	Race Winner	Make	Speed	Pole Winner	Make	Pole Speed
359	29	7/12/58	Asheville, NC	0.25	P	37.5	Jim Paschal	Chevy	46.440	Jim Paschal	Chevy	50.336
360	30	7/16/58	Busti, NY	0.333	D	49.95	Shorty Rollins	Ford	47.110	Lee Petty	Olds	N/A
361	31	7/18/58	Toronto, CAN	0.333	P	49.95	Lee Petty	Olds	43.184	Rex White	Chevy	51.406
362	32	7/19/58	Buffalo, NY	0.25	P	25	Jim Reed	Ford	46.972	Rex White	Chevy	38.593
363	33	7/25/58	Rochester, NY	0.5	D	100	Cotton Owens	Pontiac	59.990	Rex White	Chevy	62.871
364	34	7/26/58	Belmar, NJ	0.333	P	99.99	Jim Reed	Ford	65.395	Rex White	Chevy	68.936
365	35	8/3/58	Bridgehampton, NY	2.85	P	99.75	Jack Smith	Chevy	80.696	Jack Smith	Chevy	82.001
366	36	8/7/58	Columbia, SC	0.5	D	100	Speedy Thompson	Chevy	54.820	Speedy Thompson	Chevy	64.240
367	37	8/10/58	Nashville, TN	0.5	P	100	Joe Weatherly	Ford	59/269	Rex White	Chevy	71.315
368	38	8/17/58	Weaverville, NC	0.5	P	250	Fireball Roberts	Chevy	66.780	Jimmy Massey	Pontiac	76.596
369	39	8/22/58	Winston-Salem, NC	0.25	P	50	Lee Petty	Olds	39.158	George Dunn	Mercury	46.680
370	40	8/23/58	Myrtle Beach, SC	0.5	D	100	Bob Welborn	Chevy	60.443	Speedy Thompson	Chevy	66.667
371	41	9/1/58	Darlington, SC	1.375	P	500.5	Fireball Roberts	Chevy	102.585	Eddie Pagen	Ford	116.952
372	42	9/5/58	Charlotte, NC	0.5	D	100	Buck Baker	Chevy	52.280	Lee Petty	Olds	57.879
373	43	9/7/58	Birmingham, AL	0.5	D	100	Fireball Roberts	Chevy	60.678	Cotton Owens	Pontiac	64.034
374	44	9/7/58	Sacramento, CA	1.0	D	100	Parnelli Jones	Ford	65.550	Parnelli Jones	Ford	77.922
375	45	9/12/58	Gastonia, NC	0.333	D	66.7	Buck Baker	Chevy	47.856	Tiny Lund	Chevy	52.650
376	46	9/14/58	Richmond, VA	0.5	D	100	Speedy Thompson	Chevy	57.878	Speedy Thompson	Chevy	62.915
377	47	9/29/58	Hillsboro, NC	0.9	D	99	Joe Eubanks	Pontiac	72.439	Tiny Lund	Chevy	87.308
378	48	10/5/58	Salisbury, NC	0.625	D	100	Lee Petty	Olds	58.271	Gober Sosebee	Chevy	72.162
379	49	10/12/58	Martinsville, VA	0.5	P	175	Fireball Roberts	Chevy	64.344	Glen Wood	Ford	67.950
380	50	10/19/58	N. Wilkesboro, NC	0.625	P	100	Junior Johnson	Ford	84.906	Glen Wood	Ford	86.805
381	51	10/26/58	Atlanta, GA	1.0	D	150	Junior Johnson	Ford	69.570	Glen Wood	Ford	81.522

1959

Cum. No.	Yr. No.	Date	Site	Track Length	Surface	Miles	Race Winner	Make	Speed	Pole Winner	Make	Pole Speed
382	1	11/9/58	Fayetteville, NC	0.333	D	49.95	Bob Welborn	Chevy	56.001	Bob Welborn	Chevy	61.985
383	2	2/20/59	Daytona Beach, FL	2.5	P	100	Bob Welborn	Chevy	143.198	Fireball Roberts	Pontiac	140.580
384	3	2/22/59	Daytona Beach, FL	2.5	P	500	Lee Petty	Olds	135.521	Bob Welborn	Chevy	140.120
385	4	3/1/59	Hillsboro, NC	0.9	D	99	Curtis Turner	T-Bird	81.612	Curtis Turner	T-Bird	87.544
386	5	3/8/59	Concord, NC	0.5	D	100	Curtis Turner	T-Bird	59.239	Buck Baker	Chevy	66.420
387	6	3/22/59	Atlanta, GA	1.0	D	100	Johnny Beauchamp	T-Bird	75.172	Buck Baker	Chevy	77.888
388	7	3/29/59	Wilson, NC	0.5	D	100	Junior Johnson	Ford	50.300	No Time Trials	NTT	NTT
389	8	3/30/59	Winston-Salem, NC	0.25	P	50	Jim Reed	Ford	43.562	Rex White	Chevy	46.296
390	9	4/4/59	Columbia, SC	0.5	D	100	Jack Smith	Chevy	87.343	Jack Smith	Chevy	60.730
391	10	4/5/59	N. Wilkesboro, NC	0.625	P	100	Lee Petty	Olds	71.985	Speedy Thompson	Chevy	85.746
392	11	4/26/59	Reading, PA	0.5	D	100	Junior Johnson	Ford	53.011	N/A	N/A	N/A
393	12	5/2/59	Hickory, NC	0.4	D	100	Junior Johnson	Ford	62.165	Junior Johnson	Ford	68.900
394	13	5/3/59	Martinsville, VA	0.5	P	250	Lee Petty	Olds	59.512	Bobby Johns	Chevry	66.030
395	14	5/17/59	Trenton, NJ	1.0	P	150	Tom Pistone	T-Bird	87.350	Bob Burdick	T-Bird	88.950
396	15	5/22/59	Charlotte, NC	0.5	D	100	Lee Petty	Olds	55.300	Bob Welborn	Chevy	57.950
397	16	5/24/59	Nashville, TN	0.5	P	100	Rex White	Chevy	71.006	Rex White	Chevy	70.890
398	17	5/30/59	Los Angeles, CA	0.4	D	200	Parnelli Jones	Ford	50.982	Jim Reed	Chevy	53.590
399	18	6/5/59	Spartanburg, SC	0.5	D	100	Jack Smith	Chevy	55.547	Cotton Owens	Pontiac	63.180
400	19	6/13/59	Greenville, SC	0.5	D	100	Junior Johnson	Ford	51.480	Jack Smith	Chevy	65.838
401	20	6/14/59	Atlanta, GA	1.0	D	150	Lee Petty	Plymouth	58.499	No Time Trials	NTT	NTT
402	21	6/18/59	Columbia, SC	0.5	D	100	Lee Petty	Plymouth	58.726	Bob Burdick	T-Bird	64.865
403	22	6/20/59	Wilson, NC	0.5	D	100	Junior Johnson	Ford	58.065	No Time Trials	NTT	NTT
404	23	6/21/59	Richmond, VA	0.5	D	100	Tom Pistone	T-Bird	56.881	Buck Baker	Chevy	66.420
405	24	6/27/59	Winston-Salem, NC	0.25	P	50	Rex White	Chevy	41.228	Lee Petty	Plymouth	47.071
406	25	6/28/59	Weaverville, NC	0.5	P	100	Rex White	Chevy	72.934	Glen Wood	Ford	76.820
407	26	7/4/59	Daytona Beach, FL	2.5	P	250	Fireball Roberts	Pontiac	140.581	Fireball Roberts	Pontiac	144.997
408	27	7/21/59	Heidelberg, PA	0.25	D	50	Jim Reed	Chevy	45.000	Dick Bailey	Plymouth	47.970
409	28	7/26/59	Charlotte, NC	0.5	D	100	Jack Smith	Chevy	49.553	Buck Baker	Chevy	63.070
410	29	8/1/59	Myrtle Beach, SC	0.5	D	100	Ned Jarrett	Ford	52.941	Bob Welborn	Chevy	66.470
411	30	8/2/59	Charlotte, NC	0.5	D	100	Ned Jarrett	Ford	52.794	Bob Welborn	Chevy	62.540
412	31	8/3/59	Nashville, TN	0.5	P	150	Joe Lee Johnson	Chevy	63.343	Rex White	Chevy	74.044
413	32	8/16/59	Weaverville, NC	0.5	P	250	Bob Welborn	Chevy	71.833	Rex White	Chevy	77.687
414	33	8/21/59	Winston-Salem, NC	0.25	P	50	Rex White	Chevy	44.085	Rex White	Chevy	47.443
415	34	8/22/59	Greenville, SC	0.5	D	100	Buck Baker	Chevy	58.055	Lee Petty	Plymouth	63.313
416	35	8/29/59	Columbia, SC	0.5	D	100	Lee Petty	Plymouth	48.264	No Time Trials	NTT	NTT
417	36	9/7/59	Darlington, SC	1.375	P	500.5	Jim Reed	Chevy	111.836	Fireball Roberts	Pontiac	123.734
418	37	9/11/59	Hickory, NC	0.4	D	100	Lee Petty	Plymouth	63.380	No Time Trials	NTT	NTT
419	38	9/13/59	Richmond, VA	0.5	D	100	Cotton Owens	T-Bird	60.382	Cotton Owens	T-Bird	62.674

Cum. No.	Yr. No.	Date	Site	Track Length	Surface	Miles	Race Winner	Make	Speed	Pole Winner	Make	Pole Speed
420	39	9/13/59	Sacramento, CA	1.0	D	100	Eddie Gray	Ford	54.753	No Time Trials	NTT	NTT
421	40	9/20/59	Hillsboro, NC	0.9	D	99	Lee Petty	Plymouth	77.868	Jack Smith	Chevy	85.533
422	41	9/27/59	Martinsville, VA	0.5	P	250	Rex White	Chevy	60.500	Glen Wood	Ford	69.471
423	42	10/11/59	Weaverville, NC	0.5	P	100	Lee Petty	Plymouth	76.433	Tommy Irwin	T-Bird	78.568
424	43	10/18/59	N. Wilkesboro, NC	0.625	P	100	Lee Petty	Plymouth	74.829	Glen Wood	Ford	86.806
425	44	10/25/59	Concord, NC	0.5	D	150	Jack Smith	Chevy	54.005	No Time Trials	NTT	NTT

1960

Cum. No.	Yr. No.	Date	Site	Track Length	Surface	Miles	Race Winner	Make	Speed	Pole Winner	Make	Pole Speed
426	1	11/8/59	Charlotte, NC	0.5	D	100	Jack Smith	Chevy	52.409	Buck Baker	Chevy	64.103
427	2	11/26/59	Columbia, SC	0.5	D	100	Ned Jarrett	Ford	55.071	Junior Johnson	Dodge	65.217
428	3	2/12/60	Daytona Beach, FL	2.5	P	100	Fireball Roberts	Pontiac	137.614	Cotton Owens	Pontiac	149.892
429	4	2/12/60	Daytona Beach, FL	2.5	P	100	Jack Smith	Pontiac	146.520	Jack Smith	Pontiac	148.157
430	5	2/14/60	Daytona Beach, FL	2.5	P	500	Junior Johnson	Chevy	124.740	Cotton Owens	Pontiac	149.892
431	6	2/28/60	Charlotte, NC	0.5	D	100	Richard Petty	Plymouth	53.404	Lee Petty	Plymouth	62.110
432	7	3/27/60	N. Wilkesboro, NC	0.625	P	100	Lee Petty	Plymouth	66.347	Junior Johnson	Chevy	83.860
433	8	4/3/60	Phoenix, AZ	1.0	D	100	John Rostek	Ford	71.889	Mel Larson	Pontiac	78.930
434	9	4/5/60	Columbia, SC	0.5	D	100	Rex White	Chevy	50.697	Doug Yates	Plymouth	66.030
435	10	4/10/60	Martinsville, VA	0.5	P	250	Richard Petty	Plymouth	63.943	Glen Wood	Ford	60.150
436	11	4/16/60	Hickory, NC	0.5	D	100	Joe Weatherly	Ford	66.347	Rex White	Chevy	71.080
437	12	4/17/60	Wilson, NC	0.5	D	100	Joe Weatherly	Ford	55.113	Emanuel Zervakis	Chevy	60.500
438	13	4/18/60	Winston Salem, NC	0.25	P	50	Glen Wood	Ford	43.082	Glen Wood	Ford	47.240
439	14	4/23/60	Greenville, SC	0.5	D	100	Ned Jarrett	Ford	62.337	Curtis Turner	Ford	64.720
440	15	4/24/60	Weaverville, NC	0.5	P	83.5	Lee Petty	Plymouth	63.368	Junior Johnson	Ford	78.090
441	16	5/14/60	Darlington, SC	1.375	P	301.125	Joe Weatherly	Ford	102.640	Fireball Roberts	Pontiac	127.750
442	17	5/28/60	Spartanburg, SC	0.5	D	100	Ned Jarrett	Ford	51.843	Jack Smith	Pontiac	64.220
443	18	5/29/60	Hillsboro, NC	0.9	D	99	Lee Petty	Plymouth	83.583	Richard Petty	Plymouth	88.190
444	19	6/5/60	Richmond, VA	0.5	D	100	Lee Petty	Plymouth	62.251	Ned Jarrett	Ford	64.560
445	20	6/12/60	Hanford, CA	1.5	P	250	Marvin Porter	Ford	88.032	Frank Secrist	Ford	93.040
446	21	6/19/60	Charlotte, NC	1.5	P	600	Joe Lee Johnson	Chevy	107.735	Fireball Roberts	Pontiac	133.904
447	22	6/26/60	Winston-Salem, NC	0.25	P	50	Glen Wood	Ford	45.872	Lee Petty	Plymouth	47.850
448	23	7/4/60	Daytona Beach, FL	2.5	P	250	Jack Smith	Pontiac	146.842	Jack Smith	Pontiac	152.129
449	24	7/10/60	Heidelberg, PA	0.5	D	94	Lee Petty	Plymouth	67.450	Lee Petty	Plymouth	91.650
450	25	7/17/60	Montgomery, NY	2.0	P	200	Rex White	Chevy	88.626	John Rostek	Ford	96.650
451	26	7/23/60	Myrtle Beach, SC	0.5	D	100	Buck Baker	Chevy	60.985	Ned Jarrett	Ford	64.610
452	27	7/31/60	Atlanta, GA	1.5	P	300.5	Fireball Roberts	Pontiac	112.652	Fireball Roberts	Pontiac	133.129
453	28	8/3/60	Birmingham, AL	0.25	P	50	Ned Jarrett	Ford	54.463	Ned Jarrett	Ford	55.866
454	29	8/7/60	Nashville, TN	0.5	P	166.5	Johnny Beauchamp	Chevy	56.966	Rex White	Chevy	74.810
455	30	8/14/60	Weaverville, NC	0.5	P	250	Rex White	Chevy	65.024	Jack Smith	Pontiac	77.850
456	31	8/16/60	Spartanburg, SC	0.5	D	100	Cotton Owens	Pontiac	59.681	Cotton Owens	Pontiac	63.250
457	32	8/18/60	Columbia, SC	0.5	D	150	Rex White	Chevy	54.265	Tommy Irwin	T-Bird	60.360
458	33	8/20/60	South Boston, VA	0.25	D	37.5	Junior Johnson	Chevy	50.732	Ned Jarrett	Ford	51.903
459	34	8/23/60	Winston-Salem, NC	0.25	P	50	Glen Wood	Ford	44.389	Glen Wood	Ford	46.970
460	35	9/5/60	Darlington, SC	1.375	P	500.5	Buck Baker	Pontiac	105.901	Fireball Roberts	Pontiac	125.549
461	36	9/9/60	Hickory, NC	0.4	D	100	Junior Johnson	Chevy	69.998	Buck Baker	Chevy	71.180
462	37	9/11/60	Sacramento, CA	1.0	D	100	Jim Cook	Dodge	70.629	Jim Cook	Dodge	78.450
463	38	9/15/60	Sumter, SC	0.25	D	50	Ned Jarrett	Ford	41.208	David Pearson	Chevy	45.070
464	39	9/18/60	Hillsboro, NC	0.9	D	99	Richard Petty	Plymouth	80.161	Richard Petty	Plymouth	75.285
465	40	9/25/60	Martinsville, VA	0.5	P	250	Rex White	Chevy	60.439	Glen Wood	Ford	68.440
466	41	10/2/60	N. Wilkesboro, NC	0.625	P	200	Rex White	Chevy	77.444	Rex White	Chevy	93.399
467	42	10/16/60	Charlotte, NC	1.5	P	400	Speedy Thompson	Ford	112.905	Fireball Roberts	Pontiac	133.465
468	43	10/23/60	Richmond, VA	0.5	D	100	Speedy Thompson	Ford	63.739	Ned Jarrett	Ford	64.410
469	44	10/30/60	Atlanta, GA	1.5	P	501	Bobby Johns	Pontiac	108.408	Fireball Roberts	Pontiac	134.596

1961

Cum. No.	Yr. No.	Date	Site	Track Length	Surface	Miles	Race Winner	Make	Speed	Pole Winner	Make	Pole Speed
470	1	11/6/60	Charlotte, NC	0.5	D	100	Joe Weatherly	Ford	59.435	Lee Petty	Plymouth	63.581
471	2	11/20/60	Jacksonville, FL	0.5	D	100	Lee Petty	Plymouth	64.400	Junior Johnson	Pontiac	68.623
472	3	2/24/61	Daytona Beach, FL	2.5	P	100	Fireball Roberts	Pontiac	133.037	Fireball Roberts	Pontiac	155.709
473	4	2/24/61	Daytona Beach, FL	2.5	P	100	Joe Weatherly	Pontiac	152.671	Joe Weatherly	Pontiac	154.122
474	5	2/26/61	Daytona Beach, FL	2.5	P	500	Marvin Panch	Pontiac	149.601	Fireball Roberts	Pontiac	155.709
475	6	3/4/61	Spartanburg, SC	0.5	D	100	Cotton Owens	Pontiac	59.152	Ned Jarrett	Ford	63.920
476	7	3/5/61	Weaverville, NC	0.5	P	100	Rex White	Chevy	72.492	Rex White	Chevy	79.295
477	8	3/12/61	Hanford, CA	1.4	P	250	Fireball Roberts	Pontiac	95.621	Bob Ross	Ford	98.370
478	9	3/26/61	Atlanta, GA	1.5	P	501	Bob Burdick	Pontiac	124.172	Marvin Panch	Pontiac	135.755

Cum. No.	Yr. No.	Date	Site	Track Length	Surface	Miles	Race Winner	Make	Speed	Pole Winner	Make	Pole Speed
479	10	4/1/61	Greenville, SC	0.5	D	100	Emanuel Zervakis	Chevy	52.189	Junior Johnson	Pontiac	62.090
480	11	4/2/61	Hillsboro, NC	0.9	D	99	Cotton Owens	Pontiac	84.695	Ned Jarrett	Chevy	91.836
481	12	4/3/61	Winston-Salem, NC	0.25	P	37.5	Rex White	Chevy	45.500	Glen Wood	Ford	48.700
482	13	4/9/61	Martinsville, VA	0.5	P	74.5	Fred Lorenzen	Ford	68.366	Rex White	Chevy	70.280
483	14	4/16/61	N. Wilkesboro, NC	0.625	P	250	Rex White	Chevy	83.248	Junior Johnson	Pontiac	95.660
484	15	4/20/61	Columbia, SC	0.5	D	100	Cotton Owens	Pontiac	51.940	Ned Jarrett	Chevy	64.380
485	16	4/22/61	Hickory, NC	0.4	D	100	Junior Johnson	Pontiac	66.654	Junior Johnson	Pontiac	74.074
486	17	4/23/61	Richmond, VA	0.5	D	100	Richard Petty	Plymouth	62.456	Richard Petty	Plymouth	66.667
487	18	4/30/61	Martinsville, VA	0.5	P	250	Junior Johnson	Pontiac	66.287	Rex White	Chevy	71.320
488	19	5/6/61	Darlington, SC	1.375	P	301.125	Fred Lorenzen	Ford	119.520	Fred Lorenzen	Ford	128.965
489	20	5/21/61	Charlotte, NC	1.5	P	100.5	Richard Petty	Plymouth	133.554	Fred Lorenzen	Ford	137.509
490	21	5/21/61	Charlotte, NC	1.5	P	100.5	Joe Weatherly	Pontiac	115.591	Junior Johnson	Pontiac	136.951
491	22	5/21/61	Riverside, CA	2.58	P	100	Lloyd Dane	Chevy	82.512	Eddie Gray	Ford	85.210
492	23	5/27/61	Los Angeles, CA	0.5	D	100	Eddie Gray	Ford	68.833	Danny Weinberg	Ford	71.940
493	24	5/28/61	Charlotte, NC	1.5	P	600	David Pearson	Pontiac	111.633	Richard Petty	Plymouth	131.611
494	25	6/2/61	Spartanburg, SC	0.5	D	100	Jim Paschal	Pontiac	55.495	Joe Weatherly	Pontiac	61.250
495	26	6/4/61	Birmingham, AL	0.5	D	100	Ned Jarrett	Chevy	61.068	Johnny Allen	Chevy	65.910
496	27	6/8/61	Greenville, SC	0.5	D	100	Jack Smith	Pontiac	58.441	Ned Jarrett	Chevy	65.480
497	28	6/10/61	Winston-Salem, NC	0.25	P	50	Rex White	Chevy	42.714	Junior Johnson	Pontiac	47.720
498	29	6/17/61	Norwood, MA	0.25	P	125	Emanuel Zervakis	Chevy	53.827	Rex White	Chevy	55.870
499	30	6/23/61	Hartsville, SC	0.333	D	50	Buck Baker	Chrysler	46.234	Emanuel Zervakis	Chevy	54.970
500	31	6/24/61	Roanoke, VA	0.25	P	37.5	Junior Johnson	Pontiac	49.907	Rex White	Chevy	53.700
501	32	7/4/61	Daytona Beach, FL	2.5	P	250	David Pearson	Pontiac	154.294	Fireball Roberts	Pontiac	157.150
502	33	7/9/61	Atlanta, GA	1.5	P	250	Fred Lorenzen	Ford	118.067	Fireball Roberts	Pontiac	136.088
503	34	7/20/61	Columbia, SC	0.5	D	100	Cotton Owens	Pontiac	62.198	Cotton Owens	Pontiac	67.650
504	35	7/22/61	Myrtle Beach, SC	0.5	D	100	Joe Weatherly	Pontiac	57.655	Joe Weatherly	Pontiac	66.690
505	36	7/29/61	Bristol, TN	0.5	P	250	Jack Smith	Pontiac	68.373	Fred Lorenzen	Ford	70.225
506	37	8/6/61	Nashville, TN	0.5	P	201.5	Jim Paschal	Pontiac	56.455	Rex White	Chevy	76.600
507	38	8/9/61	Winston-Salem, NC	0.25	P	37.5	Rex White	Chevy	42.452	Junior Johnson	Pntiac	48.050
508	39	8/13/61	Weaverville, NC	0.5	P	129	Junior Johnson	Pontiac	64.704	Jim Paschal	Pontiac	80.430
509	40	8/18/61	Richmond, VA	0.333	D	37.5	Junior Johnson	Pontiac	51.605	Junior Johnson	Pontiac	52.630
510	41	8/27/61	South Boston, VA	0.25	P	50	Junior Johnson	Pontiac	48.348	Cotton Owens	Pntiac	52.630
511	42	9/4/61	Darlington, SC	1.375	P	500.5	Nelson Stacy	Ford	117.787	Fireball Roberts	Pontiac	128.680
512	43	9/8/61	Hickory, NC	0.4	D	100	Rex White	Chevy	67.529	Rex White	Chevy	72.290
513	44	9/10/61	Richmond, VA	0.5	D	125	Joe Weatherly	Pontiac	61.677	Junior Johnson	Pontiac	65.010
514	45	9/10/61	Sacramento, CA	1.0	D	100	Eddie Gray	Ford	None	Bill Amick	Pontiac	79.260
515	46	9/17/61	Atlanta, GA	1.5	P	400.5	David Pearson	Pontiac	125.384	Fireball Roberts	Pontiac	136.294
516	47	9/24/61	Martinsville, VA	0.5	P	250	Joe Weatherly	Pontiac	62.586	Fred Lorenzen	Ford	70.730
517	48	10/1/61	N. Wilkesboro, NC	0.625	P	200	Rex White	Chevy	84.675	Junior Johnson	Pontiac	94.540
518	49	10/15/61	Charlotte, NC	1.5	P	400.5	Joe Weatherly	Pontiac	119.950	David Pearson	Pontiac	138.577
519	50	10/22/61	Bristol, TN	0.5	P	250	Joe Weatherly	Pontiac	72.452	Bobby Johns	Pontiac	80.645
520	51	10/28/61	Greenville, SC	0.5	D	100	Junior Johnson	Pontiac	63.346	Buck Baker	Chrysler	66.667
521	52	10/29/61	Hillsboro, NC	0.9	D	148.5	Joe Weatherly	Pontiac	85.249	Joe Weatherly	Pontiac	95.154

1962

Cum. No.	Yr. No.	Date	Site	Track Length	Surface	Miles	Race Winner	Make	Speed	Pole Winner	Make	Pole Speed
522	1	11/5/61	Concord, NC	0.5	D	100	Jack Smith	Pontiac	59.405	Joe Weatherly	Pontiac	68.543
523	2	11/12/61	Weaverville, NC	0.5	P	100	Rex White	Chevy	68.467	Joe Weatherly	Pontiac	81.743
524	3	2/16/61	Daytona Beach, FL	2.5	P	100	Fireball Roberts	Pontiac	156.999	Fireball Roberts	Pontiac	155.774
525	4	2/16/62	Daytona Beach, FL	2.5	P	100	Joe Weatherly	Pontiac	145.395	Darel Dieringer	Pontiac	155.086
526	5	2/18/62	Daytona Beach, FL	2.5	P	500	Fireball Roberts	Pontiac	152.529	Fireball Roberts	Pontiac	158.774
527	6	2/25/62	Concord, NC	0.5	D	39	Joe Weatherly	Pontiac	53.161	Joe Weatherly	Pontiac	N/A
528	7	3/4/62	Weaverville, NC	0.5	P	100	Joe Weatherly	Pontiac	75.471	Rex White	Chevy	80.460
529	8	3/17/62	Savannah, GA	0.5	D	100	Jack Smith	Pontiac	58.775	Rex White	Chevy	70.588
530	9	3/18/62	Hillsboro, NC	0.9	D	99	Rex White	Chevy	86.948	Joe Weatherly	Pontiac	96.588
531	10	4/1/62	Richmond, VA	0.5	D	90	Rex White	Chevy	51.363	No Time Trials	NTT	NTT
532	11	4/13/62	Columbia, SC	0.5	D	100	Ned Jarrett	Chevy	56.710	Joe Weatherly	Pontiac	64.423
533	12	4/15/62	N. Wilkesboro, NC	0.625	P	250	Richard Petty	Plymouth	84.737	Junior Johnson	Pontiac	94.142
534	13	4/19/62	Greenville, SC	0.5	D	100	Ned Jarrett	Chevy	57.480	Ned Jarrett	Chevy	66.568
535	14	4/21/62	Myrtle Beach, SC	0.5	D	100	Jack Smith	Pontiac	63.036	Ned Jarrett	Chevy	68.939
536	15	4/22/62	Martinsville, VA	0.5	P	250	Richard Petty	Plymouth	66.425	Fred Lorenzen	Ford	71.287
537	16	4/23/62	Winston-Salem, NC	0.25	P	27	Rex White	Chevy	43.392	Rex White	Chevy	48.417
538	17	4/29/62	Bristol, TN	0.5	P	250	Bobby Johns	Pontiac	73.397	Fireball Roberts	Pontiac	81.374
539	18	5/4/62	Richmond, VA	0.5	P	66.7	Jimmy Pardue	Pontiac	67.747	Rex White	Chevy	71.145

Cum. No.	Yr. No.	Date	Site	Track Length	Surface	Miles	Race Winner	Make	Speed	Pole Winner	Make	Pole Speed
540	19	5/5/62	Hickory, NC	0.4	D	100	Jack Smith	Pontiac	71.216	Jack Smith	Pontiac	74.074
541	20	5/6/62	Concord, NC	0.5	D	100	Joe Weatherly	Pontiac	57.052	Not Time Trials	NTT	NTT
542	21	5/12/62	Darlington, SC	1.375	P	301.125	Nelson Stacy	Ford	117.429	Fred Lorenzen	Ford	129.810
543	22	5/19/62	Spartanburg, SC	0.5	D	100	Ned Jarrett	Chevy	60.080	Cotton Owens	Pontiac	64.423
544	23	5/27/62	Charlotte, NC	1.5	P	600	Nelson Stacy	Ford	125.552	Fireball Roberts	Pontiac	140.150
545	24	6/10/62	Atlanta, GA	1.5	P	328.5	Fred Lorenzen	Ford	101.983	Banjo Matthews	Pontiac	137.640
546	25	6/16/62	Winston-Salem, NC	0.25	P	50	Johnny Allen	Pontiac	45.466	Rex White	Chevy	48.179
547	26	6/19/62	Augusta, GA	0.5	P	100	Joe Weatherly	Pontiac	59.850	Joe Weatherly	Pontiac	63.069
548	27	6/22/62	Richmond, VA	0.333	P	99.9	Jim Paschal	Pontiac	66.293	Rex White	Chevy	70.435
549	28	6/23/62	South Boston, VA	0.375	P	100	Rex White	Chevy	72.540	Jack Smith	Pontiac	79.458
550	29	7/4/62	Daytona Beach, FL	2.5	P	250	Fireball Roberts	Pontiac	153.688	Banjo Matthews	Pontiac	160.499
551	30	7/7/62	Columbia, SC	0.5	D	100	Rex White	Chevy	62.370	Jack Smith	Pontiac	66.667
552	31	7/13/62	Asheville, NC	0.4	P	100	Jack Smith	Pontiac	78.294	Rex White	Chevy	82.885
553	32	7/14/62	Greensville, SC	0.5	D	100	Richard Petty	Plymouth	62.219	Rex White	Chevy	66.055
554	33	7/17/62	Augusta, GA	0.5	D	100	Joe Weatherly	Pontiac	55.104	Jack Smith	Pontiac	65.885
555	34	7/20/62	Savannah, GA	0.5	D	100	Joe Weatherly	Pontiac	67.239	Wendell Scott	Chevy	71.627
556	35	7/21/62	Myrtle Beach, SC	0.5	D	100	Ned Jarrett	Chevy	64.171	Ned Jarrett	Chevy	68.467
557	37	7/29/62	Bristol, TN	0.5	P	250	Jim Paschal	Plymouth	75.276	Fireball Roberts	Pontiac	80.321
558	37	8/3/62	Chattanooga, TN	0.333	P	66.7	Joe Weatherly	Pontiac	71.145	Richard Petty	Plymouth	73.365
559	38	8/5/62	Nashville, TN	0.5	P	250	Jim Paschal	Plymouth	64.469	Johnny Allen	Pontiac	77.854
560	39	8/8/62	Huntsville, AL	0.25	P	50	Richard Petty	Plymouth	54.644	Richard Petty	Plymouth	54.086
561	40	8/12/62	Weaverville, NC	0.5	P	250	Jim Paschal	Plymouth	77.492	Jack Smith	Pontiac	82.720
562	41	8/15/62	Roanoke, VA	0.25	P	50	Richard Petty	Plymouth	51.165	Jack Smith	Pontiac	54.086
563	42	8/18/62	Winston-Salem, NC	0.25	P	50	Richard Petty	Plymouth	46.875	Jack Smith	Pontiac	48.102
564	43	8/21/62	Spartanburg, SC	0.5	D	100	Richard Petty	Plymouth	59.870	Richard Petty	Plymouth	61.590
565	44	8/25/62	Valdosta, GA	0.5	D	100	Ned Jarrett	Chevy	61.454	Richard Petty	Plymouth	59.386
566	45	9/3/62	Darlington, SC	1.375	P	500.5	Larry Frank	Ford	117.965	Fireball Roberts	Pontiac	130.246
567	46	9/7/62	Hickory, NC	0.4	D	100	Rex White	Chevrolet	70.574	Junior Johnson	Pontiac	71.357
568	47	9/9/62	Richmond, VA	0.5	D	100	Joe Weatherly	Pontiac	64.981	Rex White	Chevy	66.127
569	48	9/11/62	Moyock, NC	0.25	D	62.5	Ned Jarrett	Chevy	43.078	Ned Jarrett	Chevy	45.569
570	49	9/13/62	Augusta, GA	0.5	D	100	Fred Lorenzen	Ford	60.759	Joe Weatherly	Pontiac	65.421
571	50	9/23/62	Martinsville, VA	0.5	P	250	Nelson Stacy	Ford	66.874	Fireball Roberts	Pontiac	71.513
572	51	9/30/62	N. Wilkesboro, NC	0.625	P	200	Richard Petty	Plymouth	86.186	Fred Lorenzen	Ford	94.657
573	52	10/14/62	Charlotte, NC	1.5	P	400.5	Junior Johnson	Pontiac	132.085	Fireball Roberts	Pontiac	140.287
574	53	10/28/62	Atlanta, GA	1.5	P	400.5	Rex White	Chevy	124.740	Fireball Roberts	Pontiac	138.978

1963

Cum. No.	Yr. No.	Date	Site	Track Length	Surface	Miles	Race Winner	Make	Speed	Pole Winner	Make	Pole Speed
575	1	11/4/62	Birmingham, AL	0.5	D	100	Jim Paschal	Plymouth	68.350	Jim Paschal	Plymouth	73.592
576	2	11/11/62	Tampa, FL	0.333	P	66.7	Richard Petty	Plymouth	57.167	Rex White	Chevy	60.090
577	3	11/22/62	Randleman, NC	0.25	P	50	Jim Paschal	Plymouth	47.544	Glen Wood	Ford	51.933
578	4	1/20/63	Riverside, CA	2.7	P	499.5	Dan Gurney	Ford	84.965	Paul Goldsmith	Pontiac	98.809
579	5	2/22/63	Daytona Beach, FL	2.5	P	100	Junior Johnson	Chevy	164.083	Fireball Roberts	Pontiac	160.943
580	6	2/22/63	Daytona Beach, FL	2.5	P	100	Johnny Rutherford	Chevy	162.969	Fred Lorenzen	Ford	161.870
581	7	2/24/63	Daytona Beach, FL	2.5	P	500	Tiny Lund	Ford	151.566	Fireball Roberts	Pontiac	160.943
582	8	3/2/63	Spartanburg, SC	0.5	D	100	Richard Petty	Plymouth	55.598	Junior Johnson	Chevy	64.670
583	9	3/3/63	Weaverville, NC	0.5	P	100	Richard Petty	Plymouth	79.664	Junior Johnson	Chevy	82.750
584	10	3/10/63	Hillsboro, NC	0.9	D	148.5	Junior Johnson	Chevy	83.129	Joe Weatherly	Pontiac	95.716
585	11	3/17/63	Atlanta, GA	1.5	P	500.5	Fred Lorenzen	Ford	130.582	Junior Johnson	Chevy	141.038
586	12	3/24/63	Hickory, NC	0.5	D	100	Junior Johnson	Chevy	67.950	Junior Johnson	Chevy	75.235
587	13	3/31/63	Bristol, TN	0.5	P	250	Fireball Roberts	Ford	76.910	Fred Lorenzen	Ford	80.681
588	14	4/4/63	Augusta, GA	0.5	D	56	Ned Jarrett	Ford	60.089	LeeRoy Yarbrough	Mercury	64.610
589	15	4/7/63	Richmond, VA	0.5	D	125	Joe Weatherly	Pontiac	58.624	Rex White	Chevy	69.151
590	16	4/13/63	Greenville, SC	0.5	D	100	Buck Baker	Pontiac	54.853	Jimmy Pardue	Ford	66.270
591	17	4/14/63	South Boston, VA	0.375	P	150	Richard Petty	Plymouth	75.229	Ned Jarrett	Ford	78.720
592	18	4/15/63	Winston-Salem, NC	0.25	P	50	Jimmy Pardue	Plymouth	46.814	Richard Petty	Plymouth	48.280
593	19	4/21/63	Martinsville, VA	0.5	P	250	Richard Petty	Plymouth	64.823	Rex White	Chevy	72.000
594	20	4/28/63	N. Wilkesboro, NC	0.625	P	160.625	Richard Petty	Plymouth	83.302	Fred Lorenzen	Ford	96.150
595	21	5/2/63	Columbia, SC	0.5	D	100	Richard Petty	Plymouth	51.650	Richard Petty	Plymouth	68.080
596	22	5/5/63	Randleman, NC	0.25	P	50	Jim Paschal	Plymouth	48.605	Ned Jarrett	Ford	50.856
597	23	5/11/63	Darlington, SC	1.375	P	302.5	Joe Weatherly	Pontiac	122.745	Fred Lorenzen	Ford	131.718
598	24	5/18/63	Manassas, VA	0.333	P	99.9	Richard Petty	Plymouth	70.275	Richard Petty	Plymouth	71.580
599	25	5/19/63	Richmond, VA	0.333	P	99.9	Ned Jarrett	Ford	65.052	Ned Jarrett	Ford	70.642
600	26	6/2/63	Charlotte, NC	1.5	P	600	Fred Lorenzen	Ford	132.417	Junior Johnson	Chevy	141.148

Cum. No.	Yr. No.	Date	Site	Track Length	Surface	Miles	Race Winner	Make	Speed	Pole Winner	Make	Pole Speed
601	27	6/9/63	Birmingham, AL	0.5	D	100	Richard Petty	Plymouth	68.195	Jack Smith	Plymouth	71.146
602	28	6/30/63	Atlanta, GA	1.5	P	400.5	Junior Johnson	Chevy	121.139	Marvin Panch	Ford	140.753
603	29	7/4/63	Daytona Beach, FL	2.5	P	400	Fireball Roberts	Ford	150.927	Junior Johnson	Chevy	166.005
604	30	7/7/63	Myrtle Beach, SC	0.5	D	100	Ned Jarrett	Ford	60.996	Richard Petty	Plymouth	68.700
605	31	7/10/63	Savannah, GA	0.5	D	100	Ned Jarrett	Ford	59.622	Richard Petty	Plymouth	71.340
606	32	7/11/63	Moyock, NC	0.25	D	62.5	Jimmy Pardue	Ford	45.464	Junior Johnson	Chevy	47.120
607	33	7/13/63	Winston-Salem, NC	0.25	P	50	Glen Wood	Ford	44.390	Glen Wood	Ford	48.387
608	34	7/14/63	Asheville, NC	0.333	P	99.9	Ned Jarrett	Ford	63.384	David Pearson	Dodge	67.235
609	35	7/19/63	Old Bridge, NJ	0.5	P	100	Fireball Roberts	Ford	73.022	Joe Weatherly	Pontiac	75.850
610	36	7/21/63	Bridgehampton, NY	2.85	P	99.75	Richard Petty	Plymouth	86.047	Richard Petty	Plymouth	86.301
611	37	7/28/63	Bristol, TN	0.5	P	250	Fred Lorenzen	Ford	74.844	Fred Lorenzen	Ford	82.229
612	38	7/30/63	Greenville, SC	0.5	D	100	Richard Petty	Plymouth	62.456	Ned Jarrett	Ford	65.526
613	39	8/4/63	Nashville, TN	0.5	P	175	Jim Paschal	Plymouth	60.126	Richard Petty	Plymouth	78.878
614	40	8/8/63	Columbia, SC	0.5	D	100	Richard Petty	Plymouth	55.1598	Richard Petty	Plymouth	60.014
615	41	8/11/63	Weaverville, NC	0.5	P	250	Fred Lorenzen	Ford	77.673	No Time Trials	NTT	NTT
616	42	8/14/63	Spartanburg, SC	0.5	D	100	Ned Jarrett	Ford	52.424`	Joe Weatherly	Pontiac	64.958
617	43	8/16/63	Winston-Salem, NC	0.25	P	50	Junior Johnson	Chevy	46.320	Junior Johnson	Chevy	66.568
618	44	8/18/63	Huntington, WV	0.375	P	112.5	Fred Lorenzen	Ford	59.340	Fred Lorenzen	Ford	66.569
619	45	9/2/63	Darlington, SC	1.375	P	500.5	Fireball Roberts	Ford	129.784	Fred Lorenzen	Ford	133.648
620	46	9/6/63	Hickory, NC	0.4	D	100	Junior Johnson	Chevy	62.926	David Pearson	Dodge	72.471
621	47	9/8/63	Richmond, VA	0.5	D	150	Ned Jarrett	Ford	66.339	Joe Weatherly	Mercury	68.104
622	48	9/22/63	Martinsville, VA	0.5	P	250	Fred Lorenzen	Ford	67.486	Junior Johnson	Chevy	73.379
623	49	9/24/63	Moyock, NC	0.25	D	75	Ned Jarrett	Ford	43.000	Joe Weatherly	Mercury	45.988
624	50	9/29/63	N. Wilkesboro, NC	0.625	P	250	Marvin Panch	Ford	89.428	Fred Lorenzen	Ford	96.566
625	51	10/5/63	Randleman, NC	0.25	P	50	Richard Petty	Plymouth	46.001	Fred Lorenzen	Ford	51.724
626	52	10/13/63	Charlotte, NC	1.5	P	400.5	Junior Johnson	Chevy	132.105	Marvin Panch	Ford	142.461
627	53	10/20/63	South Boston, VA	0.375	P	150	Richard Petty	Plymouth	76.325	Jack Smith	Plymouth	81.081
628	54	10/27/63	Hillsboro, NC	0.9	D	150	Joe Weatherly	Pontiac	85.559	Joe Weatherly	Pontiac	93.156
629	55	11/3/63	Riverside, CA	2.7	P	399.6	Darel Dieringer	Mercury	91.465	Dan Gurney	Ford	101.050

1964

Cum. No.	Yr. No.	Date	Site	Track Length	Surface	Miles	Race Winner	Make	Speed	Pole Winner	Make	Pole Speed
630	1	11/10/63	Concord, NC	0.5	D	125	Ned Jarrett	Ford	56.897	David Pearson	Dodge	69.257
631	2	11/10/63	Augusta, GA	3.0	P	417	Fireball Roberts	Ford	86.320	Fred Lorenzen	Ford	88.590
632	3	12/1/63	Jacksonville, FL	0.5	D	101	Wendell Scott	Chevy	58.252	Jack Smith	Plymouth	70.921
633	4	12/29/63	Savannah, GA	0.5	D	100	Richard Petty	Plymouth	68.143	Ned Jarrett	Ford	73.529
634	5	1/19/64	Riverside, CA	2.7	P	499.5	Dan Gurney	Ford	91.245	Fred Lorenzen	Ford	102.433
635	6	2/21/64	Daytona Beach, FL	2.5	P	100	Junior Johnson	Dodge	170.777	Paul Goldsmith	Plymouth	173.910
636	7	2/21/64	Daytona Beach, FL	2.5	P	100	Bobby Isaac	Dodge	169.811	Richard Petty	Plymouth	174.418
637	8	2/23/64	Daytona Beach, FL	2.5	P	500	Richard Petty	Plymouth	154.334	Paul Goldsmith	Plymouth	174.910
638	9	3/10/64	Richmond, VA	0.5	D	125	David Pearson	Dodge	60.233	Ned Jarrett	Ford	69.070
639	10	3/22/64	Bristol, TN	0.5	P	250	Fred Lorenzen	Ford	72.196	Marvin Panch	Ford	80.640
640	11	3/28/64	Greenville, SC	0.5	D	100	David Pearson	Dodge	57.554	Dick Hutcherson	Ford	66.740
641	12	3/30/64	Winston-Salem, NC	0.25	P	50	Marvin Panch	Ford	47.796	Marvin Panch	Ford	49.830
642	13	4/5/64	Atlanta, GA	1.5	P	500	Fred Lorenzen	Ford	134.137	Fred Lorenzen	Ford	146.470
643	14	4/11/64	Weaverville, NC	0.5	P	100	Marvin Panch	Ford	81.669	Marvin Panch	Ford	84.905
644	15	4/12/64	Hillsboro, NC	0.9	D	150	David Pearson	Dodge	83.319	David Pearson	Dodge	99.784
645	16	4/14/64	Spartanburg, SC	0.5	D	100	Ned Jarrett	Ford	58.852	Dick Hutcherson	Ford	69.044
646	17	4/16/64	Columbia, SC	0.5	D	100	Ned Jarrett	Ford	64.412	David Pearson	Dodge	71.485
647	18	4/19/64	N. Wilkesboro, NC	0.625	P	250	Fred Lorenzen	Ford	81.930	Fred Lorenzen	Ford	94.024
648	19	4/26/64	Martinsville, VA	0.5	P	250	Fred Lorenzen	Ford	70.098	Fred Lorenzen	Ford	74.472
649	20	5/1/64	Savannah, GA	0.5	D	100	LeeRoy Yarbrough	Plymouth	70.326	Jimmy Pardue	Plymouth	73.111
650	21	5/9/64	Darlington, SC	1.375	P	301.125	Fred Lorenzen	Ford	130.013	Fred Lorenzen	Ford	135.727
651	22	5/15/64	Hampton, VA	0.4	D	100	Ned Jarrett	Ford	65.300	David Pearson	Dodge	67.542
652	23	5/16/64	Hickory, NC	0.4	D	100	Ned Jarrett	Ford	69.364	Junior Johnson	Ford	76.882
653	24	5/17/64	South Boston, VA	0.333	P	99.9	Richard Petty	Plymouth	72.957	Marvin Panch	Ford	80.023
654	25	5/24/64	Charlotte, NC	1.5	P	600	Jim Paschal	Plymouth	125.772	Jimmy Pardue	Plymouth	144.346
655	26	5/30/64	Greenville, SC	0.5	D	99.5	LeeRoy Yarbrough	Plymouth	56.559	Marvin Panch	Ford	68.050
656	27	5/31/64	Asheville, NC	0.333	P	99.9	Ned Jarrett	Ford	66.538	Richard Petty	Plymouth	69.889
657	28	6/7/64	Atlanta, GA	1.5	P	400.5	Ned Jarrett	Ford	112.535	Junior Johnson	Ford	145.906
658	29	6/11/64	Concord, NC	0.5	D	100	Richard Petty	Plymouth	66.352	Richard Petty	Plymouth	68.233
659	30	6/14/64	Nashville, TN	0.5	P	100	Richard Petty	Plymouth	76.498	David Pearson	Dodge	80.142
660	31	6/19/64	Chattanooga, TN	0.333	P	99.9	David Pearson	Dodge	70.051	Richard Petty	Plymouth	75.235
661	32	6/21/64	Birmingham, AL	0.5	P	100	Ned Jarrett	Ford	67.643	David Pearson	Dodge	72.115

Cum. No.	Yr. No.	Date	Site	Track Length	Surface	Miles	Race Winner	Make	Speed	Pole Winner	Make	Pole Speed
662	33	6/23/64	Valdosta, GA	0.5	D	100	Buck Baker	Dodge	61.328	Ned Jarrett	Ford	65.146
663	34	6/26/64	Spartanburg, SC	0.5	D	100	Richard Petty	Plymouth	58.233	David Pearson	Dodge	66.939
664	35	7/4/64	Daytona Beach, FL	2.5	P	400	A. J. Foyt	Dodge	151.451	Darel Dieringer	Mercury	172.678
665	36	7/8/64	Manassas, VA	0.375	P	150	Ned Jarrett	Ford	67.652	Ned Jarrett	Ford	73.609
666	37	7/10/64	Old Bridge, NJ	0.5	P	100	Billy Wade	Mercury	73.891	Billy Wade	Mercury	76.660
667	38	7/12/64	Bridgehampton, NY	2.85	P	142.5	Billy Wade	Mercury	87.707	Richard Petty	Plymouth	90.600
668	39	7/15/64	Islip, NY	0.2	P	60	Billy Wade	Mercury	46.252	Billy Wade	Mercury	51.100
669	40	7/19/64	Watkins Glen, NY	2.3	P	151.8	Billy Wade	Mercury	97.988	Billy Wade	Mercury	102.222
670	41	7/21/64	New Oxford, PA	0.5	D	100	David Pearson	Dodge	82.568	David Pearson	Dodge	86.289
671	42	7/26/64	Bristol, TN	0.5	P	250	Fred Lorenzen	Ford	78.044	Richard Petty	Plymouth	82.910
672	43	8/2/64	Nashville, TN	0.5	P	200	Richard Petty	Plymouth	73.208	Richard Petty	Plymouth	80.826
673	44	8/7/64	Myrtle Beach, SC	0.5	D	100	David Pearson	Dodge	61.750	David Pearson	Dodge	69.659
674	45	8/9/64	Weaverville, NC	0.5	P	250	Ned Jarrett	Ford	77.600	Junior Johnson	Ford	84.626
675	46	8/13/64	Moyock, NC	0.333	P	99.9	Ned Jarrett	Ford	63.965	Ned Jarrett	Ford	67.643
676	47	8/16/64	Huntington, WV	0.375	P	218.75	Richard Petty	Plymouth	70.488	Billy Wade	Mercury	79.505
677	48	8/21/64	Columbia, SC	0.5	P	100	David Pearson	Dodge	61.697	Ned Jarrett	Ford	69.150
678	49	8/22/64	Winston-Salem, NC	0.25	P	62.5	Junior Johnson	Ford	46.192	Junior Johnson	Ford	49.846
679	50	8/23/64	Roanoke, VA	0.25	P	50	Junior Johnson	Ford	49.847	Glen Wood	Ford	55.970
680	51	9/7/64	Darlington, SC	1.375	P	500.5	Buck Baker	Dodge	117.757	Richard Petty	Plymouth	136.815
681	52	9/11/64	Hickory, NC	0.4	D	100	David Pearson	Dodge	67.797	David Pearson	Dodge	74.418
682	53	9/14/64	Richmond, VA	0.5	D	150	Cotton Owens	Dodge	61.955	Ned Jarrett	Ford	66.890
683	54	9/18/64	Manassas, VA	0.375	P	187.5	Ned Jarrett	Ford	68.842	David Pearson	Dodge	74.626
684	55	9/20/64	Hillsboro, NC	0.9	D	150.3	Ned Jarrett	Ford	86.725	David Pearson	Dodge	89.280
685	56	9/27/64	Martinsville, VA	0.5	P	250	Fred Lorenzen	Ford	67.320	Fred Lorenzen	Ford	74.196
686	57	10/9/64	Savannah, GA	0.5	D	100	Ned Jarrett	Ford	68.663	Ned Jarrett	Ford	68.886
687	58	10/11/64	N. Wilkesboro, NC	0.625	P	250	Marvin Panch	Ford	91.398	Junior Johnson	Ford	100.761
688	59	10/18/64	Charlotte, NC	1.5	P	400.5	Fred Lorenzen	Ford	134.475	Richard Petty	Plymouth	150.711
689	60	10/25/64	Harris, NC	0.3	P	100.2	Richard Petty	Plymouth	59.009	Billy Wade	Mercury	64.787
690	61	11/1/64	Augusta, GA	0.5	P	150	Darel Dieringer	Mercury	68.641	Ned Jarrett	Ford	82.455
691	62	11/8/64	Jacksonville, NC	0.5	D	100	Ned Jarrett	Ford	57.535	Doug Yates	Plymouth	64.285

1965

Cum. No.	Yr. No.	Date	Site	Track Length	Surface	Miles	Race Winner	Make	Speed	Pole Winner	Make	Pole Speed
692	1	1/17/65	Riverside, CA	2.7	P	499.5	Dan Gurney	Ford	87.708	Junior Johnson	Ford	102.846
693	2	2/12/65	Daytona Beach, FL	2.5	P	100	Darel Dieringer	Mercury	165.669	Darel Dieringer	Mercury	171.151
694	3	2/12/65	Daytona Beach, FL	2.5	P	100	Junior Johnson	Ford	111.706	Junior Johnson	Ford	168.444
695	4	2/14/65	Daytona Beach, FL	2.5	P	332.5	Fred Lorenzen	Ford	141.539	Darel Dieringer	Mercury	171.151
696	5	2/27/65	Spartanburg, SC	0.5	D	100	Ned Jarrett	Ford	66.367	Dick Hutcherson	Ford	70.644
697	6	2/28/65	Weaverville, NC	0.5	P	100	Ned Jarrett	Ford	75.678	Ned Jarrett	Ford	84.230
698	7	3/7/65	Richmond, VA	0.5	D	125	Junior Johnson	Ford	61.416	Junior Johnson	Ford	67.847
699	8	3/14/65	Hillsboro, NC	0.9	D	150	Ned Jarrett	Ford	90.663	Junior Johnson	Ford	98.570
700	9	4/11/65	Atlanta, GA	1.5	P	501	Marvin Panch	Ford	129.410	Marvin Panch	Ford	145.581
701	10	4/17/65	Greenville, SC	0.5	D	100	Dick Hutcherson	Ford	56.899	Bud Moore	Plymouth	67.695
702	11	4/18/65	N. Wilkesboro, NC	0.625	P	250	Junior Johnson	Ford	95.047	Junior Johnson	Ford	101.033
703	12	4/25/65	Martinsville, VA	0.5	P	250	Fred Lorenzen	Ford	66.765	Junior Johnson	Ford	74.503
704	13	4/28/65	Columbia, SC	0.5	D	62	Tiny Lund	Ford	55.591	Ned Jarrett	Ford	71.061
705	14	5/2/65	Bristol, TN	0.5	P	250	Junior Johnson	Ford	74.937	Marvin Panch	Ford	84.626
706	15	5/8/65	Darlington, SC	1.375	P	301.125	Junior Johnson	Ford	111.849	Fred Lorenzen	Ford	138.133
707	16	5/14/65	Hampton, VA	0.4	D	100	Ned Jarrett	Ford	57.815	Dick Hutcherson	Ford	66.790
708	17	5/15/65	Winston-Salem, NC	0.25	P	50	Junior Johnson	Ford	47.911	Junior Johnson	Ford	49.261
709	18	5/16/65	Hickory, NC	0.4	D	100	Junior Johnson	Ford	72.130	G. C. Spencer	Ford	76.312
710	19	5/23/65	Charlotte, NC	1.5	P	600	Fred Lorenzen	Ford	121.722	Fred Lorenzen	Ford	145.268
711	20	5/27/65	Shelby, NC	0.5	D	100	Ned Jarrett	Ford	63.909	Dick Hutcherson	Ford	65.862
712	21	5/29/65	Asheville, NC	0.333	P	99.9	Junior Johnson	Ford	66.293	Junior Johnson	Ford	70.601
713	22	5/30/65	Harris, NC	0.3	P	100	Ned Jarrett	Ford	56.851	Paul Lewis	Ford	61.644
714	23	6/3/65	Nashville, TN	0.5	P	100	Dick Hutcherson	Ford	71.386	Tom Pistone	Ford	79.155
715	24	6/6/65	Birmingham, AL	0.5	P	54	Ned Jarrett	Ford	56.364	Ned Jarrett	Ford	71.575
716	25	6/13/65	Atlanta, GA	1.5	P	400	Marvin Panch	Ford	110.120	Fred Lorenzen	Ford	143.407
717	26	6/19/65	Greenville, SC	0.5	D	100	Dick Hutcherson	Ford	55.274	Ned Jarrett	Ford	65.574
718	27	6/24/65	Myrtle Beach, SC	0.5	D	100	Dick Hutcherson	Ford	59.701	Dick Hutcherson	Ford	66.421
719	28	6/27/65	Valdosta, GA	0.5	D	100	Cale Yarborough	Ford	58.862	Dick Hutcherson	Ford	64.540
720	29	7/4/65	Daytona Beach, FL	2.5	P	400	A. J. Foyt	Ford	150.046	Marvin Panch	Ford	171.510
721	30	7/8/65	Manassas, VA	0.375	P	150	Junior Johnson	Ford	68.165	Ned Jarrett	Ford	73.569
722	31	7/9/65	Old Bridge, NJ	0.5	P	100	Junior Johnson	Ford	72.087	Marvin Panch	Ford	77.286

Cum. No.	Yr. No.	Date	Site	Track Length	Surface	Miles	Race Winner	Make	Speed	Pole Winner	Make	Pole Speed
723	32	7/14/65	Islip, NY	0.2	P	50	Marvin Panch	Ford	43.838	Marvin Panch	Ford	51.246
724	33	7/18/65	Watkins Glen, NY	2.3	P	151.8	Marvin Panch	Ford	98.182	No Time Trials	NTT	NTT
725	34	7/25/65	Bristol, TN	0.5	P	250	Ned Jarrett	Ford	61.826	Fred Lorenzen	Ford	84.348
726	35	7/31/65	Nashville, TN	0.5	P	200	Richard Petty	Plymouth	72.383	Richard Petty	Plymouth	82.117
727	36	8/5/65	Shelby, NC	0.5	D	100	Ned Jarrett	Ford	64.748	David Pearson	Dodge	67.797
728	37	8/8/65	Weaverville, NC	0.5	P	250	Richard Petty	Plymouth	74.343	Richard Petty	Plymouth	86.455
729	38	8/13/65	Maryville, TN	0.5	D	100	Dick Hutcherson	Ford	65.455	Ned Jarrett	Ford	77.620
730	39	8/14/65	Spartanburg, SC	0.5	D	100	Ned Jarrett	Ford	56.926	Dick Hutcherson	Ford	66.890
731	40	8/15/65	Augusta, GA	0.5	D	100	Dick Hutcherson	Ford	71.499	Ned Jarrett	Ford	81.118
732	41	8/19/65	Columbia, SC	0.5	D	100	David Pearson	Dodge	57.361	Dick Hutcherson	Ford	71.343
733	42	8/24/65	Moyock, NC	0.333	P	99.9	Dick Hutcherson	Ford	63.047	Richard Petty	Plymouth	68.493
734	43	8/25/65	Beltsville, MD	0.5	P	100	Ned Jarrett	Ford	74.165	Ned Jarrett	Ford	79.260
735	44	8/28/65	Winston-Salem, NC	0.25	P	62.5	Junior Johnson	Ford	46.632	Richard Petty	Plymouth	50.195
736	45	9/6/65	Darlington, SC	1.375	P	500.5	Ned Jarrett	Ford	115.878	Junior Johnson	Ford	137.571
737	46	9/10/65	Hickory, NC	0.4	D	100	Richard Petty	Plymouth	74.365	Junior Johnson	Ford	74.766
738	47	9/14/65	New Oxford, PA	0.5	D	100	Dick Hutcherson	Ford	82.607	Richard Petty	Plymouth	86.705
739	48	9/17/65	Manassas, VA	0.375	P	150	Richard Petty	Plymouth	67.890	Ned Jarrett	Ford	73.851
740	49	9/18/65	Richmond, VA	0.5	D	150	David Pearson	Dodge	60.983	Dick Hutcherson	Ford	67.340
741	50	9/26/65	Martinsville, VA	0.5	P	250	Junior Johnson	Ford	67.056	Richard Petty	Plymouth	74.503
742	51	10/3/65	N. Wilkesboro, NC	0.625	P	250	Junior Johnson	Ford	88.801	Fred Lorenzen	Ford	101.580
743	52	10/17/65	Charlotte, NC	1.5	P	400.5	Fred Lorenzen	Ford	119.117	Fred Lorenzen	Ford	147.773
744	53	10/24/65	Hillsboro, NC	0.9	D	100.8	Dick Hutcherson	Ford	87.462	Dick Hutcherson	Ford	98.810
745	54	10/31/65	Rockingham, NC	1.0	P	500	Curtis Turner	Ford	101.942	Richard Petty	Plymouth	116.260
746	55	11/7/65	Moyock, NC	0.333	P	99.9	Ned Jarrett	Ford	63.773	Bobby Isaac	Ford	68.143

1966

Cum. No.	Yr. No.	Date	Site	Track Length	Surface	Miles	Race Winner	Make	Speed	Pole Winner	Make	Pole Speed
747	1	11/14/65	Augusta, GA	0.5	P	150	Richard Petty	Plymouth	73.569	Richard Petty	Plymouth	82.987
748	2	1/23/66	Riverside, CA	2.7	P	499.5	Dan Gurney	Ford	97.952	David Pearson	Dodge	106.078
749	3	2/25/66	Daytona Beach, FL	2.5	P	100	Paul Goldsmith	Plymouth	160.427	Richard Petty	Plymouth	175.165
750	4	2/25/66	Daytona Beach, FL	2.5	P	100	Earl Balmer	Dodge	153.191	Dick Hutcherson	Ford	174.317
751	5	2/27/66	Daytona Beach, FL	2.5	P	495	Richard Petty	Plymouth	160.627	Richard Petty	Plymouth	175.165
752	6	3/13/66	Rockingham, NC	1.0	P	500	Paul Goldsmith	Plymouth	100.027	Paul Goldsmith	Plymouth	116.684
753	7	3/20/66	Bristol, TN	0.5	P	250	Dick Hutcherson	Ford	69.952	David Pearson	Dodge	86.248
754	8	3/27/66	Atlanta, GA	1.5	P	501	Jim Hurtubise	Plymouth	131.247	Richard Petty	Plymouth	147.742
755	9	4/3/66	Hickory, NC	0.4	D	100	David Pearson	Dodge	68.428	Elmo Langley	Ford	75.117
756	10	4/7/66	Columbia, SC	0.5	D	100	David Pearson	Dodge	65.574	Tom Pistone	Ford	72.202
757	11	4/9/66	Greenville, SC	0.5	D	100	David Pearson	Dodge	65.850	Tiny Lund	Ford	68.208
758	12	4/11/66	Winston-Salem, NC	0.25	P	50	David Pearson	Dodge	51.341	David Pearson	Dodge	54.479
759	13	4/17/66	N. Wilkesboro, NC	0.625	P	250	Jim Paschal	Plymouth	89.045	Jim Paschal	Plymouth	102.693
760	14	4/24/66	Martinsville, VA	0.5	P	250	Jim Paschal	Plymouth	69.156	Jim Paschal	Plymouth	76.345
761	15	4/30/66	Darlington, SC	1.375	P	400.125	Richard Petty	Plymouth	131.993	Richard Petty	Plymouth	140.815
762	16	5/7/66	Hampton, VA	0.4	D	100	Richard Petty	Plymouth	60.616	Richard Petty	Plymouth	66.812
763	17	5/10/66	Macon, GA	0.5	P	100	Richard Petty	Plymouth	82.023	Richard Petty	Plymouth	85.026
764	18	5/13/66	Monroe, NC	0.5	D	100	Darel Dieringer	Ford	60.140	James Hylton	Dodge	65.099
765	19	5/15/66	Richmond, VA	0.5	D	125	David Pearson	Dodge	66.539	Tom Pistone	Ford	70.978
766	20	5/22/66	Charlotte, NC	1.5	P	600	Marvin Panch	Plymouth	135.042	Richard Petty	Plymouth	148.637
767	21	5/29/66	Moyock, NC	0.333	P	99.9	David Pearson	Dodge	61.913	Richard Petty	Plymouth	69.164
768	22	6/2/66	Asheville, NC	0.333	P	99.9	David Pearson	Dodge	64.917	Richard Petty	Plymouth	72.964
769	23	6/4/66	Spartanburg, SC	0.5	D	100	Elmo Langley	Ford	60.050	David Pearson	Dodge	68.027
770	24	6/9/66	Maryville, TN	0.5	D	100	David Pearson	Dodge	71.986	Tom Pistone	Ford	78.947
771	25	6/12/66	Weaverville, NC	0.5	P	150	Richard Petty	Plymouth	81.423	Richard Petty	Plymouth	86.455
772	26	6/15/66	Beltsville, MD	0.5	P	100	Tiny Lund	Ford	73.409	Richard Petty	Plymouth	80.250
773	27	6/25/66	Greensville, SC	0.5	D	100	David Pearson	Dodge	66.286	David Pearson	Dodge	69.364
774	28	7/4/66	Daytona Beach, FL	2.5	P	400	Sam McQuagg	Dodge	153.813	Lee Roy Yarbrough	Dodge	176.660
775	29	7/7/66	Manassas, VA	0.375	P	150	Elmo Langley	Ford	68.079	Bobby Allison	Chevy	73.973
776	30	8/10/66	Bridgehampton, NY	2.85	P	148.2	David Pearson	Dodge	86.949	David Pearson	Dodge	Qual. Race
777	31	7/12/66	Oxford, ME	0.333	P	99.9	Bobby Allison	Chevy	56.782	Bobby Allison	Chevy	65.681
778	32	7/14/66	Fonda, NY	0.5	D	100	David Pearson	Dodge	61.010	Richard Petty	Plymouth	71.514
779	33	7/16/66	Islip, NY	0.2	P	60	Bobby Allison	Chevy	47.285	Tom Pistone	Ford	55.919
780	34	7/24/66	Bristol, TN	0.5	P	250	Paul Goldsmith	Plymouth	77.693	Curtis Turner	Chevy	84.309
781	35	7/28/66	Maryville, TN	0.5	D	100	Paul Lewis	Plymouth	69.822	Buddy Baker	Dodge	77.821
782	36	7/30/66	Nashville, TN	0.5	P	200	Richard Petty	Plymouth	71.770	Richard Petty	Plymouth	82.493
783	37	8/7/66	Atlanta, GA	1.5	P	501	Richard Petty	Plymouth	130.244	Curtis Turner	Chevy	148.331

Cum. No.	Yr. No.	Date	Site	Track Length	Surface	Miles	Race Winner	Make	Speed	Pole Winner	Make	Pole Speed
784	38	8/18/66	Columbia, SC	0.5	D	100	David Pearson	Dodge	66.128	Bobby Allison	Chevy	73.469
785	39	8/21/66	Weaverville, NC	0.5	P	250	Darel Dieringer	Mercury	76.700	Junior Johnson	Ford	86.831
786	40	8/24/66	Beltsville, MD	0.5	P	100	Bobby Allison	Chevy	68.899	Bobby Allison	Chevy	79.330
787	41	8/27/66	Winston-Salem, NC	0.25	P	62.5	David Pearson	Dodge	45.928	Richard Petty	Plymouth	54.348
788	42	9/5/66	Darlington, SC	1.375	P	500.5	Darel Dieringer	Mercury	114.830	LeeRoy Yarbrough	Dodge	140.058
789	43	9/9/66	Hickory, NC	0.4	D	100	David Pearson	Dodge	70.533	Richard Petty	Plymouth	76.923
790	44	9/11/66	Richmond, VA	0.5	D	150	David Pearson	Dodge	62.886	David Pearson	Dodge	70.644
791	45	9/18/66	Hillsboro, NC	0.9	D	150	Dick Hutcherson	Ford	90.603	Dick Hutcherson	Ford	95.716
792	46	9/25/66	Martinsville, VA	0.5	P	250	Fred Lorenzen	Ford	69.177	Junior Johnson	Ford	75.598
793	47	10/2/66	N. Wilkesboro, NC	0.625	P	250	Dick Hutcherson	Ford	89.012	Junior Johnson	Ford	103.069
794	48	10/16/66	Charlotte, NC	1.5	P	501	LeeRoy Yarbrough	Dodge	130.576	Fred Lorenzen	Ford	150.533
795	49	10/30/66	Rockingham, NC	1.0	P	500	Fred Lorenzen	Ford	104.348	Fred Lorenzen	Ford	115.988

1967

Cum. No.	Yr. No.	Date	Site	Track Length	Surface	Miles	Race Winner	Make	Speed	Pole Winner	Make	Pole Speed
796	1	11/13/66	Augusta, GA	0.5	P	150	Richard Petty	Plymouth	71.809	Dick Hutcherson	Ford	84.112
797	2	1/22/67	Riverside, CA	2.7	P	499.5	Parnelli Jones	Ford	91.080	Dick Hutcherson	Ford	106.951
798	3	2/24/67	Daytona Beach, FL	2.5	P	100	LeeRoy Yarbrough	Dodge	163.934	Curtis Turner	Chevy	180.831
799	4	2/24/67	Daytona Beach, FL	2.5	P	100	Fred Lorenzen	Ford	174.587	Richard Petty	Plymouth	179.068
800	5	2/26/67	Daytona Beach, FL	2.5	P	500	Mario Andretti	Ford	146.926	Curtis Turner	Chevy	180.831
801	6	3/5/67	Weaverville, NC	0.5	P	150	Richard Petty	Plymouth	83.360	Darel Dieringer	Ford	88.626
802	7	3/19/67	Bristol, TN	0.5	P	250	David Pearson	Dodge	77.937	Darel Dieringer	Ford	87.124
803	8	3/25/67	Greenville, SC	0.5	D	100	David Pearson	Dodge	61.824	Dick Hutcherson	Ford	70.313
804	9	3/27/67	Winston-Salem, NC	0.25	P	50	Bobby Allison	Chevy	49.248	Bobby Allison	Chevy	53.476
805	10	4/2/67	Atlanta, GA	1.5	P	501	Cale Yarborough	Ford	131.238	Cale Yarborough	Ford	148.996
806	11	4/6/67	Columbia, SC	0.5	D	100	Richard Petty	Plymouth	65.455	Dick Hutcherson	Ford	74.166
807	12	4/9/67	Hickory, NC	0.4	D	100	Richard Petty	Plymouth	69.699	Richard Petty	Plymouth	79.120
808	13	4/16/67	N. Wilkesboro, NC	0.625	P	250	Darel Dieringer	Ford	93.594	Darel Dieringer	Ford	104.603
809	14	4/23/67	Martinsville, VA	0.5	P	250	Richard Petty	Plymouth	67.446	Darel Dieringer	Ford	77.319
810	15	4/28/67	Savannah, GA	0.5	D	100	Bobby Allison	Chevy	66.802	John Sears	Ford	72.173
811	16	4/30/67	Richmond, VA	0.5	D	125	Richard Petty	Plymouth	65.982	Richard Petty	Plymouth	70.038
812	17	5/13/67	Darlington, SC	1.375	P	400.125	Richard Petty	Plymouth	125.738	David Pearson	Ford	144.536
813	18	5/19/67	Beltsville, MD	0.5	P	100	Jim Paschal	Plymouth	71.036	Richard Petty	Plymouth	80.286
814	19	5/20/67	Hampton, VA	0.4	D	100	Richard Petty	Plymouth	66.704	Richard Petty	Plymouth	68.214
815	20	5/28/67	Charlotte, NC	1.5	P	600	Jim Paschal	Plymouth	135.832	Cale Yarborough	Ford	154.385
816	21	6/2/67	Asheville, NC	0.333	P	99.9	Jim Paschal	Plymouth	63.080	Richard Petty	Plymouth	73.710
817	22	6/6/67	Macon, GA	0.5	P	150	Richard Petty	Plymouth	80.321	Richard Petty	Plymouth	86.538
818	23	6/8/67	Maryville, TN	0.5	D	100	Richard Petty	Plymouth	72.919	Jim Hunter	Chevy	79.051
819	24	6/10/67	Birmingham, AL	0.5	P	100	Bobby Allison	Dodge	88.999	Jim Paschal	Plymouth	94.142
820	25	6/18/67	Rockingham, NC	1.0	P	500	Richard Petty	Plymouth	104.682	Dick Hutcherson	Ford	116.486
821	26	6/24/67	Greenville, SC	0.5	P	100	Richard Petty	Plymouth	61.781	Richard Petty	Plymouth	69.498
822	27	6/27/67	Montgomery, AL	0.5	P	100	Jim Paschal	Plymouth	72.435	Richard Petty	Plymouth	77.088
823	28	7/4/67	Daytona Beach, FL	2.5	P	400	Cale Yarborough	Ford	143.583	Darel Dieringer	Ford	179.802
824	29	7/9/67	Trenton, NJ	1.5	P	300	Richard Petty	Plymouth	95.322	Richard Petty	Plymouth	101.208
825	30	7/11/67	Oxford, ME	0.333	P	99.9	Bobby Allison	Chevy	61.697	James Hylton	Dodge	66.043
826	31	7/13/67	Fonda, NY	0.5	D	100	Richard Petty	Plymouth	65.826	Richard Petty	Plymouth	72.173
827	32	7/15/67	Islip, NY	0.2	P	60	Richard Petty	Plymouth	42.428	Richard Petty	Plymouth	51.136
828	33	7/23/67	Bristol, TN	0.5	P	250	Richard Petty	Plymouth	78.705	Richard Petty	Plymouth	86.621
829	34	7/27/67	Maryville, TN	0.5	D	100	Dick Hutcherson	Ford	65.765	Dick Hutcherson	Ford	79.540
830	35	7/29/67	Nashville, TN	0.5	P	200	Richard Petty	Plymouth	70.866	Dick Hutcherson	Ford	84.260
831	36	8/6/67	Atlanta, GA	1.5	P	501	Dick Hutcherson	Ford	132.286	Darel Dieringer	Ford	150.417
832	37	8/12/67	Winston-Salem, NC	0.25	P	62.5	Richard Petty	Plymouth	50.893	Richard Petty	Plymouth	53.160
833	38	8/17/67	Columbia, SC	0.5	D	100	Richard Petty	Plymouth	64.274	Richard Petty	Plymouth	74.968
834	39	8/25/67	Savannah, GA	0.5	D	100	Richard Petty	Plymouth	65.041	Richard Petty	Plymouth	71.942
835	40	9/4/67	Darlington, SC	1.375	P	500.5	Richard Petty	Plymouth	130.423	Richard Petty	Plymouth	143.436
836	41	9/8/67	Hickory, NC	0.4	P	100	Richard Petty	Plymouth	71.414	Dick Hutcherson	Ford	86.538
837	42	9/10/67	Richmond, VVA	0.5	D	150	Richard Petty	Plymouth	57.631	No Time Trials	NTT	NTT
838	43	9/15/67	Beltsville, MD	0.5	P	150	Richard Petty	Plymouth	76.563	Richard Petty	Plymouth	81.044
839	44	9/17/67	Hillsboro, NC	0.9	D	150	Richard Petty	Plymouth	81.574	Richard Petty	Plymouth	94.159
840	45	9/24/67	Martinsville, VA	0.5	P	250	Richard Petty	Plymouth	69.605	Cale Yarborough	Ford	77.386
841	46	10/1/67	N. Wilkesboro, NC	0.625	P	250	Richard Petty	Plymouth	94.837	Dick Hutcherson	Ford	104.312
842	47	10/15/67	Charlotte, NC	1.5	P	501	Buddy Baker	Dodge	130.317	Cale Yarborough	Ford	154.872
843	48	10/29/67	Rockingham, NC	1.0	P	500	Bobby Allison	Ford	98.420	David Pearson	Ford	117.120
844	49	11/5/67	Weaverville, NC	0.5	P	250	Bobby Allison	Ford	76.291	Bobby Allison	Ford	90.407

Cum. No.	Yr. No.	Date	Site	Track Length	Surface	Miles	Race Winner	Make	Speed	Pole Winner	Make	Pole Speed
1968												
845	1	11/12/67	Macon, GA	0.5	P	267	Bobby Allison	Ford	81.001	LeeRoy Yarbrough	Ford	94.323
846	2	11/26/67	Montgomery, AL	0.5	P	100	Richard Petty	Plymouth	70.644	Richard Petty	Plymouth	79.694
847	3	1/21/68	Riverside, CA	2.7	P	502.2	Dan Gurney	Ford	100.598	Dan Gurney	Ford	110.971
848	4	2/25/68	Daytona Beach, FL	2.5	P	500	Cale Yarborough	Mercury	143.251	Cale Yarborough	Mercury	189.222
849	5	3/17/68	Bristol, TN	0.5	P	250	David Pearson	Ford	77.247	Richard Petty	Plymouth	88.582
850	6	3/24/68	Richmond, VA	0.5	D	125	David Pearson	Ford	65.217	Bobby Isaac	Dodge	67.822
851	7	3/31/68	Atlanta, GA	1.5	P	501	Cale Yarborough	Mercury	125.564	LeeRoy Yarbrough	Mercury	155.646
852	8	4/7/68	Hickory, NC	0.4	P	100	Richard Petty	Plymouth	79.435	David Pearson	Ford	86.957
853	9	4/13/68	Greenville, SC	0.5	D	100	Richard Petty	Plymouth	63.347	David Pearson	Ford	67.848
854	10	4/18/68	Columbia, SC	0.5	D	100	Bobby Isaac	Dodge	71.358	Richard Petty	Plymouth	75.282
855	11	4/21/68	N. Wilkesboro, NC	0.625	P	250	David Pearson	Ford	90.425	David Pearson	Ford	104.993
856	12	4/28/68	Martinsville, VA	0.5	P	250	Cale Yarborough	Mercury	66.686	David Pearson	Ford	78.230
857	13	5/3/68	Augusta, GA	0.5	P	125	Bobby Isaac	Dodge	73.099	Bobby Isaac	Dodge	83.877
858	14	5/5/68	Weaverville, NC	0.5	P	150	David Pearson	Ford	75.167	David Pearson	Ford	89.708
859	15	5/11/68	Darlington, SC	1.375	P	400.125	David Pearson	Ford	132.699	LeeRoy Yarbrough	Ford	148.850
860	16	5/17/68	Beltsville, MD	0.5	P	150	David Pearson	Ford	74.844	Richard Petty	Plymouth	83.604
861	17	5/18/68	Hampton, VA	0.4	P	100	David Pearson	Ford	71.457	Richard Petty	Plymouth	80.801
862	18	5/26/68	Charlotte, NC	1.5	P	382.5	Buddy Baker	Dodge	104.207	Donnie Allison	Ford	159.223
863	19	5/31/68	Asheville, NC	0.333	P	99.9	Richard Petty	Plymouth	64.741	Richard Petty	Plymouth	74.349
864	20	6/2/68	Macon, GA	0.5	P	150	David Pearson	Ford	79.342	David Pearson	Ford	86.873
865	21	6/6/68	Maryville, TN	0.5	P	100	Richard Petty	Plymouth	76.743	David Pearson	Ford	88.583
866	22	6/8/68	Birmingham, AL	0.5	P	100	Richard Petty	Plymouth	89.153	David Pearson	Ford	97.784
867	23	6/16/68	Rockingham, NC	1.0	P	500	Donnie Allison	Ford	99.338	LeeRoy Yarbrough	Ford	118.644
868	24	6/22/68	Greenville, SC	0.5	D	100	Richard Petty	Plymouth	64.609	David Pearson	Ford	68.834
869	25	7/4/68	Daytona Beach, FL	2.5	P	400	Cale Yarborough	Mercury	167.247	Charlie Glotzbach	Dodge	185.156
870	26	7/7/68	Islip, NY	0.2	P	60	Bobby Allison	Chevy	48.561	Buddy Baker	Dodge	51.873
871	27	7/9/68	Oxford, ME	0.333	P	99.9	Richard Petty	Plymouth	63.717	Buddy Baker	Dodge	67.835
872	28	7/11/68	Fonda, NY	0.5	P	100	Richard Petty	Plymouth	64.935	David Pearson	Ford	73.800
873	29	7/14/68	Trenton, NJ	1.5	P	300	LeeRoy Yarbrough	Ford	89.079	LeeRoy Yarbrough	Ford	103.717
874	30	7/21/68	Bristol, TN	0.5	P	250	David Pearson	Ford	76.310	LeeRoy Yarbrough	Ford	87.421
875	31	7/25/68	Maryville, TN	0.5	P	100	Richard Petty	Plymouth	72.513	Bobby Isaac	Dodge	86.538
876	32	7/27/68	Nashville, TN	0.5	P	151.5	David Pearson	Ford	72.980	Richard Petty	Plymouth	85.066
877	33	8/4/68	Atlanta, GA	1.5	P	501	LeeRoy Yarbrough	Mercury	127.068	Buddy Baker	Dodge	153.361
878	34	8/8/68	Columbia, SC	0.5	D	100	David Pearson	Ford	67.039	Buddy Baker	Dodge	74.196
879	35	8/10/68	Winston-Salem, NC	0.25	P	62.5	David Pearson	Ford	42.940	Richard Petty	Plymouth	53.828
880	36	8/17/68	Weaverville, NC	0.5	P	250	David Pearson	Ford	73.686	Darel Dieringer	Plymouth	88.409
881	37	8/23/68	South Boston, VA	0.375	P	100.125	Richard Petty	Plymouth	75.916	Richard Petty	Plymouth	84.428
882	38	8/24/68	Hampton, VA	0.4	P	100	David Pearson	Ford	75.582	David Pearson	Ford	78.007
883	39	9/2/68	Darlington, SC	1.375	P	500.5	Cale Yarborough	Mercury	126.132	Charlie Glotzbach	Dodge	144.830
884	40	9/6/68	Hickory, NC	0.4	P	100	David Pearson	Ford	80.357	Richard Petty	Plymouth	85.868
885	41	9/8/68	Richmond, VA	0.5	P	187.5	Richard Petty	Plymouth	85.659	Richard Petty	Plymouth	103.178
886	42	9/13/68	Beltsville, MD	0.5	P	150	Bobby Isaac	Dodge	71.033	Cale Yarborough	Mercury	81.311
887	43	9/15/68	Hillsboro, NC	0.9	P	150	Richard Petty	Plymouth	87.681	Richard Petty	Plymouth	93.245
888	44	9/22/68	Martinsville, VA	0.5	P	250	Richard Petty	Plymouth	64.808	Cale Yarborough	Mercury	77.279
889	45	9/29/68	N. Wilkesboro, NC	0.625	P	250	Richard Petty	Plymouth	94.103	Bobby Allison	Plymouth	104.525
890	46	10/5/68	Augusta, GA	0.5	P	100	David Pearson	Ford	75.821	Bobby Allison	Plymouth	84.822
891	47	10/20/68	Charlotte, NC	1.5	P	501	Charlie Glotzbach	Dodge	135.324	Charlie Glotzbach	Dodge	156.060
892	48	10/27/68	Rockingham, NC	1.0	P	500	Richard Petty	Plymouth	105.060	Cale Yarborough	Mercury	118.717
893	49	11/3/68	Jefferson, GA	0.5	P	100	Cale Yarborough	Mercury	77.737	David Pearson	Ford	90.694
1969												
894	1	11/17/68	Macon, GA	0.5	P	250	Richard Petty	Plymouth	85.121	David Pearson	Ford	95.472
895	2	12/8/68	Montgomery, AL	0.5	P	100	Bobby Allison	Plymouth	73.200	Richard Petty	Plymouth	80.899
896	3	2/1/69	Riverside, CA	2.7	P	502.2	Richard Petty	Ford	105.498	A. J. Foyt	Ford	110.323
897	4	2/20/69	Daytona Beach, FL	2.5	P	125	David Pearson	Ford	152.181	Buddy Baker	Dodge	188.901
898	5	2/20/69	Daytona Beach, FL	2.5	P	125	Bobby Isaac	Dodge	151.668	Bobby Isaac	Dodge	188.726
899	6	2/23/69	Daytona Beach, FL	2.5	P	500	LeeRoy Yarbrough	Ford	157.950	Buddy Baker	Dodge	188.901
900	7	3/9/69	Rockingham, NC	1.0	P	500	David Pearson	Ford	102.569	David Pearson	Ford	119.619
901	8	3/16/69	Augusta, GA	0.5	P	100	David Pearson	Ford	77.586	Bobby Isaac	Dodge	86.901
902	9	3/23/69	Bristol, TN	0.5	P	250	Bobby Allison	Dodge	81.455	Bobby Isaac	Dodge	88.669
903	10	3/30/69	Atlanta, GA	1.5	P	501	Cale Yarborough	Mercury	132.191	David Pearson	Ford	156.794
904	11	4/3/69	Columbia, SC	0.5	D	100	Bobby Isaac	Dodge	68.558	Bobby Isaac	Dodge	73.806

Cum. No.	Yr. No.	Date	Site	Track Length	Surface	Miles	Race Winner	Make	Speed	Pole Winner	Make	Pole Speed
905	12	4/6/69	Hickory, NC	0.4	P	100	Bobby Isaac	Dodge	79.086	Bobby Isaac	Dodge	85.612
906	13	4/8/69	Greenville, SC	0.5	D	100	Bobby Isaac	Dodge	64.389	David Pearson	Ford	70.359
907	14	4/13/69	Richamond, VA	0.5	P	250	David Pearson	Ford	73.752	David Pearson	Ford	82.538
908	15	4/20/69	N. Wilkesboro, NC	0.625	P	250	Bobby Allison	Dodge	95.268	Bobby Isaac	Dodge	106.731
909	16	4/27/69	Martinsville, VA	0.5	P	250	Richard Petty	Ford	64.405	Bobby Allison	Dodge	78.260
910	17	5/4/69	Weaverville, NC	0.5	P	150	Bobby Isaac	Dodge	72.581	Bobby Isaac	Dodge	90.361
911	18	5/10/69	Darlington, SC	1.375	P	400.125	LeeRoy Yarbrough	Mercury	131.572	Cale Yarborough	Mercury	152.293
912	19	5/16/69	Beltsville, MD	0.5	P	150	Bobby Isaac	Dodge	73.059	Bobby Isaac	Dodge	83.329
913	20	5/17/69	Hampton, VA	0.4	P	150	David Pearson	Ford	75.789	David Pearson	Ford	80.236
914	21	5/25/69	Charlotte, NC	1.5	P	600	LeeRoy Yarbrough	Mercury	134.361	Donnie Allison	Ford	159.296
915	22	6/1/69	Macon, GA	0.5	P	150	Bobby Isaac	Dodge	73.717	David Pearson	Ford	87.946
916	23	6/5/69	Maryville, TN	0.5	P	150	Bobby Isaac	Dodge	81.706	David Pearson	Ford	87.976
917	24	6/15/69	Brooklyn, MI	2.0	P	500	Cale Yarborough	Mercury	139.254	Donnie Allison	Ford	160.135
918	25	6/19/69	Kingsport, TN	0.4	P	100	Richard Petty	Ford	73.619	Bobby Isaac	Dodge	90.112
919	26	6/21/69	Greenville, SC	0.5	D	100	Bobby Isaac	Dodge	61.813	Bobby Isaac	Dodge	66.030
920	27	6/26/69	Raleigh, NC	0.5	D	100	David Pearson	Ford	65.418	Bobby Isaac	Dodge	72.942
921	28	7/4/69	Daytona Beach, FL	2.5	P	400	LeeRoy Yarbrough	Ford	160.875	Cale Yarborough	Mercury	190.706
922	29	7/6/69	Dover, DE	1.0	P	300	Richard Petty	Ford	115.772	David Pearson	Ford	130.430
923	30	7/10/69	Thompson, CT	0.625	P	125	David Pearson	Ford	89.498	David Pearson	Ford	99.800
924	31	7/13/69	Trenton, NJ	1.5	P	300	David Pearson	Ford	121.008	Bobby Isaac	Dodge	132.668
925	32	7/15/69	Beltsville, MD	0.5	P	150	Richard Petty	Ford	77.253	Richard Petty	Ford	82.094
926	33	7/20/69	Bristol, TN	0.5	P	250	David Pearson	Ford	79.737	Cale Yarborough	Mercury	103.432
927	34	7/26/69	Nashville, TN	0.5	P	200	Richard Petty	Ford	78.740	Richard Petty	Ford	84.918
928	35	7/27/69	Maryville, TN	0.5	P	200	Richard Petty	Ford	82.417	David Pearson	Ford	87.434
929	36	8/10/69	Atlanta, GA	1.5	P	501	LeeRoy Yarbrough	Ford	133.001	Cale Yarborough	Mercury	155.413
930	37	8/17/69	Brooklyn, MI	2.0	P	330	David Pearson	Ford	115.508	David Pearson	Ford	161.714
931	38	8/21/69	South Boston, VA	0.5	P	100	Bobby Isaac	Dodge	76.906	Bobby Isaac	Dodge	84.959
932	39	8/22/69	Winston-Salem, NC	0.25	P	62.5	Richard Petty	Ford	47.458	Richard Petty	Ford	54.253
933	40	8/24/69	Weaverville, NC	0.5	P	250	Bobby Isaac	Dodge	80.450	Bobby Isaac	Dodge	89.000
934	41	9/1/69	Darlington, SC	1.375	P	316.25	LeeRoy Yarbrough	Ford	105.612	Cale Yarborough	Mercury	151.985
935	42	9/5/69	Hickory, NC	0.4	P	100	Bobby Isaac	Dodge	80.519	Bobby Isaac	Dodge	86.212
936	43	9/7/69	Richmond, VA	0.563	P	250.404	Bobby Allison	Dodge	76.388	Richard Petty	Ford	91.257
937	44	9/14/69	Talladega, AL	2.66	P	500.08	Richard Brickhouse	Dodge	153.778	Bobby Isaac	Dodge	196.386
938	45	9/18/69	Columbia, SC	0.5	D	100	Bobby Isaac	Dodge	70.230	Richard Petty	Ford	73.108
939	46	9/28/69	Martinsville, VA	0.5	P	250	Richard Petty	Ford	63.127	David Pearson	Ford	83.197
940	47	10/5/69	N. Wilkesboro, NC	0.625	P	250	David Pearson	Ford	93.429	Bobby Isaac	Dodge	106.032
941	48	10/12/69	Charlotte, NC	1.5	P	501	Donnie Allison	Ford	131.271	Cale Yarborough	Mercury	162.162
942	49	10/17/69	Savannah, GA	0.5	P	100	Bobby Isaac	Dodge	78.432	Bobby Isaac	Dodge	86.095
943	50	10/19/69	Augusta, GA	0.5	P	100	Bobby Isaac	Dodge	78.740	Bobby Isaac	Dodge	85.689
944	51	10/26/69	Rockingham, NC	1.017	P	500.364	LeeRoy Yarbrough	Ford	111.938	Charlie Glotzbach	Dodge	136.972
945	52	11/2/69	Jefferson, GA	0.5	P	100	Bobby Isaac	Dodge	85.106	David Pearson	Ford	89.565
946	53	11/9/69	Macon, GA	0.548	P	274	Bobby Allison	Dodge	81.079	Bobby Isaac	Dodge	98.148
947	54	12/7/69	College Station, TX	2.0	P	500	Bobby Isaac	Dodge	144.277	Buddy Baker	Dodge	176.284

1970

Cum. No.	Yr. No.	Date	Site	Track Length	Surface	Miles	Race Winner	Make	Speed	Pole Winner	Make	Pole Speed
948	1	1/18/70	Riverside, CA	2.7	P	500.42	A. J. Foyt	Ford	97.450	Dan Gurney	Plymouth	112.060
949	2	2/19/70	Daytona Beach, FL	2.5	P	125	Cale Yarborough	Mercury	183.295	Cale Yarborough	Mercury	194.015
950	3	2/19/70	Daytona Beach, FL	2.5	P	125	Charlie Glotzbach	Dodge	147.734	Buddy Baker	Dodge	192.624
951	4	2/22/70	Daytona Beach, FL	2.5	P	500	Pete Hamilton	Plymouth	149.601	Cale Yarborough	Mercury	194.015
952	5	3/1/70	Richmond, VA	0.542	P	271	James Hylton	Ford	82.044	Richard Petty	Plymouth	89.137
953	6	3/8/70	Rockingham, NC	1.017	P	500.364	Richard Petty	Plymouth	116.117	Bobby Allison	Dodge	139.048
954	7	3/15/70	Savannah, GA	0.5	P	100	Richard Petty	Plymouth	82.418	Richard Petty	Plymouth	85.874
955	8	3/29/70	Atlanta, GA	1.522	P	499.216	Bobby Allison	Dodge	139.554	Cale Yarborough	Mercury	159.929
956	9	4/5/70	Bristol, TN	0.533	P	266.5	Donnie Allison	Ford	87.543	David Pearson	Ford	107.079
957	10	4/12/70	Talladega, AL	2.66	P	500.08	Pete Hamilton	Plymouth	152.321	Bobby Isaac	Dodge	199.658
958	11	4/18/70	N. Wilkesboro, NC	0.625	P	250	Richard Petty	Plymouth	94.246	Bobby Isaac	Dodge	107.041
959	12	4/30/70	Columbia, SC	0.5	D	100	Richard Petty	Plymouth	62.685	Larry Baumel	Ford	72.329
960	13	5/9/70	Darlington, SC	1.366	P	397.506	David Pearson	Ford	129.668	Charlie Glotzbach	Dodge	153.822
961	14	5/15/70	Beltsville, MD	0.5	P	150	Bobby Isaac	Dodge	76.370	James Hylton	Ford	83.128
962	15	5/18/70	Hampton, VA	0.4	P	120	Bobby Isaac	Dodge	73.245	Bobby Isaac	Dodge	79.659
963	16	5/24/70	Charlotte, NC	1.5	P	600	Donnie Allison	Ford	129.680	Bobby Isaac	Dodge	159.277

Cum. No.	Yr. No.	Date	Site	Track Length	Surface	Miles	Race Winner	Make	Speed	Pole Winner	Make	Pole Speed
964	17	5/28/70	Maryville, TN	0.52	P	104	Bobby Isaac	Dodge	82.558	Bobby Allison	Dodge	92.094
965	18	5/31/70	Martinsville, VA	0.525	P	197.9	Bobby Isaac	Dodge	68.584	Donnie Allison	Ford	82.609
966	19	6/7/70	Brooklyn, MI	2.04	P	400.88	Cale Yarborough	Mercury	138.302	Pete Hamilton	Plymouth	162.737
967	20	6/14/70	Riverside, CA	2.62	P	400.86	Richard Petty	Plymouth	101.120	Bobby Allison	Dodge	111.621
968	21	6/20/70	Hickory, NC	0.363	P	100.188	Bobby Isaac	Dodge	68.011	Bobby Isaac	Dodge	79.596
969	22	6/26/70	Kingsport, TN	0.337	P	100.089	Richard Petty	Plymouth	65.583	Richard Petty	Plymouth	75.056
970	23	6/27/70	Greenville, SC	0.5	P	100	Bobby Isaac	Dodge	75.345	Bobby Isaac	Dodge	82.327
971	24	7/4/70	Daytona Beach, FL	2.5	P	400	Donnie Allison	Ford	162.235	Cale Yarborough	Mercury	191.640
972	25	7/7/70	Malta, NY	0.362	P	90.5	Richard Petty	Plymouth	68.589	Bobby Isaac	Dodge	73.213
973	26	7/9/70	Thompson, CT	0.542	P	108.4	Bobby Isaac	Dodge	80.296	Bobby Isaac	Dodge	87.029
974	27	7/12/70	Trenton, NJ	1.5	P	300	Richard Petty	Plymouth	120.724	Bobby Isaac	Dodge	131.749
975	28	7/19/70	Bristol, TN	0.533	P	266.5	Bobby Allison	Dodge	84.880	Cale Yarborough	Mercury	107.375
976	29	7/24/70	Maryville, TN	0.52	P	104	Richard Petty	Plymouth	84.956	Richard Petty	Plymouth	91.264
977	30	7/25/70	Nashville, TN	0.596	P	250.32	Bobby Isaac	Dodge	87.943	LeeRoy Yarbrough	Ford	114.115
978	31	8/2/70	Atlanta, GA	1.522	P	499.216	Richard Petty	Plymouth	142.712	Fred Lorenzen	Dodge	157.625
979	32	8/6/70	Columbia, SC	0.5	D	100	Bobby Isaac	Dodge	67.101	Richard Petty	Plymouth	72.695
980	33	8/11/70	Ona, WV	0.455	P	131.1	Richard Petty	Plymouth	78.358	Bobby Allison	Ford	150.555
981	34	8/16/70	Brooklyn, MI	2.04	P	401.88	Charlie Glotzbach	Dodge	147.571	Charlie Glotzbach	Dodge	157.363
982	35	8/23/70	Talladega, AL	2.66	P	500.08	Pete Hamilton	Plymouth	158.517	Bobby Isaac	Dodge	186.834
983	36	8/28/70	Winston-Salem, NC	0.25	P	62.5	Richard Petty	Plymouth	51.527	Richard Petty	Plymouth	54.553
984	37	8/29/70	South Boston, VA	0.357	P	100.317	Richard Petty	Plymouth	73.060	Richard Petty	Plymouth	81.187
985	38	9/7/70	Darlington, SC	1.366	P	501.322	Buddy Baker	Dodge	128.817	David Pearson	Ford	150.555
986	39	9/11/70	Hickory, NC	0.363	P	100.188	Bobby Isaac	Dodge	73.365	Bobby Isaac	Dodge	78.411
987	40	9/13/70	Richmond, VA	0.542	P	271	Richard Petty	Plymouth	81.476	Richard Petty	Plymouth	87.014
988	41	9/20/70	Dover, DE	1.0	P	300	Richard Petty	Plymouth	112.103	Bobby Isaac	Dodge	129.538
989	42	9/30/70	Raleigh, NC	0.5	D	100	Richard Petty	Plymouth	68.376	John Sears	Ford	71.380
990	43	10/4/70	N. Wilkesboro, NC	0.625	P	250	Bobby Isaac	Dodge	90.162	Bobby Isaac	Dodge	105.406
991	44	10/11/70	Charlotte, NC	1.5	P	501	LeeRoy Yarbrough	Mercury	123.246	Charlie Glotzbach	Dodge	147.273
992	45	10/18/70	Martinsville, VA	0.525	P	262.5	Richard Petty	Plymouth	72.235	Bobby Allison	Dodge	82.167
993	46	11/8/70	Macon, GA	0.548	P	274	Richard Petty	Plymouth	83.284	Richard Petty	Plymouth	94.064
994	47	11/15/70	Rockingham, NC	1.017	P	500.364	Cale Yarborough	Mercury	117.811	Charlie Glotzbach	Dodge	136.498
995	48	11/22/70	Hampton, VA	0.395	P	118.5	Bobby Allison	Dodge	69.585	Benny Parsons	Ford	78.239

1971

Cum. No.	Yr. No.	Date	Site	Track Length	Surface	Miles	Race Winner	Make	Speed	Pole Winner	Make	Pole Speed
996	1	1/10/71	Riverside, CA	2.62	P	500.42	Ray Elder	Dodge	100.783	Richard Petty	Plymouth	107.084
997	2	2/11/71	Dayton Beach, FL	2.5	P	125	Pete Hamilton	Plymouth	175.029	A. J. Foyt	Mercury	182.744
998	2	2/11/71	Daytona Beach, FL	2.5	P	125	David Pearson	Mercury	168.278	Bobby Isaac	Dodge	180.050
999	4	2/14/71	Daytona Beach, FL	2.5	P	500	Richard Petty	Plymouth	144.744	A. J. Foyt	Mercury	182.744
1000	5	2/28/71	Ontario, CA	2.5	P	500	A. J. Foyt	Mercury	134.168	A. J. Foyt	Mercury	151.711
1001	6	3/7/71	Richmond, VA	0.542	P	271	Richard Petty	Plymouth	79.838	Dave Marcis	Dodge	87.178
1002	7	3/14/71	Rockingham, NC	1.017	P	500.364	Richard Petty	Plymouth	118.696	Fred Lorenzen	Plymouth	133.892
1003	8	3/21/71	Hickory, NC	0.363	P	100.188	Richard Petty	Plymouth	67.700	Bobby Allison	Dodge	79.001
1004	9	3/28/71	Bristol, TN	0.533	P	266.5	David Pearson	Ford	91.704	David Pearson	Ford	105.525
1005	10	4/4/71	Atlanta, GA	1.522	P	499.216	A. J. Foyt	Mercury	131.375	A. J. Foyt	Mercury	155.152
1006	11	4/8/71	Columbia, SC	0.5	P	100	Richard Petty	Plymouth	76.513	James Hylton	Ford	84.229
1007	12	4/10/71	Greenville, SC	0.5	P	100	Bobby Isaac	Dodge	78.159	David Pearson	Ford	82.257
1008	13	4/15/71	Maryville, TN	0.52	P	104	Richard Petty	Plymouth	88.697	Friday Hassler	Chevy	91.464
1009	14	4/18/71	N. Wilkesboro, NC	0.625	P	250	Richard Petty	Plymouth	98.479	Bobby Isaac	Dodge	106.217
1010	15	4/25/71	Martinsville, VA	0.525	P	262.5	Richard Petty	Plymouth	77.707	Donnie Allison	Mercury	82.529
1011	16	5/2/71	Darlington, SC	1.366	P	400.238	Buddy Baker	Dodge	130.678	Donnie Allison	Mercury	149.826
1012	17	5/9/71	South Boston, VA	0.357	P	100.317	Benny Parsons	Ford	72.271	Bobby Isaac	Dodge	81.548
1013	18	5/16/71	Talladega, AL	2.66	P	500.08	Donnie Allison	Mercury	147.419	Donnie Allison	Mercury	185.869
1014	19	5/21/71	Asheville, NC	0.333	P	99.9	Richard Petty	Plymouth	71.231	Richard Petty	Plymouth	79.598
1015	20	5/23/71	Kingsport, TN	0.337	P	101.1	Bobby Isaac	Dodge	63.242	Bobby Isaac	Dodge	75.167
1016	21	5/30/71	Charlotte, NC	1.5	P	600	Bobby Allison	Mercury	140.422	Charlie Glotzbach	Chevy	157.788
1017	22	6/6/71	Dover, DE	1.0	P	500	Bobby Allison	Mercury	123.119	Richard Petty	Plymouth	129.486
1018	23	6/13/71	Brooklyn, MI	2.0	P	401.88	Bobby Allison	Mercury	149.567	Bobby Allison	Mercury	161.190
1019	24	6/20/71	Riverside, CA	2.62	P	400.86	Bobby Allison	Dodge	93.427	Bobby Allison	Dodge	107.315
1020	25	6/23/71	Houston, TX	0.5	P	150	Bobby Allison	Dodge	73.489	Bobby Allison	Dodge	78.226
1021	26	6/26/71	Greenville, SC	0.5	P	100	Richard Petty	Plymouth	74.297	Bobby Allison	Ford	81.555
1022	27	7/4/71	Daytona Beach, FL	2.5	P	400	Bobby Isaac	Dodge	161.947	Donnie Allison	Mercury	183.228

Cum. No.	Yr. No.	Date	Site	Track Length	Surface	Miles	Race Winner	Make	Speed	Pole Winner	Make	Pole Speed
1023	28	7/11/71	Bristol, TN	0.533	P	266.5	Charlie Glotzbach	Chevy	101.074	Richard Petty	Plymouth	104.589
1024	29	7/14/71	Malta, NY	0.362	P	90.5	Richard Petty	Plymouth	66.748	Richard Petty	Plymouth	74.896
1025	30	7/15/71	Islip, NY	0.2	P	46	Richard Petty	Plymouth	49.925	Richard Petty	Plymouth	46.133
1026	31	7/18/71	Trenton, NJ	1.5	P	300	Richard Petty	Plymouth	120.347	Friday Hassler	Chevy	129.134
1027	32	7/24/71	Nashville, TN	0.596	P	250.32	Richard Petty	Plymouth	89.667	Richard Petty	Plymouth	114.628
1028	33	8/1/71	Atlanta, GA	1.522	P	499.216	Richard Petty	Plymouth	129.061	Buddy Baker	Dodge	155.796
1029	34	8/6/71	Winston-Salem, NC	0.25	P	62.5	Bobby Allison	Mustang	44.792	Richard Petty	Plymouth	55.283
1030	35	8/8/71	Ona, WV	0.455	P	227.5	Richard Petty	Plymouth	83.805	Bobby Allison	Mustang	84.053
1031	36	8/15/71	Brooklyn, MI	2.0	P	401.88	Bobby Allison	Mercury	149.862	Pete Hamilton	Plymouth	161.901
1032	37	8/22/71	Talladega, AL	2.66	P	500.08	Bobby Allison	Mercury	145.945	Donnie Allison	Mercury	187.323
1033	38	8/27/71	Columbia, SC	0.5	P	102	Richard Petty	Plymouth	64.831	Richard Petty	Plymouth	85.137
1034	39	8/28/71	Hickory, NC	0.363	P	100.188	Tiny Lund	Camaro	72.937	Dave Marcis	Dodge	80.147
1035	40	9/6/71	Darlington, SC	1.366	P	501.32	Bobby Allison	Mercury	131.398	Bobby Allison	Mercury	147.915
1036	41	9/26/71	Martinsville, VA	0.525	P	262.5	Bobby Isaac	Dodge	73.681	Bobby Isaac	Dodge	83.635
1037	42	10/10/71	Charlotte, NC	1.5	P	357.00	Bobby Allison	Mercury	126.140	Charlie Glotzbach	Chevy	157.085
1038	43	10/17/71	Dover, DE	1.0	P	500	Richard Petty	Plymouth	123.254	Bobby Allison	Mercury	132.811
1039	44	10/24/71	Rockingham, NC	1.017	P	500.364	Richard Petty	Plymouth	113.405	Charlie Glotzbach	Chevy	135.167
1040	45	11/7/71	Macon, GA	0.548	P	274	Bobby Allison	Ford	80.859	Bobby Allison	Ford	95.334
1041	46	11/14/71	Richmond, VA	0.542	P	271	Richard Petty	Plymouth	80.025	Bill Dennis	Mercury	—
1042	47	11/21/71	N. Wilkesboro, NC	0.625	P	250	Tiny Lund	Camaro	96.174	Charlie Glotzbach	Chevy	107.558
1043	48	12/12/71	College Station, TX	2.0	P	500	Richard Petty	Plymouth	144.000	Pete Hamilton	Plymouth	170.830

1972

Cum. No.	Yr. No.	Date	Site	Track Length	Surface	Miles	Race Winner	Make	Speed	Pole Winner	Make	Pole Speed
1044	1	1/23/72	Riverside, CA	2.62	P	387.76	Richard Petty	Plymouth	104.016	A. J. Foyt	Mercury	110.033
1045	2	2/20/72	Daytona Beach, FL	2.5	P	500	A. J. Foyt	Mercury	161.550	Bobby Isaac	Dodge	186.632
1046	3	2/27/72	Richmond, VA	0.542	P	271	Richard Petty	Plymouth	76.258	Bobby Allison	Chevy	90.573
1047	4	3/5/72	Ontario, CA	2.5	P	500	A. J. Foyt	Mercury	127.082	A. J. Foyt	Mercury	153.217
1048	5	3/12/72	Rockingham, NC	1.017	P	500.364	Bobby Isaac	Dodge	113.895	Bobby Allison	Chevy	137.539
1049	6	3/26/72	Atlanta, GA	1.522	P	499.216	Bobby Allison	Chevy	128.214	Bobby Allison	Chevy	156.245
1050	7	4/9/72	Bristol, TN	0.533	P	266.5	Bobby Allison	Chevy	92.826	Bobby Allison	Chevy	106.875
1051	8	4/16/72	Darlington, SC	1.366	P	501.322	David Pearson	Mercury	124.406	David Pearson	Mercury	148.209
1052	9	4/23/72	N. Wilkesboro, NC	0.625	P	250	Richard Petty	Plymouth	86.381	Bobby Isaac	Dodge	107.506
1053	10	4/30/72	Martinsville, VA	0.525	P	262.5	Richard Petty	Plymouth	72.657	Bobby Allison	Chevy	84.163
1054	11	5/7/72	Talladega, AL	2.66	P	500.08	David Pearson	Mercury	134.400	Bobby Isaac	Dodge	192.428
1055	12	5/28/72	Charlotte, NC	1.5	P	600	Buddy Baker	Dodge	142.255	Bobby Allison	Chevy	158.162
1056	13	6/4/72	Dover, DE	1.0	P	500	Bobby Allison	Chevy	118.019	Bobby Isaac	Dodge	130.809
1057	14	6/11/72	Brooklyn, MI	2.0	P	400	David Pearson	Mercury	146.639	Bobby Isaac	Dodge	160.764
1058	15	6/18/72	Riverside, CA	2.62	P	400.86	Ray Elder	Dodge	98.761	Richard Petty	Plymouth	108.688
1059	16	6/25/72	College Station, TX	2.0	P	500	Richard Petty	Plymouth	144.185	Richard Petty	Plymouth	169.412
1060	17	7/4/72	Daytona Beach, FL	2.5	P	400	David Pearson	Mercury	160.821	Bobby Isaac	Dodge	186.277
1061	18	7/9/72	Bristol, TN	0.533	P	266.5	Bobby Allison	Chevy	92.735	Bobby Allison	Chevy	107.279
1062	19	7/16/72	Trenton, NJ	1.5	P	300	Bobby Allison	Chevy	114.030	Bobby Isaac	Dodge	133.126
1063	20	7/23/72	Atlanta, GA	1.522	P	499.216	Bobby Allison	Chevy	131.295	David Pearson	Mercury	158.353
1064	21	8/6/72	Talladega, AL	2.66	P	500.08	James Hylton	Mercury	148.728	Bobby Isaac	Dodge	190.677
1065	22	8/20/72	Brooklyn, MI	2.0	P	400	David Pearson	Mercury	134.416	Richard Petty	Dodge	157.607
1066	23	8/27/72	Nashville, TN	0.596	P	250.32	Bobby Allison	Chevy	92.578	Bobby Allison	Chevy	116.932
1067	24	9/4/72	Darlington, SC	1.366	P	501.322	Bobby Allison	Chevy	128.124	Bobby Allison	Chevy	152.228
1068	25	9/10/72	Richmond, VA	0.542	P	271	Richard Petty	Plymouth	75.899	Bobby Allison	Chevy	89.669
1069	26	9/17/72	Dover, DE	1.0	P	500	David Pearson	Mercury	120.506	Bobby Allison	Chevy	133.323
1070	27	9/24/72	Martinsville, VA	0.525	P	262.5	Richard Petty	Plymouth	69.989	Bobby Allison	Chevy	85.890
1071	28	10/1/72	N. Wilkesboro, NC	0.625	P	250	Richard Petty	Plymouth	95.816	Buddy Baker	Dodge	105.922
1072	29	10/8/72	Charlotte, NC	1.5	P	501	Bobby Allison	Chevy	133.234	David Pearson	Mercury	158.539
1073	30	10/22/72	Rockingham, NC	1.017	P	500.364	Bobby Allison	Chevy	118.275	David Pearson	Mercury	127.528
1074	31	11/12/72	College Station, TX	2.0	P	500	Buddy Baker	Dodge	147.059	A. J. Foyt	Mercury	170.273

1973

Cum. No.	Yr. No.	Date	Site	Track Length	Surface	Miles	Race Winner	Make	Speed	Pole Winner	Make	Pole Speed
1075	1	1/21/73	Riverside, CA	2.62	P	500.42	Mark Donohue	Matador	104.055	David Pearson	Mercury	110.856
1076	2	2/18/73	Daytona Beach, FL	2.5	P	500	Richard Petty	Dodge	157.205	Buddy Baker	Dodge	185.662
1077	3	2/25/73	Richmond, VA	0.542	P	271	Richard Petty	Dodge	74.764	Bobby Allison	Chevy	90.952
1078	4	3/18/73	Rockingham, NC	1.017	P	500.364	David Pearson	Mercury	118.649	David Pearson	Mercury	134.021
1079	5	3/25/73	Bristol, TN	0.533	P	266.5	Cale Yarborough	Chevy	88.952	Cale Yarborough	Chevy	107.608
1080	6	4/1/73	Atlanta, GA	1.522	P	499.216	David Pearson	Mercury	139.351	No Time Trials	NTT	NTT

Cum. No.	Yr. No.	Date	Site	Track Length	Surface	Miles	Race Winner	Make	Speed	Pole Winner	Make	Pole Speed
1081	7	4/8/73	N. Wilkesboro, NC	0.625	P	250	Richard Petty	Dodge	97.224	Bobby Allison	Chevy	106.750
1082	8	4/15/73	Darlington, SC	1.366	P	501.322	David Pearson	Mercury	122.655	David Pearson	Mercury	153.463
1083	9	4/29/73	Martinsville, VA	0.525	P	262.5	David Pearson	Mercury	70.251	David Pearson	Mercury	86.369
1084	10	5/6/73	Talladega, AL	2.66	P	500.08	David Pearson	Mercury	131.956	Buddy Baker	Dodge	193.435
1085	11	5/12/73	Nashville, TN	0.596	P	250.32	Cale Yarborough	Chevy	98.419	Cale Yarborough	Chevy	105.741
1086	12	5/27/73	Charlotte, NC	1.5	P	600	Buddy Baker	Dodge	124.890	Buddy Baker	Dodge	158.051
1087	13	6/3/73	Dover, DE	1.0	P	500	David Pearson	Mercury	119.745	David Pearson	Mercury	133.111
1088	14	6/10/73	College Station, TX	2.0	P	500	Richard Petty	Dodge	142.114	Buddy Baker	Dodge	169.248
1089	15	6/17/73	Riverside, CA	2.62	P	400.86	Bobby Allison	Chevy	100.215	Richard Petty	Dodge	110.027
1090	16	6/24/73	Brooklyn Mi	2.0	P	400	David Pearson	Mercury	153.485	Buddy Baker	Dodge	158.273
1091	17	7/4/73	Daytona Beach, FL	2.5	P	400	David Pearson	Mercury	158.468	Bobby Allison	Chevy	179.619
1092	18	7/8/73	Bristol, TN	0.533	P	266.5	Benny Parsons	Chevy	91.342	Cale Yarborough	Chevy	106.472
1093	19	7/22/73	Atlanta, GA	1.522	P	499.216	David Pearson	Mercury	130.211	Richard Petty	Dodge	157.163
1094	20	8/12/73	Talladega, AL	2.66	P	500.08	Dick Brooks	Plymouth	145.454	Bobby Allison	Chevy	187.064
1095	21	8/25/73	Nashville, TN	0.596	P	250.32	Buddy Baker	Dodge	89.310	Cale Yarborough	Chevy	103.024
1096	22	9/3/73	Darlington, SC	1.366	P	501.322	Cale Yarborough	Chevy	134.033	David Pearson	Mercury	150.366
1097	23	9/9/73	Richmond, VA	0.542	P	271	Richard Petty	Dodge	63.215	Bobby Allison	Chevy	90.245
1098	24	9/16/73	Dover, DE	1.0	P	500	David Pearson	Mercury	112.852	David Pearson	Mercury	124.649
1099	25	9/23/73	N. Wilkesboro, NC	0.625	P	250	Bobby Allison	Chevy	95.198	Bobby Allison	Chevy	105.619
1100	26	9/30/73	Martinsville, VA	0.525	P	252	Richard Petty	Dodge	68.831	Cale Yarborough	Chevy	85.922
1101	27	10/7/73	Charlotte, NC	1.5	P	501	Cale Yarborough	Chevy	145.240	David Pearson	Mercury	158.315
1102	28	10/21/73	Rockingham, NC	1.017	P	500	David Pearson	Mercury	117.749	Richard Petty	Dodge	135.748

1974

Cum. No.	Yr. No.	Date	Site	Track Length	Surface	Miles	Race Winner	Make	Speed	Pole Winner	Make	Pole Speed
1103	1	1/26/74	Riverside, CA	2.62	P	500.42	Cale Yarborough	Chevy	101.140	David Pearson	Mercury	110.098
1104	2	2/17/74	Daytona Beach, FL	2.5	P	450	Richard Petty	Dodge	140.894	David Pearson	Mercury	185.817
1105	3	2/24/74	Richmond, VA	0.542	P	243.9	Bobby Allison	Chevy	80.095	Bobby Allison	Chevy	90.353
1106	4	3/3/74	Rockingham, NC	1.017	P	450.53	Richard Petty	Dodge	121.622	Cale Yarborough	Chevy	134.868
1107	5	3/17/74	Bristol, TN	0.533	P	239.85	Cale Yarborough	Chevy	64.533	Donnie Allison	Chevy	107.785
1108	6	3/24/74	Atlanta, GA	1.522	P	450.51	Cale Yarborough	Chevy	136.910	David Pearson	Mercury	159.242
1109	7	4/7/74	Darlington, SC	1.366	P	450.78	David Pearson	Mercury	117.543	Donnie Allison	Chevy	150.689
1110	8	4/21/74	N. Wilkesboro, NC	0.625	P	225	Richard Petty	Dodge	96.200	Bobby Allison	Chevy	105.669
1111	9	4/28/74	Martinsville, VA	0.525	P	236.25	Cale Yarborough	Chevy	70.427	Cale Yarborough	Chevy	84.362
1112	10	5/5/74	Talladega, AL	2.66	P	452.2	David Pearson	Mercury	130.220	David Pearson	Mercury	186.086
1113	11	5/11/74	Nashville, TN	0.596	P	238.4	Richard Petty	Dodge	84.240	Bobby Allison	Chevy	100.088
1114	12	5/19/74	Dover, DE	1.0	P	450	Cale Yarborough	Chevy	119.990	David Pearson	Mercury	134.403
1115	13	5/26/74	Charlotte, NC	1.5	P	540	David Pearson	Mercury	135.720	David Pearson	Mercury	157.498
1116	14	6/9/74	Riverside, CA	2.62	P	361.56	Cale Yarborough	Chevy	102.489	George Follmer	Matador	109.093
1117	15	6/16/74	Brooklyn, MI	2.0	P	360	Richard Petty	Dodge	127.098	David Pearson	Mercury	156.426
1118	16	7/4/74	Daytona Beach, FL	2.5	P	400	David Pearson	Mercury	138.310	David Pearson	Mercury	180.759
1119	17	7/14/74	Bristol, TN	0.533	P	266.5	Cale Yarborough	Chevy	75.430	Richard Petty	Dodge	107.351
1120	18	7/20/74	Nashville, TN	0.596	P	250.32	Cale Yarborough	Chevy	76.368	Darrell Waltrip	Chevy	101.274
1121	19	7/28/74	Atlanta, GA	1.522	P	499.216	Richard Petty	Dodge	131.651	Cale Yarborough	Chevy	156.750
1122	20	8/4/74	Pocono, PA	2.5	P	480	Richard Petty	Dodge	115.593	Buddy Baker	Ford	144.122
1123	21	8/11/74	Talladega, AL	2.66	P	500.08	Richard Petty	Dodge	148.637	David Pearson	Mercury	184.926
1124	22	8/25/74	Brooklyn Mi	2.0	P	400	David Pearson	Mercury	133.045	David Pearson	Mercury	157.946
1125	23	9/2/74	Darlington, SC	1.366	P	501.322	Cale Yarborough	Chevy	111.075	Richard Petty	Dodge	150.132
1126	24	9/8/74	Richmond, VA	0.542	P	271	Richard Petty	Dodge	64.430	Richard Petty	Dodge	88.852
1127	25	9/15/74	Dover, DE	1.0	P	500	Richard Petty	Dodge	113.640	Buddy Baker	Ford	133.640
1128	26	9/22/74	N. Wilkesboro, NC	0.625	P	250	Cale Yarborough	Chevy	80.782	Richard Petty	Dodge	105.087
1129	27	9/29/74	Martinsville, VA	0.525	P	262.5	Earl Ross	Chevy	66.232	Richard Petty	Dodge	84.119
1130	28	10/6/74	Charlotte, NC	1.5	P	501	David Pearson	Mercury	119.912	David Pearson	Mercury	158.749
1131	29	10/20/74	Rockingham, NC	1.017	P	500.364	David Pearson	Mercury	118.493	Richard Petty	Dodge	135.297
1132	30	11/24/74	Ontario, CA	2.5	P	500	Bobby Allison	Matador	134.963	Richard Petty	Dodge	149.940

1975

Cum. No.	Yr. No.	Date	Site	Track Length	Surface	Miles	Race Winner	Make	Speed	Pole Winner	Make	Pole Speed
1133	1	1/19/75	Riverside, CA	2.62	P	500.42	Bobby Allison	Matador	98.627	Bobby Allison	Matador	110.382
1134	2	2/16/75	Daytona Beach, FL	2.5	P	500	Benny Parsons	Chevy	153.649	Donnie Allison	Chevy	185.827
1135	3	2/23/75	Richmond, VA	0.542	P	271	Richard Petty	Dodge	74.913	Richard Petty	Dodge	93.340
1136	4	3/2/75	Rockingham, NC	1.017	P	500.364	Cale Yarborough	Chevy	117.588	Buddy Baker	Ford	137.611
1137	5	3/16/75	Bristol, TN	0.533	P	266.5	Richard Petty	Dodge	97.053	Buiddy Baker	Ford	110.951
1138	6	3/25/75	Atlanta, GA	1.522	P	499.216	Richard Petty	Dodge	133.496	Richard Petty	Dodge	159.029

Cum. No.	Yr. No.	Date	Site	Track Length	Surface	Miles	Race Winner	Make	Speed	Pole Winner	Make	Pole Speed
1139	7	4/6/75	N. Wilkesboro, NC	0.625	P	250	Richard Petty	Dodge	90.009	Darrell Waltrip	Chevy	105.520
1140	8	4/13/75	Darlington, SC	1.366	P	501.322	Bobby Allison	Matador	117.597	David Pearson	Mercury	155.433
1141	9	4/27/75	Martinsville, VA	0.525	P	262.5	Richard Petty	Dodge	69.282	Benny Parsons	Chevy	85.789
1142	10	5/4/75	Talladega, AL	2.66	P	500.08	Buddy Baker	Ford	144.948	Buddy Baker	Ford	189.947
1143	11	5/10/75	Nashville, TN	0.596	P	250.32	Darrell Waltrip	Chevy	94.107	Darrell Waltrip	Chevy	103.793
1144	12	5/19/75	Dover, DE	1.0	P	500	David Pearson	Mercury	100.820	David Pearson	Mercury	136.612
1145	13	5/25/75	Charlotte, NC	1.5	P	600	Richard Petty	Dodge	145.327	David Pearson	Mercury	159.353
1146	14	6/8/75	Riverside, CA	2.62	P	400.86	Richard Petty	Dodge	101.028	Bobby Allison	Matador	110.353
1147	15	6/15/75	Brooklyn, MI	2.0	P	400	David Pearson	Mercury	131.398	Cale Yarborough	Chevy	158.541
1148	16	7/4/75	Daytona Beach, FL	2.5	P	400	Richard Petty	Dodge	158.381	Donnie Allison	Chevy	186.737
1149	17	7/20/75	Nashville, TN	0.596	P	250.32	Cale Yarborough	Chevy	89.792	Benny Parsons	Chevy	103.247
1150	18	8/3/75	Pocono, PA	2.5	P	500	David Pearson	Mercury	111.179	Bobby Allison	Matador	146.491
1151	19	8/17/75	Talladega, AL	2.66	P	500.08	Buddy Baker	Ford	130.892	Dave Marcis	Dodge	191.340
1152	20	8/24/75	Brooklyn, MI	2.0	P	400	Richard Petty	Dodge	107.583	David Pearson	Mercury	159.798
1153	21	9/1/75	Darlington, SC	1.366	P	501.322	Bobby Allison	Matador	116.825	David Pearson	Mercury	153.401
1154	22	9/14/75	Dover, DE	1.0	P	500	Richard Petty	Dodge	111.372	Dave Marcis	Dodge	133.953
1155	23	9/21/75	N. Wilkesboro, NC	0.625	P	250	Richard Petty	Dodge	88.986	Richard Petty	Dodge	105.500
1156	24	9/28/75	Martinsville, VA	0.525	P	262.5	Dave Marcis	Dodge	75.819	Cale Yarborough	Chevy	86.199
1157	25	10/5/75	Charlotte, NC	1.5	P	501	Richard Petty	Dodge	132.209	David Pearson	Mercury	161.071
1158	26	10/12/75	Richmond, VA	0.542	P	271	Darrell Waltrip	Chevy	81.886	Benny Parsons	Chevy	91.071
1159	27	10/19/75	Rockingham, NC	1.017	P	500.364	Cale Yarborough	Chevy	120.129	Dave Marcis	Dodge	132.021
1160	28	11/2/75	Bristol, TN	0.533	P	266.5	Richard Petty	Dodge	97.016	Cale Yarborough	Chevy	110.162
1161	29	11/9/75	Atlanta, GA	1.522	P	499.216	Buddy Baker	Ford	130.990	Dave Marcis	Dodge	160.662
1162	30	11/23/75	Ontario, CA	2.5	P	500	Buddy Baker	Ford	140.712	David Pearson	Mercury	153.525

1976

Cum. No.	Yr. No.	Date	Site	Track Length	Surface	Miles	Race Winner	Make	Speed	Pole Winner	Make	Pole Speed
1163	1	1/18/76	Riverside, CA	2.62	P	500.42	David Pearson	Mercury	99.180	Bobby Allison	Matador	112.416
1164	2	2/15/76	Daytona Beach, FL	2.5	P	500	David Pearson	Mercury	152.181	Ramo Stott	Chevy	183.456
1165	3	2/29/76	Rockingham, NC	1.017	P	500.364	Richard Petty	Dodge	113.665	Dave Marcis	Dodge	138.287
1166	4	3/7/76	Richmond, VA	0.542	P	216.8	Dave Marcis	Dodge	72.792	Bobby Allison	Mercury	92.715
1167	5	3/14/76	Bristol, TN	0.533	P	213.2	Cale Yarborough	Chevy	87.377	Buddy Baker	Ford	110.720
1168	6	3/21/76	Atlanta, GA	1.522	P	499.216	David Pearson	Mercury	128.904	Dave Marcis	Dodge	160.709
1169	7	4/4/76	N. Wilkesboro, NC	0.625	P	250	Cale Yarborough	Chevy	96.858	Dave Marcis	Dodge	108.585
1170	8	4/11/76	Darlington, SC	1.366	P	501.322	David Pearson	Mercury	122.973	David Pearson	Mercury	154.171
1171	9	4/25/76	Martinsville, VA	0.525	P	262.5	Darrell Waltrip	Chevy	71.759	Dave Marcis	Dodge	86.286
1172	10	5/2/76	Talladega, AL	2.66	P	500.08	Buddy Baker	Ford	169.887	Dave Marcis	Dodge	189.197
1173	11	5/8/76	Nashville, TN	0.596	P	250.32	Cale Yarborough	Chevy	84.512	Benny Parsons	Chevy	104.328
1174	12	5/16/76	Dover, DE	1.0	P	500	Benny Parsons	Chevy	115.436	Dave Marcis	Dodge	136.013
1175	13	5/30/76	Charlotte, NC	1.5	P	600	David Pearson	Mercury	137.352	David Pearson	Mercury	159.132
1176	14	6/6/76	Riverside, CA	2.62	P	248.9	David Pearson	Mercury	106.279	David Pearson	Mercury	111.437
1177	15	6/13/76	Brooklyn, MI	2.0	P	400	David Pearson	Mercury	141.148	Richard Petty	Dodge	158.569
1178	16	7/4/76	Daytona Beach, FL	2.5	P	400	Cale Yarborough	Chevy	160.966	A. J. Foyt	Chevy	183.090
1179	17	7/16/76	Nashville, TN	0.596	P	250.32	Benny Parsons	Chevy	86.908	Neil Bonnett	Mercury	103.049
1180	18	8/1/76	Pocono, PA	2.5	P	500	Richard Petty	Dodge	115.875	Cale Yarborough	Chevy	147.865
1181	19	8/8/76	Talladega, AL	2.66	P	500.08	Dave Marcis	Dodge	157.547	Dave Marcis	Dodge	190.651
1182	20	8/22/76	Brooklyn, MI	2.0	P	400	David Pearson	Mercury	140.078	David Pearson	Mercury	160.875
1183	21	8/29/76	Bristol, TN	0.533	P	213.2	Cale Yarborough	Chevy	99.175	Darrell Waltrip	Chevy	110.300
1184	22	9/6/76	Darlington, SC	1.366	P	501.322	David Pearson	Mercury	120.534	David Pearson	Mercury	154.699
1185	23	9/12/76	Richmond, VA	0.542	P	216.8	Cale Yarborough	Chevy	77.993	Benny Parsons	Chevy	92.460
1186	24	9/19/76	Dover, DE	1.0	P	500	Cale Yarborough	Chevy	115.740	Cale Yarborough	Chevy	133.377
1187	25	9/26/76	Martinsville, VA	0.525	P	178.5	Cale Yarborough	Chevy	75.370	Darrell Waltrip	Chevy	88.484
1188	26	10/3/76	N. Wilkesboro, NC	0.625	P	250	Cale Yarborough	Chevy	96.380	Darrell Waltrip	Chevy	107.449
1189	27	10/10/76	Charlotte, NC	1.5	P	501	Donnie Allison	Chevy	141.266	David Pearson	Mercury	161.223
1190	28	10/24/76	Rockingham, NC	1.017	P	500.364	Richard Petty	Dodge	117.718	David Pearson	Mercury	139.117
1191	29	11/7/76	Atlanta, GA	1.522	P	499.216	Dave Marcis	Dodge	127.396	Buddy Baker	Ford	161.652
1192	30	11/21/76	Ontario, CA	2.5	P	500	David Pearson	Mercury	137.101	David Pearson	Mercury	153.964

1977

Cum. No.	Yr. No.	Date	Site	Track Length	Surface	Miles	Race Winner	Make	Speed	Pole Winner	Make	Pole Speed
1193	1	1/16/77	Riverside, CA	2.62	P	311.78	David Pearson	Mercury	107.038	Cale Yarborough	Chevy	112.686
1194	2	2/20/77	Daytona Beach, FL	2.5	P	500	Cale Yarborough	Chevy	153.218	Donnie Allison	Chevy	188.048
1195	3	2/27/77	Richmond, VA	0.542	P	132.79	Cale Yarborough	Chevy	73.084	Neil Bonnett	Dodge	93.632
1196	4	3/13/77	Rockingham, NC	1.017	P	500.364	Richard Petty	Dodge	97.860	Donnie Allison	Chevy	135.387

Cum. No.	Yr. No.	Date	Site	Track Length	Surface	Miles	Race Winner	Make	Speed	Pole Winner	Make	Pole Speed
1197	5	3/20/77	Atlanta, GA	1.522	P	499.216	Richard Petty	Dodge	144.093	Richard Petty	Dodge	162.501
1198	6	3/27/77	N. Wilkesboro, NC	0.625	P	250	Cale Yarborough	Chevy	88.950	Neil Bonnett	Dodge	107.537
1199	7	4/3/77	Darlington, SC	1.366	P	501.322	Darrell Waltrip	Chevy	128.817	David Pearson	Mercury	151.269
1200	8	4/17/77	Bristol, TN	0.533	P	266.5	Cale Yarborough	Chevy	100.989	Cale Yarborough	Chevy	110.168
1201	9	4/24/77	Martinsville, VA	0.525	P	201.984	Cale Yarborough	Chevy	77.405	Neil Bonnett	Dodge	88.923
1202	10	5/1/77	Talladega, AL	2.66	P	500.08	Darrell Waltrip	Chevy	164.877	A. J. Foyt	Chevy	192.424
1203	11	5/7/77	Nashville, TN	0.596	P	250.32	Benny Parsons	Chevy	87.490	Darrell Waltrip	Chevy	103.643
1294	12	5/15/77	Dover, DE	1.0	P	500	Cale Yarborough	Chevy	123.327	Richard Petty	Dodge	136.033
1205	13	5/29/77	Charlotte, NC	1.5	P	600	Richard Petty	Dodge	137.676	David Pearson	Mercury	161.435
1206	14	6/12/77	Riverside, CA	2.62	P	248.9	Richard Petty	Dodge	105.021	Richard Petty	Dodge	112.432
1207	15	6/19/77	Brooklyn, MI	2.0	P	400	Cale Yarborough	Chevy	135.033	David Pearson	Mercury	159.175
1208	16	7/4/77	Daytona Beach, FL	2.5	P	400	Richard Petty	Dodge	142.716	Neil Bonnett	Dodge	187.191
1209	17	7/16/77	Nashville, TN	0.596	P	250.32	Darrell Waltrip	Chevy	78.999	Benny Parsons	Chevy	104.210
1210	18	7/31/77	Pocono, PA	2.5	P	500	Benny Parsons	Chevy	128.379	Darrell Waltrip	Chevy	147.591
1211	19	8/7/77	Talladega, AL	2.66	P	500.08	Donnie Allison	Chevy	162.524	Benny Parsons	Chevy	192.684
1212	20	8/22/77	Brooklyn, MI	2.0	P	400	Darrell Waltrip	Chevy	137.944	David Pearson	Mercury	160.346
1213	21	8/28/77	Bristol, TN	0.533	P	213.2	Cale Yarborough	Chevy	79.726	Cale Yarborough	Chevy	109.746
1214	22	9/5/77	Darlington, SC	1.366	P	501.322	David Pearson	Mercury	106.797	Darrell Waltrip	Chevy	153.493
1215	23	9/11/77	Richmond, VA	0.542	P	216.8	Neil Bonnett	Dodge	80.644	Benny Parsons	Chevy	92.281
1216	24	9/18/77	Dover, DE	1.0	P	500	Benny Parsons	Chevy	114.708	Neil Bonnett	Dodge	134.233
1217	25	9/25/77	Martinsville, VA	0.525	P	262.5	Cale Yarborough	Chevy	73.447	Neil Bonnett	Dodge	87.637
1218	26	10/2/77	N. Wilkesboro, NC	0.625	P	250	Darrell Waltrip	Chevy	86.713	Richard Petty	Dodge	108.350
1219	27	10/9/77	Charlotte, NC	1.5	P	501	Benny Parsons	Chevy	142.780	David Pearson	Mercury	160.892
1220	28	10/23/77	Rockingham, NC	1.017	P	500	Donnie Allison	Chevy	113.584	Donnie Allison	Chevy	138.685
1221	29	11/6/77	Atlanta, GA	1.522	P	407.896	Darrell Waltrip	Chevy	110.052	Sam Sommers	Chevy	160.229
1222	30	11/20/77	Ontario, CA	2.5	P	500	Neil Bonnett	Dodge	128.296	Richard Petty	Dodge	154.905

1978

Cum. No.	Yr. No.	Date	Site	Track Length	Surface	Miles	Race Winner	Make	Speed	Pole Winner	Make	Pole Speed
1223	1	1/22/78	Riverside, CA	2.62	P	311.78	Cale Yarborough	Olds	102.269	David Pearson	Mercury	113.204
1224	2	2/19/78	Daytona Beach, FL	2.5	P	500	Bobby Allison	Ford	159.730	Cale Yarborough	Olds	187.536
1225	3	2/26/78	Richmond, VA	0.542	P	216.8	Benny Parsons	Chevy	80.304	Neil Bonnett	Dodge	93.382
1226	4	3/5/78	Rockingham, NC	1.017	P	500.364	David Pearson	Mercury	116.681	Neil Bonnett	Dodge	141.940
1227	5	3/19/78	Atlanta, GA	1.522	P	499.216	Bobby Allison	Ford	142.520	Cale Yarborough	Olds	162.006
1228	6	4/2/78	Bristol, TN	0.533	P	266.5	Darrell Waltrip	Chevy	92.401	Neil Bonnett	Dodge	110.409
1229	7	4/9/78	Darlington, SC	1.366	P	501.322	Benny Parsons	Chevy	127.544	Bobby Allison	Ford	151.862
1230	8	4/16/78	N. Wilkesboro, NC	0.625	P	250	Darrell Waltrip	Chevy	92.345	Benny Parsons	Chevy	108.510
1231	9	4/23/78	Martinsville, VA	0.525	P	262.5	Darrell Waltrip	Chevy	77.971	Lennie Pond	Chevy	88.637
1232	10	5/14/78	Talladega, AL	2.66	P	500.08	Cale Yarborough	Olds	159.699	Cale Yarborough	Olds	191.904
1233	11	5/21/78	Dover, DE	1.0	P	500	David Pearson	Mercury	114.664	Buddy Baker	Chevy	135.452
1234	12	5/28/78	Charlotte, NC	1.5	P	600	Darrell Waltrip	Chevy	138.355	David Pearson	Mercury	160.551
1235	13	6/3/78	Nashville, TN	0.596	P	250.32	Cale Yarborough	Olds	87.541	Lennie Pond	Chevy	105.094
1236	14	6/11/78	Riverside, CA	2.62	P	248.9	Benny Parsons	Chevy	104.311	David Pearson	Mercury	112.882
1237	15	6/18/78	Brooklyn, MI	2.0	P	400	Cale Yarborough	Olds	149.563	David Pearson	Mercury	163.036
1238	16	7/4/78	Daytona Beach, FL	2.5	P	400	David Pearson	Mercury	154.340	Cale Yarborough	Olds	186.803
1239	17	7/15/78	Nashville, TN	0.596	P	250.32	Cale Yarborough	Olds	88.924	Lennie Pond	Chevy	104.257
1240	18	7/30/78	Pocono, PA	2.5	P	500	Darrell Waltrip	Chevy	142.540	Benny Parsons	Chevy	149.917
1241	19	8/6/78	Talladega, AL	2.66	P	500.08	Lennie Pond	Olds	174.700	Cale Yarborough	Olds	192.917
1242	20	8/20/78	Brooklyn, MI	2.0	P	400	David Pearson	Mercury	129.566	David Pearson	Mercury	164.073
1243	21	8/26/78	Bristol, TN	0.533	P	266.5	Cale Yarborough	Olds	88.628	Lennie Pond	Olds	110.958
1244	22	9/4/78	Darlington, SC	1.266	P	501.322	Cale Yarborough	Olds	116.828	David Pearson	Mercury	153.685
1245	23	9/10/78	Richmond, VA	0.542	P	216.8	Darrell Waltrip	Chevy	79.568	Darrell Waltrip	Chevy	92.964
1246	24	9/17/78	Dover, DE	1.0	P	500	Bobby Allison	Ford	119.323	J. D. McDufffie	Chevy	135.480
1247	25	9/24/78	Martinsville, VA	0.525	P	262.5	Cale Yarborough	Olds	79.185	Lennie Pond	Chevy	86.558
1248	26	10/1/78	N. Wilkesboro, NC	0.625	P	150	Cale Yarborough	Olds	97.847	Darrell Waltrip	Chevy	109.397
1249	27	10/8/78	Charlotte, NC	1.5	P	501	Bobby Allison	Ford	141.826	David Pearson	Mercury	161.355
1250	28	10/22/78	Rockingham, NC	1.017	P	500.364	Cale Yarborough	Olds	117.288	Cale Yarborough	Olds	142.067
1251	29	11/5/78	Atlanta, GA	1.522	P	499.216	Donnie Allison	Chevy	124.312	Cale Yarborough	Olds	168.425
1252	30	11/19/78	Ontario, CA	2.5	P	500	Bobby Allison	Ford	137.783	Cale Yarborough	Olds	156.190

1979

Cum. No.	Yr. No.	Date	Site	Track Length	Surface	Miles	Race Winner	Make	Speed	Pole Winner	Make	Pole Speed
1253	1	1/14/79	Riverside, CA	2.62	P	311.78	Darrell Waltrip	Chevy	107.820	David Pearson	Mercury	113.659
1254	2	2/18/79	Daytona Beach, FL	2.5	P	500	Richard Petty	Olds	143.977	Buddy Baker	Olds	196.049

Cum. No.	Yr. No.	Date	Site	Track Length	Surface	Miles	Race Winner	Make	Speed	Pole Winner	Make	Pole Speed
1255	3	3/4/79	Rockingham, NC	1.017	P	500.364	Bobby Allison	Ford	121.727	Bobby Allison	Ford	136.790
1256	4	3/11/79	Richmond, VA	0.542	P	216.8	Cale Yarborough	Olds	83.608	Bobby Allison	Ford	92.957
1257	5	3/18/79	Atlanta, GA	1.522	P	499.216	Buddy Baker	Olds	135.136	Buddy Baker	Olds	165.951
1258	6	3/25/79	N. Wilkesborough, NC	0.625	P	0.625	Bobby Allison	Ford	88.400	Benny Parsons	Chevy	108.136
1259	7	4/1/79	Bristol, TN	0.533	P	266.5	Dale Earnhardt	Chevy	91.033	Buddy Baker	Chevy	111.610
1260	8	4/8/79	Darlington, SC	1.366	P	501.322	Darrell Waltrip	Chevy	121.721	Donnie Allison	Chevy	154.797
1261	9	4/22/79	Martinsville, VA	0.525	P	262.5	Richard Petty	Chevy	76.562	Darrell Waltrip	Chevy	87.383
1262	10	5/6/79	Talladega, AL	2.66	P	500.08	Bobby Allison	Ford	154.770	Darrell Waltrip	Olds	195.644
1263	11	5/12/79	Nashville, TN	0.596	P	250.32	Cale Yarborough	Olds	88.652	Joe Millikan	Chevy	104.155
1264	12	5/20/79	Dover, DE	1.0	P	500	Neil Bonnett	Mercury	111.269	Darrell Waltrip	Chevy	136.103
1265	13	5/27/79	Charlotte, NC	1.5	P	600	Darrell Waltrip	Chevy	136.674	Neil Bonnett	Mercury	160.125
1266	14	6/3/79	College Station, TX	2.0	P	400	Darrell Waltrip	Chevy	156.216	Buddy Baker	Chevy	167.903
1267	15	6/10/79	Riverside, CA	2.62	P	248.9	Bobby Allison	Ford	103.732	Dale Earnhardt	Chevy	113.039
1268	16	6/17/79	Brooklyn, MI	2.0	P	400	Buddy Baker	Chevy	135.798	Neil Bonnett	Mercury	162.371
1269	17	7/4/79	Daytona Beach, FL	2.5	P	400	Neil Bonnett	Mercury	172.890	Buddy Baker	Olds	193.196
1270	18	7/14/79	Nashville, TN	0.596	P	250.32	Darrell Waltrip	Chevy	92.227	Darrell Waltrip	Chevy	105.430
1271	19	7/30/79	Pocono, PA	2.5	P	500	Cale Yarborough	Chevy	115.207	Harry Gant	Chevy	148.711
1272	20	8/5/79	Talladega, AL	2.66	P	500.08	Darrell Waltrip	Olds	161.229	Neil Bonnett	Mercury	193.600
1273	21	8/19/79	Brooklyn, MI	2.0	P	400	Richard Petty	Chevy	130.376	David Pearson	Chevy	162.992
1274	22	8/25/79	Bristol, TN	0.533	P	266.5	Darrell Waltrip	Chevy	91.493	Richard Petty	Chevy	110.524
1275	23	9/3/79	Darlington, SC	1.366	P	501.322	David Pearson	Chevy	126.259	Bobby Allison	Ford	154.880
1276	24	9/9/79	Richmond, VA	0.542	P	216.8	Bobby Allison	Ford	80.604	Dale Earnhardt	Chevy	92.605
1277	25	9/16/79	Dover, DE	1.0	P	500	Richard Petty	Chevy	114.366	Dale Earnhardt	Chevy	135.726
1278	26	9/23/79	Martinsville, VA	0.525	P	262.5	Buddy Baker	Chevy	75.119	Darrell Waltrip	Chevy	88.265
1279	27	10/7/79	Charlotte, NC	1.5	P	501	Cale Yarborough	Chevy	134.266	Neil Bonnett	Mercury	164.304
1280	28	10/14/79	N. Wilkesboro, NC	0.625	P	250	Benny Parsons	Chevy	91.454	Dale Earnhardt	Chevy	112.783
1281	29	10/21/79	Rockingham, NC	1.017	P	500.364	Richard Petty	Chevy	108.356	Buddy Baker	Chevy	141.315
1282	30	11/4/79	Atlanta, GA	1.522	P	499.216	Neil Bonnett	Mercury	140.120	Buddy Baker	Chevy	164.813
1283	31	11/18/79	Ontario, CA	2.5	P	500	Benny Parsons	Chevy	132.822	Cale Yarborough	Olds	154.902

1980

Cum. No.	Yr. No.	Date	Site	Track Length	Surface	Miles	Race Winner	Make	Speed	Pole Winner	Make	Pole Speed
1284	1	1/19/80	Riverside, CA	2.62	P	311.78	Darrell Waltrip	Chevy	94.974	Darrell Waltrip	Chevy	113.404
1285	2	2/17/80	Daytona Beach, FL	2.5	P	500	Buddy Baker	Olds	177.602	Buddy Baker	Olds	194.009
1286	3	2/24/80	Richmond, VA	0.542	P	216.8	Darrell Waltrip	Chevy	67.703	Darrell Waltrip	Chevy	93.695
1287	4	3/9/80	Rockingham, NC	1.017	P	500.364	Cale Yarborough	Olds	108.735	Darrell Waltrip	Chevy	136.765
1288	5	3/16/80	Atlanta, GA	1.522	P	499.216	Dale Earnhardt	Chevy	134.808	Buddy Baker	Olds	166.212
1289	6	3/30/80	Bristol, TN	0.533	P	266.5	Dale Earnhardt	Chevy	96.977	Cale Yarborough	Chevy	111.688
1290	7	4/13/80	Darlington, SC	1.366	P	258.17	David Pearson	Chevy	112.397	Benny Parsons	Chevy	155.866
1291	8	4/20/80	N. Wilkesboro, NC	0.625	P	250	Richard Petty	Chevy	95.501	Bobby Allison	Ford	113.797
1292	9	4/27/80	Martinsville, VA	0.525	P	262.5	Darrell Waltrip	Chevy	69.049	Darrell Waltrip	Chevy	88.566
1293	10	5/4/80	Talladega, AL	2.66	P	500.08	Buddy Baker	Olds	170.481	David Pearson	Olds	197.704
1294	11	5/10/80	Nashville, TN	0.596	P	250.32	Richard Petty	Chevy	89.471	Cale Yarborough	Chevy	106.581
1295	12	5/18/80	Dover, DE	1.0	P	500	Bobby Allison	Ford	113.866	Cale Yarborough	Chevy	138.814
1296	13	5/15/80	Charlotte, NC	1.5	P	600	Benny Parsons	Chevy	119.265	Cale Yarborough	Chevy	165.194
1297	14	6/1/80	College Station, TX	2.0	P	400	Cale Yarborough	Chevy	159.046	Cale Yarborough	Chevy	170.709
1298	15	6/8/80	Riverside, CA	2.62	P	248.9	Darrell Waltrip	Chevy	101.846	Cale Yarborough	Chevy	113.792
1299	16	6/15/80	Brooklyn, MI	2.0	P	400	Benny Parsons	Chevy	131.808	Benny Parsons	Chevy	163.662
1300	17	7/4/80	Daytona Beach, FL	2.5	P	400	Bobby Allison	Ford	173.473	Cale Yarborough	Olds	194.670
1301	18	7/12/80	Nashville, TN	0.596	P	250.32	Dale Earnhardt	Chevy	93.821	Cale Yarborough	Chevy	104.817
1302	19	7/27/80	Pocono, PA	2.5	P	500	Neil Bonnett	Mercury	124.395	Cale Yarborough	Chevy	151.469
1303	20	8/3/80	Talladega, AL	2.66	P	500.08	Neil Bonnett	Mercury	166.894	Buddy Baker	Olds	198.545
1304	21	8/17/80	Brooklyn, MI	2.0	P	400	Cale Yarborough	Chevy	145.352	Buddy Baker	Chevy	162.693
1305	22	8/23/80	Bristol, TN	0.533	P	266.5	Cale Yarborough	Chevy	86.973	Cale Yarborough	Chevy	110.990
1306	23	9/1/80	Darlington, SC	1.366	P	501.322	Terry Labonte	Chevy	115.210	Darrell Waltrip	Chevy	153.838
1307	24	9/7/80	Richmond, VA	0.542	P	216.8	Bobby Allison	Ford	79.722	Cale Yarborough	Chevy	93.466
1308	25	9/14/80	Dover, DE	1.0	P	500	Darrell Waltrip	Chevy	116.024	Cale Yarborough	Chevy	137.583
1309	26	9/21/80	N. Wilkesboro, NC	0.625	P	250	Bobby Allison	Ford	75.510	Cale Yarborough	Chevy	111.996
1310	27	9/28/80	Martinsville, VA	0.525	P	262.5	Dale Earnhardt	Chevy	69.654	Buddy Baker	Chevy	88.500
1311	28	10/5/80	Charlotte, NC	1.5	P	501	Dale Earnhardt	Chevy	135.243	Buddy Baker	Buick	165.634
1312	29	10/19/80	Rockingham, NC	1.017	P	500	Cale Yarborough	Chevy	114.159	Donnie Allison	Chevy	142.648
1313	30	11/2/80	Atlanta, GA	1.522	P	499.216	Cale Yarborough	Chevy	131.190	Bobby Allison	Mercury	165.620
1314	31	11/15/80	Ontario, CA	2.5	P	500	Benny Parsons	Chevy	129.441	Cale Yarborough	Chevy	155.499

Cum. No.	Yr. No.	Date	Site	Track Length	Surface	Miles	Race Winner	Make	Speed	Pole Winner	Make	Pole Speed
1981
1315	1	1/11/81	Riverside, CA	2.62	P	311.78	Bobby Allison	Chevy	95.263	Darrell Waltrip	Chevy	114.711
1316	2	2/15/81	Daytona Beach, FL	2.5	P	500	Richard Petty	Buick	169.651	Bobby Allison	Pontiac	194.624
1317	3	2/22/81	Richmond, VA	0.542	P	216.8	Darrell Waltrip	Buick	76.570	Morgan Shepherd	Pontiac	92.821
1318	4	3/1/81	Rockingham, NC	1.017	P	500.364	Darrell Waltrip	Buick	114.594	Cale Yarborough	Buick	140.448
1319	5	3/15/81	Atlanta, GA	1.522	P	499.216	Cale Yarborough	Buick	133.619	Terry Labonte	Buick	162.940
1320	6	3/29/81	Bristol, TN	0.533	P	266.5	Darrell Waltrip	Buick	85.530	Darrell Waltrip	Buick	112.125
1321	7	4/5/81	N. Wilkesboro, NC	0.625	P	250	Richard Petty	Buick	85.381	Dave Marcis	Chevy	114.647
1322	8	4/12/81	Darlington, SC	1.366	P	501.322	Darrell Waltrip	Buick	126.703	Bill Elliott	Ford	153.896
1323	9	4/26/81	Martinsville, VA	0.525	P	262.5	Morgan Shepherd	Pontiac	75.019	Ricky Rudd	Buick	89.056
1324	10	5/3/81	Talladega, AL	2.66	P	500.08	Bobby Allison	Buick	149.376	Bobby Allison	Buick	195.864
1325	11	5/9/81	Nashville, TN	0.596	P	250.32	Benny Parsons	Ford	89.756	Ricky Rudd	Buick	104.409
1326	12	5/17/81	Dover, DE	1.0	P	500	Jody Ridley	Ford	116.595	David Pearson	Olds	138.475
1327	13	5/24/81	Charlotte, NC	1.5	P	600	Bobby Allison	Buick	129.326	Neil Bonnett	Ford	158.115
1328	14	6/7/81	College Station, TX	2.0	P	400	Benny Parsons	Ford	132.475	Terry Labonte	Buick	167.543
1329	15	6/17/81	Riverside, CA	2.62	P	248.9	Darrell Waltrip	Buick	93.957	Darrell Waltrip	Buick	114.378
1330	16	6/21/81	Brooklyn, MI	2.0	P	400	Bobby Allison	Buick	130.589	Darrell Waltrip	Buick	160.471
1331	17	7/4/81	Daytona Beach, FL	2.5	P	400	Cale Yarborough	Buick	142.588	Cale Yarborough	Buick	192.852
1332	18	7/11/81	Nashville, TN	0.596	P	250.32	Darrell Waltrip	Buick	90.052	Mark Martin	Pontiac	104.353
1333	19	7/26/81	Pocono, PA	2.5	P	500	Darrell Waltrip	Buick	119.111	Darrell Waltrip	Buick	150.148
1334	20	8/2/81	Talladega, AL	2.66	P	500.08	Ron Bouchard	Buick	156.737	Harry Gant	Buick	195.897
1335	21	8/16/81	Brooklyn, MI	2.0	P	400	Richard Petty	Buick	123.457	Ron Bouchard	Buick	161.501
1336	22	8/22/81	Bristol, TN	0.533	P	266.5	Darrell Waltrip	Buick	84.723	Darrell Waltrip	Buick	110.818
1337	23	9/7/81	Darlington, SC	1.366	P	501.322	Neil Bonnett	Ford	126.446	Harry Gant	Pontiac	152.693
1338	24	9/13/81	Richmond, VA	0.542	P	216.8	Benny Parsons	Ford	69.998	Mark Martin	Pontiac	93.435
1339	25	9/20/81	Dover, DE	1.0	P	500	Neil Bonnett	Ford	119.561	Ricky Rudd	Chevy	136.757
1340	26	9/27/81	Martinsville, VA	0.525	P	262.5	Darrell Waltrip	Buick	70.089	Darrell Waltrip	Buick	89.014
1341	27	10/4/81	N. Wilkesboro, NC	0.625	P	250	Darrell Waltrip	Buick	93.091	Darrell Waltrip	Buick	113.065
1342	28	10/11/81	Charlotte, NC	1.5	P	501	Darrell Waltrip	Buick	117.483	Darrell Waltrip	Buick	162.744
1343	29	1/1/81	Rockingham, NC	1.017	P	500.364	Darrell Waltrip	Buick	107.399	Darrell Waltrip	Buick	136.164
1344	30	11/8/81	Atlanta, GA	1.522	P	499.216	Neil Bonnett	Ford	130.391	Harry Gant	Pontiac	163.266
1345	31	11/22/81	Riverside, CA	2.62	P	311.78	Bobby Allison	Buick	95.288	Darrell Waltrip	Buick	114.981
1982
1346	1	2/14/82	Daytona Beach, FL	2.5	P	500	Bobby Allison	Buick	153.991	Benny Parsons	Pontiac	196.317
1347	2	2/21/82	Richmond, VA	0.533	P	135.5	Dave Marcis	Chevy	72.914	Darrell Waltrip	Buick	93.256
1348	3	3/14/82	Bristol, TN	0.533	P	266.5	Darrell Waltrip	Buick	94.025	Darrell Waltrip	Buick	111.068
1349	4	3/21/82	Atlanta, GA	1.522	P	436.814	Darrell Waltrip	Buick	124.824	Dale Earnhardt	Ford	163.774
1350	5	3/28/82	Rockingham, NC	1.017	P	500.364	Cale Yarborough	Buick	108.992	Benny Parsons	Pontiac	141.577
1351	6	4/4/82	Darlington, SC	1.366	P	501.322	Dale Earnhardt	Ford	123.554	Buddy Baker	Buick	153.979
1352	7	4/18/82	N. Wilkesboro, NC	0.625	P	250	Darrell Waltrip	Buick	97.646	Darrell Waltrip	Buick	114.801
1353	8	4/25/82	Martinsville, VA	0.525	P	262.5	Harry Gant	Buick	75.073	Terry Labonte	Chevy	89.988
1354	9	5/2/82	Talladega, AL	2.66	P	500.08	Darrell Waltrip	Buick	156.697	Benny Parsons	Pontiac	200.176
1355	10	5/8/82	Nashville, TN	0.596	P	250.32	Darrell Waltrip	Buick	83.502	Darrell Waltrip	Buick	102.773
1356	11	5/16/82	Dover, DE	1.0	P	500	Bobby Allison	Chevy	120.136	Darrell Waltrip	Buick	139.308
1357	12	5/30/82	Charlotte, NC	1.5	P	600	Neil Bonnett	Ford	130.058	David Pearson	Buick	162.511
1358	13	6/6/82	Pocono, PA	2.5	P	500	Bobby Allison	Buick	113.579	No Time Trials	NTT	NTT
1359	14	6/13/82	Riverside, CA	2.62	P	248.9	Tim Richmond	Buick	103.816	Terry Labonte	Buick	114.352
1360	15	6/20/82	Brooklyn, MI	2.0	P	400	Cale Yarborough	Buick	118.101	Ron Bouchard	Buick	162.404
1361	16	7/4/82	Daytona Beach, FL	2.5	P	400	Bobby Allison	Buick	163.099	Geoff Bodine	Pontiac	194.721
1362	17	7/10/82	Nashville, TN	0.596	P	250.32	Darrell Waltrip	Buick	86.524	Morgan Shepherd	Pontiac	103.959
1363	18	7/25/82	Pocono, PA	2.5	P	500	Bobby Allison	Buick	115.496	Cale Yarborough	Buick	150.764
1364	19	8/1/82	Talladega, AL	2.66	P	500.08	Darrell Waltrip	Buick	168.157	Geoff Bodine	Pontiac	199.400
1365	20	8/22/82	Brooklyn, MI	2.0	P	400	Bobby Allison	Buick	136.454	Bill Elliott	Ford	162.173
1366	21	8/28/82	Bristol, TN	0.533	P	266.5	Darrell Waltrip	Buick	94.318	Tim Richmond	Buick	112.507
1367	22	9/6/82	Darlington, SC	1.366	P	501.322	Cale Yarborough	Buick	115.224	David Pearson	Buick	155.739
1368	23	9/12/82	Richmond, VA	0.542	P	216.8	Bobby Allison	Chevy	82.800	Bobby Allison	Chevy	93.435
1369	24	9/19/82	Dover, DE	1.0	P	500	Darrell Waltrip	Buick	107.642	Ricky Rudd	Pontiac	139.384
1370	25	10/3/82	N. Wilkesboro, NC	0.625	P	250	Darrell Waltrip	Buick	98.071	Darrell Waltrip	Buick	113.860
1371	26	10/10/82	Charlotte, NC	1.5	P	501	Harry Gant	Buick	137.208	Harry Gant	Buick	164.694
1372	27	10/17/82	Martinsville, VA	0.525	P	262.5	Darrell Waltrip	Buick	71.315	Ricky Rudd	Pontiac	89.132
1373	28	10/31/82	Rockingham, NC	1.017	P	500.364	Darrell Waltrip	Buick	115.122	Cale Yarborough	Buick	143.220

Cum. No.	Yr. No.	Date	Site	Track Length	Surface	Miles	Race Winner	Make	Speed	Pole Winner	Make	Pole Speed
1374	29	11/7/82	Atlanta, GA	1.522	P	499.216	Bobby Allison	Buick	130.884	Morgan Shepherd	Buick	166.779
1375	30	11/21/82	Riverside, CA	2.62	P	311.78	Tim Richmond	Buick	99.823	Darrell Waltrip	Buick	122.021

1983

Cum. No.	Yr. No.	Date	Site	Track Length	Surface	Miles	Race Winner	Make	Speed	Pole Winner	Make	Pole Speed
1376	1	2/20/83	Daytona Beach, FL	2.5	P	500	Cale Yarborough	Pontiac	155.979	Ricky Rudd	Chevy	198.864
1377	2	2/27/83	Richmond, VA	0.542	P	216.8	Bobby Allison	Chevy	79.584	Ricky Rudd	Chevy	93.439
1378	3	3/13/83	Rockingham, NC	1.017	P	500.364	Richard Petty	Pontiac	113.055	Ricky Rudd	Chevy	143.413
1379	4	3/27/83	Atlanta, GA	1.522	P	499.216	Cale Yarborough	Chevy	124.055	Geoff Bodine	Pontiac	167.703
1380	5	4/10/83	Darlington, SC	1.366	P	501.322	Harry Gant	Buick	130.406	Tim Richmond	Pontiac	157.818
1381	6	4/17/83	N. Wilkesboro, NC	0.625	P	250	Darrell Waltrip	Chevy	91.436	Neil Bonnett	Chevy	112.332
1382	7	4/24/83	Martinsville, VA	0.525	P	262.5	Darrell Waltrip	Chevy	66.460	Ricky Rudd	Chevy	89.910
1383	8	5/1/83	Talladega, AL	2.66	P	500.08	Richard Petty	Pontiac	153.936	Cale Yarborough	Chevy	202.650
1384	9	5/7/83	Nashville, TN	0.596	P	250.32	Darrell Waltrip	Chevy	70.717	Darrell Waltrip	Chevy	103.119
1385	10	5/15/83	Dover, DE	1.0	P	500	Bobby Allison	Buick	114.847	Joe Ruttman	Buick	139.616
1386	11	5/21/83	Bristol, TN	0.533	P	266.5	Darrell Waltrip	Chevy	93.445	Neil Bonnett	Chevy	110.409
1387	12	5/29/83	Charlotte, NC	1.5	P	600	Neil Bonnett	Chevy	140.707	Buddy Baker	Ford	162.841
1388	13	6/5/83	Riverside, CA	2.62	P	248.9	Ricky Rudd	Chevy	88.063	Darrell Waltrip	Chevy	116.421
1389	14	6/12/83	Pocono, PA	2.5	P	500	Bobby Allison	Buick	128.636	Darrell Waltrip	Chevy	152.315
1390	15	6/19/83	Brooklyn, MI	2.0	P	400	Cale Yarborough	Chevy	138.728	Terry Labonte	Chevy	161.965
1391	16	7/4/83	Daytona Beach, FL	2.5	P	400	Buddy Baker	Ford	167.442	Cale Yarborough	Chevy	196.635
1392	17	7/16/83	Nashville, TN	0.596	P	250.32	Dale Earnhardt	Ford	85.726	Ron Bouchard	Buick	103.020
1393	18	7/24/83	Pocono, PA	2.5	P	500	Tim Richmond	Pontiac	114.818	Tim Richmond	Pontiac	151.981
1394	19	7/31/83	Talladega, AL	2.66	P	500.08	Dale Earnhardt	Ford	170.611	Cale Yarborough	Chevy	201.981
1395	20	8/21/83	Brooklyn, MI	2.0	P	400	Cale Yarborough	Chevy	147.511	Terry Labonte	Chevy	162.437
1396	21	8/27/83	Bristol, TN	0.533	P	223.327	Darrell Waltrip	Chevy	89.430	Joe Ruttman	Pontiac	111.437
1397	22	9/5/83	Darlington, SC	1.366	P	501.322	Bobby Allison	Buick	123.343	Neil Bonnett	Chevy	157.187
1398	23	9/11/83	Richmond, VA	0.542	P	216.8	Bobby Allison	Buick	79.381	Darrell Waltrip	Buick	96.069
1399	24	9/18/83	Dover, DE	1.0	P	500	Bobby Allison	Buick	116.077	Terry Labonte	Chevy	139.573
1400	25	9/25/83	Martinsville, VA	0.525	P	262.5	Ricky Rudd	Chevy	76.134	Darrell Waltrip	Chevy	89.342
1401	26	10/2/83	N. Wilkesboro, NC	0.625	P	250	Darrell Waltrip	Chevy	100.716	Darrell Waltrip	Chevy	114.539
1402	27	10/9/83	Charlotte, NC	1.5	P	501	Richard Petty	Pontiac	139.998	Tim Richmond	Pontiac	163.073
1403	28	10/30/83	Rockingham, NC	1.017	P	500.364	Terry Labonte	Chevy	119.324	Neil Bonnett	Chevy	143.876
1404	29	11/6/83	Atlanta, GA	1.522	P	499.216	Neil Bonnett	Chevy	137.643	Tim Richmond	Pontiac	168.151
1405	30	11/20/83	Riverside, CA	2.62	P	311.78	Bill Elliott	Ford	95.859	Darrell Waltrip	Chevy	116.782

1984

Cum. No.	Yr. No.	Date	Site	Track Length	Surface	Miles	Race Winner	Make	Speed	Pole Winner	Make	Pole Speed
1406	1	2/19/84	Daytona Beach, FL	2.5	P	500	Cale Yarborough	Chevy	150.994	Cale Yarborough	Chevy	102.848
1407	2	2/26/84	Richmond, VA	0.542	P	216.8	Ricky Rudd	Ford	76.736	Darrell Waltrip	Chevy	95.817
1408	3	3/4/84	Rockingham, NC	1.017	P	500.364	Bobby Allison	Buick	122.931	Harry Gant	Chevy	145.084
1409	4	3/18/84	Atlanta, GA	1.522	P	499.216	Benny Parsons	Chevy	144.945	Buddy Baker	Ford	166.642
1410	5	4/1/84	Bristol, TN	0.533	P	266.5	Darrell Waltrip	Chevy	93.967	Ricky Rudd	Ford	111.390
1411	6	4/8/84	N. Wilkesboro, NC	0.625	P	250	Tim Richmond	Pontiac	97.830	Ricky Rudd	Ford	113.487
1412	7	4/15/84	Darlington, SC	1.366	P	501.322	Darrell Waltrip	Chevy	119.925	Benny Parsons	Chevy	156.328
1413	8	4/29/84	Martinsville, VA	0.525	P	262.5	Geoff Bodine	Chevy	73.264	Joe Ruttman	Chevy	89.426
1414	9	5/6/84	Talladega, AL	2.66	P	500.08	Cale Yarborough	Chevy	172.988	Cale Yarborough	Chevy	202.692
1415	10	5/12/84	Nashville, TN	0.596	P	250.32	Darrell Waltrip	Chevy	85.702	Darrell Waltrip	Chevy	104.439
1416	11	5/20/84	Dover, DE	1.0	P	500	Richard Petty	Pontiac	118.717	Ricky Rudd	Ford	140.807
1417	12	5/27/84	Charlotte, NC	1.5	P	600	Bobby Allison	Buick	129.233	Harry Gant	Chevy	162.496
1418	13	6/3/84	Riverside, CA	2.62	P	248.9	Terry Labonte	Chevy	102.910	Terry Labonte	Chevy	115.921
1419	14	6/10/84	Pocono, PA	2.5	P	500	Cale Yarborough	Chevy	138.164	David Pearson	Chevy	150.921
1420	15	6/17/84	Brooklyn, MI	2.0	P	400	Bill Elliott	Ford	134.705	Bill Elliott	Ford	164.339
1421	16	7/4/84	Daytona Beach, FL	2.5	P	400	Richard Petty	Pontiac	171.204	Cale Yarborough	Chevy	199.743
1422	17	7/14/84	Nashville, TN	0.596	P	250.32	Geoff Bodine	Chevy	80.908	Ricky Rudd	Ford	104.120
1423	18	7/22/84	Pocono, PA	2.5	P	500	Harry Gant	Chevy	121.351	Bill Elliott	Ford	152.184
1424	19	7/29/84	Talladega, AL	2.66	P	500.08	Dale Earnhardt	Chevy	155.485	Cale Yarborough	Chevy	202.474
1425	20	8/12/84	Brooklyn, MI	2.0	P	400	Darrell Waltrip	Chevy	153.863	Bill Elliott	Ford	165.217
1426	21	8/25/84	Bristol, TN	0.533	P	266.5	Terry Labonte	Chevy	85.365	Geoff Bodine	Chevy	111.734
1427	22	9/2/84	Darlington, SC	1.366	P	501.322	Harry Gant	Chevy	128.270	Harry Gant	Chevy	155.502
1428	23	9/9/84	Richmond, VA	0.542	P	216.8	Darrell Waltrip	Chevy	74.780	Darrell Waltrip	Chevy	92.518
1429	24	9/16/84	Dover, DE	1.0	P	500	Harry Gant	Chevy	111.856	No Time Trials	NTT	NTT
1430	25	9/23/84	Martinsville, VA	0.525	P	262.5	Darrell Waltrip	Chevy	75.532	Geoff Bodine	Chevy	89.523
1431	26	10/7/84	Charlotte, NC	1.5	P	501	Bill Elliott	Ford	146.861	Benny Parsons	Chevy	165.579

Cum. No.	Yr. No.	Date	Site	Track Length	Surface	Miles	Race Winner	Make	Speed	Pole Winner	Make	Pole Speed
1432	27	10/14/84	N. Wilkesboro, NC	0.625	P	250	Darrell Waltrip	Chevy	90.525	Darrell Waltrip	Chevy	113.304
1433	28	10/21/84	Rockingham, NC	1.017	P	500.364	Bill Elliott	Ford	112.617	Geoff Bodine	Chevy	144.415
1434	29	11/11/84	Atlanta, GA	1.522	P	499.216	Dale Earnhardt	Chevy	134.610	Bill Elliott	Ford	170.198
1435	30	11/18/84	Riverside, CA	2.62	P	311.78	Geoff Bodine	Chevy	98.448	Terry Labonte	Chevy	116.714

1985

Cum. No.	Yr. No.	Date	Site	Track Length	Surface	Miles	Race Winner	Make	Speed	Pole Winner	Make	Pole Speed
1436	1	2/17/85	Daytona Beach, FL	2.5	P	500	Bill Elliott	Ford	172.265	Bill Elliott	Ford	205.114
1437	2	2/24/85	Richmond, VA	0.542	P	216.8	Dale Earnhardt	Chevy	67.945	Darrell Waltrip	Chevy	95.218
1438	3	3/3/85	Rockingham, NC	1.017	P	500.364	Neil Bonnett	Chevy	114.953	Terry Labonte	Chevy	145.067
1439	4	3/17/85	Atlanta, GA	1.522	P	499.216	Bill Elliott	Ford	140.273	Neil Bonnett	Chevy	170.278
1440	5	4/6/85	Bristol, TN	0.533	P	266.5	Dale Earnhardt	Chevy	81.790	Harry Gant	Chevy	112.778
1441	6	4/14/85	Darlington, SC	1.366	P	501.322	Bill Elliott	Ford	126.295	Bill Elliott	Ford	157.454
1442	7	4/21/85	N. Wilkesboro, NC	0.625	P	250	Neil Bonnett	Chevy	93.818	Darrell Waltrip	Chevy	111.899
1443	8	4/28/85	Martinsville, VA	0.525	P	262.5	Harry Gant	Chevy	73.022	Darrell Waltrip	Chevy	90.279
1444	9	5/5/85	Talladega, AL	2.66	P	500.08	Bill Elliott	Ford	186.288	Bill Elliott	Ford	209.398
1445	10	5/19/85	Dover, DE	1.0	P	500	Bill Elliott	Ford	123.094	Terry Labonte	Chevy	138.106
1446	11	5/26/85	Charlotte, NC	1.5	P	600	Darrell Waltrip	Chevy	141.807	Bill Elliott	Ford	164.703
1447	12	6/2/85	Riverside, CA	2.62	P	248.9	Terry Labonte	Chevy	104.276	Darrell Waltrip	Chevy	115.533
1448	13	6/9/85	Pocono, PA	2.5	P	500	Bill Elliott	Ford	138.974	Bill Elliott	Ford	152.563
1449	14	6/15/85	Brooklyn, MI	2.0	P	400	Bill Elliott	Ford	144.724	No Time Trials	NTT	NTT
1450	15	7/4/85	Daytona Beach, FL	2.5	P	400	Greg Sacks	Chevy	158.730	Bill Elliott	Ford	201.523
1451	16	7/21/85	Pocono, PA	2.5	P	500	Bill Elliott	Ford	134.008	Bill Elliott	Ford	151.973
1452	17	7/28/85	Talladega, AL	2.66	P	500.08	Cale Yarborough	Ford	148.772	Bill Elliott	Ford	107.578
1453	18	8/11/85	Brooklyn, MI	2.0	P	400	Bill Elliott	Ford	137.430	Bill Elliott	Ford	165.479
1454	19	8/24/85	Bristol, TN	0.533	P	266.5	Dale Earnhardt	Chevy	82.388	Dale Earnhardt	Chevy	113.586
1455	20	9/1/85	Darlington, SC	1.366	P	501.322	Bill Elliott	Ford	121.254	Bill Elliott	Ford	156.641
1456	21	9/8/85	Richmond, VA	0.542	P	216.8	Darrell Waltrip	Chevy	72.508	Geoff Bodine	Chevy	94.535
1457	22	9/15/85	Dover, DE	1.0	P	500	Harry Gant	Chevy	120.538	Bill Elliott	Ford	141.543
1458	23	9/22/85	Martinsville, VA	0.525	P	262.5	Dale Earnhardt	Chevy	70.694	Geoff Bodine	Chevy	90.521
1459	24	9/29/85	N. Wilkesboro, NC	0.625	P	250	Harry Gant	Chevy	95.077	Geoff Bodine	Chevy	113.967
1460	25	10/6/85	Charlotte, NC	1.5	P	501	Cale Yarborough	Ford	136.761	Harry Gant	Chevy	166.139
1461	26	10/25/85	Rockingham, NC	1.017	P	500.364	Darrell Waltrip	Chevy	118.344	Terry Labonte	Chevy	141.841
1462	27	11/3/85	Atlanta, GA	1.522	P	499.22	Bill Elliott	Ford	139.597	Harry Gant	Chevy	167.940
1463	28	11/17/85	Riverside, CA	2.62	P	311.78	Ricky Rudd	Ford	105.065	Terry Labonte	Chevy	116.938

1986

Cum. No.	Yr. No.	Date	Site	Track Length	Surface	Miles	Race Winner	Make	Speed	Pole Winner	Make	Pole Speed
1464	1	2/16/86	Daytona Beach, FL	2.5	P	500	Geoff Bodine	Chevy	148.124	Bill Elliott	Ford	205.039
1465	2	2/23/86	Richmond, VA	0.542	P	216.8	Kyle Petty	Ford	71.078	No Time Trials	NTT	NTT
1466	3	3/2/86	Rockingham, NC	1.017	P	500.364	Terry Labonte	Olds	120.488	Terry Labonte	Olds	146.348
1467	4	3/16/86	Atlanta, GA	1.522	P	499.216	Morgan Shepherd	Buick	132.126	Dale Earnhardt	Chevy	170.713
1468	5	4/6/86	Bristol, TN	0.533	P	266.5	Rusty Wallace	Pontiac	89.747	Geoff Bodine	Chevy	114.850
1469	6	4/13/86	Darlington, SC	1.366	P	501.322	Dale Earnhardt	Chevy	128.994	Geoff Bodine	Chevy	159.197
1470	7	4/20/86	N. Wilkesboro, NC	0.625	P	250	Dale Earnhardt	Chevy	86.408	Geoff Bodine	Chevy	112.419
1471	8	4/27/86	Martinsville, VA	0.525	P	262.5	Ricky Rudd	Ford	76.882	Tim Richmond	Chevy	90.716
1472	9	5/4/86	Talladega, AL	2.66	P	500.08	Bobby Allison	Buick	157.698	Bill Elliott	Ford	212.229
1473	10	5/18/86	Dover, DE	1.0	P	500	Geoff Bodine	Chevy	115.009	Ricky Rudd	Ford	138.217
1474	11	5/15/86	Charlotte, NC	1.5	P	600	Dale Earnhardt	Chevy	140.406	Geoff Bodine	Chevy	164.511
1475	12	6/1/86	Riverside, CA	2.62	P	248.9	Darrell Waltrip	Chevy	105.083	Darrell Waltrip	Chevy	117.006
1476	13	6/8/86	Pocono, PA	2.5	P	500	Tim Richmond	Chevy	113.279	Geoff Bodine	Chevy	153.625
1477	14	6/15/86	Brooklyn, MI	2.0	P	400	Bill Elliott	Ford	138.581	Tim Richmond	Chevy	172.031
1478	15	7/4/86	Daytona Beach, FL	2.5	P	400	Tim Richmond	Chevy	131.916	Cale Yarborough	Ford	203.519
1479	16	7/20/86	Pocono, PA	2.5	P	375	Tim Richmond	Chevy	124.218	Harry Gant	Chevy	154.392
1480	17	7/27/86	Talladega, AL	2.66	P	500.08	Bobby Hillin Jr	Buick	151.552	Bill Elliott	Ford	209.005
1481	18	8/10/86	Watkins Glen, NY	2.438	P	218.52	Tim Richmond	Chevy	90.463	Tim Richmond	Chevy	117.563
1482	19	8/17/86	Brooklyn, MI	2.0	P	400	Bill Elliott	Ford	135.376	Benny Parsons	Olds	171.924
1483	20	8/23/86	Bristol, TN	0.533	P	266.5	Darrell Waltrip	Chevy	86.934	Geoff Bodine	Chevy	114.665
1484	21	8/31/86	Darlington, SC	1.366	P	501.322	Tim Richmond	Chevy	121.068	Tim Richmond	Chevy	158.489
1485	22	9/7/86	Richmond, VA	0.542	P	216.8	Tim Richmond	Chevy	70.161	Harry Gant	Chevy	93.966
1486	23	9/14/86	Dover, DE	1.0	P	500	Ricky Rudd	Ford	114.329	Geoff Bodine	Chevy	146.205
1487	24	9/21/86	Martinsville, VA	0.525	P	262.5	Rusty Wallace	Pontiac	73.191	Geoff Bodine	Chevy	90.599
1488	25	9/28/86	N. Wilkesboro, NC	0.625	P	250	Darrell Waltrip	Chevy	95.612	Tim Richmond	Chevy	113.447
1489	26	10/3/86	Charlotte, NC	1.5	P	501	Dale Earnhardt	Chevy	132.403	Tim Richmond	Chevy	167.078

Cum. No.	Yr. No.	Date	Site	Track Length	Surface	Miles	Race Winner	Make	Speed	Pole Winner	Make	Pole Speed
1490	27	10/10/86	Rockingham, NC	1.017	P	500.364	Neil Bonnett	Chevy	126.381	Tim Richmond	Chevy	146.948
1491	28	11/2/86	Atlanta, GA	1.522	P	499.216	Dale Earnhardt	Chevy	152.523	Bill Elliott	Ford	172.905
1492	29	11/16/86	Riverside, CA	2.62	P	311.78	Tim Richmond	Chevy	101.246	Tim Richmond	Chevy	118.247

1987

Cum. No.	Yr. No.	Date	Site	Track Length	Surface	Miles	Race Winner	Make	Speed	Pole Winner	Make	Pole Speed
1493	1	2/15/87	Daytona Beach, FL	2.5	P	500	Bill Elliott	Ford	176.263	Bill Elliott	Ford	210.364
1494	2	3/1/87	Rockingham, NC	1.017	P	500.364	Dale Earnhardt	Chevy	117.556	Davey Allison	Ford	146.989
1495	3	3/8/87	Richmond, VA	0.542	P	216.80	Dale Earnhardt	Chevy	81.420	Alan Kulwicki	Ford	95.153
1496	4	3/15/87	Atlanta, GA	1.522	P	499.216	Ricky Rudd	Ford	133.689	Dale Earnhardt	Chevy	175.497
1497	5	3/29/87	Darlington, SC	1.366	P	501.322	Dale Earnhardt	Chevy	122.540	Ken Schrader	Ford	158.387
1498	6	4/5/87	N. Wilkesboro, NC	0.625	P	250	Dale Earnhardt	Chevy	94.103	Bill Elliott	Ford	116.003
1499	7	4/12/87	Bristol, TN	0.533	P	266.5	Dale Earnhardt	Chevy	75.621	Harry Gant	Chevy	115.674
1500	8	4/26/87	Martinsville, VA	0.525	P	262.5	Dale Earnhardt	Chevy	72.808	Morgan Shepherd	Buick	92.355
1501	9	5/3/87	Talladega, AL	2.66	P	473.48	Davey Allison	Ford	154.228	Bill Elliott	Ford	212.809
1502	10	5/24/87	Charlotte, NC	1.5	P	600	Kyle Petty	Ford	131.483	Bill Elliott	Ford	170.901
1503	11	5/31/87	Dover, DE	1.0	P	500	Davey Allison	Ford	112.958	Bill Elliott	Ford	145.056
1504	12	6/14/87	Pocono, PA	2.5	P	500	Tim Richmond	Chevy	122.166	Terry Labonte	Chevy	155.502
1505	13	6/21/87	Riverside, CA	2.62	P	248.9	Tim Richmond	Chevy	102.183	Terry Labonte	Chevy	117.541
1506	14	6/28/87	Brooklyn, MI	2.0	P	400	Dale Earnhardt	Chevy	148.454	Rusty Wallace	Pontiac	170.746
1507	15	7/4/87	Daytona Beach, FL	2.5	P	400	Bobby Allison	Buick	161.074	Davey Allison	Ford	198.085
1508	16	7/9/87	Pocono, PA	2.5	P	500	Dale Earnhardt	Chevy	121.745	Tim Richmond	Chevy	155.979
1509	17	7/16/87	Talladega, AL	2.66	P	500.08	Bill Elliott	Ford	171.293	Bill Elliott	Ford	203.827
1510	18	8/10/87	Watkins Glen, NY	2.438	P	218.52	Rusty Wallace	Pontiac	90.682	Terry Labonte	Chevy	117.956
1511	19	8/16/87	Brooklyn, MI	2.0	P	400	Bill Elliott	Ford	138.648	Davey Allison	Ford	170.705
1512	20	8/22/87	Bristol, TN	0.533	P	266.5	Dale Earnhardt	Chevy	90.373	Terry Labonte	Chevy	115.758
1513	21	9/6/87	Darlington, SC	1.366	P	275.9	Dale Earnhardt	Chevy	115.520	Davey Allison	Ford	157.232
1514	22	9/13/87	Richmond, VA	0.542	P	216.8	Dale Earnhardt	Chevy	67.074	Alan Kulwicki	Ford	94.052
1515	23	9/20/87	Dover, DE	1.0	P	500	Ricky Rudd	Ford	124.706	Alan Kulwicki	Ford	145.826
1516	24	9/27/87	Martinsville, VA	0.525	P	262.5	Darrell Waltrip	Chevy	76.410	Geoff Bodine	Chevy	91.218
1517	25	10/4/87	N. Wilkesboro, NC	0.625	P	250	Terry Labonte	Chevy	96.051	Bill Elliott	Ford	115.196
1518	26	10/11/87	Charlotte, NC	1.5	P	501	Bill Elliott	Ford	128.443	Bobby Allison	Buick	145.609
1519	27	10/25/87	Rockingham, NC	1.017	P	500.364	Bill Elliott	Ford	118.258	Davey Allison	Ford	145.609
1520	28	11/8/87	Riverside, CA	2.62	P	311.78	Rusty Wallace	Pontiac	98.035	Geoff Bodine	Chevy	117.934
1521	29	11/22/87	Atlanta, GA	1.522	P	499.216	Bill Elliott	Ford	139.047	Bill Elliott	Ford	174.341

1988

Cum. No.	Yr. No.	Date	Site	Track Length	Surface	Miles	Race Winner	Make	Speed	Pole Winner	Make	Pole Speed
1522	1	2/14/88	Daytona Beach, FL	2.5	P	500	Bobby Allison	Buick	137.531	Ken Schrader	Chevy	193.823
1523	2	2/21/88	Richmond, VA	0.542	P	216.8	Neil Bonnett	Pontiac	66.401	Morgan Shepherd	Buick	96.645
1524	3	3/6/88	Rockingham, NC	1.017	P	500.364	Neil Bonnett	Pontiac	120.159	Bill Elliott	Ford	146.612
1525	4	3/20/88	Atlanta, GA	1.522	P	499.216	Dale Earnhardt	Chevy	137.588	Geoff Bodine	Chevy	176.623
1526	5	3/27/88	Darlington, SC	1.366	P	501.322	Lake Speed	Olds	131.284	Ken Schrader	Chevy	162.657
1527	6	4/10/88	Bristol, TN	0.533	P	266.5	Bill Elliott	Ford	83.115	Rick Wilson	Olds	117.522
1528	7	4/17/88	N. Wilkesboro, NC	0.625	P	250	Terry Labonte	Chevy	99.075	Terry Labonte	Chevy	117.322
1529	8	4/24/88	Martinsville, VA	0.525	P	263	Dale Earnhardt	Chevy	74.740	Ricky Rudd	Buick	91.328
1530	9	5/1/88	Talladega, AL	2.66	P	500.08	Phil Parsons	Olds	156.547	Davey Allison	Ford	198.969
1531	10	5/29/88	Charlotte, NC	1.5	P	600	Darrell Waltrip	Chevy	124.460	Davey Allison	Ford	173.594
1532	11	6/5/88	Dover, DE	1.0	P	500	Bill Elliott	Ford	118.726	Alan Kulwicki	Ford	146.681
1533	12	6/12/88	Riverside, CA	2.62	P	248.9	Rusty Wallace	Pontiac	88.341	Ricky Rudd	Buick	118.484
1534	13	6/19/88	Pocono, PA	2.5	P	500	Geoff Bodine	Chevy	126.147	Alan Kulwicki	Ford	158.806
1535	14	6/26/88	Brooklyn, MI	2.0	P	400	Rusty Wallace	Pontiac	153.551	Bill Elliott	Ford	172.687
1536	15	7/2/88	Daytona Beach, FL	2.5	P	400	Bill Elliott	Ford	163.302	Darrell Waltrip	Chevy	193.819
1537	16	7/24/88	Pocono, PA	2.5	P	500	Bill Elliott	Ford	122.866	Morgan Shepherd	Pontiac	157.153
1538	17	7/31/88	Talladega, AL	2.66	P	500.08	Ken Schrader	Chevy	154.505	Darrell Waltrip	Chevy	196.274
1539	18	8/14/88	Watkins Glen, NY	2.428	P	218.52	Ricky Rudd	Buick	74.096	Geoff Bodine	Chevy	120.501
1540	19	8/21/88	Brooklyn, MI	2.0	P	400	Davey Allison	Ford	156.863	Bill Elliott	Ford	174.940
1541	20	8/27/88	Bristol, TN	0.533	P	266.5	Dale Earnhardt	Chevy	78.755	Alan Kulwicki	Ford	116.893
1542	21	9/4/88	Darlington, SC	1.366	P	501.322	Bill Elliott	Ford	128.297	Bill Elliott	Ford	160.827
1543	22	9/11/88	Richmond, VA	0.75	P	300	Davey Allison	Ford	95.770	Davey Allison	Ford	122.850
1544	23	9/18/88	Dover, DE	1.0	P	500	Bill Elliott	Ford	109.349	Mark Martin	Ford	148.075
1545	24	9/25/88	Martinsville, VA	0.525	P	263	Darrell Waltrip	Chevy	74.988	Rusty Wallace	Pontiac	91.372
1546	25	10/9/88	Charlotte, NC	1.5	P	501	Rusty Wallace	Pontiac	130.677	Alan Kulwicki	Ford	175.896
1547	26	10/16/88	N. Wilkesboro, NC	0.625	P	250	Rusty Wallace	Pontiac	94.192	Bill Elliott	Ford	116.901

Cum. No.	Yr. No.	Date	Site	Track Length	Surface	Miles	Race Winner	Make	Speed	Pole Winner	Make	Pole Speed
1548	27	10/23/88	Rockingham, NC	1.017	P	500.364	Rusty Wallace	Pontiac	111.557	Bill Elliott	Ford	148.359
1549	28	11/6/88	Phoenix, AZ	1.0	P	312	Alan Kulwicki	Ford	90.457	Geoff Bodine	Chevy	123.203
1550	29	11/20/88	Atlanta, GA	1.522	P	499.216	Rusty Wallace	Pontiac	129.024	Rusty Wallace	Pontiac	179.499

1989

Cum. No.	Yr. No.	Date	Site	Track Length	Surface	Miles	Race Winner	Make	Speed	Pole Winner	Make	Pole Speed
1551	1	2/19/89	Daytona Beach, FL	2.5	P	500	Darrell Waltrip	Chevy	148.466	Ken Schrader	Chevy	196.996
1552	2	3/5/89	Rockingham, NC	1.017	P	500.364	Rusty Wallace	Pontiac	115.122	Rusty Wallace	Pontiac	148.793
1553	3	3/19/89	Atlanta, GA	1.522	P	499.216	Darrell Waltrip	Chevy	139.684	Alan Kulwicki	ford	176.925
1554	4	3/26/89	Richmond, VA	0.75	P	300	Rusty Wallace	Pontiac	86.619	Geoff Bodine	Chevy	120.573
1555	5	4/2/89	Darlington, SC	1.366	P	501.322	Harry Gant	Olds	115.475	Mark Martin	Ford	161.111
1556	6	4/9/89	Bristol, TN	0.533	P	266.5	Rusty Wallace	Pontiac	76.034	Mark Martin	Ford	120.278
1557	7	4/16/89	N. Wilkesboro, NC	0.625	P	250	Dale Earnhardt	Chevy	89.937	Rusty Wallace	Pontiac	120.278
1558	8	4/23/89	Martinsville, VA	0.525	P	262.5	Darrell Waltrip	Chevy	79.025	Geoff Bodine	Chevy	93.097
1559	9	5/7/89	Talladega, AL	2.66	P	500.08	Davey Allison	Ford	155.869	Mark Martin	Ford	193.061
1560	10	5/28/89	Charlotte, NC	1.5	P	600	Darrell Waltrip	Chevy	144.077	Alan Kulwicki	Ford	173.021
1561	11	6/4/89	Dover, DE	1.0	P	500	Dale Earnhardt	Chevy	121.670	Mark Martin	Ford	144.387
1562	12	6/11/89	Sonoma, CA	2.52	P	186.48	Ricky Rudd	Buick	76.088	Rusty Wallace	Pontiac	90.041
1563	13	6/18/89	Pocono, PA	2.5	P	500	Terry Labonte	Ford	131.320	Rusty Wallace	Pontiac	157.489
1564	14	6/25/89	Brooklyn, MI	2.0	P	400	Bill Elliott	Ford	139.023	Ken Schrader	Chevy	174.728
1565	15	7/1/89	Daytona Beach, FL	2.5	P	400	Davey Allison	Ford	132.207	Mark Martin	Ford	191.861
1566	16	7/23/89	Pocono, PA	2.5	P	500	Bill Elliott	Ford	117.847	Ken Schrader	Chevy	157.809
1567	17	7/30/89	Talladega, AL	2.66	P	500.08	Terry Labonte	Ford	157.354	Mark Martin	Ford	194.800
1568	18	8/13/89	Watkins Glen, NY	2.428	P	218.52	Rusty Wallace	Chevy	87.242	Morgan Shepherd	Pontiac	120.456
1569	19	8/20/89	Brooklyn, MI	2.0	P	400	Rusty Wallace	Pontiac	157.704	Geoff Bodine	Chevy	175.692
1570	20	8/26/89	Bristol, TN	0.533	P	266.5	Darrell Waltrip	Chevy	85.554	Alan Kulwicki	Ford	117.043
1571	21	9/3/89	Darlington, SC	1.366	P	501.322	Dale Earnhardt	Chevy	135.462	Alan Kulwicki	Ford	160.156
1572	22	9/10/89	Richmond, VA	0.75	P	300	Rusty Wallace	Pontiac	88.380	Bill Elliott	Ford	121.136
1573	23	9/17/89	Dover, DE	1.0	P	500	Dale Earnhardt	Chevy	122.909	Davey Allison	Ford	146.169
1574	24	9/24/89	Martinsville, VA	0.525	P	262.5	Darrell Waltrip	Chevy	76.571	Jimmy Hensley	Chevy	91.913
1575	25	10/8/89	Charlotte, NC	1.5	P	501	Ken Schrader	Chevy	149.863	Bill Elliott	Foprd	174.081
1576	26	10/15/89	N. Wilkesboro, NC	0.625	P	250	Geoff Bodine	Chevy	90.289	No Time Trials	NTT	NTT
1577	27	10/22/89	Rockingham, NC	1.017	P	500.364	Mark Martin	Ford	114.079	Alan Kulwicki	Ford	148.624
1578	28	11/5/89	Phoenix, AZ	1.0	P	312	Bill Elliott	Ford	105.683	Ken Schrader	Chevy	124.645
1579	29	11/19/89	Atlanta, GA	1.522	P	499.216	Dale Earnhardt	Chevy	140.229	Alan Kulwicki	Ford	179.112

1990

Cum. No.	Yr. No.	Date	Site	Track Length	Surface	Miles	Race Winner	Make	Speed	Pole Winner	Make	Pole Speed
1580	1	2/18/90	Daytona Beach, FL	2.5	P	500	Derrike Cope	Chevy	165.761	Ken Schrader	Chevy	196.515
1581	2	2/25/90	Richmond, VA	0.75	P	300	Mark Martin	Ford	92.158	Ricky Rudd	Chevy	119.617
1582	3	3/4/90	Rockingham, NC	1.017	P	500.364	Kyle Petty	Pontiac	122.864	Kyle Petty	Pontiac	148.751
1583	4	3/18/90	Atlanta, GA	1.522	P	499.216	Dale Earnhardt	Chevy	156.849	No Time Trials	NTT	NTT
1584	5	4/1/90	Darlington, SC	1.366	P	501.322	Dale Earnhardt	Chevy	124.073	Geoff Bodine	Ford	162.996
1585	6	4/8/90	Bristol, TN	0.533	P	266.5	Davey Allison	Ford	87.258	Ernie Irvan	Olds	116.157
1586	7	4/22/90	N. Wilkesboro	0.625	P	250	Brett Bodine	Buick	83.908	Mark Martin	Ford	117.475
1587	8	4/29/90	Martinsville, VA	0.526	P	263	Geoff Bodine	Ford	77.423	Geoff Bodine	Ford	91.726
1588	9	5/6/90	Talladega, AL	2.66	P	500.08	Dale Earnhardt	Chevy	159.571	Bill Elliott	Ford	199.388
1589	10	5/27/90	Charlotte, NC	1.5	P	600	Rusty Wallace	Pontiac	137.650	Ken Schrader	Chevy	173.963
1590	11	6/3/90	Dover, DE	1.0	P	500	Derrike Cope	Chevy	123.960	Dick Trickle	Pontiac	145.814
1591	12	6/10/90	Sonoma, CA	2.52	P	186.48	Rusty Wallace	Pontiac	69.245	Ricky Rudd	Chevy	99.743
1592	13	6/17/90	Pocono, PA	2.5	P	500	Harry Gant	Olds	120.600	Ernie Irvan	Olds	158.750
1593	14	6/24/90	Brooklyn, MI	2.0	P	400	Dale Earnhardt	Chevy	150.219	No Time Trials	NTT	NTT
1594	15	7/7/90	Daytona Beach, FL	2.5	P	400	Dale Earnhardt	Chevy	160.894	Greg Sacks	Chevy	195.533
1595	16	7/22/90	Pocono, PA	2.5	P	500	Geoff Bodine	Ford	124.070	Mark Martin	Ford	158.264
1596	17	7/29/90	Talladega, AL	2.66	P	500.08	Dale Earnhardt	Chevy	174.430	Dale Earnhardt	Chevy	192.513
1597	18	8/12/90	Watkins Glen, NY	2.428	P	218.52	Ricky Rudd	Chevy	92.452	Dale Earnhardt	Chevy	121.190
1598	19	8/19/90	Brooklyn, MI	2.0	P	400	Mark Martin	Ford	138.822	Alan Kulwicki	Ford	174.982
1599	20	8/25/90	Bristol, TN	0.533	P	266.5	Ernie Irvan	Olds	91.782	Dale Earnhardt	Chevy	115.604
1600	21	9/2/90	Darlington, SC	1.366	P	501.322	Dale Earnhardt	Chevy	123.141	Dale Earnhardt	Chevy	158.448
1601	22	9/9/90	Richmond, VA	0.75	P	300	Dale Earnhardt	Chevy	95.567	Ernie Irvan	Chevy	119.872
1602	23	9/16/90	Dover, DE	1.0	P	500	Bill Elliott	Ford	125.945	Bill Elliott	Ford	144.928
1603	24	9/23/90	Martinsville, VA	0.526	P	263	Geoff Bodine	Ford	76.386	Mark Martin	Ford	91.571
1604	25	9/30/90	N. Wilkesboro, NC	0.625	P	250	Mark Martin	Ford	93.818	Kyle Petty	Pontiac	116.387
1605	26	10/7/90	Charlotte, NC	1.5	P	501	Davey Allison	Ford	137.428	Brett Bodine	Buick	174.385

Cum. No.	Yr. No.	Date	Site	Track Length	Surface	Miles	Race Winner	Make	Speed	Pole Winner	Make	Pole Speed
1606	27	10/21/90	Rockingham, NC	1.017	P	500.364	Alan Kulwicki	Ford	126.452	Ken Schrader	Chevy	147.814
1607	28	11/4/90	Phoenix, AZ	1.0	P	312	Dale Earnhardt	Chevy	96.786	Rusty Wallace	Pontiac	124.443
1608	29	11/18/90	Atlanta, GA	1.522	P	499.216	Morgan Shepherd	Ford	140.911	Rusty Wallace	Pontiac	175.222

1991

Cum. No.	Yr. No.	Date	Site	Track Length	Surface	Miles	Race Winner	Make	Speed	Pole Winner	Make	Pole Speed
1609	1	2/17/91	Daytona Beach, FL	2.5	P	500	Ernie Irvan	Chevy	148.148	Davey Allison	Ford	195.955
1610	2	2/24/91	Richmond, VA	0.75	P	300	Dale Earnhardt	Chevy	105.397	Davey Allison	Ford	120.428
1611	3	3/3/91	Rockingham, NC	1.017	P	500.364	Kyle Petty	Pontiac	124.083	Kyle Petty	Pontiac	149.205
1612	4	3/18/91	Atlanta, GA	1.522	P	499.216	Ken Schrader	Chevy	140.470	Alan Kulwicki	Ford	174.413
1613	5	4/7/91	Darlington, SC	1.366	P	501.322	Ricky Rudd	Chevy	135.594	Geoff Bodine	Ford	161.939
1614	6	4/14/91	Bristol, TN	0.533	P	266.5	Rusty Wallace	Pontiac	72.809	Rusty Wallace	Pontiac	118.051
1615	7	4/21/91	N. Wilkesboro, NC	0.625	P	250	Darrell Waltrip	Chevy	79.604	Brett Bodine	Buick	116.237
1616	8	4/28/91	Martinsville, VA	0.526	P	263	Dale Earnhardt	Chevy	75.139	Mark Martin	Ford	91.949
1617	9	5/6/91	Talladega, AL	2.66	P	500.08	Harry Gant	Olds	165.620	Ernie Irvan	Chevy	195.186
1618	10	5/26/91	Charlotte, NC	1.5	P	600	Davey Allison	Ford	138.951	Mark Martin	Ford	174.820
1619	11	6/2/91	Dover, DE	1.0	P	500	Ken Schrader	Chevy	120.152	Michael Waltrip	Pontiac	143.392
1620	12	6/9/91	Sonoma, CA	2.52	P	186.48	Davey Allison	Ford	72.970	Ricky Rudd	Chevy	90.634
1621	13	6/16/91	Pocono, PA	2.5	P	500	Darrell Waltrip	Chevy	122.666	Mark Martin	Ford	161.996
1622	14	6/23/91	Brooklyn, MI	2.0	P	400	Davey Allison	Ford	160.912	Michael Waltrip	Pontiac	174.351
1623	15	7/6/91	Daytona Beach, FL	2.5	P	400	Bill Elliott	Ford	159.116	Sterling Marlin	Ford	190.331
1624	16	7/21/91	Pocono, PA	2.5	P	447.5	Rusty Wallace	Pontiac	115.459	Alan Kulwicki	Ford	161.473
1625	17	7/28/91	Talladega, AL	2.66	P	500.08	Dale Earnhardt	Chevy	147.383	Sterling Marlin	Ford	192.085
1626	18	8/11/91	Watkins Glen, NY	2.428	P	218.52	Ernie Irvan	Chevy	98.977	Terry Labonte	Olds	121.652
1627	19	8/18/91	Brooklyn, MI	2.0	P	400	Dale Jarrett	Ford	142.972	Alan Kulwicki	Ford	173.431
1628	20	8/24/91	Bristol, TN	0.533	P	266.5	Alan Kulwicki	Ford	82.028	Bill Elliott	Ford	116.957
1629	21	9/1/91	Darlington, SC	1.366	P	501.322	Harry Gant	Olds	133.508	Davey Allison	Ford	162.506
1630	22	9/7/91	Richmond, VA	0.75	P	300	Harry Gant	Olds	101.361	Rusty Wallace	Pontiac	120.590
1631	23	9/15/91	Dover, DE	1.0	P	500	Harry Gant	Olds	110.179	Alan Kulwicki	Ford	146.825
1632	24	9/22/91	Martinsville, VA	0.526	P	263	Harry Gant	Olds	74.535	Mark Martin	Ford	93.171
1633	25	9/29/91	N. Wilkesboro, NC	0.625	P	250	Dale Earnhardt	Chevy	94.113	Harry Gant	Olds	116.871
1634	26	10/6/91	Charlotte, NC	1.5	P	501	Geoff Bodine	Ford	138.984	Mark Martin	Ford	176.499
1635	27	10/20/91	Rockingham, NC	1.017	P	500.364	Davey Allison	Ford	127.292	Kyle Petty	Pontiac	149.461
1636	28	11/3/91	Phoenix, AZ	1.0	P	312	Davey Allison	Ford	95.746	Geoff Bodine	Ford	127.589
1637	29	11/17/91	Atlanta, GA	1.522	P	499.216	Mark Martin	Ford	137.968	Bill Elliott (41	Ford	177.937

1992

Cum. No.	Yr. No.	Date	Site	Track Length	Surface	Miles	Race Winner	Make	Speed	Pole Winner	Make	Pole Speed
1638	1	2/16/92	Daytona Beach, FL	2.5	P	500	Davey Allison	Ford	160.256	Sterling Marlin	Ford	192.213
1639	2	3/1/92	Rockingham, NC	1.017	P	500.364	Bill Elliott	Ford	126.125	Kyle Petty	Pontiac	149.926
1640	3	3/8/92	Richmond, VA	0.75	P	300	Bill Elliott	Ford	104.378	Bill Elliott	Ford	121.337
1641	4	3/15/92	Atlanta, GA	1.522	P	499.216	Bill Elliott	Ford	147.746	Mark Martin	Ford	179.923
1642	5	3/29/92	Darlington, SC	1.366	P	501.322	Bill Elliott	Ford	139.364	Sterling Marlin	Ford	163.067
1643	6	4/5/92	Bristol, TN	0.533	P	266.5	Alan Kulwicki	Ford	86.316	Alan Kulwicki	Ford	122.474
1644	7	4/12/92	N. Wilkesboro, NC	0.625	P	250	Davey Allison	Ford	90.653	Alan Kulwicki	Ford	117.242
1645	8	4/26/92	Martinsville, VA	0.526	P	263	Mark Martin	Ford	78.086	Darrell Waltrip	Chevy	92.956
1646	9	5/3/92	Talladega, AL	2.66	P	500.08	Davey Allison	Ford	167.609	Ernie Irvan	Chevy	192.831
1647	10	5/24/92	Charlotte, NC	1.5	P	600	Dale Earnhardt	Chevy	132.980	Bill Elliott	Ford	175.479
1648	11	5/31/92	Dover, DE	1.0	P	500	Harry Gant	Chevy	109.456	Brett Bodine	Ford	147.408
1649	12	6/7/92	Sonoma, CA	2.52	P	186.48	Ernie Irvan	Chevy	81.413	Ricky Rudd	Chevy	90.985
1650	13	6/14/92	Pocono, PA	2.5	P	500	Alan Kulwicki	Ford	144.023	Ken Schrader	Chevy	162.499
1651	14	6/21/92	Brooklyn, MI	2.0	P	400	Davey Allison	Ford	152.672	Davey Allison	Ford	176.258
1652	15	7/4/92	Daytona Beach, FL	2.5	P	400	Ernie Irvan	Chevy	170.457	Sterling Marlin	Ford	189.366
1653	16	7/19/92	Pocono, PA	2.5	P	500	Darrell Waltrip	Chevy	134.058	Davey Allison	Ford	162.022
1654	17	7/26/92	Talladega, AL	2.66	P	500.08	Ernie Irvan	Chevy	176.309	Sterling Marlin	Ford	190.586
1655	18	8/9/92	Watkins Glen, NY	2.45	P	124.95	Kyle Petty	Pontiac	88.980	Dale Earnhardt	Chevy	116.882
1656	19	8/16/92	Brooklyn, MI	2.0	P	400	Harry Gant	Olds	146.056	Alan Kulwicki	Ford	178.196
1657	20	8/29/92	Bristol, TN	0.533	P	266.5	Darrell Waltrip	Chevy	91.198	Ernie Irvan	Chevy	120.535
1658	21	9/6/92	Darlington, SC	1.366	P	501.322	Darrell Waltrip	Chevy	129.114	Sterling Marlin	Ford	162.249
1659	22	9/12/92	Richmond, VA	0.75	P	300	Rusty Wallace	Pontiac	104.661	Ernie Irvan	Chevy	120.784
1660	23	9/20/92	Dover, DE	1.0	P	500	Ricky Rudd	Chevy	115.289	Alan Kulwicki	Ford	145.267
1661	24	9/28/92	Martinsville, VA	0.526	P	263	Geoff Bodine	Ford	75.424	Kyle Petty	Pontiac	92.497
1662	25	10/5/92	N. Wilkesboro, NC	0.625	P	250	Geoff Bodine	Ford	107.360	Alan Kulwicki	Ford	117.133
1663	26	10/11/92	Charlotte, NC	1.5	P	501	Mark Martin	Ford	153.537	Alan Kulwicki	Ford	179.027

Cum. No.	Yr. No.	Date	Site	Track Length	Surface	Miles	Race Winner	Make	Speed	Pole Winner	Make	Pole Speed
1664	27	10/25/92	Rockingham, NC	1.017	P	500.364	Kyle Petty	Pontiac	130.748	Kyle Petty	Pontiac	149.675
1665	28	11/1/92	Phoenix, AZ	1.0	P	312	Davey Allison	Ford	103.885	Rusty Wallace	Pontiac	128.141
1666	29	11/15/92	Atlanta, GA	1.522	P	499.216	Bill Elliott	Ford	133.322	Rick Mast	Olds	180.813

1993

Cum. No.	Yr. No.	Date	Site	Track Length	Surface	Miles	Race Winner	Make	Speed	Pole Winner	Make	Pole Speed
1667	1	2/14/93	Daytona Beach, FL	2.5	P	500	Dale Jarrett	Chevy	154.972	Kyle Petty	Pontiac	189.426
1668	2	2/28/93	Rockingham, NC	1.017	P	500.364	Rusty Wallace	Pontiac	124.486	Mark Martin	Ford	149.547
1669	3	3/7/93	Richmond, VA	0.75	P	300	Davey Allison	Ford	107.709	Ken Schrader	Chevy	123.164
1670	4	3/20/93	Atlanta, GA	1.522	P	499.216	Morgan Shepherd	Ford	150.442	Rusty Wallace	Pontiac	178.749
1671	5	3/28/93	Darlington, SC	1.366	P	501.322	Dale Earnhardt	Chevy	139.958	No Time Trials	NTT	NTT
1672	6	4/4/93	Bristol, TN	0.533	P	266.5	Rusty Wallace	Pontiac	84.730	Rusty Wallace	Pontiac	120.938
1673	7	4/18/93	N. Wilkesboro, NC	0.625	P	250	Rusty Wallace	Pontiac	92.602	Brett Bodine	Ford	117.017
1674	8	4/25/93	Martinsville, VA	0.526	P	263	Rusty Wallace	Pontiac	79.078	Geoff Bodine	Ford	93.887
1675	9	5/2/93	Talladega, AL	2.66	P	500.08	Ernie Irvan	Chevy	155.412	Dale Earnhardt	Chevy	192.355
1676	10	5/16/93	Sonoma, CA	2.52	P	186.48	Geoff Bodine	Ford	77.013	Dale Earnhardt	Chevy	91.838
1677	11	5/30/93	Charlotte, NC	1.5	P	600	Dale Earnhardt	Chevy	145.504	Ken Schrader	Chevy	177.352
1678	12	6/6/93	Dover, DE	1.0	P	500	Dale Earnhardt	Chevy	105.600	Ernie Irvan	Chevy	151.541
1679	13	6/13/93	Pocono, PA	2.5	P	500	Kyle Petty	Pontiac	138.005	Ken Schrader	Chevy	162.816
1680	14	6/20/93	Brooklyn, MI	2.0	P	400	Ricky Rudd	Chevy	148.484	Brett Bodine	Ford	175.456
1681	15	7/3/93	Daytona Beach, FL	2.5	P	400	Dale Earnhardt	Chevy	151.755	Ernie Irvan	Chevy	190.327
1682	16	7/11/93	Loudon, NH	1.058	P	317.4	Rusty Wallace	Pontiac	105.947	Mark Martin	Ford	126.871
1683	17	7/18/93	Pocono, PA	2.5	P	500	Dale Earnhardt	Chevy	133.343	Ken Schrader	Chevy	162.934
1684	18	7/25/93	Talladega, AL	2.66	P	500.08	Dale Earnhardt	Chevy	153.858	Bill Elliott	Ford	192.397
1685	19	8/8/93	Watkins Glen, NY	2.45	P	220.5	Mark Martin	Ford	84.771	Mark Martin	Ford	119.118
1686	20	8/15/93	Brooklyn, MI	2.0	P	400	Mark Martin	Ford	144.564	Ken Schrader	Chevy	180.750
1687	21	8/28/93	Bristol, TN	0.533	P	266.5	Mark Martin	Ford	88.172	Mark Martin	Ford	121.405
1688	22	9/5/93	Darlington, SC	1.366	P	479.47	Mark Martin	Ford	137.932	Ken Schrader	Chevy	161.259
1689	23	9/11/93	Richmond, VA	0.75	P	300	Rusty Wallace	Pontiac	99.917	Bobby Labonte	Ford	122.006
1690	24	9/19/93	Dover, DE	1.0	P	500	Rusty Wallace	Pontiac	100.334	Rusty Wallace	Pontiac	151.464
1691	25	9/26/93	Martinsville, VA	0.526	P	263	Ernie Irvan	Ford	74.101	Ernie Irvan	Ford	92.583
1692	26	10/3/93	N. Wilkesboro, NC	0.625	P	250	Rusty Wallace	Pontiac	96.920	Ernie Irvan	Ford	116.786
1693	27	10/10/93	Charlotte, NC	1.5	P	501	Ernie Irvan	Ford	154.537	Jeff Gordon	Chevy	177.684
1694	28	10/24/93	Rockingham, NC	1.017	P	500.36	Rusty Wallace	Pontiac	114.036	Mark Martin	Ford	148.353
1695	29	10/31/93	Phoenix, AZ	1.0	P	312	Mark Martin	Ford	100.375	Bill Elliott	Ford	129.482
1696	30	11/14/93	Atlanta, GA	1.522	P	499.22	Rusty Wallace	Pontiac	125.221	Harry Gant	Chevy	176.902

1994

Cum. No.	Yr. No.	Date	Site	Track Length	Surface	Miles	Race Winner	Make	Speed	Pole Winner	Make	Pole Speed
1697	1	2/20/94	Daytona Beach, FL	2.5	P	500	Sterling Marlin	Chevy	156.931	Loy Allen, Jr.	Ford	190.158
1698	2	2/27/94	Rockingham, NC	1.017	P	500.364	Rusty Wallace	Ford	125.239	Geoff Bodine	Ford	151.716
1699	3	3/6/94	Richmond, VA	0.75	P	300	Ernie Irvan	Ford	98.334	Ted Musgrave	Ford	123.474
1700	4	3/13/94	Atlanta, GA	1.522	P	499.216	Ernie Irvan	Ford	146.131	Loy Allen, Jr.	Ford	180.207
1701	5	3/27/94	Darlington, SC	1.366	P	501.322	Dale Earnhardt	Chevy	132.432	Bill Elliott	Ford	165.553
1702	6	4/10/94	Bristol, TN	0.533	P	266.5	Dale Earnhardt	Chevy	89.647	Chuck Bown	Ford	124.946
1703	7	4/17/94	N. Wilkesboro, NC	0.625	P	250	Terry Labonte	Chevy	95.816	Ernie Irvan	Ford	119.016
1704	8	4/24/94	Martinsville, VA	0.526	P	263	Rusty Wallace	Ford	76.700	Rusty Wallace	Ford	92.942
1705	9	5/1/94	Talladega, AL	2.66	P	500.08	Dale Earnhardt	Chevy	157.478	Ernie Irvan	Ford	193.298
1706	10	5/15/94	Sonoma, CA	2.52	P	186.48	Ernie Irvan	Ford	77.458	Ernie Irvan	Ford	91.514
1707	11	5/29/94	Charlotte, NC	1.5	P	600	Jeff Gordon	Chevy	139.445	Jeff Gordon	Chevy	181.439
1708	12	6/5/94	Dover, DE	1.0	P	500	Rusty Wallace	Ford	102.529	Ernie Irvan	Ford	102.529
1709	13	6/12/94	Pocono, PA	2.5	P	500	Rusty Wallace	Ford	128.801	Rusty Wallace	Ford	164.558
1710	14	6/19/94	Brooklyn, MI	2.0	P	400	Rusty Wallace	Ford	125.022	Loy Allen, Jr.	Ford	180.641
1711	15	7/2/94	Daytona Beach, FL	2.5	P	400	Jimmy Spencer	Ford	155.558	Dale Earnhardt	Chevy	191.339
1712	16	7/10/94	Loudon, NH	1.058	P	317.4	Ricky Rudd	Ford	87.599	Ernie Irvan	Ford	127.197
1713	17	7/17/94	Pocono, PA	2.5	P	500	Geoff Bodine	Ford	136.075	Geoff Bodine	Ford	163.869
1714	18	7/24/94	Talladega, AL	2.66	P	500.08	Jimmy Spencer	Ford	163.217	Dale Earnhardt	Chevy	193.470
1715	19	8/6/94	Indianapolis, IN	2.5	P	400	Jeff Gordon	Chevy	131.977	Rick Mast	Ford	172.414
1716	20	8/14/94	Watkins Glen, NY	2.45	P	220.5	Mark Martin	Ford	93.752	Mark Martin	Ford	118.326
1717	21	8/21/94	Brooklyn, MI	2.0	P	400	Geoff Bodine	Ford	139.914	Geoff Bodine	Ford	181.082
1718	22	8/27/94	Bristol, TN	0.533	P	266.50	Rusty Wallace	Ford	91.363	Harry Gant	Chevy	124.186
1719	23	9/4/94	Darlington, SC	1.366	P	479.466	Bill Elliott	Ford	127.952	Geoff Bodine	Ford	166.998
1720	24	9/10/94	Richmond, VA	0.75	P	300	Terry Labonte	Chevy	104.156	Ted Musgrave	Ford	124.052
1721	25	9/18/94	Dover, DE	1.0	P	500	Rusty Wallace	Ford	112.556	Geoff Bodine	Ford	152.840

Cum. No.	Yr. No.	Date	Site	Track Length	Surface	Miles	Race Winner	Make	Speed	Pole Winner	Make	Pole Speed
1722	26	9/25/94	Martinsville, VA	0.526	P	263	Rusty Wallace	Ford	77.139	Ted Musgrave	Ford	94.129
1723	27	10/2/94	N. Wilkesboro, NC	0.625	P	250	Geoff Bodine	Ford	98.522	Jimmy Spencer	Ford	118.558
1724	28	10/9/94	Charlotte, NC	1.5	P	501	Dale Jarrett	Chevy	145.922	Ward Burton	Chevy	185.759
1725	29	10/23/94	Rockingham, NC	1.017	P	500.364	Dale Earnhardt	Chevy	126.408	Ricky Rudd	Ford	157.099
1726	30	10/30/94	Phoenix, AZ	1.0	P	312	Terry Labonte	Chevy	107.463	Sterling Marlin	Chevy	129.833
1727	31	11/13/94	Atlanta, GA	1.522	P	499.216	Mark Martin	Ford	148.982	Greg Sacks	Ford	185.830

1995

Cum. No.	Yr. No.	Date	Site	Track Length	Surface	Miles	Race Winner	Make	Speed	Pole Winner	Make	Pole Speed
1728	1	2/19/95	Daytona Beach, FL	2.5	P	500	Sterling Marlin	Chevy	141.710	Dale Jarrett	Ford	193.498
1729	2	2/26/95	Rockingham, NC	1.017	P	500	Jeff Gordon	Chevy	125.305	Jeff Gordon	Chevy	157.620
1730	3	3/5/95	Richmond, VA	0.75	P	300	Terry Labonte	Chevy	106.425	Jeff Gordon	Chevy	124.757
1731	4	3/12/95	Atlanta, GA	1.522	P	499.216	Jeff Gordon	Chevy	150.115	Dale Earnhardt	Chevy	185.077
1732	5	3/26/95	Darlington, SC	1.366	P	400.238	Sterling Marlin	Chevy	111.392	Jeff Gordon	Chevy	170.833
1733	6	4/2/95	Bristol, TN	0.533	P	266.5	Jeff Gordon	Chevy	92.011	Mark Martin	Ford	124.605
1734	7	4/9/95	N. Wilkesboro, NC	0.625	P	250	Dale Earnhardt	Chevy	102.424	Jeff Gordon	Chevy	118.765
1735	8	4/23/95	Martinsville, VA	0.526	P	187.26	Rusty Wallace	Ford	72.145	Bobby Labonte	Chevy	93.308
1736	9	4/30/95	Talladega, AL	2.66	P	500.08	Mark Martin	Ford	178.902	Terry Labonte	Chevy	196.532
1737	10	5/7/95	Sonoma, CA	2.52	P	186.48	Dale Earnhardt	Chevy	70.681	Ricky Rudd	Ford	92.132
1738	11	5/28/95	Charlotte, NC	1.5	P	600	Bobby Labonte	Chevy	151.952	Jeff Gordon	Chevy	183.861
1739	12	6/4/95	Dover, DE	1.0	P	500	Kyle Petty	Pontiac	119.880	Jeff Gordon	Chevy	153.669
1740	13	6/11/95	Pocono, PA	2.5	P	500	Terry Labonte	Chevy	137.720	Ken Schrader	Chevy	163.375
1741	14	6/18/95	Brooklyn, MI	2.0	P	400	Bobby Labonte	Chevy	134.141	Jeff Gordon	Chevy	186.611
1742	15	7/1/95	Daytona Beach, FL	2.5	P	400	Jeff Gordon	Chevy	166.976	Dale Earnhardt	Chevy	191.355
1743	16	7/9/95	Loudon, NH	1.058	P	317.4	Jeff Gordon	Chevy	107.029	Mark Martin	Ford	128.815
1744	17	7/16/95	Pocono, PA	2.5	P	500	Dale Jarrett	Ford	134.038	Bill Elliott	Ford	162.496
1745	18	7/23/95	Talladega, AL	2.66	P	500.08	Sterling Marlin	Chevy	173.188	Sterling Marlin	Chevy	194.212
1746	19	8/5/95	Indianapolis, IN	2.5	P	400	Dale Earnhardt	Chevy	155.206	Jeff Gordon	Chevy	172.536
1747	20	8/13/95	Watkins Glen, NY	2.45	P	220.5	Mark Martin	Ford	103.030	Mark Martin	Ford	120.411
1748	21	8/20/95	Brooklyn, MI	2.0	P	400	Bobby Labonte	Chevy	157.739	Bobby Labonte	Chevy	184.403
1749	22	8/26/95	Bristol, TN	0.533	P	266.5	Terry Labonte	Chevy	81.979	Mark Martin	Ford	125.093
1750	23	9/3/95	Darlington, SC	1.366	P	501.322	Jeff Gordon	Chevy	121.231	John Andretti	Ford	167.379
1751	24	9/9/95	Richmond, VA	0.75	P	300	Rusty Wallace	Ford	104.459	Dale Earnhardt	Chevy	122.543
1752	25	9/17/95	Dover, DE	1.0	P	500	Jeff Gordon	Chevy	124.740	Rick Mast	Ford	153.446
1753	26	9/24/95	Martinsville, VA	0.526	P	263	Dale Earnhardt	Chevy	73.946	No Time Trials	NTT	NTT
1754	27	10/1/95	N. Wilkesboro, NC	0.625	P	250	Mark Martin	Ford	102.998	Ted Musgrave	Ford	118.396
1755	28	10/8/95	Charlotte, NC	1.5	P	501	Mark Martin	Ford	145.358	Ricky Rudd	Ford	180.578
1756	29	10/22/95	Rockingham, NC	1.017	P	399.681	Ward Burton	Pontiac	114.778	Hut Stricklin	Ford	155.379
1757	30	10/29/95	Phoenix, AZ	1.0	P	312	Ricky Rudd	Ford	102.128	Bill Elliott	Ford	130.020
1758	31	11/12/95	Atlanta, GA	1.522	P	499.216	Dale Earnhardt	Chevy	163.633	Darrell Waltrip	Chevy	185.046

1996

Cum. No.	Yr. No.	Date	Site	Track Length	Surface	Miles	Race Winner	Make	Speed	Pole Winner	Make	Pole Speed
1759	1	2/18/96	Daytona Beach, FL	2.5	P	500	Dale Jarrett	Ford	154.308	Dale Earnhardt	Chevy	189.510
1760	2	2/25/96	Rockingham, NC	1.017	P	399.681	Dale Earnhardt	Chevy	113.959	Terry Labonte	Chevy	156.870
1761	3	3/3/96	Richmond, VA	0.75	P	300	Jeff Gordon	Chevy	102.750	Terry Labonte	Chevy	123.728
1762	4	3/10/96	Atlanta, GA	1.522	P	499.216	Dale Earnhardt	Chevy	161.298	Johnny Benson, Jr.	Pontiac	185.434
1763	5	3/24/96	Darlington, SC	1.366	P	400.238	Jeff Gordon	Chevy	124.792	Ward Burton	Pontiac	173.797
1764	6	3/31/96	Bristol, TN	0.533	P	182.286	Jeff Gordon	Chevy	91.308	Mark Martin	Ford	123.578
1765	7	4/14/96	N. Wilkesboro, NC	0.625	P	250	Terry Labonte	Chevy	96.370	Terry Labonte	Chevy	116.659
1766	8	4/21/96	Martinsville, VA	0.526	P	263	Rusty Wallace	Ford	81.410	Ricky Craven	Chevy	93.079
1767	9	4/28/96	Talladega, AL	2.66	P	500.08	Sterling Marlin	Chevy	149.999	Ernie Irvan	Ford	192.855
1768	10	5/5/96	Sonoma, CA	2.52	P	186.48	Rusty Wallace	Ford	77.673	Terry Labonte	Chevy	92.524
1769	11	5/26/96	Charlotte, NC	1.5	P	600	Dale Jarrett	Ford	147.581	Jeff Gordon	Chevy	183.773
1770	12	6/2/96	Dover, DE	1.0	P	500	Jeff Gordon	Chevy	122.741	Jeff Gordon	Chevy	154.785
1771	13	6/16/96	Pocono, PA	2.5	P	500	Jeff Gordon	Chevy	139.104	Jeff Gordon	Chevy	169.725
1772	14	6/23/96	Brooklyn, MI	2.0	P	400	Rusty Wallace	Ford	166.033	Bobby Hamilton	Pontiac	185.166
1773	15	7/6/96	Daytona Beach, FL	2.5	P	292.5	Sterling Marlin	Chevy	161.602	Jeff Gordon	Chevy	188.869
1774	16	7/14/96	Loudon, NH	1.058	P	317.4	Ernie Irvan	Ford	98.930	Ricky Craven	Chevy	129.379
1775	17	7/21/96	Pocono, PA	2.5	P	500	Rusty Wallace	Ford	144.892	Mark Martin	Ford	168.410
1776	18	7/28/96	Talladega, AL	2.66	P	343.14	Jeff Gordon	Chevy	133.387	Jeremy Mayfield	Ford	192.370
1777	19	8/3/96	Indianapolis, IN	2.5	P	400	Dale Jarrett	Ford	139.508	Jeff Gordon	Chevy	176.419
1778	20	8/11/96	Watkins Glen, NY	2.450	P	220.5	Geoff Bodine	Ford	92.334	Dale Earnhardt	Chevy	120.733
1779	21	8/18/96	Brooklyn, MI	2.0	P	400	Dale Jarrett	Ford	139.792	Jeff Burton	Ford	185.395

Cum. No.	Yr. No.	Date	Site	Track Length	Surface	Miles	Race Winner	Make	Speed	Pole Winner	Make	Pole Speed
1780	22	8/24/96	Bristol, TN	0.533	P	266.5	Rusty Wallace	Ford	91.267	Mark Martin	Ford	124.857
1781	23	9/1/96	Darlington, SC	1.366	P	501.322	Jeff Gordon	Chevy	135.757	Dale Jarrett	Ford	170.934
1782	24	9/7/96	Richmond, VA	0.75	P	300	Ernie Irvan	Ford	105.469	Mark Martin	Ford	122.744
1783	25	9/15/96	Dover, DE	1.0	P	500	Jeff Gordon	Chevy	105.646	Bobby Labonte	Chevy	155.086
1784	26	9/22/96	Martinsville, VA	0.526	P	263	Jeff Gordon	Chevy	82.223	Bobby Hamilton	Pontiac	94.120
1785	27	9/29/96	N. Wilkesboro, NC	0.625	P	250	Jeff Gordon	Chevy	96.837	Ted Musgrave	Ford	118.054
1786	28	10/6/96	Charlotte, NC	1.5	P	501	Terry Labonte	Chevy	143.143	Bobby Labonte	Chevy	184.068
1787	29	10/20/96	Rockingham, NC	1.017	P	399.681	Ricky Rudd	Ford	122.320	Dale Jarrett	Ford	157.194
1788	30	10/27/96	Phoenix, AZ	1.0	P	312	Bobby Hamilton	Pontiac	109.709	Bobby Labonte	Chevy	131.076
1789	31	11/10/96	Atlanta, GA	1.522	P	499.216	Bobby Labonte	Chevy	134.661	Bobby Labonte	Chevy	185.887

Selected Race Histories

Asheville-Weaverville Speedway
Western North Carolina 500

Atlanta Int'l Raceway
Spring 500-Miler
Fall 500-Miler
Festival 250

Bristol Motor Speedway
Spring Race
Summer Race

Charlotte Motor Speedway
600-Miler
Fall 500-Miler

Darlington Raceway
Southern 500
Spring Race

Daytona Int'l Speedway
Daytona 500
Firecracker/Pepsi 250/400

Dover Downs Int'l Speedway
Spring Race
Fall Race

Martinsville Speedway
Spring 500-Lapper
Fall 500-Lapper

Michigan Int'l Speedway
June 500/400-Miler
August 600/400-Miler

North Carolina Motor Speedway
Spring 500/400-Miler
Fall 500/400-Miler

North Wilkesboro Speedway
Spring Race
Fall Race

Pocono Int'l Raceway
June 500-Miler
July 500-Miler

Talladega Superspeedway
Alabama/Winston 500
Talladega/DieHard 500

Virginia State Fairgrounds
Spring Race
Fall Race

Race	Date		Winner	Start Pos.	Make	Speed	Lead Ch.	No. Lds.	No. Caut.	Caut. Laps	Owner		Pole Winner	Pole Speed
ATLANTA INT'L RACEWAY *Spring 500-Miler*														
Atlanta 500	3/26/61		Bob Burdick	7	Pontiac	124.172	6	6	2		Roy Burdick Gar		Marvin Panch	135.755
Atlanta 500	6/10/62		Fred Lorenzen	7	Ford	101.983	23	7	3	3	Holman-Moody		Banjo Matthews	137.64
Atlanta 500	3/17/63		Fred Lorenzen	2	Ford	130.582	12	8			Holman-Moody		Junior Johnson	141.038
Atlanta 500	4/5/64		Fred Lorenzen	1	Ford	134.137	11	6	4	4	Holman-Moody		Fred Lorenzen	146.47
Atlanta 500	4/11/65		Marvin Panch	1	Ford	129.41	8	5	5	5	Wood Brothers		Marvin Panch	145.581
Atlanta 500	3/27/66		Jim Hurtubise	5	Plymouth	131.247	23	9	5	5	Norm Nelson		Richard Petty	147.742
Atlanta 500	4/2/67		Cale Yarborough	1	Ford	131.238	9	5	6	6	Wood Brothers		Cale Yarborough	148.996
Atlanta 500	3/31/68		Cale Yarborough	4	Mercury	125.564	15	6	11	11	Wood Brothers		LeeRoy Yarbrough	155.646

Key

START POS.	Position where winner started
MAKE	Car manufacturer
SPEED	Average speed
LEAD CH.	Number of lead changes in race
NO LDS.	Number of race leaders
NO CAUT.	Number of cautions issued during race
CAUT. LAPS	Number of laps run under caution
NTT	No time trial

Please note that blank fields indicate that the information is unavailable.

Race	Date	Winner	Start Pos.	Make	Speed	Lead Ch.	No. Lds.	No. Caut.	Caut. Laps	Owner	Pole Winner	Pole Speed

SELECTED RACE HISTORIES

ASHEVILLE-WEAVERVILLE SPEEDWAY
Western North Carolina 500

Race	Date	Winner	Start Pos.	Make	Speed	Lead Ch.	No. Lds.	No. Caut.	Caut. Laps	Owner	Pole Winner	Pole Speed
Western North Carolina 500	8/17/58	Fireball Roberts	2	Chevrolet	66.78					Frank Strickland	Jimmy Massey	76.596
Western North Carolina 500	8/16/59	Bob Welborn	4	Chevrolet	71.833					Bob Welborn	Rex White	77.687
Western North Carolina 500	8/14/60	Rex White	2	Chevrolet	65.024	8	6			Rex White	Jack Smith	77.85
Western North Carolina 500	8/13/61	Junior Johnson	2	Pontiac	65.704	1	1			Rex Lovette	Jim Paschal	80.43
Western North Carolina 500	8/12/62	Jim Paschal	2	Plymouth	77.492	1	2	2		Petty Enterprises	Jack Smith	82.72
Western North Carolina 500	8/11/63	Fred Lorenzen	2	Ford	77.673	3	3	2		Holman-Moody	NTT	
Western North Carolina 500	8/9/64	Ned Jarrett	4	Ford	77.6	5	3	2		Bondy Long	Junior Johnson	84.626
Western North Carolina 500	8/8/65	Richard Petty	1	Plymouth	74.343	8	4	5		Petty Enterprises	Richard Petty	86.455
Western North Carolina 500	8/21/66	Darel Dieringer	2	Mercury	76.7	8	4	3	23	Bud Moore	Junior Johnson	86.831
Western North Carolina 500	11/5/67	Bobby Allison	1	Ford	76.291	21	4	10	73	Holman-Moody	Bobby Allison	90.407
Western North Carolina 500	8/18/68	David Pearson	2	Ford	73.686	7	4	7	90	Holman-Moody	Darel Dieringer	88.409
Western North Carolina 500	8/24/69	Bobby Isaac	1	Dodge	80.45	7	3	4	17	Nord Krauskopf	Bobby Isaac	89.0

ATLANTA MOTOR SPEEDWAY
Spring 500-Miler

Race	Date	Winner	Start Pos.	Make	Speed	Lead Ch.	No. Lds.	No. Caut.	Caut. Laps	Owner	Pole Winner	Pole Speed
Atlanta 500	10/30/60	Bobby Johns	5	Pontiac	108.408	7	4			Cotton Owens	Fireball Roberts	134.596
Atlanta 500	3/26/61	Bob Burdick	7	Pontiac	124.172		6	2		Roy Burdick Gar	Marvin Panch	135.755
Atlanta 500	6/10/62	Fred Lorenzen	7	Ford	101.983	23	7	3	61	Holman-Moody	Banjo Matthews	137.64
Atlanta 500	3/17/63	Fred Lorenzen	2	Ford	130.582	12	8			Holman-Moody	Junior Johnson	141.038
Atlanta 500	4/5/64	Fred Lorenzen	1	Ford	134.137	11	6	4	19	Holman-Moody	Fred Lorenzen	146.47
Atlanta 500	4/11/65	Marvin Panch	1	Ford	129.41	8	5	5	26	Wood Brothers	Marvin Panch	145.581
Atlanta 500	3/27/66	Jim Hurtubise	5	Plymouth	131.247	23	9	5	31	Norm Nelson	Richard Petty	147.742
Atlanta 500	4/2/67	Cale Yarborough	1	Ford	131.238	9	5	6	39	Wood Brothers	Cale Yarborough	148.996
Atlanta 500	3/31/68	Cale Yarborough	4	Mercury	125.564	15	6	11	73	Wood Brothers	LeeRoy Yarbrough	155.646
Atlanta 500	3/30/69	Cale Yarborough	5	Mercury	132.191	10	4	5	53	Wood Brothers	David Pearson	156.794
Atlanta 500	3/29/70	Bobby Allison	9	Dodge	139.554	20	8	4	23	Mario Rossi	Cale Yarborough	159.929
Atlanta 500	4/4/71	A. J. Foyt	1	Mercury	131.375	23	6	4	31	Wood Brothers	A. J. Foyt	155.152
Atlanta 500	3/26/72	Bobby Allison	1	Chevrolet	128.214	18	6	6	47	Richard Howard	Bobby Allison	156.245
Atlanta 500	4/1/73	David Pearson	9	Mercury	139.351	23	4	4	31	Wood Brothers	NTT	
Atlanta 500	3/24/74	Cale Yarborough	9	Chevrolet	136.91	13	7	3	24	Richard Howard	David Pearson	159.242
Atlanta 500	3/23/75	Richard Petty	1	Dodge	133.496	22	7	5	43	Petty Enterprises	Richard Petty	159.029
Atlanta 500	3/21/76	David Pearson	2	Mercury	128.904	33	10	8	47	Wood Brothers	Dave Marcis	160.709
Atlanta 500	3/20/77	Richard Petty	1	Dodge	144.093	15	3	2	11	Petty Enterprises	Richard Petty	162.501
Atlanta 500	3/19/78	Bobby Allison	4	Ford	142.52	9	6	4	16	Bud Moore	Cale Yarborough	162.006
Atlanta 500	3/18/79	Buddy Baker	1	Oldsmobile	135.136	29	6	5	42	Harry Ranier	Buddy Baker	165.951
Atlanta 500	3/16/80	Dale Earnhardt	31	Chevrolet	134.808	27	11	7	45	Rod Osterlund	Buddy Baker	166.212
Coca-Cola 500	3/15/81	Cale Yarborough	17	Buick	133.619	23	9	5	39	M C Anderson	Terry Labonte	162.94
Coca-Cola 500	3/21/82	Darrell Waltrip	14	Buick	124.824	31	8	7	47	Junior Johnson	Dale Earnhardt	163.774
Coca-Cola 500	3/27/83	Cale Yarborough	22	Chevrolet	124.055	21	10	7	62	Harry Ranier	Geoff Bodine	167.703
Coca-Cola 500	3/18/84	Benny Parsons	8	Chevrolet	144.945	20	4	3	17	Johnny Hayes	Buddy Baker	166.642
Coca-Cola 500	3/17/85	Bill Elliott	3	Ford	140.273	17	10	6	31	Harry Melling	Neil Bonnett	170.278
Motorcraft 500	3/16/86	Morgan Shepherd	3	Buick	132.126	18	7	9	56	Jack Beebe	Dale Earnhardt	170.713
Motorcraft Quality Parts 500	3/15/87	Ricky Rudd	6	Ford	133.689	32	10	9	51	Bud Moore	Dale Earnhardt	175.497
Motorcraft Quality Parts 500	3/20/88	Dale Earnhardt	2	Chevrolet	137.588	19	10	7	40	Richard Childress	Geoff Bodine	176.623

Race	Date	Winner	Start Pos.	Make	Speed	Lead Ch.	No. Lds.	No. Caut.	Caut. Laps	Owner	Pole Winner	Pole Speed
Motorcraft Quality Parts 500	3/19/89	Darrell Waltrip	4	Chevrolet	139.684	29	11	6	41	Rick Hendrick	Alan Kulwicki	176.925
Motorcraft Quality Parts 500	3/18/90	Dale Earnhardt	1	Chevrolet	156.849	21	9	3	10	Richard Childress	NTT	
Motorcraft Quality Parts 500	3/18/91	Ken Schrader	5	Chevrolet	140.47	16	9	4	33	Rick Hendrick	Alan Kulwicki	174.413
Motorcraft Quality Parts 500	3/15/92	Bill Elliott	4	Ford	147.746	10	6	7	24	Junior Johnson	Mark Martin	179.923
Motorcraft Quality Parts 500	3/20/93	Morgan Shepherd	7	Ford	150.442	19	9	4	19	Wood Brothers	Rusty Wallace	178.749
Motorcraft Quality Parts 500	3/13/94	Ernie Irvan	7	Ford	146.136	19	7	5	27	Robert Yates	Loy Allen Jr.	180.207
Purolator 500	3/12/95	Jeff Gordon	3	Chevrolet	150.115	9	7	5	27	Rick Hendrick	Dale Earnhardt	185.077
Purolator 500	3/10/96	Dale Earnhardt	18	Chevrolet	161.298	30	12	3	13	Richard Childress	Johnny Benson Jr.	185.434

Fall 500-Miler

Race	Date	Winner	Start Pos.	Make	Speed	Lead Ch.	No. Lds.	No. Caut.	Caut. Laps	Owner	Pole Winner	Pole Speed
Dixie 300	7/31/60	Fireball Roberts	1	Pontiac	112.652	12	6			John Hines	Fireball Roberts	133.870
Dixie 400	9/17/61	David Pearson	5	Pontiac	125.384	7	5			John Masoni	Fireball Roberts	136.294
Dixie 400	10/28/62	Rex White	5	Chevrolet	124.74	16	6	3		Rex White	Fireball Roberts	138.978
Dixie 400	6/30/63	Junior Johnson	2	Chevrolet	121.139	7	6	2	32	Ray Fox	Marvin Panch	140.753
Dixie 400	6/7/64	Ned Jarrett	17	Ford	112.535	35	13	3	63	Bondy Long	Junior Johnson	145.906
Dixie 400	6/13/65	Marvin Panch	2	Ford	110.120	16	7	8	98	Wood Brothers	Fred Lorenzen	143.407
Dixie 400	8/7/66	Richard Petty	5	Plymouth	130.244	18	7	6	37	Petty Enterprises	Curtis Turner	148.331
Dixie 500	8/6/67	Dick Hutcherson	8	Ford	132.286	13	6	6	38	Bondy Long	Darel Dieringer	150.669
Dixie 500	8/4/68	LeeRoy Yarbrough	5	Mercury	127.068	29	9	11	67	Junior Johnson	Buddy Baker	153.361
Dixie 500	8/10/69	LeeRoy Yarbrough	2	Ford	133.001	19	7	3	31	Junior Johnson	Cale Yarborough	155.413
Dixie 500	8/2/70	Richard Petty	6	Plymouth	142.712	10	4	1	10	Petty Enterprises	Fred Lorenzen	157.625
Dixie 500	8/1/71	Richard Petty	3	Plymouth	129.061	27	4	5	48	Petty Enterprises	Buddy Baker	155.796
Dixie 500	7/23/72	Bobby Allison	3	Chevrolet	131.295	24	9	5	40	Richard Howard	David Pearson	158.353
Dixie 500	7/22/73	David Pearson	5	Mercury	130.211	14	5	6	47	Wood Brothers	Richard Petty	157.163
Dixie 500	7/28/74	Richard Petty	2	Dodge	131.651	23	7	5	38	Petty Enterprises	Cale Yarborough	156.75
Dixie 500	11/9/75	Buddy Baker	3	Ford	130.99	19	8	2	40	Bud Moore	Dave Marcis	160.662
Dixie 500	11/7/76	Dave Marcis	2	Dodge	127.396	17	5	4	41	Nord Krauskopf	Buddy Baker	161.652
Dixie 500	11/6/77	Darrell Waltrip	8	Chevrolet	110.052	12	6	5	22	DiGard	Sam Sommers	160.229
Dixie 500	11/5/78	Donnie Allison	13	Chevrolet	124.312	25	8	7	63	Hoss Ellington	Cale Yarborough	168.425
Dixie 500	11/4/79	Neil Bonnett	4	Mercury	140.12	25	7	5	24	Wood Brothers	Buddy Baker	164.813
Atlanta Journal 500	11/2/80	Cale Yarborough	12	Chevrolet	131.19	28	13	6	49	Junior Johnson	Bobby Allison	165.62
Atlanta Journal 500	11/8/81	Neil Bonnett	5	Ford	130.391	36	11	7	50	Wood Brothers	Harry Gant	163.266
Atlanta Journal 500	11/7/82	Bobby Allison	9	Buick	130.884	45	14	10	56	DiGard	Morgan Shepherd	166.779
Atlanta Journal 500	11/6/83	Neil Bonnett	15	Chevrolet	137.643	28	8	6	39	B. Rahilly & B. Mock	Tim Richmond	168.151
Atlanta Journal 500	11/11/84	Dale Earnhardt	10	Chevrolet	134.61	26	11	7	44	Richard Childress	Bill Elliott	170.198
Atlanta Journal 500	11/3/85	Bill Elliott	3	Ford	139.597	12	4	6	39	Harry Melling	Harry Gant	167.94
Atlanta Journal 500	11/2/86	Dale Earnhardt	4	Chevrolet	152.523	19	8	2	7	Richard Childress	Bill Elliott	172.905
Atlanta Journal 500	11/22/87	Bill Elliott	1	Ford	139.047	12	8	5	33	Harry Melling	Bill Elliott	174.341
Atlanta Journal 500	11/20/88	Rusty Wallace	1	Pontiac	129.024	33	15	9	55	Raymond Beadle	Rusty Wallace	179.499
Atlanta Journal 500	11/19/89	Dale Earnhardt	3	Chevrolet	140.229	21	8	6	35	Richard Childress	Alan Kulwicki	179.112
Atlanta Journal 500	11/18/90	Morgan Shepherd	20	Ford	140.911	19	9	3	34	Bud Moore	Rusty Wallace	175.222
Hardee's 500	11/17/91	Mark Martin	4	Ford	137.968	21	12	6	37	Jack Roush	Bill Elliott	177.937
Hooters 500	11/15/92	Bill Elliott	11	Ford	133.322	20	9	7	45	Junior Johnson	Rick Mast	180.183
Hooters 500	11/14/93	Rusty Wallace	20	Pontiac	125.221	26	12	11	58	Roger Penske	Harry Gant	176.902
Hooters 500	11/13/94	Mark Martin	5	Ford	148.982	30	13	4	27	Jack Roush	Greg Sacks	185.83
NAPA 500	11/12/95	Dale Earnhardt	11	Chevrolet	163.633	22	8	2	11	Richard Childress	Darrell Waltrip	185.046
NAPA 500	11/10/96	Bobby Labonte	1	Chevrolet	134.661	27	12	8	47	Joe Gibbs	Bobby Labonte	185.887

Festival 250

Race	Date	Winner	Start Pos.	Make	Speed	Lead Ch.	No. Lds.	No. Caut.	Caut. Laps	Owner	Pole Winner	Pole Speed
Festival 250	7/9/61	Fred Lorenzen	5	Ford	118.067	6	7	1	12	Holman-Moody	Fireball Roberts	136.088

BRISTOL MOTOR SPEEDWAY
Spring Race

Race	Date	Winner	Start Pos.	Make	Speed	Lead Ch.	No. Lds.	No. Caut.	Caut. Laps	Owner	Pole Winner	Pole Speed
Volunteer 500	4/29/62	Bobby Johns	6	Pontiac	73.397	5	3	4	37	Shorty Johns	Fireball Roberts	81.374
Southeastern 500	3/31/63	Fireball Roberts	3	Ford	76.91	8	5	1	9	Holman-Moody	Fred Lorenzen	80.681
Southeastern 500	3/22/64	Fred Lorenzen	2	Ford	72.196	1	2	4	54	Holman-Moody	Marvin Panch	80.64
Southeastern 500	5/2/65	Junior Johnson	3	Ford	74.937	8	4	7	39	Rex Lovette	Marvin Panch	84.626

Race	Date	Winner	Start Pos.	Make	Speed	Lead Ch.	No. Lds.	No. Caut.	Caut. Laps	Owner	Pole Winner	Pole Speed
Southeastern 500	3/20/66	Dick Hutcherson	6	Ford	69.952	7	4	7	92	Holman-Moody	David Pearson	86.248
Southeastern 500	3/19/67	David Pearson	14	Dodge	75.937	13	6	6	59	Cotton Owens	Darel Dieringer	87.124
Southeastern 500	3/17/68	David Pearson	2	Ford	77.247	18	4	11	81	Holman-Moody	Richard Petty	88.582
Southeastern 500	3/23/69	Bobby Allison	4	Dodge	81.455	9	3	4	32	Mario Rossi	Bobby Isaac	88.669
Southeastern 500	4/5/70	Donnie Allison	2	Ford	87.543	10	6	6	58	Banjo Matthews	David Pearson	107.079
Southeastern 500	3/28/71	David Pearson	1	Ford	91.704	9	5	5	45	Holman-Moody	David Pearson	105.525
Southeastern 500	4/9/72	Bobby Allison	1	Chevrolet	92.826	6	4	2	25	Richard Howard	Bobby Allison	106.875
Southeastern 500	3/25/73	Cale Yarborough	1	Chevrolet	88.952	0	1	7	56	Richard Howard	Cale Yarborough	107.608
Southeastern 500	3/17/74	Cale Yarborough	3	Chevrolet	64.533	6	5	3	28	Richard Howard	Donnie Allison	107.785
Southeastern 500	3/16/75	Richard Petty	2	Dodge	97.053	6	4	2	27	Petty Enterprises	Buddy Baker	110.951
Southeastern 400	3/14/76	Cale Yarborough	3	Chevrolet	87.377	16	7	6	79	Junior Johnson	Buddy Baker	110.72
Southeastern 500	4/17/77	Cale Yarborough	1	Chevrolet	100.989	6	4	2	9	Junior Johnson	Cale Yarborough	110.168
Southeastern 500	4/2/78	Darrell Waltrip	7	Chevrolet	92.401	13	3	4	40	DiGard	Neil Bonnett	110.409
Southeastern 500	4/1/79	Dale Earnhardt	9	Chevrolet	91.033	8	6	6	44	Rod Osterlund	Buddy Baker	111.668
Valleydale Southeastern 500	3/30/80	Dale Earnhardt	4	Chevrolet	96.977	15	6	3	14	Rod Osterlund	Cale Yarborough	111.688
Valleydale 500	3/29/81	Darrell Waltrip	1	Buick	89.53	21	11	8	44	Junior Johnson	Darrell Waltrip	112.125
Valleydale 500	3/14/82	Darrell Waltrip	1	Buick	94.025	10	6	3	25	Junior Johnson	Darrell Waltrip	111.068
Valleydale 500	5/21/83	Darrell Waltrip	13	Chevrolet	93.445	12	5	4	22	Junior Johnson	Neil Bonnett	110.409
Valleydale 500	4/1/84	Darrell Waltrip	3	Chevrolet	93.967	17	7	4	19	Junior Johnson	Ricky Rudd	111.39
Valleydale 500	4/6/85	Dale Earnhardt	12	Chevrolet	81.79	18	10	14	90	Richard Childress	Harry Gant	112.778
Valleydale 500	4/6/86	Rusty Wallace	14	Pontiac	89.747	14	8	7	56	Raymond Beadle	Geoff Bodine	114.85
Valleydale Meats 500	4/12/87	Dale Earnhardt	3	Chevrolet	75.621	19	11	13	125	Richard Childress	Harry Gant	115.674
Valleydale Meats 500	4/10/88	Bill Elliott	13	Ford	83.115	11	8	12	70	Harry Melling	Rick Wilson	117.552
Valleydale Meats 500	4/9/89	Rusty Wallace	8	Pontiac	76.034	34	16	20	98	Raymond Beadle	Mark Martin	120.278
Valleydale Meats 500	4/8/90	Davey Allison	19	Ford	87.258	11	9	13	65	Robert Yates	Ernie Irvan	116.157
Valleydale Meats 500	4/14/91	Rusty Wallace	1	Pontiac	72.809	40	8	19	133	Roger Penske	Rusty Wallace	118.051
Food City 500	4/5/92	Alan Kulwicki	1	Ford	86.316	11	7	10	75	Alan Kulwicki	Alan Kulwicki	122.474
Food City 500	4/4/93	Rusty Wallace	1	Pontiac	84.73	19	10	17	87	Roger Penske	Rusty Wallace	120.938
Food City 500	4/10/94	Dale Earnhardt	24	Chevrolet	89.647	11	5	10	75	Richard Childress	Chuck Bown	124.946
Food City 500	4/2/95	Jeff Gordon	2	Chevrolet	92.011	12	5	7	65	Rick Hendrick	Mark Martin	124.605
Food City 500	3/31/96	Jeff Gordon	8	Chevrolet	91.308	7	7	5	37	Rick Hendrick	Mark Martin	123.578

Summer Race

Race	Date	Winner	Start Pos.	Make	Speed	Lead Ch.	No. Lds.	No. Caut.	Caut. Laps	Owner	Pole Winner	Pole Speed
Volunteer 500	7/30/61	Jack Smith	12	Pontiac	68.373	7	5	8		Jack Smith	Fred Lorenzen	79.225
Southeastern 500	10/22/61	Joe Weatherly	2	Pontiac	72.452	6	5	3		Bud Moore	Bobby Johns	80.645
Southeastern 500	7/29/62	Jim Paschal	12	Plymouth	75.276	12	6	4	21	Petty Enterprises	Fireball Roberts	80.321
Volunteer 500	7/28/63	Fred Lorenzen	1	Ford	74.844	6	4	7	36	Holman-Moody	Fred Lorenzen	82.229
Volunteer 500	7/26/64	Fred Lorenzen	8	Ford	78.044	5	4	1	14	Holman-Moody	Richard Petty	82.91
Volunteer 500	7/25/65	Ned Jarrett	6	Ford	61.826	9	4	8	167	Bondy Long	Fred Lorenzen	84.348
Volunteer 500	7/24/66	Paul Goldsmith	4	Plymouth	77.963	3	3	2	24	Ray Nichels	Curtis Turner	84.309
Volunteer 500	7/23/67	Richard Petty	1	Plymouth	78.705	11	3	6	42	Petty Enterprises	Richard Petty	86.621
Volunteer 500	7/21/68	David Pearson	6	Ford	76.31	8	5	13	92	Holman-Moody	LeeRoy Yarbrough	87.421
Volunteer 500	7/20/69	David Pearson	3	Ford	79.737	9	7	8	58	Holman-Moody	Cale Yarborough	103.432
Volunteer 500	7/19/70	Bobby Allison	10	Dodge	84.88	9	2	8	54	Bobby Allison	Cale Yarborough	107.375
Volunteer 500	7/11/71	Charlie Glotzbach	2	Chevrolet	101.074	7	3	0	0	Richard Howard	Richard Petty	104.589
Volunteer 500	7/9/72	Bobby Allison	1	Chevrolet	92.735	4	3	5	30	Richard Howard	Bobby Allison	107.279
Volunteer 500	7/8/73	Benny Parsons	2	Chevrolet	91.342	5	3	5	33	L. G. DeWitt	Cale Yarborough	106.472
Volunteer 500	7/14/74	Cale Yarborough	3	Chevrolet	75.43	22	5	9	105	Junior Johnson	Richard Petty	107.351
Volunteer 400	8/29/76	Cale Yarborough	2	Chevrolet	99.175	1	2	2	13	Junior Johnson	Darrell Waltrip	110.3
Volunteer 400	8/28/77	Cale Yarborough	1	Chevrolet	79.726	14	6	6	42	Junior Johnson	Cale Yarborough	109.746
Volunteer 500	8/26/78	Cale Yarborough	4	Oldsmobile	88.628	16	7	10	59	Junior Johnson	Lennie Pond	110.958
Volunteer 500	8/25/79	Darrell Waltrip	5	Chevrolet	91.493	18	6	6	60	DiGard	Richard Petty	120.524
Busch Volunteer 500	8/23/80	Cale Yarborough	1	Chevrolet	86.973	19	8	10	57	Junior Johnson	Cale Yarborough	110.99
Busch 500	8/22/81	Darrell Waltrip	1	Buick	84.723	11	5	7	52	Junior Johnson	Darrell Waltrip	110.818
Busch 500	8/28/82	Darrell Waltrip	8	Buick	94.318	15	8	3	15	Junior Johnson	Tim Richmond	112.507
Busch 500	8/27/83	Darrell Waltrip	2	Chevrolet	89.43	12	6	5	31	Junior Johnson	Joe Ruttman	111.923
Busch 500	8/25/84	Terry Labonte	6	Chevrolet	85.365	12	6	12	66	Billy Hagan	Geoff Bodine	111.734
Busch 500	8/24/85	Dale Earnhardt	1	Chevrolet	81.388	18	8	11	82	Richard Childress	Dale Earnhardt	113.586
Busch 500	8/23/86	Darrell Waltrip	10	Chevrolet	86.934	15	9	6	56	Junior Johnson	Geoff Bodine	114.665
Busch 500	8/22/87	Dale Earnhardt	6	Chevrolet	90.373	12	7	8	49	Richard Childress	Terry Labonte	115.758
Busch 500	8/27/88	Dale Earnhardt	5	Chevrolet	78.775	23	13	14	83	Richard Childress	Alan Kulwicki	116.893
Busch 500	8/26/89	Darrell Waltrip	9	Chevrolet	85.554	11	5	11	69	Rick Hendrick	Alan Kulwicki	117.043

Race	Date	Winner	Start Pos.	Make	Speed	Lead Ch.	No. Lds.	No. Caut.	Caut. Laps	Owner	Pole Winner	Pole Speed
Busch 500	8/25/90	Ernie Irvan	6	Chevrolet	91.782	9	4	10	47	Larry McClure	Dale Earnhardt	115.604
Bud 500	8/24/91	Alan Kulwicki	5	Ford	82.028	14	8	11	81	Alan Kulwicki	Bill Elliott	116.957
Bud 500	8/29/92	Darrell Waltrip	9	Chevrolet	91.198	14	8	10	55	Darrell Waltrip	Ernie Irvan	120.0
Bud 500	8/28/93	Mark Martin	1	Ford	88.172	8	4	11	71	Jack Roush	Mark Martin	121.405
Goody's 500	8/27/94	Rusty Wallace	4	Ford	91.363	16	10	12	73	Roger Penske	Harry Gant	124.186
Goody's 500	8/26/95	Terry Labonte	2	Chevrolet	81.979	16	10	15	106	Rick Hendrick	Mark Martin	125.093
Goody's 500	8/24/96	Rusty Wallace	5	Ford	91.267	8	5	8	67	Roger Penske	Mark Martin	124.857

CHARLOTTE MOTOR SPEEDWAY
600-Miler

Race	Date	Winner	Start Pos.	Make	Speed	Lead Ch.	No. Lds.	No. Caut.	Caut. Laps	Owner	Pole Winner	Pole Speed
World 600	6/19/60	Joe Lee Johnson	20	Chevrolet	107.735	11	6	8	45	Paul McDuffie	Fireball Roberts	133.904
World 600	5/28/61	David Pearson	3	Pontiac	111.633	17	7	7	57	John Masoni	Richard Petty	131.611
World 600	5/27/62	Nelson Stacy	18	Ford	125.552	18	7	2	14	Holman-Moody	Fireball Roberts	140.15
World 600	6/2/63	Fred Lorenzen	2	Ford	132.417	15	6	2	14	Holman-Moody	Junior Johnson	141.148
World 600	5/24/64	Jim Paschal	12	Plymouth	125.772	14	8	7	48	Petty Enterprises	Jimmy Pardue	144.346
World 600	5/23/65	Fred Lorenzen	1	Ford	121.722	22	6	11	80	Holman-Moody	Fred Lorenzen	145.268
World 600	5/22/66	Marvin Panch	7	Plymouth	135.042	14	8	5	18	Petty Enterprises	Richard Petty	148.637
World 600	5/28/67	Jim Paschal	10	Plymouth	135.832	11	7	5	32	Tom Friedkin	Cale Yarborough	154.385
World 600	5/26/68	Buddy Baker	12	Dodge	104.207	16	8	6	110	Ray Fox	Donnie Allison	159.223
World 600	5/25/69	LeeRoy Yarbrough	2	Mercury	134.361	13	7	5	45	Junior Johnson	Donnie Allison	159.296
World 600	5/24/70	Donnie Allison	9	Ford	129.68	28	11	10	66	Banjo Matthews	Bobby Isaac	159.277
World 600	5/30/71	Bobby Allison	2	Mercury	140.422	13	5	3	24	Holman-Moody	Charlie Glotzbach	157.788
World 600	5/28/72	Buddy Baker	6	Dodge	142.255	22	4	3	24	Petty Enterprises	Bobby Allison	158.162
World 600	5/27/73	Buddy Baker	1	Dodge	134.89	23	6	6	48	Nord Krauskopf	Buddy Baker	158.051
World 600	5/26/74	David Pearson	1	Mercury	135.72	38	5	8	48	Wood Brothers	David Pearson	157.498
World 600	5/25/75	Richard Petty	3	Dodge	145.327	17	5	3	12	Petty Enterprises	David Pearson	159.353
World 600	5/30/76	David Pearson	1	Mercury	137.352	37	5	7	38	Wood Brothers	David Pearson	159.132
World 600	5/29/77	Richard Petty	2	Dodge	137.676	25	8	6	31	Petty Enterprises	David Pearson	161.435
World 600	5/28/78	Darrell Waltrip	17	Chevrolet	138.355	43	6	6	32	DiGard	David Pearson	160.551
World 600	5/27/79	Darrell Waltrip	3	Chevrolet	136.674	59	10	9	48	DiGard	Neil Bonnett	160.125
World 600	5/25/80	Benny Parsons	6	Chevrolet	119.265	47	12	14	113	M C Anderson	Cale Yarborough	165.194
World 600	5/24/81	Bobby Allison	7	Buick	129.326	32	7	7	50	Harry Ranier	Neil Bonnett	158.115
World 600	5/30/82	Neil Bonnett	13	Ford	130.058	47	12	10	62	Wood Brothers	David Pearson	162.511
World 600	5/29/83	Neil Bonnett	5	Chevrolet	140.707	23	9	5	28	B. Rahilly & B. Mock	Buddy Baker	162.841
World 600	5/27/84	Bobby Allison	16	Buick	129.233	22	6	5	48	DiGard	Harry Gant	162.496
Coca-Cola World 600	5/26/85	Darrell Waltrip	4	Chevrolet	141.807	29	8	7	34	Junior Johnson	Bill Elliott	164.703
Coca-Cola 600	5/25/86	Dale Earnhardt	3	Chevrolet	140.406	38	15	6	32	Richard Childress	Geoff Bodine	164.511
Coca-Cola 600	5/24/87	Kyle Petty	7	Ford	131.483	23	10	12	68	Wood Brothers	Bill Elliott	170.901
Coca-Cola 600	5/29/88	Darrell Waltrip	5	Chevrolet	124.46	43	18	13	89	Rick Hendrick	Davey Allison	173.594
Coca-Cola 600	5/28/89	Darrell Waltrip	4	Chevrolet	144.077	22	12	7	36	Rick Hendrick	Alan Kulwicki	173.021
Coca-Cola 600	5/27/90	Rusty Wallace	9	Pontiac	137.65	15	10	11	48	Raymond Beadle	Ken Schrader	173.963
Coca-Cola 600	5/26/91	Davey Allison	10	Ford	138.951	22	10	9	54	Robert Yates	Mark Martin	174.82
Coca-Cola 600	5/24/92	Dale Earnhardt	13	Chevrolet	132.98	28	14	12	62	Richard Childress	Bill Elliott	175.479
Coca-Cola 600	5/30/93	Dale Earnhardt	14	Chevrolet	145.504	29	10	7	33	Richard Childress	Ken Schrader	177.352
Coca-Cola 600	5/29/94	Jeff Gordon	1	Chevrolet	139.445	24	8	9	47	Rick Hendrick	Jeff Gordon	181.439
Coca-Cola 600	5/28/95	Bobby Labonte	2	Chevrolet	151.952	32	12	7	33	Joe Gibbs	Jeff Gordon	183.861
Coca-Cola 600	5/26/96	Dale Jarrett	15	Ford	147.581	20	8	6	35	Robert Yates	Jeff Gordon	183.733

Fall 500-Miler

Race	Date	Winner	Start Pos.	Make	Speed	Lead Ch.	No. Lds.	No. Caut.	Caut. Laps	Owner	Pole Winner	Pole Speed
National 400	10/16/60	Speedy Thompson	3	Ford	112.905	8	5	7	34	Wood Brothers	Fireball Roberts	133.465
National 400	10/15/61	Joe Weatherly	6	Pontiac	119.95	13	5	3	18	Bud Moore	David Pearson	138.577
National 400	10/14/62	Junior Johnson	3	Pontiac	132.085	10	4	1	6	Ray Fox	Fireball Roberts	140.287
National 400	10/13/63	Junior Johnson	2	Chevrolet	132.105	13	5	3	12	Ray Fox	Marvin Panch	143.017
National 400	10/18/64	Fred Lorenzen	3	Ford	134.475	10	4	4	21	Holman-Moody	Richard Petty	150.711
National 400	10/17/65	Fred Lorenzen	1	Ford	119.117	28	9	6	47	Holman-Moody	Fred Lorenzen	147.773
National 500	10/16/66	LeeRoy Yarbrough	17	Dodge	130.576	14	6	6	46	Jon Thorne	Fred Lorenzen	150.533
National 500	10/15/67	Buddy Baker	4	Dodge	130.317	22	7	9	64	Ray Fox	Cale Yarborough	154.872
National 500	10/20/68	Charlie Glotzbach	1	Dodge	156.324	26	9	6	49	Cotton Owens	Charlie Glotzbach	156.06
National 500	10/12/69	Donnie Allison	3	Ford	131.271	28	6	9	50	Banjo Matthews	Cale Yarborough	162.162
National 500	10/11/70	LeeRoy Yarbrough	5	Mercury	123.246	23	8	8	63	Junior Johnson	Charlie Glotzbach	157.273
National 500	10/10/71	Bobby Allison	3	Mercury	126.14	10	5	6	37	Holman-Moody	Charlie Glotzbach	157.085
National 500	10/8/72	Bobby Allison	4	Chevrolet	133.234	21	6	6	40	Richard Howard	David Pearson	158.539

Race	Date	Winner	Start Pos.	Make	Speed	Lead Ch.	No. Lds.	No. Caut.	Caut. Laps	Owner	Pole Winner	Pole Speed
National 500	10/7/73	Cale Yarborough	2	Chevrolet	145.24	12	7	2	16	Richard Howard	David Pearson	158.315
National 500	10/6/74	David Pearson	1	Mercury	119.912	47	11	9	79	Wood Brothers	David Pearson	158.749
National 500	10/5/75	Richard Petty	9	Dodge	132.209	29	13	7	53	Petty Enterprises	David Pearson	161.701
National 500	10/10/76	Donnie Allison	15	Chevrolet	141.226	26	7	3	18	Hoss Ellington	David Pearson	161.223
NAPA National 500	10/9/77	Benny Parsons	8	Chevrolet	142.78	18	7	4	18	L. G. DeWitt	David Pearson	160.892
NAPA National 500	10/8/78	Bobby Allison	8	Ford	141.826	40	9	4	21	Bud Moore	David Pearson	161.355
NAPA National 500	10/7/79	Cale Yarborough	4	Chevrolet	134.266	28	14	8	40	Junior Johnson	Neil Bonnett	164.304
National 500	10/5/80	Dale Earnhardt	4	Chevrolet	135.243	43	11	8	44	Rod Osterlund	Buddy Baker	165.634
National 500	10/11/81	Darrell Waltrip	1	Buick	117.483	27	13	12	78	Junior Johnson	Darrell Waltrip	162.744
National 500	10/10/82	Harry Gant	1	Buick	137.208	12	6	6	34	Hal Needham	Harry Gant	164.694
Miller High Life 500	10/9/83	Richard Petty	20	Pontiac	139.998	31	13	8	35	Petty Enterprises	Tim Richmond	163.073
Miller High Life 500	10/7/84	Bill Elliott	2	Ford	148.861	22	7	3	15	Harry Melling	Benny Parsons	165.579
Miller High Life 500	10/6/85	Cale Yarborough	7	Ford	136.761	15	6	6	41	Harry Ranier	Harry Gant	166.139
Oakwood Homes 500	10/5/86	Dale Earnhardt	3	Chevrolet	132.403	26	9	6	44	Richard Childress	Tim Richmond	167.078
Oakwood Homes 500	10/11/87	Bill Elliott	7	Ford	128.443	29	17	7	59	Harry Melling	Bobby Allison	171.636
Oakwood Homes 500	10/9/88	Rusty Wallace	3	Pontiac	130.677	36	15	10	63	Raymond Beadle	Alan Kulwicki	175.896
All Pro Auto Parts 500	10/8/89	Ken Schrader	2	Chevrolet	149.863	19	9	4	21	Rick Hendrick	Bill Elliott	174.081
Mello Yello 500	10/7/90	Davey Allison	5	Ford	137.428	14	10	6	37	Robert Yates	Brett Bodine	174.385
Mello Yello 500	10/6/91	Geoff Bodine	6	Ford	138.984	10	4	6	38	Junior Johnson	Mark Martin	176.499
Mello Yello 500	10/11/92	Mark Martin	4	Ford	153.537	20	8	3	12	Jack Roush	Alan Kulwicki	179.027
Mello Yello 500	10/10/93	Ernie Irvan	2	Ford	154.537	9	4	2	11	Robert Yates	Jeff Gordon	177.684
Mello Yello 500	10/10/94	Dale Jarrett	22	Chevrolet	145.922	30	16	7	34	Joe Gibbs	Ward Burton	185.759
UAW-GM Quality 500	10/8/95	Mark Martin	5	Ford	145.358	19	11	7	35	Jack Roush	Ricky Rudd	180.578
UAW-GM Quality 500	10/6/96	Terry Labonte	16	Chevrolet	143.143	21	9	5	37	Rick Hendrick	Bobby Labonte	184.068

DARLINGTON RACEWAY
Southern 500

Race	Date	Winner	Start Pos.	Make	Speed	Lead Ch.	No. Lds.	No. Caut.	Caut. Laps	Owner	Pole Winner	Pole Speed
Southern 500	9/4/50	Johnny Mantz	43	Plymouth	75.25	4	4	2	13	Hubert Westmoreland	Curtis Turner	82.034
Southern 500	9/3/51	Herb Thomas	2	Hudson	76.906	6	5	4	26	Herb Thomas	Frank Mundy	84.173
Southern 500	9/1/52	Fonty Flock	1	Oldsmobile	74.512	6	4	7	40	Frank Christian	Fonty Flock	88.55
Southern 500	9/7/53	Buck Baker	7	Oldsmobile	92.881		4	4	17	Griffin Motors	Fonty Flock	107.983
Southern 500	9/5/55	Herb Thomas	8	Chevrolet	92.281	10	7	8	51	Herb Thomas	Fireball Roberts	110.682
Southern 500	9/3/56	Curtis Turner	11	Ford	95.167	14	6	7	68	Charlie Schwam	Buck Baker	119.659
Southern 500	9/2/57	Speedy Thompson	7	Chevrolet	100.094	13	8	6	23	Speedy Thompson	Cotton Owens	117.416
Southern 500	9/1/58	Fireball Roberts	2	Chevrolet	102.585	8	6	6	28	Frank Strickland	Eddie Pagan	116.952
Southern 500	9/7/59	Jim Reed	14	Chevrolet	111.836	11	8	2	12	Jim Reed	Fireball Roberts	123.734
Southern 500	9/5/60	Buck Baker	2	Pontiac	105.901	14	7	5	61	Jack Smith	Fireball Roberts	125.459
Southern 500	9/4/61	Nelson Stacy	3	Ford	117.787	19	6	6	21	Dudley Farrell	Fireball Roberts	128.68
Southern 500	9/3/62	Larry Frank	10	Ford	117.965	9	7	4	27	Ratus Walters	Fireball Roberts	130.246
Southern 500	9/2/63	Fireball Roberts	10	Ford	129.784	9	4	0	0	Holman-Moody	Fred Lorenzen	133.648
Southern 500	9/7/64	Buck Baker	6	Dodge	117.757	12	7	7	50	Ray Fox	Richard Petty	136.815
Southern 500	9/6/65	Ned Jarrett	10	Ford	115.878	23	8	7	44	Bondy Long	Junior Johnson	137.571
Southern 500	9/5/66	Darel Dieringer	3	Mercury	114.83	28	10	8	80	Bud Moore	LeeRoy Yarbrough	140.058
Southern 500	9/4/67	Richard Petty	1	Plymouth	130.423	6	4	3	25	Petty Enterprises	Richard Petty	143.436
Southern 500	9/2/68	Cale Yarborough	2	Mercury	126.132	13	6	7	65	Wood Brothers	Charlie Glotzbach	144.83
Southern 500	9/1/69	LeeRoy Yarbrough	4	Ford	105.612	20	8	7	85	Junior Johnson	Cale Yarborough	151.985
Southern 500	9/7/70	Buddy Baker	2	Dodge	128.817	19	8	9	50	Cotton Owens	David Pearson	150.555
Southern 500	9/6/71	Bobby Allison	1	Mercury	131.398	14	3	5	32	Holman-Moody	Bobby Allison	147.915
Southern 500	9/4/72	Bobby Allison	1	Chevrolet	128.124	30	7	5	43	Richard Howard	Bobby Allison	152.228
Southern 500	9/3/73	Cale Yarborough	8	Chevrolet	134.033	25	5	7	38	Richard Howard	David Pearson	150.366
Southern 500	9/2/74	Cale Yarborough	4	Chevrolet	111.075	26	13	11	101	Junior Johnson	Richard Petty	150.132
Southern 500	9/1/75	Bobby Allison	3	AMC	116.825	20	8	10	72	Roger Penske	David Pearson	153.401
Southern 500	9/6/76	David Pearson	1	Mercury	120.534	31	10	8	65	Wood Brothers	David Pearson	154.699
Southern 500	9/5/77	David Pearson	5	Mercury	106.797	32	7	6	93	Wood Brothers	Darrell Waltrip	153.493
Southern 500	9/4/78	Cale Yarborough	6	Oldsmobile	116.828	21	10	9	72	Junior Johnson	David Pearson	153.685
Southern 500	9/3/79	David Pearson	5	Chevrolet	126.259	18	7	9	52	Rod Osterlund	Bobby Allison	154.88
Southern 500	9/1/80	Terry Labonte	10	Chevrolet	115.21	27	12	14	79	Billy Hagan	Darrell Waltrip	153.838
Southern 500	9/7/81	Neil Bonnett	3	Ford	126.41	23	9	8	45	Wood Brothers	Harry Gant	152.693
Southern 500	9/6/82	Cale Yarborough	9	Buick	115.224	41	17	14	87	M C Anderson	David Pearson	155.739
Southern 500	9/5/83	Bobby Allison	14	Buick	123.343	17	9	9	60	DiGard	Neil Bonnett	157.187
Southern 500	9/2/84	Harry Gant	1	Chevrolet	128.27	17	9	8	51	Hal Needham	Harry Gant	155.502
Southern 500	9/1/85	Bill Elliott	1	Ford	121.254	20	9	14	70	Harry Melling	Bill Elliott	156.641

Race	Date	Winner	Start Pos.	Make	Speed	Lead Ch.	No. Lds.	No. Caut.	Caut. Laps	Owner	Pole Winner	Pole Speed
Southern 500	8/31/86	Tim Richmond	1	Chevrolet	121.068	16	9	12	79	Rick Hendrick	Tim Richmond	158.489
Southern 500	9/6/87	Dale Earnhardt	5	Chevrolet	115.52	13	6	5	50	Richard Childress	Davey Allison	157.232
Southern 500	9/4/88	Bill Elliott	1	Ford	128.297	24	12	10	39	Harry Melling	Bill Elliott	160.827
Heinz Southern 500	9/3/89	Dale Earnhardt	10	Chevrolet	135.462	26	10	4	24	Richard Childress	Alan Kulwicki	160.156
Heinz Southern 500	9/2/90	Dale Earnhardt	1	Chevrolet	123.141	20	8	10	51	Richard Childress	Dale Earnhardt	158.448
Heinz Southern 500	9/1/91	Harry Gant	5	Oldsmobile	133.508	20	10	8	43	Leo Jackson	Davey Allison	162.506
Mountain Dew Southern 500	9/6/92	Darrell Waltrip	5	Chevrolet	129.114	23	11	5	28	Darrell Waltrip	Sterling Marlin	162.249
Mountain Dew Southern 500	9/5/93	Mark Martin	4	Ford	137.932	21	10	3	16	Jack Roush	Ken Schrader	161.259
Mountain Dew Southern 500	9/4/94	Bill Elliott	9	Ford	127.952	28	10	6	42	Junior Johnson	Geoff Bodine	166.998
Mountain Dew Southern 500	9/3/95	Jeff Gordon	5	Chevrolet	121.231	21	11	12	94	Rick Hendrick	John Andretti	167.379
Mountain Dew Southern 500	9/1/96	Jeff Gordon	2	Chevrolet	135.757	29	14	6	37	Rick Hendrick	Dale Jarrett	170.934

Spring Race

Race	Date	Winner	Start Pos.	Make	Speed	Lead Ch.	No. Lds.	No. Caut.	Caut. Laps	Owner	Pole Winner	Pole Speed
	5/10/52	Dick Rathmann	4	Hudson	83.818	8	5			Walt Chapman		
Rebel 300*	5/12/57	Fireball Roberts	4	Ford	107.941	10	5			Pete DePaolo	Paul Goldsmith	115.324
Rebel 300*	5/10/58	Curtis Turner	12	Ford	109.624	14	5	2	4	Holman-Moody	Fireball	116.299
Rebel 300*	5/9/59	Fireball Roberts	10	Chevrolet	115.817	6	4	0	0	W. J. Ridgeway	Curtis Turner	116.326
Rebel 300	5/7 & 14/60	Joe Weatherly	2	Ford	102.640	7	4	4		Fireball Roberts		127.750
Rebel 300	5/6/61	Fred Lorenzen	1	Ford	119.52	16	8	1		Holman-Moody	Fred Lorenzen	128.965
Rebel 300	5/12/62	Nelson Stacy	3	Ford	117.429	9	7			Holman-Moody	Fred Lorenzen	129.813
Rebel 300	5/11/63	Joe Weatherly	6	Pontiac	122.745	9	6	1	6	Bud Moore	Fred Lorenzen	131.718
Rebel 300	5/9/64	Fred Lorenzen	1	Ford	130.013	10	2	1	5	Holman-Moody	Fred Lorenzen	135.727
Rebel 300	5/8/65	Junior Johnson	3	Ford	111.849	11	7	6	50	Rex Lovette	Fred Lorenzen	138.133
Rebel 400	4/30/66	Richard Petty	1	Plymouth	131.993	6	5	1	5	Petty Enterprises	Richard Petty	140.815
Rebel 300	5/13/67	Richard Petty	2	Plymouth	125.738	12	6	5	31	Petty Enterprises	David Pearson	144.536
Rebel 400	5/11/68	David Pearson	2	Ford	132.699	13	7	4	23	Holman-Moody	LeeRoy Yarbrough	148.85
Rebel 400	5/10/69	LeeRoy Yarbrough	4	Mercury	131.572	11	6	4	24	Junior Johnson	Cale Yarborough	152.293
Rebel 400	5/9/70	David Pearson	3	Ford	129.668	20	7	4	37	Holman-Moody	Charlie Glotzbach	153.822
Rebel 400	5/2/71	Buddy Baker	5	Dodge	130.678	13	6	5	30	Petty Enterprises	Donnie Allison	149.826
Rebel 400	4/16/72	David Pearson	1	Mercury	124.406	14	7	5	37	Wood Brothers	David Pearson	148.209
Rebel 500	4/15/73	David Pearson	1	Mercury	122.655	21	5	11	71	Wood Brothers	David Pearson	153.463
Rebel 450	4/7/74	David Pearson	2	Mercury	117.543	29	8	7	66	Wood Brothers	Donnie Allison	150.689
Rebel 500	4/13/75	Bobby Allison	5	AMC	117.597	22	10	11	79	Roger Penske	David Pearson	155.433
Rebel 500	4/11/76	David Pearson	1	Mercury	122.973	32	10	8	54	Wood Brothers	David Pearson	154.171
Rebel 500	4/3/77	Darrell Waltrip	4	Chevrolet	128.817	28	7	6	39	DiGard	David Pearson	151.269
Rebel 500	4/9/78	Benny Parsons	8	Chevrolet	127.544	24	9	7	44	L. G. DeWitt	Bobby Allison	151.862
CRC Chemicals Rebel 500	4/8/79	Darrell Waltrip	2	Chevrolet	121.721	25	8	6	53	DiGard	Donnie Allison	154.797
CRC Chemicals Rebel 500	4/13/80	David Pearson	2	Chevrolet	112.397	12	7	7	47	Hoss Ellington	Benny Parsons	155.866
CRC Chemicals Rebel 500	4/12/81	Darrell Waltrip	3	Buick	126.703	20	5	6	40	Junior Johnson	Bill Elliott	153.896
CRC Chemicals Rebel 500	4/4/82	Dale Earnhardt	5	Ford	123.554	30	11	8	53	Bud Moore	Buddy Baker	153.979
TranSouth 500	4/10/83	Harry Gant	5	Buick	130.406	20	8	5	37	Hal Needham	Tim Richmond	157.818
TranSouth 500	4/15/84	Darrell Waltrip	9	Chevrolet	119.925	19	11	9	65	Junior Johnson	Benny Parsons	156.328
TranSouth 500	4/14/85	Bill Elliott	1	Ford	126.295	22	9	7	51	Harry Melling	Bill Elliott	157.454
TranSouth 500	4/13/86	Dale Earnhardt	4	Chevrolet	128.994	17	8	11	54	Richard Childress	Geoff Bodine	159.197
TranSouth 500	3/29/87	Dale Earnhardt	2	Chevrolet	122.54	27	11	10	71	Richard Childress	Ken Schrader	158.387
TranSouth 500	3/27/88	Lake Speed	8	Oldsmobile	131.284	18	11	8	42	Lake Speed	Ken Schrader	162.657
TranSouth 500	4/2/89	Harry Gant	10	Oldsmobile	115.475	14	9	7	68	Leo Jackson	Mark Martin	161.111
TranSouth 500	4/1/90	Dale Earnhardt	15	Chevrolet	124.073	20	10	10	51	Richard Childress	Geoff Bodine	162.996
TranSouth 500	4/7/91	Ricky Rudd	13	Chevrolet	135.594	15	7	3	19	Rick Hendrick	Geoff Bodine	161.939
TranSouth 500	3/29/92	Bill Elliott	2	Ford	139.364	21	7	4	21	Junior Johnson	Sterling Marlin	163.067
TranSouth 500	3/28/93	Dale Earnhardt	1	Chevrolet	139.958	19	11	3	14	Richard Childress		
TranSouth 500	3/27/94	Dale Earnhardt	9	Chevrolet	132.432	28	10	5	26	Richard Childress	Bill Elliott	165.553
TranSouth 400	3/26/95	Sterling Marlin	5	Chevrolet	111.392	16	11	15	87	Larry McClure	Jeff Gordon	170.833
TranSouth 400	3/24/96	Jeff Gordon	2	Chevrolet	124.792	15	9	11	56	Rick Hendrick	Ward Burton	172.797

*Please note that these races were NASCAR Convertible races, not Winston Cup or Grand National races.

Race	Date	Winner	Start Pos.	Make	Speed	Lead Ch.	No. Lds.	No. Caut.	Caut. Laps	Owner	Pole Winner	Pole Speed

Daytona Int'l Speedway
Daytona 500

Race	Date	Winner	Start Pos.	Make	Speed	Lead Ch.	No. Lds.	No. Caut.	Caut. Laps	Owner	Pole Winner	Pole Speed
Daytona 500	2/22/59	Lee Petty	15	Oldsmobile	135.521	33	7	0	0	Petty Enterprises	Bob Welborn	140.121
Daytona 500	2/14/60	Junior Johnson	9	Chevrolet	124.740	13	8	4	32	John Masoni	Cotton Owens	149.892
Daytona 500	2/26/61	Marvin Panch	4	Pontiac	149.601	9	5	0	0	Smokey Yunick	Fireball Roberts	155.709
Daytona 500	2/18/62	Fireball Roberts	1	Pontiac	152.529	22	5	0	0	Jim Stephens	Fireball Roberts	156.999
Daytona 500	2/24/63	Tiny Lund	12	Ford	151.566	29	10	2	10	Wood Brothers	Fireball Roberts	160.943
Daytona 500	2/23/64	Richard Petty	2	Plymouth	154.334	6	4	3	19	Petty Enterprises	Paul Goldsmith	174.91
Daytona 500	2/14/65	Fred Lorenzen	4	Ford	141.539	7	4	3	43	Holman-Moody	Darel Dieringer	171.151
Daytona 500	2/27/66	Richard Petty	1	Plymouth	160.627	14	6	4	22	Petty Enterprises	Richard Petty	175.165
Daytona 500	2/26/67	Mario Andretti	12	Ford	146.926	36	9	9	54	Holman-Moody	Curtis Turner	180.831
Daytona 500	2/25/68	Cale Yarborough	1	Mercury	143.251	21	9	11	60	Wood Brothers	Cale Yarborough	189.222
Daytona 500	2/23/69	LeeRoy Yarbrough	19	Ford	157.95	17	8	5	38	Junior Johnson	Buddy Baker	188.901
Daytona 500	2/22/70	Pete Hamilton	9	Plymouth	149.601	24	10	6	45	Petty Enterprises	Cale Yarborough	194.015
Daytona 500	2/14/71	Richard Petty	5	Plymouth	144.462	48	11	7	41	Petty Enterprises	A. J. Foyt	182.744
Daytona 500	2/20/72	A.J. Foyt	2	Mercury	161.55	13	3	3	17	Wood Brothers	Bobby Isaac	186.632
Daytona 500	2/18/73	Richard Petty	7	Dodge	157.205	20	5	4	28	Petty Enterprises	Buddy Baker	185.662
Daytona 500	2/17/74	Richard Petty	2	Dodge	140.894	60	16	10	53	Petty Enterprises	David Pearson	185.817
Daytona 500	2/16/75	Benny Parsons	32	Chevrolet	153.649	19	7	3	21	L. G. DeWitt	Donnie Allison	185.827
Daytona 500	2/15/76	David Pearson	7	Mercury	152.181	36	11	7	35	Wood Brothers	Ramo Stott	183.456
Daytona 500	2/20/77	Cale Yarborough	4	Chevrolet	153.218	30	10	6	37	Junior Johnson	Donnie Allison	188.048
Daytona 500	2/19/78	Bobby Allison	33	Ford	159.73	37	6	5	24	Bud Moore	Cale Yarborough	187.536
Daytona 500	2/18/79	Richard Petty	13	Oldsmobile	143.977	36	13	7	57	Petty Enterprises	Buddy Baker	196.049
Daytona 500	2/17/80	Buddy Baker	1	Oldsmobile	177.602	29	7	5	15	Harry Ranier	Buddy Baker	194.009
Daytona 500	2/15/81	Richard Petty	8	Buick	169.651	49	9	4	18	Petty Enterprises	Bobby Allison	194.624
Daytona 500	2/14/82	Bobby Allison	7	Buick	153.991	31	10	5	34	DiGard	Benny Parsons	196.317
Daytona 500	2/20/83	Cale Yarborough	8	Pontiac	155.979	58	11	6	36	Harry Ranier	Ricky Rudd	198.864
Daytona 500	2/19/84	Cale Yarborough	1	Chevrolet	150.994	34	9	7	39	Harry Ranier	Cale Yarborough	201.848
Daytona 500	2/17/85	Bill Elliott	1	Ford	172.265	22	9	5	18	Harry Melling	Bill Elliott	205.114
Daytona 500	2/16/86	Geoff Bodine	2	Chevrolet	148.124	27	12	8	46	Rick Hendrick	Bill Elliott	205.039
Daytona 500	2/15/87	Bill Elliott	1	Ford	176.263	28	10	4	15	Harry Melling	Bill Elliott	210.364
Daytona 500	2/14/88	Bobby Allison	3	Buick	137.531	26	12	7	42	Stavola Brothers	Ken Schrader	193.823
Daytona 500	2/19/89	Darrell Waltrip	2	Chevrolet	148.466	30	15	7	30	Rick Hendrick	Ken Schrader	196.996
Daytona 500	2/18/90	Derrike Cope	12	Chevrolet	165.761	27	13	3	15	Bob Whitcomb	Ken Schrader	196.515
Daytona 500	2/19/91	Ernie Irvan	2	Chevrolet	148.148	21	9	9	36	Larry McClure	Davey Allison	195.955
Daytona 500	2/16/92	Davey Allison	6	Ford	160.256	15	7	4	22	Robert Yates	Sterling Marlin	192.213
Daytona 500	2/14/93	Dale Jarrett	2	Chevrolet	154.972	38	13	7	30	Joe Gibbs	Kyle Petty	189.426
Daytona 500	2/20/94	Sterling Marlin	4	Chevrolet	156.931	33	13	4	23	Larry McClure	Loy Allen Jr.	190.158
Daytona 500	2/19/95	Sterling Marlin	3	Chevrolet	141.71	12	7	10	41	Larry McClure	Dale Jarrett	193.498
Daytona 500	2/18/96	Dale Jarrett	7	Ford	154.308	32	15	6	26	Robert Yates	Dale Earnhardt	189.51

Firecracker/Pepsi 250/400

Race	Date	Winner	Start Pos.	Make	Speed	Lead Ch.	No. Lds.	No. Caut.	Caut. Laps	Owner	Pole Winner	Pole Speed
Firecracker 250	7/4/59	Fireball Roberts	1	Pontiac	140.581	7	4	0	0	Jim Stephens	Fireball Roberts	144.997
Firecracker 250	7/4/60	Jack Smith	1	Pontiac	146.842	10	3	0	0	Jack Smith	Jack Smith	152.129
Firecracker 250	7/4/61	David Pearson	2	Pontiac	154.294	12	6	0	0	John Masoni	Fireball Roberts	157.15
Firecracker 250	7/4/62	Fireball Roberts	4	Pontiac	153.688	14	3	2	7	Banjo Matthews	Banjo Matthews	160.499
Firecracker 400	7/4/63	Fireball Roberts	3	Ford	150.927	39	6	3	19	Holman-Moody	Junior Johnson	166.005
Firecracker 400	7/4/64	A. J. Foyt	19	Dodge	151.451	19	4	5	25	Ray Nichels	Darel Dieringer	172.678
Firecracker 400	7/4/65	A. J. Foyt	11	Ford	150.046	19	7	3	20	Wood Brothers	Marvin Panch	171.51
Firecracker 400	7/4/66	Sam McQuagg	4	Dodge	153.613	17	6	4	23	Ray Nichels	LeeRoy Yarbrough	176.66
Firecracker 400	7/4/67	Cale Yarborough	2	Ford	143.583	41	8	4	43	Wood Brothers	Darel Dieringer	179.802
Firecracker 400	7/4/68	Cale Yarborough	4	Mercury	167.247	9	4	2	14	Wood Brothers	Charlie Glotzbach	185.156
Firecracker 400	7/4/69	LeeRoy Yarbrough	9	Ford	160.875	16	7	2	27	Junior Johnson	Cale Yarborough	190.706
Firecracker 400	7/4/70	Donnie Allison	15	Ford	162.235	32	10	3	17	Banjo Matthews	Cale Yarborough	191.64
Firecracker 400	7/4/71	Bobby Isaac	21	Dodge	161.947	34	8	2	11	Nord Krauskopf	Donnie Allison	183.228
Firecracker 400	7/4/72	David Pearson	2	Mercury	160.821	23	6	2	14	Wood Brothers	Bobby Isaac	186.277
Firecracker 400	7/4/73	David Pearson	6	Mercury	158.468	25	5	2	17	Wood Brothers	Bobby Allison	179.619
Firecracker 400	7/4/74	David Pearson	1	Mercury	138.31	48	9	6	41	Wood Brothers	David Pearson	180.759
Firecracker 400	7/4/75	Richard Petty	13	Dodge	158.381	16	6	3	17	Petty Enterprises	Donnie Allison	186.737
Firecracker 400	7/4/76	Cale Yarborough	2	Chevrolet	160.966	41	8	2	14	Junior Johnson	A. J. Foyt	183.09
Firecracker 400	7/4/77	Richard Petty	5	Dodge	142.716	34	8	2	26	Petty Enterprises	Neil Bonnett	187.191
Firecracker 400	7/4/78	David Pearson	3	Mercury	154.34	29	10	4	21	Wood Brothers	Cale Yarborough	186.803
Firecracker 400	7/4/79	Neil Bonnett	2	Mercury	172.89	28	8	2	11	Wood Brothers	Buddy Baker	193.196
Firecracker 400	7/4/80	Bobby Allison	14	Ford	173.473	40	8	3	11	Bud Moore	Cale Yarborough	194.67

Race	Date	Winner	Start Pos.	Make	Speed	Lead Ch.	No. Lds.	No. Caut.	Caut. Laps	Owner	Pole Winner	Pole Speed
Firecracker 400	7/4/81	Cale Yarborough	1	Buick	142.588	35	10	6	37	M C Anderson	Cale Yarborough	192.852
Firecracker 400	7/4/82	Bobby Allison	9	Buick	163.099	28	8	5	25	DiGard	Geoff Bodine	194.721
Firecracker 400	7/4/83	Buddy Baker	8	Ford	167.442	39	11	3	16	Wood Brothers	Cale Yarborough	196.635
Pepsi Firecracker 400	7/4/84	Richard Petty	6	Pontiac	171.204	29	8	3	15	Mike Curb	Cale Yarborough	199.743
Pepsi Firecracker 400	7/4/85	Greg Sacks	9	Chevrolet	158.73	19	10	6	26	DiGard	Bill Elliott	201.523
Pepsi Firecracker 400	7/4/86	Tim Richmond	9	Chevrolet	131.916	31	14	8	58	Rick Hendrick	Cale Yarborough	203.519
Pepsi Firecracker 400	7/4/87	Bobby Allison	11	Buick	161.074	24	12	4	20	Stavola Brothers	Davey Allison	198.085
Pepsi Firecracker 400	7/2/88	Bill Elliott	38	Ford	163.302	22	10	3	15	Harry Melling	Darrell Waltrip	193.819
Pepsi 400	7/1/89	Davey Allison	8	Ford	132.207	28	11	12	42	Robert Yates	Mark Martin	191.861
Pepsi 400	7/7/90	Dale Earnhardt	3	Chevrolet	160.0	15	8	4	14	Richard Childress	Greg Sacks	195.533
Pepsi 400	7/6/91	Bill Elliott	10	Ford	159.116	18	11	4	18	Harry Melling	Sterling Marlin	190.331
Pepsi 400	7/4/92	Ernie Irvan	6	Chevrolet	170.457	17	8	2	8	Larry McClure	Sterling Marlin	189.366
Pepsi 400	7/3/93	Dale Earnhardt	5	Chevrolet	151.755	28	13	6	22	Richard Childress	Ernie Irvan	190.327
Pepsi 400	7/2/94	Jimmy Spencer	3	Ford	155.558	18	10	4	19	Junior Johnson	Dale Earnhardt	191.339
Pepsi 400	7/1/95	Jeff Gordon	3	Chevrolet	166.976	8	4	3	11	Rick Hendrick	Dale Earnhardt	191.355
Pepsi 400	7/6/96	Sterling Marlin	2	Chevrolet	161.602	9	6	3	11	Larry McClure	Jeff Gordon	188.869

DOVER DOWNS INT'L SPEEDWAY
Spring Race

Race	Date	Winner	Start Pos.	Make	Speed	Lead Ch.	No. Lds.	No. Caut.	Caut. Laps	Owner	Pole Winner	Pole Speed
Mason-Dixon 300	7/6/69	Richard Petty	3	Ford	115.772	7	3	4	27	Petty Enterprises	David Pearson	130.43
Mason-Dixon 300	9/20/70	Richard Petty	2	Plymouth	112.103	10	3	4	27	Petty Enterprises	Bobby Isaac	129.538
Mason-Dixon 500	6/6/71	Bobby Allison	2	Ford	123.119	21	6	0	0	Holman-Moody	Richard Petty	129.486
Mason-Dixon 500	6/4/72	Bobby Allison	2	Chevrolet	118.019	13	4	3	25	Richard Howard	Bobby Isaac	130.809
Mason-Dixon 500	6/3/73	David Pearson	1	Mercury	119.745	13	4	3	22	Wood Brothers	David Pearson	133.111
Mason-Dixon 500	5/19/74	Cale Yarborough	3	Chevrolet	115.057	10	3	3	25	Richard Howard	David Pearson	134.403
Mason-Dixon 500	5/18 & 19/75	David Pearson	1	Mercury	100.826	26	5	8	103	Wood Brothers	David Pearson	136.612
Mason-Dixon 500	5/16/76	Benny Parsons	7	Chevrolet	115.436	17	5	6	38	L. G. DeWitt	Dave Marcis	136.013
Mason-Dixon 500	5/15/77	Cale Yarborough	6	Chevrolet	123.327	11	5	2	10	Junior Johnson	Richard Petty	136.033
Mason-Dixon 500	5/21/78	David Pearson	3	Mercury	114.664	18	9	6	37	Wood Brothers	Buddy Baker	135.452
Mason-Dixon 500	5/20/79	Neil Bonnett	5	Mercury	111.269	26	8	6	48	Wood Brothers	Darrell Waltrip	136.103
Mason-Dixon 500	5/18/80	Bobby Allison	8	Ford	113.866	17	6	9	67	Bud Moore	Cale Yarborough	138.814
Mason-Dixon 500	5/17/81	Jody Ridley	11	Ford	116.595	12	5	2	24	Junie Donlavey	David Pearson	138.425
Mason-Dixon 500	5/16/82	Bobby Allison	3	Chevrolet	120.136	9	3	6	32	DiGard	Darrell Waltrip	139.308
Mason-Dixon 500	5/15/83	Bobby Allison	10	Buick	114.847	28	9	9	53	DiGard	Joe Ruttman	139.616
Budweiser 500	5/20/84	Richard Petty	5	Pontiac	118.717	26	7	6	40	Mike Curb	Ricky Rudd	140.807
Budweiser 500	5/19/85	Bill Elliott	4	Ford	123.094	7	4	5	37	Harry Melling	Terry Labonte	138.106
Budweiser 500	5/18/86	Geoff Bodine	3	Chevrolet	115.009	29	10	8	67	Rick Hendrick	Ricky Rudd	138.217
Budweiser 500	5/31/87	Davey Allison	2	Ford	112.958	18	8	9	59	Harry Ranier	Bill Elliott	145.056
Budweiser 500	6/5/88	Bill Elliott	17	Ford	118.726	25	11	7	45	Harry Melling	Alan Kulwicki	146.681
Budweiser 500	6/4/89	Dale Earnhardt	2	Chevrolet	121.67	20	7	6	36	Richard Childress	Mark Martin	144.387
Budweiser 500	6/3/90	Derrike Cope	15	Chevrolet	123.96	21	9	5	32	Bob Whitcomb	Dick Trickle	145.814
Budweiser 500	6/2/91	Ken Schrader	19	Chevrolet	120.152	22	9	6	42	Rick Hendrick	Michael Waltrip	143.392
Budweiser 500	5/31/92	Harry Gant	15	Oldsmobile	109.456	20	11	7	98	Leo Jackson	Brett Bodine	147.408
Budweiser 500	6/6/93	Dale Earnhardt	8	Chevrolet	105.6	25	12	14	78	Richard Childress	Ernie Irvan	151.541
Budweiser 500	6/6/94	Rusty Wallace	6	Ford	102.529	22	8	12	99	Roger Penske	Ernie Irvan	151.956
Miller Genuine Draft 500	6/4/95	Kyle Petty	37	Pontiac	119.88	20	8	5	38	Felix Sabates	Jeff Gordon	153.669
Miller 500	6/2/96	Jeff Gordon	1	Chevrolet	122.741	19	6	5	38	Rick Hendrick	Jeff Gordon	154.785

Fall Race

Race	Date	Winner	Start Pos.	Make	Speed	Lead Ch.	No. Lds.	No. Caut.	Caut. Laps	Owner	Pole Winner	Pole Speed
Delaware 500	10/17/71	Richard Petty	4	Plymouth	123.254	3	3	2	9	Petty Enterprises	Bobby Allison	132.811
Delaware 500	9/17/72	David Pearson	2	Mercury	120.506	14	4	2	22	Wood Brothers	Bobby Allison	133.323
Delaware 500	9/16/73	David Pearson	1	Mercury	112.852	23	5	7	56	Wood Brothers	David Pearson	124.649
Delaware 500	9/15/74	Richard Petty	2	Dodge	113.64	6	6	7	55	Petty Enterprises	Buddy Baker	133.64
Delaware 500	9/14/75	Richard Petty	3	Dodge	111.372	18	7	5	41	Petty Enterprises	Dave Marcis	133.953
Delaware 500	9/19/76	Cale Yarborough	1	Chevrolet	115.74	21	6	2	27	Junior Johnson	Cale Yarborough	115.74
Delaware 500	9/18/77	Benny Parsons	7	Chevrolet	114.708	9	4	3	25	L. G. DeWitt	Neil Bonnett	134.233
Delaware 500	9/17/78	Bobby Allison	2	Ford	119.323	7	5	3	18	Bud Moore	J. D. McDuffie	135.48
CRC Chemicals 500	9/16/79	Richard Petty	4	Chevrolet	114.366	27	7	11	49	Petty Enterprises	Dale Earnhardt	135.726
CRC Chemicals 500	9/14/80	Darrell Waltrip	2	Chevrolet	116.024	29	11	8	39	DiGard	Cale Yarborough	137.583
CRC Chemicals 500	9/20/81	Neil Bonnett	3	Ford	119.561	17	9	4	22	Wood Brothers	Ricky Rudd	136.757
CRC Chemicals 500	9/19/82	Darrell Waltrip	3	Buick	107.642	26	11	9	67	Junior Johnson	Ricky Rudd	139.384
Budweiser 500	9/18/83	Bobby Allison	7	Buick	116.077	21	8	7	51	DiGard	Terry Labonte	139.573

Race	Date	Winner	Start Pos.	Make	Speed	Lead Ch.	No. Lds.	No. Caut.	Caut. Laps	Owner	Pole Winner	Pole Speed
Delaware 500	9/16/84	Harry Gant	3	Chevrolet	111.856	20	9	10	73	Hal Needham		
Delaware 500	9/15/85	Harry Gant	4	Chevrolet	120.538	16	6	6	45	Hal Needham	Bill Elliott	141.543
Delaware 500	9/14/86	Ricky Rudd	11	Ford	114.329	27	11	13	88	Bud Moore	Geoff Bodine	146.205
Delaware 500	9/20/87	Ricky Rudd	13	Ford	124.706	19	7	6	31	Bud Moore	Alan Kulwicki	145.826
Delaware 500	9/18/88	Bill Elliott	3	Ford	109.349	22	8	14	84	Harry Melling	Mark Martin	148.075
Peak Performance 500	9/17/89	Dale Earnhardt	15	Chevrolet	122.909	18	7	5	31	Richard Childress	Davey Allison	146.169
Peak AntiFreeze 500	9/16/90	Bill Elliott	1	Ford	125.945	11	5	6	29	Harry Melling	Bill Elliott	144.928
Peak AntiFreeze 500	9/15/91	Harry Gant	10	Oldsmobile	110.179	10	7	9	70	Leo Jackson	Alan Kulwicki	146.825
Peak AntiFreeze 500	9/20/92	Ricky Rudd	6	Chevrolet	115.289	13	7	9	48	Rick Hendrick	Alan Kulwicki	145.267
SplitFire Spark Plug 500	9/19/93	Rusty Wallace	1	Pontiac	100.334	18	8	16	103	Roger Penske	Rusty Wallace	151.564
SplitFire Spark Plug 500	9/18/94	Rusty Wallace	10	Ford	112.556	26	12	13	72	Roger Penske	Geoff Bodine	152.84
MBNA 500	9/17/95	Jeff Gordon	2	Chevrolet	124.74	10	7	5	34	Rick Hendrick	Rick Mast	153.466
MBNA 500	9/15/96	Jeff Gordon	3	Chevrolet	105.646	28	12	14	91	Rick Hendrick	Bobby Labonte	155.086

MARTINSVILLE SPEEDWAY
Spring 500-Lapper

Race	Date	Winner	Start Pos.	Make	Speed	Lead Ch.	No. Lds.	No. Caut.	Caut. Laps	Owner	Pole Winner	Pole Speed
	5/21/50	Curtis Turner		Oldsmobile		1	2			John Eanes	Buck Baker	54.216
	5/6/51	Curtis Turner	7	Oldsmobile		7	4			John Eanes	Tim Flock	55.062
	4/6/52	Dick Rathmann	9	Hudson	42.862	7	5	5		Walt Chapman	Buck Baker	54.945
	5/17/53	Lee Petty		Dodge		3	3			Petty Enterprises	NTT	
	5/16/54	Jim Paschal		Oldsmobile	46.153	2	2	3		Griffin Motors	NTT	
	5/15/55	Tim Flock	4	Chrysler	52.554	2	2	2		Carl Kiekhaefer	Jim Paschal	58.823
Virginia 500	5/20/56	Buck Baker	1	Dodge	60.824	5	3	7	20	Carl Kiekhaefer	Buck Baker	66.103
Virginia 500	5/19/57	Buck Baker	14	Chevrolet	57.318	5	4	3	51	Hugh Babb	Paul Goldsmith	65.693
Virginia 500	4/20/58	Bob Welborn	20	Chevrolet	66.007	5	4	4		J.H. Petty	Buck Baker	61.166
Virginia 500	5/3/59	Lee Petty	24	Oldsmobile	59.512	4	4	3		Petty Enterprises	Bobby Johns	66.03
Virginia 500	4/10/60	Richard Petty	4	Plymouth	63.943	8	6	8		Petty Enterprises	Glen Wood	69.15
Virginia 500	4/9/61	Fred Lorenzen	2	Ford	68.366	1	2	2		Holman-Moody	Rex White	70.28
Virginia 500 Sweepstakes	4/30/61	Junior Johnson	17	Pontiac	66.278	2	3	1	6	Rex Lovette	Rex White	71.32
Virginia 500	4/22/62	Richard Petty	7	Plymouth	66.425	6	6	2		Petty Enterprises	Fred Lorenzen	71.287
Virginia 500	4/21/63	Richard Petty	8	Plymouth	64.823	3	3	5		Petty Enterprises	Rex White	72.0
Virginia 500	4/26/64	Fred Lorenzen	1	Ford	70.098	5	3	2	14	Holman-Moody	Fred Lorenzen	74.472
Virginia 500	4/25/65	Fred Lorenzen	2	Ford	66.765	6	3	5	49	Holman-Moody	Junior Johnson	74.503
Virginia 500	4/24/66	Jim Paschal	1	Plymouth	69.156	6	4	1	6	Tom Friedkin	Jim Paschal	76.345
Virginia 500	4/23/67	Richard Petty	2	Plymouth	67.446	11	4	8	57	Petty Enterprises	Darel Dieringer	77.319
Virginia 500	4/28/68	Cale Yarborough	3	Mercury	66.686	9	5	10	72	Wood Brothers	David Pearson	78.23
Virginia 500	4/27/69	Richard Petty	6	Ford	64.405	11	5	8	61	Petty Enterprises	Bobby Allison	78.26
Virginia 500	5/31/70	Bobby Isaac	2	Dodge	68.584	5	3	7	46	Nord Krauskopf	Donnie Allison	82.609
Virginia 500	4/25/71	Richard Petty	3	Plymouth	77.707	10	4	1	3	Petty Enterprises	Donnie Allison	82.529
Virginia 500	4/30/72	Richard Petty	3	Plymouth	72.657	15	5	4	24	Petty Enterprises	Bobby Allison	84.163
Virginia 500	4/29/73	David Pearson	1	Mercury	70.251	11	3	7	49	Wood Brothers	David Pearson	86.369
Virginia 500	4/28/74	Cale Yarborough	1	Chevrolet	70.427	6	3	12	70	Richard Howard	Cale Yarborough	84.362
Virginia 500	4/27/75	Richard Petty	6	Dodge	69.282	18	7	4	58	Petty Enterprises	Benny Parsons	85.789
Virginia 500	4/25/76	Darrell Waltrip	4	Chevrolet	71.759	11	4	6	47	DiGard	Dave Marcis	86.286
Virginia 500	4/24/77	Cale Yarborough	5	Chevrolet	77.405	8	5	3	22	Junior Johnson	Neil Bonnett	88.923
Virginia 500	4/23/78	Darrell Waltrip	3	Chevrolet	77.971	6	3	4	27	DiGard	Lennie Pond	88.637
Virginia 500	4/22/79	Richard Petty	2	Chevrolet	76.562	11	5	5	32	Petty Enterprises	Darrell Waltrip	87.383
Virginia 500	4/27/80	Darrell Waltrip	1	Chevrolet	69.049	5	5	8	91	DiGard	Darrell Waltrip	88.566
Virginia 500	4/26/81	Morgan Shepherd	12	Pontiac	75.019	13	6	5	38	Cliff Stewart	Ricky Rudd	89.056
Virginia National Bank 500	4/25/82	Harry Gant	3	Buick	75.073	14	7	9	46	Hal Needham	Terry Labonte	89.988
Virginia National Bank 500	4/24/83	Darrell Waltrip	3	Chevrolet	66.46	13	7	9	105	Junior Johnson	Ricky Rudd	89.91
Sovran Bank 500	4/29/84	Geoff Bodine	6	Chevrolet	73.264	13	6	11	54	Rick Hendrick	Joe Ruttman	89.426
Sovran Bank 500	4/28/85	Harry Gant	13	Chevrolet	73.022	12	7	10	57	Hal Needham	Darrell Waltrip	90.279
Sovran Bank 500	4/27/86	Ricky Rudd	4	Ford	76.882	15	8	7	33	Bud Moore	Tim Richmond	90.716
Sovran Bank 500	4/26/87	Dale Earnhardt	4	Chevrolet	72.808	14	7	11	65	Richard Childress	Morgan Shepherd	92.355
Pannill Sweatshirts 500	4/24/88	Dale Earnhardt	14	Chevrolet	74.74	10	7	7	46	Richard Childress	Ricky Rudd	91.328
Pannill Sweatshirts 500	4/23/89	Darrell Waltrip	10	Chevrolet	79.025	12	6	5	31	Rick Hendrick	Geoff Bodine	93.097
Hanes Activewear 500	4/29/90	Geoff Bodine	1	Ford	77.423	12	5	10	44	Junior Johnson	Geoff Bodine	91.726
Hanes 500	4/28/91	Dale Earnhardt	10	Chevrolet	75.139	13	4	11	53	Richard Childress	Mark Martin	91.949
Hanes 500	4/26/92	Mark Martin	12	Ford	78.086	11	6	11	59	Jack Roush	Darrell Waltrip	92.956

Race	Date	Winner	Start Pos.	Make	Speed	Lead Ch.	No. Lds.	No. Caut.	Caut. Laps	Owner	Pole Winner	Pole Speed
Hanes 500	4/25/93	Rusty Wallace	5	Pontiac	79.078	10	4	8	49	Roger Penske	Geoff Bodine	93.887
Hanes 500	4/24/94	Rusty Wallace	1	Ford	76.7	11	5	11	65	Roger Penske	Rusty Wallace	92.942
Hanes 500	4/23/95	Rusty Wallace	15	Ford	72.145	8	5	7	84	Roger Penske	Bobby Labonte	93.308
Goody's 500	4/21/96	Rusty Wallace	5	Ford	81.41	18	7	6	36	Roger Penske	Ricky Craven	93.079

Fall 500-Lapper

Race	Date	Winner	Start Pos.	Make	Speed	Lead Ch.	No. Lds.	No. Caut.	Caut. Laps	Owner	Pole Winner	Pole Speed
	9/25/49	Red Byron	3	Oldsmobile		2	3			Raymond Parks	Curtis Turner	
	10/15/50	Herb Thomas	19	Plymouth		2	3			Herb Thomas	Fonty Flock	54.761
	10/14/51	Frank Mundy	3	Oldsmobile		4	5	1		Ted Chester	Herb Thomas	56.109
	10/19/52	Herb Thomas	2	Hudson	47.556	7	3			Herb Thomas	Perk Brown	55.333
	10/18/53	Jim Paschal		Dodge	56.013	2	2			George Hutchens	Fonty Flock	58.958
	10/17/54	Lee Petty	1	Chrysler	44.547	4	2	3		Petty Enterprises	Lee Petty	53.191
	10/16/55	Speedy Thompson	17	Chrysler		7	5	3		Carl Kiekhaefer	Gwyn Staley	
Mixed 400	10/28/56	Jack Smith	23	Dodge	61.136	7	6	4		Carl Kiekhaefer	Buck Baker	67.643
Sweepstakes 500	10/6/57	Bob Welborn	2	Chevrolet	63.025	6	4	4		Bob Welborn	Eddie Pagan	65.837
Old Dominion 500	10/12/58	Fireball Roberts	4	Chevrolet	64.344	1	2			Frank Strickland	Glen Wood	67.95
Virginia Sweepstakes 500	9/27/59	Rex White	14	Chevrolet	60.5	6	5	7		Rex White	Glen Wood	69.471
Old Dominion 500	9/25/60	Rex White	4	Chevrolet	60.439	2	2			Rex White	Glen Wood	68.442
Old Dominion 500	9/24/61	Joe Weatherly	3	Pontiac	62.586	9	6	7		Bud Moore	Fred Lorenzen	70.73
Old Dominion 500	9/23/62	Nelson Stacy	3	Ford	66.874	4	4	2		Holman-Moody	Fireball Roberts	71.51
Old Dominion 500	9/22/63	Fred Lorenzen	2	Ford	67.486	3	2	5	18	Holman-Moody	Junior Johnson	73.379
Old Dominion 500	9/27/64	Fred Lorenzen	1	Ford	67.32	6	4	6	28	Holman-Moody	Fred Lorenzen	74.196
Old Dominion 500	9/26/65	Junior Johnson	3	Ford	67.056	5	2	3	19	Rex Lovette	Richard Petty	74.503
Old Dominion 500	9/25/66	Fred Lorenzen	2	Ford	69.177	6	4	4	26	Holman-Moody	Junior Johnson	75.598
Old Dominion 500	9/24/67	Richard Petty	5	Plymouth	69.605	3	3	7	43	Petty Enterprises	Cale Yarborough	77.386
Old Dominion 500	9/22/68	Richard Petty	6	Plymouth	65.808	11	5	7	60	Petty Enterprises	Cale Yarborough	77.279
Old Dominion 500	9/28/69	Richard Petty	6	Ford	63.127	11	6	11	61	Petty Enterprises	David Pearson	83.197
Old Dominion 500	10/18/70	Richard Petty	4	Plymouth	72.235	5	4	5	32	Petty Enterprises	Bobby Allison	82.167
Old Dominion 500	9/26/71	Bobby Isaac	1	Dodge	73.681	10	3	3	33	Nord Krauskopf	Bobby Isaac	83.635
Old Dominion 500	9/24/72	Richard Petty	4	Plymouth	69.989	13	3	8	58	Petty Enterprises	Bobby Allison	85.89
Old Dominion 500	9/30/73	Richard Petty	6	Dodge	68.831	6	3	6	69	Petty Enterprises	Cale Yarborough	85.922
Old Dominion 500	9/29/74	Earl Ross	11	Chevrolet	66.232	11	7	10	78	Junior Johnson	Richard Petty	84.119
Old Dominion 500	9/28/75	Dave Marcis	7	Dodge	75.819	19	7	7	40	Nord Krauskopf	Cale Yarborough	86.199
Old Dominion 500	9/26/76	Cale Yarborough	4	Chevrolet	75.37	7	2	3	27	Junior Johnson	Darrell Waltrip	88.484
Old Dominion 500	9/25/77	Cale Yarborough	3	Chevrolet	73.447	13	5	9	57	Junior Johnson	Neil Bonnett	87.637
Old Dominion 500	9/24/78	Cale Yarborough	6	Oldsmobile	79.185	6	4	4	19	Junior Johnson	Lennie Pond	86.558
Old Dominion 500	9/23/79	Buddy Baker	7	Chevrolet	75.119	12	5	10	54	Harry Ranier	Darrell Waltrip	88.265
Old Dominion 500	9/28/80	Dale Earnhardt	7	Chevrolet	69.654	25	9	17	79	Rod Osterlund	Buddy Baker	88.5
Old Dominion 500	9/27/81	Darrell Waltrip	1	Buick	70.089	14	9	11	72	Junior Johnson	Darrell Waltrip	89.014
Old Dominion 500	10/17/82	Darrell Waltrip	3	Buick	71.315	23	11	10	70	Junior Johnson	Ricky Rudd	89.132
Goody's 500	9/25/83	Ricky Rudd	2	Chevrolet	76.134	6	5	6	37	Richard Childress	Darrell Waltrip	89.342
Goody's 500	9/23/84	Darrell Waltrip	3	Chevrolet	75.532	11	8	8	39	Junior Johnson	Geoff Bodine	89.523
Goody's 500	9/22/85	Dale Earnhardt	11	Chevrolet	70.694	11	7	12	65	Richard Childress	Geoff Bodine	90.521
Goody's 500	9/21/86	Rusty Wallace	8	Pontiac	73.191	15	9	12	54	Raymond Beadle	Geoff Bodine	90.599
Goody's 500	9/27/87	Darrell Waltrip	14	Chevrolet	76.41	13	6	8	35	Rick Hendrick	Geoff Bodine	91.218
Goody's 500	9/25/88	Darrell Waltrip	20	Chevrolet	74.988	11	6	11	53	Rick Hendrick	Rusty Wallace	91.372
Goody's 500	9/24/89	Darrell Waltrip	2	Chevrolet	76.571	19	7	8	46	Rick Hendrick	Jimmy Hensley	91.913
Goody's 500	9/23/90	Geoff Bodine	14	Ford	76.386	16	10	11	57	Junior Johnson	Mark Martin	91.571
Goody's 500	9/22/91	Harry Gant	12	Oldsmobile	74.535	20	12	15	81	Leo Jackson	Mark Martin	93.171
Goody's 500	9/28/92	Geoff Bodine	7	Ford	75.424	16	8	12	67	Bud Moore	Kyle Petty	92.497
Goody's 500	9/26/93	Ernie Irvan	1	Ford	74.102	10	4	11	73	Robert Yates	Ernie Irvan	92.583
Goody's 500	9/25/94	Rusty Wallace	7	Ford	77.139	18	9	11	62	Roger Penske	Ted Musgrave	94.129
Goody's 500	9/24/95	Dale Earnhardt	2	Chevrolet	73.946	16	8	10	85	Richard Childress		
Hanes 500	9/22/96	Jeff Gordon	10	Chevrolet	82.223	11	4	7	35	Rick Hendrick	Bobby Hamilton	94.12

MICHIGAN INT'L SPEEDWAY
June 500/400-Miler

Race	Date	Winner	Start Pos.	Make	Speed	Lead Ch.	No. Lds.	No. Caut.	Caut. Laps	Owner	Pole Winner	Pole Speed
Motor State 500	6/15/69	Cale Yarborough	4	Mercury	139.254	35	9	7	35	Wood Brothers	Donnie Allison	160.135
Motor State 400	6/7/70	Cale Yarborough	4	Mercury	138.302	15	6	3	28	Wood Brothers	Pete Hamilton	162.737
Motor State 400	6/13/71	Bobby Allison	1	Mercury	149.567	32	5	2	13	Holman-Moody	Bobby Allison	161.19
Motor State 400	6/11/72	David Pearson	3	Mercury	146.639	20	6	2	12	Wood Brothers	Bobby Isaac	160.764

Race	Date	Winner	Start Pos.	Make	Speed	Lead Ch.	No. Lds.	No. Caut.	Caut. Laps	Owner	Pole Winner	Pole Speed
Motor State 400	6/24/73	David Pearson	2	Mercury	153.485	25	5	0	0	Wood Brothers	Buddy Baker	158.273
Motor State 400	6/16/74	Richard Petty	4	Dodge	127.098	50	9	6	40	Petty Enterprises	David Pearson	156.426
Motor State 400	6/15/75	David Pearson	3	Mercury	131.398	44	9	5	36	Wood Brothers	Cale Yarborough	158.541
Cam 2 Motor Oil 400	6/20/76	David Pearson	8	Mercury	141.148	17	7	3	20	Wood Brothers	Richard Petty	158.569
Cam 2 Motor Oil 400	6/19/77	Cale Yarborough	4	Chevrolet	135.033	19	8	4	25	Junior Johnson	David Pearson	159.175
Gabriel 400	6/18/78	Cale Yarborough	3	Oldsmobile	149.563	25	7	1	8	Junior Johnson	David Pearson	163.936
Gabriel 400	6/17/79	Buddy Baker	3	Chevrolet	135.798	47	12	6	33	Harry Ranier	Neil Bonnett	162.371
Gabriel 400	6/15/80	Benny Parsons	1	Chevrolet	131.808	25	5	7	43	M C Anderson	Benny Parsons	163.662
Gabriel 400	6/21/81	Bobby Allison	4	Buick	130.589	47	11	7	36	Harry Ranier	Darrell Waltrip	160.471
Gabriel 400	6/20/82	Cale Yarborough	4	Buick	118.101	24	15	3	42	M C Anderson	Ron Bouchard	162.404
Gabriel 400	6/19/83	Cale Yarborough	9	Chevrolet	138.728	15	6	5	23	Harry Ranier	Terry Labonte	161.965
Miller High Life 400	6/17/84	Bill Elliott	1	Ford	134.705	20	10	6	28	Harry Melling	Bill Elliott	164.339
Miller 400	6/16/85	Bill Elliott	1	Ford	144.724	20	9	2	15	Harry Melling		
Miller American 400	6/15/86	Bill Elliott	8	Ford	138.851	34	12	8	39	Harry Melling	Tim Richmond	172.031
Miller American 400	6/28/87	Dale Earnhardt	5	Chevrolet	148.454	13	7	5	18	Richard Childress	Rusty Wallace	170.746
Miller High Life 400	6/26/88	Rusty Wallace	5	Pontiac	153.551	13	9	4	16	Raymond Beadle	Bill Elliott	172.687
Miller High Life 400	6/25/89	Bill Elliott	2	Ford	139.023	13	6	5	23	Harry Melling	Ken Schrader	174.728
Miller Genuine Draft 400	6/24/90	Dale Earnhardt	5	Chevrolet	150.219	17	7	4	16	Richard Childress		
Miller Genuine Draft 400	6/23/91	Davey Allison	4	Ford	160.912	31	11	1	4	Robert Yates	Michael Waltrip	174.351
Miller Genuine Draft 400	6/21/92	Davey Allison	1	Ford	152.672	14	6	4	13	Robert Yates	Davey Allison	176.258
Miller Genuine Draft 400	6/20/93	Ricky Rudd	2	Chevrolet	148.484	16	8	5	20	Rick Hendrick	Brett Bodine	175.456
Miller Genuine Draft 400	6/19/94	Rusty Wallace	5	Ford	125.022	13	7	7	52	Roger Penske	Loy Allen Jr.	180.641
Miller Genuine Draft 400	6/18/95	Bobby Labonte	19	Chevrolet	134.141	20	10	8	44	Joe Gibbs	Jeff Gordon	186.611
Miller Genuine Draft 400	6/23/96	Rusty Wallace	18	Ford	166.033	17	9	2	8	Roger Penske	Bobby Hamilton	185.166

August 600/400-Miler

Race	Date	Winner	Start Pos.	Make	Speed	Lead Ch.	No. Lds.	No. Caut.	Caut. Laps	Owner	Pole Winner	Pole Speed
Yankee 600	8/17/69	David Pearson	1	Ford	115.508	26	12	7	78	Holman-Moody	David Pearson	161.714
Yankee 400	8/16/70	Charlie Glotzbach	1	Dodge	147.571	18	8	1	9	Ray Nichels	Charlie Glotzbach	157.363
Yankee 400	8/15/71	Bobby Allison	2	Mercury	149.862	29	5	2	12	Holman-Moody	Pete Hamilton	161.901
Yankee 400	8/20/72	David Pearson	4	Mercury	134.416	19	7	3	26	Wood Brothers	Richard Petty	157.607
Yankee 400	8/25/74	David Pearson	1	Mercury	133.045	45	8	5	30	Wood Brothers	David Pearson	157.946
Champion Spark Plug 400	8/24/75	Richard Petty	4	Dodge	107.583	25	13	6	63	Petty Enterprises	David Pearson	159.798
Champion Spark Plug 400	8/22/76	David Pearson	1	Mercury	140.078	34	10	4	20	Wood Brothers	David Pearson	160.875
Champion Spark Plug 400	8/22/77	Darrell Waltrip	3	Chevrolet	137.944	31	6	5	24	DiGard	David Pearson	160.346
Champion Spark Plug 400	8/20/78	David Pearson	1	Mercury	129.566	34	10	7	35	Wood Brothers	David Pearson	164.073
Champion Spark Plug 400	8/19/79	Richard Petty	5	Chevrolet	130.376	21	8	5	35	Petty Enterprises	David Pearson	162.992
Champion Spark Plug 400	8/17/80	Cale Yarborough	2	Chevrolet	145.352	31	9	4	17	Junior Johnson	Buddy Baker	162.693
Champion Spark Plug 400	8/16/81	Richard Petty	7	Buick	123.457	65	14	9	51	Petty Enterprises	Ron Bouchard	161.501
Champion Spark Plug 400	8/22/82	Bobby Allison	10	Buick	136.454	31	12	5	29	DiGard	Bill Elliott	162.995
Champion Spark Plug 400	8/21/83	Cale Yarborough	7	Chevrolet	147.511	27	11	2	27	Harry Ranier	Terry Labonte	162.437
Champion Spark Plug 400	8/12/84	Darrell Waltrip	7	Chevrolet	153.863	7	5	0	0	Junior Johnson	Bill Elliott	165.217
Champion Spark Plug 400	8/11/85	Bill Elliott	1	Ford	137.43	14	7	5	28	Harry Melling	Bill Elliott	165.479
Champion Spark Plug 400	8/17/86	Bill Elliott	3	Ford	135.376	23	10	5	38	Harry Melling	Benny Parsons	171.924
Champion Spark Plug 400	8/16/87	Bill Elliott	3	Ford	138.648	16	9	5	25	Harry Melling	Davey Allison	170.705
Champion Spark Plug 400	8/21/88	Davey Allison	4	Ford	156.863	21	9	2	9	Harry Ranier	Bill Elliott	174.94
Champion Spark Plug 400	8/20/89	Rusty Wallace	2	Pontiac	157.704	20	11	2	8	Raymond Beadle	Geoff Bodine	175.962
Champion Spark Plug 400	8/19/90	Mark Martin	5	Ford	138.822	23	11	6	26	Jack Roush	Alan Kulwicki	174.982

Race	Date	Winner	Start Pos.	Make	Speed	Lead Ch.	No. Lds.	No. Caut.	Caut. Laps	Owner	Pole Winner	Pole Speed
Champion Spark Plug 400	8/18/91	Dale Jarrett	11	Ford	142.972	24	12	4	22	Wood Brothers	Alan Kulwicki	173.431
Champion Spark Plug 400	8/16/92	Harry Gant	24	Oldsmobile	146.056	16	8	5	25	Leo Jackson	Alan Kulwicki	178.196
Champion Spark Plug 400	8/15/93	Mark Martin	12	Ford	144.564	15	8	8	27	Jack Roush	Ken Schrader	180.75
GM Goodwrench Dealers 400	8/21/94	Geoff Bodine	1	Ford	139.914	14	8	5	30	Geoff Bodine	Geoff Bodine	181.082
GM Goodwrench Dealers 400	8/20/95	Bobby Labonte	1	Chevrolet	157.739	17	8	3	16	Joe Gibbs	Bobby Labonte	184.403
GM Goodwrench Dealers 400	8/18/96	Dale Jarrett	11	Ford	139.792	13	8	8	36	Robert Yates	Jeff Burton	185.395

NORTH CAROLINA MOTOR SPEEDWAY
Spring 500/400-Miler

Race	Date	Winner	Start Pos.	Make	Speed	Lead Ch.	No. Lds.	No. Caut.	Caut. Laps	Owner	Pole Winner	Pole Speed
Peach Blossom 500	3/13/66	Paul Goldsmith	1	Plymouth	100.027	26	10	10	70	Ray Nichels	Paul Goldsmith	116.684
Carolina 500	6/18/67	Richard Petty	2	Plymouth	104.682	20	5	9	45	Petty Enterprises	Dick Hutcherson	116.486
Carolina 500	6/16/68	Donnie Allison	7	Ford	99.338	20	5	8	74	Banjo Matthews	LeeRoy Yarbrough	118.644
Carolina 500	3/9/69	David Pearson	1	Ford	102.569	23	7	10	82	Holman-Moody	David Pearson	119.619
Carolina 500	3/8/70	Richard Petty	8	Plymouth	116.117	24	7	9	67	Petty Enterprises	Bobby Allison	139.048
Carolina 500	3/14/71	Richard Petty	2	Plymouth	118.696	19	7	7	36	Petty Enterprises	Fred Lorenzen	133.892
Carolina 500	3/12/72	Bobby Isaac	1	Dodge	113.895	13	4	8	57	Nord Krauskopf	Bobby Allison	137.539
Carolina 500	3/18/73	David Pearson	1	Mercury	118.649	2	2	7	47	Wood Brothers	David Pearson	134.021
Carolina 500	3/3/74	Richard Petty	2	Dodge	121.622	10	3	2	15	Petty Enterprises	Cale Yarborough	134.868
Carolina 500	3/2/75	Cale Yarborough	7	Chevrolet	117.588	15	5	4	34	Junior Johnson	Buddy Baker	137.611
Carolina 500	2/29/76	Richard Petty	3	Dodge	113.665	13	5	5	45	Petty Enterprises	Dave Marcis	138.287
Carolina 500	3/13/77	Richard Petty	2	Dodge	97.86	30	10	11	118	Petty Enterprises	Donnie Allison	135.387
Carolina 500	3/5/78	David Pearson	9	Mercury	116.681	24	9	8	62	Wood Brothers	Neil Bonnett	141.94
Carolina 500	3/4/79	Bobby Allison	1	Ford	122.727	13	5	7	39	Bud Moore	Bobby Allison	136.79
Carolina 500	3/9/80	Cale Yarborough	21	Oldsmobile	108.735	18	6	12	93	Junior Johnson	Darrell Waltrip	139.905
Carolina 500	3/1/81	Darrell Waltrip	4	Buick	114.594	36	10	14	75	Junior Johnson	Cale Yarborough	140.448
Warner W. Hodgdon Carolina 500	3/28/82	Cale Yarborough	11	Buick	108.992	31	12	9	86	M C Anderson	Benny Parsons	141.577
Warner W. Hodgdon Carolina 500	3/13/83	Richard Petty	12	Pontiac	113.055	30	11	10	94	Petty Enterprises	Ricky Rudd	143.413
Warner W. Hodgdon Carolina 500	3/4/84	Bobby Allison	15	Buick	122.931	23	6	6	42	DiGard	Harry Gant	145.084
Carolina 500	3/3/85	Neil Bonnett	4	Chevrolet	114.953	29	6	10	76	Junior Johnson	Terry Labonte	145.067
Goodwrench 500	3/2/86	Terry Labonte	1	Oldsmobile	120.488	22	10	9	50	Billy Hagan	Terry Labonte	146.348
Goodwrench 500	3/1/87	Dale Earnhardt	14	Chevrolet	117.556	26	10	10	55	Richard Childress	Davey Allison	146.989
Goodwrench 500	3/6/88	Neil Bonnett	30	Pontiac	120.159	23	9	7	40	B. Rahilly & B. Mock	Bill Elliott	146.612
Goodwrench 500	3/5/89	Rusty Wallace	1	Pontiac	115.122	29	11	10	64	Raymond Beadle	Rusty Wallace	148.793
GM Goodwrench 500	3/4/90	Kyle Petty	1	Pontiac	122.864	18	9	8	36	Felix Sabates	Kyle Petty	148.751
GM Goodwrench 500	3/3/91	Kyle Petty	1	Pontiac	124.083	13	5	7	29	Felix Sabates	Kyle Petty	149.205
GM Goodwrench 500	3/1/92	Bill Elliott	2	Ford	126.125	11	5	7	28	Junior Johnson	Kyle Petty	149.926
GM Goodwrench 500	2/28/93	Rusty Wallace	10	Pontiac	124.486	20	9	7	40	Roger Penske	Mark Martin	149.547
GM Goodwrench 500	2/27/94	Rusty Wallace	15	Ford	125.239	19	8	5	38	Roger Penske	Geoff Bodine	151.716
GM Goodwrench 500	2/26/95	Jeff Gordon	1	Chevrolet	125.305	19	7	11	58	Rick Hendrick	Jeff Gordon	157.62
Goodwrench Service 400	2/25/96	Dale Earnhardt	18	Chevrolet	113.959	22	6	10	66	Richard Childress	Terry Labonte	156.87

Fall 500/400-Miler

Race	Date	Winner	Start Pos.	Make	Speed	Lead Ch.	No. Lds.	No. Caut.	Caut. Laps	Owner	Pole Winner	Pole Speed
American 500	10/31/65	Curtis Turner	4	Ford	101.942	16	6	8	55	Wood Brothers	Richard Petty	116.26
American 500	10/30/66	Fred Lorenzen	1	Ford	104.348	20	2	4	35	Holman-Moody	Fred Lorenzen	115.988
American 500	10/29/67	Bobby Allison	3	Ford	98.42	26	11	9	81	Holman-Moody	David Pearson	117.12
American 500	10/27/68	Richard Petty	4	Plymouth	105.06	18	7	6	46	Petty Enterprises	Cale Yarborough	118.717
American 500	10/26/69	LeeRoy Yarbrough	9	Ford	111.938	25	7	7	66	Junior Johnson	Charlie Glotzbach	136.972
American 500	11/15/70	Cale Yarborough	2	Mercury	117.811	13	5	7	46	Wood Brothers	Charlie Glotzbach	136.498
American 500	10/24/71	Richard Petty	5	Plymouth	113.405	14	5	9	58	Petty Enterprises	Charlie Glotzbach	135.167
American 500	10/22/72	Bobby Allison	5	Chevrolet	118.275	20	8	4	35	Richard Howard	David Pearson	137.528
American 500	10/21/73	David Pearson	2	Mercury	117.749	20	6	5	36	Wood Brothers	Richard Petty	135.748
American 500	10/20/74	David Pearson	3	Mercury	118.493	23	5	4	37	Wood Brothers	Richard Petty	135.297
American 500	10/19/75	Cale Yarborough	4	Chevrolet	120.129	15	4	4	23	Junior Johnson	Dave Marcis	132.021
American 500	10/24/76	Richard Petty	4	Dodge	117.718	15	5	6	35	Petty Enterprises	David Pearson	139.117

Race	Date	Winner	Start Pos.	Make	Speed	Lead Ch.	No. Lds.	No. Caut.	Caut. Laps	Owner	Pole Winner	Pole Speed
American 500	10/23/77	Donnie Allison	1	Chevrolet	113.584	24	5	9	75	Hoss Ellington	Donnie Allison	138.685
American 500	10/22/78	Cale Yarborough	1	Oldsmobile	117.288	19	13	5	52	Junior Johnson	Cale Yarborough	142.067
American 500	10/21/79	Richard Petty	7	Chevrolet	108.356	23	8	12	82	Petty Enterprises	Buddy Baker	141.315
American 500	10/19/80	Cale Yarborough	2	Chevrolet	114.159	35	12	9	61	Junior Johnson	Donnie Allison	142.648
American 500	11/1/81	Darrell Waltrip	1	Buick	107.399	33	11	12	97	Junior Johnson	Darrell Waltrip	138.164
Warner W. Hodgdon American 500	10/31/82	Darrell Waltrip	4	Buick	115.122	33	10	8	55	Junior Johnson	Cale Yarborough	143.22
Warner W. Hodgdon American 500	10/30/83	Terry Labonte	3	Chevrolet	119.324	36	10	10	63	Billy Hagan	Neil Bonnett	143.876
Warner W. Hodgdon American 500	10/21/84	Bill Elliott	2	Ford	112.617	28	12	10	91	Harry Melling	Geoff Bodine	144.415
Nationwise 500	10/20/85	Darrell Waltrip	20	Chevrolet	118.344	27	9	10	64	Junior Johnson	Terry Labonte	141.841
Nationwise 500	10/19/86	Neil Bonnett	6	Chevrolet	126.381	22	8	6	29	Junior Johnson	Tim Richmond	146.948
AC Delco 500	10/25/87	Bill Elliott	3	Ford	118.258	31	11	8	46	Harry Melling	Davey Allison	145.609
AC Delco 500	10/23/88	Rusty Wallace	3	Pontiac	111.557	18	10	11	76	Raymond Beadle	Bill Elliott	148.359
AC Delco 500	10/22/89	Mark Martin	7	Ford	114.079	35	10	14	69	Jack Roush	Alan Kulwicki	148.624
AC Delco 500	10/21/90	Alan Kulwicki	3	Ford	126.452	21	8	7	28	Alan Kulwicki	Ken Schrader	147.814
AC Delco 500	10/20/91	Davey Allison	10	Ford	127.292	26	6	5	24	Robert Yates	Kyle Petty	149.461
AC Delco 500	10/25/92	Kyle Petty	1	Pontiac	130.748	9	4	2	12	Felix Sabates	Kyle Petty	149.675
AC Delco 500	10/24/93	Rusty Wallace	18	Pontiac	114.036	23	11	8	54	Roger Penske	Mark Martin	148.353
AC Delco 500	10/23/94	Dale Earnhardt	20	Chevrolet	126.408	26	12	10	52	Richard Childress	Ricky Rudd	157.099
AC Delco 500	10/22/95	Ward Burton	3	Pontiac	114.778	14	10	7	64	Bill Davis	Hut Stricklin	155.379
AC Delco 400	10/20/96	Ricky Rudd	2	Ford	122.32	21	10	7	46	Ricky Rudd	Dale Jarrett	157.194

NORTH WILKESBORO SPEEDWAY
Spring Race

Race	Date	Winner	Start Pos.	Make	Speed	Lead Ch.	No. Lds.	No. Caut.	Caut. Laps	Owner	Pole Winner	Pole Speed
	4/29/51	Fonty Flock	1	Oldsmobile						Frank Christian	Fonty Flock	72.184
	3/30/52	Herb Thomas	1	Hudson	58.597					Herb Thomas	Herb Thomas	75.075
	3/29/53	Herb Thomas	1	Hudson	71.907	6	5			Herb Thomas	Herb Thomas	78.424
	4/4/54	Dick Rathmann	3	Hudson	68.545	3	2			John Ditz	Gober Sosebee	78.698
	4/3/55	Buck Baker	2	Oldsmobile	73.126	1	1			Griffin Motors	Dink Widenhouse	77.72
	4/8/56	Tim Flock	3	Chrysler	71.034	2	3			Carl Kiekhaefer	Junior Johnson	78.37
	4/7/57	Fireball Roberts	1	Ford	75.015		1	2	5	Pete DePaolo	Fireball Roberts	81.5
	5/18/58	Junior Johnson	3	Ford	78.636	3	3			Paul Spaulding	Jack Smith	82.056
	4/5/59	Lee Petty	4	Oldsmobile	71.985	2	3	4	9	Petty Enterprises	Speedy Thompson	85.746
	3/27/60	Lee Petty	8	Plymouth	66.347	3	3	6		Petty Enterprises	Junior Johnson	83.86
	4/16/61	Rex White	2	Chevrolet	83.248	4	4	6	33	Rex White	Junior Johnson	95.66
Gwyn Staley 400	4/15/62	Richard Petty	15	Plymouth	84.737	5	5	5		Petty Enterprises	Junior Johnson	94.142
Gwyn Staley 400	4/28/63	Richard Petty	7	Plymouth	83.301	4	4			Petty Enterprises	Fred Lorenzen	96.15
Gwyn Staley 400	4/19/64	Fred Lorenzen	1	Ford	81.93	5	4	7	35	Holman-Moody	Fred Lorenzen	94.024
Gwyn Staley 400	4/18/65	Junior Johnson	1	Ford	95.047	5	3	3	9	Rex Lovette	Junior Johnson	101.033
Gwyn Staley 400	4/17/66	Jim Paschal	1	Plymouth	89.045	6	2	8	48	Tom Friedkin	Jim Paschal	102.693
Gwyn Staley 400	4/16/67	Darel Dieringer	1	Ford	93.594		1	6	33	Junior Johnson	Darel Dieringer	104.603
Gwyn Staley 400	4/21/68	David Pearson	1	Ford	90.425	13	6	10	67	Holman-Moody	David Pearson	104.993
Gwyn Staley 400	4/20/69	Bobby Allison	11	Dodge	95.268	11	4	4	30	Mario Rossi	Bobby Isaac	106.731
Gwyn Staley 400	4/18/70	Richard Petty	16	Plymouth	94.246	1	2	3	21	Petty Enterprises	Bobby Isaac	107.041
Gwyn Staley 400	4/18/71	Richard Petty	3	Plymouth	98.479	6	4	0	0	Petty Enterprises	Bobby Isaac	106.217
Gwyn Staley 400	4/23/72	Richard Petty	3	Plymouth	86.381	17	3	5	45	Petty Enterprises	Bobby Isaac	107.506
Gwyn Staley 400	4/8/73	Richard Petty	2	Dodge	97.224	5	3	1	9	Petty Enterprises	Bobby Allison	106.75
Gwyn Staley 400	4/21/74	Richard Petty	4	Dodge	96.2	4	3	2	11	Petty Enterprises	Bobby Allison	105.669
Gwyn Staley 400	4/6/75	Richard Petty	2	Dodge	90.009	15	7	4	36	Petty Enterprises	Darrell Waltrip	105.52
Gwyn Staley 400	4/4/76	Cale Yarborough	5	Chevrolet	96.858	8	3	2	8	Junior Johnson	Dave Marcis	108.585
Gwyn Staley 400	3/27/77	Cale Yarborough	2	Chevrolet	88.95	12	6	6	42	Junior Johnson	Neil Bonnett	107.537
Gwyn Staley 400	4/16/78	Darrell Waltrip	2	Chevrolet	92.345	18	7	4	25	DiGard	Benny Parsons	108.51
Northwestern Bank 400	3/25/79	Bobby Allison	3	Ford	88.4	20	11	4	32	Bud Moore	Benny Parsons	108.136
Northwestern Bank 400	4/20/80	Richard Petty	7	Chevrolet	95.501	9	4	5	32	Petty Enterprises	Bobby Allison	113.797
Northwestern Bank 400	4/5/81	Richard Petty	13	Buick	85.381	12	4	10	87	Petty Enterprises	Dave Marcis	114.647
Northwestern Bank 400	4/18/82	Darrell Waltrip	1	Buick	97.646	9	5	6	34	Junior Johnson	Darrell Waltrip	114.801
Northwestern Bank 400	4/17/83	Darrell Waltrip	10	Chevrolet	91.436	12	7	7	49	Junior Johnson	Neil Bonnett	112.332
Northwestern Bank 400	4/8/84	Tim Richmond	17	Pontiac	97.83	13	7	5	23	Raymond Beadle	Ricky Rudd	113.487
Northwestern Bank 400	4/21/85	Neil Bonnett	5	Chevrolet	93.818	10	6	6	36	Junior Johnson	Darrell Waltrip	111.899
First Union 400	4/20/86	Dale Earnhardt	5	Chevrolet	88.408	10	6	8	70	Richard Childress	Geoff Bodine	112.419
First Union 400	4/5/87	Dale Earnhardt	3	Chevrolet	94.103	11	7	8	49	Richard Childress	Bill Elliott	116.003
First Union 400	4/17/88	Terry Labonte	1	Chevrolet	99.075	12	5	5	20	Junior Johnson	Terry Labonte	117.322

Race	Date	Winner	Start Pos.	Make	Speed	Lead Ch.	No. Lds.	No. Caut.	Caut. Laps	Owner	Pole Winner	Pole Speed
First Union 400	4/16/89	Dale Earnhardt	3	Chevrolet	89.937	10	5	10	49	Richard Childress	Rusty Wallace	117.524
First Union 400	4/22/90	Brett Bodine	20	Buick	83.908	6	4	10	68	Kenny Bernstein	Mark Martin	117.475
First Union 400	4/21/91	Darrell Waltrip	13	Chevrolet	79.604	8	8	17	87	Darrell Waltrip	Brett Bodine	116.237
First Union 400	4/12/92	Davey Allison	7	Ford	90.653	8	6	9	55	Robert Yates	Alan Kulwicki	117.242
First Union 400	4/18/93	Rusty Wallace	9	Pontiac	92.602	12	9	4	38	Roger Penske	Brett Bodine	117.017
First Union 400	4/17/94	Terry Labonte	10	Chevrolet	95.816	8	6	6	35	Rick Hendrick	Ernie Irvan	119.016
First Union 400	4/9/95	Dale Earnhardt	5	Chevrolet	102.424	19	7	3	14	Richard Childress	Jeff Gordon	118.765
First Union 400	4/14/96	Terry Labonte	1	Chevrolet	96.37	17	9	3	25	Rick Hendrick	Terry Labonte	116.659

Fall Race

Race	Date	Winner	Start Pos.	Make	Speed	Lead Ch.	No. Lds.	No. Caut.	Caut. Laps	Owner	Pole Winner	Pole Speed
	10/16/49	Bob Flock	7	Oldsmobile	53.364	2	2			Frank Christian	Ken Wagner	57.563
	9/24/50	Leon Sales	11	Plymouth		5	4			Hubert Westmoreland	Fireball Roberts	73.266
	10/21/51	Fonty Flock	4	Oldsmobile	67.791	1	2			Ted Chester	Herb Thomas	68.828
	10/26/52	Herb Thomas	1	Hudson	67.044	2	2	3	12	Herb Thomas	Herb Thomas	76.013
	10/11/53	Speedy Thompson	12	Oldsmobile	71.202	13	4	3	16	Buckshot Morris	Buck Baker	78.288
	10/24/54	Hershel McGriff	1	Oldsmobile	65.175	4	2	4		Frank Christian	Hershel McGriff	77.612
	10/23/55	Buck Baker	1	Ford	72.347		1	3		Pete DePaolo	Buck Baker	79.815
	10/20/57	Jack Smith	4	Chevrolet	69.902	5	3	2		Jack Smith	Fireball Roberts	81.644
	10/19/58	Junior Johnson	2	Ford	84.906		2	0	0	Paul Spaulding	Glen Wood	86.805
	10/18/59	Lee Petty	2	Plymouth	74.829	1	1	3		Petty Enterprises	Glen Wood	86.806
Wilkes 200	10/2/60	Rex White	1	Chevrolet	77.444	2	2	5		Rex White	Rex White	93.399
Wilkes 200	10/1/61	Rex White	3	Chevrolet	84.675	3	3	4	23	Rex White	Junior Johnson	94.54
Wilkes 320	9/30/62	Richard Petty	5	Plymouth	86.186	2	3	3		Petty Enterprises	Fred Lorenzen	94.657
Wilkes 250	9/29/63	Marvin Panch	3	Ford	89.428	9	4	2	17	Wood Brothers	Fred Lorenzen	96.566
Wilkes 400	10/11/64	Marvin Panch	5	Ford	91.398	9	4	2	28	Wood Brothers	Junior Johnson	100.761
Wilkes 400	10/3/65	Junior Johnson	5	Ford	88.801	3	3	5	36	Rex Lovette	Fred Lorenzen	101.58
Wilkes 400	10/2/66	Dick Hutcherson	4	Ford	89.012	4	3	5	52	Bondy Long	Junior Johnson	103.069
Wilkes 400	10/1/67	Richard Petty	5	Plymouth	94.837	6	5	3	20	Petty Enterprises	Dick Hutcherson	104.312
Wilkes 400	9/29/68	Richard Petty	3	Plymouth	94.103	8	4	3	25	Petty Enterprises	Bobby Allison	104.525
Wilkes 400	10/5/69	David Pearson	2	Ford	93.429	6	4	3	23	Holman-Moody	Bobby Isaac	106.032
Wilkes 400	10/4/70	Bobby Isaac	1	Dodge	90.162	12	3	4	32	Nord Krauskopf	Bobby Isaac	105.406
Wilkes 400	11/21/71	Tiny Lund	6	Camero	96.174	8	4	3	19	Ronnie Hopkins	Charlie Glotzbach	107.558
Wilkes 400	10/1/72	Richard Petty	3	Plymouth	95.816	16	3	1	12	Petty Enterprises	Buddy Baker	105.922
Wilkes 400	9/23/73	Bobby Allison	1	Chevrolet	95.198	12	4	2	9	Bobby Allison	Bobby Allison	105.619
Wilkes 400	9/22/74	Cale Yarborough	2	Chevrolet	80.782	11	4	6	11	Junior Johnson	Richard Petty	105.087
Wilkes 400	9/21/75	Richard Petty	1	Dodge	88.986	11	3	7	34	Petty Enterprises	Richard Petty	105.5
Wilkes 400	10/3/76	Cale Yarborough	4	Chevrolet	96.38	5	5	2	9	Junior Johnson	Darrell Waltrip	107.449
Wilkes 400	10/2/77	Darrell Waltrip	3	Chevrolet	86.713	10	4	3	32	DiGard	Richard Petty	108.35
Wilkes 400	10/1/78	Cale Yarborough	3	Oldsmobile	97.847	1	2	1	4	Junior Johnson	Darrell Waltrip	109.397
Holly Farms 400	10/14/79	Benny Parsons	5	Chevrolet	91.454	12	5	9	48	M C Anderson	Dale Earnhardt	112.783
Holly Farms 400	9/21/80	Bobby Allison	2	Ford	75.51	14	5	8	113	Bud Moore	Cale Yarborough	111.996
Holly Farms 400	10/4/81	Darrell Waltrip	1	Buick	93.091	10	5	8	49	Junior Johnson	Darrell Waltrip	114.065
Holly Farms 400	10/3/82	Darrell Waltrip	1	Buick	98.071	4	2	4	26	Junior Johnson	Darrell Waltrip	113.86
Holly Farms 400	10/2/83	Darrell Waltrip	1	Chevrolet	100.716	8	5	1	4	Junior Johnson	Darrell Waltrip	114.539
Holly Farms 400	10/14/84	Darrell Waltrip	1	Chevrolet	90.525	7	5	7	35	Junior Johnson	Darrell Waltrip	113.304
Holly Farms 400	9/29/85	Harry Gant	11	Chevrolet	95.077	10	5	6	31	Hal Needham	Geoff Bodine	113.967
Holly Farms 400	9/28/86	Darrell Waltrip	4	Chevrolet	95.612	15	9	4	22	Junior Johnson	Tim Richmond	113.447
Holly Farms 400	10/4/87	Terry Labonte	4	Chevrolet	96.051	5	5	4	24	Junior Johnson	Bill Elliott	115.196
Holly Farms 400	10/16/88	Rusty Wallace	12	Pontiac	94.192	15	7	9	34	Raymond Beadle	Bill Elliott	116.901
Holly Farms 400	10/15/89	Geoff Bodine	11	Chevrolet	90.289	8	4	11	60	Rick Hendrick		
Tyson/Holly Farms 400	9/30/90	Mark Martin	2	Ford	93.818	6	4	9	40	Jack Roush	Kyle Petty	116.387
Tyson/Holly Farms 400	9/29/91	Dale Earnhardt	16	Chevrolet	94.113	3	3	8	43	Richard Childress	Harry Gant	116.871
Tyson/Holly Farms 400	10/5/92	Geoff Bodine	3	Ford	107.36	12	7	0	0	Bud Moore	Alan Kulwicki	117.133
Tyson/Holly Farms 400	10/3/93	Rusty Wallace	11	Pontiac	96.92	15	10	4	26	Roger Penske	Ernie Irvan	116.786
Tyson/Holly Farms 400	10/2/94	Geoff Bodine	18	Ford	98.522	6	6	4	25	Geoff Bodine	Jimmy Spencer	118.558
Tyson/Holly Farms 400	10/1/95	Mark Martin	2	Ford	102.998	28	13	2	10	Jack Roush	Ted Musgrave	118.396
Tyson/Holly Farms 400	9/29/96	Jeff Gordon	2	Chevrolet	96.837	18	8	4	29	Rick Hendrick	Ted Musgrave	118.054

POCONO INT'L RACEWAY
June 500-Miler

Race	Date	Winner	Start Pos.	Make	Speed	Lead Ch.	No. Lds.	No. Caut.	Caut. Laps	Owner	Pole Winner	Pole Speed
Van Scoy Diamond Mine 500	6/6/82	Bobby Allison	3	Buick	113.579	45	11	7	51	DiGard		
Van Scoy Diamond Mine 500	6/12/83	Bobby Allison	7	Buick	128.636	22	11	6	25	DiGard	Darrell Waltrip	152.315

Race	Date	Winner	Start Pos.	Make	Speed	Lead Ch.	No. Lds.	No. Caut.	Caut. Laps	Owner	Pole Winner	Pole Speed
Van Scoy Diamond Mine 500	6/10/84	Cale Yarborough	12	Chevrolet	138.164	33	12	3	12	Harry Ranier	David Pearson	150.921
Van Scoy Diamond Mine 500	6/9/85	Bill Elliott	1	Ford	138.974	13	4	3	10	Harry Melling	Bill Elliott	152.563
Miller High Life 500	6/8/86	Tim Richmond	3	Chevrolet	113.279	18	11	9	53	Rick Hendrick	Geoff Bodine	153.625
Miller High Life 500	6/14/87	Tim Richmond	3	Chevrolet	122.166	17	9	9	45	Rick Hendrick	Terry Labonte	155.502
Miller High Life 500	6/19/88	Geoff Bodine	3	Chevrolet	126.147	17	7	6	31	Rick Hendrick	Alan Kulwicki	158.806
Miller High Life 500	6/18/89	Terry Labonte	23	Ford	131.32	23	12	6	23	Junior Johnson	Rusty Wallace	157.489
Miller Genuine Draft 500	6/17/90	Harry Gant	16	Oldsmobile	120.6	26	16	13	44	Leo Jackson	Ernie Irvan	158.75
Champion Spark Plug 500	6/16/91	Darrell Waltrip	13	Chevrolet	122.666	23	14	7	37	Darrell Waltrip	Mark Martin	161.996
Champion Spark Plug 500	6/14/92	Alan Kulwicki	6	Ford	144.023	26	11	3	13	Alan Kulwicki	Ken Schrader	162.499
Champion Spark Plug 500	6/13/93	Kyle Petty	8	Pontiac	138.005	22	13	6	24	Felix Sabates	Ken Schrader	162.816
UAW-GM Teamwork 500	6/12/94	Rusty Wallace	1	Ford	128.801	22	12	5	35	Roger Penske	Rusty Wallace	164.558
UAW-GM Teamwork 500	6/11/95	Terry Labonte	27	Chevrolet	137.72	24	11	6	20	Rick Hendrick	Ken Schrader	163.375
UAW-GM Teamwork 500	6/16/96	Jeff Gordon	1	Chevrolet	139.104	26	12	4	23	Rick Hendrick	Jeff Gordon	169.125

July 500-Miler

Race	Date	Winner	Start Pos.	Make	Speed	Lead Ch.	No. Lds.	No. Caut.	Caut. Laps	Owner	Pole Winner	Pole Speed
Purolator 500	8/4/74	Richard Petty	3	Dodge	115.593	20	5	4	42	Petty Enterprises	Buddy Baker	144.122
Purolator 500	8/3/75	David Pearson	2	Mercury	111.179	44	6	5	47	Wood Brothers	Bobby Allison	146.491
Purolator 500	8/1/76	Richard Petty	5	Dodge	115.875	48	8	7	38	Petty Enterprises	Cale Yarborough	147.865
Coca-Cola 500	7/31/77	Benny Parsons	4	Chevrolet	128.379	47	6	4	22	L. G. DeWitt	Darrell Waltrip	147.591
Coca-Cola 500	7/30/78	Darrell Waltrip	4	Chevrolet	142.54	37	4	1	3	DiGard	Benny Parsons	149.236
Coca-Cola 500	7/30/79	Cale Yarborough	2	Chevrolet	115.207	56	8	7	46	Junior Johnson	Harry Gant	148.711
Coca-Cola 500	7/27/80	Neil Bonnett	2	Mercury	124.395	49	11	5	26	Wood Brothers	Cale Yarborough	151.469
Mountain Dew 500	7/26/81	Darrell Waltrip	1	Buick	119.111	27	10	6	39	Junior Johnson	Darrell Waltrip	150.148
Mountain Dew 500	7/25/82	Bobby Allison	4	Buick	115.496	46	11	6	43	DiGard	Cale Yarborough	150.764
Like Cola 500	7/24/83	Tim Richmond	1	Pontiac	114.818	41	11	5	52	Raymond Beadle	Tim Richmond	151.981
Like Cola 500	7/22/84	Harry Gant	3	Chevrolet	121.351	27	11	9	41	Hal Needham	Bill Elliott	152.184
Summer 500	7/21/85	Bill Elliott	2	Ford	134.008	37	12	6	24	Harry Melling	Bill Elliott	151.973
Summer 500	7/20/86	Tim Richmond	5	Chevrolet	124.218	20	6	8	33	Rick Hendrick	Harry Gant	154.392
Summer 500	7/19/87	Dale Earnhardt	16	Chevrolet	121.745	35	15	9	46	Richard Childress	Tim Richmond	155.979
AC Spark Plug 500	7/24/88	Bill Elliott	2	Ford	122.866	22	9	5	42	Harry Melling	Morgan Shepherd	157.153
AC Spark Plug 500	7/23/89	Bill Elliott	14	Ford	117.847	28	14	9	42	Harry Melling	Ken Schrader	157.809
AC Spark Plug 500	7/22/90	Geoff Bodine	4	Ford	124.07	22	9	10	35	Junior Johnson	Mark Martin	158.264
Miller Genuine Draft 500	7/21/91	Rusty Wallace	10	Pontiac	115.459	21	11	11	48	Roger Penske	Alan Kulwicki	161.473
Miller Genuine Draft 500	7/19/92	Darrell Waltrip	8	Chevrolet	134.058	13	7	3	23	Darrell Waltrip	Davey Allison	162.022
Miller Genuine Draft 500	7/18/93	Dale Earnhardt	11	Chevrolet	133.343	24	12	8	27	Richard Childress	Ken Schrader	162.934
Miller Genuine Draft 500	7/17/94	Geoff Bodine	1	Ford	136.075	18	9	5	23	Geoff Bodine	Geoff Bodine	163.869
Miller Genuine Draft 500	7/16/95	Dale Jarrett	15	Ford	134.038	37	13	5	25	Robert Yates	Bill Elliott	162.496
Miller Genuine Draft 500	7/21/96	Rusty Wallace	13	Ford	144.892	23	12	4	17	Roger Penske	Mark Martin	168.41

TALLADEGA SUPERSPEEDWAY
Alabama/Winston 500

Race	Date	Winner	Start Pos.	Make	Speed	Lead Ch.	No. Lds.	No. Caut.	Caut. Laps	Owner	Pole Winner	Pole Speed
Alabama 500	4/12/70	Pete Hamilton	6	Plymouth	152.321	32	8	6	42	Petty Enterprises	Bobby Isaac	199.658
Winston 500	5/16/71	Donnie Allison	1	Mercury	147.419	45	4	7	45	Wood Brothers	Donnie Allison	185.869
Winston 500	5/7/72	David Pearson	2	Mercury	134.4	53	7	9	62	Wood Brothers	Bobby Isaac	192.428
Winston 500	5/6/73	David Pearson	2	Mercury	131.956	14	10	4	54	Wood Brothers		
Winston 500	5/5/74	David Pearson	1	Mercury	130.22	52	13	6	60	Wood Brothers	David Pearson	186.086
Winston 500	5/4/75	Buddy Baker	1	Ford	144.948	51	12	5	45	Bud Moore	Buddy Baker	189.947
Winston 500	5/2/76	Buddy Baker	12	Ford	169.887	24	8	3	14	Bud Moore	Dave Marcis	189.197
Winston 500	5/1/77	Darrell Waltrip	11	Chevrolet	164.877	63	11	6	27	DiGard	A. J. Foyt	192.424
Winston 500	5/14/78	Cale Yarborough	1	Oldsmobile	155.699	44	8	5	30	Junior Johnson	Cale Yarborough	191.904
Winston 500	5/6/79	Bobby Allison	12	Ford	154.77	21	8	4	30	Bud Moore	Darrell Waltrip	195.644
Winston 500	5/4/80	Buddy Baker	2	Oldsmobile	170.481	40	12	6	28	Harry Ranier	David Pearson	197.704
Winston 500	5/3/81	Bobby Allison	1	Buick	149.376	43	10	7	44	Harry Ranier	Bobby Allison	195.864
Winston 500	5/2/82	Darrell Waltrip	2	Buick	156.697	51	13	8	39	Junior Johnson	Benny Parsons	200.176
Winston 500	5/1/83	Richard Petty	15	Pontiac	153.936	27	13	7	42	Petty Enterprises	Cale Yarborough	202.65

Race	Date	Winner	Start Pos.	Make	Speed	Lead Ch.	No. Lds.	No. Caut.	Caut. Laps	Owner	Pole Winner	Pole Speed
Winston 500	5/6/84	Cale Yarborough	1	Chevrolet	172.988	75	13	4	17	Harry Ranier	Cale Yarborough	202.692
Winston 500	5/5/85	Bill Elliott	1	Ford	186.288	28	10	2	8	Harry Melling	Bill Elliott	209.398
Winston 500	5/4/86	Bobby Allison	2	Buick	157.698	24	9	9	41	Stavola Brothers	Bill Elliott	212.229
Winston 500	5/3/87	Davey Allison	3	Ford	154.228	18	10	9	39	Harry Ranier	Bill Elliott	212.809
Winston 500	5/1/88	Phil Parsons	3	Oldsmobile	156.547	23	9	7	29	Richard Jackson	Davey Allison	198.969
Winston 500	5/7/89	Davey Allison	2	Ford	155.869	28	9	7	26	Robert Yates	Mark Martin	193.061
Winston 500	5/6/90	Dale Earnhardt	5	Chevrolet	159.571	25	12	7	28	Richard Childress	Bill Elliott	199.388
Winston 500	5/6/91	Harry Gant	2	Oldsmobile	165.62	24	11	3	18	Leo Jackson	Ernie Irvan	195.186
Winston 500	5/3/92	Davey Allison	2	Ford	167.609	16	6	5	21	Robert Yates	Ernie Irvan	192.831
Winston 500	5/2/93	Ernie Irvan	16	Chevrolet	155.412	22	7	4	25	Larry McClure	Dale Earnhardt	192.355
Winston Select 500	5/1/94	Dale Earnhardt	4	Chevrolet	157.478	30	11	4	23	Richard Childress	Ernie Irvan	193.298
Winston Select 500	4/30/95	Mark Martin	3	Ford	178.902	24	10	2	8	Jack Roush	Terry Labonte	196.532
Winston Select 500	4/28/96	Sterling Marlin	4	Chevrolet	149.999	25	14	6	31	Larry McClure	Ernie Irvan	192.855

Talladega/DieHard 500

Race	Date	Winner	Start Pos.	Make	Speed	Lead Ch.	No. Lds.	No. Caut.	Caut. Laps	Owner	Pole Winner	Pole Speed
Talladega 500	9/14/69	Richard Brickhouse	9	Dodge	153.778	35	7	7	38	Ray Nichels	Bobby Isaac	196.386
Talladega 500	8/23/70	Pete Hamilton	4	Plymouth	158.517	23	9	4	29	Petty Enterprises	Bobby Isaac	186.834
Talladega 500	8/22/71	Bobby Allison	2	Mercury	145.945	54	6	5	43	Holman-Moody	Donnie Allison	187.323
Talladega 500	8/6/72	James Hylton	22	Mercury	148.728	30	9	5	34	James Hylton	Bobby Isaac	190.677
Talladega 500	8/12/73	Dick Brooks	24	Plymouth	145.454	64	15	7	52	Crawford Brothers	Bobby Allison	187.064
Talladega 500	8/11/74	Richard Petty	3	Dodge	148.637	34	11	6	40	Petty Enterprises	David Pearson	184.926
Talladega 500	8/17/75	Buddy Baker	2	Ford	130.892	60	17	8	61	Bud Moore	Dave Marcis	191.34
Talladega 500	8/8/76	Dave Marcis	1	Dodge	157.547	58	8	3	25	Nord Krauskopf	Dave Marcis	190.651
Talladega 500	8/7/77	Donnie Allison	2	Chevrolet	162.524	49	9	5	27	Hoss Ellington	Benny Parsons	192.684
Talladega 500	8/6/78	Lennie Pond	5	Oldsmobile	174.7	67	9	4	27	Harry Ranier	Cale Yarborough	192.917
Talladega 500	8/5/79	Darrell Waltrip	8	Oldsmobile	161.229	34	8	5	28	DiGard	Neil Bonnett	193.6
Talladega 500	8/3/80	Neil Bonnett	2	Mercury	166.894	36	11	5	25	Wood Brothers	Buddy Baker	198.545
Talladega 500	8/2/81	Ron Bouchard	10	Buick	156.737	39	10	8	36	Jack Beebe	Harry Gant	195.897
Talladega 500	8/1/82	Darrell Waltrip	2	Buick	168.157	38	11	5	25	Junior Johnson	Geoff Bodine	199.4
Talladega 500	7/31/83	Dale Earnhardt	4	Ford	170.611	46	10	2	16	Bud Moore	Cale Yarborough	201.744
Talladega 500	7/29/84	Dale Earnhardt	3	Chevrolet	155.485	68	16	7	37	Richard Childress	Cale Yarborough	202.474
Talladega 500	7/28/85	Cale Yarborough	2	Ford	148.772	30	12	7	44	Harry Ranier	Bill Elliott	207.578
Talladega 500	7/27/86	Bobby Hillin Jr.	13	Buick	151.522	49	26	9	44	Stavola Brothers	Bill Elliott	209.005
Talladega 500	7/26/87	Bill Elliott	1	Ford	171.293	23	9	4	18	Harry Melling	Bill Elliott	203.827
Talladega DieHard 500	7/31/88	Ken Schrader	7	Chevrolet	154.505	30	14	8	31	Rick Hendrick	Darrell Waltrip	196.274
Talladega DieHard 500	7/30/89	Terry Labonte	5	Ford	157.354	48	9	6	25	Junior Johnson	Mark Martin	194.8
DieHard 500	7/29/90	Dale Earnhardt	1	Chevrolet	174.43	23	13	2	12	Richard Childress	Dale Earnhardt	192.513
DieHard 500	7/28/91	Dale Earnhardt	4	Chevrolet	147.383	32	13	7	43	Richard Childress	Sterling Marlin	192.085
DieHard 500	7/26/92	Ernie Irvan	7	Chevrolet	176.309	17	8	2	11	Larry McClure	Sterling Marlin	190.586
DieHard 500	7/25/93	Dale Earnhardt	11	Chevrolet	153.858	26	10	5	27	Richard Childress	Bill Elliott	192.397
DieHard 500	7/24/94	Jimmy Spencer	2	Ford	163.217	24	10	5	20	Junior Johnson	Dale Earnhardt	193.47
DieHard 500	7/23/95	Sterling Marlin	1	Chevrolet	173.188	21	9	2	11	Larry McClure	Sterling Marlin	194.212
DieHard 500	7/28/96	Jeff Gordon	2	Chevrolet	133.387	24	10	5	35	Rick Hendrick	Jeremy Mayfield	192.37

VIRGINIA STATE FAIRGROUNDS
Spring Race

Race	Date	Winner	Start Pos.	Make	Speed	Lead Ch.	No. Lds.	No. Caut.	Caut. Laps	Owner	Pole Winner	Pole Speed
	4/19/53	Lee Petty	42	Dodge	45.535					Petty Enterprises	Buck Baker	48.465
	5/22/55	Tim Flock	22	Chrysler	54.298	4	3			Carl Kiekhaefer		
	4/29/56	Buck Baker	1	Dodge	56.232	2	2			Carl Kiekhaefer	Buck Baker	67.091
	5/5/57	Paul Goldsmith	7	Ford	62.445	2	2			Pete DePaolo	Russ Hepler	64.239
	6/21/59	Tom Pistone	12	Ford	56.881					Carl Rupert	Buck Baker	66.42
	6/5/60	Lee Petty	10	Plymouth	62.251	7	6	1	5	Petty Enterprises	Ned Jarrett	64.56
	4/23/61	Richard Petty	1	Plymouth	62.456	2	2			Petty Enterprises	Richard Petty	66.667
Richmond 250	4/1/62	Rex White	20	Chevrolet	51.363	7	6	5	32	Rex White		
Richmond 250	4/7/63	Joe Weatherly	3	Pontiac	58.624	11	4	6	37	Bud Moore	Rex White	69.151
Richmond 250	3/8 & 10/64	David Pearson	10	Dodge	60.233	5	4	2		Cotton Owens	Ned Jarrett	69.07
Richmond 250	3/7/65	Junior Johnson	1	Ford	61.416	5	4	8	45	Rex Lovette	Junior Johnson	67.847
Richmond 250	5/15/66	David Pearson	4	Dodge	66.539	5	4	2	14	Cotton Owens	Tom Pistone	70.978
Richmond 250	4/30/67	Richard Petty	1	Plymouth	65.982	6	3	6	32	Petty Enterprises	Richard Petty	70.038
Richmond 250	3/24/68	David Pearson	16	Ford	65.217	7	4			Holman-Moody	Bobby Isaac	67.822
Richmond 500	4/13/69	David Pearson	1	Ford	73.752	6	4	6	40	Holman-Moody	David Pearson	82.538
Richmond 500	3/1/70	James Hylton	3	Ford	82.044	2	3	1	7	James Hylton	Richard Petty	89.137
Richmond 500	3/7/71	Richard Petty	30	Plymouth	79.836	6	4	3	18	Petty Enterprises	Dave Marcis	87.178

Race	Date	Winner	Start Pos.	Make	Speed	Lead Ch.	No. Lds.	No. Caut.	Caut. Laps	Owner	Pole Winner	Pole Speed
Richmond 500	2/27/72	Richard Petty	3	Plymouth	76.258	13	3	3	46	Petty Enterprises	Bobby Allison	90.573
Richmond 500	2/25/73	Richard Petty	8	Dodge	74.764	19	7	8	78	Petty Enterprises	Bobby Allison	90.952
Richmond 500	2/24/74	Bobby Allison	1	Chevrolet	80.095	11	4	3	16	Bobby Allison	Bobby Allison	90.353
Richmond 500	2/23/75	Richard Petty	1	Dodge	74.913	2	2	7	89	Petty Enterprises	Richard Petty	93.34
Richmond 400	3/7/76	Dave Marcis	2	Dodge	72.792	19	5	7	66	Nord Krauskopf	Bobby Allison	92.715
Richmond 400	2/27/77	Cale Yarborough	7	Chevrolet	73.084	9	7	4	35	Junior Johnson	Neil Bonnett	93.632
Richmond 400	2/26/78	Benny Parsons	3	Chevrolet	80.304	10	6	5	33	L. G. DeWitt	Neil Bonnett	93.382
Richmond 400	3/11/79	Cale Yarborough	9	Oldsmobile	83.608	3	2	2	8	Junior Johnson	Bobby Allison	92.957
Richmond 400	2/24/80	Darrell Waltrip	1	Chevrolet	67.703	19	7	9	72	DiGard	Darrell Waltrip	93.695
Richmond 400	2/22/81	Darrell Waltrip	7	Buick	76.57	6	4	7	50	Junior Johnson	Morgan Shepherd	92.821
Richmond 400	2/21/82	Dave Marcis	6	Chevrolet	72.914	11	7	6	33	Dave Marcis	Darrell Waltrip	93.256
Richmond 400	2/27/83	Bobby Allison	6	Chevrolet	79.584	15	8	5	25	DiGard	Ricky Rudd	93.439
Miller High Life 400	2/26/84	Ricky Rudd	4	Ford	76.736	11	4	9	40	Bud Moore	Darrell Waltrip	93.817
Miller High Life 400	2/24/85	Dale Earnhardt	4	Chevrolet	67.945	9	6	10	74	Richard Childress	Darrell Waltrip	95.218
Miller High Life 400	2/23/86	Kyle Petty	12	Ford	71.078	12	8	8	63	Wood Brothers		
Miller High Life 400	3/8/87	Dale Earnhardt	3	Chevrolet	81.52	12	8	6	35	Richard Childress	Alan Kulwicki	95.153
Pontiac Excitement 400	2/21/88	Neil Bonnett	3	Pontiac	66.401	11	6	14	83	B. Rahilly & B. Mock	Morgan Shepherd	94.645
Pontiac Excitement 400	3/26/89	Rusty Wallace	2	Pontiac	89.619	19	7	12	67	Raymond Beadle	Geoff Bodine	120.573
Pontiac Excitement 400	2/25/90	Mark Martin	6	Ford	92.158	18	8	12	75	Jack Roush	Ricky Rudd	119.617
Pontiac Excitement 400	2/24/91	Dale Earnhardt	19	Chevrolet	105.937	25	7	6	23	Richard Childress	Davey Allison	120.428
Pontiac Excitement 400	3/8/92	Bill Elliott	1	Ford	104.378	5	4	4	23	Junior Johnson	Bill Elliott	121.337
Pontiac Excitement 400	3/7/93	Davey Allison	14	Ford	107.0	12	6	3	19	Robert Yates	Ken Schrader	123.164
Pontiac Excitement 400	3/4/94	Ernie Irvan	7	Ford	98.334	15	8	8	51	Robert Yates	Ted Musgrave	123.474
Pontiac Excitement 400	3/5/95	Terry Labonte	24	Chevrolet	106.425	17	6	5	28	Rick Hendrick	Jeff Gordon	124.757
Pontiac Excitement 400	3/3/96	Jeff Gordon	2	Chevrolet	102.75	25	11	8	36	Rick Hendrick	Terry Labonte	123.728

Fall Race

Race	Date	Winner	Start Pos.	Make	Speed	Lead Ch.	No. Lds.	No. Caut.	Caut. Laps	Owner	Pole Winner	Pole Speed
	9/14/58	Speedy Thompson	1	Chevrolet	57.878	4	3			Speedy Thompson	Speedy Thompson	62.915
	9/13/59	Cotton Owens	1	Ford	60.382					Cotton Owens	Cotton Owens	62.674
	10/23/60	Speedy Thompson	3	Ford	63.739	3	3			Wood Brothers	Ned Jarrett	64.41
	9/10/61	Joe Weatherly	7	Pontiac	61.677					Bud Moore	Junior Johnson	65.01
Capital City 300	9/9/62	Joe Weatherly	2	Pontiac	64.981	8	4	1	9	Bud Moore	Rex White	66.127
Capital City 300	9/8/63	Ned Jarrett	7	Ford	66.339	4	3			Charles Robinson	Joe Weatherly	68.104
Capital City 300	9/14/64	Cotton Owens	3	Dodge	61.955	7	3	5	23	Cotton Owens	Ned Jarrett	66.89
Capital City 300	9/18/65	David Pearson	2	Dodge	60.983	10	5			Cotton Owens	Dick Hutcherson	67.34
Capital City 300	9/11/66	David Pearson	1	Dodge	62.886	4	3	5	29	Cotton Owens	David Pearson	70.644
Capital City 300	9/10/67	Richard Petty	2	Plymouth	57.631	10	6	10	71	Petty Enterprises		
Capital City 300	9/8/68	Richard Petty	1	Plymouth	85.659	13	5	10	52	Petty Enterprises	Richard Petty	103.178
Capital City 250	9/7/69	Bobby Allison	25	Dodge	76.388	3	2	6	39	Mario Rossi	Richard Petty	91.257
Capital City 500	9/13/70	Richard Petty	1	Plymouth	81.476	2	2	2	9	Petty Enterprises	Richard Petty	87.014
Capital City 500	11/14/71	Richard Petty	11	Plymouth	80.025	9	4	4	24	Petty Enterprises	Bill Dennis	
Capital City 500	9/10/72	Richard Petty	3	Plymouth	75.899	18	5	8	57	Petty Enterprises	Bobby Allison	89.669
Capital City 500	9/9/73	Richard Petty	5	Dodge	63.215	6	3	5	123	Petty Enterprises	Bobby Allison	90.245
Capital City 500	9/8/74	Richard Petty	1	Dodge	64.43	6	4	13	123	Petty Enterprises	Richard Petty	88.852
Capital City 500	10/12/75	Darrell Waltrip	2	Chevrolet	81.886	10	5	4	23	DiGard	Benny Parsons	91.071
Capital City 400	9/12/76	Cale Yarborough	6	Chevrolet	77.993	12	5	2	37	Junior Johnson	Benny Parsons	92.46
Capital City 400	9/11/77	Neil Bonnett	2	Dodge	80.644	12	6	5	30	Jim Stacy	Benny Parsons	92.281
Capital City 400	9/10/78	Darrell Waltrip	1	Chevrolet	79.568	15	6	5	27	DiGard	Darrell Waltrip	91.964
Capital City 400	9/9/79	Bobby Allison	2	Ford	80.604	6	4	2	20	Bud Moore	Dale Earnhardt	92.605
Capital City 400	9/7/80	Bobby Allison	2	Ford	79.722	18	8	7	31	Bud Moore	Cale Yarborough	93.466
Wrangler Sanfor-Set 400	9/13/81	Benny Parsons	4	Ford	69.998	18	8	9	63	Bud Moore	Mark Martin	93.435
Wrangler Sanfor-Set 400	9/12/82	Bobby Allison	1	Chevrolet	82.8	6	4	2	12	DiGard	Bobby Allison	93.435
Wrangler Sanfor-Set 400	9/11/83	Bobby Allison	6	Buick	79.381	6	4	4	22	DiGard	Darrell Waltrip	96.069
Wrangler Sanfor-Set 400	9/9/84	Darrell Waltrip	1	Chevrolet	74.78	9	5	9	42	Junior Johnson	Darrell Waltrip	92.518
Wrangler Sanfor-Set 400	9/8/85	Darrell Waltrip	22	Chevrolet	72.508	14	7	7	65	Junior Johnson	Geoff Bodine	94.535
Wrangler Jeans Indigo 400	9/7/86	Tim Richmond	4	Chevrolet	70.161	15	12	12	75	Rick Hendrick	Harry Gant	93.966
Wrangler Jeans Indigo 400	9/13/87	Dale Earnhardt	8	Chevrolet	67.074	13	7	12	82	Richard Childress	Alan Kulwicki	94.052
Miller High Life 400	9/11/88	Davey Allison	1	Ford	95.77	14	7	5	42	Harry Ranier	Davey Allison	122.85
Miller High Life 400	9/10/89	Rusty Wallace	6	Pontiac	88.38	9	7	14	76	Raymond Beadle	Bill Elliott	121.136
Miller Genuine Draft 400	9/9/90	Dale Earnhardt	6	Chevrolet	95.567	17	6	9	55	Richard Childress	Ernie Irvan	119.872

Race	Date	Winner	Start Pos.	Make	Speed	Lead Ch.	No. Lds.	No. Caut.	Caut. Laps	Owner	Pole Winner	Pole Speed
Miller Genuine Draft 400	9/7/91	Harry Gant	13	Oldsmobile	101.361	15	9	9	43	Leo Jackson	Rusty Wallace	120.59
Miller Genuine Draft 400	9/12/92	Rusty Wallace	3	Pontiac	104.661	12	6	3	20	Roger Penske	Ernie Irvan	120.784
Miller Genuine Draft 400	9/11/93	Rusty Wallace	3	Pontiac	99.917	12	6	8	47	Roger Penske	Bobby Labonte	122.006
Miller Genuine Draft 400	9/10/94	Terry Labonte	3	Chevrolet	104.156	17	8	5	35	Rick Hendrick	Ted Musgrave	124.052
Miller Genuine Draft 400	9/9/95	Rusty Wallace	7	Ford	104.459	15	7	4	30	Roger Penske	Dale Earnhardt	122.543
Miller Genuine Draft 400	9/7/96	Ernie Irvan	16	Ford	105.469	16	9	4	24	Robert Yates	Mark Martin	122.744